Family of Faith Library

Property of
FAMILY OF FAITH
LIBRARY

W9-BIR-248

The College Board College Cost & Financial Aid Handbook 2004

The College Board College Cost & Financial Aid Handbook 2004

Twenty-Fourth Edition

The College Board
New York

METROPOLITAN LIBRARY SYSTEM
SERVING OKLAHOMA COUNTY

DISCARDED

The College Board is a national nonprofit membership association whose mission is to prepare, inspire, and connect students to college and opportunity. Founded in 1900, the association is composed of more than 4,300 schools, colleges, universities, and other educational organizations. Each year, the College Board serves over three million students and their parents, 23,000 high schools, and 3,500 colleges, through major programs and services in college admissions, guidance, assessment, financial aid, enrollment, and teaching and learning. Among its best-known programs are the SAT®, the PSAT/NMSQT®, and the Advanced Placement Program® (AP®). The College Board is committed to the principles of excellence and equity, and that commitment is embodied in all of its programs, services, activities, and concerns.

For further information, visit www.collegeboard.com.

Editorial inquiries regarding this book should be directed to College Planning Services, The College Board, 45 Columbus Avenue, New York, New York 10023-6992; or telephone 212 713-8000.

Copies of this book may be ordered from your local bookseller, or from College Board Publications, P.O. Box 869010, Plano, TX 75074-0998. This book may also be ordered online through the College Board Store at www.collegeboard.com. The price is $23.95.

Copyright © 2003 by College Entrance Examination Board. All rights reserved. College Board, Advanced Placement Program, AP, CollegeCredit, College-Level Examination Program, CLEP, College Scholarship Service, CSS, CSS/Financial Aid PROFILE, SAT, and the acorn logo are registered trademarks of the College Entrance Examination Board. English Language Proficiency Test and ELPT are trademarks owned by the College Entrance Examination Board. PSAT/NMSQT is a registered trademark of the College Entrance Examination Board and the National Merit Scholarship Corporation. Other products and services may be trademarks of their respective owners. Visit College Board on the Web: www.collegeboard.com.

This publication contains material related to Federal Title IV student aid programs. While the College Board believes that the information contained herein is accurate and factual, this publication has not been reviewed or approved by the U.S. Department of Education.

Library of Congress Catalog Number: 80-648095
International Standard Book Number: 0-87447-697-6

Printed in the United States of America

Contents

Dear Friend,

The College Board is dedicated to preparing, inspiring, and connecting students to college and opportunity, while emphasizing the principles of excellence and equity. With the College Board's Handbook series, we hope to put an authoritative source of college information at your fingertips and help connect you to a college education.

College is a dream for many, a dream worth working hard to achieve. I've been a businessman, a governor, and now the president of the College Board, but nothing makes me prouder than to say that I graduated from college. With perseverance, anyone who desires a college education can attain one. College Board publications can help you get there.

Gaston Caperton
President
The College Board

How to use this book

You may have doubted that education or training after high school is within your family's reach. That is probably not true.

You may have assumed that there is nothing you can do to help yourself or improve your chances of finding the outside help you need. That is definitely not true.

This book is designed to help students and their families understand and meet college costs. If you are worried about your family's ability to pay future educational expenses, early planning can help. The purpose of planning is twofold:

- to get as much mileage as you can out of your own resources
  - —the information you provided on financial aid applications will be used to calculate your expected family contribution, an amount assumed to be available from parents *and* from you, the student, to contribute toward your family's share of college costs.
- to secure the additional outside help—the "financial aid" you may need
  - —last year, nearly $85 billion dollars was available in financial aid (scholarships, grants, loans, and part-time employment opportunities) to help students pay their share of college costs; although most of the money is available from *need-based* financial aid programs (eligibility determined by subtracting your expected family contribution from the total cost of college), a considerable amount of support is available from *merit-based* programs (money awarded based on academic achievement, athletic ability, musical talent, and any number of other non-need-based criteria). When you consider Federal Education Tax Credits claimed by families last year, almost $90 billion was committed to education support.

Getting started

Planning to meet college costs involves several different kinds of activities. This book will:

- show you how to estimate the full costs of attending the colleges you are considering
  - —the *total cost of college* includes more than what you find listed in a catalog for annual tuition; you also need to estimate room and board, books and supplies, transportation, and miscellaneous/personal expenses for each college.
- help you estimate what share of those costs you and your family will probably be expected to bear
  - —very few families pay the full "sticker price" for education beyond high school; financial aid programs and financing options help supplement the amount a family is able to pay toward the total cost of college.
- prove that you can make time work for you in covering your share of the costs
  - —when it comes to planning and paying for college, it's true that *time is money*: the earlier a family begins to think about paying for college, the more options a student will have available.
- describe different ways that families can make their costs more manageable
  - —saving, borrowing, and using current income provides families with a combination of strategies to pay their share of college costs.
- help you estimate your own probable need and eligibility for financial aid
  - —information you provide on the Free Application for Federal Student Aid (FAFSA) will be used to determine your eligibility for federal financial aid according to the Federal Methodology (FM), a formula established by the United States Congress; some colleges will ask you to complete an additional application such as the CSS/Financial Aid PROFILE® to calculate your financial need for nonfederal financial aid programs using Institutional Methodology (IM), a more comprehensive "need analysis" formula used by many colleges and private scholarship programs.

- explain the various types and sources of available financial aid and what you need to do to apply
  —as noted above, last year nearly $85 billion in *scholarships, grants, student loans, and part-time employment* opportunities were available to millions of students from *federal, state, institutional,* and *private financial aid programs.*

Next to buying a home, the money that you and your family pay toward college costs may well be the largest financial investment you ever make in your lifetime. You owe it to yourself to investigate all your options beforehand, and then to manage that investment as carefully as you would any other.

Using the *Handbook* figures

The 2004 edition of *The College Board College Cost & Financial Aid Handbook* continues to include the most up-to-date financial aid and scholarship information available. Each college description provides itemized costs in separate columns for students living on campus and those living at home. Out-of-state/out-of-district costs are given as well as costs for state/community colleges. Among the other data are: average financial aid packages for full- and part-time undergraduates, percentages of need=based aid awarded as grants and loans/jobs, bases for non-need-based scholarships and number of students receiving them, average indebtedness of graduating class, and percentage of those who borrowed to fund their education. Also included are sections detailing: freshman need-based and non-need-based aid, policies to reduce costs, payment plans, and application procedures.

The figures and details provided in this book serve as a helpful starting point in exploring college opportunities, comparing one college to another, and shaping your plans for continuing education beyond high school. Be sure to note that many of these figures and details are provided as averages, meaning many students will be above or below these benchmarks. Use this information to develop general guidelines to evaluate your college choices. However, be aware that information varies from college to college and from year to year.

Throughout this book, information is presented in accordance with the Common Data Set initiative, in which the College Board has taken a leading role. The goal of this ongoing collaborative effort with other publishers and college administrators is to provide students with the most accurate, consistently comparable data available.

The author gratefully acknowledges the contributions of the many individuals who assisted in the development of this book. The focus and framework of this annual publication were developed by Kathleen Brouder. College cost and financial aid data were collected by the editorial staff of College Planning Services under the direction of Renée Gernand, using information collected through the College Board's Annual Survey of Colleges. Susan McCrackin was responsible for the analysis of these data and for the development of numerous college cost tables. Tom Vanderberg was responsible for the overall editorial direction of this book.

At the time this book went to press, little or no change was expected in the financial aid application and delivery systems for academic year 2004-05. However, since changes in program, application, and eligibility rules are always possible, it is very important that students seeking aid for the fall of 2004 take steps, early on, to ensure that they fully understand and comply with all application requirements.

To improve your chances of getting the help you need, you must know what you have to do, when you have to do it, and how to do it right—the first time. The more information you are able to provide up front about your family's situation, the easier it will be for the financial aid office to identify and address your need and eligibility for assistance.

Don't make the mistake of trying to simply negotiate a financial aid award without providing a complete explanation of your family situation. But be sure to understand what needs to be done to *appeal* a financial aid award by providing new or more complete information so that the financial aid office can take all of your family circumstances into account.

Missed deadlines, incomplete or inaccurate answers, and messy or illegible forms can hurt you. If you have any doubts at all about which forms to file, which questions to complete, or what deadlines to meet, contact the financial aid offices at the colleges to which you are applying. Every college has a staff of financial aid professionals to help you make their college affordable and to address your needs from admission to graduation.

Get online

We invite you to visit the College Board's Web site at www.collegeboard.com and let us know what you think about *The College Board College Cost & Financial Aid Handbook* and about our products and services in general. While you are there, you can also register for the College Board's SAT® examinations, sample actual SAT questions, register for CSS/Financial Aid PROFILE (or complete the entire application using PROFILE online), use our free Scholarship Search, calculate financial need, or order publications. We welcome any comments and suggestions that will help us make our publications and services more useful to you. Please feel free to contact us by e-mail at guidance@collegeboard.org.

Jack Joyce
Director, College Planning Services
The College Board

Twenty questions about college financing

Here is a list of what you need to know, and when you need to know it:

Phase 1: Applying to college

As soon as you have compiled a list of colleges that match your academic and personal criteria, you should begin to consider financial assistance. You can find much of this information in this book, or by calling the college's admission and financial aid advisers:

1. What are the average costs for tuition and fees, books and supplies, room and board, transportation, and other personal expenses for the first year? What are the ranges of room (single, double) costs, board costs (21 meals?), and special tuition rates (flat rate 15–18 credits, etc.)? By how much will total costs increase each year? (A three- to five-year printed history of tuition and fee increases as well as room and board increases should be available.)

2. Does financial need have an impact on admission decisions?

3. Does the decision to apply for early admission affect financial aid?

4. Does the institution offer financial aid programs as well as merit or other scholarships that do not include consideration of financial need? How and when should applications for need based and merit aid be completed?

5. What noninstitutional sources of aid and information are available? (Check with the financial aid office regarding fee-based sources.)

6. What application forms are required to complete the financial aid process? What is the priority deadline for applying for financial aid? When will the student be notified about financial aid decisions?

Phase 2: Choosing a college

During this phase, you will be deciding which college has the best academic, social, and financial fit. To make this decision, the college financial aid offices should supply the following information:

7. How much financial aid will the student receive? Will he or she be billed for his or her share of the costs? Are there any other costs not accounted for in the aid offer that the student should plan for, such as expenses for books, room and board, transportation, or personal needs?

8. If the student (or parents) cannot meet the financial responsibilities from current income or assets, what financing options are available to help them pay their share?

9. Will the financial aid office provide each student with an explanation of how his or her expected family contribution, financial need, and award package was determined?

10. If the financial aid award package is insufficient to make it possible for the student to attend this college, under what conditions, if any, will the aid office reconsider their offer?

11. What are the terms and conditions of the aid programs included in the student's award package (e.g., treatment of outside scholarships, loan repayment policies, renewal criteria, etc.)? Regarding renewal, what are the academic requirements or other conditions for the renewal of financial aid, including scholarships?

12. How will the student's aid package change from year to year? Will loan amounts increase? What impact will cost increases have on the aid package? What will happen if the student's financial situation changes? What will happen if the student's or another family member's enrollment status changes?

13. What amount of student loan debt does your typical student borrower have once he or she finishes college?

Phase 3: Before leaving home

By the end of this phase, it should be clear to you what your financial obligations are and how you will meet them. The financial aid and/or business office of your chosen college should be helpful in answering the following questions:

14. When can the student/family expect to receive bills from the college? How many times a year will they be billed? If the bill is not paid by the deadline, will there be penalties? Does the college accept payment by credit card? Is there an option to pay monthly?

15. Is all financial aid credited to the student's account, or will the student receive checks for some or all of the financial aid awarded? What about student employment earnings? If aid exceeds billed charges, how does the student receive the funds?

16. How much money will the student need during the first week of school for things such as books, a parking permit, etc.? Can the student use financial aid to pay for books and supplies? Can books and supplies be charged to the student's account? What typical out-of-pocket expenses do most students have during the year?

17. Is information provided to students regarding budgeting resources, money management, and credit card usage?

18. Are there banking services with fee-free ATMs and/or check cashing on or near campus? Does the campus have a debit card?

19. Will the college be responsive to mid-year changes in family financial situations?

20. Regarding student employment, including federal work-study: How are jobs assigned? How many hours per week will a student be expected to or allowed to work? How often and in what manner will students receive earnings payments? Will earnings be automatically credited to the student's account?

Planning pay for co ge

What ge cost?

Th provides detailed information about osts at over 2,700 colleges and universi- 03-04 academic year (AY) to help you those costs at the college you choose to

omponents of college costs

ver you enroll, your expenses include direct edu- al expenses and living expenses, and typically sist of five parts:

- tuition and fees
- room and board
- books and supplies
- personal expenses
- transportation

Tuition and fees

Tuition and fees charged by a particular college depend on many factors, but the most significant is what kind of college it is.

Tuition and fees at public institutions are generally the lowest, because they receive funds from taxes. Most four-year and two-year public colleges charge higher tuition for nonresidents than for legal residents of the state or district in which the college is located. This "out-of-state" tuition (or "out-of-district" tuition, in the case of two-year community colleges) often can make the cost of attending a public institution as high as the cost of attending many private institutions. Tuition at private colleges is usually much higher than public institutions because private colleges must charge a larger percentage of the real costs. Private institutions often have more financial aid resources that can help you make up the difference between costs and financial aid. The greater your overall expense, the greater the possibility of your demonstrating need for financial aid. Tuition at proprietary or profit-making institutions (such as many trade and technical schools) is usually set at a level to recover all of their operating costs plus a profit.

Whether you're looking at a public, private, or proprietary college, fees may be charged for services such as the library, student activities, or the health center.

The college descriptions show the tuition and fees charged to most first-time, full-time students. Part-time charges, usually set by credit or semester hour, may work out to be higher per unit. Tuition and fees for upper-division students and graduate or professional students may also vary.

Books and supplies

Every college student has to buy books, pencils, paper, and other supplies. The amount you spend for books and supplies will vary only slightly by type of institution but is generally related to the curriculum or courses you select. In some academic fields, for instance, you may have to spend a good deal more than the averages cited in Table 3 (page 33).

Room and board

Room and board means basic living expenses for food and housing. Regardless of the kind of institution you choose, you will have to consider these expenses.

In this book, if you plan to live in college-owned housing, whether on- or off-campus, you're considered an on-campus resident, and your costs differ from those who live at home with their families.

Colleges with their own housing typically charge you on a nine-month basis for room and most meals, excluding holiday and vacation periods. The room and board charge is built into your student expense budget. Colleges also expect that students living in privately owned, off-campus housing have a similar level of expense.

If you plan to live at home, you're generally assumed to have somewhat lower expenses than on-campus students because you don't have to pay for housing. However, you or your parents will still need to factor in the cost of your food and other normal living expenses.

The estimated cost of food and other expenses at home is usually built into commuter student expense budgets for financial aid purposes. Take these costs into account in your planning.

Personal expenses

No matter what kind of institution you choose, you'll have some personal expenses for things such as clothing, laundry, toiletries, recreation, medical insurance and care, and perhaps incidental furnishings for your dormitory room.

Transportation

All students spend some money for travel. If you live on or near campus, you have to travel to get there at the start of the academic year and to return home at the end. Most students also go home at least once during the year. For financial aid purposes, colleges often budget students for two round-trips home per year by the lowest-cost means of travel possible.

If you're a commuter student, you'll also have travel expenses, whether you use public transportation or a private car to get to and from college several days a week. These costs, too, are built into student expense budgets by colleges for financial aid purposes.

Total expense budget

The total expense budget for a particular college is determined by adding up these five categories of expenses. The tables and worksheets beginning on page 33 reflect sample total expenses for both on-campus and commuter students. For your own estimates, remember to consider any additional costs that might result from medical bills or other extraordinary personal expenses.

How much will you be expected to pay?

Your family is the first source of funds for education. All colleges, government agencies, and private student aid programs expect you to pay something toward college costs according to your ability. Financial aid often makes up the difference between the costs of attending college and what a family can afford to pay. Estimating your "expected family contribution" toward educational expenses is a major part of understanding financial aid—and a critical aspect of goal setting.

What does "expected family contribution" actually mean?

The expected family contribution has traditionally been considered to be a measure of your family's overall capacity to pay some portion of educational expenses. However, depending upon which application(s) your college or programs use to determine financial aid eligibility, your "expected family contribution" will mean different things.

The "expected family contribution" used to determine *federal* financial aid eligibility is calculated according to the Federal Methodology (FM), a formula established by the U.S. Congress and administered by the U.S. Department of Education. This formula takes into consideration income, assets, expenses, family size, and other factors to help evaluate a family's financial strength.

Many colleges and programs use a more comprehensive formula, referred to as the Institutional Methodology (IM), to determine student need for *non-federal* financial aid programs. This alternate guideline differs from the Federal Methodology in several respects. For instance, it takes home equity into account and includes a minimum expected contribution from students in calculating a family's ability to pay, but it also permits more generous treatment of medical/dental expenses, elementary and secondary school tuition payments, and other special circumstances. Since IM uses information on family income, assets, and expenses that is not collected on the Free Application for Federal Student Aid (FAFSA), you may find that you need to complete an additional application, such as the CSS/Financial Aid PROFILE, in order to be considered for all available forms of financial assistance.

The FM and IM "expected family contribution" results are subtracted from the total cost of college to determine *federal eligibility* and *financial need,* respectively.

Estimating your expected family contribution

Your family's "share" is the sum of what your parents can contribute and what you can contribute from your earnings, savings, and so forth:

	Parents' contribution from income
+	Parents' contribution from assets
+	Student's contribution from income
+	Student's contribution from assets
=	Expected family contribution

Table 5, Estimated parents' contribution, on page 34 will give you a sense of what is expected of parents at different income and asset levels. You can estimate what might be expected of you and your family by fully completing Worksheets 2, 3, and 4 on pages 37 and 38.

You're usually eligible for financial aid equal to the amount of your demonstrated financial need. But whether you're awarded all the financial aid for which you're eligible depends on a variety of factors, such as the availability of funds in any given year.

Evaluating a family's income and assets

A family's financial strength is evaluated based on total income for the previous calendar year. Parents' wages and all other income (such as dividends, social security, or welfare benefits) are included, but not all of this income can be used to pay for college. The largest part of annual income must be used to provide for the family's basic living expenses—housing, food, medical care, clothing, and so forth.

Financial aid administrators also take into account other demands on the parents' income, such as taxes or unusually large medical or dental bills. Even the costs of working—clothing, transportation, meals away from home, and so forth—are taken into consideration.

After all these expenses are taken into account, the amount remaining for other uses is considerably smaller than the family's original income. This remaining amount is called "available income." A family is expected to use some of this remaining income to help pay college costs.

Also considered are family assets—the value of a business or farm, cash, savings and checking accounts, stocks and bonds, and so forth. At lower income levels, assets are not considered in determining federal eligibility, and home equity is not a factor in the Federal Methodology.

A family can't be expected to spend all its income on education, nor is it expected to use all its assets to pay for college. The financial aid formulas "protect" a portion of parents' assets for their use in retirement. The amount parents can protect increases as the age of the primary wage earner increases because an older worker has fewer years than a younger person to save for retirement. The system also "protects" a substantial portion of family assets tied up in a business or farm, since those are also sources of income.

Even when the various allowances are subtracted, a family isn't expected to convert all its remaining assets into cash for college—only a portion called "income supplement from assets."

Available income (the discretionary part of a family's annual income) is added to the income supplement from assets to get a dollar amount called "adjusted available income." If more than one family member is in college at the same time, the amount parents are expected to pay is divided by the number of students to determine the expected contribution per student. This means that a family may not be eligible for aid when the first child goes to college but becomes eligible later when a younger brother or sister starts college while the older one is still a student.

Evaluating a student's ability to pay

You are usually expected to contribute toward your college expenses, too, from savings and summer earnings. While *federal* student aid rules don't set a minimum contribution from students, many colleges expect a freshman to contribute at least $1,150 a year from summer job earnings when it comes to awarding their own private funds. Upper-division students are often expected to contribute even more from summer and part-time jobs—upward of $1,400 a year at many colleges, and more than that at some.

Special note on independent (self-supporting) students

If you are truly financially independent of your parents, you are called an "independent," or "self-supporting," student. Your ability as a self-supporting student to contribute toward college costs is evaluated on the basis of your own income, assets, and expenses. You may have extra expenses, such as child care, which may be considered in the student expense budget developed by a college for self-supporting financial aid applicants.

Who is considered self-supporting and who is not? According to federal criteria, you are automatically considered to be independent if you are:

- at least 24 years old by December 31 of the award year (e.g., by December 31, 2003, for the 2003–2004 award year)
- a veteran of the United States Armed Forces, regardless of age
- an orphan or a ward of the court
- have legal dependents of your own other than a spouse
- married
- studying for a graduate or professional degree

Financial aid administrators can make exceptions for students who do not meet these criteria but are nonetheless self-supporting. Contact the financial aid offices at the colleges you're considering if you need more information about dependency status.

Even if you meet the federal criteria for independent student status, however, you may have to submit parents' financial data as part of the aid application process at some colleges. Some colleges may also ask you to provide additional documentation of your income and expenses if you claim self-supporting status. Some private sponsors may use different definitions than the federal government for determining self-supporting status.

Special circumstances

Colleges try to take into account the unique circumstances of each applicant, for example, a family with a handicapped child who requires special medical care or education. The formulas also take into account higher costs of living in certain residential areas. In the section on applying for financial aid there's advice on how to make sure that the colleges you are considering fully understand your situation. Whether they'll be able to give you extra help depends on a variety of factors, one of the most important being how much money they have available to help students in any given year.

How to make time work for you

Keep in mind that you aren't necessarily expected to pay college costs out of your current earnings alone. No matter how large your expected family contribution may seem to you, it can be made smaller if you break it into monthly amounts.

Financing the parents' contribution

If you started early enough, you may have saved your entire share, or more, by now. One of the advantages of starting early is that you *earn* interest toward your goal. If you started late, you may have to borrow. The downside is that you are *paying* interest, not earning it. If your family is like many others, you probably will use a combination of saving and borrowing, and perhaps "leverage" your money by borrowing against your own savings. The toughest way to cover your share of educational expenses is to force them into your current household budget.

At any point on the income level chart in Table 1, you can see that the expected parents' share requires a pretty large percentage of income—if you're trying to cover it all out of current income. At the $60,000 annual income level, for example, the expected parents' contribution would require 9 percent of gross income, and a whopping 12 percent of after-tax income. As Table 2 demonstrates, that translates into a pretty big chunk of the monthly household budget.

Spreading the expense out over time has a much smaller impact on your monthly budget. This is true whether you save, borrow, or both.

Table 1. Relationship of Family Income to Parent Contribution (2003–2004 Federal Methodology)

Annual family income	*Net income (after tax)*	*Parents' contribution (annual)*	*Percentage of total*	*Percentage of net*
$10,000	$8,435	$0	0.0%	0.0%
15,000	12,653	0	0.0	0.0
20,000	16,855	0	0.0	0.0
25,000	20,573	0	0.0	0.0
30,000	24,290	128	0.4	0.5
35,000	27,850	911	2.6	3.3
40,000	31,317	1,674	4.2	5.3
45,000	34,785	2,436	5.4	7.0
50,000	38,252	3,276	6.6	8.6
55,000	41,720	4,259	7.7	10.2
60,000	45,187	5,445	9.1	12.1
65,000	48,655	6,877	10.6	14.1
70,000	51,708	8,312	11.9	16.1
75,000	54,576	9,660	12.9	17.7
80,000	57,443	11,008	13.8	19.2
85,000	59,086	12,358	14.5	20.9
90,000	62,263	13,852	15.4	22.3
95,000	65,441	15,345	16.2	23.5
100,000	68,618	16,838	16.8	24.5

Note: Estimated parents' contributions in Tables 1 and 2 assume four family members; one in college; one parent is employed; income only from employment; no unusual circumstances; standard deductions on U.S. income tax; asset neutrality (assets equal to total asset protection allowance). Values are approximate.

Table 2. Parents' contribution related to monthly net income (2003–2004 Federal Methodology)

Annual family income	*Annual net income (after taxes)*	*Parents' contribution (annual)*	*Monthly net income (after taxes)*	*Monthly net required to pay parents' contribution*
$ 10,000	$8,435	$0	$703	$0
15,000	12,653	0	1,054	0
20,000	16,855	0	1,405	0
25,000	20,573	0	1,714	0
30,000	24,290	128	2,024	11
35,000	27,850	911	2,321	76
40,000	31,317	1,674	2,610	139
45,000	34,785	2,436	2,899	203
50,000	38,252	3,276	3,188	273
55,000	41,720	4,259	3,477	355
60,000	45,187	5,445	3,766	454
65,000	48,655	6,877	4,055	573
70,000	51,708	8,312	4,309	693
75,000	54,576	9,660	4,548	805
80,000	57,443	11,008	4,787	917
85,000	59,086	12,358	4,924	1,030
90,000	62,263	13,852	5,189	1,154
95,000	65,441	15,345	5,453	1,279
100,000	68,618	16,838	5,718	1,403

Look again at the $60,000 annual income band in Tables 1 and 2. Paying the parents' contribution entirely from current income would mean cutting other expenses by $454 a month. Some families may be able to accommodate this change in their budget and many institutions provide a monthly payment plan option to accommodate them. However, other families would find it difficult to reduce their expenses so dramatically, and need to find other ways to fund their contribution. Generally this means drawing on accumulated **savings** or **borrowing** the funds needed to pay educational costs.

Research shows that families that have been able to save even a small monthly amount for college expenses are better able to manage the expense when the time comes for the child to start school. One of the myths about college planning is that accumulated savings will significantly increase the expected family contribution. This is generally not true: the need analysis systems place far more weight on current income then on accumulated savings or assets. Families that save for education have more flexibility about how to manage the expense when the time comes.

If a family with a $60,000 income also had just $10,000 in accumulated savings at the time their child started college, they could supplement their monthly cash flow so that the tuition payments were more comfortable. By drawing down just $2,500 dollars annually from their accumulated savings this family could reduce the monthly amount needed from their current monthly budget to just $250. For many families, this scenario would prove to be far more comfortable than one in which they had to pay the total contribution from current income.

In order to reach the $10,000 savings goal, a family could have saved just $20 each week, earning 6 percent interest if they started when their college-bound child turned 10 years of age. If this same family had started saving at the same rate when their child was born ($20 weekly at 6 percent) they would have accrued over $30,000 in savings: an amount equal to more than two years of costs at the average public four-year institution ($12,841 per year.) More information about savings options can be found at the College Board Web site, www.collegeboard.com/paying. The interactive savings calculators found there provide a valuable tool for helping families estimate how much to save to reach their long-term goals.

If a family has limited savings and does not want to pay their contribution from current income, financing remains a viable option. Today's low interest rates on education loans provide the opportunity for families to comfortably borrow all or a portion of their education expenses. As with the example above, an education loan can reduce the short-term out-of-pocket costs. For instance, a family with an expected family contribution of $5,445 could borrow the entire amount and incur a monthly payment of about $56 for 10 years. Of course, in this scenario the total repayment amount would be $6,808—a substantial increase over the $5,445 expected family contribution. If the family chooses to finance their contribution for four years the monthly expense will quadruple. But for some families, borrowing provides a reasonable payment option because it lowers monthly costs and puts educational opportunity within reach. More information about loan options can be found on page 15 or at www.collegeboard.com/paying.

Making the most of available resources

Are you concerned that your family can't come up with enough cash to cover your expected contribution? What if a college can't give you any aid or enough to meet your full need? What if you decide to attend college late in the year and financial aid has run out by the time you apply for admission?

This section reviews some of the strategies and options that students and families can use to meet their share of college costs, including recent income tax provisions to help families cover college costs. Several commercial and not-for-profit organizations' programs are described to illustrate the wide and growing array of options available to families in meeting college costs, but this doesn't imply any endorsement whatsoever. This section also describes some of the ways that colleges are trying to help families finance educational expenses.

Education tax benefits

The credits described below are among recent changes in the tax laws that are designed to make a college education more affordable for middle-income families. You'll find eligibility guidelines explained in U.S. Internal Revenue Service (IRS) tax form instructions: IRS Publication 970 (Tax Benefits for Higher Education) and Publication 520 (Scholarships and Fellowships) available from the IRS Web site (www.irs.gov). The following information will give you a general overview.

The Hope Education Tax Credit

Eligible taxpayers can claim the Hope Education tax credit based on the following guidelines:

- The income tax credit is for tuition and fees during the first two years of undergraduate study. The student must have a high school diploma or its equivalent, be enrolled in a degree program, and attend college at least half-time for one academic period.
- This credit may be claimed for more than one student in a family if several are college undergraduates at the same time. The maximum yearly credit per student is $1,500.

Lifetime Learning Tax Credit

Eligible taxpayers can claim the Lifetime Learning tax credit based on the following guidelines:

- An income tax credit of 20 percent may be claimed for expenses incurred for tuition and fees only for the student, a spouse, and dependents. The credit is not applicable for the cost of books or room and board.
- The maximum yearly credit per family is $2,000.

This credit covers a broad range of schooling. The student may:

- Be enrolled full-time, half-time, or less than half-time.
- Take undergraduate or graduate courses.
- Take a training program to acquire or improve job skills.

The following guidelines apply to both the Hope Education Tax Credit and the Lifetime Learning Tax Credit:

- Those credits may be claimed for tuition and fees only, for the student, a spouse, and dependents. They can't be claimed for the cost of books or room and board.
- The credits are taken in the year the expenses are paid and study either begins that year, continues in that year, or in the first three months of the following year. Expenses paid with a loan are eligible, even if the loan is still outstanding.
- The credits are available to taxpayers whose income is under $100,000 if filing a joint return, or $50,000

if filing a single return. The amount of the credit is gradually reduced for those with an income of $80,000 to $100,000 on a joint return, and $40,000 to $50,000 on a single return.

- Before calculating either credit, the taxpayer must deduct any scholarships and other tax-free financial aid, including Pell Grants and employer-provided educational assistance.
- Either credit may be claimed in the same year the student pays for other qualified education expenses (books, equipment, room and board) using a tax-free withdrawal from a Coverdell ESA (see below).
- A student convicted of a felony for possession or distribution of a controlled substance is not eligible for either credit.

Education Savings Accounts and higher education expenses

Recent changes in the tax laws provide for early withdrawal of funds from existing IRAs and establishing a new Education Savings Account (ESA). Here are the guidelines:

Early withdrawal from existing IRAs

- Taxpayers may withdraw funds from an IRA and the new Roth IRA to cover qualified higher education expenses without incurring a 10 percent penalty charge, but are liable for any regular income taxes due on the amount withdrawn.
- Qualified expenses include tuition, fees, room and board, books, supplies, and equipment required for enrollment in, or attendance at, an undergraduate or graduate school.

Coverdell Education Savings Account (ESA) [formerly known as the Education IRA]

- This is a custodial account intended to help pay the education expenses of a child beneficiary. The maximum annual contribution is $2,000 per child within income guidelines.
- It is available to anyone who wants to contribute toward a child's postsecondary education.
- To be eligible for the maximum annual contribution, taxpayers filing a joint return must have income of under $190,000 or, if filing a single return, income under $95,000. Taxpayers with income above $220,000 for a joint return, and $110,000 for a single return, cannot contribute to anyone's Coverdell ESA.
- An individual or family may contribute to both a Coverdell ESA and a state sponsored "Section 529" college savings plan (see below).
- Contributions to a Coverdell ESA are not tax deductible; must be in cash; must end when the beneficiary reaches age 18.
- The maximum annual aggregate contributions to all ESA accounts for a particular child beneficiary is $2,000.
- Anyone, including a parent, grandparent, friend, or the beneficiary, may contribute to a Coverdell ESA.
- Withdrawals are tax-free if used for qualified higher education expenses.
- The beneficiary may be enrolled full-time, half-time, or less than half-time at a college, university, or other postsecondary school. (The funds may also be used for elementary or secondary school.)
- Funds must be used or transferred to another family member's Coverdell ESA by the time the beneficiary reaches age 30.

411 on 529s

Provisions of the Taxpayer Relief Act of 1997 and subsequent federal tax relief legislation provided the impetus for states to sponsor college savings and investment plans to help families plan and pay for education beyond high school. Frequently referred to as "**Section 529 plans**" (referring to the section of the Internal Revenue Service tax code that describes the plans), these Qualified State Tuition Programs (QSTPs) provide families with tax-advantaged opportunities to save for college. While investment policies and performance vary from state to state, the 529 plans share many characteristics:

- *Anyone*—parents, grandparents, uncles, aunts, friends—can establish a 529 account for *anyone*. An account owner can designate a beneficiary of the 529 plan without regard to relationship or residency.
- Tax-advantaged 529 plans can be opened with an initial deposit of as little as $25 and contributions can total as much as $100,000 or more.

- Accounts can be opened *anytime*; as with any saving strategy, earlier is better, but a 529 plan must be open for at least 36 months before funds can be withdrawn for qualified higher education expenses.
- Earnings and accumulations in the account grow tax-free and recent tax law provisions also make withdrawals to pay for college exempt from federal tax.
- Money in the account can be used to pay for qualified education expenses, including tuition and fees, room and board, books, supplies, and equipment required for enrollment at undergraduate, graduate, or professional institutions of higher education.
- Withdrawals from a 529 plan can be used at eligible schools and colleges anywhere, not only in the account owner's or beneficiary's state of residence.
- Funds in a 529 account can be transferred to another family member if the beneficiary for whom the account was established decides not to go to college.
- Account balances can be transferred from a 529 plan in one state to a 529 plan in another state for the same beneficiary; this tax-free "roll over" provision adds to the flexibility of Section 529 plans.

As noted above, policies and performance vary from state to state so account policies and rate of return on investment may also vary from state to state. Most states rely upon established money-management firms to operate and administer their 529 plans so application, maintenance, management, or transaction fees may apply to a given account. Many states also offer their own tax breaks in addition to the federal tax benefits. To learn more about the availability and operation of Section 529 plans in your state, the College Savings Plan Network (www.collegesavings.org) provides information and an opportunity to compare your state-sponsored plan with others across the country.

Exploring immediate options

Federal PLUS Loan

Currently, parents may borrow up to the total cost of education minus any student aid awarded, per child. The interest rate on a Federal PLUS Loan is variable and monthly repayment begins within 60 days of disbursement, although some lenders may let borrowers make interest-only payments while the student is enrolled in college. This type of loan isn't based on financial need, but borrowers must demonstrate that they are creditworthy.

Because repayment generally must begin within 60 days, Federal PLUS Loans are primarily a help in meeting the cash-flow problems caused by college bills. Some parents borrow under the program to meet all or part of the expected parental contribution, while others borrow to make up the difference between costs and their contribution plus available financial aid.

This type of loan is widely available through programs like CollegeCredit®, sponsored by the College Board, as well as many banks, credit unions, and savings and loan associations.

Privately sponsored supplemental loans

Many organizations, banks, and credit unions sponsor special education loan programs that have more favorable interest rates and/or special features that make the loans more attractive than other consumer borrowing options. Eligibility generally relates more to demonstrated creditworthiness than financial need, and parents rather than students are usually the borrowers (although creditworthy students may be eligible as well).

For example, the College Board sponsors two private supplemental loans as part of its CollegeCredit program, in partnership with Sallie Mae. The Student Signature Education loan offers low interest rates, deferred repayment while in school, and a ¼ percentage point interest rate reduction for repaying electronically through Sallie Mae's Direct Repay™ Plan. Borrowers have up to 25 years to repay and can borrow up to $25,000. For more information call 800 695-3317. The CollegeCredit Private Parent Loan allows parents to borrow up to the full cost of their child's education with up to 15 years to repay, and the loan also covers students who are enrolled part-time or in non-degree programs. For information call 800 831-5626.

A few private supplemental loan programs let students and parents borrow jointly. For instance, under the MEFA loan, sponsored by the Massachusetts Educational Financing Authority, parents and students from any state may jointly borrow up to 100 percent of the costs of attendance minus any financial aid at 63 participating Massachusetts colleges and universities. Two options are available: a fixed-interest-rate plan and a variable-interest-rate plan. Both have repayment terms of 15 years. Borrowers who secure their loans with a home mortgage may be able to take advantage of the tax deductibility of interest payments. (For information about the MEFA loan, call 800 449-6332.)

Combination savings/loan plans

A participating bank will "leverage," or multiply, a customer's balance to give a family a line of credit for meeting college costs that is, in effect, a long-term loan. The interest on savings substantially offsets the interest on the loan.

Terms and conditions of these and similar programs can vary considerably from sponsor to sponsor, so you should shop around and find out about the availability of programs at banks in your community.

College-sponsored financing programs

Many colleges offer a tuition budgeting plan that lets families spread out their payments over a longer period of time. Because of the interest, insurance, and service fees involved in such programs, you'll typically end up spending more money than if the charges had been paid outright. Information about the options available at a particular college usually are published in its catalog or financial aid bulletin.

Some insurance companies offer tuition budgeting programs. Insurance features on plans like these generally guarantee that the tuition will continue to be paid in the event of a parent's death or total disability.

In evaluating these approaches to stretching your resources, get all the facts before you sign any contracts, promissory notes, or loan agreements. Look at both what you pay and what you get back to ensure that you are getting the best possible deal.

Not every college and university has financing plans or tuition installment plans. Some public colleges, for instance, are prohibited by state law from extending credit to anyone. However, they may be able to direct you to commercial budgeting or installment plans offered by outside companies.

Guaranteed or stabilized tuition plans

You can expect increases in tuition charges at least once, and probably annually, while you're in college. A few colleges guarantee their tuition for four years at the time of enrollment, at no obligation to the student. Under other plans, families can prepay tuition for four years in one lump sum and avoid subsequent tuition increases.

For families who don't have enough disposable income to pay the entire sum at once, some colleges offer a borrowing option that lets you pay in monthly installments over a period of years.

Strategies for cutting costs

Another approach to making a college education affordable is to reduce the overall costs. Each college description in this book lists the cost-reducing policies available at that college. They include:

Reducing the time involved in earning a degree

By reducing the length of time you spend earning a degree, you can reduce the overall costs. There are several ways you can do this. For instance, many colleges award advanced placement and/or academic credit to students who earn qualifying grades on Advanced Placement Program® (AP®) Exams or College-Level Examination Program® (CLEP®) exams sponsored by the College Board. When you earn credit by examination, you can reduce the number of courses you have to take in college, which reduces your overall costs. The college descriptions in this book include information about each college's credit-by-examination policy.

Some colleges also grant placement and/or credit to students who can demonstrate proficiency because of prior independent study and "life experience." College requirements for documenting prior learning tend to be rigorous, but if you can meet them, you can reduce both your time and your financial investment.

Some students also compress the number of years spent in college by taking more courses than the average student and/or going to summer school. Completing a bachelor's degree in less than four years is possible if you're highly motivated. Check with colleges you're considering to find out if they have an accelerated program, since some colleges have policies limiting the number of credits a student can carry per semester.

Reducing indirect costs

Living at home instead of on campus has helped many students reduce their overall costs. You might decide to commute from home to college for the entire course of your studies. Or you might consider alternating between living on campus and living at home. Another possibility is going to a less expensive community college for the first two years and then transferring to a higher cost public or private four-year college to complete your degree.

Buying secondhand textbooks is another way to reduce your expenses. So is opting for a less-expensive meal plan if the college offers more than one, or shopping at a food co-op if you decide to live in private, off-campus housing. If you have dependents of your own, find out if the colleges you're considering offer low-cost, on-campus day care. Colleges recognize that you need recreational activities, too, and many provide free or low-cost entertainment programs to help you have fun even if you're living on a tight budget.

Strategies for working your way through college

Some students earn enough money through part-time employment to meet their costs. Many work part-time while enrolled full-time, without interfering with their studies. The Federal Work-Study Program provides employment opportunities for many students with demonstrated financial need.

Some colleges have instituted special programs to help students find part-time employment. Check with the financial aid and student employment offices at the colleges you're considering. You might be able to tailor some of your precollege courses or summer job experiences to improve your chances in the job market once you're enrolled.

Cooperative education

Some students choose to alternate periods of full-time work and full-time study. A number of colleges have even formalized such arrangements through cooperative education programs. In addition to helping you finance your studies, cooperative education programs give you a chance to develop job skills and experience that are valuable after graduation. About 1,000 colleges and universities offer some form of cooperative education.

Deferred enrollment

Another possibility is working for a year or two after high school to earn money before starting college. Some colleges have formalized this, too, in a policy called "deferred enrollment." You apply while in high school and are accepted, but don't actually start going to college until the following year. You might keep this in mind as a question to ask about the various colleges you investigate.

Employee fringe benefits

Still another option is working full-time and attending college part-time at your employer's expense. Many employers offer educational opportunities as fringe benefits. In some cases, you're reimbursed, in whole or in part, for successfully completed course work; other programs pay tuition expenses up front. Keep in mind, too, that some unreimbursed educational expenses may be tax deductible.

How financial aid can help

Financial aid is help for meeting the costs of tuition, fees, room and board, books, personal expenses, and transportation. Even colleges with comparatively low tuition, such as community colleges, give qualified students some help in covering costs.

Who gets financial aid?

Most financial aid today is awarded on the basis of need. Sometimes your academic performance and other factors are considered in addition to demonstrated need. Students are usually eligible for aid equal to the amount of their demonstrated financial need.

Since the amount a family can afford to pay stays the same whether the costs are high or low, you can see that your need or eligibility will be different at different colleges. In fact, if you get all the financial aid for which you are eligible, you could end up paying the same amount at a high-cost college as you would at a low-cost one.

That's a pretty big "if." In academic year 2001-02, millions of students shared an estimated $89.6 billion in various forms of student aid and education tax credits. Large as that amount seems, it still was not enough to meet the full need of all the students who could have used some help. And remember, financial aid doesn't just happen to you. You have to take an active part in the process.

Types of financial aid

- **Grants and scholarships.** Grants and scholarships are sometimes called gift aid, because you do not have to repay them or work to earn them. Grants are usually awarded on the basis of need alone, while scholarship recipients may have to meet criteria other than, or in addition to, need (academic achievement, for example).
- **Educational loans.** A form of self-help aid, educational loans are usually subsidized by the state or federal government or by colleges themselves and carry lower interest rates than commercial loans. They have to be repaid, generally after you have graduated or left college.
- Student employment or work aid. The Federal Work-Study Program is perhaps the best known example of this kind of financial aid. Students work, usually 10 to 15 hours a week, to "earn" their aid.

Financial aid comes from a variety of sources:

- Federal government
- State governments
- Colleges
- Private organizations

Most students with need get a combination of grants, loans, and work-study aids. This is called a financial aid package, determined by the financial aid administrator at the college to which you apply.

Eligibility for student financial aid

To be eligible for many programs, you are required to attend at least half-time (usually six semester hours of courses per semester or the equivalent). Students attending less than half-time may be eligible for some federal funds, but other programs often require full-time enrollment, usually at least 12 hours per semester.

You must be enrolled in an eligible program at an eligible institution. More than 9,500 institutions, including colleges, universities, and vocational and technical schools, are considered eligible for some federal aid programs. Many state aid programs are limited to accredited colleges and universities. Some programs have restrictions on aid to students in certain fields of study (for example, religious studies) or in vocational or technical courses (those that are shorter than six months in duration). Most programs require that you:

- Maintain satisfactory academic progress toward a degree or certification.
- Be in good standing with the institution you attend.

Federal programs require that you be either a United States citizen or a noncitizen who is a permanent resident. Refugees or persons granted political asylum may be eligible, too. State programs are usually restricted to legal residents of their particular state, although there are exceptions, especially in loan programs. College-sponsored and private programs usually require that you be a United States citizen, too, except for a few programs designed for international students.

Financial aid from the federal government

The federal government is the largest single source of support, providing over $62 billion—or nearly 70 percent of all available financial aid dollars—in academic year 2001-02 (see Figure 1). Despite real growth over the past decade, federal funding of student aid programs hasn't kept pace with college costs. There are many reasons why, but the net result is that federal funds—and indeed, all student aid funds—are being stretched further and further to meet growing needs.

Federal Pell Grant Program

This is the largest need-based student aid program. Over 4.3 million undergraduates received Pell Grants for the 2001-02 academic year. The amount students receive depends on need, the costs at the particular college they attend, the length of the program in which they're enrolled, and whether enrollment is full or part time. Graduate students aren't eligible, nor are students who have previously received a bachelor's degree. The maximum Pell Grant for 2003-04 is estimated to be $4,050.

Federal Supplemental Educational Opportunity Grant Program (FSEOG)

This is one of three federal campus-based programs, meaning that while the money comes from the federal government, it is distributed by accredited colleges and universities to students with demonstrated need. Recipients must be United States citizens enrolled at least half-time in an undergraduate program.

Figure 1. Estimated student aid by source for academic year 2001–2002 (current dollars in billions)

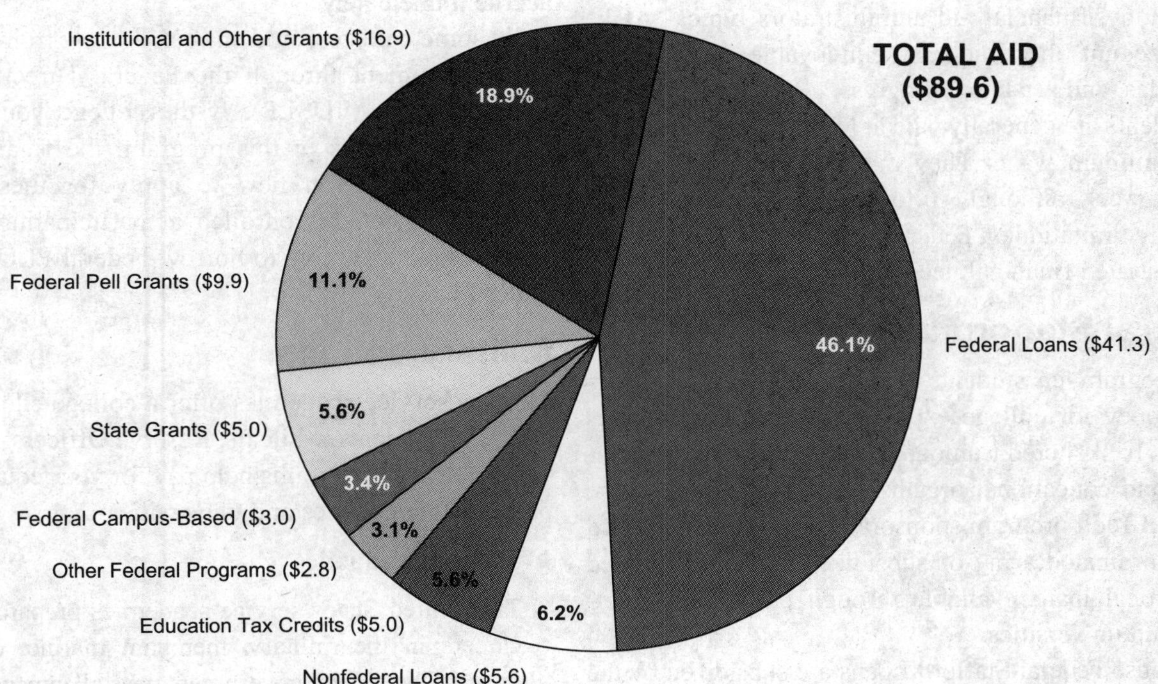

Note: "Federal Loans" include Federal Family Education Loans and Ford Direct Student Loans. "Other Federal Programs" include SSIG, Military, Other Grants, and Other Loans.

Federal Perkins Loan Program

This is another federal campus-based program administered by colleges and universities. Undergraduate and graduate students enrolled at least half-time are eligible for Perkins Loans. These carry the lowest interest rate of any educational loans and repayment is deferred until a student graduates or leaves school. Nine months after completing or leaving college, regular repayments are required over a maximum period of 10 years until the total amount (including interest) is repaid.

Repayment can sometimes be further deferred for up to three years for service in the military, the Peace Corps, or approved comparable organizations, or if study is resumed on at least a half-time basis. A student who wants to have repayment of a Federal Perkins Loan deferred for any reason must complete and submit a request form to the college from which the loan was originally borrowed. Perkins Loans are canceled outright if a student dies or is totally disabled.

Federal Work-Study Program (FWS)

This is also a federal campus-based program for students with demonstrated need who are enrolled at least half-time at either the undergraduate or graduate level. Students are employed on- or off-campus. In assigning work-study, financial aid administrators typically take into account the students' employable skills, class schedules, and academic progress.

Students are generally paid at least the prevailing federal minimum wage. They may work as many as 40 hours a week, although 10 to 15 hours is more typical. The only limitation on Federal Work-Study is a student's demonstrated financial need.

Federal Stafford Loan Program

This program lets students with demonstrated need borrow money for college expenses from private sources such as banks, credit unions, savings and loan associations, and educational organizations. For example, the CollegeCredit program sponsored by the College Board is a coordinated array of subsidized and unsubsidized educational loans available through participating colleges and universities.

Because Federal Stafford Loans are subsidized by the government, the interest rate is lower than most commercially available loans (but higher than Perkins Loans). The government pays the interest while you're enrolled—another big advantage. The interest rate is variable and repayment of both interest and principal is deferred until six months after you graduate or leave college.

Stafford Loans are insured against the student's death or total disability, but there are no provisions for cancellation of any part of a loan for other reasons. Under certain circumstances (such as full-time study or service in the military or Peace Corps), repayment can be deferred temporarily. The schedule for repayment is worked out between the student and the lender; the borrower usually has between 5 and 10 years to repay, with the amount of monthly payments and the length of the repayment period depending on the total amount borrowed.

The unsubsidized Federal Stafford Loan Program is another resource for students—intended for use by those who don't qualify for a Federal Stafford Loan and/or who need additional funds. The amounts, interest rates, and terms are generally the same as for subsidized Federal Stafford Student Loans, with a couple of important differences. For example, repayment begins when the loan is disbursed instead of when the student graduates or leaves college; the borrower may opt to postpone payments until leaving school, but interest begins to accrue immediately.

At some colleges, students can borrow from the federal government through the Federal Direct Student Loan Program (FDSLP). If the college you plan to attend participates in this program, the financial aid office will tell you how to apply for these loans. (Parents of students enrolled at participating institutions will also be able to borrow Federal PLUS Loans under FDSLP.)

Military options

Military service academies offer a college education at no cost to students, while the Reserve Officers' Training Corps (ROTC) programs help pay for your education at participating colleges and universities.

- **Service academies**

  The United States service academies prepare you for careers in the military, merchant marine, or Coast Guard. The federal government pays all expenses associated with attending a U.S. service academy and provides a monthly stipend for incidental expenses as well. Appointments to the academies (with the exception of the Coast Guard) are made through nominations from members of Congress. If you are interested, contact your senator or congressional representative early in the spring of your junior year in high school. Appointments to the Coast Guard Academy are based on national competition for admission. For information, write to one of the following:

Director of Admission
United States Air Force Academy
HQ USAFA
Colorado Springs, Colorado 80840-5025

Director of Admission
Building 606
United States Military Academy
West Point, New York 10996

Candidate Guidance Office
United States Naval Academy
117 Decatur Road
Annapolis, Maryland 21402-5018

Director of Admission
United States Merchant Marine Academy
300 Steamboat Road
Kings Point, New York 11024

Director of Admission
United States Coast Guard Academy
31 Mohegan Avenue
New London, Connecticut 06320-8103

- **Reserve Officers' Training Corps (ROTC)**

  Graduating seniors may apply for competitive four-year ROTC scholarships, which typically cover the costs of tuition, fees, and books, and provide a monthly stipend. To qualify, you have to meet certain physical and academic requirements and agree to accept an appointment as a commissioned officer in the military after graduation. (A minimum of four years' active and two years' reserve duty is required.) Some ROTC in-college scholarships are also available for students who decide to join as sophomores or even juniors, as well as for students who originally joined ROTC units as nonscholarship students. The requirements and obligations may vary.

There are different procedures, requirements, and benefits associated with each of the three military services offering ROTC programs. In addition to ROTC programs, there are other special programs that provide financial aid for education to students who promise to fulfill a term of military service after graduation. In those programs, officer training occurs during summer vacations or after college.

Financial aid from state governments

Every state has a scholarship or grant program that provides some form of financial aid to eligible students who are legal residents of the state. Eligibility criteria vary from state to state. Most programs require that students attend a postsecondary institution within the state. For information, check with your high school counselor or contact your state's office of higher education.

Financial aid from colleges

Another important resource is financial aid provided by colleges and universities themselves. College-sponsored aid usually comes from one of two sources: tuition revenues and contributions from private donors.

Some scholarships and grants-in-aid are based on demonstrated need, while others are awarded to students who meet criteria other than or in addition to need (such as academic performance, special achievements, etc.). The criteria and application procedures for college financial aid vary considerably, as you can see from the college descriptions in this book. For more detailed information consult the catalogs or Web sites of colleges you're considering. Private colleges often have more college-sponsored aid available than do public institutions; proprietary or profit-making institutions generally have very little or none at all.

Financial aid from private sources

While the total funds available through private student aid programs are comparatively small, they can be a significant help. For some students, they can mean the difference between going to the college you like best and the college you can afford. So it's well worth investigating the privately funded awards for which you may be eligible.

Among the thousands of private student aid programs that award grants, scholarships, and low-interest loans to help students pay for college or training after high school, one of the best known is the National Merit Scholarship Program. High school juniors enter the competition for these awards by taking the Preliminary SAT/National Merit Scholarship Qualifying Test (PSAT/NMSQT®), which is administered each October at more than 20,000 high schools around the country.

Eligibility criteria, application procedures, number of awards given annually, and average amounts awarded by private programs vary tremendously. Some base awards on financial need, others on need plus additional criteria, and still others don't consider need at all. You might qualify because of your:

- academic achievement
- religious affiliation
- ethnic or racial heritage
- community activities
- talents
- leadership potential
- athletic ability
- career plans
- proposed field of study
- hobbies and special interests
- parents' employers or union membership
- parents' membership in a civic or fraternal group

Since virtually everyone can meet one of these general criteria, it's important to have a realistic perspective on the subject. Stories appear in the press frequently about the "millions of scholarship dollars that go begging every year." Strictly speaking, that may be true, but it doesn't mean that you will necessarily get any.

Many of the scholarships have very detailed and restrictive eligibility requirements—you might, for instance, have to live in a certain state or region, attend a particular college, pursue a particular course of study, meet certain high academic standards, and demonstrate financial need. If you do not meet them all, you won't qualify. Nevertheless, it makes good sense to investigate all possible sources of funds for which you might be eligible. A good starting point is *The College Board Scholarship Handbook*. The book includes information about over 2,100 scholarship, internship, and loan programs for undergraduate study, representing over two million awards. The programs are indexed by general eligibility categories for easy reference. Use the *Real Stuff* CD-ROM to link to the scholarship search on **collegeboard.com**, where you can do quick, targeted searches to zero in on the programs for which you meet eligibility requirements. Realize, though, that there is no guarantee you'll receive a scholarship because the number of qualified applicants often exceeds the amount of money available.

Searching the Internet for scholarships

The Internet is another good source of financial aid information. Be sure to visit the College Board's Web site, **www.collegeboard.com**, where you'll be able to do free scholarship searches, estimate your expected family contribution, register for the CSS/Financial Aid PROFILE, and get lots of sound advice on planning for college.

If you're considering using the services of a commercial scholarship search company, the Student Advisory Committee of the College Scholarship Service® developed this advice about questions to ask when evaluating a service:

- If the company suggests that large amounts of aid currently are not being used, how does it document the statement?
- How many financial aid sources are in the company's database? Does the company maintain its own file of sources, or does it use another company's database?
- What kinds of financial aid sources are provided by the company? Do they include scholarships, work, internships, loans, contests? Do they include federal and state programs for which you'll be considered through the regular financial aid application process?
- How often does the company update its list of aid sources to determine that each of the sources still exists, and that application deadlines and eligibility criteria are current?
- Can you apply directly to the aid sources provided by the company, or must you be recommended for

consideration by some other person or group? Are there application fees for the sources provided?

- How long will you have to wait for the information? Do they guarantee that you'll receive the list of aid sources prior to application deadlines?
- What characteristics are used to match you with aid sources?
- How successful have previous participants been in obtaining funds from aid sources identified by the company?
- Will the company refund the fee if aid sources are incorrectly matched with your qualifications, if aid sources no longer exist or fail to reply to you, or if application deadlines have already passed when the information is received?

Keep in mind that, if you're awarded a scholarship from a private source, the financial aid package offered by your college may be reduced by the amount of the outside scholarship. That will depend primarily on whether the college has already met your financial need (based on their need analysis). If the college has not been able to cover your full financial need, an outside scholarship may not affect the institution's aid award. Policies differ from one institution to another so it's best to consult the financial aid officer at the college you plan to attend.

Applying for financial aid

The process of applying for financial aid can be confusing and time-consuming, especially if you're doing it for the first time. (Yes, you have to reapply for aid every year, but it really does seem a lot simpler the second time around.) Application requirements differ from college to college (and program to program), but the good news is that you don't really have to file separate applications for each and every one.

To improve your chances of getting the aid you need, you have to know three things:

- What you have to do
- When you have to do it
- How to do it right—the first time

What you have to do

All applicants for federal student aid, including Federal Stafford Loans, *must* complete the Free Application for Federal Student Aid (FAFSA). The FAFSA is available from high school guidance offices and college financial aid offices, generally in the late fall. Depending on where you are applying for admission, this may be the only form you need to complete. Detailed information on how to complete each question on the FAFSA is available on the Web: www.studentaid.ed.gov/completefafsa.

Your high school counselor can probably tell you what form you need to complete to apply for state scholarship or grant programs. In some states, your FAFSA information is enough to establish your eligibility; in other states, a separate form may be required.

The FAFSA may also be sufficient to apply for aid at many colleges and universities. However, many other colleges and most private scholarship programs require the completion of *additional* forms. Check with each college and private scholarship program from which you are looking for assistance.

For purposes of awarding their own private funds, many colleges and universities require the CSS/Financial Aid PROFILE. If a college you are considering advises you to complete the PROFILE process, ask your guidance counselor or the financial aid office for information about how to register for a complete PROFILE application. *Note: You can complete both the FAFSA and PROFILE forms electronically if you have access to the Internet.*

Note that PROFILE is not the same as a federal form and may not be used to establish eligibility for federal student aid programs. If you want to apply for federal student aid, you must complete a FAFSA.

Some colleges, universities, and private scholarship programs may ask you to complete their own financial aid application in order to be considered for private funds. If a college wants you to complete its application, it will send you the form directly. Private programs sometimes have other requirements as well, such as personal essays or biographical statements.

If you aren't sure what forms a particular college wants you to complete, don't guess. Contact the financial aid office and ask.

Later in the process, colleges or other aid sponsors may ask you for clarification of information you provided on your original forms. For example, you might be asked for copies of your own or your parents' most recent tax return. Or you might get a letter requesting additional information about some aspect of your application.

Respond to any such inquiries promptly and in as much detail as is requested. Don't assume that something is "wrong" with your application just because you're asked for more details. Colleges that administer federal funds are required to verify information from at least a portion of their applicants; some routinely request tax returns from all their aid applicants.

When you need to do it

Here again the key is to find out what colleges and programs want from you, and to follow their instructions as closely as possible. Some colleges have deadlines for receiving all application materials; others have preferred filing dates; still others will accept applications at any time.

For most types of aid, you start the application process in the fall or winter preceding the academic

What is the CSS/Financial Aid PROFILE®?

Many colleges, universities, graduate and professional schools, and scholarship programs use the information collected on PROFILE to help them award *nonfederal* student aid funds.

The PROFILE Application is customized based on the information given when the student registers for the service. PROFILE provides an opportunity for students to give a complete picture of their families' financial circumstances, including explanations about special circumstances, on a single application.

You can register for the customized PROFILE application by connecting to College Board on the Web: www.collegeboard.com, or by calling the toll-free PROFILE number (800 778-6888 for students living in the United States, Canada, or Puerto Rico; or 305 816-2550 for students living elsewhere).

The online version of the PROFILE application is available to students who register for PROFILE through collegeboard.com. The paper version is available to students who register via collegeboard.com or telephone. Within 7 to 10 work days after registering, the student receives a personalized PROFILE packet from CSS® with instructions about how and when to complete the PROFILE application.

When you register for PROFILE, you'll answer a few questions about yourself and where you are applying for aid. That information forms the basis for your personal record in the CSS processing system, and also lets CSS customize the application and instructions for you personally. The first part of the PROFILE application contains questions for all filers, but Section Q includes questions unique to the particular colleges and private scholarship programs to which you are applying. If a particular college or program wants you to complete additional CSS supplemental forms, copies will be included with your paper application. If you complete the online version of the application, you will be instructed to download the appropriate supplemental forms and print them.

To find out if the colleges you're considering require or accept the CSS/Financial Aid PROFILE, check the college descriptions section. That information is also listed in a special CSS Code List printed as part of the PROFILE Registration Guide. Some colleges may use PROFILE only for certain of their applicants, such as Early Admission candidates. Use the four-digit CSS codes when you register for PROFILE (not the six-digit federal codes you list on the FAFSA). There is a fee for the CSS/Financial Aid PROFILE service to cover the costs of processing your information and sending it to the colleges and programs from which you are seeking aid.

year for which help is needed. Try to submit your FAFSA at least four weeks before the earliest college deadline you need to meet—but not before January 1. If one or more of the colleges and programs you're applying to require PROFILE, determine what your earliest deadline is and plan accordingly.

Some colleges have different PROFILE completion deadlines for different groups of applicants. For instance, if you're applying for Early Decision, you may have a completed PROFILE application to CSS by November 15. The deadline for all other first-time applicants may not be until January 15, and for all renewal applicants by April 15.

PROFILE Online offers students the opportunity to print out a FAFSA worksheet containing selected responses from their PROFILE online application that are also asked on the Free Application for Federal Student Aid. By referring to the worksheet when completing the FAFSA, applicants can be sure that they are providing consistent answers to both applications, thereby reducing the number of errors to be addressed later in the cycle.

Many private scholarship programs, including the National Merit Scholarship Corporation, use CSS/Financial Aid PROFILE. Some programs decide not to be listed on the CSS code list, but will provide you with the four-digit CSS code privately.

Still other private scholarship programs use their own applications, and some have deadlines that are far earlier than college deadlines. Some entail substantial effort, such as writing an essay, entering a competition, or compiling a portfolio of materials.

Once you've started the application process, it's important to respond promptly to any follow-up requests for information that you receive from a college or a program. Also, don't wait until you've been offered admission to a college before applying for financial aid. There are two reasons for not waiting:

- Most colleges try to let you know what financial aid is available before you have to accept their offer of admission. If you need financial aid, colleges understand that you need information about it before you can make an informed decision about where to enroll.
- If you wait until after you've received offers of admission, the colleges' grant and scholarship funds may be exhausted. Many colleges don't have enough money to meet the full needs of all the students who could use some help, and grants and scholarships usually run out first.

How to do it right

The forms you complete as part of the application process collect information about income, assets, family size, unusual circumstances, and so forth. Detailed step-by-step instructions are provided.

Read the instructions. Then read them again. If any instruction isn't clear, ask your counselor or call the financial aid office. Enough said.

Get organized. Gather together the records you and your parents will need before you sit down to complete your forms. These include income tax returns, W-2 forms, pay stubs, interest statements, home mortgage debt information, records of medical and dental expenses, business or farm records, notices of social security payments for veterans benefits, and other financial records. You will need the records for the calendar year preceding the academic year for which you are applying for aid. If you're applying for the 2004-05 academic year, you will need information for calendar year 2003.

Know which federal income tax forms you plan to file, and draft your responses. The tax form you'll file is one of the factors that affect how your eligibility for federal aid will be determined. You don't actually have to file your tax return before you complete financial aid applications, but it's a good idea to at least rough it out. Some FAFSA and PROFILE questions are cross-referenced to the most common IRS forms to make them easier to complete. Also, drafting your IRS forms in advance helps to ensure that the answers on your financial aid applications will match the answers on your tax forms.

Complete all forms accurately, completely, and legibly. Inaccurate or missing information, or unreadable answers, can result in costly delays in processing your documents.

Provide all the information requested in the form. For instance, if the answer calls for a zero, enter a zero. Don't just leave the question blank. (A blank and a zero and a "not applicable" may seem like the same thing to you, but a computer may not interpret them the same way.)

Don't provide more information than is requested. If there is something you want to communicate to a college, and there doesn't seem to be any place to enter it on the form, don't try to force the information into another answer. Send the college a letter. (If you are completing a CSS/Financial Aid PROFILE form, a blank space is provided for explaining special circumstances.) The financial aid office will be able to take special circumstances into account if that information is explained. This is especially important if your college relies on only FAFSA information to determine your eligibility. "Special circumstances" include any change in your family's financial situation, especially loss of income, change in employment, death, divorce, etc.

Keep photocopies of every form you complete. If you are asked for follow-up information, you may need to refer to your original answers. Don't trust your memory.

Identify yourself consistently on all forms you complete. If you call yourself "John James Doe" on one form, do so on all forms. Be particularly careful about giving your correct social security number. Colleges and programs sometimes have to match records from multiple sources in order to complete your file; incorrect social security numbers and variations on your name can slow the process down.

Carefully review all the communications that you receive back from programs and colleges. For example, within a few weeks of completing a FAFSA, you'll receive a Student Aid Report (SAR). If there are errors in the information, make corrections directly on the special page provided, and mail it back to the processor. Within another few weeks, you'll get a revised SAR. If you complete a CSS/Financial Aid PROFILE form, within a few weeks you will receive an Acknowledgment and a Data Confirmation Report. Check it carefully and follow the instructions provided about correcting information or adding more listings to your original request. You may also receive letters from colleges or private programs requesting additional information.

Be sure that all of your colleges and programs receive all of your information. If you want your financial aid application(s) sent to more colleges or programs than space allows, you should list your top choices first, and

(a) when completing the FAFSA, wait until you receive your SAR, contact the colleges or programs you were unable to list on the original application, and arrange to provide a photocopy of your SAR to each college or program not listed;

(b) if you want to have your PROFILE results sent to more than 10 schools or programs, you can call the toll-free PROFILE number at 800 778-6888, refer to the CSS ID Number provided during registration, and tell CSS which codes to add to your record (remember that PROFILE is not required by all colleges or programs—follow instructions provided by your college[s]). An additional processing fee will be required for each additional listing.

Respond promptly. If you're asked for additional information, send it as soon as possible. If you find errors, correct them quickly. When it comes to applying for aid, time is money.

Understanding financial aid awards

How the financial aid process works

In mid spring you'll begin to receive financial aid award letters from colleges to which you have applied for financial aid. The award letter will describe the financial aid package a college is offering.

Because award letters are mailed early in the year, some colleges may not give you the exact amount of state and federal aid they will offer. In these cases, you will receive a preliminary letter with estimated awards and another letter in the summer that gives you exact figures.

- If you are considering more than one college, wait until you have received a letter from each one before you make a decision. Each award letter will include the deadline for accepting your financial aid package. Pay close attention to the deadline for each award package because it can be different for each school. If you miss a deadline, your financial aid package could be offered to another student. On the other hand, don't let yourself be pressured into making an immediate decision. If necessary, ask the financial aid administrator to extend the deadline for your financial aid offer — in most cases, colleges are happy to do so.
- If you have questions about your financial aid award or the financial aid package does not meet your needs, call the college and ask to speak with a financial aid administrator. Review any special circumstances you feel may have been overlooked. It is possible that the financial aid administrator can adjust your award based on new information. Most colleges do not negotiate or match offers from other schools. Each institution has different priorities and policies that govern how its financial aid is distributed.
- For awards that involve federal aid programs, financial aid administrators must adhere closely to guidelines established by the government for determining eligibility and financial need. Very few schools have enough federal or private funds available to meet every applicant's full need. Although you may have a legitimate and demonstrated need for aid, there may be other students who have even greater needs, and they may receive aid first.

What to look for in a financial aid award letter

The financial aid award letter worksheet at the end of the next section will help you put information from your award letters into a common format.

- Look for the "bottom line"— your net cost to attend each institution. Don't be dazzled by the amount of money a particular college offers—focus on how the awards affect the costs you have to pay. A $5,000 award may cover your need completely at one school, while a $10,000 award at another could leave you short.
- Look at the combination of awards in each financial aid package. Your aid offer will probably include a mix of several types and sources of aid—"gift aid" (grants and scholarships that don't have to be repaid) and "self help" (jobs a school offers so you can earn part of your award and/or loans that must be repaid).
- Finally, look for special conditions or requirements stated in the financial aid package. For example, many institutions require scholarship recipients to maintain a certain grade point average before their award is renewed. Other institutions may require continued enrollment in an academic program.
- Once you choose a college and have been awarded financial aid, follow instructions in your award letter. You may be asked to provide more information or select a lender for a student or parent loan. Complete any forms that come with the award letter, sign the letter, and return it by the due date. Be sure to notify other schools where you have been accepted that you will not attend, so any funds you may have been awarded can be given to students who will attend.

Appealing your award package

If you think the financial aid package offered by your first choice college won't meet your needs, you may want to ask the financial aid office to review it. Inquire about how your expense budget was estimated and how your family contribution and financial need were determined. If there are special circumstances that you think were overlooked, bring them to the aid administrator's attention. It's possible that the aid administrator can take your particular situation into account and adjust your award offer.

If, after meeting with the aid administrator, you still feel that your aid package isn't adequate or that you've been treated unfairly, you might consider appealing your award. You should understand the distinction between "negotiating" and "appealing" a financial aid award offer. Your appeal should provide information not previously available to the financial aid office. Some colleges have a formal procedure with a review board to hear your appeal. Others have a less formal process: the award decision is reviewed by the aid administrator's superior to see that institutional policies have been followed. To find out what the appeal procedures are, contact the financial aid office.

Understand, though, that most colleges have never had sufficient funds to meet the full needs of all students who could use some extra help, and at this time resources are shrinking, not expanding. You have a right to a full explanation of a college's policies and practices with regard to determining need, eligibility, and priorities for distribution of funds, and a college will probably be happy to provide you with this information. However, the answers to your questions won't necessarily provide the answers to your financial problems.

Loans and your aid award package

If your financial aid award letter recommends that you borrow from the Federal Stafford Student Loan Program as part of your aid package, you may need to complete a separate application to obtain the loan.

Follow the instructions completely and promptly. If there's anything you don't understand, call or write the aid office for clarification.

Your aid package may also include an award of a Federal Perkins Loan, for which you won't have to complete a separate loan application. However, you will have to sign a promissory note for each loan advance. You'll receive a copy of the promissory note and other loan information in accordance with federal loan disclosure laws.

Work and your aid award package

Many students receive a work-study job as part of their aid package, generally through the Federal Work-Study Program (although some colleges also sponsor work-study programs of their own). Your aid award notice will tell you how much of the package you are expected to earn through a work-study job, but won't typically tell you what kind of job you'll get. It will also explain how to find out about and apply for eligible jobs, usually on campus.

Private scholarships and your aid award package

Sometimes there is confusion—and even bad feelings—on the part of students and scholarship sponsors about the way colleges treat these outside awards. Often students receive outside scholarships after they have received notification about colleges' financial aid awards. If a student's package was designed to meet full demonstrated financial need, the college *must* make adjustments in the original award to comply with federal regulations that prohibit recipients of federal aid from getting more money than they need.

Even if their original awards from colleges didn't fully meet their demonstrated need, students awarded outside scholarships sometimes find that their college financial aid package is reduced by the amount of the scholarship. Some colleges have a policy of doing this to maximize their limited resources. It's a good idea to review the college's policy in advance to avoid misunderstanding and disappointment about an unexpectedly reduced aid package.

A few years ago, an advisory committee was convened by the College Board's New England Regional Office to look at some of the problems that were occurring in that particular area of the country. The committee found wide differences in college policies regarding financial aid packaging—a diversity repeated across the country—and helped create a pamphlet of advice to high school students. Here is summary of their advice in question and answer form:

Q If I receive financial aid from the college I'm planning to attend, and then I am awarded a scholarship from a civic group or business organization, how do I know if the college will change its financial aid award?

A The only way to know is to check the policy of the college you plan to attend. The financial aid officer there is your best source of information. A quick review of the college's financial aid materials might also provide the answers. Remember, policies differ greatly among colleges. What may be true for your classmate's college may not be true for yours.

Q Is it true that my college financial aid can be reduced by as much as the full amount of any outside scholarship I receive?

A That depends primarily on whether or not your college has already met your financial need (as measured by the institution). The answer: probably yes if the college met your full need; probably no if only a percentage of your need has been met.

Q What if I decide to avoid all this and not report an outside scholarship to my college?

A That's a bad idea. College policies and state and federal regulations require that if you are a candidate for financial aid, you must report your outside scholarships to the financial aid office of the college you're planning to attend. The information you and your parents provide about your financial situation and your outside scholarships must be complete and accurate. If it's not, you risk losing your entire financial aid package.

So what happens if your need has already been fully met and you receive an outside scholarship? The committee found that different colleges have different ways of handling the situation.

- Some reduce the grants or scholarship aid in their offer by the same amount as the outside award.
- Others reduce the work and/or loan portion of the package.
- Still others adjust both portions.
- If a student's need has not been fully met, the committee found that many colleges would apply the amount of the outside award against the student's remaining unmet need, and not reduce the aid package until the student's need was fully met.

The New England–based committee found that it was still to your advantage to receive outside scholarships, even if your college awards were reduced. The reason is that "only a small number of New England institutions will reduce your institutional gift aid by the full value of your outside scholarship," a situation that holds true in most areas of the country.

Student rights

You have a right to receive the following information from a college:

- what financial aid is available, including information about federal, state, and institutional programs
- deadlines for applying for each kind of aid
- the cost of attendance, and what the refund policies are if you withdraw
- criteria used to select aid recipients
- how your financial need is determined, including how student expenses are figured in your budget
- what resources, such as parents' contribution, other financial aid and benefits, assets, and so on, are considered in determining your need
- how much of your financial need has been met
- what aid resources make up your financial package
- what part of the aid must be repaid and what part is grant aid
- the interest rate on your student loan, the total amount that must be repaid, the procedures for paying back the loan, how long you have to repay, and when repayment is to begin
- procedures for appealing a financial aid decision if you feel you have been treated unfairly
- how the college determines whether or not you are making satisfactory academic progress, and what happens if you are not

Student responsibilities

You have a responsibility to:

- review and consider all information about a college's program before you enroll
- complete your application for student financial aid accurately and submit it on time to the right place

(Errors can delay your getting aid, and intentional misreporting of information is a violation of law subject to penalties under the United States Criminal Code.)

- return all additional documentation, verification, corrections, and/or new information requested either by the financial aid administrator or the agency to which you submitted your application
- read and understand all forms that you are asked to sign, keep copies of them, and accept responsibility for all agreements signed by you
- notify the lender of a loan you receive about any change in your name, address, or school status
- satisfactorily perform the work associated with aid in the form of student employment
- know and comply with the deadlines for applying and reapplying for aid
- know and comply with your college's refund policies and procedures

Financial aid checklist

☐ Develop a list of colleges that match your educational and career goals. You may want to use a comprehensive guide such as *The College Board College Handbook* to help you zero in on the colleges that have all the features you want. It's available in bookstores and in many high school guidance offices.

☐ Contact the admission office at each college on your list by mail, fax, or via the Internet for admission and financial aid application forms. It's best to do this early in the fall of your senior year of high school.

☐ Register for CSS/Financial Aid PROFILE if one or more of the colleges you're applying to request it. You can register (or complete PROFILE online) via the Internet (www.collegeboard.com) any day, any time or by calling toll-free (800 778-6888) between 8 a.m. and 10 p.m. (Eastern Time), Sunday through Friday from September 15 through April 1 (after April 1, registration hours are 8 a.m. to 6 p.m. [Eastern Time], Monday through Friday). Remember, you can register electronically for a paper PROFILE application or you can complete PROFILE online. Be sure to register for PROFILE at least four weeks in advance of your earliest financial aid deadline.

☐ Make sure your FAFSA is fully, correctly completed; then mail it as soon after January 1 as possible. The form should be sent for processing at least four weeks before the earliest financial aid deadline set by the colleges or state programs to which you are applying (but no earlier than January 1).

☐ Apply for all forms of student financial aid. Find out well in advance of any deadlines whether you have to fill out additional application forms and make certain you file the appropriate forms on time.

☐ Respond promptly to any requests for additional information so that there will be no delay in processing your request for aid.

☐ Review the acknowledgment you receive. Make certain that all entries on the acknowledgment are correct.

☐ Review your award letters carefully. The director of financial aid at each college and scholarship program is responsible for:

- determining a student's need
- knowing the funds for which a student is eligible
- deciding who will be offered financial aid and how much
- sending award letters to students describing the contents of their financial aid package and outlining any conditions attached to the award

☐ Find out if other financial aid application forms are required by the colleges to which you're applying and what the deadlines are for each. Complete these forms as early as possible.

☐ Check with your guidance office, high school library, and public library for books, pamphlets, and software about other aid sources. One reliable, annually updated publication that describes over 2,100 private scholarship, internship, and loan programs is *The College Board Scholarship Handbook*. You may qualify for one or more awards because of your:

- academic achievement
- religious affiliation
- ethnic or racial heritage
- community activities
- hobbies or special interests
- organizational memberships
- artistic talents, athletic abilities, or other special skills
- career plans or proposed field of study

☐ Find out if your parents' employers, professional associations, or labor unions sponsor any aid programs.

☐ Investigate community organizations and civic, cultural, and fraternal groups to see if they sponsor scholarship programs at the local, state, or national level. Also check with local religious organizations, veterans' posts, businesses, and industries.

☐ If you or either of your parents is a military veteran, you may be eligible for special assistance. Contact the nearest office of the Veterans Administration for information.

☐ Ask about benefits from vocational rehabilitation or other social service agencies if you think you qualify for assistance.

☐ Pay close attention to award notices from state and federal student financial aid programs. Review your federal Student Aid Report (SAR) carefully.

☐ Learn how the payments from each aid source will be made. Generally, payment of financial aid awards is made at the time you actually enroll. Also find out if there are additional procedures you should be aware of or forms you must fill out in order to receive aid.

☐ Explore alternatives. Some colleges offer tuition and/or fee waivers to certain categories of students, such as adults, children of alumni, or family members enrolled simultaneously. The college descriptions in this book include information about the types of policies to reduce costs available at each college. There are also indexes of colleges that offer tuition and/or fee waivers, special tuition payment plans, or tuition discounts for prepayment.

☐ Educate yourself about loans. Investigate all the options before you borrow, and make sure that you understand the interest rates, repayment requirements, and other terms and conditions for each loan program you are considering. Give yourself plenty of time—at least six weeks—before the start of the semester to have your loan application processed.

☐ Once you've decided which college to attend, notify that college and let other colleges know that you're declining their offer so that the financial aid they reserved for you can be freed for other applicants.

Tables and worksheets

Table 3 provides average college costs for the 2002-03 academic year. Costs are based on information from all colleges that provided data for two consecutive years.

- Average tuition and fees are weighted by total undergraduate enrollment.
- Room and board charges for resident students are weighted by the percentage of undergraduates living in college housing.
- Additional out-of-state tuition and fees are the mean charges reported by public institutions; they are not weighted by enrollment. (Private colleges rarely have additional nonresident tuition and fees.)
- Average costs for books and supplies are weighted by total undergraduate enrollment.

Table 3. Average student expenses, by College Board Region, 2002–03 (Enrollment-Weighted)

	Tuition & fees		*Books*	*Resident*			*Commuter*		
	in-state	*out-of-state*	*and supplies*	*Room and board*	*Trans-portation*	*Personal expenses*	*Board only*	*Trans-portation*	*Personal expenses*
National									
2-yr public	$1,735	$3,630	$727	—	—	—	$5,327	$1,104	$1,462
2-yr private	9,890		766	$5,327	$633	$1,221	—	1,086	1,478
4-yr public	4,081	6,347	786	5,582	749	1,643	5,730	1,013	1,853
4-yr private	18,273		807	6,779	645	1,173	6,239	957	1,419
New England									
2-yr public	2,643	4,657	703	—	—	—	5,418	1,093	1,632
2-yr private	16,390		709	8,089	480	763	—	*578*	*1,870*
4-yr public	5,484	6,684	709	6,063	519	1,294	5,736	828	1,516
4-yr private	23,289		786	8,134	529	1,122	7,191	863	1,090
Middle States									
2-yr public	2,886	3,060	687	—	—	—	5,535	966	1,385
2-yr private	9,224		881	—	—	—	—	1,209	1,780
4-yr public	5,202	5,104	779	6,267	533	1,457	5,785	798	1,783
4-yr private	19,685		784	7,750	500	1,082	7,049	897	1,295
South									
2-yr public	1,616	3,552	696	—	—	—	4,617	1,310	1,177
2-yr private	9,567		714	4,625	630	1,364	—	1,037	1,259
4-yr public	3,446	6,471	796	4,744	984	1,597	5,243	1,222	1,783
4-yr private	15,753		772	5,904	846	1,264	5,714	1,144	1,501
Midwest									
2-yr public	2,197	4,288	727	—	—	—	4,931	1,114	1,404
2-yr private	8,978		761	4,530	682	1,263	5,353	1,288	1,235
4-yr public	4,803	6,302	715	5,177	626	1,757	5,334	926	1,992
4-yr private	17,225		812	5,780	627	1,113	5,337	879	1,552
Southwest									
2-yr public	1,186	1,762	691	3,140	783	1,129	—	1,330	1,393
2-yr private	*6,369*		676	*4,084*	921	1,405	5,178	1,877	1,500
4-yr public	3,516	5,255	760	4,920	1,039	1,767	4,898	1,271	1,667
4-yr private	14,310		821	5,319	778	1,382	5,127	1,065	1,446
West									
2-yr public	967	4,104	795	—	—	—	6,173	930	1,804
2-yr private	—		—	—	—	—	—	—	—
4-yr public	3,074	8,163	892	6,694	827	1,844	6,793	932	1,950
4-yr private	17,124		921	6,951	738	1,416	6,317	986	1,505

Note: Averages in *italicized type* indicate that while the number of institutions reporting data on this item was large enough to support an analysis, the sample size was marginal. Dashes indicate that the sample was too small to provide meaningful information. Data are enrollment-weighted, with the exception of out-of-state tuition and fees (unweighted).

* Room and board costs for commuter students are average estimated living expenses for students living off-campus but not with parents.

- Personal expenses and transportation for resident students are weighted by the percentage of undergraduates living in college housing.
- Board, personal expenses, and transportation for commuters are weighted by the percentage of undergraduates who commute.

Table 4 gives sample expense budgets based on the average 2002-03 costs for resident students and commuters at different types of colleges. You can use this table to get a rough estimate of your expenses to complete Worksheet 1, or go to the college descriptions to get specific costs at the colleges you're considering.

Table 4. Sample expense budgets

	Resident	Commuter
2-year public	—	$10,548
2-year private	$17,837	—
4-year public	12,841	13,463
4-year private	27,677	27,695

Table 5 shows estimates used to determine how much parents would be expected to pay based on income and family size according to the 2003-04 Federal Methodology. (Average costs and estimated parental contributions are likely to be different for students enrolling in subsequent years. The 2004-05 Federal Methodology may be similar to the 2003-04 Federal Methodology, but adjusted for inflation.)

Table 5. 2003-04 Estimated parents' contribution

Net assets	$25,000				$50,000			
Family size	3	4	5	6	3	4	5	6
2002 income before taxes								
$ 10,000	$0	$0	$0	$0	$0	$0	$0	$0
20,000	0	0	0	0	0	0	0	0
30,000	916	128	0	0	1,122	334	0	0
40,000	2,441	1,674	952	140	2,648	1,879	1,158	346
50,000	4,265	3,276	2,478	1,666	4,575	3,525	2,690	1,872
60,000	6,887	5,445	4,313	3,267	7,327	5,819	4,631	3,514
70,000	9,783	8,312	6,940	5,431	10,223	8,752	7,380	5,805
80,000	12,479	11,008	9,635	8,070	12,919	11,447	10,075	8,510
90,000	15,323	13,852	12,479	10,914	15,763	14,291	12,919	11,354
100,000	18,310	16,838	15,466	13,901	18,749	17,278	15,906	14,341

Net assets	$100,000				$150,000			
Family size	3	4	5	6	3	4	5	6
2002 income before taxes								
$10,000	$0	$0	$0	$0	$352	$0	$0	$0
20,000	819	18	0	0	2,139	1,338	521	0
30,000	2,442	1,654	899	54	3,994	3,019	2,219	1,374
40,000	4,266	3,276	2,478	1,666	6,467	5,111	4,042	3,033
50,000	6,888	5,445	4,313	3,267	9,708	8,068	6,533	5,099
60,000	10,147	8,507	6,966	5,431	12,967	11,327	9,786	8,051
70,000	13,043	11,572	10,200	8,491	15,863	14,392	13,020	11,311
80,000	15,739	14,267	12,895	11,330	18,559	17,087	15,715	14,150
90,000	18,583	17,111	15,739	14,174	21,403	19,931	18,559	16,994
100,000	21,569	$20,098	18,726	17,161	24,389	22,918	21,546	19,981

Note: The figures shown are parents' contribution under Federal Methodology (FM), assuming the older parent is age 45; both parents are employed (equal wages); income is only from employment; no unusual circumstances; standard deductions on U.S. income tax; 1040 tax return filed; and one undergraduate child enrolled in college. Net assets exclude primary place of residence and family farms.

Tables 6 to 10 will enable you to complete Worksheets 2 to 5.

Table 6. Social Security (FICA) Tax Allowance

(Items 6 and 19)

When individual's yearly wage total equals	Allowance per wage earner for wage Social Security (FICA) tax is:
$1 to $84,900	7.65% of income earned by each wage earner (maximum $6,494.85 per person)
$84,901 or more	$6,494.85 + 1.45% of income earned above $84,900 by each wage earner

Table 7. Income protection allowance (Item 9)

Family size (including student)*	*Number in college***				
	1	2	3	4	5
2	$13,470	$11,160			
3	16,770	14,480	$12,170		
4	20,710	18,410	16,120	$13,810	
5	24,440	22,130	19,840	17,540	$15,240
6	28,580	26,280	23,990	21,680	19,390

* For each additional family member, add $3,230.
** For each additional college student, subtract $2,290.

Table 8. Business or farm adjustments (Item 11)

Net worth (NW)	*Adjusted net worth*
Less than $1	$ 0
$1 to 95,000	$ 0 + 40% of NW
$95,001 to 290,000	$ 38,000 + 50% of NW over $95,000
$290,001 to 480,000	$135,500 + 60% of NW over $290,000
$480,001 or more	$249,500 + 100% of NW over $480,000

Table 9. Parents' expected contribution (Item J)

Available income (AI) (Item I)	*Total parents' contribution*
Less than $3,409	$ 750
$ 3,409 to 12,000	22% of AI
$12,001 to 15,100	$2,640+ 25% of AI over $12,000
$15,101 to 18,200	$3,415 + 29% of AI over $15,100
$18,201 to 21,200	$4,314 + 34% of AI over $18,200
$21,201 to 24,300	$5,334 + 40% of AI over $21,200
$24,301 or more	$6,574 + 47% of AI over $24,200

Table 10. Asset protection allowance (Item F)

Older parent's age	*Two-parent family*	*One-parent family*
25 or under	$0	$0
26	2,500	1,200
27	5,000	2,500
28	7,500	3,700
29	9,900	5,000
30	12,400	6,200
31	14,900	7,400
32	17,400	8,700
33	19,900	9,900
34	22,400	11,200
35	24,900	12,400
36	27,400	13,600
37	29,800	14,900
38	32,300	16,100
39	34,800	17,400
40	37,300	18,600
41	38,200	19,000
42	39,200	19,400
43	40,200	19,800
44	41,200	20,300
45	42,200	20,700
46	43,300	21,100
47	44,300	21,600
48	45,400	22,200
49	46,600	22,600
50	47,700	23,100
51	49,200	23,700
52	50,400	24,200
53	51,700	24,800
54	53,200	25,400
55	54,500	26,200
56	56,200	26,800
57	57,900	27,400
58	59,600	28,200
59	61,400	28,900
60	63,200	29,700
61	65,100	30,500
62	67,300	31,200
63	69,200	32,100
64	71,600	33,100
65 or over	74,000	34,100

Your personal plan

You can begin to get a sense of your need at specific colleges by completing Worksheets 1–5. These will take you through the steps of comparing total expenses at several colleges (Worksheet 1), estimating parents' expected contribution (Worksheet 2), estimating your own contribution (Worksheet 3), combining the total family contribution (Worksheet 4), and finding the difference between the contribution and the costs at each of the colleges you are considering (Worksheet 5)—that is, your financial need.

Worksheet 1: Estimating student expenses	*College A*	*College B*	*College C*
1. Tuition and fees	$	$	$
2. Books and supplies			
3. Student's room			
4. Student's board/meals*			
5. Personal (clothing, laundry, recreation, medical)			
6. Transportation**			
7. Other (such as costs of child care, extra expenses because of handicap)			
A. Total college expense budget (Add 1–7.)	$	$	$

* You will want to consider these expenses to your family if you live at home.

** If you are planning to live on campus, estimate the costs of the round-trips you will have to make to your home. Colleges usually estimate a student makes two or three round-trips during the year. Students living at home should figure the costs of daily transportation to college.

Worksheet 2: Parents' expected contribution (2003-04 Federal Methodology)	
2002 income:	
1. Father's yearly wages, salaries, tips, and other compensation	$
2. Mother's yearly wages, salaries, tips, and other compensation	
3. All other income of mother and father (dividends, interest, social security, pensions, welfare, child support, etc.) Include IRA/Keogh payments and 401(K) and 403(B) contributions.	
4. IRS allowable adjustments to income (business expenses, interest penalties, alimony paid, etc.) Do not include IRA/Keogh payments.	
B. Total income (Add 1, 2, 3, and subtract 4.)	
Expenses:	
5. U.S. income tax parents paid on their 2002 income (not amount withheld from paycheck)	$
6. Social Security (FICA) tax (See Table 6.)	
7. State and other taxes (Enter 8% of B.)	
8. Employment allowance. If two-parent family and both parents work, or if one-parent family, allow 35% of lower salary to a maximum of $3,000. No allowance for a two-parent family in which only one parent works.	
9. Income protection allowance (See Table 7.)	
C. Total allowance against income (Add 5, 6, 7, 8, 9.)	
D. Available income (Subtract C from B.)	
Assets:	
10. Other real estate equity (value minus unpaid balance on mortgage)	$
11. Business or farm (Figure total value minus indebtedness and then take percentage shown in Table 8.) If your family is only part owner of the farm or business, list only your share of the net value.	
12. Cash, savings, and checking accounts	
13. Other investments (current net value)	
E. Total assets	
Deductions:	
F. Asset protection allowance (See Table 10.)	
G. Remaining assets (Subtract F from E.)	
H. Income supplement from assets (Multiply G by 12%; if value is negative, enter 0.)	
I. Adjusted available income (Add D and H.)	
J. Parents' expected contribution (Multiply I by taxation rate amount given in Table 9.)	
K. Parents' expected contribution if more than one family member is in college (Divide J by number of family members in college at least half time.)	

Students, too, are expected to contribute toward college costs when they are employed and/or have accumulated assets. Worksheet 3 will allow you to estimate what your contribution will be for your first year in college based on the Federal Methodology. It is important to note, however, that many colleges will expect a minimum contribution, such as $1,150 for a freshman and $1,400 for an upperclassman, when consideration is given for nonfederal funds.*

** Minimum student contribution according to the 2003-04 Institutional Methodology (IM).*

Worksheet 3: Student's expected contribution	
Student's 2002 income:	
14. Student's yearly wages, salaries, tips, and other compensation	$
15. Spouse's yearly wages, salaries, tips, and other compensation	
16. All other income of student (dividends, interest, untaxed income, and benefits)	
L. Total income (Add 14, 15, and 16.)	**$**
Allowances:	
17. U.S. income tax student (and spouse) paid on 2002 income (not amount withheld from paychecks)	
18. State and other taxes (enter 4% of L.)	
19. Social security (FICA) tax (See Table 6.)	
20. Dependent student income protection allowance	$2,380
M. Total allowances against student's income (Add 17, 18, 19, and 20.)	
N. Available income (Subtract M from L.)	
Resources:	
21. Contribution from income (Line N x 50%. Cannot be less than $0.)	
22. Contribution from assets (Multiply the total savings and other assets, such as stocks and bonds, excluding home equity, by 35%.)	
23. Other gifts and scholarships already received	
O. Total student resources (Add lines 21, 22, and 23.)	

Total family contribution

Use Worksheet 4 to transfer figures from Worksheet 2 (line J, or line K if there will be more than one family member in college), and Worksheet 3 (line O). By adding together these two figures, you can determine your total estimated family contribution.

Worksheet 4: Total family contribution	
J. Parents' expected contribution (Use figure for K instead of J if there is more than one family member in college.)	$
O. Student's expected contribution from resources	
P. Total family contribution (Add J and O.)	$

Are you potentially eligible for financial aid? Use Worksheet 5 to compare your family contribution with the cost of going to college. Record the total college expense budgets at the colleges that interest you (from line A in Worksheet 1). Enter your total family contribution (from line P in Worksheet 4) and subtract it from each of the student expense budgets. If your family contribution is less than the student expense budget, you have demonstrated financial need and may be eligible for financial aid equal to this estimate of your need.

It's important to remember that the figure you arrive at in line R is an *estimate*, and you should consider this figure to be only a rough approximation of your eligibility for financial aid. It is also important to remember that this estimate of need is based on 2003-04 need analysis methodology for federal financial aid programs. Colleges that award significant amounts of nonfederal funds may use a different methodology.

Your eligibility for financial aid, and the amount and type of aid you receive, will be determined by the financial aid administrator at each college. Many colleges lack sufficient funds to provide aid to all needy students, regardless of the methodology used. So it's very important to apply for financial aid as early as possible and meet all deadlines.

Worksheet 5: Estimated financial need

	College A	*College B*	*College C*
A. Total college expense budget	$	$	$
P. Total family contribution			
Q. Student need (Subtract P from A.)	$	$	$

Comparing financial aid award letters

Use Worksheet 6 to record and compare your financial aid awards. List the award deadline date and the total college expense budget (from line A in Worksheet 1).

The award deadline date and the total cost of attendance will probably be included in your award letter. If you have not received an award letter, find the figures in this book or the college catalog for estimating the cost of attendance, or call the school's financial aid office.

Worksheet 6: Comparing financial aid award letters

	College A	*College B*	*College C*
Award deadline date			
A Total college expense budget	$	$	$
Grants and scholarships:			
1. Pell	$	$	$
2. SEOG	$	$	$
3. State	$	$	$
4. College	$	$	$
5. Other	$	$	$
6. Other	$	$	$
R. Total grants and scholarships	$	$	$
S. Work-study programs	$	$	$
Loans:			
7. Stafford	$	$	$
8. Perkins	$	$	$
9. Other	$	$	$
10. Other	$	$	$
T. Total loans	$	$	$
U. Total financial aid award			
Grants and scholarships + Work-study + Loans =	$	$	$
A Total college expense budget	$	$	$
Minus			
U. Total financial aid award	$	$	$
Equals			
V. Net cost to attend	$	$	$

Compare your financial aid awards online

A free online service called *Compare Your Financial Aid Awards* is available on www.collegeboard.com to help students and parents understand, compare, and evaluate aid offers from institutions to which they were admitted. The tool is free and easy to use and will help families:

- Calculate how much they will be expected to pay at each college
- Get advice about college costs, education loans, and college work-study offers
- Learn helpful strategies for evaluating and comparing offers
- Get practical tips and information for paying the bill

The service also provides practical advice and information about understanding costs, asking the right questions, and interpreting the award letter. With links to College Board loan repayment calculators, families can figure out what their loan debt and repayments will be.

This service also includes a special section on paying the bill, with financing strategies and helpful information about the most popular financing options.

What's in the college descriptions

The descriptions provide information supplied by the colleges themselves on the College Board's Annual Survey of Colleges 2003-04 and are organized alphabetically by state. A team of data editors verified the facts and figures and every effort was made to ensure that they are as complete and accurate as possible. But changes may have occurred at individual colleges after the survey was completed, so we recommend that you contact colleges you're considering directly to confirm the information.

The college. Each description begins with the college's official name—which isn't always the one in popular use. An acorn logo after the college's name indicates that it is a member of the College Board. The heading includes the college's city, state, and Internet address. Most colleges now have Web sites that are invaluable resources in your college search. The last line of the heading indicates whether the college is a two-, three-, four-, or five-year institution and whether it is public or private. Most college headings also include the Federal Code number, which is required on the FAFSA. If that number doesn't appear in the lower right corner, you can get the the Federal School Codes via the Internet at: www.fafsa.ed.gov.

Detailed cost facts. This list itemizes the expenses for first-year, full-time students living at home or on campus.

- Tuition and fees charged by the college for a nine-month academic year of 30 semester hours or 45 quarter hours. If those costs were not yet set but a reliable forecast was available, projected figures are given. If a reliable forecast couldn't be made, 2002-03 figures are given. If the college combines tuition, fees, and room and board expenses, that single figure is given as a comprehensive fee.
- Out-of-district/state tuition and fees indicate costs at public colleges for students who do not meet district or state residency requirements.
- Room and board for students living on campus in a double room with a full meal plan. Single rooms or rooms for three or more could be a lot more or less than the figures reported here.
- Board only shows average meal costs for dependent students living at home.
- Books and supplies—the average cost of those items for the normal course load. Supplies may be more expensive for students in certain areas of study (art, architecture, or engineering, for example).
- Personal expenses include items such as clothing, laundry, entertainment, and furnishings. Those expenses will vary widely depending on your lifestyle.
- Transportation cost are estimated for a typical full-time undergraduate student, based on two round-trips home per year for a student living on campus, and on average commuting expenses for students living at home.

Undergraduate aid. This section includes information about:

- Need-based aid—whether a college bases all aid on need; average financial aid package for full-time and part-time students; percentages awarded as gift aid and self-help.
- Non-need-based aid—percentages awarded as gift aid and self-help; basis for scholarship awards. Be sure to check the indexes in the back of this book for colleges listed by type of scholarship available.
- Student debt—percent of graduating class who borrowed to fund education and average total debt for those who borrowed.

Freshman aid. This section includes information about:

- Need-based aid—number of full-time freshmen who applied for aid; number judged to have need; number of students judged to have need who received aid; percent of need met by average financial aid package; number of freshmen who had full need met; and average scholarship/grant and average loan amounts awarded to freshmen.

- Non-need-based aid—number of full-time freshmen with need who received non-need scholarships; number without need receiving awards of any type; special merit scholarships unique to the college.

Merit scholarships. This section describes any non-need-based merit scholarship opportunities offered by the college.

Policies to reduce costs. This section indicates whether the college offers tuition/fee waivers, credit by examination, prepayment discount, etc.

Payment plans. If a college offers credit card, installment, or deferred payment, that is indicated here.

Application procedures. This is where you'll find information about required forms and priority, closing, notification, and reply dates for freshmen as well as transfer students. If a college offers early decision, that closing date is included, as that date will also be the deadline for early decision applicants to submit their financial aid forms.

Contact. Look here for the financial aid office phone number, name of the person to contact, and mailing address.

Glossary

The following definitions of terms commonly used by colleges to describe their programs, admission procedures, and financial aid policies are necessarily general. You should consult the catalogs of specific colleges and financial aid programs to get more detailed descriptions of their programs and procedures.

Accelerated program. A college program of study completed in less time than is usually required, most often by attending classes in summer or by taking extra courses during the regular academic terms. Completion of a bachelor's degree program in three years is an example of acceleration.

Advanced placement. Admission or assignment of a freshman to an advanced course in a certain subject on the basis of evidence that the student has already completed the equivalent of the college's freshman course in that subject.

Advanced Placement Program® (AP®). A service of the College Board that provides high schools with course descriptions of college subjects and Advanced Placement Examinations in those subjects. High schools implement the courses and administer the examinations to interested students, who are then eligible for advanced placement, college credit, or both, on the basis of satisfactory grades.

ACT Assessment. Test battery of ACT, Inc., formerly known as the American College Testing Program, given at test centers in the United States and other countries on specified dates throughout the year. It includes tests in English, mathematics, reading, and science reasoning.

Associate degree. A degree granted by a college or university after the satisfactory completion of a two-year, full-time program of study or its part-time equivalent. In general, the associate of arts (A.A.) or associate of science (A.S.) degree is granted after students complete a program of study similar to the first two years of a four-year college curriculum. The associate in applied science (A.A.S.) is awarded by many colleges on completion of technological or vocational programs of study.

Bachelor's, or baccalaureate, degree. A degree received after the satisfactory completion of a four- or five-year, full-time program of study (or its part-time equivalent) at a college or university. The bachelor of arts (B.A.) and bachelor of science (B.S.) are the most common baccalaureates. There is no absolute difference between the degrees, and policies concerning their award vary from college to college.

Campus-based programs. The three federally funded student financial aid programs that are directly administered by colleges: Federal Supplemental Educational Opportunity Grant Program, Federal Perkins Loan Program, and Federal Work-Study Program.

Candidates Reply Date Agreement (CRDA). A college subscribing to this College Board-sponsored agreement will not require any applicants offered admission as freshmen to notify the college of their decision to attend (or to accept an offer of financial aid) before May 1 of the year the applicant applies. The purpose of the agreement is to give applicants time to hear from all the colleges to which they have applied before having to make a commitment to any of them.

Certificate. An award for completing a particular program or course of study, sometimes given by two-year colleges or vocational or technical schools.

College-Level Examination Program® (CLEP®). A series of examinations in undergraduate college courses that provides students of any age the opportunity to demonstrate college-level achievement, thereby reducing costs and time to degree completion. The examinations, which are sponsored by the College Board, are administered at colleges year-round. All CLEP exams are delivered on computer, providing test-takers instant score results.

CollegeCredit® Education Loans. An array of government and private loans sponsored by the College Scholarship Service of the College Board. Federal Stafford Loans, Federal PLUS Loans, and privately sponsored Student Signature Education and Private Parent loans are available to students and parents in 31 states and the District of Columbia.

College Scholarship Service® (CSS®). A unit of the College Board that assists postsecondary institutions, state scholarship programs, and private scholarship organizations in the equitable and efficient distribution of student financial aid funds.

Comprehensive fee. If the college combines tuition, fees, room, and board expenses, that single figure is called a comprehensive fee.

Consumer Price Index (CPI). A measure of inflation or deflation at the consumer level, updated monthly by the U.S. Bureau of Labor Statistics.

Cooperative education. A program that provides for alternative class attendance and employment in business, industry, or government. Students are typically paid for their work. Under a cooperative plan, five years are normally required to complete a bachelor's degree, but graduates have the advantage of about a year's practical work experience in addition to their studies.

Coverdell Education Savings Account (ESA). Formerly referred to as the Education ERA, this federal income tax provision enables taxpayers to establish a college savings plan. A maximum of $2,000 may be contributed annually, according to income.

Credit by examination. Academic credit granted by a college to entering students who have demonstrated proficiency in college-level studies through examinations such as those sponsored by the College Board's AP and CLEP programs. This is a means of cutting college costs by reducing the number of courses needed to earn a degree.

CSS/Financial Aid PROFILE®. A form and service offered by the College Board and used by some colleges, universities, and private scholarship programs to award their own private financial aid funds. Students pay a fee to register for PROFILE and send reports to institutions and programs that use it. Students register with CSS by calling a toll-free telephone service or by connecting to the College Board Web site: www.collegeboard.com. CSS provides a customized application for each registrant, based on the individual's information and the requirements of the colleges and programs from which she or he is seeking aid. Students complete and submit the customized application and supplements, if required, to CSS for processing and reporting to institutions. CSS/Financial Aid PROFILE is not a federal form and may not be used to apply for federal student aid.

Dependent student. One who is dependent on his/her parents for financial support. Dependency status is determined by guidelines established by the federal government.

Early decision. Students who apply under early decision commit to enroll at the college if admitted and offered a satisfactory financial aid package. Application deadlines are usually in November or December with a mid-to-late December notification date. Some colleges have two rounds of early decision.

Early Decision Plan (EDPA). Colleges that subscribe to this College Board-sponsored plan agree to follow a common schedule for early decision applicants. A student applying under EDPA must withdraw applications from all other colleges as soon as he or she is notified of acceptance by the first-choice college. Applications (including financial aid applications) must be received by a specified date no later than November 15, and the college agrees to notify the applicant by a specified date no later than December 15.

Education IRA. (See Coverdell ESA.)

Expected family contribution. The total amount students and their families are expected to pay toward college costs from their income and assets. The amount is derived from a need analysis of the family's overall financial circumstances. A Federal Methodology is used to determine a student's eligibility for federal student aid. Colleges, state agencies, and private aid programs may use a different methodology to determine eligibility for nonfederal financial aid.

FAFSA. See Free Application for Federal Student Aid.

FAFSA on the Web. An electronic option for completing the Free Application for Federal Student Aid (www.fafsa.ed.gov).

Federal Pell Grant Program. A federally sponsored and administered program that provides grants based on need to undergraduate students. Congress annually sets the dollar range. Currently a Pell Grant cannot exceed $3,600 per year.

Federal Perkins Loan Program. A federally funded program based on need, administered by colleges, that provides low-interest (5 percent) loans of up to $4,000 per year during undergraduate study and up to $20,000 for the total undergraduate program. The combined cumulative total of loan funds available to an individual for undergraduate and graduate education is $40,000. Repayment need not begin until completion of the student's education or after limited periods of service in the military, Peace Corps, or approved comparable organizations.

Federal PLUS Loan. The federal PLUS loan program permits parents of undergraduate students to borrow up to the full cost of education less any other financial aid the student may have received. The interest rate is variable and is adjusted annually.

Federal code number. A six-digit federal code number that identifies a specific college to which you want your FAFSA form submitted. (Formerly known as Title IV number.)

Federal Stafford Loan. This is a federal program based on need that allows students to borrow money for educational expenses directly from banks and other lending institutions (sometimes from the colleges themselves). The amounts that may be borrowed depend on the student's year in school. Interest rates are variable.

Federal Supplemental Educational Opportunity Grant Program (FSEOG). A federal program administered by colleges that provides grants of up to $4,000 a year for undergraduate students on the basis of exceptional financial need.

Federal Work-Study Program. An arrangement by which a student combines employment and college study. The employment may be an integral part of the academic program (as in cooperative education or internships) or simply a means of paying for college.

Financial aid award letter. A notice from a college or other financial aid sponsor that tells you how much aid is being offered. The award letter also usually explains how your financial need was determined, describes the contents of the financial aid package, and outlines any conditions attached to the award.

Financial aid package. Your total financial aid award. It may be made up of a combination or "package" that includes both gift aid and self-help. Many colleges try to meet a student's full financial need, but availability of funds, institutional aid policies, and the number of students who need assistance all influence the composition and amount of a financial aid package.

Financial need. The amount by which your family contribution falls short of covering your expense budget. Assessments of need may differ depending on the need-analysis methodology used. (See Expected family contribution.)

Free Application for Federal Student Aid (FAFSA). A form completed by all applicants for federal student aid. In many states, completion of the FAFSA is also sufficient to establish eligibility for state-sponsored aid programs. There is no charge to students for completing the FAFSA. Forms are widely available in high schools and colleges, and may be filed any time after January 1 of the year for which one is seeking aid (e.g., after January 1, 2004, for academic year 2004–2005 assistance).

Gift aid. Scholarships and grants, which do not have to be repaid.

HOPE Education Tax Credit. A federal income tax credit of as much as $1,500 per student dependent annually; available to eligible taxpayers based on "out-of-pocket" tuition and fee expenditures, according to income eligibility guidelines.

Independent student. For financial aid purposes, a student who is not dependent on financial support from his or her parents. Also called self-supporting student.

International Baccalaureate (IB). A comprehensive and rigorous two-year curriculum (usually taken in the final two years of high school) that is similar to the final year of secondary school in Europe. Some colleges award credit or advanced placement to students who have completed an IB program.

Lifetime Learning Tax Credit. A federal income tax credit of as much as $1,000 per household annually; available to eligible taxpayers based on "out-of-pocket" tuition and fee expenditures, according to income eligibility guidelines.

Need analysis form. The starting point in applying for financial aid. All students must file the federally sponsored Free Application for Federal Student Aid (FAFSA) to apply for federal financial aid programs. For many colleges, this may be the only need analysis form you will need to file. For other schools, particularly private colleges, additional forms, such as the CSS/Financial Aid PROFILE, may be required. To apply for state financial aid programs, the FAFSA may be all you need to file, but check with your state agency to find out if other application forms are required.

Need-based financial aid. Gift and/or self-help financial aid given to students who have demonstrated financial need, calculated by subtracting the student's expected family contribution from a college's total costs.

Open admission. The college admission policy of admitting high school graduates and other adults generally without regard to conventional academic qualifications, such as high school subjects, high school grades, and admission test scores. Virtually all applicants with high school diplomas or their equivalent are accepted.

Parents' contribution. The amount your parents are expected to pay toward college costs from their income and assets. It is derived from need analysis of the parents' overall financial situation. Your parents' contribution and your contribution together constitute the total family contribution, which, when subtracted from your college expense budget, equals your financial need. Generally, you are eligible for financial aid equal to your financial need.

Parent's Loan for Undergraduate Students. (See Federal PLUS Loan.)

PROFILE Online: An electronic application option available for students required to complete the CSS/Financial Aid PROFILE. By connecting to collegeboard.com, students can choose to register for a paper PROFILE application or complete the entire application online.

PSAT/NMSQT® (Preliminary SAT/National Merit Scholarship Qualifying Test). A shorter version of the SAT I with an additional writing skills section as well as a diagnostic component providing skills feedback. Administered by high schools to sophomores and juniors each year in October, the PSAT/NMSQT aids high schools in the early guidance of students planning for college and serves as the qualifying test for scholarships awarded by the National Merit Scholarship Corporation.

Reserve Officers' Training Corps (ROTC). Programs conducted by certain colleges in cooperation with the United States Air Force, Army, and Navy. Naval ROTC includes the Marine Corps (the Coast Guard and Merchant Marine do not sponsor ROTC programs). Local recruiting offices of the services themselves can supply detailed information about these programs, as can participating colleges.

SAT® I: Reasoning Test. The College Board's test of developed verbal and mathematical reasoning abilities, given on specified dates throughout the year at test centers in the United States and other countries. The SAT I is required by many colleges and sponsors of financial aid programs.

SAT II: Subject Tests. College Board tests in specific subjects, given at test centers in the United States and other countries on specified dates throughout the year. Used by colleges not only to help with decisions about admission but also in course placement and exemption of enrolled freshmen. Includes ELPT™ (English Language Proficiency Test™).

Scholarship or grant. A type of financial aid that doesn't have to be repaid. Grants are often based on financial need. Scholarships may be based on need, on need combined with other criteria, or solely on other criteria such as academic achievement, artistic ability, talent in the performing arts, and the like.

Section 529 Plans. State sponsored college savings programs commonly referred to as "529 Plans" after the section of the Internal Revenue Code that provides the plan's tax breaks.

Self-help. Student financial aid, such as loans and jobs, that require repayment or employment.

Student Aid Report (SAR). A report produced by the U.S. Department of Education and sent to students in response to their having filed the Free Application for Federal Student Aid (FAFSA). The SAR contains information the student provided on the FAFSA as well as the federally calculated result, which the financial aid office will use to determine the student's eligibility for the Federal Pell Grant and other federal student aid programs.

Student expense budget. A calculation of the annual cost of attending college that is used to determine your financial need. Student expense budgets usually include tuition and fees, books and supplies, room and board, personal expenses, and transportation. Sometimes additional expenses are included for students with special education needs, students who have a disability, or students who are married or have children.

Student's contribution. The amount you are expected to pay toward college costs from your income, assets, and benefits. The amount is derived from need analysis of your resources. Your contribution and your parents' contribution constitute the total family contribution, which, when subtracted from the student budget, equals financial need. Generally, you are eligible for financial aid equal to your financial need.

Title IV number. (See Federal code number.)

Tuition and fee waivers. Some colleges waive the tuition or tuition and fees for some categories of students, such as adults, senior citizens, or children of alumni. Colleges with such plans are listed in a separate section in this book.

Sources of information about state grant programs

Alabama
Alabama Commission on Higher Education
P.O. Box 302000
100 North Union Street
Montgomery, AL 36130-2000
334 242-1998; www.ache.state.al.us

Alaska
Alaska Commission on Postsecondary Education
3030 Vintage Boulevard
Juneau, AK 99801-7109
800 141-2962; www.state.ak.us/acpe

Arizona
Department of Education
P.O. Box 6490
Phoenix, AZ 85005
602 542-4361; www.ade.state.az.us

Arkansas
Department of Higher Education
114 East Capitol
Little Rock, AR 72201
501 371-2000; www.arkansashighered.com

California
California Student Aid Commission
P.O. Box 419026
Rancho Cordova, CA 95741-9026
916 526-7590; www.csac.ca.gov

Colorado
Department of Education
201 East Colfax Avenue
Denver, CO 80203
303 866-6600; www.cde.state.co.us

Connecticut
Department of Higher Education
61 Woodland Street
Hartford, CT 06105
860 947-1800; www.ctdhe.org

Delaware
Delaware Higher Education Commission
820 North French Street
Fourth Floor
Wilmington, DE 19801
800 292-7935; www.doe.state.de.us/high-ed

Florida
Florida Department of Education, Office of Student Financial Assistance
325 West Gaines Street
Tallahassee, FL 32399-0400
850 487-1785; www.firn.edu/doe

Georgia
Georgia Student Finance Authority
2082 East Exchange Place
Suite 100
Tucker, GA 30084
770 724-9000; www.hope.gsfc.org

Hawaii
Hawaii Department of Education
P.O. Box 2360
Honolulu, HI 96804
808 586-3230; www.doe.k12.hi.us

Idaho
Office of the State Board of Education
P.O. Box 83720
650 West State Street
Boise, ID 83720-0037
208 334-2270; www.sde.state.id.us

Illinois
Illinois Student Assistance Commission
1755 Lake Cook Road
Deerfield, IL 60015
800 899-4722; www.isac-online.org

Indiana
State Student Assistance Commission of Indiana
150 W. Market Street
Suite 500
Indianapolis, IN 46204
888 528-4719; www.ai.org/ssaci

Iowa
Iowa College Student Aid Commission
200 Tenth Street
Fourth Floor
Des Moines, IA 50309-2036
515 242-3344; www.state.ia.us/collegeaid

Kansas
Board of Regents
1000 SW Jackson Street
Suite 520
Topeka, KS 66612-1368
785 296-3421; www.kansasregents.org

Kentucky
KHEAA Student Aid Branch
1050 U.S. 127 South
Frankfort, KY 40601
800 928-8926; www.kheaa.com

Louisiana
Office of Student Financial Assistance for Louisiana
Scholarship/Grant Division
P.O. Box 91202
Baton Rouge, LA 70821-9202
800 259-5626; www.osfa.state.la.us

Maine
Finance Authority of Maine
Maine Education Assistance Division
P.O. Box 949
5 Community Drive
Augusta, ME 04333
800 228-3734; www.famemaine.com

Maryland
Maryland Higher Education Commission/
State Scholarship Administration
839 Bestgate Road
Suite 400
Annapolis, MD 21401-1781
800 974-0203; www.mhec.state.md.us

Massachusetts
Board of Higher Education,
Office of Student Financial Assistance
One Ashburton Place, Rm 1401
Boston, MA 02108-1696
617 994-6950; www.mass.edu

Michigan
Michigan Higher Education Assistance Authority,
Office of Scholarships and Grants
P.O. Box 30008
Lansing, MI 48909
517 373-3394; www.michigan.gov

Minnesota
Minnesota Higher Education Services Office
1450 Energy Park Drive
Suite 350
St. Paul, MN 55101
651 642-0533; www.mheso.state.mn.us

Mississippi
Mississippi Office of State Student Financial Aid
3825 Ridgewood Road
Jackson, MS 39211-6453
800 327-2980; www.mde.k12.ms.us

Missouri
Missouri Coordinating Board for Higher Education
3515 Amazonas Drive
Jefferson City, MO 65109
573 751-2361; www.mocbhe.gov

Montana
Montana Board of Regents of Higher Education
P.O. Box 203101
2500 Broadway
Helena, MT 59620-3101
406 444-6570; www.montana.edu/wwwbor

Nebraska
Nebraska Department of Education
P.O. Box 95005
Lincoln, NE 68509-5005
402 471-2847; www.ccpe.state.ne.us

Nevada
Nevada Department of Education, Financial Aid
700 East 5th Street
Capitol Complex
Carson City, NV 89701
775 687-9200; www.nde.state.nv.us

New Hampshire
New Hampshire Postsecondary Education Commission
3 Barrell Court
Suite 300
Concord, NH 03301-8512
603 271-2555; www.state.nh.us/postsecondary

New Jersey
New Jersey Higher Education Student Assistance Authority
4 Quakerbridge Plaza
P.O. Box 540
Trenton, NJ 08625
800 792-8670; www.hesaa.org

New Mexico
Commission on Higher Education
1068 Cerillos Road
Santa Fe, NM 87505
505 476-6500; www.nmche.org

New York
Higher Education Services Corporation,
Student Information
99 Washington Avenue
14th Floor
Albany, NY 12255
888 697-4372; www.hesc.state.ny.us

North Carolina
North Carolina State Education Assistance Authority
P.O. Box 14103
Research Triangle Park, NC 27709-3663
919 549-8614; www.ncseaa.edu

North Dakota
North Dakota University System
10th Floor, State Capitol
600 East Boulevard
Dept. 215
Bismarck, ND 58505
701 328-2960; www.ndus.nodak.edu

Ohio
Ohio Board of Regents
30 East Broad Street, 36th floor
Columbus, OH 43215-3414
614 466-7420; www.regents.state.oh.us

Oklahoma
Oklahoma State Regents for Higher Education,
Tuition Aid Grant Program
655 Research Parkway
Suite 200
Oklahoma City, OK 73104
405 225-9100; www.okhighered.org

Oregon
Oregon State Scholarship Commission,
Valley River Office Park
1500 Valley River Drive
Suite 100
Eugene, OR 97401
800 452-8807; www.ossc.state.or.us

Pennsylvania
Pennsylvania Higher Education Assistance Agency
1200 N. Seventh St.
Harrisburg, PA 17102
877 603-6010; www.pheaa.org

Puerto Rico
Departmento de Educacion
P.O. Box 190759
San Juan, PR 00919-0759
787 724-7100

Rhode Island
Rhode Island Higher Education Assistance Authority
560 Jefferson Boulevard
Warwick, RI 02886
401 736-1100; www.riheaa.org

South Carolina
South Carolina Tuition Grants Commission
1333 Main Street
Suite 200
Columbia, SC 29201
803 737-2260; www.che400.state.sc.us

South Dakota
Department of Education and Cultural Affairs,
Office of the Secretary
700 Governors Drive
Pierre, SD 57501-2291
605 773-3426; www.state.sd.us/deca

Tennessee
Tennessee Student Assistance Corporation
Parkway Towers
Suite 1950
404 James Robertson Parkway
Nashville, TN 37243-0820
615 313-0300; www.state.tn.us/thec

Texas
Texas Higher Education Coordinating Board
Division of Student Services
P.O. Box 12788, Capital Station
Austin, TX 78711
512 427-6101; www.thecb.state.tx.us

Utah
Utah Higher Education Assistance Authority
Board of Regents Building, The Gateway
60 South 400 West
Salt Lake City, UT 84101-1284
801 321-7200; www.uheaa.org

Vermont
Vermont Student Assistance Corporation
Champlain Mill, P.O. Box 2000
Winooski, VT 05404-2601
802 655-9602; www.vsac.org

Virginia
Virginia Council of Higher Education
James Monroe Building
101 North 14th Street
Richmond, VA 23219
804 225-2600; www.schev.edu

Washington
Washington State Higher Education Coordination Board
917 Lakeridge Way
P.O. Box 43430
Olympia, WA 98504-3430
360 753-7800; www.hecb.wa.gov

West Virginia
West Virginia Higher Education Policy Commission
Central Office, Higher Education Grant Program
1018 Kanawha Boulevard East
Suite 700
Charleston, WV 25301-2827
304 558-2101; www.hepc.wvnet.edu

Wisconsin
Wisconsin Higher Educational Aids Board
131 West Wilson
Suite 902
Madison, WI 53707
608 267-2206; www.heab.state.wi.us

Wyoming
Wyoming State Department of Education
2300 Capitol Avenue
Cheyenne, WY 82002
307 777-7673; www.k12.wy.us

Guam
Student Financial Aid Office UOG Station, 40G Station
Mangilao, GU 96923
671 735-2283; www.uog.edu

Virgin Islands
Financial Aid Office, Virgin Islands Board of Education
P.O. Box 11900
St. Thomas, VI 00801
340 774-4546

Alabama

Alabama Agricultural and Mechanical University
Normal, Alabama
aamu.edu
Four-year public **Federal Code: 001002**

College costs. Cost of rooms ranges from $700-$1,300 for double occupancy.

	Living at home	On-campus
Tuition and fees (2002-2003):	$4,190	$4,190
Out-of-state:	$7,340	$7,340
Room and board:		$3,300
Books and supplies:	$850	$850
Personal expenses:	$950	$950
Transportation:	$1,000	$1,000

Undergraduate aid. Need-based: Need-based aid available for full-time and part-time students. **Non-need-based:** Scholarships based on athletics, minority status.

Merit scholarships. Presidential scholarship for students with 4.0 GPA, pays tuition and fees.

Policies to reduce costs. Tuition/fee waivers for minority students, employees and their families. Credit/placement for qualifying scores on AP, CLEP examinations. Work study available weekends.

Payment plans. Credit card, installment, deferred payment.

Application procedures. FAFSA, institutional form required. Priority date 1/1; closing date 3/17. Applicants notified on rolling basis, must reply within 2 week(s) of notification. **Transfers:** Priority date 3/17.

Contact. **Financial aid office:** (256) 851-5400
Carlos Clark, Director of Financial Aid
Box 908
Normal, AL 35762

Alabama Southern Community College
Monroeville, Alabama
www.ascc.edu
Two-year public **Federal Code: 001034**

	Living at home
Tuition and fees (2002-2003):	$2,280
Out-of-state:	$4,080
Per-credit charge:	$60
Per-credit out-of-state:	$120
Books and supplies:	$750
Transportation:	$600

Policies to reduce costs. Tuition/fee waivers for senior citizens. Credit/placement for qualifying scores on AP, CLEP examinations.

Payment plans. Credit card payment.

Application procedures. FAFSA required. Priority date 7/15; no closing date. Applicants notified on rolling basis, must reply within 4 week(s) of notification.

Contact. Roger Chandler, Dean of Finance
Box 2000
Monroeville, AL 36461

Alabama State University
Montgomery, Alabama
www.alasu.edu
Four-year public **Federal Code: 001005**

College costs. Students pay a one time $150 property damage fee, this fee is refundable.

	Living at home	On-campus
Tuition and fees:	$3,600	$3,600
Out-of-state:	$7,200	$7,200
Room and board:		$3,600
Board only:	$2,070	
Books and supplies:	$800	$800
Personal expenses:	$1,380	$1,380
Transportation:	$1,440	$930

Undergraduate aid. Need-based: Average financial aid package for full-time students was $9,148; for part-time $9,071. 47% awarded as scholarships/grants, 53% as loans/jobs. **Non-need-based:** 37% awarded as scholarships/grants, 63% as loans/jobs. Scholarships based on academics, athletics. **Student debt:** 72% of graduating class borrowed to fund education; average debt was $34,430.

Freshman aid. Need-based: Out of 1,401 full-time freshmen, 1,309 applied for aid; 1,208 were judged to have need; of these 1,171 received aid. Average package met 70% of need. 164 students had full need met. Average scholarship/grant was $3,590; average loan $2,688. **Non-need based:** 247 full-time freshmen with need received non-need scholarships; 31 without need received awards; 40 received athletic scholarships.

Policies to reduce costs. Tuition/fee waivers for minority students, employees and their families. Credit/placement for qualifying scores on AP, CLEP examinations.

Payment plans. Credit card, installment, deferred payment.

Application procedures. FAFSA required. Priority date 5/1; no closing date. Applicants notified on rolling basis starting 6/1. **Transfers:** Priority date 5/1; no deadline. Financial aid transcript required.

Contact. **Financial aid office:** (334) 229-4323
Dorenda Adams, Director of Financial Aid
915 South Jackson Street
Montgomery, AL 36101-0271

American College of Computer and Information Sciences
Birmingham, Alabama
www.accis.edu
Four-year proprietary

College costs. $130 per credit hour charge.

Contact. 2101 Magnolia Avenue, Suite 200
Birmingham, AL 35205-2827

Andrew Jackson University
Birmingham, Alabama
www.aju.edu
Four-year proprietary

	Living at home
Tuition and fees:	$3,900

Contact. 10 Old Montgomery Highway
Birmingham, AL 35209

Athens State University
Athens, Alabama
www.athens.edu
Upper-division public **Federal Code: 001008**

	Living at home	On-campus
Tuition and fees (2002-2003):	$2,730	$2,730
Out-of-state:	$5,280	$5,280
Room only:		$900
Books and supplies:	$800	$800
Transportation:	$3,000	

Undergraduate aid. Need-based: Need-based aid available for full-time and part-time students. **Non-need-based:** Scholarships based on academics, alumni affiliation, art, athletics, leadership, minority status.

Policies to reduce costs. Tuition/fee waivers for senior citizens, employees and their families. Credit/placement for qualifying scores on CLEP examinations. Work study available nights, weekends and for part-time students.

Payment plans. Credit card payment.

Application procedures. FAFSA required. No deadline. Applicants notified on rolling basis starting 6/1, must reply within 30 week(s) of notification. **Transfers:** Tax returns required.

Contact. **Financial aid office:** (256) 233-8122
Sarah McAbee, Director of Financial Aid
300 North Beaty Street
Athens, AL 35611

Auburn University

Auburn, Alabama
www.auburn.edu
Four-year public **Federal Code: 001009**

College costs. Part-time per-credit-hour charge accompanied by registration fee. Per-credit-hour charges above 15 credits differ.

	Living at home	On-campus
Tuition and fees (2002-2003):	$3,784	$3,784
Out-of-state:	$11,084	$11,084
Room and board:		$5,586
Books and supplies:	$900	$900
Personal expenses:		$1,640
Transportation:		$805

Undergraduate aid. Need-based: Average financial aid package for full-time students was $6,400; for part-time $5,942. 36% awarded as scholarships/grants, 64% as loans/jobs. **Non-need-based:** 10% awarded as scholarships/grants, 90% as loans/jobs. Scholarships based on academics, athletics. **Student debt:** 63% of graduating class borrowed to fund education; average debt was $18,585. **Additional information:** State of Alabama has pre-paid college tuition plan for residents.

Freshman aid. Need-based: Out of 3,713 full-time freshmen, 2,211 applied for aid; 1,137 were judged to have need; of these 1,059 received aid. Average package met 52% of need. 112 students had full need met. Average scholarship/grant was $2,894; average loan $2,880. **Non-need based:** 602 full-time freshmen with need received non-need scholarships; 504 without need received awards; 53 received athletic scholarships.

Merit scholarships. Entering Freshmen Academic Scholarship requires minimum 29 ACT or 1280 SAT and 3.5 GPA; up to full tuition awarded. National Merit and National Achievement Finalists, renewable with maintenance of 3.0 GPA; full tuition plus $750-$2,000. General and departmental scholarships, minimum 27 ACT or 1200 SAT and 3.5 GPA required for freshmen, 3.5 GPA for transfers, 3.0 GPA for other students, financial need considered.

Policies to reduce costs. Tuition/fee waivers for children of alumni, employees and their families. Credit/placement for qualifying scores on AP, CLEP examinations.

Payment plans. Installment payment.

Application procedures. FAFSA, institutional form required. Priority date 3/1; no closing date. Applicants notified on rolling basis starting 5/1, must reply within 2 week(s) of notification.

Contact. Mike Reynolds, Director of Student Financial Aid
202 Mary Martin Hall
Auburn, AL 36849-5145

Auburn University at Montgomery

Montgomery, Alabama
www.aum.edu
Four-year public **Federal Code: 008310**

College costs. Cost for room only is dependent on where students are housed. East housing costs $2,160 per year and West housing costs $2,960 per year.

	Living at home	On-campus
Tuition and fees (projected):	$3,873	$3,873
Out-of-state:	$11,128	$11,128
Room and board:		$5,104
Books and supplies:	$600	$600
Personal expenses:	$1,060	$1,060
Transportation:	$850	$850

Undergraduate aid. Need-based: 39% awarded as scholarships/grants, 61% as loans/jobs. Need-based aid available for part-time students. **Non-need-based:** 16% awarded as scholarships/grants, 84% as loans/jobs. Scholarships based on academics, alumni affiliation, art, athletics, job skills, leadership, minority status, music/drama, state/district residency.

Policies to reduce costs. Tuition/fee waivers for employees and their families. Credit/placement for qualifying scores on AP, IB, CLEP examinations. Work study available nights, weekends and for part-time students.

Payment plans. Credit card, installment payment.

Application procedures. FAFSA, institutional form required. Priority date 3/1; no closing date. Applicants notified on rolling basis, must reply within 2 week(s) of notification. **Transfers:** No deadline. Aid awarded based on need and the availability of funds.

Contact. **Financial aid office:** (334) 244-3571
Anthony Richey, Director of Financial Aid
Box 244023
Montgomery, AL 36124-4023

Bevill State Community College

Sumiton, Alabama
www.bevillst.cc.al.us
Two-year public

College costs. Annual room price $1,100 for Sumiton and $1,350 for Fayette campuses, $900 for Hamilton, $990 for Jasper.

	Living at home
Tuition and fees (2002-2003):	$1,950
Out-of-state:	$3,750
Per-credit charge:	$60
Per-credit out-of-state:	$120
Books and supplies:	$900
Personal expenses:	$2,125
Transportation:	$1,125

Policies to reduce costs. Tuition/fee waivers for senior citizens, employees and their families. Credit/placement for qualifying scores on CLEP examinations.

Payment plans. Credit card payment.

Application procedures. FAFSA required. Priority date 5/1; closing date 8/25. Applicants notified on rolling basis starting 7/1.

Contact. Susanne Bush
Box 800
Sumiton, AL 35148

Birmingham-Southern College

Birmingham, Alabama
www.bsc.edu
Four-year private **Federal Code: 001012**

	Living at home	On-campus
Tuition and fees (2002-2003):	$18,050	$18,050
Room and board:		$6,720
Books and supplies:	$600	$600
Personal expenses:	$900	$500
Transportation:	$500	$500

Undergraduate aid. Need-based: Average financial aid package for full-time students was $15,639; for part-time $9,130. 42% awarded as scholarships/grants, 58% as loans/jobs. **Non-need-based:** 92% awarded as scholarships/grants, 8% as loans/jobs. Scholarships based on academics, alumni affiliation, art, athletics, job skills, leadership, minority status, music/drama, religious affiliation, state/district residency. **Student debt:** 41% of graduating class borrowed to fund education; average debt was $12,000. **Additional information:** Auditions required for music, theater, dance applicants seeking scholarships. Portfolios required for art applicants seeking scholarships, and essays recommended for all applicants seeking scholarships.

Freshman aid. Need-based: Out of 340 full-time freshmen, 222 applied for aid; 163 were judged to have need; of these 163 received aid. Average package met 82% of need. 55 students had full need met. Average scholarship/grant was $11,807; average loan $3,898. **Non-need based:** 46 full-time freshmen with need received non-need scholarships; 167 without need received awards; 63 received athletic scholarships.

Merit scholarships. McWane Honors Award; full tuition plus $11,000 per year stipend; based on academic achievement; 1 awarded. Neal and Anne Berte Scholarship; full tuition; academic achievement; 1 awarded. Blount-Monaghan/Vulcan Materials Company Scholarship; full tuition; academic achievement; 1 awarded. William Jones and Elizabeth Perry Rushton Scholarship; full tuition; based on academic achievement; 1 awarded. Phi Beta Kappa; full tuition; based on academic achievement. United Methodist Scholarship; $1,000-$2500; awarded to United Methodist with recommendation from senior United Methodist Minister.

Policies to reduce costs. Tuition/fee waivers for children of alumni, family of clergy, employees and their families. Credit/placement for qualifying scores on AP, IB, CLEP examinations. Work study available nights and weekends.

Payment plans. Credit card, installment, deferred payment.

Application procedures. Priority date 3/1; closing date 5/1. Applicants notified on rolling basis starting 2/1, must reply by 5/1.

Contact. **Financial aid office:** (205) 226-4688
Ron Day, Director of Financial Aid
900 Arkadelphia Road
Birmingham, AL 35254

Bishop State Community College

Mobile, Alabama
www.bishop.edu
Two-year public **Federal Code: 001030**

	Living at home
Tuition and fees (2002-2003):	$2,280
Out-of-state:	$4,080
Per-credit charge:	$60
Per-credit out-of-state:	$120
Board only:	$1,500
Books and supplies:	$700
Personal expenses:	$1,033
Transportation:	$1,260

Undergraduate aid. Non-need-based: Scholarships based on academics, athletics.

Policies to reduce costs. Tuition/fee waivers for senior citizens, employees and their families. Credit/placement for qualifying scores on CLEP examinations.

Payment plans. Credit card, deferred payment.

Application procedures. FAFSA, institutional form required. Priority date 6/15; closing date 7/31. Applicants notified on rolling basis, must reply within 2 week(s) of notification. **Transfers:** Priority date 6/15; closing date 7/31.

Contact. Charles Holloway, Manager of Student Financial Aid and Veterans Services
351 North Broad Street
Mobile, AL 36603-5898

Calhoun Community College

Decatur, Alabama
www.calhoun.edu
Two-year public **Federal Code: 001013**

	Living at home
Tuition and fees (2002-2003):	$2,010
Out-of-state:	$3,810
Per-credit charge:	$60
Per-credit out-of-state:	$120
Books and supplies:	$1,500
Personal expenses:	$1,000
Transportation:	$1,200

Undergraduate aid. Non-need-based: Scholarships based on academics.

Policies to reduce costs. Tuition/fee waivers for senior citizens, employees and their families. Credit/placement for qualifying scores on AP, CLEP examinations. Work study available nights and for part-time students.

Payment plans. Credit card payment.

Application procedures. FAFSA, institutional form required. Priority date 5/1; no closing date. Applicants notified on rolling basis starting 7/1, must reply within 2 week(s) of notification. **Transfers:** Closing date 3/15.

Contact. **Financial aid office:** (256) 306-2623
Deborah Byrd, Director of Student Financial Services
Box 2216
Decatur, AL 35609-2216

Central Alabama Community College

Alexander City, Alabama
www.cacc.cc.al.us
Two-year public **Federal Code: 001007**

	Living at home
Tuition and fees (2002-2003):	$2,040
Out-of-state:	$3,840
Per-credit charge:	$60
Per-credit out-of-state:	$120
Books and supplies:	$300
Personal expenses:	$500
Transportation:	$600

Undergraduate aid. Non-need-based: Scholarships based on academics, athletics, state/district residency.

Policies to reduce costs. Tuition/fee waivers for senior citizens. Credit/placement for qualifying scores on AP, CLEP examinations.

Payment plans. Credit card payment.

Application procedures. FAFSA, institutional form required. Priority date 7/15; no closing date. Applicants notified on rolling basis. **Transfers:** No deadline.

Contact. Lynn Spraggins, Financial Aid Officer
Box 699
Alexander City, AL 35011

Chattahoochee Valley Community College

Phenix City, Alabama
www.cvcc.cc.al.us
Two-year public **Federal Code: 012182**

	Living at home
Tuition and fees (2002-2003):	$2,100
Out-of-state:	$3,900
Per-credit charge:	$60
Per-credit out-of-state:	$120
Board only:	$5,400
Books and supplies:	$800
Personal expenses:	$750
Transportation:	$900

Undergraduate aid. Need-based: Need-based aid available for full-time and part-time students. **Non-need-based:** Scholarships based on academics, art, athletics, leadership, music/drama.

Policies to reduce costs. Tuition/fee waivers for senior citizens, employees and their families. Credit/placement for qualifying scores on AP, CLEP examinations. Work study available nights, weekends and for part-time students.

Payment plans. Credit card, deferred payment.

Application procedures. FAFSA required. Priority date 7/1; no closing date. Applicants notified on rolling basis, must reply within 1 week(s) of notification. **Transfers:** No deadline.

Contact. Joan Waters, Director of Financial Aid
2602 College Drive
Phenix City, AL 36869

Columbia Southern University

Orange Beach, Alabama
www.columbiasouthern.edu
Four-year proprietary

	Living at home
Tuition and fees (projected):	$1,900

Contact. 24847 Commercial Avenue
Orange Beach, AL 36561

Community College of the Air Force

Maxwell AFB, Alabama
www.au.af.mil/au/ccaf
Two-year public **Federal Code: 012308**

College costs. Students pay no tuition or fees for Air Force technical courses.

Undergraduate aid. Additional information: Air Force Tuition Assistance program available for general and technical education courses taken at civilian colleges and universities. Pays 75% of tuition costs.

Policies to reduce costs. Credit/placement for qualifying scores on AP, CLEP examinations.

Application procedures. No deadline.

Contact. Marshell Cobb
130 West Maxwell Boulevard
Maxwell AFB, AL 36112-6613

Concordia College

Selma, Alabama
www.concordiaselma.edu
Four-year private **Federal Code: 010554**

	Living at home	On-campus
Tuition and fees:	$6,364	$6,364
Room and board:		$3,200
Books and supplies:	$400	$400

Undergraduate aid. All financial aid based on need. Need-based aid available for full-time and part-time students.

Policies to reduce costs. Tuition/fee waivers for adults, employees and their families.

Payment plans. Installment payment.

Application procedures. FAFSA, institutional form, CSS PROFILE required. No deadline. Applicants notified on rolling basis starting 6/15, must reply within 2 week(s) of notification.

Contact. Tharsteen Bridges, Financial Aid Administrator
1804 Green Street
Selma, AL 36701

Douglas MacArthur State Technical College

Opp, Alabama
www.mstc.cc.al.us
Two-year public **Federal Code: 005698**

	Living at home
Tuition and fees (2002-2003):	$1,920
Out-of-state:	$3,720
Per-credit charge:	$60
Per-credit out-of-state:	$120
Books and supplies:	$845
Personal expenses:	$668
Transportation:	$1,560

Policies to reduce costs. Tuition/fee waivers for senior citizens, employees and their families.

Application procedures. FAFSA required. Priority date 6/1; no closing date. Applicants notified on rolling basis. **Transfers:** No deadline.

Contact. Financial aid office: (334) 493-3573 ext. 238
Wanda Bass, Financial Aid Officer/ Executive Assistant
Drawer 910
Opp, AL 36467

Enterprise State Junior College

Enterprise, Alabama
www.esjc.cc.al.us
Two-year public **Federal Code: 001015**

College costs. Distance learning students pay $76 per credit hour tuition.

	Living at home
Tuition and fees (2002-2003):	$2,040
Out-of-state:	$3,840
Per-credit charge:	$60
Per-credit out-of-state:	$120
Board only:	$1,800
Books and supplies:	$500
Personal expenses:	$500
Transportation:	$600

Undergraduate aid. Non-need-based: Scholarships based on academics, art, athletics, leadership, music/drama, state/district residency.

Policies to reduce costs. Tuition/fee waivers for senior citizens, employees and their families. Credit/placement for qualifying scores on AP, CLEP examinations. Work study available for part-time students.

Payment plans. Credit card, installment, deferred payment.

Application procedures. FAFSA, institutional form required. Priority date 6/11; no closing date. Applicants notified on rolling basis starting 7/1, must reply within 2 week(s) of notification. **Transfers:** No deadline.

Contact. Financial aid office: (334) 347-2623 ext. 214
Henry Quisenberry, Director, Student Financial Aid
Box 1300
Enterprise, AL 36331

Faulkner University

Montgomery, Alabama
www.faulkner.edu
Four-year private **Federal Code: 001003**

	Living at home
Tuition and fees:	$9,750
Books and supplies:	$900
Personal expenses:	$1,200
Transportation:	$1,000

Undergraduate aid. Need-based: Average financial aid package for full-time students was $6,800; for part-time $3,500. 33% awarded as scholarships/grants, 67% as loans/jobs. **Non-need-based:** 26% awarded as scholarships/grants, 74% as loans/jobs. Scholarships based on academics, alumni affiliation, athletics, leadership, music/drama, religious affiliation, state/district residency. **Student debt:** 78% of graduating class borrowed to fund education; average debt was $18,100.

Freshman aid. Need-based: Out of 232 full-time freshmen, 220 applied for aid; 183 were judged to have need; of these 183 received aid. Average package met 63% of need. 22 students had full need met. Average scholarship/grant was $2,400; average loan $2,625. **Non-need based:** 115 full-time freshmen with need received non-need scholarships; 12 without need received awards; 185 received athletic scholarships.

Policies to reduce costs. Tuition/fee waivers for adults, senior citizens, minority students, unemployed or children of unemployed, family of clergy, employees and their families. Tuition at time of enrollment guaranteed for 4 years; prepayment discount; credit/placement for qualifying scores on AP, CLEP examinations. Work study available nights, weekends and for part-time students.

Payment plans. Credit card, installment payment.

Application procedures. FAFSA, institutional form required. Priority date 5/1; no closing date. Applicants notified on rolling basis starting 6/1, must reply within 3 week(s) of notification. **Transfers:** No deadline.

Contact. Financial aid office: (334) 386-7195
William Jackson, Director of Financial Aid
5345 Atlanta Highway
Montgomery, AL 36109-3398

Gadsden State Community College

Gadsden, Alabama
www.gadsdenstate.edu
Two-year public **Federal Code: 001017**

	Living at home	On-campus
Tuition and fees (2002-2003):	$2,280	$2,280
Out-of-state:	$4,080	$4,080
Per-credit charge:	$60	$60
Per-credit out-of-state:	$120	$120
Room and board:		$2,350
Books and supplies:	$600	$600
Personal expenses:	$400	$400
Transportation:	$1,700	$900

Undergraduate aid. Need-based: Average financial aid package for full-time students was $4,200; for part-time $2,075. 98% awarded as scholarships/grants, 2% as loans/jobs. **Non-need-based:** Scholarships based on academics, athletics, state/district residency.

Policies to reduce costs. Tuition/fee waivers for senior citizens, unemployed or children of unemployed, employees and their families. Credit/placement for qualifying scores on IB, CLEP examinations. Work study available for part-time students.

Payment plans. Credit card payment.

Application procedures. FAFSA, institutional form required. Priority date 4/15; no closing date. Applicants notified on rolling basis starting 6/10, must reply within 2 week(s) of notification.

Contact. Kim Carter, Coordinator of Financial Aid
1001 George Wallace Drive
Gadsden, AL 35902-0227

George C. Wallace State Community College at Dothan

Dothan, Alabama
www.wallace.edu
Two-year public **Federal Code: 001018**

	Living at home
Tuition and fees (2002-2003):	$2,040
Out-of-state:	$3,840
Per-credit charge:	$60
Per-credit out-of-state:	$120
Books and supplies:	$600
Personal expenses:	$300
Transportation:	$720

Policies to reduce costs. Tuition/fee waivers for senior citizens. Credit/placement for qualifying scores on AP, CLEP examinations.

Payment plans. Credit card payment.

Application procedures. FAFSA required. No deadline. Applicants notified on rolling basis.

Contact. Erma Perry, Director of Financial Aid
1141 Wallace Drive
Dothan, AL 36303-9234

George C. Wallace State Community College at Selma

Selma, Alabama
www.wccs.edu
Two-year public **Federal Code: 005699**

	Living at home
Tuition and fees (2002-2003):	$2,040
Out-of-state:	$3,840
Per-credit charge:	$60
Per-credit out-of-state:	$120
Books and supplies:	$690
Personal expenses:	$976
Transportation:	$577

Undergraduate aid. Non-need-based: Scholarships based on academics, athletics.

Policies to reduce costs. Tuition/fee waivers for senior citizens, employees and their families. Credit/placement for qualifying scores on AP, CLEP examinations.

Payment plans. Credit card payment.

Application procedures. FAFSA required. Priority date 6/1; no closing date. Applicants notified on rolling basis starting 6/15. **Transfers:** No deadline.

Contact. Financial aid office: (334) 876-9290
Corey Bowie, Director of Financial Aid
PO Box 2530
Selma, AL 36702-2530

Harry M. Ayers State Technical College

Anniston, Alabama
www.ayers.cc.al.us
Two-year public **Federal Code: 005705**

College costs. Some Georgia residents pay in-state tuition.

	Living at home
Tuition and fees (2002-2003):	$2,040
Out-of-state:	$3,840
Per-credit charge:	$60
Per-credit out-of-state:	$120
Books and supplies:	$400
Transportation:	$1,200

Undergraduate aid. Need-based: Need-based aid available for full-time and part-time students. **Non-need-based:** Scholarships based on academics, leadership. **Additional information:** 50% tuition wavers available to some workers dislocated by layoffs or plant closures.

Merit scholarships. Ambassador Scholarships; tuition, fees, books. Presidential Technical Scholarship; tuition and fees for 12 or 8 semester hours each term.

Policies to reduce costs. Tuition/fee waivers for senior citizens, employees and their families. Credit/placement for qualifying scores on AP examinations.

Payment plans. Credit card, deferred payment.

Application procedures. FAFSA required. No deadline. Applicants notified on rolling basis starting 7/1.

Contact. Financial aid office: (205) 835-5420
Carol Tidwell, Director of Financial Aid
PO Box 1647
Anniston, AL 36202

Heritage Christian University

Florence, Alabama
www.hcu.edu
Four-year private **Federal Code: 015370**

	Living at home
Tuition and fees:	$7,710

Policies to reduce costs. Tuition/fee waivers for family members, family of clergy, employees and their families.

Payment plans. Credit card payment.

Application procedures. FAFSA required. Priority date 6/1; no closing date. Applicants notified on rolling basis starting 6/1, must reply within 2 week(s) of notification. **Transfers:** Priority date 6/1; no deadline.

Contact. James Collins, Director of Financial Aid
3625 Helton Drive
Florence, AL 35630

Herzing College

Homewood, Alabama
www.herzing.edu
Four-year proprietary **Federal Code: 010193**

College costs. Per-credit hour charge ranges from $220 to $270 depending on program. Full-time tuition ranges from $6,400 to $7,800 per academic year, including books.

Undergraduate aid. All financial aid based on need. Need-based aid available for full-time students.

Application procedures. FAFSA required.

Contact. Kentray Sims, Director, Financial Services
280 West Valley Avenue
Homewood, AL 35209

Huntingdon College

Montgomery, Alabama
www.huntingdon.edu
Four-year private **Federal Code: 001019**

	Living at home	On-campus
Tuition and fees:	$14,560	$14,560
Room and board:		$5,820
Board only:	$450	
Books and supplies:	$700	$700
Personal expenses:	$665	$865
Transportation:	$300	$500

Undergraduate aid. Need-based: Need-based aid available for full-time and part-time students. **Non-need-based:** Scholarships based on academics, alumni affiliation, art, leadership, music/drama, religious affiliation, state/district residency.

Merit scholarships. Merit scholarships based upon academic achievement range from $3,000 to full tuition. Special grants awarded in recognition of visual or performing arts talent.

Policies to reduce costs. Tuition/fee waivers for children of alumni, family of clergy, employees and their families. Tuition at time of enrollment guaranteed for 4 years; credit/placement for qualifying scores on AP, IB, CLEP examinations. Work study available nights and weekends.

Payment plans. Credit card, installment, deferred payment.

Application procedures. FAFSA, institutional form required. Priority date 4/15; no closing date. Applicants notified on rolling basis starting 3/1, must reply by 5/1 or within 4 week(s) of notification. **Transfers:** Scholarships range from $3,000 to half-tuition per year, based on academic credentials and evidence of character and leadership ability.

Contact. Financial aid office: (334) 833-4428
Lisa Lilley, Director of Financial Aid
1500 East Fairview Avenue
Montgomery, AL 36106-2148

ITT Technical Institute: Birmingham

Birmingham, Alabama
www.itt-tech.edu
Three-year proprietary **Federal Code: 030734**

College costs. Total program varies depending on course of study. Per-credit-hour charge: $347.

Policies to reduce costs. Tuition/fee waivers for employees and their families.

Payment plans. Credit card, installment payment.

Application procedures. FAFSA, institutional form required. No deadline. Applicants notified on rolling basis.

Contact. Steve Meeks, Director of Finance
500 Riverhills Business Park
Birmingham, AL 35242

J. F. Drake State Technical College

Huntsville, Alabama
www.dstc.cc.al.us
Two-year public **Federal Code: 00526**

	Living at home
Tuition and fees (2002-2003):	$2,280
Out-of-state:	$4,080
Per-credit charge:	$60
Per-credit out-of-state:	$120
Transportation:	$550

Undergraduate aid. Need-based: 95% awarded as scholarships/grants, 5% as loans/jobs. Need-based aid available for part-time students. **Non-need-based:** Scholarships based on academics, state/district residency.

Policies to reduce costs. Tuition/fee waivers for senior citizens. Work study available for part-time students.

Payment plans. Credit card payment.

Application procedures. FAFSA required. Priority date 7/1; no closing date. Applicants notified on rolling basis.

Contact. Financial aid office: (256) 551-3127
Joylyn Trotman, Financial Aid Officer
3421 Meridian Street, North
Huntsville, AL 35811

Jacksonville State University

Jacksonville, Alabama
www.jsucc.jsu.edu
Four-year public **Federal Code: 001020**

College costs. Students residing in northwest Georgia counties bordering upon Alabama not charged out-of-state tuition.

	Living at home	On-campus
Tuition and fees:	$3,240	$3,240
Out-of-state:	$6,480	$6,480
Room and board:		$3,470
Books and supplies:	$900	$900
Personal expenses:	$2,400	$2,400
Transportation:	$1,800	$1,100

Undergraduate aid. Need-based: Need-based aid available for full-time and part-time students. **Non-need-based:** Scholarships based on academics, alumni affiliation, art, athletics, music/drama.

Merit scholarships. Entering freshman from Alabama with ACT of 28 or 1230 SAT can apply for 4 year tuition scholarship.

Policies to reduce costs. Tuition/fee waivers for employees and their families. Credit/placement for qualifying scores on AP, CLEP examinations. Work study available nights, weekends and for part-time students.

Payment plans. Credit card payment.

Application procedures. FAFSA, institutional form required. Priority date 3/15; no closing date. Applicants notified on rolling basis starting 5/15, must reply within 2 week(s) of notification.

Contact. Financial aid office: (256) 782-5006
Vickie Adams, Director of Financial Aid
700 Pelham Road North
Jacksonville, AL 36265-1602

James H. Faulkner State Community College

Bay Minette, Alabama
www.faulknerstate.edu
Two-year public **Federal Code: 001060**

	Living at home	On-campus
Tuition and fees (2002-2003):	$2,370	$2,370
Out-of-state:	$4,170	$4,170
Per-credit charge:	$60	$60
Per-credit out-of-state:	$120	$120
Room and board:		$2,931
Books and supplies:	$450	$450
Personal expenses:	$700	$800
Transportation:	$950	$550

Policies to reduce costs. Tuition/fee waivers for senior citizens. Credit/placement for qualifying scores on AP examinations.

Payment plans. Credit card payment.

Application procedures. FAFSA, institutional form required. Priority date 7/1; closing date 8/1. Applicants notified on rolling basis starting 8/1.

Contact. Financial aid office: (334) 580-2151
Sam Chuks, Financial Aid Coordinator
1900 Highway 31 South
Bay Minette, AL 36507

Jefferson Davis Community College

Brewton, Alabama
www.jeffdavis.cc.al.us
Two-year public **Federal Code: 001021**

College costs. $76 per credit hour tuition for distance learning students.

	Living at home	On-campus
Tuition and fees (2002-2003):	$2,040	$2,040
Out-of-state:	$3,840	$3,840
Per-credit charge:	$60	$60
Per-credit out-of-state:	$120	$120
Room only:		$1,866
Books and supplies:	$800	$800
Personal expenses:	$800	$400
Transportation:	$400	$300

Undergraduate aid. Non-need-based: Scholarships based on academics, athletics.

Policies to reduce costs. Tuition/fee waivers for senior citizens.

Payment plans. Credit card payment.

Application procedures. FAFSA required. No deadline. Applicants notified on rolling basis.

Contact. Vanessa Kyles, Director of Financial Aid
Box 958
Brewton, AL 36427

Jefferson State Community College

Birmingham, Alabama
www.jscc.cc.al.us
Two-year public **Federal Code: 001022**

	Living at home
Tuition and fees (2002-2003):	$2,280
Out-of-state:	$4,080
Per-credit charge:	$60
Per-credit out-of-state:	$120
Books and supplies:	$960
Personal expenses:	$2,700

Undergraduate aid. **Need-based:** Need-based aid available for full-time and part-time students. **Non-need-based:** Scholarships based on academics, art, athletics, leadership, music/drama. **Additional information:** Any Alabama resident over age 60 may attend classes tuition free.

Policies to reduce costs. Tuition/fee waivers for senior citizens, employees and their families. Credit/placement for qualifying scores on AP, CLEP examinations. Work study available nights and for part-time students.

Payment plans. Credit card payment.

Application procedures. FAFSA, institutional form required. Priority date 5/1; no closing date. Applicants notified on rolling basis starting 6/1. **Transfers:** No deadline. Transfer students are not eligible for academic scholarships until they have completed 12 hours at JSCC.

Contact. **Financial aid office:** (205) 856-7704
Tracy Adams, Director, Financial Aid
2601 Carson Road
Birmingham, AL 35215-3098

Judson College

Marion, Alabama
www.judson.edu
Four-year private **Federal Code: 001023**

	Living at home	On-campus
Tuition and fees (projected):	$9,027	$9,027
Room and board:		$5,649
Books and supplies:	$700	$700
Personal expenses:	$1,600	$1,600
Transportation:	$400	$400

Undergraduate aid. **Need-based:** Average financial aid package for full-time students was $10,078; for part-time $3,994. 61% awarded as scholarships/grants, 39% as loans/jobs. **Non-need-based:** 84% awarded as scholarships/grants, 16% as loans/jobs. Scholarships based on academics, art, athletics, job skills, music/drama, religious affiliation, state/district residency. **Student debt:** 73% of graduating class borrowed to fund education; average debt was $11,793.

Freshman aid. **Need-based:** Out of 93 full-time freshmen, 93 applied for aid; 73 were judged to have need; of these 73 received aid. Average package met 86% of need. 18 students had full need met. Average scholarship/grant was $9,083; average loan $2,535. **Non-need based:** 8 full-time freshmen with need received non-need scholarships; 21 without need received awards; 2 received athletic scholarships.

Merit scholarships. Garner-Webb Honors Scholarship, full tuition, up to 5 given to applicants who are National Merit Finalists or have ACT of 30 or above. Lockhart Competitive Scholarships: 1 full tuition, 2 for $2,500, 3 for $2,000; awarded based on exam scores. Music scholarships: $1,500; awarded based on audition.

Policies to reduce costs. Tuition/fee waivers for family of clergy, employees and their families. Credit/placement for qualifying scores on AP, IB, CLEP examinations.

Payment plans. Credit card, installment payment.

Application procedures. FAFSA, institutional form required. Priority date 3/1; no closing date. Applicants notified on rolling basis starting 1/15, must reply within 2 week(s) of notification. **Transfers:** Priority date 3/1; no deadline.

Contact. **Financial aid office:** (334) 683-5157
Doris Wilson, Financial Aid Officer
Box 120
Marion, AL 36756

Lawson State Community College

Birmingham, Alabama
www.lawsonstate.edu
Two-year public **Federal Code: 001059**

	Living at home
Tuition and fees (2002-2003):	$2,040
Out-of-state:	$3,840
Per-credit charge:	$60
Per-credit out-of-state:	$120
Books and supplies:	$450
Personal expenses:	$900
Transportation:	$850

Undergraduate aid. All financial aid based on need. 97% awarded as scholarships/grants, 3% as loans/jobs. Need-based aid available for part-time students.

Policies to reduce costs. Tuition/fee waivers for children of alumni, senior citizens, employees and their families. Work study available nights and for part-time students.

Payment plans. Credit card payment.

Application procedures. FAFSA required. Priority date 6/1; no closing date. Applicants notified on rolling basis starting 8/1, must reply within 2 week(s) of notification. **Transfers:** No deadline.

Contact. **Financial aid office:** (205) 929-6380
Cassandra Matthews, Director of Financial Aid
3060 Wilson Road SW
Birmingham, AL 35221

Lurleen B. Wallace Junior College

Andalusia, Alabama
www.alaweb.com
Two-year public **Federal Code: 008988**

	Living at home
Tuition and fees (2002-2003):	$2,040
Out-of-state:	$3,840
Per-credit charge:	$60
Per-credit out-of-state:	$120
Books and supplies:	$450
Personal expenses:	$600
Transportation:	$600

Undergraduate aid. **Non-need-based:** Scholarships based on academics, art, athletics, leadership, music/drama, state/district residency.

Policies to reduce costs. Tuition/fee waivers for senior citizens. Credit/placement for qualifying scores on AP, CLEP examinations.

Payment plans. Credit card payment.

Application procedures. Priority date 5/1; no closing date. Applicants notified on rolling basis starting 7/1, must reply within 2 week(s) of notification. **Transfers:** No deadline.

Contact. Donna Bass, Coordinator of Admissions and Financial Aid
Box 1418
Andalusia, AL 36420-1418

Marion Military Institute

Marion, Alabama
www.marionmilitary.org
Two-year private **Federal Code: 001026**

	Living at home	On-campus
Tuition and fees (projected):	$12,000	$12,000
Out-of-state:	$13,000	$13,000
Room and board:		$3,000
Books and supplies:	$900	$900
Personal expenses:	$1,900	$3,400
Transportation:	$500	$1,200

Undergraduate aid. All financial aid based on need. 93% awarded as scholarships/grants, 7% as loans/jobs. Need-based aid available for part-time students. **Student debt:** 27% of graduating class borrowed to fund education; average debt was $2,505.

Policies to reduce costs. Tuition/fee waivers for family members, employees and their families. Tuition at time of enrollment guaranteed for 2 years. Work study available nights and weekends.

Payment plans. Installment, deferred payment.

Application procedures. FAFSA required. Priority date 6/15; no closing date. Applicants notified on rolling basis starting 6/15, must reply within 6 week(s) of notification. **Transfers:** Priority date 5/15; no deadline.

Contact. **Financial aid office:** (334) 683-2309
Joe Wood, Chief Financial Aid Officer
1101 Washington Street
Marion, AL 36756-0420

Miles College

Fairfield, Alabama
www.miles.edu
Four-year private **Federal Code: 001028**

	Living at home	On-campus
Tuition and fees:	$5,028	$5,028
Room and board:		$3,470
Books and supplies:	$400	$400
Personal expenses:	$1,000	$1,000
Transportation:	$500	$500

Undergraduate aid. All financial aid based on need. Need-based aid available for full-time and part-time students.

Policies to reduce costs. Tuition/fee waivers for family of clergy, employees and their families.

Payment plans. Installment payment.

Application procedures. FAFSA required. Priority date 4/15; no closing date. Applicants notified on rolling basis starting 7/15, must reply within 2 week(s) of notification.

Contact. P.N. Lanier, Financial Aid Administrator
5500 Myron-Massey Boulevard
Fairfield, AL 35064

Northeast Alabama Community College

Rainsville, Alabama
www.nacc.edu
Two-year public **Federal Code: 001031**

	Living at home
Tuition and fees (2002-2003):	$2,040
Out-of-state:	$3,840
Per-credit charge:	$60
Per-credit out-of-state:	$120
Personal expenses:	$1,500
Transportation:	$750

Undergraduate aid. **Need-based:** 96% awarded as scholarships/grants, 4% as loans/jobs. Need-based aid available for part-time students. **Non-need-based:** Scholarships based on academics, art, leadership, music/drama.

Policies to reduce costs. Tuition/fee waivers for senior citizens, employees and their families. Credit/placement for qualifying scores on AP, CLEP examinations. Work study available for part-time students.

Application procedures. FAFSA required. No deadline. Applicants notified on rolling basis.

Contact. **Financial aid office:** (256) 228-6001 ext. 227
Harold Brookshire, Director of Financial Aid
Admissions Office, NACC
Rainsville, AL 35986

Northwest-Shoals Community College

Muscle Shoals, Alabama
www.nwscc.edu
Two-year public **Federal Code: 005697**

	Living at home	On-campus
Tuition and fees (2002-2003):	$2,040	$2,040
Out-of-state:	$3,840	$3,840
Per-credit charge:	$60	$60
Per-credit out-of-state:	$120	$120
Room only:		$1,450
Books and supplies:	$700	$700
Personal expenses:	$900	
Transportation:	$1,207	

Undergraduate aid. **Need-based:** 65% awarded as scholarships/grants, 35% as loans/jobs. Need-based aid available for part-time students. **Non-need-based:** Scholarships based on academics, art, athletics, leadership, minority status, music/drama.

Policies to reduce costs. Tuition/fee waivers for senior citizens, employees and their families. Tuition at time of enrollment guaranteed for 2 years; credit/placement for qualifying scores on AP, CLEP examinations. Work study available nights and for part-time students.

Payment plans. Credit card payment.

Application procedures. FAFSA, institutional form required. Priority date 4/1; no closing date. Applicants notified on rolling basis, must reply within 2 week(s) of notification. **Transfers:** Priority date 3/1; closing date 6/1. Students without 1-year Alabama residency before fall term ineligible for state grant.

Contact. **Financial aid office:** (256) 331-5368
Joel Parris, Director of Student Financial Aid Services
Box 2545
Muscle Shoals, AL 35662

Oakwood College

Huntsville, Alabama
www.oakwood.edu
Four-year private **Federal Code: 001033**

	Living at home	On-campus
Tuition and fees:	$10,708	$10,708
Room and board:		$6,128

Undergraduate aid. **Need-based:** Need-based aid available for full-time students. **Non-need-based:** Scholarships based on academics, leadership, religious affiliation, state/district residency.

Policies to reduce costs. Credit/placement for qualifying scores on AP, CLEP examinations.

Payment plans. Credit card, installment payment.

Application procedures. FAFSA required. Priority date 3/31; no closing date. Applicants notified on rolling basis starting 4/1. **Transfers:** Priority date 3/30; no deadline.

Contact. **Financial aid office:** (256) 726-7208
Fred Stennis, Director of Financial Aid
7000 Adventist Boulevard, NW
Huntsville, AL 35896

Prince Institute of Professional Studies

Montgomery, Alabama
www.princeinstitute.com
Two-year proprietary **Federal Code: 022960**

College costs. Additional required fees vary per program.

	Living at home
Tuition and fees:	$5,898
Books and supplies:	$272
Personal expenses:	$1,674
Transportation:	$1,386

Undergraduate aid. All financial aid based on need. 20% awarded as scholarships/grants, 80% as loans/jobs. Need-based aid available for part-time students.

Payment plans. Installment payment.

Application procedures. FAFSA required. No deadline.

Contact. **Financial aid office:** (334) 271-1670
Tracie Campbell, Financial Aid Administrator
7735 Atlanta Highway
Montgomery, AL 36117-4231

Reid State Technical College

Evergreen, Alabama
www.rstc.cc.al.us
Two-year public **Federal Code: 005692**

	Living at home
Tuition and fees (2002-2003):	$2,040
Out-of-state:	$3,840
Per-credit charge:	$60
Per-credit out-of-state:	$120
Books and supplies:	$400

Undergraduate aid. Need-based: 98% awarded as scholarships/grants, 2% as loans/jobs. Need-based aid available for part-time students.

Policies to reduce costs. Tuition/fee waivers for senior citizens, employees and their families. Credit/placement for qualifying scores on CLEP examinations. Work study available nights and for part-time students.

Payment plans. Credit card payment.

Application procedures. FAFSA required. No deadline. Applicants notified on rolling basis. **Transfers:** No deadline.

Contact. Linda Brantley, Financial Aid Officer
Box 588
Evergreen, AL 36401

Remington College: Southeast College of Technology

Mobile, Alabama
www.educationamerica.com
Two-year private

College costs. Tuition varies according to program. All required fees included in tuition cost.

	Living at home
Tuition and fees (2002-2003):	$12,936
Per-credit charge:	$270

Undergraduate aid. All financial aid based on need. Need-based aid available for full-time students.

Policies to reduce costs. Work study available nights.

Application procedures. FAFSA required.

Contact. **Financial aid office:** (251) 343-8200
Linda Calvanese, Financial Aid Director
828 Downtowner Loop West
Mobile, AL 36609-5404

Samford University

Birmingham, Alabama
www.samford.edu
Four-year private **Federal Code: 001036**

	Living at home	On-campus
Tuition and fees:	$13,154	$13,154
Room and board:		$5,494
Books and supplies:	$840	$840
Personal expenses:	$2,642	$2,642
Transportation:	$990	$890

Undergraduate aid. Need-based: Average financial aid package for full-time students was $9,708; for part-time $4,888. 58% awarded as scholarships/grants, 42% as loans/jobs. **Non-need-based:** 52% awarded as scholarships/grants, 48% as loans/jobs. Scholarships based on academics, athletics, leadership, music/drama, religious affiliation, state/district residency. **Student debt:** 46% of graduating class borrowed to fund education; average debt was $15,863. **Additional information:** Consideration for merit scholarships automatically given to students with admission files completed by December 15.

Freshman aid. Need-based: Out of 654 full-time freshmen, 442 applied for aid; 266 were judged to have need; of these 264 received aid. Average package met 77% of need. 73 students had full need met. Average scholarship/grant was $7,527; average loan $2,389. **Non-need based:** 277 without need received awards; 45 received athletic scholarships.

Policies to reduce costs. Tuition/fee waivers for family of clergy, employees and their families. Credit/placement for qualifying scores on AP, IB, CLEP examinations.

Payment plans. Credit card payment.

Application procedures. FAFSA required. Priority date 3/15; no closing date. Applicants notified on rolling basis starting 3/1.

Contact. **Financial aid office:** (205) 726-2905
Ann Waller, Director of Financial Aid
800 Lakeshore Drive
Birmingham, AL 35229

Selma University

Selma, Alabama
Four-year private
Federal Code: 001037

	Living at home
Tuition and fees:	$3,130
Books and supplies:	$600
Personal expenses:	$600

Policies to reduce costs. Tuition/fee waivers for family of clergy.

Payment plans. Installment payment.

Application procedures. FAFSA required. Priority date 9/15; no closing date. Applicants notified on rolling basis starting 8/23, must reply within 2 week(s) of notification.

Contact. Marva White, Director of Financial Aid
1501 Lapsley Street
Selma, AL 36701

Shelton State Community College

Tuscaloosa, Alabama
www.sheltonstate.edu
Two-year public **Federal Code: 005691**

	Living at home
Tuition and fees (2002-2003):	$2,280
Out-of-state:	$4,080
Per-credit charge:	$60
Per-credit out-of-state:	$120
Books and supplies:	$739
Personal expenses:	$200
Transportation:	$500

Undergraduate aid. All financial aid based on need. Need-based aid available for full-time and part-time students.

Policies to reduce costs. Tuition/fee waivers for senior citizens, employees and their families. Credit/placement for qualifying scores on AP, IB examinations. Work study available nights.

Payment plans. Credit card payment.

Application procedures. FAFSA required. Priority date 6/30; no closing date. Applicants notified on rolling basis starting 7/30.

Contact. **Financial aid office:** (205) 391-2376
Betty Brown-Bogan, Financial Aid Coordinator
9500 Old Greensboro Road
Tuscaloosa, AL 35405

Snead State Community College

Boaz, Alabama
www.snead.edu
Two-year public **Federal Code: 001038**

	Living at home	On-campus
Tuition and fees (2002-2003):	$2,040	$2,040
Out-of-state:	$3,840	$3,840
Per-credit charge:	$60	$60
Per-credit out-of-state:	$120	$120
Room and board:		$1,724
Board only:	$1,000	
Books and supplies:	$800	$800
Personal expenses:	$1,000	$1,000
Transportation:	$1,200	$600

Undergraduate aid. Need-based: Need-based aid available for full-time and part-time students. **Non-need-based:** Scholarships based on academics, alumni affiliation, art, athletics, leadership, music/drama.

Policies to reduce costs. Tuition/fee waivers for senior citizens, employees and their families. Credit/placement for qualifying scores on AP, CLEP examinations. Work study available nights and for part-time students.

Payment plans. Credit card payment.

Application procedures. FAFSA required. Priority date 4/15; no closing date. Applicants notified on rolling basis starting 4/15. **Transfers:** Priority date 4/15; no deadline.

Contact. Financial aid office: (256) 840-4127
Melissa Rice, Financial Aid Director
Box 734
Boaz, AL 35957-0734

South University

Montgomery, Alabama
www.southuniversity.edu
Four-year proprietary **Federal Code: 004463**

College costs. Information technology and physical therapy assistant programs cost $11,085 per academic year.

	Living at home
Tuition and fees (projected):	$9,585
Books and supplies:	$600
Personal expenses:	$1,622
Transportation:	$1,206

Undergraduate aid. All financial aid based on need. Need-based aid available for full-time and part-time students.

Policies to reduce costs. Tuition/fee waivers for employees and their families. Work study available for part-time students.

Payment plans. Credit card, installment, deferred payment.

Application procedures. FAFSA required. No deadline. Applicants notified on rolling basis starting 6/1.

Contact. Financial aid office: (334) 395-8800
James Berry, Director of Financial Aid
5355 Vaughn Road
Montgomery, AL 36116-1120

Southeastern Bible College

Birmingham, Alabama
www.sebc.edu
Four-year private **Federal Code: 013857**

	Living at home	On-campus
Tuition and fees (projected):	$6,580	$6,580
Out-of-state:	$6,580	$6,580
Room and board:		$3,640
Books and supplies:	$500	$500
Transportation:	$720	$400

Undergraduate aid. Need-based: Average financial aid package for full-time students was $6,457; for part-time $2,625. 31% awarded as scholarships/grants, 69% as loans/jobs. **Non-need-based:** 89% awarded as scholarships/grants, 11% as loans/jobs. Scholarships based on academics. **Student debt:** 50% of graduating class borrowed to fund education; average debt was $20,000.

Freshman aid. Need-based: Out of 40 full-time freshmen, 40 applied for aid; 39 were judged to have need; of these 39 received aid. Average package met 60% of need. 6 students had full need met. Average scholarship/grant was $1,500; average loan $2,625. **Non-need based:** 24 full-time freshmen with need received non-need scholarships.

Policies to reduce costs. Tuition/fee waivers for family of clergy, employees and their families. Credit/placement for qualifying scores on AP, CLEP examinations.

Payment plans. Credit card, installment payment.

Application procedures. FAFSA, institutional form required. Priority date 5/1; closing date 8/15. Applicants notified by 7/15, must reply within 2 week(s) of notification.

Contact. Joanne Belin, Financial Aid Officer
3001 Highway 280 East
Birmingham, AL 35243-4181

Southern Christian University

Montgomery, Alabama
www.southernchristian.edu
Four-year private **Federal Code: 016885**

	Living at home
Tuition and fees:	$11,600
Books and supplies:	$800
Personal expenses:	$1,739
Transportation:	$1,730

Undergraduate aid. Need-based: Need-based aid available for full-time and part-time students. **Non-need-based:** Scholarships based on academics, leadership. **Additional information:** Scholarships based on need and grades. Half-tuition scholarship is available for full-time undergraduate students.

Policies to reduce costs. Tuition/fee waivers for senior citizens, employees and their families. Credit/placement for qualifying scores on AP, CLEP examinations.

Payment plans. Credit card payment.

Application procedures. FAFSA, institutional form required. Priority date 5/1; closing date 6/30. Applicants notified by 6/30, must reply by 8/15 or within 2 week(s) of notification. **Transfers:** No deadline.

Contact. Financial aid office: (800) 351-4040 ext. 227
Rosemary Kennington, Financial Aid Officer
1200 Taylor Road
Montgomery, AL 36117-3553

Southern Union State Community College

Wadley, Alabama
suscc.cc.al.us
Two-year public **Federal Code: 001040**

	Living at home	On-campus
Tuition and fees (2002-2003):	$2,280	$2,280
Out-of-state:	$4,080	$4,080
Per-credit charge:	$60	$60
Per-credit out-of-state:	$120	$120
Room and board:		$2,400
Books and supplies:	$400	$400
Personal expenses:	$600	$1,100
Transportation:	$600	$600

Undergraduate aid. Need-based: Need-based aid available for full-time and part-time students.

Application procedures. FAFSA required. No deadline. Applicants notified on rolling basis.

Contact. Ben Jordan, Business Manager
750 Roberts Street
Wadley, AL 36276

Spring Hill College

Mobile, Alabama
www.shc.edu
Four-year private **Federal Code: 001041**

	Living at home	On-campus
Tuition and fees:	$19,000	$19,000
Room and board:		$6,868
Board only:	$800	
Books and supplies:	$1,100	$1,100
Personal expenses:	$990	$990
Transportation:	$1,440	$990

Undergraduate aid. Need-based: Average financial aid package for full-time students was $16,254; for part-time $7,337. 63% awarded as scholarships/grants, 37% as loans/jobs. **Non-need-based:** 64% awarded as scholarships/grants, 36% as loans/jobs. Scholarships based on academics, alumni affiliation, athletics, leadership, minority status, state/district residency. **Student debt:** 69% of graduating class borrowed to fund education; average debt was $17,214.

Freshman aid. Need-based: Out of 288 full-time freshmen, 284 applied for aid; 196 were judged to have need; of these 196 received aid. Average package met 89% of need. 45 students had full need met. Average scholarship/grant was $7,948; average loan $3,557. **Non-need based:** 131 full-time freshmen with need received non-need scholarships; 93 without need received awards; 58 received athletic scholarships.

Merit scholarships. 4 Spring Hill Scholars scholarships; $23,000 awarded each fall to incoming freshmen who have demonstrated academic excellence, leadership, and service; 3.4 high school GPA, and a 27 ACT or 1200 SAT. Trustee Honors Scholarship; $12,500-$14,000; 3.4 high school GPA and 27 ACT. Presidential Honors Scholarship; $6,000-$10,000; 3.25 high school GPA and 26 ACT. Faculty Honors Scholarship; $4,000-$7,000; 3.25 high school GPA and 24 ACT. Academic Honors Scholarship; $1,000-$4,000; 3.0 high school GPA and 22 ACT. 10 AHANA Leadership Scholarships; $4,000; awarded to African American, Hispanic, Asian or Native American students who have demonstrated exceptional leadership qualities.

Policies to reduce costs. Tuition/fee waivers for family members, employees and their families. Credit/placement for qualifying scores on AP, IB, CLEP examinations. Work study available for part-time students.

Payment plans. Credit card, deferred payment.

Application procedures. FAFSA, institutional form required. Priority date 3/1; no closing date. Applicants notified on rolling basis starting 3/1, must reply by 5/1 or within 2 week(s) of notification. **Transfers:** Priority date 6/15; no deadline. Transfer students must submit a financial aid transcript from each higher education institution previously attended. Transfer Honors Scholarships are awarded to transfer students with a cumulative 3.2 college GPA and a minimum of 20 transferable semester hours.

Contact. Financial aid office: (251) 380-3460
Betty Harlan, Director of Financial Aid
4000 Dauphin Street
Mobile, AL 36608

Stillman College

Tuscaloosa, Alabama
www.stillman.edu
Four-year private **Federal Code: 001044**

	Living at home	On-campus
Tuition and fees (projected):	$7,848	$7,848
Room and board:		$4,236

Undergraduate aid. All financial aid based on need. Need-based aid available for full-time and part-time students.

Policies to reduce costs. Tuition/fee waivers for employees and their families. Credit/placement for qualifying scores on AP, CLEP examinations.

Payment plans. Installment payment.

Application procedures. FAFSA, institutional form required. Priority date 6/1; no closing date. Applicants notified on rolling basis, must reply within 4 week(s) of notification. **Transfers:** Priority date 6/1.

Contact. Financial aid office: (205) 366-8950
Jacqueline Morris, Director of Financial Aid
3600 Stillman Boulevard
Tuscaloosa, AL 35403

Talladega College

Talladega, Alabama
www.talladega.edu
Four-year private **Federal Code: 001046**

	Living at home	On-campus
Tuition and fees (projected):	$6,232	$6,232
Room and board:		$3,622
Board only:	$1,200	
Books and supplies:	$100	$100
Personal expenses:	$500	$900
Transportation:	$1,000	$1,000

Undergraduate aid. All financial aid based on need. Need-based aid available for full-time and part-time students.

Policies to reduce costs. Tuition/fee waivers for employees and their families. Credit/placement for qualifying scores on AP examinations. Work study available for part-time students.

Payment plans. Credit card, installment payment.

Application procedures. FAFSA, institutional form required. Priority date 5/1; closing date 6/10. Applicants notified by 5/1, must reply within 2 week(s) of notification.

Contact. Financial aid office: (256) 761-6256
Melvin Jefferson, Director of Financial Aid
627 West Battle Street
Talladega, AL 35160

Trenholm State Technical College

Montgomery, Alabama
www.trenholmtech.cc.al.us
Two-year public **Federal Code: 005734**

	Living at home
Tuition and fees (2002-2003):	$2,040
Out-of-state:	$3,840
Per-credit charge:	$60
Per-credit out-of-state:	$120
Books and supplies:	$850
Personal expenses:	$800
Transportation:	$200

Undergraduate aid. Need-based: Need-based aid available for full-time and part-time students. **Non-need-based:** Scholarships based on state/district residency.

Merit scholarships. Leadership Scholarships; $2,000-$2,800 annually.

Policies to reduce costs. Tuition/fee waivers for senior citizens, employees and their families. Tuition at time of enrollment guaranteed for 2 years; credit/placement for qualifying scores on CLEP examinations. Work study available for part-time students.

Payment plans. Credit card, installment, deferred payment.

Application procedures. FAFSA required. No deadline. Applicants notified on rolling basis.

Contact. Betty Edwards, Director of Financial Aid
1225 Air Base Boulevard
Montgomery, AL 36108

Troy State University

Troy, Alabama
www.troyst.edu
Four-year public **Federal Code: 001047**

	Living at home	On-campus
Tuition and fees:	$4,056	$4,056
Out-of-state:	$7,476	$7,476
Room and board:		$4,770
Books and supplies:	$360	$360

Undergraduate aid. Need-based: Need-based aid available for full-time and part-time students. **Non-need-based:** Scholarships based on academics, athletics.

Policies to reduce costs. Tuition/fee waivers for employees and their families. Credit/placement for qualifying scores on AP, CLEP examinations.

Payment plans. Credit card, deferred payment.

Application procedures. FAFSA, institutional form required. Priority date 5/1; no closing date. Applicants notified on rolling basis starting 5/1, must reply within 2 week(s) of notification.

Contact. **Financial aid office:** (334) 670-3186
Carol Supri, Director of Financial Aid
University Avenue, Adams Administration 111
Troy, AL 36082

Troy State University Dothan

Dothan, Alabama
www.tsud.edu
Four-year public **Federal Code: 001048**

	Living at home
Tuition and fees (projected):	$3,743
Out-of-state:	$7,156
Board only:	$3,480
Books and supplies:	$600
Personal expenses:	$1,975
Transportation:	$2,305

Undergraduate aid. **Need-based:** 33% awarded as scholarships/grants, 67% as loans/jobs. Need-based aid available for part-time students. **Non-need-based:** Scholarships based on academics.

Policies to reduce costs. Tuition/fee waivers for senior citizens, employees and their families. Credit/placement for qualifying scores on AP, CLEP examinations. Work study available for part-time students.

Payment plans. Credit card, installment payment.

Application procedures. FAFSA, institutional form required. Priority date 5/1; no closing date. Applicants notified on rolling basis starting 2/1, must reply within 2 week(s) of notification. **Transfers:** No deadline.

Contact. **Financial aid office:** (334) 983-6556 ext. 255
Jonua Byrd, Financial Aid Officer
PO Box 8368
Dothan, AL 36304

Troy State University in Montgomery

Montgomery, Alabama
www.tsum.edu
Four-year public **Federal Code: 001049**

	Living at home
Tuition and fees (2002-2003):	$3,290
Out-of-state:	$6,510
Books and supplies:	$840
Transportation:	$1,050

Undergraduate aid. All financial aid based on need. Average financial aid package for full-time students was $5,000. 32% awarded as scholarships/grants, 68% as loans/jobs. Need-based aid available for part-time students.

Freshman aid. Out of 86 full-time freshmen, 86 applied for aid; 56 were judged to have need; of these 47 received aid. Average package met 50% of need. Average scholarship/grant was $4,000; average loan $2,625.

Policies to reduce costs. Tuition/fee waivers for employees and their families. Credit/placement for qualifying scores on CLEP examinations.

Payment plans. Credit card, deferred payment.

Application procedures. FAFSA, institutional form required. Priority date 5/1; no closing date. Applicants notified on rolling basis, must reply within 2 week(s) of notification.

Contact. **Financial aid office:** (334) 241-9520
John Brown, Director of Financial Aid
PO Drawer 4419
Montgomery, AL 36103-4419

Tuskegee University

Tuskegee, Alabama
www.tusk.edu
Four-year private **Federal Code: 001050**

	Living at home	On-campus
Tuition and fees (2002-2003):	$10,784	$10,784
Room and board:		$5,680
Board only:	$2,400	
Books and supplies:	$848	$848
Personal expenses:	$826	$2,000
Transportation:	$370	$888

Undergraduate aid. **Need-based:** Average financial aid package for full-time students was $13,666. 37% awarded as scholarships/grants, 63% as loans/jobs. Need-based aid available for part-time students. **Non-need-based:** 23% awarded as scholarships/grants, 77% as loans/jobs. Scholarships based on academics, athletics, state/district residency. **Student debt:** 91% of graduating class borrowed to fund education; average debt was $30,000.

Freshman aid. **Need-based:** Out of 661 full-time freshmen, 601 applied for aid; 510 were judged to have need; of these 433 received aid. Average package met 85% of need. 324 students had full need met. Average scholarship/grant was $8,000; average loan $5,625. **Non-need based:** 368 full-time freshmen with need received non-need scholarships; 198 without need received awards; 52 received athletic scholarships.

Policies to reduce costs. Tuition/fee waivers for family members, employees and their families. Credit/placement for qualifying scores on AP, CLEP examinations.

Payment plans. Installment payment.

Application procedures. FAFSA, institutional form, CSS PROFILE required. Closing date 3/31. Applicants notified on rolling basis starting 5/15, must reply within 2 week(s) of notification.

Contact. Leslie Porter, Vice President for Business and Fiscal Affairs
102 Old Administration Building
Tuskegee, AL 36088

University of Alabama

Tuscaloosa, Alabama
www.ua.edu
Four-year public **Federal Code: 001051**

	Living at home	On-campus
Tuition and fees (2002-2003):	$3,556	$3,556
Out-of-state:	$9,624	$9,624
Room and board:		$4,232
Board only:	$3,026	
Books and supplies:	$700	$700
Personal expenses:	$1,690	$1,690
Transportation:	$634	$634

Undergraduate aid. **Need-based:** Average financial aid package for full-time students was $7,622; for part-time $5,409. 34% awarded as scholarships/grants, 66% as loans/jobs. **Non-need-based:** 44% awarded as scholarships/grants, 56% as loans/jobs. Scholarships based on academics, alumni affiliation, art, athletics, leadership, minority status, music/drama, state/district residency. **Student debt:** 49% of graduating class borrowed to fund education; average debt was $18,978.

Freshman aid. **Need-based:** Out of 2,404 full-time freshmen, 1,518 applied for aid; 727 were judged to have need; of these 717 received aid. Average package met 75% of need. 200 students had full need met. Average scholarship/grant was $3,005; average loan $2,866. **Non-need based:** 318 full-time freshmen with need received non-need scholarships; 650 without need received awards; 44 received athletic scholarships.

Merit scholarships. National Merit, Achievement, Hispanic Finalist and Semi-Finalist Award programs available, award based leadership skills program available.

Policies to reduce costs. Tuition/fee waivers for employees and their families. Credit/placement for qualifying scores on AP, IB, CLEP examinations. Work study available nights, weekends and for part-time students.

Payment plans. Credit card, installment, deferred payment.

Application procedures. FAFSA required. Priority date 3/1; no closing date. Applicants notified on rolling basis starting 4/1, must reply within 3 week(s) of notification. **Transfers:** Priority date 3/1; no deadline. Scholarship opportunities for transfer students.

Contact. **Financial aid office:** (205) 348-5666
Lisa Harris, Assistant Vice President for Admissions and Financial Aid
Box 870132
Tuscaloosa, AL 35487-0132

University of Alabama at Birmingham

Birmingham, Alabama
www.uab.edu
Four-year public **Federal Code: 001052**

	Living at home	On-campus
Tuition and fees (2002-2003):	$3,880	$3,880
Out-of-state:	$7,810	$7,810
Room only:		$2,588
Books and supplies:	$900	$900
Personal expenses:	$1,500	$1,500
Transportation:	$1,875	$938

Undergraduate aid. Need-based: Average financial aid package for full-time students was $9,357; for part-time $5,991. 27% awarded as scholarships/grants, 73% as loans/jobs. **Non-need-based:** 22% awarded as scholarships/grants, 78% as loans/jobs. Scholarships based on academics, alumni affiliation, art, athletics, leadership, minority status, music/drama, state/district residency. **Student debt:** 48% of graduating class borrowed to fund education; average debt was $16,852.

Freshman aid. Need-based: Out of 1,224 full-time freshmen, 861 applied for aid; 607 were judged to have need; of these 602 received aid. Average package met 34% of need. 110 students had full need met. Average scholarship/grant was $2,965; average loan $2,663. **Non-need based:** 329 full-time freshmen with need received non-need scholarships; 195 without need received awards; 52 received athletic scholarships.

Policies to reduce costs. Tuition/fee waivers for employees and their families. Credit/placement for qualifying scores on AP, IB, CLEP examinations.

Payment plans. Credit card payment.

Application procedures. FAFSA, institutional form required. Priority date 4/1; no closing date. Applicants notified by 4/15, must reply within 2 week(s) of notification.

Contact. **Financial aid office:** (205) 934-8223
Jan May, Director of Financial Aid
260 HUC, 1530 3rd Avenue South
Birmingham, AL 35294-1150

University of Alabama in Huntsville

Huntsville, Alabama
www.uah.edu
Four-year public **Federal Code: 001055**

	Living at home	On-campus
Tuition and fees (2002-2003):	$3,764	$3,764
Out-of-state:	$7,940	$7,940
Room and board:		$4,380
Board only:	$2,645	
Books and supplies:	$720	$720
Personal expenses:	$900	$1,200
Transportation:	$1,350	$900

Undergraduate aid. Need-based: Average financial aid package for full-time students was $5,702; for part-time $4,872. 41% awarded as scholarships/grants, 59% as loans/jobs. **Non-need-based:** 31% awarded as scholarships/grants, 69% as loans/jobs. Scholarships based on academics, art, athletics, leadership, minority status, music/drama. **Student debt:** 54% of graduating class borrowed to fund education; average debt was $17,309. **Additional information:** Application deadline for institutional scholarships is February 1.

Freshman aid. Need-based: Out of 610 full-time freshmen, 554 applied for aid; 272 were judged to have need; of these 260 received aid. Average package met 50% of need. 47 students had full need met. Average scholarship/grant was $3,179; average loan $2,405. **Non-need based:** 184 full-time freshmen with need received non-need scholarships; 229 without need received awards; 60 received athletic scholarships.

Policies to reduce costs. Tuition/fee waivers for employees and their families. Credit/placement for qualifying scores on AP, IB, CLEP examinations.

Payment plans. Credit card, deferred payment.

Application procedures. FAFSA, institutional form required. Priority date 4/1; closing date 7/31. Applicants notified on rolling basis starting 7/1, must reply within 2 week(s) of notification.

Contact. **Financial aid office:** (256) 824-6241
Andy Weaver, Director of Financial Aid
301 Sparkman Drive
Huntsville, AL 35899

University of Mobile

Mobile, Alabama
www.umobile.edu
Four-year private **Federal Code: 001029**

	Living at home	On-campus
Tuition and fees (2002-2003):	$9,040	$9,040
Room and board:		$5,230
Books and supplies:	$500	$500
Personal expenses:	$400	$1,000
Transportation:	$450	$250

Undergraduate aid. Need-based: Average financial aid package for full-time students was $7,000; for part-time $2,331. 52% awarded as scholarships/grants, 48% as loans/jobs. **Non-need-based:** 41% awarded as scholarships/grants, 59% as loans/jobs. Scholarships based on academics, alumni affiliation, art, athletics, leadership, minority status, music/drama, religious affiliation, state/district residency.

Freshman aid. Need-based: Average package met 54% of need. Average scholarship/grant was $3,201; average loan $2,625.

Policies to reduce costs. Tuition/fee waivers for family of clergy, employees and their families. Credit/placement for qualifying scores on AP, IB, CLEP examinations.

Payment plans. Credit card, installment, deferred payment.

Application procedures. FAFSA, institutional form required. Priority date 3/31; no closing date. Applicants notified on rolling basis, must reply within 2 week(s) of notification. **Transfers:** No deadline.

Contact. **Financial aid office:** (251) 442-2252
Lydia Houck, Director of Financial Aid
Box 13220
Mobile, AL 36663-0220

University of Montevallo

Montevallo, Alabama
www.montevallo.edu
Four-year public **Federal Code: 001004**

	Living at home	On-campus
Tuition and fees (2002-2003):	$4,334	$4,334
Out-of-state:	$8,384	$8,384
Room and board:		$3,638
Books and supplies:	$600	$600
Personal expenses:	$1,622	$1,622
Transportation:	$1,334	$982

Undergraduate aid. Need-based: Average financial aid package for full-time students was $6,650; for part-time $5,129. 40% awarded as scholarships/grants, 60% as loans/jobs. **Non-need-based:** 49% awarded as scholarships/grants, 51% as loans/jobs. Scholarships based on academics, art, athletics, leadership, minority status, music/drama. **Student debt:** 56% of graduating class borrowed to fund education; average debt was $16,321. **Additional information:** All low-income applicants eligible for financial assistance.

Freshman aid. Need-based: Out of 522 full-time freshmen, 432 applied for aid; 306 were judged to have need; of these 304 received aid. Average package met 68% of need. 109 students had full need met. Average scholarship/grant was $5,018; average loan $1,561. **Non-need based:** 56 full-time freshmen with need received non-need scholarships; 113 without need received awards; 19 received athletic scholarships.

Policies to reduce costs. Tuition/fee waivers for senior citizens, employees and their families. Credit/placement for qualifying scores on AP, CLEP examinations.

Payment plans. Credit card, installment payment.

Application procedures. FAFSA required. Priority date 4/15; no closing date. Applicants notified by 6/1, must reply within 2 week(s) of notification. **Transfers:** Priority date 4/15; no deadline.

Contact. Clark Aldridge, Director of Financial Aid
Station 6030
Montevallo, AL 35115-6030

University of North Alabama

Florence, Alabama
www.una.edu
Four-year public **Federal Code: 001016**

	Living at home	On-campus
Tuition and fees (2002-2003):	$3,262	$3,262
Out-of-state:	$7,300	$7,300
Room and board:		$4,034
Board only:	$2,274	
Books and supplies:	$830	$830

Undergraduate aid. Need-based: Average financial aid package for full-time students was $3,945; for part-time $395. 34% awarded as scholarships/grants, 66% as loans/jobs. **Non-need-based:** 42% awarded as scholarships/grants, 58% as loans/jobs. Scholarships based on academics, art, athletics, leadership, minority status, music/drama, state/district residency. **Student debt:** 38% of graduating class borrowed to fund education; average debt was $15,835.

Freshman aid. Need-based: Out of 732 full-time freshmen, 535 applied for aid; 408 were judged to have need; of these 389 received aid. 130 students had full need met. **Non-need based:** 43 received athletic scholarships.

Policies to reduce costs. Tuition/fee waivers for senior citizens, employees and their families. Credit/placement for qualifying scores on AP, CLEP examinations. Work study available nights and weekends.

Payment plans. Credit card payment.

Application procedures. FAFSA required. Priority date 4/1; no closing date. Applicants notified on rolling basis starting 5/31, must reply within 2 week(s) of notification.

Contact. Financial aid office: (256) 765-4590
Ben Baker, Director of Student Financial Services
UNA - Box 5011
Florence, AL 35632-0001

University of South Alabama

Mobile, Alabama
www.southalabama.edu
Four-year public **Federal Code: 001057**

	Living at home	On-campus
Tuition and fees (2002-2003):	$3,410	$3,410
Out-of-state:	$6,500	$6,500
Room and board:		$3,910
Books and supplies:	$600	$600

Undergraduate aid. Need-based: Average financial aid package for full-time students was $5,702. 25% awarded as scholarships/grants, 75% as loans/jobs. Need-based aid available for part-time students. **Non-need-based:** Scholarships based on academics, alumni affiliation, art, athletics, job skills, leadership, minority status, music/drama, state/district residency. **Student debt:** 65% of graduating class borrowed to fund education; average debt was $9,000.

Freshman aid. Need-based: Out of 1,003 full-time freshmen, 887 applied for aid; 884 were judged to have need; of these 822 received aid. Average package met 45% of need. 45 students had full need met. **Non-need based:** 296 full-time freshmen with need received non-need scholarships; 699 without need received awards.

Policies to reduce costs. Tuition/fee waivers for children of alumni, employees and their families. Credit/placement for qualifying scores on AP, CLEP examinations. Work study available for part-time students.

Payment plans. Credit card, installment payment.

Application procedures. FAFSA, institutional form required. Priority date 5/1; no closing date. Applicants notified on rolling basis starting 5/15. **Transfers:** No deadline.

Contact. Financial aid office: (251) 460-6231
Emily Johnston, Director of Financial Aid
AD 182
Mobile, AL 36688-0002

University of West Alabama

Livingston, Alabama
www.uwa.edu
Four-year public **Federal Code: 001024**

	Living at home	On-campus
Tuition and fees (2002-2003):	$3,510	$3,510
Out-of-state:	$6,582	$6,582
Room and board:		$2,924
Books and supplies:	$700	$700
Personal expenses:	$1,200	$1,200
Transportation:	$1,500	$900

Undergraduate aid. Need-based: Average financial aid package for full-time students was $7,793. 38% awarded as scholarships/grants, 62% as loans/jobs. Need-based aid available for part-time students. **Non-need-based:** Scholarships based on academics, alumni affiliation, athletics, leadership, music/drama, state/district residency.

Policies to reduce costs. Tuition/fee waivers for employees and their families. Credit/placement for qualifying scores on AP, CLEP examinations. Work study available nights, weekends and for part-time students.

Payment plans. Credit card, installment, deferred payment.

Application procedures. FAFSA required. Priority date 4/1; no closing date. Applicants notified on rolling basis starting 6/1, must reply within 2 week(s) of notification.

Contact. Financial aid office: (205) 652-3576
Patsy Reedy, Director of Financial Aid
Station 4
Livingston, AL 35470

Virginia College

Birmingham, Alabama
www.vc.edu
Four-year proprietary **Federal Code: 030106**

College costs. $235 per credit hour charge represents networking program. Tuition and charges for other programs vary. Charge includes books.

	Living at home
Tuition and fees (2002-2003):	$7,150
Personal expenses:	$100
Transportation:	$100

Policies to reduce costs. Tuition/fee waivers for family members, employees and their families.

Payment plans. Credit card, installment payment.

Application procedures. No deadline.

Contact. Financial aid office: (205) 802-1200
Monica Gauker, Director of Financial Aid
Box 19249
Birmingham, AL 35219

Wallace Community College: Sparks Campus

Eufaula, Alabama
www.wallace.edu
Two-year public

	Living at home
Tuition and fees (2002-2003):	$2,040
Out-of-state:	$3,840
Per-credit charge:	$60
Per-credit out-of-state:	$120
Books and supplies:	$820

Policies to reduce costs. Tuition/fee waivers for senior citizens, employees and their families.

Payment plans. Credit card payment.

Application procedures. FAFSA required. Priority date 8/1; no closing date. Applicants notified on rolling basis starting 7/31. **Transfers:** No deadline.

Contact. **Financial aid office:** (334) 687-3543 ext. 4285
Erma Perry, Financial Aid Director
PO Drawer 580
Eufaula, AL 36072-0580

Wallace State Community College at Hanceville

Hanceville, Alabama
www.wallacestatehanceville.edu
Two-year public **Federal Code: 007871**

	Living at home	On-campus
Tuition and fees (2002-2003):	$1,860	$1,860
Out-of-state:	$3,660	$3,660
Per-credit charge:	$60	$60
Per-credit out-of-state:	$120	$120
Room only:		$1,450
Books and supplies:	$600	$600
Personal expenses:	$900	$2,650
Transportation:	$1,155	$675

Undergraduate aid. All financial aid based on need. Need-based aid available for full-time and part-time students.

Policies to reduce costs. Tuition/fee waivers for senior citizens, employees and their families. Credit/placement for qualifying scores on AP, CLEP examinations. Work study available nights.

Payment plans. Credit card payment.

Application procedures. FAFSA, institutional form required. Priority date 6/1; closing date 5/1. Applicants notified on rolling basis starting 7/15, must reply within 2 week(s) of notification. **Transfers:** Priority date 6/1; no deadline.

Contact. **Financial aid office:** (256) 352-8182
Allison Rice, Director of Student Financial Aid
Box 2000
Hanceville, AL 35077-2000

Alaska

Alaska Bible College

Glennallen, Alaska
www.akbible.edu
Four-year private **Federal Code: 014325**

	Living at home	On-campus
Tuition and fees:	$5,300	$5,300
Room and board:		$4,200
Books and supplies:	$400	$400
Personal expenses:	$700	$1,000
Transportation:	$750	$1,000

Undergraduate aid. Additional information: All full-time faculty and staff are missionaries, and salaries are not charged to students.

Freshman aid. Average package met 45% of need. Average scholarship/grant was $2,250.

Policies to reduce costs. Tuition/fee waivers for employees and their families. Prepayment discount; credit/placement for qualifying scores on AP, CLEP examinations. Work study available nights and weekends.

Payment plans. Installment payment.

Application procedures. Institutional form required. Priority date 4/30; closing date 8/1. Applicants notified on rolling basis, must reply within 2 week(s) of notification. **Transfers:** Priority date 4/30; closing date 8/1.

Contact. Rick Knight, Vice President of Business Affairs
Box 289
Glennallen, AK 99588-0289

Alaska Pacific University

Anchorage, Alaska
www.alaskapacific.edu
Four-year private **Federal Code: 001061**

	Living at home	On-campus
Tuition and fees:	$12,380	$12,380
Out-of-state:	$16,298	$16,298
Room and board:		$5,600
Books and supplies:	$1,000	$1,000
Personal expenses:	$1,500	$1,500
Transportation:	$350	$350

Undergraduate aid. Need-based: Average financial aid package for full-time students was $8,803. 43% awarded as scholarships/grants, 57% as loans/jobs. Need-based aid available for part-time students. **Non-need-based:** 40% awarded as scholarships/grants, 60% as loans/jobs. Scholarships based on academics, leadership, state/district residency. **Student debt:** 68% of graduating class borrowed to fund education; average debt was $20,151.

Freshman aid. Need-based: Out of 20 full-time freshmen, 20 applied for aid; 16 were judged to have need; of these 16 received aid. Average package met 35% of need. Average scholarship/grant was $4,250; average loan $2,625. **Non-need based:** 16 full-time freshmen with need received non-need scholarships; 4 without need received awards.

Policies to reduce costs. Tuition/fee waivers for employees and their families. Tuition at time of enrollment guaranteed for 4 years; credit/placement for qualifying scores on AP, CLEP examinations.

Payment plans. Credit card, installment, deferred payment.

Application procedures. FAFSA required. Priority date 3/15; no closing date. Applicants notified on rolling basis starting 4/1, must reply within 4 week(s) of notification. Early decision closing date 12/1.

Contact. Peter Miller, Director of Financial Aid
4101 University Drive
Anchorage, AK 99508-4672

Charter College

Anchorage, Alaska
www.chartercollege.edu
Four-year private **Federal Code: 017377**

College costs (2002-2003). Tuition ranges from $19,000 to $23,000 for associates and from $38,000 to $44,000 for bachelors depending on program; includes books and supplies. Students enrolling on full-time basis receive 10% discount. Books/supplies: $700.

Undergraduate aid. Need-based: Need-based aid available for full-time and part-time students.

Policies to reduce costs. Tuition/fee waivers for employees and their families.

Payment plans. Credit card, installment payment.

Application procedures. FAFSA required. No deadline. Applicants notified on rolling basis, must reply within 5 week(s) of notification.

Contact. Janell McIntyre, Director of Student Services
2221 East Northern Lights Boulevard, Suite 120
Anchorage, AK 99508

Prince William Sound Community College

Valdez, Alaska
www.uaa.alaska.edu/pwscc
Two-year public **Federal Code: 011462**

College costs. $91 per credit hour charge for upper-division students.

	Living at home	On-campus
Tuition and fees (2002-2003):	$2,208	$2,208
Per-credit charge:	$70	$70
Room only:		$2,800
Books and supplies:	$550	$550
Personal expenses:	$100	$100
Transportation:	$100	

Undergraduate aid. Need-based: Need-based aid available for full-time and part-time students. **Non-need-based:** Scholarships based on state/district residency.

Policies to reduce costs. Tuition/fee waivers for senior citizens, employees and their families. Credit/placement for qualifying scores on AP, IB, CLEP examinations.

Payment plans. Credit card, installment, deferred payment.

Application procedures. FAFSA required. Priority date 4/1; no closing date. Applicants notified on rolling basis. **Transfers:** Priority date 4/1; closing date 5/1.

Contact. Financial aid office: (907) 834-1666
Douglas Desorcie, Dean of Instruction
Box 97
Valdez, AK 99686

Sheldon Jackson College

Sitka, Alaska
sj-alaska.edu
Four-year private **Federal Code: 001062**

	Living at home	On-campus
Tuition and fees:	$10,450	$10,450
Room and board:		$6,920
Board only:	$2,100	
Books and supplies:	$750	$750
Personal expenses:	$1,000	$1,000
Transportation:	$1,000	$1,500

Undergraduate aid. Need-based: Need-based aid available for full-time students. **Additional information:** Financial aid available from Bureau of Indian Affairs and Alaska State Loan Program.

Policies to reduce costs. Tuition/fee waivers for employees and their families. Credit/placement for qualifying scores on AP, CLEP examinations.

Payment plans. Credit card, deferred payment.

Application procedures. FAFSA required. Priority date 5/2; no closing date. Applicants notified on rolling basis starting 4/2, must reply within 3 week(s) of notification.

Contact. **Financial aid office:** (907) 747-5207
Louise Driver, Financial Aid Director and Director of Admissions
801 Lincoln Street
Sitka, AK 99835

University of Alaska Anchorage

Anchorage, Alaska
www.uaa.alaska.edu
Four-year public **Federal Code: 011462**

College costs. Per-credit-hour charges for upper-division students: $87 in-state, $261 out-of-state.

	Living at home	On-campus
Tuition and fees (2002-2003):	$2,920	$2,920
Out-of-state:	$7,990	$7,990
Room and board:		$7,030
Board only:	$1,467	
Books and supplies:	$891	$891
Personal expenses:	$1,172	$1,172
Transportation:	$1,557	$483

Undergraduate aid. **Need-based:** Average financial aid package for full-time students was $7,614; for part-time $3,927. **Non-need-based:** Scholarships based on academics, athletics. **Student debt:** 47% of graduating class borrowed to fund education; average debt was $15,621.

Freshman aid. **Need-based:** Average package met 93% of need. Average scholarship/grant was $3,413; average loan $2,771.

Policies to reduce costs. Tuition/fee waivers for children of alumni, senior citizens, employees and their families. Credit/placement for qualifying scores on AP, IB, CLEP examinations. Work study available nights and weekends.

Payment plans. Credit card, installment payment.

Application procedures. FAFSA, institutional form required. Priority date 4/1; closing date 8/1. Applicants notified on rolling basis. **Transfers:** Priority date 4/1; closing date 8/30.

Contact. Ted Malone, Director of Financial Aid
3211 Providence Drive, #158
Anchorage, AK 99508-8046

University of Alaska Fairbanks

Fairbanks, Alaska
www.uaf.edu
Four-year public **Federal Code: 001063**

College costs. per-credit-hour charges for upper division students: $93 in-state, $267 out-of-state.

	Living at home	On-campus
Tuition and fees (2002-2003):	$3,402	$3,402
Out-of-state:	$8,622	$8,622
Room and board:		$4,950
Books and supplies:	$650	$650
Personal expenses:		$2,160
Transportation:		$324

Undergraduate aid. **Need-based:** Average financial aid package for full-time students was $8,082; for part-time $4,928. 30% awarded as scholarships/grants, 70% as loans/jobs. **Non-need-based:** 40% awarded as scholarships/grants, 60% as loans/jobs. Scholarships based on academics, art, athletics, job skills. **Student debt:** 52% of graduating class borrowed to fund education; average debt was $11,080.

Freshman aid. **Need-based:** Out of 751 full-time freshmen, 612 applied for aid; 314 were judged to have need; of these 286 received aid. Average package met 68% of need. 94 students had full need met. Average scholarship/grant was $4,085; average loan $5,325. **Non-need based:** 34 full-time freshmen with need received non-need scholarships; 160 without need received awards; 15 received athletic scholarships.

Policies to reduce costs. Tuition/fee waivers for children of alumni, senior citizens, employees and their families. Credit/placement for qualifying scores on AP, IB, CLEP examinations.

Payment plans. Credit card, installment, deferred payment.

Application procedures. FAFSA required. Priority date 7/1; no closing date. Applicants notified on rolling basis starting 3/1, must reply within 2 week(s) of notification.

Contact. **Financial aid office:** (907) 474-7256
Donald Scheaffer, Director of Financial Aid
PO Box 757480
Fairbanks, AK 99775-7480

University of Alaska Southeast

Juneau, Alaska
www.uas.alaska.edu
Four-year public **Federal Code: 001065**

College costs. Per-credit-hour charges for upper-division students: $93 in-state, $267 out-of-state.

	Living at home	On-campus
Tuition and fees (2002-2003):	$2,883	$2,883
Out-of-state:	$8,103	$8,103
Room and board:		$5,610
Books and supplies:	$412	$412
Personal expenses:	$1,035	$1,035
Transportation:	$595	

Undergraduate aid. **Need-based:** Need-based aid available for full-time and part-time students. **Additional information:** Transfer, continuing, and freshman scholarship deadline March 1.

Policies to reduce costs. Tuition/fee waivers for senior citizens, employees and their families. Credit/placement for qualifying scores on AP, CLEP examinations. Work study available nights, weekends and for part-time students.

Payment plans. Credit card, installment, deferred payment.

Application procedures. FAFSA required. Applicants notified on rolling basis. **Transfers:** Transfer scholarships available.

Contact. **Financial aid office:** (817) 465-4827
B. Carlson-Burnett, Financial Aid Officer
11120 Glacier Highway
Juneau, AK 99801-8681

Arizona

American Indian College of the Assemblies of God

Phoenix, Arizona
Four-year private
Federal Code: 015550

	Living at home	On-campus
Tuition and fees (2002-2003):	$4,975	$4,975
Room and board:		$3,500
Books and supplies:	$500	$500
Personal expenses:	$1,400	$1,400
Transportation:	$1,100	$1,100

Policies to reduce costs. Tuition/fee waivers for employees and their families. Credit/placement for qualifying scores on CLEP examinations.

Payment plans. Installment payment.

Application procedures. FAFSA required. Priority date 4/1; closing date 8/23. Applicants notified on rolling basis starting 7/15.

Contact. M. Nadine Waldrop, Director of Student Financial Aid
10020 North 15th Avenue
Phoenix, AZ 85021-2199

Arizona Automotive Institute

Glendale, Arizona
www.azautoinst.com
Two-year proprietary
Federal Code: 010847

College costs. Total cost of associate degree program: $17,995 including tuition, books, supplies, tools. Other non-degree programs available at minimum of $13,550.

Application procedures. FAFSA, institutional form required. No deadline. Applicants notified on rolling basis.

Contact. Kimberly Richter, Financial Aid Director
6829 North 46th Avenue
Glendale, AZ 85301

Arizona State University

Tempe, Arizona
www.asu.edu
Four-year public
Federal Code: 001081

	Living at home	On-campus
Tuition and fees (2002-2003):	$2,585	$2,585
Out-of-state:	$11,105	$11,105
Room and board:		$5,706
Board only:	$1,000	
Books and supplies:	$700	$700
Personal expenses:	$2,992	$2,992
Transportation:	$1,000	$1,000

Undergraduate aid. Need-based: Average financial aid package for full-time students was $7,309; for part-time $5,661. 41% awarded as scholarships/grants, 59% as loans/jobs. **Non-need-based:** 36% awarded as scholarships/grants, 64% as loans/jobs. Scholarships based on academics, art, athletics, music/drama. **Student debt:** 40% of graduating class borrowed to fund education; average debt was $17,357.

Freshman aid. Need-based: Out of 5,983 full-time freshmen, 3,886 applied for aid; 1,888 were judged to have need; of these 1,888 received aid. Average package met 68% of need. 323 students had full need met. Average scholarship/grant was $4,638; average loan $2,532. **Non-need based:** 201 full-time freshmen with need received non-need scholarships; 1,911 without need received awards; 72 received athletic scholarships.

Policies to reduce costs. Tuition/fee waivers for employees and their families. Credit/placement for qualifying scores on AP, IB, CLEP examinations.

Payment plans. Credit card, installment payment.

Application procedures. FAFSA required. Priority date 3/1; no closing date. Applicants notified on rolling basis starting 3/15, must reply within 4 week(s) of notification.

Contact. Diane Stemper, Director of Student Financial Assistance
Box 870112
Tempe, AZ 85287-0112

Arizona Western College

Yuma, Arizona
www.azwestern.edu
Two-year public
Federal Code: 001071

	Living at home	On-campus
Tuition and fees (2002-2003):	$1,020	$1,020
Out-of-state:	$5,580	$5,580
Per-credit charge:	$34	$34
Per-credit out-of-state:	$40	$40
Room and board:		$3,848
Books and supplies:	$990	$990
Personal expenses:	$1,800	$1,800
Transportation:	$2,300	$850

Undergraduate aid. Need-based: 88% awarded as scholarships/grants, 12% as loans/jobs. Need-based aid available for part-time students. **Non-need-based:** Scholarships based on academics, athletics.

Policies to reduce costs. Tuition/fee waivers for senior citizens, employees and their families. Credit/placement for qualifying scores on AP, CLEP examinations. Work study available nights, weekends and for part-time students.

Payment plans. Credit card payment.

Application procedures. FAFSA, institutional form required. Priority date 4/20; no closing date. Applicants notified on rolling basis starting 5/2.

Contact. Luis Barajas, Director of Financial Aid
PO Box 929
Yuma, AZ 85366-0929

Art Institute of Phoenix

Phoenix, Arizona
www.aipx.edu
Four-year private

	Living at home	On-campus
Tuition and fees (2002-2003):	$14,304	$14,304
Room only:		$3,750
Books and supplies:	$1,323	$1,323
Personal expenses:	$2,880	$3,630
Transportation:		$1,065

Undergraduate aid. Need-based: Need-based aid available for full-time and part-time students.

Policies to reduce costs. Tuition/fee waivers for employees and their families. Credit/placement for qualifying scores on AP, IB, CLEP examinations. Work study available nights and weekends.

Application procedures. FAFSA required. No deadline.

Contact. Paula Cady, Director of Student Financial Services
2233 West Dunlap Avenue
Phoenix, AZ 85021-2859

Central Arizona College

Coolidge, Arizona
www.centralaz.edu
Two-year public
Federal Code: 007283

College costs. Students in Western Undergraduate Education Program pay 150% of Arizona resident tuition.

	Living at home	On-campus
Tuition and fees (2002-2003):	$1,050	$1,050
Out-of-state:	$5,838	$5,838
Per-credit charge:	$37	$37
Per-credit out-of-state:	$74	$74
Room and board:		$3,820
Books and supplies:	$400	$400
Personal expenses:	$1,500	$1,500
Transportation:	$700	$700

Undergraduate aid. Need-based: Need-based aid available for full-time and part-time students.

Policies to reduce costs. Tuition/fee waivers for senior citizens, employees and their families. Credit/placement for qualifying scores on CLEP examinations. Work study available nights, weekends and for part-time students.

Payment plans. Credit card payment.

Application procedures. FAFSA required. Priority date 5/1; closing date 7/15. Applicants notified by 5/30, must reply within 3 week(s) of notification.

Contact. Financial aid office: (520) 426-4425
Greg Mason, Director of Student Financial Aid
8470 North Overfield Road
Coolidge, AZ 85228

Cochise College

Douglas, Arizona
www.cochise.edu
Two-year public **Federal Code: 001072**

	Living at home	On-campus
Tuition and fees (2002-2003):	$1,050	$1,050
Out-of-state:	$5,700	$5,700
Per-credit charge:	$33	$33
Per-credit out-of-state:	$188	$188
Room and board:		$3,228
Books and supplies:	$600	$600
Personal expenses:	$675	$1,125
Transportation:	$800	$680

Undergraduate aid. Need-based: Need-based aid available for full-time and part-time students.

Policies to reduce costs. Tuition/fee waivers for senior citizens, employees and their families. Credit/placement for qualifying scores on CLEP examinations.

Payment plans. Credit card payment.

Application procedures. FAFSA required. Priority date 4/15; no closing date. Applicants notified on rolling basis starting 6/15, must reply within 2 week(s) of notification.

Contact. Dartle Atherton, Director of Financial Aid
4190 West Highway 80
Douglas, AZ 85607-6190

Collins College

Tempe, Arizona
www.collinscollege.edu
Four-year proprietary **Federal Code: 015333**

College costs (2002-2003). Cost of tuition vary according to program. Tuition ranges from $16,000 to $20,800. Books/supplies: $1,800.

Contact. Carol Clapp, Financial Aid Director
1140 South Priest Drive
Tempe, AZ 85281

DeVry University: Phoenix

Phoenix, Arizona
www.devry-phx.edu
Four-year proprietary **Federal Code: 008322**

	Living at home
Tuition and fees:	$10,155
Books and supplies:	$1,100
Personal expenses:	$1,996
Transportation:	$1,612

Undergraduate aid. All financial aid based on need. Average financial aid package for full-time students was $8,069; for part-time $5,438. 22% awarded as scholarships/grants, 78% as loans/jobs.

Freshman aid. Average package met 39% of need. Average scholarship/grant was $3,576; average loan $3,883.

Policies to reduce costs. Tuition/fee waivers for employees and their families.

Payment plans. Credit card, installment, deferred payment.

Application procedures. FAFSA required. No deadline. Applicants notified on rolling basis starting 7/2.

Contact. Kathy Wyse, Dean of Student Finances
2149 West Dunlap
Phoenix, AZ 85021-2995

Eastern Arizona College

Thatcher, Arizona
www.eac.edu
Two-year public **Federal Code: 001073**

	Living at home	On-campus
Tuition and fees (2002-2003):	$788	$788
Out-of-state:	$4,908	$4,908
Per-credit charge:	$32	$32
Per-credit out-of-state:	$57	$57
Room and board:		$3,580
Board only:	$2,119	
Books and supplies:	$600	$600
Personal expenses:	$1,550	$1,550
Transportation:	$1,034	$1,059

Undergraduate aid. Need-based: Average financial aid package for full-time students was $3,408; for part-time $1,757. 95% awarded as scholarships/grants, 5% as loans/jobs. **Non-need-based:** 68% awarded as scholarships/grants, 32% as loans/jobs. Scholarships based on academics, art, athletics, leadership, music/drama, state/district residency.

Freshman aid. Need-based: Average package met 33% of need. Average scholarship/grant was $3,125.

Merit scholarships. Departmental Scholarships; in-state tuition, based on 2.5 minimum GPA. Academic Scholarships; in-state tuition, based on 3.0 minimum GPA. Performing Arts Scholarships; amounts vary, based on 2.5 minimum GPA, audition.

Policies to reduce costs. Tuition/fee waivers for senior citizens, employees and their families. Credit/placement for qualifying scores on AP, IB, CLEP examinations. Work study available nights and weekends.

Payment plans. Credit card, deferred payment.

Application procedures. FAFSA, institutional form required. Priority date 3/1; no closing date. Applicants notified on rolling basis starting 3/15. **Transfers:** No deadline.

Contact. Financial aid office: (928) 428-8287
Geraldine Covert, Director of Financial Aid
615 North Stadium Avenue
Thatcher, AZ 85552

Embry-Riddle Aeronautical University: Prescott Campus

Prescott, Arizona
www.embryriddle.edu
Four-year private **Federal Code: 014797**

	Living at home	On-campus
Tuition and fees:	$21,330	$21,330
Room and board:		$5,808
Board only:	$1,010	
Books and supplies:	$900	$900
Personal expenses:	$1,220	$1,220
Transportation:	$1,590	$2,070

Undergraduate aid. Need-based: Average financial aid package for full-time students was $11,025; for part-time $8,968. 22% awarded as scholarships/grants, 78% as loans/jobs. **Non-need-based:** Scholarships based on academics, athletics, leadership. **Student debt:** 87% of graduating class borrowed to fund education; average debt was $31,312.

Freshman aid. Need-based: Out of 308 full-time freshmen, 240 applied for aid; 196 were judged to have need; of these 196 received aid. Average scholarship/grant was $7,089; average loan $3,526. **Non-need based:** 8 received athletic scholarships.

Policies to reduce costs. Tuition/fee waivers for employees and their families. Credit/placement for qualifying scores on AP, IB, CLEP examinations.

Payment plans. Credit card, installment, deferred payment.

Application procedures. FAFSA required. Priority date 4/15; closing date 6/30. Applicants notified on rolling basis starting 2/1, must reply within 4 week(s) of notification. Early decision closing date 12/1.

Contact. Financial aid office: (928) 777-3765
Daniel Lupin, Director of Financial Aid
3200 North Willow Creek Road
Prescott, AZ 86301-3720

Estrella Mountain Community College

Avondale, Arizona
www.emc.maricopa.edu
Two-year public **Federal Code: 031563**

	Living at home
Tuition and fees (2002-2003):	$1,390
Out-of-state:	$6,340
Per-credit charge:	$46
Per-credit out-of-state:	$211
Books and supplies:	$848
Transportation:	$1,986

Undergraduate aid. Need-based: 70% awarded as scholarships/grants, 30% as loans/jobs. Need-based aid available for part-time students. **Non-need-based:** 34% awarded as scholarships/grants, 66% as loans/jobs. Scholarships based on leadership.

Policies to reduce costs. Credit/placement for qualifying scores on AP, IB, CLEP examinations. Work study available nights and for part-time students.

Payment plans. Credit card payment.

Application procedures. Priority date 4/1; no closing date. Applicants notified on rolling basis starting 4/15.

Contact. Financial aid office: (623) 935-8940
Lauren Shellenbarger, Director, Financial Aid
3000 North Dysart Road
Avondale, AZ 85323

Gateway Community College

Phoenix, Arizona
www.gwc.maricopa.edu
Two-year public **Federal Code: 008303**

College costs. Out-of-county students pay same as out-of-state students for under 7 credits per semester, $6,210 full-time for the year. Distance learning $125 per-credit-hour.

	Living at home
Tuition and fees (2002-2003):	$1,390
Out-of-state:	$6,340
Per-credit charge:	$46
Per-credit out-of-state:	$211

Undergraduate aid. Need-based: Need-based aid available for full-time and part-time students.

Policies to reduce costs. Tuition/fee waivers for employees and their families. Credit/placement for qualifying scores on AP, IB, CLEP examinations. Work study available nights, weekends and for part-time students.

Payment plans. Credit card, installment, deferred payment.

Application procedures. FAFSA, institutional form required. Priority date 4/15; no closing date. Applicants notified on rolling basis starting 7/1, must reply within 4 week(s) of notification. **Transfers:** Priority date 4/15; no deadline.

Contact. Financial aid office: (602) 392-5132
Bradley Honius, Director of Financial Aid
108 North 40th Street
Phoenix, AZ 85034

Glendale Community College

Glendale, Arizona
www.gc.maricopa.edu
Two-year public **Federal Code: 001076**

College costs. Students from Apache, Gila, Greenlee, and Santa Cruz counties pay $5,850 full-time tuition per year, $195 per-credit-hour.

	Living at home
Tuition and fees (2002-2003):	$1,390
Out-of-state:	$6,340
Per-credit charge:	$46
Per-credit out-of-state:	$211
Books and supplies:	$820
Personal expenses:	$1,150
Transportation:	$1,930

Undergraduate aid. All financial aid based on need. Need-based aid available for full-time and part-time students.

Policies to reduce costs. Tuition/fee waivers for employees and their families. Credit/placement for qualifying scores on AP, CLEP examinations. Work study available nights.

Payment plans. Credit card, installment payment.

Application procedures. FAFSA, institutional form required. Priority date 5/1; no closing date. Applicants notified on rolling basis starting 5/1, must reply within 2 week(s) of notification.

Contact. Financial aid office: (623) 845-3366
Ellen Neel, Director of Financial Aid
6000 West Olive Avenue
Glendale, AZ 85302

High-Tech Institute

Phoenix, Arizona
www.hightechschools.com
Two-year proprietary **Federal Code: 022631**

College costs (2002-2003). Total costs of associate degree programs including books and supplies range from $17,650-$24,950. Personal expenses: $205.

Undergraduate aid. All financial aid based on need. Need-based aid available for full-time students.

Application procedures. No deadline.

Contact. Financial aid office: (602) 279-9700
Dana Niswander, Financial Director
1515 East Indian School Road
Phoenix, AZ 85014-4901

ITT Technical Institute: Phoenix

Phoenix, Arizona
www.itt-tech.edu
Three-year proprietary **Federal Code: 013928**

College costs. Total program varies depending on course of study. Per-credit-hour charge: $347.

Policies to reduce costs. Tuition/fee waivers for employees and their families.

Payment plans. Credit card, installment payment.

Application procedures. FAFSA, institutional form required. No deadline. Applicants notified on rolling basis.

Contact. Laurie Robbins, Director of Finance
4837 East McDowell Road
Phoenix, AZ 85008

ITT Technical Institute: Tucson

Tucson, Arizona
www.itt-tech.edu
Two-year proprietary **Federal Code: 016776**

College costs. Total program varies depending on course of study. Per-credit-hour charge: $347.

Policies to reduce costs. Tuition/fee waivers for employees and their families. Tuition at time of enrollment guaranteed for 2 years.

Payment plans. Credit card, installment payment.

Application procedures. FAFSA, institutional form required. No deadline. Applicants notified on rolling basis.

Contact. Betty Marchant, Director of Finance
1455 West River Road
Tucson, AZ 85704

International Institute of the Americas: Phoenix

Phoenix, Arizona
www.aibt.edu
Two-year private **Federal Code: 022188**

College costs. 7-month diploma programs range from $8,650 to $10,050. 16-month associate degree programs range from $17,300 to $19,200. 60-week bachelor's degree program costs $17,300.

Undergraduate aid. All financial aid based on need. Average financial aid package for full-time students was $4,000. 50% awarded as scholarships/grants, 50% as loans/jobs.

Payment plans. Credit card, installment payment.

Application procedures. FAFSA, institutional form required. No deadline.

Contact. **Financial aid office:** (623) 873-5429
Melba Moore, Financial Aid Director
6049 North 43rd Avenue
Phoenix, AZ 85019

International Institute of the Americas: Tucson

Tucson, Arizona
www.aibt.edu
Four-year private **Federal Code: 022188**

College costs (2002-2003). Diploma $8,000, AA $16,300, BA $31,850.

Undergraduate aid. All financial aid based on need. Average financial aid package for full-time students was $4,000. 50% awarded as scholarships/grants, 50% as loans/jobs. Need-based aid available for part-time students.

Payment plans. Credit card, installment payment.

Application procedures. FAFSA, institutional form required. No deadline.

Contact. **Financial aid office:** (623) 873-5429
Melba Moore, Financial Aid Director
5441 East 22nd Street, Suite 125
Tucson, AZ 85711

Northern Arizona University

Flagstaff, Arizona
www.nau.edu
Four-year public **Federal Code: 001082**

	Living at home	On-campus
Tuition and fees (2002-2003):	$2,586	$2,586
Out-of-state:	$11,106	$11,106
Room and board:		$4,910
Books and supplies:	$750	$750
Personal expenses:	$1,494	$1,965
Transportation:	$852	$1,200

Undergraduate aid. Need-based: Average financial aid package for full-time students was $8,004; for part-time $5,561. 41% awarded as scholarships/grants, 59% as loans/jobs. **Non-need-based:** 49% awarded as scholarships/grants, 51% as loans/jobs. Scholarships based on academics, alumni affiliation, art, athletics, music/drama, state/district residency. **Student debt:** 55% of graduating class borrowed to fund education; average debt was $15,795.

Freshman aid. Need-based: Out of 2,153 full-time freshmen, 1,661 applied for aid; 809 were judged to have need; of these 776 received aid. Average package met 78% of need. 283 students had full need met. Average scholarship/grant was $4,273; average loan $2,613. **Non-need based:** 506 full-time freshmen with need received non-need scholarships; 417 without need received awards; 50 received athletic scholarships.

Policies to reduce costs. Tuition/fee waivers for employees and their families. Credit/placement for qualifying scores on AP, IB, CLEP examinations. Work study available for part-time students.

Payment plans. Credit card, deferred payment.

Application procedures. FAFSA required. Priority date 2/14; no closing date. Applicants notified on rolling basis.

Contact. **Financial aid office:** (928) 523-4951
Jim Pritchard, Director of Student Financial Aid
Box 4084
Flagstaff, AZ 86011-4084

Paradise Valley Community College

Phoenix, Arizona
www.pvc.maricopa.edu
Two-year public **Federal Code: 026236**

	Living at home
Tuition and fees (2002-2003):	$1,390
Out-of-state:	$6,340
Per-credit charge:	$46
Per-credit out-of-state:	$211
Books and supplies:	$700
Personal expenses:	$1,185
Transportation:	$1,185

Policies to reduce costs. Tuition/fee waivers for employees and their families. Credit/placement for qualifying scores on CLEP examinations.

Payment plans. Credit card, deferred payment.

Application procedures. FAFSA required. No deadline. Applicants notified on rolling basis starting 6/1. **Transfers:** No deadline.

Contact. JoAnn Caufield, Director, Financial Aid
18401 North 32nd Street
Phoenix, AZ 85032

Phoenix College

Phoenix, Arizona
www.pc.maricopa.edu
Two-year public **Federal Code: 001078**

	Living at home
Tuition and fees (2002-2003):	$1,390
Out-of-state:	$6,340
Per-credit charge:	$46
Per-credit out-of-state:	$211
Books and supplies:	$700
Personal expenses:	$3,654
Transportation:	$1,150

Policies to reduce costs. Tuition/fee waivers for employees and their families. Credit/placement for qualifying scores on CLEP examinations. Work study available weekends.

Payment plans. Credit card, installment, deferred payment.

Application procedures. FAFSA required. Priority date 6/30; no closing date. Applicants notified on rolling basis starting 5/1.

Contact. **Financial aid office:** (602) 285-7404
Genevieve Watson, Director of Financial Aid
1202 West Thomas Road
Phoenix, AZ 85013

Pima Community College

Tucson, Arizona
www.pima.edu
Two-year public **Federal Code: 007266**

	Living at home
Tuition and fees (2002-2003):	$1,024
Out-of-state:	$5,794
Per-credit charge:	$39
Per-credit out-of-state:	$67
Books and supplies:	$720
Personal expenses:	$2,734
Transportation:	$1,650

Undergraduate aid. **Need-based:** Need-based aid available for full-time and part-time students. **Non-need-based:** Scholarships based on academics, alumni affiliation, art, athletics, minority status, music/drama.

Policies to reduce costs. Tuition/fee waivers for employees and their families. Credit/placement for qualifying scores on CLEP examinations.

Payment plans. Credit card payment.

Application procedures. FAFSA required. Priority date 4/1; no closing date. Applicants notified on rolling basis starting 7/1, must reply within 2 week(s) of notification.

Contact. **Financial aid office:** (520) 206-4950
Lupita Murphy, Director of Financial Aid
4905B East Broadway
Tucson, AZ 85709-1120

Prescott College

Prescott, Arizona
www.prescott.edu
Four-year private **Federal Code: 013659**

College costs. Student insurance for RDP program.

	Living at home
Tuition and fees (2002-2003):	$13,990
Books and supplies:	$600
Personal expenses:	$1,600
Transportation:	$1,500

Undergraduate aid. **Need-based:** Average financial aid package for full-time students was $4,542; for part-time $3,723. 29% awarded as scholarships/grants, 71% as loans/jobs. **Non-need-based:** 0% awarded as scholarships/grants, 100% as loans/jobs. Scholarships based on academics, state/district residency. **Student debt:** 66% of graduating class borrowed to fund education; average debt was $14,255.

Freshman aid. **Need-based:** Out of 23 full-time freshmen, 21 applied for aid; 19 were judged to have need; of these 19 received aid. Average package met 26% of need. Average scholarship/grant was $2,432. **Non-need based:** 3 full-time freshmen with need received non-need scholarships.

Policies to reduce costs. Tuition/fee waivers for employees and their families. Work study available nights and weekends.

Payment plans. Credit card, installment payment.

Application procedures. FAFSA, institutional form required. No deadline. Applicants notified on rolling basis starting 4/1, must reply within 3 week(s) of notification.

Contact. **Financial aid office:** (928) 778-2090
Sheri Sterling, Director of Financial Aid
220 Grove Avenue
Prescott, AZ 86301

Refrigeration School

Phoenix, Arizona
www.refrigerationschool.com
One-year proprietary **Federal Code: 011689**

College costs. Tuition $5,000 to $15,000 depending on program.

Contact. 4210 East Washington Street
Phoenix, AZ 85034-1816

Rio Salado College

Tempe, Arizona
www.rio.maricopa.edu
Two-year public **Federal Code: 014483**

College costs. Students from Apache, Gila, Greenlee, and Santa Cruz counties pay $6,210 tuition, $207 per-credit-hour.

	Living at home
Tuition and fees (2002-2003):	$1,390
Out-of-state:	$6,340
Per-credit charge:	$46
Per-credit out-of-state:	$211
Books and supplies:	$800
Personal expenses:	$1,275
Transportation:	$1,275

Policies to reduce costs. Tuition/fee waivers for employees and their families. Credit/placement for qualifying scores on CLEP examinations.

Payment plans. Credit card, deferred payment.

Application procedures. FAFSA, institutional form required. Priority date 6/30; no closing date. Applicants notified on rolling basis starting 6/30.

Contact. **Financial aid office:** (480) 517-8310
Linda Ross, Director of Financial Aid
2323 West 14th Street
Tempe, AZ 85281

Scottsdale Community College

Scottsdale, Arizona
www.sc.maricopa.edu
Two-year public **Federal Code: 008304**

	Living at home
Tuition and fees (2002-2003):	$1,390
Out-of-state:	$6,340
Per-credit charge:	$46
Per-credit out-of-state:	$211
Books and supplies:	$848
Personal expenses:	$4,194
Transportation:	$1,185

Undergraduate aid. **Non-need-based:** Scholarships based on academics, athletics. **Additional information:** Athletic scholarships offered in rodeo. All athletic scholarships limited to county residents.

Policies to reduce costs. Tuition/fee waivers for adults, minority students, employees and their families. Credit/placement for qualifying scores on AP, CLEP examinations.

Payment plans. Credit card, installment, deferred payment.

Application procedures. FAFSA, institutional form required. Priority date 6/30; no closing date. Applicants notified on rolling basis starting 4/1, must reply by 7/15 or within 3 week(s) of notification.

Contact. **Financial aid office:** (480) 423-6549
Dee Shipley, Director of Placement and Financial Aid
9000 East Chaparral Road
Scottsdale, AZ 85256

South Mountain Community College

Phoenix, Arizona
www.smc.maricopa.edu
Two-year public **Federal Code: 015001**

	Living at home
Tuition and fees (2002-2003):	$1,390
Out-of-state:	$6,340
Per-credit charge:	$46
Per-credit out-of-state:	$211
Board only:	$1,365
Books and supplies:	$760
Personal expenses:	$1,250
Transportation:	$1,275

Undergraduate aid. Need-based: Average financial aid package for full-time students was $1,375. 92% awarded as scholarships/grants, 8% as loans/jobs. Need-based aid available for part-time students. **Non-need-based:** Scholarships based on academics, athletics, minority status, music/drama.

Policies to reduce costs. Tuition/fee waivers for employees and their families. Credit/placement for qualifying scores on AP, IB examinations. Work study available nights, weekends and for part-time students.

Payment plans. Credit card, installment payment.

Application procedures. FAFSA required. Priority date 5/1; no closing date. Applicants notified on rolling basis starting 5/15, must reply within 3 week(s) of notification. **Transfers:** No deadline.

Contact. **Financial aid office:** (602) 243-8130
Inez Moreno-Weinert, Director of Financial Aid and Placement
7050 South 24th Street
Phoenix, AZ 85042

Southwestern College

Phoenix, Arizona
www.swcaz.edu
Four-year private **Federal Code: 007113**

	Living at home	On-campus
Tuition and fees:	$10,460	$10,460
Room and board:		$4,020
Board only:	$1,000	
Books and supplies:	$800	$800
Personal expenses:	$1,300	$1,300
Transportation:	$2,000	$2,000

Undergraduate aid. Need-based: Average financial aid package for full-time students was $6,500; for part-time $4,500. 40% awarded as scholarships/grants, 60% as loans/jobs. **Non-need-based:** Scholarships based on academics, alumni affiliation, leadership, music/drama, religious affiliation. **Student debt:** 74% of graduating class borrowed to fund education; average debt was $17,125.

Freshman aid. Need-based: Out of 55 full-time freshmen, 55 applied for aid; 46 were judged to have need; of these 46 received aid. **Non-need based:** 41 received athletic scholarships.

Policies to reduce costs. Tuition/fee waivers for employees and their families. Credit/placement for qualifying scores on AP, CLEP examinations.

Payment plans. Credit card, installment, deferred payment.

Application procedures. FAFSA required. Priority date 3/15; closing date 8/31. Applicants notified on rolling basis.

Contact. **Financial aid office:** (602) 992-6101 Ext.114
Pete Leonard, Director of Financial Aid
2625 East Cactus Road
Phoenix, AZ 85032-7042

University of Arizona

Tucson, Arizona
www.arizona.edu
Four-year public **Federal Code: 001083**

	Living at home	On-campus
Tuition and fees (2002-2003):	$2,594	$2,594
Out-of-state:	$11,114	$11,114
Room and board:		$6,124
Board only:	$1,710	
Books and supplies:	$714	$714
Personal expenses:	$2,212	$2,212
Transportation:	$930	$520

Undergraduate aid. Need-based: Average financial aid package for full-time students was $9,502. 31% awarded as scholarships/grants, 69% as loans/jobs. Need-based aid available for part-time students. **Non-need-based:** 29% awarded as scholarships/grants, 71% as loans/jobs. Scholarships based on academics, art, athletics, leadership, minority status, music/drama, state/district residency. **Student debt:** 44% of graduating class borrowed to fund education; average debt was $17,340.

Freshman aid. Need-based: Out of 5,727 full-time freshmen, 3,074 applied for aid; 2,058 were judged to have need; of these 2,058 received aid.

Merit scholarships. Over $3 million in merit scholarships available to freshmen. National Merit scholarship packages range from $6,000 - $10,000 a year.

Policies to reduce costs. Tuition/fee waivers for minority students, employees and their families. Credit/placement for qualifying scores on AP, IB, CLEP examinations. Work study available nights and weekends.

Payment plans. Credit card, deferred payment.

Application procedures. FAFSA required. Priority date 3/1; no closing date. Applicants notified on rolling basis starting 4/1, must reply within 3 week(s) of notification. **Transfers:** No deadline. Some waivers available for Arizona Community College transfer students with 3.2 GPA who are Arizona residents.

Contact. Phyllis Bannister, Executive Director of Student Financial Aid
Robert L. Nugent Building
Tucson, AZ 85721-0040

University of Phoenix

Phoenix, Arizona
www.phoenix.edu
Four-year proprietary **Federal Code: 014593**

College costs. Quoted prices are representative costs in Arizona for 30 credits in business-related degree programs; costs vary by program, by campus and by state.

	Living at home
Tuition and fees (2002-2003):	$8,400
Books and supplies:	$525
Transportation:	$300

Undergraduate aid. Need-based: 6% awarded as scholarships/grants, 94% as loans/jobs.

Policies to reduce costs. Tuition/fee waivers for employees and their families. Credit/placement for qualifying scores on AP, CLEP examinations.

Payment plans. Credit card payment.

Application procedures. FAFSA, institutional form required. No deadline. Applicants notified on rolling basis.

Contact. Robert Collins, Vice President, Student Financial Aid
4615 East Elwood Street
Phoenix, AZ 85040-1958

Yavapai College

Prescott, Arizona
www.yavapai.cc.az.us
Two-year public **Federal Code: 001079**

	Living at home	On-campus
Tuition and fees (2002-2003):	$930	$930
Out-of-state:	$5,930	$5,930
Per-credit charge:	$31	$31
Per-credit out-of-state:	$239	$239
Room and board:		$4,000
Books and supplies:	$600	$600
Personal expenses:	$950	$1,180
Transportation:	$670	$670

Undergraduate aid. Need-based: Need-based aid available for full-time students. **Non-need-based:** Scholarships based on academics, athletics.

Policies to reduce costs. Tuition/fee waivers for senior citizens, employees and their families. Credit/placement for qualifying scores on AP, IB, CLEP examinations.

Payment plans. Credit card payment.

Application procedures. FAFSA required. Priority date 4/15; no closing date. Applicants notified on rolling basis.

Contact. Financial aid office: (928) 776-2152
Vikki Gill, Director of Financial Aid
1100 East Sheldon Street
Prescott, AZ 86301

Arkansas

Arkansas Baptist College

Little Rock, Arkansas
Four-year private
Federal Code: 001087

	Living at home	On-campus
Tuition and fees (2002-2003):	$2,875	$2,875
Room and board:		$4,200
Books and supplies:	$700	$700
Personal expenses:	$1,000	$850
Transportation:	$1,000	$1,000

Undergraduate aid. All financial aid based on need. Need-based aid available for full-time and part-time students.

Policies to reduce costs. Tuition/fee waivers for senior citizens.

Payment plans. Installment, deferred payment.

Application procedures. FAFSA required. Closing date 5/1. Applicants notified on rolling basis starting 6/15.

Contact. Evelyn Thomas-Jones, Director of Financial Aid
1600 Bishop Street
Little Rock, AR 72202

Arkansas State University

State University, Arkansas
www.astate.edu
Four-year public
Federal Code: 001090

	Living at home	On-campus
Tuition and fees (2002-2003):	$4,480	$4,480
Out-of-state:	$10,090	$10,090
Room and board:		$3,410
Board only:	$1,800	
Books and supplies:	$900	$900
Personal expenses:	$450	$1,350
Transportation:	$2,000	$1,350

Undergraduate aid. Need-based: Average financial aid package for full-time students was $2,900. 62% awarded as scholarships/grants, 38% as loans/jobs. Need-based aid available for part-time students. **Non-need-based:** Scholarships based on academics, alumni affiliation, art, athletics, leadership, minority status, music/drama, state/district residency. **Student debt:** 60% of graduating class borrowed to fund education; average debt was $13,350.

Freshman aid. Need-based: Out of 1,546 full-time freshmen, 1,406 applied for aid; 1,392 were judged to have need; of these 1,354 received aid. Average package met 65% of need. 567 students had full need met. Average scholarship/grant was $2,400; average loan $1,200. **Non-need based:** 463 full-time freshmen with need received non-need scholarships; 45 without need received awards; 65 received athletic scholarships.

Policies to reduce costs. Tuition/fee waivers for children of alumni, senior citizens, employees and their families. Credit/placement for qualifying scores on AP, CLEP examinations. Work study available nights, weekends and for part-time students.

Payment plans. Credit card, installment payment.

Application procedures. FAFSA, institutional form required. Priority date 2/15; closing date 7/2. Applicants notified on rolling basis starting 6/1, must reply within 2 week(s) of notification.

Contact. Financial aid office: (870) 972-2310
Greg Thornburg, Director of Financial Aid
Box 1630
State University, AR 72467

Arkansas State University: Beebe

Beebe, Arkansas
Two-year public
Federal Code: 001090

	Living at home	On-campus
Tuition and fees (2002-2003):	$1,830	$1,830
Out-of-state:	$3,000	$3,000
Per-credit charge:	$56	$56
Per-credit out-of-state:	$95	$95
Room and board:		$2,380
Board only:	$2,300	
Books and supplies:	$800	$800
Personal expenses:	$1,800	$1,900
Transportation:	$1,300	$1,300

Undergraduate aid. Need-based: Need-based aid available for full-time and part-time students. **Non-need-based:** Scholarships based on academics, leadership, minority status, music/drama.

Policies to reduce costs. Tuition/fee waivers for senior citizens, employees and their families. Credit/placement for qualifying scores on AP, CLEP examinations. Work study available nights, weekends and for part-time students.

Payment plans. Credit card payment.

Application procedures. FAFSA, institutional form required. Priority date 7/1; no closing date. Applicants notified on rolling basis starting 6/1, must reply within 2 week(s) of notification.

Contact. Financial aid office: (501) 882-8245
Dena Prior, Director of Student Aid
PO Box 1000
Beebe, AR 72012-1000

Arkansas State University: Mountain Home

Mountain Home, Arkansas
www.asumh.edu
Two-year public
Federal Code: 001090

	Living at home
Tuition and fees (projected):	$1,920
Out-of-state:	$3,090
Per-credit charge:	$56
Per-credit out-of-state:	$95
Books and supplies:	$500
Transportation:	$500

Undergraduate aid. Need-based: Need-based aid available for full-time and part-time students. **Non-need-based:** Scholarships based on academics, state/district residency.

Policies to reduce costs. Tuition/fee waivers for senior citizens. Credit/placement for qualifying scores on AP, CLEP examinations.

Payment plans. Credit card, installment payment.

Application procedures. FAFSA, institutional form required. Priority date 7/1; no closing date. Applicants notified on rolling basis starting 5/1, must reply within 2 week(s) of notification.

Contact. Financial aid office: (870) 508-6127
Lyndle McCurley, Vice Chancellor Administrative Affairs
1600 South College Street
Mountain Home, AR 72653

Arkansas Tech University

Russellville, Arkansas
www.atu.edu
Four-year public
Federal Code: 001089

	Living at home	On-campus
Tuition and fees (2002-2003):	$3,256	$3,256
Out-of-state:	$6,152	$6,152
Room and board:		$3,576
Board only:	$1,686	
Books and supplies:	$1,000	$1,000
Personal expenses:	$1,000	$1,000
Transportation:	$790	$790

Undergraduate aid. Need-based: Average financial aid package for full-time students was $4,593; for part-time $3,675. 57% awarded as scholarships/grants, 43% as loans/jobs. **Non-need-based:** 56% awarded as scholarships/grants, 44% as loans/jobs. Scholarships based on academics, art, athletics, leadership, minority status, music/drama. **Student debt:** 53% of graduating class borrowed to fund education; average debt was $13,947.

Freshman aid. Need-based: Out of 1,306 full-time freshmen, 935 applied for aid; 772 were judged to have need; of these 763 received aid. Average package met 53% of need. 254 students had full need met. Average scholarship/grant was $2,838; average loan $814. **Non-need based:** 388 full-time freshmen with need received non-need scholarships; 345 without need received awards; 42 received athletic scholarships.

Policies to reduce costs. Tuition/fee waivers for senior citizens, employees and their families. Credit/placement for qualifying scores on AP, CLEP examinations.

Payment plans. Credit card, installment payment.

Application procedures. FAFSA required. Priority date 4/15; no closing date. Applicants notified on rolling basis starting 5/1, must reply within 2 week(s) of notification. **Transfers:** Must have academic transcript on file with the registrar's office.

Contact. Financial aid office: (479) 968-0399
Shirley Goines, Director of Student Financial Aid
Doc Bryan Student Services Building
Russellville, AR 72801-2222

Black River Technical College

Pocahontas, Arkansas
www.blackrivertech.org
Two-year public **Federal Code: 011948**

	Living at home
Tuition and fees:	$1,650
Out-of-state:	$2,070
Per-credit charge:	$52
Per-credit out-of-district:	$66
Per-credit out-of-state:	$178

Contact. Carolyn Collins, Director of Financial Aid
Highway 304 East
Pocahontas, AR 72455

Central Baptist College

Conway, Arkansas
www.cbc.edu
Four-year private **Federal Code: 001093**

	Living at home	On-campus
Tuition and fees (2002-2003):	$6,984	$6,984
Room and board:		$4,398
Books and supplies:	$600	$600
Personal expenses:	$800	$800
Transportation:	$800	$600

Undergraduate aid. Need-based: Need-based aid available for full-time students. **Non-need-based:** Scholarships based on academics, state/district residency.

Policies to reduce costs. Tuition/fee waivers for family of clergy, employees and their families. Credit/placement for qualifying scores on AP, CLEP examinations.

Payment plans. Installment payment.

Application procedures. FAFSA required. Priority date 7/1; closing date 8/15. Applicants notified on rolling basis starting 4/1. **Transfers:** No deadline.

Contact. Christie Bell, Director, Financial Aid
1501 College Avenue
Conway, AR 72034

Cossatot Community College of the University of Arkansas

De Queen, Arkansas
www.cccua.edu
Two-year public **Federal Code: 012432**

College costs. Residents of bordering out-of-state counties may qualify for in-state tuition.

	Living at home
Tuition and fees (2002-2003):	$1,274
Out-of-state:	$4,124
Per-credit charge:	$40
Per-credit out-of-state:	$135
Books and supplies:	$747
Personal expenses:	$2,365
Transportation:	$546

Undergraduate aid. Need-based: Need-based aid available for full-time and part-time students.

Policies to reduce costs. Tuition/fee waivers for senior citizens, employees and their families. Credit/placement for qualifying scores on CLEP examinations. Work study available nights and for part-time students.

Payment plans. Credit card, installment payment.

Application procedures. FAFSA, institutional form required. Priority date 6/1; no closing date. Applicants notified on rolling basis starting 3/1.

Contact. Financial aid office: (870) 584-4471
Denise Hammond, Director of Financial Aid
183 Highway 399
De Queen, AR 71832

Crowley's Ridge College

Paragould, Arkansas
www.crowleysridgecollege.edu
Two-year private **Federal Code: 001095**

	Living at home	On-campus
Tuition and fees:	$6,400	$6,400
Per-credit charge:	$189	$189
Room and board:		$3,800
Books and supplies:	$300	$300

Policies to reduce costs. Tuition/fee waivers for adults. Work study available nights and weekends.

Payment plans. Credit card, installment payment.

Application procedures. FAFSA required.

Contact. David Goff
100 College Drive
Paragould, AR 72450

East Arkansas Community College

Forrest City, Arkansas
www.eacc.cc.ar.us
Two-year public **Federal Code: 012260**

	Living at home
Tuition and fees (2002-2003):	$1,380
Out-of-district:	$1,620
Out-of-state:	$1,950
Per-credit charge:	$41
Per-credit out-of-district:	$49
Per-credit out-of-state:	$60
Board only:	$1,500
Books and supplies:	$700
Personal expenses:	$1,000
Transportation:	$700

Undergraduate aid. All financial aid based on need. Need-based aid available for full-time and part-time students.

Policies to reduce costs. Tuition/fee waivers for senior citizens, employees and their families. Credit/placement for qualifying scores on CLEP examinations.

Payment plans. Credit card payment.

Application procedures. FAFSA required. Priority date 3/1; closing date 7/1. Applicants notified on rolling basis starting 5/15, must reply within 2 week(s) of notification.

Contact. Alvin Coleman, Director of Financial Aid
1700 Newcastle Road
Forrest City, AR 72335-9598

Harding University

Searcy, Arkansas
www.harding.edu
Four-year private **Federal Code: 001097**

College costs. Additional $142 required fees for campus residents.

	Living at home	On-campus
Tuition and fees:	$10,266	$10,266
Room and board:		$4,770
Board only:	$2,530	
Books and supplies:	$800	$800
Personal expenses:		$980
Transportation:		$900

Undergraduate aid. Need-based: Average financial aid package for full-time students was $8,673. 39% awarded as scholarships/grants, 61% as loans/jobs. Need-based aid available for part-time students. **Non-need-based:** 66% awarded as scholarships/grants, 34% as loans/jobs. Scholarships based on academics, art, athletics, music/drama, religious affiliation, state/district residency. **Student debt:** 67% of graduating class borrowed to fund education; average debt was $21,153. **Additional information:** Music scholarships available, audition required.

Freshman aid. Need-based: Out of 1,039 full-time freshmen, 982 applied for aid; 568 were judged to have need; of these 568 received aid. Average package met 69% of need. 48 students had full need met. Average scholarship/grant was $5,828; average loan $3,892. **Non-need based:** 372 without need received awards; 15 received athletic scholarships.

Policies to reduce costs. Tuition/fee waivers for senior citizens, employees and their families. Credit/placement for qualifying scores on AP, IB, CLEP examinations.

Payment plans. Credit card, installment payment.

Application procedures. FAFSA, institutional form required. Priority date 4/1; no closing date. Applicants notified on rolling basis starting 2/15, must reply within 2 week(s) of notification. **Transfers:** Priority date 4/1; no deadline.

Contact. Financial aid office: (501) 279-4257
Jon Roberts, Director of Financial Aid
900 East Center
Searcy, AR 72149-0001

Henderson State University

Arkadelphia, Arkansas
www.hsu.edu
Four-year public **Federal Code: 001098**

	Living at home	On-campus
Tuition and fees (2002-2003):	$3,252	$3,252
Out-of-state:	$6,204	$6,204
Room and board:		$3,936
Board only:	$875	
Books and supplies:	$800	$800
Personal expenses:	$1,600	$2,000
Transportation:	$1,400	$800

Undergraduate aid. Need-based: Need-based aid available for full-time and part-time students. **Non-need-based:** Scholarships based on academics, alumni affiliation, art, athletics, leadership, minority status, music/drama, state/district residency.

Policies to reduce costs. Tuition/fee waivers for senior citizens, employees and their families. Credit/placement for qualifying scores on AP, CLEP examinations.

Payment plans. Credit card payment.

Application procedures. FAFSA required. Priority date 6/1; no closing date. Applicants notified on rolling basis starting 3/1, must reply within 2 week(s) of notification. **Transfers:** No deadline.

Contact. Financial aid office: (870) 230-5094
Jo Holland, Director of Financial Aid
1100 Henderson Street
Arkadelphia, AR 71999-0001

Hendrix College

Conway, Arkansas
www.hendrix.edu
Four-year private **Federal Code: 001099**

	Living at home	On-campus
Tuition and fees:	$15,630	$15,630
Room and board:		$5,340
Board only:	$2,986	
Books and supplies:	$800	$800
Personal expenses:	$1,080	$1,080
Transportation:	$1,080	$1,080

Undergraduate aid. Need-based: Average financial aid package for full-time students was $13,738; for part-time $7,143. 71% awarded as scholarships/grants, 29% as loans/jobs. **Non-need-based:** 83% awarded as scholarships/grants, 17% as loans/jobs. Scholarships based on academics, art, leadership, music/drama, religious affiliation. **Student debt:** 43% of graduating class borrowed to fund education; average debt was $14,291.

Freshman aid. Need-based: Out of 317 full-time freshmen, 235 applied for aid; 164 were judged to have need; of these 164 received aid. Average package met 92% of need. 68 students had full need met. Average scholarship/grant was $10,945; average loan $3,287. **Non-need based:** 36 full-time freshmen with need received non-need scholarships; 139 without need received awards.

Merit scholarships. Hays Memorial Scholarship; full tuition, room, board, mandatory fees; based on academic excellence. Visual and Performing Arts Scholarships (music, theatre, art); $1,000 to $5,000 per year; auditions/portfolios required. Leadership and United Methodist (UMYF) scholarships; $1,000 to $3,500.

Policies to reduce costs. Tuition/fee waivers for family of clergy, employees and their families. Credit/placement for qualifying scores on AP, IB, CLEP examinations. Work study available nights and weekends.

Payment plans. Credit card, installment, deferred payment.

Application procedures. FAFSA required. Priority date 2/15; no closing date. Applicants notified on rolling basis starting 3/1, must reply by 5/1 or within 2 week(s) of notification. **Transfers:** No deadline.

Contact. Financial aid office: (501) 450-1368
Tammy Robbins, Director of Financial Aid
1600 Washington Avenue
Conway, AR 72032-3080

ITT Technical Institute: Little Rock

Little Rock, Arkansas
www.itt-tech.edu
Two-year proprietary **Federal Code: 023217**

College costs. Total program varies depending on course of study. Per-credit-hour charge: $347.

Policies to reduce costs. Tuition/fee waivers for employees and their families. Tuition at time of enrollment guaranteed for 2 years.

Payment plans. Credit card, installment payment.

Application procedures. FAFSA, institutional form required. No deadline. Applicants notified on rolling basis.

Contact. Tresa Smith, Director of Finance
4520 S. University Avenue
Little Rock, AR 72204

John Brown University

Siloam Springs, Arkansas
www.jbu.edu
Four-year private **Federal Code: 001100**

	Living at home	On-campus
Tuition and fees:	$13,716	$13,716
Room and board:		$5,070
Board only:	$2,500	
Books and supplies:	$700	$700
Personal expenses:	$1,350	$1,350
Transportation:	$1,500	$1,500

Undergraduate aid. Need-based: Average financial aid package for full-time students was $11,178. 62% awarded as scholarships/grants, 38% as loans/jobs. **Non-need-based:** 56% awarded as scholarships/grants, 44% as loans/jobs. Scholarships based on academics, alumni affiliation, athletics, leadership, music/drama. **Student debt:** 63% of graduating class borrowed to fund education; average debt was $12,815.

Freshman aid. Need-based: Out of 307 full-time freshmen, 259 applied for aid; 210 were judged to have need; of these 210 received aid. Average package met 74% of need. 36 students had full need met. Average scholarship/grant was $7,037; average loan $3,953. **Non-need based:** 27 full-time freshmen with need received non-need scholarships; 76 without need received awards.

Policies to reduce costs. Tuition/fee waivers for adults, senior citizens, family of clergy, employees and their families. Credit/placement for qualifying scores on AP, CLEP examinations.

Payment plans. Installment payment.

Application procedures. FAFSA required. Priority date 3/1; closing date 5/1. Applicants notified on rolling basis starting 4/1, must reply by 5/1 or within 4 week(s) of notification.

Contact. Financial aid office: (877) 528-4636
Kim Eldridge, Director of Financial Aid
2000 West University Street
Siloam Springs, AR 72761-2121

Lyon College

Batesville, Arkansas
www.lyon.edu
Four-year private **Federal Code: 001088**

	Living at home	On-campus
Tuition and fees:	$12,395	$12,395
Room and board:		$5,600
Board only:	$3,300	
Books and supplies:	$700	$700
Personal expenses:	$900	$900
Transportation:	$900	$900

Undergraduate aid. Need-based: Average financial aid package for full-time students was $13,006; for part-time $5,378. 69% awarded as scholarships/grants, 31% as loans/jobs. **Non-need-based:** 65% awarded as scholarships/grants, 35% as loans/jobs. Scholarships based on academics, art, athletics, leadership, minority status, music/drama, religious affiliation, state/district residency. **Student debt:** 93% of graduating class borrowed to fund education; average debt was $11,639.

Freshman aid. Need-based: Out of 113 full-time freshmen, 90 applied for aid; 70 were judged to have need; of these 70 received aid. Average package met 90% of need. 26 students had full need met. Average scholarship/grant was $9,820; average loan $3,210. **Non-need based:** 19 full-time freshmen with need received non-need scholarships; 35 without need received awards; 22 received athletic scholarships.

Merit scholarships. Brown Scholarship; full tuition, room and board, based on high school record, standardized test scores, interview, 4 awards. Anderson Scholarship; up to $10,000, based on high school record, test scores, interview, 4 awards. Lyon Fellowship; $10,000, based on high school record, test scores, interview, career interest in business or public service, 8 awards.

Policies to reduce costs. Tuition/fee waivers for employees and their families. Credit/placement for qualifying scores on AP examinations.

Payment plans. Credit card, installment payment.

Application procedures. FAFSA required. Priority date 3/15; no closing date. Applicants notified on rolling basis starting 3/1, must reply by 8/15. **Transfers:** No deadline.

Contact. Financial aid office: (870) 698-4257
Amber Schubert, Director of Student Financial Assistance
PO Box 2317
Batesville, AR 72503-2317

Mid-South Community College

West Memphis, Arkansas
www.midsouthcc.edu
Two-year public **Federal Code: 015862**

	Living at home
Tuition and fees (2002-2003):	$1,272
Out-of-district:	$1,572
Out-of-state:	$1,872
Per-credit charge:	$40
Per-credit out-of-district:	$50
Per-credit out-of-state:	$60
Personal expenses:	$2,238
Transportation:	$2,376

Undergraduate aid. Need-based: Average financial aid package for full-time students was $2,056; for part-time $1,304. 98% awarded as scholarships/grants, 2% as loans/jobs. **Non-need-based:** Scholarships based on academics, state/district residency.

Freshman aid. Need-based: Out of 44 full-time freshmen, 30 applied for aid; 29 were judged to have need; of these 25 received aid. Average package met 17% of need. Average scholarship/grant was $1,858. **Non-need based:** 2 full-time freshmen with need received non-need scholarships; 6 without need received awards.

Policies to reduce costs. Tuition/fee waivers for senior citizens, employees and their families. Credit/placement for qualifying scores on AP, CLEP examinations. Work study available nights and for part-time students.

Payment plans. Credit card, installment payment.

Application procedures. FAFSA, institutional form required. No deadline. Applicants notified on rolling basis starting 6/1, must reply within 2 week(s) of notification. **Transfers:** No deadline.

Contact. Jackie Brubaker, Director of FInancial Aid
2000 West Broadway
West Memphis, AR 72301

Mississippi County Community College

Blytheville, Arkansas
www.mccc.cc.ar.us
Two-year public **Federal Code: 012860**

	Living at home
Tuition and fees (2002-2003):	$1,124
Out-of-district:	$1,364
Out-of-state:	$2,564
Per-credit charge:	$43
Per-credit out-of-district:	$53
Per-credit out-of-state:	$103
Board only:	$1,500
Books and supplies:	$514
Personal expenses:	$3,402
Transportation:	$1,099

Undergraduate aid. Need-based: Average financial aid package for full-time students was $3,932; for part-time $3,158. 92% awarded as scholarships/grants, 8% as loans/jobs. **Non-need-based:** 92% awarded as scholarships/grants, 8% as loans/jobs. Scholarships based on academics, minority status, music/drama, state/district residency. **Student debt:** 9% of graduating class borrowed to fund education; average debt was $2,924.

Freshman aid. Need-based: Average package met 39% of need. Average scholarship/grant was $3,877; average loan $1,128.

Policies to reduce costs. Tuition/fee waivers for senior citizens, employees and their families. Credit/placement for qualifying scores on AP, CLEP examinations. Work study available nights and for part-time students.

Payment plans. Credit card, installment, deferred payment.

Application procedures. FAFSA, institutional form required. Priority date 4/15; no closing date. Applicants notified on rolling basis starting 5/1, must reply within 2 week(s) of notification.

Contact. Financial aid office: (870) 762-1020 ext. 1161
Laura Yarbrough, Director of Financial Aid
Box 1109
Blytheville, AR 72316-1109

North Arkansas College

Harrison, Arkansas
www.northark.edu
Two-year public **Federal Code: 012261**

	Living at home
Tuition and fees (2002-2003):	$1,008
Out-of-district:	$1,248
Out-of-state:	$2,448
Per-credit charge:	$42
Per-credit out-of-district:	$52
Per-credit out-of-state:	$102
Board only:	$1,630
Books and supplies:	$569
Personal expenses:	$982
Transportation:	$1,097

Undergraduate aid. Need-based: 80% awarded as scholarships/grants, 20% as loans/jobs. Need-based aid available for part-time students. **Non-need-based:** Scholarships based on academics, alumni affiliation, art, athletics, leadership, music/drama, state/district residency.

Policies to reduce costs. Tuition/fee waivers for senior citizens, employees and their families. Credit/placement for qualifying scores on AP, CLEP examinations. Work study available nights and for part-time students.

Payment plans. Credit card, installment payment.

Application procedures. FAFSA, institutional form required. Priority date 5/1; no closing date. Applicants notified on rolling basis starting 5/15, must reply within 4 week(s) of notification. **Transfers:** Priority date 5/1.

Contact. Financial aid office: (870) 391-3266
Nancy Fountain, Director of Financial Aid
1515 Pioneer Drive
Harrison, AR 72601

Northwest Arkansas Community College

Bentonville, Arkansas
www.nwacc.edu
Two-year public **Federal Code: 030633**

	Living at home
Tuition and fees (2002-2003):	$1,440
Out-of-district:	$2,820
Out-of-state:	$3,570
Per-credit charge:	$46
Per-credit out-of-district:	$92
Per-credit out-of-state:	$117
Books and supplies:	$675
Personal expenses:	$2,660
Transportation:	$1,444

Undergraduate aid. Need-based: Need-based aid available for full-time and part-time students. **Non-need-based:** Scholarships based on academics, leadership, music/drama, state/district residency.

Policies to reduce costs. Tuition/fee waivers for senior citizens, employees and their families. Credit/placement for qualifying scores on AP, CLEP examinations. Work study available nights, weekends and for part-time students.

Payment plans. Credit card, installment payment.

Application procedures. FAFSA, institutional form required. Priority date 4/1; no closing date. Applicants notified on rolling basis starting 4/1, must reply within 2 week(s) of notification.

Contact. Carolyn Jines, Financial Aid Director
One College Drive
Bentonville, AR 72712

Ouachita Baptist University

Arkadelphia, Arkansas
www.obu.edu
Four-year private **Federal Code: 001102**

	Living at home	On-campus
Tuition and fees (2002-2003):	$12,800	$12,800
Room and board:		$4,600
Books and supplies:	$700	$700
Personal expenses:	$1,000	$1,000
Transportation:	$800	$800

Undergraduate aid. Need-based: Average financial aid package for full-time students was $12,033. 72% awarded as scholarships/grants, 28% as loans/jobs. Need-based aid available for part-time students. **Non-need-based:** 66% awarded as scholarships/grants, 34% as loans/jobs. Scholarships based on academics, alumni affiliation, art, athletics. **Student debt:** 53% of graduating class borrowed to fund education; average debt was $13,334.

Freshman aid. Need-based: Out of 396 full-time freshmen, 360 applied for aid; 227 were judged to have need; of these 227 received aid. Average package met 100% of need. 119 students had full need met. Average scholarship/grant was $7,242; average loan $1,682. **Non-need based:** 36 full-time freshmen with need received non-need scholarships; 107 without need received awards.

Policies to reduce costs. Tuition/fee waivers for family of clergy, employees and their families. Credit/placement for qualifying scores on AP, IB, CLEP examinations. Work study available nights, weekends and for part-time students.

Payment plans. Credit card, installment payment.

Application procedures. FAFSA, institutional form required. Priority date 2/15; closing date 6/1. Applicants notified on rolling basis starting 12/1, must reply within 4 week(s) of notification. **Transfers:** Priority date 2/15; closing date 6/1.

Contact. Financial aid office: (870) 245-5570
Susan Hurst, Director of Financial Aid
OBU Box 3776
Arkadelphia, AR 71998

Ouachita Technical College

Malvern, Arkansas
www.otcweb.edu
Two-year public **Federal Code: 009976**

	Living at home
Tuition and fees (2002-2003):	$1,680
Out-of-state:	$4,380
Per-credit charge:	$45
Per-credit out-of-state:	$135
Books and supplies:	$600
Personal expenses:	$1,433

Undergraduate aid. Need-based: Need-based aid available for full-time and part-time students.

Policies to reduce costs. Tuition/fee waivers for senior citizens, family members. Credit/placement for qualifying scores on AP, CLEP examinations. Work study available nights.

Payment plans. Credit card, installment payment.

Application procedures. FAFSA required. Closing date 6/30. Applicants notified on rolling basis starting 7/1, must reply within 6 week(s) of notification.

Contact. Financial aid office: (501) 332-3658
Teresa Avery, Director of Financial Aid
One College Circle
Malvern, AR 72104

Ozarka College

Melbourne, Arkansas
www.ozarka.edu
Two-year public **Federal Code: 013217**

	Living at home
Tuition and fees (2002-2003):	$1,865
Out-of-state:	$5,255
Per-credit charge:	$50
Per-credit out-of-state:	$168
Books and supplies:	$800
Personal expenses:	$4,900

Undergraduate aid. Need-based: Need-based aid available for full-time and part-time students.

Application procedures. FAFSA required. No deadline. Applicants notified on rolling basis, must reply within 2 week(s) of notification.

Contact. Joyce Gott, Financial Aid Officer
PO Box 10
Melbourne, AR 72556-0010

Philander Smith College

Little Rock, Arkansas
www.philander.edu
Four-year private **Federal Code: 001103**

	Living at home	On-campus
Tuition and fees:	$5,375	$5,375
Room and board:		$5,090
Board only:	$700	
Books and supplies:	$650	$650
Personal expenses:	$600	$600
Transportation:	$775	$775

Undergraduate aid. All financial aid based on need. Need-based aid available for full-time and part-time students.

Policies to reduce costs. Tuition/fee waivers for family members, family of clergy, employees and their families. Prepayment discount; credit/placement for qualifying scores on CLEP examinations.

Payment plans. Credit card, installment payment.

Application procedures. FAFSA, institutional form required. Priority date 5/1; no closing date. Applicants notified on rolling basis starting 5/1, must reply within 2 week(s) of notification. **Transfers:** Priority date 3/1; closing date 6/30.

Contact. **Financial aid office:** (501) 370-5350
Terri Powers, Director of Financial Aid
One Trudie Kibbe Reed Drive
Little Rock, AR 72202-3718

Phillips Community College of the University of Arkansas

Helena, Arkansas
www.pccua.edu
Two-year public **Federal Code: 001104**

College costs. Students from some Mississippi counties near state line qualify for out-of-district costs: Coahoma County; Tunica County; Quitman County; Bolivar County.

	Living at home
Tuition and fees (2002-2003):	$1,460
Out-of-district:	$1,730
Out-of-state:	$2,870
Per-credit charge:	$44
Per-credit out-of-district:	$53
Per-credit out-of-state:	$91
Board only:	$1,600
Books and supplies:	$800
Personal expenses:	$3,025
Transportation:	$1,600

Undergraduate aid. All financial aid based on need. 85% awarded as scholarships/grants, 15% as loans/jobs. Need-based aid available for part-time students.

Policies to reduce costs. Tuition/fee waivers for senior citizens, employees and their families. Credit/placement for qualifying scores on CLEP examinations. Work study available nights and for part-time students.

Payment plans. Credit card, installment payment.

Application procedures. FAFSA required. Priority date 4/1; closing date 5/1. Applicants notified on rolling basis starting 4/1, must reply within 2 week(s) of notification.

Contact. Barbra Stevenson, Director of Financial Aid
Campus Drive
Helena, AR 72342

Pulaski Technical College

North Little Rock, Arkansas
www.pulaskitech.edu
Two-year public **Federal Code: 014167**

	Living at home
Tuition and fees:	$2,010
Out-of-state:	$2,520
Per-credit charge:	$63
Per-credit out-of-state:	$80
Board only:	$3,200
Books and supplies:	$800
Personal expenses:	$2,732
Transportation:	$1,425

Undergraduate aid. Need-based: Need-based aid available for full-time and part-time students.

Policies to reduce costs. Tuition/fee waivers for senior citizens. Credit/placement for qualifying scores on AP, CLEP examinations.

Application procedures. FAFSA, institutional form required. Priority date 5/15; no closing date. Applicants notified on rolling basis starting 5/1, must reply within 2 week(s) of notification.

Contact. Kris Buford, Director Financial Aid
3000 West Scenic Drive
North Little Rock, AR 72118

Rich Mountain Community College

Mena, Arkansas
www.rmcc.edu
Two-year public **Federal Code: 012435**

	Living at home
Tuition and fees:	$1,170
Out-of-district:	$1,740
Out-of-state:	$4,200
Per-credit charge:	$37
Per-credit out-of-district:	$46
Per-credit out-of-state:	$138
Board only:	$1,149
Books and supplies:	$800
Personal expenses:	$3,000
Transportation:	$800

Undergraduate aid. Need-based: 98% awarded as scholarships/grants, 2% as loans/jobs. Need-based aid available for part-time students. **Non-need-based:** Scholarships based on academics.

Policies to reduce costs. Tuition/fee waivers for senior citizens, employees and their families. Credit/placement for qualifying scores on AP, CLEP examinations. Work study available for part-time students.

Payment plans. Credit card, installment payment.

Application procedures. FAFSA, institutional form required. Priority date 7/31; no closing date. Applicants notified on rolling basis starting 6/1, must reply within 2 week(s) of notification. **Transfers:** No deadline.

Contact. **Financial aid office:** (501) 394-7622 ext. 1420
Louise Dunn, Financial Aid Officer
1100 College Drive
Mena, AR 71953

South Arkansas Community College
El Dorado, Arkansas
www.SouthArk.edu
Two-year public **Federal Code: 013858**

College costs. $25 lab fee for most courses.

	Living at home
Tuition and fees (2002-2003):	$1,760
Out-of-district:	$2,090
Out-of-state:	$3,740
Per-credit charge:	$54
Per-credit out-of-district:	$65
Per-credit out-of-state:	$120
Books and supplies:	$600
Personal expenses:	$550

Undergraduate aid. Need-based: Need-based aid available for full-time and part-time students.

Policies to reduce costs. Tuition/fee waivers for senior citizens, employees and their families. Credit/placement for qualifying scores on AP, IB, CLEP examinations.

Payment plans. Credit card, installment payment.

Application procedures. FAFSA, institutional form required. Priority date 7/1; no closing date. Applicants notified on rolling basis starting 7/1, must reply within 2 week(s) of notification. **Transfers:** No deadline.

Contact. Financial aid office: (870) 864-7133
John Jefferson, Director of Financial Aid
Box 7010
El Dorado, AR 71731-7010

Southeast Arkansas College
Pine Bluff, Arkansas
www.seark.edu
Two-year public **Federal Code: 005707**

College costs. $3 per credit hour technology fee. $5 assessment fee.

	Living at home
Tuition and fees:	$1,600
Out-of-state:	$3,100
Per-credit charge:	$50
Per-credit out-of-state:	$100
Board only:	$750
Books and supplies:	$700
Personal expenses:	$2,450
Transportation:	$1,000

Undergraduate aid. Need-based: Need-based aid available for full-time and part-time students. **Non-need-based:** Scholarships based on academics, leadership, state/district residency.

Policies to reduce costs. Tuition/fee waivers for senior citizens, employees and their families. Credit/placement for qualifying scores on AP, CLEP examinations. Work study available nights, weekends and for part-time students.

Payment plans. Credit card, installment, deferred payment.

Application procedures. FAFSA required. Priority date 6/1; no closing date. Applicants notified on rolling basis starting 5/1, must reply within 2 week(s) of notification.

Contact. Financial aid office: (870) 543-5968
Donna Cox, Director of Financial Aid
1900 Hazel Street
Pine Bluff, AR 71603

Southern Arkansas University
Magnolia, Arkansas
www.saumag.edu
Four-year public **Federal Code: 001107**

	Living at home	On-campus
Tuition and fees (2002-2003):	$3,064	$3,064
Out-of-state:	$4,552	$4,552
Room and board:		$3,220
Board only:	$2,100	
Books and supplies:	$800	$800
Personal expenses:	$1,600	$2,000
Transportation:	$1,400	$800

Undergraduate aid. Need-based: Average financial aid package for full-time students was $6,011; for part-time $6,228. 48% awarded as scholarships/grants, 52% as loans/jobs. **Non-need-based:** 51% awarded as scholarships/grants, 49% as loans/jobs. Scholarships based on academics, alumni affiliation, art, athletics, leadership, minority status, music/drama, state/district residency. **Student debt:** 43% of graduating class borrowed to fund education; average debt was $24,050.

Freshman aid. Need-based: Out of 563 full-time freshmen, 399 applied for aid; 341 were judged to have need; of these 294 received aid. Average package met 100% of need. 294 students had full need met. Average scholarship/grant was $3,333; average loan $2,076. **Non-need based:** 189 full-time freshmen with need received non-need scholarships; 116 without need received awards; 39 received athletic scholarships.

Policies to reduce costs. Tuition/fee waivers for children of alumni, senior citizens, employees and their families. Credit/placement for qualifying scores on AP, CLEP examinations. Work study available nights, weekends and for part-time students.

Payment plans. Credit card, installment payment.

Application procedures. FAFSA required. Priority date 7/1; no closing date. Applicants notified on rolling basis starting 4/15, must reply within 2 week(s) of notification.

Contact. Financial aid office: (870) 235-4023
Bronwyn Sneed, Director of Financial Aid
Box 9382
Magnolia, AR 71754-9382

Southern Arkansas University Tech
Camden, Arkansas
www.sautech.edu
Two-year public **Federal Code: 007738**

	Living at home
Tuition and fees (2002-2003):	$1,815
Out-of-state:	$2,295
Per-credit charge:	$55
Per-credit out-of-state:	$75
Board only:	$2,000
Books and supplies:	$700
Personal expenses:	$2,000
Transportation:	$1,300

Undergraduate aid. Need-based: Average financial aid package for full-time students was $4,283; for part-time $3,295. 86% awarded as scholarships/grants, 14% as loans/jobs. **Non-need-based:** 55% awarded as scholarships/grants, 45% as loans/jobs. Scholarships based on academics. **Student debt:** 17% of graduating class borrowed to fund education; average debt was $5,738.

Freshman aid. Need-based: Out of 89 full-time freshmen, 59 applied for aid; 56 were judged to have need; of these 54 received aid. Average package met 54% of need. 3 students had full need met. Average scholarship/grant was $3,584; average loan $2,388. **Non-need based:** 3 full-time freshmen with need received non-need scholarships; 3 without need received awards.

Policies to reduce costs. Tuition/fee waivers for senior citizens, employees and their families. Credit/placement for qualifying scores on AP, CLEP examinations. Work study available for part-time students.

Payment plans. Credit card payment.

Application procedures. FAFSA, institutional form required. Closing date 6/1. Applicants notified on rolling basis starting 5/1.

Contact. Financial aid office: (870) 574-4511
Vicki Taylor, Director of Financial Aid
PO Box 3499
Camden, AR 71711-1599

University of Arkansas

Fayetteville, Arkansas
www.uark.edu
Four-year public **Federal Code: 001108**

College costs. Members of Native American tribes that formerly resided in Arkansas (Caddo, Cherokee, Choctaw, Osage and Quapaw) are classified as in-state students for tuition and fee purposes. College fees vary depending on student's field of study.

	Living at home	On-campus
Tuition and fees (2002-2003):	$4,228	$4,228
Out-of-state:	$10,600	$10,600
Room and board:		$4,728
Board only:	$1,700	
Books and supplies:	$800	$800
Personal expenses:	$1,100	$1,100
Transportation:	$1,100	$1,100

Undergraduate aid. Need-based: Average financial aid package for full-time students was $8,028; for part-time $5,791. 45% awarded as scholarships/grants, 55% as loans/jobs. **Non-need-based:** 67% awarded as scholarships/grants, 33% as loans/jobs. Scholarships based on academics, alumni affiliation, art, athletics, leadership, minority status, music/drama, state/district residency. **Student debt:** 48% of graduating class borrowed to fund education; average debt was $7,597.

Freshman aid. Need-based: Out of 2,235 full-time freshmen, 1,487 applied for aid; 969 were judged to have need; of these 934 received aid. Average package met 82% of need. 402 students had full need met. Average scholarship/grant was $3,225; average loan $2,285. **Non-need based:** 772 full-time freshmen with need received non-need scholarships; 674 without need received awards; 67 received athletic scholarships.

Merit scholarships. Sturgis Fellowship; $11,500, based on exceptional academic performance, 10 awards available to arts and sciences majors. Badenhamer Fellowship; $11,000, based on strong academic performance and leadership. Chancellor's Scholarships; tuition, fees, room and board. University Scholarships; $4,000, based on rank in top 5-10% of high school class. Nonresident Tuition Award; non-resident tuition, for entering freshmen from neighboring states, based on minimum ACT score of 24 or SAT of 1090 and 3.0 high school GPA.

Policies to reduce costs. Tuition/fee waivers for children of alumni, senior citizens, employees and their families. Credit/placement for qualifying scores on AP, IB, CLEP examinations. Work study available nights, weekends and for part-time students.

Payment plans. Credit card, installment payment.

Application procedures. FAFSA required. Priority date 3/15; no closing date. Applicants notified on rolling basis starting 4/1, must reply by 5/1 or within 2 week(s) of notification.

Contact. Financial aid office: (479) 575-3806
Ed Schroeder, Director of Student Financial Services
200 Silas Hunt Hall
Fayetteville, AR 72701

University of Arkansas - Fort Smith

Fort Smith, Arkansas
www.uafortsmith.edu
Four-year public **Federal Code: 001110**

	Living at home
Tuition and fees (2002-2003):	$1,830
Out-of-district:	$2,100
Out-of-state:	$6,480
Books and supplies:	$900
Personal expenses:	$2,100

Undergraduate aid. Need-based: Need-based aid available for full-time and part-time students. **Non-need-based:** Scholarships based on academics, athletics, job skills, leadership, music/drama. **Student debt:** 1% of graduating class borrowed to fund education; average debt was $2,793. **Additional information:** Scholarship deadline February 1.

Merit scholarships. Academic scholarships available to high school seniors in institution's service area; honors scholarships, technical scholarships also available.

Policies to reduce costs. Tuition/fee waivers for senior citizens, employees and their families. Credit/placement for qualifying scores on AP, CLEP examinations. Work study available nights, weekends and for part-time students.

Payment plans. Credit card, installment, deferred payment.

Application procedures. FAFSA, institutional form required. Priority date 4/1; no closing date. Applicants notified on rolling basis starting 3/1, must reply within 4 week(s) of notification. **Transfers:** No deadline.

Contact. Financial aid office: (479) 788-7090
Mary Cogbill, Director of Financial Aid
Box 3649
Fort Smith, AR 72913-3649

University of Arkansas at Little Rock

Little Rock, Arkansas
www.ualr.edu
Four-year public **Federal Code: 001161**

College costs. Technology fees vary from $2 to $10 per-credit-hour depending on student's field of study.

	Living at home	On-campus
Tuition and fees (2002-2003):	$4,210	$4,210
Out-of-state:	$9,827	$9,827
Room only:		$2,600
Books and supplies:	$1,000	$1,000
Personal expenses:	$800	$800
Transportation:	$800	$800

Undergraduate aid. Need-based: Need-based aid available for full-time and part-time students.

Policies to reduce costs. Tuition/fee waivers for senior citizens, employees and their families. Credit/placement for qualifying scores on AP, CLEP examinations.

Payment plans. Credit card, installment payment.

Application procedures. FAFSA required. Closing date 3/15. Applicants notified on rolling basis starting 5/1.

Contact. Financial aid office: (501) 569-3035
John Noah, Director of Admissions and Financial Aid
208 Administration South
Little Rock, AR 72204

University of Arkansas at Monticello

Monticello, Arkansas
www.uamont.edu
Four-year public **Federal Code: 001085**

	Living at home	On-campus
Tuition and fees (2002-2003):	$3,175	$3,175
Out-of-state:	$6,415	$6,415
Room and board:		$3,204
Board only:	$900	
Books and supplies:	$800	$800
Personal expenses:	$1,800	$1,800
Transportation:	$1,800	$1,125

Undergraduate aid. Need-based: Need-based aid available for full-time and part-time students. **Non-need-based:** Scholarships based on academics, athletics, job skills, leadership, music/drama, state/district residency.

Policies to reduce costs. Tuition/fee waivers for senior citizens, employees and their families. Credit/placement for qualifying scores on AP, IB, CLEP examinations. Work study available nights, weekends and for part-time students.

Payment plans. Credit card payment.

Application procedures. FAFSA, institutional form required. No deadline. Applicants notified on rolling basis starting 4/1, must reply within 2 week(s) of notification. **Transfers:** No deadline.

Contact. Financial aid office: (870) 460-1050
Susan Brewer, Director of Financial Aid
Box 3600
Monticello, AR 71656

University of Arkansas at Pine Bluff

Pine Bluff, Arkansas
www.uapb.edu
Four-year public **Federal Code: 001086**

College costs. Courses at North Little Rock site $116 per-credit-hour, $234 per credit hour out-of-state.

	Living at home	On-campus
Tuition and fees (2002-2003):	$3,458	$3,458
Out-of-state:	$6,989	$6,989
Room and board:		$4,744
Books and supplies:	$800	$800
Personal expenses:	$700	$800
Transportation:	$800	$700

Undergraduate aid. Need-based: Need-based aid available for full-time and part-time students. **Non-need-based:** Scholarships based on academics, alumni affiliation, art, athletics, leadership, minority status, music/drama, religious affiliation, state/district residency.

Policies to reduce costs. Tuition/fee waivers for senior citizens, minority students, employees and their families. Credit/placement for qualifying scores on AP, IB, CLEP examinations. Work study available weekends and for part-time students.

Payment plans. Credit card, installment, deferred payment.

Application procedures. FAFSA required. Priority date 4/15; no closing date. Applicants notified on rolling basis starting 3/1. **Transfers:** No deadline. Must supply financial aid transcript from prior college or university.

Contact. **Financial aid office:** (870) 575-8302
Ray Watley, Director of Financial Aid
1200 North University Drive, Mail Slot 4981
Pine Bluff, AR 71601-2799

University of Arkansas for Medical Sciences

Little Rock, Arkansas
www.uams.edu
Four-year public **Federal Code: 001109**

College costs. Required fees vary widely among several programs offered; tuition varies according to program.

	Living at home	On-campus
Tuition and fees (2002-2003):	$3,265	$3,265
Out-of-state:	$7,801	$7,801
Room only:		$1,531
Books and supplies:	$400	$400
Personal expenses:	$1,800	$1,800
Transportation:	$1,206	$1,206

Undergraduate aid. Need-based: Need-based aid available for full-time and part-time students.

Policies to reduce costs. Tuition/fee waivers for senior citizens, employees and their families.

Payment plans. Credit card payment.

Application procedures. FAFSA required. No deadline. Applicants notified on rolling basis starting 5/1, must reply within 2 week(s) of notification.

Contact. Paul Carter, Assistant Dean for Graduate Studies
4301 West Markham Street
Little Rock, AR 72205

University of Arkansas: Community College at Batesville

Batesville, Arkansas
www.uaccb.edu
Two-year public **Federal Code: 020735**

	Living at home
Tuition and fees (2002-2003):	$1,450
Out-of-district:	$1,750
Out-of-state:	$3,190
Per-credit charge:	$40
Per-credit out-of-district:	$50
Per-credit out-of-state:	$98
Books and supplies:	$700
Personal expenses:	$2,100

Undergraduate aid. All financial aid based on need. Average financial aid package for full-time students was $4,000; for part-time $2,000. 90% awarded as scholarships/grants, 10% as loans/jobs. **Student debt:** 10% of graduating class borrowed to fund education; average debt was $925.

Freshman aid. Average package met 55% of need. Average scholarship/grant was $1,500; average loan $970.

Policies to reduce costs. Tuition/fee waivers for senior citizens, employees and their families. Credit/placement for qualifying scores on AP, CLEP examinations. Work study available nights, weekends and for part-time students.

Payment plans. Credit card payment.

Application procedures. FAFSA required. No deadline. Applicants notified on rolling basis starting 3/1, must reply within 2 week(s) of notification.

Contact. **Financial aid office:** (870) 612-2036
Kristen Cross, Director of Financial Aid
Box 3350
Batesville, AR 72503

University of Arkansas: Community College at Hope

Hope, Arkansas
www.uacch.edu
Two-year public **Federal Code: 005732**

	Living at home
Tuition and fees (2002-2003):	$1,610
Out-of-district:	$1,760
Out-of-state:	$3,290
Per-credit charge:	$49
Per-credit out-of-district:	$54
Per-credit out-of-state:	$105
Board only:	$1,500
Books and supplies:	$900
Personal expenses:	$500
Transportation:	$540

Undergraduate aid. Need-based: Need-based aid available for full-time students. **Non-need-based:** Scholarships based on academics.

Policies to reduce costs. Tuition/fee waivers for senior citizens, employees and their families. Work study available nights and for part-time students.

Payment plans. Credit card payment.

Application procedures. FAFSA, institutional form required. Priority date 7/1; no closing date. Applicants notified on rolling basis starting 1/1, must reply within 4 week(s) of notification.

Contact. **Financial aid office:** (870) 722-8264
Jerald Barber, Vice Chancellor for Finance
2500 South Main
Hope, AR 71802-0140

University of Central Arkansas

Conway, Arkansas
www.uca.edu
Four-year public **Federal Code: 001092**

	Living at home	On-campus
Tuition and fees (2002-2003):	$3,990	$3,990
Out-of-state:	$7,302	$7,302
Room and board:		$3,600
Books and supplies:	$600	$600

Undergraduate aid. Need-based: Need-based aid available for full-time students. **Non-need-based:** Scholarships based on academics, athletics, music/drama, state/district residency. **Additional information:** Room and board may be paid monthly.

Policies to reduce costs. Tuition/fee waivers for senior citizens, employees and their families. Credit/placement for qualifying scores on AP, CLEP examinations.

Payment plans. Credit card payment.

Application procedures. FAFSA required. Priority date 2/15; no closing date. Applicants notified on rolling basis starting 5/1.

Contact. Financial aid office: (501) 450-3140
Cheryl Lyons, Director of Student Financial Aid
201 Donaghey Avenue
Conway, AR 72035-0001

University of the Ozarks

Clarksville, Arkansas
www.ozarks.edu
Four-year private **Federal Code: 001094**

	Living at home	On-campus
Tuition and fees:	$11,880	$11,880
Room and board:		$4,540
Board only:	$1,668	
Books and supplies:	$600	$600
Personal expenses:	$1,413	$2,357
Transportation:	$857	$862

Undergraduate aid. Need-based: Average financial aid package for full-time students was $12,667; for part-time $6,048. 77% awarded as scholarships/grants, 23% as loans/jobs. **Non-need-based:** 73% awarded as scholarships/grants, 27% as loans/jobs. Scholarships based on academics, alumni affiliation, art, leadership, minority status, music/drama, religious affiliation. **Student debt:** 40% of graduating class borrowed to fund education; average debt was $13,600.

Freshman aid. Need-based: Out of 203 full-time freshmen, 176 applied for aid; 120 were judged to have need; of these 120 received aid. Average package met 76% of need. 38 students had full need met. Average scholarship/grant was $10,959; average loan $2,378. **Non-need based:** 111 full-time freshmen with need received non-need scholarships; 56 without need received awards.

Policies to reduce costs. Tuition/fee waivers for children of alumni, minority students, family members, family of clergy, employees and their families. Credit/placement for qualifying scores on AP, CLEP examinations. Work study available nights and weekends.

Payment plans. Installment, deferred payment.

Application procedures. FAFSA required. Priority date 2/15; no closing date. Applicants notified on rolling basis starting 3/15, must reply within 2 week(s) of notification.

Contact. Financial aid office: (479) 979-1221
Jana Hart, Director of Financial Aid
415 College Avenue
Clarksville, AR 72830

Williams Baptist College

Walnut Ridge, Arkansas
www.wbcoll.edu
Four-year private **Federal Code: 001106**

	Living at home	On-campus
Tuition and fees:	$8,120	$8,120
Room and board:		$3,800
Board only:	$2,600	
Books and supplies:	$850	$850
Personal expenses:	$800	$800
Transportation:	$950	$750

Undergraduate aid. Need-based: Average financial aid package for full-time students was $8,435; for part-time $4,628. 53% awarded as scholarships/grants, 47% as loans/jobs. **Non-need-based:** 68% awarded as scholarships/grants, 32% as loans/jobs. Scholarships based on academics, art, athletics, leadership, minority status, music/drama, state/district residency. **Student debt:** 69% of graduating class borrowed to fund education; average debt was $14,863. **Additional information:** Art scholarship applicants must submit portfolio.

Freshman aid. Need-based: Out of 144 full-time freshmen, 141 applied for aid; 107 were judged to have need; of these 107 received aid. Average scholarship/grant was $2,491; average loan $2,024. **Non-need based:** 107 full-time freshmen with need received non-need scholarships; 33 without need received awards; 32 received athletic scholarships.

Merit scholarships. Trustee's Scholarship; up to full tuition and room and board, based on minimum composite score of 30 on Enhanced ACT and minimum 3.5 sixth or seventh semester high school cumulative GPA, 1 award, deadline March 1, renewable for 4 years with 3.25 minimum cumulative GPA on at least 15 credit hours per semester.

Policies to reduce costs. Tuition/fee waivers for senior citizens, family of clergy, employees and their families. Credit/placement for qualifying scores on AP, CLEP examinations. Work study available nights, weekends and for part-time students.

Payment plans. Credit card, installment payment.

Application procedures. FAFSA required. Priority date 5/1; no closing date. Applicants notified on rolling basis starting 3/1, must reply within 2 week(s) of notification. **Transfers:** Priority date 4/1; no deadline.

Contact. Financial aid office: (870) 759-4112
Barbara Turner, Director of Financial Aid
Box 3665
Walnut Ridge, AR 72476

California

Academy of Art College

San Francisco, California
www.academyart.edu
Four-year proprietary **Federal Code: 007531**

	Living at home	On-campus
Tuition and fees:	$16,780	$16,780
Room only:		$8,400
Board only:	$3,168	
Books and supplies:	$1,224	$1,224
Personal expenses:	$2,418	$1,959
Transportation:	$828	$594

Undergraduate aid. Need-based: Average financial aid package for full-time students was $6,319; for part-time $5,034. 35% awarded as scholarships/grants, 65% as loans/jobs. **Student debt:** 48% of graduating class borrowed to fund education; average debt was $30,000. **Additional information:** Presidential scholarships and numerous summer grant programs available.

Freshman aid. Need-based: Out of 307 full-time freshmen, 181 applied for aid; 158 were judged to have need; of these 143 received aid. Average package met 27% of need. 2 students had full need met. Average scholarship/grant was $5,152; average loan $2,584. **Non-need based:** 10 full-time freshmen with need received non-need scholarships; 20 without need received awards.

Policies to reduce costs. Credit/placement for qualifying scores on AP, IB examinations. Work study available weekends and for part-time students.

Payment plans. Credit card, installment, deferred payment.

Application procedures. FAFSA, institutional form required. Priority date 7/10; no closing date. Applicants notified on rolling basis.

Contact. Financial aid office: (415) 274-2223
Joe Vollaro, Executive Vice President for Financial Aid/Compliance
79 New Montgomery Street
San Francisco, CA 94105-3410

Antelope Valley College

Lancaster, California
www.avc.edu
Two-year public **Federal Code: 001113**

	Living at home
Tuition and fees (projected):	$330
Out-of-state:	$4,350
Per-credit charge:	$11
Per-credit out-of-state:	$145
Board only:	$2,988
Personal expenses:	$2,250
Transportation:	$990

Undergraduate aid. Need-based: 81% awarded as scholarships/grants, 19% as loans/jobs. Need-based aid available for part-time students. **Non-need-based:** 16% awarded as scholarships/grants, 84% as loans/jobs.

Policies to reduce costs. Credit/placement for qualifying scores on AP, CLEP examinations. Work study available for part-time students.

Payment plans. Credit card, installment payment.

Application procedures. FAFSA, institutional form required. Priority date 3/2; no closing date. Applicants notified on rolling basis starting 7/15, must reply within 2 week(s) of notification.

Contact. Financial aid office: (661) 722-6336
Sherrie Padilla, Assistant Director of Financial Aid
3041 West Avenue K
Lancaster, CA 93536-5426

Antioch Southern California at Los Angeles

Marina del Rey, California
www.antiochla.edu
Upper-division private **Federal Code: E00554**

	Living at home
Tuition and fees (2002-2003):	$17,415
Books and supplies:	$1,500

Policies to reduce costs. Tuition/fee waivers for minority students, employees and their families. Credit/placement for qualifying scores on AP, CLEP examinations.

Payment plans. Credit card, installment, deferred payment.

Application procedures. FAFSA, institutional form required. Priority date 8/1; no closing date. Applicants notified on rolling basis starting 8/30, must reply within 2 week(s) of notification.

Contact. Financial aid office: (310) 578-1080
Rebecca Santillan, Director of Financial Aid
13274 Fiji Way
Marina del Rey, CA 90292-7090

Antioch Southern California at Santa Barbara

Santa Barbara, California
www.antiochsb.edu
Upper-division private **Federal Code: 003010**

	Living at home
Tuition and fees (projected):	$12,018
Books and supplies:	$990

Undergraduate aid. Need-based: Need-based aid available for full-time and part-time students.

Policies to reduce costs. Tuition/fee waivers for employees and their families. Credit/placement for qualifying scores on AP, IB examinations. Work study available nights, weekends and for part-time students.

Payment plans. Credit card, installment payment.

Application procedures. FAFSA, institutional form required. No deadline. Applicants notified on rolling basis, must reply within 4 week(s) of notification. **Transfers:** Priority date 4/1; no deadline.

Contact. Financial aid office: (805) 962-8179
Karen Morgan, Financial Aid Director
801 Garden Street
Santa Barbara, CA 93101

Art Center College of Design

Pasadena, California
www.artcenter.edu
Four-year private **Federal Code: 001116**

	Living at home
Tuition and fees (projected):	$22,148
Books and supplies:	$5,900
Transportation:	$850

Undergraduate aid. All financial aid based on need. Average financial aid package for full-time students was $18,675. 52% awarded as scholarships/grants, 48% as loans/jobs. **Student debt:** 61% of graduating class borrowed to fund education; average debt was $51,864. **Additional information:** Students may apply for scholarships after they enroll while progressing through the program.

Policies to reduce costs. Tuition/fee waivers for employees and their families. Credit/placement for qualifying scores on AP, IB examinations.

Payment plans. Credit card, installment payment.

Application procedures. FAFSA required. Priority date 3/1; no closing date. Applicants notified on rolling basis starting 5/15, must reply within 4 week(s) of notification.

Contact. Financial aid office: (626) 396-2215
Clema McKenzie, Director of Financial Aid
1700 Lida Street
Pasadena, CA 91103

Art Institute of California
San Diego, California
www.aicasd.artinstitutes.edu
Four-year proprietary **Federal Code: 016471**

	Living at home
Tuition and fees (projected):	$16,464

Undergraduate aid. Need-based: Need-based aid available for full-time students.

Contact. Financial aid office: (858) 598-1399
Debra Spindler
7650 Mission Valley Road
San Diego, CA 92108-4423

Art Institute of California - Orange County
Santa Ana, California
www.aicaoc.artinstitutes.edu
Four-year proprietary **Federal Code: 007236**

	Living at home
Tuition and fees:	$16,374
Books and supplies:	$1,100
Personal expenses:	$2,280
Transportation:	$1,068

Undergraduate aid. Need-based: 45% awarded as scholarships/grants, 55% as loans/jobs. Need-based aid available for part-time students. **Non-need-based:** 9% awarded as scholarships/grants, 91% as loans/jobs. Scholarships based on academics, art.

Policies to reduce costs. Tuition/fee waivers for employees and their families. Tuition at time of enrollment guaranteed for 4 years; prepayment discount; credit/placement for qualifying scores on AP, IB examinations. Work study available nights, weekends and for part-time students.

Payment plans. Credit card, installment payment.

Application procedures. FAFSA required. Priority date 3/2; no closing date. Applicants notified on rolling basis starting 3/1, must reply within 2 week(s) of notification. **Transfers:** Priority date 3/2; no deadline.

Contact. Financial aid office: (714) 830-0200
Gary Byers, Director of Student Financial Services
3601 West Sunflower Avenue
Santa Ana, CA 92794

Art Institute of California - San Francisco
San Francisco, California
www.aicasf.aii.edu
Four-year proprietary **Federal Code: 007236**

	Living at home
Tuition and fees:	$16,896
Books and supplies:	$1,000

Policies to reduce costs. Tuition/fee waivers for family members, employees and their families. Credit/placement for qualifying scores on IB examinations.

Payment plans. Installment payment.

Application procedures. FAFSA required. No deadline. Applicants notified on rolling basis.

Contact. Financial aid office: (415) 865-0198
Troy Ward, Director of Student Financial Services
1170 Market Street
San Francisco, CA 94102

Art Institute of California: Los Angeles
Santa Monica, California
www.aila.artinstitutes.edu
Two-year proprietary **Federal Code: 007470**

	Living at home	On-campus
Tuition and fees (2002-2003):	$15,988	$15,988
Per-credit charge:	$331	$331
Room only:		$6,522
Books and supplies:	$1,733	$1,733
Personal expenses:	$1,500	$1,500

Undergraduate aid. Need-based: Need-based aid available for full-time and part-time students. **Non-need-based:** Scholarships based on academics.

Policies to reduce costs. Tuition/fee waivers for employees and their families. Tuition at time of enrollment guaranteed for 2 years; credit/placement for qualifying scores on AP examinations. Work study available nights, weekends and for part-time students.

Payment plans. Credit card, installment payment.

Application procedures. FAFSA required. No deadline. Applicants notified on rolling basis.

Contact. Financial aid office: (310) 751-4700
Brian Cronkright, Director of Stuent Financial Services
2900 31st Street
Santa Monica, CA 90405-3035

Azusa Pacific University
Azusa, California
www.apu.edu
Four-year private **Federal Code: 001117**

	Living at home	On-campus
Tuition and fees (2002-2003):	$17,218	$17,218
Room and board:		$5,690
Board only:	$2,592	
Books and supplies:	$846	$846
Personal expenses:	$4,800	
Transportation:	$756	

Undergraduate aid. Need-based: 56% awarded as scholarships/grants, 44% as loans/jobs. Need-based aid available for part-time students. **Non-need-based:** 66% awarded as scholarships/grants, 34% as loans/jobs. Scholarships based on academics, athletics, leadership, minority status, music/drama, religious affiliation.

Freshman aid. Need-based: Average package met 73% of need. Average scholarship/grant was $9,718; average loan $5,658.

Policies to reduce costs. Tuition/fee waivers for minority students, family members, family of clergy, employees and their families. Credit/placement for qualifying scores on AP, IB, CLEP examinations. Work study available nights, weekends and for part-time students.

Payment plans. Credit card, installment payment.

Application procedures. FAFSA, institutional form required. Priority date 7/1; closing date 3/2. Applicants notified on rolling basis starting 3/1, must reply within 3 week(s) of notification. **Transfers:** Cal Grants not available to first time applicants who are seniors.

Contact. Financial aid office: (626) 812-3009
Ginny Dadaian, Director of Student Financial Services
901 East Alosta Avenue
Azusa, CA 91702-7000

Bakersfield College
Bakersfield, California
www.bakersfieldcollege.edu
Two-year public **Federal Code: 001118**

	Living at home
Tuition and fees (2002-2003):	$362
Out-of-state:	$4,592
Per-credit charge:	$11
Per-credit out-of-state:	$152
Books and supplies:	$650
Personal expenses:	$1,420
Transportation:	$670

Payment plans. Deferred payment.

Application procedures. FAFSA required. Priority date 3/2; no closing date. Applicants notified on rolling basis starting 6/1, must reply within 2 week(s) of notification.

Contact. Financial aid office: (661) 395-4011
Joan Wegner, Director, Financial Aid
1801 Panorama Drive
Bakersfield, CA 93305

Barstow College

Barstow, California
www.barstow.edu
Two-year public **Federal Code: 001119**

	Living at home
Tuition and fees (projected):	$330
Out-of-state:	$4,560
Per-credit charge:	$11
Per-credit out-of-state:	$152
Books and supplies:	$685
Personal expenses:	$1,500
Transportation:	$576

Undergraduate aid. All financial aid based on need. Need-based aid available for full-time and part-time students.

Policies to reduce costs. Tuition/fee waivers for adults, unemployed or children of unemployed. Credit/placement for qualifying scores on CLEP examinations.

Payment plans. Installment payment.

Application procedures. FAFSA required. Closing date 5/22. Applicants notified on rolling basis starting 7/1.

Contact. Financial aid office: (760) 252-2411
Della King, Financial Aid Coordinator
2700 Barstow Road
Barstow, CA 92311-9984

Bethany College

Scotts Valley, California
www.bethany.edu
Four-year private **Federal Code: 001121**

College costs. $500 per-credit-hour charge for less than 12 credits; $360 for more than 17 credits.

	Living at home	On-campus
Tuition and fees:	$12,552	$12,552
Room and board:		$5,340
Books and supplies:	$1,079	$1,079
Personal expenses:	$2,136	$2,136
Transportation:	$2,247	$2,247

Undergraduate aid. Need-based: Need-based aid available for full-time and part-time students. **Non-need-based:** Scholarships based on academics, alumni affiliation, athletics, leadership, minority status, music/drama, religious affiliation.

Policies to reduce costs. Tuition/fee waivers for family of clergy, employees and their families. Credit/placement for qualifying scores on AP, CLEP examinations. Work study available nights, weekends and for part-time students.

Payment plans. Credit card, installment payment.

Application procedures. FAFSA, institutional form required. Priority date 3/2; no closing date. Applicants notified on rolling basis starting 4/15, must reply within 2 week(s) of notification.

Contact. Financial aid office: (831) 438-3800 ext. 147
Debi Snow, Director of Financial Aid
800 Bethany Drive
Scotts Valley, CA 95066-2898

Bethesda Christian University

Anaheim, California
www.bcu.edu/english
Four-year private **Federal Code: 032663**

	Living at home
Tuition and fees:	$5,000
Books and supplies:	$1,000
Personal expenses:	$500

Undergraduate aid. All financial aid based on need. Need-based aid available for part-time students. **Student debt:** 33% of graduating class borrowed to fund education; average debt was $7,000.

Policies to reduce costs. Tuition/fee waivers for family of clergy. Credit/placement for qualifying scores on IB examinations.

Payment plans. Credit card, installment, deferred payment.

Application procedures. FAFSA, institutional form required. Closing date 6/30. Applicants notified on rolling basis starting 6/30. **Transfers:** No deadline.

Contact. Financial aid office: (714) 517-1945
730 North Euclid Street
Anaheim, CA 92801

Biola University

La Mirada, California
www.biola.edu
Four-year private **Federal Code: 001122**

	Living at home	On-campus
Tuition and fees:	$19,564	$19,564
Room and board:		$5,967
Books and supplies:	$846	$846
Personal expenses:	$1,656	$1,476
Transportation:	$756	$558

Undergraduate aid. Need-based: Average financial aid package for full-time students was $13,701; for part-time $9,315. 64% awarded as scholarships/grants, 36% as loans/jobs. **Non-need-based:** 36% awarded as scholarships/grants, 64% as loans/jobs. Scholarships based on academics, alumni affiliation, athletics, leadership, minority status, music/drama. **Student debt:** 77% of graduating class borrowed to fund education; average debt was $21,220.

Freshman aid. Need-based: Out of 605 full-time freshmen, 495 applied for aid; 382 were judged to have need; of these 382 received aid. Average package met 75% of need. 69 students had full need met. Average scholarship/grant was $8,695; average loan $2,578. **Non-need based:** 296 full-time freshmen with need received non-need scholarships; 116 without need received awards; 17 received athletic scholarships.

Merit scholarships. Scholarships for Underrepresented Groups of Ethnicity; $4,000-$6,000; based on GPA and ethnicity. Community Service Scholarship; $2,500; based on demonstration of outstanding spiritual leadership. Alumni Dependent Scholarship; $500; given to children whose parents completed 30 units of coursework at Biola University.

Policies to reduce costs. Tuition/fee waivers for family of clergy, employees and their families. Credit/placement for qualifying scores on AP, IB, CLEP examinations.

Payment plans. Credit card, installment, deferred payment.

Application procedures. FAFSA, institutional form required. Closing date 3/2. Applicants notified on rolling basis starting 3/1, must reply by 5/1. **Transfers:** Priority date 3/2.

Contact. Financial aid office: (562) 903-4742
Les Butler, Assistant Director of Student Financial Services
13800 Biola Avenue
La Mirada, CA 90639

Cabrillo College

Aptos, California
www.cabrillo.cc.ca.us
Two-year public **Federal Code: 001124**

	Living at home
Tuition and fees (projected):	$366
Out-of-state:	$4,596
Per-credit charge:	$11
Per-credit out-of-state:	$152
Books and supplies:	$846
Personal expenses:	$1,595
Transportation:	$600

Policies to reduce costs. Credit/placement for qualifying scores on AP examinations.

Payment plans. Credit card payment.

Application procedures. FAFSA, institutional form required. No deadline. Applicants notified on rolling basis starting 7/31, must reply within 3 week(s) of notification. **Transfers:** Academic transcript required.

Contact. Financial aid office: (831) 479-6100
Debbie Soria, Director, Financial Aid
6500 Soquel Drive
Aptos, CA 95003

California Baptist University
Riverside, California
www.calbaptist.edu
Four-year private **Federal Code: 001125**

	Living at home	On-campus
Tuition and fees (2002-2003):	$12,790	$12,790
Room and board:		$5,360
Board only:	$2,304	
Books and supplies:	$752	$752
Personal expenses:	$2,032	$1,808
Transportation:	$756	$558

Undergraduate aid. Need-based: Average financial aid package for full-time students was $10,700; for part-time $5,700. 35% awarded as scholarships/grants, 65% as loans/jobs. **Non-need-based:** 24% awarded as scholarships/grants, 76% as loans/jobs. Scholarships based on academics, art, athletics, leadership, music/drama, religious affiliation. **Student debt:** 94% of graduating class borrowed to fund education; average debt was $19,200.

Freshman aid. Need-based: Out of 187 full-time freshmen, 176 applied for aid; 170 were judged to have need; of these 170 received aid. Average package met 86% of need. 146 students had full need met. Average scholarship/grant was $6,600; average loan $2,600. **Non-need based:** 31 full-time freshmen with need received non-need scholarships; 13 without need received awards; 7 received athletic scholarships.

Policies to reduce costs. Tuition/fee waivers for family members, family of clergy, employees and their families. Credit/placement for qualifying scores on AP, IB, CLEP examinations. Work study available for part-time students.

Payment plans. Credit card, installment payment.

Application procedures. FAFSA required. Priority date 3/2; no closing date. Applicants notified on rolling basis starting 3/1, must reply by 4/1 or within 2 week(s) of notification.

Contact. Financial aid office: (909) 343-4236
Eileen Terry, Director, Financial Aid
8432 Magnolia Avenue
Riverside, CA 92504-3297

California College of Arts and Crafts
San Francisco, California
www.ccac-art.edu
Four-year private **Federal Code: 001127**

	Living at home	On-campus
Tuition and fees:	$23,250	$23,250
Room only:		$5,600
Board only:	$2,448	
Books and supplies:	$810	$810
Personal expenses:	$1,548	$1,368
Transportation:	$738	$558

Undergraduate aid. Need-based: Average financial aid package for full-time students was $16,423; for part-time $6,923. 66% awarded as scholarships/grants, 34% as loans/jobs. **Non-need-based:** 14% awarded as scholarships/grants, 86% as loans/jobs. Scholarships based on academics, art, minority status. **Student debt:** 60% of graduating class borrowed to fund education; average debt was $25,361. **Additional information:** Application deadline for merit scholarships February 15.

Freshman aid. Need-based: Out of 122 full-time freshmen, 104 applied for aid; 69 were judged to have need; of these 69 received aid. Average package met 72% of need. 17 students had full need met. Average scholarship/grant was $9,801; average loan $2,764. **Non-need based:** 58 full-time freshmen with need received non-need scholarships; 9 without need received awards.

Merit scholarships. Creative Achievement Scholarship; $3,500-$12,000; renewable; based on academic achievement and strength of admissions portfolios.

Policies to reduce costs. Tuition/fee waivers for employees and their families. Credit/placement for qualifying scores on AP, IB examinations.

Payment plans. Credit card, installment, deferred payment.

Application procedures. FAFSA required. Priority date 2/15; no closing date. Applicants notified on rolling basis starting 4/1, must reply by 5/1 or within 3 week(s) of notification. **Transfers:** Scholarships available for community college transfer students.

Contact. Financial aid office: (415) 703-9528
Don Crewell, Director of Financial Aid
1111 Eighth Street
San Francisco, CA 94107

California Culinary Academy
San Francisco, California
www.baychef.com
Two-year proprietary **Federal Code: 015698**

College costs (2002-2003). $31,754 for complete 18-month program includes all fees and supplies. Additional $2,430 for 4 months' board, including $450 refundable security deposit.

Undergraduate aid. Need-based: Need-based aid available for full-time students. **Additional information:** Financial aid forms due 60 days prior to first day of classes.

Payment plans. Credit card, installment payment.

Application procedures. FAFSA required. No deadline. Applicants notified on rolling basis, must reply within 1 week(s) of notification. **Transfers:** No deadline.

Contact. Financial aid office: (415) 771-3500
Dean Riling, Director of Financial Aid
625 Polk Street
San Francisco, CA 94102

California Institute of Integral Studies
San Francisco, California
www.ciis.edu
Four-year private **Federal Code: 012154**

College costs. 3 semesters for bachelor's completion program: $16,200 tuition ($5,400 per semester); $450 registration fee ($150 per semester). Books/supplies: $945.

Contact. Financial aid office: (415) 575-6122
Cynthia Mitchell, Financial Aid Counselor
1453 Mission Street
San Francisco, CA 94103

California Institute of Technology
Pasadena, California
www.caltech.edu
Four-year private **Federal Code: 001131**

	Living at home	On-campus
Tuition and fees:	$24,117	$24,117
Room and board:		$7,560
Board only:	$3,261	
Books and supplies:	$1,005	$1,005
Personal expenses:	$2,061	$3,945

Undergraduate aid. Need-based: Average financial aid package for full-time students was $23,427. 90% awarded as scholarships/grants, 10% as loans/jobs. **Non-need-based:** 97% awarded as scholarships/grants, 3% as loans/jobs. Scholarships based on academics. **Student debt:** 55% of graduating class borrowed to fund education; average debt was $10,244.

Freshman aid. Need-based: Out of 252 full-time freshmen, 190 applied for aid; 136 were judged to have need; of these 136 received aid. Average package met 100% of need. 136 students had full need met. Average scholarship/grant was $20,485; average loan $1,404. **Non-need based:** 7 full-time freshmen with need received non-need scholarships; 60 without need received awards.

Policies to reduce costs. Tuition/fee waivers for employees and their families. Credit/placement for qualifying scores on AP examinations. Work study available nights, weekends and for part-time students.

Payment plans. Installment payment.

Application procedures. FAFSA, CSS PROFILE required. Priority date 1/15; no closing date. Applicants notified by 4/1, must reply by 5/1 or within 2 week(s) of notification. **Transfers:** Priority date 3/2; no deadline.

Contact. Financial aid office: (626) 395-6280
David Levy, Director of Financial Aid
1200 East California Boulevard
Pasadena, CA 91125

California Institute of the Arts

Valencia, California
www.calarts.edu
Four-year private **Federal Code: 001132**

	Living at home	On-campus
Tuition and fees (projected):	$24,741	$24,741
Room and board:		$6,400
Board only:	$2,150	
Books and supplies:	$1,000	$1,000
Personal expenses:	$1,000	$1,000
Transportation:	$700	$700

Undergraduate aid. Need-based: Average financial aid package for full-time students was $20,466. 52% awarded as scholarships/grants, 48% as loans/jobs. Need-based aid available for part-time students. **Non-need-based:** 56% awarded as scholarships/grants, 44% as loans/jobs. Scholarships based on academics, art, minority status, music/drama. **Student debt:** 68% of graduating class borrowed to fund education; average debt was $29,694.

Freshman aid. Need-based: Out of 116 full-time freshmen, 93 applied for aid; 76 were judged to have need; of these 76 received aid. Average package met 77% of need. 10 students had full need met. Average scholarship/grant was $10,167; average loan $3,842. **Non-need based:** 13 without need received awards.

Policies to reduce costs. Tuition/fee waivers for employees and their families. Credit/placement for qualifying scores on AP, IB examinations. Work study available nights, weekends and for part-time students.

Payment plans. Credit card, installment payment.

Application procedures. FAFSA required. Priority date 3/2; no closing date. Applicants notified on rolling basis starting 4/15, must reply within 3 week(s) of notification.

Contact. Financial aid office: (661) 255-1050
Bobbi Heuer, Financial Aid Director
24700 McBean Parkway
Valencia, CA 91355

California Maritime Academy

Vallejo, California
www.csum.edu
Four-year public **Federal Code: 001134**

College costs. Mandatory cruise fee for freshmen $2,800; uniform costs for freshman $1,450.

	Living at home	On-campus
Tuition and fees (2002-2003):	$2,268	$2,268
Out-of-state:	$9,300	$9,300
Room and board:		$6,180
Board only:	$2,592	
Books and supplies:	$846	$846
Personal expenses:	$1,840	$1,640
Transportation:	$672	$496

Undergraduate aid. All financial aid based on need. Need-based aid available for full-time and part-time students. **Additional information:** US Maritime Administration provides annual incentive payment of $3,000 per student, with certain conditions. Tuition waiver for children of deceased or disabled California veterans.

Policies to reduce costs. Tuition/fee waivers for senior citizens, employees and their families. Credit/placement for qualifying scores on AP, CLEP examinations.

Payment plans. Credit card, installment payment.

Application procedures. FAFSA required. Priority date 3/2; no closing date. Applicants notified on rolling basis starting 4/1.

Contact. Financial aid office: (707) 654-1275
Karen Neal, Director of Financial Aid
PO Box 1392
Vallejo, CA 94590-0644

California Polytechnic State University: San Luis Obispo

San Luis Obispo, California
www.calpoly.edu
Four-year public **Federal Code: 001143**

College costs. Other fees vary by college.

	Living at home	On-campus
Tuition and fees (2002-2003):	$2,180	$2,180
Out-of-state:	$10,640	$10,640
Room and board:		$7,106
Board only:	$1,296	
Books and supplies:	$1,080	$1,080
Personal expenses:	$1,800	$1,800
Transportation:	$828	$828

Undergraduate aid. Need-based: Need-based aid available for full-time and part-time students. **Non-need-based:** Scholarships based on academics, alumni affiliation, art, athletics, job skills, leadership, music/drama, state/district residency.

Policies to reduce costs. Tuition/fee waivers for senior citizens, employees and their families. Credit/placement for qualifying scores on AP, CLEP examinations. Work study available nights and weekends.

Payment plans. Installment payment.

Application procedures. FAFSA, institutional form required. Priority date 3/2; closing date 6/30. Applicants notified on rolling basis starting 4/15, must reply within 8 week(s) of notification. Early decision closing date 10/31.

Contact. Financial aid office: (805) 756-1111
John Anderson, Director of Financial Aid
Admissions Office, Cal Poly
San Luis Obispo, CA 93407

California State Polytechnic University: Pomona

Pomona, California
www.csupomona.edu
Four-year public **Federal Code: 001144**

	Living at home	On-campus
Tuition and fees (2002-2003):	$1,815	$1,815
Out-of-state:	$10,275	$10,275
Room and board:		$6,843
Books and supplies:	$846	$846
Personal expenses:	$1,432	$1,181
Transportation:	$756	$558

Undergraduate aid. Need-based: Average financial aid package for full-time students was $7,276; for part-time $6,546. 57% awarded as scholarships/grants, 43% as loans/jobs. **Non-need-based:** 6% awarded as scholarships/grants, 94% as loans/jobs. Scholarships based on academics, alumni affiliation, art, athletics, leadership, music/drama, state/district residency. **Student debt:** 63% of graduating class borrowed to fund education; average debt was $9,851.

Freshman aid. Need-based: Out of 2,156 full-time freshmen, 1,819 applied for aid; 1,264 were judged to have need; of these 1,227 received aid. Average package met 82% of need. 328 students had full need met. Average scholarship/grant was $4,952; average loan $2,327. **Non-need based:** 150 full-time freshmen with need received non-need scholarships; 51 without need received awards; 24 received athletic scholarships.

Policies to reduce costs. Tuition/fee waivers for senior citizens, employees and their families. Credit/placement for qualifying scores on AP, CLEP examinations.

Payment plans. Credit card, installment payment.

Application procedures. FAFSA required. Priority date 3/2; no closing date. Applicants notified on rolling basis starting 4/1.

Contact. Financial aid office: (909) 869-3700
Melanie Saracco, Director of Financial Aid
3801 West Temple Avenue
Pomona, CA 91768-4019

California State University: Bakersfield

Bakersfield, California
www.csub.edu
Four-year public **Federal Code: 007993**

	Living at home	On-campus
Tuition and fees (2002-2003):	$1,797	$1,797
Out-of-state:	$10,257	$10,257
Room and board:		$4,802
Books and supplies:	$630	$630
Personal expenses:	$925	$1,164
Transportation:	$530	$530

Undergraduate aid. All financial aid based on need. Average financial aid package for full-time students was $5,897. 66% awarded as scholarships/grants, 34% as loans/jobs. Need-based aid available for part-time students. **Student debt:** 12% of graduating class borrowed to fund education; average debt was $3,525.

Freshman aid. Out of 634 full-time freshmen, 493 applied for aid; 397 were judged to have need; of these 382 received aid. Average package met 85% of need. 52 students had full need met. Average scholarship/grant was $4,989; average loan $2,034.

Policies to reduce costs. Tuition/fee waivers for senior citizens, employees and their families. Credit/placement for qualifying scores on AP, CLEP examinations.

Payment plans. Credit card, installment payment.

Application procedures. FAFSA required. Priority date 3/2; closing date 4/1. Applicants notified on rolling basis, must reply within 2 week(s) of notification.

Contact. **Financial aid office:** (661) 664-2011
Steve Herndon, Associate Dean of Financial Aid
9001 Stockdale Highway
Bakersfield, CA 93311-1099

California State University: Chico

Chico, California
www.csuchico.edu
Four-year public **Federal Code: 001146**

	Living at home	On-campus
Tuition and fees (2002-2003):	$2,114	$2,114
Out-of-state:	$10,574	$10,574
Room and board:		$6,973
Books and supplies:	$846	$846
Personal expenses:	$1,671	$1,601
Transportation:	$746	$644

Undergraduate aid. Need-based: 47% awarded as scholarships/grants, 53% as loans/jobs. Need-based aid available for part-time students. **Non-need-based:** 15% awarded as scholarships/grants, 85% as loans/jobs. Scholarships based on academics, art, athletics, leadership, minority status, music/drama, religious affiliation.

Merit scholarships. President's Scholar Award; 10 awards at $12,000 each and 12 awards at $1,000 each.

Policies to reduce costs. Tuition/fee waivers for senior citizens, employees and their families. Credit/placement for qualifying scores on AP, IB, CLEP examinations. Work study available nights and for part-time students.

Payment plans. Credit card, installment, deferred payment.

Application procedures. FAFSA required. Priority date 3/2; no closing date. Applicants notified on rolling basis starting 2/15. **Transfers:** Priority date 3/2; no deadline.

Contact. **Financial aid office:** (530) 898-6451
Annette Edwards, Director of Financial Aid
Chico, CA 95929-0720

California State University: Dominguez Hills

Carson, California
www.csudh.edu
Four-year public **Federal Code: 001141**

	Living at home	On-campus
Tuition and fees (2002-2003):	$1,850	$1,850
Out-of-state:	$10,310	$10,310
Room only:		$3,690
Books and supplies:	$630	$630
Personal expenses:	$1,600	$1,600
Transportation:	$576	$540

Undergraduate aid. Non-need-based: Scholarships based on academics, minority status.

Policies to reduce costs. Tuition/fee waivers for adults, senior citizens. Credit/placement for qualifying scores on AP, CLEP examinations.

Payment plans. Credit card payment.

Application procedures. FAFSA, CSS PROFILE required. Priority date 4/15; no closing date. Applicants notified on rolling basis starting 2/15, must reply within 4 week(s) of notification.

Contact. **Financial aid office:** (310) 243-3696
Dolores Lee, Director of Financial Aid
1000 East Victoria Street
Carson, CA 90747

California State University: Fresno

Fresno, California
www.csufresno.edu
Four-year public **Federal Code: 001147**

	Living at home	On-campus
Tuition and fees (2002-2003):	$1,796	$1,796
Out-of-state:	$10,256	$10,256
Room and board:		$6,221
Books and supplies:	$405	$405
Personal expenses:	$1,096	$1,216
Transportation:	$692	$552

Undergraduate aid. Need-based: Average financial aid package for full-time students was $6,277; for part-time $4,108. 66% awarded as scholarships/grants, 34% as loans/jobs. **Non-need-based:** 31% awarded as scholarships/grants, 69% as loans/jobs. Scholarships based on academics, alumni affiliation, athletics, leadership, music/drama, state/district residency. **Student debt:** 53% of graduating class borrowed to fund education; average debt was $14,004.

Freshman aid. Need-based: Out of 1,949 full-time freshmen, 1,356 applied for aid; 1,090 were judged to have need; of these 1,050 received aid. Average package met 29% of need. 283 students had full need met. Average scholarship/grant was $2,401; average loan $2,050. **Non-need based:** 334 full-time freshmen with need received non-need scholarships; 252 without need received awards; 118 received athletic scholarships.

Policies to reduce costs. Tuition/fee waivers for senior citizens, employees and their families. Credit/placement for qualifying scores on AP, CLEP examinations.

Payment plans. Credit card, installment payment.

Application procedures. FAFSA required. Priority date 3/1; no closing date. Applicants notified on rolling basis starting 4/1, must reply within 3 week(s) of notification.

Contact. **Financial aid office:** (559) 278-6557
Maria Hernandez, Director of Financial Aid
5150 North Maple Avenue, M/S JA 57
Fresno, CA 93740-8026

California State University: Fullerton

Fullerton, California
www.fullerton.edu
Four-year public **Federal Code: 001137**

	Living at home	On-campus
Tuition and fees (2002-2003):	$1,881	$1,881
Out-of-state:	$9,261	$9,261
Room and board:		$6,545
Books and supplies:	$846	$846
Personal expenses:	$2,466	$2,214
Transportation:	$738	$558

Undergraduate aid. Need-based: Average financial aid package for full-time students was $5,871; for part-time $5,131. **Non-need-based:** Scholarships based on academics, athletics. **Student debt:** 41% of graduating class borrowed to fund education; average debt was $12,000. **Additional information:** Fee waiver for children of veterans killed in action or with service-connected disability whose annual income is $5,000 or less.

Freshman aid. Need-based: Out of 2,772 full-time freshmen, 1,929 applied for aid; 1,314 were judged to have need; of these 964 received aid. Average package met 73% of need. 62 students had full need met. Average scholarship/grant was $5,079; average loan $2,173. **Non-need based:** 323 without need received awards; 39 received athletic scholarships.

Policies to reduce costs. Tuition/fee waivers for employees and their families. Credit/placement for qualifying scores on AP, IB, CLEP examinations. Work study available nights, weekends and for part-time students.

Payment plans. Credit card, installment, deferred payment.

Application procedures. FAFSA required. Priority date 11/1; no closing date. Applicants notified on rolling basis starting 3/1, must reply within 3 week(s) of notification.

Contact. Financial aid office: (714) 278-3125
Deborah McCracken, Director of Financial Aid
Box 6900
Fullerton, CA 92834-6900

California State University: Hayward

Hayward, California
www.csuhayward.edu
Four-year public **Federal Code: 001138**

	Living at home	On-campus
Tuition and fees (2002-2003):	$1,800	$1,800
Out-of-state:	$9,180	$9,180
Room only:		$3,700
Board only:	$2,376	
Books and supplies:	$864	$864
Personal expenses:	$1,584	$1,656
Transportation:	$720	$540

Undergraduate aid. Need-based: Need-based aid available for full-time and part-time students.

Policies to reduce costs. Tuition/fee waivers for senior citizens, employees and their families. Credit/placement for qualifying scores on AP, IB, CLEP examinations. Work study available for part-time students.

Payment plans. Credit card, installment payment.

Application procedures. FAFSA required. Priority date 3/3; no closing date. Applicants notified on rolling basis, must reply within 3 week(s) of notification.

Contact. Financial aid office: (510) 885-3616
Anita Patino, Financial Aid Department
25800 Carlos Bee Boulevard
Hayward, CA 94542-3035

California State University: Long Beach

Long Beach, California
www.csulb.edu
Four-year public **Federal Code: 001139**

	Living at home	On-campus
Tuition and fees (2002-2003):	$1,744	$1,744
Out-of-state:	$10,204	$10,204
Room and board:		$5,747
Books and supplies:	$1,000	$1,000
Personal expenses:	$1,642	$1,513
Transportation:	$756	$572

Undergraduate aid. Need-based: Average financial aid package for full-time students was $6,692. 55% awarded as scholarships/grants, 45% as loans/jobs. Need-based aid available for part-time students. **Non-need-based:** 0% awarded as scholarships/grants, 100% as loans/jobs. Scholarships based on academics, art, athletics, music/drama. **Student debt:** 29% of graduating class borrowed to fund education; average debt was $5,923.

Freshman aid. Need-based: Out of 2,909 full-time freshmen, 2,082 applied for aid; 1,452 were judged to have need; of these 1,403 received aid. Average package met 89% of need. 406 students had full need met. Average scholarship/grant was $3,909; average loan $2,099. **Non-need based:** 8 full-time freshmen with need received non-need scholarships; 384 without need received awards.

Merit scholarships. President's Scholar Award: 101 awarded, full payment of tuition and fees, campus housing, books.

Policies to reduce costs. Tuition/fee waivers for senior citizens, employees and their families. Credit/placement for qualifying scores on AP, IB, CLEP examinations.

Payment plans. Credit card, installment payment.

Application procedures. FAFSA required. Priority date 3/2; no closing date. Applicants notified on rolling basis starting 4/15, must reply within 3 week(s) of notification. **Transfers:** Community college EOPS students may apply as EOP students and thus be eligible for an EOP Grant.

Contact. Financial aid office: (562) 985-4641
Dean Kulju, Director of Financial Aid
1250 Bellflower Boulevard
Long Beach, CA 90840-0106

California State University: Los Angeles

Los Angeles, California
www.calstatela.edu
Four-year public **Federal Code: 001140**

	Living at home	On-campus
Tuition and fees (2002-2003):	$1,787	$1,787
Out-of-state:	$10,247	$10,247
Room and board:		$6,201
Books and supplies:	$846	$846
Personal expenses:	$1,710	$1,584
Transportation:	$756	$630

Undergraduate aid. Need-based: Need-based aid available for full-time and part-time students.

Policies to reduce costs. Tuition/fee waivers for senior citizens. Credit/placement for qualifying scores on AP, CLEP examinations. Work study available for part-time students.

Payment plans. Credit card, installment payment.

Application procedures. FAFSA required. Priority date 3/1; no closing date. Applicants notified on rolling basis starting 5/1, must reply within 3 week(s) of notification.

Contact. Financial aid office: (323) 343-1784
Lindy Fong, Director of Center for Student Financial Aid
5151 State University Drive SA101
Los Angeles, CA 90032

California State University: Monterey Bay

Seaside, California
www.csumb.edu
Four-year public **Federal Code: 032603**

	Living at home	On-campus
Tuition and fees (2002-2003):	$1,855	$1,855
Out-of-state:	$9,235	$9,235
Room and board:		$5,700
Books and supplies:	$2,500	$2,500

Undergraduate aid. All financial aid based on need. Average financial aid package for full-time students was $6,391; for part-time $5,158. 52% awarded as scholarships/grants, 48% as loans/jobs. **Student debt:** 75% of graduating class borrowed to fund education; average debt was $7,115.

Freshman aid. Out of 502 full-time freshmen, 394 applied for aid; 321 were judged to have need; of these 321 received aid. Average package met 64% of need. 66 students had full need met. Average scholarship/grant was $5,576; average loan $2,207.

Policies to reduce costs. Tuition/fee waivers for senior citizens. Credit/placement for qualifying scores on AP, CLEP examinations. Work study available nights, weekends and for part-time students.

Payment plans. Credit card payment.

Application procedures. FAFSA required. Priority date 3/2; no closing date. Applicants notified on rolling basis starting 4/15. **Transfers:** No deadline.

Contact. **Financial aid office:** (831) 582-4074
Bonnie Brown, Director of Financial Aid
100 Campus Center, Building 47
Seaside, CA 93955-8001

California State University: Northridge

Northridge, California
www.csun.edu
Four-year public **Federal Code: 001153**

	Living at home	On-campus
Tuition and fees (2002-2003):	$1,814	$1,814
Out-of-state:	$9,194	$9,194
Room and board:		$7,000
Books and supplies:	$630	$630
Personal expenses:	$1,400	$1,592
Transportation:	$594	$576

Undergraduate aid. Need-based: Need-based aid available for full-time and part-time students. **Non-need-based:** Scholarships based on academics, athletics, state/district residency.

Policies to reduce costs. Tuition/fee waivers for senior citizens, employees and their families. Credit/placement for qualifying scores on AP, CLEP examinations.

Payment plans. Deferred payment.

Application procedures. Priority date 3/2; no closing date. Applicants notified on rolling basis starting 5/1.

Contact. **Financial aid office:** (818) 677-1200
Diane Ryan, Director of Financial Aid
Box 1286
Northridge, CA 91328

California State University: Sacramento

Sacramento, California
www.csus.edu
Four-year public **Federal Code: 001233**

	Living at home	On-campus
Tuition and fees (2002-2003):	$1,891	$1,891
Out-of-state:	$10,351	$10,351
Room and board:		$6,123
Books and supplies:	$810	$810
Personal expenses:	$1,548	$1,386
Transportation:	$738	$558

Undergraduate aid. Need-based: Average financial aid package for full-time students was $7,541; for part-time $6,131. 59% awarded as scholarships/grants, 41% as loans/jobs. **Non-need-based:** 0% awarded as scholarships/grants, 100% as loans/jobs. **Student debt:** 35% of graduating class borrowed to fund education; average debt was $11,181.

Freshman aid. Need-based: Out of 1,724 full-time freshmen, 1,174 applied for aid; 887 were judged to have need; of these 836 received aid. Average package met 75% of need. 81 students had full need met. Average scholarship/grant was $1,793; average loan $217. **Non-need based:** 105 without need received awards.

Policies to reduce costs. Tuition/fee waivers for senior citizens, employees and their families. Credit/placement for qualifying scores on AP, IB, CLEP examinations. Work study available nights, weekends and for part-time students.

Payment plans. Credit card, installment, deferred payment.

Application procedures. FAFSA required. Priority date 3/2; no closing date. Applicants notified on rolling basis starting 4/1.

Contact. **Financial aid office:** (916) 278-6011
Linda Joy Clemons, Financial Aid Director
6000 J Street
Sacramento, CA 95819-6048

California State University: San Bernardino

San Bernardino, California
www.csusb.edu
Four-year public **Federal Code: 001142**

	Living at home	On-campus
Tuition and fees (2002-2003):	$2,078	$2,078
Out-of-state:	$10,538	$10,538
Room and board:		$8,607
Books and supplies:	$846	$846
Personal expenses:	$1,530	$1,584
Transportation:	$720	$576

Policies to reduce costs. Tuition/fee waivers for senior citizens, employees and their families. Credit/placement for qualifying scores on AP, CLEP examinations.

Payment plans. Credit card payment.

Application procedures. FAFSA required. Priority date 3/1; no closing date. Applicants notified on rolling basis starting 5/1.

Contact. **Financial aid office:** (909) 880-7800
Ted Krug, Director of Financial Aid
5500 University Parkway
San Bernardino, CA 92407-2397

California State University: San Marcos

San Marcos, California
www.csusm.edu
Four-year public **Federal Code: 030113**

	Living at home
Tuition and fees (2002-2003):	$1,796
Out-of-state:	$10,256
Board only:	$2,644
Books and supplies:	$1,000
Personal expenses:	$1,738
Transportation:	$738

Undergraduate aid. Need-based: Average financial aid package for full-time students was $6,199. 58% awarded as scholarships/grants, 42% as loans/jobs. **Non-need-based:** 0% awarded as scholarships/grants, 100% as loans/jobs. **Student debt:** 53% of graduating class borrowed to fund education; average debt was $14,602.

Merit scholarships. Fenstermaker scholarships, up to $6,000 a year, renewable, to outstanding chemistry, biology, or computer science majors.

Policies to reduce costs. Tuition/fee waivers for senior citizens, employees and their families. Credit/placement for qualifying scores on AP, IB, CLEP examinations.

Payment plans. Credit card, installment payment.

Application procedures. FAFSA required. Priority date 3/2; no closing date. Applicants notified by 4/15.

Contact. **Financial aid office:** (760) 750-4850
Paul Phillips, Director Financial Aid
CSU San Marcos
San Marcos, CA 92096-0001

California State University: Stanislaus

Turlock, California
www.csustan.edu
Four-year public **Federal Code: 001157**

	Living at home	On-campus
Tuition and fees (2002-2003):	$1,714	$1,714
Out-of-state:	$10,174	$10,174
Room and board:		$6,764
Board only:	$832	
Books and supplies:	$846	$846
Personal expenses:	$1,656	$1,476
Transportation:	$756	$558

Undergraduate aid. All financial aid based on need. Average financial aid package for full-time students was $6,503; for part-time $5,370. 57% awarded as scholarships/grants, 43% as loans/jobs. **Student debt:** 30% of graduating class borrowed to fund education; average debt was $12,750. **Additional information:** Every student must complete 2 winter terms, 4 weeks at $164, to fullfill graduation requirements.

Freshman aid. Out of 550 full-time freshmen, 449 applied for aid; 338 were judged to have need; of these 324 received aid. Average package met 63% of need. 41 students had full need met. Average scholarship/grant was $4,548; average loan $2,330.

Policies to reduce costs. Tuition/fee waivers for senior citizens, employees and their families. Credit/placement for qualifying scores on AP, CLEP examinations.

Payment plans. Credit card, installment, deferred payment.

Application procedures. FAFSA required. Priority date 3/2; no closing date. Applicants notified on rolling basis starting 3/15, must reply within 3 week(s) of notification. Early decision closing date 11/30. **Transfers:** No deadline.

Contact. **Financial aid office:** (209) 667-3336
Joan Hillery, Director of Financial Aid
801 West Monte Vista Avenue
Turlock, CA 95382

Cerritos Community College

Norwalk, California
www.cerritos.edu
Two-year public **Federal Code: 001161**

	Living at home
Tuition and fees (projected):	$816
Out-of-state:	$4,964
Per-credit charge:	$26
Per-credit out-of-state:	$164
Books and supplies:	$648
Personal expenses:	$1,710
Transportation:	$702

Policies to reduce costs. Tuition/fee waivers for adults, senior citizens, minority students, family members, unemployed or children of unemployed.

Payment plans. Deferred payment.

Application procedures. FAFSA required. Priority date 5/8; no closing date. Applicants notified on rolling basis, must reply within 2 week(s) of notification. **Transfers:** No deadline.

Contact. **Financial aid office:** (562) 860-2451 ext. 2397
Phil Rodriguez, Coordinator of Student Affairs
11110 Alondra Boulevard
Norwalk, CA 90650

Cerro Coso Community College

Ridgecrest, California
www.cc.cc.ca.us
Two-year public **Federal Code: 010111**

	Living at home
Tuition and fees (projected):	$330
Out-of-state:	$4,560
Per-credit charge:	$11
Per-credit out-of-state:	$152
Board only:	$1,100
Books and supplies:	$882
Personal expenses:	$1,656
Transportation:	$792

Undergraduate aid. Need-based: Need-based aid available for full-time and part-time students.

Policies to reduce costs. Credit/placement for qualifying scores on AP, CLEP examinations. Work study available nights and for part-time students.

Payment plans. Installment payment.

Application procedures. FAFSA required. Priority date 5/15; no closing date. Applicants notified on rolling basis starting 6/1, must reply within 2 week(s) of notification.

Contact. **Financial aid office:** (760) 384-6221
Bob Weisenthal, Director of Student Aid
3000 College Heights Boulevard
Ridgecrest, CA 93555-7777

Chabot College

Hayward, California
www.chabotcollege.edu
Two-year public **Federal Code: 001162**

	Living at home
Tuition and fees (2002-2003):	$638
Out-of-state:	$5,078
Per-credit charge:	$11
Per-credit out-of-state:	$159
Board only:	$2,997
Books and supplies:	$1,206
Personal expenses:	$2,340
Transportation:	$864

Undergraduate aid. Additional information: Tuition and/or fee waivers for low-income students.

Policies to reduce costs. Credit/placement for qualifying scores on AP examinations. Work study available nights, weekends and for part-time students.

Payment plans. Credit card, installment payment.

Application procedures. FAFSA, institutional form required. Priority date 8/1; no closing date. Applicants notified on rolling basis.

Contact. **Financial aid office:** (510) 723-6746
Kathryn Linzmeyer, Director of Financial Aid
25555 Hesperian Boulevard
Hayward, CA 94545

Chapman University

Orange, California
www.chapman.edu
Four-year private **Federal Code: 001164**

	Living at home	On-campus
Tuition and fees:	$24,576	$24,576
Room and board:		$9,260
Board only:	$1,800	
Books and supplies:	$900	$900
Personal expenses:	$1,390	$1,390
Transportation:	$1,294	$566

Undergraduate aid. Need-based: Average financial aid package for full-time students was $17,066; for part-time $11,483. 71% awarded as scholarships/grants, 29% as loans/jobs. **Non-need-based:** 86% awarded as scholarships/grants, 14% as loans/jobs. Scholarships based on academics, alumni affiliation,

art, music/drama, religious affiliation. **Student debt:** 52% of graduating class borrowed to fund education; average debt was $18,122.

Freshman aid. Need-based: Out of 763 full-time freshmen, 701 applied for aid; 476 were judged to have need; of these 475 received aid. Average package met 100% of need. 474 students had full need met. Average scholarship/grant was $15,667; average loan $3,276. **Non-need based:** 210 without need received awards.

Policies to reduce costs. Tuition/fee waivers for employees and their families. Credit/placement for qualifying scores on AP, IB, CLEP examinations. Work study available nights, weekends and for part-time students.

Payment plans. Credit card, installment payment.

Application procedures. FAFSA required. Priority date 3/2; no closing date. Applicants notified on rolling basis starting 4/1, must reply within 3 week(s) of notification.

Contact. Financial aid office: 714) 997-6815
Gregory Ball, Director of Financial Aid
One University Drive
Orange, CA 92866

Christian Heritage College

El Cajon, California
www.christianheritage.edu
Four-year private **Federal Code: 012031**

	Living at home	On-campus
Tuition and fees:	$14,000	$14,000
Room and board:		$5,990
Board only:	$3,168	
Books and supplies:	$1,224	$1,224
Personal expenses:	$2,286	$1,872
Transportation:	$828	$594

Undergraduate aid. Need-based: Average financial aid package for full-time students was $9,194; for part-time $6,625. 57% awarded as scholarships/grants, 43% as loans/jobs. **Non-need-based:** 45% awarded as scholarships/grants, 55% as loans/jobs. Scholarships based on academics, athletics, leadership, music/drama, religious affiliation. **Student debt:** 82% of graduating class borrowed to fund education; average debt was $15,124.

Freshman aid. Need-based: Out of 194 full-time freshmen, 189 applied for aid; 113 were judged to have need; of these 113 received aid. Average package met 42% of need. 43 students had full need met. Average scholarship/grant was $4,074; average loan $2,532. **Non-need based:** 77 full-time freshmen with need received non-need scholarships; 9 without need received awards; 20 received athletic scholarships.

Policies to reduce costs. Tuition/fee waivers for family of clergy, employees and their families. Prepayment discount; credit/placement for qualifying scores on AP, IB, CLEP examinations.

Payment plans. Credit card, installment, deferred payment.

Application procedures. FAFSA required. Priority date 3/2; closing date 9/1. Applicants notified on rolling basis starting 4/1, must reply by 5/1 or within 4 week(s) of notification. **Transfers:** Priority date 3/2; closing date 9/1.

Contact. Financial aid office: (619) 590-1786
Nancy Demars, Financial Aid Director
2100 Greenfield Drive
El Cajon, CA 92019-1157

Citrus College

Glendora, California
www.citruscollege.edu
Two-year public **Federal Code: 001166**

	Living at home
Tuition and fees (projected):	$354
Out-of-state:	$4,644
Per-credit charge:	$11
Per-credit out-of-state:	$154
Board only:	$4,682
Books and supplies:	$1,224
Personal expenses:	$2,200
Transportation:	$950

Undergraduate aid. Need-based: 78% awarded as scholarships/grants, 22% as loans/jobs. Need-based aid available for part-time students.

Policies to reduce costs. Tuition/fee waivers for senior citizens. Credit/placement for qualifying scores on AP, CLEP examinations. Work study available nights, weekends and for part-time students.

Payment plans. Credit card payment.

Application procedures. FAFSA required. Priority date 3/2; no closing date. Applicants notified on rolling basis, must reply within 2 week(s) of notification.

Contact. Financial aid office: (626) 914-8592
Lois Papner, Financial Aid Director
1000 West Foothill Boulevard
Glendora, CA 91741-1899

Claremont McKenna College

Claremont, California
www.claremontmckenna.edu
Four-year private **Federal Code: 001170**

	Living at home	On-campus
Tuition and fees:	$27,700	$27,700
Room and board:		$9,180
Board only:	$2,988	
Books and supplies:	$850	$850
Personal expenses:	$2,250	$1,000
Transportation:	$864	

Undergraduate aid. All financial aid based on need. Average financial aid package for full-time students was $23,059. 87% awarded as scholarships/grants, 13% as loans/jobs. Need-based aid available for part-time students. **Student debt:** 63% of graduating class borrowed to fund education; average debt was $16,914.

Freshman aid. Out of 250 full-time freshmen, 170 applied for aid; 142 were judged to have need; of these 142 received aid. Average package met 100% of need. 140 students had full need met. Average scholarship/grant was $20,885; average loan $2,499.

Policies to reduce costs. Tuition/fee waivers for employees and their families. Credit/placement for qualifying scores on AP, IB examinations.

Payment plans. Credit card, installment payment.

Application procedures. FAFSA, CSS PROFILE required. Closing date 2/1. Applicants notified by 4/1, must reply by 5/1. Early decision closing date 11/15. **Transfers:** Closing date 3/2.

Contact. Financial aid office: (909) 621-8088
Georgette DeVeres, Director of Financial Aid
890 Columbia Avenue
Claremont, CA 91711-6425

Coastline Community College

Fountain Valley, California
coastline.cccd.edu
Two-year public **Federal Code: 013536**

	Living at home
Tuition and fees (projected):	$350
Out-of-state:	$4,580
Per-credit charge:	$11
Per-credit out-of-state:	$152
Books and supplies:	$648
Personal expenses:	$1,566
Transportation:	$576

Undergraduate aid. All financial aid based on need. Need-based aid available for full-time and part-time students. **Additional information:** Board of Governor's Grant: statewide fee waiver program for students or dependents receiving HFOL/TANF, SSI, General Relief, or whose income meets set standards or who are considered eligible through Federal needs analysis.

Policies to reduce costs. Tuition/fee waivers for unemployed or children of unemployed. Credit/placement for qualifying scores on AP, CLEP examinations.

Payment plans. Credit card payment.

Application procedures. FAFSA, institutional form required. Priority date 3/2; no closing date. Applicants notified on rolling basis starting 8/1, must reply within 2 week(s) of notification. **Transfers:** No deadline.

Contact. **Financial aid office:** (714) 241-6239
Cynthia Pienkowski, Director of Financial Aid
11460 Warner Avenue
Fountain Valley, CA 92708

Cogswell Polytechnical College

Sunnyvale, California
Four-year private
Federal Code: 001177

	Living at home
Tuition and fees:	$11,320
Books and supplies:	$1,224
Personal expenses:	$1,300
Transportation:	$650

Policies to reduce costs. Tuition/fee waivers for employees and their families. Credit/placement for qualifying scores on AP, IB, CLEP examinations.

Payment plans. Credit card, deferred payment.

Application procedures. FAFSA, institutional form required. Priority date 3/2; no closing date. Applicants notified on rolling basis starting 4/30, must reply within 4 week(s) of notification. **Transfers:** No deadline. No closing date for financial aid application. However, tuition and fees are due upon registration for portion not covered by completed financial aid.

Contact. **Financial aid office:** (408) 541-0100
Matt Clemons, Director of Enrollment Services
1175 Bordeaux Drive
Sunnyvale, CA 94089-1299

Coleman College

La Mesa, California
www.coleman.edu
Four-year private
Federal Code: 009273

College costs. Cited tuition is annual for associate degree program in computer information science. Costs for other programs vary with program.

	Living at home
Tuition and fees (2002-2003):	$12,000
Board only:	$2,394
Books and supplies:	$425
Personal expenses:	$1,206
Transportation:	$558

Policies to reduce costs. Tuition/fee waivers for employees and their families. Tuition at time of enrollment guaranteed for 4 years; credit/placement for qualifying scores on CLEP examinations.

Payment plans. Credit card payment.

Application procedures. FAFSA, institutional form required. Priority date 3/2; no closing date. Applicants notified on rolling basis. **Transfers:** No deadline.

Contact. **Financial aid office:** (619) 465-3990
Gloria Aguillar, Director of Financial Aid
7380 Parkway Drive
La Mesa, CA 91942-1500

College of Alameda

Alameda, California
www.peralta.cc.ca.us
Two-year public
Federal Code: 006720

	Living at home
Tuition and fees (projected):	$330
Out-of-state:	$5,250
Per-credit charge:	$11
Per-credit out-of-state:	$175
Books and supplies:	$630
Personal expenses:	$1,584
Transportation:	$720

Payment plans. Credit card, installment, deferred payment.

Application procedures. FAFSA required. Priority date 3/2; no closing date. Applicants notified on rolling basis starting 7/1, must reply within 2 week(s) of notification.

Contact. **Financial aid office:** (510) 522-7221
Angelita Finlayson, Financial Aid Coordinator
555 Atlantic Avenue
Alameda, CA 94501

College of Marin: Kentfield

Kentfield, California
www.marin.cc.ca.us
Two-year public
Federal Code: 001178

	Living at home
Tuition and fees (2002-2003):	$354
Out-of-state:	$4,734
Per-credit charge:	$11
Per-credit out-of-state:	$157
Books and supplies:	$650
Personal expenses:	$2,021
Transportation:	$680

Undergraduate aid. Need-based: Need-based aid available for full-time and part-time students.

Payment plans. Credit card payment.

Application procedures. FAFSA required. Priority date 3/1; no closing date. Applicants notified on rolling basis starting 5/15.

Contact. **Financial aid office:** (415) 457-8811
David Cook, Director of Financial Aid
835 College Avenue
Kentfield, CA 94904

College of Oceaneering

Wilmington, California
www.diveco.com
Two-year proprietary
Federal Code: 011696

	Living at home
Tuition and fees:	$16,100

Undergraduate aid. Need-based: Need-based aid available for full-time students.

Policies to reduce costs. Prepayment discount.

Payment plans. Credit card, installment payment.

Application procedures. FAFSA, institutional form required. No deadline. Applicants notified on rolling basis, must reply within 3 week(s) of notification. **Transfers:** No deadline.

Contact. **Financial aid office:** (310) 834-2501
Lida Castillo, Financial Aid Officer
272 South Fries Avenue
Wilmington, CA 90744

College of the Canyons

Santa Clarita, California
www.canyons.edu
Two-year public
Federal Code: 008903

	Living at home
Tuition and fees (projected):	$366
Out-of-state:	$4,006
Personal expenses:	$2,250
Transportation:	$864

Undergraduate aid. Need-based: Need-based aid available for full-time and part-time students. **Non-need-based:** Scholarships based on academics, alumni affiliation, art, athletics, leadership, music/drama, state/district residency. **Additional information:** Enrollment waived for students enrolled concurrently in high school and COC. School has own payment plan.

Policies to reduce costs. Credit/placement for qualifying scores on AP, CLEP examinations. Work study available nights and for part-time students.

Payment plans. Credit card payment.

Application procedures. FAFSA required. Closing date 3/2. Applicants notified on rolling basis starting 6/1, must reply within 4 week(s) of notification. **Transfers:** No deadline.

Contact. **Financial aid office:** (661) 362-3242
Beth Asmus, Director, Financial Aid
26455 Rockwell Canyon Road
Santa Clarita, CA 91355

College of the Redwoods

Eureka, California
www.redwoods.edu
Two-year public **Federal Code: 001185**

	Living at home	On-campus
Tuition and fees (projected):	$350	$350
Out-of-state:	$4,880	$4,880
Per-credit charge:	$11	$11
Per-credit out-of-state:	$162	$162
Room and board:		$5,310
Board only:	$2,682	
Books and supplies:	$882	$882
Personal expenses:	$1,656	$1,476
Transportation:	$792	$594

Undergraduate aid. Need-based: Need-based aid available for full-time and part-time students.

Policies to reduce costs. Credit/placement for qualifying scores on AP examinations. Work study available for part-time students.

Payment plans. Credit card, installment, deferred payment.

Application procedures. FAFSA, institutional form required. Priority date 4/15; no closing date. Applicants notified on rolling basis starting 5/1, must reply within 6 week(s) of notification.

Contact. **Financial aid office:** (707) 476-4182
Karen Johnson, Financial Aid Director
7351 Tompkins Hill Road
Eureka, CA 95501-9300

College of the Sequoias

Visalia, California
www.cos.edu
Two-year public **Federal Code: 001186**

	Living at home
Tuition and fees (2002-2003):	$352
Out-of-state:	$4,252
Per-credit charge:	$11
Per-credit out-of-state:	$145
Books and supplies:	$846

Policies to reduce costs. Credit/placement for qualifying scores on AP examinations.

Payment plans. Credit card, installment payment.

Application procedures. FAFSA, institutional form required. Priority date 3/2; no closing date. Applicants notified on rolling basis starting 6/1, must reply within 2 week(s) of notification.

Contact. **Financial aid office:** (559) 730-3879
J. Hays, Dean of Special Student Services
915 South Mooney Boulevard
Visalia, CA 93277

College of the Siskiyous

Weed, California
www.siskiyous.edu
Two-year public **Federal Code: 001187**

	Living at home	On-campus
Tuition and fees (2002-2003):	$356	$356
Out-of-state:	$4,616	$4,616
Per-credit charge:	$11	$11
Per-credit out-of-state:	$158	$158
Room and board:		$5,204
Board only:	$2,592	
Books and supplies:	$846	$846
Personal expenses:	$1,650	$1,500
Transportation:	$756	$558

Undergraduate aid. All financial aid based on need. Average financial aid package for full-time students was $3,614. 81% awarded as scholarships/grants, 19% as loans/jobs. Need-based aid available for part-time students.

Freshman aid. Out of 280 full-time freshmen, 231 applied for aid; 199 were judged to have need; of these 168 received aid. Average package met 48% of need. 4 students had full need met. Average scholarship/grant was $3,333; average loan $2,462.

Policies to reduce costs. Credit/placement for qualifying scores on AP examinations. Work study available nights, weekends and for part-time students.

Payment plans. Credit card payment.

Application procedures. FAFSA required. Priority date 4/30; no closing date. Applicants notified on rolling basis starting 6/1, must reply within 2 week(s) of notification. **Transfers:** Academic transcripts required.

Contact. **Financial aid office:** (530) 938-5501
Vicki Wrobel, Director of Financial Aid
800 College Avenue
Weed, CA 96094

Columbia College

Sonora, California
www.gocolumbia.org
Two-year public **Federal Code: 007707**

	Living at home
Tuition and fees (2002-2003):	$364
Out-of-state:	$4,594
Per-credit charge:	$11
Per-credit out-of-state:	$152
Board only:	$1,300
Books and supplies:	$882
Personal expenses:	$1,656
Transportation:	$792

Undergraduate aid. Need-based: Need-based aid available for full-time and part-time students. **Non-need-based:** Scholarships based on academics.

Policies to reduce costs. Credit/placement for qualifying scores on AP examinations.

Payment plans. Credit card payment.

Application procedures. FAFSA, institutional form required. Priority date 3/2; closing date 12/15. Applicants notified on rolling basis starting 6/15, must reply within 2 week(s) of notification.

Contact. **Financial aid office:** (209) 588-5105
Cass Larkin, Financial Aid Officer
11600 Columbia College Drive
Sonora, CA 95370

Concordia University

Irvine, California
www.cui.edu
Four-year private **Federal Code: 013885**

	Living at home	On-campus
Tuition and fees:	$17,990	$17,990
Room and board:		$6,430
Board only:	$2,470	
Books and supplies:	$700	$700
Personal expenses:	$1,400	$1,400
Transportation:	$900	$580

Undergraduate aid. Need-based: Average financial aid package for full-time students was $13,500. 62% awarded as scholarships/grants, 38% as loans/jobs. **Non-need-based:** 50% awarded as scholarships/grants, 50% as loans/jobs. Scholarships based on academics, art, athletics, music/drama. **Student debt:** 61% of graduating class borrowed to fund education; average debt was $15,900.

Freshman aid. Need-based: Out of 251 full-time freshmen, 235 applied for aid; 163 were judged to have need; of these 163 received aid. Average package met 89% of need. 52 students had full need met. Average scholarship/grant was $8,500; average loan $2,500. **Non-need based:** 146 full-time freshmen with need received non-need scholarships; 57 without need received awards; 25 received athletic scholarships.

Merit scholarships. Regents Scholarship; $4,000; GPA 3.8 and higher. Dean's Scholarship; $2,500; GPA 3.5 to 3.79. Merit Scholarship; $1,500;

GPA 3.2 to 3.49. Various other academic, music, theatre, athletic scholarships; amounts vary from $1,500 to $4,000.

Policies to reduce costs. Tuition/fee waivers for minority students, family members, family of clergy, employees and their families. Credit/placement for qualifying scores on AP, IB, CLEP examinations. Work study available weekends.

Payment plans. Credit card, installment payment.

Application procedures. FAFSA, institutional form required. Priority date 3/1; closing date 4/30. Applicants notified on rolling basis starting 3/1, must reply within 4 week(s) of notification. **Transfers:** Priority date 3/2; closing date 4/30.

Contact. **Financial aid office:** (949) 854-8002 ext. 1136
Gary McDaniel, Vice President, Student Services
1530 Concordia West
Irvine, CA 92612-3299

Contra Costa College

San Pablo, California
www.contracosta.cc.ca.us
Two-year public **Federal Code: 001190**

	Living at home
Tuition and fees (2002-2003):	$330
Out-of-state:	$4,800
Per-credit charge:	$11
Per-credit out-of-state:	$148
Books and supplies:	$680
Personal expenses:	$1,620
Transportation:	$700

Policies to reduce costs. Tuition/fee waivers for adults, unemployed or children of unemployed. Credit/placement for qualifying scores on AP examinations.

Payment plans. Credit card payment.

Application procedures. Priority date 3/2; no closing date. Applicants notified on rolling basis, must reply within 2 week(s) of notification.

Contact. **Financial aid office:** (510) 235-7800
Mickey Mathews, Financial Aid Officer
2600 Mission Bell Drive
San Pablo, CA 94806

Copper Mountain College

Joshua Tree, California
www.cmccd.edu
Two-year public **Federal Code: 035424**

	Living at home
Tuition and fees (2002-2003):	$330
Out-of-state:	$4,170
Per-credit charge:	$11
Per-credit out-of-state:	$139

Undergraduate aid. **Need-based:** Need-based aid available for full-time and part-time students.

Application procedures. FAFSA required. Priority date 3/2; no closing date.

Contact. **Financial aid office:** (760) 366-3791
Kathryn Verseman, Director of Financial Aid
6162 Rotary Way
Joshua Tree, CA 92252

Cuesta College

San Luis Obispo, California
www.cuesta.org
Two-year public **Federal Code: 001192**

	Living at home
Tuition and fees (2002-2003):	$364
Out-of-state:	$4,984
Per-credit charge:	$11
Per-credit out-of-state:	$165
Books and supplies:	$810
Personal expenses:	$1,625
Transportation:	$828

Policies to reduce costs. Credit/placement for qualifying scores on AP, CLEP examinations.

Application procedures. FAFSA required. Priority date 3/2; no closing date. Applicants notified on rolling basis starting 4/15.

Contact. **Financial aid office:** (805) 546-3100
Robin Crawford, Director of Financial Aid
Box 8106
San Luis Obispo, CA 93403

Cuyamaca College

El Cajon, California
www.cuyamaca.net
Two-year public **Federal Code: 014435**

	Living at home
Tuition and fees (projected):	$382
Out-of-state:	$4,282
Per-credit charge:	$11
Per-credit out-of-state:	$141
Books and supplies:	$450
Personal expenses:	$700
Transportation:	$600

Policies to reduce costs. Tuition/fee waivers for employees and their families. Credit/placement for qualifying scores on CLEP examinations. Work study available nights, weekends and for part-time students.

Payment plans. Credit card, deferred payment.

Application procedures. FAFSA required. Priority date 7/21; no closing date. Applicants notified on rolling basis, must reply within 2 week(s) of notification.

Contact. **Financial aid office:** (619) 660-4201
Carmen Solom, Dean
900 Rancho San Diego Parkway
El Cajon, CA 92019-4304

De Anza College

Cupertino, California
www.deanza.edu
Two-year public **Federal Code: 004480**

	Living at home
Tuition and fees (2002-2003):	$387
Out-of-state:	$4,707
Per-credit charge:	$7
Per-credit out-of-state:	$103
Board only:	$1,296
Books and supplies:	$846
Personal expenses:	$1,719
Transportation:	$756

Undergraduate aid. All financial aid based on need. Need-based aid available for full-time and part-time students.

Policies to reduce costs. Credit/placement for qualifying scores on AP, CLEP examinations.

Payment plans. Credit card, installment, deferred payment.

Application procedures. FAFSA required. Priority date 3/2; no closing date. Applicants notified on rolling basis starting 5/15, must reply within 2 week(s) of notification.

Contact. **Financial aid office:** (408) 864-8718
Cindy Castillo, Director of Financial Aid
21250 Stevens Creek Boulevard
Cupertino, CA 95014

DeVry University: Fremont

Fremont, California
www.fre.devry.edu
Four-year proprietary **Federal Code: 008322**

	Living at home
Tuition and fees:	$11,265
Books and supplies:	$1,100
Personal expenses:	$1,996
Transportation:	$1,612

Undergraduate aid. All financial aid based on need. Average financial aid package for full-time students was $8,956; for part-time $6,681. 26% awarded as scholarships/grants, 74% as loans/jobs.

Freshman aid. Average package met 43% of need. Average scholarship/grant was $4,199; average loan $4,187.

Policies to reduce costs. Tuition/fee waivers for employees and their families.

Payment plans. Credit card, installment, deferred payment.

Application procedures. FAFSA required. No deadline. Applicants notified on rolling basis starting 7/2. **Transfers:** No deadline.

Contact. Financial aid office: (510) 574-1100
Kim Kane, Director of Financial Aid
6600 Dumbarton Circle
Fremont, CA 94555

DeVry University: Long Beach

Long Beach, California
www.lb.devry.edu
Four-year proprietary **Federal Code: 023329**

	Living at home
Tuition and fees:	$10,755
Books and supplies:	$1,100
Personal expenses:	$1,996
Transportation:	$1,612

Undergraduate aid. All financial aid based on need. Average financial aid package for full-time students was $7,440; for part-time $5,798. 26% awarded as scholarships/grants, 74% as loans/jobs.

Freshman aid. Average package met 29% of need. Average scholarship/grant was $2,747; average loan $2,903.

Policies to reduce costs. Tuition/fee waivers for employees and their families.

Payment plans. Credit card, installment, deferred payment.

Application procedures. FAFSA required. No deadline. Applicants notified on rolling basis starting 7/1. **Transfers:** No deadline.

Contact. Financial aid office: (562) 427-0861
Brenda Woods, Assistant Director of Financial Aid
3880 Kilroy Airport Way
Long Beach, CA 90806

DeVry University: Pomona

Pomona, California
www.pom.devry.edu
Four-year proprietary **Federal Code: 023329**

	Living at home
Tuition and fees:	$10,755
Books and supplies:	$1,100
Personal expenses:	$1,996
Transportation:	$1,612

Undergraduate aid. All financial aid based on need. Average financial aid package for full-time students was $7,521; for part-time $5,510. 26% awarded as scholarships/grants, 74% as loans/jobs.

Freshman aid. Average package met 32% of need. Average scholarship/grant was $2,886; average loan $2,928.

Policies to reduce costs. Tuition/fee waivers for employees and their families.

Payment plans. Credit card, installment, deferred payment.

Application procedures. FAFSA required. No deadline. Applicants notified on rolling basis starting 7/2. **Transfers:** No deadline.

Contact. Financial aid office: (909) 622-8866
Kathy Odom, Director of Financial Aid
901 Corporate Center Drive
Pomona, CA 91768

DeVry University: West Hills

West Hills, California
www.wh.devry.edu
Four-year proprietary **Federal Code: 016219**

	Living at home
Tuition and fees:	$10,755
Books and supplies:	$1,100
Personal expenses:	$1,996
Transportation:	$1,612

Undergraduate aid. All financial aid based on need. Average financial aid package for full-time students was $7,405; for part-time $4,725. 24% awarded as scholarships/grants, 76% as loans/jobs.

Freshman aid. Average package met 26% of need. Average scholarship/grant was $2,727; average loan $3,023.

Policies to reduce costs. Tuition/fee waivers for employees and their families.

Payment plans. Credit card, installment, deferred payment.

Application procedures. FAFSA required. No deadline. Applicants notified on rolling basis. **Transfers:** No deadline.

Contact. Financial aid office: (818) 932-3001
Ann Logan, Assistant Director of Financial Aid
22801 Roscoe Boulevard
West Hills, CA 91304

Deep Springs College

Deep Springs, California
Two-year private **Federal Code: 015483**

College costs (2002-2003). All students receive a full scholarship (typically renewed for second year) covering tuition, room, and board. Books/supplies: $1,500.

Undergraduate aid. Non-need-based: Scholarships based on academics.

Policies to reduce costs. Tuition at time of enrollment guaranteed for 2 years. Work study available nights and weekends.

Application procedures. No deadline. **Transfers:** No deadline.

Contact. Financial aid office: (760) 872-2000
L. Jackson Newell, President
HC 72, Box 45001
Dyer, NV 89010-9803

Diablo Valley College

Pleasant Hill, California
www.dvc.edu
Two-year public **Federal Code: 001191**

	Living at home
Tuition and fees (2002-2003):	$340
Out-of-state:	$4,690
Per-credit charge:	$11
Per-credit out-of-state:	$156
Board only:	$2,484
Books and supplies:	$882
Personal expenses:	$1,656
Transportation:	$792

Undergraduate aid. Need-based: 91% awarded as scholarships/grants, 9% as loans/jobs. Need-based aid available for part-time students. **Non-need-based:** 50% awarded as scholarships/grants, 50% as loans/jobs.

Policies to reduce costs. Credit/placement for qualifying scores on AP examinations.

Payment plans. Credit card payment.

Application procedures. FAFSA, institutional form required. Priority date 3/2; closing date 5/1. Applicants notified on rolling basis starting 6/1, must reply within 2 week(s) of notification.

Contact. Financial aid office: (925) 685-1230 ext. 290
Brenda Jerez, Financial Aid Director
321 Golf Club Road
Pleasant Hill, CA 94523

Dominican School of Philosophy and Theology

Berkeley, California
www.dspt.edu
Upper-division private **Federal Code: 016673**

College costs. Required medical insurance for otherwise uninsured students costs approximately $610 per semester.

	Living at home
Tuition and fees:	$11,870
Board only:	$2,880
Books and supplies:	$1,020
Personal expenses:	$3,048
Transportation:	$1,530

Undergraduate aid. All financial aid based on need. 6% awarded as scholarships/grants, 94% as loans/jobs. Need-based aid available for part-time students. **Additional information:** Limited financial aid. Support available from religious orders.

Policies to reduce costs. Work study available for part-time students.

Payment plans. Installment payment.

Application procedures. FAFSA, institutional form required. Priority date 5/1; no closing date. Applicants notified on rolling basis starting 5/15. **Transfers:** Closing date 4/1.

Contact. **Financial aid office:** (510) 649-2469
Priscilla Muha, Director of Financial Aid
2401 Ridge Road
Berkeley, CA 94709-1295

Dominican University of California

San Rafael, California
www.dominican.edu
Four-year private **Federal Code: 001196**

	Living at home	On-campus
Tuition and fees (2002-2003):	$20,670	$20,670
Room and board:		$9,400
Board only:	$2,682	
Books and supplies:	$882	$882
Personal expenses:	$1,656	$1,476
Transportation:	$792	$594

Undergraduate aid. Need-based: Average financial aid package for full-time students was $15,289; for part-time $10,713. 94% awarded as scholarships/grants, 6% as loans/jobs. **Non-need-based:** Scholarships based on academics, athletics, minority status, music/drama. **Student debt:** 92% of graduating class borrowed to fund education; average debt was $12,135. **Additional information:** Four-year guarantee program.

Freshman aid. Need-based: Out of 127 full-time freshmen, 126 applied for aid; 88 were judged to have need; of these 88 received aid. Average package met 86% of need. 22 students had full need met. Average scholarship/grant was $10,305; average loan $2,505. **Non-need based:** 48 without need received awards; 16 received athletic scholarships.

Merit scholarships. President Scholarship based on academic and leadership record; $11,500. ALANA Scholarship based on academic and leadership record; $11,500. Music Scholarship based on academic and musical ability; 4 awarded; $8,000.

Policies to reduce costs. Tuition/fee waivers for employees and their families. Credit/placement for qualifying scores on AP, IB, CLEP examinations. Work study available nights, weekends and for part-time students.

Payment plans. Credit card, installment, deferred payment.

Application procedures. FAFSA, institutional form required. Priority date 3/2; no closing date. Applicants notified on rolling basis starting 3/15. **Transfers:** Priority date 3/1.

Contact. **Financial aid office:** (415) 485-3294
Karen Shepherd, Director of Financial Aid
50 Acacia Avenue
San Rafael, CA 94901-2298

Don Bosco Technical Institute

Rosemead, California
www.boscotech.org
Two-year private **Federal Code: 009158**

	Living at home
Tuition and fees:	$6,430
Board only:	$3,168
Books and supplies:	$1,224
Personal expenses:	$2,286
Transportation:	$828

Undergraduate aid. All financial aid based on need. Average financial aid package for full-time students was $3,976; for part-time $2,009.

Freshman aid. Out of 101 full-time freshmen, 28 applied for aid; 24 were judged to have need; of these 15 received aid. Average package met 36% of need. Average scholarship/grant was $4,409.

Policies to reduce costs. Tuition/fee waivers for employees and their families. Credit/placement for qualifying scores on AP, IB, CLEP examinations.

Payment plans. Credit card payment.

Application procedures. FAFSA required. Priority date 3/2; no closing date. Applicants notified by 5/1, must reply within 2 week(s) of notification.

Contact. **Financial aid office:** (626) 940-2020
Bill Rice, Registrar, Director of Student Financial Aid
1151 San Gabriel Boulevard
Rosemead, CA 91770-4299

East Los Angeles College

Monterey Park, California
www.elac.cc.ca.us
Two-year public **Federal Code: 001222**

	Living at home
Tuition and fees (projected):	$352
Out-of-state:	$4,372
Per-credit charge:	$11
Per-credit out-of-state:	$145
Board only:	$2,400
Books and supplies:	$500
Personal expenses:	$1,300
Transportation:	$576

Undergraduate aid. Need-based: Need-based aid available for full-time and part-time students. **Non-need-based:** Scholarships based on academics. **Additional information:** Need-based enrollment fee waivers available through a state aid program.

Policies to reduce costs. Credit/placement for qualifying scores on CLEP examinations.

Application procedures. FAFSA required. Closing date 3/2. Applicants notified on rolling basis, must reply within 2 week(s) of notification. **Transfers:** No deadline.

Contact. **Financial aid office:** (323) 265-8738
Robert Zuniga, Director of Financial Aid
1301 Avenida Cesar Chavez
Monterey Park, CA 91754

Everest College

Rancho Cucamonga, California
www.everest-college.com
Four-year proprietary

	Living at home
Tuition and fees:	$10,015
Books and supplies:	$750

Application procedures. FAFSA required. Applicants notified on rolling basis.

Contact. 9616 Archibald Avenue, Suite 100
Rancho Cucamonga, CA 91730

Fashion Institute of Design and Merchandising

Los Angeles, California
www.fidm.com
Two-year proprietary **Federal Code: 011112**

College costs. Tuition may vary depending on program. Additional $150 acceptance fee for out of state applicants; additional $300 acceptance fee for international students.

	Living at home
Tuition and fees (2002-2003):	$14,500
Books and supplies:	$1,630

Undergraduate aid. Non-need-based: Scholarships based on academics. **Additional information:** Tuition/fee expenses may be reduced by applying for admission by December 31 of year before student plans to attend.

Policies to reduce costs. Tuition/fee waivers for employees and their families. Credit/placement for qualifying scores on AP, IB, CLEP examinations.

Payment plans. Credit card, installment, deferred payment.

Application procedures. FAFSA, institutional form required. Priority date 3/1; no closing date. Applicants notified on rolling basis starting 3/15, must reply within 3 week(s) of notification.

Contact. Financial aid office: (213) 624-1200
Chris Jennings, Executive Marketing Liaison
919 South Grand Avenue
Los Angeles, CA 90015

Fashion Institute of Design and Merchandising: San Diego

San Diego, California
www.fidm.edu
Two-year proprietary **Federal Code: 011112**

College costs (2002-2003). Tuition ranges from $14,700 to $20,000; required fees range from $450 to $600; estimated books and supplies expenses range from $1,400 to $3,500.

Undergraduate aid. Non-need-based: Scholarships based on academics.

Policies to reduce costs. Tuition/fee waivers for employees and their families. Credit/placement for qualifying scores on AP, IB examinations.

Payment plans. Credit card, installment, deferred payment.

Application procedures. FAFSA, institutional form required. Priority date 3/2; no closing date. Applicants notified on rolling basis, must reply within 3 week(s) of notification.

Contact. Financial aid office: (213) 624-1200
1010 Second Avenue, Suite 2000
San Diego, CA 92101

Fashion Institute of Design and Merchandising: San Francisco

San Francisco, California
Two-year proprietary **Federal Code: 011112**

College costs (2002-2003). Tuition ranges from $14,760 to $15,500 depending on program. Fees, $500. Books/supplies: $2,140.

Undergraduate aid. Non-need-based: Scholarships based on academics.

Policies to reduce costs. Tuition/fee waivers for employees and their families. Credit/placement for qualifying scores on AP, CLEP examinations.

Payment plans. Credit card, installment, deferred payment.

Application procedures. FAFSA, institutional form required. Priority date 3/2; no closing date. Applicants notified on rolling basis.

Contact. Financial aid office: (800) 711-7175
55 Stockton Street
San Francisco, CA 94108-5805

Feather River College

Quincy, California
www.frcc.edu
Two-year public **Federal Code: 008597**

College costs. Students from selected counties in Nevada pay per-credit-hour charge of $42. Required fees: $12 per semester for health, $1 per-credit-hour charge for transit, $1.50 per-credit-hour charge for parking; some can be waived.

	Living at home
Tuition and fees (projected):	$435
Out-of-state:	$4,935
Per-credit charge:	$11
Per-credit out-of-state:	$161
Books and supplies:	$800
Personal expenses:	$1,700
Transportation:	$700

Undergraduate aid. Need-based: 81% awarded as scholarships/grants, 19% as loans/jobs. Need-based aid available for part-time students.

Policies to reduce costs. Tuition/fee waivers for adults, unemployed or children of unemployed. Credit/placement for qualifying scores on AP, IB, CLEP examinations. Work study available nights, weekends and for part-time students.

Payment plans. Installment, deferred payment.

Application procedures. FAFSA required. No deadline. Applicants notified on rolling basis starting 7/30, must reply within 3 week(s) of notification. **Transfers:** No deadline.

Contact. Financial aid office: (530) 283-0202
Virginia Cokor, Financial Aid Supervisor
570 Golden Eagle Avenue
CA, 95971

Foothill College

Los Altos Hills, California
www.foothill.edu
Two-year public **Federal Code: 001199**

	Living at home
Tuition and fees (2002-2003):	$369
Out-of-state:	$3,969
Per-credit charge:	$7
Per-credit out-of-state:	$87
Books and supplies:	$750
Transportation:	$750

Undergraduate aid. All financial aid based on need. Need-based aid available for full-time and part-time students.

Policies to reduce costs. Credit/placement for qualifying scores on AP examinations.

Payment plans. Credit card payment.

Application procedures. FAFSA, institutional form required. Priority date 3/30; no closing date. Applicants notified on rolling basis, must reply within 2 week(s) of notification. **Transfers:** Application required for CDL grants, March 2 due date for CAL grant application.

Contact. Financial aid office: (650) 949-7245
John Bostic, Financial Aid Officer
12345 El Monte Road
Los Altos Hills, CA 94022

Foundation College of San Diego

San Diego, California
www.foundationcollege.org
Two-year private **Federal Code: 032713**

College costs. Reported tuition includes books.

	Living at home
Tuition and fees (2002-2003):	$14,070
Per-credit charge:	$260

Contact. **Financial aid office:** (619) 683-3273
Patricia McKee, Financial Aid Administrator
5353 Mission Center Road, Suite 100
San Diego, CA 92108-1306

Fresno Pacific University

Fresno, California
www.fresno.edu
Four-year private **Federal Code: 001253**

	Living at home	On-campus
Tuition and fees:	$17,592	$17,592
Room and board:		$4,870
Board only:	$2,990	
Books and supplies:	$1,224	$1,224
Personal expenses:	$2,286	$1,872
Transportation:	$828	$594

Undergraduate aid. **Need-based:** 41% awarded as scholarships/grants, 59% as loans/jobs. Need-based aid available for part-time students.

Freshman aid. **Need-based:** Out of 209 full-time freshmen, 209 applied for aid; 188 were judged to have need; of these 188 received aid. **Non-need based:** 18 full-time freshmen with need received non-need scholarships.

Merit scholarships. Paragon Scholarship; 2 awarded; full tuition; requires 3.65 GPA, demonstrated Christian leadership, SAT combined score 1150 or higher. President's Scholarship; 40 awarded; $6,500-$9,500; requires 3.65 GPA, demonstrated Christian leadership, SAT combined score 1150 or higher. Provost Scholarship; 20 awarded; $4,000-$8,000; for transfer students with 3.5 GPA and demonstrated Christian leadership.

Policies to reduce costs. Tuition/fee waivers for senior citizens, family of clergy, employees and their families. Credit/placement for qualifying scores on AP, IB, CLEP examinations. Work study available nights, weekends and for part-time students.

Payment plans. Credit card, installment payment.

Application procedures. FAFSA, institutional form required. Priority date 3/2; no closing date. Applicants notified on rolling basis starting 2/15, must reply by 7/30 or within 3 week(s) of notification. **Transfers:** No deadline.

Contact. **Financial aid office:** (559) 453-2041
Amber Blodgett, Director of Financial Aid
1717 South Chestnut Avenue
Fresno, CA 93702

Gavilan Community College

Gilroy, California
www.gavilan.edu
Two-year public **Federal Code: 001202**

	Living at home
Tuition and fees (2002-2003):	$350
Out-of-state:	$4,580
Per-credit charge:	$11
Per-credit out-of-state:	$152
Books and supplies:	$1,206
Personal expenses:	$2,250
Transportation:	$864

Policies to reduce costs. Credit/placement for qualifying scores on AP, CLEP examinations.

Payment plans. Credit card payment.

Application procedures. FAFSA required. Priority date 6/30; no closing date. Applicants notified on rolling basis starting 7/15, must reply within 2 week(s) of notification.

Contact. **Financial aid office:** (408) 847-1400
Audren Morris, Financial Aid and Veterans Officer
5055 Santa Teresa Boulevard
Gilroy, CA 95020

Glendale Community College

Glendale, California
www.glendale.edu
Two-year public **Federal Code: 001203**

	Living at home
Tuition and fees (2002-2003):	$359
Out-of-state:	$4,259
Per-credit charge:	$11
Per-credit out-of-state:	$141
Board only:	$2,448
Books and supplies:	$810
Personal expenses:	$1,548
Transportation:	$738

Undergraduate aid. All financial aid based on need. Need-based aid available for full-time and part-time students.

Policies to reduce costs. Credit/placement for qualifying scores on AP, CLEP examinations. Work study available nights, weekends and for part-time students.

Payment plans. Deferred payment.

Application procedures. FAFSA, institutional form required. Priority date 4/15; no closing date. Applicants notified on rolling basis starting 6/15, must reply within 2 week(s) of notification. **Transfers:** No deadline.

Contact. **Financial aid office:** (818) 240-1000 ext. 5916
Patricia Hurley, Director of Financial Aid
1500 North Verdugo Road
Glendale, CA 91208

Golden Gate University

San Francisco, California
www.ggu.edu
Four-year private **Federal Code: 001205**

	Living at home
Tuition and fees (2002-2003):	$12,000

Undergraduate aid. **Need-based:** Average financial aid package for full-time students was $2,931. 98% awarded as scholarships/grants, 2% as loans/jobs. **Non-need-based:** 86% awarded as scholarships/grants, 14% as loans/jobs. Scholarships based on academics, alumni affiliation. **Student debt:** 53% of graduating class borrowed to fund education; average debt was $17,522.

Freshman aid. **Need-based:** Out of 13 full-time freshmen, 3 applied for aid; 3 were judged to have need; of these 1 received aid. Average package met 31% of need. 1 students had full need met. Average scholarship/grant was $1,200; average loan $1,374.

Policies to reduce costs. Tuition/fee waivers for employees and their families. Credit/placement for qualifying scores on AP, CLEP examinations.

Payment plans. Credit card, installment, deferred payment.

Application procedures. FAFSA, institutional form required. No deadline. Applicants notified on rolling basis starting 4/1, must reply within 3 week(s) of notification. **Transfers:** No deadline.

Contact. **Financial aid office:** (415) 442-7000
Ken Walsh, Director of Financial Aid
536 Mission Street
San Francisco, CA 94105-2968

Golden West College

Huntington Beach, California
www.gwc.cccd.edu
Two-year public **Federal Code: 001206**

	Living at home
Tuition and fees (2002-2003):	$365
Out-of-state:	$4,595
Per-credit charge:	$11
Per-credit out-of-state:	$152
Books and supplies:	$810
Personal expenses:	$1,530
Transportation:	$720

Undergraduate aid. **Non-need-based:** Scholarships based on academics.

Policies to reduce costs. Credit/placement for qualifying scores on AP, CLEP examinations.

Payment plans. Credit card payment.

Application procedures. FAFSA, institutional form required. Priority date 6/1; no closing date. Applicants notified on rolling basis starting 7/1, must reply within 3 week(s) of notification. **Transfers:** Priority date 6/1; no deadline.

Contact. **Financial aid office:** (714) 892-7711
15744 Golden West Street, Box 2748
Huntington Beach, CA 92647-2748

Grossmont Community College

El Cajon, California
www.grossmont.net
Two-year public **Federal Code: 001208**

	Living at home
Tuition and fees (2002-2003):	$354
Out-of-state:	$4,584
Per-credit charge:	$11
Per-credit out-of-state:	$152
Board only:	$2,600
Books and supplies:	$850
Personal expenses:	$1,100
Transportation:	$800

Undergraduate aid. All financial aid based on need. 84% awarded as scholarships/grants, 16% as loans/jobs. Need-based aid available for part-time students.

Policies to reduce costs. Credit/placement for qualifying scores on AP, CLEP examinations. Work study available nights, weekends and for part-time students.

Application procedures. FAFSA required. Priority date 2/1; no closing date. Applicants notified on rolling basis starting 7/15, must reply within 2 week(s) of notification.

Contact. **Financial aid office:** (619) 644-7129
Susan Lipsmeyer, Director of Financial Aid
8800 Grossmont College Drive
El Cajon, CA 92020

Harvey Mudd College

Claremont, California
www.hmc.edu
Four-year private **Federal Code: 001171**

	Living at home	On-campus
Tuition and fees:	$28,660	$28,660
Room and board:		$9,420
Board only:	$2,988	
Books and supplies:	$800	$800
Personal expenses:	$900	$900

Undergraduate aid. **Need-based:** Average financial aid package for full-time students was $21,358; for part-time $8,044. 75% awarded as scholarships/grants, 25% as loans/jobs. **Non-need-based:** 75% awarded as scholarships/grants, 25% as loans/jobs. Scholarships based on academics. **Student debt:** 68% of graduating class borrowed to fund education; average debt was $20,219.

Freshman aid. **Need-based:** Out of 187 full-time freshmen, 135 applied for aid; 108 were judged to have need; of these 108 received aid. Average package met 100% of need. 108 students had full need met. Average scholarship/grant was $17,993; average loan $3,103. **Non-need based:** 37 full-time freshmen with need received non-need scholarships; 61 without need received awards.

Merit scholarships. Harvey S. Mudd Scholarship for first-time freshmen in science and technology programs, must maintain minimum 2.75 GPA; $5,000 annually for 4 years. Harvey Mudd College sponsored National Merit Scholarships from $750 to $2,000 based on need. Nova Scholar Award; 1/2 tuition renewable; must be in top 10% of high school graduating class with 1450 SAT I.

Policies to reduce costs. Credit/placement for qualifying scores on AP examinations. Work study available nights, weekends and for part-time students.

Payment plans. Installment payment.

Application procedures. FAFSA, CSS PROFILE required. Closing date 2/1. Applicants notified on rolling basis starting 4/1, must reply by 5/1 or within 2 week(s) of notification. Early decision closing date 11/15. **Transfers:** Priority date 3/15; no deadline.

Contact. **Financial aid office:** (909) 621-8055
Youlonda Copeland-Morgan, Associate Vice President/Admission and Financial Aid
Kingston Hall, 301 East 12th Street
Claremont, CA 91711-5901

Heald College: Hayward

Hayward, California
www.heald.edu
Two-year private **Federal Code: 008532**

College costs (2002-2003). Cost of 18-month associate degree program: $17,100.

Undergraduate aid. All financial aid based on need. Need-based aid available for full-time and part-time students.

Policies to reduce costs. Work study available nights, weekends and for part-time students.

Application procedures. FAFSA required.

Contact. **Financial aid office:** (510) 783-2100
25500 Industrial Boulevard
Hayward, CA 94545

Heald College: Milpitas

Milpitas, California
www.heald.edu
Two-year private **Federal Code: 025932**

College costs (2002-2003). Cost of 18-month associate degree program: $17,100. Books/supplies: $1,200.

Undergraduate aid. All financial aid based on need. Need-based aid available for full-time and part-time students.

Policies to reduce costs. Tuition/fee waivers for employees and their families. Credit/placement for qualifying scores on CLEP examinations. Work study available nights, weekends and for part-time students.

Payment plans. Credit card, installment payment.

Application procedures. FAFSA required. Priority date 6/1; no closing date. Applicants notified on rolling basis starting 6/15, must reply within 2 week(s) of notification.

Contact. **Financial aid office:** (408) 934-4900
341 Great Mall Parkway
Milpitas, CA 95035

Holy Names College

Oakland, California
www.hnc.edu
Four-year private **Federal Code: 001183**

	Living at home	On-campus
Tuition and fees:	$20,180	$20,180
Room and board:		$7,800
Board only:	$2,448	
Books and supplies:	$946	$946
Personal expenses:	$1,800	$1,800
Transportation:	$846	$846

Undergraduate aid. **Need-based:** Average financial aid package for full-time students was $20,582; for part-time $12,349. 66% awarded as scholarships/grants, 34% as loans/jobs. **Non-need-based:** 68% awarded as scholarships/grants, 32% as loans/jobs. Scholarships based on academics, alumni affiliation, athletics, leadership, music/drama, religious affiliation.

Freshman aid. **Need-based:** Out of 63 full-time freshmen, 51 applied for aid; 46 were judged to have need; of these 42 received aid. Average package met 78% of need. Average scholarship/grant was $9,918; average loan $2,625. **Non-need based:** 42 full-time freshmen with need received non-need scholarships.

Merit scholarships. Regents' Scholarships for students with a minimum 3.5 high school or transfer GPA, based on leadership and contributions to school or community, as well as academic achievement; award renewed annually if the recipient maintains a 3.0 GPA each semester and completes 30 units each academic year; 5 awarded; up to full tuition for students living on campus or up to 75% of tuition for students living off campus. Presidents' Scholarships based on contributions to school or community, as well as academic achievement; renewed annually if the recipient maintains a 3.0 GPA each semester and completes 30 units each academic year; 10 awarded; up to 50% of tuition.

Policies to reduce costs. Tuition/fee waivers for family of clergy, employees and their families. Credit/placement for qualifying scores on AP, IB, CLEP examinations.

Payment plans. Credit card, installment, deferred payment.

Application procedures. FAFSA, institutional form required. Priority date 3/2; no closing date. Applicants notified on rolling basis starting 4/15, must reply by 5/1 or within 2 week(s) of notification. **Transfers:** Priority date 3/2; no deadline.

Contact. **Financial aid office:** (510) 436-1327
Loretta Williams, Director of Financial Aid
3500 Mountain Boulevard
Oakland, CA 94619-1699

Hope International University

Fullerton, California
www.hiu.edu
Four-year private **Federal Code: 001252**

	Living at home	On-campus
Tuition and fees (projected):	$15,290	$15,290
Room and board:		$5,202
Board only:	$810	
Books and supplies:	$648	$648
Personal expenses:	$1,485	$1,215
Transportation:	$693	$549

Undergraduate aid. Need-based: Need-based aid available for full-time and part-time students. **Non-need-based:** Scholarships based on academics, athletics.

Policies to reduce costs. Tuition/fee waivers for senior citizens, family members, family of clergy, employees and their families. Prepayment discount; credit/placement for qualifying scores on AP, IB, CLEP examinations. Work study available nights and weekends.

Payment plans. Credit card, installment payment.

Application procedures. FAFSA, institutional form required. Applicants notified on rolling basis, must reply within 4 week(s) of notification. **Transfers:** Priority date 3/2; no deadline.

Contact. **Financial aid office:** (714) 879-3901
Mai Bui, Director of Student Financial Aid
2500 East Nutwood Avenue
Fullerton, CA 92831-3199

Humboldt State University

Arcata, California
www.humboldt.edu
Four-year public **Federal Code: 001149**

	Living at home	On-campus
Tuition and fees (2002-2003):	$1,894	$1,894
Out-of-state:	$10,354	$10,354
Room and board:		$6,618
Board only:	$2,988	
Books and supplies:	$1,030	$1,030
Personal expenses:	$1,826	$1,760
Transportation:	$864	$628

Undergraduate aid. Need-based: Average financial aid package for full-time students was $8,430; for part-time $3,469. 50% awarded as scholarships/grants, 50% as loans/jobs. **Non-need-based:** Scholarships based on academics.

Freshman aid. Need-based: Out of 834 full-time freshmen, 647 applied for aid; 441 were judged to have need; of these 413 received aid. Average package met 85% of need. 122 students had full need met. Average scholarship/grant was $5,100; average loan $3,200.

Policies to reduce costs. Tuition/fee waivers for senior citizens, employees and their families. Credit/placement for qualifying scores on AP, IB, CLEP examinations.

Payment plans. Credit card, installment payment.

Application procedures. FAFSA required. No deadline. Applicants notified on rolling basis starting 3/1, must reply within 6 week(s) of notification. **Transfers:** Need is most salient factor for some programs.

Contact. **Financial aid office:** (707) 826-3011
Don Scheaffer, Director of Financial Aid
Arcata, CA 95521-8299

ITT Technical Institute: Anaheim

Anaheim, California
www.itt-tech.edu
Three-year proprietary **Federal Code: 023219**

College costs. Total cost of program varies depending on course of study. Per-credit-hour charge: $347.

Policies to reduce costs. Tuition/fee waivers for employees and their families.

Payment plans. Credit card, installment payment.

Application procedures. FAFSA, institutional form required. No deadline. Applicants notified on rolling basis.

Contact. **Financial aid office:** (714) 535-3700
Janice Richards, Director of Finance
525 North Muller
Anaheim, CA 92801

ITT Technical Institute: Lathrop

Lathrop, California
www.itt-tech.edu
Two-year proprietary **Federal Code: 022915**

College costs. Total cost of program varies depending on course of study. Per-credit-hour charge: $347.

Policies to reduce costs. Tuition/fee waivers for employees and their families. Tuition at time of enrollment guaranteed for 2 years.

Payment plans. Credit card, installment payment.

Application procedures. FAFSA, institutional form required. No deadline. Applicants notified on rolling basis.

Contact. **Financial aid office:** (209) 858-0077
Lourena Deggins, Director of Finance
16916 South Harlan Road
Lathrop, CA 95330

ITT Technical Institute: Oxnard

Oxnard, California
www.itt-tech.edu
Three-year proprietary **Federal Code: 023218**

College costs. Total cost of program varies depending on course of study. Per-credit-hour charge: $347.

Policies to reduce costs. Tuition/fee waivers for employees and their families.

Payment plans. Credit card, installment payment.

Application procedures. FAFSA, institutional form required. No deadline. Applicants notified on rolling basis.

Contact. **Financial aid office:** (805) 988-0143
Nancy Lopez, Director of Finance
2051 Solar Drive, Building B
Oxnard, CA 93036

ITT Technical Institute: Rancho Cordova

Rancho Cordova, California
www.itt-tech.edu
Three-year proprietary **Federal Code: 014685**

College costs. Total cost of program varies depending on course of study. Per-credit-hour charge: $347.

Policies to reduce costs. Tuition/fee waivers for employees and their families.

Payment plans. Credit card, installment payment.

Application procedures. FAFSA, institutional form required. No deadline. Applicants notified on rolling basis.

Contact. Financial aid office: (916) 851-3900
Dale Gerger, Director of Finance
10863 Gold Center Drive
Rancho Cordova, CA 95670

ITT Technical Institute: San Bernardino

San Bernardino, California
www.itt-tech.edu
Three-year proprietary **Federal Code: 030704**

College costs. Total cost of program varies depending on course of study. Per-credit-hour charge: $347.

Policies to reduce costs. Tuition/fee waivers for employees and their families.

Payment plans. Credit card, installment payment.

Application procedures. FAFSA, institutional form required. No deadline. Applicants notified on rolling basis.

Contact. Financial aid office: (909) 889-3800
Annie Chen, Director of Finance
630 E Brier Drive
San Bernardino, CA 92408-2800

ITT Technical Institute: San Diego

San Diego, California
www.itt-tech.edu
Three-year proprietary **Federal Code: 016205**

College costs. Total cost of program varies depending on course of study. Per-credit-hour charge: $347.

Policies to reduce costs. Tuition/fee waivers for employees and their families.

Payment plans. Credit card, installment payment.

Application procedures. FAFSA, institutional form required. No deadline. Applicants notified on rolling basis.

Contact. Financial aid office: (858) 571-8500
Kurt Johnson, Director of Finance
9680 Granite Ridge Drive
San Diego, CA 92123

ITT Technical Institute: Sylmar

Sylmar, California
www.itt-tech.edu
Three-year proprietary **Federal Code: 023218**

College costs. Total cost of program varies depending on course of study. Per-credit-hour charge: $347.

Policies to reduce costs. Tuition/fee waivers for employees and their families.

Payment plans. Credit card, installment payment.

Application procedures. FAFSA, institutional form required. No deadline. Applicants notified on rolling basis.

Contact. Financial aid office: (818) 364-5151
Willetta Collins, Director of Finance
12669 Encinitas Avenue
Sylmar, CA 91342-3664

ITT Technical Institute: Torrance

Torrance, California
www.itt-tech.edu
Two-year proprietary **Federal Code: 030874**

College costs. Total cost of program varies depending on course of study. Per-credit-hour charge: $347.

Policies to reduce costs. Tuition/fee waivers for employees and their families. Tuition at time of enrollment guaranteed for 2 years.

Payment plans. Credit card, installment payment.

Application procedures. FAFSA, institutional form required. No deadline. Applicants notified on rolling basis.

Contact. Financial aid office: (310) 380-1555
Wylodin Banez, Director of Finance
20050 South Vermont Avenue
Torrance, CA 90502

ITT Technical Institute: West Covina

West Covina, California
www.itt-tech.edu
Three-year proprietary **Federal Code: 016206**

College costs. Total cost of program varies depending on course of study. Per-credit-hour charge: $347.

Policies to reduce costs. Tuition/fee waivers for employees and their families.

Payment plans. Credit card, installment payment.

Application procedures. FAFSA, institutional form required. No deadline. Applicants notified on rolling basis.

Contact. Financial aid office: (626) 960-8681
Cheryl Lebleu, Director of Finance
1530 West Cameron Avenue
West Covina, CA 91790

Imperial Valley College

Imperial, California
Two-year public **Federal Code: 001214**

	Living at home
Tuition and fees (2002-2003):	$330
Out-of-state:	$4,560
Per-credit charge:	$11
Per-credit out-of-state:	$152
Books and supplies:	$1,206
Personal expenses:	$2,250
Transportation:	$864

Policies to reduce costs. Credit/placement for qualifying scores on AP examinations.

Payment plans. Credit card payment.

Application procedures. FAFSA required. Priority date 3/2; no closing date. Applicants notified on rolling basis starting 5/1. **Transfers:** Academic transcripts from previous institutions required.

Contact. Financial aid office: (760) 355-6266
Janis Magno, Director of Financial Aid
Box 158
Imperial, CA 92251-0158

Irvine Valley College

Irvine, California
www.ivc.edu
Two-year public **Federal Code: 025395**

	Living at home
Tuition and fees (2002-2003):	$340
Out-of-state:	$4,540
Per-credit charge:	$11
Per-credit out-of-state:	$133
Books and supplies:	$630

Undergraduate aid. All financial aid based on need. 67% awarded as scholarships/grants, 33% as loans/jobs. Need-based aid available for part-time students. **Student debt:** 17% of graduating class borrowed to fund education; average debt was $5,250.

Policies to reduce costs. Tuition/fee waivers for minority students, family members. Credit/placement for qualifying scores on AP, CLEP examinations. Work study available nights and for part-time students.

Payment plans. Credit card payment.

Application procedures. FAFSA, institutional form required. No deadline. Applicants notified on rolling basis starting 4/30.

Contact. Financial aid office: (949) 451-5287
Darryl Cox, Director of Financial Aid
5500 Irvine Center Drive
Irvine, CA 92618-4399

John F. Kennedy University

Orinda, California
www.jfku.edu
Four-year private **Federal Code: 004484**

	Living at home
Tuition and fees (2002-2003):	$11,637
Books and supplies:	$1,080
Transportation:	$1,104

Undergraduate aid. All financial aid based on need. Need-based aid available for full-time and part-time students.

Policies to reduce costs. Tuition/fee waivers for employees and their families. Credit/placement for qualifying scores on AP, CLEP examinations.

Payment plans. Credit card, installment payment.

Application procedures. FAFSA, institutional form required. Priority date 4/1; no closing date. Applicants notified on rolling basis, must reply within 4 week(s) of notification. **Transfers:** Priority date 4/1; no deadline.

Contact. **Financial aid office:** (925) 258-2385
Mindy Bergeron, Director of Financial Aid
12 Altarinda Road
Orinda, CA 94563-2603

LIFE Pacific College

San Dimas, California
www.lifepacific.edu
Four-year private **Federal Code: 016029**

	Living at home	On-campus
Tuition and fees:	$7,300	$7,300
Room and board:		$4,000
Board only:	$300	
Books and supplies:	$700	$700
Personal expenses:	$475	$475
Transportation:	$700	

Undergraduate aid. Need-based: Need-based aid available for full-time and part-time students. **Non-need-based:** Scholarships based on state/district residency.

Policies to reduce costs. Tuition/fee waivers for children of alumni, family members, family of clergy, employees and their families. Credit/placement for qualifying scores on AP, CLEP examinations.

Payment plans. Credit card, installment payment.

Application procedures. FAFSA required. Closing date 7/15. Applicants notified on rolling basis, must reply by 8/15.

Contact. **Financial aid office:** (909) 599-5433
Becky Huyck, Director of Financial Aid
1100 Covina Boulevard
San Dimas, CA 91773

La Sierra University

Riverside, California
www.lasierra.edu
Four-year private **Federal Code: 001215**

	Living at home	On-campus
Tuition and fees:	$16,740	$16,740
Room and board:		$4,680
Books and supplies:	$900	$900
Transportation:	$1,101	$540

Undergraduate aid. Need-based: Need-based aid available for full-time and part-time students. **Non-need-based:** Scholarships based on academics, leadership, music/drama, religious affiliation.

Policies to reduce costs. Tuition/fee waivers for family members, unemployed or children of unemployed, family of clergy, employees and their families. Prepayment discount; credit/placement for qualifying scores on AP, IB, CLEP examinations. Work study available nights, weekends and for part-time students.

Payment plans. Credit card, installment payment.

Application procedures. FAFSA, institutional form required. Priority date 3/2; no closing date. Applicants notified on rolling basis. **Transfers:** No deadline.

Contact. **Financial aid office:** (909) 785-2175
William Chunestudy, Director of Student Aid
4700 Pierce Street
Riverside, CA 92515-8247

Laney College

Oakland, California
www.peralta.cc.ca.us
Two-year public **Federal Code: 001266**

	Living at home
Tuition and fees (projected):	$334
Out-of-state:	$5,254
Per-credit charge:	$11
Per-credit out-of-state:	$175
Books and supplies:	$648
Personal expenses:	$1,620
Transportation:	$738

Policies to reduce costs. Tuition/fee waivers for unemployed or children of unemployed.

Payment plans. Credit card payment.

Application procedures. FAFSA, institutional form required. Priority date 4/1; no closing date. Applicants notified on rolling basis, must reply within 2 week(s) of notification.

Contact. **Financial aid office:** (510) 834-5740
Judith Cohen, Financial Aid Officer
900 Fallon Street
Oakland, CA 94607

Las Positas College

Livermore, California
www.laspositas.cc.ca.us
Two-year public **Federal Code: 030357**

	Living at home
Tuition and fees (2002-2003):	$352
Out-of-state:	$4,432
Per-credit charge:	$11
Per-credit out-of-state:	$147
Books and supplies:	$810
Personal expenses:	$1,548
Transportation:	$702

Undergraduate aid. Need-based: Need-based aid available for full-time students.

Policies to reduce costs. Tuition/fee waivers for unemployed or children of unemployed. Credit/placement for qualifying scores on AP examinations.

Application procedures. Institutional form required. Priority date 5/1; no closing date. Applicants notified on rolling basis starting 7/1, must reply within 2 week(s) of notification.

Contact. **Financial aid office:** (925) 373-5800
Andi Schreibman, Financial Aid Officer
3033 Collier Canyon Road
Livermore, CA 94551

Loma Linda University

Loma Linda, California
www.llu.edu
Upper-division private **Federal Code: 001218**

College costs. Tuition quoted is for nursing program. Full-time tuition for dental hygiene program: $16,090. For allied health program: $420 per credit hour for first 8 credits; $252 per credit hour after 8 credits.

	Living at home	On-campus
Tuition and fees (2002-2003):	$20,640	$20,640
Room only:		$2,043
Board only:	$1,665	
Books and supplies:	$1,100	$1,100
Personal expenses:	$1,260	$1,260
Transportation:	$2,835	$2,835

Undergraduate aid. Need-based: Need-based aid available for full-time and part-time students.

Payment plans. Credit card, installment payment.

Application procedures. FAFSA required. Applicants notified on rolling basis. **Transfers:** No deadline.

Contact. Financial aid office: (909) 558-4509
Verdell Schaefer, Director of Financial Aid
Loma Linda, CA 92350

Long Beach City College

Long Beach, California
www.lbcc.edu
Two-year public **Federal Code: 001219**

	Living at home
Tuition and fees (projected):	$358
Out-of-state:	$3,662
Per-credit charge:	$11
Per-credit out-of-state:	$140
Board only:	$711
Books and supplies:	$1,560
Personal expenses:	$1,955
Transportation:	$828

Undergraduate aid. All financial aid based on need. 87% awarded as scholarships/grants, 13% as loans/jobs. Need-based aid available for part-time students.

Policies to reduce costs. Credit/placement for qualifying scores on AP, IB examinations. Work study available for part-time students.

Payment plans. Credit card, deferred payment.

Application procedures. FAFSA, institutional form required. Priority date 5/1; no closing date. Applicants notified on rolling basis starting 7/1, must reply within 2 week(s) of notification.

Contact. Financial aid office: (562) 938-4257
Toni Dubois, Director of Financial Aid and Veterans Affairs
4901 East Carson Street
Long Beach, CA 90808

Los Angeles Harbor College

Wilmington, California
www.lahc.edu
Two-year public **Federal Code: 001224**

	Living at home
Tuition and fees (2002-2003):	$354
Out-of-state:	$4,254
Per-credit charge:	$11
Per-credit out-of-state:	$145
Books and supplies:	$650
Personal expenses:	$1,620
Transportation:	$594

Undergraduate aid. All financial aid based on need. Need-based aid available for full-time and part-time students.

Policies to reduce costs. Tuition/fee waivers for senior citizens. Work study available nights, weekends and for part-time students.

Payment plans. Credit card, deferred payment.

Application procedures. FAFSA, institutional form required. Priority date 3/2; no closing date. Applicants notified on rolling basis, must reply within 2 week(s) of notification. **Transfers:** Closing date 5/15.

Contact. Financial aid office: (310) 233-4320
Sheila Millman, Financial Aid Manager
1111 Figueroa Place
Wilmington, CA 90744

Los Angeles Pierce College

Woodland Hills, California
www.piercecollege.com
Two-year public **Federal Code: 001226**

	Living at home
Tuition and fees (projected):	$354
Out-of-state:	$4,374
Per-credit charge:	$11
Per-credit out-of-state:	$145
Books and supplies:	$1,200

Undergraduate aid. All financial aid based on need. Need-based aid available for full-time and part-time students.

Policies to reduce costs. Credit/placement for qualifying scores on AP, CLEP examinations.

Payment plans. Credit card payment.

Application procedures. FAFSA, institutional form required. Priority date 5/1; no closing date. Applicants notified on rolling basis starting 8/1. **Transfers:** Priority date 3/2; no deadline.

Contact. Financial aid office: (818) 719-6428
Jeremy Villar, Manager of Financial Aid
6201 Winnetka Avenue
Woodland Hills, CA 91371

Los Angeles Southwest College

Los Angeles, California
Two-year public **Federal Code: 007047**

	Living at home
Tuition and fees (projected):	$352
Out-of-state:	$4,372
Per-credit charge:	$11
Per-credit out-of-state:	$145
Books and supplies:	$630
Personal expenses:	$1,530
Transportation:	$576

Undergraduate aid. Need-based: Need-based aid available for full-time and part-time students. **Additional information:** Board of Governors Enrollment Fee Waiver available to students receiving AFDC, SSI/SSP, or General Assistance. May also qualify on basis of income.

Payment plans. Deferred payment.

Application procedures. FAFSA required. No deadline. Applicants notified on rolling basis, must reply within 2 week(s) of notification.

Contact. Financial aid office: (323) 241-5225
Marilyn Moy, Associate Dean, Student Services
1600 West Imperial Highway
Los Angeles, CA 90047

Los Angeles Trade and Technical College

Los Angeles, California
www.lattc.edu
Two-year public **Federal Code: 001227**

	Living at home
Tuition and fees (2002-2003):	$372
Out-of-state:	$4,522
Per-credit charge:	$12
Per-credit out-of-state:	$150
Books and supplies:	$708
Personal expenses:	$1,620
Transportation:	$594

Undergraduate aid. All financial aid based on need. Need-based aid available for full-time and part-time students.

Policies to reduce costs. Credit/placement for qualifying scores on AP, CLEP examinations. Work study available nights, weekends and for part-time students.

Payment plans. Credit card, deferred payment.

Application procedures. FAFSA required. Priority date 5/1; no closing date. Applicants notified on rolling basis. **Transfers:** No deadline.

Contact. **Financial aid office:** (213) 744-9016
Leann Roque, Financial Aid Manager
400 West Washington Boulevard
Los Angeles, CA 90015-4181

Los Medanos College

Pittsburg, California
www.losmedanos.net
Two-year public **Federal Code: 010340**

	Living at home
Tuition and fees (2002-2003):	$332
Out-of-state:	$4,322
Per-credit charge:	$11
Per-credit out-of-state:	$144
Board only:	$2,484
Books and supplies:	$648
Personal expenses:	$1,485
Transportation:	$693

Policies to reduce costs. Credit/placement for qualifying scores on AP examinations.

Payment plans. Credit card, deferred payment.

Application procedures. FAFSA required. Priority date 3/2; no closing date. Applicants notified on rolling basis starting 7/1, must reply within 2 week(s) of notification.

Contact. **Financial aid office:** (925) 439-2181
Felipe Torres, Director
2700 East Leland Road
Pittsburg, CA 94565

Loyola Marymount University

Los Angeles, California
www.lmu.edu
Four-year private **Federal Code: 001234**

	Living at home	On-campus
Tuition and fees (2002-2003):	$22,098	$22,098
Room and board:		$7,730
Board only:	$2,448	
Books and supplies:	$810	$810
Personal expenses:	$1,548	$1,386
Transportation:	$738	$558

Undergraduate aid. **Need-based:** Average financial aid package for full-time students was $19,970. 38% awarded as scholarships/grants, 62% as loans/jobs. **Non-need-based:** 21% awarded as scholarships/grants, 79% as loans/jobs.

Freshman aid. **Need-based:** Average package met 77% of need. Average scholarship/grant was $12,339; average loan $5,301.

Policies to reduce costs. Tuition/fee waivers for employees and their families. Credit/placement for qualifying scores on AP examinations. Work study available nights and weekends.

Payment plans. Credit card, installment, deferred payment.

Application procedures. FAFSA, CSS PROFILE required. Priority date 2/15; no closing date. Applicants notified on rolling basis starting 4/10, must reply within 4 week(s) of notification.

Contact. **Financial aid office:** (310) 338-2700
Donna Palmer, Director of Financial Aid
Admissions, One LMU Drive
Los Angeles, CA 90045-8350

MTI College of Business and Technology

Sacramento, California
www.mticollege.com
Two-year proprietary **Federal Code: 012912**

	Living at home
Tuition and fees (2002-2003):	$8,575
Books and supplies:	$1,019
Personal expenses:	$184

Undergraduate aid. **Need-based:** Need-based aid available for full-time students.

Policies to reduce costs. Work study available nights and weekends.

Payment plans. Credit card, installment payment.

Contact. **Financial aid office:** (916) 339-1500
Dawn Gerak, Director of Financial Aid
5221 Madison Avenue
Sacramento, CA 95841

Marymount College

Rancho Palos Verdes, California
www.marymountpv.edu
Two-year private **Federal Code: 010474**

	Living at home	On-campus
Tuition and fees (2002-2003):	$16,570	$16,570
Room and board:		$8,400
Books and supplies:	$800	$800
Personal expenses:	$1,600	$1,300
Transportation:	$720	

Undergraduate aid. **Need-based:** Average financial aid package for full-time students was $10,215. 81% awarded as scholarships/grants, 19% as loans/jobs. **Non-need-based:** 47% awarded as scholarships/grants, 53% as loans/jobs. Scholarships based on academics, athletics, leadership. **Student debt:** 30% of graduating class borrowed to fund education; average debt was $6,000.

Freshman aid. **Need-based:** Out of 392 full-time freshmen, 139 applied for aid; 102 were judged to have need; of these 102 received aid. Average package met 80% of need. 30 students had full need met. Average scholarship/grant was $12,125; average loan $2,625. **Non-need based:** 17 full-time freshmen with need received non-need scholarships; 15 without need received awards; 1 received athletic scholarships.

Policies to reduce costs. Tuition/fee waivers for employees and their families. Credit/placement for qualifying scores on AP, IB, CLEP examinations.

Payment plans. Credit card, installment payment.

Application procedures. FAFSA, institutional form required. Priority date 3/2; no closing date. Applicants notified on rolling basis starting 4/30, must reply by 5/1 or within 2 week(s) of notification. **Transfers:** No deadline. Financial aid transcripts from previous institutions required for midyear transfers.

Contact. **Financial aid office:** (310) 377-5501
David Carnevale, Director of Financial Aid
30800 Palos Verdes Drive East
Rancho Palos Verdes, CA 90275-6299

Master's College

Santa Clarita, California
www.masters.edu
Four-year private **Federal Code: 001220**

	Living at home	On-campus
Tuition and fees:	$17,200	$17,200
Room and board:		$6,050
Board only:	$2,106	
Books and supplies:	$1,224	$1,224
Personal expenses:	$2,286	$1,872
Transportation:	$828	$594

Undergraduate aid. **Need-based:** Average financial aid package for full-time students was $13,872; for part-time $8,485. 61% awarded as scholarships/grants, 39% as loans/jobs. **Non-need-based:** 49% awarded as scholarships/grants, 51% as loans/jobs. Scholarships based on academics, alumni affiliation, art, athletics, leadership, music/drama. **Student debt:** 43% of graduating class borrowed to fund education; average debt was $13,131.

Freshman aid. **Need-based:** Out of 204 full-time freshmen, 169 applied for aid; 139 were judged to have need; of these 139 received aid. Average package met 75% of need. 32 students had full need met. Average scholarship/grant was $11,062; average loan $2,877. **Non-need based:** 19 full-time freshmen with need received non-need scholarships; 56 without need received awards; 21 received athletic scholarships.

Policies to reduce costs. Tuition/fee waivers for family of clergy, employees and their families. Credit/placement for qualifying scores on AP, IB, CLEP examinations. Work study available nights and weekends.

Payment plans. Credit card, installment, deferred payment.

Application procedures. FAFSA, institutional form required. Priority date 3/2; no closing date. Applicants notified on rolling basis starting 3/17, must reply within 2 week(s) of notification. **Transfers:** Closing date 3/2.

Contact. **Financial aid office:** (661) 259-3540
Karen Bosworth, Director of Financial Aid
21726 Placerita Canyon Road
Santa Clarita, CA 91321-1200

Menlo College

Atherton, California
www.menlo.edu
Four-year private **Federal Code: 001236**

	Living at home	On-campus
Tuition and fees (2002-2003):	$20,600	$20,600
Room and board:		$8,650
Board only:	$2,988	
Books and supplies:	$850	$850
Personal expenses:	$1,410	$1,410
Transportation:	$584	$584

Undergraduate aid. Need-based: Need-based aid available for full-time and part-time students. **Non-need-based:** Scholarships based on academics.

Merit scholarships. President's Scholarship for students with 3.5 GPA or higher, up to $10,000 annually. Dean's Scholarship for students with 3.25-3.49 GPA, up to $6,500 annually. Leadership and Service Grant for students with a minimum 2.8 GPA who have demonstrated outstanding leadership potential, up to $5,000 annually.

Policies to reduce costs. Tuition/fee waivers for employees and their families. Credit/placement for qualifying scores on AP, IB examinations. Work study available nights, weekends and for part-time students.

Payment plans. Credit card, installment payment.

Application procedures. FAFSA, institutional form required. Priority date 3/2; closing date 8/1. Applicants notified on rolling basis starting 2/1. **Transfers:** No deadline.

Contact. **Financial aid office:** (650) 543-3880
Elinore Burkhardt, Director of Financial Aid
1000 El Camino Real
Atherton, CA 94027

Mills College

Oakland, California
www.mills.edu
Four-year private **Federal Code: 001238**

	Living at home	On-campus
Tuition and fees (2002-2003):	$21,634	$21,634
Room and board:		$8,500
Books and supplies:	$890	$890
Personal expenses:	$1,506	$1,506
Transportation:	$950	

Undergraduate aid. Need-based: Need-based aid available for full-time students. **Non-need-based:** Scholarships based on academics.

Merit scholarships. Audition or audiotape required for consideration for Music Scholarship. Presidential Scholarships for entering freshmen with strong academic records; $5,000-$7,500 annually. Dean's Scholarships for entering transfers with strong academic records; $2,500-$3,500 annually.

Policies to reduce costs. Tuition/fee waivers for employees and their families. Credit/placement for qualifying scores on AP, IB, CLEP examinations.

Payment plans. Installment payment.

Application procedures. FAFSA, institutional form required. Priority date 2/1; closing date 2/15. Applicants notified by 4/1, must reply by 5/1 or within 2 week(s) of notification. **Transfers:** Priority date 3/2. Applications by March 2 for California residents, April 1 for out-of-state students.

Contact. **Financial aid office:** (510) 430-2000
David Gin, Director of Financial Aid
5000 MacArthur Boulevard
Oakland, CA 94613

MiraCosta College

Oceanside, California
www.miracosta.edu
Two-year public **Federal Code: 001239**

	Living at home
Tuition and fees (2002-2003):	$364
Out-of-state:	$4,384
Per-credit charge:	$11
Per-credit out-of-state:	$145
Board only:	$2,592
Books and supplies:	$846
Personal expenses:	$1,720
Transportation:	$756

Undergraduate aid. Need-based: Need-based aid available for full-time and part-time students. **Additional information:** Waiver of in-state fees for eligible low-income students.

Policies to reduce costs. Tuition/fee waivers for employees and their families. Credit/placement for qualifying scores on AP, IB, CLEP examinations.

Payment plans. Credit card, deferred payment.

Application procedures. FAFSA required. Priority date 3/3; no closing date. Applicants notified on rolling basis.

Contact. **Financial aid office:** (760) 795-6711
JoAnn Bernard, Financial Aid Director
One Barnard Drive
Oceanside, CA 92056-3899

Modesto Junior College

Modesto, California
www.gomjc.org
Two-year public **Federal Code: 001240**

College costs. Fees vary depending on course.

	Living at home
Tuition and fees (projected):	$366
Out-of-state:	$4,596
Per-credit charge:	$11
Per-credit out-of-state:	$152
Books and supplies:	$630
Personal expenses:	$1,584
Transportation:	$576

Undergraduate aid. All financial aid based on need. 95% awarded as scholarships/grants, 5% as loans/jobs. Need-based aid available for part-time students.

Policies to reduce costs. Credit/placement for qualifying scores on AP examinations. Work study available nights, weekends and for part-time students.

Payment plans. Credit card payment.

Application procedures. FAFSA, institutional form required. Priority date 3/1; no closing date. Applicants notified on rolling basis starting 5/1, must reply within 2 week(s) of notification.

Contact. **Financial aid office:** (209) 575-6023
Myra Rush, Director Financial Aid, Scholarships
435 College Avenue
Modesto, CA 95350

Monterey Institute of International Studies

Monterey, California
www.miis.edu
Upper-division private **Federal Code: 001241**

	Living at home
Tuition and fees:	$22,380
Books and supplies:	$600
Personal expenses:	$1,575
Transportation:	$787

Undergraduate aid. Need-based: Need-based aid available for full-time and part-time students. **Non-need-based:** Scholarships based on academics, job skills, minority status.

Merit scholarships. Wide variety of competitive scholarships based on merit and international experience offered.

Policies to reduce costs. Tuition/fee waivers for minority students, employees and their families. Credit/placement for qualifying scores on CLEP examinations. Work study available weekends and for part-time students.

Payment plans. Credit card payment.

Application procedures. FAFSA, institutional form required. Priority date 3/1; no closing date. Applicants notified on rolling basis starting 3/15, must reply within 6 week(s) of notification. **Transfers:** Priority date 3/15; no deadline. Competitive scholarships available to transfer students based partly on academic record.

Contact. **Financial aid office:** (831) 647-4100
Michael Benson, Financial Aid Officer
460 Pierce Street
Monterey, CA 93940

Monterey Peninsula College

Monterey, California
www.mpc.edu
Two-year public **Federal Code: 001242**

	Living at home
Tuition and fees (2002-2003):	$372
Out-of-state:	$4,272
Per-credit charge:	$11
Per-credit out-of-state:	$141
Books and supplies:	$846
Personal expenses:	$1,719
Transportation:	$756

Undergraduate aid. Need-based: Need-based aid available for full-time and part-time students.

Policies to reduce costs. Tuition/fee waivers for adults, senior citizens, minority students, family members, unemployed or children of unemployed, family of clergy, employees and their families. Credit/placement for qualifying scores on AP, CLEP examinations.

Payment plans. Credit card, installment, deferred payment.

Application procedures. FAFSA, institutional form required. Priority date 3/2; no closing date. Applicants notified on rolling basis starting 6/1.

Contact. **Financial aid office:** (831) 646-4000
Claudia Martin, Director of Financial Aid
980 Fremont Street
Monterey, CA 93940-4799

Moorpark College

Moorpark, California
www.moorpark.net
Two-year public **Federal Code: 007115**

	Living at home
Tuition and fees (projected):	$340
Out-of-state:	$4,570
Per-credit charge:	$11
Per-credit out-of-state:	$152
Board only:	$2,682
Books and supplies:	$882
Personal expenses:	$1,656
Transportation:	$792

Policies to reduce costs. Tuition/fee waivers for unemployed or children of unemployed. Credit/placement for qualifying scores on AP examinations.

Payment plans. Credit card payment.

Application procedures. FAFSA required. Priority date 5/16; no closing date. Applicants notified on rolling basis starting 6/15, must reply within 2 week(s) of notification.

Contact. **Financial aid office:** (805) 378-1462
Teri Hernandez, Financial Aid Officer
7075 Campus Road
Moorpark, CA 93021

Mount St. Mary's College

Los Angeles, California
www.msmc.la.edu
Four-year private **Federal Code: 001243**

	Living at home	On-campus
Tuition and fees (2002-2003):	$19,774	$19,774
Room and board:		$7,832
Books and supplies:	$648	$648
Personal expenses:	$1,440	$1,170
Transportation:	$702	$558

Policies to reduce costs. Tuition/fee waivers for children of alumni, employees and their families. Credit/placement for qualifying scores on AP, IB, CLEP examinations.

Payment plans. Credit card, installment, deferred payment.

Application procedures. FAFSA required. Priority date 3/1; no closing date. Applicants notified on rolling basis starting 2/1. **Transfers:** No deadline.

Contact. **Financial aid office:** (310) 954-4195
Jonathan Choy, Director of Financial Aid
12001 Chalon Road
Los Angeles, CA 90049

Mount San Antonio College

Walnut, California
www.mtsac.edu
Two-year public **Federal Code: 001245**

	Living at home
Tuition and fees (projected):	$376
Out-of-state:	$4,666
Per-credit charge:	$11
Per-credit out-of-state:	$152
Books and supplies:	$1,100
Personal expenses:	$5,174

Undergraduate aid. All financial aid based on need. Need-based aid available for full-time and part-time students.

Policies to reduce costs. Credit/placement for qualifying scores on CLEP examinations.

Payment plans. Deferred payment.

Application procedures. FAFSA, institutional form required. Priority date 3/2; no closing date. Applicants notified on rolling basis starting 6/29, must reply within 4 week(s) of notification.

Contact. **Financial aid office:** (909) 594-5611
Susanna Jones, Director Financial Aid
1100 North Grand Avenue
Walnut, CA 91789

Mount San Jacinto College

San Jacinto, California
www.msjc.cc.ca.us
Two-year public **Federal Code: 001246**

	Living at home
Tuition and fees (projected):	$330
Out-of-state:	$4,260
Per-credit charge:	$11
Per-credit out-of-state:	$142
Board only:	$2,998
Books and supplies:	$1,206
Personal expenses:	$2,250
Transportation:	$864

Undergraduate aid. All financial aid based on need. 79% awarded as scholarships/grants, 21% as loans/jobs. Need-based aid available for part-time students. **Additional information:** Board of Governors Grant Program for state residents to defray cost of enrollment fee.

Policies to reduce costs. Credit/placement for qualifying scores on AP, CLEP examinations. Work study available nights and for part-time students.

Payment plans. Credit card, installment payment.

Application procedures. FAFSA, institutional form required. Priority date 3/2; no closing date. Applicants notified on rolling basis starting 5/1, must reply within 3 week(s) of notification. **Transfers:** No deadline.

Contact. **Financial aid office:** (909) 487-6752 ext.1432
Mary Ellen Muehring, Financial Aid Director
1499 North State Street
San Jacinto, CA 92583

Napa Valley College

Napa, California
www.napavalley.edu
Two-year public **Federal Code: 001247**

	Living at home
Tuition and fees (2002-2003):	$332
Out-of-state:	$4,352
Per-credit charge:	$11
Per-credit out-of-state:	$145
Books and supplies:	$630
Personal expenses:	$1,476
Transportation:	$702

Policies to reduce costs. Tuition/fee waivers for adults, minority students. Credit/placement for qualifying scores on AP, CLEP examinations.

Payment plans. Installment, deferred payment.

Application procedures. FAFSA required. Priority date 4/1; no closing date. Applicants notified on rolling basis starting 6/1, must reply within 3 week(s) of notification.

Contact. **Financial aid office:** (702) 253-3020
Jill Schrutz, Dean, Financial Aid
2277 Napa-Vallejo Highway
Napa, CA 94558

National Hispanic University

San Jose, California
www.nhu.edu
Four-year private **Federal Code: 016968**

	Living at home
Tuition and fees (2002-2003):	$3,950

Undergraduate aid. **Need-based:** Average financial aid package for full-time students was $4,000; for part-time $2,000. 87% awarded as scholarships/grants, 13% as loans/jobs. **Non-need-based:** 96% awarded as scholarships/grants, 4% as loans/jobs. Scholarships based on academics. **Student debt:** 10% of graduating class borrowed to fund education; average debt was $5,000.

Freshman aid. **Need-based:** Out of 48 full-time freshmen, 48 applied for aid; 40 were judged to have need; of these 45 received aid. Average package met 50% of need. Average scholarship/grant was $1,500. **Non-need based:** 5 full-time freshmen with need received non-need scholarships; 3 without need received awards.

Application procedures. FAFSA required. No deadline.

Contact. **Financial aid office:** (408) 254-6900
Takeo Kubo, Director, Office of Financial Aid and Scholarship
14271 Story Road
San Jose, CA 95127-3823

National University

La Jolla, California
www.nu.edu
Four-year private **Federal Code: 011460**

	Living at home
Tuition and fees (2002-2003):	$7,965
Books and supplies:	$810
Transportation:	$650

Undergraduate aid. **Need-based:** Need-based aid available for full-time and part-time students.

Policies to reduce costs. Tuition/fee waivers for employees and their families. Credit/placement for qualifying scores on AP, CLEP examinations.

Payment plans. Credit card payment.

Application procedures. FAFSA, institutional form required. No deadline. Applicants notified on rolling basis. **Transfers:** No deadline.

Contact. **Financial aid office:** (800) 628-8648
Matt Levine, Director, Financial Aid
11255 North Torrey Pines Road
La Jolla, CA 92037

Northrop-Rice Aviation Institute of Technology

Inglewood, California
www.nrait.edu
Four-year proprietary

College costs (projected). Cost of 27-month full-time program leading to BS degree: $42,500 including tuition and books. Cost of 6-month full-time program leading to AA degree: $9,500 including tuition and books.

Contact. **Financial aid office:** (310) 568-8541
1155 West Arbor Vitae Street, Suite 115
Inglewood, CA 90301

Northwestern Polytechnic University

Fremont, California
www.npu.edu
Four-year private

	Living at home
Tuition and fees:	$6,040
Books and supplies:	$500

Undergraduate aid. **Additional information:** Federal aid not yet available. Work-study, co-op program, internships available. Many students work for engineering firms that help with costs.

Policies to reduce costs. Tuition/fee waivers for employees and their families. Work study available for part-time students.

Payment plans. Credit card, installment, deferred payment.

Contact. **Financial aid office:** (510) 657-5911
117 Fourier Avenue
Fremont, CA 94539

Occidental College

Los Angeles, California
www.oxy.edu
Four-year private **Federal Code: 001249**

	Living at home	On-campus
Tuition and fees:	$28,298	$28,298
Room and board:		$7,830
Board only:	$3,168	
Books and supplies:	$870	$870
Personal expenses:	$1,520	$1,520
Transportation:	$300	$300

Undergraduate aid. **Need-based:** Need-based aid available for full-time and part-time students. **Non-need-based:** Scholarships based on academics, leadership, music/drama.

Merit scholarships. Margaret Bundy Scott Scholarship: $17,500. President's Scholarship: $12,500. Trustee Scholarship: $10,000. All awarded to top 10-15% of incoming class based on academic achievement, leadership, and citizenship.

Policies to reduce costs. Tuition/fee waivers for employees and their families. Credit/placement for qualifying scores on AP, IB examinations.

Payment plans. Credit card, installment payment.

Application procedures. FAFSA, CSS PROFILE required. Closing date 2/1. Applicants notified by 4/1, must reply by 5/1. Early decision closing date 11/15. **Transfers:** California residents must apply for Cal Grant by completing FAFSA and CSAC's GPA verification form by March 2.

Contact. **Financial aid office:** (323) 259-2500
Maureen Levy, Director of Financial Aid
1600 Campus Road
Los Angeles, CA 90041-3393

Ohlone College
Fremont, California
www.ohlone.cc.ca.us
Two-year public **Federal Code: 004481**

	Living at home
Tuition and fees (projected):	$354
Out-of-state:	$4,374
Per-credit charge:	$11
Per-credit out-of-state:	$145
Board only:	$3,168
Books and supplies:	$810
Personal expenses:	$2,616
Transportation:	$828

Undergraduate aid. Need-based: Need-based aid available for full-time and part-time students. **Non-need-based:** Scholarships based on academics.

Policies to reduce costs. Tuition/fee waivers for adults, children of alumni, senior citizens, minority students, family members, unemployed or children of unemployed, family of clergy, employees and their families. Credit/placement for qualifying scores on AP, IB examinations. Work study available for part-time students.

Payment plans. Deferred payment.

Application procedures. FAFSA, institutional form required. Priority date 7/1; no closing date. Applicants notified on rolling basis starting 7/30, must reply within 2 week(s) of notification.

Contact. Financial aid office: (510) 659-6150
Dennis Putnam, Financial Aid Director
43600 Mission Boulevard
Fremont, CA 94539-0390

Orange Coast College
Costa Mesa, California
www.occ.cccd.edu
Two-year public **Federal Code: 001250**

	Living at home
Tuition and fees (projected):	$378
Out-of-state:	$4,398
Per-credit charge:	$11
Per-credit out-of-state:	$145
Books and supplies:	$1,206
Personal expenses:	$3,150
Transportation:	$864

Undergraduate aid. Need-based: 85% awarded as scholarships/grants, 15% as loans/jobs. Need-based aid available for part-time students. **Non-need-based:** Scholarships based on academics.

Freshman aid. Need-based: Out of 844 full-time freshmen, 844 applied for aid; 832 were judged to have need; of these 832 received aid. 38 students had full need met.

Policies to reduce costs. Tuition/fee waivers for adults, senior citizens, minority students, unemployed or children of unemployed. Credit/placement for qualifying scores on AP, CLEP examinations. Work study available for part-time students.

Payment plans. Credit card payment.

Application procedures. FAFSA, institutional form required. Priority date 3/2; no closing date. Applicants notified on rolling basis, must reply within 2 week(s) of notification.

Contact. Financial aid office: (714) 432-5508
Melissa Moser, Financial Aid Director
2701 Fairview Road
Costa Mesa, CA 92628-5005

Otis College of Art and Design
Los Angeles, California
www.otis.edu
Four-year private **Federal Code: 001251**

	Living at home
Tuition and fees (projected):	$22,892
Books and supplies:	$2,400
Personal expenses:	$1,500
Transportation:	$1,400

Undergraduate aid. Need-based: Average financial aid package for full-time students was $13,042. 59% awarded as scholarships/grants, 41% as loans/jobs. Need-based aid available for part-time students. **Non-need-based:** 61% awarded as scholarships/grants, 39% as loans/jobs. Scholarships based on academics, art. **Student debt:** 78% of graduating class borrowed to fund education; average debt was $24,935.

Freshman aid. Need-based: Out of 143 full-time freshmen, 120 applied for aid; 100 were judged to have need; of these 100 received aid. Average package met 49% of need. Average scholarship/grant was $9,775; average loan $2,386. **Non-need based:** 20 without need received awards.

Policies to reduce costs. Tuition/fee waivers for employees and their families. Credit/placement for qualifying scores on AP examinations. Work study available nights and weekends.

Payment plans. Credit card, installment payment.

Application procedures. FAFSA, institutional form required. Priority date 2/15; no closing date. Applicants notified on rolling basis starting 2/15, must reply within 2 week(s) of notification.

Contact. Financial aid office: (310) 665-6880
Ji Choi, Director of Financial Aid
9045 Lincoln Boulevard
Los Angeles, CA 90045-9785

Pacific Oaks College
Pasadena, California
www.pacificoaks.edu
Upper-division private **Federal Code: 001255**

	Living at home
Tuition and fees (2002-2003):	$17,310
Board only:	$3,600
Books and supplies:	$400
Personal expenses:	$2,700
Transportation:	$1,800

Undergraduate aid. All financial aid based on need. Average financial aid package for full-time students was $10,500; for part-time $10,500. 28% awarded as scholarships/grants, 72% as loans/jobs. **Student debt:** 45% of graduating class borrowed to fund education; average debt was $10,500.

Policies to reduce costs. Tuition/fee waivers for employees and their families. Credit/placement for qualifying scores on CLEP examinations. Work study available nights, weekends and for part-time students.

Payment plans. Credit card, installment payment.

Application procedures. FAFSA, institutional form required. Closing date 4/15. Applicants notified on rolling basis starting 5/1, must reply by 5/15 or within 4 week(s) of notification. **Transfers:** Closing date 4/15.

Contact. Financial aid office: (626) 397-1350
Tracie Matthews, Director of Financial Aid
5 Westmoreland Place
Pasadena, CA 91103

Pacific States University
Los Angeles, California
www.psuca.edu
Four-year private **Federal Code: 031633**

	Living at home
Tuition and fees:	$10,560
Books and supplies:	$800

Undergraduate aid. All financial aid based on need. Need-based aid available for full-time and part-time students.

Policies to reduce costs. Credit/placement for qualifying scores on IB examinations.

Payment plans. Credit card, installment payment.

Application procedures. FAFSA required. No deadline.

Contact. Financial aid office: (323) 731-2383
Mai Diep, Financial Aid Officer
1516 South Western Avenue
Los Angeles, CA 90006

Pacific Union College
Angwin, California
www.puc.edu
Four-year private **Federal Code: 001258**

	Living at home	On-campus
Tuition and fees (projected):	$17,355	$17,355
Room and board:		$4,902
Board only:	$3,168	
Books and supplies:	$1,224	$1,224
Personal expenses:	$2,286	$1,872
Transportation:	$828	$594

Undergraduate aid. All financial aid based on need. 59% awarded as scholarships/grants, 41% as loans/jobs. Need-based aid available for part-time students.

Policies to reduce costs. Tuition/fee waivers for family members, employees and their families. Prepayment discount; credit/placement for qualifying scores on AP, CLEP examinations.

Payment plans. Credit card, deferred payment.

Application procedures. FAFSA, institutional form required. No deadline. Applicants notified on rolling basis, must reply within 3 week(s) of notification.

Contact. **Financial aid office:** (707) 965-7200
Glen Bobst, Director of Student Financial Services
Enrollment Services
Angwin, CA 94508

Palomar College
San Marcos, California
www.palomar.edu
Two-year public **Federal Code: 001260**

	Living at home
Tuition and fees (projected):	$360
Out-of-state:	$4,380
Per-credit charge:	$11
Per-credit out-of-state:	$145
Books and supplies:	$648
Personal expenses:	$1,620
Transportation:	$594

Undergraduate aid. All financial aid based on need. Need-based aid available for full-time and part-time students.

Policies to reduce costs. Credit/placement for qualifying scores on AP, CLEP examinations. Work study available nights and for part-time students.

Application procedures. FAFSA, institutional form required. Priority date 4/1; no closing date. Applicants notified on rolling basis starting 6/1. **Transfers:** No deadline.

Contact. **Financial aid office:** (760) 744-1150
Mary San Agustin, Financial Aid Director
1140 West Mission Road
San Marcos, CA 92069

Patten University
Oakland, California
www.patten.edu
Four-year private **Federal Code: 004490**

	Living at home	On-campus
Tuition and fees:	$9,840	$9,840
Room and board:		$5,800
Books and supplies:	$550	$550
Personal expenses:	$1,595	$1,100
Transportation:	$330	$440

Undergraduate aid. **Need-based:** Need-based aid available for full-time and part-time students. **Non-need-based:** Scholarships based on academics, athletics, state/district residency.

Policies to reduce costs. Tuition/fee waivers for children of alumni, family members, family of clergy, employees and their families. Credit/placement for qualifying scores on AP, CLEP examinations.

Payment plans. Credit card, installment, deferred payment.

Application procedures. FAFSA, institutional form required. Priority date 3/2; closing date 7/15. Applicants notified on rolling basis starting 5/31. **Transfers:** No deadline.

Contact. **Financial aid office:** (510) 261-8500
Dennis Clark, Financial Aid Director
2433 Coolidge Avenue
Oakland, CA 94601-2699

Pepperdine University
Malibu, California
www.pepperdine.edu
Four-year private **Federal Code: 001264**

	Living at home	On-campus
Tuition and fees (2002-2003):	$26,370	$26,370
Room and board:		$7,930
Board only:	$1,000	
Books and supplies:	$500	$500
Personal expenses:	$500	$500
Transportation:	$600	$600

Undergraduate aid. **Need-based:** Average financial aid package for full-time students was $22,611; for part-time $10,642. 68% awarded as scholarships/grants, 32% as loans/jobs. **Non-need-based:** 75% awarded as scholarships/grants, 25% as loans/jobs. Scholarships based on academics, athletics. **Student debt:** 59% of graduating class borrowed to fund education; average debt was $31,179.

Freshman aid. **Need-based:** Out of 607 full-time freshmen, 416 applied for aid; 337 were judged to have need; of these 335 received aid. Average package met 94% of need. 92 students had full need met. Average scholarship/grant was $17,511; average loan $4,181. **Non-need based:** 80 full-time freshmen with need received non-need scholarships; 58 without need received awards; 38 received athletic scholarships.

Policies to reduce costs. Tuition/fee waivers for employees and their families. Credit/placement for qualifying scores on AP, IB, CLEP examinations.

Payment plans. Credit card, installment, deferred payment.

Application procedures. FAFSA, institutional form required. Closing date 2/15. Applicants notified by 4/1, must reply within 2 week(s) of notification.

Contact. **Financial aid office:** (506) 506-4301
Cathy Marcus, Director of Financial Aid
24255 Pacific Coast Highway
Malibu, CA 90263-4392

Pitzer College
Claremont, California
www.pitzer.edu
Four-year private **Federal Code: 001172**

	Living at home	On-campus
Tuition and fees (2002-2003):	$28,256	$28,256
Room and board:		$7,370
Books and supplies:	$900	$900
Personal expenses:	$1,000	$1,000
Transportation:		$500

Undergraduate aid. All financial aid based on need. Average financial aid package for full-time students was $25,947. 75% awarded as scholarships/grants, 25% as loans/jobs. Need-based aid available for part-time students. **Student debt:** 60% of graduating class borrowed to fund education; average debt was $20,900.

Freshman aid. Out of 235 full-time freshmen, 105 applied for aid; 81 were judged to have need; of these 81 received aid. Average package met 100% of need. 81 students had full need met. Average scholarship/grant was $19,326; average loan $2,626.

Policies to reduce costs. Tuition/fee waivers for employees and their families. Credit/placement for qualifying scores on AP, IB examinations.

Payment plans. Credit card, installment payment.

Application procedures. FAFSA, CSS PROFILE required. Closing date 2/1. Applicants notified by 4/1, must reply by 5/1. **Transfers:** Closing date 3/1.

Contact. **Financial aid office:** (909) 621-8208
Margaret Carothers, Director of Financial Aid
1050 North Mills Avenue
Claremont, CA 91711-6101

Platt College: Newport Beach

Newport Beach, California
plattcollege.edu
Two-year proprietary **Federal Code: 026203**

College costs (projected). Full academic program tuition ranges from $8,300 to $22,000.

Undergraduate aid. **Need-based:** Need-based aid available for full-time and part-time students.

Policies to reduce costs. Tuition at time of enrollment guaranteed for 2 years. Work study available nights.

Payment plans. Credit card, installment, deferred payment.

Application procedures. FAFSA, institutional form required. Priority date 3/2; no closing date. Applicants notified on rolling basis starting 1/1.

Contact. **Financial aid office:** (949) 833-2300
Tracy Karp, Corporate Financial Aid Officer
3901 MacArthur Boulevard
Newport Beach, CA 92660

Platt College: Ontario

Ontario, California
plattcollege.edu
Two-year proprietary **Federal Code: 030627**

College costs (2002-2003). Full academic program tuition ranges from $8,300 to $22,000.

Undergraduate aid. **Need-based:** Average financial aid package for full-time students was $14,125. 26% awarded as scholarships/grants, 74% as loans/jobs. Need-based aid available for part-time students. **Student debt:** 68% of graduating class borrowed to fund education; average debt was $14,125.

Merit scholarships. Presidential scholarship: $1,000; based on application and essay; varying number available.

Policies to reduce costs. Tuition/fee waivers for employees and their families. Tuition at time of enrollment guaranteed for 2 years. Work study available nights.

Payment plans. Credit card, installment, deferred payment.

Application procedures. FAFSA, institutional form required. Priority date 3/2; no closing date. Applicants notified on rolling basis starting 1/1. **Transfers:** No deadline.

Contact. **Financial aid office:** (909) 941-9410
Tracy Karp, Corporate Financial Aid Officer
3700 Inland Empire Boulevard
Ontario, CA 91764

Point Loma Nazarene University

San Diego, California
www.ptloma.edu
Four-year private **Federal Code: 001262**

	Living at home	On-campus
Tuition and fees (2002-2003):	$16,260	$16,260
Room and board:		$6,630
Books and supplies:	$1,210	$1,210
Personal expenses:	$2,250	$1,850
Transportation:	$1,090	$720

Undergraduate aid. **Need-based:** Average financial aid package for full-time students was $11,509; for part-time $9,052. 65% awarded as scholarships/grants, 35% as loans/jobs. **Non-need-based:** 55% awarded as scholarships/grants, 45% as loans/jobs. Scholarships based on academics, alumni affiliation, art, athletics, leadership, music/drama, religious affiliation, state/district residency. **Student debt:** 89% of graduating class borrowed to fund education; average debt was $15,022.

Freshman aid. **Need-based:** Out of 995 full-time freshmen, 623 applied for aid; 382 were judged to have need; of these 382 received aid. Average package met 69% of need. 104 students had full need met. Average scholarship/grant was $8,950; average loan $2,338. **Non-need based:** 48 full-time freshmen with need received non-need scholarships; 461 without need received awards.

Policies to reduce costs. Tuition/fee waivers for senior citizens, family members, family of clergy, employees and their families. Credit/placement for qualifying scores on AP, IB, CLEP examinations.

Payment plans. Credit card, installment payment.

Application procedures. FAFSA, institutional form required. Priority date 3/15; no closing date. Applicants notified by 5/30, must reply within 4 week(s) of notification. **Transfers:** No deadline.

Contact. **Financial aid office:** (619) 849-2200
Mary Jane Towne-Denton, Director of Financial Aid
3900 Lomaland Drive
San Diego, CA 92106-2899

Pomona College

Claremont, California
www.pomona.edu
Four-year private **Federal Code: 001173**

	Living at home	On-campus
Tuition and fees:	$27,150	$27,150
Room and board:		$9,980
Board only:	$3,000	
Books and supplies:	$850	$850
Personal expenses:	$1,000	$1,000
Transportation:	$600	$600

Undergraduate aid. All financial aid based on need. Need-based aid available for full-time and part-time students.

Policies to reduce costs. Tuition/fee waivers for employees and their families. Credit/placement for qualifying scores on AP, IB examinations.

Payment plans. Installment payment.

Application procedures. FAFSA, CSS PROFILE required. Closing date 2/1. Applicants notified by 4/10, must reply by 5/1 or within 1 week(s) of notification. Early decision closing date 11/15. **Transfers:** Closing date 3/1. Candidates required to submit finanical aid transcript from previous institution directly to the college.

Contact. **Financial aid office:** (909) 621-8205
Patricia Coye, Director of Financial Aid
333 North College Way
Claremont, CA 91711-6312

Queen of the Holy Rosary College

Fremont, California
www.msjdominicans.org
Two-year private **Federal Code: 030189**

	Living at home
Tuition and fees (projected):	$2,815
Per-credit charge:	$100
Books and supplies:	$150

Undergraduate aid. **Additional information:** Full-time students receive financial aid based on need.

Policies to reduce costs. Tuition/fee waivers for children of alumni, family members.

Application procedures. No deadline.

Contact. **Financial aid office:** (510) 657-2468
Diane Adams, Treasurer
43326 Mission Boulevard
Fremont, CA 94539

Reedley College

Reedley, California
www.reedleycollege.edu
Two-year public **Federal Code: 001308**

	Living at home	On-campus
Tuition and fees (2002-2003):	$354	$354
Out-of-state:	$4,584	$4,584
Per-credit charge:	$11	$11
Per-credit out-of-state:	$152	$152
Room and board:		$4,200
Books and supplies:	$648	$648
Personal expenses:	$1,450	$1,550
Transportation:	$684	$738

Undergraduate aid. All financial aid based on need. Need-based aid available for full-time and part-time students.

Policies to reduce costs. Tuition/fee waivers for adults, minority students, unemployed or children of unemployed. Credit/placement for qualifying scores on AP, CLEP examinations. Work study available for part-time students.

Payment plans. Credit card, installment, deferred payment.

Application procedures. FAFSA required. Priority date 3/2; no closing date. Applicants notified on rolling basis starting 3/2, must reply within 3 week(s) of notification. **Transfers:** Priority date 4/15. March 2 deadline for California grants.

Contact. Financial aid office: (559) 638-3641
Christina Cortes, Director, Financial Aid
995 North Reed
Reedley, CA 93654

Riverside Community College

Riverside, California
rccd.cc.ca.us
Two-year public **Federal Code: 001270**

	Living at home
Tuition and fees (projected):	$370
Out-of-state:	$4,390
Per-credit charge:	$11
Per-credit out-of-state:	$145
Books and supplies:	$1,080
Personal expenses:	$2,250
Transportation:	$864

Undergraduate aid. Need-based: 98% awarded as scholarships/grants, 2% as loans/jobs. Need-based aid available for part-time students. **Non-need-based:** Scholarships based on academics, alumni affiliation, art, leadership, minority status, music/drama, state/district residency.

Policies to reduce costs. Tuition/fee waivers for adults, family members, unemployed or children of unemployed. Credit/placement for qualifying scores on AP, CLEP examinations. Work study available nights, weekends and for part-time students.

Payment plans. Credit card, deferred payment.

Application procedures. FAFSA, institutional form required. Priority date 3/2; no closing date. Applicants notified on rolling basis starting 7/1. **Transfers:** Students who received financial aid at another institution and earned less than 2.0 GPA ineligible for aid during first semester. Students must complete 6 units and earn 2.0 GPA to be eligible.

Contact. Financial aid office: (909) 222-8709
Eugenia Vincent, Director, Financial Aid
4800 Magnolia Avenue
Riverside, CA 92506

St. Mary's College of California

Moraga, California
www.stmarys-ca.edu
Four-year private **Federal Code: 001302**

	Living at home	On-campus
Tuition and fees:	$23,775	$23,775
Room and board:		$9,075
Board only:	$2,592	
Books and supplies:	$846	$846
Personal expenses:	$1,656	$1,476
Transportation:	$756	$558

Undergraduate aid. Need-based: Average financial aid package for full-time students was $20,096; for part-time $8,527. 66% awarded as scholarships/grants, 34% as loans/jobs. **Non-need-based:** 48% awarded as scholarships/grants, 52% as loans/jobs. Scholarships based on academics, alumni affiliation, athletics. **Student debt:** 60% of graduating class borrowed to fund education; average debt was $19,334.

Freshman aid. Need-based: Out of 644 full-time freshmen, 500 applied for aid; 430 were judged to have need; of these 427 received aid. Average package met 85% of need. 126 students had full need met. Average scholarship/grant was $16,090; average loan $2,879. **Non-need based:** 32 full-time freshmen with need received non-need scholarships; 23 without need received awards; 20 received athletic scholarships.

Merit scholarships. Honors at Entrance Scholarship Awards awarded automatically for freshmen with a 3.7 GPA or higher and a combined SAT score of at least 1200, or transfers with over 30 semester units or the equivalent and a 3.5 GPA; for fall term applicants must be admitted by March 1; $6,000 annually. Presidential Scholars Scholarship for freshmen with a 3.8 GPA or higher and a combined SAT score of at least 1350.

Policies to reduce costs. Tuition/fee waivers for family members, employees and their families. Prepayment discount; credit/placement for qualifying scores on AP, IB, CLEP examinations. Work study available nights and weekends.

Payment plans. Credit card, installment payment.

Application procedures. FAFSA required. Priority date 3/2; no closing date. Applicants notified on rolling basis starting 4/15, must reply by 5/1 or within 2 week(s) of notification. **Transfers:** Priority date 3/2. To receive consideration for all types of financial aid, transfer students must be admitted by March 1 prior to enrolling in the following fall term.

Contact. Financial aid office: (925) 631-4370
Billie Jones, Director of Financial Aid
Box 4800
Moraga, CA 94575-4800

Samuel Merritt College

Oakland, California
www.samuelmerritt.edu
Four-year private **Federal Code: 007012**

	Living at home	On-campus
Tuition and fees (2002-2003):	$19,814	$19,814
Room only:		$3,307
Board only:	$2,592	
Books and supplies:	$864	$864
Personal expenses:	$1,800	$1,800
Transportation:	$1,161	$1,161

Undergraduate aid. Need-based: Need-based aid available for full-time and part-time students. **Non-need-based:** Scholarships based on academics. **Additional information:** Ongoing private scholarships available. Students eligible to work in Medical Center (associated with college).

Policies to reduce costs. Credit/placement for qualifying scores on AP, CLEP examinations. Work study available nights, weekends and for part-time students.

Payment plans. Credit card, installment, deferred payment.

Application procedures. FAFSA required. Priority date 3/2; no closing date. Applicants notified on rolling basis starting 4/15, must reply within 2 week(s) of notification. **Transfers:** Priority date 3/2.

Contact. Financial aid office: (510) 869-6511
Mary Robinson, Director of Financial Aid
370 Hawthorne Avenue
Oakland, CA 94609-9954

San Diego City College

San Diego, California
www.sdccd.net
Two-year public **Federal Code: 001273**

	Living at home
Tuition and fees (projected):	$354
Out-of-state:	$4,254
Per-credit charge:	$11
Per-credit out-of-state:	$141
Board only:	$2,457
Books and supplies:	$1,206
Personal expenses:	$1,620
Transportation:	$792

Undergraduate aid. All financial aid based on need. Need-based aid available for full-time and part-time students.

Policies to reduce costs. Tuition/fee waivers for unemployed or children of unemployed, employees and their families. Credit/placement for qualifying scores on AP, CLEP examinations. Work study available for part-time students.

Payment plans. Credit card payment.

Application procedures. FAFSA required. Priority date 4/1; no closing date. Applicants notified on rolling basis starting 7/1, must reply within 4 week(s) of notification. **Transfers:** No deadline. Aid is limited to remaining eligibility based on receipt of aid from previous college.

Contact. **Financial aid office:** (619) 388-3501
Greg Sanchez, Financial Aid Manager
1313 12th Avenue
San Diego, CA 92101

San Diego Mesa College

San Diego, California
www.sandiegomesacollege.net
Two-year public **Federal Code: 001275**

	Living at home
Tuition and fees (projected):	$354
Out-of-state:	$3,954
Per-credit charge:	$11
Per-credit out-of-state:	$131
Board only:	$899
Books and supplies:	$1,206
Personal expenses:	$1,584
Transportation:	$864

Policies to reduce costs. Credit/placement for qualifying scores on AP, CLEP examinations.

Payment plans. Credit card payment.

Application procedures. FAFSA required. Priority date 3/2; no closing date. Applicants notified on rolling basis starting 6/15, must reply within 3 week(s) of notification. **Transfers:** No deadline.

Contact. **Financial aid office:** (619) 388-2817
Gilda Maldonado, Financial Aid Officer
7250 Mesa College Drive
San Diego, CA 92111

San Diego State University

San Diego, California
www.sdsu.edu
Four-year public **Federal Code: 001151**

	Living at home	On-campus
Tuition and fees (2002-2003):	$1,870	$1,870
Out-of-state:	$10,330	$10,330
Room and board:		$7,970
Board only:	$2,443	
Books and supplies:	$810	$810
Personal expenses:	$2,026	$1,885
Transportation:	$661	$641

Undergraduate aid. **Need-based:** Average financial aid package for full-time students was $8,000; for part-time $7,200. 43% awarded as scholarships/grants, 57% as loans/jobs. **Non-need-based:** 31% awarded as scholarships/grants, 69% as loans/jobs. Scholarships based on academics, alumni affiliation, art, athletics, leadership, music/drama, state/district residency. **Student debt:** 48% of graduating class borrowed to fund education; average debt was $13,000.

Freshman aid. **Need-based:** Average package met 65% of need. Average scholarship/grant was $4,500; average loan $2,500.

Merit scholarships. First Time Freshman Awards: 8-10 awarded; $1,250 per semester for 4 years; based on 3.5 overall GPA. Grant Trust Scholarship Award: 2 awarded; includes costs of campus housing, fees, and books; based on incoming freshman status, intended biology major with 3.5 overall GPA. Field Family Scholarship: 2 awarded each 2 years; includes costs of campus housing, fees and books for up to 5 years; based on maintenance of satisfactory student performance. Conrad Klement Memorial Scholarship: 2-6 awarded; $2,500 - $10,000 per year; permanent resident of San Diego County; parents and students must be U.S. citizens at birth; 3.0 GPA.

Policies to reduce costs. Tuition/fee waivers for senior citizens, employees and their families. Credit/placement for qualifying scores on AP, IB, CLEP examinations. Work study available nights, weekends and for part-time students.

Payment plans. Installment, deferred payment.

Application procedures. FAFSA required. No deadline. Applicants notified on rolling basis starting 2/15. **Transfers:** Priority date 3/2; no deadline.

Contact. **Financial aid office:** (619) 594-6323
Chrys Dutton, Director of Financial Aid
5500 Campanile Drive
San Diego, CA 92182-7455

San Francisco State University

San Francisco, California
www.sfsu.edu
Four-year public **Federal Code: 001154**

	Living at home	On-campus
Tuition and fees (2002-2003):	$1,826	$1,826
Out-of-state:	$10,286	$10,286
Room and board:		$7,830
Board only:	$2,468	
Books and supplies:	$810	$810
Personal expenses:	$2,020	$2,020
Transportation:	$810	$810

Undergraduate aid. All financial aid based on need. Average financial aid package for full-time students was $8,202; for part-time $6,520. 43% awarded as scholarships/grants, 57% as loans/jobs. **Student debt:** 39% of graduating class borrowed to fund education; average debt was $31,491.

Freshman aid. Out of 2,133 full-time freshmen, 1,318 applied for aid; 1,002 were judged to have need; of these 926 received aid. Average package met 69% of need. 150 students had full need met. Average scholarship/grant was $5,204; average loan $2,671.

Policies to reduce costs. Tuition/fee waivers for senior citizens. Credit/placement for qualifying scores on AP, IB, CLEP examinations.

Payment plans. Credit card, installment payment.

Application procedures. FAFSA required. Priority date 3/2; no closing date. Applicants notified on rolling basis starting 1/31, must reply within 3 week(s) of notification.

Contact. **Financial aid office:** (415) 338-1111
Barbara Hubler, Director of Financial Aid
1600 Holloway Avenue
San Francisco, CA 94132

San Joaquin Delta College

Stockton, California
www.deltacollege.edu
Two-year public **Federal Code: 001280**

	Living at home
Tuition and fees (projected):	$330
Out-of-state:	$4,470
Per-credit charge:	$11
Per-credit out-of-state:	$149
Board only:	$280
Books and supplies:	$800
Personal expenses:	$1,400
Transportation:	$900

Undergraduate aid. All financial aid based on need. Average financial aid package for full-time students was $1,595; for part-time $3,134. 96% awarded as scholarships/grants, 4% as loans/jobs. **Student debt:** 100% of graduating class borrowed to fund education; average debt was $2,940. **Additional information:** Enrollment fee waivers available for low-income California residents.

Freshman aid. Out of 655 full-time freshmen, 653 applied for aid; 651 were judged to have need; of these 651 received aid. Average package met 30% of need. 11 students had full need met. Average scholarship/grant was $1,609; average loan $343.

Policies to reduce costs. Tuition/fee waivers for employees and their families. Credit/placement for qualifying scores on AP, IB, CLEP examinations. Work study available nights, weekends and for part-time students.

Payment plans. Credit card, installment payment.

Application procedures. FAFSA, institutional form required. Priority date 4/15; no closing date. Applicants notified on rolling basis starting 5/1, must reply within 3 week(s) of notification.

Contact. **Financial aid office:** (209) 954-5115
Ena Hull, Director of Financial Aid
5151 Pacific Avenue
Stockton, CA 95207-6370

San Jose Christian College

San Jose, California
www.christianity.edu
Four-year private **Federal Code: 001281**

	Living at home	On-campus
Tuition and fees (2002-2003):	$10,755	$10,755
Room and board:		$5,475
Books and supplies:	$648	$648
Personal expenses:	$1,485	$1,215
Transportation:	$693	$549

Policies to reduce costs. Tuition/fee waivers for employees and their families. Credit/placement for qualifying scores on AP, CLEP examinations.

Payment plans. Installment payment.

Application procedures. FAFSA, institutional form required. Priority date 3/2; closing date 8/1. Applicants notified on rolling basis starting 6/1, must reply within 3 week(s) of notification.

Contact. **Financial aid office:** (408) 278-4300
Judi Carpenter, Director of Financial Aid
790 South 12th Street
San Jose, CA 95112

San Jose State University

San Jose, California
www.sjsu.edu
Four-year public **Federal Code: 001155**

	Living at home	On-campus
Tuition and fees (2002-2003):	$1,915	$1,915
Out-of-state:	$10,375	$10,375
Room and board:		$8,136
Books and supplies:	$810	$810
Personal expenses:	$2,281	$1,914
Transportation:	$738	$558

Undergraduate aid. All financial aid based on need. Average financial aid package for full-time students was $7,562; for part-time $6,238. 70% awarded as scholarships/grants, 30% as loans/jobs. **Student debt:** 30% of graduating class borrowed to fund education; average debt was $9,739.

Freshman aid. Out of 2,517 full-time freshmen, 1,682 applied for aid; 1,227 were judged to have need; of these 1,132 received aid. Average package met 80% of need. 345 students had full need met. Average scholarship/grant was $5,538; average loan $2,394.

Policies to reduce costs. Tuition/fee waivers for senior citizens, employees and their families. Credit/placement for qualifying scores on AP, IB, CLEP examinations. Work study available nights, weekends and for part-time students.

Payment plans. Credit card, installment payment.

Application procedures. FAFSA required. Priority date 3/2; no closing date. Applicants notified on rolling basis starting 4/15, must reply within 2 week(s) of notification. **Transfers:** No deadline.

Contact. **Financial aid office:** (408) 283-7500
Colleen Brown, Director of Financial Aid
One Washington Square
San Jose, CA 95192-0009

Santa Barbara Business College

Santa Barbara, California
www.sbbcollege.net
Two-year proprietary

College costs. Full cost of typical associate degree program including tuition, books and fees; $15,825.

Application procedures. FAFSA required. Applicants notified on rolling basis.

Contact. **Financial aid office:** (805) 967-9677
Mary Castodio, Financial Aid Official
5266 Hollister Avenue
Santa Barbara, CA 93111

Santa Barbara Business College: Bakersfield

Bakersfield, California
www.sbbcollege.com
Two-year proprietary

College costs. Full cost of typical associate degree program including tuition, books, fees: $15,825.

Application procedures. FAFSA required. Applicants notified on rolling basis.

Contact. **Financial aid office:** (661) 835-1100
Mary Castodio, Financial Aid Officer
211 South Real Road
Bakersfield, CA 93309

Santa Barbara Business College: Santa Maria

Santa Maria, California
www.sbbcollege.com
Two-year proprietary

College costs. Full cost of typical associate degree program including tuition, books and fees; $15,825.

Application procedures. Applicants notified on rolling basis.

Contact. **Financial aid office:** (805) 922-8256
Mary Castodio, Financial Aid Officer
303 East Plaza Drive
Santa Maria, CA 93454

Santa Barbara City College

Santa Barbara, California
www.sbcc.edu
Two-year public **Federal Code: 001285**

	Living at home
Tuition and fees (projected):	$395
Out-of-state:	$4,625
Per-credit charge:	$11
Per-credit out-of-state:	$145
Books and supplies:	$1,206
Personal expenses:	$1,962
Transportation:	$803

Undergraduate aid. Need-based: 76% awarded as scholarships/grants, 24% as loans/jobs. Need-based aid available for part-time students. **Additional information:** California residents may qualify for Board of Governor's Financial Assistance Program which will allow institutions to waive enrollment fee.

Policies to reduce costs. Tuition/fee waivers for unemployed or children of unemployed. Credit/placement for qualifying scores on AP, IB examinations.

Payment plans. Deferred payment.

Application procedures. FAFSA required. No deadline. Applicants notified on rolling basis starting 5/1, must reply within 2 week(s) of notification.

Contact. **Financial aid office:** (805) 965-0581 ext. 2716
Brad Hardison, Director, Financial Aid
721 Cliff Drive
Santa Barbara, CA 93109-2394

Santa Clara University

Santa Clara, California
www.scu.edu
Four-year private **Federal Code: 001326**

	Living at home	On-campus
Tuition and fees:	$25,625	$25,625
Room and board:		$9,336
Board only:	$3,168	
Books and supplies:	$1,224	$1,224
Personal expenses:	$2,286	$1,872
Transportation:	$828	$594

Undergraduate aid. Need-based: Average financial aid package for full-time students was $14,718. 80% awarded as scholarships/grants, 20% as loans/jobs. Need-based aid available for part-time students. **Non-need-based:** 48% awarded as scholarships/grants, 52% as loans/jobs. Scholarships based on academics, alumni affiliation, athletics, music/drama. **Student debt:** 61% of graduating class borrowed to fund education; average debt was $22,869.

Freshman aid. Need-based: Out of 1,018 full-time freshmen, 768 applied for aid; 523 were judged to have need; of these 484 received aid. Average package met 83% of need. 247 students had full need met. Average scholarship/grant was $12,292; average loan $3,104. **Non-need based:** 85 full-time freshmen with need received non-need scholarships; 354 without need received awards; 53 received athletic scholarships.

Merit scholarships. Dean's Scholarship: $5,000; to students admitted with distinction. Ignation Scholarship: $7,500; to 1 student from each of the 5 western province Jesuit high schools. Bannan Merit Scholarship: $1,000; based on high academic achievement. Jesuit Scholars Award; $1,000 to $5,000, based on being in top 50 outstanding Jesuit High School graduates.

Policies to reduce costs. Tuition/fee waivers for children of alumni, family members, employees and their families. Credit/placement for qualifying scores on AP, IB examinations.

Payment plans. Credit card, installment, deferred payment.

Application procedures. FAFSA, CSS PROFILE required. Priority date 2/1; no closing date. Applicants notified on rolling basis starting 4/1, must reply by 5/1 or within 2 week(s) of notification. **Transfers:** Priority date 3/2; no deadline.

Contact. **Financial aid office:** (408) 554-4505
Richard Toomey, Dean of Enrollment Services
500 El Camino Real
Santa Clara, CA 95053

Santa Monica College

Santa Monica, California
www.smc.edu
Two-year public **Federal Code: 001286**

College costs. Students may also pay annual $16 I.D. card, $20 associated student fees.

	Living at home
Tuition and fees (projected):	$354
Out-of-state:	$4,584
Per-credit charge:	$11
Per-credit out-of-state:	$152
Books and supplies:	$670

Undergraduate aid. Need-based: 90% awarded as scholarships/grants, 10% as loans/jobs. Need-based aid available for part-time students.

Policies to reduce costs. Credit/placement for qualifying scores on AP, CLEP examinations.

Payment plans. Credit card, deferred payment.

Application procedures. FAFSA, institutional form required. No deadline. Applicants notified on rolling basis starting 7/1, must reply within 2 week(s) of notification. **Transfers:** No deadline.

Contact. **Financial aid office:** (310) 434-4343
Heidi Granger, Director of Financial Aid
1900 Pico Boulevard
Santa Monica, CA 90405-1628

Santa Rosa Junior College

Santa Rosa, California
www.santarosa.edu
Two-year public **Federal Code: 001287**

	Living at home	On-campus
Tuition and fees (2002-2003):	$354	$354
Out-of-state:	$5,004	$5,004
Per-credit charge:	$11	$11
Per-credit out-of-state:	$166	$166
Room only:		$2,680
Board only:	$2,988	
Books and supplies:	$1,206	$1,206
Personal expenses:	$2,250	$2,250
Transportation:	$864	$864

Undergraduate aid. All financial aid based on need. 72% awarded as scholarships/grants, 28% as loans/jobs. Need-based aid available for part-time students. **Additional information:** California's Board of Governors Program (BOG) provides fee waivers for applicants with need, welfare recipients, and families with low income levels.

Policies to reduce costs. Credit/placement for qualifying scores on AP, IB examinations. Work study available nights, weekends and for part-time students.

Payment plans. Credit card, installment, deferred payment.

Application procedures. FAFSA required. Priority date 3/2; no closing date. Applicants notified on rolling basis starting 3/28, must reply within 4 week(s) of notification.

Contact. **Financial aid office:** (707) 527-4478
Kristin Shear, Director of Financial Aid
1501 Mendocino Avenue
Santa Rosa, CA 95401

Scripps College

Claremont, California
www.scrippscollege.edu
Four-year private **Federal Code: 001174**

	Living at home	On-campus
Tuition and fees (2002-2003):	$25,700	$25,700
Room and board:		$8,300
Board only:	$2,464	
Books and supplies:	$800	$800
Personal expenses:	$1,550	$1,000

Undergraduate aid. Need-based: Average financial aid package for full-time students was $23,802. 81% awarded as scholarships/grants, 19% as loans/jobs. Need-based aid available for part-time students. **Non-need-based:** 51% awarded as scholarships/grants, 49% as loans/jobs. Scholarships based on academics, leadership. **Student debt:** 52% of graduating class borrowed to fund education; average debt was $12,941.

Freshman aid. Need-based: Out of 224 full-time freshmen, 140 applied for aid; 110 were judged to have need; of these 110 received aid. Average package met 100% of need. 110 students had full need met. Average scholarship/grant was $20,140; average loan $2,998. **Non-need based:** 23 full-time freshmen with need received non-need scholarships; 19 without need received awards.

Merit scholarships. James E. Scripps Scholarship for distinguished young women whose intellectual and personal promise can be developed with a Scripps education; financial aid available to recipients exhibiting further need.

Policies to reduce costs. Tuition/fee waivers for employees and their families. Credit/placement for qualifying scores on AP, IB, CLEP examinations.

Payment plans. Credit card, installment payment.

Application procedures. FAFSA, CSS PROFILE required. Priority date 2/1; no closing date. Applicants notified by 4/1, must reply by 5/1 or within 2 week(s) of notification. Early decision closing date 11/1. **Transfers:** Priority date 3/1; no deadline. Students applying for admission as a transfer student should be aware that financial aid may be limited or unavailable.

Contact. **Financial aid office:** (909) 621-8275
Sean Smith, Director of Financial Aid
1030 North Columbia Avenue
Claremont, CA 91711

Shasta College

Redding, California
www.shastacollege.edu
Two-year public **Federal Code: 001289**

	Living at home	On-campus
Tuition and fees (2002-2003):	$385	$385
Out-of-state:	$4,975	$4,975
Per-credit charge:	$11	$11
Per-credit out-of-state:	$164	$164
Room only:		$3,200
Books and supplies:	$810	$810
Personal expenses:	$1,500	$1,350
Transportation:	$738	$558

Undergraduate aid. All financial aid based on need. 76% awarded as scholarships/grants, 24% as loans/jobs. Need-based aid available for part-time students.

Policies to reduce costs. Credit/placement for qualifying scores on AP examinations.

Payment plans. Credit card payment.

Application procedures. FAFSA, institutional form required. Priority date 3/2; no closing date. Applicants notified on rolling basis starting 7/1.

Contact. **Financial aid office:** (530) 225-4735
Benna Starrett, Financial Aid Office Manager
Box 496006
Redding, CA 96049-6006

Sierra College

Rocklin, California
www.sierracollege.edu
Two-year public **Federal Code: 001290**

	Living at home	On-campus
Tuition and fees (projected):	$354	$354
Out-of-state:	$4,524	$4,524
Per-credit charge:	$11	$11
Per-credit out-of-state:	$150	$150
Room and board:		$5,990
Board only:	$2,592	
Books and supplies:	$1,206	$1,206
Personal expenses:	$1,574	$1,574
Transportation:	$612	$612

Undergraduate aid. Need-based: Need-based aid available for full-time and part-time students.

Policies to reduce costs. Tuition/fee waivers for unemployed or children of unemployed. Credit/placement for qualifying scores on AP examinations. Work study available nights, weekends and for part-time students.

Payment plans. Installment, deferred payment.

Application procedures. FAFSA required. Priority date 3/2; closing date 4/22. Applicants notified on rolling basis starting 4/15. **Transfers:** No deadline.

Contact. **Financial aid office:** (916) 781-0568
Craig Yamamoto, Financial Services Program Manager
5000 Rocklin Road
Rocklin, CA 95677

Simpson College

Redding, California
www.simpsonca.edu
Four-year private **Federal Code: 001291**

	Living at home	On-campus
Tuition and fees (2002-2003):	$12,550	$12,550
Room and board:		$5,410
Board only:	$2,484	
Books and supplies:	$725	$725
Personal expenses:	$1,485	$1,215
Transportation:	$616	$488

Undergraduate aid. All financial aid based on need. Need-based aid available for full-time students.

Policies to reduce costs. Tuition/fee waivers for family members, family of clergy, employees and their families. Credit/placement for qualifying scores on AP, CLEP examinations.

Payment plans. Credit card, installment, deferred payment.

Application procedures. FAFSA, institutional form required. Priority date 3/1; no closing date. Applicants notified on rolling basis starting 3/30, must reply within 3 week(s) of notification. **Transfers:** Priority date 3/2; no deadline.

Contact. **Financial aid office:** (530) 226-4606
Jim Herberger, Director of Student Financial Services
2211 College View Drive
Redding, CA 96003-8606

Sonoma State University

Rohnert Park, California
www.sonoma.edu
Four-year public **Federal Code: 001156**

	Living at home	On-campus
Tuition and fees (2002-2003):	$2,226	$2,226
Out-of-state:	$10,866	$10,866
Room and board:		$7,545
Books and supplies:	$846	$846
Personal expenses:	$1,710	$1,584
Transportation:	$756	$630

Undergraduate aid. Need-based: Average financial aid package for full-time students was $8,411; for part-time $8,078. 42% awarded as scholarships/grants, 58% as loans/jobs. **Non-need-based:** 11% awarded as scholarships/grants, 89% as loans/jobs. Scholarships based on academics, alumni affiliation, art, athletics, leadership, minority status, music/drama, state/district residency. **Student debt:** 85% of graduating class borrowed to fund education; average debt was $15,000.

Freshman aid. Need-based: Out of 1,204 full-time freshmen, 791 applied for aid; 611 were judged to have need; of these 598 received aid. Average package met 39% of need. 239 students had full need met. Average scholarship/grant was $5,629; average loan $3,077. **Non-need based:** 147 full-time freshmen with need received non-need scholarships; 173 without need received awards; 11 received athletic scholarships.

Policies to reduce costs. Tuition/fee waivers for employees and their families. Credit/placement for qualifying scores on AP, CLEP examinations.

Payment plans. Credit card, deferred payment.

Application procedures. FAFSA required. Priority date 1/31; no closing date. Applicants notified on rolling basis starting 3/15, must reply within 4 week(s) of notification.

Contact. **Financial aid office:** (707) 664-2880
Susan Gutierrez, Interim Director, Financial Aid
1801 East Cotati Avenue
Rohnert Park, CA 94928

Southern California Institute of Architecture

Los Angeles, California
www.sciarc.edu
Five-year private **Federal Code: 014073**

	Living at home
Tuition and fees (2002-2003):	$17,406
Board only:	$3,474
Books and supplies:	$1,502
Personal expenses:	$2,048
Transportation:	$1,232

Policies to reduce costs. Credit/placement for qualifying scores on AP, CLEP examinations.

Payment plans. Credit card payment.

Application procedures. Institutional form required. Priority date 3/2; closing date 5/1. Applicants notified on rolling basis starting 5/1, must reply within 2 week(s) of notification.

Contact. **Financial aid office:** (213) 613-2200
Odessa Mathis, Coordinator of Financial Aid
960 East 3rd Street
Los Angeles, CA 90013

Southwestern College

Chula Vista, California
www.swc.cc.ca.us
Two-year public **Federal Code: 001294**

	Living at home
Tuition and fees (projected):	$364
Out-of-state:	$4,384
Per-credit charge:	$11
Per-credit out-of-state:	$145
Books and supplies:	$887
Personal expenses:	$1,656
Transportation:	$738

Undergraduate aid. **Need-based:** 90% awarded as scholarships/grants, 10% as loans/jobs. Need-based aid available for part-time students.

Policies to reduce costs. Credit/placement for qualifying scores on AP, IB, CLEP examinations. Work study available nights, weekends and for part-time students.

Payment plans. Credit card payment.

Application procedures. FAFSA required. Priority date 3/1; no closing date. Applicants notified on rolling basis starting 7/1.

Contact. **Financial aid office:** (619) 482-6359
Arthur Lopez, Director of Financial Aid
900 Otay Lakes Road
Chula Vista, CA 91910

Stanford University

Stanford, California
www.stanford.edu
Four-year private **Federal Code: 001305**

	Living at home	On-campus
Tuition and fees (2002-2003):	$27,549	$27,549
Room and board:		$8,680
Books and supplies:	$1,155	$1,155

Undergraduate aid. All financial aid based on need. Average financial aid package for full-time students was $24,648. 85% awarded as scholarships/grants, 15% as loans/jobs. **Student debt:** 45% of graduating class borrowed to fund education; average debt was $15,782.

Freshman aid. Out of 1,618 full-time freshmen, 1,019 applied for aid; 767 were judged to have need; of these 760 received aid. Average package met 100% of need. 747 students had full need met. Average scholarship/grant was $22,839; average loan $2,089.

Policies to reduce costs. Credit/placement for qualifying scores on AP, IB examinations.

Payment plans. Installment, deferred payment.

Application procedures. FAFSA, CSS PROFILE required. Priority date 2/1; no closing date. Applicants notified on rolling basis starting 4/2, must reply by 5/1. Early decision closing date 11/1. **Transfers:** Closing date 3/15.

Contact. **Financial aid office:** (650) 723-3058
Robin Mamlet, Dean, Undergraduate Admissions/Financial Aid
Old Union, Second Floor
Stanford, CA 94305-3005

Taft College

Taft, California
www.taft.cc.ca.us
Two-year public **Federal Code: 001309**

	Living at home	On-campus
Tuition and fees (projected):	$405	$405
Out-of-state:	$4,635	$4,635
Per-credit charge:	$11	$11
Per-credit out-of-state:	$152	$152
Room and board:		$2,720
Board only:	$2,782	
Books and supplies:	$500	$500
Personal expenses:	$1,656	$1,476
Transportation:	$792	$684

Undergraduate aid. **Need-based:** 84% awarded as scholarships/grants, 16% as loans/jobs. Need-based aid available for part-time students. **Non-need-based:** Scholarships based on academics.

Merit scholarships. Taft College Merit Awards; $250; available for 2 years; based on GPA of 3.0 or higher; for students from local high schools. Taft College High School Merit Award; $600; for students from local high schools. Taft College Nonresident Awards; $4,230; available for 1 year; based on GPA of 3.0 or higher and is applied to nonresident tuition.

Policies to reduce costs. Credit/placement for qualifying scores on AP examinations. Work study available nights, weekends and for part-time students.

Payment plans. Credit card, installment, deferred payment.

Application procedures. FAFSA, institutional form required. Priority date 1/1; no closing date. Applicants notified on rolling basis starting 7/1, must reply within 4 week(s) of notification. **Transfers:** Priority date 1/1; no deadline.

Contact. **Financial aid office:** (661) 763-7762
Gayle Roberts, Director of Financial Aid and Admissions
29 Emmons Park Drive
Taft, CA 93268

Thomas Aquinas College

Santa Paula, California
www.thomasaquinas.edu
Four-year private **Federal Code: G23580**

	Living at home	On-campus
Tuition and fees:	$17,000	$17,000
Room and board:		$5,000
Books and supplies:	$450	$450
Personal expenses:	$2,286	$1,872
Transportation:	$828	$594

Undergraduate aid. All financial aid based on need. Average financial aid package for full-time students was $13,480. 61% awarded as scholarships/grants, 39% as loans/jobs. **Student debt:** 75% of graduating class borrowed to fund education; average debt was $13,250.

Freshman aid. Out of 102 full-time freshmen, 81 applied for aid; 74 were judged to have need; of these 74 received aid. Average package met 100% of need. 74 students had full need met. Average scholarship/grant was $9,371; average loan $2,697.

Policies to reduce costs. Prepayment discount. Work study available nights and weekends.

Payment plans. Credit card, installment payment.

Application procedures. FAFSA, institutional form required. No deadline. Applicants notified on rolling basis starting 11/1, must reply within 4 week(s) of notification.

Contact. **Financial aid office:** (800) 634-9797
Gregory Becher, Director of Financial Aid
10000 North Ojai Road
Santa Paula, CA 93060

Travel University International

San Diego, California
www.traveluniversity.edu
Two-year proprietary **Federal Code: 016799**

College costs. Reported costs are for associate degree programs. Cost of certificate programs is $3,995 including all tuition, textbooks, supplies through conclusion of program.

	Living at home
Tuition and fees:	$7,100
Per-credit charge:	$125
Board only:	$2,176
Books and supplies:	$550
Personal expenses:	$1,376
Transportation:	$656

Undergraduate aid. All financial aid based on need. Need-based aid available for full-time and part-time students.

Policies to reduce costs. Tuition at time of enrollment guaranteed for 2 years.

Payment plans. Credit card, installment payment.

Application procedures. FAFSA required. No deadline. Applicants notified on rolling basis. **Transfers:** No deadline.

Contact. **Financial aid office:** (858) 292-9755
Senol Sahin, Financial Aid
3870 Murphy Canyon Road, Suite 310
San Diego, CA 92123

University of California: Berkeley

Berkeley, California
www.berkeley.edu
Four-year public **Federal Code: 001312**

	Living at home	On-campus
Tuition and fees (2002-2003):	$4,091	$4,091
Out-of-state:	$15,163	$15,163
Room and board:		$9,682
Board only:	$1,274	
Books and supplies:	$1,108	$1,108
Personal expenses:	$1,390	$1,156
Transportation:	$994	$604

Undergraduate aid. **Need-based:** Average financial aid package for full-time students was $11,952; for part-time $10,202. 67% awarded as scholarships/grants, 33% as loans/jobs. **Non-need-based:** 39% awarded as scholarships/grants, 61% as loans/jobs. Scholarships based on academics, athletics. **Student debt:** 36% of graduating class borrowed to fund education; average debt was $14,990.

Freshman aid. **Need-based:** Out of 3,578 full-time freshmen, 2,740 applied for aid; 1,732 were judged to have need; of these 1,706 received aid. Average package met 93% of need. 983 students had full need met. Average scholarship/grant was $9,663; average loan $4,103. **Non-need based:** 70 full-time freshmen with need received non-need scholarships; 643 without need received awards; 83 received athletic scholarships.

Merit scholarships. University Scholarship, President's Undergraduate Fellowships, Regents and Chancellor's Scholarships, Alumni Scholarships, and Institutional National Merit Scholarships.

Policies to reduce costs. Credit/placement for qualifying scores on AP, IB examinations.

Payment plans. Installment payment.

Application procedures. FAFSA required. Closing date 3/2. Applicants notified on rolling basis starting 4/15.

Contact. **Financial aid office:** (510) 642-6000
Richard Black, Director, Financial Aid
110 Sproul Hall, #5800
Berkeley, CA 94720

University of California: Davis

Davis, California
www.ucdavis.edu
Four-year public **Federal Code: 001313**

	Living at home	On-campus
Tuition and fees (2002-2003):	$4,601	$4,601
Out-of-state:	$15,674	$15,674
Room and board:		$7,892
Board only:	$3,471	
Books and supplies:	$1,214	$1,214
Personal expenses:	$1,982	$1,792
Transportation:	$1,477	$945

Policies to reduce costs. Credit/placement for qualifying scores on AP examinations.

Payment plans. Credit card, installment payment.

Application procedures. FAFSA required. Closing date 3/1. Applicants notified on rolling basis starting 4/1, must reply within 3 week(s) of notification.

Contact. **Financial aid office:** (530) 752-1011
Patricia Kearney, Director, Financial Aid
175 Mrak Hall
Davis, CA 95616

University of California: Irvine

Irvine, California
www.uci.edu
Four-year public **Federal Code: 001314**

	Living at home	On-campus
Tuition and fees (2002-2003):	$4,556	$4,556
Out-of-state:	$15,630	$15,630
Room and board:		$7,032
Board only:	$2,180	
Books and supplies:	$1,355	$1,355
Personal expenses:	$1,515	$1,330
Transportation:	$1,855	$1,120

Undergraduate aid. **Need-based:** Need-based aid available for full-time and part-time students. **Non-need-based:** Scholarships based on academics, athletics, state/district residency.

Policies to reduce costs. Credit/placement for qualifying scores on AP, IB examinations. Work study available nights, weekends and for part-time students.

Payment plans. Installment payment.

Application procedures. FAFSA required. Priority date 3/2; closing date 5/1. Applicants notified by 4/15, must reply by 5/1 or within 3 week(s) of notification.

Contact. **Financial aid office:** (949) 824-8262
Brent Yunek, Director of Financial Aid
204 Administration Building
Irvine, CA 92697-1075

University of California: Los Angeles

Los Angeles, California
www.ucla.edu
Four-year public **Federal Code: 001315**

	Living at home	On-campus
Tuition and fees (2002-2003):	$4,230	$4,230
Out-of-state:	$15,303	$15,303
Room and board:		$8,991
Board only:	$2,874	
Books and supplies:	$1,290	$1,290
Personal expenses:	$1,569	$1,368
Transportation:	$1,821	$747

Undergraduate aid. **Need-based:** Average financial aid package for full-time students was $10,905; for part-time $9,751. 66% awarded as scholarships/grants, 34% as loans/jobs. **Non-need-based:** 28% awarded as scholarships/grants, 72% as loans/jobs. Scholarships based on academics, athletics. **Student debt:** 44% of graduating class borrowed to fund education; average debt was $12,886.

Freshman aid. **Need-based:** Out of 4,091 full-time freshmen, 2,753 applied for aid; 1,997 were judged to have need; of these 1,997 received aid. Average package met 84% of need. 1160 students had full need met. Average scholarship/grant was $8,534; average loan $3,996. **Non-need based:** 47 full-time freshmen with need received non-need scholarships; 570 without need received awards; 43 received athletic scholarships.

Policies to reduce costs. Credit/placement for qualifying scores on AP, IB examinations.

Payment plans. Credit card payment.

Application procedures. FAFSA required. Priority date 3/2; no closing date. Applicants notified on rolling basis starting 3/15, must reply within 3 week(s) of notification.

Contact. **Financial aid office:** (310) 825-4321
Ronald Johnson, Director, Financial Aid Office
1147 Murphy Hall
Los Angeles, CA 90095

University of California: Riverside

Riverside, California
www.ucr.edu
Four-year public **Federal Code: 001316**

	Living at home	On-campus
Tuition and fees (2002-2003):	$4,379	$4,379
Out-of-state:	$15,449	$15,449
Room and board:		$7,200
Board only:	$2,000	
Books and supplies:	$1,300	$1,300
Personal expenses:	$1,800	$1,800
Transportation:	$1,500	$1,100

Undergraduate aid. **Need-based:** Average financial aid package for full-time students was $9,274; for part-time $6,239. 62% awarded as scholarships/grants, 38% as loans/jobs. **Non-need-based:** 28% awarded as scholarships/grants, 72% as loans/jobs. Scholarships based on academics, art, athletics, leadership, music/drama. **Student debt:** 72% of graduating class borrowed to fund education; average debt was $13,226.

Freshman aid. **Need-based:** Out of 2,609 full-time freshmen, 2,127 applied for aid; 1,656 were judged to have need; of these 1,574 received aid. Average package met 82% of need. 584 students had full need met. Average scholarship/grant was $7,648; average loan $2,467. **Non-need based:** 369 full-time freshmen with need received non-need scholarships; 464 without need received awards; 31 received athletic scholarships.

Policies to reduce costs. Credit/placement for qualifying scores on AP, IB examinations. Work study available nights, weekends and for part-time students.

Payment plans. Installment, deferred payment.

Application procedures. FAFSA required. Priority date 3/2; no closing date. Applicants notified on rolling basis starting 3/1, must reply by 5/1 or within 3 week(s) of notification.

Contact. **Financial aid office:** (909) 787-3878
Sheryl Hayes, Director of Financial Aid
1138 Hinderaker Hall
Riverside, CA 92521

University of California: San Diego

La Jolla, California
www.ucsd.edu
Four-year public **Federal Code: 001317**

College costs. Required $936 insurance fee for international students.

	Living at home	On-campus
Tuition and fees (2002-2003):	$4,358	$4,358
Out-of-state:	$15,878	$15,878
Room and board:		$8,172
Books and supplies:	$1,225	$1,225
Personal expenses:	$1,943	$1,786
Transportation:	$1,580	$951

Undergraduate aid. **Need-based:** Average financial aid package for full-time students was $10,407. 54% awarded as scholarships/grants, 46% as loans/jobs. Need-based aid available for part-time students. **Non-need-based:** 46% awarded as scholarships/grants, 54% as loans/jobs. Scholarships based on academics, art, leadership, music/drama. **Student debt:** 54% of graduating class borrowed to fund education; average debt was $13,275.

Freshman aid. **Need-based:** Average package met 97% of need. Average scholarship/grant was $6,737; average loan $2,991.

Policies to reduce costs. Tuition/fee waivers for employees and their families. Credit/placement for qualifying scores on AP, IB examinations.

Payment plans. Deferred payment.

Application procedures. FAFSA required. Priority date 3/2; no closing date. Applicants notified on rolling basis starting 3/15.

Contact. **Financial aid office:** (858) 534-3800
Vincent De Anda, Director of Financial Aid Office
9500 Gilman Drive, 0021
La Jolla, CA 92093

University of California: Santa Barbara

Santa Barbara, California
www.ucsb.edu
Four-year public **Federal Code: 001320**

	Living at home	On-campus
Tuition and fees (2002-2003):	$3,841	$3,841
Out-of-state:	$14,915	$14,915
Room and board:		$7,891
Books and supplies:	$1,225	$1,225
Personal expenses:		$1,913
Transportation:		$863

Undergraduate aid. **Need-based:** Average financial aid package for full-time students was $10,285; for part-time $10,006. 62% awarded as scholarships/grants, 38% as loans/jobs. **Non-need-based:** 17% awarded as scholarships/grants, 83% as loans/jobs.

Freshman aid. **Need-based:** Out of 3,625 full-time freshmen, 2,217 applied for aid; 1,550 were judged to have need; of these 1,550 received aid. Average package met 92% of need. 1137 students had full need met. Average scholarship/grant was $8,479; average loan $3,742. **Non-need based:** 48 full-time freshmen with need received non-need scholarships; 415 without need received awards; 44 received athletic scholarships.

Policies to reduce costs. Tuition/fee waivers for employees and their families. Credit/placement for qualifying scores on AP examinations.

Payment plans. Deferred payment.

Application procedures. FAFSA required. Priority date 3/2; closing date 5/31. Applicants notified on rolling basis starting 3/15, must reply within 2 week(s) of notification. **Transfers:** California residents must apply for a CAL grant from the California Student Aid Commission; must complete and submit FAFSA by March 2.

Contact. **Financial aid office:** (805) 893-2432
Ron Andrade, Director of Financial Aid
1234 Cheadle Hall
Santa Barbara, CA 93106-2014

University of California: Santa Cruz

Santa Cruz, California
www.ucsc.edu
Four-year public **Federal Code: 001321**

	Living at home	On-campus
Tuition and fees (2002-2003):	$3,870	$3,870
Out-of-state:	$14,944	$14,944
Room and board:		$8,661
Books and supplies:	$1,203	$1,203
Personal expenses:	$1,463	$1,370
Transportation:	$1,489	$887

Undergraduate aid. **Need-based:** Average financial aid package for full-time students was $11,334. 63% awarded as scholarships/grants, 37% as loans/jobs. Need-based aid available for part-time students. **Non-need-based:** 32% awarded as scholarships/grants, 68% as loans/jobs. Scholarships based on academics, art, leadership, music/drama, religious affiliation, state/district residency. **Student debt:** 55% of graduating class borrowed to fund education; average debt was $13,282.

Freshman aid. **Need-based:** Out of 3,048 full-time freshmen, 1,671 applied for aid; 1,237 were judged to have need; of these 1,235 received aid. Average package met 94% of need. 889 students had full need met. Average scholarship/grant was $7,243; average loan $3,544. **Non-need based:** 15

full-time freshmen with need received non-need scholarships; 219 without need received awards.

Merit scholarships. Merit Scholarships, up to $2,000 per year, awarded on basis of geographic residence, family background, majors, classes, colleges.

Policies to reduce costs. Tuition/fee waivers for unemployed or children of unemployed. Credit/placement for qualifying scores on AP, IB examinations.

Payment plans. Installment, deferred payment.

Application procedures. FAFSA required. Priority date 3/2; closing date 5/2. Applicants notified on rolling basis starting 4/1, must reply within 3 week(s) of notification.

Contact. **Financial aid office:** (831) 459-4342
Esperanza Nee, Director of Financial Aid
Cook House, 1156 High Street
Santa Cruz, CA 95064

University of La Verne

La Verne, California
www.ulv.edu
Four-year private **Federal Code: 001216**

	Living at home	On-campus
Tuition and fees (projected):	$20,500	$20,500
Room and board:		$7,750
Board only:	$3,500	
Books and supplies:	$1,206	$1,206
Personal expenses:	$2,330	$1,934
Transportation:	$864	$864

Undergraduate aid. Need-based: Average financial aid package for full-time students was $19,477; for part-time $9,583. 78% awarded as scholarships/grants, 22% as loans/jobs. **Non-need-based:** 26% awarded as scholarships/grants, 74% as loans/jobs. Scholarships based on academics, alumni affiliation, art, leadership, minority status, music/drama, religious affiliation, state/district residency.

Freshman aid. Need-based: Out of 295 full-time freshmen, 287 applied for aid; 269 were judged to have need; of these 269 received aid. Average package met 88% of need. 79 students had full need met. Average scholarship/grant was $11,224; average loan $3,581. **Non-need based:** 224 full-time freshmen with need received non-need scholarships; 15 without need received awards; 9 received athletic scholarships.

Merit scholarships. Trustee Award, $10,000; based on GPA of 3.8, SAT of 1100; Founders Award, $9,000; based on GPA of 3.5, SAT of 1000. 1891 Award, $8,000; based on GPA of 3.0, SAT of 850 with neither verbal nor math score below 400.

Policies to reduce costs. Tuition/fee waivers for employees and their families. Credit/placement for qualifying scores on AP, CLEP examinations.

Payment plans. Credit card, installment, deferred payment.

Application procedures. FAFSA required. Priority date 3/2; no closing date. Applicants notified on rolling basis starting 3/15, must reply by 5/1 or within 2 week(s) of notification. **Transfers:** Priority date 3/2; no deadline. Trustee Award, $6,000, based on college GPA of 3.3; Founders Award, $5,000, based on college GPA of 2.8-3.29; 1891 Award, $3000, based on GPA of 2.5.

Contact. **Financial aid office:** (909) 593-3511
Leatha Webster, Director of Financial Aid
1950 Third Street
La Verne, CA 91750-4443

University of Redlands

Redlands, California
www.redlands.edu
Four-year private **Federal Code: 001322**

	Living at home	On-campus
Tuition and fees (2002-2003):	$22,750	$22,750
Room and board:		$8,114
Books and supplies:	$800	$800
Personal expenses:	$1,550	$1,550

Undergraduate aid. Need-based: Average financial aid package for full-time students was $22,020; for part-time $18,226. 73% awarded as scholarships/grants, 27% as loans/jobs. **Non-need-based:** 72% awarded as scholarships/grants, 28% as loans/jobs. Scholarships based on academics, art, leadership, music/drama. **Student debt:** 77% of graduating class borrowed to fund education; average debt was $18,956.

Freshman aid. Need-based: Out of 601 full-time freshmen, 515 applied for aid; 410 were judged to have need; of these 410 received aid. Average package met 94% of need. 201 students had full need met. Average scholarship/grant was $13,019; average loan $3,854. **Non-need based:** 229 full-time freshmen with need received non-need scholarships; 57 without need received awards.

Policies to reduce costs. Tuition/fee waivers for employees and their families. Prepayment discount; credit/placement for qualifying scores on AP, IB, CLEP examinations.

Payment plans. Credit card, installment payment.

Application procedures. FAFSA required. Priority date 3/2; no closing date. Applicants notified on rolling basis starting 2/28. **Transfers:** No deadline.

Contact. **Financial aid office:** (909) 793-2121
Bethann Corey, Director of Financial Aid
1200 East Colton Avenue
Redlands, CA 92373-0999

University of San Diego

San Diego, California
www.sandiego.edu
Four-year private **Federal Code: 010395**

	Living at home	On-campus
Tuition and fees:	$23,518	$23,518
Room and board:		$9,130
Board only:	$2,986	
Books and supplies:	$1,206	$1,206
Personal expenses:	$2,250	$1,854
Transportation:	$860	$612

Undergraduate aid. Need-based: Average financial aid package for full-time students was $19,700; for part-time $8,624. 71% awarded as scholarships/grants, 29% as loans/jobs. **Non-need-based:** 82% awarded as scholarships/grants, 18% as loans/jobs. Scholarships based on academics, art, athletics, music/drama, religious affiliation. **Student debt:** 42% of graduating class borrowed to fund education; average debt was $26,900.

Freshman aid. Need-based: Out of 1,051 full-time freshmen, 751 applied for aid; 511 were judged to have need; of these 511 received aid. Average package met 98% of need. 413 students had full need met. Average scholarship/grant was $17,402; average loan $2,664. **Non-need based:** 283 full-time freshmen with need received non-need scholarships; 180 without need received awards; 36 received athletic scholarships.

Merit scholarships. Available for freshmen only.

Policies to reduce costs. Tuition/fee waivers for employees and their families. Prepayment discount; credit/placement for qualifying scores on AP, IB, CLEP examinations. Work study available nights, weekends and for part-time students.

Payment plans. Installment payment.

Application procedures. FAFSA, institutional form required. Closing date 2/20. Applicants notified on rolling basis starting 3/1, must reply by 5/1 or within 3 week(s) of notification. **Transfers:** Priority date 2/20; no deadline. Entering transfer students not eligible for institutional merit-based scholarships.

Contact. **Financial aid office:** (619) 260-4514
Judith Lewis Logue, Director of Financial Aid Services
5998 Alcala Park
San Diego, CA 92110

University of San Francisco

San Francisco, California
www.usfca.edu
Four-year private **Federal Code: 001325**

	Living at home	On-campus
Tuition and fees (projected):	$23,340	$23,340
Room and board:		$9,350
Board only:	$2,600	
Books and supplies:	$800	$800
Personal expenses:	$2,400	$2,400
Transportation:	$650	$800

Undergraduate aid. Need-based: Need-based aid available for full-time and part-time students. **Non-need-based:** Scholarships based on academics, athletics. **Additional information:** Individualized installment plans available.

Merit scholarships. University Scholars Program; 75% of tuition for four years; student must have 3.8 weighted GPA and combined SAT of 1320 or ACT composite of 24. Applicants must apply through early action program.

Policies to reduce costs. Tuition/fee waivers for family members, family of clergy, employees and their families. Prepayment discount; credit/placement for qualifying scores on AP, IB, CLEP examinations.

Payment plans. Credit card, installment, deferred payment.

Application procedures. FAFSA required. Priority date 2/15; no closing date. Applicants notified on rolling basis starting 4/1, must reply within 4 week(s) of notification.

Contact. Financial aid office: (415) 422-6303
Susan Murphy, Director of Financial Aid
2130 Fulton Street
San Francisco, CA 94117

University of Southern California

Los Angeles, California
www.usc.edu
Four-year private **Federal Code: 001328**

	Living at home	On-campus
Tuition and fees (2002-2003):	$26,954	$26,954
Room and board:		$8,512
Board only:	$1,580	
Books and supplies:	$650	$650
Personal expenses:	$1,600	$1,600
Transportation:	$580	$580

Undergraduate aid. Need-based: Average financial aid package for full-time students was $24,941; for part-time $12,124. 73% awarded as scholarships/grants, 27% as loans/jobs. **Non-need-based:** 44% awarded as scholarships/grants, 56% as loans/jobs. Scholarships based on academics, alumni affiliation, art, athletics, leadership, minority status, music/drama. **Student debt:** 59% of graduating class borrowed to fund education; average debt was $19,651.

Freshman aid. Need-based: Out of 2,770 full-time freshmen, 1,732 applied for aid; 1,203 were judged to have need; of these 1,203 received aid. Average package met 99% of need. 1165 students had full need met. Average scholarship/grant was $20,866; average loan $3,016. **Non-need based:** 743 full-time freshmen with need received non-need scholarships; 602 without need received awards; 54 received athletic scholarships.

Policies to reduce costs. Tuition/fee waivers for employees and their families. Prepayment discount; credit/placement for qualifying scores on AP, IB examinations.

Payment plans. Credit card, installment, deferred payment.

Application procedures. FAFSA, CSS PROFILE required. Priority date 1/21; closing date 2/28. Applicants notified on rolling basis starting 3/15, must reply by 5/1 or within 2 week(s) of notification.

Contact. Financial aid office: (213) 740-1111
Catherine Thomas, Associate Dean of Financial Aid
University Park
Los Angeles, CA 90089

University of West Los Angeles

Inglewood, California
www.uwla.edu
Upper-division private **Federal Code: 009170**

College costs (projected). School of law $535 per-credit-hour charge; $650 annual fee. School of paralegal studies $225 per-credit-hour charge; $360 annual fee. Books/supplies: $927. Personal expenses: $1,545. Transportation: $1,030.

Undergraduate aid. Need-based: Average financial aid package for full-time students was $8,150. 4% awarded as scholarships/grants, 96% as loans/jobs. Need-based aid available for part-time students. **Non-need-based:** 1% awarded as scholarships/grants, 99% as loans/jobs.

Policies to reduce costs. Credit/placement for qualifying scores on CLEP examinations. Work study available nights and for part-time students.

Payment plans. Credit card, installment payment.

Application procedures. FAFSA required. Priority date 6/1; no closing date. Applicants notified on rolling basis starting 6/1, must reply within 4 week(s) of notification.

Contact. Financial aid office: (310) 342-5268
Ed Mervine, Financial Aid Officer
1155 West Arbor Vitae Street
Inglewood, CA 90301

University of the Pacific

Stockton, California
www.uop.edu
Four-year private **Federal Code: 001329**

	Living at home	On-campus
Tuition and fees:	$23,600	$23,600
Room and board:		$7,490
Board only:	$2,592	
Books and supplies:	$1,206	$1,206
Personal expenses:	$2,250	$1,854
Transportation:	$756	$558

Undergraduate aid. Need-based: Average financial aid package for full-time students was $21,837; for part-time $17,052. 74% awarded as scholarships/grants, 26% as loans/jobs. **Non-need-based:** 79% awarded as scholarships/grants, 21% as loans/jobs. Scholarships based on academics, athletics, music/drama.

Freshman aid. Need-based: Out of 698 full-time freshmen, 561 applied for aid; 451 were judged to have need; of these 451 received aid. 207 students had full need met. Average scholarship/grant was $17,283; average loan $3,107. **Non-need based:** 114 without need received awards; 37 received athletic scholarships.

Policies to reduce costs. Tuition/fee waivers for employees and their families. Credit/placement for qualifying scores on AP, CLEP examinations.

Payment plans. Credit card, installment payment.

Application procedures. FAFSA required. Priority date 2/15; no closing date. Applicants notified on rolling basis starting 3/15.

Contact. Financial aid office: (209) 946-2011
Lynn Fox, Director of Financial Aid
3601 Pacific Avenue
Stockton, CA 95211

Vanguard University of Southern California

Costa Mesa, California
www.vanguard.edu
Four-year private **Federal Code: 001293**

	Living at home	On-campus
Tuition and fees (2002-2003):	$15,328	$15,328
Room and board:		$5,488
Board only:	$2,448	
Books and supplies:	$850	$850
Personal expenses:	$1,548	$1,386
Transportation:	$738	$558

Undergraduate aid. Need-based: Average financial aid package for full-time students was $12,651; for part-time $6,759. 62% awarded as scholarships/grants, 38% as loans/jobs. **Non-need-based:** 31% awarded as scholarships/grants, 69% as loans/jobs. Scholarships based on academics, athletics. **Student debt:** 70% of graduating class borrowed to fund education; average debt was $16,000.

Freshman aid. Need-based: Out of 322 full-time freshmen, 305 applied for aid; 235 were judged to have need; of these 234 received aid. Average package met 75% of need. 32 students had full need met. Average scholarship/grant was $11,076; average loan $2,420. **Non-need based:** 22 full-time freshmen with need received non-need scholarships; 43 without need received awards; 12 received athletic scholarships.

Policies to reduce costs. Tuition/fee waivers for family of clergy, employees and their families. Prepayment discount; credit/placement for qualifying scores on AP, IB, CLEP examinations.

Payment plans. Credit card, installment payment.

Application procedures. FAFSA required. Priority date 3/2; no closing date. Applicants notified on rolling basis starting 4/1, must reply by 5/1 or within 3 week(s) of notification. **Transfers:** Priority date 3/2.

Contact. **Financial aid office:** (714) 556-3610 ext. 355
Amy Kasper, Director of Financial Aid
55 Fair Drive
Costa Mesa, CA 92626-9601

Ventura College

Ventura, California
www.venturacollege.edu
Two-year public **Federal Code: 001334**

	Living at home
Tuition and fees (projected):	$354
Out-of-state:	$4,584
Per-credit charge:	$11
Per-credit out-of-state:	$152
Books and supplies:	$600
Personal expenses:	$1,300
Transportation:	$700

Policies to reduce costs. Credit/placement for qualifying scores on AP examinations.

Payment plans. Deferred payment.

Application procedures. FAFSA required. Priority date 3/3; no closing date. Applicants notified on rolling basis.

Contact. **Financial aid office:** (805) 654-6369
Dora Washington, Director, Financial Aid
4667 Telegraph Road
Ventura, CA 93003

Victor Valley College

Victorville, California
www.victor.cc.ca.us
Two-year public **Federal Code: 001335**

College costs. Nevada residents pay $42 per credit hour.

	Living at home
Tuition and fees (2002-2003):	$340
Out-of-state:	$4,360
Per-credit charge:	$11
Per-credit out-of-state:	$145
Books and supplies:	$648
Personal expenses:	$1,566
Transportation:	$738

Undergraduate aid. **Need-based:** Need-based aid available for full-time and part-time students. **Additional information:** Board of Governors grant pays enrollment fee in full for low-income students.

Policies to reduce costs. Credit/placement for qualifying scores on AP examinations. Work study available for part-time students.

Payment plans. Credit card, installment, deferred payment.

Application procedures. FAFSA, institutional form, CSS PROFILE required. Priority date 3/2; no closing date. Applicants notified on rolling basis starting 8/1, must reply within 4 week(s) of notification.

Contact. **Financial aid office:** (760) 245-4271 ext. 2277
Sandy Clark, Financial Aid
18422 Bear Valley Road
Victorville, CA 92392-5849

Vista Community College

Berkeley, California
www.peralta.cc.ca.us
Two-year public **Federal Code: 014311**

	Living at home
Tuition and fees (projected):	$330
Out-of-state:	$5,250
Per-credit charge:	$11
Per-credit out-of-state:	$175
Books and supplies:	$630
Personal expenses:	$1,584
Transportation:	$720

Undergraduate aid. All financial aid based on need. Need-based aid available for full-time and part-time students.

Policies to reduce costs. Work study available for part-time students.

Payment plans. Credit card payment.

Application procedures. No deadline. Applicants notified on rolling basis.

Contact. **Financial aid office:** (510) 981-2800
Robert Vergas, Financial Aid Coordinator
2020 Milvia Street
Berkeley, CA 94704-1183

West Valley College

Saratoga, California
www.westvalley.edu
Two-year public **Federal Code: 001338**

	Living at home
Tuition and fees (projected):	$390
Out-of-state:	$4,740
Per-credit charge:	$11
Per-credit out-of-state:	$156
Books and supplies:	$612
Personal expenses:	$1,566
Transportation:	$810

Undergraduate aid. All financial aid based on need. Need-based aid available for full-time and part-time students.

Policies to reduce costs. Tuition/fee waivers for senior citizens, unemployed or children of unemployed, employees and their families. Credit/placement for qualifying scores on CLEP examinations.

Payment plans. Credit card, deferred payment.

Application procedures. FAFSA required. Priority date 5/31; no closing date. Applicants notified on rolling basis starting 7/16.

Contact. **Financial aid office:** (408) 867-2200
Maureen Kent, Financial Aid Coordinator
14000 Fruitvale Avenue
Saratoga, CA 95070-5698

Westwood College of Technology

Anaheim, California
www.westwood.edu
Four-year proprietary

College costs. Total cost of tuition plus fees for 17-month, 7-term associate degree program: $24,855. Cost of books, supplies will vary with program.

Application procedures. FAFSA required. Applicants notified on rolling basis.

Contact. **Financial aid office:** (714) 226-9990
Angeles Ramirez, Director of Financial Aid
2461 West La Palma Avenue
Anaheim, CA 92801

Westwood College of Technology: Inland Empire

Upland, California
www.westwood.edu
Four-year proprietary **Federal Code: 007548-03**

	Living at home
Tuition and fees (projected):	$10,794
Board only:	$522
Books and supplies:	$1,464
Personal expenses:	$1,840
Transportation:	$616

Undergraduate aid. **Need-based:** Need-based aid available for full-time and part-time students. **Non-need-based:** Scholarships based on academics.

Policies to reduce costs. Tuition/fee waivers for employees and their families. Credit/placement for qualifying scores on AP, IB examinations. Work study available nights and for part-time students.

Payment plans. Credit card, installment payment.

Application procedures. FAFSA, institutional form required. No deadline. Must reply within 1 week(s) of notification. **Transfers:** No deadline.

Contact. **Financial aid office:** (909) 931-7599
Michael Hauser, Director of Business Affairs
20 West Seventh Street
Upland, CA 91786

Westwood College of Technology: Los Angeles

Los Angeles, California
www.westwood.edu
Two-year proprietary

College costs. Total cost of tuition plus fees for 17-month, 7-term associate degree program: $24,855. Cost of tuition plus fees for 14-term, 34-month bachelor program: $49,635. Cost of books, supplies will vary with program.

Application procedures. FAFSA required. Applicants notified on rolling basis.

Contact. **Financial aid office:** (213) 739-9999
Amy Consolacion, Director of Financial Aid
3460 Wilshire Boulevard, Suite 700
Los Angeles, CA 90010

Whittier College

Whittier, California
www.whittier.edu
Four-year private **Federal Code: 001342**

	Living at home	On-campus
Tuition and fees:	$23,492	$23,492
Room and board:		$7,778
Board only:	$1,607	
Books and supplies:	$656	$656
Personal expenses:	$1,630	$1,380
Transportation:	$602	$584

Undergraduate aid. Need-based: Need-based aid available for full-time students. **Non-need-based:** Scholarships based on academics, alumni affiliation, art, music/drama. **Additional information:** Auditions required for talent scholarship applicants.

Policies to reduce costs. Tuition/fee waivers for employees and their families. Credit/placement for qualifying scores on AP, IB examinations.

Payment plans. Credit card, installment payment.

Application procedures. FAFSA, CSS PROFILE required. Priority date 2/1; no closing date. Applicants notified on rolling basis starting 2/1, must reply by 5/2 or within 4 week(s) of notification. **Transfers:** Priority date 2/1.

Contact. **Financial aid office:** (562) 907-4285
Nina Martinez, Director of Student Financing
13406 East Philadelphia Street
Whittier, CA 90608-0634

Woodbury University

Burbank, California
www.woodbury.edu
Four-year private **Federal Code: 001343**

College costs. Architecture program tuition: full-time $20,116; interior architecture tuition: full-time $19,717.

	Living at home	On-campus
Tuition and fees (2002-2003):	$19,254	$19,254
Room and board:		$6,646
Board only:	$2,988	
Books and supplies:	$1,206	$1,206
Personal expenses:	$2,250	$1,854
Transportation:	$864	$612

Undergraduate aid. Non-need-based: Scholarships based on academics.

Policies to reduce costs. Tuition/fee waivers for employees and their families. Credit/placement for qualifying scores on AP, IB, CLEP examinations.

Payment plans. Credit card, installment, deferred payment.

Application procedures. FAFSA, institutional form required. Priority date 3/3; no closing date. Applicants notified on rolling basis starting 4/1, must reply by 5/1 or within 2 week(s) of notification. **Transfers:** Priority date 3/2; no deadline.

Contact. **Financial aid office:** (818) 767-0888 ext. 273
Celeastia Williams, Director of Financial Aid
7500 Glenoaks Boulevard
Burbank, CA 91510-7846

Yuba Community College District

Marysville, California
www.yccd.edu
Two-year public **Federal Code: 001344**

	Living at home	On-campus
Tuition and fees (2002-2003):	$342	$342
Out-of-state:	$4,782	$4,782
Per-credit charge:	$11	$11
Per-credit out-of-state:	$159	$159
Room and board:		$5,745
Books and supplies:	$1,646	$1,646
Personal expenses:	$1,656	$1,440
Transportation:	$756	$558

Undergraduate aid. Need-based: Need-based aid available for full-time and part-time students. **Non-need-based:** Scholarships based on academics, athletics, job skills, minority status, music/drama. **Additional information:** Tuition fee waiver based on Board of Governors Grant.

Policies to reduce costs. Tuition/fee waivers for adults. Credit/placement for qualifying scores on AP, CLEP examinations. Work study available for part-time students.

Payment plans. Installment, deferred payment.

Application procedures. FAFSA required. Closing date 3/1. Applicants notified on rolling basis starting 4/1. **Transfers:** Closing date 3/1.

Contact. **Financial aid office:** (530) 741-6781
Marisela Arce, Associate Dean for EOP&S and Financial Aid
2088 North Beale Road
Marysville, CA 95901

Colorado

Arapahoe Community College

Littleton, Colorado
www.arapahoe.edu
Two-year public **Federal Code: 001346**

	Living at home
Tuition and fees (2002-2003):	$1,664
Out-of-state:	$7,684
Per-credit charge:	$63
Per-credit out-of-state:	$314
Board only:	$1,526
Books and supplies:	$825
Personal expenses:	$2,142
Transportation:	$990

Undergraduate aid. Need-based: Need-based aid available for full-time and part-time students. **Non-need-based:** Scholarships based on academics, leadership, state/district residency.

Merit scholarships. President's Scholarship, based on minimum 3.0 GPA, references; College Bound Scholarship, based on high GED score; all awards $750 for full-time students, $375 for half-time, $563 for three-quarters time. Awards made on first-come first-served basis.

Policies to reduce costs. Prepayment discount; credit/placement for qualifying scores on AP, CLEP examinations. Work study available nights, weekends and for part-time students.

Payment plans. Credit card, installment payment.

Application procedures. FAFSA, institutional form required. Priority date 5/1; no closing date. Applicants notified on rolling basis starting 5/1, must reply within 3 week(s) of notification. **Transfers:** Priority date 5/1.

Contact. Financial aid office: (303) 797-5661
Jim Contreras, Director of Financial Aid
Box 9002
Littleton, CO 80160-9002

Art Institute of Colorado

Denver, Colorado
www.aic.artinstitutes.edu
Four-year proprietary **Federal Code: 013961**

	Living at home	On-campus
Tuition and fees (2002-2003):	$15,360	$15,360
Room and board:		$5,760
Board only:	$3,504	
Books and supplies:	$2,250	$2,250
Personal expenses:	$900	$900
Transportation:	$900	$500

Undergraduate aid. Need-based: 21% awarded as scholarships/grants, 79% as loans/jobs. Need-based aid available for part-time students. **Additional information:** Tuition at time of first enrollment guaranteed to students for 4 years providing student maintains continuous attendance and completes program within 150% of program length.

Policies to reduce costs. Tuition/fee waivers for employees and their families. Tuition at time of enrollment guaranteed for 4 years; credit/placement for qualifying scores on AP, IB, CLEP examinations.

Payment plans. Credit card, installment, deferred payment.

Application procedures. FAFSA, institutional form required. No deadline. Applicants notified on rolling basis. **Transfers:** No deadline.

Contact. Financial aid office: (303)824-4757
Shannon May, Director of Student Financial Services
1200 Lincoln Street
Denver, CO 80203

Bel-Rea Institute of Animal Technology

Denver, Colorado
www.bel-rea.com
Two-year proprietary **Federal Code: 012670**

College costs. Tuition for full associate program $18,000 including fees; estimated cost of books $1,300. Personal expenses: $1,100. Transportation: $1,000.

Undergraduate aid. All financial aid based on need. Need-based aid available for full-time students.

Policies to reduce costs. Tuition at time of enrollment guaranteed for 2 years; credit/placement for qualifying scores on AP examinations.

Payment plans. Installment payment.

Application procedures. FAFSA required. Priority date 8/31; no closing date. Applicants notified on rolling basis starting 8/15. **Transfers:** No deadline.

Contact. Stasi Botinelli, Financial Aid Director
1681 South Dayton Street
Denver, CO 80231

Blair Junior College

Colorado Springs, Colorado
www.cci.edu
Two-year proprietary **Federal Code: 004503**

	Living at home
Tuition and fees (projected):	$9,765
Per-credit charge:	$238
Books and supplies:	$1,025
Transportation:	$1,020

Undergraduate aid. Need-based: Average financial aid package for full-time students was $6,000; for part-time $5,000. 30% awarded as scholarships/grants, 70% as loans/jobs. **Student debt:** 90% of graduating class borrowed to fund education; average debt was $10,000.

Freshman aid. Need-based: Out of 46 full-time freshmen, 44 applied for aid; 43 were judged to have need; of these 43 received aid. Average package met 71% of need. 30 students had full need met. Average scholarship/grant was $1,500; average loan $2,625. **Non-need based:** 2 without need received awards.

Policies to reduce costs. Tuition/fee waivers for employees and their families. Tuition at time of enrollment guaranteed for 2 years; credit/placement for qualifying scores on CLEP examinations. Work study available nights and for part-time students.

Payment plans. Installment, deferred payment.

Application procedures. FAFSA, institutional form required. No deadline. Applicants notified on rolling basis starting 7/1. **Transfers:** No deadline.

Contact. Loretta Roth, Student Financial Director
828 Wooten Road
Colorado Springs, CO 80915

Colorado Christian University

Lakewood, Colorado
www.ccu.edu
Four-year private **Federal Code: 009401**

	Living at home	On-campus
Tuition and fees:	$15,040	$15,040
Room and board:		$5,990
Books and supplies:	$1,000	$1,000
Personal expenses:	$1,170	$1,170

Undergraduate aid. Need-based: Average financial aid package for full-time students was $8,850; for part-time $5,590. 45% awarded as scholarships/grants, 55% as loans/jobs. **Non-need-based:** 37% awarded as scholarships/grants, 63% as loans/jobs. Scholarships based on academics, art, athletics, leadership, music/drama, religious affiliation.

Freshman aid. Need-based: Average package met 55% of need. Average scholarship/grant was $6,223; average loan $3,290.

Policies to reduce costs. Tuition/fee waivers for children of alumni, family members, family of clergy, employees and their families. Credit/placement for qualifying scores on AP, IB, CLEP examinations.

Payment plans. Credit card, installment payment.

Application procedures. FAFSA required. Priority date 3/15; no closing date. Applicants notified on rolling basis starting 4/1, must reply by 5/1 or within 4 week(s) of notification.

Contact. **Financial aid office:** (303) 963-3230
Steve Woodburn, Director Financial Aid
180 South Garrison Street
Lakewood, CO 80226

Colorado College

Colorado Springs, Colorado
www.coloradocollege.edu
Four-year private **Federal Code: 001347**

	Living at home	On-campus
Tuition and fees:	$27,270	$27,270
Room and board:		$6,840
Board only:	$3,344	
Books and supplies:	$730	$730
Personal expenses:	$756	$756
Transportation:	$900	$900

Undergraduate aid. Need-based: Average financial aid package for full-time students was $21,385. 79% awarded as scholarships/grants, 21% as loans/jobs. Need-based aid available for part-time students. **Non-need-based:** 75% awarded as scholarships/grants, 25% as loans/jobs. Scholarships based on academics, athletics, state/district residency. **Student debt:** 38% of graduating class borrowed to fund education; average debt was $13,500. **Additional information:** Need-based financial aid available only to students enrolled half-time or more.

Freshman aid. Need-based: Out of 482 full-time freshmen, 233 applied for aid; 198 were judged to have need; of these 198 received aid. Average package met 96% of need. 116 students had full need met. Average scholarship/grant was $18,181; average loan $2,701. **Non-need based:** 17 full-time freshmen with need received non-need scholarships; 68 without need received awards; 11 received athletic scholarships.

Merit scholarships. Barnes Scholarship, full tuition, available in all natural sciences, based on selection by departments, 4 or 5 awarded in chemistry, 4 available in remaining natural sciences; Trustee Scholarship, $7,000, based on highly rated entering students,10 awards; Merit Awards, up to $2,000, for National Merit finalists; Men's Ice Hockey and Women's Soccer merit awards, Colorado College Scholars, 10 merit awards for highly rated entering students from Colorado.

Policies to reduce costs. Tuition/fee waivers for employees and their families. Credit/placement for qualifying scores on AP, IB examinations. Work study available nights and weekends.

Payment plans. Installment payment.

Application procedures. FAFSA, CSS PROFILE required. Closing date 2/15. Applicants notified by 3/25, must reply by 5/1. **Transfers:** Closing date 4/1. Transfer students might not receive full-need package during first year.

Contact. **Financial aid office:** (719) 389-6651
James Swanson, Director of Financial Aid
14 East Cache La Poudre
Colorado Springs, CO 80903

Colorado Mountain College: Alpine Campus

Glenwood Springs, Colorado
www.coloradomtn.edu
Two-year public **Federal Code: 004506**

	Living at home	On-campus
Tuition and fees (2002-2003):	$1,410	$1,410
Out-of-district:	$2,250	$2,250
Out-of-state:	$6,780	$6,780
Per-credit charge:	$41	$41
Per-credit out-of-district:	$69	$69
Per-credit out-of-state:	$220	$220
Room and board:		$5,700
Books and supplies:	$700	$700
Personal expenses:	$900	$2,050
Transportation:	$280	$570

Undergraduate aid. Need-based: Need-based aid available for full-time and part-time students. **Non-need-based:** Scholarships based on academics, athletics, state/district residency.

Policies to reduce costs. Tuition/fee waivers for senior citizens, employees and their families. Credit/placement for qualifying scores on AP, CLEP examinations. Work study available nights, weekends and for part-time students.

Payment plans. Credit card, deferred payment.

Application procedures. FAFSA required. Priority date 3/31; no closing date. Applicants notified on rolling basis starting 5/15, must reply within 4 week(s) of notification. **Transfers:** Priority date 3/31; no deadline. Transfer scholarships available to Colorado residents with 3.0 GPA and minimum 20 credits from prior institution.

Contact. **Financial aid office:** (970) 870-4444
Gary Lewis, Director of Financial Aid
Box 10001
Glenwood Springs, CO 81602

Colorado Mountain College: Spring Valley Campus

Glenwood Springs, Colorado
www.coloradomtn.edu
Two-year public **Federal Code: 004506**

	Living at home	On-campus
Tuition and fees (2002-2003):	$1,410	$1,410
Out-of-district:	$2,250	$2,250
Out-of-state:	$6,780	$6,780
Per-credit charge:	$41	$41
Per-credit out-of-district:	$69	$69
Per-credit out-of-state:	$220	$220
Room and board:		$5,700
Books and supplies:	$650	$650
Personal expenses:	$900	$2,050
Transportation:	$280	$570

Undergraduate aid. All financial aid based on need. Need-based aid available for full-time and part-time students.

Policies to reduce costs. Tuition/fee waivers for senior citizens, employees and their families. Credit/placement for qualifying scores on AP, CLEP examinations. Work study available nights, weekends and for part-time students.

Payment plans. Credit card payment.

Application procedures. FAFSA required. Priority date 3/31; no closing date. Applicants notified on rolling basis starting 5/15, must reply within 4 week(s) of notification. **Transfers:** Priority date 3/31; no deadline. Transfer scholarships available for Colorado residents with 3.0 GPA and minimum 20 credit hours from previous schools.

Contact. **Financial aid office:** (970) 947-8277
Gary Lewis, Director of Student Financial Aid
3000 County Road 114, Dept. CB
Glenwood Springs, CO 81601

Colorado Mountain College: Timberline Campus

Leadville, Colorado
www.coloradomtn.edu
Two-year public **Federal Code: 004506**

	Living at home	On-campus
Tuition and fees (2002-2003):	$1,410	$1,410
Out-of-district:	$2,250	$2,250
Out-of-state:	$6,780	$6,780
Per-credit charge:	$41	$41
Per-credit out-of-district:	$69	$69
Per-credit out-of-state:	$220	$220
Room and board:		$5,700
Books and supplies:	$650	$650
Personal expenses:	$900	$2,050
Transportation:	$280	$570

Undergraduate aid. Non-need-based: Scholarships based on academics, athletics, state/district residency.

Policies to reduce costs. Tuition/fee waivers for senior citizens, employees and their families. Credit/placement for qualifying scores on AP, CLEP examinations. Work study available nights, weekends and for part-time students.

Payment plans. Credit card, deferred payment.

Application procedures. FAFSA required. Priority date 3/31; no closing date. Applicants notified on rolling basis starting 5/15, must reply within 4 week(s) of notification. **Transfers:** Priority date 3/31; no deadline. Transfer scholarships available for Colorado residents with 3.0 GPA and at least 20 credits from previous colleges.

Contact. **Financial aid office:** (719) 486-4293
Gary Lewis, Director of Financial Aid
901 South Highway 24, Dept. CB
Leadville, CO 80461

Colorado School of Mines

Golden, Colorado
www.mines.edu
Four-year public **Federal Code: 001348**

	Living at home	On-campus
Tuition and fees (2002-2003):	$5,952	$5,952
Out-of-state:	$18,222	$18,222
Room and board:		$5,860
Board only:	$2,280	
Books and supplies:	$1,200	$1,200
Personal expenses:	$1,700	$1,700
Transportation:	$1,100	

Undergraduate aid. Need-based: Average financial aid package for full-time students was $5,200. 58% awarded as scholarships/grants, 42% as loans/jobs. Need-based aid available for part-time students. **Non-need-based:** 35% awarded as scholarships/grants, 65% as loans/jobs. Scholarships based on academics, alumni affiliation, athletics, minority status, music/drama, state/district residency. **Student debt:** 70% of graduating class borrowed to fund education; average debt was $17,500.

Freshman aid. Need-based: Out of 564 full-time freshmen, 367 applied for aid; 338 were judged to have need; of these 338 received aid. Average package met 100% of need. 338 students had full need met. Average scholarship/grant was $5,248; average loan $3,000. **Non-need based:** 202 full-time freshmen with need received non-need scholarships; 65 without need received awards; 35 received athletic scholarships.

Policies to reduce costs. Tuition/fee waivers for senior citizens, employees and their families. Credit/placement for qualifying scores on AP, IB examinations.

Payment plans. Credit card, installment, deferred payment.

Application procedures. FAFSA required. Priority date 3/1; no closing date. Applicants notified by 3/15, must reply by 5/1 or within 2 week(s) of notification. **Transfers:** Limited aid available for second undergraduate degree candidates.

Contact. **Financial aid office:** (303) 273-3301
Roger Koester, Director of Financial Aid
1600 Maple Street
Golden, CO 80401

Colorado State University

Fort Collins, Colorado
www.colostate.edu
Four-year public **Federal Code: 001350**

	Living at home	On-campus
Tuition and fees (2002-2003):	$3,435	$3,435
Out-of-state:	$12,705	$12,705
Room and board:		$5,780
Board only:	$1,800	
Books and supplies:	$680	$680
Personal expenses:	$1,700	$2,100

Undergraduate aid. Need-based: Average financial aid package for full-time students was $7,522; for part-time $5,816. 37% awarded as scholarships/grants, 63% as loans/jobs. **Non-need-based:** 31% awarded as scholarships/grants, 69% as loans/jobs. Scholarships based on academics, art, athletics, leadership, music/drama. **Student debt:** 51% of graduating class borrowed to fund education; average debt was $16,042.

Freshman aid. Need-based: Out of 3,637 full-time freshmen, 2,312 applied for aid; 1,415 were judged to have need; of these 1,404 received aid. Average package met 87% of need. 527 students had full need met. Average scholarship/grant was $4,115; average loan $3,443. **Non-need based:** 830 without need received awards; 45 received athletic scholarships.

Policies to reduce costs. Tuition/fee waivers for employees and their families. Credit/placement for qualifying scores on AP, IB, CLEP examinations.

Payment plans. Credit card, installment payment.

Application procedures. FAFSA required. Priority date 3/1; no closing date. Applicants notified on rolling basis starting 3/1.

Contact. Sandra Calhoun, Director of Financial Aid
Spruce Hall
Fort Collins, CO 80523-0015

Colorado State University: Pueblo

Pueblo, Colorado
www.uscolo.edu
Four-year public **Federal Code: 001365**

College costs. Students from Alaska, Arizona, Hawaii, Idaho, Montana, Nevada, Oregon, South Dakota, North Dakota, Utah, New Mexico, and Wyoming pay $146 per credit hour; $2,910 full time.

	Living at home	On-campus
Tuition and fees (2002-2003):	$2,450	$2,450
Out-of-state:	$9,730	$9,730
Room and board:		$5,164
Books and supplies:	$540	$540
Personal expenses:	$1,013	$1,013
Transportation:	$1,216	$1,216

Undergraduate aid. All financial aid based on need. Need-based aid available for full-time and part-time students.

Policies to reduce costs. Tuition/fee waivers for senior citizens, employees and their families. Credit/placement for qualifying scores on AP, IB, CLEP examinations. Work study available nights and weekends.

Payment plans. Credit card, installment, deferred payment.

Application procedures. FAFSA required. Priority date 3/1; no closing date. Applicants notified on rolling basis starting 3/1, must reply within 2 week(s) of notification. **Transfers:** Priority date 3/1; no deadline.

Contact. **Financial aid office:** (719) 549-2753
Ofelia Morales, Director of Student Financial Services
2200 Bonforte Boulevard
Pueblo, CO 81001-4901

Colorado Technical University

Colorado Springs, Colorado
www.coloradotech.edu
Four-year proprietary **Federal Code: 010148**

College costs. Lab fees $50 per lab class.

	Living at home
Tuition and fees (2002-2003):	$8,982
Board only:	$4,437
Books and supplies:	$1,300
Personal expenses:	$1,215
Transportation:	$1,215

Undergraduate aid. Need-based: 35% awarded as scholarships/grants, 65% as loans/jobs. Need-based aid available for part-time students. **Non-need-based:** 1% awarded as scholarships/grants, 99% as loans/jobs. Scholarships based on academics.

Policies to reduce costs. Tuition/fee waivers for employees and their families. Credit/placement for qualifying scores on AP, CLEP examinations. Work study available nights, weekends and for part-time students.

Payment plans. Credit card, installment payment.

Application procedures. FAFSA required. No deadline. Applicants notified on rolling basis starting 6/30. **Transfers:** No deadline.

Contact. **Financial aid office:** (719) 598-0200
Pat Hollenbeck, Director, Financial Aid
4435 North Chestnut Street
Colorado Springs, CO 80907

Community College of Aurora

Aurora, Colorado
www.ccaurora.edu
Two-year public **Federal Code: 016058**

College costs. Room and board available on Lowry campus.

	Living at home	On-campus
Tuition and fees (2002-2003):	$1,987	$1,987
Out-of-state:	$9,513	$9,513
Per-credit charge:	$63	$63
Per-credit out-of-state:	$314	$314
Room and board:		$5,800
Books and supplies:	$400	$400

Undergraduate aid. Need-based: Need-based aid available for full-time and part-time students.

Policies to reduce costs. Tuition/fee waivers for senior citizens. Credit/placement for qualifying scores on AP, IB, CLEP examinations. Work study available nights and for part-time students.

Payment plans. Credit card, installment payment.

Application procedures. FAFSA, institutional form required. Priority date 6/1; no closing date. Applicants notified on rolling basis starting 7/15.

Contact. **Financial aid office:** (303) 360-4709
Terry Campbell-Caron, Executive Director, Financial Aid
16000 East CentreTech Parkway
Aurora, CO 80011-9036

DeVry University: Colorado Springs

Colorado Springs, Colorado
www.cs.devry.edu
Four-year proprietary **Federal Code: 007648**

	Living at home
Tuition and fees:	$10,755
Books and supplies:	$1,100
Personal expenses:	$1,996
Transportation:	$1,612

Undergraduate aid. All financial aid based on need. Average financial aid package for full-time students was $4,467; for part-time $2,975. 16% awarded as scholarships/grants, 84% as loans/jobs.

Freshman aid. Average package met 31% of need. Average scholarship/grant was $2,941; average loan $2,984.

Policies to reduce costs. Tuition/fee waivers for employees and their families.

Payment plans. Credit card, installment, deferred payment.

Application procedures. FAFSA required. No deadline. Applicants notified on rolling basis starting 7/1. **Transfers:** No deadline.

Contact. 225 South Union Boulevard
Colorado Springs, CO 80910

DeVry University: Denver

Denver, Colorado
www.den.devry.edu
Four-year proprietary **Federal Code: 014831**

	Living at home
Tuition and fees:	$10,755
Books and supplies:	$1,100
Personal expenses:	$1,996
Transportation:	$1,612

Undergraduate aid. All financial aid based on need. Average financial aid package for full-time students was $5,040; for part-time $3,421. 17% awarded as scholarships/grants, 83% as loans/jobs.

Freshman aid. Average package met 36% of need. Average scholarship/grant was $3,453; average loan $3,121.

Policies to reduce costs. Tuition/fee waivers for employees and their families.

Payment plans. Credit card, installment, deferred payment.

Application procedures. FAFSA, institutional form required. No deadline. Applicants notified on rolling basis starting 7/2.

Contact. Terry Bargas, Director of Financial Aid
925 South Niagara Street
Denver, CO 80224

Fort Lewis College

Durango, Colorado
www.fortlewis.edu
Four-year public **Federal Code: 001353**

College costs. Credits in excess of 19: $60 per credit hour; out-of-state $313 per credit hour. Fees for part-time students $79.

	Living at home	On-campus
Tuition and fees (2002-2003):	$2,632	$2,632
Out-of-state:	$10,330	$10,330
Room and board:		$5,446
Board only:	$1,800	
Books and supplies:	$750	$750
Personal expenses:	$2,100	$2,210
Transportation:	$840	$1,284

Undergraduate aid. Need-based: Average financial aid package for full-time students was $7,251; for part-time $3,116. 58% awarded as scholarships/grants, 42% as loans/jobs. **Non-need-based:** 74% awarded as scholarships/grants, 26% as loans/jobs. Scholarships based on academics, alumni affiliation, art, athletics, leadership, music/drama. **Student debt:** 52% of graduating class borrowed to fund education; average debt was $13,850. **Additional information:** Tuition waived for Native Americans of federally recognized tribes; census number and CIB (Certificate of Indian Blood) must accompany application.

Freshman aid. Need-based: Out of 1,059 full-time freshmen, 682 applied for aid; 596 were judged to have need; of these 444 received aid. Average package met 77% of need. 102 students had full need met. Average scholarship/grant was $3,965; average loan $3,118. **Non-need based:** 199 full-time freshmen with need received non-need scholarships; 188 without need received awards; 53 received athletic scholarships.

Policies to reduce costs. Tuition/fee waivers for employees and their families. Credit/placement for qualifying scores on AP, IB, CLEP examinations. Work study available nights and weekends.

Payment plans. Credit card, installment, deferred payment.

Application procedures. FAFSA required. Priority date 2/15; no closing date. Applicants notified on rolling basis starting 4/1, must reply within 2 week(s) of notification. **Transfers:** Closing date 2/15.

Contact. **Financial aid office:** (970) 247-7142
Richard Willis, Director of Financial Aid
1000 Rim Drive
Durango, CO 81301-3999

Front Range Community College

Westminster, Colorado
www.frcc.cc.co.us
Two-year public **Federal Code: 007933**

College costs. Full-time students at Larimer campus pay additional $60 student-approved fees.

	Living at home
Tuition and fees (2002-2003):	$2,077
Out-of-state:	$9,602
Per-credit charge:	$63
Per-credit out-of-state:	$314
Books and supplies:	$1,100

Undergraduate aid. Need-based: Need-based aid available for full-time and part-time students. **Non-need-based:** Scholarships based on academics, job skills, leadership, state/district residency.

Policies to reduce costs. Tuition/fee waivers for senior citizens, employees and their families. Credit/placement for qualifying scores on CLEP examinations. Work study available nights, weekends and for part-time students.

Payment plans. Credit card, deferred payment.

Application procedures. FAFSA, institutional form required. Priority date 5/1; no closing date. Applicants notified on rolling basis starting 7/1, must reply within 3 week(s) of notification.

Contact. **Financial aid office:** (303) 439-9454
Elaine Redwine, Director of Financial Aid
3645 West 112th Avenue
Westminster, CO 80031

Heritage College

Denver, Colorado
www.heritage-education.com
Two-year proprietary **Federal Code: 0261100**

	Living at home
Tuition and fees:	$14,495

Undergraduate aid. All financial aid based on need. Need-based aid available for full-time students.

Policies to reduce costs. Work study available nights and weekends.

Payment plans. Installment payment.

Application procedures. FAFSA required. No deadline. Applicants notified on rolling basis.

Contact. **Financial aid office:** (720) 855-6014
Donna Blea, Director of Financial Aid
12 Lakeside Lane
Denver, CO 80212-7413

ITT Technical Institute: Thornton

Thornton, Colorado
www.itt-tech.edu
Three-year proprietary **Federal Code: 016500**

College costs. Total program varies depending on course of study. Per-credit-hour charge: $347.

Policies to reduce costs. Tuition/fee waivers for employees and their families.

Payment plans. Credit card, installment payment.

Application procedures. FAFSA, institutional form required. No deadline. Applicants notified on rolling basis.

Contact. Brad Hettich, Director of Finance
500 East 84th Avenue
Thornton, CO 80229

IntelliTec College

Colorado Springs, Colorado
www.intelliteccollege.com
Two-year proprietary **Federal Code: 008635**

	Living at home
Tuition and fees:	$13,000
Books and supplies:	$1,000

Undergraduate aid. All financial aid based on need. Need-based aid available for full-time and part-time students.

Policies to reduce costs. Tuition/fee waivers for employees and their families. Tuition at time of enrollment guaranteed for 2 years. Work study available nights.

Payment plans. Credit card, installment payment.

Application procedures. FAFSA, institutional form required. No deadline. Applicants notified on rolling basis. **Transfers:** No deadline.

Contact. **Financial aid office:** (719) 632-7626
Taffi Wright, Financial Services Representative
2315 East Pikes Peak Avenue
Colorado Springs, CO 80909

IntelliTec College, Grand Junction

Grand Junction, Colorado
www.intelliteccollege.com/grandjunction/
Two-year proprietary **Federal Code: 030669**

College costs. Lab fees vary per program; average $865.

	Living at home
Tuition and fees (2002-2003):	$10,560
Books and supplies:	$1,140
Transportation:	$135

Undergraduate aid. All financial aid based on need. Need-based aid available for full-time students.

Policies to reduce costs. Tuition/fee waivers for employees and their families. Tuition at time of enrollment guaranteed for 2 years.

Payment plans. Credit card, installment payment.

Application procedures. FAFSA required. No deadline. Applicants notified on rolling basis. **Transfers:** No deadline.

Contact. Sherry Martin, Financial Services Representative
772 Horizon Drive
Grand Junction, CO 81506

Johnson & Wales University

Denver, Colorado
www.jwu.edu
Four-year proprietary **Federal Code: 003404**

College costs (2002-2003). Culinary arts program $16,893 per year; business programs $13,740 per year. Fees $600. Room/board: $8,259.

Contact. C. F. Simmons
7150 Montview Boulevard
Denver, CO 80220

Jones International University

Englewood, Colorado
www.jonesinternational.edu
Upper-division proprietary

College costs (projected). Tuition: $835 per course for Bachelor's degrees. Tuition for certificate programs range from $400 to $925 per course depending on programs. $40 technology fee per course.

Undergraduate aid. **Additional information:** Loans available through Sallie Mae and PLATO. Most students have costs reimbursed by employers. GI Bill and VA benefits are also accepted.

Policies to reduce costs. Credit/placement for qualifying scores on AP, CLEP examinations.

Contact. Candice Morrissey, Associate Director of Admissions
9697 East Mineral Avenue
Englewood, CO 80112

Mesa State College

Grand Junction, Colorado
www.mesastate.edu
Four-year public **Federal Code: 001358**

	Living at home	On-campus
Tuition and fees (2002-2003):	$2,373	$2,373
Out-of-state:	$7,623	$7,623
Room and board:		$6,037
Board only:	$1,852	
Books and supplies:	$850	$850
Personal expenses:	$1,980	$1,980
Transportation:	$764	$764

Undergraduate aid. **Need-based:** Average financial aid package for full-time students was $5,871. 48% awarded as scholarships/grants, 52% as loans/jobs. Need-based aid available for part-time students. **Non-need-based:** 25% awarded as scholarships/grants, 75% as loans/jobs. Scholarships based on academics, art, athletics, leadership, minority status, music/drama. **Student debt:** 49% of graduating class borrowed to fund education; average debt was $13,935.

Freshman aid. **Need-based:** Out of 1,004 full-time freshmen, 665 applied for aid; 605 were judged to have need; of these 605 received aid. Average package met 56% of need. Average scholarship/grant was $2,986; average loan $2,250. **Non-need based:** 182 full-time freshmen with need received non-need scholarships.

Policies to reduce costs. Tuition/fee waivers for senior citizens. Credit/placement for qualifying scores on AP, IB, CLEP examinations. Work study available nights and weekends.

Payment plans. Credit card payment.

Application procedures. FAFSA required. Priority date 3/1; no closing date. Applicants notified on rolling basis starting 4/1, must reply within 5 week(s) of notification.

Contact. **Financial aid office:** (970) 248-1396
Curt Martin, Director of Financial Aid
Grand Junction, CO 81501

Metropolitan State College of Denver

Denver, Colorado
www.mscd.edu
Four-year public **Federal Code: 001360**

	Living at home
Tuition and fees (projected):	$2,668
Out-of-state:	$9,275
Books and supplies:	$1,163
Personal expenses:	$1,025
Transportation:	$568

Undergraduate aid. **Need-based:** Average financial aid package for full-time students was $6,819; for part-time $4,379. 34% awarded as scholarships/ grants, 66% as loans/jobs. **Non-need-based:** 30% awarded as scholarships/ grants, 70% as loans/jobs. Scholarships based on academics, art, athletics, job skills, music/drama, state/district residency. **Student debt:** 48% of graduating class borrowed to fund education; average debt was $18,149.

Freshman aid. **Need-based:** Out of 1,784 full-time freshmen, 1,016 applied for aid; 711 were judged to have need; of these 632 received aid. Average package met 65% of need. 20 students had full need met. Average scholarship/grant was $3,797; average loan $2,400. **Non-need based:** 53 full-time freshmen with need received non-need scholarships; 106 without need received awards; 23 received athletic scholarships.

Policies to reduce costs. Tuition/fee waivers for senior citizens, employees and their families. Credit/placement for qualifying scores on AP, IB, CLEP examinations. Work study available for part-time students.

Payment plans. Credit card, installment, deferred payment.

Application procedures. FAFSA required. Priority date 3/1; no closing date. Applicants notified on rolling basis starting 5/1. **Transfers:** No deadline.

Contact. Cindy Hejl, Director of Financial Aid
Campus Box 16
Denver, CO 80217

Morgan Community College

Fort Morgan, Colorado
www.mcc.cccoes.edu
Two-year public **Federal Code: 009981**

College costs. Out-of-state students pay in-state tuition after first quarter.

	Living at home
Tuition and fees (2002-2003):	$2,042
Out-of-state:	$9,567
Per-credit charge:	$63
Per-credit out-of-state:	$314
Books and supplies:	$675
Transportation:	$1,150

Undergraduate aid. **Need-based:** Need-based aid available for full-time and part-time students. **Non-need-based:** Scholarships based on academics, state/district residency.

Policies to reduce costs. Tuition/fee waivers for senior citizens, employees and their families. Credit/placement for qualifying scores on CLEP examinations. Work study available nights, weekends and for part-time students.

Payment plans. Credit card, installment payment.

Application procedures. FAFSA required. Priority date 6/1; no closing date. Applicants notified on rolling basis.

Contact. **Financial aid office:** (503) 977-4934
Kent Bauer, Director of Financial Aid
17800 Road 20
Fort Morgan, CO 80701

Naropa University

Boulder, Colorado
www.naropa.edu
Four-year private **Federal Code: 014652**

	Living at home	On-campus
Tuition and fees (2002-2003):	$15,860	$15,860
Room and board:		$8,400
Board only:	$2,924	
Books and supplies:	$600	$600
Personal expenses:	$1,500	$1,500
Transportation:	$1,200	$1,200

Undergraduate aid. All financial aid based on need. Average financial aid package for full-time students was $19,818; for part-time $9,605. 36% awarded as scholarships/grants, 64% as loans/jobs. **Student debt:** 66% of graduating class borrowed to fund education; average debt was $20,167.

Freshman aid. Out of 34 full-time freshmen, 27 applied for aid; 26 were judged to have need; of these 26 received aid. Average package met 64% of need. 3 students had full need met. Average scholarship/grant was $7,088; average loan $4,992.

Policies to reduce costs. Tuition/fee waivers for employees and their families. Credit/placement for qualifying scores on AP, IB, CLEP examinations.

Payment plans. Credit card, installment payment.

Application procedures. FAFSA required. Priority date 3/1; no closing date. Applicants notified on rolling basis starting 4/1, must reply within 4 week(s) of notification. **Transfers:** Priority date 3/1.

Contact. **Financial aid office:** (303) 546-3534
Cheryl Barbour, Assistant Vice President of Student Administrative Services
2130 Arapahoe Avenue
Boulder, CO 80302

National American University: Denver

Denver, Colorado
www.national.edu
Four-year proprietary **Federal Code: 004057**

	Living at home
Tuition and fees (2002-2003):	$7,695
Books and supplies:	$1,200

Policies to reduce costs. Tuition/fee waivers for employees and their families.

Payment plans. Installment, deferred payment.

Application procedures. No deadline. Applicants notified on rolling basis. **Transfers:** No deadline.

Contact. Jeanne Girod, Branch Financial Aid Coordinator
1325 South Colorado Boulevard, Suite 100
Denver, CO 80222

Nazarene Bible College

Colorado Springs, Colorado
www.nbc.edu
Four-year private **Federal Code: 013007**

	Living at home
Tuition and fees (projected):	$7,265
Books and supplies:	$500

Undergraduate aid. **Need-based:** Need-based aid available for full-time and part-time students. **Non-need-based:** Scholarships based on religious affiliation. **Additional information:** Tuition waiver available to students serving as student body officers.

Policies to reduce costs. Tuition/fee waivers for employees and their families.

Payment plans. Credit card, installment, deferred payment.

Application procedures. FAFSA required. Priority date 6/1; no closing date. Applicants notified on rolling basis starting 6/15, must reply within 2 week(s) of notification.

Contact. Mal Britton, Director of Financial Aid
1111 Academy Park Loop
Colorado Springs, CO 80910-3717

Otero Junior College

La Junta, Colorado
www.ojc.edu
Two-year public **Federal Code: 001362**

	Living at home	On-campus
Tuition and fees (2002-2003):	$2,057	$2,057
Out-of-state:	$7,700	$7,700
Per-credit charge:	$63	$63
Per-credit out-of-state:	$251	$251
Room and board:		$4,010
Board only:	$1,600	
Books and supplies:	$650	$650
Personal expenses:	$2,750	$2,500
Transportation:	$650	$650

Undergraduate aid. Need-based: 75% awarded as scholarships/grants, 25% as loans/jobs. Need-based aid available for part-time students. **Non-need-based:** 48% awarded as scholarships/grants, 52% as loans/jobs. Scholarships based on academics, athletics, state/district residency.

Policies to reduce costs. Credit/placement for qualifying scores on AP examinations.

Payment plans. Credit card, installment payment.

Application procedures. FAFSA required. Priority date 4/15; no closing date. Applicants notified on rolling basis, must reply within 2 week(s) of notification.

Contact. Jeff Paolucci, Director of Financial Aid
1802 Colorado Avenue
La Junta, CO 81050

Parks College

Denver, Colorado
www.cci.edu
Two-year proprietary **Federal Code: 004507**

College costs (projected). Per-credit-hour: 1-11 $241; 12-15 $220; 16 or more $204.

Undergraduate aid. Need-based: Need-based aid available for full-time and part-time students.

Policies to reduce costs. Tuition/fee waivers for employees and their families.

Payment plans. Installment payment.

Application procedures. FAFSA, institutional form required. No deadline. Applicants notified on rolling basis starting 8/1.

Contact. Joyce Sitton, Director of Financial Services
9065 Grant Street
Denver, CO 80229

Platt College: Aurora

Aurora, Colorado
www.plattcolorado.edu
Two-year proprietary **Federal Code: 030149**

College costs. Total cost of typical associate degree program: $27,000; bachelor's degree program: $44,000. Costs include tuition, registration fee, lab fees, supplies. Cost of books, art kit vary with program.

Undergraduate aid. All financial aid based on need. Need-based aid available for full-time students.

Application procedures. FAFSA, institutional form required. No deadline. Applicants notified on rolling basis.

Contact. Nancy Black, Assistant Director, Financial Aid
3100 South Parker Road
Aurora, CO 80014

Red Rocks Community College

Lakewood, Colorado
www.rrcc.cccoes.edu
Two-year public **Federal Code: 009543**

	Living at home
Tuition and fees (2002-2003):	$2,099
Out-of-state:	$9,625
Per-credit charge:	$63
Per-credit out-of-state:	$314

Undergraduate aid. Need-based: 57% awarded as scholarships/grants, 43% as loans/jobs. Need-based aid available for part-time students.

Policies to reduce costs. Tuition/fee waivers for senior citizens, employees and their families. Credit/placement for qualifying scores on AP, CLEP examinations. Work study available nights, weekends and for part-time students.

Payment plans. Credit card, installment, deferred payment.

Application procedures. FAFSA, institutional form required. Priority date 4/1; no closing date. Applicants notified on rolling basis starting 6/1, must reply within 2 week(s) of notification. **Transfers:** No deadline.

Contact. Financial aid office: (303) 914-6256
Linda Crook, Director of Financial Aid
13300 West Sixth Avenue
Lakewood, CO 80228-1255

Regis University

Denver, Colorado
www.regis.edu
Four-year private **Federal Code: 001363**

	Living at home	On-campus
Tuition and fees:	$20,900	$20,900
Room and board:		$7,600
Board only:	$3,300	
Books and supplies:	$400	$400
Personal expenses:	$882	$882
Transportation:	$765	$765

Undergraduate aid. Need-based: Need-based aid available for full-time and part-time students. **Non-need-based:** Scholarships based on academics, athletics, state/district residency. **Additional information:** Regis guarantees that a student carrying required amount of credit hours will graduate in 4 years or tuition is free.

Policies to reduce costs. Tuition/fee waivers for employees and their families. Credit/placement for qualifying scores on AP, IB, CLEP examinations.

Payment plans. Credit card, installment, deferred payment.

Application procedures. FAFSA required. Priority date 3/5; no closing date. Applicants notified on rolling basis starting 3/31, must reply by 5/1 or within 2 week(s) of notification.

Contact. Financial aid office: (800) 388-2366 ext. 4066
Lydia MacMillan, Director of Financial Aid
3333 Regis Boulevard, Mail Code A12
Denver, CO 80221-1099

Remington College: Colorado Springs

Colorado Springs, Colorado
www.educationamerica.com
Two-year proprietary **Federal Code: 030121**

College costs (2002-2003). $27,840 for all programs. Tuition covers costs of all books, lab fees, laptop computer.

Undergraduate aid. Need-based: Average financial aid package for full-time students was $4,833; for part-time $4,499. **Non-need-based:** Scholarships based on academics. **Student debt:** 85% of graduating class borrowed to fund education; average debt was $14,000.

Freshman aid. Need-based: Average scholarship/grant was $1,092; average loan $2,625.

Policies to reduce costs. Tuition at time of enrollment guaranteed for 2 years.

Payment plans. Credit card, installment payment.

Application procedures. FAFSA required. No deadline. Applicants notified on rolling basis, must reply within 3 week(s) of notification.

Contact. **Financial aid office:** (719) 532-1234 ext. 228
Shirley McCray, Director of Financial Services
6050 Erin Park Drive, Suite 250
Colorado Springs, CO 80918

Rocky Mountain College of Art & Design

Denver, Colorado
www.rmcad.edu
Four-year proprietary **Federal Code: 013991**

	Living at home	On-campus
Tuition and fees (2002-2003):	$12,366	$12,366
Room only:		$2,900
Board only:	$2,310	
Books and supplies:	$1,200	$1,200
Personal expenses:	$300	$300
Transportation:	$800	$800

Undergraduate aid. **Need-based:** Average financial aid package for full-time students was $3,033; for part-time $3,204. 23% awarded as scholarships/grants, 77% as loans/jobs. **Non-need-based:** 60% awarded as scholarships/grants, 40% as loans/jobs. Scholarships based on academics, art, state/district residency.

Freshman aid. **Need-based:** Out of 32 full-time freshmen, 25 applied for aid; 19 were judged to have need; of these 11 received aid. Average package met 58% of need. Average scholarship/grant was $395; average loan $1,283. **Non-need based:** 6 full-time freshmen with need received non-need scholarships; 6 without need received awards.

Policies to reduce costs. Tuition/fee waivers for employees and their families. Credit/placement for qualifying scores on AP, CLEP examinations. Work study available nights, weekends and for part-time students.

Payment plans. Credit card, installment payment.

Application procedures. FAFSA, institutional form required. Priority date 3/15; no closing date. Applicants notified on rolling basis starting 4/15, must reply within 2 week(s) of notification. **Transfers:** No deadline.

Contact. **Financial aid office:** (303) 753-6046
Julia Alexander, Director of Financial Aid
6875 East Evans Avenue
Denver, CO 80224-2359

Trinidad State Junior College

Trinidad, Colorado
www.tsjc.cccoes.edu
Two-year public **Federal Code: 001368**

College costs. Fees shown are for Trinidad Campus. Fees lower at Alamosa campus.

	Living at home	On-campus
Tuition and fees (2002-2003):	$2,249	$2,249
Out-of-state:	$7,892	$7,892
Per-credit charge:	$63	$63
Per-credit out-of-state:	$251	$251
Room and board:		$4,214
Board only:	$3,842	
Books and supplies:	$800	$800
Personal expenses:	$972	$972
Transportation:	$2,286	$2,286

Undergraduate aid. **Need-based:** 81% awarded as scholarships/grants, 19% as loans/jobs. Need-based aid available for part-time students. **Non-need-based:** 22% awarded as scholarships/grants, 78% as loans/jobs. Scholarships based on academics, athletics, state/district residency.

Policies to reduce costs. Tuition/fee waivers for senior citizens, employees and their families. Credit/placement for qualifying scores on AP, CLEP examinations. Work study available nights and for part-time students.

Payment plans. Credit card, installment, deferred payment.

Application procedures. FAFSA, institutional form required. Priority date 5/1; no closing date. Applicants notified on rolling basis starting 6/15. **Transfers:** Priority date 5/1; no deadline.

Contact. **Financial aid office:** (719) 846-5553
Gary Fresquez, Financial Aid Director
600 Prospect Street
Trinidad, CO 81082

United States Air Force Academy

USAF Academy, Colorado
www.usafa.edu
Four-year public **Federal Code: 001369**

College costs. Tuition, room, board, medical and dental care paid by U.S. government. Each cadet receives monthly salary to pay for uniforms, supplies and personal expenses. Entering freshmen required to deposit $2,500 to defray the initial cost of uniforms and equipment. A government loan of up to $5,000 is advanced to each member of the freshman class.

Policies to reduce costs. Credit/placement for qualifying scores on AP examinations.

Contact. HQ USAF/RRS, 2304 Cadet Drive, Suite 200
USAF Academy, CO 80840

University of Colorado Health Sciences Center

Denver, Colorado
www.uchsc.edu
Upper-division public **Federal Code: 004508**

College costs. Reported costs are for nursing bachelor's programs; costs of other programs may vary.

	Living at home
Tuition and fees (2002-2003):	$5,685
Out-of-state:	$18,645
Books and supplies:	$1,960

Undergraduate aid. **Need-based:** Need-based aid available for full-time and part-time students. **Non-need-based:** Scholarships based on academics, leadership.

Policies to reduce costs. Tuition/fee waivers for employees and their families. Credit/placement for qualifying scores on AP, CLEP examinations. Work study available nights and weekends.

Payment plans. Deferred payment.

Application procedures. FAFSA, institutional form required. Closing date 3/15. Applicants notified on rolling basis. **Transfers:** Priority date 3/15; no deadline.

Contact. **Financial aid office:** (303) 315-8364
Jane Nakata, Director of Financial Aid
4200 East Ninth Avenue
Denver, CO 80262

University of Colorado at Boulder

Boulder, Colorado
www.colorado.edu
Four-year public **Federal Code: 001370**

	Living at home	On-campus
Tuition and fees (2002-2003):	$3,601	$3,601
Out-of-state:	$18,945	$18,945
Room and board:		$6,272
Board only:	$1,953	
Books and supplies:	$1,100	$1,100
Personal expenses:	$2,493	$2,493
Transportation:	$765	$765

Undergraduate aid. **Need-based:** Average financial aid package for full-time students was $9,591; for part-time $8,087. 48% awarded as scholarships/grants, 52% as loans/jobs. **Non-need-based:** 28% awarded as scholarships/grants, 72% as loans/jobs. Scholarships based on academics, alumni affiliation, art, athletics, leadership, minority status, music/drama, state/district residency. **Student debt:** 46% of graduating class borrowed to fund education; average debt was $16,737. **Additional information:** Over 50 scholarship programs available.

Freshman aid. **Need-based:** Out of 5,380 full-time freshmen, 3,328 applied for aid; 1,401 were judged to have need; of these 1,399 received aid. Average package met 65% of need. 362 students had full need met. Average scholarship/grant was $4,302; average loan $2,599. **Non-need based:** 368

full-time freshmen with need received non-need scholarships; 1,484 without need received awards; 74 received athletic scholarships.

Merit scholarships. Arnold Scholarship, $1,000, based on academic excellence, leadership and community involvement, renewable for 4 years with 2.50 GPA (automatic consideration without application to students admitted by March 1). Parents Association Scholarship, $1,000, 15-30 awarded annually based on full-time entering freshman status with 3.5 GPA, academic excellence and extracurricular activities, nonrenewable. Norlin Scholars Program, $2,000, based on excellent academic or creative ability, 20 awards, renewable for 2 or 4 years contingent upon academic progress.

Policies to reduce costs. Tuition/fee waivers for senior citizens, employees and their families. Credit/placement for qualifying scores on AP, IB, CLEP examinations. Work study available for part-time students.

Payment plans. Deferred payment.

Application procedures. FAFSA required. Priority date 4/1; no closing date. Applicants notified on rolling basis starting 2/1, must reply within 3 week(s) of notification.

Contact. **Financial aid office:** (303) 492-5091
Karon Johnson, Director of Financial Aid
552 UCB
Boulder, CO 80309-0552

University of Colorado at Colorado Springs

Colorado Springs, Colorado
www.uccs.edu
Four-year public **Federal Code: 004509**

	Living at home	On-campus
Tuition and fees (2002-2003):	$4,082	$4,082
Out-of-state:	$17,306	$17,306
Room and board:		$5,893
Board only:	$1,162	
Books and supplies:	$700	$700
Personal expenses:	$520	$1,174
Transportation:	$1,180	$1,180

Undergraduate aid. Need-based: Average financial aid package for full-time students was $6,875; for part-time $4,786. 37% awarded as scholarships/grants, 63% as loans/jobs. **Non-need-based:** 58% awarded as scholarships/grants, 42% as loans/jobs. Scholarships based on academics, alumni affiliation, art, athletics, leadership, minority status, religious affiliation. **Student debt:** 30% of graduating class borrowed to fund education; average debt was $13,939.

Freshman aid. Need-based: Average package met 59% of need. Average scholarship/grant was $4,313; average loan $2,545.

Policies to reduce costs. Credit/placement for qualifying scores on AP, CLEP examinations. Work study available nights and for part-time students.

Payment plans. Credit card, installment payment.

Application procedures. FAFSA required. Priority date 4/1; no closing date. Applicants notified on rolling basis starting 4/15, must reply within 3 week(s) of notification.

Contact. Lee Noble, Director of Financial Aid
PO Box 7150
Colorado Springs, CO 80933-7150

University of Colorado at Denver

Denver, Colorado
www.cudenver.edu
Four-year public **Federal Code: 006740**

	Living at home
Tuition and fees (2002-2003):	$3,265
Out-of-state:	$13,839
Board only:	$1,800
Books and supplies:	$1,100
Personal expenses:	$855
Transportation:	$765

Undergraduate aid. All financial aid based on need. Average financial aid package for full-time students was $6,628; for part-time $4,866. **Student debt:** 41% of graduating class borrowed to fund education; average debt was $15,706.

Freshman aid. Out of 478 full-time freshmen, 318 applied for aid; 206 were judged to have need; of these 184 received aid. Average package met 64% of need. 38 students had full need met. Average scholarship/grant was $3,950; average loan $2,120.

Policies to reduce costs. Tuition/fee waivers for senior citizens, employees and their families. Credit/placement for qualifying scores on AP, IB, CLEP examinations. Work study available nights, weekends and for part-time students.

Payment plans. Credit card, installment, deferred payment.

Application procedures. FAFSA, institutional form required. Closing date 4/1. Applicants notified on rolling basis starting 5/1, must reply within 2 week(s) of notification.

Contact. **Financial aid office:** (303) 556-2886
Ellie Miller, Director of Financial Aid
Box 173364, Campus Box 167
Denver, CO 80217-3364

University of Denver

Denver, Colorado
www.du.edu
Four-year private **Federal Code: 001371**

	Living at home	On-campus
Tuition and fees (projected):	$24,873	$24,873
Room and board:		$7,275
Board only:	$2,175	
Books and supplies:	$630	$630
Personal expenses:	$1,350	
Transportation:	$1,200	

Undergraduate aid. Need-based: Average financial aid package for full-time students was $19,074; for part-time $8,252. 61% awarded as scholarships/grants, 39% as loans/jobs. **Non-need-based:** 86% awarded as scholarships/grants, 14% as loans/jobs. Scholarships based on academics, alumni affiliation, art, athletics, leadership, minority status, music/drama. **Student debt:** 48% of graduating class borrowed to fund education; average debt was $19,656.

Freshman aid. Need-based: Out of 940 full-time freshmen, 721 applied for aid; 379 were judged to have need; of these 375 received aid. Average package met 88% of need. 150 students had full need met. Average scholarship/grant was $7,496; average loan $3,758. **Non-need based:** 335 full-time freshmen with need received non-need scholarships; 225 without need received awards; 48 received athletic scholarships.

Policies to reduce costs. Tuition/fee waivers for employees and their families. Credit/placement for qualifying scores on AP, CLEP examinations.

Payment plans. Credit card, installment, deferred payment.

Application procedures. FAFSA required. Priority date 2/15; no closing date. Applicants notified by 4/1, must reply within 3 week(s) of notification.

Contact. Tammy Dybdahl, Director of Financial Aid
Mary Reed Building 107G
Denver, CO 80208-0132

University of Northern Colorado

Greeley, Colorado
www.unco.edu
Four-year public **Federal Code: 001349**

	Living at home	On-campus
Tuition and fees (2002-2003):	$2,984	$2,984
Out-of-state:	$11,278	$11,278
Room and board:		$6,160
Books and supplies:	$800	$800
Personal expenses:	$972	$972
Transportation:	$765	$765

Undergraduate aid. Need-based: Average financial aid package for full-time students was $7,356; for part-time $6,554. 38% awarded as scholarships/grants, 62% as loans/jobs. **Non-need-based:** 38% awarded as scholarships/grants, 62% as loans/jobs. Scholarships based on academics, athletics, music/drama.

Freshman aid. Need-based: Out of 2,110 full-time freshmen, 1,788 applied for aid; 893 were judged to have need; of these 708 received aid. Average package met 73% of need. 161 students had full need met. Average scholarship/grant was $2,868; average loan $2,675. **Non-need based:** 408 full-time freshmen with need received non-need scholarships; 245 without need received awards; 25 received athletic scholarships.

Policies to reduce costs. Tuition/fee waivers for senior citizens. Credit/placement for qualifying scores on AP, IB, CLEP examinations. Work study available nights, weekends and for part-time students.

Payment plans. Credit card, installment payment.

Application procedures. FAFSA required. Priority date 3/1; no closing date. Applicants notified on rolling basis starting 4/15, must reply within 4 week(s) of notification.

Contact. Donni Clark, Director of Student Financial Resources
Campus Box 10
Greeley, CO 80639

Westwood College of Technology: South

Denver, Colorado
www.westwood.edu
Four-year proprietary **Federal Code: 00754801**

	Living at home
Tuition and fees (2002-2003):	$17,325

Undergraduate aid. Need-based: 42% awarded as scholarships/grants, 58% as loans/jobs. Need-based aid available for part-time students. **Non-need-based:** 78% awarded as scholarships/grants, 22% as loans/jobs. **Student debt:** 90% of graduating class borrowed to fund education; average debt was $24,125.

Policies to reduce costs. Tuition/fee waivers for employees and their families. Credit/placement for qualifying scores on AP, CLEP examinations. Work study available nights and for part-time students.

Payment plans. Credit card, installment payment.

Application procedures. FAFSA, institutional form required. No deadline. Applicants notified on rolling basis, must reply within 2 week(s) of notification.

Contact. **Financial aid office:** (303) 934-1122
Allison Dean, Director of Financial Aid
3150 South Sheridan Boulevard
Denver, CO 80227-5507

Connecticut

Albertus Magnus College
New Haven, Connecticut
www.albertus.edu
Four-year private **Federal Code: 001374**

	Living at home	On-campus
Tuition and fees (2002-2003):	$15,712	$15,712
Room and board:		$7,116
Board only:	$2,190	
Books and supplies:	$620	$620
Personal expenses:	$1,240	$940
Transportation:	$840	$600

Undergraduate aid. Non-need-based: Scholarships based on academics, art, athletics, leadership, music/drama, state/district residency.

Policies to reduce costs. Tuition/fee waivers for children of alumni, senior citizens, family members, employees and their families. Credit/placement for qualifying scores on AP, CLEP examinations.

Payment plans. Credit card, installment payment.

Application procedures. FAFSA, institutional form required. Priority date 3/15; no closing date. Applicants notified on rolling basis starting 4/1, must reply within 2 week(s) of notification. **Transfers:** Priority date 3/15; no deadline. Scholarships for transfer students with 3.0 GPA and 30 completed credits.

Contact. Richard LoLatte, Director of Financial Aid
700 Prospect Street
New Haven, CT 06511-1189

Asnuntuck Community College
Enfield, Connecticut
www.acc.commnet.edu
Two-year public **Federal Code: 011150**

College costs. Out-of-state students pay additional $392 required fees. New England Regional Student Program: $2,960 annual tuition/fees, $110 per credit-hour.

	Living at home
Tuition and fees (2002-2003):	$1,980
Out-of-state:	$5,508
Per-credit charge:	$74
Per-credit out-of-state:	$221
Board only:	$3,290
Books and supplies:	$1,000
Personal expenses:	$1,146
Transportation:	$997

Undergraduate aid. All financial aid based on need. Need-based aid available for full-time and part-time students.

Policies to reduce costs. Tuition/fee waivers for senior citizens, employees and their families. Credit/placement for qualifying scores on AP, CLEP examinations.

Payment plans. Credit card payment.

Application procedures. FAFSA, institutional form required. Priority date 6/1; no closing date. Applicants notified on rolling basis starting 7/1, must reply within 2 week(s) of notification. **Transfers:** Financial Aid Transcript (FAT) required.

Contact. Donna Jones-Searle, Director of Financial Aid
170 Elm Street
Enfield, CT 06082

Briarwood College
Southington, Connecticut
www.briarwood.edu
Two-year proprietary **Federal Code: 009407**

College costs. $725 required fees for resident students; $525 for commuters.

	Living at home	On-campus
Tuition and fees (2002-2003):	$13,600	$13,600
Room only:		$2,800
Board only:	$500	
Books and supplies:	$1,000	$1,000
Personal expenses:	$1,400	$2,400
Transportation:	$1,463	$975

Undergraduate aid. Need-based: Need-based aid available for full-time and part-time students. **Non-need-based:** Scholarships based on academics, alumni affiliation, leadership.

Policies to reduce costs. Tuition/fee waivers for family members, employees and their families. Tuition at time of enrollment guaranteed for 2 years; credit/placement for qualifying scores on IB, CLEP examinations. Work study available nights, weekends and for part-time students.

Payment plans. Credit card, installment payment.

Application procedures. FAFSA required. Priority date 4/30; no closing date. Applicants notified on rolling basis starting 3/15, must reply within 2 week(s) of notification. **Transfers:** Priority date 4/15; no deadline.

Contact. Financial aid office: (860) 628-4751 ext. 129
Deborah Flinn, Director of Financial Aid
2279 Mount Vernon Road
Southington, CT 06489-1057

Capital Community College
Hartford, Connecticut
webster.commnet.edu
Two-year public **Federal Code: 007635**

College costs. Out-of-state students pay additional $392 required fees. New England Regional Student Program: $2,960 annual tuition/fees, $110 per credit-hour.

	Living at home
Tuition and fees (2002-2003):	$1,980
Out-of-state:	$5,508
Per-credit charge:	$74
Per-credit out-of-state:	$221
Board only:	$2,200
Books and supplies:	$800
Personal expenses:	$1,870
Transportation:	$902

Undergraduate aid. All financial aid based on need. Need-based aid available for full-time and part-time students.

Policies to reduce costs. Tuition/fee waivers for senior citizens, employees and their families. Credit/placement for qualifying scores on CLEP examinations. Work study available nights and for part-time students.

Payment plans. Credit card, installment, deferred payment.

Application procedures. FAFSA, institutional form required. Priority date 7/15; no closing date. Applicants notified on rolling basis starting 7/15, must reply within 2 week(s) of notification.

Contact. Margaret Wolf, Director of Financial Aid
950 Main Street
Hartford, CT 06103

Central Connecticut State University
New Britain, Connecticut
www.ccsu.edu
Four-year public **Federal Code: 001378**

College costs. Out-of-state students pay additional $1,010 in required fees. New England Regional Student Program tuition $3,471.

	Living at home	On-campus
Tuition and fees (2002-2003):	$4,770	$4,770
Out-of-state:	$9,942	$9,942
Room and board:		$6,280
Board only:	$2,640	
Books and supplies:	$750	$750
Personal expenses:	$1,440	$1,440
Transportation:	$872	$350

Undergraduate aid. All financial aid based on need. Average financial aid package for full-time students was $5,838; for part-time $4,011. 49% awarded as scholarships/grants, 51% as loans/jobs.

Freshman aid. Out of 1,495 full-time freshmen, 874 applied for aid; 579 were judged to have need; of these 554 received aid. Average package met 76% of need. 126 students had full need met. Average scholarship/grant was $3,878; average loan $2,652.

Policies to reduce costs. Tuition/fee waivers for senior citizens, employees and their families. Credit/placement for qualifying scores on AP, IB, CLEP examinations.

Payment plans. Credit card, deferred payment.

Application procedures. FAFSA required. Priority date 2/15; closing date 9/24. Applicants notified on rolling basis starting 3/15, must reply within 2 week(s) of notification.

Contact. **Financial aid office:** (860) 832-2200
Richard Bishop, Director of Financial Aid
1615 Stanley Street
New Britain, CT 06050

Charter Oak State College

New Britain, Connecticut
www.charteroak.edu
Four-year public **Federal Code: 032343**

College costs. After first year of enrollment, all students must pay annual advisement, records maintenance, technology and activity fee of $352 in-state, $506 out-of-state. Baccalaureate planning fee $260; graduation fee $150. Other fees vary by program.

	Living at home
Tuition and fees:	$610
Out-of-state:	$850

Undergraduate aid. All financial aid based on need. 81% awarded as scholarships/grants, 19% as loans/jobs.

Policies to reduce costs. Credit/placement for qualifying scores on AP, CLEP examinations.

Payment plans. Credit card, installment, deferred payment.

Application procedures. FAFSA, institutional form required. No deadline. Applicants notified on rolling basis starting 8/15.

Contact. **Financial aid office:** (860) 832-3872
Velma Walters, Director of Financial Aid
55 Paul Manafort Drive
New Britain, CT 06053-2142

Connecticut College

New London, Connecticut
conncoll.edu
Four-year private **Federal Code: 001379**

	On-campus
Comprehensive fee:	$37,900

Undergraduate aid. All financial aid based on need. Average financial aid package for full-time students was $23,586; for part-time $10,338. 81% awarded as scholarships/grants, 19% as loans/jobs. **Student debt:** 43% of graduating class borrowed to fund education; average debt was $17,250. **Additional information:** School meets full demonstrated need.

Freshman aid. Out of 499 full-time freshmen, 252 applied for aid; 205 were judged to have need; of these 205 received aid. Average package met 100% of need. 205 students had full need met. Average scholarship/grant was $21,782; average loan $2,700.

Policies to reduce costs. Tuition/fee waivers for employees and their families. Credit/placement for qualifying scores on AP, IB examinations.

Payment plans. Installment, deferred payment.

Application procedures. FAFSA, CSS PROFILE required. Closing date 1/15. Applicants notified by 4/1, must reply by 5/1 or within 2 week(s) of notification. Early decision closing date 11/15. **Transfers:** Closing date 4/1.

Contact. Elaine Solinga, Director of Financial Aid
270 Mohegan Avenue
New London, CT 06320

Eastern Connecticut State University

Willimantic, Connecticut
www.easternct.edu
Four-year public **Federal Code: 001425**

College costs. Additional $1,030 required fees for out-of-state residents. New England Regional Student Program tuition $3,470.

	Living at home	On-campus
Tuition and fees (2002-2003):	$4,831	$4,831
Out-of-state:	$10,003	$10,003
Room and board:		$6,450
Board only:	$2,914	
Books and supplies:	$906	$906
Personal expenses:	$1,422	$2,160
Transportation:	$1,880	$848

Undergraduate aid. **Need-based:** Need-based aid available for full-time and part-time students. **Non-need-based:** Scholarships based on academics, alumni affiliation, art, leadership, minority status, music/drama, state/district residency. **Additional information:** Tuition waiver for veterans and members of National Guard.

Policies to reduce costs. Tuition/fee waivers for senior citizens, employees and their families. Credit/placement for qualifying scores on AP, CLEP examinations.

Payment plans. Credit card, installment payment.

Application procedures. FAFSA, institutional form required. Closing date 3/15. Applicants notified on rolling basis starting 2/15, must reply within 3 week(s) of notification.

Contact. **Financial aid office:** (860) 465-5205
Richard Savage, Director of Financial Aid
83 Windham Street
Willimantic, CT 06226-2295

Fairfield University

Fairfield, Connecticut
www.fairfield.edu
Four-year private **Federal Code: 001385**

	Living at home	On-campus
Tuition and fees:	$26,585	$26,585
Room and board:		$8,920
Board only:	$3,600	
Books and supplies:	$800	$800
Personal expenses:	$1,200	$1,200
Transportation:	$1,000	$1,000

Undergraduate aid. **Need-based:** Average financial aid package for full-time students was $17,013; for part-time $6,586. 69% awarded as scholarships/grants, 31% as loans/jobs. **Non-need-based:** 28% awarded as scholarships/grants, 72% as loans/jobs. Scholarships based on academics, alumni affiliation, art, athletics, leadership, minority status, music/drama. **Student debt:** 59% of graduating class borrowed to fund education; average debt was $17,446.

Freshman aid. **Need-based:** Out of 814 full-time freshmen, 571 applied for aid; 434 were judged to have need; of these 420 received aid. Average package met 82% of need. 98 students had full need met. Average scholarship/grant was $10,506; average loan $3,288. **Non-need based:** 75 full-time freshmen with need received non-need scholarships; 54 without need received awards.

Merit scholarships. University Fellow Scholarships for students in top 5% of class and high SAT score, admission application with writing sample required by December 1; $13,000 annual grant/computer/research stipend. Presidential Scholarships for students in top 10% of class and with high SAT score; $10,000 annual grant/research stipend. Dean's Scholarship for students in top 20% of class; $8,000 annual grant. Approximately 100-160 scholarships available.

Policies to reduce costs. Tuition/fee waivers for family members, family of clergy, employees and their families. Credit/placement for qualifying scores on AP, IB, CLEP examinations. Work study available nights and weekends.

Payment plans. Installment payment.

Application procedures. FAFSA, CSS PROFILE required. Closing date 2/15. Applicants notified by 4/5, must reply by 5/1 or within 2 week(s) of notification. Early decision closing date 11/15. **Transfers:** Closing date 3/15. Students eligible for federal aid during first academic year of enrollment and may receive university and federal aid thereafter. Scholarships available for Phi Theta Kappa members.

Contact. Susan Kadir, Director of Financial Aid
1073 North Benson Road
Fairfield, CT 06824-5195

Gateway Community College

New Haven, Connecticut
www.gwcc.commnet.edu
Two-year public **Federal Code: 008303**

College costs. Out-of-state students pay additional $392 required fees. New England Regional Student Program: $2,960 annual tuition/fees, $110 per credit-hour.

	Living at home
Tuition and fees (2002-2003):	$1,980
Out-of-state:	$5,508
Per-credit charge:	$74
Per-credit out-of-state:	$221
Board only:	$786
Books and supplies:	$800
Personal expenses:	$1,100
Transportation:	$500

Undergraduate aid. All financial aid based on need. Need-based aid available for full-time and part-time students.

Policies to reduce costs. Tuition/fee waivers for senior citizens, employees and their families. Credit/placement for qualifying scores on AP, CLEP examinations. Work study available nights, weekends and for part-time students.

Payment plans. Credit card, deferred payment.

Application procedures. FAFSA, institutional form required. No deadline. Applicants notified on rolling basis, must reply within 2 week(s) of notification. **Transfers:** No deadline.

Contact. **Financial aid office:** (203) 285-2030
Cheryl Pegues, Director of Financial Aid
60 Sargent Drive
New Haven, CT 06511-5970

Gibbs College

Norwalk, Connecticut
www.gibbscollege.com
Two-year proprietary **Federal Code: 012877**

College costs. Cost of 18-month program: $26,976.

	Living at home
Tuition and fees (2002-2003):	$13,488
Books and supplies:	$900

Application procedures. FAFSA, institutional form required. No deadline. Applicants notified on rolling basis.

Contact. Alex Ormeno, Financial Aid Director
142 East Avenue
Norwalk, CT 06851

Holy Apostles College and Seminary

Cromwell, Connecticut
www.holyapostles.edu
Four-year private **Federal Code: 001389**

	Living at home	On-campus
Tuition and fees (2002-2003):	$8,310	$8,310
Room and board:		$6,600
Books and supplies:	$630	$630
Personal expenses:	$580	$735
Transportation:	$890	$420

Payment plans. Credit card, installment payment.

Application procedures. No deadline. Applicants notified on rolling basis starting 9/15.

Contact. Henry Miller, Financial Aid Director
33 Prospect Hill Road
Cromwell, CT 06416-2005

Housatonic Community College

Bridgeport, Connecticut
www.hcc.commnet.edu
Two-year public **Federal Code: 004513**

College costs. Out-of-state students pay additional $392 required fees. New England Regional Student Program: $2,960 annual tuition/fees, $110 per credit-hour.

	Living at home
Tuition and fees (2002-2003):	$1,980
Out-of-state:	$5,508
Per-credit charge:	$74
Per-credit out-of-state:	$221
Books and supplies:	$700

Undergraduate aid. All financial aid based on need. Need-based aid available for full-time and part-time students.

Policies to reduce costs. Tuition/fee waivers for senior citizens. Credit/placement for qualifying scores on CLEP examinations.

Payment plans. Credit card, installment payment.

Application procedures. FAFSA required. Priority date 5/1; no closing date. Applicants notified on rolling basis starting 6/1.

Contact. Paul Marchelli, Director of Financial Aid
900 Lafayette Boulevard
Bridgeport, CT 06604-4704

International College of Hospitality Management

Washington, Connecticut
www.ichm.ritz.edu
Two-year proprietary **Federal Code: 031575**

	Living at home	On-campus
Tuition and fees (2002-2003):	$14,000	$14,000
Per-credit charge:	$550	$550
Room and board:		$4,250
Personal expenses:	$1,000	$1,000

Undergraduate aid. Need-based: Need-based aid available for full-time and part-time students. **Non-need-based:** Scholarships based on academics. **Additional information:** Financial aid notification usually within 24 hours of application.

Policies to reduce costs. Tuition/fee waivers for children of alumni, family members, employees and their families. Tuition at time of enrollment guaranteed for 2 years. Work study available nights, weekends and for part-time students.

Payment plans. Credit card, installment, deferred payment.

Application procedures. No deadline. Applicants notified on rolling basis starting 1/1.

Contact. Carrie Ablamsky, Director of Financial Affairs
101 Wykeham Road
Washington, CT 06793

Manchester Community College

Manchester, Connecticut
www.mcc.commnet.edu
Two-year public **Federal Code: 001392**

College costs. Out-of-state students pay additional $392 required fees. New England Regional Student Program: $2,960 annual tuition/fees, $110 per credit-hour.

	Living at home
Tuition and fees (2002-2003):	$2,034
Out-of-state:	$5,562
Per-credit charge:	$74
Per-credit out-of-state:	$221
Books and supplies:	$800
Personal expenses:	$1,596
Transportation:	$1,479

Undergraduate aid. Need-based: Need-based aid available for full-time and part-time students.

Policies to reduce costs. Tuition/fee waivers for senior citizens, employees and their families. Credit/placement for qualifying scores on AP, CLEP examinations.

Payment plans. Credit card, deferred payment.

Application procedures. FAFSA, institutional form required. Closing date 5/15. Applicants notified on rolling basis starting 5/1, must reply within 2 week(s) of notification. **Transfers:** No deadline.

Contact. Financial aid office: (860) 512-3380
Ivette Rivera-Dreyer, Director of Financial Aid
Great Path PO Box 1046, MS 12
Manchester, CT 06040-1046

Middlesex Community College

Middletown, Connecticut
www.mxctc.commnet.edu
Two-year public **Federal Code: 008038**

College costs. Out-of-state students pay additional $392 required fees. New England Regional Student Program: $2,960 annual tuition/fees, $110 per credit-hour.

	Living at home
Tuition and fees (2002-2003):	$1,980
Out-of-state:	$5,508
Per-credit charge:	$74
Per-credit out-of-state:	$221
Books and supplies:	$400
Personal expenses:	$700
Transportation:	$1,500

Undergraduate aid. All financial aid based on need. Need-based aid available for full-time and part-time students. **Additional information:** Tuition and/or fee waiver for veterans.

Policies to reduce costs. Tuition/fee waivers for senior citizens, employees and their families. Credit/placement for qualifying scores on CLEP examinations.

Payment plans. Credit card payment.

Application procedures. FAFSA, institutional form required. Priority date 6/1; no closing date. Applicants notified on rolling basis starting 7/1, must reply within 2 week(s) of notification. **Transfers:** Priority date 6/1; closing date 9/1.

Contact. Sharon Thomas, Director of Financial Aid
100 Training Hill Road
Middletown, CT 06457

Mitchell College

New London, Connecticut
www.mitchell.edu
Four-year private **Federal Code: 001393**

College costs. $5,500 additional fee for students in comprehensive program at learning center for learning disabilities.

	Living at home	On-campus
Tuition and fees:	$18,128	$18,128
Room and board:		$8,268
Books and supplies:	$900	$900
Personal expenses:	$1,050	$1,050
Transportation:	$1,050	$1,000

Undergraduate aid. Need-based: Average financial aid package for full-time students was $10,000; for part-time $1,800. 49% awarded as scholarships/grants, 51% as loans/jobs. **Non-need-based:** Scholarships based on academics, alumni affiliation, athletics, leadership.

Freshman aid. Need-based: Average package met 80% of need. Average scholarship/grant was $6,400; average loan $4,000.

Policies to reduce costs. Tuition/fee waivers for employees and their families. Credit/placement for qualifying scores on AP, CLEP examinations. Work study available nights and weekends.

Payment plans. Credit card, installment payment.

Application procedures. FAFSA required. Priority date 3/1; no closing date. Applicants notified on rolling basis starting 2/15, must reply within 2 week(s) of notification. Early decision closing date 11/15. **Transfers:** No deadline.

Contact. Financial aid office: (860) 701-5040
Jacklyn Stoltz, Director of Financial Aid
437 Pequot Avenue
New London, CT 06320

Naugatuck Valley Community College

Waterbury, Connecticut
www.nvcc.commnet.edu
Two-year public **Federal Code: 006982**

College costs. Out-of-state students pay additional $392 required fees. New England Regional Student Program: $2,960 annual tuition/fees, $110 per credit-hour.

	Living at home
Tuition and fees (2002-2003):	$2,034
Out-of-state:	$5,562
Per-credit charge:	$74
Per-credit out-of-state:	$221
Board only:	$1,500
Books and supplies:	$1,000
Personal expenses:	$1,970
Transportation:	$1,100

Undergraduate aid. All financial aid based on need. Average financial aid package for full-time students was $2,647; for part-time $1,588. 93% awarded as scholarships/grants, 7% as loans/jobs.

Policies to reduce costs. Tuition/fee waivers for senior citizens, minority students, employees and their families. Credit/placement for qualifying scores on AP, CLEP examinations. Work study available for part-time students.

Payment plans. Credit card, installment payment.

Application procedures. FAFSA, institutional form required. Priority date 4/7; no closing date. Applicants notified on rolling basis starting 6/1. **Transfers:** No deadline. Financial aid transcripts from all previous schools attended.

Contact. Financial aid office: (203) 575-8007
Rodney Butler, Director of Financial Aid Services
750 Chase Parkway
Waterbury, CT 06708-3089

Northwestern Connecticut Community College

Winsted, Connecticut
www.nwctc.commnet.edu
Two-year public **Federal Code: 001398**

College costs. Out-of-state students pay additional $392 required fees. New England Regional Student Program: $2,960 annual tuition/fees, $110 per credit-hour.

	Living at home
Tuition and fees (2002-2003):	$1,980
Out-of-state:	$5,508
Per-credit charge:	$74
Per-credit out-of-state:	$221
Books and supplies:	$600
Personal expenses:	$1,000
Transportation:	$950

Policies to reduce costs. Tuition/fee waivers for senior citizens, employees and their families. Credit/placement for qualifying scores on AP, CLEP examinations.

Payment plans. Credit card payment.

Application procedures. FAFSA required. Applicants notified on rolling basis.

Contact. Dennis Williams, Financial Aid Officer
Park Place East
Winsted, CT 06098

Norwalk Community College

Norwalk, Connecticut
www.ncc.commnet.edu
Two-year public **Federal Code: 001399**

College costs. Out-of-state students pay additional $392 required fees. New England Regional Student Program: $2,960 annual tuition/fees, $110 per credit-hour.

	Living at home
Tuition and fees (2002-2003):	$1,980
Out-of-state:	$5,508
Per-credit charge:	$74
Per-credit out-of-state:	$221
Books and supplies:	$800
Personal expenses:	$2,000
Transportation:	$2,400

Undergraduate aid. Need-based: Need-based aid available for full-time and part-time students. **Non-need-based:** Scholarships based on academics, alumni affiliation.

Policies to reduce costs. Tuition/fee waivers for senior citizens, employees and their families. Credit/placement for qualifying scores on AP, IB, CLEP examinations. Work study available for part-time students.

Payment plans. Credit card payment.

Application procedures. FAFSA, institutional form required. Priority date 4/1; no closing date. Applicants notified on rolling basis starting 7/1, must reply within 2 week(s) of notification. **Transfers:** No deadline.

Contact. **Financial aid office:** (203) 857-7023
Norma McNerney, Director of Financial Aid
188 Richards Avenue
Norwalk, CT 06854-1655

Paier College of Art

Hamden, Connecticut
www.www.paierart.com
Four-year proprietary **Federal Code: 007459**

	Living at home
Tuition and fees:	$11,565
Books and supplies:	$600
Personal expenses:	$600
Transportation:	$1,200

Undergraduate aid. Need-based: Average financial aid package for full-time students was $6,727; for part-time $3,552. 51% awarded as scholarships/grants, 49% as loans/jobs. **Student debt:** 80% of graduating class borrowed to fund education; average debt was $14,011.

Freshman aid. Need-based: Out of 45 full-time freshmen, 31 applied for aid; 24 were judged to have need; of these 24 received aid. Average package met 70% of need. 2 students had full need met. Average scholarship/grant was $3,627; average loan $2,914.

Policies to reduce costs. Tuition/fee waivers for children of alumni, senior citizens, employees and their families. Credit/placement for qualifying scores on AP, IB examinations.

Payment plans. Credit card, installment payment.

Application procedures. FAFSA required. Priority date 4/15; no closing date. Applicants notified on rolling basis starting 6/1, must reply within 3 week(s) of notification. **Transfers:** No deadline.

Contact. **Financial aid office:** (203) 287-3034
Jonathan Paier, President
20 Gorham Avenue
Hamden, CT 06514-3902

Quinebaug Valley Community College

Danielson, Connecticut
www.qvcc.commnet.edu
Two-year public **Federal Code: 010530**

College costs. Out-of-state students pay additional $392 required fees. New England Regional Student Program: $2,960 annual tuition/fees, $110 per credit-hour.

	Living at home
Tuition and fees (2002-2003):	$1,980
Out-of-state:	$5,508
Per-credit charge:	$74
Per-credit out-of-state:	$221
Books and supplies:	$800
Personal expenses:	$1,000
Transportation:	$1,600

Undergraduate aid. All financial aid based on need. Need-based aid available for full-time and part-time students.

Policies to reduce costs. Tuition/fee waivers for senior citizens, employees and their families. Credit/placement for qualifying scores on AP, CLEP examinations. Work study available nights, weekends and for part-time students.

Payment plans. Credit card, installment payment.

Application procedures. FAFSA required. Closing date 10/1. Applicants notified on rolling basis starting 5/1.

Contact. Monica Mattscheck, Director of Financial Aid
742 Upper Maple Street
Danielson, CT 06239-1440

Quinnipiac University

Hamden, Connecticut
www.quinnipiac.edu
Four-year private **Federal Code: 001402**

	Living at home	On-campus
Tuition and fees:	$21,120	$21,120
Room and board:		$9,000
Board only:	$1,670	
Books and supplies:	$600	$600
Personal expenses:	$900	$900
Transportation:	$300	$300

Undergraduate aid. Need-based: Average financial aid package for full-time students was $12,555; for part-time $5,511. 60% awarded as scholarships/grants, 40% as loans/jobs. **Non-need-based:** 59% awarded as scholarships/grants, 41% as loans/jobs. Scholarships based on academics, athletics, minority status. **Student debt:** 71% of graduating class borrowed to fund education; average debt was $16,719. **Additional information:** Foreign students eligible for academic scholarships.

Freshman aid. Need-based: Out of 1,347 full-time freshmen, 1,060 applied for aid; 819 were judged to have need; of these 818 received aid. Average package met 67% of need. 124 students had full need met. Average scholarship/grant was $8,502; average loan $2,795. **Non-need based:** 359 full-time freshmen with need received non-need scholarships; 151 without need received awards; 78 received athletic scholarships.

Merit scholarships. Over 800 merit-based scholarships for admitted freshmen. Amounts based on a combination of class rank and SAT or ACT scores.

Policies to reduce costs. Tuition/fee waivers for senior citizens, family members, employees and their families. Credit/placement for qualifying scores on AP, IB, CLEP examinations. Work study available nights and weekends.

Payment plans. Credit card, installment, deferred payment.

Application procedures. FAFSA required. Priority date 3/1; no closing date. Applicants notified on rolling basis starting 3/1, must reply by 5/1 or within 2 week(s) of notification. **Transfers:** No deadline.

Contact. **Financial aid office:** (800) 462-1944
Dominic Yoia, Director of Financial Aid
275 Mount Carmel Avenue
Hamden, CT 06518-1908

Sacred Heart University

Fairfield, Connecticut
www.sacredheart.edu
Four-year private **Federal Code: 001403**

College costs. Tuition includes cost of laptop computer.

	Living at home	On-campus
Tuition and fees (2002-2003):	$19,260	$19,260
Room and board:		$9,050
Board only:	$2,260	
Books and supplies:	$600	$600
Transportation:	$700	$700

Undergraduate aid. Need-based: Need-based aid available for full-time and part-time students. **Non-need-based:** Scholarships based on academics, alumni affiliation, art, athletics, leadership, minority status, music/drama.

Policies to reduce costs. Tuition/fee waivers for minority students, family members, employees and their families. Credit/placement for qualifying scores on AP, IB, CLEP examinations. Work study available nights and weekends.

Payment plans. Credit card, installment, deferred payment.

Application procedures. FAFSA, CSS PROFILE required. Priority date 2/15; no closing date. Applicants notified on rolling basis starting 3/1, must reply within 2 week(s) of notification. Early decision closing date 10/1. **Transfers:** Priority date 5/1; no deadline.

Contact. **Financial aid office:** (203) 371-7980
Julie Savino, Dean of University Financial Assistance
5151 Park Avenue
Fairfield, CT 06825

St. Joseph College

West Hartford, Connecticut
www.sjc.edu
Four-year private **Federal Code: 001409**

	Living at home	On-campus
Tuition and fees:	$20,900	$20,900
Room and board:		$8,785
Books and supplies:	$850	$850
Personal expenses:	$700	$700
Transportation:	$2,000	$200

Undergraduate aid. Need-based: Average financial aid package for full-time students was $18,304; for part-time $9,340. 62% awarded as scholarships/grants, 38% as loans/jobs. **Non-need-based:** 47% awarded as scholarships/grants, 53% as loans/jobs. Scholarships based on academics, leadership. **Student debt:** 73% of graduating class borrowed to fund education; average debt was $14,550.

Freshman aid. Need-based: Average package met 73% of need. Average scholarship/grant was $12,707; average loan $2,625.

Merit scholarships. Variety of Merit Scholarships based on High School academic record for first-year students and college academic record for transfer students.

Policies to reduce costs. Tuition/fee waivers for family members, employees and their families. Credit/placement for qualifying scores on AP, CLEP examinations. Work study available nights and weekends.

Payment plans. Credit card, installment payment.

Application procedures. FAFSA required. Priority date 2/15; closing date 6/30. Applicants notified on rolling basis starting 2/1, must reply within 2 week(s) of notification. **Transfers:** Priority date 6/1; closing date 7/15.

Contact. **Financial aid office:** (860) 231-5223
Philip Malinoski, Director of Student Financial Services
1678 Asylum Avenue
West Hartford, CT 06117-2700

Southern Connecticut State University

New Haven, Connecticut
www.scsu.ctstateu.edu
Four-year public **Federal Code: 001406**

College costs. Additional $1,030 in required fees for out-of-state residents. New England Regional tuition $3,471.

	Living at home	On-campus
Tuition and fees (2002-2003):	$4,444	$4,444
Out-of-state:	$9,616	$9,616
Room and board:		$6,446
Books and supplies:	$750	$750
Personal expenses:	$300	$300
Transportation:	$1,300	$300

Undergraduate aid. Need-based: Need-based aid available for full-time and part-time students. **Non-need-based:** Scholarships based on academics, athletics.

Merit scholarships. General Academic Achievement Awards; 90 awarded; total of $260,000.

Policies to reduce costs. Tuition/fee waivers for senior citizens, employees and their families. Credit/placement for qualifying scores on AP, IB, CLEP examinations.

Payment plans. Credit card payment.

Application procedures. FAFSA, institutional form required. Must reply within 2 week(s) of notification.

Contact. Avon Dennis, Director of Financial Aid
131 Farnham Avenue
New Haven, CT 06515-1202

Teikyo Post University

Waterbury, Connecticut
www.teikyopost.edu
Four-year private **Federal Code: 001401**

	Living at home	On-campus
Tuition and fees:	$17,600	$17,600
Room and board:		$7,375
Books and supplies:	$1,000	$1,000
Personal expenses:	$1,200	$1,200

Undergraduate aid. Need-based: Need-based aid available for full-time and part-time students. **Additional information:** Academic merit scholarships available based on GPA and test scores. Renewable contingent upon maintaining specific GPA.

Policies to reduce costs. Tuition/fee waivers for senior citizens, family members, employees and their families. Credit/placement for qualifying scores on AP, CLEP examinations. Work study available nights, weekends and for part-time students.

Payment plans. Credit card, installment payment.

Application procedures. FAFSA required. Priority date 3/15; no closing date. Applicants notified on rolling basis starting 4/15, must reply by 5/1 or within 3 week(s) of notification. **Transfers:** Priority date 3/15; no deadline.

Contact. **Financial aid office:** (203) 596-4527
Patricia DelBuono, Associate Director of Financial Aid
800 Country Club Road
Waterbury, CT 06723-2540

Three Rivers Community College

Norwich, Connecticut
www.trcc.commnet.edu
Two-year public **Federal Code: 009765**

College costs. Out-of-state students pay additional $392 required fees. New England Regional Student Program: $2,960 annual tuition/fees, $110 per credit-hour.

	Living at home
Tuition and fees (2002-2003):	$2,014
Out-of-state:	$5,542
Per-credit charge:	$74
Per-credit out-of-state:	$221
Books and supplies:	$500
Transportation:	$500

Merit scholarships. Available for continuing students; ranging from $75 to $500.

Policies to reduce costs. Tuition/fee waivers for senior citizens, employees and their families. Credit/placement for qualifying scores on AP, CLEP examinations.

Payment plans. Credit card, installment payment.

Application procedures. FAFSA required. Priority date 7/15; no closing date. Applicants notified on rolling basis, must reply within 2 week(s) of notification. **Transfers:** No deadline.

Contact. **Financial aid office:** (860) 823-2870
Dan Zaneski, Financial Aid Director
7 Mahan Drive
Norwich, CT 06360-2479

Trinity College

Hartford, Connecticut
www.trincoll.edu
Four-year private **Federal Code: 001414**

	Living at home	On-campus
Tuition and fees:	$30,230	$30,230
Room and board:		$7,810
Board only:	$2,884	
Books and supplies:	$850	$850
Personal expenses:	$850	$850
Transportation:		$207

Undergraduate aid. All financial aid based on need. Average financial aid package for full-time students was $24,367; for part-time $30,339. 83% awarded as scholarships/grants, 17% as loans/jobs. **Student debt:** 43% of graduating class borrowed to fund education; average debt was $15,402.

Freshman aid. Out of 550 full-time freshmen, 278 applied for aid; 240 were judged to have need; of these 240 received aid. Average package met 98% of need. 227 students had full need met. Average scholarship/grant was $21,469; average loan $3,521.

Policies to reduce costs. Tuition/fee waivers for adults, employees and their families. Credit/placement for qualifying scores on AP, IB examinations. Work study available nights, weekends and for part-time students.

Payment plans. Installment payment.

Application procedures. FAFSA, CSS PROFILE required. Closing date 2/1. Applicants notified by 4/1, must reply by 5/1 or within 2 week(s) of notification. Early decision closing date 11/15. **Transfers:** Closing date 4/1.

Contact. **Financial aid office:** (860) 297-2046
Kelly O'Brien, Director of Financial Aid
300 Summit Street
Hartford, CT 06106

Tunxis Community College

Farmington, Connecticut
www.tunxis.commnet.edu
Two-year public **Federal Code: 009764**

College costs. Out-of-state students pay additional $392 required fees. New England Regional Student Program: $2,960 annual tuition/fees, $110 per credit-hour.

	Living at home
Tuition and fees (2002-2003):	$1,980
Out-of-state:	$5,508
Per-credit charge:	$74
Per-credit out-of-state:	$221
Books and supplies:	$420
Personal expenses:	$1,210
Transportation:	$1,400

Undergraduate aid. **Need-based:** 79% awarded as scholarships/grants, 21% as loans/jobs. Need-based aid available for part-time students. **Non-need-based:** Scholarships based on academics, leadership. **Student debt:** 5% of graduating class borrowed to fund education; average debt was $3,500. **Additional information:** Financial aid available to all students showing need. Part-time students encouraged to apply.

Policies to reduce costs. Tuition/fee waivers for senior citizens, employees and their families. Credit/placement for qualifying scores on CLEP examinations. Work study available nights, weekends and for part-time students.

Payment plans. Credit card, installment, deferred payment.

Application procedures. FAFSA, institutional form required. No deadline. Applicants notified on rolling basis starting 3/1, must reply within 2 week(s) of notification. **Transfers:** No deadline.

Contact. **Financial aid office:** (860) 679-9558
David Welsh, Director of Financial Aid
271 Scott Swamp Road
Farmington, CT 06032-3187

United States Coast Guard Academy

New London, Connecticut
www.cga.edu
Four-year public **Federal Code: 001415**

College costs. All tuition, room and board paid for by U.S. government. Students make one-time entrance deposit of $3,000 to help defray cost of uniforms, books, supplies and personal computer. All students paid monthly stipend of $734.

Application procedures. No deadline.

Contact. 31 Mohegan Avenue
New London, CT 06320

University of Bridgeport

Bridgeport, Connecticut
www.bridgeport.edu
Four-year private **Federal Code: 001416**

	Living at home	On-campus
Tuition and fees (2002-2003):	$16,504	$16,504
Room and board:		$7,760
Board only:	$1,800	
Books and supplies:	$850	$850
Personal expenses:	$750	$750
Transportation:	$700	$700

Undergraduate aid. **Non-need-based:** Scholarships based on academics, athletics, state/district residency.

Merit scholarships. Academic Excellence and Leadership Scholarship for students ranking in the top quarter of high school class with SAT score greater than 1200; up to full tuition, room, and board. Academic Scholarship for students in the top quarter of class and SAT score greater than 1100; up to full tuition. Academic Grant for students in top half of class and SAT greater than 1100; up to half of tuition costs. Challenge Grant for students in the top half of class and SAT greater than 1000; $3,000.

Policies to reduce costs. Tuition/fee waivers for family members, employees and their families. Credit/placement for qualifying scores on AP, IB, CLEP examinations.

Payment plans. Credit card, installment, deferred payment.

Application procedures. FAFSA, institutional form required. Priority date 4/1; no closing date. Applicants notified on rolling basis starting 4/1, must reply within 4 week(s) of notification.

Contact. **Financial aid office:** (203) 576-4568
Garrick Campbell, Director of Financial Aid
126 Park Avenue/Wahlstrom Library
Bridgeport, CT 06601

University of Connecticut

Storrs, Connecticut
www.uconn.edu
Four-year public **Federal Code: 007997**

College costs. Out-of-state New England residents pay 150% of in-state tuition rate for programs of study not offered at their home state university.

	Living at home	On-campus
Tuition and fees:	$6,800	$6,800
Out-of-state:	$17,584	$17,584
Room and board:		$6,888
Board only:	$3,218	
Books and supplies:	$725	$725
Personal expenses:	$1,800	$1,800
Transportation:	$900	$900

Undergraduate aid. **Need-based:** Average financial aid package for full-time students was $8,313; for part-time $8,174. 50% awarded as scholarships/grants, 50% as loans/jobs. **Non-need-based:** 30% awarded as scholarships/grants, 70% as loans/jobs. Scholarships based on academics, art, athletics, leadership, minority status, music/drama. **Student debt:** 61% of graduating class borrowed to fund education; average debt was $16,093. **Additional**

information: Institution offers variety of need-based financial aid programs. Financial assistance packages may include grants, loans and work-study awards.

Freshman aid. Need-based: Out of 3,164 full-time freshmen, 2,474 applied for aid; 1,561 were judged to have need; of these 1,516 received aid. Average package met 74% of need. 465 students had full need met. Average scholarship/grant was $5,124; average loan $3,108. **Non-need based:** 859 full-time freshmen with need received non-need scholarships; 457 without need received awards; 79 received athletic scholarships.

Merit scholarships. Incoming freshmen apply for university merit scholarships automatically as part of application process; no other applications necessary. Two other scholarships for CT residents -- Day of Pride and Nutmeg -- require supplementary applications.

Policies to reduce costs. Tuition/fee waivers for senior citizens, employees and their families. Credit/placement for qualifying scores on AP, IB examinations. Work study available nights, weekends and for part-time students.

Payment plans. Credit card payment.

Application procedures. FAFSA required. Priority date 3/1; no closing date. Applicants notified on rolling basis starting 3/1, must reply within 4 week(s) of notification.

Contact. Jean Main, Director of Financial Aid
2131 Hillside Road, Unit 3088
Storrs, CT 06269-3088

University of Hartford

West Hartford, Connecticut
www.hartford.edu
Four-year private **Federal Code: 001422**

	Living at home	On-campus
Tuition and fees:	$22,470	$22,470
Room and board:		$8,610
Board only:	$3,300	
Books and supplies:	$800	$800
Personal expenses:	$1,350	$1,350
Transportation:	$1,553	$800

Undergraduate aid. Need-based: Average financial aid package for full-time students was $17,368; for part-time $5,633. 64% awarded as scholarships/grants, 36% as loans/jobs. **Non-need-based:** 54% awarded as scholarships/grants, 46% as loans/jobs. Scholarships based on academics, art, athletics, music/drama, state/district residency. **Student debt:** 66% of graduating class borrowed to fund education; average debt was $23,040.

Freshman aid. Need-based: Out of 1,398 full-time freshmen, 1,019 applied for aid; 880 were judged to have need; of these 880 received aid. Average package met 76% of need. 201 students had full need met. Average scholarship/grant was $9,654; average loan $4,400. **Non-need based:** 856 full-time freshmen with need received non-need scholarships; 453 without need received awards; 13 received athletic scholarships.

Policies to reduce costs. Tuition/fee waivers for minority students, family members, employees and their families. Credit/placement for qualifying scores on AP, CLEP examinations. Work study available nights, weekends and for part-time students.

Payment plans. Credit card, installment payment.

Application procedures. FAFSA, institutional form required. Priority date 2/1; no closing date. Applicants notified on rolling basis starting 3/1, must reply by 5/1.

Contact. Financial aid office: (860) 768-4296
Suzanne Peters, Director of Student Financial Assistance
Bates House
West Hartford, CT 06117-1599

University of New Haven

West Haven, Connecticut
www.newhaven.edu
Four-year private **Federal Code: 001397**

	Living at home	On-campus
Tuition and fees:	$20,660	$20,660
Room and board:		$8,500
Board only:	$1,500	
Books and supplies:	$750	$750
Personal expenses:	$1,000	$1,000
Transportation:	$1,500	$300

Undergraduate aid. Need-based: Average financial aid package for full-time students was $12,884; for part-time $4,545. 54% awarded as scholarships/grants, 46% as loans/jobs. **Non-need-based:** 19% awarded as scholarships/grants, 81% as loans/jobs. Scholarships based on academics, athletics. **Student debt:** 67% of graduating class borrowed to fund education; average debt was $16,868. **Additional information:** Tuition-free program for selected outstanding high school seniors.

Freshman aid. Need-based: Out of 503 full-time freshmen, 426 applied for aid; 383 were judged to have need; of these 383 received aid. Average package met 79% of need. 94 students had full need met. Average scholarship/grant was $9,588; average loan $4,424. **Non-need based:** 25 full-time freshmen with need received non-need scholarships; 61 without need received awards; 11 received athletic scholarships.

Merit scholarships. Half-tuition Presidential Scholarship awards to applicants in top 15% of class with 1200 SAT I combined score or ACT equivalent. Academic Achievement Awards range from $5,000-$7,500 to applicants with a minimum 1050 SAT and top 35% of class.

Policies to reduce costs. Tuition/fee waivers for senior citizens, employees and their families. Credit/placement for qualifying scores on AP, IB, CLEP examinations. Work study available nights and weekends.

Payment plans. Credit card, installment payment.

Application procedures. FAFSA, institutional form required. Closing date 3/2. Applicants notified on rolling basis starting 3/15, must reply by 5/2 or within 2 week(s) of notification.

Contact. Financial aid office: (203) 932-7315
Karen Flynn, Director of Financial Aid
300 Orange Avenue
West Haven, CT 06516

Wesleyan University

Middletown, Connecticut
www.wesleyan.edu
Four-year private **Federal Code: 001424**

	Living at home	On-campus
Tuition and fees (projected):	$28,320	$28,320
Room and board:		$7,610
Books and supplies:	$2,010	$2,010
Transportation:		$275

Undergraduate aid. All financial aid based on need. Average financial aid package for full-time students was $24,532. 72% awarded as scholarships/grants, 28% as loans/jobs. Need-based aid available for part-time students. **Additional information:** Loan debt capped for students at $20,000 over 4 years.

Freshman aid. Out of 719 full-time freshmen, 420 applied for aid; 336 were judged to have need; of these 336 received aid. Average package met 100% of need. 336 students had full need met. Average scholarship/grant was $21,003; average loan $2,770.

Policies to reduce costs. Tuition/fee waivers for employees and their families. Credit/placement for qualifying scores on AP, IB examinations. Work study available nights and weekends.

Payment plans. Installment, deferred payment.

Application procedures. FAFSA, CSS PROFILE required. Closing date 2/1. Applicants notified by 4/1, must reply by 5/1 or within 2 week(s) of notification. Early decision closing date 11/15. **Transfers:** Priority date 2/15; closing date 3/15. No financial aid available for international transfer candidates.

Contact. Financial aid office: (860) 685-2800
Elizabeth McCormick, Director of Financial Aid
The Stewart Reid House, 70 Wyllys Avenue
Middletown, CT 06459-0260

Western Connecticut State University

Danbury, Connecticut
www.wcsu.edu
Four-year public **Federal Code: 001380**

College costs. New England residents in select programs of study pay $3,471 tuition. Out-of-state students pay additional $1,030 in fees.

	Living at home	On-campus
Tuition and fees (2002-2003):	$4,456	$4,456
Out-of-state:	$9,628	$9,628
Room and board:		$6,224
Board only:	$1,100	
Books and supplies:	$1,000	$1,000
Personal expenses:	$1,985	$1,750
Transportation:	$903	$730

Undergraduate aid. Need-based: Average financial aid package for full-time students was $6,314; for part-time $3,361. 46% awarded as scholarships/grants, 54% as loans/jobs. **Non-need-based:** 14% awarded as scholarships/grants, 86% as loans/jobs. Scholarships based on academics.

Freshman aid. Need-based: Out of 848 full-time freshmen, 632 applied for aid; 385 were judged to have need; of these 361 received aid. Average package met 63% of need. 103 students had full need met. Average scholarship/grant was $3,959; average loan $2,639. **Non-need based:** 52 full-time freshmen with need received non-need scholarships; 43 without need received awards.

Policies to reduce costs. Tuition/fee waivers for senior citizens, employees and their families. Credit/placement for qualifying scores on AP, IB, CLEP examinations. Work study available nights, weekends and for part-time students.

Payment plans. Credit card, installment payment.

Application procedures. FAFSA, institutional form required. Priority date 3/15; closing date 4/15. Applicants notified on rolling basis starting 3/15, must reply by 5/1 or within 2 week(s) of notification.

Contact. Financial aid office: (203) 837-8580
William Hawkins, Director, Financial Aid/Veterans Affairs
181 White Street
Danbury, CT 06810

Yale University

New Haven, Connecticut
www.yale.edu
Four-year private **Federal Code: 001426**

	Living at home	On-campus
Tuition and fees:	$28,400	$28,400
Room and board:		$8,600
Board only:	$3,900	
Books and supplies:	$2,520	$2,520

Undergraduate aid. All financial aid based on need. Average financial aid package for full-time students was $25,501. 86% awarded as scholarships/grants, 14% as loans/jobs. Need-based aid available for part-time students. **Student debt:** 43% of graduating class borrowed to fund education; average debt was $19,228. **Additional information:** All scholarships based on demonstrated need.

Freshman aid. Out of 1,300 full-time freshmen, 787 applied for aid; 560 were judged to have need; of these 560 received aid. Average package met 100% of need. 560 students had full need met. Average scholarship/grant was $23,212; average loan $1,170.

Policies to reduce costs. Tuition/fee waivers for employees and their families. Credit/placement for qualifying scores on AP, IB examinations. Work study available nights and weekends.

Payment plans. Installment payment.

Application procedures. FAFSA, CSS PROFILE required. Closing date 3/1. Applicants notified by 4/1, must reply by 5/1. Early decision closing date 11/1. **Transfers:** Closing date 3/1.

Contact. Financial aid office: (203) 432-0360
Myra Smith, Director of University Financial Aid
Box 208234
New Haven, CT 06520-8234

Delaware

Delaware State University

Dover, Delaware
www.dsc.edu
Four-year public **Federal Code: 001428**

	Living at home	On-campus
Tuition and fees:	$4,296	$4,296
Out-of-state:	$9,276	$9,276
Room and board:		$5,966
Books and supplies:	$1,050	$1,050
Personal expenses:		$777
Transportation:		$1,576

Undergraduate aid. All financial aid based on need. Average financial aid package for full-time students was $7,691; for part-time $6,096. 44% awarded as scholarships/grants, 56% as loans/jobs.

Freshman aid. Out of 761 full-time freshmen, 717 applied for aid; 627 were judged to have need; of these 613 received aid. Average package met 63% of need. 219 students had full need met.

Policies to reduce costs. Tuition/fee waivers for senior citizens, employees and their families. Credit/placement for qualifying scores on AP, IB, CLEP examinations.

Payment plans. Credit card, installment, deferred payment.

Application procedures. FAFSA required. Priority date 3/1; no closing date. Applicants notified on rolling basis starting 4/1. **Transfers:** Closing date 2/15.

Contact. **Financial aid office:** (302) 857-6250
Carylin Brinkley, Director of Financial Aid
1200 North DuPont Highway
Dover, DE 19901

Delaware Technical and Community College: Owens Campus

Georgetown, Delaware
www.dtcc.edu
Two-year public **Federal Code: 007053**

College costs. Lab fees vary depending on program.

	Living at home
Tuition and fees (2002-2003):	$1,806
Out-of-state:	$4,290
Per-credit charge:	$69
Per-credit out-of-state:	$173
Board only:	$2,000
Books and supplies:	$800
Personal expenses:	$400
Transportation:	$800

Undergraduate aid. **Non-need-based:** Scholarships based on academics, athletics.

Policies to reduce costs. Tuition/fee waivers for senior citizens, employees and their families. Credit/placement for qualifying scores on CLEP examinations.

Payment plans. Credit card, installment, deferred payment.

Application procedures. FAFSA required. Priority date 6/15; no closing date. Applicants notified on rolling basis, must reply within 2 week(s) of notification.

Contact. Kristine Collins, Financial Aid Officer
Box 610
Georgetown, DE 19947

Delaware Technical and Community College: Stanton/Wilmington Campus

Newark, Delaware
www.dtcc.edu
Two-year public **Federal Code: 021449**

College costs. Lab fees vary depending on program.

	Living at home
Tuition and fees (2002-2003):	$1,806
Out-of-state:	$4,290
Per-credit charge:	$69
Per-credit out-of-state:	$173
Board only:	$2,000
Books and supplies:	$800
Personal expenses:	$400
Transportation:	$800

Undergraduate aid. **Need-based:** Need-based aid available for full-time and part-time students. **Non-need-based:** Scholarships based on academics, athletics. **Additional information:** Male Delaware residents must be registered for Selective Service to be eligible for state financial aid.

Policies to reduce costs. Tuition/fee waivers for senior citizens, employees and their families. Credit/placement for qualifying scores on AP, IB, CLEP examinations.

Payment plans. Credit card, installment, deferred payment.

Application procedures. FAFSA, institutional form required. Priority date 7/1; no closing date. Applicants notified on rolling basis, must reply within 2 week(s) of notification. **Transfers:** Priority date 11/15; no deadline.

Contact. **Financial aid office:** (302) 571-5380
Lawrence Digregorio, Student Financial Aid Officer
400 Stanton-Christiana Road
Newark, DE 19713

Delaware Technical and Community College: Terry Campus

Dover, Delaware
www.dtcc.edu
Two-year public **Federal Code: 011727**

College costs. Lab fees vary per program.

	Living at home
Tuition and fees (2002-2003):	$1,806
Out-of-state:	$4,290
Per-credit charge:	$69
Per-credit out-of-state:	$173
Board only:	$2,000
Books and supplies:	$800
Personal expenses:	$400
Transportation:	$800

Undergraduate aid. **Need-based:** Need-based aid available for full-time and part-time students.

Policies to reduce costs. Tuition/fee waivers for senior citizens, employees and their families. Credit/placement for qualifying scores on CLEP examinations.

Payment plans. Credit card, installment, deferred payment.

Application procedures. FAFSA required. No deadline. Applicants notified on rolling basis starting 7/1, must reply within 2 week(s) of notification.

Contact. Jennifer Grunden, Financial Aid Director
100 Campus Drive
Dover, DE 19901

Goldey-Beacom College

Wilmington, Delaware
goldey.gbc.edu
Four-year private **Federal Code: 001429**

	Living at home	On-campus
Tuition and fees:	$9,720	$9,720
Room only:		$3,996
Books and supplies:	$600	$600
Personal expenses:	$1,068	$1,068
Transportation:	$819	$819

Undergraduate aid. All financial aid based on need. Need-based aid available for full-time and part-time students. **Additional information:** Essays required for scholarship applicants.

Policies to reduce costs. Tuition/fee waivers for family members, employees and their families. Credit/placement for qualifying scores on AP, IB, CLEP examinations.

Payment plans. Credit card, installment, deferred payment.

Application procedures. FAFSA required. Priority date 4/1; no closing date. Applicants notified on rolling basis starting 2/15, must reply within 2 week(s) of notification. **Transfers:** No deadline.

Contact. **Financial aid office:** (302) 225-6265
Jane Lysle, Director of Financial Aid and Advisement
4701 Limestone Road
Wilmington, DE 19808

University of Delaware

Newark, Delaware
www.udel.edu
Four-year public **Federal Code: 001431**

	Living at home	On-campus
Tuition and fees (2002-2003):	$5,680	$5,680
Out-of-state:	$15,210	$15,210
Room and board:		$5,822
Books and supplies:	$800	$800
Personal expenses:	$1,300	$1,500

Undergraduate aid. All financial aid based on need. Average financial aid package for full-time students was $9,750; for part-time $7,150. 48% awarded as scholarships/grants, 52% as loans/jobs. **Student debt:** 33% of graduating class borrowed to fund education; average debt was $13,610. **Additional information:** January 15 application deadline to receive scholarship consideration. Sibling/parent tuition credit plan. Senior citizen tuition credit for state residents over 60.

Freshman aid. Out of 3,402 full-time freshmen, 2,512 applied for aid; 1,455 were judged to have need; of these 1,455 received aid. Average package met 80% of need. 682 students had full need met. Average scholarship/grant was $5,650; average loan $3,500.

Policies to reduce costs. Tuition/fee waivers for senior citizens, employees and their families. Credit/placement for qualifying scores on AP, IB examinations.

Payment plans. Installment payment.

Application procedures. FAFSA required. Priority date 2/1; closing date 3/15. Applicants notified on rolling basis starting 3/15, must reply by 5/1 or within 3 week(s) of notification. Early decision closing date 11/15. **Transfers:** No deadline. Aid usualy limited to federal and state programs.

Contact. **Financial aid office:** (302) 831-8761
Johnie Burton, Director of Financial Aid
116 Hullihen Hall
Newark, DE 19716

Wilmington College

New Castle, Delaware
www.wilmcoll.edu
Four-year private **Federal Code: 007948**

	Living at home
Tuition and fees (2002-2003):	$6,740
Books and supplies:	$800
Personal expenses:	$1,500
Transportation:	$2,000

Undergraduate aid. **Need-based:** Average financial aid package for full-time students was $5,136; for part-time $3,887. 22% awarded as scholarships/grants, 78% as loans/jobs. **Non-need-based:** 8% awarded as scholarships/grants, 92% as loans/jobs. Scholarships based on academics, athletics. **Student debt:** 31% of graduating class borrowed to fund education; average debt was $15,400.

Freshman aid. **Need-based:** Average package met 67% of need. Average scholarship/grant was $2,557; average loan $2,423.

Policies to reduce costs. Tuition/fee waivers for children of alumni, employees and their families. Credit/placement for qualifying scores on AP, CLEP examinations. Work study available nights, weekends and for part-time students.

Payment plans. Credit card, installment payment.

Application procedures. FAFSA required. Priority date 4/15; no closing date. Applicants notified on rolling basis, must reply within 2 week(s) of notification. **Transfers:** No deadline.

Contact. Lynn Iocono, Financial Aid Coordinator
320 Dupont Highway
New Castle, DE 19720

District of Columbia

American University

Washington, District of Columbia
www.american.edu
Four-year private **Federal Code: 001434**

	Living at home	On-campus
Tuition and fees:	$24,839	$24,839
Room and board:		$9,916
Board only:	$1,646	
Books and supplies:	$600	$600
Personal expenses:	$600	$600
Transportation:	$700	$700

Undergraduate aid. Need-based: Average financial aid package for full-time students was $21,266; for part-time $10,783. 56% awarded as scholarships/grants, 44% as loans/jobs. **Non-need-based:** 52% awarded as scholarships/grants, 48% as loans/jobs. Scholarships based on academics, alumni affiliation, athletics, leadership, minority status, music/drama, religious affiliation, state/district residency. **Student debt:** 50% of graduating class borrowed to fund education; average debt was $19,953. **Additional information:** ED applicants must submit estimated AU Institutional financial aid application by 11/15.

Freshman aid. Need-based: Out of 1,303 full-time freshmen, 886 applied for aid; 642 were judged to have need; of these 642 received aid. Average package met 72% of need. 303 students had full need met. Average scholarship/grant was $12,061; average loan $5,791. **Non-need based:** 178 full-time freshmen with need received non-need scholarships; 189 without need received awards; 32 received athletic scholarships.

Policies to reduce costs. Tuition/fee waivers for family of clergy, employees and their families. Credit/placement for qualifying scores on AP, IB, CLEP examinations.

Payment plans. Credit card, installment, deferred payment.

Application procedures. FAFSA, institutional form required. Closing date 3/1. Applicants notified by 4/1, must reply by 5/1 or within 4 week(s) of notification. Early decision closing date 11/15. **Transfers:** Priority date 3/1. Transfer filing deadline for financial aid forms is 3/01 for fall, spring or summer semester.

Contact. Brian Lee-Sang, Director of Financial Aid
4400 Massachusetts Avenue NW
Washington, DC 20016-8001

Catholic University of America

Washington, District of Columbia
www.cua.edu
Four-year private **Federal Code: 001437**

College costs. New student fee (one-time fee required of all students): Undergraduate $350; Graduate $175

	Living at home	On-campus
Tuition and fees (projected):	$23,250	$23,250
Room and board:		$9,002
Books and supplies:	$925	$925
Personal expenses:	$1,700	$1,700
Transportation:	$800	$800

Undergraduate aid. Need-based: Average financial aid package for full-time students was $19,390; for part-time $9,494. 64% awarded as scholarships/grants, 36% as loans/jobs. **Non-need-based:** 72% awarded as scholarships/grants, 28% as loans/jobs. Scholarships based on academics, alumni affiliation, leadership, music/drama, religious affiliation, state/district residency.

Freshman aid. Need-based: Out of 700 full-time freshmen, 683 applied for aid; 563 were judged to have need; of these 544 received aid. Average package met 52% of need. 242 students had full need met. Average scholarship/grant was $4,008; average loan $3,206. **Non-need based:** 525 full-time freshmen with need received non-need scholarships; 132 without need received awards.

Merit scholarships. Award of Excellence $10,000; available to early decision applicants with 3.5 GPA, 1300 SAT (28 ACT), and top 20% of HS class. Leadership/Service Scholarship $5,000; for outstanding contribution to school, church or community, and 3.4 GPA and 1200 SAT (26 ACT).

Policies to reduce costs. Tuition/fee waivers for adults, children of alumni, family members, employees and their families. Credit/placement for qualifying scores on AP, IB examinations. Work study available for part-time students.

Payment plans. Credit card, installment payment.

Application procedures. FAFSA required. Priority date 1/15; closing date 2/1. Applicants notified on rolling basis starting 4/1, must reply by 5/1. Early decision closing date 12/1. **Transfers:** Priority date 1/15; no deadline.

Contact. **Financial aid office:** (202) 319-5307
Doris Torosian, Director of Financial Aid
102 McMahon Hall
Washington, DC 20064

Corcoran College of Art and Design

Washington, District of Columbia
www.corcoran.edu
Four-year private **Federal Code: 011950**

	Living at home	On-campus
Tuition and fees:	$19,900	$19,900
Room only:		$5,800
Books and supplies:	$2,250	$2,250
Personal expenses:	$1,054	$1,500
Transportation:	$1,050	

Undergraduate aid. Need-based: Need-based aid available for full-time students. **Non-need-based:** Scholarships based on academics, art.

Merit scholarships. Dean's Merit Scholarship, up to 70 awards, based on art portfolio and academics, $500-3,000. Dean's Merit Writing Scholarship, up to 10 awards, by competition, $500-3,000. Award of Excellence, up to 40 awards, based on high school GPA, $2,000-14,000.

Policies to reduce costs. Tuition/fee waivers for employees and their families. Credit/placement for qualifying scores on AP, IB examinations.

Payment plans. Credit card, installment payment.

Application procedures. FAFSA, institutional form required. Priority date 3/15; no closing date. Applicants notified on rolling basis starting 4/1, must reply by 5/1 or within 2 week(s) of notification.

Contact. **Financial aid office:** (202) 639-1818
Diane Morris, Director of Financial Aid
500 17th Street, N.W.
Washington, DC 20006-4804

Gallaudet University

Washington, District of Columbia
www.gallaudet.edu
Four-year private **Federal Code: 001443**

College costs. Certain non-resident aliens may apply for tuition reduction.

	Living at home	On-campus
Tuition and fees (projected):	$9,330	$9,330
Room and board:		$8,030
Board only:	$825	
Books and supplies:	$704	$704
Personal expenses:	$2,165	$2,486
Transportation:	$1,024	$1,024

Undergraduate aid. Need-based: Average financial aid package for full-time students was $12,626. 84% awarded as scholarships/grants, 16% as loans/jobs. Need-based aid available for part-time students. **Non-need-based:** 97% awarded as scholarships/grants, 3% as loans/jobs. Scholarships based on academics. **Student debt:** 39% of graduating class borrowed to fund education; average debt was $9,333. **Additional information:** Institution receives substantial aid from state vocational rehabilitation agencies, supplemented by institutional grants when needed.

Freshman aid. Need-based: Out of 218 full-time freshmen, 171 applied for aid; 156 were judged to have need; of these 153 received aid. Average package met 82% of need. 44 students had full need met. Average scholarship/grant was $12,480; average loan $2,246. **Non-need based:** 36 full-time fresh-

men with need received non-need scholarships; 15 without need received awards.

Policies to reduce costs. Tuition/fee waivers for employees and their families. Credit/placement for qualifying scores on AP, CLEP examinations.

Payment plans. Credit card, installment, deferred payment.

Application procedures. FAFSA, institutional form required. Priority date 7/1; no closing date. Applicants notified on rolling basis starting 4/1, must reply within 4 week(s) of notification.

Contact. **Financial aid office:** (202) 651-5290
Nancy Goodman, Director of Financial Aid
800 Florida Avenue, NE
Washington, DC 20002

George Washington University

Washington, District of Columbia
www.gwu.edu
Four-year private **Federal Code: 001444**

	Living at home	On-campus
Tuition and fees:	$29,350	$29,350
Room and board:		$1,004
Board only:	$2,000	
Books and supplies:	$850	$850
Personal expenses:	$950	$950

Undergraduate aid. Need-based: Average financial aid package for full-time students was $25,695; for part-time $12,047. 72% awarded as scholarships/grants, 28% as loans/jobs. **Non-need-based:** 98% awarded as scholarships/grants, 2% as loans/jobs. Scholarships based on academics, art, athletics, music/drama. **Student debt:** 52% of graduating class borrowed to fund education; average debt was $22,854. **Additional information:** Auditions required for performing arts scholarships.

Freshman aid. Need-based: Out of 2,566 full-time freshmen, 1,556 applied for aid; 1,029 were judged to have need; of these 1,023 received aid. Average package met 95% of need. 856 students had full need met. Average scholarship/grant was $15,182; average loan $3,460. **Non-need based:** 371 full-time freshmen with need received non-need scholarships; 404 without need received awards; 42 received athletic scholarships.

Policies to reduce costs. Tuition/fee waivers for family members, employees and their families. Credit/placement for qualifying scores on AP, IB, CLEP examinations.

Payment plans. Installment, deferred payment.

Application procedures. FAFSA, CSS PROFILE required. Priority date 1/31; no closing date. Applicants notified by 3/20, must reply by 5/1 or within 2 week(s) of notification. Early decision closing date 12/1. **Transfers:** Priority date 4/1; closing date 5/1.

Contact. **Financial aid office:** (202) 994-6620
Daniel Small, Director of Student Financial Assistance
2121 I Street NW, Suite 201
Washington, DC 20052

Georgetown University

Washington, District of Columbia
www.georgetown.edu
Four-year private **Federal Code: 001445**

	Living at home	On-campus
Tuition and fees (2002-2003):	$26,853	$26,853
Room and board:		$9,692
Board only:	$1,562	
Books and supplies:	$940	$940
Personal expenses:	$1,040	$1,040
Transportation:	$410	$410

Undergraduate aid. Need-based: Average financial aid package for full-time students was $21,650. 69% awarded as scholarships/grants, 31% as loans/jobs. Need-based aid available for part-time students. **Non-need-based:** 28% awarded as scholarships/grants, 72% as loans/jobs. Scholarships based on athletics. **Student debt:** 45% of graduating class borrowed to fund education; average debt was $20,000.

Freshman aid. Need-based: Out of 1,477 full-time freshmen, 800 applied for aid; 605 were judged to have need; of these 605 received aid. Average package met 100% of need. 605 students had full need met. Average scholarship/grant was $16,300; average loan $2,250. **Non-need based:** 10 full-time freshmen with need received non-need scholarships; 70 without need received awards; 40 received athletic scholarships.

Policies to reduce costs. Tuition/fee waivers for employees and their families. Credit/placement for qualifying scores on AP, IB examinations. Work study available nights, weekends and for part-time students.

Payment plans. Installment, deferred payment.

Application procedures. FAFSA, CSS PROFILE required. Closing date 2/1. Applicants notified by 4/1, must reply by 5/1 or within 2 week(s) of notification. **Transfers:** Closing date 3/1.

Contact. **Financial aid office:** (202) 687-4547
Patricia McWade, Dean of Student Financial Services
37th and P Streets NW
Washington, DC 20057-1002

Howard University

Washington, District of Columbia
www.howard.edu
Four-year private **Federal Code: 001448**

	Living at home	On-campus
Tuition and fees (2002-2003):	$10,320	$10,320
Room and board:		$5,410
Board only:	$1,500	
Books and supplies:	$1,020	$1,020
Personal expenses:	$2,000	$2,000
Transportation:	$893	$893

Undergraduate aid. All financial aid based on need. Need-based aid available for full-time and part-time students.

Policies to reduce costs. Tuition/fee waivers for employees and their families. Credit/placement for qualifying scores on AP examinations.

Payment plans. Credit card, deferred payment.

Application procedures. FAFSA, institutional form required. Closing date 4/1. Applicants notified by 5/1, must reply within 4 week(s) of notification.

Contact. **Financial aid office:** (202) 806-2820
Sheryl Spiney, Director of Admission and Student Financial Services
2400 Sixth Street Northwest
Washington, DC 20059

Potomac College

Washington, District of Columbia
www.potomac.edu
Three-year proprietary **Federal Code: 032183**

	Living at home
Tuition and fees (2002-2003):	$10,970
Books and supplies:	$630

Undergraduate aid. Need-based: Need-based aid available for full-time and part-time students.

Policies to reduce costs. Tuition/fee waivers for employees and their families.

Payment plans. Credit card, installment payment.

Application procedures. FAFSA, institutional form required. No deadline. Applicants notified on rolling basis, must reply within 4 week(s) of notification. **Transfers:** No deadline.

Contact. Phyllis Crews, Financial Aid Officer
4000 Chesapeake Street NW
Washington, DC 20016

Strayer University

Washington, District of Columbia
www.strayer.edu
Four-year proprietary **Federal Code: 001459**

College costs. Loan fees $253 to $555.

	Living at home
Tuition and fees (2002-2003):	$8,930
Books and supplies:	$1,000

Undergraduate aid. Additional information: October 3 closing date for academic scholarship applications.

Policies to reduce costs. Tuition/fee waivers for employees and their families. Credit/placement for qualifying scores on AP, CLEP examinations.

Payment plans. Credit card, installment, deferred payment.

Application procedures. FAFSA required. No deadline. Applicants notified on rolling basis, must reply within 2 week(s) of notification.

Contact. Marjorie Arrington, Director of Financial Aid
1025 15th Street, NW
Washington, DC 20005

Trinity College

Washington, District of Columbia
www.trinitydc.edu
Four-year private **Federal Code: 001460**

	Living at home	On-campus
Tuition and fees (projected):	$16,380	$16,380
Room and board:		$7,170
Board only:	$3,720	
Books and supplies:	$600	$600
Personal expenses:	$1,500	$1,500
Transportation:	$500	$500

Undergraduate aid. Need-based: Average financial aid package for full-time students was $16,313. 52% awarded as scholarships/grants, 48% as loans/jobs. **Non-need-based:** 45% awarded as scholarships/grants, 55% as loans/jobs. Scholarships based on academics, alumni affiliation, leadership, religious affiliation, state/district residency. **Student debt:** 75% of graduating class borrowed to fund education; average debt was $26,448.

Freshman aid. Need-based: Out of 120 full-time freshmen, 109 applied for aid; 102 were judged to have need; of these 102 received aid. Average package met 79% of need. 16 students had full need met. Average scholarship/grant was $11,573; average loan $3,153. **Non-need based:** 8 full-time freshmen with need received non-need scholarships; 6 without need received awards.

Policies to reduce costs. Tuition/fee waivers for children of alumni, family members, employees and their families. Credit/placement for qualifying scores on AP, CLEP examinations.

Payment plans. Credit card, installment, deferred payment.

Application procedures. FAFSA, institutional form required. Priority date 4/1; no closing date. Applicants notified on rolling basis starting 1/15, must reply within 3 week(s) of notification.

Contact. Financial aid office: (202) 884-9530
Janet Pearlman, Director of Financial Services
125 Michigan Avenue, NE
Washington, DC 20017-1094

University of the District of Columbia

Washington, District of Columbia
www.udc.edu
Four-year public **Federal Code: 007015**

	Living at home
Tuition and fees:	$2,520
Out-of-state:	$4,710
Books and supplies:	$800
Personal expenses:	$1,600
Transportation:	$1,260

Undergraduate aid. All financial aid based on need. Average financial aid package for full-time students was $3,346; for part-time $2,497. 62% awarded as scholarships/grants, 38% as loans/jobs. **Student debt:** 24% of graduating class borrowed to fund education; average debt was $8,624.

Freshman aid. Out of 474 full-time freshmen, 381 applied for aid; 286 were judged to have need; of these 202 received aid. Average package met 48% of need. 46 students had full need met. Average scholarship/grant was $1,947; average loan $2,625.

Policies to reduce costs. Tuition/fee waivers for employees and their families. Credit/placement for qualifying scores on IB, CLEP examinations. Work study available nights, weekends and for part-time students.

Payment plans. Credit card, installment, deferred payment.

Application procedures. FAFSA required. Priority date 3/15; no closing date. Applicants notified on rolling basis starting 5/1, must reply within 2 week(s) of notification. **Transfers:** Priority date 3/15.

Contact. Financial aid office: (202) 274-5060
James Lockwood, Director of Financial Aid
4200 Connecticut Avenue NW
Washington, DC 20008

Florida

ATI Health Education Center

Miami, Florida
www.aticareertraining.com
Two-year proprietary **Federal Code: 014612**

College costs (projected). $15,895 tuition for medical assistant program and pharmacy technician program; $32,895 tuition for diagnostic ultrasound program and respiratory therapist program. Personal expenses: $2,064.

Undergraduate aid. All financial aid based on need. Need-based aid available for full-time and part-time students.

Application procedures. FAFSA, institutional form, CSS PROFILE required. No deadline. Applicants notified on rolling basis.

Contact. **Financial aid office:** (305) 628-1000
Aida Claro, Financial Aid Director
1395 NW 167th Street, Suite 200
Miami, FL 33169-5745

Art Institute of Fort Lauderdale

Ft. Lauderdale, Florida
www.artinstitute.edu
Four-year proprietary **Federal Code: 010195**

	Living at home
Tuition and fees (projected):	$15,075
Board only:	$2,820
Books and supplies:	$1,227
Personal expenses:	$1,980
Transportation:	$1,065

Undergraduate aid. All financial aid based on need. 30% awarded as scholarships/grants, 70% as loans/jobs. Need-based aid available for part-time students. **Additional information:** Internal scholarships available. Financial planning program allows personalized service to budget and meet college costs through individualized payment plans.

Policies to reduce costs. Tuition/fee waivers for family members, employees and their families. Tuition at time of enrollment guaranteed for 4 years; credit/placement for qualifying scores on AP, IB, CLEP examinations. Work study available nights, weekends and for part-time students.

Payment plans. Credit card, installment, deferred payment.

Application procedures. FAFSA required. No deadline. **Transfers:** No deadline.

Contact. **Financial aid office:** (954) 463-3000 ext. 479
Melissa Ziselman, Director of Student Financial Service
1799 Southeast 17th Street
Fort Lauderdale, FL 33316

Baptist College of Florida

Graceville, Florida
www.baptistcollege.edu
Four-year private **Federal Code: 013001**

	Living at home	On-campus
Tuition and fees (projected):	$5,600	$5,600
Room and board:		$3,150
Books and supplies:	$600	$600
Personal expenses:	$350	$350
Transportation:	$1,000	$400

Undergraduate aid. Need-based: Average financial aid package for full-time students was $3,500; for part-time $1,500. 58% awarded as scholarships/grants, 42% as loans/jobs. **Non-need-based:** 68% awarded as scholarships/grants, 32% as loans/jobs. Scholarships based on academics, state/district residency. **Student debt:** 75% of graduating class borrowed to fund education; average debt was $11,500.

Freshman aid. Need-based: Average package met 59% of need. 3 students had full need met. Average loan $1,313.

Policies to reduce costs. Tuition/fee waivers for employees and their families. Credit/placement for qualifying scores on AP, IB, CLEP examinations.

Payment plans. Credit card, installment, deferred payment.

Application procedures. FAFSA, institutional form required. Priority date 4/1; closing date 4/15. Applicants notified on rolling basis starting 6/15, must reply within 4 week(s) of notification. **Transfers:** Priority date 4/1; no deadline.

Contact. **Financial aid office:** (850) 263-3261 ext. 461
Angela Rathel, Director of Financial Aid
5400 College Drive
Graceville, FL 32440-3306

Barry University

Miami Shores, Florida
www.barry.edu
Four-year private **Federal Code: 001466**

College costs. Additional required fees for campus residents: $200 room deposit, $439 health insurance.

	Living at home	On-campus
Tuition and fees (projected):	$20,320	$20,320
Room and board:		$7,300

Undergraduate aid. Need-based: Average financial aid package for full-time students was $16,391; for part-time $5,435. 45% awarded as scholarships/grants, 55% as loans/jobs. **Non-need-based:** 60% awarded as scholarships/grants, 40% as loans/jobs. Scholarships based on academics, art, athletics, music/drama. **Student debt:** 63% of graduating class borrowed to fund education; average debt was $16,657.

Freshman aid. Need-based: Out of 461 full-time freshmen, 372 applied for aid; 338 were judged to have need; of these 337 received aid. Average package met 82% of need. 42 students had full need met. Average scholarship/grant was $8,119; average loan $2,576. **Non-need based:** 336 full-time freshmen with need received non-need scholarships; 105 without need received awards; 443 received athletic scholarships.

Policies to reduce costs. Tuition/fee waivers for family members, employees and their families. Credit/placement for qualifying scores on AP, IB, CLEP examinations. Work study available nights and weekends.

Payment plans. Credit card, installment, deferred payment.

Application procedures. FAFSA required. No deadline. Applicants notified on rolling basis starting 1/25. **Transfers:** No deadline.

Contact. **Financial aid office:** (305) 899-3673
H. Dart Humeston, Director of Financial Aid
11300 Northeast Second Avenue
Miami Shores, FL 33161-6695

Beacon College

Leesburg, Florida
www.beaconcollege.edu
Four-year private **Federal Code: 032513**

	Living at home	On-campus
Tuition and fees:	$19,700	$19,700
Room and board:		$6,200
Books and supplies:	$400	$400

Undergraduate aid. All financial aid based on need. Average financial aid package for full-time students was $12,336. 76% awarded as scholarships/grants, 24% as loans/jobs. **Additional information:** Work-study programs offered based on financial need.

Freshman aid. Average package met 100% of need.

Policies to reduce costs. Tuition/fee waivers for minority students, family members, unemployed or children of unemployed. Work study available nights.

Payment plans. Installment payment.

Application procedures. FAFSA, institutional form required. Priority date 4/1; closing date 5/1. Applicants notified by 5/31, must reply within 3 week(s) of notification.

Contact. **Financial aid office:** (352) 787-7660
Financial Aid Officer
105 East Main Street
Leesburg, FL 34748

Bethune-Cookman College

Daytona Beach, Florida
www.bethune.cookman.edu
Four-year private **Federal Code: 001467**

	Living at home	On-campus
Tuition and fees:	$10,106	$10,106
Room and board:		$6,374
Board only:	$1,500	
Books and supplies:	$730	$730
Personal expenses:	$1,200	$2,200
Transportation:	$1,110	$710

Undergraduate aid. All financial aid based on need. Average financial aid package for full-time students was $13,612; for part-time $8,415. 65% awarded as scholarships/grants, 35% as loans/jobs. **Student debt:** 78% of graduating class borrowed to fund education; average debt was $25,940.

Freshman aid. Out of 607 full-time freshmen, 604 applied for aid; 595 were judged to have need; of these 591 received aid. Average package met 83% of need. 169 students had full need met. Average scholarship/grant was $7,165; average loan $2,603.

Policies to reduce costs. Tuition/fee waivers for employees and their families. Credit/placement for qualifying scores on AP, IB, CLEP examinations. Work study available nights, weekends and for part-time students.

Payment plans. Credit card, installment payment.

Application procedures. FAFSA required. Priority date 4/1; no closing date. Applicants notified on rolling basis starting 4/1, must reply within 3 week(s) of notification.

Contact. **Financial aid office:** (800) 553-9369
Joseph Coleman, Financial Aid Director
Dr. Mary McLeod Bethune Boulevard
Daytona Beach, FL 32114-3099

Broward Community College

Ft. Lauderdale, Florida
www.broward.edu
Two-year public **Federal Code: 001500**

College costs. Additional $259 required fees for out-of-state students.

	Living at home
Tuition and fees (2002-2003):	$1,536
Out-of-state:	$5,505
Per-credit charge:	$44
Per-credit out-of-state:	$176
Books and supplies:	$1,000
Personal expenses:	$1,134
Transportation:	$2,155

Undergraduate aid. Need-based: Need-based aid available for full-time and part-time students. **Non-need-based:** Scholarships based on academics, art, athletics, leadership, minority status, music/drama, state/district residency.

Policies to reduce costs. Tuition/fee waivers for senior citizens, minority students, employees and their families. Credit/placement for qualifying scores on AP, CLEP examinations. Work study available nights, weekends and for part-time students.

Payment plans. Credit card, deferred payment.

Application procedures. FAFSA required. Priority date 4/15; no closing date. Applicants notified on rolling basis starting 7/15, must reply within 5 week(s) of notification. **Transfers:** No deadline.

Contact. **Financial aid office:** (954) 201-6575
Marcia Conliffe, Director of Financial Aid
225 East Las Olas Boulevard
Fort Lauderdale, FL 33301

Carlos Albizu University

Miami, Florida
www.albizu.edu
Four-year private **Federal Code: 010724**

	Living at home
Tuition and fees (projected):	$11,469
Board only:	$4,425
Books and supplies:	$690
Personal expenses:	$1,800
Transportation:	$2,700

Undergraduate aid. All financial aid based on need. Average financial aid package for full-time students was $7,925; for part-time $6,331. 58% awarded as scholarships/grants, 42% as loans/jobs. **Student debt:** 85% of graduating class borrowed to fund education; average debt was $23,500.

Freshman aid. Out of 55 full-time freshmen, 54 applied for aid; 54 were judged to have need; of these 54 received aid. Average package met 55% of need. Average scholarship/grant was $5,300; average loan $3,549.

Policies to reduce costs. Tuition/fee waivers for employees and their families. Credit/placement for qualifying scores on IB, CLEP examinations. Work study available nights and for part-time students.

Payment plans. Credit card payment.

Application procedures. FAFSA, institutional form required. Priority date 6/1; no closing date. Applicants notified on rolling basis starting 2/1.

Contact. **Financial aid office:** (305) 593-1223 ext. 153
Carmen Freire, Financial Aid Director
2173 NW 99th Avenue
Miami, FL 33172

Chipola Junior College

Marianna, Florida
www.chipola.edu
Two-year public **Federal Code: 001472**

	Living at home
Tuition and fees (2002-2003):	$1,579
Out-of-state:	$4,864
Per-credit charge:	$42
Per-credit out-of-state:	$152
Board only:	$720
Books and supplies:	$600
Personal expenses:	$1,400
Transportation:	$1,300

Undergraduate aid. Need-based: 93% awarded as scholarships/grants, 7% as loans/jobs. Need-based aid available for part-time students. **Non-need-based:** 99% awarded as scholarships/grants, 1% as loans/jobs. Scholarships based on academics, alumni affiliation, art, athletics, job skills, leadership, minority status, music/drama. **Additional information:** Over 100 scholarships and 200 grants awarded.

Policies to reduce costs. Credit/placement for qualifying scores on AP, CLEP examinations. Work study available nights and for part-time students.

Payment plans. Credit card, deferred payment.

Application procedures. FAFSA, institutional form required. Priority date 5/1; no closing date. Applicants notified on rolling basis starting 1/2, must reply within 2 week(s) of notification. **Transfers:** Priority date 5/1; no deadline.

Contact. **Financial aid office:** (850) 718-2223
Sybil Cloud, Director of Financial Aid
3094 Indian Circle
Marianna, FL 32446

City College: Casselberry

Casselberry, Florida
Two-year proprietary

	Living at home
Tuition and fees:	$6,525
Per-credit charge:	$145

Contact. 853 Semoran Boulevard
Casselberry, FL 32707-5353

City College: Miami

Miami, Florida
www.citycollege.edu
Two-year proprietary **Federal Code: 025154**

	Living at home
Tuition and fees:	$6,525
Per-credit charge:	$145
Books and supplies:	$1,044
Personal expenses:	$1,692
Transportation:	$1,359

Undergraduate aid. All financial aid based on need. Need-based aid available for full-time and part-time students.

Application procedures. FAFSA, institutional form required. No deadline. Applicants notified on rolling basis.

Contact. **Financial aid office:** (305) 666-9242
Director of Financial Aid
9300 South Dadeland Boulevard
Miami, FL 33156

Cooper Career Institute

West Palm Beach, Florida
www.coopercareer.com
Two-year proprietary **Federal Code: 030327**

College costs (2002-2003). Tuition for 15-month associate programs: medical assistance $12,500, lab fees $200/quarter; paralegal $12,500; computer systems administration $15,000. Tuition for 10-month diploma programs: $5,000 to $9,000. Required fees $50 for all students.

Undergraduate aid. Need-based: Need-based aid available for full-time and part-time students.

Payment plans. Credit card, installment payment.

Application procedures. FAFSA, institutional form required. No deadline. Applicants notified on rolling basis.

Contact. **Financial aid office:** (561) 640-6999
Catherine Sternlicht, Financial Aid Administrator
2247 Palm Beach Lakes Boulevard, Suite 110
West Palm Beach, FL 33409

Daytona Beach Community College

Daytona Beach, Florida
www.dbcc.cc.fl.us
Two-year public **Federal Code: 001475**

College costs. Additional $401 in required fees for out-of-state students.

	Living at home
Tuition and fees (2002-2003):	$1,649
Out-of-state:	$5,710
Per-credit charge:	$45
Per-credit out-of-state:	$180
Books and supplies:	$485
Personal expenses:	$1,000
Transportation:	$1,000

Undergraduate aid. Need-based: 61% awarded as scholarships/grants, 39% as loans/jobs. Need-based aid available for part-time students. **Non-need-based:** 17% awarded as scholarships/grants, 83% as loans/jobs. Scholarships based on athletics, music/drama.

Policies to reduce costs. Tuition/fee waivers for senior citizens, employees and their families. Credit/placement for qualifying scores on AP, IB, CLEP examinations. Work study available for part-time students.

Payment plans. Credit card payment.

Application procedures. FAFSA required. No deadline. Applicants notified on rolling basis starting 2/15.

Contact. Elly Will, Director of Financial Aid
Box 2811
Daytona Beach, FL 32120

DeVry University: Miramar

Miramar, Florida
www.mir.devry.edu
Four-year proprietary

	Living at home
Tuition and fees:	$10,755
Books and supplies:	$1,100
Personal expenses:	$1,816
Transportation:	$1,438

Undergraduate aid. All financial aid based on need. Need-based aid available for full-time and part-time students.

Policies to reduce costs. Tuition/fee waivers for employees and their families.

Payment plans. Credit card, installment, deferred payment.

Application procedures. FAFSA required. No deadline. Applicants notified on rolling basis starting 7/2. **Transfers:** No deadline.

Contact. Scott Howard, Assistant Director of Student Finance
2300 Southwest 145th Avenue
Miramar, FL 33027

DeVry University: Orlando

Orlando, Florida
www.orl.devry.edu
Four-year proprietary **Federal Code: 022966**

	Living at home
Tuition and fees (2002-2003):	$10,040
Books and supplies:	$1,100
Personal expenses:	$1,750
Transportation:	$1,422

Undergraduate aid. All financial aid based on need. Average financial aid package for full-time students was $6,175; for part-time $4,679. 17% awarded as scholarships/grants, 83% as loans/jobs.

Freshman aid. Average package met 33% of need. Average scholarship/grant was $3,253; average loan $3,907.

Policies to reduce costs. Tuition/fee waivers for employees and their families.

Payment plans. Credit card, installment, deferred payment.

Application procedures. FAFSA required. No deadline. Applicants notified on rolling basis starting 7/2. **Transfers:** No deadline.

Contact. Estrella Velasquez Domenech, Director of Student Finance
400 Millennia Drive
Orlando, FL 32839

Eckerd College

St. Petersburg, Florida
www.eckerd.edu
Four-year private **Federal Code: 001487**

	Living at home	On-campus
Tuition and fees:	$22,774	$22,774
Room and board:		$5,970
Board only:	$2,165	
Books and supplies:	$946	$946
Personal expenses:	$1,166	$1,166
Transportation:	$1,410	$1,410

Undergraduate aid. Need-based: Average financial aid package for full-time students was $17,208. 65% awarded as scholarships/grants, 35% as loans/jobs. **Non-need-based:** 76% awarded as scholarships/grants, 24% as loans/jobs. Scholarships based on academics, art, athletics, leadership, music/drama, religious affiliation, state/district residency. **Student debt:** 57% of graduating class borrowed to fund education; average debt was $17,500.

Freshman aid. Need-based: Out of 440 full-time freshmen, 316 applied for aid; 265 were judged to have need; of these 265 received aid. Average package met 85% of need. 225 students had full need met. **Non-need based:** 79 full-time freshmen with need received non-need scholarships.

Merit scholarships. Presidential Scholarships; based on academic credentials, leadership and service; 25 awarded; $8,000-10,000 annually. Special Honors Scholarships; awarded on competitive basis to National Merit, National Achievement, and National Hispanic finalists and semi-finalists; 15 awarded; full tuition.

Policies to reduce costs. Tuition/fee waivers for employees and their families. Credit/placement for qualifying scores on AP, IB, CLEP examinations.

Payment plans. Credit card, installment payment.

Application procedures. FAFSA required. Priority date 4/1; no closing date. Applicants notified on rolling basis starting 2/1, must reply by 5/1 or within 4 week(s) of notification.

Contact. Margaret Morris, Director of Financial Aid
4200 54th Avenue South
St. Petersburg, FL 33711-4700

Edward Waters College

Jacksonville, Florida
www.ewc.edu
Four-year private **Federal Code: 001478**

	Living at home	On-campus
Tuition and fees (2002-2003):	$8,724	$8,724
Room and board:		$4,930
Books and supplies:	$500	$500
Personal expenses:	$550	$750
Transportation:	$600	$500

Undergraduate aid. **Need-based:** Need-based aid available for full-time and part-time students. **Non-need-based:** Scholarships based on academics, athletics, minority status, state/district residency.

Policies to reduce costs. Tuition/fee waivers for employees and their families. Credit/placement for qualifying scores on AP, CLEP examinations. Work study available nights, weekends and for part-time students.

Payment plans. Credit card, installment, deferred payment.

Application procedures. FAFSA, institutional form required. Closing date 4/15. Applicants notified on rolling basis starting 5/1, must reply within 2 week(s) of notification.

Contact. **Financial aid office:** (904) 366-2733
MiBomeh Gabriel, Director of Financial Aid
1658 Kings Road
Jacksonville, FL 32209

Embry Riddle Aeronautical University-Extended Campus

Daytona Beach, Florida
www.embryriddle.edu
Four-year private **Federal Code: 001479**

College costs (2002-2003). Per-credit-hour charges range from $150 to $190.

Undergraduate aid. **Need-based:** Average financial aid package for full-time students was $4,901; for part-time $4,556. 33% awarded as scholarships/grants, 67% as loans/jobs. **Student debt:** 16% of graduating class borrowed to fund education; average debt was $13,205.

Application procedures. FAFSA required. Priority date 4/15; closing date 6/30. Applicants notified on rolling basis starting 4/1, must reply within 4 week(s) of notification.

Contact. **Financial aid office:** (386) 226-6300
Director of Financial Aid
600 South Clyde Morris Boulevard
Daytona Beach, FL 32114-3900

Embry-Riddle Aeronautical University

Daytona Beach, Florida
www.embryriddle.edu
Four-year private **Federal Code: 001479**

	Living at home	On-campus
Tuition and fees:	$21,360	$21,360
Room and board:		$6,370
Board only:	$940	
Books and supplies:	$800	$800
Personal expenses:	$1,540	$1,540
Transportation:	$1,440	$1,920

Undergraduate aid. **Need-based:** Average financial aid package for full-time students was $11,350; for part-time $8,829. 25% awarded as scholarships/grants, 75% as loans/jobs. **Non-need-based:** Scholarships based on academics, athletics, leadership. **Student debt:** 66% of graduating class borrowed to fund education; average debt was $34,546.

Freshman aid. **Need-based:** Out of 873 full-time freshmen, 706 applied for aid; 582 were judged to have need; of these 582 received aid. Average scholarship/grant was $7,013; average loan $3,067. **Non-need based:** 11 received athletic scholarships.

Policies to reduce costs. Tuition/fee waivers for employees and their families. Credit/placement for qualifying scores on AP, IB, CLEP examinations.

Payment plans. Credit card, installment, deferred payment.

Application procedures. FAFSA required. Priority date 4/15; closing date 6/30. Applicants notified on rolling basis starting 2/1, must reply within 4 week(s) of notification. Early decision closing date 12/1.

Contact. **Financial aid office:** (386) 226-6300
Director of Financial Aid
600 South Clyde Morris Boulevard
Daytona Beach, FL 32114-3900

Everglades College

Fort Lauderdale, Florida
www.evergladescollege.edu
Four-year proprietary **Federal Code: 031085**

College costs. $145 registration fee, $400 per semester education fee (encompasses all other fees such as lab fee) required.

	Living at home
Tuition and fees:	$10,906
Books and supplies:	$700
Personal expenses:	$500
Transportation:	$500

Undergraduate aid. **Need-based:** Need-based aid available for full-time students. **Additional information:** Federal Pell Grant, Federal Direct Stafford Student Loan, Federal Family Education Loan (Stafford Student Loan), Unsubsidized Federal Direct and FFEL Stafford Loans and Federal Plus Loans offered.

Application procedures. FAFSA required. No deadline. Applicants notified on rolling basis.

Contact. **Financial aid office:** (954) 772-2655
Seeta Singh, Director of Financial Aid
1500 NW 49th Street, Suite 600
Fort Lauderdale, FL 33309

Flagler College

St. Augustine, Florida
www.flagler.edu
Four-year private **Federal Code: 007893**

	Living at home	On-campus
Tuition and fees (projected):	$7,100	$7,100
Room and board:		$4,250
Board only:	$2,800	
Books and supplies:	$750	$750
Personal expenses:	$2,300	$2,300
Transportation:	$1,500	$1,500

Undergraduate aid. **Need-based:** Average financial aid package for full-time students was $6,930; for part-time $5,047. 58% awarded as scholarships/grants, 42% as loans/jobs. **Non-need-based:** 61% awarded as scholarships/grants, 39% as loans/jobs. Scholarships based on academics, athletics, job skills, leadership, minority status, state/district residency. **Student debt:** 55% of graduating class borrowed to fund education; average debt was $14,496.

Freshman aid. **Need-based:** Out of 472 full-time freshmen, 432 applied for aid; 170 were judged to have need; of these 168 received aid. Average package met 71% of need. 54 students had full need met. Average scholarship/grant was $2,486; average loan $2,175. **Non-need based:** 127 full-time freshmen with need received non-need scholarships; 253 without need received awards; 23 received athletic scholarships.

Merit scholarships. Lewis-Wiley Scholarship for freshmen who demonstrate exceptional leadership and academic achievement; 4 awarded; tuition, fees, room and board for 4 years.

Policies to reduce costs. Tuition/fee waivers for employees and their families. Credit/placement for qualifying scores on AP, IB, CLEP examinations. Work study available weekends.

Payment plans. Credit card payment.

Application procedures. FAFSA, institutional form required. Priority date 5/1; no closing date. Applicants notified on rolling basis starting 3/1, must reply within 2 week(s) of notification. Early decision closing date 12/1. **Transfers:** Transfer students receiving Florida-sponsored aid must notify Florida Office of Student Financial Assistance (OSFA) of their transfer.

Contact. **Financial aid office:** (800) 304-4208 ext. 225
Robert Sterling, Director of Financial Aid
74 King Street
St. Augustine, FL 32085

Florida Agricultural and Mechanical University

Tallahassee, Florida
www.famu.edu
Four-year public **Federal Code: 001480**

College costs. Additional $454 required fees for out-of-state students.

	Living at home	On-campus
Tuition and fees (2002-2003):	$2,759	$2,759
Out-of-state:	$11,849	$11,849
Room and board:		$4,680
Books and supplies:	$800	$800
Personal expenses:	$2,400	$2,400
Transportation:	$780	$880

Undergraduate aid. Need-based: Average financial aid package for full-time students was $7,807; for part-time $6,489. 48% awarded as scholarships/grants, 52% as loans/jobs. **Non-need-based:** 50% awarded as scholarships/grants, 50% as loans/jobs. Scholarships based on academics, art, leadership. **Student debt:** 78% of graduating class borrowed to fund education; average debt was $21,633.

Freshman aid. Need-based: Average package met 59% of need. Average scholarship/grant was $3,090; average loan $2,262.

Policies to reduce costs. Tuition/fee waivers for senior citizens, employees and their families. Credit/placement for qualifying scores on AP, IB, CLEP examinations.

Payment plans. Deferred payment.

Application procedures. FAFSA required. Priority date 3/1; closing date 6/30. Applicants notified on rolling basis starting 3/1, must reply within 2 week(s) of notification.

Contact. **Financial aid office:** (850) 599-3730
Deloris Davis, Director of Financial Aid
FHAC, G-9
Tallahassee, FL 32307

Florida Atlantic University

Boca Raton, Florida
www.fau.edu
Four-year public **Federal Code: 001481**

College costs. Additional $438 required fees for out-of-state students.

	Living at home	On-campus
Tuition and fees (2002-2003):	$2,838	$2,838
Out-of-state:	$11,928	$11,928
Room and board:		$5,836
Board only:	$1,990	
Books and supplies:	$636	$636
Personal expenses:	$1,284	$1,284
Transportation:	$2,031	$1,393

Undergraduate aid. Need-based: 42% awarded as scholarships/grants, 58% as loans/jobs. Need-based aid available for part-time students. **Non-need-based:** 37% awarded as scholarships/grants, 63% as loans/jobs. Scholarships based on academics, athletics, state/district residency.

Policies to reduce costs. Tuition/fee waivers for senior citizens, employees and their families. Credit/placement for qualifying scores on AP, IB, CLEP examinations.

Payment plans. Credit card, installment, deferred payment.

Application procedures. FAFSA required. Priority date 3/1; no closing date. Applicants notified on rolling basis starting 5/1, must reply within 2 week(s) of notification. **Transfers:** Scholarships available.

Contact. **Financial aid office:** (561) 297-2738
Carol Pfeilsticker, Director of Financial Aid
777 Glades Road
Boca Raton, FL 33431

Florida Christian College

Kissimmee, Florida
www.fcc.edu
Four-year private **Federal Code: 015192**

	Living at home	On-campus
Tuition and fees:	$7,365	$7,365
Room and board:		$3,795
Board only:	$2,055	
Books and supplies:	$850	$850
Personal expenses:	$895	$895
Transportation:	$890	$720

Undergraduate aid. All financial aid based on need. Average financial aid package for full-time students was $5,947; for part-time $3,390. 47% awarded as scholarships/grants, 53% as loans/jobs. **Student debt:** 77% of graduating class borrowed to fund education; average debt was $15,353.

Freshman aid. Out of 49 full-time freshmen, 46 applied for aid; 46 were judged to have need; of these 46 received aid. Average package met 35% of need. 1 students had full need met. Average scholarship/grant was $2,278; average loan $2,123.

Policies to reduce costs. Tuition/fee waivers for family members, family of clergy, employees and their families. Credit/placement for qualifying scores on AP, CLEP examinations. Work study available weekends and for part-time students.

Payment plans. Credit card, installment, deferred payment.

Application procedures. FAFSA, institutional form required. Priority date 5/1; closing date 7/15. Applicants notified on rolling basis starting 6/1. **Transfers:** Available only if funding remains.

Contact. **Financial aid office:** (407) 847-8966 ext. 365
Sandra Peppard, Director of Student Financial Aid
1011 Bill Beck Boulevard
Kissimmee, FL 34744-4402

Florida College

Temple Terrace, Florida
www.floridacollege.edu
Four-year private **Federal Code: 001482**

	Living at home	On-campus
Tuition and fees:	$9,640	$9,640
Room and board:		$5,012
Books and supplies:	$1,200	$1,200
Personal expenses:	$2,000	$2,000
Transportation:	$1,500	$2,200

Undergraduate aid. Need-based: Average financial aid package for full-time students was $4,620; for part-time $225. 61% awarded as scholarships/grants, 39% as loans/jobs. **Non-need-based:** 72% awarded as scholarships/grants, 28% as loans/jobs. Scholarships based on academics, athletics, state/district residency. **Student debt:** 46% of graduating class borrowed to fund education; average debt was $6,000. **Additional information:** Music and forensic scholarships available. Audition required for music scholarships.

Freshman aid. Need-based: Out of 203 full-time freshmen, 185 applied for aid; 117 were judged to have need; of these 117 received aid. Average package met 44% of need. 10 students had full need met. Average scholarship/grant was $3,201; average loan $1,296. **Non-need based:** 78 full-time freshmen with need received non-need scholarships; 47 without need received awards; 15 received athletic scholarships.

Policies to reduce costs. Tuition/fee waivers for employees and their families. Credit/placement for qualifying scores on AP, IB, CLEP examinations.

Payment plans. Credit card payment.

Application procedures. FAFSA, institutional form required. Priority date 4/1; closing date 6/1. Applicants notified on rolling basis starting 3/1, must reply within 2 week(s) of notification. **Transfers:** No deadline.

Contact. **Financial aid office:** (813) 899-6774
Darrel McCann, Financial Aid Director
119 North Glen Arven Avenue
Temple Terrace, FL 33617

Florida Gulf Coast University

Ft. Myers, Florida
www.fgcu.edu
Four-year public **Federal Code: 032553**

College costs. Additional required fees $455 for out-of-state students.

	Living at home	On-campus
Tuition and fees (2002-2003):	$2,628	$2,628
Out-of-state:	$11,717	$11,717
Room only:		$3,420
Books and supplies:	$700	$700
Personal expenses:	$1,400	$1,400
Transportation:	$1,440	$1,440

Undergraduate aid. Need-based: Average financial aid package for full-time students was $6,618; for part-time $4,867. 34% awarded as scholarships/grants, 66% as loans/jobs. **Non-need-based:** 48% awarded as scholarships/grants, 52% as loans/jobs. Scholarships based on academics, job skills, state/district residency. **Student debt:** 47% of graduating class borrowed to fund education; average debt was $13,119.

Freshman aid. Need-based: Out of 491 full-time freshmen, 434 applied for aid; 187 were judged to have need; of these 180 received aid. Average package met 70% of need. 37 students had full need met. Average scholarship/grant was $3,322; average loan $2,442. **Non-need based:** 130 full-time freshmen with need received non-need scholarships; 206 without need received awards; 10 received athletic scholarships.

Policies to reduce costs. Tuition/fee waivers for senior citizens, employees and their families. Credit/placement for qualifying scores on AP, IB, CLEP examinations. Work study available nights, weekends and for part-time students.

Application procedures. FAFSA required. Priority date 5/1; no closing date. Applicants notified on rolling basis starting 3/1, must reply within 2 week(s) of notification. **Transfers:** Priority date 4/1; no deadline.

Contact. **Financial aid office:** (239) 590-7920
Venita Jones, Director of Financial Aid
10501 FGCU Boulevard South
Ft. Myers, FL 33965-6565

Florida Hospital College of Health Sciences

Orlando, Florida
www.fhchs.edu
Four-year private **Federal Code: 031155**

	Living at home
Tuition and fees (projected):	$6,250
Board only:	$908
Books and supplies:	$900
Personal expenses:	$1,112
Transportation:	$4,177

Undergraduate aid. Need-based: 17% awarded as scholarships/grants, 83% as loans/jobs. Need-based aid available for part-time students. **Non-need-based:** 75% awarded as scholarships/grants, 25% as loans/jobs. **Student debt:** 56% of graduating class borrowed to fund education; average debt was $10,963.

Policies to reduce costs. Tuition/fee waivers for employees and their families. Work study available nights, weekends and for part-time students.

Payment plans. Credit card, installment, deferred payment.

Application procedures. FAFSA, institutional form required. Closing date 4/12. Applicants notified on rolling basis starting 3/15, must reply within 2 week(s) of notification.

Contact. **Financial aid office:** (407) 303-8016
Starr Bender, Director of Financial Aid
800 Lake Estelle Drive
Orlando, FL 32803

Florida Institute of Technology

Melbourne, Florida
www.fit.edu
Four-year private **Federal Code: 001469**

College costs. Tuition $19,600 for aeronautics, business, psychology, and humanities programs.

	Living at home	On-campus
Tuition and fees:	$22,600	$22,600
Room and board:		$6,140
Board only:	$2,890	
Books and supplies:	$1,000	$1,000
Personal expenses:	$1,400	$1,400
Transportation:	$1,600	$1,600

Undergraduate aid. Need-based: Average financial aid package for full-time students was $17,050; for part-time $9,142. 71% awarded as scholarships/grants, 29% as loans/jobs. **Non-need-based:** 96% awarded as scholarships/grants, 4% as loans/jobs. Scholarships based on academics, alumni affiliation, athletics, leadership. **Student debt:** 46% of graduating class borrowed to fund education; average debt was $20,221.

Freshman aid. Need-based: Out of 519 full-time freshmen, 509 applied for aid; 369 were judged to have need; of these 369 received aid. Average package met 86% of need. 109 students had full need met. Average scholarship/grant was $14,233; average loan $3,498. **Non-need based:** 369 full-time freshmen with need received non-need scholarships; 140 without need received awards; 5 received athletic scholarships.

Policies to reduce costs. Tuition/fee waivers for children of alumni, senior citizens, employees and their families. Credit/placement for qualifying scores on AP, IB, CLEP examinations. Work study available nights and weekends.

Payment plans. Credit card, installment payment.

Application procedures. FAFSA required. Priority date 3/15; no closing date. Applicants notified on rolling basis starting 3/1, must reply by 5/1 or within 4 week(s) of notification.

Contact. **Financial aid office:** (321) 674-8070
Director of Financial Aid
150 West University Boulevard
Melbourne, FL 32901-6975

Florida International University

Miami, Florida
www.fiu.edu
Four-year public **Federal Code: 009635**

College costs. Additional $451 required fees for out-of-state students.

	Living at home	On-campus
Tuition and fees (2002-2003):	$2,696	$2,696
Out-of-state:	$12,161	$12,161
Room and board:		$7,180
Board only:	$1,638	
Books and supplies:	$1,080	$1,080
Personal expenses:	$1,690	$2,100
Transportation:	$2,528	$1,912

Undergraduate aid. Need-based: Average financial aid package for full-time students was $6,351. 50% awarded as scholarships/grants, 50% as loans/jobs. Need-based aid available for part-time students. **Non-need-based:** 42% awarded as scholarships/grants, 58% as loans/jobs. Scholarships based on academics, art, athletics, minority status, music/drama, state/district residency. **Student debt:** 37% of graduating class borrowed to fund education; average debt was $4,547.

Freshman aid. Need-based: Out of 1,492 full-time freshmen, 866 applied for aid; 746 were judged to have need; of these 723 received aid. Average package met 64% of need. 113 students had full need met. Average scholarship/grant was $1,695; average loan $2,545. **Non-need based:** 561 full-time freshmen with need received non-need scholarships; 463 without need received awards.

Policies to reduce costs. Tuition/fee waivers for senior citizens, minority students, employees and their families. Credit/placement for qualifying scores on AP, IB, CLEP examinations.

Payment plans. Deferred payment.

Application procedures. FAFSA required. Priority date 3/1; no closing date. Applicants notified on rolling basis starting 4/15, must reply within 4 week(s) of notification.

Contact. **Financial aid office:** (305) 348-1500
Ana Sarasti, Director of Financial Aid
University Park Campus, PC 140
Miami, FL 33199

Florida Keys Community College

Key West, Florida
www.firn.edu/fkcc
Two-year public **Federal Code: 001485**

College costs. Additional $451 required fees for out-of-state students.

	Living at home
Tuition and fees (2002-2003):	$1,645
Out-of-state:	$5,706
Per-credit charge:	$45
Per-credit out-of-state:	$180
Books and supplies:	$1,100
Personal expenses:	$500
Transportation:	$800

Undergraduate aid. **Need-based:** Need-based aid available for full-time and part-time students. **Non-need-based:** Scholarships based on academics, art, leadership, minority status.

Policies to reduce costs. Tuition/fee waivers for minority students, unemployed or children of unemployed, employees and their families. Credit/placement for qualifying scores on AP, IB, CLEP examinations. Work study available nights and for part-time students.

Payment plans. Credit card payment.

Application procedures. FAFSA, institutional form required. Priority date 5/1; no closing date. Applicants notified on rolling basis starting 6/15, must reply within 2 week(s) of notification. **Transfers:** Closing date 5/1. Florida Student Assistance Grant available to students paying Florida resident tuition.

Contact. **Financial aid office:** (505) 296-9081ext. 260
Jean Mark, Director of Financial Aid
5901 College Road
Key West, FL 33040

Florida Metropolitan University: Melbourne Campus

Melbourne, Florida
www.cci.edu
Four-year proprietary **Federal Code: 001499**

College costs. $255 per-credit-hour charge for film and video program

	Living at home
Tuition and fees:	$10,815
Books and supplies:	$600
Personal expenses:	$1,764
Transportation:	$1,890

Undergraduate aid. **Need-based:** Need-based aid available for full-time and part-time students. **Non-need-based:** Scholarships based on academics.

Policies to reduce costs. Tuition/fee waivers for employees and their families. Work study available nights and for part-time students.

Payment plans. Credit card, installment payment.

Application procedures. FAFSA required. No deadline. Applicants notified on rolling basis, must reply within 3 week(s) of notification. **Transfers:** No deadline.

Contact. Rhonda Nabb, Director of Student Finance Office
2401 North Harbor City Boulevard
Melbourne, FL 32935

Florida Metropolitan University: Orlando College North

Orlando, Florida
www.cci.edu
Four-year proprietary **Federal Code: 001499**

	Living at home
Tuition and fees:	$10,775
Books and supplies:	$700
Personal expenses:	$1,764
Transportation:	$1,242

Undergraduate aid. **Need-based:** Need-based aid available for full-time and part-time students.

Policies to reduce costs. Tuition/fee waivers for employees and their families. Credit/placement for qualifying scores on CLEP examinations.

Payment plans. Credit card, installment payment.

Application procedures. FAFSA required. No deadline. Applicants notified on rolling basis starting 6/1. **Transfers:** No deadline.

Contact. Linda Kaisrlik, Senior Financial Aid Administrator
5421 Diplomat Circle
Orlando, FL 32810

Florida Metropolitan University: Orlando College South

Orlando, Florida
www.fmu.edu
Four-year proprietary

	Living at home
Tuition and fees (projected):	$10,326
Books and supplies:	$800
Personal expenses:	$1,764
Transportation:	$1,215

Contact. 2411 Sand Lake Road
Orlando, FL 32809

Florida Metropolitan University: Tampa College

Tampa, Florida
www.fmu.edu
Four-year proprietary **Federal Code: 001534**

College costs. Cost of tuition may vary with program.

	Living at home
Tuition and fees:	$10,815
Books and supplies:	$540
Personal expenses:	$1,710
Transportation:	$369

Undergraduate aid. All financial aid based on need. Need-based aid available for full-time and part-time students.

Policies to reduce costs. Tuition/fee waivers for employees and their families. Credit/placement for qualifying scores on CLEP examinations.

Payment plans. Credit card, installment, deferred payment.

Application procedures. FAFSA required. No deadline. Applicants notified on rolling basis.

Contact. Rod Kirkwood, Director of Financial Aid
3319 West Hillsborough Avenue
Tampa, FL 33614

Florida Metropolitan University: Tampa College Lakeland

Lakeland, Florida
www.cci.edu
Four-year private **Federal Code: 025998**

College costs. Institution tuition on sliding scale depending on program and number of credits. $185-$270 per credit for undergraduates, $297-$315 per credit for graduate candidates.

	Living at home
Tuition and fees (2002-2003):	$7,405

Undergraduate aid. All financial aid based on need. Need-based aid available for full-time and part-time students.

Application procedures. No deadline.

Contact. Linda Wagner
995 East Memorial Boulevard, Suite 110
Lakeland, FL 33801-1919

Florida National College

Hialeah, Florida
www.fnc.edu
Two-year proprietary **Federal Code: 017069**

	Living at home
Tuition and fees:	$8,216
Per-credit charge:	$260
Books and supplies:	$850

Undergraduate aid. All financial aid based on need. Need-based aid available for full-time and part-time students.

Payment plans. Installment payment.

Application procedures. FAFSA, institutional form required. No deadline.

Contact. **Financial aid office:** (305) 821-3333 ext.1003
Omar Sanchez, Vice President for Planning and Research
4162 West 12th Avenue
Hialeah, FL 33012

Florida Southern College

Lakeland, Florida
www.flsouthern.edu
Four-year private **Federal Code: 001488**

	Living at home	On-campus
Tuition and fees:	$17,542	$17,542
Room and board:		$6,050
Board only:	$2,700	
Books and supplies:	$800	$800
Personal expenses:	$800	$800
Transportation:	$600	$600

Undergraduate aid. **Need-based:** Average financial aid package for full-time students was $13,648; for part-time $5,196. 74% awarded as scholarships/grants, 26% as loans/jobs. **Non-need-based:** 75% awarded as scholarships/grants, 25% as loans/jobs. Scholarships based on academics, alumni affiliation, art, athletics, job skills, leadership, minority status, music/drama, religious affiliation, state/district residency.

Freshman aid. **Need-based:** Average package met 68% of need. Average scholarship/grant was $11,401; average loan $3,888. **Non-need based:** 60 without need received awards; 11 received athletic scholarships.

Policies to reduce costs. Tuition/fee waivers for children of alumni, family members, family of clergy, employees and their families. Credit/placement for qualifying scores on AP, IB, CLEP examinations. Work study available nights and weekends.

Payment plans. Credit card, installment payment.

Application procedures. FAFSA, institutional form required. Priority date 4/1; closing date 8/1. Applicants notified on rolling basis starting 3/15.

Contact. **Financial aid office:** (863) 680-4140
David Bodwell, Director of Student Financial Aid
111 Lake Hollingsworth Drive
Lakeland, FL 33801-5698

Florida State University

Tallahassee, Florida
www.fsu.edu
Four-year public **Federal Code: 001489**

College costs. Additional $454 required fees for out-of-state students.

	Living at home	On-campus
Tuition and fees (2002-2003):	$2,684	$2,684
Out-of-state:	$11,774	$11,774
Room and board:		$5,909
Books and supplies:	$702	$702
Personal expenses:	$1,000	$1,000
Transportation:	$1,000	$1,000

Undergraduate aid. **Need-based:** Average financial aid package for full-time students was $6,529; for part-time $5,121. 51% awarded as scholarships/grants, 49% as loans/jobs. **Non-need-based:** 41% awarded as scholarships/grants, 59% as loans/jobs. Scholarships based on academics, athletics, state/district residency. **Student debt:** 64% of graduating class borrowed to fund education; average debt was $16,372. **Additional information:** Out-of-state tuition costs waived for National Merit and National Achievement students and National Hispanic Scholars, and some southwest Georgia residents.

Freshman aid. **Need-based:** Average package met 21% of need. Average scholarship/grant was $4,033; average loan $2,511.

Merit scholarships. National Merit/Achievement Scholarship awarded to all finalists who name FSU as their first choice institution; renewable package covers the basic costs of tuition, room and board. National Hispanic Scholars for all scholars who enroll; renewable package covers basic cost of tuition, room and board. University Scholarship for Freshmen for best admitted students based on high school grades and test scores; $8,000 over 4 years. Incentive Scholarship for best minority freshmen admitted based on high school grades and test scores; $8,000 over 4 years.

Policies to reduce costs. Tuition/fee waivers for senior citizens, employees and their families. Credit/placement for qualifying scores on AP, IB, CLEP examinations.

Payment plans. Installment, deferred payment.

Application procedures. FAFSA required. Priority date 2/15; no closing date. Applicants notified on rolling basis starting 3/15, must reply within 2 week(s) of notification.

Contact. **Financial aid office:** (850) 644-5871
Daryl Marshall, Director of Financial Aid
A2500 University Center
Tallahassee, FL 32306-2400

Florida Technical College

Orlando, Florida
www.flatech.edu
Two-year proprietary **Federal Code: 015670**

College costs. Network administration/programming $14,664 annually. Tuition includes cost of books and supplies.

	Living at home
Tuition and fees (2002-2003):	$13,822
Transportation:	$1,440

Undergraduate aid. All financial aid based on need. Need-based aid available for full-time and part-time students.

Payment plans. Credit card, installment payment.

Application procedures. FAFSA, institutional form required. No deadline. Applicants notified on rolling basis.

Contact. **Financial aid office:** (407) 678-5600
Shalanda Jones, Director of Financial Aid
1819 North Semoran Boulevard
Orlando, FL 32807

Florida Technical College: Auburndale

Auburndale, Florida
www.flatech.edu
Two-year proprietary

College costs (2002-2003). Tuition, including cost of books and supplies, ranges from $3,333 to $3,666 per quarter. Fees, $490. Transportation: $1,440.

Undergraduate aid. All financial aid based on need. Need-based aid available for full-time and part-time students.

Application procedures. FAFSA, institutional form required. No deadline. Applicants notified on rolling basis.

Contact. Robbin Lowe, Financial Aid Administrator
298 Havendale Boulevard
Auburndale, FL 33823

Florida Technical College: Deland

Deland, Florida
www.flatech.edu
Two-year proprietary

College costs. $3,600 tuition per quarter for medical assistant, business, computer drafting & design, electronic program; $3,960 tuition per quarter for network hardware, network programming, e-commerce, web-design program. Required fees $1,000. Tuition includes cost of books and supplies. Transportation: $1,440.

Undergraduate aid. All financial aid based on need. Need-based aid available for full-time and part-time students.

Payment plans. Credit card, installment payment.

Application procedures. FAFSA required. No deadline. Applicants notified on rolling basis.

Contact. Shalanda Jones
1450 South Woodland Boulevard
Deland, FL 32720

Florida Technical College: Jacksonville

Jacksonville, Florida
www.flatech.edu
Two-year proprietary **Federal Code: 025982**

College costs. Network administration/programming $12,100 annually. Tuition includes cost of books and supplies.

	Living at home
Tuition and fees:	$10,834
Transportation:	$1,440

Application procedures. FAFSA required. No deadline.

Contact. Lisa Dozier, Head of Financial Aid
8711 Lone Star Road
Jacksonville, FL 32211

Full Sail Real World Education

Winter Park, Florida
www.fullsail.com
Two-year proprietary **Federal Code: 016812**

College costs (2002-2003). Tuition ranges from $30,000 to $35,000 for entire degree programs. Books and supplies included in tuition.

Undergraduate aid. Need-based: Need-based aid available for full-time students.

Policies to reduce costs. Work study available nights and weekends.

Payment plans. Credit card, installment payment.

Application procedures. FAFSA required. No deadline. Applicants notified on rolling basis, must reply within 2 week(s) of notification.

Contact. Debbie Magruder
3300 University Boulevard
Winter Park, FL 32792-7429

Gulf Coast Community College

Panama City, Florida
www.gulfcoast.edu
Two-year public **Federal Code: 001490**

College costs. Additional $398 required fees for out-of-state students.

	Living at home
Tuition and fees (2002-2003):	$1,558
Out-of-state:	$5,437
Per-credit charge:	$42
Per-credit out-of-state:	$172
Board only:	$1,800
Books and supplies:	$800
Personal expenses:	$1,500
Transportation:	$800

Undergraduate aid. Need-based: 85% awarded as scholarships/grants, 15% as loans/jobs. Need-based aid available for part-time students. **Non-need-based:** Scholarships based on academics, athletics, job skills, leadership, minority status, music/drama, state/district residency. **Student debt:** 15% of graduating class borrowed to fund education; average debt was $4,000.

Merit scholarships. GCCC Foundation based on academic performance, financial need and other criteria; more than $350,000 total annually.

Policies to reduce costs. Credit/placement for qualifying scores on AP, IB, CLEP examinations. Work study available nights, weekends and for part-time students.

Payment plans. Credit card, deferred payment.

Application procedures. FAFSA required. Priority date 4/1; closing date 7/1. Applicants notified on rolling basis starting 7/1. **Transfers:** Priority date 11/1; no deadline.

Contact. Financial aid office: (850) 872-3845
Judy Mitchell, Director of Financial Aid
5230 West Highway 98
Panama City, FL 32401-1041

Herzing College: Orlando

Winter Park, Florida
www.herzing.edu
Two-year proprietary **Federal Code: 014030**

College costs. Tuition is $1,080 per class. Students typically take 3 to 4 classes per semester.

	Living at home
Tuition and fees:	$8,765

Contact. Karyn Fahey, Financial Aid Director
1595 South Semoran Boulevard, Suite 1501
Winter Park, FL 32792-5509

Hillsborough Community College

Tampa, Florida
www.hcc.cc.fl.us
Two-year public **Federal Code: 007870**

College costs. Additional $268 required fees for out-of-state students.

	Living at home
Tuition and fees (2002-2003):	$1,628
Out-of-state:	$5,797
Per-credit charge:	$46
Per-credit out-of-state:	$185
Books and supplies:	$741
Personal expenses:	$2,353
Transportation:	$1,930

Undergraduate aid. Need-based: Need-based aid available for full-time students.

Policies to reduce costs. Tuition/fee waivers for senior citizens, employees and their families. Credit/placement for qualifying scores on AP, IB, CLEP examinations. Work study available nights, weekends and for part-time students.

Payment plans. Credit card payment.

Application procedures. FAFSA required. Priority date 4/15; no closing date. Applicants notified on rolling basis starting 7/1, must reply within 2 week(s) of notification. **Transfers:** No deadline. Transfer students must submit academic transcripts prior to obtaining student loans at sophomore level.

Contact. **Financial aid office:** (813) 253-7235
Charlotte Johns, Financial Aid Officer
Box 31127
Tampa, FL 33631-3127

Hobe Sound Bible College

Hobe Sound, Florida
www.hsbc.edu
Four-year private **Federal Code: 015463**

	Living at home	On-campus
Tuition and fees (2002-2003):	$4,240	$4,240
Room and board:		$3,010
Board only:	$1,350	
Books and supplies:	$450	$450
Personal expenses:	$2,000	$2,000
Transportation:	$500	$1,000

Undergraduate aid. Need-based: Need-based aid available for full-time and part-time students. **Non-need-based:** Scholarships based on academics, leadership.

Policies to reduce costs. Tuition/fee waivers for family of clergy, employees and their families. Prepayment discount.

Payment plans. Credit card, installment payment.

Application procedures. No deadline. **Transfers:** No deadline.

Contact. **Financial aid office:** (772) 546-5534 ext. 1003
Phillip Gray, Director of Financial Aid
Box 1065
Hobe Sound, FL 33475

ITT Technical Institute: Ft. Lauderdale

Ft. Lauderdale, Florida
www.itt-tech.edu
Three-year proprietary

College costs. Total program varies depending on course of study. Per-credit-hour charge: $347.

Policies to reduce costs. Tuition/fee waivers for employees and their families.

Payment plans. Credit card, installment payment.

Application procedures. FAFSA, institutional form required. No deadline. Applicants notified on rolling basis.

Contact. Lara Gates, Director of Finance
3401 S. University Drive
Ft. Lauderdale, FL 33328

ITT Technical Institute: Jacksonville

Jacksonville, Florida
www.itt-tech.edu
Three-year proprietary **Federal Code: 022865**

College costs. Total program varies depending on course of study. Per-credit-hour charge: $347.

Policies to reduce costs. Tuition/fee waivers for employees and their families.

Payment plans. Credit card, installment payment.

Application procedures. FAFSA, institutional form required. No deadline. Applicants notified on rolling basis.

Contact. Roberta Wilson, Director of Finance
6600-10 Youngerman Circle
Jacksonville, FL 32244

ITT Technical Institute: Maitland

Maitland, Florida
www.itt-tech.edu
Three-year proprietary **Federal Code: 030876**

College costs. Total program varies depending on course of study. Per-credit-hour charge: $347.

Policies to reduce costs. Tuition/fee waivers for employees and their families.

Payment plans. Credit card, installment payment.

Application procedures. FAFSA, institutional form required. No deadline. Applicants notified on rolling basis.

Contact. Rebecca Lydick, Director of Finance
2600 Lake Lucien Drive
Maitland, FL 32751-9754

ITT Technical Institute: Miami

Miami, Florida
www.itt-tech.edu
Two-year proprietary **Federal Code: 030876**

College costs. Total program varies depending on course of study. Per-credit-hour charge: $347.

Policies to reduce costs. Tuition/fee waivers for employees and their families. Tuition at time of enrollment guaranteed for 2 years.

Payment plans. Credit card, installment payment.

Application procedures. FAFSA, institutional form required. No deadline. Applicants notified on rolling basis.

Contact. Carlos Alayon, Director of Finance
7955 12th Street, Suite 119
Miami, FL 33126

ITT Technical Institute: Tampa

Tampa, Florida
www.itt-tech.edu
Three-year proprietary **Federal Code: 016204**

College costs. Total program varies depending on course of study. Per-credit-hour charge: $347.

Policies to reduce costs. Tuition/fee waivers for employees and their families.

Payment plans. Credit card, installment payment.

Application procedures. FAFSA, institutional form required. No deadline. Applicants notified on rolling basis.

Contact. Julie Cummings, Director of Finance
4809 Memorial Highway
Tampa, FL 33634

Indian River Community College

Fort Pierce, Florida
www.ircc.edu
Two-year public **Federal Code: 001493**

College costs. Additional $315 required fees for out-of-state students.

	Living at home	On-campus
Tuition and fees (2002-2003):	$1,602	$1,602
Out-of-state:	$5,281	$5,281
Per-credit charge:	$52	$52
Per-credit out-of-state:	$193	$193
Room only:		$2,700
Board only:	$1,250	
Books and supplies:	$700	$700
Personal expenses:	$856	
Transportation:	$1,150	

Undergraduate aid. Need-based: Need-based aid available for full-time and part-time students. **Non-need-based:** Scholarships based on academics, athletics, minority status, music/drama, state/district residency.

Policies to reduce costs. Credit/placement for qualifying scores on AP, IB, CLEP examinations. Work study available for part-time students.

Payment plans. Credit card payment.

Application procedures. FAFSA, institutional form required. Priority date 6/30; no closing date. Applicants notified on rolling basis starting 5/15.

Contact. Steven Payne, Director of Financial Aid
3209 Virginia Avenue
Fort Pierce, FL 34981-5596

Institute of Career Education

West Palm Beach, Florida
www.vocedu.com
One-year proprietary

College costs. Tuition for medical assisting diploma (9-month program): $8,873; tuition for full 13-month medical assisting degree certificate: $11,688. Other costs vary by program.

	Living at home
Tuition and fees (2002-2003):	$9,000
Books and supplies:	$600

Contact. Rich Dombrowski, Financial Aid Director
1750 45th Street
West Palm Beach, FL 33407

International Academy of Design and Technology

Tampa, Florida
www.academy.edu
Four-year proprietary **Federal Code: 030314**

College costs. $270 per-credit-hour for fashion, interior design and merchandising programs; $295 per-credit-hour for computer-related programs.

	Living at home
Tuition and fees (2002-2003):	$13,920
Books and supplies:	$1,200
Personal expenses:	$1,665
Transportation:	$2,169

Policies to reduce costs. Tuition/fee waivers for employees and their families. Tuition at time of enrollment guaranteed for 4 years; credit/placement for qualifying scores on AP examinations.

Payment plans. Credit card, installment, deferred payment.

Application procedures. FAFSA, institutional form required. No deadline. Applicants notified on rolling basis.

Contact. James Friend, Financial Aid Director
5225 Memorial Highway
Tampa, FL 33634

International College

Naples, Florida
www.internationalcollege.edu
Four-year private **Federal Code: 030375**

	Living at home
Tuition and fees (2002-2003):	$9,970
Board only:	$1,000
Books and supplies:	$900
Personal expenses:	$944
Transportation:	$1,464

Undergraduate aid. Need-based: Average financial aid package for full-time students was $7,600; for part-time $4,200. 28% awarded as scholarships/grants, 72% as loans/jobs. **Non-need-based:** 40% awarded as scholarships/grants, 60% as loans/jobs. Scholarships based on academics, leadership, state/district residency. **Student debt:** 82% of graduating class borrowed to fund education; average debt was $17,000.

Freshman aid. Need-based: Out of 100 full-time freshmen, 88 applied for aid; 75 were judged to have need; of these 75 received aid. Average package met 48% of need. 38 students had full need met. Average scholarship/grant was $2,000; average loan $2,600. **Non-need based:** 68 full-time freshmen with need received non-need scholarships; 11 without need received awards; 8 received athletic scholarships.

Policies to reduce costs. Tuition/fee waivers for employees and their families. Credit/placement for qualifying scores on AP, IB, CLEP examinations. Work study available nights and weekends.

Payment plans. Credit card, installment payment.

Application procedures. FAFSA required. No deadline. Applicants notified on rolling basis.

Contact. Financial aid office: (239) 513-1122
Joe Gilchrist, Director of Financial Aid
2655 Northbrooke Drive
Naples, FL 34119

Jacksonville University

Jacksonville, Florida
www.ju.edu
Four-year private **Federal Code: 001495**

	Living at home	On-campus
Tuition and fees:	$17,940	$17,940
Room and board:		$5,900
Board only:	$1,410	
Books and supplies:	$600	$600
Personal expenses:	$600	$600
Transportation:	$800	$800

Undergraduate aid. Need-based: Average financial aid package for full-time students was $14,786; for part-time $4,901. 61% awarded as scholarships/grants, 39% as loans/jobs. **Non-need-based:** 86% awarded as scholarships/grants, 14% as loans/jobs. Scholarships based on academics, alumni affiliation, art, athletics, leadership, music/drama, state/district residency.

Freshman aid. Need-based: Out of 381 full-time freshmen, 369 applied for aid; 239 were judged to have need; of these 239 received aid. Average package met 83% of need. 71 students had full need met. Average scholarship/grant was $13,345; average loan $3,694. **Non-need based:** 102 without need received awards; 22 received athletic scholarships.

Policies to reduce costs. Tuition/fee waivers for family members, employees and their families. Credit/placement for qualifying scores on AP, IB, CLEP examinations.

Payment plans. Credit card, installment, deferred payment.

Application procedures. FAFSA, institutional form required. Priority date 1/15; no closing date. Applicants notified on rolling basis starting 10/15, must reply within 3 week(s) of notification.

Contact. Catherine Huntress, Director of Financial Assistance
2800 University Boulevard North
Jacksonville, FL 32211

Jones College

Jacksonville, Florida
www.jones.edu
Four-year private **Federal Code: 001497**

	Living at home
Tuition and fees (projected):	$6,840
Books and supplies:	$750
Personal expenses:	$1,700
Transportation:	$950

Undergraduate aid. All financial aid based on need. Need-based aid available for full-time and part-time students.

Policies to reduce costs. Tuition/fee waivers for employees and their families. Prepayment discount; credit/placement for qualifying scores on CLEP examinations. Work study available nights, weekends and for part-time students.

Payment plans. Credit card, installment payment.

Application procedures. FAFSA required. No deadline. Applicants notified on rolling basis.

Contact. Financial aid office: (904) 743-1122 ext. 100
Becky Davis, Financial Assistance Director
5353 Arlington Expressway
Jacksonville, FL 32211

Jones College: Miami

Miami, Florida
www.jones.edu
Four-year private **Federal Code: 001497**

	Living at home
Tuition and fees:	$6,840
Books and supplies:	$750
Personal expenses:	$1,700
Transportation:	$950

Undergraduate aid. All financial aid based on need. Need-based aid available for full-time and part-time students.

Application procedures. FAFSA required. No deadline. Applicants notified on rolling basis.

Contact. Rainford Bowles, Dean of the College
11430 North Kendall Drive, Suite 200
Miami, FL 33176

Lake City Community College

Lake City, Florida
www.lakecitycc.edu
Two-year public **Federal Code: 001501**

College costs. Additional $454 required fees for out-of-state students.

	Living at home	On-campus
Tuition and fees (2002-2003):	$1,499	$1,499
Out-of-state:	$5,149	$5,149
Per-credit charge:	$41	$41
Per-credit out-of-state:	$162	$162
Room and board:		$4,239
Board only:	$3,690	
Books and supplies:	$800	$800
Personal expenses:	$750	$750
Transportation:	$600	$600

Undergraduate aid. Need-based: 79% awarded as scholarships/grants, 21% as loans/jobs. Need-based aid available for part-time students. **Non-need-based:** 78% awarded as scholarships/grants, 22% as loans/jobs. Scholarships based on academics, athletics.

Freshman aid. Need-based: Out of 279 full-time freshmen, 209 applied for aid; 195 were judged to have need; of these 176 received aid. Average package met 75% of need. **Non-need based:** 84 full-time freshmen with need received non-need scholarships; 16 received athletic scholarships.

Policies to reduce costs. Tuition/fee waivers for minority students, employees and their families. Credit/placement for qualifying scores on AP, IB, CLEP examinations. Work study available for part-time students.

Payment plans. Credit card, deferred payment.

Application procedures. FAFSA, institutional form required. Priority date 6/1; no closing date. Applicants notified on rolling basis starting 6/1, must reply within 2 week(s) of notification.

Contact. Financial aid office: (386) 754-4282
Debberin Tunsil, Director of Financial Aid
Route 19, Box 1030
Lake City, FL 32025-8703

Lake-Sumter Community College

Leesburg, Florida
www.lscc.cc.fl.us
Two-year public **Federal Code: 001502**

College costs. Additional $369 required fees for out-of-state students.

	Living at home
Tuition and fees (2002-2003):	$1,585
Out-of-state:	$5,572
Per-credit charge:	$44
Per-credit out-of-state:	$177
Board only:	$2,400
Books and supplies:	$800
Personal expenses:	$1,975

Undergraduate aid. Need-based: Need-based aid available for full-time and part-time students. **Non-need-based:** Scholarships based on academics, alumni affiliation, art, athletics, leadership, minority status, music/drama, state/district residency.

Policies to reduce costs. Tuition/fee waivers for employees and their families. Credit/placement for qualifying scores on AP, CLEP examinations. Work study available nights, weekends and for part-time students.

Payment plans. Credit card payment.

Application procedures. FAFSA, institutional form required. Priority date 6/1; no closing date. Applicants notified on rolling basis starting 7/1. **Transfers:** No deadline.

Contact. Financial aid office: (352) 365-3512
Audrey Maxwell, Director of Financial Aid
9501 U.S. Highway 441
Leesburg, FL 34788-8751

Manatee Community College

Bradenton, Florida
www.mccfl.us
Two-year public **Federal Code: 001504**

College costs. Additional $269 required fees for out-of-state students.

	Living at home
Tuition and fees (2002-2003):	$1,622
Out-of-state:	$5,791
Per-credit charge:	$46
Per-credit out-of-state:	$185
Board only:	$2,000
Books and supplies:	$708
Personal expenses:	$1,266
Transportation:	$1,394

Undergraduate aid. Need-based: 72% awarded as scholarships/grants, 28% as loans/jobs. Need-based aid available for part-time students. **Non-need-based:** 46% awarded as scholarships/grants, 54% as loans/jobs. Scholarships based on academics, art, athletics, music/drama, state/district residency. **Student debt:** 35% of graduating class borrowed to fund education; average debt was $4,000.

Policies to reduce costs. Tuition/fee waivers for employees and their families. Credit/placement for qualifying scores on AP, CLEP examinations. Work study available nights, weekends and for part-time students.

Payment plans. Credit card payment.

Application procedures. FAFSA required. Priority date 6/1; no closing date. Applicants notified on rolling basis starting 3/15.

Contact. Financial aid office: (941) 752-5309
Anders Nilsen, Director of Financial Aid
Box 1849
Bradenton, FL 34206-1849

Miami-Dade Community College

Miami, Florida
www.mdcc.edu
Two-year public **Federal Code: 001506**

College costs. Additional required fees $349 for out-of-state students.

	Living at home
Tuition and fees (2002-2003):	$1,583
Out-of-state:	$5,180
Per-credit charge:	$44
Per-credit out-of-state:	$164
Board only:	$1,748
Books and supplies:	$1,168
Personal expenses:	$2,220
Transportation:	$2,190

Undergraduate aid. Need-based: Average financial aid package for full-time students was $5,322; for part-time $3,694. 62% awarded as scholarships/grants, 38% as loans/jobs. **Non-need-based:** Scholarships based on academics, art, athletics, music/drama, state/district residency.

Freshman aid. Need-based: Out of 2,998 full-time freshmen, 2,391 applied for aid; 2,226 were judged to have need; of these 2,156 received aid. Average package met 46% of need. 2040 students had full need met. Average scholarship/grant was $3,265; average loan $2,428. **Non-need based:** 220 full-time freshmen with need received non-need scholarships; 26 without need received awards; 1 received athletic scholarships.

Policies to reduce costs. Tuition/fee waivers for employees and their families. Credit/placement for qualifying scores on AP, IB, CLEP examinations. Work study available nights, weekends and for part-time students.

Payment plans. Credit card payment.

Application procedures. FAFSA, institutional form required. Priority date 3/15; no closing date. Applicants notified on rolling basis starting 5/15.

Contact. Financial aid office: (305) 237-7461
James McMillan, District Director of Financial Aid
300 Northeast Second Avenue
Miami, FL 33132-2297

New College of Florida

Sarasota, Florida
www.ncf.edu
Four-year public **Federal Code: 001537 04**

	Living at home	On-campus
Tuition and fees (2002-2003):	$3,026	$3,026
Out-of-state:	$13,816	$13,816
Room and board:		$5,395
Board only:	$283	
Books and supplies:	$700	$700
Personal expenses:	$2,500	$2,500
Transportation:		$1,100

Undergraduate aid. Need-based: Average financial aid package for full-time students was $7,669. 51% awarded as scholarships/grants, 49% as loans/jobs. **Non-need-based:** 86% awarded as scholarships/grants, 14% as loans/jobs. Scholarships based on academics, leadership, state/district residency.

Freshman aid. Need-based: Average package met 87% of need. Average scholarship/grant was $5,443; average loan $2,181.

Policies to reduce costs. Tuition/fee waivers for senior citizens. Prepayment discount.

Application procedures. FAFSA required. Priority date 3/1; no closing date. Applicants notified on rolling basis starting 10/1, must reply by 5/1 or within 4 week(s) of notification.

Contact. Financial aid office: (941) 359-4255
Joel Bauman, Dean of Admissions and Financial Aid
5700 North Tamiami Trail
Sarasota, FL 34243-2197

New England Institute of Technology

West Palm Beach, Florida
www.newenglandtech.com
Two-year proprietary **Federal Code: 016095**

College costs. Tuition and lab fees for full associate degree programs range from $7,400 to $32,800. Registration fee $125. Board: $2,997. Books/supplies: $558. Personal expenses: $1,863. Transportation: $936.

Undergraduate aid. Need-based: 49% awarded as scholarships/grants, 51% as loans/jobs.

Policies to reduce costs. Tuition at time of enrollment guaranteed for 2 years. Work study available nights and weekends.

Payment plans. Credit card, installment payment.

Application procedures. FAFSA, institutional form required. No deadline. Applicants notified on rolling basis.

Contact. Financial aid office: (561) 842-8324
Elizabeth Layton, Director of Student Financial Services
2410 Metrocentre Boulevard
West Palm Beach, FL 33407

Northwood University: Florida Campus

West Palm Beach, Florida
www.northwood.edu
Four-year private **Federal Code: 013040**

	Living at home	On-campus
Tuition and fees:	$13,995	$13,995
Room and board:		$7,045
Books and supplies:	$1,200	$1,200
Transportation:	$834	$602

Undergraduate aid. Need-based: Average financial aid package for full-time students was $12,153; for part-time $5,295. 65% awarded as scholarships/grants, 35% as loans/jobs. **Non-need-based:** 80% awarded as scholarships/grants, 20% as loans/jobs. Scholarships based on academics, alumni affiliation, athletics, state/district residency. **Student debt:** 23% of graduating class borrowed to fund education; average debt was $16,370.

Freshman aid. Need-based: Out of 132 full-time freshmen, 92 applied for aid; 81 were judged to have need; of these 80 received aid. Average package met 71% of need. 17 students had full need met. Average scholarship/grant was $9,500; average loan $2,401. **Non-need based:** 63 full-time freshmen with need received non-need scholarships; 5 without need received awards; 7 received athletic scholarships.

Merit scholarships. Merit Scholarships, $3,000-$5,000, unlimited number awarded, based on test scores and GPA.

Policies to reduce costs. Tuition/fee waivers for children of alumni, family members, employees and their families. Credit/placement for qualifying scores on AP, IB, CLEP examinations. Work study available nights, weekends and for part-time students.

Payment plans. Installment payment.

Application procedures. FAFSA required. Priority date 3/1; no closing date. Applicants notified on rolling basis starting 3/1, must reply within 2 week(s) of notification.

Contact. Joan Begin, Director of Financial Aid
2600 North Military Trail
West Palm Beach, FL 33409

Nova Southeastern University

Fort Lauderdale, Florida
www.nova.edu
Four-year private **Federal Code: 001509**

	Living at home	On-campus
Tuition and fees:	$15,535	$15,535
Room and board:		$8,126
Books and supplies:	$856	$856
Personal expenses:	$1,800	$1,800
Transportation:	$2,540	$2,540

Undergraduate aid. Need-based: Average financial aid package for full-time students was $14,846; for part-time $12,604. 44% awarded as scholarships/grants, 56% as loans/jobs. **Non-need-based:** 45% awarded as scholarships/grants, 55% as loans/jobs. Scholarships based on academics, athletics, leadership, minority status, state/district residency. **Student debt:** 58% of graduating class borrowed to fund education; average debt was $23,405.

Freshman aid. Need-based: Out of 310 full-time freshmen, 299 applied for aid; 226 were judged to have need; of these 226 received aid. Average package met 57% of need. 13 students had full need met. Average scholarship/grant was $9,968; average loan $3,120. **Non-need based:** 210 full-time freshmen with need received non-need scholarships; 64 without need received awards; 39 received athletic scholarships.

Policies to reduce costs. Tuition/fee waivers for employees and their families. Credit/placement for qualifying scores on AP, IB, CLEP examinations. Work study available nights, weekends and for part-time students.

Payment plans. Credit card, installment, deferred payment.

Application procedures. FAFSA, institutional form required. Priority date 4/15; no closing date. Applicants notified on rolling basis, must reply within 4 week(s) of notification.

Contact. Financial aid office: (954) 262-3380
Peggy Loewy-Wellisch, Director of Financial Aid
3301 College Avenue
Fort Lauderdale, FL 33314

Okaloosa-Walton Community College

Niceville, Florida
www.owcc.edu
Two-year public **Federal Code: 001510**

	Living at home
Tuition and fees (2002-2003):	$1,337
Out-of-state:	$5,156
Per-credit charge:	$42
Per-credit out-of-state:	$170
Books and supplies:	$688
Personal expenses:	$1,280
Transportation:	$2,850

Undergraduate aid. Need-based: Need-based aid available for full-time and part-time students. **Non-need-based:** Scholarships based on academics, art, athletics, leadership, minority status, music/drama.

Policies to reduce costs. Tuition/fee waivers for minority students, employees and their families. Credit/placement for qualifying scores on AP, CLEP examinations. Work study available nights and for part-time students.

Payment plans. Credit card, installment, deferred payment.

Application procedures. FAFSA, institutional form required. Priority date 4/1; no closing date. Applicants notified on rolling basis starting 2/1, must reply within 2 week(s) of notification. **Transfers:** Academic transcript evaluated to determine student eligibility for financial aid.

Contact. Doug Savage, Director of Financial Aid
100 College Boulevard
Niceville, FL 32578

Palm Beach Atlantic University

West Palm Beach, Florida
www.pba.edu
Four-year private **Federal Code: 008849**

College costs. Per-credit-hour charge ranges from $330 to $545 depending on number of credits.

	Living at home	On-campus
Tuition and fees:	$14,890	$14,890
Room and board:		$5,434
Board only:	$1,900	
Books and supplies:	$800	$800
Personal expenses:	$1,200	$1,200
Transportation:	$2,000	$2,000

Undergraduate aid. Need-based: Average financial aid package for full-time students was $11,065; for part-time $5,353. 67% awarded as scholarships/grants, 33% as loans/jobs. **Non-need-based:** 68% awarded as scholarships/grants, 32% as loans/jobs. Scholarships based on academics, alumni affiliation, art, athletics, leadership, minority status, music/drama, religious affiliation, state/district residency. **Student debt:** 51% of graduating class borrowed to fund education; average debt was $12,645.

Freshman aid. Need-based: Out of 426 full-time freshmen, 326 applied for aid; 268 were judged to have need; of these 268 received aid. Average package met 66% of need. 46 students had full need met. Average scholarship/grant was $8,732; average loan $2,595. **Non-need based:** 37 full-time freshmen with need received non-need scholarships; 205 without need received awards; 19 received athletic scholarships.

Policies to reduce costs. Tuition/fee waivers for adults, children of alumni, senior citizens, family members, family of clergy, employees and their families. Credit/placement for qualifying scores on AP, IB, CLEP examinations. Work study available weekends and for part-time students.

Payment plans. Credit card, installment payment.

Application procedures. FAFSA, institutional form required. Priority date 4/1; no closing date. Applicants notified on rolling basis starting 3/1, must reply within 4 week(s) of notification.

Contact. Financial aid office: (561) 803-2126
Margherite Powell, Student Financial Planning
Box 24708
West Palm Beach, FL 33416-4708

Palm Beach Community College

Lake Worth, Florida
www.pbcc.edu
Two-year public **Federal Code: 001512**

College costs. Additional $286 required fees for out-of-state students.

	Living at home	On-campus
Tuition and fees (2002-2003):	$1,530	$1,530
Out-of-state:	$5,450	$5,450
Per-credit charge:	$44	$44
Per-credit out-of-state:	$174	$174
Room only:		$3,735
Board only:	$3,160	
Books and supplies:	$600	$600
Personal expenses:	$400	$800
Transportation:	$928	$928

Undergraduate aid. Non-need-based: Scholarships based on academics, alumni affiliation, athletics, leadership, state/district residency.

Policies to reduce costs. Tuition/fee waivers for employees and their families. Credit/placement for qualifying scores on AP, IB, CLEP examinations. Work study available nights, weekends and for part-time students.

Payment plans. Credit card payment.

Application procedures. FAFSA, institutional form required. Priority date 7/1; no closing date. Applicants notified on rolling basis, must reply within 2 week(s) of notification.

Contact. Lauren Peavler, Director of Student Financial Aid
4200 Congress Avenue
Lake Worth, FL 33461

Pasco-Hernando Community College

New Port Richey, Florida
phcc.edu
Two-year public **Federal Code: 010652**

College costs. Additional $433 required fees for out-of-state students.

	Living at home
Tuition and fees (2002-2003):	$1,561
Out-of-state:	$5,347
Per-credit charge:	$42
Per-credit out-of-state:	$168
Books and supplies:	$1,050
Personal expenses:	$1,571
Transportation:	$1,114

Undergraduate aid. Need-based: 84% awarded as scholarships/grants, 16% as loans/jobs. Need-based aid available for part-time students. **Non-need-based:** 32% awarded as scholarships/grants, 68% as loans/jobs. Scholarships based on academics, athletics, minority status. **Additional information:** Childcare assistance grants available to eligible students.

Policies to reduce costs. Tuition/fee waivers for employees and their families. Credit/placement for qualifying scores on AP, IB, CLEP examinations. Work study available nights, weekends and for part-time students.

Payment plans. Credit card, deferred payment.

Application procedures. FAFSA required. Priority date 4/1; no closing date. Applicants notified on rolling basis starting 3/1. **Transfers:** Priority date 3/1.

Contact. Financial aid office: (727) 816-3463
Rebecca Shanafelt, Director of Financial Aid/Veterans Services
10230 Ridge Road
New Port Richey, FL 34654-5199

Pensacola Junior College

Pensacola, Florida
www.pjc.edu
Two-year public **Federal Code: 001513**

College costs. Additional $259 required fees for out-of-state students.

	Living at home
Tuition and fees (2002-2003):	$1,556
Out-of-state:	$5,543
Per-credit charge:	$44
Per-credit out-of-state:	$177
Board only:	$1,800
Books and supplies:	$800
Personal expenses:	$1,100
Transportation:	$986

Undergraduate aid. Non-need-based: Scholarships based on academics, athletics, state/district residency.

Policies to reduce costs. Tuition/fee waivers for senior citizens, employees and their families. Credit/placement for qualifying scores on AP, IB, CLEP examinations.

Payment plans. Credit card payment.

Application procedures. FAFSA, institutional form required. Priority date 4/1; no closing date. Applicants notified on rolling basis starting 7/1, must reply within 2 week(s) of notification.

Contact. Financial aid office: (850) 484-1680
1000 College Boulevard
Pensacola, FL 32504-8998

Polk Community College

Winter Haven, Florida
www.polk.cc.fl.us
Two-year public **Federal Code: 001514**

College costs. Additional $260 required fees for out-of-state students.

	Living at home
Tuition and fees (2002-2003):	$1,558
Out-of-state:	$5,545
Per-credit charge:	$44
Per-credit out-of-state:	$177
Books and supplies:	$800
Personal expenses:	$600
Transportation:	$1,000

Undergraduate aid. Need-based: 84% awarded as scholarships/grants, 16% as loans/jobs. Need-based aid available for part-time students. **Non-need-based:** Scholarships based on academics, athletics, leadership, state/district residency. **Student debt:** 1% of graduating class borrowed to fund education; average debt was $2,613.

Policies to reduce costs. Tuition/fee waivers for employees and their families. Credit/placement for qualifying scores on AP, IB, CLEP examinations.

Payment plans. Credit card payment.

Application procedures. FAFSA required. Priority date 5/15; no closing date. Applicants notified on rolling basis. **Transfers:** No deadline.

Contact. **Financial aid office:** (863) 297-1004
L. Porter, Director of Financial Aid
999 Avenue H Northeast
Winter Haven, FL 33881-4299

Ringling School of Art and Design

Sarasota, Florida
www.rsad.edu
Four-year private **Federal Code: 012574**

College costs. Technology fees vary from $800-$2,000 according to program.

	Living at home	On-campus
Tuition and fees (2002-2003):	$16,430	$16,430
Room and board:		$7,844
Board only:	$3,922	
Books and supplies:	$1,800	$1,800
Personal expenses:	$1,890	$1,890
Transportation:	$640	$640

Undergraduate aid. All financial aid based on need. Average financial aid package for full-time students was $8,454; for part-time $4,642. 35% awarded as scholarships/grants, 65% as loans/jobs. **Student debt:** 53% of graduating class borrowed to fund education; average debt was $25,370.

Freshman aid. Out of 193 full-time freshmen, 145 applied for aid; 119 were judged to have need; of these 119 received aid. Average package met 37% of need. 5 students had full need met. Average scholarship/grant was $6,487; average loan $2,482.

Policies to reduce costs. Tuition/fee waivers for employees and their families. Credit/placement for qualifying scores on AP, IB, CLEP examinations.

Payment plans. Credit card payment.

Application procedures. FAFSA required. Priority date 3/1; no closing date. Applicants notified on rolling basis starting 5/1, must reply by 8/1.

Contact. **Financial aid office:** (941) 359-7534
Kurt Wolf, Director of Financial Aid
2700 North Tamiami Trail
Sarasota, FL 34234

Rollins College

Winter Park, Florida
www.rollins.edu
Four-year private **Federal Code: 001515**

	Living at home	On-campus
Tuition and fees (2002-2003):	$24,958	$24,958
Room and board:		$7,652
Board only:	$4,400	
Books and supplies:	$530	$530
Personal expenses:	$480	$2,018
Transportation:	$435	$750

Undergraduate aid. Need-based: Average financial aid package for full-time students was $26,716. 83% awarded as scholarships/grants, 17% as loans/jobs. **Non-need-based:** 60% awarded as scholarships/grants, 40% as loans/jobs. Scholarships based on academics, art, athletics, leadership, music/drama. **Student debt:** 48% of graduating class borrowed to fund education; average debt was $14,719. **Additional information:** Audition required for theater arts and music scholarship applicants. Portfolio required for art scholarships.

Freshman aid. Need-based: Out of 467 full-time freshmen, 232 applied for aid; 184 were judged to have need; of these 184 received aid. Average package met 92% of need. 74 students had full need met. Average scholarship/grant was $19,665; average loan $3,604. **Non-need based:** 29 full-time freshmen with need received non-need scholarships; 98 without need received awards; 14 received athletic scholarships.

Merit scholarships. Presidential, Alonzo Rollins; $4,000-$15,000 per year; based on academic record; 130 available per year. Donald Cram; $3,000-$5,000 per year; based on academic record, science major; 10 available per year. Crosby & Cornell Leadership; $10,000-$20,000 per year; based on leadership record; 6 available per year.

Policies to reduce costs. Tuition/fee waivers for employees and their families. Credit/placement for qualifying scores on AP, IB, CLEP examinations. Work study available nights and weekends.

Payment plans. Credit card, installment payment.

Application procedures. FAFSA, institutional form required. Priority date 2/15; closing date 3/1. Applicants notified on rolling basis starting 3/1. Early decision closing date 11/15. **Transfers:** Priority date 4/15; no deadline.

Contact. **Financial aid office:** (407) 646-2395
Phil Asbury, Director of Financial Aid
1000 Holt Avenue
Winter Park, FL 32789

St. John Vianney College Seminary

Miami, Florida
www.sjvcs.edu
Four-year private **Federal Code: 008075**

	Living at home	On-campus
Tuition and fees:	$11,000	$11,000
Room and board:		$4,000
Books and supplies:	$600	$600
Personal expenses:		$990
Transportation:		$900

Policies to reduce costs. Credit/placement for qualifying scores on AP, CLEP examinations.

Payment plans. Installment, deferred payment.

Application procedures. FAFSA required. No deadline. Applicants notified on rolling basis.

Contact. Maria DeAngulo, Financial Aid Officer
2900 Southwest 87 Avenue
Miami, FL 33165-3244

St. Leo University

St. Leo, Florida
www.saintleo.edu
Four-year private **Federal Code: 001526**

	Living at home	On-campus
Tuition and fees (2002-2003):	$12,970	$12,970
Room and board:		$6,834
Board only:	$2,500	
Books and supplies:	$1,200	$1,200
Personal expenses:	$800	$900
Transportation:	$1,100	$900

Undergraduate aid. Need-based: Average financial aid package for full-time students was $17,695. 63% awarded as scholarships/grants, 37% as loans/jobs. Need-based aid available for part-time students. **Non-need-based:** 70% awarded as scholarships/grants, 30% as loans/jobs. Scholarships based on academics, alumni affiliation, art, athletics, leadership, minority status, music/drama, religious affiliation, state/district residency. **Student debt:** 75% of graduating class borrowed to fund education; average debt was $12,000.

Freshman aid. Need-based: Out of 283 full-time freshmen, 260 applied for aid; 199 were judged to have need; of these 199 received aid. Average package met 78% of need. 68 students had full need met. Average scholarship/grant was $10,381; average loan $2,625. **Non-need based:** 77 without need received awards; 5 received athletic scholarships.

Policies to reduce costs. Tuition/fee waivers for family members, employees and their families. Credit/placement for qualifying scores on AP, IB, CLEP examinations. Work study available nights and weekends.

Payment plans. Credit card, deferred payment.

Application procedures. FAFSA required. Priority date 3/1; no closing date. Applicants notified on rolling basis starting 3/1, must reply within 2 week(s) of notification.

Contact. Financial aid office: (800) 240-7658
Pat Watkins, Director of Financial Aid
Office of Admission
St. Leo, FL 33574-6665

St. Petersburg College

St. Petersburg, Florida
www.spcollege.edu
Two-year public **Federal Code: 001528**

College costs. Additional $268 required fees for out-of-state students.

	Living at home
Tuition and fees (2002-2003):	$1,628
Out-of-state:	$5,797
Per-credit charge:	$46
Per-credit out-of-state:	$185
Books and supplies:	$800
Personal expenses:	$915
Transportation:	$1,015

Undergraduate aid. Need-based: Need-based aid available for full-time and part-time students. **Non-need-based:** Scholarships based on academics, art, athletics, minority status, music/drama.

Policies to reduce costs. Tuition/fee waivers for senior citizens, employees and their families. Credit/placement for qualifying scores on AP, IB, CLEP examinations. Work study available nights and for part-time students.

Payment plans. Credit card payment.

Application procedures. FAFSA, institutional form required. Priority date 4/15; no closing date. Applicants notified on rolling basis starting 5/15, must reply within 2 week(s) of notification. **Transfers:** No deadline.

Contact. Financial aid office: (727) 791-2443
Ray Pranske, Director of Financial Aid
Box 13489
St. Petersburg, FL 33733

St. Thomas University

Miami, Florida
www.stu.edu
Four-year private **Federal Code: 001468**

	Living at home	On-campus
Tuition and fees (2002-2003):	$15,450	$15,450
Room and board:		$5,040
Board only:	$500	
Books and supplies:	$750	$750
Personal expenses:	$1,000	$1,200
Transportation:	$1,000	$1,200

Undergraduate aid. Need-based: 37% awarded as scholarships/grants, 63% as loans/jobs. **Non-need-based:** 14% awarded as scholarships/grants, 86% as loans/jobs. Scholarships based on academics, athletics.

Freshman aid. Need-based: Out of 164 full-time freshmen, 118 applied for aid; 113 were judged to have need; of these 113 received aid. **Non-need based:** 113 full-time freshmen with need received non-need scholarships; 39 without need received awards; 18 received athletic scholarships.

Policies to reduce costs. Tuition/fee waivers for family of clergy, employees and their families. Credit/placement for qualifying scores on AP, CLEP examinations.

Payment plans. Credit card, installment, deferred payment.

Application procedures. FAFSA required. Priority date 4/1; no closing date. Applicants notified on rolling basis starting 3/15, must reply within 2 week(s) of notification. **Transfers:** Priority date 4/15; no deadline.

Contact. Financial aid office: (305) 628-6547
Andres Marrero, Assistant Director of Financial Aid
1540 Northwest 32nd Avenue
Miami, FL 33054

Santa Fe Community College

Gainesville, Florida
www.santafe.sfcc.edu
Two-year public **Federal Code: 001519**

College costs. Additional $259 required fees for out-of-state students.

	Living at home
Tuition and fees (2002-2003):	$1,557
Out-of-state:	$5,544
Per-credit charge:	$44
Per-credit out-of-state:	$177
Board only:	$2,720
Books and supplies:	$552
Personal expenses:	$1,008
Transportation:	$928

Undergraduate aid. Need-based: Need-based aid available for full-time and part-time students. **Non-need-based:** Scholarships based on academics, art, athletics, leadership, minority status, music/drama, state/district residency.

Policies to reduce costs. Tuition/fee waivers for senior citizens, minority students, family members, employees and their families. Credit/placement for qualifying scores on AP, CLEP examinations.

Payment plans. Credit card, deferred payment.

Application procedures. FAFSA required. Priority date 3/15; closing date 6/30. Applicants notified by 8/1. **Transfers:** Must have minimum 2.0 GPA to be eligible for financial aid.

Contact. Financial aid office: (352) 395-5480
Steven Fisher, Director of Financial Aid
3000 NW 83rd Street
Gainesville, FL 32606

Schiller International University

Dunedin, Florida
www.schiller.edu
Four-year proprietary **Federal Code: 023141**

	Living at home	On-campus
Tuition and fees:	$14,880	$14,880
Room and board:		$6,500
Books and supplies:	$1,250	$1,250
Personal expenses:	$2,600	$2,600
Transportation:	$950	$950

Undergraduate aid. Need-based: Need-based aid available for full-time and part-time students. **Non-need-based:** Scholarships based on academics, alumni affiliation, leadership, minority status, state/district residency. **Additional information:** Special scholarship program for U.S. college students studying abroad at European campuses of Schiller. Work-study available to students taking 2 or more courses.

Policies to reduce costs. Tuition/fee waivers for children of alumni, family members, employees and their families. Credit/placement for qualifying scores on AP, IB, CLEP examinations. Work study available weekends and for part-time students.

Payment plans. Deferred payment.

Application procedures. FAFSA, institutional form required. Closing date 4/1. Applicants notified on rolling basis starting 5/1, must reply within 3 week(s) of notification.

Contact. Financial aid office: (727) 736-5082
Teri Reeves, Financial Aid Officer
453 Edgewater Drive
Dunedin, FL 34698

Seminole Community College

Sanford, Florida
www.scc-fl.edu
Two-year public **Federal Code: 001520**

College costs. Additional $371 required fees for out-of-state students.

	Living at home
Tuition and fees (2002-2003):	$1,619
Out-of-state:	$5,680
Per-credit charge:	$45
Per-credit out-of-state:	$180
Board only:	$1,800
Books and supplies:	$775
Personal expenses:	$900
Transportation:	$1,710

Undergraduate aid. Non-need-based: Scholarships based on academics, art, athletics, leadership, minority status, music/drama, state/district residency.

Policies to reduce costs. Tuition/fee waivers for senior citizens, employees and their families. Credit/placement for qualifying scores on AP, IB, CLEP examinations. Work study available for part-time students.

Payment plans. Credit card, deferred payment.

Application procedures. FAFSA, institutional form required. No deadline. Applicants notified on rolling basis starting 4/1. **Transfers:** No deadline.

Contact. Robert Lynn, Director of Financial Aid
100 Weldon Boulevard
Sanford, FL 32773-6199

South Florida Community College

Avon Park, Florida
www.sfcc.cc
Two-year public **Federal Code: 001522**

College costs. Additional $339 required fees for out-of-state students.

	Living at home	On-campus
Tuition and fees (2002-2003):	$1,585	$1,585
Out-of-state:	$5,572	$5,572
Per-credit charge:	$44	$44
Per-credit out-of-state:	$177	$177
Room only:		$1,620
Board only:	$1,050	
Books and supplies:	$800	$800
Personal expenses:	$1,500	$1,500
Transportation:	$1,454	$1,454

Undergraduate aid. Need-based: Need-based aid available for full-time and part-time students. **Non-need-based:** Scholarships based on academics, athletics, leadership, minority status, music/drama, state/district residency.

Policies to reduce costs. Tuition/fee waivers for minority students, employees and their families. Credit/placement for qualifying scores on AP, IB, CLEP examinations. Work study available for part-time students.

Payment plans. Credit card payment.

Application procedures. FAFSA, institutional form required. Priority date 6/1; no closing date. Applicants notified on rolling basis starting 4/1. **Transfers:** Students must maintain satisfactory academic progress.

Contact. Financial aid office: (863) 453-6661 ext. 7108
Susie Johnson, Director, Financial Aid
600 West College Drive
Avon Park, FL 33825

Southeastern College of the Assemblies of God

Lakeland, Florida
www.secollege.edu
Four-year private **Federal Code: 001521**

	Living at home	On-campus
Tuition and fees (2002-2003):	$8,184	$8,184
Room and board:		$4,606
Books and supplies:	$800	$800
Personal expenses:	$800	$800
Transportation:	$800	$800

Undergraduate aid. Need-based: Need-based aid available for full-time students. **Non-need-based:** Scholarships based on academics, leadership, music/drama.

Policies to reduce costs. Tuition/fee waivers for family members, employees and their families. Credit/placement for qualifying scores on AP, IB, CLEP examinations.

Payment plans. Credit card, installment payment.

Application procedures. FAFSA, institutional form required. Priority date 5/1; no closing date. Applicants notified on rolling basis starting 5/10, must reply within 3 week(s) of notification. **Transfers:** No deadline.

Contact. Carol Bradley, Financial Aid Director
1000 Longfellow Boulevard
Lakeland, FL 33801

Southwest Florida College

Ft. Myers, Florida
www.swfc.edu
Two-year private **Federal Code: 016068**

College costs (2002-2003). MSCE program $265 per credit-hour; $9,540 per year, including fees and books. Books/supplies: $1,685. Personal expenses: $1,260. Transportation: $1,148.

Undergraduate aid. Need-based: Need-based aid available for full-time and part-time students.

Policies to reduce costs. Work study available nights and for part-time students.

Payment plans. Credit card, installment payment.

Application procedures. FAFSA required. Priority date 4/15; no closing date. Applicants notified on rolling basis.

Contact. **Financial aid office:** (941) 939-4766
Ingrid Sprandel, Director, Student Finance
1685 Medical Lane
Ft. Myers, FL 33907-1108

Stetson University

DeLand, Florida
www.stetson.edu
Four-year private **Federal Code: 001531**

	Living at home	On-campus
Tuition and fees:	$22,640	$22,640
Room and board:		$6,855
Board only:	$3,010	
Books and supplies:	$800	$800
Personal expenses:	$1,620	$1,620

Undergraduate aid. **Need-based:** Average financial aid package for full-time students was $18,988; for part-time $11,482. 60% awarded as scholarships/grants, 40% as loans/jobs. **Non-need-based:** 82% awarded as scholarships/grants, 18% as loans/jobs. Scholarships based on academics, art, athletics, leadership, music/drama, state/district residency.

Freshman aid. **Need-based:** Out of 529 full-time freshmen, 509 applied for aid; 314 were judged to have need; of these 313 received aid. Average package met 88% of need. 131 students had full need met. Average scholarship/grant was $12,504; average loan $3,827. **Non-need based:** 309 full-time freshmen with need received non-need scholarships; 165 without need received awards; 22 received athletic scholarships.

Policies to reduce costs. Tuition/fee waivers for employees and their families. Credit/placement for qualifying scores on AP, IB, CLEP examinations.

Payment plans. Credit card, installment payment.

Application procedures. FAFSA, institutional form required. Priority date 3/15; no closing date. Applicants notified on rolling basis starting 2/1. Early decision closing date 11/1.

Contact. Terry Whittum, Dean of Admissions and Financial Aid
Campus Box 8378
DeLand, FL 32723

Tallahassee Community College

Tallahassee, Florida
www.tcc.fl.edu
Two-year public **Federal Code: 001533**

College costs. Additional $258 required fees for out-of-state students.

	Living at home
Tuition and fees (2002-2003):	$1,520
Out-of-state:	$5,372
Per-credit charge:	$43
Per-credit out-of-state:	$171
Books and supplies:	$740
Personal expenses:	$1,600
Transportation:	$1,200

Undergraduate aid. **Need-based:** Average financial aid package for full-time students was $4,232; for part-time $2,085. **Non-need-based:** Scholarships based on academics, art, athletics, leadership, music/drama, state/district residency.

Freshman aid. **Need-based:** Average package met 2% of need. Average scholarship/grant was $3,538; average loan $2,364.

Policies to reduce costs. Tuition/fee waivers for senior citizens, employees and their families. Credit/placement for qualifying scores on AP, IB, CLEP examinations.

Payment plans. Credit card payment.

Application procedures. FAFSA, institutional form required. Priority date 5/1; no closing date. Applicants notified on rolling basis starting 5/15.

Contact. **Financial aid office:** (850) 201-8399
William Spiers, Director of Financial Aid
444 Appleyard Drive
Tallahassee, FL 32304

Talmudic College of Florida

Miami Beach, Florida
www.talmudicu.edu
Four-year private **Federal Code: 013814**

College costs (2002-2003). Costs for 11 months: tuition $6,500, fees $200, room and board $4,300. Board: $1,800. Books/supplies: $900.

Undergraduate aid. All financial aid based on need. Need-based aid available for full-time and part-time students.

Policies to reduce costs. Tuition/fee waivers for family of clergy, employees and their families. Tuition at time of enrollment guaranteed for 4 years; prepayment discount. Work study available nights, weekends and for part-time students.

Payment plans. Credit card, installment payment.

Application procedures. FAFSA, institutional form required. No deadline. Applicants notified on rolling basis.

Contact. Ira Hill, Chief Financial Officer
1910 Alton Road
Miami Beach, FL 33139

Tampa Technical Institute

Tampa, Florida
tampatech.edu
Three-year proprietary **Federal Code: 007586**

College costs. Tuition includes cost of books. Some programs have additional fees that cover cost of a laptop computer.

	Living at home
Tuition and fees (2002-2003):	$6,450
Personal expenses:	$1,200
Transportation:	$1,500

Undergraduate aid. **Need-based:** Need-based aid available for full-time students.

Policies to reduce costs. Credit/placement for qualifying scores on CLEP examinations.

Application procedures. FAFSA, institutional form required. No deadline.

Contact. Jean Hawk, Director of Student Financial Services
2410 East Busch Boulevard
Tampa, FL 33612

University of Central Florida

Orlando, Florida
www.ucf.edu
Four-year public **Federal Code: 003954**

College costs. Additional $394 required fees for out-of-state students.

	Living at home	On-campus
Tuition and fees (2002-2003):	$2,830	$2,830
Out-of-state:	$11,845	$11,845
Room and board:		$6,165
Board only:	$899	
Books and supplies:	$800	$800
Personal expenses:	$1,868	$1,868
Transportation:	$1,934	$450

Undergraduate aid. **Need-based:** Average financial aid package for full-time students was $7,109; for part-time $6,078. 48% awarded as scholarships/grants, 52% as loans/jobs. **Non-need-based:** 62% awarded as scholarships/grants, 38% as loans/jobs. Scholarships based on academics, alumni affiliation, athletics, leadership, state/district residency. **Student debt:** 49% of graduating class borrowed to fund education; average debt was $14,927.

Freshman aid. **Need-based:** Out of 5,323 full-time freshmen, 3,671 applied for aid; 2,111 were judged to have need; of these 2,093 received aid. Average package met 74% of need. 1737 students had full need met. Average scholarship/grant was $2,462; average loan $2,530. **Non-need based:** 1,699 full-time freshmen with need received non-need scholarships; 1,034 without need received awards; 44 received athletic scholarships.

Merit scholarships. Academic scholarships, $2,000-$24,000 over 4-year period. Freshmen automatically considered.

Policies to reduce costs. Tuition/fee waivers for senior citizens, employees and their families. Credit/placement for qualifying scores on AP, IB, CLEP examinations.

Payment plans. Deferred payment.

Application procedures. FAFSA required. Priority date 3/1; closing date 6/30. Applicants notified on rolling basis starting 3/15, must reply within 3 week(s) of notification. **Transfers:** Priority date 3/1.

Contact. **Financial aid office:** (407) 823-2827
Mary McKinney, Director of Financial Aid
Box 160111
Orlando, FL 32816-0111

University of Florida

Gainesville, Florida
www.ufl.edu
Four-year public **Federal Code: 001535**

College costs. Additional $451 required fees for out-of-state students.

	Living at home	On-campus
Tuition and fees (2002-2003):	$2,581	$2,581
Out-of-state:	$11,595	$11,595
Room and board:		$5,599
Board only:	$1,530	
Books and supplies:	$770	$770
Personal expenses:	$2,280	$2,280
Transportation:	$310	$310

Undergraduate aid. Need-based: Average financial aid package for full-time students was $9,082. 59% awarded as scholarships/grants, 41% as loans/jobs. Need-based aid available for part-time students. **Non-need-based:** 73% awarded as scholarships/grants, 27% as loans/jobs. Scholarships based on academics, leadership, minority status, music/drama, state/district residency. **Student debt:** 45% of graduating class borrowed to fund education; average debt was $14,449.

Freshman aid. Need-based: Out of 6,337 full-time freshmen, 3,423 applied for aid; 2,133 were judged to have need; of these 2,124 received aid. Average package met 82% of need. 698 students had full need met. Average scholarship/grant was $4,036; average loan $2,004. **Non-need based:** 1,986 full-time freshmen with need received non-need scholarships; 3,915 without need received awards; 86 received athletic scholarships.

Policies to reduce costs. Tuition/fee waivers for senior citizens, minority students, employees and their families. Credit/placement for qualifying scores on AP, CLEP examinations.

Payment plans. Deferred payment.

Application procedures. FAFSA required. Priority date 3/15; no closing date. Applicants notified on rolling basis starting 4/1. Early decision closing date 10/1.

Contact. Karen Fooks, Director of Student Financial Aid
201 Criser Hall
Gainesville, FL 32611-4000

University of Miami

Coral Gables, Florida
www.miami.edu
Four-year private **Federal Code: 001536**

	Living at home	On-campus
Tuition and fees:	$26,280	$26,280
Room and board:		$8,328
Board only:	$1,800	
Books and supplies:	$775	$775
Personal expenses:	$1,215	$1,215
Transportation:	$1,115	$1,115

Undergraduate aid. Need-based: Average financial aid package for full-time students was $22,399; for part-time $13,996. 67% awarded as scholarships/grants, 33% as loans/jobs. **Non-need-based:** 73% awarded as scholarships/grants, 27% as loans/jobs. Scholarships based on academics, alumni affiliation, art, athletics, job skills, leadership, minority status, music/drama. **Student debt:** 58% of graduating class borrowed to fund education; average debt was $25,093.

Freshman aid. Need-based: Out of 2,047 full-time freshmen, 1,419 applied for aid; 1,157 were judged to have need; of these 1,157 received aid. Average package met 84% of need. 35 students had full need met. Average scholarship/grant was $16,573; average loan $3,581. **Non-need based:** 240 full-time freshmen with need received non-need scholarships; 585 without need received awards; 47 received athletic scholarships.

Merit scholarships. Isaac Bashevis Singer Scholarship, full tuition, based on minimum 1400 SAT I or 32 ACT, 4.0 GPA, rank in top 1% of high school graduating class; Bowman Foster Ashe Scholarship, three-quarters tuition, based on minimum 1360 SAT I or 31 ACT, 3.9 cumulative GPA, class rank in top 5%; Henry King Stanford Scholarship, half-tuition, renewable, based on minimum SAT I score of 1280 or 28 ACT, 3.8 cumulative GPA, class rank in top 10%; George E. Merrick Scholarship, one-third tuition, 1220 SAT I or 27 ACT, 3.7 cumulative GPA, class rank in top 10%; George W. Jenkins Scholarship, full tuition, fees and stipend, for US citizen, Florida resident, with strong school/community involvement, 3.2 GPA, demonstrated high financial need; Jay F.W. Pearson Scholarship, one-quarter tuition, top 10% in high school class, 3.7 GPA, 1220 SAT or 27 ACT; Golden Drum Ronald M. Hammond Scholarships, full tuition, renewable, for exceptionally well-qualified high school seniors of African descent in Dade and Broward counties; music scholarships, based on performance ability, academic achievement and financial need; National Merit Scholarships, $750-$2,000, for National Merit finalist.

Policies to reduce costs. Tuition/fee waivers for employees and their families. Prepayment discount; credit/placement for qualifying scores on AP, IB, CLEP examinations. Work study available nights, weekends and for part-time students.

Payment plans. Installment, deferred payment.

Application procedures. FAFSA required. Priority date 2/15; no closing date. Applicants notified on rolling basis starting 3/1, must reply by 5/1. Early decision closing date 11/15. **Transfers:** Priority date 3/1; no deadline.

Contact. **Financial aid office:** (305) 284-5212
James Bauer, Director of Financial Assistance Services
132 Ashe Building
Coral Gables, FL 33124-4616

University of North Florida

Jacksonville, Florida
www.unf.edu
Four-year public **Federal Code: 009841**

College costs. Additional $428 required fees for out-of-state students.

	Living at home	On-campus
Tuition and fees (2002-2003):	$2,757	$2,757
Out-of-state:	$11,321	$11,321
Room and board:		$5,212
Board only:	$1,994	
Books and supplies:	$600	$600
Personal expenses:	$785	$785
Transportation:	$2,081	$2,081

Undergraduate aid. Need-based: Average financial aid package for full-time students was $2,253; for part-time $2,509. 56% awarded as scholarships/grants, 44% as loans/jobs. **Non-need-based:** 46% awarded as scholarships/grants, 54% as loans/jobs. Scholarships based on academics, athletics, leadership, minority status, music/drama, state/district residency. **Student debt:** 39% of graduating class borrowed to fund education; average debt was $15,079.

Freshman aid. Need-based: Out of 1,827 full-time freshmen, 1,569 applied for aid; 1,146 were judged to have need; of these 1,127 received aid. Average package met 77% of need. 246 students had full need met. Average scholarship/grant was $1,732; average loan $2,386. **Non-need based:** 971 full-time freshmen with need received non-need scholarships; 371 without need received awards; 40 received athletic scholarships.

Policies to reduce costs. Tuition/fee waivers for senior citizens, employees and their families. Credit/placement for qualifying scores on AP, IB, CLEP examinations. Work study available for part-time students.

Payment plans. Credit card, deferred payment.

Application procedures. FAFSA required. Priority date 4/1; no closing date. Applicants notified on rolling basis starting 3/15, must reply within 2 week(s) of notification.

Contact. **Financial aid office:** (904) 620-2604
Janice Nowak, Financial Aid Director
4567 St. Johns Bluff Road, South
Jacksonville, FL 32224-2645

University of South Florida

Tampa, Florida
www.usf.edu
Four-year public **Federal Code: 001537**

College costs. Additional $455 required fees for out-of-state students.

	Living at home	On-campus
Tuition and fees (2002-2003):	$2,734	$2,734
Out-of-state:	$11,823	$11,823
Room and board:		$5,594
Board only:	$2,560	
Books and supplies:	$700	$700
Personal expenses:	$2,640	$2,640
Transportation:	$960	$960

Undergraduate aid. Need-based: Average financial aid package for full-time students was $8,211; for part-time $7,517. 45% awarded as scholarships/grants, 55% as loans/jobs. **Non-need-based:** 57% awarded as scholarships/grants, 43% as loans/jobs. Scholarships based on academics, alumni affiliation, art, leadership, minority status, music/drama, state/district residency. **Student debt:** 48% of graduating class borrowed to fund education; average debt was $16,645. **Additional information:** Deferred tuition payment plan available for late financial aid recipients.

Freshman aid. Need-based: Out of 2,311 full-time freshmen, 1,702 applied for aid; 1,697 were judged to have need; of these 962 received aid. Average package met 18% of need. Average scholarship/grant was $3,854; average loan $2,330. **Non-need based:** 283 full-time freshmen with need received non-need scholarships; 519 without need received awards; 49 received athletic scholarships.

Policies to reduce costs. Tuition/fee waivers for senior citizens, employees and their families. Credit/placement for qualifying scores on AP, IB, CLEP examinations.

Payment plans. Installment payment.

Application procedures. FAFSA required. Priority date 3/1; no closing date. Applicants notified on rolling basis starting 3/15, must reply within 2 week(s) of notification.

Contact. Financial aid office: (813) 974-4700
Leonard Gude, Director, Student Financial Aid
4202 East Fowler Avenue, SVC 1036
Tampa, FL 33620-9951

University of Tampa

Tampa, Florida
www.ut.edu
Four-year private **Federal Code: 001538**

	Living at home	On-campus
Tuition and fees:	$17,572	$17,572
Room and board:		$6,410
Board only:	$1,350	
Books and supplies:	$765	$765
Personal expenses:	$1,406	$1,127
Transportation:	$907	$600

Undergraduate aid. Need-based: Average financial aid package for full-time students was $14,099; for part-time $4,790. 67% awarded as scholarships/grants, 33% as loans/jobs. **Non-need-based:** 53% awarded as scholarships/grants, 47% as loans/jobs. Scholarships based on academics, alumni affiliation, art, athletics, leadership, music/drama, state/district residency. **Student debt:** 71% of graduating class borrowed to fund education; average debt was $21,013. **Additional information:** Early aid estimator service.

Freshman aid. Need-based: Out of 933 full-time freshmen, 852 applied for aid; 535 were judged to have need; of these 535 received aid. Average package met 84% of need. 119 students had full need met. Average scholarship/grant was $5,460; average loan $2,615. **Non-need based:** 432 full-time freshmen with need received non-need scholarships; 282 without need received awards; 13 received athletic scholarships.

Merit scholarships. Presidential Scholarships; up to $7,000; 3.5 GPA. Dean's Scholarships; up to $6,500; 3.0 GPA. Departmental scholarships; athletic scholarships.

Policies to reduce costs. Tuition/fee waivers for employees and their families. Credit/placement for qualifying scores on AP, IB, CLEP examinations. Work study available nights and weekends.

Payment plans. Credit card, installment payment.

Application procedures. FAFSA required. No deadline. Applicants notified on rolling basis starting 2/1, must reply within 3 week(s) of notification. **Transfers:** Transfer scholarships available; Phi Theta Kappa Scholarships.

Contact. Financial aid office: (813) 253-6239
John Marsh, Director of Financial Aid
401 West Kennedy Boulevard
Tampa, FL 33606-1490

University of West Florida

Pensacola, Florida
www.uwf.edu
Four-year public **Federal Code: 003955**

College costs. Additional $361 required fees for out-of-state students.

	Living at home	On-campus
Tuition and fees (2002-2003):	$2,638	$2,638
Out-of-state:	$10,902	$10,902
Room only:		$2,920
Board only:	$1,995	
Books and supplies:	$766	$766
Personal expenses:	$1,638	$1,638
Transportation:	$1,300	$770

Undergraduate aid. Need-based: 32% awarded as scholarships/grants, 68% as loans/jobs. Need-based aid available for part-time students. **Non-need-based:** 69% awarded as scholarships/grants, 31% as loans/jobs. Scholarships based on academics, alumni affiliation, art, athletics, minority status, music/drama, state/district residency.

Merit scholarships. John C. Pace Scholars, 8 awards, based on high school record and leadership, $16,000 total. John C. Pace Honors and Presidential Scholarships, based on high school record, $4,000 total. Both available to Florida residents only. Non-Florida tuition reduction scholarships available to non-Florida residents.

Policies to reduce costs. Tuition/fee waivers for senior citizens, employees and their families. Credit/placement for qualifying scores on AP, IB, CLEP examinations. Work study available nights, weekends and for part-time students.

Payment plans. Credit card, installment payment.

Application procedures. FAFSA, institutional form required. Priority date 3/1; no closing date. Applicants notified on rolling basis starting 2/1.

Contact. Financial aid office: (850) 474-2400
Cathy Brown, Director of Student Financial Aid
11000 University Parkway
Pensacola, FL 32514

Valencia Community College

Orlando, Florida
www.valencia.edu
Two-year public **Federal Code: 006750**

College costs. Additional $268 required fees for out-of-state students.

	Living at home
Tuition and fees (2002-2003):	$1,610
Out-of-state:	$5,779
Per-credit charge:	$46
Per-credit out-of-state:	$185
Board only:	$1,500
Books and supplies:	$800
Personal expenses:	$100
Transportation:	$1,500

Undergraduate aid. Need-based: Need-based aid available for full-time and part-time students.

Policies to reduce costs. Tuition/fee waivers for senior citizens, employees and their families. Credit/placement for qualifying scores on AP, IB, CLEP examinations. Work study available nights and for part-time students.

Payment plans. Credit card payment.

Application procedures. FAFSA, institutional form required. Closing date 5/15. Applicants notified on rolling basis starting 5/1, must reply within 2 week(s) of notification. **Transfers:** No deadline.

Contact. **Financial aid office:** (407) 299-5000
Linda Downing, Director of Financial Aid
PO Box 3028
Orlando, FL 32802-3028

Warner Southern College

Lake Wales, Florida
www.warner.edu
Four-year private **Federal Code: 008848**

College costs. One-time $50 security deposit for incoming freshmen living on campus.

	Living at home	On-campus
Tuition and fees (projected):	$11,380	$11,380
Room and board:		$4,952
Board only:	$2,900	
Books and supplies:	$796	$796
Personal expenses:	$1,737	$1,737
Transportation:	$675	$675

Undergraduate aid. **Need-based:** Average financial aid package for full-time students was $10,091; for part-time $5,408. 38% awarded as scholarships/grants, 62% as loans/jobs. **Non-need-based:** 65% awarded as scholarships/grants, 35% as loans/jobs. Scholarships based on academics, alumni affiliation, athletics, leadership, music/drama, religious affiliation, state/district residency. **Student debt:** 48% of graduating class borrowed to fund education; average debt was $6,046.

Freshman aid. **Need-based:** Out of 116 full-time freshmen, 113 applied for aid; 66 were judged to have need; of these 66 received aid. Average scholarship/grant was $1,813; average loan $1,760. **Non-need based:** 62 full-time freshmen with need received non-need scholarships; 47 without need received awards; 73 received athletic scholarships.

Policies to reduce costs. Tuition/fee waivers for family members, family of clergy, employees and their families. Credit/placement for qualifying scores on AP, IB, CLEP examinations.

Payment plans. Credit card, installment, deferred payment.

Application procedures. FAFSA required. Priority date 5/1; no closing date. Applicants notified on rolling basis starting 2/1, must reply within 2 week(s) of notification. **Transfers:** Priority date 10/1; closing date 5/15.

Contact. **Financial aid office:** (863) 638-7202
Lorrie White, Financial Aid Director
13895 Hwy. 27
Lake Wales, FL 33859

Webber International University

Babson Park, Florida
www.webber.edu
Four-year private **Federal Code: 001540**

	Living at home	On-campus
Tuition and fees (projected):	$11,600	$11,600
Room and board:		$4,510
Board only:	$2,422	
Books and supplies:	$650	$650
Personal expenses:	$1,351	$2,530
Transportation:	$906	$906

Undergraduate aid. **Need-based:** Average financial aid package for full-time students was $10,639; for part-time $5,223. 57% awarded as scholarships/grants, 43% as loans/jobs. **Non-need-based:** 84% awarded as scholarships/grants, 16% as loans/jobs. Scholarships based on academics, alumni affiliation, athletics, leadership, music/drama, state/district residency. **Student debt:** 46% of graduating class borrowed to fund education; average debt was $11,200.

Freshman aid. **Need-based:** Out of 142 full-time freshmen, 139 applied for aid; 88 were judged to have need; of these 88 received aid. Average package met 72% of need. 40 students had full need met. Average scholarship/grant was $11,319; average loan $2,546. **Non-need based:** 48 full-time freshmen with need received non-need scholarships; 12 without need received awards; 38 received athletic scholarships.

Policies to reduce costs. Tuition/fee waivers for adults, children of alumni, senior citizens, family members, employees and their families. Prepayment discount; credit/placement for qualifying scores on AP, IB, CLEP examinations. Work study available nights and weekends.

Payment plans. Credit card, installment, deferred payment.

Application procedures. FAFSA required. Priority date 5/1; no closing date. Applicants notified on rolling basis starting 3/15, must reply within 4 week(s) of notification. **Transfers:** No deadline. Eligibility for academic scholarships predicated on 30 hours of transferable credit.

Contact. **Financial aid office:** (863) 638-2929
Kathleen Wilson, Registrar/Director of Financial Aid
1201 North Scenic Highway
Babson Park, FL 33827-0096

Webster College

Ocala, Florida
www.webstercollege.com
Two-year proprietary **Federal Code: 008501**

College costs. $20 enrollment fee included in tuition.

	Living at home
Tuition and fees:	$9,585
Personal expenses:	$2,856
Transportation:	$2,247

Undergraduate aid. **Need-based:** Need-based aid available for full-time and part-time students.

Application procedures. Institutional form required. Applicants notified on rolling basis, must reply within 1 week(s) of notification.

Contact. 2221 Southwest 19th Avenue Road
Ocala, FL 34474-7051

Webster College: Holiday

Holiday, Florida
www.webstercollege.com
Two-year proprietary **Federal Code: 008501**

	Living at home
Tuition and fees:	$9,585
Books and supplies:	$203
Personal expenses:	$2,448
Transportation:	$1,926

Undergraduate aid. All financial aid based on need. Need-based aid available for full-time and part-time students.

Application procedures. FAFSA, institutional form required. No deadline.

Contact. **Financial aid office:** (727) 942-0069
Tina Fisher, Financial Aid Director
2127 Grand Boulevard
Holiday, FL 34691

Georgia

Abraham Baldwin Agricultural College

Tifton, Georgia
www.abac.edu
Two-year public **Federal Code: 001541**

	Living at home	On-campus
Tuition and fees (2002-2003):	$1,756	$1,756
Out-of-state:	$5,740	$5,740
Per-credit charge:	$56	$56
Per-credit out-of-state:	$222	$222
Room and board:		$3,500
Books and supplies:	$775	$775
Personal expenses:	$1,500	$1,500
Transportation:	$680	$680

Policies to reduce costs. Tuition/fee waivers for senior citizens. Credit/placement for qualifying scores on AP, CLEP examinations.

Payment plans. Credit card payment.

Application procedures. FAFSA, institutional form required. Priority date 5/1; no closing date. Applicants notified on rolling basis starting 5/15, must reply within 2 week(s) of notification.

Contact. Jenelle Louder, Director of Financial Aid
ABAC Station, Box 4
Tifton, GA 31794-2693

Agnes Scott College

Atlanta/Decatur, Georgia
www.agnesscott.edu
Four-year private **Federal Code: 001542**

	Living at home	On-campus
Tuition and fees (2002-2003):	$19,000	$19,000
Room and board:		$7,500
Board only:	$1,500	
Books and supplies:	$700	$700
Personal expenses:	$900	$900
Transportation:	$650	$950

Undergraduate aid. Need-based: Average financial aid package for full-time students was $17,925; for part-time $7,862. 77% awarded as scholarships/grants, 23% as loans/jobs. **Non-need-based:** 78% awarded as scholarships/grants, 22% as loans/jobs. Scholarships based on academics, leadership, music/drama, state/district residency. **Student debt:** 63% of graduating class borrowed to fund education; average debt was $17,602. **Additional information:** Middle Income Assistance Grants available. Auditions required for music scholarship applicants.

Freshman aid. Need-based: Out of 234 full-time freshmen, 192 applied for aid; 151 were judged to have need; of these 151 received aid. Average package met 95% of need. 123 students had full need met. Average scholarship/grant was $14,757; average loan $2,459. **Non-need based:** 60 full-time freshmen with need received non-need scholarships; 60 without need received awards.

Merit scholarships. Presidential and Honor Scholarships; $8,750 to full tuition, room and board. College will match HOPE Scholarship for HOPE-eligible Georgia residents who meet college admission criteria. Leadership and community service awards also available.

Policies to reduce costs. Tuition/fee waivers for employees and their families. Credit/placement for qualifying scores on AP, IB examinations. Work study available nights and weekends.

Payment plans. Credit card, installment payment.

Application procedures. FAFSA, institutional form required. CSS PROFILE required of Early Decision applicants. Priority date 2/15; closing date 5/1. Applicants notified on rolling basis starting 3/1, must reply by 5/1 or within 2 week(s) of notification. Early decision closing date 11/15. **Transfers:** Closing date 5/1. Merit Scholarships available.

Contact. Financial aid office: (404) 471-6395
Karen Smith, Director of Financial Aid
141 East College Avenue
Atlanta/Decatur, GA 30030-3797

Albany State University

Albany, Georgia
www.asurams.edu
Four-year public **Federal Code: 001544**

	Living at home	On-campus
Tuition and fees (2002-2003):	$2,564	$2,564
Out-of-state:	$8,594	$8,594
Room and board:		$3,280
Board only:	$988	
Books and supplies:	$750	$750
Personal expenses:	$920	$925
Transportation:	$462	$760

Undergraduate aid. Need-based: Need-based aid available for full-time and part-time students. **Non-need-based:** Scholarships based on academics, athletics, state/district residency.

Merit scholarships. State of Georgia Hope Scholarship Award.

Policies to reduce costs. Tuition/fee waivers for senior citizens.

Payment plans. Credit card payment.

Application procedures. FAFSA, institutional form required. Priority date 4/15; no closing date. Applicants notified on rolling basis starting 7/1, must reply within 2 week(s) of notification. **Transfers:** Closing date 7/1.

Contact. Financial aid office: (229) 430-4650
Kathleen Caldwell, Director of Financial Aid
504 College Drive
Albany, GA 31705-2796

Albany Technical College

Albany, Georgia
www.albanytech.org
Two-year public **Federal Code: 005601**

	Living at home
Tuition and fees:	$1,112
Out-of-state:	$2,516
Per-credit charge:	$26
Per-credit out-of-state:	$52

Contact. 1704 South Slappy Boulevard
Albany, GA 31701

Andrew College

Cuthbert, Georgia
www.andrewcollege.edu
Two-year private **Federal Code: 001545**

	Living at home	On-campus
Tuition and fees:	$8,150	$8,150
Per-credit charge:	$375	$375
Room and board:		$5,130
Books and supplies:	$600	$600
Personal expenses:	$1,100	$1,200
Transportation:	$200	$700

Undergraduate aid. Need-based: Need-based aid available for full-time and part-time students. **Non-need-based:** Scholarships based on academics, art, athletics, leadership, music/drama, religious affiliation, state/district residency.

Policies to reduce costs. Tuition/fee waivers for family of clergy, employees and their families. Credit/placement for qualifying scores on AP, CLEP examinations.

Payment plans. Credit card, installment, deferred payment.

Application procedures. FAFSA, institutional form required. Priority date 4/1; closing date 8/1. Applicants notified on rolling basis starting 4/15.

Contact. Financial aid office: (229) 732-5938
Amy Thompson, Financial Aid Administrator
413 College Street
Cuthbert, GA 39840-1395

Armstrong Atlantic State University

Savannah, Georgia
www.armstrong.edu
Four-year public **Federal Code: 001546**

	Living at home	On-campus
Tuition and fees (2002-2003):	$2,400	$2,400
Out-of-state:	$8,430	$8,430
Room only:		$3,375
Books and supplies:	$800	$800
Personal expenses:	$1,232	$1,232
Transportation:	$2,652	$2,652

Undergraduate aid. Need-based: Need-based aid available for full-time and part-time students. **Non-need-based:** Scholarships based on academics, athletics, state/district residency.

Policies to reduce costs. Tuition/fee waivers for senior citizens, employees and their families. Credit/placement for qualifying scores on AP, IB, CLEP examinations. Work study available nights and weekends.

Payment plans. Credit card payment.

Application procedures. FAFSA required. Priority date 3/15; no closing date. Applicants notified on rolling basis starting 2/1.

Contact. Financial aid office: (912) 927-5272
Lee Ann Kirkland, Financial Aid Director
11935 Abercorn Street
Savannah, GA 31419-1997

Art Institute of Atlanta

Atlanta, Georgia
www.aia.artinstitute.edu
Four-year proprietary **Federal Code: 009270**

	Living at home	On-campus
Tuition and fees (2002-2003):	$14,880	$14,880
Room only:		$5,490
Books and supplies:	$1,401	$1,401
Personal expenses:	$3,690	$3,680
Transportation:	$1,038	$1,038

Undergraduate aid. Need-based: Need-based aid available for full-time and part-time students. **Non-need-based:** Scholarships based on academics, art, state/district residency.

Merit scholarships. Art Institutes Scholarship Competition awards $2,000 - $56,064 depending on program to winning high school seniors selected on merits of written essay, original artwork, resume, letter(s) of recommendation, and high school academic achievement; up to 1 full-tuition, 2 half-tuition, and 24 partial-tuition scholarships available. Art Institutes Culinary Scholarship Competition awards $2,000 - $32,704 to winning high school seniors selected through three-part elimination-style competition to prove academic ability, culinary expertise, and commitment to succeed; up to 1 full-tuition or 2 partial-tuition scholarships available. Various other scholarships and awards available.

Policies to reduce costs. Tuition/fee waivers for family members, employees and their families. Tuition at time of enrollment guaranteed for 4 years; credit/placement for qualifying scores on AP, IB, CLEP examinations. Work study available nights, weekends and for part-time students.

Payment plans. Credit card, installment payment.

Application procedures. FAFSA required. No deadline. Applicants notified on rolling basis starting 3/15. **Transfers:** No deadline.

Contact. Financial aid office: (770) 394-8300
Rena Marroquin, Director of Student Financial Services
6600 Peachtree Dunwoody Road, 100 Embassy Row
Atlanta, GA 30328

Athens Technical College

Athens, Georgia
www.aati.edu
Two-year public **Federal Code: 005600**

	Living at home
Tuition and fees (2002-2003):	$1,212
Out-of-state:	$2,292
Per-credit charge:	$24
Per-credit out-of-state:	$48
Books and supplies:	$600
Personal expenses:	$1,000
Transportation:	$1,000

Undergraduate aid. Need-based: Need-based aid available for full-time and part-time students.

Payment plans. Credit card payment.

Application procedures. FAFSA, institutional form required. No deadline. Applicants notified on rolling basis starting 6/15, must reply within 2 week(s) of notification.

Contact. Financial aid office: (706) 355-5009
Wanda Hicks, Director of Financial Aid and Admissions
800 U.S. Highway 29 North
Athens, GA 30601-1500

Atlanta College of Art

Atlanta, Georgia
www.aca.edu
Four-year private **Federal Code: 001549**

	Living at home	On-campus
Tuition and fees:	$16,700	$16,700
Room only:		$4,950
Board only:	$1,575	
Books and supplies:	$900	$900
Personal expenses:	$1,245	$1,245
Transportation:	$525	

Undergraduate aid. All financial aid based on need. Average financial aid package for full-time students was $11,701; for part-time $5,966. 52% awarded as scholarships/grants, 48% as loans/jobs. **Student debt:** 53% of graduating class borrowed to fund education; average debt was $20,492.

Freshman aid. Out of 59 full-time freshmen, 41 applied for aid; 36 were judged to have need; of these 36 received aid. Average package met 65% of need. 4 students had full need met. Average scholarship/grant was $9,712; average loan $2,537.

Policies to reduce costs. Tuition/fee waivers for employees and their families. Credit/placement for qualifying scores on AP, IB examinations.

Payment plans. Credit card, installment payment.

Application procedures. FAFSA, institutional form required. Priority date 3/15; closing date 7/15. Applicants notified on rolling basis starting 4/1, must reply by 5/1 or within 2 week(s) of notification.

Contact. Teresa Tantillo, Director of Financial Aid
1280 Peachtree Street NE
Atlanta, GA 30309

Atlanta Metropolitan College

Atlanta, Georgia
www.atlm.edu
Two-year public **Federal Code: 012165**

	Living at home
Tuition and fees (2002-2003):	$1,522
Out-of-state:	$5,518
Per-credit charge:	$56
Per-credit out-of-state:	$222
Board only:	$1,800
Books and supplies:	$500
Transportation:	$900

Undergraduate aid. Need-based: Need-based aid available for full-time and part-time students. **Non-need-based:** Scholarships based on athletics.

Policies to reduce costs. Tuition/fee waivers for senior citizens. Credit/placement for qualifying scores on AP, CLEP examinations. Work study available for part-time students.

Payment plans. Credit card, installment payment.

Application procedures. FAFSA required. Closing date 4/1. Applicants notified on rolling basis, must reply within 2 week(s) of notification.

Contact. **Financial aid office:** (404) 756-4002
Vera Brooks, Financial Aid Officer
1630 Metropolitan Parkway, Southwest
Atlanta, GA 30310

Augusta State University

Augusta, Georgia
www.aug.edu
Four-year public **Federal Code: 001552**

	Living at home
Tuition and fees (2002-2003):	$2,384
Out-of-state:	$8,414
Board only:	$1,980
Books and supplies:	$778
Personal expenses:	$3,080
Transportation:	$1,100

Undergraduate aid. **Need-based:** Average financial aid package for full-time students was $7,070; for part-time $3,556. 49% awarded as scholarships/grants, 51% as loans/jobs. **Non-need-based:** 56% awarded as scholarships/grants, 44% as loans/jobs. Scholarships based on academics, art, athletics, leadership, music/drama, state/district residency. **Student debt:** 42% of graduating class borrowed to fund education; average debt was $14,274.

Freshman aid. **Need-based:** Out of 1,845 full-time freshmen, 1,299 applied for aid; 916 were judged to have need; of these 894 received aid. Average package met 70% of need. 14 students had full need met. Average scholarship/grant was $3,915; average loan $2,458. **Non-need based:** 13 full-time freshmen with need received non-need scholarships; 27 without need received awards; 111 received athletic scholarships.

Policies to reduce costs. Tuition/fee waivers for senior citizens, employees and their families. Credit/placement for qualifying scores on AP, CLEP examinations. Work study available nights, weekends and for part-time students.

Payment plans. Credit card payment.

Application procedures. FAFSA, institutional form required. Priority date 4/15; no closing date. Applicants notified on rolling basis starting 3/31, must reply within 4 week(s) of notification.

Contact. **Financial aid office:** (706) 737-1431
Willene Holmes, Director of Financial Aid
2500 Walton Way
Augusta, GA 30904-2200

Bainbridge College

Bainbridge, Georgia
www.bainbridge.edu
Two-year public **Federal Code: 011074**

	Living at home
Tuition and fees (2002-2003):	$1,456
Out-of-state:	$5,452
Per-credit charge:	$56
Per-credit out-of-state:	$222
Books and supplies:	$600
Personal expenses:	$450
Transportation:	$1,734

Undergraduate aid. **Need-based:** 43% awarded as scholarships/grants, 57% as loans/jobs. **Additional information:** 30-day loans available for tuition and fees.

Merit scholarships. Small number of merit scholarships available.

Policies to reduce costs. Tuition/fee waivers for senior citizens. Credit/placement for qualifying scores on AP, CLEP examinations.

Payment plans. Credit card payment.

Application procedures. FAFSA, institutional form required. Priority date 6/1; closing date 8/1. Applicants notified on rolling basis starting 6/1, must reply within 2 week(s) of notification.

Contact. **Financial aid office:** (229) 248-2505
Linda Casey, Director of Finacial Aid
PO Box 953
Bainbridge, GA 39818-0990

Bauder College

Atlanta, Georgia
www.bauder.edu
Two-year proprietary **Federal Code: 011574**

College costs. Cost of tuition for 21-month associate degree program in fashion design $24,296; books $2,300; $50 administrative fee, $200 graduation fee. Tuition only for the associate degree programs varies from $20,377-$24,296. Room: $3,750. Books/supplies: $900. Personal expenses: $1,100. Transportation: $1,000.

Undergraduate aid. All financial aid based on need. Need-based aid available for full-time and part-time students.

Policies to reduce costs. Tuition/fee waivers for employees and their families. Work study available nights and weekends.

Payment plans. Credit card, installment payment.

Application procedures. FAFSA, institutional form required. No deadline. Applicants notified on rolling basis starting 7/15.

Contact. Rhonda Staines, Director of Finance
3500 Peachtree Road NE
Atlanta, GA 30326-9975

Berry College

Mount Berry, Georgia
www.berry.edu
Four-year private **Federal Code: 001554**

	Living at home	On-campus
Tuition and fees:	$15,220	$15,220
Room and board:		$6,190
Board only:	$1,266	
Books and supplies:	$800	$800
Personal expenses:	$2,644	$2,290
Transportation:	$984	$366

Undergraduate aid. **Need-based:** Average financial aid package for full-time students was $11,684. 76% awarded as scholarships/grants, 24% as loans/jobs. Need-based aid available for part-time students. **Non-need-based:** 67% awarded as scholarships/grants, 33% as loans/jobs. Scholarships based on academics, art, athletics, minority status, music/drama, state/district residency. **Student debt:** 46% of graduating class borrowed to fund education; average debt was $11,506. **Additional information:** All students are encouraged to work on-campus up to 20 hours per week. Jobs available in over 100 different areas.

Freshman aid. **Need-based:** Out of 536 full-time freshmen, 536 applied for aid; 323 were judged to have need; of these 323 received aid. Average package met 87% of need. 110 students had full need met. Average scholarship/grant was $9,914; average loan $2,976. **Non-need based:** 230 full-time freshmen with need received non-need scholarships; 221 without need received awards; 31 received athletic scholarships.

Merit scholarships. HOPE Scholarship for entering freshmen based on legal residence in Georgia and graduation from eligible high school with at least a B average in college preparatory coursework; $3,000 annually.

Policies to reduce costs. Tuition/fee waivers for adults, senior citizens, minority students, family members, employees and their families. Credit/placement for qualifying scores on AP, IB, CLEP examinations. Work study available nights, weekends and for part-time students.

Payment plans. Credit card, installment payment.

Application procedures. FAFSA, institutional form required. Priority date 4/1; closing date 5/15. Applicants notified on rolling basis starting 4/1, must reply within 4 week(s) of notification. **Transfers:** Priority date 4/1; closing date 5/15.

Contact. **Financial aid office:** (706) 236-1714
William Fron, Director of Student Financial Aid
2277 Martha Berry Highway, Northwest
Mount Berry, GA 30149-0159

Beulah Heights Bible College

Atlanta, Georgia
www.beulah.org
Four-year private **Federal Code: 030763**

	Living at home
Tuition and fees:	$5,340

Contact. Patricia Banks, Director of Financial Aid
892 Berne Street SE
Atlanta, GA 30316

Brenau University

Gainesville, Georgia
www.brenau.edu
Four-year private **Federal Code: 001556**

	Living at home	On-campus
Tuition and fees (2002-2003):	$13,440	$13,440
Room and board:		$7,320
Board only:	$1,800	
Books and supplies:	$700	$700
Personal expenses:	$1,200	$1,100
Transportation:	$900	$700

Undergraduate aid. Need-based: Average financial aid package for full-time students was $13,057; for part-time $16,302. 81% awarded as scholarships/grants, 19% as loans/jobs. **Non-need-based:** 63% awarded as scholarships/grants, 37% as loans/jobs. Scholarships based on academics, art, athletics, leadership, music/drama.

Freshman aid. Need-based: Out of 108 full-time freshmen, 107 applied for aid; 86 were judged to have need; of these 86 received aid. Average package met 91% of need. 36 students had full need met. Average scholarship/grant was $13,079; average loan $2,086. **Non-need based:** 22 full-time freshmen with need received non-need scholarships; 20 without need received awards; 5 received athletic scholarships.

Policies to reduce costs. Tuition/fee waivers for family members, employees and their families. Credit/placement for qualifying scores on AP, IB, CLEP examinations.

Payment plans. Credit card payment.

Application procedures. FAFSA required. Priority date 5/1; no closing date. Applicants notified on rolling basis starting 3/15. **Transfers:** Priority date 5/1.

Contact. Financial aid office: (770) 534-6152
Pam Barrett, Director of Scholarships and Financial Assistance
One Centennial Circle
Gainesville, GA 30501

Brewton-Parker College

Mount Vernon, Georgia
www.bpc.edu
Four-year private **Federal Code: 001557**

College costs. Applied music majors pay additional $110 per-credit.

	Living at home	On-campus
Tuition and fees:	$9,850	$9,850
Room and board:		$4,900
Board only:	$1,200	
Books and supplies:	$750	$750
Personal expenses:	$1,200	$1,200
Transportation:	$600	$600

Undergraduate aid. Need-based: Average financial aid package for full-time students was $8,028; for part-time $6,018. 67% awarded as scholarships/grants, 33% as loans/jobs. **Non-need-based:** 34% awarded as scholarships/grants, 66% as loans/jobs. Scholarships based on academics, athletics, religious affiliation, state/district residency. **Student debt:** 74% of graduating class borrowed to fund education; average debt was $7,443.

Freshman aid. Need-based: Out of 260 full-time freshmen, 242 applied for aid; 205 were judged to have need; of these 205 received aid. Average package met 69% of need. 48 students had full need met. Average scholarship/grant was $5,918; average loan $2,126. **Non-need based:** 41 full-time freshmen with need received non-need scholarships; 55 without need received awards; 3 received athletic scholarships.

Merit scholarships. Scholarships available for academic achievement and SAT scores for incoming freshman transfer students, ranging from $1,500-$3,000 per academic year, available for four years.

Policies to reduce costs. Tuition/fee waivers for senior citizens, unemployed or children of unemployed, employees and their families. Credit/placement for qualifying scores on AP, CLEP examinations. Work study available nights, weekends and for part-time students.

Payment plans. Credit card, installment payment.

Application procedures. FAFSA, institutional form required. Priority date 4/1; no closing date. Applicants notified on rolling basis starting 3/1. **Transfers:** No deadline.

Contact. Financial aid office: (912) 583-3213
Ione Maze, Director of Financial Aid
Highway 280
Mount Vernon, GA 30445

Central Georgia Technical College

Macon, Georgia
www.cgtcollege.org
Two-year public **Federal Code: 005763**

	Living at home
Tuition and fees:	$1,061
Out-of-state:	$1,997
Per-credit charge:	$26
Per-credit out-of-state:	$52
Books and supplies:	$750

Contact. Financial aid office: (478) 757-3422
Director, Financial Aid
3300 Macon Tech Drive
Macon, GA 31206

Chattahoochee Technical College

Marietta, Georgia
www.chat-tec.com
Two-year public **Federal Code: 005620**

	Living at home
Tuition and fees (2002-2003):	$1,095
Out-of-state:	$2,031
Per-credit charge:	$26
Per-credit out-of-state:	$52
Books and supplies:	$1,020
Personal expenses:	$1,300
Transportation:	$1,300

Undergraduate aid. Need-based: Need-based aid available for full-time and part-time students. **Non-need-based:** Scholarships based on state/district residency.

Policies to reduce costs. Tuition/fee waivers for senior citizens. Work study available nights, weekends and for part-time students.

Payment plans. Credit card payment.

Application procedures. FAFSA, institutional form required. Priority date 7/15; no closing date. Applicants notified on rolling basis starting 6/15. **Transfers:** No deadline.

Contact. Financial aid office: (770) 528-4531
Lori Burnette, Director of Financial Aid
980 South Cobb Drive
Marietta, GA 30060

Clark Atlanta University

Atlanta, Georgia
www.cau.edu
Four-year private **Federal Code: 001559**

	Living at home	On-campus
Tuition and fees:	$12,862	$12,862
Room and board:		$6,438
Books and supplies:	$800	$800
Personal expenses:	$1,832	$1,832
Transportation:	$225	$1,306

Undergraduate aid. All financial aid based on need. Average financial aid package for full-time students was $3,206; for part-time $3,327. 48%

awarded as scholarships/grants, 52% as loans/jobs. **Student debt:** 9% of graduating class borrowed to fund education; average debt was $11,795.

Freshman aid. Out of 911 full-time freshmen, 865 applied for aid; 805 were judged to have need; of these 791 received aid. Average package met 19% of need. 27 students had full need met. Average scholarship/grant was $3,614; average loan $2,568.

Policies to reduce costs. Tuition/fee waivers for employees and their families. Tuition at time of enrollment guaranteed for 4 years; credit/placement for qualifying scores on AP, IB, CLEP examinations. Work study available weekends.

Payment plans. Credit card, installment, deferred payment.

Application procedures. FAFSA, institutional form required. Priority date 3/1; closing date 4/1. Applicants notified on rolling basis starting 2/1, must reply by 7/31. **Transfers:** Priority date 3/1; closing date 4/1.

Contact. **Financial aid office:** (404) 880-6018
Thelma Ross, Associate Director of Financial Aid
223 James P. Brawley Drive, SW
Atlanta, GA 30314

Clayton College and State University

Morrow, Georgia
www.clayton.edu
Four-year public **Federal Code: 008976**

	Living at home
Tuition and fees (2002-2003):	$2,436
Out-of-state:	$8,466
Books and supplies:	$826
Personal expenses:	$2,576

Undergraduate aid. Non-need-based: Scholarships based on academics, athletics, leadership, music/drama, state/district residency.

Policies to reduce costs. Tuition/fee waivers for senior citizens, employees and their families. Credit/placement for qualifying scores on AP, CLEP examinations.

Payment plans. Credit card payment.

Application procedures. FAFSA, institutional form required. Priority date 4/1; no closing date.

Contact. **Financial aid office:** (770) 961-3511
Catherine McClarin, Director of Financial Aid
5900 North Lee Street
Morrow, GA 30260-0285

Coastal Georgia Community College

Brunswick, Georgia
www.cgcc.edu
Two-year public **Federal Code: 001558**

	Living at home
Tuition and fees (2002-2003):	$1,544
Out-of-state:	$5,540
Per-credit charge:	$56
Per-credit out-of-state:	$222
Books and supplies:	$600
Personal expenses:	$500
Transportation:	$1,000

Undergraduate aid. Need-based: Need-based aid available for full-time students. **Non-need-based:** Scholarships based on state/district residency.

Policies to reduce costs. Tuition/fee waivers for senior citizens. Credit/placement for qualifying scores on AP, CLEP examinations.

Payment plans. Credit card payment.

Application procedures. FAFSA required. Priority date 5/1; no closing date. Applicants notified on rolling basis starting 7/1. **Transfers:** No deadline.

Contact. Betty Coen, Financial Aid Director
3700 Altama Avenue
Brunswick, GA 31520

Columbus State University

Columbus, Georgia
www.colstate.edu
Four-year public **Federal Code: 001561**

	Living at home	On-campus
Tuition and fees (2002-2003):	$2,466	$2,466
Out-of-state:	$8,496	$8,496
Room and board:		$5,170
Books and supplies:	$650	$650
Personal expenses:	$600	
Transportation:	$600	

Undergraduate aid. Need-based: Need-based aid available for full-time students. **Non-need-based:** Scholarships based on academics.

Policies to reduce costs. Tuition/fee waivers for senior citizens, minority students, employees and their families. Credit/placement for qualifying scores on AP, IB, CLEP examinations.

Payment plans. Credit card payment.

Application procedures. FAFSA, institutional form required. Priority date 5/1; no closing date. Applicants notified by 8/1, must reply by 6/1 or within 4 week(s) of notification. **Transfers:** No deadline.

Contact. **Financial aid office:** (706) 568-2036
Janis Bowles, Director of Financial Aid
4225 University Avenue
Columbus, GA 31907-5645

Columbus Technical College

Columbus, Georgia
www.columbustech.org
Two-year public **Federal Code: 005624**

College costs. Varies by program on per-credit-hour charges.

	Living at home
Tuition and fees:	$1,388
Out-of-state:	$2,636
Per-credit charge:	$26
Per-credit out-of-state:	$52
Books and supplies:	$1,600
Personal expenses:	$1,100

Undergraduate aid. Need-based: Need-based aid available for full-time and part-time students.

Policies to reduce costs. Tuition/fee waivers for senior citizens, employees and their families. Credit/placement for qualifying scores on AP, CLEP examinations.

Payment plans. Credit card payment.

Application procedures. FAFSA required. No deadline. Applicants notified on rolling basis. **Transfers:** No deadline.

Contact. Shirley Walton, Director, Financial Aid
928 Manchester Expressway
Columbus, GA 31904-6572

Covenant College

Lookout Mountain, Georgia
www.covenant.edu
Four-year private **Federal Code: 003484**

	Living at home	On-campus
Tuition and fees:	$18,170	$18,170
Room and board:		$5,600
Board only:	$930	
Books and supplies:	$600	$600
Personal expenses:	$560	$560
Transportation:	$560	$560

Undergraduate aid. Need-based: Average financial aid package for full-time students was $15,903; for part-time $7,212. 70% awarded as scholarships/grants, 30% as loans/jobs. **Non-need-based:** 93% awarded as scholarships/grants, 7% as loans/jobs. Scholarships based on academics, alumni affiliation, art, athletics, leadership, minority status, music/drama, religious affiliation, state/district residency. **Student debt:** 45% of graduating class borrowed to fund education; average debt was $13,565.

Freshman aid. **Need-based:** Average package met 83% of need. Average scholarship/grant was $7,396; average loan $3,693.

Merit scholarships. Maclellan Scholars Program: minimum SAT 1200 (or ACT 27), high school GPA 3.3; Presidential Scholarship based on GPA, leadership, Christian commitment, extracurricular activities, work experience, references.

Policies to reduce costs. Tuition/fee waivers for employees and their families. Credit/placement for qualifying scores on AP, IB, CLEP examinations. Work study available nights, weekends and for part-time students.

Payment plans. Credit card, installment payment.

Application procedures. FAFSA, institutional form required. Priority date 3/1; closing date 3/31. Applicants notified on rolling basis starting 4/15, must reply within 3 week(s) of notification. **Transfers:** Priority date 3/1; closing date 3/31. Some scholarships may be depleted for mid-semester transfers, such as athletic, diversity or music.

Contact. **Financial aid office:** (706) 419-1126
Rebecca Morton, Financial Aid Director
14049 Scenic Highway
Lookout Mountain, GA 30750

Dalton State College

Dalton, Georgia
www.daltonstate.edu
Four-year public **Federal Code: 003956**

	Living at home
Tuition and fees (2002-2003):	$1,446
Out-of-state:	$5,442
Books and supplies:	$950
Personal expenses:	$1,150
Transportation:	$2,080

Undergraduate aid. **Need-based:** Need-based aid available for full-time and part-time students. **Non-need-based:** Scholarships based on academics, state/district residency.

Policies to reduce costs. Credit/placement for qualifying scores on CLEP examinations.

Payment plans. Credit card payment.

Application procedures. Priority date 7/1; no closing date. Applicants notified on rolling basis starting 7/1. **Transfers:** Priority date 7/1.

Contact. **Financial aid office:** (706) 272-4545
Jodi Johnson, Vice President for Enrollment Services
213 North College Drive
Dalton, GA 30720-3797

Darton College

Albany, Georgia
www.darton.edu
Two-year public **Federal Code: 001543**

	Living at home
Tuition and fees (2002-2003):	$1,566
Out-of-state:	$5,562
Per-credit charge:	$56
Per-credit out-of-state:	$222
Books and supplies:	$1,100
Personal expenses:	$1,200
Transportation:	$900

Undergraduate aid. **Need-based:** Need-based aid available for full-time and part-time students. **Non-need-based:** Scholarships based on academics, alumni affiliation, art, athletics, music/drama, state/district residency. **Additional information:** Auditions, portfolios, essays, extracurricular activities impact scholarship decisions.

Merit scholarships. Talent scholarships offered for art, music, science, literary skills, and mathematics. Each academic division can recommend talent scholarship recipients.

Policies to reduce costs. Tuition/fee waivers for senior citizens, employees and their families. Credit/placement for qualifying scores on AP, CLEP examinations. Work study available nights, weekends and for part-time students.

Payment plans. Credit card payment.

Application procedures. FAFSA, institutional form required. No deadline. Applicants notified on rolling basis, must reply within 3 week(s) of notification.

Contact. **Financial aid office:** (229) 430-6746
Martha Whittle, Director of Financial Aid
2400 Gillionville Road
Albany, GA 31707-3098

DeKalb Technical College

Clarkston, Georgia
www.dekalbtech.org
Two-year public **Federal Code: 016582**

College costs. Per-credit-hour rate is capped at 12 credits per quarter, though students permitted to take more than 12 credits per quarter. Some programs have additional charges.

	Living at home
Tuition and fees (2002-2003):	$1,119
Out-of-state:	$2,055
Per-credit charge:	$26
Per-credit out-of-state:	$52
Books and supplies:	$600
Personal expenses:	$900
Transportation:	$900

Undergraduate aid. **Need-based:** Need-based aid available for full-time and part-time students. **Non-need-based:** Scholarships based on academics, leadership, state/district residency.

Policies to reduce costs. Tuition/fee waivers for senior citizens. Credit/placement for qualifying scores on AP, CLEP examinations. Work study available nights, weekends and for part-time students.

Payment plans. Credit card payment.

Application procedures. FAFSA, institutional form required. Priority date 7/15; closing date 8/20. Applicants notified on rolling basis starting 6/1, must reply by 8/30. **Transfers:** No deadline.

Contact. **Financial aid office:** (404) 297-9522 ext. 1166
Gary Mann, Director of Financial Aid
495 North Indian Creek Drive
Clarkston, GA 30021

DeVry University: Alpharetta

Alpharetta, Georgia
www.atl.devry.edu
Four-year proprietary **Federal Code: 009224**

	Living at home
Tuition and fees:	$10,155
Books and supplies:	$1,100
Personal expenses:	$1,750
Transportation:	$1,422

Undergraduate aid. All financial aid based on need. Average financial aid package for full-time students was $7,054; for part-time $6,025. 27% awarded as scholarships/grants, 73% as loans/jobs.

Freshman aid. Average package met 36% of need. Average scholarship/grant was $2,905; average loan $3,021.

Policies to reduce costs. Tuition/fee waivers for employees and their families.

Payment plans. Credit card, installment, deferred payment.

Application procedures. FAFSA required. No deadline. Applicants notified on rolling basis starting 7/2. **Transfers:** No deadline.

Contact. David Pickett, Assistant Director of Financial Aid
2555 Northwinds Parkway
Alpharetta, GA 30004

DeVry University: Atlanta

Decatur, Georgia
www.atl.devry.edu
Four-year proprietary **Federal Code: 009224**

	Living at home
Tuition and fees:	$10,155
Books and supplies:	$1,100
Personal expenses:	$1,750
Transportation:	$1,422

Undergraduate aid. All financial aid based on need. Average financial aid package for full-time students was $12,676; for part-time $11,475. 45% awarded as scholarships/grants, 55% as loans/jobs.

Freshman aid. Average package met 51% of need. Average scholarship/grant was $6,237; average loan $4,255.

Policies to reduce costs. Tuition/fee waivers for employees and their families.

Payment plans. Credit card, installment, deferred payment.

Application procedures. FAFSA required. No deadline. Applicants notified on rolling basis starting 7/2. **Transfers:** No deadline.

Contact. Robin Winston, Director of Financial Aid
250 North Arcadia Avenue
Decatur, GA 30030-2198

East Georgia College

Swainsboro, Georgia
www.ega.peachnet.edu
Two-year public **Federal Code: 010997**

	Living at home
Tuition and fees (2002-2003):	$1,428
Out-of-state:	$5,424
Per-credit charge:	$56
Per-credit out-of-state:	$222
Books and supplies:	$600
Personal expenses:	$900
Transportation:	$1,800

Undergraduate aid. Need-based: 76% awarded as scholarships/grants, 24% as loans/jobs. Need-based aid available for part-time students. **Non-need-based:** Scholarships based on academics, leadership, state/district residency.

Policies to reduce costs. Tuition/fee waivers for senior citizens. Credit/placement for qualifying scores on CLEP examinations.

Application procedures. FAFSA, institutional form required. Priority date 6/15; no closing date. Applicants notified on rolling basis starting 6/15, must reply within 2 week(s) of notification. **Transfers:** No deadline.

Contact. Financial aid office: (478) 289-2009
Barbara Green, Director of Financial Aid
131 College Circle
Swainsboro, GA 30401-2699

Emmanuel College

Franklin Springs, Georgia
www.emmanuelcollege.edu
Four-year private **Federal Code: 001563**

	Living at home	On-campus
Tuition and fees:	$9,344	$9,344
Room and board:		$4,136
Books and supplies:	$600	$600
Personal expenses:	$750	$900
Transportation:	$700	$500

Undergraduate aid. Need-based: Average financial aid package for full-time students was $8,948; for part-time $4,540. 32% awarded as scholarships/grants, 68% as loans/jobs. **Non-need-based:** 62% awarded as scholarships/grants, 38% as loans/jobs. Scholarships based on academics, art, athletics, leadership, music/drama, religious affiliation, state/district residency. **Student debt:** 73% of graduating class borrowed to fund education; average debt was $17,600.

Freshman aid. Need-based: Out of 156 full-time freshmen, 147 applied for aid; 118 were judged to have need; of these 118 received aid. Average package met 44% of need. 31 students had full need met. Average scholarship/grant was $3,057; average loan $2,407. **Non-need based:** 112 full-time freshmen with need received non-need scholarships; 29 without need received awards; 4 received athletic scholarships.

Policies to reduce costs. Tuition/fee waivers for adults, senior citizens, family of clergy, employees and their families. Credit/placement for qualifying scores on AP, CLEP examinations.

Payment plans. Credit card, deferred payment.

Application procedures. FAFSA, institutional form required. Priority date 5/1; no closing date. Applicants notified on rolling basis starting 3/15, must reply within 2 week(s) of notification. **Transfers:** Priority date 5/1; no deadline. Students on probation at previous institution may be accepted and funded for one semester. Continued funding dependent on satisfactory performance.

Contact. Mary Beadles, Financial Aid Director
181 Spring Street
Franklin Springs, GA 30639-0129

Emory University

Atlanta, Georgia
www.emory.edu
Four-year private **Federal Code: 001564**

	Living at home	On-campus
Tuition and fees (2002-2003):	$26,957	$26,957
Room and board:		$8,498
Books and supplies:	$700	$700
Personal expenses:	$700	$700
Transportation:	$600	$600

Undergraduate aid. Need-based: Need-based aid available for full-time and part-time students. **Non-need-based:** Scholarships based on academics, art, athletics, leadership, music/drama, religious affiliation, state/district residency. **Additional information:** Private Emory loan programs assist families in financing tuition. Fixed tuition program also available.

Merit scholarships. Emory Scholars, deadline Nov. 15, all merit-based scholarships are through Emory Scholars; scholarships range from 2/3 tuition, to tuition, books, fees, room and board.

Policies to reduce costs. Tuition/fee waivers for family of clergy, employees and their families. Credit/placement for qualifying scores on AP, IB examinations. Work study available nights and weekends.

Payment plans. Installment payment.

Application procedures. FAFSA, CSS PROFILE required. All applicants wishing to be considered for institutionally funded need-based grant aid must file CSS PROFILE. Priority date 2/15; closing date 4/1. Applicants notified by 4/15, must reply by 5/1. Early decision closing date 11/1. **Transfers:** Priority date 2/15; closing date 4/1. Limitations on aid available to transfer students. Financial aid filing deadline for transfers is 30 days following transfer student application for admission admit date.

Contact. Julia Perreault, Director of Financial Aid
200 Boisfeuillet Jones Center
Atlanta, GA 30322

Floyd College

Rome, Georgia
www.fc.peachnet.edu
Two-year public **Federal Code: 009507**

	Living at home
Tuition and fees (2002-2003):	$1,516
Out-of-state:	$5,512
Per-credit charge:	$56
Per-credit out-of-state:	$222
Books and supplies:	$450
Personal expenses:	$250
Transportation:	$200

Undergraduate aid. Non-need-based: Scholarships based on academics, art.

Merit scholarships. Bartow Service Scholarship: commit to 80 hours community service, Bartow County resident, essay required, March 15 deadline.

Policies to reduce costs. Tuition/fee waivers for senior citizens, employees and their families. Credit/placement for qualifying scores on AP examinations. Work study available nights and for part-time students.

Payment plans. Credit card payment.

Application procedures. FAFSA required. Closing date 4/2. Applicants notified on rolling basis starting 4/2, must reply within 2 week(s) of notification. **Transfers:** Priority date 4/2.

Contact. **Financial aid office:** (706) 295-6311
Wendy Shapiro, Director of Financial Aid
3175 Cedartown Highway
Rome, GA 30162-1864

Fort Valley State University

Fort Valley, Georgia
www.fvsu.edu
Four-year public **Federal Code: 001566**

	Living at home	On-campus
Tuition and fees (2002-2003):	$2,580	$2,580
Out-of-state:	$8,610	$8,610
Room and board:		$4,078
Books and supplies:	$790	$790
Personal expenses:	$945	$1,425
Transportation:	$1,904	$1,200

Undergraduate aid. Need-based: Need-based aid available for full-time and part-time students. **Non-need-based:** Scholarships based on academics, athletics, state/district residency.

Policies to reduce costs. Tuition/fee waivers for senior citizens. Credit/placement for qualifying scores on CLEP examinations.

Payment plans. Credit card, deferred payment.

Application procedures. FAFSA, institutional form required. Priority date 2/15; closing date 4/15. Applicants notified by 6/15, must reply within 1 week(s) of notification. **Transfers:** Financial aid transcripts must be received from former institutions before application for aid will be considered complete and reviewed for awards.

Contact. **Financial aid office:** (478) 825-6351
Baetricia King, Director of Financial Aid
1005 State University Drive
Fort Valley, GA 31030-4313

Gainesville College

Gainesville, Georgia
www.gc.peachnet.edu
Two-year public **Federal Code: 001567**

	Living at home
Tuition and fees (2002-2003):	$1,470
Out-of-state:	$5,466
Per-credit charge:	$56
Per-credit out-of-state:	$222
Books and supplies:	$630
Personal expenses:	$1,000
Transportation:	$1,900

Undergraduate aid. Need-based: Need-based aid available for full-time and part-time students.

Policies to reduce costs. Tuition/fee waivers for senior citizens, minority students, employees and their families. Credit/placement for qualifying scores on AP, CLEP examinations.

Payment plans. Credit card payment.

Application procedures. FAFSA, institutional form required. Priority date 4/15; no closing date. Applicants notified on rolling basis starting 7/1, must reply within 3 week(s) of notification. **Transfers:** Must have minimum 2.0 GPA to be eligible for financial aid.

Contact. Stephen Langston, Financial Aid Director
PO Box 1358
Gainesville, GA 30503

Georgia College and State University

Milledgeville, Georgia
www.gcsu.edu
Four-year public **Federal Code: 001602**

	Living at home	On-campus
Tuition and fees (2002-2003):	$3,138	$3,138
Out-of-state:	$10,968	$10,968
Room and board:		$5,776
Board only:	$1,880	
Books and supplies:	$600	$600
Personal expenses:	$1,888	$1,888
Transportation:	$940	$940

Undergraduate aid. Need-based: 28% awarded as scholarships/grants, 72% as loans/jobs. Need-based aid available for part-time students. **Non-need-based:** 64% awarded as scholarships/grants, 36% as loans/jobs. Scholarships based on academics, alumni affiliation, art, athletics, job skills, minority status, music/drama, religious affiliation, state/district residency. **Student debt:** 51% of graduating class borrowed to fund education; average debt was $14,053.

Freshman aid. Need-based: Out of 852 full-time freshmen, 820 applied for aid; 527 were judged to have need; of these 521 received aid. **Non-need based:** 475 full-time freshmen with need received non-need scholarships; 101 without need received awards; 22 received athletic scholarships.

Merit scholarships. Presidential Scholarship: up to $2,000 per year; 1200 SAT or equivalent ACT, 3.5 high school GPA. Outstanding Student: up to $1,500 a year; 1100 SAT or ACT equivalent, 3.3 high school GPA, demonstrated ability in athletics, debate, theater, music, nursing, biology, chemistry, music therapy, education, business or community service. Valedictorian/Salutatorian/STAR Student: one-time amount of $1,000 awarded.

Policies to reduce costs. Tuition/fee waivers for senior citizens, employees and their families. Credit/placement for qualifying scores on AP, CLEP examinations.

Payment plans. Credit card payment.

Application procedures. FAFSA required. Priority date 3/1; no closing date. Applicants notified on rolling basis starting 4/15, must reply within 2 week(s) of notification. **Transfers:** Priority date 3/1.

Contact. **Financial aid office:** (478) 445-5149
Suzanne Price-Buttram, Director of Financial Aid
Campus Box 23
Milledgeville, GA 31061-0490

Georgia Institute of Technology

Atlanta, Georgia
www.gatech.edu
Four-year public **Federal Code: 001569**

	Living at home	On-campus
Tuition and fees (2002-2003):	$3,616	$3,616
Out-of-state:	$13,986	$13,986
Room and board:		$5,922
Books and supplies:	$1,278	$1,278
Personal expenses:	$1,500	$1,500

Undergraduate aid. Need-based: Average financial aid package for full-time students was $7,141; for part-time $5,127. 50% awarded as scholarships/grants, 50% as loans/jobs. **Non-need-based:** 71% awarded as scholarships/grants, 29% as loans/jobs. Scholarships based on academics, alumni affiliation, art, athletics, job skills, leadership, minority status, music/drama, religious affiliation, state/district residency. **Student debt:** 41% of graduating class borrowed to fund education; average debt was $17,221.

Freshman aid. Need-based: Out of 2,277 full-time freshmen, 2,230 applied for aid; 709 were judged to have need; of these 693 received aid. Average package met 73% of need. 378 students had full need met. Average scholarship/grant was $5,910; average loan $3,063. **Non-need based:** 548 full-time freshmen with need received non-need scholarships; 978 without need received awards; 49 received athletic scholarships.

Merit scholarships. President's Scholarship Program for freshmen with outstanding academic/leadership qualities; over 80 each in the last 2 years awarded; 4-year awards range from half to full tuition.

Policies to reduce costs. Credit/placement for qualifying scores on AP, IB examinations. Work study available nights, weekends and for part-time students.

Payment plans. Credit card, installment, deferred payment.

Application procedures. FAFSA, institutional form required. Closing date 3/1. Applicants notified by 4/1, must reply by 5/1. **Transfers:** Priority date 4/15.

Contact. **Financial aid office:** (404) 894-4160
Marie Mons, Director of Student Financial Planning and Services
225 North Avenue, NW
Atlanta, GA 30332-0320

Georgia Military College
Milledgeville, Georgia
www.gmc.cc.ga.us
Two-year public **Federal Code: 001571**

College costs. Quoted full-time tuition and fees are for cadet students. Additonal $1,025 for uniforms.

	Living at home	On-campus
Tuition and fees (projected):	$10,806	$10,806
Room and board:		$3,600
Books and supplies:	$600	$600
Personal expenses:	$1,050	$300
Transportation:	$900	$300

Undergraduate aid. Need-based: 79% awarded as scholarships/grants, 21% as loans/jobs. Need-based aid available for part-time students. **Non-need-based:** 88% awarded as scholarships/grants, 12% as loans/jobs. **Additional information:** Institutional aid offered to those enrolled in Cadet Corps who reside in on-campus housing.

Freshman aid. Need-based: Out of 314 full-time freshmen, 310 applied for aid; 202 were judged to have need; of these 202 received aid. 40 students had full need met. **Non-need based:** 174 full-time freshmen with need received non-need scholarships; 24 received athletic scholarships.

Policies to reduce costs. Tuition/fee waivers for senior citizens, employees and their families. Credit/placement for qualifying scores on CLEP examinations. Work study available nights, weekends and for part-time students.

Payment plans. Credit card, deferred payment.

Application procedures. FAFSA, institutional form required. Priority date 4/1; no closing date. Applicants notified on rolling basis starting 8/15.

Contact. **Financial aid office:** (478) 445-0840
Alisa Stephens, Director of Financial Aid
201 East Greene Street
Milledgeville, GA 31061

Georgia Perimeter College
Clarkston, Georgia
www.gpc.edu
Two-year public **Federal Code: 001562**

	Living at home
Tuition and fees (2002-2003):	$1,576
Out-of-state:	$5,572
Per-credit charge:	$56
Per-credit out-of-state:	$222
Books and supplies:	$900
Transportation:	$1,500

Undergraduate aid. Need-based: Need-based aid available for full-time and part-time students.

Policies to reduce costs. Tuition/fee waivers for senior citizens. Credit/placement for qualifying scores on AP, CLEP examinations.

Payment plans. Credit card payment.

Application procedures. FAFSA, institutional form required. Closing date 7/2. Applicants notified on rolling basis, must reply within 3 week(s) of notification. **Transfers:** Priority date 3/31; no deadline.

Contact. Mary Sanders, Director of Financial Aid
555 North Indian Creek Drive
Clarkston, GA 30021

Georgia Southern University
Statesboro, Georgia
www.gasou.edu
Four-year public **Federal Code: 001572**

	Living at home	On-campus
Tuition and fees (2002-2003):	$2,694	$2,694
Out-of-state:	$8,724	$8,724
Room and board:		$4,550
Board only:	$1,590	
Books and supplies:	$968	$968
Personal expenses:	$1,692	$1,692
Transportation:	$800	$800

Undergraduate aid. Need-based: Average financial aid package for full-time students was $6,056; for part-time $4,475. 47% awarded as scholarships/grants, 53% as loans/jobs. **Non-need-based:** 48% awarded as scholarships/grants, 52% as loans/jobs. Scholarships based on academics, alumni affiliation, art, athletics, leadership, music/drama, state/district residency. **Student debt:** 71% of graduating class borrowed to fund education; average debt was $16,926.

Freshman aid. Need-based: Out of 2,628 full-time freshmen, 2,432 applied for aid; 1,136 were judged to have need; of these 1,114 received aid. Average package met 76% of need. 322 students had full need met. Average scholarship/grant was $4,297; average loan $2,398. **Non-need based:** 145 full-time freshmen with need received non-need scholarships; 1,200 without need received awards; 52 received athletic scholarships.

Policies to reduce costs. Tuition/fee waivers for senior citizens, employees and their families. Credit/placement for qualifying scores on AP, IB, CLEP examinations. Work study available nights, weekends and for part-time students.

Payment plans. Credit card payment.

Application procedures. FAFSA required. Priority date 3/31; no closing date. Applicants notified by 4/15. **Transfers:** Priority date 3/31; no deadline.

Contact. **Financial aid office:** (912) 681-5413
Connie Murphey, Director of Financial Aid
PO Box 8024
Statesboro, GA 30460

Georgia Southwestern State University
Americus, Georgia
www.gsw.edu
Four-year public **Federal Code: 001573**

	Living at home	On-campus
Tuition and fees (2002-2003):	$2,564	$2,564
Out-of-state:	$8,594	$8,594
Room and board:		$3,926
Board only:	$1,530	
Books and supplies:	$500	$500

Undergraduate aid. Need-based: Need-based aid available for full-time and part-time students. **Non-need-based:** Scholarships based on academics, athletics, leadership.

Merit scholarships. Wheatley Scholarship awards $2,000-2,500, requires separate application, 40-50 available each year. Student must have 3.0 in college preparatory course and either 1100 SAT or 24 ACT.

Policies to reduce costs. Tuition/fee waivers for senior citizens. Credit/placement for qualifying scores on AP, CLEP examinations.

Payment plans. Credit card, installment payment.

Application procedures. FAFSA, institutional form required. Priority date 4/1; closing date 6/1. Applicants notified on rolling basis starting 3/1. Early decision closing date 12/15.

Contact. **Financial aid office:** (229) 928-1378
Freida Jones, Director of Financial Aid
800 Wheatly Street
Americus, GA 31709-9957

Georgia State University

Atlanta, Georgia
www.gsu.edu
Four-year public **Federal Code: 001574**

	Living at home	On-campus
Tuition and fees (2002-2003):	$3,472	$3,472
Out-of-state:	$11,842	$11,842
Room only:		$4,680
Books and supplies:	$1,320	$1,320
Transportation:	$1,740	$828

Undergraduate aid. All financial aid based on need. Need-based aid available for full-time and part-time students.

Policies to reduce costs. Tuition/fee waivers for senior citizens, employees and their families. Credit/placement for qualifying scores on AP, IB, CLEP examinations. Work study available weekends and for part-time students.

Payment plans. Credit card, installment payment.

Application procedures. FAFSA required. Priority date 4/1; no closing date. Applicants notified on rolling basis starting 5/1, must reply within 2 week(s) of notification.

Contact. **Financial aid office:** (404) 651-2227
Dane Bledsoe, Director of Student Financial Aid
Box 4009
Atlanta, GA 30302-4009

Gordon College

Barnesville, Georgia
www.gdn.edu
Two-year public **Federal Code: 001575**

	Living at home	On-campus
Tuition and fees (2002-2003):	$1,512	$1,512
Out-of-state:	$5,508	$5,508
Per-credit charge:	$56	$56
Per-credit out-of-state:	$222	$222
Room and board:		$2,992
Books and supplies:	$950	$950
Personal expenses:	$903	$903
Transportation:	$1,130	$521

Undergraduate aid. Need-based: Need-based aid available for full-time and part-time students.

Policies to reduce costs. Tuition/fee waivers for senior citizens. Credit/placement for qualifying scores on AP, CLEP examinations.

Payment plans. Credit card payment.

Application procedures. Institutional form required. Priority date 5/1; no closing date. Applicants notified on rolling basis starting 5/1.

Contact. Larry Micham, Director of Financial Aid
419 College Drive
Barnesville, GA 30204

Griffin Technical College

Griffin, Georgia
www.griftec.org
Two-year public **Federal Code: 005621**

College costs. Cost of specialized programs provided at registration.

	Living at home
Tuition and fees (projected):	$1,068
Out-of-state:	$2,004
Per-credit charge:	$26
Per-credit out-of-state:	$52
Books and supplies:	$150
Personal expenses:	$587

Application procedures. FAFSA, institutional form required. Applicants notified on rolling basis.

Contact. Debbie Bowles, Director of Financial Aid
501 Varsity Road
Griffin, GA 30223

Gupton Jones College of Funeral Service

Decatur, Georgia
www.gupton-jones.edu
Two-year private **Federal Code: 010771**

	Living at home
Tuition and fees:	$6,100
Per-credit charge:	$150
Board only:	$600
Personal expenses:	$500
Transportation:	$1,000

Payment plans. Installment payment.

Application procedures. FAFSA required. No deadline. Applicants notified on rolling basis.

Contact. James Hinz, Dean
5141 Snapfinger Woods Drive
Decatur, GA 30035

Herzing College

Atlanta, Georgia
www.herzing.com
Three-year proprietary **Federal Code: 014030**

College costs. Tuition includes use of books. One-time $100 fee for technology programs; one-time $300 fee for engineering programs.

	Living at home
Tuition and fees:	$8,000

Undergraduate aid. Need-based: Need-based aid available for full-time and part-time students. **Non-need-based:** Scholarships based on academics.

Policies to reduce costs. Credit/placement for qualifying scores on IB examinations. Work study available nights.

Payment plans. Credit card, installment payment.

Application procedures. FAFSA, institutional form required. No deadline. Applicants notified on rolling basis.

Contact. **Financial aid office:** (404) 816-4533
Debbie Price-Harris, Financial Aid Director
3355 Lenox Road, Suite 100
Atlanta, GA 30326

High-Tech Institute: Atlanta

Marietta, Georgia
www.high-techinstitute.com
Two-year proprietary

College costs. Total costs of associate degree programs including books and supplies range from $17,950-$26,550.

Contact. Vinita Simpson, Chief Financial Aid Officer
1090 Northchase Parkway
Marietta, GA 30067

Kennesaw State University

Kennesaw, Georgia
www.kennesaw.edu
Four-year public **Federal Code: 001577**

College costs. Room rate reflects standard 12-month contract.

	Living at home	On-campus
Tuition and fees (2002-2003):	$2,516	$2,516
Out-of-state:	$8,546	$8,546
Room only:		$4,140
Board only:	$2,780	
Books and supplies:	$812	$812
Personal expenses:	$1,180	
Transportation:	$1,650	

Undergraduate aid. Need-based: Need-based aid available for full-time students. **Non-need-based:** Scholarships based on academics, athletics, leadership, music/drama.

Policies to reduce costs. Tuition/fee waivers for senior citizens. Credit/placement for qualifying scores on AP, IB, CLEP examinations. Work study available nights and for part-time students.

Payment plans. Credit card payment.

Application procedures. FAFSA required. Priority date 4/1; no closing date. Applicants notified by 5/1.

Contact. **Financial aid office:** (770) 423-6074
Terry Faust, Director of Financial Aid
1000 Chastain Road/Box 444
Kennesaw, GA 30144-5591

LaGrange College

LaGrange, Georgia
www.lagrange.edu
Four-year private **Federal Code: 001578**

	Living at home	On-campus
Tuition and fees (2002-2003):	$13,226	$13,226
Room and board:		$5,494
Books and supplies:	$750	$750
Personal expenses:	$1,800	$1,800

Undergraduate aid. **Need-based:** Average financial aid package for full-time students was $12,269; for part-time $6,203. 63% awarded as scholarships/grants, 37% as loans/jobs. **Non-need-based:** 68% awarded as scholarships/grants, 32% as loans/jobs. Scholarships based on academics, art, leadership, minority status, music/drama, religious affiliation. **Student debt:** 67% of graduating class borrowed to fund education; average debt was $15,972.

Freshman aid. **Need-based:** Out of 235 full-time freshmen, 226 applied for aid; 161 were judged to have need; of these 161 received aid. Average package met 86% of need. 52 students had full need met. Average scholarship/grant was $10,702; average loan $2,520. **Non-need based:** 35 full-time freshmen with need received non-need scholarships; 65 without need received awards.

Merit scholarships. Presidential Scholarship: competitive, full tuition. Cunningham Scholarship: competitive; $3,500 per year. Academic Achievement Awards: minimum GPA 3.0; $1,000-$4,500. Methodist Scholarship: minimum of 2 of the following criteria: 3.2 GPA, 1100 SAT, 24 ACT; up to $1,000.

Policies to reduce costs. Tuition/fee waivers for family of clergy, employees and their families. Credit/placement for qualifying scores on AP, IB, CLEP examinations. Work study available nights and weekends.

Payment plans. Credit card, installment, deferred payment.

Application procedures. FAFSA, institutional form required. Closing date 3/15. Applicants notified on rolling basis starting 3/1, must reply by 8/15 or within 2 week(s) of notification.

Contact. **Financial aid office:** (706) 880-8241
Sylvia Smith, Director of Financial Aid
601 Broad Street
LaGrange, GA 30240-2999

Life University

Marietta, Georgia
www.life.edu
Four-year private **Federal Code: 014170**

College costs. Out-of-state tuition: $4,250.

	Living at home
Tuition and fees (projected):	$2,490
Books and supplies:	$760

Undergraduate aid. **Need-based:** Need-based aid available for full-time students.

Application procedures. FAFSA, institutional form, CSS PROFILE required.

Contact. Kim James, Director of Financial Aid
1269 Barclay Circle
Marietta, GA 30060

Macon State College

Macon, Georgia
www.mc.peachnet.edu
Four-year public **Federal Code: 007728**

	Living at home
Tuition and fees (2002-2003):	$1,490
Out-of-state:	$5,486
Board only:	$2,700
Books and supplies:	$800
Personal expenses:	$3,000
Transportation:	$900

Undergraduate aid. All financial aid based on need. 51% awarded as scholarships/grants, 49% as loans/jobs. Need-based aid available for part-time students. **Student debt:** 40% of graduating class borrowed to fund education; average debt was $10,000.

Policies to reduce costs. Tuition/fee waivers for senior citizens. Credit/placement for qualifying scores on AP, IB, CLEP examinations. Work study available nights, weekends and for part-time students.

Payment plans. Credit card payment.

Application procedures. FAFSA required. Priority date 4/1; no closing date. Applicants notified on rolling basis starting 4/15, must reply within 2 week(s) of notification. **Transfers:** Priority date 4/1; no deadline.

Contact. **Financial aid office:** (912) 471-2717
Pat Simmons, Director of Financial Aid
100 College Station Drive
Macon, GA 31206-5144

Medical College of Georgia

Augusta, Georgia
www.mcg.edu
Upper-division public **Federal Code: 001579**

College costs. Tuition/fees including summer: $4,981; $17,536 out-of-state. Up to $1,240 in additional, education-related costs (e.g. uniforms, vaccinations). Other fees or expenses may vary by program.

	Living at home	On-campus
Tuition and fees (2002-2003):	$3,356	$3,356
Out-of-state:	$11,726	$11,726
Room only:		$1,280
Board only:	$1,980	
Books and supplies:	$800	$800
Personal expenses:	$1,917	$1,917
Transportation:	$1,890	$1,665

Undergraduate aid. **Need-based:** Average financial aid package for full-time students was $8,407; for part-time $8,113. 32% awarded as scholarships/grants, 68% as loans/jobs. **Non-need-based:** 45% awarded as scholarships/grants, 55% as loans/jobs. Scholarships based on academics, state/district residency. **Student debt:** 60% of graduating class borrowed to fund education; average debt was $15,555.

Policies to reduce costs. Tuition/fee waivers for employees and their families. Work study available nights, weekends and for part-time students.

Application procedures. FAFSA, institutional form required. Priority date 3/31; no closing date. Applicants notified on rolling basis starting 4/30, must reply within 2 week(s) of notification. **Transfers:** State Hope scholarships only available to Georgia residents.

Contact. **Financial aid office:** (706) 721-4901
John Powell, Director of Financial Aid
Office of Academic Admissions, Room 170 Kelly Building
Augusta, GA 30912-7310

Mercer University

Macon, Georgia
www.mercer.edu
Four-year private **Federal Code: 001580**

	Living at home	On-campus
Tuition and fees (2002-2003):	$19,728	$19,728
Room and board:		$6,420
Board only:	$750	
Books and supplies:	$650	$650
Personal expenses:	$715	$715
Transportation:	$500	$500

Undergraduate aid. Need-based: Average financial aid package for full-time students was $19,833; for part-time $10,503. 70% awarded as scholarships/grants, 30% as loans/jobs. **Non-need-based:** 80% awarded as scholarships/grants, 20% as loans/jobs. Scholarships based on academics, art, athletics, job skills, leadership, music/drama, religious affiliation, state/district residency.

Freshman aid. Need-based: Out of 612 full-time freshmen, 541 applied for aid; 414 were judged to have need; of these 414 received aid. Average package met 91% of need. 229 students had full need met. Average scholarship/grant was $13,646; average loan $2,993. **Non-need based:** 165 full-time freshmen with need received non-need scholarships; 181 without need received awards; 39 received athletic scholarships.

Policies to reduce costs. Tuition/fee waivers for family members, family of clergy, employees and their families. Credit/placement for qualifying scores on AP, IB, CLEP examinations. Work study available nights and weekends.

Payment plans. Credit card, installment payment.

Application procedures. FAFSA, institutional form required. Priority date 4/1; no closing date. Applicants notified on rolling basis starting 3/15, must reply within 2 week(s) of notification. **Transfers:** Priority date 7/1; no deadline.

Contact. **Financial aid office:** (478) 301-2670
Carol Kennedy Williams, Director of Financial Aid
1400 Coleman Avenue
Macon, GA 31207-0001

Middle Georgia College

Cochran, Georgia
www.mgc.edu
Two-year public **Federal Code: 001581**

College costs. Vehicle registration fee $8 per semester, $15 per-lab course fee.

	Living at home	On-campus
Tuition and fees (2002-2003):	$1,778	$1,778
Out-of-state:	$5,774	$5,774
Per-credit charge:	$56	$56
Per-credit out-of-state:	$222	$222
Room and board:		$3,692
Books and supplies:	$700	$700
Personal expenses:	$600	$600
Transportation:	$309	$288

Undergraduate aid. Need-based: Average financial aid package for full-time students was $5,125; for part-time $4,450. 69% awarded as scholarships/grants, 31% as loans/jobs. **Non-need-based:** 64% awarded as scholarships/grants, 36% as loans/jobs. Scholarships based on academics, alumni affiliation, art, athletics, job skills, leadership, minority status, music/drama, state/district residency. **Student debt:** 21% of graduating class borrowed to fund education; average debt was $3,876.

Freshman aid. Need-based: Out of 580 full-time freshmen, 474 applied for aid; 455 were judged to have need; of these 416 received aid. Average package met 80% of need. 307 students had full need met. Average scholarship/grant was $2,912; average loan $2,625. **Non-need based:** 168 full-time freshmen with need received non-need scholarships; 147 without need received awards; 22 received athletic scholarships.

Policies to reduce costs. Tuition/fee waivers for senior citizens, employees and their families. Credit/placement for qualifying scores on AP, CLEP examinations. Work study available nights, weekends and for part-time students.

Payment plans. Credit card payment.

Application procedures. FAFSA, institutional form required. Priority date 4/1; no closing date. Applicants notified on rolling basis starting 5/1.

Contact. Charlene Morgan, Director of Financial Aid
1100 Second Street SE
Cochran, GA 31014

Middle Georgia Technical College

Warner Robins, Georgia
www.mgtc.org
Two-year public **Federal Code: 014625**

College costs. Technical certificate tuition rates vary by program. Annual required fees $44.

Application procedures. FAFSA required.

Contact. 80 Cohen Walker Drive
Warner Robins, GA 31088

Morehouse College

Atlanta, Georgia
www.morehouse.edu
Four-year private **Federal Code: 001582**

	Living at home	On-campus
Tuition and fees (2002-2003):	$13,760	$13,760
Room and board:		$8,172
Board only:	$3,160	
Books and supplies:	$750	$750
Personal expenses:	$2,272	$2,772

Undergraduate aid. Need-based: Average financial aid package for full-time students was $6,416. 24% awarded as scholarships/grants, 76% as loans/jobs. Need-based aid available for part-time students. **Non-need-based:** 68% awarded as scholarships/grants, 32% as loans/jobs. Scholarships based on academics, athletics, state/district residency.

Freshman aid. Need-based: Out of 664 full-time freshmen, 644 applied for aid; 644 were judged to have need; of these 644 received aid. Average package met 48% of need. 5 students had full need met. Average scholarship/grant was $2,229; average loan $1,702. **Non-need based:** 491 full-time freshmen with need received non-need scholarships; 385 without need received awards; 159 received athletic scholarships.

Policies to reduce costs. Tuition/fee waivers for employees and their families.

Payment plans. Credit card, installment, deferred payment.

Application procedures. FAFSA, institutional form, CSS PROFILE required. Closing date 4/1. Applicants notified by 5/1.

Contact. **Financial aid office:** (404) 215-2638
James Stotts, Director of Financial Aid
830 Westview Drive SW
Atlanta, GA 30314

Morris Brown College

Atlanta, Georgia
www.morrisbrown.edu
Four-year private **Federal Code: 001583**

	Living at home	On-campus
Tuition and fees (2002-2003):	$10,188	$10,188
Room and board:		$5,262
Books and supplies:	$508	$508
Personal expenses:	$1,100	$1,100
Transportation:	$1,526	$794

Undergraduate aid. Need-based: Need-based aid available for full-time students. **Non-need-based:** Scholarships based on academics, alumni affiliation, art, leadership.

Policies to reduce costs. Tuition/fee waivers for family members, employees and their families. Credit/placement for qualifying scores on CLEP examinations.

Payment plans. Credit card, installment, deferred payment.

Application procedures. FAFSA, CSS PROFILE required. Priority date 3/31; no closing date. Applicants notified by 6/1, must reply within 2 week(s) of notification.

Contact. **Financial aid office:** (404) 739-1050
Parvesh Singh, Director of Financial Aid
643 Martin Luther King Jr. Drive Northwest
Atlanta, GA 30314

North Georgia College & State University

Dahlonega, Georgia
www.ngcsu.edu
Four-year public **Federal Code: 001585**

	Living at home	On-campus
Tuition and fees (2002-2003):	$2,594	$2,594
Out-of-state:	$8,624	$8,624
Room and board:		$4,016
Board only:	$520	
Books and supplies:	$500	$500
Personal expenses:		$1,000

Undergraduate aid. **Need-based:** 49% awarded as scholarships/grants, 51% as loans/jobs. Need-based aid available for part-time students. **Non-need-based:** 72% awarded as scholarships/grants, 28% as loans/jobs. Scholarships based on academics, alumni affiliation, art, athletics, leadership, music/drama, state/district residency. **Additional information:** Aid to international students limited to fee waiver for cadets.

Merit scholarships. ROTC grant available to Georgia residents, $1,500 a year. Student must participate in Corps of Cadets; no military service commitment required after graduation. ROTC out-of-state tuition waiver of $5,628 per year available to qualified non-Georgia US citizens. Participation in Corps of Cadets required; no military service commitment required after graduation.

Policies to reduce costs. Tuition/fee waivers for senior citizens, employees and their families. Credit/placement for qualifying scores on AP, CLEP examinations. Work study available for part-time students.

Payment plans. Credit card payment.

Application procedures. FAFSA, institutional form required. Priority date 5/1; no closing date. Applicants notified on rolling basis starting 5/15, must reply within 3 week(s) of notification.

Contact. **Financial aid office:** (706) 864-1412
Deborah Barbone, Director of Financial Aid
32 College Circle
Dahlonega, GA 30597

Oglethorpe University

Atlanta, Georgia
www.oglethorpe.edu
Four-year private **Federal Code: 001586**

	Living at home	On-campus
Tuition and fees (2002-2003):	$19,440	$19,440
Room and board:		$6,360
Books and supplies:	$600	$600
Personal expenses:	$1,200	$1,200
Transportation:	$1,000	$1,000

Undergraduate aid. **Need-based:** Average financial aid package for full-time students was $15,650. 72% awarded as scholarships/grants, 28% as loans/jobs. **Non-need-based:** 94% awarded as scholarships/grants, 6% as loans/jobs. Scholarships based on academics, leadership, music/drama, state/district residency. **Student debt:** 62% of graduating class borrowed to fund education; average debt was $19,885.

Freshman aid. **Need-based:** Average package met 85% of need. Average scholarship/grant was $13,918; average loan $2,287.

Policies to reduce costs. Tuition/fee waivers for family members, employees and their families. Prepayment discount; credit/placement for qualifying scores on AP, CLEP examinations.

Payment plans. Credit card, installment, deferred payment.

Application procedures. FAFSA, institutional form required. Priority date 3/1; no closing date. Applicants notified on rolling basis starting 1/1, must reply by 5/1 or within 4 week(s) of notification. **Transfers:** No deadline.

Contact. Patrick Bonones, Director of Financial Aid
4484 Peachtree Road NE
Atlanta, GA 30319-2797

Oxford College of Emory University

Oxford, Georgia
www.emory.edu/OXFORD
Two-year private **Federal Code: 001565**

	Living at home	On-campus
Tuition and fees:	$20,840	$20,840
Per-credit charge:	$859	$859
Room and board:		$6,352
Board only:	$1,810	
Books and supplies:	$700	$700
Personal expenses:	$1,400	$1,400
Transportation:	$750	$350

Undergraduate aid. **Need-based:** Average financial aid package for full-time students was $10,764. 81% awarded as scholarships/grants, 19% as loans/jobs. Need-based aid available for part-time students. **Non-need-based:** Scholarships based on academics, leadership, state/district residency. **Student debt:** 51% of graduating class borrowed to fund education; average debt was $6,125.

Freshman aid. **Need-based:** Average loan $2,625. **Non-need based:** 23 without need received awards.

Merit scholarships. Deadline of November 15 to apply for Oxford College Scholars Program along with admission application. Finalists invited to campus to compete for Woodruff Scholarships (covering full tuition and room and board), Dean's Scholarships (covering full tuition), and Faculty Scholarships (covering half the tuition), all of which are for 4 years. 2-year scholarships which range from $3,000 to $6,000 a year are also awarded.

Policies to reduce costs. Tuition/fee waivers for family of clergy, employees and their families. Credit/placement for qualifying scores on AP, IB examinations. Work study available nights and weekends.

Payment plans. Installment payment.

Application procedures. FAFSA, CSS PROFILE required. CSS PROFILE required of those applying for institutional need based aid. Priority date 2/15; closing date 4/1. Applicants notified by 4/1, must reply by 5/1 or within 2 week(s) of notification. **Transfers:** Priority date 2/15.

Contact. **Financial aid office:** (770) 784-8303
Jennifer Taylor, Associate Dean of Admission and Financial Aid
100 Hamill Street
Oxford, GA 30054-1418

Paine College

Augusta, Georgia
www.paine.edu
Four-year private **Federal Code: 001587**

	Living at home	On-campus
Tuition and fees (2002-2003):	$8,640	$8,640
Room and board:		$3,752
Board only:	$1,125	
Books and supplies:	$600	$600
Personal expenses:	$1,484	$1,484
Transportation:	$1,826	$2,434

Undergraduate aid. **Non-need-based:** Scholarships based on academics, alumni affiliation, athletics, music/drama, religious affiliation.

Policies to reduce costs. Tuition/fee waivers for children of alumni, family members, family of clergy, employees and their families. Credit/placement for qualifying scores on AP, CLEP examinations. Work study available nights, weekends and for part-time students.

Payment plans. Installment payment.

Application procedures. FAFSA, institutional form required. Priority date 3/15; closing date 4/15. Applicants notified on rolling basis starting 3/15, must reply within 2 week(s) of notification.

Contact. **Financial aid office:** (706) 821-8262
Gerri Bogan, Director of Financial Aid
1235 15th Street
Augusta, GA 30901-3182

Piedmont College

Demorest, Georgia
www.piedmont.edu
Four-year private **Federal Code: 001588**

	Living at home	On-campus
Tuition and fees (2002-2003):	$12,500	$12,500
Room and board:		$4,400
Board only:	$900	
Books and supplies:	$850	$850
Personal expenses:	$5,025	$2,910
Transportation:	$1,680	$1,400

Undergraduate aid. Need-based: Average financial aid package for full-time students was $7,681; for part-time $1,924. 37% awarded as scholarships/grants, 63% as loans/jobs. **Non-need-based:** 70% awarded as scholarships/grants, 30% as loans/jobs. Scholarships based on academics, alumni affiliation, art, leadership, minority status, music/drama, religious affiliation, state/district residency. **Student debt:** 74% of graduating class borrowed to fund education; average debt was $13,614. **Additional information:** College meets 100% of unmet direct financial need for early applicants.

Freshman aid. Need-based: Out of 141 full-time freshmen, 140 applied for aid; 122 were judged to have need; of these 122 received aid. Average package met 65% of need. 79 students had full need met. Average scholarship/grant was $2,492; average loan $2,142. **Non-need based:** 107 full-time freshmen with need received non-need scholarships; 23 without need received awards.

Merit scholarships. Each year high school seniors superior in academics, leadership, and extracurricular activities are invited to campus for an overnight scholarship competition.

Policies to reduce costs. Tuition/fee waivers for family of clergy, employees and their families. Credit/placement for qualifying scores on AP, CLEP examinations.

Payment plans. Credit card, installment payment.

Application procedures. FAFSA, institutional form required. Priority date 5/1; no closing date. Applicants notified on rolling basis starting 3/1, must reply within 2 week(s) of notification. **Transfers:** Priority date 5/1; no deadline.

Contact. Financial aid office: (706) 776-0103
Kimberly Lovell, Director of Financial Aid
Box 10
Demorest, GA 30535-0010

Reinhardt College

Waleska, Georgia
www.reinhardt.edu
Four-year private **Federal Code: 001589**

	Living at home	On-campus
Tuition and fees (2002-2003):	$8,875	$8,875
Room and board:		$5,030
Books and supplies:	$300	$300

Undergraduate aid. Need-based: Need-based aid available for full-time and part-time students. **Non-need-based:** Scholarships based on academics, alumni affiliation, art, athletics.

Policies to reduce costs. Credit/placement for qualifying scores on AP, CLEP examinations.

Payment plans. Credit card, installment, deferred payment.

Application procedures. FAFSA, institutional form required. Priority date 5/1; no closing date. Applicants notified on rolling basis starting 4/1, must reply within 2 week(s) of notification.

Contact. Financial aid office: (770) 720-5667
Mary Parker, Director for Financial Aid
7300 Reinhardt College Circle
Waleska, GA 30183

Savannah College of Art and Design

Savannah, Georgia
www.scad.edu
Four-year private **Federal Code: 015022**

	Living at home	On-campus
Tuition and fees:	$19,535	$19,535
Room and board:		$8,175
Board only:	$500	
Books and supplies:	$1,500	$1,500
Personal expenses:	$1,500	$1,500
Transportation:	$1,000	$500

Undergraduate aid. Need-based: Average financial aid package for full-time students was $8,206; for part-time $7,816. 52% awarded as scholarships/grants, 48% as loans/jobs. **Non-need-based:** 58% awarded as scholarships/grants, 42% as loans/jobs. Scholarships based on academics, art, music/drama, state/district residency. **Additional information:** Degree-seeking students may be awarded maximum of one scholarship from college, but may receive additional scholarships from other sources, as well as additional forms of financial aid. Scholarships based on academic achievement are awarded through admission office based on certain criteria.

Freshman aid. Need-based: Out of 1,043 full-time freshmen, 670 applied for aid; 525 were judged to have need; of these 503 received aid. Average package met 46% of need. 170 students had full need met. Average scholarship/grant was $3,735; average loan $2,509. **Non-need based:** 171 full-time freshmen with need received non-need scholarships; 41 without need received awards.

Merit scholarships. May and Paul Poetter Scholarship: $7,500 per year; National Merit finalist, valedictorian or salutatorian, 1450 SAT or composite 33 ACT. Academic Honors Scholarship: $3,000; National Merit semifinalist or 1250-1440 SAT or 27-32 ACT. Academic Merit Scholarship; $1,500; 1100-1240 SAT or 24-26 ACT. SCAD Scholars (deadline March 1); $7,500; outstanding academic achievement; excellence in art and design; 3.0 GPA, 1250 SAT/27 ACT or International Baccalaureate diploma program. Transfer Scholars; $7,500; for transfer students; outstanding academic achievement, honors, awards. Combined Merit Scholarships; undergraduate students who have shown outstanding ability in both academic and artistic endeavors. HOPE scholarship; Georgia applicants. Frances Larkin McCommon Scholarship; $7,500; superior artistic ability through portfolio presentation. Artistic Honors Scholarship; $3,000; first place in the Congressional Art Competition, Governor's Honors Programs, Governor's Schools, or other similar approved programs.

Policies to reduce costs. Tuition/fee waivers for employees and their families. Credit/placement for qualifying scores on AP examinations. Work study available nights and weekends.

Payment plans. Credit card, installment, deferred payment.

Application procedures. FAFSA, institutional form required. Priority date 4/1; no closing date. Applicants notified on rolling basis starting 7/1, must reply within 4 week(s) of notification. **Transfers:** No deadline. Transfer students eligible to apply for academic and portfolio scholarships.

Contact. Financial aid office: (912) 525-6109
Cindy Bradley, Director of Financial Aid
Admission Department
Savannah, GA 31402

Savannah State University

Savannah, Georgia
www.savstate.edu
Four-year public **Federal Code: 001590**

	Living at home	On-campus
Tuition and fees (2002-2003):	$2,628	$2,628
Out-of-state:	$8,658	$8,658
Room and board:		$4,386
Books and supplies:	$750	$750
Personal expenses:	$800	$800
Transportation:	$700	$700

Undergraduate aid. Non-need-based: Scholarships based on academics, alumni affiliation, music/drama.

Merit scholarships. TIGER-Award, amount varies, must demonstrate academic promise. SSU-Award, amount varies, 3.0 GPA, 1000 SAT, 19 ACT. Presidential Scholar-full tuition, exceptional academic achievement.

Policies to reduce costs. Tuition/fee waivers for senior citizens. Credit/placement for qualifying scores on AP, CLEP examinations.

Application procedures. FAFSA required. Priority date 5/1; closing date 8/1. Applicants notified on rolling basis starting 4/15, must reply within 2 week(s) of notification. **Transfers:** Transfer students must submit financial aid transcripts from previous institution.

Contact. **Financial aid office:** (912) 356-2253
Jerrie Huewitt, Assistant Director of Financial Aid
State College Branch
Savannah, GA 31404

Savannah Technical College

Savannah, Georgia
www.savtec.org
Two-year public **Federal Code: 005618**

	Living at home
Tuition and fees (2002-2003):	$1,077
Out-of-state:	$1,977
Per-credit charge:	$25
Per-credit out-of-state:	$50
Books and supplies:	$600

Undergraduate aid. Non-need-based: Scholarships based on academics, leadership, minority status, state/district residency.

Policies to reduce costs. Tuition/fee waivers for senior citizens. Credit/placement for qualifying scores on CLEP examinations.

Payment plans. Credit card payment.

Application procedures. No deadline. Applicants notified on rolling basis. **Transfers:** No deadline.

Contact. Carol Jones, Financial Aid Specialist
5717 White Bluff Road
Savannah, GA 31405

Shorter College

Rome, Georgia
www.shorter.edu
Four-year private **Federal Code: 001591**

	Living at home	On-campus
Tuition and fees:	$10,640	$10,640
Room and board:		$5,565
Board only:	$2,200	
Books and supplies:	$700	$700
Personal expenses:	$3,300	$2,300
Transportation:	$2,100	$1,000

Undergraduate aid. Need-based: Average financial aid package for full-time students was $9,416; for part-time $6,739. 67% awarded as scholarships/grants, 33% as loans/jobs. **Non-need-based:** 73% awarded as scholarships/grants, 27% as loans/jobs. Scholarships based on academics, alumni affiliation, art, athletics, leadership, minority status, music/drama, religious affiliation, state/district residency. **Additional information:** Cost is reduced for all in-state students by state tuition equalization grant program. College matches this for out-of-state full-time students.

Freshman aid. Need-based: Out of 218 full-time freshmen, 184 applied for aid; 140 were judged to have need; of these 140 received aid. Average package met 72% of need. 44 students had full need met. Average scholarship/grant was $7,602; average loan $2,495. **Non-need based:** 34 full-time freshmen with need received non-need scholarships; 66 without need received awards; 12 received athletic scholarships.

Merit scholarships. Presidential Scholarship; 20 awarded; full tuition for 4 years. Provost Scholarship; 40 awarded; full tuition but applicants must cover any tuition increases.

Policies to reduce costs. Tuition/fee waivers for senior citizens, family members, family of clergy, employees and their families. Credit/placement for qualifying scores on AP, IB, CLEP examinations.

Payment plans. Credit card, installment payment.

Application procedures. FAFSA, institutional form required. Priority date 4/1; no closing date. Applicants notified on rolling basis starting 3/1, must reply within 2 week(s) of notification.

Contact. **Financial aid office:** (706) 233-7227
Philip Hawkins, Director for Financial Aid
315 Shorter Avenue
Rome, GA 30165

South Georgia College

Douglas, Georgia
www.sga.edu
Two-year public **Federal Code: 001592**

	Living at home	On-campus
Tuition and fees (2002-2003):	$1,588	$1,588
Out-of-state:	$5,584	$5,584
Per-credit charge:	$56	$56
Per-credit out-of-state:	$222	$222
Room and board:		$3,190
Books and supplies:	$660	$660
Personal expenses:	$825	$825
Transportation:	$660	$660

Undergraduate aid. Need-based: Need-based aid available for full-time and part-time students. **Non-need-based:** Scholarships based on academics.

Policies to reduce costs. Tuition/fee waivers for senior citizens. Credit/placement for qualifying scores on AP, IB, CLEP examinations.

Payment plans. Credit card payment.

Application procedures. FAFSA, institutional form required. Priority date 6/1; no closing date. Applicants notified on rolling basis starting 7/6, must reply within 2 week(s) of notification.

Contact. Gregory Fowler, Director of Financial Aid
100 West College Park Drive
Douglas, GA 31533-5098

South University

Savannah, Georgia
www.southuniversity.edu
Four-year proprietary **Federal Code: 013039**

College costs. Academic year tuition for physical therapy assistant program $10,165; for physician assistant program $13,800.

	Living at home
Tuition and fees:	$9,585
Books and supplies:	$750

Undergraduate aid. Non-need-based: Scholarships based on state/district residency.

Merit scholarships. South College Academic Scholarship; 1 awarded full-tuition, 1 awarded half-tuition. Youth Futures Scholarship Program for students recommended through Youth Futures Authority; 2 awarded.

Policies to reduce costs. Tuition/fee waivers for employees and their families. Credit/placement for qualifying scores on AP, IB, CLEP examinations.

Payment plans. Credit card, installment, deferred payment.

Application procedures. FAFSA required. No deadline. Applicants notified on rolling basis starting 9/1. **Transfers:** No deadline.

Contact. Director of Financial Aid
709 Mall Boulevard
Savannah, GA 31406

Southern Polytechnic State University

Marietta, Georgia
www.spsu.edu
Four-year public **Federal Code: 001570**

	Living at home	On-campus
Tuition and fees (2002-2003):	$2,452	$2,452
Out-of-state:	$8,482	$8,482
Room and board:		$4,806
Board only:	$774	
Books and supplies:	$1,000	$1,000
Personal expenses:	$1,356	$1,356
Transportation:	$1,224	$724

Undergraduate aid. Need-based: Average financial aid package for full-time students was $4,463; for part-time $2,872. 40% awarded as scholarships/grants, 60% as loans/jobs. **Non-need-based:** 50% awarded as scholarships/grants, 50% as loans/jobs. Scholarships based on academics, athletics. **Student debt:** 43% of graduating class borrowed to fund education; average debt was $16,585.

Freshman aid. **Need-based:** Out of 389 full-time freshmen, 270 applied for aid; 154 were judged to have need; of these 143 received aid. Average package met 65% of need. 43 students had full need met. Average scholarship/grant was $2,700; average loan $2,430. **Non-need based:** 50 full-time freshmen with need received non-need scholarships; 33 without need received awards; 3 received athletic scholarships.

Policies to reduce costs. Tuition/fee waivers for senior citizens, employees and their families. Credit/placement for qualifying scores on AP, IB, CLEP examinations. Work study available nights, weekends and for part-time students.

Payment plans. Credit card payment.

Application procedures. FAFSA required. Priority date 3/15; no closing date. Applicants notified on rolling basis starting 5/15, must reply within 2 week(s) of notification.

Contact. **Financial aid office:** (770) 528-7290
Helen Spivak, Director of Financial Aid
1100 South Marietta Parkway
Marietta, GA 30060-2896

Southwest Georgia Technical College

Thomasville, Georgia
www.swgtc.net
Two-year public **Federal Code: 005615**

	Living at home
Tuition and fees (projected):	$1,416
Per-credit charge:	$26
Books and supplies:	$800
Personal expenses:	$3,200

Undergraduate aid. **Need-based:** 97% awarded as scholarships/grants, 3% as loans/jobs. Need-based aid available for part-time students. **Non-need-based:** Scholarships based on state/district residency.

Merit scholarships. Hope Scholarship pays tuition. Available to GA residents with 3.0 minimum GPA.

Policies to reduce costs. Tuition/fee waivers for senior citizens. Work study available nights.

Payment plans. Credit card payment.

Application procedures. FAFSA, institutional form required. No deadline. Applicants notified on rolling basis starting 7/1. **Transfers:** No deadline.

Contact. **Financial aid office:** (229) 225-5221
Michael Rayburn, Director of Financial Aid
15689 US Highway 19N
Thomasville, GA 31729

Spelman College

Atlanta, Georgia
www.spelman.edu
Four-year private **Federal Code: 001594**

	Living at home	On-campus
Tuition and fees (2002-2003):	$12,525	$12,525
Room and board:		$7,450
Books and supplies:	$1,150	$1,150
Personal expenses:	$2,100	$2,100
Transportation:	$1,044	$1,044

Undergraduate aid. All financial aid based on need. Need-based aid available for full-time and part-time students.

Policies to reduce costs. Tuition/fee waivers for employees and their families. Credit/placement for qualifying scores on AP, IB, CLEP examinations. Work study available nights, weekends and for part-time students.

Payment plans. Installment, deferred payment.

Application procedures. FAFSA, institutional form, CSS PROFILE required. Priority date 4/1; closing date 4/15. Applicants notified on rolling basis starting 2/15, must reply within 2 week(s) of notification. **Transfers:** Closing date 10/1. No special aid for transfer students for the first year.

Contact. Lenora Jackson, Director of Student Financial Services
350 Spelman Lane Southwest Campus Box 277
Atlanta, GA 30314

State University of West Georgia

Carrollton, Georgia
www.westga.edu
Four-year public **Federal Code: 001601**

	Living at home	On-campus
Tuition and fees (2002-2003):	$2,558	$2,558
Out-of-state:	$8,588	$8,588
Room and board:		$4,044
Books and supplies:	$600	$600

Undergraduate aid. **Need-based:** Average financial aid package for full-time students was $6,425; for part-time $2,865. 60% awarded as scholarships/grants, 40% as loans/jobs. **Non-need-based:** 58% awarded as scholarships/grants, 42% as loans/jobs. Scholarships based on academics, alumni affiliation, athletics, leadership, minority status.

Freshman aid. **Need-based:** Out of 1,657 full-time freshmen, 1,549 applied for aid; 859 were judged to have need; of these 844 received aid. Average package met 76% of need. 266 students had full need met. Average scholarship/grant was $4,268; average loan $1,640. **Non-need based:** 784 full-time freshmen with need received non-need scholarships; 729 without need received awards; 29 received athletic scholarships.

Policies to reduce costs. Tuition/fee waivers for senior citizens, employees and their families. Credit/placement for qualifying scores on AP, IB, CLEP examinations. Work study available nights.

Payment plans. Credit card payment.

Application procedures. FAFSA required. Priority date 4/1; no closing date. Applicants notified on rolling basis starting 5/15, must reply within 4 week(s) of notification. **Transfers:** Priority date 4/1; no deadline.

Contact. Kimberly Jordan, Director of Financial Aid
1600 Maple Street
Carrollton, GA 30118-0001

Thomas University

Thomasville, Georgia
www.thomasu.edu
Four-year private **Federal Code: 001555**

	Living at home	On-campus
Tuition and fees:	$9,020	$9,020
Room only:		$2,400
Board only:	$2,400	
Books and supplies:	$900	$900
Personal expenses:	$1,000	$1,000
Transportation:	$1,600	$1,600

Undergraduate aid. **Need-based:** Average financial aid package for full-time students was $5,372; for part-time $6,900. 44% awarded as scholarships/grants, 56% as loans/jobs. **Non-need-based:** 40% awarded as scholarships/grants, 60% as loans/jobs. Scholarships based on academics, athletics, state/district residency. **Student debt:** 53% of graduating class borrowed to fund education; average debt was $11,451.

Freshman aid. **Need-based:** Out of 56 full-time freshmen, 53 applied for aid; 53 were judged to have need; of these 53 received aid. Average package met 34% of need. 36 students had full need met. Average scholarship/grant was $3,124; average loan $2,581. **Non-need based:** 19 full-time freshmen with need received non-need scholarships; 11 without need received awards; 16 received athletic scholarships.

Policies to reduce costs. Tuition/fee waivers for senior citizens, employees and their families. Credit/placement for qualifying scores on AP, CLEP examinations.

Payment plans. Credit card, installment, deferred payment.

Application procedures. FAFSA, institutional form required. Priority date 7/1; no closing date. Applicants notified on rolling basis. **Transfers:** No deadline. Previous college attended must submit academic transcripts. Financial aid received during current academic year from previous school will be verified through NSLDS.

Contact. **Financial aid office:** (229) 227-6931
Debbie Wiggins, Director of Financial Aid
1501 Millpond Road
Thomasville, GA 31792-7499

Toccoa Falls College

Toccoa Falls, Georgia
www.tfc.edu
Four-year private **Federal Code: 001596**

	Living at home	On-campus
Tuition and fees:	$11,300	$11,300
Room and board:		$4,300
Books and supplies:	$800	$800

Undergraduate aid. Need-based: Need-based aid available for full-time and part-time students. **Non-need-based:** Scholarships based on academics, leadership, music/drama, religious affiliation.

Merit scholarships. Music and Leadership scholarships available to qualified students as well as scholarships for entering freshman who were valedictorians of their high school classes. Honors scholarships covering up to full tuition and renewable yearly for students with qualifying ACT/SAT scores who maintain a GPA of at least 3.3 also available.

Policies to reduce costs. Tuition/fee waivers for senior citizens, family members, family of clergy, employees and their families. Prepayment discount; credit/placement for qualifying scores on AP, IB, CLEP examinations.

Payment plans. Credit card, installment payment.

Application procedures. FAFSA, institutional form required. Priority date 3/1; no closing date. Applicants notified on rolling basis starting 3/1. **Transfers:** Need based aid awarded to students based on documented need reflected in information submitted to the federal government.

Contact. **Financial aid office:** (706) 886-6831 ext. 5234
Vince Welch, Financial Aid Director
Office of Admissions
Toccoa Falls, GA 30598-0368

Truett-McConnell College

Cleveland, Georgia
www.truett.edu
Two-year private **Federal Code: 001597**

	Living at home	On-campus
Tuition and fees (2002-2003):	$7,800	$7,800
Per-credit charge:	$260	$260
Room and board:		$3,800
Board only:	$2,000	
Books and supplies:	$800	$800
Personal expenses:	$875	$900
Transportation:	$1,075	$750

Undergraduate aid. Need-based: Need-based aid available for full-time and part-time students. **Non-need-based:** Scholarships based on academics, athletics, music/drama, religious affiliation, state/district residency.

Policies to reduce costs. Tuition/fee waivers for family members, family of clergy, employees and their families. Credit/placement for qualifying scores on AP, CLEP examinations.

Payment plans. Credit card, installment payment.

Application procedures. FAFSA, institutional form required. Priority date 6/1; no closing date. Applicants notified on rolling basis starting 4/1, must reply within 2 week(s) of notification. **Transfers:** No deadline.

Contact. **Financial aid office:** (800) 226-8621
Robert Gregory, Director of Financial Aid
100 Alumni Drive
Cleveland, GA 30528

University of Georgia

Athens, Georgia
www.uga.edu
Four-year public **Federal Code: 001598**

	Living at home	On-campus
Tuition and fees (2002-2003):	$3,616	$3,616
Out-of-state:	$12,986	$12,986
Room and board:		$5,216
Board only:	$2,276	
Books and supplies:	$610	$610
Personal expenses:	$2,424	$1,682

Undergraduate aid. Need-based: Average financial aid package for full-time students was $6,874; for part-time $5,493. 60% awarded as scholarships/grants, 40% as loans/jobs. **Non-need-based:** 76% awarded as scholarships/grants, 24% as loans/jobs. Scholarships based on academics, art, athletics, leadership, music/drama, state/district residency.

Freshman aid. Need-based: Out of 4,295 full-time freshmen, 3,891 applied for aid; 1,190 were judged to have need; of these 1,179 received aid. Average package met 81% of need. 525 students had full need met. Average scholarship/grant was $5,670; average loan $2,270. **Non-need based:** 416 full-time freshmen with need received non-need scholarships; 2,639 without need received awards; 98 received athletic scholarships.

Policies to reduce costs. Tuition/fee waivers for senior citizens, employees and their families. Credit/placement for qualifying scores on AP, IB, CLEP examinations. Work study available nights, weekends and for part-time students.

Payment plans. Credit card payment.

Application procedures. FAFSA required. Priority date 3/3; closing date 8/1. Applicants notified on rolling basis starting 5/1, must reply within 2 week(s) of notification.

Contact. Ray Tripp, Director, Student Financial Aid
212 Terrell Hall
Athens, GA 30602

Valdosta State University

Valdosta, Georgia
www.valdosta.edu
Four-year public **Federal Code: 001599**

	Living at home	On-campus
Tuition and fees (2002-2003):	$2,634	$2,634
Out-of-state:	$8,664	$8,664
Room and board:		$4,680
Board only:	$1,125	
Books and supplies:	$750	$750
Personal expenses:	$1,355	$1,355
Transportation:	$1,355	$1,355

Undergraduate aid. Need-based: Average financial aid package for full-time students was $8,366; for part-time $7,150. 51% awarded as scholarships/grants, 49% as loans/jobs. **Non-need-based:** 35% awarded as scholarships/grants, 65% as loans/jobs. Scholarships based on academics, athletics. **Student debt:** 64% of graduating class borrowed to fund education; average debt was $16,681.

Freshman aid. Need-based: Out of 1,584 full-time freshmen, 1,468 applied for aid; 725 were judged to have need; of these 725 received aid. Average package met 87% of need. 318 students had full need met. Average scholarship/grant was $2,944; average loan $2,204. **Non-need based:** 592 full-time freshmen with need received non-need scholarships; 435 without need received awards; 43 received athletic scholarships.

Policies to reduce costs. Tuition/fee waivers for senior citizens, employees and their families. Credit/placement for qualifying scores on AP, IB, CLEP examinations.

Payment plans. Credit card payment.

Application procedures. FAFSA, institutional form required. Priority date 4/1; no closing date. Applicants notified on rolling basis starting 6/1, must reply within 2 week(s) of notification. **Transfers:** Priority date 6/1; no deadline.

Contact. Doug Tanner, Director of Financial Aid
1500 North Patterson Street
Valdosta, GA 31698

Waycross College

Waycross, Georgia
www.waycross.edu
Two-year public **Federal Code: 013537**

	Living at home
Tuition and fees (2002-2003):	$1,478
Out-of-state:	$5,474
Per-credit charge:	$56
Per-credit out-of-state:	$222
Books and supplies:	$500
Personal expenses:	$900
Transportation:	$600

Undergraduate aid. Non-need-based: Scholarships based on academics, alumni affiliation, leadership.

Policies to reduce costs. Tuition/fee waivers for adults, senior citizens, employees and their families. Credit/placement for qualifying scores on AP, CLEP examinations. Work study available nights, weekends and for part-time students.

Payment plans. Credit card payment.

Application procedures. FAFSA, institutional form required. Priority date 5/1; no closing date. Applicants notified on rolling basis, must reply within 2 week(s) of notification. **Transfers:** No deadline.

Contact. Debbie Howard, Assistant Director of Financial Aid
2001 South Georgia Parkway
Waycross, GA 31503

Wesleyan College

Macon, Georgia
www.wesleyancollege.edu
Four-year private **Federal Code: 001600**

	Living at home	On-campus
Tuition and fees:	$10,420	$10,420
Room and board:		$7,450
Books and supplies:	$600	$600
Personal expenses:	$1,500	$1,500

Undergraduate aid. Need-based: Average financial aid package for full-time students was $11,432; for part-time $9,954. 65% awarded as scholarships/grants, 35% as loans/jobs. **Non-need-based:** 63% awarded as scholarships/grants, 37% as loans/jobs. Scholarships based on academics, alumni affiliation, art, job skills, leadership, music/drama. **Student debt:** 76% of graduating class borrowed to fund education; average debt was $20,627.

Freshman aid. Need-based: Out of 151 full-time freshmen, 110 applied for aid; 88 were judged to have need; of these 88 received aid. Average package met 86% of need. 22 students had full need met. Average scholarship/grant was $9,920; average loan $3,383. **Non-need based:** 15 full-time freshmen with need received non-need scholarships; 81 without need received awards.

Merit scholarships. Academic Scholarships based on minimum 1100 SAT or 25 ACT and 3.75 GPA; or 1200 SAT/27 ACT and 3.5 GPA; range in value from 50% to 100% of tuition. Special $3,000 grant available to students who have at least a 1050 SAT/23 ACT and a 3.25 GPA. Talent Awards in music, art and theater ranging from $500-$5,000.

Policies to reduce costs. Tuition/fee waivers for adults, children of alumni, senior citizens, family members, family of clergy, employees and their families. Credit/placement for qualifying scores on AP, IB, CLEP examinations. Work study available nights, weekends and for part-time students.

Payment plans. Credit card, installment payment.

Application procedures. FAFSA, institutional form required. No deadline. Applicants notified on rolling basis starting 2/1, must reply by 5/1 or within 2 week(s) of notification. Early decision closing date 11/15. **Transfers:** Fellowships available based on number of hours and cumulative GPA transferred in, with minimum 30 semester or 45 quarter hours and 3.0 GPA required.

Contact. Financial aid office: (478) 757-5205
Wendy Newingham, Director of Financial Aid
4760 Forsyth Road
Macon, GA 31210-4462

West Georgia Technical College

LaGrange, Georgia
www.westgatech.org
Two-year public **Federal Code: 005614**

College costs. Alabama residents pay in-state costs.

	Living at home
Tuition and fees (projected):	$1,424
Out-of-state:	$2,672
Per-credit charge:	$26
Per-credit out-of-state:	$52
Books and supplies:	$600
Transportation:	$1,707

Undergraduate aid. Need-based: Need-based aid available for full-time and part-time students. **Non-need-based:** Scholarships based on academics, state/district residency.

Merit scholarships. Coca-Cola Scholarship awards $1,000. WGTC Foundation awards $100.

Policies to reduce costs. Tuition/fee waivers for senior citizens, family of clergy, employees and their families. Work study available nights and for part-time students.

Payment plans. Credit card, deferred payment.

Application procedures. FAFSA, institutional form required. Closing date 6/7. Applicants notified on rolling basis, must reply within 1 week(s) of notification. **Transfers:** Priority date 12/1; closing date 2/16. Hold placed on all students with incomplete files at pre-registration for the next quarter. Student can only have financial aid one quarter without complete file. Financial aid forms to be filed 30 days prior to quarter.

Contact. Financial aid office: (706) 845-4323
Dorothy Cantor, Financial Aid Coordinator
303 Fort Drive
LaGrange, GA 30240

Young Harris College

Young Harris, Georgia
www.yhc.edu
Two-year private **Federal Code: 001604**

	Living at home	On-campus
Tuition and fees:	$12,400	$12,400
Per-credit charge:	$472	$472
Room and board:		$4,318
Board only:	$2,474	
Books and supplies:	$650	$650
Personal expenses:	$1,650	$1,050
Transportation:	$900	$600

Undergraduate aid. Need-based: Need-based aid available for full-time and part-time students. **Non-need-based:** Scholarships based on academics, art, athletics, job skills, music/drama, state/district residency.

Merit scholarships. Academic Scholarships $3,000-$5,000, based on index including GPA and SAT/ACT; additional upgrades to a percentage of recipients range from additional $1,000 to full tuition, room and board.

Policies to reduce costs. Tuition/fee waivers for family of clergy, employees and their families. Tuition at time of enrollment guaranteed for 2 years; credit/placement for qualifying scores on AP, IB, CLEP examinations. Work study available nights.

Payment plans. Installment payment.

Application procedures. FAFSA, institutional form required. Priority date 4/1; no closing date. Applicans notified on rolling basis starting 3/1, must reply within 2 week(s) of notification. **Transfers:** No deadline.

Contact. Financial aid office: (706) 379-3111 ext. 5117
Joanne Putnam, Financial Aid Director
Box 116
Young Harris, GA 30582-0116

Hawaii

Brigham Young University-Hawaii

Laie, Hawaii
www.byuh.edu
Four-year private **Federal Code: 001606**

College costs. 50% higher tuition and per-credit-hour charges for students who are not members of Church of Jesus Christ of Latter-Day Saints.

	Living at home	On-campus
Tuition and fees:	$2,589	$2,589
Out-of-district:	$3,877	$3,877
Room and board:		$4,660
Books and supplies:	$875	$875
Personal expenses:	$1,590	$1,590

Undergraduate aid. Need-based: 29% awarded as scholarships/grants, 71% as loans/jobs. Need-based aid available for part-time students. **Non-need-based:** 22% awarded as scholarships/grants, 78% as loans/jobs. Scholarships based on academics, art, athletics, leadership, music/drama, state/district residency. **Additional information:** Closing date for scholarship applications May 1.

Policies to reduce costs. Tuition/fee waivers for employees and their families. Credit/placement for qualifying scores on AP, IB, CLEP examinations.

Payment plans. Credit card, installment payment.

Application procedures. FAFSA required. Closing date 4/30. Applicants notified by 6/1, must reply by 8/31. **Transfers:** Closing date 3/15.

Contact. Financial aid office: (808) 293-3749
William Oldroyd, Director of Financial Aid
P.O. Box 1973
Laie, HI 96762-1294

Chaminade University of Honolulu

Honolulu, Hawaii
www.chaminade.edu
Four-year private **Federal Code: 001605**

	Living at home	On-campus
Tuition and fees:	$13,380	$13,380
Room and board:		$7,380
Books and supplies:	$720	$720
Personal expenses:	$1,350	$1,350
Transportation:	$246	$246

Undergraduate aid. Need-based: Average financial aid package for full-time students was $9,918; for part-time $3,211. 34% awarded as scholarships/grants, 66% as loans/jobs. **Non-need-based:** 57% awarded as scholarships/grants, 43% as loans/jobs. Scholarships based on academics, athletics. **Additional information:** For students whose eligibility for federal and institutional aid does not meet entire costs, alternative student loans may be secured for eligible applicants.

Freshman aid. Need-based: Average package met 51% of need. Average scholarship/grant was $5,203; average loan $2,340.

Policies to reduce costs. Tuition/fee waivers for family members, employees and their families. Prepayment discount; credit/placement for qualifying scores on IB, CLEP examinations.

Payment plans. Credit card, installment payment.

Application procedures. FAFSA, institutional form required. Priority date 3/1; no closing date. Applicants notified on rolling basis, must reply within 2 week(s) of notification.

Contact. Financial aid office: (808) 735-4780
Eric Nemoto, Director of Financial Aid
3140 Waialae Avenue
Honolulu, HI 96816

Hawaii Business College

Honolulu, Hawaii
www.hbc.edu
Two-year proprietary **Federal Code: 013615**

	Living at home
Tuition and fees:	$8,390
Per-credit charge:	$218
Books and supplies:	$900
Personal expenses:	$2,835
Transportation:	$1,017

Undergraduate aid. All financial aid based on need. Need-based aid available for full-time and part-time students.

Policies to reduce costs. Tuition/fee waivers for employees and their families. Work study available nights, weekends and for part-time students.

Payment plans. Credit card, installment payment.

Application procedures. FAFSA required. No deadline. Applicants notified on rolling basis, must reply within 3 week(s) of notification.

Contact. Financial aid office: (808) 524-4014
Roxann Bedra, Director of Financial Aid
33 South King Street, Suite 405
Honolulu, HI 96817

Hawaii Pacific University

Honolulu, Hawaii
www.hpu.edu
Four-year private **Federal Code: 007279**

	Living at home	On-campus
Tuition and fees:	$10,368	$10,368
Room and board:		$8,770
Books and supplies:	$1,200	$1,200
Personal expenses:	$600	$600
Transportation:	$400	$1,000

Undergraduate aid. Need-based: Average financial aid package for full-time students was $10,713; for part-time $8,921. 24% awarded as scholarships/grants, 76% as loans/jobs. **Non-need-based:** Scholarships based on academics, athletics, job skills, leadership, music/drama, religious affiliation. **Student debt:** 32% of graduating class borrowed to fund education; average debt was $17,946.

Freshman aid. Need-based: Out of 584 full-time freshmen, 435 applied for aid; 249 were judged to have need; of these 247 received aid. Average package met 70% of need. 43 students had full need met. Average scholarship/grant was $3,662; average loan $2,774. **Non-need based:** 100 full-time freshmen with need received non-need scholarships; 190 without need received awards; 23 received athletic scholarships.

Merit scholarships. Makana Scholarship: $1,800, for graduate of U.S. high school with GPA of 3.5 or higher; Phi Theta Kappa Scholarship: $4,230, for member of Phi Theta Kappa.

Policies to reduce costs. Tuition/fee waivers for family of clergy, employees and their families. Credit/placement for qualifying scores on AP, IB, CLEP examinations. Work study available nights, weekends and for part-time students.

Payment plans. Credit card, installment payment.

Application procedures. FAFSA required. Priority date 3/1; no closing date. Applicants notified on rolling basis starting 4/1, must reply within 3 week(s) of notification. **Transfers:** No deadline.

Contact. Financial aid office: (808) 544-0253
Josephine Stenberg, Director of Financial Aid
1164 Bishop Street
Honolulu, HI 96813

Hawaii Tokai International College

Honolulu, Hawaii
www.tokai.edu
Two-year private

	Living at home	On-campus
Tuition and fees (projected):	$9,800	$9,800
Per-credit charge:	$300	$300
Room and board:		$6,000
Books and supplies:	$800	$800
Personal expenses:		$1,200

Contact. Wanda T. Sako, Director, External Relations
2241 Kapiolani Boulevard
Honolulu, HI 96826

Heald College: Honolulu

Honolulu, Hawaii
www.heald.edu
Two-year private **Federal Code: E00886**

College costs (2002-2003). Cost of 18-month associate degree program (6 quarters): $17,100.

Undergraduate aid. All financial aid based on need. Need-based aid available for full-time and part-time students.

Policies to reduce costs. Tuition/fee waivers for employees and their families. Work study available nights, weekends and for part-time students.

Payment plans. Credit card, installment payment.

Application procedures. FAFSA required. No deadline. **Transfers:** No deadline.

Contact. 1500 Kapiolani Boulevard
Honolulu, HI 96814-3715

Remington College: Honolulu

Honolulu, Hawaii
www.remingtoncollege.edu
Two-year proprietary **Federal Code: 030121**

	Living at home
Tuition and fees:	$12,425
Per-credit charge:	$275
Personal expenses:	$1,764
Transportation:	$837

Undergraduate aid. All financial aid based on need. Need-based aid available for full-time students.

Policies to reduce costs. Tuition/fee waivers for employees and their families. Tuition at time of enrollment guaranteed for 2 years.

Payment plans. Credit card, installment payment.

Application procedures. FAFSA required. No deadline. Applicants notified on rolling basis. **Transfers:** No deadline.

Contact. Erwin Ramello, Director of Financial Services
1111 Bishop Street, Suite 400
Honolulu, HI 96813

University of Hawaii at Hilo

Hilo, Hawaii
www.uhh.hawaii.edu
Four-year public **Federal Code: 001611**

	Living at home	On-campus
Tuition and fees (2002-2003):	$2,060	$2,060
Out-of-state:	$9,080	$9,080
Room and board:		$6,043
Board only:	$1,585	
Books and supplies:	$1,017	$1,017
Personal expenses:	$991	$1,166
Transportation:	$243	$243

Undergraduate aid. Need-based: Average financial aid package for full-time students was $6,372; for part-time $5,735. 67% awarded as scholarships/grants, 33% as loans/jobs. **Non-need-based:** 18% awarded as scholarships/grants, 82% as loans/jobs. **Student debt:** 41% of graduating class borrowed to fund education; average debt was $11,236. **Additional information:** Hawaii student incentive grants and tuition waivers (merit and need-based) available to Hawaii residents at participating institutions.

Freshman aid. Need-based: Out of 542 full-time freshmen, 246 applied for aid; 238 were judged to have need; of these 200 received aid. Average package met 56% of need. 57 students had full need met. Average scholarship/grant was $2,390; average loan $1,287. **Non-need based:** 19 full-time freshmen with need received non-need scholarships.

Policies to reduce costs. Tuition/fee waivers for employees and their families. Tuition at time of enrollment guaranteed for 4 years; credit/placement for qualifying scores on AP, IB, CLEP examinations. Work study available nights and weekends.

Payment plans. Credit card payment.

Application procedures. FAFSA, institutional form required. Priority date 3/1; no closing date. Applicants notified on rolling basis starting 4/12, must reply within 2 week(s) of notification.

Contact. Financial aid office: (808) 974-7324
Jeff Schofield, Financial Aid Director
200 West Kawili Street
Hilo, HI 96720-4091

University of Hawaii at Manoa

Honolulu, Hawaii
www.uhm.hawaii.edu
Four-year public **Federal Code: 001610**

	Living at home	On-campus
Tuition and fees (2002-2003):	$4,153	$4,153
Out-of-state:	$12,253	$12,253
Room and board:		$6,043
Board only:	$2,615	
Books and supplies:	$1,017	$1,017
Personal expenses:	$991	$1,166
Transportation:	$243	$243

Undergraduate aid. All financial aid based on need. Average financial aid package for full-time students was $5,947; for part-time $5,422. 55% awarded as scholarships/grants, 45% as loans/jobs. **Student debt:** 33% of graduating class borrowed to fund education; average debt was $13,629. **Additional information:** Hawaii student incentive grants and tuition waivers (merit and need-based) available to Hawaii residents at participating institutions.

Freshman aid. Average package met 70% of need. Average scholarship/grant was $3,303; average loan $1,362.

Policies to reduce costs. Tuition/fee waivers for minority students, employees and their families. Credit/placement for qualifying scores on AP, IB examinations.

Payment plans. Credit card payment.

Application procedures. FAFSA, institutional form required. Priority date 3/15; no closing date. Applicants notified on rolling basis starting 4/1, must reply within 4 week(s) of notification. **Transfers:** Priority date 3/15.

Contact. Gail Koki, Director of Financial Aid
2600 Campus Road, RM 001
Honolulu, HI 96822-9978

University of Hawaii: Hawaii Community College

Hilo, Hawaii
www.hawcc.hawaii.edu
Two-year public **Federal Code: 005258**

	Living at home
Tuition and fees (2002-2003):	$1,340
Out-of-state:	$7,310
Per-credit charge:	$43
Per-credit out-of-state:	$242
Books and supplies:	$672
Personal expenses:	$953
Transportation:	$457

Undergraduate aid. All financial aid based on need. Need-based aid available for full-time and part-time students. **Additional information:** Hawaii student incentive grants and tuition waivers (merit and need-based) available to Hawaii residents.

Policies to reduce costs. Tuition/fee waivers for senior citizens, employees and their families. Credit/placement for qualifying scores on AP examinations.

Payment plans. Credit card payment.

Application procedures. FAFSA required. Priority date 4/1; no closing date. Applicants notified on rolling basis starting 5/1, must reply within 2 week(s) of notification. **Transfers:** Residents of Guam, Federated States of Micronesia, Palau, Marianas Islands and certain other island nations considered residents for tuition purpose.

Contact. Sheryl Lundberg-Spregue, Financial Aid Officer
200 West Kawili Street
Hilo, HI 96720-4091

University of Hawaii: Honolulu Community College

Honolulu, Hawaii
www.hcc.hawaii.edu
Two-year public **Federal Code: 001612**

	Living at home
Tuition and fees (2002-2003):	$1,320
Out-of-state:	$7,290
Per-credit charge:	$43
Per-credit out-of-state:	$242
Board only:	$1,585
Books and supplies:	$773
Personal expenses:	$1,166
Transportation:	$225

Undergraduate aid. Need-based: Need-based aid available for full-time and part-time students. **Non-need-based:** Scholarships based on academics, state/district residency. **Additional information:** Hawaii student incentive grants and tuition waivers (merit and need-based) available to Hawaii residents at participating institutions.

Policies to reduce costs. Tuition/fee waivers for employees and their families. Credit/placement for qualifying scores on AP, CLEP examinations. Work study available for part-time students.

Payment plans. Credit card payment.

Application procedures. FAFSA required. Priority date 4/1; no closing date. Applicants notified on rolling basis starting 7/1, must reply within 3 week(s) of notification.

Contact. Financial aid office: (808) 845-9116
Jannine Dyama, Financial Aid Officer
874 Dillingham Boulevard
Honolulu, HI 96817

University of Hawaii: Kauai Community College

Lihue, Hawaii
www.kauaicc.hawaii.edu
Two-year public **Federal Code: 001614**

	Living at home
Tuition and fees (2002-2003):	$1,315
Out-of-state:	$7,285
Per-credit charge:	$43
Per-credit out-of-state:	$242
Board only:	$2,550
Books and supplies:	$750
Personal expenses:	$1,000
Transportation:	$250

Undergraduate aid. Additional information: Hawaii student incentive grants and tuition waivers (merit and need-based) available to Hawaii residents.

Policies to reduce costs. Tuition/fee waivers for employees and their families. Credit/placement for qualifying scores on AP examinations. Work study available nights and for part-time students.

Payment plans. Credit card payment.

Application procedures. FAFSA, institutional form required. Priority date 3/1; closing date 5/1. Applicants notified on rolling basis starting 5/1. **Transfers:** Academic transcript evaluation by end of first semester is required.

Contact. Frances Dinnan, Financial Aid Officer
3-1901 Kaumualii Highway
Lihue, HI 96766

University of Hawaii: Leeward Community College

Pearl City, Hawaii
www.lcc.hawaii.edu
Two-year public **Federal Code: 004549**

	Living at home
Tuition and fees (2002-2003):	$1,315
Out-of-state:	$7,285
Per-credit charge:	$43
Per-credit out-of-state:	$242
Board only:	$2,515
Books and supplies:	$672
Personal expenses:	$953
Transportation:	$225

Undergraduate aid. Need-based: Need-based aid available for full-time and part-time students. **Additional information:** Leveraging Educational Assistance Partnership (LEAP) funds or tuition waivers available to students with financial need.

Policies to reduce costs. Credit/placement for qualifying scores on AP, IB, CLEP examinations.

Payment plans. Credit card payment.

Application procedures. FAFSA required. Priority date 4/15; no closing date. Applicants notified on rolling basis starting 6/1, must reply within 2 week(s) of notification.

Contact. Valerie Chun, Financial Aid Officer
96-045 Ala Ike
Pearl City, HI 96782

University of Hawaii: Maui Community College

Kahului, Hawaii
mauicc.hawaii.edu
Two-year public **Federal Code: 001615**

	Living at home	On-campus
Tuition and fees (2002-2003):	$1,308	$1,308
Out-of-state:	$7,278	$7,278
Per-credit charge:	$43	$43
Per-credit out-of-state:	$242	$242
Room only:		$1,994
Board only:	$2,576	
Books and supplies:	$796	$796
Transportation:	$457	$933

Undergraduate aid. Need-based: Need-based aid available for full-time and part-time students.

Policies to reduce costs. Tuition/fee waivers for minority students, employees and their families. Credit/placement for qualifying scores on CLEP examinations. Work study available nights and for part-time students.

Payment plans. Credit card payment.

Application procedures. FAFSA, institutional form required. Priority date 4/1; no closing date. Must reply within 4 week(s) of notification.

Contact. Financial aid office: (808) 984-3277
Paula Purdy, Financial Aid Officer
310 Kaahumanu Avenue
Kahului, HI 96732

University of Hawaii: West Oahu

Pearl City, Hawaii
www.uhwo.hawaii.edu
Upper-division public **Federal Code: 014315**

College costs. Foreign students pay out-of-state tuition rates, except for applicants from countries with reciprocity agreements.

	Living at home
Tuition and fees (2002-2003):	$2,560
Out-of-state:	$8,980
Board only:	$1,585
Books and supplies:	$940
Personal expenses:	$991
Transportation:	$225

Undergraduate aid. Need-based: Average financial aid package for full-time students was $3,961; for part-time $4,084. 57% awarded as scholarships/grants, 43% as loans/jobs. **Non-need-based:** 1% awarded as scholarships/grants, 99% as loans/jobs. Scholarships based on academics, state/district residency. **Additional information:** Hawaii student incentive grants and tuition waivers (merit and need-based) available to Hawaii residents.

Policies to reduce costs. Tuition/fee waivers for employees and their families. Credit/placement for qualifying scores on CLEP examinations.

Payment plans. Credit card payment.

Application procedures. FAFSA required. **Transfers:** Priority date 5/1; no deadline.

Contact. Jennifer Bradley, Student Services Specialist
96-129 Ala Ike
Pearl City, HI 96782

Albertson College of Idaho

Caldwell, Idaho
www.albertson.edu
Four-year private **Federal Code: 001617**

	Living at home	On-campus
Tuition and fees:	$14,400	$14,400
Room and board:		$5,358
Board only:	$1,900	
Books and supplies:	$700	$700
Personal expenses:	$700	$700
Transportation:	$550	$550

Undergraduate aid. Need-based: Average financial aid package for full-time students was $14,738; for part-time $9,987. 49% awarded as scholarships/grants, 51% as loans/jobs. **Non-need-based:** 76% awarded as scholarships/grants, 24% as loans/jobs. Scholarships based on academics, alumni affiliation, art, athletics, job skills, leadership, minority status, music/drama, religious affiliation. **Student debt:** 71% of graduating class borrowed to fund education; average debt was $17,181.

Freshman aid. Need-based: Average package met 81% of need. Average scholarship/grant was $3,851; average loan $2,114.

Policies to reduce costs. Tuition/fee waivers for adults, children of alumni, senior citizens, minority students, family members, employees and their families. Prepayment discount; credit/placement for qualifying scores on AP, IB examinations. Work study available for part-time students.

Payment plans. Credit card, installment payment.

Application procedures. FAFSA, institutional form required. Priority date 2/15; no closing date. Applicants notified on rolling basis starting 4/1, must reply within 3 week(s) of notification.

Contact. Financial aid office: (208) 459-5308
Juanita Pearson, Director of Student Financial Services
2112 Cleveland Boulevard
Caldwell, ID 83605

Boise Bible College

Boise, Idaho
www.boisebible.edu
Four-year private **Federal Code: 015783**

	Living at home	On-campus
Tuition and fees (2002-2003):	$5,700	$5,700
Room and board:		$4,200
Board only:	$2,420	
Books and supplies:	$605	$605
Personal expenses:	$935	$1,210
Transportation:	$1,210	$1,320

Undergraduate aid. Need-based: Need-based aid available for full-time and part-time students. **Non-need-based:** Scholarships based on academics, leadership, music/drama, religious affiliation.

Policies to reduce costs. Tuition/fee waivers for family of clergy, employees and their families. Prepayment discount; credit/placement for qualifying scores on IB examinations.

Payment plans. Credit card, installment payment.

Application procedures. FAFSA, institutional form required. Priority date 5/1; no closing date. Applicants notified on rolling basis starting 5/2, must reply by 8/1 or within 2 week(s) of notification. **Transfers:** Financial aid and academic transcripts must be on file before federal aid is awarded.

Contact. Financial aid office: (800) 893-7755
Joyce Anderson, Financial Aid Officer
8695 W. Marigold Street
Boise, ID 83714-1220

Boise State University

Boise, Idaho
www.boisestate.edu
Four-year public **Federal Code: 001616**

College costs. Western Undergraduate Exchange tuition: $4,476

	Living at home	On-campus
Tuition and fees (2002-2003):	$2,984	$2,984
Out-of-state:	$9,384	$9,384
Room and board:		$4,179
Board only:	$1,898	
Books and supplies:	$920	$920
Personal expenses:	$1,123	$2,258
Transportation:	$970	$970

Undergraduate aid. Need-based: Need-based aid available for full-time and part-time students. **Non-need-based:** Scholarships based on academics, athletics, music/drama, state/district residency.

Policies to reduce costs. Tuition/fee waivers for senior citizens, employees and their families. Credit/placement for qualifying scores on AP, CLEP examinations.

Payment plans. Credit card, deferred payment.

Application procedures. FAFSA required. Priority date 4/1; no closing date. Applicants notified on rolling basis starting 6/1, must reply within 2 week(s) of notification. **Transfers:** Priority date 4/1; no deadline. Financial aid transcripts required from all postsecondary schools attended whether or not financial aid was received.

Contact. Financial aid office: (208) 426-1664
David Tolman, Director of Financial Aid
1910 University Drive
Boise, ID 83725

Brigham Young University - Idaho

Rexburg, Idaho
www.byui.edu
Four-year private **Federal Code: 001625**

College costs. Tuition for students who are not members of The Church of Jesus Christ of Latter-day Saints is $3,830 per academic year, $160 per credit hour.

	Living at home	On-campus
Tuition and fees:	$2,866	$2,866
Room and board:		$4,500
Books and supplies:	$920	$920
Personal expenses:	$1,300	$1,300
Transportation:	$1,200	$1,200

Undergraduate aid. Need-based: Need-based aid available for full-time and part-time students. **Non-need-based:** Scholarships based on academics, athletics, leadership. **Additional information:** Application deadline for merit scholarships March 1.

Policies to reduce costs. Tuition/fee waivers for employees and their families. Credit/placement for qualifying scores on AP, IB, CLEP examinations.

Payment plans. Credit card payment.

Application procedures. FAFSA required. Priority date 5/1; no closing date. Applicants notified on rolling basis starting 2/1.

Contact. Financial aid office: (208) 496-1013
Dan Gulbransen, Director of Financial Aid
120 Kimball Building
Rexburg, ID 83460-1615

College of Southern Idaho

Twin Falls, Idaho
www.csi.edu
Two-year public **Federal Code: 001619**

	Living at home	On-campus
Tuition and fees (2002-2003):	$1,550	$1,550
Out-of-state:	$4,300	$4,300
Per-credit charge:	$78	$78
Per-credit out-of-state:	$215	$215
Room and board:		$3,890
Books and supplies:	$800	$800
Personal expenses:	$1,900	$1,900
Transportation:	$1,600	$1,600

Undergraduate aid. Need-based: Need-based aid available for full-time and part-time students. **Additional information:** Out-of-state tuition waivers based on GPA and activities.

Policies to reduce costs. Tuition/fee waivers for senior citizens, employees and their families. Credit/placement for qualifying scores on AP, CLEP examinations.

Payment plans. Credit card, deferred payment.

Application procedures. FAFSA required. Priority date 3/1; no closing date. Applicants notified on rolling basis starting 4/30, must reply within 3 week(s) of notification. **Transfers:** No deadline.

Contact. Colin Randolph, Director of Student Financial Aid
Box 1238
Twin Falls, ID 83303-1238

Eastern Idaho Technical College

Idaho Falls, Idaho
www.eitc.edu
Two-year public **Federal Code: 011133**

	Living at home
Tuition and fees (2002-2003):	$1,350
Out-of-state:	$4,948
Per-credit charge:	$68
Per-credit out-of-state:	$136
Books and supplies:	$964
Personal expenses:	$1,344

Undergraduate aid. Need-based: 89% awarded as scholarships/grants, 11% as loans/jobs. Need-based aid available for part-time students. **Non-need-based:** Scholarships based on academics, job skills, state/district residency.

Policies to reduce costs. Tuition/fee waivers for employees and their families. Work study available for part-time students.

Payment plans. Credit card payment.

Application procedures. FAFSA, institutional form required. Priority date 6/1; no closing date. Applicants notified on rolling basis starting 6/1, must reply within 4 week(s) of notification.

Contact. Financial aid office: (208) 524-3000 ext. 3311
Tony Siebers, Financial Aid Officer
1600 South 25th East
Idaho Falls, ID 83404

ITT Technical Institute: Boise

Boise, Idaho
www.itt-tech.edu
Three-year proprietary **Federal Code: 004553**

College costs. Total program varies depending on course of study. Per-credit-hour charge: $347.

Policies to reduce costs. Tuition/fee waivers for employees and their families.

Payment plans. Credit card, installment payment.

Application procedures. FAFSA, institutional form required. No deadline. Applicants notified on rolling basis.

Contact. Larry Hallam, Director of Finance
12302 West Explorer Drive
Boise, ID 83713-1529

Idaho State University

Pocatello, Idaho
www.isu.edu
Four-year public **Federal Code: 001620**

College costs. Western Undergraduate Exchange tuition plus fees: $4,704

	Living at home	On-campus
Tuition and fees (2002-2003):	$3,136	$3,136
Out-of-state:	$9,376	$9,376
Room and board:		$4,410
Board only:	$2,214	
Books and supplies:	$600	$600
Personal expenses:	$1,890	$1,890
Transportation:	$810	$810

Undergraduate aid. Need-based: Need-based aid available for full-time and part-time students. **Non-need-based:** Scholarships based on academics, alumni affiliation, art, athletics, leadership, minority status, music/drama.

Policies to reduce costs. Tuition/fee waivers for senior citizens, employees and their families. Credit/placement for qualifying scores on AP, IB, CLEP examinations. Work study available nights, weekends and for part-time students.

Payment plans. Deferred payment.

Application procedures. FAFSA required. Priority date 3/15; closing date 6/30.

Contact. Financial aid office: (208) 282-2756
Doug Severs, Director of Financial Aid
PO Box 8270
Pocatello, ID 83209

Lewis-Clark State College

Lewiston, Idaho
www.lcsc.edu
Four-year public **Federal Code: 001621**

College costs. Western Undergraduate Exchange tuition plus fees: $4,278

	Living at home	On-campus
Tuition and fees (2002-2003):	$2,852	$2,852
Out-of-state:	$8,562	$8,562
Room and board:		$3,880
Board only:	$1,538	
Books and supplies:	$750	$750
Personal expenses:	$1,446	$1,446
Transportation:	$1,768	

Undergraduate aid. Need-based: Average financial aid package for full-time students was $5,008; for part-time $3,861. 47% awarded as scholarships/grants, 53% as loans/jobs. **Non-need-based:** 14% awarded as scholarships/grants, 86% as loans/jobs. Scholarships based on academics, alumni affiliation, art, athletics, job skills, leadership, minority status, music/drama.

Freshman aid. Need-based: Out of 395 full-time freshmen, 315 applied for aid; 270 were judged to have need; of these 269 received aid. Average package met 30% of need. 80 students had full need met. Average scholarship/grant was $2,781; average loan $2,621. **Non-need based:** 63 full-time freshmen with need received non-need scholarships; 95 without need received awards; 51 received athletic scholarships.

Policies to reduce costs. Tuition/fee waivers for senior citizens, employees and their families. Credit/placement for qualifying scores on AP examinations. Work study available nights, weekends and for part-time students.

Payment plans. Credit card, deferred payment.

Application procedures. FAFSA required. Priority date 3/1; no closing date. Applicants notified on rolling basis starting 3/13, must reply within 3 week(s) of notification. **Transfers:** No deadline.

Contact. Financial aid office: (208) 792-2224
Laura Hughes, Director of Financial Aid
500 Eighth Avenue
Lewiston, ID 83501-2698

North Idaho College

Coeur d'Alene, Idaho
www.nic.edu
Two-year public **Federal Code: 001623**

	Living at home	On-campus
Tuition and fees:	$1,696	$1,696
Out-of-district:	$2,696	$2,696
Out-of-state:	$5,788	$5,788
Room and board:		$5,300
Board only:	$1,700	
Books and supplies:	$600	$600
Personal expenses:	$926	$926
Transportation:	$600	$300

Undergraduate aid. Need-based: Need-based aid available for full-time and part-time students. **Non-need-based:** Scholarships based on academics, athletics, minority status, music/drama.

Policies to reduce costs. Tuition/fee waivers for senior citizens, minority students, employees and their families. Credit/placement for qualifying scores on AP, CLEP examinations. Work study available weekends and for part-time students.

Payment plans. Credit card, deferred payment.

Application procedures. FAFSA, institutional form required. Priority date 3/1; no closing date. Applicants notified on rolling basis starting 3/1, must reply by 8/1 or within 2 week(s) of notification. **Transfers:** No deadline.

Contact. Financial aid office: (208) 769-3368
Connie Dawson, Director of Financial Aid
1000 West Garden Avenue
Coeur d'Alene, ID 83814-2199

Northwest Nazarene University

Nampa, Idaho
www.nnu.edu
Four-year private **Federal Code: 001624**

	Living at home	On-campus
Tuition and fees:	$15,920	$15,920
Room and board:		$4,440
Board only:	$2,484	
Books and supplies:	$760	$760
Personal expenses:	$850	$870
Transportation:	$740	$770

Undergraduate aid. Need-based: Average financial aid package for full-time students was $11,942; for part-time $7,445. 50% awarded as scholarships/grants, 50% as loans/jobs. **Non-need-based:** 56% awarded as scholarships/grants, 44% as loans/jobs. Scholarships based on academics, athletics, job skills, state/district residency. **Student debt:** 83% of graduating class borrowed to fund education; average debt was $19,203.

Freshman aid. Need-based: Average package met 79% of need. Average scholarship/grant was $2,708; average loan $3,607.

Merit scholarships. Merit scholarships for freshmen based primarily on cumulative high school GPA and ACT test scores.

Policies to reduce costs. Tuition/fee waivers for senior citizens, family members, family of clergy, employees and their families. Credit/placement for qualifying scores on AP, IB, CLEP examinations. Work study available nights, weekends and for part-time students.

Payment plans. Credit card, installment payment.

Application procedures. FAFSA, institutional form required. Priority date 3/1; no closing date. Applicants notified on rolling basis starting 4/1, must reply within 3 week(s) of notification. **Transfers:** No deadline.

Contact. Financial aid office: (208) 467-8347
Wes Maggard, Director of Financial Aid
623 Holly Street
Nampa, ID 83686-5897

University of Idaho

Moscow, Idaho
www.its.uidaho.edu/uihome/
Four-year public **Federal Code: 001626**

College costs. Western Undergraduate Exchange tuition plus fees: $4,566

	Living at home	On-campus
Tuition and fees (2002-2003):	$3,044	$3,044
Out-of-state:	$9,764	$9,764
Room and board:		$4,680
Books and supplies:	$1,130	$1,130
Personal expenses:	$1,996	$1,996
Transportation:	$998	$998

Undergraduate aid. Need-based: Average financial aid package for full-time students was $8,072; for part-time $6,822. **Non-need-based:** Scholarships based on academics, alumni affiliation, leadership, minority status, music/drama, state/district residency. **Student debt:** 67% of graduating class borrowed to fund education; average debt was $18,413.

Freshman aid. Need-based: Out of 1,646 full-time freshmen, 1,256 applied for aid; 881 were judged to have need; of these 878 received aid. Average package met 80% of need. 309 students had full need met. Average scholarship/grant was $2,836; average loan $3,159. **Non-need based:** 805 full-time freshmen with need received non-need scholarships; 673 without need received awards; 45 received athletic scholarships.

Policies to reduce costs. Tuition/fee waivers for minority students, employees and their families. Credit/placement for qualifying scores on AP, IB, CLEP examinations.

Payment plans. Credit card, installment, deferred payment.

Application procedures. FAFSA required. Priority date 2/15; no closing date. Applicants notified by 3/28, must reply within 3 week(s) of notification.

Contact. Financial aid office: (208) 885-6312
Dan Davenport, Director of Admissions and Financial Aid
PO Box 444264
Moscow, ID 83844-4264

Illinois

American Academy of Art

Chicago, Illinois
www.aaart.edu
Four-year proprietary **Federal Code: 001628**

College costs. Electronic design specialty computer lab fees range from $200 to $800.

	Living at home
Tuition and fees (2002-2003):	$16,680
Books and supplies:	$800
Transportation:	$720

Undergraduate aid. Non-need-based: Scholarships based on art.

Policies to reduce costs. Tuition/fee waivers for employees and their families. Work study available nights.

Payment plans. Credit card, installment payment.

Application procedures. FAFSA, institutional form required. No deadline. Applicants notified on rolling basis. **Transfers:** No deadline. Financial aid transcript from previously attended college required.

Contact. Ione Fitzgerald, Financial Aid Director
332 South Michigan Avenue
Chicago, IL 60604-4302

Augustana College

Rock Island, Illinois
www.augustana.edu
Four-year private **Federal Code: 001633**

	Living at home	On-campus
Tuition and fees:	$20,829	$20,829
Room and board:		$5,781
Board only:	$2,736	
Books and supplies:	$675	$675
Personal expenses:	$800	$800
Transportation:	$400	$400

Undergraduate aid. Need-based: Average financial aid package for full-time students was $15,068. 62% awarded as scholarships/grants, 38% as loans/jobs. **Non-need-based:** Scholarships based on academics, alumni affiliation, art, music/drama, religious affiliation. **Student debt:** 71% of graduating class borrowed to fund education; average debt was $16,985.

Freshman aid. Need-based: Out of 601 full-time freshmen, 593 applied for aid; 407 were judged to have need; of these 406 received aid. Average package met 91% of need. 157 students had full need met. Average scholarship/grant was $11,118; average loan $3,674. **Non-need based:** 340 full-time freshmen with need received non-need scholarships; 106 without need received awards.

Policies to reduce costs. Tuition/fee waivers for family members, employees and their families. Tuition at time of enrollment guaranteed for 4 years; credit/placement for qualifying scores on AP, IB examinations.

Payment plans. Installment payment.

Application procedures. FAFSA, institutional form required. Priority date 4/1; no closing date. Applicants notified on rolling basis starting 2/15, must reply by 5/1. **Transfers:** Priority date 5/1; no deadline. Financial aid transcripts from previous institutions required.

Contact. Sue Standley, Director of Financial Aid
639 38th Street
Rock Island, IL 61201-2296

Aurora University

Aurora, Illinois
www.aurora.edu
Four-year private **Federal Code: 001634**

	Living at home	On-campus
Tuition and fees:	$14,810	$14,810
Room and board:		$5,514
Board only:	$2,566	
Books and supplies:	$750	$750
Personal expenses:	$1,152	$1,542
Transportation:	$1,419	$1,243

Undergraduate aid. Need-based: Average financial aid package for full-time students was $12,256; for part-time $7,555. 61% awarded as scholarships/grants, 39% as loans/jobs. **Non-need-based:** 64% awarded as scholarships/grants, 36% as loans/jobs. Scholarships based on academics, alumni affiliation, leadership, minority status, music/drama, religious affiliation. **Student debt:** 87% of graduating class borrowed to fund education; average debt was $11,257.

Freshman aid. Need-based: Out of 209 full-time freshmen, 208 applied for aid; 169 were judged to have need; of these 169 received aid. Average package met 88% of need. 61 students had full need met. Average scholarship/grant was $6,006; average loan $2,259. **Non-need based:** 167 full-time freshmen with need received non-need scholarships; 82 without need received awards.

Merit scholarships. Board of Trustees scholarships: $8,000; James E. Crimi Presidential Scholarships: $6,500; Dean's scholarships: $6,000; Aurora University Opportunity Grants: $3,000-$5,000.

Policies to reduce costs. Tuition/fee waivers for children of alumni, senior citizens, employees and their families. Credit/placement for qualifying scores on AP, CLEP examinations. Work study available nights, weekends and for part-time students.

Payment plans. Credit card, installment, deferred payment.

Application procedures. FAFSA required. Priority date 4/15; no closing date. Applicants notified on rolling basis starting 3/1, must reply by 5/1 or within 4 week(s) of notification. **Transfers:** No deadline.

Contact. Financial aid office: (630) 844-5149
Heather Gutierrez, Dean of Student Financial Services
347 South Gladstone Avenue
Aurora, IL 60506-4892

Benedictine University

Lisle, Illinois
www.ben.edu
Four-year private **Federal Code: 001767**

	Living at home	On-campus
Tuition and fees (2002-2003):	$16,660	$16,660
Room and board:		$5,940
Books and supplies:	$700	$700
Personal expenses:	$1,500	$1,500
Transportation:	$900	$900

Undergraduate aid. All financial aid based on need. Average financial aid package for full-time students was $10,986; for part-time $8,215. **Additional information:** Need-based financial aid available to part-time students who are enrolled at least half-time.

Freshman aid. Average package met 100% of need. Average scholarship/grant was $9,472; average loan $2,759.

Policies to reduce costs. Tuition/fee waivers for children of alumni, family members, family of clergy, employees and their families. Credit/placement for qualifying scores on AP, CLEP examinations. Work study available nights, weekends and for part-time students.

Payment plans. Credit card, deferred payment.

Application procedures. FAFSA, institutional form required. Priority date 4/15; no closing date. Applicants notified on rolling basis starting 3/1, must reply within 2 week(s) of notification.

Contact. Maria Lee, Director of Financial Aid
5700 College Road
Lisle, IL 60532

Black Hawk College

Moline, Illinois
www.bhc.edu
Two-year public **Federal Code: 001638**

	Living at home
Tuition and fees (2002-2003):	$1,650
Out-of-district:	$4,320
Out-of-state:	$7,890
Per-credit charge:	$51
Per-credit out-of-district:	$140
Per-credit out-of-state:	$259
Board only:	$1,998
Books and supplies:	$770
Personal expenses:	$1,842
Transportation:	$1,690

Undergraduate aid. Need-based: Average financial aid package for full-time students was $3,260; for part-time $2,405. 88% awarded as scholarships/grants, 12% as loans/jobs. **Non-need-based:** 34% awarded as scholarships/grants, 66% as loans/jobs. Scholarships based on academics, art, athletics, leadership, music/drama, state/district residency. **Student debt:** 13% of graduating class borrowed to fund education; average debt was $3,853.

Freshman aid. Need-based: Out of 788 full-time freshmen, 610 applied for aid; 545 were judged to have need; of these 492 received aid. Average package met 83% of need. 290 students had full need met. Average scholarship/grant was $3,232; average loan $1,820. **Non-need based:** 151 full-time freshmen with need received non-need scholarships; 105 without need received awards; 31 received athletic scholarships.

Merit scholarships. Scholarship program funded by college foundations and community donors. Awards based on need and/or merit. Application deadline is 5/15.

Policies to reduce costs. Tuition/fee waivers for senior citizens, employees and their families. Credit/placement for qualifying scores on AP, CLEP examinations. Work study available for part-time students.

Payment plans. Credit card, installment, deferred payment.

Application procedures. FAFSA required. Priority date 5/15; no closing date. Applicants notified on rolling basis starting 5/1.

Contact. Financial aid office: (309) 796-5400
Bob Bopp, Director, Financial Aid
6600 34th Avenue
Moline, IL 61265-5899

Black Hawk College: East Campus

Kewanee, Illinois
www.bhc.edu
Two-year public **Federal Code: 001638**

	Living at home
Tuition and fees (2002-2003):	$1,650
Out-of-district:	$4,320
Out-of-state:	$7,890
Per-credit charge:	$51
Per-credit out-of-district:	$140
Per-credit out-of-state:	$259
Books and supplies:	$600

Policies to reduce costs. Tuition/fee waivers for senior citizens, employees and their families. Credit/placement for qualifying scores on CLEP examinations.

Payment plans. Credit card, installment, deferred payment.

Application procedures. FAFSA required. Priority date 6/1; no closing date. Applicants notified on rolling basis, must reply within 2 week(s) of notification. **Transfers:** No deadline.

Contact. Financial aid office: (309) 852-5671 ext. 6242
Juanita Zertuche, Coordinator of Financial Aid
1501 State Highway 78
Kewanee, IL 61443-0630

Blackburn College

Carlinville, Illinois
www.blackburn.edu
Four-year private **Federal Code: 001639**

	Living at home	On-campus
Tuition and fees (2002-2003):	$9,420	$9,420
Room and board:		$4,270
Books and supplies:	$600	$600
Personal expenses:	$800	$800
Transportation:	$50	$250

Undergraduate aid. Need-based: Average financial aid package for full-time students was $8,053; for part-time $4,203. 87% awarded as scholarships/grants, 13% as loans/jobs. **Non-need-based:** 50% awarded as scholarships/grants, 50% as loans/jobs. Scholarships based on academics, state/district residency. **Student debt:** 84% of graduating class borrowed to fund education; average debt was $11,900. **Additional information:** Each resident student works 10 hours weekly on campus.

Freshman aid. Need-based: Out of 193 full-time freshmen, 184 applied for aid; 184 were judged to have need; of these 184 received aid. Average package met 100% of need. 184 students had full need met. Average scholarship/grant was $5,546; average loan $1,490. **Non-need based:** 87 full-time freshmen with need received non-need scholarships; 27 without need received awards.

Policies to reduce costs. Tuition/fee waivers for employees and their families. Credit/placement for qualifying scores on AP, CLEP examinations.

Payment plans. Credit card, installment, deferred payment.

Application procedures. FAFSA required. Priority date 4/1; no closing date. Applicants notified on rolling basis starting 3/1, must reply within 4 week(s) of notification. **Transfers:** Priority date 4/1.

Contact. Jane Kelsey, Financial Aid Administrator
700 College Avenue
Carlinville, IL 62626

Blessing-Reiman College of Nursing

Quincy, Illinois
www.brcn.edu
Four-year private **Federal Code: 006214**

College costs (2002-2003). Blessing-Reiman is partnered with two other schools, Quincy University and Culver-Stockton. Freshmen and sophomores pay tuition at partnering school's rate: $15,910 at Quincy, $11,600 at Culver Stockton. Juniors and seniors pay tuition at BRCN rate, $7,875. Fees at BRCN for all $363. Board: $1,800. Books/supplies: $800. Personal expenses: $1,725. Transportation: $720.

Undergraduate aid. Need-based: Need-based aid available for full-time and part-time students. **Additional information:** Financial aid for freshmen and sophomores is administered by Culver-Stockton College and Quincy University.

Policies to reduce costs. Tuition/fee waivers for employees and their families. Credit/placement for qualifying scores on AP, CLEP examinations.

Payment plans. Installment payment.

Application procedures. FAFSA required. Priority date 3/1; no closing date. Applicants notified on rolling basis starting 7/1.

Contact. Financial aid office: (217) 228-5520 ext. 6993
Sara Brehm, Financial Aid Officer
PO Box 7005
Quincy, IL 62305-7005

Bradley University

Peoria, Illinois
www.bradley.edu
Four-year private **Federal Code: 001641**

	Living at home	On-campus
Tuition and fees:	$16,910	$16,910
Room and board:		$5,980
Personal expenses:	$1,500	$1,500

Undergraduate aid. Need-based: Need-based aid available for full-time and part-time students. **Non-need-based:** Scholarships based on academics, alumni affiliation, art, athletics, leadership, music/drama, state/district residency. **Student debt:** 81% of graduating class borrowed to fund education; average debt was $16,531.

Policies to reduce costs. Tuition/fee waivers for children of alumni, senior citizens, employees and their families. Credit/placement for qualifying scores on AP, IB, CLEP examinations. Work study available nights and weekends.

Payment plans. Credit card, installment, deferred payment.

Application procedures. FAFSA required. Priority date 3/1; no closing date. Applicants notified on rolling basis starting 2/15, must reply by 5/1.

Contact. **Financial aid office:** (309) 677-3089
Gary Anna, Vice President for Business Affairs
1501 West Bradley Avenue
Peoria, IL 61625

Carl Sandburg College

Galesburg, Illinois
www.sandburg.edu
Two-year public **Federal Code: 007265**

	Living at home
Tuition and fees (2002-2003):	$1,965
Out-of-district:	$5,280
Out-of-state:	$7,320
Per-credit charge:	$58
Per-credit out-of-district:	$168
Per-credit out-of-state:	$236
Board only:	$1,600
Books and supplies:	$710
Personal expenses:	$880
Transportation:	$1,340

Undergraduate aid. **Need-based:** Need-based aid available for full-time students. **Non-need-based:** Scholarships based on academics, art, athletics.

Policies to reduce costs. Tuition/fee waivers for senior citizens, employees and their families. Credit/placement for qualifying scores on AP, CLEP examinations. Work study available for part-time students.

Payment plans. Credit card, installment, deferred payment.

Application procedures. FAFSA, institutional form required. Priority date 5/1; no closing date. Applicants notified on rolling basis starting 6/15, must reply within 2 week(s) of notification.

Contact. **Financial aid office:** (309) 341-5283
Lisa Hanson, Director of Financial Aid
2400 Tom L. Wilson Boulevard
Galesburg, IL 61401

Chicago State University

Chicago, Illinois
www.csu.edu
Four-year public **Federal Code: 001694**

	Living at home
Tuition and fees (2002-2003):	$3,823
Out-of-state:	$9,379
Books and supplies:	$1,400
Personal expenses:	$3,300

Undergraduate aid. **Need-based:** 72% awarded as scholarships/grants, 28% as loans/jobs. **Non-need-based:** Scholarships based on academics, athletics, state/district residency. **Additional information:** Freshmen of outstanding academic ability and talent eligible for Scholars Program full-tuition scholarship.

Policies to reduce costs. Tuition/fee waivers for children of alumni, senior citizens, employees and their families. Credit/placement for qualifying scores on AP, CLEP examinations.

Payment plans. Credit card, deferred payment.

Application procedures. FAFSA, institutional form required. No deadline. **Transfers:** Priority date 3/31; no deadline. Transfer students must have valid financial aid transcripts from previous institutions whether or not they received aid.

Contact. **Financial aid office:** (773) 995-2304
Brenda Hooker, Director
9501 South King Drive
Chicago, IL 60628

City Colleges of Chicago: Harold Washington College

Chicago, Illinois
www.ccc.edu
Two-year public **Federal Code: 001652**

	Living at home
Tuition and fees (2002-2003):	$1,810
Out-of-district:	$5,485
Out-of-state:	$7,879
Per-credit charge:	$52
Per-credit out-of-district:	$175
Per-credit out-of-state:	$254
Books and supplies:	$600
Personal expenses:	$1,761
Transportation:	$540

Undergraduate aid. All financial aid based on need. Need-based aid available for full-time and part-time students.

Policies to reduce costs. Tuition/fee waivers for senior citizens, employees and their families. Work study available nights and for part-time students.

Payment plans. Credit card, installment, deferred payment.

Application procedures. FAFSA required. Priority date 5/1; closing date 6/30. Applicants notified on rolling basis starting 7/1, must reply within 2 week(s) of notification.

Contact. **Financial aid office:** (312) 553-6041
Francois Hasouk, Director of Financial Aid
30 East Lake Street
Chicago, IL 60601

City Colleges of Chicago: Kennedy-King College

Chicago, Illinois
www.ccc.edu
Two-year public **Federal Code: 001654**

College costs. Lab fees for technical and vocational courses.

	Living at home
Tuition and fees (2002-2003):	$1,810
Out-of-district:	$5,485
Out-of-state:	$7,879
Per-credit charge:	$52
Per-credit out-of-district:	$175
Per-credit out-of-state:	$254
Board only:	$3,600
Books and supplies:	$1,000
Personal expenses:	$2,000
Transportation:	$910

Undergraduate aid. All financial aid based on need. 96% awarded as scholarships/grants, 4% as loans/jobs. Need-based aid available for part-time students.

Policies to reduce costs. Tuition/fee waivers for senior citizens, employees and their families. Credit/placement for qualifying scores on CLEP examinations.

Payment plans. Credit card, installment, deferred payment.

Application procedures. FAFSA required. Priority date 8/1; no closing date. Applicants notified on rolling basis starting 8/15, must reply within 2 week(s) of notification.

Contact. **Financial aid office:** (773) 602-5133
Alicia Williams, Financial Aid Supervisor
6800 South Wentworth Avenue
Chicago, IL 60621

City Colleges of Chicago: Malcolm X College

Chicago, Illinois
www.ccc.edu/malcolmx
Two-year public **Federal Code: 001650**

College costs. Some courses require a $20 lab fee.

	Living at home
Tuition and fees (2002-2003):	$1,810
Out-of-district:	$5,485
Out-of-state:	$7,879
Per-credit charge:	$52
Per-credit out-of-district:	$175
Per-credit out-of-state:	$254
Books and supplies:	$800

Undergraduate aid. All financial aid based on need. Need-based aid available for full-time and part-time students.

Policies to reduce costs. Tuition/fee waivers for senior citizens, employees and their families. Credit/placement for qualifying scores on AP, IB, CLEP examinations. Work study available nights, weekends and for part-time students.

Payment plans. Credit card, installment, deferred payment.

Application procedures. FAFSA, institutional form required. Priority date 7/1; no closing date. Applicants notified on rolling basis starting 7/1, must reply within 2 week(s) of notification.

Contact. **Financial aid office:** (312) 850-7146
Patricia Burke, Director, Financial Aid
1900 West Van Buren Street
Chicago, IL 60612

City Colleges of Chicago: Olive-Harvey College

Chicago, Illinois
www.ccc.edu
Two-year public **Federal Code: 009767**

	Living at home
Tuition and fees (2002-2003):	$1,810
Out-of-district:	$5,485
Out-of-state:	$7,879
Per-credit charge:	$52
Per-credit out-of-district:	$175
Per-credit out-of-state:	$254
Books and supplies:	$600
Transportation:	$70

Undergraduate aid. **Need-based:** Need-based aid available for full-time and part-time students.

Policies to reduce costs. Tuition/fee waivers for senior citizens, employees and their families. Credit/placement for qualifying scores on AP, CLEP examinations.

Payment plans. Credit card, installment, deferred payment.

Application procedures. FAFSA required. Priority date 8/15; no closing date. Applicants notified on rolling basis, must reply within 3 week(s) of notification.

Contact. Michael Shields, Director of Financial Aid
10001 South Woodlawn Avenue
Chicago, IL 60628

City Colleges of Chicago: Richard J. Daley College

Chicago, Illinois
www.ccc.edu/daley
Two-year public **Federal Code: 001649**

	Living at home
Tuition and fees (2002-2003):	$1,810
Out-of-district:	$5,485
Out-of-state:	$7,879
Per-credit charge:	$52
Per-credit out-of-district:	$175
Per-credit out-of-state:	$254
Books and supplies:	$800
Personal expenses:	$320
Transportation:	$640

Undergraduate aid. **Need-based:** Need-based aid available for full-time students.

Policies to reduce costs. Tuition/fee waivers for senior citizens, employees and their families. Credit/placement for qualifying scores on AP examinations.

Payment plans. Credit card, deferred payment.

Application procedures. FAFSA required. No deadline. Applicants notified on rolling basis. **Transfers:** College workstudy jobs and Federal Supplemental Educational Opportunity Grant (SEOG) may not be available to transfers.

Contact. **Financial aid office:** (773) 838-7579
Thelma Barnes, Dean of Student Services
7500 South Pulaski Road
Chicago, IL 60652

City Colleges of Chicago: Wright College

Chicago, Illinois
www.ccc.edu
Two-year public **Federal Code: 001655**

	Living at home
Tuition and fees (2002-2003):	$1,810
Out-of-district:	$5,485
Out-of-state:	$7,879
Per-credit charge:	$52
Per-credit out-of-district:	$175
Per-credit out-of-state:	$254
Books and supplies:	$630
Personal expenses:	$1,280
Transportation:	$600

Undergraduate aid. **Need-based:** Need-based aid available for full-time and part-time students.

Policies to reduce costs. Tuition/fee waivers for senior citizens, employees and their families. Tuition at time of enrollment guaranteed for 2 years; credit/placement for qualifying scores on AP, IB, CLEP examinations. Work study available nights, weekends and for part-time students.

Payment plans. Credit card, installment payment.

Application procedures. FAFSA, institutional form required. Priority date 6/1; no closing date. Applicants notified on rolling basis starting 7/15.

Contact. **Financial aid office:** (773) 481-8100
Marco Sepulveda, Financial Aid Director
4300 N. Narragansett Avenue
Chicago, IL 60634-4276

College of DuPage
Glen Ellyn, Illinois
www.cod.edu
Two-year public **Federal Code: 006656**

	Living at home
Tuition and fees (2002-2003):	$2,036
Out-of-district:	$5,924
Out-of-state:	$8,180
Per-credit charge:	$43
Per-credit out-of-district:	$124
Per-credit out-of-state:	$171
Board only:	$1,874
Books and supplies:	$978
Personal expenses:	$1,278
Transportation:	$1,617

Undergraduate aid. **Need-based:** 69% awarded as scholarships/grants, 31% as loans/jobs. Need-based aid available for part-time students. **Non-need-based:** 30% awarded as scholarships/grants, 70% as loans/jobs. Scholarships based on academics, art, leadership, minority status, music/drama, religious affiliation, state/district residency.

Policies to reduce costs. Tuition/fee waivers for senior citizens, employees and their families. Credit/placement for qualifying scores on AP, CLEP examinations. Work study available nights and for part-time students.

Payment plans. Credit card, installment, deferred payment.

Application procedures. FAFSA, institutional form required. Priority date 5/2; no closing date. Applicants notified on rolling basis starting 8/2, must reply within 2 week(s) of notification. **Transfers:** No deadline. Must have financial aid transcript on file.

Contact. **Financial aid office:** (630) 942-2251
Marilyn Comer, Director of Student Financial Aid
425 Fawell Boulevard
Glen Ellyn, IL 60137-6599

College of Lake County
Grayslake, Illinois
www.clcillinois.edu
Two-year public **Federal Code: 007694**

	Living at home
Tuition and fees (projected):	$1,680
Out-of-district:	$5,460
Out-of-state:	$7,590
Per-credit charge:	$51
Per-credit out-of-district:	$177
Per-credit out-of-state:	$248
Personal expenses:	$1,200
Transportation:	$1,000

Undergraduate aid. **Need-based:** Average financial aid package for full-time students was $2,988; for part-time $2,560. 79% awarded as scholarships/grants, 21% as loans/jobs. **Non-need-based:** 35% awarded as scholarships/grants, 65% as loans/jobs. Scholarships based on academics, alumni affiliation, athletics, leadership, minority status, music/drama. **Student debt:** 6% of graduating class borrowed to fund education; average debt was $1,962.

Freshman aid. **Need-based:** Average package met 59% of need. Average scholarship/grant was $1,190; average loan $571.

Merit scholarships. Academic Achievement Scholarship based on GPA and student essay; tuition and fees.

Policies to reduce costs. Tuition/fee waivers for senior citizens, employees and their families. Credit/placement for qualifying scores on AP, CLEP examinations. Work study available nights and for part-time students.

Payment plans. Credit card, installment, deferred payment.

Application procedures. FAFSA required. Priority date 6/1; no closing date. Applicants notified on rolling basis starting 6/15, must reply within 2 week(s) of notification. **Transfers:** No deadline.

Contact. **Financial aid office:** (847) 543-2062
Brian Pomeroy, Director of Financial Aid
19351 West Washington Street
Grayslake, IL 60030-1198

College of Office Technology
Chicago, Illinois
Two-year proprietary **Federal Code: 017378**

College costs. Tuition includes books and supplies.

	Living at home
Tuition and fees (2002-2003):	$15,105
Personal expenses:	$4,574
Transportation:	$920

Application procedures. FAFSA required. No deadline. Applicants notified on rolling basis.

Contact. 1520 West Division Street
Chicago, IL 60622-3312

Columbia College Chicago
Chicago, Illinois
www.colum.edu
Four-year private **Federal Code: 001665**

	Living at home	On-campus
Tuition and fees (2002-2003):	$14,104	$14,104
Room only:		$6,305
Board only:	$1,963	
Books and supplies:	$796	$796
Personal expenses:	$2,480	$3,193
Transportation:	$803	$803

Undergraduate aid. **Need-based:** 39% awarded as scholarships/grants, 61% as loans/jobs. Need-based aid available for part-time students. **Non-need-based:** Scholarships based on academics, art, leadership, music/drama.

Policies to reduce costs. Tuition/fee waivers for minority students, employees and their families. Prepayment discount; credit/placement for qualifying scores on AP, IB, CLEP examinations.

Payment plans. Credit card, installment payment.

Application procedures. FAFSA, institutional form required. Priority date 8/15; no closing date. Applicants notified on rolling basis. **Transfers:** Relevant Title IV regulations and Illinois Student Assistance Commission regulations.

Contact. **Financial aid office:** (312) 344-7140
John Olino, Director of Financial Aid
600 South Michigan Avenue
Chicago, IL 60605-1996

Concordia University
River Forest, Illinois
www.curf.edu
Four-year private **Federal Code: 001666**

	Living at home	On-campus
Tuition and fees:	$18,200	$18,200
Room and board:		$5,400
Board only:	$3,100	
Books and supplies:	$600	$600
Personal expenses:		$400
Transportation:	$600	$600

Undergraduate aid. **Need-based:** Need-based aid available for full-time students. **Non-need-based:** Scholarships based on academics, alumni affiliation, minority status, music/drama.

Policies to reduce costs. Tuition/fee waivers for employees and their families. Credit/placement for qualifying scores on AP, IB, CLEP examinations.

Payment plans. Credit card, installment payment.

Application procedures. FAFSA, institutional form required. Closing date 4/1. Applicants notified on rolling basis, must reply within 4 week(s) of notification. **Transfers:** No deadline.

Contact. **Financial aid office:** (708) 209-3113
Deborah Ness, Dean of Student Financial Planning
7400 Augusta Street
River Forest, IL 60305-1499

Cooking & Hospitality Institute of Chicago

Chicago, Illinois
www.chicnet.org
Two-year proprietary **Federal Code: 016758**

College costs. Cost of tuition for 16-month associate degree program: $38,500; per-credit-hour charge; $775. Books/supplies: $3,200. Personal expenses: $1,000.

Undergraduate aid. Need-based: Need-based aid available for full-time and part-time students.

Policies to reduce costs. Tuition/fee waivers for employees and their families. Tuition at time of enrollment guaranteed for 2 years; credit/placement for qualifying scores on IB examinations. Work study available nights, weekends and for part-time students.

Payment plans. Credit card payment.

Application procedures. FAFSA, institutional form required. No deadline. Applicants notified on rolling basis, must reply within 3 week(s) of notification.

Contact. Financial aid office: (312) 944-0882
Maria Calafiore, Director of Financial Services
361 West Chestnut Street
Chicago, IL 60610-3050

Danville Area Community College

Danville, Illinois
www.dacc.cc.il.us
Two-year public **Federal Code: 001669**

	Living at home
Tuition and fees (2002-2003):	$1,440
Out-of-district:	$6,765
Out-of-state:	$11,356
Per-credit charge:	$48
Per-credit out-of-district:	$226
Per-credit out-of-state:	$379
Board only:	$1,700
Books and supplies:	$700
Personal expenses:	$1,575
Transportation:	$1,536

Undergraduate aid. Need-based: 88% awarded as scholarships/grants, 12% as loans/jobs. Need-based aid available for part-time students. **Non-need-based:** Scholarships based on academics, athletics, minority status.

Policies to reduce costs. Tuition/fee waivers for senior citizens, employees and their families. Credit/placement for qualifying scores on AP, CLEP examinations. Work study available nights, weekends and for part-time students.

Payment plans. Credit card, installment, deferred payment.

Application procedures. FAFSA, institutional form required. Priority date 6/1; no closing date. Applicants notified on rolling basis starting 6/1. **Transfers:** No deadline. NSLDS reviewed before aid disbursed.

Contact. Janet Ingargiola, Director of Financial Aid
2000 East Main Street
Danville, IL 61832

De Paul University

Chicago, Illinois
www.depaul.edu
Four-year private **Federal Code: 001671**

	Living at home	On-campus
Tuition and fees (2002-2003):	$18,020	$18,020
Room and board:		$8,750
Books and supplies:	$900	$900

Undergraduate aid. Need-based: Need-based aid available for full-time and part-time students. **Non-need-based:** Scholarships based on academics, art, athletics, leadership, minority status, music/drama.

Merit scholarships. Students in top 10% of class, with SAT scores of at least 1100 or ACT of 26, and active in student/community organizations should inquire about scholarships.

Policies to reduce costs. Tuition/fee waivers for employees and their families. Credit/placement for qualifying scores on AP, IB, CLEP examinations. Work study available for part-time students.

Payment plans. Credit card, installment, deferred payment.

Application procedures. FAFSA required. Closing date 5/1. Applicants notified on rolling basis starting 2/15, must reply by 5/1 or within 4 week(s) of notification. **Transfers:** Priority date 4/1; closing date 5/1.

Contact. Financial aid office: 312-362-8091
John Schoultz, Director of Financial Aid
1 East Jackson Boulevard
Chicago, IL 60604-2287

DeVry University: Addison

Addison, Illinois
www.dpg.devry.edu
Four-year proprietary **Federal Code: 016219**

	Living at home
Tuition and fees:	$10,265
Books and supplies:	$1,100
Personal expenses:	$1,750
Transportation:	$1,438

Undergraduate aid. All financial aid based on need. Average financial aid package for full-time students was $8,374; for part-time $6,454. 33% awarded as scholarships/grants, 67% as loans/jobs.

Freshman aid. Average package met 49% of need. Average scholarship/grant was $5,292; average loan $3,462.

Policies to reduce costs. Tuition/fee waivers for employees and their families.

Payment plans. Credit card, installment, deferred payment.

Application procedures. FAFSA required. No deadline. Applicants notified on rolling basis starting 7/2. **Transfers:** No deadline.

Contact. Sajel Anin, Director of Student Finance
1221 North Swift Road
Addison, IL 60101-6106

DeVry University: Chicago

Chicago, Illinois
www.chi.devry.edu
Four-year proprietary **Federal Code: 010727**

	Living at home
Tuition and fees:	$10,265
Books and supplies:	$1,100
Personal expenses:	$1,816
Transportation:	$1,438

Undergraduate aid. All financial aid based on need. Average financial aid package for full-time students was $10,268; for part-time $7,627. 45% awarded as scholarships/grants, 55% as loans/jobs.

Freshman aid. Average package met 54% of need. Average scholarship/grant was $6,174; average loan $3,288.

Policies to reduce costs. Tuition/fee waivers for employees and their families.

Payment plans. Credit card, installment, deferred payment.

Application procedures. FAFSA required. No deadline. Applicants notified on rolling basis starting 7/2.

Contact. Milena Dobrina, Director of Financial Aid
3300 North Campbell Avenue
Chicago, IL 60618-5994

DeVry University: Tinley Park

Tinley Park, Illinois
www.tp.devry.edu
Four-year proprietary **Federal Code: 022966**

	Living at home
Tuition and fees:	$10,265
Books and supplies:	$1,100
Personal expenses:	$1,816
Transportation:	$1,438

Undergraduate aid. All financial aid based on need. Average financial aid package for full-time students was $8,382; for part-time $6,526. 39% awarded as scholarships/grants, 61% as loans/jobs.

Freshman aid. Average package met 52% of need. Average scholarship/grant was $5,606; average loan $3,274.

Policies to reduce costs. Tuition/fee waivers for employees and their families.

Payment plans. Credit card, installment, deferred payment.

Application procedures. FAFSA required. No deadline. Applicants notified on rolling basis starting 7/2. **Transfers:** No deadline.

Contact. Sejal Amin, Director of Student Finance
18624 West Creek Drive
Tinley Park, IL 60477

Dominican University

River Forest, Illinois
www.dom.edu
Four-year private **Federal Code: 001750**

	Living at home	On-campus
Tuition and fees:	$17,950	$17,950
Out-of-state:	$17,950	$17,950
Room and board:		$5,700
Books and supplies:	$750	$750
Personal expenses:	$2,400	$900
Transportation:	$500	$500

Undergraduate aid. Need-based: Average financial aid package for full-time students was $11,208; for part-time $6,708. 70% awarded as scholarships/grants, 30% as loans/jobs. **Non-need-based:** 47% awarded as scholarships/grants, 53% as loans/jobs. Scholarships based on academics, alumni affiliation, leadership. **Student debt:** 72% of graduating class borrowed to fund education; average debt was $14,758.

Freshman aid. Need-based: Out of 224 full-time freshmen, 188 applied for aid; 159 were judged to have need; of these 159 received aid. Average package met 84% of need. 38 students had full need met. Average scholarship/grant was $10,371; average loan $2,140. **Non-need based:** 29 full-time freshmen with need received non-need scholarships; 30 without need received awards.

Merit scholarships. Parish Leadership Awards for qualified students involved in parish volunteer work; $500. Annual Presidential Scholarship Competition winners; full-tuition. Honor Scholarships ($7,250), Achievement Awards ($5,500), Incentive Awards ($3,500) available based on ACT/SAT scores and grades. Ida Brechtel Scholarships for students majoring in chemistry or biology/chemistry, $5,000 to full tuition, 5 awards per year, must have 26 ACT.

Policies to reduce costs. Tuition/fee waivers for children of alumni, family members, employees and their families. Credit/placement for qualifying scores on AP, IB, CLEP examinations. Work study available nights and weekends.

Payment plans. Credit card, installment payment.

Application procedures. FAFSA required. Priority date 6/1; no closing date. Applicants notified on rolling basis starting 2/15, must reply by 5/1 or within 2 week(s) of notification. **Transfers:** Priority date 6/1; no deadline. Merit scholarships available to full-time students with GPA of 3.3 from previous institution. Phi Theta Kappa scholarships available to students with 3.5 from last school attended. Students must apply by June 1.

Contact. Financial aid office: (708) 524-6809
Howard Florine, Director of Financial Aid
7900 West Division
River Forest, IL 60305-1099

East-West University

Chicago, Illinois
www.eastwest.edu
Four-year private **Federal Code: 015310**

	Living at home
Tuition and fees:	$10,395
Books and supplies:	$1,000
Personal expenses:	$1,800
Transportation:	$700

Undergraduate aid. Need-based: Need-based aid available for full-time and part-time students. **Non-need-based:** Scholarships based on academics.

Additional information: Foreign students eligible for institutional scholarship.

Policies to reduce costs. Tuition/fee waivers for employees and their families. Credit/placement for qualifying scores on CLEP examinations.

Payment plans. Credit card, installment, deferred payment.

Application procedures. FAFSA required. No deadline. Applicants notified on rolling basis starting 1/4, must reply within 4 week(s) of notification. **Transfers:** Closing date 4/1.

Contact. Financial aid office: (312) 939-0111
Elizabeth Guzman, Director of Financial Aid
816 South Michigan Avenue
Chicago, IL 60605

Eastern Illinois University

Charleston, Illinois
www.eiu.edu
Four-year public **Federal Code: 001674**

College costs. Fees include $186 textbook rental, $130 health and accident insurance.

	Living at home	On-campus
Tuition and fees (2002-2003):	$4,648	$4,648
Out-of-state:	$11,155	$11,155
Room and board:		$5,800
Board only:	$3,000	
Books and supplies:	$120	$120
Personal expenses:	$1,240	$1,460
Transportation:	$1,350	$670

Undergraduate aid. All financial aid based on need. Average financial aid package for full-time students was $8,472; for part-time $7,201. 46% awarded as scholarships/grants, 54% as loans/jobs. **Student debt:** 57% of graduating class borrowed to fund education; average debt was $13,075.

Freshman aid. Out of 2,060 full-time freshmen, 1,998 applied for aid; 1,505 were judged to have need; of these 969 received aid. Average package met 16% of need. 737 students had full need met. Average scholarship/grant was $2,528; average loan $2,177.

Policies to reduce costs. Tuition/fee waivers for senior citizens, employees and their families. Credit/placement for qualifying scores on AP, CLEP examinations. Work study available nights, weekends and for part-time students.

Payment plans. Installment payment.

Application procedures. FAFSA required. Priority date 4/15; no closing date. Applicants notified on rolling basis starting 5/1, must reply within 2 week(s) of notification.

Contact. Financial aid office: (217) 581-3714
Jone Zieren, Director of Financial Aid
600 Lincoln Avenue
Charleston, IL 61920-3099

Elgin Community College

Elgin, Illinois
www.elgin.edu
Two-year public **Federal Code: 001675**

	Living at home
Tuition and fees (2002-2003):	$1,350
Out-of-district:	$5,200
Out-of-state:	$6,362
Per-credit charge:	$48
Per-credit out-of-district:	$214
Per-credit out-of-state:	$266
Books and supplies:	$700
Transportation:	$850

Undergraduate aid. Need-based: Need-based aid available for full-time and part-time students. **Non-need-based:** Scholarships based on academics, alumni affiliation, art, athletics, job skills, leadership, minority status, music/drama, religious affiliation, state/district residency.

Policies to reduce costs. Tuition/fee waivers for senior citizens, employees and their families. Credit/placement for qualifying scores on AP, CLEP examinations. Work study available nights and weekends.

Payment plans. Credit card, installment, deferred payment.

Application procedures. FAFSA, institutional form required. Priority date 5/15; no closing date. Applicants notified on rolling basis starting 4/7, must reply within 3 week(s) of notification. **Transfers:** No deadline.

Contact. **Financial aid office:** (847) 214-7360
Robert Laws, Associate Dean of Financial Aid and Records
1700 Spartan Drive
Elgin, IL 60123-7193

Elmhurst College

Elmhurst, Illinois
www.elmhurst.edu
Four-year private **Federal Code: 001676**

	Living at home	On-campus
Tuition and fees:	$18,600	$18,600
Room and board:		$6,030
Board only:	$2,000	
Books and supplies:	$600	$600
Personal expenses:	$1,000	$1,000
Transportation:	$1,400	$1,400

Undergraduate aid. Need-based: Need-based aid available for full-time and part-time students. **Non-need-based:** Scholarships based on academics, art, minority status, music/drama, religious affiliation.

Merit scholarships. Presidential Scholarship, 70 awarded, two-thirds tuition. Academic Achievement, 80 awarded, one-half tuition. Students qualify through a combination of class rank, test scores, and GPA, must be admitted to the college by January 15 to be considered.

Policies to reduce costs. Tuition/fee waivers for senior citizens, employees and their families. Credit/placement for qualifying scores on AP, IB, CLEP examinations. Work study available nights and weekends.

Payment plans. Credit card, installment, deferred payment.

Application procedures. FAFSA, institutional form required. Priority date 4/15; no closing date. Applicants notified on rolling basis starting 2/20, must reply within 3 week(s) of notification. **Transfers:** No deadline.

Contact. **Financial aid office:** (630) 617-3075
Gary Rold, Director of Financial Aid
190 Prospect Avenue
Elmhurst, IL 60126-3296

Eureka College

Eureka, Illinois
www.eureka.edu
Four-year private **Federal Code: 001678**

	Living at home	On-campus
Tuition and fees (2002-2003):	$17,930	$17,930
Room and board:		$5,565
Books and supplies:	$600	$600
Personal expenses:	$770	$510
Transportation:	$675	$160

Undergraduate aid. Need-based: Average financial aid package for full-time students was $13,802. 79% awarded as scholarships/grants, 21% as loans/jobs. Need-based aid available for part-time students. **Non-need-based:** 44% awarded as scholarships/grants, 56% as loans/jobs. Scholarships based on academics, alumni affiliation, leadership, religious affiliation, state/district residency. **Student debt:** 80% of graduating class borrowed to fund education; average debt was $13,688.

Freshman aid. Need-based: Out of 133 full-time freshmen, 133 applied for aid; 129 were judged to have need; of these 129 received aid. Average package met 81% of need. 119 students had full need met. Average scholarship/grant was $10,903; average loan $2,248. **Non-need based:** 9 full-time freshmen with need received non-need scholarships; 4 without need received awards.

Policies to reduce costs. Tuition/fee waivers for children of alumni, family members, employees and their families. Credit/placement for qualifying scores on AP, CLEP examinations. Work study available nights, weekends and for part-time students.

Payment plans. Credit card payment.

Application procedures. FAFSA required. Priority date 4/15; no closing date. Applicants notified on rolling basis starting 2/15, must reply by 5/1 or within 3 week(s) of notification. **Transfers:** Priority date 4/15; no deadline.

Contact. **Financial aid office:** (309) 467-6311
Ellen Rigsby, Director of Financial Aid
300 College Avenue
Eureka, IL 61530

Finch University of Health Sciences/The Chicago Medical School

North Chicago, Illinois
www.finchcms.edu
Upper-division private **Federal Code: 001659**

	Living at home
Tuition and fees (2002-2003):	$15,456
Books and supplies:	$1,057

Undergraduate aid. All financial aid based on need. Need-based aid available for full-time and part-time students.

Policies to reduce costs. Tuition/fee waivers for employees and their families. Credit/placement for qualifying scores on AP examinations.

Payment plans. Credit card, installment payment.

Application procedures. FAFSA, institutional form required. Applicants notified on rolling basis. **Transfers:** No deadline.

Contact. **Financial aid office:** (847) 578-3217
Maryann DeCaire, Director of Financial Aid
3333 Green Bay Road
North Chicago, IL 60064

Fox College

Oak Lawn, Illinois
www.foxcollege.com
Two-year proprietary **Federal Code: 016924**

	Living at home
Tuition and fees:	$11,480
Books and supplies:	$905

Application procedures. No deadline.

Contact. Steffani Fitzpatrick
4201 West 93rd Street
Oak Lawn, IL 60453

Gem City College

Quincy, Illinois
www.gemcitycollege.com
Two-year proprietary **Federal Code: 004560**

	Living at home
Tuition and fees (2002-2003):	$8,400
Books and supplies:	$600
Personal expenses:	$1,350
Transportation:	$400

Policies to reduce costs. Tuition at time of enrollment guaranteed for 2 years.

Payment plans. Credit card payment.

Application procedures. FAFSA required. No deadline. Applicants notified on rolling basis. **Transfers:** No deadline.

Contact. Joan Manzke, Director of Financial Aid
700 State Street
Quincy, IL 62306

Governors State University

University Park, Illinois
www.govst.edu
Upper-division public **Federal Code: 009145**

	Living at home
Tuition and fees (2002-2003):	$2,823
Out-of-state:	$7,863
Books and supplies:	$550
Personal expenses:	$800
Transportation:	$800

Undergraduate aid. Need-based: Need-based aid available for full-time and part-time students. **Non-need-based:** Scholarships based on academics, state/district residency.

Policies to reduce costs. Tuition/fee waivers for senior citizens, minority students, employees and their families. Credit/placement for qualifying scores on CLEP examinations. Work study available nights, weekends and for part-time students.

Payment plans. Credit card, installment, deferred payment.

Application procedures. FAFSA required. Priority date 5/1; closing date 10/1. Applicants notified on rolling basis. **Transfers:** Priority date 5/1; no deadline. No aid for second bachelor's or second master's degree.

Contact. Financial aid office: (708) 534-4480
Freda Whisenton-Comer, Office of Financial Aid
University Parkway
University Park, IL 60466

Greenville College

Greenville, Illinois
www.greenville.edu
Four-year private **Federal Code: 001684**

	Living at home	On-campus
Tuition and fees (2002-2003):	$14,860	$14,860
Room and board:		$5,620
Books and supplies:	$600	$600
Personal expenses:	$2,800	$1,200
Transportation:		$600

Undergraduate aid. Need-based: Need-based aid available for full-time and part-time students. **Non-need-based:** Scholarships based on academics, alumni affiliation, art, leadership, minority status, music/drama, religious affiliation, state/district residency.

Merit scholarships. Presidential Scholarships requiring cumulative GPA of 3.3, ACT of 27 or SAT of 1210 and leadership qualities; $4,000 to competitors, $7,000 to winners. Dean's Scholarships for GPA of 3.3, ACT of 22 or SAT of 1030 and leadership qualities; $3,000 to competitors, $5,000 to winners. Leadership Scholarships for GPA of 2.5, ACT of 18 or SAT 860 and leadership qualities; $500-$4,000.

Policies to reduce costs. Tuition/fee waivers for children of alumni, senior citizens, family members, family of clergy, employees and their families. Credit/placement for qualifying scores on AP, CLEP examinations. Work study available nights and weekends.

Payment plans. Credit card, installment, deferred payment.

Application procedures. FAFSA required. Priority date 5/1; no closing date. Applicants notified on rolling basis starting 3/15, must reply within 4 week(s) of notification. **Transfers:** Targeted Major Transfer Scholarship of $2,500 available to junior transfer students majoring in targeted areas-art, art education, chemistry, chemistry education, French, history/political science, mathematics, philosophy, physics, physics education, recreation, social work and Spanish.

Contact. Karl Somerville, Director of Financial Aid
315 East College Avenue
Greenville, IL 62246-0159

Harrington Institute of Interior Design

Chicago, Illinois
www.harringtoninstitute.com
Four-year proprietary **Federal Code: 013601**

	Living at home
Tuition and fees (2002-2003):	$12,127
Board only:	$3,060
Personal expenses:	$2,500
Transportation:	$1,000

Undergraduate aid. All financial aid based on need. Need-based aid available for full-time and part-time students.

Policies to reduce costs. Tuition/fee waivers for employees and their families.

Payment plans. Credit card, installment payment.

Application procedures. FAFSA required. No deadline. Applicants notified on rolling basis, must reply within 2 week(s) of notification. **Transfers:** No deadline. Aid received at other schools may reduce or limit financial aid award.

Contact. Renee Darosky, Director of Financial Aid
410 South Michigan Avenue
Chicago, IL 60605

Heartland Community College

Normal, Illinois
www.hcc.cc.il.us
Two-year public **Federal Code: 030838**

	Living at home
Tuition and fees (2002-2003):	$1,500
Out-of-district:	$3,000
Out-of-state:	$4,500
Per-credit charge:	$50
Per-credit out-of-district:	$100
Per-credit out-of-state:	$150

Undergraduate aid. All financial aid based on need. Need-based aid available for full-time and part-time students.

Policies to reduce costs. Tuition/fee waivers for senior citizens, employees and their families. Credit/placement for qualifying scores on AP examinations. Work study available nights, weekends and for part-time students.

Payment plans. Credit card, installment payment.

Application procedures. FAFSA, institutional form required. No deadline.

Contact. 1500 West Raab Road
Normal, IL 61761

Highland Community College

Freeport, Illinois
www.highland.edu
Two-year public **Federal Code: 001681**

College costs. $80 per-credt-hour charge for border counties in Iowa and Wisconsin.

	Living at home
Tuition and fees:	$1,710
Out-of-district:	$2,430
Out-of-state:	$2,670
Per-credit charge:	$57
Per-credit out-of-district:	$81
Per-credit out-of-state:	$89
Board only:	$2,025
Books and supplies:	$1,140
Personal expenses:	$1,000
Transportation:	$1,800

Undergraduate aid. Need-based: Need-based aid available for full-time and part-time students. **Non-need-based:** Scholarships based on academics, athletics.

Policies to reduce costs. Tuition/fee waivers for senior citizens, employees and their families. Credit/placement for qualifying scores on AP, CLEP examinations. Work study available nights and for part-time students.

Payment plans. Credit card, deferred payment.

Application procedures. FAFSA, institutional form required. Priority date 6/1; no closing date. Applicants notified on rolling basis starting 8/1, must reply within 2 week(s) of notification.

Contact. Financial aid office: (815) 599-3519
Marcia Wells, Director of Financial Aid and Veteran Affairs
Pearl City Road
Freeport, IL 61032-9341

ITT Technical Institute: Burr Ridge

Burr Ridge, Illinois
www.itt-tech.edu
Two-year proprietary **Federal Code: 008329**

College costs. Total program varies depending on course of study. Per-credit-hour charge: $347. Books/supplies: $3,100.

Policies to reduce costs. Tuition/fee waivers for employees and their families. Tuition at time of enrollment guaranteed for 2 years.

Payment plans. Credit card, installment payment.

Application procedures. FAFSA, institutional form required. No deadline. Applicants notified on rolling basis.

Contact. Jim Garrett, Director of Finance
7040 High Grove Boulevard
Burr Ridge, IL 60521

ITT Technical Institute: Matteson

Matteson, Illinois
www.itt-tech.edu
Two-year proprietary **Federal Code: 010627**

College costs. Total program varies depending on course of study. Per-credit-hour charge: $347.

Policies to reduce costs. Tuition/fee waivers for employees and their families. Tuition at time of enrollment guaranteed for 2 years.

Payment plans. Credit card, installment payment.

Application procedures. FAFSA, institutional form required. No deadline. Applicants notified on rolling basis.

Contact. Linda Pappas, Director of Finance
600 Holiday Plaza Drive
Matteson, IL 60443

ITT Technical Institute: Mount Prospect

Mount Prospect, Illinois
www.itt-tech.edu
Three-year proprietary **Federal Code: 007329**

College costs. Total program varies depending on course of study. Per-credit-hour charge: $347.

Policies to reduce costs. Tuition/fee waivers for employees and their families.

Payment plans. Credit card, installment payment.

Application procedures. FAFSA, institutional form required. No deadline. Applicants notified on rolling basis.

Contact. Jose Navarro, Director of Finance
1401 Feehanville Drive
Mount Prospect, IL 60056

Illinois Central College

East Peoria, Illinois
www.icc.edu
Two-year public **Federal Code: 006753**

	Living at home
Tuition and fees:	$1,620
Out-of-district:	$3,600
Out-of-state:	$3,600
Per-credit charge:	$54
Per-credit out-of-district:	$120
Per-credit out-of-state:	$120
Books and supplies:	$600
Personal expenses:	$2,335
Transportation:	$1,344

Undergraduate aid. Non-need-based: Scholarships based on athletics.

Policies to reduce costs. Tuition/fee waivers for senior citizens, employees and their families. Credit/placement for qualifying scores on AP, CLEP examinations.

Payment plans. Credit card, deferred payment.

Application procedures. FAFSA, institutional form required. Priority date 4/15; no closing date. Applicants notified on rolling basis starting 6/1, must reply within 2 week(s) of notification. **Transfers:** No deadline.

Contact. Amy Ziegler, Coordinator of Financial Assistance
One College Drive
East Peoria, IL 61635-0001

Illinois College

Jacksonville, Illinois
www.ic.edu
Four-year private **Federal Code: 001688**

	Living at home	On-campus
Tuition and fees:	$13,300	$13,300
Room and board:		$5,800
Board only:	$800	
Books and supplies:	$700	$700
Personal expenses:	$800	$800
Transportation:	$700	$300

Undergraduate aid. Need-based: Average financial aid package for full-time students was $12,508; for part-time $3,594. 63% awarded as scholarships/grants, 37% as loans/jobs. **Non-need-based:** 76% awarded as scholarships/grants, 24% as loans/jobs. Scholarships based on academics, art, minority status, music/drama. **Student debt:** 75% of graduating class borrowed to fund education; average debt was $9,656.

Freshman aid. Need-based: Out of 306 full-time freshmen, 304 applied for aid; 232 were judged to have need; of these 232 received aid. Average package met 98% of need. 139 students had full need met. Average scholarship/grant was $6,113; average loan $2,991. **Non-need based:** 222 full-time freshmen with need received non-need scholarships; 63 without need received awards.

Policies to reduce costs. Tuition/fee waivers for minority students, family of clergy, employees and their families. Credit/placement for qualifying scores on AP, IB, CLEP examinations. Work study available nights, weekends and for part-time students.

Payment plans. Installment payment.

Application procedures. FAFSA required. Priority date 3/15; no closing date. Applicants notified on rolling basis starting 3/15, must reply within 2 week(s) of notification. **Transfers:** College transfer scholarship available with 24 transferable credit hours and minimum 3.0 GPA.

Contact. Financial aid office: (217) 245-3035
Katherine Taylor, Director of Financial Aid
1101 West College Avenue
Jacksonville, IL 62650

Illinois Eastern Community Colleges: Frontier Community College

Fairfield, Illinois
www.iecc.edu/fcc
Two-year public **Federal Code: 014090**

	Living at home
Tuition and fees (2002-2003):	$1,350
Out-of-district:	$5,653
Out-of-state:	$7,085
Per-credit charge:	$42
Per-credit out-of-district:	$185
Per-credit out-of-state:	$233
Books and supplies:	$600
Personal expenses:	$800
Transportation:	$1,200

Undergraduate aid. Need-based: Need-based aid available for full-time and part-time students. **Non-need-based:** Scholarships based on academics, state/district residency.

Policies to reduce costs. Tuition/fee waivers for senior citizens, employees and their families. Credit/placement for qualifying scores on AP, CLEP examinations.

Payment plans. Credit card payment.

Application procedures. FAFSA, institutional form required. No deadline. Applicants notified on rolling basis starting 8/1, must reply within 2 week(s) of notification. **Transfers:** No deadline.

Contact. Financial aid office: (618) 842-3711
Carroll Hilliard, Director of Financial Assistance and Community Services
Frontier Drive
Fairfield, IL 62837-9801

Illinois Eastern Community Colleges: Lincoln Trail College

Robinson, Illinois
www.iecc.edu/ltc
Two-year public **Federal Code: 009786**

	Living at home
Tuition and fees (2002-2003):	$1,350
Out-of-district:	$5,653
Out-of-state:	$7,085
Per-credit charge:	$42
Per-credit out-of-district:	$185
Per-credit out-of-state:	$233
Books and supplies:	$600
Personal expenses:	$800
Transportation:	$1,200

Undergraduate aid. Need-based: Need-based aid available for full-time and part-time students. **Non-need-based:** Scholarships based on academics, athletics, state/district residency.

Policies to reduce costs. Tuition/fee waivers for senior citizens, employees and their families. Credit/placement for qualifying scores on AP, CLEP examinations.

Payment plans. Credit card payment.

Application procedures. FAFSA, institutional form required. No deadline. Applicants notified on rolling basis starting 8/1, must reply within 2 week(s) of notification. **Transfers:** No deadline.

Contact. Financial aid office: (618) 544-8657
Deborah Kull, Director of Financial Aid
11220 State Highway 1
Robinson, IL 62454-5707

Illinois Eastern Community Colleges: Olney Central College

Olney, Illinois
www.iecc.edu/occ
Two-year public **Federal Code: 001742**

	Living at home
Tuition and fees (2002-2003):	$1,350
Out-of-district:	$5,653
Out-of-state:	$7,085
Per-credit charge:	$42
Per-credit out-of-district:	$185
Per-credit out-of-state:	$233
Books and supplies:	$600
Personal expenses:	$800
Transportation:	$1,200

Undergraduate aid. Need-based: Need-based aid available for full-time and part-time students. **Non-need-based:** Scholarships based on academics, athletics, state/district residency.

Policies to reduce costs. Tuition/fee waivers for senior citizens, employees and their families. Credit/placement for qualifying scores on AP, CLEP examinations.

Payment plans. Credit card payment.

Application procedures. FAFSA, institutional form required. No deadline. Applicants notified on rolling basis starting 8/1, must reply within 2 week(s) of notification. **Transfers:** No deadline.

Contact. Financial aid office: (618) 395-7777
Vicki Stuckey, Financial Aid Coordinator
305 North West Street
Olney, IL 62450

Illinois Eastern Community Colleges: Wabash Valley College

Mount Carmel, Illinois
www.iecc.edu/wvc
Two-year public **Federal Code: 001779**

	Living at home
Tuition and fees (2002-2003):	$1,350
Out-of-district:	$5,357
Out-of-state:	$6,616
Per-credit charge:	$42
Per-credit out-of-district:	$185
Per-credit out-of-state:	$233
Books and supplies:	$600
Personal expenses:	$800
Transportation:	$1,200

Undergraduate aid. Need-based: Need-based aid available for full-time and part-time students. **Non-need-based:** Scholarships based on academics, athletics, state/district residency.

Policies to reduce costs. Tuition/fee waivers for senior citizens, employees and their families. Credit/placement for qualifying scores on AP, CLEP examinations.

Payment plans. Credit card payment.

Application procedures. FAFSA, institutional form required. No deadline. Applicants notified on rolling basis starting 8/1, must reply within 2 week(s) of notification. **Transfers:** No deadline.

Contact. Financial aid office: (618) 262-8641
Melinda Silvernale, Financial Aid Coordinator
2200 College Drive
Mount Carmel, IL 62863-2657

Illinois Institute of Art

Chicago, Illinois
www.ilic.artinstitutes.edu
Four-year proprietary **Federal Code: 012584**

College costs. Fees range from $285-$710 depending on program.

	Living at home
Tuition and fees:	$15,264
Books and supplies:	$1,000
Personal expenses:	$1,260
Transportation:	$540

Undergraduate aid. Need-based: Need-based aid available for full-time and part-time students.

Policies to reduce costs. Credit/placement for qualifying scores on AP examinations.

Payment plans. Credit card, installment payment.

Application procedures. FAFSA required. Priority date 5/1; no closing date. Applicants notified on rolling basis.

Contact. Gina Lackland, Financial Aid Officer
350 North Orleans, Suite 136-L
Chicago, IL 60654

Illinois Institute of Art

Schaumburg, Illinois
www.ilis.aii.edu
Four-year proprietary **Federal Code: 012584**

	Living at home	On-campus
Tuition and fees (2002-2003):	$13,230	$13,230
Room and board:		$6,612
Books and supplies:	$987	$987
Personal expenses:	$2,628	$1,788

Undergraduate aid. Need-based: Need-based aid available for full-time and part-time students. **Non-need-based:** Scholarships based on art. **Additional information:** Merit scholarships based on GPA; talent-based scholarships.

Policies to reduce costs. Tuition/fee waivers for family members, employees and their families. Tuition at time of enrollment guaranteed for 4 years; prepayment discount. Work study available nights, weekends and for part-time students.

Payment plans. Credit card, installment payment.

Application procedures. FAFSA required. No deadline.

Contact. **Financial aid office:** (800) 314-3450
Joe Payne, Director of Student Financial Services
1000 North Plaza Drive, Suite 100
Schaumburg, IL 60173-4913

Illinois Institute of Technology

Chicago, Illinois
www.iit.edu
Four-year private **Federal Code: 001691**

College costs. Tuition and fees cover unlimited number of courses during academic year and include library and computer usage fees.

	Living at home	On-campus
Tuition and fees:	$20,331	$20,331
Room and board:		$6,282
Books and supplies:	$1,000	$1,000
Personal expenses:		$2,000
Transportation:		$1,200

Undergraduate aid. Need-based: Average financial aid package for full-time students was $18,232; for part-time $6,377. 73% awarded as scholarships/grants, 27% as loans/jobs. **Non-need-based:** 85% awarded as scholarships/grants, 15% as loans/jobs. Scholarships based on academics, alumni affiliation, athletics, leadership, minority status. **Student debt:** 53% of graduating class borrowed to fund education; average debt was $15,402.

Freshman aid. Need-based: Out of 293 full-time freshmen, 207 applied for aid; 184 were judged to have need; of these 184 received aid. Average package met 87% of need. 79 students had full need met. Average scholarship/grant was $7,901; average loan $4,404. **Non-need based:** 182 full-time freshmen with need received non-need scholarships; 24 without need received awards; 12 received athletic scholarships.

Merit scholarships. Henry Heald Scholarship based on ACT/SAT scores; $3,000-$15,000. Camras/Next Scholarship; $13,000, full tuition and room. Cyrus Tang and Chinese American Service League (CASL) Scholarship based on community service, essay, GPA and test scores, CASL only open to Chinese Americans; $4,500.

Policies to reduce costs. Tuition/fee waivers for employees and their families. Credit/placement for qualifying scores on AP, IB, CLEP examinations.

Payment plans. Credit card, installment payment.

Application procedures. FAFSA required. Closing date 4/15. Applicants notified on rolling basis starting 3/15, must reply by 5/1 or within 2 week(s) of notification. **Transfers:** Closing date 4/15.

Contact. **Financial aid office:** (312) 567-7219
Virginia Foster, Director for Student Finance Center
10 West 33rd Street, Room 101
Chicago, IL 60616

Illinois State University

Normal, Illinois
www.ilstu.edu
Four-year public **Federal Code: 001692**

	Living at home	On-campus
Tuition and fees (2002-2003):	$5,036	$5,036
Out-of-state:	$9,227	$9,227
Room and board:		$5,062
Board only:	$2,331	
Books and supplies:	$668	$668
Personal expenses:	$2,746	$2,231
Transportation:	$581	$261

Undergraduate aid. Need-based: Average financial aid package for full-time students was $7,675; for part-time $7,908. 50% awarded as scholarships/grants, 50% as loans/jobs. **Non-need-based:** 25% awarded as scholarships/grants, 75% as loans/jobs. Scholarships based on academics, art, athletics, leadership, music/drama. **Student debt:** 60% of graduating class borrowed to fund education; average debt was $13,921.

Freshman aid. Need-based: Out of 3,101 full-time freshmen, 2,383 applied for aid; 1,257 were judged to have need; of these 1,211 received aid. Average package met 80% of need. 503 students had full need met. Average scholarship/grant was $5,369; average loan $2,701. **Non-need based:** 354 full-time freshmen with need received non-need scholarships; 392 without need received awards; 48 received athletic scholarships.

Merit scholarships. Various non-need based merit scholarships available, including Presidential Scholars' Program, Provost's Scholarship, and Dean's Scholarship.

Policies to reduce costs. Tuition/fee waivers for senior citizens, employees and their families. Credit/placement for qualifying scores on AP, CLEP examinations. Work study available for part-time students.

Payment plans. Credit card, installment payment.

Application procedures. FAFSA required. Priority date 3/1; no closing date. Applicants notified on rolling basis starting 4/1, must reply within 2 week(s) of notification.

Contact. **Financial aid office:** (309) 438-2231
Charles Boudreau, Director of Financial Aid
Campus Box 2200
Normal, IL 61790-2200

Illinois Valley Community College

Oglesby, Illinois
www.ivcc.edu
Two-year public **Federal Code: 001705**

	Living at home
Tuition and fees (2002-2003):	$1,742
Out-of-district:	$5,977
Out-of-state:	$7,237
Per-credit charge:	$60
Per-credit out-of-district:	$192
Per-credit out-of-state:	$234
Books and supplies:	$650
Personal expenses:	$1,107
Transportation:	$1,466

Policies to reduce costs. Tuition/fee waivers for senior citizens. Credit/placement for qualifying scores on AP, CLEP examinations.

Application procedures. FAFSA required. Priority date 5/1; no closing date. Applicants notified on rolling basis starting 5/1. **Transfers:** No deadline.

Contact. **Financial aid office:** (815) 224-0438
Steve Crick, Director, Financial Aid
815 North Orlando Smith Avenue
Oglesby, IL 61348-9693

Illinois Wesleyan University

Bloomington, Illinois
www.iwu.edu
Four-year private **Federal Code: 001696**

	Living at home	On-campus
Tuition and fees:	$24,540	$24,540
Room and board:		$6,140
Board only:	$1,630	
Books and supplies:	$650	$650
Personal expenses:	$780	$780
Transportation:	$370	

Undergraduate aid. Need-based: Average financial aid package for full-time students was $16,671. 70% awarded as scholarships/grants, 30% as loans/jobs. **Non-need-based:** 64% awarded as scholarships/grants, 36% as loans/jobs. Scholarships based on academics, art, music/drama. **Student debt:** 69% of graduating class borrowed to fund education; average debt was $17,722.

Freshman aid. Need-based: Out of 582 full-time freshmen, 399 applied for aid; 327 were judged to have need; of these 327 received aid. Average package met 95% of need. 216 students had full need met. Average scholarship/grant was $13,214; average loan $2,816. **Non-need based:** 19 full-time freshmen with need received non-need scholarships; 186 without need received awards.

Merit scholarships. Alumni scholarships granted to students based on their high school academic performance, recommendations, testing and extracurricular activities, ranging from $5,000 to $15,700. Talent awards available in Schools of Music, Art and Music Theatre, ranging from $6,400 to $24,390.

Policies to reduce costs. Tuition/fee waivers for employees and their families. Credit/placement for qualifying scores on AP, IB, CLEP examinations. Work study available nights and weekends.

Payment plans. Credit card, installment payment.

Application procedures. FAFSA, institutional form required. Priority date 3/1; no closing date. Applicants notified on rolling basis starting 4/15, must reply within 4 week(s) of notification.

Contact. Financial aid office: (309) 556-3096
Lynn Nichelson, Director of Financial Aid
1312 North Park
Bloomington, IL 61702-2900

International Academy of Design and Technology

Chicago, Illinois
www.iadtchicago.com
Four-year proprietary **Federal Code: 021603**

College costs. Tuition higher for certain programs.

	Living at home
Tuition and fees (projected):	$17,200
Books and supplies:	$1,125
Personal expenses:	$1,428
Transportation:	$750

Undergraduate aid. All financial aid based on need. 36% awarded as scholarships/grants, 64% as loans/jobs.

Policies to reduce costs. Tuition/fee waivers for employees and their families. Credit/placement for qualifying scores on AP, IB, CLEP examinations.

Payment plans. Credit card, installment, deferred payment.

Application procedures. FAFSA, institutional form required. Priority date 9/1; no closing date. Applicants notified on rolling basis starting 3/1, must reply within 2 week(s) of notification. **Transfers:** Closing date 10/1.

Contact. Financial aid office: (312) 980-9200
Andrea Watkins, Director of Financial Aid
One North State Street
Chicago, IL 60602

John A. Logan College

Carterville, Illinois
www.jal.cc.il.us.
Two-year public **Federal Code: 008076**

	Living at home
Tuition and fees (2002-2003):	$1,470
Out-of-district:	$4,961
Out-of-state:	$7,201
Per-credit charge:	$49
Per-credit out-of-district:	$165
Per-credit out-of-state:	$240
Books and supplies:	$1,000
Personal expenses:	$800
Transportation:	$312

Undergraduate aid. All financial aid based on need. 88% awarded as scholarships/grants, 12% as loans/jobs. Need-based aid available for part-time students.

Policies to reduce costs. Tuition/fee waivers for senior citizens, employees and their families. Credit/placement for qualifying scores on AP, CLEP examinations.

Application procedures. FAFSA required. Priority date 5/1; no closing date. Applicants notified on rolling basis starting 8/1. **Transfers:** No deadline.

Contact. Stacy Holloway, Director for Student Financial Assistance
700 Logan College Road
Carterville, IL 62918

John Wood Community College

Quincy, Illinois
www.jwcc.edu
Two-year public **Federal Code: 012813**

	Living at home
Tuition and fees (2002-2003):	$1,890
Out-of-state:	$4,890
Per-credit charge:	$58
Per-credit out-of-district:	$158
Per-credit out-of-state:	$158
Books and supplies:	$956
Personal expenses:	$720
Transportation:	$864

Undergraduate aid. Need-based: Need-based aid available for full-time and part-time students.

Policies to reduce costs. Tuition/fee waivers for senior citizens, employees and their families. Credit/placement for qualifying scores on AP, CLEP examinations. Work study available nights and weekends.

Payment plans. Credit card, installment payment.

Application procedures. FAFSA required. No deadline. Applicants notified on rolling basis starting 3/1. **Transfers:** No deadline.

Contact. Financial aid office: (217) 224-6564 ext. 4312
D. Denny, Director of Financial Aid
1301 South 48th Street
Quincy, IL 62305-8736

Joliet Junior College

Joliet, Illinois
www.jjc.cc.il.us
Two-year public **Federal Code: 001699**

	Living at home
Tuition and fees (2002-2003):	$1,680
Out-of-district:	$5,547
Out-of-state:	$6,858
Per-credit charge:	$49
Per-credit out-of-district:	$178
Per-credit out-of-state:	$221
Board only:	$1,420
Personal expenses:	$1,500
Transportation:	$1,280

Undergraduate aid. Need-based: 79% awarded as scholarships/grants, 21% as loans/jobs. Need-based aid available for part-time students. **Non-need-based:** 50% awarded as scholarships/grants, 50% as loans/jobs. Scholarships based on academics.

Policies to reduce costs. Tuition/fee waivers for senior citizens, employees and their families. Credit/placement for qualifying scores on AP, CLEP examinations. Work study available nights, weekends and for part-time students.

Payment plans. Credit card, deferred payment.

Application procedures. FAFSA, institutional form required. Priority date 6/1; no closing date. Applicants notified on rolling basis starting 5/15.

Contact. Financial aid office: (815) 729-9020 ext. 2414
Jennifer Kloberdanz, Director of Financial Aid
1215 Houbolt Road
Joliet, IL 60431-8938

Judson College

Elgin, Illinois
www.judsoncollege.edu
Four-year private **Federal Code: 001700**

	Living at home	On-campus
Tuition and fees:	$16,050	$16,050
Room and board:		$6,000
Books and supplies:	$700	$700
Personal expenses:	$1,000	$1,000
Transportation:	$750	$500

Undergraduate aid. Need-based: Average financial aid package for full-time students was $15,439; for part-time $6,097. 58% awarded as scholarships/

grants, 42% as loans/jobs. **Non-need-based:** 41% awarded as scholarships/grants, 59% as loans/jobs. Scholarships based on academics, athletics, music/drama. **Student debt:** 79% of graduating class borrowed to fund education; average debt was $12,386.

Freshman aid. Need-based: Out of 105 full-time freshmen, 90 applied for aid; 74 were judged to have need; of these 74 received aid. Average package met 40% of need. 26 students had full need met. Average scholarship/grant was $11,576; average loan $2,132. **Non-need based:** 25 full-time freshmen with need received non-need scholarships; 11 without need received awards; 17 received athletic scholarships.

Policies to reduce costs. Tuition/fee waivers for senior citizens, family members, employees and their families. Credit/placement for qualifying scores on AP, CLEP examinations.

Payment plans. Credit card, deferred payment.

Application procedures. FAFSA required. No deadline. Applicants notified on rolling basis starting 1/1, must reply within 4 week(s) of notification.

Contact. Thomas Rueger, Director of Financial Aid
1151 North State Street
Elgin, IL 60123

Kankakee Community College

Kankakee, Illinois
www.kcc.cc.il.us
Two-year public **Federal Code: 007690**

	Living at home
Tuition and fees (2002-2003):	$1,320
Out-of-district:	$4,206
Out-of-state:	$9,375
Per-credit charge:	$42
Per-credit out-of-district:	$138
Per-credit out-of-state:	$310
Board only:	$1,325
Books and supplies:	$648
Personal expenses:	$720
Transportation:	$864

Undergraduate aid. Need-based: Need-based aid available for full-time and part-time students. **Non-need-based:** Scholarships based on athletics.

Policies to reduce costs. Tuition/fee waivers for senior citizens, employees and their families. Credit/placement for qualifying scores on CLEP examinations.

Payment plans. Credit card, deferred payment.

Application procedures. FAFSA, institutional form required. Priority date 6/1; no closing date. Applicants notified on rolling basis, must reply within 4 week(s) of notification.

Contact. Financial aid office: (815) 933-0218
Al Widhalm, Director of Financial Aid
PO Box 888
Kankakee, IL 60901

Kaskaskia College

Centralia, Illinois
www.kaskaskia.edu
Two-year public **Federal Code: 001701**

	Living at home
Tuition and fees:	$1,570
Out-of-district:	$4,704
Out-of-state:	$8,224
Per-credit charge:	$47
Per-credit out-of-district:	$142
Per-credit out-of-state:	$252
Books and supplies:	$1,080
Personal expenses:	$1,618
Transportation:	$1,750

Undergraduate aid. Need-based: 95% awarded as scholarships/grants, 5% as loans/jobs. Need-based aid available for part-time students. **Non-need-based:** Scholarships based on academics, athletics, state/district residency.

Policies to reduce costs. Tuition/fee waivers for senior citizens, employees and their families. Credit/placement for qualifying scores on CLEP examinations. Work study available for part-time students.

Payment plans. Credit card, installment, deferred payment.

Application procedures. FAFSA, institutional form required. Priority date 5/15; no closing date. Applicants notified on rolling basis starting 4/1, must reply within 2 week(s) of notification. **Transfers:** No deadline.

Contact. Financial aid office: (618) 545-3080
Sherry Summary, Director of Financial Aid
27210 College Road
Centralia, IL 62801

Kendall College

Evanston, Illinois
www.kendall.edu
Four-year private **Federal Code: 001703**

College costs (2002-2003). There are four degree programs offered. Tuition costs range from $9,360 to $16,185 per academic year. Per credit hour charges range from $260 to $415. Fees, $225. Room and board, $7,200.

Undergraduate aid. Need-based: Need-based aid available for full-time and part-time students. **Non-need-based:** Scholarships based on academics, athletics, religious affiliation.

Policies to reduce costs. Tuition/fee waivers for senior citizens, family members, family of clergy, employees and their families. Credit/placement for qualifying scores on AP, IB, CLEP examinations. Work study available nights, weekends and for part-time students.

Payment plans. Credit card, installment payment.

Application procedures. FAFSA required. Priority date 6/1; no closing date. Applicants notified on rolling basis starting 4/1, must reply within 2 week(s) of notification.

Contact. Financial aid office: (847) 866-1300 ext. 2349
L. Denise Coleman, Director of Financial Aid
2408 Orrington Avenue
Evanston, IL 60201-2899

Kishwaukee College

Malta, Illinois
www.kishwaukeecollege.edu
Two-year public **Federal Code: 007684**

	Living at home
Tuition and fees (2002-2003):	$1,940
Out-of-district:	$6,360
Out-of-state:	$7,560
Per-credit charge:	$54
Per-credit out-of-district:	$200
Per-credit out-of-state:	$241
Books and supplies:	$760
Personal expenses:	$1,020
Transportation:	$1,440

Undergraduate aid. Need-based: 77% awarded as scholarships/grants, 23% as loans/jobs. Need-based aid available for part-time students. **Non-need-based:** Scholarships based on academics, athletics, music/drama.

Policies to reduce costs. Tuition/fee waivers for senior citizens, employees and their families. Credit/placement for qualifying scores on AP, CLEP examinations. Work study available nights.

Payment plans. Credit card, installment, deferred payment.

Application procedures. FAFSA, institutional form required. Priority date 5/1; no closing date. Applicants notified on rolling basis starting 5/1, must reply within 2 week(s) of notification.

Contact. Financial aid office: (815) 825-2086
Pamela Siegfried Wagener, Coordinator of Financial Aid
21193 Malta Road
Malta, IL 60150-9699

Knox College

Galesburg, Illinois
www.knox.edu
Four-year private **Federal Code: 001704**

	Living at home	On-campus
Tuition and fees:	$24,369	$24,369
Room and board:		$5,925
Board only:	$1,000	
Books and supplies:	$600	$600
Personal expenses:	$600	$600
Transportation:	$200	$200

Undergraduate aid. Need-based: Average financial aid package for full-time students was $20,356. 76% awarded as scholarships/grants, 24% as loans/jobs. Need-based aid available for part-time students. **Non-need-based:** 58% awarded as scholarships/grants, 42% as loans/jobs. Scholarships based on academics, art, music/drama. **Student debt:** 60% of graduating class borrowed to fund education; average debt was $16,920.

Freshman aid. Need-based: Out of 300 full-time freshmen, 263 applied for aid; 212 were judged to have need; of these 212 received aid. Average package met 98% of need. 127 students had full need met. Average scholarship/grant was $15,957; average loan $4,306. **Non-need based:** 29 full-time freshmen with need received non-need scholarships; 72 without need received awards.

Merit scholarships. Academic scholarships; up to $15,000 ; award based upon high school academic performance and class rank. Visual and performing arts scholarships (in music, art, theater, dance, writing); up to $3,500; award based upon auditions or submission of portfolios. Social Concerns Scholarships; up to $3,500; award based upon community service activity.

Policies to reduce costs. Tuition/fee waivers for employees and their families. Credit/placement for qualifying scores on AP, IB, CLEP examinations. Work study available nights, weekends and for part-time students.

Payment plans. Credit card, installment payment.

Application procedures. FAFSA, institutional form required. Priority date 3/1; no closing date. Applicants notified on rolling basis starting 3/15, must reply by 5/1 or within 2 week(s) of notification. **Transfers:** Priority date 4/1.

Contact. **Financial aid office:** (309) 341-7149
Teresa Jackson, Director of Financial Aid
Campus Box 148
Galesburg, IL 61401-4999

Lake Forest College

Lake Forest, Illinois
www.lakeforest.edu
Four-year private **Federal Code: 001706**

	Living at home	On-campus
Tuition and fees:	$24,406	$24,406
Room and board:		$5,764
Board only:	$1,500	
Books and supplies:	$600	$600
Personal expenses:	$1,794	$730
Transportation:	$1,200	

Undergraduate aid. Need-based: Average financial aid package for full-time students was $20,020. 81% awarded as scholarships/grants, 19% as loans/jobs. **Non-need-based:** 92% awarded as scholarships/grants, 8% as loans/jobs. Scholarships based on academics, alumni affiliation, art, leadership, music/drama, state/district residency. **Student debt:** 61% of graduating class borrowed to fund education; average debt was $15,486.

Freshman aid. Need-based: Out of 358 full-time freshmen, 283 applied for aid; 251 were judged to have need; of these 251 received aid. Average package met 100% of need. 251 students had full need met. Average scholarship/grant was $17,496; average loan $2,691. **Non-need based:** 71 without need received awards.

Merit scholarships. Trustee Scholarship awards up to full tuition without regard to financial need. Deerpath Scholarships awarded in art, leadership, music, science, theater, and writing without regard to financial need. Awards range from $1,000-$5,000.

Policies to reduce costs. Tuition/fee waivers for employees and their families. Credit/placement for qualifying scores on AP, IB examinations.

Payment plans. Installment payment.

Application procedures. FAFSA, CSS PROFILE required. Priority date 3/1; no closing date. Applicants notified on rolling basis starting 3/15, must reply by 5/1. Early decision closing date 1/1. **Transfers:** Priority date 3/1; closing date 7/1.

Contact. Jerry Cebrzynski, Director of Financial Aid
555 North Sheridan Road
Lake Forest, IL 60045-2399

Lake Land College

Mattoon, Illinois
www.lakelandcollege.edu
Two-year public **Federal Code: 007644**

	Living at home
Tuition and fees:	$1,770
Out-of-district:	$3,480
Out-of-state:	$7,320
Per-credit charge:	$48
Per-credit out-of-district:	$105
Per-credit out-of-state:	$233
Books and supplies:	$318

Undergraduate aid. Need-based: 82% awarded as scholarships/grants, 18% as loans/jobs. Need-based aid available for part-time students. **Non-need-based:** 87% awarded as scholarships/grants, 13% as loans/jobs. Scholarships based on academics, athletics.

Policies to reduce costs. Tuition/fee waivers for senior citizens, employees and their families. Credit/placement for qualifying scores on CLEP examinations. Work study available nights, weekends and for part-time students.

Payment plans. Credit card, deferred payment.

Application procedures. FAFSA, institutional form required. Closing date 5/1. Applicants notified on rolling basis starting 6/1, must reply within 2 week(s) of notification. **Transfers:** No deadline.

Contact. Tynia Kessler, Director of Financial Aid and Veteran Services
5001 Lake Land Boulevard
Mattoon, IL 61938-9366

Lakeview College of Nursing

Danville, Illinois
www.lakeviewcol.edu
Upper-division private **Federal Code: 010501**

	Living at home
Tuition and fees:	$9,300
Books and supplies:	$582

Undergraduate aid. All financial aid based on need. Need-based aid available for full-time and part-time students.

Policies to reduce costs. Credit/placement for qualifying scores on CLEP examinations.

Payment plans. Installment, deferred payment.

Application procedures. FAFSA, institutional form required. Closing date 4/15. **Transfers:** Priority date 4/15; no deadline.

Contact. Janet Ingargiola, Financial Aid Officer
903 North Logan Avenue
Danville, IL 61832

Lewis University

Romeoville, Illinois
www.lewisu.edu
Four-year private **Federal Code: 001707**

	Living at home	On-campus
Tuition and fees:	$15,950	$15,950
Room and board:		$7,250
Board only:	$2,500	
Books and supplies:	$500	$500
Personal expenses:	$1,320	$1,320
Transportation:	$1,350	$570

Undergraduate aid. Need-based: Average financial aid package for full-time students was $13,422; for part-time $6,915. 51% awarded as scholarships/grants, 49% as loans/jobs. **Non-need-based:** 60% awarded as scholarships/grants, 40% as loans/jobs. Scholarships based on academics, alumni affiliation,

art, athletics, music/drama. **Student debt:** 72% of graduating class borrowed to fund education; average debt was $17,648.

Freshman aid. Need-based: Out of 367 full-time freshmen, 363 applied for aid; 263 were judged to have need; of these 263 received aid. Average package met 87% of need. 110 students had full need met. Average scholarship/grant was $6,552; average loan $2,356. **Non-need based:** 187 full-time freshmen with need received non-need scholarships; 90 without need received awards; 52 received athletic scholarships.

Policies to reduce costs. Tuition/fee waivers for employees and their families. Credit/placement for qualifying scores on AP examinations. Work study available nights, weekends and for part-time students.

Payment plans. Credit card, installment payment.

Application procedures. FAFSA required. Priority date 5/1; no closing date. Applicants notified on rolling basis starting 3/15, must reply by 2/1. **Transfers:** No deadline.

Contact. **Financial aid office:** (815) 836-5262
Janeen Decharinte, Director of Financial Aid
One University Parkway
Romeoville, IL 60446-2200

Lewis and Clark Community College

Godfrey, Illinois
www.lc.cc.il.us
Two-year public **Federal Code: 010020**

	Living at home
Tuition and fees:	$1,890
Out-of-district:	$5,310
Out-of-state:	$7,020
Per-credit charge:	$57
Per-credit out-of-district:	$171
Per-credit out-of-state:	$228
Books and supplies:	$435
Personal expenses:	$1,100
Transportation:	$900

Undergraduate aid. Need-based: 85% awarded as scholarships/grants, 15% as loans/jobs. Need-based aid available for part-time students.

Policies to reduce costs. Tuition/fee waivers for senior citizens, employees and their families. Credit/placement for qualifying scores on AP, CLEP examinations.

Payment plans. Credit card, installment, deferred payment.

Application procedures. FAFSA, institutional form required. Priority date 6/1; no closing date. Applicants notified on rolling basis starting 8/1, must reply within 3 week(s) of notification. **Transfers:** No deadline.

Contact. **Financial aid office:** (618) 468-2223
Khaneetah Cunningham, Director of Financial Aid
5800 Godfrey Road
Godfrey, IL 62035-2466

Lexington College

Chicago, Illinois
www.lexingtoncollege.edu
Two-year private **Federal Code: 016942**

	Living at home
Tuition and fees (2002-2003):	$10,940
Per-credit charge:	$640
Books and supplies:	$1,500
Personal expenses:	$400
Transportation:	$800

Undergraduate aid. All financial aid based on need. Average financial aid package for full-time students was $6,568; for part-time $4,378. 81% awarded as scholarships/grants, 19% as loans/jobs. **Student debt:** 36% of graduating class borrowed to fund education; average debt was $4,000.

Freshman aid. Out of 29 full-time freshmen, 28 applied for aid; 28 were judged to have need; of these 28 received aid. Average package met 89% of need. 12 students had full need met. Average scholarship/grant was $4,126.

Policies to reduce costs. Tuition/fee waivers for employees and their families. Credit/placement for qualifying scores on AP examinations.

Payment plans. Credit card, installment payment.

Application procedures. FAFSA required. Priority date 6/1; no closing date. Applicants notified on rolling basis starting 7/1, must reply within 2 week(s) of notification. **Transfers:** Closing date 6/1. Can only receive Illinois state aid at one institution per academic year if student enrolls and then withdraws to transfer to another college within term.

Contact. **Financial aid office:** (312) 226-6294
Andrew Addy, Director of Financial Aid
310 South Peoria Street, Suite 512
Chicago, IL 60607-3534

Lincoln Christian College and Seminary

Lincoln, Illinois
www.lccs.edu
Four-year private **Federal Code: 001708**

	Living at home	On-campus
Tuition and fees:	$9,568	$9,568
Room and board:		$4,468
Books and supplies:	$600	$600
Personal expenses:	$1,700	$1,700
Transportation:	$500	$500

Undergraduate aid. Need-based: Need-based aid available for full-time and part-time students.

Policies to reduce costs. Tuition/fee waivers for employees and their families. Credit/placement for qualifying scores on AP, CLEP examinations. Work study available nights, weekends and for part-time students.

Payment plans. Credit card, installment, deferred payment.

Application procedures. FAFSA required. Priority date 8/10; no closing date. Applicants notified on rolling basis starting 3/1, must reply within 2 week(s) of notification.

Contact. **Financial aid office:** (217) 732-3168 ext. 2226
Jack Getchel, Director of Student Financial Aid
100 Campus View Drive
Lincoln, IL 62656

Lincoln College

Lincoln, Illinois
www.lincolncollege.edu
Two-year private **Federal Code: 001709**

	Living at home	On-campus
Tuition and fees:	$13,210	$13,210
Per-credit charge:	$100	$100
Room and board:		$5,200
Books and supplies:	$240	$240
Personal expenses:	$1,000	$1,000
Transportation:	$500	$200

Undergraduate aid. Need-based: Need-based aid available for full-time and part-time students. **Non-need-based:** Scholarships based on academics, art, athletics, music/drama. **Additional information:** Auditions recommended for music, speech, theater, broadcasting, and dance scholarship candidates, portfolios recommended for art and technical theater scholarship candidates.

Policies to reduce costs. Tuition/fee waivers for employees and their families. Tuition at time of enrollment guaranteed for 2 years; credit/placement for qualifying scores on CLEP examinations. Work study available nights and weekends.

Payment plans. Credit card, installment, deferred payment.

Application procedures. FAFSA required. Priority date 6/1; closing date 7/1. Applicants notified on rolling basis starting 6/1, must reply within 3 week(s) of notification.

Contact. **Financial aid office:** (217) 732-3155 ext. 230
Kevin Stephens, Director of Financial Aid
300 Keokuk
Lincoln, IL 62656

Lincoln Land Community College

Springfield, Illinois
www.lincolnland.net
Two-year public **Federal Code: 007170**

	Living at home
Tuition and fees (2002-2003):	$1,380
Out-of-district:	$4,334
Out-of-state:	$15,472
Per-credit charge:	$42
Per-credit out-of-district:	$140
Per-credit out-of-state:	$256
Books and supplies:	$550
Personal expenses:	$3,100
Transportation:	$630

Undergraduate aid. Need-based: 86% awarded as scholarships/grants, 14% as loans/jobs. Need-based aid available for part-time students. **Non-need-based:** Scholarships based on academics, athletics, minority status, state/district residency.

Policies to reduce costs. Tuition/fee waivers for senior citizens, minority students, employees and their families. Credit/placement for qualifying scores on AP, CLEP examinations.

Payment plans. Credit card, installment, deferred payment.

Application procedures. FAFSA, institutional form required. Priority date 5/1; no closing date. Applicants notified on rolling basis starting 4/15, must reply within 2 week(s) of notification. **Transfers:** No deadline.

Contact. Financial aid office: (217) 786-2237
Lee Bursi, Director of Financial Aid
5250 Shepherd Road
Springfield, IL 62794-9256

Loyola University of Chicago

Chicago, Illinois
www.luc.edu
Four-year private **Federal Code: 001710**

	Living at home	On-campus
Tuition and fees:	$21,054	$21,054
Room and board:		$7,900
Board only:	$800	
Books and supplies:	$800	$800
Personal expenses:	$1,600	$1,600
Transportation:	$930	$450

Undergraduate aid. Need-based: Average financial aid package for full-time students was $20,087; for part-time $7,237. 62% awarded as scholarships/grants, 38% as loans/jobs. **Non-need-based:** 60% awarded as scholarships/grants, 40% as loans/jobs. Scholarships based on academics, art, athletics, leadership, music/drama. **Student debt:** 63% of graduating class borrowed to fund education; average debt was $18,000.

Freshman aid. Need-based: Out of 1,623 full-time freshmen, 1,530 applied for aid; 1,151 were judged to have need; of these 1,147 received aid. Average package met 90% of need. 348 students had full need met. Average scholarship/grant was $13,093; average loan $3,958. **Non-need based:** 411 full-time freshmen with need received non-need scholarships; 341 without need received awards; 8 received athletic scholarships.

Policies to reduce costs. Tuition/fee waivers for senior citizens, employees and their families. Credit/placement for qualifying scores on AP, CLEP examinations. Work study available nights, weekends and for part-time students.

Payment plans. Credit card, installment payment.

Application procedures. FAFSA required. Priority date 3/1; no closing date. Applicants notified on rolling basis starting 3/1, must reply within 3 week(s) of notification. **Transfers:** No deadline. FAFSA must be filed by July 1 to receive Illinois map grant.

Contact. Financial aid office: (773) 508-3155
Terry Richards, Associate Vice President for Operations
820 North Michigan Avenue
Chicago, IL 60611

MacMurray College

Jacksonville, Illinois
www.mac.edu
Four-year private **Federal Code: 001717**

	Living at home	On-campus
Tuition and fees (2002-2003):	$14,500	$14,500
Room and board:		$5,165
Books and supplies:	$750	$750
Personal expenses:	$655	$655
Transportation:	$500	$500

Undergraduate aid. Need-based: Average financial aid package for full-time students was $11,433; for part-time $3,133. 70% awarded as scholarships/grants, 30% as loans/jobs. **Non-need-based:** 17% awarded as scholarships/grants, 83% as loans/jobs. Scholarships based on academics, alumni affiliation, art, leadership, minority status, music/drama, religious affiliation. **Student debt:** 94% of graduating class borrowed to fund education; average debt was $14,461. **Additional information:** Merit scholarships for accepted, enrolled freshman based on academic record. Need-based program meets 100% of direct tuition charges after family contribution and financial aid.

Freshman aid. Need-based: Out of 127 full-time freshmen, 127 applied for aid; 123 were judged to have need; of these 123 received aid. Average package met 71% of need. 80 students had full need met. Average scholarship/grant was $5,806; average loan $3,309. **Non-need based:** 5 full-time freshmen with need received non-need scholarships; 4 without need received awards.

Merit scholarships. $500-$1,4000 academic scholarships based on merit. Music performance and Art competition scholarships available. Transfer scholarships to $10,000 based on academic merit. Leadership scholarships available based on committee selection.

Policies to reduce costs. Tuition/fee waivers for children of alumni, senior citizens, employees and their families. Prepayment discount; credit/placement for qualifying scores on AP, IB, CLEP examinations. Work study available nights, weekends and for part-time students.

Payment plans. Credit card, installment, deferred payment.

Application procedures. FAFSA required. Priority date 5/1; closing date 8/1. Applicants notified on rolling basis starting 3/1, must reply by 5/1 or within 4 week(s) of notification. **Transfers:** Priority date 5/1; no deadline.

Contact. Financial aid office: (217) 479-7041
Rhonda Cors, Director of Financial Aid
447 East College Avenue
Jacksonville, IL 62650-2590

McHenry County College

Crystal Lake, Illinois
www.mchenry.edu
Two-year public **Federal Code: 007691**

	Living at home
Tuition and fees (2002-2003):	$1,724
Out-of-district:	$7,603
Out-of-state:	$8,861
Per-credit charge:	$49
Per-credit out-of-district:	$237
Per-credit out-of-state:	$278
Board only:	$1,342
Books and supplies:	$750
Personal expenses:	$1,304
Transportation:	$1,370

Undergraduate aid. Need-based: 66% awarded as scholarships/grants, 34% as loans/jobs. Need-based aid available for part-time students. **Non-need-based:** 74% awarded as scholarships/grants, 26% as loans/jobs. Scholarships based on academics, athletics, leadership, music/drama, state/district residency. **Additional information:** Students can apply throughout the award year for federal and state aid. Students with physical handicaps or learning disabilities may apply for Special Needs Scholarship (full tuition for one year).

Merit scholarships. President's Scholarship, full tuition for two years, based on talent in academic areas; students must complete portfolio and have 3.0 GPA. Applications available at high school guidance offices. Founding Faculty Scholarship, full tuition for 2 years based on GPA and essay.

Policies to reduce costs. Tuition/fee waivers for senior citizens, employees and their families. Credit/placement for qualifying scores on AP, CLEP examinations. Work study available nights, weekends and for part-time students.

Payment plans. Credit card, installment payment.

Application procedures. FAFSA, institutional form required. Priority date 6/1; no closing date. Applicants notified on rolling basis starting 5/1. **Transfers:** No deadline.

Contact. **Financial aid office:** (815) 455-8767
Marianne Devenny, Director, Office of Financial Aid and Records
8900 U.S. Highway 14
Crystal Lake, IL 60012-2761

McKendree College

Lebanon, Illinois
www.mckendree.edu
Four-year private **Federal Code: 001722**

	Living at home	On-campus
Tuition and fees (2002-2003):	$14,200	$14,200
Room and board:		$5,440
Books and supplies:	$900	$900
Personal expenses:	$835	$835
Transportation:	$600	$280

Undergraduate aid. Need-based: Average financial aid package for full-time students was $11,368; for part-time $4,338. 68% awarded as scholarships/grants, 32% as loans/jobs. **Non-need-based:** 57% awarded as scholarships/grants, 43% as loans/jobs. Scholarships based on academics, art, athletics, leadership, minority status, music/drama, religious affiliation. **Student debt:** 39% of graduating class borrowed to fund education; average debt was $14,647.

Freshman aid. Need-based: Out of 262 full-time freshmen, 250 applied for aid; 212 were judged to have need; of these 211 received aid. Average package met 89% of need. 80 students had full need met. Average scholarship/grant was $9,807; average loan $2,024. **Non-need based:** 56 full-time freshmen with need received non-need scholarships; 50 without need received awards; 32 received athletic scholarships.

Merit scholarships. Presidential Scholarship candidates must be interviewed final weekend in January and meet at least 1 of following critieria: 25 ACT composite, 3.4 GPA, rank in upper 20% of class; unlimited number awarded; $1,000 to full tuition.

Policies to reduce costs. Tuition/fee waivers for employees and their families. Credit/placement for qualifying scores on AP, CLEP examinations. Work study available nights and weekends.

Payment plans. Credit card, installment payment.

Application procedures. FAFSA, institutional form required. Priority date 5/31; no closing date. Applicants notified on rolling basis, must reply within 4 week(s) of notification. **Transfers:** Priority date 5/31.

Contact. **Financial aid office:** (618) 537-6829
Mark Campbell, Vice President for Admissions and Financial Aid
701 College Road
Lebanon, IL 62254

Midstate College

Peoria, Illinois
www.midstate.edu
Four-year proprietary **Federal Code: 004568**

College costs. Fees vary according to courses taken and range from $60-$120.

	Living at home
Tuition and fees (2002-2003):	$8,400
Books and supplies:	$940
Transportation:	$1,500

Policies to reduce costs. Tuition/fee waivers for employees and their families. Credit/placement for qualifying scores on CLEP examinations.

Payment plans. Credit card, installment, deferred payment.

Application procedures. FAFSA, institutional form required. No deadline. Applicants notified on rolling basis, must reply within 4 week(s) of notification. **Transfers:** No deadline.

Contact. Janet Ozuna, Director of Financial Aid
411 West Northmoor Road
Peoria, IL 61614-3558

Millikin University

Decatur, Illinois
www.millikin.edu
Four-year private **Federal Code: 001724**

	Living at home	On-campus
Tuition and fees:	$19,309	$19,309
Room and board:		$6,123
Board only:	$1,000	
Books and supplies:	$800	$800
Transportation:	$1,200	$200

Undergraduate aid. Need-based: Average financial aid package for full-time students was $15,641; for part-time $3,862. 76% awarded as scholarships/grants, 24% as loans/jobs. **Non-need-based:** 59% awarded as scholarships/grants, 41% as loans/jobs. Scholarships based on academics, art, leadership, music/drama, state/district residency.

Freshman aid. Need-based: Out of 637 full-time freshmen, 633 applied for aid; 563 were judged to have need; of these 551 received aid. Average package met 93% of need. 372 students had full need met. Average scholarship/grant was $11,313; average loan $2,913. **Non-need based:** 169 full-time freshmen with need received non-need scholarships; 173 without need received awards.

Merit scholarships. Millikin awards 5 full-tuition scholarships to students with outstanding academic records who demonstrate leadership qualities in their community and school activities. Scholarships are awarded following an on-campus interview. Students selected to the Freshman Honors Scholar Program receive an annual scholarship no less than $8,500 and may qualify for more based on financial aid.

Policies to reduce costs. Tuition/fee waivers for family of clergy, employees and their families. Credit/placement for qualifying scores on AP, IB, CLEP examinations. Work study available nights and weekends.

Payment plans. Credit card, installment payment.

Application procedures. FAFSA required. Priority date 4/15; closing date 6/1. Applicants notified on rolling basis starting 3/1, must reply within 4 week(s) of notification.

Contact. **Financial aid office:** (217) 424-6343
Jeanne Puckett, Director of Financial Aid
1184 West Main St.
Decatur, IL 62522-2084

Monmouth College

Monmouth, Illinois
www.monm.edu
Four-year private **Federal Code: 001725**

	Living at home	On-campus
Tuition and fees:	$18,600	$18,600
Room and board:		$5,000
Board only:	$750	
Books and supplies:	$600	$600
Personal expenses:	$110	$400
Transportation:	$500	$350

Undergraduate aid. Need-based: Average financial aid package for full-time students was $15,376. **Non-need-based:** Scholarships based on academics, art, music/drama, state/district residency. **Student debt:** 81% of graduating class borrowed to fund education; average debt was $17,145. **Additional information:** Monmouth Plan: if family annual income less than $250,000, at least $9,000 in gift assistance available.

Freshman aid. Need-based: Out of 269 full-time freshmen, 269 applied for aid; 212 were judged to have need; of these 212 received aid. Average package met 94% of need. 97 students had full need met. Average scholarship/grant was $11,207; average loan $2,972. **Non-need based:** 56 full-time freshmen with need received non-need scholarships; 55 without need received awards.

Merit scholarships. Unlimited merit awards to top 25% of class with 25 ACT: up to $5,000. Talent scholarships available (amount varies) for drama, art, theatre, Latin, bagpipes.

Policies to reduce costs. Tuition/fee waivers for family members, employees and their families. Credit/placement for qualifying scores on AP, IB examinations.

Payment plans. Installment payment.

Application procedures. FAFSA required. Priority date 4/15; no closing date. Applicants notified on rolling basis starting 3/1, must reply by 8/25. **Transfers:** Priority date 4/15.

Contact. Jayne Whitside, Director of Financial Aid
700 East Broadway
Monmouth, IL 61462-9989

Moody Bible Institute

Chicago, Illinois
www.moody.edu
Four-year private **Federal Code: 001727**

College costs (2002-2003). Undergraduate students are not charged tuition because tuition is paid from external funding. Students must pay fees of $2,228 and room and board costs of $6,010. Books/supplies: $600. Personal expenses: $500. Transportation: $500.

Undergraduate aid. All financial aid based on need. Need-based aid available for full-time students. **Additional information:** Aid available to upperclassmen is based on private and not federal/state sources.

Policies to reduce costs. Tuition/fee waivers for employees and their families. Tuition at time of enrollment guaranteed for 4 years; credit/placement for qualifying scores on AP, IB, CLEP examinations.

Payment plans. Credit card, installment payment.

Application procedures. No deadline. Early decision closing date 12/1. **Transfers:** No deadline. Students should complete two semesters of study in residence before applying for aid.

Contact. **Financial aid office:** (312) 329-4178
Daniel Ward, Financial Aid Coordinator
820 North La Salle Boulevard
Chicago, IL 60610

Moraine Valley Community College

Palos Hills, Illinois
www.morainevalley.edu
Two-year public **Federal Code: 007692**

	Living at home
Tuition and fees (2002-2003):	$1,682
Out-of-district:	$6,062
Out-of-state:	$7,322
Per-credit charge:	$51
Per-credit out-of-district:	$197
Per-credit out-of-state:	$239
Board only:	$1,800
Books and supplies:	$1,000
Personal expenses:	$1,488
Transportation:	$1,513

Undergraduate aid. **Need-based:** 84% awarded as scholarships/grants, 16% as loans/jobs. Need-based aid available for part-time students. **Non-need-based:** Scholarships based on academics, athletics, leadership.

Policies to reduce costs. Tuition/fee waivers for senior citizens, employees and their families. Credit/placement for qualifying scores on AP, CLEP examinations. Work study available nights and for part-time students.

Payment plans. Credit card, installment, deferred payment.

Application procedures. FAFSA, institutional form required. Priority date 6/2; no closing date. Applicants notified on rolling basis starting 2/2, must reply within 4 week(s) of notification.

Contact. **Financial aid office:** (708) 974-5726
Laurie Anema, Director of Financial Aid
10900 South 88th Avenue
Palos Hills, IL 60465-0937

Morrison Institute of Technology

Morrison, Illinois
www.morrison.tec.il.us
Two-year private **Federal Code: 008880**

College costs. Computer account fee $100, recreational center/activity fee $30.

	Living at home	On-campus
Tuition and fees:	$9,990	$9,990
Per-credit charge:	$416	$416
Room only:		$1,600
Books and supplies:	$575	$575
Personal expenses:	$900	$900
Transportation:	$400	$200

Undergraduate aid. **Non-need-based:** Scholarships based on academics.

Policies to reduce costs. Tuition/fee waivers for children of alumni.

Payment plans. Credit card, installment payment.

Application procedures. FAFSA, institutional form required. No deadline. Applicants notified on rolling basis, must reply within 2 week(s) of notification.

Contact. Julie Damhoff, Financial Aid Officer
701 Portland Avenue
Morrison, IL 61270-2959

NAES College

Chicago, Illinois
www.naes.edu
Four-year private **Federal Code: 016088**

	Living at home
Tuition and fees:	$5,140
Books and supplies:	$250

Payment plans. Credit card, installment, deferred payment.

Application procedures. FAFSA required. Priority date 6/1; no closing date. Applicants notified on rolling basis starting 6/1.

Contact. Tim Murphy, Financial Aid Officer
2838 West Peterson Avenue
Chicago, IL 60659

National University of Health Sciences

Lombard, Illinois
www.nuhs.edu
Four-year private **Federal Code: 001732**

	Living at home	On-campus
Tuition and fees (2002-2003):	$21,200	$21,200
Room and board:		$5,000
Books and supplies:	$1,000	$1,000

Undergraduate aid. **Need-based:** Need-based aid available for full-time students. **Additional information:** Massage Therapy certificate program is eligible for Title IV financial aid. Program is half-time and qualifies for half-time and less-than-half-time Pell grants, federal work-study, FSEOG, federal Perkins grants, and prorated federal Stafford loans.

Policies to reduce costs. Tuition/fee waivers for family members. Work study available nights and for part-time students.

Payment plans. Credit card, installment, deferred payment.

Contact. **Financial aid office:** (630) 889-6700
Sarah Adams, Director of Financial Aid
200 East Roosevelt Road
Lombard, IL 60148

National-Louis University

Chicago, Illinois
www.nl.edu
Four-year private **Federal Code: E00787**

	Living at home	On-campus
Tuition and fees (2002-2003):	$14,715	$14,715
Room and board:		$6,013
Board only:	$2,511	
Books and supplies:	$900	$900
Personal expenses:	$1,305	$1,305
Transportation:	$1,521	$432

Undergraduate aid. **Non-need-based:** Scholarships based on academics.

Policies to reduce costs. Tuition/fee waivers for employees and their families. Prepayment discount; credit/placement for qualifying scores on AP, CLEP examinations.

Payment plans. Credit card, installment, deferred payment.

Application procedures. FAFSA, institutional form required. Priority date 4/15; no closing date. Applicants notified on rolling basis starting 5/1, must reply within 2 week(s) of notification.

Contact. **Financial aid office:** (847) 465-0575 ext. 5693
Rebecca Babel, Director of Student Finance
122 South Michigan Avenue
Chicago, IL 60603

North Central College

Naperville, Illinois
www.noctrl.edu
Four-year private **Federal Code: 001734**

	Living at home	On-campus
Tuition and fees:	$19,446	$19,446
Room and board:		$6,375
Books and supplies:	$900	$900
Personal expenses:	$2,350	$1,150
Transportation:	$1,050	$320

Undergraduate aid. Need-based: Average financial aid package for full-time students was $16,323; for part-time $8,455. 74% awarded as scholarships/grants, 26% as loans/jobs. **Non-need-based:** 45% awarded as scholarships/grants, 55% as loans/jobs. Scholarships based on academics, art, music/drama, religious affiliation. **Student debt:** 57% of graduating class borrowed to fund education; average debt was $13,638.

Freshman aid. Need-based: Out of 443 full-time freshmen, 387 applied for aid; 312 were judged to have need; of these 312 received aid. Average package met 90% of need. 159 students had full need met. Average scholarship/grant was $11,943; average loan $3,380. **Non-need based:** 101 full-time freshmen with need received non-need scholarships; 101 without need received awards.

Merit scholarships. Numerous merit and talent scholarship opportunities available.

Policies to reduce costs. Tuition/fee waivers for senior citizens, family of clergy, employees and their families. Credit/placement for qualifying scores on AP, IB, CLEP examinations. Work study available nights and weekends.

Payment plans. Credit card, installment payment.

Application procedures. FAFSA, institutional form required. Priority date 4/1; no closing date. Applicants notified on rolling basis starting 3/1, must reply within 4 week(s) of notification. **Transfers:** No deadline. Part-time students not needing financial assistance may apply for special student status at discounted rate.

Contact. **Financial aid office:** (630) 637-5600
Kathy Edmunds, Financial Aid Director
PO Box 3065
Naperville, IL 60566

North Park University

Chicago, Illinois
www.northpark.edu
Four-year private **Federal Code: 001735**

	Living at home	On-campus
Tuition and fees (projected):	$19,470	$19,470
Room and board:		$6,710
Books and supplies:	$950	$950
Personal expenses:	$925	$925
Transportation:	$900	

Undergraduate aid. Need-based: Need-based aid available for full-time students. **Non-need-based:** Scholarships based on academics, art, music/drama.

Policies to reduce costs. Tuition/fee waivers for family of clergy, employees and their families. Credit/placement for qualifying scores on AP, CLEP examinations.

Payment plans. Credit card, installment payment.

Application procedures. FAFSA required. Priority date 4/1; closing date 8/1. Applicants notified on rolling basis starting 3/10. **Transfers:** Priority date 5/15; closing date 8/1.

Contact. **Financial aid office:** (773) 244-5525
Alex Shu, Director of Financial Aid
3225 West Foster Avenue
Chicago, IL 60625-4895

Northeastern Illinois University

Chicago, Illinois
www.neiu.edu
Four-year public **Federal Code: 001693**

	Living at home
Tuition and fees (2002-2003):	$3,330
Out-of-state:	$8,346
Board only:	$2,124
Books and supplies:	$960
Personal expenses:	$2,376
Transportation:	$918

Undergraduate aid. Need-based: Average financial aid package for full-time students was $5,426; for part-time $3,485. 79% awarded as scholarships/grants, 21% as loans/jobs. **Non-need-based:** 38% awarded as scholarships/grants, 62% as loans/jobs. Scholarships based on academics, art, leadership, minority status, music/drama, state/district residency. **Student debt:** 25% of graduating class borrowed to fund education; average debt was $11,765.

Freshman aid. Need-based: Out of 977 full-time freshmen, 702 applied for aid; 519 were judged to have need; of these 506 received aid. Average package met 72% of need. 71 students had full need met. Average scholarship/grant was $5,514; average loan $1,291. **Non-need based:** 31 full-time freshmen with need received non-need scholarships; 19 without need received awards.

Policies to reduce costs. Tuition/fee waivers for senior citizens, employees and their families. Credit/placement for qualifying scores on AP, IB, CLEP examinations.

Payment plans. Credit card, deferred payment.

Application procedures. FAFSA, institutional form required. Priority date 4/1; no closing date. Applicants notified on rolling basis starting 4/1, must reply within 3 week(s) of notification.

Contact. J. Jennings, Director of Financial Aid
5500 North St. Louis Avenue
Chicago, IL 60625

Northern Illinois University

DeKalb, Illinois
www.niu.edu
Four-year public **Federal Code: 001737**

	Living at home	On-campus
Tuition and fees (2002-2003):	$4,484	$4,484
Out-of-state:	$7,776	$7,776
Room and board:		$5,826
Books and supplies:	$700	$700
Personal expenses:		$1,584
Transportation:		$450

Undergraduate aid. Non-need-based: Scholarships based on academics, athletics.

Policies to reduce costs. Tuition/fee waivers for minority students, employees and their families. Credit/placement for qualifying scores on AP, CLEP examinations.

Payment plans. Installment payment.

Application procedures. FAFSA, institutional form required. Priority date 3/1; no closing date. Applicants notified on rolling basis starting 4/15.

Contact. **Financial aid office:** (815) 753-1395
Kathleen Brunson, Director of Student Financial Aid
DeKalb, IL 60115-2854

Northwestern Business College

Chicago, Illinois
northwesternbc.edu
Two-year proprietary **Federal Code: 012362**

	Living at home
Tuition and fees (2002-2003):	$12,870
Board only:	$6,029
Books and supplies:	$835
Personal expenses:	$1,000

Undergraduate aid. All financial aid based on need. Need-based aid available for full-time and part-time students. **Additional information:** State grant programs for Illinois residents and alternative loans offered.

Policies to reduce costs. Tuition/fee waivers for employees and their families. Credit/placement for qualifying scores on IB examinations. Work study available nights and for part-time students.

Payment plans. Credit card, installment payment.

Application procedures. FAFSA, institutional form required. Priority date 6/30; no closing date. Applicants notified on rolling basis starting 8/15, must reply within 4 week(s) of notification. **Transfers:** No deadline. Students transferring in must have financial aid prorated based on what they used at former school.

Contact. **Financial aid office:** (773) 777-4220
Kevin Sullivan, Director of Financial Assistance
4839 North Milwaukee Avenue
Chicago, IL 60630

Northwestern University

Evanston, Illinois
www.northwestern.edu
Four-year private **Federal Code: 001739**

	Living at home	On-campus
Tuition and fees:	$28,524	$28,524
Room and board:		$8,967
Board only:	$1,215	
Books and supplies:	$1,326	$1,326
Personal expenses:	$1,566	$1,566
Transportation:	$984	$510

Undergraduate aid. All financial aid based on need. Average financial aid package for full-time students was $23,382. 77% awarded as scholarships/grants, 23% as loans/jobs. **Student debt:** 48% of graduating class borrowed to fund education; average debt was $14,551.

Freshman aid. Out of 2,005 full-time freshmen, 1,177 applied for aid; 899 were judged to have need; of these 899 received aid. Average package met 100% of need. 899 students had full need met. Average scholarship/grant was $19,106; average loan $2,660.

Policies to reduce costs. Tuition/fee waivers for employees and their families. Credit/placement for qualifying scores on AP, IB examinations.

Payment plans. Installment payment.

Application procedures. FAFSA, CSS PROFILE required. Closing date 2/1. Applicants notified by 4/15, must reply by 5/1. Early decision closing date 11/1. **Transfers:** Closing date 6/1. Transfer student aid limited for first year.

Contact. **Financial aid office:** (847) 491-7400
Carolyn Lindley, Director of Financial Aid
1801 Hinman Avenue
Evanston, IL 60204-3060

Oakton Community College

Des Plaines, Illinois
www.oakton.edu
Two-year public **Federal Code: 009896**

	Living at home
Tuition and fees:	$1,878
Out-of-district:	$5,358
Out-of-state:	$7,098
Per-credit charge:	$58
Per-credit out-of-district:	$174
Per-credit out-of-state:	$232
Board only:	$1,525
Books and supplies:	$800
Personal expenses:	$1,000
Transportation:	$1,200

Undergraduate aid. **Need-based:** Average financial aid package for full-time students was $1,517. 94% awarded as scholarships/grants, 6% as loans/jobs. Need-based aid available for part-time students. **Non-need-based:** 21% awarded as scholarships/grants, 79% as loans/jobs. Scholarships based on academics, leadership, state/district residency. **Student debt:** 2% of graduating class borrowed to fund education; average debt was $2,315. **Additional information:** Foundation Scholarships applications available in January through mid-March.

Policies to reduce costs. Tuition/fee waivers for senior citizens, employees and their families. Credit/placement for qualifying scores on AP, CLEP examinations. Work study available nights, weekends and for part-time students.

Payment plans. Credit card, installment payment.

Application procedures. FAFSA, institutional form required. Priority date 5/1; no closing date. Applicants notified on rolling basis starting 6/1, must reply within 2 week(s) of notification.

Contact. Cheryl Warmann, Director of Financial Aid
1600 East Golf Road
Des Plaines, IL 60016

Olivet Nazarene University

Bourbonnais, Illinois
www.olivet.edu
Four-year private **Federal Code: 001741**

	Living at home	On-campus
Tuition and fees:	$14,980	$14,980
Room and board:		$5,500
Books and supplies:	$800	$800
Personal expenses:	$400	$400
Transportation:		$800

Undergraduate aid. **Need-based:** Need-based aid available for full-time and part-time students. **Non-need-based:** Scholarships based on academics, art, athletics, leadership, music/drama, religious affiliation, state/district residency.

Policies to reduce costs. Tuition/fee waivers for family members, family of clergy, employees and their families. Credit/placement for qualifying scores on AP, IB, CLEP examinations. Work study available nights, weekends and for part-time students.

Payment plans. Credit card, installment, deferred payment.

Application procedures. FAFSA, institutional form required. Priority date 3/1; no closing date. Applicants notified on rolling basis starting 1/15, must reply within 2 week(s) of notification. **Transfers:** Priority date 3/1; no deadline.

Contact. **Financial aid office:** (815) 939-5249
Greg Bruner, Director of Financial Aid
One University Avenue
Bourbonnais, IL 60914

Parkland College

Champaign, Illinois
www.parkland.edu
Two-year public **Federal Code: 007118**

College costs. For internet classes in-district students pay $55 per-credit-hour, all others pay $95 per-credit-hour.

	Living at home
Tuition and fees (projected):	$1,800
Out-of-district:	$6,450
Out-of-state:	$7,800
Per-credit charge:	$57
Per-credit out-of-district:	$205
Per-credit out-of-state:	$248
Board only:	$2,100
Books and supplies:	$800
Personal expenses:	$950
Transportation:	$950

Undergraduate aid. Need-based: 78% awarded as scholarships/grants, 22% as loans/jobs. **Non-need-based:** Scholarships based on academics, art, athletics, job skills, leadership, minority status, music/drama, state/district residency. **Student debt:** 26% of graduating class borrowed to fund education; average debt was $1,839.

Freshman aid. Need-based: Average package met 78% of need. **Non-need based:** 18 received athletic scholarships.

Policies to reduce costs. Tuition/fee waivers for senior citizens, employees and their families. Credit/placement for qualifying scores on AP, CLEP examinations. Work study available nights.

Payment plans. Credit card, installment, deferred payment.

Application procedures. FAFSA, institutional form required. Priority date 3/1; no closing date. Applicants notified on rolling basis starting 6/1, must reply within 2 week(s) of notification. **Transfers:** No deadline.

Contact. Financial aid office: (217) 351-2222
Jack Lyons, Director of Financial Aid and Veterans Affairs
2400 West Bradley Avenue
Champaign, IL 61821-1899

Prairie State College

Chicago Heights, Illinois
www.prairiestate.edu
Two-year public **Federal Code: 001640**

	Living at home
Tuition and fees (2002-2003):	$2,120
Out-of-district:	$6,020
Out-of-state:	$9,020
Per-credit charge:	$70
Per-credit out-of-district:	$200
Per-credit out-of-state:	$300
Books and supplies:	$750
Personal expenses:	$1,700
Transportation:	$1,100

Undergraduate aid. Need-based: Need-based aid available for full-time and part-time students.

Policies to reduce costs. Tuition/fee waivers for senior citizens, employees and their families. Credit/placement for qualifying scores on AP examinations. Work study available nights, weekends and for part-time students.

Payment plans. Credit card, installment, deferred payment.

Application procedures. FAFSA, institutional form required. Priority date 7/1; no closing date. Applicants notified on rolling basis, must reply within 2 week(s) of notification.

Contact. Financial aid office: (708) 709-3523
Alice Cabriales, Coordinator of Financial Aid
202 South Halsted Street
Chicago Heights, IL 60411

Principia College

Elsah, Illinois
www.prin.edu/college
Four-year private **Federal Code: 001744**

	Living at home	On-campus
Tuition and fees:	$18,540	$18,540
Room and board:		$6,504
Books and supplies:	$900	$900
Personal expenses:		$750
Transportation:		$750

Undergraduate aid. Need-based: Average financial aid package for full-time students was $16,399. 80% awarded as scholarships/grants, 20% as loans/jobs. Need-based aid available for part-time students. **Non-need-based:** Scholarships based on academics, alumni affiliation. **Student debt:** 47% of graduating class borrowed to fund education; average debt was $12,000. **Additional information:** Need-based Tuition Reduction Work Plan combines job with grant. No external finance company for current students to use to pay current tuition.

Freshman aid. Need-based: Average package met 90% of need. Average scholarship/grant was $11,373; average loan $3,350.

Merit scholarships. Trustee Scholarship, full tuition; Presidential Scholarship, $8,700; Dean's Scholarship, $5,800; Academic Scholarship, $3,000; Arthur Schulz, Jr. Alumni Scholarship, $4,500; 4-year scholarships based on high school GPA and test scores. Dean's and Academic Scholarships for transfer students who meet the above criteria with a minimum 3.4 GPA. Children and grandchildren of alumni eligible for 4-year scholarships based on high school or transfer GPA.

Policies to reduce costs. Tuition/fee waivers for employees and their families. Credit/placement for qualifying scores on AP, IB, CLEP examinations.

Payment plans. Credit card, installment payment.

Application procedures. Institutional form, CSS PROFILE required. Closing date 4/15. Applicants notified on rolling basis starting 5/1.

Contact. Financial aid office: (800) 277-4648
Ruth Schoch, Director of Financial Aid
1 Maybeck Place
Elsah, IL 62028-9799

Quincy University

Quincy, Illinois
www.quincy.edu
Four-year private **Federal Code: 001745**

	Living at home	On-campus
Tuition and fees:	$16,850	$16,850
Room and board:		$5,480
Books and supplies:	$800	$800
Personal expenses:	$800	$800
Transportation:	$1,320	$750

Undergraduate aid. Need-based: Average financial aid package for full-time students was $14,207; for part-time $6,520. 70% awarded as scholarships/grants, 30% as loans/jobs. **Non-need-based:** 51% awarded as scholarships/grants, 49% as loans/jobs. Scholarships based on academics, art, athletics, music/drama. **Student debt:** 81% of graduating class borrowed to fund education; average debt was $15,465.

Freshman aid. Need-based: Out of 229 full-time freshmen, 212 applied for aid; 170 were judged to have need; of these 170 received aid. Average package met 87% of need. 50 students had full need met. Average scholarship/grant was $10,860; average loan $3,329. **Non-need based:** 33 full-time freshmen with need received non-need scholarships; 59 without need received awards; 39 received athletic scholarships.

Merit scholarships. Academic scholarships based on ACT and high school GPA; unlimited number awarded; $2,500-$9,000 per year.

Policies to reduce costs. Tuition/fee waivers for senior citizens, employees and their families. Credit/placement for qualifying scores on AP, IB, CLEP examinations. Work study available nights and weekends.

Payment plans. Credit card, installment payment.

Application procedures. FAFSA required. Priority date 4/15; no closing date. Applicants notified on rolling basis starting 2/15, must reply by 5/1 or within 2 week(s) of notification. **Transfers:** No deadline.

Contact. Financial aid office: (217) 228-5260
Shann Doerr, Director of Financial Aid
1800 College Avenue
Quincy, IL 62301-2699

Rend Lake College

Ina, Illinois
www.rlc.edu
Two-year public **Federal Code: 007119**

	Living at home
Tuition and fees (projected):	$1,536
Out-of-district:	$2,352
Out-of-state:	$4,800
Per-credit charge:	$48
Per-credit out-of-district:	$74
Per-credit out-of-state:	$150
Board only:	$1,374
Books and supplies:	$500
Personal expenses:	$1,636
Transportation:	$1,616

Undergraduate aid. Need-based: 82% awarded as scholarships/grants, 18% as loans/jobs. Need-based aid available for part-time students. **Non-need-based:** 62% awarded as scholarships/grants, 38% as loans/jobs. Scholarships based on academics, art, athletics, leadership, music/drama, state/district residency.

Policies to reduce costs. Tuition/fee waivers for senior citizens, employees and their families. Credit/placement for qualifying scores on AP, CLEP examinations.

Payment plans. Credit card, installment, deferred payment.

Application procedures. FAFSA required. No deadline. Applicants notified on rolling basis starting 3/15, must reply within 4 week(s) of notification.

Contact. Financial aid office: (618) 437-5321 ext. 385
Doug Carlson, Director of Financial Aid
468 North Ken Gray Parkway
Ina, IL 62846

Richland Community College

Decatur, Illinois
www.richland.edu
Two-year public **Federal Code: 010879**

	Living at home
Tuition and fees (2002-2003):	$1,580
Out-of-district:	$5,131
Out-of-state:	$9,289
Per-credit charge:	$48
Per-credit out-of-district:	$166
Per-credit out-of-state:	$305
Books and supplies:	$600
Transportation:	$1,000

Undergraduate aid. Need-based: Average financial aid package for full-time students was $3,851; for part-time $2,327. 91% awarded as scholarships/grants, 9% as loans/jobs. **Non-need-based:** 88% awarded as scholarships/grants, 12% as loans/jobs. Scholarships based on academics. **Student debt:** 7% of graduating class borrowed to fund education; average debt was $3,418.

Freshman aid. Need-based: Out of 260 full-time freshmen, 133 applied for aid; 94 were judged to have need; of these 76 received aid. Average package met 56% of need. 8 students had full need met. Average scholarship/grant was $3,265; average loan $1,848. **Non-need based:** 28 full-time freshmen with need received non-need scholarships; 14 without need received awards.

Policies to reduce costs. Tuition/fee waivers for senior citizens, employees and their families. Credit/placement for qualifying scores on AP, CLEP examinations. Work study available nights and for part-time students.

Payment plans. Credit card, installment, deferred payment.

Application procedures. FAFSA required. No deadline. Applicants notified on rolling basis starting 3/20. **Transfers:** No deadline.

Contact. Financial aid office: (217) 875-7200
Deborah McGee, Director of Financial Aid
One College Park
Decatur, IL 62521

Robert Morris College: Chicago

Chicago, Illinois
www.robertmorris.edu
Four-year private **Federal Code: 001746**

	Living at home
Tuition and fees:	$13,500
Board only:	$1,239
Personal expenses:	$1,044
Transportation:	$858

Undergraduate aid. Need-based: Average financial aid package for full-time students was $10,032; for part-time $7,443. 67% awarded as scholarships/grants, 33% as loans/jobs. **Non-need-based:** 22% awarded as scholarships/grants, 78% as loans/jobs. Scholarships based on academics, art, athletics, state/district residency. **Student debt:** 91% of graduating class borrowed to fund education; average debt was $12,857.

Freshman aid. Need-based: Out of 1,189 full-time freshmen, 907 applied for aid; 889 were judged to have need; of these 889 received aid. Average package met 63% of need. 28 students had full need met. Average scholarship/grant was $8,493; average loan $2,581. **Non-need based:** 17 full-time freshmen with need received non-need scholarships; 18 without need received awards; 12 received athletic scholarships.

Policies to reduce costs. Tuition/fee waivers for employees and their families. Credit/placement for qualifying scores on AP, CLEP examinations. Work study available nights, weekends and for part-time students.

Payment plans. Installment payment.

Application procedures. FAFSA required. No deadline. Applicants notified on rolling basis. **Transfers:** No deadline.

Contact. Financial aid office: (312) 935-4076
Karen LeVeque, Director of Financial Services
401 South State Street
Chicago, IL 60605

Rock Valley College

Rockford, Illinois
www.rvc.cc.il.us
Two-year public **Federal Code: 001747**

College costs. Fees vary according to the courses taken. Registration fee is $2 per semester and lab fee is $1 per course.

	Living at home
Tuition and fees:	$1,560
Out-of-district:	$5,880
Out-of-state:	$8,730
Per-credit charge:	$45
Per-credit out-of-district:	$189
Per-credit out-of-state:	$284
Books and supplies:	$900
Transportation:	$1,536

Undergraduate aid. Need-based: Need-based aid available for full-time and part-time students. **Non-need-based:** Scholarships based on academics.

Policies to reduce costs. Tuition/fee waivers for senior citizens, employees and their families. Credit/placement for qualifying scores on AP, CLEP examinations. Work study available nights and for part-time students.

Payment plans. Credit card, deferred payment.

Application procedures. FAFSA required. Priority date 6/15; no closing date. Applicants notified on rolling basis starting 4/1, must reply within 2 week(s) of notification.

Contact. Financial aid office: (815) 921-4150
Sue Ullrick, Coordinator of Financial Aid/Scholarships
3301 North Mulford Road
Rockford, IL 61114-5699

Rockford Business College

Rockford, Illinois
www.rbcsuccess.com
Two-year proprietary **Federal Code: 008545**

College costs. Tuition $485 per class; $25 additional fee per class. Students typically take 4-5 classes per term. Books/supplies: $2,000. Personal expenses: $2,880. Transportation: $1,000.

Undergraduate aid. Need-based: Need-based aid available for full-time and part-time students.

Policies to reduce costs. Tuition/fee waivers for employees and their families. Credit/placement for qualifying scores on IB examinations. Work study available nights.

Application procedures. FAFSA required. No deadline. Applicants notified on rolling basis. **Transfers:** No deadline.

Contact. Ed Hastings, Director of Financial Aid
730 North Church Street
Rockford, IL 61103

Rockford College

Rockford, Illinois
www.rockford.edu
Four-year private **Federal Code: 001748**

	Living at home	On-campus
Tuition and fees:	$20,210	$20,210
Room and board:		$6,581
Board only:	$1,600	
Books and supplies:	$880	$880
Personal expenses:	$1,745	$1,745
Transportation:	$1,025	$615

Undergraduate aid. Need-based: Need-based aid available for full-time and part-time students. **Non-need-based:** Scholarships based on academics, alumni affiliation. **Additional information:** Will attempt to meet 100% of student's demonstrated financial need. Full tuition scholarships available, separate application and interview process required.

Policies to reduce costs. Tuition/fee waivers for family members, employees and their families. Credit/placement for qualifying scores on AP, IB, CLEP examinations. Work study available nights and weekends.

Payment plans. Credit card, installment, deferred payment.

Application procedures. FAFSA, institutional form required. Priority date 4/15; no closing date. Applicants notified on rolling basis starting 4/15, must reply within 3 week(s) of notification. **Transfers:** No deadline.

Contact. **Financial aid office:** (815) 226-3383
Todd Free, Director of Student Administrative Services
5050 East State Street
Rockford, IL 61108-2393

Roosevelt University

Chicago, Illinois
www.roosevelt.edu
Four-year private **Federal Code: 001749**

	Living at home	On-campus
Tuition and fees (2002-2003):	$13,970	$13,970
Room and board:		$6,270
Books and supplies:	$600	$600

Undergraduate aid. Need-based: Need-based aid available for full-time students. **Non-need-based:** Scholarships based on academics.

Merit scholarships. Presidential Award based on GPA, SAT or ACT test scores, and involvement; 5 awarded; full tuition. Honors Program for 3.5 GPA, ACT of 23, and involvement; 20-30 awarded; $14,000-$42,000 over 4 years. Recognition Award for transfers and freshmen; 60 awarded; $1,500-$6,000 annually. Music and Theater Scholarships for transfers and freshmen based on talent; approximately 90 awarded; tuition and housing.

Policies to reduce costs. Tuition/fee waivers for senior citizens, employees and their families. Credit/placement for qualifying scores on AP, CLEP examinations.

Payment plans. Credit card, installment, deferred payment.

Application procedures. FAFSA required. Priority date 5/1; no closing date. Applicants notified on rolling basis, must reply within 1 week(s) of notification.

Contact. **Financial aid office:** (312) 341-3565
Walter O'Neill, Director of Financial Aid
430 South Michigan Avenue
Chicago, IL 60605-1394

Rush University

Chicago, Illinois
www.rushu.rush.edu
Upper-division private **Federal Code: 009800**

College costs. Costs listed are for nursing and pre-med students. Costs vary greatly for different programs.

	Living at home
Tuition and fees (2002-2003):	$14,175
Books and supplies:	$650
Personal expenses:	$1,200
Transportation:	$550

Undergraduate aid. All financial aid based on need. Need-based aid available for full-time and part-time students.

Policies to reduce costs. Tuition/fee waivers for employees and their families. Credit/placement for qualifying scores on AP, CLEP examinations. Work study available nights and weekends.

Payment plans. Credit card, installment, deferred payment.

Application procedures. FAFSA, institutional form required. Priority date 5/1; no closing date. Applicants notified on rolling basis starting 4/1, must reply within 4 week(s) of notification.

Contact. Robert Dame, Director of Student Financial Aid
600 South Paulina, Suite 440
Chicago, IL 60612

Saint Anthony College of Nursing

Rockford, Illinois
www.sacn.edu
Upper-division private **Federal Code: 009987**

	Living at home
Tuition and fees:	$13,650
Books and supplies:	$1,500

Application procedures. Priority date 5/1; no closing date.

Contact. Lisa Ruch
5658 East State Street
Rockford, IL 61108-2468

St. Augustine College

Chicago, Illinois
www.staugustinecollege.edu
Four-year private **Federal Code: 021854**

College costs. Cost includes tuition, fees, books.

	Living at home
Tuition and fees (projected):	$8,400

Policies to reduce costs. Tuition/fee waivers for employees and their families. Credit/placement for qualifying scores on IB, CLEP examinations.

Payment plans. Credit card, installment payment.

Application procedures. FAFSA, institutional form required. No deadline. Applicants notified on rolling basis.

Contact. **Financial aid office:** (773) 878-8756
Maria Zambonino, Financial Aid Office Director
1333 West Argyle
Chicago, IL 60640-3501

St. Francis Medical Center College of Nursing

Peoria, Illinois
www.sfmccon.edu
Upper-division private **Federal Code: 006240**

	Living at home	On-campus
Tuition and fees:	$10,088	$10,088
Room only:		$1,680
Board only:	$1,238	
Books and supplies:	$1,192	$1,192
Personal expenses:	$2,035	$2,107
Transportation:	$763	$763

Undergraduate aid. Need-based: Average financial aid package for full-time students was $9,543; for part-time $5,425. 65% awarded as scholarships/grants, 35% as loans/jobs. **Non-need-based:** 80% awarded as scholarships/grants, 20% as loans/jobs. Scholarships based on academics, alumni affiliation. **Student debt:** 55% of graduating class borrowed to fund education; average debt was $10,647. **Additional information:** Modified Education Employment Program available to full-time students on a limited basis. Tuition waiver program for hospital employees available.

Policies to reduce costs. Tuition/fee waivers for employees and their families.

Payment plans. Credit card, installment payment.

Application procedures. FAFSA, institutional form required. Priority date 6/1; no closing date. Applicants notified on rolling basis starting 5/15, must reply within 2 week(s) of notification. **Transfers:** Priority date 6/1; no deadline.

Contact. **Financial aid office:** (309) 655-2291
Kathy Casey, Director of Financial Aid
511 NE Greenleaf Street
Peoria, IL 61603-3783

St. Xavier University

Chicago, Illinois
www.sxu.edu
Four-year private **Federal Code: 001768**

	Living at home	On-campus
Tuition and fees:	$16,670	$16,670
Room and board:		$6,484
Board only:	$1,872	
Books and supplies:	$900	$900
Personal expenses:	$1,318	$862
Transportation:	$862	$354

Undergraduate aid. Need-based: Average financial aid package for full-time students was $13,849; for part-time $7,141. 59% awarded as scholarships/grants, 41% as loans/jobs. **Non-need-based:** 64% awarded as scholarships/grants, 36% as loans/jobs. Scholarships based on academics, athletics, music/drama. **Student debt:** 63% of graduating class borrowed to fund education; average debt was $17,271.

Freshman aid. Need-based: Out of 375 full-time freshmen, 357 applied for aid; 322 were judged to have need; of these 322 received aid. Average package met 89% of need. 84 students had full need met. Average scholarship/grant was $8,271; average loan $3,081. **Non-need based:** 315 full-time freshmen with need received non-need scholarships; 42 without need received awards; 35 received athletic scholarships.

Policies to reduce costs. Tuition/fee waivers for senior citizens, employees and their families. Credit/placement for qualifying scores on AP, CLEP examinations.

Payment plans. Credit card, installment, deferred payment.

Application procedures. FAFSA required. Priority date 3/1; no closing date. Applicants notified on rolling basis starting 2/1, must reply by 5/1 or within 2 week(s) of notification.

Contact. **Financial aid office:** (773) 298-3070
Susan Swisher, Director of Financial Aid
3700 West 103rd Street
Chicago, IL 60655

Sauk Valley Community College

Dixon, Illinois
www.svcc.edu
Two-year public **Federal Code: 001752**

College costs. For internet courses tuition $54 in-state, $88 out-of-state.

	Living at home
Tuition and fees (2002-2003):	$1,770
Out-of-district:	$6,600
Out-of-state:	$8,220
Per-credit charge:	$54
Per-credit out-of-district:	$215
Per-credit out-of-state:	$269
Books and supplies:	$500
Personal expenses:	$900
Transportation:	$1,000

Undergraduate aid. Need-based: Need-based aid available for full-time and part-time students. **Non-need-based:** Scholarships based on academics, athletics, leadership, minority status, state/district residency.

Policies to reduce costs. Tuition/fee waivers for senior citizens, employees and their families. Credit/placement for qualifying scores on AP, CLEP examinations. Work study available nights and for part-time students.

Payment plans. Credit card, deferred payment.

Application procedures. FAFSA, institutional form required. Priority date 3/1; no closing date. Applicants notified on rolling basis starting 5/1. **Transfers:** There is a state filing deadline for state-aid programs, begins June 1.

Contact. **Financial aid office:** (815) 288-5511 ext. 339
David Peterson, Director of Financial Aid
173 Illinois Route 2
Dixon, IL 61021

School of the Art Institute of Chicago

Chicago, Illinois
www.artic.edu/saic
Four-year private **Federal Code: 001753**

	Living at home
Tuition and fees (2002-2003):	$21,300
Board only:	$2,100
Books and supplies:	$2,220
Personal expenses:	$1,420
Transportation:	$910

Undergraduate aid. Need-based: Average financial aid package for full-time students was $23,600; for part-time $15,426. 57% awarded as scholarships/grants, 43% as loans/jobs. **Non-need-based:** 33% awarded as scholarships/grants, 67% as loans/jobs. Scholarships based on academics, art, state/district residency. **Student debt:** 55% of graduating class borrowed to fund education; average debt was $17,004.

Freshman aid. Need-based: Out of 292 full-time freshmen, 211 applied for aid; 159 were judged to have need; of these 159 received aid. Average package met 75% of need. 27 students had full need met. Average scholarship/grant was $11,409; average loan $6,513. **Non-need based:** 17 full-time freshmen with need received non-need scholarships; 31 without need received awards.

Policies to reduce costs. Tuition/fee waivers for employees and their families. Credit/placement for qualifying scores on AP, IB, CLEP examinations. Work study available nights, weekends and for part-time students.

Payment plans. Credit card, installment, deferred payment.

Application procedures. FAFSA, institutional form required. Priority date 3/15; no closing date. Applicants notified on rolling basis starting 5/1.

Contact. **Financial aid office:** (312) 899-5106
Patrick James, Director of Financial Aid
37 South Wabash Avenue
Chicago, IL 60603

Shawnee Community College

Ullin, Illinois
www.shawneecc.edu
Two-year public **Federal Code: 007693**

	Living at home
Tuition and fees:	$1,350
Out-of-district:	$2,220
Out-of-state:	$2,220
Per-credit charge:	$45
Per-credit out-of-district:	$74
Per-credit out-of-state:	$74
Books and supplies:	$500
Personal expenses:	$680
Transportation:	$1,414

Undergraduate aid. All financial aid based on need. Need-based aid available for full-time and part-time students.

Policies to reduce costs. Tuition/fee waivers for senior citizens, employees and their families. Credit/placement for qualifying scores on AP, CLEP examinations.

Payment plans. Installment payment.

Application procedures. FAFSA required. Priority date 9/1; no closing date. Applicants notified on rolling basis, must reply within 2 week(s) of notification.

Contact. Tammy Capps, Director of Financial Aid
8364 Shawnee College Road
Ullin, IL 62992

Shimer College

Waukegan, Illinois
www.shimer.edu
Four-year private **Federal Code: 001756**

	Living at home	On-campus
Tuition and fees:	$17,150	$17,150
Room and board:		$2,530
Books and supplies:	$940	$940

Policies to reduce costs. Tuition/fee waivers for adults, children of alumni, senior citizens, employees and their families.

Payment plans. Credit card, installment payment.

Application procedures. FAFSA, institutional form required. Priority date 6/1; closing date 7/31. Applicants notified by 7/31, must reply by 9/1.

Contact. Bob Morris, Director of Financial Aid
414 North Sheridan Road
Waukegan, IL 60079-0500

South Suburban College of Cook County

South Holland, Illinois
www.southsuburbancollege.edu
Two-year public **Federal Code: 001769**

College costs. Some out-of-state students in nearby states may qualify for tuition reduction under regional tuition plan.

	Living at home
Tuition and fees:	$2,040
Out-of-district:	$6,870
Out-of-state:	$7,470
Per-credit charge:	$59
Per-credit out-of-district:	$220
Per-credit out-of-state:	$240
Books and supplies:	$500
Personal expenses:	$1,000
Transportation:	$300

Undergraduate aid. Need-based: Need-based aid available for full-time and part-time students. **Non-need-based:** Scholarships based on academics, art, athletics, music/drama, state/district residency.

Policies to reduce costs. Tuition/fee waivers for adults, senior citizens, employees and their families. Credit/placement for qualifying scores on CLEP examinations. Work study available nights and for part-time students.

Payment plans. Credit card, deferred payment.

Application procedures. FAFSA required. Priority date 6/1; no closing date. Applicants notified on rolling basis starting 7/1.

Contact. Financial aid office: (708) 596-2000 ext. 2321
John Semple, Director of Financial Aid
15800 South State Street
South Holland, IL 60473

Southeastern Illinois College

Harrisburg, Illinois
www.sic.edu
Two-year public **Federal Code: 001757**

	Living at home
Tuition and fees (2002-2003):	$1,470
Out-of-district:	$6,210
Out-of-state:	$7,830
Per-credit charge:	$49
Per-credit out-of-district:	$207
Per-credit out-of-state:	$261
Board only:	$2,500
Books and supplies:	$450
Personal expenses:	$1,400
Transportation:	$1,200

Undergraduate aid. Need-based: 91% awarded as scholarships/grants, 9% as loans/jobs. Need-based aid available for part-time students. **Non-need-based:** Scholarships based on academics, alumni affiliation, art, athletics, music/drama.

Policies to reduce costs. Tuition/fee waivers for senior citizens, employees and their families. Credit/placement for qualifying scores on AP, CLEP examinations. Work study available for part-time students.

Payment plans. Credit card, installment, deferred payment.

Application procedures. FAFSA required. No deadline. Applicants notified on rolling basis starting 4/15, must reply within 2 week(s) of notification. **Transfers:** No deadline.

Contact. Financial aid office: (618) 252-5400 ext. 2450
Kelli Mahoney, Director of Financial Aid
3575 College Road
Harrisburg, IL 62946

Southern Illinois University Carbondale

Carbondale, Illinois
www.siuc.edu
Four-year public **Federal Code: 001758**

	Living at home	On-campus
Tuition and fees (2002-2003):	$4,865	$4,865
Out-of-state:	$8,525	$8,525
Room and board:		$4,627
Books and supplies:	$660	$660
Personal expenses:	$3,603	$2,546

Undergraduate aid. Need-based: Average financial aid package for full-time students was $7,892; for part-time $4,873. 53% awarded as scholarships/grants, 47% as loans/jobs. **Non-need-based:** 42% awarded as scholarships/grants, 58% as loans/jobs. Scholarships based on academics, alumni affiliation, art, athletics, leadership, minority status, music/drama, state/district residency. **Student debt:** 39% of graduating class borrowed to fund education; average debt was $12,366. **Additional information:** Need-based financial aid available to part-time students enrolled in minimum of 6 semester hours.

Freshman aid. Need-based: Out of 2,054 full-time freshmen, 1,542 applied for aid; 1,048 were judged to have need; of these 1,022 received aid. Average package met 95% of need. 859 students had full need met. Average scholarship/grant was $4,660; average loan $2,129. **Non-need based:** 592 full-time freshmen with need received non-need scholarships; 139 without need received awards; 39 received athletic scholarships.

Policies to reduce costs. Tuition/fee waivers for senior citizens, employees and their families. Credit/placement for qualifying scores on AP, IB, CLEP examinations. Work study available nights, weekends and for part-time students.

Payment plans. Credit card, installment payment.

Application procedures. FAFSA required. Priority date 4/1; no closing date. Applicants notified on rolling basis starting 2/15, must reply within 3 week(s) of notification. **Transfers:** Priority date 4/1.

Contact. Dan Mann, Director of Financial Aid
Mailcode 4701
Carbondale, IL 62901-4701

Southern Illinois University Edwardsville

Edwardsville, Illinois
www.siue.edu
Four-year public **Federal Code: 001759**

College costs. Required fees include book rental.

	Living at home	On-campus
Tuition and fees (2002-2003):	$3,709	$3,709
Out-of-state:	$6,679	$6,679
Room and board:		$4,714
Board only:	$2,802	
Books and supplies:	$610	$610
Personal expenses:	$1,284	$1,284
Transportation:	$1,463	$1,463

Undergraduate aid. All financial aid based on need. Average financial aid package for full-time students was $7,500; for part-time $5,782. 57% awarded as scholarships/grants, 43% as loans/jobs. **Student debt:** 20% of graduating class borrowed to fund education; average debt was $15,534.

Freshman aid. Out of 1,629 full-time freshmen, 1,169 applied for aid; 824 were judged to have need; of these 767 received aid. Average package met 79% of need. 141 students had full need met. Average scholarship/grant was $4,831; average loan $2,068.

Policies to reduce costs. Tuition/fee waivers for senior citizens, employees and their families. Credit/placement for qualifying scores on AP, CLEP examinations. Work study available nights, weekends and for part-time students.

Payment plans. Credit card, installment, deferred payment.

Application procedures. FAFSA required. Priority date 3/1; closing date 6/1. Applicants notified on rolling basis starting 3/15, must reply within 2 week(s) of notification. **Transfers:** No deadline.

Contact. **Financial aid office:** (618) 650-3880
Marian Smithson, Director of Student Financial Aid
PO Box 1600
Edwardsville, IL 62026-1600

Southwestern Illinois College

Belleville, Illinois
www.swic.edu
Two-year public **Federal Code: 001636**

	Living at home
Tuition and fees (2002-2003):	$1,470
Out-of-district:	$4,260
Out-of-state:	$7,140
Per-credit charge:	$49
Per-credit out-of-district:	$142
Per-credit out-of-state:	$238
Board only:	$2,000
Books and supplies:	$500
Personal expenses:	$1,320
Transportation:	$1,310

Undergraduate aid. **Need-based:** Need-based aid available for full-time and part-time students. **Non-need-based:** Scholarships based on academics, athletics.

Policies to reduce costs. Tuition/fee waivers for senior citizens, employees and their families. Credit/placement for qualifying scores on AP, CLEP examinations.

Payment plans. Credit card, installment, deferred payment.

Application procedures. FAFSA required. Priority date 5/31; no closing date. Applicants notified on rolling basis starting 7/1, must reply within 2 week(s) of notification.

Contact. Robert Clement, Director of Financial Aid
2500 Carlyle Avenue
Belleville, IL 62221-9989

Spoon River College

Canton, Illinois
www.spoonrivercollege.net
Two-year public **Federal Code: 001643**

	Living at home
Tuition and fees (2002-2003):	$1,710
Per-credit charge:	$50
Books and supplies:	$600

Undergraduate aid. **Non-need-based:** Scholarships based on academics, athletics.

Policies to reduce costs. Tuition/fee waivers for senior citizens, employees and their families. Credit/placement for qualifying scores on AP, CLEP examinations.

Payment plans. Credit card, installment payment.

Application procedures. FAFSA required. No deadline. Applicants notified on rolling basis starting 3/15.

Contact. Louise White, Director of Financial Aid
23235 North County Road 22
Canton, IL 61520

Springfield College in Illinois

Springfield, Illinois
www.sci.edu
Two-year private **Federal Code: 001761**

	Living at home	On-campus
Tuition and fees:	$7,338	$7,338
Per-credit charge:	$297	$297
Room only:		$2,120
Board only:	$3,000	
Books and supplies:	$700	$700
Personal expenses:	$860	$1,210
Transportation:	$850	$450

Undergraduate aid. **Need-based:** 84% awarded as scholarships/grants, 16% as loans/jobs. Need-based aid available for part-time students. **Non-need-based:** 54% awarded as scholarships/grants, 46% as loans/jobs. Scholarships based on academics, art, athletics, leadership, music/drama, religious affiliation.

Policies to reduce costs. Tuition/fee waivers for senior citizens, family of clergy, employees and their families. Credit/placement for qualifying scores on AP, IB, CLEP examinations. Work study available nights, weekends and for part-time students.

Payment plans. Credit card, installment, deferred payment.

Application procedures. FAFSA, institutional form required. Priority date 3/1; no closing date. Applicants notified on rolling basis starting 3/15, must reply within 2 week(s) of notification.

Contact. **Financial aid office:** (217) 525-1420 ext. 244
Karla Keizer, Director of Financial Aid
1500 North Fifth Street
Springfield, IL 62702-2694

Taylor Business Institute

Chicago, Illinois
www.tbiil.org
Two-year proprietary **Federal Code: 011810**

College costs (2002-2003). Tuition for non degree programs is $14,400; fees $250; associate degree program in electronic technology and medical billing $21,375; fees $250.

Application procedures. FAFSA required.

Contact. **Financial aid office:** (312) 658-5100
Florence Davis, Financial Aid Director
200 North Michigan Avenue, Suite 301
Chicago, IL 60601

Trinity Christian College
Palos Heights, Illinois
www.trnty.edu
Four-year private **Federal Code: 001771**

	Living at home	On-campus
Tuition and fees:	$15,490	$15,490
Room and board:		$5,790
Board only:	$2,109	
Books and supplies:	$650	$650
Personal expenses:	$1,700	$1,700
Transportation:	$2,006	$1,182

Undergraduate aid. Need-based: Average financial aid package for full-time students was $9,875; for part-time $8,192. 61% awarded as scholarships/grants, 39% as loans/jobs. **Non-need-based:** 42% awarded as scholarships/grants, 58% as loans/jobs. Scholarships based on academics, alumni affiliation, art, athletics, leadership, minority status, music/drama, religious affiliation. **Student debt:** 78% of graduating class borrowed to fund education; average debt was $15,728.

Freshman aid. Need-based: Out of 208 full-time freshmen, 178 applied for aid; 149 were judged to have need; of these 149 received aid. Average package met 68% of need. 19 students had full need met. Average scholarship/grant was $2,680; average loan $3,450. **Non-need based:** 124 full-time freshmen with need received non-need scholarships; 18 without need received awards; 32 received athletic scholarships.

Policies to reduce costs. Tuition/fee waivers for senior citizens, employees and their families. Credit/placement for qualifying scores on AP, IB, CLEP examinations. Work study available nights, weekends and for part-time students.

Payment plans. Installment, deferred payment.

Application procedures. FAFSA, institutional form required. Priority date 2/15; no closing date. Applicants notified on rolling basis starting 4/1, must reply by 5/1 or within 2 week(s) of notification. **Transfers:** Submit high school transcripts and ACT or SAT scores for merit scholarships.

Contact. **Financial aid office:** (708) 239-4706
Luke Egolf, Financial Aid Officer
6601 West College Drive
Palos Heights, IL 60463

Trinity International University
Deerfield, Illinois
www.tiu.edu
Four-year private **Federal Code: 001772**

	Living at home	On-campus
Tuition and fees:	$17,150	$17,150
Room and board:		$5,830
Books and supplies:	$840	$840
Personal expenses:	$1,050	$1,050
Transportation:	$1,050	$1,050

Undergraduate aid. Need-based: Average financial aid package for full-time students was $12,955; for part-time $6,388. 62% awarded as scholarships/grants, 38% as loans/jobs. **Non-need-based:** 40% awarded as scholarships/grants, 60% as loans/jobs. Scholarships based on academics, alumni affiliation, athletics, minority status, music/drama, religious affiliation. **Additional information:** Monthly payment plan to spread cost of the semester evenly over 4 months.

Freshman aid. Need-based: Out of 250 full-time freshmen, 174 applied for aid; 156 were judged to have need; of these 149 received aid. Average package met 37% of need. 37 students had full need met. Average scholarship/grant was $5,433; average loan $2,930. **Non-need based:** 123 full-time freshmen with need received non-need scholarships; 23 without need received awards; 70 received athletic scholarships.

Policies to reduce costs. Tuition/fee waivers for family members, family of clergy, employees and their families. Prepayment discount; credit/placement for qualifying scores on AP, IB, CLEP examinations. Work study available nights, weekends and for part-time students.

Payment plans. Credit card, installment, deferred payment.

Application procedures. FAFSA required. Priority date 4/1; no closing date. Applicants notified on rolling basis starting 2/15, must reply within 4 week(s) of notification.

Contact. **Financial aid office:** (847) 317-8060
Ron Anderson, Director of Financial Aid
2065 Half Day Road
Deerfield, IL 60015

Triton College
River Grove, Illinois
www.triton.edu
Two-year public **Federal Code: 001773**

	Living at home
Tuition and fees (2002-2003):	$1,690
Out-of-district:	$4,190
Out-of-state:	$6,390
Per-credit charge:	$48
Per-credit out-of-district:	$170
Per-credit out-of-state:	$259

Undergraduate aid. Need-based: 83% awarded as scholarships/grants, 17% as loans/jobs. Need-based aid available for part-time students. **Non-need-based:** Scholarships based on academics, athletics.

Merit scholarships. Board of Trustees Honor Scholarship; for in-district high school students in top 10% of graduating class; covers tuition and fees.

Policies to reduce costs. Tuition/fee waivers for senior citizens, employees and their families. Credit/placement for qualifying scores on AP, CLEP examinations.

Payment plans. Credit card, installment payment.

Application procedures. FAFSA, institutional form required. No deadline. Applicants notified on rolling basis starting 4/1, must reply within 2 week(s) of notification.

Contact. **Financial aid office:** (708) 456-0300 ext. 3441
Patty Williamson, Director of Financial Aid
2000 North Fifth Avenue
River Grove, IL 60171

University of Chicago
Chicago, Illinois
www.uchicago.edu
Four-year private **Federal Code: 001774**

	Living at home	On-campus
Tuition and fees:	$30,336	$30,336
Room and board:		$9,315
Books and supplies:	$900	$900
Personal expenses:	$3,725	$1,069

Undergraduate aid. Need-based: Average financial aid package for full-time students was $20,993. 73% awarded as scholarships/grants, 27% as loans/jobs. **Non-need-based:** 80% awarded as scholarships/grants, 20% as loans/jobs. Scholarships based on academics, leadership.

Freshman aid. Need-based: Out of 1,017 full-time freshmen, 721 applied for aid; 587 were judged to have need; of these 587 received aid. Average package met 100% of need. 587 students had full need met. Average scholarship/grant was $16,399; average loan $3,660.

Policies to reduce costs. Tuition/fee waivers for employees and their families. Credit/placement for qualifying scores on AP, IB examinations.

Payment plans. Credit card, installment payment.

Application procedures. FAFSA, institutional form, CSS PROFILE required. Closing date 2/1. Applicants notified by 4/5, must reply by 5/1.

Contact. Alicia Reyes, Director of Financial Aid
1116 East 59th Street
Chicago, IL 60637

University of Illinois at Chicago
Chicago, Illinois
www.uic.edu
Four-year public **Federal Code: 001776**

College costs. Tuition surcharges applicable to engineering program.

	Living at home	On-campus
Tuition and fees (2002-2003):	$6,592	$6,592
Out-of-state:	$13,920	$13,920
Room and board:		$6,428
Books and supplies:	$850	$850
Personal expenses:	$1,500	$2,000
Transportation:	$150	$150

Undergraduate aid. Need-based: Average financial aid package for full-time students was $11,900. 73% awarded as scholarships/grants, 27% as loans/jobs. Need-based aid available for part-time students. **Non-need-based:** 14% awarded as scholarships/grants, 86% as loans/jobs. Scholarships based on academics, athletics, state/district residency. **Student debt:** 45% of graduating class borrowed to fund education; average debt was $17,000.

Freshman aid. Need-based: Out of 2,692 full-time freshmen, 1,700 applied for aid; 1,530 were judged to have need; of these 1,455 received aid. Average package met 85% of need. 655 students had full need met. Average scholarship/grant was $7,980; average loan $2,300. **Non-need based:** 210 full-time freshmen with need received non-need scholarships; 800 without need received awards.

Policies to reduce costs. Tuition/fee waivers for senior citizens, minority students, employees and their families. Credit/placement for qualifying scores on AP, IB, CLEP examinations. Work study available for part-time students.

Payment plans. Credit card payment.

Application procedures. FAFSA required. Priority date 3/1; no closing date. Applicants notified on rolling basis starting 4/15, must reply within 2 week(s) of notification.

Contact. Financial aid office: (312) 996-5563
Marsha Weiss, Director of the Office of Student Financial Aid
PO Box 5220
Chicago, IL 60680

University of Illinois at Urbana-Champaign

Urbana, Illinois
www.uiuc.edu
Four-year public **Federal Code: 001775**

College costs. Tuition surcharges applicable for engineering, chemistry, life sciences, and selected fine arts programs.

	Living at home	On-campus
Tuition and fees (2002-2003):	$6,704	$6,704
Out-of-state:	$15,308	$15,308
Room and board:		$6,360
Books and supplies:	$740	$740
Personal expenses:	$1,610	$1,610
Transportation:	$440	$440

Undergraduate aid. Need-based: Average financial aid package for full-time students was $9,263; for part-time $1,699. 54% awarded as scholarships/grants, 46% as loans/jobs. **Non-need-based:** 43% awarded as scholarships/grants, 57% as loans/jobs. Scholarships based on academics, athletics, leadership, minority status, state/district residency.

Freshman aid. Need-based: Out of 6,366 full-time freshmen, 4,341 applied for aid; 2,657 were judged to have need; of these 2,657 received aid. Average package met 94% of need. 1291 students had full need met. Average scholarship/grant was $6,025; average loan $3,570. **Non-need based:** 1,347 without need received awards; 83 received athletic scholarships.

Policies to reduce costs. Tuition/fee waivers for senior citizens, employees and their families. Credit/placement for qualifying scores on AP, IB, CLEP examinations. Work study available nights, weekends and for part-time students.

Payment plans. Installment payment.

Application procedures. FAFSA required. Priority date 3/15; no closing date. Applicants notified on rolling basis starting 4/1, must reply within 2 week(s) of notification. **Transfers:** Closing date 3/15.

Contact. Financial aid office: (217) 333-0100
Orlo Austin, Director of Student Financial Aid
901 West Illinois
Urbana, IL 61801

University of Illinois: Springfield

Springfield, Illinois
www.uis.edu
Four-year public **Federal Code: 009333**

	Living at home	On-campus
Tuition and fees (2002-2003):	$4,009	$4,009
Out-of-state:	$10,579	$10,579
Room only:		$4,170
Books and supplies:	$800	$800
Personal expenses:	$1,575	$1,575
Transportation:	$1,400	

Undergraduate aid. Need-based: Need-based aid available for full-time and part-time students. **Non-need-based:** Scholarships based on academics, athletics, leadership, minority status.

Policies to reduce costs. Tuition/fee waivers for senior citizens, employees and their families. Credit/placement for qualifying scores on CLEP examinations. Work study available nights, weekends and for part-time students.

Payment plans. Credit card, installment, deferred payment.

Application procedures. FAFSA, institutional form required. Priority date 4/1; no closing date. Applicants notified on rolling basis starting 4/1, must reply within 2 week(s) of notification. **Transfers:** Priority date 4/1; no deadline. International students must be at the university one year before they are eligible for tuition waivers.

Contact. Financial aid office: (217) 206-6724
Gerard Joseph, Director of Financial Aid
Shepherd Road
Springfield, IL 62794

University of St. Francis

Joliet, Illinois
www.stfrancis.edu
Four-year private **Federal Code: 001664**

	Living at home	On-campus
Tuition and fees:	$16,820	$16,820
Room and board:		$6,030
Books and supplies:	$410	$410
Personal expenses:	$900	$900
Transportation:	$710	$340

Undergraduate aid. Need-based: Average financial aid package for full-time students was $14,279; for part-time $7,123. 68% awarded as scholarships/grants, 32% as loans/jobs. **Non-need-based:** 30% awarded as scholarships/grants, 70% as loans/jobs. Scholarships based on academics, alumni affiliation, art, athletics, leadership, religious affiliation, state/district residency. **Student debt:** 63% of graduating class borrowed to fund education; average debt was $16,563.

Freshman aid. Need-based: Out of 148 full-time freshmen, 147 applied for aid; 117 were judged to have need; of these 117 received aid. Average package met 87% of need. 90 students had full need met. Average scholarship/grant was $6,883; average loan $2,986. **Non-need based:** 110 full-time freshmen with need received non-need scholarships; 21 without need received awards; 9 received athletic scholarships.

Policies to reduce costs. Tuition/fee waivers for children of alumni, family members, employees and their families. Credit/placement for qualifying scores on AP, CLEP examinations.

Payment plans. Credit card, installment, deferred payment.

Application procedures. FAFSA, institutional form required. Priority date 5/1; no closing date. Applicants notified on rolling basis starting 2/15, must reply within 3 week(s) of notification. **Transfers:** Priority date 5/1.

Contact. Financial aid office: (866) 890-8331
Mary Shaw, Director of Financial Aid
500 Wilcox Street
Joliet, IL 60435-6188

VanderCook College of Music

Chicago, Illinois
www.vandercook.edu
Four-year private **Federal Code: 001778**

	Living at home	On-campus
Tuition and fees:	$15,290	$15,290
Room and board:		$6,300
Books and supplies:	$350	$350

Undergraduate aid. Non-need-based: Scholarships based on academics, music/drama. **Additional information:** Musical talent considered for partial tuition waiver.

Policies to reduce costs. Credit/placement for qualifying scores on AP, CLEP examinations.

Payment plans. Credit card, installment, deferred payment.

Application procedures. FAFSA required. Priority date 3/1; no closing date. Applicants notified on rolling basis, must reply within 2 week(s) of notification. **Transfers:** No deadline. Title IV funding is pro-rated by semester.

Contact. Financial aid office: (312) 225-6288
Susan Frost, Financial Aid Administrator
3140 South Federal Street
Chicago, IL 60616-3731

Waubonsee Community College

Sugar Grove, Illinois
www.waubonsee.edu
Two-year public **Federal Code: 006931**

	Living at home
Tuition and fees (projected):	$1,670
Out-of-district:	$5,812
Out-of-state:	$7,014
Per-credit charge:	$51
Per-credit out-of-district:	$181
Per-credit out-of-state:	$218
Board only:	$1,950
Books and supplies:	$950
Personal expenses:	$1,076
Transportation:	$1,752

Undergraduate aid. All financial aid based on need. 82% awarded as scholarships/grants, 18% as loans/jobs. Need-based aid available for part-time students.

Policies to reduce costs. Tuition/fee waivers for senior citizens, employees and their families. Credit/placement for qualifying scores on AP, CLEP examinations. Work study available nights and for part-time students.

Payment plans. Credit card, installment, deferred payment.

Application procedures. FAFSA, institutional form required. Priority date 7/1; closing date 12/5. Applicants notified on rolling basis.

Contact. Financial aid office: (630) 466-7900 ext. 5774
Douglas McCoy, Associate Dean for Admissions, Recruitment and Financial Aid
Route 47 at Waubonsee Drive
Sugar Grove, IL 60554-9454

West Suburban College of Nursing

Oak Park, Illinois
www.wscn.edu
Upper-division private **Federal Code: 006250**

	Living at home
Tuition and fees:	$17,745
Books and supplies:	$400
Personal expenses:	$600

Undergraduate aid. Need-based: Need-based aid available for full-time and part-time students. **Additional information:** Financial aid administered through Concordia University.

Payment plans. Installment payment.

Application procedures. FAFSA required. Applicants notified on rolling basis.

Contact. Financial aid office: (708) 763-6530
Ruth Rehwaldt, Financial Aid Director
3 Erie Court
Oak Park, IL 60302

Western Illinois University

Macomb, Illinois
www.wiu.edu
Four-year public **Federal Code: 001780**

College costs. Residents of nearby counties in Iowa and Missouri pay in-state tuition during first year.

	Living at home	On-campus
Tuition and fees:	$4,997	$4,997
Out-of-state:	$8,912	$8,912
Room and board:		$5,366
Board only:	$2,130	
Books and supplies:	$800	$800
Personal expenses:	$2,032	$1,515
Transportation:	$1,321	$809

Undergraduate aid. Need-based: Average financial aid package for full-time students was $7,220; for part-time $5,256. 54% awarded as scholarships/grants, 46% as loans/jobs. **Non-need-based:** 23% awarded as scholarships/grants, 77% as loans/jobs. Scholarships based on academics, alumni affiliation, art, athletics, leadership, minority status, music/drama. **Student debt:** 61% of graduating class borrowed to fund education; average debt was $13,360.

Freshman aid. Need-based: Out of 1,929 full-time freshmen, 1,601 applied for aid; 1,025 were judged to have need; of these 994 received aid. Average package met 68% of need. 310 students had full need met. Average scholarship/grant was $5,083; average loan $2,454. **Non-need based:** 505 without need received awards; 83 received athletic scholarships.

Policies to reduce costs. Tuition/fee waivers for senior citizens, employees and their families. Tuition at time of enrollment guaranteed for 4 years; credit/placement for qualifying scores on AP, IB, CLEP examinations.

Payment plans. Credit card, deferred payment.

Application procedures. FAFSA required. Priority date 2/15; no closing date. Applicants notified on rolling basis starting 2/15. **Transfers:** Priority date 2/15; no deadline.

Contact. Financial aid office: (309) 298-2446
William Bushaw, Director of Financial Aid
One University Circle, 115 Sherman Hall
Macomb, IL 61455-1390

Westwood College of Technology: O'Hare

Schiller Park, Illinois
www.westwood.edu
Two-year proprietary

College costs. Total cost of Associate degree program including books, supplies and fees: $25,000, graphic design; $31,000, networking program.

Application procedures. FAFSA required.

Contact. 4825 North Scott Street, Suite 100
Schiller Park, IL 60176

Wheaton College

Wheaton, Illinois
www.wheaton.edu
Four-year private **Federal Code: 001781**

	Living at home	On-campus
Tuition and fees:	$18,500	$18,500
Room and board:		$6,100
Board only:	$2,380	
Books and supplies:	$680	$680
Personal expenses:	$1,796	

Undergraduate aid. Need-based: Average financial aid package for full-time students was $14,830; for part-time $6,454. 63% awarded as scholarships/grants, 37% as loans/jobs. **Non-need-based:** 73% awarded as scholarships/grants, 27% as loans/jobs. Scholarships based on academics, alumni affiliation, art, minority status, music/drama. **Student debt:** 53% of graduating class borrowed to fund education; average debt was $15,864.

Freshman aid. Need-based: Out of 569 full-time freshmen, 438 applied for aid; 276 were judged to have need; of these 265 received aid. Average package met 86% of need. 58 students had full need met. Average scholarship/grant was $11,191; average loan $3,754. **Non-need based:** 125 full-time freshmen with need received non-need scholarships; 131 without need received awards.

Policies to reduce costs. Tuition/fee waivers for employees and their families. Credit/placement for qualifying scores on AP, IB examinations.

Payment plans. Installment, deferred payment.

Application procedures. FAFSA, institutional form required. Priority date 2/15; no closing date. Applicants notified on rolling basis starting 3/1. **Transfers:** Priority date 3/1; no deadline.

Contact. Financial aid office: (630) 752-5021
Donna Peltz, Director of Financial Aid
501 College Avenue
Wheaton, IL 60187-5593

William Rainey Harper College

Palatine, Illinois
www.harpercollege.edu
Two-year public **Federal Code: 003961**

College costs. In-district tuition rates available to employees of in-district companies who reside outside college district.

	Living at home
Tuition and fees:	$2,292
Out-of-district:	$8,682
Out-of-state:	$11,082
Per-credit charge:	$67
Per-credit out-of-district:	$280
Per-credit out-of-state:	$360
Books and supplies:	$600
Personal expenses:	$1,492
Transportation:	$1,225

Undergraduate aid. Need-based: 82% awarded as scholarships/grants, 18% as loans/jobs. Need-based aid available for part-time students. **Non-need-based:** 24% awarded as scholarships/grants, 76% as loans/jobs. Scholarships based on academics, art, leadership, minority status, music/drama, state/district residency.

Freshman aid. Need-based: Out of 1,420 full-time freshmen, 437 applied for aid; 306 were judged to have need; of these 243 received aid. Average scholarship/grant was $863. **Non-need based:** 20 full-time freshmen with need received non-need scholarships.

Merit scholarships. Distinguished Scholar Award available to full-time students during regular academic year who graduate in top 10% of class from district high school, with full tuition and fees renewable for second year.

Policies to reduce costs. Tuition/fee waivers for senior citizens, employees and their families. Credit/placement for qualifying scores on AP, CLEP examinations. Work study available nights and weekends.

Payment plans. Credit card, installment, deferred payment.

Application procedures. FAFSA, institutional form required. Priority date 5/1; no closing date. Applicants notified on rolling basis starting 5/2, must reply within 2 week(s) of notification.

Contact. Financial aid office: (847) 925-6248
Maria Moten, Registrar
1200 West Algonquin Road
Palatine, IL 60067-7398

Indiana

American Conservatory of Music

Hammond, Indiana
www.americanconservatory.edu
Four-year private

College costs. Annual full-time cost ranges from $10,000-$18,000 depending on teacher.

	Living at home
Tuition and fees (2002-2003):	$11,000
Books and supplies:	$500
Personal expenses:	$1,200

Undergraduate aid. Non-need-based: Scholarships based on music/drama.

Policies to reduce costs. Credit/placement for qualifying scores on IB examinations.

Payment plans. Credit card, installment payment.

Application procedures. FAFSA required. No deadline. Applicants notified on rolling basis.

Contact. Mary Ellen Newsom, Registrar
252 Wildwood Road
Hammond, IN 46324

American Trans Air Aviation Training Academy

Indianapolis, Indiana
www.aviationtraining.net
Two-year proprietary **Federal Code: 031763**

College costs. Tuition for 15-month associate program $17,729; includes books, tools, and mandatory uniform.

Undergraduate aid. Need-based: Need-based aid available for full-time students.

Application procedures. FAFSA required.

Contact. Financial aid office: (317) 243-4514
Donna Reddick, Director of Financial Aid
7251 West McCarty Street
Indianapolis, IN 46241

Ancilla College

Donaldson, Indiana
www.ancilla.edu
Two-year private **Federal Code: 001784**

	Living at home
Tuition and fees:	$7,850
Per-credit charge:	$255
Board only:	$1,365
Books and supplies:	$712
Personal expenses:	$612
Transportation:	$780

Undergraduate aid. Need-based: Need-based aid available for full-time and part-time students. **Non-need-based:** Scholarships based on academics, athletics, job skills, leadership.

Policies to reduce costs. Tuition/fee waivers for employees and their families. Credit/placement for qualifying scores on AP, CLEP examinations. Work study available for part-time students.

Payment plans. Credit card, installment, deferred payment.

Application procedures. FAFSA, institutional form required. Priority date 3/1; no closing date. Applicants notified on rolling basis starting 3/1, must reply within 2 week(s) of notification. **Transfers:** No deadline.

Contact. Financial aid office: (574) 936-8898 ext. 307
Director of Financial Aid
9001 Union Road
Donaldson, IN 46513

Anderson University

Anderson, Indiana
www.anderson.edu
Four-year private **Federal Code: 001785**

	Living at home	On-campus
Tuition and fees:	$17,050	$17,050
Room and board:		$5,560
Board only:	$3,300	
Books and supplies:	$700	$700
Personal expenses:	$1,200	$1,200
Transportation:	$500	$500

Undergraduate aid. Need-based: Need-based aid available for full-time and part-time students. **Non-need-based:** Scholarships based on academics, leadership, minority status, music/drama, state/district residency.

Policies to reduce costs. Tuition/fee waivers for adults, senior citizens, family of clergy, employees and their families. Prepayment discount; credit/placement for qualifying scores on AP, IB, CLEP examinations. Work study available nights and weekends.

Payment plans. Installment, deferred payment.

Application procedures. FAFSA required. Priority date 3/1; no closing date. Applicants notified on rolling basis starting 3/1.

Contact. Kenneth Nieman, Director of Financial Aid
1100 East Fifth
Anderson, IN 46012

Ball State University

Muncie, Indiana
www.bsu.edu
Four-year public **Federal Code: 001786**

College costs. $50 residence hall technology fee for on-campus residents.

	Living at home	On-campus
Tuition and fees (2002-2003):	$4,700	$4,700
Out-of-state:	$12,480	$12,480
Room and board:		$5,546
Board only:	$1,280	
Books and supplies:	$830	$830
Personal expenses:	$1,300	$1,300
Transportation:	$1,460	$610

Undergraduate aid. Need-based: Average financial aid package for full-time students was $6,368; for part-time $5,914. 45% awarded as scholarships/grants, 55% as loans/jobs. **Non-need-based:** 26% awarded as scholarships/grants, 74% as loans/jobs. Scholarships based on academics, athletics, leadership, minority status, music/drama. **Student debt:** 60% of graduating class borrowed to fund education; average debt was $15,926.

Freshman aid. Need-based: Out of 4,016 full-time freshmen, 3,337 applied for aid; 2,224 were judged to have need; of these 2,216 received aid. Average package met 69% of need. 703 students had full need met. Average scholarship/grant was $3,906; average loan $2,612. **Non-need based:** 1,480 full-time freshmen with need received non-need scholarships; 503 without need received awards; 73 received athletic scholarships.

Policies to reduce costs. Tuition/fee waivers for senior citizens, employees and their families. Credit/placement for qualifying scores on AP, CLEP examinations. Work study available nights, weekends and for part-time students.

Payment plans. Installment payment.

Application procedures. FAFSA required. Priority date 3/1; no closing date. Applicants notified on rolling basis starting 4/15. **Transfers:** Priority date 3/1; no deadline.

Contact. Robert Zellers, Director of Scholarships/Financial Aid
Office of Admissions
Muncie, IN 47306-0855

Bethel College

Mishawaka, Indiana
www.bethelcollege.edu
Four-year private **Federal Code: 001787**

	Living at home	On-campus
Tuition and fees:	$15,060	$15,060
Room and board:		$5,000
Books and supplies:	$600	$600
Personal expenses:	$700	$700
Transportation:	$1,000	$600

Undergraduate aid. Need-based: Average financial aid package for full-time students was $12,041; for part-time $12,431. 41% awarded as scholarships/grants, 59% as loans/jobs. **Non-need-based:** 95% awarded as scholarships/grants, 5% as loans/jobs. Scholarships based on academics, art, athletics, minority status, music/drama, state/district residency. **Student debt:** 65% of graduating class borrowed to fund education; average debt was $14,500.

Freshman aid. Need-based: Out of 253 full-time freshmen, 250 applied for aid; 214 were judged to have need; of these 214 received aid. Average package met 90% of need. 92 students had full need met. Average scholarship/grant was $4,404; average loan $3,179. **Non-need based:** 214 full-time freshmen with need received non-need scholarships; 19 without need received awards.

Policies to reduce costs. Tuition/fee waivers for adults, minority students, family members, family of clergy, employees and their families. Credit/placement for qualifying scores on AP, IB, CLEP examinations.

Payment plans. Installment, deferred payment.

Application procedures. Institutional form, CSS PROFILE required. Priority date 3/1; no closing date. Applicants notified on rolling basis starting 2/15, must reply within 2 week(s) of notification. **Transfers:** Priority date 3/1.

Contact. Financial aid office: (574) 257-3316
Guy Fisher, Director of Financial Aid
1001 West McKinley Avenue
Mishawaka, IN 46545

Butler University

Indianapolis, Indiana
www.butler.edu
Four-year private **Federal Code: 001788**

College costs. Full time tuition for pharmacy and health sciences $21,360; per credit hour charge $890.

	Living at home	On-campus
Tuition and fees:	$21,210	$21,210
Room and board:		$7,250
Books and supplies:	$750	$750
Personal expenses:	$1,300	$1,300
Transportation:	$450	$450

Undergraduate aid. Need-based: Average financial aid package for full-time students was $15,534; for part-time $6,734. 67% awarded as scholarships/grants, 33% as loans/jobs. **Non-need-based:** 63% awarded as scholarships/grants, 37% as loans/jobs. Scholarships based on academics, athletics, minority status.

Freshman aid. Need-based: Out of 939 full-time freshmen, 879 applied for aid; 600 were judged to have need; of these 600 received aid. Average package met 84% of need. 134 students had full need met. Average scholarship/grant was $12,392; average loan $3,193. **Non-need based:** 158 full-time freshmen with need received non-need scholarships; 244 without need received awards; 24 received athletic scholarships.

Policies to reduce costs. Tuition/fee waivers for employees and their families. Prepayment discount; credit/placement for qualifying scores on AP, CLEP examinations.

Payment plans. Credit card, installment payment.

Application procedures. FAFSA, institutional form required. Priority date 3/1; no closing date. Applicants notified on rolling basis starting 3/15, must reply within 3 week(s) of notification. **Transfers:** Priority date 3/15; no deadline.

Contact. Financial aid office: (317) 940-8200
Richard Bellows, Director of Financial Aid
4600 Sunset Avenue
Indianapolis, IN 46208

Calumet College of St. Joseph

Whiting, Indiana
www.ccsj.edu
Four-year private **Federal Code: 001834**

	Living at home
Tuition and fees (2002-2003):	$7,800
Board only:	$6,020
Books and supplies:	$800
Personal expenses:	$1,149
Transportation:	$822

Undergraduate aid. Need-based: Need-based aid available for full-time and part-time students. **Non-need-based:** Scholarships based on academics, alumni affiliation, religious affiliation. **Additional information:** Immediate computerized estimate of financial aid eligibility available to students applying in person.

Policies to reduce costs. Tuition/fee waivers for senior citizens, family of clergy, employees and their families. Credit/placement for qualifying scores on CLEP examinations. Work study available for part-time students.

Payment plans. Credit card, installment payment.

Application procedures. FAFSA required. Priority date 3/1; closing date 9/1. Applicants notified on rolling basis, must reply within 2 week(s) of notification. **Transfers:** No deadline.

Contact. Financial aid office: (219) 473-4296
Richard Miller, Director of Financial Aid
2400 New York Avenue
Whiting, IN 46394-2195

College of Court Reporting

Hobart, Indiana
www.ccredu.com
Three-year private **Federal Code: 026158**

	Living at home
Tuition and fees (2002-2003):	$4,860

Contact. 111 West 10th Street, Suite 111
Hobart, IN 46342

Commonwealth Business College: Michigan City

Michigan City, Indiana
www.cbcaec.com
Two-year proprietary **Federal Code: 21032-01**

	Living at home
Tuition and fees (2002-2003):	$7,580
Per-credit charge:	$148
Books and supplies:	$630
Personal expenses:	$2,664

Contact. Financial aid office: (219) 877-3100
Pat Zinsmeister, Director of Financial Aid
325 East US Highway 20
Michigan City, IN 46360-7362

DePauw University

Greencastle, Indiana
www.depauw.edu
Four-year private **Federal Code: 001792**

	Living at home	On-campus
Tuition and fees:	$24,450	$24,450
Room and board:		$7,050
Board only:	$750	
Books and supplies:	$600	$600
Personal expenses:	$400	$750
Transportation:	$700	$300

Undergraduate aid. Need-based: Average financial aid package for full-time students was $20,223; for part-time $2,750. 82% awarded as scholarships/grants, 18% as loans/jobs. **Non-need-based:** 90% awarded as scholarships/grants, 10% as loans/jobs. Scholarships based on academics, alumni affiliation, leadership, minority status, religious affiliation, state/district residency. **Student debt:** 55% of graduating class borrowed to fund education; average debt was $15,048.

Freshman aid. **Need-based:** Out of 685 full-time freshmen, 446 applied for aid; 363 were judged to have need; of these 363 received aid. Average package met 98% of need. 333 students had full need met. Average scholarship/grant was $14,958; average loan $3,141. **Non-need based:** 238 full-time freshmen with need received non-need scholarships; 266 without need received awards.

Merit scholarships. Holton Scholarships recognizing exceptional leadership and/or service, ranging from $1,000 to full tuition, 50 awarded.

Policies to reduce costs. Tuition/fee waivers for employees and their families. Credit/placement for qualifying scores on AP, IB examinations. Work study available nights, weekends and for part-time students.

Payment plans. Deferred payment.

Application procedures. FAFSA, institutional form required. Closing date 2/15. Applicants notified by 3/31, must reply by 5/1. Early decision closing date 11/1. **Transfers:** Closing date 2/15.

Contact. **Financial aid office:** (765) 658-4030
Anna Sinnet, Director of Financial Aid
101 East Seminary Street
Greencastle, IN 46135-1611

Earlham College

Richmond, Indiana
www.earlham.edu
Four-year private **Federal Code: 001793**

	Living at home	On-campus
Tuition and fees:	$24,560	$24,560
Room and board:		$5,416
Board only:	$750	
Books and supplies:	$550	$550
Personal expenses:	$600	$600
Transportation:	$500	$500

Undergraduate aid. **Need-based:** Average financial aid package for full-time students was $20,439. 78% awarded as scholarships/grants, 22% as loans/jobs. Need-based aid available for part-time students. **Non-need-based:** 70% awarded as scholarships/grants, 30% as loans/jobs. Scholarships based on academics, minority status, religious affiliation, state/district residency. **Student debt:** 64% of graduating class borrowed to fund education; average debt was $15,444.

Freshman aid. **Need-based:** Out of 282 full-time freshmen, 222 applied for aid; 186 were judged to have need; of these 185 received aid. Average package met 94% of need. 45 students had full need met. Average scholarship/grant was $12,651; average loan $3,168. **Non-need based:** 120 full-time freshmen with need received non-need scholarships; 41 without need received awards.

Merit scholarships. Wilkinson Scholarships for Quaker applicants; $3,000. Cunningham Scholarships for selected minority applicants; $5,000. National Merit Award; $750-$2,000. Honors Scholarships; $7,000.

Policies to reduce costs. Tuition/fee waivers for employees and their families. Credit/placement for qualifying scores on AP, IB examinations. Work study available nights, weekends and for part-time students.

Payment plans. Installment, deferred payment.

Application procedures. FAFSA, institutional form required. Priority date 3/1; no closing date. Applicants notified by 4/1, must reply by 5/1 or within 3 week(s) of notification. Early decision closing date 12/1. **Transfers:** Priority date 3/1; no deadline.

Contact. **Financial aid office:** (765) 983-1217
Robert Arnold, Director of Financial Aid
801 National Road West
Richmond, IN 47374-4095

Franklin College

Franklin, Indiana
www.franklincollege.edu
Four-year private **Federal Code: 001798**

	Living at home	On-campus
Tuition and fees:	$17,130	$17,130
Room and board:		$5,270
Books and supplies:	$700	$700
Personal expenses:	$1,695	$1,695

Undergraduate aid. **Need-based:** Average financial aid package for full-time students was $12,302; for part-time $10,207. 77% awarded as scholarships/grants, 23% as loans/jobs. **Non-need-based:** 58% awarded as scholarships/grants, 42% as loans/jobs. Scholarships based on academics, alumni affiliation, leadership, minority status, religious affiliation, state/district residency. **Student debt:** 76% of graduating class borrowed to fund education; average debt was $5,694.

Freshman aid. **Need-based:** Out of 316 full-time freshmen, 275 applied for aid; 228 were judged to have need; of these 228 received aid. Average package met 87% of need. 67 students had full need met. Average scholarship/grant was $9,582; average loan $2,855. **Non-need based:** 56 full-time freshmen with need received non-need scholarships; 78 without need received awards.

Policies to reduce costs. Tuition/fee waivers for senior citizens, employees and their families. Credit/placement for qualifying scores on AP, CLEP examinations. Work study available for part-time students.

Payment plans. Credit card, installment payment.

Application procedures. FAFSA, institutional form required. Closing date 3/1. Applicants notified on rolling basis starting 4/1, must reply by 5/1 or within 4 week(s) of notification.

Contact. **Financial aid office:** (317) 738-8075
Richard Nash, Director of Financial Aid
501 East Monroe Street
Franklin, IN 46131

Goshen College

Goshen, Indiana
www.goshen.edu
Four-year private **Federal Code: 001799**

	Living at home	On-campus
Tuition and fees:	$16,650	$16,650
Room and board:		$5,800
Board only:	$753	
Books and supplies:	$700	$700
Transportation:	$360	$360

Undergraduate aid. **Need-based:** Average financial aid package for full-time students was $13,629. 69% awarded as scholarships/grants, 31% as loans/jobs. Need-based aid available for part-time students. **Non-need-based:** 57% awarded as scholarships/grants, 43% as loans/jobs. Scholarships based on academics, athletics, leadership, minority status, music/drama, state/district residency. **Student debt:** 69% of graduating class borrowed to fund education; average debt was $15,689.

Freshman aid. **Need-based:** Out of 135 full-time freshmen, 135 applied for aid; 95 were judged to have need; of these 95 received aid. Average package met 90% of need. 38 students had full need met. Average scholarship/grant was $9,559; average loan $3,624. **Non-need based:** 90 full-time freshmen with need received non-need scholarships; 15 without need received awards; 6 received athletic scholarships.

Merit scholarships. Yoder Honors Scholarship; predicted college GPA of 3.2 to 3.39 or 1110 SAT or 24 ACT or top 15% of class, $3,000, renews at 3.0 GPA. Menno Simons Scholarship; predicted college GPA of 3.6 or greater or 1270 SAT or 29 ACT or top 5% of class, $6,000, renews at 3.2 GPA. President's Leadership Award; must meet 2 of the following: predicted college GPA 3.8, 1270 SAT, 28 ACT, top 5% of class, must be a National Merit finalist; $7,500, 10 awarded, renews at 3.2 or higher GPA. Wens Honors Scholarship; predicted college GPA of 3.4 to 3.59, $4,500, unlimited, renewable with 3.0 GPA. Grebel Scholarship; predicted college GPA of 3.0 to 3.19, $2,200, renewable with 3.0 GPA.

Policies to reduce costs. Tuition/fee waivers for children of alumni, family of clergy, employees and their families. Prepayment discount; credit/placement for qualifying scores on AP, IB, CLEP examinations. Work study available nights and weekends.

Payment plans. Credit card, installment, deferred payment.

Application procedures. FAFSA, institutional form required. Priority date 2/15; no closing date. Applicants notified by 3/15, must reply by 5/1 or within 2 week(s) of notification. **Transfers:** Scholarships available to transfers.

Contact. **Financial aid office:** (574) 535-7525
Galen Graber, Director of Student Financial Aid
1700 South Main Street
Goshen, IN 46526

Grace College

Winona Lake, Indiana
www.grace.edu
Four-year private **Federal Code: 001800**

	Living at home	On-campus
Tuition and fees:	$14,070	$14,070
Room and board:		$5,755
Board only:	$1,500	
Books and supplies:	$500	$500
Personal expenses:	$800	$800
Transportation:	$1,200	$600

Undergraduate aid. Need-based: Average financial aid package for full-time students was $11,521; for part-time $6,509. 55% awarded as scholarships/grants, 45% as loans/jobs. **Non-need-based:** 40% awarded as scholarships/grants, 60% as loans/jobs. Scholarships based on academics, art, athletics, music/drama. **Student debt:** 76% of graduating class borrowed to fund education; average debt was $18,865.

Freshman aid. Need-based: Out of 288 full-time freshmen, 212 applied for aid; 186 were judged to have need; of these 186 received aid. Average package met 85% of need. 61 students had full need met. Average scholarship/grant was $7,514; average loan $4,071. **Non-need based:** 24 full-time freshmen with need received non-need scholarships; 43 without need received awards; 32 received athletic scholarships.

Policies to reduce costs. Tuition/fee waivers for family of clergy, employees and their families. Credit/placement for qualifying scores on AP, IB, CLEP examinations.

Payment plans. Credit card payment.

Application procedures. FAFSA required. Priority date 3/1; no closing date. Applicants notified on rolling basis starting 3/15.

Contact. Financial aid office: (574) 327-5100 ext. 6162
Dawn Weaver, Director of Student Aid
200 Seminary Drive
Winona Lake, IN 46590

Hanover College

Hanover, Indiana
www.hanover.edu
Four-year private **Federal Code: 001801**

College costs. Per-unit charge of $1,335 for part-time students only.

	Living at home	On-campus
Tuition and fees (projected):	$13,500	$13,500
Room and board:		$5,500
Books and supplies:	$800	$800

Undergraduate aid. Need-based: Average financial aid package for full-time students was $12,050. 80% awarded as scholarships/grants, 20% as loans/jobs. Need-based aid available for part-time students. **Non-need-based:** 66% awarded as scholarships/grants, 34% as loans/jobs. Scholarships based on academics, leadership, minority status, music/drama, religious affiliation, state/district residency. **Student debt:** 78% of graduating class borrowed to fund education; average debt was $11,583.

Freshman aid. Need-based: Out of 280 full-time freshmen, 234 applied for aid; 171 were judged to have need; of these 171 received aid. Average package met 96% of need. 132 students had full need met. Average scholarship/grant was $10,101; average loan $1,616. **Non-need based:** 38 full-time freshmen with need received non-need scholarships; 98 without need received awards.

Policies to reduce costs. Tuition/fee waivers for senior citizens, employees and their families. Credit/placement for qualifying scores on AP, IB examinations.

Payment plans. Installment payment.

Application procedures. FAFSA required. Priority date 3/10; no closing date. Applicants notified on rolling basis starting 3/10, must reply by 5/1. **Transfers:** No deadline.

Contact. Financial aid office: (812) 866-7030
Jon Riester, Chief Financial Officer
PO Box 108
Hanover, IN 47243-0108

Holy Cross College

Notre Dame, Indiana
www.hcc-nd.edu
Two-year private **Federal Code: 007263**

	Living at home	On-campus
Tuition and fees (projected):	$9,700	$9,700
Per-credit charge:	$323	$323
Room and board:		$7,400
Books and supplies:	$500	$500
Personal expenses:	$1,460	
Transportation:	$2,060	

Undergraduate aid. Need-based: Need-based aid available for full-time and part-time students.

Policies to reduce costs. Tuition/fee waivers for employees and their families. Credit/placement for qualifying scores on AP, CLEP examinations. Work study available nights, weekends and for part-time students.

Payment plans. Credit card payment.

Application procedures. FAFSA required. Priority date 3/15; no closing date. Applicants notified on rolling basis starting 5/1, must reply within 2 week(s) of notification.

Contact. Doug Irvine, Director of Financial Aid
54515 State Road 933N
Notre Dame, IN 46556-0308

Huntington College

Huntington, Indiana
www.huntington.edu
Four-year private **Federal Code: 001803**

	Living at home	On-campus
Tuition and fees:	$17,700	$17,700
Room and board:		$5,890
Board only:	$3,160	
Books and supplies:	$750	$750
Personal expenses:	$1,050	$1,150
Transportation:	$1,000	$750

Undergraduate aid. Need-based: Need-based aid available for full-time and part-time students. **Non-need-based:** Scholarships based on academics, alumni affiliation, art, athletics, music/drama, religious affiliation.

Policies to reduce costs. Tuition/fee waivers for senior citizens, family members, family of clergy, employees and their families. Credit/placement for qualifying scores on AP, CLEP examinations. Work study available nights, weekends and for part-time students.

Payment plans. Credit card, installment payment.

Application procedures. FAFSA required. Priority date 3/1; no closing date. Applicants notified on rolling basis starting 3/1, must reply by 5/1 or within 2 week(s) of notification.

Contact. Financial aid office: (260) 359-4015
Sharon Woods, Financial Aid Director
2303 College Avenue
Huntington, IN 46750

ITT Technical Institute: Fort Wayne

Fort Wayne, Indiana
www.itt-tech.edu
Three-year proprietary **Federal Code: 008329**

College costs. Total program varies depending on course of study. Per-credit-hour charge: $347.

Policies to reduce costs. Tuition/fee waivers for employees and their families.

Payment plans. Credit card, installment payment.

Application procedures. FAFSA, institutional form required. No deadline. Applicants notified on rolling basis.

Contact. Alois Johnson, Director of Finance
4919 Coldwater Road
Fort Wayne, IN 46825-5532

ITT Technical Institute: Indianapolis

Indianapolis, Indiana
www.itt-tech.edu
Three-year proprietary **Federal Code: 007329**

College costs. Total program varies depending on course of study. Per-credit-hour charge: $347.

Policies to reduce costs. Tuition/fee waivers for employees and their families.

Payment plans. Credit card, installment payment.

Application procedures. FAFSA, institutional form required. No deadline. Applicants notified on rolling basis.

Contact. Michele Hurst, Director of Finance
9511 Angola Court
Indianapolis, IN 46268-1119

Indiana Business College

Indianapolis, Indiana
www.ibcschools.com
Two-year proprietary **Federal Code: 015218**

College costs. Tuition and fees vary by program. Per-credit-hour charge ranges from $139-$204.

Undergraduate aid. Need-based: Need-based aid available for full-time and part-time students.

Application procedures. Applicants notified on rolling basis.

Contact. 550 E. Washington Street
Indianapolis, IN 46204

Indiana Business College: Anderson

Anderson, Indiana
www.ibcschools.com
Two-year proprietary **Federal Code: 021584**

College costs. Tuition and fees vary by program. Per-credit-hour charge ranges from $139-$204.

Undergraduate aid. Need-based: Need-based aid available for full-time and part-time students.

Contact. 140 East 53rd Street
Anderson, IN 46013

Indiana Business College: Columbus

Columbus, Indiana
Two-year proprietary
Federal Code: 021584

College costs. Tuition and fees vary by program. Per-credit-hour charge ranges from $139-$204.

Undergraduate aid. Need-based: Need-based aid available for full-time and part-time students.

Contact. 2222 Poshard Drive
Columbus, IN 47203-9988

Indiana Business College: Evansville

Evansville, Indiana
www.ibcschools.com
Two-year proprietary **Federal Code: 021584**

College costs. Tuition and fees vary by program. Per-credit-hour charge ranges from $139-$204.

Undergraduate aid. Need-based: Need-based aid available for full-time and part-time students.

Contact. 4601 Theatre Drive
Evansville, IN 47715

Indiana Business College: Fort Wayne

Fort Wayne, Indiana
www.ibcschools.com
Two-year proprietary

College costs. Tuition and fees vary by program. Per-credit-hour charge ranges from $139-$204.

Undergraduate aid. Need-based: Need-based aid available for full-time and part-time students.

Contact. Pam Pace, Financial Aid Analyst
Fort Wayne, IN 46825

Indiana Business College: Lafayette

Lafayette, Indiana
www.ibcschools.com
Two-year proprietary **Federal Code: 021584**

College costs. Tuition varies by program: $139-$204 per-credit-hour charge. Books/supplies: $1,800.

Undergraduate aid. Need-based: Need-based aid available for full-time and part-time students.

Contact. 2 Executive Drive
Lafayette, IN 47905-4859

Indiana Business College: Marion

Marion, Indiana
www.ibcschools.com
Two-year proprietary **Federal Code: 021584**

College costs. Tuition and fees vary by program. Per-credit-hour charge ranges from $139-$204.

Undergraduate aid. Need-based: Need-based aid available for full-time and part-time students.

Contact. 830 North Miller Avenue
Marion, IN 46952

Indiana Business College: Medical

Indianapolis, Indiana
www.ibcschools.com
Two-year private **Federal Code: 021584**

College costs (2002-2003). Tuition and fees vary by program. Per-credit-hour charge ranges from $139-$204. Books/supplies: $1,200.

Contact. Jason Reed, Director of Financial Aid
8150 Brookville Road
Indianapolis, IN 46239

Indiana Business College: Muncie

Muncie, Indiana
www.ibcschools.com
Two-year proprietary **Federal Code: 030097**

College costs. Tuition and fees vary by program. Per-credit-hour charge ranges from $139-$204.

Undergraduate aid. Need-based: Need-based aid available for full-time and part-time students.

Contact. 411 West Riggin Road
Muncie, IN 47303

Indiana Business College: Terre Haute

Terre Haute, Indiana
www.ibcschools.com
Two-year proprietary **Federal Code: 021584**

College costs. Tuition and fees vary by program. Per-credit-hour charge ranges from $139-$204.

Undergraduate aid. Need-based: Need-based aid available for full-time and part-time students.

Contact. 3175 South Third Place
Terre Haute, IN 47802

Indiana Institute of Technology

Fort Wayne, Indiana
www.indtech.edu
Four-year private **Federal Code: 001805**

	Living at home	On-campus
Tuition and fees:	$15,590	$15,590
Room and board:		$6,030
Books and supplies:	$1,000	$1,000
Transportation:	$1,050	

Undergraduate aid. Need-based: Average financial aid package for full-time students was $8,889; for part-time $3,334. 60% awarded as scholarships/grants, 40% as loans/jobs. **Non-need-based:** 40% awarded as scholarships/grants, 60% as loans/jobs. Scholarships based on academics, alumni affiliation, athletics, minority status, music/drama, state/district residency. **Student debt:** 72% of graduating class borrowed to fund education; average debt was $14,305.

Freshman aid. Need-based: Out of 254 full-time freshmen, 235 applied for aid; 211 were judged to have need; of these 211 received aid. Average package met 78% of need. 25 students had full need met. Average scholarship/grant was $8,739; average loan $2,988. **Non-need based:** 10 full-time freshmen with need received non-need scholarships; 23 without need received awards; 18 received athletic scholarships.

Policies to reduce costs. Tuition/fee waivers for adults, family members, employees and their families. Credit/placement for qualifying scores on AP, CLEP examinations. Work study available nights and weekends.

Payment plans. Credit card, installment, deferred payment.

Application procedures. FAFSA, institutional form required. Priority date 3/10; closing date 3/10. Must reply within 2 week(s) of notification. **Transfers:** Priority date 3/10; no deadline.

Contact. **Financial aid office:** (260) 422-5561ext. 2208
Teresa Vasquez, Coordinator of Financial Aid
1600 East Washington Boulevard
Fort Wayne, IN 46803-1297

Indiana State University

Terre Haute, Indiana
web.indstate.edu
Four-year public **Federal Code: 001807**

	Living at home	On-campus
Tuition and fees (2002-2003):	$4,216	$4,216
Out-of-state:	$10,376	$10,376
Room and board:		$4,998
Board only:	$2,251	
Books and supplies:	$750	$750
Personal expenses:	$1,656	$1,656
Transportation:	$1,532	$540

Undergraduate aid. All financial aid based on need. Average financial aid package for full-time students was $5,838; for part-time $7,225. 41% awarded as scholarships/grants, 59% as loans/jobs. **Additional information:** Financial aid application deadline March 1 for Indiana residents applying for state grant.

Freshman aid. Out of 2,164 full-time freshmen, 1,644 applied for aid; 1,206 were judged to have need; of these 1,075 received aid. Average package met 74% of need. 196 students had full need met. Average scholarship/grant was $4,019; average loan $2,903.

Policies to reduce costs. Tuition/fee waivers for children of alumni, employees and their families. Credit/placement for qualifying scores on AP, CLEP examinations.

Payment plans. Credit card, deferred payment.

Application procedures. FAFSA required. Priority date 3/1; no closing date. Applicants notified on rolling basis starting 4/15.

Contact. **Financial aid office:** (812) 237-2215
Norman Hayes, Director of Student Financial Aid
Office of Admissions, Tirey Hall
Terre Haute, IN 47809

Indiana University Bloomington

Bloomington, Indiana
www.indiana.edu
Four-year public **Federal Code: 001809**

	Living at home	On-campus
Tuition and fees (2002-2003):	$5,315	$5,315
Out-of-state:	$15,926	$15,926
Room and board:		$6,238
Books and supplies:	$740	$740
Personal expenses:	$2,200	$2,200
Transportation:	$1,720	$750

Undergraduate aid. Need-based: Average financial aid package for full-time students was $7,079; for part-time $5,683. 42% awarded as scholarships/grants, 58% as loans/jobs. **Non-need-based:** 56% awarded as scholarships/grants, 44% as loans/jobs. Scholarships based on academics, art, athletics, leadership, minority status, music/drama, religious affiliation. **Student debt:** 47% of graduating class borrowed to fund education; average debt was $16,930. **Additional information:** Majority of institutional gift aid merit-based. Some need-based grants go to merit winners with financial need.

Freshman aid. Need-based: Out of 7,020 full-time freshmen, 4,663 applied for aid; 2,959 were judged to have need; of these 2,922 received aid. Average package met 63% of need. 463 students had full need met. Average scholarship/grant was $4,699; average loan $2,937. **Non-need based:** 1,227 full-time freshmen with need received non-need scholarships; 1,888 without need received awards.

Merit scholarships. Wells Scholarship; all costs for 4 years; individual schools nominate students; 25 students selected each year. Honors College Scholarship; $1,000-$6,000; 1300 SAT (30 ACT), top 10% class rank. Minority Achievers Program; $3,000-$4,000; 1000 SAT (25 ACT), top 20% class rank, 3.00+ GPA, based on African, Hispanic, Native American ethnicity. Mathematics and Science Scholarship; $5,000-$6,000; 1000 SAT (25 ACT), top 20% class rank, 3.00+ GPA. E.W. Kelley Scholars Program; tuition, room and board, books (overseas study funding, if requested); business major, 1300 SAT (30 ACT), top 10% class rank. School of Music Dean's Award; competitive awards, varying in amount; exceptional talent displayed in audition. Residence Scholarship (via Honors College); $1,500; 1100 SAT (27 ACT), top 10% class rank. Faculty Scholarship; competitive awards, varying in amount; out-of-state residence; superior test scores and class rank. Valedictorian Award; $1,000; Indiana residence, highest ranking in high school class. 21st Century Scholars Award; in-state instructional fees; Indiana residence, fulfilled terms of pledged in eighth grade, filed FAFSA before March 1 of senior year. Army and Air Force ROTC Scholarships; tuition, fees, books, $200 monthly; Army: 850 SAT (19 ACT), Air Force: 1030 SAT (22 ACT).

Policies to reduce costs. Tuition/fee waivers for senior citizens, employees and their families. Credit/placement for qualifying scores on AP, CLEP examinations. Work study available nights, weekends and for part-time students.

Payment plans. Credit card, deferred payment.

Application procedures. FAFSA required. Priority date 3/1; no closing date. Applicants notified on rolling basis starting 5/1. **Transfers:** Except for school of music, no merit-based aid for transfer students.

Contact. **Financial aid office:** (812) 855-0321
Susan Pugh, Director of Student Financial Assistance
107 South Indiana Avenue
Bloomington, IN 47405

Indiana University East

Richmond, Indiana
www.indiana.edu
Four-year public **Federal Code: 001811**

	Living at home
Tuition and fees (2002-2003):	$3,789
Out-of-state:	$9,511
Books and supplies:	$800
Personal expenses:	$1,300
Transportation:	$1,400

Undergraduate aid. Need-based: Average financial aid package for full-time students was $4,786; for part-time $3,179. 56% awarded as scholarships/grants, 44% as loans/jobs. **Non-need-based:** 24% awarded as scholarships/grants, 76% as loans/jobs. Scholarships based on academics, alumni affiliation, minority status. **Student debt:** 68% of graduating class borrowed to fund education; average debt was $17,237.

Freshman aid. **Need-based:** Out of 304 full-time freshmen, 271 applied for aid; 208 were judged to have need; of these 191 received aid. Average package met 50% of need. 6 students had full need met. Average scholarship/grant was $4,024; average loan $2,211. **Non-need based:** 51 full-time freshmen with need received non-need scholarships; 15 without need received awards.

Policies to reduce costs. Tuition/fee waivers for employees and their families. Credit/placement for qualifying scores on AP, CLEP examinations. Work study available nights, weekends and for part-time students.

Payment plans. Credit card, installment, deferred payment.

Application procedures. FAFSA, institutional form required. Priority date 3/1; no closing date. Applicants notified on rolling basis starting 5/1, must reply within 2 week(s) of notification. **Transfers:** Priority date 3/1.

Contact. **Financial aid office:** (765) 973-8206
James Bland, Director of Financial Aid
2325 Chester Boulevard
Richmond, IN 47374-1289

Indiana University Kokomo

Kokomo, Indiana
www.indiana.edu
Four-year public **Federal Code: 001814**

	Living at home
Tuition and fees (2002-2003):	$3,824
Out-of-state:	$9,546
Books and supplies:	$900
Personal expenses:	$1,000
Transportation:	$1,110

Undergraduate aid. **Need-based:** Average financial aid package for full-time students was $5,128; for part-time $3,510. 57% awarded as scholarships/grants, 43% as loans/jobs. **Non-need-based:** 38% awarded as scholarships/grants, 62% as loans/jobs. Scholarships based on academics. **Student debt:** 44% of graduating class borrowed to fund education; average debt was $11,511.

Freshman aid. **Need-based:** Out of 339 full-time freshmen, 188 applied for aid; 113 were judged to have need; of these 111 received aid. Average package met 66% of need. 18 students had full need met. Average scholarship/grant was $3,789; average loan $2,074. **Non-need based:** 38 full-time freshmen with need received non-need scholarships; 33 without need received awards.

Policies to reduce costs. Tuition/fee waivers for senior citizens, employees and their families. Credit/placement for qualifying scores on AP, CLEP examinations. Work study available for part-time students.

Payment plans. Credit card, deferred payment.

Application procedures. FAFSA, institutional form required. Closing date 3/1. Applicants notified on rolling basis starting 5/1, must reply within 4 week(s) of notification.

Contact. Jackie Kennedy-Fletcher, Director of Financial Aid
Box 9003, KC 230A
Kokomo, IN 46904-9003

Indiana University Northwest

Gary, Indiana
www.indiana.edu
Four-year public **Federal Code: 001815**

	Living at home
Tuition and fees (2002-2003):	$3,895
Out-of-state:	$9,617
Books and supplies:	$750
Personal expenses:	$1,120
Transportation:	$1,120

Undergraduate aid. **Need-based:** Average financial aid package for full-time students was $5,877; for part-time $4,144. 54% awarded as scholarships/grants, 46% as loans/jobs. **Non-need-based:** 26% awarded as scholarships/grants, 74% as loans/jobs. Scholarships based on academics, athletics. **Student debt:** 53% of graduating class borrowed to fund education; average debt was $13,855.

Freshman aid. **Need-based:** Out of 604 full-time freshmen, 423 applied for aid; 233 were judged to have need; of these 228 received aid. Average package met 70% of need. 50 students had full need met. Average scholarship/grant was $4,290; average loan $2,049. **Non-need based:** 26 full-time freshmen with need received non-need scholarships; 24 without need received awards.

Policies to reduce costs. Tuition/fee waivers for employees and their families. Credit/placement for qualifying scores on AP, CLEP examinations.

Payment plans. Credit card, installment, deferred payment.

Application procedures. FAFSA, institutional form required. Priority date 3/1; no closing date. Applicants notified on rolling basis starting 5/1, must reply within 2 week(s) of notification.

Contact. **Financial aid office:** (219) 980-6778
Chuck Carothers, Financial Aid Director
3400 Broadway
Gary, IN 46408

Indiana University South Bend

South Bend, Indiana
www.indiana.edu
Four-year public **Federal Code: 001816**

	Living at home
Tuition and fees (2002-2003):	$3,930
Out-of-state:	$10,269
Books and supplies:	$976
Personal expenses:	$1,604
Transportation:	$1,512

Undergraduate aid. **Need-based:** Average financial aid package for full-time students was $4,854; for part-time $3,919. 49% awarded as scholarships/grants, 51% as loans/jobs. **Non-need-based:** 35% awarded as scholarships/grants, 65% as loans/jobs. Scholarships based on academics, athletics. **Student debt:** 56% of graduating class borrowed to fund education; average debt was $15,141.

Freshman aid. **Need-based:** Out of 659 full-time freshmen, 485 applied for aid; 317 were judged to have need; of these 279 received aid. Average package met 53% of need. 20 students had full need met. Average scholarship/grant was $3,256; average loan $2,506. **Non-need based:** 59 full-time freshmen with need received non-need scholarships; 50 without need received awards.

Merit scholarships. Honors Scholarship: $1,200 per academic year (full-time); entering freshman, 1200 or more SAT (27 ACT), rank top 10 percent, 3.5 GPA; renewable up to 8 semesters. Alumni Scholarship: $3,500 freshman year; first-time freshman from Northern Indiana, meet Honors Scholarship criteria, submit essay and 3 letters of recommendation.

Policies to reduce costs. Tuition/fee waivers for employees and their families. Credit/placement for qualifying scores on AP, IB, CLEP examinations. Work study available nights, weekends and for part-time students.

Payment plans. Credit card, deferred payment.

Application procedures. FAFSA, institutional form required. Closing date 3/1. Applicants notified on rolling basis starting 5/1. **Transfers:** No deadline.

Contact. **Financial aid office:** (574) 237-4357
Lisa Shaffer, Dean of Enrollment Management
1700 Mishawaka Avenue
South Bend, IN 46634-7111

Indiana University Southeast

New Albany, Indiana
www.indiana.edu
Four-year public **Federal Code: 001817**

	Living at home
Tuition and fees (2002-2003):	$3,865
Out-of-state:	$9,587
Books and supplies:	$720
Personal expenses:	$1,470
Transportation:	$1,240

Undergraduate aid. **Need-based:** Average financial aid package for full-time students was $5,053; for part-time $3,624. 56% awarded as scholarships/grants, 44% as loans/jobs. **Non-need-based:** 36% awarded as scholarships/grants, 64% as loans/jobs. Scholarships based on academics, art, athletics, leadership, minority status, music/drama. **Student debt:** 44% of graduating class borrowed to fund education; average debt was $13,197.

Freshman aid. **Need-based:** Out of 679 full-time freshmen, 563 applied for aid; 306 were judged to have need; of these 265 received aid. Average package met 62% of need. 28 students had full need met. Average scholarship/grant was $3,673; average loan $2,471. **Non-need based:** 79 full-time freshmen with need received non-need scholarships; 79 without need received awards.

Policies to reduce costs. Tuition/fee waivers for senior citizens, employees and their families. Credit/placement for qualifying scores on AP, IB, CLEP examinations.

Payment plans. Credit card, deferred payment.

Application procedures. FAFSA, institutional form required. Closing date 3/1. Applicants notified on rolling basis starting 5/1.

Contact. Patrick Mrozowski, Director of Scholarships and Financial Aid
4201 Grant Line Road
New Albany, IN 47150-6405

Indiana University-Purdue University Fort Wayne

Fort Wayne, Indiana
www.ipfw.edu
Four-year public **Federal Code: 001828**

	Living at home
Tuition and fees (2002-2003):	$4,865
Out-of-state:	$10,650
Books and supplies:	$655
Personal expenses:	$1,500
Transportation:	$1,219

Undergraduate aid. Need-based: Average financial aid package for full-time students was $4,601; for part-time $3,125. 49% awarded as scholarships/grants, 51% as loans/jobs. **Non-need-based:** 16% awarded as scholarships/grants, 84% as loans/jobs. Scholarships based on academics, alumni affiliation, art, athletics. **Student debt:** 59% of graduating class borrowed to fund education; average debt was $13,764.

Freshman aid. Need-based: Out of 1,411 full-time freshmen, 938 applied for aid; 894 were judged to have need; of these 722 received aid. Average package met 71% of need. 131 students had full need met. Average scholarship/grant was $3,322; average loan $2,478. **Non-need based:** 199 full-time freshmen with need received non-need scholarships; 105 without need received awards; 48 received athletic scholarships.

Policies to reduce costs. Tuition/fee waivers for senior citizens, employees and their families. Credit/placement for qualifying scores on AP, IB, CLEP examinations. Work study available nights and weekends.

Payment plans. Credit card, installment, deferred payment.

Application procedures. FAFSA required. Priority date 3/1; no closing date. Applicants notified by 4/30, must reply within 4 week(s) of notification. **Transfers:** Priority date 3/1; closing date 5/1.

Contact. Financial aid office: (260) 481-6820
Mark Franke, Director of Financial Aid
2101 East Coliseum Boulevard
Fort Wayne, IN 46805-1499

Indiana University-Purdue University Indianapolis

Indianapolis, Indiana
www.indiana.edu
Four-year public **Federal Code: 001813**

	Living at home	On-campus
Tuition and fees (2002-2003):	$4,715	$4,715
Out-of-state:	$13,545	$13,545
Room only:		$2,080
Board only:	$1,754	
Books and supplies:	$768	$768
Personal expenses:	$3,462	$3,694
Transportation:	$2,448	$1,962

Undergraduate aid. Need-based: Average financial aid package for full-time students was $6,139; for part-time $3,995. 57% awarded as scholarships/grants, 43% as loans/jobs. **Non-need-based:** 37% awarded as scholarships/grants, 63% as loans/jobs. Scholarships based on academics. **Student debt:** 60% of graduating class borrowed to fund education; average debt was $18,640.

Freshman aid. Need-based: Out of 2,243 full-time freshmen, 1,568 applied for aid; 1,222 were judged to have need; of these 1,066 received aid. Average package met 51% of need. 97 students had full need met. Average scholarship/grant was $4,465; average loan $2,304. **Non-need based:** 364 full-time freshmen with need received non-need scholarships; 254 without need received awards.

Policies to reduce costs. Tuition/fee waivers for employees and their families. Credit/placement for qualifying scores on AP, CLEP examinations. Work study available nights and weekends.

Payment plans. Credit card, installment, deferred payment.

Application procedures. FAFSA required. Priority date 3/1; no closing date. Applicants notified on rolling basis starting 4/1. **Transfers:** Student must present financial aid transcripts from previous schools.

Contact. Barbara Thompson, Director of Scholarships and Financial Aid
425 North University Boulevard, Cavanaugh Hall R129
Indianapolis, IN 46202-5143

Indiana Wesleyan University

Marion, Indiana
www.indwes.edu
Four-year private **Federal Code: 001822**

College costs. Required fees vary on program.

	Living at home	On-campus
Tuition and fees:	$14,420	$14,420
Room and board:		$5,480
Board only:	$1,752	
Books and supplies:	$800	$800
Personal expenses:	$800	$800
Transportation:	$590	$590

Undergraduate aid. Need-based: Need-based aid available for full-time and part-time students. **Non-need-based:** Scholarships based on academics, alumni affiliation, art, athletics, music/drama.

Merit scholarships. Academic Scholarships with awards ranging from $750 to $6,000, 3.2 GPA and 1050 SAT/23 ACT

Policies to reduce costs. Tuition/fee waivers for senior citizens, family members, family of clergy, employees and their families. Credit/placement for qualifying scores on AP, CLEP examinations.

Payment plans. Credit card payment.

Application procedures. FAFSA required. Closing date 3/1. Applicants notified by 4/1.

Contact. Financial aid office: (765) 677-2116
Lois Kelly, Assistant Vice President for Financial Aid
4201 South Washington Street
Marion, IN 46953-4999

International Business College

Fort Wayne, Indiana
Four-year proprietary **Federal Code: 004579**

College costs. Fee for medical assisting program $960. Total for 2-1/2 semester program $12,000.

	Living at home	On-campus
Tuition and fees (2002-2003):	$9,600	$9,600
Room only:		$4,100
Books and supplies:	$900	$900

Policies to reduce costs. Tuition/fee waivers for employees and their families.

Payment plans. Credit card, installment payment.

Application procedures. Closing date 5/1. Applicants notified by 9/15.

Contact. Roxanna Shull, Director of Financial Aid
5699 Coventry Lane
Fort Wayne, IN 46804

International Business College: Indianapolis

Indianapolis, Indiana
www.intlbusinesscollege.com
Two-year proprietary **Federal Code: 004579**

	Living at home
Tuition and fees (2002-2003):	$9,600
Books and supplies:	$1,400

Contact. 7205 Shadeland Station
Indianapolis, IN 46256

Ivy Tech State College: Bloomington

Bloomington, Indiana
www.ivytech.edu
Two-year public **Federal Code: 035213**

	Living at home
Tuition and fees (2002-2003):	$2,264
Out-of-state:	$4,513
Per-credit charge:	$74
Per-credit out-of-state:	$149
Board only:	$2,485
Books and supplies:	$726
Personal expenses:	$1,584
Transportation:	$1,104

Undergraduate aid. Need-based: 67% awarded as scholarships/grants, 33% as loans/jobs. Need-based aid available for part-time students.

Policies to reduce costs. Tuition/fee waivers for senior citizens, employees and their families. Credit/placement for qualifying scores on CLEP examinations. Work study available nights and for part-time students.

Payment plans. Credit card, deferred payment.

Application procedures. FAFSA required. Priority date 3/1; no closing date. Applicants notified on rolling basis starting 7/1.

Contact. Peg Creech, Director of Financial Aid
Bloomington, IN 47404-1511

Ivy Tech State College: Central Indiana

Indianapolis, Indiana
www.ivytech.edu
Two-year public **Federal Code: 009917**

	Living at home
Tuition and fees (2002-2003):	$2,264
Out-of-state:	$4,513
Per-credit charge:	$74
Per-credit out-of-state:	$149
Board only:	$2,485
Books and supplies:	$726
Personal expenses:	$1,584
Transportation:	$1,104

Undergraduate aid. Need-based: 66% awarded as scholarships/grants, 34% as loans/jobs. Need-based aid available for part-time students.

Policies to reduce costs. Tuition/fee waivers for senior citizens, employees and their families. Credit/placement for qualifying scores on CLEP examinations. Work study available nights, weekends and for part-time students.

Payment plans. Credit card, deferred payment.

Application procedures. FAFSA required. Priority date 3/1; no closing date. Applicants notified on rolling basis starting 7/1.

Contact. Financial aid office: (317) 921-4777
Mildrid Williamson, Director of Financial Aid
One West 26th Street
Indianapolis, IN 46206-1763

Ivy Tech State College: Columbus

Columbus, Indiana
www.ivytech.edu
Two-year public **Federal Code: 010038**

	Living at home
Tuition and fees (2002-2003):	$2,264
Out-of-state:	$4,513
Per-credit charge:	$74
Per-credit out-of-state:	$149
Board only:	$2,485
Books and supplies:	$726
Personal expenses:	$1,584
Transportation:	$1,104

Undergraduate aid. Need-based: 73% awarded as scholarships/grants, 27% as loans/jobs. Need-based aid available for part-time students.

Policies to reduce costs. Tuition/fee waivers for senior citizens, employees and their families. Credit/placement for qualifying scores on CLEP examinations. Work study available nights and for part-time students.

Payment plans. Credit card, deferred payment.

Application procedures. FAFSA required. Priority date 3/1; no closing date. Applicants notified on rolling basis starting 7/1, must reply within 3 week(s) of notification.

Contact. Financial aid office: (812) 372-9925
Doug Hess, Director of Financial Aid
4475 Central Avenue
Columbus, IN 47203-1868

Ivy Tech State College: Eastcentral

Muncie, Indiana
www.ivytech.edu
Two-year public **Federal Code: 009924**

	Living at home
Tuition and fees (2002-2003):	$2,264
Out-of-state:	$4,513
Per-credit charge:	$74
Per-credit out-of-state:	$149
Board only:	$2,485
Books and supplies:	$726
Personal expenses:	$1,584
Transportation:	$1,104

Undergraduate aid. Need-based: 79% awarded as scholarships/grants, 21% as loans/jobs. Need-based aid available for part-time students. **Additional information:** Higher Education Aid (HEA), Child of Disabled/Deceased Veterans (CDV), Ivy Tech Scholarships (IVTC) and grants, vocational rehabilitation and veteran's assistance available. None require repayment.

Policies to reduce costs. Tuition/fee waivers for senior citizens, employees and their families. Credit/placement for qualifying scores on CLEP examinations. Work study available nights and for part-time students.

Payment plans. Credit card, deferred payment.

Application procedures. FAFSA required. Priority date 3/1; no closing date. Applicants notified on rolling basis starting 7/1.

Contact. Financial aid office: (765) 289-2291 ext. 386
Sylvia Bogle, Director of Financial Aid
4301 South Cowan Road
Muncie, IN 47302-9448

Ivy Tech State College: Kokomo

Kokomo, Indiana
www.ivytech.edu
Two-year public **Federal Code: 010041**

	Living at home
Tuition and fees (2002-2003):	$2,264
Out-of-state:	$4,513
Per-credit charge:	$74
Per-credit out-of-state:	$149
Board only:	$2,485
Books and supplies:	$726
Personal expenses:	$1,584
Transportation:	$1,104

Undergraduate aid. Need-based: 75% awarded as scholarships/grants, 25% as loans/jobs. Need-based aid available for part-time students.

Policies to reduce costs. Tuition/fee waivers for senior citizens, employees and their families. Credit/placement for qualifying scores on CLEP examinations. Work study available nights and for part-time students.

Payment plans. Credit card, deferred payment.

Application procedures. FAFSA required. Priority date 3/1; no closing date. Applicants notified on rolling basis starting 7/1, must reply within 4 week(s) of notification.

Contact. Financial aid office: (765) 459-0561 ext. 308
Christina Coon, Director of Financial Aid
1815 East Morgan Street
Kokomo, IN 46903-1373

Ivy Tech State College: Lafayette

Lafayette, Indiana
www.ivytech.edu
Two-year public **Federal Code: 010039**

	Living at home
Tuition and fees (2002-2003):	$2,264
Out-of-state:	$4,513
Per-credit charge:	$74
Per-credit out-of-state:	$149
Board only:	$2,485
Books and supplies:	$726
Personal expenses:	$1,584
Transportation:	$1,104

Undergraduate aid. Need-based: 59% awarded as scholarships/grants, 41% as loans/jobs. Need-based aid available for part-time students.

Policies to reduce costs. Tuition/fee waivers for senior citizens, employees and their families. Credit/placement for qualifying scores on CLEP examinations. Work study available nights and for part-time students.

Payment plans. Credit card, deferred payment.

Application procedures. FAFSA required. Priority date 3/1; no closing date. Applicants notified on rolling basis starting 7/1.

Contact. Financial aid office: (765) 772-9112
Kirsten Reynolds, Director of Financial Aid
3101 South Creasy Lane
Lafayette, IN 47905-5266

Ivy Tech State College: Northcentral

South Bend, Indiana
www.ivytech.edu
Two-year public **Federal Code: 008423**

	Living at home
Tuition and fees (2002-2003):	$2,264
Out-of-state:	$4,513
Per-credit charge:	$74
Per-credit out-of-state:	$149
Board only:	$2,485
Books and supplies:	$726
Personal expenses:	$1,584
Transportation:	$1,104

Undergraduate aid. Need-based: 81% awarded as scholarships/grants, 19% as loans/jobs. Need-based aid available for part-time students.

Policies to reduce costs. Tuition/fee waivers for senior citizens, employees and their families. Credit/placement for qualifying scores on CLEP examinations. Work study available nights and for part-time students.

Payment plans. Credit card, deferred payment.

Application procedures. FAFSA required. Priority date 3/1; no closing date. Applicants notified on rolling basis starting 7/1.

Contact. Financial aid office: (219) 289-7001 ext. 5306
Jeff Fisher, Director of Financial Aid
220 Dean Johnson Boulevard
South Bend, IN 46601-3415

Ivy Tech State College: Northeast

Fort Wayne, Indiana
www.ivytech.edu
Two-year public **Federal Code: 009926**

	Living at home
Tuition and fees (2002-2003):	$2,264
Out-of-state:	$4,513
Per-credit charge:	$74
Per-credit out-of-state:	$149
Board only:	$2,485
Books and supplies:	$726
Personal expenses:	$1,584
Transportation:	$1,104

Undergraduate aid. Need-based: 63% awarded as scholarships/grants, 37% as loans/jobs. Need-based aid available for part-time students.

Policies to reduce costs. Tuition/fee waivers for senior citizens, employees and their families. Credit/placement for qualifying scores on CLEP examinations. Work study available nights and for part-time students.

Payment plans. Credit card, deferred payment.

Application procedures. FAFSA required. Priority date 3/1; no closing date. Applicants notified on rolling basis starting 7/1.

Contact. Financial aid office: (219) 480-4136
Tom Liggett, Director of Financial Aid
3800 North Anthony Boulevard
Fort Wayne, IN 46805-1489

Ivy Tech State College: Northwest

Gary, Indiana
www.ivytech.edu
Two-year public **Federal Code: 010040**

	Living at home
Tuition and fees (2002-2003):	$2,264
Out-of-state:	$4,513
Per-credit charge:	$74
Per-credit out-of-state:	$149
Board only:	$2,485
Books and supplies:	$726
Personal expenses:	$1,584
Transportation:	$1,104

Undergraduate aid. Need-based: 83% awarded as scholarships/grants, 17% as loans/jobs. Need-based aid available for part-time students.

Policies to reduce costs. Tuition/fee waivers for senior citizens, employees and their families. Credit/placement for qualifying scores on CLEP examinations. Work study available nights and for part-time students.

Payment plans. Credit card, deferred payment.

Application procedures. FAFSA required. Priority date 3/1; no closing date. Applicants notified on rolling basis starting 7/1.

Contact. Financial aid office: (219) 981-4417
Bash Jerzyk, Director of Financial Aid
1440 East 35th Avenue
Gary, IN 46409-1499

Ivy Tech State College: Southcentral

Sellersburg, Indiana
www.ivytech.edu
Two-year public **Federal Code: 010109**

	Living at home
Tuition and fees (2002-2003):	$2,264
Out-of-state:	$4,513
Per-credit charge:	$74
Per-credit out-of-state:	$149
Board only:	$2,485
Books and supplies:	$726
Personal expenses:	$1,584
Transportation:	$1,104

Undergraduate aid. Need-based: 73% awarded as scholarships/grants, 27% as loans/jobs. Need-based aid available for part-time students.

Policies to reduce costs. Tuition/fee waivers for senior citizens, employees and their families. Credit/placement for qualifying scores on CLEP examinations. Work study available nights and for part-time students.

Payment plans. Credit card, deferred payment.

Application procedures. FAFSA required. Priority date 3/1; no closing date. Applicants notified on rolling basis starting 7/1.

Contact. Financial aid office: (812) 246-3301 ext. 4114
Gary Cottrill, Director of Financial Aid
8204 Highway 311
Sellersburg, IN 47172-1897

Ivy Tech State College: Southeast

Madison, Indiana
www.ivytech.edu
Two-year public **Federal Code: 009923**

	Living at home
Tuition and fees (2002-2003):	$2,264
Out-of-state:	$4,513
Per-credit charge:	$74
Per-credit out-of-state:	$149
Board only:	$2,485
Books and supplies:	$726
Personal expenses:	$1,584
Transportation:	$1,104

Undergraduate aid. Need-based: 67% awarded as scholarships/grants, 33% as loans/jobs. Need-based aid available for part-time students.

Policies to reduce costs. Tuition/fee waivers for senior citizens, employees and their families. Credit/placement for qualifying scores on CLEP examinations. Work study available nights and for part-time students.

Payment plans. Credit card, deferred payment.

Application procedures. FAFSA required. Priority date 3/1; no closing date. Applicants notified on rolling basis starting 7/1, must reply within 4 week(s) of notification.

Contact. Financial aid office: (812) 265-2580 ext. 4148
Richard Hill, Director of Financial Aid
590 Ivy Tech Drive
Madison, IN 47250-1881

Ivy Tech State College: Southwest

Evansville, Indiana
www.ivytech.edu
Two-year public **Federal Code: 009925**

	Living at home
Tuition and fees (2002-2003):	$2,264
Out-of-state:	$4,513
Per-credit charge:	$74
Per-credit out-of-state:	$149
Board only:	$2,485
Books and supplies:	$726
Personal expenses:	$1,584
Transportation:	$1,104

Undergraduate aid. Need-based: 69% awarded as scholarships/grants, 31% as loans/jobs. Need-based aid available for part-time students.

Policies to reduce costs. Tuition/fee waivers for senior citizens, employees and their families. Credit/placement for qualifying scores on CLEP examinations. Work study available nights and for part-time students.

Payment plans. Credit card, deferred payment.

Application procedures. FAFSA required. Priority date 3/1; no closing date. Applicants notified on rolling basis starting 7/1.

Contact. Financial aid office: (812) 429-1429
Lois Rini, Director of Financial Aid
3501 First Avenue
Evansville, IN 47710-3398

Ivy Tech State College: Wabash Valley

Terre Haute, Indiana
www.ivytech.edu
Two-year public **Federal Code: 008547**

	Living at home
Tuition and fees (2002-2003):	$2,264
Out-of-state:	$4,513
Per-credit charge:	$74
Per-credit out-of-state:	$149
Board only:	$2,485
Books and supplies:	$726
Personal expenses:	$1,584
Transportation:	$1,104

Undergraduate aid. Need-based: 80% awarded as scholarships/grants, 20% as loans/jobs. Need-based aid available for part-time students.

Policies to reduce costs. Tuition/fee waivers for senior citizens, employees and their families. Credit/placement for qualifying scores on CLEP examinations. Work study available nights and for part-time students.

Payment plans. Credit card, deferred payment.

Application procedures. FAFSA required. Priority date 3/1; no closing date. Applicants notified on rolling basis starting 7/1.

Contact. Financial aid office: (812) 298-2293
Julie Wonderlin, Director of Financial Aid
7999 US Highway 41 South
Terre Haute, IN 47802-4898

Ivy Tech State College: Whitewater

Richmond, Indiana
www.ivytech.edu
Two-year public **Federal Code: 010037**

	Living at home
Tuition and fees (2002-2003):	$2,264
Out-of-state:	$4,513
Per-credit charge:	$74
Per-credit out-of-state:	$149
Board only:	$2,485
Books and supplies:	$726
Personal expenses:	$1,584
Transportation:	$1,104

Undergraduate aid. Need-based: 75% awarded as scholarships/grants, 25% as loans/jobs. Need-based aid available for part-time students.

Policies to reduce costs. Tuition/fee waivers for senior citizens, employees and their families. Credit/placement for qualifying scores on CLEP examinations. Work study available nights and for part-time students.

Payment plans. Credit card, deferred payment.

Application procedures. FAFSA required. Priority date 3/1; no closing date. Applicants notified on rolling basis starting 7/1, must reply within 3 week(s) of notification.

Contact. Financial aid office: (765) 966-2656 ext. 308
Ann Franzen-Roha, Director of Financial Aid
2325 Chester Boulevard
Richmond, IN 47374-1298

Lincoln Technical Institute

Indianapolis, Indiana
www.lincolntech.com
Two-year proprietary **Federal Code: 007938**

College costs (2002-2003). Tuition $20,000 for auto-diesel management program, $16,000 for technology programs, $16,000 for drafting program. Books/supplies: $1,815.

Contact. 1201 Stadium Drive
Indianapolis, IN 46202

Manchester College

North Manchester, Indiana
www.manchester.edu
Four-year private **Federal Code: 001820**

	Living at home	On-campus
Tuition and fees:	$17,050	$17,050
Room and board:		$6,340
Books and supplies:	$550	$550
Personal expenses:	$900	$900
Transportation:	$550	$550

Undergraduate aid. Need-based: Average financial aid package for full-time students was $15,435; for part-time $6,733. 74% awarded as scholarships/grants, 26% as loans/jobs. **Non-need-based:** 79% awarded as scholarships/grants, 21% as loans/jobs. Scholarships based on academics, alumni affiliation, art, minority status, music/drama, religious affiliation, state/district residency. **Student debt:** 75% of graduating class borrowed to fund education; average debt was $12,050. **Additional information:** Students are automatically considered for all scholarship programs.

Freshman aid. Need-based: Out of 309 full-time freshmen, 289 applied for aid; 257 were judged to have need; of these 257 received aid. Average package met 97% of need. 165 students had full need met. Average scholarship/grant was $12,953; average loan $3,050. **Non-need based:** 186 full-time freshmen with need received non-need scholarships; 17 without need received awards.

Merit scholarships. Honors Fellowships based on academics; 2 awarded; full tuition. Presidential Leadership Awards; 3 awarded; $2,500 travel grant. Trustee Scholarships based on merit, $8,500; 40 awarded to each incoming class. Presidential Scholarships based on merit; $7,000. Arts, Service, Modern Language Scholarships based on merit/ability; $7,000.

Policies to reduce costs. Tuition/fee waivers for employees and their families. Credit/placement for qualifying scores on AP, IB, CLEP examinations. Work study available nights, weekends and for part-time students.

Payment plans. Credit card, installment payment.

Application procedures. FAFSA required. Priority date 3/1; no closing date. Applicants notified on rolling basis starting 2/15, must reply by 5/1 or within 2 week(s) of notification. **Transfers:** No deadline. Aid eligibility remaining determined by reviewing total credit hours transferred and financial aid transcripts.

Contact. Financial aid office: (260) 982-5066
Gina Voelz, Director of Financial Aid
604 E College Avenue
North Manchester, IN 46962-0365

Marian College

Indianapolis, Indiana
www.marian.edu
Four-year private **Federal Code: 001821**

College costs. Tuition includes required fees.

	Living at home	On-campus
Tuition and fees:	$17,460	$17,460
Room and board:		$5,800
Board only:	$2,400	
Books and supplies:	$700	$700
Personal expenses:	$900	$900
Transportation:	$640	$360

Undergraduate aid. Need-based: Average financial aid package for full-time students was $14,322; for part-time $5,782. 67% awarded as scholarships/grants, 33% as loans/jobs. **Non-need-based:** 47% awarded as scholarships/grants, 53% as loans/jobs. Scholarships based on academics, alumni affiliation, art, athletics, leadership, minority status, music/drama, religious affiliation. **Student debt:** 80% of graduating class borrowed to fund education; average debt was $14,815.

Freshman aid. Need-based: Out of 231 full-time freshmen, 215 applied for aid; 191 were judged to have need; of these 191 received aid. 115 students had full need met. Average scholarship/grant was $9,156; average loan $3,014. **Non-need based:** 125 full-time freshmen with need received non-need scholarships; 24 without need received awards; 55 received athletic scholarships.

Policies to reduce costs. Tuition/fee waivers for children of alumni, senior citizens, family members, family of clergy, employees and their families. Credit/placement for qualifying scores on AP, IB, CLEP examinations.

Payment plans. Credit card, installment payment.

Application procedures. FAFSA, institutional form required. Priority date 3/1; no closing date. Applicants notified on rolling basis starting 3/15, must reply within 3 week(s) of notification. **Transfers:** Priority date 5/1.

Contact. Financial aid office: (317) 955-6040
John Shelton, Assistant Dean for Financial Aid
3200 Cold Spring Road
Indianapolis, IN 46222

Martin University

Indianapolis, Indiana
www.martin.edu
Four-year private **Federal Code: 014975**

	Living at home
Tuition and fees:	$10,320
Books and supplies:	$820
Personal expenses:	$1,114
Transportation:	$1,114

Policies to reduce costs. Tuition/fee waivers for senior citizens, employees and their families. Credit/placement for qualifying scores on CLEP examinations.

Payment plans. Credit card, installment payment.

Application procedures. FAFSA required. Priority date 5/1; no closing date. Applicants notified on rolling basis starting 6/1, must reply within 2 week(s) of notification.

Contact. Andrea Watkins, Director of Financial Aid
2171 Avondale Place
Indianapolis, IN 46218

Michiana College

South Bend, Indiana
www.michianacollege.com
Two-year proprietary **Federal Code: 004583**

	Living at home
Tuition and fees (2002-2003):	$5,976
Per-credit charge:	$156
Books and supplies:	$1,200

Undergraduate aid. All financial aid based on need. Need-based aid available for full-time and part-time students.

Policies to reduce costs. Tuition/fee waivers for employees and their families. Tuition at time of enrollment guaranteed for 2 years; credit/placement for qualifying scores on AP examinations.

Payment plans. Credit card, installment payment.

Application procedures. FAFSA required. No deadline. Applicants notified on rolling basis, must reply within 1 week(s) of notification. **Transfers:** No deadline.

Contact. Matt Soucy, Financial Aid Director
1030 East Jefferson Boulevard
South Bend, IN 46617

Michiana College: Fort Wayne

Fort Wayne, Indiana
www.michianacollege.com
Two-year proprietary **Federal Code: 004583**

College costs (2002-2003). Tuition and fees $15,936 for 24-month associate programs; $11,952 for 18-month certificate and diploma programs. Books/supplies: $1,100.

Contact. Financial aid office: (260) 484-4400
Fabio Vegas, Senior Financial Aid
4422 East State Boulevard
Fort Wayne, IN 46815

Mid-America College of Funeral Service

Jeffersonville, Indiana
www.mid-america.edu
Two-year proprietary **Federal Code: 010618**

College costs. Tuition includes books. Online courses $600 per course.

	Living at home
Tuition and fees:	$8,000
Personal expenses:	$2,520
Transportation:	$1,920

Payment plans. Installment payment.

Application procedures. FAFSA required. No deadline. Applicants notified on rolling basis.

Contact. Richard Nelson, Director of Financial Aid
3111 Hamburg Pike
Jeffersonville, IN 47130

Oakland City University

Oakland City, Indiana
www.oak.edu
Four-year private **Federal Code: 001824**

	Living at home	On-campus
Tuition and fees:	$12,320	$12,320
Room and board:		$4,560
Books and supplies:	$1,000	$1,000
Personal expenses:	$1,500	$1,000
Transportation:	$2,000	$500

Undergraduate aid. Need-based: 32% awarded as scholarships/grants, 68% as loans/jobs. Need-based aid available for part-time students. **Non-need-based:** Scholarships based on academics, alumni affiliation, art, athletics, minority status, music/drama, religious affiliation.

Policies to reduce costs. Tuition/fee waivers for children of alumni, senior citizens, minority students, unemployed or children of unemployed, family of clergy, employees and their families. Credit/placement for qualifying scores on AP, IB, CLEP examinations. Work study available nights, weekends and for part-time students.

Payment plans. Credit card, installment, deferred payment.

Application procedures. FAFSA required. Closing date 3/1. Applicants notified on rolling basis starting 6/1. **Transfers:** Closing date 3/1.

Contact. Financial aid office: (812) 749-1224
Caren Richeson, Director of Financial Aid
143 N. Lucretia Street
Oakland City, IN 47660

Professional Careers Institute

Indianapolis, Indiana
www.pcicareers.com
Two-year proprietary **Federal Code: 009777**

College costs. Tuition for full associate degree program in computer programming $16,000; for paralegal/legal assisting program $15,000. Lab fees and books vary per program.

	Living at home
Tuition and fees (2002-2003):	$7,350
Books and supplies:	$500
Personal expenses:	$1,472

Undergraduate aid. All financial aid based on need. Need-based aid available for full-time students.

Contact. Financial aid office: (317) 299-6001 ext. 320
Phyllis Robbins
7302 Woodland Drive
Indianapolis, IN 46278-1736

Purdue University

West Lafayette, Indiana
www.purdue.edu
Four-year public **Federal Code: 001825**

College costs. Engineering students pay additional $488 fee.

	Living at home	On-campus
Tuition and fees (2002-2003):	$5,580	$5,580
Out-of-state:	$16,260	$16,260
Room and board:		$6,340
Board only:	$2,280	
Books and supplies:	$830	$830
Personal expenses:	$1,040	$1,040
Transportation:	$1,260	$210

Undergraduate aid. Need-based: Average financial aid package for full-time students was $7,387; for part-time $5,054. 52% awarded as scholarships/grants, 48% as loans/jobs. **Non-need-based:** 18% awarded as scholarships/grants, 82% as loans/jobs. Scholarships based on academics, athletics, leadership, minority status, music/drama, state/district residency. **Student debt:** 50% of graduating class borrowed to fund education; average debt was $15,677. **Additional information:** Cooperative work for credit available in many programs.

Freshman aid. Need-based: Out of 6,242 full-time freshmen, 4,424 applied for aid; 2,668 were judged to have need; of these 2,357 received aid. Average package met 90% of need. 807 students had full need met. Average scholarship/grant was $7,650; average loan $3,021. **Non-need based:** 608 full-time freshmen with need received non-need scholarships; 1,137 without need received awards; 70 received athletic scholarships.

Policies to reduce costs. Tuition/fee waivers for senior citizens, employees and their families. Credit/placement for qualifying scores on AP, IB, CLEP examinations.

Payment plans. Installment, deferred payment.

Application procedures. FAFSA required. Priority date 3/1; no closing date. Applicants notified by 4/15. **Transfers:** Priority date 3/1.

Contact. Financial aid office: (765) 494-5050
Joyce Hall, Director of Financial Aid
475 Stadum Mall Dr.
West Lafayette, IN 47907-2050

Purdue University: Calumet

Hammond, Indiana
www.calumet.purdue.edu
Four-year public **Federal Code: 001827**

	Living at home
Tuition and fees (2002-2003):	$4,393
Out-of-state:	$9,846
Books and supplies:	$700
Personal expenses:	$1,064
Transportation:	$1,263

Undergraduate aid. All financial aid based on need. Need-based aid available for full-time and part-time students.

Policies to reduce costs. Tuition/fee waivers for employees and their families. Credit/placement for qualifying scores on AP, CLEP examinations. Work study available nights, weekends and for part-time students.

Payment plans. Credit card payment.

Application procedures. FAFSA required. Priority date 3/1; no closing date. Applicants notified on rolling basis starting 5/1, must reply within 2 week(s) of notification.

Contact. Financial aid office: (219) 989-2302
Mary Ann Bishel, Director of Financial Aid
171 Street and Woodmar Avenue
Hammond, IN 46323-2094

Purdue University: North Central Campus

Westville, Indiana
www.purduenc.edu
Four-year public **Federal Code: 001825**

College costs. Additional $50 per course fee for classes at Valparaiso Academic Center.

	Living at home
Tuition and fees (2002-2003):	$4,487
Out-of-state:	$10,019
Books and supplies:	$600
Personal expenses:	$1,200
Transportation:	$1,300

Undergraduate aid. All financial aid based on need. Average financial aid package for full-time students was $4,893; for part-time $3,753. 56% awarded as scholarships/grants, 44% as loans/jobs. **Student debt:** 39% of graduating class borrowed to fund education; average debt was $8,270.

Freshman aid. Out of 573 full-time freshmen, 427 applied for aid; 361 were judged to have need; of these 336 received aid. Average package met 63% of need. 87 students had full need met. Average scholarship/grant was $4,285; average loan $2,243.

Policies to reduce costs. Tuition/fee waivers for senior citizens, minority students, employees and their families. Credit/placement for qualifying scores on AP, CLEP examinations.

Payment plans. Credit card, deferred payment.

Application procedures. FAFSA required. Priority date 3/1; no closing date. Applicants notified on rolling basis starting 5/31, must reply within 2 week(s) of notification. **Transfers:** Priority date 3/1; no deadline. Transfer students are not considered for campus-based financial aid.

Contact. Gerald Lewis, Director of Financial Aid
1401 South US Highway 421
Westville, IN 46391-9528

Rose-Hulman Institute of Technology

Terre Haute, Indiana
www.rose-hulman.edu
Four-year private **Federal Code: 001830**

College costs. Laptop computer $3,125.

	Living at home	On-campus
Tuition and fees:	$24,705	$24,705
Room and board:		$6,720
Board only:	$1,800	
Books and supplies:	$900	$900
Transportation:	$1,200	$1,200

Undergraduate aid. Need-based: Average financial aid package for full-time students was $14,471; for part-time $7,338. 59% awarded as scholarships/ grants, 41% as loans/jobs. **Non-need-based:** 78% awarded as scholarships/ grants, 22% as loans/jobs. Scholarships based on academics, minority status. **Student debt:** 85% of graduating class borrowed to fund education; average debt was $27,000.

Freshman aid. Need-based: Out of 403 full-time freshmen, 366 applied for aid; 310 were judged to have need; of these 310 received aid. Average package met 93% of need. 29 students had full need met. Average scholarship/ grant was $4,993; average loan $5,501. **Non-need based:** 47 full-time freshmen with need received non-need scholarships; 87 without need received awards.

Policies to reduce costs. Tuition/fee waivers for employees and their families. Credit/placement for qualifying scores on AP, IB examinations. Work study available nights, weekends and for part-time students.

Payment plans. Credit card payment.

Application procedures. FAFSA required. Priority date 3/1; no closing date. Applicants notified on rolling basis starting 3/10. **Transfers:** Priority date 3/1; no deadline.

Contact. Financial aid office: (800) 248-7448
Melinda Middleton, Director of Financial Aid
Office of Admissions, 5500 Wabash Avenue
Terre Haute, IN 47803-3999

St. Joseph's College

Rensselaer, Indiana
www.saintjoe.edu
Four-year private **Federal Code: 001833**

	Living at home	On-campus
Tuition and fees (projected):	$18,060	$18,060
Room and board:		$6,190
Books and supplies:	$700	$700
Personal expenses:	$4,705	$650
Transportation:	$2,226	$400

Undergraduate aid. Need-based: Average financial aid package for full-time students was $12,500; for part-time $5,000. 72% awarded as scholarships/ grants, 28% as loans/jobs. **Non-need-based:** 42% awarded as scholarships/ grants, 58% as loans/jobs. Scholarships based on academics, alumni affiliation, athletics, minority status, music/drama. **Student debt:** 74% of graduating class borrowed to fund education; average debt was $18,668.

Freshman aid. Need-based: Out of 213 full-time freshmen, 207 applied for aid; 174 were judged to have need; of these 174 received aid. Average package met 80% of need. 70 students had full need met. Average scholarship/ grant was $9,000; average loan $2,900. **Non-need based:** 148 full-time freshmen with need received non-need scholarships; 10 without need received awards; 30 received athletic scholarships.

Policies to reduce costs. Tuition/fee waivers for children of alumni, minority students, family members, employees and their families. Credit/ placement for qualifying scores on AP, CLEP examinations.

Application procedures. FAFSA required. Priority date 3/1; no closing date. Applicants notified on rolling basis starting 3/1, must reply by 6/1 or within 2 week(s) of notification. Early decision closing date 10/1. **Transfers:** Limited institutional academic scholarship.

Contact. Financial aid office: (219) 866-6163
Dianne Mickey, Director of Financial Aid
Box 815
Rensselaer, IN 47978

Saint Mary's College

Notre Dame, Indiana
www.saintmarys.edu
Four-year private **Federal Code: 001836**

	Living at home	On-campus
Tuition and fees:	$21,974	$21,974
Room and board:		$7,289
Books and supplies:	$1,000	$1,000
Personal expenses:	$1,150	$1,150
Transportation:	$425	$275

Undergraduate aid. Need-based: Average financial aid package for full-time students was $16,507. 65% awarded as scholarships/grants, 35% as loans/jobs. Need-based aid available for part-time students. **Non-need-based:** 57% awarded as scholarships/grants, 43% as loans/jobs. Scholarships based on academics. **Student debt:** 58% of graduating class borrowed to fund education; average debt was $15,436.

Freshman aid. Need-based: Out of 376 full-time freshmen, 299 applied for aid; 232 were judged to have need; of these 232 received aid. Average package met 86% of need. 55 students had full need met. Average scholarship/ grant was $12,719; average loan $3,307. **Non-need based:** 76 full-time freshmen with need received non-need scholarships; 126 without need received awards.

Merit scholarships. A variety of endowed and specific purpose scholarships are available. Contact the office of financial aid for more information.

Policies to reduce costs. Tuition/fee waivers for family members, employees and their families. Credit/placement for qualifying scores on AP, IB, CLEP examinations. Work study available nights and weekends.

Application procedures. FAFSA, CSS PROFILE required. Priority date 3/1; no closing date. Applicants notified on rolling basis starting 12/15, must reply by 5/1. Early decision closing date 11/15. **Transfers:** Priority date 5/15; no deadline. To meet Indiana grant deadlines, Indiana residents must submit FAFSA by March 1.

Contact. Financial aid office: (574) 284-4557
Mary Nucciarone, Director of Financial Aid
Notre Dame, IN 46556-5001

St. Mary-of-the-Woods College

St. Mary-of-the-Woods, Indiana
www.smwc.edu
Four-year private **Federal Code: 001835**

College costs. External degree program tuition $307 per credit hour.

	Living at home	On-campus
Tuition and fees:	$17,030	$17,030
Room and board:		$6,100
Board only:	$3,200	
Books and supplies:	$980	$980
Personal expenses:	$700	$900
Transportation:	$900	$900

Undergraduate aid. Need-based: Average financial aid package for full-time students was $12,000; for part-time $6,000. 58% awarded as scholarships/ grants, 42% as loans/jobs. **Non-need-based:** 37% awarded as scholarships/ grants, 63% as loans/jobs. Scholarships based on academics, alumni affiliation, art, athletics, leadership, minority status, music/drama, state/district residency. **Student debt:** 70% of graduating class borrowed to fund education; average debt was $1,300. **Additional information:** Portfolio or audition required of applicants who wish to be considered for Creative Arts Scholarship.

Freshman aid. Need-based: Out of 97 full-time freshmen, 97 applied for aid; 54 were judged to have need; of these 54 received aid. Average package met 61% of need. 5 students had full need met. Average scholarship/grant was $5,000; average loan $2,625. **Non-need based:** 47 full-time freshmen with need received non-need scholarships; 9 without need received awards; 14 received athletic scholarships.

Policies to reduce costs. Tuition/fee waivers for children of alumni, minority students, family members, employees and their families. Credit/ placement for qualifying scores on AP, IB, CLEP examinations. Work study available nights, weekends and for part-time students.

Payment plans. Credit card, installment, deferred payment.

Application procedures. FAFSA required. Priority date 3/1; no closing date. Applicants notified on rolling basis starting 12/1, must reply within 6 week(s) of notification. **Transfers:** Priority date 7/1; no deadline.

Contact. **Financial aid office:** (812) 535-5109
Jan Benton, Director of Financial Aid
Guerin Hall, SMWC
St. Mary-of-the-Woods, IN 47876

Sawyer College

Hammond, Indiana
www.sawyercollege.com
Two-year proprietary **Federal Code: 022018**

	Living at home
Tuition and fees:	$7,875
Per-credit charge:	$175

Policies to reduce costs. Credit/placement for qualifying scores on AP examinations.

Payment plans. Installment payment.

Application procedures. FAFSA required. Applicants notified on rolling basis. **Transfers:** No deadline.

Contact. **Financial aid office:** (219) 931-0436
Denise Edwards, Financial Aid Coordinator
6040 Hohman Avenue
Hammond, IN 46320

Sawyer College: Merrillville

Merrillville, Indiana
www.sawyercollege.com
Two-year proprietary **Federal Code: 022018**

College costs (2002-2003). Per-credit hour charge $145 to $195 depending on program. Full program costs: $15,000 to $19,000 for 2-year associate programs; $6,000 to $9,000 for 9-month certificate programs. Books/supplies: $1,292. Personal expenses: $2,862.

Contact. 3803 East Lincoln Highway
Merrillville, IN 46410

Taylor University

Upland, Indiana
www.tayloru.edu
Four-year private **Federal Code: 001838**

	Living at home	On-campus
Tuition and fees:	$18,528	$18,528
Room and board:		$5,292
Board only:	$1,800	
Books and supplies:	$700	$700
Personal expenses:	$1,500	$1,500

Undergraduate aid. Need-based: Average financial aid package for full-time students was $12,425; for part-time $4,124. 65% awarded as scholarships/grants, 35% as loans/jobs. **Non-need-based:** 68% awarded as scholarships/grants, 32% as loans/jobs. Scholarships based on academics, alumni affiliation, art, athletics, leadership, minority status, music/drama, religious affiliation, state/district residency. **Student debt:** 51% of graduating class borrowed to fund education; average debt was $15,117. **Additional information:** Reduced rates for high school students during academic year. Tuition waivers for children of alumni during summer session.

Freshman aid. Need-based: Out of 455 full-time freshmen, 338 applied for aid; 255 were judged to have need; of these 255 received aid. Average package met 78% of need. 51 students had full need met. Average scholarship/grant was $9,146; average loan $2,859. **Non-need based:** 20 full-time freshmen with need received non-need scholarships; 130 without need received awards; 13 received athletic scholarships.

Merit scholarships. Dean's Scholarship for minimum SAT of 1200 or minimum ACT of 27 and top 15% of class; unlimited number awarded; 10-15% of tuition. President's Scholarship for SAT 1300 or ACT 29 and top 10% of class; unlimited number awarded; 15-25% of tuition. Ethnic Student Scholarship based on Christian commitment, leadership potential, willingness to contribute to the Taylor community; 10 awarded; 25% of tuition. Christian Leadership Scholarship based on leadership characteristics as determined by application and interview; 20 awarded; 25% of tuition.

Policies to reduce costs. Tuition/fee waivers for senior citizens, employees and their families. Credit/placement for qualifying scores on AP, CLEP examinations. Work study available nights, weekends and for part-time students.

Payment plans. Installment payment.

Application procedures. FAFSA, institutional form required. Closing date 3/1. Applicants notified on rolling basis starting 3/1, must reply by 5/1.

Contact. **Financial aid office:** (765) 998-5358
Tim Nace, Director of Financial Aid
236 West Reade Avenue
Upland, IN 46989-1001

Taylor University: Fort Wayne

Fort Wayne, Indiana
www.tayloru.edu/fw
Four-year private **Federal Code: 001838**

	Living at home	On-campus
Tuition and fees:	$15,904	$15,904
Room and board:		$4,680
Books and supplies:	$700	$700
Personal expenses:		$1,500

Undergraduate aid. Need-based: Average financial aid package for full-time students was $13,470; for part-time $4,006. 75% awarded as scholarships/grants, 25% as loans/jobs. **Non-need-based:** 36% awarded as scholarships/grants, 64% as loans/jobs. Scholarships based on academics, alumni affiliation, leadership, state/district residency. **Student debt:** 62% of graduating class borrowed to fund education; average debt was $12,269.

Freshman aid. Need-based: Out of 130 full-time freshmen, 112 applied for aid; 99 were judged to have need; of these 99 received aid. Average package met 87% of need. 19 students had full need met. Average scholarship/grant was $10,750; average loan $2,714. **Non-need based:** 10 full-time freshmen with need received non-need scholarships; 12 without need received awards.

Policies to reduce costs. Tuition/fee waivers for children of alumni, senior citizens, family of clergy, employees and their families. Credit/placement for qualifying scores on AP, CLEP examinations. Work study available nights and weekends.

Payment plans. Installment payment.

Application procedures. FAFSA, institutional form required. Priority date 3/1; closing date 3/1. Applicants notified on rolling basis starting 3/1, must reply by 5/1 or within 2 week(s) of notification.

Contact. **Financial aid office:** (800) 233-3922
Paul Johnston, Director of Financial Aid
1025 West Rudisill Boulevard
Fort Wayne, IN 46807

Tri-State University

Angola, Indiana
www.tristate.edu
Four-year private **Federal Code: 001839**

	Living at home	On-campus
Tuition and fees:	$18,000	$18,000
Room and board:		$5,600
Books and supplies:	$700	$700
Personal expenses:	$3,562	$1,322

Undergraduate aid. Need-based: Average financial aid package for full-time students was $11,128; for part-time $4,108. 61% awarded as scholarships/grants, 39% as loans/jobs. **Non-need-based:** 84% awarded as scholarships/grants, 16% as loans/jobs. Scholarships based on academics. **Student debt:** 67% of graduating class borrowed to fund education; average debt was $16,695.

Freshman aid. Need-based: Out of 269 full-time freshmen, 269 applied for aid; 266 were judged to have need; of these 266 received aid. Average package met 95% of need. 266 students had full need met. Average scholarship/grant was $4,095; average loan $2,452. **Non-need based:** 266 full-time freshmen with need received non-need scholarships; 12 without need received awards.

Policies to reduce costs. Tuition/fee waivers for employees and their families. Credit/placement for qualifying scores on AP, CLEP examinations. Work study available nights and weekends.

Payment plans. Credit card payment.

Application procedures. FAFSA required. Priority date 3/1; no closing date. Applicants notified on rolling basis starting 2/1, must reply by 5/1 or within 2 week(s) of notification. **Transfers:** Priority date 3/1; no deadline.

Contact. **Financial aid office:** (260) 665-4116
Kim Bennett, Director of Admission and Financial Aid
One University Avenue
Angola, IN 46703

University of Evansville

Evansville, Indiana
www.evansville.edu
Four-year private **Federal Code: 001795**

	Living at home	On-campus
Tuition and fees:	$19,230	$19,230
Room and board:		$5,830
Board only:	$1,650	
Books and supplies:	$700	$700
Personal expenses:	$746	$746
Transportation:	$1,650	$550

Undergraduate aid. Need-based: Average financial aid package for full-time students was $16,197; for part-time $6,523. 72% awarded as scholarships/grants, 28% as loans/jobs. **Non-need-based:** 86% awarded as scholarships/grants, 14% as loans/jobs. Scholarships based on academics, alumni affiliation, art, athletics, leadership, minority status, music/drama, religious affiliation, state/district residency. **Student debt:** 54% of graduating class borrowed to fund education; average debt was $18,661. **Additional information:** Early financial planning service allows prospective students to get free estimate of aid available to them.

Freshman aid. Need-based: Out of 603 full-time freshmen, 600 applied for aid; 439 were judged to have need; of these 439 received aid. 186 students had full need met. Average scholarship/grant was $14,935; average loan $3,361. **Non-need based:** 211 full-time freshmen with need received non-need scholarships; 137 without need received awards; 22 received athletic scholarships.

Policies to reduce costs. Tuition/fee waivers for children of alumni, family members, family of clergy, employees and their families. Credit/placement for qualifying scores on AP, IB, CLEP examinations.

Payment plans. Credit card, installment payment.

Application procedures. FAFSA required. CSS PROFILE accepted but not required. Priority date 3/1; no closing date. Applicants notified on rolling basis starting 3/1, must reply by 5/1.

Contact. **Financial aid office:** (812) 479-2364
JoAnn Laugel, Director of Financial Aid
1800 Lincoln Avenue
Evansville, IN 47722

University of Indianapolis

Indianapolis, Indiana
www.uindy.edu
Four-year private **Federal Code: 001804**

	Living at home	On-campus
Tuition and fees:	$16,620	$16,620
Room and board:		$5,940
Books and supplies:	$600	$600
Personal expenses:	$3,000	$1,200
Transportation:	$1,000	$500

Undergraduate aid. Need-based: Average financial aid package for full-time students was $13,688; for part-time $5,203. 45% awarded as scholarships/grants, 55% as loans/jobs. **Non-need-based:** 55% awarded as scholarships/grants, 45% as loans/jobs. Scholarships based on academics, alumni affiliation, art, athletics, job skills, leadership, minority status, music/drama, religious affiliation, state/district residency. **Student debt:** 73% of graduating class borrowed to fund education; average debt was $16,809.

Freshman aid. Need-based: Out of 563 full-time freshmen, 518 applied for aid; 450 were judged to have need; of these 450 received aid. Average package met 79% of need. 116 students had full need met. Average scholarship/grant was $7,353; average loan $473. **Non-need based:** 432 full-time freshmen with need received non-need scholarships; 76 without need received awards; 61 received athletic scholarships.

Merit scholarships. Presidential Scholarship; upper 5% of class, 1270 SAT/29 ACT, strong college prep; full tuition. Dean's Scholarship; upper 7% of class, 1270 SAT/29 ACT, demonstrated leadership, strong college prep; 50% tuition. Alumni Scholarship; upper 15% of class, 1100 SAT/24 ACT, alumnus connection to school; 30% tuition. Service Award; demonstrated commitment to community volunteerism; $2,500. United Methodist Award; demonstrated commitment to church, activities; $2,500.

Policies to reduce costs. Tuition/fee waivers for senior citizens, family of clergy, employees and their families. Credit/placement for qualifying scores on AP, IB, CLEP examinations.

Payment plans. Credit card, installment, deferred payment.

Application procedures. FAFSA, institutional form required. Closing date 3/1. Applicants notified by 4/1, must reply within 3 week(s) of notification.

Contact. **Financial aid office:** (317) 788-3217
Linda Handy, Director of Financial Aid
1400 East Hanna Avenue
Indianapolis, IN 46227-3697

University of Notre Dame

Notre Dame, Indiana
www.nd.edu
Four-year private **Federal Code: 001840**

	Living at home	On-campus
Tuition and fees (2002-2003):	$25,852	$25,852
Room and board:		$6,510
Books and supplies:	$850	$850
Personal expenses:	$900	$900
Transportation:	$500	$500

Undergraduate aid. Need-based: Average financial aid package for full-time students was $23,432. 74% awarded as scholarships/grants, 26% as loans/jobs. Need-based aid available for part-time students. **Non-need-based:** 37% awarded as scholarships/grants, 63% as loans/jobs. Scholarships based on athletics. **Student debt:** 56% of graduating class borrowed to fund education; average debt was $25,595. **Additional information:** ROTC scholarships and athletic grants are available to qualified applicants on competitive basis.

Freshman aid. Need-based: Out of 1,946 full-time freshmen, 1,237 applied for aid; 888 were judged to have need; of these 888 received aid. Average package met 100% of need. 874 students had full need met. Average scholarship/grant was $18,379; average loan $3,231. **Non-need based:** 374 full-time freshmen with need received non-need scholarships; 258 without need received awards; 83 received athletic scholarships.

Policies to reduce costs. Credit/placement for qualifying scores on AP, IB examinations.

Payment plans. Installment payment.

Application procedures. FAFSA, CSS PROFILE required. Closing date 2/15. Applicants notified by 4/1, must reply by 5/1.

Contact. **Financial aid office:** (574) 631-6436
Joseph Russo, Director of Financial Aid
220 Main Building
Notre Dame, IN 46556

University of St. Francis

Fort Wayne, Indiana
www.sf.edu
Four-year private **Federal Code: 001832**

	Living at home	On-campus
Tuition and fees:	$15,488	$15,488
Room and board:		$5,450
Board only:	$2,140	
Books and supplies:	$600	$600
Personal expenses:	$1,500	$1,100
Transportation:	$1,000	$1,000

Undergraduate aid. Need-based: Average financial aid package for full-time students was $12,146; for part-time $5,694. 54% awarded as scholarships/grants, 46% as loans/jobs. **Non-need-based:** 20% awarded as scholarships/grants, 80% as loans/jobs. Scholarships based on academics, alumni affiliation, art, athletics. **Student debt:** 65% of graduating class borrowed to fund education; average debt was $15,180.

Freshman aid. Need-based: Out of 267 full-time freshmen, 264 applied for aid; 231 were judged to have need; of these 231 received aid. Average package met 81% of need. 64 students had full need met. Average scholarship/grant was $9,463; average loan $2,521. **Non-need based:** 23 full-time fresh-

men with need received non-need scholarships; 35 without need received awards; 17 received athletic scholarships.

Policies to reduce costs. Tuition/fee waivers for adults, children of alumni, senior citizens, family members, employees and their families. Credit/placement for qualifying scores on AP, CLEP examinations. Work study available nights, weekends and for part-time students.

Payment plans. Credit card, installment payment.

Application procedures. FAFSA required. Priority date 3/1; no closing date. Applicants notified on rolling basis starting 3/1.

Contact. **Financial aid office:** (260) 434-3283
Sherri Shockey, Director of Financial Aid
2701 Spring Street
Fort Wayne, IN 46808

University of Southern Indiana

Evansville, Indiana
www.usi.edu
Four-year public **Federal Code: 001808**

	Living at home	On-campus
Tuition and fees (2002-2003):	$3,630	$3,630
Out-of-state:	$8,528	$8,528
Room and board:		$5,632
Board only:	$2,300	
Books and supplies:	$750	$750
Personal expenses:	$1,736	$1,736
Transportation:	$1,500	$720

Undergraduate aid. Need-based: Average financial aid package for full-time students was $5,658; for part-time $4,305. 49% awarded as scholarships/grants, 51% as loans/jobs. **Non-need-based:** 31% awarded as scholarships/grants, 69% as loans/jobs. Scholarships based on academics, alumni affiliation, art, athletics, job skills, leadership, music/drama, state/district residency. **Student debt:** 56% of graduating class borrowed to fund education; average debt was $13,933.

Freshman aid. Need-based: Out of 1,891 full-time freshmen, 1,633 applied for aid; 1,154 were judged to have need; of these 1,078 received aid. Average package met 40% of need. 165 students had full need met. Average scholarship/grant was $3,713; average loan $2,895. **Non-need based:** 145 full-time freshmen with need received non-need scholarships; 204 without need received awards; 13 received athletic scholarships.

Policies to reduce costs. Tuition/fee waivers for senior citizens, employees and their families. Credit/placement for qualifying scores on AP, CLEP examinations. Work study available nights, weekends and for part-time students.

Payment plans. Credit card, installment payment.

Application procedures. FAFSA, institutional form required. Priority date 3/1; no closing date. Applicants notified on rolling basis starting 4/15.

Contact. James Patton, Director of Student Financial Assistance
8600 University Boulevard
Evansville, IN 47712

Valparaiso University

Valparaiso, Indiana
www.valpo.edu
Four-year private **Federal Code: 001842**

	Living at home	On-campus
Tuition and fees (projected):	$20,638	$20,638
Room and board:		$5,480
Board only:	$750	
Books and supplies:	$600	$600
Personal expenses:	$870	$870
Transportation:	$500	$200

Undergraduate aid. Need-based: Average financial aid package for full-time students was $16,448; for part-time $7,667. 73% awarded as scholarships/grants, 27% as loans/jobs. **Non-need-based:** 57% awarded as scholarships/grants, 43% as loans/jobs. Scholarships based on academics, alumni affiliation, art, athletics, leadership, minority status, music/drama, religious affiliation. **Student debt:** 64% of graduating class borrowed to fund education; average debt was $19,418. **Additional information:** Financial assistance based on need, academic record, talent, etc., available through University.

Freshman aid. Need-based: Out of 721 full-time freshmen, 721 applied for aid; 501 were judged to have need; of these 501 received aid. Average package met 95% of need. 302 students had full need met. Average scholarship/grant was $12,300; average loan $4,201. **Non-need based:** 192 full-time freshmen with need received non-need scholarships; 188 without need received awards; 19 received athletic scholarships.

Merit scholarships. Merit scholarships; minimum 1100 SAT or 24 ACT and class rank in top 30%; awards range up to full tuition and are renewable for up to 3 more years with a minimum recalculated GPA of 2.75.

Policies to reduce costs. Tuition/fee waivers for children of alumni, minority students, family members, family of clergy, employees and their families. Credit/placement for qualifying scores on AP, IB, CLEP examinations.

Payment plans. Credit card, installment payment.

Application procedures. FAFSA required. Priority date 3/1; no closing date. Applicants notified on rolling basis starting 3/1, must reply by 5/1. **Transfers:** Priority date 3/1. Merit scholarships awarded only to first-time freshmen. Institutional grants available to transfer students without prior degree.

Contact. **Financial aid office:** (219) 464-5015
David Fevig, Director of Financial Aid
Kretzmann Hall, 1700 Chapel Drive
Valparaiso, IN 46383-6493

Vincennes University

Vincennes, Indiana
www.vinu.edu
Two-year public **Federal Code: 001843**

College costs. Students from Crawford, Richland, Lawrence and Wabash counties in Illinois pay tuition of $3,978, $133 per credit.

	Living at home	On-campus
Tuition and fees (2002-2003):	$2,822	$2,822
Out-of-state:	$6,930	$6,930
Per-credit charge:	$92	$92
Per-credit out-of-state:	$229	$229
Room and board:		$5,288
Books and supplies:	$500	$500
Personal expenses:	$550	$550
Transportation:	$700	$700

Undergraduate aid. Need-based: Need-based aid available for full-time and part-time students. **Non-need-based:** Scholarships based on academics, art, athletics, leadership, music/drama, state/district residency.

Merit scholarships. Presidential Scholarship for 1100 SAT and rank in upper 10% of class; 10 awarded; $2,000 annually. Blue & Gold Scholarship for 1010 SAT and rank in upper half of class; 40 awarded; $1,100 annually. Indiana Academic Honors Diploma, $900 annually. Walters Scholarship for candidates in good standing; tuition and room and board. Education Scholarship for education majors based on SAT scores and rank in upper 10% of class; 1 awarded. Validictorian/Salutatorian scholarships.

Policies to reduce costs. Tuition/fee waivers for senior citizens, employees and their families. Credit/placement for qualifying scores on AP, IB, CLEP examinations. Work study available nights, weekends and for part-time students.

Payment plans. Credit card, installment payment.

Application procedures. FAFSA required. Priority date 3/1; closing date 5/1. Applicants notified on rolling basis starting 5/1, must reply by 8/24. **Transfers:** Transfer students must notify state student assistance commission, within 30 days of start of term.

Contact. **Financial aid office:** (812) 888-4361
Robert Gunter, Director of Financial Aid
1002 North First Street
Vincennes, IN 47591

Wabash College

Crawfordsville, Indiana
www.wabash.edu
Four-year private **Federal Code: 001844**

	Living at home	On-campus
Tuition and fees:	$21,215	$21,215
Room and board:		$6,717
Books and supplies:	$600	$600
Personal expenses:	$900	$900

Undergraduate aid. Need-based: Average financial aid package for full-time students was $18,585. 76% awarded as scholarships/grants, 24% as loans/jobs. Need-based aid available for part-time students. **Non-need-based:** 67% awarded as scholarships/grants, 33% as loans/jobs. Scholarships based on academics, art, leadership, music/drama. **Student debt:** 61% of graduating class borrowed to fund education; average debt was $16,473. **Additional information:** Unlimited President's Scholarships based on class rank, SAT I scores. Extensive merit awards including Leadership Scholarships, Fine Arts Fellowships, Lilly Awards.

Freshman aid. Need-based: Out of 279 full-time freshmen, 243 applied for aid; 215 were judged to have need; of these 215 received aid. Average package met 100% of need. 215 students had full need met. Average scholarship/grant was $15,052; average loan $1,597. **Non-need based:** 55 full-time freshmen with need received non-need scholarships; 55 without need received awards.

Merit scholarships. Lilly Awards Program recognizes outstanding personal achievement and potential for leadership, covers full tuition, room, board, fees and travel stipend. Approximately 16 Fine Arts Fellows named each year, based on creativity/ability. Awards, ranging up to $12,000. Approximately 40 Honor Scholars named each year, based on competitive exams. Awards, ranging up to $12,000.

Policies to reduce costs. Tuition/fee waivers for employees and their families. Credit/placement for qualifying scores on AP, CLEP examinations.

Payment plans. Credit card, installment payment.

Application procedures. FAFSA, CSS PROFILE required. Priority date 2/15; closing date 3/1. Applicants notified by 4/1, must reply by 5/1 or within 2 week(s) of notification. Early decision closing date 11/15. **Transfers:** No deadline.

Contact. Financial aid office: (800) 718-9746
Clint Gasaway, Director of Financial Aid
PO Box 352
Crawfordsville, IN 47933

Iowa

Allen College

Waterloo, Iowa
www.allencollege.edu
Four-year private **Federal Code: 030691**

College costs. Room and board paid to University of Northern Iowa, part of tuition and fees paid to UNI. Tuition for nursing program: $6,256 full time; $1,994 paid to Allen College, $4,312 paid to UNI. Required fees $798; $426 paid to Allen, $372 to UNI. Per-credit-hour charges: $324 paid to Allen; additional per-credit-hour charges of $154 in-state, $417 out-of-state paid to UNI. Room and board $4,606. Tuition for associate degree program in radiography: full-year cost $10,256 tuition, $828 required fees (includes $2,156 tuition, $185 fees, plus $6,141 room and board paid to UNI).

	Living at home
Tuition and fees (projected):	$10,543
Board only:	$2,303
Books and supplies:	$797
Personal expenses:	$2,433
Transportation:	$863

Undergraduate aid. Need-based: Average financial aid package for full-time students was $8,246; for part-time $5,807. 52% awarded as scholarships/grants, 48% as loans/jobs. **Non-need-based:** 6% awarded as scholarships/grants, 94% as loans/jobs. Scholarships based on academics, leadership, minority status. **Student debt:** 75% of graduating class borrowed to fund education; average debt was $15,291. **Additional information:** Scholarship application at www.allencollege.edu may be accessed and submitted online.

Freshman aid. Need-based: Out of 19 full-time freshmen, 19 applied for aid; 14 were judged to have need; of these 14 received aid. Average package met 78% of need. 5 students had full need met. Average scholarship/grant was $3,767; average loan $2,588. **Non-need based:** 3 full-time freshmen with need received non-need scholarships; 3 without need received awards.

Policies to reduce costs. Credit/placement for qualifying scores on AP, IB examinations. Work study available weekends.

Payment plans. Credit card, installment, deferred payment.

Application procedures. FAFSA, institutional form required. Priority date 6/1; no closing date. Applicants notified on rolling basis starting 4/1, must reply within 2 week(s) of notification. **Transfers:** No deadline.

Contact. Financial aid office: (319) 226-2003
Kathie Walters, Financial Aid Director
1825 Logan Avenue
Waterloo, IA 50703

American Institute of Business

Des Moines, Iowa
www.aib.edu
Two-year private **Federal Code: 003963**

	Living at home	On-campus
Tuition and fees:	$8,109	$8,109
Per-credit charge:	$225	$225
Room and board:		$3,495
Board only:	$630	
Books and supplies:	$780	$780
Personal expenses:	$1,080	$1,080
Transportation:	$945	$540

Undergraduate aid. Need-based: Average financial aid package for full-time students was $7,359; for part-time $3,378. 61% awarded as scholarships/grants, 39% as loans/jobs. **Non-need-based:** 15% awarded as scholarships/grants, 85% as loans/jobs. Scholarships based on academics, alumni affiliation, leadership. **Student debt:** 66% of graduating class borrowed to fund education; average debt was $2,411.

Freshman aid. Need-based: Out of 271 full-time freshmen, 271 applied for aid; 242 were judged to have need; of these 241 received aid. Average package met 65% of need. 37 students had full need met. Average scholarship/grant was $5,306; average loan $3,145. **Non-need based:** 155 full-time freshmen with need received non-need scholarships; 29 without need received awards.

Merit scholarships. Founder's Tuition Scholarship, a full-tuition scholarship, awarded to top 15% of high school graduating class.

Policies to reduce costs. Tuition/fee waivers for children of alumni, family members, employees and their families. Tuition at time of enrollment guaranteed for 2 years; credit/placement for qualifying scores on AP, CLEP examinations. Work study available nights, weekends and for part-time students.

Payment plans. Credit card, installment payment.

Application procedures. FAFSA, institutional form required. Priority date 4/1; no closing date. Applicants notified on rolling basis starting 3/15, must reply within 2 week(s) of notification. **Transfers:** Priority date 4/1; no deadline. If student has received aid at prior institution, we will take prior aid into consideration.

Contact. Financial aid office: (515) 244-4221
Connie Jensen, Financial Aid Director
2500 Fleur Drive
Des Moines, IA 50321

Briar Cliff University

Sioux City, Iowa
www.briarcliff.edu
Four-year private **Federal Code: 001846**

	Living at home	On-campus
Tuition and fees:	$16,350	$16,350
Room and board:		$5,310
Board only:	$2,604	
Books and supplies:	$700	$700
Personal expenses:	$1,050	$1,050
Transportation:	$1,050	$510

Undergraduate aid. Need-based: Average financial aid package for full-time students was $15,950. 43% awarded as scholarships/grants, 57% as loans/jobs. Need-based aid available for part-time students. **Non-need-based:** Scholarships based on academics, athletics, state/district residency. **Student debt:** 83% of graduating class borrowed to fund education; average debt was $18,900.

Freshman aid. Need-based: Out of 195 full-time freshmen, 195 applied for aid; 146 were judged to have need; of these 146 received aid. Average package met 94% of need. 142 students had full need met. Average scholarship/grant was $4,980; average loan $3,150. **Non-need based:** 146 full-time freshmen with need received non-need scholarships; 192 without need received awards; 192 received athletic scholarships.

Policies to reduce costs. Tuition/fee waivers for adults, senior citizens, minority students, employees and their families. Credit/placement for qualifying scores on AP, IB, CLEP examinations.

Payment plans. Credit card, installment, deferred payment.

Application procedures. FAFSA required. Priority date 3/15; no closing date. Applicants notified on rolling basis starting 3/15, must reply by 5/1 or within 2 week(s) of notification.

Contact. Financial aid office: (712) 279-5200
Robert Piechota, Director of Financial Aid
3303 Rebecca Street
Sioux City, IA 51104-2100

Buena Vista University

Storm Lake, Iowa
www.bvu.edu
Four-year private **Federal Code: 001847**

	Living at home	On-campus
Tuition and fees (2002-2003):	$18,738	$18,738
Room and board:		$5,230
Books and supplies:	$500	$500
Personal expenses:	$1,000	$1,000

Undergraduate aid. Need-based: Need-based aid available for full-time and part-time students. **Non-need-based:** Scholarships based on academics, state/district residency. **Additional information:** Portfolio required of art scholarship applicants, audition required of music and drama scholarship applicants.

Policies to reduce costs. Tuition/fee waivers for family members, employees and their families. Credit/placement for qualifying scores on AP, IB, CLEP examinations. Work study available nights and weekends.

Payment plans. Credit card, installment payment.

Application procedures. FAFSA, institutional form required. Priority date 6/1; no closing date. Applicants notified on rolling basis starting 2/20, must reply by 5/1 or within 2 week(s) of notification. **Transfers:** Priority date 6/1; no deadline.

Contact. Leanne Valentine, Director of Financial Aid
610 West Fourth Street
Storm Lake, IA 50588

Central College

Pella, Iowa
www.central.edu
Four-year private **Federal Code: 001850**

	Living at home	On-campus
Tuition and fees:	$17,753	$17,753
Room and board:		$6,145
Board only:	$2,954	
Books and supplies:	$750	$750
Personal expenses:	$1,500	$1,500
Transportation:	$200	$750

Undergraduate aid. Need-based: Need-based aid available for full-time and part-time students. **Non-need-based:** Scholarships based on academics, alumni affiliation, art, leadership, minority status, music/drama, religious affiliation, state/district residency. **Additional information:** Institutional parent loan program and interest-earning, tuition prepayment savings account available. Auditions required for music and theater scholarships, portfolios required for art scholarships. Monthly payment plan available.

Policies to reduce costs. Tuition/fee waivers for employees and their families. Credit/placement for qualifying scores on AP, IB, CLEP examinations. Work study available nights, weekends and for part-time students.

Payment plans. Credit card, installment payment.

Application procedures. FAFSA required. Priority date 3/1; no closing date. Applicants notified on rolling basis starting 3/10, must reply by 5/1 or within 2 week(s) of notification. **Transfers:** Priority date 3/1; no deadline. Transfers only eligible for total of 4 years of state funds.

Contact. Financial aid office: (641) 628-5336
Jean VanderWert, Director of Student Financial Planning
812 University Street
Pella, IA 50219-1999

Clarke College

Dubuque, Iowa
www.clarke.edu
Four-year private **Federal Code: 001852**

	Living at home	On-campus
Tuition and fees (2002-2003):	$16,190	$16,190
Room and board:		$5,765
Board only:	$750	
Books and supplies:	$600	$600
Personal expenses:	$700	$700
Transportation:	$200	$200

Undergraduate aid. Need-based: Average financial aid package for full-time students was $13,913; for part-time $5,044. 68% awarded as scholarships/grants, 32% as loans/jobs. **Non-need-based:** 27% awarded as scholarships/grants, 73% as loans/jobs. Scholarships based on academics, alumni affiliation, art, leadership, music/drama. **Student debt:** 73% of graduating class borrowed to fund education; average debt was $17,833.

Freshman aid. Need-based: Out of 175 full-time freshmen, 166 applied for aid; 142 were judged to have need; of these 142 received aid. Average package met 100% of need. 35 students had full need met. Average scholarship/grant was $12,076; average loan $2,917. **Non-need based:** 136 full-time freshmen with need received non-need scholarships; 32 without need received awards.

Policies to reduce costs. Tuition/fee waivers for children of alumni, senior citizens, family members, employees and their families. Credit/placement for qualifying scores on AP, IB, CLEP examinations. Work study available nights and weekends.

Payment plans. Credit card, installment payment.

Application procedures. FAFSA required. Priority date 4/15; no closing date. Applicants notified on rolling basis starting 3/1, must reply by 5/1 or within 2 week(s) of notification. **Transfers:** Priority date 4/15; no deadline.

Contact. Michael Pope, Director of Financial Aid
1550 Clarke Drive
Dubuque, IA 52001-3198

Clinton Community College

Clinton, Iowa
www.eicc.org
Two-year public **Federal Code: 001853**

	Living at home
Tuition and fees (2002-2003):	$2,250
Out-of-state:	$3,375
Per-credit charge:	$75
Per-credit out-of-state:	$113
Board only:	$1,500
Books and supplies:	$900
Personal expenses:	$900
Transportation:	$900

Policies to reduce costs. Tuition/fee waivers for senior citizens, employees and their families. Credit/placement for qualifying scores on AP, CLEP examinations.

Payment plans. Credit card payment.

Application procedures. FAFSA, institutional form required. Priority date 4/20; no closing date. Applicants notified on rolling basis starting 5/15, must reply within 2 week(s) of notification.

Contact. Teresa Thiede, Financial Aid Officer
1000 Lincoln Boulevard
Clinton, IA 52732

Coe College

Cedar Rapids, Iowa
www.coe.edu
Four-year private **Federal Code: 001854**

	Living at home	On-campus
Tuition and fees:	$21,605	$21,605
Room and board:		$5,780
Books and supplies:	$600	$600
Personal expenses:	$1,100	$1,100
Transportation:	$500	$500

Undergraduate aid. Need-based: Average financial aid package for full-time students was $18,365; for part-time $7,696. 71% awarded as scholarships/grants, 29% as loans/jobs. **Non-need-based:** 64% awarded as scholarships/grants, 36% as loans/jobs. Scholarships based on academics, alumni affiliation, art, leadership, music/drama. **Student debt:** 77% of graduating class borrowed to fund education; average debt was $19,925.

Freshman aid. Need-based: Out of 302 full-time freshmen, 299 applied for aid; 250 were judged to have need; of these 250 received aid. Average package met 92% of need. 196 students had full need met. Average scholarship/grant was $14,152; average loan $4,249. **Non-need based:** 90 full-time freshmen with need received non-need scholarships; 63 without need received awards.

Merit scholarships. Scholarships for business/economics, music, art, theater, writing, foreign language, science; based on portfolio or audition; available for non-majors except in science and business/economics. Academic Awards; $3,500-$10,500; based on high school achievement.

Policies to reduce costs. Tuition/fee waivers for adults, children of alumni, employees and their families. Credit/placement for qualifying scores on AP, IB, CLEP examinations. Work study available nights and weekends.

Payment plans. Credit card, installment payment.

Application procedures. FAFSA required. Priority date 3/1; closing date 4/30. Applicants notified on rolling basis starting 3/1, must reply by 5/1 or within 2 week(s) of notification.

Contact. Financial aid office: (319) 399-8540
Barb Hoffman, Director of Financial Aid
1220 First Avenue Northeast
Cedar Rapids, IA 52402-9983

Cornell College

Mount Vernon, Iowa
www.cornellcollege.edu
Four-year private **Federal Code: 001856**

	Living at home	On-campus
Tuition and fees:	$21,790	$21,790
Room and board:		$6,035
Books and supplies:	$920	$920
Personal expenses:	$950	$950

Undergraduate aid. Need-based: Average financial aid package for full-time students was $18,795; for part-time $8,570. 80% awarded as scholarships/grants, 20% as loans/jobs. **Non-need-based:** 65% awarded as scholarships/grants, 35% as loans/jobs. Scholarships based on academics, art, leadership, music/drama, state/district residency. **Student debt:** 73% of graduating class borrowed to fund education; average debt was $17,650. **Additional information:** Portfolio required for art scholarship applicants. Audition required for music scholarship applicants.

Freshman aid. Need-based: Out of 314 full-time freshmen, 295 applied for aid; 261 were judged to have need; of these 261 received aid. Average package met 98% of need. 99 students had full need met. Average scholarship/grant was $16,145; average loan $3,745. **Non-need based:** 79 full-time freshmen with need received non-need scholarships; 67 without need received awards.

Policies to reduce costs. Tuition/fee waivers for adults, senior citizens, family of clergy, employees and their families. Credit/placement for qualifying scores on AP, IB, CLEP examinations. Work study available nights and weekends.

Application procedures. FAFSA, institutional form required. Closing date 3/1. Applicants notified on rolling basis starting 3/1, must reply by 5/1 or within 2 week(s) of notification.

Contact. **Financial aid office:** (319) 895-4216
Cindi Reints, Director of Financial Assistance
600 First Street West
Mount Vernon, IA 52314-1098

Des Moines Area Community College

Ankeny, Iowa
www.dmacc.org
Two-year public **Federal Code: 004589**

	Living at home
Tuition and fees (2002-2003):	$2,412
Out-of-state:	$4,572
Per-credit charge:	$72
Per-credit out-of-state:	$144
Books and supplies:	$620
Personal expenses:	$740
Transportation:	$1,388

Undergraduate aid. Need-based: Average financial aid package for full-time students was $4,788; for part-time $2,991. 51% awarded as scholarships/grants, 49% as loans/jobs. **Non-need-based:** 10% awarded as scholarships/grants, 90% as loans/jobs. Scholarships based on academics, athletics, state/district residency.

Freshman aid. Need-based: Average package met 57% of need. Average scholarship/grant was $2,706; average loan $2,325.

Merit scholarships. DMACC Foundation Freshmen Scholar Award: Competitive award; full tuition, fees and books for first year at DMACC for maximum of 15 credit hours per semester; based on available funds, offered fall term; open to all high school seniors in top 10% of graduating class.

Policies to reduce costs. Tuition/fee waivers for senior citizens. Credit/placement for qualifying scores on AP, CLEP examinations. Work study available nights, weekends and for part-time students.

Payment plans. Credit card, installment payment.

Application procedures. FAFSA required. Priority date 4/1; no closing date. Applicants notified on rolling basis starting 4/1, must reply within 2 week(s) of notification.

Contact. **Financial aid office:** (515) 964-6282
DeLores Hawkins, Director of Financial Aid
2006 South Ankeny Boulevard
Ankeny, IA 50021

Divine Word College

Epworth, Iowa
Four-year private
Federal Code: 001858

	Living at home	On-campus
Tuition and fees:	$9,150	$9,150
Room and board:		$2,100
Books and supplies:	$500	$500
Transportation:		$900

Policies to reduce costs. Tuition/fee waivers for employees and their families. Credit/placement for qualifying scores on AP, CLEP examinations.

Payment plans. Installment payment.

Application procedures. Priority date 8/31; no closing date. Applicants notified on rolling basis starting 8/1.

Contact. Carolyn Waechter, Director of Student Financial Aid
102 Jacoby Drive Southwest
Epworth, IA 52045

Dordt College

Sioux Center, Iowa
www.dordt.edu
Four-year private **Federal Code: 001859**

	Living at home	On-campus
Tuition and fees (2002-2003):	$14,880	$14,880
Room and board:		$4,160
Board only:	$3,300	
Books and supplies:	$650	$650
Personal expenses:	$1,900	$1,900
Transportation:	$1,600	$1,100

Undergraduate aid. Need-based: Average financial aid package for full-time students was $13,323; for part-time $6,955. 48% awarded as scholarships/grants, 52% as loans/jobs. **Non-need-based:** 57% awarded as scholarships/grants, 43% as loans/jobs. Scholarships based on academics, alumni affiliation, art, athletics, leadership, minority status, music/drama, religious affiliation, state/district residency. **Student debt:** 97% of graduating class borrowed to fund education; average debt was $16,010.

Freshman aid. Need-based: Average package met 76% of need. Average scholarship/grant was $8,030; average loan $3,813.

Policies to reduce costs. Tuition/fee waivers for children of alumni, employees and their families. Credit/placement for qualifying scores on AP, IB, CLEP examinations. Work study available nights and weekends.

Payment plans. Installment payment.

Application procedures. FAFSA, institutional form required. Priority date 4/1; no closing date. Applicants notified on rolling basis starting 3/15, must reply within 3 week(s) of notification. **Transfers:** Priority date 4/1; no deadline.

Contact. Michael Epema, Director of Financial Aid
498 Fourth Avenue, Northeast
Sioux Center, IA 51250

Drake University

Des Moines, Iowa
www.drake.edu
Four-year private **Federal Code: 001860**

	Living at home	On-campus
Tuition and fees (2002-2003):	$18,510	$18,510
Room and board:		$5,490
Board only:	$1,600	
Books and supplies:	$700	$700
Personal expenses:	$1,500	$1,800
Transportation:	$500	$175

Undergraduate aid. Need-based: Average financial aid package for full-time students was $15,701; for part-time $8,815. 66% awarded as scholarships/grants, 34% as loans/jobs. **Non-need-based:** 55% awarded as scholarships/grants, 45% as loans/jobs. Scholarships based on academics, alumni affiliation, art, athletics, music/drama, state/district residency. **Student debt:** 58% of graduating class borrowed to fund education; average debt was $22,115.

Freshman aid. Need-based: Out of 763 full-time freshmen, 615 applied for aid; 465 were judged to have need; of these 458 received aid. Average

package met 90% of need. 89 students had full need met. Average scholarship/grant was $11,236; average loan $4,292. **Non-need based:** 100 full-time freshmen with need received non-need scholarships; 273 without need received awards; 31 received athletic scholarships.

Merit scholarships. Drake University Presidential Scholarship; $7,000-$9,000. Drake University Achievement Award; $5,000-$7,000. Both based on academic merit and awards; unlimited available. National Alumni Scholarship Competition; 6 full-time tuition, room&board and 10 full-time tuition scholarships; available to top students.

Policies to reduce costs. Tuition/fee waivers for children of alumni, senior citizens, employees and their families. Credit/placement for qualifying scores on AP, IB, CLEP examinations. Work study available nights and weekends.

Payment plans. Credit card, installment, deferred payment.

Application procedures. FAFSA required. Priority date 3/1; no closing date. Applicants notified on rolling basis starting 3/1, must reply by 5/1 or within 3 week(s) of notification. **Transfers:** FAFSA must be filed by July 1 for Iowa Tuition Grant deadline.

Contact. **Financial aid office:** (515) 271-2905
Tom Willoughby, Dean of Admission and Financial Aid
2507 University Avenue
Des Moines, IA 50311-4505

Ellsworth Community College

Iowa Falls, Iowa
www.ellsworthcollege.edu
Two-year public **Federal Code: 001862**

	Living at home	On-campus
Tuition and fees (projected):	$3,075	$3,075
Out-of-state:	$4,290	$4,290
Room and board:		$3,550
Board only:	$1,000	
Books and supplies:	$700	$700
Personal expenses:	$1,400	$1,400
Transportation:	$1,350	$850

Undergraduate aid. **Need-based:** Need-based aid available for full-time and part-time students. **Non-need-based:** Scholarships based on academics, art, athletics, leadership, minority status, music/drama.

Merit scholarships. Academic scholarships based upon ACT score and GPA; unlimited number offered; $500-$1,800. Directors Scholarship-1st or 2nd in class; $2,300; unlimited number offered. For freshman and sophomore years.

Policies to reduce costs. Tuition/fee waivers for adults, senior citizens, employees and their families. Credit/placement for qualifying scores on AP, CLEP examinations. Work study available nights, weekends and for part-time students.

Payment plans. Credit card, installment, deferred payment.

Application procedures. FAFSA, institutional form required. Priority date 4/1; no closing date. Applicants notified on rolling basis starting 2/15, must reply within 4 week(s) of notification. **Transfers:** Priority date 4/15; no deadline.

Contact. Tara Miller, Financial Aid Administrator
1100 College Avenue
Iowa Falls, IA 50126

Emmaus Bible College

Dubuque, Iowa
www.emmaus.edu
Four-year private **Federal Code: 016487**

	Living at home	On-campus
Tuition and fees (2002-2003):	$6,326	$6,326
Room and board:		$3,480
Books and supplies:	$450	$450
Personal expenses:	$850	$850
Transportation:	$550	$850

Undergraduate aid. **Need-based:** Need-based aid available for full-time and part-time students. **Non-need-based:** Scholarships based on academics, music/drama.

Policies to reduce costs. Tuition/fee waivers for employees and their families. Prepayment discount; credit/placement for qualifying scores on AP, IB, CLEP examinations.

Payment plans. Installment, deferred payment.

Application procedures. FAFSA, institutional form required. Priority date 5/15; closing date 7/1. Applicants notified on rolling basis starting 3/1, must reply within 2 week(s) of notification.

Contact. **Financial aid office:** (563) 588-8000, ext 1117
Angela DeArment, Financial Aid Officer
2570 Asbury Road
Dubuque, IA 52001

Faith Baptist Bible College and Theological Seminary

Ankeny, Iowa
www.faith.edu
Four-year private **Federal Code: 007121**

	Living at home	On-campus
Tuition and fees (2002-2003):	$9,692	$9,692
Room and board:		$3,726
Board only:	$2,450	
Books and supplies:	$600	$600
Personal expenses:	$1,600	$1,600
Transportation:	$1,100	$1,100

Undergraduate aid. **Need-based:** Average financial aid package for full-time students was $6,440; for part-time $3,724. 56% awarded as scholarships/grants, 44% as loans/jobs. **Non-need-based:** 72% awarded as scholarships/grants, 28% as loans/jobs. Scholarships based on academics, leadership.

Freshman aid. **Need-based:** Out of 109 full-time freshmen, 109 applied for aid; 88 were judged to have need; of these 86 received aid. Average package met 49% of need. 1 students had full need met. Average scholarship/grant was $4,226; average loan $2,472. **Non-need based:** 62 full-time freshmen with need received non-need scholarships; 9 without need received awards.

Policies to reduce costs. Tuition/fee waivers for family of clergy, employees and their families. Credit/placement for qualifying scores on AP, CLEP examinations.

Payment plans. Credit card, installment payment.

Application procedures. FAFSA required. Priority date 4/1; no closing date. Applicants notified on rolling basis starting 3/15.

Contact. **Financial aid office:** (515) 964-0601 ext. 216
Breck Appell, Financial Assistance Director
1900 Northwest Fourth Street
Ankeny, IA 50021

Franciscan University

Clinton, Iowa
www.clare.edu
Four-year private **Federal Code: 001881**

	Living at home	On-campus
Tuition and fees:	$13,920	$13,920
Room and board:		$5,000
Board only:	$200	
Books and supplies:	$600	$600
Personal expenses:	$600	$600
Transportation:	$600	$400

Undergraduate aid. **Need-based:** Average financial aid package for full-time students was $10,654; for part-time $5,609. 61% awarded as scholarships/grants, 39% as loans/jobs. **Non-need-based:** 29% awarded as scholarships/grants, 71% as loans/jobs. Scholarships based on academics, alumni affiliation, art, athletics, leadership, minority status, music/drama, religious affiliation. **Student debt:** 80% of graduating class borrowed to fund education; average debt was $15,139.

Freshman aid. **Need-based:** Out of 47 full-time freshmen, 44 applied for aid; 44 were judged to have need; of these 44 received aid. Average package met 81% of need. 11 students had full need met. Average scholarship/grant was $8,466; average loan $2,815. **Non-need based:** 7 full-time freshmen with need received non-need scholarships; 1 without need received awards; 7 received athletic scholarships.

Merit scholarships. Divisional Awards; high school GPA of at least 3.2 and ACT score between 23 and 26; up to full tuition. Presidential Scholarships; rank in top 20% of high school class, or ACT composite of 26 or higher, or have GPA of at least 3.2; $1,500-$5,000. Departmental Awards; competitive exams in various departments; maximum $1,500. Leadership Awards; extracurricular activities and GPA of at least 2.3; maximum $1,000. St. Francis Awards; GPA of at least 2.3 and involvement in parish activities; $500. Counselor's Choice Awards; recommendation from high school guidance counselor, GPA between 2.50 and 3.19, ACT composite between 19 and 25, and at least one extracurricular activity; $500.

Policies to reduce costs. Tuition/fee waivers for children of alumni, senior citizens, minority students, family members, unemployed or children of unemployed, family of clergy, employees and their families. Credit/placement for qualifying scores on AP, CLEP examinations. Work study available nights, weekends and for part-time students.

Payment plans. Credit card, installment, deferred payment.

Application procedures. FAFSA required. Priority date 3/1; closing date 8/1. Applicants notified on rolling basis starting 3/15, must reply within 3 week(s) of notification. **Transfers:** Students with GPA of 3.0 or higher eligible for Presidential Scholarship.

Contact. **Financial aid office:** (563) 242-4023 ext. 1242
Lisa Kramer, Director of Financial Aid
400 North Bluff Boulevard
Clinton, IA 52733-2967

Graceland University

Lamoni, Iowa
www.graceland.edu
Four-year private **Federal Code: 001866**

	Living at home	On-campus
Tuition and fees:	$14,800	$14,800
Room and board:		$4,750
Board only:	$2,980	
Books and supplies:	$900	$900
Personal expenses:	$1,300	$1,300
Transportation:	$400	$400

Undergraduate aid. Need-based: Average financial aid package for full-time students was $13,203; for part-time $5,393. 62% awarded as scholarships/grants, 38% as loans/jobs. **Non-need-based:** 40% awarded as scholarships/grants, 60% as loans/jobs. Scholarships based on academics, alumni affiliation, art, athletics, job skills, leadership, music/drama, religious affiliation. **Student debt:** 64% of graduating class borrowed to fund education; average debt was $17,884.

Freshman aid. Need-based: Out of 272 full-time freshmen, 231 applied for aid; 197 were judged to have need; of these 196 received aid. Average package met 92% of need. 73 students had full need met. Average scholarship/grant was $11,588; average loan $3,941. **Non-need based:** 100 full-time freshmen with need received non-need scholarships; 58 without need received awards; 37 received athletic scholarships.

Policies to reduce costs. Tuition/fee waivers for senior citizens, employees and their families. Credit/placement for qualifying scores on AP, IB, CLEP examinations. Work study available nights, weekends and for part-time students.

Payment plans. Credit card, installment payment.

Application procedures. FAFSA required. Priority date 3/1; no closing date. Applicants notified on rolling basis starting 2/1, must reply within 2 week(s) of notification. **Transfers:** No deadline.

Contact. **Financial aid office:** (641) 784-5140
Sharon Mesle-Morain, Director of Student Finance
1 University Place
Lamoni, IA 50140

Grand View College

Des Moines, Iowa
www.gvc.edu
Four-year private **Federal Code: 001867**

	Living at home	On-campus
Tuition and fees:	$14,740	$14,740
Room and board:		$5,008
Board only:	$1,500	
Books and supplies:	$600	$600
Personal expenses:	$2,000	$2,000
Transportation:	$1,200	$600

Undergraduate aid. Need-based: Average financial aid package for full-time students was $12,192; for part-time $5,736. 56% awarded as scholarships/grants, 44% as loans/jobs. **Non-need-based:** 23% awarded as scholarships/grants, 77% as loans/jobs. Scholarships based on academics, alumni affiliation, art, athletics, leadership, music/drama, religious affiliation. **Student debt:** 84% of graduating class borrowed to fund education; average debt was $18,611.

Freshman aid. Need-based: Out of 189 full-time freshmen, 189 applied for aid; 167 were judged to have need; of these 167 received aid. Average package met 86% of need. 27 students had full need met. Average scholarship/grant was $9,430; average loan $3,903. **Non-need based:** 19 full-time freshmen with need received non-need scholarships; 40 without need received awards; 14 received athletic scholarships.

Merit scholarships. Grand View Honor Scholarship; $4,000-5,000; new, full-time freshman. Viking Incentive Scholarship (VIP); $3,000-4,000; new, full-time freshmen. Presidential Scholarship; $5,000-6,500, new, full-time freshmen.

Policies to reduce costs. Tuition/fee waivers for senior citizens, family of clergy, employees and their families. Credit/placement for qualifying scores on AP, IB, CLEP examinations. Work study available nights, weekends and for part-time students.

Payment plans. Credit card, installment, deferred payment.

Application procedures. FAFSA required. Priority date 3/1; no closing date. Applicants notified by 3/1, must reply by 5/1 or within 4 week(s) of notification. **Transfers:** No deadline.

Contact. **Financial aid office:** (515) 263-2963
Christina Hlas, Director of Financial Aid
1200 Grandview Avenue
Des Moines, IA 50316-1599

Grinnell College

Grinnell, Iowa
www.grinnell.edu
Four-year private **Federal Code: 001868**

	Living at home	On-campus
Tuition and fees:	$24,490	$24,490
Room and board:		$6,570
Books and supplies:	$400	$400
Personal expenses:		$400
Transportation:		$500

Undergraduate aid. Need-based: Average financial aid package for full-time students was $19,611. 76% awarded as scholarships/grants, 24% as loans/jobs. **Non-need-based:** 94% awarded as scholarships/grants, 6% as loans/jobs. Scholarships based on academics. **Student debt:** 58% of graduating class borrowed to fund education; average debt was $13,854. **Additional information:** Students may apply financial aid to off-campus study programs.

Freshman aid. Need-based: Out of 368 full-time freshmen, 343 applied for aid; 214 were judged to have need; of these 214 received aid. Average package met 100% of need. 214 students had full need met. Average scholarship/grant was $13,934; average loan $4,211. **Non-need based:** 33 full-time freshmen with need received non-need scholarships; 100 without need received awards.

Policies to reduce costs. Tuition/fee waivers for employees and their families. Credit/placement for qualifying scores on AP, IB examinations.

Payment plans. Credit card, installment payment.

Application procedures. FAFSA, institutional form required. Closing date 2/1. Applicants notified by 4/1, must reply by 5/1. Early decision closing date 11/20. **Transfers:** Closing date 2/1.

Contact. **Financial aid office:** (641) 269-3250
Arnold Woods, Director of Student Financial Aid
Office of Admission
Grinnell, IA 50112-1690

Hamilton College

Urbandale, Iowa
www.hamiltonia.edu
Four-year proprietary **Federal Code: 004220**

College costs. Tuition includes books and fees.

	Living at home
Tuition and fees (2002-2003):	$9,735
Board only:	$1,000
Personal expenses:	$1,500
Transportation:	$600

Undergraduate aid. All financial aid based on need. Need-based aid available for full-time and part-time students.

Policies to reduce costs. Tuition/fee waivers for employees and their families. Credit/placement for qualifying scores on AP examinations. Work study available nights and weekends.

Payment plans. Credit card, installment payment.

Application procedures. FAFSA, institutional form required. No deadline. **Transfers:** No deadline.

Contact. **Financial aid office:** (515) 727-2100
Melissa Prichard, Director of Student Finance
4655 121st Street
Urbandale, IA 50323

Hamilton College: Cedar Falls

Cedar Falls, Iowa
www.hamiltoncf.com
Four-year proprietary

College costs. Costs vary by program.

Undergraduate aid. All financial aid based on need. Need-based aid available for full-time and part-time students. **Additional information:** Freshman deadline for filing required financial aid forms is 30 days after start of classes.

Contact. Brenda Biersner, Director of Finance
2302 West First Street
Cedar Falls, IA 50613

Hamilton College: Cedar Rapids

Cedar Rapids, Iowa
www.hamiltonia.edu
Four-year proprietary **Federal Code: 004220**

	Living at home
Tuition and fees (projected):	$13,017
Board only:	$2,727
Personal expenses:	$1,692
Transportation:	$207

Undergraduate aid. **Need-based:** Average financial aid package for full-time students was $2,645; for part-time $1,358. 53% awarded as scholarships/grants, 47% as loans/jobs. **Non-need-based:** 6% awarded as scholarships/grants, 94% as loans/jobs. Scholarships based on academics. **Student debt:** 93% of graduating class borrowed to fund education; average debt was $5,350.

Freshman aid. **Need-based:** Out of 55 full-time freshmen, 54 applied for aid; 54 were judged to have need; of these 54 received aid. Average package met 49% of need. 4 students had full need met. Average scholarship/grant was $1,123; average loan $910. **Non-need based:** 3 full-time freshmen with need received non-need scholarships.

Policies to reduce costs. Tuition/fee waivers for employees and their families. Credit/placement for qualifying scores on AP, CLEP examinations. Work study available nights, weekends and for part-time students.

Payment plans. Credit card, installment payment.

Application procedures. FAFSA, institutional form required. Priority date 6/30; no closing date. Applicants notified on rolling basis. **Transfers:** No deadline.

Contact. **Financial aid office:** (319) 363-0481
Dennis Kurtz, Financial Manager
3165 Edgewood Parkway SW
Cedar Rapids, IA 52404

Hamilton College: Mason City

Mason City, Iowa
www.hamiltoncollegemc.com
Four-year proprietary **Federal Code: 004220**

College costs. Tuition and fees for full programs range from $9,000 to $36,000 (including books) depending on program.

	Living at home
Tuition and fees:	$10,620

Undergraduate aid. **Non-need-based:** Scholarships based on academics.

Payment plans. Deferred payment.

Application procedures. FAFSA required. Closing date 6/1. Applicants notified on rolling basis.

Contact. Cathy Gomez, Director of Financial Aid
100 First Street NW
Mason City, IA 50401

Hamilton Technical College

Davenport, Iowa
www.hamiltontechcollege.com
Three-year proprietary **Federal Code: 012064**

College costs. Tuition includes all fees, books and materials.

	Living at home
Tuition and fees (2002-2003):	$6,300

Payment plans. Installment payment.

Application procedures. FAFSA, institutional form required. No deadline. Applicants notified on rolling basis. **Transfers:** No deadline.

Contact. Lisa Boyd, Financial Aid Director
1011 East 53rd Street
Davenport, IA 52807

Hawkeye Community College

Waterloo, Iowa
www.hawkeyecollege.edu
Two-year public **Federal Code: 004595**

	Living at home
Tuition and fees (2002-2003):	$2,730
Out-of-state:	$5,160
Per-credit charge:	$81
Per-credit out-of-state:	$162
Books and supplies:	$750
Personal expenses:	$4,304
Transportation:	$2,080

Undergraduate aid. **Need-based:** Need-based aid available for full-time students. **Non-need-based:** Scholarships based on academics, state/district residency.

Policies to reduce costs. Tuition/fee waivers for employees and their families. Credit/placement for qualifying scores on AP, CLEP examinations.

Payment plans. Credit card, installment payment.

Application procedures. FAFSA, institutional form required. Priority date 3/15; no closing date. Applicants notified on rolling basis starting 4/25, must reply within 2 week(s) of notification.

Contact. **Financial aid office:** (319) 296-4020
Brian Will, Director of Financial Aid
Box 8015
Waterloo, IA 50704-8015

Indian Hills Community College

Ottumwa, Iowa
www.ihcc.cc.ia.us
Two-year public **Federal Code: 008298**

	Living at home	On-campus
Tuition and fees (2002-2003):	$2,130	$2,130
Out-of-state:	$3,180	$3,180
Per-credit charge:	$79	$79
Per-credit out-of-state:	$119	$119
Room and board:		$3,380
Books and supplies:	$675	$675
Personal expenses:	$750	$750
Transportation:	$1,361	$1,361

Undergraduate aid. **Need-based:** Need-based aid available for full-time and part-time students. **Non-need-based:** Scholarships based on athletics, state/district residency.

Policies to reduce costs. Tuition/fee waivers for senior citizens, employees and their families. Credit/placement for qualifying scores on AP, CLEP examinations.

Payment plans. Credit card, installment, deferred payment.

Application procedures. FAFSA, institutional form required. Priority date 4/1; no closing date. Applicants notified on rolling basis starting 6/1, must reply within 2 week(s) of notification. **Transfers:** No deadline.

Contact. Gail Lockridge, Enrollment Services Chair/Registrar
525 Grandview
Ottumwa, IA 52501

Iowa Central Community College

Fort Dodge, Iowa
www.iccc.cc.ia.us
Two-year public **Federal Code: 004597**

	Living at home	On-campus
Tuition and fees (2002-2003):	$2,528	$2,528
Out-of-state:	$3,653	$3,653
Per-credit charge:	$75	$75
Per-credit out-of-state:	$113	$113
Room and board:		$3,990
Board only:	$1,500	
Books and supplies:	$750	$750
Personal expenses:	$945	$1,240
Transportation:	$750	$750

Undergraduate aid. All financial aid based on need. Need-based aid available for full-time and part-time students.

Policies to reduce costs. Tuition/fee waivers for employees and their families. Credit/placement for qualifying scores on AP, CLEP examinations. Work study available nights, weekends and for part-time students.

Payment plans. Credit card, installment, deferred payment.

Application procedures. FAFSA required. No deadline. Applicants notified on rolling basis starting 4/15, must reply within 2 week(s) of notification.

Contact. Angie Martin, Director of Financial Aid
330 Avenue M
Fort Dodge, IA 50501

Iowa Lakes Community College

Estherville, Iowa
www.iowalakes.edu
Two-year public **Federal Code: 001864**

	Living at home	On-campus
Tuition and fees (2002-2003):	$2,905	$2,905
Out-of-state:	$2,965	$2,965
Per-credit charge:	$82	$82
Per-credit out-of-state:	$84	$84
Room and board:		$3,350
Books and supplies:	$600	$600
Personal expenses:	$500	$500
Transportation:	$850	$850

Undergraduate aid. Need-based: Need-based aid available for full-time students.

Policies to reduce costs. Credit/placement for qualifying scores on AP, CLEP examinations.

Payment plans. Credit card, installment payment.

Application procedures. FAFSA, institutional form required. Priority date 4/22; no closing date. Applicants notified on rolling basis starting 4/15.

Contact. Financial aid office: (712) 362-7917
John Beneke, Director of Financial Aid
300 South 18th Street
Estherville, IA 51334-2725

Iowa State University

Ames, Iowa
www.iastate.edu
Four-year public **Federal Code: 001869**

College costs. Engineering program pays additional $206 fees, computer science and management information systems programs pay additional $128.

	Living at home	On-campus
Tuition and fees (2002-2003):	$4,110	$4,110
Out-of-state:	$12,802	$12,802
Room and board:		$5,020
Board only:	$1,934	
Books and supplies:	$754	$754
Personal expenses:	$2,532	$2,320
Transportation:	$1,294	$424

Undergraduate aid. Need-based: Average financial aid package for full-time students was $6,772; for part-time $8,431. 33% awarded as scholarships/grants, 67% as loans/jobs. **Non-need-based:** 23% awarded as scholarships/grants, 77% as loans/jobs. Scholarships based on academics, art, athletics, leadership, minority status, music/drama, state/district residency. **Student debt:** 66% of graduating class borrowed to fund education; average debt was $17,119. **Additional information:** Short-term loan program available to meet unplanned needs. Financial counseling clinic provides budget and credit education assistance.

Freshman aid. Need-based: Out of 4,015 full-time freshmen, 3,575 applied for aid; 2,327 were judged to have need; of these 2,303 received aid. Average package met 100% of need. 1200 students had full need met. Average scholarship/grant was $3,160; average loan $2,976. **Non-need based:** 1,240 full-time freshmen with need received non-need scholarships; 1,123 without need received awards; 51 received athletic scholarships.

Merit scholarships. Current award information available on our website.

Policies to reduce costs. Credit/placement for qualifying scores on AP, IB, CLEP examinations. Work study available nights, weekends and for part-time students.

Payment plans. Installment, deferred payment.

Application procedures. FAFSA required. Priority date 3/1; no closing date. Applicants notified on rolling basis starting 4/1, must reply by 5/1. **Transfers:** Priority date 2/15; no deadline.

Contact. Financial aid office: (515) 294-0066
Roberta Johnson, Director of Student Financial Aid
100 Alumni Hall
Ames, IA 50011-2011

Iowa Wesleyan College

Mt. Pleasant, Iowa
www.iwc.edu
Four-year private **Federal Code: 001871**

	Living at home	On-campus
Tuition and fees (2002-2003):	$14,380	$14,380
Room and board:		$4,460
Books and supplies:	$735	$735
Personal expenses:	$3,800	$1,200
Transportation:	$900	$600

Undergraduate aid. Need-based: Average financial aid package for full-time students was $10,775; for part-time $3,204. 52% awarded as scholarships/grants, 48% as loans/jobs. **Non-need-based:** 49% awarded as scholarships/grants, 51% as loans/jobs. Scholarships based on academics, art, athletics, job skills, minority status, music/drama, religious affiliation, state/district residency. **Student debt:** 77% of graduating class borrowed to fund education; average debt was $14,428.

Freshman aid. Need-based: Out of 124 full-time freshmen, 120 applied for aid; 113 were judged to have need; of these 113 received aid. Average package met 76% of need. 7 students had full need met. Average scholarship/grant was $6,900; average loan $2,502. **Non-need based:** 18 full-time freshmen with need received non-need scholarships; 3 without need received awards; 1 received athletic scholarships.

Merit scholarships. Goodell Scholarship for music majors, $1,000-$6,000, based on audition; Academic Achievement, $1,000-$3,000, based on rank in top 25%, 3.0 GPA, or 21 ACT; Athletic Scholarship, up to $5,000, based on coaches' recommendations; Music Performance Award, $1,000-$2,000, based on participation by nonmusic majors. Jericho Scholarships (2 out of 3 requirements), 3.6 GPA, top 5% of class, 30 ACT/1310 SAT and personal interview. Presidential Scholarships of 100% tuition, 30 ACT/1310 SAT, 3.6 GPA and personal interview.

Policies to reduce costs. Tuition/fee waivers for children of alumni, senior citizens, employees and their families. Credit/placement for qualifying scores on AP, IB, CLEP examinations.

Payment plans. Credit card, installment payment.

Application procedures. FAFSA required. Priority date 4/1; no closing date. Applicants notified on rolling basis starting 3/1, must reply within 3 week(s) of notification.

Contact. Financial aid office: (319) 385-6242
Director of Financial Aid
601 North Main Street
Mount Pleasant, IA 52641-1398

Iowa Western Community College

Council Bluffs, Iowa
www.iwcc.edu
Two-year public **Federal Code: 004598**

	Living at home	On-campus
Tuition and fees (2002-2003):	$2,880	$2,880
Out-of-state:	$4,170	$4,170
Per-credit charge:	$86	$86
Per-credit out-of-state:	$129	$129
Room and board:		$3,920
Books and supplies:	$800	$800
Personal expenses:	$1,440	$1,440
Transportation:	$1,900	$1,000

Undergraduate aid. Need-based: Need-based aid available for full-time and part-time students. **Non-need-based:** Scholarships based on athletics, music/drama.

Policies to reduce costs. Tuition/fee waivers for senior citizens, employees and their families. Credit/placement for qualifying scores on CLEP examinations.

Payment plans. Credit card, installment, deferred payment.

Application procedures. FAFSA required. Priority date 5/1; no closing date. Applicants notified on rolling basis starting 3/1, must reply within 3 week(s) of notification. **Transfers:** Priority date 5/1; no deadline.

Contact. Financial aid office: (800) 432-5852 ext. 292
Blaine Duistermars, Director of Financial Aid
2700 College Road
Council Bluffs, IA 51502-3004

Kaplan College

Davenport, Iowa
www.kaplancollegeia.com
Two-year proprietary **Federal Code: 004586**

College costs. Tuition figure includes fees and books.

	Living at home
Tuition and fees:	$10,620
Personal expenses:	$1,485
Transportation:	$1,206

Undergraduate aid. All financial aid based on need. Average financial aid package for full-time students was $9,792; for part-time $9,792. 37% awarded as scholarships/grants, 63% as loans/jobs. **Student debt:** 76% of graduating class borrowed to fund education; average debt was $10,125.

Freshman aid. Out of 111 full-time freshmen, 111 applied for aid; 110 were judged to have need; of these 110 received aid. Average package met 60% of need. Average loan $2,625.

Policies to reduce costs. Tuition/fee waivers for employees and their families. Tuition at time of enrollment guaranteed for 2 years. Work study available nights.

Payment plans. Credit card, installment payment.

Application procedures. FAFSA, institutional form required. Priority date 5/15; no closing date. Applicants notified on rolling basis starting 1/1, must reply within 2 week(s) of notification. **Transfers:** No deadline.

Contact. Financial aid office: (563) 355-3500
Sue McCabe, Director of Financial Aid
1801 East Kimberly Road, Suite 1
Davenport, IA 52807-2095

Kirkwood Community College

Cedar Rapids, Iowa
www.kirkwood.cc.ia.us
Two-year public **Federal Code: 004076**

	Living at home
Tuition and fees (2002-2003):	$2,340
Out-of-state:	$4,680
Per-credit charge:	$78
Per-credit out-of-state:	$156
Board only:	$3,086
Books and supplies:	$500
Personal expenses:	$900
Transportation:	$1,000

Undergraduate aid. Need-based: Need-based aid available for full-time and part-time students. **Non-need-based:** Scholarships based on art, athletics, leadership, music/drama.

Policies to reduce costs. Tuition/fee waivers for senior citizens, employees and their families. Credit/placement for qualifying scores on AP, IB, CLEP examinations. Work study available nights, weekends and for part-time students.

Payment plans. Credit card, installment payment.

Application procedures. FAFSA required. Priority date 7/1; no closing date. Applicants notified on rolling basis starting 4/1. **Transfers:** No deadline.

Contact. Financial aid office: (319) 398-1274
Peg Julius, Director of Financial Aid
6301 Kirkwood Boulevard SW
Cedar Rapids, IA 52406

Loras College

Dubuque, Iowa
www.loras.edu
Four-year private **Federal Code: 001873**

	Living at home	On-campus
Tuition and fees (2002-2003):	$17,949	$17,949
Room and board:		$5,895
Board only:	$2,995	
Books and supplies:	$1,000	$1,000
Personal expenses:	$600	$600
Transportation:	$600	$600

Undergraduate aid. Need-based: Average financial aid package for full-time students was $16,812; for part-time $7,932. 53% awarded as scholarships/grants, 47% as loans/jobs. **Non-need-based:** 84% awarded as scholarships/grants, 16% as loans/jobs. Scholarships based on academics, alumni affiliation, music/drama. **Student debt:** 81% of graduating class borrowed to fund education; average debt was $17,748. **Additional information:** Audition or portfolio recommended for music and art financial aid applicants.

Freshman aid. Need-based: Out of 371 full-time freshmen, 328 applied for aid; 274 were judged to have need; of these 274 received aid. Average package met 97% of need. 91 students had full need met. Average scholarship/grant was $6,001; average loan $4,385. **Non-need based:** 243 full-time freshmen with need received non-need scholarships; 46 without need received awards.

Policies to reduce costs. Tuition/fee waivers for children of alumni, family members, employees and their families. Credit/placement for qualifying scores on AP, IB, CLEP examinations. Work study available nights, weekends and for part-time students.

Payment plans. Credit card, installment payment.

Application procedures. FAFSA required. Priority date 4/15; no closing date. Applicants notified on rolling basis starting 3/1, must reply within 3 week(s) of notification.

Contact. Financial aid office: (563) 588-7136
Julie Dunn, Director of Financial Planning
1450 Alta Vista Street
Dubuque, IA 52004-0178

Luther College

Decorah, Iowa
www.luther.edu
Four-year private **Federal Code: 001874**

	Living at home	On-campus
Tuition and fees:	$21,600	$21,600
Room and board:		$4,100
Board only:	$2,100	
Books and supplies:	$710	$710
Personal expenses:	$1,440	$1,440
Transportation:	$815	$815

Undergraduate aid. Need-based: Average financial aid package for full-time students was $16,554; for part-time $4,001. 69% awarded as scholarships/grants, 31% as loans/jobs. **Non-need-based:** 62% awarded as scholarships/grants, 38% as loans/jobs. Scholarships based on academics, alumni affiliation, art, minority status, music/drama, religious affiliation. **Student debt:** 70% of graduating class borrowed to fund education; average debt was $16,245.

Freshman aid. Need-based: Out of 612 full-time freshmen, 550 applied for aid; 409 were judged to have need; of these 409 received aid. Average package met 87% of need. 103 students had full need met. Average scholarship/grant was $11,785; average loan $3,601. **Non-need based:** 327 full-time freshmen with need received non-need scholarships.

Merit scholarships. Modest art scholarships; $150-$500; determined by evaluation of portfolio. Music scholarships; $750-$3,500; based on audition. Academic scholarships; $2,000-$10,500; based on class rank and SAT/ACT.

Policies to reduce costs. Tuition/fee waivers for employees and their families. Credit/placement for qualifying scores on AP, IB, CLEP examinations. Work study available nights, weekends and for part-time students.

Payment plans. Installment payment.

Application procedures. FAFSA, institutional form required. Priority date 3/1; no closing date. Applicants notified on rolling basis starting 3/15, must reply by 5/1 or within 4 week(s) of notification. **Transfers:** Priority date 3/1; no deadline.

Contact. Financial aid office: (563) 387-1018
Janice Cordell, Director of Student Financial Planning
700 College Drive
Decorah, IA 52101-1042

Maharishi University of Management

Fairfield, Iowa
www.mum.edu
Four-year private **Federal Code: 011113**

	Living at home	On-campus
Tuition and fees (projected):	$24,030	$24,030
Room and board:		$5,200
Board only:	$2,480	
Books and supplies:	$800	$800
Personal expenses:	$1,500	$1,500
Transportation:	$900	$900

Undergraduate aid. Need-based: Average financial aid package for full-time students was $29,462; for part-time $7,452. 75% awarded as scholarships/grants, 25% as loans/jobs. **Non-need-based:** 55% awarded as scholarships/grants, 45% as loans/jobs. Scholarships based on academics, alumni affiliation, music/drama, state/district residency. **Student debt:** 83% of graduating class borrowed to fund education; average debt was $19,626. **Additional information:** Students may earn scholarships through volunteer staff program.

Freshman aid. Need-based: Out of 37 full-time freshmen, 36 applied for aid; 36 were judged to have need; of these 36 received aid. Average package met 93% of need. 22 students had full need met. Average scholarship/grant was $18,657; average loan $5,313. **Non-need based:** 4 full-time freshmen with need received non-need scholarships.

Merit scholarships. Shelley Hoffman Scholarship; $500-$900; based on creative writing and/or cerebral palsy; 7 awarded. National Merit Scholarship; full tuition; for NMS finalists; 4 awarded. Ray Prat Scholarship; $500-$1,750; for musically-talented undergraduates; 4 awarded. Girl Scout Gold Award Scholarship; $1,500 renewable; for GS Gold Award recipients; 5 awarded. DeRoy D. Thomas Scholarship; $3,000 each; open to outstanding African American; 1 awarded.

Policies to reduce costs. Tuition/fee waivers for children of alumni, senior citizens, employees and their families. Credit/placement for qualifying scores on AP, IB, CLEP examinations.

Payment plans. Credit card, installment payment.

Application procedures. FAFSA required. Priority date 4/15; no closing date. Applicants notified on rolling basis starting 3/1, must reply within 4 week(s) of notification. **Transfers:** No deadline.

Contact. Tom Rowe, Director of Financial Aid
Fairfield, IA 52557

Marshalltown Community College

Marshalltown, Iowa
www.marshalltowncommunitycollege.com
Two-year public **Federal Code: 001875**

	Living at home
Tuition and fees (projected):	$3,075
Out-of-state:	$5,505
Per-credit charge:	$81
Per-credit out-of-state:	$162
Books and supplies:	$425
Personal expenses:	$760
Transportation:	$630

Policies to reduce costs. Tuition/fee waivers for senior citizens. Credit/placement for qualifying scores on CLEP examinations.

Payment plans. Credit card, installment, deferred payment.

Application procedures. Institutional form required. Priority date 3/15; no closing date. Applicants notified on rolling basis starting 6/1, must reply within 2 week(s) of notification.

Contact. Chloe Webb, Chief Financial Aid Officer
3700 South Center Street
Marshalltown, IA 50158

Mercy College of Health Sciences

Des Moines, Iowa
www.mchs.edu
Four-year proprietary **Federal Code: 006273**

	Living at home	On-campus
Tuition and fees (projected):	$9,990	$9,990
Room and board:		$5,250
Books and supplies:	$400	$400
Personal expenses:		$733
Transportation:		$438

Undergraduate aid. Need-based: 38% awarded as scholarships/grants, 62% as loans/jobs. Need-based aid available for part-time students. **Non-need-based:** 47% awarded as scholarships/grants, 53% as loans/jobs. Scholarships based on academics.

Policies to reduce costs. Credit/placement for qualifying scores on AP, CLEP examinations. Work study available nights and for part-time students.

Payment plans. Credit card, installment payment.

Application procedures. FAFSA required. Closing date 7/1. **Transfers:** Students must submit information by 07/01 to be eligible for Iowa Tuition Grant.

Contact. Sara Pratt, Financial Aid Officer
928 6th Avenue
Des Moines, IA 50309

Morningside College

Sioux City, Iowa
www.morningside.edu
Four-year private **Federal Code: 001879**

College costs. 1-7 per credit hour is $300; 8-11 per credit hour charge is $500. Full-time students receive laptop computer as part of required fees.

	Living at home	On-campus
Tuition and fees:	$16,350	$16,350
Room and board:		$5,260
Board only:	$1,500	
Books and supplies:	$800	$800
Personal expenses:	$1,400	$1,400
Transportation:	$800	$800

Undergraduate aid. Need-based: Average financial aid package for full-time students was $15,516; for part-time $4,385. 56% awarded as scholarships/grants, 44% as loans/jobs. **Non-need-based:** 62% awarded as scholarships/grants, 38% as loans/jobs. Scholarships based on academics, alumni affiliation, art, athletics, leadership, music/drama, religious affiliation, state/district residency. **Student debt:** 85% of graduating class borrowed to fund education; average debt was $17,340.

Freshman aid. Need-based: Out of 245 full-time freshmen, 239 applied for aid; 220 were judged to have need; of these 220 received aid. Average package met 88% of need. 127 students had full need met. Average scholarship/grant was $5,189; average loan $3,627. **Non-need based:** 219 full-time freshmen with need received non-need scholarships; 24 without need received awards; 143 received athletic scholarships.

Merit scholarships. President's Scholarship; $6,000 to $10,000; ACT 29 and top 10% of class. Dean's Scholarship; $3,000 to $6,000; ACT 23 or top 20% of class. Mustang Co-Curricular Award; up to $3,000; based on leadership and involvement. Unlimited number awarded in all categories.

Policies to reduce costs. Tuition/fee waivers for adults, children of alumni, senior citizens, family of clergy, employees and their families. Credit/placement for qualifying scores on AP, IB, CLEP examinations. Work study available nights and weekends.

Payment plans. Credit card, installment payment.

Application procedures. FAFSA required. Priority date 3/1; no closing date. Applicants notified on rolling basis starting 3/31. **Transfers:** Priority date 3/1; no deadline.

Contact. Financial aid office: (712) 274-5159
Karen Gagnon, Director Student Financial Planning
1501 Morningside Avenue
Sioux City, IA 51106

Mount Mercy College

Cedar Rapids, Iowa
www.mtmercy.edu
Four-year private — **Federal Code: 001880**

	Living at home	On-campus
Tuition and fees:	$16,070	$16,070
Room and board:		$5,330
Board only:	$1,880	
Books and supplies:	$700	$700
Personal expenses:	$1,690	$1,924
Transportation:	$1,470	$832

Undergraduate aid. Need-based: Average financial aid package for full-time students was $13,305; for part-time $7,205. 60% awarded as scholarships/grants, 40% as loans/jobs. **Non-need-based:** 31% awarded as scholarships/grants, 69% as loans/jobs. Scholarships based on academics, art, leadership, music/drama. **Student debt:** 76% of graduating class borrowed to fund education; average debt was $20,426.

Freshman aid. Need-based: Out of 160 full-time freshmen, 154 applied for aid; 137 were judged to have need; of these 137 received aid. Average package met 85% of need. 56 students had full need met. Average scholarship/grant was $9,796; average loan $3,230. **Non-need based:** 13 full-time freshmen with need received non-need scholarships; 23 without need received awards.

Policies to reduce costs. Tuition/fee waivers for family of clergy, employees and their families. Credit/placement for qualifying scores on AP, CLEP examinations. Work study available nights, weekends and for part-time students.

Payment plans. Credit card, installment payment.

Application procedures. FAFSA required. Priority date 3/1; no closing date. Applicants notified on rolling basis starting 3/15, must reply by 5/1 or within 3 week(s) of notification.

Contact. Financial aid office: (319) 368-6467
Lois Mulbrook, Director of Financial Aid
1330 Elmhurst Drive Northeast
Cedar Rapids, IA 52402-4797

Muscatine Community College

Muscatine, Iowa
www.eicc.edu
Two-year public — **Federal Code: 001882**

	Living at home
Tuition and fees (2002-2003):	$2,250
Out-of-state:	$3,375
Per-credit charge:	$75
Per-credit out-of-state:	$113
Board only:	$1,500
Books and supplies:	$900
Personal expenses:	$900
Transportation:	$900

Policies to reduce costs. Tuition/fee waivers for senior citizens, employees and their families. Credit/placement for qualifying scores on AP, CLEP examinations.

Payment plans. Credit card payment.

Application procedures. FAFSA required. Priority date 4/20; no closing date. Applicants notified on rolling basis starting 5/15, must reply within 2 week(s) of notification.

Contact. Debbie Beatty, Financial Aid Officer
152 Colorado Street
Muscatine, IA 52761-5396

North Iowa Area Community College

Mason City, Iowa
www.niacc.com
Two-year public — **Federal Code: 001877**

	Living at home	On-campus
Tuition and fees (projected):	$2,772	$2,772
Out-of-state:	$3,976	$3,976
Per-credit charge:	$81	$81
Per-credit out-of-state:	$122	$122
Room and board:		$3,660
Books and supplies:	$697	$697
Personal expenses:	$1,440	$1,440
Transportation:	$1,165	$384

Undergraduate aid. Need-based: Average financial aid package for full-time students was $3,235; for part-time $2,270. 59% awarded as scholarships/grants, 41% as loans/jobs. **Non-need-based:** Scholarships based on academics, alumni affiliation, art, athletics, leadership, music/drama. **Student debt:** 38% of graduating class borrowed to fund education; average debt was $5,562.

Freshman aid. Need-based: Average package met 38% of need. Average scholarship/grant was $2,559; average loan $2,191.

Policies to reduce costs. Tuition/fee waivers for employees and their families. Credit/placement for qualifying scores on AP examinations. Work study available nights and for part-time students.

Payment plans. Credit card, installment, deferred payment.

Application procedures. FAFSA, institutional form required. Priority date 3/1; no closing date. Applicants notified on rolling basis starting 4/1, must reply within 2 week(s) of notification.

Contact. Financial aid office: (641) 422-4351
Mary Bloomingdale, Director of Financial Aid
500 College Drive
Mason City, IA 50401

Northeast Iowa Community College

Calmar, Iowa
www.nicc.edu
Two-year public — **Federal Code: 004587**

	Living at home
Tuition and fees (2002-2003):	$3,136
Per-credit charge:	$86
Books and supplies:	$1,200
Personal expenses:	$1,225
Transportation:	$1,400

Undergraduate aid. Need-based: 43% awarded as scholarships/grants, 57% as loans/jobs. Need-based aid available for part-time students. **Non-**

need-based: Scholarships based on academics, leadership. **Student debt:** 57% of graduating class borrowed to fund education; average debt was $8,684.

Policies to reduce costs. Tuition/fee waivers for senior citizens, employees and their families. Credit/placement for qualifying scores on CLEP examinations. Work study available nights and for part-time students.

Payment plans. Credit card, installment, deferred payment.

Application procedures. FAFSA required. Priority date 7/1; no closing date. Applicants notified on rolling basis starting 5/1.

Contact. **Financial aid office:** (563) 556-5110 ext. 401
Kim Baumler, Financial Aid Officer
Box 400
Calmar, IA 52132

Northwest Iowa Community College

Sheldon, Iowa
www.nwicc.cc.ia.us
Two-year public **Federal Code: 004600**

College costs. Fees vary per program ($6, $9 or $12 per credit hour).

	Living at home	On-campus
Tuition and fees (2002-2003):	$2,400	$2,400
Out-of-state:	$3,600	$3,600
Per-credit charge:	$80	$80
Per-credit out-of-state:	$120	$120
Room only:		$1,900
Books and supplies:	$716	$716
Personal expenses:	$854	$854
Transportation:	$2,450	$724

Undergraduate aid. **Need-based:** Need-based aid available for full-time and part-time students.

Payment plans. Credit card, deferred payment.

Application procedures. FAFSA, institutional form required. Priority date 4/20; no closing date. Applicants notified on rolling basis starting 5/1. **Transfers:** No deadline.

Contact. Karna Hofmeyer, Financial Aid Coordinator
603 West Park Street
Sheldon, IA 51201

Northwestern College

Orange City, Iowa
www.nwciowa.edu
Four-year private **Federal Code: 001883**

College costs. 1-4 credits $320 per credit hour; 5-8 credits $480 per credit hour; 9-11 credits $640 per credit hour.

	Living at home	On-campus
Tuition and fees:	$15,290	$15,290
Room and board:		$4,350
Books and supplies:	$500	$500
Personal expenses:	$1,200	$1,200
Transportation:	$1,000	$400

Undergraduate aid. **Need-based:** Average financial aid package for full-time students was $11,598; for part-time $4,803. 45% awarded as scholarships/grants, 55% as loans/jobs. **Non-need-based:** 83% awarded as scholarships/grants, 17% as loans/jobs. Scholarships based on academics, athletics, state/district residency. **Student debt:** 87% of graduating class borrowed to fund education; average debt was $16,500.

Freshman aid. **Need-based:** Out of 346 full-time freshmen, 346 applied for aid; 344 were judged to have need; of these 344 received aid. Average package met 69% of need. 156 students had full need met. Average scholarship/grant was $5,100; average loan $5,029. **Non-need based:** 312 full-time freshmen with need received non-need scholarships; 18 without need received awards; 1 received athletic scholarships.

Policies to reduce costs. Tuition/fee waivers for adults, children of alumni, family members, employees and their families. Credit/placement for qualifying scores on AP, IB, CLEP examinations.

Payment plans. Installment payment.

Application procedures. FAFSA, institutional form required. Priority date 6/30; closing date 4/1. Applicants notified on rolling basis starting 3/15, must reply within 3 week(s) of notification. **Transfers:** No deadline.

Contact. **Financial aid office:** (712) 707-7131
Carol Bogaard, Director of Financial Aid
101 7th St. SW
Orange City, IA 51041

St. Ambrose University

Davenport, Iowa
www.sau.edu
Four-year private **Federal Code: 00188900**

College costs. $322 per credit for ACCEL program.

	Living at home	On-campus
Tuition and fees:	$16,540	$16,540
Room and board:		$5,840
Board only:	$1,323	
Books and supplies:	$756	$756
Personal expenses:	$1,134	$1,071
Transportation:	$1,890	$473

Undergraduate aid. **Need-based:** Average financial aid package for full-time students was $12,696; for part-time $6,835. 57% awarded as scholarships/grants, 43% as loans/jobs. **Non-need-based:** 13% awarded as scholarships/grants, 87% as loans/jobs. Scholarships based on academics, alumni affiliation, art, athletics, job skills, music/drama. **Student debt:** 13% of graduating class borrowed to fund education; average debt was $16,697. **Additional information:** Iowa applicants must apply for financial aid by March 15. Audition required for music, drama scholarship applicants.

Freshman aid. **Need-based:** Out of 391 full-time freshmen, 359 applied for aid; 293 were judged to have need; of these 290 received aid. Average package met 41% of need. 87 students had full need met. Average scholarship/grant was $4,849; average loan $2,906. **Non-need based:** 290 full-time freshmen with need received non-need scholarships; 82 without need received awards; 25 received athletic scholarships.

Merit scholarships. Ambrose Scholarship: 4.0 GPA and 30 ACT or 1320 SAT score required. Presidential Scholarship: 3.8 GPA and ACT 26-29 or SAT 1170-1319 required.

Policies to reduce costs. Tuition/fee waivers for adults, children of alumni, senior citizens, minority students, family members, family of clergy, employees and their families. Credit/placement for qualifying scores on AP, IB, CLEP examinations. Work study available nights and weekends.

Payment plans. Credit card, installment, deferred payment.

Application procedures. FAFSA required. Priority date 3/15; no closing date. Applicants notified on rolling basis starting 2/1, must reply within 2 week(s) of notification. **Transfers:** No deadline.

Contact. **Financial aid office:** (563) 333-6314
Julie Haack, Director of Financial Aid
518 West Locust Street
Davenport, IA 52803-2898

St. Luke's College

Sioux City, Iowa
www.stlukes.org
Two-year private **Federal Code: 007291**

College costs. Summer general fee: $125

	Living at home	On-campus
Tuition and fees:	$10,650	$10,650
Per-credit charge:	$280	$280
Room and board:		$3,470
Board only:	$1,587	
Books and supplies:	$1,200	$1,200
Personal expenses:	$1,074	$1,074
Transportation:	$1,653	$1,653

Undergraduate aid. **Need-based:** Average financial aid package for full-time students was $11,557; for part-time $8,793. 38% awarded as scholarships/grants, 62% as loans/jobs. **Non-need-based:** 50% awarded as scholarships/grants, 50% as loans/jobs. Scholarships based on academics, job skills, leadership. **Student debt:** 95% of graduating class borrowed to fund education; average debt was $11,746.

Freshman aid. **Need-based:** Average package met 12% of need. Average scholarship/grant was $2,400; average loan $6,320.

Policies to reduce costs. Tuition/fee waivers for employees and their families. Credit/placement for qualifying scores on CLEP examinations. Work study available nights, weekends and for part-time students.

Payment plans. Credit card, installment payment.

Application procedures. FAFSA required. Priority date 5/1; closing date 7/15. Applicants notified on rolling basis starting 1/1, must reply within 2 week(s) of notification.

Contact. **Financial aid office:** (712) 279-3377
Danelle Johannsen, Coordinator, Financial Aid/Registrar
2720 Stone Park Boulevard
Sioux City, IA 51104

Scott Community College

Bettendorf, Iowa
www.eicc.edu
Two-year public **Federal Code: 004074**

	Living at home
Tuition and fees (2002-2003):	$2,250
Out-of-state:	$3,375
Per-credit charge:	$75
Per-credit out-of-state:	$113
Board only:	$1,500
Books and supplies:	$900
Personal expenses:	$900
Transportation:	$900

Policies to reduce costs. Tuition/fee waivers for senior citizens, employees and their families. Credit/placement for qualifying scores on AP, CLEP examinations.

Payment plans. Credit card payment.

Application procedures. FAFSA required. Priority date 4/20; no closing date. Applicants notified on rolling basis starting 5/15, must reply within 2 week(s) of notification.

Contact. Jeannine Ingleson, Financial Aid Officer
500 Belmont Road
Bettendorf, IA 52722-6804

Simpson College

Indianola, Iowa
www.simpson.edu
Four-year private **Federal Code: 001887**

	Living at home	On-campus
Tuition and fees:	$18,097	$18,097
Room and board:		$5,561
Board only:	$2,892	
Books and supplies:	$800	$800
Personal expenses:	$1,300	$1,300
Transportation:	$800	$700

Undergraduate aid. **Need-based:** Average financial aid package for full-time students was $17,200; for part-time $5,502. 71% awarded as scholarships/grants, 29% as loans/jobs. **Non-need-based:** 38% awarded as scholarships/grants, 62% as loans/jobs. Scholarships based on academics, alumni affiliation, art, leadership, minority status, music/drama, religious affiliation, state/district residency. **Additional information:** Music and theater scholarships based on audition. Art scholarships based on portfolio.

Freshman aid. **Need-based:** Out of 381 full-time freshmen, 381 applied for aid; 330 were judged to have need; of these 330 received aid. Average package met 91% of need. 107 students had full need met. Average scholarship/grant was $12,096; average loan $2,845. **Non-need based:** 50 full-time freshmen with need received non-need scholarships; 49 without need received awards.

Policies to reduce costs. Tuition/fee waivers for adults, children of alumni, senior citizens, family members, family of clergy, employees and their families. Credit/placement for qualifying scores on AP, IB, CLEP examinations.

Payment plans. Credit card, installment payment.

Application procedures. FAFSA required. Priority date 4/1; no closing date. Applicants notified on rolling basis starting 3/15, must reply by 5/1 or within 3 week(s) of notification.

Contact. Tracie Pavon, Director of Financial Assistance
701 North C Street
Indianola, IA 50125

Southeastern Community College: North Campus

West Burlington, Iowa
www.secc.cc.ia.us
Two-year public **Federal Code: 001848**

	Living at home	On-campus
Tuition and fees (2002-2003):	$2,220	$2,220
Out-of-state:	$2,693	$2,693
Per-credit charge:	$73	$73
Per-credit out-of-state:	$90	$90
Room and board:		$2,860
Books and supplies:	$600	$600
Transportation:	$1,000	

Undergraduate aid. All financial aid based on need. Need-based aid available for full-time and part-time students.

Policies to reduce costs. Tuition/fee waivers for senior citizens, employees and their families. Credit/placement for qualifying scores on AP, CLEP examinations.

Payment plans. Credit card, deferred payment.

Application procedures. FAFSA, institutional form required. Priority date 6/1; no closing date. Applicants notified on rolling basis starting 6/1, must reply within 4 week(s) of notification.

Contact. Gwen Scholer, Financial Aid Officer
1500 West Agency Road
West Burlington, IA 52655-0605

Southeastern Community College: South Campus

Keokuk, Iowa
www.scciowa.edu
Two-year public **Federal Code: 004603**

	Living at home
Tuition and fees (2002-2003):	$2,400
Out-of-state:	$2,760
Per-credit charge:	$80
Per-credit out-of-state:	$92
Books and supplies:	$600

Undergraduate aid. **Need-based:** Need-based aid available for full-time and part-time students.

Policies to reduce costs. Tuition/fee waivers for employees and their families. Credit/placement for qualifying scores on AP, CLEP examinations. Work study available nights.

Payment plans. Credit card, installment, deferred payment.

Application procedures. FAFSA, institutional form required. Priority date 8/1; no closing date. Applicants notified on rolling basis starting 6/1, must reply within 2 week(s) of notification.

Contact. James Bowles, Financial Aid Officer
Box 6007
Keokuk, IA 52632-6007

Southwestern Community College

Creston, Iowa
www.swcc.cc.ia.us
Two-year public **Federal Code: 001857**

	Living at home	On-campus
Tuition and fees (projected):	$2,730	$2,730
Out-of-state:	$3,735	$3,735
Per-credit charge:	$79	$79
Per-credit out-of-state:	$113	$113
Room and board:		$3,400
Books and supplies:	$600	$600
Personal expenses:	$1,500	$1,500
Transportation:	$2,400	$648

Undergraduate aid. **Need-based:** 9% awarded as scholarships/grants, 91% as loans/jobs. **Non-need-based:** 32% awarded as scholarships/grants, 68% as loans/jobs. Scholarships based on athletics, leadership, music/drama, state/district residency.

Freshman aid. **Need-based:** Out of 245 full-time freshmen, 227 applied for aid; 210 were judged to have need; of these 210 received aid. 3 students had full need met. **Non-need based:** 34 full-time freshmen with need received non-need scholarships; 30 without need received awards.

Policies to reduce costs. Tuition/fee waivers for employees and their families. Credit/placement for qualifying scores on AP, CLEP examinations. Work study available nights, weekends and for part-time students.

Payment plans. Credit card, installment payment.

Application procedures. FAFSA, institutional form required. Priority date 6/1; no closing date. Applicants notified on rolling basis starting 2/1, must reply within 2 week(s) of notification.

Contact. **Financial aid office:** (641) 782-1333
Tracy Sleep, Financial Aid Officer
1501 West Townline Street
Creston, IA 50801

University of Dubuque

Dubuque, Iowa
www.dbq.edu
Four-year private **Federal Code: 001891**

	Living at home	On-campus
Tuition and fees:	$16,260	$16,260
Room and board:		$5,430
Board only:	$1,500	
Books and supplies:	$750	$750
Transportation:	$900	$900

Undergraduate aid. **Need-based:** Average financial aid package for full-time students was $13,294; for part-time $11,498. **Non-need-based:** 18% awarded as scholarships/grants, 82% as loans/jobs. Scholarships based on academics, alumni affiliation, leadership, minority status, music/drama, religious affiliation. **Student debt:** 89% of graduating class borrowed to fund education; average debt was $17,622.

Freshman aid. **Need-based:** Out of 148 full-time freshmen, 144 applied for aid; 132 were judged to have need; of these 132 received aid. Average package met 88% of need. 56 students had full need met. Average scholarship/grant was $7,412; average loan $7,602. **Non-need based:** 6 full-time freshmen with need received non-need scholarships; 16 without need received awards.

Merit scholarships. Presidential; 6,000 per annum for 4 years; top 20% of high school graduation class and top 20% of ACT. Academic scholarships available for environmental science, business, education, aviation.

Policies to reduce costs. Tuition/fee waivers for employees and their families. Credit/placement for qualifying scores on AP, IB, CLEP examinations. Work study available nights and weekends.

Payment plans. Credit card, installment, deferred payment.

Application procedures. FAFSA required. Priority date 4/1; no closing date. Applicants notified on rolling basis starting 3/1, must reply within 3 week(s) of notification. **Transfers:** No deadline. Iowa Tuition Grant available to Iowa residents.

Contact. **Financial aid office:** (563) 589-3396
Timothy Kremer, Director of Financial Aid
2000 University Avenue
Dubuque, IA 52001-5099

University of Iowa

Iowa City, Iowa
www.uiowa.edu
Four-year public **Federal Code: 001892**

	Living at home	On-campus
Tuition and fees (2002-2003):	$4,191	$4,191
Out-of-state:	$13,833	$13,833
Room and board:		$5,492
Books and supplies:	$840	$840
Personal expenses:	$2,170	$2,170
Transportation:	$960	$620

Undergraduate aid. **Need-based:** Average financial aid package for full-time students was $6,806. 44% awarded as scholarships/grants, 56% as loans/jobs. Need-based aid available for part-time students. **Non-need-based:** 32% awarded as scholarships/grants, 68% as loans/jobs. Scholarships based on academics, minority status. **Student debt:** 54% of graduating class borrowed to fund education; average debt was $15,335.

Freshman aid. **Need-based:** Out of 3,924 full-time freshmen, 2,800 applied for aid; 1,691 were judged to have need; of these 1,622 received aid. Average package met 90% of need. 678 students had full need met. Average scholarship/grant was $2,128; average loan $2,089. **Non-need based:** 931 full-time freshmen with need received non-need scholarships; 1,103 without need received awards; 90 received athletic scholarships.

Merit scholarships. Presidential Scholarship: based on ACT/SAT, GPA, essay; 50 awarded, $28,000. Dean's Scholarship: awarded to runners up for Presidential Scholarship; 70 awarded, $4,000. Opportunity at Iowa: members of underrepresented groups (African-American, Hispanic/Latin, Native American, Alaskan Native) with ACT of 25 and 3.5 GPA automatically considered, $20,000. National Scholars Award for non-residents based on admission index; awards range from $5,500-$9,900. Iowa Scholars Award to residents in top 15 percent of class, $2,000.

Policies to reduce costs. Credit/placement for qualifying scores on AP, IB, CLEP examinations. Work study available nights, weekends and for part-time students.

Payment plans. Installment, deferred payment.

Application procedures. FAFSA, institutional form required. Priority date 1/1; no closing date. Applicants notified on rolling basis starting 3/1.

Contact. **Financial aid office:** (319) 335-1450
Mark Warner, Director of Financial Aid
107 Calvin Hall
Iowa City, IA 52242

University of Northern Iowa

Cedar Falls, Iowa
www.uni.edu
Four-year public **Federal Code: 001890**

	Living at home	On-campus
Tuition and fees (2002-2003):	$4,118	$4,118
Out-of-state:	$10,426	$10,426
Room and board:		$4,640
Board only:	$2,388	
Books and supplies:	$776	$776
Personal expenses:	$2,426	$2,426
Transportation:	$532	$532

Undergraduate aid. **Need-based:** Average financial aid package for full-time students was $6,222; for part-time $5,231. 29% awarded as scholarships/grants, 71% as loans/jobs. **Non-need-based:** 20% awarded as scholarships/grants, 80% as loans/jobs. Scholarships based on academics, art, athletics, leadership, minority status, music/drama. **Student debt:** 69% of graduating class borrowed to fund education; average debt was $15,786.

Freshman aid. **Need-based:** Out of 1,821 full-time freshmen, 1,525 applied for aid; 1,033 were judged to have need; of these 1,024 received aid. Average package met 72% of need. 247 students had full need met. Average scholarship/grant was $2,714; average loan $2,537. **Non-need based:** 496 full-time freshmen with need received non-need scholarships; 288 without need received awards; 54 received athletic scholarships.

Merit scholarships. Presidential Scholarship and Provost Scholarship for rank in upper 10% of high school class or rank in top 5 of class of 50 or less and ACT composite of 29 or above, selection based on academic excellence, extracurricular achievements, leadership and demonstrated potential for making a significant contribution to society; deadline October 1; 15 of each scholarship awarded; tuition and fees, room and board.

Policies to reduce costs. Credit/placement for qualifying scores on AP, IB, CLEP examinations.

Payment plans. Installment, deferred payment.

Application procedures. FAFSA required. No deadline. Applicants notified on rolling basis starting 3/1, must reply within 2 week(s) of notification.

Contact. **Financial aid office:** (319) 273-2700
Roland Carrillo, Director Financial Aid and Student Employment
120 Gilchrist Hall
Cedar Falls, IA 50614-0018

Upper Iowa University

Fayette, Iowa
www.uiu.edu
Four-year private **Federal Code: 001893**

	Living at home	On-campus
Tuition and fees:	$15,056	$15,056
Room and board:		$5,020
Board only:	$2,244	
Books and supplies:	$1,050	$1,050
Personal expenses:	$1,600	$1,600
Transportation:	$560	$560

Undergraduate aid. Need-based: Need-based aid available for full-time and part-time students. **Non-need-based:** Scholarships based on academics.

Policies to reduce costs. Tuition/fee waivers for children of alumni, family members, employees and their families. Credit/placement for qualifying scores on AP, IB, CLEP examinations.

Payment plans. Installment payment.

Application procedures. FAFSA required. Priority date 6/1; no closing date. Applicants notified on rolling basis starting 4/1.

Contact. Financial aid office: (800) 553-4150 ext. 3
Jobyna Johnston, Director of Financial Aid
Parker Fox Hall
Fayette, IA 52142

Vatterott College

Des Moines, Iowa
www.vatterott-college.edu
Two-year proprietary **Federal Code: 026092**

College costs (2002-2003). Tuition ranges from $7,706 to $23,458. Costs vary depending on program for each campus. Fees included in costs.

Undergraduate aid. All financial aid based on need. Need-based aid available for full-time students.

Payment plans. Credit card, installment payment.

Application procedures. FAFSA required. No deadline. Applicants notified on rolling basis.

Contact. Financial aid office: (515) 309-9000
Scott Graves, Financial Aid Administrator
6100 Thornton, Suite 290
Des Moines, IA 50321

Vennard College

University Park, Iowa
www.vennard.edu
Four-year private **Federal Code: 001894**

	Living at home	On-campus
Tuition and fees:	$9,020	$9,020
Room and board:		$4,600
Books and supplies:	$500	$500
Personal expenses:	$1,390	$1,390
Transportation:	$1,435	$875

Undergraduate aid. Need-based: Need-based aid available for full-time and part-time students.

Policies to reduce costs. Tuition/fee waivers for children of alumni, family members, family of clergy, employees and their families. Credit/placement for qualifying scores on AP, CLEP examinations.

Payment plans. Installment, deferred payment.

Application procedures. Institutional form required. Priority date 5/1; no closing date. Applicants notified on rolling basis starting 3/1. **Transfers:** Academic scholarships available to full-time new transfer students. 3.5 minimum college GPA for 2 consecutive semesters of credit work in degree granting program required.

Contact. John Olson, Financial Aid Director
Box 29
University Park, IA 52595

Waldorf College

Forest City, Iowa
www.waldorf.edu
Three-year private **Federal Code: 001895**

	Living at home	On-campus
Tuition and fees:	$13,662	$13,662
Room and board:		$4,200
Board only:	$2,100	
Books and supplies:	$730	$730
Personal expenses:	$1,465	$1,465
Transportation:	$875	$875

Undergraduate aid. Need-based: Average financial aid package for full-time students was $15,218; for part-time $10,803. 63% awarded as scholarships/grants, 37% as loans/jobs. **Non-need-based:** 53% awarded as scholarships/grants, 47% as loans/jobs. Scholarships based on academics, art, athletics, job skills, leadership, music/drama, religious affiliation, state/district residency.

Freshman aid. Need-based: Out of 217 full-time freshmen, 192 applied for aid; 177 were judged to have need; of these 177 received aid. Average package met 83% of need. 43 students had full need met. Average scholarship/grant was $9,479; average loan $3,611. **Non-need based:** 8 full-time freshmen with need received non-need scholarships; 32 without need received awards; 17 received athletic scholarships.

Policies to reduce costs. Tuition/fee waivers for employees and their families. Credit/placement for qualifying scores on AP, CLEP examinations. Work study available nights and weekends.

Payment plans. Credit card, installment, deferred payment.

Application procedures. FAFSA required. Priority date 5/1; no closing date. Applicants notified on rolling basis starting 3/1, must reply within 2 week(s) of notification. **Transfers:** No deadline.

Contact. Financial aid office: (641) 585-8120
Duane Polsdofer, Director of Student Financial Aid
106 South Sixth Street
Forest City, IA 50436

Wartburg College

Waverly, Iowa
www.wartburg.edu
Four-year private **Federal Code: 001896**

	Living at home	On-campus
Tuition and fees:	$18,550	$18,550
Room and board:		$5,080
Board only:	$2,500	
Books and supplies:	$600	$600
Personal expenses:	$700	$700
Transportation:	$600	$600

Undergraduate aid. Need-based: Average financial aid package for full-time students was $16,135; for part-time $11,076. 65% awarded as scholarships/grants, 35% as loans/jobs. **Non-need-based:** 24% awarded as scholarships/grants, 76% as loans/jobs. Scholarships based on academics, alumni affiliation, job skills, leadership, music/drama, religious affiliation, state/district residency. **Student debt:** 97% of graduating class borrowed to fund education; average debt was $18,226.

Freshman aid. Need-based: Out of 511 full-time freshmen, 467 applied for aid; 402 were judged to have need; of these 402 received aid. Average package met 95% of need. 283 students had full need met. Average scholarship/grant was $11,944; average loan $4,911. **Non-need based:** 50 full-time freshmen with need received non-need scholarships; 109 without need received awards.

Merit scholarships. Regents scholarship: up to full tuition, fees, room and board, to students with minimum ACT score of 28, (1240 SAT) or rank in top 10 percent of class; renewable for 4 years, based on maintaining 3.0 cumulative GPA. Students who participate in Regents Scholarship competition not eligible for Presidential scholarship. Presidential scholarship: up to $6,000 per year, to students with minimum ACT score of 25 (1140 SAT) or rank in top 20 percent of class or have cumulative GPA of 3.5 or above. Renewable for 4 years, based on maintaining 2.7 cumulative GPA.

Policies to reduce costs. Tuition/fee waivers for employees and their families. Credit/placement for qualifying scores on AP, CLEP examinations.

Payment plans. Installment, deferred payment.

Application procedures. FAFSA required. Priority date 3/1; no closing date. Applicants notified on rolling basis starting 3/22, must reply within 2 week(s) of notification.

Contact. **Financial aid office:** (319) 352-8262
Jennifer Sassman, Director of Financial Aid
100 Wartburg Blvd.
Waverly, IA 50677-0903

Western Iowa Tech Community College

Sioux City, Iowa
www.witcc.com
Two-year public **Federal Code: 004590**

	Living at home	On-campus
Tuition and fees (2002-2003):	$2,760	$2,760
Out-of-state:	$4,380	$4,380
Per-credit charge:	$79	$79
Per-credit out-of-state:	$133	$133
Room only:		$2,340
Board only:	$900	
Books and supplies:	$800	$800
Personal expenses:	$990	$990
Transportation:	$1,350	$1,350

Undergraduate aid. Need-based: 46% awarded as scholarships/grants, 54% as loans/jobs. Need-based aid available for part-time students. **Non-need-based:** 48% awarded as scholarships/grants, 52% as loans/jobs. Scholarships based on academics, job skills, leadership, state/district residency.

Freshman aid. Need-based: Out of 485 full-time freshmen, 385 applied for aid; 316 were judged to have need; of these 300 received aid. 316 students had full need met.

Policies to reduce costs. Credit/placement for qualifying scores on AP, CLEP examinations. Work study available nights, weekends and for part-time students.

Payment plans. Credit card, deferred payment.

Application procedures. FAFSA required. No deadline. Applicants notified on rolling basis starting 3/1. **Transfers:** No deadline.

Contact. **Financial aid office:** (712) 274-6402
Donald Duzik, Director of Financial Aid
Box 5199
Sioux City, IA 51102-5199

William Penn University

Oskaloosa, Iowa
www.wmpenn.edu
Four-year private **Federal Code: 001900**

	Living at home	On-campus
Tuition and fees:	$14,190	$14,190
Room and board:		$4,610
Board only:	$1,350	
Books and supplies:	$800	$800
Personal expenses:	$901	$900
Transportation:	$1,000	$1,000

Undergraduate aid. Need-based: 58% awarded as scholarships/grants, 42% as loans/jobs. Need-based aid available for part-time students. **Non-need-based:** 15% awarded as scholarships/grants, 85% as loans/jobs. Scholarships based on academics, alumni affiliation, athletics, leadership, music/drama, religious affiliation. **Student debt:** 74% of graduating class borrowed to fund education; average debt was $18,624.

Merit scholarships. Athletic scholarships: determined by coaches. Participation awards: up to $3,000 per year, for music, drama, media, cheerleading, religious leadership. Academic scholarships based on high school GPA, ACT or SAT, class rank.

Policies to reduce costs. Tuition/fee waivers for children of alumni, senior citizens, employees and their families. Prepayment discount; credit/placement for qualifying scores on AP, IB, CLEP examinations.

Payment plans. Credit card, installment, deferred payment.

Application procedures. FAFSA required. Priority date 7/1; no closing date. Applicants notified on rolling basis starting 1/1, must reply within 2 week(s) of notification. **Transfers:** Priority date 4/1.

Contact. **Financial aid office:** (641) 673-1060
Cyndi Peiffer, Director of Financial Aid
201 Trueblood Avenue
Oskaloosa, IA 52577

Kansas

Allen County Community College

Iola, Kansas
www.allencc.edu
Two-year public **Federal Code: 001901**

College costs. Fees include $270 book rental fee.

	Living at home	On-campus
Tuition and fees (2002-2003):	$1,350	$1,350
Out-of-state:	$1,350	$1,350
Per-credit charge:	$31	$31
Per-credit out-of-state:	$31	$31
Room and board:		$3,250
Board only:	$2,500	
Books and supplies:	$300	$300
Personal expenses:	$1,620	$1,620
Transportation:	$550	$550

Undergraduate aid. Need-based: Average financial aid package for full-time students was $4,801; for part-time $2,280. 68% awarded as scholarships/grants, 32% as loans/jobs. **Non-need-based:** 44% awarded as scholarships/grants, 56% as loans/jobs. Scholarships based on academics, art, athletics, music/drama, state/district residency. **Student debt:** 22% of graduating class borrowed to fund education; average debt was $3,442. **Additional information:** Scholarships for livestock judging, cheerleading, choir, dance, drama, art, academic challenge, and student ambassadors.

Freshman aid. Need-based: Out of 375 full-time freshmen, 324 applied for aid; 169 were judged to have need; of these 163 received aid. Average package met 100% of need. 163 students had full need met. Average scholarship/grant was $2,990; average loan $1,804. **Non-need based:** 95 full-time freshmen with need received non-need scholarships; 94 without need received awards; 45 received athletic scholarships.

Policies to reduce costs. Tuition/fee waivers for senior citizens. Credit/placement for qualifying scores on AP, CLEP examinations. Work study available nights and weekends.

Payment plans. Credit card payment.

Application procedures. FAFSA required. Priority date 6/1; closing date 8/1. Applicants notified on rolling basis starting 6/1, must reply within 2 week(s) of notification.

Contact. Barbara Leavitt, Director of Financial Aid/Registrar
1801 North Cottonwood
Iola, KS 66749

Baker University

Baldwin City, Kansas
www.bakeru.edu
Four-year private **Federal Code: 001903**

	Living at home	On-campus
Tuition and fees:	$14,640	$14,640
Room and board:		$5,300
Board only:	$2,840	
Books and supplies:	$900	$900
Personal expenses:	$1,260	$1,260
Transportation:	$450	$1,500

Undergraduate aid. Need-based: Average financial aid package for full-time students was $10,900; for part-time $5,126. 45% awarded as scholarships/grants, 55% as loans/jobs. **Non-need-based:** 67% awarded as scholarships/grants, 33% as loans/jobs. Scholarships based on academics, art, athletics, music/drama, religious affiliation. **Student debt:** 72% of graduating class borrowed to fund education; average debt was $17,682. **Additional information:** Special loan program available at College of Arts and Sciences to returning students filing FAFSA statements and meeting grade criteria. Loans advanced annually become grants upon graduation and do not have to be repaid.

Freshman aid. Need-based: Out of 231 full-time freshmen, 231 applied for aid; 173 were judged to have need; of these 173 received aid. Average scholarship/grant was $4,254; average loan $4,037. **Non-need based:** 128 full-time freshmen with need received non-need scholarships; 58 without need received awards; 196 received athletic scholarships.

Merit scholarships. Presidential Scholarship Criteria: $6,000, 28 ACT composite and 3.70 GPA, $5,000, 25 ACT composite and 3.40 GPA, $4,000, 22 ACT composite and 3.10 GPA

Policies to reduce costs. Tuition/fee waivers for senior citizens, employees and their families. Credit/placement for qualifying scores on AP, IB examinations. Work study available nights and weekends.

Payment plans. Credit card, installment payment.

Application procedures. FAFSA, institutional form required. Priority date 3/1; no closing date. Applicants notified on rolling basis starting 2/15, must reply by 5/1 or within 6 week(s) of notification. **Transfers:** Priority date 3/1.

Contact. Financial aid office: (785) 594-4595
Jeanne Mott, Director of Financial Aid
618 Eighth Street
Baldwin City, KS 66006

Barclay College

Haviland, Kansas
www.barclaycollege.edu
Four-year private **Federal Code: 001917**

	Living at home	On-campus
Tuition and fees (projected):	$8,250	$8,250
Room and board:		$4,200
Board only:	$2,250	
Books and supplies:	$500	$500
Personal expenses:	$1,210	$1,435
Transportation:	$450	$300

Undergraduate aid. Need-based: Average financial aid package for full-time students was $10,055; for part-time $900. 56% awarded as scholarships/grants, 44% as loans/jobs. **Non-need-based:** 16% awarded as scholarships/grants, 84% as loans/jobs. Scholarships based on academics, alumni affiliation, leadership, music/drama, state/district residency.

Freshman aid. Need-based: Out of 17 full-time freshmen, 17 applied for aid; 17 were judged to have need; of these 17 received aid. Average package met 83% of need. 6 students had full need met. Average scholarship/grant was $5,328; average loan $2,047. **Non-need based:** 4 full-time freshmen with need received non-need scholarships.

Merit scholarships. President's Academic Award, $2,600, for 3.8 GPA or ACT score of 30; Dean's Academic Award, $2,000, for 3.6 GPA or ACT scores of 27-29; Trustees Academic Award, $1,600, for 3.4 GPA or ACT scores of 25-26.

Policies to reduce costs. Tuition/fee waivers for children of alumni, family of clergy, employees and their families. Credit/placement for qualifying scores on AP, IB, CLEP examinations. Work study available nights, weekends and for part-time students.

Payment plans. Credit card, installment payment.

Application procedures. FAFSA, institutional form required. Priority date 3/15; closing date 7/15. Applicants notified by 4/15, must reply within 4 week(s) of notification. **Transfers:** Priority date 3/15.

Contact. Financial aid office: (620) 862-5252
Richard Sandstrom, Financial Aid Director
607 North Kingman
Haviland, KS 67059

Barton County Community College

Great Bend, Kansas
www.bartonccc.edu
Two-year public **Federal Code: 004608**

College costs. Out-of-state first-time freshmen pay in-state tuition; other out-of-state students pay $68 per-credit-hour, $2,040 full-time. Edukan online courses $115 per-credit-hour, BartOnline courses $125 per-credit-hour, BCCC online courses $71 per-credit-hour.

	Living at home	On-campus
Tuition and fees (2002-2003):	$1,560	$1,560
Out-of-state:	$1,560	$1,560
Per-credit charge:	$34	$34
Per-credit out-of-state:	$34	$34
Room and board:		$3,054
Board only:	$2,730	
Books and supplies:	$700	$700
Personal expenses:	$2,500	$2,500
Transportation:	$800	$800

Undergraduate aid. Need-based: 65% awarded as scholarships/grants, 35% as loans/jobs. Need-based aid available for part-time students. **Non-need-based:** 61% awarded as scholarships/grants, 39% as loans/jobs. Scholarships based on academics, athletics.

Policies to reduce costs. Tuition/fee waivers for senior citizens, employees and their families. Credit/placement for qualifying scores on CLEP examinations.

Payment plans. Credit card, installment payment.

Application procedures. FAFSA, institutional form required. Priority date 3/1; no closing date. Applicants notified on rolling basis starting 6/1, must reply within 4 week(s) of notification.

Contact. Financial aid office: (620) 792-9270
Myrna Perkins, Director of Financial Aid
245 NE 30th Road
Great Bend, KS 67530-9283

Benedictine College

Atchison, Kansas
www.benedictine.edu
Four-year private **Federal Code: 010256**

	Living at home	On-campus
Tuition and fees (2002-2003):	$14,900	$14,900
Room and board:		$5,900
Books and supplies:	$900	$900
Personal expenses:	$1,200	$1,200
Transportation:	$600	$800

Undergraduate aid. Need-based: Average financial aid package for full-time students was $13,523; for part-time $6,503. 35% awarded as scholarships/grants, 65% as loans/jobs. **Non-need-based:** 66% awarded as scholarships/grants, 34% as loans/jobs. Scholarships based on academics, athletics, leadership, music/drama, religious affiliation. **Student debt:** 83% of graduating class borrowed to fund education; average debt was $21,000.

Freshman aid. Need-based: Out of 240 full-time freshmen, 240 applied for aid; 206 were judged to have need; of these 206 received aid. Average package met 83% of need. 83 students had full need met. Average scholarship/grant was $4,131; average loan $3,842. **Non-need based:** 201 full-time freshmen with need received non-need scholarships; 23 without need received awards; 107 received athletic scholarships.

Merit scholarships. Presidential Scholarship, full tuition; Dean's Scholarship, partial tuition. Both renewable every year, 5 recipients each, must maintain 3.5 GPA. Application deadline Jan. 15. Academic Scholarships (unlimited number) renewable every year, ranging from $2,500-$7,500 depending on ACT scores.

Policies to reduce costs. Tuition/fee waivers for employees and their families. Prepayment discount; credit/placement for qualifying scores on AP, IB, CLEP examinations. Work study available nights and weekends.

Payment plans. Credit card, installment, deferred payment.

Application procedures. FAFSA, institutional form required. Priority date 3/1; no closing date. Applicants notified on rolling basis starting 2/1, must reply by 5/1 or within 4 week(s) of notification. **Transfers:** Scholarship available for students transferring with a minimum of 24 hours and 2.5 cumulative GPA.

Contact. Financial aid office: (913) 367-5340 ext. 2485
Keith Jaloma, Director of Student Financial Aid
1020 North Second Street
Atchison, KS 66002-1499

Bethany College

Lindsborg, Kansas
www.bethanylb.edu
Four-year private **Federal Code: 001904**

	Living at home	On-campus
Tuition and fees:	$14,140	$14,140
Room and board:		$4,570
Books and supplies:	$550	$550
Transportation:	$600	$600

Undergraduate aid. Need-based: Average financial aid package for full-time students was $14,465; for part-time $8,243. 49% awarded as scholarships/grants, 51% as loans/jobs. **Non-need-based:** 29% awarded as scholarships/grants, 71% as loans/jobs. Scholarships based on academics, art, athletics, leadership, music/drama, religious affiliation. **Student debt:** 21% of graduating class borrowed to fund education; average debt was $5,747. **Additional information:** State financial aid deadline March 15.

Freshman aid. Need-based: Out of 139 full-time freshmen, 130 applied for aid; 107 were judged to have need; of these 107 received aid. Average package met 95% of need. 40 students had full need met. Average scholarship/grant was $5,446; average loan $3,970. **Non-need based:** 14 full-time freshmen with need received non-need scholarships; 11 without need received awards; 14 received athletic scholarships.

Policies to reduce costs. Tuition/fee waivers for family of clergy, employees and their families. Credit/placement for qualifying scores on AP, IB, CLEP examinations. Work study available for part-time students.

Payment plans. Credit card, installment payment.

Application procedures. FAFSA required. Priority date 3/15; closing date 8/1. Applicants notified on rolling basis starting 2/1, must reply within 3 week(s) of notification.

Contact. Financial aid office: (785) 227-3311 ext. 8114
Brenda Meagher, Director of Financial Aid
421 North First Street
Lindsborg, KS 67456-1897

Bethel College

North Newton, Kansas
www.bethelks.edu
Four-year private **Federal Code: 001905**

	Living at home	On-campus
Tuition and fees:	$13,900	$13,900
Room and board:		$5,900
Board only:	$2,000	
Books and supplies:	$800	$800
Personal expenses:	$1,800	$1,800
Transportation:	$600	$600

Undergraduate aid. Need-based: Average financial aid package for full-time students was $13,599; for part-time $7,905. 38% awarded as scholarships/grants, 62% as loans/jobs. **Non-need-based:** 71% awarded as scholarships/grants, 29% as loans/jobs. Scholarships based on academics, alumni affiliation, art, athletics, music/drama, religious affiliation, state/district residency. **Student debt:** 78% of graduating class borrowed to fund education; average debt was $15,530.

Freshman aid. Need-based: Out of 121 full-time freshmen, 117 applied for aid; 106 were judged to have need; of these 106 received aid. Average package met 90% of need. 39 students had full need met. Average scholarship/grant was $3,802; average loan $3,130. **Non-need based:** 89 full-time freshmen with need received non-need scholarships; 14 without need received awards; 47 received athletic scholarships.

Merit scholarships. Scholarships for academically talented students, ranging from 10%-60% of tuition.

Policies to reduce costs. Tuition/fee waivers for children of alumni, senior citizens, family of clergy, employees and their families. Credit/placement for qualifying scores on AP, IB, CLEP examinations.

Payment plans. Credit card, installment, deferred payment.

Application procedures. FAFSA required. No deadline. Applicants notified on rolling basis starting 3/1, must reply within 2 week(s) of notification. **Transfers:** No deadline.

Contact. Financial aid office: (800) 522-1887 ext. 232
Tony Graber, Director of Financial Aid
300 East 27th Street
North Newton, KS 67117-0531

Butler County Community College

Eldorado, Kansas
www.butlercc.edu
Two-year public **Federal Code: 001906**

	Living at home	On-campus
Tuition and fees (2002-2003):	$1,590	$1,590
Out-of-state:	$2,850	$2,850
Per-credit charge:	$41	$41
Per-credit out-of-state:	$83	$83
Room and board:		$4,000
Books and supplies:	$1,000	$1,000
Personal expenses:	$1,350	$1,350
Transportation:	$1,200	$1,200

Undergraduate aid. Need-based: Need-based aid available for full-time and part-time students. **Non-need-based:** Scholarships based on academics, athletics.

Policies to reduce costs. Tuition/fee waivers for senior citizens, unemployed or children of unemployed, employees and their families. Credit/placement for qualifying scores on AP, CLEP examinations. Work study available nights, weekends and for part-time students.

Payment plans. Credit card, installment, deferred payment.

Application procedures. FAFSA, institutional form required. Priority date 4/1; no closing date. Applicants notified on rolling basis starting 5/1, must reply within 2 week(s) of notification. **Transfers:** Students with 90 hours or more must have classes validated by degree-granting 4-year institution.

Contact. Susie Edwards, Director of Financial Aid
901 South Haverhill Road
Eldorado, KS 67042-3280

Central Christian College

McPherson, Kansas
www.centralchristian.edu
Four-year private **Federal Code: 001908**

	Living at home	On-campus
Tuition and fees:	$12,500	$12,500
Room and board:		$4,100
Board only:	$2,200	
Books and supplies:	$500	$500
Personal expenses:	$700	$700
Transportation:		$800

Undergraduate aid. Need-based: Average financial aid package for full-time students was $10,414; for part-time $5,430. 38% awarded as scholarships/grants, 62% as loans/jobs. **Non-need-based:** 64% awarded as scholarships/grants, 36% as loans/jobs. Scholarships based on academics, athletics, leadership, music/drama, religious affiliation. **Student debt:** 75% of graduating class borrowed to fund education; average debt was $20,000.

Freshman aid. Need-based: Out of 100 full-time freshmen, 100 applied for aid; 92 were judged to have need; of these 92 received aid. Average package met 88% of need. 2 students had full need met. Average scholarship/grant was $3,702; average loan $4,999. **Non-need based:** 87 full-time freshmen with need received non-need scholarships; 8 without need received awards; 28 received athletic scholarships.

Merit scholarships. National Merit Scholarship, full tuition, for National Merit semifinalists; Trustees Scholarship, 2/3 tuition, based on minimum score of 30 on ACT/1340 on SAT and minimum 3.5 high school GPA; Valedictorian Scholarship, half tuition, for students who are first in their class, with minimum 27 ACT/1220 SAT and 3.5 GPA.

Policies to reduce costs. Tuition/fee waivers for family of clergy, employees and their families. Credit/placement for qualifying scores on AP, IB, CLEP examinations. Work study available nights and weekends.

Payment plans. Credit card, installment payment.

Application procedures. FAFSA required. Priority date 3/1; no closing date. Applicants notified on rolling basis starting 3/1, must reply within 4 week(s) of notification. **Transfers:** No deadline.

Contact. Financial aid office: (316) 241-0723 ext. 333
Mike Reimer, Director of Financial Aid
1200 South Main
McPherson, KS 67460-5740

Cloud County Community College

Concordia, Kansas
www.cloud.edu
Two-year public **Federal Code: 001909**

College costs. Geary County campus pays in-state tuition and $570 annual required fees. Nebraska tuition: $54.50 per-credit-hour, $1,635 full-time. Out-of-state and Nebraska required fees $540.

	Living at home	On-campus
Tuition and fees (2002-2003):	$1,680	$1,680
Out-of-state:	$3,150	$3,150
Per-credit charge:	$38	$38
Per-credit out-of-state:	$87	$87
Room and board:		$3,240
Board only:	$1,980	
Books and supplies:	$600	$600
Personal expenses:	$2,300	$2,300

Undergraduate aid. Need-based: Average financial aid package for full-time students was $4,588; for part-time $3,206. 64% awarded as scholarships/grants, 36% as loans/jobs. **Non-need-based:** 16% awarded as scholarships/grants, 84% as loans/jobs.

Freshman aid. Need-based: Out of 301 full-time freshmen, 255 applied for aid; 143 were judged to have need; of these 143 received aid. Average package met 70% of need. 34 students had full need met. Average scholarship/grant was $2,671; average loan $1,917. **Non-need based:** 96 full-time freshmen with need received non-need scholarships.

Policies to reduce costs. Tuition/fee waivers for employees and their families. Credit/placement for qualifying scores on CLEP examinations. Work study available nights, weekends and for part-time students.

Payment plans. Credit card, installment, deferred payment.

Application procedures. FAFSA required. Priority date 4/1; no closing date. Applicants notified on rolling basis starting 5/1, must reply within 4 week(s) of notification. **Transfers:** No deadline.

Contact. Financial aid office: (785) 243-1435 ext. 280
Sherry Campbell, Director of Student Financial Aid
2221 Campus Drive
Concordia, KS 66901-1002

Dodge City Community College

Dodge City, Kansas
www.dccc.cc.ks.us
Two-year public **Federal Code: 001913**

	Living at home	On-campus
Tuition and fees (2002-2003):	$1,500	$1,500
Out-of-state:	$1,710	$1,710
Per-credit charge:	$33	$33
Per-credit out-of-state:	$40	$40
Room and board:		$3,560
Board only:	$2,500	
Books and supplies:	$600	$600
Personal expenses:	$1,000	$1,000
Transportation:	$1,000	$1,000

Undergraduate aid. Need-based: Need-based aid available for full-time and part-time students. **Non-need-based:** Scholarships based on academics, athletics, state/district residency.

Policies to reduce costs. Tuition/fee waivers for senior citizens, employees and their families. Credit/placement for qualifying scores on AP, CLEP examinations. Work study available nights, weekends and for part-time students.

Payment plans. Credit card, installment, deferred payment.

Application procedures. FAFSA, institutional form required. Priority date 4/1; no closing date. Applicants notified on rolling basis, must reply within 2 week(s) of notification.

Contact. Financial aid office: (620) 227-9336
Anthony Lyons, Director of Financial Assistance
2501 North 14th
Dodge City, KS 67801-2399

Donnelly College

Kansas City, Kansas
www.donnelly.cc.ks.us
Two-year private **Federal Code: 001914**

	Living at home
Tuition and fees:	$3,780
Per-credit charge:	$145
Books and supplies:	$575
Personal expenses:	$1,800
Transportation:	$800

Undergraduate aid. All financial aid based on need. Average financial aid package for full-time students was $3,973; for part-time $2,113. 91% awarded as scholarships/grants, 9% as loans/jobs. **Student debt:** 42% of graduating class borrowed to fund education; average debt was $7,242.

Freshman aid. Out of 43 full-time freshmen, 43 applied for aid; 41 were judged to have need; of these 41 received aid. Average package met 64% of need. 2 students had full need met. Average scholarship/grant was $1,324; average loan $2,147.

Policies to reduce costs. Tuition/fee waivers for senior citizens, employees and their families. Credit/placement for qualifying scores on CLEP examinations. Work study available for part-time students.

Payment plans. Installment payment.

Application procedures. FAFSA required. Priority date 6/1; no closing date. Applicants notified on rolling basis starting 7/1. **Transfers:** No deadline.

Contact. **Financial aid office:** (913) 621-8741
Paul London, Director of Financial Aid
608 North 18th Street
Kansas City, KS 66102-4210

Emporia State University

Emporia, Kansas
www.emporia.edu
Four-year public **Federal Code: 001927**

	Living at home	On-campus
Tuition and fees (2002-2003):	$2,454	$2,454
Out-of-state:	$7,746	$7,746
Room and board:		$4,056
Board only:	$1,998	
Books and supplies:	$700	$700
Personal expenses:	$1,692	$1,692
Transportation:	$622	$622

Undergraduate aid. Need-based: Average financial aid package for full-time students was $5,141; for part-time $3,671. 43% awarded as scholarships/grants, 57% as loans/jobs. **Non-need-based:** 21% awarded as scholarships/grants, 79% as loans/jobs. Scholarships based on academics, alumni affiliation, art, athletics, job skills, leadership, minority status, music/drama, religious affiliation, state/district residency. **Student debt:** 43% of graduating class borrowed to fund education; average debt was $13,252. **Additional information:** Additional school's own payment plan is available.

Freshman aid. Need-based: Out of 1,206 full-time freshmen, 538 applied for aid; 379 were judged to have need; of these 379 received aid. Average package met 75% of need. 110 students had full need met. Average scholarship/grant was $2,861; average loan $1,929. **Non-need based:** 37 full-time freshmen with need received non-need scholarships; 248 without need received awards; 37 received athletic scholarships.

Merit scholarships. Presidential Academic Awards; $800 to $1,500; unlimited number. Challenge Awards; $500; unlimited number. Transfer President's Academic Award; $500 to $1,500; based on cumulative GPA or Phi Theta Kappa membership. Guaranteed GPA Scholarship; $500 to $1,200; based on GPA for continuing full-time undergraduates.

Policies to reduce costs. Tuition/fee waivers for senior citizens, employees and their families. Credit/placement for qualifying scores on AP, IB, CLEP examinations. Work study available nights, weekends and for part-time students.

Payment plans. Credit card, installment, deferred payment.

Application procedures. FAFSA required. Priority date 3/15; no closing date. Applicants notified on rolling basis starting 2/2, must reply within 2 week(s) of notification. **Transfers:** No deadline.

Contact. **Financial aid office:** (620) 341-5457
Wilma Kasnic, Director of Financial Aid
1200 Commercial
Emporia, KS 66801-5087

Fort Hays State University

Hays, Kansas
www.fhsu.edu
Four-year public **Federal Code: 001915**

	Living at home	On-campus
Tuition and fees (2002-2003):	$2,328	$2,328
Out-of-state:	$7,488	$7,488
Room and board:		$4,300
Board only:	$2,005	
Books and supplies:	$700	$700
Personal expenses:	$1,450	$2,670
Transportation:	$298	$918

Undergraduate aid. Need-based: Need-based aid available for full-time and part-time students.

Policies to reduce costs. Tuition/fee waivers for adults, employees and their families. Credit/placement for qualifying scores on AP, CLEP examinations. Work study available nights, weekends and for part-time students.

Payment plans. Credit card, installment, deferred payment.

Application procedures. FAFSA required. Priority date 3/15; no closing date. Applicants notified on rolling basis starting 3/15, must reply within 2 week(s) of notification.

Contact. **Financial aid office:** (785) 628-4408
Craig Karlin, Director of Student Financial Aid
600 Park Street
Hays, KS 67601

Fort Scott Community College

Fort Scott, Kansas
www.ftscott.cc.ks.us
Two-year public **Federal Code: 001916**

College costs. Students from adjoining states Oklahoma, Nebraska, Missouri, and Colorado pay $1,770 tuition, $59 per-credit-hour.

	Living at home	On-campus
Tuition and fees (2002-2003):	$1,500	$1,500
Out-of-state:	$3,180	$3,180
Per-credit charge:	$31	$31
Per-credit out-of-state:	$87	$87
Room and board:		$3,420
Board only:	$1,900	
Books and supplies:	$550	$550
Personal expenses:	$1,020	$1,020
Transportation:	$500	$850

Policies to reduce costs. Credit/placement for qualifying scores on CLEP examinations.

Payment plans. Credit card, installment, deferred payment.

Application procedures. Priority date 5/1; no closing date. Applicants notified on rolling basis starting 10/1.

Contact. Bonnie Quick, Financial Aid Officer
2108 South Horton
Fort Scott, KS 66701

Friends University

Wichita, Kansas
www.friends.edu
Four-year private **Federal Code: 001918**

	Living at home	On-campus
Tuition and fees (2002-2003):	$12,935	$12,935
Room and board:		$3,810
Books and supplies:	$750	$750
Personal expenses:	$2,765	$2,765

Undergraduate aid. Need-based: Need-based aid available for full-time and part-time students. **Additional information:** Scholarships for clergy/family of clergy available.

Policies to reduce costs. Tuition/fee waivers for senior citizens, employees and their families. Credit/placement for qualifying scores on CLEP examinations.

Payment plans. Credit card, installment payment.

Application procedures. FAFSA, institutional form required. Priority date 4/1; no closing date. Applicants notified on rolling basis, must reply within 3 week(s) of notification.

Contact. **Financial aid office:** (316) 295-5200
Myra Pfannenstiel, Director of Financial Aid
2100 University
Wichita, KS 67213

Garden City Community College

Garden City, Kansas
www.gcccks.edu
Two-year public **Federal Code: 001919**

	Living at home	On-campus
Tuition and fees (2002-2003):	$1,500	$1,500
Out-of-state:	$2,430	$2,430
Per-credit charge:	$34	$34
Per-credit out-of-state:	$65	$65
Room and board:		$4,400
Board only:	$1,500	
Books and supplies:	$600	$600
Personal expenses:	$1,000	$1,500
Transportation:	$1,000	$1,500

Undergraduate aid. Need-based: 66% awarded as scholarships/grants, 34% as loans/jobs. Need-based aid available for part-time students. **Non-need-based:** 74% awarded as scholarships/grants, 26% as loans/jobs. Scholarships based on academics, art, athletics, leadership, music/drama, state/district residency.

Policies to reduce costs. Tuition/fee waivers for senior citizens, employees and their families. Credit/placement for qualifying scores on AP, IB, CLEP examinations. Work study available nights, weekends and for part-time students.

Payment plans. Credit card, installment, deferred payment.

Application procedures. FAFSA, institutional form required. Priority date 6/1; no closing date. Applicants notified on rolling basis starting 4/15, must reply within 2 week(s) of notification.

Contact. **Financial aid office:** (620) 276-9519
Kathleen Blau, Director of Financial Aid
801 Campus Drive
Garden City, KS 67846

Haskell Indian Nations University

Lawrence, Kansas
www.haskell.edu
Four-year public **Federal Code: 010438**

College costs. No tuition; federal college for Native American students. Required fees $140; room and board $70. Books/supplies: $220. Transportation: $668.

Undergraduate aid. Need-based: Need-based aid available for full-time and part-time students. **Additional information:** Some personal expenses may be offset by Bureau of Indian Affairs grants. Most students qualify for only minimum Pell grant.

Policies to reduce costs. Work study available nights, weekends and for part-time students.

Payment plans. Credit card, deferred payment.

Application procedures. FAFSA required. Priority date 5/15; no closing date. Applicants notified on rolling basis starting 3/15, must reply within 9 week(s) of notification. **Transfers:** Priority date 11/8; closing date 4/15.

Contact. **Financial aid office:** (785) 830-2718
Reta Beaver, Financial Aid Officer
155 Indian Avenue #5031
Lawrence, KS 66046-4800

Hesston College

Hesston, Kansas
www.hesston.edu
Two-year private **Federal Code: 001920**

	Living at home	On-campus
Tuition and fees:	$13,798	$13,798
Per-credit charge:	$568	$568
Room and board:		$5,200
Board only:	$3,120	
Books and supplies:	$800	$800
Personal expenses:	$1,500	$1,500
Transportation:	$200	$500

Undergraduate aid. Need-based: 58% awarded as scholarships/grants, 42% as loans/jobs. Need-based aid available for part-time students. **Non-need-based:** Scholarships based on academics, alumni affiliation, athletics, job skills, music/drama. **Student debt:** 65% of graduating class borrowed to fund education; average debt was $5,600.

Policies to reduce costs. Tuition/fee waivers for senior citizens, employees and their families. Prepayment discount; credit/placement for qualifying scores on AP, CLEP examinations. Work study available nights, weekends and for part-time students.

Payment plans. Credit card, installment payment.

Application procedures. FAFSA required. Priority date 5/1; no closing date. Applicants notified on rolling basis starting 2/1, must reply within 4 week(s) of notification.

Contact. **Financial aid office:** (800) 995-2757
Marcia Mendez, Financial Aid Director
Box 3000
Hesston, KS 67062

Highland Community College

Highland, Kansas
www.highlandcc.edu
Two-year public **Federal Code: 001921**

College costs. Required fees include textbook rental. Doniphan County residents pay $31 per credit hour, $930 tuition.

	Living at home	On-campus
Tuition and fees (2002-2003):	$1,680	$1,680
Out-of-state:	$3,180	$3,180
Per-credit charge:	$38	$38
Per-credit out-of-state:	$88	$88
Room and board:		$4,108
Board only:	$1,500	
Books and supplies:	$275	$275
Personal expenses:	$845	$845
Transportation:	$449	$449

Undergraduate aid. Non-need-based: Scholarships based on academics, alumni affiliation, art, athletics, leadership, minority status, music/drama. **Additional information:** Auditions and portfolios important for certain scholarship candidates.

Policies to reduce costs. Credit/placement for qualifying scores on AP, CLEP examinations. Work study available nights, weekends and for part-time students.

Payment plans. Credit card, installment, deferred payment.

Application procedures. FAFSA required. Priority date 4/1; no closing date. Applicants notified on rolling basis starting 4/15.

Contact. Kelly Twombly, Director of Student Financial Aid
606 West Main Street
Highland, KS 66035-0068

Hutchinson Community College

Hutchinson, Kansas
www.hutchcc.edu
Two-year public **Federal Code: 001923**

	Living at home	On-campus
Tuition and fees (2002-2003):	$1,620	$1,620
Out-of-state:	$2,940	$2,940
Per-credit charge:	$42	$42
Per-credit out-of-state:	$86	$86
Room and board:		$3,440
Board only:	$1,500	
Books and supplies:	$700	$700
Personal expenses:	$900	$900
Transportation:	$1,000	$600

Undergraduate aid. Need-based: Average financial aid package for full-time students was $8,886; for part-time $6,318. 65% awarded as scholarships/grants, 35% as loans/jobs. **Non-need-based:** 39% awarded as scholarships/grants, 61% as loans/jobs. Scholarships based on academics, athletics, minority status, state/district residency. **Student debt:** 34% of graduating class borrowed to fund education; average debt was $5,753.

Freshman aid. Need-based: Out of 935 full-time freshmen, 644 applied for aid; 476 were judged to have need; of these 402 received aid. Average package met 78% of need. 118 students had full need met. Average scholarship/grant was $2,860; average loan $2,184. **Non-need based:** 98 full-time freshmen with need received non-need scholarships; 283 without need received awards; 78 received athletic scholarships.

Policies to reduce costs. Tuition/fee waivers for senior citizens, employees and their families. Credit/placement for qualifying scores on AP, CLEP examinations.

Payment plans. Credit card payment.

Application procedures. FAFSA required. Priority date 2/1; no closing date. Applicants notified on rolling basis starting 5/1, must reply within 2 week(s) of notification.

Contact. Financial aid office: (620) 665-3400
Kathie Tyrell, Financial Aid Director
1300 North Plum
Hutchinson, KS 67501

Independence Community College

Independence, Kansas
www.indy.cc.ks.edu
Two-year public **Federal Code: 001924**

College costs. Montgomery County residents pay $810 tuition, $510 required fees.

	Living at home	On-campus
Tuition and fees (2002-2003):	$1,590	$1,590
Per-credit charge:	$30	$30
Per-credit out-of-state:	$30	$30
Room and board:		$4,000
Books and supplies:	$500	$500

Undergraduate aid. Need-based: Need-based aid available for full-time and part-time students. **Non-need-based:** Scholarships based on academics, athletics.

Policies to reduce costs. Tuition/fee waivers for senior citizens, employees and their families. Credit/placement for qualifying scores on AP examinations.

Payment plans. Credit card, installment payment.

Application procedures. FAFSA required. Priority date 4/1; no closing date. Applicants notified on rolling basis. **Transfers:** No deadline.

Contact. Sheila Jarrett, Director of Financial Aid
Box 708
Independence, KS 67301

Johnson County Community College

Overland Park, Kansas
www.jccc.net
Two-year public **Federal Code: 008244**

	Living at home
Tuition and fees (2002-2003):	$1,740
Out-of-district:	$2,190
Out-of-state:	$4,170
Per-credit charge:	$58
Per-credit out-of-district:	$73
Per-credit out-of-state:	$139
Board only:	$4,500
Books and supplies:	$840
Personal expenses:	$1,170
Transportation:	$1,620

Undergraduate aid. Need-based: Need-based aid available for full-time and part-time students. **Non-need-based:** Scholarships based on academics.

Policies to reduce costs. Tuition/fee waivers for senior citizens, employees and their families. Credit/placement for qualifying scores on AP, CLEP examinations.

Payment plans. Credit card payment.

Application procedures. FAFSA required. Priority date 4/1; no closing date. Applicants notified on rolling basis starting 4/15, must reply within 2 week(s) of notification.

Contact. Financial aid office: (913) 469-3840
Julie Cooper, Program Director for Student Financial Aid
12345 College Boulevard
Overland Park, KS 66210-1299

Kansas City Kansas Community College

Kansas City, Kansas
www.kckcc.edu
Two-year public **Federal Code: 001925**

	Living at home
Tuition and fees (2002-2003):	$1,500
Out-of-state:	$4,020
Per-credit charge:	$42
Per-credit out-of-state:	$126
Books and supplies:	$740
Personal expenses:	$2,025
Transportation:	$1,173

Undergraduate aid. Need-based: 58% awarded as scholarships/grants, 42% as loans/jobs. Need-based aid available for part-time students. **Non-need-based:** Scholarships based on academics, art, athletics, music/drama, state/district residency.

Policies to reduce costs. Tuition/fee waivers for employees and their families. Credit/placement for qualifying scores on AP, IB, CLEP examinations. Work study available nights, weekends and for part-time students.

Payment plans. Credit card, installment, deferred payment.

Application procedures. FAFSA required. Priority date 4/15; no closing date. Applicants notified on rolling basis starting 5/1, must reply within 4 week(s) of notification.

Contact. Mary Dorr, Director of Financial Aid
7250 State Avenue
Kansas City, KS 66112

Kansas State University

Manhattan, Kansas
www.ksu.edu
Four-year public **Federal Code: 001928**

	Living at home	On-campus
Tuition and fees (2002-2003):	$3,436	$3,436
Out-of-state:	$10,696	$10,696
Room and board:		$4,500
Board only:	$2,446	
Books and supplies:	$684	$684
Personal expenses:	$2,520	$2,520
Transportation:	$302	$302

Undergraduate aid. Need-based: Average financial aid package for full-time students was $4,882; for part-time $4,818. 38% awarded as scholarships/grants, 62% as loans/jobs. **Non-need-based:** 13% awarded as scholarships/grants, 87% as loans/jobs. Scholarships based on academics, alumni affiliation, art, athletics, job skills, leadership, minority status, music/drama, religious affiliation, state/district residency. **Student debt:** 55% of graduating class borrowed to fund education; average debt was $17,000.

Freshman aid. Need-based: Out of 3,472 full-time freshmen, 2,814 applied for aid; 1,939 were judged to have need; of these 1,905 received aid. Average package met 75% of need. 337 students had full need met. Average scholarship/grant was $2,550; average loan $2,504. **Non-need based:** 1,300 full-time freshmen with need received non-need scholarships; 465 without need received awards; 57 received athletic scholarships.

Policies to reduce costs. Tuition/fee waivers for employees and their families. Credit/placement for qualifying scores on AP, IB, CLEP examinations.

Payment plans. Credit card, installment, deferred payment.

Application procedures. FAFSA required. Priority date 3/1; no closing date. Applicants notified on rolling basis starting 4/15, must reply within 2 week(s) of notification.

Contact. Larry Moeder, Director of Student Financial Assistance
119 Anderson Hall
Manhattan, KS 66506

Kansas Wesleyan University

Salina, Kansas
www.kwu.edu
Four-year private **Federal Code: 001929**

	Living at home	On-campus
Tuition and fees:	$14,200	$14,200
Room and board:		$4,700
Board only:	$1,500	
Books and supplies:	$500	$500
Personal expenses:	$500	$500
Transportation:	$400	$400

Undergraduate aid. Need-based: Average financial aid package for full-time students was $14,506. 50% awarded as scholarships/grants, 50% as loans/jobs. Need-based aid available for part-time students. **Non-need-based:** 64% awarded as scholarships/grants, 36% as loans/jobs. Scholarships based on academics, alumni affiliation, art, athletics, music/drama, state/district residency. **Student debt:** 72% of graduating class borrowed to fund education; average debt was $10,786. **Additional information:** Awards available for residence hall students: minimum $7,000 for 3.0 GPA plus ACT score of 22 or SAT of 950; minimum $8,000 for 3.5 GPA plus ACT score of 22 or SAT score of 1030; minimum $9,000 for 3.75 GPA plus ACT score of 25 or SAT score of 1140. Application deadline March 15.

Freshman aid. Need-based: Out of 155 full-time freshmen, 155 applied for aid; 140 were judged to have need; of these 140 received aid. Average package met 95% of need. 48 students had full need met. Average scholarship/grant was $5,098; average loan $4,468. **Non-need based:** 109 full-time freshmen with need received non-need scholarships; 13 without need received awards; 83 received athletic scholarships.

Policies to reduce costs. Tuition/fee waivers for adults, children of alumni, senior citizens, family members, employees and their families. Credit/placement for qualifying scores on AP, CLEP examinations.

Payment plans. Installment payment.

Application procedures. FAFSA required. Closing date 3/15. Applicants notified on rolling basis starting 1/1, must reply by 8/1 or within 3 week(s) of notification. **Transfers:** Academic scholarships based upon cumulative GPA of transferring credit hours.

Contact. Financial aid office: (785) 827-5541 ext. 1130
Glenna Alexander, Director of Financial Assistance
100 East Claflin Avenue
Salina, KS 67401-6196

Labette Community College

Parsons, Kansas
www.labette.edu
Two-year public **Federal Code: 001930**

	Living at home	On-campus
Tuition and fees (2002-2003):	$1,590	$1,590
Out-of-state:	$3,240	$3,240
Per-credit charge:	$37	$37
Per-credit out-of-state:	$92	$92
Room and board:		$3,040
Board only:	$1,800	
Books and supplies:	$550	$550
Personal expenses:	$2,000	$2,000
Transportation:	$450	$250

Undergraduate aid. Need-based: 30% awarded as scholarships/grants, 70% as loans/jobs. Need-based aid available for part-time students. **Non-need-based:** Scholarships based on academics, leadership. **Additional information:** Students seeking financial aid must process FAFSA prior to issuance of aid.

Merit scholarships. Foundation Scholarships

Policies to reduce costs. Tuition/fee waivers for adults, senior citizens, minority students, unemployed or children of unemployed, employees and their families. Credit/placement for qualifying scores on AP, CLEP examinations. Work study available nights.

Payment plans. Credit card, installment, deferred payment.

Application procedures. FAFSA required. No deadline. Applicants notified on rolling basis starting 4/1, must reply within 2 week(s) of notification.

Contact. Financial aid office: (620) 820-1219
Wayne Hatcher, Dean of Student Services
200 South 14th Street
Parsons, KS 67357

McPherson College

McPherson, Kansas
www.mcpherson.edu
Four-year private **Federal Code: 001933**

	Living at home	On-campus
Tuition and fees:	$14,090	$14,090
Room and board:		$5,450
Board only:	$1,800	
Books and supplies:	$720	$720
Personal expenses:	$1,500	$2,400
Transportation:	$2,290	$940

Undergraduate aid. Need-based: Average financial aid package for full-time students was $14,357. 40% awarded as scholarships/grants, 60% as loans/jobs. Need-based aid available for part-time students. **Non-need-based:** 76% awarded as scholarships/grants, 24% as loans/jobs. Scholarships based on academics, art, athletics, religious affiliation, state/district residency. **Student debt:** 85% of graduating class borrowed to fund education; average debt was $19,472.

Freshman aid. Need-based: Out of 75 full-time freshmen, 72 applied for aid; 68 were judged to have need; of these 68 received aid. Average package met 83% of need. 15 students had full need met. Average scholarship/grant was $4,111; average loan $3,537. **Non-need based:** 66 full-time freshmen with need received non-need scholarships; 5 without need received awards; 23 received athletic scholarships.

Policies to reduce costs. Tuition/fee waivers for senior citizens, employees and their families. Prepayment discount; credit/placement for qualifying scores on AP, IB, CLEP examinations. Work study available nights and weekends.

Payment plans. Credit card, installment payment.

Application procedures. FAFSA required. Priority date 4/1; no closing date. Applicants notified on rolling basis starting 3/1, must reply within 4 week(s) of notification.

Contact. Financial aid office: (620) 241-0731 ext. 1239
Dale Minnich, Chief Financial Officer
1600 East Euclid Street
McPherson, KS 67460-1402

MidAmerica Nazarene University

Olathe, Kansas
www.mnu.edu
Four-year private **Federal Code: 007032**

	Living at home	On-campus
Tuition and fees:	$12,910	$12,910
Room and board:		$6,110
Books and supplies:	$600	$600
Personal expenses:	$2,500	$2,500
Transportation:	$1,427	$1,427

Undergraduate aid. Need-based: Need-based aid available for full-time and part-time students. **Non-need-based:** Scholarships based on academics, art, athletics, leadership, music/drama, religious affiliation.

Policies to reduce costs. Tuition/fee waivers for senior citizens, family of clergy, employees and their families. Credit/placement for qualifying scores on AP, IB, CLEP examinations.

Payment plans. Credit card, installment payment.

Application procedures. FAFSA, institutional form required. Priority date 3/1; no closing date. Applicants notified on rolling basis starting 3/30, must reply within 2 week(s) of notification. **Transfers:** Priority date 3/1; no deadline.

Contact. **Financial aid office:** (913) 791-3298
Rhonda Cole, Director of Student Financial Services
2030 East College Way
Olathe, KS 66062

Newman University

Wichita, Kansas
www.newmanu.edu
Four-year private **Federal Code: 001939**

	Living at home	On-campus
Tuition and fees:	$13,348	$13,348
Room and board:		$4,820
Books and supplies:	$750	$750
Personal expenses:	$5,416	$3,964

Undergraduate aid. Need-based: Need-based aid available for full-time and part-time students. **Non-need-based:** Scholarships based on academics, alumni affiliation, athletics, leadership, minority status, music/drama, religious affiliation.

Merit scholarships. Full tuition to any National Merit Finalist.

Policies to reduce costs. Tuition/fee waivers for adults, children of alumni, family members, employees and their families. Credit/placement for qualifying scores on AP, IB, CLEP examinations. Work study available nights, weekends and for part-time students.

Payment plans. Credit card, installment payment.

Application procedures. FAFSA, institutional form required. Priority date 3/1; no closing date. Applicants notified on rolling basis starting 2/1.

Contact. Kelli Hartman, Director of Financial Aid
3100 McCormick Avenue
Wichita, KS 67213-2097

North Central Kansas Technical College

Beloit, Kansas
www.ncktc.tec.ks.us
Two-year public

College costs (2002-2003). Tool expenses $350-$4,000 depending on program. Board: $990. Books/supplies: $800. Transportation: $1,200.

Undergraduate aid. All financial aid based on need. Average financial aid package for full-time students was $5,625; for part-time $5,625. 46% awarded as scholarships/grants, 54% as loans/jobs. **Student debt:** 99% of graduating class borrowed to fund education; average debt was $3,190.

Freshman aid. Out of 54 full-time freshmen, 46 applied for aid; 46 were judged to have need; of these 46 received aid. Average package met 85% of need. 20 students had full need met. Average scholarship/grant was $3,000; average loan $2,625.

Policies to reduce costs. Work study available nights and for part-time students.

Payment plans. Credit card, deferred payment.

Application procedures. FAFSA required.

Contact. PO Box 507
Beloit, KS 67420

Ottawa University

Ottawa, Kansas
www.ottawa.edu
Four-year private **Federal Code: 001937**

	Living at home	On-campus
Tuition and fees:	$13,060	$13,060
Room and board:		$5,360
Board only:	$2,442	
Books and supplies:	$609	$609
Personal expenses:	$1,601	$1,800
Transportation:	$1,100	$1,100

Undergraduate aid. Need-based: Need-based aid available for full-time and part-time students. **Non-need-based:** Scholarships based on academics, alumni affiliation, art, athletics, leadership, minority status, music/drama, religious affiliation.

Policies to reduce costs. Tuition/fee waivers for children of alumni, minority students, family members, employees and their families. Credit/placement for qualifying scores on AP, IB, CLEP examinations. Work study available for part-time students.

Payment plans. Credit card payment.

Application procedures. FAFSA, institutional form required. Priority date 3/15; no closing date. Applicants notified on rolling basis starting 2/1, must reply within 4 week(s) of notification.

Contact. **Financial aid office:** (785) 242-5200
Howard Fischer, Director of Financial Aid
1001 South Cedar Street, #17
Ottawa, KS 66067-3399

Pittsburg State University

Pittsburg, Kansas
www.pittstate.edu
Four-year public **Federal Code: 001926**

	Living at home	On-campus
Tuition and fees (2002-2003):	$2,534	$2,534
Out-of-state:	$7,946	$7,946
Room and board:		$4,006
Board only:	$4,270	
Books and supplies:	$500	$500
Personal expenses:	$1,578	$1,578
Transportation:	$1,428	$778

Undergraduate aid. All financial aid based on need. Average financial aid package for full-time students was $6,439; for part-time $4,756. 44% awarded as scholarships/grants, 56% as loans/jobs. **Student debt:** 89% of graduating class borrowed to fund education; average debt was $9,670.

Freshman aid. Out of 868 full-time freshmen, 608 applied for aid; 446 were judged to have need; of these 430 received aid. Average package met 82% of need. 74 students had full need met. Average scholarship/grant was $3,602; average loan $2,401.

Policies to reduce costs. Tuition/fee waivers for senior citizens, minority students, employees and their families. Credit/placement for qualifying scores on AP, CLEP examinations.

Payment plans. Credit card, installment, deferred payment.

Application procedures. FAFSA required. Priority date 3/1; no closing date. Applicants notified on rolling basis starting 4/1, must reply within 2 week(s) of notification. **Transfers:** Transfer student scholarships available.

Contact. **Financial aid office:** (620) 235-4240
Marilyn Haverly, Director of Student Financial Assistance
1701 South Broadway
Pittsburg, KS 66762

Pratt Community College

Pratt, Kansas
www.pcc.cc.ks.us
Two-year public **Federal Code: 001938**

College costs. $100 per semester additional resident fee for non-Kansas students.

	Living at home	On-campus
Tuition and fees (2002-2003):	$1,590	$1,590
Out-of-state:	$1,590	$1,590
Per-credit charge:	$33	$33
Per-credit out-of-state:	$33	$33
Room and board:		$3,390
Board only:	$1,000	
Books and supplies:	$450	$450
Personal expenses:	$600	$600
Transportation:	$400	$200

Undergraduate aid. Need-based: Need-based aid available for full-time and part-time students. **Non-need-based:** Scholarships based on academics, art, athletics, leadership, music/drama, state/district residency.

Policies to reduce costs. Tuition/fee waivers for senior citizens, employees and their families. Credit/placement for qualifying scores on CLEP examinations. Work study available for part-time students.

Payment plans. Credit card, installment, deferred payment.

Application procedures. FAFSA, institutional form required. Priority date 5/1; no closing date. Applicants notified on rolling basis starting 2/1, must reply within 2 week(s) of notification. **Transfers:** No deadline.

Contact. Financial aid office: (620) 672-9800 ext. 248
Debbie Boley, Director of Financial Aid
348 NE SR 61
Pratt, KS 67124

St. Mary College

Leavenworth, Kansas
www.smcks.edu
Four-year private **Federal Code: 001943**

	Living at home	On-campus
Tuition and fees (2002-2003):	$12,928	$12,928
Room and board:		$5,122
Board only:	$2,300	
Books and supplies:	$750	$750
Personal expenses:	$1,490	$1,490
Transportation:	$1,280	$820

Undergraduate aid. Need-based: Average financial aid package for full-time students was $10,225. 58% awarded as scholarships/grants, 42% as loans/jobs. Need-based aid available for part-time students. **Non-need-based:** 37% awarded as scholarships/grants, 63% as loans/jobs. Scholarships based on academics, art, athletics, leadership, music/drama. **Student debt:** 91% of graduating class borrowed to fund education; average debt was $13,275. **Additional information:** Essays may be required for scholarship applicants. Auditions recommended for music and drama scholarship applicants. Portfolio reviews for art award applicants.

Freshman aid. Need-based: Out of 91 full-time freshmen, 91 applied for aid; 70 were judged to have need; of these 82 received aid. Average package met 81% of need. 48 students had full need met. Average scholarship/grant was $3,810; average loan $2,425. **Non-need based:** 78 full-time freshmen with need received non-need scholarships; 20 without need received awards.

Policies to reduce costs. Tuition/fee waivers for children of alumni, senior citizens, family members, employees and their families. Credit/placement for qualifying scores on AP, IB, CLEP examinations. Work study available nights and weekends.

Payment plans. Credit card, installment, deferred payment.

Application procedures. FAFSA required. Priority date 4/3; no closing date. Applicants notified on rolling basis starting 2/3, must reply within 2 week(s) of notification. **Transfers:** No deadline.

Contact. Financial aid office: (913) 682-5151 ext. 6450
Judy Wiedower, Director of Admissions and Financial Aid
4100 South Fourth Street Trafficway
Leavenworth, KS 66048

Seward County Community College

Liberal, Kansas
www.sccc.edu
Two-year public **Federal Code: 008228**

College costs. Non-resident border counties tuition $46 per-credit-hour, $1,380 full-time. Online classes $115 per-credit-hour with no required fees.

	Living at home	On-campus
Tuition and fees (2002-2003):	$1,530	$1,530
Out-of-state:	$2,220	$2,220
Per-credit charge:	$36	$36
Per-credit out-of-state:	$59	$59
Room and board:		$3,900
Books and supplies:	$600	$600
Personal expenses:	$1,000	$1,000
Transportation:	$250	$350

Undergraduate aid. Need-based: Need-based aid available for full-time and part-time students. **Non-need-based:** Scholarships based on academics, athletics.

Policies to reduce costs. Tuition/fee waivers for senior citizens, employees and their families. Prepayment discount; credit/placement for qualifying scores on AP, CLEP examinations.

Payment plans. Credit card, installment, deferred payment.

Application procedures. FAFSA, institutional form required. Priority date 5/1; no closing date. Applicants notified on rolling basis starting 6/15, must reply within 4 week(s) of notification.

Contact. Bea Rosales, Financial Aid Director
1801 North Kansas Avenue
Liberal, KS 67905-1137

Southwestern College

Winfield, Kansas
www.sckans.edu
Four-year private **Federal Code: 001940**

	Living at home	On-campus
Tuition and fees (2002-2003):	$13,922	$13,922
Room and board:		$4,736
Books and supplies:	$600	$600
Personal expenses:	$1,055	$1,055
Transportation:	$600	$600

Undergraduate aid. Need-based: Average financial aid package for full-time students was $14,054; for part-time $8,204. 43% awarded as scholarships/grants, 57% as loans/jobs. **Non-need-based:** 40% awarded as scholarships/grants, 60% as loans/jobs. Scholarships based on academics, alumni affiliation, athletics, leadership, minority status, music/drama, religious affiliation, state/district residency. **Student debt:** 57% of graduating class borrowed to fund education; average debt was $14,533. **Additional information:** Academic and activity grants available.

Freshman aid. Need-based: Out of 106 full-time freshmen, 99 applied for aid; 91 were judged to have need; of these 91 received aid. Average package met 87% of need. 32 students had full need met. Average scholarship/grant was $9,543; average loan $4,647. **Non-need based:** 91 full-time freshmen with need received non-need scholarships; 15 without need received awards; 1 received athletic scholarships.

Merit scholarships. Presidential Scholarship based on GPA, SAT/ACT scores, essay, resume, leadership, community service; full tuition. Scholarships for major based on GPA, SAT scores, essay, interview; 3 awarded.

Policies to reduce costs. Tuition/fee waivers for children of alumni, senior citizens, family members, family of clergy, employees and their families. Credit/placement for qualifying scores on AP, CLEP examinations. Work study available nights and weekends.

Payment plans. Credit card, installment payment.

Application procedures. Institutional form required. Priority date 7/1; closing date 8/1. Applicants notified on rolling basis starting 4/1, must reply within 2 week(s) of notification. **Transfers:** Activity grants and scholarships, except for presidential scholarship and premier scholarships, available to transfer students. Phi Theta Kappa scholarship available for transfer students who are members.

Contact. **Financial aid office:** (620) 229-6215
Brenda Hicks, Director of Financial Aid
100 College Street
Winfield, KS 67156

Sterling College

Sterling, Kansas
www.sterling.edu
Four-year private **Federal Code: 001945**

	Living at home	On-campus
Tuition and fees (2002-2003):	$12,875	$12,875
Room and board:		$5,240
Books and supplies:	$600	$600
Personal expenses:		$650
Transportation:	$1,250	

Undergraduate aid. **Need-based:** Average financial aid package for full-time students was $10,346; for part-time $5,663. 76% awarded as scholarships/grants, 24% as loans/jobs. **Non-need-based:** 63% awarded as scholarships/grants, 37% as loans/jobs. Scholarships based on academics, alumni affiliation, art, athletics, leadership, minority status, music/drama, religious affiliation. **Student debt:** 63% of graduating class borrowed to fund education; average debt was $10,583. **Additional information:** Twins enrolled at institution pay single tuition.

Freshman aid. **Need-based:** Out of 96 full-time freshmen, 96 applied for aid; 79 were judged to have need; of these 79 received aid. Average package met 70% of need. 17 students had full need met. Average scholarship/grant was $6,308; average loan $2,185. **Non-need based:** 15 without need received awards; 5 received athletic scholarships.

Policies to reduce costs. Tuition/fee waivers for senior citizens, employees and their families. Credit/placement for qualifying scores on AP, CLEP examinations. Work study available nights, weekends and for part-time students.

Payment plans. Credit card, installment payment.

Application procedures. FAFSA required. Priority date 3/15; no closing date. Applicants notified on rolling basis starting 3/1, must reply within 2 week(s) of notification. **Transfers:** Priority date 3/15; no deadline.

Contact. **Financial aid office:** (620) 278-4226
Anne Norwood, Director of Financial Aid
Box 98
Sterling, KS 67579-0098

Tabor College

Hillsboro, Kansas
www.tabor.edu
Four-year private **Federal Code: 001946**

	Living at home	On-campus
Tuition and fees:	$14,350	$14,350
Room and board:		$5,150
Board only:	$2,000	
Books and supplies:	$600	$600
Personal expenses:	$880	$1,920
Transportation:	$270	$1,000

Undergraduate aid. **Need-based:** Average financial aid package for full-time students was $13,731; for part-time $7,826. 32% awarded as scholarships/grants, 68% as loans/jobs. **Non-need-based:** Scholarships based on academics, alumni affiliation, art, athletics, music/drama, religious affiliation. **Student debt:** 79% of graduating class borrowed to fund education; average debt was $18,493.

Freshman aid. **Need-based:** Out of 108 full-time freshmen, 98 applied for aid; 82 were judged to have need; of these 82 received aid. Average package met 87% of need. 24 students had full need met. Average scholarship/grant was $3,700; average loan $4,191. **Non-need based:** 82 full-time freshmen with need received non-need scholarships; 26 without need received awards; 72 received athletic scholarships.

Policies to reduce costs. Tuition/fee waivers for adults, children of alumni, senior citizens, family members, family of clergy, employees and their families. Credit/placement for qualifying scores on AP, IB, CLEP examinations.

Payment plans. Credit card, installment payment.

Application procedures. FAFSA required. Priority date 3/1; closing date 8/15. Applicants notified on rolling basis starting 3/1, must reply within 4 week(s) of notification. **Transfers:** Transfer students not eligible for Presidential, National Merit or Dean's scholarships.

Contact. **Financial aid office:** (620) 947-3121 ext. 1726
Bruce Jost, Director of Student Financial Assistance
400 South Jefferson
Hillsboro, KS 67063

University of Kansas

Lawrence, Kansas
www.ku.edu
Four-year public **Federal Code: 001948**

	Living at home	On-campus
Tuition and fees (2002-2003):	$3,484	$3,484
Out-of-state:	$10,687	$10,687
Room and board:		$4,642
Books and supplies:	$750	$750
Personal expenses:	$1,904	$1,904
Transportation:	$1,222	$1,222

Undergraduate aid. **Need-based:** Average financial aid package for full-time students was $6,173; for part-time $4,020. 45% awarded as scholarships/grants, 55% as loans/jobs. **Non-need-based:** 34% awarded as scholarships/grants, 66% as loans/jobs. Scholarships based on academics, alumni affiliation, art, athletics, leadership, minority status, music/drama, state/district residency. **Student debt:** 37% of graduating class borrowed to fund education; average debt was $17,347. **Additional information:** Work study available weekdays.

Freshman aid. **Need-based:** Out of 4,031 full-time freshmen, 2,089 applied for aid; 1,311 were judged to have need; of these 1,289 received aid. Average package met 71% of need. 343 students had full need met. Average scholarship/grant was $3,777; average loan $2,502. **Non-need based:** 8 full-time freshmen with need received non-need scholarships; 548 without need received awards; 45 received athletic scholarships.

Policies to reduce costs. Tuition/fee waivers for senior citizens, employees and their families. Credit/placement for qualifying scores on AP, IB, CLEP examinations.

Payment plans. Credit card, installment, deferred payment.

Application procedures. FAFSA required. Priority date 3/1; no closing date. Applicants notified on rolling basis starting 4/1, must reply within 2 week(s) of notification.

Contact. **Financial aid office:** (785) 864-4700
Brenda Maigaard, Director of Student Financial Aid
1502 Iowa Street
Lawrence, KS 66045-7576

University of Kansas Medical Center

Kansas City, Kansas
www.kumc.edu
Upper-division public **Federal Code: 004605**

	Living at home
Tuition and fees (2002-2003):	$3,181
Out-of-state:	$11,972
Board only:	$2,821
Books and supplies:	$750
Personal expenses:	$5,784
Transportation:	$2,208

Undergraduate aid. **Need-based:** Average financial aid package for full-time students was $7,632; for part-time $5,012. 32% awarded as scholarships/grants, 68% as loans/jobs. **Non-need-based:** 4% awarded as scholarships/grants, 96% as loans/jobs. Scholarships based on academics, leadership, minority status, state/district residency.

Policies to reduce costs. Tuition/fee waivers for employees and their families. Credit/placement for qualifying scores on AP examinations. Work study available nights, weekends and for part-time students.

Payment plans. Credit card, deferred payment.

Application procedures. Priority date 2/14; no closing date.

Contact. **Financial aid office:** (913) 588-5170
Jack Taylor, Director of Student Financial Aid
3901 Rainbow Boulevard
Kansas City, KS 66160

Washburn University of Topeka

Topeka, Kansas
www.washburn.edu
Four-year public **Federal Code: 001949**

	Living at home	On-campus
Tuition and fees (2002-2003):	$3,656	$3,656
Out-of-state:	$8,186	$8,186
Room and board:		$4,486
Board only:	$4,300	
Books and supplies:	$690	$690
Personal expenses:	$1,300	$1,300
Transportation:	$1,540	$1,540

Undergraduate aid. Need-based: Average financial aid package for full-time students was $4,300; for part-time $3,100. 31% awarded as scholarships/grants, 69% as loans/jobs. **Non-need-based:** 28% awarded as scholarships/grants, 72% as loans/jobs. Scholarships based on academics. **Student debt:** 67% of graduating class borrowed to fund education; average debt was $11,000.

Freshman aid. Need-based: Out of 705 full-time freshmen, 585 applied for aid; 349 were judged to have need; of these 302 received aid. Average package met 55% of need. 45 students had full need met. Average scholarship/grant was $2,100; average loan $2,325. **Non-need based:** 114 full-time freshmen with need received non-need scholarships; 439 without need received awards; 62 received athletic scholarships.

Policies to reduce costs. Tuition/fee waivers for children of alumni, senior citizens, employees and their families. Credit/placement for qualifying scores on AP, CLEP examinations. Work study available nights, weekends and for part-time students.

Payment plans. Credit card, installment, deferred payment.

Application procedures. FAFSA required. Priority date 3/1; no closing date. Applicants notified on rolling basis, must reply within 2 week(s) of notification. **Transfers:** Priority date 3/1.

Contact. Financial aid office: (785) 231-1151
Annita Huff, Director of Financial Aid
1700 SW College Avenue
Topeka, KS 66621

Wichita State University

Wichita, Kansas
www.wichita.edu
Four-year public **Federal Code: 001950**

	Living at home	On-campus
Tuition and fees (2002-2003):	$3,085	$3,085
Out-of-state:	$9,832	$9,832
Room and board:		$4,420
Board only:	$2,550	
Books and supplies:	$800	$800
Personal expenses:	$1,570	$1,570
Transportation:	$1,570	$1,570

Undergraduate aid. Need-based: Average financial aid package for full-time students was $5,516; for part-time $4,006. 32% awarded as scholarships/grants, 68% as loans/jobs. **Non-need-based:** 24% awarded as scholarships/grants, 76% as loans/jobs. Scholarships based on academics, alumni affiliation, art, athletics, leadership, minority status, music/drama, state/district residency. **Student debt:** 52% of graduating class borrowed to fund education; average debt was $16,282. **Additional information:** Top freshman applicants admitted by October 1 invited to university scholarship competition.

Freshman aid. Need-based: Out of 1,557 full-time freshmen, 986 applied for aid; 763 were judged to have need; of these 694 received aid. Average package met 44% of need. 84 students had full need met. Average scholarship/grant was $3,143; average loan $2,265. **Non-need based:** 380 full-time freshmen with need received non-need scholarships; 231 without need received awards; 23 received athletic scholarships.

Policies to reduce costs. Tuition/fee waivers for senior citizens. Credit/placement for qualifying scores on AP, IB, CLEP examinations. Work study available nights, weekends and for part-time students.

Payment plans. Credit card, installment payment.

Application procedures. FAFSA required. Closing date 3/15. Applicants notified on rolling basis starting 3/15, must reply within 2 week(s) of notification.

Contact. Deborah Byers, Director of Financial Aid
1845 Fairmount
Wichita, KS 67260-0124

Kentucky

Alice Lloyd College

Pippa Passes, Kentucky
www.alc.edu
Four-year private **Federal Code: 001951**

College costs. Guaranteed tuition, room and board for Pell Grant-eligible students from 108-county central Appalachian service area in Kentucky, West Virginia, Virginia, Tennessee, and Ohio; guaranteed tuition for non-Pell-eligible students from this area; $4,790 tuition for students outside area.

	Living at home	On-campus
Tuition and fees (2002-2003):	$7,150	$7,150
Room and board:		$3,180
Books and supplies:	$850	$850
Personal expenses:	$1,240	$1,240
Transportation:	$1,600	$640

Undergraduate aid. Need-based: Average financial aid package for full-time students was $7,871. 77% awarded as scholarships/grants, 23% as loans/jobs. Need-based aid available for part-time students. **Non-need-based:** 68% awarded as scholarships/grants, 32% as loans/jobs. Scholarships based on athletics, minority status, state/district residency. **Student debt:** 28% of graduating class borrowed to fund education; average debt was $4,235. **Additional information:** All students receive financial aid through student work program. No student denied admission because of inability to pay. All full-time students required to work minimum of 10 hours per week.

Freshman aid. Need-based: Out of 188 full-time freshmen, 188 applied for aid; 157 were judged to have need; of these 157 received aid. Average package met 70% of need. 17 students had full need met. Average scholarship/grant was $6,456; average loan $209. **Non-need based:** 11 full-time freshmen with need received non-need scholarships; 30 without need received awards; 6 received athletic scholarships.

Merit scholarships. Students meeting admissions criteria from one of 108 counties in West Virginia, Virginia, Tennessee, Ohio and Kentucky are guaranteed free tuition. Students chosen based on admission application.

Policies to reduce costs. Tuition/fee waivers for minority students, employees and their families. Credit/placement for qualifying scores on AP, IB, CLEP examinations. Work study available nights and weekends.

Payment plans. Credit card payment.

Application procedures. FAFSA required. Priority date 3/15; no closing date. Applicants notified on rolling basis starting 4/1, must reply within 6 week(s) of notification. **Transfers:** Closing date 3/15. Tuition guarantee only for total of 10 semesters of course work from all schools attended.

Contact. **Financial aid office:** (606) 368-6059
Nancy Melton, Director of Financial Aid
100 Purpose Road
Pippa Passes, KY 41844

Asbury College

Wilmore, Kentucky
www.asbury.edu
Four-year private **Federal Code: 001952**

	Living at home	On-campus
Tuition and fees:	$16,500	$16,500
Room and board:		$4,204
Board only:	$1,155	
Books and supplies:	$500	$500
Personal expenses:	$940	$940
Transportation:	$410	$865

Undergraduate aid. Need-based: Average financial aid package for full-time students was $10,317; for part-time $5,520. 48% awarded as scholarships/grants, 52% as loans/jobs. **Non-need-based:** 64% awarded as scholarships/grants, 36% as loans/jobs. Scholarships based on academics, alumni affiliation, leadership, minority status, music/drama. **Student debt:** 67% of graduating class borrowed to fund education; average debt was $18,101.

Freshman aid. Need-based: Out of 331 full-time freshmen, 281 applied for aid; 222 were judged to have need; of these 221 received aid. Average package met 74% of need. 37 students had full need met. Average scholarship/grant was $5,952; average loan $3,143. **Non-need based:** 90 full-time freshmen with need received non-need scholarships; 55 without need received awards.

Policies to reduce costs. Tuition/fee waivers for children of alumni, senior citizens, minority students, family members, employees and their families. Credit/placement for qualifying scores on AP, IB, CLEP examinations. Work study available nights, weekends and for part-time students.

Payment plans. Installment, deferred payment.

Application procedures. FAFSA, institutional form required. Priority date 3/1; no closing date. Applicants notified on rolling basis starting 3/1, must reply within 2 week(s) of notification.

Contact. **Financial aid office:** (859) 858-3511 ext. 2195
Patricia Burns, Director of Financial Aid
One Macklem Drive
Wilmore, KY 40390-1198

Beckfield College

Florence, Kentucky
www.beckfieldcollege.com
Two-year proprietary **Federal Code: 016726**

College costs. Technology fee, where applicable, varies with program.

	Living at home
Tuition and fees:	$7,191
Books and supplies:	$950

Undergraduate aid. All financial aid based on need. Need-based aid available for full-time and part-time students. **Additional information:** Deadline for filing of financial aid forms is end of first week of classes.

Policies to reduce costs. Credit/placement for qualifying scores on IB examinations.

Payment plans. Credit card, installment payment.

Application procedures. FAFSA required. Applicants notified on rolling basis. **Transfers:** No deadline.

Contact. **Financial aid office:** (859) 371-9393
Robert Beck, President
PO Box 143
Florence, KY 41022-0143

Bellarmine University

Louisville, Kentucky
www.bellarmine.edu
Four-year private **Federal Code: 001954**

	Living at home	On-campus
Tuition and fees:	$18,490	$18,490
Room and board:		$5,620
Board only:	$1,500	
Books and supplies:	$700	$700
Personal expenses:	$1,100	$1,100
Transportation:	$770	$600

Undergraduate aid. Need-based: Need-based aid available for full-time and part-time students. **Non-need-based:** Scholarships based on academics, alumni affiliation, art, athletics, leadership, minority status, music/drama, religious affiliation, state/district residency.

Merit scholarships. Merit Awards available to all applicants meeting academic requirements; ranging from $3,000 to full-tuition annually.

Policies to reduce costs. Tuition/fee waivers for senior citizens, employees and their families. Credit/placement for qualifying scores on AP, IB, CLEP examinations. Work study available nights and weekends.

Payment plans. Credit card, deferred payment.

Application procedures. FAFSA required. Priority date 3/1; no closing date. Applicants notified on rolling basis starting 3/15, must reply by 5/1 or within 3 week(s) of notification. **Transfers:** No deadline.

Contact. **Financial aid office:** (502) 452-8124
David Wuinee, Assistant Vice President for Enrollment Management
2001 Newburg Road
Louisville, KY 40205

Berea College

Berea, Kentucky
www.berea.edu
Four-year private **Federal Code: 001955**

College costs (2002-2003). Only those with financial need admitted. All students receive 4-year full tuition scholarship. Students required to earn a portion of their expenses by working a minimum of 10 hours per week on campus. Required fees, $207. Room/board: $4,303. Books/supplies: $675. Personal expenses: $1,425. Transportation: $290.

Undergraduate aid. All financial aid based on need. Average financial aid package for full-time students was $21,438. 93% awarded as scholarships/grants, 7% as loans/jobs. **Student debt:** 78% of graduating class borrowed to fund education; average debt was $6,233.

Freshman aid. Out of 356 full-time freshmen, 356 applied for aid; 356 were judged to have need; of these 356 received aid. Average package met 92% of need. 125 students had full need met. Average scholarship/grant was $23,529; average loan $1,144.

Policies to reduce costs. Credit/placement for qualifying scores on AP, IB, CLEP examinations.

Application procedures. FAFSA required. Priority date 4/15; closing date 8/1. Applicants notified on rolling basis starting 5/1. **Transfers:** Financial aid transcript from previous school(s) must be received before awarding aid.

Contact. **Financial aid office:** (859) 985-3310
Bryan Erslan, Director of Student Financial Services
CPO 2220
Berea, KY 40404

Brescia University

Owensboro, Kentucky
www.brescia.edu
Four-year private **Federal Code: 001958**

	Living at home	On-campus
Tuition and fees (2002-2003):	$10,130	$10,130
Room and board:		$4,540
Board only:	$2,280	
Books and supplies:	$800	$800
Personal expenses:	$1,800	$1,800
Transportation:	$755	$754

Undergraduate aid. Need-based: Need-based aid available for full-time and part-time students. **Non-need-based:** Scholarships based on academics, athletics, state/district residency.

Policies to reduce costs. Tuition/fee waivers for children of alumni, senior citizens, employees and their families. Credit/placement for qualifying scores on AP, CLEP examinations. Work study available nights and weekends.

Payment plans. Credit card, installment, deferred payment.

Application procedures. FAFSA required. Priority date 3/1; no closing date. Applicants notified on rolling basis, must reply within 2 week(s) of notification. **Transfers:** No deadline.

Contact. **Financial aid office:** (270) 686-4290
Martie Ruxer-Boyken, Director of Financial Aid
717 Frederica Street
Owensboro, KY 42301-3023

Campbellsville University

Campbellsville, Kentucky
www.campbellsville.edu
Four-year private **Federal Code: 001959**

	Living at home	On-campus
Tuition and fees (2002-2003):	$11,340	$11,340
Room and board:		$4,740
Board only:	$3,600	
Books and supplies:	$800	$800
Personal expenses:	$1,330	$1,330
Transportation:	$1,150	$550

Undergraduate aid. Need-based: Average financial aid package for full-time students was $8,798; for part-time $9,083. 66% awarded as scholarships/grants, 34% as loans/jobs. **Non-need-based:** 74% awarded as scholarships/grants, 26% as loans/jobs. **Additional information:** Matching scholarships available for students whose church contributes $200 annually. Performance grants available to members of marching band.

Freshman aid. Need-based: Out of 327 full-time freshmen, 291 applied for aid; 244 were judged to have need; of these 244 received aid. Average package met 71% of need. 39 students had full need met. Average scholarship/grant was $7,019; average loan $2,154. **Non-need based:** 23 full-time freshmen with need received non-need scholarships; 82 without need received awards; 49 received athletic scholarships.

Policies to reduce costs. Tuition/fee waivers for adults, senior citizens, family of clergy, employees and their families. Credit/placement for qualifying scores on AP, CLEP examinations. Work study available nights and weekends.

Payment plans. Credit card, installment, deferred payment.

Application procedures. FAFSA required. Priority date 4/1; no closing date. Applicants notified on rolling basis starting 5/15.

Contact. **Financial aid office:** (270) 789-5013
Chris Tolson, Director of Financial Aid
1University Drive
Campbellsville, KY 42718-2799

Centre College

Danville, Kentucky
www.centre.edu
Four-year private **Federal Code: 001961**

	Living at home	On-campus
Tuition and fees:	$20,400	$20,400
Room and board:		$6,900
Board only:	$1,050	
Books and supplies:	$700	$700
Personal expenses:	$350	$700
Transportation:	$200	

Undergraduate aid. Need-based: Average financial aid package for full-time students was $19,585; for part-time $16,541. 79% awarded as scholarships/grants, 21% as loans/jobs. **Non-need-based:** 80% awarded as scholarships/grants, 20% as loans/jobs. Scholarships based on academics, alumni affiliation, minority status, music/drama. **Student debt:** 54% of graduating class borrowed to fund education; average debt was $14,300.

Freshman aid. Need-based: Out of 298 full-time freshmen, 249 applied for aid; 210 were judged to have need; of these 210 received aid. Average package met 100% of need. 119 students had full need met. Average scholarship/grant was $13,949; average loan $2,702. **Non-need based:** 183 full-time freshmen with need received non-need scholarships; 40 without need received awards.

Merit scholarships. Institutional Merit Award; applications must be on file by February 1; ranging from $4,500 to full tuition; renewable. Program of Music and Drama Scholarships; $4,500; available to Centre Fellows and Kentucky Governor's Scholars.

Policies to reduce costs. Tuition/fee waivers for employees and their families. Credit/placement for qualifying scores on AP, IB examinations.

Payment plans. Credit card, installment payment.

Application procedures. FAFSA, institutional form required. Closing date 3/1. Applicants notified by 4/1, must reply by 5/1 or within 2 week(s) of notification. **Transfers:** Priority date 3/1; no deadline. Financial aid transcript required.

Contact. **Financial aid office:** (859) 238-5365
Elaine Larson, Director of Student Financial Planning
600 West Walnut Street
Danville, KY 40422-1394

Clear Creek Baptist Bible College

Pineville, Kentucky
www.ccbbc.edu
Four-year private **Federal Code: 017044**

	Living at home	On-campus
Tuition and fees (2002-2003):	$4,340	$4,340
Room and board:		$3,500
Board only:	$750	
Books and supplies:	$200	$200
Personal expenses:	$960	$1,600
Transportation:	$3,840	$3,840

Undergraduate aid. Need-based: Need-based aid available for full-time students. **Non-need-based:** Scholarships based on academics.

Policies to reduce costs. Tuition/fee waivers for employees and their families.

Payment plans. Credit card, installment payment.

Application procedures. FAFSA, institutional form required. Priority date 6/30; no closing date. Applicants notified on rolling basis, must reply by 8/1. **Transfers:** Priority date 7/1; no deadline.

Contact. Financial aid office: (606) 337-3196 ext. 142
Sam Risner, Director of Financial Aid
300 Clear Creek Road
Pineville, KY 40977-9754

Cumberland College

Williamsburg, Kentucky
www.cumberlandcollege.edu
Four-year private **Federal Code: 001962**

	Living at home	On-campus
Tuition and fees:	$11,458	$11,458
Room and board:		$4,926
Books and supplies:	$800	$800
Transportation:	$700	$700

Undergraduate aid. Need-based: Average financial aid package for full-time students was $11,750; for part-time $9,272. 53% awarded as scholarships/grants, 47% as loans/jobs. **Non-need-based:** 78% awarded as scholarships/grants, 22% as loans/jobs. Scholarships based on academics, alumni affiliation, art, athletics, leadership, music/drama, religious affiliation, state/district residency. **Student debt:** 68% of graduating class borrowed to fund education; average debt was $16,709.

Freshman aid. Need-based: Out of 393 full-time freshmen, 393 applied for aid; 330 were judged to have need; of these 330 received aid. Average package met 90% of need. 131 students had full need met. Average scholarship/grant was $4,725; average loan $3,038. **Non-need based:** 320 full-time freshmen with need received non-need scholarships; 48 without need received awards; 125 received athletic scholarships.

Policies to reduce costs. Tuition/fee waivers for children of alumni, senior citizens, minority students, family members, unemployed or children of unemployed, family of clergy, employees and their families. Credit/placement for qualifying scores on AP, IB, CLEP examinations. Work study available nights and weekends.

Payment plans. Credit card, installment, deferred payment.

Application procedures. FAFSA required. Priority date 3/1; no closing date. Applicants notified on rolling basis starting 4/1, must reply within 2 week(s) of notification.

Contact. Financial aid office: (800) 532-0828
Jack Stanfill, Director of Financial Planning
6178 College Station Drive
Williamsburg, KY 40769

Daymar College

Owensboro, Kentucky
www.daymarcollege.com
Two-year proprietary **Federal Code: 009313**

College costs. $65 technology fee per course.

	Living at home
Tuition and fees (2002-2003):	$6,425
Per-credit charge:	$175
Books and supplies:	$933
Transportation:	$493

Undergraduate aid. All financial aid based on need. Average financial aid package for full-time students was $5,425. 33% awarded as scholarships/grants, 67% as loans/jobs. Need-based aid available for part-time students. **Student debt:** 65% of graduating class borrowed to fund education; average debt was $15,000.

Policies to reduce costs. Tuition/fee waivers for senior citizens, employees and their families. Tuition at time of enrollment guaranteed for 2 years; credit/placement for qualifying scores on AP examinations. Work study available for part-time students.

Payment plans. Credit card, installment payment.

Application procedures. FAFSA required. No deadline. Applicants notified on rolling basis. **Transfers:** No deadline.

Contact. Financial aid office: (270) 926-4040
Linda Blackburn, Financial Aid Director
Box 1350
Owensboro, KY 42301

Daymar College: Louisville

Louisville, Kentucky
Two-year proprietary **Federal Code: 009313**

	Living at home
Tuition and fees (2002-2003):	$6,210
Books and supplies:	$950

Contact. Al Clements, Director
4400 Breckinridge Lane, Suite 415
Louisville, KY 40218

Elizabethtown Community College

Elizabethtown, Kentucky
www.elizabethtown.kctcs.edu
Two-year public **Federal Code: 001991**

	Living at home
Tuition and fees (2002-2003):	$1,920
Out-of-state:	$5,760
Per-credit charge:	$64
Per-credit out-of-state:	$192
Books and supplies:	$400

Undergraduate aid. Need-based: Need-based aid available for full-time and part-time students.

Policies to reduce costs. Tuition/fee waivers for senior citizens, employees and their families. Credit/placement for qualifying scores on AP, CLEP examinations.

Payment plans. Credit card, deferred payment.

Application procedures. FAFSA required. Priority date 4/1; no closing date. Applicants notified on rolling basis starting 6/1, must reply within 2 week(s) of notification.

Contact. Betty Pierce, Director of Financial Aid
600 College Street Road
Elizabethtown, KY 42701

Georgetown College

Georgetown, Kentucky
www.georgetowncollege.edu
Four-year private **Federal Code: 001964**

	Living at home	On-campus
Tuition and fees:	$16,370	$16,370
Room and board:		$5,180
Board only:	$1,825	
Books and supplies:	$650	$650
Personal expenses:	$1,000	$1,000
Transportation:	$450	$450

Undergraduate aid. Need-based: Average financial aid package for full-time students was $14,518. 79% awarded as scholarships/grants, 21% as loans/jobs. **Non-need-based:** 67% awarded as scholarships/grants, 33% as loans/jobs. Scholarships based on academics, art, athletics, leadership, minority status, music/drama, religious affiliation. **Student debt:** 69% of graduating class borrowed to fund education; average debt was $14,582.

Freshman aid. Need-based: Out of 327 full-time freshmen, 324 applied for aid; 220 were judged to have need; of these 220 received aid. Average package met 91% of need. 88 students had full need met. Average scholarship/grant was $11,054; average loan $2,629. **Non-need based:** 216 full-time freshmen with need received non-need scholarships; 104 without need received awards; 41 received athletic scholarships.

Policies to reduce costs. Tuition/fee waivers for employees and their families. Credit/placement for qualifying scores on AP, IB, CLEP examinations.

Payment plans. Credit card, installment, deferred payment.

Application procedures. FAFSA required. Priority date 2/15; no closing date. Applicants notified on rolling basis starting 3/15, must reply by 5/1. Early decision closing date 11/15.

Contact. Rhyan Conyers, Director of Student Financial Planning
400 East College Street
Georgetown, KY 40324

Hazard Community College

Hazard, Kentucky
www.hazard.kctcs.edu
Two-year public **Federal Code: 006962**

	Living at home
Tuition and fees (2002-2003):	$1,920
Out-of-state:	$5,760
Per-credit charge:	$64
Per-credit out-of-state:	$192
Board only:	$3,440
Books and supplies:	$800
Personal expenses:	$800
Transportation:	$1,040

Undergraduate aid. All financial aid based on need. Need-based aid available for full-time and part-time students.

Policies to reduce costs. Tuition/fee waivers for senior citizens. Credit/placement for qualifying scores on AP, CLEP examinations.

Payment plans. Credit card, installment payment.

Application procedures. FAFSA required. Priority date 4/1; no closing date. Applicants notified on rolling basis starting 6/15, must reply within 2 week(s) of notification.

Contact. **Financial aid office:** (606) 436-5721 ext. 327
Chuck Anderson, Financial Aid Director
One Community College Drive
Hazard, KY 41701

Henderson Community College

Henderson, Kentucky
www.hencc.kctcs.edu
Two-year public **Federal Code: 001993**

	Living at home
Tuition and fees (2002-2003):	$1,920
Out-of-state:	$5,760
Per-credit charge:	$64
Per-credit out-of-state:	$192
Books and supplies:	$500

Policies to reduce costs. Tuition/fee waivers for senior citizens. Credit/placement for qualifying scores on AP, CLEP examinations.

Application procedures. FAFSA required. No deadline. Applicants notified on rolling basis starting 5/1.

Contact. **Financial aid office:** (270) 827-1867
Fern Bishop, Coordinator of Financial Aid
2660 South Green Street
Henderson, KY 42420

Hopkinsville Community College

Hopkinsville, Kentucky
www.hopkinsville.kctcs.edu
Two-year public **Federal Code: 001994**

	Living at home
Tuition and fees (2002-2003):	$1,920
Out-of-state:	$5,760
Per-credit charge:	$64
Per-credit out-of-state:	$192
Books and supplies:	$450
Personal expenses:	$1,840

Undergraduate aid. **Need-based:** Need-based aid available for full-time and part-time students. **Non-need-based:** Scholarships based on academics, leadership, minority status, state/district residency. **Additional information:** ACT required for academic scholarships.

Policies to reduce costs. Tuition/fee waivers for senior citizens, employees and their families. Credit/placement for qualifying scores on AP, CLEP examinations.

Payment plans. Credit card, installment payment.

Application procedures. FAFSA required. No deadline. Applicants notified on rolling basis starting 7/1. **Transfers:** No deadline.

Contact. **Financial aid office:** (270) 886-3921 ext. 6189
Vincent Shykes, Director
PO Box 2100
Hopkinsville, KY 42241

ITT Technical Institute: Louisville

Louisville, Kentucky
www.itt-tech.edu
Two-year proprietary

College costs. Total program varies depending on course of study. Per-credit-hour charge: $347.

Policies to reduce costs. Tuition/fee waivers for employees and their families. Tuition at time of enrollment guaranteed for 2 years.

Payment plans. Credit card, installment payment.

Application procedures. FAFSA, institutional form required. No deadline. Applicants notified on rolling basis.

Contact. Karen Myers, Director of Finance
10509 Timberwood Circle
Louisville, KY 40223

Jefferson Community College

Louisville, Kentucky
www.jcc.kctcs.edu
Two-year public **Federal Code: 006961**

	Living at home
Tuition and fees (2002-2003):	$1,920
Out-of-state:	$5,760
Per-credit charge:	$64
Per-credit out-of-state:	$192
Books and supplies:	$450
Personal expenses:	$848
Transportation:	$460

Undergraduate aid. **Need-based:** Need-based aid available for full-time and part-time students. **Non-need-based:** Scholarships based on academics, art, minority status.

Policies to reduce costs. Tuition/fee waivers for senior citizens, employees and their families. Credit/placement for qualifying scores on AP, CLEP examinations.

Payment plans. Credit card, installment payment.

Application procedures. FAFSA, institutional form required. Priority date 3/15; no closing date. Applicants notified on rolling basis starting 6/15, must reply within 3 week(s) of notification. **Transfers:** No deadline.

Contact. **Financial aid office:** (502) 213-2141
Angela Johnson, Financial Aid Officer
109 East Broadway
Louisville, KY 40202

Kentucky Christian College

Grayson, Kentucky
www.kcc.edu
Four-year private **Federal Code: 001965**

	Living at home	On-campus
Tuition and fees (2002-2003):	$8,774	$8,774
Room and board:		$4,128
Books and supplies:	$800	$800
Personal expenses:	$1,086	$1,696
Transportation:	$1,107	$834

Undergraduate aid. **Need-based:** Need-based aid available for full-time and part-time students. **Non-need-based:** Scholarships based on academics, alumni affiliation, leadership, music/drama, religious affiliation.

Policies to reduce costs. Prepayment discount; credit/placement for qualifying scores on AP, CLEP examinations.

Payment plans. Credit card, installment payment.

Application procedures. FAFSA, institutional form required. Priority date 4/1; no closing date. Applicants notified on rolling basis starting 5/1, must reply within 2 week(s) of notification. **Transfers:** No deadline.

Contact. **Financial aid office:** (606) 474-3226
Jennie Bender, Director of Financial Aid
100 Academic Parkway
Grayson, KY 41143-2205

Kentucky Mountain Bible College

Vancleve, Kentucky
www.kmbc.edu
Four-year private **Federal Code: 030021**

	Living at home	On-campus
Tuition and fees (2002-2003):	$4,630	$4,630
Room and board:		$3,000
Books and supplies:	$400	$400
Personal expenses:	$250	$250
Transportation:	$900	$900

Undergraduate aid. All financial aid based on need. Need-based aid available for full-time students.

Policies to reduce costs. Credit/placement for qualifying scores on CLEP examinations.

Application procedures. FAFSA required. Priority date 4/1; closing date 6/30. Applicants notified on rolling basis, must reply by 7/1. **Transfers:** No deadline.

Contact. **Financial aid office:** (606) 693-5000 ext. 142
Jewel MacGregor, Director of Financial Aid
Box 10
Vancleve, KY 41385

Kentucky Wesleyan College

Owensboro, Kentucky
www.kwc.edu
Four-year private **Federal Code: 001969**

	Living at home	On-campus
Tuition and fees (2002-2003):	$11,400	$11,400
Room and board:		$5,910
Board only:	$3,060	
Books and supplies:	$800	$800
Personal expenses:	$850	$850
Transportation:	$850	$350

Undergraduate aid. **Need-based:** Average financial aid package for full-time students was $10,676; for part-time $4,601. 75% awarded as scholarships/grants, 25% as loans/jobs. **Non-need-based:** 63% awarded as scholarships/grants, 37% as loans/jobs.

Freshman aid. **Need-based:** Average package met 88% of need. Average scholarship/grant was $9,289; average loan $22.

Merit scholarships. On-campus scholarship competitions (held in fall and spring) allow students to compete for scholarships that range from $1,000 to full tuition. Music and theater students must audition on campus. Art scholarship candidates must provide portfolio for review.

Policies to reduce costs. Tuition/fee waivers for senior citizens, family of clergy, employees and their families. Credit/placement for qualifying scores on AP, IB, CLEP examinations.

Payment plans. Credit card, installment, deferred payment.

Application procedures. FAFSA, institutional form required. Priority date 3/1; no closing date. Applicants notified on rolling basis starting 3/15, must reply within 3 week(s) of notification. **Transfers:** Priority date 3/15; no deadline.

Contact. **Financial aid office:** (800) 999-0592
Vivian Rinaldo, Financial Aid Officer
3000 Frederica Street
Owensboro, KY 42302-1039

Lexington Community College

Lexington, Kentucky
www.uky.edu/lcc
Two-year public **Federal Code: 009707**

	Living at home
Tuition and fees (2002-2003):	$2,684
Out-of-state:	$7,904
Per-credit charge:	$73
Per-credit out-of-state:	$247
Books and supplies:	$500
Personal expenses:	$1,070
Transportation:	$500

Undergraduate aid. **Need-based:** Need-based aid available for full-time and part-time students. **Non-need-based:** Scholarships based on academics, minority status.

Policies to reduce costs. Tuition/fee waivers for senior citizens, employees and their families. Credit/placement for qualifying scores on AP, CLEP examinations. Work study available nights and for part-time students.

Payment plans. Credit card, installment payment.

Application procedures. FAFSA, institutional form required. Priority date 4/1; no closing date. Applicants notified on rolling basis starting 6/1, must reply within 3 week(s) of notification.

Contact. **Financial aid office:** (859) 257-4872
Michael Barlow, Director of Financial Aid
200 Oswald Building, Cooper Drive
Lexington, KY 40506-0235

Lindsey Wilson College

Columbia, Kentucky
www.lindsey.edu
Four-year private **Federal Code: 001972**

	Living at home	On-campus
Tuition and fees:	$12,602	$12,602
Room and board:		$5,484
Books and supplies:	$400	$400
Personal expenses:	$800	$800
Transportation:	$975	$500

Undergraduate aid. All financial aid based on need. Need-based aid available for full-time and part-time students.

Policies to reduce costs. Tuition/fee waivers for family of clergy, employees and their families. Credit/placement for qualifying scores on AP, CLEP examinations.

Payment plans. Installment, deferred payment.

Application procedures. FAFSA, institutional form required. Priority date 4/15; no closing date. Applicants notified on rolling basis starting 5/1, must reply within 2 week(s) of notification.

Contact. Denise Fudge, Vice President of Enrollment Management
210 Lindsey Wilson Street
Columbia, KY 42728

Louisville Technical Institute

Louisville, Kentucky
www.louisvilletech.com
Two-year proprietary **Federal Code: 012088**

College costs. Computer graphic design program tuition: $12,285; fees: $1,400.

	Living at home
Tuition and fees (2002-2003):	$11,995
Books and supplies:	$950
Transportation:	$1,200

Undergraduate aid. **Need-based:** Need-based aid available for full-time and part-time students. **Non-need-based:** Scholarships based on art, job skills.

Merit scholarships. Academic Scholarships; based on class rank, high school GPA, essay; up to $4,000. Scholarship Day Competition; based upon testing scores; up to $2,000. Skills Competition; based upon open competition in electronics, drafting, and art skills; up to $4,000.

Policies to reduce costs. Tuition/fee waivers for employees and their families. Tuition at time of enrollment guaranteed for 2 years; credit/placement for qualifying scores on AP, CLEP examinations. Work study available nights.

Payment plans. Credit card, installment, deferred payment.

Application procedures. FAFSA required. No deadline. Applicants notified on rolling basis, must reply within 2 week(s) of notification. **Transfers:** No deadline.

Contact. **Financial aid office:** (502) 456-6509
Lisa Bailey, Financial Planning Director
3901 Atkinson Square Drive
Louisville, KY 40218-4524

Madisonville Community College

Madisonville, Kentucky
www.madcc.kctcs.net
Two-year public **Federal Code: 009010**

	Living at home
Tuition and fees (2002-2003):	$1,920
Out-of-state:	$5,760
Per-credit charge:	$64
Per-credit out-of-state:	$192
Books and supplies:	$500
Personal expenses:	$1,000
Transportation:	$540

Undergraduate aid. **Need-based:** Need-based aid available for full-time and part-time students. **Non-need-based:** Scholarships based on minority status. **Additional information:** Students are encouraged to file early and visit financial aid department for advance calculations.

Merit scholarships. Valedictorian Scholarship, $2,500/year, based on GPA, class rank, number awarded varies. John T. Smith Scholarship, $1,060/year, number awarded varies.

Policies to reduce costs. Tuition/fee waivers for senior citizens, minority students, unemployed or children of unemployed, employees and their families. Credit/placement for qualifying scores on AP, CLEP examinations. Work study available nights, weekends and for part-time students.

Payment plans. Credit card, deferred payment.

Application procedures. FAFSA, institutional form required. Priority date 3/15; no closing date. Applicants notified on rolling basis, must reply within 3 week(s) of notification. **Transfers:** Priority date 3/15; no deadline.

Contact. **Financial aid office:** (270) 821-6514
Stanley Lewis, Director of Financial Aid
2000 College Drive
Madisonville, KY 42431

Maysville Community College

Maysville, Kentucky
www.maycc.kctcs.net
Two-year public **Federal Code: 006960**

	Living at home
Tuition and fees (2002-2003):	$1,920
Out-of-state:	$5,760
Per-credit charge:	$64
Per-credit out-of-state:	$192
Books and supplies:	$800
Personal expenses:	$950
Transportation:	$514

Undergraduate aid. **Need-based:** 95% awarded as scholarships/grants, 5% as loans/jobs. Need-based aid available for part-time students. **Non-need-based:** 83% awarded as scholarships/grants, 17% as loans/jobs. Scholarships based on academics.

Policies to reduce costs. Tuition/fee waivers for senior citizens, employees and their families. Credit/placement for qualifying scores on AP, CLEP examinations. Work study available nights.

Payment plans. Credit card, deferred payment.

Application procedures. FAFSA, institutional form required. Priority date 4/1; no closing date. Applicants notified on rolling basis starting 3/1, must reply within 3 week(s) of notification.

Contact. **Financial aid office:** (606) 759-7141 ext. 6179
Linda Cook, Financial Aid Coordinator
1755 US 68
Maysville, KY 41056

Mid-Continent College

Mayfield, Kentucky
www.midcontinent.edu
Four-year private **Federal Code: 025762**

	Living at home	On-campus
Tuition and fees (2002-2003):	$9,000	$9,000
Room and board:		$4,900
Books and supplies:	$800	$800
Personal expenses:	$2,400	$2,400
Transportation:	$1,000	$1,000

Undergraduate aid. **Need-based:** Average financial aid package for full-time students was $5,685; for part-time $4,591. 57% awarded as scholarships/grants, 43% as loans/jobs. **Non-need-based:** 10% awarded as scholarships/grants, 90% as loans/jobs. Scholarships based on academics. **Student debt:** 75% of graduating class borrowed to fund education; average debt was $12,000.

Freshman aid. **Need-based:** Out of 77 full-time freshmen, 77 applied for aid; 50 were judged to have need; of these 50 received aid. Average package met 42% of need. 5 students had full need met. Average scholarship/grant was $4,070; average loan $1,938. **Non-need based:** 2 full-time freshmen with need received non-need scholarships; 16 without need received awards.

Policies to reduce costs. Tuition/fee waivers for employees and their families. Credit/placement for qualifying scores on AP, CLEP examinations. Work study available nights, weekends and for part-time students.

Payment plans. Credit card payment.

Application procedures. FAFSA, institutional form required. Priority date 3/15; closing date 5/30. Applicants notified on rolling basis starting 4/1. **Transfers:** No deadline. Scholarship priority given to students who return FAFSA by March 15.

Contact. Andy Stratton, Vice President for Business Operations
99 Powell Road East
Mayfield, KY 42066-0357

Morehead State University

Morehead, Kentucky
www.moreheadstate.edu
Four-year public **Federal Code: 001976**

	Living at home	On-campus
Tuition and fees (2002-2003):	$2,926	$2,926
Out-of-state:	$7,780	$7,780
Room and board:		$4,000
Books and supplies:	$500	$500
Personal expenses:	$800	$800
Transportation:	$850	$300

Undergraduate aid. **Need-based:** Average financial aid package for full-time students was $6,387; for part-time $4,428. 63% awarded as scholarships/grants, 37% as loans/jobs. **Non-need-based:** 51% awarded as scholarships/grants, 49% as loans/jobs. Scholarships based on academics, alumni affiliation, athletics, leadership, minority status, music/drama, state/district residency. **Student debt:** 55% of graduating class borrowed to fund education; average debt was $13,647.

Freshman aid. **Need-based:** Out of 1,492 full-time freshmen, 1,309 applied for aid; 988 were judged to have need; of these 984 received aid. Average package met 92% of need. 434 students had full need met. Average scholarship/grant was $3,723; average loan $2,174. **Non-need based:** 752 full-time freshmen with need received non-need scholarships; 360 without need received awards; 34 received athletic scholarships.

Policies to reduce costs. Tuition/fee waivers for children of alumni, senior citizens, family members, employees and their families. Credit/placement for qualifying scores on AP, CLEP examinations.

Payment plans. Credit card, installment, deferred payment.

Application procedures. FAFSA, institutional form required. Priority date 3/15; no closing date. Applicants notified on rolling basis. **Transfers:** Transfer scholarships available.

Contact. **Financial aid office:** (606) 783-2011
Carol Becker, Director of Financial Aid
HM 301
Morehead, KY 40351

Murray State University

Murray, Kentucky
www.murraystate.edu
Four-year public **Federal Code: 001977**

College costs. Regional tuition plan available for new students from Illinois, Indiana, Missouri, Tennessee (costs vary with region).

	Living at home	On-campus
Tuition and fees (2002-2003):	$3,032	$3,032
Out-of-state:	$8,112	$8,112
Room and board:		$4,420
Board only:	$2,320	
Books and supplies:	$700	$700
Personal expenses:	$790	$790
Transportation:	$350	$350

Undergraduate aid. **Need-based:** Average financial aid package for full-time students was $4,575; for part-time $4,005. 42% awarded as scholarships/grants, 58% as loans/jobs. **Non-need-based:** 46% awarded as scholarships/grants, 54% as loans/jobs. Scholarships based on academics, alumni affiliation, art, athletics, leadership, minority status, music/drama, state/district residency. **Student debt:** 54% of graduating class borrowed to fund education; average debt was $14,152. **Additional information:** Tuition discount for children and grandchildren of out-of-state alumni.

Freshman aid. **Need-based:** Average package met 95% of need. Average scholarship/grant was $2,140; average loan $1,845.

Merit scholarships. Tuition discount for children and grandchildren of out-of-state alumni; $2,750. Regional Tuition for students from certain counties in Illinois, Tennessee, Missouri, and Indiana who meet admission requirements.

Policies to reduce costs. Tuition/fee waivers for children of alumni, senior citizens, minority students, employees and their families. Credit/placement for qualifying scores on AP, CLEP examinations. Work study available nights, weekends and for part-time students.

Payment plans. Credit card, installment, deferred payment.

Application procedures. FAFSA, institutional form required. Priority date 4/1; no closing date. Applicants notified on rolling basis starting 4/15. **Transfers:** Priority date 4/1; no deadline.

Contact. **Financial aid office:** (270) 762-2546
Charles Vinson, Director of Financial Aid
PO Box 9
Murray, KY 42071

National College of Business & Technology: Danville

Danville, Kentucky
www.ncbt.edu
Two-year proprietary **Federal Code: 010489**

	Living at home
Tuition and fees (projected):	$6,236
Per-credit charge:	$162
Books and supplies:	$1,200

Undergraduate aid. All financial aid based on need. Need-based aid available for full-time and part-time students.

Policies to reduce costs. Tuition/fee waivers for employees and their families.

Payment plans. Credit card payment.

Application procedures. FAFSA required. No deadline. Applicants notified on rolling basis. **Transfers:** No deadline.

Contact. **Financial aid office:** (540) 986-1800
Pamela Cotton, Director of Financial Aid and Compliance Officer
PO Box 6400
Roanoke, VA 24017

National College of Business & Technology: Florence

Florence, Kentucky
www.ncbt.edu
Two-year proprietary **Federal Code: 010489**

	Living at home
Tuition and fees (projected):	$6,186
Per-credit charge:	$162
Books and supplies:	$1,200

Undergraduate aid. All financial aid based on need. Need-based aid available for full-time and part-time students.

Policies to reduce costs. Tuition/fee waivers for employees and their families.

Payment plans. Credit card payment.

Application procedures. FAFSA required. No deadline. Applicants notified on rolling basis. **Transfers:** No deadline.

Contact. **Financial aid office:** (540) 986-1800
Pamela Cotton, Director of Financial Aid and Compliance Officer
PO Box 6400
Roanoke, VA 24017

National College of Business & Technology: Lexington

Lexington, Kentucky
www.ncbt.edu
Two-year proprietary **Federal Code: 010489**

	Living at home
Tuition and fees (projected):	$6,186
Per-credit charge:	$162
Books and supplies:	$1,200

Undergraduate aid. All financial aid based on need. Need-based aid available for full-time and part-time students.

Policies to reduce costs. Tuition/fee waivers for employees and their families.

Payment plans. Credit card payment.

Application procedures. FAFSA required. No deadline. Applicants notified on rolling basis. **Transfers:** No deadline.

Contact. Pamela Cotton, Director of Financial Aid and Compliance Officer
PO Box 6400
Roanoke, VA 24017

National College of Business & Technology: Pikeville

Pikeville, Kentucky
www.ncbt.edu
Two-year proprietary **Federal Code: 010489**

	Living at home
Tuition and fees (projected):	$6,186
Per-credit charge:	$162
Books and supplies:	$1,200

Undergraduate aid. All financial aid based on need. Need-based aid available for full-time and part-time students.

Policies to reduce costs. Tuition/fee waivers for employees and their families.

Payment plans. Credit card payment.

Application procedures. FAFSA required. No deadline. **Transfers:** No deadline.

Contact. **Financial aid office:** (540) 986-1800
Pamela Cotton, Director of Financial Aid and Compliance Officer
PO Box 6400
Roanoke, VA 24017

National College of Business & Technology: Richmond

Richmond, Kentucky
www.ncbt.edu
Two-year proprietary **Federal Code: 010489**

	Living at home
Tuition and fees (projected):	$6,186
Per-credit charge:	$162
Books and supplies:	$1,200

Undergraduate aid. All financial aid based on need. Need-based aid available for full-time and part-time students.

Policies to reduce costs. Tuition/fee waivers for employees and their families.

Payment plans. Credit card payment.

Application procedures. FAFSA required. No deadline. Applicants notified on rolling basis. **Transfers:** No deadline.

Contact. **Financial aid office:** (540) 986-1800
Pamela Cotton, Director of Financial Aid and Compliance Officer
PO Box 6400
Roanoke, VA 24017

Paducah Community College

Paducah, Kentucky
www.uky.edu/communitycolleges
Two-year public **Federal Code: 001979**

	Living at home
Tuition and fees (2002-2003):	$1,920
Out-of-state:	$5,760
Per-credit charge:	$64
Per-credit out-of-state:	$192
Books and supplies:	$400
Personal expenses:	$425
Transportation:	$975

Undergraduate aid. **Need-based:** Need-based aid available for full-time and part-time students.

Policies to reduce costs. Tuition/fee waivers for senior citizens. Credit/placement for qualifying scores on AP, CLEP examinations.

Payment plans. Credit card, deferred payment.

Application procedures. FAFSA required. Priority date 4/1; no closing date. Applicants notified on rolling basis starting 7/15, must reply within 4 week(s) of notification.

Contact. Betsy Irby, Financial Aid Officer
Box 7380
Paducah, KY 42002-7380

Paducah Technical College

Paducah, Kentucky
www.ptc-ky.com
Two-year proprietary **Federal Code: 013661**

College costs (2002-2003). $18,975 for 3-year program includes books, fees, tools. Personal expenses: $2,000. Transportation: $827.

Undergraduate aid. **Need-based:** Need-based aid available for full-time students.

Policies to reduce costs. Tuition at time of enrollment guaranteed for 2 years.

Payment plans. Installment payment.

Application procedures. CSS PROFILE required. No deadline. Applicants notified on rolling basis, must reply within 3 week(s) of notification.

Contact. Carolyn Watson, Financial Aid Officer
509 South 30th Street
Paducah, KY 42001

Pikeville College

Pikeville, Kentucky
www.pc.edu
Four-year private **Federal Code: 001980**

	Living at home	On-campus
Tuition and fees (2002-2003):	$9,000	$9,000
Room and board:		$4,600
Board only:	$4,500	
Books and supplies:	$1,000	$1,000
Personal expenses:	$1,500	$1,500
Transportation:	$1,500	$1,100

Undergraduate aid. **Need-based:** Average financial aid package for full-time students was $10,108; for part-time $5,539. 62% awarded as scholarships/grants, 38% as loans/jobs. **Non-need-based:** 97% awarded as scholarships/grants, 3% as loans/jobs. Scholarships based on academics, alumni affiliation, athletics, minority status, music/drama, state/district residency.

Freshman aid. **Need-based:** Out of 226 full-time freshmen, 214 applied for aid; 188 were judged to have need; of these 188 received aid. Average package met 72% of need. 42 students had full need met. Average scholarship/grant was $5,174; average loan $2,648. **Non-need based:** 200 full-time freshmen with need received non-need scholarships; 23 without need received awards; 43 received athletic scholarships.

Policies to reduce costs. Tuition/fee waivers for senior citizens, employees and their families. Credit/placement for qualifying scores on AP, CLEP examinations. Work study available nights, weekends and for part-time students.

Payment plans. Credit card, installment payment.

Application procedures. FAFSA, institutional form required. Priority date 3/15; closing date 8/23. Applicants notified on rolling basis starting 1/15, must reply within 2 week(s) of notification. **Transfers:** No deadline.

Contact. **Financial aid office:** (606) 218-5253
Judy Bradley, Financial Aid Administrator
147 Sycamore Street
Pikeville, KY 41501-1194

Prestonsburg Community College

Prestonsburg, Kentucky
www.uky.edu/communitycolleges
Two-year public **Federal Code: 001996**

	Living at home
Tuition and fees (2002-2003):	$1,920
Out-of-state:	$5,760
Per-credit charge:	$64
Per-credit out-of-state:	$192
Books and supplies:	$450
Personal expenses:	$3,000
Transportation:	$500

Undergraduate aid. **Need-based:** Need-based aid available for full-time and part-time students. **Non-need-based:** Scholarships based on academics.

Policies to reduce costs. Tuition/fee waivers for senior citizens, employees and their families. Credit/placement for qualifying scores on AP, CLEP examinations.

Payment plans. Credit card payment.

Application procedures. FAFSA, institutional form required. Priority date 4/1; no closing date. Applicants notified on rolling basis, must reply within 2 week(s) of notification. **Transfers:** Kentucky State Grant must be transferred by August 1 for fall semester, December 1 for spring semester.

Contact. Denese Atkinson, Financial Aid Director/Counselor
One Bert T. Combs Drive
Prestonsburg, KY 41653

RETS Institute of Technology

Louisville, Kentucky
www.retsaec.com
Two-year proprietary **Federal Code: 021082**

College costs (2002-2003). Cost of 23-month associate degree programs $14,720 ($640 per month). Cost of books and supplies varies with program. Personal expenses: $896. Transportation: $750.

Policies to reduce costs. Tuition/fee waivers for employees and their families. Tuition at time of enrollment guaranteed for 2 years.

Payment plans. Installment payment.

Application procedures. FAFSA required. No deadline. Applicants notified on rolling basis. **Transfers:** No deadline.

Contact. Beverly Sensenb, Financial Aid Officer
300 High Rise Drive
Louisville, KY 40213-3206

RETS Medical and Business Institute

Hopkinsville, Kentucky
Two-year proprietary
Federal Code: 014493

	Living at home
Tuition and fees (2002-2003):	$6,105
Per-credit charge:	$125
Books and supplies:	$500

Undergraduate aid. Need-based: Need-based aid available for full-time students.

Application procedures. FAFSA required. No deadline. Applicants notified on rolling basis. **Transfers:** No deadline.

Contact. Financial aid office: (800) 359-4753
Pat Bailey, Director of Financial Aid
4001 Fort Campbell Boulevard
Hopkinsville, KY 42240

St. Catharine College

St. Catharine, Kentucky
Two-year private
Federal Code: 001983

College costs. Health sciences associate degree programs: $9900 annual tuition; fees vary with program.

	Living at home	On-campus
Tuition and fees (2002-2003):	$7,180	$7,180
Per-credit charge:	$230	$230
Room and board:		$4,820
Books and supplies:	$700	$700
Personal expenses:	$1,080	$1,080
Transportation:	$850	$500

Undergraduate aid. All financial aid based on need. Need-based aid available for full-time and part-time students.

Policies to reduce costs. Tuition/fee waivers for senior citizens, employees and their families. Credit/placement for qualifying scores on AP, CLEP examinations.

Payment plans. Credit card, installment payment.

Application procedures. FAFSA, institutional form required. Priority date 3/15; no closing date. Applicants notified on rolling basis, must reply by 8/15.

Contact. Jane Moore, Financial Aid Director
2735 Bardstown Road
St. Catharine, KY 40061

Somerset Community College

Somerset, Kentucky
www.somerset.kctcs.edu
Two-year public
Federal Code: 001997

	Living at home
Tuition and fees (2002-2003):	$1,920
Out-of-state:	$5,760
Per-credit charge:	$64
Per-credit out-of-state:	$192
Books and supplies:	$500

Undergraduate aid. All financial aid based on need. Need-based aid available for full-time and part-time students.

Policies to reduce costs. Tuition/fee waivers for senior citizens, employees and their families. Credit/placement for qualifying scores on AP, CLEP examinations.

Payment plans. Credit card, installment, deferred payment.

Application procedures. FAFSA required. Priority date 4/1; no closing date. Applicants notified on rolling basis starting 6/30, must reply within 2 week(s) of notification.

Contact. Financial aid office: (606) 679-8501
Shawn Anderson, Chief Financial Aid Officer
808 Monticello Street
Somerset, KY 42501

Southeast Community College

Cumberland, Kentucky
www.uky.edu/communitycolleges/sou
Two-year public
Federal Code: 001998

	Living at home
Tuition and fees (2002-2003):	$1,920
Out-of-state:	$5,760
Per-credit charge:	$64
Per-credit out-of-state:	$192
Board only:	$1,175
Books and supplies:	$450
Personal expenses:	$1,100
Transportation:	$514

Undergraduate aid. All financial aid based on need. Need-based aid available for full-time and part-time students. **Additional information:** March 15 deadline for state financial aid.

Policies to reduce costs. Tuition/fee waivers for senior citizens. Credit/placement for qualifying scores on AP, CLEP examinations. Work study available for part-time students.

Payment plans. Credit card, installment, deferred payment.

Application procedures. FAFSA required. Priority date 3/15; no closing date. Applicants notified by 6/15, must reply within 2 week(s) of notification. **Transfers:** No deadline.

Contact. Financial aid office: (606) 589-2145
Charles Sellars, Dean of Student Affairs/Director Financial Aid
700 College Road
Cumberland, KY 40823

Southern Ohio College: Fort Mitchell

Fort Mitchell, Kentucky
www.socaec.com
Two-year proprietary
Federal Code: 005127

	Living at home
Tuition and fees (2002-2003):	$6,336
Per-credit charge:	$166
Books and supplies:	$1,116
Personal expenses:	$1,764
Transportation:	$1,854

Contact. Tracy Bumgardner, Financial Aid Officer
309 Buttermilk Pike
Fort Mitchell, KY 41017

Southwestern College of Business

Crestview Hills, Kentucky
www.southwesterncollegeofbusiness.8k.com
Two-year proprietary
Federal Code: 012128

	Living at home
Tuition and fees (2002-2003):	$6,048
Per-credit charge:	$85

Payment plans. Installment payment.

Application procedures. FAFSA required. No deadline.

Contact. Financial aid office: (859) 341-6633
Kay Boone, Director of Financial Aid
2929 South Dixie Highway
Crestview Hills, KY 41017

Spalding University

Louisville, Kentucky
www.spalding.edu
Four-year private **Federal Code: 001960**

	Living at home	On-campus
Tuition and fees (2002-2003):	$12,946	$12,946
Room and board:		$3,100
Books and supplies:	$700	$700
Transportation:	$900	

Undergraduate aid. Need-based: 53% awarded as scholarships/grants, 47% as loans/jobs. Need-based aid available for part-time students. **Non-need-based:** 50% awarded as scholarships/grants, 50% as loans/jobs. Scholarships based on academics, athletics.

Freshman aid. Need-based: Out of 239 full-time freshmen, 239 applied for aid; 171 were judged to have need; of these 90 received aid. **Non-need based:** 16 without need received awards; 20 received athletic scholarships.

Merit scholarships. Angela Garcia Residence Hall Scholarship: covers cost of a double room on campus; up to 12 awards per year; awarded to students who demonstrate leadership in campus activites, especially in residence halls.

Policies to reduce costs. Tuition/fee waivers for children of alumni, senior citizens, family members, employees and their families. Credit/placement for qualifying scores on AP, CLEP examinations. Work study available for part-time students.

Payment plans. Credit card, installment, deferred payment.

Application procedures. FAFSA required. Priority date 3/1; no closing date. Applicants notified on rolling basis starting 3/31, must reply within 2 week(s) of notification. **Transfers:** Student must not be in default on any student loan.

Contact. Lisa Flack, Director of Financial Aid
851 South Fourth Street
Louisville, KY 40203

Spencerian College

Louisville, Kentucky
www.spencerian.edu
Two-year proprietary **Federal Code: 004618**

	Living at home	On-campus
Tuition and fees (2002-2003):	$10,355	$10,355
Room only:		$3,375
Books and supplies:	$700	$700
Personal expenses:	$2,619	$2,619

Policies to reduce costs. Tuition/fee waivers for employees and their families.

Payment plans. Credit card, installment, deferred payment.

Contact. 4627 Dixie Highway
Louisville, KY 40216

Spencerian College: Lexington

Lexington, Kentucky
www.spencerian.edu
Two-year proprietary **Federal Code: 004618**

College costs (2002-2003). Tuition for full 18-month associate programs ranges from $21,840 to $23,400; tuition for diploma programs ranges from $10,920 to $14,560. General fee $395; additional $1,200 fee for computer graphic design program. On-campus housing $6,750 for full associate program. Room: $3,375. Books/supplies: $1,100. Personal expenses: $2,313. Transportation: $2,682.

Undergraduate aid. All financial aid based on need. Need-based aid available for full-time and part-time students.

Payment plans. Credit card payment.

Application procedures. FAFSA, institutional form, CSS PROFILE required. Priority date 5/1; no closing date. **Transfers:** No deadline.

Contact. Melody McClain, Director of Financial Planning
2355 Harrodsburg Road
Lexington, KY 40504

Sullivan University

Louisville, Kentucky
www.sullivan.edu
Four-year proprietary **Federal Code: 004619**

College costs (2002-2003). Tuition, fees and per-credit-hour charges vary by program. Tuition costs range from $11,280 to $12,240 per academic year. Required fees are $415. Books/supplies: $900. Personal expenses: $1,305. Transportation: $814.

Undergraduate aid. All financial aid based on need. Need-based aid available for full-time and part-time students.

Policies to reduce costs. Tuition/fee waivers for employees and their families. Credit/placement for qualifying scores on CLEP examinations.

Payment plans. Credit card, installment, deferred payment.

Application procedures. FAFSA, institutional form required. No deadline. Applicants notified on rolling basis starting 1/2. **Transfers:** No deadline.

Contact. Financial aid office: (502) 456-6504
Charlene Geiser, Financial Aid Director
3101 Bardstown Road
Louisville, KY 40232

Thomas More College

Crestview Hills, Kentucky
www.thomasmore.edu
Four-year private **Federal Code: 002001**

	Living at home	On-campus
Tuition and fees (2002-2003):	$14,600	$14,600
Room and board:		$5,300
Books and supplies:	$700	$700
Personal expenses:	$4,320	$2,870

Undergraduate aid. Need-based: Average financial aid package for full-time students was $10,671. 39% awarded as scholarships/grants, 61% as loans/jobs. Need-based aid available for part-time students. **Non-need-based:** 39% awarded as scholarships/grants, 61% as loans/jobs. Scholarships based on academics, state/district residency. **Student debt:** 39% of graduating class borrowed to fund education; average debt was $21,133.

Freshman aid. Need-based: Out of 287 full-time freshmen, 258 applied for aid; 219 were judged to have need; of these 219 received aid. Average package met 92% of need. 189 students had full need met. Average scholarship/grant was $4,648; average loan $4,632. **Non-need based:** 65 full-time freshmen with need received non-need scholarships; 57 without need received awards.

Policies to reduce costs. Tuition/fee waivers for children of alumni, minority students, employees and their families. Credit/placement for qualifying scores on AP, IB, CLEP examinations. Work study available nights and weekends.

Payment plans. Credit card payment.

Application procedures. FAFSA required. Priority date 3/15; no closing date. Applicants notified on rolling basis starting 3/15, must reply within 2 week(s) of notification.

Contact. Financial aid office: (859) 344-3319
Tim Ring, Director of Financial Aid
333 Thomas More Parkway
Crestview Hills, KY 41017-3495

Transylvania University

Lexington, Kentucky
www.transy.edu
Four-year private **Federal Code: 001987**

	Living at home	On-campus
Tuition and fees (2002-2003):	$16,790	$16,790
Room and board:		$5,940
Board only:	$1,500	
Books and supplies:	$500	$500
Personal expenses:	$1,000	$1,000
Transportation:	$600	$200

Undergraduate aid. Need-based: Average financial aid package for full-time students was $14,175. 74% awarded as scholarships/grants, 26% as loans/jobs. Need-based aid available for part-time students. **Non-need-based:** 78% awarded as scholarships/grants, 22% as loans/jobs. Scholarships based on academics, art, leadership, minority status, music/drama, religious affiliation, state/district residency. **Student debt:** 48% of graduating class borrowed to fund education; average debt was $13,989. **Additional information:** Auditions and portfolios required for music and art scholarships respectively. Essays required for other scholarship programs. Applications for William T. Young, scholarships must be received by December 1.

Freshman aid. **Need-based:** Out of 343 full-time freshmen, 260 applied for aid; 194 were judged to have need; of these 194 received aid. Average package met 87% of need. 58 students had full need met. Average scholarship/grant was $10,867; average loan $3,296. **Non-need based:** 43 full-time freshmen with need received non-need scholarships; 130 without need received awards.

Merit scholarships. William T. Young Merit Scholarships; 25 awarded; tuition and fees.

Policies to reduce costs. Tuition/fee waivers for minority students, family of clergy, employees and their families. Credit/placement for qualifying scores on AP, IB examinations. Work study available nights and weekends.

Payment plans. Installment, deferred payment.

Application procedures. FAFSA required. Priority date 3/1; no closing date. Applicants notified on rolling basis starting 3/15, must reply within 2 week(s) of notification. **Transfers:** No deadline.

Contact. **Financial aid office:** (859) 233-8239
Dave Cecil, Director of Financial Aid
300 North Broadway
Lexington, KY 40508-1797

Union College

Barbourville, Kentucky
www.unionky.edu
Four-year private **Federal Code: 001988**

	Living at home	On-campus
Tuition and fees (2002-2003):	$12,480	$12,480
Room and board:		$4,250
Board only:	$2,500	
Books and supplies:	$550	$550
Personal expenses:	$600	$600
Transportation:	$900	$900

Undergraduate aid. **Need-based:** Average financial aid package for full-time students was $12,163. 64% awarded as scholarships/grants, 36% as loans/jobs. Need-based aid available for part-time students. **Non-need-based:** 17% awarded as scholarships/grants, 83% as loans/jobs. Scholarships based on academics, alumni affiliation, art, athletics, minority status, music/drama, religious affiliation, state/district residency. **Student debt:** 90% of graduating class borrowed to fund education; average debt was $19,928.

Freshman aid. **Need-based:** Out of 137 full-time freshmen, 135 applied for aid; 117 were judged to have need; of these 117 received aid. Average package met 74% of need. 29 students had full need met. Average scholarship/grant was $7,501; average loan $3,459. **Non-need based:** 46 full-time freshmen with need received non-need scholarships; 18 without need received awards; 29 received athletic scholarships.

Policies to reduce costs. Tuition/fee waivers for children of alumni, senior citizens, family members, family of clergy, employees and their families. Credit/placement for qualifying scores on AP, CLEP examinations. Work study available nights and weekends.

Payment plans. Credit card, installment payment.

Application procedures. FAFSA required. Priority date 3/15; no closing date. Applicants notified on rolling basis starting 4/1, must reply within 2 week(s) of notification.

Contact. **Financial aid office:** (606) 546-1618
Sue Buttery, Director of Financial Aid
310 College Street
Barbourville, KY 40906

University of Kentucky

Lexington, Kentucky
www.uky.edu
Four-year public **Federal Code: 001989**

	Living at home	On-campus
Tuition and fees (2002-2003):	$3,975	$3,975
Out-of-state:	$10,527	$10,527
Room and board:		$4,050
Board only:	$1,600	
Books and supplies:	$600	$600
Personal expenses:	$1,148	$1,148
Transportation:	$560	$560

Undergraduate aid. **Need-based:** Average financial aid package for full-time students was $8,538; for part-time $7,042. 48% awarded as scholarships/grants, 52% as loans/jobs. **Non-need-based:** Scholarships based on academics, alumni affiliation, athletics, leadership, minority status, music/drama, state/district residency.

Freshman aid. **Need-based:** Out of 3,692 full-time freshmen, 2,236 applied for aid; 1,386 were judged to have need; of these 1,380 received aid. Average package met 86% of need. 747 students had full need met. Average scholarship/grant was $3,604; average loan $2,468. **Non-need based:** 732 full-time freshmen with need received non-need scholarships; 1,972 without need received awards; 98 received athletic scholarships.

Policies to reduce costs. Tuition/fee waivers for adults, senior citizens, minority students, employees and their families. Credit/placement for qualifying scores on AP, IB, CLEP examinations. Work study available weekends and for part-time students.

Payment plans. Credit card, installment payment.

Application procedures. FAFSA required. Priority date 2/15; no closing date. Applicants notified on rolling basis starting 4/1, must reply within 3 week(s) of notification. **Transfers:** Priority date 4/1.

Contact. **Financial aid office:** (859) 257-3172
Lynda George, Director of Student Financial Aid
100 W.D. Funkhouser Building
Lexington, KY 40506-0054

University of Louisville

Louisville, Kentucky
www.louisville.edu
Four-year public **Federal Code: 001999**

	Living at home	On-campus
Tuition and fees (2002-2003):	$4,082	$4,082
Out-of-state:	$11,162	$11,162
Room and board:		$3,872
Books and supplies:	$700	$700
Personal expenses:	$2,004	$2,004
Transportation:	$1,176	$1,176

Undergraduate aid. **Need-based:** Average financial aid package for full-time students was $4,799; for part-time $3,236. 40% awarded as scholarships/grants, 60% as loans/jobs. **Non-need-based:** 79% awarded as scholarships/grants, 21% as loans/jobs. Scholarships based on academics, art, athletics, leadership, minority status, music/drama, state/district residency.

Freshman aid. **Need-based:** Out of 2,250 full-time freshmen, 1,474 applied for aid; 1,185 were judged to have need; of these 1,158 received aid. Average package met 52% of need. 190 students had full need met. Average scholarship/grant was $3,695; average loan $1,041. **Non-need based:** 137 full-time freshmen with need received non-need scholarships; 17 received athletic scholarships.

Policies to reduce costs. Tuition/fee waivers for senior citizens, employees and their families. Credit/placement for qualifying scores on AP, IB, CLEP examinations.

Payment plans. Credit card, installment payment.

Application procedures. FAFSA required. Priority date 3/15; no closing date. Applicants notified on rolling basis starting 4/1, must reply by 5/1. **Transfers:** Priority date 3/1; no deadline.

Contact. Patricia Arauz, Director of Student Financial Aid
2211 South Brook Street
Louisville, KY 40292

Louisiana

American School of Business

Shreveport, Louisiana
www.americanschoolofbusiness.com
One-year proprietary **Federal Code: 026010**

	Living at home
Tuition and fees:	$7,300
Personal expenses:	$2,429

Application procedures. FAFSA, institutional form required.

Contact. Patty Donovan, Director of Financial Aid
702 Professional Drive North
Shreveport, LA 71105

Baton Rouge Community College

Baton Rouge, Louisiana
www.mybr.cc
Two-year public

	Living at home
Tuition and fees (2002-2003):	$1,452
Out-of-state:	$4,020

Contact. 5310 Florida Boulevard
Baton Rouge, LA 70806

Centenary College of Louisiana

Shreveport, Louisiana
www.centenary.edu
Four-year private **Federal Code: 002003**

	Living at home	On-campus
Tuition and fees (2002-2003):	$16,450	$16,450
Room and board:		$5,550
Board only:	$2,350	
Books and supplies:	$900	$900
Personal expenses:	$1,400	$1,400
Transportation:	$1,200	$800

Undergraduate aid. Need-based: Average financial aid package for full-time students was $12,815; for part-time $5,643. 82% awarded as scholarships/grants, 18% as loans/jobs. **Non-need-based:** 77% awarded as scholarships/grants, 23% as loans/jobs. Scholarships based on academics, art, athletics, leadership, music/drama, religious affiliation, state/district residency. **Student debt:** 55% of graduating class borrowed to fund education; average debt was $15,019.

Freshman aid. Need-based: Out of 272 full-time freshmen, 271 applied for aid; 183 were judged to have need; of these 183 received aid. Average package met 89% of need. 87 students had full need met. Average scholarship/grant was $11,992; average loan $2,518. **Non-need based:** 56 full-time freshmen with need received non-need scholarships; 71 without need received awards; 41 received athletic scholarships.

Policies to reduce costs. Tuition/fee waivers for family of clergy, employees and their families. Credit/placement for qualifying scores on AP, IB, CLEP examinations. Work study available nights, weekends and for part-time students.

Payment plans. Credit card, installment payment.

Application procedures. FAFSA, institutional form required. Priority date 2/15; no closing date. Applicants notified by 3/15, must reply by 5/1. Early decision closing date 12/1. **Transfers:** No deadline.

Contact. Mary Sue Rix, Director of Financial Aid
Box 41188
Shreveport, LA 71134-1188

Delgado Community College

New Orleans, Louisiana
www.dcc.edu
Two-year public **Federal Code: 004626**

	Living at home
Tuition and fees (2002-2003):	$1,544
Out-of-state:	$4,524
Books and supplies:	$500
Personal expenses:	$930
Transportation:	$860

Undergraduate aid. Need-based: Average financial aid package for full-time students was $5,077; for part-time $4,225. 57% awarded as scholarships/grants, 43% as loans/jobs. **Non-need-based:** 10% awarded as scholarships/grants, 90% as loans/jobs. Scholarships based on academics, athletics, state/district residency.

Freshman aid. Need-based: Average package met 54% of need. Average scholarship/grant was $3,312; average loan $1,150.

Policies to reduce costs. Tuition/fee waivers for senior citizens, employees and their families. Credit/placement for qualifying scores on IB, CLEP examinations. Work study available weekends and for part-time students.

Payment plans. Credit card, installment payment.

Application procedures. FAFSA, institutional form required. Priority date 5/1; closing date 7/17. Applicants notified on rolling basis starting 4/1, must reply within 2 week(s) of notification.

Contact. Diane Jackson, Director of Student Financial Assistance
City Park Campus/Building 1, 615 City Park Drive
New Orleans, LA 70119-4399

Dillard University

New Orleans, Louisiana
www.dillard.edu
Four-year private **Federal Code: 002004**

College costs. $700 additional tuition for nursing program per year.

	Living at home	On-campus
Tuition and fees (2002-2003):	$10,759	$10,759
Room and board:		$6,156
Books and supplies:	$1,000	$1,000
Transportation:	$824	$824

Undergraduate aid. All financial aid based on need. Average financial aid package for full-time students was $12,708; for part-time $5,078. 62% awarded as scholarships/grants, 38% as loans/jobs. **Student debt:** 98% of graduating class borrowed to fund education; average debt was $22,508.

Freshman aid. Out of 624 full-time freshmen, 570 applied for aid; 536 were judged to have need; of these 536 received aid. Average package met 85% of need. 601 students had full need met. Average scholarship/grant was $3,180; average loan $3,152.

Policies to reduce costs. Tuition/fee waivers for family members, employees and their families. Credit/placement for qualifying scores on AP, IB, CLEP examinations. Work study available nights and weekends.

Payment plans. Credit card, installment, deferred payment.

Application procedures. FAFSA, institutional form required. Priority date 3/1; closing date 6/1. Applicants notified on rolling basis starting 3/15, must reply by 5/1 or within 2 week(s) of notification. **Transfers:** Priority date 3/1; no deadline.

Contact. Financial aid office: (800) 216-8094
Cynthia Thornton, Director of Financial Aid
2601 Gentilly Boulevard
New Orleans, LA 70122-3097

Grambling State University

Grambling, Louisiana
www.gram.edu
Four-year public **Federal Code: 002006**

	Living at home	On-campus
Tuition and fees (2002-2003):	$2,716	$2,716
Out-of-state:	$8,066	$8,066
Room and board:		$2,936
Board only:	$2,204	
Books and supplies:	$702	$702
Personal expenses:	$1,365	$1,365
Transportation:	$1,187	$487

Policies to reduce costs. Tuition/fee waivers for children of alumni, senior citizens, minority students, employees and their families. Credit/placement for qualifying scores on AP, CLEP examinations.

Payment plans. Credit card, deferred payment.

Application procedures. FAFSA required. Priority date 6/1; closing date 7/1. Applicants notified on rolling basis starting 4/1, must reply within 1 week(s) of notification.

Contact. Alvina Thomas, Director of Student Financial Aid
Box 864
Grambling, LA 71245

Grantham University

Slidell, Louisiana
www.grantham.edu
Four-year proprietary **Federal Code: 004283**

College costs. Tuition includes books, software, supplies.

	Living at home
Tuition and fees:	$4,996

Undergraduate aid. Additional information: Defense Activity for Non Traditional Education Support (DANTES) and some employer reimbursement programs available. Department of Defense tuition assistance.

Merit scholarships. Military scholarships for free books, software, 25 percent tuition discount.

Policies to reduce costs. Tuition at time of enrollment guaranteed for 4 years; prepayment discount; credit/placement for qualifying scores on IB, CLEP examinations.

Payment plans. Credit card, installment payment.

Application procedures. FAFSA required.

Contact. Admissions Officer
34641 Grantham College Road
Slidell, LA 70460

Herzing College

Kenner, Louisiana
www.herzing.edu
Four-year proprietary **Federal Code: 020897**

College costs. Cost per 4-hour course in associate or bachelor's program $1,144 (includes fees). Cost per 4-hour course in general education program $880 (includes fees).

Policies to reduce costs. Credit/placement for qualifying scores on IB examinations. Work study available nights and weekends.

Payment plans. Credit card, installment payment.

Contact. Ava Gomez, Financial Aid Director
2400 Veterans Boulevard, Suite 410
Kenner, LA 70062

ITI Technical College

Baton Rouge, Louisiana
www.iticollege.org
Two-year proprietary **Federal Code: 015270**

College costs (projected). Tuition varies by program from $5,000 to $10,000.

Contact. 13944 Airline Highway
Baton Rouge, LA 70817-5998

ITT Technical Institute: St. Rose

St. Rose, Louisiana
www.itt-tech.edu
Two-year proprietary **Federal Code: 023611**

College costs. Total program varies depending on course of study. Per-credit-hour charge: $347.

Policies to reduce costs. Tuition/fee waivers for employees and their families. Tuition at time of enrollment guaranteed for 2 years.

Payment plans. Credit card, installment payment.

Application procedures. FAFSA, institutional form required. No deadline. Applicants notified on rolling basis.

Contact. Michelle Phelps, Director of Finance
140 James Drive East
St. Rose, LA 70087

Louisiana College

Pineville, Louisiana
www.lacollege.edu
Four-year private **Federal Code: 002007**

	Living at home	On-campus
Tuition and fees (2002-2003):	$9,050	$9,050
Room and board:		$3,486
Books and supplies:	$535	$535
Personal expenses:	$1,040	$1,040
Transportation:	$970	$410

Undergraduate aid. Need-based: Average financial aid package for full-time students was $10,591; for part-time $5,801. **Non-need-based:** Scholarships based on academics, art, leadership, music/drama. **Student debt:** 67% of graduating class borrowed to fund education; average debt was $14,265.

Freshman aid. Need-based: Out of 309 full-time freshmen, 308 applied for aid; 201 were judged to have need; of these 201 received aid. Average package met 33% of need. 56 students had full need met. Average scholarship/grant was $1,181; average loan $1,312. **Non-need based:** 200 full-time freshmen with need received non-need scholarships; 100 without need received awards.

Policies to reduce costs. Tuition/fee waivers for senior citizens, employees and their families. Tuition at time of enrollment guaranteed for 4 years; credit/placement for qualifying scores on AP, CLEP examinations. Work study available nights, weekends and for part-time students.

Payment plans. Installment payment.

Application procedures. FAFSA, institutional form required. Priority date 3/31; no closing date. Applicants notified on rolling basis starting 4/15, must reply within 4 week(s) of notification. **Transfers:** Priority date 3/31. Scholarships available.

Contact. Financial aid office: (318) 487-7386
Shelly Jinks, Director of Financial Aid
1140 College Drive
Pineville, LA 71359

Louisiana State University and Agricultural and Mechanical College

Baton Rouge, Louisiana
www.lsu.edu
Four-year public **Federal Code: 002010**

	Living at home	On-campus
Tuition and fees (2002-2003):	$3,540	$3,540
Out-of-state:	$8,840	$8,840
Room and board:		$5,136
Books and supplies:	$1,000	$1,000
Personal expenses:	$1,427	$1,427
Transportation:	$1,206	$822

Undergraduate aid. Need-based: Average financial aid package for full-time students was $6,354; for part-time $4,790. 49% awarded as scholarships/grants, 51% as loans/jobs. **Non-need-based:** 61% awarded as scholarships/grants, 39% as loans/jobs. Scholarships based on academics, alumni affiliation,

art, athletics, leadership, music/drama, state/district residency. **Student debt:** 48% of graduating class borrowed to fund education; average debt was $17,569.

Freshman aid. Need-based: Out of 5,358 full-time freshmen, 4,773 applied for aid; 2,350 were judged to have need; of these 2,320 received aid. Average package met 69% of need. 573 students had full need met. Average scholarship/grant was $2,716; average loan $2,276. **Non-need based:** 2,258 full-time freshmen with need received non-need scholarships; 2,561 without need received awards; 95 received athletic scholarships.

Merit scholarships. Merit-based scholarships for entering freshmen include Chancellor's Alumni Scholarship, LSU Alumni Association Scholarship, LSU Merit Achievement, Nonresident Fee Waiver, and Centennial Awards. Scholarships range from $2,000 to $26,720 over 4-year period and are based on standardized test scores as well as high school record. Application for admission to university serves as initial application for these scholarship programs.

Policies to reduce costs. Tuition/fee waivers for children of alumni, senior citizens, employees and their families. Credit/placement for qualifying scores on AP, IB, CLEP examinations. Work study available for part-time students.

Payment plans. Credit card, installment, deferred payment.

Application procedures. FAFSA, institutional form required. Applicants notified on rolling basis starting 3/1, must reply within 3 week(s) of notification. **Transfers:** No deadline.

Contact. **Financial aid office:** (225) 578-3103
Kim Dudley, Associate Director of Student Aid and Scholarships
110 Thomas Boyd Hall
Baton Rouge, LA 70803-2750

Louisiana State University at Alexandria

Alexandria, Louisiana
www.lsua.edu
Two-year public **Federal Code: 002011**

	Living at home
Tuition and fees (2002-2003):	$1,513
Out-of-state:	$3,985
Board only:	$2,167
Books and supplies:	$690
Personal expenses:	$1,342
Transportation:	$1,167

Undergraduate aid. Need-based: Average financial aid package for full-time students was $3,021; for part-time $2,947. 45% awarded as scholarships/grants, 55% as loans/jobs. **Non-need-based:** Scholarships based on academics, state/district residency.

Freshman aid. Need-based: Out of 455 full-time freshmen, 384 applied for aid; 241 were judged to have need; of these 106 received aid. Average scholarship/grant was $3,465; average loan $2,109. **Non-need based:** 64 full-time freshmen with need received non-need scholarships; 86 without need received awards.

Policies to reduce costs. Tuition/fee waivers for senior citizens, employees and their families. Credit/placement for qualifying scores on AP, CLEP examinations. Work study available nights.

Payment plans. Credit card, deferred payment.

Application procedures. FAFSA, institutional form required. Priority date 4/1; no closing date. Applicants notified on rolling basis starting 4/20, must reply within 3 week(s) of notification.

Contact. **Financial aid office:** (318) 473-6423
Kenn Posey, Director of Student Aid and Scholarships
8100 Highway 71 South
Alexandria, LA 71302

Louisiana State University at Eunice

Eunice, Louisiana
www.lsue.edu
Two-year public **Federal Code: 002012**

	Living at home
Tuition and fees (2002-2003):	$1,456
Out-of-state:	$4,456
Per-credit charge:	$61
Per-credit out-of-state:	$187
Books and supplies:	$1,000

Undergraduate aid. Need-based: Need-based aid available for full-time and part-time students.

Policies to reduce costs. Tuition/fee waivers for senior citizens, family of clergy, employees and their families. Credit/placement for qualifying scores on AP, CLEP examinations.

Payment plans. Deferred payment.

Application procedures. FAFSA, institutional form required. Priority date 6/1; no closing date. Applicants notified on rolling basis starting 4/1, must reply within 2 week(s) of notification.

Contact. **Financial aid office:** (337) 550-1282
Jacqueline Lachapelle, Director
Box 1129
Eunice, LA 70535

Louisiana State University in Shreveport

Shreveport, Louisiana
www.lsus.edu
Four-year public **Federal Code: 002013**

	Living at home
Tuition and fees (2002-2003):	$2,554
Out-of-state:	$6,884
Board only:	$2,204
Books and supplies:	$702
Personal expenses:	$1,365
Transportation:	$1,200

Undergraduate aid. Need-based: Need-based aid available for full-time and part-time students.

Policies to reduce costs. Tuition/fee waivers for children of alumni, senior citizens, employees and their families. Credit/placement for qualifying scores on AP, CLEP examinations. Work study available nights and weekends.

Payment plans. Credit card, deferred payment.

Application procedures. No deadline. Applicants notified on rolling basis.

Contact. **Financial aid office:** (318) 797-5363
Betty McCrary, Director of Student Financial Aid
One University Place
Shreveport, LA 71115-2399

Louisiana Tech University

Ruston, Louisiana
www.latech.edu
Four-year public **Federal Code: 002008**

	Living at home	On-campus
Tuition and fees (2002-2003):	$3,138	$3,138
Out-of-state:	$9,138	$9,138
Room and board:		$3,555
Board only:	$2,169	
Books and supplies:	$660	$660
Personal expenses:	$1,440	$1,440
Transportation:	$1,200	$600

Undergraduate aid. Need-based: Average financial aid package for full-time students was $5,473. 48% awarded as scholarships/grants, 52% as loans/jobs. Need-based aid available for part-time students. **Non-need-based:** 54% awarded as scholarships/grants, 46% as loans/jobs. **Student debt:** 71% of graduating class borrowed to fund education; average debt was $13,286.

Freshman aid. Need-based: Out of 1,772 full-time freshmen, 1,525 applied for aid; 846 were judged to have need; of these 846 received aid. Average package met 66% of need. 167 students had full need met. Average scholarship/grant was $3,673; average loan $1,554. **Non-need based:** 155 full-time freshmen with need received non-need scholarships; 481 without need received awards; 7 received athletic scholarships.

Policies to reduce costs. Tuition/fee waivers for children of alumni, senior citizens, employees and their families. Credit/placement for qualifying scores on AP, CLEP examinations.

Payment plans. Credit card payment.

Application procedures. FAFSA, institutional form required. No deadline. Applicants notified on rolling basis starting 4/18, must reply within 6 week(s) of notification.

Contact. Roger Vick, Director of Student Financial Aid
Box 3178
Ruston, LA 71272

Loyola University New Orleans

New Orleans, Louisiana
www.loyno.edu
Four-year private **Federal Code: 002016**

	Living at home	On-campus
Tuition and fees:	$22,180	$22,180
Room and board:		$7,660
Books and supplies:	$1,000	$1,000
Personal expenses:	$1,424	$1,424
Transportation:	$1,239	

Undergraduate aid. Need-based: Average financial aid package for full-time students was $15,288; for part-time $5,451. 69% awarded as scholarships/grants, 31% as loans/jobs. **Non-need-based:** 79% awarded as scholarships/grants, 21% as loans/jobs. Scholarships based on academics, alumni affiliation, art, music/drama. **Student debt:** 60% of graduating class borrowed to fund education; average debt was $16,591.

Freshman aid. Need-based: Out of 878 full-time freshmen, 664 applied for aid; 497 were judged to have need; of these 497 received aid. Average package met 89% of need. 382 students had full need met. Average scholarship/grant was $13,805; average loan $2,696. **Non-need based:** 72 full-time freshmen with need received non-need scholarships; 304 without need received awards.

Merit scholarships. Interview recommended of scholarship applicants.

Policies to reduce costs. Tuition/fee waivers for senior citizens, employees and their families. Credit/placement for qualifying scores on AP, IB, CLEP examinations. Work study available nights, weekends and for part-time students.

Payment plans. Credit card payment.

Application procedures. FAFSA required. Priority date 2/15; no closing date. Applicants notified on rolling basis starting 3/1, must reply by 5/1 or within 2 week(s) of notification. **Transfers:** Priority date 3/1; closing date 5/1. Transfer scholarship deadline June 1.

Contact. Financial aid office: (504) 865-3231
Cathy Simoneaux, Director of Scholarships and Financial Aid
6363 St. Charles Avenue
New Orleans, LA 70118-6195

McNeese State University

Lake Charles, Louisiana
www.mcneese.edu
Four-year public **Federal Code: 002017**

	Living at home	On-campus
Tuition and fees (2002-2003):	$2,545	$2,545
Out-of-state:	$9,256	$9,256
Room and board:		$2,770
Books and supplies:	$1,000	$1,000
Personal expenses:	$2,668	$2,250
Transportation:	$1,239	$822

Undergraduate aid. Need-based: Need-based aid available for full-time and part-time students. **Non-need-based:** Scholarships based on academics, alumni affiliation, athletics, job skills, leadership. **Additional information:** Books may be charged and paid in 2 installments during semester.

Policies to reduce costs. Tuition/fee waivers for children of alumni, senior citizens, employees and their families. Credit/placement for qualifying scores on AP, CLEP examinations. Work study available nights, weekends and for part-time students.

Payment plans. Credit card, installment, deferred payment.

Application procedures. FAFSA, institutional form required. Priority date 5/1; no closing date. Applicants notified on rolling basis starting 4/15, must reply within 2 week(s) of notification. **Transfers:** Transfer students must exhibit satisfactory academic progress at school most recently attended to be eligible for financial aid.

Contact. Taina Savoit, Director of Financial Aid
Box 92495
Lake Charles, LA 70609-2495

New Orleans Baptist Theological Seminary: School of Christian Education

New Orleans, Louisiana
www.nobts.edu
Four-year private **Federal Code: G02019**

College costs. Tuition varies from $120 to $240 per credit-hour. Fees vary and are subject to change. Room: $1,500. Books/supplies: $500.

Application procedures. Closing date 6/1. Applicants notified by 8/1.

Contact. Shane Baker, Director of Financial Aid
3939 Gentilly Boulevard
New Orleans, LA 70126-4858

Nicholls State University

Thibodaux, Louisiana
www.nicholls.edu
Four-year public **Federal Code: 002005**

College costs. Per-credit-hour charge varies greatly with number of credits taken.

	Living at home	On-campus
Tuition and fees (2002-2003):	$2,477	$2,477
Out-of-state:	$7,924	$7,924
Room and board:		$3,352
Board only:	$2,299	
Books and supplies:	$1,000	$1,000
Personal expenses:	$1,427	$1,427
Transportation:	$1,239	$822

Undergraduate aid. Need-based: Average financial aid package for full-time students was $2,714; for part-time $1,767. 42% awarded as scholarships/grants, 58% as loans/jobs. **Non-need-based:** 49% awarded as scholarships/grants, 51% as loans/jobs. Scholarships based on academics, athletics, state/district residency.

Freshman aid. Need-based: Out of 1,402 full-time freshmen, 1,170 applied for aid; 676 were judged to have need; of these 655 received aid. Average package met 64% of need. 53 students had full need met. Average scholarship/grant was $1,731; average loan $1,327. **Non-need based:** 53 full-time freshmen with need received non-need scholarships; 348 without need received awards; 26 received athletic scholarships.

Policies to reduce costs. Tuition/fee waivers for senior citizens, employees and their families. Credit/placement for qualifying scores on AP, CLEP examinations.

Payment plans. Credit card, deferred payment.

Application procedures. FAFSA, institutional form required. Priority date 4/6; no closing date. Applicants notified on rolling basis, must reply within 2 week(s) of notification. **Transfers:** Priority date 5/1; no deadline.

Contact. Financial aid office: (985) 448-4048
Colette Lagarde, Director of Financial Aid
PO Box 2004-NSU
Thibodaux, LA 70310

Northwestern State University

Natchitoches, Louisiana
www.nsula.edu
Four-year public **Federal Code: 002021**

College costs. Students living on-campus pay $70 health services fee. Per-credit-hour charges vary greatly.

	Living at home	On-campus
Tuition and fees (2002-2003):	$2,642	$2,642
Out-of-state:	$8,516	$8,516
Room and board:		$3,266
Board only:	$1,457	
Books and supplies:	$1,000	$1,000
Personal expenses:	$1,342	$1,342
Transportation:	$1,316	$1,316

Undergraduate aid. Need-based: Average financial aid package for full-time students was $5,306; for part-time $3,127. 49% awarded as scholarships/grants, 51% as loans/jobs. **Non-need-based:** 51% awarded as scholarships/grants, 49% as loans/jobs. Scholarships based on academics, alumni affiliation, art, athletics, leadership, music/drama.

Freshman aid. Need-based: Average scholarship/grant was $2,912; average loan $2,135. **Non-need based:** 908 full-time freshmen with need received non-need scholarships.

Policies to reduce costs. Tuition/fee waivers for senior citizens, employees and their families. Credit/placement for qualifying scores on AP, CLEP examinations.

Payment plans. Installment, deferred payment.

Application procedures. FAFSA, institutional form required. No deadline. Applicants notified on rolling basis.

Contact. Financial aid office: (318) 357-5961
Misti Chelette, Director of Financial Aid
Roy Hall, Room 209
Natchitoches, LA 71497

Nunez Community College

Chalmette, Louisiana
www.nunez.cc.la.us
Two-year public **Federal Code: 015130**

	Living at home
Tuition and fees (2002-2003):	$1,418
Out-of-state:	$3,938
Board only:	$1,199
Books and supplies:	$617
Personal expenses:	$1,424
Transportation:	$1,239

Undergraduate aid. Need-based: 59% awarded as scholarships/grants, 41% as loans/jobs. Need-based aid available for part-time students. **Non-need-based:** 5% awarded as scholarships/grants, 95% as loans/jobs. **Additional information:** Pell Grants, Stafford Loans, campus workstudy, and tuition waiver scholarships available. Louisiana National Guard tuition exemption, teacher tuition exemption, dependents of injured fire-police tuition waivers.

Policies to reduce costs. Tuition/fee waivers for senior citizens, employees and their families. Credit/placement for qualifying scores on CLEP examinations.

Payment plans. Credit card, installment, deferred payment.

Application procedures. FAFSA, institutional form required. Priority date 4/1; closing date 7/1. Applicants notified by 8/1, must reply by 8/15. **Transfers:** Applicant must supply academic transcripts from every postsecondary school attended.

Contact. Financial aid office: (504) 680-2428
John Whisnant, Financial Aid Officer
3710 Paris Road
Chalmette, LA 70043

Our Lady of Holy Cross College

New Orleans, Louisiana
www.olhcc.edu
Four-year private **Federal Code: 002023**

College costs. Tuition for undergraduate nursing program (BSN) $235 per credit hour.

	Living at home
Tuition and fees (2002-2003):	$6,850
Books and supplies:	$700
Personal expenses:	$1,264
Transportation:	$1,167

Undergraduate aid. Need-based: Average financial aid package for full-time students was $4,603; for part-time $5,618. 24% awarded as scholarships/grants, 76% as loans/jobs. **Non-need-based:** Scholarships based on academics, state/district residency. **Student debt:** 88% of graduating class borrowed to fund education; average debt was $20,000.

Freshman aid. Need-based: Out of 229 full-time freshmen, 108 applied for aid; 70 were judged to have need; of these 70 received aid. Average package met 46% of need. 13 students had full need met. Average scholarship/grant was $2,683; average loan $2,140. **Non-need based:** 10 full-time freshmen with need received non-need scholarships; 137 without need received awards.

Policies to reduce costs. Tuition/fee waivers for senior citizens, family of clergy, employees and their families. Credit/placement for qualifying scores on CLEP examinations. Work study available nights, weekends and for part-time students.

Payment plans. Credit card, installment payment.

Application procedures. FAFSA, institutional form required. Priority date 4/16; no closing date. Applicants notified on rolling basis starting 5/15, must reply within 2 week(s) of notification. **Transfers:** Priority date 4/15; no deadline.

Contact. Financial aid office: (504) 394-7744
Johnell Armer, Director of Financial Aid
4123 Woodland Drive
New Orleans, LA 70131-7399

Remington College

Lafayette, Louisiana
www.educationamerica.com
Two-year proprietary **Federal Code: 005203**

College costs (2002-2003). Total cost of associate degree programs in electronics, computer networking, business information technology $19,250 (includes tuition, fees, books, supplies, laptop computer, software).

Undergraduate aid. All financial aid based on need. Need-based aid available for full-time students.

Policies to reduce costs. Work study available nights.

Payment plans. Installment payment.

Application procedures. FAFSA, institutional form required. No deadline.

Contact. Jo Ann Boudreax, Director of Financial Aid
303 Rue Louis XIV
Lafayette, LA 70508

Remington College: Baton Rouge

Baton Rouge, Louisiana
www.educationamerica.com
Two-year proprietary **Federal Code: E00907**

College costs (2002-2003). Total cost of typical associate degree program: $25,872. Required fees, $150.

Undergraduate aid. All financial aid based on need. 99% awarded as scholarships/grants, 1% as loans/jobs.

Policies to reduce costs. Tuition/fee waivers for family members, employees and their families. Work study available nights.

Payment plans. Credit card, installment payment.

Application procedures. FAFSA required. No deadline. Applicants notified on rolling basis, must reply within 1 week(s) of notification.

Contact. Bob Lutz, Chief Financial Officer
1900 N. Lobdell Boulevard
Baton Rouge, LA 70806

St. Joseph Seminary College

St. Benedict, Louisiana
www.sjasc.edu
Four-year private **Federal Code: 002027**

	Living at home	On-campus
Tuition and fees (2002-2003):	$11,500	$11,500
Room and board:		$5,700
Books and supplies:	$1,000	$1,000
Personal expenses:		$1,387
Transportation:		$800

Undergraduate aid. Need-based: Need-based aid available for full-time and part-time students. **Non-need-based:** Scholarships based on academics, leadership.

Policies to reduce costs. Credit/placement for qualifying scores on AP, IB, CLEP examinations.

Payment plans. Installment payment.

Application procedures. FAFSA required. Priority date 3/15; no closing date. Applicants notified on rolling basis starting 7/1, must reply within 4 week(s) of notification. **Transfers:** Closing date 5/1.

Contact. **Financial aid office:** (985) 867-2229
Betty Ann Burns, Director of Student Aid
St. Benedict, LA 70457-9990

Southeastern Louisiana University

Hammond, Louisiana
www.selu.edu
Four-year public **Federal Code: 002024**

	Living at home	On-campus
Tuition and fees (2002-2003):	$2,618	$2,618
Out-of-state:	$7,946	$7,946
Room and board:		$3,720

Undergraduate aid. Need-based: Need-based aid available for full-time and part-time students. **Non-need-based:** Scholarships based on academics, athletics, job skills, leadership, music/drama, state/district residency.

Policies to reduce costs. Tuition/fee waivers for senior citizens, employees and their families. Credit/placement for qualifying scores on AP, CLEP examinations.

Payment plans. Credit card, installment, deferred payment.

Application procedures. FAFSA, institutional form required. Priority date 5/1; no closing date. Applicants notified on rolling basis starting 3/15, must reply within 2 week(s) of notification. **Transfers:** Financial aid is available for transfer students, including those admitted on probation.

Contact. **Financial aid office:** (985) 549-2244
Sam Domiano, Director, Admissions and Financial Aid
SLU 10752
Hammond, LA 70402

Southern University and Agricultural and Mechanical College

Baton Rouge, Louisiana
www.subr.edu
Four-year public **Federal Code: 002025**

	Living at home	On-campus
Tuition and fees (2002-2003):	$2,702	$2,702
Out-of-state:	$8,494	$8,494
Room and board:		$3,624
Books and supplies:	$900	$900
Personal expenses:		$22

Undergraduate aid. Need-based: Average financial aid package for full-time students was $7,098; for part-time $6,850. 40% awarded as scholarships/grants, 60% as loans/jobs. **Non-need-based:** 95% awarded as scholarships/grants, 5% as loans/jobs. Scholarships based on academics, athletics. **Student debt:** 75% of graduating class borrowed to fund education; average debt was $17,000.

Freshman aid. Need-based: Out of 1,178 full-time freshmen, 1,120 applied for aid; 1,010 were judged to have need; of these 910 received aid. Average package met 65% of need. 85 students had full need met. Average scholarship/grant was $3,100; average loan $2,625. **Non-need based:** 335 full-time freshmen with need received non-need scholarships; 15 without need received awards; 15 received athletic scholarships.

Policies to reduce costs. Tuition/fee waivers for children of alumni, senior citizens, employees and their families. Credit/placement for qualifying scores on AP, CLEP examinations.

Payment plans. Credit card payment.

Application procedures. FAFSA required. Closing date 5/31. Applicants notified on rolling basis starting 6/30, must reply within 3 week(s) of notification. **Transfers:** Priority date 5/31.

Contact. **Financial aid office:** (225) 771-2790
Philip Rogers, Director of Financial Aid
Box 9901
Baton Rouge, LA 70813

Southern University at New Orleans

New Orleans, Louisiana
Four-year public **Federal Code: 002026**

	Living at home
Tuition and fees (2002-2003):	$2,198
Out-of-state:	$5,936
Books and supplies:	$400

Application procedures. FAFSA required. Closing date 4/1. Applicants notified by 5/15, must reply within 1 week(s) of notification.

Contact. Ursula Shorty, Director of Financial Aid
6400 Press Drive
New Orleans, LA 70126

Southern University in Shreveport

Shreveport, Louisiana
www.susla.edu
Two-year public **Federal Code: 007686**

	Living at home
Tuition and fees (2002-2003):	$1,662
Out-of-state:	$2,792
Books and supplies:	$600
Personal expenses:	$1,420
Transportation:	$1,076

Policies to reduce costs. Tuition/fee waivers for senior citizens.

Payment plans. Credit card, installment, deferred payment.

Application procedures. FAFSA required. No deadline. Applicants notified on rolling basis.

Contact. Patricia Flanagan, Director of Financial Aid
3050 Martin Luther King, Jr. Drive
Shreveport, LA 71107

Tulane University

New Orleans, Louisiana
www.tulane.edu
Four-year private **Federal Code: 002029**

	Living at home	On-campus
Tuition and fees (2002-2003):	$28,310	$28,310
Room and board:		$7,378
Books and supplies:	$600	$600
Personal expenses:	$800	$800
Transportation:		$1,250

Undergraduate aid. Need-based: Average financial aid package for full-time students was $23,918; for part-time $7,244. 74% awarded as scholarships/grants, 26% as loans/jobs. **Non-need-based:** 82% awarded as scholarships/grants, 18% as loans/jobs. Scholarships based on academics, athletics, state/district residency. **Student debt:** 50% of graduating class borrowed to fund education; average debt was $20,685. **Additional information:** Application deadline for merit scholarships December 1.

Freshman aid. Need-based: Out of 1,540 full-time freshmen, 1,031 applied for aid; 709 were judged to have need; of these 708 received aid. Average package met 94% of need. 464 students had full need met. Average scholarship/grant was $16,568; average loan $4,328. **Non-need based:** 250 full-time freshmen with need received non-need scholarships; 469 without need received awards; 37 received athletic scholarships.

Policies to reduce costs. Tuition/fee waivers for employees and their families. Credit/placement for qualifying scores on AP, IB examinations.

Application procedures. FAFSA, CSS PROFILE required. Priority date 1/15; closing date 2/1. Applicants notified on rolling basis starting 2/1, must reply by 5/1 or within 2 week(s) of notification. Early decision closing date 11/1.

Contact. **Financial aid office:** (504) 865-5723
Elaine Rivera, Director of Financial Aid
210 Gibson Hall, 6823 St. Charles Avenue
New Orleans, LA 70118-5680

University of Louisiana at Lafayette

Lafayette, Louisiana
www.louisiana.edu
Four-year public **Federal Code: 002031**

	Living at home	On-campus
Tuition and fees (2002-2003):	$2,428	$2,428
Out-of-state:	$8,628	$8,628
Room and board:		$2,896
Books and supplies:	$1,000	$1,000
Personal expenses:	$1,166	$1,166
Transportation:	$1,076	$442

Undergraduate aid. All financial aid based on need. Average financial aid package for full-time students was $4,500; for part-time $3,594. 37% awarded as scholarships/grants, 63% as loans/jobs. **Student debt:** 43% of graduating class borrowed to fund education; average debt was $15,000.

Freshman aid. Average package met 90% of need. Average scholarship/grant was $2,200; average loan $1,800.

Policies to reduce costs. Tuition/fee waivers for senior citizens, employees and their families. Credit/placement for qualifying scores on AP, CLEP examinations. Work study available nights, weekends and for part-time students.

Payment plans. Credit card payment.

Application procedures. FAFSA, institutional form required. Priority date 5/1; no closing date. Applicants notified on rolling basis starting 4/1, must reply within 2 week(s) of notification.

Contact. Cindy Perez, Director, Student Financial Aid
Box 41210
Lafayette, LA 70504

University of Louisiana at Monroe

Monroe, Louisiana
www.ulm.edu
Four-year public **Federal Code: 002020**

	Living at home	On-campus
Tuition and fees (2002-2003):	$2,453	$2,453
Out-of-state:	$8,405	$8,405
Room and board:		$2,870
Books and supplies:	$600	$600
Personal expenses:	$1,264	$1,264
Transportation:	$1,167	$479

Undergraduate aid. Non-need-based: Scholarships based on academics, alumni affiliation, art, athletics, job skills, leadership, minority status, music/drama, religious affiliation, state/district residency.

Policies to reduce costs. Tuition/fee waivers for senior citizens, employees and their families. Credit/placement for qualifying scores on AP, CLEP examinations.

Payment plans. Credit card, installment payment.

Application procedures. FAFSA required. Priority date 4/1; no closing date. Applicants notified on rolling basis starting 6/1, must reply within 2 week(s) of notification.

Contact. Ralph Perri, Director of Financial Aid Services and Scholarships
700 University Avenue
Monroe, LA 71209-1160

University of New Orleans

New Orleans, Louisiana
www.uno.edu
Four-year public **Federal Code: 002015**

	Living at home	On-campus
Tuition and fees (2002-2003):	$3,026	$3,026
Out-of-state:	$10,070	$10,070
Room only:		$3,672
Books and supplies:	$1,150	$1,150
Personal expenses:	$1,490	$1,490
Transportation:	$882	$882

Undergraduate aid. Need-based: Average financial aid package for full-time students was $4,493; for part-time $3,960. 43% awarded as scholarships/grants, 57% as loans/jobs. **Non-need-based:** 38% awarded as scholarships/grants, 62% as loans/jobs. Scholarships based on academics, athletics. **Additional information:** Students in good academic and financial standing eligible to participate in Extended Payment Plan option.

Freshman aid. Need-based: Out of 1,685 full-time freshmen, 1,230 applied for aid; 861 were judged to have need; of these 448 received aid. Average package met 64% of need. 18 students had full need met. Average scholarship/grant was $2,492; average loan $2,284. **Non-need based:** 85 full-time freshmen with need received non-need scholarships; 17 without need received awards; 51 received athletic scholarships.

Policies to reduce costs. Tuition/fee waivers for adults, children of alumni, senior citizens, employees and their families. Credit/placement for qualifying scores on AP, IB, CLEP examinations.

Payment plans. Credit card, deferred payment.

Application procedures. FAFSA, institutional form required. Priority date 5/15; no closing date. Applicants notified on rolling basis starting 4/20, must reply within 4 week(s) of notification. **Transfers:** Mid-year transfers must submit financial aid transcript from all post-secondary schools attended. Others submit NSLDS.

Contact. Emily London, Director of Student Financial Aid
Administrative Building Room 103
New Orleans, LA 70148-2135

Xavier University of Louisiana

New Orleans, Louisiana
www.xula.edu
Four-year private **Federal Code: 002032**

	Living at home	On-campus
Tuition and fees (2002-2003):	$11,000	$11,000
Room and board:		$6,000
Books and supplies:	$1,000	$1,000
Personal expenses:	$1,476	$1,476
Transportation:	$1,281	$850

Undergraduate aid. Need-based: Average financial aid package for full-time students was $9,091; for part-time $6,840. 21% awarded as scholarships/grants, 79% as loans/jobs. **Non-need-based:** Scholarships based on academics, art, athletics, music/drama, religious affiliation. **Student debt:** 13% of graduating class borrowed to fund education; average debt was $3,426.

Freshman aid. Need-based: Out of 976 full-time freshmen, 927 applied for aid; 816 were judged to have need; of these 815 received aid. Average package met 14% of need. 184 students had full need met. Average scholarship/grant was $3,621; average loan $4,288. **Non-need based:** 428 full-time freshmen with need received non-need scholarships; 59 without need received awards.

Policies to reduce costs. Tuition/fee waivers for senior citizens, family of clergy, employees and their families. Credit/placement for qualifying scores on AP, CLEP examinations. Work study available nights and weekends.

Payment plans. Credit card, installment, deferred payment.

Application procedures. FAFSA required. Closing date 1/1. Applicants notified on rolling basis starting 4/1, must reply within 2 week(s) of notification.

Contact. Mildred Higgins, Director of Financial Aid
1 Drexel Drive
New Orleans, LA 70125-1098

Maine

Andover College

Portland, Maine
www.andovercollege.edu
Two-year proprietary **Federal Code: 009292**

	Living at home
Tuition and fees:	$5,640
Books and supplies:	$700
Personal expenses:	$1,115
Transportation:	$1,175

Undergraduate aid. Additional information: Work-study positions available.

Policies to reduce costs. Tuition/fee waivers for employees and their families. Tuition at time of enrollment guaranteed for 2 years; credit/placement for qualifying scores on AP, CLEP examinations.

Payment plans. Credit card payment.

Application procedures. FAFSA required. No deadline. Applicants notified on rolling basis. **Transfers:** No deadline.

Contact. Adrienne Amari, Director of Student Finances
901 Washington Avenue
Portland, ME 04103

Bates College

Lewiston, Maine
www.bates.edu
Four-year private **Federal Code: 002036**

	On-campus
Comprehensive fee:	$35,750
Books and supplies:	$1,750
Transportation:	$350

Undergraduate aid. All financial aid based on need. Average financial aid package for full-time students was $24,193. 84% awarded as scholarships/grants, 16% as loans/jobs. **Student debt:** 48% of graduating class borrowed to fund education; average debt was $17,045.

Freshman aid. Out of 415 full-time freshmen, 236 applied for aid; 201 were judged to have need; of these 190 received aid. Average package met 100% of need. 190 students had full need met. Average scholarship/grant was $21,160; average loan $2,431.

Policies to reduce costs. Tuition/fee waivers for employees and their families. Credit/placement for qualifying scores on AP, IB examinations.

Application procedures. FAFSA, CSS PROFILE required. Closing date 2/1. Applicants notified by 4/2, must reply by 5/1. Early decision closing date 11/15.

Contact. Financial aid office: (207) 786-6096
Meredith Braz, Registrar & Director of Student Financial Services
Lindholm House, 23 Campus Avenue
Lewiston, ME 04240-9917

Beal College

Bangor, Maine
bealcollege.com
Two-year proprietary **Federal Code: 005204**

	Living at home
Tuition and fees (2002-2003):	$4,705
Per-credit charge:	$130
Books and supplies:	$900
Personal expenses:	$700
Transportation:	$1,500

Policies to reduce costs. Tuition/fee waivers for employees and their families.

Payment plans. Credit card, installment, deferred payment.

Application procedures. FAFSA, institutional form required. Priority date 5/1; no closing date. Applicants notified on rolling basis starting 6/15, must reply within 2 week(s) of notification. **Transfers:** Priority date 5/1; no deadline.

Contact. Beth Lausier, Financial Aid Director
629 Main Street
Bangor, ME 04401

Bowdoin College

Brunswick, Maine
www.bowdoin.edu
Four-year private **Federal Code: 002038**

	Living at home	On-campus
Tuition and fees:	$30,120	$30,120
Room and board:		$7,670
Board only:	$4,220	
Books and supplies:	$850	$850
Personal expenses:	$1,160	$1,160

Undergraduate aid. Need-based: Average financial aid package for full-time students was $24,675. 82% awarded as scholarships/grants, 18% as loans/jobs. **Non-need-based:** 26% awarded as scholarships/grants, 74% as loans/jobs. Scholarships based on academics, leadership. **Student debt:** 45% of graduating class borrowed to fund education; average debt was $15,307. **Additional information:** Regardless of financial circumstances, students admitted to college will receive money they need to attend.

Freshman aid. Need-based: Out of 458 full-time freshmen, 268 applied for aid; 205 were judged to have need; of these 205 received aid. Average package met 100% of need. 205 students had full need met. Average scholarship/grant was $22,660; average loan $2,375. **Non-need based:** 3 full-time freshmen with need received non-need scholarships; 4 without need received awards.

Merit scholarships. National Merit Scholarship ($1,000); Posse & Chamberlain Scholarships for leadership (amounts vary)

Policies to reduce costs. Tuition/fee waivers for employees and their families. Credit/placement for qualifying scores on AP, IB examinations.

Payment plans. Installment, deferred payment.

Application procedures. FAFSA, institutional form, CSS PROFILE required. Closing date 2/15. Applicants notified by 4/5, must reply by 5/1 or within 1 week(s) of notification. Early decision closing date 11/15. **Transfers:** Closing date 3/1. Transfers aided on funds-available basis after meeting aid commitments to entering first-year students and returning upperclass students.

Contact. Financial aid office: (207) 725-3273
Stephen Joyce, Director of Student Aid
5000 College Station
Brunswick, ME 04011-8441

Central Maine Medical Center School of Nursing

Lewiston, Maine
www.cmmcson.org
Two-year private **Federal Code: 006305**

	Living at home	On-campus
Tuition and fees (2002-2003):	$6,054	$6,054
Per-credit charge:	$113	$113
Room only:		$1,500
Board only:	$1,500	
Books and supplies:	$1,217	$1,217
Personal expenses:	$700	$700
Transportation:	$780	

Undergraduate aid. All financial aid based on need. Average financial aid package for full-time students was $4,978; for part-time $2,987.

Freshman aid. Out of 4 full-time freshmen, 4 applied for aid; 4 were judged to have need; of these 4 received aid. Average package met 65% of need. Average scholarship/grant was $4,094; average loan $2,625.

Policies to reduce costs. Credit/placement for qualifying scores on AP, CLEP examinations.

Payment plans. Credit card payment.

Application procedures. FAFSA required. Priority date 3/15; closing date 7/1. Applicants notified on rolling basis starting 4/1, must reply within 2 week(s) of notification.

Contact. **Financial aid office:** (207) 795-2270
Keith Bourgault, Financial Aid Director
70 Middle Street
Lewiston, ME 04240

Central Maine Technical College

Auburn, Maine
www.cmtc.net
Two-year public **Federal Code: 005276**

College costs. New England Regional tuition: $3,060 full-time, $102 per-credit-hour.

	Living at home	On-campus
Tuition and fees (2002-2003):	$2,290	$2,290
Out-of-state:	$4,720	$4,720
Per-credit charge:	$68	$68
Per-credit out-of-state:	$149	$149
Room and board:		$4,590
Books and supplies:	$800	$800
Personal expenses:	$1,300	$1,300
Transportation:	$1,500	$750

Undergraduate aid. All financial aid based on need. 60% awarded as scholarships/grants, 40% as loans/jobs. Need-based aid available for part-time students. **Additional information:** Tuition and/or fee waivers may be available to orphans, Native Americans, fire fighters, police, disabled veterans, dependents or survivors of veterans killed in line of duty.

Freshman aid. Out of 601 full-time freshmen, 272 applied for aid; 224 were judged to have need; of these 210 received aid.

Policies to reduce costs. Tuition/fee waivers for minority students, employees and their families. Credit/placement for qualifying scores on IB, CLEP examinations. Work study available nights, weekends and for part-time students.

Payment plans. Credit card, installment payment.

Application procedures. FAFSA, institutional form required. Priority date 5/1; no closing date. Applicants notified on rolling basis starting 3/15, must reply within 2 week(s) of notification.

Contact. Linda Bolton, Financial Aid Director
1250 Turner Street
Auburn, ME 04210

Colby College

Waterville, Maine
www.colby.edu
Four-year private **Federal Code: 002039**

	On-campus
Comprehensive fee:	$37,570
Books and supplies:	$650
Personal expenses:	$800
Transportation:	$500

Undergraduate aid. All financial aid based on need. Average financial aid package for full-time students was $22,055. 85% awarded as scholarships/grants, 15% as loans/jobs. **Student debt:** 41% of graduating class borrowed to fund education; average debt was $17,270.

Freshman aid. Out of 471 full-time freshmen, 273 applied for aid; 203 were judged to have need; of these 203 received aid. Average package met 100% of need. 203 students had full need met. Average scholarship/grant was $21,966; average loan $3,243.

Policies to reduce costs. Tuition/fee waivers for senior citizens, employees and their families. Credit/placement for qualifying scores on AP, IB examinations. Work study available nights and weekends.

Payment plans. Installment payment.

Application procedures. FAFSA required. Closing date 2/1. Applicants notified by 4/1, must reply by 5/1. Early decision closing date 11/15. **Transfers:** Priority date 2/1; closing date 3/1.

Contact. Lucia Whittelsey, Director of Financial Aid
4800 Mayflower Hill
Waterville, ME 04901-8848

College of the Atlantic

Bar Harbor, Maine
www.coa.edu
Four-year private **Federal Code: 011385**

	Living at home	On-campus
Tuition and fees (2002-2003):	$22,535	$22,535
Room and board:		$6,060
Board only:	$2,220	
Books and supplies:	$500	$500
Personal expenses:	$500	$560

Undergraduate aid. **Need-based:** Average financial aid package for full-time students was $19,800; for part-time $10,900. 75% awarded as scholarships/grants, 25% as loans/jobs. **Non-need-based:** 13% awarded as scholarships/grants, 87% as loans/jobs. Scholarships based on academics. **Student debt:** 58% of graduating class borrowed to fund education; average debt was $12,992.

Freshman aid. **Need-based:** Average package met 95% of need. Average scholarship/grant was $16,800; average loan $3,175.

Policies to reduce costs. Tuition/fee waivers for employees and their families. Credit/placement for qualifying scores on AP, IB, CLEP examinations.

Payment plans. Credit card, installment payment.

Application procedures. FAFSA, institutional form required. Closing date 2/15. Applicants notified by 4/1, must reply by 5/1 or within 2 week(s) of notification. Early decision closing date 12/1.

Contact. Bruce Hazam, Director of Financial Aid
105 Eden Street
Bar Harbor, ME 04609

Husson College

Bangor, Maine
www.husson.edu
Four-year private **Federal Code: 002043**

	Living at home	On-campus
Tuition and fees (2002-2003):	$10,290	$10,290
Room and board:		$5,510
Board only:	$900	
Books and supplies:	$900	$900
Personal expenses:	$900	$900
Transportation:	$1,000	$450

Undergraduate aid. **Need-based:** Average financial aid package for full-time students was $8,554; for part-time $5,233. 52% awarded as scholarships/grants, 48% as loans/jobs. **Non-need-based:** 24% awarded as scholarships/grants, 76% as loans/jobs. Scholarships based on academics, leadership. **Student debt:** 96% of graduating class borrowed to fund education; average debt was $20,250.

Freshman aid. **Need-based:** Out of 642 full-time freshmen, 355 applied for aid; 324 were judged to have need; of these 324 received aid. Average package met 69% of need. 34 students had full need met. Average scholarship/grant was $6,373; average loan $2,185. **Non-need based:** 12 full-time freshmen with need received non-need scholarships; 103 without need received awards.

Merit scholarships. Scholarships awarded based on academics and leadership, ranging from $1,000 to full tuition. Number available varies year to year. Also offer full-tuition scholarships to graduates ranked 1st or 2nd in their senior class at public comprehensive or public academic high schools in Maine.

Policies to reduce costs. Tuition/fee waivers for senior citizens, employees and their families. Credit/placement for qualifying scores on AP, CLEP examinations. Work study available nights and weekends.

Payment plans. Credit card, installment payment.

Application procedures. FAFSA required. Priority date 4/15; no closing date. Applicants notified on rolling basis starting 4/1, must reply by 5/1 or within 2 week(s) of notification.

Contact. **Financial aid office:** (207) 941-7156
Linda Conant, Director of Financial Aid
One College Circle
Bangor, ME 04401-7935

Maine College of Art

Portland, Maine
www.meca.edu
Four-year private **Federal Code: 011673**

College costs. Studio fees vary per class.

	Living at home	On-campus
Tuition and fees (2002-2003):	$19,878	$19,878
Room and board:		$7,140
Books and supplies:	$1,714	$1,714
Personal expenses:	$1,174	$1,174
Transportation:	$918	$582

Undergraduate aid. Need-based: Average financial aid package for full-time students was $12,135; for part-time $6,751. 55% awarded as scholarships/grants, 45% as loans/jobs. **Non-need-based:** 46% awarded as scholarships/grants, 54% as loans/jobs. Scholarships based on academics, art. **Student debt:** 77% of graduating class borrowed to fund education; average debt was $25,012.

Freshman aid. Need-based: Out of 98 full-time freshmen, 86 applied for aid; 77 were judged to have need; of these 77 received aid. Average package met 54% of need. 5 students had full need met. Average scholarship/grant was $8,830; average loan $2,946. **Non-need based:** 1 full-time freshmen with need received non-need scholarships; 18 without need received awards.

Policies to reduce costs. Tuition/fee waivers for employees and their families. Credit/placement for qualifying scores on AP, IB, CLEP examinations. Work study available nights, weekends and for part-time students.

Payment plans. Credit card, installment payment.

Application procedures. FAFSA required. Priority date 3/1; closing date 4/15. Applicants notified on rolling basis starting 2/15, must reply within 2 week(s) of notification. **Transfers:** Priority date 3/1; closing date 4/15.

Contact. Michelle LeClerc, Director of Financial Aid
97 Spring Street
Portland, ME 04101

New England School of Communications

Bangor, Maine
www.nescom.edu
Two-year private **Federal Code: 023471**

College costs. $14,790 per year for residential students, $9,280 for commuters. $275 per-credit-hour charge.

	Living at home	On-campus
Tuition and fees:	$9,280	$9,280
Per-credit charge:	$275	$275
Room and board:		$5,510
Books and supplies:	$550	$550
Personal expenses:	$150	$150
Transportation:	$500	$500

Undergraduate aid. Need-based: Need-based aid available for full-time and part-time students. **Non-need-based:** Scholarships based on academics, leadership.

Merit scholarships. Scholarships are merit based for second semester.

Policies to reduce costs. Tuition/fee waivers for employees and their families. Tuition at time of enrollment guaranteed for 2 years; credit/placement for qualifying scores on AP examinations.

Payment plans. Credit card, installment payment.

Application procedures. FAFSA, institutional form required. Priority date 4/15; closing date 8/15. Applicants notified on rolling basis.

Contact. Financial aid office: (207) 941-7176
Nicole Rediker, Director of Financial Aid
One College Circle
Bangor, ME 04401

St. Joseph's College

Standish, Maine
www.sjcme.edu
Four-year private **Federal Code: 002051**

	Living at home	On-campus
Tuition and fees (2002-2003):	$16,590	$16,590
Room and board:		$6,650
Books and supplies:	$600	$600
Personal expenses:	$1,050	$1,050
Transportation:	$550	$400

Undergraduate aid. Need-based: Average financial aid package for full-time students was $13,886; for part-time $5,913. 62% awarded as scholarships/grants, 38% as loans/jobs. **Non-need-based:** 33% awarded as scholarships/grants, 67% as loans/jobs. Scholarships based on academics, leadership, religious affiliation. **Student debt:** 95% of graduating class borrowed to fund education; average debt was $19,860.

Freshman aid. Need-based: Out of 290 full-time freshmen, 284 applied for aid; 257 were judged to have need; of these 257 received aid. Average package met 81% of need. 65 students had full need met. Average scholarship/grant was $9,932; average loan $4,247. **Non-need based:** 24 full-time freshmen with need received non-need scholarships; 26 without need received awards.

Policies to reduce costs. Tuition/fee waivers for family members, employees and their families. Credit/placement for qualifying scores on AP, CLEP examinations.

Payment plans. Credit card payment.

Application procedures. FAFSA, institutional form required. Priority date 3/1; no closing date. Applicants notified on rolling basis starting 3/1, must reply by 5/1 or within 2 week(s) of notification. **Transfers:** Priority date 3/1.

Contact. Financial aid office: (207) 892-6612
Andrea Cross, Director of Financial Aid
278 Whites Bridge Road
Standish, ME 04084

Thomas College

Waterville, Maine
www.thomas.edu
Four-year private **Federal Code: 002052**

	Living at home	On-campus
Tuition and fees (2002-2003):	$13,890	$13,890
Room and board:		$6,070
Board only:	$800	
Books and supplies:	$700	$700
Personal expenses:	$1,000	$1,000
Transportation:	$1,500	$800

Undergraduate aid. Need-based: Average financial aid package for full-time students was $11,575; for part-time $2,365. 60% awarded as scholarships/grants, 40% as loans/jobs. **Non-need-based:** 46% awarded as scholarships/grants, 54% as loans/jobs. Scholarships based on academics, leadership, state/district residency. **Student debt:** 78% of graduating class borrowed to fund education; average debt was $19,125.

Freshman aid. Need-based: Out of 200 full-time freshmen, 189 applied for aid; 185 were judged to have need; of these 185 received aid. Average package met 85% of need. 6 students had full need met. Average scholarship/grant was $8,114; average loan $3,376. **Non-need based:** 84 full-time freshmen with need received non-need scholarships; 7 without need received awards.

Policies to reduce costs. Tuition/fee waivers for employees and their families. Credit/placement for qualifying scores on AP, CLEP examinations. Work study available nights and weekends.

Payment plans. Credit card, installment payment.

Application procedures. FAFSA required. Priority date 2/15; no closing date. Applicants notified on rolling basis starting 3/15, must reply within 2 week(s) of notification. **Transfers:** No deadline.

Contact. Financial aid office: (207) 859-1105
Angela Dostie, Director of Student Financial Services
180 West River Road
Waterville, ME 04901

University of Maine

Orono, Maine
www.umaine.edu
Four-year public **Federal Code: 002053**

College costs. New England Regional Student Program tuition is 150% of public in-district tuition.

	Living at home	On-campus
Tuition and fees (2002-2003):	$5,550	$5,550
Out-of-state:	$13,620	$13,620
Room and board:		$5,922
Board only:	$1,500	
Books and supplies:	$700	$700
Personal expenses:	$1,100	$1,100
Transportation:	$1,100	$500

Undergraduate aid. Need-based: Average financial aid package for full-time students was $7,829; for part-time $5,983. 45% awarded as scholarships/grants, 55% as loans/jobs. **Non-need-based:** 43% awarded as scholarships/grants, 57% as loans/jobs. Scholarships based on academics, alumni affiliation, art, athletics, job skills, leadership, minority status, music/drama, religious affiliation, state/district residency. **Student debt:** 70% of graduating class borrowed to fund education; average debt was $17,917.

Freshman aid. Need-based: Out of 1,715 full-time freshmen, 1,475 applied for aid; 1,278 were judged to have need; of these 1,258 received aid. Average package met 74% of need. 411 students had full need met. Average scholarship/grant was $5,329; average loan $2,974. **Non-need based:** 193 full-time freshmen with need received non-need scholarships; 276 without need received awards; 10 received athletic scholarships.

Merit scholarships. Academic merit scholarships range from $1,000, one-time to full tuition waivers for in-state students and full tuition differential for out-of-state students.

Policies to reduce costs. Tuition/fee waivers for senior citizens, employees and their families. Credit/placement for qualifying scores on AP, IB, CLEP examinations. Work study available nights, weekends and for part-time students.

Payment plans. Credit card, installment payment.

Application procedures. FAFSA required. Priority date 3/1; no closing date. Applicants notified on rolling basis starting 3/15, must reply by 5/1 or within 2 week(s) of notification. **Transfers:** Spring transfer aid packages subject to availability of funds.

Contact. **Financial aid office:** (207) 581-1324
Peggy Crawford, Director of Student Financial Aid
5713 Chadbourne Hall
Orono, ME 04469-5713

University of Maine at Augusta

Augusta, Maine
www.uma.maine.edu
Four-year public **Federal Code: 006760**

College costs. New England Regional Student Program tuition is 150% of public in-district tuition.

	Living at home
Tuition and fees (2002-2003):	$3,855
Out-of-state:	$8,745
Board only:	$1,850
Books and supplies:	$702
Personal expenses:	$1,600
Transportation:	$1,200

Undergraduate aid. Need-based: Average financial aid package for full-time students was $6,976; for part-time $3,589. 57% awarded as scholarships/grants, 43% as loans/jobs. **Non-need-based:** 9% awarded as scholarships/grants, 91% as loans/jobs. Scholarships based on academics, alumni affiliation, art, athletics, leadership, music/drama, state/district residency. **Student debt:** 63% of graduating class borrowed to fund education; average debt was $12,462.

Freshman aid. Need-based: Out of 627 full-time freshmen, 361 applied for aid; 332 were judged to have need; of these 310 received aid. Average package met 64% of need. 43 students had full need met. Average scholarship/grant was $4,005; average loan $2,581. **Non-need based:** 6 full-time freshmen with need received non-need scholarships; 19 without need received awards.

Policies to reduce costs. Tuition/fee waivers for senior citizens, employees and their families. Credit/placement for qualifying scores on AP, IB, CLEP examinations. Work study available nights, weekends and for part-time students.

Payment plans. Credit card, installment, deferred payment.

Application procedures. FAFSA required. Priority date 3/1; no closing date. Applicants notified on rolling basis starting 3/15, must reply by 5/1 or within 2 week(s) of notification. **Transfers:** No deadline.

Contact. **Financial aid office:** (207) 621-3455
Lisa Bongiovanni, Financial Aid Director
46 University Drive
Augusta, ME 04330

University of Maine at Farmington

Farmington, Maine
www.umf.maine.edu
Four-year public **Federal Code: 002040**

College costs. New England Regional Student Program tuition is 150% of public in-district tuition.

	Living at home	On-campus
Tuition and fees (2002-2003):	$4,482	$4,482
Out-of-state:	$10,242	$10,242
Room and board:		$5,064
Board only:	$2,074	
Books and supplies:	$560	$560
Personal expenses:	$2,122	$2,122
Transportation:	$468	$468

Undergraduate aid. Need-based: Average financial aid package for full-time students was $7,816; for part-time $5,242. 45% awarded as scholarships/grants, 55% as loans/jobs. **Non-need-based:** 27% awarded as scholarships/grants, 73% as loans/jobs. Scholarships based on academics, leadership, minority status, state/district residency. **Student debt:** 80% of graduating class borrowed to fund education; average debt was $14,321. **Additional information:** FAFSA must arrive at Federal processor by March 1.

Freshman aid. Need-based: Out of 453 full-time freshmen, 381 applied for aid; 298 were judged to have need; of these 298 received aid. Average package met 85% of need. 62 students had full need met. Average scholarship/grant was $4,235; average loan $2,605. **Non-need based:** 54 full-time freshmen with need received non-need scholarships; 15 without need received awards.

Merit scholarships. Presidential Scholarships; for non-residents graduating in top half of high school class; $2,000 renewable annually.

Policies to reduce costs. Tuition/fee waivers for senior citizens, minority students, employees and their families. Credit/placement for qualifying scores on AP, IB, CLEP examinations. Work study available nights, weekends and for part-time students.

Payment plans. Credit card, installment payment.

Application procedures. FAFSA required. Priority date 3/1; no closing date. Applicants notified on rolling basis starting 3/15, must reply within 2 week(s) of notification. **Transfers:** Priority date 3/1.

Contact. Ronald Milliken, Director of Financial Aid
246 Main Street
Farmington, ME 04938-1994

University of Maine at Fort Kent

Fort Kent, Maine
www.umfk.maine.edu
Four-year public **Federal Code: 002041**

College costs. New England Regional tuition is 150% of public in-district tuition.

	Living at home	On-campus
Tuition and fees (2002-2003):	$3,844	$3,844
Out-of-state:	$8,734	$8,734
Room and board:		$4,436
Books and supplies:	$660	$660
Personal expenses:	$1,000	$1,000
Transportation:	$1,000	$800

Undergraduate aid. Need-based: Average financial aid package for full-time students was $4,764; for part-time $3,129. 56% awarded as scholarships/

grants, 44% as loans/jobs. **Non-need-based:** 11% awarded as scholarships/ grants, 89% as loans/jobs. Scholarships based on academics. **Student debt:** 81% of graduating class borrowed to fund education; average debt was $10,483.

Freshman aid. Need-based: Average package met 82% of need. Average scholarship/grant was $4,229; average loan $2,345.

Policies to reduce costs. Tuition/fee waivers for senior citizens, minority students, employees and their families. Credit/placement for qualifying scores on AP, IB, CLEP examinations. Work study available nights, weekends and for part-time students.

Payment plans. Credit card, installment, deferred payment.

Application procedures. FAFSA required. Priority date 3/15; no closing date. Applicants notified on rolling basis starting 3/15, must reply within 2 week(s) of notification. **Transfers:** Priority date 3/15; no deadline.

Contact. Financial aid office: (207) 834-7605
Lisa Lipe, Director of Financial Aid
23 University Drive
Fort Kent, ME 04743

University of Maine at Machias

Machias, Maine
www.umm.maine.edu
Four-year public **Federal Code: 002055**

College costs. New England Regional Student Program tuition is 150% of public in-district tuition.

	Living at home	On-campus
Tuition and fees (2002-2003):	$4,390	$4,390
Out-of-state:	$9,700	$9,700
Room and board:		$4,880
Books and supplies:	$650	$650
Personal expenses:	$1,600	$1,600
Transportation:	$900	$900

Undergraduate aid. Need-based: Average financial aid package for full-time students was $8,182; for part-time $4,265. 57% awarded as scholarships/ grants, 43% as loans/jobs. **Non-need-based:** 42% awarded as scholarships/ grants, 58% as loans/jobs. Scholarships based on academics, alumni affiliation, art, job skills, leadership, minority status, music/drama, state/district residency. **Student debt:** 69% of graduating class borrowed to fund education; average debt was $14,873.

Freshman aid. Need-based: Out of 154 full-time freshmen, 131 applied for aid; 112 were judged to have need; of these 110 received aid. Average package met 74% of need. 18 students had full need met. Average scholarship/ grant was $5,099; average loan $2,700. **Non-need based:** 7 full-time freshmen with need received non-need scholarships; 15 without need received awards.

Policies to reduce costs. Tuition/fee waivers for senior citizens, minority students, employees and their families. Credit/placement for qualifying scores on AP, CLEP examinations.

Payment plans. Credit card, installment payment.

Application procedures. FAFSA required. Priority date 3/1; no closing date. Applicants notified on rolling basis starting 2/15, must reply within 2 week(s) of notification.

Contact. Financial aid office: (207) 255-1203
Stephanie Larrabee, Director of Financial Aid
9 O'Brien Avenue
Machias, ME 04654

University of Maine at Presque Isle

Presque Isle, Maine
www.umpi.maine.edu
Four-year public **Federal Code: 002033**

College costs. New England Regional tuition is 150% of public in-district tuition. New England Board of Higher Education/Canadian tuition for participating qualifying Canadian students, $4,905.

	Living at home	On-campus
Tuition and fees (2002-2003):	$3,850	$3,850
Out-of-state:	$9,010	$9,010
Room and board:		$4,494
Board only:	$2,000	
Books and supplies:	$650	$650
Personal expenses:	$1,100	$1,100
Transportation:	$1,100	$1,100

Undergraduate aid. Need-based: Average financial aid package for full-time students was $6,730; for part-time $3,337. 63% awarded as scholarships/ grants, 37% as loans/jobs. **Non-need-based:** 23% awarded as scholarships/ grants, 77% as loans/jobs. Scholarships based on academics, alumni affiliation, art, job skills, leadership, minority status, music/drama, state/district residency. **Student debt:** 40% of graduating class borrowed to fund education; average debt was $11,742.

Freshman aid. Need-based: Out of 253 full-time freshmen, 218 applied for aid; 193 were judged to have need; of these 185 received aid. Average package met 89% of need. 78 students had full need met. Average scholarship/ grant was $5,074; average loan $2,275. **Non-need based:** 14 full-time freshmen with need received non-need scholarships; 22 without need received awards.

Policies to reduce costs. Tuition/fee waivers for senior citizens, minority students, family members, employees and their families. Credit/ placement for qualifying scores on AP, IB, CLEP examinations. Work study available nights, weekends and for part-time students.

Payment plans. Credit card, installment payment.

Application procedures. FAFSA required. Priority date 4/1; no closing date. Applicants notified on rolling basis starting 3/1, must reply within 2 week(s) of notification. **Transfers:** No deadline.

Contact. Financial aid office: (207) 768-9510
Barbara Bridges, Director of Financial Aid
181 Main Street
Presque Isle, ME 04769

University of New England

Biddeford, Maine
www.une.edu
Four-year private **Federal Code: 002050**

	Living at home	On-campus
Tuition and fees (2002-2003):	$18,460	$18,460
Room and board:		$7,100
Board only:	$3,150	
Books and supplies:	$820	$820
Personal expenses:	$930	$930
Transportation:	$1,390	$1,030

Undergraduate aid. Need-based: Average financial aid package for full-time students was $13,705; for part-time $10,985. 43% awarded as scholarships/ grants, 57% as loans/jobs. **Non-need-based:** 65% awarded as scholarships/ grants, 35% as loans/jobs. Scholarships based on academics, alumni affiliation, leadership. **Student debt:** 87% of graduating class borrowed to fund education; average debt was $26,723.

Freshman aid. Need-based: Out of 302 full-time freshmen, 279 applied for aid; 250 were judged to have need; of these 249 received aid. Average package met 71% of need. 6 students had full need met. Average scholarship/ grant was $6,331; average loan $4,802. **Non-need based:** 202 full-time freshmen with need received non-need scholarships; 39 without need received awards.

Policies to reduce costs. Tuition/fee waivers for employees and their families. Credit/placement for qualifying scores on AP, CLEP examinations. Work study available nights, weekends and for part-time students.

Payment plans. Credit card, installment payment.

Application procedures. FAFSA, institutional form required. Priority date 3/1; no closing date. Applicants notified on rolling basis starting 3/15, must reply within 2 week(s) of notification. Early decision closing date 11/ 15.

Contact. Financial aid office: (207) 283-0170 ext. 2342
John Bowie, Director of Financial Aid
Hills Beach Road
Biddeford, ME 04005

University of Southern Maine

Gorham, Maine
www.usm.maine.edu
Four-year public **Federal Code: 009762**

College costs. New England Regional Student Program tuition is 150% of public in-district tuition.

	Living at home	On-campus
Tuition and fees (2002-2003):	$4,796	$4,796
Out-of-state:	$11,966	$11,966
Room and board:		$5,738
Books and supplies:	$800	$800
Personal expenses:	$2,000	$2,000
Transportation:	$1,000	$1,000

Undergraduate aid. Need-based: Average financial aid package for full-time students was $8,621. 37% awarded as scholarships/grants, 63% as loans/jobs. Need-based aid available for part-time students. **Non-need-based:** 12% awarded as scholarships/grants, 88% as loans/jobs. Scholarships based on academics, music/drama. **Student debt:** 61% of graduating class borrowed to fund education; average debt was $19,023.

Freshman aid. Need-based: Out of 902 full-time freshmen, 771 applied for aid; 631 were judged to have need; of these 604 received aid. Average package met 75% of need. 96 students had full need met. Average scholarship/grant was $4,022; average loan $3,051. **Non-need based:** 23 full-time freshmen with need received non-need scholarships; 91 without need received awards.

Merit scholarships. Merit Scholarships based on academic record, school/community leadership, and potential for intellectual/social contribution; $2,950 in-state, $5,100 out-of-state.

Policies to reduce costs. Tuition/fee waivers for senior citizens, minority students, employees and their families. Credit/placement for qualifying scores on AP, IB, CLEP examinations. Work study available nights, weekends and for part-time students.

Payment plans. Credit card, installment payment.

Application procedures. FAFSA required. Priority date 2/15; no closing date. Applicants notified on rolling basis starting 3/15, must reply by 5/1 or within 2 week(s) of notification. **Transfers:** Priority date 2/15; no deadline.

Contact. Financial aid office: (207) 780-5250
Keith Dubois, Financial Aid Office, Director
37 College Avenue
Gorham, ME 04038

Maryland

Allegany College

Cumberland, Maryland
www.allegany.edu
Two-year public **Federal Code: 002057**

	Living at home
Tuition and fees (2002-2003):	$2,720
Out-of-district:	$5,180
Out-of-state:	$6,080
Per-credit charge:	$85
Per-credit out-of-district:	$167
Per-credit out-of-state:	$197
Board only:	$1,980
Books and supplies:	$700
Personal expenses:	$1,200
Transportation:	$100

Undergraduate aid. Need-based: Need-based aid available for full-time and part-time students. **Non-need-based:** Scholarships based on academics, athletics. **Student debt:** 46% of graduating class borrowed to fund education; average debt was $7,293.

Policies to reduce costs. Tuition/fee waivers for senior citizens, employees and their families. Credit/placement for qualifying scores on AP, CLEP examinations. Work study available nights and for part-time students.

Payment plans. Credit card, deferred payment.

Application procedures. FAFSA required. Priority date 3/15; no closing date. Applicants notified on rolling basis starting 5/15, must reply within 2 week(s) of notification.

Contact. **Financial aid office:** (301) 784-5213
Cynthia Harbel, Director of Financial Aid
12401 Willowbrook Road, SE
Cumberland, MD 21502

Anne Arundel Community College

Arnold, Maryland
www.aacc.edu
Two-year public **Federal Code: 002058**

	Living at home
Tuition and fees (2002-2003):	$1,990
Out-of-district:	$3,580
Out-of-state:	$6,250
Per-credit charge:	$62
Per-credit out-of-district:	$115
Per-credit out-of-state:	$204
Board only:	$2,090
Books and supplies:	$900
Personal expenses:	$1,300
Transportation:	$1,600

Undergraduate aid. Need-based: 23% awarded as scholarships/grants, 77% as loans/jobs. Need-based aid available for part-time students.

Policies to reduce costs. Tuition/fee waivers for senior citizens, employees and their families. Credit/placement for qualifying scores on AP, CLEP examinations. Work study available nights, weekends and for part-time students.

Payment plans. Credit card, deferred payment.

Application procedures. FAFSA, institutional form required. Priority date 4/15; no closing date. Applicants notified on rolling basis starting 7/1, must reply within 2 week(s) of notification. **Transfers:** No deadline.

Contact. **Financial aid office:** (410) 777-2203
Rich Heath, Director of Student Financial Services
101 College Parkway
Arnold, MD 21012-1895

Baltimore Hebrew University

Baltimore, Maryland
www.bhu.edu
Four-year private **Federal Code: 002060**

	Living at home
Tuition and fees (2002-2003):	$7,230
Books and supplies:	$400
Personal expenses:	$1,300
Transportation:	$400

Undergraduate aid. Need-based: Average financial aid package for full-time students was $4,800; for part-time $2,000. 99% awarded as scholarships/grants, 1% as loans/jobs. **Non-need-based:** Scholarships based on academics.

Freshman aid. Need-based: Out of 2 full-time freshmen, 2 applied for aid; 2 were judged to have need; of these 2 received aid. Average package met 50% of need. 1 students had full need met. **Non-need based:** 1 without need received awards.

Merit scholarships. 25% tuition subsidy for teachers employed at any Jewish congregational day school, nursery or kindergarten; 50% tuition subsidy for teachers employed at a school affiliated with Center for Jewish Education; 25% tuition discount for full-time employees of the Associated Jewish Community Federation of Baltimore

Policies to reduce costs. Tuition/fee waivers for senior citizens, employees and their families. Credit/placement for qualifying scores on AP, IB, CLEP examinations.

Payment plans. Credit card, installment payment.

Application procedures. FAFSA, institutional form required. Priority date 3/1; closing date 9/9. Applicants notified on rolling basis starting 7/15, must reply by 9/9. **Transfers:** No deadline.

Contact. **Financial aid office:** (410) 578-6913
Yelena Feldman, Financial Aid Counselor
5800 Park Heights Avenue
Baltimore, MD 21215

Baltimore International College

Baltimore, Maryland
www.bic.edu
Four-year private **Federal Code: 016376**

College costs. Fees shown are for the culinary school and include use of computer, culinary supplies, upgrading and maintenance of kitchen equipment and facilities. Day students provided one full meal daily. Business program students pay lower fees.

	Living at home	On-campus
Tuition and fees:	$19,039	$19,039
Room and board:		$5,996
Board only:	$3,744	
Books and supplies:	$1,500	$1,500
Transportation:	$1,800	$1,800

Undergraduate aid. Need-based: 50% awarded as scholarships/grants, 50% as loans/jobs. **Non-need-based:** 74% awarded as scholarships/grants, 26% as loans/jobs. Scholarships based on academics, alumni affiliation, athletics, job skills, leadership, state/district residency. **Student debt:** 80% of graduating class borrowed to fund education; average debt was $14,125.

Policies to reduce costs. Tuition/fee waivers for employees and their families. Tuition at time of enrollment guaranteed for 4 years; credit/placement for qualifying scores on CLEP examinations. Work study available nights and weekends.

Payment plans. Credit card, installment payment.

Application procedures. FAFSA, institutional form required. Priority date 3/1; no closing date. Applicants notified on rolling basis, must reply within 2 week(s) of notification. **Transfers:** Priority date 7/1; no deadline.

Contact. **Financial aid office:** (410) 752-0490
Kim Wittler, Director of Student Financial Planning
Commerce Exchange, 17 Commerce Street
Baltimore, MD 21202-3230

Bowie State University

Bowie, Maryland
www.umsa.umd.edu
Four-year public **Federal Code: 002062**

	Living at home	On-campus
Tuition and fees (2002-2003):	$3,944	$3,944
Out-of-state:	$10,360	$10,360
Room and board:		$5,030
Board only:	$2,762	
Books and supplies:	$1,172	$1,172
Personal expenses:	$1,937	$1,785
Transportation:	$1,910	$850

Undergraduate aid. Need-based: Average financial aid package for full-time students was $6,839. 53% awarded as scholarships/grants, 47% as loans/jobs. Need-based aid available for part-time students. **Non-need-based:** 45% awarded as scholarships/grants, 55% as loans/jobs. Scholarships based on academics, art, athletics, music/drama, state/district residency.

Freshman aid. Need-based: Out of 592 full-time freshmen, 527 applied for aid; 394 were judged to have need; of these 370 received aid. Average package met 60% of need. 57 students had full need met. Average scholarship/grant was $3,572; average loan $2,538. **Non-need based:** 199 full-time freshmen with need received non-need scholarships; 56 without need received awards.

Policies to reduce costs. Tuition/fee waivers for senior citizens, employees and their families. Credit/placement for qualifying scores on AP, CLEP examinations. Work study available nights and weekends.

Payment plans. Credit card, installment, deferred payment.

Application procedures. FAFSA, institutional form required. Priority date 4/1; no closing date. Applicants notified on rolling basis starting 5/1, must reply within 1 week(s) of notification. **Transfers:** Priority date 4/1; no deadline. Financial aid transcripts required from previous institutions.

Contact. Veronica Pickett, Director of Financial Aid
14000 Jericho Park Road
Bowie, MD 20715

Capitol College

Laurel, Maryland
www.capitol-college.edu
Four-year private **Federal Code: 001436**

	Living at home	On-campus
Tuition and fees:	$17,450	$17,450
Room only:		$3,710
Books and supplies:	$800	$800
Personal expenses:	$1,900	$1,900
Transportation:	$1,600	$1,400

Undergraduate aid. Need-based: Average financial aid package for full-time students was $6,630; for part-time $6,937. 49% awarded as scholarships/grants, 51% as loans/jobs. **Non-need-based:** 30% awarded as scholarships/grants, 70% as loans/jobs. Scholarships based on academics, alumni affiliation, leadership, minority status.

Freshman aid. Need-based: Out of 379 full-time freshmen, 92 applied for aid; 83 were judged to have need; of these 83 received aid. Average package met 27% of need. 3 students had full need met. Average scholarship/grant was $4,879; average loan $2,124. **Non-need based:** 16 without need received awards.

Policies to reduce costs. Tuition/fee waivers for employees and their families. Tuition at time of enrollment guaranteed for 4 years; credit/placement for qualifying scores on AP, CLEP examinations.

Payment plans. Credit card, installment, deferred payment.

Application procedures. FAFSA, institutional form required. Priority date 2/1; no closing date. Applicants notified on rolling basis starting 6/3, must reply by 5/1 or within 3 week(s) of notification.

Contact. Financial aid office: (301) 369-2800 ext. 3039
Sue Thompson, Director of Financial Aid
11301 Springfield Road
Laurel, MD 20708

Carroll Community College

Westminster, Maryland
www.carrollcc.edu
Two-year public **Federal Code: 031007**

College costs. Required fees: 15% of tuition plus $2 per credit.

	Living at home
Tuition and fees:	$2,460
Out-of-district:	$3,840
Out-of-state:	$5,850
Per-credit charge:	$82
Per-credit out-of-district:	$128
Per-credit out-of-state:	$195
Board only:	$1,500
Books and supplies:	$800
Personal expenses:	$1,000
Transportation:	$1,500

Undergraduate aid. Need-based: 97% awarded as scholarships/grants, 3% as loans/jobs. Need-based aid available for part-time students. **Non-need-based:** Scholarships based on academics.

Policies to reduce costs. Tuition/fee waivers for senior citizens, employees and their families. Credit/placement for qualifying scores on AP, CLEP examinations. Work study available nights, weekends and for part-time students.

Payment plans. Credit card, deferred payment.

Application procedures. FAFSA required. Priority date 3/1; no closing date. Applicants notified on rolling basis starting 6/1, must reply within 2 week(s) of notification.

Contact. Financial aid office: (410) 386-8437
Robert Koermer, Senior Director of Enrollment Services
1601 Washington Road
Westminster, MD 21157

Cecil Community College

North East, Maryland
www.cecilcc.edu
Two-year public **Federal Code: 008308**

	Living at home
Tuition and fees (2002-2003):	$2,303
Out-of-district:	$5,003
Out-of-state:	$6,353
Per-credit charge:	$70
Per-credit out-of-district:	$155
Per-credit out-of-state:	$200
Books and supplies:	$700
Personal expenses:	$1,500
Transportation:	$1,500

Undergraduate aid. Need-based: Average financial aid package for full-time students was $872; for part-time $604. 57% awarded as scholarships/grants, 43% as loans/jobs. **Non-need-based:** Scholarships based on academics, athletics, state/district residency.

Freshman aid. Need-based: Average scholarship/grant was $1,126.

Policies to reduce costs. Tuition/fee waivers for senior citizens, employees and their families. Tuition at time of enrollment guaranteed for 2 years; credit/placement for qualifying scores on AP, CLEP examinations.

Payment plans. Credit card, installment, deferred payment.

Application procedures. Institutional form required. Priority date 8/1; no closing date. Applicants notified on rolling basis, must reply within 2 week(s) of notification.

Contact. Kate Lockhart, Director of Financial Aid
One Seahawk Drive
North East, MD 21901

Chesapeake College

Wye Mills, Maryland
www.chesapeake.edu
Two-year public **Federal Code: 004650**

College costs. Additional capital improvement fee per semester is $10 in-district and $25 out-of-district.

	Living at home
Tuition and fees:	$2,564
Out-of-district:	$3,824
Out-of-state:	$5,384
Per-credit charge:	$75
Per-credit out-of-district:	$117
Per-credit out-of-state:	$169
Board only:	$660
Books and supplies:	$1,200
Personal expenses:	$1,000
Transportation:	$3,128

Undergraduate aid. Need-based: Need-based aid available for full-time and part-time students. **Non-need-based:** Scholarships based on academics, art, athletics, state/district residency.

Policies to reduce costs. Tuition/fee waivers for senior citizens, employees and their families. Credit/placement for qualifying scores on AP, CLEP examinations.

Payment plans. Credit card, installment payment.

Application procedures. FAFSA, institutional form required. Priority date 5/1; no closing date. Applicants notified on rolling basis starting 5/1, must reply within 2 week(s) of notification. **Transfers:** No deadline.

Contact. Financial aid office: (410) 822-5400 ext. 252
Mindy Schaffer, Director of Financial Aid
PO Box 8
Wye Mills, MD 21679-0008

College of Notre Dame of Maryland

Baltimore, Maryland
www.ndm.edu
Four-year private **Federal Code: 002065**

	Living at home	On-campus
Tuition and fees:	$19,075	$19,075
Room and board:		$7,600
Books and supplies:	$800	$800
Personal expenses:	$800	$800
Transportation:	$400	$400

Undergraduate aid. Need-based: Average financial aid package for full-time students was $18,300; for part-time $5,500. 60% awarded as scholarships/grants, 40% as loans/jobs. **Non-need-based:** Scholarships based on academics, alumni affiliation, art, leadership, music/drama. **Student debt:** 82% of graduating class borrowed to fund education; average debt was $16,000. **Additional information:** Maximum consideration for financial aid if application received by February 15. Auditions and portfolios in areas of art, music and writing considered for scholarships.

Freshman aid. Need-based: Out of 119 full-time freshmen, 104 applied for aid; 104 were judged to have need; of these 104 received aid. Average package met 97% of need. 72 students had full need met. Average scholarship/grant was $7,000; average loan $3,200. **Non-need based:** 91 full-time freshmen with need received non-need scholarships; 25 without need received awards.

Merit scholarships. Academic/achievement awards $4,000 to full tuition; endowed scholarships $1,000 to $8,000, variable criteria, usually 20-35 awards. Transfer scholarships range from $4,000 to $9,350.

Policies to reduce costs. Tuition/fee waivers for family members, employees and their families. Credit/placement for qualifying scores on AP, IB examinations.

Payment plans. Credit card, installment payment.

Application procedures. FAFSA required. Priority date 2/15; no closing date. Applicants notified on rolling basis starting 3/15, must reply by 5/1 or within 2 week(s) of notification. **Transfers:** Specific non-need based merit scholarships available for transfer students.

Contact. Financial aid office: (410) 532-5369
Rick Staisloff, Vice President, Financial Affairs
4701 North Charles Street
Baltimore, MD 21210

College of Southern Maryland

La Plata, Maryland
www.csmd.edu
Two-year public **Federal Code: 002064**

College costs. Additional required fees are 20% of per credit hour rate.

	Living at home
Tuition and fees (2002-2003):	$2,916
Out-of-district:	$4,986
Out-of-state:	$6,486
Per-credit charge:	$81
Per-credit out-of-district:	$150
Per-credit out-of-state:	$200
Board only:	$750
Books and supplies:	$650
Personal expenses:	$900
Transportation:	$900

Undergraduate aid. Need-based: 93% awarded as scholarships/grants, 7% as loans/jobs. Need-based aid available for part-time students. **Non-need-based:** 61% awarded as scholarships/grants, 39% as loans/jobs. Scholarships based on academics, athletics, state/district residency.

Policies to reduce costs. Tuition/fee waivers for senior citizens, employees and their families. Credit/placement for qualifying scores on AP, CLEP examinations. Work study available nights, weekends and for part-time students.

Payment plans. Credit card, installment payment.

Application procedures. FAFSA, institutional form required. Priority date 3/1; no closing date. Applicants notified on rolling basis starting 5/15, must reply within 2 week(s) of notification.

Contact. Financial aid office: (301) 934-7533
Chad Norcross, Director of Financial Assistance
8730 Mitchell Road
La Plata, MD 20646-0910

Columbia Union College

Takoma Park, Maryland
www.cuc.edu
Four-year private **Federal Code: 002067**

	Living at home	On-campus
Tuition and fees (2002-2003):	$14,548	$14,548
Room and board:		$5,043
Books and supplies:	$945	$945

Undergraduate aid. Need-based: Need-based aid available for full-time and part-time students. **Non-need-based:** Scholarships based on academics, athletics, leadership, music/drama, state/district residency.

Policies to reduce costs. Tuition/fee waivers for family of clergy, employees and their families. Credit/placement for qualifying scores on AP, CLEP examinations.

Payment plans. Installment payment.

Application procedures. FAFSA, institutional form required. Priority date 3/1; closing date 3/31. Applicants notified on rolling basis starting 5/31, must reply within 4 week(s) of notification. **Transfers:** No deadline.

Contact. Financial aid office: (301) 891-4005
Elaine Oliver, Director of Financial Aid
7600 Flower Avenue
Takoma Park, MD 20912

Community College of Baltimore County - Catonsville

Baltimore, Maryland
www.ccbcmd.edu
Two-year public **Federal Code: 002063**

	Living at home
Tuition and fees (2002-2003):	$2,446
Out-of-district:	$4,096
Out-of-state:	$5,746
Per-credit charge:	$71
Per-credit out-of-district:	$126
Per-credit out-of-state:	$181
Books and supplies:	$800
Personal expenses:	$1,610
Transportation:	$1,800

Undergraduate aid. Need-based: Need-based aid available for full-time and part-time students. **Additional information:** On-campus employment typically available.

Policies to reduce costs. Tuition/fee waivers for senior citizens, employees and their families. Credit/placement for qualifying scores on AP, CLEP examinations.

Payment plans. Credit card, installment, deferred payment.

Application procedures. FAFSA required. Priority date 4/15; no closing date. Applicants notified on rolling basis starting 7/1, must reply within 2 week(s) of notification.

Contact. Jerome Lovick, Director of Financial Aid
800 South Rolling Road
Baltimore, MD 21228

Community College of Baltimore County - Dundalk

Baltimore, Maryland
www.ccbcmd.edu
Two-year public **Federal Code: 009935**

	Living at home
Tuition and fees (2002-2003):	$2,446
Out-of-district:	$4,096
Out-of-state:	$5,746
Per-credit charge:	$71
Per-credit out-of-district:	$126
Per-credit out-of-state:	$181
Books and supplies:	$800
Personal expenses:	$1,610
Transportation:	$1,800

Undergraduate aid. Need-based: Need-based aid available for full-time and part-time students.

Policies to reduce costs. Tuition/fee waivers for senior citizens, employees and their families. Credit/placement for qualifying scores on AP, CLEP examinations.

Payment plans. Credit card, installment, deferred payment.

Application procedures. FAFSA required. Priority date 4/15; no closing date. Applicants notified on rolling basis starting 5/1, must reply within 2 week(s) of notification. **Transfers:** Priority date 7/1.

Contact. Barbara Miller, Director of Financial Aid
7200 Sollers Point Road
Baltimore, MD 21222-4692

Community College of Baltimore County - Essex

Baltimore, Maryland
www.ccbc.cc.md.us
Two-year public **Federal Code: 002070**

	Living at home
Tuition and fees (2002-2003):	$2,446
Out-of-district:	$4,096
Out-of-state:	$5,746
Per-credit charge:	$71
Per-credit out-of-district:	$126
Per-credit out-of-state:	$181
Books and supplies:	$800
Personal expenses:	$1,610
Transportation:	$1,800

Undergraduate aid. Need-based: Need-based aid available for full-time and part-time students. **Non-need-based:** Scholarships based on academics, alumni affiliation, art, athletics, job skills, leadership, music/drama, state/district residency. **Additional information:** Tuition waiver for handicapped applicants.

Policies to reduce costs. Tuition/fee waivers for senior citizens, employees and their families. Credit/placement for qualifying scores on AP, CLEP examinations.

Payment plans. Credit card, installment, deferred payment.

Application procedures. FAFSA required. Priority date 4/15; no closing date. Applicants notified on rolling basis starting 5/1, must reply within 2 week(s) of notification. **Transfers:** Priority date 7/1; no deadline.

Contact. Financial aid office: (410) 780-6975
Marica Amaio, Director of Financial Aid
7201 Rossville Boulevard
Baltimore, MD 21237-3899

Coppin State College

Baltimore, Maryland
www.coppin.edu
Four-year public **Federal Code: 002068**

	Living at home	On-campus
Tuition and fees (2002-2003):	$3,959	$3,959
Out-of-state:	$9,368	$9,368
Room and board:		$5,814
Board only:	$1,800	
Books and supplies:	$600	$600
Personal expenses:	$2,785	$2,785
Transportation:	$900	$300

Undergraduate aid. Need-based: Average financial aid package for full-time students was $6,316. 60% awarded as scholarships/grants, 40% as loans/jobs. Need-based aid available for part-time students. **Non-need-based:** 18% awarded as scholarships/grants, 82% as loans/jobs. Scholarships based on academics, athletics, state/district residency. **Student debt:** 96% of graduating class borrowed to fund education; average debt was $13,905. **Additional information:** Funds allocated by State of Maryland for minority students enrolled for at least 6 credits who are Maryland residents and U.S. citizens (Other Race Grant).

Freshman aid. Need-based: Out of 524 full-time freshmen, 511 applied for aid; 423 were judged to have need; of these 383 received aid. Average package met 53% of need. 25 students had full need met. Average scholarship/grant was $3,876; average loan $2,522. **Non-need based:** 56 full-time freshmen with need received non-need scholarships; 31 received athletic scholarships.

Merit scholarships. Gold Freshman Merit Award; $1,200 per year; awarded to freshmen with 950 combined SAT and 2.5 high school GPA. Gold Transfer Merit Award; $1,200 per year; awarded to Maryland Community College transfer students with 2.8 GPA and successful completion of 56 credits. Blue Freshman Merit Award; $800 per year; awarded to freshman with 900 combined SAT and 2.5 GPA. Blue Transfer Merit Award; $600 per year; awarded to Maryland Community College transfer students with 2.5 GPA and successful completion of 25 credits.

Policies to reduce costs. Tuition/fee waivers for senior citizens, family members, employees and their families. Credit/placement for qualifying scores on AP, CLEP examinations. Work study available for part-time students.

Payment plans. Credit card, deferred payment.

Application procedures. FAFSA, institutional form required. Priority date 3/1; no closing date. Applicants notified on rolling basis starting 6/1, must reply within 2 week(s) of notification. **Transfers:** Priority date 3/1; no deadline.

Contact. **Financial aid office:** (410) 951-3636
Lady Jenkins, Director of Financial Aid
2500 West North Avenue
Baltimore, MD 21216

Frederick Community College

Frederick, Maryland
www.frederick.edu
Two-year public **Federal Code: 002071**

	Living at home
Tuition and fees (2002-2003):	$2,632
Out-of-district:	$5,332
Out-of-state:	$7,252
Per-credit charge:	$77
Per-credit out-of-district:	$167
Per-credit out-of-state:	$231
Books and supplies:	$700
Personal expenses:	$850
Transportation:	$1,100

Undergraduate aid. **Need-based:** Need-based aid available for full-time and part-time students. **Non-need-based:** Scholarships based on academics, athletics, state/district residency.

Policies to reduce costs. Tuition/fee waivers for senior citizens, employees and their families. Credit/placement for qualifying scores on AP, CLEP examinations. Work study available for part-time students.

Payment plans. Credit card, installment, deferred payment.

Application procedures. FAFSA, institutional form required. Priority date 6/15; no closing date. Applicants notified on rolling basis starting 5/15, must reply within 2 week(s) of notification. **Transfers:** Financial aid transcripts from prior institutions must be submitted before awards are made.

Contact. Brenda Dayhoff, Director, Financial Aid
7932 Opossumtown Pike
Frederick, MD 21702

Frostburg State University

Frostburg, Maryland
www.frostburg.edu
Four-year public **Federal Code: 002072**

	Living at home	On-campus
Tuition and fees (2002-2003):	$4,618	$4,618
Out-of-state:	$10,424	$10,424
Room and board:		$5,522
Board only:	$2,694	
Books and supplies:	$750	$750
Personal expenses:	$900	$900
Transportation:	$500	

Undergraduate aid. **Need-based:** Average financial aid package for full-time students was $6,602. 52% awarded as scholarships/grants, 48% as loans/jobs. Need-based aid available for part-time students. **Non-need-based:** Scholarships based on academics, leadership, minority status. **Student debt:** 58% of graduating class borrowed to fund education; average debt was $14,180.

Freshman aid. **Need-based:** Out of 999 full-time freshmen, 769 applied for aid; 474 were judged to have need; of these 463 received aid. Average package met 74% of need. 154 students had full need met. Average scholarship/grant was $4,087; average loan $2,367. **Non-need based:** 151 full-time freshmen with need received non-need scholarships; 145 without need received awards.

Policies to reduce costs. Tuition/fee waivers for senior citizens, employees and their families. Credit/placement for qualifying scores on AP, IB, CLEP examinations.

Payment plans. Credit card, installment, deferred payment.

Application procedures. FAFSA required. Priority date 3/1; no closing date. Applicants notified on rolling basis starting 3/15, must reply within 3 week(s) of notification.

Contact. **Financial aid office:** (301) 687-4301
Marjorie Robison, Director of Financial Aid
101 Braddock Road
Frostburg, MD 21532-1099

Garrett College

McHenry, Maryland
www.garrettcollege.edu
Two-year public **Federal Code: 010014**

	Living at home	On-campus
Tuition and fees:	$2,790	$2,790
Out-of-district:	$5,460	$5,460
Out-of-state:	$6,750	$6,750
Per-credit charge:	$76	$76
Per-credit out-of-district:	$165	$165
Per-credit out-of-state:	$208	$208
Room and board:		$4,870
Board only:	$1,200	
Books and supplies:	$2,000	$2,000
Personal expenses:	$2,000	$1,000
Transportation:	$2,400	$1,600

Undergraduate aid. **Additional information:** Many local scholarships both merit and need based.

Policies to reduce costs. Tuition/fee waivers for senior citizens, employees and their families. Credit/placement for qualifying scores on AP, CLEP examinations.

Payment plans. Installment, deferred payment.

Application procedures. Priority date 4/1; no closing date. Applicants notified on rolling basis starting 5/15, must reply within 3 week(s) of notification.

Contact. **Financial aid office:** (301) 387-3012
Patricia Bennett, Associate Director of Financial Aid and Veterans Affairs
687 Mosser Road
McHenry, MD 21541

Goucher College

Baltimore, Maryland
www.goucher.edu
Four-year private **Federal Code: 002073**

	Living at home	On-campus
Tuition and fees:	$24,450	$24,450
Room and board:		$8,200
Books and supplies:	$800	$800
Personal expenses:	$1,300	$1,300
Transportation:	$850	$530

Undergraduate aid. **Need-based:** Average financial aid package for full-time students was $16,661; for part-time $3,886. 80% awarded as scholarships/grants, 20% as loans/jobs. **Non-need-based:** 50% awarded as scholarships/grants, 50% as loans/jobs. Scholarships based on academics, art, music/drama. **Student debt:** 91% of graduating class borrowed to fund education; average debt was $15,376.

Freshman aid. **Need-based:** Average package met 85% of need. Average scholarship/grant was $11,674; average loan $1,820.

Merit scholarships. Merit scholarships ranging from $5,000-full tuition, based on strong high school academic records, special artistic talents and/or potential for leadership and personal achievement; criteria vary, but students with 3.0 high school GPA and SAT scores of 1100 and above can qualify.

Policies to reduce costs. Tuition/fee waivers for employees and their families. Credit/placement for qualifying scores on AP, IB, CLEP examinations.

Payment plans. Installment payment.

Application procedures. FAFSA, CSS PROFILE required. Priority date 2/15; no closing date. Applicants notified by 4/1, must reply by 5/1 or within 2 week(s) of notification. Early decision closing date 11/15.

Contact. **Financial aid office:** (410) 337-6500
Sharon Hassan, Director of Financial Aid
1021 Dulaney Valley Road
Baltimore, MD 21204

Hagerstown Community College

Hagerstown, Maryland
www.hagerstowncc.edu
Two-year public **Federal Code: 002074**

	Living at home
Tuition and fees (projected):	$2,530
Out-of-district:	$3,940
Out-of-state:	$5,110
Per-credit charge:	$77
Per-credit out-of-district:	$124
Per-credit out-of-state:	$163
Board only:	$2,250
Books and supplies:	$600
Personal expenses:	$200
Transportation:	$578

Undergraduate aid. All financial aid based on need. Need-based aid available for full-time and part-time students.

Policies to reduce costs. Tuition/fee waivers for senior citizens, employees and their families. Credit/placement for qualifying scores on AP, CLEP examinations. Work study available nights, weekends and for part-time students.

Payment plans. Credit card, installment, deferred payment.

Application procedures. FAFSA required. No deadline. Applicants notified on rolling basis starting 5/1.

Contact. **Financial aid office:** (301) 790-2800 ext. 473
Carolyn Cox, Director of Financial Aid
11400 Robinwood Drive
Hagerstown, MD 21742-6590

Harford Community College

Bel Air, Maryland
www.harford.cc.md.us
Two-year public **Federal Code: 002075**

	Living at home
Tuition and fees:	$2,145
Out-of-district:	$4,095
Out-of-state:	$6,045
Per-credit charge:	$65
Per-credit out-of-district:	$130
Per-credit out-of-state:	$195
Board only:	$1,500
Books and supplies:	$500
Personal expenses:	$500
Transportation:	$1,200

Policies to reduce costs. Tuition/fee waivers for adults, senior citizens, employees and their families. Credit/placement for qualifying scores on AP, CLEP examinations. Work study available for part-time students.

Payment plans. Credit card payment.

Application procedures. FAFSA, institutional form required. Priority date 3/1; no closing date. Applicants notified on rolling basis starting 4/1, must reply within 2 week(s) of notification. **Transfers:** No deadline. Maryland state application deadline March 1.

Contact. Lynn Lee, Director of Financial Aid
401 Thomas Run Road
Bel Air, MD 21015

Hood College

Frederick, Maryland
www.hood.edu
Four-year private **Federal Code: 002076**

	Living at home	On-campus
Tuition and fees:	$20,275	$20,275
Room and board:		$7,520
Board only:	$900	
Books and supplies:	$800	$800
Personal expenses:	$700	$700
Transportation:	$600	$400

Undergraduate aid. **Need-based:** Average financial aid package for full-time students was $16,619; for part-time $7,458. 74% awarded as scholarships/grants, 26% as loans/jobs. **Non-need-based:** 67% awarded as scholarships/grants, 33% as loans/jobs. Scholarships based on academics, alumni affiliation, leadership, minority status. **Student debt:** 68% of graduating class borrowed to fund education; average debt was $16,938.

Freshman aid. **Need-based:** Out of 179 full-time freshmen, 178 applied for aid; 135 were judged to have need; of these 135 received aid. Average package met 93% of need. 53 students had full need met. Average scholarship/grant was $15,341; average loan $4,154. **Non-need based:** 43 full-time freshmen with need received non-need scholarships; 41 without need received awards.

Merit scholarships. Hood Trust Academic Scholarship, amount varies; Hodson Scholarship, amount varies; Project Excellence Scholarship, up to full tuition; Presidential Scholarship, $10,000-$13,000; Trustee Scholarship, $8,000-$10,000

Policies to reduce costs. Tuition/fee waivers for senior citizens, family members, employees and their families. Credit/placement for qualifying scores on AP, IB, CLEP examinations. Work study available nights and weekends.

Payment plans. Credit card payment.

Application procedures. FAFSA required. Priority date 2/15; no closing date. Applicants notified on rolling basis starting 3/1, must reply within 3 week(s) of notification. **Transfers:** No deadline.

Contact. **Financial aid office:** (301) 696-3411
Jamie Lowthert, Director of Financial Aid
401 Rosemont Avenue
Frederick, MD 21701-8575

Howard Community College

Columbia, Maryland
www.howardcc.edu
Two-year public **Federal Code: 008175**

	Living at home
Tuition and fees (2002-2003):	$2,915
Out-of-district:	$5,675
Out-of-state:	$7,025
Per-credit charge:	$86
Per-credit out-of-district:	$178
Per-credit out-of-state:	$223
Board only:	$4,280
Books and supplies:	$450
Personal expenses:	$200
Transportation:	$960

Undergraduate aid. **Need-based:** 86% awarded as scholarships/grants, 14% as loans/jobs. Need-based aid available for part-time students. **Non-need-based:** 7% awarded as scholarships/grants, 93% as loans/jobs.

Policies to reduce costs. Tuition/fee waivers for senior citizens, employees and their families. Credit/placement for qualifying scores on AP, IB, CLEP examinations. Work study available nights and for part-time students.

Payment plans. Credit card, installment payment.

Application procedures. FAFSA, institutional form required. Priority date 3/1; no closing date. Applicants notified on rolling basis starting 4/1. **Transfers:** Priority date 3/1; no deadline.

Contact. **Financial aid office:** (410) 772-4912
Stephanie Pina, Director of Financial Aid
10901 Little Patuxent Parkway
Columbia, MD 21044

Johns Hopkins University

Baltimore, Maryland
www.jhu.edu
Four-year private **Federal Code: 002077**

	Living at home	On-campus
Tuition and fees:	$29,230	$29,230
Room and board:		$9,158
Books and supplies:	$800	$800
Personal expenses:	$800	$800

Undergraduate aid. **Need-based:** Average financial aid package for full-time students was $25,210; for part-time $23,732. 81% awarded as scholarships/grants, 19% as loans/jobs. **Non-need-based:** 75% awarded as scholarships/grants, 25% as loans/jobs. Scholarships based on academics, athletics, leadership.

Student debt: 54% of graduating class borrowed to fund education; average debt was $13,600. **Additional information:** Selected students receive aid packages without loan expectation, grants to full need. Private merit aid does not reduce Hopkins grant.

Freshman aid. Need-based: Out of 1,127 full-time freshmen, 721 applied for aid; 493 were judged to have need; of these 488 received aid. Average package met 100% of need. 457 students had full need met. Average scholarship/grant was $21,375; average loan $2,529. **Non-need based:** 198 full-time freshmen with need received non-need scholarships; 38 without need received awards; 10 received athletic scholarships.

Merit scholarships. Trust Hodson Scholarship, for candidates nominated by teacher or counselor for academic excellence and leadership by January 1, no special application required, $20,000 annually for 4 years, 20 awards; Westgate Scholarship for engineering freshmen, tuition plus $5,000 for 4 years, academic excellence, leadership, demonstrated research experience required, 2 offered per year per class. Wilson Research grants; $10,000.

Policies to reduce costs. Tuition/fee waivers for employees and their families. Prepayment discount; credit/placement for qualifying scores on AP, IB examinations. Work study available nights, weekends and for part-time students.

Payment plans. Installment, deferred payment.

Application procedures. FAFSA, institutional form required. Priority date 2/1; closing date 2/15. Applicants notified by 4/1, must reply by 5/1. Early decision closing date 11/15. **Transfers:** Closing date 4/1. Aid on funds-available basis. School of nursing has no closing date for financial aid applications.

Contact. **Financial aid office:** (410) 516-8028
Ellen Frishberg, University Director of Student Financial Services
3400 North Charles Street, 140 Garland Hall
Baltimore, MD 21218

Johns Hopkins University: Peabody Conservatory of Music

Baltimore, Maryland
www.peabody.jhu.edu
Four-year private **Federal Code: E00233**

	Living at home	On-campus
Tuition and fees:	$26,825	$26,825
Room and board:		$8,950
Books and supplies:	$625	$625
Personal expenses:	$1,000	$1,000
Transportation:	$800	$800

Undergraduate aid. Need-based: Need-based aid available for full-time and part-time students. **Non-need-based:** Scholarships based on academics, music/drama.

Policies to reduce costs. Tuition/fee waivers for employees and their families. Credit/placement for qualifying scores on AP, IB examinations. Work study available for part-time students.

Application procedures. FAFSA, institutional form required. Closing date 2/1. Applicants notified by 4/7, must reply by 5/1 or within 2 week(s) of notification.

Contact. Anita Goodwin, Director of Financial Aid
One East Mount Vernon Place
Baltimore, MD 21202

Loyola College in Maryland

Baltimore, Maryland
www.loyola.edu
Four-year private **Federal Code: 002078**

	Living at home	On-campus
Tuition and fees:	$25,743	$25,743
Room and board:		$8,630
Books and supplies:	$740	$740
Personal expenses:	$950	$950
Transportation:	$720	$320

Undergraduate aid. Need-based: Average financial aid package for full-time students was $16,950; for part-time $6,120. 69% awarded as scholarships/grants, 31% as loans/jobs. **Non-need-based:** 65% awarded as scholarships/grants, 35% as loans/jobs. Scholarships based on academics, athletics, minority status, state/district residency. **Student debt:** 68% of graduating class borrowed to fund education; average debt was $15,835.

Freshman aid. Need-based: Out of 901 full-time freshmen, 608 applied for aid; 414 were judged to have need; of these 414 received aid. Average package met 96% of need. 399 students had full need met. Average scholarship/grant was $10,960; average loan $5,200. **Non-need based:** 200 full-time freshmen with need received non-need scholarships; 152 without need received awards; 43 received athletic scholarships.

Policies to reduce costs. Tuition/fee waivers for employees and their families. Credit/placement for qualifying scores on AP, IB, CLEP examinations.

Payment plans. Credit card payment.

Application procedures. FAFSA, CSS PROFILE required. Closing date 2/10. Applicants notified by 4/5, must reply by 5/1. **Transfers:** Academic (merit-based) scholarships not available to transfer students.

Contact. Mark Lindenmeyer, Director of Financial Aid
4501 North Charles Street
Baltimore, MD 21210-2699

Maryland College of Art and Design

Silver Spring, Maryland
www.mcadmd.org
Two-year private **Federal Code: 014173**

	Living at home
Tuition and fees (2002-2003):	$10,875
Per-credit charge:	$435
Books and supplies:	$1,000

Undergraduate aid. Need-based: Average financial aid package for full-time students was $3,386; for part-time $711. 46% awarded as scholarships/grants, 54% as loans/jobs. **Non-need-based:** 24% awarded as scholarships/grants, 76% as loans/jobs. Scholarships based on art.

Freshman aid. Need-based: Average package met 100% of need. Average scholarship/grant was $2,675.

Merit scholarships. Annual merit scholarship competition, 16 recipients, ($500-$5,000). Must submit artwork.

Policies to reduce costs. Tuition/fee waivers for employees and their families. Credit/placement for qualifying scores on AP examinations.

Payment plans. Credit card, installment, deferred payment.

Application procedures. FAFSA required. Priority date 4/1; no closing date. Applicants notified on rolling basis starting 6/1, must reply within 2 week(s) of notification.

Contact. **Financial aid office:** (301) 649-4454
Belva Hill, Director of Financial Aid
10500 Georgia Avenue
Silver Spring, MD 20902-4111

Maryland Institute College of Art

Baltimore, Maryland
www.mica.edu
Four-year private **Federal Code: 002080**

	Living at home	On-campus
Tuition and fees:	$23,710	$23,710
Room and board:		$7,180
Board only:	$1,600	
Books and supplies:	$1,400	$1,400
Personal expenses:	$600	$600
Transportation:	$1,000	$700

Undergraduate aid. Need-based: Need-based aid available for full-time and part-time students. **Non-need-based:** Scholarships based on academics, art.

Policies to reduce costs. Tuition/fee waivers for senior citizens, employees and their families. Credit/placement for qualifying scores on AP, IB examinations. Work study available nights and weekends.

Payment plans. Credit card, installment payment.

Application procedures. FAFSA, institutional form required. Closing date 3/1. Applicants notified by 4/15, must reply by 5/1. Early decision closing date 11/15. **Transfers:** Closing date 3/15.

Contact. **Financial aid office:** (410) 225-2285
Diane Prengaman, Associate Vice President for Financial Aid
1300 Mount Royal Avenue
Baltimore, MD 21217

McDaniel College
Westminster, Maryland
www.mcdaniel.edu
Four-year private **Federal Code: 002109**

	Living at home	On-campus
Tuition and fees:	$22,860	$22,860
Room and board:		$5,280
Board only:	$1,500	
Books and supplies:	$600	$600
Personal expenses:	$970	$970
Transportation:	$600	$400

Undergraduate aid. Need-based: Average financial aid package for full-time students was $17,589; for part-time $5,838. 70% awarded as scholarships/grants, 30% as loans/jobs. **Non-need-based:** 77% awarded as scholarships/grants, 23% as loans/jobs. Scholarships based on academics, leadership. **Student debt:** 52% of graduating class borrowed to fund education; average debt was $17,663.

Freshman aid. Need-based: Out of 440 full-time freshmen, 358 applied for aid; 306 were judged to have need; of these 306 received aid. Average package met 94% of need. 92 students had full need met. Average scholarship/grant was $7,641; average loan $3,892. **Non-need based:** 108 without need received awards.

Policies to reduce costs. Tuition/fee waivers for adults, family members, employees and their families. Credit/placement for qualifying scores on AP, IB, CLEP examinations.

Payment plans. Credit card, installment payment.

Application procedures. FAFSA, institutional form required. Priority date 3/1; no closing date. Applicants notified on rolling basis starting 3/1, must reply by 5/1 or within 2 week(s) of notification. **Transfers:** No deadline. Academic transfer scholarships and nontraditional student reduced tuition grants available.

Contact. Financial aid office: (410) 857-2233
Patricia Williams, Director of Financial Aid
2 College Hill
Westminster, MD 21157-4390

Montgomery College: Rockville Campus
Rockville, Maryland
www.montgomerycollege.edu
Two-year public **Federal Code: 006911**

	Living at home
Tuition and fees (2002-2003):	$3,054
Out-of-district:	$6,078
Out-of-state:	$7,950
Per-credit charge:	$79
Per-credit out-of-district:	$163
Per-credit out-of-state:	$215
Board only:	$1,500
Books and supplies:	$800
Personal expenses:	$1,000
Transportation:	$1,700

Undergraduate aid. Need-based: 91% awarded as scholarships/grants, 9% as loans/jobs. Need-based aid available for part-time students. **Non-need-based:** 49% awarded as scholarships/grants, 51% as loans/jobs. Scholarships based on academics, alumni affiliation, art, music/drama, state/district residency.

Merit scholarships. Board of Trustees Academic Potential Scholarship. First year of tuition. 125 awards available to students with high GPAs, nominated by high school.

Policies to reduce costs. Tuition/fee waivers for senior citizens, employees and their families. Credit/placement for qualifying scores on AP, IB, CLEP examinations. Work study available nights, weekends and for part-time students.

Payment plans. Credit card, installment, deferred payment.

Application procedures. FAFSA, institutional form required. Priority date 5/15; no closing date. Applicants notified on rolling basis starting 5/30. **Transfers:** No deadline.

Contact. Financial aid office: (301) 279-5100
Melissa Gregory, Director of Financial Aid
51 Mannakee Street, Room 105
Rockville, MD 20850

Morgan State University
Baltimore, Maryland
www.morgan.edu
Four-year public **Federal Code: 002083**

	Living at home	On-campus
Tuition and fees (projected):	$4,644	$4,644
Out-of-state:	$11,040	$11,040
Room and board:		$6,129
Board only:	$773	
Books and supplies:	$721	$721
Personal expenses:	$1,185	$2,369
Transportation:	$361	$361

Undergraduate aid. Need-based: Average financial aid package for full-time students was $7,670; for part-time $4,583. 37% awarded as scholarships/grants, 63% as loans/jobs. **Non-need-based:** 66% awarded as scholarships/grants, 34% as loans/jobs. **Student debt:** 89% of graduating class borrowed to fund education; average debt was $17,062.

Freshman aid. Need-based: Out of 1,206 full-time freshmen, 1,108 applied for aid; 951 were judged to have need; of these 925 received aid. Average package met 62% of need. 21 students had full need met. Average scholarship/grant was $3,456. **Non-need based:** 4 full-time freshmen with need received non-need scholarships; 7 without need received awards; 43 received athletic scholarships.

Policies to reduce costs. Tuition/fee waivers for senior citizens, minority students, employees and their families. Credit/placement for qualifying scores on AP, CLEP examinations.

Payment plans. Credit card, installment, deferred payment.

Application procedures. FAFSA required. Priority date 4/1; no closing date. Applicants notified on rolling basis starting 6/1, must reply within 2 week(s) of notification.

Contact. Reginald Cureton, Director of Financial Aid
1700 East Coldspring Lane
Baltimore, MD 21251

Mount St. Mary's College
Emmitsburg, Maryland
www.msmary.edu
Four-year private **Federal Code: 002086**

	Living at home	On-campus
Tuition and fees:	$21,000	$21,000
Room and board:		$7,400
Board only:	$2,100	
Books and supplies:	$800	$800
Personal expenses:	$700	$600
Transportation:	$650	$300

Undergraduate aid. Need-based: Average financial aid package for full-time students was $14,020; for part-time $4,500. 71% awarded as scholarships/grants, 29% as loans/jobs. **Non-need-based:** 64% awarded as scholarships/grants, 36% as loans/jobs. Scholarships based on academics, athletics, job skills, leadership, minority status. **Student debt:** 78% of graduating class borrowed to fund education; average debt was $15,940.

Freshman aid. Need-based: Out of 400 full-time freshmen, 335 applied for aid; 275 were judged to have need; of these 275 received aid. Average package met 82% of need. 88 students had full need met. Average scholarship/grant was $9,320; average loan $3,133. **Non-need based:** 54 full-time freshmen with need received non-need scholarships; 107 without need received awards; 37 received athletic scholarships.

Merit scholarships. Kuderer Scholarship; full-tuition scholarship for 4 years; based on competitive examinations, strong academic records and SAT scores of 1180 or higher; 3 awards.

Policies to reduce costs. Tuition/fee waivers for family members, employees and their families. Prepayment discount; credit/placement for qualifying scores on AP, IB, CLEP examinations. Work study available nights and weekends.

Payment plans. Credit card, installment payment.

Application procedures. FAFSA, CSS PROFILE required. Closing date 2/15. Applicants notified on rolling basis starting 2/15, must reply by 5/1. **Transfers:** Scholarships available based on GPA at previous institution.

Contact. **Financial aid office:** (800) 448-4347
David Reeder, Director of Financial Aid
16300 Old Emmitsburg Road
Emmitsburg, MD 21727

Ner Israel Rabbinical College

Baltimore, Maryland
Four-year private
Federal Code: 002087

	Living at home	On-campus
Tuition and fees (2002-2003):	$6,000	$6,000
Room and board:		$6,000

Contact. Moshe Pelberg, Financial Aid Administrator
400 Mount Wilson Lane
Baltimore, MD 21208

St. John's College

Annapolis, Maryland
www.sjca.edu
Four-year private
Federal Code: 002092

	Living at home	On-campus
Tuition and fees:	$29,040	$29,040
Room and board:		$7,320
Books and supplies:	$280	$280
Personal expenses:	$750	$750
Transportation:	$350	$350

Undergraduate aid. All financial aid based on need. Average financial aid package for full-time students was $22,262. 73% awarded as scholarships/grants, 27% as loans/jobs. Need-based aid available for part-time students. **Student debt:** 65% of graduating class borrowed to fund education; average debt was $18,125.

Freshman aid. Out of 124 full-time freshmen, 90 applied for aid; 69 were judged to have need; of these 69 received aid. Average package met 90% of need. 59 students had full need met. Average scholarship/grant was $17,264; average loan $2,800.

Policies to reduce costs. Tuition/fee waivers for employees and their families. Work study available nights and weekends.

Payment plans. Credit card, installment payment.

Application procedures. FAFSA, CSS PROFILE required. Priority date 2/15; no closing date. Applicants notified on rolling basis starting 1/15, must reply by 5/1.

Contact. **Financial aid office:** (410) 626-2502
Caroline Christensen, Director of Financial Aid
PO Box 2800
Annapolis, MD 21404

St. Mary's College of Maryland

St. Mary's City, Maryland
www.smcm.edu
Four-year public
Federal Code: 002095

	Living at home	On-campus
Tuition and fees:	$8,740	$8,740
Out-of-state:	$15,060	$15,060
Room and board:		$7,105
Board only:	$1,570	
Books and supplies:	$1,000	$1,000
Personal expenses:	$1,800	$1,800
Transportation:	$1,000	$300

Undergraduate aid. **Need-based:** Average financial aid package for full-time students was $6,695; for part-time $4,698. 58% awarded as scholarships/grants, 42% as loans/jobs. **Non-need-based:** 61% awarded as scholarships/grants, 39% as loans/jobs. Scholarships based on academics, art, leadership, music/drama. **Student debt:** 68% of graduating class borrowed to fund education; average debt was $17,125.

Freshman aid. **Need-based:** Out of 425 full-time freshmen, 318 applied for aid; 178 were judged to have need; of these 178 received aid. Average package met 58% of need. Average scholarship/grant was $3,500; average loan $2,625. **Non-need based:** 80 full-time freshmen with need received non-need scholarships; 128 without need received awards.

Policies to reduce costs. Tuition/fee waivers for senior citizens, employees and their families. Credit/placement for qualifying scores on AP, IB, CLEP examinations. Work study available nights, weekends and for part-time students.

Payment plans. Credit card, installment payment.

Application procedures. FAFSA required. Closing date 3/1. Applicants notified by 4/1, must reply by 5/1. Early decision closing date 12/1. **Transfers:** Priority date 3/1; closing date 6/1. All financial aid recipients must have GED or high school diploma. Financial aid transcript required from previous colleges attended.

Contact. **Financial aid office:** (240) 895-3000
Tim Wolfe, Director of Financial Aid
18952 East Fisher Road
St. Mary's City, MD 20686-3001

Salisbury University

Salisbury, Maryland
www.salisbury.edu
Four-year public
Federal Code: 002091

	Living at home	On-campus
Tuition and fees (2002-2003):	$4,804	$4,804
Out-of-state:	$10,568	$10,568
Room and board:		$6,800
Board only:	$1,470	
Books and supplies:	$650	$650
Personal expenses:	$1,250	$1,250
Transportation:	$850	$850

Undergraduate aid. **Need-based:** Average financial aid package for full-time students was $5,654; for part-time $3,164. 40% awarded as scholarships/grants, 60% as loans/jobs. **Non-need-based:** 40% awarded as scholarships/grants, 60% as loans/jobs. Scholarships based on academics, alumni affiliation, art, leadership, music/drama, state/district residency. **Student debt:** 54% of graduating class borrowed to fund education; average debt was $14,773. **Additional information:** Job opportunities provided for almost 30% of full-time undergraduate students (over 900 jobs). Students can expect to earn $1500 per academic year by working 10 to 15 hours per week.

Freshman aid. **Need-based:** Out of 900 full-time freshmen, 710 applied for aid; 400 were judged to have need; of these 388 received aid. Average package met 71% of need. 114 students had full need met. Average scholarship/grant was $3,925; average loan $2,330. **Non-need based:** 208 full-time freshmen with need received non-need scholarships; 154 without need received awards.

Merit scholarships. Scholarships based on outstanding scholastic achievement, extra-curricular activities, geographic residence, degree program and additional factors; over 20 awarded.

Policies to reduce costs. Tuition/fee waivers for senior citizens, employees and their families. Credit/placement for qualifying scores on AP, IB, CLEP examinations. Work study available nights and weekends.

Payment plans. Credit card, installment payment.

Application procedures. FAFSA required. Priority date 2/1; no closing date. Applicants notified on rolling basis starting 4/1, must reply by 5/1 or within 2 week(s) of notification. Early decision closing date 12/15. **Transfers:** No deadline. Financial aid transcripts from previous schools required.

Contact. **Financial aid office:** (410) 543-6165
Beverly Horner, Director of Financial Aid
1200 Camden Avenue
Salisbury, MD 21801-6862

Sojourner-Douglass College

Baltimore, Maryland
www.sdc.edu
Four-year private
Federal Code: 021279

	Living at home
Tuition and fees:	$5,590
Books and supplies:	$800
Personal expenses:	$2,800
Transportation:	$416

Undergraduate aid. **Need-based:** Need-based aid available for full-time and part-time students.

Policies to reduce costs. Tuition/fee waivers for employees and their families.

Payment plans. Installment payment.

Application procedures. FAFSA, institutional form required. Priority date 3/1; no closing date. Applicants notified on rolling basis, must reply within 2 week(s) of notification.

Contact. Rebecca Chalk, Financial Aid Administrator
500 North Caroline Street
Baltimore, MD 21205

Towson University

Towson, Maryland
www.towson.edu
Four-year public **Federal Code: 002099**

	Living at home	On-campus
Tuition and fees (2002-2003):	$5,401	$5,401
Out-of-state:	$12,753	$12,753
Room and board:		$6,322
Board only:	$1,200	
Books and supplies:	$790	$790
Personal expenses:	$930	$1,450
Transportation:	$1,680	$1,500

Undergraduate aid. Need-based: Average financial aid package for full-time students was $8,109; for part-time $6,156. 37% awarded as scholarships/grants, 63% as loans/jobs. **Non-need-based:** 49% awarded as scholarships/grants, 51% as loans/jobs. Scholarships based on academics, alumni affiliation, art, athletics, leadership, minority status, music/drama, state/district residency. **Student debt:** 48% of graduating class borrowed to fund education; average debt was $15,530.

Freshman aid. Need-based: Out of 2,209 full-time freshmen, 1,635 applied for aid; 1,066 were judged to have need; of these 989 received aid. Average package met 79% of need. 493 students had full need met. Average scholarship/grant was $4,393; average loan $2,883. **Non-need based:** 798 full-time freshmen with need received non-need scholarships; 335 without need received awards; 64 received athletic scholarships.

Merit scholarships. Towson Scholar Award; full tuition, fees, room and board. Presidential Scholarship; full tuition and fees. University Scholarship; full tuition. Provost Scholarship; $1,000-$6,000. Selection based on GPA and combined SAT score.

Policies to reduce costs. Tuition/fee waivers for senior citizens, employees and their families. Credit/placement for qualifying scores on AP, IB, CLEP examinations. Work study available nights, weekends and for part-time students.

Payment plans. Credit card payment.

Application procedures. FAFSA required. Priority date 3/1; no closing date. Applicants notified on rolling basis starting 3/15, must reply within 2 week(s) of notification. **Transfers:** Priority date 3/1; no deadline.

Contact. Vincent Pecora, Director of Financial Aid
8000 York Road
Towson, MD 21252-0001

United States Naval Academy

Annapolis, Maryland
www.usna.edu
Four-year public **Federal Code: 002101**

College costs (projected). First-year students pay deposit of $2,200 for initial outfitting of uniforms and other supplies. Tuition, room and board, and medical and dental care provided by United States Government. Each midshipman receives monthly salary of about $764 to cover costs of books, supplies, uniforms, laundry, and equipment, including microcomputer.

Undergraduate aid. Additional information: Naval Academy does not charge for tuition, room or board.

Policies to reduce costs. Credit/placement for qualifying scores on AP examinations.

Contact. 117 Decatur Road
Annapolis, MD 21402-5018

University of Baltimore

Baltimore, Maryland
www.ubalt.edu
Upper-division public **Federal Code: 002102**

	Living at home
Tuition and fees (2002-2003):	$4,996
Out-of-state:	$13,766
Books and supplies:	$730

Undergraduate aid. Need-based: Need-based aid available for full-time and part-time students. **Additional information:** Full need met for dependent students only.

Policies to reduce costs. Tuition/fee waivers for senior citizens, employees and their families. Credit/placement for qualifying scores on AP, CLEP examinations.

Payment plans. Credit card, installment, deferred payment.

Application procedures. FAFSA, institutional form required. No deadline. Applicants notified on rolling basis. **Transfers:** Priority date 4/1; no deadline. Scholarship application deadline, March 1.

Contact. Financial aid office: (410) 837-4763
Barbara Miller, Director, Financial Aid
1420 North Charles Street
Baltimore, MD 21201-5779

University of Maryland: Baltimore

Baltimore, Maryland
www.umaryland.edu
Upper-division public **Federal Code: 002104**

	Living at home	On-campus
Tuition and fees (2002-2003):	$5,566	$5,566
Out-of-state:	$13,221	$13,221
Room only:		$2,143
Books and supplies:	$1,530	$1,530
Personal expenses:	$1,596	$1,596
Transportation:	$1,331	

Undergraduate aid. All financial aid based on need. Average financial aid package for full-time students was $6,496. 36% awarded as scholarships/grants, 64% as loans/jobs. Need-based aid available for part-time students.

Policies to reduce costs. Tuition/fee waivers for employees and their families. Credit/placement for qualifying scores on AP, CLEP examinations. Work study available nights, weekends and for part-time students.

Payment plans. Credit card, installment payment.

Application procedures. FAFSA required. Priority date 3/15; no closing date. Applicants notified on rolling basis starting 4/15, must reply within 2 week(s) of notification. **Transfers:** Priority date 3/15; no deadline. Maryland state deadline is March 1.

Contact. Financial aid office: (410) 706-7347
Cissy VanSickle, Director of Financial Aid
Office of Records and Registration, Baltimore Student Union, Room 326; 621 West Lombard Street
Baltimore, MD 21201-1575

University of Maryland: Baltimore County

Baltimore, Maryland
www.umbc.edu
Four-year public **Federal Code: 00215**

	Living at home	On-campus
Tuition and fees (2002-2003):	$6,362	$6,362
Out-of-state:	$12,546	$12,546
Room and board:		$6,780
Board only:	$2,695	
Books and supplies:	$800	$800
Personal expenses:	$1,312	$1,312
Transportation:	$2,268	$545

Undergraduate aid. Need-based: Average financial aid package for full-time students was $6,212; for part-time $4,500. 46% awarded as scholarships/grants, 54% as loans/jobs. **Non-need-based:** 61% awarded as scholarships/grants, 39% as loans/jobs. Scholarships based on academics, art, music/drama.

Freshman aid. **Need-based:** Out of 1,333 full-time freshmen, 4,066 applied for aid; 878 were judged to have need; of these 708 received aid. Average package met 61% of need. 509 students had full need met. Average scholarship/grant was $2,925; average loan $2,566. **Non-need based:** 358 full-time freshmen with need received non-need scholarships; 227 without need received awards; 92 received athletic scholarships.

Merit scholarships. Meyerhoff Scholarship Program for outstanding students committed to promoting minority careers in science, math, engineering; full scholarships, computers, stipends, academic support services. University Scholarships, Honors College Fellowships: tuition, fees, room and board. President's Fellowships: $5,000 per year. UMBC Merit Awards; $500-$2,500 per year. Scholastic Achievement Awards President's Scholarships; $3,500 per year. Honors College Scholarships; $1,000 per year. Center for Women and Information Technology supports careers in government and politics. The Humanities Scholars Program supports study in literature, history, philosophy and language.

Policies to reduce costs. Tuition/fee waivers for senior citizens, employees and their families. Credit/placement for qualifying scores on AP, IB, CLEP examinations.

Payment plans. Credit card, installment, deferred payment.

Application procedures. FAFSA required. Priority date 3/1; no closing date. Applicants notified on rolling basis starting 3/15, must reply within 3 week(s) of notification. **Transfers:** Two-year merit scholarships available for transfer students from community colleges.

Contact. **Financial aid office:** (410) 455-2387
Rachel Brinkley, Director of Financial Aid
1000 Hilltop Circle
Baltimore, MD 21250

University of Maryland: College Park

College Park, Maryland
www.maryland.edu
Four-year public **Federal Code: 002103**

	Living at home	On-campus
Tuition and fees (2002-2003):	$5,670	$5,670
Out-of-state:	$14,434	$14,434
Room and board:		$7,101
Books and supplies:	$785	$785
Personal expenses:	$1,940	$1,940
Transportation:	$604	$604

Undergraduate aid. **Need-based:** Average financial aid package for full-time students was $8,051; for part-time $6,211. 41% awarded as scholarships/grants, 59% as loans/jobs. **Non-need-based:** 62% awarded as scholarships/grants, 38% as loans/jobs. Scholarships based on academics, art, athletics, leadership, music/drama, state/district residency. **Student debt:** 22% of graduating class borrowed to fund education; average debt was $15,566. **Additional information:** Prepaid tuition plans available through state but not university.

Freshman aid. **Need-based:** Out of 4,358 full-time freshmen, 3,589 applied for aid; 1,693 were judged to have need; of these 1,600 received aid. Average package met 74% of need. 531 students had full need met. Average scholarship/grant was $4,818; average loan $2,383. **Non-need based:** 846 full-time freshmen with need received non-need scholarships; 1,155 without need received awards; 87 received athletic scholarships.

Policies to reduce costs. Tuition/fee waivers for senior citizens, employees and their families. Credit/placement for qualifying scores on AP, IB, CLEP examinations. Work study available nights, weekends and for part-time students.

Payment plans. Credit card, installment, deferred payment.

Application procedures. FAFSA required. Priority date 2/15; no closing date. Applicants notified on rolling basis starting 4/1, must reply within 2 week(s) of notification.

Contact. **Financial aid office:** (301) 314-9000
William Leith, Director of Student Financial Aid
Mitchell Building
College Park, MD 20742-5235

University of Maryland: University College

Adelphi, Maryland
www.umuc.edu
Four-year public **Federal Code: 011644**

	Living at home
Tuition and fees (2002-2003):	$6,330
Out-of-state:	$11,670

Undergraduate aid. **Need-based:** Average financial aid package for full-time students was $1,631; for part-time $1,429. 24% awarded as scholarships/grants, 76% as loans/jobs. **Non-need-based:** 1% awarded as scholarships/grants, 99% as loans/jobs. Scholarships based on academics. **Student debt:** 89% of graduating class borrowed to fund education; average debt was $1,977.

Freshman aid. **Need-based:** Out of 52 full-time freshmen, 35 applied for aid; 31 were judged to have need; of these 24 received aid. Average package met 22% of need. Average scholarship/grant was $1,324; average loan $1,236.

Policies to reduce costs. Tuition/fee waivers for senior citizens, employees and their families. Credit/placement for qualifying scores on AP, IB, CLEP examinations. Work study available nights, weekends and for part-time students.

Payment plans. Credit card payment.

Application procedures. FAFSA, institutional form required. Priority date 6/1; no closing date. Applicants notified on rolling basis starting 5/1, must reply within 3 week(s) of notification.

Contact. **Financial aid office:** (301) 985-7000
Dawn Mosisa, Assistant Vice President, Financial Aid
3501 University Boulevard East
Adelphi, MD 20783

Villa Julie College

Stevenson, Maryland
www.vjc.edu
Four-year private **Federal Code: 002107**

	Living at home	On-campus
Tuition and fees (2002-2003):	$12,800	$12,800
Room only:		$4,450
Books and supplies:	$900	$900
Personal expenses:	$2,376	$1,824

Undergraduate aid. **Need-based:** Average financial aid package for full-time students was $17,560; for part-time $9,177. 53% awarded as scholarships/grants, 47% as loans/jobs. **Non-need-based:** 70% awarded as scholarships/grants, 30% as loans/jobs. Scholarships based on academics, art, leadership, music/drama. **Student debt:** 33% of graduating class borrowed to fund education; average debt was $16,591. **Additional information:** Cooperative Education Program allows students to work in their field of study with area corporations.

Freshman aid. **Need-based:** Out of 487 full-time freshmen, 456 applied for aid; 359 were judged to have need; of these 347 received aid. Average package met 49% of need. 161 students had full need met. Average scholarship/grant was $2,318; average loan $2,636. **Non-need based:** 222 full-time freshmen with need received non-need scholarships; 120 without need received awards.

Policies to reduce costs. Tuition/fee waivers for employees and their families. Credit/placement for qualifying scores on AP, IB, CLEP examinations. Work study available nights, weekends and for part-time students.

Payment plans. Credit card, installment payment.

Application procedures. FAFSA, institutional form required. Priority date 3/1; no closing date. Applicants notified on rolling basis starting 3/15, must reply within 2 week(s) of notification. **Transfers:** Limited number of scholarships available based on merit.

Contact. **Financial aid office:** (410) 602-6559
Debra Bottoms, Director of Student Financial Aid
1525 Greenspring Valley Road
Stevenson, MD 21153

Washington Bible College

Lanham, Maryland
www.bible.edu
Four-year private **Federal Code: 001462**

College costs. 1-12 hours cost $325 per credit hour; 13+ hours cost $100 per credit hour

	Living at home	On-campus
Tuition and fees:	$8,030	$8,030
Room and board:		$5,250
Board only:	$1,575	
Books and supplies:	$500	$500
Personal expenses:	$1,300	$1,300
Transportation:	$500	$500

Undergraduate aid. Need-based: Need-based aid available for full-time and part-time students. **Non-need-based:** Scholarships based on academics, leadership.

Policies to reduce costs. Tuition/fee waivers for family of clergy, employees and their families. Prepayment discount; credit/placement for qualifying scores on AP, CLEP examinations.

Payment plans. Installment payment.

Application procedures. FAFSA, institutional form required. Priority date 3/1; no closing date. Applicants notified on rolling basis starting 7/1, must reply within 2 week(s) of notification.

Contact. Nancy Minton, Administrator of Financial Aid
6511 Princess Garden Parkway
Lanham, MD 20706-3599

Washington College

Chestertown, Maryland
www.washcoll.edu
Four-year private **Federal Code: 002108**

	Living at home	On-campus
Tuition and fees:	$24,800	$24,800
Room and board:		$5,740
Board only:	$750	
Books and supplies:	$1,500	$1,500
Personal expenses:	$800	$800

Undergraduate aid. Need-based: Average financial aid package for full-time students was $18,409. 55% awarded as scholarships/grants, 45% as loans/jobs. Need-based aid available for part-time students. **Non-need-based:** 87% awarded as scholarships/grants, 13% as loans/jobs. Scholarships based on academics, leadership. **Student debt:** 60% of graduating class borrowed to fund education; average debt was $17,711.

Freshman aid. Need-based: Out of 339 full-time freshmen, 204 applied for aid; 199 were judged to have need; of these 199 received aid. Average package met 89% of need. 92 students had full need met. Average scholarship/grant was $15,404; average loan $2,625. **Non-need based:** 123 full-time freshmen with need received non-need scholarships.

Merit scholarships. National Honor Society Scholarship, $40,000 over 4 years; applicant must be member of NHS.

Policies to reduce costs. Tuition/fee waivers for employees and their families. Credit/placement for qualifying scores on AP, IB, CLEP examinations. Work study available nights and weekends.

Payment plans. Credit card, installment payment.

Application procedures. FAFSA, institutional form required. Priority date 2/15; closing date 4/1. Applicants notified on rolling basis starting 3/1, must reply by 5/1 or within 3 week(s) of notification. Early decision closing date 11/15.

Contact. **Financial aid office:** (410) 778-7214
Jean Narcum, Director of Financial Aid
300 Washington Avenue
Chestertown, MD 21620-1197

Wor-Wic Community College

Salisbury, Maryland
www.worwic.edu
Two-year public **Federal Code: 013842**

	Living at home
Tuition and fees (2002-2003):	$1,914
Out-of-district:	$4,704
Out-of-state:	$5,514
Per-credit charge:	$62
Per-credit out-of-district:	$155
Per-credit out-of-state:	$182
Board only:	$3,600
Books and supplies:	$1,200
Personal expenses:	$500
Transportation:	$1,200

Undergraduate aid. Need-based: Average financial aid package for full-time students was $1,908; for part-time $1,027. 87% awarded as scholarships/grants, 13% as loans/jobs. **Non-need-based:** 33% awarded as scholarships/grants, 67% as loans/jobs. Scholarships based on academics, state/district residency.

Freshman aid. Need-based: Out of 275 full-time freshmen, 149 applied for aid; 126 were judged to have need; of these 103 received aid. Average package met 19% of need. 1 students had full need met. Average scholarship/grant was $1,680; average loan $1,227. **Non-need based:** 1 full-time freshmen with need received non-need scholarships; 7 without need received awards.

Policies to reduce costs. Tuition/fee waivers for senior citizens, employees and their families. Work study available nights, weekends and for part-time students.

Payment plans. Credit card, deferred payment.

Application procedures. FAFSA, institutional form required. Priority date 6/1; no closing date. Applicants notified on rolling basis starting 4/1.

Contact. **Financial aid office:** (410) 334-2905
Deborah Jenkins, Director of Financial Aid
32000 Campus Drive
Salisbury, MD 21804

Massachusetts

Ai The New England Institute of Art and Design

Brookline, Massachusetts
www.aine.artinstitutes.edu
Four-year proprietary **Federal Code: 007486**

	Living at home
Tuition and fees (projected):	$15,575
Books and supplies:	$800
Personal expenses:	$2,800
Transportation:	$324

Undergraduate aid. Need-based: Average financial aid package for full-time students was $4,373; for part-time $3,279. 24% awarded as scholarships/grants, 76% as loans/jobs. **Non-need-based:** Scholarships based on academics. **Student debt:** 75% of graduating class borrowed to fund education; average debt was $17,125. **Additional information:** Institutional scholarships (need and non-need based) available; separate application required.

Freshman aid. Need-based: Out of 353 full-time freshmen, 321 applied for aid; 292 were judged to have need; of these 292 received aid. Average package met 23% of need. Average scholarship/grant was $2,958; average loan $3,103. **Non-need based:** 12 full-time freshmen with need received non-need scholarships.

Policies to reduce costs. Tuition/fee waivers for employees and their families. Tuition at time of enrollment guaranteed for 4 years; prepayment discount. Work study available nights, weekends and for part-time students.

Payment plans. Credit card, installment payment.

Application procedures. FAFSA required. Priority date 5/1; no closing date. Applicants notified on rolling basis starting 3/1.

Contact. Financial aid office: (617) 582-4407
Deana Coady, Director of Student Financial Services
10 Brookline Place West
Brookline, MA 02445-7295

American International College

Springfield, Massachusetts
www.aic.edu
Four-year private **Federal Code: 002114**

College costs. Required fees are included in tuition.

	Living at home	On-campus
Tuition and fees:	$16,700	$16,700
Room and board:		$7,990
Books and supplies:	$600	$600
Personal expenses:	$2,600	$1,000
Transportation:	$1,000	$450

Undergraduate aid. Need-based: Average financial aid package for full-time students was $17,643; for part-time $8,785. 44% awarded as scholarships/grants, 56% as loans/jobs. **Non-need-based:** Scholarships based on academics, athletics. **Student debt:** 85% of graduating class borrowed to fund education; average debt was $17,125.

Freshman aid. Need-based: Out of 247 full-time freshmen, 229 applied for aid; 201 were judged to have need; of these 201 received aid. Average package met 84% of need. 51 students had full need met. Average scholarship/grant was $9,993; average loan $3,733. **Non-need based:** 76 full-time freshmen with need received non-need scholarships; 30 without need received awards; 28 received athletic scholarships.

Merit scholarships. Presidential, Provost, Opportunity Scholarships; $5,000 to $9,000; based on class rank, SAT scores, GPA.

Policies to reduce costs. Tuition/fee waivers for senior citizens, family members, employees and their families. Prepayment discount; credit/placement for qualifying scores on AP, IB, CLEP examinations. Work study available nights and weekends.

Payment plans. Credit card, installment, deferred payment.

Application procedures. FAFSA required. Priority date 4/1; no closing date. Applicants notified on rolling basis starting 3/15, must reply by 5/1 or within 2 week(s) of notification.

Contact. Financial aid office: (413) 737-7000
Irene Martin, Director of Financial Aid
1000 State Street
Springfield, MA 01109

Amherst College

Amherst, Massachusetts
www.amherst.edu
Four-year private **Federal Code: 002115**

College costs. Health insurance fee $548 for students who do not have own insurance. Residence life fee $104 for campus residents.

	Living at home	On-campus
Tuition and fees:	$29,624	$29,624
Room and board:		$7,740
Books and supplies:	$850	$850
Personal expenses:	$1,500	$1,500

Undergraduate aid. All financial aid based on need. Average financial aid package for full-time students was $26,080. 87% awarded as scholarships/grants, 13% as loans/jobs. **Student debt:** 44% of graduating class borrowed to fund education; average debt was $11,544.

Freshman aid. Out of 408 full-time freshmen, 243 applied for aid; 192 were judged to have need; of these 192 received aid. Average package met 100% of need. 192 students had full need met. Average scholarship/grant was $23,725; average loan $2,150.

Policies to reduce costs. Credit/placement for qualifying scores on IB examinations.

Application procedures. FAFSA, CSS PROFILE required. Closing date 2/15. Applicants notified by 4/8, must reply by 5/1. Early decision closing date 11/15. **Transfers:** Closing date 2/15. Candidates for spring admission must apply for financial aid by November 1.

Contact. Financial aid office: (413) 542-2296
Joe Paul Case, Dean of Financial Aid
Campus Box 2231
Amherst, MA 01002

Anna Maria College

Paxton, Massachusetts
www.annamaria.edu
Four-year private **Federal Code: 002117**

College costs. Music programs pay $18,410 tuition, $614 per-credit-hour.

	Living at home	On-campus
Tuition and fees (2002-2003):	$17,860	$17,860
Room and board:		$6,550
Board only:	$2,000	
Books and supplies:	$600	$600
Personal expenses:	$1,000	$1,000
Transportation:	$1,000	$1,000

Undergraduate aid. Need-based: Average financial aid package for full-time students was $13,565; for part-time $4,424. 65% awarded as scholarships/grants, 35% as loans/jobs. **Non-need-based:** 27% awarded as scholarships/grants, 73% as loans/jobs. Scholarships based on academics, alumni affiliation, music/drama, religious affiliation, state/district residency. **Student debt:** 48% of graduating class borrowed to fund education; average debt was $15,648.

Freshman aid. Need-based: Out of 160 full-time freshmen, 152 applied for aid; 137 were judged to have need; of these 137 received aid. Average package met 84% of need. 43 students had full need met. Average scholarship/grant was $12,037; average loan $3,896. **Non-need based:** 19 full-time freshmen with need received non-need scholarships; 26 without need received awards.

Policies to reduce costs. Tuition/fee waivers for children of alumni, senior citizens, family members, employees and their families. Tuition at time of enrollment guaranteed for 4 years; credit/placement for qualifying scores on AP, CLEP examinations. Work study available nights and weekends.

Payment plans. Credit card, installment, deferred payment.

Application procedures. FAFSA required. No deadline. Applicants notified on rolling basis starting 3/15, must reply within 4 week(s) of notification. **Transfers:** Deadline May 1 for state aid.

Contact. **Financial aid office:** (508) 849-3366
Laurie Peltier, Director of Financial Aid
50 Sunset Lane, Box O
Paxton, MA 01612

Art Institute of Boston at Lesley University

Boston, Massachusetts
www.aiboston.edu
Four-year private **Federal Code: 008174**

	Living at home	On-campus
Tuition and fees:	$17,110	$17,110
Room and board:		$8,700
Board only:	$2,790	
Books and supplies:	$1,575	$1,575
Personal expenses:	$1,025	$2,125
Transportation:	$900	$450

Undergraduate aid. **Need-based:** Average financial aid package for full-time students was $7,834. 40% awarded as scholarships/grants, 60% as loans/jobs. Need-based aid available for part-time students. **Non-need-based:** 46% awarded as scholarships/grants, 54% as loans/jobs. Scholarships based on academics, art, leadership, minority status. **Student debt:** 75% of graduating class borrowed to fund education; average debt was $13,990.

Freshman aid. **Need-based:** Out of 116 full-time freshmen, 103 applied for aid; 75 were judged to have need; of these 75 received aid. Average package met 65% of need. 7 students had full need met. Average scholarship/grant was $4,005; average loan $3,225. **Non-need based:** 25 full-time freshmen with need received non-need scholarships; 8 without need received awards.

Merit scholarships. Merit Scholarship; $2,000-8,000 per year; 80 awarded. Presidential Scholarship; full tuition; 1 awarded. Alan Scholarship; $10,000; based on minority status and academic accomplishment; 1-3 awarded.

Policies to reduce costs. Tuition/fee waivers for employees and their families. Credit/placement for qualifying scores on AP examinations.

Payment plans. Credit card, installment payment.

Application procedures. FAFSA, institutional form required. Priority date 3/12; no closing date. Applicants notified on rolling basis starting 4/1, must reply within 2 week(s) of notification. **Transfers:** Priority date 3/18; no deadline.

Contact. **Financial aid office:** (617) 349-8710
Paul Henderson, Director of Financial Aid
700 Beacon Street
Boston, MA 02215-2598

Assumption College

Worcester, Massachusetts
www.assumption.edu
Four-year private **Federal Code: 002118**

	Living at home	On-campus
Tuition and fees:	$21,165	$21,165
Room and board:		$8,210
Board only:	$3,120	
Books and supplies:	$700	$700
Personal expenses:	$1,130	$1,130
Transportation:	$1,000	$400

Undergraduate aid. **Need-based:** Average financial aid package for full-time students was $13,958; for part-time $5,769. 66% awarded as scholarships/grants, 34% as loans/jobs. **Non-need-based:** 55% awarded as scholarships/grants, 45% as loans/jobs. Scholarships based on academics, athletics. **Student debt:** 83% of graduating class borrowed to fund education; average debt was $18,291.

Freshman aid. **Need-based:** Out of 621 full-time freshmen, 520 applied for aid; 439 were judged to have need; of these 439 received aid. Average package met 78% of need. 126 students had full need met. Average scholarship/grant was $10,343; average loan $3,720. **Non-need based:** 71 full-time freshmen with need received non-need scholarships; 117 without need received awards; 13 received athletic scholarships.

Merit scholarships. Lyceum, Milleret, Aquinas Presidential Scholarships; $7,500-$15,000; based on academic achievement and leadership potential, renewable depending on maintenance of GPA.

Policies to reduce costs. Tuition/fee waivers for family members, employees and their families. Credit/placement for qualifying scores on AP, IB examinations.

Payment plans. Credit card, installment payment.

Application procedures. FAFSA required. Priority date 2/1; closing date 3/1. Applicants notified on rolling basis starting 2/15, must reply by 5/1 or within 2 week(s) of notification. Early decision closing date 11/1. **Transfers:** Closing date 5/1.

Contact. **Financial aid office:** (508) 767-7368
Shelley John, Director of Financial Aid
500 Salisbury Street
Worcester, MA 01609

Atlantic Union College

South Lancaster, Massachusetts
www.atlanticuc.edu
Four-year private **Federal Code: 002119**

College costs. Required fees for nursing program $280.

	Living at home	On-campus
Tuition and fees (2002-2003):	$13,584	$13,584
Room and board:		$4,788
Board only:	$2,000	
Books and supplies:	$1,000	$1,000
Personal expenses:	$2,300	$2,300
Transportation:	$800	$800

Undergraduate aid. **Need-based:** Need-based aid available for full-time and part-time students. **Non-need-based:** Scholarships based on academics, athletics, job skills, leadership, music/drama.

Policies to reduce costs. Tuition/fee waivers for adults, senior citizens, family members, employees and their families. Prepayment discount; credit/placement for qualifying scores on AP, IB, CLEP examinations. Work study available nights, weekends and for part-time students.

Payment plans. Credit card, installment, deferred payment.

Application procedures. FAFSA, institutional form required. Priority date 4/1; no closing date. Applicants notified on rolling basis starting 4/1, must reply within 2 week(s) of notification. **Transfers:** No deadline.

Contact. **Financial aid office:** (978) 368-2275
Dwight Carnegie, Financial Aid Director
Main Street
South Lancaster, MA 01561

Babson College

Babson Park, Massachusetts
www.babson.edu
Four-year private **Federal Code: 002121**

	Living at home	On-campus
Tuition and fees:	$27,248	$27,248
Room and board:		$9,978
Board only:	$2,300	
Books and supplies:	$688	$688
Personal expenses:	$1,546	$1,546
Transportation:	$1,150	

Undergraduate aid. **Need-based:** Average financial aid package for full-time students was $22,004. 78% awarded as scholarships/grants, 22% as loans/jobs. **Non-need-based:** 26% awarded as scholarships/grants, 74% as loans/jobs. Scholarships based on academics, leadership, minority status.

Freshman aid. **Need-based:** Out of 402 full-time freshmen, 218 applied for aid; 178 were judged to have need; of these 178 received aid. Average package met 98% of need. 156 students had full need met. Average scholarship/grant was $18,439; average loan $2,833. **Non-need based:** 42 full-time freshmen with need received non-need scholarships; 26 without need received awards.

Merit scholarships. Presidential Scholarship; $10,000 per year. Women's Leadership Award; $5,000 per year. Multicultural Leadership Award; $10,000 per year.

Policies to reduce costs. Tuition/fee waivers for employees and their families. Credit/placement for qualifying scores on IB examinations. Work study available nights and weekends.

Payment plans. Installment payment.

Application procedures. FAFSA, CSS PROFILE required. Closing date 2/15. Applicants notified by 4/1, must reply by 5/1. Early decision closing date 12/1. **Transfers:** Closing date 4/15.

Contact. **Financial aid office:** (781) 239-4219
Melissa Shaak, Student Financial Services Team Leader
Mustard Hall
Babson Park, MA 02457-0310

Bay Path College

Longmeadow, Massachusetts
www.baypath.edu
Four-year private **Federal Code: 002122**

	Living at home	On-campus
Tuition and fees (2002-2003):	$15,934	$15,934
Room and board:		$7,416
Books and supplies:	$600	$600
Personal expenses:	$900	$900
Transportation:	$1,000	$300

Undergraduate aid. Need-based: Average financial aid package for full-time students was $9,958; for part-time $4,739. 53% awarded as scholarships/grants, 47% as loans/jobs. **Non-need-based:** 30% awarded as scholarships/grants, 70% as loans/jobs. Scholarships based on academics, state/district residency. **Student debt:** 69% of graduating class borrowed to fund education; average debt was $18,250.

Freshman aid. Need-based: Average package met 79% of need. Average scholarship/grant was $8,775; average loan $4,270.

Policies to reduce costs. Tuition/fee waivers for family members, employees and their families. Credit/placement for qualifying scores on AP, IB, CLEP examinations. Work study available nights and weekends.

Payment plans. Credit card, installment payment.

Application procedures. FAFSA, institutional form required. Priority date 3/15; no closing date. Applicants notified on rolling basis, must reply within 2 week(s) of notification. **Transfers:** No deadline.

Contact. **Financial aid office:** (413) 565-1345
Stephanie King, Director of Financial Aid
588 Longmeadow Street
Longmeadow, MA 01106

Bay State College

Boston, Massachusetts
www.baystate.edu
Two-year private **Federal Code: 003965**

	Living at home	On-campus
Tuition and fees:	$14,500	$14,500
Per-credit charge:	$473	$473
Room and board:		$8,925
Board only:	$1,800	
Books and supplies:	$810	$810
Personal expenses:	$2,745	
Transportation:	$513	$513

Undergraduate aid. Need-based: Need-based aid available for full-time and part-time students.

Merit scholarships. Scholarship Day award; $1,000-$5,000; based on examination held on last Saturday of January; amount of award determined by score.

Policies to reduce costs. Tuition/fee waivers for employees and their families. Credit/placement for qualifying scores on IB examinations. Work study available nights, weekends and for part-time students.

Payment plans. Credit card, installment payment.

Application procedures. FAFSA, institutional form required. Priority date 3/1; no closing date. Applicants notified on rolling basis starting 3/15, must reply within 3 week(s) of notification.

Contact. **Financial aid office:** (617) 236-8038
Melissa Holster, Director of Financial Aid
122 Commonwealth Avenue
Boston, MA 02116

Becker College

Worcester, Massachusetts
www.beckercollege.edu
Four-year private **Federal Code: 002123**

College costs. Campus residents pay $50 security deposit.

	Living at home	On-campus
Tuition and fees (2002-2003):	$15,190	$15,190
Room and board:		$7,550
Books and supplies:	$1,000	$1,000
Personal expenses:	$700	$700
Transportation:	$700	$300

Undergraduate aid. Need-based: Average financial aid package for full-time students was $10,111. 43% awarded as scholarships/grants, 57% as loans/jobs. Need-based aid available for part-time students. **Non-need-based:** 6% awarded as scholarships/grants, 94% as loans/jobs. Scholarships based on academics, leadership. **Student debt:** 100% of graduating class borrowed to fund education; average debt was $16,724.

Freshman aid. Need-based: Out of 195 full-time freshmen, 185 applied for aid; 168 were judged to have need; of these 168 received aid. Average package met 64% of need. 39 students had full need met. Average scholarship/grant was $5,038; average loan $4,504. **Non-need based:** 6 full-time freshmen with need received non-need scholarships; 27 without need received awards.

Policies to reduce costs. Tuition/fee waivers for senior citizens, family members, employees and their families. Credit/placement for qualifying scores on AP, CLEP examinations. Work study available nights, weekends and for part-time students.

Payment plans. Credit card, installment payment.

Application procedures. FAFSA required. Priority date 3/1; no closing date. Applicants notified on rolling basis starting 4/1, must reply within 2 week(s) of notification. **Transfers:** No deadline.

Contact. **Financial aid office:** (508) 791-9241 ext. 242
Denise Lawrie, Director of Financial Aid
61 Sever Street
Worcester, MA 01609

Benjamin Franklin Institute of Technology

Boston, Massachusetts
www.bfit.edu
Two-year private **Federal Code: 002151**

	Living at home
Tuition and fees (2002-2003):	$11,150
Per-credit charge:	$465
Books and supplies:	$600
Transportation:	$550

Undergraduate aid. Need-based: Need-based aid available for full-time and part-time students. **Non-need-based:** Scholarships based on academics.

Policies to reduce costs. Tuition/fee waivers for employees and their families. Credit/placement for qualifying scores on AP, IB, CLEP examinations.

Payment plans. Credit card, installment payment.

Application procedures. FAFSA required. Priority date 4/1; no closing date. Applicants notified on rolling basis starting 3/1, must reply by 6/1 or within 4 week(s) of notification.

Contact. **Financial aid office:** (617) 423-4630
Kevin Sullivan, Director of Financial Aid
41 Berkeley Street
Boston, MA 02116

Bentley College

Waltham, Massachusetts
www.bentley.edu
Four-year private **Federal Code: 002124**

	Living at home	On-campus
Tuition and fees:	$24,324	$24,324
Room and board:		$9,580
Board only:	$2,140	
Books and supplies:	$900	$900
Personal expenses:	$960	$960
Transportation:	$1,440	

Undergraduate aid. Need-based: Average financial aid package for full-time students was $21,514; for part-time $12,469. 70% awarded as scholarships/grants, 30% as loans/jobs. **Non-need-based:** 39% awarded as scholarships/grants, 61% as loans/jobs. Scholarships based on academics, athletics, leadership, minority status. **Student debt:** 60% of graduating class borrowed to fund education; average debt was $18,929. **Additional information:** Filing deadlines for CSS PROFILE: Early Decision November 1, regular decision January 1.

Freshman aid. Need-based: Out of 908 full-time freshmen, 670 applied for aid; 522 were judged to have need; of these 514 received aid. Average package met 95% of need. 172 students had full need met. Average scholarship/grant was $15,170; average loan $2,810. **Non-need based:** 60 full-time freshmen with need received non-need scholarships; 99 without need received awards; 7 received athletic scholarships.

Merit scholarships. Trustee Scholarships; full tuition; based on superior record of academic accomplishment; 10 awarded. Chancellor's Scholarships; full tuition; for ALANA students with excellent academic records; 7 awarded. President's Scholarships; full tuition (renewable to 3 years); based on excellent academic records. Bentley's Service Learning Scholarships; $5,000; for students with excellent academic records who have demonstrated commitment to service learning.

Policies to reduce costs. Tuition/fee waivers for employees and their families. Credit/placement for qualifying scores on AP, IB, CLEP examinations.

Payment plans. Credit card, installment payment.

Application procedures. FAFSA, CSS PROFILE required. Closing date 2/1. Applicants notified on rolling basis starting 3/25. Early decision closing date 12/1. **Transfers:** Priority date 5/15; no deadline.

Contact. Financial aid office: (781) 891-3341
Donna Kendall, Director of Financial Assistance
175 Forest Street
Waltham, MA 02452-4705

Berklee College of Music

Boston, Massachusetts
www.berklee.edu
Four-year private **Federal Code: 002126**

College costs. Room and board on-campus cost $10,280.

	Living at home
Tuition and fees:	$19,644
Books and supplies:	$500

Undergraduate aid. All financial aid based on need. Need-based aid available for full-time students.

Policies to reduce costs. Tuition/fee waivers for employees and their families. Work study available nights and weekends.

Payment plans. Credit card, installment payment.

Application procedures. FAFSA, institutional form required. Priority date 3/1; no closing date. **Transfers:** Financial aid transcripts required from all colleges previously attended.

Contact. Financial aid office: (800) 538-3844
Julie Poorman, Director of Financial Aid
1140 Boylston Street
Boston, MA 02215

Berkshire Community College

Pittsfield, Massachusetts
www.berkshirecc.edu
Two-year public **Federal Code: 002167**

College costs. $116 per-credit-hour: New England Regional tuition, New York residents.

	Living at home
Tuition and fees (2002-2003):	$3,090
Out-of-state:	$10,110
Per-credit charge:	$103
Per-credit out-of-state:	$337
Board only:	$2,519
Books and supplies:	$750
Personal expenses:	$1,792
Transportation:	$900

Undergraduate aid. Need-based: Average financial aid package for full-time students was $3,599. 77% awarded as scholarships/grants, 23% as loans/jobs. Need-based aid available for part-time students. **Non-need-based:** Scholarships based on academics, leadership, state/district residency. **Additional information:** Tuition waivers for veterans and National Guard available.

Policies to reduce costs. Tuition/fee waivers for senior citizens, employees and their families. Credit/placement for qualifying scores on AP, IB, CLEP examinations. Work study available nights, weekends and for part-time students.

Payment plans. Credit card, installment, deferred payment.

Application procedures. FAFSA required. Priority date 5/1; no closing date. Applicants notified on rolling basis starting 5/15, must reply within 2 week(s) of notification.

Contact. Financial aid office: (413) 499-4660 ext. 279
Anne Moore, Director of Financial Aid
1350 West Street
Pittsfield, MA 01201

Boston Architectural Center

Boston, Massachusetts
www.the-bac.edu
Six-year private **Federal Code: 003966**

	Living at home
Tuition and fees (projected):	$7,818
Board only:	$1,390
Books and supplies:	$628
Personal expenses:	$2,657
Transportation:	$943

Undergraduate aid. All financial aid based on need. Average financial aid package for full-time students was $3,310. 12% awarded as scholarships/grants, 88% as loans/jobs. **Student debt:** 65% of graduating class borrowed to fund education; average debt was $22,864.

Freshman aid. Out of 43 full-time freshmen, 39 applied for aid; 39 were judged to have need; of these 39 received aid. Average package met 33% of need. Average scholarship/grant was $3,042; average loan $2,229.

Policies to reduce costs. Tuition/fee waivers for employees and their families.

Payment plans. Credit card, installment payment.

Application procedures. FAFSA required. Priority date 4/15; no closing date. Applicants notified on rolling basis, must reply within 2 week(s) of notification. **Transfers:** Priority date 4/15; no deadline.

Contact. Financial aid office: (617) 585-0125
Maureen Samways, Director of Financial Aid
320 Newbury Street
Boston, MA 02115-2795

Boston College

Chestnut Hill, Massachusetts
www.bc.edu
Four-year private **Federal Code: 002128**

	Living at home	On-campus
Tuition and fees:	$27,522	$27,522
Room and board:		$9,300
Board only:	$1,500	
Books and supplies:	$600	$600
Personal expenses:	$500	$1,000
Transportation:	$1,000	

Undergraduate aid. Need-based: Need-based aid available for full-time students. **Non-need-based:** Scholarships based on academics, athletics.

Policies to reduce costs. Tuition/fee waivers for family of clergy, employees and their families. Prepayment discount; credit/placement for qualifying scores on AP examinations.

Payment plans. Installment payment.

Application procedures. FAFSA, CSS PROFILE required. Priority date 2/1; no closing date. Applicants notified by 4/15, must reply by 5/1. **Transfers:** Priority date 5/1; no deadline.

Contact. Financial aid office: (617) 552-3300
Bernard Pekala, Director of Financial Strategies
140 Commonwealth Avenue, Devlin Hall 208
Chestnut Hill, MA 02467-3809

Boston Conservatory

Boston, Massachusetts
www.bostonconservatory.edu
Four-year private **Federal Code: 002129**

College costs. Tuition for conservatory diploma program $20,100. Health insurance fee $876 required of international students and students who do not have own insurance.

	Living at home	On-campus
Tuition and fees (2002-2003):	$21,395	$21,395
Room and board:		$9,840
Books and supplies:	$500	$500
Personal expenses:	$1,250	$1,250
Transportation:	$800	$500

Undergraduate aid. Need-based: Average financial aid package for full-time students was $14,250. 24% awarded as scholarships/grants, 76% as loans/jobs. Need-based aid available for part-time students.

Freshman aid. Need-based: Out of 119 full-time freshmen, 100 applied for aid; 71 were judged to have need; of these 68 received aid. Average package met 50% of need. 26 students had full need met. Average scholarship/grant was $3,109; average loan $2,600. **Non-need based:** 40 full-time freshmen with need received non-need scholarships; 10 without need received awards.

Policies to reduce costs. Tuition/fee waivers for employees and their families. Credit/placement for qualifying scores on AP, CLEP examinations.

Payment plans. Installment payment.

Application procedures. FAFSA, institutional form required. Closing date 2/1. Applicants notified by 4/1, must reply by 5/1 or within 4 week(s) of notification.

Contact. Financial aid office: (617) 912-9147
James Bynum, Director of Financial Aid
8 The Fenway
Boston, MA 02215

Boston University

Boston, Massachusetts
www.bu.edu
Four-year private **Federal Code: 002130**

	Living at home	On-campus
Tuition and fees:	$28,906	$28,906
Room and board:		$9,288
Board only:	$1,843	
Books and supplies:	$686	$686
Personal expenses:	$1,108	$1,108
Transportation:	$1,649	$314

Undergraduate aid. Need-based: Need-based aid available for full-time and part-time students. **Non-need-based:** Scholarships based on academics, alumni affiliation, art, athletics, music/drama, religious affiliation, state/district residency. **Student debt:** 59% of graduating class borrowed to fund education; average debt was $17,491.

Merit scholarships. Trustee Scholar Program; full tuition and fees (renewable); candidates nominated by high school principals, headmasters, or students. University Scholarships; half tuition (renewable); based on exceptionally strong high school academic record. Dean's Scholarships; $7,500 towards tuition (renewable); based on strong academic credentials; for students who have applied for need-based financial aid but according to standard calculations have significant financial resources which exceed, but not significantly, cost of attendance. Presidential Scholarships for School of Education. Engineering Scholar Award. Competitive scholarship exams in engineering, Latin, Greek.

Policies to reduce costs. Tuition/fee waivers for senior citizens, family of clergy, employees and their families. Prepayment discount; credit/placement for qualifying scores on AP, IB examinations. Work study available nights, weekends and for part-time students.

Payment plans. Installment, deferred payment.

Application procedures. FAFSA, CSS PROFILE required. Priority date 2/15; no closing date. Applicants notified on rolling basis starting 3/15, must reply by 5/1 or within 2 week(s) of notification. Early decision closing date 11/1. **Transfers:** Priority date 4/1; no deadline. Transfer students cannot receive duplicate disbursements simultaneously from different institutions.

Contact. Financial aid office: (617) 353-2965
Christine McGuire, Director of Financial Assistance
121 Bay State Road
Boston, MA 02215

Brandeis University

Waltham, Massachusetts
www.brandeis.edu
Four-year private **Federal Code: 002133**

	Living at home	On-campus
Tuition and fees:	$29,875	$29,875
Room and board:		$8,323
Board only:	$820	
Books and supplies:	$700	$700
Personal expenses:	$1,000	$1,000
Transportation:	$900	

Undergraduate aid. Need-based: Average financial aid package for full-time students was $21,053. 69% awarded as scholarships/grants, 31% as loans/jobs. Need-based aid available for part-time students. **Non-need-based:** 68% awarded as scholarships/grants, 32% as loans/jobs. Scholarships based on academics, leadership, minority status.

Freshman aid. Need-based: Out of 837 full-time freshmen, 569 applied for aid; 420 were judged to have need; of these 420 received aid. Average package met 86% of need. 142 students had full need met. Average scholarship/grant was $16,844; average loan $4,090. **Non-need based:** 55 full-time freshmen with need received non-need scholarships; 180 without need received awards.

Merit scholarships. Justice Brandeis Scholarship; $27,000 (renewable for 4 years). Presidential Awards; $20,000 (renewable for 4 years). Dean Awards; $10,000. Up to 25% of entering class receives non-need based merit awards.

Policies to reduce costs. Tuition/fee waivers for employees and their families. Credit/placement for qualifying scores on AP, IB examinations.

Payment plans. Installment payment.

Application procedures. FAFSA required. CSS PROFILE required of all applicants for institutional aid. Priority date 1/31; no closing date. Applicants notified on rolling basis starting 4/1, must reply by 5/1. Early decision closing date 1/1. **Transfers:** Priority date 4/1; no deadline. International transfer students seeking scholarship or need-based financial assistance must apply by 2/1.

Contact. **Financial aid office:** (781) 736-3700
Peter Giumette, Director of Financial Aid
Box 9110
Waltham, MA 02454-9110

Bridgewater State College

Bridgewater, Massachusetts
www.bridgew.edu
Four-year public **Federal Code: 002183**

	Living at home	On-campus
Tuition and fees (2002-2003):	$3,735	$3,735
Out-of-state:	$9,875	$9,875
Room and board:		$5,366
Board only:	$2,100	
Books and supplies:	$600	$600
Personal expenses:	$1,332	$1,332
Transportation:	$1,250	$500

Undergraduate aid. Need-based: Average financial aid package for full-time students was $6,470; for part-time $5,084. 58% awarded as scholarships/grants, 42% as loans/jobs. **Non-need-based:** 12% awarded as scholarships/grants, 88% as loans/jobs. Scholarships based on academics, leadership, minority status. **Student debt:** 41% of graduating class borrowed to fund education; average debt was $8,658.

Freshman aid. Need-based: Out of 1,012 full-time freshmen, 775 applied for aid; 467 were judged to have need; of these 459 received aid. Average package met 75% of need. 237 students had full need met. Average scholarship/grant was $3,710; average loan $1,922. **Non-need based:** 182 full-time freshmen with need received non-need scholarships; 182 without need received awards.

Policies to reduce costs. Tuition/fee waivers for senior citizens, unemployed or children of unemployed, employees and their families. Credit/placement for qualifying scores on AP, IB, CLEP examinations.

Payment plans. Credit card, installment payment.

Application procedures. FAFSA required. Priority date 3/1; no closing date. Applicants notified on rolling basis starting 3/15.

Contact. **Financial aid office:** (508) 531-1341
Janet Gumbris, Director of Financial Aid
Gates House
Bridgewater, MA 02325

Bunker Hill Community College

Boston, Massachusetts
www.bhcc.mass.edu
Two-year public **Federal Code: 011210**

College costs. New England Regional Tuition: $87 per-credit-hour.

	Living at home
Tuition and fees (2002-2003):	$2,250
Out-of-state:	$8,430
Per-credit charge:	$75
Per-credit out-of-state:	$281
Board only:	$2,170
Books and supplies:	$1,000
Personal expenses:	$1,150
Transportation:	$800

Undergraduate aid. Need-based: Need-based aid available for full-time and part-time students.

Policies to reduce costs. Tuition/fee waivers for senior citizens, employees and their families. Credit/placement for qualifying scores on AP, IB, CLEP examinations.

Payment plans. Credit card payment.

Application procedures. FAFSA, institutional form required. Priority date 4/15; no closing date. Applicants notified on rolling basis starting 6/1, must reply within 2 week(s) of notification.

Contact. **Financial aid office:** (508) 362-2131 ext. 4393
Scott Jewell, Director of Financial Aid
250 New Rutherford Avenue
Boston, MA 02129-2925

Cape Cod Community College

West Barnstable, Massachusetts
www.capecod.mass.edu
Two-year public **Federal Code: 002168**

College costs. Additional required fees: $50 for nursing; $100 for dental hygiene.

	Living at home
Tuition and fees (2002-2003):	$2,760
Out-of-state:	$8,940
Per-credit charge:	$92
Per-credit out-of-state:	$298
Board only:	$2,000
Books and supplies:	$600
Personal expenses:	$1,000
Transportation:	$1,500

Undergraduate aid. Need-based: Average financial aid package for full-time students was $3,752; for part-time $2,689. 82% awarded as scholarships/grants, 18% as loans/jobs. **Non-need-based:** 22% awarded as scholarships/grants, 78% as loans/jobs. Scholarships based on academics, leadership, music/drama, state/district residency. **Student debt:** 43% of graduating class borrowed to fund education; average debt was $7,674.

Freshman aid. Need-based: Out of 481 full-time freshmen, 171 applied for aid; 149 were judged to have need; of these 149 received aid. Average package met 59% of need. 10 students had full need met. Average scholarship/grant was $3,075; average loan $1,502. **Non-need based:** 1 full-time freshmen with need received non-need scholarships; 22 without need received awards.

Policies to reduce costs. Tuition/fee waivers for senior citizens, employees and their families. Credit/placement for qualifying scores on AP, CLEP examinations. Work study available for part-time students.

Payment plans. Credit card, installment payment.

Application procedures. FAFSA required. Priority date 4/1; no closing date. Applicants notified on rolling basis starting 4/1.

Contact. **Financial aid office:** (508) 362-2131 ext. 4393
Sherry Andersen, Director of Financial Aid
2240 Iyanough Road
West Barnstable, MA 02668-1599

Clark University

Worcester, Massachusetts
www.clarku.edu
Four-year private **Federal Code: 002139**

College costs. Fifth-year tuition waived for eligible undergraduates admitted to accelerated bachelor's/master's programs.

	Living at home	On-campus
Tuition and fees:	$26,965	$26,965
Room and board:		$5,150
Board only:	$2,500	
Books and supplies:	$800	$800
Personal expenses:	$700	$700
Transportation:	$250	$200

Undergraduate aid. Need-based: Average financial aid package for full-time students was $20,515. 71% awarded as scholarships/grants, 29% as loans/jobs. Need-based aid available for part-time students. **Non-need-based:** 56% awarded as scholarships/grants, 44% as loans/jobs. Scholarships based on academics. **Student debt:** 86% of graduating class borrowed to fund education; average debt was $17,875.

Freshman aid. Need-based: Out of 576 full-time freshmen, 419 applied for aid; 331 were judged to have need; of these 323 received aid. Average package met 95% of need. 231 students had full need met. Average scholarship/grant was $10,920; average loan $3,618. **Non-need based:** 277 full-time freshmen with need received non-need scholarships; 74 without need received awards.

Merit scholarships. Scholarships; $8,000-$11,000; based on superior academic achievement or community service involvement.

Policies to reduce costs. Tuition/fee waivers for employees and their families. Credit/placement for qualifying scores on AP, IB examinations.

Payment plans. Credit card, installment payment.

Application procedures. FAFSA, CSS PROFILE required. Priority date 2/1; no closing date. Applicants notified by 3/31, must reply by 5/1 or within 2 week(s) of notification. Early decision closing date 11/15. **Transfers:** Priority date 4/1; no deadline. Financial aid transcript from previous institution(s) attended required.

Contact. **Financial aid office:** (508) 793-7478
Mary Ellen Severance, Director of Financial Aid and Student Employment
950 Main Street
Worcester, MA 01610-1477

College of the Holy Cross

Worcester, Massachusetts
www.holycross.edu
Four-year private **Federal Code: 002141**

	Living at home	On-campus
Tuition and fees:	$28,011	$28,011
Room and board:		$8,440
Board only:	$2,135	
Books and supplies:	$400	$400
Personal expenses:	$900	$900
Transportation:	$550	$350

Undergraduate aid. **Need-based:** Average financial aid package for full-time students was $18,427. 75% awarded as scholarships/grants, 25% as loans/jobs. **Non-need-based:** 50% awarded as scholarships/grants, 50% as loans/jobs. Scholarships based on academics, athletics. **Student debt:** 57% of graduating class borrowed to fund education; average debt was $16,063.

Freshman aid. **Need-based:** Out of 696 full-time freshmen, 446 applied for aid; 370 were judged to have need; of these 370 received aid. Average package met 100% of need. 370 students had full need met. Average scholarship/grant was $13,433; average loan $4,521. **Non-need based:** 52 without need received awards; 7 received athletic scholarships.

Policies to reduce costs. Tuition/fee waivers for employees and their families. Credit/placement for qualifying scores on AP, IB examinations. Work study available nights and weekends.

Payment plans. Installment payment.

Application procedures. FAFSA, CSS PROFILE required. CSS PROFILE required of all students applying for institutional aid. Closing date 2/1. Applicants notified by 4/1, must reply by 5/1. **Transfers:** Priority date 4/15; no deadline.

Contact. Lynne Myers, Director of Financial Aid
One College Street
Worcester, MA 01610-2395

Dean College

Franklin, Massachusetts
www.dean.edu
Two-year private **Federal Code: 002144**

	Living at home	On-campus
Tuition and fees (2002-2003):	$19,110	$19,110
Room and board:		$8,360
Board only:	$2,880	
Books and supplies:	$600	$600
Personal expenses:	$600	$600
Transportation:	$800	$300

Undergraduate aid. **Need-based:** Need-based aid available for full-time and part-time students. **Non-need-based:** Scholarships based on academics, athletics. **Additional information:** If aid must be reduced due to receipt of outside scholarship, loans will be reduced or eliminated before any reduction of grants.

Merit scholarships. Oliver Dean Recognition Award; $1,500-$3,000. Community Service Scholarship; $2,000; based on service background; 40-50 awarded.

Policies to reduce costs. Tuition/fee waivers for senior citizens, employees and their families. Tuition at time of enrollment guaranteed for 2 years; credit/placement for qualifying scores on AP, IB, CLEP examinations.

Payment plans. Credit card, installment, deferred payment.

Application procedures. FAFSA, institutional form required. Priority date 3/1; no closing date. Applicants notified on rolling basis starting 4/1, must reply within 3 week(s) of notification.

Contact. **Financial aid office:** (508) 541-1900
Nancy Amaral, Director of Financial Aid
99 Main Street
Franklin, MA 02038-1994

Elms College

Chicopee, Massachusetts
www.elms.edu
Four-year private **Federal Code: 002140**

	Living at home	On-campus
Tuition and fees (2002-2003):	$17,160	$17,160
Room and board:		$6,490
Books and supplies:	$525	$525
Personal expenses:	$2,200	$900
Transportation:	$800	$500

Undergraduate aid. **Need-based:** Average financial aid package for full-time students was $14,477. 60% awarded as scholarships/grants, 40% as loans/jobs. Need-based aid available for part-time students. **Non-need-based:** 27% awarded as scholarships/grants, 73% as loans/jobs. Scholarships based on academics, alumni affiliation, leadership, state/district residency.

Freshman aid. **Need-based:** Out of 143 full-time freshmen, 124 applied for aid; 117 were judged to have need; of these 117 received aid. Average package met 88% of need. 33 students had full need met. Average scholarship/grant was $11,887; average loan $4,152. **Non-need based:** 6 full-time freshmen with need received non-need scholarships; 12 without need received awards.

Policies to reduce costs. Tuition/fee waivers for senior citizens, family members, employees and their families. Prepayment discount; credit/placement for qualifying scores on AP, IB, CLEP examinations. Work study available nights and weekends.

Payment plans. Credit card, installment, deferred payment.

Application procedures. FAFSA, institutional form required. Priority date 3/1; no closing date. Applicants notified on rolling basis starting 2/15, must reply by 5/1 or within 2 week(s) of notification. **Transfers:** No deadline.

Contact. **Financial aid office:** (413) 592-3189
Troy Davis, Director of Student Financial Aid Services
291 Springfield Street
Chicopee, MA 01013

Emerson College

Boston, Massachusetts
www.emerson.edu
Four-year private **Federal Code: 002146**

	Living at home	On-campus
Tuition and fees:	$22,663	$22,663
Room and board:		$9,858
Books and supplies:	$600	$600
Personal expenses:	$165	$165
Transportation:	$1,215	$900

Undergraduate aid. **Need-based:** Average financial aid package for full-time students was $12,543; for part-time $8,950. 51% awarded as scholarships/grants, 49% as loans/jobs. **Non-need-based:** 27% awarded as scholarships/grants, 73% as loans/jobs. Scholarships based on academics, music/drama. **Student debt:** 68% of graduating class borrowed to fund education; average debt was $10,550. **Additional information:** Massachusetts Loan Plan available for parents of dependent undergraduates.

Freshman aid. **Need-based:** Out of 651 full-time freshmen, 537 applied for aid; 481 were judged to have need; of these 458 received aid. Average package met 64% of need. 274 students had full need met. Average scholarship/grant was $11,853; average loan $2,927. **Non-need based:** 29 full-time freshmen with need received non-need scholarships; 149 without need received awards.

Merit scholarships. Trustee's Scholarships (honors program); half tuition. Dean's Scholarships; $7,500. Emerson Stage Scholarships; based on performing arts audition.

Policies to reduce costs. Tuition/fee waivers for employees and their families. Credit/placement for qualifying scores on AP, IB, CLEP examinations. Work study available weekends.

Payment plans. Credit card, installment, deferred payment.

Application procedures. FAFSA, institutional form, CSS PROFILE required. Priority date 3/1; no closing date. Applicants notified on rolling basis starting 4/1, must reply by 5/1 or within 3 week(s) of notification. **Transfers:** Priority date 4/1; no deadline.

Contact. **Financial aid office:** (617) 824-8655
Michelle Smith, Director of Student Financial Services
120 Boylston Street
Boston, MA 02116-4624

Emmanuel College

Boston, Massachusetts
www.emmanuel.edu
Four-year private **Federal Code: 002147**

	Living at home	On-campus
Tuition and fees:	$19,300	$19,300
Room and board:		$8,400
Board only:	$1,890	
Books and supplies:	$750	$750
Personal expenses:	$1,710	$1,710
Transportation:	$1,035	$270

Undergraduate aid. **Need-based:** Average financial aid package for full-time students was $15,971; for part-time $7,221. 71% awarded as scholarships/grants, 29% as loans/jobs. **Non-need-based:** 30% awarded as scholarships/grants, 70% as loans/jobs. Scholarships based on academics, alumni affiliation, leadership, religious affiliation, state/district residency. **Student debt:** 67% of graduating class borrowed to fund education; average debt was $15,325.

Freshman aid. **Need-based:** Out of 322 full-time freshmen, 283 applied for aid; 262 were judged to have need; of these 262 received aid. Average package met 77% of need. 43 students had full need met. Average scholarship/grant was $8,913; average loan $3,191. **Non-need based:** 139 full-time freshmen with need received non-need scholarships; 29 without need received awards.

Policies to reduce costs. Tuition/fee waivers for children of alumni, family members, employees and their families. Credit/placement for qualifying scores on AP, IB examinations. Work study available nights, weekends and for part-time students.

Payment plans. Credit card, installment, deferred payment.

Application procedures. FAFSA, institutional form required. Priority date 4/1; no closing date. Applicants notified on rolling basis starting 3/15, must reply within 2 week(s) of notification. Early decision closing date 11/1.

Contact. **Financial aid office:** (617) 735-9938
Jennifer Porter, Director of Student Financial Services
400 The Fenway
Boston, MA 02115

Endicott College

Beverly, Massachusetts
www.endicott.edu
Four-year private **Federal Code: 002148**

College costs. Additional technology fee: $364 for campus residents, $150 for commuters. $634 per-credit-hour charge for nursing and physical therapy.

	Living at home	On-campus
Tuition and fees:	$17,044	$17,044
Room and board:		$8,858
Board only:	$2,250	
Books and supplies:	$600	$600
Personal expenses:	$1,000	$1,000
Transportation:	$1,000	$1,000

Undergraduate aid. **Need-based:** Average financial aid package for full-time students was $12,742; for part-time $6,349. 54% awarded as scholarships/grants, 46% as loans/jobs. **Non-need-based:** 73% awarded as scholarships/grants, 27% as loans/jobs. Scholarships based on academics, alumni affiliation, art, leadership. **Student debt:** 74% of graduating class borrowed to fund education; average debt was $17,125.

Freshman aid. **Need-based:** Out of 484 full-time freshmen, 441 applied for aid; 337 were judged to have need; of these 333 received aid. Average package met 65% of need. 34 students had full need met. Average scholarship/grant was $5,096; average loan $3,134. **Non-need based:** 204 full-time freshmen with need received non-need scholarships; 61 without need received awards.

Policies to reduce costs. Tuition/fee waivers for family members, employees and their families. Credit/placement for qualifying scores on AP, IB examinations. Work study available nights and weekends.

Payment plans. Credit card, installment payment.

Application procedures. FAFSA, institutional form required. Priority date 3/15; no closing date. Applicants notified on rolling basis starting 3/15, must reply within 2 week(s) of notification.

Contact. **Financial aid office:** (978) 232-2060
Marcia Toomey, Director of Financial Aid
376 Hale Street
Beverly, MA 01915-9985

Fisher College

Boston, Massachusetts
www.fisher.edu
Two-year private **Federal Code: 002150**

	Living at home	On-campus
Tuition and fees (2002-2003):	$16,000	$16,000
Per-credit charge:	$483	$483
Room and board:		$8,500
Books and supplies:	$800	$800
Personal expenses:	$800	$800
Transportation:	$750	$750

Undergraduate aid. **Need-based:** Need-based aid available for full-time and part-time students. **Non-need-based:** Scholarships based on academics, alumni affiliation, state/district residency.

Merit scholarships. Fisher Honor Scholarship,$2,500 (renewable with 3.0 GPA), based on outstanding academic and personal achievement, contribution to school and community; Business Administration and Computer Technology Scholarship for students enrolling in associate programs in business administration or computer technology, $1,500 for 2.5-2.99 GPA, $3,000 for minimum 3.0 GPA, renewable.

Policies to reduce costs. Tuition/fee waivers for employees and their families. Credit/placement for qualifying scores on AP, CLEP examinations. Work study available nights, weekends and for part-time students.

Payment plans. Credit card, installment payment.

Application procedures. FAFSA required. Priority date 3/1; no closing date. Applicants notified on rolling basis starting 3/1, must reply within 2 week(s) of notification. **Transfers:** No deadline.

Contact. **Financial aid office:** (617) 236-4418
Michelle Miller, Director of Financial Aid
118 Beacon Street
Boston, MA 02116

Fitchburg State College

Fitchburg, Massachusetts
www.fsc.edu
Four-year public **Federal Code: 002184**

	Living at home	On-campus
Tuition and fees (2002-2003):	$3,688	$3,688
Out-of-state:	$9,768	$9,768
Room and board:		$5,120
Books and supplies:	$600	$600
Personal expenses:	$1,500	$1,500
Transportation:	$500	$350

Undergraduate aid. **Need-based:** Need-based aid available for full-time and part-time students. **Non-need-based:** Scholarships based on academics, leadership.

Merit scholarships. Renewable merit scholarships; awarded on basis of high school record and test scores; details available at admissions office.

Policies to reduce costs. Tuition/fee waivers for senior citizens, employees and their families. Credit/placement for qualifying scores on AP, CLEP examinations. Work study available nights, weekends and for part-time students.

Payment plans. Credit card, installment payment.

Application procedures. FAFSA, institutional form required. Priority date 3/1; no closing date. Applicants notified on rolling basis starting 4/1.

Contact. **Financial aid office:** (978) 345-2151
Pamela McCafferty, Director of Financial Aid
160 Pearl Street
Fitchburg, MA 01420-2697

Framingham State College

Framingham, Massachusetts
www.framingham.edu
Four-year public **Federal Code: 002185**

College costs. New England Regional tuition: $3,825 full-time.

	Living at home	On-campus
Tuition and fees (2002-2003):	$3,334	$3,334
Out-of-state:	$9,414	$9,414
Room and board:		$4,651
Board only:	$1,860	
Books and supplies:	$700	$700
Personal expenses:	$1,200	$1,200
Transportation:	$1,000	$700

Undergraduate aid. Need-based: Average financial aid package for full-time students was $4,646; for part-time $4,926. 60% awarded as scholarships/grants, 40% as loans/jobs. **Non-need-based:** 5% awarded as scholarships/grants, 95% as loans/jobs. Scholarships based on academics, state/district residency. **Student debt:** 42% of graduating class borrowed to fund education; average debt was $10,863.

Freshman aid. Need-based: Out of 727 full-time freshmen, 508 applied for aid; 273 were judged to have need; of these 273 received aid. Average package met 82% of need. 105 students had full need met. Average scholarship/grant was $3,304; average loan $1,662. **Non-need based:** 12 full-time freshmen with need received non-need scholarships; 46 without need received awards.

Merit scholarships. Senator Paul E. Tsongas Scholarship; full tuition and fees; available to Massachusetts residents; based on 3.75 high school GPA and test scores; 5 awarded. Merit scholarships available to students majoring in education, natural or physical sciences; based on GPA and test scores.

Policies to reduce costs. Tuition/fee waivers for senior citizens, employees and their families. Credit/placement for qualifying scores on AP, CLEP examinations. Work study available nights and weekends.

Payment plans. Credit card, installment payment.

Application procedures. FAFSA required. Priority date 2/15; no closing date. Applicants notified on rolling basis starting 4/1, must reply by 5/1 or within 2 week(s) of notification.

Contact. **Financial aid office:** (508) 626-4534
Susan Lanzillo, Director of Financial Aid
100 State Street
Framingham, MA 01701-9101

Franklin W. Olin College of Engineering

Needham, Massachusetts
www.olin.edu
Four-year private

College costs. Every admitted student receives full 4-year scholarship covering tuition. Board $3,400; student activity fee $100; computer $1,250. Books/supplies: $750.

Undergraduate aid. Need-based: Need-based aid available for full-time students. **Additional information:** No financial aid forms necessary.

Merit scholarships. All students receive full tuition scholarships.

Contact. **Financial aid office:** (781) 292-2300
Charles Nolan, Dean of Admission
Olin Way
Needham, MA 02492

Gordon College

Wenham, Massachusetts
www.gordon.edu
Four-year private **Federal Code: 002153**

	Living at home	On-campus
Tuition and fees:	$20,234	$20,234
Room and board:		$5,748
Board only:	$1,768	
Books and supplies:	$800	$800
Personal expenses:	$1,000	$1,000
Transportation:	$400	$400

Undergraduate aid. Need-based: Average financial aid package for full-time students was $13,922; for part-time $10,615. 61% awarded as scholarships/grants, 39% as loans/jobs. **Non-need-based:** 56% awarded as scholarships/grants, 44% as loans/jobs. Scholarships based on academics, alumni affiliation, leadership, minority status, music/drama, religious affiliation.

Freshman aid. Need-based: Average package met 74% of need. Average scholarship/grant was $4,872; average loan $3,105.

Merit scholarships. A.J. Gordon Scholarship; $12,000 (renewable annually); based on academic achievement and leadership. Dean's Scholarships; $8,000 (renewable); based on academic record. Choral Scholars Program; $6,000 (renewable); for students with excellent ability/academic performance seeking career in vocal music field.

Policies to reduce costs. Tuition/fee waivers for employees and their families. Credit/placement for qualifying scores on AP, IB, CLEP examinations. Work study available nights, weekends and for part-time students.

Payment plans. Installment payment.

Application procedures. FAFSA, CSS PROFILE required. Closing date 3/1. Applicants notified on rolling basis starting 4/15, must reply by 5/1 or within 2 week(s) of notification. Early decision closing date 12/1.

Contact. **Financial aid office:** (800) 343-1379
Barbara Layne, Director of Financial Aid
255 Grapevine Road
Wenham, MA 01984-1899

Greenfield Community College

Greenfield, Massachusetts
www.gcc.mass.edu
Two-year public **Federal Code: 002169**

College costs. New England regional tuition: $110 per-credit-hour, $3,285 full-time.

	Living at home
Tuition and fees (2002-2003):	$3,017
Out-of-state:	$10,667
Per-credit charge:	$97
Per-credit out-of-state:	$352
Board only:	$2,218
Books and supplies:	$850
Personal expenses:	$1,560
Transportation:	$950

Undergraduate aid. All financial aid based on need. Average financial aid package for full-time students was $3,464; for part-time $3,036. 72% awarded as scholarships/grants, 28% as loans/jobs.

Freshman aid. Out of 620 full-time freshmen, 414 applied for aid; 310 were judged to have need; of these 276 received aid. Average package met 59% of need. 6 students had full need met. Average scholarship/grant was $3,860; average loan $1,200.

Policies to reduce costs. Tuition/fee waivers for senior citizens, unemployed or children of unemployed, employees and their families. Credit/placement for qualifying scores on AP, CLEP examinations. Work study available nights, weekends and for part-time students.

Payment plans. Credit card, installment, deferred payment.

Application procedures. FAFSA, institutional form required. Priority date 4/15; no closing date. Applicants notified on rolling basis starting 5/15, must reply within 3 week(s) of notification. **Transfers:** No deadline.

Contact. **Financial aid office:** (413) 775-1109
Jane Abbott, Director of Financial Aid
One College Drive
Greenfield, MA 01301

Hampshire College

Amherst, Massachusetts
www.hampshire.edu
Four-year private **Federal Code: 004661**

	Living at home	On-campus
Tuition and fees (2002-2003):	$27,870	$27,870
Room and board:		$7,294
Books and supplies:	$400	$400
Personal expenses:	$450	$450

Undergraduate aid. Need-based: Average financial aid package for full-time students was $27,015. 76% awarded as scholarships/grants, 24% as loans/jobs. **Non-need-based:** 34% awarded as scholarships/grants, 66% as loans/jobs. Scholarships based on academics. **Student debt:** 45% of graduating class borrowed to fund education; average debt was $16,200.

Freshman aid. Need-based: Out of 304 full-time freshmen, 212 applied for aid; 162 were judged to have need; of these 160 received aid. Average package met 100% of need. 137 students had full need met. Average scholarship/grant was $16,615; average loan $2,625. **Non-need based:** 51 full-time freshmen with need received non-need scholarships; 11 without need received awards.

Policies to reduce costs. Tuition/fee waivers for employees and their families. Credit/placement for qualifying scores on AP, IB examinations. Work study available nights and weekends.

Application procedures. FAFSA, institutional form, CSS PROFILE required. Closing date 2/1. Applicants notified by 4/1, must reply by 5/1 or within 2 week(s) of notification. Early decision closing date 11/15. **Transfers:** Closing date 3/1.

Contact. Financial aid office: (413) 559-5484
Kathleen Methot, Director of Financial Aid
893 West Street
Amherst, MA 01002-9988

Harvard College

Cambridge, Massachusetts
www.fas.harvard.edu
Four-year private **Federal Code: 002155**

	Living at home	On-campus
Tuition and fees:	$29,060	$29,060
Room and board:		$8,868
Board only:	$4,162	
Books and supplies:	$873	$873
Personal expenses:	$2,638	$2,638

Undergraduate aid. All financial aid based on need. Average financial aid package for full-time students was $23,739. 88% awarded as scholarships/grants, 12% as loans/jobs. **Student debt:** 53% of graduating class borrowed to fund education; average debt was $10,465. **Additional information:** Institution meets full need of all admitted students.

Freshman aid. Out of 1,645 full-time freshmen, 917 applied for aid; 787 were judged to have need; of these 787 received aid. Average package met 100% of need. 787 students had full need met. Average scholarship/grant was $22,140; average loan $2,340.

Policies to reduce costs. Credit/placement for qualifying scores on AP, IB examinations.

Payment plans. Installment payment.

Application procedures. FAFSA, CSS PROFILE required. Priority date 2/1; no closing date. Applicants notified by 4/1, must reply by 5/1 or within 2 week(s) of notification. **Transfers:** Priority date 3/1; no deadline.

Contact. Financial aid office: (617) 495-1000
Sally Donahue, Director of Financial Aid
Byerly Hall, 8 Garden Street
Cambridge, MA 02138

Hebrew College

Newton Centre, Massachusetts
www.hebrewcollege.edu
Four-year private **Federal Code: G02157**

College costs. Tuition charged per-credit-hour.

	Living at home
Tuition and fees (2002-2003):	$17,100
Books and supplies:	$600
Transportation:	$300

Undergraduate aid. Need-based: Need-based aid available for full-time and part-time students.

Policies to reduce costs. Tuition/fee waivers for employees and their families.

Payment plans. Credit card, installment payment.

Application procedures. FAFSA, institutional form required. Priority date 5/1; no closing date. Applicants notified on rolling basis starting 7/1, must reply within 3 week(s) of notification.

Contact. Financial aid office: (617) 559-8612
Norma Frankel, Registrar
160 Herrick Road
Newton Centre, MA 02459

Hellenic College/Holy Cross

Brookline, Massachusetts
www.hchc.edu
Four-year private **Federal Code: 002154**

	Living at home	On-campus
Tuition and fees (2002-2003):	$10,275	$10,275
Room and board:		$7,800
Books and supplies:	$500	$500
Personal expenses:	$1,500	$1,500
Transportation:	$1,000	$1,000

Undergraduate aid. Need-based: 42% awarded as scholarships/grants, 58% as loans/jobs. Need-based aid available for part-time students. **Non-need-based:** Scholarships based on academics, alumni affiliation, athletics, religious affiliation. **Student debt:** 25% of graduating class borrowed to fund education; average debt was $18,000.

Policies to reduce costs. Tuition/fee waivers for children of alumni, minority students, family of clergy, employees and their families. Credit/placement for qualifying scores on AP, CLEP examinations.

Payment plans. Credit card, installment payment.

Application procedures. FAFSA, institutional form required. Closing date 5/1. Applicants notified on rolling basis starting 6/1, must reply within 2 week(s) of notification.

Contact. Financial aid office: (617) 850-1297
George Georgenes, Director of Financial Aid
50 Goddard Avenue
Brookline, MA 02445

ITT Technical Institute: Norwood

Norwood, Massachusetts
www.itt-tech.edu
Two-year proprietary **Federal Code: 007327**

College costs. Total program varies depending on course of study. Per-credit-hour charge: $347.

Policies to reduce costs. Tuition/fee waivers for employees and their families. Tuition at time of enrollment guaranteed for 2 years.

Payment plans. Credit card, installment payment.

Application procedures. FAFSA, institutional form required. Applicants notified on rolling basis.

Contact. Financial aid office: (781) 278-7200
Maureen Renzoni, Director of Finance
333 Providence Highway
Norwood, MA 02062

ITT Technical Institute: Woburn

Woburn, Massachusetts
www.itt-tech.edu
Two-year proprietary

College costs. Total program varies depending on course of study. Per-credit-hour charge: $347.

Contact. **Financial aid office:** (781) 937-8324
Steve Hoover, Director of Finance
10 Forbes Road
Woburn, MA 01801

Katharine Gibbs School

Boston, Massachusetts
www.gibbsboston.com
Two-year proprietary **Federal Code: 007481**

	Living at home
Tuition and fees:	$13,500
Books and supplies:	$1,200

Undergraduate aid. All financial aid based on need. Need-based aid available for full-time and part-time students.

Policies to reduce costs. Tuition/fee waivers for employees and their families. Credit/placement for qualifying scores on CLEP examinations.

Payment plans. Credit card, installment payment.

Application procedures. FAFSA, institutional form required. No deadline. Applicants notified on rolling basis.

Contact. **Financial aid office:** (617) 578-7100
Lisa Howard, Director of Financial Planning
126 Newbury Street
Boston, MA 02116

Laboure College

Boston, Massachusetts
www.laboure.edu
Two-year private **Federal Code: 006324**

	Living at home
Tuition and fees (2002-2003):	$11,180
Per-credit charge:	$360
Board only:	$2,300
Books and supplies:	$800
Personal expenses:	$1,000
Transportation:	$1,000

Undergraduate aid. Need-based: Need-based aid available for full-time and part-time students. **Non-need-based:** Scholarships based on academics, alumni affiliation, leadership, religious affiliation. **Additional information:** Allied Health Scholarship covers cost of general education courses for students enrolled in electroneurodiagnostic technology, health information technology, and nutrition and food management programs; constitutes significant reduction in tuition. Caritas Christi Scholarship for students who work 16 hours per week at a Caritas Christi healthcare agency; covers 25% of tuition for nursing and radiation therapy courses; also covers 50% of cost of nursing courses for students with LPN credential. Evening LPN Scholarship discounts tuition 75% for evening nursing majors with LPN credential.

Policies to reduce costs. Tuition/fee waivers for children of alumni, family of clergy, employees and their families. Work study available nights and for part-time students.

Payment plans. Credit card, installment payment.

Application procedures. FAFSA, institutional form required. Priority date 5/1; no closing date. Applicants notified on rolling basis starting 5/15, must reply within 2 week(s) of notification. **Transfers:** Priority date 12/1; no deadline.

Contact. **Financial aid office:** (617) 296-8300 ext. 4066
Mark Virello, Chief Financial Officer
2120 Dorchester Avenue
Boston, MA 02124-5698

Lasell College

Newton, Massachusetts
www.lasell.edu
Four-year private **Federal Code: 002158**

	Living at home	On-campus
Tuition and fees (2002-2003):	$16,700	$16,700
Room and board:		$8,300
Board only:	$2,500	
Books and supplies:	$750	$750
Personal expenses:	$2,000	$2,000
Transportation:	$500	$500

Undergraduate aid. Need-based: Need-based aid available for full-time students. **Non-need-based:** Scholarships based on academics, alumni affiliation, leadership.

Policies to reduce costs. Tuition/fee waivers for children of alumni, family members, employees and their families. Credit/placement for qualifying scores on AP, CLEP examinations. Work study available nights and weekends.

Payment plans. Credit card, installment payment.

Application procedures. FAFSA, institutional form required. Priority date 4/1; no closing date. Applicants notified on rolling basis starting 2/20, must reply by 5/1 or within 4 week(s) of notification. **Transfers:** No deadline.

Contact. **Financial aid office:** (617) 243-2000
Michele Kosboth, Director of Financial Planning
1844 Commonwealth Avenue
Newton, MA 02466

Lesley University

Cambridge, Massachusetts
www.lesley.edu
Four-year private **Federal Code: 002160**

College costs. Resident students must pay $826 University Health Services fee.

	Living at home	On-campus
Tuition and fees:	$19,700	$19,700
Room and board:		$8,800
Board only:	$2,790	
Books and supplies:	$700	$700
Personal expenses:	$1,025	$2,125
Transportation:	$900	$450

Undergraduate aid. Need-based: Average financial aid package for full-time students was $11,390. 64% awarded as scholarships/grants, 36% as loans/jobs. Need-based aid available for part-time students. **Non-need-based:** 63% awarded as scholarships/grants, 37% as loans/jobs. Scholarships based on academics, alumni affiliation, leadership, minority status. **Student debt:** 86% of graduating class borrowed to fund education; average debt was $14,125.

Freshman aid. Need-based: Out of 118 full-time freshmen, 117 applied for aid; 115 were judged to have need; of these 115 received aid. Average package met 94% of need. 8 students had full need met. Average scholarship/grant was $8,891; average loan $4,025. **Non-need based:** 42 full-time freshmen with need received non-need scholarships; 2 without need received awards.

Merit scholarships. Number scholarships for freshmen with strong academic backgrounds who have shown a commitment to community service and made a difference in the lives of others; $5,000 to full tuition.

Policies to reduce costs. Tuition/fee waivers for employees and their families. Credit/placement for qualifying scores on AP, IB, CLEP examinations. Work study available nights and weekends.

Payment plans. Installment payment.

Application procedures. FAFSA, institutional form required. Priority date 2/1; no closing date. Applicants notified on rolling basis starting 3/15, must reply within 2 week(s) of notification. **Transfers:** Priority date 3/15; no deadline.

Contact. **Financial aid office:** (617) 349-8710
Paul Henderson, Director of Financial Aid
29 Everett Street
Cambridge, MA 02138

Marian Court College

Swampscott, Massachusetts
www.mariancourt.edu
Two-year private **Federal Code: 006873**

	Living at home
Tuition and fees (2002-2003):	$10,360
Board only:	$2,035
Books and supplies:	$600
Personal expenses:	$1,957
Transportation:	$1,409

Undergraduate aid. Need-based: Need-based aid available for full-time and part-time students. **Non-need-based:** Scholarships based on academics.

Policies to reduce costs. Tuition/fee waivers for adults, senior citizens, employees and their families. Prepayment discount; credit/placement for qualifying scores on CLEP examinations.

Payment plans. Credit card, installment payment.

Application procedures. FAFSA, institutional form required. Priority date 4/1; no closing date. Applicants notified on rolling basis starting 4/15.

Contact. **Financial aid office:** (781) 595-6768
Melissa Faye, Director of Financial Aid
35 Little's Point Road
Swampscott, MA 01907-2896

Massachusetts Bay Community College

Wellesley Hills, Massachusetts
www.massbay.edu
Two-year public **Federal Code: 002171**

College costs. New England Regional tuition: $125 per-credit-hour, $3,760 full-time.

	Living at home
Tuition and fees (2002-2003):	$2,900
Out-of-state:	$9,080
Per-credit charge:	$94
Per-credit out-of-state:	$300
Board only:	$1,977
Books and supplies:	$800
Personal expenses:	$2,966
Transportation:	$1,242

Undergraduate aid. Need-based: Need-based aid available for full-time and part-time students.

Policies to reduce costs. Tuition/fee waivers for senior citizens, family members, unemployed or children of unemployed, employees and their families. Credit/placement for qualifying scores on AP, IB, CLEP examinations.

Payment plans. Credit card, deferred payment.

Application procedures. FAFSA, institutional form required. Priority date 8/30; no closing date. Applicants notified on rolling basis starting 4/1.

Contact. **Financial aid office:** (781) 239-2600
Paula Ogden, Director of Financial Aid/Assistant Dean of Students
50 Oakland Street
Wellesley Hills, MA 02481

Massachusetts College of Art

Boston, Massachusetts
www.massart.edu
Four-year public **Federal Code: 002180**

College costs. New England Regional tuition: $5,974.

	Living at home	On-campus
Tuition and fees (2002-2003):	$4,778	$4,778
Out-of-state:	$14,788	$14,788
Room and board:		$7,846
Books and supplies:	$2,000	$2,000
Personal expenses:	$3,150	$1,150
Transportation:	$700	$700

Undergraduate aid. Need-based: Need-based aid available for full-time students. **Non-need-based:** Scholarships based on academics, art, leadership, minority status. **Additional information:** Tuition waiver available to Vietnam veterans.

Policies to reduce costs. Tuition/fee waivers for senior citizens, unemployed or children of unemployed, employees and their families. Credit/placement for qualifying scores on AP, IB, CLEP examinations.

Payment plans. Credit card payment.

Application procedures. FAFSA required. Priority date 3/15; no closing date. Applicants notified on rolling basis starting 3/15, must reply within 3 week(s) of notification. Early decision closing date 12/1. **Transfers:** Priority date 5/1; no deadline. Financial aid transcripts required.

Contact. **Financial aid office:** (617) 232-1555 ext. 524
Kenneth Berryhill, Director of Financial Aid
621 Huntington Avenue
Boston, MA 02115-5882

Massachusetts College of Liberal Arts

North Adams, Massachusetts
www.mcla.mass.edu
Four-year public **Federal Code: 002187**

College costs. New England Regional tuition: $172 per-credit-hour, $4,712 full-time.

	Living at home	On-campus
Tuition and fees (2002-2003):	$4,197	$4,197
Out-of-state:	$13,142	$13,142
Room and board:		$5,846
Books and supplies:	$600	$600
Personal expenses:	$800	$800
Transportation:	$500	$250

Undergraduate aid. Need-based: Need-based aid available for full-time and part-time students. **Non-need-based:** Scholarships based on academics, alumni affiliation, art, leadership, minority status, music/drama.

Policies to reduce costs. Tuition/fee waivers for senior citizens, unemployed or children of unemployed, employees and their families. Credit/placement for qualifying scores on AP, IB, CLEP examinations.

Payment plans. Credit card, installment payment.

Application procedures. FAFSA, institutional form required. Priority date 4/1; no closing date. Applicants notified on rolling basis starting 4/1, must reply within 2 week(s) of notification. **Transfers:** Priority date 4/1; no deadline.

Contact. **Financial aid office:** (413) 662-5000
Beth Petri, Director of Financial Aid
375 Church Street
North Adams, MA 01247

Massachusetts College of Pharmacy and Health Sciences

Boston, Massachusetts
www.mcp.edu
Four-year private **Federal Code: 002165**

	Living at home	On-campus
Tuition and fees (2002-2003):	$18,550	$18,550
Room and board:		$9,580
Board only:	$1,500	
Books and supplies:	$450	$450
Personal expenses:	$1,700	$1,700
Transportation:	$900	$300

Undergraduate aid. Need-based: Average financial aid package for full-time students was $11,631; for part-time $7,259. 26% awarded as scholarships/grants, 74% as loans/jobs. **Non-need-based:** 6% awarded as scholarships/grants, 94% as loans/jobs. Scholarships based on academics. **Student debt:** 76% of graduating class borrowed to fund education; average debt was $43,300.

Freshman aid. Need-based: Out of 223 full-time freshmen, 186 applied for aid; 174 were judged to have need; of these 174 received aid. Average package met 71% of need. 15 students had full need met. Average scholarship/grant was $10,019; average loan $4,855. **Non-need based:** 6 full-time freshmen with need received non-need scholarships; 20 without need received awards.

Policies to reduce costs. Tuition/fee waivers for employees and their families. Credit/placement for qualifying scores on AP, IB, CLEP examinations.

Application procedures. FAFSA required. Closing date 3/15. Applicants notified on rolling basis starting 2/1, must reply by 5/1 or within 2 week(s) of notification. Early decision closing date 11/1. **Transfers:** Massachusetts State Grant deadline 5/1.

Contact. **Financial aid office:** (617) 732-2864
Carrie Glass, Director of Student Financial Services
179 Longwood Avenue
Boston, MA 02115

Massachusetts Institute of Technology

Cambridge, Massachusetts
web.mit.edu
Four-year private **Federal Code: 002178**

	Living at home	On-campus
Tuition and fees:	$29,600	$29,600
Room and board:		$8,710
Books and supplies:	$2,720	$2,720

Undergraduate aid. All financial aid based on need. Average financial aid package for full-time students was $22,983; for part-time $21,470. 79% awarded as scholarships/grants, 21% as loans/jobs. **Student debt:** 56% of graduating class borrowed to fund education; average debt was $22,855. **Additional information:** Filing deadline 2/1 for CSS Profile.

Freshman aid. Out of 1,027 full-time freshmen, 721 applied for aid; 587 were judged to have need; of these 587 received aid. Average package met 100% of need. 587 students had full need met. Average scholarship/grant was $19,367; average loan $3,084.

Policies to reduce costs. Tuition/fee waivers for employees and their families. Credit/placement for qualifying scores on AP, IB examinations.

Payment plans. Installment payment.

Application procedures. FAFSA, CSS PROFILE required. Closing date 2/1. Applicants notified by 3/15, must reply by 5/1. **Transfers:** Access to MIT funds may be limited to fewer than 8 terms.

Contact. **Financial aid office:** (617) 253-4971
Elizabeth Hicks, Director of Student Financial Services
77 Massachusetts Avenue, 3-108
Cambridge, MA 02139

Massachusetts Maritime Academy

Buzzards Bay, Massachusetts
www.maritime.edu
Four-year public **Federal Code: 002181**

College costs. Sea term tuition $2,386. New England Regional tuition $3,978.

	Living at home	On-campus
Tuition and fees (2002-2003):	$3,663	$3,663
Out-of-state:	$14,143	$14,143
Room and board:		$5,500
Books and supplies:	$550	$550
Personal expenses:	$1,200	$1,200
Transportation:	$1,300	$350

Undergraduate aid. Need-based: Average financial aid package for full-time students was $7,007. 20% awarded as scholarships/grants, 80% as loans/jobs. Need-based aid available for part-time students. **Non-need-based:** Scholarships based on academics. **Student debt:** 82% of graduating class borrowed to fund education; average debt was $12,125.

Freshman aid. Need-based: Out of 261 full-time freshmen, 261 applied for aid; 149 were judged to have need; of these 149 received aid. Average package met 19% of need. 28 students had full need met. Average scholarship/grant was $1,943; average loan $2,625. **Non-need based:** 12 full-time freshmen with need received non-need scholarships; 12 without need received awards.

Policies to reduce costs. Tuition/fee waivers for senior citizens, employees and their families. Credit/placement for qualifying scores on AP, IB, CLEP examinations.

Application procedures. FAFSA, institutional form required. Priority date 4/30; no closing date. Applicants notified on rolling basis starting 3/1.

Contact. **Financial aid office:** (508) 830-5086
Elizabeth Benway, Financial Aid Director
101 Academy Drive
Buzzards Bay, MA 02532-1803

Massasoit Community College

Brockton, Massachusetts
www.massasoit.mass.edu
Two-year public **Federal Code: 002177**

	Living at home
Tuition and fees (2002-2003):	$2,640
Out-of-state:	$8,820
Per-credit charge:	$85
Per-credit out-of-state:	$291
Board only:	$1,700
Books and supplies:	$600
Personal expenses:	$900
Transportation:	$900

Undergraduate aid. Need-based: Need-based aid available for full-time students.

Policies to reduce costs. Tuition/fee waivers for adults, senior citizens, unemployed or children of unemployed, employees and their families. Credit/placement for qualifying scores on CLEP examinations.

Payment plans. Credit card, installment payment.

Application procedures. FAFSA required. Priority date 4/15; no closing date. Applicants notified on rolling basis starting 6/1.

Contact. **Financial aid office:** (508) 588-9100
Sharon McLaughlin, Director of Financial Aid
One Massasoit Boulevard
Brockton, MA 02302

Merrimack College

North Andover, Massachusetts
www.merrimack.edu
Four-year private **Federal Code: 002120**

College costs. Lab fees vary per course. $1,500 laptop user fee for business majors.

	Living at home	On-campus
Tuition and fees:	$20,875	$20,875
Room and board:		$8,750
Board only:	$3,200	
Books and supplies:	$700	$700
Personal expenses:	$500	$500
Transportation:	$1,050	$1,000

Undergraduate aid. Need-based: Average financial aid package for full-time students was $15,500. 72% awarded as scholarships/grants, 28% as loans/jobs. Need-based aid available for part-time students. **Non-need-based:** 30% awarded as scholarships/grants, 70% as loans/jobs. Scholarships based on academics, athletics, leadership, music/drama, religious affiliation. **Student debt:** 66% of graduating class borrowed to fund education; average debt was $18,000.

Freshman aid. Need-based: Out of 525 full-time freshmen, 440 applied for aid; 400 were judged to have need; of these 400 received aid. Average package met 75% of need. 340 students had full need met. Average scholarship/grant was $8,500; average loan $4,125. **Non-need based:** 45 full-time freshmen with need received non-need scholarships; 40 without need received awards; 20 received athletic scholarships.

Policies to reduce costs. Tuition/fee waivers for senior citizens, family members, family of clergy, employees and their families. Credit/placement for qualifying scores on AP, IB, CLEP examinations. Work study available nights and weekends.

Payment plans. Credit card, installment, deferred payment.

Application procedures. FAFSA, CSS PROFILE required. Closing date 2/15. Applicants notified on rolling basis starting 3/1, must reply by 5/1 or within 2 week(s) of notification. **Transfers:** Priority date 3/15; closing date 4/30.

Contact. **Financial aid office:** (978) 837-5186
Christine Mordach, Director of Financial Aid
315 Turnpike Street
North Andover, MA 01845

Montserrat College of Art

Beverly, Massachusetts
www.montserrat.edu
Four-year private **Federal Code: 013774**

College costs. Freshmen encouraged to get $595 starter kit.

	Living at home	On-campus
Tuition and fees:	$17,755	$17,755
Room only:		$4,640
Books and supplies:	$825	$825
Personal expenses:	$900	$900
Transportation:	$1,500	$800

Undergraduate aid. All financial aid based on need. Average financial aid package for full-time students was $6,527. 42% awarded as scholarships/ grants, 58% as loans/jobs. Need-based aid available for part-time students. **Student debt:** 64% of graduating class borrowed to fund education; average debt was $8,757. **Additional information:** Limited on-campus employment for students not receiving financial aid.

Freshman aid. Average package met 47% of need. Average scholarship/ grant was $6,327; average loan $4,702.

Policies to reduce costs. Tuition/fee waivers for children of alumni, family members, employees and their families. Credit/placement for qualifying scores on AP, IB examinations. Work study available for part-time students.

Payment plans. Credit card, installment payment.

Application procedures. FAFSA required. Closing date 3/2. Applicants notified on rolling basis starting 12/20, must reply within 2 week(s) of notification.

Contact. Financial aid office: (978) 922-8222
Creda Carney, Director of Financial Aid
Box 26
Beverly, MA 01915

Mount Holyoke College

South Hadley, Massachusetts
www.mtholyoke.edu
Four-year private **Federal Code: 002192**

	Living at home	On-campus
Tuition and fees:	$29,338	$29,338
Room and board:		$8,580
Books and supplies:	$750	$750
Transportation:		$1,500

Undergraduate aid. Need-based: Average financial aid package for full-time students was $25,500; for part-time $17,400. 76% awarded as scholarships/ grants, 24% as loans/jobs. **Non-need-based:** 28% awarded as scholarships/ grants, 72% as loans/jobs. Scholarships based on academics, leadership. **Student debt:** 88% of graduating class borrowed to fund education; average debt was $14,200. **Additional information:** Parent loan plans include MASS-PLAN, Achievers and PLUS. 10-month payment plan offered.

Freshman aid. Need-based: Out of 574 full-time freshmen, 434 applied for aid; 373 were judged to have need; of these 373 received aid. Average package met 100% of need. 373 students had full need met. Average scholarship/ grant was $21,087; average loan $2,700. **Non-need based:** 53 without need received awards.

Merit scholarships. Mount Holyoke College Leadership Awards; limited number; based on high school scholarship and extracurricular achievement; conditional annual renewal.

Policies to reduce costs. Tuition/fee waivers for employees and their families. Credit/placement for qualifying scores on AP, IB examinations. Work study available nights, weekends and for part-time students.

Payment plans. Installment, deferred payment.

Application procedures. FAFSA, CSS PROFILE required. Closing date 2/1. Applicants notified by 3/25, must reply by 5/1. Early decision closing date 11/15. **Transfers:** Priority date 2/1; closing date 5/31. Financial aid transcripts from all schools previously attended required.

Contact. Financial aid office: (413) 538-2291
Jill Cashman, Director of Financial Assistance
50 College Street
South Hadley, MA 01075-1488

Mount Ida College

Newton Centre, Massachusetts
www.mountida.edu
Four-year private **Federal Code: 002193**

College costs. Campus residents pay $420 comprehensive fee; commuters pay $240 comprehensive fee.

	Living at home	On-campus
Tuition and fees:	$16,696	$16,696
Room and board:		$9,000
Books and supplies:	$800	$800
Personal expenses:	$525	$525
Transportation:	$2,880	$650

Undergraduate aid. Need-based: Need-based aid available for full-time and part-time students.

Policies to reduce costs. Tuition/fee waivers for senior citizens, employees and their families. Credit/placement for qualifying scores on CLEP examinations.

Payment plans. Credit card, installment payment.

Application procedures. FAFSA, institutional form required. Priority date 5/1; no closing date. Applicants notified on rolling basis starting 3/1, must reply within 3 week(s) of notification. **Transfers:** No deadline.

Contact. Financial aid office: (617) 928-4785
Linda Mularczyk, Director of Financial Aid
777 Dedham Street
Newton Centre, MA 02459

Mount Wachusett Community College

Gardner, Massachusetts
www.mwcc.mass.edu
Two-year public **Federal Code: 002172**

College costs. New England resident tuition: $138.50 per-credit-hour, $4,155 full-time.

	Living at home
Tuition and fees (2002-2003):	$3,930
Out-of-state:	$10,080
Per-credit charge:	$126
Per-credit out-of-state:	$331
Board only:	$2,500
Books and supplies:	$700
Personal expenses:	$1,380
Transportation:	$1,500

Undergraduate aid. Need-based: Need-based aid available for full-time and part-time students.

Policies to reduce costs. Tuition/fee waivers for senior citizens, employees and their families. Credit/placement for qualifying scores on AP, CLEP examinations. Work study available nights and for part-time students.

Payment plans. Credit card, installment payment.

Application procedures. FAFSA, institutional form required. Priority date 4/1; no closing date. Applicants notified on rolling basis starting 5/1.

Contact. Financial aid office: (978) 632-6600 ext. 169
Kelly Morrissey, Director of Financial Aid
444 Green Street
Gardner, MA 01440-1000

New England Conservatory of Music

Boston, Massachusetts
www.newenglandconservatory.edu
Four-year private **Federal Code: 002194**

College costs. On-campus residents pay $300 health fee.

	Living at home	On-campus
Tuition and fees:	$24,750	$24,750
Room and board:		$10,250
Board only:	$2,000	
Books and supplies:	$700	$700
Personal expenses:	$2,000	$2,000
Transportation:	$1,600	$316

Undergraduate aid. Need-based: Average financial aid package for full-time students was $17,173. 63% awarded as scholarships/grants, 37% as loans/jobs. Need-based aid available for part-time students. **Non-need-based:** 72% awarded as scholarships/grants, 28% as loans/jobs. Scholarships based on academics, music/drama. **Student debt:** 66% of graduating class borrowed to fund education; average debt was $15,000.

Freshman aid. Need-based: Out of 121 full-time freshmen, 56 applied for aid; 45 were judged to have need; of these 45 received aid. Average package met 59% of need. 6 students had full need met. Average scholarship/grant was $10,403; average loan $3,096. **Non-need based:** 6 full-time freshmen with need received non-need scholarships; 24 without need received awards.

Policies to reduce costs. Tuition/fee waivers for employees and their families. Credit/placement for qualifying scores on AP, IB, CLEP examinations. Work study available nights, weekends and for part-time students.

Payment plans. Credit card payment.

Application procedures. FAFSA, institutional form required. Closing date 2/2. Applicants notified on rolling basis starting 3/2, must reply by 5/1 or within 2 week(s) of notification.

Contact. Financial aid office: (617) 585-1110
Ken Ferreira, Director of Financial Aid
290 Huntington Avenue
Boston, MA 02115

Newbury College

Brookline, Massachusetts
www.newbury.edu
Four-year private **Federal Code: 007484**

	Living at home	On-campus
Tuition and fees:	$15,500	$15,500
Room and board:		$7,575
Books and supplies:	$630	$630
Personal expenses:	$1,000	$1,000
Transportation:	$700	$520

Undergraduate aid. All financial aid based on need. Average financial aid package for full-time students was $8,580. 49% awarded as scholarships/grants, 51% as loans/jobs. Need-based aid available for part-time students.

Freshman aid. Out of 272 full-time freshmen, 211 applied for aid; 200 were judged to have need; of these 200 received aid. 32 students had full need met. Average scholarship/grant was $4,500; average loan $2,625.

Policies to reduce costs. Tuition/fee waivers for employees and their families. Credit/placement for qualifying scores on AP, IB, CLEP examinations. Work study available nights.

Payment plans. Credit card, installment payment.

Application procedures. FAFSA required. Priority date 3/1; no closing date. Applicants notified on rolling basis starting 4/1, must reply within 2 week(s) of notification. **Transfers:** No deadline.

Contact. Financial aid office: (617) 730-7196
Jeanne Gonzalez, Director of Financial Assistance
129 Fisher Avenue
Brookline, MA 02445

Nichols College

Dudley, Massachusetts
www.nichols.edu
Four-year private **Federal Code: 002197**

College costs. Tuition includes laptop for each student.

	Living at home	On-campus
Tuition and fees:	$19,650	$19,650
Room and board:		$7,912
Board only:	$2,500	
Books and supplies:	$800	$800
Personal expenses:	$1,171	$1,171
Transportation:	$1,000	$500

Undergraduate aid. Need-based: Average financial aid package for full-time students was $12,921; for part-time $2,795. 55% awarded as scholarships/grants, 45% as loans/jobs. **Non-need-based:** 46% awarded as scholarships/grants, 54% as loans/jobs. Scholarships based on academics. **Student debt:** 75% of graduating class borrowed to fund education; average debt was $21,175.

Freshman aid. Need-based: Out of 267 full-time freshmen, 257 applied for aid; 219 were judged to have need; of these 219 received aid. Average package met 71% of need. 62 students had full need met. Average scholarship/grant was $8,331; average loan $4,575. **Non-need based:** 72 without need received awards.

Policies to reduce costs. Tuition/fee waivers for children of alumni, senior citizens, family members, employees and their families. Credit/placement for qualifying scores on AP, IB, CLEP examinations. Work study available nights and weekends.

Payment plans. Credit card, installment payment.

Application procedures. FAFSA, CSS PROFILE required. Closing date 3/1. Applicants notified on rolling basis starting 3/15, must reply within 2 week(s) of notification.

Contact. Financial aid office: (508) 213-2276
Diane Gillespie, Director of Financial Aid
Office of Admissions
Dudley, MA 01571-5000

Northeastern University

Boston, Massachusetts
www.northeastern.edu
Five-year private **Federal Code: 002199**

	Living at home	On-campus
Tuition and fees (projected):	$24,467	$24,467
Room and board:		$9,660
Board only:	$2,250	
Books and supplies:	$900	$900
Personal expenses:	$540	$900
Transportation:	$900	$900

Undergraduate aid. Need-based: Average financial aid package for full-time students was $14,925. 54% awarded as scholarships/grants, 46% as loans/jobs. **Non-need-based:** 37% awarded as scholarships/grants, 63% as loans/jobs. Scholarships based on academics, athletics, music/drama.

Freshman aid. Need-based: Out of 2,974 full-time freshmen, 2,372 applied for aid; 1,988 were judged to have need; of these 1,988 received aid. Average package met 67% of need. 265 students had full need met. Average scholarship/grant was $12,321; average loan $3,028. **Non-need based:** 172 full-time freshmen with need received non-need scholarships; 485 without need received awards; 51 received athletic scholarships.

Policies to reduce costs. Tuition/fee waivers for senior citizens, employees and their families. Credit/placement for qualifying scores on AP, IB examinations. Work study available nights and weekends.

Payment plans. Credit card, installment payment.

Application procedures. FAFSA, CSS PROFILE required. Priority date 2/15; no closing date. Applicants notified on rolling basis starting 2/15, must reply by 5/1. **Transfers:** Institutional application and financial aid transcript from all previously attended colleges required.

Contact. Financial aid office: (617) 373-3190
M. Seamus Harreys, Dean and Director of Student Financial Services
360 Huntington Avenue, 150 Richards Hall
Boston, MA 02115-9959

Pine Manor College

Chestnut Hill, Massachusetts
www.pmc.edu
Four-year private **Federal Code: 002201**

	Living at home	On-campus
Tuition and fees (2002-2003):	$12,964	$12,964
Room and board:		$8,120
Board only:	$1,000	
Books and supplies:	$600	$600
Personal expenses:	$900	$900
Transportation:	$360	$360

Undergraduate aid. Need-based: Average financial aid package for full-time students was $13,837. 65% awarded as scholarships/grants, 35% as loans/jobs. Need-based aid available for part-time students. **Non-need-based:** 39% awarded as scholarships/grants, 61% as loans/jobs. Scholarships based on academics, alumni affiliation, leadership. **Student debt:** 60% of graduating class borrowed to fund education; average debt was $14,312.

Freshman aid. Need-based: Out of 155 full-time freshmen, 136 applied for aid; 130 were judged to have need; of these 130 received aid. Average

package met 78% of need. 25 students had full need met. Average scholarship/grant was $9,926; average loan $2,887. **Non-need based:** 2 full-time freshmen with need received non-need scholarships; 16 without need received awards.

Merit scholarships. Distinguished Scholar Award; 3.5 GPA from accredited secondary school; no grade below C; 1100 combined SAT. Presidential Scholar Award; 3.2 GPA from accredited secondary school; no grade below C; 1000 combined SAT. Leadership Award; demonstrated leadership roles; 2.75 GPA at accredited high school or college; no grade lower than D. For transfers: Phi Theta Kappa Scholarship; $3,000. Collegiate Articulation Transfer Award; $2,000; successful completion of AA with 2.0 GPA from community college with which Pine Manor College has articulation agreement.

Policies to reduce costs. Tuition/fee waivers for employees and their families. Credit/placement for qualifying scores on AP, IB, CLEP examinations.

Payment plans. Credit card, installment payment.

Application procedures. FAFSA, institutional form required. No deadline. Applicants notified on rolling basis starting 3/1, must reply by 5/1 or within 2 week(s) of notification. **Transfers:** Priority date 5/1; no deadline.

Contact. **Financial aid office:** (617) 731-7053
Linda Schoendorf, Financial Aid Director
400 Heath Street
Chestnut Hill, MA 02467

Quinsigamond Community College

Worcester, Massachusetts
www.qcc.mass.edu
Two-year public **Federal Code: 002175**

	Living at home
Tuition and fees (2002-2003):	$2,730
Out-of-state:	$8,910
Per-credit charge:	$91
Per-credit out-of-state:	$297
Board only:	$2,500
Books and supplies:	$680
Personal expenses:	$1,748
Transportation:	$766

Undergraduate aid. All financial aid based on need. 92% awarded as scholarships/grants, 8% as loans/jobs. Need-based aid available for part-time students. **Student debt:** 7% of graduating class borrowed to fund education; average debt was $3,606.

Policies to reduce costs. Tuition/fee waivers for senior citizens, employees and their families. Credit/placement for qualifying scores on AP, IB, CLEP examinations. Work study available weekends and for part-time students.

Payment plans. Credit card, installment payment.

Application procedures. FAFSA required. Priority date 4/1; no closing date. Applicants notified on rolling basis starting 4/1.

Contact. **Financial aid office:** (508) 854-4261
Iris Godes, Director of Financial Aid
670 West Boylston Street
Worcester, MA 01606

Regis College

Weston, Massachusetts
www.regiscollege.edu
Four-year private **Federal Code: 002206**

	Living at home	On-campus
Tuition and fees:	$19,910	$19,910
Room and board:		$9,090
Board only:	$1,500	
Books and supplies:	$900	$900
Personal expenses:	$1,680	$1,680
Transportation:	$1,200	$300

Undergraduate aid. **Need-based:** Average financial aid package for full-time students was $18,143; for part-time $6,325. 51% awarded as scholarships/grants, 49% as loans/jobs. **Non-need-based:** 57% awarded as scholarships/grants, 43% as loans/jobs. Scholarships based on academics, alumni affiliation, art, leadership, minority status, music/drama, religious affiliation. **Student debt:** 82% of graduating class borrowed to fund education; average debt was $19,913.

Freshman aid. **Need-based:** Out of 137 full-time freshmen, 122 applied for aid; 107 were judged to have need; of these 107 received aid. Average package met 80% of need. 6 students had full need met. Average scholarship/grant was $11,752; average loan $4,279. **Non-need based:** 62 full-time freshmen with need received non-need scholarships; 21 without need received awards.

Policies to reduce costs. Tuition/fee waivers for employees and their families. Credit/placement for qualifying scores on AP, IB, CLEP examinations. Work study available nights, weekends and for part-time students.

Payment plans. Credit card, installment payment.

Application procedures. FAFSA, institutional form required. Priority date 3/1; no closing date. Applicants notified on rolling basis starting 3/1, must reply within 2 week(s) of notification.

Contact. **Financial aid office:** (781) 768-7180
Dolores Ludwick, Director of Financial Aid
235 Wellesley Street
Weston, MA 02493-1571

Roxbury Community College

Roxbury Crossing, Massachusetts
www.rcc.mass.edu
Two-year public **Federal Code: 011930**

	Living at home
Tuition and fees (2002-2003):	$2,550
Out-of-state:	$9,180
Per-credit charge:	$75
Per-credit out-of-state:	$296
Board only:	$2,800
Books and supplies:	$800
Personal expenses:	$1,800
Transportation:	$720

Undergraduate aid. All financial aid based on need. Need-based aid available for full-time and part-time students.

Policies to reduce costs. Tuition/fee waivers for senior citizens, employees and their families.

Payment plans. Credit card payment.

Application procedures. FAFSA, institutional form required. Priority date 5/1; no closing date. Applicants notified on rolling basis starting 6/15, must reply within 2 week(s) of notification.

Contact. **Financial aid office:** (617) 541-5322
Ray O'Rourke, Director of Financial Aid
1234 Columbus Avenue
Roxbury Crossing, MA 02120-3400

St. John's Seminary College

Brighton, Massachusetts
www.sjs.edu
Four-year private **Federal Code: 002214**

	Living at home	On-campus
Tuition and fees (projected):	$8,000	$8,000
Room and board:		$4,500
Books and supplies:	$500	$500
Personal expenses:		$600
Transportation:		$400

Undergraduate aid. **Need-based:** Average financial aid package for full-time students was $8,000. **Non-need-based:** Scholarships based on state/district residency.

Policies to reduce costs. Tuition/fee waivers for minority students.

Application procedures. FAFSA required. No deadline. Applicants notified on rolling basis, must reply within 3 week(s) of notification. **Transfers:** No deadline.

Contact. **Financial aid office:** (617) 254-2610
John Lynch, Business Manager, Financial Aid Officer
127 Lake Street
Brighton, MA 02135

Salem State College

Salem, Massachusetts
www.salemstate.edu
Four-year public **Federal Code: 002188**

College costs. New England Regional tuition: $4,339 per year. Campus resident activity fee $20.

	Living at home	On-campus
Tuition and fees (2002-2003):	$3,938	$3,938
Out-of-state:	$10,078	$10,078
Room and board:		$5,290
Board only:	$1,620	
Books and supplies:	$800	$800
Personal expenses:	$900	$900
Transportation:	$1,440	$540

Undergraduate aid. Need-based: Need-based aid available for full-time and part-time students. **Non-need-based:** Scholarships based on academics, alumni affiliation, art, leadership, music/drama, state/district residency. **Additional information:** Tuition waivers for qualified veterans and National Guard members. Grant assistance available for eligible adult students.

Policies to reduce costs. Tuition/fee waivers for senior citizens, unemployed or children of unemployed, employees and their families. Credit/placement for qualifying scores on AP, CLEP examinations.

Payment plans. Installment payment.

Application procedures. FAFSA required. Priority date 4/1; no closing date. Applicants notified on rolling basis starting 4/1, must reply within 2 week(s) of notification.

Contact. Financial aid office: (978) 542-6112
Mary Benda, Director of Financial Aid
352 Lafayette Street
Salem, MA 01970

School of the Museum of Fine Arts

Boston, Massachusetts
www.smfa.edu
Four-year private **Federal Code: 004667**

	Living at home	On-campus
Tuition and fees (2002-2003):	$20,853	$20,853
Room and board:		$10,425
Books and supplies:	$1,250	$1,250
Personal expenses:	$1,600	$1,600
Transportation:	$1,600	$1,600

Undergraduate aid. Need-based: Need-based aid available for full-time and part-time students.

Policies to reduce costs. Tuition/fee waivers for employees and their families. Credit/placement for qualifying scores on AP examinations.

Payment plans. Credit card, installment, deferred payment.

Application procedures. FAFSA, institutional form, CSS PROFILE required. Priority date 3/15; no closing date. Applicants notified on rolling basis starting 4/15.

Contact. Financial aid office: (617) 267-6100
Beth Goreham, Director of Financial Aid
230 The Fenway
Boston, MA 02115

Simmons College

Boston, Massachusetts
www.simmons.edu
Four-year private **Federal Code: 002208**

	Living at home	On-campus
Tuition and fees:	$23,550	$23,550
Room and board:		$9,450
Books and supplies:	$600	$600
Personal expenses:	$1,250	$1,250
Transportation:	$620	

Undergraduate aid. Need-based: Average financial aid package for full-time students was $16,119; for part-time $6,966. 69% awarded as scholarships/grants, 31% as loans/jobs. **Non-need-based:** 78% awarded as scholarships/grants, 22% as loans/jobs. Scholarships based on academics, alumni affiliation, leadership, minority status. **Student debt:** 88% of graduating class borrowed to fund education; average debt was $19,820.

Freshman aid. Need-based: Out of 266 full-time freshmen, 204 applied for aid; 167 were judged to have need; of these 162 received aid. Average package met 93% of need. 10 students had full need met. Average scholarship/grant was $12,229; average loan $2,606. **Non-need based:** 31 full-time freshmen with need received non-need scholarships; 11 without need received awards.

Policies to reduce costs. Tuition/fee waivers for adults, employees and their families. Credit/placement for qualifying scores on AP, IB, CLEP examinations. Work study available for part-time students.

Payment plans. Credit card, installment payment.

Application procedures. FAFSA required. Closing date 2/1. Applicants notified by 4/1, must reply by 5/1 or within 4 week(s) of notification. **Transfers:** Closing date 4/1. Combination of grants, loans, employment opportunities available.

Contact. Financial aid office: (617) 521-2036
Diane Hallisey, Director of Student Financial Services
300 The Fenway
Boston, MA 02115-5898

Simon's Rock College of Bard

Great Barrington, Massachusetts
www.simons-rock.edu
Four-year private **Federal Code: 009645**

	Living at home	On-campus
Tuition and fees (2002-2003):	$27,415	$27,415
Room and board:		$7,160
Board only:	$705	
Books and supplies:	$1,000	$1,000
Personal expenses:	$400	$225
Transportation:	$1,000	$1,000

Undergraduate aid. Need-based: Average financial aid package for full-time students was $15,763. 72% awarded as scholarships/grants, 28% as loans/jobs. Need-based aid available for part-time students. **Non-need-based:** 87% awarded as scholarships/grants, 13% as loans/jobs. Scholarships based on academics, minority status. **Student debt:** 80% of graduating class borrowed to fund education; average debt was $17,000.

Freshman aid. Need-based: Average package met 70% of need. Average scholarship/grant was $13,200; average loan $3,571.

Merit scholarships. Acceleration to Excellence Program (AEP); 2 years full tuition; based on excellent grades, community service, maturity; 20-25 awarded. Special application process.

Policies to reduce costs. Tuition/fee waivers for employees and their families. Credit/placement for qualifying scores on AP examinations. Work study available nights and weekends.

Payment plans. Installment payment.

Application procedures. FAFSA, CSS PROFILE required. Priority date 4/30; closing date 6/15. Applicants notified on rolling basis starting 4/30, must reply within 2 week(s) of notification. **Transfers:** No deadline.

Contact. Financial aid office: (413) 528-7297
Eve Caimano, Director of Financial Aid
84 Alford Road
Great Barrington, MA 01230

Smith College

Northampton, Massachusetts
www.smith.edu
Four-year private **Federal Code: 002209**

	Living at home	On-campus
Tuition and fees:	$27,544	$27,544
Room and board:		$9,490
Board only:	$4,705	
Books and supplies:	$1,590	$1,590
Personal expenses:	$1,120	$1,120
Transportation:	$510	$510

Undergraduate aid. Need-based: Average financial aid package for full-time students was $25,647; for part-time $17,429. 78% awarded as scholarships/grants, 22% as loans/jobs. **Non-need-based:** 28% awarded as scholarships/grants, 72% as loans/jobs. Scholarships based on academics. **Student debt:**

68% of graduating class borrowed to fund education; average debt was $19,911. **Additional information:** Committed to very generous financial aid policy that guarantees to meet full financial need, as calculated by college, of all admitted students. Evaluation and ratings based strictly on academic and personal qualities of each applicant, with no consideration of financial need. Full aid packages offered to students with highest ratings until aid budget exhausted. College is need-blind for 96% to 99% of applicants.

Freshman aid. Need-based: Out of 679 full-time freshmen, 540 applied for aid; 415 were judged to have need; of these 415 received aid. Average package met 100% of need. 415 students had full need met. Average scholarship/grant was $21,874; average loan $2,674. **Non-need based:** 36 without need received awards.

Merit scholarships. Zollman Scholarships; half-tuition; for academic excellence; 5 to 10 awarded. STRIDE scholarship; $2,500 per year; for academic excellence; about 35 awarded. Springfield Partnership; full-tuition; for academic excellence in Springfield, MA, public high school; up to 3 awarded. Picker Scholarships; partial tuition; for students enrolling in engineering program. Ford Motor Company; full tuition; for engineering students; 4 awarded.

Policies to reduce costs. Tuition/fee waivers for employees and their families. Credit/placement for qualifying scores on AP, IB examinations. Work study available nights, weekends and for part-time students.

Payment plans. Installment, deferred payment.

Application procedures. FAFSA, institutional form, CSS PROFILE required. Closing date 2/1. Applicants notified by 4/1, must reply by 5/1 or within 4 week(s) of notification. Early decision closing date 11/15. **Transfers:** Closing date 2/15. Applicants who apply after admission decision is made cannot receive college aid until they reach junior standing and complete at least 32 credits at Smith.

Contact. **Financial aid office:** (413) 585-2530
Linda Dagradi, Director of Student Financial Services
7 College Lane
Northampton, MA 01063

Springfield College

Springfield, Massachusetts
www.spfldcol.edu
Four-year private **Federal Code: 002211**

	Living at home	On-campus
Tuition and fees (2002-2003):	$18,690	$18,690
Room and board:		$7,240
Books and supplies:	$900	$900
Personal expenses:	$1,000	$1,000
Transportation:	$1,600	$400

Undergraduate aid. Need-based: Need-based aid available for full-time students. **Additional information:** Co-operative education program available to students after freshman year.

Policies to reduce costs. Tuition/fee waivers for children of alumni, family members, employees and their families. Credit/placement for qualifying scores on AP, CLEP examinations.

Payment plans. Credit card, installment payment.

Application procedures. FAFSA, CSS PROFILE required. Priority date 3/15; no closing date. Applicants notified on rolling basis starting 3/15, must reply by 5/1 or within 2 week(s) of notification. Early decision closing date 12/1. **Transfers:** Priority date 4/15; no deadline.

Contact. **Financial aid office:** (413) 748-3000
Linda Dagradi, Director of Financial Aid
263 Alden Street
Springfield, MA 01109

Springfield Technical Community College

Springfield, Massachusetts
www.stcc.edu
Two-year public **Federal Code: 005549**

College costs. New England Regional tuition $98.50 per-credit-hour, $2,955 full-time.

	Living at home
Tuition and fees (2002-2003):	$2,734
Out-of-state:	$9,244
Per-credit charge:	$86
Per-credit out-of-state:	$303
Board only:	$1,200
Books and supplies:	$700
Personal expenses:	$900
Transportation:	$1,650

Undergraduate aid. All financial aid based on need. 88% awarded as scholarships/grants, 12% as loans/jobs. Need-based aid available for part-time students.

Policies to reduce costs. Tuition/fee waivers for senior citizens, employees and their families. Credit/placement for qualifying scores on AP, CLEP examinations. Work study available for part-time students.

Payment plans. Credit card, installment payment.

Application procedures. FAFSA, institutional form required. Priority date 4/1; no closing date. Applicants notified on rolling basis starting 7/1.

Contact. **Financial aid office:** (413) 755-4214
Mary Forni, Coordinator of Financial Aid Services
One Armory Square
Springfield, MA 01105

Stonehill College

Easton, Massachusetts
www.stonehill.edu
Four-year private **Federal Code: 002217**

	Living at home	On-campus
Tuition and fees:	$21,302	$21,302
Room and board:		$9,450
Board only:	$2,500	
Books and supplies:	$740	$740
Personal expenses:	$764	$764
Transportation:	$1,014	$180

Undergraduate aid. Need-based: Average financial aid package for full-time students was $13,923; for part-time $4,744. 66% awarded as scholarships/grants, 34% as loans/jobs. **Non-need-based:** 47% awarded as scholarships/grants, 53% as loans/jobs. Scholarships based on academics, athletics, job skills, leadership, minority status, music/drama.

Freshman aid. Need-based: Out of 566 full-time freshmen, 492 applied for aid; 398 were judged to have need; of these 398 received aid. Average package met 81% of need. 84 students had full need met. Average scholarship/grant was $11,561; average loan $3,481. **Non-need based:** 54 full-time freshmen with need received non-need scholarships; 138 without need received awards; 16 received athletic scholarships.

Policies to reduce costs. Tuition/fee waivers for family members, family of clergy, employees and their families. Credit/placement for qualifying scores on AP, IB, CLEP examinations. Work study available nights, weekends and for part-time students.

Payment plans. Installment payment.

Application procedures. FAFSA, CSS PROFILE required. Closing date 2/1. Applicants notified by 4/1, must reply by 5/1. Early decision closing date 11/1. **Transfers:** Priority date 4/1; no deadline.

Contact. **Financial aid office:** (508) 565-1088
Eileen O'Leary, Director of Student Aid and Finance
320 Washington Street
Easton, MA 02357-5610

Suffolk University

Boston, Massachusetts
www.suffolk.edu
Four-year private **Federal Code: 002218**

College costs. Additional $80 computer fee for School of Management.

	Living at home	On-campus
Tuition and fees (2002-2003):	$17,690	$17,690
Room and board:		$10,290
Board only:	$1,800	
Books and supplies:	$500	$500
Personal expenses:	$2,622	$2,622
Transportation:	$700	$150

Undergraduate aid. Need-based: Average financial aid package for full-time students was $12,645; for part-time $7,499. 47% awarded as scholarships/grants, 53% as loans/jobs. **Non-need-based:** 28% awarded as scholarships/grants, 72% as loans/jobs. Scholarships based on academics, alumni affiliation. **Additional information:** Foreign students may apply for institutional employment awards.

Freshman aid. Need-based: Out of 787 full-time freshmen, 651 applied for aid; 508 were judged to have need; of these 507 received aid. Average package met 77% of need. 89 students had full need met. Average scholarship/grant was $7,073; average loan $3,689. **Non-need based:** 181 full-time freshmen with need received non-need scholarships; 59 without need received awards.

Merit scholarships. Merit scholarships; amounts vary; based on academic achievement, talent, and contribution to applicant's school and community.

Policies to reduce costs. Tuition/fee waivers for children of alumni, senior citizens, family members, employees and their families. Credit/placement for qualifying scores on AP, IB, CLEP examinations. Work study available nights, weekends and for part-time students.

Payment plans. Credit card, installment, deferred payment.

Application procedures. FAFSA, institutional form required. Priority date 3/1; no closing date. Applicants notified on rolling basis starting 3/1, must reply within 2 week(s) of notification.

Contact. Financial aid office: (617) 720-3579
Christine Perry, Director of Financial Aid
8 Ashburton Place
Boston, MA 02108

Tufts University

Medford, Massachusetts
www.tufts.edu
Four-year private **Federal Code: 002219**

	Living at home	On-campus
Tuition and fees:	$29,630	$29,630
Room and board:		$8,640
Board only:	$3,000	
Books and supplies:	$800	$800
Personal expenses:	$1,135	$1,135

Undergraduate aid. All financial aid based on need. Average financial aid package for full-time students was $22,334. 78% awarded as scholarships/grants, 22% as loans/jobs. **Student debt:** 34% of graduating class borrowed to fund education; average debt was $15,499.

Freshman aid. Out of 1,271 full-time freshmen, 669 applied for aid; 458 were judged to have need; of these 458 received aid. Average package met 100% of need. 458 students had full need met. Average scholarship/grant was $19,183; average loan $3,356.

Policies to reduce costs. Tuition/fee waivers for employees and their families. Credit/placement for qualifying scores on AP, IB examinations.

Payment plans. Installment payment.

Application procedures. FAFSA, CSS PROFILE required. Priority date 2/1; closing date 2/15. Applicants notified by 4/10, must reply by 5/1. Early decision closing date 11/15. **Transfers:** Closing date 3/1.

Contact. Financial aid office: (617) 628-5000
Patricia Reilly, Director of Financial Aid
Bendetson Hall
Medford, MA 02155-5555

University of Massachusetts Amherst

Amherst, Massachusetts
www.umass.edu
Four-year public **Federal Code: 002221**

College costs. New England Regional tuition: $107 per-credit-hour, $7,339 full-time.

	Living at home	On-campus
Tuition and fees (2002-2003):	$6,482	$6,482
Out-of-state:	$15,335	$15,335
Room and board:		$5,994
Board only:	$1,800	
Books and supplies:	$500	$500
Personal expenses:	$1,000	$1,000
Transportation:	$600	$400

Undergraduate aid. Need-based: Average financial aid package for full-time students was $8,439; for part-time $7,195. 53% awarded as scholarships/grants, 47% as loans/jobs. **Non-need-based:** 26% awarded as scholarships/grants, 74% as loans/jobs. Scholarships based on academics, art, athletics, music/drama, state/district residency. **Student debt:** 48% of graduating class borrowed to fund education; average debt was $15,321.

Freshman aid. Need-based: Out of 4,302 full-time freshmen, 3,496 applied for aid; 1,975 were judged to have need; of these 1,864 received aid. Average package met 80% of need. 296 students had full need met. Average scholarship/grant was $4,773; average loan $2,772. **Non-need based:** 162 full-time freshmen with need received non-need scholarships; 380 without need received awards; 66 received athletic scholarships.

Merit scholarships. All applicants automatically reviewed for merit scholarships.

Policies to reduce costs. Tuition/fee waivers for senior citizens, employees and their families. Credit/placement for qualifying scores on AP, IB, CLEP examinations. Work study available nights, weekends and for part-time students.

Payment plans. Credit card payment.

Application procedures. FAFSA required. Priority date 3/1; no closing date. Applicants notified on rolling basis starting 4/1. **Transfers:** Financial aid transcripts required.

Contact. Financial aid office: (413) 545-0801
Kenneth Burnham, Director of Financial Aid
University Admissions Center, 37 Mather Drive
Amherst, MA 01003-9291

University of Massachusetts Boston

Boston, Massachusetts
www.umb.edu
Four-year public **Federal Code: 002222**

College costs. New England residents pay 150% of in-state tuition for programs not available at their home state institutions.

	Living at home
Tuition and fees (2002-2003):	$5,227
Out-of-state:	$14,887
Board only:	$2,000
Books and supplies:	$680
Personal expenses:	$2,420

Undergraduate aid. Need-based: Need-based aid available for full-time and part-time students. **Non-need-based:** Scholarships based on academics, art, leadership, music/drama. **Additional information:** Some Massachusetts state employees and Massachusetts Vietnam veterans eligible for tuition waiver. Some waivers available based on talent and academic excellence.

Policies to reduce costs. Tuition/fee waivers for senior citizens, minority students, employees and their families. Credit/placement for qualifying scores on AP, CLEP examinations. Work study available for part-time students.

Application procedures. FAFSA required. Priority date 3/1; no closing date. Applicants notified on rolling basis starting 4/1, must reply within 4 week(s) of notification. **Transfers:** Priority date 6/1; no deadline.

Contact. Financial aid office: (617) 287-6300
Director of Financial Aid Services
100 Morrissey Boulevard
Boston, MA 02125-3393

University of Massachusetts Dartmouth

North Dartmouth, Massachusetts
www.umassd.edu
Four-year public **Federal Code: 002210**

	Living at home	On-campus
Tuition and fees (2002-2003):	$5,164	$5,164
Out-of-state:	$13,664	$13,664
Room and board:		$6,526
Board only:	$700	
Books and supplies:	$600	$600
Personal expenses:	$1,156	$1,156
Transportation:	$1,300	$494

Undergraduate aid. Need-based: Need-based aid available for full-time and part-time students. **Non-need-based:** Scholarships based on academics.

Merit scholarships. Chancellor's Merit Scholarship; approximately $2,000; for Massachusetts high school seniors with combined SAT 1250 and above and in top 25% of class, 50 awarded. Solveig E.J. Balestracci Scholarship; $1,000; for academic achievement in marine-related area for residents of New Bedford, Dartmouth, Acushnet, Westport, Mattapoisett, Marion, Rochester or Lakeville; 1 awarded. Donald E. & Anne L. Walker Merit Scholarship; $750-$1,000 (renewable); based on superior SAT score and high school rank, essay and interview; 2-4 awarded. Boivon Scholarship; $1,000; based on academic involvement in French language and culture. Wal-Mart Scholarship; $5,000 per year (renewable); for certain engineering and science majors; 2 awarded.

Policies to reduce costs. Tuition/fee waivers for senior citizens, employees and their families. Credit/placement for qualifying scores on AP, IB, CLEP examinations. Work study available nights, weekends and for part-time students.

Payment plans. Credit card, installment payment.

Application procedures. FAFSA required. Priority date 3/1; no closing date. Applicants notified on rolling basis starting 4/1. Early decision closing date 11/15.

Contact. Financial aid office: (508) 999-8632
Bruce Palmer, Director of Financial Aid
285 Old Westport Road
North Dartmouth, MA 02747-2300

University of Massachusetts Lowell

Lowell, Massachusetts
www.uml.edu
Four-year public **Federal Code: 002161**

College costs. New England Regional tuition: $217 per-credit-hour, $4,982 full-time.

	Living at home	On-campus
Tuition and fees (2002-2003):	$5,213	$5,213
Out-of-state:	$14,651	$14,651
Room and board:		$5,464
Board only:	$1,500	
Books and supplies:	$500	$500
Personal expenses:	$800	$800
Transportation:	$900	$200

Undergraduate aid. Need-based: Average financial aid package for full-time students was $6,728; for part-time $5,500. 49% awarded as scholarships/grants, 51% as loans/jobs. **Non-need-based:** 19% awarded as scholarships/grants, 81% as loans/jobs. Scholarships based on academics, art, athletics. **Student debt:** 65% of graduating class borrowed to fund education; average debt was $15,979.

Freshman aid. Need-based: Out of 967 full-time freshmen, 703 applied for aid; 413 were judged to have need; of these 396 received aid. Average package met 96% of need. 248 students had full need met. Average scholarship/grant was $3,745; average loan $1,936. **Non-need based:** 58 full-time freshmen with need received non-need scholarships; 48 without need received awards; 31 received athletic scholarships.

Policies to reduce costs. Tuition/fee waivers for senior citizens, employees and their families. Credit/placement for qualifying scores on AP, CLEP examinations.

Payment plans. Installment payment.

Application procedures. FAFSA required. Priority date 3/1; no closing date. Applicants notified on rolling basis starting 3/24.

Contact. Financial aid office: (978) 934-4220
Judy Keyes, Director of Financial Aid
883 Broadway Street, Room 110
Lowell, MA 01854-5104

Urban College of Boston

Boston, Massachusetts
www.urbancollege.edu
Two-year private **Federal Code: 031305**

	Living at home
Tuition and fees:	$3,020
Per-credit charge:	$100
Board only:	$2,100
Books and supplies:	$400
Personal expenses:	$2,340
Transportation:	$448

Undergraduate aid. All financial aid based on need. Need-based aid available for full-time and part-time students.

Policies to reduce costs. Credit/placement for qualifying scores on IB examinations.

Payment plans. Credit card payment.

Application procedures. FAFSA required. No deadline. Applicants notified on rolling basis starting 3/15.

Contact. Financial aid office: (617) 292-4723 ext.6220
Patricia Harden, Financial Aid Coordinator
178 Tremont Street, Seventh Floor
Boston, MA 02111

Wellesley College

Wellesley, Massachusetts
www.wellesley.edu
Four-year private **Federal Code: 002224**

	Living at home	On-campus
Tuition and fees:	$27,904	$27,904
Room and board:		$8,612
Books and supplies:	$800	$800
Personal expenses:		$1,200
Transportation:		$1,000

Undergraduate aid. All financial aid based on need. Average financial aid package for full-time students was $22,614. 84% awarded as scholarships/grants, 16% as loans/jobs. Need-based aid available for part-time students. **Student debt:** 51% of graduating class borrowed to fund education; average debt was $15,697.

Freshman aid. Out of 593 full-time freshmen, 409 applied for aid; 334 were judged to have need; of these 334 received aid. Average package met 100% of need. 334 students had full need met. Average scholarship/grant was $21,701; average loan $2,360.

Policies to reduce costs. Tuition/fee waivers for employees and their families. Credit/placement for qualifying scores on AP, IB examinations.

Payment plans. Installment, deferred payment.

Application procedures. FAFSA, institutional form, CSS PROFILE required. Closing date 1/15. Applicants notified by 4/1, must reply by 5/1. Early decision closing date 11/1. **Transfers:** Closing date 2/10.

Contact. Financial aid office: (781) 283-2360
Kathryn Osmond, Director of Student Financial Services
106 Central Street
Wellesley, MA 02481-8203

Wentworth Institute of Technology

Boston, Massachusetts
www.wit.edu
Four-year private **Federal Code: 002225**

	Living at home	On-campus
Tuition and fees:	$15,000	$15,000
Room and board:		$8,200
Books and supplies:	$1,000	$1,000
Personal expenses:	$1,000	$1,000
Transportation:	$1,500	$1,000

Undergraduate aid. Need-based: Average financial aid package for full-time students was $7,475; for part-time $3,740. 44% awarded as scholarships/grants, 56% as loans/jobs. **Non-need-based:** Scholarships based on academics, leadership. **Student debt:** 81% of graduating class borrowed to fund education; average debt was $13,516.

Freshman aid. Need-based: Out of 1,168 full-time freshmen, 1,168 applied for aid; 691 were judged to have need; of these 691 received aid. Average package met 41% of need. 23 students had full need met. Average scholarship/grant was $604; average loan $2,503. **Non-need based:** 697 full-time freshmen with need received non-need scholarships; 183 without need received awards.

Merit scholarships. Applicants for admission automatically considered for merit scholarships.

Policies to reduce costs. Tuition/fee waivers for employees and their families. Credit/placement for qualifying scores on AP, CLEP examinations. Work study available nights and weekends.

Payment plans. Credit card, installment payment.

Application procedures. FAFSA required. Priority date 3/1; no closing date. Applicants notified on rolling basis starting 3/15, must reply within 2 week(s) of notification. **Transfers:** Review of NSLDS history within 30 days of beginning of enrollment required.

Contact. Financial aid office: (617) 989-4020
Traci Cady, Director of Financial Aid
550 Huntington Avenue
Boston, MA 02115

Western New England College

Springfield, Massachusetts
www.wnec.edu
Four-year private **Federal Code: 002226**

	Living at home	On-campus
Tuition and fees:	$20,824	$20,824
Room and board:		$8,100
Board only:	$2,130	
Books and supplies:	$660	$660
Personal expenses:	$1,490	$1,110
Transportation:	$1,210	$390

Undergraduate aid. Need-based: Need-based aid available for full-time and part-time students. **Non-need-based:** Scholarships based on academics.

Policies to reduce costs. Tuition/fee waivers for senior citizens, family members, employees and their families. Credit/placement for qualifying scores on AP, IB, CLEP examinations. Work study available nights and weekends.

Payment plans. Installment, deferred payment.

Application procedures. FAFSA required. Priority date 4/1; no closing date. Applicants notified on rolling basis starting 3/15, must reply by 5/1 or within 2 week(s) of notification.

Contact. Financial aid office: (413) 782-3111
Kathy Chambers, Associate Director of Financial Aid
1215 Wilbraham Road
Springfield, MA 01119-2688

Westfield State College

Westfield, Massachusetts
www.wsc.ma.edu
Four-year public **Federal Code: 002189**

College costs. New England Regional tuition $3,940.

	Living at home	On-campus
Tuition and fees (2002-2003):	$3,455	$3,455
Out-of-state:	$9,535	$9,535
Room and board:		$4,762
Board only:	$1,560	
Books and supplies:	$650	$650
Personal expenses:	$1,442	$1,442
Transportation:	$1,250	$400

Undergraduate aid. Need-based: Average financial aid package for full-time students was $4,561; for part-time $3,787. 57% awarded as scholarships/grants, 43% as loans/jobs. **Non-need-based:** 8% awarded as scholarships/grants, 92% as loans/jobs. Scholarships based on academics. **Student debt:** 88% of graduating class borrowed to fund education; average debt was $12,759.

Freshman aid. Need-based: Out of 967 full-time freshmen, 784 applied for aid; 418 were judged to have need; of these 418 received aid. Average package met 78% of need. 120 students had full need met. Average scholarship/grant was $3,439; average loan $1,615. **Non-need based:** 25 full-time freshmen with need received non-need scholarships; 364 without need received awards.

Policies to reduce costs. Tuition/fee waivers for senior citizens, employees and their families. Credit/placement for qualifying scores on AP, CLEP examinations.

Payment plans. Installment payment.

Application procedures. FAFSA required. Priority date 3/1; no closing date. Applicants notified on rolling basis starting 4/15.

Contact. Financial aid office: (413) 572-5218
Catherine Ryan, Director of Student Administrative Services Center
577 Western Avenue
Westfield, MA 01086-1630

Wheaton College

Norton, Massachusetts
www.wheatoncollege.edu
Four-year private **Federal Code: 002227**

College costs. Freshman pay one-time $50 general fee that is refunded at the end of their senior year.

	Living at home	On-campus
Tuition and fees:	$28,900	$28,900
Room and board:		$7,430
Board only:	$1,200	
Books and supplies:	$1,060	$1,060
Personal expenses:	$640	$640
Transportation:	$600	$300

Undergraduate aid. Need-based: Average financial aid package for full-time students was $20,390. 72% awarded as scholarships/grants, 28% as loans/jobs. Need-based aid available for part-time students. **Non-need-based:** 47% awarded as scholarships/grants, 53% as loans/jobs. Scholarships based on academics. **Student debt:** 63% of graduating class borrowed to fund education; average debt was $18,348.

Freshman aid. Need-based: Out of 416 full-time freshmen, 262 applied for aid; 211 were judged to have need; of these 211 received aid. Average package met 95% of need. 118 students had full need met. Average scholarship/grant was $16,188; average loan $3,602. **Non-need based:** 1 full-time freshmen with need received non-need scholarships; 51 without need received awards.

Merit scholarships. Balfour Scholarship; $10,000 annually plus laptop computer. Trustee Scholarship; $6,000 annually plus $4,000 total in research/internship/community service stipends. Community Scholarship; $5,000 annually plus $3,000 total in research/internship/community service stipends. All selected from top 15% of applicant pool.

Policies to reduce costs. Tuition/fee waivers for employees and their families. Credit/placement for qualifying scores on AP, IB examinations. Work study available nights, weekends and for part-time students.

Payment plans. Installment payment.

Application procedures. FAFSA, CSS PROFILE required. Closing date 2/1. Applicants notified by 4/1, must reply by 5/1. Early decision closing date 11/15. **Transfers:** Very limited institutional grant funds available for late transfer applicants.

Contact. Financial aid office: (508) 286-7722
Robin Randall, Assistant VP for Enrollment and Student Financial Services
26 East Main Street
Norton, MA 02766

Williams College

Williamstown, Massachusetts
www.williams.edu
Four-year private **Federal Code: 002229**

	Living at home	On-campus
Tuition and fees:	$28,090	$28,090
Room and board:		$7,660
Books and supplies:	$800	$800
Personal expenses:		$1,200
Transportation:		$600

Undergraduate aid. All financial aid based on need. Average financial aid package for full-time students was $24,390. 86% awarded as scholarships/grants, 14% as loans/jobs. Need-based aid available for part-time students. **Student debt:** 46% of graduating class borrowed to fund education; average debt was $12,316.

Freshman aid. Out of 540 full-time freshmen, 298 applied for aid; 241 were judged to have need; of these 241 received aid. Average package met 100% of need. 241 students had full need met. Average scholarship/grant was $23,724; average loan $1,875.

Policies to reduce costs. Tuition/fee waivers for employees and their families. Credit/placement for qualifying scores on AP, IB examinations. Work study available nights, weekends and for part-time students.

Payment plans. Installment payment.

Application procedures. FAFSA, CSS PROFILE required. Closing date 2/1. Applicants notified by 4/1, must reply by 5/1. Early decision closing date 11/15. **Transfers:** Closing date 3/1.

Contact. **Financial aid office:** (413) 597-3131
Paul Boyer, Director of Financial Aid
33 Stetson Court
Williamstown, MA 01267

Worcester Polytechnic Institute

Worcester, Massachusetts
www.wpi.edu
Four-year private **Federal Code: 002233**

	Living at home	On-campus
Tuition and fees:	$28,420	$28,420
Room and board:		$8,984
Books and supplies:	$692	$692
Personal expenses:	$1,100	$1,100

Undergraduate aid. Need-based: Average financial aid package for full-time students was $19,334; for part-time $5,079. 72% awarded as scholarships/grants, 28% as loans/jobs. **Non-need-based:** 42% awarded as scholarships/grants, 58% as loans/jobs. Scholarships based on academics, minority status. **Student debt:** 81% of graduating class borrowed to fund education; average debt was $25,609.

Freshman aid. Need-based: Out of 714 full-time freshmen, 667 applied for aid; 557 were judged to have need; of these 552 received aid. Average package met 95% of need. 189 students had full need met. Average scholarship/grant was $16,228; average loan $4,340. **Non-need based:** 115 full-time freshmen with need received non-need scholarships; 55 without need received awards.

Merit scholarships. Dean's Scholarship; $5,000; 125 awarded. Presidential Scholarship; $10,000; 60 awarded. Trustees' Scholarship; full tuition; 10 awarded. All based on academic excellence.

Policies to reduce costs. Tuition/fee waivers for employees and their families. Credit/placement for qualifying scores on AP, IB examinations.

Payment plans. Credit card, installment, deferred payment.

Application procedures. FAFSA, CSS PROFILE required. Closing date 3/1. Applicants notified by 4/1, must reply by 5/1. Early decision closing date 11/15.

Contact. **Financial aid office:** (508) 831-5469
Michael Curley, Director, Financial Aid
100 Institute Road
Worcester, MA 01609-2280

Michigan

Adrian College

Adrian, Michigan
www.adrian.edu
Four-year private **Federal Code: 002234**

	Living at home	On-campus
Tuition and fees (2002-2003):	$15,660	$15,660
Room and board:		$5,440
Board only:	$2,760	
Books and supplies:	$400	$400
Personal expenses:	$928	$928
Transportation:	$647	$647

Undergraduate aid. Need-based: Average financial aid package for full-time students was $14,697; for part-time $7,186. 65% awarded as scholarships/grants, 35% as loans/jobs. **Non-need-based:** 71% awarded as scholarships/grants, 29% as loans/jobs. Scholarships based on academics, alumni affiliation, art, music/drama, religious affiliation. **Student debt:** 75% of graduating class borrowed to fund education; average debt was $13,245.

Freshman aid. Need-based: Out of 302 full-time freshmen, 299 applied for aid; 253 were judged to have need; of these 253 received aid. Average package met 98% of need. 236 students had full need met. Average scholarship/grant was $9,601; average loan $3,220. **Non-need based:** 122 full-time freshmen with need received non-need scholarships; 44 without need received awards.

Merit scholarships. Academic scholarships; based on ACT score of 20 and GPA of 3.0.

Policies to reduce costs. Tuition/fee waivers for employees and their families. Credit/placement for qualifying scores on AP, CLEP examinations. Work study available nights and weekends.

Payment plans. Credit card, installment payment.

Application procedures. FAFSA required. Closing date 3/1. Applicants notified on rolling basis starting 3/15, must reply by 5/1 or within 2 week(s) of notification. **Transfers:** Closing date 3/1.

Contact. Financial aid office: (517) 265-5161
Mike Hague, Associate Vice President for Financial Services
110 South Madison Street
Adrian, MI 49221-2575

Alma College

Alma, Michigan
www.alma.edu
Four-year private **Federal Code: 002236**

	Living at home	On-campus
Tuition and fees (2002-2003):	$17,582	$17,582
Room and board:		$6,336
Board only:	$1,528	
Books and supplies:	$700	$700
Personal expenses:	$700	$700
Transportation:	$750	$750

Undergraduate aid. Need-based: Average financial aid package for full-time students was $15,914; for part-time $9,368. 76% awarded as scholarships/grants, 24% as loans/jobs. **Non-need-based:** 58% awarded as scholarships/grants, 42% as loans/jobs. Scholarships based on academics, alumni affiliation, art, leadership, music/drama. **Student debt:** 94% of graduating class borrowed to fund education; average debt was $15,862.

Freshman aid. Need-based: Out of 333 full-time freshmen, 324 applied for aid; 244 were judged to have need; of these 244 received aid. Average package met 94% of need. 104 students had full need met. Average scholarship/grant was $14,545; average loan $3,615. **Non-need based:** 67 full-time freshmen with need received non-need scholarships; 80 without need received awards.

Merit scholarships. Auditions required for music, drama, dance scholarship candidates. Portfolios required for art scholarship candidates. Distinguished Scholar Award to designated National Merit Scholarship Finalist, up to full tuition. Alma College Merit Scholarship awarded to National Merit Scholarship Finalist, up to $2000. Distinguished Trustee Honors Scholarship awarded on basis of campus interview, superior academic achievement, national test scores, up to $7,500. Presidential Scholarships awarded on basis of outstanding scholarship and high national test scores, up to $6,000. Tartan Awards based on academic achievement or high national test scores, up to $5,000. Performance Scholarships: $1,000 during the first and second years; $1,500 during the third year and $2,000 during the fourth year.

Policies to reduce costs. Tuition/fee waivers for employees and their families. Prepayment discount; credit/placement for qualifying scores on AP, IB examinations.

Payment plans. Credit card, installment, deferred payment.

Application procedures. FAFSA required. Priority date 2/15; no closing date. Applicants notified on rolling basis starting 3/1, must reply within 3 week(s) of notification. **Transfers:** No deadline.

Contact. Financial aid office: (989) 463-7347
Christopher Brown, Director of Financial Aid
614 West Superior Street
Alma, MI 48801-1599

Alpena Community College

Alpena, Michigan
www.alpenacc.edu
Two-year public **Federal Code: 002237**

	Living at home	On-campus
Tuition and fees (2002-2003):	$2,330	$2,330
Out-of-district:	$3,230	$3,230
Out-of-state:	$4,160	$4,160
Per-credit charge:	$58	$58
Per-credit out-of-district:	$86	$86
Per-credit out-of-state:	$115	$115
Room only:		$2,600
Board only:	$1,300	
Books and supplies:	$500	$500
Personal expenses:	$600	
Transportation:	$500	

Undergraduate aid. Need-based: 78% awarded as scholarships/grants, 22% as loans/jobs. Need-based aid available for part-time students. **Non-need-based:** 62% awarded as scholarships/grants, 38% as loans/jobs. Scholarships based on academics, art, athletics, job skills, leadership, music/drama.

Policies to reduce costs. Tuition/fee waivers for senior citizens, employees and their families. Credit/placement for qualifying scores on AP, CLEP examinations. Work study available for part-time students.

Payment plans. Credit card payment.

Application procedures. FAFSA required. Priority date 5/15; no closing date. Applicants notified on rolling basis starting 5/15, must reply within 3 week(s) of notification.

Contact. Financial aid office: (989) 358-7205
Max Lindsay, Dean of Students
666 Johnson Street
Alpena, MI 49707

Andrews University

Berrien Springs, Michigan
www.andrews.edu
Four-year private **Federal Code: 002238**

	Living at home	On-campus
Tuition and fees (2002-2003):	$13,746	$13,746
Room and board:		$4,840
Board only:	$1,570	
Books and supplies:	$1,400	$1,400
Personal expenses:	$945	$945
Transportation:	$750	$750

Undergraduate aid. Need-based: Average financial aid package for full-time students was $16,236; for part-time $17,660. 66% awarded as scholarships/grants, 34% as loans/jobs. **Non-need-based:** Scholarships based on academics, alumni affiliation, leadership, music/drama, religious affiliation. **Student debt:** 38% of graduating class borrowed to fund education; average debt was $15,833.

Freshman aid. Need-based: Out of 252 full-time freshmen, 247 applied for aid; 163 were judged to have need; of these 163 received aid. Average

package met 86% of need. 48 students had full need met. Average scholarship/grant was $6,348; average loan $2,552. **Non-need based:** 156 full-time freshmen with need received non-need scholarships; 78 without need received awards.

Policies to reduce costs. Tuition/fee waivers for senior citizens, family members, employees and their families. Prepayment discount; credit/placement for qualifying scores on AP, IB, CLEP examinations.

Payment plans. Credit card, installment payment.

Application procedures. FAFSA, institutional form required. Priority date 3/31; no closing date. Applicants notified on rolling basis starting 3/15.

Contact. **Financial aid office:** (269) 471-7771
Jerri Gifford, Director of Student Financial Services
Berrien Springs, MI 49104

Aquinas College

Grand Rapids, Michigan
www.aquinas.edu
Four-year private **Federal Code: 002239**

	Living at home	On-campus
Tuition and fees (2002-2003):	$15,620	$15,620
Room and board:		$5,436
Board only:	$1,575	
Books and supplies:	$628	$628
Personal expenses:	$661	$661
Transportation:	$1,125	$628

Undergraduate aid. **Need-based:** Average financial aid package for full-time students was $14,634; for part-time $9,435. 83% awarded as scholarships/grants, 17% as loans/jobs. **Non-need-based:** 68% awarded as scholarships/grants, 32% as loans/jobs. Scholarships based on academics, alumni affiliation, art, athletics, leadership, religious affiliation. **Student debt:** 65% of graduating class borrowed to fund education; average debt was $13,262.

Freshman aid. **Need-based:** Out of 349 full-time freshmen, 307 applied for aid; 263 were judged to have need; of these 263 received aid. Average package met 98% of need. 117 students had full need met. Average scholarship/grant was $12,523; average loan $2,078. **Non-need based:** 87 full-time freshmen with need received non-need scholarships; 83 without need received awards; 64 received athletic scholarships.

Merit scholarships. Spectrum Scholarship; awarded to students who have excelled in academics, leadership or community service. Renewable scholarships; $3,000 to full tuition.

Policies to reduce costs. Tuition/fee waivers for adults, children of alumni, senior citizens, family of clergy, employees and their families. Credit/placement for qualifying scores on AP, CLEP examinations.

Payment plans. Credit card, installment, deferred payment.

Application procedures. FAFSA required. Priority date 2/15; no closing date. Applicants notified on rolling basis starting 4/1, must reply within 2 week(s) of notification. **Transfers:** Priority date 4/15; closing date 7/1.

Contact. **Financial aid office:** (616) 459-8281
David Steffee, Director of Financial Aid
1607 Robinson Road Southeast
Grand Rapids, MI 49506-1799

Baker College of Auburn Hills

Auburn Hills, Michigan
www.baker.edu
Four-year private **Federal Code: E00466**

	Living at home
Tuition and fees (2002-2003):	$7,680
Books and supplies:	$900

Undergraduate aid. **Need-based:** 52% awarded as scholarships/grants, 48% as loans/jobs. **Non-need-based:** Scholarships based on academics, alumni affiliation. **Student debt:** 70% of graduating class borrowed to fund education; average debt was $11,684.

Policies to reduce costs. Tuition/fee waivers for employees and their families. Credit/placement for qualifying scores on AP, IB, CLEP examinations. Work study available nights, weekends and for part-time students.

Payment plans. Credit card, installment, deferred payment.

Application procedures. FAFSA, institutional form required. Priority date 2/21; closing date 9/1. Applicants notified on rolling basis starting 4/1. **Transfers:** Closing date 9/1. Must have been deemed financial aid-eligible at previous school.

Contact. Greg Little, Financial Aid Director
1500 University Drive
Auburn Hills, MI 48326

Baker College of Cadillac

Cadillac, Michigan
www.baker.edu
Four-year private **Federal Code: E00461**

	Living at home
Tuition and fees (2002-2003):	$7,680
Books and supplies:	$1,000

Undergraduate aid. **Need-based:** 60% awarded as scholarships/grants, 40% as loans/jobs. Need-based aid available for part-time students. **Non-need-based:** 8% awarded as scholarships/grants, 92% as loans/jobs. Scholarships based on academics.

Merit scholarships. Baker College Career Scholarships; $400 per term for 4 years; based on 2.5 GPA after junior year of high school. Board of Regents Scholarships; half tuition for 4 years; based on 3.5 GPA through grade 11.

Policies to reduce costs. Tuition/fee waivers for employees and their families. Credit/placement for qualifying scores on AP, IB, CLEP examinations. Work study available nights, weekends and for part-time students.

Payment plans. Credit card, installment payment.

Application procedures. FAFSA, institutional form required. Priority date 2/21; no closing date. Applicants notified on rolling basis starting 5/1. **Transfers:** Priority date 3/20; closing date 9/1.

Contact. **Financial aid office:** (231) 876-3118
Kristin Bonney, Financial Aid Officer
9600 East 13th Street
Cadillac, MI 49601

Baker College of Clinton Township

Clinton Township, Michigan
www.baker.edu
Four-year private **Federal Code: E00462**

	Living at home
Tuition and fees (projected):	$7,200
Books and supplies:	$1,000
Personal expenses:	$2,000
Transportation:	$1,600

Undergraduate aid. **Need-based:** 64% awarded as scholarships/grants, 36% as loans/jobs. Need-based aid available for part-time students. **Non-need-based:** Scholarships based on academics, minority status. **Student debt:** 70% of graduating class borrowed to fund education; average debt was $12,022.

Policies to reduce costs. Tuition/fee waivers for employees and their families. Credit/placement for qualifying scores on AP, IB, CLEP examinations. Work study available nights, weekends and for part-time students.

Payment plans. Credit card, installment, deferred payment.

Application procedures. FAFSA, institutional form required. Priority date 2/21; closing date 9/1. Applicants notified on rolling basis starting 4/1. **Transfers:** Priority date 2/21; closing date 9/1.

Contact. **Financial aid office:** (586) 790-9589
Lisa Harvener, Vice President of Student Services
34950 Little Mack Avenue
Clinton Township, MI 48035

Baker College of Jackson

Jackson, Michigan
www.baker.edu
Two-year private **Federal Code: E00733**

	Living at home
Tuition and fees (projected):	$7,440
Per-credit charge:	$155
Books and supplies:	$975

Undergraduate aid. **Non-need-based:** Scholarships based on academics, minority status.

Policies to reduce costs. Tuition/fee waivers for employees and their families. Credit/placement for qualifying scores on AP, IB, CLEP examinations.

Payment plans. Credit card, installment, deferred payment.

Application procedures. FAFSA, institutional form required. Priority date 2/21; closing date 9/1. Applicants notified on rolling basis starting 4/1. **Transfers:** Priority date 3/21; closing date 9/1.

Contact. **Financial aid office:** (517) 789-6123
Robert Nelson, Director of Financial Aid
2800 Springport Road
Jackson, MI 49202

Baker College of Muskegon

Muskegon, Michigan
www.baker.edu
Four-year private **Federal Code: E00463**

College costs. Students provide own meals, no meal plan.

	Living at home	On-campus
Tuition and fees:	$7,700	$7,700
Room only:		$2,025
Books and supplies:	$975	$975
Personal expenses:	$2,000	$2,000
Transportation:	$900	$450

Undergraduate aid. Need-based: Average financial aid package for full-time students was $6,650; for part-time $5,070. 60% awarded as scholarships/grants, 40% as loans/jobs. **Non-need-based:** 17% awarded as scholarships/grants, 83% as loans/jobs. Scholarships based on academics, minority status. **Student debt:** 70% of graduating class borrowed to fund education; average debt was $11,684.

Freshman aid. Need-based: Out of 699 full-time freshmen, 525 applied for aid; 475 were judged to have need; of these 475 received aid. Average package met 75% of need. Average scholarship/grant was $3,350; average loan $2,625. **Non-need based:** 235 full-time freshmen with need received non-need scholarships; 70 without need received awards.

Merit scholarships. Career Scholarship; $4,800 over 4 years; based on incoming freshman status, high school GPA over 3.0. Board Regents Scholarship; one-half tuition for 4 years; based on incoming freshman status, GPA over 3.5. Alternative Scholarship; one-half tuition for 2 years; based on academic success in alternative high school education program.

Policies to reduce costs. Tuition/fee waivers for employees and their families. Credit/placement for qualifying scores on AP, IB, CLEP examinations. Work study available nights, weekends and for part-time students.

Payment plans. Credit card, installment, deferred payment.

Application procedures. FAFSA, institutional form required. Priority date 2/21; no closing date. Applicants notified on rolling basis starting 4/1. **Transfers:** Priority date 3/21. State grant deadline for attending private, non-profit colleges in Michigan.

Contact. **Financial aid office:** (231) 777-5231
Aaron Maike, Director of Financial Aid
1903 Marquette Avenue
Muskegon, MI 49442

Baker College of Owosso

Owosso, Michigan
www.baker.edu
Four-year private **Federal Code: E00464**

	Living at home	On-campus
Tuition and fees (2002-2003):	$7,200	$7,200
Room only:		$1,950
Books and supplies:	$900	$900

Undergraduate aid. Need-based: Need-based aid available for full-time and part-time students. **Non-need-based:** Scholarships based on academics, minority status.

Policies to reduce costs. Tuition/fee waivers for employees and their families. Credit/placement for qualifying scores on AP, IB, CLEP examinations.

Payment plans. Credit card, installment payment.

Application procedures. FAFSA, institutional form required. Priority date 2/21; closing date 9/1. Applicants notified on rolling basis starting 4/1. **Transfers:** Priority date 3/21; closing date 9/1.

Contact. David Lewis, Financial Aid Director
1020 South Washington Street
Owosso, MI 48867

Baker College of Port Huron

Port Huron, Michigan
www.baker.edu
Four-year private **Federal Code: E00465**

	Living at home
Tuition and fees (2002-2003):	$7,440
Board only:	$1,800
Books and supplies:	$1,000
Personal expenses:	$2,000
Transportation:	$2,700

Undergraduate aid. All financial aid based on need. 58% awarded as scholarships/grants, 42% as loans/jobs. Need-based aid available for part-time students.

Policies to reduce costs. Tuition/fee waivers for employees and their families. Credit/placement for qualifying scores on AP, IB, CLEP examinations. Work study available nights and for part-time students.

Payment plans. Credit card, installment payment.

Application procedures. FAFSA, institutional form required. Priority date 2/21; no closing date. Applicants notified on rolling basis starting 4/1. **Transfers:** Priority date 3/21; closing date 9/1.

Contact. **Financial aid office:** (810) 985-7000
Wendi Hickman, Financial Aid Director
3403 Lapeer Road
Port Huron, MI 48060-2597

Bay de Noc Community College

Escanaba, Michigan
www.baydenoc.cc.mi.us
Two-year public **Federal Code: 002240**

College costs. Tuition and instructional fee charged on per-contact-hour basis.

	Living at home	On-campus
Tuition and fees (2002-2003):	$1,900	$1,900
Out-of-district:	$2,600	$2,600
Out-of-state:	$3,819	$3,819
Per-credit charge:	$57	$57
Per-credit out-of-district:	$79	$79
Per-credit out-of-state:	$124	$124
Room only:		$1,600
Books and supplies:	$350	$350
Personal expenses:	$500	$500
Transportation:	$940	$470

Undergraduate aid. Need-based: 77% awarded as scholarships/grants, 23% as loans/jobs. Need-based aid available for part-time students. **Non-need-based:** Scholarships based on academics.

Policies to reduce costs. Tuition/fee waivers for senior citizens, employees and their families. Credit/placement for qualifying scores on AP examinations. Work study available nights, weekends and for part-time students.

Application procedures. FAFSA required. Priority date 4/1; no closing date. Applicants notified on rolling basis starting 2/1, must reply within 2 week(s) of notification.

Contact. **Financial aid office:** (906) 786-5802
Gloria Seney, Director of Financial Aid
2001 North Lincoln Road
Escanaba, MI 49829-2511

Calvin College

Grand Rapids, Michigan
www.calvin.edu
Four-year private **Federal Code: 002241**

	Living at home	On-campus
Tuition and fees:	$16,775	$16,775
Room and board:		$5,840
Board only:	$2,290	
Books and supplies:	$680	$680
Personal expenses:	$875	$875
Transportation:	$1,960	$670

Undergraduate aid. Need-based: Average financial aid package for full-time students was $12,252; for part-time $8,973. 63% awarded as scholarships/grants, 37% as loans/jobs. **Non-need-based:** 65% awarded as scholarships/grants, 35% as loans/jobs. Scholarships based on academics, alumni affiliation, art, leadership, minority status, music/drama, religious affiliation, state/district residency. **Student debt:** 67% of graduating class borrowed to fund education; average debt was $17,000.

Freshman aid. Need-based: Out of 1,046 full-time freshmen, 850 applied for aid; 666 were judged to have need; of these 662 received aid. Average package met 94% of need. 170 students had full need met. Average scholarship/grant was $8,912; average loan $4,332. **Non-need based:** 90 full-time freshmen with need received non-need scholarships; 317 without need received awards.

Merit scholarships. Calvin merit-based scholarships; awarded to more than 50% of prospective first-year students, more than 45% of undergraduates.

Policies to reduce costs. Tuition/fee waivers for employees and their families. Credit/placement for qualifying scores on AP, IB, CLEP examinations. Work study available nights, weekends and for part-time students.

Payment plans. Installment payment.

Application procedures. FAFSA, institutional form required. Priority date 2/15; no closing date. Applicants notified on rolling basis starting 3/15. **Transfers:** Priority date 3/15; no deadline. Considered for same types of merit-based scholarship as freshman.

Contact. Financial aid office: (616) 957-6000
Edward Kerestley, Director of Scholarships and Financial Aid
3201 Burton Street SE
Grand Rapids, MI 49546

Central Michigan University

Mount Pleasant, Michigan
www.cmich.edu
Four-year public **Federal Code: 002243**

	Living at home	On-campus
Tuition and fees (2002-2003):	$4,747	$4,747
Out-of-state:	$11,119	$11,119
Room and board:		$5,524
Board only:	$2,414	
Books and supplies:	$650	$650
Personal expenses:	$1,621	$1,621
Transportation:	$600	$600

Undergraduate aid. Need-based: Average financial aid package for full-time students was $8,495; for part-time $8,108. 44% awarded as scholarships/grants, 56% as loans/jobs. **Non-need-based:** 31% awarded as scholarships/grants, 69% as loans/jobs. Scholarships based on academics, alumni affiliation, art, athletics, leadership, minority status, music/drama, state/district residency. **Student debt:** 65% of graduating class borrowed to fund education; average debt was $15,937. **Additional information:** Tuition waiver for Native American students qualifying under state program criteria.

Freshman aid. Need-based: Out of 3,545 full-time freshmen, 2,746 applied for aid; 1,866 were judged to have need; of these 1,863 received aid. Average package met 100% of need. 1159 students had full need met. Average scholarship/grant was $4,726; average loan $1,735. **Non-need based:** 378 full-time freshmen with need received non-need scholarships; 1,351 without need received awards; 60 received athletic scholarships.

Merit scholarships. President's Award; for out-of-state students; based on high school GPA of 3.0 or higher; awarded differential between in and out-of-state tuition.

Policies to reduce costs. Tuition/fee waivers for children of alumni, employees and their families. Credit/placement for qualifying scores on AP, CLEP examinations.

Payment plans. Credit card payment.

Application procedures. FAFSA required. Priority date 2/21; no closing date. Applicants notified on rolling basis starting 4/1, must reply within 4 week(s) of notification. **Transfers:** No deadline.

Contact. Financial aid office: (989) 774-3674
Terry Viau, Director, Scholarships and Financial Aid
105 Warriner Hall
Mount Pleasant, MI 48859

Cleary University

Ann Arbor, Michigan
www.cleary.edu
Four-year private **Federal Code: 002246-00**

College costs. Annual costs $11,960, including tuition, fees, books. Board: $3,258. Transportation: $1,159.

Undergraduate aid. Need-based: Average financial aid package for full-time students was $4,598. 39% awarded as scholarships/grants, 61% as loans/jobs. Need-based aid available for part-time students. **Non-need-based:** 0% awarded as scholarships/grants, 100% as loans/jobs. Scholarships based on academics. **Student debt:** 36% of graduating class borrowed to fund education; average debt was $10,500. **Additional information:** Filing electronically preferred; paper applications available.

Policies to reduce costs. Tuition/fee waivers for senior citizens, employees and their families. Tuition at time of enrollment guaranteed for 4 years; prepayment discount; credit/placement for qualifying scores on AP, IB, CLEP examinations. Work study available nights and for part-time students.

Payment plans. Credit card, installment, deferred payment.

Application procedures. FAFSA, institutional form required. Priority date 3/15; closing date 8/15. Applicants notified on rolling basis starting 4/31, must reply within 2 week(s) of notification.

Contact. Financial aid office: (517) 548-3670
Vesta Smith-Campbell, Director of Financial Aid
3750 Cleary Drive
Howell, MI 48843

College for Creative Studies

Detroit, Michigan
www.ccscad.edu
Four-year private **Federal Code: 006771**

	Living at home	On-campus
Tuition and fees (projected):	$19,798	$19,798
Room only:		$3,300
Books and supplies:	$2,500	$2,500
Personal expenses:	$1,500	$1,800
Transportation:	$1,200	$1,200

Undergraduate aid. Need-based: Need-based aid available for full-time and part-time students. **Non-need-based:** Scholarships based on academics, art. **Student debt:** 75% of graduating class borrowed to fund education; average debt was $26,240.

Policies to reduce costs. Tuition/fee waivers for employees and their families. Credit/placement for qualifying scores on AP, IB, CLEP examinations. Work study available nights, weekends and for part-time students.

Payment plans. Credit card, installment, deferred payment.

Application procedures. FAFSA required. Priority date 2/21; no closing date. Applicants notified on rolling basis starting 3/15, must reply within 3 week(s) of notification. **Transfers:** Priority date 3/21; no deadline.

Contact. Financial aid office: (313) 664-7497
Debra Kollenberg, Director of Financial Aid
201 East Kirby
Detroit, MI 48202-4034

Concordia University

Ann Arbor, Michigan
www.cuaa.edu
Four-year private **Federal Code: 002247**

	Living at home	On-campus
Tuition and fees (2002-2003):	$16,650	$16,650
Room and board:		$6,600
Books and supplies:	$800	$800
Personal expenses:	$1,055	$1,100
Transportation:	$200	$200

Undergraduate aid. Need-based: Need-based aid available for full-time and part-time students. **Non-need-based:** Scholarships based on academics, alumni affiliation, art, athletics, leadership, music/drama, religious affiliation.

Policies to reduce costs. Tuition/fee waivers for employees and their families. Credit/placement for qualifying scores on AP, CLEP examinations. Work study available nights and weekends.

Payment plans. Credit card, installment payment.

Application procedures. FAFSA, institutional form required. Closing date 5/1. Applicants notified on rolling basis starting 3/1, must reply within 3 week(s) of notification. **Transfers:** Closing date 5/1.

Contact. Financial aid office: (734) 995-7408
David Houle, Director of Student Financial Aid
4090 Geddes Road
Ann Arbor, MI 48105

Cornerstone University

Grand Rapids, Michigan
www.cornerstone.edu
Four-year private **Federal Code: 002266**

	Living at home	On-campus
Tuition and fees (2002-2003):	$13,770	$13,770
Room and board:		$5,218
Board only:	$800	
Books and supplies:	$800	$800
Personal expenses:	$1,546	$1,546
Transportation:	$1,252	$954

Undergraduate aid. Need-based: Average financial aid package for full-time students was $11,570; for part-time $8,028. 55% awarded as scholarships/grants, 45% as loans/jobs. **Non-need-based:** 31% awarded as scholarships/grants, 69% as loans/jobs. Scholarships based on academics, athletics, leadership, music/drama, state/district residency. **Student debt:** 81% of graduating class borrowed to fund education; average debt was $16,817. **Additional information:** Audition required for music scholarship applicants.

Freshman aid. Need-based: Out of 291 full-time freshmen, 290 applied for aid; 231 were judged to have need; of these 231 received aid. Average package met 82% of need. 48 students had full need met. Average scholarship/grant was $7,162; average loan $2,947. **Non-need based:** 224 full-time freshmen with need received non-need scholarships; 52 without need received awards; 33 received athletic scholarships.

Merit scholarships. Academic scholarships; based on high school GPA and ACT scores.

Policies to reduce costs. Tuition/fee waivers for employees and their families. Credit/placement for qualifying scores on AP, CLEP examinations. Work study available nights, weekends and for part-time students.

Payment plans. Credit card, installment payment.

Application procedures. FAFSA required. Priority date 2/21; no closing date. Applicants notified on rolling basis starting 3/15, must reply within 2 week(s) of notification. **Transfers:** No deadline.

Contact. Financial aid office: (616) 222-1424
Geoff Marsh, Director of Student Financial aid Services
1001 East Beltline Northeast
Grand Rapids, MI 49525

Davenport University - Eastern Region

Dearborn, Michigan
www.davenport.edu
Four-year private **Federal Code: 002253**

College costs. Listed tuition for Dearborn and Warren campuses. Tuition for Flint campuses $6,615 per year, $147 per-credit-hour.

	Living at home
Tuition and fees (2002-2003):	$9,720
Board only:	$2,895
Books and supplies:	$900
Personal expenses:	$921
Transportation:	$1,072

Undergraduate aid. Need-based: Need-based aid available for full-time and part-time students. **Non-need-based:** Scholarships based on academics.

Policies to reduce costs. Tuition/fee waivers for children of alumni, employees and their families. Credit/placement for qualifying scores on AP, CLEP examinations. Work study available nights, weekends and for part-time students.

Payment plans. Credit card, installment, deferred payment.

Application procedures. FAFSA, institutional form required. Priority date 3/21; no closing date. Applicants notified on rolling basis starting 5/1. **Transfers:** Priority date 3/15.

Contact. Financial aid office: (313) 581-4400
Zeena Skinner, Financial Aid Director
4801 Oakman Boulevard
Dearborn, MI 48126-3799

Davenport University - Midland

Midland, Michigan
www.davenport.edu
Four-year private **Federal Code: 006770**

College costs. Nursing program $7,980 tuition, $266 per-credit-hour. Distance learning courses: $872 per class.

	Living at home
Tuition and fees (2002-2003):	$7,300
Board only:	$3,069
Books and supplies:	$800
Personal expenses:	$990
Transportation:	$2,400

Undergraduate aid. All financial aid based on need. Need-based aid available for full-time and part-time students.

Policies to reduce costs. Tuition/fee waivers for employees and their families. Prepayment discount; credit/placement for qualifying scores on AP, CLEP examinations. Work study available nights, weekends and for part-time students.

Payment plans. Credit card, installment, deferred payment.

Application procedures. FAFSA required. No deadline. Applicants notified on rolling basis starting 5/15, must reply within 4 week(s) of notification. **Transfers:** No deadline.

Contact. Financial aid office: (989) 755-3445
Patricia Finerty, Financial Aid Director
3555 East Patrick
Midland, MI 48642

Davenport University - Western Region

Grand Rapids, Michigan
www.davenport.edu
Four-year private **Federal Code: 015260**

	Living at home	On-campus
Tuition and fees (2002-2003):	$10,005	$10,005
Room only:		$4,050
Books and supplies:	$1,180	$1,180
Personal expenses:	$942	$942
Transportation:	$1,097	$1,097

Undergraduate aid. Non-need-based: Scholarships based on academics. **Additional information:** Institutional tuition plan available.

Policies to reduce costs. Tuition/fee waivers for employees and their families. Credit/placement for qualifying scores on AP, CLEP examinations.

Payment plans. Credit card, installment payment.

Application procedures. FAFSA required. Priority date 3/15; no closing date. Applicants notified on rolling basis starting 7/1, must reply within 2 week(s) of notification. Early decision closing date 3/24.

Contact. Financial aid office: (616) 732-7120
Mary Bethune, Vice President of Financial Aid
415 East Fulton Street
Grand Rapids, MI 49503

Eastern Michigan University

Ypsilanti, Michigan
www.emich.edu
Four-year public **Federal Code: 002259**

	Living at home	On-campus
Tuition and fees (2002-2003):	$5,027	$5,027
Out-of-state:	$13,760	$13,760
Room and board:		$5,597
Board only:	$2,668	
Books and supplies:	$600	$600
Personal expenses:	$700	$700
Transportation:	$1,200	$600

Undergraduate aid. Need-based: Average financial aid package for full-time students was $10,495. 39% awarded as scholarships/grants, 61% as loans/jobs. Need-based aid available for part-time students. **Non-need-based:** 37% awarded as scholarships/grants, 63% as loans/jobs. Scholarships based on academics, alumni affiliation, art, athletics, leadership, music/drama, state/district residency. **Student debt:** 44% of graduating class borrowed to fund education; average debt was $20,580.

Freshman aid. Need-based: Out of 2,583 full-time freshmen, 1,524 applied for aid; 1,343 were judged to have need; of these 1,020 received aid. Average package met 52% of need. 479 students had full need met. Average scholarship/grant was $3,730; average loan $2,768. **Non-need based:** 326 full-time freshmen with need received non-need scholarships; 598 without need received awards; 83 received athletic scholarships.

Policies to reduce costs. Tuition/fee waivers for employees and their families. Credit/placement for qualifying scores on AP, IB, CLEP examinations. Work study available nights, weekends and for part-time students.

Payment plans. Credit card, installment, deferred payment.

Application procedures. FAFSA required. Priority date 3/15; no closing date. Applicants notified on rolling basis starting 3/2. **Transfers:** No deadline.

Contact. Financial aid office: (734) 487-1849
Bernice Lindke, Director of Financial Aid
400 Pierce Hall
Ypsilanti, MI 48197

Ferris State University

Big Rapids, Michigan
www.ferris.edu
Four-year public **Federal Code: 002260**

College costs. Midwest Compact states of Illinois, Indiana, Kansas, Minnesota, Missouri, Nebraska, Ohio, and Wisconsin pay $7,508 full-time tuition, $335 per-credit-hour.

	Living at home	On-campus
Tuition and fees (2002-2003):	$5,442	$5,442
Out-of-state:	$10,934	$10,934
Room and board:		$5,968
Books and supplies:	$850	$850
Personal expenses:	$1,440	$1,440
Transportation:	$704	$438

Undergraduate aid. Need-based: Average financial aid package for full-time students was $7,800; for part-time $4,000. 34% awarded as scholarships/grants, 66% as loans/jobs. **Non-need-based:** 25% awarded as scholarships/grants, 75% as loans/jobs. Scholarships based on academics, alumni affiliation, art, athletics, leadership, minority status, music/drama, religious affiliation. **Student debt:** 85% of graduating class borrowed to fund education; average debt was $14,000.

Freshman aid. Need-based: Out of 2,138 full-time freshmen, 1,988 applied for aid; 1,790 were judged to have need; of these 1,701 received aid. Average package met 75% of need. 103 students had full need met. Average scholarship/grant was $2,900; average loan $1,400. **Non-need based:** 228 full-time freshmen with need received non-need scholarships; 205 without need received awards; 65 received athletic scholarships.

Policies to reduce costs. Tuition/fee waivers for employees and their families. Prepayment discount; credit/placement for qualifying scores on AP, CLEP examinations. Work study available nights, weekends and for part-time students.

Payment plans. Deferred payment.

Application procedures. FAFSA required. Priority date 3/15; no closing date. Applicants notified on rolling basis starting 3/15, must reply within 2 week(s) of notification.

Contact. Financial aid office: (231) 591-2110
Phillip Tetsworth, Associate Director of Financial Aid
1201 S. State Street, CSS 201
Big Rapids, MI 49307-2714

Finlandia University

Hancock, Michigan
www.finlandia.edu
Four-year private **Federal Code: 002322**

	Living at home	On-campus
Tuition and fees (projected):	$13,750	$13,750
Room and board:		$4,870
Books and supplies:	$1,300	$1,300
Personal expenses:		$100
Transportation:		$800

Undergraduate aid. Need-based: Need-based aid available for full-time and part-time students. **Non-need-based:** Scholarships based on academics, leadership. **Additional information:** Work/study program available for up to $2,400 per year.

Policies to reduce costs. Tuition/fee waivers for family members, employees and their families. Prepayment discount; credit/placement for qualifying scores on AP, IB, CLEP examinations. Work study available nights, weekends and for part-time students.

Payment plans. Credit card, installment, deferred payment.

Application procedures. FAFSA, institutional form required. Priority date 2/15; closing date 8/1. Applicants notified on rolling basis starting 3/1. **Transfers:** Priority date 3/21.

Contact. Financial aid office: (906) 487-7261
Deborah Aho, Director of Financial Aid
601 Quincy Street
Hancock, MI 49930-1882

Glen Oaks Community College

Centreville, Michigan
www.glenoaks.cc.mi.us
Two-year public **Federal Code: 002263**

	Living at home
Tuition and fees:	$2,090
Out-of-district:	$2,450
Out-of-state:	$2,960
Per-credit charge:	$63
Per-credit out-of-district:	$75
Per-credit out-of-state:	$92
Board only:	$800
Books and supplies:	$480
Personal expenses:	$775
Transportation:	$1,320

Undergraduate aid. Need-based: Need-based aid available for full-time and part-time students. **Non-need-based:** Scholarships based on academics, art, athletics, leadership, minority status, music/drama.

Policies to reduce costs. Tuition/fee waivers for senior citizens, employees and their families. Credit/placement for qualifying scores on AP, CLEP examinations. Work study available nights and for part-time students.

Payment plans. Credit card, deferred payment.

Application procedures. FAFSA, institutional form required. No deadline. Applicants notified on rolling basis. **Transfers:** No deadline.

Contact. **Financial aid office:** (269) 467-9945 ext. 250
Matthew Soucy, Director of Financial Aid and Scholarship
62249 Shimmel Road
Centreville, MI 49032-9719

Gogebic Community College

Ironwood, Michigan
www.gogebic.cc.mi.us
Two-year public **Federal Code: 002264**

College costs. Wisconsin reciprocity tuition: $67 per-credit-hour, $2,010 full-time.

	Living at home
Tuition and fees (2002-2003):	$1,739
Out-of-district:	$2,297
Out-of-state:	$3,072
Per-credit charge:	$47
Per-credit out-of-district:	$65
Per-credit out-of-state:	$90
Books and supplies:	$500
Personal expenses:	$700
Transportation:	$750

Undergraduate aid. **Need-based:** Need-based aid available for full-time and part-time students. **Non-need-based:** Scholarships based on academics, art, athletics, job skills, leadership, music/drama, state/district residency.

Policies to reduce costs. Tuition/fee waivers for senior citizens, employees and their families. Credit/placement for qualifying scores on AP, CLEP examinations. Work study available nights, weekends and for part-time students.

Payment plans. Credit card payment.

Application procedures. FAFSA required. Priority date 5/1; no closing date. Applicants notified on rolling basis starting 3/15, must reply within 2 week(s) of notification.

Contact. **Financial aid office:** (906) 932-4231 ext. 206
Sue Forbes, Director of Financial Aid
E4946 Jackson Road
Ironwood, MI 49938

Grace Bible College

Grand Rapids, Michigan
www.gbcol.edu
Four-year private **Federal Code: 002265**

	Living at home	On-campus
Tuition and fees:	$9,730	$9,730
Room and board:		$6,160
Books and supplies:	$465	$465
Personal expenses:	$865	$865
Transportation:	$1,159	$979

Undergraduate aid. All financial aid based on need. Average financial aid package for full-time students was $6,873; for part-time $3,137. 63% awarded as scholarships/grants, 37% as loans/jobs. **Student debt:** 68% of graduating class borrowed to fund education; average debt was $12,261.

Freshman aid. Out of 29 full-time freshmen, 29 applied for aid; 26 were judged to have need; of these 26 received aid. Average package met 57% of need. 2 students had full need met. Average scholarship/grant was $9,454; average loan $2,071.

Policies to reduce costs. Tuition/fee waivers for family of clergy, employees and their families. Credit/placement for qualifying scores on AP, CLEP examinations.

Payment plans. Credit card, installment payment.

Application procedures. FAFSA required. Priority date 2/15; no closing date. Applicants notified on rolling basis starting 5/15.

Contact. **Financial aid office:** (616) 261-8557
Marlene DeVries, Financial Aid Director
PO Box 910
Grand Rapids, MI 49509

Grand Rapids Community College

Grand Rapids, Michigan
www.grcc.edu
Two-year public **Federal Code: 002267**

College costs. Tuition charged per contact hour.

	Living at home
Tuition and fees (2002-2003):	$1,935
Out-of-district:	$2,790
Out-of-state:	$3,390
Per-credit charge:	$62
Per-credit out-of-district:	$90
Per-credit out-of-state:	$110
Books and supplies:	$1,368
Personal expenses:	$515
Transportation:	$1,159

Undergraduate aid. **Need-based:** Average financial aid package for full-time students was $2,752; for part-time $1,925. 71% awarded as scholarships/grants, 29% as loans/jobs. **Non-need-based:** 60% awarded as scholarships/grants, 40% as loans/jobs. Scholarships based on academics, alumni affiliation, art, athletics, leadership, minority status, music/drama, state/district residency. **Additional information:** Tuition reimbursement and/or child-care services for single parents and displaced homemakers who meet Perkins guidelines.

Freshman aid. **Need-based:** Out of 2,260 full-time freshmen, 1,791 applied for aid; 1,403 were judged to have need; of these 1,234 received aid. 220 students had full need met. Average scholarship/grant was $2,729; average loan $1,196. **Non-need based:** 797 full-time freshmen with need received non-need scholarships; 216 without need received awards; 44 received athletic scholarships.

Merit scholarships. Michigan Merit Award; $2,500; based on Michigan Educational Assessment Program scores.

Policies to reduce costs. Prepayment discount; credit/placement for qualifying scores on AP, CLEP examinations. Work study available nights, weekends and for part-time students.

Payment plans. Credit card, installment payment.

Application procedures. FAFSA required. Priority date 4/1; no closing date. Applicants notified on rolling basis starting 5/1, must reply within 3 week(s) of notification. **Transfers:** No deadline.

Contact. **Financial aid office:** (616) 234-4030
Jill Nutt, Executive Director of Student Financial Services
143 Bostwick NE
Grand Rapids, MI 49503-3295

Grand Valley State University

Allendale, Michigan
www.gvsu.edu
Four-year public **Federal Code: 002268**

College costs. Annual tuition for undergraduate upper division (55+ credits) students: $4,830 in-state; $10,420 out-of-state. Upper divison per-credit-hour charges: $212 in state; $445 out-of-state.

	Living at home	On-campus
Tuition and fees (2002-2003):	$5,056	$5,056
Out-of-state:	$10,936	$10,936
Room and board:		$5,380
Books and supplies:	$600	$600
Personal expenses:	$550	$450
Transportation:	$950	$550

Undergraduate aid. **Need-based:** Average financial aid package for full-time students was $6,428; for part-time $2,398. 31% awarded as scholarships/grants, 69% as loans/jobs. **Non-need-based:** 38% awarded as scholarships/grants, 62% as loans/jobs. Scholarships based on academics, alumni affiliation, art, athletics, minority status, music/drama, state/district residency. **Student debt:** 70% of graduating class borrowed to fund education; average debt was $13,745. **Additional information:** College traditionally funds 100% of each student's demonstrated need.

Freshman aid. **Need-based:** Out of 2,870 full-time freshmen, 2,601 applied for aid; 1,820 were judged to have need; of these 1,820 received aid. Average package met 100% of need. 1820 students had full need met. Average scholarship/grant was $4,013; average loan $2,272. **Non-need based:**

1,403 full-time freshmen with need received non-need scholarships; 1,050 without need received awards; 86 received athletic scholarships.

Policies to reduce costs. Tuition/fee waivers for children of alumni, minority students, employees and their families. Credit/placement for qualifying scores on AP, IB, CLEP examinations.

Payment plans. Credit card, installment, deferred payment.

Application procedures. FAFSA required. Priority date 2/15; no closing date. Applicants notified on rolling basis starting 4/1, must reply within 3 week(s) of notification. **Transfers:** Priority date 2/15; no deadline.

Contact. Financial aid office: (616) 331-3234
Ken Fridsma, Director of Financial Aid
One Campus Drive
Allendale, MI 49401

Hillsdale College

Hillsdale, Michigan
www.hillsdale.edu
Four-year private **Federal Code: 002272**

	Living at home	On-campus
Tuition and fees (2002-2003):	$15,800	$15,800
Room and board:		$6,086
Books and supplies:	$800	$800
Personal expenses:		$500
Transportation:		$500

Undergraduate aid. Need-based: Average financial aid package for full-time students was $14,000. 67% awarded as scholarships/grants, 33% as loans/jobs. **Non-need-based:** 83% awarded as scholarships/grants, 17% as loans/jobs. Scholarships based on academics, art, athletics, leadership, music/drama. **Student debt:** 62% of graduating class borrowed to fund education; average debt was $14,000.

Freshman aid. Need-based: Out of 329 full-time freshmen, 239 applied for aid; 239 were judged to have need; of these 239 received aid. Average package met 77% of need. 50 students had full need met. Average scholarship/grant was $6,800; average loan $2,500. **Non-need based:** 79 full-time freshmen with need received non-need scholarships; 69 without need received awards.

Merit scholarships. Distinct Honor Scholarship; full tuition; 2 awarded. Presidential Scholarship; half tuition; 25 awarded. Trustee Scholarship; up to $7,000; 30 awarded.

Policies to reduce costs. Tuition/fee waivers for employees and their families. Credit/placement for qualifying scores on AP, IB, CLEP examinations.

Payment plans. Credit card, installment payment.

Application procedures. FAFSA, institutional form required. Priority date 3/1; no closing date. Applicants notified on rolling basis starting 2/15, must reply by 5/1 or within 3 week(s) of notification.

Contact. Financial aid office: (517) 607-2350
Connie Bricker, Director of Financial Aid
33 East College Street
Hillsdale, MI 49242

Hope College

Holland, Michigan
www.hope.edu
Four-year private **Federal Code: 002273**

	Living at home	On-campus
Tuition and fees (2002-2003):	$18,268	$18,268
Room and board:		$5,688
Board only:	$1,500	
Books and supplies:	$640	$640
Personal expenses:	$610	$1,040
Transportation:	$580	$295

Undergraduate aid. All financial aid based on need. Average financial aid package for full-time students was $15,673; for part-time $8,506. 72% awarded as scholarships/grants, 28% as loans/jobs. **Student debt:** 89% of graduating class borrowed to fund education; average debt was $17,022.

Freshman aid. Out of 721 full-time freshmen, 599 applied for aid; 478 were judged to have need; of these 478 received aid. Average package met 90% of need. 150 students had full need met. Average scholarship/grant was $12,012; average loan $3,495.

Policies to reduce costs. Tuition/fee waivers for employees and their families. Credit/placement for qualifying scores on AP, IB, CLEP examinations. Work study available nights, weekends and for part-time students.

Payment plans. Installment payment.

Application procedures. FAFSA, institutional form required. Priority date 2/15; no closing date. Applicants notified on rolling basis starting 3/16, must reply by 5/1 or within 2 week(s) of notification. **Transfers:** Priority date 5/1; no deadline.

Contact. Financial aid office: (888) 439-8907
Phyllis Hooyman, Director of Financial Aid
69 East 10th Street
Holland, MI 49422-9000

ITT Technical Institute: Grand Rapids

Grand Rapids, Michigan
www.itt-tech.edu
Two-year proprietary **Federal Code: 010627**

College costs. Total program varies depending on course of study. Per-credit-hour charge: $347.

Policies to reduce costs. Tuition/fee waivers for employees and their families. Tuition at time of enrollment guaranteed for 2 years.

Payment plans. Credit card, installment payment.

Application procedures. FAFSA, institutional form required. No deadline. Applicants notified on rolling basis.

Contact. Financial aid office: (616) 956-1060
Beth Berggren, Director of Finance
4020 Sparks Drive S.E.
Grand Rapids, MI 49546

ITT Technical Institute: Troy

Troy, Michigan
www.itt-tech.edu
Two-year proprietary **Federal Code: 008329**

College costs. Total program varies depending on course of study. Per-credit-hour charge: $347.

Policies to reduce costs. Tuition/fee waivers for employees and their families. Tuition at time of enrollment guaranteed for 2 years.

Payment plans. Credit card, installment payment.

Application procedures. FAFSA, institutional form required. No deadline. Applicants notified on rolling basis.

Contact. Financial aid office: (248) 524-1800
Matt Deimling, Director of Finance
1522 E. Big Beaver Road
Troy, MI 48083-1905

Jackson Community College

Jackson, Michigan
www.jccmi.us
Two-year public **Federal Code: 002274**

	Living at home
Tuition and fees (projected):	$1,654
Out-of-district:	$2,086
Out-of-state:	$2,542
Per-credit charge:	$64
Per-credit out-of-district:	$82
Per-credit out-of-state:	$101
Board only:	$3,330
Books and supplies:	$648
Personal expenses:	$702
Transportation:	$1,161

Undergraduate aid. Need-based: 86% awarded as scholarships/grants, 14% as loans/jobs. Need-based aid available for part-time students. **Non-need-based:** 69% awarded as scholarships/grants, 31% as loans/jobs. Scholarships based on academics, art, leadership, music/drama, state/district residency.

Policies to reduce costs. Tuition/fee waivers for senior citizens, employees and their families. Credit/placement for qualifying scores on AP, IB examinations. Work study available nights, weekends and for part-time students.

Payment plans. Credit card payment.

Application procedures. FAFSA, institutional form required. Priority date 4/1; no closing date. Applicants notified on rolling basis starting 3/1.

Contact. **Financial aid office:** (517) 796-8410
Janet Zukowski, Director of Financial Aid
2111 Emmons Road
Jackson, MI 49201

Kalamazoo College

Kalamazoo, Michigan
www.kzoo.edu
Four-year private **Federal Code: 002275**

	Living at home	On-campus
Tuition and fees (2002-2003):	$21,683	$21,683
Room and board:		$6,354
Board only:	$3,360	
Books and supplies:	$750	$750
Personal expenses:	$828	$828
Transportation:	$300	$300

Undergraduate aid. Need-based: Average financial aid package for full-time students was $19,000. 75% awarded as scholarships/grants, 25% as loans/jobs. **Non-need-based:** 77% awarded as scholarships/grants, 23% as loans/jobs. Scholarships based on academics, alumni affiliation, art, leadership, music/drama, religious affiliation. **Student debt:** 65% of graduating class borrowed to fund education; average debt was $20,000. **Additional information:** Many students are paid for career development internship and senior project experiences. Earnings can be used for college expenses.

Freshman aid. Need-based: Out of 337 full-time freshmen, 256 applied for aid; 195 were judged to have need; of these 195 received aid. 144 students had full need met. Average scholarship/grant was $14,010; average loan $4,230. **Non-need based:** 139 without need received awards.

Merit scholarships. Honors Scholarship; $2,000-$11,000; based on academic and co-curricular record and accomplishments; varied number awarded. Competitive Scholarships; $2,000-$3,000; based on written exam in a subject area or a fine arts audition.

Policies to reduce costs. Tuition/fee waivers for employees and their families. Credit/placement for qualifying scores on AP, IB examinations. Work study available nights and weekends.

Payment plans. Installment, deferred payment.

Application procedures. FAFSA, institutional form required. Priority date 2/15; no closing date. Applicants notified on rolling basis starting 3/21, must reply by 5/1. Early decision closing date 11/15. **Transfers:** Priority date 3/15; no deadline.

Contact. **Financial aid office:** (616) 337-7192
Marian Conrad, Director of Financial Aid
1200 Academy Street
Kalamazoo, MI 49006-3295

Kellogg Community College

Battle Creek, Michigan
www.kellogg.edu
Two-year public **Federal Code: 002276**

	Living at home
Tuition and fees (projected):	$1,740
Out-of-district:	$2,820
Out-of-state:	$4,260
Per-credit charge:	$53
Per-credit out-of-district:	$89
Per-credit out-of-state:	$137
Books and supplies:	$750
Personal expenses:	$4,190
Transportation:	$1,200

Undergraduate aid. Need-based: 75% awarded as scholarships/grants, 25% as loans/jobs. Need-based aid available for part-time students. **Non-need-based:** Scholarships based on academics, alumni affiliation, athletics.

Policies to reduce costs. Tuition/fee waivers for senior citizens, employees and their families. Credit/placement for qualifying scores on AP, IB, CLEP examinations. Work study available nights and for part-time students.

Payment plans. Credit card, installment, deferred payment.

Application procedures. FAFSA, institutional form required. Priority date 4/2; no closing date. Applicants notified on rolling basis starting 4/2. **Transfers:** Priority date 4/3; no deadline.

Contact. **Financial aid office:** (269) 965-4123
Patricia Stephenson, Director of Financial Aid
450 North Avenue
Battle Creek, MI 49017-3397

Kettering University

Flint, Michigan
www.kettering.edu
Five-year private **Federal Code: 002262**

	Living at home	On-campus
Tuition and fees (projected):	$21,549	$21,549
Room and board:		$4,924
Books and supplies:	$800	$800

Undergraduate aid. Need-based: Average financial aid package for full-time students was $8,661. 42% awarded as scholarships/grants, 58% as loans/jobs. **Non-need-based:** 60% awarded as scholarships/grants, 40% as loans/jobs. Scholarships based on academics, alumni affiliation, leadership, minority status, state/district residency. **Additional information:** All undergraduate students participate in paid professional co-op work experience in industry that typically begins in freshman year. Average total student earnings over 4 1/2-year program typically range from $40,000 to $65,000.

Freshman aid. Need-based: Out of 571 full-time freshmen, 525 applied for aid; 459 were judged to have need; of these 444 received aid. Average package met 48% of need. 26 students had full need met. Average scholarship/grant was $8,654; average loan $2,470. **Non-need based:** 329 full-time freshmen with need received non-need scholarships; 111 without need received awards.

Merit scholarships. Various scholarships; $6,000-$60,000 for 4 years; based on merit. Special scholarships, including Society of Women's Engineers (SWE), US FIRST Robotics, Society of Automotive Engineers (SAE), DECA, Science Olympiad; $250-full tuition.

Policies to reduce costs. Tuition/fee waivers for employees and their families. Credit/placement for qualifying scores on AP, IB examinations. Work study available nights and weekends.

Payment plans. Credit card, installment payment.

Application procedures. FAFSA, institutional form required. Priority date 2/14; no closing date. Applicants notified on rolling basis starting 3/1, must reply within 5 week(s) of notification. **Transfers:** No deadline.

Contact. **Financial aid office:** (810) 762-7859
Diane Bice, Director of Financial Aid
1700 West Third Avenue
Flint, MI 48504-4898

Kirtland Community College

Roscommon, Michigan
www.kirtland.edu
Two-year public **Federal Code: 007171**

	Living at home
Tuition and fees (2002-2003):	$1,863
Out-of-district:	$2,664
Out-of-state:	$3,384
Per-credit charge:	$54
Per-credit out-of-district:	$81
Per-credit out-of-state:	$105
Books and supplies:	$450

Undergraduate aid. Need-based: Need-based aid available for full-time and part-time students.

Policies to reduce costs. Tuition/fee waivers for senior citizens, employees and their families. Prepayment discount; credit/placement for qualifying scores on AP, CLEP examinations.

Payment plans. Credit card, deferred payment.

Application procedures. FAFSA required. Priority date 5/15; no closing date. Applicants notified on rolling basis.

Contact. **Financial aid office:** (989) 275-5121
Christine Oestrike, Director of Financial Aid
10775 North St. Helen Road
Roscommon, MI 48653

Lansing Community College

Lansing, Michigan
www.lansing.cc.mi.us
Two-year public **Federal Code: 002278**

	Living at home
Tuition and fees (2002-2003):	$1,615
Out-of-district:	$2,485
Out-of-state:	$3,355
Per-credit charge:	$50
Per-credit out-of-district:	$79
Per-credit out-of-state:	$108
Board only:	$2,310
Books and supplies:	$660
Personal expenses:	$1,020
Transportation:	$1,020

Undergraduate aid. **Need-based:** 53% awarded as scholarships/grants, 47% as loans/jobs. Need-based aid available for part-time students. **Non-need-based:** 29% awarded as scholarships/grants, 71% as loans/jobs. Scholarships based on academics, athletics.

Policies to reduce costs. Tuition/fee waivers for senior citizens, employees and their families. Credit/placement for qualifying scores on AP, IB examinations. Work study available nights, weekends and for part-time students.

Payment plans. Credit card payment.

Application procedures. FAFSA required. Priority date 7/3; no closing date. Applicants notified on rolling basis starting 4/3. **Transfers:** Priority date 7/15; no deadline.

Contact. **Financial aid office:** (517) 483-1296
Barbara Larson, Vice President, Administrative Services
422 North Washington Square
Lansing, MI 48901

Lawrence Technological University

Southfield, Michigan
www.ltu.edu
Four-year private **Federal Code: 002279**

	Living at home	On-campus
Tuition and fees (2002-2003):	$13,290	$13,290
Room only:		$2,925
Board only:	$1,800	
Books and supplies:	$1,300	$1,300
Personal expenses:	$800	$800
Transportation:	$1,200	$1,000

Undergraduate aid. **Need-based:** Average financial aid package for full-time students was $9,149; for part-time $7,420. 28% awarded as scholarships/grants, 72% as loans/jobs. **Non-need-based:** Scholarships based on academics, alumni affiliation, job skills, minority status, state/district residency.

Freshman aid. **Need-based:** Out of 385 full-time freshmen, 312 applied for aid; 238 were judged to have need; of these 232 received aid. Average package met 90% of need. 97 students had full need met. Average scholarship/grant was $2,712; average loan $1,723. **Non-need based:** 155 full-time freshmen with need received non-need scholarships; 79 without need received awards.

Policies to reduce costs. Tuition/fee waivers for employees and their families. Credit/placement for qualifying scores on AP, IB, CLEP examinations. Work study available nights, weekends and for part-time students.

Payment plans. Credit card, installment, deferred payment.

Application procedures. FAFSA required. Priority date 5/1; no closing date. Applicants notified on rolling basis starting 4/1, must reply within 4 week(s) of notification.

Contact. **Financial aid office:** (248) 204-2120
Mark Martin, Director of Student Financial Aid
21000 West Ten Mile Road
Southfield, MI 48075-1058

Macomb Community College

Warren, Michigan
www.macomb.edu
Two-year public **Federal Code: 008906**

	Living at home
Tuition and fees (2002-2003):	$1,797
Out-of-district:	$2,665
Out-of-state:	$3,130
Per-credit charge:	$56
Per-credit out-of-district:	$84
Per-credit out-of-state:	$99
Books and supplies:	$578
Personal expenses:	$791
Transportation:	$1,003

Undergraduate aid. **Need-based:** Need-based aid available for full-time and part-time students. **Non-need-based:** Scholarships based on academics, athletics, leadership, music/drama, state/district residency.

Policies to reduce costs. Tuition/fee waivers for senior citizens, employees and their families. Credit/placement for qualifying scores on AP, CLEP examinations. Work study available nights, weekends and for part-time students.

Payment plans. Credit card payment.

Application procedures. FAFSA, institutional form required. Priority date 4/15; no closing date. Applicants notified on rolling basis starting 5/15, must reply within 2 week(s) of notification. **Transfers:** Must submit financial aid transcripts from all institutions attended after 7/1.

Contact. **Financial aid office:** (586) 445-7228
Judy Florian, Director of Financial Aid
14500 East Twelve Mile Road
Warren, MI 48088-3896

Madonna University

Livonia, Michigan
www.madonna.edu
Four-year private **Federal Code: 002282**

College costs. Nursing students pay $9,630 full-time tuition, $321 per-credit-hour. Non-resident aliens pay $2,500 deposit.

	Living at home	On-campus
Tuition and fees (2002-2003):	$8,350	$8,350
Room and board:		$5,252
Board only:	$2,443	
Books and supplies:	$646	$646
Personal expenses:	$725	$725
Transportation:	$1,025	$585

Undergraduate aid. **Need-based:** Average financial aid package for full-time students was $6,258; for part-time $5,420. 48% awarded as scholarships/grants, 52% as loans/jobs. **Non-need-based:** 15% awarded as scholarships/grants, 85% as loans/jobs. Scholarships based on academics, alumni affiliation, art, athletics, minority status, music/drama, religious affiliation, state/district residency. **Student debt:** 65% of graduating class borrowed to fund education; average debt was $15,365.

Freshman aid. **Need-based:** Out of 203 full-time freshmen, 152 applied for aid; 122 were judged to have need; of these 122 received aid. Average package met 42% of need. 26 students had full need met. Average scholarship/grant was $4,891; average loan $1,919. **Non-need based:** 19 full-time freshmen with need received non-need scholarships; 53 without need received awards; 19 received athletic scholarships.

Policies to reduce costs. Tuition/fee waivers for senior citizens, employees and their families. Credit/placement for qualifying scores on AP, IB, CLEP examinations. Work study available nights, weekends and for part-time students.

Payment plans. Credit card, installment, deferred payment.

Application procedures. FAFSA required. Priority date 2/21; no closing date. Applicants notified on rolling basis starting 4/1, must reply by 9/1 or within 2 week(s) of notification. **Transfers:** No deadline. Deadline for state aid is September 1.

Contact. **Financial aid office:** (734) 432-5664
Chris Ziegler, Director of Financial Aid
36600 Schoolcraft Road
Livonia, MI 48150

Marygrove College

Detroit, Michigan
www.marygrove.edu
Four-year private **Federal Code: 002284**

	Living at home	On-campus
Tuition and fees (2002-2003):	$11,250	$11,250
Room and board:		$5,600
Books and supplies:	$700	$700
Personal expenses:	$1,745	
Transportation:	$1,576	

Undergraduate aid. All financial aid based on need. Need-based aid available for full-time and part-time students.

Policies to reduce costs. Tuition/fee waivers for senior citizens, family members, employees and their families. Prepayment discount; credit/placement for qualifying scores on AP, CLEP examinations.

Payment plans. Credit card, installment, deferred payment.

Application procedures. FAFSA, institutional form required. Priority date 3/15; no closing date. Applicants notified on rolling basis starting 5/15, must reply within 2 week(s) of notification.

Contact. **Financial aid office:** (313) 927-1245
Patricia Chaplin, Director of Financial Aid
8425 West McNichols Road
Detroit, MI 48221

Michigan State University

East Lansing, Michigan
www.msu.edu
Four-year public **Federal Code: 002290**

	Living at home	On-campus
Tuition and fees (2002-2003):	$6,101	$6,101
Out-of-state:	$15,168	$15,168
Room and board:		$4,678
Board only:	$2,652	
Books and supplies:	$778	$778
Personal expenses:	$1,314	$1,314

Undergraduate aid. All financial aid based on need. Average financial aid package for full-time students was $9,355; for part-time $8,642. 58% awarded as scholarships/grants, 42% as loans/jobs. **Student debt:** 52% of graduating class borrowed to fund education; average debt was $18,663.

Freshman aid. Out of 6,833 full-time freshmen, 5,908 applied for aid; 3,713 were judged to have need; of these 3,702 received aid. Average package met 97% of need. 1125 students had full need met. Average scholarship/grant was $4,311; average loan $2,380.

Policies to reduce costs. Tuition/fee waivers for employees and their families. Credit/placement for qualifying scores on AP, IB, CLEP examinations.

Payment plans. Deferred payment.

Application procedures. FAFSA, institutional form required. Priority date 2/21; closing date 6/30. Applicants notified on rolling basis starting 3/15, must reply within 4 week(s) of notification.

Contact. **Financial aid office:** (517) 353-5940
Richard Shipman, Director of Financial Aid
250 Administration Building
East Lansing, MI 48824-1046

Michigan Technological University

Houghton, Michigan
www.mtu.edu
Four-year public **Federal Code: 002292**

	Living at home	On-campus
Tuition and fees (2002-2003):	$5,887	$5,887
Out-of-state:	$13,165	$13,165
Room and board:		$5,201
Board only:	$2,904	
Books and supplies:	$900	$900
Personal expenses:	$800	$800
Transportation:	$600	$600

Undergraduate aid. Need-based: Average financial aid package for full-time students was $7,855. 49% awarded as scholarships/grants, 51% as loans/jobs. Need-based aid available for part-time students. **Non-need-based:** 48% awarded as scholarships/grants, 52% as loans/jobs. Scholarships based on academics, alumni affiliation, athletics, leadership, minority status, state/district residency. **Student debt:** 62% of graduating class borrowed to fund education; average debt was $15,711.

Freshman aid. Need-based: Out of 1,190 full-time freshmen, 1,190 applied for aid; 570 were judged to have need; of these 562 received aid. Average package met 86% of need. 291 students had full need met. Average scholarship/grant was $5,537; average loan $3,296. **Non-need based:** 423 full-time freshmen with need received non-need scholarships; 402 without need received awards; 51 received athletic scholarships.

Merit scholarships. Michigan Technological University Scholar Awards; full-time tuition, room and board, allowance for books; based on merit, Michigan residency, membership in current year's graduating class of Michigan high schools, recommendation by high school teacher by mid-October of senior year. Board of Control Scholarships; $1,000 to full-time tuition; based on merit, Michigan residency, membership in current year's graduating class in Michigan high schools. Michigan Technological University Merit Scholarships; $1,000-$2,000; based on merit and need, U.S. citizenship, membership in current year's high school graduating class, finalist status in National Merit Scholarship Qualifying Test. United States Scholarships; award equal to the difference between resident and non-resident tuition; based on merit, U.S. residency in any state or territory except Michigan; membership in current year's high school graduating class. Academic Excellence Award; merit-based for non-Michigan resident of U.S. or Canada; entering freshmen must rank in top 25% of high school class; award equal to the difference between resident and non-resident tuition. Alumni Legacy Award; non-Michigan residents; must be children or grandchildren of Michigan Technological University alumni; award equal to the difference between resident and non-resident tuition. Michigan Tech Alumni Legacy Award; for Michigan residents; must be children or grandchildren of Michigan Technological University alumni; $250 per year for maximum of 4 years.

Policies to reduce costs. Tuition/fee waivers for children of alumni, senior citizens, minority students, employees and their families. Credit/placement for qualifying scores on AP, IB, CLEP examinations. Work study available nights, weekends and for part-time students.

Payment plans. Credit card, installment, deferred payment.

Application procedures. FAFSA required. Priority date 2/21; no closing date. Applicants notified on rolling basis starting 2/28, must reply within 4 week(s) of notification.

Contact. **Financial aid office:** (906) 987-2622
Timothy Malette, Director of Financial Aid
1400 Townsend Drive
Houghton, MI 49931-1295

Mid Michigan Community College

Harrison, Michigan
www.midmich.edu
Two-year public **Federal Code: 006768**

	Living at home
Tuition and fees (2002-2003):	$1,867
Out-of-district:	$3,074
Out-of-state:	$4,753
Per-credit charge:	$54
Per-credit out-of-district:	$88
Per-credit out-of-state:	$126
Board only:	$1,458
Books and supplies:	$766
Personal expenses:	$698
Transportation:	$1,125

Undergraduate aid. Need-based: 56% awarded as scholarships/grants, 44% as loans/jobs. Need-based aid available for part-time students. **Non-need-based:** Scholarships based on academics.

Merit scholarships. Scholastic Incentive Scholarships; $350 per semester; for any student who completes full-time semester, is enrolled full-time for next regular semester, maintains GPA of 3.5 through 3.89; $500 per semester; for students meeting above criteria, maintaining a cumulative GPA of 3.9 through 4.0.

Policies to reduce costs. Tuition/fee waivers for adults, senior citizens, employees and their families. Credit/placement for qualifying scores on AP, CLEP examinations. Work study available for part-time students.

Payment plans. Credit card, installment, deferred payment.

Application procedures. FAFSA, institutional form required. Priority date 5/1; no closing date. Applicants notified on rolling basis starting 4/1, must reply within 2 week(s) of notification.

Contact. Financial aid office: (989) 386-6622
Gale Crandell, Financial Aid Director
1375 South Clare Avenue
Harrison, MI 48625

Monroe County Community College

Monroe, Michigan
www.monroeccc.edu
Two-year public **Federal Code: 002294**

	Living at home
Tuition and fees (projected):	$1,758
Out-of-district:	$2,778
Out-of-state:	$3,018
Per-credit charge:	$54
Per-credit out-of-district:	$87
Per-credit out-of-state:	$95
Board only:	$2,090
Books and supplies:	$700
Personal expenses:	$560
Transportation:	$500

Undergraduate aid. Need-based: 87% awarded as scholarships/grants, 13% as loans/jobs. Need-based aid available for part-time students. **Non-need-based:** 72% awarded as scholarships/grants, 28% as loans/jobs. Scholarships based on academics, alumni affiliation, art, leadership, music/drama, state/district residency.

Policies to reduce costs. Tuition/fee waivers for senior citizens, employees and their families. Credit/placement for qualifying scores on AP, CLEP examinations. Work study available nights, weekends and for part-time students.

Payment plans. Credit card, deferred payment.

Application procedures. FAFSA, institutional form required. Priority date 4/1; no closing date. Applicants notified on rolling basis starting 4/1, must reply within 2 week(s) of notification. **Transfers:** No deadline.

Contact. Financial aid office: (734) 384-4135
Tracy Kominek, Director of Financial Aid/Placement
1555 South Raisinville Road
Monroe, MI 48161

Montcalm Community College

Sidney, Michigan
www.montcalm.edu
Two-year public **Federal Code: 002295**

	Living at home
Tuition and fees (projected):	$1,900
Out-of-district:	$2,745
Out-of-state:	$3,412
Per-credit charge:	$57
Per-credit out-of-district:	$87
Per-credit out-of-state:	$111
Board only:	$1,629
Personal expenses:	$1,912
Transportation:	$1,159

Undergraduate aid. Need-based: Need-based aid available for full-time and part-time students. **Non-need-based:** Scholarships based on academics, state/district residency.

Policies to reduce costs. Tuition/fee waivers for senior citizens, employees and their families. Credit/placement for qualifying scores on AP, CLEP examinations. Work study available for part-time students.

Payment plans. Credit card, installment payment.

Application procedures. FAFSA, institutional form required. Priority date 2/15; no closing date. Applicants notified on rolling basis starting 6/15, must reply within 2 week(s) of notification. **Transfers:** Priority date 4/1; no deadline.

Contact. Financial aid office: (989) 328-1226
Rebecca Powell, Director of Financial Aid
2800 College Drive
Sidney, MI 48885

Mott Community College

Flint, Michigan
www.mcc.edu
Two-year public **Federal Code: 002261**

	Living at home
Tuition and fees (2002-2003):	$1,974
Out-of-district:	$2,809
Out-of-state:	$3,718
Per-credit charge:	$61
Per-credit out-of-district:	$88
Per-credit out-of-state:	$118
Books and supplies:	$672
Personal expenses:	$703
Transportation:	$1,178

Undergraduate aid. Need-based: 83% awarded as scholarships/grants, 17% as loans/jobs. Need-based aid available for part-time students. **Non-need-based:** 35% awarded as scholarships/grants, 65% as loans/jobs. Scholarships based on academics, athletics.

Policies to reduce costs. Tuition/fee waivers for senior citizens, employees and their families. Credit/placement for qualifying scores on AP, CLEP examinations. Work study available nights, weekends and for part-time students.

Payment plans. Credit card, installment payment.

Application procedures. FAFSA required. No deadline. Applicants notified on rolling basis starting 5/1. **Transfers:** No deadline. Pell Grants adjusted for amount used at another institution.

Contact. Financial aid office: (810) 762-0144
Carlos Cisneros, Director of Financial Aid
1401 East Court Street
Flint, MI 48503

Muskegon Community College

Muskegon, Michigan
www.muskegon.edu
Two-year public **Federal Code: 002297**

College costs. Students also assessed contact hour fees, which vary according to residency status, and course fees, which vary.

	Living at home
Tuition and fees (2002-2003):	$1,530
Out-of-district:	$2,220
Out-of-state:	$2,715
Per-credit charge:	$50
Per-credit out-of-district:	$73
Per-credit out-of-state:	$90
Board only:	$1,600
Books and supplies:	$700
Personal expenses:	$800
Transportation:	$1,000

Policies to reduce costs. Tuition/fee waivers for senior citizens. Credit/placement for qualifying scores on AP, CLEP examinations.

Payment plans. Credit card payment.

Application procedures. FAFSA, institutional form required. Priority date 5/1; no closing date. Applicants notified on rolling basis starting 6/1, must reply within 2 week(s) of notification.

Contact. Financial aid office: (231) 773-9131
Mary McCann, Director of Financial Aid
221 South Quarterline Road
Muskegon, MI 49442

North Central Michigan College

Petoskey, Michigan
www.ncmc.cc.mi.us
Two-year public **Federal Code: 002299**

	Living at home	On-campus
Tuition and fees:	$1,890	$1,890
Out-of-district:	$2,850	$2,850
Out-of-state:	$3,510	$3,510
Per-credit charge:	$58	$58
Per-credit out-of-district:	$90	$90
Per-credit out-of-state:	$112	$112
Room and board:		$2,100
Books and supplies:	$750	$750
Transportation:	$1,060	$605

Undergraduate aid. Need-based: Need-based aid available for full-time and part-time students.

Policies to reduce costs. Tuition/fee waivers for senior citizens, employees and their families. Credit/placement for qualifying scores on AP, IB, CLEP examinations. Work study available nights, weekends and for part-time students.

Payment plans. Credit card, installment payment.

Application procedures. FAFSA, institutional form required. Priority date 4/15; no closing date. Applicants notified on rolling basis starting 4/30.

Contact. Financial aid office: (231) 348-6627
Sharron Hemme, Director of Financial Aid
1515 Howard Street
Petoskey, MI 49770

Northern Michigan University

Marquette, Michigan
www.nmu.edu
Four-year public **Federal Code: 002301**

	Living at home	On-campus
Tuition and fees (2002-2003):	$4,880	$4,880
Out-of-state:	$7,832	$7,832
Room and board:		$5,630
Board only:	$2,100	
Books and supplies:	$500	$500
Personal expenses:	$759	$759
Transportation:	$713	$603

Undergraduate aid. Need-based: Average financial aid package for full-time students was $7,054; for part-time $3,938. 40% awarded as scholarships/grants, 60% as loans/jobs. **Non-need-based:** 54% awarded as scholarships/grants, 46% as loans/jobs. Scholarships based on academics, alumni affiliation, art, athletics, leadership, minority status, music/drama, religious affiliation, state/district residency. **Student debt:** 71% of graduating class borrowed to fund education; average debt was $14,012. **Additional information:** Audition or portfolio required for music, drama, and art scholarship applicants. Alumni Dependent Tuition Program gives resident tuition rates to non-resident dependents of NMU alumni who received master's, bacccalaureate, or associate degree; renewable.

Freshman aid. Need-based: Out of 1,557 full-time freshmen, 1,552 applied for aid; 906 were judged to have need; of these 889 received aid. Average package met 83% of need. 149 students had full need met. Average scholarship/grant was $3,385; average loan $2,534. **Non-need based:** 8 full-time freshmen with need received non-need scholarships; 3 received athletic scholarships.

Merit scholarships. Talent recognition awards available in art and design, music, and theatre. Freshman Fellowship: based on minimum high school 3.5 GPA and ACT 24+, awards $1,000 student employment; Dr. Edgar L. Harden Scholarship: based on minimum 3.5 GPA and ACT 24+; National Academics Award: minimum 3.0 GPA and ACT 19+, awards $2,000 per year to an unlimited number of non-Michigan residents; NMU Merit Excellence Award: based on minimum 3.0 GPA and ACT 33+, awards $2,750 per year or $3,500 on campus; NMU Merit Award: minimum 3.0 GPA and ACT 30-32, awards $2,250 or $3,000 on campus; NMU Scholars Award: minimum 3.0 GPA and ACT 27-29, awards $1,250 or $2,000 on campus; NMU Outstanding Achievement: minimum 3.0 GPA and ACT 25-26, awards $750 or $1,500.

Policies to reduce costs. Tuition/fee waivers for children of alumni, senior citizens, minority students, employees and their families. Credit/placement for qualifying scores on AP, IB, CLEP examinations.

Payment plans. Credit card, installment payment.

Application procedures. FAFSA required. Priority date 2/20; no closing date. Applicants notified on rolling basis starting 4/1, must reply within 2 week(s) of notification. **Transfers:** Priority date 3/1; no deadline.

Contact. Financial aid office: (906) 227-2327
Mark Delorey, Director, Financial Aid
1401 Presque Isle Avenue
Marquette, MI 49855

Northwestern Michigan College

Traverse City, Michigan
www.nmc.edu
Two-year public **Federal Code: 002302**

	Living at home	On-campus
Tuition and fees:	$2,151	$2,151
Out-of-district:	$3,588	$3,588
Out-of-state:	$4,405	$4,405
Per-credit charge:	$62	$62
Per-credit out-of-district:	$110	$110
Per-credit out-of-state:	$137	$137
Room and board:		$5,700
Books and supplies:	$608	$608
Personal expenses:	$607	$607
Transportation:	$1,060	$592

Undergraduate aid. Need-based: Need-based aid available for full-time and part-time students. **Non-need-based:** Scholarships based on academics, art, music/drama, state/district residency.

Policies to reduce costs. Tuition/fee waivers for minority students, unemployed or children of unemployed, employees and their families. Credit/placement for qualifying scores on AP, CLEP examinations. Work study available nights, weekends and for part-time students.

Payment plans. Credit card, deferred payment.

Application procedures. FAFSA required. Priority date 4/1; no closing date. Applicants notified on rolling basis starting 5/1, must reply within 2 week(s) of notification.

Contact. Financial aid office: (231) 995-1035
Deb Faas, Coordinator of Financial Aid
1701 East Front Street
Traverse City, MI 49686

Northwood University

Midland, Michigan
www.northwood.edu
Four-year private **Federal Code: 004072**

	Living at home	On-campus
Tuition and fees (2002-2003):	$13,461	$13,461
Room and board:		$6,006
Books and supplies:	$1,271	$1,271
Transportation:	$860	$736

Undergraduate aid. Need-based: Average financial aid package for full-time students was $10,556; for part-time $4,950. 62% awarded as scholarships/grants, 38% as loans/jobs. **Non-need-based:** 60% awarded as scholarships/grants, 40% as loans/jobs. Scholarships based on academics, alumni affiliation, athletics. **Student debt:** 44% of graduating class borrowed to fund education; average debt was $11,191.

Freshman aid. Need-based: Out of 489 full-time freshmen, 370 applied for aid; 311 were judged to have need; of these 311 received aid. Average package met 55% of need. 54 students had full need met. Average scholarship/grant was $8,968; average loan $2,120. **Non-need based:** 251 full-time freshmen with need received non-need scholarships; 19 without need received awards; 4 received athletic scholarships.

Merit scholarships. Merit Scholarships; $3,000 - $5,000; unlimited number awarded; all based on test scores, GPA.

Policies to reduce costs. Tuition/fee waivers for children of alumni, family members, employees and their families. Credit/placement for qualifying scores on AP, IB, CLEP examinations. Work study available nights, weekends and for part-time students.

Payment plans. Installment payment.

Application procedures. FAFSA required. No deadline. Applicants notified on rolling basis starting 4/1, must reply within 2 week(s) of notification. **Transfers:** No deadline.

Contact. **Financial aid office:** (989) 837-4230
William Healy, Financial Aid Director
4000 Whiting Drive
Midland, MI 48640

Oakland Community College

Bloomfield Hills, Michigan
www.oakland.cc.edu
Two-year public **Federal Code: 002303**

College costs. Many students earn associate degree in 2 years by taking 31 credits over two semesters and summer. Related tuition/fees: $1,699.

	Living at home
Tuition and fees (2002-2003):	$1,579
Out-of-district:	$2,626
Out-of-state:	$3,655
Per-credit charge:	$50
Per-credit out-of-district:	$85
Per-credit out-of-state:	$120
Books and supplies:	$700
Personal expenses:	$570
Transportation:	$1,160

Undergraduate aid. **Need-based:** 85% awarded as scholarships/grants, 15% as loans/jobs. Need-based aid available for part-time students. **Non-need-based:** 58% awarded as scholarships/grants, 42% as loans/jobs. Scholarships based on academics, athletics.

Policies to reduce costs. Tuition/fee waivers for employees and their families. Credit/placement for qualifying scores on AP, CLEP examinations. Work study available for part-time students.

Payment plans. Credit card payment.

Application procedures. FAFSA required. Priority date 4/15; no closing date. Applicants notified on rolling basis starting 4/15. **Transfers:** Michigan residency required for aid to transfer students.

Contact. **Financial aid office:** (248) 232-4347
Wilma Porter, Director of Financial Assistance and Scholarships
2480 Opdyke Road
Bloomfield Hills, MI 48304-2266

Oakland University

Rochester, Michigan
www.oakland.edu
Four-year public **Federal Code: 002307**

	Living at home	On-campus
Tuition and fees (2002-2003):	$4,814	$4,814
Out-of-state:	$11,406	$11,406
Room and board:		$5,252
Books and supplies:	$580	$580
Personal expenses:	$594	$594
Transportation:	$1,020	$1,020

Undergraduate aid. **Need-based:** Average financial aid package for full-time students was $5,866; for part-time $3,657. 39% awarded as scholarships/grants, 61% as loans/jobs. **Non-need-based:** 16% awarded as scholarships/grants, 84% as loans/jobs. Scholarships based on academics, athletics.

Freshman aid. **Need-based:** Out of 1,815 full-time freshmen, 1,021 applied for aid; 631 were judged to have need; of these 616 received aid. Average package met 93% of need. 201 students had full need met. Average scholarship/grant was $3,166; average loan $2,386. **Non-need based:** 391 full-time freshmen with need received non-need scholarships; 680 without need received awards; 51 received athletic scholarships.

Policies to reduce costs. Tuition/fee waivers for senior citizens, employees and their families. Credit/placement for qualifying scores on AP, IB, CLEP examinations.

Payment plans. Credit card, installment, deferred payment.

Application procedures. FAFSA required. Priority date 2/21; no closing date. Applicants notified on rolling basis starting 3/15, must reply by 7/1 or within 2 week(s) of notification. **Transfers:** Closing date 4/1.

Contact. **Financial aid office:** (248) 370-2550
Cindy Hermsen, Director of Financial Aid
101 North Foundation Hall
Rochester, MI 48309-4475

Reformed Bible College

Grand Rapids, Michigan
www.reformed.edu
Four-year private **Federal Code: 002311**

	Living at home	On-campus
Tuition and fees (2002-2003):	$9,275	$9,275
Room and board:		$4,900
Books and supplies:	$455	$455
Personal expenses:	$725	$725
Transportation:	$575	$575

Undergraduate aid. **Need-based:** Need-based aid available for full-time and part-time students. **Non-need-based:** Scholarships based on academics, leadership, minority status.

Merit scholarships. Christian Leadership Scholarship; $1,500 renewable annually; based on Christian service activities, 3.2 cumulative GPA; 2 awarded.

Policies to reduce costs. Tuition/fee waivers for senior citizens, family members, employees and their families. Credit/placement for qualifying scores on AP, CLEP examinations. Work study available nights, weekends and for part-time students.

Payment plans. Credit card, installment payment.

Application procedures. FAFSA, institutional form required. Priority date 2/15; no closing date. Applicants notified on rolling basis starting 5/1, must reply within 2 week(s) of notification. **Transfers:** Priority date 4/1.

Contact. **Financial aid office:** (616) 988-3656
Agnes Russell, Financial Aid Administrator
3333 East Beltline NE
Grand Rapids, MI 49525-9749

Sacred Heart Major Seminary

Detroit, Michigan
www.shmsonline.org
Four-year private **Federal Code: 002313**

	Living at home	On-campus
Tuition and fees (projected):	$7,429	$7,429
Room and board:		$4,914
Books and supplies:	$1,436	$1,436

Undergraduate aid. **Need-based:** Average financial aid package for full-time students was $10,000. 90% awarded as scholarships/grants, 10% as loans/jobs. Need-based aid available for part-time students. **Non-need-based:** Scholarships based on religious affiliation, state/district residency.

Freshman aid. **Need-based:** Out of 2 full-time freshmen, 2 applied for aid; 2 were judged to have need; of these 2 received aid. 2 students had full need met. Average scholarship/grant was $10,000.

Policies to reduce costs. Work study available nights and weekends.

Payment plans. Credit card, installment, deferred payment.

Application procedures. FAFSA, institutional form required. Priority date 2/15; no closing date. Applicants notified on rolling basis starting 6/1, must reply within 3 week(s) of notification. **Transfers:** Priority date 4/1; no deadline. Must submit certified high school transcript, copy of high school diploma, copy of GED certificate showing passing score, or college transcript showing associate degree as certification of eligibility; must submit financial aid transcripts from all previous post-secondary institutions attended.

Contact. **Financial aid office:** (313) 883-8500
Anne-Marie Fry, Financial Aid Officer
2701 Chicago Boulevard
Detroit, MI 48226

Saginaw Valley State University

University Center, Michigan
www.svsu.edu
Four-year public **Federal Code: 002314**

	Living at home	On-campus
Tuition and fees (2002-2003):	$4,940	$4,940
Out-of-state:	$9,846	$9,846
Room and board:		$5,485
Board only:	$2,159	
Books and supplies:	$600	$600
Personal expenses:	$614	$741
Transportation:	$1,060	$592

Undergraduate aid. Need-based: Average financial aid package for full-time students was $3,576; for part-time $500. 42% awarded as scholarships/grants, 58% as loans/jobs. **Non-need-based:** 42% awarded as scholarships/grants, 58% as loans/jobs. Scholarships based on academics, alumni affiliation, athletics, leadership, minority status, music/drama.

Freshman aid. Need-based: Out of 1,044 full-time freshmen, 999 applied for aid; 533 were judged to have need; of these 412 received aid. Average package met 80% of need. 164 students had full need met. Average scholarship/grant was $2,044; average loan $2,147. **Non-need based:** 288 full-time freshmen with need received non-need scholarships.

Merit scholarships. Presidential Scholarships; full tuition/fees and books; 1st or 2nd in high school class. Award for Excellence; full tuition and fees; 3.7 GPA, 28 ACT. University Scholarship; full tuition and fees; 3.5 GPA. Math Olympics; top 2 scores in Math Olympics; 2 awarded. Various private scholarships also available.

Policies to reduce costs. Tuition/fee waivers for employees and their families. Credit/placement for qualifying scores on AP, IB, CLEP examinations. Work study available nights, weekends and for part-time students.

Payment plans. Credit card, installment payment.

Application procedures. FAFSA required. Priority date 2/14; no closing date. Applicants notified on rolling basis starting 3/20. **Transfers:** Community college scholarship, private scholarships, and Transfer Deans' scholarships available.

Contact. Financial aid office: (989) 964-4103
James Dwyer, Director of Scholarships, Financial Aid, Undergraduate Admissions
7400 Bay Road
University Center, MI 48710

St. Clair County Community College

Port Huron, Michigan
www.sc4.edu
Two-year public **Federal Code: 002310**

College costs. Residents of Lambton County, Canada pay in-state, out-of-district rate for tuition. Lambton County residents pay in-district tuition rate if enrolled in program of study not offered at Lambton College.

	Living at home
Tuition and fees:	$2,075
Out-of-district:	$2,945
Out-of-state:	$3,875
Per-credit charge:	$65
Per-credit out-of-district:	$94
Per-credit out-of-state:	$125
Books and supplies:	$850
Personal expenses:	$439
Transportation:	$1,125

Policies to reduce costs. Tuition/fee waivers for senior citizens, employees and their families. Credit/placement for qualifying scores on AP, CLEP examinations.

Payment plans. Credit card, deferred payment.

Application procedures. FAFSA required. Priority date 6/1; no closing date. Applicants notified on rolling basis starting 5/15, must reply within 2 week(s) of notification. **Transfers:** No deadline.

Contact. Financial aid office: (810) 989-5530
Josephine Cassar, Director of Financial Aid
323 Erie Street
Port Huron, MI 48061-5015

Schoolcraft College

Livonia, Michigan
www.schoolcraft.cc.mi.us
Two-year public **Federal Code: 002315**

	Living at home
Tuition and fees (2002-2003):	$1,820
Out-of-district:	$2,660
Out-of-state:	$3,890
Per-credit charge:	$57
Per-credit out-of-district:	$85
Per-credit out-of-state:	$126
Books and supplies:	$680
Personal expenses:	$648
Transportation:	$1,159

Undergraduate aid. Need-based: 74% awarded as scholarships/grants, 26% as loans/jobs. **Non-need-based:** Scholarships based on academics, athletics, leadership, music/drama, state/district residency.

Merit scholarships. Trustee Scholarships; $1,000-$1,200; renewable for 2nd year; based on essay, placement test, trustee application, graduation from local high school; 80 awarded.

Policies to reduce costs. Tuition/fee waivers for senior citizens, employees and their families. Credit/placement for qualifying scores on AP, CLEP examinations. Work study available nights, weekends and for part-time students.

Payment plans. Credit card payment.

Application procedures. FAFSA required. No deadline. Applicants notified on rolling basis starting 6/1.

Contact. Financial aid office: (734) 462-4433
Julieanne Tobin, Director Enrollment Management
18600 Haggerty Road
Livonia, MI 48152-2696

Siena Heights University

Adrian, Michigan
www.sienahts.edu
Four-year private **Federal Code: 002316**

	Living at home	On-campus
Tuition and fees:	$14,630	$14,630
Room and board:		$5,220
Books and supplies:	$600	$600
Personal expenses:	$900	$900
Transportation:	$200	$200

Undergraduate aid. Non-need-based: Scholarships based on academics, art, athletics, music/drama, religious affiliation.

Policies to reduce costs. Tuition/fee waivers for employees and their families. Credit/placement for qualifying scores on AP, CLEP examinations.

Payment plans. Credit card, installment, deferred payment.

Application procedures. FAFSA, institutional form, CSS PROFILE required. Priority date 3/15; closing date 8/15. Applicants notified on rolling basis starting 2/15. **Transfers:** No deadline. Transfer scholarship available.

Contact. Financial aid office: (517) 264-7130
Kevin Kucera, Dean of Admissions and Enrollment Services
1247 East Siena Heights Drive
Adrian, MI 49221-1796

Southwestern Michigan College

Dowagiac, Michigan
www.swmich.edu
Two-year public **Federal Code: 002317**

	Living at home
Tuition and fees (2002-2003):	$2,085
Out-of-district:	$2,348
Out-of-state:	$3,022
Per-credit charge:	$55
Per-credit out-of-district:	$64
Per-credit out-of-state:	$86
Board only:	$500
Books and supplies:	$800
Personal expenses:	$800
Transportation:	$1,500

Undergraduate aid. Need-based: Need-based aid available for full-time and part-time students. **Non-need-based:** Scholarships based on academics, art, leadership, music/drama.

Policies to reduce costs. Tuition/fee waivers for senior citizens, employees and their families. Credit/placement for qualifying scores on AP, CLEP examinations. Work study available nights, weekends and for part-time students.

Payment plans. Credit card, installment payment.

Application procedures. FAFSA, institutional form required. Priority date 8/1; no closing date. Applicants notified on rolling basis starting 4/1, must reply within 4 week(s) of notification. **Transfers:** No deadline.

Contact. Financial aid office: (269) 782-1313
Rob Wirt, Director of Financial Aid
58900 Cherry Grove Road
Dowagiac, MI 49047-9793

Spring Arbor University

Spring Arbor, Michigan
www.arbor.edu
Four-year private **Federal Code: 002318**

	Living at home	On-campus
Tuition and fees (2002-2003):	$14,016	$14,016
Room and board:		$5,080
Books and supplies:	$580	$580
Personal expenses:		$709
Transportation:		$628

Undergraduate aid. Need-based: Average financial aid package for full-time students was $11,293; for part-time $4,753. 65% awarded as scholarships/grants, 35% as loans/jobs. **Non-need-based:** 16% awarded as scholarships/grants, 84% as loans/jobs. Scholarships based on academics, art, athletics. **Student debt:** 78% of graduating class borrowed to fund education; average debt was $9,953.

Freshman aid. Need-based: Out of 292 full-time freshmen, 268 applied for aid; 148 were judged to have need; of these 148 received aid. Average package met 98% of need. 112 students had full need met. Average scholarship/grant was $8,118; average loan $3,867. **Non-need based:** 115 full-time freshmen with need received non-need scholarships; 144 without need received awards; 25 received athletic scholarships.

Policies to reduce costs. Tuition/fee waivers for family of clergy, employees and their families. Credit/placement for qualifying scores on AP, CLEP examinations.

Payment plans. Credit card, installment, deferred payment.

Application procedures. FAFSA required. Priority date 2/15; no closing date. Applicants notified on rolling basis starting 4/1. **Transfers:** No deadline. Financial aid transcript required from each college previously attended.

Contact. Financial aid office: (517) 750-1200
Lois Hardy, Director of Financial Aid
106 East Main Street
Spring Arbor, MI 49283-9799

University of Michigan

Ann Arbor, Michigan
www.umich.edu
Four-year public **Federal Code: 002325**

College costs. Commuter living at home: estimated expense for room, board and transportation, $1,780. Commuter not living at home: estimated cost for rent, utilities, and food $7,155. Part-time students pay $400 in-state/ $1,061 out-of-state for the first credit hour.

	Living at home	On-campus
Tuition and fees (2002-2003):	$7,411	$7,411
Out-of-state:	$23,289	$23,289
Room and board:		$6,496
Books and supplies:	$756	$756
Personal expenses:	$2,060	$2,060

Undergraduate aid. Need-based: Average financial aid package for full-time students was $10,022. 46% awarded as scholarships/grants, 54% as loans/jobs. Need-based aid available for part-time students. **Non-need-based:** 72% awarded as scholarships/grants, 28% as loans/jobs. Scholarships based on academics, alumni affiliation, art, athletics, leadership, minority status, music/drama, religious affiliation, state/district residency.

Freshman aid. Need-based: Out of 5,637 full-time freshmen, 2,960 applied for aid; 1,896 were judged to have need; of these 1,896 received aid. Average package met 90% of need. 1706 students had full need met. Average scholarship/grant was $8,481; average loan $1,920. **Non-need based:** 1,328 full-time freshmen with need received non-need scholarships; 1,790 without need received awards; 128 received athletic scholarships.

Policies to reduce costs. Tuition/fee waivers for employees and their families. Credit/placement for qualifying scores on AP, IB, CLEP examinations.

Payment plans. Installment payment.

Application procedures. FAFSA required. Priority date 2/15; closing date 9/30. Applicants notified on rolling basis starting 3/15, must reply by 9/30 or within 2 week(s) of notification. **Transfers:** Community College Scholarship available for qualified students.

Contact. Financial aid office: (734) 763-6600
Pamela Fowler, Director for Office of Financial Aid
1220 Student Activities Building
Ann Arbor, MI 48109-1316

University of Michigan: Dearborn

Dearborn, Michigan
www.umd.umich.edu
Four-year public **Federal Code: 002326**

College costs. In-state students pay $43 per credit-hour above 12 each semester. Out-of-state students pay $95. Engineering students pay additional $72.60 technology assessment.

	Living at home
Tuition and fees (2002-2003):	$5,452
Out-of-state:	$13,012
Books and supplies:	$800
Personal expenses:	$1,603
Transportation:	$1,176

Undergraduate aid. Need-based: Average financial aid package for full-time students was $7,252. 26% awarded as scholarships/grants, 74% as loans/jobs. **Non-need-based:** 91% awarded as scholarships/grants, 9% as loans/jobs. Scholarships based on academics, alumni affiliation, art, athletics, job skills, leadership, minority status, music/drama, state/district residency. **Student debt:** 39% of graduating class borrowed to fund education; average debt was $14,614.

Freshman aid. Need-based: Out of 738 full-time freshmen, 619 applied for aid; 221 were judged to have need; of these 212 received aid. Average package met 43% of need. 28 students had full need met. Average scholarship/grant was $3,104; average loan $816. **Non-need based:** 168 full-time freshmen with need received non-need scholarships; 528 without need received awards; 10 received athletic scholarships.

Policies to reduce costs. Tuition/fee waivers for senior citizens, employees and their families. Credit/placement for qualifying scores on AP examinations.

Payment plans. Credit card, installment, deferred payment.

Application procedures. FAFSA required. Priority date 4/1; no closing date. Applicants notified on rolling basis starting 5/1, must reply within 3 week(s) of notification.

Contact. **Financial aid office:** (313) 593-5000
John Mason, Director of Financial Aid
4901 Evergreen Road
Dearborn, MI 48128-1491

University of Michigan: Flint

Flint, Michigan
www.umflint.edu
Four-year public **Federal Code: 002327**

	Living at home
Tuition and fees (2002-2003):	$4,752
Out-of-state:	$9,246
Board only:	$2,272
Personal expenses:	$1,229
Transportation:	$1,412

Undergraduate aid. **Need-based:** Average financial aid package for full-time students was $6,562; for part-time $5,758. 28% awarded as scholarships/grants, 72% as loans/jobs. **Non-need-based:** Scholarships based on academics, art, minority status, music/drama. **Additional information:** SAT/ACT scores must be submitted for scholarship consideration.

Freshman aid. **Need-based:** Out of 467 full-time freshmen, 324 applied for aid; 219 were judged to have need; of these 218 received aid. 107 students had full need met. Average scholarship/grant was $3,920; average loan $2,447. **Non-need based:** 153 full-time freshmen with need received non-need scholarships; 100 without need received awards.

Policies to reduce costs. Tuition/fee waivers for senior citizens, employees and their families. Credit/placement for qualifying scores on AP, CLEP examinations. Work study available nights, weekends and for part-time students.

Payment plans. Credit card, deferred payment.

Application procedures. FAFSA required. Priority date 2/23; no closing date. Applicants notified on rolling basis starting 3/15. **Transfers:** No deadline. Must not be in default or owe refunds for Title IV aid.

Contact. **Financial aid office:** (810) 762-3444
Lori Veddar, Director of Financial Aid
303 East Kearsley Street
Flint, MI 48502-1950

Walsh College of Accountancy and Business Administration

Troy, Michigan
www.walshcollege.edu
Upper-division private **Federal Code: 004071**

	Living at home
Tuition and fees (2002-2003):	$6,530
Board only:	$7,332
Books and supplies:	$2,016

Undergraduate aid. **Need-based:** Average financial aid package for full-time students was $10,937; for part-time $8,607. 45% awarded as scholarships/grants, 55% as loans/jobs. **Non-need-based:** 84% awarded as scholarships/grants, 16% as loans/jobs. Scholarships based on academics. **Student debt:** 41% of graduating class borrowed to fund education; average debt was $8,006.

Policies to reduce costs. Tuition/fee waivers for employees and their families. Credit/placement for qualifying scores on IB, CLEP examinations. Work study available for part-time students.

Payment plans. Credit card, installment, deferred payment.

Application procedures. FAFSA required. Priority date 3/23; no closing date. Applicants notified on rolling basis. **Transfers:** Priority date 3/23; no deadline.

Contact. **Financial aid office:** (248) 689-8282
Howard Thomas, Director, Financial Aid
PO Box 7006
Troy, MI 48007-7006

Washtenaw Community College

Ann Arbor, Michigan
www.washtenaw.cc.mi.us
Two-year public **Federal Code: 002328**

	Living at home
Tuition and fees (2002-2003):	$1,726
Out-of-district:	$2,476
Out-of-state:	$3,106
Per-credit charge:	$52
Per-credit out-of-district:	$77
Per-credit out-of-state:	$98
Books and supplies:	$550
Personal expenses:	$600
Transportation:	$600

Undergraduate aid. **Non-need-based:** Scholarships based on academics.

Policies to reduce costs. Tuition/fee waivers for senior citizens, employees and their families. Credit/placement for qualifying scores on AP, CLEP examinations.

Payment plans. Credit card, deferred payment.

Application procedures. FAFSA, institutional form required. Priority date 6/1; closing date 7/1. Applicants notified on rolling basis. **Transfers:** No deadline.

Contact. **Financial aid office:** (734) 973-3543
Guy Hower, Financial Aids Officer
4800 East Huron River Drive
Ann Arbor, MI 48106-1610

Wayne County Community College

Detroit, Michigan
www.wccc.edu
Two-year public **Federal Code: 009230**

	Living at home
Tuition and fees (2002-2003):	$1,790
Out-of-district:	$2,270
Out-of-state:	$2,840
Per-credit charge:	$54
Per-credit out-of-district:	$70
Per-credit out-of-state:	$89
Books and supplies:	$400
Personal expenses:	$495
Transportation:	$915

Undergraduate aid. **Additional information:** High school diploma, GED, or passing grade on ABT required for financial aid.

Policies to reduce costs. Tuition/fee waivers for senior citizens, employees and their families.

Payment plans. Credit card, installment, deferred payment.

Application procedures. FAFSA required. Priority date 8/1; no closing date. Applicants notified on rolling basis starting 7/1.

Contact. **Financial aid office:** (313) 496-2500
Bernadette Spencer, Financial Aid Administrator
801 West Fort Street
Detroit, MI 48226

Wayne State University

Detroit, Michigan
www.wayne.edu
Four-year public **Federal Code: 002329**

	Living at home	On-campus
Tuition and fees (2002-2003):	$4,723	$4,723
Out-of-state:	$10,201	$10,201
Room only:		$5,607
Board only:	$2,390	
Books and supplies:	$590	$590
Personal expenses:	$1,750	$1,750
Transportation:	$1,410	$1,410

Undergraduate aid. **Need-based:** Average financial aid package for full-time students was $6,488; for part-time $5,370. **Non-need-based:** Scholarships based on academics, athletics, job skills, leadership, minority status, music/drama, state/district residency. **Student debt:** 43% of graduating class borrowed to fund education; average debt was $16,452.

Freshman aid. Need-based: Out of 1,401 full-time freshmen, 1,185 applied for aid; 961 were judged to have need; of these 935 received aid. Average package met 57% of need. 123 students had full need met. Average scholarship/grant was $3,398; average loan $2,378. **Non-need based:** 685 full-time freshmen with need received non-need scholarships; 182 without need received awards; 58 received athletic scholarships.

Policies to reduce costs. Tuition/fee waivers for senior citizens, employees and their families. Credit/placement for qualifying scores on AP, IB, CLEP examinations.

Payment plans. Credit card payment.

Application procedures. FAFSA required. Priority date 3/1; no closing date. Applicants notified on rolling basis starting 4/1, must reply within 2 week(s) of notification.

Contact. Financial aid office: (313) 577-3378
Bryan Terry, Interim Director of Scholarships and Financial Aid
HNJ, 3 East
Detroit, MI 48202

West Shore Community College

Scottville, Michigan
www.westshore.edu
Two-year public **Federal Code: 007950**

	Living at home
Tuition and fees (2002-2003):	$1,839
Out-of-district:	$2,627
Out-of-state:	$3,264
Per-credit charge:	$59
Per-credit out-of-district:	$91
Per-credit out-of-state:	$114
Books and supplies:	$700
Personal expenses:	$650
Transportation:	$1,150

Undergraduate aid. Need-based: Need-based aid available for full-time and part-time students.

Policies to reduce costs. Tuition/fee waivers for senior citizens, employees and their families. Credit/placement for qualifying scores on AP, CLEP examinations. Work study available nights, weekends and for part-time students.

Payment plans. Credit card, deferred payment.

Application procedures. FAFSA required. Priority date 3/1; no closing date. Applicants notified on rolling basis starting 5/15, must reply within 2 week(s) of notification. **Transfers:** Priority date 3/1; no deadline.

Contact. Financial aid office: (231) 845-6211
Victoria Oddo, Director of Student Services
3000 North Stiles Road
Scottville, MI 49454-0277

Western Michigan University

Kalamazoo, Michigan
www.wmich.edu
Four-year public **Federal Code: 002330**

	Living at home	On-campus
Tuition and fees (2002-2003):	$4,499	$4,499
Out-of-state:	$10,255	$10,255
Room and board:		$5,517
Books and supplies:	$804	$804
Personal expenses:	$1,736	$1,736
Transportation:	$1,830	$526

Undergraduate aid. Need-based: Average financial aid package for full-time students was $7,006. 31% awarded as scholarships/grants, 69% as loans/jobs. Need-based aid available for part-time students. **Non-need-based:** 61% awarded as scholarships/grants, 39% as loans/jobs. Scholarships based on academics, art, athletics, minority status, music/drama, state/district residency. **Student debt:** 44% of graduating class borrowed to fund education; average debt was $16,013.

Freshman aid. Need-based: Average package met 67% of need. Average scholarship/grant was $4,200; average loan $2,370.

Merit scholarships. Medallion Scholarship Program; $1,200-$8,000 annually; based on academic performance in high school (3.8 GPA, minimum 25 ACT or 1130 SAT); renewable for students maintaining full-time enrollment and 3.25 minimum GPA; Minority Scholarship; $2,000-$8,000 renewable annually; based on 3.5 GPA, test scores, high school, community activities.

Policies to reduce costs. Tuition/fee waivers for senior citizens, employees and their families. Credit/placement for qualifying scores on AP, IB, CLEP examinations.

Payment plans. Credit card payment.

Application procedures. FAFSA required. Priority date 4/1; no closing date. Applicants notified on rolling basis starting 3/15. **Transfers:** No deadline.

Contact. Financial aid office: (269) 387-6000
Susan O'Flaherty, Executive Director of Student Services
1903 West Michigan Avenue
Kalamazoo, MI 49008

William Tyndale College

Farmington Hills, Michigan
williamtyndale.edu
Four-year private **Federal Code: 002252**

	Living at home	On-campus
Tuition and fees (2002-2003):	$8,650	$8,650
Room and board:		$3,520
Books and supplies:	$1,289	$1,289
Transportation:	$1,125	$1,125

Undergraduate aid. Need-based: Average financial aid package for full-time students was $6,912; for part-time $2,864. 58% awarded as scholarships/grants, 42% as loans/jobs. **Non-need-based:** 66% awarded as scholarships/grants, 34% as loans/jobs. Scholarships based on academics, alumni affiliation, leadership, music/drama, religious affiliation. **Student debt:** 32% of graduating class borrowed to fund education; average debt was $15,341.

Freshman aid. Need-based: Out of 50 full-time freshmen, 50 applied for aid; 37 were judged to have need; of these 37 received aid. Average package met 78% of need. 29 students had full need met. Average scholarship/grant was $3,180. **Non-need based:** 13 without need received awards.

Policies to reduce costs. Tuition/fee waivers for children of alumni, senior citizens, employees and their families. Credit/placement for qualifying scores on AP, CLEP examinations. Work study available weekends and for part-time students.

Payment plans. Credit card, installment, deferred payment.

Application procedures. FAFSA, institutional form required. Priority date 2/15; closing date 5/1. Applicants notified by 8/15, must reply within 4 week(s) of notification. **Transfers:** No deadline.

Contact. Financial aid office: (877) 499-6800, ext. 815
Kim Zwierzchowski, Director of Financial Aid
35700 West 12 Mile Road
Farmington Hills, MI 48331-3147

Minnesota

Academy College

Bloomington, Minnesota
www.academycollege.edu
Two-year proprietary **Federal Code: 013505**

College costs (2002-2003). Tuition ranges from $210 to $320 per credit depending on program. Full program costs range from $12,000 to $61,000. Books/supplies: $550. Personal expenses: $2,200.

Undergraduate aid. Need-based: Need-based aid available for full-time and part-time students.

Policies to reduce costs. Work study available nights and for part-time students.

Payment plans. Credit card payment.

Application procedures. FAFSA, institutional form required.

Contact. Financial aid office: (952) 851-0066
Mary Erickson, Director of Administration
3050 Metro Drive, Suite 200
Bloomington, MN 55425-1554

Alexandria Technical College

Alexandria, Minnesota
www.alextech.org
Two-year public **Federal Code: 005544**

	Living at home
Tuition and fees (2002-2003):	$2,874
Out-of-state:	$5,529
Per-credit charge:	$89
Per-credit out-of-state:	$177
Books and supplies:	$750
Personal expenses:	$900
Transportation:	$1,350

Undergraduate aid. All financial aid based on need. Need-based aid available for full-time and part-time students.

Policies to reduce costs. Tuition/fee waivers for senior citizens, employees and their families. Credit/placement for qualifying scores on AP, CLEP examinations. Work study available for part-time students.

Payment plans. Credit card, deferred payment.

Application procedures. FAFSA, institutional form required. Priority date 5/1; no closing date. Applicants notified on rolling basis starting 6/30, must reply within 2 week(s) of notification. **Transfers:** No deadline.

Contact. Financial aid office: (320) 762-4540
Gary McFarland, Financial Aid Coordinator
1601 Jefferson Street
Alexandria, MN 56308-3799

Anoka-Ramsey Community College

Coon Rapids, Minnesota
www.anokaramsey.edu
Two-year public **Federal Code: 002332**

College costs. Various reciprocity agreements with some neighboring states provide tuition reduction to out-of-state students.

	Living at home
Tuition and fees (2002-2003):	$2,958
Out-of-state:	$5,532
Per-credit charge:	$85
Per-credit out-of-state:	$169
Books and supplies:	$600
Personal expenses:	$600
Transportation:	$500

Policies to reduce costs. Tuition/fee waivers for senior citizens, employees and their families. Credit/placement for qualifying scores on AP, CLEP examinations. Work study available nights, weekends and for part-time students.

Payment plans. Credit card, deferred payment.

Application procedures. FAFSA, institutional form required. Priority date 6/1; no closing date. Applicants notified on rolling basis, must reply within 2 week(s) of notification.

Contact. Financial aid office: (763) 427-2600
Karla Seymour, Financial Aid Officer
11200 Mississippi Boulevard NW
Coon Rapids, MN 55433

Art Institutes International Minnesota

Minneapolis, Minnesota
www.aim.artinstitutes.edu
Four-year proprietary **Federal Code: 010248**

College costs. Tuition for full bachelor's degree program $57,558; tuition for full associate degree programs range from $33,638 to $38,422. Starter kits for most programs $485; for culinary arts program $625; lab fee for culinary arts program $275 per quarter.

	Living at home
Tuition and fees (2002-2003):	$18,788
Books and supplies:	$1,649
Personal expenses:	$2,880

Undergraduate aid. Need-based: Need-based aid available for full-time students.

Policies to reduce costs. Tuition/fee waivers for employees and their families. Tuition at time of enrollment guaranteed for 4 years; prepayment discount.

Payment plans. Credit card, installment payment.

Application procedures. FAFSA required.

Contact. Financial aid office: (612) 332-3361
Director of Administrative and Financial Services
15 South Ninth Street
Minneapolis, MN 55402

Augsburg College

Minneapolis, Minnesota
www.augsburg.edu
Four-year private **Federal Code: 002334**

	Living at home	On-campus
Tuition and fees (2002-2003):	$18,193	$18,193
Room and board:		$5,690
Books and supplies:	$900	$900
Personal expenses:	$1,070	$1,070

Undergraduate aid. Need-based: Average financial aid package for full-time students was $12,808; for part-time $11,174. 57% awarded as scholarships/grants, 43% as loans/jobs. **Non-need-based:** 26% awarded as scholarships/grants, 74% as loans/jobs. Scholarships based on academics, alumni affiliation, art, leadership, minority status, music/drama, religious affiliation. **Student debt:** 68% of graduating class borrowed to fund education; average debt was $20,892.

Freshman aid. Need-based: Out of 346 full-time freshmen, 279 applied for aid; 233 were judged to have need; of these 233 received aid. Average package met 90% of need. 119 students had full need met. Average scholarship/grant was $11,316; average loan $3,915. **Non-need based:** 40 full-time freshmen with need received non-need scholarships; 77 without need received awards.

Merit scholarships. President's Scholarships; up to full tuition annually; 3.7 GPA and ACT/SAT score 27 or higher; number awarded determined annually. Regents Scholarships; $3,000-$9,000; top 30% of class rank or test scores. Must apply before 5/1 for both scholarships.

Policies to reduce costs. Tuition/fee waivers for children of alumni, senior citizens, employees and their families. Credit/placement for qualifying scores on AP, IB, CLEP examinations.

Payment plans. Credit card, installment payment.

Application procedures. FAFSA, institutional form required. Priority date 4/15; no closing date. Applicants notified on rolling basis starting 3/1, must reply within 3 week(s) of notification.

Contact. **Financial aid office:** (612) 330-1046
Paul Terrio, Director of Student Financial Services
2211 Riverside Avenue
Minneapolis, MN 55454

Bemidji State University

Bemidji, Minnesota
www.bemidjistate.edu
Four-year public **Federal Code: 002336**

College costs. Various reciprocal tuition plans with some neighboring states and Manitoba, Canada provide tuition reduction for out-of-state students.

	Living at home	On-campus
Tuition and fees (2002-2003):	$4,475	$4,475
Out-of-state:	$8,715	$8,715
Room and board:		$4,597
Board only:	$800	
Books and supplies:	$700	$700
Personal expenses:	$250	$250
Transportation:	$100	$100

Undergraduate aid. Need-based: Average financial aid package for full-time students was $7,189; for part-time $5,655. 56% awarded as scholarships/grants, 44% as loans/jobs. **Non-need-based:** 35% awarded as scholarships/grants, 65% as loans/jobs. Scholarships based on academics, alumni affiliation, art, music/drama. **Student debt:** 69% of graduating class borrowed to fund education; average debt was $13,187.

Freshman aid. Need-based: Out of 590 full-time freshmen, 478 applied for aid; 336 were judged to have need; of these 332 received aid. Average package met 81% of need. 168 students had full need met. Average scholarship/grant was $4,212; average loan $2,370. **Non-need based:** 185 full-time freshmen with need received non-need scholarships; 130 without need received awards; 46 received athletic scholarships.

Policies to reduce costs. Tuition/fee waivers for senior citizens, minority students, employees and their families. Credit/placement for qualifying scores on AP, CLEP examinations. Work study available nights and weekends.

Payment plans. Credit card, installment, deferred payment.

Application procedures. FAFSA, institutional form required. Priority date 5/15; no closing date. Applicants notified on rolling basis starting 5/15. **Transfers:** No deadline.

Contact. **Financial aid office:** (218) 755-2034
Paul Lindseth, Director of Financial Aid
1500 Birchmont Drive Northeast, D-102
Bemidji, MN 56601

Bethany Lutheran College

Mankato, Minnesota
www.blc.edu
Four-year private **Federal Code: 002337**

	Living at home	On-campus
Tuition and fees:	$14,150	$14,150
Room and board:		$4,688
Board only:	$2,970	
Books and supplies:	$750	$750
Personal expenses:	$1,000	$1,000

Undergraduate aid. Need-based: Average financial aid package for full-time students was $10,794; for part-time $5,899. 70% awarded as scholarships/grants, 30% as loans/jobs. **Non-need-based:** 27% awarded as scholarships/grants, 73% as loans/jobs. Scholarships based on academics, art, athletics, music/drama.

Freshman aid. Need-based: Out of 165 full-time freshmen, 131 applied for aid; 117 were judged to have need; of these 117 received aid. Average package met 91% of need. 56 students had full need met. Average scholarship/grant was $7,857; average loan $3,228. **Non-need based:** 13 full-time freshmen with need received non-need scholarships; 37 without need received awards; 14 received athletic scholarships.

Policies to reduce costs. Tuition/fee waivers for employees and their families. Credit/placement for qualifying scores on AP, IB, CLEP examinations. Work study available nights, weekends and for part-time students.

Payment plans. Credit card, installment payment.

Application procedures. FAFSA, institutional form required. Priority date 5/1; no closing date. Applicants notified on rolling basis starting 3/1, must reply within 2 week(s) of notification.

Contact. **Financial aid office:** (507) 344-7328
Jeffrey Younge, Financial Aid Director
700 Luther Drive
Mankato, MN 56001-4490

Bethel College

St. Paul, Minnesota
www.bethel.edu
Four-year private **Federal Code: 002338**

	Living at home	On-campus
Tuition and fees (2002-2003):	$17,700	$17,700
Room and board:		$6,200
Books and supplies:	$400	$400
Personal expenses:	$1,500	$1,500

Undergraduate aid. Need-based: Average financial aid package for full-time students was $14,097; for part-time $9,366. 59% awarded as scholarships/grants, 41% as loans/jobs. **Non-need-based:** Scholarships based on academics, alumni affiliation, art, leadership, minority status, music/drama, religious affiliation, state/district residency. **Student debt:** 77% of graduating class borrowed to fund education; average debt was $20,965.

Freshman aid. Need-based: Average package met 85% of need. Average scholarship/grant was $9,098; average loan $3,610.

Policies to reduce costs. Tuition/fee waivers for family of clergy, employees and their families. Prepayment discount; credit/placement for qualifying scores on AP, CLEP examinations. Work study available nights, weekends and for part-time students.

Payment plans. Credit card, installment payment.

Application procedures. FAFSA, institutional form required. Priority date 4/15; no closing date. Applicants notified on rolling basis starting 3/1, must reply by 5/1 or within 3 week(s) of notification.

Contact. **Financial aid office:** (651) 638-6241
Dan Nelson, Senior Director of Financial Aid/Coordinator of Institutional Research/Planning
3900 Bethel Drive
St. Paul, MN 55112-6999

Brown College

Mendota Heights, Minnesota
www.browncollege.edu
Two-year proprietary **Federal Code: 007351**

College costs. Tuition varies by program.

	Living at home
Tuition and fees (2002-2003):	$27,500
Books and supplies:	$1,800
Personal expenses:	$1,520
Transportation:	$674

Undergraduate aid. Non-need-based: Scholarships based on academics.

Merit scholarships. Scholarships for graduating high school seniors who score in the top 20 in institution's competency test; up to $50,000 total in $1,000, $2,500 and $5,000 awards. Upper Midwest Communications Conclave-Brown Institute Broadcasting Scholarship for high school senior or graduate from the greater Midwest area; 1 awarded; tuition.

Policies to reduce costs. Tuition/fee waivers for employees and their families. Tuition at time of enrollment guaranteed for 2 years.

Payment plans. Credit card, installment payment.

Application procedures. FAFSA, institutional form required. Priority date 7/1; no closing date. Applicants notified on rolling basis starting 1/1, must reply within 2 week(s) of notification.

Contact. **Financial aid office:** (651) 905-3400
Darrell Rhoten, Director of Financial Aid
1440 Northland Drive
Mendota Heights, MN 55120

Capella University
Minneapolis, Minnesota
www.capellauniversity.edu
Upper-division proprietary **Federal Code: 032673**

	Living at home
Tuition and fees:	$12,000

Undergraduate aid. Need-based: Need-based aid available for full-time and part-time students.

Policies to reduce costs. Tuition/fee waivers for employees and their families. Credit/placement for qualifying scores on IB examinations.

Payment plans. Credit card payment.

Contact. **Financial aid office:** (888) 227-3552
Financial Aid Office
222 South 9th Street, 20th Floor
Minneapolis, MN 55402

Carleton College
Northfield, Minnesota
www.carleton.edu
Four-year private **Federal Code: 002340**

	Living at home	On-campus
Tuition and fees (2002-2003):	$26,910	$26,910
Room and board:		$5,535
Books and supplies:	$1,200	$1,200
Personal expenses:		$100
Transportation:		$500

Undergraduate aid. Need-based: Average financial aid package for full-time students was $18,832. 74% awarded as scholarships/grants, 26% as loans/jobs. **Non-need-based:** 38% awarded as scholarships/grants, 62% as loans/jobs. Scholarships based on academics. **Student debt:** 53% of graduating class borrowed to fund education; average debt was $14,543. **Additional information:** Full financial need of all admitted applicants met through combination of work, loans, grants.

Freshman aid. Need-based: Out of 516 full-time freshmen, 414 applied for aid; 286 were judged to have need; of these 286 received aid. Average package met 100% of need. 286 students had full need met. Average scholarship/grant was $15,207; average loan $1,597. **Non-need based:** 48 full-time freshmen with need received non-need scholarships; 68 without need received awards.

Merit scholarships. Carleton sponsors National Merit, National Achievement, National Hispanic Scholars Awards; $2,000 per year; based on outstanding academic achievement and promise.

Policies to reduce costs. Tuition/fee waivers for employees and their families. Credit/placement for qualifying scores on AP, IB examinations. Work study available nights and weekends.

Payment plans. Installment payment.

Application procedures. FAFSA, CSS PROFILE required. Closing date 2/15. Applicants notified by 4/15, must reply by 5/1 or within 2 week(s) of notification. Early decision closing date 11/15. **Transfers:** Closing date 3/15.

Contact. **Financial aid office:** (507) 646-4138
Rod Oto, Director of Student Financial Services
100 South College Street
Northfield, MN 55057

Central Lakes College
Brainerd, Minnesota
www.clc.mnscu.edu
Two-year public **Federal Code: 002339**

College costs. Various reciprocity agreements with some neighboring states provide tuition reduction to out-of-state students.

	Living at home
Tuition and fees (2002-2003):	$2,668
Out-of-state:	$5,012
Per-credit charge:	$78
Per-credit out-of-state:	$156
Books and supplies:	$600
Personal expenses:	$1,500
Transportation:	$1,100

Undergraduate aid. Need-based: Need-based aid available for full-time and part-time students.

Policies to reduce costs. Tuition/fee waivers for senior citizens, employees and their families. Credit/placement for qualifying scores on AP, CLEP examinations. Work study available for part-time students.

Payment plans. Credit card, installment, deferred payment.

Application procedures. FAFSA, institutional form required. Priority date 6/1; no closing date. Applicants notified on rolling basis starting 6/10, must reply within 2 week(s) of notification. **Transfers:** Priority date 6/1; no deadline.

Contact. **Financial aid office:** (218) 855-8025
Mike Barnaby, Director of Financial Aid
501 West College Drive
Brainerd, MN 56401

Century Community and Technical College
White Bear Lake, Minnesota
www.century.mnscu.edu
Two-year public **Federal Code: 010546**

College costs. Various reciprocity agreements with some neighboring states provide tuition reduction to out-of-state students.

	Living at home
Tuition and fees (2002-2003):	$2,873
Out-of-state:	$5,442
Per-credit charge:	$86
Per-credit out-of-state:	$171
Books and supplies:	$960

Undergraduate aid. All financial aid based on need. 54% awarded as scholarships/grants, 46% as loans/jobs. Need-based aid available for part-time students. **Additional information:** Minnesota resident out of high school or not enrolled in college for 7 years without bachelor's or other higher degree offered cost of tuition and books for 1 course in 1 semester up to maximum of 5 credits.

Policies to reduce costs. Tuition/fee waivers for senior citizens, employees and their families. Credit/placement for qualifying scores on AP, IB, CLEP examinations. Work study available for part-time students.

Payment plans. Credit card, deferred payment.

Application procedures. FAFSA required. Priority date 6/15; closing date 6/30. Applicants notified on rolling basis starting 6/15.

Contact. **Financial aid office:** (612) 779-3305
Lois Larson, Financial Aid Director
3300 Century Avenue North
White Bear Lake, MN 55110

College of St. Benedict
St. Joseph, Minnesota
www.csbsju.edu
Four-year private **Federal Code: 002341**

	Living at home	On-campus
Tuition and fees (2002-2003):	$19,226	$19,226
Room and board:		$5,789
Board only:	$1,500	
Books and supplies:	$600	$600
Personal expenses:	$700	$700
Transportation:	$200	$200

Undergraduate aid. Need-based: Average financial aid package for full-time students was $16,190; for part-time $6,341. 58% awarded as scholarships/grants, 42% as loans/jobs. **Non-need-based:** 79% awarded as scholarships/grants, 21% as loans/jobs. Scholarships based on academics, art, leadership, music/drama. **Student debt:** 72% of graduating class borrowed to fund education; average debt was $20,412. **Additional information:** Special travel allowance for out-of-state students.

Freshman aid. **Need-based:** Out of 516 full-time freshmen, 508 applied for aid; 356 were judged to have need; of these 356 received aid. Average package met 98% of need. 332 students had full need met. Average scholarship/grant was $11,643; average loan $4,069. **Non-need based:** 331 full-time freshmen with need received non-need scholarships; 146 without need received awards.

Merit scholarships. Regents/Trustees Scholarships, $10,000; Minimum 3.6 GPA, ACT composite 30, SAT 1320, demonstrated leadership and service, faculty interview. President's Scholarships, $5,500-$8,000; GPA, high school rank, ACT/SAT scores, leadership and service. Dean's Scholarships, $2,000-$5,000; GPA, high school rank, ACT/SAT scores, leadership and service. Art, Music and Theater Scholarships, up to $2,000; Excelled in these subjects in high school, portfolio, tape, audition. Diversity Leadership Scholarships, up to $5,000; Demonstrated diversity leadership and service in the area of cultural and ethnic diversity, personal statement on topic. Wasie Scholarships, $1,000 - $10, 000; eligible applicants must have Polish ancestry, financial need, and demonstrated academic achievement. Army ROTC and ROTC Nursing Scholarships, $17,000; Demonstrated leadership potential. High school GPA, class standing, and ACT/SAT scores considered, high achievement with broad interests and willingness to take on challenges.

Policies to reduce costs. Tuition/fee waivers for employees and their families. Prepayment discount; credit/placement for qualifying scores on AP, IB, CLEP examinations.

Payment plans. Credit card, installment payment.

Application procedures. FAFSA, institutional form required. Priority date 3/15; no closing date. Applicants notified on rolling basis starting 3/1, must reply by 5/1.

Contact. **Financial aid office:** (320) 363-5388
Jane Haugen, Executive Director of Financial Aid
37 South College Avenue
St. Joseph, MN 56374-2099

College of St. Catherine

St. Paul, Minnesota
www.stkate.edu
Four-year private **Federal Code: 002342**

	Living at home	On-campus
Tuition and fees (2002-2003):	$18,362	$18,362
Room and board:		$5,170
Books and supplies:	$625	$625
Personal expenses:	$500	$400
Transportation:	$600	$300

Undergraduate aid. **Need-based:** Average financial aid package for full-time students was $18,319; for part-time $11,569. 54% awarded as scholarships/grants, 46% as loans/jobs. **Non-need-based:** 34% awarded as scholarships/grants, 66% as loans/jobs. Scholarships based on academics, leadership. **Student debt:** 81% of graduating class borrowed to fund education; average debt was $24,602. **Additional information:** Audition required for music scholarships.

Freshman aid. **Need-based:** Average package met 95% of need. Average scholarship/grant was $7,658; average loan $3,559.

Merit scholarships. St. Catherine of Alexandria Merit Scholarships; $2,000-$6,000; for high school seniors in top 15% of class, evidence of academic preparation, outstanding leadership abilities, involvement in extracurricular activities and community service; renewable for 3 years.

Policies to reduce costs. Tuition/fee waivers for senior citizens, family of clergy, employees and their families. Credit/placement for qualifying scores on AP, IB, CLEP examinations. Work study available nights, weekends and for part-time students.

Payment plans. Credit card, installment, deferred payment.

Application procedures. FAFSA, institutional form required. Priority date 4/1; no closing date. Applicants notified on rolling basis starting 3/15, must reply within 2 week(s) of notification.

Contact. **Financial aid office:** (651) 690-6540
Pam Johnson, Director of Financial Aid
2004 Randolph Avenue
St. Paul, MN 55105

College of St. Scholastica

Duluth, Minnesota
www.css.edu
Four-year private **Federal Code: 002343**

	Living at home	On-campus
Tuition and fees:	$19,302	$19,302
Room and board:		$6,456
Books and supplies:	$750	$750
Personal expenses:	$780	$780
Transportation:	$550	$208

Undergraduate aid. **Need-based:** Average financial aid package for full-time students was $15,908; for part-time $7,312. 57% awarded as scholarships/grants, 43% as loans/jobs. **Non-need-based:** 64% awarded as scholarships/grants, 36% as loans/jobs. Scholarships based on academics, alumni affiliation, art, music/drama. **Student debt:** 70% of graduating class borrowed to fund education; average debt was $23,233.

Freshman aid. **Need-based:** Average package met 78% of need. Average scholarship/grant was $4,983; average loan $3,382.

Merit scholarships. Benedictine Scholarship; $4,000-$10,000 per year for up to 4 years; based on GPA, SAT/ACT score; unlimited number awarded.

Policies to reduce costs. Tuition/fee waivers for children of alumni, senior citizens, minority students, family members, employees and their families. Credit/placement for qualifying scores on AP, IB, CLEP examinations. Work study available nights, weekends and for part-time students.

Payment plans. Credit card, installment payment.

Application procedures. FAFSA, institutional form required. Priority date 3/15; no closing date. Applicants notified on rolling basis starting 3/1, must reply by 5/1 or within 2 week(s) of notification. **Transfers:** Priority date 3/15; no deadline.

Contact. **Financial aid office:** (218) 723-6397
Jon Erickson, Director of Financial Aid
1200 Kenwood Avenue
Duluth, MN 55811-4199

College of Visual Arts

St. Paul, Minnesota
www.cva.edu
Four-year private **Federal Code: 007462**

	Living at home
Tuition and fees (2002-2003):	$14,388
Board only:	$2,823
Books and supplies:	$2,000
Personal expenses:	$1,774
Transportation:	$300

Undergraduate aid. **Need-based:** Average financial aid package for full-time students was $8,625; for part-time $8,647. 47% awarded as scholarships/grants, 53% as loans/jobs. **Non-need-based:** 12% awarded as scholarships/grants, 88% as loans/jobs. Scholarships based on academics, art. **Student debt:** 27% of graduating class borrowed to fund education; average debt was $6,255.

Freshman aid. **Need-based:** Out of 46 full-time freshmen, 37 applied for aid; 30 were judged to have need; of these 30 received aid. Average scholarship/grant was $4,298; average loan $2,123. **Non-need based:** 11 full-time freshmen with need received non-need scholarships; 2 without need received awards.

Policies to reduce costs. Tuition/fee waivers for employees and their families. Credit/placement for qualifying scores on AP examinations. Work study available nights, weekends and for part-time students.

Application procedures. FAFSA, institutional form required. Priority date 4/15; no closing date. Applicants notified by 5/15, must reply within 2 week(s) of notification.

Contact. **Financial aid office:** (651) 224-3416
Bonnie Clayton, Director of Financial Aid
344 Summit Avenue
St. Paul, MN 55102-2199

Concordia College: Moorhead

Moorhead, Minnesota
www.concordiacollege.edu
Four-year private **Federal Code: 002346**

	Living at home	On-campus
Tuition and fees (2002-2003):	$15,635	$15,635
Room and board:		$4,310
Books and supplies:	$600	$600
Personal expenses:	$795	$795
Transportation:	$200	$200

Undergraduate aid. All financial aid based on need. Need-based aid available for full-time and part-time students. **Additional information:** Students in ACCORD program (age 25 and older) may apply for tuition reductions for first 4 courses.

Policies to reduce costs. Tuition/fee waivers for employees and their families. Prepayment discount; credit/placement for qualifying scores on AP, IB, CLEP examinations. Work study available nights, weekends and for part-time students.

Payment plans. Installment payment.

Application procedures. FAFSA, institutional form required. Priority date 4/15; no closing date. Applicants notified on rolling basis starting 3/1. **Transfers:** No deadline.

Contact. **Financial aid office:** (218) 299-3010
Dale Thornton, Director of Financial Aid
901 South Eighth Street
Moorhead, MN 56562-9981

Concordia University: St. Paul

St. Paul, Minnesota
www.csp.edu
Four-year private **Federal Code: 002347**

	Living at home	On-campus
Tuition and fees (2002-2003):	$17,326	$17,326
Room and board:		$5,530
Books and supplies:	$1,000	$1,000
Personal expenses:	$750	$750

Undergraduate aid. **Need-based:** Average financial aid package for full-time students was $11,051; for part-time $9,346. 54% awarded as scholarships/grants, 46% as loans/jobs. **Non-need-based:** 48% awarded as scholarships/grants, 52% as loans/jobs. Scholarships based on academics, athletics, music/drama. **Additional information:** Church districts and local congregations major sources of aid for church-vocation students.

Freshman aid. **Need-based:** Out of 175 full-time freshmen, 171 applied for aid; 145 were judged to have need; of these 145 received aid. Average package met 89% of need. 50 students had full need met. Average scholarship/grant was $9,739; average loan $3,569. **Non-need based:** 24 without need received awards; 9 received athletic scholarships.

Policies to reduce costs. Tuition/fee waivers for senior citizens, employees and their families. Credit/placement for qualifying scores on AP, IB, CLEP examinations. Work study available nights, weekends and for part-time students.

Payment plans. Credit card, installment payment.

Application procedures. FAFSA, institutional form required. Priority date 4/15; no closing date. Applicants notified on rolling basis starting 3/1, must reply within 3 week(s) of notification. **Transfers:** Priority date 4/15; no deadline.

Contact. **Financial aid office:** (651) 641-8204
Brian Heinemann, Financial Aid Director
275 North Syndicate Street
St. Paul, MN 55104-5494

Crossroads College

Rochester, Minnesota
www.crossroads.edu
Four-year private **Federal Code: 002366**

	Living at home	On-campus
Tuition and fees (2002-2003):	$6,560	$6,560
Room only:		$1,600
Board only:	$1,500	
Books and supplies:	$450	$450
Personal expenses:	$1,500	$1,500
Transportation:	$400	$400

Undergraduate aid. **Need-based:** Average financial aid package for full-time students was $7,326; for part-time $3,249. 53% awarded as scholarships/grants, 47% as loans/jobs. **Non-need-based:** 42% awarded as scholarships/grants, 58% as loans/jobs. Scholarships based on academics, leadership, music/drama, religious affiliation. **Student debt:** 78% of graduating class borrowed to fund education; average debt was $14,811.

Freshman aid. **Need-based:** Out of 17 full-time freshmen, 17 applied for aid; 10 were judged to have need; of these 10 received aid. Average package met 84% of need. 4 students had full need met. Average scholarship/grant was $4,750; average loan $2,366. **Non-need based:** 1 full-time freshmen with need received non-need scholarships; 8 without need received awards.

Merit scholarships. Home-Educated Grant: $500 per semester (home-schooled for two years, grades 9-12. Travel Grant: $500 per semester for student who resides in states other than Minnesota, Iowa, Wisconsin. Crossroads Matching Grant: up to $500 per semester, first year of enrollment (church sends funds we will match)

Policies to reduce costs. Tuition/fee waivers for senior citizens, family members, employees and their families. Credit/placement for qualifying scores on AP, CLEP examinations. Work study available nights and for part-time students.

Payment plans. Installment payment.

Application procedures. FAFSA, institutional form required. Priority date 4/1; no closing date. Applicants notified on rolling basis starting 2/1, must reply within 4 week(s) of notification. **Transfers:** No deadline. Mid-year transfer students will have financial aid calculated with the prior school term award in mind.

Contact. **Financial aid office:** (507) 288-4563 ext. 308
Kimberly Hudson, Director of Financial Aid
920 Mayowood Road SW
Rochester, MN 55902

Crown College

St. Bonifacius, Minnesota
www.crown.edu
Four-year private **Federal Code: 002383**

	Living at home	On-campus
Tuition and fees (2002-2003):	$11,982	$11,982
Room and board:		$4,980
Board only:	$1,350	
Books and supplies:	$800	$800
Personal expenses:	$1,890	$1,890
Transportation:	$800	$800

Undergraduate aid. **Need-based:** Average financial aid package for full-time students was $10,286; for part-time $5,516. 48% awarded as scholarships/grants, 52% as loans/jobs. **Non-need-based:** 46% awarded as scholarships/grants, 54% as loans/jobs. Scholarships based on academics, alumni affiliation, leadership, music/drama, religious affiliation.

Freshman aid. **Need-based:** Out of 132 full-time freshmen, 124 applied for aid; 118 were judged to have need; of these 118 received aid. Average package met 45% of need. 7 students had full need met. Average scholarship/grant was $5,090; average loan $3,880. **Non-need based:** 101 full-time freshmen with need received non-need scholarships; 6 without need received awards.

Policies to reduce costs. Tuition/fee waivers for family of clergy, employees and their families. Credit/placement for qualifying scores on AP, IB, CLEP examinations. Work study available nights, weekends and for part-time students.

Payment plans. Credit card, installment payment.

Application procedures. FAFSA, institutional form required. Priority date 5/1; closing date 8/1. Applicants notified on rolling basis starting 4/1, must reply within 4 week(s) of notification. **Transfers:** No deadline. Cannot have attended more than 5 years of college to receive MN state grant.

Contact. **Financial aid office:** (952) 446-4177
Cheryl Fernandez, Director of Financial Aid
6425 County Road 30
St. Bonifacius, MN 55375-9001

Dakota County Technical College

Rosemount, Minnesota
www.dctc.mnscu.edu
Two-year public **Federal Code: 010402**

College costs. Various reciprocity agreements with some neighboring states provide tuition reduction to out-of-state students.

	Living at home
Tuition and fees (2002-2003):	$3,252
Out-of-state:	$6,000
Per-credit charge:	$92
Per-credit out-of-state:	$183
Board only:	$750
Books and supplies:	$600
Personal expenses:	$1,000
Transportation:	$2,750

Undergraduate aid. All financial aid based on need. Need-based aid available for full-time and part-time students.

Policies to reduce costs. Tuition/fee waivers for senior citizens, employees and their families. Credit/placement for qualifying scores on AP examinations. Work study available nights, weekends and for part-time students.

Payment plans. Credit card, installment payment.

Application procedures. FAFSA, institutional form required. No deadline. Applicants notified on rolling basis starting 3/15. **Transfers:** No deadline.

Contact. **Financial aid office:** (651) 423-8299
Scott Roelke, Financial Aid Coordinator
1300 East 145th Street
Rosemount, MN 55068

Fergus Falls Community College

Fergus Falls, Minnesota
www.ffcc.edu
Two-year public **Federal Code: 002352**

College costs. Various reciprocity agreements with some neighboring states provide tuition reduction to out-of-state students.

	Living at home	On-campus
Tuition and fees (2002-2003):	$3,299	$3,299
Out-of-state:	$6,071	$6,071
Per-credit charge:	$92	$92
Per-credit out-of-state:	$185	$185
Room only:		$1,840
Board only:	$1,220	
Books and supplies:	$600	$600
Personal expenses:	$900	
Transportation:	$500	

Undergraduate aid. **Need-based:** Need-based aid available for full-time and part-time students. **Non-need-based:** Scholarships based on academics, leadership, minority status, music/drama.

Merit scholarships. Academic and leadership scholarships; $400-$1,000 each; available to 1st and 2nd year students; over 150 awarded annually.

Policies to reduce costs. Tuition/fee waivers for adults, senior citizens. Credit/placement for qualifying scores on AP, IB, CLEP examinations.

Application procedures. FAFSA, institutional form required. Priority date 6/1; no closing date. Applicants notified on rolling basis starting 7/1.

Contact. **Financial aid office:** (218) 739-7520
Robert Anderson, Director of Financial Aid
1414 College Way
Fergus Falls, MN 56537-1000

Globe College

Oakdale, Minnesota
www.globecollege.com
Four-year proprietary **Federal Code: 004642**

	Living at home
Tuition and fees:	$13,050
Board only:	$5,580
Transportation:	$765

Undergraduate aid. **Need-based:** Average financial aid package for full-time students was $4,600; for part-time $3,350. 33% awarded as scholarships/grants, 67% as loans/jobs. **Student debt:** 30% of graduating class borrowed to fund education; average debt was $5,925.

Freshman aid. **Need-based:** Out of 132 full-time freshmen, 125 applied for aid; 125 were judged to have need; of these 91 received aid. Average package met 47% of need. 12 students had full need met. Average scholarship/grant was $1,200; average loan $2,450.

Policies to reduce costs. Tuition/fee waivers for employees and their families.

Payment plans. Credit card, installment payment.

Application procedures. FAFSA, institutional form required. No deadline. Applicants notified on rolling basis starting 5/1.

Contact. **Financial aid office:** (651) 730-5100
Sally Mickelson, Financial Aid Director
7166 10th Street North
Oakdale, MN 55128-5939

Gustavus Adolphus College

St. Peter, Minnesota
www.gustavus.edu
Four-year private **Federal Code: 002353**

	Living at home	On-campus
Tuition and fees:	$21,735	$21,735
Room and board:		$5,460
Board only:	$2,370	
Books and supplies:	$700	$700
Personal expenses:	$930	$930

Undergraduate aid. **Need-based:** Average financial aid package for full-time students was $14,501. **Non-need-based:** Scholarships based on academics, alumni affiliation, music/drama. **Student debt:** 66% of graduating class borrowed to fund education; average debt was $17,400.

Freshman aid. **Need-based:** Out of 670 full-time freshmen, 660 applied for aid; 438 were judged to have need; of these 437 received aid. Average package met 92% of need. 185 students had full need met. Average scholarship/grant was $11,133; average loan $3,531. **Non-need based:** 70 full-time freshmen with need received non-need scholarships; 215 without need received awards.

Merit scholarships. Partners in Scholarship; $9,000; academic; 35 awarded. Presidential Scholarship; $12,500; National Merit finalist; 25 awarded. Trustee Scholarship; $1,000-$6,500; academic. Alumni Scholarship; $1,500; academic for children of alumni. Jussi Bjorling Scholarship; $3,000; music; 40 awarded. Anderson Theatre and Dance Scholarship; $2,000; theatre and dance; 15 awarded. Norelius Service Award; $500-1,500; volunteer leadership. Gustavus State Scholarship; $12,000; academic; 1 awarded. Dean's Scholarship; $7,500; 35 awarded.

Policies to reduce costs. Tuition/fee waivers for senior citizens, employees and their families. Tuition at time of enrollment guaranteed for 4 years; prepayment discount; credit/placement for qualifying scores on AP, IB examinations. Work study available nights and weekends.

Payment plans. Installment payment.

Application procedures. FAFSA, institutional form required. CSS PROFILE required of students desiring a financial aid award before February 15 of their applicant year. Priority date 4/15; closing date 6/15. Applicants notified on rolling basis starting 3/1, must reply by 5/1 or within 2 week(s) of notification. **Transfers:** Priority date 2/15; closing date 5/1. Phi Theta Kappa Scholarships for eligible community college graduates.

Contact. **Financial aid office:** (507) 933-7527
Robert Helgeson, Director of Student Financial Assistance
800 West College Avenue
St. Peter, MN 56082

Hamline University

St. Paul, Minnesota
www.hamline.edu
Four-year private **Federal Code: 002354**

	Living at home	On-campus
Tuition and fees:	$20,832	$20,832
Room and board:		$6,220
Books and supplies:	$1,400	$1,400
Personal expenses:	$1,000	$1,000
Transportation:	$1,000	$800

Undergraduate aid. Need-based: Average financial aid package for full-time students was $16,865; for part-time $8,209. 81% awarded as scholarships/grants, 19% as loans/jobs. **Non-need-based:** 31% awarded as scholarships/grants, 69% as loans/jobs. Scholarships based on academics, state/district residency. **Student debt:** 78% of graduating class borrowed to fund education; average debt was $19,925.

Freshman aid. Need-based: Out of 417 full-time freshmen, 399 applied for aid; 319 were judged to have need; of these 319 received aid. Average package met 70% of need. 69 students had full need met. Average scholarship/grant was $10,928; average loan $574. **Non-need based:** 76 without need received awards.

Merit scholarships. Presidential Scholarship; $5,000-$12,500; for students with excellent academic ability, strong sense of motivation. Hamline Honors Scholarship; $4,000; to students with successful academic record, involvement in school and community activities. Hamline Trustee Scholarship; $2,500; to new first year students who have excelled academically.

Policies to reduce costs. Tuition/fee waivers for family of clergy, employees and their families. Prepayment discount; credit/placement for qualifying scores on AP, IB, CLEP examinations. Work study available nights, weekends and for part-time students.

Payment plans. Installment payment.

Application procedures. FAFSA, institutional form required. Priority date 3/15; no closing date. Applicants notified on rolling basis starting 3/1, must reply within 2 week(s) of notification.

Contact. Financial aid office: (651) 523-3000
Richard Manderfeld, Director, Financial Aid
1536 Hewitt Avenue
St. Paul, MN 55104-1284

Hennepin Technical College

Brooklyn Park, Minnesota
www.htc.mnscu.edu
Two-year public **Federal Code: 010491**

College costs. Different reciprocity agreements for different states.

	Living at home
Tuition and fees (2002-2003):	$2,698
Out-of-state:	$5,213
Per-credit charge:	$84
Per-credit out-of-state:	$168

Payment plans. Credit card payment.

Application procedures. FAFSA, institutional form required. No deadline. Applicants notified on rolling basis starting 3/1.

Contact. Financial aid office: (763) 425-3800
Patricia Berktold, Director
9000 Brooklyn Boulevard
Brooklyn Park, MN 55455

Herzing College: Minneapolis Drafting School

Crystal, Minnesota
www.herzing.edu
Two-year proprietary **Federal Code: 011017**

	Living at home
Tuition and fees (projected):	$9,000
Per-credit charge:	$300

Contact. Financial aid office: (763) 535-3000
5700 West Broadway
Crystal, MN 55428-3548

Hibbing Community College: A Technical and Community College

Hibbing, Minnesota
www.hcc.mnscu.edu
Two-year public **Federal Code: 002355**

College costs. Different reciprocity agreements for different states.

	Living at home
Tuition and fees (2002-2003):	$2,994
Out-of-state:	$2,994
Per-credit charge:	$86
Per-credit out-of-state:	$86
Books and supplies:	$600
Transportation:	$900

Payment plans. Deferred payment.

Application procedures. Institutional form required. Priority date 7/1; no closing date. Applicants notified on rolling basis starting 6/30, must reply within 2 week(s) of notification.

Contact. Financial aid office: (218) 262-7200
Paul Hatch, Financial Aid Director
1515 East 25th Street
Hibbing, MN 55746

High-Tech Institute

Brooklyn Center, Minnesota
www.hightechschools.org
Two-year proprietary **Federal Code: 022631**

College costs. Costs for full associate programs range from $15,950 to $24,500; diploma programs range from $7,650 to $20,250. Fees, books, uniforms and tools included. Estimated cost of other supplies $50.

Contact. Financial aid office: (763) 560-9700
Ronnie Hinton-Rivera, Director of Financial Aid
5701 Shingle Creek Parkway North, Suite 200
Brooklyn Center, MN 55430

Inver Hills Community College

Inver Grove Heights, Minnesota
www.inverhills.mnscu.edu
Two-year public **Federal Code: 006935**

College costs. Different reciprocity agreements for different states.

	Living at home
Tuition and fees (2002-2003):	$3,172
Out-of-state:	$5,886
Per-credit charge:	$90
Per-credit out-of-state:	$181
Books and supplies:	$800
Personal expenses:	$900
Transportation:	$1,800

Undergraduate aid. All financial aid based on need. Need-based aid available for full-time and part-time students.

Policies to reduce costs. Tuition/fee waivers for senior citizens, employees and their families. Credit/placement for qualifying scores on AP examinations. Work study available nights, weekends and for part-time students.

Payment plans. Credit card, deferred payment.

Application procedures. FAFSA, institutional form required. Priority date 5/1; no closing date. Applicants notified on rolling basis starting 6/1. **Transfers:** No deadline.

Contact. Financial aid office: (651) 450- 8518
John Pogue, Financial Aid Officer
2500 East 80 Street
Inver Grove Heights, MN 55076-3209

Itasca Community College

Grand Rapids, Minnesota
www.itascacc.edu
Two-year public **Federal Code: 002356**

College costs. Different reciprocity agreements for different states.

	Living at home
Tuition and fees (2002-2003):	$3,139
Out-of-state:	$5,825
Per-credit charge:	$90
Per-credit out-of-state:	$179
Books and supplies:	$800
Personal expenses:	$1,284
Transportation:	$770

Undergraduate aid. Need-based: 71% awarded as scholarships/grants, 29% as loans/jobs. Need-based aid available for part-time students. **Non-need-based:** 42% awarded as scholarships/grants, 58% as loans/jobs. Scholarships based on academics, leadership.

Policies to reduce costs. Tuition/fee waivers for senior citizens, employees and their families. Credit/placement for qualifying scores on AP, IB, CLEP examinations. Work study available nights and for part-time students.

Payment plans. Credit card payment.

Application procedures. FAFSA required. Priority date 5/1; no closing date. Applicants notified on rolling basis starting 4/1.

Contact. Financial aid office: (218) 327-4460
Patty Holycross, Director of Financial Aid
1851 Highway 169 East
Grand Rapids, MN 55744

Lake Superior College: A Community and Technical College

Duluth, Minnesota
www.lsc.mnscu.edu
Two-year public **Federal Code: 005757**

College costs. Various reciprocity plans for residents of neighboring states may reduce tuition for out-of-state students.

	Living at home
Tuition and fees (2002-2003):	$2,972
Out-of-state:	$5,484
Per-credit charge:	$84
Per-credit out-of-state:	$168
Board only:	$2,646
Books and supplies:	$600
Personal expenses:	$900
Transportation:	$900

Undergraduate aid. Need-based: Need-based aid available for full-time and part-time students.

Policies to reduce costs. Tuition/fee waivers for senior citizens, employees and their families. Credit/placement for qualifying scores on AP, IB, CLEP examinations. Work study available nights, weekends and for part-time students.

Payment plans. Credit card, installment, deferred payment.

Application procedures. FAFSA, institutional form required. Priority date 6/30; no closing date. Applicants notified on rolling basis starting 4/1. **Transfers:** No deadline.

Contact. Financial aid office: (218) 733-7616
Sandra Olin, Director of Financial Aid
2101 Trinity Road
Duluth, MN 55811

Lakeland Medical-Dental Academy

Crystal, Minnesota
www.herzing.edu
Two-year proprietary **Federal Code: 007590**

College costs. Cost of full programs ranges from $11,710 to $17,190, including fees and books. Required fees vary by program.

Application procedures. FAFSA required.

Contact. Financial aid office: (763) 535-3000
5700 West Broadway
Crystal, MN 55428

Macalester College

St. Paul, Minnesota
www.macalester.edu
Four-year private **Federal Code: 002358**

	Living at home	On-campus
Tuition and fees:	$25,070	$25,070
Room and board:		$6,874
Books and supplies:	$750	$750
Personal expenses:	$700	$700

Undergraduate aid. Need-based: Average financial aid package for full-time students was $20,539; for part-time $14,770. 80% awarded as scholarships/grants, 20% as loans/jobs. **Non-need-based:** 24% awarded as scholarships/grants, 76% as loans/jobs. Scholarships based on academics, minority status. **Additional information:** College meets full need for all admitted students. Minnesota Self Loan available to qualified students.

Freshman aid. Need-based: Average package met 100% of need. Average scholarship/grant was $18,009; average loan $1,422.

Merit scholarships. Macalester College National Merit Scholarships; $5,000; to National Merit Finalists whose first choice college is Macalester and who are offered admission. DeWitt Wallace Distinguished Scholarships; minimum $3,000; competitive, open to National Merit semifinalists, commended students, and finalists not awarded National Merit Scholarship. DeWitt Wallace Scholarships; minimum $3,000; to selected middle-income students who need assistance to attend Macalester and whose academic records have shown them to be worthy of recognition. Catherine Lealtad Scholarships; minimum $3,000; to African American, Latino, and Native American students with strong high school records. Students who are National Achievement or National Hispanic Scholarship finalists and who have achieved a strong high school record will receive a minimum annual award of $5,000.

Policies to reduce costs. Credit/placement for qualifying scores on AP examinations.

Payment plans. Installment payment.

Application procedures. FAFSA, CSS PROFILE required. Priority date 2/7; closing date 4/15. Applicants notified by 4/1, must reply by 5/1 or within 1 week(s) of notification. Early decision closing date 11/15. **Transfers:** Closing date 4/15.

Contact. Financial aid office: (651) 696-6214
Brian Lindeman, Director of Financial Aid
1600 Grand Avenue
St. Paul, MN 55105-1899

Martin Luther College

New Ulm, Minnesota
www.mlc-wels.edu
Four-year private **Federal Code: 002361**

	Living at home	On-campus
Tuition and fees (2002-2003):	$5,820	$5,820
Room and board:		$2,530
Books and supplies:	$1,050	$1,050
Personal expenses:	$955	$920
Transportation:	$525	$760

Undergraduate aid. Need-based: Average financial aid package for full-time students was $6,131. 71% awarded as scholarships/grants, 29% as loans/jobs. Need-based aid available for part-time students. **Non-need-based:** Scholarships based on academics, alumni affiliation, leadership, music/drama, religious affiliation. **Student debt:** 48% of graduating class borrowed to fund education; average debt was $8,676.

Freshman aid. Need-based: Out of 255 full-time freshmen, 240 applied for aid; 180 were judged to have need; of these 180 received aid. Average package met 70% of need. 74 students had full need met. Average scholarship/grant was $4,311; average loan $2,064. **Non-need based:** 91 full-time freshmen with need received non-need scholarships; 37 without need received awards.

Merit scholarships. Academic scholarship: $500, 3.75 GPA after 6 semesters of high school or 27 ACT. Presidential scholarship: $1,000, to student selected as high school valedictorian or ranked first in class after 7 semesters.

Policies to reduce costs. Prepayment discount; credit/placement for qualifying scores on AP examinations. Work study available nights, weekends and for part-time students.

Payment plans. Installment payment.

Application procedures. FAFSA, institutional form required. Closing date 4/15. Applicants notified by 5/15.

Contact. Financial aid office: (507) 354-8221
Gene Slettedahl, Director of Financial Aid
1995 Luther Court
New Ulm, MN 56073-3965

Mesabi Range Community and Technical College

Virginia, Minnesota
www.mr.mnscu.edu
Two-year public **Federal Code: 004009**

College costs. Different reciprocity agreements for different states.

	Living at home	On-campus
Tuition and fees (2002-2003):	$3,116	$3,116
Per-credit charge:	$90	$90
Room only:		$2,178
Books and supplies:	$600	$600
Personal expenses:	$1,000	$1,000
Transportation:	$470	

Undergraduate aid. Need-based: Need-based aid available for full-time and part-time students. **Non-need-based:** Scholarships based on state/district residency.

Policies to reduce costs. Tuition/fee waivers for senior citizens, employees and their families. Credit/placement for qualifying scores on AP examinations.

Payment plans. Credit card payment.

Application procedures. FAFSA, institutional form required. Priority date 4/22; no closing date. Applicants notified on rolling basis starting 5/1, must reply within 2 week(s) of notification. **Transfers:** No deadline.

Contact. Financial aid office: (218) 741-3095
George Walters, Director of Financial Aid
1001 Chestnut Street West
Virginia, MN 55792-3448

Metropolitan State University

St. Paul, Minnesota
www.metrostate.edu
Four-year public **Federal Code: 010374**

	Living at home
Tuition and fees (2002-2003):	$3,359
Out-of-state:	$7,152
Books and supplies:	$975
Personal expenses:	$3,198

Undergraduate aid. All financial aid based on need. 19% awarded as scholarships/grants, 81% as loans/jobs. Need-based aid available for part-time students.

Freshman aid. Out of 57 full-time freshmen, 45 applied for aid; 45 were judged to have need; of these 45 received aid. Average package met 28% of need. Average scholarship/grant was $1,250; average loan $1,800.

Policies to reduce costs. Tuition/fee waivers for senior citizens, employees and their families. Credit/placement for qualifying scores on AP, IB, CLEP examinations. Work study available nights, weekends and for part-time students.

Payment plans. Credit card, installment payment.

Application procedures. FAFSA required. Priority date 5/1; closing date 8/1. Applicants notified on rolling basis starting 5/1, must reply within 2 week(s) of notification. **Transfers:** Priority date 5/1; no deadline.

Contact. Financial aid office: (651) 772-7670
Jim Cleaveland, Director of Financial Aid
700 East Seventh Street
St. Paul, MN 55106-5000

Minneapolis Community and Technical College

Minneapolis, Minnesota
www.mctc.mnscu.edu
Two-year public **Federal Code: 002362**

College costs. Various reciprocity agreements with some neighboring states and Manitoba, Canada provide tuition reduction to out-of-state students.

	Living at home
Tuition and fees (2002-2003):	$3,100
Out-of-state:	$5,837
Per-credit charge:	$91
Per-credit out-of-state:	$183
Books and supplies:	$850
Personal expenses:	$2,000
Transportation:	$2,700

Undergraduate aid. All financial aid based on need. Need-based aid available for full-time and part-time students.

Policies to reduce costs. Tuition/fee waivers for senior citizens, employees and their families. Credit/placement for qualifying scores on AP, CLEP examinations. Work study available nights and weekends.

Payment plans. Credit card payment.

Application procedures. FAFSA required. Priority date 6/1; no closing date. Applicants notified on rolling basis starting 7/15, must reply within 2 week(s) of notification.

Contact. Financial aid office: (612) 341-7033
Beth Stephens, Director of Financial Aid
1501 Hennepin Avenue
Minneapolis, MN 55403-1779

Minnesota School of Business

Richfield, Minnesota
www.msbcollege.edu
Two-year proprietary **Federal Code: 017145**

	Living at home
Tuition and fees:	$13,100
Per-credit charge:	$290
Board only:	$675
Books and supplies:	$1,400
Personal expenses:	$2,637
Transportation:	$657

Undergraduate aid. All financial aid based on need. Need-based aid available for full-time and part-time students.

Payment plans. Credit card payment.

Application procedures. FAFSA, institutional form required. No deadline.

Contact. Financial aid office: (612) 861-2000
Tim Jacobson, Financial Aid Director
1401 West 76 Street, Suite 500
Richfield, MN 55423

Minnesota School of Business: Brooklyn Center

Brooklyn Center, Minnesota
www.msbcollege.edu
Two-year proprietary **Federal Code: 004646**

	Living at home
Tuition and fees:	$13,050
Per-credit charge:	$290
Books and supplies:	$1,800
Personal expenses:	$5,940
Transportation:	$1,890

Undergraduate aid. All financial aid based on need. Need-based aid available for full-time and part-time students.

Application procedures. FAFSA required.

Contact. **Financial aid office:** (763) 566-7777
Tom Hensch, Director, Financial Aid
5910 Shingle Creek Parkway
Brooklyn Center, MN 55430

Minnesota State College - Southeast Technical

Winona, Minnesota
www.southeastmn.edu
Two-year public **Federal Code: 002393**

College costs. Various reciprocity agreements with some neighboring states provide tuition reduction to out-of-state students.

	Living at home
Tuition and fees (2002-2003):	$3,025
Out-of-state:	$5,708
Per-credit charge:	$89
Per-credit out-of-state:	$179
Books and supplies:	$600
Personal expenses:	$1,800
Transportation:	$1,800

Undergraduate aid. Need-based: Need-based aid available for full-time and part-time students. **Non-need-based:** Scholarships based on academics, state/district residency. **Additional information:** Many scholarships available throughout year.

Merit scholarships. Rose Tandeski Memorial Scholarship; $2,500; based on submission of autobiography; number awarded varies annually.

Policies to reduce costs. Work study available nights, weekends and for part-time students.

Payment plans. Credit card payment.

Application procedures. FAFSA, institutional form required. No deadline. Applicants notified by 6/1, must reply by 5/1 or within 3 week(s) of notification. **Transfers:** Priority date 5/15; closing date 6/30. Mid-year transfer application forms must be accompanied by financial aid transcript.

Contact. **Financial aid office:** (507) 453-2710
Anne Dahlen, Director of Financial Aid
1250 Homer Road
Winona, MN 55987-0409

Minnesota State University Moorhead

Moorhead, Minnesota
www.mnstate.edu
Four-year public **Federal Code: 002367**

	Living at home	On-campus
Tuition and fees (2002-2003):	$3,690	$3,690
Room and board:		$4,171
Board only:	$800	
Books and supplies:	$600	$600
Personal expenses:	$1,900	$1,900
Transportation:	$600	$600

Undergraduate aid. Need-based: Need-based aid available for full-time and part-time students. **Non-need-based:** Scholarships based on academics, athletics, state/district residency.

Policies to reduce costs. Tuition/fee waivers for senior citizens, employees and their families. Credit/placement for qualifying scores on AP, CLEP examinations.

Payment plans. Credit card, installment payment.

Application procedures. FAFSA, institutional form required. Priority date 3/1; no closing date. Applicants notified on rolling basis starting 5/1, must reply within 2 week(s) of notification. **Transfers:** No deadline.

Contact. **Financial aid office:** (218) 236-2251
Carolyn Zehren, Director of Financial Aid and Scholarships
Owens Hall
Moorhead, MN 56563

Minnesota State University, Mankato

Mankato, Minnesota
www.mnsu.edu
Four-year public **Federal Code: 002360**

	Living at home	On-campus
Tuition and fees (2002-2003):	$3,981	$3,981
Out-of-state:	$7,691	$7,691
Room and board:		$4,018
Books and supplies:	$750	$750
Personal expenses:		$1,500
Transportation:		$700

Undergraduate aid. All financial aid based on need. Need-based aid available for full-time students. **Student debt:** 75% of graduating class borrowed to fund education; average debt was $13,600.

Policies to reduce costs. Tuition/fee waivers for senior citizens, employees and their families. Credit/placement for qualifying scores on AP, IB, CLEP examinations.

Payment plans. Credit card, installment payment.

Application procedures. FAFSA required. Priority date 3/15; closing date 6/30. Applicants notified on rolling basis starting 3/15, must reply within 2 week(s) of notification.

Contact. **Financial aid office:** (507) 389-1185
Sandra Loerts, Director of Financial Aid
122 Taylor Center
Mankato, MN 56001

Minnesota West Community and Technical College: Worthington Campus

Worthington, Minnesota
www.mnwest.mnscu.edu
Two-year public **Federal Code: 005263**

College costs. Various reciprocity agreements with neighboring states.

	Living at home
Tuition and fees (2002-2003):	$3,047
Out-of-state:	$3,047
Per-credit charge:	$91
Per-credit out-of-state:	$91
Books and supplies:	$600

Undergraduate aid. Need-based: Need-based aid available for full-time and part-time students.

Policies to reduce costs. Credit/placement for qualifying scores on AP, CLEP examinations.

Application procedures. FAFSA required. Priority date 6/1; no closing date. Applicants notified on rolling basis starting 7/1, must reply within 2 week(s) of notification.

Contact. **Financial aid office:** (507) 372-2107
Faith Drent, Financial Aid Officer
1450 Collegeway
Worthington, MN 56187

National American University: St. Paul

Bloomington, Minnesota
www.national.edu
Four-year proprietary **Federal Code: E00640**

	Living at home
Tuition and fees (2002-2003):	$12,020
Books and supplies:	$1,000

Undergraduate aid. Need-based: Need-based aid available for full-time and part-time students. **Non-need-based:** Scholarships based on academics.

Policies to reduce costs. Tuition/fee waivers for employees and their families. Credit/placement for qualifying scores on AP, IB, CLEP examinations. Work study available nights, weekends and for part-time students.

Payment plans. Credit card, installment payment.

Application procedures. FAFSA required. Priority date 8/21; no closing date. Applicants notified on rolling basis.

Contact. Lynn Roth, Financial Aid Coordinator
Mall of America West 112 West Market
Bloomington, MN 55425

Normandale Community College

Bloomington, Minnesota
www.normandale.mnscu.edu
Two-year public **Federal Code: 007954**

College costs. Various reciprocity agreements with some neighboring states provide tuition reduction to out-of-state students.

	Living at home
Tuition and fees (2002-2003):	$3,235
Out-of-state:	$6,047
Per-credit charge:	$94
Per-credit out-of-state:	$189
Books and supplies:	$400
Personal expenses:	$2,000
Transportation:	$1,350

Undergraduate aid. Need-based: Average financial aid package for full-time students was $7,000. 43% awarded as scholarships/grants, 57% as loans/jobs. Need-based aid available for part-time students. **Non-need-based:** 9% awarded as scholarships/grants, 91% as loans/jobs.

Freshman aid. Need-based: Average package met 85% of need.

Policies to reduce costs. Tuition/fee waivers for senior citizens, employees and their families. Credit/placement for qualifying scores on AP, IB, CLEP examinations. Work study available nights and for part-time students.

Payment plans. Credit card, installment, deferred payment.

Application procedures. FAFSA required. Priority date 5/15; no closing date. Applicants notified on rolling basis starting 4/15.

Contact. **Financial aid office:** (952) 487-8202
Catherine Breuer, Director of Financial Aid
9700 France Avenue South
Bloomington, MN 55431

North Central University

Minneapolis, Minnesota
www.northcentral.edu
Four-year private **Federal Code: 002369**

	Living at home	On-campus
Tuition and fees:	$10,594	$10,594
Room and board:		$4,400
Books and supplies:	$600	$600
Transportation:	$240	$240

Undergraduate aid. Need-based: Need-based aid available for full-time students. **Non-need-based:** Scholarships based on academics, music/drama.

Merit scholarships. Christian leadership scholarship; $6,000 per year; renewable up to 4 years; GPA 2.5 or above, ministry and community involvement.

Policies to reduce costs. Tuition/fee waivers for senior citizens, family of clergy, employees and their families. Prepayment discount; credit/placement for qualifying scores on AP, CLEP examinations.

Payment plans. Credit card, installment payment.

Application procedures. FAFSA, institutional form required. Priority date 4/1; closing date 5/1. Applicants notified on rolling basis starting 3/15, must reply within 2 week(s) of notification. **Transfers:** No deadline.

Contact. **Financial aid office:** (800) 289-4488
Donna Jager, Director of Financial Aid
910 Elliot Avenue
Minneapolis, MN 55404

North Hennepin Community College

Minneapolis, Minnesota
www.nh.cc.edu
Two-year public **Federal Code: 002370**

College costs. Various reciprocity agreements with some neighboring states provide tuition reduction to out-of-state students.

	Living at home
Tuition and fees (2002-2003):	$3,164
Out-of-state:	$5,490
Per-credit charge:	$91
Per-credit out-of-state:	$169
Books and supplies:	$639
Personal expenses:	$1,000
Transportation:	$1,500

Undergraduate aid. Non-need-based: Scholarships based on academics. **Additional information:** Computerized financial aid application.

Policies to reduce costs. Tuition/fee waivers for senior citizens, employees and their families. Credit/placement for qualifying scores on AP, CLEP examinations.

Payment plans. Credit card payment.

Application procedures. FAFSA, institutional form required. Priority date 5/15; no closing date. Applicants notified on rolling basis starting 6/1. **Transfers:** No deadline.

Contact. **Financial aid office:** (763) 424-0702
Dennis Stukenborg, Director of Financial Aid
7411 85th Avenue North
Minneapolis, MN 55445

Northland Community & Technical College

Thief River Falls, Minnesota
Two-year public
Federal Code: 002385

College costs. Various reciprocity agreements with some neighboring states.

	Living at home
Tuition and fees (2002-2003):	$3,138
Out-of-state:	$3,138
Per-credit charge:	$91
Per-credit out-of-state:	$91
Books and supplies:	$600
Personal expenses:	$1,350
Transportation:	$900

Undergraduate aid. Need-based: 48% awarded as scholarships/grants, 52% as loans/jobs. Need-based aid available for part-time students. **Non-need-based:** Scholarships based on academics.

Policies to reduce costs. Tuition/fee waivers for senior citizens, employees and their families. Credit/placement for qualifying scores on AP, CLEP examinations. Work study available nights.

Payment plans. Credit card, installment, deferred payment.

Application procedures. FAFSA required. Priority date 5/1; no closing date. Applicants notified on rolling basis starting 5/15. **Transfers:** Priority date 5/1; no deadline.

Contact. Donna Quam, Financial Aid Director
1101 Highway 1 East
Thief River Falls, MN 56701

Northwest Technical Institute

Eden Prairie, Minnesota
www.nw-ti.com
Two-year proprietary **Federal Code: 014044**

	Living at home
Tuition and fees:	$12,745
Per-credit charge:	$383
Per-credit out-of-state:	$383
Books and supplies:	$500
Personal expenses:	$2,234
Transportation:	$1,867

Undergraduate aid. Need-based: Average financial aid package for full-time students was $9,000. 25% awarded as scholarships/grants, 75% as loans/jobs.

Freshman aid. Need-based: Out of 37 full-time freshmen, 35 applied for aid; 35 were judged to have need; of these 35 received aid. Average package met 50% of need. Average scholarship/grant was $1,700; average loan $7,125.

Policies to reduce costs. Tuition at time of enrollment guaranteed for 2 years.

Payment plans. Installment payment.

Application procedures. FAFSA, institutional form required. No deadline. Applicants notified on rolling basis, must reply within 2 week(s) of notification. **Transfers:** No deadline.

Contact. **Financial aid office:** (952) 944-0080
Michael Kotchevar, Financial Aid Officer
11995 Singletree Lane
Eden Prairie, MN 55344-5351

Northwestern College

St. Paul, Minnesota
www.nwc.edu
Four-year private **Federal Code: 002371**

	Living at home	On-campus
Tuition and fees:	$17,400	$17,400
Room and board:		$5,620
Board only:	$500	
Books and supplies:	$500	$500
Personal expenses:	$1,250	$2,550
Transportation:	$1,500	$980

Undergraduate aid. Need-based: Average financial aid package for full-time students was $13,183; for part-time $8,543. 57% awarded as scholarships/grants, 43% as loans/jobs. **Non-need-based:** 62% awarded as scholarships/grants, 38% as loans/jobs. Scholarships based on academics, alumni affiliation, leadership, music/drama. **Student debt:** 72% of graduating class borrowed to fund education; average debt was $18,132.

Freshman aid. Need-based: Out of 401 full-time freshmen, 394 applied for aid; 332 were judged to have need; of these 331 received aid. Average package met 75% of need. 27 students had full need met. Average scholarship/grant was $9,800; average loan $3,422. **Non-need based:** 309 full-time freshmen with need received non-need scholarships; 62 without need received awards.

Merit scholarships. Eagle Scholars Program scholarships, $10,000 per year (renewable), 20 awards, for applicants meeting at least one of following criteria: National Merit finalist or semifinalist; minimum ACT composite score of 30 (or SAT equivalent); minimum 3.98 high school GPA; high school rank in top 2%.

Policies to reduce costs. Tuition/fee waivers for senior citizens, family members, family of clergy, employees and their families. Credit/placement for qualifying scores on AP, IB, CLEP examinations.

Payment plans. Credit card, installment payment.

Application procedures. FAFSA, institutional form required. Priority date 3/1; closing date 7/1. Applicants notified on rolling basis starting 3/1, must reply within 2 week(s) of notification.

Contact. **Financial aid office:** (651) 631-5212
Richard Blatchley, Director of Financial Aid
3003 Snelling Avenue North
St. Paul, MN 55113

Oak Hills Christian College

Bemidji, Minnesota
www.oakhills.edu
Four-year private **Federal Code: 016116**

	Living at home	On-campus
Tuition and fees (2002-2003):	$9,900	$9,900
Room and board:		$3,580
Board only:	$2,475	
Books and supplies:	$650	$650
Personal expenses:	$2,625	$2,625
Transportation:	$1,350	$1,050

Undergraduate aid. Need-based: Average financial aid package for full-time students was $8,481; for part-time $5,754. 69% awarded as scholarships/grants, 31% as loans/jobs. **Non-need-based:** Scholarships based on academics, alumni affiliation. **Student debt:** 83% of graduating class borrowed to fund education; average debt was $22,713.

Freshman aid. Need-based: Out of 33 full-time freshmen, 31 applied for aid; 30 were judged to have need; of these 30 received aid. Average package met 60% of need. 2 students had full need met. Average scholarship/grant was $5,007; average loan $2,209. **Non-need based:** 1 without need received awards.

Policies to reduce costs. Tuition/fee waivers for children of alumni, family members, employees and their families. Credit/placement for qualifying scores on AP, CLEP examinations. Work study available nights, weekends and for part-time students.

Payment plans. Installment payment.

Application procedures. FAFSA, institutional form required. No deadline. Applicants notified on rolling basis starting 1/3. **Transfers:** No deadline.

Contact. **Financial aid office:** (218) 751-8672 ext.1220
Dan Hovestol, Financial Aid Director
1600 Oak Hills Road, SW
Bemidji, MN 56601

Pine Technical College

Pine City, Minnesota
www.ptc.tec.mn.us
Two-year public **Federal Code: 005535**

College costs. Various reciprocity agreements with some neighboring states provide tuition reduction to out-of-state students.

	Living at home
Tuition and fees (2002-2003):	$3,122
Out-of-state:	$5,822
Per-credit charge:	$90
Per-credit out-of-state:	$180
Board only:	$4,500
Books and supplies:	$675
Personal expenses:	$600
Transportation:	$1,800

Undergraduate aid. Need-based: Need-based aid available for full-time and part-time students. **Non-need-based:** Scholarships based on academics, state/district residency.

Policies to reduce costs. Tuition/fee waivers for children of alumni, senior citizens, employees and their families. Work study available for part-time students.

Payment plans. Deferred payment.

Application procedures. FAFSA, institutional form required. No deadline. Applicants notified on rolling basis starting 6/1. **Transfers:** No deadline.

Contact. **Financial aid office:** (320) 629-5100
Susan Pixley, Financial Aid Director
900 Fourth Street SE
Pine City, MN 55063

Rainy River Community College

International Falls, Minnesota
www.rrcc.mnscu.edu
Two-year public **Federal Code: 006775**

College costs. Various reciprocity agreements with some nearby states.

	Living at home	On-campus
Tuition and fees (2002-2003):	$3,148	$3,148
Out-of-state:	$3,148	$3,148
Per-credit charge:	$88	$88
Per-credit out-of-state:	$88	$88
Room and board:		$3,440
Books and supplies:	$600	$600
Personal expenses:	$900	$1,200
Transportation:	$650	$650

Undergraduate aid. Need-based: Need-based aid available for full-time and part-time students. **Non-need-based:** Scholarships based on academics, alumni affiliation, minority status, state/district residency. **Additional information:** Many scholarship and employment opportunities for applicants showing little or no need.

Policies to reduce costs. Tuition/fee waivers for senior citizens, family members, unemployed or children of unemployed, employees and their families. Credit/placement for qualifying scores on AP, IB, CLEP examinations. Work study available nights, weekends and for part-time students.

Payment plans. Credit card, installment, deferred payment.

Application procedures. FAFSA, institutional form required. Priority date 6/1; no closing date. Applicants notified on rolling basis starting 5/1, must reply within 3 week(s) of notification. **Transfers:** Priority date 6/1; no deadline.

Contact. **Financial aid office:** (218) 285-7722
Scott Riley, Director of Financial Aid
1501 Highway 71
International Falls, MN 56649

Rasmussen College-Mankato

Mankato, Minnesota
www.rasmussen.edu
Two-year proprietary **Federal Code: 016845**

College costs. Some variation in cost depending on program.

	Living at home
Tuition and fees (projected):	$7,710
Per-credit charge:	$255
Books and supplies:	$450
Personal expenses:	$1,575
Transportation:	$900

Undergraduate aid. **Non-need-based:** Scholarships based on academics.

Policies to reduce costs. Tuition/fee waivers for employees and their families.

Payment plans. Credit card payment.

Application procedures. FAFSA, institutional form required. Priority date 2/1; no closing date. Applicants notified on rolling basis.

Contact. **Financial aid office:** (507) 625-6556
Toni Hobbs, Financial Aid Director
501 Holly Lane
Mankato, MN 56001

Rasmussen College-Minnetonka

Minnetonka, Minnesota
www.rasmussen.edu
Two-year proprietary **Federal Code: 011686**

College costs. Costs vary depending on program.

	Living at home
Tuition and fees:	$11,475
Per-credit charge:	$255

Undergraduate aid. **Need-based:** Need-based aid available for full-time and part-time students.

Policies to reduce costs. Tuition/fee waivers for family members, employees and their families. Tuition at time of enrollment guaranteed for 2 years.

Payment plans. Credit card, installment payment.

Application procedures. FAFSA, institutional form required. Priority date 6/1; no closing date. Applicants notified on rolling basis. **Transfers:** No deadline.

Contact. **Financial aid office:** (952) 545-2000
Dan Vega, Financial Aid Director
12450 Wayzata Boulevard
Minnetonka, MN 55305-9845

Rasmussen College-St. Cloud

St. Cloud, Minnesota
www.rasmussen.edu
Two-year proprietary **Federal Code: 008694**

	Living at home
Tuition and fees (projected):	$7,710
Per-credit charge:	$255
Board only:	$1,575
Books and supplies:	$900
Personal expenses:	$1,575
Transportation:	$1,800

Undergraduate aid. **Need-based:** 34% awarded as scholarships/grants, 66% as loans/jobs. Need-based aid available for part-time students. **Non-need-based:** Scholarships based on academics. **Student debt:** 64% of graduating class borrowed to fund education; average debt was $10,550.

Policies to reduce costs. Tuition/fee waivers for employees and their families. Work study available nights, weekends and for part-time students.

Payment plans. Credit card, installment payment.

Application procedures. FAFSA, institutional form required. No deadline. Applicants notified on rolling basis starting 1/1. **Transfers:** No deadline.

Contact. **Financial aid office:** (320) 251-5600
Carol Dockendorf, Financial Aid Officer
226 Park Avenue South
St Cloud, MN 56301-3713

Ridgewater College: A Community and Technical College

Willmar, Minnesota
www.ridgewater.mnscu.edu
Two-year public **Federal Code: 005252**

College costs. Various reciprocity agreements with some neighboring states provide tuition reduction to out-of-state students.

	Living at home
Tuition and fees (2002-2003):	$3,194
Out-of-state:	$5,931
Per-credit charge:	$91
Per-credit out-of-state:	$183
Board only:	$2,516
Books and supplies:	$650
Personal expenses:	$900
Transportation:	$1,800

Undergraduate aid. **Additional information:** Special funds (first 4 credits free) available for adult transfer students returning or continuing education after 7-year absence from academic training.

Policies to reduce costs. Tuition/fee waivers for adults, senior citizens, employees and their families. Credit/placement for qualifying scores on AP, CLEP examinations.

Payment plans. Credit card, deferred payment.

Application procedures. FAFSA, institutional form required. No deadline. Applicants notified on rolling basis.

Contact. **Financial aid office:** (320) 231-5102
Jim Rice, Director of Financial Aid
2101 15th Avenue NW
Willmar, MN 56201

Riverland Community College: A Technical and Community College

Austin, Minnesota
www.riverland.cc.mn.us
Two-year public **Federal Code: 002335**

College costs. Various reciprocity agreements with some neighboring states provide tuition reduction to out-of-state students.

	Living at home	On-campus
Tuition and fees (2002-2003):	$3,084	$3,084
Out-of-state:	$5,739	$5,739
Per-credit charge:	$89	$89
Per-credit out-of-state:	$177	$177
Room only:		$2,565
Books and supplies:	$650	$650
Personal expenses:	$1,800	
Transportation:	$1,800	

Undergraduate aid. All financial aid based on need. Need-based aid available for full-time and part-time students. **Student debt:** 37% of graduating class borrowed to fund education; average debt was $2,600. **Additional information:** One class tuition-free for Minnesota residents over 25 who have not attended college for at least 7 years.

Policies to reduce costs. Tuition/fee waivers for senior citizens, employees and their families. Credit/placement for qualifying scores on AP examinations. Work study available for part-time students.

Payment plans. Credit card, installment payment.

Application procedures. FAFSA required. Priority date 5/15; no closing date. Applicants notified on rolling basis, must reply within 5 week(s) of notification. **Transfers:** No deadline.

Contact. Financial aid office: (507) 433-0511
Judy Robeck, Financial Aid Director
1900 Eighth Avenue Northwest
Austin, MN 55912-1407

Rochester Community and Technical College

Rochester, Minnesota
www.roch.edu
Two-year public **Federal Code: 002373**

College costs. Various reciprocity agreements with some neighboring states provide tuition reduction to out-of-state students.

	Living at home
Tuition and fees (2002-2003):	$3,116
Out-of-state:	$5,760
Per-credit charge:	$88
Per-credit out-of-state:	$176
Personal expenses:	$1,860
Transportation:	$1,542

Policies to reduce costs. Tuition/fee waivers for senior citizens, employees and their families. Credit/placement for qualifying scores on AP, CLEP examinations.

Payment plans. Credit card payment.

Application procedures. FAFSA, institutional form required. No deadline.

Contact. Financial aid office: (507) 285-7210
Rosemary Hicks, Director of Financial Aid
851 30th Avenue SE
Rochester, MN 55904-4999

St. Cloud State University

St. Cloud, Minnesota
www.stcloudstate.edu
Four-year public **Federal Code: 002377**

College costs. Various reciprocity agreements with some nearby states provide tuition reduction to out-of-state students.

	Living at home	On-campus
Tuition and fees (2002-2003):	$3,998	$3,998
Out-of-state:	$8,049	$8,049
Room and board:		$3,788
Board only:	$1,494	
Books and supplies:	$655	$655
Personal expenses:	$1,300	$1,300
Transportation:	$750	

Undergraduate aid. Additional information: State loan program for students who do not qualify for other programs or who need additional aid.

Merit scholarships. Foundation scholarships; $1,000 per year; to applicants in top 10% of class; awards made in order applications received. Special Merit Scholarships; $8,800 per year covering all tuition, fees room and board, other expenses; to National Merit Finalists who name SCSU as 1st choice school. Richard Green Scholarships; $1,000 per year; to new students who contribute to cultural diversity of SCSU. Applicants should rank in top 25% of class, test scores, curriculum, activities, community service considered. Variety of endowed scholarships; $250-1,500; top 25% of class.

Policies to reduce costs. Tuition/fee waivers for senior citizens, employees and their families. Credit/placement for qualifying scores on AP, IB, CLEP examinations.

Application procedures. FAFSA, institutional form required. Priority date 5/1; no closing date. Applicants notified on rolling basis starting 6/15. **Transfers:** No deadline.

Contact. Financial aid office: (320) 255-2244
Frank Loncorich, Financial Aid Director
720 Fourth Avenue South
St. Cloud, MN 56301-4498

St. Cloud Technical College

St. Cloud, Minnesota
sctc.edu
Two-year public **Federal Code: 005534**

College costs. Various reciprocity agreements with some neighboring states provide tuition reduction to out-of-state students.

	Living at home
Tuition and fees (2002-2003):	$2,878
Out-of-state:	$5,540
Per-credit charge:	$89
Per-credit out-of-state:	$178
Board only:	$1,003
Books and supplies:	$900
Personal expenses:	$1,200
Transportation:	$600

Undergraduate aid. Need-based: 51% awarded as scholarships/grants, 49% as loans/jobs. Need-based aid available for part-time students. **Non-need-based:** 6% awarded as scholarships/grants, 94% as loans/jobs. Scholarships based on academics, leadership.

Policies to reduce costs. Tuition/fee waivers for senior citizens, employees and their families. Work study available nights, weekends and for part-time students.

Payment plans. Credit card payment.

Application procedures. FAFSA, institutional form required. Priority date 5/15; no closing date. Applicants notified on rolling basis starting 6/1. **Transfers:** No deadline.

Contact. Financial aid office: (320) 654-5961
Anita Baugh, Financial Aid Director
1540 Northway Drive
St. Cloud, MN 56303

St. John's University

Collegeville, Minnesota
www.csbsju.edu
Four-year private **Federal Code: 002379**

	Living at home	On-campus
Tuition and fees (2002-2003):	$19,226	$19,226
Room and board:		$5,852
Board only:	$1,500	
Books and supplies:	$600	$600
Personal expenses:	$700	$700
Transportation:	$200	$200

Undergraduate aid. Need-based: Average financial aid package for full-time students was $16,895. 59% awarded as scholarships/grants, 41% as loans/jobs. **Non-need-based:** 76% awarded as scholarships/grants, 24% as loans/jobs. Scholarships based on academics, art, leadership, music/drama. **Student debt:** 68% of graduating class borrowed to fund education; average debt was $20,680.

Freshman aid. Need-based: Out of 467 full-time freshmen, 454 applied for aid; 299 were judged to have need; of these 299 received aid. Average package met 96% of need. 219 students had full need met. Average scholarship/grant was $11,669; average loan $3,748. **Non-need based:** 238 full-time freshmen with need received non-need scholarships; 131 without need received awards.

Merit scholarships. Regents/Trustees Scholarship: $10,000; minimum GPA of 3.6 and minimum ACT composite score 30 or minimum SAT combined score of 1320. Demonstrated leadership and service. Faculty interview. President's Scholarships: $5,500-$8,000; GPA, high school rank, ACT/SAT scores; leadership and service. Dean's Scholarships: $2,000-$5,000; GPA, high school rank, ACT/SAT scores; leadership and service. Art: up to $2,000; Music: up to $2,000; Theater: up to $2,000; all based on excellence in subject area. Art requires review; Music requires review and audition; Theater requires interview.

Policies to reduce costs. Prepayment discount; credit/placement for qualifying scores on AP, IB, CLEP examinations.

Payment plans. Installment payment.

Application procedures. FAFSA, institutional form required. Priority date 3/15; no closing date. Applicants notified on rolling basis starting 3/1, must reply within 3 week(s) of notification.

Contact. **Financial aid office:** (320) 363-2189
Stuart Perry, Director of Financial Aid
Box 7155
Collegeville, MN 56321-7155

St. Mary's University of Minnesota

Winona, Minnesota
www.smumn.edu
Four-year private **Federal Code: 002380**

	Living at home	On-campus
Tuition and fees (2002-2003):	$15,675	$15,675
Room and board:		$4,940
Books and supplies:	$650	$650
Personal expenses:	$845	$845
Transportation:	$130	$130

Undergraduate aid. **Need-based:** Average financial aid package for full-time students was $14,588. 55% awarded as scholarships/grants, 45% as loans/jobs. Need-based aid available for part-time students. **Non-need-based:** Scholarships based on academics, art, leadership, music/drama.

Freshman aid. **Need-based:** Out of 396 full-time freshmen, 299 applied for aid; 246 were judged to have need; of these 246 received aid. Average package met 79% of need. 185 students had full need met. Average scholarship/grant was $8,700; average loan $3,734. **Non-need based:** 81 without need received awards.

Policies to reduce costs. Tuition/fee waivers for family of clergy, employees and their families. Credit/placement for qualifying scores on AP, IB, CLEP examinations. Work study available nights and weekends.

Payment plans. Credit card, installment payment.

Application procedures. FAFSA, institutional form required. Priority date 3/15; no closing date. Applicants notified on rolling basis starting 3/1, must reply within 3 week(s) of notification.

Contact. **Financial aid office:** (507) 457-1437
Jayne Wobig, Director of Financial Aid
700 Terrace Heights, #2
Winona, MN 55987-1399

St. Olaf College

Northfield, Minnesota
www.stolaf.edu
Four-year private **Federal Code: 002382**

	Living at home	On-campus
Tuition and fees (projected):	$23,650	$23,650
Room and board:		$4,850
Board only:	$2,600	
Books and supplies:	$850	$850
Personal expenses:	$700	$700

Undergraduate aid. **Need-based:** Average financial aid package for full-time students was $16,873. 71% awarded as scholarships/grants, 29% as loans/jobs. **Non-need-based:** 51% awarded as scholarships/grants, 49% as loans/jobs. Scholarships based on academics. **Student debt:** 64% of graduating class borrowed to fund education; average debt was $18,806. **Additional information:** Limited number of music lesson fee waivers available for music majors, awarded on audition basis only.

Freshman aid. **Need-based:** Out of 779 full-time freshmen, 692 applied for aid; 468 were judged to have need; of these 468 received aid. Average package met 100% of need. 468 students had full need met. Average scholarship/grant was $12,210; average loan $3,680. **Non-need based:** 212 full-time freshmen with need received non-need scholarships; 183 without need received awards.

Merit scholarships. All are 4-year renewable; number varies per year. Buntrock Academic Awards: $4,000-$9,000; St. Olaf Scholarships: $500-$12,000; National Merit Scholarships: $7,500; Winston Cassler Music Scholarships: $470-$3,500; National Merit Commended Scholarships: $1,500; Awards for leadership in Community and Church: $3,000; TRIO Scholarships: $5,000

Policies to reduce costs. Tuition/fee waivers for adults, senior citizens, employees and their families. Prepayment discount; credit/placement for qualifying scores on AP, IB examinations. Work study available nights and weekends.

Payment plans. Installment payment.

Application procedures. FAFSA, CSS PROFILE required. Priority date 2/15; no closing date. Applicants notified on rolling basis starting 3/1, must reply by 5/1 or within 2 week(s) of notification. Early decision closing date 11/15. **Transfers:** No deadline.

Contact. **Financial aid office:** (507) 646-2222
Katharine Ruby, Director of Financial Aid
1520 St. Olaf Avenue
Northfield, MN 55057-1098

St. Paul College - A Community and Technical College

St. Paul, Minnesota
www.saintpaul.edu
Two-year public **Federal Code: 005533**

College costs. Various reciprocity agreements with some neighboring states provide tuition reduction to out-of-state students.

	Living at home
Tuition and fees (2002-2003):	$2,816
Out-of-state:	$5,396
Per-credit charge:	$86
Per-credit out-of-state:	$172
Books and supplies:	$700
Personal expenses:	$1,485
Transportation:	$450

Undergraduate aid. **Need-based:** 66% awarded as scholarships/grants, 34% as loans/jobs. Need-based aid available for part-time students. **Non-need-based:** 3% awarded as scholarships/grants, 97% as loans/jobs. Scholarships based on leadership.

Policies to reduce costs. Tuition/fee waivers for senior citizens, employees and their families. Credit/placement for qualifying scores on IB examinations. Work study available nights and for part-time students.

Payment plans. Credit card, installment payment.

Application procedures. FAFSA, institutional form required. No deadline. Applicants notified on rolling basis starting 6/1. **Transfers:** No deadline.

Contact. **Financial aid office:** (651) 846-1386
Susan Prater, Financial Aid Director
235 Marshall Avenue
St. Paul, MN 55102-1800

South Central Technical College

North Mankato, Minnesota
www.sctc.mnscu.edu
Two-year public **Federal Code: 009891**

College costs. Various reciprocity agreements with some neighboring states provide tuition reduction to out-of-state students.

	Living at home
Tuition and fees (2002-2003):	$2,837
Out-of-state:	$5,334
Per-credit charge:	$83
Per-credit out-of-state:	$167
Books and supplies:	$650
Personal expenses:	$1,050

Undergraduate aid. **Need-based:** Need-based aid available for full-time and part-time students.

Policies to reduce costs. Tuition/fee waivers for senior citizens.

Application procedures. FAFSA, institutional form required. No deadline. Applicants notified on rolling basis.

Contact. **Financial aid office:** (507) 389-7200
Jayne Dinse, Financial Aid Director
1920 Lee Boulevard
North Mankato, MN 56003

Southwest State University

Marshall, Minnesota
www.southwest.msus.edu
Four-year public **Federal Code: 002375**

College costs. Various reciprocity agreements with nearby states to reduce cost of out-of-state tuition.

	Living at home	On-campus
Tuition and fees (2002-2003):	$4,092	$4,092
Room and board:		$4,368
Books and supplies:	$800	$800
Personal expenses:	$1,800	$1,000
Transportation:	$200	$200

Undergraduate aid. Need-based: Average financial aid package for full-time students was $5,757; for part-time $3,497. 34% awarded as scholarships/grants, 66% as loans/jobs. **Non-need-based:** 40% awarded as scholarships/grants, 60% as loans/jobs. Scholarships based on academics, art, athletics, leadership, minority status, music/drama, state/district residency.

Freshman aid. Need-based: Out of 530 full-time freshmen, 517 applied for aid; 489 were judged to have need; of these 489 received aid. Average package met 73% of need. 309 students had full need met. Average scholarship/grant was $2,907; average loan $2,278. **Non-need based:** 275 full-time freshmen with need received non-need scholarships; 55 without need received awards; 52 received athletic scholarships.

Policies to reduce costs. Tuition/fee waivers for senior citizens, employees and their families. Credit/placement for qualifying scores on CLEP examinations.

Payment plans. Installment, deferred payment.

Application procedures. FAFSA, institutional form required. Priority date 4/1; no closing date. Applicants notified on rolling basis starting 5/15. **Transfers:** Priority date 4/1; no deadline.

Contact. Financial aid office: (507) 537-7021
Scott Crowell, Director of Financial Aid
1501 State Street
Marshall, MN 56258-1598

University of Minnesota: Crookston

Crookston, Minnesota
www.crk.umn.edu
Four-year public **Federal Code: 004069**

	Living at home	On-campus
Tuition and fees (2002-2003):	$6,098	$6,098
Room and board:		$4,510
Books and supplies:	$565	$565
Personal expenses:	$800	$800
Transportation:	$400	$400

Undergraduate aid. Need-based: Average financial aid package for full-time students was $8,524; for part-time $5,233. 44% awarded as scholarships/grants, 56% as loans/jobs. **Non-need-based:** 30% awarded as scholarships/grants, 70% as loans/jobs. Scholarships based on academics, leadership, minority status.

Freshman aid. Need-based: Out of 264 full-time freshmen, 218 applied for aid; 174 were judged to have need; of these 172 received aid. Average package met 84% of need. 90 students had full need met. Average scholarship/grant was $5,154; average loan $5,064. **Non-need based:** 69 full-time freshmen with need received non-need scholarships; 58 without need received awards.

Policies to reduce costs. Tuition/fee waivers for adults, senior citizens, minority students, employees and their families. Credit/placement for qualifying scores on AP examinations.

Payment plans. Installment payment.

Application procedures. FAFSA required. Priority date 3/31; no closing date. Applicants notified on rolling basis starting 3/1, must reply within 3 week(s) of notification.

Contact. Financial aid office: (218) 281-8569
Heidi Patterson, Director of Financial Aid
2900 University Avenue, 170 Owen Hall
Crookston, MN 56716

University of Minnesota: Duluth

Duluth, Minnesota
www.d.umn.edu
Four-year public **Federal Code: 002388**

College costs. Course fees vary per program.

	Living at home	On-campus
Tuition and fees (2002-2003):	$6,259	$6,259
Out-of-state:	$16,517	$16,517
Room and board:		$4,960
Books and supplies:	$882	$882
Personal expenses:	$1,600	$1,600
Transportation:	$706	$706

Undergraduate aid. Need-based: Average financial aid package for full-time students was $7,371; for part-time $5,925. 38% awarded as scholarships/grants, 62% as loans/jobs. **Non-need-based:** 38% awarded as scholarships/grants, 62% as loans/jobs. Scholarships based on academics, athletics. **Student debt:** 65% of graduating class borrowed to fund education; average debt was $15,866.

Freshman aid. Need-based: Average package met 70% of need. Average scholarship/grant was $4,619; average loan $2,957.

Policies to reduce costs. Tuition/fee waivers for senior citizens, employees and their families. Credit/placement for qualifying scores on AP, IB, CLEP examinations. Work study available nights, weekends and for part-time students.

Payment plans. Installment payment.

Application procedures. FAFSA required. Priority date 3/31; no closing date. Applicants notified on rolling basis starting 3/1, must reply within 2 week(s) of notification. **Transfers:** Priority date 3/31.

Contact. Financial aid office: (218) 726-8000
Brenda Herzig, Director of Financial Aid
23 Solon Campus Center, 1117 University Drive
Duluth, MN 55812-2496

University of Minnesota: Morris

Morris, Minnesota
www.mrs.umn.edu
Four-year public **Federal Code: 002389**

	Living at home	On-campus
Tuition and fees (2002-2003):	$7,154	$7,154
Out-of-state:	$13,535	$13,535
Room and board:		$4,580
Books and supplies:	$600	$600
Personal expenses:	$1,200	$1,200
Transportation:	$500	$500

Undergraduate aid. Need-based: Need-based aid available for full-time and part-time students. **Non-need-based:** Scholarships based on academics, state/district residency. **Additional information:** Land-grant program waiving tuition for Native Americans.

Merit scholarships. Chancellor Scholarship; $2,000 (renewable for 4 years); top 5% of high school class. Deans Scholarship; $1,500 (renewable for 4 years); top 10% of high school class. Founders Scholarship; $500 (renewable for 4 years); top 20% of high school class. Transfer Academic Scholarships; $2,000 for students with a cumulative GPA 3.75 or higher; $1,000 for transfer students with a cumulative GPA of at least 3.5. Presidential Scholarship supplements Freshman Automatic Academic Scholarship for outstanding students. National Merit Scholarship Commended for "commended" status; $1,000 (renewable for 4 years).

Policies to reduce costs. Tuition/fee waivers for minority students. Tuition at time of enrollment guaranteed for 4 years; credit/placement for qualifying scores on AP, IB, CLEP examinations.

Payment plans. Installment payment.

Application procedures. FAFSA, institutional form required. Priority date 4/1; no closing date. Applicants notified on rolling basis starting 4/15, must reply within 3 week(s) of notification. **Transfers:** Priority date 4/1; closing date 5/1.

Contact. Financial aid office: (800) 992-8863
Pam Engebretson, Director of Financial Aid
600 East 4th Street
Morris, MN 56267

University of Minnesota: Twin Cities

Minneapolis, Minnesota
www.umn.edu/tc
Four-year public **Federal Code: 003969**

	Living at home	On-campus
Tuition and fees (2002-2003):	$6,280	$6,280
Out-of-state:	$16,853	$16,853
Room and board:		$5,696
Books and supplies:	$730	$730
Personal expenses:	$2,392	$2,392
Transportation:	$750	

Undergraduate aid. Need-based: Average financial aid package for full-time students was $8,496; for part-time $6,266. 47% awarded as scholarships/grants, 53% as loans/jobs. **Non-need-based:** 41% awarded as scholarships/grants, 59% as loans/jobs. Scholarships based on academics, art, athletics, leadership, minority status, music/drama, religious affiliation, state/district residency.

Freshman aid. Need-based: Out of 5,162 full-time freshmen, 3,671 applied for aid; 2,511 were judged to have need; of these 2,452 received aid. Average package met 84% of need. 1166 students had full need met. Average scholarship/grant was $6,346; average loan $3,874. **Non-need based:** 348 full-time freshmen with need received non-need scholarships; 741 without need received awards.

Merit scholarships. A variety of merit-based scholarships offered including scholarships specifically for Minnesota residents and for non-residents.

Policies to reduce costs. Tuition/fee waivers for employees and their families. Credit/placement for qualifying scores on AP, IB, CLEP examinations. Work study available nights, weekends and for part-time students.

Payment plans. Installment, deferred payment.

Application procedures. FAFSA required. Priority date 1/15; no closing date. Applicants notified on rolling basis starting 2/15. **Transfers:** No deadline.

Contact. Financial aid office: (612) 624-1665
Kris Wright, Director of Financial Aid
240 Williamson Hall, 231 Pillsbury Drive SE
Minneapolis, MN 55455-0115

University of St. Thomas

St. Paul, Minnesota
www.stthomas.edu
Four-year private **Federal Code: 002345**

	Living at home	On-campus
Tuition and fees:	$20,608	$20,608
Room and board:		$6,310

Undergraduate aid. Need-based: Average financial aid package for full-time students was $15,313; for part-time $8,250. 58% awarded as scholarships/grants, 42% as loans/jobs. **Non-need-based:** 51% awarded as scholarships/grants, 49% as loans/jobs. Scholarships based on academics, music/drama. **Student debt:** 67% of graduating class borrowed to fund education; average debt was $22,073.

Freshman aid. Need-based: Out of 1,099 full-time freshmen, 814 applied for aid; 597 were judged to have need; of these 596 received aid. Average package met 87% of need. 161 students had full need met. Average scholarship/grant was $9,291; average loan $3,067. **Non-need based:** 75 full-time freshmen with need received non-need scholarships; 211 without need received awards.

Policies to reduce costs. Tuition/fee waivers for senior citizens, family members, employees and their families. Credit/placement for qualifying scores on AP, IB, CLEP examinations. Work study available nights, weekends and for part-time students.

Payment plans. Credit card, installment, deferred payment.

Application procedures. FAFSA required. Priority date 4/1; no closing date. Applicants notified on rolling basis starting 3/1, must reply within 3 week(s) of notification. **Transfers:** Recognition scholarship available for Minnesota community college transfer students.

Contact. Financial aid office: (651) 962-6550
Kris Getting, Director of Enrollment
2115 Summit Avenue, 32F-1
St. Paul, MN 55455-0115

Vermilion Community College

Ely, Minnesota
www.vcc.mnscu.edu
Two-year public **Federal Code: 002350**

College costs. Various reciprocity agreements with some neighboring states provide tuition reduction to out-of-state students.

	Living at home	On-campus
Tuition and fees (2002-2003):	$3,171	$3,171
Out-of-state:	$5,872	$5,872
Per-credit charge:	$90	$90
Per-credit out-of-state:	$180	$180
Room and board:		$4,380
Books and supplies:	$600	$600
Personal expenses:	$1,500	$1,500
Transportation:	$200	$365

Undergraduate aid. Need-based: Average financial aid package for full-time students was $4,625. 33% awarded as scholarships/grants, 67% as loans/jobs. Need-based aid available for part-time students. **Non-need-based:** Scholarships based on academics. **Student debt:** 80% of graduating class borrowed to fund education; average debt was $10,625.

Freshman aid. Need-based: Average loan $2,625.

Merit scholarships. Academic Excellence Scholarship

Policies to reduce costs. Tuition/fee waivers for children of alumni, senior citizens. Credit/placement for qualifying scores on AP examinations. Work study available nights and weekends.

Payment plans. Credit card, installment, deferred payment.

Application procedures. FAFSA, institutional form required. No deadline. Applicants notified on rolling basis starting 4/1.

Contact. Financial aid office: (218) 365-7200
Peter Wielinski, Financial Aid Director
1900 East Camp Street
Ely, MN 55731-9989

Winona State University

Winona, Minnesota
www.winona.edu
Four-year public **Federal Code: 002394**

College costs. Laptop computer leasing and support: $1,000.

	Living at home	On-campus
Tuition and fees (2002-2003):	$4,261	$4,261
Out-of-state:	$8,141	$8,141
Room and board:		$4,180
Books and supplies:	$500	$500
Personal expenses:	$600	$600
Transportation:	$300	$300

Undergraduate aid. Need-based: Average financial aid package for full-time students was $5,406. 41% awarded as scholarships/grants, 59% as loans/jobs. Need-based aid available for part-time students. **Non-need-based:** 16% awarded as scholarships/grants, 84% as loans/jobs. Scholarships based on academics, alumni affiliation, art, athletics, leadership, minority status, music/drama. **Student debt:** 85% of graduating class borrowed to fund education; average debt was $10,762.

Freshman aid. Need-based: Average package met 60% of need. Average scholarship/grant was $2,812; average loan $2,376.

Merit scholarships. Outstanding Academics Honors Award; $2,500; renewable, top 5% of class, ACT 32 or above. WSU Foundation Board Scholarship; $2,000 renewable; top 15% of class, ACT 28-31, essay/interview. Presidential Honor Scholarships; $1,500 renewable; top 15% of class, ACT 28-31; $1,000 renewable; top 10% of class, ACT 27; $750 renewable; top 15% of class, ACT 26. Resident Tuition Scholarships; $3,400 renewable; to out-of-state students; top 15% of class or ACT 25.

Policies to reduce costs. Tuition/fee waivers for senior citizens, employees and their families. Credit/placement for qualifying scores on AP, IB, CLEP examinations. Work study available nights, weekends and for part-time students.

Application procedures. FAFSA required. Priority date 3/1; no closing date. Applicants notified on rolling basis starting 3/1, must reply within 2 week(s) of notification. **Transfers:** No deadline.

Contact. Financial aid office: (800) 342-5978
Greg Peterson, Director of Financial Aid
Office of Admissions
Winona, MN 55987

Mississippi

Alcorn State University

Alcorn State, Mississippi
www.alcorn.edu
Four-year public **Federal Code: 002396**

	Living at home	On-campus
Tuition and fees (2002-2003):	$3,459	$3,459
Out-of-state:	$7,965	$7,965
Room and board:		$3,538
Board only:	$1,333	
Books and supplies:	$1,000	$1,000
Personal expenses:	$1,711	$1,500
Transportation:	$2,396	$1,500

Undergraduate aid. Need-based: Average financial aid package for full-time students was $9,500; for part-time $1,700. 47% awarded as scholarships/grants, 53% as loans/jobs. **Non-need-based:** 61% awarded as scholarships/grants, 39% as loans/jobs. Scholarships based on academics, athletics. **Student debt:** 67% of graduating class borrowed to fund education; average debt was $7,500.

Freshman aid. Need-based: Average package met 69% of need. Average scholarship/grant was $4,200; average loan $2,625.

Policies to reduce costs. Tuition/fee waivers for employees and their families. Credit/placement for qualifying scores on AP, CLEP examinations. Work study available nights and for part-time students.

Payment plans. Credit card payment.

Application procedures. FAFSA, institutional form required. Priority date 4/1; no closing date. Applicants notified on rolling basis starting 4/1, must reply within 4 week(s) of notification.

Contact. Financial aid office: (601) 877-6190
Juanita Russell, Director of Financial Aid
1000 ASU Drive #300
Alcorn State, MS 39096

Antonelli College: Hattiesburg

Hattiesburg, Mississippi
www.antonellic.com
Two-year proprietary **Federal Code: 012891**

College costs (2002-2003). Total cost of tuition for 2-year associate degree program in medical assisting $16,400, additional required fees $600, part-time per credit hour charge $175; for 2-year associate degree program in graphic design $19,960, additional required fees $965, part-time per credit hour charge $210; for 2-year associate degree program in health information technology $17,040, additional required fees $600, part-time per credit hour charge $180. Books/supplies: $900.

Contact. Financial aid office: (601) 583-4100
1500 North 31st Avenue
Hattiesburg, MS 39401

Antonelli College: Jackson

Jackson, Mississippi
www.antonellic.com
Two-year proprietary **Federal Code: 012891**

College costs (2002-2003). Total cost of tuition for 2-year associate degree program in medical assisting $16,400, additional required fees $600, part-time per credit hour charge $175; for 2-year associate degree program in graphic design $19,960, additional required fees $965, part-time per credit hour charge $210; for 2-year associate degree program in health information technology $17,040, additional required fees $600, part-time per credit hour charge $180. Books/supplies: $900.

Contact. Financial aid office: (601) 362-9991
Barbara Warren, Director of Financial Aid
2323 Lakeland Drive
Jackson, MS 39232

Blue Mountain College

Blue Mountain, Mississippi
www.bmc.edu
Four-year private **Federal Code: 002398**

	Living at home	On-campus
Tuition and fees (2002-2003):	$6,870	$6,870
Room and board:		$3,120
Board only:	$920	
Books and supplies:	$550	$550
Personal expenses:	$981	$792
Transportation:	$3,422	$552

Undergraduate aid. Need-based: 39% awarded as scholarships/grants, 61% as loans/jobs. Need-based aid available for part-time students. **Non-need-based:** 75% awarded as scholarships/grants, 25% as loans/jobs. Scholarships based on academics, athletics, state/district residency. **Student debt:** 46% of graduating class borrowed to fund education; average debt was $10,000.

Freshman aid. Need-based: Out of 50 full-time freshmen, 49 applied for aid; 43 were judged to have need; of these 43 received aid. Average package met 20% of need. 6 students had full need met. Average scholarship/grant was $2,428; average loan $2,326. **Non-need based:** 32 full-time freshmen with need received non-need scholarships; 6 without need received awards; 3 received athletic scholarships.

Policies to reduce costs. Tuition/fee waivers for family members, employees and their families. Credit/placement for qualifying scores on AP, CLEP examinations.

Payment plans. Credit card, installment, deferred payment.

Application procedures. FAFSA required. Priority date 6/1; closing date 8/1. Applicants notified on rolling basis starting 5/1, must reply within 2 week(s) of notification. **Transfers:** Priority date 6/1; no deadline.

Contact. Financial aid office: (662) 685-4771 ext. 141
Brenda Paganelli, Financial Aid Director
PO Box 160
Blue Mountain, MS 38610-0160

Coahoma Community College

Clarksdale, Mississippi
www.ccc.cc.ms.us
Two-year public **Federal Code: 002401**

College costs. Out of state students pay surcharge.

	Living at home	On-campus
Tuition and fees:	$1,600	$1,600
Out-of-state:	$2,100	$2,100
Per-credit charge:	$80	$80
Room and board:		$2,900
Board only:	$3,600	
Books and supplies:	$800	$800
Personal expenses:	$700	$700
Transportation:	$400	$400

Undergraduate aid. All financial aid based on need. Need-based aid available for full-time and part-time students.

Policies to reduce costs. Tuition/fee waivers for employees and their families.

Payment plans. Installment, deferred payment.

Application procedures. FAFSA, institutional form required. Priority date 4/1; no closing date. Applicants notified on rolling basis starting 7/1.

Contact. Financial aid office: (662) 627-2571
Patricia Brooks, Director of Financial Aid
3240 Friars Point Road
Clarksdale, MS 38614-9799

Delta State University

Cleveland, Mississippi
www.deltastate.edu
Four-year public **Federal Code: 002403**

	Living at home	On-campus
Tuition and fees (2002-2003):	$3,348	$3,348
Out-of-state:	$7,965	$7,965
Room and board:		$3,180
Books and supplies:	$500	$500

Undergraduate aid. Need-based: 38% awarded as scholarships/grants, 62% as loans/jobs. Need-based aid available for part-time students. **Non-need-based:** 68% awarded as scholarships/grants, 32% as loans/jobs. Scholarships based on academics, alumni affiliation, art, athletics, leadership, music/drama, religious affiliation, state/district residency.

Policies to reduce costs. Tuition/fee waivers for children of alumni, senior citizens, employees and their families. Credit/placement for qualifying scores on AP, CLEP examinations. Work study available nights and weekends.

Payment plans. Credit card, installment payment.

Application procedures. FAFSA, institutional form required. Priority date 4/1; no closing date. Applicants notified on rolling basis starting 5/1, must reply within 2 week(s) of notification.

Contact. Financial aid office: (662) 846-4670
Ann Mullins, Director of Student Financial Assistance
Highway 8 West
Cleveland, MS 38733

Holmes Community College

Goodman, Mississippi
www.holmes.cc.ms.us
Two-year public **Federal Code: 002408**

	Living at home	On-campus
Tuition and fees (2002-2003):	$1,430	$1,430
Out-of-state:	$2,930	$2,930
Per-credit charge:	$65	$65
Per-credit out-of-state:	$65	$65
Room and board:		$1,750
Books and supplies:	$600	$600
Personal expenses:	$1,600	$1,600
Transportation:	$600	$600

Undergraduate aid. Non-need-based: Scholarships based on academics, athletics.

Merit scholarships. President's Scholarship for full-time students provides full tuition, requires ACT of 20 or higher; Board of Trustees Scholarship for full-time students provides tuition, room and board, requires ACT of 28 or higher.

Policies to reduce costs. Tuition/fee waivers for senior citizens, family members, employees and their families. Credit/placement for qualifying scores on AP, CLEP examinations.

Payment plans. Credit card, installment payment.

Application procedures. FAFSA, institutional form required. Priority date 6/1; no closing date. Applicants notified on rolling basis.

Contact. Financial aid office: (662) 472-2312
Wirt Hayes, Director of Financial Aid
Box 369
Goodman, MS 39079

Itawamba Community College

Fulton, Mississippi
www.icc.cc.ms.us
Two-year public **Federal Code: 002409**

	Living at home	On-campus
Tuition and fees:	$1,270	$1,270
Out-of-state:	$3,020	$3,020
Per-credit charge:	$65	$65
Per-credit out-of-state:	$65	$65
Room and board:		$1,990
Board only:	$750	
Books and supplies:	$900	$900
Personal expenses:		$180
Transportation:	$1,740	$710

Undergraduate aid. Need-based: 74% awarded as scholarships/grants, 26% as loans/jobs. Need-based aid available for part-time students. **Non-need-based:** 69% awarded as scholarships/grants, 31% as loans/jobs. Scholarships based on academics, art, athletics, leadership, music/drama, state/district residency.

Policies to reduce costs. Tuition/fee waivers for senior citizens, employees and their families. Credit/placement for qualifying scores on AP, CLEP examinations. Work study available for part-time students.

Payment plans. Credit card, installment, deferred payment.

Application procedures. FAFSA, institutional form required. Priority date 4/30; no closing date. Applicants notified on rolling basis starting 4/15.

Contact. Financial aid office: (662) 862-8222
Bobby Walker, Director of Financial Aid
602 West Hill Street
Fulton, MS 38843

Magnolia Bible College

Kosciusko, Mississippi
Four-year private
Federal Code: 016788

	Living at home	On-campus
Tuition and fees (projected):	$4,590	$4,590
Room and board:		$1,120
Books and supplies:	$400	$400
Personal expenses:	$1,000	$1,000
Transportation:	$750	$400

Undergraduate aid. Need-based: 85% awarded as scholarships/grants, 15% as loans/jobs. Need-based aid available for part-time students. **Non-need-based:** 89% awarded as scholarships/grants, 11% as loans/jobs. Scholarships based on academics, leadership, religious affiliation.

Freshman aid. Need-based: Out of 4 full-time freshmen, 4 applied for aid; 1 were judged to have need; of these 1 received aid. Average package met 70% of need. Average scholarship/grant was $4,665. **Non-need based:** 3 full-time freshmen with need received non-need scholarships; 3 without need received awards.

Policies to reduce costs. Tuition/fee waivers for family members, employees and their families. Credit/placement for qualifying scores on AP, CLEP examinations.

Payment plans. Credit card, installment, deferred payment.

Application procedures. FAFSA, institutional form required. Priority date 8/1; no closing date. Applicants notified on rolling basis starting 4/15, must reply within 4 week(s) of notification.

Contact. Financial aid office: (662) 289-3658
Sharon Paseur, Financial Aid Officer
PO Box 1109
Kosciusko, MS 39090

Mary Holmes College

West Point, Mississippi
www.maryholmes.edu
Two-year private **Federal Code: 002412**

	Living at home	On-campus
Tuition and fees:	$4,225	$4,225
Per-credit charge:	$141	$141
Room and board:		$3,890
Books and supplies:	$400	$400
Personal expenses:	$500	$700
Transportation:	$1,500	$500

Undergraduate aid. Need-based: Need-based aid available for full-time students.

Policies to reduce costs. Tuition/fee waivers for employees and their families. Credit/placement for qualifying scores on CLEP examinations.

Payment plans. Credit card, installment, deferred payment.

Application procedures. Priority date 4/1; no closing date. Applicants notified on rolling basis starting 8/1, must reply by 8/28.

Contact. Financial aid office: (662) 495-5100
Maria Thomas, Director of Financial Aid
Drawer 1257
West Point, MS 39773-1257

Millsaps College

Jackson, Mississippi
www.millsaps.edu
Four-year private **Federal Code: 002414**

	Living at home	On-campus
Tuition and fees (2002-2003):	$17,372	$17,372
Room and board:		$6,364
Board only:	$2,600	
Books and supplies:	$800	$800
Personal expenses:	$900	$900
Transportation:	$450	$450

Undergraduate aid. Need-based: Average financial aid package for full-time students was $16,072; for part-time $4,613. 74% awarded as scholarships/grants, 26% as loans/jobs. **Non-need-based:** 76% awarded as scholarships/grants, 24% as loans/jobs. Scholarships based on academics, art, leadership, music/drama, religious affiliation, state/district residency. **Student debt:** 68% of graduating class borrowed to fund education; average debt was $11,582.

Freshman aid. Need-based: Out of 251 full-time freshmen, 174 applied for aid; 128 were judged to have need; of these 128 received aid. Average package met 88% of need. 44 students had full need met. Average scholarship/grant was $12,880; average loan $3,111. **Non-need based:** 28 full-time freshmen with need received non-need scholarships; 110 without need received awards.

Policies to reduce costs. Tuition/fee waivers for employees and their families. Credit/placement for qualifying scores on AP, IB, CLEP examinations.

Payment plans. Credit card, installment payment.

Application procedures. FAFSA, institutional form required. Priority date 3/1; no closing date. Applicants notified on rolling basis starting 3/15, must reply by 5/1 or within 2 week(s) of notification.

Contact. Financial aid office: (601) 974-1220
Patrick James, Director of Financial Aid
1701 North State Street
Jackson, MS 39210

Mississippi College

Clinton, Mississippi
www.mc.edu
Four-year private **Federal Code: 002415**

	Living at home	On-campus
Tuition and fees (2002-2003):	$10,712	$10,712
Room and board:		$4,680
Books and supplies:	$700	$700
Personal expenses:	$1,500	$1,500
Transportation:	$1,250	$710

Undergraduate aid. Need-based: Average financial aid package for full-time students was $12,602; for part-time $10,881. 51% awarded as scholarships/grants, 49% as loans/jobs. **Non-need-based:** 88% awarded as scholarships/grants, 12% as loans/jobs. Scholarships based on academics, leadership. **Student debt:** 20% of graduating class borrowed to fund education; average debt was $23,430. **Additional information:** Student reply date for institutional scholarships: May 1.

Freshman aid. Need-based: Out of 272 full-time freshmen, 267 applied for aid; 147 were judged to have need; of these 147 received aid. Average package met 75% of need. 66 students had full need met. Average scholarship/grant was $9,518; average loan $3,369. **Non-need based:** 60 full-time freshmen with need received non-need scholarships; 120 without need received awards.

Merit scholarships. Merit Scholarships; up to $10,000; various awards based on various criteria including leadership, academics, church and community involvement; extensive number of scholarships awarded including some specifically available to transfers.

Policies to reduce costs. Tuition/fee waivers for children of alumni, family of clergy, employees and their families. Credit/placement for qualifying scores on AP, IB, CLEP examinations. Work study available for part-time students.

Payment plans. Credit card, installment, deferred payment.

Application procedures. FAFSA, institutional form required. Priority date 3/1; no closing date. Applicants notified on rolling basis starting 2/1. Early decision closing date 12/15.

Contact. Financial aid office: (601) 925-3800
Mary Givhan, Director of Financial Aid
Box 4026
Clinton, MS 39058

Mississippi Gulf Coast Community College: Jackson County Campus

Gautier, Mississippi
www.mgccc.edu
Two-year public **Federal Code: 002418**

College costs. $15 required book rental fee per course.

	Living at home
Tuition and fees (2002-2003):	$1,372
Out-of-state:	$3,546
Per-credit charge:	$65
Per-credit out-of-state:	$142
Personal expenses:	$410
Transportation:	$1,530

Policies to reduce costs. Credit/placement for qualifying scores on AP examinations.

Application procedures. Priority date 6/1; no closing date. Applicants notified on rolling basis starting 7/1, must reply within 2 week(s) of notification.

Contact. Lashanda Chamberlan-Mitchell, Director of Financial Aid
Box 100
Gautier, MS 39553

Mississippi Gulf Coast Community College: Jefferson Davis Campus

Gulfport, Mississippi
www.mgccc.cc.ms.us
Two-year public **Federal Code: 002419**

College costs. $15 required book rental fee per course.

	Living at home
Tuition and fees (2002-2003):	$1,372
Out-of-state:	$3,546
Per-credit charge:	$65
Per-credit out-of-state:	$142
Books and supplies:	$280
Personal expenses:	$600
Transportation:	$1,870

Contact. 2226 Switzer Road
Gulfport, MS 39507-3894

Mississippi Gulf Coast Community College: Perkinston

Perkinston, Mississippi
www.mgccc.edu
Two-year public **Federal Code: 002417**

College costs. $15 required book rental fee per course.

	Living at home	On-campus
Tuition and fees (2002-2003):	$1,372	$1,372
Out-of-state:	$3,546	$3,546
Per-credit charge:	$65	$65
Per-credit out-of-state:	$142	$142
Room and board:		$3,810
Books and supplies:	$150	$150

Undergraduate aid. All financial aid based on need. Need-based aid available for full-time students.

Policies to reduce costs. Tuition/fee waivers for senior citizens, employees and their families. Credit/placement for qualifying scores on AP, CLEP examinations.

Payment plans. Credit card, installment, deferred payment.

Application procedures. Institutional form required. Priority date 6/1; no closing date. Applicants notified on rolling basis starting 7/1, must reply within 2 week(s) of notification.

Contact. **Financial aid office:** (601) 928-6225
Sheree Bond, Director of Financial Aid
Box 508
Perkinston, MS 39573

Mississippi State University

Miss. State, Mississippi
www.msstate.edu
Four-year public **Federal Code: 002423**

	Living at home	On-campus
Tuition and fees (2002-2003):	$3,873	$3,873
Out-of-state:	$8,778	$8,778
Room and board:		$5,704
Board only:	$3,035	
Books and supplies:	$750	$750
Personal expenses:	$799	$799
Transportation:	$1,000	$1,000

Undergraduate aid. All financial aid based on need. Average financial aid package for full-time students was $7,142. 40% awarded as scholarships/grants, 60% as loans/jobs. Need-based aid available for part-time students. **Student debt:** 46% of graduating class borrowed to fund education; average debt was $15,081. **Additional information:** No institutional closing date for FAFSA.

Freshman aid. Out of 1,734 full-time freshmen, 1,616 applied for aid; 1,172 were judged to have need; of these 1,059 received aid. Average package met 69% of need. 336 students had full need met. Average scholarship/grant was $2,864; average loan $2,542.

Policies to reduce costs. Tuition/fee waivers for children of alumni, senior citizens, employees and their families. Credit/placement for qualifying scores on AP, IB, CLEP examinations.

Payment plans. Credit card, installment payment.

Application procedures. FAFSA required. Closing date 4/1. Applicants notified on rolling basis starting 2/15, must reply within 3 week(s) of notification.

Contact. **Financial aid office:** (662) 325-2450
Bruce Crain, Director of Financial Aid
Box 6305
Mississippi State, MS 39762

Mississippi University for Women

Columbus, Mississippi
www.muw.edu
Four-year public **Federal Code: 002422**

	Living at home	On-campus
Tuition and fees (2002-2003):	$3,298	$3,298
Out-of-state:	$7,965	$7,965
Room and board:		$3,230
Books and supplies:	$600	$600
Personal expenses:	$1,200	$1,200
Transportation:	$500	$500

Undergraduate aid. **Need-based:** Need-based aid available for full-time and part-time students. **Non-need-based:** Scholarships based on academics, athletics, state/district residency.

Policies to reduce costs. Tuition/fee waivers for adults, children of alumni, senior citizens, minority students, employees and their families. Credit/placement for qualifying scores on AP, CLEP examinations.

Payment plans. Credit card, installment, deferred payment.

Application procedures. FAFSA required. Priority date 4/1; no closing date. Applicants notified on rolling basis starting 3/15, must reply within 2 week(s) of notification. **Transfers:** Closing date 4/1.

Contact. **Financial aid office:** (662) 329-7114
Don Rainer, Director of Financial Aid
Box W-1613
Columbus, MS 39701

Mississippi Valley State University

Itta Bena, Mississippi
www.mvsu.edu
Four-year public **Federal Code: 002424**

	Living at home	On-campus
Tuition and fees (2002-2003):	$3,411	$3,411
Out-of-state:	$7,965	$7,965
Room and board:		$3,192
Books and supplies:	$700	$700
Personal expenses:	$1,000	$1,200
Transportation:	$2,000	$1,500

Undergraduate aid. **Non-need-based:** Scholarships based on academics, athletics, minority status.

Policies to reduce costs. Tuition/fee waivers for minority students, employees and their families. Credit/placement for qualifying scores on AP, CLEP examinations.

Payment plans. Installment, deferred payment.

Application procedures. Closing date 4/1. Applicants notified on rolling basis starting 8/15, must reply within 2 week(s) of notification. **Transfers:** No deadline.

Contact. **Financial aid office:** (601) 254-3335
Darrel Boyd, Director of Financial Aid
14000 Highway 82 West
Itta Bena, MS 38941-1400

Northwest Mississippi Community College

Senatobia, Mississippi
www.northwestms.edu
Two-year public **Federal Code: 002427**

College costs. Lab fees range from $15 to $25 per course.

	Living at home	On-campus
Tuition and fees (2002-2003):	$1,200	$1,200
Out-of-state:	$3,200	$3,200
Per-credit charge:	$55	$55
Per-credit out-of-state:	$100	$100
Room and board:		$2,250
Books and supplies:	$600	$600
Personal expenses:	$375	$375

Undergraduate aid. **Need-based:** 85% awarded as scholarships/grants, 15% as loans/jobs.

Policies to reduce costs. Tuition/fee waivers for senior citizens, employees and their families. Credit/placement for qualifying scores on AP examinations.

Payment plans. Credit card, installment, deferred payment.

Application procedures. FAFSA required. Closing date 8/9. Applicants notified by 8/16.

Contact. **Financial aid office:** (662) 562-3271
Joe Boyles, Director of Financial Aid
4975 Highway 51 North
Senatobia, MS 38668

Pearl River Community College

Poplarville, Mississippi
www.prcc.edu
Two-year public **Federal Code: 002430**

	Living at home	On-campus
Tuition and fees (2002-2003):	$1,472	$1,472
Out-of-state:	$3,870	$3,870
Per-credit charge:	$63	$63
Per-credit out-of-state:	$163	$163
Room and board:		$2,418
Books and supplies:	$500	$500

Undergraduate aid. **Need-based:** Average financial aid package for full-time students was $2,311; for part-time $2,063. 77% awarded as scholarships/grants, 23% as loans/jobs. **Non-need-based:** 14% awarded as scholarships/grants, 86% as loans/jobs. Scholarships based on academics, alumni affiliation, athletics, leadership, music/drama, state/district residency.

Freshman aid. **Need-based:** Out of 907 full-time freshmen, 832 applied for aid; 517 were judged to have need; of these 503 received aid. Average package met 59% of need. 161 students had full need met. Average scholarship/grant was $2,249; average loan $1,091. **Non-need based:** 136 full-time freshmen with need received non-need scholarships; 5 without need received awards; 79 received athletic scholarships.

Policies to reduce costs. Tuition/fee waivers for senior citizens, employees and their families. Credit/placement for qualifying scores on AP, CLEP examinations.

Payment plans. Credit card, installment, deferred payment.

Application procedures. FAFSA, institutional form required. Priority date 5/1; no closing date. Applicants notified on rolling basis.

Contact. **Financial aid office:** (601) 403-1000
Peggy Shoemake, Director of Financial Aid
101 Highway 11 North
Poplarville, MS 39470

Rust College

Holly Springs, Mississippi
www.rustcollege.edu
Four-year private **Federal Code: 002433**

	Living at home	On-campus
Tuition and fees:	$5,800	$5,800
Room and board:		$2,600
Board only:	$900	
Books and supplies:	$500	$500
Personal expenses:	$2,350	$1,450
Transportation:	$1,000	$1,000

Undergraduate aid. **Need-based:** Average financial aid package for full-time students was $5,886; for part-time $5,353. 60% awarded as scholarships/grants, 40% as loans/jobs. **Non-need-based:** 74% awarded as scholarships/grants, 26% as loans/jobs. Scholarships based on academics, leadership, music/drama, religious affiliation, state/district residency. **Student debt:** 67% of graduating class borrowed to fund education; average debt was $8,105.

Freshman aid. **Need-based:** Out of 292 full-time freshmen, 256 applied for aid; 256 were judged to have need; of these 256 received aid. Average package met 47% of need. 173 students had full need met. Average scholarship/grant was $4,224; average loan $1,452. **Non-need based:** 226 full-time freshmen with need received non-need scholarships.

Merit scholarships. Honor Track based on top 10% of high school graduating class, GPA 3.5 and above, ACT 22 or above, SAT 1030 or above, 3 letters of recommendation, essay; 17 awarded; full tuition. Presidential for top 10% of high school graduating class, GPA 3.25 and above, ACT 19 and above, SAT 910 and above; 17 awarded; $2,000. Academic Dean's Scholarship for top 10% of high school graduating class, GPA 3.0 or above, ACT 17 and above, SAT 830 and above; 17 awarded.

Policies to reduce costs. Tuition/fee waivers for adults, senior citizens, family members, family of clergy, employees and their families. Prepayment discount. Work study available for part-time students.

Payment plans. Credit card, installment, deferred payment.

Application procedures. FAFSA, institutional form required. Priority date 5/1; closing date 3/1. Applicants notified on rolling basis starting 5/1, must reply within 2 week(s) of notification. **Transfers:** No deadline. Financial aid transcripts from previous schools required.

Contact. **Financial aid office:** (662) 252-8000 ext. 4062
Helen Street, Director of Financial Aid
150 Rust Avenue
Holly Springs, MS 38635-2328

University of Mississippi

University, Mississippi
www.olemiss.edu
Four-year public **Federal Code: 002440**

College costs. Law and pharmacy students pay different tuition rate. Law students in-state pay $311 per credit hour; out-of-state $607 per credit hour; 10-15 credits in-state $6,215; out-of-state $12,142 per academic year. Pharmacy I & II students pay $190 in-state, OOS $413. Pharmacy III & IV in-state $228, OOS $453. Pharmacy V & VI in-state $280, OOS $557.

	Living at home	On-campus
Tuition and fees (2002-2003):	$3,916	$3,916
Out-of-state:	$8,826	$8,826
Room and board:		$4,090
Board only:	$2,800	
Books and supplies:	$750	$750
Personal expenses:	$2,000	$2,000
Transportation:	$600	$600

Undergraduate aid. **Need-based:** Need-based aid available for full-time and part-time students. **Non-need-based:** Scholarships based on academics, alumni affiliation, art, athletics, leadership, minority status, music/drama, state/district residency.

Policies to reduce costs. Tuition/fee waivers for children of alumni, senior citizens, minority students, family members, employees and their families. Credit/placement for qualifying scores on AP, IB, CLEP examinations.

Payment plans. Credit card, installment, deferred payment.

Application procedures. FAFSA required. Priority date 3/15; no closing date. Applicants notified on rolling basis starting 4/15, must reply within 3 week(s) of notification. **Transfers:** Priority date 3/15; no deadline.

Contact. **Financial aid office:** (662) 915-7175
Laura Diver-Brown, Director
145 Martindale
University, MS 38677-1848

University of Mississippi Medical Center

Jackson, Mississippi
Upper-division public **Federal Code: 004688**

College costs. Tuition and fees quoted are for nursing program. Required fees vary per program. Occupational therapy and physical therapy programs require summer session (at an additional cost).

	Living at home	On-campus
Tuition and fees (2002-2003):	$3,202	$3,202
Out-of-state:	$6,704	$6,704
Room only:		$1,890
Books and supplies:	$2,378	$2,378
Personal expenses:	$2,475	$2,475
Transportation:	$900	$900

Undergraduate aid. All financial aid based on need. Average financial aid package for full-time students was $6,500. 45% awarded as scholarships/grants, 55% as loans/jobs. Need-based aid available for part-time students. **Student debt:** 65% of graduating class borrowed to fund education; average debt was $5,936.

Policies to reduce costs. Tuition/fee waivers for employees and their families. Credit/placement for qualifying scores on AP examinations.

Payment plans. Installment, deferred payment.

Application procedures. FAFSA, institutional form required. Priority date 4/1; no closing date. Applicants notified by 7/15, must reply within 2 week(s) of notification. **Transfers:** Priority date 4/1.

Contact. **Financial aid office:** (601) 984-1117
Rebecca Dalton, Director of Student Financial Aid
2500 North State Street
Jackson, MS 39216

University of Southern Mississippi

Hattiesburg, Mississippi
www.usm.edu
Four-year public **Federal Code: 002441**

	Living at home	On-campus
Tuition and fees (2002-2003):	$3,782	$3,782
Out-of-state:	$8,660	$8,660
Room and board:		$4,450
Board only:	$1,000	
Books and supplies:	$700	$700
Personal expenses:	$1,840	$1,840
Transportation:	$970	$380

Undergraduate aid. Need-based: Average financial aid package for full-time students was $5,805. 41% awarded as scholarships/grants, 59% as loans/jobs. Need-based aid available for part-time students. **Non-need-based:** 27% awarded as scholarships/grants, 73% as loans/jobs. **Student debt:** 51% of graduating class borrowed to fund education; average debt was $14,442.

Freshman aid. Need-based: Out of 1,631 full-time freshmen, 1,093 applied for aid; 854 were judged to have need; of these 854 received aid. 357 students had full need met. Average scholarship/grant was $2,750. **Non-need based:** 182 full-time freshmen with need received non-need scholarships.

Policies to reduce costs. Tuition/fee waivers for children of alumni, senior citizens, employees and their families. Credit/placement for qualifying scores on AP, CLEP examinations.

Payment plans. Credit card, installment, deferred payment.

Application procedures. FAFSA, institutional form required. Priority date 3/15; no closing date. Applicants notified on rolling basis starting 4/1, must reply within 4 week(s) of notification. **Transfers:** Priority date 3/15; no deadline. Merit scholarships available to community college transfer students based on college GPA.

Contact. **Financial aid office:** (601) 266-4111
Kristi Motter, Director of Financial Aid
Southern Station Box 5166
Hattiesburg, MS 39406-5166

Wesley College

Florence, Mississippi
www.wesleycollege.com
Four-year private **Federal Code: 011461**

	Living at home	On-campus
Tuition and fees (2002-2003):	$4,400	$4,400
Room and board:		$2,900
Books and supplies:	$700	$700
Personal expenses:	$1,150	$650
Transportation:	$500	$400

Undergraduate aid. Need-based: Average financial aid package for full-time students was $3,000; for part-time $2,200. 45% awarded as scholarships/grants, 55% as loans/jobs. **Student debt:** 4% of graduating class borrowed to fund education; average debt was $15,517.

Freshman aid. Need-based: Out of 8 full-time freshmen, 7 applied for aid; 7 were judged to have need; of these 7 received aid. Average package met 57% of need. Average scholarship/grant was $3,125; average loan $1,313. **Non-need based:** 1 full-time freshmen with need received non-need scholarships; 1 without need received awards.

Policies to reduce costs. Tuition/fee waivers for employees and their families. Credit/placement for qualifying scores on AP, CLEP examinations. Work study available nights and weekends.

Payment plans. Installment payment.

Application procedures. FAFSA required. Closing date 5/15. Applicants notified on rolling basis starting 7/1, must reply within 2 week(s) of notification.

Contact. **Financial aid office:** (601) 845-2265
William Devore, Director of Financial Aid
Box 1070
Florence, MS 39073-0070

Missouri

Avila University

Kansas City, Missouri
www.avila.edu
Four-year private **Federal Code: 002449**

	Living at home	On-campus
Tuition and fees (2002-2003):	$14,160	$14,160
Room and board:		$5,300
Board only:	$4,400	
Books and supplies:	$800	$800
Personal expenses:	$2,000	$2,200
Transportation:	$1,400	$600

Undergraduate aid. Need-based: Need-based aid available for full-time and part-time students. **Non-need-based:** Scholarships based on academics, alumni affiliation, art, athletics, music/drama, religious affiliation. **Additional information:** Financial aid adjusted for increases in tuition based on need.

Policies to reduce costs. Tuition/fee waivers for children of alumni, senior citizens, family members, family of clergy, employees and their families. Credit/placement for qualifying scores on AP, IB, CLEP examinations. Work study available nights, weekends and for part-time students.

Payment plans. Credit card, installment, deferred payment.

Application procedures. FAFSA required. Priority date 4/1; no closing date. Applicants notified on rolling basis starting 2/1, must reply within 3 week(s) of notification. **Transfers:** Non-need-based academic scholarship available for transfer students.

Contact. **Financial aid office:** (816) 501-3600
Angie Comstock, Director of Financial Aid
11901 Wornall Road
Kansas City, MO 64145-1698

Baptist Bible College

Springfield, Missouri
Four-year private **Federal Code: 013208**

College costs. Quoted costs are for Bible-related majors. For education program: full-time tuition $3,688, required fees $742, per-credit-hour charge $157.

	Living at home	On-campus
Tuition and fees (2002-2003):	$3,760	$3,760
Room and board:		$4,590
Books and supplies:	$800	$800
Personal expenses:	$2,164	$2,164

Undergraduate aid. Need-based: Need-based aid available for full-time and part-time students.

Policies to reduce costs. Credit/placement for qualifying scores on AP, CLEP examinations.

Payment plans. Credit card, installment payment.

Application procedures. FAFSA, institutional form required. Closing date 5/1. Applicants notified on rolling basis, must reply within 2 week(s) of notification.

Contact. Shirley Cutburth, Financial Aid Director
628 East Kearney Street
Springfield, MO 65803

Blue River Community College

Blue Springs, Missouri
www.kcmetro.cc.mo.us/blueriver/brhome.html
Two-year public **Federal Code: 009140**

	Living at home
Tuition and fees (projected):	$1,980
Out-of-district:	$3,420
Out-of-state:	$4,650
Per-credit charge:	$61
Per-credit out-of-district:	$109
Per-credit out-of-state:	$150
Books and supplies:	$700
Personal expenses:	$1,500
Transportation:	$1,690

Undergraduate aid. Need-based: Average financial aid package for full-time students was $2,618; for part-time $1,544. 89% awarded as scholarships/grants, 11% as loans/jobs. **Non-need-based:** Scholarships based on academics, athletics, leadership.

Freshman aid. Need-based: Average package met 33% of need. Average scholarship/grant was $2,414; average loan $2,068.

Policies to reduce costs. Tuition/fee waivers for senior citizens, employees and their families. Credit/placement for qualifying scores on AP examinations. Work study available nights and for part-time students.

Payment plans. Credit card, installment payment.

Application procedures. FAFSA, institutional form required. Priority date 5/30; closing date 8/20. Applicants notified on rolling basis starting 4/8. **Transfers:** No deadline.

Contact. **Financial aid office:** (816) 672-2066
Rosemarie Lozano, Student Financial Aid Advisor
1501 West Jefferson Street
Blue Springs, MO 64015-7242

Calvary Bible College

Kansas City, Missouri
www.calvary.edu
Four-year private **Federal Code: 002450**

	Living at home	On-campus
Tuition and fees (2002-2003):	$5,986	$5,986
Room and board:		$3,600
Books and supplies:	$225	$225
Personal expenses:	$350	$350
Transportation:	$800	$800

Undergraduate aid. Need-based: 49% awarded as scholarships/grants, 51% as loans/jobs. Need-based aid available for part-time students. **Non-need-based:** Scholarships based on academics, alumni affiliation, minority status.

Policies to reduce costs. Tuition/fee waivers for children of alumni, minority students, family members, unemployed or children of unemployed, family of clergy, employees and their families. Prepayment discount; credit/placement for qualifying scores on AP, IB, CLEP examinations.

Payment plans. Credit card, installment payment.

Application procedures. FAFSA, institutional form required. Closing date 3/31. Applicants notified on rolling basis starting 5/1.

Contact. Robert E. Cranck, Director of Financial Aid
15800 Calvary Road
Kansas City, MO 64147

Central Bible College

Springfield, Missouri
www.cbcag.edu
Four-year private **Federal Code: 002452**

	Living at home	On-campus
Tuition and fees:	$7,536	$7,536
Room and board:		$3,942
Board only:	$1,500	
Books and supplies:	$550	$550
Personal expenses:	$2,000	$1,000
Transportation:	$850	$400

Policies to reduce costs. Tuition/fee waivers for family members, family of clergy, employees and their families. Prepayment discount; credit/placement for qualifying scores on AP, CLEP examinations.

Payment plans. Installment payment.

Application procedures. FAFSA required. Priority date 5/1; no closing date. Applicants notified on rolling basis starting 5/15, must reply within 3 week(s) of notification. **Transfers:** No deadline.

Contact. **Financial aid office:** (800) 831-4222 ext. 1205
Rick Woolverton, Financial Aid Director
3000 North Grant Avenue
Springfield, MO 65803-1069

Central Christian College of the Bible

Moberly, Missouri
www.cccb.edu
Four-year private **Federal Code: TG51656**

College costs. Full-time students receive full scholarship for the $5,070 tuition.

	Living at home	On-campus
Tuition and fees:	$5,070	$5,070
Room and board:		$3,860
Books and supplies:	$484	$484
Personal expenses:	$3,846	$1,446
Transportation:	$1,729	$1,039

Undergraduate aid. **Need-based:** Need-based aid available for full-time and part-time students.

Policies to reduce costs. Tuition/fee waivers for children of alumni, family members, family of clergy, employees and their families.

Payment plans. Installment, deferred payment.

Application procedures. FAFSA required. Priority date 3/15; closing date 4/1. Applicants notified by 5/15, must reply within 2 week(s) of notification.

Contact. Rhonda Dunham, Financial Aid Director
911 East Urbandale Drive
Moberly, MO 65270-1997

Central Methodist College

Fayette, Missouri
www.cmc.edu
Four-year private **Federal Code: E00605**

	Living at home	On-campus
Tuition and fees:	$13,762	$13,762
Room and board:		$4,920
Board only:	$2,350	
Books and supplies:	$650	$650
Personal expenses:	$1,750	$2,250
Transportation:	$600	$600

Undergraduate aid. **Need-based:** Need-based aid available for full-time and part-time students. **Non-need-based:** Scholarships based on academics, alumni affiliation, athletics, music/drama, religious affiliation.

Policies to reduce costs. Tuition/fee waivers for children of alumni, senior citizens, employees and their families. Credit/placement for qualifying scores on AP, CLEP examinations.

Payment plans. Credit card, installment, deferred payment.

Application procedures. FAFSA required. Priority date 4/1; no closing date. Applicants notified on rolling basis starting 1/30, must reply within 2 week(s) of notification. **Transfers:** No deadline. Institutional financial assistance based on merit is determined by college transfer GPA.

Contact. Courtney Siebert, Director of Financial Aid
411 Central Methodist Square
Fayette, MO 65248-1198

Central Missouri State University

Warrensburg, Missouri
www.cmsu.edu
Four-year public **Federal Code: 02454**

	Living at home	On-campus
Tuition and fees (2002-2003):	$4,110	$4,110
Out-of-state:	$7,869	$7,869
Room and board:		$4,630
Board only:	$1,800	
Books and supplies:	$450	$450
Personal expenses:	$900	$1,400
Transportation:	$900	$900

Undergraduate aid. **Need-based:** Average financial aid package for full-time students was $5,929; for part-time $4,826. 41% awarded as scholarships/grants, 59% as loans/jobs. **Non-need-based:** 41% awarded as scholarships/grants, 59% as loans/jobs. Scholarships based on academics, alumni affiliation, art, athletics, leadership, minority status, music/drama, state/district residency. **Student debt:** 58% of graduating class borrowed to fund education; average debt was $9,975.

Freshman aid. **Need-based:** Out of 1,438 full-time freshmen, 1,095 applied for aid; 715 were judged to have need; of these 700 received aid. Average package met 76% of need. 192 students had full need met. Average scholarship/grant was $3,342; average loan $2,189. **Non-need based:** 507 full-time freshmen with need received non-need scholarships; 488 without need received awards; 66 received athletic scholarships.

Policies to reduce costs. Tuition/fee waivers for children of alumni, senior citizens, employees and their families. Credit/placement for qualifying scores on AP, IB, CLEP examinations. Work study available nights, weekends and for part-time students.

Payment plans. Credit card, installment, deferred payment.

Application procedures. FAFSA required. Priority date 3/1; no closing date. Applicants notified on rolling basis starting 3/1, must reply within 2 week(s) of notification. **Transfers:** Priority date 3/1.

Contact. **Financial aid office:** (660) 543-8080
Phil Shreves, Director, Student Financial Assistance
WOE 1401
Warrensburg, MO 64093

College of the Ozarks

Point Lookout, Missouri
www.cofo.edu
Four-year private **Federal Code: 002500**

College costs. Full-time students are required to work 15 hours per week for 16 weeks and one 40-hour work week per semester to help defray the cost of education. Part-time students (commuters only) pay $250 per-credit-hour. Required fees, $250. Room and board $3,250. Board: $1,560. Books/supplies: $600. Transportation: $2,840.

Undergraduate aid. **Need-based:** Average financial aid package for full-time students was $12,484; for part-time $6,501. 78% awarded as scholarships/grants, 22% as loans/jobs. **Non-need-based:** 43% awarded as scholarships/grants, 57% as loans/jobs. Scholarships based on athletics, leadership.

Freshman aid. **Need-based:** Out of 269 full-time freshmen, 269 applied for aid; 242 were judged to have need; of these 242 received aid. Average package met 90% of need. 101 students had full need met. Average scholarship/grant was $7,716. **Non-need based:** 22 full-time freshmen with need received non-need scholarships; 27 without need received awards; 28 received athletic scholarships.

Policies to reduce costs. Credit/placement for qualifying scores on AP, CLEP examinations.

Payment plans. Credit card, installment payment.

Application procedures. FAFSA required. Priority date 3/15; no closing date. Applicants notified by 7/1.

Contact. **Financial aid office:** (417) 334-6411 ext. 4290
Kyla McCarty, Financial Aid Director
PO Box 17
Point Lookout, MO 65726-0017

Columbia College

Columbia, Missouri
www.ccis.edu
Four-year private **Federal Code: 002456**

	Living at home	On-campus
Tuition and fees:	$11,362	$11,362
Room and board:		$4,770
Books and supplies:	$600	$600
Personal expenses:	$900	$900
Transportation:	$200	$1,000

Undergraduate aid. Need-based: Average financial aid package for full-time students was $12,167. 61% awarded as scholarships/grants, 39% as loans/jobs. Need-based aid available for part-time students. **Non-need-based:** 81% awarded as scholarships/grants, 19% as loans/jobs. Scholarships based on academics, alumni affiliation, art, athletics, leadership, music/drama, religious affiliation, state/district residency.

Freshman aid. Need-based: Out of 137 full-time freshmen, 120 applied for aid; 94 were judged to have need; of these 94 received aid. Average package met 76% of need. 32 students had full need met. Average scholarship/grant was $3,562; average loan $2,608. **Non-need based:** 80 full-time freshmen with need received non-need scholarships; 21 without need received awards; 6 received athletic scholarships.

Merit scholarships. Columbia College Scholarships, full tuition and room, minimum 3.5 high school GPA required. Awarded on competitive basis; selection process includes campus visit, interview, essay. Renewable with minimum 3.5 GPA. Half-tuition scholarships, minimum 3.4 high school GPA and ACT score of 24 required, renewable for 3 years with minimum 3.4 GPA.

Policies to reduce costs. Tuition/fee waivers for children of alumni, senior citizens, family members, employees and their families. Credit/placement for qualifying scores on AP, IB, CLEP examinations. Work study available nights and weekends.

Payment plans. Credit card, installment, deferred payment.

Application procedures. FAFSA, institutional form required. Priority date 3/15; no closing date. Applicants notified on rolling basis starting 3/1, must reply within 2 week(s) of notification.

Contact. Financial aid office: (573) 875-7360
Sharon Abernathy, Director of Financial Aid
1001 Rogers Street
Columbia, MO 65216

Conception Seminary College

Conception, Missouri
www.conceptionabbey.org
Four-year private **Federal Code: 002467**

	Living at home	On-campus
Tuition and fees (2002-2003):	$9,890	$9,890
Room and board:		$5,790
Books and supplies:	$450	$450
Personal expenses:		$800
Transportation:		$550

Undergraduate aid. Need-based: Need-based aid available for full-time and part-time students. **Non-need-based:** Scholarships based on academics.

Policies to reduce costs. Work study available nights, weekends and for part-time students.

Payment plans. Installment, deferred payment.

Application procedures. FAFSA required. No deadline. Applicants notified on rolling basis starting 8/1, must reply by 8/20.

Contact. Financial aid office: (660) 944-2851
Justin Hernandez, Financial Aid Officer
Box 502
Conception, MO 64433

Concorde Career Institute

Kansas City, Missouri
www.concordecareercolleges.com
Two-year proprietary **Federal Code: 023616**

College costs (2002-2003). Cost of full programs: associate degree programs $16,000, diploma programs $8,000 to $9,000; includes fees, books, uniforms. Books/supplies: $348.

Contact. Sharon Baldwin, Director of Financial Aid
3239 Broadway
Kansas City, MO 64111

Cottey College

Nevada, Missouri
www.cottey.edu
Two-year private **Federal Code: 002458**

	Living at home	On-campus
Tuition and fees (2002-2003):	$10,030	$10,030
Room and board:		$4,600
Books and supplies:	$800	$800
Personal expenses:	$1,600	$900
Transportation:		$1,000

Undergraduate aid. Need-based: Need-based aid available for full-time and part-time students. **Non-need-based:** Scholarships based on academics, alumni affiliation, art, athletics, music/drama.

Policies to reduce costs. Tuition/fee waivers for employees and their families. Credit/placement for qualifying scores on AP, IB examinations.

Payment plans. Credit card payment.

Application procedures. FAFSA required. Priority date 3/30; no closing date. Applicants notified on rolling basis starting 3/15, must reply by 5/1. **Transfers:** Priority date 3/30.

Contact. Sherry Pennington, Coordinator of Financial Aid
1000 West Austin Boulevard
Nevada, MO 64772

Crowder College

Neosho, Missouri
www.crowder.edu
Two-year public **Federal Code: 002459**

	Living at home	On-campus
Tuition and fees (2002-2003):	$1,710	$1,710
Out-of-district:	$2,320	$2,320
Out-of-state:	$3,060	$3,060
Per-credit charge:	$46	$46
Per-credit out-of-district:	$67	$67
Per-credit out-of-state:	$87	$87
Room and board:		$3,750
Board only:	$1,650	
Books and supplies:	$700	$700
Personal expenses:	$1,100	$1,100
Transportation:	$1,050	$1,050

Undergraduate aid. All financial aid based on need. 64% awarded as scholarships/grants, 36% as loans/jobs. Need-based aid available for part-time students. **Student debt:** 12% of graduating class borrowed to fund education; average debt was $4,900.

Policies to reduce costs. Tuition/fee waivers for senior citizens, employees and their families. Credit/placement for qualifying scores on AP, CLEP examinations. Work study available nights, weekends and for part-time students.

Payment plans. Credit card, installment payment.

Application procedures. FAFSA, institutional form required. Priority date 7/1; no closing date. Applicants notified on rolling basis starting 5/15. **Transfers:** Priority date 7/1; no deadline.

Contact. Financial aid office: (417) 451-3223 ext. 5566
Michelle Paul, Director of Financial Aid
601 LaClede
Neosho, MO 64850

Culver-Stockton College

Canton, Missouri
www.culver.edu
Four-year private **Federal Code: 002460**

	Living at home	On-campus
Tuition and fees:	$12,400	$12,400
Room and board:		$5,450
Board only:	$2,800	
Books and supplies:	$600	$600
Personal expenses:	$1,946	$1,946

Undergraduate aid. Need-based: Average financial aid package for full-time students was $11,614; for part-time $2,371. 64% awarded as scholarships/grants, 36% as loans/jobs. **Non-need-based:** 39% awarded as scholarships/grants, 61% as loans/jobs. Scholarships based on academics, alumni affiliation, art, athletics, job skills, leadership, music/drama, religious affiliation, state/district residency. **Student debt:** 81% of graduating class borrowed to fund education; average debt was $14,895. **Additional information:** Interview required for scholarships; audition also required for music students, portfolio for art students.

Freshman aid. Need-based: Out of 224 full-time freshmen, 215 applied for aid; 183 were judged to have need; of these 183 received aid. Average package met 81% of need. 52 students had full need met. Average scholarship/grant was $8,647; average loan $2,485. **Non-need based:** 34 full-time freshmen with need received non-need scholarships; 39 without need received awards; 24 received athletic scholarships.

Policies to reduce costs. Tuition/fee waivers for adults, children of alumni, senior citizens, family of clergy, employees and their families. Credit/placement for qualifying scores on AP, IB, CLEP examinations. Work study available nights, weekends and for part-time students.

Payment plans. Credit card, installment payment.

Application procedures. FAFSA required. Priority date 4/1; closing date 6/15. Applicants notified on rolling basis starting 2/15, must reply within 2 week(s) of notification.

Contact. Financial aid office: (217) 231-6306
Carla Boren, Director of Financial Aid
One College Hill
Canton, MO 63435-1299

DeVry University: Kansas City

Kansas City, Missouri
www.kc.devry.edu
Four-year proprietary **Federal Code: 002455**

	Living at home
Tuition and fees:	$10,155
Books and supplies:	$1,100
Personal expenses:	$1,816
Transportation:	$1,438

Undergraduate aid. All financial aid based on need. Average financial aid package for full-time students was $7,095; for part-time $5,448. 19% awarded as scholarships/grants, 81% as loans/jobs.

Freshman aid. Average package met 37% of need. Average scholarship/grant was $4,277; average loan $3,835.

Policies to reduce costs. Tuition/fee waivers for employees and their families.

Payment plans. Credit card, installment, deferred payment.

Application procedures. FAFSA required. No deadline. Applicants notified on rolling basis starting 7/2. **Transfers:** No deadline.

Contact. Maureen Kelly, Senior Associate Director of Financial Aid
11224 Holmes Street
Kansas City, MO 64131

Deaconess College of Nursing

St. Louis, Missouri
www.deaconess.edu
Four-year proprietary **Federal Code: 006385**

College costs. Students enrolled in web-based program pay $416 per credit-hour.

	Living at home	On-campus
Tuition and fees:	$10,680	$10,680
Room and board:		$3,800
Board only:	$2,330	
Books and supplies:	$1,100	$1,100
Personal expenses:	$550	$1,140
Transportation:	$1,970	$1,290

Undergraduate aid. Need-based: Need-based aid available for full-time and part-time students. **Non-need-based:** Scholarships based on academics.

Merit scholarships. Tenet Nurse Citizen Award, full tuition, based on application, essay, interview, renewable with 3.25 GPA, 1 awarded; Chancellor's Award, half tuition, for students with 24 ACT, 3.5 GPA, number awarded subject to fund availability; Merit Scholarships, up to $3,000, based on academic achievement, number awarded subject to fund availability.

Policies to reduce costs. Tuition/fee waivers for employees and their families. Credit/placement for qualifying scores on AP, CLEP examinations.

Payment plans. Credit card, installment, deferred payment.

Application procedures. FAFSA, institutional form required. Priority date 4/1; closing date 7/1. Applicants notified on rolling basis starting 4/1, must reply within 2 week(s) of notification. **Transfers:** No deadline.

Contact. Financial aid office: (314) 768-5604
Michelle Mohn, Financial Counselor
6150 Oakland Avenue
St. Louis, MO 63139

Drury University

Springfield, Missouri
www.drury.edu
Four-year private **Federal Code: 002461**

	Living at home	On-campus
Tuition and fees:	$13,411	$13,411
Room and board:		$5,007
Books and supplies:	$1,000	$1,000
Personal expenses:	$1,500	$1,500
Transportation:	$1,600	$1,600

Undergraduate aid. Need-based: Average financial aid package for full-time students was $7,985; for part-time $2,500. 46% awarded as scholarships/grants, 54% as loans/jobs. **Non-need-based:** 78% awarded as scholarships/grants, 22% as loans/jobs. Scholarships based on academics, alumni affiliation, art, athletics, job skills, leadership, minority status, music/drama, religious affiliation. **Student debt:** 38% of graduating class borrowed to fund education; average debt was $14,570.

Freshman aid. Need-based: Average package met 83% of need. Average scholarship/grant was $6,045; average loan $3,600.

Merit scholarships. Trustee Scholarship; 10 awarded; room and board. Presidential Scholarship; 10 awarded; $10,000 a year. Academic Honor Scholarship; $500 to $5,000 a year. Peter Hudson Ethnic Diversity Scholarship; 2 awarded; $8,000 a year. Samuel Drury Award; $8,000 a year. Leadership Award; $1,000 a year. Dean Award; 2% of high school class awarded; $1,000 a year. International Baccalaureate Award; $1,000 a year. Alumni Children's Scholarship; $500 a year.

Policies to reduce costs. Tuition/fee waivers for senior citizens, employees and their families. Credit/placement for qualifying scores on AP, IB, CLEP examinations.

Payment plans. Installment, deferred payment.

Application procedures. FAFSA, institutional form required. Priority date 3/15; no closing date. Applicants notified on rolling basis starting 3/30, must reply within 2 week(s) of notification. **Transfers:** No deadline.

Contact. Financial aid office: (417) 873-7312
Annette Avery, Director of Financial Aid
900 North Benton Ave.
Springfield, MO 65802

East Central College

Union, Missouri
www.eastcentral.edu
Two-year public **Federal Code: 008862**

	Living at home
Tuition and fees (2002-2003):	$1,965
Out-of-district:	$2,655
Out-of-state:	$3,735
Per-credit charge:	$56
Per-credit out-of-district:	$79
Per-credit out-of-state:	$115
Board only:	$1,561
Books and supplies:	$600
Personal expenses:	$600
Transportation:	$2,165

Undergraduate aid. Need-based: Average financial aid package for full-time students was $1,800. 68% awarded as scholarships/grants, 32% as loans/jobs. Need-based aid available for part-time students. **Non-need-based:** 96% awarded as scholarships/grants, 4% as loans/jobs. Scholarships based on academics, athletics, music/drama, state/district residency.

Policies to reduce costs. Tuition/fee waivers for senior citizens, employees and their families. Credit/placement for qualifying scores on AP, CLEP examinations.

Payment plans. Credit card, installment, deferred payment.

Application procedures. FAFSA required. Priority date 3/30; no closing date. Applicants notified on rolling basis starting 4/15, must reply within 2 week(s) of notification.

Contact. Financial aid office: (636) 583-5195 ext. 2211
1964 Prairie Dell Road
Union, MO 63084-0529

Evangel University

Springfield, Missouri
www.evangel.edu
Four-year private **Federal Code: 002463**

	Living at home	On-campus
Tuition and fees:	$11,305	$11,305
Room and board:		$4,130
Board only:	$2,500	
Books and supplies:	$800	$800
Personal expenses:	$1,500	$1,500
Transportation:	$1,500	$1,500

Undergraduate aid. All financial aid based on need. Average financial aid package for full-time students was $7,795; for part-time $8,435. 34% awarded as scholarships/grants, 66% as loans/jobs. **Student debt:** 99% of graduating class borrowed to fund education; average debt was $22,192.

Freshman aid. Out of 484 full-time freshmen, 301 applied for aid; 256 were judged to have need; of these 256 received aid. Average package met 59% of need. 27 students had full need met. Average scholarship/grant was $4,958; average loan $2,981.

Policies to reduce costs. Tuition/fee waivers for employees and their families. Prepayment discount; credit/placement for qualifying scores on AP, IB, CLEP examinations. Work study available nights, weekends and for part-time students.

Payment plans. Credit card, installment payment.

Application procedures. FAFSA required. Priority date 3/1; no closing date. Applicants notified on rolling basis starting 4/1, must reply within 3 week(s) of notification.

Contact. Financial aid office: (417) 865-2811
Kathy White, Director of Financial Aid
1111 North Glenstone
Springfield, MO 65802

Fontbonne College

St. Louis, Missouri
www.fontbonne.edu
Four-year private **Federal Code: 002464**

	Living at home	On-campus
Tuition and fees (projected):	$13,715	$13,715
Room and board:		$5,629
Books and supplies:	$650	$650
Personal expenses:	$2,212	$1,500
Transportation:	$2,288	$958

Undergraduate aid. Need-based: Average financial aid package for full-time students was $15,600; for part-time $4,200. 38% awarded as scholarships/grants, 62% as loans/jobs. **Non-need-based:** Scholarships based on academics, alumni affiliation, art, leadership, minority status, music/drama, religious affiliation, state/district residency. **Student debt:** 80% of graduating class borrowed to fund education; average debt was $14,000.

Freshman aid. Need-based: Out of 167 full-time freshmen, 151 applied for aid; 105 were judged to have need; of these 105 received aid. Average package met 86% of need. 23 students had full need met. Average scholarship/grant was $8,150; average loan $3,625. **Non-need based:** 50 full-time freshmen with need received non-need scholarships; 32 without need received awards.

Merit scholarships. Dean's Scholarship: GPA, ACT, rank criteria, $6,000-$8,000. Alumni Scholarship: GPA, ACT and class rank criteria, $1,000-$6,000. Presidential Scholarship: up to full tuition. Campus Service Scholarship: activities, leadership, $500-$3,000. Art, theater, English, writing and computer science scholarships also available.

Policies to reduce costs. Tuition/fee waivers for senior citizens, family members, employees and their families. Credit/placement for qualifying scores on AP, CLEP examinations. Work study available nights and weekends.

Payment plans. Credit card, installment, deferred payment.

Application procedures. FAFSA, institutional form required. Priority date 4/30; closing date 4/1. Applicants notified on rolling basis starting 3/1, must reply within 2 week(s) of notification. **Transfers:** Priority date 4/3; no deadline.

Contact. Financial aid office: (314) 889-1414
Nicole Moore, Director of Financial Aid
6800 Wydown Boulevard
St. Louis, MO 63105

Global University

Springfield, Missouri
www.globaluniversity.edu
Four-year private

College costs. Quoted tuition is for U.S. students. Tuition for international students varies per country.

	Living at home
Tuition and fees (2002-2003):	$2,720
Books and supplies:	$600

Contact. 1112 South Glenstone Avenue
Springfield, MO 65804

Hannibal-LaGrange College

Hannibal, Missouri
www.hlg.edu
Four-year private **Federal Code: 009089**

	Living at home	On-campus
Tuition and fees (projected):	$9,960	$9,960
Room and board:		$3,710
Board only:	$1,561	
Books and supplies:	$700	$700
Personal expenses:	$1,260	$1,260

Undergraduate aid. Need-based: Average financial aid package for full-time students was $5,310. 54% awarded as scholarships/grants, 46% as loans/jobs. **Non-need-based:** Scholarships based on academics, art, athletics, music/drama, religious affiliation. **Student debt:** 57% of graduating class borrowed to fund education; average debt was $15,928.

Policies to reduce costs. Tuition/fee waivers for senior citizens, family of clergy, employees and their families. Credit/placement for qualifying scores on AP, CLEP examinations.

Payment plans. Credit card, installment, deferred payment.

Application procedures. FAFSA, institutional form required. Closing date 7/1. Applicants notified on rolling basis.

Contact. Amy Blackwell, Associate Dean of Financial Aid
2800 Palmyra Road
Hannibal, MO 63401

Harris Stowe State College

St. Louis, Missouri
www.hssc.edu
Four-year public **Federal Code: 002466**

	Living at home
Tuition and fees (2002-2003):	$3,760
Out-of-state:	$7,252
Board only:	$800
Books and supplies:	$600
Personal expenses:	$1,700
Transportation:	$315

Undergraduate aid. **Need-based:** Average financial aid package for full-time students was $10,650; for part-time $8,775. 71% awarded as scholarships/grants, 29% as loans/jobs. **Non-need-based:** 41% awarded as scholarships/grants, 59% as loans/jobs. Scholarships based on academics, athletics, music/drama, state/district residency. **Student debt:** 82% of graduating class borrowed to fund education; average debt was $14,000.

Freshman aid. **Need-based:** Out of 103 full-time freshmen, 89 applied for aid; 67 were judged to have need; of these 67 received aid. Average package met 65% of need. 20 students had full need met. **Non-need based:** 12 full-time freshmen with need received non-need scholarships; 21 without need received awards; 10 received athletic scholarships.

Policies to reduce costs. Tuition/fee waivers for employees and their families. Credit/placement for qualifying scores on AP examinations. Work study available nights, weekends and for part-time students.

Payment plans. Credit card, installment, deferred payment.

Application procedures. FAFSA, institutional form required. Priority date 4/1; no closing date. Applicants notified on rolling basis starting 4/1, must reply within 3 week(s) of notification.

Contact. **Financial aid office:** (314)340-3500
Angela Davis, Director of Financial Aid
3026 Laclede Avenue
St. Louis, MO 63103-2199

Hickey College

St. Louis, Missouri
www.hickeycollege.com
Two-year proprietary **Federal Code: 014209**

	Living at home	On-campus
Tuition and fees:	$9,960	$9,960
Room and board:		$4,560
Books and supplies:	$1,000	$1,000

Undergraduate aid. **Need-based:** Need-based aid available for full-time students.

Application procedures. FAFSA required. No deadline. Applicants notified on rolling basis.

Contact. **Financial aid office:** (314) 434-2212 ext. 128
Deana Pecoroni, Director, Student Services
940 West Port Plaza
St. Louis, MO 63146

ITT Technical Institute: Arnold

Arnold, Missouri
www.itt-tech.edu
Two-year proprietary **Federal Code: 007327**

College costs. Total program varies depending on course of study. Per-credit-hour charge: $347. Books/supplies: $3,100.

Policies to reduce costs. Tuition/fee waivers for employees and their families. Tuition at time of enrollment guaranteed for 2 years.

Payment plans. Credit card, installment payment.

Application procedures. FAFSA, institutional form required. No deadline. Applicants notified on rolling basis.

Contact. Michele Brown, Director of Finance
1930 Meyer Drury Drive
Arnold, MO 63010

ITT Technical Institute: Earth City

Earth City, Missouri
www.itt-tech.edu
Three-year proprietary **Federal Code: 007557**

College costs. Total program varies depending on course of study. Per-credit-hour charge: $347.

Policies to reduce costs. Tuition/fee waivers for employees and their families.

Payment plans. Credit card, installment payment.

Application procedures. FAFSA, institutional form required. No deadline. Applicants notified on rolling basis.

Contact. Cheryl Pace, Director of Finance
13505 Lakefront Drive
Earth City, MO 63045

Jefferson College

Hillsboro, Missouri
www.jeffco.edu
Two-year public **Federal Code: 002468**

	Living at home	On-campus
Tuition and fees (projected):	$1,620	$1,620
Out-of-district:	$2,310	$2,310
Out-of-state:	$3,030	$3,030
Per-credit charge:	$47	$47
Per-credit out-of-district:	$70	$70
Per-credit out-of-state:	$94	$94
Room and board:		$5,794
Board only:	$1,608	
Books and supplies:	$718	$718
Personal expenses:	$1,000	$1,000
Transportation:	$1,837	$870

Undergraduate aid. **Need-based:** Average financial aid package for full-time students was $1,955; for part-time $937. 69% awarded as scholarships/grants, 31% as loans/jobs. **Non-need-based:** 55% awarded as scholarships/grants, 45% as loans/jobs. Scholarships based on academics, art, athletics, leadership, state/district residency. **Student debt:** 23% of graduating class borrowed to fund education; average debt was $6,287.

Freshman aid. **Need-based:** Out of 818 full-time freshmen, 616 applied for aid; 366 were judged to have need; of these 348 received aid. Average package met 28% of need. 10 students had full need met. Average scholarship/grant was $1,401; average loan $1,156. **Non-need based:** 142 full-time freshmen with need received non-need scholarships; 172 without need received awards; 20 received athletic scholarships.

Policies to reduce costs. Tuition/fee waivers for senior citizens, employees and their families. Credit/placement for qualifying scores on AP, CLEP examinations. Work study available nights and for part-time students.

Payment plans. Credit card, deferred payment.

Application procedures. FAFSA required. Priority date 4/1; no closing date. Applicants notified on rolling basis starting 4/15, must reply within 2 week(s) of notification.

Contact. **Financial aid office:** (636) 797-3000 Ext. 212
Amy Martin - Small, Director of Admissions and Financial Aid
1000 Viking Drive
Hillsboro, MO 63050-2441

Kansas City Art Institute

Kansas City, Missouri
www.kcai.edu
Four-year private **Federal Code: 002473**

	Living at home	On-campus
Tuition and fees:	$20,310	$20,310
Room and board:		$6,540
Board only:	$2,400	
Books and supplies:	$2,500	$2,500
Personal expenses:	$1,680	$1,680
Transportation:	$1,320	$1,320

Undergraduate aid. Need-based: Average financial aid package for full-time students was $15,661; for part-time $5,282. 54% awarded as scholarships/grants, 46% as loans/jobs. **Non-need-based:** 57% awarded as scholarships/grants, 43% as loans/jobs. Scholarships based on academics, art. **Student debt:** 85% of graduating class borrowed to fund education; average debt was $17,125. **Additional information:** February 15 and March 15 priority application dates for merit scholarships; deadline July 1.

Freshman aid. Need-based: Average package met 70% of need. Average scholarship/grant was $10,411; average loan $5,292.

Policies to reduce costs. Credit/placement for qualifying scores on AP examinations. Work study available nights, weekends and for part-time students.

Payment plans. Credit card, installment payment.

Application procedures. FAFSA, institutional form required. Priority date 3/15; closing date 8/1. Applicants notified on rolling basis starting 3/31, must reply within 2 week(s) of notification. **Transfers:** Priority date 3/15; no deadline. March 1 priority application date for transfer student competitive scholarship.

Contact. Financial aid office: (816) 474-5224
Christal Williams, Director of Financial Aid
4415 Warwick Boulevard
Kansas City, MO 64111-1762

Kansas City College of Legal Studies

Kansas City, Missouri
www.metropolitancollege.edu
Four-year private **Federal Code: 030993**

College costs. Quoted tuition is for bachelor's degree in court reporting. Machine $1,050; estimated cost of books $200. Tuition for associate paralegal program $6,593 per academic year; estimated cost of books $500.

	Living at home
Tuition and fees (2002-2003):	$6,534
Board only:	$750
Books and supplies:	$1,000
Transportation:	$700

Undergraduate aid. All financial aid based on need. Need-based aid available for full-time and part-time students. **Student debt:** 100% of graduating class borrowed to fund education; average debt was $12,000.

Payment plans. Installment payment.

Application procedures. FAFSA, institutional form required. No deadline. **Transfers:** No deadline.

Contact. Financial aid office: (816) 444-2232
Jeanna Blakely, Financial Aid Director
402 East Bannister Road Suite A
Kansas City, MO 64131

Lincoln University

Jefferson City, Missouri
www.lincolnu.edu
Four-year public **Federal Code: 002479**

	Living at home	On-campus
Tuition and fees (2002-2003):	$3,730	$3,730
Out-of-state:	$7,270	$7,270
Room and board:		$3,790
Board only:	$2,120	
Books and supplies:	$800	$800
Transportation:	$2,647	$1,724

Undergraduate aid. Need-based: Average financial aid package for full-time students was $5,000; for part-time $3,000. 49% awarded as scholarships/grants, 51% as loans/jobs. **Non-need-based:** 0% awarded as scholarships/grants, 100% as loans/jobs. Scholarships based on academics, alumni affiliation, art, athletics, job skills, leadership, minority status, music/drama, religious affiliation, state/district residency. **Student debt:** 65% of graduating class borrowed to fund education; average debt was $9,000.

Freshman aid. Need-based: Out of 427 full-time freshmen, 250 applied for aid; 195 were judged to have need; of these 180 received aid. Average package met 30% of need. 70 students had full need met. Average scholarship/grant was $1,000; average loan $2,625. **Non-need based:** 30 full-time freshmen with need received non-need scholarships; 50 without need received awards; 50 received athletic scholarships.

Policies to reduce costs. Tuition/fee waivers for senior citizens, employees and their families. Credit/placement for qualifying scores on AP, CLEP examinations.

Payment plans. Credit card, installment, deferred payment.

Application procedures. FAFSA required. Priority date 3/1; no closing date. Applicants notified on rolling basis starting 2/1, must reply within 2 week(s) of notification.

Contact. Alfred Robinson, Director of Financial Aid and Student Employment
820 Chestnut Street
Jefferson City, MO 65102-0029

Lindenwood University

St. Charles, Missouri
www.lindenwood.edu
Four-year private **Federal Code: 002480**

	Living at home	On-campus
Tuition and fees:	$11,650	$11,650
Room and board:		$5,400
Books and supplies:	$2,250	$2,250
Transportation:	$2,550	$1,750

Undergraduate aid. Need-based: 64% awarded as scholarships/grants, 36% as loans/jobs. Need-based aid available for part-time students. **Non-need-based:** 59% awarded as scholarships/grants, 41% as loans/jobs. Scholarships based on academics, alumni affiliation, art, athletics, job skills, leadership, minority status, music/drama.

Policies to reduce costs. Tuition/fee waivers for senior citizens. Prepayment discount; credit/placement for qualifying scores on AP, IB, CLEP examinations. Work study available nights and weekends.

Payment plans. Credit card, installment, deferred payment.

Application procedures. FAFSA required. Priority date 4/1; no closing date. Applicants notified on rolling basis, must reply within 2 week(s) of notification.

Contact. Financial aid office: (636) 949-4923
David Williams, Dean of Financial Aid
209 South Kingshighway
St. Charles, MO 63301-1695

Longview Community College

Lee's Summit, Missouri
www.kcmetro.cc.mo.us
Two-year public **Federal Code: 009140**

	Living at home
Tuition and fees (projected):	$1,980
Out-of-district:	$3,420
Out-of-state:	$4,650
Per-credit charge:	$61
Per-credit out-of-district:	$109
Per-credit out-of-state:	$150
Books and supplies:	$700
Personal expenses:	$1,500
Transportation:	$1,690

Undergraduate aid. Need-based: Average financial aid package for full-time students was $2,618; for part-time $1,544. 83% awarded as scholarships/grants, 17% as loans/jobs. **Non-need-based:** Scholarships based on academics, athletics, leadership.

Freshman aid. Need-based: Average package met 33% of need. Average scholarship/grant was $2,414; average loan $2,068.

Policies to reduce costs. Tuition/fee waivers for senior citizens, employees and their families. Credit/placement for qualifying scores on AP, CLEP examinations. Work study available nights and for part-time students.

Payment plans. Credit card, installment payment.

Application procedures. FAFSA, institutional form required. Priority date 5/30; no closing date. Applicants notified on rolling basis starting 4/8. **Transfers:** No deadline.

Contact. **Financial aid office:** (816) 672-2066
Lisa Fannan, Director of Financial Aid
500 Longview Road
Lee's Summit, MO 64081-2105

Maple Woods Community College

Kansas City, Missouri
www.kcmetro.cc.mo.us/maplewoods
Two-year public **Federal Code: 004432**

	Living at home
Tuition and fees (projected):	$1,980
Out-of-district:	$3,420
Out-of-state:	$4,650
Per-credit charge:	$61
Per-credit out-of-district:	$109
Per-credit out-of-state:	$150
Books and supplies:	$700
Personal expenses:	$1,500
Transportation:	$1,690

Undergraduate aid. **Need-based:** Average financial aid package for full-time students was $2,618; for part-time $1,544. 83% awarded as scholarships/grants, 17% as loans/jobs. **Non-need-based:** Scholarships based on academics, athletics, leadership.

Freshman aid. **Need-based:** Average package met 33% of need. Average scholarship/grant was $2,414; average loan $2,068.

Policies to reduce costs. Tuition/fee waivers for senior citizens, employees and their families. Credit/placement for qualifying scores on AP, CLEP examinations. Work study available nights and for part-time students.

Payment plans. Credit card, installment payment.

Application procedures. FAFSA, institutional form required. Priority date 5/30; no closing date. Applicants notified on rolling basis starting 4/8. **Transfers:** No deadline.

Contact. **Financial aid office:** (816) 437-3066
Hula Howard-Stevenson, Financial Aid Specialist
2601 Northeast Barry Road
Kansas City, MO 64156-1299

Maryville University of Saint Louis

St. Louis, Missouri
www.maryville.edu
Four-year private **Federal Code: 002482**

	Living at home	On-campus
Tuition and fees (2002-2003):	$14,720	$14,720
Room and board:		$6,300
Board only:	$2,196	
Books and supplies:	$830	$830
Personal expenses:	$1,270	$1,270
Transportation:	$2,500	$1,380

Undergraduate aid. **Need-based:** Average financial aid package for full-time students was $8,110; for part-time $3,500. 45% awarded as scholarships/grants, 55% as loans/jobs. **Non-need-based:** 67% awarded as scholarships/grants, 33% as loans/jobs. Scholarships based on academics, art, leadership, minority status, religious affiliation, state/district residency. **Student debt:** 54% of graduating class borrowed to fund education; average debt was $9,617.

Freshman aid. **Need-based:** Out of 280 full-time freshmen, 270 applied for aid; 194 were judged to have need; of these 194 received aid. Average package met 90% of need. 122 students had full need met. Average scholarship/grant was $9,470; average loan $2,252. **Non-need based:** 55 full-time freshmen with need received non-need scholarships; 47 without need received awards.

Merit scholarships. University Scholars Program: full-time freshmen with composite ACT score of 28 or SAT I combined 1170; high school GPA 3.5-4.0. Special application and interview required.

Policies to reduce costs. Tuition/fee waivers for senior citizens, family members, employees and their families. Credit/placement for qualifying scores on AP, IB, CLEP examinations. Work study available weekends and for part-time students.

Payment plans. Credit card, installment, deferred payment.

Application procedures. FAFSA, institutional form required. Priority date 4/1; no closing date. Applicants notified on rolling basis starting 1/15, must reply by 5/1 or within 2 week(s) of notification. **Transfers:** Priority date 4/1; no deadline. Outstanding Transfer Student Awards.

Contact. **Financial aid office:** (314) 529-9360
Martha Harbaugh, Director of Financial Aid
13550 Conway Road
St. Louis, MO 63141-7299

Mineral Area College

Park Hills, Missouri
www.mineralarea.edu
Two-year public **Federal Code: 002486**

	Living at home
Tuition and fees (projected):	$1,740
Out-of-district:	$2,460
Out-of-state:	$3,180
Per-credit charge:	$58
Per-credit out-of-district:	$82
Per-credit out-of-state:	$106
Board only:	$1,561
Books and supplies:	$900
Transportation:	$2,754

Undergraduate aid. **Need-based:** 72% awarded as scholarships/grants, 28% as loans/jobs. Need-based aid available for part-time students. **Non-need-based:** 35% awarded as scholarships/grants, 65% as loans/jobs. Scholarships based on academics, alumni affiliation, art, athletics, leadership, music/drama, state/district residency.

Policies to reduce costs. Tuition/fee waivers for senior citizens, employees and their families. Credit/placement for qualifying scores on AP, CLEP examinations. Work study available for part-time students.

Payment plans. Credit card, deferred payment.

Application procedures. FAFSA required. Priority date 4/15; no closing date. Applicants notified on rolling basis starting 2/15, must reply within 4 week(s) of notification.

Contact. **Financial aid office:** (573) 518-2133
Denise Sebastian, Financial Aid Director
PO Box 1000
Park Hills, MO 63601-1000

Missouri Baptist University

St. Louis, Missouri
www.mobap.edu
Four-year private **Federal Code: 007540**

	Living at home	On-campus
Tuition and fees:	$12,230	$12,230
Room and board:		$5,800
Board only:	$1,700	
Books and supplies:	$1,500	$1,500
Personal expenses:	$1,450	$1,450
Transportation:	$4,250	$4,250

Undergraduate aid. **Need-based:** Need-based aid available for full-time and part-time students. **Non-need-based:** Scholarships based on academics, alumni affiliation, athletics, leadership, music/drama, religious affiliation.

Policies to reduce costs. Tuition/fee waivers for children of alumni, senior citizens, family members, family of clergy, employees and their families. Credit/placement for qualifying scores on AP, CLEP examinations.

Payment plans. Credit card, installment, deferred payment.

Application procedures. FAFSA, institutional form required. Priority date 4/1; no closing date. Applicants notified on rolling basis starting 4/15, must reply within 2 week(s) of notification. **Transfers:** Institutional academic scholarships available.

Contact. **Financial aid office:** (314) 392-2368
Robert Miller, Director of Financial Aid
One College Park Drive
St. Louis, MO 63141

Missouri College

St. Louis, Missouri
www.missouricollege.com
Two-year proprietary **Federal Code: 009795**

	Living at home
Tuition and fees:	$9,382
Per-credit charge:	$309
Books and supplies:	$1,409

Undergraduate aid. Need-based: Need-based aid available for full-time and part-time students.

Policies to reduce costs. Work study available nights.

Payment plans. Credit card, installment payment.

Application procedures. FAFSA required. No deadline.

Contact. **Financial aid office:** (314) 821-7700
Leslie Harmon, Director of Financial Aid
10121 Manchester Road
St. Louis, MO 63122-1583

Missouri Southern State College

Joplin, Missouri
www.mssc.edu
Four-year public **Federal Code: 002488**

	Living at home	On-campus
Tuition and fees (2002-2003):	$2,868	$2,868
Out-of-state:	$5,568	$5,568
Room and board:		$3,800
Books and supplies:	$500	$500
Personal expenses:	$700	$1,000
Transportation:	$900	$450

Undergraduate aid. Need-based: Average financial aid package for full-time students was $4,682; for part-time $2,259. 43% awarded as scholarships/grants, 57% as loans/jobs. **Non-need-based:** 39% awarded as scholarships/grants, 61% as loans/jobs. Scholarships based on academics, alumni affiliation, art, athletics, job skills, leadership, minority status, music/drama, state/district residency. **Student debt:** 36% of graduating class borrowed to fund education; average debt was $15,168.

Freshman aid. Need-based: Average package met 70% of need. Average scholarship/grant was $6,634; average loan $2,601.

Merit scholarships. Performance Award in Foreign Language; for students majoring in French, German or Spanish, average award $1,000; for students minoring in French, German, Spanish, Japanese or Russian, average award $500; awards are competitive; based on academic credentials and prior participation in language study.

Policies to reduce costs. Tuition/fee waivers for senior citizens, employees and their families. Credit/placement for qualifying scores on AP, IB, CLEP examinations.

Payment plans. Credit card, installment payment.

Application procedures. FAFSA required. Priority date 2/15; no closing date. Applicants notified on rolling basis starting 2/15, must reply within 3 week(s) of notification. **Transfers:** Priority date 2/15; no deadline.

Contact. **Financial aid office:** (417) 625-9325
James Gilbert, Director of Student Financial Aid
3950 East Newman Road
Joplin, MO 64801-1595

Missouri Technical School

St. Louis, Missouri
www.motech.edu
Four-year proprietary **Federal Code: 016272**

College costs (2002-2003). Costs for calendar year: full-time tuition $14,625, required fees $180, average lab fees $340, on campus housing $4,500. Books/supplies: $800. Transportation: $1,565.

Undergraduate aid. All financial aid based on need. Need-based aid available for full-time and part-time students.

Policies to reduce costs. Credit/placement for qualifying scores on IB examinations.

Payment plans. Credit card, installment payment.

Application procedures. FAFSA required. No deadline. Applicants notified on rolling basis. **Transfers:** No deadline.

Contact. Terry Todd, Financial Aid Director
1167 Corporate Lake Drive
St. Louis, MO 63132-2907

Missouri Valley College

Marshall, Missouri
www.moval.edu
Four-year private **Federal Code: 002489**

	Living at home	On-campus
Tuition and fees:	$13,100	$13,100
Room and board:		$5,200
Books and supplies:	$1,300	$1,300
Personal expenses:		$2,900
Transportation:		$1,700

Undergraduate aid. Need-based: Need-based aid available for full-time and part-time students. **Non-need-based:** Scholarships based on academics, state/district residency.

Merit scholarships. Talent scholarships, 100 awards ranging from $1,000 to $13,000 (average $5,000) for general achievement (academic, athletic, artistic, other).

Policies to reduce costs. Tuition/fee waivers for children of alumni, senior citizens, family members, employees and their families. Credit/placement for qualifying scores on AP, CLEP examinations. Work study available nights and weekends.

Payment plans. Credit card, installment payment.

Application procedures. FAFSA required. Priority date 3/1; no closing date. Applicants notified on rolling basis starting 2/1, must reply within 6 week(s) of notification. **Transfers:** Closing date 3/1.

Contact. **Financial aid office:** (660) 831-4176
Bette Gorrell, Director of Financial Aid
500 East College Street
Marshall, MO 65340

Missouri Western State College

St. Joseph, Missouri
www.mwsc.edu
Four-year public **Federal Code: 002490**

	Living at home	On-campus
Tuition and fees (2002-2003):	$4,064	$4,064
Out-of-state:	$7,370	$7,370
Room and board:		$3,804
Books and supplies:	$600	$600
Personal expenses:	$1,500	$1,500
Transportation:	$600	$600

Undergraduate aid. Need-based: Average financial aid package for full-time students was $6,677; for part-time $3,499. 46% awarded as scholarships/grants, 54% as loans/jobs. **Non-need-based:** 37% awarded as scholarships/grants, 63% as loans/jobs. Scholarships based on academics, alumni affiliation, art, athletics, job skills, leadership, minority status, music/drama, state/district residency.

Freshman aid. Need-based: Out of 1,099 full-time freshmen, 886 applied for aid; 651 were judged to have need; of these 618 received aid. Average package met 15% of need. 89 students had full need met. Average scholarship/grant was $480. **Non-need based:** 315 full-time freshmen with need received non-need scholarships; 143 without need received awards; 32 received athletic scholarships.

Policies to reduce costs. Tuition/fee waivers for senior citizens, employees and their families. Credit/placement for qualifying scores on AP, CLEP examinations.

Payment plans. Credit card, installment, deferred payment.

Application procedures. FAFSA, institutional form required. Priority date 4/1; no closing date. Applicants notified on rolling basis starting 4/5, must reply within 3 week(s) of notification.

Contact. **Financial aid office:** (816) 271-4361
Angela Beam, Director of Student Financial Aid
4525 Downs Drive
St. Joseph, MO 64507

Moberly Area Community College

Moberly, Missouri
www.macc.edu
Two-year public **Federal Code: 002491**

	Living at home	On-campus
Tuition and fees (projected):	$1,650	$1,650
Out-of-district:	$2,430	$2,430
Out-of-state:	$3,840	$3,840
Per-credit charge:	$47	$47
Per-credit out-of-district:	$73	$73
Per-credit out-of-state:	$120	$120
Room only:		$1,700
Board only:	$800	
Books and supplies:	$600	$600
Personal expenses:	$1,500	$1,500
Transportation:	$1,700	$980

Undergraduate aid. Need-based: Average financial aid package for full-time students was $4,115; for part-time $4,115. 72% awarded as scholarships/grants, 28% as loans/jobs. **Non-need-based:** 71% awarded as scholarships/grants, 29% as loans/jobs. Scholarships based on academics, alumni affiliation, athletics, leadership, music/drama. **Student debt:** 18% of graduating class borrowed to fund education; average debt was $7,500.

Freshman aid. Need-based: Out of 540 full-time freshmen, 314 applied for aid; 222 were judged to have need; of these 222 received aid. Average package met 25% of need. 52 students had full need met. Average scholarship/grant was $2,074; average loan $1,631. **Non-need based:** 151 full-time freshmen with need received non-need scholarships; 72 without need received awards; 13 received athletic scholarships.

Policies to reduce costs. Tuition/fee waivers for senior citizens, employees and their families. Credit/placement for qualifying scores on AP, IB, CLEP examinations. Work study available nights, weekends and for part-time students.

Payment plans. Credit card, installment payment.

Application procedures. FAFSA required. Priority date 4/1; no closing date. Applicants notified on rolling basis starting 4/1, must reply by 7/15 or within 2 week(s) of notification.

Contact. Amy Hager, Director of Financial Aid
101 College Avenue
Moberly, MO 65270

National American University: Kansas City

Kansas City, Missouri
www.national.edu
Four-year proprietary **Federal Code: E00639**

	Living at home
Tuition and fees (2002-2003):	$9,575
Books and supplies:	$900
Transportation:	$500

Undergraduate aid. All financial aid based on need. Need-based aid available for full-time and part-time students.

Policies to reduce costs. Tuition/fee waivers for family members, employees and their families. Credit/placement for qualifying scores on CLEP examinations. Work study available nights, weekends and for part-time students.

Payment plans. Credit card, installment payment.

Application procedures. FAFSA required. No deadline. Applicants notified on rolling basis starting 6/4. **Transfers:** No deadline.

Contact. Mary Anderson, Financial Aid Officer
4200 Blue Ridge Boulevard
Kansas City, MO 64133

North Central Missouri College

Trenton, Missouri
www.ncmc.cc.mo.us
Two-year public **Federal Code: 002514**

	Living at home	On-campus
Tuition and fees (2002-2003):	$1,770	$1,770
Out-of-district:	$2,520	$2,520
Out-of-state:	$3,390	$3,390
Per-credit charge:	$44	$44
Per-credit out-of-district:	$69	$69
Per-credit out-of-state:	$98	$98
Room and board:		$3,260
Board only:	$1,500	
Books and supplies:	$600	$600
Personal expenses:	$1,278	$1,278
Transportation:	$1,500	$1,200

Undergraduate aid. Need-based: Need-based aid available for full-time and part-time students. **Non-need-based:** Scholarships based on academics, athletics, minority status, music/drama.

Policies to reduce costs. Tuition/fee waivers for adults, senior citizens, minority students, employees and their families. Credit/placement for qualifying scores on AP, CLEP examinations. Work study available nights, weekends and for part-time students.

Payment plans. Credit card, installment payment.

Application procedures. FAFSA, institutional form required. Priority date 3/15; no closing date. Applicants notified on rolling basis starting 3/15. **Transfers:** Transfer students may not receive same awards after transferring since some funds campus-based.

Contact. **Financial aid office:** (660) 359-3948 ext. 402
John Brandt, Financial Aid Officer
1301 Main Street
Trenton, MO 64683

Northwest Missouri State University

Maryville, Missouri
www.nwmissouri.edu
Four-year public **Federal Code: 002496**

College costs. Primary textbooks free of charge.

	Living at home	On-campus
Tuition and fees (2002-2003):	$3,600	$3,600
Out-of-state:	$6,067	$6,067
Room and board:		$4,322
Books and supplies:	$400	$400
Personal expenses:	$1,350	$1,350
Transportation:	$800	$800

Undergraduate aid. Need-based: Need-based aid available for full-time and part-time students. **Non-need-based:** Scholarships based on academics, athletics, state/district residency.

Policies to reduce costs. Tuition/fee waivers for children of alumni, senior citizens, minority students, employees and their families. Credit/placement for qualifying scores on AP, CLEP examinations. Work study available nights.

Payment plans. Credit card, installment payment.

Application procedures. FAFSA required. Priority date 3/1; no closing date. Applicants notified on rolling basis starting 4/10, must reply within 2 week(s) of notification. **Transfers:** Priority date 4/1; no deadline. Transfer scholarship based on academic record.

Contact. Del Morley, Director of Financial Assistance
800 University Drive
Maryville, MO 64468-6001

Ozark Christian College
Joplin, Missouri
www.occ.edu
Four-year private **Federal Code: 015569**

	Living at home	On-campus
Tuition and fees (2002-2003):	$5,350	$5,350
Room and board:		$3,830
Books and supplies:	$600	$600
Personal expenses:	$1,500	$1,500
Transportation:	$1,350	$1,350

Undergraduate aid. Need-based: 49% awarded as scholarships/grants, 51% as loans/jobs. Need-based aid available for part-time students. **Non-need-based:** 77% awarded as scholarships/grants, 23% as loans/jobs. Scholarships based on academics.

Policies to reduce costs. Tuition/fee waivers for senior citizens, family of clergy, employees and their families.

Payment plans. Credit card, installment payment.

Application procedures. FAFSA, institutional form required. Priority date 4/1; no closing date. Applicants notified on rolling basis starting 6/1. **Transfers:** No deadline. Academic transcripts required. ACT scores may qualify student for grants or scholarships.

Contact. Debi Mayfield, Director of Financial Aid
1111 North Main Street
Joplin, MO 64801

Ozarks Technical Community College
Springfield, Missouri
www.otc.edu
Two-year public **Federal Code: 030830**

	Living at home
Tuition and fees (2002-2003):	$2,160
Out-of-district:	$2,760
Out-of-state:	$3,660
Per-credit charge:	$62
Per-credit out-of-district:	$82
Per-credit out-of-state:	$112
Board only:	$2,022
Books and supplies:	$600
Personal expenses:	$1,100
Transportation:	$1,380

Undergraduate aid. All financial aid based on need. Need-based aid available for full-time and part-time students.

Policies to reduce costs. Tuition/fee waivers for senior citizens, employees and their families. Credit/placement for qualifying scores on AP, IB, CLEP examinations.

Payment plans. Credit card, installment, deferred payment.

Application procedures. FAFSA, institutional form required. Priority date 5/1; closing date 7/16. Applicants notified on rolling basis starting 5/16.

Contact. Financial aid office: (417) 895-7142
Jeff Ford, Director of Financial Aid
Box 5958
Springfield, MO 65801

Patricia Stevens College
St. Louis, Missouri
www.patriciastevenscollege.com
Two-year proprietary **Federal Code: 008552**

College costs. Books included in tuition.

	Living at home
Tuition and fees (2002-2003):	$8,993
Per-credit charge:	$160

Undergraduate aid. All financial aid based on need. Need-based aid available for full-time and part-time students.

Policies to reduce costs. Tuition/fee waivers for family members. Tuition at time of enrollment guaranteed for 2 years.

Payment plans. Credit card, installment payment.

Application procedures. FAFSA required. No deadline. Applicants notified on rolling basis.

Contact. Greg Elsenrath, Financial Aid Director
330 North Fourth Street Suite 306
St. Louis, MO 63102

Penn Valley Community College
Kansas City, Missouri
www.kcmetro.cc.mo.us/pennvalley
Two-year public **Federal Code: 002484**

College costs. Lab fees $25 per-credit hour.

	Living at home
Tuition and fees (projected):	$1,980
Out-of-district:	$3,420
Out-of-state:	$4,650
Per-credit charge:	$61
Per-credit out-of-district:	$109
Per-credit out-of-state:	$150
Books and supplies:	$700
Personal expenses:	$1,500
Transportation:	$1,690

Undergraduate aid. Need-based: Average financial aid package for full-time students was $2,618; for part-time $1,544. 86% awarded as scholarships/grants, 14% as loans/jobs. **Non-need-based:** Scholarships based on academics, athletics, leadership.

Freshman aid. Need-based: Average package met 33% of need. Average scholarship/grant was $2,414; average loan $2,068.

Policies to reduce costs. Tuition/fee waivers for senior citizens, employees and their families. Credit/placement for qualifying scores on AP, CLEP examinations. Work study available nights and for part-time students.

Payment plans. Credit card, installment payment.

Application procedures. FAFSA, institutional form required. Priority date 5/30; no closing date. Applicants notified on rolling basis starting 4/8. **Transfers:** No deadline.

Contact. Financial aid office: (816) 759-4066
Toni Alexander, Financial Aid Director
3201 Southwest Trafficway
Kansas City, MO 64111-2429

Pinnacle Career Institute
Kansas City, Missouri
www.electronicsinstitute.com
Two-year proprietary **Federal Code: 010405**

College costs. Per credit hour charge for computer program $170; lab fees $120 for first academic year.

	Living at home
Tuition and fees:	$8,565
Books and supplies:	$965

Contact. Debbie Fajen, Director of Financial Aid
15329 Kensington Avenue
Kansas City, MO 64147-1212

Ranken Technical College
St. Louis, Missouri
www.ranken.org
Two-year private **Federal Code: 012500**

	Living at home	On-campus
Tuition and fees (2002-2003):	$8,550	$8,550
Per-credit charge:	$354	$354
Room and board:		$4,000
Board only:	$3,078	
Books and supplies:	$1,700	$1,700
Personal expenses:	$1,774	$1,774
Transportation:	$2,482	$1,241

Undergraduate aid. Need-based: Need-based aid available for full-time and part-time students.

Policies to reduce costs. Tuition/fee waivers for employees and their families. Credit/placement for qualifying scores on IB examinations.

Payment plans. Credit card, installment payment.

Application procedures. FAFSA required. No deadline. Applicants notified on rolling basis starting 4/1.

Contact. **Financial aid office:** (314) 286-4866
Michelle Williams, Director, Financial Aid
4431 Finney Avenue
St. Louis, MO 63113

Research College of Nursing

Kansas City, Missouri
www.researchcollege.edu
Four-year private **Federal Code: 006392**

	Living at home	On-campus
Tuition and fees (2002-2003):	$16,580	$16,580
Room and board:		$5,240
Board only:	$500	
Books and supplies:	$720	$720
Personal expenses:	$915	$915
Transportation:	$1,250	$825

Undergraduate aid. Need-based: Need-based aid available for full-time and part-time students. **Additional information:** Financial aid handled by Rockhurst University for freshmen and sophomores.

Policies to reduce costs. Tuition/fee waivers for children of alumni, family members, employees and their families. Prepayment discount; credit/placement for qualifying scores on AP, CLEP examinations.

Payment plans. Credit card, installment, deferred payment.

Application procedures. FAFSA, institutional form required. Priority date 3/15; no closing date. Applicants notified on rolling basis starting 3/15.

Contact. **Financial aid office:** (816) 276-4728
Stacie Withers, Director of Financial Aid
2300 East Meyer Boulevard
Kansas City, MO 64132-1199

Rockhurst University

Kansas City, Missouri
www.rockhurst.edu
Four-year private **Federal Code: 002499**

	Living at home	On-campus
Tuition and fees (2002-2003):	$16,380	$16,380
Room and board:		$5,200
Board only:	$5,794	
Books and supplies:	$778	$778
Personal expenses:	$2,430	$2,874
Transportation:	$1,020	$1,816

Undergraduate aid. Need-based: Average financial aid package for full-time students was $14,306; for part-time $8,725. 45% awarded as scholarships/grants, 55% as loans/jobs. **Non-need-based:** 57% awarded as scholarships/grants, 43% as loans/jobs. Scholarships based on academics, alumni affiliation, athletics, leadership, minority status, music/drama. **Student debt:** 55% of graduating class borrowed to fund education; average debt was $13,443. **Additional information:** Scholarships available to students from Catholic and Jesuit high schools. Auditions, portfolios required for some scholarships.

Freshman aid. Need-based: Out of 214 full-time freshmen, 207 applied for aid; 182 were judged to have need; of these 179 received aid. Average package met 89% of need. 2 students had full need met. Average scholarship/grant was $5,652; average loan $5,668. **Non-need based:** 179 full-time freshmen with need received non-need scholarships; 17 without need received awards; 15 received athletic scholarships.

Policies to reduce costs. Tuition/fee waivers for children of alumni, senior citizens, family members, family of clergy, employees and their families. Credit/placement for qualifying scores on AP, IB, CLEP examinations.

Payment plans. Credit card, installment, deferred payment.

Application procedures. FAFSA, institutional form required. Priority date 3/1; no closing date. Applicants notified on rolling basis starting 2/15, must reply within 4 week(s) of notification. **Transfers:** Scholarships awarded to qualified first-time transfers.

Contact. **Financial aid office:** (816) 501-4100
Carla Boren, Director of Financial Aid
1100 Rockhurst Road
Kansas City, MO 64110-2561

St. Charles Community College

St. Peters, Missouri
www.stchas.edu
Two-year public **Federal Code: 025306**

	Living at home
Tuition and fees:	$1,740
Out-of-district:	$2,370
Out-of-state:	$3,510
Per-credit charge:	$48
Per-credit out-of-district:	$69
Per-credit out-of-state:	$107
Board only:	$1,800
Books and supplies:	$600
Personal expenses:	$1,280
Transportation:	$800

Undergraduate aid. Need-based: 73% awarded as scholarships/grants, 27% as loans/jobs. Need-based aid available for part-time students. **Non-need-based:** 58% awarded as scholarships/grants, 42% as loans/jobs. Scholarships based on academics, art, athletics, leadership, music/drama.

Policies to reduce costs. Tuition/fee waivers for senior citizens, employees and their families. Credit/placement for qualifying scores on AP, IB, CLEP examinations. Work study available for part-time students.

Payment plans. Credit card payment.

Application procedures. FAFSA, institutional form required. Priority date 6/1; no closing date. Applicants notified on rolling basis starting 4/1, must reply within 3 week(s) of notification.

Contact. **Financial aid office:** (636) 922-8270
Karen Vossenkemper, Director of Financial Assistance
4601 Mid Rivers Mall Drive
St. Peters, MO 63376

St. Louis Christian College

Florissant, Missouri
www.slcc4ministry.edu
Four-year private **Federal Code: 012580**

	Living at home	On-campus
Tuition and fees (2002-2003):	$5,910	$5,910
Room and board:		$3,380
Books and supplies:	$350	$350
Personal expenses:	$1,200	$600
Transportation:	$405	$400

Undergraduate aid. Need-based: Average financial aid package for full-time students was $6,332; for part-time $3,453. 51% awarded as scholarships/grants, 49% as loans/jobs. **Non-need-based:** 41% awarded as scholarships/grants, 59% as loans/jobs. Scholarships based on academics, alumni affiliation, leadership, music/drama, religious affiliation. **Student debt:** 48% of graduating class borrowed to fund education; average debt was $13,390.

Freshman aid. Need-based: Out of 23 full-time freshmen, 23 applied for aid; 16 were judged to have need; of these 15 received aid. Average package met 38% of need. Average scholarship/grant was $2,425; average loan $1,781. **Non-need based:** 9 full-time freshmen with need received non-need scholarships; 6 without need received awards.

Merit scholarships. President's Scholarship; full tuition, ACT score 30 or higher, 1 available. Chancellor's Scholarships; two-thirds tuition, ACT 28 or higher, 2 available. Dean's Scholarships; half tuition, ACT 28 or higher, unlimited number available.

Policies to reduce costs. Tuition/fee waivers for children of alumni, employees and their families. Credit/placement for qualifying scores on AP, CLEP examinations. Work study available for part-time students.

Payment plans. Credit card, installment payment.

Application procedures. FAFSA, institutional form required. Priority date 7/1; no closing date. Applicants notified on rolling basis starting 7/20, must reply within 2 week(s) of notification. **Transfers:** No deadline.

Contact. Cathi Wilhoit, Financial Aid Director
1360 Grandview Drive
Florissant, MO 63033

St. Louis College of Pharmacy

St. Louis, Missouri
www.stlcop.edu
Six-year private **Federal Code: 002504**

	Living at home	On-campus
Tuition and fees:	$16,450	$16,450
Room and board:		$6,750
Board only:	$3,520	
Books and supplies:	$1,000	$1,000
Personal expenses:	$1,250	$1,700
Transportation:	$1,250	$630

Undergraduate aid. Need-based: Average financial aid package for full-time students was $8,737; for part-time $4,901. 23% awarded as scholarships/grants, 77% as loans/jobs. **Non-need-based:** 32% awarded as scholarships/grants, 68% as loans/jobs. Scholarships based on academics, state/district residency. **Student debt:** 83% of graduating class borrowed to fund education; average debt was $51,193. **Additional information:** Missouri Advantage Program awards need-based grant of $2,500 to students who agree to work in state of Missouri for at least one year after graduation; grant becomes loan if student works out of state.

Freshman aid. Need-based: Out of 201 full-time freshmen, 200 applied for aid; 172 were judged to have need; of these 172 received aid. Average package met 44% of need. 1 students had full need met. Average scholarship/grant was $5,400; average loan $3,934. **Non-need based:** 170 full-time freshmen with need received non-need scholarships; 28 without need received awards.

Policies to reduce costs. Tuition/fee waivers for employees and their families. Credit/placement for qualifying scores on AP examinations. Work study available nights and weekends.

Payment plans. Installment payment.

Application procedures. FAFSA, institutional form required. Priority date 3/1; no closing date. Applicants notified on rolling basis starting 2/1, must reply within 2 week(s) of notification. **Transfers:** No deadline.

Contact. Financial aid office: (314) 367-8700
David Rice, Director of Financial Aid
4588 Parkview Place
St. Louis, MO 63110

St. Louis Community College at Florissant Valley

St. Louis, Missouri
www.stlcc.edu
Two-year public **Federal Code: 002471**

	Living at home
Tuition and fees (2002-2003):	$1,680
Out-of-district:	$2,190
Out-of-state:	$3,090
Per-credit charge:	$48
Per-credit out-of-district:	$65
Per-credit out-of-state:	$95
Board only:	$3,000
Books and supplies:	$800
Personal expenses:	$2,000
Transportation:	$960

Policies to reduce costs. Tuition/fee waivers for employees and their families. Credit/placement for qualifying scores on CLEP examinations.

Payment plans. Credit card payment.

Application procedures. FAFSA required. Priority date 8/1; no closing date. Applicants notified on rolling basis starting 5/1.

Contact. Financial aid office: (314) 595-4231
Jim Camparo, Manager
3400 Pershall Road
St. Louis, MO 63135

St. Louis Community College at Forest Park

St. Louis, Missouri
www.stlcc.edu
Two-year public **Federal Code: 6226**

	Living at home
Tuition and fees (2002-2003):	$1,680
Out-of-district:	$2,190
Out-of-state:	$3,090
Per-credit charge:	$48
Per-credit out-of-district:	$65
Per-credit out-of-state:	$95
Board only:	$3,000
Books and supplies:	$800
Personal expenses:	$2,300
Transportation:	$700

Undergraduate aid. Need-based: Need-based aid available for full-time and part-time students. **Non-need-based:** Scholarships based on academics, art, athletics, leadership, music/drama.

Policies to reduce costs. Tuition/fee waivers for senior citizens, employees and their families. Credit/placement for qualifying scores on AP, CLEP examinations.

Payment plans. Credit card payment.

Application procedures. FAFSA required. Priority date 3/15; no closing date. Applicants notified by 7/2. **Transfers:** Priority date 3/15; no deadline.

Contact. Financial aid office: (314) 644-9117
Herb Gross, Manager of Financial Aid
5600 Oakland
St. Louis, MO 63110

St. Louis Community College at Meramec

St. Louis, Missouri
www.stlcc.edu
Two-year public **Federal Code: 002471**

	Living at home
Tuition and fees (2002-2003):	$1,680
Out-of-district:	$2,190
Out-of-state:	$3,090
Per-credit charge:	$48
Per-credit out-of-district:	$65
Per-credit out-of-state:	$95
Board only:	$3,500
Books and supplies:	$800
Personal expenses:	$2,100
Transportation:	$1,200

Undergraduate aid. Need-based: Need-based aid available for full-time and part-time students.

Policies to reduce costs. Tuition/fee waivers for senior citizens, employees and their families. Credit/placement for qualifying scores on AP, CLEP examinations.

Payment plans. Credit card payment.

Application procedures. FAFSA, institutional form required. Closing date 6/30. Applicants notified on rolling basis starting 2/1.

Contact. Helen Nauman, Manager of Student Aid
11333 Big Bend Boulevard
Kirkwood, MO 63122-5799

St. Louis University

St. Louis, Missouri
www.imagine.slu.edu
Four-year private **Federal Code: 002506**

	Living at home	On-campus
Tuition and fees (2002-2003):	$21,000	$21,000
Room and board:		$7,310
Board only:	$3,270	
Books and supplies:	$1,040	$1,040
Personal expenses:	$1,000	$1,000
Transportation:	$1,500	$1,500

Undergraduate aid. Need-based: Average financial aid package for full-time students was $20,707; for part-time $12,517. 64% awarded as scholarships/grants, 36% as loans/jobs. **Non-need-based:** 88% awarded as scholarships/grants, 12% as loans/jobs. Scholarships based on academics, alumni affiliation, art, athletics, job skills, leadership, minority status, music/drama, religious affiliation, state/district residency. **Student debt:** 59% of graduating class borrowed to fund education; average debt was $14,989. **Additional information:** Physical therapy scholarship candidates must apply by December 15. Occupational therapy students should apply earlier.

Freshman aid. Need-based: Average package met 75% of need. Average scholarship/grant was $14,787; average loan $5,728.

Policies to reduce costs. Tuition/fee waivers for adults, children of alumni, minority students, family members, unemployed or children of unemployed, family of clergy, employees and their families. Credit/placement for qualifying scores on AP, IB, CLEP examinations. Work study available nights, weekends and for part-time students.

Payment plans. Credit card, installment, deferred payment.

Application procedures. FAFSA required. Priority date 4/1; closing date 5/1. Applicants notified on rolling basis starting 1/15, must reply by 5/1. **Transfers:** No deadline. Students should file FAFSA by April 1 for Missouri state funds.

Contact. **Financial aid office:** (314) 977-2350
Harold Deuser, Financial Aid Director
221 North Grand Boulevard
St. Louis, MO 63103-2097

St. Luke's College

Kansas City, Missouri
www.saint-lukes.org/about/slc
Upper-division private **Federal Code: 009782**

	Living at home
Tuition and fees (projected):	$8,710
Books and supplies:	$900

Undergraduate aid. Need-based: Average financial aid package for full-time students was $9,500. 25% awarded as scholarships/grants, 75% as loans/jobs. Need-based aid available for part-time students. **Student debt:** 90% of graduating class borrowed to fund education; average debt was $25,000.

Policies to reduce costs. Tuition/fee waivers for employees and their families. Credit/placement for qualifying scores on CLEP examinations.

Payment plans. Credit card payment.

Application procedures. FAFSA, institutional form required. No deadline. Applicants notified by 5/1.

Contact. Jeff Gannon, Director of Financial Aid
4426 Wornall Road
Kansas City, MO 64111

Sanford-Brown College

Fenton, Missouri
www.sanfordbrown.com
Two-year proprietary **Federal Code: 022052**

College costs. Business program tuition: $8,850 per year.

	Living at home
Tuition and fees (2002-2003):	$9,150
Books and supplies:	$1,714

Undergraduate aid. Need-based: Need-based aid available for full-time and part-time students.

Policies to reduce costs. Tuition/fee waivers for employees and their families. Work study available nights and weekends.

Application procedures. FAFSA required. No deadline.

Contact. Karen Koenig-Griffin, Director of Financial Aid
1203 Smizer Mill Road
Fenton, MO 63026

Southeast Missouri State University

Cape Girardeau, Missouri
www.semo.edu
Four-year public **Federal Code: 002501**

	Living at home	On-campus
Tuition and fees (2002-2003):	$4,035	$4,035
Out-of-state:	$7,110	$7,110
Room and board:		$4,938
Board only:	$2,060	
Books and supplies:	$350	$350
Personal expenses:	$1,855	$1,855
Transportation:	$1,052	$765

Undergraduate aid. Need-based: Average financial aid package for full-time students was $5,506; for part-time $3,900. 45% awarded as scholarships/grants, 55% as loans/jobs. **Non-need-based:** 30% awarded as scholarships/grants, 70% as loans/jobs. Scholarships based on academics, alumni affiliation, art, athletics, job skills, leadership, minority status, music/drama, state/district residency. **Student debt:** 56% of graduating class borrowed to fund education; average debt was $13,854.

Freshman aid. Need-based: Out of 1,458 full-time freshmen, 1,242 applied for aid; 687 were judged to have need; of these 680 received aid. Average package met 80% of need. 387 students had full need met. Average scholarship/grant was $3,483; average loan $2,589. **Non-need based:** 65 full-time freshmen with need received non-need scholarships; 395 without need received awards; 38 received athletic scholarships.

Policies to reduce costs. Tuition/fee waivers for senior citizens, employees and their families. Credit/placement for qualifying scores on AP, CLEP examinations. Work study available nights, weekends and for part-time students.

Payment plans. Credit card, installment payment.

Application procedures. FAFSA required. Priority date 3/1; no closing date. Applicants notified on rolling basis starting 4/1, must reply within 3 week(s) of notification.

Contact. **Financial aid office:** (573) 651-2253
Karen Walker, Director of Financial Aid Services
One University Plaza
Cape Girardeau, MO 63701

Southwest Baptist University

Bolivar, Missouri
www.sbuniv.edu
Four-year private **Federal Code: 002502**

	Living at home	On-campus
Tuition and fees:	$11,550	$11,550
Room and board:		$3,500
Board only:	$1,350	
Books and supplies:	$800	$800
Personal expenses:	$1,000	$1,000
Transportation:	$1,000	$1,000

Undergraduate aid. Need-based: Need-based aid available for full-time and part-time students. **Non-need-based:** Scholarships based on academics, alumni affiliation, art, athletics, job skills, leadership, minority status, music/drama, religious affiliation, state/district residency.

Policies to reduce costs. Tuition/fee waivers for employees and their families. Credit/placement for qualifying scores on AP, IB, CLEP examinations.

Payment plans. Credit card, installment, deferred payment.

Application procedures. FAFSA, institutional form required. Priority date 3/15; no closing date. Applicants notified on rolling basis starting 3/1, must reply within 2 week(s) of notification. **Transfers:** No deadline.

Contact. **Financial aid office:** (417) 328-1822
Brad Gamble, Director of Financial Aid
1600 University Avenue
Bolivar, MO 65613-2597

Southwest Missouri State University

Springfield, Missouri
www.smsu.edu
Four-year public **Federal Code: 002503**

	Living at home	On-campus
Tuition and fees:	$4,636	$4,636
Out-of-state:	$8,776	$8,776
Room and board:		$4,850
Board only:	$1,300	
Books and supplies:	$400	$400
Personal expenses:	$1,276	$1,276
Transportation:	$2,000	$2,000

Undergraduate aid. Need-based: Average financial aid package for full-time students was $7,253; for part-time $5,871. 37% awarded as scholarships/grants, 63% as loans/jobs. **Non-need-based:** 53% awarded as scholarships/grants, 47% as loans/jobs. Scholarships based on academics, alumni affiliation, art, athletics, job skills, leadership, minority status, music/drama, state/district residency. **Student debt:** 60% of graduating class borrowed to fund education; average debt was $12,993. **Additional information:** Extensive scholarship program offered to freshmen and transfer students. Out-of-state fee stipends available. Student employment service available to assist students in securing employment on campus and in community.

Freshman aid. Need-based: Out of 2,707 full-time freshmen, 1,874 applied for aid; 1,282 were judged to have need; of these 1,219 received aid. Average package met 63% of need. 162 students had full need met. Average scholarship/grant was $3,149; average loan $2,274. **Non-need based:** 634 full-time freshmen with need received non-need scholarships; 197 without need received awards; 60 received athletic scholarships.

Merit scholarships. Presidential Scholarships, full tuition, room and board, based on ACT score 30 or higher and rank in top 10% of class, 40 awarded, application deadline January 15; Board of Governors Scholarships, cover; required student fees, based on ACT score of 28 or higher and either top 10% class rank or GPA of 3.8 or higher, unlimited number of awards; Freshman Academic Scholarships, $2,000 per year, based on ACT score of 26 or higher and either top 20% class rank or GPA of 3.6 or higher, unlimited number of awards; Freshman Recognition Scholarships, $1,000 per year, based on ACT score of 24 or 25 and either top 10% class rank or GPA of 3.8 or higher, unlimited number of awards; Multicultural Leadership Scholarships, cover; required student fees, for students in top half of class who have demonstrated leadership in minority community, 40 awarded.

Policies to reduce costs. Tuition/fee waivers for children of alumni, senior citizens, employees and their families. Credit/placement for qualifying scores on AP, IB, CLEP examinations. Work study available nights, weekends and for part-time students.

Payment plans. Credit card, deferred payment.

Application procedures. FAFSA required. Priority date 3/30; no closing date. **Transfers:** Priority date 3/31; no deadline.

Contact. Financial aid office: (417) 836-5262
Billie Jo Hamilton, Director of Financial Aid
901 South National
Springfield, MO 65804-0094

Southwest Missouri State University: West Plains Campus

West Plains, Missouri
www.wp.smsu.edu
Two-year public **Federal Code: 031060**

	Living at home	On-campus
Tuition and fees (2002-2003):	$2,680	$2,680
Out-of-state:	$5,170	$5,170
Per-credit charge:	$83	$83
Per-credit out-of-state:	$166	$166
Room and board:		$4,350
Books and supplies:	$700	$700

Undergraduate aid. Need-based: Need-based aid available for full-time and part-time students.

Policies to reduce costs. Tuition/fee waivers for senior citizens, employees and their families. Credit/placement for qualifying scores on AP, IB, CLEP examinations. Work study available nights, weekends and for part-time students.

Payment plans. Deferred payment.

Application procedures. FAFSA required. Priority date 3/31; no closing date. Applicants notified on rolling basis, must reply within 4 week(s) of notification.

Contact. Financial aid office: (417) 255-7243
Donna Basham, Coordinator of Financial Aid
128 Garfield
West Plains, MO 65775

Springfield College

Springfield, Missouri
Two-year proprietary
Federal Code: 022506

	Living at home
Tuition and fees (2002-2003):	$9,468
Per-credit charge:	$191
Books and supplies:	$1,000
Personal expenses:	$1,260
Transportation:	$2,025

Undergraduate aid. All financial aid based on need. Need-based aid available for full-time and part-time students.

Policies to reduce costs. Tuition at time of enrollment guaranteed for 2 years; credit/placement for qualifying scores on AP examinations.

Payment plans. Credit card, installment payment.

Application procedures. No deadline. Applicants notified on rolling basis.

Contact. Shawn Shelton, Financial Aid Director
1010 West Sunshine Avenue
Springfield, MO 65807

Stephens College

Columbia, Missouri
www.stephens.edu
Four-year private **Federal Code: 002512**

	Living at home	On-campus
Tuition and fees (2002-2003):	$16,715	$16,715
Room and board:		$6,050
Board only:	$960	
Books and supplies:	$600	$600
Personal expenses:	$1,835	$1,835
Transportation:	$700	$700

Undergraduate aid. Need-based: Average financial aid package for full-time students was $17,694; for part-time $8,931. 80% awarded as scholarships/grants, 20% as loans/jobs. **Non-need-based:** 58% awarded as scholarships/grants, 42% as loans/jobs. Scholarships based on academics, alumni affiliation, leadership. **Student debt:** 78% of graduating class borrowed to fund education; average debt was $16,455.

Freshman aid. Need-based: Out of 122 full-time freshmen, 103 applied for aid; 89 were judged to have need; of these 89 received aid. Average package met 84% of need. 27 students had full need met. Average scholarship/grant was $11,167; average loan $2,525. **Non-need based:** 13 full-time freshmen with need received non-need scholarships; 14 without need received awards.

Policies to reduce costs. Tuition/fee waivers for employees and their families. Credit/placement for qualifying scores on AP, IB, CLEP examinations. Work study available nights and weekends.

Payment plans. Credit card, installment payment.

Application procedures. FAFSA required. Priority date 3/15; no closing date. Applicants notified on rolling basis starting 3/1, must reply within 2 week(s) of notification. **Transfers:** No deadline. Phi Theta Kappa students transferring from 2-year institutions eligible for Phi Theta Kappa scholarship.

Contact. Financial aid office: (800) 876-7207
Rachel Touchatt, Director of Financial Aid
1200 East Broadway, Box 2121
Columbia, MO 65215

Three Rivers Community College

Poplar Bluff, Missouri
www.trcc.cc.mo.us
Two-year public **Federal Code: 004713**

College costs. Book rental $12 per book. Refundable book deposit fee $25 per semester. Lab fees vary per course.

	Living at home
Tuition and fees:	$1,860
Out-of-district:	$2,820
Out-of-state:	$3,480
Per-credit charge:	$54
Per-credit out-of-district:	$86
Per-credit out-of-state:	$108
Board only:	$1,800
Books and supplies:	$400
Personal expenses:	$1,040
Transportation:	$1,612

Undergraduate aid. Need-based: Need-based aid available for full-time and part-time students. **Non-need-based:** Scholarships based on academics, athletics, state/district residency.

Policies to reduce costs. Tuition/fee waivers for senior citizens, employees and their families. Credit/placement for qualifying scores on AP, CLEP examinations. Work study available for part-time students.

Payment plans. Credit card, installment payment.

Application procedures. FAFSA, institutional form required. Priority date 5/1; no closing date. Applicants notified on rolling basis starting 6/1, must reply within 2 week(s) of notification. **Transfers:** No deadline.

Contact. Financial aid office: (573) 840-9607
Pauletta Burns, Director of Financial Aid
2080 Three Rivers Boulevard
Poplar Bluff, MO 63901-1308

Truman State University

Kirksville, Missouri
www.truman.edu
Four-year public **Federal Code: 002495**

	Living at home	On-campus
Tuition and fees (2002-2003):	$4,350	$4,350
Out-of-state:	$7,750	$7,750
Room and board:		$4,928
Books and supplies:	$600	$600
Personal expenses:	$1,800	$1,800
Transportation:	$200	$500

Undergraduate aid. Need-based: Average financial aid package for full-time students was $5,263. 33% awarded as scholarships/grants, 67% as loans/jobs. Need-based aid available for part-time students. **Non-need-based:** 70% awarded as scholarships/grants, 30% as loans/jobs. Scholarships based on academics, alumni affiliation, art, athletics, leadership, music/drama. **Student debt:** 46% of graduating class borrowed to fund education; average debt was $14,382. **Additional information:** Out-of-state students whose parents work in Missouri may deduct $1 for every dollar paid in Missouri income taxes from out-of-state tuition.

Freshman aid. Need-based: Out of 1,459 full-time freshmen, 760 applied for aid; 399 were judged to have need; of these 383 received aid. Average package met 88% of need. 230 students had full need met. Average scholarship/grant was $2,955; average loan $2,677. **Non-need based:** 341 full-time freshmen with need received non-need scholarships; 932 without need received awards; 56 received athletic scholarships.

Merit scholarships. Pershing Scholarship: awards 12 full scholarships for tuition and residence hall room and board to outstanding scholars & leaders; provides up to $4,000 for a Study-Abroad experience. Truman Leadership Award: provides amounts up to full tuition, room & board for Missouri residents; awarded to high school seniors who demonstrate energetic leadership in the classroom, school, and community as well as academic acheivement.

Policies to reduce costs. Tuition/fee waivers for senior citizens, employees and their families. Credit/placement for qualifying scores on AP, IB, CLEP examinations. Work study available nights, weekends and for part-time students.

Payment plans. Credit card, installment payment.

Application procedures. FAFSA, institutional form required. Priority date 4/1; no closing date. Applicants notified on rolling basis starting 4/15, must reply within 4 week(s) of notification. **Transfers:** Limited number of automatic and competitive awards offered to transfer students.

Contact. Financial aid office: (660) 785-4130
Melinda Wood, Financial Aid Director
McClain Hall 205
Kirksville, MO 63501-9980

University of Missouri: Columbia

Columbia, Missouri
www.missouri.edu
Four-year public **Federal Code: 002516**

	Living at home	On-campus
Tuition and fees (2002-2003):	$5,552	$5,552
Out-of-state:	$14,705	$14,705
Room and board:		$5,335
Board only:	$3,125	
Books and supplies:	$835	$835
Personal expenses:	$2,436	$2,436

Undergraduate aid. Need-based: Average financial aid package for full-time students was $7,544; for part-time $6,457. 53% awarded as scholarships/grants, 47% as loans/jobs. **Non-need-based:** 52% awarded as scholarships/grants, 48% as loans/jobs. Scholarships based on academics, alumni affiliation, art, athletics, leadership, minority status, music/drama, state/district residency. **Student debt:** 42% of graduating class borrowed to fund education; average debt was $17,137. **Additional information:** Scholarship available for international students based on written competition.

Freshman aid. Need-based: Out of 4,383 full-time freshmen, 3,689 applied for aid; 1,937 were judged to have need; of these 1,937 received aid. Average package met 89% of need. 672 students had full need met. Average scholarship/grant was $5,492; average loan $2,742. **Non-need based:** 197 full-time freshmen with need received non-need scholarships; 1,304 without need received awards; 84 received athletic scholarships.

Policies to reduce costs. Tuition/fee waivers for senior citizens, employees and their families. Credit/placement for qualifying scores on AP, IB, CLEP examinations.

Payment plans. Credit card, installment, deferred payment.

Application procedures. FAFSA required. Priority date 3/1; no closing date. Applicants notified on rolling basis starting 4/1, must reply within 4 week(s) of notification. **Transfers:** No deadline.

Contact. Financial aid office: (573) 882-7506
Joe Camille, Director of Student Financial Aid
230 Jesse Hall
Columbia, MO 65211

University of Missouri: Kansas City

Kansas City, Missouri
www.umkc.edu
Four-year public **Federal Code: 002518**

	Living at home	On-campus
Tuition and fees (2002-2003):	$5,573	$5,573
Out-of-state:	$14,726	$14,726
Room and board:		$5,785
Books and supplies:	$825	$825
Personal expenses:	$2,810	$2,810
Transportation:	$2,840	$990

Undergraduate aid. Need-based: Average financial aid package for full-time students was $10,778; for part-time $6,588. 28% awarded as scholarships/grants, 72% as loans/jobs. **Non-need-based:** 34% awarded as scholarships/grants, 66% as loans/jobs. Scholarships based on academics, alumni affiliation, art, athletics, leadership, minority status, music/drama. **Student debt:** 80% of graduating class borrowed to fund education; average debt was $14,642.

Freshman aid. Need-based: Out of 736 full-time freshmen, 645 applied for aid; 426 were judged to have need; of these 426 received aid. Average package met 74% of need. 336 students had full need met. Average scholarship/grant was $4,881; average loan $4,206. **Non-need based:** 289 full-time freshmen with need received non-need scholarships; 155 without need received awards; 24 received athletic scholarships.

Policies to reduce costs. Tuition/fee waivers for employees and their families. Credit/placement for qualifying scores on AP, IB, CLEP examinations.

Payment plans. Credit card, installment payment.

Application procedures. FAFSA required. Priority date 3/1; no closing date. Must reply within 2 week(s) of notification.

Contact. Patrick McTee, Director of Student Financial Aid
5100 Rockhill Rd.
Kansas City, MO 64110-2499

University of Missouri: Rolla

Rolla, Missouri
www.umr.edu
Four-year public **Federal Code: 002517**

College costs. Additional $43 per credit hour for engineering courses.

	Living at home	On-campus
Tuition and fees (2002-2003):	$5,661	$5,661
Out-of-state:	$14,814	$14,814
Room and board:		$5,230
Board only:	$2,060	
Books and supplies:	$850	$850
Personal expenses:	$1,812	$1,812

Undergraduate aid. Need-based: Need-based aid available for full-time and part-time students. **Non-need-based:** Scholarships based on academics, alumni affiliation, athletics, job skills, leadership, minority status, music/drama, state/district residency.

Policies to reduce costs. Tuition/fee waivers for children of alumni, senior citizens, minority students, employees and their families. Credit/placement for qualifying scores on AP, IB, CLEP examinations. Work study available nights, weekends and for part-time students.

Payment plans. Credit card, installment, deferred payment.

Application procedures. FAFSA required. No deadline. Applicants notified on rolling basis, must reply within 3 week(s) of notification. **Transfers:** Priority date 3/1. Special scholarships available to transfer students.

Contact. Financial aid office: (573) 341-4282
Robert Whites, Director of Financial Assistance
102 Parker Hall
Rolla, MO 65409

University of Missouri: St. Louis

St. Louis, Missouri
www.umsl.edu
Four-year public **Federal Code: 002519**

	Living at home	On-campus
Tuition and fees (2002-2003):	$5,813	$5,813
Out-of-state:	$14,966	$14,966
Room and board:		$4,920
Board only:	$1,600	
Books and supplies:	$824	$824
Personal expenses:	$2,326	$2,394
Transportation:	$1,000	$500

Undergraduate aid. Need-based: Average financial aid package for full-time students was $6,680; for part-time $5,579. **Non-need-based:** Scholarships based on academics, alumni affiliation, art, athletics, music/drama, state/district residency.

Freshman aid. Need-based: Out of 426 full-time freshmen, 268 applied for aid; 191 were judged to have need; of these 185 received aid. Average package met 47% of need. 12 students had full need met. Average scholarship/grant was $4,407; average loan $2,538. **Non-need based:** 96 full-time freshmen with need received non-need scholarships; 187 without need received awards; 25 received athletic scholarships.

Merit scholarships. Curator's Scholarships for freshmen with high test scores and class rank; unlimited awarded; $3,500 renewable annually. Chancellor's Scholarships for freshmen with strong test scores and class rank; unlimited awarded; $2,500 annually. Pierre Laclede Honors College Scholarships for freshmen and transfer students; varying amounts.

Policies to reduce costs. Tuition/fee waivers for senior citizens, employees and their families. Credit/placement for qualifying scores on AP, CLEP examinations.

Payment plans. Credit card, installment, deferred payment.

Application procedures. FAFSA required. Priority date 4/1; no closing date. Applicants notified on rolling basis starting 4/1, must reply within 2 week(s) of notification.

Contact. Financial aid office: (314) 516-5526
Tony Georges, Director of Student Financial Aid
8001 Natural Bridge Road
St. Louis, MO 63121-4499

Vatterott College: St. Joseph

St. Joseph, Missouri
www.vatterott-college.edu
Two-year proprietary **Federal Code: 025997**

College costs (2002-2003). Tuition for 90-week associate programs ranges from $24,600 to $26,900 depending on major. Books/supplies: $500. Personal expenses: $1,288. Transportation: $840.

Undergraduate aid. Need-based: Need-based aid available for full-time and part-time students.

Merit scholarships. Make the Grade Scholarship for first 12 months after high school graduation, up to $1,000. Total based on high school grades.

Policies to reduce costs. Tuition/fee waivers for employees and their families.

Payment plans. Credit card, installment payment.

Application procedures. FAFSA required.

Contact. Anna Schwarz, Regional Financial Aid Director
3131 Frederick Avenue
St. Joseph, MO 64506

Vatterott College: Sunset Hills

Sunset Hills, Missouri
www.vatterott-college.com
Two-year proprietary **Federal Code: 025997**

College costs (2002-2003). Costs vary per program. 170-week bachelor's degree: tuition $50,713, required fees $3,240, books and supplies $2,229; total cost $56,295 including taxes. Associate degree programs (90 weeks): tuition $25,913; required fees range from $1,250 to $1,850; books and supplies range from $752 to $1,548; total costs up to $28,847 including taxes. Diploma programs (60 weeks): tuition $16,935; required fees range from $900 to $1,450; books and supplies range from $587 to $1,400; total costs up to $19,196 including taxes.

Contact. J.C. Wheeler, Financial Aid Officer
12970 Maurer Industrial Drive
Sunset Hills, MO 63127

Washington University in St. Louis

St. Louis, Missouri
www.wustl.edu
Four-year private **Federal Code: 002520**

	Living at home	On-campus
Tuition and fees:	$29,053	$29,053
Room and board:		$9,240
Board only:	$1,800	
Books and supplies:	$960	$960
Personal expenses:	$3,800	$1,530

Undergraduate aid. Need-based: Average financial aid package for full-time students was $22,979. 75% awarded as scholarships/grants, 25% as loans/jobs. Need-based aid available for part-time students. **Non-need-based:** 87% awarded as scholarships/grants, 13% as loans/jobs. Scholarships based on academics.

Freshman aid. Need-based: Out of 1,330 full-time freshmen, 919 applied for aid; 557 were judged to have need; of these 541 received aid. Average package met 100% of need. 541 students had full need met. Average scholarship/grant was $19,969; average loan $4,849. **Non-need based:** 78 full-time freshmen with need received non-need scholarships; 258 without need received awards.

Merit scholarships. Numerous scholarships available, ranging up to full tuition plus stipend, renewable for 4 years, based on exceptional academic promise.

Policies to reduce costs. Tuition/fee waivers for employees and their families. Prepayment discount; credit/placement for qualifying scores on AP, IB examinations. Work study available nights and weekends.

Payment plans. Installment, deferred payment.

Application procedures. FAFSA, CSS PROFILE required. Closing date 2/15. Applicants notified by 4/1, must reply by 5/1. Early decision closing date 11/15. **Transfers:** Closing date 4/1.

Contact. Financial aid office: (314) 935-5900
William Witbrodt, Director of Student Financial Services
Campus Box 1089, One Brookings Drive
St. Louis, MO 63130-4899

Webster University

Webster Groves, Missouri
www.websteruniv.edu
Four-year private **Federal Code: 002521**

College costs. Tuition $17,600 for theater conservatory students.

	Living at home	On-campus
Tuition and fees (2002-2003):	$14,600	$14,600
Room and board:		$6,120
Books and supplies:	$800	$800
Personal expenses:	$1,500	$1,500
Transportation:	$500	$1,500

Undergraduate aid. Need-based: 59% awarded as scholarships/grants, 41% as loans/jobs. Need-based aid available for part-time students. **Non-need-based:** 22% awarded as scholarships/grants, 78% as loans/jobs. Scholarships based on academics, art, music/drama.

Merit scholarships. Daniel Webster Scholarships for students with 3.8 GPA, top 10% class rank, 29 ACT and interview; 5 awarded; full tuition. Webster Academic Scholarships for students with minimum 3.0 GPA and 23 ACT; unlimited awarded; ranging from $2,000-$10,000. Leadership Scholarships based on minimum 3.3 GPA and 24 ACT, resume of activities; 15 awarded; $1,500.

Policies to reduce costs. Tuition/fee waivers for employees and their families. Credit/placement for qualifying scores on AP, IB, CLEP examinations.

Payment plans. Credit card, installment, deferred payment.

Application procedures. FAFSA, institutional form required. Priority date 4/1; no closing date. Applicants notified on rolling basis starting 2/9, must reply within 2 week(s) of notification.

Contact. Financial aid office: (314) 968-6992
Jonathan Gruett, Director of Financial Aid
470 East Lockwood Avenue
St. Louis, MO 63119

Wentworth Military Academy

Lexington, Missouri
www.wma1880.org
Two-year private **Federal Code: 002522**

College costs. Uniform: $2,060 for men, $2,317 for women. International students pay $1,000 international fee, plus additional $460 for insurance.

	Living at home	On-campus
Tuition and fees (2002-2003):	$13,360	$13,360
Room and board:		$3,680
Board only:	$2,400	
Books and supplies:	$450	$450

Policies to reduce costs. Tuition/fee waivers for family members, employees and their families. Prepayment discount; credit/placement for qualifying scores on AP, CLEP examinations.

Payment plans. Credit card, installment, deferred payment.

Application procedures. FAFSA required. Priority date 4/30; closing date 6/30. Applicants notified on rolling basis. **Transfers:** No deadline.

Contact. Financial aid office: (660) 259-2221 ext. 302
Pam Fuenfhausen, Director
1880 Washington Avenue
Lexington, MO 64067-1799

Westminster College

Fulton, Missouri
www.westminster-mo.edu
Four-year private **Federal Code: 002523**

	Living at home	On-campus
Tuition and fees:	$12,540	$12,540
Room and board:		$5,430
Board only:	$1,608	
Books and supplies:	$800	$800
Personal expenses:	$2,842	$1,900

Undergraduate aid. Need-based: Average financial aid package for full-time students was $14,906; for part-time $11,352. 86% awarded as scholarships/grants, 14% as loans/jobs. **Non-need-based:** Scholarships based on academics, alumni affiliation, leadership, minority status, state/district residency. **Student debt:** 52% of graduating class borrowed to fund education; average debt was $14,910.

Freshman aid. Need-based: Out of 208 full-time freshmen, 171 applied for aid; 141 were judged to have need; of these 141 received aid. Average package met 95% of need. 93 students had full need met. Average scholarship/grant was $13,496; average loan $2,096. **Non-need based:** 60 without need received awards.

Policies to reduce costs. Tuition/fee waivers for children of alumni, minority students, family members, family of clergy, employees and their families. Credit/placement for qualifying scores on AP, IB, CLEP examinations. Work study available nights, weekends and for part-time students.

Payment plans. Credit card, installment payment.

Application procedures. FAFSA required. Priority date 2/14; no closing date. Applicants notified on rolling basis starting 2/14, must reply within 3 week(s) of notification. **Transfers:** Priority date 2/28; no deadline.

Contact. Financial aid office: (573) 592-5365
Aimee Bristow, Director of Financial Aid
501 Westminster Avenue
Fulton, MO 65251-1299

William Jewell College

Liberty, Missouri
www.jewell.edu
Four-year private **Federal Code: 002524**

	Living at home	On-campus
Tuition and fees (2002-2003):	$15,400	$15,400
Room and board:		$4,550
Board only:	$1,650	
Books and supplies:	$650	$650
Personal expenses:	$1,800	$1,800
Transportation:	$1,000	$800

Undergraduate aid. Need-based: Average financial aid package for full-time students was $11,899; for part-time $2,669. 67% awarded as scholarships/grants, 33% as loans/jobs. **Non-need-based:** 57% awarded as scholarships/grants, 43% as loans/jobs. Scholarships based on academics, alumni affiliation, art, athletics, music/drama, religious affiliation.

Freshman aid. Need-based: Out of 348 full-time freshmen, 288 applied for aid; 241 were judged to have need; of these 241 received aid. Average loan $4,073. **Non-need based:** 46 received athletic scholarships.

Merit scholarships. Distinguished Scholar Award, full tuition, competitive academic scholarship offered annually by invitation only to qualified high school seniors, 4 awarded annually; Oxbridge Scholar Award, $9,000, for students accepted into Oxbridge Honors Program.

Policies to reduce costs. Tuition/fee waivers for children of alumni, senior citizens, family of clergy, employees and their families. Credit/placement for qualifying scores on AP, IB, CLEP examinations. Work study available nights, weekends and for part-time students.

Payment plans. Credit card, installment, deferred payment.

Application procedures. FAFSA required. Priority date 3/1; no closing date. Applicants notified on rolling basis starting 3/15, must reply within 2 week(s) of notification. **Transfers:** No deadline.

Contact. Susan Armstrong, Director of Student Financial Planning
500 College Hill
Liberty, MO 64068

William Woods University

Fulton, Missouri
www.williamwoods.edu
Four-year private **Federal Code: 002525**

College costs. Resident students pay additional $50 fee per year.

	Living at home	On-campus
Tuition and fees:	$14,370	$14,370
Room and board:		$5,700
Board only:	$1,850	
Books and supplies:	$700	$700
Personal expenses:	$1,350	$2,700
Transportation:	$900	$1,500

Undergraduate aid. Need-based: Average financial aid package for full-time students was $14,162; for part-time $4,138. 36% awarded as scholarships/grants, 64% as loans/jobs. **Non-need-based:** 75% awarded as scholarships/grants, 25% as loans/jobs. Scholarships based on academics, alumni affiliation, art, athletics, leadership, music/drama, religious affiliation. **Student debt:** 60% of graduating class borrowed to fund education; average debt was $15,070.

Freshman aid. Need-based: Out of 241 full-time freshmen, 197 applied for aid; 166 were judged to have need; of these 166 received aid. Average package met 75% of need. 46 students had full need met. Average scholarship/grant was $2,295; average loan $1,996. **Non-need based:** 166 full-time freshmen with need received non-need scholarships; 84 without need received awards; 11 received athletic scholarships.

Merit scholarships. LEAD (Leading, Educating, Achieving and Developing) Award, $5,000 for campus residents, $2,500 for commuters; based on commitment to campus and community involvement. Renewable each year if commitment has been met in previous year.

Policies to reduce costs. Tuition/fee waivers for children of alumni, senior citizens, family members, family of clergy, employees and their families. Credit/placement for qualifying scores on AP, IB, CLEP examinations. Work study available nights and weekends.

Payment plans. Credit card, installment payment.

Application procedures. FAFSA, institutional form required. Priority date 3/1; no closing date. Applicants notified on rolling basis starting 3/15, must reply within 2 week(s) of notification.

Contact. Financial aid office: (573) 592-4232
Liz Bennett, Director of Financial Aid
One University Avenue
Fulton, MO 65251-2388

Montana

Carroll College

Helena, Montana
www.carroll.edu
Four-year private **Federal Code: 002526**

	Living at home	On-campus
Tuition and fees (projected):	$14,028	$14,028
Room and board:		$5,566
Board only:	$2,924	
Books and supplies:	$600	$600
Personal expenses:	$700	$700
Transportation:	$350	$350

Undergraduate aid. Need-based: Average financial aid package for full-time students was $13,047; for part-time $9,393. 65% awarded as scholarships/grants, 35% as loans/jobs. **Non-need-based:** 53% awarded as scholarships/grants, 47% as loans/jobs. Scholarships based on academics, athletics, leadership, music/drama, religious affiliation. **Student debt:** 71% of graduating class borrowed to fund education; average debt was $22,297.

Freshman aid. Need-based: Out of 277 full-time freshmen, 276 applied for aid; 185 were judged to have need; of these 185 received aid. Average package met 91% of need. 58 students had full need met. Average scholarship/grant was $8,196; average loan $3,918. **Non-need based:** 24 full-time freshmen with need received non-need scholarships; 82 without need received awards; 17 received athletic scholarships.

Policies to reduce costs. Tuition/fee waivers for senior citizens, family members, employees and their families. Credit/placement for qualifying scores on AP, IB, CLEP examinations. Work study available nights, weekends and for part-time students.

Payment plans. Credit card, installment payment.

Application procedures. FAFSA required. Priority date 3/1; no closing date. Applicants notified on rolling basis starting 3/1, must reply within 4 week(s) of notification. **Transfers:** No deadline.

Contact. **Financial aid office:** (406) 447-5425
Richard Franz, Director of Financial Aid
1601 North Benton Avenue
Helena, MT 59625

Chief Dull Knife College

Lame Deer, Montana
www.cdkc.edu
Two-year private **Federal Code: 014878**

	Living at home
Tuition and fees (2002-2003):	$1,720
Per-credit charge:	$50
Books and supplies:	$600
Personal expenses:	$656
Transportation:	$455

Undergraduate aid. Need-based: Need-based aid available for full-time and part-time students.

Policies to reduce costs. Tuition/fee waivers for senior citizens, employees and their families. Work study available nights and for part-time students.

Payment plans. Installment payment.

Application procedures. FAFSA, institutional form required. No deadline. Applicants notified on rolling basis, must reply within 2 week(s) of notification.

Contact. Donna Small, Financial Aid Director
Box 98
Lame Deer, MT 59043

Dawson Community College

Glendive, Montana
www.dawson.edu
Two-year public **Federal Code: 002529**

College costs. Western Undergraduate Exchange tuition: $83 per credit hour, $2,331 full-time.

	Living at home	On-campus
Tuition and fees (2002-2003):	$1,666	$1,666
Out-of-district:	$2,310	$2,310
Out-of-state:	$5,012	$5,012
Per-credit charge:	$33	$33
Per-credit out-of-district:	$56	$56
Per-credit out-of-state:	$152	$152
Room only:		$1,650
Board only:	$1,500	
Books and supplies:	$660	$660
Personal expenses:	$1,048	$1,048
Transportation:	$1,049	$1,049

Undergraduate aid. Non-need-based: Scholarships based on academics, art, athletics, music/drama.

Policies to reduce costs. Tuition/fee waivers for senior citizens, employees and their families. Credit/placement for qualifying scores on AP, CLEP examinations. Work study available nights, weekends and for part-time students.

Payment plans. Credit card, installment, deferred payment.

Application procedures. FAFSA required. Priority date 3/1; no closing date. Applicants notified on rolling basis starting 5/15, must reply within 2 week(s) of notification.

Contact. Jolene Myers, Director of Admissions
300 College Drive
Glendive, MT 59330

Flathead Valley Community College

Kalispell, Montana
www.fvcc.edu
Two-year public **Federal Code: 006777**

	Living at home
Tuition and fees (2002-2003):	$1,922
Out-of-district:	$2,769
Out-of-state:	$6,041
Per-credit charge:	$47
Per-credit out-of-district:	$78
Per-credit out-of-state:	$194
Board only:	$630
Books and supplies:	$500
Personal expenses:	$900
Transportation:	$900

Undergraduate aid. Need-based: 80% awarded as scholarships/grants, 20% as loans/jobs. Need-based aid available for part-time students. **Non-need-based:** Scholarships based on academics, athletics. **Student debt:** 21% of graduating class borrowed to fund education; average debt was $5,275.

Policies to reduce costs. Tuition/fee waivers for senior citizens, employees and their families. Credit/placement for qualifying scores on AP, CLEP examinations.

Payment plans. Credit card, installment, deferred payment.

Application procedures. FAFSA, institutional form required. Priority date 3/1; no closing date. Applicants notified by 4/15, must reply within 2 week(s) of notification.

Contact. **Financial aid office:** (406) 756-3949
Bonnie Whitehouse, Financial Aid Director
777 Grandview Drive
Kalispell, MT 59901

Fort Belknap College
Harlem, Montana
www.fortbelknap.cc.mt.us
Two-year public **Federal Code: 016967**

	Living at home
Tuition and fees (2002-2003):	$2,280
Per-credit charge:	$45
Books and supplies:	$910
Personal expenses:	$960
Transportation:	$1,765

Application procedures. No deadline. Applicants notified on rolling basis. **Transfers:** Students must reply to financial aid notifice by first week of every quarter.

Contact. Wayne Birdtail, Financial Aid Officer
Box 159
Harlem, MT 59526-0159

Miles Community College
Miles City, Montana
www.milescc.edu
Two-year public **Federal Code: 002528**

	Living at home	On-campus
Tuition and fees:	$2,550	$2,550
Out-of-district:	$3,300	$3,300
Out-of-state:	$5,250	$5,250
Per-credit charge:	$52	$52
Per-credit out-of-district:	$77	$77
Per-credit out-of-state:	$142	$142
Room and board:		$2,200
Books and supplies:	$650	$650
Personal expenses:	$630	$630
Transportation:	$600	$600

Undergraduate aid. Non-need-based: Scholarships based on academics, athletics, leadership, music/drama.

Policies to reduce costs. Tuition/fee waivers for senior citizens, employees and their families. Credit/placement for qualifying scores on AP, IB, CLEP examinations. Work study available nights, weekends and for part-time students.

Payment plans. Credit card, installment, deferred payment.

Application procedures. FAFSA required. Priority date 3/1; no closing date. Applicants notified on rolling basis starting 4/15, must reply within 4 week(s) of notification. **Transfers:** Priority date 3/1; no deadline.

Contact. Financial aid office: (406) 234-3525
Jessie Dufner, Financial Aid Officer
2715 Dickinson Street
Miles City, MT 59301

Montana State University: Billings
Billings, Montana
www.msubillings.edu
Four-year public **Federal Code: 002530**

	Living at home	On-campus
Tuition and fees (2002-2003):	$3,799	$3,799
Out-of-state:	$10,381	$10,381
Room only:		$2,380
Board only:	$1,500	
Books and supplies:	$800	$800
Personal expenses:	$2,200	$2,200
Transportation:	$900	$900

Undergraduate aid. Need-based: Average financial aid package for full-time students was $6,804; for part-time $4,630. 52% awarded as scholarships/grants, 48% as loans/jobs. **Non-need-based:** 42% awarded as scholarships/grants, 58% as loans/jobs. Scholarships based on academics, alumni affiliation, art, athletics, job skills, leadership, minority status, music/drama, state/district residency. **Student debt:** 67% of graduating class borrowed to fund education; average debt was $11,675. **Additional information:** Veteran's and honors fee waivers offered.

Freshman aid. Need-based: Out of 638 full-time freshmen, 556 applied for aid; 447 were judged to have need; of these 420 received aid. Average package met 54% of need. 58 students had full need met. Average scholarship/grant was $3,237; average loan $2,102. **Non-need based:** 138 full-time freshmen with need received non-need scholarships; 25 without need received awards; 18 received athletic scholarships.

Policies to reduce costs. Tuition/fee waivers for senior citizens, minority students, employees and their families. Credit/placement for qualifying scores on AP, CLEP examinations. Work study available nights, weekends and for part-time students.

Payment plans. Credit card, installment, deferred payment.

Application procedures. FAFSA, institutional form required. Priority date 3/1; no closing date. Applicants notified on rolling basis starting 5/1, must reply within 4 week(s) of notification. **Transfers:** No deadline.

Contact. Melina Hawkins, Director of Financial Aid
1500 University Drive
Billings, MT 59101-0298

Montana State University: Billings College of Technology
Billings, Montana
www.msubillings.edu/cot
Two-year public **Federal Code: 002530**

	Living at home
Tuition and fees (2002-2003):	$3,510
Out-of-state:	$5,926
Books and supplies:	$500
Transportation:	$600

Policies to reduce costs. Work study available nights, weekends and for part-time students.

Payment plans. Installment payment.

Application procedures. FAFSA required. Priority date 3/1; no closing date. Applicants notified on rolling basis starting 4/1.

Contact. Melina Hawkins, Director of Financial Aid and Scholarships
3803 Central Avenue
Billings, MT 59102

Montana State University: Bozeman
Bozeman, Montana
www.montana.edu
Four-year public **Federal Code: 002532**

College costs. $582 in health insurance required of uninsured students.

	Living at home	On-campus
Tuition and fees (2002-2003):	$3,759	$3,759
Out-of-state:	$11,396	$11,396
Room and board:		$5,120
Board only:	$4,650	
Books and supplies:	$750	$750
Transportation:	$2,300	$2,300

Undergraduate aid. Need-based: Need-based aid available for full-time and part-time students. **Non-need-based:** Scholarships based on academics, alumni affiliation, art, athletics, job skills, leadership, minority status, music/drama, state/district residency.

Policies to reduce costs. Tuition/fee waivers for senior citizens, minority students, employees and their families. Credit/placement for qualifying scores on AP, IB, CLEP examinations. Work study available for part-time students.

Payment plans. Credit card, installment payment.

Application procedures. FAFSA required. Priority date 3/1; no closing date. Applicants notified on rolling basis starting 4/1, must reply within 3 week(s) of notification.

Contact. Financial aid office: (406) 994-2845
Thomas Stump, Director of Auxiliaries and Financial Aid Services
PO Box 172190
Bozeman, MT 59717-2190

Montana Tech of the University of Montana

Butte, Montana
www.mtech.edu
Four-year public **Federal Code: 002531**

	Living at home	On-campus
Tuition and fees (2002-2003):	$3,833	$3,833
Out-of-state:	$10,866	$10,866
Room and board:		$4,740
Books and supplies:	$700	$700
Personal expenses:	$1,500	$1,500
Transportation:	$1,100	$1,600

Undergraduate aid. All financial aid based on need. Average financial aid package for full-time students was $5,000; for part-time $3,500. 20% awarded as scholarships/grants, 80% as loans/jobs. **Student debt:** 75% of graduating class borrowed to fund education; average debt was $12,000.

Freshman aid. Average package met 75% of need. Average scholarship/grant was $2,000; average loan $2,500.

Policies to reduce costs. Tuition/fee waivers for adults, senior citizens, minority students, employees and their families. Credit/placement for qualifying scores on AP, IB, CLEP examinations. Work study available nights and weekends.

Payment plans. Credit card, deferred payment.

Application procedures. FAFSA, institutional form required. Priority date 3/1; no closing date. Applicants notified on rolling basis starting 4/1, must reply within 2 week(s) of notification. **Transfers:** Priority date 3/1.

Contact. **Financial aid office:** (406) 496-4212
Mike Richardson, Director of Financial Aid
1300 West Park Street
Butte, MT 59701-8997

Rocky Mountain College

Billings, Montana
www.rocky.edu
Four-year private **Federal Code: 002534**

	Living at home	On-campus
Tuition and fees (2002-2003):	$13,455	$13,455
Room and board:		$4,800
Board only:	$2,628	
Books and supplies:	$780	$780
Personal expenses:	$725	$725
Transportation:	$725	$725

Undergraduate aid. Need-based: Average financial aid package for full-time students was $9,919; for part-time $5,683. 53% awarded as scholarships/grants, 47% as loans/jobs. **Non-need-based:** 85% awarded as scholarships/grants, 15% as loans/jobs. Scholarships based on academics, alumni affiliation, art, athletics, music/drama, religious affiliation, state/district residency. **Student debt:** 72% of graduating class borrowed to fund education; average debt was $21,338.

Freshman aid. Need-based: Out of 156 full-time freshmen, 156 applied for aid; 144 were judged to have need; of these 144 received aid. Average package met 78% of need. 27 students had full need met. Average scholarship/grant was $5,681; average loan $1,791. **Non-need based:** 20 full-time freshmen with need received non-need scholarships; 12 without need received awards; 9 received athletic scholarships.

Merit scholarships. Presidential Award: $6,000, 2 awarded; Trustee Award: $10,000, 1 awarded. Renewable up to 4 years, 27 ACT, 1200 SAT, 3.7 GPA. Valedictorian, $8,000, 2 awarded; Business Leadership Scholarship, $2,500, 8 awarded.

Policies to reduce costs. Tuition/fee waivers for employees and their families. Credit/placement for qualifying scores on AP, IB, CLEP examinations. Work study available nights and weekends.

Payment plans. Credit card, installment payment.

Application procedures. FAFSA, institutional form required. Priority date 4/1; no closing date. Applicants notified on rolling basis starting 2/1, must reply within 4 week(s) of notification.

Contact. Lisa Browning, Director of Financial Aid
1511 Poly Drive
Billings, MT 59102-1796

Salish Kootenai College

Pablo, Montana
www.skc.edu
Four-year private **Federal Code: 015023**

College costs (2002-2003). Tuition for Indian students $58 per-credit hour, $2,079 full-time; for students of Indian descent $71 per-credit hour, $2,577 full-time; for non-Indian in-state students $90 per-credit hour, $3,246 full-time; for non-Indian out-of-state students $243 per-credit hour, $8,733 full-time. Required fees $687. Board: $2,700. Books/supplies: $750. Personal expenses: $1,800. Transportation: $600.

Undergraduate aid. Need-based: Need-based aid available for full-time and part-time students.

Policies to reduce costs. Tuition/fee waivers for senior citizens, minority students, employees and their families. Work study available nights, weekends and for part-time students.

Payment plans. Installment, deferred payment.

Application procedures. FAFSA required. Priority date 3/31; no closing date. Applicants notified on rolling basis starting 7/15, must reply within 6 week(s) of notification. **Transfers:** No deadline.

Contact. **Financial aid office:** (406) 675-4800
Jeannie Burland, Financial Aid Director
Box 117
Pablo, MT 59855

University of Great Falls

Great Falls, Montana
www.ugf.edu
Four-year private **Federal Code: 002527**

	Living at home	On-campus
Tuition and fees (2002-2003):	$10,960	$10,960
Room and board:		$5,100
Board only:	$1,000	
Books and supplies:	$750	$750
Personal expenses:	$900	$900
Transportation:	$750	$750

Undergraduate aid. Need-based: Need-based aid available for full-time and part-time students. **Non-need-based:** Scholarships based on academics, leadership, religious affiliation, state/district residency.

Merit scholarships. $4,500 renewable scholarship, based on 3.95 to 4.0 high school GPA. $4,000 renewable scholarship, based on 3.8 to 3.94 high school GPA. $3,500 renewable scholarship, based on 3.6 to 3.79 high school GPA. $3,000 renewable scholarship, based on 3.0 to 3.59 high school GPA. $2,000 renewable grant, based on 2.5 to 2.99 high school GPA. $1,500 renewable grant, based on 2.0 to 2.49 high school GPA.

Policies to reduce costs. Tuition/fee waivers for senior citizens, family members, employees and their families. Credit/placement for qualifying scores on AP, IB, CLEP examinations. Work study available nights, weekends and for part-time students.

Payment plans. Credit card, installment, deferred payment.

Application procedures. FAFSA required. No deadline. Applicants notified on rolling basis starting 3/1. **Transfers:** No deadline.

Contact. Sandy Kiehnau, Director of Financial Aid
1301 20th Street South
Great Falls, MT 59405

University of Montana-Missoula

Missoula, Montana
www.umt.edu
Four-year public **Federal Code: 002536**

	Living at home	On-campus
Tuition and fees (2002-2003):	$3,920	$3,920
Out-of-state:	$10,704	$10,704
Room and board:		$5,090
Board only:	$2,760	
Books and supplies:	$750	$750
Personal expenses:	$2,030	$2,030
Transportation:	$700	

Undergraduate aid. **Need-based:** Need-based aid available for full-time and part-time students. **Non-need-based:** Scholarships based on academics, art, athletics, leadership, music/drama, state/district residency.

Policies to reduce costs. Tuition/fee waivers for senior citizens, minority students, employees and their families. Credit/placement for qualifying scores on AP, CLEP examinations. Work study available nights, weekends and for part-time students.

Payment plans. Credit card, installment payment.

Application procedures. FAFSA, institutional form, CSS PROFILE required. Priority date 3/1; no closing date. Applicants notified on rolling basis starting 4/1, must reply by 8/1 or within 4 week(s) of notification. **Transfers:** Priority date 3/1; no deadline.

Contact. **Financial aid office:** (406) 243-5373
Myron Hanson, Director of Financial Aid
Lommasson Center 103
Missoula, MT 59812

University of Montana: Western

Dillon, Montana
www.umwestern.edu
Four-year public **Federal Code: 002537**

	Living at home	On-campus
Tuition and fees (2002-2003):	$2,930	$2,930
Out-of-state:	$9,842	$9,842
Room and board:		$4,300
Board only:	$1,500	
Books and supplies:	$700	$700
Personal expenses:	$2,000	$2,000
Transportation:	$300	$1,000

Undergraduate aid. **Need-based:** Average financial aid package for full-time students was $2,549; for part-time $2,328. 47% awarded as scholarships/grants, 53% as loans/jobs. **Non-need-based:** 10% awarded as scholarships/grants, 90% as loans/jobs. Scholarships based on academics, alumni affiliation, art, athletics, job skills, leadership, minority status, music/drama, religious affiliation, state/district residency. **Additional information:** Tuition and/or fee waiver for veterans and Native Americans.

Freshman aid. **Need-based:** Average package met 18% of need. Average scholarship/grant was $2,424; average loan $2,439.

Policies to reduce costs. Tuition/fee waivers for senior citizens, minority students, employees and their families. Credit/placement for qualifying scores on AP, CLEP examinations. Work study available nights, weekends and for part-time students.

Payment plans. Credit card, installment, deferred payment.

Application procedures. FAFSA required. Priority date 3/1; no closing date. Applicants notified on rolling basis starting 3/1, must reply within 2 week(s) of notification.

Contact. **Financial aid office:** (406) 683-7511
Arlene Williams, Director of Financial Aid
710 South Atlantic
Dillon, MT 59725-3598

Nebraska

Bellevue University

Bellevue, Nebraska
www.bellevue.edu
Four-year private **Federal Code: 002538**

	Living at home
Tuition and fees (projected):	$4,275
Books and supplies:	$900
Personal expenses:	$1,485
Transportation:	$1,080

Undergraduate aid. Need-based: 15% awarded as scholarships/grants, 85% as loans/jobs. Need-based aid available for part-time students. **Non-need-based:** Scholarships based on academics, athletics, state/district residency.

Policies to reduce costs. Tuition/fee waivers for employees and their families. Credit/placement for qualifying scores on AP, IB, CLEP examinations. Work study available nights, weekends and for part-time students.

Payment plans. Credit card, installment, deferred payment.

Application procedures. FAFSA, institutional form required. Priority date 4/15; no closing date. Applicants notified on rolling basis starting 4/15, must reply within 2 week(s) of notification. **Transfers:** No deadline.

Contact. Jon Dotterer, Director of Financial Aid
1000 Galvin Road South
Bellevue, NE 68005-3098

Central Community College

Grand Island, Nebraska
www.cccneb.edu
Two-year public **Federal Code: 014468**

	Living at home	On-campus
Tuition and fees:	$1,620	$1,620
Out-of-state:	$2,370	$2,370
Per-credit charge:	$50	$50
Per-credit out-of-state:	$75	$75
Room and board:		$3,276
Board only:	$1,500	
Books and supplies:	$800	$800
Personal expenses:	$500	$1,180
Transportation:	$800	$600

Undergraduate aid. Need-based: Need-based aid available for full-time and part-time students. **Non-need-based:** Scholarships based on academics, art, athletics, job skills, leadership, music/drama.

Policies to reduce costs. Tuition/fee waivers for employees and their families. Credit/placement for qualifying scores on CLEP examinations. Work study available nights and for part-time students.

Payment plans. Credit card, installment, deferred payment.

Application procedures. FAFSA, institutional form required. Priority date 6/1; no closing date. Applicants notified on rolling basis starting 3/1, must reply within 1 week(s) of notification.

Contact. Financial aid office: (308) 398-7407
Dennis Tyson, Vice President of Educational Services
3134 West Highway 34
Grand Island, NE 68802-4903

Chadron State College

Chadron, Nebraska
www.csc.edu
Four-year public **Federal Code: 002539**

	Living at home	On-campus
Tuition and fees (2002-2003):	$2,907	$2,907
Out-of-state:	$5,194	$5,194
Room and board:		$3,754
Board only:	$1,029	
Books and supplies:	$600	$600
Personal expenses:	$460	$972
Transportation:	$229	$689

Undergraduate aid. Need-based: Need-based aid available for full-time and part-time students. **Non-need-based:** Scholarships based on academics, alumni affiliation, art, athletics, leadership, minority status, music/drama, state/district residency.

Policies to reduce costs. Tuition/fee waivers for adults, senior citizens, employees and their families. Credit/placement for qualifying scores on AP, CLEP examinations. Work study available nights and weekends.

Payment plans. Credit card, installment, deferred payment.

Application procedures. FAFSA, institutional form required. Priority date 6/1; no closing date. Applicants notified on rolling basis starting 4/1, must reply within 2 week(s) of notification.

Contact. Financial aid office: (308) 432-6230
Sherry Douglas, Director of Financial Aid
1000 Main Street
Chadron, NE 69337

Clarkson College

Omaha, Nebraska
www.clarksoncollege.edu
Four-year private **Federal Code: 009862**

College costs. Distance learning fee: $10 per credit-hour.

	Living at home	On-campus
Tuition and fees (2002-2003):	$8,835	$8,835
Room only:		$2,800
Board only:	$1,200	
Books and supplies:	$600	$600
Personal expenses:	$1,500	$1,500
Transportation:	$600	$300

Undergraduate aid. Need-based: Average financial aid package for full-time students was $8,291; for part-time $7,917. 50% awarded as scholarships/grants, 50% as loans/jobs. **Non-need-based:** 35% awarded as scholarships/grants, 65% as loans/jobs. Scholarships based on academics, alumni affiliation, minority status, religious affiliation. **Student debt:** 74% of graduating class borrowed to fund education; average debt was $13,931.

Freshman aid. Need-based: Out of 27 full-time freshmen, 26 applied for aid; 22 were judged to have need; of these 22 received aid. Average package met 73% of need. 4 students had full need met. Average scholarship/grant was $5,489; average loan $3,159. **Non-need based:** 2 full-time freshmen with need received non-need scholarships; 4 without need received awards.

Policies to reduce costs. Tuition/fee waivers for employees and their families. Credit/placement for qualifying scores on AP, CLEP examinations. Work study available nights, weekends and for part-time students.

Payment plans. Credit card, installment, deferred payment.

Application procedures. FAFSA, institutional form required. Priority date 4/1; no closing date. Applicants notified on rolling basis starting 4/13, must reply within 3 week(s) of notification.

Contact. Financial aid office: (402) 552-2749
Pam Shelton, Director of Financial Aid
101 South 42nd Street
Omaha, NE 68131-2739

College of Saint Mary

Omaha, Nebraska
www.csm.edu
Four-year private **Federal Code: 002540**

	Living at home	On-campus
Tuition and fees (2002-2003):	$13,750	$13,750
Room and board:		$4,976
Board only:	$1,381	
Books and supplies:	$600	$600
Personal expenses:	$1,946	$1,946
Transportation:	$1,452	$726

Undergraduate aid. Need-based: Average financial aid package for full-time students was $11,164; for part-time $6,693. 36% awarded as scholarships/grants, 64% as loans/jobs. **Non-need-based:** Scholarships based on academics, athletics, music/drama. **Student debt:** 62% of graduating class borrowed to fund education; average debt was $13,326.

Freshman aid. Need-based: Out of 64 full-time freshmen, 41 applied for aid; 36 were judged to have need; of these 36 received aid. Average package met 74% of need. 8 students had full need met. Average scholarship/grant was $8,443; average loan $3,509. **Non-need based:** 5 full-time freshmen with need received non-need scholarships; 5 without need received awards; 3 received athletic scholarships.

Policies to reduce costs. Tuition/fee waivers for senior citizens, employees and their families. Credit/placement for qualifying scores on AP, IB, CLEP examinations. Work study available nights and weekends.

Payment plans. Credit card, installment, deferred payment.

Application procedures. FAFSA required. Priority date 4/1; no closing date. Applicants notified on rolling basis starting 3/15, must reply within 2 week(s) of notification. **Transfers:** Priority date 4/1. Scholarships available for transfer students.

Contact. **Financial aid office:** (402) 399-2362
Jenny Mosher, Director of Financial Aid
1901 South 72nd Street
Omaha, NE 68124

Concordia University

Seward, Nebraska
www.cune.edu
Four-year private **Federal Code: 002541**

	Living at home	On-campus
Tuition and fees (2002-2003):	$14,546	$14,546
Room and board:		$4,388
Books and supplies:	$1,200	$1,200
Personal expenses:	$1,200	$1,200
Transportation:	$900	$900

Undergraduate aid. Need-based: Average financial aid package for full-time students was $13,280; for part-time $5,035. 52% awarded as scholarships/grants, 48% as loans/jobs. **Non-need-based:** 70% awarded as scholarships/grants, 30% as loans/jobs. Scholarships based on academics, athletics. **Student debt:** 86% of graduating class borrowed to fund education; average debt was $13,140.

Freshman aid. Need-based: Out of 305 full-time freshmen, 305 applied for aid; 256 were judged to have need; of these 256 received aid. Average package met 94% of need. 232 students had full need met. Average scholarship/grant was $3,588; average loan $2,457. **Non-need based:** 255 full-time freshmen with need received non-need scholarships; 48 without need received awards; 87 received athletic scholarships.

Policies to reduce costs. Tuition/fee waivers for adults, children of alumni, employees and their families. Credit/placement for qualifying scores on AP, IB, CLEP examinations. Work study available nights, weekends and for part-time students.

Payment plans. Credit card payment.

Application procedures. FAFSA, institutional form required. Priority date 3/1; closing date 5/1. Applicants notified on rolling basis starting 3/1, must reply within 4 week(s) of notification.

Contact. **Financial aid office:** (402) 643-7270
Gloria Hennig, Director of Financial Aid
800 North Columbia Avenue
Seward, NE 68434-9989

Creative Center

Omaha, Nebraska
thecreativecenter.com
Two-year proprietary **Federal Code: 031643**

College costs. Supplies and room & board are not included in tuition and are the responsibility of students.

	Living at home
Tuition and fees:	$14,900

Undergraduate aid. Need-based: Need-based aid available for full-time students. **Non-need-based:** Scholarships based on academics, art.

Merit scholarships. Pro Award-$250, President's Award-$500, Founder's Award-$1,000

Policies to reduce costs. Tuition/fee waivers for employees and their families.

Application procedures. FAFSA required. No deadline. Applicants notified on rolling basis starting 1/1. **Transfers:** No deadline.

Contact. **Financial aid office:** (402) 898-1000 ext. 203
Sandra LaRocca, Director of Financial Aid
10850 Emmet Street
Omaha, NE 68164

Creighton University

Omaha, Nebraska
www.creighton.edu
Four-year private **Federal Code: 002542**

	Living at home	On-campus
Tuition and fees (2002-2003):	$18,882	$18,882
Room and board:		$6,438
Board only:	$1,500	
Books and supplies:	$900	$900
Personal expenses:	$1,375	$1,375
Transportation:	$600	$600

Undergraduate aid. Need-based: Average financial aid package for full-time students was $17,552. 63% awarded as scholarships/grants, 37% as loans/jobs. Need-based aid available for part-time students. **Non-need-based:** 70% awarded as scholarships/grants, 30% as loans/jobs. Scholarships based on academics, alumni affiliation, art, athletics, leadership, minority status. **Student debt:** 65% of graduating class borrowed to fund education; average debt was $21,494. **Additional information:** For academic scholarship consideration, student must be admitted by January 1 of fall matriculation.

Freshman aid. Need-based: Out of 802 full-time freshmen, 591 applied for aid; 452 were judged to have need; of these 450 received aid. Average package met 87% of need. 149 students had full need met. Average scholarship/grant was $13,052; average loan $4,890. **Non-need based:** 331 full-time freshmen with need received non-need scholarships; 324 without need received awards; 15 received athletic scholarships.

Merit scholarships. Scott Scholarship for top students admitted to School of Business; 4 awarded; full tuition. Presidential Scholarship for valedictorian of high school class with 30 or better ACT score; 20 awarded; 75% of tuition. Creighton scholarship for students with 3.75 GPA and 25 or better ACT score; $3,000-$8,500.

Policies to reduce costs. Tuition/fee waivers for family members, employees and their families. Credit/placement for qualifying scores on AP, IB, CLEP examinations. Work study available nights and weekends.

Payment plans. Installment payment.

Application procedures. FAFSA, institutional form required. Priority date 4/1; no closing date. Applicants notified on rolling basis starting 3/15, must reply by 5/1 or within 4 week(s) of notification. **Transfers:** No deadline. If transferring 24 or more hours of credit, student not eligible for academic (no-need) scholarships.

Contact. Robert Walker, Director of Financial Aid
2500 California Plaza
Omaha, NE 68178

Dana College

Blair, Nebraska
www.dana.edu
Four-year private **Federal Code: 002543**

	Living at home	On-campus
Tuition and fees:	$15,750	$15,750
Room and board:		$4,880
Board only:	$1,200	
Books and supplies:	$600	$600
Personal expenses:	$1,150	$1,150
Transportation:	$300	$300

Undergraduate aid. Need-based: Average financial aid package for full-time students was $13,887; for part-time $6,684. 43% awarded as scholarships/grants, 57% as loans/jobs. **Non-need-based:** 83% awarded as scholarships/grants, 17% as loans/jobs. Scholarships based on academics, alumni affiliation, art, athletics, music/drama, religious affiliation, state/district residency. **Student debt:** 83% of graduating class borrowed to fund education; average debt was $16,604. **Additional information:** Auditions recommended for music, drama, scholarship applicants. Portfolios recommended for art and graphic design scholarship applicants.

Freshman aid. Need-based: Out of 140 full-time freshmen, 140 applied for aid; 122 were judged to have need; of these 121 received aid. Average package met 91% of need. 25 students had full need met. Average scholarship/grant was $4,727; average loan $4,442. **Non-need based:** 86 full-time freshmen with need received non-need scholarships; 18 without need received awards; 82 received athletic scholarships.

Merit scholarships. EC Hunt SR Scholarships; $1,700; 10-17 awards. Leadership Scholarships; $2,000; 20 awards.

Policies to reduce costs. Tuition/fee waivers for employees and their families. Credit/placement for qualifying scores on AP, IB, CLEP examinations. Work study available nights and weekends.

Payment plans. Credit card, installment, deferred payment.

Application procedures. FAFSA, institutional form required. Priority date 3/15; no closing date. Applicants notified on rolling basis starting 3/1, must reply within 3 week(s) of notification. **Transfers:** No deadline. Academic scholarships awarded on basis of high school GPA, rank and test scores for students with 1 year or less as full time college student. Transfers with 27 credits or more will be based on college GPA.

Contact. Amy Lyons, Director of Financial Aid
2848 College Drive
Blair, NE 68008-1099

Doane College

Crete, Nebraska
www.doane.edu
Four-year private **Federal Code: 002544**

College costs. Per-credit-hour charge at Lincoln campus $170.

	Living at home	On-campus
Tuition and fees:	$15,400	$15,400
Room and board:		$4,600
Board only:'	$480	
Books and supplies:	$700	$700
Personal expenses:	$500	$1,030
Transportation:	$570	$570

Undergraduate aid. Need-based: Average financial aid package for full-time students was $12,570. Need-based aid available for part-time students. **Non-need-based:** Scholarships based on academics, art, athletics, leadership, music/drama, religious affiliation.

Freshman aid. Need-based: Out of 275 full-time freshmen, 259 applied for aid; 231 were judged to have need; of these 230 received aid. Average package met 99% of need. 156 students had full need met. Average scholarship/grant was $9,520; average loan $2,651. **Non-need based:** 9 full-time freshmen with need received non-need scholarships; 38 without need received awards.

Policies to reduce costs. Tuition/fee waivers for senior citizens, employees and their families. Credit/placement for qualifying scores on AP, IB, CLEP examinations.

Payment plans. Credit card, installment payment.

Application procedures. FAFSA, institutional form required. Priority date 3/1; no closing date. Applicants notified on rolling basis starting 2/1, must reply within 2 week(s) of notification.

Contact. Financial aid office: (402) 826-8260
Janet Dodson, Director of Financial Aid
1014 Boswell Avenue
Crete, NE 68333

Grace University

Omaha, Nebraska
www.graceu.edu
Four-year private **Federal Code: 002547**

	Living at home	On-campus
Tuition and fees:	$10,680	$10,680
Room and board:		$5,000

Undergraduate aid. Need-based: Need-based aid available for full-time and part-time students. **Non-need-based:** Scholarships based on academics, alumni affiliation, music/drama, religious affiliation.

Policies to reduce costs. Tuition/fee waivers for children of alumni, senior citizens, family members, family of clergy, employees and their families. Tuition at time of enrollment guaranteed for 4 years; credit/placement for qualifying scores on AP, CLEP examinations. Work study available nights and for part-time students.

Payment plans. Credit card, installment, deferred payment.

Application procedures. FAFSA, institutional form required. Priority date 2/1; no closing date. Applicants notified on rolling basis starting 4/15, must reply within 2 week(s) of notification.

Contact. Financial aid office: (402) 449-2810
Lydia Thompson, Financial Aid Officer
1311 South Ninth Street
Omaha, NE 68108

Hastings College

Hastings, Nebraska
www.hastings.edu
Four-year private **Federal Code: 002548**

	Living at home	On-campus
Tuition and fees (2002-2003):	$14,554	$14,554
Room and board:		$4,398
Board only:	$2,500	
Books and supplies:	$650	$650
Personal expenses:	$2,050	$2,050
Transportation:	$500	$500

Undergraduate aid. Need-based: Average financial aid package for full-time students was $11,597; for part-time $6,734. 62% awarded as scholarships/grants, 38% as loans/jobs. **Non-need-based:** 62% awarded as scholarships/grants, 38% as loans/jobs. Scholarships based on academics, art, athletics, leadership, music/drama, religious affiliation. **Student debt:** 83% of graduating class borrowed to fund education; average debt was $16,869.

Freshman aid. Need-based: Out of 281 full-time freshmen, 242 applied for aid; 197 were judged to have need; of these 197 received aid. Average package met 77% of need. 42 students had full need met. Average scholarship/grant was $8,710; average loan $3,313. **Non-need based:** 28 full-time freshmen with need received non-need scholarships; 76 without need received awards; 48 received athletic scholarships.

Merit scholarships. The Walter Scott Scholarship Competition identifies 3 freshmen for full-tuition scholarships and 20 others for approximately $12,000 each year. Similar scholarships are Trustees Scholarships worth approximately $10,000 per year, and President's Scholarships worth approximately $8,000 per year.

Policies to reduce costs. Tuition/fee waivers for adults, senior citizens, family members, family of clergy, employees and their families. Credit/placement for qualifying scores on AP, IB, CLEP examinations. Work study available nights, weekends and for part-time students.

Payment plans. Installment, deferred payment.

Application procedures. FAFSA, institutional form required. Priority date 5/1; closing date 9/1. Applicants notified on rolling basis starting 2/15, must reply within 3 week(s) of notification. **Transfers:** No deadline. Stafford loans based on number of transferable credits.

Contact. **Financial aid office:** (402) 461-7391
Ian Roberts, Director of Financial Aid
800 Turner Avenue
Hastings, NE 68901-7696

ITT Technical Institute: Omaha

Omaha, Nebraska
www.itt-tech.edu
Two-year proprietary **Federal Code: 007557**

College costs. Total program varies depending on course of study. Per-credit-hour charge: $347.

Policies to reduce costs. Tuition/fee waivers for employees and their families. Tuition at time of enrollment guaranteed for 2 years.

Payment plans. Credit card, installment payment.

Application procedures. FAFSA, institutional form required. No deadline. Applicants notified on rolling basis.

Contact. Carrie Burns, Director of Finance
9814 M Street
Omaha, NE 68127

Lincoln School of Commerce

Lincoln, Nebraska
www.lincolnschoolofcommerce.com
Two-year proprietary **Federal Code: 004721**

	Living at home	On-campus
Tuition and fees:	$10,000	$10,000
Room only:		$3,125

Undergraduate aid. All financial aid based on need. Need-based aid available for full-time and part-time students.

Policies to reduce costs. Tuition at time of enrollment guaranteed for 2 years.

Payment plans. Credit card, installment payment.

Application procedures. FAFSA, institutional form required. No deadline. Applicants notified on rolling basis. **Transfers:** No deadline.

Contact. **Financial aid office:** (402) 474-5315
Roberta Pettinger, Director of Financial Services
1821 K Street
Lincoln, NE 68501

Little Priest Tribal College

Winnebago, Nebraska
www.lptc.bia.edu
Two-year private **Federal Code: 033233**

	Living at home
Tuition and fees:	$2,805
Per-credit charge:	$74
Books and supplies:	$700

Undergraduate aid. All financial aid based on need. Need-based aid available for full-time and part-time students.

Policies to reduce costs. Tuition/fee waivers for senior citizens, employees and their families. Work study available for part-time students.

Application procedures. FAFSA, institutional form required. No deadline. **Transfers:** No deadline.

Contact. **Financial aid office:** (402) 878-2380 ext. 104
Darla Wingett, Financial Aid Director
PO Box 270
Winnebago, NE 68071

Metropolitan Community College

Omaha, Nebraska
www.mccneb.edu
Two-year public **Federal Code: 004432**

	Living at home
Tuition and fees (projected):	$1,553
Out-of-state:	$2,025
Per-credit charge:	$35
Per-credit out-of-state:	$45
Board only:	$1,638
Books and supplies:	$900
Personal expenses:	$270
Transportation:	$1,050

Undergraduate aid. **Need-based:** 89% awarded as scholarships/grants, 11% as loans/jobs. Need-based aid available for part-time students. **Non-need-based:** 38% awarded as scholarships/grants, 62% as loans/jobs. Scholarships based on academics.

Policies to reduce costs. Tuition/fee waivers for senior citizens, employees and their families. Credit/placement for qualifying scores on AP, CLEP examinations.

Payment plans. Credit card payment.

Application procedures. FAFSA, institutional form required. Priority date 3/15; no closing date. Applicants notified on rolling basis starting 4/15.

Contact. **Financial aid office:** (402) 457-2330
Danni Warrick, Director of Financial Aid
Box 3777
Omaha, NE 68103-3777

Mid Plains Community College Area

North Platte, Nebraska
www.mpcca.cc.ne.us
Two-year public **Federal Code: 002557**

College costs. Course fees vary according to program.

	Living at home	On-campus
Tuition and fees (2002-2003):	$1,500	$1,500
Out-of-state:	$1,560	$1,560
Per-credit charge:	$50	$50
Per-credit out-of-state:	$52	$52
Room and board:		$2,900
Board only:	$1,500	
Books and supplies:	$600	$600
Personal expenses:	$750	$750
Transportation:	$700	$700

Undergraduate aid. **Need-based:** Need-based aid available for full-time and part-time students. **Non-need-based:** Scholarships based on academics, art, athletics, music/drama.

Policies to reduce costs. Tuition/fee waivers for senior citizens, employees and their families. Credit/placement for qualifying scores on AP, CLEP examinations. Work study available nights.

Payment plans. Credit card, installment payment.

Application procedures. FAFSA, institutional form required. Priority date 5/1; no closing date. Applicants notified on rolling basis starting 7/1, must reply within 3 week(s) of notification.

Contact. **Financial aid office:** (800) 658-4348
Ted Fellers, Director of Financial Aid
1101 Halligan Drive
North Platte, NE 69101-0001

Midland Lutheran College

Fremont, Nebraska
www.mlc.edu
Four-year private **Federal Code: 002553**

	Living at home	On-campus
Tuition and fees:	$16,310	$16,310
Room and board:		$4,420
Books and supplies:	$600	$600
Personal expenses:	$2,350	$1,430
Transportation:	$80	$200

Undergraduate aid. Need-based: Need-based aid available for full-time and part-time students. **Non-need-based:** Scholarships based on academics, alumni affiliation, art, athletics, leadership, minority status, music/drama, religious affiliation.

Policies to reduce costs. Tuition/fee waivers for senior citizens, minority students, family members, family of clergy, employees and their families. Credit/placement for qualifying scores on AP, CLEP examinations. Work study available nights, weekends and for part-time students.

Payment plans. Credit card, installment, deferred payment.

Application procedures. FAFSA required. Priority date 5/1; no closing date. Applicants notified on rolling basis starting 3/1, must reply within 4 week(s) of notification. **Transfers:** No deadline.

Contact. Doug Watson, Associate Vice President for Financial Aid and Enrollment Management
900 North Clarkson
Fremont, NE 68025

Nebraska Christian College

Norfolk, Nebraska
www.nechristian.edu
Four-year private **Federal Code: 012976**

	Living at home	On-campus
Tuition and fees:	$5,980	$5,980
Room and board:		$3,630
Board only:	$2,700	
Books and supplies:	$600	$600
Personal expenses:	$1,900	$1,900
Transportation:	$500	$500

Undergraduate aid. Need-based: Need-based aid available for full-time and part-time students. **Non-need-based:** Scholarships based on academics, leadership.

Policies to reduce costs. Tuition/fee waivers for family of clergy, employees and their families.

Payment plans. Credit card, installment payment.

Application procedures. FAFSA, institutional form required. Priority date 6/1; no closing date. Applicants notified on rolling basis starting 5/1. **Transfers:** No deadline.

Contact. Linda Bigbee, Financial Aid Officer
1800 Syracuse Avenue
Norfolk, NE 68701

Nebraska College of Business

Omaha, Nebraska
www.ncbedu.com
Two-year proprietary **Federal Code: 008491**

	Living at home
Tuition and fees (2002-2003):	$9,000
Books and supplies:	$100

Undergraduate aid. All financial aid based on need. Need-based aid available for full-time and part-time students.

Application procedures. FAFSA required. No deadline. Applicants notified on rolling basis.

Contact. Sharon McDonald, Director Of Financial Aid
3350 North 90th Street
Omaha, NE 68134

Nebraska College of Technical Agriculture

Curtis, Nebraska
www.ncta.unl.edu
Two-year public **Federal Code: 007358**

	Living at home	On-campus
Tuition and fees (2002-2003):	$2,134	$2,134
Out-of-state:	$4,002	$4,002
Per-credit charge:	$63	$63
Per-credit out-of-state:	$125	$125
Room and board:		$3,526
Books and supplies:	$1,000	$1,000
Personal expenses:	$1,375	$1,375
Transportation:	$1,100	$550

Undergraduate aid. All financial aid based on need. 45% awarded as scholarships/grants, 55% as loans/jobs. Need-based aid available for part-time students.

Policies to reduce costs. Tuition/fee waivers for employees and their families.

Payment plans. Deferred payment.

Application procedures. FAFSA required. Priority date 4/2; no closing date. Applicants notified on rolling basis starting 5/1, must reply within 2 week(s) of notification.

Contact. Financial aid office: (308) 367-4124 ext. 207
Mary Ann Mercer, Director of Financial Aid
Route 3, Box 23A
Curtis, NE 69025-0069

Nebraska Indian Community College

Macy, Nebraska
Two-year public **Federal Code: 015339**

	Living at home
Tuition and fees (2002-2003):	$2,660
Per-credit charge:	$50

Policies to reduce costs. Tuition/fee waivers for senior citizens, employees and their families.

Payment plans. Installment, deferred payment.

Application procedures. FAFSA required. Priority date 7/15; no closing date. Applicants notified on rolling basis starting 8/30, must reply within 2 week(s) of notification. **Transfers:** No deadline.

Contact. Shelley Baxter, Director of Financial Aid
Box 428
Macy, NE 68039

Nebraska Methodist College of Nursing and Allied Health

Omaha, Nebraska
www.methodistcollege.edu
Four-year private **Federal Code: 009937**

College costs. $1,600 for semi-private room

	Living at home	On-campus
Tuition and fees:	$10,200	$10,200
Room and board:		$3,600
Board only:	$1,197	
Books and supplies:	$712	$712
Personal expenses:	$1,183	$1,183
Transportation:	$1,324	$662

Undergraduate aid. Need-based: Average financial aid package for full-time students was $6,021; for part-time $7,861. 44% awarded as scholarships/grants, 56% as loans/jobs. **Non-need-based:** 29% awarded as scholarships/grants, 71% as loans/jobs. Scholarships based on academics, leadership, religious affiliation. **Student debt:** 83% of graduating class borrowed to fund education; average debt was $20,565.

Freshman aid. Need-based: Out of 15 full-time freshmen, 13 applied for aid; 11 were judged to have need; of these 11 received aid. Average package met 74% of need. 3 students had full need met. Average scholarship/grant was $3,875; average loan $2,416. **Non-need based:** 2 full-time freshmen with need received non-need scholarships; 13 without need received awards.

Merit scholarships. President's Leadership Scholarship, 3 awards, $5,000 per year for 4 years; Horizon Scholarship, 45 awards, $2,500 per year; based on academic and personal merit.

Policies to reduce costs. Tuition/fee waivers for employees and their families. Credit/placement for qualifying scores on AP, CLEP examinations.

Payment plans. Credit card, installment, deferred payment.

Application procedures. FAFSA, institutional form required. Priority date 5/1; no closing date. Applicants notified on rolling basis starting 3/1, must reply by 5/1 or within 4 week(s) of notification.

Contact. Financial aid office: (402) 354-4874
Brenda Boyd, Director of Financial Aid
8501 West Dodge Road
Omaha, NE 68114

Nebraska Wesleyan University
Lincoln, Nebraska
www.nebrwesleyan.edu
Four-year private **Federal Code: 002555**

	Living at home	On-campus
Tuition and fees (projected):	$16,424	$16,424
Room and board:		$4,530
Board only:	$2,500	
Books and supplies:	$800	$800
Personal expenses:	$1,800	$1,800
Transportation:	$900	$400

Undergraduate aid. Need-based: Average financial aid package for full-time students was $11,866; for part-time $2,456. 65% awarded as scholarships/grants, 35% as loans/jobs. **Non-need-based:** 61% awarded as scholarships/grants, 39% as loans/jobs. Scholarships based on academics, art, music/drama. **Student debt:** 72% of graduating class borrowed to fund education; average debt was $16,666.

Freshman aid. Need-based: Out of 336 full-time freshmen, 299 applied for aid; 259 were judged to have need; of these 259 received aid. Average package met 75% of need. 22 students had full need met. Average scholarship/grant was $9,567; average loan $3,381. **Non-need based:** 6 full-time freshmen with need received non-need scholarships; 60 without need received awards.

Policies to reduce costs. Tuition/fee waivers for adults, senior citizens, family of clergy, employees and their families. Credit/placement for qualifying scores on AP, IB, CLEP examinations. Work study available nights and weekends.

Payment plans. Installment, deferred payment.

Application procedures. FAFSA required. Priority date 11/15; no closing date. Applicants notified on rolling basis starting 12/15, must reply by 1/15 or within 4 week(s) of notification. Early decision closing date 11/15.

Contact. Claire Fredstrom, Director of Financial Aid
5000 St. Paul Avenue
Lincoln, NE 68504

Northeast Community College
Norfolk, Nebraska
www.northeastcollege.com
Two-year public **Federal Code: 002556**

	Living at home	On-campus
Tuition and fees:	$1,785	$1,785
Out-of-state:	$2,175	$2,175
Room and board:		$3,374
Board only:	$1,700	
Books and supplies:	$600	$600
Personal expenses:	$900	$900
Transportation:	$850	$650

Undergraduate aid. Need-based: Need-based aid available for full-time and part-time students. **Non-need-based:** Scholarships based on academics, art, athletics.

Policies to reduce costs. Tuition/fee waivers for employees and their families. Credit/placement for qualifying scores on AP, CLEP examinations. Work study available nights and for part-time students.

Payment plans. Credit card payment.

Application procedures. FAFSA, institutional form required. No deadline. Applicants notified on rolling basis, must reply within 2 week(s) of notification. **Transfers:** No deadline.

Contact. Financial aid office: (402) 844-7285
Joan Zanders, Director of Financial Aid
801 East Benjamin Avenue
Norfolk, NE 68702-0469

Peru State College
Peru, Nebraska
www.peru.edu
Four-year public **Federal Code: 002559**

	Living at home	On-campus
Tuition and fees (2002-2003):	$2,908	$2,908
Out-of-state:	$5,195	$5,195
Room and board:		$4,010
Board only:	$750	
Books and supplies:	$600	$600
Personal expenses:	$500	$1,000
Transportation:	$1,300	$800

Undergraduate aid. All financial aid based on need. Need-based aid available for full-time and part-time students. **Student debt:** 52% of graduating class borrowed to fund education; average debt was $16,251.

Policies to reduce costs. Tuition/fee waivers for employees and their families. Credit/placement for qualifying scores on AP examinations.

Payment plans. Credit card payment.

Application procedures. FAFSA, institutional form required. Priority date 3/1; no closing date. Applicants notified on rolling basis starting 3/1, must reply within 2 week(s) of notification. **Transfers:** Must have financial aid transcripts from all previous schools sent to college.

Contact. Financial aid office: (402) 872-2228
Diana Lind, Director of Financial Aid
Box 10
Peru, NE 68421-0010

Southeast Community College: Beatrice Campus
Beatrice, Nebraska
www.southeast.edu
Two-year public **Federal Code: 002546**

	Living at home	On-campus
Tuition and fees (2002-2003):	$1,493	$1,493
Out-of-state:	$1,718	$1,718
Per-credit charge:	$47	$47
Per-credit out-of-state:	$55	$55
Room only:		$1,512
Board only:	$162	
Books and supplies:	$600	$600
Personal expenses:	$900	$2,538
Transportation:	$1,000	$1,000

Undergraduate aid. Non-need-based: Scholarships based on academics, art, athletics, leadership, minority status, music/drama.

Policies to reduce costs. Tuition/fee waivers for employees and their families.

Payment plans. Credit card, installment payment.

Application procedures. FAFSA required. Priority date 4/1; no closing date. Applicants notified on rolling basis starting 6/1, must reply within 2 week(s) of notification.

Contact. Financial aid office: (402) 228-8212
Dave Sonenberg, Dean of Student Services, Lincoln Campus
4771 West Scott Road
Beatrice, NE 68310

Southeast Community College: Lincoln Campus

Lincoln, Nebraska
www.southeast.edu
Two-year public **Federal Code: 007591**

	Living at home
Tuition and fees (2002-2003):	$1,463
Out-of-state:	$1,688
Per-credit charge:	$32
Per-credit out-of-state:	$37
Board only:	$2,400
Books and supplies:	$1,000
Personal expenses:	$1,200
Transportation:	$1,500

Undergraduate aid. Need-based: Need-based aid available for full-time and part-time students. **Non-need-based:** Scholarships based on academics.

Policies to reduce costs. Tuition/fee waivers for senior citizens, employees and their families. Credit/placement for qualifying scores on CLEP examinations. Work study available nights, weekends and for part-time students.

Payment plans. Credit card payment.

Application procedures. FAFSA, institutional form required. No deadline. Applicants notified on rolling basis, must reply within 2 week(s) of notification. **Transfers:** No deadline.

Contact. Financial aid office: (402) 437-2610
Donna Bargen, Director of Financial Aid
8800 O Street
Lincoln, NE 68520

Southeast Community College: Milford Campus

Milford, Nebraska
www.southeast.edu
Two-year public **Federal Code: 004723**

	Living at home	On-campus
Tuition and fees (2002-2003):	$1,463	$1,463
Out-of-state:	$1,688	$1,688
Per-credit charge:	$32	$32
Per-credit out-of-state:	$37	$37
Room and board:		$2,922
Books and supplies:	$750	$750
Personal expenses:		$900
Transportation:	$900	$900

Undergraduate aid. Need-based: 46% awarded as scholarships/grants, 54% as loans/jobs. Need-based aid available for part-time students. **Non-need-based:** 35% awarded as scholarships/grants, 65% as loans/jobs. Scholarships based on academics.

Policies to reduce costs. Tuition/fee waivers for employees and their families.

Payment plans. Credit card, installment payment.

Application procedures. FAFSA, institutional form required. Priority date 4/1; no closing date. Applicants notified on rolling basis, must reply within 2 week(s) of notification.

Contact. Financial aid office: (402) 761-8250
Merlyn Williams, Associate Director of Financial Aid
600 State Street
Milford, NE 68405-8498

Union College

Lincoln, Nebraska
www.ucollege.edu
Four-year private **Federal Code: 002563**

College costs. Technology fee of $6 per credit hour.

	Living at home	On-campus
Tuition and fees:	$12,950	$12,950
Room and board:		$4,210
Board only:	$1,500	
Books and supplies:	$800	$800
Personal expenses:	$1,200	$1,200
Transportation:	$1,200	$1,200

Undergraduate aid. Need-based: Average financial aid package for full-time students was $8,376. 45% awarded as scholarships/grants, 55% as loans/jobs. Need-based aid available for part-time students. **Non-need-based:** 65% awarded as scholarships/grants, 35% as loans/jobs. Scholarships based on academics. **Student debt:** 64% of graduating class borrowed to fund education; average debt was $23,379. **Additional information:** Special institutional grants offered to all freshmen and sophomores demonstrating exceptional financial need.

Freshman aid. Need-based: Average package met 45% of need. Average scholarship/grant was $5,508; average loan $3,623.

Policies to reduce costs. Tuition/fee waivers for family members, family of clergy, employees and their families. Prepayment discount; credit/placement for qualifying scores on AP, IB, CLEP examinations. Work study available for part-time students.

Payment plans. Credit card, installment payment.

Application procedures. FAFSA required. Priority date 5/1; no closing date. Applicants notified on rolling basis starting 3/1, must reply within 3 week(s) of notification.

Contact. Financial aid office: (402) 486-2505
Dan Duff, Director of Financial Aid
3800 South 48th Street
Lincoln, NE 68506-4300

University of Nebraska - Kearney

Kearney, Nebraska
www.unk.edu
Four-year public **Federal Code: 002551**

	Living at home	On-campus
Tuition and fees (2002-2003):	$3,413	$3,413
Out-of-state:	$6,248	$6,248
Room and board:		$4,156
Board only:	$2,154	
Books and supplies:	$720	$720
Personal expenses:	$2,204	$2,204
Transportation:	$690	$690

Undergraduate aid. Need-based: Need-based aid available for full-time and part-time students. **Non-need-based:** Scholarships based on academics, athletics, state/district residency.

Policies to reduce costs. Tuition/fee waivers for employees and their families. Credit/placement for qualifying scores on AP, CLEP examinations.

Application procedures. FAFSA, institutional form required. Priority date 3/1; no closing date. Applicants notified on rolling basis starting 5/1, must reply within 3 week(s) of notification.

Contact. Financial aid office: (308) 865-8520
Mary Sommers, Director of Financial Aid
905 West 25th
Kearney, NE 68849

University of Nebraska - Lincoln

Lincoln, Nebraska
www.unl.edu
Four-year public **Federal Code: 002565**

College costs. Reciprocity agreement for selected programs with University of Missouri-Columbia, Kansas State University, University of South Dakota.

	Living at home	On-campus
Tuition and fees (2002-2003):	$4,145	$4,145
Out-of-state:	$10,738	$10,738
Room and board:		$4,875
Board only:	$2,350	
Books and supplies:	$720	$720
Personal expenses:	$2,206	$2,356

Undergraduate aid. All financial aid based on need. Average financial aid package for full-time students was $6,234; for part-time $4,960. 41% awarded as scholarships/grants, 59% as loans/jobs. **Student debt:** 59% of graduating class borrowed to fund education; average debt was $15,682.

Freshman aid. Out of 3,617 full-time freshmen, 2,258 applied for aid; 1,508 were judged to have need; of these 1,475 received aid. Average package met 84% of need. 400 students had full need met. Average scholarship/grant was $3,716; average loan $2,501.

Policies to reduce costs. Tuition/fee waivers for senior citizens, employees and their families. Credit/placement for qualifying scores on AP, IB, CLEP examinations.

Payment plans. Credit card, deferred payment.

Application procedures. FAFSA required. Priority date 4/1; no closing date. Applicants notified on rolling basis starting 4/15. **Transfers:** Priority application date of April 1 for scholarship consideration.

Contact. **Financial aid office:** (402) 472-2030
Craig Munier, Director of Scholarships and Financial Aid
Alexander Building, 1410 Q Street
Lincoln, NE 68588-0417

University of Nebraska - Omaha

Omaha, Nebraska
www.unomaha.edu
Four-year public **Federal Code: 002554**

	Living at home	On-campus
Tuition and fees (2002-2003):	$3,576	$3,576
Out-of-state:	$9,524	$9,524
Room and board:		$4,517
Board only:	$2,050	
Books and supplies:	$650	$650
Personal expenses:	$2,790	$2,790
Transportation:	$850	$850

Undergraduate aid. **Need-based:** 37% awarded as scholarships/grants, 63% as loans/jobs. Need-based aid available for part-time students. **Non-need-based:** 40% awarded as scholarships/grants, 60% as loans/jobs. Scholarships based on academics, alumni affiliation, art, athletics, leadership, minority status, music/drama, state/district residency. **Student debt:** 48% of graduating class borrowed to fund education; average debt was $16,900.

Freshman aid. **Need-based:** Out of 1,556 full-time freshmen, 1,121 applied for aid; 735 were judged to have need; of these 732 received aid. **Non-need based:** 716 full-time freshmen with need received non-need scholarships.

Policies to reduce costs. Tuition/fee waivers for employees and their families. Credit/placement for qualifying scores on AP, CLEP examinations. Work study available nights, weekends and for part-time students.

Payment plans. Credit card, deferred payment.

Application procedures. FAFSA required. Priority date 3/1; no closing date. Applicants notified on rolling basis starting 4/15, must reply within 2 week(s) of notification.

Contact. Randall Sell, Director of Financial Aid
6001 Dodge Street
Omaha, NE 68182-0005

University of Nebraska Medical Center

Omaha, Nebraska
www.unmc.edu
Upper-division public **Federal Code: 006895**

College costs. Nursing program: $141 per-credit-hour in-state, $414 out-of-state, additional $25 fees per semester.

	Living at home
Tuition and fees (2002-2003):	$3,605
Out-of-state:	$10,197
Books and supplies:	$900
Personal expenses:	$1,500
Transportation:	$500

Undergraduate aid. **Need-based:** Average financial aid package for full-time students was $6,949; for part-time $5,231. 21% awarded as scholarships/grants, 79% as loans/jobs. **Non-need-based:** 64% awarded as scholarships/grants, 36% as loans/jobs. **Additional information:** Parental data collected from applicants for certain types of aid.

Policies to reduce costs. Tuition/fee waivers for children of alumni, employees and their families. Credit/placement for qualifying scores on AP, IB, CLEP examinations.

Payment plans. Credit card payment.

Application procedures. FAFSA, institutional form required. No deadline. **Transfers:** Priority date 4/1; no deadline.

Contact. **Financial aid office:** (402) 559-4199
Judith Walker, Director Financial Aid
984230 Nebraska Medical Center
Omaha, NE 68198-4230

Vatterott College

Omaha, Nebraska
www.vatterott-college.edu
Two-year proprietary **Federal Code: 030233**

College costs (2002-2003). Associate degree programs range in cost from $23,248 to $26,418. Diploma programs range in cost from $15,193 to $17,612.

Undergraduate aid. All financial aid based on need. Need-based aid available for full-time students.

Policies to reduce costs. Tuition at time of enrollment guaranteed for 2 years.

Payment plans. Credit card, installment payment.

Application procedures. FAFSA required. No deadline.

Contact. **Financial aid office:** (402) 891-9411
5318 South 136th St
Omaha, NE 68137

Vatterott College: Dodge Campus

Omaha, Nebraska
www.vatterott-college.edu
Two-year proprietary **Federal Code: 030233**

College costs. First year of veterinary technician program: $31,665. One time $150 registration fee also required in all programs except for veterinary technician; registration fees for this program is $250. Cost of books and supplies varies per program.

	Living at home
Tuition and fees (projected):	$21,978
Books and supplies:	$750

Undergraduate aid. All financial aid based on need. Need-based aid available for full-time and part-time students.

Application procedures. FAFSA, institutional form required. No deadline.

Contact. **Financial aid office:** (402) 392-1300
Sheri Ford, Financial Aid Administrator
225 North 80th Street
Omaha, NE 68114

Vatterott College: Spring Valley

Omaha, Nebraska
www.vatterott-college.com
Two-year proprietary

College costs. First year of veterinary technician program, $31,665. One time $150 registration fee required in all programs, except for veterinary technician; registration fees for that program are $250.

	Living at home
Tuition and fees (projected):	$21,978

Contact. Sheri Ford, Financial Aid Administrator
5141 F Street
Omaha, NE 68117

Wayne State College

Wayne, Nebraska
www.wsc.edu
Four-year public **Federal Code: 002566**

	Living at home	On-campus
Tuition and fees (2002-2003):	$3,014	$3,014
Out-of-state:	$5,301	$5,301
Room and board:		$3,760
Books and supplies:	$600	$600
Personal expenses:	$713	$713
Transportation:	$587	$587

Undergraduate aid. Need-based: Average financial aid package for full-time students was $2,996; for part-time $2,573. 43% awarded as scholarships/grants, 57% as loans/jobs. **Non-need-based:** 29% awarded as scholarships/grants, 71% as loans/jobs. Scholarships based on academics, art, athletics, leadership, minority status, music/drama, religious affiliation, state/district residency.

Freshman aid. Need-based: Out of 602 full-time freshmen, 517 applied for aid; 409 were judged to have need; of these 403 received aid. Average package met 38% of need. 74 students had full need met. Average scholarship/grant was $1,407; average loan $1,436. **Non-need based:** 138 full-time freshmen with need received non-need scholarships.

Policies to reduce costs. Tuition/fee waivers for employees and their families. Credit/placement for qualifying scores on AP, CLEP examinations.

Payment plans. Credit card, installment payment.

Application procedures. FAFSA, institutional form required. Priority date 6/1; no closing date. Applicants notified on rolling basis starting 4/1, must reply within 3 week(s) of notification.

Contact. Kyle Rose, Director of Financial Aid
1111 Main Street
Wayne, NE 68787

Western Nebraska Community College

Scottsbluff, Nebraska
www.wncc.net
Two-year public **Federal Code: 002560**

	Living at home	On-campus
Tuition and fees (2002-2003):	$1,560	$1,560
Out-of-state:	$1,800	$1,800
Per-credit charge:	$46	$46
Per-credit out-of-state:	$54	$54
Room and board:		$3,300
Board only:	$1,200	
Books and supplies:	$650	$650
Personal expenses:	$600	$900
Transportation:	$500	$500

Undergraduate aid. Need-based: Average financial aid package for full-time students was $4,711; for part-time $3,598. 70% awarded as scholarships/grants, 30% as loans/jobs. **Non-need-based:** 15% awarded as scholarships/grants, 85% as loans/jobs. Scholarships based on academics, art, athletics, music/drama, state/district residency.

Freshman aid. Need-based: Out of 361 full-time freshmen, 317 applied for aid; 199 were judged to have need; of these 193 received aid. Average package met 75% of need. Average scholarship/grant was $3,104; average loan $2,310.

Policies to reduce costs. Tuition/fee waivers for senior citizens, employees and their families. Credit/placement for qualifying scores on AP, CLEP examinations. Work study available nights, weekends and for part-time students.

Payment plans. Credit card, installment, deferred payment.

Application procedures. FAFSA required. Priority date 3/1; no closing date. Applicants notified on rolling basis starting 3/15. **Transfers:** Priority date 3/1.

Contact. Financial aid office: (308) 635-6011
Penny Jones, Director of Financial Aid
1601 East 27th Street
Scottsbluff, NE 69361

York College

York, Nebraska
www.york.edu
Four-year private **Federal Code: 002567**

	Living at home	On-campus
Tuition and fees:	$11,500	$11,500
Room and board:		$3,475
Books and supplies:	$700	$700
Personal expenses:	$1,600	$1,600
Transportation:	$350	$600

Undergraduate aid. Need-based: 54% awarded as scholarships/grants, 46% as loans/jobs. Need-based aid available for part-time students. **Non-need-based:** Scholarships based on academics, alumni affiliation, athletics, leadership, music/drama.

Policies to reduce costs. Tuition/fee waivers for children of alumni, family members, employees and their families. Credit/placement for qualifying scores on AP, IB, CLEP examinations. Work study available nights and weekends.

Payment plans. Credit card, installment, deferred payment.

Application procedures. FAFSA required. Priority date 4/30; no closing date. Applicants notified on rolling basis starting 3/1, must reply within 4 week(s) of notification. **Transfers:** No deadline.

Contact. Deb Lowry, Comptroller
1125 East Eighth Street
York, NE 68467

Nevada

Academy of Healing Arts

Las Vegas, Nevada
Two-year proprietary
Federal Code: 031100

College costs (2002-2003). Tuition and fees for 52-week medical office administration program: $41,000.

Contact. William Paul, President
901 Rancho Lane, Suite 190
Las Vegas, NV 89106

Art Institute of Las Vegas

Henderson, Nevada
www.ailv.artinstitutes.edu
Two-year proprietary
Federal Code: 030846

College costs. Tuition ranges from $11,250 to $13,250 depending on program.

	Living at home
Tuition and fees:	$12,164
Per-credit charge:	$327
Books and supplies:	$550
Personal expenses:	$2,527

Contact. Dan Shellenberger, Director of Student Financial Services
2350 Corporate Circle
Henderson, NV 89074

Career College of Northern Nevada

Reno, Nevada
www.ccnn4u.com
Two-year proprietary
Federal Code: 026215

College costs (2002-2003). Tuition for full associate programs ranges from $14,830 to $18,813; diploma programs $9,887 to $11,085. Fees and books range from $120 to $624. Personal expenses: $1,832.

Undergraduate aid. All financial aid based on need. Need-based aid available for full-time students.

Application procedures. FAFSA required. Closing date 5/30. Applicants notified on rolling basis.

Contact. **Financial aid office:** (775) 856-2266
L. Nathan Clark, President
1195 A Corporate Boulevard
Reno, NV 89502-2331

Community College of Southern Nevada

North Las Vegas, Nevada
www.ccsn.nevada.edu
Two-year public
Federal Code: 010362

College costs. Good Neighbor tuition: $2,055 full-time, $69 per-credit-hour.

	Living at home
Tuition and fees (2002-2003):	$1,365
Out-of-state:	$4,430
Per-credit charge:	$46
Per-credit out-of-state:	$69
Board only:	$1,500
Books and supplies:	$600
Personal expenses:	$1,480
Transportation:	$1,000

Undergraduate aid. Non-need-based: Scholarships based on state/district residency.

Policies to reduce costs. Tuition/fee waivers for senior citizens, employees and their families. Credit/placement for qualifying scores on AP, CLEP examinations. Work study available nights, weekends and for part-time students.

Payment plans. Credit card, installment, deferred payment.

Application procedures. FAFSA required. Priority date 4/15; closing date 6/30. Applicants notified on rolling basis starting 7/15, must reply within 2 week(s) of notification.

Contact. **Financial aid office:** (702) 651-4047
Chemene Crawford, Financial Aid Director
3200 East Cheyenne Avenue
North Las Vegas, NV 89030

Great Basin College

Elko, Nevada
www.gbcnv.edu
Four-year public
Federal Code: 006977

	Living at home
Tuition and fees (2002-2003):	$1,365
Out-of-state:	$4,430
Board only:	$1,800
Books and supplies:	$800
Personal expenses:	$1,200
Transportation:	$1,000

Undergraduate aid. Need-based: Need-based aid available for full-time and part-time students.

Policies to reduce costs. Tuition/fee waivers for senior citizens, employees and their families. Credit/placement for qualifying scores on CLEP examinations. Work study available nights, weekends and for part-time students.

Payment plans. Credit card, deferred payment.

Application procedures. FAFSA required. Priority date 6/1; no closing date. Applicants notified on rolling basis starting 7/1. **Transfers:** Priority date 4/1; no deadline.

Contact. **Financial aid office:** (775) 753-2267
Joan Williams, Director of Financial Aid
1500 College Parkway
Elko, NV 89801

Heritage College

Las Vegas, Nevada
www.heritagecollege.com
Two-year proprietary
Federal Code: 030432

College costs. Cost of full programs: associate degree programs $20,404, diploma programs $10,204, including fees and books. Personal expenses: $380.

Undergraduate aid. Need-based: Need-based aid available for full-time students.

Application procedures. FAFSA, institutional form required. No deadline.

Contact. **Financial aid office:** (702) 368-2338
Melissa Hughes, Financial Aid Director
3315 Spring Mountain Road
Las Vegas, NV 89102

ITT Technical Institute: Henderson

Santa Fe, Nevada
www.itt-tech.edu
Two-year proprietary
Federal Code: 023610

College costs. Total program varies depending on course of study. Per-credit-hour charge: $347.

Policies to reduce costs. Tuition/fee waivers for employees and their families. Tuition at time of enrollment guaranteed for 2 years.

Payment plans. Credit card, installment payment.

Application procedures. FAFSA, institutional form required. Applicants notified on rolling basis.

Contact. Kathy Henson, Director of Finance
168 North Gibson Road
Henderson, NV 89014

Las Vegas College

Las Vegas, Nevada
www.cci.edu
Two-year proprietary **Federal Code: 015804**

	Living at home
Tuition and fees:	$11,647
Per-credit charge:	$239
Board only:	$296
Books and supplies:	$300
Personal expenses:	$124
Transportation:	$124

Undergraduate aid. All financial aid based on need. Need-based aid available for full-time and part-time students.

Policies to reduce costs. Work study available nights and weekends.

Payment plans. Credit card, installment payment.

Application procedures. FAFSA required. Applicants notified on rolling basis, must reply within 2 week(s) of notification.

Contact. Michael Holmes, Finance Director
4100 West Flamingo Road
Las Vegas, NV 89103

Morrison University

Reno, Nevada
www.morrison.edu
Four-year proprietary **Federal Code: 009948**

College costs. Full cost of bachelor's degree programs (180 credits) $30,600; associate degree programs (90 credits) $15,300; diploma programs (64 credits) $10,880; certificate programs 32 credits) $5,440.

	Living at home
Tuition and fees:	$6,559
Books and supplies:	$825
Personal expenses:	$1,800
Transportation:	$1,000

Undergraduate aid. Need-based: Need-based aid available for full-time students.

Policies to reduce costs. Tuition/fee waivers for employees and their families. Tuition at time of enrollment guaranteed for 4 years; prepayment discount; credit/placement for qualifying scores on IB, CLEP examinations. Work study available nights and for part-time students.

Payment plans. Credit card, installment payment.

Application procedures. FAFSA required. No deadline. Applicants notified on rolling basis starting 7/1. **Transfers:** No deadline.

Contact. Financial aid office: (775) 323-4145
Lisa Brown, Financial Aid Director
140 Washington Street
Reno, NV 89503

Sierra Nevada College

Incline Village, Nevada
www.sierranevada.edu
Four-year private **Federal Code: 009192**

	Living at home	On-campus
Tuition and fees:	$18,870	$18,870
Room and board:		$7,236
Board only:	$3,356	
Books and supplies:	$700	$700

Undergraduate aid. Need-based: Average financial aid package for full-time students was $15,900. 46% awarded as scholarships/grants, 54% as loans/jobs. Need-based aid available for part-time students. **Non-need-based:** Scholarships based on academics, art, athletics.

Freshman aid. Need-based: Out of 80 full-time freshmen, 75 applied for aid; 70 were judged to have need; of these 70 received aid. Average package met 95% of need. 65 students had full need met. **Non-need based:** 65 full-time freshmen with need received non-need scholarships; 8 without need received awards; 3 received athletic scholarships.

Merit scholarships. Academic scholarships available ranging from $2,000-$10,000 per year, renewable.

Policies to reduce costs. Tuition/fee waivers for employees and their families. Credit/placement for qualifying scores on AP, IB, CLEP examinations.

Payment plans. Credit card, installment payment.

Application procedures. FAFSA, institutional form required. Closing date 4/1. Applicants notified on rolling basis starting 8/15, must reply by 5/1 or within 4 week(s) of notification. **Transfers:** Priority date 3/15; closing date 4/1.

Contact. Dorothy Caruso, Director of Financial Aid
999 Tahoe Boulevard
Incline Village, NV 89450-4269

Truckee Meadows Community College

Reno, Nevada
www.tmcc.edu
Two-year public **Federal Code: 010363**

College costs. Good Neighbor tuition: $2,055 full-time, $69 per-credit-hour.

	Living at home
Tuition and fees (2002-2003):	$1,485
Out-of-state:	$4,550
Per-credit charge:	$46
Per-credit out-of-state:	$69
Books and supplies:	$800
Personal expenses:	$1,000
Transportation:	$700

Undergraduate aid. Need-based: 53% awarded as scholarships/grants, 47% as loans/jobs. **Non-need-based:** 38% awarded as scholarships/grants, 62% as loans/jobs. Scholarships based on academics, art, leadership, minority status, music/drama, state/district residency. **Additional information:** Institutional grants to state residents, short-term emergency loans available. Work-study applications must reply within 10 days of notification.

Policies to reduce costs. Tuition/fee waivers for senior citizens, employees and their families. Credit/placement for qualifying scores on CLEP examinations. Work study available nights, weekends and for part-time students.

Payment plans. Credit card, deferred payment.

Application procedures. FAFSA, institutional form required. No deadline. Applicants notified by 5/15. **Transfers:** No deadline. Must provide academic transcript from previous institution.

Contact. Financial aid office: (775) 673-7072
Mona Buckheart, Director of Student Financial Aid
7000 Dandini Boulevard
Reno, NV 89512

University of Nevada: Las Vegas

Las Vegas, Nevada
www.unlv.edu
Four-year public **Federal Code: 002569**

	Living at home	On-campus
Tuition and fees (2002-2003):	$2,490	$2,490
Out-of-state:	$10,275	$10,275
Room and board:		$6,910
Board only:	$1,430	
Books and supplies:	$850	$850
Personal expenses:	$1,900	$1,900
Transportation:	$1,400	$530

Undergraduate aid. Need-based: Average financial aid package for full-time students was $6,889; for part-time $5,272. 28% awarded as scholarships/grants, 72% as loans/jobs. **Non-need-based:** 53% awarded as scholarships/grants, 47% as loans/jobs. Scholarships based on academics, alumni affiliation, art, athletics, job skills, leadership, minority status, music/drama, state/district residency. **Student debt:** 47% of graduating class borrowed to fund education; average debt was $12,900. **Additional information:** Tuition reduction for state residents through consortium programs and for out-of-state students graduating from high schools in designated counties bordering Nevada, for military dependents residing in-state, and for dependents of dues-paying alumni not residing in-state.

Freshman aid. **Need-based:** Out of 2,360 full-time freshmen, 2,122 applied for aid; 1,108 were judged to have need; of these 1,028 received aid. Average package met 66% of need. 641 students had full need met. Average scholarship/grant was $2,710; average loan $2,505. **Non-need based:** 607 full-time freshmen with need received non-need scholarships; 1,180 without need received awards; 100 received athletic scholarships.

Policies to reduce costs. Tuition/fee waivers for children of alumni, senior citizens, employees and their families. Credit/placement for qualifying scores on AP, IB, CLEP examinations.

Payment plans. Credit card, installment, deferred payment.

Application procedures. FAFSA, institutional form required. Priority date 2/1; no closing date. Applicants notified on rolling basis starting 4/1, must reply within 2 week(s) of notification. **Transfers:** Priority date 10/15; no deadline.

Contact. **Financial aid office:** (702) 895-3424
Judy Belanger, Director of Student Financial Services
4505 Maryland Parkway
Las Vegas, NV 89154-1021

University of Nevada: Reno

Reno, Nevada
www.unr.edu
Four-year public **Federal Code: 002568**

	Living at home	On-campus
Tuition and fees (2002-2003):	$2,672	$2,672
Out-of-state:	$10,122	$10,122
Room and board:		$6,952
Board only:	$2,810	
Books and supplies:	$1,000	$1,000
Personal expenses:	$2,114	$2,582
Transportation:	$2,700	$1,800

Undergraduate aid. All financial aid based on need. Average financial aid package for full-time students was $6,288; for part-time $3,295. 45% awarded as scholarships/grants, 55% as loans/jobs. **Student debt:** 44% of graduating class borrowed to fund education; average debt was $15,788. **Additional information:** Reduced out-of-state tuition available for children of alumni and for non-residents from some neighboring counties in California.

Freshman aid. Out of 1,956 full-time freshmen, 948 applied for aid; 641 were judged to have need; of these 623 received aid. Average package met 60% of need. 111 students had full need met. Average scholarship/grant was $2,754; average loan $2,299.

Policies to reduce costs. Tuition/fee waivers for children of alumni, senior citizens, employees and their families. Credit/placement for qualifying scores on AP, CLEP examinations. Work study available for part-time students.

Payment plans. Credit card, installment, deferred payment.

Application procedures. FAFSA required. Priority date 2/1; no closing date. Applicants notified on rolling basis starting 4/1, must reply within 2 week(s) of notification. **Transfers:** No deadline. Transfer GPA must be 2.0 or higher to be eligible for aid.

Contact. **Financial aid office:** (775) 784-4666
Nancee Langley, Director, Student Financial Services
Mail Stop 120
Reno, NV 89557

Western Nevada Community College

Carson City, Nevada
www.wncc.edu
Two-year public **Federal Code: 013896**

College costs. Good Neighbor tuition: $69 per-credit-hour, $2,055 full-time.

	Living at home
Tuition and fees (2002-2003):	$1,485
Out-of-state:	$4,550
Per-credit charge:	$46
Per-credit out-of-state:	$69
Books and supplies:	$1,000
Personal expenses:	$1,000
Transportation:	$1,300

Undergraduate aid. **Need-based:** 74% awarded as scholarships/grants, 26% as loans/jobs. Need-based aid available for part-time students. **Non-need-based:** 92% awarded as scholarships/grants, 8% as loans/jobs. Scholarships based on academics, state/district residency.

Policies to reduce costs. Tuition/fee waivers for senior citizens, employees and their families. Credit/placement for qualifying scores on AP, CLEP examinations.

Payment plans. Credit card, deferred payment.

Application procedures. FAFSA, institutional form required. Priority date 7/1; no closing date. Applicants notified on rolling basis starting 7/1. **Transfers:** No deadline. Maximum loan debt of $14,125 allowed. Loans received at other schools counted toward limit.

Contact. **Financial aid office:** (775) 445-3264
Dan Dreves, Director of Financial Aid
2201 West College Parkway
Carson City, NV 89703-7399

New Hampshire

Chester College of New England

Chester, New Hampshire
www.chestercollege.edu
Four-year private **Federal Code: 004733**

College costs. Lab fees vary per student; average $500.

	Living at home	On-campus
Tuition and fees:	$13,130	$13,130
Room and board:		$6,900
Books and supplies:	$1,100	$1,100
Personal expenses:	$1,000	$1,000
Transportation:	$1,000	$500

Undergraduate aid. Need-based: Average financial aid package for full-time students was $6,837. 54% awarded as scholarships/grants, 46% as loans/jobs. Need-based aid available for part-time students. **Non-need-based:** 4% awarded as scholarships/grants, 96% as loans/jobs. Scholarships based on academics, art, state/district residency.

Freshman aid. Need-based: Out of 54 full-time freshmen, 41 applied for aid; 37 were judged to have need; of these 34 received aid. **Non-need based:** 2 without need received awards.

Policies to reduce costs. Tuition/fee waivers for family members, employees and their families. Credit/placement for qualifying scores on AP, CLEP examinations. Work study available nights and weekends.

Payment plans. Credit card, installment payment.

Application procedures. FAFSA required. Priority date 3/15; no closing date. Applicants notified on rolling basis starting 12/1, must reply within 2 week(s) of notification. **Transfers:** No deadline.

Contact. **Financial aid office:** (603) 887-7404
Katie Weddle, Director of Financial Aid
40 Chester Street
Chester, NH 03036-4331

Colby-Sawyer College

New London, New Hampshire
www.colby-sawyer.edu
Four-year private **Federal Code: 002572**

	Living at home	On-campus
Tuition and fees:	$22,200	$22,200
Room and board:		$8,520
Board only:	$3,600	
Books and supplies:	$700	$700
Personal expenses:	$900	$900
Transportation:	$750	

Undergraduate aid. Need-based: Need-based aid available for full-time and part-time students. **Non-need-based:** Scholarships based on academics, art, leadership, music/drama.

Merit scholarships. All students accepted to the college prior to February 1 who have 2.5 GPA with 950 SAT or 20 composite ACT score or higher will be considered for scholarship program. Selection based on demonstrated involvement in the areas of leadership, community service, music, art, or creative writing. Awards are renewable and range between $1,500 and $5,000.

Policies to reduce costs. Tuition/fee waivers for employees and their families. Credit/placement for qualifying scores on AP, IB, CLEP examinations. Work study available nights and weekends.

Payment plans. Credit card payment.

Application procedures. FAFSA, institutional form required. Closing date 3/1. Applicants notified on rolling basis starting 3/25, must reply by 5/1 or within 3 week(s) of notification.

Contact. **Financial aid office:** (603) 526-3717
Jolene Mitchell, Dean Financial Aid
541 Main Street
New London, NH 03257

College for Lifelong Learning

Concord, New Hampshire
Four-year public
Federal Code: 031013

	Living at home
Tuition and fees (2002-2003):	$5,610
Out-of-state:	$6,210
Books and supplies:	$650

Policies to reduce costs. Tuition/fee waivers for senior citizens, employees and their families. Credit/placement for qualifying scores on AP, CLEP examinations.

Payment plans. Credit card, installment payment.

Application procedures. No deadline. Applicants notified on rolling basis.

Contact. **Financial aid office:** (603) 228-3000
Juanita Plourde, Director of Financial Aid
125 North State Street
Concord, NH 03301

Daniel Webster College

Nashua, New Hampshire
www.dwc.edu
Four-year private **Federal Code: 004731**

	Living at home	On-campus
Tuition and fees (2002-2003):	$19,200	$19,200
Room and board:		$7,440
Board only:	$2,250	
Books and supplies:	$800	$800
Personal expenses:	$1,500	$1,500
Transportation:	$1,500	$1,200

Undergraduate aid. Need-based: Average financial aid package for full-time students was $13,680. 54% awarded as scholarships/grants, 46% as loans/jobs. Need-based aid available for part-time students. **Non-need-based:** 95% awarded as scholarships/grants, 5% as loans/jobs. Scholarships based on academics, leadership. **Student debt:** 83% of graduating class borrowed to fund education; average debt was $48,000.

Freshman aid. Need-based: Out of 165 full-time freshmen, 163 applied for aid; 151 were judged to have need; of these 151 received aid. Average package met 73% of need. Average scholarship/grant was $5,751; average loan $2,625. **Non-need based:** 112 full-time freshmen with need received non-need scholarships; 12 without need received awards.

Merit scholarships. Scholarships, based on GPA and test scores, leadership, guidance counselor recommendation, awarded in amounts ranging from $500 to $7,500. Alumni and other scholarships range from $500 to full tuition.

Policies to reduce costs. Tuition/fee waivers for employees and their families. Credit/placement for qualifying scores on AP, IB, CLEP examinations. Work study available nights, weekends and for part-time students.

Payment plans. Credit card, installment payment.

Application procedures. FAFSA, institutional form required. Priority date 3/1; no closing date. Applicants notified on rolling basis starting 3/15, must reply within 2 week(s) of notification. **Transfers:** Priority date 3/1.

Contact. **Financial aid office:** (603) 577-6590
Anne Marie Caruso, Director of Financial Assistance
20 University Drive
Nashua, NH 03063

Dartmouth College

Hanover, New Hampshire
www.dartmouth.edu
Four-year private **Federal Code: 002573**

	Living at home	On-campus
Tuition and fees:	$29,256	$29,256
Room and board:		$8,740

Undergraduate aid. All financial aid based on need. Average financial aid package for full-time students was $25,549. 77% awarded as scholarships/grants, 23% as loans/jobs. Need-based aid available for part-time students. **Student debt:** 51% of graduating class borrowed to fund education; average debt was $15,543.

Freshman aid. Out of 1,130 full-time freshmen, 733 applied for aid; 576 were judged to have need; of these 576 received aid. Average package met 100% of need. 576 students had full need met. Average scholarship/grant was $21,968; average loan $2,950.

Policies to reduce costs. Prepayment discount; credit/placement for qualifying scores on AP, IB examinations.

Payment plans. Installment payment.

Application procedures. FAFSA, CSS PROFILE required. Closing date 2/1. Applicants notified by 4/2, must reply by 5/1. Early decision closing date 11/1. **Transfers:** Closing date 3/15. Grant budget for transfer students is limited. Some admitted transfer students may not have their full needs met.

Contact. **Financial aid office:** (603) 646-1110
Virginia Hazen, Director of Financial Aid
6016 McNutt Hall
Hanover, NH 03755

Franklin Pierce College

Rindge, New Hampshire
www.fpc.edu
Four-year private **Federal Code: 002575**

	Living at home	On-campus
Tuition and fees (projected):	$21,380	$21,380
Room and board:		$7,250
Board only:	$3,150	
Books and supplies:	$786	$786
Personal expenses:	$1,122	$1,122
Transportation:	$890	$280

Undergraduate aid. Need-based: Average financial aid package for full-time students was $16,296; for part-time $18,418. 62% awarded as scholarships/grants, 38% as loans/jobs. **Non-need-based:** 60% awarded as scholarships/grants, 40% as loans/jobs. Scholarships based on academics, alumni affiliation, athletics, music/drama, state/district residency. **Student debt:** 71% of graduating class borrowed to fund education; average debt was $21,802.

Freshman aid. Need-based: Out of 606 full-time freshmen, 440 applied for aid; 395 were judged to have need; of these 395 received aid. Average package met 71% of need. 31 students had full need met. Average scholarship/grant was $11,423; average loan $3,592. **Non-need based:** 24 full-time freshmen with need received non-need scholarships; 126 without need received awards; 12 received athletic scholarships.

Merit scholarships. Marlin Fitzwater Mass Communication; 6 awarded; $2,000. Robert Alvin Performing Arts-Theatre, Music, Dance; 2 awarded in each category; $2,000.

Policies to reduce costs. Tuition/fee waivers for children of alumni, senior citizens, family members, employees and their families. Credit/placement for qualifying scores on AP, IB, CLEP examinations. Work study available nights, weekends and for part-time students.

Payment plans. Credit card, installment, deferred payment.

Application procedures. FAFSA required. No deadline. Applicants notified on rolling basis starting 2/15, must reply within 2 week(s) of notification. **Transfers:** No deadline.

Contact. **Financial aid office:** (603) 899-4180
JoEllen Soucier, Director of Financial Aid
20 College Road
Rindge, NH 03461-0060

Hesser College

Manchester, New Hampshire
www.hesser.edu
Two-year proprietary **Federal Code: 004729**

	Living at home	On-campus
Tuition and fees (2002-2003):	$11,110	$11,110
Per-credit charge:	$373	$373
Room and board:		$6,200
Books and supplies:	$1,200	$1,200
Personal expenses:	$450	$550
Transportation:	$495	$500

Undergraduate aid. All financial aid based on need. Need-based aid available for full-time and part-time students. **Additional information:** Two private loans available to assist students in paying their balance; Tree Loan, SLM Loan.

Policies to reduce costs. Tuition/fee waivers for family members, employees and their families. Credit/placement for qualifying scores on AP, IB, CLEP examinations. Work study available nights, weekends and for part-time students.

Payment plans. Credit card, installment payment.

Application procedures. FAFSA, institutional form required. Priority date 5/1; no closing date. Applicants notified on rolling basis starting 3/1, must reply within 3 week(s) of notification. **Transfers:** No deadline.

Contact. **Financial aid office:** (603) 668-6660
Donna Wells, Director of Financial Aid
3 Sundial Avenue
Manchester, NH 03103

Keene State College

Keene, New Hampshire
www.keene.edu
Four-year public **Federal Code: 002590**

College costs. New England Regional tuition is 150% of in-state public institution tuition.

	Living at home	On-campus
Tuition and fees (2002-2003):	$6,142	$6,142
Out-of-state:	$11,802	$11,802
Room and board:		$5,430
Books and supplies:	$600	$600
Personal expenses:	$1,300	$750
Transportation:	$750	$800

Undergraduate aid. Need-based: Average financial aid package for full-time students was $6,967; for part-time $5,237. 42% awarded as scholarships/grants, 58% as loans/jobs. **Non-need-based:** 21% awarded as scholarships/grants, 79% as loans/jobs. Scholarships based on academics, alumni affiliation, art, music/drama. **Student debt:** 70% of graduating class borrowed to fund education; average debt was $17,560.

Freshman aid. Need-based: Out of 946 full-time freshmen, 784 applied for aid; 532 were judged to have need; of these 519 received aid. Average package met 82% of need. 163 students had full need met. Average scholarship/grant was $4,012; average loan $2,805. **Non-need based:** 152 full-time freshmen with need received non-need scholarships; 133 without need received awards.

Policies to reduce costs. Tuition/fee waivers for senior citizens, employees and their families. Credit/placement for qualifying scores on AP, CLEP examinations. Work study available nights and weekends.

Payment plans. Credit card payment.

Application procedures. FAFSA required. Closing date 3/1. Applicants notified on rolling basis starting 5/15, must reply within 4 week(s) of notification.

Contact. **Financial aid office:** (603) 358-2280
Patricia Blodgett, Director of Financial Aid
229 Main Street
Keene, NH 03435-2604

Magdalen College

Warner, New Hampshire
www.magdalen.edu
Four-year private

	Living at home	On-campus
Tuition and fees:	$8,000	$8,000
Room and board:		$5,250
Books and supplies:	$300	$300
Personal expenses:		$200

Undergraduate aid. All financial aid based on need. Average financial aid package for full-time students was $6,000. 34% awarded as scholarships/grants, 66% as loans/jobs. Need-based aid available for part-time students. **Student debt:** 60% of graduating class borrowed to fund education; average debt was $11,500.

Freshman aid. Out of 28 full-time freshmen, 22 applied for aid; 22 were judged to have need; of these 22 received aid. Average package met 90% of need. 20 students had full need met. Average scholarship/grant was $2,000; average loan $3,000.

Policies to reduce costs. Tuition/fee waivers for family members, employees and their families.

Application procedures. Institutional form required. Closing date 6/30. Applicants notified by 7/1, must reply by 7/1 or within 4 week(s) of notification.

Contact. **Financial aid office:** (603) 456-2656
Donald Regan, Vice President
511 Kearsarge Mountain Road
Warner, NH 03278

New England College

Henniker, New Hampshire
www.nec.edu
Four-year private **Federal Code: 002579**

	Living at home	On-campus
Tuition and fees (2002-2003):	$20,326	$20,326
Room and board:		$7,434
Books and supplies:	$450	$450
Personal expenses:	$450	$450
Transportation:	$600	$600

Undergraduate aid. **Need-based:** Average financial aid package for full-time students was $23,601; for part-time $6,898. 65% awarded as scholarships/grants, 35% as loans/jobs. **Non-need-based:** 38% awarded as scholarships/grants, 62% as loans/jobs. Scholarships based on academics, alumni affiliation, art, job skills, leadership, music/drama. **Student debt:** 87% of graduating class borrowed to fund education; average debt was $23,207.

Freshman aid. **Need-based:** Out of 238 full-time freshmen, 175 applied for aid; 154 were judged to have need; of these 154 received aid. Average package met 79% of need. 1 students had full need met. Average scholarship/grant was $9,849; average loan $8,969. **Non-need based:** 1 full-time freshmen with need received non-need scholarships; 56 without need received awards.

Policies to reduce costs. Tuition/fee waivers for adults, children of alumni, senior citizens, family members, employees and their families. Prepayment discount; credit/placement for qualifying scores on AP, IB, CLEP examinations. Work study available nights and weekends.

Payment plans. Credit card, installment payment.

Application procedures. FAFSA required. Priority date 4/1; no closing date. Applicants notified on rolling basis starting 4/15, must reply within 2 week(s) of notification. **Transfers:** Priority date 4/1; no deadline. May 1 deadline for state grant consideration.

Contact. **Financial aid office:** (603) 428-2284
Paul Miller, Director of Admissions and Financial Aid
26 Bridge Street
Henniker, NH 03242

New Hampshire Community Technical College: Berlin

Berlin, New Hampshire
www.berlin.nhctc.edu
Two-year public **Federal Code: 005291**

College costs. New England Regional tuition: 150% of in-state tuition.

	Living at home
Tuition and fees (2002-2003):	$3,780
Out-of-state:	$8,610
Per-credit charge:	$124
Per-credit out-of-state:	$285
Books and supplies:	$500
Personal expenses:	$1,500
Transportation:	$1,700

Undergraduate aid. All financial aid based on need. Need-based aid available for full-time and part-time students.

Policies to reduce costs. Tuition/fee waivers for senior citizens, employees and their families. Credit/placement for qualifying scores on CLEP examinations.

Payment plans. Credit card, installment, deferred payment.

Application procedures. FAFSA, institutional form required. Priority date 5/1; no closing date. Applicants notified on rolling basis starting 5/1, must reply within 2 week(s) of notification.

Contact. **Financial aid office:** (603) 752-1113
Jacqueline Catello, Financial Aid Officer
2020 Riverside Drive
Berlin, NH 03570

New Hampshire Community Technical College: Claremont

Claremont, New Hampshire
www.ncctc.edu
Two-year public **Federal Code: 007560**

College costs. New England Regional tuition: 150% of in-state tuition.

	Living at home
Tuition and fees (2002-2003):	$3,810
Out-of-state:	$8,640
Per-credit charge:	$124
Per-credit out-of-state:	$285
Books and supplies:	$550
Personal expenses:	$1,100
Transportation:	$1,600

Undergraduate aid. All financial aid based on need. Need-based aid available for full-time and part-time students.

Policies to reduce costs. Tuition/fee waivers for senior citizens, employees and their families. Credit/placement for qualifying scores on CLEP examinations.

Payment plans. Credit card payment.

Application procedures. FAFSA required. Priority date 5/1; no closing date. Applicants notified on rolling basis, must reply within 2 week(s) of notification.

Contact. **Financial aid office:** (603) 542-7744
Rita Wolfe, Financial Aid Officer
One College Drive
Claremont, NH 03743-9707

New Hampshire Community Technical College: Laconia

Laconia, New Hampshire
www.laco.tec.nh.us
Two-year public **Federal Code: 00839**

College costs. New England Regional tuition: 150% of in-state tuition.

	Living at home
Tuition and fees (2002-2003):	$3,780
Out-of-state:	$8,610
Per-credit charge:	$124
Per-credit out-of-state:	$285
Books and supplies:	$500
Personal expenses:	$800
Transportation:	$1,400

Undergraduate aid. All financial aid based on need. Need-based aid available for full-time and part-time students.

Policies to reduce costs. Tuition/fee waivers for senior citizens, employees and their families. Credit/placement for qualifying scores on AP, IB, CLEP examinations. Work study available nights.

Payment plans. Credit card, installment, deferred payment.

Application procedures. FAFSA, institutional form required. Priority date 5/1; no closing date. Applicants notified on rolling basis starting 4/1, must reply within 2 week(s) of notification. **Transfers:** No deadline.

Contact. Financial aid office: (603) 524-3207
Susan Jacobs, Financial Aid Officer
379 New Prescott Hill Road
Laconia, NH 03246-9204

New Hampshire Community Technical College: Manchester

Manchester, New Hampshire
www.manchester.nhctc.edu
Two-year public **Federal Code: 002582**

College costs. New England Regional tuition: 150% of in-state tuition.

	Living at home
Tuition and fees (2002-2003):	$3,810
Out-of-state:	$8,640
Per-credit charge:	$124
Per-credit out-of-state:	$285
Books and supplies:	$550
Personal expenses:	$1,770
Transportation:	$1,000

Undergraduate aid. Additional information: 100% of direct educational expenses met for all financial aid applicants.

Policies to reduce costs. Tuition/fee waivers for senior citizens, employees and their families. Credit/placement for qualifying scores on CLEP examinations. Work study available nights, weekends and for part-time students.

Payment plans. Credit card, installment, deferred payment.

Application procedures. FAFSA, institutional form required. Priority date 5/1; no closing date. Applicants notified on rolling basis starting 4/15, must reply within 2 week(s) of notification.

Contact. Financial aid office: (603) 668-6706
Marcia Gillis, Financial Aid Officer
1066 Front Street
Manchester, NH 03102-8518

New Hampshire Community Technical College: Nashua

Nashua, New Hampshire
www.ncctc.edu
Two-year public **Federal Code: 009236**

College costs. New England Regional tuition: 150% of in-state tuition.

	Living at home
Tuition and fees (2002-2003):	$3,810
Out-of-state:	$8,640
Per-credit charge:	$124
Per-credit out-of-state:	$285
Books and supplies:	$500
Personal expenses:	$500
Transportation:	$1,000

Undergraduate aid. All financial aid based on need. 32% awarded as scholarships/grants, 68% as loans/jobs. Need-based aid available for part-time students.

Policies to reduce costs. Tuition/fee waivers for senior citizens, employees and their families. Credit/placement for qualifying scores on AP examinations. Work study available nights and for part-time students.

Payment plans. Credit card, installment, deferred payment.

Application procedures. FAFSA required. Priority date 5/1; no closing date. Applicants notified on rolling basis starting 3/1, must reply within 2 week(s) of notification.

Contact. Financial aid office: (603) 882-6923
Julie Burns, Financial Aid Officer
505 Amherst Street
Nashua, NH 03063

New Hampshire Community Technical College: Stratham

Stratham, New Hampshire
www.stratham.nhctc.edu
Two-year public **Federal Code: 002583**

College costs. New England Regional tuition: 150% of in-state tuition.

	Living at home
Tuition and fees (2002-2003):	$3,840
Out-of-state:	$8,670
Per-credit charge:	$124
Per-credit out-of-state:	$285
Books and supplies:	$600
Personal expenses:	$1,000
Transportation:	$1,500

Policies to reduce costs. Tuition/fee waivers for senior citizens, employees and their families. Credit/placement for qualifying scores on CLEP examinations.

Payment plans. Credit card, installment payment.

Application procedures. FAFSA, institutional form required. Priority date 5/1; no closing date. Applicants notified on rolling basis, must reply within 2 week(s) of notification.

Contact. Financial aid office: (603) 772-1194
Elaine Scovill, Financial Aid Officer
277 Portsmouth Avenue
Stratham, NH 03885

New Hampshire Technical Institute

Concord, New Hampshire
www.nhti.edu
Two-year public **Federal Code: 002581**

College costs. New England Regional tuition: 150% of in-state tuition.

	Living at home	On-campus
Tuition and fees (2002-2003):	$4,080	$4,080
Out-of-state:	$8,910	$8,910
Per-credit charge:	$124	$124
Per-credit out-of-state:	$285	$285
Room and board:		$5,070
Books and supplies:	$400	$400
Personal expenses:	$1,600	$1,600
Transportation:	$1,500	$750

Undergraduate aid. All financial aid based on need. Need-based aid available for full-time and part-time students.

Policies to reduce costs. Credit/placement for qualifying scores on AP, IB, CLEP examinations. Work study available nights, weekends and for part-time students.

Payment plans. Credit card, installment payment.

Application procedures. FAFSA, institutional form required. Priority date 5/1; no closing date. Applicants notified on rolling basis starting 6/1, must reply within 2 week(s) of notification. **Transfers:** Priority date 5/1; no deadline.

Contact. Financial aid office: (603) 271-7136
Paula Marsh, Financial Aid Officer
31 College Drive
Concord, NH 03301

Plymouth State College

Plymouth, New Hampshire
www.plymouth.edu
Four-year public **Federal Code: 002591**

College costs. New England Regional tuition is 150% of in-state public institution tuition.

	Living at home	On-campus
Tuition and fees (2002-2003):	$5,857	$5,857
Out-of-state:	$11,517	$11,517
Room and board:		$5,768
Board only:	$2,000	
Books and supplies:	$700	$700
Personal expenses:	$1,070	$1,170
Transportation:	$1,100	$300

Undergraduate aid. Need-based: Average financial aid package for full-time students was $7,677; for part-time $6,220. 35% awarded as scholarships/grants, 65% as loans/jobs. **Non-need-based:** 30% awarded as scholarships/grants, 70% as loans/jobs. Scholarships based on academics, minority status, music/drama. **Student debt:** 72% of graduating class borrowed to fund education; average debt was $17,629.

Freshman aid. Need-based: Out of 940 full-time freshmen, 773 applied for aid; 558 were judged to have need; of these 558 received aid. Average package met 77% of need. 65 students had full need met. Average scholarship/grant was $4,016; average loan $2,806. **Non-need based:** 199 full-time freshmen with need received non-need scholarships; 63 without need received awards.

Merit scholarships. Presidents' Scholars: $3,000 based on outstanding academic performance and overall achievement; 20 awarded. PSC Scholars: $2,000 based on overall merit and past achievement; 75 awarded. Aspire Awards: $1,000 for first year students, based on high class rank and SAT scores, 40 awarded. Excel Scholarship: $1,500 award for first year based on high school rank and SAT scores, 100 awarded. New Hampshire Top Scholars: $2,500 to New Hampshire residents in top 15%. Music/theatre talent grants: $2,500 based on talent and audition.

Policies to reduce costs. Tuition/fee waivers for senior citizens, employees and their families. Credit/placement for qualifying scores on AP, CLEP examinations. Work study available nights, weekends and for part-time students.

Payment plans. Installment payment.

Application procedures. FAFSA required. Priority date 3/1; no closing date. Applicants notified on rolling basis starting 3/1, must reply by 5/1. **Transfers:** Priority date 3/1.

Contact. Financial aid office: (603) 535-5000
Robert Tuveson, Director of Financial Aid
17 High Street
Plymouth, NH 03264-1595

Rivier College

Nashua, New Hampshire
www.rivier.edu
Four-year private **Federal Code: 002586**

	Living at home	On-campus
Tuition and fees (2002-2003):	$18,155	$18,155
Room and board:		$6,916
Board only:	$2,900	
Books and supplies:	$800	$800
Personal expenses:	$1,000	$1,500
Transportation:	$1,000	$450

Undergraduate aid. Need-based: Average financial aid package for full-time students was $11,932; for part-time $4,414. 38% awarded as scholarships/grants, 62% as loans/jobs. **Non-need-based:** 57% awarded as scholarships/grants, 43% as loans/jobs. Scholarships based on academics, alumni affiliation, minority status.

Freshman aid. Need-based: Out of 330 full-time freshmen, 330 applied for aid; 330 were judged to have need; of these 330 received aid. Average package met 74% of need. 33 students had full need met. Average scholarship/grant was $8,587; average loan $3,280. **Non-need based:** 98 full-time freshmen with need received non-need scholarships; 21 without need received awards.

Merit scholarships. Dean's Scholarship for high school seniors with minimum 1000 SAT and 3.0 GPA; renewable annually with minimum 2.67 cumulative GPA; $6,000 for residents, $5,000 for commuters. Presidential Scholarship for high school seniors with minimum 1150 SAT and 3.4 GPA; renewable annually with minimum 3.0 cumulative GPA; $7,000 for residents, $6,000 for commuters. Catholic High School Grant for students graduating from Catholic high school, renewable annually with 2.5 cumulative GPA; $4,000 for residents, $3,000 for commuters. Honors Scholarship for honors program participants; $10,000 for residents, $2,000 for commuters. Alumni Scholarship for children of Rivier alumni, renewable annually with minimum 2.0 cumulative GPA; $2,000. Trustee Scholarship for high school seniors with minimum 1200 SAT and 3.4 GPA, renewable annually with minimum 3.0 cumulative GPA; $8,000 for residents, $7,000 for commuters. Founders Scholarship for National Merit Finalists; full tuition, renewable with minimum 3.0 cumulative GPA.

Policies to reduce costs. Tuition/fee waivers for children of alumni, senior citizens, family members, family of clergy, employees and their families. Credit/placement for qualifying scores on AP, CLEP examinations. Work study available nights and weekends.

Payment plans. Credit card, installment, deferred payment.

Application procedures. FAFSA required. Priority date 2/1; no closing date. Applicants notified on rolling basis starting 3/1, must reply by 5/1 or within 2 week(s) of notification. **Transfers:** Priority date 3/1; no deadline. Scholarship for transfer students with minimum 3.0 GPA and 15 transferable credits.

Contact. Financial aid office: (603) 897-8510
John Caiazza, Director of Financial Aid
420 Main Street
Nashua, NH 03060-5086

St. Anselm College

Manchester, New Hampshire
www.anselm.edu
Four-year private **Federal Code: 002587**

College costs. Minimum required lab fees $200 for freshmen. Lab fees vary per course. $75 dorm deposit required for campus residents.

	Living at home	On-campus
Tuition and fees:	$22,160	$22,160
Room and board:		$8,090
Books and supplies:	$750	$750

Undergraduate aid. Need-based: Average financial aid package for full-time students was $21,933. 71% awarded as scholarships/grants, 29% as loans/jobs. Need-based aid available for part-time students. **Non-need-based:** 71% awarded as scholarships/grants, 29% as loans/jobs. Scholarships based on academics, athletics, state/district residency. **Student debt:** 80% of graduating class borrowed to fund education; average debt was $19,139.

Freshman aid. Need-based: Out of 572 full-time freshmen, 532 applied for aid; 522 were judged to have need; of these 522 received aid. Average package met 82% of need. 76 students had full need met. Average scholarship/grant was $7,696; average loan $2,427. **Non-need based:** 212 full-time freshmen with need received non-need scholarships; 212 without need received awards; 7 received athletic scholarships.

Merit scholarships. Presidential Scholarships; 350 awarded; based on academic performance (grades, class rank, SAT results) and extracurricular experience; $6,000 to $11,500.

Policies to reduce costs. Tuition/fee waivers for senior citizens, minority students, family members, family of clergy, employees and their families. Credit/placement for qualifying scores on AP, IB, CLEP examinations. Work study available nights and weekends.

Payment plans. Installment payment.

Application procedures. FAFSA, CSS PROFILE required. Priority date 3/1; no closing date. Applicants notified on rolling basis starting 3/10, must reply by 5/1. Early decision closing date 12/1. **Transfers:** Merit scholarships are not available for transfer students.

Contact. Financial aid office: (603) 641-7110
Elizabeth Keuffel, Director of Financial Aid
100 Saint Anselm Drive
Manchester, NH 03102-1310

Southern New Hampshire University

Manchester, New Hampshire
www.snhu.edu
Four-year private **Federal Code: 002580**

	Living at home	On-campus
Tuition and fees (projected):	$18,594	$18,594
Room and board:		$7,648
Board only:	$1,500	
Books and supplies:	$700	$700
Personal expenses:	$900	$900
Transportation:	$750	$350

Undergraduate aid. **Need-based:** Need-based aid available for full-time and part-time students. **Non-need-based:** Scholarships based on academics, athletics.

Policies to reduce costs. Tuition/fee waivers for children of alumni, family members, employees and their families. Credit/placement for qualifying scores on AP, IB, CLEP examinations.

Payment plans. Credit card, installment, deferred payment.

Application procedures. FAFSA required. Priority date 3/15; no closing date. Applicants notified on rolling basis starting 2/15, must reply within 2 week(s) of notification. **Transfers:** Priority date 6/15.

Contact. **Financial aid office:** (603) 668-2211
Tim Dryer, Director of Financial Aid
2500 North River Road
Manchester, NH 03106

Thomas More College of Liberal Arts

Merrimack, New Hampshire
www.thomasmorecollege.edu
Four-year private **Federal Code: 030431**

	Living at home	On-campus
Tuition and fees (projected):	$10,400	$10,400
Room and board:		$7,700
Books and supplies:	$500	$500
Personal expenses:		$100
Transportation:		$1,500

Undergraduate aid. **Need-based:** Average financial aid package for full-time students was $9,198. 79% awarded as scholarships/grants, 21% as loans/jobs. **Non-need-based:** 51% awarded as scholarships/grants, 49% as loans/jobs. Scholarships based on academics. **Student debt:** 72% of graduating class borrowed to fund education; average debt was $17,648.

Freshman aid. **Need-based:** Out of 20 full-time freshmen, 20 applied for aid; 15 were judged to have need; of these 15 received aid. Average package met 80% of need. Average scholarship/grant was $5,664; average loan $2,625. **Non-need based:** 1 full-time freshmen with need received non-need scholarships; 5 without need received awards.

Merit scholarships. Thomas More Scholarship; several awarded; based on superior academic achievement, exceptional promise or potential; full and/or partial tuition. Commuter Grants; offered to full-time students within commuting distance of the college; 25% of tuition. Faith and Reason Essay Contest; 4 awarded; based on essay; half tuition for four years. Summer Program Scholarship; for students who have attended the Thomas More College Summer Program for high-school students; $1,000 per year.

Policies to reduce costs. Tuition/fee waivers for employees and their families.

Payment plans. Credit card, installment payment.

Application procedures. FAFSA required. Priority date 5/1; no closing date. Applicants notified on rolling basis starting 5/15, must reply within 2 week(s) of notification. **Transfers:** Priority date 5/1; no deadline.

Contact. **Financial aid office:** (603) 880-8308
Catherine Alcarez, Director of Financial Aid
6 Manchester Street
Merrimack, NH 03054

University of New Hampshire

Durham, New Hampshire
www.unh.edu
Four-year public **Federal Code: 002589**

College costs. New England Regional Student Program tuition is 150% of in-state public institution tuition.

	Living at home	On-campus
Tuition and fees (2002-2003):	$8,130	$8,130
Out-of-state:	$17,830	$17,830
Room and board:		$5,882
Board only:	$750	
Books and supplies:	$1,100	$1,100
Personal expenses:	$2,000	$1,800
Transportation:	$1,100	$300

Undergraduate aid. **Need-based:** Average financial aid package for full-time students was $13,429; for part-time $9,231. 40% awarded as scholarships/grants, 60% as loans/jobs. **Non-need-based:** 43% awarded as scholarships/grants, 57% as loans/jobs. Scholarships based on academics, art, athletics, leadership, music/drama. **Student debt:** 69% of graduating class borrowed to fund education; average debt was $20,701.

Freshman aid. **Need-based:** Out of 2,709 full-time freshmen, 2,017 applied for aid; 1,490 were judged to have need; of these 1,476 received aid. Average package met 89% of need. 360 students had full need met. Average scholarship/grant was $2,475; average loan $2,309. **Non-need based:** 162 full-time freshmen with need received non-need scholarships; 505 without need received awards; 38 received athletic scholarships.

Merit scholarships. Presidential Scholarship; half tuition. Various other awards recognizing outstanding high school achievement determined during freshmen candidate application review process, no additional application materials required.

Policies to reduce costs. Tuition/fee waivers for senior citizens, employees and their families. Credit/placement for qualifying scores on AP, IB, CLEP examinations. Work study available nights, weekends and for part-time students.

Application procedures. FAFSA required. Priority date 3/1; no closing date. Applicants notified on rolling basis starting 3/1.

Contact. **Financial aid office:** (603) 862-3600
Susan Allen, Director of Financial Aid
Grant House, 4 Garrison Avenue
Durham, NH 03824

University of New Hampshire at Manchester

Manchester, New Hampshire
www.unh.edu/unhm
Four-year public **Federal Code: 002589**

College costs. New England Regional Student is 150% of in-state public institution tuition.

	Living at home
Tuition and fees (2002-2003):	$5,544
Out-of-state:	$13,784
Board only:	$750
Books and supplies:	$700
Personal expenses:	$2,020
Transportation:	$1,100

Undergraduate aid. **Non-need-based:** Scholarships based on academics, state/district residency.

Policies to reduce costs. Tuition/fee waivers for senior citizens, employees and their families. Credit/placement for qualifying scores on AP, IB, CLEP examinations. Work study available nights, weekends and for part-time students.

Payment plans. Credit card, installment payment.

Application procedures. FAFSA required. Closing date 5/1. Applicants notified on rolling basis starting 4/1, must reply within 2 week(s) of notification.

Contact. **Financial aid office:** (603) 641-4189
Jodi Abad, Director of Financial Aid
400 Commercial Street
Manchester, NH 03101-1113

New Jersey

Assumption College for Sisters

Mendham, New Jersey
www.asccollegeforsisters.org
Two-year private **Federal Code: 002595**

	Living at home	On-campus
Tuition and fees:	$2,400	$2,400
Per-credit charge:	$100	$100
Room and board:		$1,100
Books and supplies:	$400	$400

Undergraduate aid. Additional information: All students receive half of tuition as scholarship.

Policies to reduce costs. Tuition at time of enrollment guaranteed for 2 years; credit/placement for qualifying scores on AP examinations.

Payment plans. Installment payment.

Application procedures. No deadline. **Transfers:** No deadline.

Contact. Financial aid office: (973) 543-6528
Mary Lawrence Cassidy, Treasurer
350 Bernardsville Road
Mendham, NJ 07945-0800

Atlantic Cape Community College

Mays Landing, New Jersey
www.atlantic.edu
Two-year public **Federal Code: 002596**

	Living at home
Tuition and fees (2002-2003):	$2,349
Out-of-district:	$4,158
Out-of-state:	$6,846
Per-credit charge:	$60
Per-credit out-of-district:	$121
Per-credit out-of-state:	$210
Books and supplies:	$800
Transportation:	$1,360

Undergraduate aid. Need-based: Need-based aid available for full-time and part-time students. **Additional information:** Installment plan available for culinary arts majors. Employees of Atlantic City casinos may attend ACCC at in-county rates regardless of where they live.

Merit scholarships. Howard Persina Scholarship for hospitality management students. Barbara Rimm Memorial Scholarship for nursing majors. William R. Cohn Memorial Scholarship for accounting students. Atlantic City Restaurant Association Scholarship for culinary arts students. Math and Science Scholarship.

Policies to reduce costs. Tuition/fee waivers for senior citizens, unemployed or children of unemployed, employees and their families. Credit/placement for qualifying scores on AP, CLEP examinations. Work study available for part-time students.

Payment plans. Credit card payment.

Application procedures. FAFSA, institutional form required. Priority date 5/1; no closing date. Applicants notified on rolling basis starting 5/1. **Transfers:** Priority date 5/1; no deadline.

Contact. Financial aid office: (609) 343-5082
Fred Mason, Director of Financial Aid
5100 Black Horse Pike
Mays Landing, NJ 08330

Bergen Community College

Paramus, New Jersey
www.bergen.edu
Two-year public **Federal Code: 004736**

	Living at home
Tuition and fees (2002-2003):	$2,708
Out-of-district:	$5,108
Out-of-state:	$5,408
Per-credit charge:	$75
Per-credit out-of-district:	$155
Per-credit out-of-state:	$165
Books and supplies:	$750
Personal expenses:	$1,800

Policies to reduce costs. Tuition/fee waivers for senior citizens, employees and their families. Credit/placement for qualifying scores on CLEP examinations.

Payment plans. Credit card payment.

Application procedures. FAFSA required. Priority date 5/15; no closing date. Applicants notified on rolling basis starting 6/1. **Transfers:** Priority date 7/1; no deadline.

Contact. Financial aid office: (201) 447-7200
Joseph Roberto, Director of Financial Aid
400 Paramus Road
Paramus, NJ 07652-1595

Berkeley College

West Paterson, New Jersey
www.berkeleycollege.edu
Four-year proprietary **Federal Code: 007502**

	Living at home	On-campus
Tuition and fees (projected):	$14,340	$14,340
Room and board:		$8,100
Books and supplies:	$900	$900
Transportation:	$1,765	

Undergraduate aid. Need-based: Need-based aid available for full-time students. **Non-need-based:** Scholarships based on academics, alumni affiliation. **Additional information:** Alumni scholarship examination given in November and December. Full and partial scholarships awarded.

Policies to reduce costs. Tuition/fee waivers for family members, employees and their families. Tuition at time of enrollment guaranteed for 4 years; credit/placement for qualifying scores on AP, CLEP examinations.

Payment plans. Credit card, installment payment.

Application procedures. FAFSA required. No deadline. Applicants notified on rolling basis starting 3/1, must reply within 6 week(s) of notification. **Transfers:** No deadline.

Contact. Financial aid office: (973) 278-5400 ext. 350
Keith Green, Vice President, Student Finance
44 Rifle Camp Road
West Paterson, NJ 07424-0440

Bloomfield College

Bloomfield, New Jersey
www.bloomfield.edu
Four-year private **Federal Code: 002597**

	Living at home	On-campus
Tuition and fees (2002-2003):	$12,250	$12,250
Room and board:		$5,850
Board only:	$350	
Books and supplies:	$500	$500
Personal expenses:	$1,315	$1,496
Transportation:	$1,135	$300

Undergraduate aid. Need-based: Average financial aid package for full-time students was $12,438. 79% awarded as scholarships/grants, 21% as loans/jobs. Need-based aid available for part-time students. **Non-need-based:** 36% awarded as scholarships/grants, 64% as loans/jobs. Scholarships based on academics, alumni affiliation, art, athletics, leadership, religious affiliation.

Freshman aid. Need-based: Out of 373 full-time freshmen, 360 applied for aid; 329 were judged to have need; of these 329 received aid. 187 students had full need met. Average scholarship/grant was $10,464; average loan $1,807. **Non-need based:** 71 full-time freshmen with need received non-need scholarships; 12 without need received awards; 25 received athletic scholarships.

Merit scholarships. Trustee Scholar Award: $5,000, high school GPA of 3.2 or higher, top 25% of graduating class, competitive SAT scores; Presidential Scholarship: $3,500, high school GPA of 3.0 or higher, top 33% of graduating class, competitive SAT scores; Academic Division Scholarships: requirements vary by division; Transfer Scholarship: $3,000, transfer students from 2-year colleges with GPA of 3.0 or higher.

Policies to reduce costs. Tuition/fee waivers for senior citizens, employees and their families. Credit/placement for qualifying scores on AP, CLEP examinations. Work study available nights, weekends and for part-time students.

Payment plans. Credit card, installment, deferred payment.

Application procedures. FAFSA, institutional form required. Priority date 3/15; no closing date. Applicants notified on rolling basis starting 3/15, must reply within 2 week(s) of notification. **Transfers:** No deadline.

Contact. **Financial aid office:** (973) 748-9000 ext. 212
Luis Gonzales, Director Of Financial Aid
One Park Place
Bloomfield, NJ 07003-9981

Brookdale Community College

Lincroft, New Jersey
www.brookdalecc.edu
Two-year public **Federal Code: 008404**

	Living at home
Tuition and fees (2002-2003):	$2,808
Out-of-district:	$5,328
Out-of-state:	$8,718
Per-credit charge:	$78
Per-credit out-of-district:	$156
Per-credit out-of-state:	$275
Board only:	$5,168
Books and supplies:	$1,000
Personal expenses:	$1,195
Transportation:	$1,462

Undergraduate aid. Need-based: Need-based aid available for full-time and part-time students. **Non-need-based:** Scholarships based on athletics.

Policies to reduce costs. Tuition/fee waivers for senior citizens, unemployed or children of unemployed, employees and their families. Credit/placement for qualifying scores on CLEP examinations.

Payment plans. Credit card, installment payment.

Application procedures. FAFSA, institutional form required. Priority date 5/1; no closing date. Applicants notified on rolling basis starting 5/1, must reply within 2 week(s) of notification.

Contact. **Financial aid office:** (732) 224-2361
Michael Bennett, Director of Financial Aid
765 Newman Springs Road
Lincroft, NJ 07738

Burlington County College

Pemberton, New Jersey
www.bcc.edu
Two-year public **Federal Code: 007730**

	Living at home
Tuition and fees (2002-2003):	$1,857
Out-of-district:	$2,595
Out-of-state:	$4,485
Per-credit charge:	$62
Per-credit out-of-district:	$77
Per-credit out-of-state:	$140
Books and supplies:	$1,000
Transportation:	$2,300

Undergraduate aid. All financial aid based on need. Need-based aid available for full-time and part-time students.

Policies to reduce costs. Tuition/fee waivers for senior citizens, family members, unemployed or children of unemployed, employees and their families. Credit/placement for qualifying scores on CLEP examinations.

Payment plans. Credit card, installment, deferred payment.

Application procedures. FAFSA, institutional form required. No deadline. Applicants notified on rolling basis starting 7/1, must reply within 3 week(s) of notification.

Contact. **Financial aid office:** (609) 894-9311 ext. 7249
Chris Pesotski, Director of Financial Aid
Route 530
Pemberton, NJ 08068-1599

Caldwell College

Caldwell, New Jersey
www.caldwell.edu
Four-year private **Federal Code: 002598**

	Living at home	On-campus
Tuition and fees (2002-2003):	$16,100	$16,100
Room and board:		$6,800
Books and supplies:	$800	$800
Personal expenses:	$1,000	$1,000
Transportation:	$1,400	$600

Undergraduate aid. Need-based: Average financial aid package for full-time students was $9,735; for part-time $6,268. 63% awarded as scholarships/grants, 37% as loans/jobs. **Non-need-based:** Scholarships based on academics, alumni affiliation, art, athletics, leadership, music/drama, religious affiliation. **Student debt:** 79% of graduating class borrowed to fund education; average debt was $15,125.

Freshman aid. Need-based: Out of 296 full-time freshmen, 278 applied for aid; 232 were judged to have need; of these 232 received aid. Average package met 74% of need. 10 students had full need met. Average scholarship/grant was $7,525; average loan $1,975.

Merit scholarships. Academic awards range from $3,750-full tuition; leadership awards range from $500-$2,000; athletic awards range from $1,000-$6,000; special interest awards range from $500-$1,500. The number of awards varies for all listed.

Policies to reduce costs. Tuition/fee waivers for children of alumni, senior citizens, family members, family of clergy, employees and their families. Credit/placement for qualifying scores on AP, IB, CLEP examinations. Work study available nights and weekends.

Payment plans. Credit card payment.

Application procedures. FAFSA, institutional form required. Priority date 4/15; no closing date. Applicants notified on rolling basis starting 3/1. **Transfers:** No deadline. Students who have filed for aid through the state before must file FAFSA by June 1 for succeeding year.

Contact. **Financial aid office:** (973) 618-3222
Lissa Anderson, Financial Aid Executive Director
9 Ryerson Avenue
Caldwell, NJ 07006-6195

Camden County College

Blackwood, New Jersey
www.camdencc.edu
Two-year public **Federal Code: 006865**

	Living at home
Tuition and fees (2002-2003):	$2,160
Out-of-district:	$2,280
Out-of-state:	$2,280
Per-credit charge:	$62
Per-credit out-of-district:	$66
Per-credit out-of-state:	$66
Books and supplies:	$650

Undergraduate aid. Need-based: Need-based aid available for full-time and part-time students.

Policies to reduce costs. Tuition/fee waivers for senior citizens, unemployed or children of unemployed, employees and their families. Credit/placement for qualifying scores on CLEP examinations. Work study available for part-time students.

Payment plans. Credit card, installment, deferred payment.

Application procedures. FAFSA, institutional form required. Priority date 7/1; no closing date. Applicants notified on rolling basis starting 7/1. **Transfers:** Must submit financial aid transcripts from all previously attended institutions.

Contact. **Financial aid office:** (856) 227-7200
James Owens, Director of Financial Aid
Box 200
Blackwood, NJ 08012

Centenary College

Hackettstown, New Jersey
www.centenarycollege.edu
Four-year private **Federal Code: 002599**

College costs. Required fee $1,600 for equine major and $1,860 for comprehensive learning support program.

	Living at home	On-campus
Tuition and fees (2002-2003):	$16,800	$16,800
Room and board:		$6,850
Books and supplies:	$660	$660
Personal expenses:	$600	$600
Transportation:	$1,500	$300

Undergraduate aid. **Need-based:** Need-based aid available for full-time students. **Non-need-based:** Scholarships based on academics, alumni affiliation, leadership, religious affiliation.

Merit scholarships. Academic awards based on minimum GPA of 2.5, SAT 800 or ACT 16. Leadership awards available based on demonstrated leadership ability and potential. Equine Award, Centenary Resident Grant, Out-of-State Centenary Grant, Skylands Centenary Grant, Centenary United Methodist Scholarship also available.

Policies to reduce costs. Tuition/fee waivers for children of alumni, senior citizens, family members, employees and their families. Credit/placement for qualifying scores on AP, IB, CLEP examinations. Work study available nights and weekends.

Payment plans. Credit card payment.

Application procedures. FAFSA, institutional form required. Priority date 5/1; closing date 8/15. Applicants notified on rolling basis starting 4/1, must reply within 2 week(s) of notification. **Transfers:** Students from New Jersey colleges who have received TAG must apply by state deadline. Students must submit financial aid transcripts from all previous institutions attended.

Contact. **Financial aid office:** (908) 852-1400 ext. 2350
Carol Strauss, Director of Financial Aid
400 Jefferson Street
Hackettstown, NJ 07840-9989

College of St. Elizabeth

Morristown, New Jersey
www.cse.edu
Four-year private **Federal Code: 002600**

	Living at home	On-campus
Tuition and fees (2002-2003):	$16,375	$16,375
Room and board:		$7,750
Board only:	$3,000	
Books and supplies:	$800	$800
Personal expenses:	$650	$650
Transportation:	$1,800	$700

Undergraduate aid. **Need-based:** Average financial aid package for full-time students was $15,328; for part-time $5,072. 81% awarded as scholarships/grants, 19% as loans/jobs. **Non-need-based:** 71% awarded as scholarships/grants, 29% as loans/jobs. Scholarships based on academics, alumni affiliation, art, leadership, state/district residency. **Student debt:** 33% of graduating class borrowed to fund education; average debt was $12,751.

Freshman aid. **Need-based:** Out of 149 full-time freshmen, 131 applied for aid; 119 were judged to have need; of these 119 received aid. Average package met 85% of need. 27 students had full need met. Average scholarship/grant was $14,258; average loan $2,693. **Non-need based:** 14 full-time freshmen with need received non-need scholarships; 36 without need received awards.

Merit scholarships. Scholarships available to students with rigorous high school academic program and significant participation in extracurricular activities; SAT score requirements varied. Presidential Scholarship for campus residents, full tuition. Elizabethan Scholarship, $8,000-$10,000 for campus residents, $8,000 for commuters. Seton Scholarship, $4,000-$7,000 for campus residents, $3,000-$5,000 for commuters. Awards guaranteed to eligible students who apply by March 1 and enroll by May 1 for fall semester. Spring semester awards dependent upon availability of funds. International scholarships awarded annually for fall semester only to first year students enrolled in Women's College; covers tuition, room and board; very competitive, based on academic record, SAT scores (if submitted) and TOEFL score.

Policies to reduce costs. Tuition/fee waivers for adults, children of alumni, senior citizens, family members, employees and their families. Credit/placement for qualifying scores on AP, IB, CLEP examinations. Work study available nights, weekends and for part-time students.

Payment plans. Credit card, installment payment.

Application procedures. FAFSA required. Priority date 3/1; no closing date. Applicants notified on rolling basis starting 11/15, must reply by 5/1 or within 2 week(s) of notification. **Transfers:** Priority date 4/15; closing date 8/20. Scholarships available for full-time students who enroll immediately following full-time enrollment at another college. Applicants must have completed minimum 32 credits and have minimum 3.0 GPA. Awards range from $3,500 to half tuition. Minimum of 5 awarded annually. Preference given to applications received by June 1 for fall semester and by December 1 for spring semester. Limited number of partial scholarships awarded to international students.

Contact. **Financial aid office:** (973) 290-4000
Camille Green-Thomas, Director of Financial Aid
Two Convent Road
Morristown, NJ 07960-6989

County College of Morris

Randolph, New Jersey
www.ccm.edu
Two-year public **Federal Code: 007106**

College costs. Tuition reciprocity agreements with neighboring counties allow some out-of-county residents to pay in-county rates. Stated amount for required fees is based on $10.50 per credit charge and reflects a 30-credit annual enrollment.

	Living at home
Tuition and fees (projected):	$2,440
Out-of-district:	$4,540
Out-of-state:	$6,130
Per-credit charge:	$70
Per-credit out-of-district:	$140
Per-credit out-of-state:	$193
Books and supplies:	$750
Personal expenses:	$1,120
Transportation:	$1,500

Undergraduate aid. **Need-based:** Average financial aid package for full-time students was $7,105; for part-time $2,011. 51% awarded as scholarships/grants, 49% as loans/jobs. **Non-need-based:** 17% awarded as scholarships/grants, 83% as loans/jobs. Scholarships based on athletics.

Freshman aid. **Need-based:** Average package met 96% of need. Average scholarship/grant was $2,000; average loan $2,830.

Policies to reduce costs. Tuition/fee waivers for senior citizens, unemployed or children of unemployed, employees and their families. Credit/placement for qualifying scores on AP, CLEP examinations. Work study available for part-time students.

Payment plans. Credit card payment.

Application procedures. FAFSA required. Priority date 3/1; no closing date. Applicants notified on rolling basis starting 5/1. **Transfers:** Priority date 3/1; no deadline.

Contact. **Financial aid office:** (973) 328-5230
Harvey Willis, Director, Financial Aid
214 Center Grove Road
Randolph, NJ 07869-2086

Cumberland County College

Vineland, New Jersey
www.cccnj.net
Two-year public **Federal Code: 002601**

College costs. $8 per-credit-hour technology fee.

	Living at home
Tuition and fees (projected):	$2,400
Out-of-district:	$4,530
Out-of-state:	$8,790
Per-credit charge:	$71
Per-credit out-of-district:	$142
Per-credit out-of-state:	$284
Books and supplies:	$600
Personal expenses:	$1,429
Transportation:	$727

Undergraduate aid. Need-based: Need-based aid available for full-time and part-time students. **Non-need-based:** Scholarships based on academics.

Policies to reduce costs. Tuition/fee waivers for senior citizens, unemployed or children of unemployed, employees and their families. Credit/placement for qualifying scores on CLEP examinations.

Payment plans. Credit card, installment, deferred payment.

Application procedures. FAFSA required. No deadline. Applicants notified on rolling basis, must reply within 3 week(s) of notification. **Transfers:** No deadline.

Contact. Financial aid office: (609) 691-8600
Kimberly Mitchell, Director, Financial Aid
Box 517
Vineland, NJ 08362-0517

DeVry College of Technology

North Brunswick, New Jersey
www.nj.devry.edu
Four-year proprietary **Federal Code: 009228**

	Living at home
Tuition and fees:	$10,265
Books and supplies:	$1,100
Personal expenses:	$1,816
Transportation:	$1,336

Undergraduate aid. All financial aid based on need. Average financial aid package for full-time students was $7,419; for part-time $5,469. 28% awarded as scholarships/grants, 72% as loans/jobs.

Freshman aid. Average package met 42% of need. Average scholarship/grant was $4,540; average loan $3,594.

Policies to reduce costs. Tuition/fee waivers for employees and their families.

Payment plans. Credit card, installment, deferred payment.

Application procedures. FAFSA required. No deadline. Applicants notified on rolling basis. **Transfers:** No deadline.

Contact. Financial aid office: (732) 435-4880
Albert Cama, Director of Financial Aid
630 US Highway One
North Brunswick, NJ 08902-3362

Drew University

Madison, New Jersey
www.drew.edu
Four-year private **Federal Code: 002603**

	Living at home	On-campus
Tuition and fees (2002-2003):	$26,346	$26,346
Room and board:		$7,228
Board only:	$2,682	
Books and supplies:	$956	$956
Personal expenses:	$1,982	$1,982
Transportation:	$1,584	

Undergraduate aid. Need-based: Average financial aid package for full-time students was $19,403. 77% awarded as scholarships/grants, 23% as loans/jobs. Need-based aid available for part-time students. **Non-need-based:** 83% awarded as scholarships/grants, 17% as loans/jobs. Scholarships based on academics, art, minority status, music/drama. **Student debt:** 60% of graduating class borrowed to fund education; average debt was $16,120.

Policies to reduce costs. Tuition/fee waivers for employees and their families. Prepayment discount; credit/placement for qualifying scores on AP, IB, CLEP examinations.

Payment plans. Credit card, installment payment.

Application procedures. FAFSA, CSS PROFILE required. Closing date 2/15. Applicants notified by 3/31, must reply by 5/1. Early decision closing date 12/1. **Transfers:** No deadline.

Contact. Financial aid office: (973) 408-3112
Joyce Farmer, Director of College Admissions and Financial Aid
36 Madison Avenue
Madison, NJ 07940-1493

Essex County College

Newark, New Jersey
www.essex.edu
Two-year public **Federal Code: 007107**

	Living at home
Tuition and fees (2002-2003):	$2,730
Out-of-state:	$4,935
Per-credit charge:	$74
Per-credit out-of-district:	$147
Per-credit out-of-state:	$147
Books and supplies:	$600
Personal expenses:	$1,061
Transportation:	$900

Undergraduate aid. Need-based: Need-based aid available for full-time and part-time students.

Policies to reduce costs. Tuition/fee waivers for senior citizens, unemployed or children of unemployed, employees and their families. Credit/placement for qualifying scores on AP, CLEP examinations.

Payment plans. Credit card, installment, deferred payment.

Application procedures. FAFSA, institutional form required. Priority date 6/30; no closing date. Applicants notified on rolling basis starting 6/15, must reply within 3 week(s) of notification.

Contact. Financial aid office: (973) 877-3000
Mildred Cofer, Director of Financial Aid
303 University Avenue
Newark, NJ 07102

Fairleigh Dickinson University: College at Florham

Madison, New Jersey
www.fdu.edu
Four-year private **Federal Code: 004738**

	Living at home	On-campus
Tuition and fees (2002-2003):	$19,074	$19,074
Room and board:		$7,904
Board only:	$2,070	
Books and supplies:	$672	$672
Personal expenses:	$2,072	$2,072
Transportation:	$2,072	$1,036

Policies to reduce costs. Credit/placement for qualifying scores on AP, IB, CLEP examinations.

Application procedures. FAFSA, institutional form required. Priority date 3/15; no closing date. Applicants notified on rolling basis starting 3/1, must reply within 2 week(s) of notification.

Contact. Financial aid office: (973) 443-8700
285 Madison Avenue
Madison, NJ 07940

Fairleigh Dickinson University: Metropolitan Campus

Teaneck, New Jersey
www.fdu.edu
Four-year private **Federal Code: 002604**

	Living at home	On-campus
Tuition and fees (2002-2003):	$19,074	$19,074
Room and board:		$7,904
Board only:	$2,070	
Books and supplies:	$672	$672
Personal expenses:	$2,072	$2,072
Transportation:	$2,072	$1,036

Policies to reduce costs. Credit/placement for qualifying scores on AP, IB, CLEP examinations.

Application procedures. FAFSA, institutional form required. Priority date 3/15; no closing date. Applicants notified on rolling basis starting 3/1, must reply within 2 week(s) of notification.

Contact. **Financial aid office:** (201) 692-2362
Theresa Coll, Director of Financial Aid
1000 River Road
Teaneck, NJ 07666-1996

Felician College

Lodi, New Jersey
www.felician.edu
Four-year private **Federal Code: 002610**

College costs. Additional $330 required fees for campus residents.

	Living at home	On-campus
Tuition and fees (2002-2003):	$13,450	$13,450
Room and board:		$6,600
Board only:	$3,000	
Books and supplies:	$600	$600
Personal expenses:	$650	$500
Transportation:	$750	$750

Undergraduate aid. **Need-based:** Need-based aid available for full-time and part-time students. **Non-need-based:** Scholarships based on academics, alumni affiliation, art, athletics, religious affiliation, state/district residency.

Policies to reduce costs. Tuition/fee waivers for adults, senior citizens, family members, employees and their families. Credit/placement for qualifying scores on AP, IB, CLEP examinations. Work study available nights, weekends and for part-time students.

Payment plans. Credit card, installment payment.

Application procedures. FAFSA required. Priority date 6/2; no closing date. Applicants notified on rolling basis starting 4/2, must reply within 2 week(s) of notification. **Transfers:** No deadline.

Contact. **Financial aid office:** (201) 559-6000
Norma Betz, Director of Financial Aid
262 South Main Street
Lodi, NJ 07644-2198

Georgian Court College

Lakewood, New Jersey
www.georgian.edu
Four-year private **Federal Code: 002608**

	Living at home	On-campus
Tuition and fees:	$16,232	$16,232
Room and board:		$6,600
Board only:	$3,174	
Books and supplies:	$600	$600
Personal expenses:	$1,500	$1,500
Transportation:	$2,432	$1,000

Undergraduate aid. **Need-based:** Average financial aid package for full-time students was $10,373; for part-time $5,886. 59% awarded as scholarships/grants, 41% as loans/jobs. **Non-need-based:** 37% awarded as scholarships/grants, 63% as loans/jobs. Scholarships based on academics, alumni affiliation, art, athletics, leadership, minority status, music/drama, religious affiliation. **Student debt:** 79% of graduating class borrowed to fund education; average debt was $14,786.

Freshman aid. **Need-based:** Out of 179 full-time freshmen, 179 applied for aid; 170 were judged to have need; of these 170 received aid. Average package met 68% of need. 25 students had full need met. Average scholarship/grant was $8,790; average loan $2,170. **Non-need based:** 14 full-time freshmen with need received non-need scholarships; 33 without need received awards.

Policies to reduce costs. Tuition/fee waivers for senior citizens, family members, family of clergy, employees and their families. Credit/placement for qualifying scores on AP, CLEP examinations.

Payment plans. Credit card, installment payment.

Application procedures. FAFSA, institutional form required. Priority date 3/1; closing date 10/1. Applicants notified on rolling basis starting 2/1, must reply within 2 week(s) of notification. **Transfers:** Transfer students who have outstanding financial obligations to previous college or who are in default are not admitted before being cleared by previous college or following federal guidelines concerning defaults.

Contact. **Financial aid office:** (732) 364-2200 ext. 258
Ann Sirico, Associate Director of Financial Aid
900 Lakewood Avenue
Lakewood, NJ 08701-2697

Gloucester County College

Sewell, New Jersey
www.gccnj.edu
Two-year public **Federal Code: 006901**

	Living at home
Tuition and fees (2002-2003):	$2,528
Out-of-district:	$2,544
Out-of-state:	$8,528
Per-credit charge:	$79
Per-credit out-of-district:	$80
Per-credit out-of-state:	$267
Books and supplies:	$750

Undergraduate aid. All financial aid based on need. Need-based aid available for full-time and part-time students.

Policies to reduce costs. Tuition/fee waivers for senior citizens, employees and their families. Credit/placement for qualifying scores on AP, CLEP examinations. Work study available nights and for part-time students.

Payment plans. Credit card payment.

Application procedures. FAFSA, institutional form required. Priority date 5/1; no closing date. Applicants notified on rolling basis starting 3/20. **Transfers:** No deadline.

Contact. **Financial aid office:** (856) 415-2210
Jeffrey Williams, Financial Aid Administrator/Veterans Affairs
1400 Tanyard Road
Sewell, NJ 08080

Hudson County Community College

Jersey City, New Jersey
www.hccc.edu
Two-year public **Federal Code: 012954**

	Living at home
Tuition and fees (2002-2003):	$2,943
Out-of-district:	$5,013
Out-of-state:	$7,083
Per-credit charge:	$69
Per-credit out-of-district:	$138
Per-credit out-of-state:	$207
Books and supplies:	$800
Personal expenses:	$1,500
Transportation:	$1,000

Undergraduate aid. All financial aid based on need. 97% awarded as scholarships/grants, 3% as loans/jobs. Need-based aid available for part-time students.

Policies to reduce costs. Tuition/fee waivers for senior citizens, employees and their families. Credit/placement for qualifying scores on IB, CLEP examinations.

Payment plans. Credit card, deferred payment.

Application procedures. FAFSA required. Priority date 4/1; no closing date. Applicants notified on rolling basis starting 6/1, must reply within 1 week(s) of notification.

Contact. **Financial aid office:** (201) 714-2145
Pamela Norris-Littles, Director of Financial Aid
162 Sip Avenue
Jersey City, NJ 07306

Kean University

Union, New Jersey
www.kean.edu
Four-year public **Federal Code: 002622**

College costs. Fees included in tuition.

	Living at home	On-campus
Tuition and fees (2002-2003):	$5,840	$5,840
Out-of-state:	$8,000	$8,000
Room and board:		$5,056
Board only:	$800	
Books and supplies:	$850	$850
Personal expenses:	$1,053	$800
Transportation:	$1,600	$650

Undergraduate aid. Need-based: Average financial aid package for full-time students was $6,836; for part-time $5,035. 54% awarded as scholarships/grants, 46% as loans/jobs. **Non-need-based:** 15% awarded as scholarships/grants, 85% as loans/jobs. Scholarships based on academics. **Student debt:** 39% of graduating class borrowed to fund education; average debt was $16,700.

Freshman aid. Need-based: Out of 970 full-time freshmen, 737 applied for aid; 571 were judged to have need; of these 526 received aid. Average package met 65% of need. 97 students had full need met. Average scholarship/grant was $4,707; average loan $2,219. **Non-need based:** 67 full-time freshmen with need received non-need scholarships; 13 without need received awards.

Policies to reduce costs. Tuition/fee waivers for senior citizens, employees and their families. Credit/placement for qualifying scores on AP, CLEP examinations. Work study available nights, weekends and for part-time students.

Payment plans. Credit card, installment, deferred payment.

Application procedures. FAFSA required. Closing date 3/15. Applicants notified on rolling basis starting 4/15, must reply within 2 week(s) of notification.

Contact. **Financial aid office:** (908) 737-3190
Sandra Bembry, Director of Financial Aid
Box 411
Union, NJ 07083

Mercer County Community College

Trenton, New Jersey
www.mccc.edu
Two-year public **Federal Code: 002641**

	Living at home
Tuition and fees (projected):	$2,400
Out-of-district:	$3,255
Out-of-state:	$5,205
Per-credit charge:	$80
Per-credit out-of-district:	$109
Per-credit out-of-state:	$174
Board only:	$2,680
Books and supplies:	$690
Personal expenses:	$1,500
Transportation:	$1,080

Undergraduate aid. Need-based: Need-based aid available for full-time and part-time students. **Non-need-based:** Scholarships based on academics, athletics, state/district residency.

Merit scholarships. MCCC Foundation Scholarship $2,500, top 25% of high school class, 15 total awards.

Policies to reduce costs. Tuition/fee waivers for senior citizens, unemployed or children of unemployed, employees and their families. Credit/placement for qualifying scores on CLEP examinations. Work study available nights and for part-time students.

Payment plans. Credit card, installment, deferred payment.

Application procedures. FAFSA required. Priority date 5/1; no closing date. Applicants notified on rolling basis starting 6/1. **Transfers:** No deadline.

Contact. **Financial aid office:** (609) 586-4800 ext. 3210
Reginald Page, Director of Financial Aid
Box B
Trenton, NJ 08690-1099

Middlesex County College

Edison, New Jersey
www.middlesexcc.edu
Two-year public **Federal Code: 002615**

College costs. Out-of-county and out-of-state students pay additional $450 in required fees.

	Living at home
Tuition and fees:	$2,655
Out-of-state:	$4,860
Per-credit charge:	$74
Per-credit out-of-district:	$147
Per-credit out-of-state:	$147
Books and supplies:	$1,162
Personal expenses:	$1,643
Transportation:	$1,921

Undergraduate aid. Need-based: Need-based aid available for full-time and part-time students.

Policies to reduce costs. Tuition/fee waivers for employees and their families. Credit/placement for qualifying scores on CLEP examinations. Work study available for part-time students.

Payment plans. Credit card, installment payment.

Application procedures. FAFSA, institutional form required. Priority date 4/1; no closing date. Applicants notified on rolling basis starting 5/4. **Transfers:** No deadline.

Contact. **Financial aid office:** (732) 906-2520
Gail Scott Bey, Director of Financial Aid
2600 Woodbridge Avenue
Edison, NJ 08818-3050

Monmouth University

West Long Branch, New Jersey
www.monmouth.edu
Four-year private **Federal Code: 002616**

	Living at home	On-campus
Tuition and fees (2002-2003):	$17,900	$17,900
Room and board:		$7,250
Board only:	$3,410	
Books and supplies:	$600	$600
Personal expenses:	$1,669	$1,669
Transportation:	$445	$445

Undergraduate aid. Need-based: Average financial aid package for full-time students was $12,768; for part-time $12,768. 49% awarded as scholarships/grants, 51% as loans/jobs. **Non-need-based:** 50% awarded as scholarships/grants, 50% as loans/jobs. Scholarships based on academics, alumni affiliation, art, athletics, leadership. **Student debt:** 64% of graduating class borrowed to fund education; average debt was $21,400.

Freshman aid. Need-based: Out of 949 full-time freshmen, 823 applied for aid; 649 were judged to have need; of these 643 received aid. Average package met 70% of need. 113 students had full need met. Average scholarship/grant was $8,006; average loan $3,121. **Non-need based:** 541 full-time freshmen with need received non-need scholarships; 243 without need received awards; 50 received athletic scholarships.

Merit scholarships. Academic Excellence Awards, range from $1,000-$10,500 based on SAT scores and high school GPA, renewable annually as long as required GPA is maintained.

Policies to reduce costs. Tuition/fee waivers for senior citizens, family members, employees and their families. Credit/placement for qualifying scores on AP, IB, CLEP examinations.

Payment plans. Credit card, installment, deferred payment.

Application procedures. FAFSA required. No deadline. Applicants notified on rolling basis starting 2/1, must reply within 2 week(s) of notification. Early decision closing date 12/1.

Contact. **Financial aid office:** (732) 571-3400
Claire Alasio, Director of Financial Aid
400 Cedar Avenue
West Long Branch, NJ 07764-1898

Montclair State University

Upper Montclair, New Jersey
www.montclair.edu
Four-year public **Federal Code: 002617**

	Living at home	On-campus
Tuition and fees (2002-2003):	$5,706	$5,706
Out-of-state:	$8,458	$8,458
Room and board:		$7,590
Board only:	$1,875	
Books and supplies:	$800	$800
Personal expenses:	$1,200	$1,500
Transportation:	$1,500	$550

Undergraduate aid. Need-based: Need-based aid available for full-time and part-time students. **Non-need-based:** Scholarships based on academics, alumni affiliation, art, leadership, minority status, music/drama, state/district residency.

Policies to reduce costs. Tuition/fee waivers for senior citizens, unemployed or children of unemployed, employees and their families. Credit/placement for qualifying scores on AP examinations. Work study available nights, weekends and for part-time students.

Payment plans. Credit card, installment payment.

Application procedures. FAFSA required. Priority date 3/1; no closing date. Applicants notified on rolling basis starting 4/1, must reply within 2 week(s) of notification. **Transfers:** Priority date 3/1; no deadline. Students will be eligible for financial aid beginning fall semester of the academic year for which they are admitted.

Contact. **Financial aid office:** (973) 655-4461
Bryan Terry, Director of Financial Aid
One Normal Avenue
Upper Montclair, NJ 07043-1624

New Jersey City University

Jersey City, New Jersey
www.njcu.edu
Four-year public **Federal Code: 002613**

	Living at home	On-campus
Tuition and fees (2002-2003):	$5,556	$5,556
Out-of-state:	$9,509	$9,509
Room and board:		$6,198
Board only:	$1,600	
Books and supplies:	$1,000	$1,000
Personal expenses:	$1,040	$1,600
Transportation:	$1,049	$1,049

Policies to reduce costs. Tuition/fee waivers for senior citizens. Credit/placement for qualifying scores on AP, IB, CLEP examinations.

Payment plans. Installment, deferred payment.

Contact. **Financial aid office:** (201) 200-3173
Carmen Pam Lilio, Director of Financial Aid
2039 Kennedy Boulevard
Jersey City, NJ 07305-1597

New Jersey Institute of Technology

Newark, New Jersey
www.njit.edu
Four-year public **Federal Code: 002621**

	Living at home	On-campus
Tuition and fees (2002-2003):	$9,054	$9,054
Out-of-state:	$14,006	$14,006
Room and board:		$7,864
Board only:	$1,500	
Books and supplies:	$900	$900
Personal expenses:	$1,100	$1,100
Transportation:	$1,000	$500

Undergraduate aid. Need-based: Need-based aid available for full-time and part-time students. **Non-need-based:** Scholarships based on academics, athletics, state/district residency. **Additional information:** Extensive co-op program for all majors.

Policies to reduce costs. Tuition/fee waivers for employees and their families. Credit/placement for qualifying scores on AP, CLEP examinations.

Payment plans. Credit card, installment payment.

Application procedures. FAFSA required. Priority date 3/15; no closing date. Applicants notified on rolling basis starting 3/1, must reply within 2 week(s) of notification. **Transfers:** Priority date 5/15.

Contact. **Financial aid office:** (973) 596-3478
Kathy Bialk, Director of Financial Aid
University Heights
Newark, NJ 07102

Ocean County College

Toms River, New Jersey
www.ocean.edu
Two-year public **Federal Code: 002624**

	Living at home
Tuition and fees:	$2,715
Out-of-district:	$3,525
Out-of-state:	$5,445
Per-credit charge:	$67
Per-credit out-of-district:	$81
Per-credit out-of-state:	$134
Board only:	$1,500
Books and supplies:	$700
Personal expenses:	$1,000
Transportation:	$1,600

Undergraduate aid. All financial aid based on need. Need-based aid available for full-time and part-time students.

Policies to reduce costs. Tuition/fee waivers for senior citizens, unemployed or children of unemployed, employees and their families. Credit/placement for qualifying scores on AP, CLEP examinations.

Payment plans. Credit card, installment payment.

Application procedures. FAFSA required. Priority date 5/31; no closing date. Applicants notified on rolling basis starting 7/15, must reply within 1 week(s) of notification. **Transfers:** No deadline.

Contact. **Financial aid office:** (732) 255-0400 ext. 2020
Susan E. Barschow, Director of Financial Aid
College Drive
Toms River, NJ 08754-2001

Passaic County Community College

Paterson, New Jersey
www.pccc.cc.nj.us
Two-year public **Federal Code: 009994**

College costs. Required fees vary by course.

	Living at home
Tuition and fees (2002-2003):	$2,405
Out-of-state:	$4,310
Per-credit charge:	$65
Per-credit out-of-state:	$127
Books and supplies:	$839
Personal expenses:	$978
Transportation:	$880

Undergraduate aid. Need-based: Need-based aid available for full-time and part-time students. **Non-need-based:** Scholarships based on academics. **Additional information:** Limited scholarship funds available for low income students eligible for federal or state aid.

Policies to reduce costs. Tuition/fee waivers for senior citizens, unemployed or children of unemployed, employees and their families. Credit/placement for qualifying scores on AP, CLEP examinations.

Payment plans. Credit card, installment, deferred payment.

Application procedures. FAFSA, CSS PROFILE required. Priority date 8/1; no closing date. Applicants notified on rolling basis starting 8/1, must reply within 2 week(s) of notification. **Transfers:** Priority date 5/15; closing date 6/30.

Contact. Financial aid office: (973) 684-6800
Sheila Attias, Director of Financial Aid
One College Boulevard
Paterson, NJ 07505-1179

Princeton University

Princeton, New Jersey
www.princeton.edu
Four-year private **Federal Code: 002627**

	Living at home	On-campus
Tuition and fees:	$28,540	$28,540
Room and board:		$8,109
Books and supplies:	$790	$790
Personal expenses:		$1,719
Transportation:		$450

Undergraduate aid. All financial aid based on need. Average financial aid package for full-time students was $23,289. 96% awarded as scholarships/grants, 4% as loans/jobs. **Student debt:** 15% of graduating class borrowed to fund education; average debt was $1,200.

Freshman aid. Out of 1,187 full-time freshmen, 672 applied for aid; 543 were judged to have need; of these 543 received aid. Average package met 100% of need. 543 students had full need met. Average scholarship/grant was $22,309.

Policies to reduce costs. Tuition/fee waivers for employees and their families. Credit/placement for qualifying scores on AP examinations.

Payment plans. Installment, deferred payment.

Application procedures. FAFSA, institutional form required. Closing date 2/1. Applicants notified by 4/1, must reply by 5/1. Early decision closing date 11/1.

Contact. Financial aid office: (609) 258-3330
Don Betterton, Director of Financial Aid
Box 430
Princeton, NJ 08544-0430

Rabbinical College of America

Morristown, New Jersey
Four-year private
Federal Code: 008609

	Living at home	On-campus
Tuition and fees:	$7,500	$7,500
Room and board:		$6,500

Payment plans. Installment payment.

Application procedures. Priority date 10/20; no closing date. Applicants notified on rolling basis starting 10/31.

Contact. Financial aid office: (973) 267-9404
Moshe Weisberg, Director of Financial Aid
226 Sussex Avenue, CN 1996
Morristown, NJ 07962-1996

Ramapo College of New Jersey

Mahwah, New Jersey
www.ramapo.edu
Four-year public **Federal Code: 009344**

College costs. Graduates of Orange County and Rockland Community Colleges in New York enrolling directly at Ramapo pay $8,725 full-time tuition/fees, $212 per credit-hour.

	Living at home	On-campus
Tuition and fees (2002-2003):	$6,775	$6,775
Out-of-state:	$10,677	$10,677
Room and board:		$7,722
Board only:	$2,422	
Books and supplies:	$750	$750
Personal expenses:	$1,900	$1,300
Transportation:	$1,200	$250

Undergraduate aid. Need-based: Average financial aid package for full-time students was $8,966; for part-time $4,174. 51% awarded as scholarships/grants, 49% as loans/jobs. **Non-need-based:** 30% awarded as scholarships/grants, 70% as loans/jobs. Scholarships based on academics. **Student debt:** 37% of graduating class borrowed to fund education; average debt was $15,576.

Freshman aid. Need-based: Out of 628 full-time freshmen, 404 applied for aid; 294 were judged to have need; of these 284 received aid. Average package met 92% of need. 50 students had full need met. Average scholarship/grant was $8,079; average loan $2,467. **Non-need based:** 125 full-time freshmen with need received non-need scholarships; 125 without need received awards.

Merit scholarships. Academic Achievement Scholarships; number and amount awarded vary annually.

Policies to reduce costs. Tuition/fee waivers for senior citizens, unemployed or children of unemployed, employees and their families. Credit/placement for qualifying scores on AP, IB, CLEP examinations. Work study available nights, weekends and for part-time students.

Payment plans. Credit card, installment payment.

Application procedures. FAFSA required. Priority date 3/1; no closing date. Applicants notified on rolling basis starting 4/1, must reply by 5/1 or within 2 week(s) of notification. **Transfers:** Priority date 3/1; no deadline.

Contact. Financial aid office: (201) 684-7549
Mark Singer, Director of Financial Aid
505 Ramapo Valley Road
Mahwah, NJ 07430-1680

Raritan Valley Community College

Somerville, New Jersey
www.raritanval.edu
Two-year public **Federal Code: 007731**

	Living at home
Tuition and fees (2002-2003):	$2,420
Per-credit charge:	$64
Books and supplies:	$750
Personal expenses:	$1,000
Transportation:	$1,080

Undergraduate aid. Need-based: 88% awarded as scholarships/grants, 12% as loans/jobs. **Non-need-based:** 18% awarded as scholarships/grants, 82% as loans/jobs.

Policies to reduce costs. Tuition/fee waivers for senior citizens, unemployed or children of unemployed, employees and their families. Credit/placement for qualifying scores on AP, CLEP examinations. Work study available for part-time students.

Payment plans. Credit card, deferred payment.

Application procedures. FAFSA required. No deadline. Applicants notified on rolling basis starting 7/1. **Transfers:** No deadline.

Contact. Financial aid office: (908) 526-1200
Thomas Carroll, Vice President of Finance and Administration
Box 3300
Somerville, NJ 08876-1265

Richard Stockton College of New Jersey

Pomona, New Jersey
www.stockton.edu
Four-year public **Federal Code: 009345**

	Living at home	On-campus
Tuition and fees (2002-2003):	$5,250	$5,250
Out-of-state:	$7,770	$7,770
Room and board:		$6,290
Books and supplies:	$825	$825
Personal expenses:	$1,225	$1,425
Transportation:	$1,250	$1,092

Undergraduate aid. Need-based: Need-based aid available for full-time and part-time students. **Non-need-based:** Scholarships based on academics, art, leadership, minority status, music/drama, state/district residency.

Policies to reduce costs. Tuition/fee waivers for senior citizens, unemployed or children of unemployed, employees and their families. Credit/placement for qualifying scores on AP, IB, CLEP examinations. Work study available nights, weekends and for part-time students.

Payment plans. Credit card, installment payment.

Application procedures. FAFSA required. Priority date 3/1; no closing date. Applicants notified on rolling basis starting 4/1, must reply within 2 week(s) of notification. **Transfers:** No deadline.

Contact. Financial aid office: (609) 652-4201
Jeanne Lewis, Director of Financial Aid
Jim Leeds Road
Pomona, NJ 08240

Rider University

Lawrenceville, New Jersey
www.rider.edu
Four-year private **Federal Code: 002628**

	Living at home	On-campus
Tuition and fees:	$21,050	$21,050
Room and board:		$8,060
Books and supplies:	$1,000	$1,000
Personal expenses:	$700	$700
Transportation:	$1,200	$1,200

Undergraduate aid. Need-based: Average financial aid package for full-time students was $17,189; for part-time $10,806. 61% awarded as scholarships/grants, 39% as loans/jobs. **Non-need-based:** 37% awarded as scholarships/grants, 63% as loans/jobs. Scholarships based on academics, alumni affiliation, art, athletics, minority status, music/drama, state/district residency. **Student debt:** 59% of graduating class borrowed to fund education; average debt was $23,500.

Freshman aid. Need-based: Out of 961 full-time freshmen, 789 applied for aid; 663 were judged to have need; of these 663 received aid. Average package met 84% of need. 87 students had full need met. Average scholarship/grant was $9,048; average loan $3,613. **Non-need based:** 477 full-time freshmen with need received non-need scholarships; 149 without need received awards; 89 received athletic scholarships.

Policies to reduce costs. Tuition/fee waivers for employees and their families. Credit/placement for qualifying scores on AP, CLEP examinations. Work study available nights and weekends.

Payment plans. Credit card, installment payment.

Application procedures. FAFSA required. Priority date 3/1; closing date 6/1. Applicants notified on rolling basis starting 4/15. **Transfers:** No deadline.

Contact. Financial aid office: (609) 896-5360
John Williams, Director of Student Financial Services
2083 Lawrenceville Road
Lawrenceville, NJ 08648-3099

Rowan University

Glassboro, New Jersey
www.rowan.edu
Four-year public **Federal Code: 002609**

	Living at home	On-campus
Tuition and fees (2002-2003):	$6,658	$6,658
Out-of-state:	$11,608	$11,608
Room and board:		$6,846
Books and supplies:	$800	$800
Personal expenses:	$1,000	$1,000
Transportation:	$1,100	$100

Undergraduate aid. Need-based: Average financial aid package for full-time students was $6,447; for part-time $4,088. 41% awarded as scholarships/grants, 59% as loans/jobs. **Non-need-based:** 22% awarded as scholarships/grants, 78% as loans/jobs. Scholarships based on academics, alumni affiliation, leadership, minority status, music/drama.

Freshman aid. Need-based: Out of 1,277 full-time freshmen, 1,178 applied for aid; 1,017 were judged to have need; of these 1,017 received aid. Average package met 94% of need. 358 students had full need met. Average scholarship/grant was $5,344; average loan $2,254. **Non-need based:** 513 full-time freshmen with need received non-need scholarships; 177 without need received awards.

Policies to reduce costs. Tuition/fee waivers for senior citizens, employees and their families. Credit/placement for qualifying scores on AP, CLEP examinations. Work study available for part-time students.

Payment plans. Credit card, installment payment.

Application procedures. FAFSA required. Closing date 3/15. Applicants notified on rolling basis starting 5/1, must reply within 2 week(s) of notification.

Contact. Financial aid office: (856) 256-4250
Louis Tavarez, Director of Financial Aid
Savitz Hall, 201 Mullica Hill Road
Glassboro, NJ 08028

Rutgers, The State University of New Jersey: Camden Regional Campus

Camden, New Jersey
www.rutgers.edu
Four-year public **Federal Code: 002629**

	Living at home	On-campus
Tuition and fees (2002-2003):	$7,126	$7,126
Out-of-state:	$13,102	$13,102
Room and board:		$7,106
Board only:	$2,000	
Books and supplies:	$733	$733
Personal expenses:	$1,480	$1,453
Transportation:	$1,289	$544

Undergraduate aid. Need-based: Average financial aid package for full-time students was $8,903; for part-time $4,712. 48% awarded as scholarships/grants, 52% as loans/jobs. **Non-need-based:** 19% awarded as scholarships/grants, 81% as loans/jobs. Scholarships based on academics, alumni affiliation, minority status, state/district residency. **Student debt:** 67% of graduating class borrowed to fund education; average debt was $15,223.

Freshman aid. Need-based: Out of 451 full-time freshmen, 385 applied for aid; 300 were judged to have need; of these 295 received aid. Average package met 90% of need. 125 students had full need met. Average scholarship/grant was $6,450; average loan $2,420. **Non-need based:** 52 full-time freshmen with need received non-need scholarships; 14 without need received awards.

Merit scholarships. Outstanding Scholarship Recruitment Program: $2,500-$7,500, for selected in-state resident applicants based on SAT scores and class rank, 2,500 awarded; Carr Scholarship: $10,000, for selected minority applicants, 150 awarded; Class of 1941 Scholarship: $1,941, descendent of 1941 alumni preferred, 1 awarded; National Merit Scholarship for National Merit finalists: $1,000-$2,000, 15 or more awarded; National Achievement Scholarship for National Achievement finalists: $1,000-$2,000, 2 awarded; Rockland County-Herman T. Hopper Scholarship: out-of-state tuition, for Rockland County, New York resident, 1 awarded; Rutgers University Academic Achievement Award: $1,000, for in- and out-of-state minority students, 20 awarded; Rutgers University Alumni Federation Scholarship: $1,000, for children of Rutgers University alumni, 20 awarded; Rutgers University National Scholarship: $5,000, for out-of-state students, about 100 awards university-wide.

Policies to reduce costs. Tuition/fee waivers for unemployed or children of unemployed, employees and their families. Credit/placement for qualifying scores on AP, IB, CLEP examinations.

Payment plans. Credit card, installment, deferred payment.

Application procedures. FAFSA required. Priority date 3/15; no closing date. Applicants notified on rolling basis starting 2/15, must reply within 2 week(s) of notification.

Contact. **Financial aid office:** (856) 225-6039
John Brugel, University Director of Financial Aid
406 Penn Street
Camden, NJ 08102

Rutgers, The State University of New Jersey: New Brunswick Regional Campus

Piscataway, New Jersey
www.rutgers.edu
Four-year public **Federal Code: 002629**

	Living at home	On-campus
Tuition and fees (2002-2003):	$7,308	$7,308
Out-of-state:	$13,284	$13,284
Room and board:		$7,500
Board only:	$2,000	
Books and supplies:	$733	$733
Personal expenses:	$1,480	$1,453
Transportation:	$1,289	$544

Undergraduate aid. Need-based: Average financial aid package for full-time students was $9,952; for part-time $4,637. 47% awarded as scholarships/grants, 53% as loans/jobs. **Non-need-based:** 51% awarded as scholarships/grants, 49% as loans/jobs. Scholarships based on academics, alumni affiliation, art, athletics, minority status, music/drama, state/district residency. **Student debt:** 57% of graduating class borrowed to fund education; average debt was $15,270.

Freshman aid. Need-based: Out of 5,070 full-time freshmen, 3,680 applied for aid; 2,522 were judged to have need; of these 2,466 received aid. Average package met 86% of need. 879 students had full need met. Average scholarship/grant was $6,598; average loan $2,668. **Non-need based:** 877 full-time freshmen with need received non-need scholarships; 405 without need received awards; 101 received athletic scholarships.

Merit scholarships. Outstanding Scholarship Recruitment Program: $2,500-$7,500, for selected in-state resident applicants based on SAT scores and class rank, 2,500 awarded; Carr Scholarship: $10,000, for selected minority applicants, 150 awarded; Class of 1941 Scholarship: $1,941, descendent of Class of 1941 alumni preferred, 1 awarded; National Merit Scholarship for National Merit finalists: $1,000-$2,000, 15 or more awarded; National Achievement Scholarship for National Achievement finalists: $1,000-$2,000, 2 awarded; Rockland County-Herman T. Hopper Scholarship: out-of-state tuition, for Rockland County, New York resident, 1 awarded; Rutgers University Academic Achievement Award for in- and out-of-state minority students: $1,000, 20 awarded; Rutgers University Alumni Federation Scholarship, $1,000, for children of Rutgers University alumni, 20 awarded; Rutgers University National Scholarship for out-of-state students: $5,000, about 100 awards university-wide.

Policies to reduce costs. Tuition/fee waivers for unemployed or children of unemployed, employees and their families. Credit/placement for qualifying scores on AP, IB, CLEP examinations.

Payment plans. Credit card, installment, deferred payment.

Application procedures. FAFSA required. Priority date 3/15; no closing date. Applicants notified on rolling basis starting 2/15, must reply within 2 week(s) of notification.

Contact. **Financial aid office:** (732) 932-1766
John Brugel, University Director of Financial Aid
65 Davidson Road, Room 202
Piscataway, NJ 08854-8097

Rutgers, The State University of New Jersey: Newark Regional Campus

Newark, New Jersey
www.rutgers.edu
Four-year public **Federal Code: 002629**

	Living at home	On-campus
Tuition and fees (2002-2003):	$7,007	$7,007
Out-of-state:	$12,983	$12,983
Room and board:		$7,570
Board only:	$2,000	
Books and supplies:	$733	$733
Personal expenses:	$1,480	$1,453
Transportation:	$1,289	$544

Undergraduate aid. Non-need-based: Scholarships based on academics, alumni affiliation, art, minority status.

Merit scholarships. Outstanding Scholarship Recruitment Program: $2,500-$7,500, for selected in-state resident applicants based on SAT scores and class rank, 2,500 awarded; Carr Scholarship: $10,000, for selected minority applicants; 150 awarded; Class of 1941 Scholarship: $1,941, descendent of Class of 1941 alumni preferred; 1 awarded; National Merit Scholarship for National Merit finalists: $1,000-$2,000, 15 or more awarded; National Achievement Scholarship for National Achievement finalists: 1,000-$2,000, 2 awarded; Rockland County-Herman T. Hopper Scholarship: out-of-state tuition, for Rockland County, New York resident; 1 awarded; Rutgers University Academic Achievement Award: $1,000, for in- and out-of-state minority students, 20 awarded; Rutgers University Alumni Federation Scholarship: $1,000, for children of Rutgers University alumni; 20 awarded; James Bryan Scholarship: $400, for selected in-state freshmen, 3 awarded; Rutgers University National Scholarship: $5,000, for out-of-state students, about 100 awards university-wide.

Policies to reduce costs. Tuition/fee waivers for senior citizens, unemployed or children of unemployed, employees and their families. Credit/placement for qualifying scores on AP, IB, CLEP examinations.

Payment plans. Credit card, installment, deferred payment.

Application procedures. FAFSA required. Priority date 3/15; no closing date. Applicants notified on rolling basis starting 2/15, must reply within 2 week(s) of notification.

Contact. **Financial aid office:** (973) 353-1766
John Brugel, University Director of Financial Aid
249 University Avenue
Newark, NJ 07102-1896

St. Peter's College

Jersey City, New Jersey
www.spc.edu
Four-year private **Federal Code: 002638**

	Living at home	On-campus
Tuition and fees (2002-2003):	$17,358	$17,358
Room and board:		$7,340
Books and supplies:	$700	$700
Personal expenses:	$600	$600
Transportation:	$650	$500

Undergraduate aid. Need-based: Need-based aid available for full-time students. **Non-need-based:** Scholarships based on academics, athletics, state/district residency. **Additional information:** Cooperative education internships available in all majors, with average salaries exceeding $5,200.

Merit scholarships. Academic Awards based on minimum SAT of 1100, minimum GPA of 3.0, and in top 20% of class; 50 awarded; full tuition. Incentive Awards for selected applicants with some qualities necessary for academic awards but who are otherwise ineligible; ranging from $500-$4,000 annually. Residential Grants based on academics and extracurricular activities; $500-$2,500 toward housing.

Policies to reduce costs. Tuition/fee waivers for family of clergy, employees and their families. Credit/placement for qualifying scores on AP, CLEP examinations.

Payment plans. Credit card, installment, deferred payment.

Application procedures. FAFSA required. Priority date 3/15; no closing date. Applicants notified on rolling basis starting 2/15, must reply by 5/1 or within 2 week(s) of notification. **Transfers:** Student and parents (if dependent students) must be New Jersey residents for at least 1 year prior to start date. Students must complete the renewal application before June 1.

Contact. **Financial aid office:** (201) 915-9308
Rebecca Royal, Director of Financial Aid
2641 Kennedy Boulevard
Jersey City, NJ 07306

Salem Community College

Carneys Point, New Jersey
www.salemcc.edu
Two-year public **Federal Code: 005461**

College costs. Any credits over 30 are free.

	Living at home
Tuition and fees (2002-2003):	$2,745
Out-of-state:	$3,060
Per-credit charge:	$70
Per-credit out-of-district:	$80
Per-credit out-of-state:	$80
Books and supplies:	$1,000
Personal expenses:	$800
Transportation:	$1,000

Undergraduate aid. All financial aid based on need. 85% awarded as scholarships/grants, 15% as loans/jobs. Need-based aid available for part-time students.

Policies to reduce costs. Tuition/fee waivers for senior citizens, unemployed or children of unemployed, employees and their families. Credit/placement for qualifying scores on CLEP examinations. Work study available for part-time students.

Payment plans. Credit card, installment, deferred payment.

Application procedures. FAFSA, institutional form required. Priority date 6/1; no closing date. Applicants notified on rolling basis starting 5/1, must reply within 2 week(s) of notification.

Contact. **Financial aid office:** (856) 351-2699
Suzanne Campo, Coordinator of Financial Aid
460 Hollywood Avenue
Carneys Point, NJ 08069-2799

Seton Hall University

South Orange, New Jersey
www.shu.edu
Four-year private **Federal Code: 002632**

College costs. Required fees include lease of laptop computer.

	Living at home	On-campus
Tuition and fees:	$21,855	$21,855
Room and board:		$8,550
Board only:	$3,260	
Books and supplies:	$950	$950
Personal expenses:	$1,476	$1,476
Transportation:	$1,254	$896

Undergraduate aid. Need-based: Need-based aid available for full-time and part-time students. **Non-need-based:** Scholarships based on academics, alumni affiliation, athletics, leadership, minority status, state/district residency.

Policies to reduce costs. Tuition/fee waivers for senior citizens, family members, family of clergy, employees and their families. Credit/placement for qualifying scores on AP, IB, CLEP examinations.

Payment plans. Credit card, installment, deferred payment.

Application procedures. FAFSA required. Priority date 4/1; no closing date. Applicants notified on rolling basis starting 3/15, must reply by 5/1 or within 4 week(s) of notification. **Transfers:** No deadline. Transfer academic scholarships available.

Contact. **Financial aid office:** (973) 761-9350
Karen Struthers, Executive Director of Financial Aid
400 South Orange Avenue
South Orange, NJ 07079-2680

Somerset Christian College

Zarephath, New Jersey
www.somerset.edu
Two-year private **Federal Code: 036663**

	Living at home
Tuition and fees (projected):	$3,920
Per-credit charge:	$160
Personal expenses:	$1,120
Transportation:	$1,800

Undergraduate aid. All financial aid based on need. Need-based aid available for full-time and part-time students.

Policies to reduce costs. Tuition/fee waivers for employees and their families.

Payment plans. Credit card, installment payment.

Application procedures. FAFSA required. No deadline. Applicants notified on rolling basis starting 1/31.

Contact. **Financial aid office:** (800) 234-9305
Ellen Johnson, Financial Aid Counselor
10 Liberty Square
Zarephath, NJ 08890

Stevens Institute of Technology

Hoboken, New Jersey
www.stevens.edu
Four-year private **Federal Code: 002639**

	Living at home	On-campus
Tuition and fees (2002-2003):	$25,700	$25,700
Room and board:		$8,100
Board only:	$1,500	
Books and supplies:	$900	$900
Personal expenses:	$750	$750

Undergraduate aid. Need-based: Average financial aid package for full-time students was $20,837. 66% awarded as scholarships/grants, 34% as loans/jobs. Need-based aid available for part-time students. **Non-need-based:** 90% awarded as scholarships/grants, 10% as loans/jobs. Scholarships based on academics, leadership, minority status. **Student debt:** 70% of graduating class borrowed to fund education; average debt was $13,175.

Freshman aid. Need-based: Out of 412 full-time freshmen, 351 applied for aid; 306 were judged to have need; of these 305 received aid. Average package met 86% of need. 49 students had full need met. Average scholarship/grant was $13,240; average loan $3,958. **Non-need based:** 203 full-time freshmen with need received non-need scholarships; 42 without need received awards.

Merit scholarships. Neupauer Scholarship: full tuition to top candidates in freshman class. Edwin A. Stevens Scholarship: $2,000-$12,000 to top candidates in freshman class. Exxon Scholarship: full costs to top 2 minority students pursuing mechanical or chemical engineering degree. Becton Dickinson Scholarship: full tuition to top student pursuing engineering degree.

Policies to reduce costs. Tuition/fee waivers for employees and their families. Credit/placement for qualifying scores on AP examinations. Work study available nights and weekends.

Payment plans. Credit card, installment payment.

Application procedures. FAFSA required. Priority date 2/15; no closing date. Applicants notified by 3/30, must reply by 5/1 or within 2 week(s) of notification. Early decision closing date 11/1. **Transfers:** No deadline. Transfer merit scholarships, Phi Theta Kappa awards.

Contact. **Financial aid office:** (201) 216-5555
David Sheridan, Dean of Enrollment Services
Castle Point on Hudson
Hoboken, NJ 07030

Sussex County Community College

Newton, New Jersey
www.sussex.cc.nj.us
Two-year public **Federal Code: 025688**

College costs. Residents of Pike County (PA): $102 per-credit-hour.

	Living at home
Tuition and fees (projected):	$2,480
Out-of-state:	$4,460
Per-credit charge:	$68
Per-credit out-of-district:	$136
Per-credit out-of-state:	$136
Board only:	$1,500
Books and supplies:	$900
Personal expenses:	$1,220
Transportation:	$2,050

Undergraduate aid. All financial aid based on need. Need-based aid available for part-time students.

Policies to reduce costs. Tuition/fee waivers for senior citizens, unemployed or children of unemployed, employees and their families. Prepayment discount; credit/placement for qualifying scores on AP, CLEP examinations.

Payment plans. Credit card, installment, deferred payment.

Application procedures. FAFSA, institutional form required. Closing date 6/1. Applicants notified on rolling basis, must reply within 2 week(s) of notification. **Transfers:** Closing date 6/1.

Contact. **Financial aid office:** (973) 300-2225
James Pegg, Director, Financial Aid
College Hill
Newton, NJ 07860

The College of New Jersey

Ewing, New Jersey
www.tcnj.edu
Four-year public **Federal Code: 002642**

	Living at home	On-campus
Tuition and fees (2002-2003):	$7,516	$7,516
Out-of-state:	$11,713	$11,713
Room and board:		$7,416
Board only:	$2,958	
Books and supplies:	$700	$700
Personal expenses:	$1,254	$1,254
Transportation:	$1,200	$200

Undergraduate aid. **Need-based:** Average financial aid package for full-time students was $2,449; for part-time $1,973. 55% awarded as scholarships/grants, 45% as loans/jobs. **Non-need-based:** 47% awarded as scholarships/grants, 53% as loans/jobs. Scholarships based on academics, minority status, music/drama, state/district residency. **Student debt:** 31% of graduating class borrowed to fund education; average debt was $5,490. **Additional information:** Merit scholarships available to New Jersey high school graduates based on academic distinction. Limited number of scholarships available to out-of-state students who demonstrate exceptional academic achievement in high school and on SAT.

Freshman aid. **Need-based:** Out of 1,262 full-time freshmen, 849 applied for aid; 523 were judged to have need; of these 523 received aid. Average package met 79% of need. 144 students had full need met. Average scholarship/grant was $2,251; average loan $2,220. **Non-need based:** 209 full-time freshmen with need received non-need scholarships; 137 without need received awards.

Policies to reduce costs. Tuition/fee waivers for senior citizens, unemployed or children of unemployed, employees and their families. Credit/placement for qualifying scores on AP, IB examinations.

Payment plans. Credit card, installment payment.

Application procedures. FAFSA required. No deadline. Applicants notified on rolling basis starting 4/1, must reply within 2 week(s) of notification. Early decision closing date 11/15. **Transfers:** Priority date 3/1; no deadline.

Contact. **Financial aid office:** (609) 771-2211
Kathy Ragan, Director of Student Financial Services
Box 7718
Ewing, NJ 08628

Thomas Edison State College

Trenton, New Jersey
www.tesc.edu
Four-year public **Federal Code: 011648**

College costs. Quoted figures are for first year comprehensive plan, including unlimited tests, portfolios and courses. Enrolled options plan also available: first year enrollment and technology fee $830 for state residents, $1,480 for out-of-state; registration fee $15 per semester; students pay for tests, portfolios, and courses as they use them. Registration fee and per-credit-hour charges shown apply only to students in enrollment options plan. Comprehensive plan and enrollment costs slightly lower for second and subsequent years.

	Living at home
Tuition and fees (2002-2003):	$3,025
Out-of-state:	$4,345

Undergraduate aid. All financial aid based on need. 30% awarded as scholarships/grants, 70% as loans/jobs.

Policies to reduce costs. Tuition/fee waivers for employees and their families. Credit/placement for qualifying scores on AP, IB, CLEP examinations.

Payment plans. Credit card payment.

Application procedures. FAFSA, institutional form required. No deadline. Applicants notified on rolling basis.

Contact. **Financial aid office:** (609) 633-9658
James Owens, Director of Financial Aid
101 West State Street
Trenton, NJ 08608-1176

Union County College

Cranford, New Jersey
www.ucc.edu
Two-year public **Federal Code: 002643**

College costs. Course fees additional; vary per course.

	Living at home
Tuition and fees (2002-2003):	$2,814
Out-of-district:	$5,004
Out-of-state:	$5,004
Per-credit charge:	$73
Per-credit out-of-district:	$146
Per-credit out-of-state:	$146
Books and supplies:	$840
Personal expenses:	$1,210
Transportation:	$1,540

Undergraduate aid. All financial aid based on need. 88% awarded as scholarships/grants, 12% as loans/jobs. Need-based aid available for part-time students.

Policies to reduce costs. Tuition/fee waivers for senior citizens, employees and their families. Credit/placement for qualifying scores on CLEP examinations.

Payment plans. Credit card, deferred payment.

Application procedures. FAFSA, institutional form required. Priority date 5/1; no closing date. Must reply within 2 week(s) of notification.

Contact. **Financial aid office:** (908) 709-7137
Elizabeth Riquez, Director of Financial Aid
1033 Springfield Avenue
Cranford, NJ 07016-1599

University of Medicine and Dentistry of New Jersey: School of Health Related Professions

Newark, New Jersey
www.umdnj.edu/shrpweb
Upper-division public

College costs. Required fees vary per program; average $10 per credit hour.

	Living at home
Tuition and fees (projected):	$6,200
Out-of-state:	$9,200
Books and supplies:	$1,000

Undergraduate aid. Need-based: Need-based aid available for full-time and part-time students.

Policies to reduce costs. Credit/placement for qualifying scores on IB, CLEP examinations.

Payment plans. Credit card, installment, deferred payment.

Application procedures. FAFSA, institutional form required. **Transfers:** Priority date 5/1; no deadline. Notification of awards on rolling basis; students must reply within 3 weeks of notification.

Contact. Financial aid office: (973) 972-4495
Michael Katz, Director of Financial Aid
65 Bergen Street
Newark, NJ 07107-3001

Warren County Community College

Washington, New Jersey
www.warren.edu
Two-year public **Federal Code: 016857**

College costs. Required fee of $13 per credit.

	Living at home
Tuition and fees:	$2,144
Out-of-district:	$4,288
Out-of-state:	$4,288
Per-credit charge:	$67
Per-credit out-of-district:	$134
Per-credit out-of-state:	$134
Board only:	$2,700
Books and supplies:	$700
Personal expenses:	$900
Transportation:	$864

Undergraduate aid. Non-need-based: Scholarships based on academics, state/district residency.

Policies to reduce costs. Tuition/fee waivers for senior citizens, unemployed or children of unemployed, employees and their families. Credit/placement for qualifying scores on AP, IB, CLEP examinations. Work study available nights, weekends and for part-time students.

Payment plans. Credit card, installment payment.

Application procedures. FAFSA, institutional form required. Closing date 7/1. Applicants notified on rolling basis starting 4/1, must reply within 2 week(s) of notification. **Transfers:** No deadline.

Contact. Financial aid office: (908) 835-2329
Jay Alexander, Director of Financial Aid
Route 57 West
Washington, NJ 07882-4343

William Paterson University of New Jersey

Wayne, New Jersey
www.wpunj.edu
Four-year public **Federal Code: 002625**

	Living at home	On-campus
Tuition and fees (2002-2003):	$6,400	$6,400
Out-of-state:	$10,200	$10,200
Room and board:		$7,030
Books and supplies:	$800	$800
Personal expenses:	$1,500	$1,500
Transportation:	$1,100	$800

Undergraduate aid. Need-based: Average financial aid package for full-time students was $7,983; for part-time $4,535. 52% awarded as scholarships/grants, 48% as loans/jobs. **Non-need-based:** 35% awarded as scholarships/grants, 65% as loans/jobs. Scholarships based on academics, alumni affiliation, minority status, music/drama. **Student debt:** 42% of graduating class borrowed to fund education; average debt was $9,681.

Freshman aid. Need-based: Out of 1,276 full-time freshmen, 983 applied for aid; 737 were judged to have need; of these 682 received aid. Average package met 81% of need. 181 students had full need met. Average scholarship/grant was $5,784; average loan $2,581. **Non-need based:** 243 full-time freshmen with need received non-need scholarships; 55 without need received awards.

Merit scholarships. Trustee Scholarship (full tuition for freshman); Residential Scholarships (full tuition for freshman and transfer student); Distinguished, Academic Excellence, and African American and Hispanic Students scholarships: $1,000 annually for 4 years.

Policies to reduce costs. Tuition/fee waivers for senior citizens, unemployed or children of unemployed, employees and their families. Credit/placement for qualifying scores on AP, CLEP examinations.

Payment plans. Credit card, installment, deferred payment.

Application procedures. FAFSA required. Closing date 4/1. Applicants notified on rolling basis starting 3/1, must reply within 2 week(s) of notification.

Contact. Financial aid office: (973) 720-2202
Robert Baumel, Director of Financial Aid
300 Pompton Road
Wayne, NJ 07470

New Mexico

Albuquerque Technical-Vocational Institute

Albuquerque, New Mexico
www.tvi.cc.nm.us
Two-year public **Federal Code: 004742**

College costs. In-state students do not pay tuition for technical courses, only arts and sciences courses.

	Living at home
Tuition and fees (2002-2003):	$914
Out-of-state:	$3,007
Per-credit charge:	$36
Per-credit out-of-state:	$123

Undergraduate aid. Need-based: 49% awarded as scholarships/grants, 51% as loans/jobs. Need-based aid available for part-time students. **Non-need-based:** Scholarships based on academics, state/district residency.

Freshman aid. Need-based: Average scholarship/grant was $1,758; average loan $3,569. **Non-need based:** 302 full-time freshmen with need received non-need scholarships.

Policies to reduce costs. Tuition/fee waivers for employees and their families. Credit/placement for qualifying scores on AP, CLEP examinations. Work study available for part-time students.

Payment plans. Credit card, deferred payment.

Application procedures. FAFSA required. Priority date 3/1; no closing date. Applicants notified by 5/1.

Contact. Financial aid office: (505) 224-3090
Eugene Padilla, Director of Financial Aid
525 Buena Vista Southeast
Albuquerque, NM 87106

Art Center Design College

Albuquerque, New Mexico
www.theartcenter.edu
Two-year proprietary **Federal Code: 024915**

College costs. Costs per calendar year: tuition $15,840; required fees $125 (one-time registration fee); estimated cost of books and supplies $1,250.

Contact. Financial aid office: (505) 254-7575
5000 Marble Ave. NE
Albuquerque, NM 87119

Clovis Community College

Clovis, New Mexico
www.clovis.edu
Two-year public **Federal Code: 004743**

College costs. Per credit hour charge for first credit: $43 in-district, $45 out-of-district. Out-of-state residents charged out-of-district per credit hour charge for under seven credits.

	Living at home
Tuition and fees (2002-2003):	$592
Out-of-district:	$640
Out-of-state:	$880
Per-credit charge:	$43
Per-credit out-of-district:	$45
Per-credit out-of-state:	$45
Books and supplies:	$600
Personal expenses:	$1,500
Transportation:	$1,000

Undergraduate aid. Need-based: 71% awarded as scholarships/grants, 29% as loans/jobs. Need-based aid available for part-time students.

Policies to reduce costs. Tuition/fee waivers for senior citizens, employees and their families. Credit/placement for qualifying scores on CLEP examinations. Work study available nights, weekends and for part-time students.

Payment plans. Credit card, deferred payment.

Application procedures. FAFSA required. Priority date 9/1; no closing date. Applicants notified on rolling basis starting 9/2.

Contact. Financial aid office: (505) 769-4060
April Dickenson, Director of Financial Aid
417 Schepps Boulevard
Clovis, NM 88101-8381

College of Santa Fe

Santa Fe, New Mexico
www.csf.edu
Four-year private **Federal Code: 002649**

	Living at home	On-campus
Tuition and fees (2002-2003):	$18,284	$18,284
Room and board:		$5,484
Board only:	$1,523	
Books and supplies:	$792	$792
Personal expenses:	$1,120	$1,120
Transportation:	$578	$578

Undergraduate aid. Need-based: Average financial aid package for full-time students was $16,429; for part-time $7,372. 14% awarded as scholarships/grants, 86% as loans/jobs. **Non-need-based:** 45% awarded as scholarships/grants, 55% as loans/jobs. Scholarships based on academics, alumni affiliation, art, leadership, minority status, music/drama. **Student debt:** 65% of graduating class borrowed to fund education; average debt was $22,000.

Freshman aid. Need-based: Out of 221 full-time freshmen, 98 applied for aid; 91 were judged to have need; of these 91 received aid. Average package met 82% of need. 11 students had full need met. Average scholarship/grant was $9,382; average loan $3,316. **Non-need based:** 58 full-time freshmen with need received non-need scholarships; 44 without need received awards.

Policies to reduce costs. Tuition/fee waivers for senior citizens, employees and their families. Prepayment discount; credit/placement for qualifying scores on AP, CLEP examinations.

Payment plans. Credit card, installment payment.

Application procedures. FAFSA required. Priority date 3/1; no closing date. Applicants notified on rolling basis starting 3/1, must reply by 5/1 or within 2 week(s) of notification. Early decision closing date 11/15. **Transfers:** No financial aid credited to student accounts until all financial aid transcripts are received.

Contact. Financial aid office: (505) 473-6453
Patty Hoban, Financial Aid Director
1600 St. Michael's Drive
Santa Fe, NM 87505

College of the Southwest

Hobbs, New Mexico
www.csw.edu
Four-year private **Federal Code: 013935**

College costs. Tuition for Carlsbad campus: $210 per credit hour, $6,720 full-time, $120 required fees.

	Living at home	On-campus
Tuition and fees (projected):	$7,150	$7,150
Room and board:		$4,400
Board only:	$3,725	
Books and supplies:	$804	$804
Personal expenses:	$814	$814
Transportation:	$484	$484

Undergraduate aid. Need-based: Average financial aid package for full-time students was $7,217; for part-time $4,749. 51% awarded as scholarships/grants, 49% as loans/jobs. **Non-need-based:** 33% awarded as scholarships/grants, 67% as loans/jobs. Scholarships based on academics, alumni affiliation, athletics, leadership, music/drama, religious affiliation, state/district residency. **Student debt:** 72% of graduating class borrowed to fund education; average debt was $18,411.

Freshman aid. Need-based: Out of 38 full-time freshmen, 38 applied for aid; 37 were judged to have need; of these 37 received aid. Average package met 31% of need. Average scholarship/grant was $3,830; average loan $926.

Non-need based: 34 full-time freshmen with need received non-need scholarships; 2 without need received awards; 2 received athletic scholarships.

Policies to reduce costs. Tuition/fee waivers for children of alumni, family of clergy, employees and their families. Credit/placement for qualifying scores on AP, IB, CLEP examinations. Work study available for part-time students.

Payment plans. Credit card, installment, deferred payment.

Application procedures. FAFSA, institutional form required. Priority date 4/2; closing date 6/2. Applicants notified on rolling basis starting 4/2, must reply within 2 week(s) of notification.

Contact. Financial aid office: (505) 392-6561
Donna Owen, Director of Financial Aid
6610 Lovington Highway
Hobbs, NM 88240

Dona Ana Branch Community College of New Mexico State University

Las Cruces, New Mexico
www.nmsu.edu
Two-year public **Federal Code: 002657**

	Living at home	On-campus
Tuition and fees (2002-2003):	$903	$903
Out-of-district:	$1,023	$1,023
Out-of-state:	$2,319	$2,319
Per-credit charge:	$37	$37
Per-credit out-of-district:	$42	$42
Per-credit out-of-state:	$96	$96
Room and board:		$4,296
Board only:	$3,345	
Books and supplies:	$664	$664
Personal expenses:	$1,215	$1,215
Transportation:	$1,023	$1,023

Undergraduate aid. Need-based: Need-based aid available for full-time and part-time students.

Policies to reduce costs. Tuition/fee waivers for senior citizens, employees and their families.

Payment plans. Credit card, installment, deferred payment.

Application procedures. FAFSA required. Priority date 3/1; no closing date. Applicants notified on rolling basis starting 5/1.

Contact. Financial aid office: (505) 527-7535
Gladys Chairez, Financial Aid Advisor
P.O. Box 30001
Las Cruces, NM 88003-8001

Eastern New Mexico University

Portales, New Mexico
www.enmu.edu
Four-year public **Federal Code: 002651**

	Living at home	On-campus
Tuition and fees (2002-2003):	$2,088	$2,088
Out-of-state:	$7,644	$7,644
Room and board:		$4,160

Undergraduate aid. Need-based: Average financial aid package for full-time students was $7,061; for part-time $5,050. 45% awarded as scholarships/grants, 55% as loans/jobs. **Non-need-based:** 99% awarded as scholarships/grants, 1% as loans/jobs. Scholarships based on academics, alumni affiliation, art, athletics, leadership, music/drama, state/district residency. **Student debt:** 44% of graduating class borrowed to fund education; average debt was $5,025. **Additional information:** Not all merit scholarships are need-based.

Freshman aid. Need-based: Out of 528 full-time freshmen, 452 applied for aid; 395 were judged to have need; of these 378 received aid. Average package met 45% of need. 63 students had full need met. Average scholarship/grant was $3,391; average loan $2,965. **Non-need based:** 250 full-time freshmen with need received non-need scholarships; 51 without need received awards; 59 received athletic scholarships.

Policies to reduce costs. Tuition/fee waivers for employees and their families. Credit/placement for qualifying scores on AP, CLEP examinations.

Payment plans. Credit card, installment payment.

Application procedures. FAFSA required. Priority date 3/1; no closing date. Applicants notified by 4/1, must reply within 3 week(s) of notification. **Transfers:** Child care grants and non-need-based college work study limited to New Mexico residents.

Contact. Financial aid office: (505) 562-2194
Theresa Beres, Director of Financial Aid
Station Seven
Portales, NM 88130

Eastern New Mexico University: Roswell Campus

Roswell, New Mexico
www.roswell.enmu.edu
Two-year public **Federal Code: 002651**

	Living at home	On-campus
Tuition and fees (2002-2003):	$804	$804
Out-of-district:	$828	$828
Out-of-state:	$2,127	$2,127
Per-credit charge:	$30	$30
Per-credit out-of-district:	$31	$31
Per-credit out-of-state:	$85	$85
Room and board:		$3,464
Books and supplies:	$659	$659
Personal expenses:	$950	$907
Transportation:	$1,300	$1,470

Undergraduate aid. Need-based: Need-based aid available for full-time and part-time students.

Merit scholarships. New Mexico Lottery Scholarship. Tuition only for New Mexico High Seniors, New Mexico residents. Must attend school full-time the semester following high school graduation or GED. Maintain 12 credit hours and 2.5 GPA.

Policies to reduce costs. Tuition/fee waivers for senior citizens, employees and their families. Credit/placement for qualifying scores on AP, IB, CLEP examinations. Work study available nights, weekends and for part-time students.

Payment plans. Credit card, deferred payment.

Application procedures. FAFSA required. Priority date 4/1; no closing date. Applicants notified on rolling basis starting 7/1, must reply within 3 week(s) of notification. **Transfers:** All students receiving state aid must be New Mexico residents and enrolled in at least 6 credit hours.

Contact. Financial aid office: (505) 624-7152
Jessie Hall, Director of Financial Aid
Box 6000
Roswell, NM 88202-6000

ITT Technical Institute: Albuquerque

Albuquerque, New Mexico
www.itt-tech.edu
Three-year proprietary **Federal Code: 020652**

College costs. Total program varies depending on course of study. Per-credit-hour charge: $347.

Policies to reduce costs. Tuition/fee waivers for employees and their families.

Payment plans. Credit card, installment payment.

Application procedures. FAFSA, institutional form required. No deadline. Applicants notified on rolling basis.

Contact. Financial aid office: (505) 828-1114
Eulalia Chavez, Director of Finance
5100 Masthead Street N.E.
Albuquerque, NM 87109

Institute of American Indian Arts

Santa Fe, New Mexico
www.iaiancad.org
Four-year public **Federal Code: 014152**

	Living at home	On-campus
Tuition and fees:	$2,470	$2,470
Room and board:		$4,536
Books and supplies:	$1,850	$1,850
Personal expenses:	$1,200	$1,200
Transportation:	$550	$550

Undergraduate aid. Need-based: Need-based aid available for full-time and part-time students. **Additional information:** For American Indian and Alaskan natives, financial aid available through Tribe or Native Corporation in which student is enrolled.

Merit scholarships. IAIA merit scholarships available to all students with GPA 3.0, $1,000; GPA 3.5, $1,500; and GPA 4.0, $2,000.

Policies to reduce costs. Work study available nights and for part-time students.

Payment plans. Deferred payment.

Application procedures. FAFSA, institutional form required. Priority date 3/15; no closing date. Applicants notified on rolling basis starting 5/1. **Transfers:** Priority date 3/15.

Contact. **Financial aid office:** (505) 424-2330
Dorothy Espinoza, Financial Aid Manager
83 Avan Nu Po Road
Santa Fe, NM 87508-1300

Luna Community College

Las Vegas, New Mexico
www.lvti.cc.nm.us
Two-year public **Federal Code: 009962**

	Living at home
Tuition and fees (2002-2003):	$644
Out-of-district:	$932
Out-of-state:	$1,868
Per-credit charge:	$25
Per-credit out-of-district:	$37
Per-credit out-of-state:	$76
Board only:	$1,722
Books and supplies:	$500
Personal expenses:	$572
Transportation:	$540

Contact. **Financial aid office:** (505) 454-2500
Donna Flores-Median, Exec. Dir./ Budget & Finance
Box 1510
Las Vegas, NM 87701

Mesalands Community College

Tucumcari, New Mexico
www.mesalands.edu
Two-year public **Federal Code: 032063**

	Living at home
Tuition and fees (2002-2003):	$970
Out-of-state:	$1,570
Per-credit charge:	$28
Per-credit out-of-state:	$48
Books and supplies:	$564
Personal expenses:	$1,427
Transportation:	$1,517

Undergraduate aid. Need-based: Need-based aid available for full-time and part-time students.

Contact. **Financial aid office:** (505) 461-4413
Jerry Klaverweyden, Director of Financial Aid
911 South Tenth Street
Tucumcari, NM 88401

Metropolitan College of Court Reporting

Albuquerque, New Mexico
Four-year proprietary **Federal Code: 030993**

College costs. 33-month court reporter bachelor's degree program tuition: $19,000. 2-year paralegal associate's degree program tuition: $10,989. Personal expenses: $1,700.

Contact. **Financial aid office:** (505) 888-3400
8100 Mountain Road NE, Suite 200
Albuquerque, NM 87110

National American University

Albuquerque, New Mexico
www.national.edu
Four-year proprietary **Federal Code: 004057**

College costs (2002-2003). Tuition $200 per credit hour for online courses. Required fees: $50 matriculation fee (one-time); technology fee $105 per quarter for full-time students. Books/supplies: $675. Transportation: $2,184.

Policies to reduce costs. Tuition/fee waivers for senior citizens. Credit/placement for qualifying scores on CLEP examinations.

Payment plans. Credit card, installment, deferred payment.

Application procedures. Institutional form required. No deadline. Applicants notified on rolling basis.

Contact. **Financial aid office:** (505) 265-7517
Brenda Graves, Financial Aid Director
4775 Indian School Road NE, Suite 200
Albuquerque, NM 87110

New Mexico Highlands University

Las Vegas, New Mexico
www.nmhu.edu
Four-year public **Federal Code: 002653**

	Living at home	On-campus
Tuition and fees (2002-2003):	$2,099	$2,099
Out-of-state:	$8,819	$8,819
Room and board:		$3,620
Board only:	$1,280	
Books and supplies:	$700	$700
Personal expenses:	$1,494	$1,494
Transportation:	$1,350	$1,950

Undergraduate aid. Need-based: Average financial aid package for full-time students was $3,830; for part-time $2,857. 42% awarded as scholarships/grants, 58% as loans/jobs. **Non-need-based:** 60% awarded as scholarships/grants, 40% as loans/jobs. Scholarships based on academics, athletics, leadership, minority status, music/drama, state/district residency. **Student debt:** 46% of graduating class borrowed to fund education; average debt was $8,792. **Additional information:** Work study funds available on no-need basis to state residents.

Freshman aid. Need-based: Average package met 30% of need. Average scholarship/grant was $2,593; average loan $2,166.

Policies to reduce costs. Tuition/fee waivers for employees and their families. Credit/placement for qualifying scores on AP, CLEP examinations.

Payment plans. Credit card, installment, deferred payment.

Application procedures. FAFSA required. Priority date 5/1; no closing date. Applicants notified on rolling basis starting 5/15, must reply within 2 week(s) of notification. **Transfers:** Priority date 3/1; closing date 6/30.

Contact. **Financial aid office:** (505) 454-3318
Eilenne Sedillo, Director of Financial Aid
Box 9000
Las Vegas, NM 87701

New Mexico Institute of Mining and Technology

Socorro, New Mexico
www.nmt.edu
Four-year public
Federal Code: 002654

	Living at home	On-campus
Tuition and fees (2002-2003):	$2,911	$2,911
Out-of-state:	$9,122	$9,122
Room and board:		$4,218
Books and supplies:	$800	$800
Personal expenses:	$1,635	$1,635
Transportation:	$500	$500

Undergraduate aid. Need-based: Average financial aid package for full-time students was $7,945; for part-time $6,762. 47% awarded as scholarships/grants, 53% as loans/jobs. **Non-need-based:** 96% awarded as scholarships/grants, 4% as loans/jobs. Scholarships based on academics, alumni affiliation, minority status, state/district residency. **Student debt:** 30% of graduating class borrowed to fund education; average debt was $9,500. **Additional information:** Campus research projects offer student employment based on merit.

Freshman aid. Need-based: Out of 358 full-time freshmen, 262 applied for aid; 108 were judged to have need; of these 105 received aid. Average package met 90% of need. 45 students had full need met. Average scholarship/grant was $3,732; average loan $3,150. **Non-need based:** 97 full-time freshmen with need received non-need scholarships; 150 without need received awards.

Merit scholarships. Merit Scholarships of up to $3,500 annually for transfer students. Must have college GPA of 3.5 and 30 degree credit hours.

Policies to reduce costs. Tuition/fee waivers for senior citizens, employees and their families. Credit/placement for qualifying scores on AP examinations.

Payment plans. Credit card, installment payment.

Application procedures. FAFSA, institutional form required. Priority date 6/1; no closing date. Applicants notified on rolling basis starting 6/1, must reply within 2 week(s) of notification. **Transfers:** Priority date 3/1; no deadline. Financial aid transcripts required from all colleges attended.

Contact. Financial aid office: (505) 835-5333
Annette Kaus, Director of Financial Aid
801 Leroy Place
Socorro, NM 87801

New Mexico Junior College

Hobbs, New Mexico
Two-year public
Federal Code: 002655

	Living at home	On-campus
Tuition and fees (2002-2003):	$362	$362
Out-of-district:	$920	$920
Out-of-state:	$1,030	$1,030
Per-credit charge:	$13	$13
Per-credit out-of-district:	$30	$30
Per-credit out-of-state:	$35	$35
Room and board:		$3,110
Books and supplies:	$700	$700
Personal expenses:	$1,575	$1,575
Transportation:	$1,060	$720

Undergraduate aid. Need-based: Need-based aid available for full-time and part-time students.

Policies to reduce costs. Tuition/fee waivers for employees and their families. Credit/placement for qualifying scores on AP, CLEP examinations.

Payment plans. Installment payment.

Application procedures. FAFSA required. Priority date 6/1; no closing date. Applicants notified on rolling basis, must reply within 2 week(s) of notification.

Contact. Financial aid office: (505) 392-4510
Linda Neal, Financial Aid Officer
5317 Lovington Highway
Hobbs, NM 88240

New Mexico Military Institute

Roswell, New Mexico
www.nmmi.edu
Two-year public
Federal Code: 002656

College costs. Tuition costs include room and board, uniform, supplies and fees.

	Living at home
Tuition and fees (2002-2003):	$7,400
Out-of-state:	$9,400
Books and supplies:	$700

Undergraduate aid. Need-based: Need-based aid available for full-time students. **Non-need-based:** Scholarships based on academics, athletics, state/district residency.

Policies to reduce costs. Tuition/fee waivers for employees and their families. Credit/placement for qualifying scores on AP, CLEP examinations.

Payment plans. Credit card, deferred payment.

Application procedures. FAFSA required. Priority date 4/1; no closing date. Applicants notified on rolling basis starting 5/1, must reply within 3 week(s) of notification. **Transfers:** New Mexico Scholars Program, New Mexico Success Scholarship.

Contact. Financial aid office: (505) 622-6250
Craig Collins, Financial Aid Director
101 West College Boulevard
Roswell, NM 88201-5173

New Mexico State University

Las Cruces, New Mexico
www.nmsu.edu
Four-year public
Federal Code: 002657

	Living at home	On-campus
Tuition and fees (2002-2003):	$3,216	$3,216
Out-of-state:	$10,788	$10,788
Room and board:		$4,422
Books and supplies:	$664	$664
Personal expenses:	$2,686	$2,686
Transportation:		$1,228

Undergraduate aid. Need-based: Average financial aid package for full-time students was $8,207; for part-time $6,362. 57% awarded as scholarships/grants, 43% as loans/jobs. **Non-need-based:** 61% awarded as scholarships/grants, 39% as loans/jobs.

Freshman aid. Need-based: Out of 2,013 full-time freshmen, 1,433 applied for aid; 1,204 were judged to have need; of these 1,185 received aid. Average package met 70% of need. 220 students had full need met. Average scholarship/grant was $5,745; average loan $2,740. **Non-need based:** 131 full-time freshmen with need received non-need scholarships; 573 without need received awards; 29 received athletic scholarships.

Policies to reduce costs. Tuition/fee waivers for senior citizens, employees and their families. Credit/placement for qualifying scores on AP, CLEP examinations.

Payment plans. Credit card, installment, deferred payment.

Application procedures. FAFSA, institutional form required. Priority date 3/1; no closing date. Applicants notified on rolling basis starting 4/1, must reply within 4 week(s) of notification.

Contact. Financial aid office: (505) 646-4105
Cydney Conway, Director of Financial Aid
Box 30001, MSC 3A
Las Cruces, NM 88003-8001

New Mexico State University at Alamogordo

Alamogordo, New Mexico
alamo.nmsu.edu
Two-year public **Federal Code: 002658**

	Living at home
Tuition and fees (2002-2003):	$912
Out-of-district:	$1,032
Out-of-state:	$2,352
Per-credit charge:	$38
Per-credit out-of-district:	$43
Per-credit out-of-state:	$98
Board only:	$4,016
Books and supplies:	$664
Personal expenses:	$1,458
Transportation:	$1,228

Undergraduate aid. Need-based: Need-based aid available for full-time and part-time students. **Non-need-based:** Scholarships based on academics, state/district residency.

Policies to reduce costs. Tuition/fee waivers for senior citizens, employees and their families. Credit/placement for qualifying scores on AP, CLEP examinations.

Payment plans. Credit card, installment, deferred payment.

Application procedures. FAFSA, institutional form required. Applicants notified by 6/1.

Contact. **Financial aid office:** (505) 439-3600
Sharon Fischer, Financial Aid Coordinator
Alamogordo, NM 88310

St. John's College

Santa Fe, New Mexico
www.sjcsf.edu
Four-year private **Federal Code: 002093**

	Living at home	On-campus
Tuition and fees (2002-2003):	$27,410	$27,410
Room and board:		$6,970
Books and supplies:	$275	$275
Personal expenses:		$900
Transportation:	$100	$600

Undergraduate aid. Need-based: Average financial aid package for full-time students was $20,424; for part-time $13,521. 73% awarded as scholarships/grants, 27% as loans/jobs. **Non-need-based:** 17% awarded as scholarships/grants, 83% as loans/jobs. Scholarships based on academics, alumni affiliation, state/district residency. **Student debt:** 75% of graduating class borrowed to fund education; average debt was $22,753. **Additional information:** 100% of need met for most of those qualified to receive aid. Families receive individual attention in determining need fairly. Independent students must submit parental data. Financial aid information also required of noncustodial parent in cases of separation or divorce. Aid awarded first-come, first-served until institutional money exhausted. Apply early by February 15; after April 1 aid difficult to obtain.

Freshman aid. Need-based: Average package met 94% of need. Average scholarship/grant was $15,788; average loan $4,825.

Policies to reduce costs. Tuition/fee waivers for employees and their families. Work study available nights, weekends and for part-time students.

Payment plans. Credit card, installment payment.

Application procedures. FAFSA, CSS PROFILE required. Priority date 2/15; no closing date. Applicants notified on rolling basis starting 12/1, must reply by 5/1 or within 2 week(s) of notification.

Contact. **Financial aid office:** (505) 984-6000
Michael Rodgriguez, Director of Financial Aid
1160 Camino Cruz Blanca
Santa Fe, NM 87505-4599

San Juan College

Farmington, New Mexico
www.sanjuancollege.edu
Two-year public **Federal Code: 002660**

	Living at home
Tuition and fees (2002-2003):	$360
Out-of-state:	$600
Per-credit charge:	$15
Per-credit out-of-state:	$25
Books and supplies:	$600

Undergraduate aid. Need-based: Need-based aid available for full-time and part-time students. **Non-need-based:** Scholarships based on academics, state/district residency.

Policies to reduce costs. Tuition/fee waivers for senior citizens, employees and their families. Credit/placement for qualifying scores on AP, CLEP examinations. Work study available nights, weekends and for part-time students.

Payment plans. Credit card payment.

Application procedures. FAFSA required. No deadline. Applicants notified on rolling basis starting 7/1, must reply within 2 week(s) of notification. **Transfers:** No deadline.

Contact. **Financial aid office:** (505) 326-3311
Roger Evans, Director of Financial Aid
4601 College Boulevard
Farmington, NM 87402

Santa Fe Community College

Santa Fe, New Mexico
www.santa-fe.cc.nm.us
Two-year public **Federal Code: 016065**

	Living at home
Tuition and fees:	$929
Out-of-district:	$1,169
Out-of-state:	$1,994
Per-credit charge:	$26
Per-credit out-of-district:	$35
Per-credit out-of-state:	$63
Board only:	$2,300
Books and supplies:	$500
Personal expenses:	$1,500
Transportation:	$1,000

Undergraduate aid. Need-based: Average financial aid package for full-time students was $2,500; for part-time $1,800. 69% awarded as scholarships/grants, 31% as loans/jobs.

Freshman aid. Need-based: Out of 213 full-time freshmen, 159 applied for aid; 132 were judged to have need; of these 128 received aid. Average package met 45% of need. 4 students had full need met. Average scholarship/grant was $3,100; average loan $2,625.

Policies to reduce costs. Tuition/fee waivers for senior citizens, employees and their families. Credit/placement for qualifying scores on AP, CLEP examinations.

Payment plans. Credit card, deferred payment.

Application procedures. FAFSA, institutional form required. Priority date 3/1; no closing date. Applicants notified on rolling basis starting 7/15, must reply within 4 week(s) of notification. **Transfers:** No deadline.

Contact. **Financial aid office:** (505) 428-1268
Willie Bachicha, Financial Aid Director
6401 Richards Avenue
Santa Fe, NM 87508-4887

Southwestern Indian Polytechnic Institute

Albuquerque, New Mexico
www.sipi.bia.edu
Two-year public **Federal Code: 011185**

College costs. Applicants must have valid membership in a U.S. federally recognized Indian tribe, and as Native Americans attend tuition-free. $20 fees and $150 refundable book deposit required. Board: $3,000. Books/supplies: $800. Personal expenses: $1,400. Transportation: $1,000.

Undergraduate aid. Need-based: Average financial aid package for full-time students was $3,000. 92% awarded as scholarships/grants, 8% as loans/jobs. Need-based aid available for part-time students. **Non-need-based:** Scholarships based on academics, leadership, minority status.

Policies to reduce costs. Tuition/fee waivers for minority students. Work study available nights and weekends.

Application procedures. FAFSA required. Closing date 6/30. Applicants notified on rolling basis starting 9/30. **Transfers:** No deadline.

Contact. Financial aid office: (505) 346-2347
Marilyn Pargas, Financial Aid Specialist
9169 Coors Road NW
Albuquerque, NM 87184

University of New Mexico

Albuquerque, New Mexico
www.unm.edu
Four-year public **Federal Code: 002663**

	Living at home	On-campus
Tuition and fees (2002-2003):	$3,562	$3,562
Out-of-state:	$11,960	$11,960
Room and board:		$5,217
Books and supplies:	$744	$744
Personal expenses:	$1,526	$1,526
Transportation:	$1,366	$1,366

Undergraduate aid. Need-based: Need-based aid available for full-time and part-time students. **Non-need-based:** Scholarships based on academics, art, athletics, leadership, music/drama, state/district residency. **Additional information:** Financial aid has priority date of March 1. Regent scholarship program has a priority date of December 1. UNM scholars program has deadline of February 1.

Merit scholarships. Bridge to Success Scholarship; $1,000 for first semester only while awaiting other scholarship aid; requires New Mexico residency, full-time status in degree-granting program; acceptable GED test score and/or requisite high school GPA per sponsor.

Policies to reduce costs. Tuition/fee waivers for senior citizens, employees and their families. Credit/placement for qualifying scores on AP, IB, CLEP examinations. Work study available nights, weekends and for part-time students.

Payment plans. Credit card, deferred payment.

Application procedures. FAFSA required. Priority date 3/1; no closing date. Applicants notified on rolling basis starting 4/15. **Transfers:** Priority date 3/1; closing date 5/30.

Contact. Financial aid office: (505) 277-2041
Ron Martinez, Director of Financial Aid
Student Services Center, Room 150
Albuquerque, NM 87131-2046

Western New Mexico University

Silver City, New Mexico
www.wnmu.edu
Four-year public **Federal Code: 002664**

	Living at home	On-campus
Tuition and fees (2002-2003):	$2,124	$2,124
Out-of-state:	$7,788	$7,788
Room and board:		$3,764
Books and supplies:	$810	$810
Personal expenses:	$2,014	$2,060

Undergraduate aid. Need-based: Average financial aid package for full-time students was $5,230; for part-time $5,163. 57% awarded as scholarships/grants, 43% as loans/jobs. **Non-need-based:** 54% awarded as scholarships/grants, 46% as loans/jobs. Scholarships based on academics, athletics, state/district residency.

Freshman aid. Need-based: Out of 442 full-time freshmen, 385 applied for aid; 285 were judged to have need; of these 285 received aid. Average package met 78% of need. 89 students had full need met. Average scholarship/grant was $1,869; average loan $2,184. **Non-need based:** 27 full-time freshmen with need received non-need scholarships; 103 without need received awards; 85 received athletic scholarships.

Policies to reduce costs. Tuition/fee waivers for senior citizens, employees and their families. Credit/placement for qualifying scores on AP, IB, CLEP examinations.

Payment plans. Credit card, installment, deferred payment.

Application procedures. FAFSA, institutional form required. Closing date 4/1. Applicants notified on rolling basis starting 4/1, must reply within 2 week(s) of notification.

Contact. Financial aid office: (505) 538-6173
Charles Kelly, Director of Financial Aid
Castorena 106
Silver City, NM 88062

New York

Adelphi University

Garden City, New York
www.adelphi.edu
Four-year private **Federal Code: 002666**

	Living at home	On-campus
Tuition and fees (2002-2003):	$16,980	$16,980
Room and board:		$7,900
Board only:	$1,500	
Books and supplies:	$1,000	$1,000
Personal expenses:	$1,800	$1,000
Transportation:	$3,000	$1,000

Undergraduate aid. Need-based: Average financial aid package for full-time students was $13,200. 56% awarded as scholarships/grants, 44% as loans/jobs. Need-based aid available for part-time students. **Non-need-based:** 46% awarded as scholarships/grants, 54% as loans/jobs. Scholarships based on academics, alumni affiliation, art, athletics, leadership, minority status, music/drama, religious affiliation.

Freshman aid. Need-based: Out of 666 full-time freshmen, 616 applied for aid; 613 were judged to have need; of these 613 received aid. Average scholarship/grant was $7,034; average loan $3,720. **Non-need based:** 107 full-time freshmen with need received non-need scholarships; 102 without need received awards; 10 received athletic scholarships.

Merit scholarships. Trustee Scholarship: 12 available, $12,500 to full tuition, top 10% of high school class, 1350 SAT, and 3.7 GPA required. Presidential Scholarship: 25 available, $10,500 to $12,000, top 10% of high school class, 1350 SAT, and 3.5 GPA required. Provost Scholarship: 55 available, $8,000 to $10,000, top 15% of high school class, 1250 SAT, and 3.3 GPA required. Dean's Scholarship: 252 available, $3,000 to $7,500, top 25% of high school class, 1000 SAT, and 3.0 GPA required.

Policies to reduce costs. Tuition/fee waivers for children of alumni, senior citizens, employees and their families. Prepayment discount; credit/placement for qualifying scores on AP, IB examinations. Work study available nights, weekends and for part-time students.

Payment plans. Credit card, installment, deferred payment.

Application procedures. FAFSA required. Priority date 3/1; no closing date. Applicants notified on rolling basis starting 3/1. **Transfers:** Priority date 3/1; no deadline.

Contact. Financial aid office: (516) 877-3080
Sheryl Mihopulos, Director of Admissions/Financial Aid
One South Avenue, Levermore 114
Garden City, NY 11530

Adirondack Community College

Queensbury, New York
www.sunyacc.edu
Two-year public **Federal Code: 002860**

	Living at home
Tuition and fees (2002-2003):	$2,660
Out-of-state:	$5,130
Per-credit charge:	$102
Per-credit out-of-state:	$204
Board only:	$945
Books and supplies:	$800
Personal expenses:	$785
Transportation:	$850

Undergraduate aid. All financial aid based on need. Need-based aid available for full-time and part-time students.

Policies to reduce costs. Tuition/fee waivers for senior citizens, employees and their families. Credit/placement for qualifying scores on AP, IB, CLEP examinations.

Payment plans. Credit card, installment payment.

Application procedures. FAFSA, institutional form required. Priority date 4/15; no closing date. Applicants notified on rolling basis starting 5/1.

Contact. Financial aid office: (518) 743-2223
Maureen Reilly, Director of Financial Aid
640 Bay Road
Queensbury, NY 12804

Albany College of Pharmacy

Albany, New York
www.acp.edu
Six-year private **Federal Code: 002885**

	Living at home	On-campus
Tuition and fees (2002-2003):	$15,550	$15,550
Room and board:		$5,200
Books and supplies:	$700	$700
Personal expenses:	$100	$700
Transportation:	$1,600	$300

Undergraduate aid. Need-based: Average financial aid package for full-time students was $12,320; for part-time $15,833. 35% awarded as scholarships/grants, 65% as loans/jobs. **Non-need-based:** 12% awarded as scholarships/grants, 88% as loans/jobs. Scholarships based on academics, state/district residency.

Freshman aid. Need-based: Out of 158 full-time freshmen, 152 applied for aid; 134 were judged to have need; of these 134 received aid. Average package met 80% of need. 64 students had full need met. Average scholarship/grant was $5,487; average loan $7,669. **Non-need based:** 8 full-time freshmen with need received non-need scholarships; 19 without need received awards.

Policies to reduce costs. Tuition/fee waivers for employees and their families. Credit/placement for qualifying scores on AP, CLEP examinations. Work study available nights and weekends.

Payment plans. Installment, deferred payment.

Application procedures. FAFSA required. Closing date 3/15. Applicants notified on rolling basis starting 3/15, must reply within 2 week(s) of notification. **Transfers:** Priority date 2/1; closing date 3/15.

Contact. Financial aid office: (518) 445-7258
Tiffany Guitierrez, Director of Financial Aid
106 New Scotland Avenue
Albany, NY 12208

Alfred University

Alfred, New York
www.alfred.edu
Four-year private **Federal Code: 002668**

	Living at home	On-campus
Tuition and fees (2002-2003):	$19,236	$19,236
Room and board:		$8,478
Board only:	$1,500	
Books and supplies:	$700	$700
Personal expenses:	$350	$350
Transportation:	$1,000	$750

Undergraduate aid. Need-based: Average financial aid package for full-time students was $18,740. 72% awarded as scholarships/grants, 28% as loans/jobs. **Non-need-based:** 45% awarded as scholarships/grants, 55% as loans/jobs. Scholarships based on academics, art, leadership, music/drama. **Student debt:** 87% of graduating class borrowed to fund education; average debt was $17,600.

Freshman aid. Need-based: Out of 473 full-time freshmen, 424 applied for aid; 381 were judged to have need; of these 381 received aid. Average package met 95% of need. 342 students had full need met. Average scholarship/grant was $15,428; average loan $3,715. **Non-need based:** 185 full-time freshmen with need received non-need scholarships; 52 without need received awards.

Policies to reduce costs. Tuition/fee waivers for employees and their families. Prepayment discount; credit/placement for qualifying scores on AP, IB, CLEP examinations.

Payment plans. Installment payment.

Application procedures. FAFSA, institutional form required. No deadline. Applicants notified on rolling basis starting 2/1, must reply by 5/1 or within 2 week(s) of notification. Early decision closing date 12/1. **Transfers:** No deadline.

Contact. **Financial aid office:** (607) 871-2159
Earl Pierce, Director of Financial Aid
One Saxon Drive
Alfred, NY 14802-1205

American Academy McAllister Institute of Funeral Service

New York, New York
Two-year private
Federal Code: 010813

	Living at home
Tuition and fees:	$8,765
Per-credit charge:	$175
Books and supplies:	$709
Personal expenses:	$2,635
Transportation:	$1,051

Undergraduate aid. All financial aid based on need. Need-based aid available for full-time students.

Policies to reduce costs. Tuition/fee waivers for employees and their families. Tuition at time of enrollment guaranteed for 2 years.

Application procedures. FAFSA required. Applicants notified on rolling basis starting 7/1, must reply by 9/1 or within 3 week(s) of notification. **Transfers:** Priority date 6/1.

Contact. **Financial aid office:** (212) 220-4275
Theresa Powell, Financial Aid Administrator
450 West 56th Street
New York, NY 10019-3602

American Academy of Dramatic Arts

New York, New York
www.aada.org
Two-year private
Federal Code: 007465

	Living at home
Tuition and fees:	$14,850
Board only:	$1,000
Books and supplies:	$1,542
Personal expenses:	$1,000
Transportation:	$600

Undergraduate aid. All financial aid based on need. Need-based aid available for full-time students. **Additional information:** Need-based incentive grants of $200-$500 for first-year students available. Merit awards of $500-$1,500. Scholarships of $500-$3,000 available for second year. Scholarships of $500-$5,000 available for post-degree third year.

Policies to reduce costs. Prepayment discount.

Payment plans. Credit card, installment, deferred payment.

Application procedures. FAFSA, institutional form required. No deadline. Applicants notified on rolling basis.

Contact. **Financial aid office:** (212) 686-9244 ext. 342
Roberto Lopez, Financial Aid Director/Registrar
120 Madison Avenue
New York, NY 10016

Bard College

Annandale-on-Hudson, New York
www.bard.edu
Four-year private
Federal Code: 002671

	Living at home	On-campus
Tuition and fees (projected):	$28,580	$28,580
Room and board:		$8,380
Board only:	$4,000	
Books and supplies:	$700	$700
Personal expenses:	$1,500	$1,500
Transportation:	$600	$550

Undergraduate aid. **Need-based:** Average financial aid package for full-time students was $21,466; for part-time $5,193. 78% awarded as scholarships/grants, 22% as loans/jobs. **Non-need-based:** 51% awarded as scholarships/grants, 49% as loans/jobs. Scholarships based on academics. **Student debt:** 58% of graduating class borrowed to fund education; average debt was $15,400. **Additional information:** Excellence and Equal Cost Program for students who graduate in top 10 of public high school class lowers fees to levels equivalent to those at home state university or college.

Freshman aid. **Need-based:** Out of 344 full-time freshmen, 239 applied for aid; 208 were judged to have need; of these 208 received aid. Average package met 85% of need. 117 students had full need met. Average scholarship/grant was $18,282; average loan $3,351. **Non-need based:** 16 without need received awards.

Merit scholarships. Distinguished Scientist Scholarship for students intending to major in math or science; 10 full tuition scholarships annually.

Policies to reduce costs. Tuition/fee waivers for employees and their families. Credit/placement for qualifying scores on AP, IB examinations.

Payment plans. Installment payment.

Application procedures. FAFSA, CSS PROFILE required. Priority date 2/1; closing date 3/15. Applicants notified by 4/1, must reply by 5/1.

Contact. **Financial aid office:** (845) 758-7526
Denise Ackerman, Director of Financial Aid
Box 5000
Annandale-on-Hudson, NY 12504-5000

Barnard College

New York, New York
www.barnard.edu
Four-year private
Federal Code: 002708

	Living at home	On-campus
Tuition and fees (2002-2003):	$25,270	$25,270
Room and board:		$10,140
Board only:	$900	
Books and supplies:	$850	$850
Personal expenses:	$1,050	$1,050
Transportation:	$570	$520

Undergraduate aid. All financial aid based on need. Average financial aid package for full-time students was $24,416. 80% awarded as scholarships/grants, 20% as loans/jobs. Need-based aid available for part-time students. **Student debt:** 52% of graduating class borrowed to fund education; average debt was $14,030.

Freshman aid. Out of 543 full-time freshmen, 305 applied for aid; 220 were judged to have need; of these 220 received aid. Average package met 100% of need. 220 students had full need met. Average scholarship/grant was $21,914; average loan $2,625.

Policies to reduce costs. Tuition/fee waivers for employees and their families. Prepayment discount; credit/placement for qualifying scores on AP, IB examinations. Work study available nights, weekends and for part-time students.

Payment plans. Credit card, installment, deferred payment.

Application procedures. FAFSA, institutional form, CSS PROFILE required. Closing date 2/1. Applicants notified by 4/1, must reply by 5/1. Early decision closing date 11/15. **Transfers:** Closing date 4/1. Transfers admitted in the spring are not eligible for institutional grant aid.

Contact. **Financial aid office:** (212) 854-2154
Suzanne Clair Guard, Director of Financial Aid
3009 Broadway
New York, NY 10027-6598

Berkeley College

White Plains, New York
www.berkeleycollege.edu
Four-year proprietary
Federal Code: 007421

	Living at home
Tuition and fees (2002-2003):	$14,340
Books and supplies:	$900

Undergraduate aid. **Need-based:** Need-based aid available for full-time students. **Non-need-based:** Scholarships based on academics, alumni affiliation. **Additional information:** Alumni scholarship examination given in November and December. Full and partial scholarships awarded.

Policies to reduce costs. Tuition/fee waivers for family members, employees and their families. Tuition at time of enrollment guaranteed for 4 years; credit/placement for qualifying scores on AP, CLEP examinations.

Payment plans. Credit card, installment payment.

Application procedures. FAFSA required. No deadline. Applicants notified on rolling basis starting 3/1, must reply within 6 week(s) of notification. **Transfers:** No deadline.

Contact. **Financial aid office:** (914) 694-1122
Catherine Boscher-Murphy, Vice President, Financial Services
99 Church Street
White Plains, NY 10601

Berkeley College of New York City

New York, New York
www.berkeleycollege.edu
Four-year proprietary **Federal Code: 008556**

	Living at home
Tuition and fees:	$15,135
Books and supplies:	$900

Undergraduate aid. Need-based: Need-based aid available for full-time students. **Non-need-based:** Scholarships based on academics, alumni affiliation. **Additional information:** Alumni scholarship examination given in November and December. Full and partial scholarships awarded.

Policies to reduce costs. Tuition/fee waivers for family members, employees and their families. Tuition at time of enrollment guaranteed for 4 years; credit/placement for qualifying scores on AP, CLEP examinations.

Payment plans. Credit card, installment payment.

Application procedures. FAFSA required. No deadline. Applicants notified on rolling basis starting 3/1, must reply within 4 week(s) of notification. **Transfers:** No deadline. New York State TAP Grant eligibility may be affected.

Contact. **Financial aid office:** (212) 986-4343
Catherine Boscher-Murphy, Associate Vice President, Student Finance
3 East 43rd Street
New York, NY 10017

Briarcliffe College

Bethpage, New York
www.briarcliffe.edu
Four-year proprietary **Federal Code: 020757**

College costs. Technical division students pay additional $400 in fees.

	Living at home
Tuition and fees (2002-2003):	$12,680
Books and supplies:	$700
Personal expenses:	$1,500
Transportation:	$1,600

Undergraduate aid. Non-need-based: Scholarships based on academics, athletics.

Policies to reduce costs. Tuition/fee waivers for senior citizens, employees and their families. Credit/placement for qualifying scores on AP examinations.

Payment plans. Credit card, installment payment.

Application procedures. FAFSA, institutional form required. No deadline. Applicants notified on rolling basis.

Contact. **Financial aid office:** (516) 918-3600
Donna Michelson, Director of Financial Aid
1055 Stewart Avenue
Bethpage, NY 11714

Broome Community College

Binghamton, New York
www.sunybroome.edu
Two-year public **Federal Code: 002862**

	Living at home
Tuition and fees (2002-2003):	$2,732
Out-of-state:	$5,232
Per-credit charge:	$105
Per-credit out-of-state:	$210
Board only:	$750
Personal expenses:	$750
Transportation:	$975

Undergraduate aid. All financial aid based on need. 61% awarded as scholarships/grants, 39% as loans/jobs. Need-based aid available for part-time students.

Policies to reduce costs. Tuition/fee waivers for senior citizens, employees and their families. Credit/placement for qualifying scores on CLEP examinations.

Payment plans. Credit card, installment, deferred payment.

Application procedures. FAFSA required. Priority date 3/1; no closing date. Applicants notified on rolling basis starting 3/15, must reply within 2 week(s) of notification.

Contact. **Financial aid office:** (607) 778-5028
Douglas Lusasik, Director of Financial Aid
Box 1017
Binghamton, NY 13902

Bryant & Stratton Business Institute: Albany

Albany, New York
www.bryantstratton.edu
Two-year proprietary **Federal Code: 004749**

College costs. Technology fee $25 per course (maximum $100 per semester).

	Living at home
Tuition and fees:	$9,900
Per-credit charge:	$330
Books and supplies:	$1,000
Transportation:	$738

Undergraduate aid. All financial aid based on need. Need-based aid available for full-time and part-time students.

Policies to reduce costs. Tuition/fee waivers for unemployed or children of unemployed, employees and their families. Work study available nights, weekends and for part-time students.

Payment plans. Credit card, installment, deferred payment.

Application procedures. FAFSA required. No deadline. Applicants notified on rolling basis. **Transfers:** No deadline.

Contact. **Financial aid office:** (518) 437-1802
Kathleen Montague, Financial Aid Director
1259 Central Avenue
Albany, NY 12205

Bryant & Stratton Business Institute: Rochester

Rochester, New York
www.bryantstratton.edu
Two-year proprietary **Federal Code: 012470**

	Living at home
Tuition and fees:	$10,100
Per-credit charge:	$330
Books and supplies:	$700

Application procedures. FAFSA required. No deadline. Applicants notified on rolling basis.

Contact. **Financial aid office:** (585) 720-0660
Sam Summerville, Financial Aid Officer
150 Bellwood Drive
Rochester, NY 14606-4227

Bryant & Stratton Business Institute: Syracuse

Syracuse, New York
www.bryantstratton.edu
Two-year proprietary **Federal Code: 008276**

College costs. Technology fee $200 per year.

	Living at home	On-campus
Tuition and fees (2002-2003):	$9,900	$9,900
Per-credit charge:	$330	$330
Room and board:		$5,466
Books and supplies:	$1,000	$1,000
Personal expenses:	$1,350	$1,350
Transportation:	$1,720	$1,720

Policies to reduce costs. Tuition/fee waivers for employees and their families. Work study available nights, weekends and for part-time students.

Payment plans. Credit card, installment payment.

Application procedures. FAFSA required. No deadline. Applicants notified on rolling basis starting 10/1, must reply by 7/1. **Transfers:** Priority date 5/1; no deadline.

Contact. Financial aid office: (315) 472-6603
Tami Eiklor, Financial Aid Supervisor
953 James Street
Syracuse, NY 13203

Canisius College

Buffalo, New York
www.canisius.edu
Four-year private **Federal Code: 002681**

	Living at home	On-campus
Tuition and fees:	$20,193	$20,193
Room and board:		$7,970
Board only:	$1,500	
Books and supplies:	$500	$500
Personal expenses:	$630	$700
Transportation:	$430	$430

Undergraduate aid. Need-based: Average financial aid package for full-time students was $16,403. 70% awarded as scholarships/grants, 30% as loans/jobs. Need-based aid available for part-time students. **Non-need-based:** 42% awarded as scholarships/grants, 58% as loans/jobs. Scholarships based on academics, alumni affiliation, art, athletics, leadership, minority status, music/drama, religious affiliation. **Student debt:** 73% of graduating class borrowed to fund education; average debt was $18,635.

Freshman aid. Need-based: Out of 849 full-time freshmen, 774 applied for aid; 683 were judged to have need; of these 682 received aid. Average package met 87% of need. 185 students had full need met. Average scholarship/grant was $12,634; average loan $3,288. **Non-need based:** 196 full-time freshmen with need received non-need scholarships; 143 without need received awards; 18 received athletic scholarships.

Merit scholarships. Dean's Academic Scholarship; $10,000; 3.7 GPA and SAT 1100 or ACT 24 required. Benefactor's Scholarship; $7,700; 3.5 GPA and SAT 1000 or ACT 22 required. Academic Incentive Scholarship; $5,700; 3.0 GPA and SAT 1000 or ACT 22 required.

Policies to reduce costs. Tuition/fee waivers for children of alumni, minority students, family members, family of clergy, employees and their families. Credit/placement for qualifying scores on AP, IB, CLEP examinations.

Payment plans. Credit card, installment, deferred payment.

Application procedures. FAFSA, institutional form required. Priority date 2/15; no closing date. Applicants notified on rolling basis starting 3/15, must reply within 2 week(s) of notification. **Transfers:** No deadline.

Contact. Financial aid office: (800) 541-6348
Curtis Gaume, Director of Student Financial Aid
2001 Main Street
Buffalo, NY 14208-1098

Cayuga County Community College

Auburn, New York
www.cayuga-cc.edu
Two-year public **Federal Code: 002861**

	Living at home
Tuition and fees (2002-2003):	$2,972
Out-of-state:	$5,572
Per-credit charge:	$95
Per-credit out-of-state:	$190
Board only:	$1,650
Books and supplies:	$800
Personal expenses:	$500

Undergraduate aid. All financial aid based on need. 60% awarded as scholarships/grants, 40% as loans/jobs. Need-based aid available for part-time students.

Policies to reduce costs. Tuition/fee waivers for senior citizens, employees and their families. Credit/placement for qualifying scores on AP, CLEP examinations. Work study available nights, weekends and for part-time students.

Payment plans. Credit card payment.

Application procedures. FAFSA required. Closing date 5/1. Applicants notified on rolling basis starting 6/1.

Contact. Financial aid office: (315) 255-1743 ext. 2470
Judi Miladin, Director of Financial Aid
197 Franklin Street
Auburn, NY 13021-3099

Cazenovia College

Cazenovia, New York
www.cazenovia.edu
Four-year private **Federal Code: 002685**

	Living at home	On-campus
Tuition and fees (2002-2003):	$15,650	$15,650
Room and board:		$6,700
Books and supplies:	$800	$800
Personal expenses:	$500	$500
Transportation:	$500	$500

Undergraduate aid. Need-based: Average financial aid package for full-time students was $13,827; for part-time $4,219. 76% awarded as scholarships/grants, 24% as loans/jobs. **Non-need-based:** 34% awarded as scholarships/grants, 66% as loans/jobs. Scholarships based on academics. **Student debt:** 73% of graduating class borrowed to fund education; average debt was $15,515.

Freshman aid. Need-based: Out of 260 full-time freshmen, 245 applied for aid; 233 were judged to have need; of these 232 received aid. Average package met 80% of need. 49 students had full need met. Average scholarship/grant was $12,294; average loan $2,568. **Non-need based:** 31 full-time freshmen with need received non-need scholarships; 30 without need received awards.

Policies to reduce costs. Tuition/fee waivers for employees and their families. Credit/placement for qualifying scores on AP, CLEP examinations. Work study available weekends.

Payment plans. Credit card, installment, deferred payment.

Application procedures. FAFSA required. Priority date 3/15; no closing date. Applicants notified on rolling basis starting 3/15, must reply within 3 week(s) of notification. **Transfers:** Priority date 1/1; no deadline.

Contact. Financial aid office: (315) 655-7208
Christine Mandel, Director of Financial Aid
13 Nickerson Street
Cazenovia, NY 13035

City University of New York: Baruch College

New York, New York
www.baruch.cuny.edu
Four-year public **Federal Code: 007273**

	Living at home
Tuition and fees (2002-2003):	$3,500
Out-of-state:	$7,100
Board only:	$1,500
Personal expenses:	$2,718
Transportation:	$578

Undergraduate aid. Need-based: Average financial aid package for full-time students was $4,705. 83% awarded as scholarships/grants, 17% as loans/jobs. Need-based aid available for part-time students. **Non-need-based:** 77% awarded as scholarships/grants, 23% as loans/jobs. Scholarships based on academics, alumni affiliation, state/district residency. **Student debt:** 19% of graduating class borrowed to fund education; average debt was $9,400.

Freshman aid. Need-based: Out of 1,425 full-time freshmen, 1,411 applied for aid; 1,325 were judged to have need; of these 1,301 received aid. Average package met 69% of need. 241 students had full need met. Average scholarship/grant was $4,630; average loan $2,100. **Non-need based:** 1,412 full-time freshmen with need received non-need scholarships; 165 without need received awards.

Merit scholarships. Honors college scholarships based on SAT scores and high school GPA.

Policies to reduce costs. Tuition/fee waivers for senior citizens, employees and their families. Credit/placement for qualifying scores on AP, IB, CLEP examinations. Work study available for part-time students.

Payment plans. Credit card, installment, deferred payment.

Application procedures. FAFSA required. Priority date 3/15; closing date 4/30. Applicants notified on rolling basis starting 4/1, must reply by 6/1 or within 6 week(s) of notification. **Transfers:** Priority date 3/15; closing date 4/30.

Contact. Financial aid office: (212) 802-2300
James Murphy, Vice President, Enrollment and Director of Undergraduate Administration and Financial Aid
One Bernard Baruch Way, Box H-0720
New York, NY 10010-5585

City University of New York: Borough of Manhattan Community College

New York, New York
www.bmcc.cuny.edu
Two-year public **Federal Code: 002691**

	Living at home
Tuition and fees (2002-2003):	$2,730
Out-of-state:	$3,306
Per-credit charge:	$105
Per-credit out-of-state:	$130
Board only:	$975
Books and supplies:	$600
Personal expenses:	$1,781
Transportation:	$578

Undergraduate aid. All financial aid based on need. Need-based aid available for full-time and part-time students.

Policies to reduce costs. Tuition/fee waivers for senior citizens, employees and their families. Credit/placement for qualifying scores on AP, CLEP examinations.

Payment plans. Installment payment.

Application procedures. FAFSA, institutional form required. No deadline. Applicants notified on rolling basis starting 8/1, must reply within 2 week(s) of notification.

Contact. Financial aid office: (212) 220-1430
Howard Entin, Director of Financial Aid
199 Chambers Street
New York, NY 10007-1097

City University of New York: Bronx Community College

Bronx, New York
www.bcc.cuny.edu
Two-year public **Federal Code: 002692**

	Living at home
Tuition and fees (2002-2003):	$2,766
Out-of-state:	$3,342
Per-credit charge:	$105
Per-credit out-of-state:	$130
Books and supplies:	$600
Personal expenses:	$2,100
Transportation:	$675

Undergraduate aid. Need-based: Need-based aid available for full-time students.

Policies to reduce costs. Tuition/fee waivers for senior citizens, employees and their families. Credit/placement for qualifying scores on CLEP examinations.

Payment plans. Deferred payment.

Application procedures. FAFSA required. Closing date 7/15. Applicants notified on rolling basis starting 8/1.

Contact. Financial aid office: (718) 289-5700
Orlando Lopez, Financial Aid Officer
West 181st Street and University Avenue
Bronx, NY 10453

City University of New York: Brooklyn College

Brooklyn, New York
www.brooklyn.cuny.edu
Four-year public **Federal Code: 002687**

	Living at home
Tuition and fees (2002-2003):	$3,403
Out-of-state:	$7,003
Books and supplies:	$700
Personal expenses:	$2,300
Transportation:	$675

Undergraduate aid. Need-based: Average financial aid package for full-time students was $4,700; for part-time $2,300. 74% awarded as scholarships/grants, 26% as loans/jobs. **Non-need-based:** 93% awarded as scholarships/grants, 7% as loans/jobs. Scholarships based on academics, art, leadership, minority status, music/drama, state/district residency. **Student debt:** 30% of graduating class borrowed to fund education; average debt was $13,200.

Freshman aid. Need-based: Out of 1,194 full-time freshmen, 736 applied for aid; 687 were judged to have need; of these 660 received aid. Average package met 99% of need. 660 students had full need met. Average scholarship/grant was $2,900; average loan $1,675. **Non-need based:** 100 full-time freshmen with need received non-need scholarships; 125 without need received awards.

Merit scholarships. Presidential Scholarship Program for 25 freshman students for 8 tuition payments totalling $13,000. Brooklyn College Freshman Scholarships for $1,000 per year of study at Brooklyn College. Many scholarships for freshman students based on degree of study, academic merit, and community service.

Policies to reduce costs. Tuition/fee waivers for senior citizens, employees and their families. Credit/placement for qualifying scores on AP, IB, CLEP examinations. Work study available nights and weekends.

Payment plans. Credit card, installment, deferred payment.

Application procedures. FAFSA required. Priority date 4/1; no closing date. Applicants notified on rolling basis starting 6/1. **Transfers:** No deadline.

Contact. Financial aid office: (718) 951-5000
Sherwood Johnson, Director of Financial Aid
2900 Bedford
Brooklyn, NY 11210

City University of New York: City College

New York, New York
www.ccny.cuny.edu
Four-year public **Federal Code: 002688**

	Living at home
Tuition and fees (2002-2003):	$3,459
Out-of-state:	$7,059
Board only:	$1,500
Books and supplies:	$670
Personal expenses:	$2,718
Transportation:	$578

Policies to reduce costs. Tuition/fee waivers for senior citizens. Credit/placement for qualifying scores on AP, IB examinations.

Payment plans. Credit card, deferred payment.

Application procedures. FAFSA required. Priority date 5/15; no closing date. Applicants notified on rolling basis starting 5/15. **Transfers:** Priority date 5/1; no deadline.

Contact. Financial aid office: (212) 650-7000
Thelma Mason, Director of Financial Aid
Convent Avenue at 138th Street
New York, NY 10031

City University of New York: College of Staten Island

Staten Island, New York
www.csi.cuny.edu
Four-year public **Federal Code: 002698**

	Living at home
Tuition and fees (2002-2003):	$3,508
Out-of-state:	$7,108
Books and supplies:	$500
Personal expenses:	$2,100
Transportation:	$675

Undergraduate aid. Need-based: Average financial aid package for full-time students was $4,804; for part-time $3,078. 77% awarded as scholarships/grants, 23% as loans/jobs. **Non-need-based:** 98% awarded as scholarships/grants, 2% as loans/jobs. Scholarships based on academics, art, leadership, music/drama.

Freshman aid. Need-based: Out of 1,743 full-time freshmen, 1,334 applied for aid; 950 were judged to have need; of these 912 received aid. Average package met 59% of need. 65 students had full need met. Average scholarship/grant was $4,625; average loan $2,309. **Non-need based:** 158 full-time freshmen with need received non-need scholarships; 113 without need received awards.

Policies to reduce costs. Tuition/fee waivers for senior citizens, employees and their families. Credit/placement for qualifying scores on AP, CLEP examinations.

Payment plans. Credit card, installment, deferred payment.

Application procedures. FAFSA required. No deadline. Applicants notified on rolling basis starting 6/30.

Contact. Financial aid office: (718) 982-2030
Sherman Whipkey, Director of Financial Aid
2800 Victory Boulevard
Staten Island, NY 10314

City University of New York: Hostos Community College

Bronx, New York
www.hostos.cuny.edu
Two-year public **Federal Code: 008611**

	Living at home
Tuition and fees (2002-2003):	$2,726
Out-of-state:	$3,302
Per-credit charge:	$105
Per-credit out-of-state:	$130
Books and supplies:	$692
Personal expenses:	$2,667
Transportation:	$578

Undergraduate aid. Need-based: Average financial aid package for full-time students was $3,250; for part-time $1,500. 86% awarded as scholarships/grants, 14% as loans/jobs.

Freshman aid. Need-based: Average package met 60% of need. Average loan $1,000.

Policies to reduce costs. Tuition/fee waivers for senior citizens, employees and their families. Work study available for part-time students.

Payment plans. Credit card, installment, deferred payment.

Application procedures. FAFSA, institutional form required. Priority date 7/1; no closing date. Applicants notified on rolling basis, must reply within 3 week(s) of notification. **Transfers:** No deadline.

Contact. Financial aid office: (718) 518-6555
Joseph Alicea, Director of Financial Aid
120 East 149th Street, Room D210
Bronx, NY 10451

City University of New York: Hunter College

New York, New York
www.hunter.cuny.edu
Four-year public **Federal Code: 002689**

College costs. Dormitory availability very limited.

	Living at home	On-campus
Tuition and fees (2002-2003):	$3,500	$3,500
Out-of-state:	$7,100	$7,100
Room only:		$1,980
Books and supplies:	$500	$500
Personal expenses:	$2,360	$2,455
Transportation:	$675	$675

Undergraduate aid. Need-based: Need-based aid available for full-time and part-time students. **Non-need-based:** Scholarships based on academics. **Additional information:** Tuition fund grants available.

Policies to reduce costs. Tuition/fee waivers for senior citizens. Credit/placement for qualifying scores on AP, IB, CLEP examinations.

Payment plans. Credit card, deferred payment.

Application procedures. FAFSA required. Priority date 5/1; no closing date. Applicants notified on rolling basis.

Contact. Financial aid office: (212) 772-4820
Kevin McGowan, Director of Financial Aid
695 Park Avenue
New York, NY 10021

City University of New York: John Jay College of Criminal Justice

New York, New York
www.jjay.cuny.edu
Four-year public **Federal Code: 002693**

	Living at home
Tuition and fees (2002-2003):	$3,459
Out-of-state:	$7,059
Books and supplies:	$875
Personal expenses:	$3,550
Transportation:	$1,075

Undergraduate aid. Need-based: Average financial aid package for full-time students was $5,100. 81% awarded as scholarships/grants, 19% as loans/jobs. Need-based aid available for part-time students. **Non-need-based:** 33% awarded as scholarships/grants, 67% as loans/jobs. Scholarships based on academics, athletics, state/district residency. **Student debt:** 50% of graduating class borrowed to fund education; average debt was $10,000.

Freshman aid. Need-based: Out of 1,697 full-time freshmen, 1,612 applied for aid; 1,612 were judged to have need; of these 1,128 received aid. Average package met 70% of need. Average loan $2,400. **Non-need based:** 14 without need received awards.

Policies to reduce costs. Tuition/fee waivers for senior citizens, employees and their families. Credit/placement for qualifying scores on AP, CLEP examinations.

Payment plans. Credit card, installment, deferred payment.

Application procedures. FAFSA required. Priority date 6/1; no closing date. Applicants notified on rolling basis starting 7/15, must reply within 2 week(s) of notification.

Contact. **Financial aid office:** (212) 237-8151
Arnold Osansky, Associate Director of Financial Aid
445 West 59th Street
New York, NY 10019

City University of New York: Kingsborough Community College

Brooklyn, New York
www.kbcc.cuny.edu
Two-year public **Federal Code: 002694**

	Living at home
Tuition and fees (2002-2003):	$2,600
Out-of-state:	$3,176
Per-credit charge:	$105
Per-credit out-of-state:	$130
Books and supplies:	$500
Personal expenses:	$2,100
Transportation:	$675

Undergraduate aid. All financial aid based on need. Need-based aid available for full-time and part-time students.

Policies to reduce costs. Tuition/fee waivers for senior citizens, employees and their families.

Payment plans. Installment, deferred payment.

Application procedures. FAFSA required. Priority date 8/1; no closing date. Applicants notified on rolling basis starting 8/15, must reply within 2 week(s) of notification.

Contact. **Financial aid office:** (718) 368-4644
Wayne Harewood, Director of Financial Aid
2001 Oriental Boulevard
Brooklyn, NY 11235

City University of New York: La Guardia Community College

Long Island City, New York
www.lagcc.cuny.edu
Two-year public **Federal Code: 010051**

	Living at home
Tuition and fees (2002-2003):	$2,772
Out-of-state:	$3,348
Per-credit charge:	$105
Per-credit out-of-state:	$130
Board only:	$2,425
Books and supplies:	$600
Personal expenses:	$1,761
Transportation:	$578

Policies to reduce costs. Tuition/fee waivers for senior citizens. Credit/placement for qualifying scores on AP, CLEP examinations. Work study available nights, weekends and for part-time students.

Payment plans. Deferred payment.

Application procedures. FAFSA required. No deadline. Applicants notified on rolling basis starting 8/1, must reply within 4 week(s) of notification.

Contact. **Financial aid office:** (718) 482-7200
Gail Baksh-Jarrett, Director of Financial Aid
31-10 Thomson Avenue
Long Island City, NY 11101

City University of New York: Medgar Evers College

Brooklyn, New York
www.mec.cuny.edu
Four-year public **Federal Code: 010097**

	Living at home
Tuition and fees (2002-2003):	$3,432
Out-of-state:	$7,032
Board only:	$1,500
Books and supplies:	$500
Personal expenses:	$2,355
Transportation:	$810

Policies to reduce costs. Tuition/fee waivers for senior citizens, employees and their families. Credit/placement for qualifying scores on AP, IB, CLEP examinations.

Payment plans. Credit card, installment, deferred payment.

Application procedures. FAFSA required. No deadline. Applicants notified on rolling basis, must reply within 2 week(s) of notification.

Contact. **Financial aid office:** (718) 270-6139
Louise Martin, Director of Financial Aid
1150 Carroll Street Room C-115
Brooklyn, NY 11225

City University of New York: Queens College

Flushing, New York
www.qc.edu
Four-year public **Federal Code: 002690**

	Living at home
Tuition and fees (2002-2003):	$3,553
Out-of-state:	$7,153
Board only:	$2,259
Books and supplies:	$670
Personal expenses:	$1,500
Transportation:	$675

Undergraduate aid. **Need-based:** Average financial aid package for full-time students was $8,600; for part-time $6,800. 67% awarded as scholarships/grants, 33% as loans/jobs. **Non-need-based:** Scholarships based on academics, athletics, minority status, music/drama, religious affiliation, state/district residency. **Student debt:** 38% of graduating class borrowed to fund education; average debt was $12,000. **Additional information:** SAT I or ACT required for scholarship applicants.

Freshman aid. **Need-based:** Out of 1,204 full-time freshmen, 1,174 applied for aid; 1,092 were judged to have need; of these 1,004 received aid. Average package met 95% of need. 953 students had full need met. Average scholarship/grant was $2,450; average loan $2,000. **Non-need based:** 145 full-time freshmen with need received non-need scholarships; 1,204 without need received awards; 21 received athletic scholarships.

Merit scholarships. Regents Award for Deceased or Disabled Veterans ($450 a year), Vietnam Veteran Tuition Aid Program (cost of tuition per semester), Regents Award for children of deceased police officers, firefighters, or corrections officers ($450 a year), Paul Douglas Teacher Scholarship Program (up to $5,000 a year), State Aid to Native Americans ($1,100 a year), SEEK Presidential Scholarship, Beinstock Memorial Scholarship for students with disabilities, CMP Publications Scholarship in Journalism or English, Daly Scholarship in the Physical Sciences, Foster Scholarship for women and minorities, Kupferberg Memorial Scholarship, Linakis Scholarship, Mitsui USA Scholarships, Nagdimon Scholarship, Queens College Scholarships, Weprin Memorial Scholarship in the Public Interest.

Policies to reduce costs. Tuition/fee waivers for senior citizens. Credit/placement for qualifying scores on AP examinations. Work study available for part-time students.

Payment plans. Credit card, installment payment.

Application procedures. FAFSA, institutional form required. Priority date 2/1; no closing date. Applicants notified on rolling basis starting 3/1, must reply within 3 week(s) of notification. **Transfers:** Priority date 5/1; no deadline.

Contact. **Financial aid office:** (718) 997-5123
Rena Smith-Kiawu, Director of Financial Aid
65-30 Kissena Boulevard, Jefferson 117
Flushing, NY 11367

City University of New York: Queensborough Community College

Bayside, New York
www.qcc.cuny.edu
Two-year public **Federal Code: 002697**

	Living at home
Tuition and fees (2002-2003):	$2,766
Out-of-state:	$3,342
Per-credit charge:	$105
Per-credit out-of-state:	$130
Books and supplies:	$500
Personal expenses:	$2,100
Transportation:	$675

Undergraduate aid. Need-based: Need-based aid available for full-time students.

Policies to reduce costs. Tuition/fee waivers for senior citizens, employees and their families. Credit/placement for qualifying scores on CLEP examinations.

Payment plans. Credit card, installment payment.

Application procedures. FAFSA, institutional form required. No deadline. Applicants notified on rolling basis starting 7/15.

Contact. Financial aid office: (718) 631-6262
Mary White, Director of Financial Aid
Springfield Boulevard & 56th Avenue
Bayside, NY 11364-1497

City University of New York: York College

Jamaica, New York
www.york.cuny.edu
Four-year public **Federal Code: 004759**

	Living at home
Tuition and fees (2002-2003):	$3,442
Out-of-state:	$7,042
Books and supplies:	$600
Personal expenses:	$4,186
Transportation:	$676

Undergraduate aid. All financial aid based on need. 86% awarded as scholarships/grants, 14% as loans/jobs. Need-based aid available for part-time students.

Policies to reduce costs. Tuition/fee waivers for senior citizens, employees and their families. Credit/placement for qualifying scores on IB, CLEP examinations. Work study available for part-time students.

Payment plans. Deferred payment.

Application procedures. FAFSA required. No deadline. Applicants notified on rolling basis starting 3/1.

Contact. Financial aid office: (718) 262-2000
Anne Balkcon, Director of Financial Aid
94-20 Guy R. Brewer Boulevard
Jamaica, NY 11451-9989

Clarkson University

Potsdam, New York
www.clarkson.edu
Four-year private **Federal Code: 002699**

	Living at home	On-campus
Tuition and fees:	$23,500	$23,500
Room and board:		$8,726
Board only:	$4,020	
Books and supplies:	$900	$900
Personal expenses:	$1,617	$1,617

Undergraduate aid. Need-based: Average financial aid package for full-time students was $15,500; for part-time $4,894. 59% awarded as scholarships/grants, 41% as loans/jobs. **Non-need-based:** 85% awarded as scholarships/grants, 15% as loans/jobs. Scholarships based on academics, alumni affiliation, leadership, minority status. **Student debt:** 83% of graduating class borrowed to fund education; average debt was $18,148.

Freshman aid. Need-based: Out of 725 full-time freshmen, 673 applied for aid; 583 were judged to have need; of these 583 received aid. Average package met 87% of need. 149 students had full need met. Average scholarship/grant was $7,600; average loan $5,500. **Non-need based:** 232 full-time freshmen with need received non-need scholarships; 100 without need received awards; 4 received athletic scholarships.

Policies to reduce costs. Tuition/fee waivers for minority students, employees and their families. Credit/placement for qualifying scores on AP, CLEP examinations. Work study available nights and weekends.

Payment plans. Installment payment.

Application procedures. FAFSA, institutional form required. Priority date 3/1; no closing date. Applicants notified on rolling basis starting 3/23, must reply by 5/1 or within 2 week(s) of notification. Early decision closing date 12/1. **Transfers:** Closing date 4/15. Presidential Scholarships, Phi Theta Kappa scholarships and Alpha Beta Gamma Awards, in addition to state and federal programs.

Contact. Financial aid office: (315) 268-6400
Suzanne Davis, Director of Financial Assistance
Holcroft House
Potsdam, NY 13699-5605

Clinton Community College

Plattsburgh, New York
www.clinton.edu
Two-year public **Federal Code: 006787**

	Living at home
Tuition and fees (2002-2003):	$2,638
Out-of-state:	$5,138
Per-credit charge:	$105
Per-credit out-of-state:	$210
Board only:	$1,200
Books and supplies:	$675
Personal expenses:	$800
Transportation:	$1,275

Undergraduate aid. All financial aid based on need. 65% awarded as scholarships/grants, 35% as loans/jobs. Need-based aid available for part-time students. **Student debt:** 65% of graduating class borrowed to fund education; average debt was $5,249.

Policies to reduce costs. Tuition/fee waivers for senior citizens. Credit/placement for qualifying scores on AP, IB, CLEP examinations. Work study available for part-time students.

Payment plans. Credit card, deferred payment.

Application procedures. FAFSA required. Priority date 6/2; no closing date. Applicants notified on rolling basis starting 5/1, must reply within 2 week(s) of notification.

Contact. Financial aid office: (518) 562-4125
Karen Goodrich, Director of Financial Aid
136 Clinton Point Drive
Plattsburgh, NY 12901-4297

Cochran School of Nursing-St. John's Riverside Hospital

Yonkers, New York
www.riversidehealth.org
Two-year private **Federal Code: 006443**

College costs. $200 for uniforms. $770 required fees include lab fees. Books/supplies: $550. Personal expenses: $2,037. Transportation: $946.

Undergraduate aid. All financial aid based on need. Need-based aid available for full-time and part-time students.

Policies to reduce costs. Credit/placement for qualifying scores on AP, CLEP examinations.

Payment plans. Credit card, installment payment.

Application procedures. FAFSA required. No deadline. Applicants notified on rolling basis. **Transfers:** No deadline.

Contact. Financial aid office: (914) 964-4265
Geraldine Bailey, Financial Aid Officer
967 North Broadway
Yonkers, NY 10701

Colgate University

Hamilton, New York
www.colgate.edu
Four-year private **Federal Code: 002701**

	Living at home	On-campus
Tuition and fees (2002-2003):	$28,355	$28,355
Room and board:		$6,775
Books and supplies:	$620	$620
Personal expenses:		$860

Undergraduate aid. All financial aid based on need. Average financial aid package for full-time students was $23,490. 88% awarded as scholarships/grants, 12% as loans/jobs. **Student debt:** 40% of graduating class borrowed to fund education; average debt was $12,984.

Freshman aid. Out of 731 full-time freshmen, 411 applied for aid; 357 were judged to have need; of these 357 received aid. Average package met 100% of need. 357 students had full need met. Average scholarship/grant was $22,001; average loan $2,331.

Policies to reduce costs. Prepayment discount; credit/placement for qualifying scores on AP, IB, CLEP examinations. Work study available nights, weekends and for part-time students.

Payment plans. Installment payment.

Application procedures. FAFSA, CSS PROFILE required. Closing date 2/1. Applicants notified by 4/1, must reply by 5/1 or within 2 week(s) of notification. Early decision closing date 11/15. **Transfers:** Closing date 3/15.

Contact. **Financial aid office:** (315) 228-7431
Marcelle Tyburski, Director of Financial Aid
13 Oak Drive
Hamilton, NY 13346-1383

College of Aeronautics

Flushing, New York
www.aero.edu
Four-year private **Federal Code: 002665**

	Living at home
Tuition and fees (2002-2003):	$9,650
Board only:	$1,000
Books and supplies:	$1,050
Personal expenses:	$1,950
Transportation:	$1,350

Undergraduate aid. All financial aid based on need. Average financial aid package for full-time students was $1,950. 68% awarded as scholarships/grants, 32% as loans/jobs. Need-based aid available for part-time students. **Student debt:** 92% of graduating class borrowed to fund education; average debt was $15,000.

Freshman aid. Out of 424 full-time freshmen, 295 applied for aid; 295 were judged to have need; of these 295 received aid. Average package met 50% of need. 108 students had full need met. Average scholarship/grant was $2,000; average loan $2,625.

Policies to reduce costs. Tuition/fee waivers for employees and their families. Credit/placement for qualifying scores on AP, CLEP examinations.

Payment plans. Credit card, installment payment.

Application procedures. FAFSA required. Priority date 3/15; closing date 7/2. Applicants notified on rolling basis. **Transfers:** No deadline.

Contact. **Financial aid office:** (800) 776-2371
Melanie Williams, Director, Financial Aid
La Guardia Airport
Flushing, NY 11369

College of Mount St. Vincent

Riverdale, New York
www.mountsaintvincent.edu
Four-year private **Federal Code: 002703**

	Living at home	On-campus
Tuition and fees (projected):	$19,000	$19,000
Room and board:		$7,800
Board only:	$1,500	
Books and supplies:	$800	$800
Personal expenses:	$850	$850
Transportation:	$750	$200

Undergraduate aid. All financial aid based on need. Average financial aid package for full-time students was $15,000. 67% awarded as scholarships/grants, 33% as loans/jobs. Need-based aid available for part-time students. **Student debt:** 80% of graduating class borrowed to fund education; average debt was $14,000.

Freshman aid. Out of 338 full-time freshmen, 325 applied for aid; 291 were judged to have need; of these 291 received aid. Average package met 78% of need. Average scholarship/grant was $9,000; average loan $2,500.

Policies to reduce costs. Tuition/fee waivers for children of alumni, senior citizens, family of clergy, employees and their families. Credit/placement for qualifying scores on AP, IB, CLEP examinations.

Payment plans. Credit card, installment payment.

Application procedures. FAFSA required. Priority date 3/15; no closing date. Applicants notified on rolling basis starting 3/1, must reply by 5/1 or within 2 week(s) of notification. Early decision closing date 11/15. **Transfers:** Priority date 5/15; no deadline.

Contact. **Financial aid office:** (718) 405-3289
Monica Simotas, Director of Financial Aid
6301 Riverdale Avenue
Riverdale, NY 10471-1093

College of New Rochelle

New Rochelle, New York
www.cnr.edu
Four-year private **Federal Code: 002704**

	Living at home	On-campus
Tuition and fees (projected):	$14,650	$14,650
Room and board:		$7,150
Books and supplies:	$600	$600
Personal expenses:	$1,000	$1,000
Transportation:	$1,000	$1,000

Undergraduate aid. All financial aid based on need. 41% awarded as scholarships/grants, 59% as loans/jobs. Need-based aid available for part-time students.

Policies to reduce costs. Tuition/fee waivers for family members, employees and their families. Credit/placement for qualifying scores on AP, CLEP examinations.

Payment plans. Credit card, installment, deferred payment.

Application procedures. FAFSA, institutional form required. Priority date 9/1; no closing date. Applicants notified on rolling basis starting 1/1, must reply within 1 week(s) of notification. Early decision closing date 11/1.

Contact. **Financial aid office:** (914) 632-5300
Ronald Pollack, Director of Financial Aid
Castle Place
New Rochelle, NY 10805-2308

College of New Rochelle: School of New Resources

New Rochelle, New York
www.cnr.edu
Four-year private **Federal Code: 002704**

	Living at home
Tuition and fees:	$6,810
Books and supplies:	$600
Personal expenses:	$500
Transportation:	$500

Undergraduate aid. All financial aid based on need. 74% awarded as scholarships/grants, 26% as loans/jobs. Need-based aid available for part-time students.

Policies to reduce costs. Tuition/fee waivers for family members, employees and their families. Credit/placement for qualifying scores on CLEP examinations.

Payment plans. Credit card, installment, deferred payment.

Application procedures. FAFSA, institutional form required. No deadline. Applicants notified on rolling basis.

Contact. **Financial aid office:** (914) 654-5224
Ronald Pollack, Director of Financial Aid
Newman Hall, Castle Place
New Rochelle, NY 10805-2339

Columbia University: Columbia College

New York, New York
www.college.columbia.edu
Four-year private **Federal Code: E00485**

	Living at home	On-campus
Tuition and fees (2002-2003):	$28,206	$28,206
Room and board:		$8,546
Books and supplies:	$1,000	$1,000
Personal expenses:		$1,060

Undergraduate aid. All financial aid based on need. Average financial aid package for full-time students was $25,327. 77% awarded as scholarships/grants, 23% as loans/jobs. **Student debt:** 41% of graduating class borrowed to fund education; average debt was $15,331.

Freshman aid. Out of 1,038 full-time freshmen, 565 applied for aid; 459 were judged to have need; of these 459 received aid. Average package met 100% of need. 459 students had full need met. Average scholarship/grant was $23,648; average loan $3,372.

Policies to reduce costs. Tuition/fee waivers for employees and their families. Prepayment discount; credit/placement for qualifying scores on AP, IB examinations. Work study available nights and weekends.

Payment plans. Credit card, installment payment.

Application procedures. FAFSA, institutional form, CSS PROFILE required. Closing date 2/10. Applicants notified by 4/1, must reply by 5/1 or within 4 week(s) of notification. Early decision closing date 11/1. **Transfers:** Closing date 4/1. Institutional financial aid for transfer candidates very limited.

Contact. **Financial aid office:** (212) 854-3711
David Charlow, Director of Student Financial Planning
1130 Amsterdam Avenue MC2807
New York, NY 10027

Columbia University: Fu Foundation School of Engineering and Applied Science

New York, New York
www.engineering.columbia.edu
Four-year private **Federal Code: E00486**

	Living at home	On-campus
Tuition and fees (2002-2003):	$28,206	$28,206
Room and board:		$8,546
Books and supplies:	$1,000	$1,000
Personal expenses:		$1,060

Undergraduate aid. All financial aid based on need. Average financial aid package for full-time students was $25,613. 76% awarded as scholarships/grants, 24% as loans/jobs. **Student debt:** 44% of graduating class borrowed to fund education; average debt was $15,391.

Freshman aid. Out of 332 full-time freshmen, 194 applied for aid; 156 were judged to have need; of these 156 received aid. Average package met 100% of need. 156 students had full need met. Average scholarship/grant was $22,441; average loan $3,325.

Policies to reduce costs. Tuition/fee waivers for employees and their families. Prepayment discount; credit/placement for qualifying scores on AP, IB examinations. Work study available nights and weekends.

Payment plans. Credit card, installment payment.

Application procedures. FAFSA, institutional form, CSS PROFILE required. Closing date 2/10. Applicants notified by 4/1, must reply by 5/1. Early decision closing date 11/1. **Transfers:** Closing date 4/1. Institutional financial aid very limited for transfer applicants.

Contact. **Financial aid office:** (212) 854-3711
David Charlow, Associate Dean of Student Affairs
1130 Amsterdam Avenue MCZ807
New York, NY 10027

Columbia University: School of Nursing

New York, New York
www.nursing.hs.columbia.edu
Upper-division private **Federal Code: E00124**

College costs. No annual meal plan; students buy meal cards in $50 increments.

	Living at home	On-campus
Tuition and fees (projected):	$27,992	$27,992
Room only:		$4,600
Books and supplies:	$1,600	$1,600
Personal expenses:	$1,200	$1,200
Transportation:	$800	$800

Undergraduate aid. **Need-based:** Need-based aid available for full-time and part-time students.

Policies to reduce costs. Tuition/fee waivers for employees and their families. Tuition at time of enrollment guaranteed for 2 years; credit/placement for qualifying scores on IB, CLEP examinations.

Payment plans. Credit card payment.

Application procedures. FAFSA required. No deadline. Applicants notified on rolling basis starting 1/1, must reply within 2 week(s) of notification.

Contact. **Financial aid office:** (212) 305-5756
Oscar Vasquez, Director of Financial Aid
617 West 168th Street
New York, NY 10032

Concordia College

Bronxville, New York
www.concordia-ny.edu
Four-year private **Federal Code: 002709**

	Living at home	On-campus
Tuition and fees (2002-2003):	$16,800	$16,800
Room and board:		$7,400
Books and supplies:	$600	$600
Personal expenses:	$850	$850
Transportation:	$350	$350

Undergraduate aid. **Need-based:** 69% awarded as scholarships/grants, 31% as loans/jobs. Need-based aid available for part-time students. **Non-need-based:** 54% awarded as scholarships/grants, 46% as loans/jobs. Scholarships based on academics, athletics, leadership, music/drama.

Merit scholarships. Fellows Scholarship at $8,000 a year for 1200 SAT and 95 average. Merit scholarships ranging between $4,000-6,000 for 80 average and above. Athletic, leadership, academic, and music scholarships and Lutheran students grants available.

Policies to reduce costs. Tuition/fee waivers for senior citizens, employees and their families. Credit/placement for qualifying scores on AP, IB, CLEP examinations. Work study available nights, weekends and for part-time students.

Payment plans. Credit card, installment, deferred payment.

Application procedures. FAFSA required. Priority date 4/1; no closing date. Applicants notified on rolling basis starting 4/1, must reply by 5/1 or within 3 week(s) of notification. Early decision closing date 11/15. **Transfers:** No deadline.

Contact. **Financial aid office:** (914) 337-9300
Kenneth Fick, Director of Financial Aid
171 White Plains Road
Bronxville, NY 10708

Cooper Union for the Advancement of Science and Art

New York, New York
www.cooper.edu
Four-year private **Federal Code: 002710**

College costs. Every student admitted receives full tuition scholarship for duration of enrollment. Tuition $28,000; required fees $1,250; room $9,000. Board: $1,500. Books/supplies: $1,800. Personal expenses: $1,575. Transportation: $720.

Undergraduate aid. **Need-based:** Average financial aid package for full-time students was $5,578. 71% awarded as scholarships/grants, 29% as loans/jobs. **Non-need-based:** Scholarships based on academics. **Student debt:** 40% of graduating class borrowed to fund education; average debt was $9,250. **Additional information:** All students receive full-tuition scholarships. Students able to document need receive financial aid package that may include combination of grants, loans, work-study, internships.

Freshman aid. **Need-based:** Out of 223 full-time freshmen, 152 applied for aid; 81 were judged to have need; of these 81 received aid. Average package met 91% of need. 62 students had full need met. Average scholarship/grant was $3,237; average loan $2,361. **Non-need based:** 81 full-time freshmen with need received non-need scholarships.

Policies to reduce costs. Tuition/fee waivers for employees and their families. Credit/placement for qualifying scores on AP examinations.

Application procedures. FAFSA, CSS PROFILE required. Priority date 4/15; closing date 6/1. Applicants notified by 6/1, must reply by 6/30 or within 2 week(s) of notification. Early decision closing date 12/1. **Transfers:** No deadline.

Contact. Financial aid office: (212) 353-4130
Mary Ruokonen, Director of Financial Aid
30 Cooper Square, Suite 300
New York, NY 10003-7183

Cornell University

Ithaca, New York
www.cornell.edu
Four-year private **Federal Code: 002711**

College costs. Tuition and fees for statutory divisions (Agriculture and Life Science, Human Ecology, and Industrial and Labor Relations): $13,150 in-state, $23,500 out-of-state.

	Living at home	On-campus
Tuition and fees (2002-2003):	$27,394	$27,394
Room and board:		$8,980
Board only:	$3,580	
Books and supplies:	$600	$600
Personal expenses:	$1,220	$1,220

Undergraduate aid. All financial aid based on need. Average financial aid package for full-time students was $23,017. 63% awarded as scholarships/grants, 37% as loans/jobs. **Student debt:** 51% of graduating class borrowed to fund education; average debt was $15,587.

Freshman aid. Out of 3,003 full-time freshmen, 1,883 applied for aid; 1,481 were judged to have need; of these 1,481 received aid. Average package met 100% of need. 1481 students had full need met. Average scholarship/grant was $17,021; average loan $5,811.

Policies to reduce costs. Tuition/fee waivers for employees and their families. Credit/placement for qualifying scores on AP, IB examinations.

Payment plans. Installment payment.

Application procedures. FAFSA, CSS PROFILE required. Closing date 2/11. Applicants notified by 4/1, must reply by 5/1 or within 2 week(s) of notification. Early decision closing date 11/10. **Transfers:** Closing date 2/11. Submit Cornell aid application forms in addition to regular required forms.

Contact. Financial aid office: (607) 255-2000
Thomas Keane, Director, Financial Aid and Student Employment
410 Thurston Avenue
Ithaca, NY 14850-2488

Corning Community College

Corning, New York
www.corning-cc.edu
Two-year public **Federal Code: 002863**

	Living at home
Tuition and fees (2002-2003):	$2,986
Out-of-state:	$5,650
Per-credit charge:	$111
Per-credit out-of-state:	$222
Personal expenses:	$425
Transportation:	$1,150

Undergraduate aid. All financial aid based on need. Need-based aid available for full-time and part-time students.

Policies to reduce costs. Tuition/fee waivers for senior citizens, employees and their families. Credit/placement for qualifying scores on AP, CLEP examinations. Work study available for part-time students.

Payment plans. Credit card, installment payment.

Application procedures. FAFSA required. Priority date 4/1; no closing date. Applicants notified on rolling basis starting 4/15, must reply within 2 week(s) of notification.

Contact. Financial aid office: (607) 962-9011
Barbara Snow, Director of Financial Aid
One Academic Drive
Corning, NY 14830

Culinary Institute of America

Hyde Park, New York
www.ciachef.edu
Four-year private **Federal Code: 007304**

College costs. Additional costs for uniforms, books, supplies: $820 for culinary program, $720 for baking and pastry program.

	Living at home	On-campus
Tuition and fees (2002-2003):	$17,360	$17,360
Room and board:		$6,200
Board only:	$3,670	
Personal expenses:	$2,550	$2,550
Transportation:	$750	$1,200

Undergraduate aid. Need-based: Average financial aid package for full-time students was $8,500. 35% awarded as scholarships/grants, 65% as loans/jobs. **Non-need-based:** 27% awarded as scholarships/grants, 73% as loans/jobs. Scholarships based on academics, job skills, leadership, minority status. **Student debt:** 91% of graduating class borrowed to fund education; average debt was $18,000.

Merit scholarships. Cream of the Crop Scholarship; up to $20,000; 10 per year; for prospective students with outstanding academic and leadership skills.

Policies to reduce costs. Tuition/fee waivers for employees and their families. Work study available nights and weekends.

Payment plans. Credit card, installment payment.

Application procedures. FAFSA, institutional form required. Closing date 2/15. Applicants notified by 4/1, must reply by 5/1 or within 4 week(s) of notification.

Contact. Financial aid office: (845) 451-1243
Patricia Arcuri, Director of Financial Aid
1946 Campus Drive
Hyde Park, NY 12538

D'Youville College

Buffalo, New York
www.dyc.edu
Four-year private **Federal Code: 002712**

	Living at home	On-campus
Tuition and fees (2002-2003):	$13,336	$13,336
Room and board:		$6,560
Books and supplies:	$680	$680
Personal expenses:	$680	$680
Transportation:	$640	$640

Undergraduate aid. Need-based: Average financial aid package for full-time students was $12,612; for part-time $17,384. 70% awarded as scholarships/grants, 30% as loans/jobs. **Non-need-based:** 46% awarded as scholarships/grants, 54% as loans/jobs. Scholarships based on academics.

Freshman aid. Need-based: Average package met 91% of need. Average scholarship/grant was $9,364; average loan $3,208.

Policies to reduce costs. Tuition/fee waivers for children of alumni, senior citizens, family members, family of clergy, employees and their families. Credit/placement for qualifying scores on AP, IB, CLEP examinations. Work study available nights, weekends and for part-time students.

Payment plans. Credit card, installment, deferred payment.

Application procedures. FAFSA required. Priority date 3/1; no closing date. Applicants notified on rolling basis starting 4/1, must reply within 3 week(s) of notification. **Transfers:** Must submit financial aid transcripts from all previously attended institutions even if no aid was received.

Contact. Financial aid office: (716) 851-7691
Lorraine Metz, Director of Financial Aid
320 Porter Avenue
Buffalo, NY 14201-1084

Daemen College

Amherst, New York
www.daemen.edu
Four-year private **Federal Code: 002808**

College costs. Part-time tuition charges include fees.

	Living at home	On-campus
Tuition and fees (2002-2003):	$14,270	$14,270
Room and board:		$6,700
Books and supplies:	$790	$790
Personal expenses:	$800	$800
Transportation:	$700	$700

Undergraduate aid. Need-based: Average financial aid package for full-time students was $10,606; for part-time $6,260. 42% awarded as scholarships/grants, 58% as loans/jobs. **Non-need-based:** 80% awarded as scholarships/grants, 20% as loans/jobs. Scholarships based on academics, alumni affiliation, art, athletics. **Student debt:** 75% of graduating class borrowed to fund education; average debt was $12,638.

Freshman aid. Need-based: Out of 340 full-time freshmen, 338 applied for aid; 313 were judged to have need; of these 313 received aid. Average package met 71% of need. 22 students had full need met. Average scholarship/grant was $6,651; average loan $3,163. **Non-need based:** 31 full-time freshmen with need received non-need scholarships; 4 without need received awards; 11 received athletic scholarships.

Merit scholarships. President's Scholarship, Dean's Scholarship and Alumni Grant; $2,000-$8,000; based on high school GPA, SAT I scores and resident status.

Policies to reduce costs. Tuition/fee waivers for senior citizens, family members, employees and their families. Credit/placement for qualifying scores on AP, IB, CLEP examinations. Work study available nights and weekends.

Payment plans. Credit card, installment payment.

Application procedures. FAFSA required. Priority date 3/15; no closing date. Applicants notified on rolling basis starting 2/15, must reply within 2 week(s) of notification. **Transfers:** No deadline.

Contact. Financial aid office: (716) 839-8254
Jeffrey Pagano, Director of Financial Aid
4380 Main Street
Amherst, NY 14226-3592

DeVry Institute of Technology: New York

Long Island City, New York
www.ny.devry.edu
Four-year proprietary **Federal Code: 003099**

	Living at home
Tuition and fees:	$11,265
Books and supplies:	$1,100
Personal expenses:	$1,816
Transportation:	$1,336

Undergraduate aid. All financial aid based on need. Average financial aid package for full-time students was $9,227; for part-time $5,925. 39% awarded as scholarships/grants, 61% as loans/jobs.

Freshman aid. Average package met 46% of need. Average scholarship/grant was $5,177; average loan $3,250.

Policies to reduce costs. Tuition/fee waivers for employees and their families.

Payment plans. Credit card, installment, deferred payment.

Application procedures. FAFSA required. No deadline. Applicants notified on rolling basis starting 7/1. **Transfers:** No deadline.

Contact. Financial aid office: (718) 472-2728
Elvira Senese, Director, Student Finance
30-20 Thompson Avenue
Long Island City, NY 11101

Dominican College of Blauvelt

Orangeburg, New York
www.dc.edu
Four-year private **Federal Code: 002713**

	Living at home	On-campus
Tuition and fees (2002-2003):	$15,650	$15,650
Room and board:		$7,770
Board only:	$1,800	
Books and supplies:	$1,800	$1,800
Personal expenses:	$1,200	$1,200
Transportation:	$1,000	$1,000

Undergraduate aid. Need-based: Average financial aid package for full-time students was $10,914; for part-time $5,686. 50% awarded as scholarships/grants, 50% as loans/jobs. **Non-need-based:** 50% awarded as scholarships/grants, 50% as loans/jobs. Scholarships based on academics, athletics. **Student debt:** 96% of graduating class borrowed to fund education; average debt was $15,000. **Additional information:** Individual financial aid counseling available.

Freshman aid. Need-based: Out of 214 full-time freshmen, 202 applied for aid; 179 were judged to have need; of these 179 received aid. Average package met 75% of need. 33 students had full need met. Average scholarship/grant was $11,446; average loan $2,625. **Non-need based:** 18 full-time freshmen with need received non-need scholarships; 32 without need received awards; 1 received athletic scholarships.

Merit scholarships. All applicants will be considered for non-need based scholarships or grants based on high school GPA and SAT/ACT scores.

Policies to reduce costs. Tuition/fee waivers for senior citizens, employees and their families. Credit/placement for qualifying scores on AP, IB, CLEP examinations. Work study available nights and weekends.

Payment plans. Credit card, installment, deferred payment.

Application procedures. FAFSA required. Priority date 2/15; no closing date. Applicants notified on rolling basis starting 2/1. **Transfers:** Priority date 2/15; no deadline. Financial aid information must be received for all prior institutions.

Contact. Financial aid office: (845) 359-7800 ext. 226
Eileen Felske, Director of Financial Aid
470 Western Highway
Orangeburg, NY 10962

Dowling College

Oakdale, New York
www.dowling.edu
Four-year private **Federal Code: 002667**

	Living at home	On-campus
Tuition and fees:	$14,700	$14,700
Room only:		$4,850
Books and supplies:	$750	$750
Personal expenses:	$1,066	$1,066
Transportation:	$1,350	$1,350

Undergraduate aid. Need-based: Average financial aid package for full-time students was $14,107; for part-time $7,531. 67% awarded as scholarships/grants, 33% as loans/jobs. **Non-need-based:** 52% awarded as scholarships/grants, 48% as loans/jobs. Scholarships based on academics, alumni affiliation, athletics, leadership. **Student debt:** 82% of graduating class borrowed to fund education; average debt was $13,500.

Freshman aid. Need-based: Out of 441 full-time freshmen, 396 applied for aid; 350 were judged to have need; of these 348 received aid. Average package met 79% of need. 58 students had full need met. Average scholarship/grant was $5,611; average loan $2,625. **Non-need based:** 105 full-time freshmen with need received non-need scholarships; 51 without need received awards; 18 received athletic scholarships.

Policies to reduce costs. Tuition/fee waivers for children of alumni, senior citizens, employees and their families. Tuition at time of enrollment guaranteed for 4 years; prepayment discount; credit/placement for qualifying scores on AP, IB, CLEP examinations. Work study available weekends and for part-time students.

Payment plans. Credit card, installment, deferred payment.

Application procedures. FAFSA, institutional form required. Priority date 5/30; no closing date. Applicants notified on rolling basis starting 3/15, must reply within 4 week(s) of notification. **Transfers:** No deadline. Academic scholarships available for transfers with associate degrees.

Contact. **Financial aid office:** (631) 244-3030
Nancy Brewer, Director of Enrollment Services and Financial Aid
Idle Hour Boulevard
Oakdale, NY 11769-1999

Dutchess Community College

Poughkeepsie, New York
www.sunydutchess.edu
Two-year public **Federal Code: 002864**

	Living at home
Tuition and fees (2002-2003):	$2,480
Out-of-state:	$4,830
Per-credit charge:	$90
Per-credit out-of-state:	$180
Board only:	$1,915
Books and supplies:	$675
Personal expenses:	$750
Transportation:	$850

Undergraduate aid. Need-based: Need-based aid available for full-time and part-time students.

Policies to reduce costs. Tuition/fee waivers for senior citizens, employees and their families. Credit/placement for qualifying scores on AP, CLEP examinations. Work study available for part-time students.

Payment plans. Credit card, installment, deferred payment.

Application procedures. FAFSA, institutional form required. Priority date 5/1; no closing date. Applicants notified on rolling basis starting 5/15, must reply within 2 week(s) of notification.

Contact. **Financial aid office:** (845) 431-8030
Susan Mead, Director of Financial Aid
53 Pendell Road
Poughkeepsie, NY 12601

Eastman School of Music of the University of Rochester

Rochester, New York
www.rochester.edu/eastman
Four-year private **Federal Code: 008124**

	Living at home	On-campus
Tuition and fees (projected):	$24,495	$24,495
Room and board:		$9,470
Board only:	$3,050	
Books and supplies:	$600	$600
Personal expenses:	$700	$700
Transportation:	$650	$650

Undergraduate aid. Need-based: Need-based aid available for full-time and part-time students. **Non-need-based:** Scholarships based on academics, alumni affiliation, music/drama.

Merit scholarships. All merit scholarships are awarded based on admission criteria, and do not require separate application, audition, or interview.

Policies to reduce costs. Tuition/fee waivers for employees and their families. Credit/placement for qualifying scores on AP examinations.

Payment plans. Installment payment.

Application procedures. FAFSA, institutional form, CSS PROFILE required. Priority date 2/1; no closing date. Applicants notified on rolling basis starting 3/15, must reply by 5/1 or within 2 week(s) of notification. **Transfers:** Priority date 2/1.

Contact. **Financial aid office:** (585) 274-1070
Mary Ellen Nugent, Director of Financial Aid
26 Gibbs Street
Rochester, NY 14604-2599

Elmira Business Institute

Elmira, New York
www.ebi-college.com
Two-year proprietary **Federal Code: 009043**

College costs (2002-2003). Program cost for 16 month associate degree in office technology (medical or legal) $17,690. Includes tuition, fees, books, graduation costs. Costs of other programs vary. Books/supplies: $2,200.

Undergraduate aid. All financial aid based on need. Need-based aid available for full-time and part-time students.

Policies to reduce costs. Tuition at time of enrollment guaranteed for 2 years.

Payment plans. Credit card, installment, deferred payment.

Application procedures. FAFSA, institutional form required. Closing date 5/1.

Contact. **Financial aid office:** (607) 733-7177
Kathy Hamilton, Executive Director
303 North Main Street
Elmira, NY 14901

Elmira College

Elmira, New York
www.elmira.edu
Four-year private **Federal Code: 002718**

	Living at home	On-campus
Tuition and fees:	$25,740	$25,740
Room and board:		$8,080
Board only:	$1,600	
Books and supplies:	$450	$450
Personal expenses:	$1,000	$550

Undergraduate aid. Need-based: Average financial aid package for full-time students was $20,242. 68% awarded as scholarships/grants, 32% as loans/jobs. Need-based aid available for part-time students. **Non-need-based:** 58% awarded as scholarships/grants, 42% as loans/jobs. Scholarships based on academics, leadership, minority status, music/drama. **Student debt:** 65% of graduating class borrowed to fund education; average debt was $20,235. **Additional information:** Sibling Scholarship program provides 50% discounts on second family member's room and board, regardless of need.

Freshman aid. Need-based: Out of 338 full-time freshmen, 313 applied for aid; 282 were judged to have need; of these 282 received aid. Average package met 90% of need. 50 students had full need met. Average scholarship/grant was $15,159; average loan $5,765. **Non-need based:** 37 full-time freshmen with need received non-need scholarships; 75 without need received awards.

Merit scholarships. Scholarships for valedictorian and salutatorian; 20 awarded; full and 75% tuition respectively, renewable. Scholarships based on GPA, test scores, and class rank; $15,000, $12,000, $10,000 or $7,000 renewable awards.

Policies to reduce costs. Tuition/fee waivers for family members, employees and their families. Prepayment discount; credit/placement for qualifying scores on AP, IB, CLEP examinations. Work study available nights and weekends.

Payment plans. Credit card, installment, deferred payment.

Application procedures. FAFSA required. Priority date 2/1; closing date 6/30. Applicants notified on rolling basis starting 2/15, must reply by 5/1 or within 2 week(s) of notification. Early decision closing date 11/15.

Contact. **Financial aid office:** (607) 735-1728
Kathleen Cohen, Dean of Financial Aid
One Park Place
Elmira, NY 14901

Erie Community College: City Campus

Buffalo, New York
www.ecc.edu
Two-year public **Federal Code: 010684**

College costs. Tuition discounts available for off-site and off-times courses.

	Living at home
Tuition and fees (2002-2003):	$2,690
Out-of-state:	$5,190
Per-credit charge:	$105
Per-credit out-of-state:	$210
Board only:	$1,008
Books and supplies:	$600
Personal expenses:	$750
Transportation:	$750

Undergraduate aid. All financial aid based on need. Need-based aid available for full-time and part-time students.

Policies to reduce costs. Tuition/fee waivers for senior citizens, employees and their families. Credit/placement for qualifying scores on AP, CLEP examinations. Work study available weekends and for part-time students.

Payment plans. Credit card, installment payment.

Application procedures. FAFSA, institutional form required. Priority date 5/1; no closing date. Applicants notified on rolling basis starting 4/1, must reply within 2 week(s) of notification. **Transfers:** No deadline.

Contact. Financial aid office: (716) 851-1182
Bernice Anson, Director of Financial Aid
121 Ellicott Street
Buffalo, NY 14203-2698

Erie Community College: North Campus

Williamsville, New York
www.ecc.edu
Two-year public **Federal Code: 010684**

College costs. Tuition discounts available for off-site and off-times courses.

	Living at home
Tuition and fees (2002-2003):	$2,690
Out-of-state:	$5,190
Per-credit charge:	$105
Per-credit out-of-state:	$210
Board only:	$1,008
Books and supplies:	$600
Personal expenses:	$750
Transportation:	$750

Undergraduate aid. All financial aid based on need. Need-based aid available for full-time and part-time students.

Policies to reduce costs. Tuition/fee waivers for senior citizens, employees and their families. Credit/placement for qualifying scores on AP, CLEP examinations. Work study available weekends and for part-time students.

Payment plans. Credit card, installment payment.

Application procedures. FAFSA, institutional form required. Priority date 5/1; no closing date. Applicants notified on rolling basis starting 4/1, must reply within 2 week(s) of notification. **Transfers:** No deadline.

Contact. Financial aid office: (716) 851-1477
Bernice Anson, Director of Financial Aid
6205 Main Street
Williamsville, NY 14221-7095

Erie Community College: South Campus

Orchard Park, New York
www.ecc.edu
Two-year public **Federal Code: 010684**

College costs. Tuition discounts available for off-site and off-times courses.

	Living at home
Tuition and fees (2002-2003):	$2,690
Out-of-state:	$5,190
Per-credit charge:	$105
Per-credit out-of-state:	$210
Board only:	$1,008
Books and supplies:	$600
Personal expenses:	$750
Transportation:	$750

Undergraduate aid. All financial aid based on need. Need-based aid available for full-time and part-time students.

Policies to reduce costs. Tuition/fee waivers for senior citizens, employees and their families. Credit/placement for qualifying scores on AP, CLEP examinations. Work study available weekends and for part-time students.

Payment plans. Credit card, installment payment.

Application procedures. FAFSA, institutional form required. Priority date 5/1; no closing date. Applicants notified on rolling basis starting 4/1, must reply within 2 week(s) of notification. **Transfers:** No deadline.

Contact. Financial aid office: (716) 851-1677
Bernice Anson, Director of Financial Aid
4041 Southwestern Boulevard
Orchard Park, NY 14127-2199

Eugene Lang College/New School University

New York, New York
www.lang.edu
Four-year private **Federal Code: 002780**

	Living at home	On-campus
Tuition and fees (2002-2003):	$22,990	$22,990
Room only:		$7,650

Undergraduate aid. Need-based: Average financial aid package for full-time students was $17,088. 74% awarded as scholarships/grants, 26% as loans/jobs. **Non-need-based:** 18% awarded as scholarships/grants, 82% as loans/jobs. Scholarships based on academics, leadership. **Student debt:** 76% of graduating class borrowed to fund education; average debt was $20,963.

Freshman aid. Need-based: Out of 173 full-time freshmen, 144 applied for aid; 119 were judged to have need; of these 119 received aid. Average package met 68% of need. 3 students had full need met. Average scholarship/grant was $14,722; average loan $3,226. **Non-need based:** 3 full-time freshmen with need received non-need scholarships; 3 without need received awards.

Policies to reduce costs. Tuition/fee waivers for employees and their families. Credit/placement for qualifying scores on AP, IB examinations.

Payment plans. Credit card, installment payment.

Application procedures. FAFSA required. Priority date 3/1; no closing date. Applicants notified on rolling basis starting 3/1, must reply within 4 week(s) of notification. Early decision closing date 11/15.

Contact. Financial aid office: (212) 229-8930
Julie Disa, Assistant Provost
65 West 11th Street (3rd floor)
New York, NY 10011-8693

Excelsior College

Albany, New York
www.excelsior.edu
Four-year private **Federal Code: 014251**

	Living at home
Tuition and fees (2002-2003):	$945

Undergraduate aid. Need-based: Need-based aid available for part-time students. **Additional information:** College is approved for all VA Educational benefit programs.

Policies to reduce costs. Tuition/fee waivers for employees and their families. Credit/placement for qualifying scores on AP, CLEP examinations.

Payment plans. Credit card payment.

Application procedures. Institutional form required. Priority date 7/1; no closing date. Applicants notified on rolling basis starting 8/1, must reply within 2 week(s) of notification.

Contact. Donna Eames, Director of Financial Aid
7 Columbia Circle
Albany, NY 12203-5159

Fashion Institute of Technology

New York, New York
www.fitnyc.edu
Four-year public **Federal Code: 002866**

	Living at home	On-campus
Tuition and fees (2002-2003):	$3,020	$3,020
Out-of-state:	$7,520	$7,520
Room and board:		$6,258
Books and supplies:	$1,200	$1,200
Personal expenses:	$900	$1,050
Transportation:	$800	$600

Undergraduate aid. All financial aid based on need. Average financial aid package for full-time students was $6,118; for part-time $3,512. 63%

awarded as scholarships/grants, 37% as loans/jobs. **Student debt:** 32% of graduating class borrowed to fund education; average debt was $9,395.

Freshman aid. Out of 1,006 full-time freshmen, 773 applied for aid; 501 were judged to have need; of these 491 received aid. Average package met 77% of need. 142 students had full need met. Average scholarship/grant was $3,477; average loan $2,460.

Policies to reduce costs. Tuition/fee waivers for employees and their families. Credit/placement for qualifying scores on CLEP examinations.

Payment plans. Credit card, installment payment.

Application procedures. FAFSA, institutional form required. Priority date 2/15; no closing date. Applicants notified on rolling basis starting 4/15, must reply within 2 week(s) of notification.

Contact. **Financial aid office:** (212) 217-7999
Mina Friedmann, Director of Financial Aid
Seventh Avenue at 27 Street
New York, NY 10001-5992

Finger Lakes Community College

Canandaigua, New York
www.flcc.edu
Two-year public **Federal Code: 007532**

	Living at home
Tuition and fees (2002-2003):	$2,670
Out-of-state:	$5,170
Per-credit charge:	$96
Per-credit out-of-state:	$192
Board only:	$800
Books and supplies:	$700
Personal expenses:	$700
Transportation:	$900

Undergraduate aid. All financial aid based on need. 56% awarded as scholarships/grants, 44% as loans/jobs. Need-based aid available for part-time students. **Student debt:** 50% of graduating class borrowed to fund education; average debt was $4,500.

Policies to reduce costs. Tuition/fee waivers for senior citizens, employees and their families. Credit/placement for qualifying scores on AP, IB, CLEP examinations. Work study available nights, weekends and for part-time students.

Payment plans. Credit card, deferred payment.

Application procedures. FAFSA, institutional form required. Priority date 4/1; no closing date. Applicants notified on rolling basis starting 3/1.

Contact. **Financial aid office:** (585) 394-3500 ext. 7275
Nancy Van Zetta, Director, Financial Aid
4355 Lake Shore Drive
Canandaigua, NY 14424-8399

Fordham University

Bronx, New York
www.fordham.edu
Four-year private **Federal Code: 002722**

	Living at home	On-campus
Tuition and fees (2002-2003):	$24,000	$24,000
Room and board:		$9,235
Board only:	$2,045	
Books and supplies:	$640	$640
Personal expenses:	$925	$1,270
Transportation:	$850	$620

Undergraduate aid. **Need-based:** Need-based aid available for full-time and part-time students. **Non-need-based:** Scholarships based on academics, athletics, state/district residency.

Policies to reduce costs. Tuition/fee waivers for employees and their families. Credit/placement for qualifying scores on AP, IB examinations.

Payment plans. Credit card, installment, deferred payment.

Application procedures. FAFSA, CSS PROFILE required. Closing date 2/1. Applicants notified by 4/1, must reply by 5/1 or within 2 week(s) of notification. Early decision closing date 11/1. **Transfers:** Priority date 2/1; closing date 5/1.

Contact. **Financial aid office:** (718) 817-5069
Angela Van Dekker, Director of Financial Aid
441 East Fordham Road
Bronx, NY 10458

Fulton-Montgomery Community College

Johnstown, New York
www.fmcc.suny.edu
Two-year public **Federal Code: 002867**

	Living at home
Tuition and fees (2002-2003):	$2,872
Out-of-state:	$5,472
Per-credit charge:	$108
Per-credit out-of-state:	$216
Books and supplies:	$500

Undergraduate aid. **Need-based:** Need-based aid available for full-time and part-time students. **Non-need-based:** Scholarships based on academics.

Merit scholarships. Academic Excellence Scholarship at $1,000 a year with limit of two years for residents of Fulton, Montgomery, or Hamilton or Galway Central School District. Applicants must have 3.5 cumulative GPA, submit an essay and list of extracurricular activities, and be enrolled full-time at college. Must maintain 3.3 cumulative GPA. CTW Scholarship at $1,000 a year with limit of two years, for Montgomery residents or applicants who attend high school in Montgomery County. Applicants must have B average. Must maintain 3.3 cumulative GPA at end of first year.

Policies to reduce costs. Tuition/fee waivers for senior citizens, employees and their families. Credit/placement for qualifying scores on AP, CLEP examinations. Work study available nights, weekends and for part-time students.

Payment plans. Credit card, installment, deferred payment.

Application procedures. FAFSA required. Priority date 6/1; no closing date. Applicants notified on rolling basis starting 6/15, must reply within 2 week(s) of notification. **Transfers:** Priority date 6/1; no deadline.

Contact. **Financial aid office:** (518) 762-4651 ext. 8201
Rebecca Swart, Coordinator of Financial Aid
2805 State Highway 67
Johnstown, NY 12095

Genesee Community College

Batavia, New York
www.genesee.suny.edu
Two-year public **Federal Code: 006782**

	Living at home
Tuition and fees (2002-2003):	$2,872
Out-of-state:	$3,222
Per-credit charge:	$99
Per-credit out-of-state:	$108
Board only:	$1,500
Books and supplies:	$600
Personal expenses:	$576
Transportation:	$702

Undergraduate aid. **Need-based:** Need-based aid available for full-time and part-time students. **Non-need-based:** Scholarships based on athletics, music/drama.

Policies to reduce costs. Tuition/fee waivers for children of alumni, employees and their families. Credit/placement for qualifying scores on AP, IB, CLEP examinations. Work study available nights, weekends and for part-time students.

Payment plans. Credit card, deferred payment.

Application procedures. FAFSA required. Priority date 3/1; closing date 5/1. Applicants notified on rolling basis starting 4/15, must reply within 2 week(s) of notification. **Transfers:** No deadline.

Contact. **Financial aid office:** (585) 345-6900
Joseph Bailey, Director of Financial Aid
One College Road
Batavia, NY 14020-9704

Globe Institute of Technology

New York, New York
www.globe.edu
Two-year proprietary **Federal Code: 025408**

	Living at home
Tuition and fees (2002-2003):	$8,620
Per-credit charge:	$280
Board only:	$2,512
Books and supplies:	$443
Personal expenses:	$1,746
Transportation:	$450

Undergraduate aid. All financial aid based on need. Need-based aid available for full-time and part-time students.

Policies to reduce costs. Tuition/fee waivers for employees and their families. Tuition at time of enrollment guaranteed for 2 years.

Payment plans. Credit card, installment payment.

Application procedures. FAFSA, institutional form required.

Contact. Financial aid office: (212) 349-4330
Marcus Browne, Director of Financial Aid
291 Broadway
New York, NY 10007

Hamilton College

Clinton, New York
www.hamilton.edu
Four-year private **Federal Code: 002728**

	Living at home	On-campus
Tuition and fees (2002-2003):	$28,760	$28,760
Room and board:		$7,040

Undergraduate aid. Need-based: Average financial aid package for full-time students was $22,460. 83% awarded as scholarships/grants, 17% as loans/jobs. **Non-need-based:** 99% awarded as scholarships/grants, 1% as loans/jobs. Scholarships based on academics. **Student debt:** 76% of graduating class borrowed to fund education; average debt was $16,856. **Additional information:** Will meet demonstrated need of all aided applicants.

Freshman aid. Need-based: Out of 491 full-time freshmen, 300 applied for aid; 248 were judged to have need; of these 248 received aid. Average package met 99% of need. 248 students had full need met. Average scholarship/grant was $20,336; average loan $2,489. **Non-need based:** 5 full-time freshmen with need received non-need scholarships; 28 without need received awards.

Merit scholarships. $10,000 and $3,000 summer research grants. 10 awards to top applicants in entering class.

Policies to reduce costs. Tuition/fee waivers for employees and their families. Credit/placement for qualifying scores on AP, IB examinations. Work study available nights and weekends.

Payment plans. Installment payment.

Application procedures. FAFSA, institutional form, CSS PROFILE required. Closing date 2/1. Applicants notified by 4/1, must reply by 5/1. Early decision closing date 11/15. **Transfers:** Closing date 2/1.

Contact. Financial aid office: (315) 859-4434
Kenneth Kogut, Director of Financial Aid
198 College Hill Road
Clinton, NY 13323-1293

Hartwick College

Oneonta, New York
www.hartwick.edu
Four-year private **Federal Code: 002729**

	Living at home	On-campus
Tuition and fees (2002-2003):	$26,615	$26,615
Room and board:		$7,050
Books and supplies:	$700	$700
Personal expenses:	$400	$400
Transportation:	$750	

Undergraduate aid. Need-based: Average financial aid package for full-time students was $20,000. 70% awarded as scholarships/grants, 30% as loans/jobs. Need-based aid available for part-time students. **Non-need-based:** 86% awarded as scholarships/grants, 14% as loans/jobs. Scholarships based on academics, alumni affiliation, art, athletics, music/drama, state/district residency. **Student debt:** 68% of graduating class borrowed to fund education; average debt was $19,400.

Freshman aid. Need-based: Average package met 85% of need. Average scholarship/grant was $10,715; average loan $3,025. **Non-need based:** 118 without need received awards; 3 received athletic scholarships.

Policies to reduce costs. Tuition/fee waivers for children of alumni, family members, employees and their families. Credit/placement for qualifying scores on AP, IB, CLEP examinations. Work study available weekends.

Payment plans. Installment payment.

Application procedures. FAFSA, institutional form required. Closing date 2/1. Applicants notified by 3/15, must reply by 5/1 or within 2 week(s) of notification. **Transfers:** Priority date 3/1; no deadline.

Contact. Financial aid office: (607) 431-4200
Barbara Pledger, Director of Financial Aid
Box 4022
Oneonta, NY 13820-4022

Helene Fuld College of Nursing

New York, New York
Two-year private **Federal Code: 015395**

	Living at home
Tuition and fees (2002-2003):	$12,125
Per-credit charge:	$216
Books and supplies:	$1,100
Personal expenses:	$1,665
Transportation:	$595

Undergraduate aid. All financial aid based on need. Need-based aid available for full-time and part-time students.

Policies to reduce costs. Credit/placement for qualifying scores on CLEP examinations.

Application procedures. FAFSA required. No deadline. Applicants notified on rolling basis. **Transfers:** No deadline.

Contact. Financial aid office: (212) 423-2771
Sandra Senior, Director of Student Services
1879 Madison Avenue
New York, NY 10035

Hilbert College

Hamburg, New York
www.hilbert.edu
Four-year private **Federal Code: 002735**

	Living at home	On-campus
Tuition and fees (projected):	$13,500	$13,500
Room and board:		$5,387
Books and supplies:	$700	$700
Personal expenses:	$800	$800
Transportation:	$600	$600

Undergraduate aid. Need-based: Average financial aid package for full-time students was $8,410; for part-time $4,856. 53% awarded as scholarships/grants, 47% as loans/jobs. **Non-need-based:** 21% awarded as scholarships/grants, 79% as loans/jobs. Scholarships based on academics, leadership, minority status, state/district residency. **Student debt:** 95% of graduating class borrowed to fund education; average debt was $9,510.

Freshman aid. Need-based: Out of 158 full-time freshmen, 154 applied for aid; 138 were judged to have need; of these 138 received aid. Average package met 69% of need. 12 students had full need met. Average scholarship/grant was $6,357; average loan $2,327. **Non-need based:** 6 full-time freshmen with need received non-need scholarships; 20 without need received awards.

Policies to reduce costs. Tuition/fee waivers for children of alumni, senior citizens, minority students, employees and their families. Credit/placement for qualifying scores on AP, IB, CLEP examinations. Work study available nights, weekends and for part-time students.

Payment plans. Credit card, installment, deferred payment.

Application procedures. FAFSA required. Priority date 2/28; no closing date. Applicants notified on rolling basis starting 3/15, must reply within 2 week(s) of notification. **Transfers:** No deadline.

Contact. **Financial aid office:** (716) 649-7900
Leigh Fiorenzo, Director, Financial Aid
5200 South Park Avenue
Hamburg, NY 14075-1597

Hobart and William Smith Colleges

Geneva, New York
www.hws.edu
Four-year private **Federal Code: 002731**

	Living at home	On-campus
Tuition and fees (2002-2003):	$27,348	$27,348
Room and board:		$7,230
Board only:	$1,500	
Books and supplies:	$850	$850
Personal expenses:	$600	$600
Transportation:	$50	$210

Undergraduate aid. Need-based: Average financial aid package for full-time students was $21,561. 79% awarded as scholarships/grants, 21% as loans/jobs. **Non-need-based:** Scholarships based on academics, art, leadership, music/drama.

Freshman aid. Need-based: Out of 532 full-time freshmen, 377 applied for aid; 328 were judged to have need; of these 328 received aid. Average package met 96% of need. 252 students had full need met. Average scholarship/grant was $17,918; average loan $2,537. **Non-need based:** 47 full-time freshmen with need received non-need scholarships; 99 without need received awards.

Merit scholarships. Cornelius and Muriel P. Wood Scholarship, full tuition for 4 years. Trustee Scholarship for Academic Excellence based on GPA, test scores, class standing, 25 awarded, $17,000 annually, for 4 years. Faculty Scholarships based on pool competing for Trustee scholarship, 25-50 awarded, ranging from $3,000-$12,000. Phi Theta Kappa Trustee Scholarship for academically qualified transfer students with 2-year degree from junior or community college, $2,500-$17,000 annually. Presidential Leaders Scholarship based on academic excellence, leadership, personal qualities, 25-50 awarded, $3,000-$10,000. Arts Scholarships for special talent in visual and performing arts, 15 awarded, $3,000-$10,000.

Policies to reduce costs. Tuition/fee waivers for employees and their families. Prepayment discount; credit/placement for qualifying scores on AP, IB examinations.

Payment plans. Installment payment.

Application procedures. FAFSA, CSS PROFILE required. Closing date 2/15. Applicants notified by 4/1, must reply by 5/1 or within 2 week(s) of notification. Early decision closing date 11/15. **Transfers:** No deadline.

Contact. **Financial aid office:** (315) 781-3315
Don Emmons, Dean of Admissions and Financial Aid
639 South Main Street
Geneva, NY 14456

Hofstra University

Hempstead, New York
www.hofstra.edu
Four-year private **Federal Code: 002732**

	Living at home	On-campus
Tuition and fees (2002-2003):	$16,916	$16,916
Room and board:		$8,450

Undergraduate aid. Need-based: Average financial aid package for full-time students was $11,197; for part-time $6,578. 53% awarded as scholarships/grants, 47% as loans/jobs. **Non-need-based:** 53% awarded as scholarships/grants, 47% as loans/jobs. Scholarships based on academics, athletics. **Student debt:** 44% of graduating class borrowed to fund education; average debt was $15,455. **Additional information:** Special financial aid funds may be available for applicants demonstrating superior academic ability, minority applicants and low/middle income applicants.

Freshman aid. Need-based: Out of 1,766 full-time freshmen, 1,435 applied for aid; 1,024 were judged to have need; of these 1,024 received aid. Average package met 68% of need. 225 students had full need met. Average scholarship/grant was $4,722; average loan $2,841. **Non-need based:** 829 full-time freshmen with need received non-need scholarships; 247 without need received awards; 71 received athletic scholarships.

Policies to reduce costs. Tuition/fee waivers for senior citizens, employees and their families. Credit/placement for qualifying scores on AP, IB, CLEP examinations. Work study available nights, weekends and for part-time students.

Payment plans. Credit card, deferred payment.

Application procedures. FAFSA required. Priority date 2/15; no closing date. Applicants notified on rolling basis starting 3/1, must reply by 5/1 or within 2 week(s) of notification. **Transfers:** No deadline.

Contact. **Financial aid office:** (516) 463-6680
Suzanne Tang, Director, Financial and Academic Records
Admissions Center, 100 Hofstra University
Hempstead, NY 11549

Holy Trinity Orthodox Seminary

Jordanville, New York
www.hts.edu
Five-year private

	Living at home	On-campus
Tuition and fees (2002-2003):	$2,025	$2,025
Room and board:		$2,000
Books and supplies:	$250	$250

Application procedures. No deadline.

Contact. **Financial aid office:** (315) 858-0945
Box 36
Jordanville, NY 13361

Houghton College

Houghton, New York
www.houghton.edu
Four-year private **Federal Code: 002734**

College costs. Tuition includes laptop computer, printer, fees.

	Living at home	On-campus
Tuition and fees:	$17,984	$17,984
Room and board:		$6,000
Board only:	$800	
Books and supplies:	$750	$750
Personal expenses:	$750	$750
Transportation:	$500	$500

Undergraduate aid. Need-based: Average financial aid package for full-time students was $13,908; for part-time $11,964. 52% awarded as scholarships/grants, 48% as loans/jobs. **Non-need-based:** 66% awarded as scholarships/grants, 34% as loans/jobs. Scholarships based on academics, alumni affiliation, art, athletics, music/drama, religious affiliation. **Student debt:** 74% of graduating class borrowed to fund education; average debt was $15,257.

Freshman aid. Need-based: Out of 333 full-time freshmen, 333 applied for aid; 291 were judged to have need; of these 291 received aid. Average package met 71% of need. 83 students had full need met. Average scholarship/grant was $10,306; average loan $3,758. **Non-need based:** 90 full-time freshmen with need received non-need scholarships; 64 without need received awards; 4 received athletic scholarships.

Merit scholarships. Academic Excellence Scholarships based on academic record, co-curricular involvement, and recommendations; ranging from $1,250-$12,500. Wesleyan Grant awards $1,000 to members of Wesley Church. Willard J. Houghton Ministerial Scholarship, based on recommendation of local District Board of Ministerial Development, awards a renewable $5,000 to a student preparing for the Wesleyan pastorate.

Policies to reduce costs. Tuition/fee waivers for children of alumni, senior citizens, family members, family of clergy, employees and their families. Credit/placement for qualifying scores on AP, IB, CLEP examinations. Work study available nights and weekends.

Payment plans. Credit card, installment payment.

Application procedures. FAFSA required. Priority date 3/1; no closing date. Applicants notified on rolling basis starting 3/15, must reply by 5/1 or within 4 week(s) of notification. **Transfers:** Priority date 3/1; no deadline.

Contact. **Financial aid office:** (585) 567-9328
Troy Martin, Director of Student Financial Services
One Willard Avenue/Box 128
Houghton, NY 14744-9989

Hudson Valley Community College

Troy, New York
www.hvcc.edu
Two-year public **Federal Code: 002868**

	Living at home
Tuition and fees (2002-2003):	$2,715
Out-of-state:	$6,500
Per-credit charge:	$98
Per-credit out-of-state:	$255
Books and supplies:	$550
Personal expenses:	$800
Transportation:	$900

Policies to reduce costs. Credit/placement for qualifying scores on CLEP examinations.

Payment plans. Credit card, installment, deferred payment.

Application procedures. FAFSA required. Priority date 5/30; no closing date. Applicants notified on rolling basis starting 5/1, must reply within 2 week(s) of notification.

Contact. Financial aid office: (518) 629-4822
Heather Wysocki, Director of Financial Aid
80 Vandenburgh Avenue
Troy, NY 12180

ITT Technical Institute: Albany

Albany, New York
www.itt-tech.edu
Two-year proprietary **Federal Code: 004553**

College costs. Total program varies depending on course of study. Per-credit-hour charge: $347. Books/supplies: $3,300.

Policies to reduce costs. Tuition/fee waivers for employees and their families. Tuition at time of enrollment guaranteed for 2 years.

Payment plans. Credit card, installment payment.

Application procedures. FAFSA, institutional form required. Applicants notified on rolling basis.

Contact. Financial aid office: (518) 452-9300
Andrea Wedler
13 Airline Drive
Albany, NY 12205

ITT Technical Institute: Getzville

Getzville, New York
www.itt-tech.edu
Two-year proprietary **Federal Code: 010627**

College costs. Total program varies depending on course of study. Per-credit-hour charge: $347.

Policies to reduce costs. Tuition/fee waivers for employees and their families. Tuition at time of enrollment guaranteed for 2 years.

Payment plans. Credit card, installment payment.

Application procedures. FAFSA, institutional form required. No deadline. Applicants notified on rolling basis.

Contact. Financial aid office: (716) 689-2200
Kristin Sidor, Director of Finance
2295 Millersport Highway
Getzville, NY 14068

ITT Technical Institute: Liverpool

Liverpool, New York
www.itt-tech.edu
Two-year proprietary **Federal Code: 023217**

College costs. Total program varies depending on course of study. Per-credit-hour charge: $347. Books/supplies: $3,300.

Policies to reduce costs. Tuition/fee waivers for employees and their families. Tuition at time of enrollment guaranteed for 2 years.

Payment plans. Credit card, installment payment.

Application procedures. FAFSA, institutional form required. No deadline. Applicants notified on rolling basis.

Contact. Financial aid office: (315) 461-8000
Marcia Todaro, Director of Finance
235 Greenfield Parkway
Liverpool, NY 13088

Institute of Design and Construction

Brooklyn, New York
www.idcbrooklyn.org
Two-year private **Federal Code: 012107**

	Living at home
Tuition and fees:	$6,050
Per-credit charge:	$200
Books and supplies:	$800
Personal expenses:	$400
Transportation:	$200

Policies to reduce costs. Credit/placement for qualifying scores on AP, CLEP examinations.

Application procedures. FAFSA, institutional form required. No deadline. Applicants notified on rolling basis starting 3/1, must reply within 4 week(s) of notification.

Contact. Financial aid office: (718) 855-3661
John Anselmo, Director of Financial Aid
141 Willoughby Street
Brooklyn, NY 11201-5380

Iona College

New Rochelle, New York
www.iona.edu
Four-year private **Federal Code: 002737**

	Living at home	On-campus
Tuition and fees (2002-2003):	$17,866	$17,866
Room and board:		$9,700
Books and supplies:	$700	$700
Personal expenses:	$1,220	$1,220
Transportation:	$1,000	$580

Undergraduate aid. All financial aid based on need. Average financial aid package for full-time students was $12,416; for part-time $3,432. 51% awarded as scholarships/grants, 49% as loans/jobs. **Student debt:** 67% of graduating class borrowed to fund education; average debt was $14,415.

Freshman aid. Out of 779 full-time freshmen, 727 applied for aid; 606 were judged to have need; of these 586 received aid. Average package met 24% of need. 119 students had full need met. Average scholarship/grant was $3,130; average loan $1,722.

Policies to reduce costs. Tuition/fee waivers for children of alumni, senior citizens, minority students, family members, employees and their families. Credit/placement for qualifying scores on AP, CLEP examinations.

Payment plans. Credit card, installment payment.

Application procedures. FAFSA, institutional form required. No deadline. Applicants notified on rolling basis starting 12/20, must reply by 5/1 or within 2 week(s) of notification. **Transfers:** Priority date 8/1; no deadline.

Contact. Financial aid office: (914) 633-2497
Mary Grant, Associate Director of Student Financial Services
715 North Avenue
New Rochelle, NY 10801-1890

Island Drafting and Technical Institute

Amityville, New York
www.islanddrafting.com
Two-year proprietary **Federal Code: 007375**

	Living at home
Tuition and fees (projected):	$10,850
Per-credit charge:	$350
Board only:	$3,137
Books and supplies:	$500

Undergraduate aid. All financial aid based on need. Need-based aid available for full-time students.

Policies to reduce costs. Tuition at time of enrollment guaranteed for 2 years.

Payment plans. Credit card, installment payment.

Application procedures. No deadline. Applicants notified on rolling basis.

Contact. **Financial aid office:** (631) 264-0465
James DiLiberto, Dean
128 Broadway
Amityville, NY 11701-2704

Ithaca College
Ithaca, New York
www.ithaca.edu
Four-year private **Federal Code: 002739**

	Living at home	On-campus
Tuition and fees (2002-2003):	$21,102	$21,102
Room and board:		$8,960
Board only:	$4,484	
Books and supplies:	$876	$876
Personal expenses:	$1,200	$1,200
Transportation:	$650	

Undergraduate aid. **Need-based:** Average financial aid package for full-time students was $19,830; for part-time $9,284. 66% awarded as scholarships/grants, 34% as loans/jobs. **Non-need-based:** 60% awarded as scholarships/grants, 40% as loans/jobs. Scholarships based on academics, alumni affiliation, leadership, music/drama.

Freshman aid. **Need-based:** Out of 1,518 full-time freshmen, 1,268 applied for aid; 1,081 were judged to have need; of these 1,080 received aid. Average package met 87% of need. 458 students had full need met. Average scholarship/grant was $13,224; average loan $4,012. **Non-need based:** 269 full-time freshmen with need received non-need scholarships; 67 without need received awards.

Merit scholarships. President's Scholarship awarded for academic achievement to approximately 10% of applicants; $7,000-$10,000. Dean's Scholarship awarded for academic ability to approximately top 11% to 25% of applicants; $3,000-$5,000. Minority Scholarship awarded for academic achievement to 25% of applicants who are representatives of minority group; $2,000-$10,000. Ithaca Leadership Scholarship awarded for demonstrated record of leadership and above average academic performance; 30 new awards available per year; $6,000 each. Ithaca Premier Talent Scholarship for selected applicants majoring in music and theater; approximately 10 available; maximum award of $10,000. Ithaca Sibling Grant awarded to students who have concurrently enrolled sibling attending Ithaca College; $1,000. Park Scholar Achievement award for outstanding achievement in communications; covers full cost of attendance; approximately 10 new scholarships available per year. Ithaca College Merit Scholarship and Ithaca College National Merit Recognition Award for students who designate Ithaca their first-choice institution to National Merit Scholarship Corporation; $2,000 scholarship plus Ithaca College President's Scholarship of $10,000. All awards renewable up to four years of undergraduate study; some restrictions apply for maintaining eligibility.

Policies to reduce costs. Tuition/fee waivers for family members, employees and their families. Credit/placement for qualifying scores on AP, IB, CLEP examinations. Work study available nights.

Payment plans. Credit card, installment, deferred payment.

Application procedures. FAFSA required. CSS Profile required of early decision applicants; deadline November 1. Priority date 2/1; no closing date. Applicants notified on rolling basis starting 2/15. Early decision closing date 11/1. **Transfers:** Priority date 2/1; no deadline. Financial aid transcripts from previous institutions must be received by July 15.

Contact. **Financial aid office:** (800) 429-4275
Larry Chambers, Director of Financial Aid
100 Job Hall
Ithaca, NY 14850-7020

Jamestown Business College
Jamestown, New York
www.jbcny.org
Two-year proprietary **Federal Code: 008495**

	Living at home
Tuition and fees (2002-2003):	$7,860
Per-credit charge:	$208
Board only:	$525
Books and supplies:	$750
Personal expenses:	$1,602
Transportation:	$2,622

Undergraduate aid. **Need-based:** 72% awarded as scholarships/grants, 28% as loans/jobs. Need-based aid available for part-time students. **Non-need-based:** Scholarships based on academics.

Application procedures. FAFSA required. No deadline. Applicants notified on rolling basis starting 2/15.

Contact. **Financial aid office:** (716) 664-5100
Diane Sturzenbecker, Financial Aid Officer
7 Fairmount Avenue
Jamestown, NY 14702-0429

Jamestown Community College
Jamestown, New York
www.sunyjcc.edu
Two-year public **Federal Code: 002869**

	Living at home
Tuition and fees (2002-2003):	$3,020
Out-of-state:	$5,720
Per-credit charge:	$113
Per-credit out-of-state:	$204
Board only:	$1,850
Books and supplies:	$700
Personal expenses:	$520
Transportation:	$800

Undergraduate aid. **Need-based:** Need-based aid available for full-time and part-time students. **Non-need-based:** Scholarships based on academics, alumni affiliation, athletics, music/drama, state/district residency. **Additional information:** 100% resident tuition scholarship (less federal and state grants) for students in top 20% of high school graduating class with Regents diploma if residents of Chautauqua, Cattaraugus, or Allegany counties. Guaranteed in-state tuition rate for students in Warren, Potter, McKean and Forest counties in Pennsylvania, in top 20% of graduating class with an academic diploma.

Policies to reduce costs. Tuition/fee waivers for senior citizens, employees and their families. Credit/placement for qualifying scores on AP examinations. Work study available nights, weekends and for part-time students.

Payment plans. Credit card, installment payment.

Application procedures. FAFSA, institutional form required. Priority date 3/1; no closing date. Applicants notified on rolling basis starting 4/15.

Contact. **Financial aid office:** (716) 665-5220 ext. 2348
Laurie Vorp, Director of Financial Aid
525 Falconer Street
Jamestown, NY 14702-0020

Jefferson Community College
Watertown, New York
www.sunyjefferson.edu
Two-year public **Federal Code: 002870**

	Living at home
Tuition and fees (2002-2003):	$2,685
Out-of-state:	$3,955
Per-credit charge:	$95
Per-credit out-of-state:	$148
Board only:	$2,250
Books and supplies:	$800
Personal expenses:	$600
Transportation:	$310

Undergraduate aid. All financial aid based on need. Average financial aid package for full-time students was $3,650; for part-time $1,340. 75% awarded as scholarships/grants, 25% as loans/jobs. **Student debt:** 43% of graduating class borrowed to fund education; average debt was $4,075.

Freshman aid. Out of 638 full-time freshmen, 482 applied for aid; 399 were judged to have need; of these 474 received aid. Average package met 76% of need. 171 students had full need met. Average scholarship/grant was $1,850; average loan $2,050.

Policies to reduce costs. Tuition/fee waivers for senior citizens. Credit/placement for qualifying scores on AP, IB, CLEP examinations. Work study available for part-time students.

Payment plans. Credit card, installment payment.

Application procedures. FAFSA, institutional form required. Priority date 4/1; closing date 8/15. Applicants notified on rolling basis starting 4/15, must reply within 2 week(s) of notification. **Transfers:** No deadline.

Contact. **Financial aid office:** (315) 786-2355
Betsy Penrose, Director of Financial Aid
1220 Coffeen Street
Watertown, NY 13601

Juilliard School

New York, New York
www.juilliard.edu
Four-year private **Federal Code: 002742**

	Living at home	On-campus
Tuition and fees (2002-2003):	$19,700	$19,700
Room and board:		$7,850
Board only:	$3,700	
Books and supplies:	$3,100	$3,100
Transportation:	$1,300	$600

Undergraduate aid. **Need-based:** Average financial aid package for full-time students was $20,791. 75% awarded as scholarships/grants, 25% as loans/jobs. Need-based aid available for part-time students. **Non-need-based:** 48% awarded as scholarships/grants, 52% as loans/jobs. **Student debt:** 66% of graduating class borrowed to fund education; average debt was $22,868.

Freshman aid. **Need-based:** Out of 113 full-time freshmen, 108 applied for aid; 76 were judged to have need; of these 76 received aid. Average package met 86% of need. 26 students had full need met. Average scholarship/grant was $16,659; average loan $3,148. **Non-need based:** 25 without need received awards.

Policies to reduce costs. Credit/placement for qualifying scores on AP examinations. Work study available nights, weekends and for part-time students.

Payment plans. Installment payment.

Application procedures. FAFSA, institutional form required. Closing date 3/1. Applicants notified by 4/1, must reply by 5/1.

Contact. **Financial aid office:** (212) 799-5000
Joan Warren, Dean for Financial Aid
60 Lincoln Center Plaza
New York, NY 10023-6588

Katharine Gibbs School: Melville

Melville, New York
www.gibbslongisland.com
Two-year proprietary **Federal Code: 011647**

College costs. Certificate and associate programs range from $5,000 to $32,000 for duration of program. Additional charges for laptop and computing-related fees in some programs. Books/supplies: $700.

Payment plans. Credit card, installment payment.

Application procedures. FAFSA required. No deadline. Applicants notified on rolling basis, must reply within 3 week(s) of notification.

Contact. **Financial aid office:** (631) 370-3300
Louis Guaman, Financial Aid Director
320 South Service Road
Melville, NY 11747

Keuka College

Keuka Park, New York
www.keuka.edu
Four-year private **Federal Code: 002744**

	Living at home	On-campus
Tuition and fees (projected):	$16,050	$16,050
Room and board:		$7,600
Books and supplies:	$800	$800
Personal expenses:	$750	$1,000
Transportation:	$750	$750

Undergraduate aid. **Need-based:** Need-based aid available for full-time and part-time students. **Non-need-based:** Scholarships based on academics, alumni affiliation, leadership.

Merit scholarships. Goals Scholarship; 1/2 tuition; 82 average and 1000 SAT or 22 ACT required. Dean's Scholarship; 1/2-full tuition; 82 average and 1000 SAT or 22 ACT required. Presidential Scholarship; full tuition; based on GPA, SAT scores, class rank.

Policies to reduce costs. Tuition/fee waivers for employees and their families. Credit/placement for qualifying scores on AP, CLEP examinations. Work study available nights and weekends.

Payment plans. Credit card, installment payment.

Application procedures. FAFSA, institutional form required. Priority date 3/15; no closing date. Applicants notified on rolling basis starting 12/1, must reply by 5/1 or within 2 week(s) of notification. **Transfers:** No deadline.

Contact. **Financial aid office:** (315) 279-5232
Jennifer Bates, Director of Financial Aid
Wagner House
Keuka Park, NY 14478

Laboratory Institute of Merchandising

New York, New York
www.limcollege.edu
Four-year proprietary **Federal Code: 007466**

	Living at home
Tuition and fees (2002-2003):	$14,150
Books and supplies:	$600
Personal expenses:	$1,000
Transportation:	$1,500

Undergraduate aid. All financial aid based on need. Average financial aid package for full-time students was $8,500. 32% awarded as scholarships/grants, 68% as loans/jobs. Need-based aid available for part-time students. **Student debt:** 65% of graduating class borrowed to fund education; average debt was $17,125.

Freshman aid. Out of 92 full-time freshmen, 74 applied for aid; 74 were judged to have need; of these 74 received aid. Average package met 85% of need. 53 students had full need met. Average scholarship/grant was $1,500; average loan $2,625.

Policies to reduce costs. Tuition/fee waivers for employees and their families. Credit/placement for qualifying scores on AP, CLEP examinations.

Payment plans. Installment payment.

Application procedures. FAFSA, institutional form required. Priority date 4/1; no closing date. Applicants notified on rolling basis, must reply within 2 week(s) of notification. **Transfers:** No deadline.

Contact. **Financial aid office:** (212) 752-1530 ext. 26
Christine Murad, Director of Financial Aid
12 East 53rd Street
New York, NY 10022

Le Moyne College

Syracuse, New York
www.lemoyne.edu
Four-year private **Federal Code: 002748**

	Living at home	On-campus
Tuition and fees:	$18,950	$18,950
Room and board:		$7,450
Board only:	$740	
Books and supplies:	$550	$550
Personal expenses:	$360	$950
Transportation:	$400	$200

Undergraduate aid. Need-based: Average financial aid package for full-time students was $14,019; for part-time $4,424. 64% awarded as scholarships/grants, 36% as loans/jobs. **Non-need-based:** 68% awarded as scholarships/grants, 32% as loans/jobs. Scholarships based on academics, alumni affiliation, athletics, leadership, minority status. **Student debt:** 82% of graduating class borrowed to fund education; average debt was $18,750. **Additional information:** Parent loan program at low interest, monthly payment plans and alternative loans for students.

Freshman aid. Need-based: Out of 502 full-time freshmen, 465 applied for aid; 414 were judged to have need; of these 408 received aid. Average package met 86% of need. 118 students had full need met. Average scholarship/grant was $11,573; average loan $3,356. **Non-need based:** 220 full-time freshmen with need received non-need scholarships; 79 without need received awards; 33 received athletic scholarships.

Merit scholarships. Presidential Scholarships, 105 awarded, $15,000; Dean Scholarships, 250 awarded, $10,500; Leadership Scholarships, 614 awarded, $3,000; based on academic criteria (GPA, rank, test scores). Loyola Scholarships for students of color based on academic criteria; 55 awarded; $10,500.

Policies to reduce costs. Tuition/fee waivers for employees and their families. Credit/placement for qualifying scores on AP, IB, CLEP examinations. Work study available nights and weekends.

Payment plans. Credit card, installment payment.

Application procedures. FAFSA, institutional form required. Priority date 2/1; no closing date. Applicants notified by 3/15, must reply by 5/1 or within 2 week(s) of notification. Early decision closing date 11/15. **Transfers:** Priority date 6/1; no deadline.

Contact. **Financial aid office:** (315) 445-4400
William C. Cheetham, Director of Financial Aid
1419 Salt Springs Road
Syracuse, NY 13214-1399

Long Island Business Institute

Commack, New York
Two-year proprietary **Federal Code: 014514**

	Living at home
Tuition and fees (projected):	$8,600
Per-credit charge:	$275
Books and supplies:	$600
Personal expenses:	$1,000
Transportation:	$1,200

Undergraduate aid. Need-based: Average financial aid package for full-time students was $2,200; for part-time $1,800. 50% awarded as scholarships/grants, 50% as loans/jobs. **Non-need-based:** 50% awarded as scholarships/grants, 50% as loans/jobs. **Student debt:** 90% of graduating class borrowed to fund education; average debt was $8,500.

Freshman aid. Need-based: Out of 35 full-time freshmen, 25 applied for aid; 18 were judged to have need; of these 18 received aid. Average package met 60% of need. 1 students had full need met. Average loan $2,400.

Policies to reduce costs. Tuition/fee waivers for employees and their families. Tuition at time of enrollment guaranteed for 2 years.

Payment plans. Credit card, installment payment.

Application procedures. FAFSA, institutional form required. No deadline. Applicants notified on rolling basis, must reply within 2 week(s) of notification. **Transfers:** No deadline.

Contact. **Financial aid office:** (631) 499-7100
Patricia Ensley, Director of Financial Aid
6500 Jericho Turnpike
Commack, NY 11725

Long Island University: C. W. Post Campus

Brookville, New York
www.liu.edu
Four-year private **Federal Code: 002751**

	Living at home	On-campus
Tuition and fees (projected):	$20,115	$20,115
Room and board:		$8,075
Board only:	$1,900	
Books and supplies:	$600	$600
Personal expenses:	$990	$2,060
Transportation:	$900	$500

Undergraduate aid. Need-based: Average financial aid package for full-time students was $8,791. 47% awarded as scholarships/grants, 53% as loans/jobs. Need-based aid available for part-time students. **Non-need-based:** Scholarships based on academics, alumni affiliation, art, athletics, music/drama. **Student debt:** 65% of graduating class borrowed to fund education; average debt was $12,500.

Freshman aid. Need-based: Out of 876 full-time freshmen, 755 applied for aid; 642 were judged to have need; of these 642 received aid. Average package met 75% of need. Average scholarship/grant was $6,200; average loan $2,500. **Non-need based:** 125 full-time freshmen with need received non-need scholarships; 190 without need received awards; 40 received athletic scholarships.

Policies to reduce costs. Tuition/fee waivers for adults, children of alumni, family members, employees and their families. Credit/placement for qualifying scores on AP, IB, CLEP examinations. Work study available nights and weekends.

Payment plans. Credit card, installment, deferred payment.

Application procedures. FAFSA, CSS PROFILE required. Priority date 3/1; no closing date. Applicants notified on rolling basis starting 3/1, must reply by 5/1 or within 2 week(s) of notification. **Transfers:** Priority date 3/1; closing date 6/1. March 1 is scholarship applicants deadline. Candidates reply within 2 weeks of notification.

Contact. **Financial aid office:** (516) 299-2338
Joanne Graziano, Director of Financial Assistance
720 Northern Boulevard
Brookville, NY 11548-1300

Long Island University: Southampton College

Southampton, New York
www.southampton.liu.edu
Four-year private **Federal Code: 002755**

	Living at home	On-campus
Tuition and fees (2002-2003):	$19,230	$19,230
Room and board:		$8,430
Board only:	$1,580	
Books and supplies:	$500	$500
Personal expenses:	$936	$840
Transportation:		$200

Undergraduate aid. Need-based: Average financial aid package for full-time students was $12,874. 65% awarded as scholarships/grants, 35% as loans/jobs. Need-based aid available for part-time students. **Non-need-based:** 85% awarded as scholarships/grants, 15% as loans/jobs. Scholarships based on academics, alumni affiliation, art, athletics, state/district residency.

Freshman aid. Need-based: Out of 332 full-time freshmen, 299 applied for aid; 260 were judged to have need; of these 250 received aid. **Non-need based:** 234 full-time freshmen with need received non-need scholarships; 23 without need received awards; 14 received athletic scholarships.

Policies to reduce costs. Tuition/fee waivers for children of alumni, family members, employees and their families. Credit/placement for qualifying scores on AP, IB, CLEP examinations. Work study available nights and weekends.

Payment plans. Credit card, installment, deferred payment.

Application procedures. FAFSA, institutional form required. No deadline. Applicants notified on rolling basis starting 3/1, must reply by 5/1 or within 4 week(s) of notification.

Contact. **Financial aid office:** (631) 283-4000
James Newell, Director of Financial Aid
239 Montauk Highway
Southampton, NY 11968

Machzikei Hadath Rabbinical College

Brooklyn, New York
Five-year private
Federal Code: 013026

	Living at home	On-campus
Tuition and fees (projected):	$5,500	$5,500
Room and board:		$1,800

Application procedures. No deadline. Applicants notified on rolling basis.

Contact. **Financial aid office:** (718) 854-8777
Dov Garfinkel, Director of Financial Aid
5407 16th Avenue
Brooklyn, NY 11204

Manhattan College

Riverdale, New York
www.manhattan.edu
Four-year private
Federal Code: 002758

College costs. Program fees range from $1,000 to $1,700 depending on program.

	Living at home	On-campus
Tuition and fees (projected):	$19,000	$19,000
Room and board:		$8,100
Board only:	$2,000	
Books and supplies:	$750	$750
Personal expenses:	$1,000	$1,000
Transportation:	$800	$500

Undergraduate aid. All financial aid based on need. Average financial aid package for full-time students was $12,454; for part-time $5,320. 62% awarded as scholarships/grants, 38% as loans/jobs. **Student debt:** 68% of graduating class borrowed to fund education; average debt was $16,250.

Freshman aid. Out of 735 full-time freshmen, 608 applied for aid; 527 were judged to have need; of these 626 received aid. Average package met 90% of need. 80 students had full need met. Average scholarship/grant was $5,844; average loan $2,480.

Policies to reduce costs. Tuition/fee waivers for children of alumni, employees and their families. Credit/placement for qualifying scores on AP, CLEP examinations. Work study available nights, weekends and for part-time students.

Payment plans. Credit card, installment, deferred payment.

Application procedures. FAFSA required. Priority date 2/15; closing date 4/15. Applicants notified on rolling basis starting 1/1, must reply by 5/1. Early decision closing date 11/15. **Transfers:** Priority date 4/15; no deadline.

Contact. **Financial aid office:** (718) 862-7300
Ed Keough, Director of Student Financial Services
Manhattan College Parkway
Riverdale, NY 10471

Manhattan School of Music

New York, New York
www.msmnyc.edu
Four-year private
Federal Code: 002759

College costs. $990 health fee unless already insured.

	Living at home	On-campus
Tuition and fees (2002-2003):	$22,700	$22,700
Room only:		$7,300
Board only:	$2,100	
Books and supplies:	$800	$800
Personal expenses:	$1,200	$1,200
Transportation:	$1,500	$1,500

Undergraduate aid. **Need-based:** Average financial aid package for full-time students was $12,921; for part-time $6,526. 59% awarded as scholarships/grants, 41% as loans/jobs. **Non-need-based:** 79% awarded as scholarships/grants, 21% as loans/jobs. Scholarships based on academics, leadership, music/drama. **Student debt:** 64% of graduating class borrowed to fund education; average debt was $17,125.

Freshman aid. **Need-based:** Out of 105 full-time freshmen, 53 applied for aid; 42 were judged to have need; of these 42 received aid. Average package met 36% of need. 3 students had full need met. Average scholarship/grant was $7,934; average loan $2,688. **Non-need based:** 3 full-time freshmen with need received non-need scholarships; 38 without need received awards.

Policies to reduce costs. Tuition/fee waivers for employees and their families. Credit/placement for qualifying scores on AP examinations. Work study available nights and weekends.

Payment plans. Deferred payment.

Application procedures. FAFSA, institutional form, CSS PROFILE required. Closing date 3/15. Applicants notified on rolling basis starting 4/1, must reply by 5/1 or within 2 week(s) of notification.

Contact. **Financial aid office:** (212) 749-2802 ext. 4463
Amy Anderson, Director of Admission and Financial Aid
120 Claremont Avenue
New York, NY 10027-4698

Manhattanville College

Purchase, New York
www.manhattanville.edu
Four-year private
Federal Code: 002760

	Living at home	On-campus
Tuition and fees:	$23,040	$23,040
Room and board:		$9,380
Board only:	$3,910	
Books and supplies:	$800	$800
Personal expenses:	$1,500	$800
Transportation:	$800	$300

Undergraduate aid. **Need-based:** Average financial aid package for full-time students was $17,432. 60% awarded as scholarships/grants, 40% as loans/jobs. Need-based aid available for part-time students. **Non-need-based:** 72% awarded as scholarships/grants, 28% as loans/jobs. Scholarships based on academics. **Additional information:** Upper level students may earn additional money and academic credit through internship program.

Freshman aid. **Need-based:** Out of 402 full-time freshmen, 366 applied for aid; 264 were judged to have need; of these 245 received aid. Average package met 89% of need. 118 students had full need met. Average scholarship/grant was $9,712; average loan $3,071. **Non-need based:** 237 full-time freshmen with need received non-need scholarships; 371 without need received awards.

Policies to reduce costs. Tuition/fee waivers for senior citizens, employees and their families. Credit/placement for qualifying scores on AP, IB, CLEP examinations. Work study available nights, weekends and for part-time students.

Payment plans. Credit card, installment, deferred payment.

Application procedures. FAFSA required. Priority date 4/15; no closing date. Applicants notified on rolling basis starting 2/1, must reply by 5/1 or within 2 week(s) of notification. Early decision closing date 12/1. **Transfers:** No deadline.

Contact. **Financial aid office:** (914) 323-5357
Maria Barlaam, Director of Financial Aid
2900 Purchase Street
Purchase, NY 10577

Mannes College of Music

New York, New York
www.mannes.edu
Four-year private
Federal Code: 002780

	Living at home	On-campus
Tuition and fees (2002-2003):	$20,250	$20,250
Room only:		$7,500
Board only:	$1,984	
Books and supplies:	$2,062	$2,062
Personal expenses:	$1,742	$1,742
Transportation:	$744	$744

Undergraduate aid. **Need-based:** Average financial aid package for full-time students was $13,625. 75% awarded as scholarships/grants, 25% as loans/jobs. **Non-need-based:** 68% awarded as scholarships/grants, 32% as loans/jobs. Scholarships based on academics, leadership, music/drama. **Student debt:** 63% of graduating class borrowed to fund education; average debt was $21,512. **Additional information:** Closing date for scholarship applications 2 weeks prior to audition date.

Freshman aid. Need-based: Average package met 48% of need. Average scholarship/grant was $8,628; average loan $3,015.

Policies to reduce costs. Tuition/fee waivers for unemployed or children of unemployed.

Payment plans. Installment, deferred payment.

Application procedures. FAFSA required. Priority date 3/1; no closing date. Applicants notified on rolling basis starting 3/1, must reply by 5/1 or within 4 week(s) of notification. **Transfers:** Priority date 3/1.

Contact. Financial aid office: (212) 580-0210 ext. 248
Ramon Verdejo, Financial Aid Director
150 West 85th Street
New York, NY 10024

Maria College

Albany, New York
www.mariacollege.edu
Two-year private **Federal Code: 002763**

	Living at home
Tuition and fees (2002-2003):	$6,450
Per-credit charge:	$230
Board only:	$1,500
Books and supplies:	$600
Personal expenses:	$500
Transportation:	$600

Undergraduate aid. All financial aid based on need. Average financial aid package for full-time students was $6,967; for part-time $4,102. 56% awarded as scholarships/grants, 44% as loans/jobs. **Student debt:** 71% of graduating class borrowed to fund education; average debt was $5,405.

Freshman aid. Out of 65 full-time freshmen, 53 applied for aid; 48 were judged to have need; of these 48 received aid. Average package met 57% of need. Average scholarship/grant was $5,083; average loan $1,863.

Policies to reduce costs. Tuition/fee waivers for senior citizens, family of clergy, employees and their families. Credit/placement for qualifying scores on AP, IB, CLEP examinations. Work study available nights, weekends and for part-time students.

Payment plans. Credit card payment.

Application procedures. FAFSA required. No deadline. Applicants notified on rolling basis starting 2/1, must reply within 2 week(s) of notification.

Contact. Financial aid office: (518) 438-3111 ext. 229
Kenneth Clough, Director of Student Records
700 New Scotland Avenue
Albany, NY 12208

Marist College

Poughkeepsie, New York
www.marist.edu
Four-year private **Federal Code: 002765**

	Living at home	On-campus
Tuition and fees (2002-2003):	$17,894	$17,894
Room and board:		$8,584
Books and supplies:	$700	$700
Personal expenses:	$575	$575
Transportation:	$637	$320

Undergraduate aid. Need-based: Average financial aid package for full-time students was $10,569; for part-time $4,082. 53% awarded as scholarships/grants, 47% as loans/jobs. **Non-need-based:** 45% awarded as scholarships/grants, 55% as loans/jobs. Scholarships based on academics, alumni affiliation, athletics, leadership, minority status, music/drama, state/district residency. **Student debt:** 59% of graduating class borrowed to fund education; average debt was $19,967.

Freshman aid. Need-based: Out of 1,020 full-time freshmen, 812 applied for aid; 812 were judged to have need; of these 803 received aid. Average package met 72% of need. 127 students had full need met. Average scholarship/grant was $7,378; average loan $3,245. **Non-need based:** 296 full-time freshmen with need received non-need scholarships; 57 without need received awards; 47 received athletic scholarships.

Merit scholarships. Merit and athletic awards for undergraduates; $4,500,000 available.

Policies to reduce costs. Tuition/fee waivers for minority students, employees and their families. Credit/placement for qualifying scores on AP, IB, CLEP examinations. Work study available nights and weekends.

Payment plans. Credit card, installment payment.

Application procedures. FAFSA, institutional form required. Closing date 2/15. Applicants notified on rolling basis starting 3/15, must reply by 5/1 or within 2 week(s) of notification. **Transfers:** No deadline. FAFSA should be filed as soon as possible after January 1.

Contact. Financial aid office: (845) 575-3230
Joe Weglarz, Director of Financial Aid
3399 North Road
Poughkeepsie, NY 12601-1387

Marymount College of Fordham University

Tarrytown, New York
www.marymt.edu
Four-year private **Federal Code: 002768**

	Living at home	On-campus
Tuition and fees (2002-2003):	$17,210	$17,210
Room and board:		$8,695
Board only:	$1,790	
Books and supplies:	$840	$840
Personal expenses:	$1,375	$1,170
Transportation:	$1,980	$1,315

Undergraduate aid. Need-based: Average financial aid package for full-time students was $14,441; for part-time $4,951. 58% awarded as scholarships/grants, 42% as loans/jobs. **Non-need-based:** 71% awarded as scholarships/grants, 29% as loans/jobs. Scholarships based on academics. **Student debt:** 61% of graduating class borrowed to fund education; average debt was $11,793.

Freshman aid. Need-based: Out of 222 full-time freshmen, 200 applied for aid; 179 were judged to have need; of these 179 received aid. Average package met 70% of need. 16 students had full need met. Average scholarship/grant was $11,365; average loan $3,245. **Non-need based:** 14 full-time freshmen with need received non-need scholarships; 21 without need received awards.

Merit scholarships. Merit Awards based on GPA and test scores, ranging from $1,500-$14,700.

Policies to reduce costs. Tuition/fee waivers for family members, employees and their families. Credit/placement for qualifying scores on AP, IB, CLEP examinations. Work study available nights.

Payment plans. Credit card, installment payment.

Application procedures. FAFSA required. Priority date 3/1; no closing date. Applicants notified on rolling basis starting 3/15, must reply within 2 week(s) of notification. **Transfers:** No deadline. Scholarships available, amount keyed to GPA at previous college.

Contact. Financial aid office: (914) 332-8345
Dianne Pepitone, Director of Financial Assistance
100 Marymount Avenue
Tarrytown, NY 10591-3796

Marymount Manhattan College

New York, New York
marymount.mmm.edu
Four-year private **Federal Code: 002769**

	Living at home	On-campus
Tuition and fees (2002-2003):	$15,535	$15,535
Room only:		$8,800
Books and supplies:	$600	$600
Personal expenses:	$1,160	$1,160
Transportation:	$450	$450

Undergraduate aid. Need-based: Need-based aid available for full-time and part-time students. **Non-need-based:** Scholarships based on academics, alumni affiliation.

Policies to reduce costs. Tuition/fee waivers for senior citizens, employees and their families. Credit/placement for qualifying scores on AP, IB,

CLEP examinations. Work study available nights, weekends and for part-time students.

Payment plans. Credit card, installment payment.

Application procedures. FAFSA required. Priority date 2/15; no closing date. Applicants notified on rolling basis starting 3/15, must reply by 5/1 or within 2 week(s) of notification. **Transfers:** Must submit academic and financial transcripts from previous institutions.

Contact. **Financial aid office:** (212) 517-0480
Breisada Rios, Director of Financial Aid
221 East 71st Street
New York, NY 10021-4597

Medaille College

Buffalo, New York
www.medaille.edu
Four-year private **Federal Code: 002777**

	Living at home	On-campus
Tuition and fees (2002-2003):	$13,030	$13,030
Room and board:		$5,950
Board only:	$2,750	
Books and supplies:	$900	$900
Personal expenses:	$1,000	$1,000
Transportation:	$1,050	$1,050

Undergraduate aid. **Need-based:** Average financial aid package for full-time students was $10,000. 46% awarded as scholarships/grants, 54% as loans/jobs. Need-based aid available for part-time students. **Non-need-based:** 2% awarded as scholarships/grants, 98% as loans/jobs. Scholarships based on academics, state/district residency.

Freshman aid. **Need-based:** Out of 235 full-time freshmen, 201 applied for aid; 197 were judged to have need; of these 197 received aid. Average package met 78% of need. 60 students had full need met. Average scholarship/grant was $2,500; average loan $2,600. **Non-need based:** 125 full-time freshmen with need received non-need scholarships; 42 without need received awards.

Merit scholarships. Trustee Scholarships; for a 92 average or higher; $5,000 per year. Presidential Scholarships; for a 90-91 average; $2,000 per year. Dean Scholarships; for an 88-89 average; $1,500 per year. Merit Scholarships; for an 85-87 average; $1,000 per year.

Policies to reduce costs. Tuition/fee waivers for adults, employees and their families. Prepayment discount; credit/placement for qualifying scores on AP, IB, CLEP examinations.

Payment plans. Credit card, installment, deferred payment.

Application procedures. FAFSA, institutional form required. Priority date 4/15; no closing date. Applicants notified on rolling basis starting 5/1, must reply within 2 week(s) of notification.

Contact. **Financial aid office:** (716) 884-3281
Rachel Barker, Director of Financial Aid
18 Agassiz Circle
Buffalo, NY 14214

Mercy College

Dobbs Ferry, New York
www.mercy.edu
Four-year private **Federal Code: 002772**

	Living at home	On-campus
Tuition and fees:	$10,844	$10,844
Room and board:		$7,700
Books and supplies:	$500	$500
Personal expenses:	$800	
Transportation:	$700	

Undergraduate aid. **Need-based:** Need-based aid available for full-time and part-time students.

Policies to reduce costs. Tuition/fee waivers for senior citizens, employees and their families. Credit/placement for qualifying scores on AP, CLEP examinations. Work study available nights, weekends and for part-time students.

Payment plans. Credit card, installment, deferred payment.

Application procedures. FAFSA required. Priority date 6/1; no closing date. Applicants notified on rolling basis starting 3/1, must reply within 4 week(s) of notification.

Contact. **Financial aid office:** (914) 674-7328
Neal Harris, Financial Aid Officer
555 Broadway
Dobbs Ferry, NY 10522

Metropolitan College of New York

New York, New York
www.metropolitan.edu
Four-year private **Federal Code: 009769**

College costs. 3 full semesters each calendar year. Students attend classes for full year.

	Living at home
Tuition and fees:	$16,635
Board only:	$6,000
Books and supplies:	$1,500
Personal expenses:	$726
Transportation:	$1,820

Undergraduate aid. **Need-based:** Need-based aid available for full-time and part-time students. **Non-need-based:** Scholarships based on academics. **Additional information:** Limited merit scholarships.

Merit scholarships. Presidential scholarships awarded on the basis of academic merit; awards up to $1300 per semester. This award given to top 10% of accepted students each semester.

Policies to reduce costs. Tuition/fee waivers for employees and their families. Tuition at time of enrollment guaranteed for 4 years; credit/placement for qualifying scores on IB, CLEP examinations. Work study available for part-time students.

Payment plans. Credit card, installment, deferred payment.

Application procedures. FAFSA required. Priority date 8/15; no closing date. Applicants notified on rolling basis. **Transfers:** Priority date 8/15; no deadline.

Contact. **Financial aid office:** (212) 343-1234 ext. 5004
Rosabel Gomez, Director of Financial Aid
75 Varick Street
New York, NY 10013-1919

Mildred Elley

Latham, New York
Two-year proprietary **Federal Code: 022195**

College costs (2002-2003). $8,640 per year includes tuition, fees, books and supplies for associate program or certificate program.

Undergraduate aid. All financial aid based on need. Need-based aid available for full-time and part-time students.

Policies to reduce costs. Tuition at time of enrollment guaranteed for 2 years. Work study available nights and for part-time students.

Payment plans. Credit card, installment, deferred payment.

Application procedures. FAFSA required.

Contact. Heidi Nocosia, Director of Financial Aid
800 New Loudon Road, Suite 5120
Latham, NY 12110

Mohawk Valley Community College

Utica, New York
www.mvcc.edu
Two-year public **Federal Code: 002871**

	Living at home	On-campus
Tuition and fees (2002-2003):	$3,054	$3,054
Out-of-state:	$5,654	$5,654
Per-credit charge:	$99	$99
Per-credit out-of-state:	$198	$198
Room and board:		$5,690
Books and supplies:	$800	$800
Personal expenses:	$720	$975
Transportation:	$910	$1,040

Undergraduate aid. **Need-based:** 59% awarded as scholarships/grants, 41% as loans/jobs. Need-based aid available for part-time students. **Student**

debt: 73% of graduating class borrowed to fund education; average debt was $6,500.

Freshman aid. Need-based: Average package met 88% of need. Average scholarship/grant was $2,364; average loan $1,313.

Policies to reduce costs. Tuition/fee waivers for senior citizens, employees and their families. Credit/placement for qualifying scores on AP examinations. Work study available nights, weekends and for part-time students.

Payment plans. Credit card payment.

Application procedures. FAFSA, institutional form required. Priority date 4/15; no closing date. Applicants notified on rolling basis starting 3/1, must reply within 2 week(s) of notification. **Transfers:** No deadline.

Contact. Financial aid office: (315) 792-5415
Annette Broski, Director, Student Financial Aid
1101 Sherman Drive
Utica, NY 13501-5394

Molloy College

Rockville Centre, New York
www.molloy.edu
Four-year private **Federal Code: 002775**

	Living at home
Tuition and fees (2002-2003):	$14,790
Board only:	$1,500
Books and supplies:	$800
Personal expenses:	$1,250
Transportation:	$1,700

Undergraduate aid. Need-based: Need-based aid available for full-time and part-time students. **Non-need-based:** Scholarships based on academics, art, athletics, leadership, music/drama.

Merit scholarships. Molloy Scholar Scholarship gives full-tuition for minimum 95 high school average and minimum 1250 SAT or 28 ACT; 10 awarded annually; renewable for 3.5 cumulative GPA. Dominican Academic Scholarship ranges from $1,000 through $8,500 for minimum 88 high school average and minimum 1000 SAT; 50 awarded annually, renewable with 3.0 cumulative GPA. Community Service Awards range from $1,000 to $3,000, renewable for 2.5 cumulative GPA, awarded to incoming freshmen demonstrating committment to community and school; 10 awarded annually.

Policies to reduce costs. Tuition/fee waivers for family members, family of clergy, employees and their families. Credit/placement for qualifying scores on AP, IB, CLEP examinations.

Payment plans. Credit card, installment, deferred payment.

Application procedures. FAFSA required. Priority date 4/15; no closing date. Applicants notified on rolling basis. **Transfers:** No deadline. All transfer applicants with a minimum of 30 credits and 3.0 GPA automatically considered for transfer scholarships ranging from $1,500-$3,000.

Contact. Financial aid office: (516) 678-5000 ext. 6249
Vincent Tunstall, Director of Financial Aid
1000 Hempstead Avenue
Rockville Centre, NY 11570

Monroe College

Bronx, New York
www.monroecollege.edu
Two-year proprietary **Federal Code: 004799**

College costs. Tuition, fees, room and board, all estimated expenses based on 3 semesters.

	Living at home	On-campus
Tuition and fees (2002-2003):	$12,690	$12,690
Per-credit charge:	$332	$332
Room and board:		$7,220
Board only:	$3,300	
Books and supplies:	$1,350	$1,350
Personal expenses:	$2,085	
Transportation:	$1,080	

Undergraduate aid. All financial aid based on need. Need-based aid available for full-time and part-time students.

Policies to reduce costs. Tuition/fee waivers for employees and their families. Credit/placement for qualifying scores on AP, IB, CLEP examinations. Work study available nights, weekends and for part-time students.

Payment plans. Credit card, installment, deferred payment.

Application procedures. FAFSA required. Closing date 3/31. Applicants notified on rolling basis starting 7/1.

Contact. Financial aid office: (718) 933-6700
Howard Leslie, Dean of Student Financial Services
Monroe College Way
Bronx, NY 10468

Monroe Community College

Rochester, New York
www.monroecc.edu
Two-year public **Federal Code: 002872**

	Living at home
Tuition and fees (2002-2003):	$2,688
Out-of-state:	$5,188
Per-credit charge:	$105
Per-credit out-of-state:	$210
Books and supplies:	$480

Undergraduate aid. All financial aid based on need. Need-based aid available for full-time and part-time students.

Policies to reduce costs. Tuition/fee waivers for senior citizens, employees and their families. Credit/placement for qualifying scores on AP, CLEP examinations. Work study available nights.

Payment plans. Credit card, installment, deferred payment.

Application procedures. FAFSA required. Priority date 5/1; no closing date. Applicants notified on rolling basis, must reply within 2 week(s) of notification.

Contact. Jerome St. Croix, Director of Financial Aid
Office of Admissions-Monroe Community College
Rochester, NY 14692-8908

Mount St. Mary College

Newburgh, New York
www.msmc.edu
Four-year private **Federal Code: 002778**

	Living at home	On-campus
Tuition and fees (2002-2003):	$13,335	$13,335
Room and board:		$6,520
Books and supplies:	$500	$500
Personal expenses:	$750	$750
Transportation:	$1,000	$300

Undergraduate aid. All financial aid based on need. Average financial aid package for full-time students was $9,115; for part-time $5,601. 58% awarded as scholarships/grants, 42% as loans/jobs. **Student debt:** 70% of graduating class borrowed to fund education; average debt was $19,070.

Freshman aid. Out of 350 full-time freshmen, 337 applied for aid; 257 were judged to have need; of these 254 received aid. Average package met 61% of need. 41 students had full need met. Average scholarship/grant was $6,073; average loan $2,480.

Policies to reduce costs. Tuition/fee waivers for employees and their families. Credit/placement for qualifying scores on AP, IB, CLEP examinations. Work study available nights and weekends.

Payment plans. Credit card, installment, deferred payment.

Application procedures. FAFSA, institutional form required. Priority date 2/15; no closing date. Applicants notified on rolling basis starting 3/15, must reply within 2 week(s) of notification. **Transfers:** Priority date 3/15; no deadline.

Contact. Financial aid office: (845) 569-3194
Susan Twomey, Director of Financial Aid
330 Powell Avenue
Newburgh, NY 12550

Nassau Community College

Garden City, New York
www.ncc.edu
Two-year public **Federal Code: 002873**

	Living at home
Tuition and fees (2002-2003):	$2,755
Out-of-state:	$5,280
Per-credit charge:	$106
Per-credit out-of-state:	$212
Books and supplies:	$720
Personal expenses:	$1,200
Transportation:	$1,272

Undergraduate aid. Need-based: Need-based aid available for full-time and part-time students. **Non-need-based:** Scholarships based on academics, art, music/drama.

Policies to reduce costs. Credit/placement for qualifying scores on AP, CLEP examinations. Work study available nights and for part-time students.

Payment plans. Credit card, installment payment.

Application procedures. FAFSA, institutional form required. Priority date 6/1; no closing date. Applicants notified on rolling basis, must reply within 1 week(s) of notification. **Transfers:** Priority date 6/1; no deadline.

Contact. Financial aid office: (516) 572-7396
Evangeline Manjares, Assistant Dean, Financial Aid
One Education Drive
Garden City, NY 11530

Nazareth College of Rochester

Rochester, New York
www.naz.edu
Four-year private **Federal Code: 002779**

College costs. Fees vary by program.

	Living at home	On-campus
Tuition and fees (2002-2003):	$16,410	$16,410
Room and board:		$6,930
Board only:	$2,460	
Books and supplies:	$800	$800
Personal expenses:	$900	$900

Undergraduate aid. Need-based: Average financial aid package for full-time students was $14,097; for part-time $5,833. 60% awarded as scholarships/grants, 40% as loans/jobs. **Non-need-based:** 39% awarded as scholarships/grants, 61% as loans/jobs. Scholarships based on academics, alumni affiliation, art, minority status, music/drama, state/district residency. **Student debt:** 81% of graduating class borrowed to fund education; average debt was $18,750.

Freshman aid. Need-based: Out of 386 full-time freshmen, 363 applied for aid; 298 were judged to have need; of these 297 received aid. Average package met 87% of need. Average scholarship/grant was $10,802; average loan $2,964. **Non-need based:** 36 full-time freshmen with need received non-need scholarships; 72 without need received awards.

Merit scholarships. Presidential Scholarship for full tuition, Dean's Scholarship for $12,500, Nazareth Scholars for $8,500, and Founders Scholarship for $6,000. Access merit scholarship available at $2,500 per year. All awarded based on grades, test scores, class rank and course load. Trustee Scholarships at $4,000 available for students who meet criteria but do not receive other merit scholarships. Campus diversity, regional, art, music, and theater scholarships also available.

Policies to reduce costs. Tuition/fee waivers for children of alumni, family members, employees and their families. Credit/placement for qualifying scores on AP, IB, CLEP examinations. Work study available nights and weekends.

Payment plans. Credit card, installment payment.

Application procedures. FAFSA required. CSS PROFILE required of early decision applicants only. Priority date 2/15; closing date 5/1. Applicants notified on rolling basis starting 2/20, must reply by 5/1 or within 2 week(s) of notification. Early decision closing date 11/15. **Transfers:** Priority date 2/15; no deadline.

Contact. Bruce Woolley, Director of Financial Aid
4245 East Avenue
Rochester, NY 14618-3790

New York Institute of Technology

Old Westbury, New York
www.nyit.edu
Four-year private **Federal Code: 002782**

College costs. Tuition for architecture, engineering, allied health, and BS/DO programs $16,000.

	Living at home	On-campus
Tuition and fees (2002-2003):	$15,950	$15,950
Room and board:		$7,680
Books and supplies:	$1,200	$1,200
Personal expenses:	$2,748	$2,748
Transportation:	$1,270	

Undergraduate aid. Need-based: Average financial aid package for full-time students was $8,323; for part-time $3,649. 46% awarded as scholarships/grants, 54% as loans/jobs. **Non-need-based:** 63% awarded as scholarships/grants, 37% as loans/jobs. Scholarships based on academics, athletics. **Student debt:** 75% of graduating class borrowed to fund education; average debt was $17,125.

Freshman aid. Need-based: Out of 840 full-time freshmen, 807 applied for aid; 670 were judged to have need; of these 629 received aid. Average scholarship/grant was $6,080. **Non-need based:** 572 full-time freshmen with need received non-need scholarships; 137 without need received awards; 38 received athletic scholarships.

Policies to reduce costs. Tuition/fee waivers for children of alumni, senior citizens, unemployed or children of unemployed, employees and their families. Prepayment discount; credit/placement for qualifying scores on AP, IB, CLEP examinations.

Payment plans. Credit card, installment, deferred payment.

Application procedures. FAFSA required. Priority date 3/1; no closing date. Applicants notified on rolling basis starting 3/15, must reply by 5/1 or within 2 week(s) of notification. **Transfers:** No deadline.

Contact. Financial aid office: (516) 686-7680
Robbie de Leur, Director of Financial Aid
Box 8000
Old Westbury, NY 11568

New York School of Interior Design

New York, New York
www.nysid.edu
Four-year private **Federal Code: 013606**

	Living at home
Tuition and fees:	$18,070
Books and supplies:	$1,000
Personal expenses:	$900
Transportation:	$1,100

Undergraduate aid. All financial aid based on need. Average financial aid package for full-time students was $8,500; for part-time $3,500. 29% awarded as scholarships/grants, 71% as loans/jobs. **Student debt:** 15% of graduating class borrowed to fund education; average debt was $13,250.

Freshman aid. Average package met 50% of need. Average scholarship/grant was $5,000; average loan $2,625.

Policies to reduce costs. Tuition/fee waivers for employees and their families. Work study available nights, weekends and for part-time students.

Payment plans. Credit card, installment, deferred payment.

Application procedures. FAFSA, institutional form required. Priority date 5/1; no closing date. Applicants notified on rolling basis starting 2/1, must reply within 2 week(s) of notification. **Transfers:** No deadline.

Contact. Financial aid office: (212) 472-1500 ext.212
Nina Bunchuk, Financial Aid Administrator
170 East 70th Street
New York, NY 10021

New York University
New York, New York
www.nyu.edu
Four-year private **Federal Code: 002785**

	Living at home	On-campus
Tuition and fees (2002-2003):	$26,646	$26,646
Room and board:		$10,430
Board only:	$1,300	
Books and supplies:	$450	$450
Personal expenses:	$500	$1,000

Undergraduate aid. Need-based: Average financial aid package for full-time students was $17,745; for part-time $6,155. 57% awarded as scholarships/grants, 43% as loans/jobs. **Non-need-based:** 60% awarded as scholarships/grants, 40% as loans/jobs. Scholarships based on academics. **Student debt:** 60% of graduating class borrowed to fund education; average debt was $21,495. **Additional information:** Both need-based and merit scholarships available to first-time students. Range from $1,000 to $25,000.

Freshman aid. Need-based: Out of 3,909 full-time freshmen, 3,018 applied for aid; 2,394 were judged to have need; of these 2,386 received aid. Average package met 72% of need. Average scholarship/grant was $13,043; average loan $4,384. **Non-need based:** 639 without need received awards.

Policies to reduce costs. Tuition/fee waivers for employees and their families. Prepayment discount; credit/placement for qualifying scores on AP, IB, CLEP examinations.

Payment plans. Credit card, installment, deferred payment.

Application procedures. FAFSA required. Closing date 2/15. Applicants notified on rolling basis starting 4/1, must reply by 5/1. Early decision closing date 11/15.

Contact. Financial aid office: (212) 998-1212
Antonio Delbono, Director of Financial Aid
22 Washington Square North
New York, NY 10011-9108

Niagara County Community College
Sanborn, New York
www.niagaracc.suny.edu
Two-year public **Federal Code: 002874**

	Living at home
Tuition and fees (2002-2003):	$2,860
Out-of-state:	$4,160
Per-credit charge:	$105
Per-credit out-of-state:	$158
Board only:	$1,980
Books and supplies:	$615
Personal expenses:	$650
Transportation:	$650

Undergraduate aid. All financial aid based on need. 63% awarded as scholarships/grants, 37% as loans/jobs. Need-based aid available for part-time students. **Additional information:** Assistance offered placing students in part-time employment. Students can charge books, food coupons, or $100 advance against anticipated financial aid.

Policies to reduce costs. Tuition/fee waivers for senior citizens, employees and their families. Credit/placement for qualifying scores on AP, IB, CLEP examinations. Work study available nights and for part-time students.

Payment plans. Credit card, installment, deferred payment.

Application procedures. FAFSA required. Priority date 4/1; no closing date. Applicants notified on rolling basis starting 5/1, must reply within 2 week(s) of notification. **Transfers:** No deadline. Must file appropriate state and federal change forms at least 4 weeks before registration date.

Contact. Financial aid office: (716) 614-6200
Randyll Bowen, Director of Enrollment Services
3111 Saunders Settlement Road
Sanborn, NY 14132

Niagara University
Niagara University, New York
www.niagara.edu
Four-year private **Federal Code: 002788**

	Living at home	On-campus
Tuition and fees:	$17,380	$17,380
Room and board:		$7,670
Books and supplies:	$700	$700
Personal expenses:	$650	$650
Transportation:	$800	$600

Undergraduate aid. Need-based: Average financial aid package for full-time students was $15,555; for part-time $5,452. 66% awarded as scholarships/grants, 34% as loans/jobs. **Non-need-based:** 51% awarded as scholarships/grants, 49% as loans/jobs. Scholarships based on academics, athletics, music/drama. **Student debt:** 75% of graduating class borrowed to fund education; average debt was $15,402. **Additional information:** Opportunity program available for academically and economically disadvantaged students.

Freshman aid. Need-based: Out of 737 full-time freshmen, 629 applied for aid; 516 were judged to have need; of these 516 received aid. Average package met 82% of need. 147 students had full need met. Average scholarship/grant was $11,607; average loan $2,925. **Non-need based:** 89 full-time freshmen with need received non-need scholarships; 66 without need received awards.

Policies to reduce costs. Tuition/fee waivers for family of clergy, employees and their families. Tuition at time of enrollment guaranteed for 4 years; credit/placement for qualifying scores on AP, CLEP examinations. Work study available nights and weekends.

Payment plans. Credit card, installment, deferred payment.

Application procedures. FAFSA required. Priority date 2/15; no closing date. Applicants notified on rolling basis starting 3/1, must reply within 3 week(s) of notification. **Transfers:** Academic scholarship available: $5,800-$6,700 per year based on minimum 3.0 GPA from transfer institution; $3,700 per year based on 2.5-2.99 GPA.

Contact. Financial aid office: (716) 286-8686
Maureen Salfi, Director of Financial Aid
Niagara University, NY 14109

North Country Community College
Saranac Lake, New York
nccc.edu
Two-year public **Federal Code: 007111**

	Living at home
Tuition and fees (2002-2003):	$2,825
Out-of-state:	$5,325
Per-credit charge:	$110
Per-credit out-of-state:	$220
Board only:	$2,450
Books and supplies:	$750
Personal expenses:	$750
Transportation:	$850

Undergraduate aid. All financial aid based on need. Average financial aid package for full-time students was $6,653; for part-time $4,258. 64% awarded as scholarships/grants, 36% as loans/jobs. **Student debt:** 60% of graduating class borrowed to fund education; average debt was $5,200.

Freshman aid. Out of 297 full-time freshmen, 278 applied for aid; 234 were judged to have need; of these 197 received aid. Average package met 84% of need. 83 students had full need met. Average scholarship/grant was $3,000; average loan $2,050.

Policies to reduce costs. Tuition/fee waivers for senior citizens, employees and their families. Credit/placement for qualifying scores on AP, CLEP examinations. Work study available nights, weekends and for part-time students.

Payment plans. Credit card, installment payment.

Application procedures. FAFSA required. Priority date 4/1; no closing date. Applicants notified on rolling basis starting 4/1, must reply within 3 week(s) of notification. Early decision closing date 11/15. **Transfers:** No deadline.

Contact. Financial aid office: (518) 891-2915 ext. 229
Edwin Trathen, Assistant to the President for Enrollment Management
20 Winona Avenue
Saranac Lake, NY 12983

Nyack College

Nyack, New York
www.nyackcollege.edu
Four-year private **Federal Code: 002790**

	Living at home	On-campus
Tuition and fees:	$14,400	$14,400
Room and board:		$7,000
Board only:	$3,750	
Books and supplies:	$750	$750
Personal expenses:	$1,720	$1,720
Transportation:	$1,970	$690

Undergraduate aid. Need-based: Average financial aid package for full-time students was $12,620; for part-time $7,610. 60% awarded as scholarships/grants, 40% as loans/jobs. **Non-need-based:** 50% awarded as scholarships/grants, 50% as loans/jobs. Scholarships based on academics, athletics, leadership, minority status, music/drama, religious affiliation, state/district residency.

Freshman aid. Need-based: Out of 477 full-time freshmen, 390 applied for aid; 365 were judged to have need; of these 365 received aid. Average package met 54% of need. 58 students had full need met. Average scholarship/grant was $8,899; average loan $2,909. **Non-need based:** 18 full-time freshmen with need received non-need scholarships; 81 without need received awards; 24 received athletic scholarships.

Merit scholarships. More than 45 non-competitive scholarships and grants are available to students. Eligibility is based on GPA and varies according to the award. Prospective students are encouraged to contact the office of financial aid for details.

Policies to reduce costs. Tuition/fee waivers for employees and their families. Prepayment discount; credit/placement for qualifying scores on AP, CLEP examinations.

Payment plans. Credit card, installment payment.

Application procedures. FAFSA required. No deadline. Applicants notified on rolling basis starting 3/1, must reply by 7/1 or within 4 week(s) of notification. **Transfers:** No deadline.

Contact. **Financial aid office:** (845) 358-1710
Andres Valenzuela, Director of Student Financial Services
One South Boulevard
Nyack, NY 10960

Ohr Somayach Tanenbaum Education Center

Monsey, New York
Five-year private **Federal Code: 016417**

	On-campus
Comprehensive fee:	$11,500
Books and supplies:	$300
Personal expenses:	$725
Transportation:	$150

Payment plans. Installment payment.

Application procedures. No deadline. Applicants notified on rolling basis starting 7/1, must reply within 4 week(s) of notification.

Contact. **Financial aid office:** (845) 425-1370
Yisroel Rokowsky, Dean
244 Route 306
Monsey, NY 10952

Olean Business Institute

Olean, New York
www.oleanbusinessinstitute.net
Two-year proprietary **Federal Code: 009003**

	Living at home
Tuition and fees (2002-2003):	$7,950
Per-credit charge:	$260
Books and supplies:	$700

Payment plans. Credit card, installment payment.

Application procedures. FAFSA required. Priority date 5/1; no closing date. Applicants notified on rolling basis.

Contact. Valerie Goodwin, Financial Aid Director
301 North Union Street
Olean, NY 14760

Onondaga Community College

Syracuse, New York
www.sunyocc.edu
Two-year public **Federal Code: 002875**

	Living at home
Tuition and fees (2002-2003):	$2,806
Out-of-district:	$5,306
Out-of-state:	$7,806
Per-credit charge:	$98
Per-credit out-of-district:	$196
Per-credit out-of-state:	$294
Books and supplies:	$730
Personal expenses:	$450
Transportation:	$1,000

Undergraduate aid. All financial aid based on need. Need-based aid available for full-time and part-time students.

Policies to reduce costs. Tuition/fee waivers for employees and their families. Credit/placement for qualifying scores on AP, CLEP examinations. Work study available for part-time students.

Payment plans. Credit card, installment, deferred payment.

Application procedures. FAFSA required. Priority date 2/15; no closing date. Applicants notified on rolling basis starting 4/15, must reply within 4 week(s) of notification. **Transfers:** No deadline.

Contact. **Financial aid office:** (315) 469-2291
Lorna Roberts, Director of Financial Aid
4941 Onondaga Road
Syracuse, NY 13215

Orange County Community College

Middletown, New York
orange.cc.ny.us
Two-year public **Federal Code: 002876**

	Living at home
Tuition and fees (2002-2003):	$2,675
Out-of-state:	$5,175
Per-credit charge:	$100
Per-credit out-of-state:	$200
Books and supplies:	$600
Personal expenses:	$475
Transportation:	$650

Undergraduate aid. Need-based: Need-based aid available for full-time and part-time students.

Policies to reduce costs. Tuition/fee waivers for senior citizens, unemployed or children of unemployed, employees and their families. Credit/placement for qualifying scores on AP, CLEP examinations.

Payment plans. Credit card, installment, deferred payment.

Application procedures. FAFSA, institutional form required. Priority date 5/1; no closing date. Applicants notified on rolling basis starting 5/1, must reply within 4 week(s) of notification.

Contact. Sue Sheehan, Director of Student Financial Assistance
115 South Street
Middletown, NY 10940-0115

Pace University

New York, New York
www.pace.edu
Four-year private **Federal Code: 002791**

	Living at home	On-campus
Tuition and fees (2002-2003):	$18,208	$18,208
Room and board:		$7,590
Board only:	$1,900	
Books and supplies:	$720	$720
Personal expenses:	$1,160	$1,160
Transportation:	$1,550	$770

Undergraduate aid. Need-based: Average financial aid package for full-time students was $11,948; for part-time $5,473. 68% awarded as scholarships/grants, 32% as loans/jobs. **Non-need-based:** 27% awarded as scholarships/grants, 73% as loans/jobs. Scholarships based on academics, athletics, leadership. **Student debt:** 68% of graduating class borrowed to fund education; average debt was $19,402.

Freshman aid. Need-based: Average package met 81% of need. Average scholarship/grant was $10,507; average loan $3,201. **Non-need based:** 135 without need received awards.

Policies to reduce costs. Tuition/fee waivers for senior citizens, employees and their families. Credit/placement for qualifying scores on AP, IB, CLEP examinations.

Payment plans. Credit card, installment payment.

Application procedures. FAFSA required. Priority date 2/15; no closing date. Applicants notified on rolling basis starting 4/1, must reply by 5/1 or within 2 week(s) of notification.

Contact. Financial aid office: (212) 346-1300
Desiree Cilmi, Associate Vice President of Enrollment Management
1 Pace Plaza
New York, NY 10038

Pace University: Pleasantville/Briarcliff

Pleasantville, New York
www.pace.edu
Four-year private **Federal Code: 002791**

	Living at home	On-campus
Tuition and fees (2002-2003):	$18,208	$18,208
Room and board:		$7,590
Board only:	$1,900	
Books and supplies:	$720	$720
Personal expenses:	$1,160	$1,160
Transportation:	$1,550	$770

Undergraduate aid. Need-based: Average financial aid package for full-time students was $11,948; for part-time $5,473. 68% awarded as scholarships/grants, 32% as loans/jobs. **Non-need-based:** 27% awarded as scholarships/grants, 73% as loans/jobs. Scholarships based on academics, athletics, leadership. **Student debt:** 68% of graduating class borrowed to fund education; average debt was $19,402.

Freshman aid. Need-based: Average package met 81% of need. Average scholarship/grant was $10,507; average loan $3,201.

Policies to reduce costs. Tuition/fee waivers for senior citizens, employees and their families. Credit/placement for qualifying scores on AP, IB, CLEP examinations.

Payment plans. Credit card, installment payment.

Application procedures. FAFSA required. Priority date 2/15; no closing date. Applicants notified on rolling basis starting 4/1, must reply by 5/1 or within 2 week(s) of notification.

Contact. Financial aid office: (914) 773-3751
Desiree Cilmi, Associate Vice President Enrollment Management
861 Bedford Road
Pleasantville, NY 10570

Parsons School of Design

New York, New York
www.parsons.edu
Four-year private **Federal Code: 002780**

	Living at home	On-campus
Tuition and fees (2002-2003):	$24,400	$24,400
Room and board:		$9,896
Books and supplies:	$1,950	$1,950
Personal expenses:		$1,516

Undergraduate aid. Need-based: Average financial aid package for full-time students was $13,156. 67% awarded as scholarships/grants, 33% as loans/jobs. Need-based aid available for part-time students. **Non-need-based:** 11% awarded as scholarships/grants, 89% as loans/jobs. Scholarships based on academics, art, leadership. **Student debt:** 55% of graduating class borrowed to fund education; average debt was $23,919.

Freshman aid. Need-based: Out of 350 full-time freshmen, 264 applied for aid; 244 were judged to have need; of these 223 received aid. Average package met 52% of need. 12 students had full need met. Average scholarship/grant was $10,061; average loan $3,704. **Non-need based:** 32 full-time freshmen with need received non-need scholarships; 14 without need received awards.

Policies to reduce costs. Tuition/fee waivers for employees and their families. Credit/placement for qualifying scores on AP, IB examinations. Work study available nights, weekends and for part-time students.

Payment plans. Credit card, installment payment.

Application procedures. FAFSA required. Priority date 3/1; no closing date. Applicants notified on rolling basis starting 3/1, must reply within 4 week(s) of notification.

Contact. Financial aid office: (212) 229-8930
Julie Disa, Assistant Provost for University Financial Aid and Enrollment Management
66 Fifth Avenue
New York, NY 10011

Paul Smith's College

Paul Smiths, New York
www.paulsmiths.edu
Four-year private **Federal Code: 002795**

College costs. Program fees range from $600 to $1,400 depending on program.

	Living at home	On-campus
Tuition and fees (2002-2003):	$14,300	$14,300
Room and board:		$6,160
Board only:	$3,080	
Books and supplies:	$750	$750
Personal expenses:	$1,000	$1,000
Transportation:	$600	$400

Undergraduate aid. Need-based: Need-based aid available for full-time and part-time students. **Non-need-based:** Scholarships based on academics, athletics.

Merit scholarships. Many $500-$8,000 annual awards based on merit available to all students.

Policies to reduce costs. Tuition/fee waivers for employees and their families. Credit/placement for qualifying scores on AP, CLEP examinations. Work study available nights and weekends.

Payment plans. Credit card, installment, deferred payment.

Application procedures. FAFSA required. Priority date 3/31; no closing date. Applicants notified on rolling basis starting 3/1, must reply within 4 week(s) of notification. **Transfers:** Priority date 3/31; no deadline.

Contact. Financial aid office: (518) 327-6220
Mary Ellen Chamberlain, Director of Financial Aid
PO Box 265, Routes 30 & 86
Paul Smiths, NY 12970-0265

Phillips Beth Israel School of Nursing

New York, New York
www.wehealny.org/bischoolofnursing
Two-year private **Federal Code: 006438**

	Living at home
Tuition and fees:	$11,620
Per-credit charge:	$240
Board only:	$3,905
Books and supplies:	$1,490
Personal expenses:	$1,490
Transportation:	$1,070

Undergraduate aid. Need-based: Average financial aid package for full-time students was $7,866; for part-time $6,247. 55% awarded as scholarships/grants, 45% as loans/jobs. **Non-need-based:** 67% awarded as scholarships/grants, 33% as loans/jobs. Scholarships based on academics. **Student debt:** 55% of graduating class borrowed to fund education; average debt was $3,500.

Freshman aid. Need-based: Out of 12 full-time freshmen, 5 applied for aid; 4 were judged to have need; of these 4 received aid. Average package met 77% of need. 1 students had full need met. Average scholarship/grant was $8,920; average loan $3,560. **Non-need based:** 1 without need received awards.

Merit scholarships. Hillman Scholarship Program; variable number awarded each year; based on academic achievement; full tuition, books, and uniforms. Karpas Scholarship Program; 15 awarded each year; based on academic achievement; $3,000 a year.

Policies to reduce costs. Tuition/fee waivers for employees and their families. Credit/placement for qualifying scores on AP, CLEP examinations.

Payment plans. Credit card, installment payment.

Application procedures. FAFSA, institutional form required. Closing date 6/1. Applicants notified by 7/1, must reply within 2 week(s) of notification.

Contact. **Financial aid office:** (212) 614-6104
Bernice Pass-Stern, Director of Student Services
310 East 22nd Street
New York, NY 10010

Plaza College

Jackson Heights, New York
www.plazacollege.edu
Two-year proprietary **Federal Code: 012358**

	Living at home
Tuition and fees:	$6,225
Books and supplies:	$600
Personal expenses:	$1,800
Transportation:	$900

Policies to reduce costs. Tuition/fee waivers for children of alumni, family members, unemployed or children of unemployed, employees and their families.

Payment plans. Credit card, installment, deferred payment.

Application procedures. FAFSA, institutional form required. No deadline. Applicants notified on rolling basis.

Contact. **Financial aid office:** (718) 779-1430
Elizabeth Callahan, Vice President, Financial Affairs
74-09 37th Avenue
Jackson Heights, NY 11372

Polytechnic University

Brooklyn, New York
www.poly.edu
Four-year private **Federal Code: 002796**

	Living at home	On-campus
Tuition and fees (2002-2003):	$25,480	$25,480
Room and board:		$8,000
Books and supplies:	$575	$575
Personal expenses:	$1,350	$1,575
Transportation:	$815	$1,389

Undergraduate aid. **Need-based:** Average financial aid package for full-time students was $18,578; for part-time $7,675. 65% awarded as scholarships/grants, 35% as loans/jobs. **Non-need-based:** 88% awarded as scholarships/grants, 12% as loans/jobs. Scholarships based on academics, state/district residency. **Student debt:** 81% of graduating class borrowed to fund education; average debt was $18,295.

Freshman aid. **Need-based:** Out of 449 full-time freshmen, 442 applied for aid; 377 were judged to have need; of these 377 received aid. Average package met 83% of need. 61 students had full need met. Average scholarship/grant was $8,694; average loan $3,747. **Non-need based:** 276 full-time freshmen with need received non-need scholarships; 65 without need received awards.

Policies to reduce costs. Tuition/fee waivers for employees and their families. Credit/placement for qualifying scores on AP, IB examinations.

Payment plans. Credit card, installment, deferred payment.

Application procedures. FAFSA, institutional form, CSS PROFILE required. Priority date 3/1; no closing date. Applicants notified on rolling basis starting 3/15, must reply within 2 week(s) of notification. **Transfers:** Priority date 5/1; no deadline.

Contact. **Financial aid office:** (718) 260-3600
Veronica Lukas, Director of Financial Aid
6 Metrotech Center
Brooklyn, NY 11201-2999

Pratt Institute

Brooklyn, New York
www.pratt.edu
Four-year private **Federal Code: 002798**

	Living at home	On-campus
Tuition and fees:	$24,198	$24,198
Room and board:		$8,186
Books and supplies:	$3,000	$3,000
Personal expenses:	$650	$650
Transportation:	$800	

Undergraduate aid. **Need-based:** Average financial aid package for full-time students was $13,705; for part-time $7,855. 56% awarded as scholarships/grants, 44% as loans/jobs. **Non-need-based:** 95% awarded as scholarships/grants, 5% as loans/jobs. Scholarships based on academics, art.

Freshman aid. **Need-based:** Out of 623 full-time freshmen, 608 applied for aid; 532 were judged to have need; of these 532 received aid. Average package met 69% of need. Average scholarship/grant was $5,030; average loan $2,690. **Non-need based:** 369 full-time freshmen with need received non-need scholarships; 76 without need received awards.

Policies to reduce costs. Tuition/fee waivers for employees and their families. Credit/placement for qualifying scores on AP, CLEP examinations.

Payment plans. Credit card, installment, deferred payment.

Application procedures. FAFSA, institutional form required. Closing date 2/1. Applicants notified on rolling basis starting 4/15. Early decision closing date 11/15.

Contact. **Financial aid office:** (718) 636-3519
Karen Price Scott, Director of Financial Aid
200 Willoughby Avenue
Brooklyn, NY 11205

Rensselaer Polytechnic Institute

Troy, New York
www.rpi.edu
Four-year private **Federal Code: 002803**

	Living at home	On-campus
Tuition and fees:	$28,496	$28,496
Room and board:		$9,083
Books and supplies:	$1,621	$1,621
Transportation:	$3,010	

Undergraduate aid. **Need-based:** Average financial aid package for full-time students was $22,791. 68% awarded as scholarships/grants, 32% as loans/jobs. **Non-need-based:** 67% awarded as scholarships/grants, 33% as loans/jobs. Scholarships based on academics, art, athletics, leadership, minority status, music/drama. **Student debt:** 77% of graduating class borrowed to fund education; average debt was $24,590.

Freshman aid. **Need-based:** Out of 1,049 full-time freshmen, 872 applied for aid; 732 were judged to have need; of these 732 received aid. Average package met 93% of need. 458 students had full need met. Average scholarship/grant was $19,532; average loan $5,819. **Non-need based:** 242 full-time freshmen with need received non-need scholarships; 175 without need received awards; 4 received athletic scholarships.

Merit scholarships. Rensselaer Medals: $15,000 scholarships awarded by participating high schools for excellence in science and mathematics. Emily Roebling Award: to top ranking female admitted students; $7,500.

Policies to reduce costs. Tuition/fee waivers for employees and their families. Credit/placement for qualifying scores on AP, IB examinations.

Payment plans. Credit card, installment payment.

Application procedures. FAFSA required. Closing date 2/15. Applicants notified by 3/20. Early decision closing date 11/15. **Transfers:** Closing date 8/31.

Contact. **Financial aid office:** (518) 276-6813
James Stevenson, Director of Financial Aid
110 Eighth Street
Troy, NY 12180

Roberts Wesleyan College

Rochester, New York
www.roberts.edu
Four-year private **Federal Code: 002805**

	Living at home	On-campus
Tuition and fees (2002-2003):	$16,012	$16,012
Room and board:		$5,746
Board only:	$1,498	
Books and supplies:	$600	$600
Personal expenses:	$1,125	$1,125
Transportation:	$2,232	$567

Undergraduate aid. Need-based: Average financial aid package for full-time students was $13,263; for part-time $8,424. 57% awarded as scholarships/grants, 43% as loans/jobs. **Non-need-based:** 47% awarded as scholarships/grants, 53% as loans/jobs. Scholarships based on academics, alumni affiliation, art, athletics, music/drama, religious affiliation, state/district residency. **Student debt:** 93% of graduating class borrowed to fund education; average debt was $5,664. **Additional information:** Dollars for Scholars offer matching grants of up to $750.

Freshman aid. Need-based: Out of 243 full-time freshmen, 209 applied for aid; 196 were judged to have need; of these 196 received aid. Average package met 85% of need. 41 students had full need met. Average scholarship/grant was $9,282; average loan $3,817. **Non-need based:** 19 full-time freshmen with need received non-need scholarships; 35 without need received awards; 10 received athletic scholarships.

Policies to reduce costs. Tuition/fee waivers for children of alumni, senior citizens, family members, family of clergy, employees and their families. Credit/placement for qualifying scores on AP, CLEP examinations. Work study available nights, weekends and for part-time students.

Payment plans. Credit card, installment payment.

Application procedures. FAFSA, institutional form required. Priority date 3/15; no closing date. Applicants notified on rolling basis starting 3/15, must reply by 5/1 or within 2 week(s) of notification.

Contact. **Financial aid office:** (585) 594-6150
Stephen Field, Director of Student Financial Services
2301 Westside Drive
Rochester, NY 14624-1997

Rochester Business Institute

Rochester, New York
www.rochester-institute.com
Two-year proprietary **Federal Code: 004811**

	Living at home
Tuition and fees (2002-2003):	$9,330
Per-credit charge:	$199
Books and supplies:	$750

Policies to reduce costs. Tuition/fee waivers for employees and their families. Credit/placement for qualifying scores on CLEP examinations.

Payment plans. Credit card, installment, deferred payment.

Application procedures. No deadline. Applicants notified on rolling basis starting 3/15, must reply within 4 week(s) of notification.

Contact. Toni Brown, Director Student Financial Services
1630 Portland Avenue
Rochester, NY 14621-3007

Rochester Institute of Technology

Rochester, New York
www.rit.edu
Four-year private **Federal Code: 002806**

College costs. Tuition for National Technical Institute for the Deaf $6,525 per year; $242 per-credit-hour.

	Living at home	On-campus
Tuition and fees (2002-2003):	$19,815	$19,815
Room and board:		$7,623
Books and supplies:	$600	$600
Personal expenses:	$2,100	$600
Transportation:	$300	$300

Undergraduate aid. Need-based: Average financial aid package for full-time students was $15,250. 67% awarded as scholarships/grants, 33% as loans/jobs. Need-based aid available for part-time students. **Non-need-based:** 35% awarded as scholarships/grants, 65% as loans/jobs. Scholarships based on academics, art, leadership. **Additional information:** Most junior and senior year students participate in cooperative education program, earning average $5,000 per year through paid employment.

Freshman aid. Need-based: Out of 2,236 full-time freshmen, 1,880 applied for aid; 1,560 were judged to have need; of these 1,560 received aid. Average package met 90% of need. 1480 students had full need met. Average scholarship/grant was $9,800; average loan $3,900. **Non-need based:** 550 full-time freshmen with need received non-need scholarships; 250 without need received awards.

Merit scholarships. Presidential Scholarships for applicants ranked in top 10th of high school class with minimum SAT combined score of 1220 and applicants in top 5th of high school class with minimum score of 1270; more than 600 awarded; up to $8,000.

Policies to reduce costs. Tuition/fee waivers for unemployed or children of unemployed, employees and their families. Prepayment discount; credit/placement for qualifying scores on AP, IB, CLEP examinations. Work study available nights, weekends and for part-time students.

Payment plans. Credit card, installment, deferred payment.

Application procedures. FAFSA required. Priority date 3/1; no closing date. Applicants notified on rolling basis starting 3/15, must reply by 5/1 or within 2 week(s) of notification. Early decision closing date 12/1. **Transfers:** Priority date 3/15. Applicant must provide financial aid transcripts from any college attended previously. Special merit scholarship programs available specifically for transfers with high GPA.

Contact. **Financial aid office:** (585) 472-2186
Verna Hazen, Director of Financial Aid
60 Lomb Memorial Drive
Rochester, NY 14623-5604

Rockland Community College

Suffern, New York
www.sunyrockland.edu
Two-year public **Federal Code: 002877**

	Living at home
Tuition and fees (2002-2003):	$2,650
Out-of-state:	$5,050
Per-credit charge:	$100
Per-credit out-of-state:	$200
Books and supplies:	$600
Personal expenses:	$600
Transportation:	$800

Undergraduate aid. Need-based: Need-based aid available for full-time and part-time students.

Merit scholarships. SUNY Empire State Honors Minority Scholarships available to African American, Latino, and Native American students; 8 awarded; $1,000 per semester for 4 semesters. Jack Watson Scholarships based on minimum 3.5 high school GPA or 94 average in Regents; 5 awarded; $1162.50 per semester, renewable for 2nd year. Alumni Scholarships for children of alumni with 75 average; varying amounts.

Policies to reduce costs. Tuition/fee waivers for senior citizens, employees and their families. Credit/placement for qualifying scores on AP, IB, CLEP examinations. Work study available nights and weekends.

Payment plans. Credit card payment.

Application procedures. FAFSA, institutional form required. Priority date 6/15; no closing date. Applicants notified on rolling basis starting 6/1, must reply within 3 week(s) of notification.

Contact. **Financial aid office:** (845) 574-4000
Marvin Oppenheim, Director of Financial Aid
145 College Road
Suffern, NY 10901

Russell Sage College

Troy, New York
www.sage.edu/rsc
Four-year private **Federal Code: 002810**

College costs. $120 annual technology fee for commuter, $320 for residents.

	Living at home	On-campus
Tuition and fees (2002-2003):	$18,820	$18,820
Room and board:		$6,526
Books and supplies:	$800	$800
Personal expenses:	$650	$650
Transportation:	$300	$300

Undergraduate aid. Need-based: 62% awarded as scholarships/grants, 38% as loans/jobs. Need-based aid available for part-time students. **Non-need-based:** 62% awarded as scholarships/grants, 38% as loans/jobs. Scholarships based on academics, alumni affiliation. **Student debt:** 87% of graduating class borrowed to fund education; average debt was $19,200.

Freshman aid. Need-based: Out of 96 full-time freshmen, 94 applied for aid; 85 were judged to have need; of these 85 received aid. **Non-need based:** 55 full-time freshmen with need received non-need scholarships; 7 without need received awards.

Policies to reduce costs. Tuition/fee waivers for children of alumni, senior citizens, family members, employees and their families. Credit/placement for qualifying scores on AP, CLEP examinations. Work study available nights, weekends and for part-time students.

Payment plans. Credit card, installment, deferred payment.

Application procedures. FAFSA required. Priority date 3/1; no closing date. Applicants notified on rolling basis starting 3/15, must reply by 5/1 or within 2 week(s) of notification. Early decision closing date 12/1.

Contact. Financial aid office: (518) 244-2341
James Dease, Director of Financial Aid
45 Ferry Street
Troy, NY 12180-4115

Sage College of Albany

Albany, New York
www.sage.edu
Four-year private **Federal Code: 002811**

College costs. Annual technology fee $100 for commuters, $300 for campus residents.

	Living at home	On-campus
Tuition and fees (2002-2003):	$14,320	$14,320
Room and board:		$6,526
Books and supplies:	$800	$800
Personal expenses:	$650	$650
Transportation:	$300	$300

Undergraduate aid. Need-based: 58% awarded as scholarships/grants, 42% as loans/jobs. Need-based aid available for part-time students. **Non-need-based:** 45% awarded as scholarships/grants, 55% as loans/jobs. Scholarships based on academics, athletics. **Student debt:** 91% of graduating class borrowed to fund education; average debt was $9,000.

Policies to reduce costs. Tuition/fee waivers for children of alumni, senior citizens, family members, employees and their families. Credit/placement for qualifying scores on AP, CLEP examinations. Work study available nights, weekends and for part-time students.

Payment plans. Credit card, installment, deferred payment.

Application procedures. FAFSA required. Priority date 3/1; no closing date. Applicants notified on rolling basis starting 3/15, must reply within 2 week(s) of notification.

Contact. Financial aid office: (518) 244-2341
James Dease, Director of Student Financial Services
140 New Scotland Avenue
Albany, NY 12208

St. Bonaventure University

St. Bonaventure, New York
www.sbu.edu
Four-year private **Federal Code: 002817**

	Living at home	On-campus
Tuition and fees (2002-2003):	$16,845	$16,845
Room and board:		$6,250
Board only:	$1,500	
Books and supplies:	$600	$600
Personal expenses:	$650	$650
Transportation:	$600	$400

Undergraduate aid. Need-based: Average financial aid package for full-time students was $14,448; for part-time $9,028. 63% awarded as scholarships/grants, 37% as loans/jobs. **Non-need-based:** 56% awarded as scholarships/grants, 44% as loans/jobs. Scholarships based on academics, art, athletics, leadership, minority status, music/drama, religious affiliation, state/district residency. **Student debt:** 72% of graduating class borrowed to fund education; average debt was $16,900.

Freshman aid. Need-based: Out of 585 full-time freshmen, 506 applied for aid; 433 were judged to have need; of these 433 received aid. Average package met 88% of need. 152 students had full need met. Average scholarship/grant was $10,283; average loan $3,311. **Non-need based:** 77 full-time freshmen with need received non-need scholarships; 116 without need received awards; 26 received athletic scholarships.

Policies to reduce costs. Tuition/fee waivers for senior citizens, minority students, family members, family of clergy, employees and their families. Credit/placement for qualifying scores on AP, IB, CLEP examinations. Work study available nights and weekends.

Payment plans. Deferred payment.

Application procedures. FAFSA, institutional form required. No deadline. Applicants notified on rolling basis starting 4/1, must reply by 5/1 or within 3 week(s) of notification. **Transfers:** Priority date 2/1; closing date 5/1.

Contact. Financial aid office: (716) 375-2400
Mary Piccioli, Director of Financial Aid
Route 417
St. Bonaventure, NY 14778-2284

St. Elizabeth College of Nursing

Utica, New York
www.stemc.org/college/edu.htm
Two-year private **Federal Code: 0064661**

College costs. Out-of-state tuition: $8,500.

	Living at home	On-campus
Tuition and fees (projected):	$7,020	$7,020
Room and board:		$4,000
Books and supplies:	$1,100	$1,100
Personal expenses:	$1,300	$1,300
Transportation:	$1,250	$1,250

Undergraduate aid. Need-based: Average financial aid package for full-time students was $6,900; for part-time $5,100. 55% awarded as scholarships/grants, 45% as loans/jobs. **Non-need-based:** 10% awarded as scholarships/grants, 90% as loans/jobs. **Student debt:** 56% of graduating class borrowed to fund education; average debt was $14,125.

Freshman aid. Need-based: Out of 6 full-time freshmen, 6 applied for aid; 5 were judged to have need; of these 5 received aid. Average package met 67% of need. 6 students had full need met. Average scholarship/grant was $2,613; average loan $2,625. **Non-need based:** 1 without need received awards.

Policies to reduce costs. Tuition/fee waivers for employees and their families. Credit/placement for qualifying scores on CLEP examinations.

Payment plans. Credit card payment.

Application procedures. FAFSA required. No deadline. Applicants notified on rolling basis starting 1/1, must reply within 2 week(s) of notification.

Contact. Financial aid office: (315) 798-8206
Sherry Gibson, Director of Financial Aid
2215 Genesee Street
Utica, NY 13501

St. John Fisher College

Rochester, New York
www.sjfc.edu
Four-year private **Federal Code: 002821**

	Living at home	On-campus
Tuition and fees (projected):	$17,550	$17,550
Room and board:		$7,500
Board only:	$2,700	
Books and supplies:	$500	$500
Personal expenses:	$600	$600
Transportation:	$200	$200

Undergraduate aid. **Need-based:** Average financial aid package for full-time students was $2,237; for part-time $480. 51% awarded as scholarships/grants, 49% as loans/jobs. **Non-need-based:** 1% awarded as scholarships/grants, 99% as loans/jobs. Scholarships based on academics, alumni affiliation, leadership, minority status. **Student debt:** 85% of graduating class borrowed to fund education; average debt was $18,400.

Freshman aid. **Need-based:** Out of 540 full-time freshmen, 522 applied for aid; 460 were judged to have need; of these 457 received aid. Average package met 83% of need. 65 students had full need met. Average scholarship/grant was $7,756; average loan $1,495. **Non-need based:** 58 full-time freshmen with need received non-need scholarships; 73 without need received awards.

Merit scholarships. Merit Awards must apply by March 1st: Founders Award $5,500, Presidential Scholarship $7,500, Trustees Scholarship $8,500. Fisher Service Scholar Program; one-third of cost of education; must be nominated. First Generation Scholars Program; $4,500 to one-third of cost of education; must be nominated. Both Honors and Science Scholars will receive a monetary award of $2,500 per year ($2,000 in scholarship and $500 in the form of a book voucher). Science Scholars will also receive a laptop computer to use throughout their four years of enrollment at Fisher.

Policies to reduce costs. Tuition/fee waivers for employees and their families. Credit/placement for qualifying scores on AP, CLEP examinations. Work study available nights, weekends and for part-time students.

Payment plans. Credit card, installment, deferred payment.

Application procedures. FAFSA required. Priority date 2/15; no closing date. Applicants notified on rolling basis starting 3/21, must reply by 5/1 or within 3 week(s) of notification. Early decision closing date 12/1. **Transfers:** No deadline.

Contact. **Financial aid office:** (585) 385-8042
Angela Monnat, Director of Financial Aid
3690 East Avenue
Rochester, NY 14618-3597

St. John's University

Jamaica, New York
www.stjohns.edu
Four-year private **Federal Code: 002823**

College costs. Tuition may vary by program and class year.

	Living at home	On-campus
Tuition and fees (projected):	$18,330	$18,330
Room and board:		$9,700
Board only:	$2,700	
Books and supplies:	$1,000	$1,000
Personal expenses:	$1,800	$1,100
Transportation:	$1,100	$2,700

Undergraduate aid. All financial aid based on need. Average financial aid package for full-time students was $13,386; for part-time $8,943. 56% awarded as scholarships/grants, 44% as loans/jobs. **Student debt:** 67% of graduating class borrowed to fund education; average debt was $17,949.

Freshman aid. Out of 2,670 full-time freshmen, 2,349 applied for aid; 2,144 were judged to have need; of these 2,144 received aid. Average package met 78% of need. 298 students had full need met. Average scholarship/grant was $12,739; average loan $3,014.

Policies to reduce costs. Tuition/fee waivers for senior citizens, family members, employees and their families. Tuition at time of enrollment guaranteed for 4 years; credit/placement for qualifying scores on AP, CLEP examinations.

Payment plans. Credit card, installment, deferred payment.

Application procedures. FAFSA required. Priority date 2/1; no closing date. Applicants notified on rolling basis starting 4/1, must reply within 2 week(s) of notification. **Transfers:** Priority date 2/1; no deadline. Scholarships available if 1 year of prior college study completed.

Contact. **Financial aid office:** (718) 990-2000
Jorge Rodriguez, Assistant Vice President/Executive Director of Financial Aid
8000 Utopia Parkway
Jamaica, NY 11439

St. Joseph's College

Brooklyn, New York
www.sjcny.edu
Four-year private **Federal Code: 002825**

	Living at home
Tuition and fees (2002-2003):	$10,400
Board only:	$600
Books and supplies:	$600
Personal expenses:	$600
Transportation:	$1,000

Undergraduate aid. **Need-based:** Need-based aid available for full-time and part-time students. **Non-need-based:** Scholarships based on academics, alumni affiliation, leadership. **Student debt:** 67% of graduating class borrowed to fund education; average debt was $15,264.

Policies to reduce costs. Tuition/fee waivers for children of alumni, family members, employees and their families. Credit/placement for qualifying scores on AP, CLEP examinations. Work study available nights, weekends and for part-time students.

Payment plans. Credit card, installment payment.

Application procedures. FAFSA, institutional form required. Priority date 2/25; no closing date. Applicants notified on rolling basis starting 4/1, must reply by 5/1 or within 2 week(s) of notification. **Transfers:** Priority date 3/15; no deadline.

Contact. **Financial aid office:** (718) 636-6808
Carol Sullivan, Director of Financial Aid
245 Clinton Avenue
Brooklyn, NY 11205-3688

St. Joseph's College: Suffolk Campus

Patchogue, New York
www.sjcny.edu
Four-year private **Federal Code: E00505**

	Living at home
Tuition and fees (2002-2003):	$10,665
Board only:	$1,600
Books and supplies:	$600
Personal expenses:	$600
Transportation:	$1,200

Undergraduate aid. **Need-based:** Average financial aid package for full-time students was $7,400. 34% awarded as scholarships/grants, 66% as loans/jobs. Need-based aid available for part-time students. **Non-need-based:** 92% awarded as scholarships/grants, 8% as loans/jobs. Scholarships based on academics.

Freshman aid. **Need-based:** Out of 399 full-time freshmen, 353 applied for aid; 240 were judged to have need; of these 240 received aid. Average package met 49% of need. 159 students had full need met. Average scholarship/grant was $5,617; average loan $2,380. **Non-need based:** 98 full-time freshmen with need received non-need scholarships; 92 without need received awards.

Merit scholarships. Board of Trustees Scholarship; full tuition less outside aid for the normal length of matriculation to entering freshmen with a 90 high school academic average and 1180 total on SAT. Alumni Scholarship; variable award on a yearly basis to the children of alumni. Scholastic Achievement Award; up to $5,000 a year for the normal length of matriculation to entering freshmen with a 86 high school academic average and 1020 total on SAT. Academic Achievement Scholarship automatically awards up to $3,000 for a 3.6 GPA or better and $1,500 for a 3.3 GPA or better to entering transfer students with a 3.3 or better and an associate degree.

Policies to reduce costs. Tuition/fee waivers for family members, employees and their families. Credit/placement for qualifying scores on AP, CLEP examinations. Work study available nights, weekends and for part-time students.

Payment plans. Credit card, installment payment.

Application procedures. FAFSA, institutional form required. Priority date 2/25; no closing date. Applicants notified by 4/15, must reply within 2 week(s) of notification. **Transfers:** Priority date 3/15; no deadline.

Contact. **Financial aid office:** (631) 447-3214
Carol Sullivan, Director of Financial Aid
155 West Roe Boulevard
Patchogue, NY 11772-2603

St. Joseph's Hospital Health Center School of Nursing

Syracuse, New York
www.sjhsyr.org/nursing
Two-year private **Federal Code: 006467**

College costs. Tuition for full two-year program is $11,846.

	Living at home	On-campus
Tuition and fees (2002-2003):	$6,488	$6,488
Per-credit charge:	$230	$230
Room only:		$2,900
Books and supplies:	$700	$700
Personal expenses:	$780	$780
Transportation:	$320	$120

Undergraduate aid. All financial aid based on need. Need-based aid available for full-time and part-time students.

Policies to reduce costs. Tuition/fee waivers for employees and their families. Credit/placement for qualifying scores on AP, CLEP examinations.

Payment plans. Credit card payment.

Application procedures. FAFSA required. Priority date 5/1; no closing date. Applicants notified on rolling basis starting 6/15. **Transfers:** Priority date 5/30; no deadline.

Contact. **Financial aid office:** (315) 448-5040
Theresa Moser, Director of Financial Aid
206 Prospect Avenue
Syracuse, NY 13203

St. Lawrence University

Canton, New York
www.stlawu.edu
Four-year private **Federal Code: 002829**

	Living at home	On-campus
Tuition and fees (2002-2003):	$26,480	$26,480
Room and board:		$7,755
Books and supplies:	$650	$650
Personal expenses:	$3,400	$800
Transportation:	$1,000	

Undergraduate aid. Need-based: Average financial aid package for full-time students was $25,373. 75% awarded as scholarships/grants, 25% as loans/jobs. **Non-need-based:** 55% awarded as scholarships/grants, 45% as loans/jobs. Scholarships based on academics, alumni affiliation, athletics, minority status. **Student debt:** 72% of graduating class borrowed to fund education; average debt was $22,132.

Freshman aid. Need-based: Out of 619 full-time freshmen, 495 applied for aid; 431 were judged to have need; of these 430 received aid. Average package met 91% of need. 164 students had full need met. Average scholarship/grant was $18,341; average loan $5,009. **Non-need based:** 68 full-time freshmen with need received non-need scholarships; 60 without need received awards; 8 received athletic scholarships.

Merit scholarships. Community Service Award, $15,000.

Policies to reduce costs. Tuition/fee waivers for employees and their families. Credit/placement for qualifying scores on AP, IB, CLEP examinations. Work study available nights and weekends.

Payment plans. Installment payment.

Application procedures. FAFSA, institutional form required. Closing date 2/15. Applicants notified by 3/31, must reply by 5/1 or within 2 week(s) of notification. Early decision closing date 11/15. **Transfers:** Closing date 3/15.

Contact. **Financial aid office:** (315) 229-5265
Patricia Farmer, Director of Financial Aid
Payson Hall
Canton, NY 13617

Sarah Lawrence College

Bronxville, New York
www.sarahlawrence.edu
Four-year private **Federal Code: 002813**

	Living at home	On-campus
Tuition and fees (2002-2003):	$29,360	$29,360
Room and board:		$10,494
Books and supplies:	$600	$600
Personal expenses:	$3,750	$800

Undergraduate aid. All financial aid based on need. Average financial aid package for full-time students was $26,289; for part-time $16,866. 78% awarded as scholarships/grants, 22% as loans/jobs. **Student debt:** 40% of graduating class borrowed to fund education; average debt was $13,042.

Freshman aid. Out of 323 full-time freshmen, 198 applied for aid; 150 were judged to have need; of these 150 received aid. Average package met 96% of need. 127 students had full need met. Average scholarship/grant was $18,268; average loan $2,370.

Policies to reduce costs. Tuition/fee waivers for employees and their families. Credit/placement for qualifying scores on AP, IB examinations. Work study available nights, weekends and for part-time students.

Payment plans. Installment payment.

Application procedures. FAFSA, CSS PROFILE required. Closing date 2/1. Applicants notified by 4/1, must reply by 5/1. Early decision closing date 11/15. **Transfers:** Closing date 3/15. Maximum institutional grant to transfer students is $24,000 a year. Loans and work study available above and beyond this grant.

Contact. **Financial aid office:** (914) 395-2570
Heather McDonnell, Director of Financial Aid
One Mead Way
Bronxville, NY 10708-5999

Schenectady County Community College

Schenectady, New York
www.sunysccc.edu
Two-year public **Federal Code: 006785**

	Living at home
Tuition and fees (2002-2003):	$2,608
Out-of-state:	$5,098
Per-credit charge:	$98
Per-credit out-of-state:	$196
Board only:	$1,750
Books and supplies:	$800
Personal expenses:	$900
Transportation:	$1,200

Undergraduate aid. All financial aid based on need. Need-based aid available for full-time and part-time students.

Policies to reduce costs. Tuition/fee waivers for senior citizens, employees and their families. Credit/placement for qualifying scores on AP, CLEP examinations. Work study available for part-time students.

Payment plans. Credit card payment.

Application procedures. FAFSA required. Priority date 5/1; no closing date. Applicants notified on rolling basis starting 4/15, must reply by 8/31. **Transfers:** No deadline.

Contact. **Financial aid office:** (518) 381-1352
Brian McGarvey, Director of Financial Aid
78 Washington Avenue
Schenectady, NY 12305

School of Visual Arts

New York, New York
www.schoolofvisualarts.edu
Four-year proprietary **Federal Code: 007468**

College costs. One-time enrollment fee of $400.

	Living at home	On-campus
Tuition and fees:	$18,330	$18,330
Room only:		$8,000
Board only:	$2,500	
Books and supplies:	$2,500	$2,500
Personal expenses:	$1,500	$1,500
Transportation:	$2,000	$2,000

Undergraduate aid. Need-based: Average financial aid package for full-time students was $8,987. 33% awarded as scholarships/grants, 67% as loans/jobs. Need-based aid available for part-time students. **Non-need-based:** 29% awarded as scholarships/grants, 71% as loans/jobs. Scholarships based on academics. **Student debt:** 77% of graduating class borrowed to fund education; average debt was $15,000.

Freshman aid. Need-based: Out of 463 full-time freshmen, 457 applied for aid; 412 were judged to have need; of these 389 received aid. Average package met 49% of need. Average scholarship/grant was $6,056; average loan $2,922. **Non-need based:** 99 full-time freshmen with need received non-need scholarships; 8 without need received awards.

Policies to reduce costs. Tuition/fee waivers for employees and their families. Credit/placement for qualifying scores on AP, CLEP examinations.

Payment plans. Credit card, installment, deferred payment.

Application procedures. FAFSA required. Priority date 2/1; closing date 5/1. Applicants notified on rolling basis starting 1/1, must reply within 3 week(s) of notification. Early decision closing date 12/1.

Contact. Javier Vega, Director of Student Financial Services
209 East 23rd Street
New York, NY 10010-3994

Skidmore College

Saratoga Springs, New York
www.skidmore.edu
Four-year private **Federal Code: 002814**

	Living at home	On-campus
Tuition and fees (2002-2003):	$27,980	$27,980
Room and board:		$7,835
Board only:	$3,055	
Books and supplies:	$650	$650
Personal expenses:	$900	$900
Transportation:	$1,720	$250

Undergraduate aid. Need-based: Average financial aid package for full-time students was $23,148. 80% awarded as scholarships/grants, 20% as loans/jobs. **Non-need-based:** 52% awarded as scholarships/grants, 48% as loans/jobs. Scholarships based on music/drama. **Student debt:** 43% of graduating class borrowed to fund education; average debt was $15,560.

Freshman aid. Need-based: Out of 637 full-time freshmen, 302 applied for aid; 253 were judged to have need; of these 253 received aid. Average package met 99% of need. 243 students had full need met. Average scholarship/grant was $18,991; average loan $2,336. **Non-need based:** 86 full-time freshmen with need received non-need scholarships; 2 without need received awards.

Merit scholarships. Based on outstanding ability and achievement in mathematics, science, or computer science; 5 awarded; $10,000 annually for 4 years. Filene Music Competition Awards based on music ability; 4 awarded; $9,000 annually for 4 years.

Policies to reduce costs. Tuition/fee waivers for employees and their families. Prepayment discount; credit/placement for qualifying scores on AP, IB, CLEP examinations. Work study available nights and weekends.

Payment plans. Installment payment.

Application procedures. FAFSA, CSS PROFILE required. CSS PROFILE required for all students applying for need-based financial aid. Closing date 1/15. Applicants notified by 4/1, must reply by 5/1. Early decision closing date 12/1. **Transfers:** Up to five transfer students eligible for need-based grant assistance. Other transfer students eligible for grant assistance after one full year of enrollment or at beginning of junior year, whichever comes first.

Contact. Financial aid office: (518) 580-5750
Robert Shorb, Director of Student Aid and Family Finance
815 North Broadway
Saratoga Springs, NY 12866

State University of New York College at Brockport

Brockport, New York
www.brockport.edu
Four-year public **Federal Code: 002841**

	Living at home	On-campus
Tuition and fees (2002-2003):	$4,127	$4,127
Out-of-state:	$9,027	$9,027
Room and board:		$6,460
Board only:	$1,750	
Books and supplies:	$800	$800
Personal expenses:	$1,158	$1,158
Transportation:	$1,620	$120

Undergraduate aid. Need-based: Average financial aid package for full-time students was $7,228; for part-time $4,751. 39% awarded as scholarships/grants, 61% as loans/jobs. **Non-need-based:** 16% awarded as scholarships/grants, 84% as loans/jobs. Scholarships based on academics, alumni affiliation, leadership, minority status, state/district residency. **Student debt:** 76% of graduating class borrowed to fund education; average debt was $16,451.

Freshman aid. Need-based: Out of 1,023 full-time freshmen, 880 applied for aid; 623 were judged to have need; of these 613 received aid. Average package met 81% of need. 217 students had full need met. Average scholarship/grant was $2,695; average loan $2,715. **Non-need based:** 120 full-time freshmen with need received non-need scholarships; 120 without need received awards.

Merit scholarships. Extraordinary Academic scholarships ranging from $1,000 to over $10,000 per year; minimum qualifications include SAT scores of 1100 (24 ACT), rank in top 25% of class and 90 or higher high school average.

Policies to reduce costs. Tuition/fee waivers for senior citizens. Tuition at time of enrollment guaranteed for 4 years; credit/placement for qualifying scores on AP, IB, CLEP examinations.

Payment plans. Credit card, installment, deferred payment.

Application procedures. FAFSA required. Priority date 2/15; no closing date. Applicants notified on rolling basis. **Transfers:** Extraordinary Academic scholarships available to transfer students based on minimum 3.75 GPA and junior status; $1,000-$4,800 per year.

Contact. Financial aid office: (585) 395-2501
Scott Atkinson, Assistant Vice President for Enrollment Management
350 New Campus Drive
Brockport, NY 14420

State University of New York College at Buffalo

Buffalo, New York
www.buffalostate.edu
Four-year public **Federal Code: 002842**

	Living at home	On-campus
Tuition and fees (2002-2003):	$4,109	$4,109
Out-of-state:	$9,009	$9,009
Room and board:		$5,640
Board only:	$1,998	
Books and supplies:	$800	$800
Personal expenses:	$900	$900
Transportation:	$900	$900

Undergraduate aid. All financial aid based on need. Average financial aid package for full-time students was $3,037; for part-time $2,968. 48% awarded as scholarships/grants, 52% as loans/jobs. **Student debt:** 65% of graduating class borrowed to fund education; average debt was $13,430.

Freshman aid. Out of 1,329 full-time freshmen, 1,079 applied for aid; 883 were judged to have need; of these 870 received aid. Average package met 62% of need. 157 students had full need met. Average scholarship/grant was $870; average loan $1,145.

Policies to reduce costs. Tuition/fee waivers for minority students. Credit/placement for qualifying scores on AP, IB, CLEP examinations.

Payment plans. Credit card, installment payment.

Application procedures. FAFSA required. No deadline. Applicants notified on rolling basis starting 4/15, must reply within 4 week(s) of notification. Early decision closing date 11/15. **Transfers:** No deadline.

Contact. **Financial aid office:** (716) 878-4000
Kent McGowan, Director of Financial Aid
1300 Elmwood Avenue
Buffalo, NY 14222-1095

State University of New York College at Cortland

Cortland, New York
www.cortland.edu/admissions/apply
Four-year public **Federal Code: 002843**

	Living at home	On-campus
Tuition and fees (2002-2003):	$4,266	$4,266
Out-of-state:	$9,166	$9,166
Room and board:		$6,700
Books and supplies:	$700	$700
Personal expenses:		$1,000
Transportation:		$500

Undergraduate aid. Need-based: Average financial aid package for full-time students was $7,880. 44% awarded as scholarships/grants, 56% as loans/jobs. Need-based aid available for part-time students. **Non-need-based:** 10% awarded as scholarships/grants, 90% as loans/jobs. Scholarships based on academics, leadership.

Freshman aid. Need-based: Out of 1,691 full-time freshmen, 1,463 applied for aid; 985 were judged to have need; of these 969 received aid. Average package met 74% of need. 126 students had full need met. Average scholarship/grant was $2,842; average loan $2,776. **Non-need based:** 100 full-time freshmen with need received non-need scholarships; 373 without need received awards.

Policies to reduce costs. Tuition/fee waivers for employees and their families. Credit/placement for qualifying scores on AP, IB, CLEP examinations.

Payment plans. Credit card, installment payment.

Application procedures. FAFSA required. Closing date 4/1. Applicants notified on rolling basis starting 3/1, must reply by 5/1 or within 2 week(s) of notification. Early decision closing date 11/15. **Transfers:** Federal regulations require financial aid transcript from each post-secondary school attended even if student did not receive aid.

Contact. **Financial aid office:** (607) 753-4717
David Canaski, Director of Financial Aid
Box 2000
Cortland, NY 13045

State University of New York College at Fredonia

Fredonia, New York
www.fredonia.edu
Four-year public **Federal Code: 002844**

	Living at home	On-campus
Tuition and fees (2002-2003):	$4,373	$4,373
Out-of-state:	$9,273	$9,273
Room and board:		$6,150
Board only:	$2,450	
Books and supplies:	$750	$750
Personal expenses:	$735	$600
Transportation:	$750	$525

Undergraduate aid. Need-based: Average financial aid package for full-time students was $6,481; for part-time $4,044. 47% awarded as scholarships/grants, 53% as loans/jobs. **Non-need-based:** Scholarships based on academics. **Student debt:** 78% of graduating class borrowed to fund education; average debt was $12,430.

Freshman aid. Need-based: Out of 987 full-time freshmen, 921 applied for aid; 626 were judged to have need; of these 623 received aid. Average package met 66% of need. 540 students had full need met. Average scholarship/grant was $3,048; average loan $2,878. **Non-need based:** 224 full-time freshmen with need received non-need scholarships; 224 without need received awards.

Merit scholarships. Foundation Freshman Award; 30 awarded; minimum 91 high school average, 1250 SAT or 28 ACT; $3,000. Fredonia Achievement Award; 60 awarded; minimum 87 high school average, 1100 SAT or 25 ACT, minimum 3.0 GPA for transfer students; $1,000. Fredonia Award for Excellence; high school valedictorians and salutatorians; $2,500 renewable for 4 years. Out-of-State Student Scholarships; 90 high school average, 1250 SAT or 28 ACT, 3.25 GPA for transfer students.

Policies to reduce costs. Tuition/fee waivers for employees and their families. Credit/placement for qualifying scores on AP, IB, CLEP examinations.

Payment plans. Credit card, installment payment.

Application procedures. FAFSA required. Priority date 2/1; no closing date. Applicants notified on rolling basis starting 3/15. Early decision closing date 11/1. **Transfers:** Financial aid transcripts required from prior institutions attended.

Contact. **Financial aid office:** (716) 673-3111
Daniel Tramuta, Director of Financial Aid
178 Central Avenue
Fredonia, NY 14063-1136

State University of New York College at Geneseo

Geneseo, New York
www.geneseo.edu
Four-year public **Federal Code: 002845**

	Living at home	On-campus
Tuition and fees (2002-2003):	$4,440	$4,440
Out-of-state:	$9,340	$9,340
Room and board:		$6,020
Books and supplies:	$600	$600
Personal expenses:	$650	$650
Transportation:	$650	$650

Undergraduate aid. Need-based: Average financial aid package for full-time students was $7,421. 42% awarded as scholarships/grants, 58% as loans/jobs. Need-based aid available for part-time students. **Non-need-based:** 11% awarded as scholarships/grants, 89% as loans/jobs. Scholarships based on academics. **Student debt:** 70% of graduating class borrowed to fund education; average debt was $15,000.

Freshman aid. Need-based: Out of 1,140 full-time freshmen, 980 applied for aid; 515 were judged to have need; of these 515 received aid. Average package met 80% of need. 412 students had full need met. Average scholarship/grant was $2,038; average loan $2,975. **Non-need based:** 161 full-time freshmen with need received non-need scholarships; 242 without need received awards.

Policies to reduce costs. Credit/placement for qualifying scores on AP, CLEP examinations. Work study available nights, weekends and for part-time students.

Payment plans. Credit card, installment, deferred payment.

Application procedures. FAFSA required. Closing date 2/15. Applicants notified on rolling basis starting 5/1. Early decision closing date 11/15.

Contact. **Financial aid office:** (585) 245-5211
Archie Cureton, Director of Financial Aid
1 College Circle
Geneseo, NY 14454-1471

State University of New York College at Old Westbury

Old Westbury, New York
www.oldwestbury.edu
Four-year public **Federal Code: 007109**

	Living at home	On-campus
Tuition and fees (2002-2003):	$4,085	$4,085
Out-of-state:	$8,985	$8,985
Room and board:		$6,900
Board only:	$404	
Books and supplies:	$675	$675
Personal expenses:	$990	$1,210
Transportation:	$1,675	$750

Undergraduate aid. Need-based: Need-based aid available for full-time and part-time students. **Non-need-based:** Scholarships based on academics.

Policies to reduce costs. Tuition/fee waivers for senior citizens. Credit/placement for qualifying scores on AP, CLEP examinations. Work study available nights, weekends and for part-time students.

Payment plans. Credit card, installment payment.

Application procedures. FAFSA, institutional form required. Closing date 4/19. Applicants notified on rolling basis starting 5/1. **Transfers:** Financial aid transcript required.

Contact. **Financial aid office:** (516) 876-3222
Delores James, Director of Financial Aid
Box 307
Old Westbury, NY 11568-0307

State University of New York College at Oneonta

Oneonta, New York
www.oneonta.edu
Four-year public **Federal Code: 002847**

	Living at home	On-campus
Tuition and fees (2002-2003):	$4,291	$4,291
Out-of-state:	$9,191	$9,191
Room and board:		$6,876
Board only:	$2,350	
Books and supplies:	$800	$800
Personal expenses:	$1,300	$1,300
Transportation:	$750	$750

Undergraduate aid. Need-based: Average financial aid package for full-time students was $7,766; for part-time $4,931. 38% awarded as scholarships/grants, 62% as loans/jobs. **Non-need-based:** 5% awarded as scholarships/grants, 95% as loans/jobs. Scholarships based on academics, athletics. **Student debt:** 50% of graduating class borrowed to fund education; average debt was $5,815.

Freshman aid. Need-based: Out of 1,117 full-time freshmen, 961 applied for aid; 662 were judged to have need; of these 640 received aid. Average package met 60% of need. 93 students had full need met. Average scholarship/grant was $2,920; average loan $2,934. **Non-need based:** 116 without need received awards; 4 received athletic scholarships.

Merit scholarships. Presidential Scholarships award $3,400 to 36 applicants for academics, service, and extracurricular activities. Organization of Ancillary Services awards $1,000 to 50 applicants for applicants for academics, service, and extracurricular activities. OAS Minority Student Merit Scholarships award $3,400 to 6 applicants for academics, service, and extracurricular activities. Mildred Haight Memorial Scholarships award $500 to 28 applicants for academics. Edward Griesmer Transfer Scholarships award $2,500 to 2 applicants for academics and residence.

Policies to reduce costs. Tuition/fee waivers for employees and their families. Credit/placement for qualifying scores on AP, IB, CLEP examinations. Work study available nights and weekends.

Payment plans. Credit card, installment payment.

Application procedures. FAFSA required. Priority date 3/15; no closing date. Applicants notified on rolling basis starting 3/1. Early decision closing date 11/1.

Contact. **Financial aid office:** (607) 436-2532
William Goodhue, Director of Student Financial Aid
Admissions, Alumni Hall
Oneonta, NY 13820-4016

State University of New York College at Plattsburgh

Plattsburgh, New York
www.plattsburgh.edu
Four-year public **Federal Code: 002849**

	Living at home	On-campus
Tuition and fees (2002-2003):	$4,229	$4,229
Out-of-state:	$9,129	$9,129
Room and board:		$5,870
Board only:	$750	
Books and supplies:	$750	$750
Personal expenses:	$2,034	$2,034
Transportation:	$2,310	$500

Undergraduate aid. Need-based: Average financial aid package for full-time students was $7,718; for part-time $4,758. 43% awarded as scholarships/grants, 57% as loans/jobs. **Non-need-based:** 38% awarded as scholarships/grants, 62% as loans/jobs. Scholarships based on academics, alumni affiliation, art, leadership, music/drama, state/district residency. **Student debt:** 72% of graduating class borrowed to fund education; average debt was $16,081.

Freshman aid. Need-based: Out of 1,011 full-time freshmen, 783 applied for aid; 552 were judged to have need; of these 547 received aid. Average package met 82% of need. 174 students had full need met. Average scholarship/grant was $4,027; average loan $3,543. **Non-need based:** 272 full-time freshmen with need received non-need scholarships; 327 without need received awards.

Policies to reduce costs. Tuition/fee waivers for employees and their families. Credit/placement for qualifying scores on AP, IB, CLEP examinations.

Payment plans. Credit card, installment payment.

Application procedures. FAFSA required. Priority date 3/1; no closing date. Applicants notified on rolling basis starting 3/15, must reply within 5 week(s) of notification. Early decision closing date 11/15. **Transfers:** Priority date 3/1; no deadline.

Contact. **Financial aid office:** (518) 564-4076
Todd Moravec, Director of Financial Aid
Kehoe Administration Building
Plattsburgh, NY 12901

State University of New York College at Potsdam

Potsdam, New York
www.potsdam.edu
Four-year public **Federal Code: 002850**

	Living at home	On-campus
Tuition and fees (2002-2003):	$4,215	$4,215
Out-of-state:	$9,115	$9,115
Room and board:		$6,620
Board only:	$900	
Books and supplies:	$900	$900
Personal expenses:	$1,200	$1,200
Transportation:	$600	$600

Undergraduate aid. Need-based: Average financial aid package for full-time students was $9,998; for part-time $7,391. 49% awarded as scholarships/grants, 51% as loans/jobs. **Non-need-based:** 34% awarded as scholarships/grants, 66% as loans/jobs. Scholarships based on academics, art, leadership, minority status, music/drama. **Student debt:** 84% of graduating class borrowed to fund education; average debt was $16,611.

Freshman aid. Need-based: Out of 738 full-time freshmen, 656 applied for aid; 508 were judged to have need; of these 504 received aid. Average package met 92% of need. 463 students had full need met. Average scholarship/grant was $4,008; average loan $3,182. **Non-need based:** 219 full-time freshmen with need received non-need scholarships; 97 without need received awards.

Merit scholarships. Unlimited number of merit-based scholarship awards offered annually through Adirondack Scholars Program. Awards range from $500 to $11,440 a year, with some scholarships renewable for up to four years.

Policies to reduce costs. Tuition/fee waivers for minority students. Credit/placement for qualifying scores on AP, IB, CLEP examinations. Work study available nights, weekends and for part-time students.

Payment plans. Credit card, installment, deferred payment.

Application procedures. FAFSA required. Priority date 3/1; no closing date. Applicants notified on rolling basis starting 2/15, must reply within 3 week(s) of notification.

Contact. **Financial aid office:** (315) 267-2000
Susan Aldrich, Director of Financial Aid
44 Pierrepont Avenue
Potsdam, NY 13676

State University of New York College of Agriculture and Technology at Cobleskill

Cobleskill, New York
www.cobleskill.edu
Two-year public **Federal Code: 002956**

College costs. Tuition for bachelor's degree: full-time in-state tuition and fees $4,532, out-of-state full-time tuition and fees $6,132; per-credit-hour $137 in-state, $209 out-of-state.

	Living at home	On-campus
Tuition and fees (2002-2003):	$4,332	$4,332
Out-of-state:	$6,132	$6,132
Per-credit charge:	$128	$128
Per-credit out-of-state:	$209	$209
Room and board:		$6,510
Books and supplies:	$900	$900
Personal expenses:	$900	$900
Transportation:	$550	

Undergraduate aid. Need-based: Average financial aid package for full-time students was $4,792; for part-time $4,651. 52% awarded as scholarships/grants, 48% as loans/jobs. **Non-need-based:** Scholarships based on academics, alumni affiliation, leadership, state/district residency.

Freshman aid. Need-based: Out of 971 full-time freshmen, 862 applied for aid; 840 were judged to have need; of these 803 received aid. Average package met 78% of need. 296 students had full need met. Average scholarship/grant was $1,376; average loan $2,393. **Non-need based:** 730 full-time freshmen with need received non-need scholarships.

Merit scholarships. Application deadline for scholarships March 15. Separate application required, which is available through the admissions office.

Policies to reduce costs. Tuition/fee waivers for senior citizens, employees and their families. Credit/placement for qualifying scores on AP, CLEP examinations. Work study available nights and weekends.

Payment plans. Credit card, installment payment.

Application procedures. FAFSA, CSS PROFILE required. Closing date 3/15. Applicants notified by 4/15, must reply within 2 week(s) of notification.

Contact. Financial aid office: (800) 295-8998
Richard Young, Director of Financial Aid
Cobleskill, NY 12043

State University of New York College of Agriculture and Technology at Morrisville

Morrisville, New York
www.morrisville.edu
Two-year public **Federal Code: 002859**

College costs. Tuition for bachelor's degree: in-state full-time tuition and fees $4,235, out-of-state tuition and fees $5,835; per-credit-hour $137 in-state, $208 out-of-state.

	Living at home	On-campus
Tuition and fees (2002-2003):	$4,035	$4,035
Out-of-state:	$5,835	$5,835
Per-credit charge:	$128	$128
Per-credit out-of-state:	$208	$208
Room and board:		$5,960
Board only:	$1,500	
Books and supplies:	$800	$800
Personal expenses:	$1,000	$800
Transportation:	$1,600	$570

Undergraduate aid. Need-based: Average financial aid package for full-time students was $6,900; for part-time $5,740. 51% awarded as scholarships/grants, 49% as loans/jobs. **Non-need-based:** 43% awarded as scholarships/grants, 57% as loans/jobs. Scholarships based on academics. **Student debt:** 93% of graduating class borrowed to fund education; average debt was $6,125.

Freshman aid. Need-based: Out of 1,085 full-time freshmen, 1,008 applied for aid; 878 were judged to have need; of these 865 received aid. Average package met 89% of need. 154 students had full need met. Average scholarship/grant was $3,355; average loan $2,220. **Non-need based:** 115 full-time freshmen with need received non-need scholarships; 19 without need received awards.

Policies to reduce costs. Credit/placement for qualifying scores on AP, CLEP examinations. Work study available nights, weekends and for part-time students.

Payment plans. Credit card, installment payment.

Application procedures. FAFSA required. Priority date 2/1; no closing date. Applicants notified on rolling basis starting 3/1. **Transfers:** No deadline.

Contact. Financial aid office: (800) 626-5844
Tom David, Director of Financial Aid
Route 20
Morrisville, NY 13408

State University of New York College of Environmental Science and Forestry

Syracuse, New York
www.esf.edu
Four-year public **Federal Code: 002851**

College costs. Room and board available through Syracuse University at $9040.

	Living at home
Tuition and fees (2002-2003):	$3,862
Out-of-state:	$8,762
Books and supplies:	$800
Personal expenses:	$450
Transportation:	$600

Undergraduate aid. Need-based: Average financial aid package for full-time students was $7,434; for part-time $4,704. 43% awarded as scholarships/grants, 57% as loans/jobs. **Non-need-based:** 28% awarded as scholarships/grants, 72% as loans/jobs. Scholarships based on academics.

Freshman aid. Need-based: Out of 197 full-time freshmen, 181 applied for aid; 119 were judged to have need; of these 118 received aid. Average package met 83% of need. 118 students had full need met. Average scholarship/grant was $5,121; average loan $2,442. **Non-need based:** 27 full-time freshmen with need received non-need scholarships; 34 without need received awards.

Policies to reduce costs. Credit/placement for qualifying scores on AP, IB, CLEP examinations. Work study available nights, weekends and for part-time students.

Payment plans. Deferred payment.

Application procedures. FAFSA required. Priority date 3/1; no closing date. Applicants notified on rolling basis starting 3/15, must reply within 2 week(s) of notification. Early decision closing date 11/15. **Transfers:** Priority date 3/1.

Contact. Financial aid office: (315) 470-6670
John View, Director of Financial Aid
106 Bray Hall, One Forestry Drive
Syracuse, NY 13210

State University of New York College of Technology at Alfred

Alfred, New York
www.alfredstate.edu
Two-year public **Federal Code: 002854**

College costs. Tuition for bachelor's degree: full-time in-state tuition and fees $4,190; out-of-state tuition and fees $5,790; per-credit-hour $137 in-state, $346 out-of-state.

	Living at home	On-campus
Tuition and fees (2002-2003):	$3,990	$3,990
Out-of-state:	$5,790	$5,790
Per-credit charge:	$128	$128
Per-credit out-of-state:	$346	$346
Room and board:		$5,746
Books and supplies:	$600	$600
Personal expenses:	$700	$700
Transportation:	$863	$438

Policies to reduce costs. Tuition/fee waivers for employees and their families. Credit/placement for qualifying scores on AP, CLEP examinations. Work study available nights, weekends and for part-time students.

Payment plans. Credit card, installment, deferred payment.

Application procedures. FAFSA required. Priority date 5/1; no closing date. Applicants notified on rolling basis starting 3/1, must reply within 3 week(s) of notification. **Transfers:** No deadline.

Contact. Financial aid office: (607) 587-4215
Valerie Nixon, Director of Financial Aid
Huntington Administration Building
Alfred, NY 14802-1196

State University of New York College of Technology at Canton

Canton, New York
www.canton.edu
Two-year public **Federal Code: 002855**

	Living at home	On-campus
Tuition and fees (2002-2003):	$4,125	$4,125
Out-of-state:	$5,925	$5,925
Per-credit charge:	$128	$128
Per-credit out-of-state:	$210	$210
Room and board:		$6,610
Books and supplies:	$800	$800
Personal expenses:	$800	$800
Transportation:	$1,500	$500

Undergraduate aid. Need-based: Need-based aid available for full-time and part-time students.

Policies to reduce costs. Tuition/fee waivers for unemployed or children of unemployed. Credit/placement for qualifying scores on AP, CLEP examinations.

Payment plans. Credit card, installment, deferred payment.

Application procedures. FAFSA required. Priority date 3/15; no closing date. Applicants notified on rolling basis starting 2/1, must reply within 4 week(s) of notification. **Transfers:** Priority date 3/15; no deadline. Financial aid transcripts required from all previously attended schools for mid-year transfers.

Contact. Financial aid office: (315) 386-7123
Kerrie Cooper, Director of Financial Aid
Cornell Drive
Canton, NY 13617-1098

State University of New York College of Technology at Delhi

Delhi, New York
www.delhi.edu
Two-year public **Federal Code: 002857**

College costs. Tuition for BBA degree: full-time in-state tuition and fees $4,265, out-of-state tuition and fees $9,165; per-credit-hour $137 in-state, $346 out-of-state.

	Living at home	On-campus
Tuition and fees (2002-2003):	$4,065	$4,065
Out-of-state:	$5,865	$5,865
Per-credit charge:	$128	$128
Per-credit out-of-state:	$346	$346
Room and board:		$6,350
Books and supplies:	$500	$500
Personal expenses:	$1,000	$1,000
Transportation:	$860	$500

Undergraduate aid. Need-based: Need-based aid available for full-time and part-time students.

Policies to reduce costs. Credit/placement for qualifying scores on AP, CLEP examinations.

Payment plans. Credit card, installment, deferred payment.

Application procedures. FAFSA required. Priority date 2/15; no closing date. Applicants notified on rolling basis starting 3/1, must reply within 2 week(s) of notification.

Contact. Financial aid office: (607) 746-4000
Dawn Sohns, Assistant Director of Enrollment Services/Financial Aid Director
Main Street
Delhi, NY 13753-1190

State University of New York Empire State College

Saratoga Springs, New York
www.esc.edu
Four-year public **Federal Code: 010286**

	Living at home
Tuition and fees (2002-2003):	$3,855
Out-of-state:	$8,755
Books and supplies:	$600
Personal expenses:	$1,500
Transportation:	$405

Policies to reduce costs. Credit/placement for qualifying scores on CLEP examinations.

Payment plans. Credit card, installment payment.

Application procedures. FAFSA required. No deadline. Applicants notified on rolling basis, must reply within 3 week(s) of notification.

Contact. Financial aid office: (518) 587-2100
Eileen Corrigan, Director of Financial Services
2 Union Avenue
Saratoga Springs, NY 12866

State University of New York Health Science Center at Brooklyn

Brooklyn, New York
www.downstate.edu
Upper-division public **Federal Code: 002839**

	Living at home	On-campus
Tuition and fees (2002-2003):	$3,715	$3,715
Out-of-state:	$8,615	$8,615
Room and board:		$10,206
Books and supplies:	$1,116	$1,116

Undergraduate aid. Need-based: Need-based aid available for full-time and part-time students.

Policies to reduce costs. Tuition/fee waivers for employees and their families. Credit/placement for qualifying scores on AP, CLEP examinations.

Application procedures. FAFSA required. Priority date 3/1; no closing date. Applicants notified on rolling basis.

Contact. Financial aid office: (718) 270-2446
Julia Clayton, Director of Financial Aid
450 Clarkson Avenue, Box 60
Brooklyn, NY 11203-2098

State University of New York Health Science Center at Stony Brook

Stony Brook, New York
www.hsc.stonybrook.edu
Upper-division public **Federal Code: 002838**

	Living at home	On-campus
Tuition and fees (2002-2003):	$4,383	$4,383
Out-of-state:	$9,283	$9,283
Room and board:		$8,594
Books and supplies:	$1,250	$1,250
Personal expenses:	$1,000	$1,000
Transportation:	$2,080	$500

Payment plans. Credit card, installment, deferred payment.

Application procedures. FAFSA required. No deadline. Applicants notified on rolling basis. **Transfers:** Priority date 3/1; no deadline.

Contact. Financial aid office: (631) 444-2109
Ana Maria Torres, Director of Financial Aid
Level 2, Room 271
Stony Brook, NY 11794-8276

State University of New York Institute of Technology at Utica/Rome

Utica, New York
www.sunyit.edu
Upper-division public **Federal Code: 011678**

	Living at home	On-campus
Tuition and fees (2002-2003):	$4,164	$4,164
Out-of-state:	$9,064	$9,064
Room and board:		$6,240
Board only:	$750	
Books and supplies:	$750	$750
Personal expenses:	$960	$1,280
Transportation:	$1,410	$470

Undergraduate aid. **Need-based:** Need-based aid available for full-time and part-time students. **Non-need-based:** Scholarships based on academics.

Policies to reduce costs. Tuition/fee waivers for senior citizens, employees and their families. Credit/placement for qualifying scores on IB, CLEP examinations. Work study available nights, weekends and for part-time students.

Payment plans. Credit card, installment payment.

Application procedures. FAFSA, institutional form required. No deadline. Applicants notified on rolling basis starting 3/17, must reply within 2 week(s) of notification. **Transfers:** No deadline.

Contact. **Financial aid office:** (315) 792-7210
Edward Hutchinson, Director of Financial Aid
Box 3050
Utica, NY 13504-3050

State University of New York Maritime College

Throggs Neck, New York
www.sunymaritime.edu
Four-year public **Federal Code: 002853**

College costs. Additional required uniform charges.

	Living at home	On-campus
Tuition and fees (2002-2003):	$5,090	$5,090
Out-of-state:	$9,990	$9,990
Room and board:		$6,770
Books and supplies:	$700	$700
Personal expenses:		$1,500
Transportation:		$500

Undergraduate aid. **Need-based:** Need-based aid available for full-time students. **Non-need-based:** Scholarships based on academics, state/district residency. **Additional information:** All cadets who are United States citizens, physically qualified for Merchant Marine license, and not yet 25 at time of enrollment are eligible to apply for Student Incentive Payment (SIP) of $3,000 per year from Maritime Administration of the Department of Transportation. Out-of-state students who elect to participate in SIP pay in-state tuition fees.

Merit scholarships. Admiral's Scholarships; full-tuition. NROTC/AFROTC Scholarships; full room and board for 4 years.

Policies to reduce costs. Tuition/fee waivers for employees and their families. Credit/placement for qualifying scores on AP, IB, CLEP examinations. Work study available nights and weekends.

Application procedures. FAFSA, institutional form required. Priority date 2/15; no closing date. Applicants notified on rolling basis starting 3/1, must reply by 3/15 or within 4 week(s) of notification. Early decision closing date 12/1.

Contact. **Financial aid office:** (718) 409-7267
Madelene Aponte, Director of Financial Aid
6 Pennyfield Avenue
Throggs Neck, NY 10465-4198

State University of New York Upstate Medical University

Syracuse, New York
www.upstate.edu
Upper-division public **Federal Code: 002840**

	Living at home	On-campus
Tuition and fees (2002-2003):	$3,925	$3,925
Out-of-state:	$8,825	$8,825
Room only:		$4,360
Books and supplies:	$760	$760
Personal expenses:	$1,130	$1,160
Transportation:	$865	$640

Undergraduate aid. All financial aid based on need. Need-based aid available for full-time and part-time students.

Policies to reduce costs. Credit/placement for qualifying scores on AP, CLEP examinations.

Application procedures. FAFSA required. Priority date 3/1; no closing date. Applicants notified on rolling basis starting 6/1, must reply within 2 week(s) of notification. **Transfers:** Priority date 3/1; no deadline.

Contact. **Financial aid office:** (315) 464-4329
Irvin Bodofsky, Director of Financial Aid
766 Irving Avenue
Syracuse, NY 13210

State University of New York at Albany

Albany, New York
www.albany.edu
Four-year public **Federal Code: 002835**

	Living at home	On-campus
Tuition and fees (2002-2003):	$4,820	$4,820
Out-of-state:	$9,720	$9,720
Room and board:		$6,768
Board only:	$1,900	
Books and supplies:	$800	$800
Personal expenses:	$1,175	$1,398
Transportation:	$500	$300

Undergraduate aid. **Need-based:** Average financial aid package for full-time students was $7,739. 49% awarded as scholarships/grants, 51% as loans/jobs. Need-based aid available for part-time students. **Non-need-based:** 36% awarded as scholarships/grants, 64% as loans/jobs. Scholarships based on academics, athletics. **Student debt:** 70% of graduating class borrowed to fund education; average debt was $15,108.

Freshman aid. **Need-based:** Out of 2,274 full-time freshmen, 1,845 applied for aid; 1,232 were judged to have need; of these 1,224 received aid. Average package met 73% of need. 324 students had full need met. Average scholarship/grant was $4,310; average loan $3,149. **Non-need based:** 180 full-time freshmen with need received non-need scholarships; 176 without need received awards; 66 received athletic scholarships.

Merit scholarships. University-level scholarships offered to incoming freshman who can be admitted as Presidential, Frederick Douglass, or College Scholars. Amounts vary. Presidential Scholars Program requires high school average of at least 90 and combined SAT score in the upper 1200s or higher. Presidential Scholars who are NY State residents can receive up to $3,400 per year and out of state students can qualify for up to $5,500 per year in renewable scholarship funding.

Policies to reduce costs. Tuition/fee waivers for senior citizens. Credit/placement for qualifying scores on AP, IB, CLEP examinations.

Payment plans. Credit card, installment, deferred payment.

Application procedures. FAFSA required. Priority date 3/15; no closing date. Applicants notified on rolling basis starting 4/1, must reply within 2 week(s) of notification.

Contact. Dennis Tillman, Director of Financial Aid
1400 Washington Avenue
Albany, NY 12222

State University of New York at Binghamton

Binghamton, New York
www.binghamton.edu
Four-year public **Federal Code: 002836**

	Living at home	On-campus
Tuition and fees (2002-2003):	$4,551	$4,551
Out-of-state:	$9,451	$9,451
Room and board:		$6,390
Board only:	$824	
Books and supplies:	$800	$800
Transportation:	$900	$250

Undergraduate aid. Need-based: Average financial aid package for full-time students was $9,136; for part-time $7,326. 37% awarded as scholarships/grants, 63% as loans/jobs. **Non-need-based:** Scholarships based on academics, art, athletics, leadership, minority status, music/drama, state/district residency. **Student debt:** 60% of graduating class borrowed to fund education; average debt was $13,915. **Additional information:** Institution awards both need and non-need funds from its own resources. Need and academic merit are considered in the awarding of funds. Institution strives to minimize out-of-pocket expenses for students.

Freshman aid. Need-based: Out of 2,076 full-time freshmen, 1,620 applied for aid; 904 were judged to have need; of these 898 received aid. Average package met 73% of need. 599 students had full need met. Average scholarship/grant was $4,271; average loan $2,812. **Non-need based:** 233 full-time freshmen with need received non-need scholarships; 193 without need received awards; 59 received athletic scholarships.

Merit scholarships. Morris Gitlitz Memorial Scholarship given annually to one freshman who has demonstrated a broad range of academic and extracurricular interests particularly in arts and letters; $4,000 per year renewable. Binghamton Scholarship given annually to up to 80 outstanding freshmen; $2,000 to $3,400 a year renewable. Phi Theta Kappa Scholarship, $250-$1,000, awarded annually admitted Phi Theta Kappa transfer students, 3.3 GPA at time of matriculation, highly selective. Binghamton University Out-of-State Scholarship, $2,500 renewable, awarded to qualified students admitted to freshman class, have permanent legal residence outside borders of New York State. Awards also based on academic merit, SAT and/or ACT scores, and extracurricular involvement.

Policies to reduce costs. Tuition/fee waivers for employees and their families. Credit/placement for qualifying scores on AP, IB, CLEP examinations. Work study available nights, weekends and for part-time students.

Payment plans. Credit card, installment payment.

Application procedures. FAFSA required. CSS PROFILE required of early decision applicants only. Priority date 3/1; no closing date. Applicants notified on rolling basis starting 3/15, must reply within 2 week(s) of notification. **Transfers:** Priority date 3/1.

Contact. Financial aid office: (607) 777-2428
Dennis Chavez, Director of Financial Aid and Employment
Box 6001
Binghamton, NY 13902-6001

State University of New York at Buffalo

Buffalo, New York
www.buffalo.edu
Four-year public **Federal Code: 002837**

	Living at home	On-campus
Tuition and fees (2002-2003):	$4,850	$4,850
Out-of-state:	$9,750	$9,750
Room and board:		$6,512
Board only:	$2,580	
Books and supplies:	$750	$750
Personal expenses:	$720	$720
Transportation:	$500	$500

Undergraduate aid. Need-based: Average financial aid package for full-time students was $7,525; for part-time $5,928. 27% awarded as scholarships/grants, 73% as loans/jobs. **Non-need-based:** 17% awarded as scholarships/grants, 83% as loans/jobs. Scholarships based on academics, athletics, minority status, music/drama, state/district residency.

Freshman aid. Need-based: Out of 3,029 full-time freshmen, 2,989 applied for aid; 1,985 were judged to have need; of these 1,961 received aid. Average package met 59% of need. 1840 students had full need met. Average scholarship/grant was $1,477; average loan $1,697. **Non-need based:** 85 full-time freshmen with need received non-need scholarships; 116 without need received awards.

Merit scholarships. Honors program includes scholarships for high academic achievement, high SAT scores.

Policies to reduce costs. Tuition/fee waivers for senior citizens, minority students. Credit/placement for qualifying scores on AP, IB, CLEP examinations. Work study available nights, weekends and for part-time students.

Payment plans. Credit card, installment payment.

Application procedures. FAFSA required. Closing date 3/1. Applicants notified on rolling basis starting 2/4, must reply by 5/1. Early decision closing date 11/1.

Contact. Financial aid office: (716) 645-2450
Shirley Walker, Director of Financial Processing Services
17 Capen Hall
Buffalo, NY 14260

State University of New York at Farmingdale

Farmingdale, New York
www.farmingdale.edu
Four-year public **Federal Code: 002858**

College costs. Tuition for associate degree: full-time in-state tuition and fees $4,035, out-of-state tuition and fees $9,135; per-credit-hour $128 in-state, $346 out-of-state.

	Living at home	On-campus
Tuition and fees (2002-2003):	$4,235	$4,235
Out-of-state:	$9,135	$9,135
Room and board:		$7,280
Books and supplies:	$600	$600
Personal expenses:	$800	$800
Transportation:	$1,200	$600

Undergraduate aid. Need-based: Need-based aid available for full-time and part-time students. **Non-need-based:** Scholarships based on academics.

Policies to reduce costs. Credit/placement for qualifying scores on AP, CLEP examinations.

Payment plans. Credit card, installment payment.

Application procedures. FAFSA, institutional form required. Priority date 4/1; no closing date. Applicants notified on rolling basis starting 4/1.

Contact. Financial aid office: (631) 420-2578
Catherine Malnichuck, Director of Financial Services
2350 Broad Hollow Road
Farmingdale, NY 11735-1021

State University of New York at New Paltz

New Paltz, New York
www.newpaltz.edu
Four-year public **Federal Code: 002846**

	Living at home	On-campus
Tuition and fees (2002-2003):	$4,165	$4,165
Out-of-state:	$9,065	$9,065
Room and board:		$5,800
Board only:	$1,983	
Books and supplies:	$1,100	$1,100
Personal expenses:	$1,057	$1,057
Transportation:	$900	$600

Undergraduate aid. Need-based: 53% awarded as scholarships/grants, 47% as loans/jobs. Need-based aid available for part-time students. **Non-need-based:** Scholarships based on academics, alumni affiliation, art, leadership, minority status, music/drama.

Freshman aid. Need-based: Out of 913 full-time freshmen, 786 applied for aid; 493 were judged to have need; of these 486 received aid. 151 students had full need met. **Non-need based:** 85 full-time freshmen with need received non-need scholarships.

Merit scholarships. Merit Scholarships; $120,000 total available.

Policies to reduce costs. Credit/placement for qualifying scores on AP, IB, CLEP examinations.

Payment plans. Credit card, installment, deferred payment.

Application procedures. FAFSA required. Closing date 3/15. Applicants notified on rolling basis starting 4/1, must reply within 2 week(s) of notification. **Transfers:** No deadline.

Contact. **Financial aid office:** (845) 257-3250
Daniel Sistarenik, Director of Financial Aid
75 South Manheim Boulevard, Suite 1
New Paltz, NY 12561-2499

State University of New York at Oswego

Oswego, New York
www.oswego.edu
Four-year public **Federal Code: 002848**

College costs. Room and board costs frozen for up to 4 years for current entering freshmen.

	Living at home	On-campus
Tuition and fees (2002-2003):	$4,194	$4,194
Out-of-state:	$9,094	$9,094
Room and board:		$6,696
Books and supplies:	$800	$800
Personal expenses:	$838	$838
Transportation:	$900	$600

Undergraduate aid. **Need-based:** Average financial aid package for full-time students was $7,649; for part-time $5,291. 39% awarded as scholarships/grants, 61% as loans/jobs. **Non-need-based:** 15% awarded as scholarships/grants, 85% as loans/jobs. Scholarships based on academics, state/district residency. **Student debt:** 76% of graduating class borrowed to fund education; average debt was $16,832.

Freshman aid. **Need-based:** Out of 1,349 full-time freshmen, 1,175 applied for aid; 878 were judged to have need; of these 859 received aid. Average package met 78% of need. 276 students had full need met. Average scholarship/grant was $3,418; average loan $2,766. **Non-need based:** 299 full-time freshmen with need received non-need scholarships; 244 without need received awards.

Merit scholarships. Scholarships based on top 15% of class rank for freshmen and 3.3 GPA for transfers: $3,400 annually for 4 years, $1,250 annually for 4 years, $500 annually for 4 years. Additional residential scholarships for out-of-state freshmen and transfers: $4,190 annually, $16,710 for 4 years (requires on-campus housing).

Policies to reduce costs. Credit/placement for qualifying scores on AP, IB, CLEP examinations. Work study available for part-time students.

Payment plans. Credit card, installment payment.

Application procedures. FAFSA required. Priority date 4/1; no closing date. Applicants notified on rolling basis starting 4/1, must reply by 5/1 or within 3 week(s) of notification. Early decision closing date 11/15. **Transfers:** Transfer students entering in January need to supply financial aid transcipts from prior colleges.

Contact. **Financial aid office:** (315) 312-2248
Mark Humbert, Director of Financial Aid
211 Culkin Hall
Oswego, NY 13126-3599

State University of New York at Purchase

Purchase, New York
www.purchase.edu
Four-year public **Federal Code: 006791**

	Living at home	On-campus
Tuition and fees (2002-2003):	$4,202	$4,202
Out-of-state:	$9,102	$9,102
Room and board:		$6,620
Board only:	$2,000	
Books and supplies:	$1,400	$1,400
Personal expenses:	$1,000	$600
Transportation:	$900	$400

Undergraduate aid. **Need-based:** Average financial aid package for full-time students was $7,235; for part-time $3,591. 41% awarded as scholarships/grants, 59% as loans/jobs. **Non-need-based:** 18% awarded as scholarships/grants, 82% as loans/jobs. Scholarships based on academics, art, minority status, music/drama. **Student debt:** 70% of graduating class borrowed to fund education; average debt was $13,873. **Additional information:** All applicants are automatically considered for scholarship upon review of their applications, essays, auditions and/or portfolio reviews and are notified if eligible.

Freshman aid. **Need-based:** Out of 689 full-time freshmen, 504 applied for aid; 338 were judged to have need; of these 338 received aid. Average package met 64% of need. 41 students had full need met. Average scholarship/grant was $3,928; average loan $2,730. **Non-need based:** 6 full-time freshmen with need received non-need scholarships; 165 without need received awards.

Policies to reduce costs. Tuition/fee waivers for senior citizens, employees and their families. Credit/placement for qualifying scores on AP, CLEP examinations.

Payment plans. Credit card, installment payment.

Application procedures. FAFSA required. Priority date 3/15; no closing date. Applicants notified on rolling basis starting 3/1, must reply within 2 week(s) of notification. Early decision closing date 11/1. **Transfers:** Financial aid transcripts required from all previously attended institutions.

Contact. **Financial aid office:** (914) 251-6350
Emilie Devine, Director of Financial Aid
735 Anderson Hill Road
Purchase, NY 10577-1400

State University of New York at Stony Brook

Stony Brook, New York
www.stonybrook.edu
Four-year public **Federal Code: 002838**

	Living at home	On-campus
Tuition and fees (2002-2003):	$4,383	$4,383
Out-of-state:	$9,283	$9,283
Room and board:		$8,594
Books and supplies:	$750	$750
Personal expenses:	$1,000	$1,000
Transportation:	$2,080	$500

Undergraduate aid. All financial aid based on need. Average financial aid package for full-time students was $7,579; for part-time $5,003. 58% awarded as scholarships/grants, 42% as loans/jobs. **Student debt:** 63% of graduating class borrowed to fund education; average debt was $15,747.

Freshman aid. Out of 2,390 full-time freshmen, 1,531 applied for aid; 1,209 were judged to have need; of these 1,197 received aid. Average package met 74% of need. 152 students had full need met. Average scholarship/grant was $4,043; average loan $2,153.

Policies to reduce costs. Tuition/fee waivers for employees and their families. Credit/placement for qualifying scores on AP, IB, CLEP examinations. Work study available nights, weekends and for part-time students.

Payment plans. Credit card, installment payment.

Application procedures. FAFSA required. Priority date 3/1; no closing date. Applicants notified on rolling basis starting 3/1, must reply by 5/1 or within 2 week(s) of notification.

Contact. **Financial aid office:** (631) 689-6000
Ana-Maria Torres, Assistant Provost for Registration and Financial Aid
Stony Brook, NY 11794-1901

Suffolk County Community College

Selden, New York
www.sunysuffolk.edu
Two-year public **Federal Code: 002878**

	Living at home
Tuition and fees (2002-2003):	$3,052
Out-of-state:	$5,552
Per-credit charge:	$105
Per-credit out-of-state:	$210
Books and supplies:	$550
Personal expenses:	$1,048
Transportation:	$1,248

Undergraduate aid. **Need-based:** Need-based aid available for full-time and part-time students. **Non-need-based:** Scholarships based on academics, minority status, state/district residency.

Policies to reduce costs. Tuition/fee waivers for senior citizens. Credit/placement for qualifying scores on AP, IB, CLEP examinations.

Payment plans. Credit card payment.

Application procedures. FAFSA required. Priority date 4/15; closing date 6/1. Applicants notified on rolling basis starting 5/15, must reply within 2 week(s) of notification.

Contact. Carl Bello, Central Director of Financial Aid
NFL Building, 533 College Road
Selden, NY 11784

Syracuse University

Syracuse, New York
www.syracuse.edu
Four-year private **Federal Code: 002882**

	Living at home	On-campus
Tuition and fees:	$25,122	$25,122
Room and board:		$9,590
Board only:	$4,340	
Books and supplies:	$1,166	$1,166
Personal expenses:	$970	$970
Transportation:	$510	$510

Undergraduate aid. Need-based: Average financial aid package for full-time students was $18,000. 67% awarded as scholarships/grants, 33% as loans/jobs. Need-based aid available for part-time students. **Non-need-based:** 76% awarded as scholarships/grants, 24% as loans/jobs. Scholarships based on academics, art, athletics, music/drama. **Student debt:** 70% of graduating class borrowed to fund education; average debt was $18,925.

Freshman aid. Need-based: Out of 2,916 full-time freshmen, 2,065 applied for aid; 1,618 were judged to have need; of these 1,618 received aid. Average package met 80% of need. Average scholarship/grant was $13,400; average loan $3,300. **Non-need based:** 116 full-time freshmen with need received non-need scholarships; 493 without need received awards; 40 received athletic scholarships.

Merit scholarships. University automatically considers all students who apply for admission for merit scholarships, regardless of financial need, based upon academic credentials, performance on standardized tests, class rank, portfolio or audition results (if relevant), community and extracurricular involvement, overall citizenship and character.

Policies to reduce costs. Tuition/fee waivers for employees and their families. Credit/placement for qualifying scores on AP, IB examinations.

Payment plans. Installment payment.

Application procedures. FAFSA, CSS PROFILE required. Closing date 2/1. Applicants notified by 4/1, must reply by 5/1. Early decision closing date 11/15. **Transfers:** Closing date 6/15. Students should apply for aid as early as possible.

Contact. Financial aid office: (315) 443-1513
Christopher Walsh, Executive Director of Financial Aid
201 Tolley Administration Building
Syracuse, NY 13244-1100

Talmudical Institute of Upstate New York

Rochester, New York
Five-year private **Federal Code: 014614**

	Living at home	On-campus
Tuition and fees:	$4,500	$4,500
Room and board:		$3,500

Payment plans. Installment payment.

Application procedures. No deadline. Applicants notified on rolling basis.

Contact. Financial aid office: (585) 473-2810
769 Park Avenue
Rochester, NY 14607

Taylor Business Institute

New York, New York
www.tbiglobal.com
Two-year proprietary **Federal Code: 004825**

	Living at home
Tuition and fees:	$9,900
Transportation:	$720

Policies to reduce costs. Tuition/fee waivers for employees and their families. Tuition at time of enrollment guaranteed for 2 years.

Payment plans. Credit card, installment payment.

Application procedures. FAFSA, institutional form required. No deadline. Applicants notified on rolling basis.

Contact. Financial aid office: (212) 229-1963
Paula Jones, Financial Aid Administrator
18th West 18th Street, 8th Floor
New York, NY 10011

Tompkins-Cortland Community College

Dryden, New York
www.sunytccc.edu
Two-year public **Federal Code: 006788**

	Living at home	On-campus
Tuition and fees (2002-2003):	$3,025	$3,025
Out-of-state:	$6,005	$6,005
Per-credit charge:	$104	$104
Per-credit out-of-state:	$218	$218
Room only:		$3,200
Board only:	$1,500	
Books and supplies:	$600	$600
Personal expenses:	$1,000	$1,000
Transportation:	$1,000	$500

Undergraduate aid. Need-based: 58% awarded as scholarships/grants, 42% as loans/jobs. Need-based aid available for part-time students. **Non-need-based:** Scholarships based on academics.

Policies to reduce costs. Tuition/fee waivers for senior citizens, employees and their families. Credit/placement for qualifying scores on AP, CLEP examinations. Work study available nights, weekends and for part-time students.

Payment plans. Credit card, installment, deferred payment.

Application procedures. FAFSA required. No deadline. Applicants notified on rolling basis.

Contact. Financial aid office: (607) 844-8211
Michael McGraw, Director of Recruitment, Admissions and Financial Aid
170 North Street
Dryden, NY 13053-0139

Touro College

New York, New York
www.touro.edu
Four-year private **Federal Code: 010142**

	Living at home	On-campus
Tuition and fees (2002-2003):	$10,150	$10,150
Room only:		$4,500
Books and supplies:	$750	$750
Personal expenses:	$1,764	$1,764
Transportation:	$570	$570

Policies to reduce costs. Tuition/fee waivers for employees and their families. Prepayment discount; credit/placement for qualifying scores on AP, CLEP examinations.

Payment plans. Credit card, installment payment.

Application procedures. FAFSA required. Priority date 5/15; closing date 6/1. Applicants notified by 8/15.

Contact. Carol Rosenbaum, Director of Financial Aid
1602 Avenue J
Brooklyn, NY 11230

Trocaire College

Buffalo, New York
www.trocaire.edu
Two-year private **Federal Code: 002812**

	Living at home
Tuition and fees:	$9,840
Per-credit charge:	$350
Board only:	$3,000
Books and supplies:	$1,000
Personal expenses:	$700
Transportation:	$700

Undergraduate aid. Need-based: Need-based aid available for full-time and part-time students. **Non-need-based:** Scholarships based on academics, alumni affiliation.

Policies to reduce costs. Tuition/fee waivers for children of alumni, senior citizens, employees and their families. Credit/placement for qualifying scores on AP, CLEP examinations.

Payment plans. Credit card, installment, deferred payment.

Application procedures. FAFSA required. Priority date 3/31; no closing date. Applicants notified on rolling basis starting 3/1, must reply within 2 week(s) of notification.

Contact. Financial aid office: (716) 826-1200
Janet McGrath, Director of Financial Aid
360 Choate Avenue
Buffalo, NY 14220

Ulster County Community College

Stone Ridge, New York
www.sunyulster.edu
Two-year public **Federal Code: 002880**

	Living at home
Tuition and fees (2002-2003):	$2,756
Out-of-state:	$5,356
Per-credit charge:	$93
Per-credit out-of-state:	$186
Books and supplies:	$650
Personal expenses:	$480
Transportation:	$700

Undergraduate aid. Need-based: Need-based aid available for full-time and part-time students.

Policies to reduce costs. Tuition/fee waivers for senior citizens, employees and their families. Credit/placement for qualifying scores on AP, CLEP examinations.

Payment plans. Credit card, installment, deferred payment.

Application procedures. FAFSA required. Priority date 6/1; no closing date. Applicants notified on rolling basis starting 6/1, must reply within 2 week(s) of notification.

Contact. Financial aid office: (845) 687-5000
Mildred Brown, Director of Financial Aid
Cottekill Road
Stone Ridge, NY 12484

Union College

Schenectady, New York
www.union.edu
Four-year private **Federal Code: 002889**

	Living at home	On-campus
Tuition and fees (2002-2003):	$27,514	$27,514
Room and board:		$6,738
Board only:	$1,539	
Books and supplies:	$450	$450
Personal expenses:	$786	$786
Transportation:	$250	$250

Undergraduate aid. Need-based: Average financial aid package for full-time students was $22,750. 80% awarded as scholarships/grants, 20% as loans/jobs. Need-based aid available for part-time students. **Non-need-based:** 39% awarded as scholarships/grants, 61% as loans/jobs. Scholarships based on academics. **Student debt:** 62% of graduating class borrowed to fund education; average debt was $15,725. **Additional information:** CAUSE program: cancellable loans, given to eligible students who engage in public service work after graduation. Loans cancellable at rate of 20 percent for each year of service.

Freshman aid. Need-based: Out of 522 full-time freshmen, 295 applied for aid; 253 were judged to have need; of these 253 received aid. Average package met 100% of need. 253 students had full need met. Average scholarship/grant was $19,846; average loan $2,745. **Non-need based:** 7 without need received awards.

Policies to reduce costs. Tuition/fee waivers for employees and their families. Prepayment discount; credit/placement for qualifying scores on AP, IB examinations.

Payment plans. Installment payment.

Application procedures. FAFSA, CSS PROFILE required. CSS PROFILE required of all undergraduate students applying for institutional aid. Priority date 2/1; no closing date. Applicants notified by 4/1, must reply by 5/1. Early decision closing date 11/15. **Transfers:** Closing date 6/1. Financial aid applicants must send financial aid transcripts from previous institutions and the Union transfer financial aid form (as well as the PROFILE and the FAFSA).

Contact. Financial aid office: (518) 388-6123
Michael Brown, Director of Financial Aid Administration
Grant Hall
Schenectady, NY 12308-2311

United States Merchant Marine Academy

Kings Point, New York
www.usmma.edu
Four-year public **Federal Code: G02892**

College costs. All midshipmen receive full tuition, room and board, and medical and dental expenses from federal government. Freshman fees include purchase of computer for $2,900. Total required fees $5,736. International students pay required fees plus $6,900 for other expenses.

Undergraduate aid. Need-based: Average financial aid package for full-time students was $4,833. **Student debt:** 33% of graduating class borrowed to fund education; average debt was $9,000. **Additional information:** Students paid by steamship companies while at sea.

Freshman aid. Need-based: Out of 282 full-time freshmen, 197 applied for aid; 82 were judged to have need; of these 76 received aid. Average package met 100% of need. Average scholarship/grant was $3,333; average loan $2,625.

Application procedures. FAFSA, institutional form required. Closing date 5/1. Applicants notified on rolling basis starting 1/31. Early decision closing date 11/1.

Contact. Financial aid office: (516) 773-5295
James Skinner, Director of Financial Aid
Kings Point, NY 11024-1699

United States Military Academy

West Point, New York
www.usma.edu
Four-year public **Federal Code: 002893**

College costs. All cadets are members of United States Army and receive salary of $699 per month. Tuition, room and board, medical and dental care provided at no cost to cadets. First-year students pay deposit of $2,400 for books, personal computer, supplies, initial uniforms and fees.

Undergraduate aid. Additional information: First-year students who cannot pay deposit of $2,400 for books, personal computer, and supplies receive no-interest loan. Payments deducted from their salary.

Contact. Financial aid office: (845) 938-4262
Debbie Earl, Treasurer
606 Thayer Road
West Point, NY 10996-1797

University of Rochester

Rochester, New York
www.rochester.edu
Four-year private **Federal Code: 002894**

	Living at home	On-campus
Tuition and fees:	$27,768	$27,768
Room and board:		$8,770
Books and supplies:	$575	$575
Personal expenses:	$1,125	$1,125
Transportation:	$800	

Undergraduate aid. Non-need-based: Scholarships based on academics, state/district residency. **Additional information:** Alternative loans and financing information available.

Policies to reduce costs. Tuition/fee waivers for children of alumni, minority students, employees and their families. Credit/placement for qualifying scores on AP, IB examinations.

Payment plans. Installment payment.

Application procedures. FAFSA, CSS PROFILE required. Closing date 2/1. Applicants notified by 4/1, must reply by 5/1. Early decision closing date 11/15. **Transfers:** Priority date 2/1; no deadline.

Contact. **Financial aid office:** (585) 275-3226
Director of Financial Aid
Wallis Hall
Rochester, NY 14627-0251

Utica College

Utica, New York
www.utica.edu
Four-year private **Federal Code: 002883**

	Living at home	On-campus
Tuition and fees (2002-2003):	$19,118	$19,118
Room and board:		$7,580
Board only:	$2,580	
Books and supplies:	$700	$700
Personal expenses:	$650	$650
Transportation:	$850	$500

Undergraduate aid. Need-based: 67% awarded as scholarships/grants, 33% as loans/jobs. Need-based aid available for part-time students. **Non-need-based:** 54% awarded as scholarships/grants, 46% as loans/jobs. Scholarships based on academics.

Freshman aid. Need-based: Out of 450 full-time freshmen, 447 applied for aid; 413 were judged to have need; of these 413 received aid. 63 students had full need met. Average scholarship/grant was $13,954; average loan $3,239. **Non-need based:** 141 full-time freshmen with need received non-need scholarships; 12 without need received awards.

Policies to reduce costs. Tuition/fee waivers for senior citizens, employees and their families. Credit/placement for qualifying scores on AP, IB, CLEP examinations. Work study available nights, weekends and for part-time students.

Payment plans. Credit card, installment, deferred payment.

Application procedures. FAFSA required. Priority date 2/15; no closing date. Applicants notified on rolling basis starting 3/1, must reply by 5/1 or within 4 week(s) of notification.

Contact. **Financial aid office:** (315) 792-3179
Elizabeth Wilson, Director of Financial Aid
1600 Burrstone Road
Utica, NY 13502-4892

Utica School of Commerce

Utica, New York
www.uscny.com
Two-year proprietary **Federal Code: 009077**

	Living at home
Tuition and fees:	$9,760
Per-credit charge:	$150
Books and supplies:	$1,185

Policies to reduce costs. Tuition at time of enrollment guaranteed for 2 years.

Payment plans. Credit card, installment payment.

Application procedures. FAFSA, institutional form required. No deadline. Applicants notified on rolling basis.

Contact. **Financial aid office:** (315) 733-2307
Fred Zuccala, Director of Student Financial Aid
201 Bleecker Street
Utica, NY 13501

Vassar College

Poughkeepsie, New York
www.vassar.edu
Four-year private **Federal Code: 002895**

	Living at home	On-campus
Tuition and fees (2002-2003):	$27,960	$27,960
Room and board:		$7,340
Board only:	$3,440	
Books and supplies:	$820	$820
Personal expenses:	$880	$880
Transportation:	$150	$470

Undergraduate aid. All financial aid based on need. Average financial aid package for full-time students was $23,655. 78% awarded as scholarships/grants, 22% as loans/jobs. **Student debt:** 61% of graduating class borrowed to fund education; average debt was $17,170.

Freshman aid. Out of 634 full-time freshmen, 450 applied for aid; 349 were judged to have need; of these 349 received aid. Average package met 100% of need. 349 students had full need met. Average scholarship/grant was $19,917; average loan $2,797.

Policies to reduce costs. Tuition/fee waivers for employees and their families. Credit/placement for qualifying scores on AP, IB examinations.

Payment plans. Installment payment.

Application procedures. FAFSA, institutional form, CSS PROFILE required. Closing date 2/1. Applicants notified by 4/3, must reply by 5/1. Early decision closing date 11/15. **Transfers:** Closing date 4/1. Limited number of need-based award packages offered to transfers.

Contact. **Financial aid office:** (845) 437-5320
Michael Fraher, Director of Financial Aid
Box 10, 124 Raymond Avenue
Poughkeepsie, NY 12604-0077

Villa Maria College of Buffalo

Buffalo, New York
www.villa.edu
Two-year private **Federal Code: 002896**

	Living at home
Tuition and fees (2002-2003):	$9,550
Per-credit charge:	$310
Books and supplies:	$1,000
Personal expenses:	$800
Transportation:	$600

Undergraduate aid. Need-based: 62% awarded as scholarships/grants, 38% as loans/jobs. Need-based aid available for part-time students. **Non-need-based:** Scholarships based on academics, alumni affiliation, art, leadership, minority status, music/drama, religious affiliation, state/district residency.

Policies to reduce costs. Tuition/fee waivers for senior citizens, family members, unemployed or children of unemployed, family of clergy, employees and their families. Credit/placement for qualifying scores on AP, CLEP examinations. Work study available nights.

Payment plans. Credit card, installment payment.

Application procedures. FAFSA required. Priority date 4/1; no closing date. Applicants notified on rolling basis starting 5/1, must reply within 3 week(s) of notification. **Transfers:** Priority date 4/1; no deadline.

Contact. **Financial aid office:** (716) 896-0700 ext. 1850
Diane Kasprzak, Director of Financial Aid and Veteran's Affairs
240 Pine Ridge Road
Buffalo, NY 14225

Wagner College

Staten Island, New York
www.wagner.edu
Four-year private **Federal Code: 002899**

	Living at home	On-campus
Tuition and fees:	$22,600	$22,600
Room and board:		$7,300
Books and supplies:	$625	$625
Personal expenses:	$1,100	$1,100
Transportation:	$525	$625

Undergraduate aid. Need-based: Average financial aid package for full-time students was $14,245. 52% awarded as scholarships/grants, 48% as loans/jobs. **Non-need-based:** 79% awarded as scholarships/grants, 21% as loans/jobs. Scholarships based on academics, athletics, music/drama.

Freshman aid. Need-based: Out of 523 full-time freshmen, 425 applied for aid; 342 were judged to have need; of these 342 received aid. Average package met 72% of need. 77 students had full need met. Average scholarship/grant was $10,209; average loan $3,115. **Non-need based:** 120 without need received awards; 28 received athletic scholarships.

Policies to reduce costs. Tuition/fee waivers for senior citizens, family members, unemployed or children of unemployed, employees and their families. Credit/placement for qualifying scores on AP, CLEP examinations. Work study available nights and weekends.

Payment plans. Credit card, installment payment.

Application procedures. FAFSA, institutional form required. Priority date 3/1; closing date 5/1. Applicants notified on rolling basis starting 3/15, must reply by 5/1 or within 3 week(s) of notification. Early decision closing date 11/15. **Transfers:** Priority date 6/1; closing date 8/1.

Contact. **Financial aid office:** (718) 390-3183
Theresa Weimer, Director of Financial Aid
One Campus Road
Staten Island, NY 10301-4495

Webb Institute

Glen Cove, New York
www.webb-institute.edu
Four-year private **Federal Code: 002900**

College costs. All students receive 4-year, full-tuition scholarships. Room/board: $6,950. Books/supplies: $600. Personal expenses: $600. Transportation: $2,000.

Undergraduate aid. All financial aid based on need. Average financial aid package for full-time students was $800. 21% awarded as scholarships/grants, 79% as loans/jobs. **Student debt:** 18% of graduating class borrowed to fund education; average debt was $5,700.

Freshman aid. Out of 17 full-time freshmen, 9 applied for aid; 9 were judged to have need; of these 9 received aid. Average package met 33% of need. 2 students had full need met. Average scholarship/grant was $1,500; average loan $2,650.

Application procedures. FAFSA required. Closing date 7/1. Applicants notified by 8/1, must reply within 2 week(s) of notification. Early decision closing date 10/15.

Contact. **Financial aid office:** (516) 671-2213
William Murray, Director of Financial Aid
Crescent Beach Road
Glen Cove, NY 11542-1398

Wells College

Aurora, New York
www.wells.edu
Four-year private **Federal Code: 002901**

	Living at home	On-campus
Tuition and fees (2002-2003):	$13,750	$13,750
Room and board:		$6,450
Board only:	$1,800	
Books and supplies:	$600	$600
Personal expenses:	$600	$600

Undergraduate aid. Need-based: Average financial aid package for full-time students was $13,131. 71% awarded as scholarships/grants, 29% as loans/jobs. Need-based aid available for part-time students. **Non-need-based:** 35% awarded as scholarships/grants, 65% as loans/jobs. Scholarships based on academics, leadership. **Student debt:** 95% of graduating class borrowed to fund education; average debt was $17,125.

Freshman aid. Need-based: Out of 100 full-time freshmen, 90 applied for aid; 80 were judged to have need; of these 80 received aid. Average package met 87% of need. 12 students had full need met. Average scholarship/grant was $9,978; average loan $3,066. **Non-need based:** 9 without need received awards.

Merit scholarships. Henry Wells Scholarship, guaranteed first-year internship or related experience and a paid $3,000 internship or experiential learning program in student's upper-class years. Applicants must have a minimum SAT score of 1150 or a 28 on the ACT, as well as a GPA of at least 3.5. 21st Century Leadership Award; $20,000 over 4 years. Applicants must have a GPA of at least 3.5 and are required to submit a leadership transcript. Applicants for both scholarships must be nominated by a guidance counselor.

Policies to reduce costs. Tuition/fee waivers for senior citizens, employees and their families. Prepayment discount; credit/placement for qualifying scores on AP, IB, CLEP examinations. Work study available nights and weekends.

Payment plans. Credit card, installment payment.

Application procedures. FAFSA required. CSS PROFILE required of Early Decision candidates. Priority date 2/15; closing date 5/1. Applicants notified on rolling basis starting 3/1, must reply by 5/30 or within 4 week(s) of notification. Early decision closing date 12/15. **Transfers:** Priority date 3/1; no deadline.

Contact. **Financial aid office:** (315) 364-3266
Cathleen Bellomo, Director of Financial Aid
170 Main Street
Aurora, NY 13026

Westchester Business Institute

White Plains, New York
www.wbi.org
Two-year proprietary **Federal Code: 005208**

	Living at home
Tuition and fees:	$16,260
Personal expenses:	$1,520
Transportation:	$2,333

Undergraduate aid. Need-based: Need-based aid available for full-time and part-time students. **Non-need-based:** Scholarships based on academics.

Policies to reduce costs. Tuition/fee waivers for unemployed or children of unemployed, employees and their families. Credit/placement for qualifying scores on AP, CLEP examinations. Work study available nights and weekends.

Payment plans. Credit card, installment, deferred payment.

Application procedures. FAFSA, institutional form required. Priority date 6/1; no closing date. Applicants notified on rolling basis starting 1/2. **Transfers:** No deadline.

Contact. **Financial aid office:** (914) 948-4442 ext. 425
Marie Bonafonte, Vice President, Student Financial Services
325 Central Park Avenue
White Plains, NY 10602

Westchester Community College

Valhalla, New York
www.sunywcc.edu
Two-year public **Federal Code: 002881**

	Living at home
Tuition and fees (2002-2003):	$2,653
Out-of-state:	$6,178
Per-credit charge:	$98
Per-credit out-of-state:	$245
Books and supplies:	$800
Personal expenses:	$515
Transportation:	$930

Undergraduate aid. All financial aid based on need. 93% awarded as scholarships/grants, 7% as loans/jobs. Need-based aid available for part-time students. **Student debt:** 9% of graduating class borrowed to fund education; average debt was $5,142.

Policies to reduce costs. Tuition/fee waivers for employees and their families. Credit/placement for qualifying scores on AP, CLEP examinations. Work study available nights, weekends and for part-time students.

Payment plans. Credit card, deferred payment.

Application procedures. FAFSA, institutional form required. No deadline. Applicants notified on rolling basis starting 4/15, must reply within 4 week(s) of notification. **Transfers:** No deadline.

Contact. **Financial aid office:** (914) 785-6773
Eleanor Hackett, Director of Financial Aid
75 Grasslands Road
Valhalla, NY 10595

Yeshiva University

New York, New York
www.yu.edu
Four-year private **Federal Code: 002903**

	Living at home	On-campus
Tuition and fees:	$22,190	$22,190
Room and board:		$6,980
Books and supplies:	$1,072	$1,072
Transportation:	$1,041	$1,041

Undergraduate aid. Additional information: Essays required of Distinguished Scholarship applicants.

Policies to reduce costs. Tuition/fee waivers for employees and their families. Credit/placement for qualifying scores on AP, CLEP examinations.

Payment plans. Installment, deferred payment.

Application procedures. FAFSA, institutional form required. Priority date 4/15; closing date 5/1. Applicants notified on rolling basis starting 4/1.

Contact. Lori Farrior, Director of Student Finances
500 West 185th Street
New York, NY 10033-3299

North Carolina

Alamance Community College

Graham, North Carolina
www.alamance.cc.nc.us
Two-year public **Federal Code: 005463**

	Living at home
Tuition and fees (2002-2003):	$1,043
Out-of-state:	$5,738
Per-credit charge:	$34
Per-credit out-of-state:	$191
Books and supplies:	$800
Personal expenses:	$800
Transportation:	$750

Undergraduate aid. Need-based: Average financial aid package for full-time students was $2,000; for part-time $2,000. 94% awarded as scholarships/grants, 6% as loans/jobs. **Non-need-based:** Scholarships based on academics, state/district residency.

Freshman aid. Need-based: Out of 357 full-time freshmen, 307 applied for aid; 301 were judged to have need; of these 301 received aid. Average package met 25% of need. Average scholarship/grant was $2,000. **Non-need based:** 6 full-time freshmen with need received non-need scholarships; 20 without need received awards.

Policies to reduce costs. Tuition/fee waivers for senior citizens, family members, employees and their families. Credit/placement for qualifying scores on AP, CLEP examinations.

Payment plans. Credit card, deferred payment.

Application procedures. FAFSA required. Priority date 5/15; no closing date. Applicants notified on rolling basis starting 3/15, must reply within 2 week(s) of notification. **Transfers:** No deadline. Supplemental educational opportunity grants limited.

Contact. Steve Reinhartsen, Coordinator of Placement and Financial Aid
Box 8000
Graham, NC 27253

Appalachian State University

Boone, North Carolina
www.appstate.edu
Four-year public **Federal Code: 002906**

	Living at home	On-campus
Tuition and fees (2002-2003):	$1,988	$1,988
Out-of-state:	$9,258	$9,258
Room and board:		$3,810
Board only:	$1,950	
Books and supplies:	$500	$500
Personal expenses:	$1,200	$1,200
Transportation:	$1,400	$1,000

Undergraduate aid. Need-based: Average financial aid package for full-time students was $5,566; for part-time $5,509. 40% awarded as scholarships/grants, 60% as loans/jobs. **Non-need-based:** 42% awarded as scholarships/grants, 58% as loans/jobs. Scholarships based on academics, alumni affiliation, art, athletics, job skills, leadership, minority status, music/drama, religious affiliation, state/district residency. **Student debt:** 45% of graduating class borrowed to fund education; average debt was $14,184.

Freshman aid. Need-based: Out of 2,417 full-time freshmen, 1,449 applied for aid; 746 were judged to have need; of these 725 received aid. Average package met 72% of need. 237 students had full need met. Average scholarship/grant was $3,383; average loan $2,511. **Non-need based:** 266 full-time freshmen with need received non-need scholarships; 288 without need received awards; 35 received athletic scholarships.

Policies to reduce costs. Tuition/fee waivers for senior citizens, employees and their families. Credit/placement for qualifying scores on AP, IB, CLEP examinations. Work study available nights, weekends and for part-time students.

Payment plans. Credit card, installment payment.

Application procedures. FAFSA required. Priority date 3/31; no closing date. Applicants notified on rolling basis starting 4/1, must reply within 3 week(s) of notification. **Transfers:** No deadline.

Contact. Financial aid office: (828) 262-2190
Esther Captain, Director of Financial Aid
ASU Box 32004
Boone, NC 28608

Art Institute of Charlotte

Charlotte, North Carolina
www.aich.artinstitutes.edu
Two-year proprietary **Federal Code: 014578**

College costs. Annual tuition varies by program, approximately $30,000.

Contact. Three LakePointe Plaza, 2110 Water Ridge Parkway
Charlotte, NC 28217

Asheville Buncombe Technical Community College

Asheville, North Carolina
www.abtech.edu
Two-year public **Federal Code: 004033**

	Living at home
Tuition and fees (2002-2003):	$1,055
Out-of-state:	$5,750
Per-credit charge:	$34
Per-credit out-of-state:	$191
Books and supplies:	$550

Undergraduate aid. Need-based: 85% awarded as scholarships/grants, 15% as loans/jobs. **Non-need-based:** 66% awarded as scholarships/grants, 34% as loans/jobs. Scholarships based on academics, leadership.

Policies to reduce costs. Tuition/fee waivers for senior citizens.

Payment plans. Deferred payment.

Application procedures. FAFSA required. Priority date 3/15; closing date 3/31. Applicants notified on rolling basis starting 5/1, must reply within 2 week(s) of notification.

Contact. Lynn Deyton, Director of Financial Aid
340 Victoria Road
Asheville, NC 28801-4897

Barber-Scotia College

Concord, North Carolina
www.b-sc.edu
Four-year private **Federal Code: 002909**

	Living at home	On-campus
Tuition and fees (2002-2003):	$9,048	$9,048
Room and board:		$3,952
Board only:	$600	
Books and supplies:	$1,000	$1,000
Personal expenses:	$560	$560
Transportation:	$825	

Undergraduate aid. Need-based: Need-based aid available for full-time and part-time students.

Policies to reduce costs. Tuition/fee waivers for family of clergy, employees and their families. Credit/placement for qualifying scores on AP, CLEP examinations.

Payment plans. Installment payment.

Application procedures. FAFSA required. Priority date 5/1; no closing date. Applicants notified on rolling basis starting 6/15, must reply within 2 week(s) of notification.

Contact. Financial aid office: (704) 789-2908
Raymond Robinson, Director of Financial Aid
145 Cabarrus Avenue - West
Concord, NC 28025

Barton College

Wilson, North Carolina
www.barton.edu
Four-year private **Federal Code: 002908**

	Living at home	On-campus
Tuition and fees (2002-2003):	$13,074	$13,074
Room and board:		$4,754
Board only:	$1,336	
Books and supplies:	$900	$900
Personal expenses:	$3,840	$1,340
Transportation:	$1,500	$1,300

Undergraduate aid. Need-based: Average financial aid package for full-time students was $12,473. 45% awarded as scholarships/grants, 55% as loans/jobs. Need-based aid available for part-time students. **Non-need-based:** 66% awarded as scholarships/grants, 34% as loans/jobs. Scholarships based on academics, alumni affiliation, art, athletics, leadership, minority status, music/drama, religious affiliation, state/district residency. **Student debt:** 70% of graduating class borrowed to fund education; average debt was $16,660.

Freshman aid. Need-based: Out of 298 full-time freshmen, 241 applied for aid; 199 were judged to have need; of these 199 received aid. Average package met 79% of need. 40 students had full need met. Average scholarship/grant was $3,971; average loan $2,537. **Non-need based:** 186 full-time freshmen with need received non-need scholarships; 59 without need received awards; 15 received athletic scholarships.

Policies to reduce costs. Tuition/fee waivers for adults, children of alumni, senior citizens, family members, family of clergy, employees and their families. Credit/placement for qualifying scores on AP, IB, CLEP examinations. Work study available nights, weekends and for part-time students.

Payment plans. Credit card, installment payment.

Application procedures. FAFSA required. Priority date 4/1; no closing date. Applicants notified on rolling basis starting 2/1, must reply within 2 week(s) of notification.

Contact. Financial aid office: (252) 399-6323
Bettie Westbrook, Director of Financial Aid
Box 5000
Wilson, NC 27893

Beaufort County Community College

Washington, North Carolina
www.beaufort.cc.nc.us
Two-year public **Federal Code: 008558**

	Living at home
Tuition and fees (2002-2003):	$1,056
Out-of-state:	$5,751
Per-credit charge:	$34
Per-credit out-of-state:	$191
Books and supplies:	$700

Undergraduate aid. Need-based: Need-based aid available for full-time and part-time students. **Non-need-based:** Scholarships based on academics, state/district residency.

Policies to reduce costs. Tuition/fee waivers for senior citizens, employees and their families.

Payment plans. Credit card payment.

Application procedures. FAFSA required. Priority date 6/1; no closing date. Applicants notified on rolling basis starting 5/1, must reply within 2 week(s) of notification.

Contact. Financial aid office: (252) 940-6222
Harold Smith, Director of Financial Aid
Box 1069
Washington, NC 27889

Belmont Abbey College

Belmont, North Carolina
www.belmontabbeycollege.edu
Four-year private **Federal Code: 002910**

	Living at home	On-campus
Tuition and fees:	$14,872	$14,872
Room and board:		$7,640
Books and supplies:	$750	$750
Personal expenses:	$1,000	$1,600
Transportation:	$1,800	$1,600

Undergraduate aid. Need-based: Average financial aid package for full-time students was $10,748; for part-time $4,970. 60% awarded as scholarships/grants, 40% as loans/jobs. **Non-need-based:** 65% awarded as scholarships/grants, 35% as loans/jobs. Scholarships based on academics, athletics, leadership. **Student debt:** 80% of graduating class borrowed to fund education; average debt was $14,000.

Freshman aid. Need-based: Out of 120 full-time freshmen, 120 applied for aid; 99 were judged to have need; of these 99 received aid. Average package met 75% of need. 28 students had full need met. Average scholarship/grant was $9,240; average loan $2,244. **Non-need based:** 21 full-time freshmen with need received non-need scholarships; 21 without need received awards; 10 received athletic scholarships.

Merit scholarships. Many merit scholarships offered, based solely on academic achievement, ranging from $500 to $10,000.

Policies to reduce costs. Tuition/fee waivers for family members, employees and their families. Credit/placement for qualifying scores on AP, IB, CLEP examinations. Work study available nights and weekends.

Payment plans. Credit card, installment payment.

Application procedures. FAFSA required. Priority date 4/1; closing date 8/1. Applicants notified on rolling basis starting 3/1, must reply by 5/1 or within 3 week(s) of notification. **Transfers:** No deadline.

Contact. Financial aid office: (704) 825-6718
Anne Stevens, Director of Enrollment Management
100 Belmont - Mt. Holly Road
Belmont, NC 28012-2795

Bennett College

Greensboro, North Carolina
www.bennett.edu
Four-year private **Federal Code: 002911**

	Living at home	On-campus
Tuition and fees (projected):	$10,978	$10,978
Room and board:		$5,162
Books and supplies:	$750	$750

Undergraduate aid. Non-need-based: Scholarships based on state/district residency.

Policies to reduce costs. Tuition/fee waivers for family of clergy, employees and their families. Credit/placement for qualifying scores on CLEP examinations.

Payment plans. Credit card, installment payment.

Application procedures. FAFSA, institutional form required. Closing date 4/15. Applicants notified by 7/15.

Contact. Financial aid office: (336) 517-2205
Stephanie Lynch, Financial Aid Officer
900 East Washington Street
Greensboro, NC 27401-3239

Bladen Community College

Dublin, North Carolina
www.bladen.cc.nc.us
Two-year public **Federal Code: 007987**

	Living at home
Tuition and fees (2002-2003):	$1,066
Out-of-state:	$5,761
Per-credit charge:	$34
Per-credit out-of-state:	$191
Board only:	$1,000
Books and supplies:	$800
Personal expenses:	$725
Transportation:	$725

Undergraduate aid. Need-based: Need-based aid available for full-time and part-time students.

Policies to reduce costs. Tuition/fee waivers for senior citizens. Work study available nights.

Payment plans. Credit card, installment, deferred payment.

Application procedures. FAFSA required. Priority date 6/1; no closing date. Applicants notified on rolling basis starting 8/1, must reply within 2 week(s) of notification. **Transfers:** No deadline.

Contact. Financial aid office: (910) 879-5562
Marva Dinkins, Financial Aid Director
Box 266
Dublin, NC 28332

Blue Ridge Community College

Flat Rock, North Carolina
www.blueridge.cc.nc.us
Two-year public **Federal Code: 009684**

	Living at home
Tuition and fees (2002-2003):	$1,059
Out-of-state:	$5,754
Per-credit charge:	$34
Per-credit out-of-state:	$191
Books and supplies:	$750
Personal expenses:	$1,717
Transportation:	$2,628

Undergraduate aid. Need-based: 95% awarded as scholarships/grants, 5% as loans/jobs. **Non-need-based:** Scholarships based on academics, state/district residency.

Policies to reduce costs. Tuition/fee waivers for senior citizens, employees and their families. Work study available nights and for part-time students.

Payment plans. Credit card payment.

Application procedures. FAFSA, institutional form required. Priority date 6/30; no closing date. Applicants notified on rolling basis starting 2/1, must reply within 4 week(s) of notification.

Contact. Financial aid office: (828) 694-1806
Wanda Bodenhamer, Financial Aid Officer
College Drive
Flat Rock, NC 28731-9624

Brevard College

Brevard, North Carolina
www.brevard.edu
Four-year private **Federal Code: 002912**

College costs. Telecommunications fee $650 for on-campus residents.

	Living at home	On-campus
Tuition and fees (2002-2003):	$12,930	$12,930
Room and board:		$5,400
Board only:	$1,500	
Books and supplies:	$800	$800
Personal expenses:	$1,000	$1,000
Transportation:	$750	$750

Undergraduate aid. Need-based: Average financial aid package for full-time students was $12,240; for part-time $4,880. 63% awarded as scholarships/grants, 37% as loans/jobs. **Non-need-based:** 66% awarded as scholarships/grants, 34% as loans/jobs. Scholarships based on academics, art, athletics, job skills, leadership, music/drama, religious affiliation, state/district residency. **Student debt:** 52% of graduating class borrowed to fund education; average debt was $16,150.

Freshman aid. Need-based: Out of 152 full-time freshmen, 116 applied for aid; 96 were judged to have need; of these 96 received aid. Average package met 82% of need. 26 students had full need met. Average scholarship/grant was $10,745; average loan $3,020. **Non-need based:** 7 full-time freshmen with need received non-need scholarships; 35 without need received awards; 5 received athletic scholarships.

Policies to reduce costs. Tuition/fee waivers for family of clergy, employees and their families. Credit/placement for qualifying scores on AP, IB, CLEP examinations. Work study available nights, weekends and for part-time students.

Payment plans. Credit card payment.

Application procedures. FAFSA required. Priority date 4/15; no closing date. Applicants notified on rolling basis starting 2/15, must reply within 4 week(s) of notification.

Contact. Financial aid office: (828) 884-8287
Lisanne Masterson, Associate Dean of Financial Aid
400 North Broad Street
Brevard, NC 28712

Brunswick Community College

Supply, North Carolina
www.brunswick.cc.nc.us
Two-year public **Federal Code: 015285**

	Living at home
Tuition and fees (2002-2003):	$1,069
Out-of-state:	$5,764
Per-credit charge:	$34
Per-credit out-of-state:	$191
Books and supplies:	$600
Personal expenses:	$800
Transportation:	$1,300

Undergraduate aid. Need-based: Need-based aid available for full-time and part-time students. **Non-need-based:** Scholarships based on academics, state/district residency. **Additional information:** Attendance required at financial aid orientation session for those receiving federal student aid.

Merit scholarships. La Dane Williamson Scholarship; must be a resident of Brunswick County for 5 years prior to application, must be a high school graduate of Brunswick County or complete GED or adult high school diploma program at Brunswick Community College, recipient must not be eligible for Pell; $1,200 per year for 2 years. Brunswick Family Scholarship for Brunswick County residents of 3 years prior to application; GED or high school graduate; recipient must not be eligible for Pell; may cover total amount of tuition and fees.

Policies to reduce costs. Tuition/fee waivers for senior citizens. Credit/placement for qualifying scores on AP, CLEP examinations. Work study available for part-time students.

Payment plans. Credit card payment.

Application procedures. FAFSA, institutional form required. Priority date 6/30; no closing date. Applicants notified on rolling basis starting 3/1, must reply within 2 week(s) of notification. **Transfers:** Priority date 6/30; no deadline.

Contact. Financial aid office: (910) 755-7422
Linda Gilliam, Coordinator of Financial Aid and Veterans Affairs
Box 30
Supply, NC 28462

Caldwell Community College and Technical Institute

Hudson, North Carolina
www.cccti.edu
Two-year public **Federal Code: 004835**

	Living at home
Tuition and fees (2002-2003):	$1,060
Out-of-state:	$5,755
Per-credit charge:	$34
Per-credit out-of-state:	$191
Books and supplies:	$925
Personal expenses:	$1,350
Transportation:	$1,260

Undergraduate aid. All financial aid based on need. Need-based aid available for full-time and part-time students.

Policies to reduce costs. Tuition/fee waivers for senior citizens. Credit/placement for qualifying scores on AP, CLEP examinations. Work study available for part-time students.

Payment plans. Credit card payment.

Application procedures. FAFSA required. Priority date 4/1; no closing date. Applicants notified on rolling basis starting 6/30.

Contact. **Financial aid office:** (828) 726-2714
Dianne Henderson, Director of Financial Aid
2855 Hickory Boulevard
Hudson, NC 28638-2672

Campbell University

Buies Creek, North Carolina
www.campbell.edu
Four-year private **Federal Code: 002913**

	Living at home	On-campus
Tuition and fees:	$13,541	$13,541
Room and board:		$4,756
Board only:	$1,210	
Books and supplies:	$850	$850
Personal expenses:	$2,034	$2,796
Transportation:	$1,347	$689

Undergraduate aid. Need-based: Average financial aid package for full-time students was $19,893; for part-time $12,755. 45% awarded as scholarships/grants, 55% as loans/jobs. **Non-need-based:** 45% awarded as scholarships/grants, 55% as loans/jobs. Scholarships based on academics, athletics, music/drama, religious affiliation, state/district residency. **Student debt:** 58% of graduating class borrowed to fund education; average debt was $13,064.

Freshman aid. Need-based: Out of 773 full-time freshmen, 773 applied for aid; 589 were judged to have need; of these 589 received aid. Average package met 100% of need. 589 students had full need met. Average scholarship/grant was $4,567; average loan $3,094. **Non-need based:** 520 full-time freshmen with need received non-need scholarships; 152 without need received awards; 49 received athletic scholarships.

Merit scholarships. Presidential Scholarships; $6,000-$11,000; must be in top 10% of class with SAT 1150 and/or ACT 25/GPA 3.2; Campbell Scholarship; $3,500-7,000; must be in top 25% of class with SAT 1000 and/or ACT 21/GPA 3.0.

Policies to reduce costs. Tuition/fee waivers for adults, family of clergy, employees and their families. Credit/placement for qualifying scores on AP, IB, CLEP examinations. Work study available nights and weekends.

Payment plans. Credit card, installment payment.

Application procedures. FAFSA required. Priority date 3/15; no closing date. Applicants notified on rolling basis starting 4/15, must reply within 2 week(s) of notification.

Contact. **Financial aid office:** (800) 334-4111 ext. 1310
Nancy Beasley, Director of Financial Aid
Box 546
Buies Creek, NC 27506

Cape Fear Community College

Wilmington, North Carolina
cfcc.net
Two-year public **Federal Code: 005320**

	Living at home
Tuition and fees (2002-2003):	$1,066
Out-of-state:	$5,761
Per-credit charge:	$34
Per-credit out-of-state:	$191
Books and supplies:	$900
Personal expenses:	$900
Transportation:	$500

Undergraduate aid. Need-based: 83% awarded as scholarships/grants, 17% as loans/jobs. Need-based aid available for part-time students. **Non-need-based:** Scholarships based on academics, job skills.

Policies to reduce costs. Tuition/fee waivers for senior citizens, employees and their families. Credit/placement for qualifying scores on AP, CLEP examinations. Work study available nights.

Payment plans. Credit card payment.

Application procedures. FAFSA required. Priority date 6/1; no closing date. Applicants notified on rolling basis starting 4/1, must reply within 2 week(s) of notification.

Contact. **Financial aid office:** (910) 362-7057
Linda Smiley, Director of Financial Aid
411 North Front Street
Wilmington, NC 28401-3993

Carteret Community College

Morehead City, North Carolina
www.carteret.cc.nc.us
Two-year public **Federal Code: 008081**

College costs. Mandatory technology fee is $20 per year.

	Living at home
Tuition and fees (2002-2003):	$1,055
Out-of-state:	$5,750
Per-credit charge:	$34
Per-credit out-of-state:	$191
Board only:	$1,500
Books and supplies:	$500
Personal expenses:	$1,665
Transportation:	$975

Undergraduate aid. Need-based: Need-based aid available for full-time and part-time students. **Non-need-based:** Scholarships based on academics, leadership, minority status, state/district residency. **Additional information:** Institutional student loan program administered by college. Student may charge up to $600 for books, supplies and tuition per quarter. Repayment due by 11th week of semester.

Policies to reduce costs. Tuition/fee waivers for senior citizens, employees and their families. Credit/placement for qualifying scores on AP, CLEP examinations.

Payment plans. Credit card, installment, deferred payment.

Application procedures. FAFSA, institutional form required. Priority date 8/1; no closing date. Applicants notified on rolling basis, must reply within 2 week(s) of notification. **Transfers:** No deadline.

Contact. **Financial aid office:** (252) 222-6147
Brenda Long, Financial Aid Officer
3505 Arendell Street
Morehead City, NC 28557-2989

Catawba College

Salisbury, North Carolina
www.catawba.edu
Four-year private **Federal Code: 002914**

	Living at home	On-campus
Tuition and fees (2002-2003):	$15,300	$15,300
Room and board:		$5,200
Books and supplies:	$750	$750
Personal expenses:	$1,300	$1,300
Transportation:	$1,500	$1,200

Undergraduate aid. Need-based: Average financial aid package for full-time students was $13,766; for part-time $6,777. 42% awarded as scholarships/grants, 58% as loans/jobs. **Non-need-based:** 78% awarded as scholarships/grants, 22% as loans/jobs. Scholarships based on academics, athletics, music/drama, state/district residency.

Freshman aid. Need-based: Out of 328 full-time freshmen, 285 applied for aid; 244 were judged to have need; of these 178 received aid. Average package met 51% of need. 123 students had full need met. Average scholarship/grant was $3,690; average loan $5,724. **Non-need based:** 224 full-time freshmen with need received non-need scholarships; 41 without need received awards; 72 received athletic scholarships.

Policies to reduce costs. Tuition/fee waivers for employees and their families. Credit/placement for qualifying scores on AP, IB, CLEP examinations. Work study available nights and weekends.

Payment plans. Credit card, installment payment.

Application procedures. FAFSA required. Priority date 3/1; no closing date. Applicants notified on rolling basis starting 2/15, must reply within 2 week(s) of notification. **Transfers:** Priority date 3/1; no deadline.

Contact. **Financial aid office:** (704) 637-4416
Melanie McCulloh, Director of Scholarships and Financial Assistance
2300 West Innes Street
Salisbury, NC 28144

Catawba Valley Community College

Hickory, North Carolina
www.cvcc.cc.nc.us
Two-year public **Federal Code: 005318**

	Living at home
Tuition and fees (2002-2003):	$1,052
Out-of-state:	$5,747
Per-credit charge:	$34
Per-credit out-of-state:	$191
Board only:	$2,358
Books and supplies:	$800
Personal expenses:	$1,386
Transportation:	$900

Undergraduate aid. Need-based: Need-based aid available for full-time students. **Non-need-based:** Scholarships based on academics, athletics.

Policies to reduce costs. Tuition/fee waivers for senior citizens, employees and their families. Credit/placement for qualifying scores on IB, CLEP examinations.

Payment plans. Credit card payment.

Application procedures. FAFSA required. Priority date 7/1; no closing date. Applicants notified on rolling basis, must reply within 2 week(s) of notification.

Contact. Debbie Barger, Director of Scholarships and Financial Aid
2550 Highway 70 SE
Hickory, NC 28602

Central Carolina Community College

Sanford, North Carolina
www.cccc.edu
Two-year public **Federal Code: 005449**

	Living at home
Tuition and fees (2002-2003):	$1,064
Out-of-state:	$5,759
Per-credit charge:	$34
Per-credit out-of-state:	$191
Books and supplies:	$666
Personal expenses:	$1,204
Transportation:	$1,342

Undergraduate aid. Need-based: Need-based aid available for full-time and part-time students. **Non-need-based:** Scholarships based on academics.

Policies to reduce costs. Tuition/fee waivers for senior citizens, employees and their families. Work study available nights and for part-time students.

Payment plans. Credit card, installment payment.

Application procedures. FAFSA, institutional form required. Priority date 3/15; closing date 5/1. Applicants notified on rolling basis starting 7/1, must reply within 2 week(s) of notification. **Transfers:** No deadline.

Contact. **Financial aid office:** (919) 718-7205
Jackie Thomas, Director of Financial Aid
1105 Kelly Drive
Sanford, NC 27330

Central Piedmont Community College

Charlotte, North Carolina
www.cpcc.edu
Two-year public **Federal Code: 002915**

	Living at home
Tuition and fees (2002-2003):	$1,090
Out-of-state:	$5,785
Per-credit charge:	$34
Per-credit out-of-state:	$191
Books and supplies:	$1,100
Personal expenses:	$596
Transportation:	$1,200

Undergraduate aid. Need-based: Need-based aid available for full-time and part-time students.

Policies to reduce costs. Tuition/fee waivers for senior citizens, employees and their families. Credit/placement for qualifying scores on AP, CLEP examinations.

Payment plans. Credit card, deferred payment.

Application procedures. FAFSA required. Priority date 4/3; closing date 6/3. Applicants notified on rolling basis.

Contact. **Financial aid office:** (704) 330-6579
Donovan Woodside, Director, Student Financial Aid
Box 35009
Charlotte, NC 28235

Chowan College

Murfreesboro, North Carolina
www.chowan.edu
Four-year private **Federal Code: 002916**

	Living at home	On-campus
Tuition and fees (2002-2003):	$12,500	$12,500
Room and board:		$5,040
Board only:	$2,680	
Books and supplies:	$725	$725
Personal expenses:	$1,000	$1,000
Transportation:	$1,540	$420

Undergraduate aid. Need-based: Need-based aid available for full-time and part-time students. **Non-need-based:** Scholarships based on academics, leadership, music/drama, religious affiliation, state/district residency.

Merit scholarships. Scholarship program for students serving as student body president who qualify for admission; full tuition.

Policies to reduce costs. Tuition/fee waivers for senior citizens, family of clergy, employees and their families. Credit/placement for qualifying scores on AP, IB, CLEP examinations. Work study available nights and weekends.

Payment plans. Credit card, deferred payment.

Application procedures. FAFSA required. Priority date 5/1; no closing date. Applicants notified on rolling basis starting 3/1, must reply within 2 week(s) of notification.

Contact. **Financial aid office:** (252) 398-1229
Stephanie Harold, Director of Financial Aid
200 Jones Drive
Murfreesboro, NC 27855-9901

Cleveland Community College

Shelby, North Carolina
www.clevelandcommunitycollege.edu
Two-year public **Federal Code: 008082**

	Living at home
Tuition and fees (2002-2003):	$1,066
Out-of-state:	$5,761
Per-credit charge:	$34
Per-credit out-of-state:	$191
Books and supplies:	$700

Undergraduate aid. Need-based: Average financial aid package for full-time students was $2,170. 99% awarded as scholarships/grants, 1% as loans/jobs. Need-based aid available for part-time students.

Policies to reduce costs. Tuition/fee waivers for senior citizens, employees and their families. Credit/placement for qualifying scores on AP, IB, CLEP examinations. Work study available for part-time students.

Payment plans. Credit card payment.

Application procedures. FAFSA required. Priority date 7/1; no closing date. Applicants notified on rolling basis.

Contact. **Financial aid office:** (704) 484-4096
Andy Gardner, Director of Financial Aid
137 South Post Road
Shelby, NC 28152

Coastal Carolina Community College

Jacksonville, North Carolina
www.coastal.cc.nc.us
Two-year public **Federal Code: 005316**

	Living at home
Tuition and fees (2002-2003):	$1,058
Out-of-state:	$5,753
Per-credit charge:	$34
Per-credit out-of-state:	$191
Board only:	$2,650
Books and supplies:	$700
Personal expenses:	$1,802
Transportation:	$1,190

Undergraduate aid. Need-based: Average financial aid package for full-time students was $2,392; for part-time $1,734. 97% awarded as scholarships/grants, 3% as loans/jobs. **Non-need-based:** Scholarships based on academics, state/district residency.

Freshman aid. Need-based: Out of 421 full-time freshmen, 187 applied for aid; 138 were judged to have need; of these 138 received aid. Average package met 23% of need. Average scholarship/grant was $333. **Non-need based:** 68 full-time freshmen with need received non-need scholarships; 68 without need received awards.

Policies to reduce costs. Tuition/fee waivers for senior citizens. Credit/placement for qualifying scores on AP, CLEP examinations. Work study available nights, weekends and for part-time students.

Payment plans. Credit card, installment payment.

Application procedures. FAFSA, institutional form required. Priority date 5/15; no closing date. Applicants notified on rolling basis starting 5/15, must reply within 4 week(s) of notification. **Transfers:** Priority date 7/15; no deadline.

Contact. **Financial aid office:** (910) 938-6247
John Kopka, Director of Financial Aid & Veterans Programs
444 Western Boulevard
Jacksonville, NC 28546

College of the Albemarle

Elizabeth City, North Carolina
www.albemarle.cc.nc.us
Two-year public **Federal Code: 002917**

	Living at home
Tuition and fees (2002-2003):	$1,066
Out-of-state:	$5,761
Per-credit charge:	$34
Per-credit out-of-state:	$191
Books and supplies:	$850
Personal expenses:	$2,100

Undergraduate aid. Need-based: Need-based aid available for full-time and part-time students. **Non-need-based:** Scholarships based on academics, art, leadership, minority status, music/drama. **Additional information:** Separate application must be submitted for COA Private Scholarships.

Policies to reduce costs. Tuition/fee waivers for senior citizens, employees and their families. Credit/placement for qualifying scores on AP, CLEP examinations. Work study available nights, weekends and for part-time students.

Payment plans. Credit card payment.

Application procedures. FAFSA required. Priority date 3/15; no closing date. Applicants notified on rolling basis starting 5/10, must reply within 2 week(s) of notification. **Transfers:** Priority date 3/15; no deadline.

Contact. Angie Dawson, Director of Scholarships and Student Aid
Box 2327
Elizabeth City, NC 27906

Craven Community College

New Bern, North Carolina
www.cravencc.edu
Two-year public **Federal Code: 008086**

	Living at home
Tuition and fees (2002-2003):	$1,056
Out-of-state:	$5,751
Per-credit charge:	$34
Per-credit out-of-state:	$191
Board only:	$4,096
Books and supplies:	$700
Personal expenses:	$1,056
Transportation:	$612

Policies to reduce costs. Tuition/fee waivers for senior citizens. Credit/placement for qualifying scores on AP, CLEP examinations.

Payment plans. Credit card payment.

Application procedures. FAFSA required. Priority date 4/1; no closing date. Applicants notified on rolling basis starting 6/1. **Transfers:** No deadline.

Contact. **Financial aid office:** (252) 638-7216
Kathy Banks, Director of Financial Aid
800 College Court
New Bern, NC 28562

Davidson College

Davidson, North Carolina
www.davidson.edu
Four-year private **Federal Code: 002918**

	Living at home	On-campus
Tuition and fees:	$25,903	$25,903
Room and board:		$7,389
Board only:	$3,223	
Books and supplies:	$1,000	$1,000
Personal expenses:	$1,176	$1,176
Transportation:	$350	$350

Undergraduate aid. Need-based: Average financial aid package for full-time students was $16,108. 81% awarded as scholarships/grants, 19% as loans/jobs. Need-based aid available for part-time students. **Non-need-based:** 69% awarded as scholarships/grants, 31% as loans/jobs. Scholarships based on academics, art, athletics, leadership, minority status, music/drama. **Student debt:** 31% of graduating class borrowed to fund education; average debt was $13,697.

Freshman aid. Need-based: Out of 465 full-time freshmen, 234 applied for aid; 150 were judged to have need; of these 150 received aid. Average package met 100% of need. 150 students had full need met. Average scholarship/grant was $15,040; average loan $2,355. **Non-need based:** 24 full-time freshmen with need received non-need scholarships; 100 without need received awards; 41 received athletic scholarships.

Merit scholarships. Thompson S./Sarah S. Baker Scholarships for first-time students with highest achievements; 3 awarded; comprehensive fees. John Montgomery Belk Scholarship for Southeast applicants with highest achievements; 6 awarded; comprehensive fees. Amos Norris Scholarship for first-time student athlete; 1 awarded; full cost. William Holt Terry Scholarships for first-year students with leadership skills and personal qualities, 2 awarded; full tuition. John I. Smith Scholars Programs for first-year students with leadership, academic excellence, and commitment to community service; 2 awarded; full tuition.

Policies to reduce costs. Tuition/fee waivers for employees and their families. Credit/placement for qualifying scores on AP, IB examinations.

Payment plans. Installment payment.

Application procedures. FAFSA, CSS PROFILE required. Closing date 2/15. Applicants notified by 4/1, must reply by 5/1. Early decision closing date 11/15. **Transfers:** Priority date 2/15; closing date 3/15.

Contact. Financial aid office: (704) 894-2232
Kathleen Stevenson-McNeely, Senior Associate Dean of Admission and Financial Aid
PO Box 7156
Davidson, NC 28035-7156

Davidson County Community College

Lexington, North Carolina
www.davidson.cc.nc.us
Two-year public **Federal Code: 002919**

	Living at home
Tuition and fees (2002-2003):	$1,069
Out-of-state:	$5,764
Per-credit charge:	$34
Per-credit out-of-state:	$191
Board only:	$1,800
Books and supplies:	$800
Personal expenses:	$540
Transportation:	$2,400

Undergraduate aid. Need-based: 93% awarded as scholarships/grants, 7% as loans/jobs. Need-based aid available for part-time students. **Non-need-based:** 83% awarded as scholarships/grants, 17% as loans/jobs. Scholarships based on academics, state/district residency. **Student debt:** 10% of graduating class borrowed to fund education; average debt was $2,219.

Policies to reduce costs. Tuition/fee waivers for senior citizens. Credit/placement for qualifying scores on AP, CLEP examinations.

Payment plans. Credit card payment.

Application procedures. FAFSA, institutional form required. Priority date 7/1; no closing date. Applicants notified on rolling basis starting 7/1, must reply within 2 week(s) of notification. **Transfers:** No deadline.

Contact. Financial aid office: (336) 249-8186 ext. 237
Anita Pennix, Coordinator, Financial Aid
PO Box 1287
Lexington, NC 27293-1287

Duke University

Durham, North Carolina
www.duke.edu
Four-year private **Federal Code: 002920**

	Living at home	On-campus
Tuition and fees:	$29,345	$29,345
Room and board:		$8,210
Books and supplies:	$875	$875
Personal expenses:	$1,590	$1,590
Transportation:	$700	$700

Undergraduate aid. Need-based: Need-based aid available for full-time students. **Non-need-based:** Scholarships based on academics, alumni affiliation, art, athletics, leadership, minority status, religious affiliation, state/district residency.

Policies to reduce costs. Tuition/fee waivers for employees and their families. Prepayment discount; credit/placement for qualifying scores on AP examinations.

Payment plans. Credit card, installment payment.

Application procedures. FAFSA, institutional form, CSS PROFILE required. Closing date 2/1. Applicants notified by 4/1, must reply by 5/1 or within 4 week(s) of notification. Early decision closing date 11/1.

Contact. Financial aid office: (919) 684-6225
Nerissa Rivera, Coordinator Financial Aid
2138 Campus Drive
Durham, NC 27708

Durham Technical Community College

Durham, North Carolina
www.durhamtech.org
Two-year public **Federal Code: 005448**

	Living at home
Tuition and fees (2002-2003):	$1,058
Out-of-state:	$5,753
Per-credit charge:	$34
Per-credit out-of-state:	$191
Board only:	$1,500
Personal expenses:	$562
Transportation:	$900

Undergraduate aid. Need-based: Need-based aid available for full-time and part-time students. **Non-need-based:** Scholarships based on academics, state/district residency. **Additional information:** Special funds available to single parents or displaced homemakers for tuition, fees, books, supplies and child care expenses.

Policies to reduce costs. Tuition/fee waivers for senior citizens, employees and their families. Credit/placement for qualifying scores on AP, CLEP examinations. Work study available nights and for part-time students.

Payment plans. Credit card payment.

Application procedures. FAFSA required. Priority date 5/31; no closing date. Applicants notified on rolling basis starting 6/15, must reply within 3 week(s) of notification. **Transfers:** Priority date 5/31; no deadline.

Contact. Cameron Murray, Financial Aid Officer
1637 Lawson Street
Durham, NC 27703

East Carolina University

Greenville, North Carolina
www.ecu.edu
Four-year public **Federal Code: 002923**

	Living at home	On-campus
Tuition and fees (2002-2003):	$2,980	$2,980
Out-of-state:	$12,636	$12,636
Room and board:		$5,090
Board only:	$2,586	
Books and supplies:	$750	$750
Personal expenses:	$1,360	$1,360
Transportation:	$680	$680

Undergraduate aid. Need-based: 44% awarded as scholarships/grants, 56% as loans/jobs. Need-based aid available for part-time students. **Non-need-based:** 23% awarded as scholarships/grants, 77% as loans/jobs. Scholarships based on academics, art, athletics, leadership, minority status, music/drama. **Student debt:** 58% of graduating class borrowed to fund education; average debt was $17,117.

Freshman aid. Need-based: Out of 3,561 full-time freshmen, 2,493 applied for aid; 1,425 were judged to have need; of these 1,347 received aid. 428 students had full need met. Average scholarship/grant was $2,397; average loan $2,773. **Non-need based:** 342 full-time freshmen with need received non-need scholarships; 681 without need received awards; 54 received athletic scholarships.

Policies to reduce costs. Tuition/fee waivers for senior citizens, employees and their families. Credit/placement for qualifying scores on AP, IB, CLEP examinations.

Payment plans. Credit card, installment, deferred payment.

Application procedures. FAFSA required. Priority date 4/15; no closing date. Applicants notified on rolling basis starting 3/15, must reply within 3 week(s) of notification.

Contact. **Financial aid office:** (252) 328-6610
Rose Mary Stelma, Director of Student Financial Aid
Office of Undergraduate Admissions
Greenville, NC 27858-4353

Edgecombe Community College

Tarboro, North Carolina
www.edgecombe.cc.nc.us
Two-year public **Federal Code: 008855**

	Living at home
Tuition and fees (2002-2003):	$1,052
Out-of-state:	$5,747
Per-credit charge:	$34
Per-credit out-of-state:	$191
Books and supplies:	$700
Personal expenses:	$1,800
Transportation:	$925

Undergraduate aid. All financial aid based on need. Average financial aid package for full-time students was $1,340; for part-time $600. 97% awarded as scholarships/grants, 3% as loans/jobs. **Student debt:** 2% of graduating class borrowed to fund education; average debt was $5,750.

Freshman aid. Out of 140 full-time freshmen, 101 applied for aid; 84 were judged to have need; of these 78 received aid. Average package met 90% of need. 73 students had full need met. Average scholarship/grant was $1,340; average loan $3,200.

Policies to reduce costs. Tuition/fee waivers for senior citizens, employees and their families. Credit/placement for qualifying scores on CLEP examinations.

Payment plans. Credit card payment.

Application procedures. FAFSA, institutional form required. Closing date 6/30. Applicants notified on rolling basis starting 8/15, must reply within 3 week(s) of notification. **Transfers:** No deadline.

Contact. Carolyn Knight, Director of Financial Aid
2009 West Wilson Street
Tarboro, NC 27886

Elizabeth City State University

Elizabeth City, North Carolina
www.ecsu.edu
Four-year public **Federal Code: 002926**

	Living at home	On-campus
Tuition and fees (2002-2003):	$1,840	$1,840
Out-of-state:	$8,836	$8,836
Room and board:		$4,172
Books and supplies:	$670	$670
Personal expenses:	$1,400	$1,200
Transportation:	$800	$700

Undergraduate aid. Need-based: Need-based aid available for full-time students. **Non-need-based:** Scholarships based on academics, athletics, state/district residency.

Policies to reduce costs. Tuition/fee waivers for senior citizens, employees and their families. Credit/placement for qualifying scores on AP, CLEP examinations.

Application procedures. FAFSA required. Priority date 4/1; no closing date. Applicants notified on rolling basis starting 6/1, must reply within 3 week(s) of notification.

Contact. **Financial aid office:** (252) 335-3283
Andre Farley, Director of Financial Aid
1704 Weeksville Road, Campus Box 901
Elizabeth City, NC 27909

Elon University

Elon, North Carolina
www.elon.edu
Four-year private **Federal Code: 002927**

	Living at home	On-campus
Tuition and fees:	$16,570	$16,570
Room and board:		$5,670
Board only:	$2,754	
Books and supplies:	$800	$800
Personal expenses:	$1,070	$1,380
Transportation:	$690	$750

Undergraduate aid. Need-based: Average financial aid package for full-time students was $10,694. 51% awarded as scholarships/grants, 49% as loans/jobs. Need-based aid available for part-time students. **Non-need-based:** 62% awarded as scholarships/grants, 38% as loans/jobs. Scholarships based on academics, art, athletics, leadership, music/drama, state/district residency. **Student debt:** 48% of graduating class borrowed to fund education; average debt was $26,663.

Freshman aid. Need-based: Out of 1,194 full-time freshmen, 709 applied for aid; 437 were judged to have need; of these 437 received aid. Average package met 78% of need. Average scholarship/grant was $5,874; average loan $2,416. **Non-need based:** 46 full-time freshmen with need received non-need scholarships; 430 without need received awards; 32 received athletic scholarships.

Merit scholarships. Presidential Scholarships based on academic credentials; ranging from $1,000-$3,000 annually. Fellows Programs (Communications, Science, Jefferson-Pilot Business, Honors, Isabella Cannon Leadership) based on merit; $1,000-$6,000 annually, North Carolina Teaching Fellows $13,000 annually; Engineering Scholarships $2,000 annually.

Policies to reduce costs. Tuition/fee waivers for family of clergy, employees and their families. Credit/placement for qualifying scores on AP, IB, CLEP examinations. Work study available nights, weekends and for part-time students.

Payment plans. Credit card, installment payment.

Application procedures. FAFSA, institutional form, CSS PROFILE required. Priority date 2/15; no closing date. Applicants notified on rolling basis starting 3/30. Early decision closing date 11/15. **Transfers:** Priority date 2/15; no deadline.

Contact. **Financial aid office:** (336) 278-7640
Pat Murphy, Associate Dean of Admissions/Director of Financial Planning
2700 Campus Box
Elon, NC 27244-2010

Fayetteville State University

Fayetteville, North Carolina
www.uncfsu.edu
Four-year public **Federal Code: 002928**

	Living at home	On-campus
Tuition and fees (2002-2003):	$1,542	$1,542
Out-of-state:	$8,812	$8,812
Room and board:		$3,800
Books and supplies:	$350	$350
Personal expenses:	$750	$750
Transportation:	$185	$190

Undergraduate aid. Non-need-based: Scholarships based on athletics.

Policies to reduce costs. Tuition/fee waivers for senior citizens, employees and their families. Credit/placement for qualifying scores on AP, CLEP examinations.

Payment plans. Credit card, installment payment.

Application procedures. Closing date 4/1. Applicants notified on rolling basis starting 7/1, must reply within 8 week(s) of notification.

Contact. Lois McKoy, Director of Financial Aid
1200 Murchison Road
Fayetteville, NC 28301-4298

Fayetteville Technical Community College

Fayetteville, North Carolina
www.faytechcc.edu
Two-year public **Federal Code: 007640**

	Living at home
Tuition and fees (2002-2003):	$1,047
Out-of-state:	$5,742
Per-credit charge:	$34
Per-credit out-of-state:	$191
Books and supplies:	$700
Personal expenses:	$525
Transportation:	$495

Undergraduate aid. Need-based: 79% awarded as scholarships/grants, 21% as loans/jobs. Need-based aid available for part-time students. **Student debt:** 8% of graduating class borrowed to fund education; average debt was $2,800.

Freshman aid. Need-based: Out of 2,122 full-time freshmen, 401 applied for aid; 401 were judged to have need; of these 401 received aid. Average package met 60% of need. 18 students had full need met. Average scholarship/grant was $322; average loan $1,742.

Policies to reduce costs. Tuition/fee waivers for senior citizens. Credit/placement for qualifying scores on AP, CLEP examinations. Work study available for part-time students.

Payment plans. Credit card payment.

Application procedures. FAFSA required. Priority date 6/2; closing date 7/15. Applicants notified on rolling basis starting 7/29, must reply by 8/8. **Transfers:** No deadline.

Contact. Janet Melvin, Financial Aid Coordinator
Box 35236
Fayetteville, NC 28303-0236

Forsyth Technical Community College

Winston-Salem, North Carolina
www.forsyth.tec.nc.us
Two-year public **Federal Code: 005317**

	Living at home
Tuition and fees (2002-2003):	$1,028
Out-of-state:	$5,723
Per-credit charge:	$34
Per-credit out-of-state:	$191
Books and supplies:	$650
Personal expenses:	$750
Transportation:	$750

Undergraduate aid. All financial aid based on need. Need-based aid available for full-time and part-time students. **Additional information:** Apply as soon after January 1 of each year as possible in order to be considered for several types of aid.

Policies to reduce costs. Tuition/fee waivers for senior citizens. Credit/placement for qualifying scores on AP examinations. Work study available nights and for part-time students.

Payment plans. Credit card, deferred payment.

Application procedures. FAFSA, institutional form required. Priority date 5/1; closing date 8/1. Applicants notified on rolling basis starting 7/1, must reply within 2 week(s) of notification. **Transfers:** Priority date 6/1; no deadline. Mid-year transfer students must submit a financial aid transcript from previous college in order for financial aid office to award any Federal Pell Grant funds to eligible students.

Contact. Regina Draughn, Director of Student Financial Services
2100 Silas Creek Parkway
Winston-Salem, NC 27103

Gardner-Webb University

Boiling Springs, North Carolina
www.gardner-webb.edu
Four-year private **Federal Code: 002929**

College costs. $75 communication fee for resident students.

	Living at home	On-campus
Tuition and fees:	$14,160	$14,160
Room and board:		$5,140
Board only:	$1,500	
Books and supplies:	$500	$500
Personal expenses:	$680	$1,090
Transportation:	$850	$510

Undergraduate aid. Need-based: Average financial aid package for full-time students was $9,921; for part-time $3,921. 56% awarded as scholarships/grants, 44% as loans/jobs. **Non-need-based:** 50% awarded as scholarships/grants, 50% as loans/jobs. Scholarships based on academics, athletics, leadership, minority status, music/drama, state/district residency. **Student debt:** 41% of graduating class borrowed to fund education; average debt was $6,059.

Freshman aid. Need-based: Out of 374 full-time freshmen, 340 applied for aid; 277 were judged to have need; of these 277 received aid. Average package met 94% of need. 121 students had full need met. Average scholarship/grant was $7,246; average loan $2,921. **Non-need based:** 120 full-time freshmen with need received non-need scholarships; 86 without need received awards; 31 received athletic scholarships.

Policies to reduce costs. Tuition/fee waivers for family of clergy, employees and their families. Credit/placement for qualifying scores on AP, IB, CLEP examinations.

Payment plans. Credit card, installment payment.

Application procedures. FAFSA required. No deadline. Applicants notified on rolling basis starting 3/1, must reply within 4 week(s) of notification. **Transfers:** No deadline.

Contact. Financial aid office: (704) 406-4243
Patricia Cope, Director of Financial Planning
Box 817
Boiling Springs, NC 28017

Gaston College

Dallas, North Carolina
www.gaston.cc.nc.us
Two-year public **Federal Code: 002973**

	Living at home
Tuition and fees (2002-2003):	$1,062
Out-of-state:	$5,757
Per-credit charge:	$34
Per-credit out-of-state:	$191
Books and supplies:	$1,000
Personal expenses:	$1,000
Transportation:	$1,000

Undergraduate aid. Need-based: Need-based aid available for full-time students. **Non-need-based:** Scholarships based on academics, state/district residency. **Additional information:** Grants/scholarships available for women pursuing nontraditional roles.

Merit scholarships. Academic Scholarship: over 30 available, $1,100, GPA of 3.0 or better. Careers Scholarship: 10 available, $1,100 each, must pursue career in specified engineering technologies or industrial technologies major and have GPA of 3.0 or better.

Policies to reduce costs. Tuition/fee waivers for senior citizens, employees and their families. Credit/placement for qualifying scores on AP examinations. Work study available for part-time students.

Payment plans. Credit card payment.

Application procedures. FAFSA, institutional form required. Priority date 3/15; no closing date. Applicants notified on rolling basis.

Contact. Financial aid office: (704) 922-6227
Peggy Oates, Director of Financial Aid and Veterans Affairs
201 Highway 321 South
Dallas, NC 28034-1499

Greensboro College

Greensboro, North Carolina
www.gborocollege.edu
Four-year private **Federal Code: 002930**

	Living at home	On-campus
Tuition and fees (2002-2003):	$13,700	$13,700
Room and board:		$5,380
Board only:	$750	
Books and supplies:	$800	$800
Personal expenses:	$900	$900
Transportation:	$400	$300

Undergraduate aid. Need-based: Average financial aid package for full-time students was $9,501; for part-time $5,320. 49% awarded as scholarships/grants, 51% as loans/jobs. **Non-need-based:** 68% awarded as scholarships/grants, 32% as loans/jobs. Scholarships based on academics, alumni affiliation, art, leadership, music/drama, religious affiliation, state/district residency. **Student debt:** 56% of graduating class borrowed to fund education; average debt was $14,324.

Freshman aid. Need-based: Out of 235 full-time freshmen, 230 applied for aid; 195 were judged to have need; of these 195 received aid. Average package met 65% of need. 25 students had full need met. Average scholarship/grant was $1,903; average loan $2,031. **Non-need based:** 191 full-time freshmen with need received non-need scholarships; 52 without need received awards.

Merit scholarships. Presidential Scholarships; full tuition, fees, room, and board; number of awards vary. Additional merit-based or talent-based scholarships awarded; number and dollar amounts vary.

Policies to reduce costs. Tuition/fee waivers for employees and their families. Credit/placement for qualifying scores on AP, IB, CLEP examinations. Work study available nights, weekends and for part-time students.

Payment plans. Credit card, installment payment.

Application procedures. FAFSA, institutional form required. Priority date 4/15; no closing date. Applicants notified on rolling basis starting 2/1, must reply within 2 week(s) of notification.

Contact. Financial aid office: (336) 272-7102
Ron Elmore, Director of Financial Aid
815 West Market Street
Greensboro, NC 27401-1875

Guilford College

Greensboro, North Carolina
www.guilford.edu
Four-year private **Federal Code: 002931**

	Living at home	On-campus
Tuition and fees:	$19,020	$19,020
Room and board:		$5,940
Books and supplies:	$700	$700
Personal expenses:	$1,000	$1,000
Transportation:	$575	$575

Undergraduate aid. Need-based: Average financial aid package for full-time students was $15,200; for part-time $2,800. 73% awarded as scholarships/grants, 27% as loans/jobs. **Non-need-based:** 89% awarded as scholarships/grants, 11% as loans/jobs. Scholarships based on academics, art, job skills, leadership, music/drama, religious affiliation, state/district residency. **Student debt:** 42% of graduating class borrowed to fund education; average debt was $17,380.

Freshman aid. Need-based: Out of 311 full-time freshmen, 220 applied for aid; 182 were judged to have need; of these 182 received aid. Average package met 90% of need. 162 students had full need met. Average scholarship/grant was $12,100; average loan $4,800. **Non-need based:** 93 full-time freshmen with need received non-need scholarships; 106 without need received awards.

Merit scholarships. Honors Scholarship; $7,500 to full tuition; merit based. Presidential Scholarship; $5,000; merit based. Incentive grants; $3,000; based on participation or leadership in school or community activities. Quaker Leadership Scholarships; $3,000; candidates must be active members of the Religious Society of Friends.

Policies to reduce costs. Tuition/fee waivers for adults, employees and their families. Credit/placement for qualifying scores on AP, IB, CLEP examinations. Work study available nights and weekends.

Payment plans. Credit card, installment payment.

Application procedures. FAFSA, CSS PROFILE required. Priority date 3/1; no closing date. Applicants notified on rolling basis starting 2/15, must reply by 5/1 or within 4 week(s) of notification. Early decision closing date 11/15. **Transfers:** Priority date 3/1; no deadline.

Contact. Financial aid office: (336) 316-2354
Anthony Gurley, Associate Dean of Enrollment
5800 West Friendly Avenue
Greensboro, NC 27410

Guilford Technical Community College

Jamestown, North Carolina
technet.gtcc.cc.nc.us
Two-year public **Federal Code: 004838**

	Living at home
Tuition and fees (2002-2003):	$1,071
Out-of-state:	$5,766
Per-credit charge:	$34
Per-credit out-of-state:	$191
Board only:	$1,553
Books and supplies:	$650
Personal expenses:	$1,151
Transportation:	$1,152

Undergraduate aid. Need-based: Need-based aid available for full-time and part-time students.

Policies to reduce costs. Tuition/fee waivers for senior citizens, employees and their families. Credit/placement for qualifying scores on AP, IB, CLEP examinations. Work study available for part-time students.

Payment plans. Installment payment.

Application procedures. FAFSA required. Priority date 3/15; no closing date. Applicants notified on rolling basis starting 7/1, must reply within 2 week(s) of notification.

Contact. Financial aid office: (336) 334-4822 ext. 2306
Lisa Koretoff, Director of Financial Aid
PO Box 309
Jamestown, NC 27282

Halifax Community College

Weldon, North Carolina
www.halfaxcc.edu
Two-year public **Federal Code: 007986**

	Living at home
Tuition and fees (2002-2003):	$1,050
Out-of-state:	$5,745
Per-credit charge:	$34
Per-credit out-of-state:	$191
Books and supplies:	$500
Personal expenses:	$896
Transportation:	$1,031

Undergraduate aid. Need-based: Need-based aid available for full-time students.

Policies to reduce costs. Tuition/fee waivers for senior citizens.

Application procedures. Priority date 7/1; no closing date. Applicants notified on rolling basis starting 8/1, must reply within 2 week(s) of notification.

Contact. Ray Barmer, Director, Financial Aid
Drawer 809
Weldon, NC 27890

Haywood Community College
Clyde, North Carolina
www.haywood.edu
Two-year public **Federal Code: 008083**

	Living at home
Tuition and fees (2002-2003):	$1,056
Out-of-state:	$5,751
Per-credit charge:	$34
Per-credit out-of-state:	$191
Board only:	$1,500
Books and supplies:	$1,000
Personal expenses:	$1,656
Transportation:	$1,682

Undergraduate aid. Need-based: Average financial aid package for full-time students was $1,747; for part-time $1,079. 81% awarded as scholarships/grants, 19% as loans/jobs. **Non-need-based:** Scholarships based on academics. **Student debt:** 12% of graduating class borrowed to fund education; average debt was $4,545. **Additional information:** Complete FAFSA by priority filing date for consideration for institutional scholarships.

Freshman aid. Need-based: Out of 507 full-time freshmen, 337 applied for aid; 317 were judged to have need; of these 310 received aid. Average package met 35% of need. Average scholarship/grant was $1,700; average loan $1,300. **Non-need based:** 6 full-time freshmen with need received non-need scholarships.

Policies to reduce costs. Tuition/fee waivers for senior citizens, employees and their families. Credit/placement for qualifying scores on AP examinations. Work study available for part-time students.

Payment plans. Credit card payment.

Application procedures. FAFSA, institutional form required. Priority date 4/1; no closing date. Applicants notified on rolling basis starting 4/15, must reply within 2 week(s) of notification. **Transfers:** No deadline.

Contact. Financial aid office: (828) 627-4506
Kathy Lovedahl, Coordinator Financial Aid
185 Freelander Drive
Clyde, NC 28721-9454

High Point University
High Point, North Carolina
www.highpoint.edu
Four-year private **Federal Code: 002933**

	Living at home	On-campus
Tuition and fees:	$14,710	$14,710
Room and board:		$6,610
Board only:	$3,000	
Books and supplies:	$1,000	$1,000
Personal expenses:	$1,050	$1,700
Transportation:	$580	$580

Undergraduate aid. Need-based: Average financial aid package for full-time students was $11,427. 55% awarded as scholarships/grants, 45% as loans/jobs. Need-based aid available for part-time students. **Non-need-based:** 67% awarded as scholarships/grants, 33% as loans/jobs. Scholarships based on academics, athletics, leadership, music/drama, religious affiliation, state/district residency. **Student debt:** 76% of graduating class borrowed to fund education; average debt was $15,000.

Freshman aid. Need-based: Out of 445 full-time freshmen, 445 applied for aid; 401 were judged to have need; of these 401 received aid. Average package met 85% of need. 17 students had full need met. Average scholarship/grant was $4,500; average loan $2,625. **Non-need based:** 107 full-time freshmen with need received non-need scholarships; 36 without need received awards; 26 received athletic scholarships.

Merit scholarships. At least 3 full tuition scholarships, at least 50 $6,400 scholarships, and at least 50 $4,000 scholarships awarded annually to entering freshmen based on Presidential Scholarship Competition. Based on academic merit. Application and interview required.

Policies to reduce costs. Tuition/fee waivers for family of clergy, employees and their families. Credit/placement for qualifying scores on AP, IB, CLEP examinations.

Application procedures. FAFSA required. Priority date 3/1; no closing date. Applicants notified on rolling basis starting 2/15, must reply by 5/1 or within 4 week(s) of notification.

Contact. Financial aid office: (336) 841-9128
Dana Kelly, Director of Financial Aid
833 Montlieu Avenue
High Point, NC 27262-3598

Isothermal Community College
Spindale, North Carolina
www.isothermal.edu
Two-year public **Federal Code: 002934**

	Living at home
Tuition and fees (2002-2003):	$1,060
Out-of-state:	$5,755
Per-credit charge:	$34
Per-credit out-of-state:	$191
Board only:	$1,500
Books and supplies:	$500
Personal expenses:	$760
Transportation:	$800

Undergraduate aid. Need-based: 98% awarded as scholarships/grants, 2% as loans/jobs. Need-based aid available for part-time students. **Non-need-based:** Scholarships based on academics, job skills, leadership, minority status, music/drama, state/district residency.

Policies to reduce costs. Tuition/fee waivers for senior citizens, employees and their families. Credit/placement for qualifying scores on AP, CLEP examinations. Work study available nights and for part-time students.

Payment plans. Credit card payment.

Application procedures. FAFSA, institutional form required. Priority date 5/31; no closing date. Applicants notified on rolling basis starting 4/30, must reply within 4 week(s) of notification.

Contact. Financial aid office: (828) 286-3636 ext.242
Jeff Boyle, Director of Financial Aid
Box 804
Spindale, NC 28160

James Sprunt Community College
Kenansville, North Carolina
www.sprunt.com
Two-year public **Federal Code: 007687**

	Living at home
Tuition and fees (2002-2003):	$1,066
Out-of-state:	$5,761
Per-credit charge:	$34
Per-credit out-of-state:	$191
Board only:	$2,400
Books and supplies:	$800
Personal expenses:	$600
Transportation:	$1,488

Undergraduate aid. All financial aid based on need. Average financial aid package for full-time students was $3,000; for part-time $2,000.

Freshman aid. Out of 118 full-time freshmen, 52 applied for aid; 52 were judged to have need; of these 52 received aid. Average package met 50% of need. Average scholarship/grant was $990; average loan $6,187.

Policies to reduce costs. Tuition/fee waivers for senior citizens, employees and their families. Credit/placement for qualifying scores on AP, CLEP examinations. Work study available nights and for part-time students.

Payment plans. Credit card payment.

Application procedures. FAFSA, institutional form required. Priority date 6/1; no closing date. Applicants notified on rolling basis starting 7/15, must reply within 2 week(s) of notification. **Transfers:** Priority date 6/1; no deadline.

Contact. Financial aid office: (910) 296-2503
Connie Taylor, Financial Aid Officer
Box 398
Kenansville, NC 28349-0398

John Wesley College

High Point, North Carolina
johnwesley.edu
Four-year private **Federal Code: 013819**

	Living at home	On-campus
Tuition and fees (2002-2003):	$7,610	$7,610
Room only:		$1,990
Books and supplies:	$600	$600
Transportation:	$875	

Undergraduate aid. Need-based: Need-based aid available for full-time and part-time students. **Additional information:** Early Acceptance Scholarships, Academic Honor Scholarships, Married Student Credit and Minister/Missionary Dependent Scholarship available.

Merit scholarships. Early Acceptance; $100. Academic Honor; 10% of tuition.

Policies to reduce costs. Tuition/fee waivers for family members, family of clergy, employees and their families. Credit/placement for qualifying scores on IB, CLEP examinations. Work study available nights, weekends and for part-time students.

Payment plans. Credit card, installment payment.

Application procedures. FAFSA required. Priority date 5/1; no closing date. Applicants notified on rolling basis starting 6/1.

Contact. Shirley Carter, Director of Financial Aid
2314 North Centennial
High Point, NC 27265-3197

Johnson C. Smith University

Charlotte, North Carolina
www.jcsu.edu
Four-year private **Federal Code: 002936**

	Living at home	On-campus
Tuition and fees (2002-2003):	$12,444	$12,444
Room and board:		$4,806
Books and supplies:	$1,000	$1,000
Personal expenses:	$2,400	$2,400
Transportation:	$1,200	$1,200

Undergraduate aid. Need-based: Average financial aid package for full-time students was $14,000; for part-time $2,000. 49% awarded as scholarships/grants, 51% as loans/jobs. **Non-need-based:** Scholarships based on academics, athletics, state/district residency. **Student debt:** 80% of graduating class borrowed to fund education; average debt was $25,000.

Freshman aid. Need-based: Out of 464 full-time freshmen, 460 applied for aid; 460 were judged to have need; of these 460 received aid. Average package met 83% of need. 400 students had full need met. Average scholarship/grant was $9,500; average loan $6,000. **Non-need based:** 154 full-time freshmen with need received non-need scholarships.

Policies to reduce costs. Tuition/fee waivers for employees and their families. Credit/placement for qualifying scores on AP examinations.

Payment plans. Credit card, installment payment.

Application procedures. FAFSA, institutional form required. Priority date 4/15; no closing date. Applicants notified on rolling basis starting 3/15, must reply within 2 week(s) of notification.

Contact. Financial aid office: (704) 378-1035
Cynthia Anderson, Director of Financial Aid
100 Beatties Ford Road
Charlotte, NC 28216-5398

Johnston Community College

Smithfield, North Carolina
www.johnston.cc.nc.us
Two-year public **Federal Code: 009336**

	Living at home
Tuition and fees (2002-2003):	$1,066
Out-of-state:	$5,761
Per-credit charge:	$34
Per-credit out-of-state:	$191
Books and supplies:	$450
Personal expenses:	$900
Transportation:	$900

Undergraduate aid. All financial aid based on need. 90% awarded as scholarships/grants, 10% as loans/jobs. Need-based aid available for part-time students.

Policies to reduce costs. Tuition/fee waivers for senior citizens, employees and their families. Credit/placement for qualifying scores on AP examinations. Work study available for part-time students.

Payment plans. Credit card, deferred payment.

Application procedures. FAFSA, institutional form required. Priority date 5/31; no closing date. Applicants notified on rolling basis starting 6/1, must reply within 2 week(s) of notification. **Transfers:** Priority date 5/31; no deadline.

Contact. Financial aid office: (919) 209-2028
Betty Woodall, Financial Aid Officer
Box 2350
Smithfield, NC 27577

King's College

Charlotte, North Carolina
www.kingscollege.org
Two-year proprietary

	Living at home	On-campus
Tuition and fees:	$9,960	$9,960
Room and board:		$4,900

Undergraduate aid. All financial aid based on need. Need-based aid available for full-time students.

Payment plans. Credit card, installment payment.

Application procedures. FAFSA required. Applicants notified on rolling basis.

Contact. Financial aid office: (704) 688-3616
Eunice Torifa, Director of Studnet Services
322 Lamar Avenue
Charlotte, NC 28204

Lees-McRae College

Banner Elk, North Carolina
www.lmc.edu
Four-year private **Federal Code: 002923**

	Living at home	On-campus
Tuition and fees:	$14,500	$14,500
Room and board:		$5,440
Books and supplies:	$760	$760
Personal expenses:	$1,800	$2,000
Transportation:	$334	$134

Undergraduate aid. Need-based: Need-based aid available for full-time and part-time students. **Non-need-based:** Scholarships based on academics, alumni affiliation, athletics, leadership, minority status, music/drama, religious affiliation, state/district residency.

Policies to reduce costs. Tuition/fee waivers for family of clergy, employees and their families. Credit/placement for qualifying scores on AP, IB, CLEP examinations. Work study available nights, weekends and for part-time students.

Payment plans. Credit card, installment payment.

Application procedures. FAFSA required. Priority date 3/15; no closing date. Applicants notified on rolling basis starting 3/1, must reply within 2 week(s) of notification.

Contact. Financial aid office: (828) 898-8793
Lester McKenzie, Director of Financial Aid
Box 128
Banner Elk, NC 28604

Lenoir Community College

Kinston, North Carolina
Two-year public **Federal Code: 002940**

College costs. Required technology fee $2 per credit, maximum $16 per semester.

	Living at home
Tuition and fees (2002-2003):	$1,066
Out-of-state:	$5,761
Per-credit charge:	$34
Per-credit out-of-state:	$191
Books and supplies:	$800
Personal expenses:	$540
Transportation:	$680

Undergraduate aid. Need-based: 89% awarded as scholarships/grants, 11% as loans/jobs. Need-based aid available for part-time students. **Non-need-based:** Scholarships based on academics, athletics, leadership, state/district residency.

Policies to reduce costs. Tuition/fee waivers for senior citizens, employees and their families. Credit/placement for qualifying scores on AP, IB, CLEP examinations. Work study available nights and for part-time students.

Payment plans. Credit card payment.

Application procedures. Institutional form required. Priority date 6/1; closing date 7/15. Applicants notified on rolling basis starting 7/1, must reply within 2 week(s) of notification.

Contact. Financial aid office: (252) 527-6223
Mary Anne Dawson, Director of Student Financial Aid
Box 188
Kinston, NC 28502-0188

Lenoir-Rhyne College

Hickory, North Carolina
www.lrc.edu
Four-year private **Federal Code: 002941**

	Living at home	On-campus
Tuition and fees:	$16,450	$16,450
Room and board:		$5,815
Board only:	$2,360	
Books and supplies:	$850	$850
Personal expenses:	$900	$1,150
Transportation:	$1,000	$700

Undergraduate aid. Need-based: Average financial aid package for full-time students was $10,277; for part-time $6,615. 55% awarded as scholarships/grants, 45% as loans/jobs. **Non-need-based:** 78% awarded as scholarships/grants, 22% as loans/jobs. Scholarships based on academics, alumni affiliation, athletics, leadership, minority status, music/drama, religious affiliation, state/district residency. **Student debt:** 86% of graduating class borrowed to fund education; average debt was $21,125.

Freshman aid. Need-based: Out of 270 full-time freshmen, 261 applied for aid; 190 were judged to have need; of these 190 received aid. Average package met 72% of need. 136 students had full need met. Average scholarship/grant was $7,366; average loan $2,733. **Non-need based:** 189 full-time freshmen with need received non-need scholarships; 148 without need received awards.

Policies to reduce costs. Tuition/fee waivers for senior citizens, minority students, family members, family of clergy, employees and their families. Credit/placement for qualifying scores on AP, IB, CLEP examinations. Work study available nights, weekends and for part-time students.

Payment plans. Credit card, installment payment.

Application procedures. FAFSA, institutional form required. Priority date 3/1; closing date 9/1. Applicants notified on rolling basis starting 3/15, must reply within 4 week(s) of notification.

Contact. Financial aid office: (828) 328-7304
Rachel Nichols, Director of Admissions and Financial Aid
PO Box 7227
Hickory, NC 28603

Livingstone College

Salisbury, North Carolina
www.livingstone.edu
Four-year private **Federal Code: 002942**

	Living at home	On-campus
Tuition and fees (2002-2003):	$9,860	$9,860
Room and board:		$4,000
Books and supplies:	$800	$800
Personal expenses:	$1,598	$1,598
Transportation:	$1,500	$1,500

Undergraduate aid. Need-based: Need-based aid available for full-time and part-time students. **Non-need-based:** Scholarships based on academics, athletics, state/district residency.

Policies to reduce costs. Tuition/fee waivers for family members, employees and their families. Work study available nights and weekends.

Payment plans. Credit card, installment payment.

Application procedures. FAFSA required. Priority date 5/15; closing date 6/1. Applicants notified on rolling basis starting 3/15, must reply within 2 week(s) of notification.

Contact. Financial aid office: (704) 216-6069
Timothy Holmes, Director of Financial Aid
701 West Monroe Street
Salisbury, NC 28144-5213

Louisburg College

Louisburg, North Carolina
www.louisburg.edu
Two-year private **Federal Code: 002943**

	Living at home	On-campus
Tuition and fees (2002-2003):	$10,450	$10,450
Per-credit charge:	$370	$370
Room and board:		$6,100
Books and supplies:	$900	$900
Personal expenses:	$1,125	$1,125
Transportation:	$1,500	$750

Undergraduate aid. Need-based: Need-based aid available for full-time students. **Additional information:** Job location and development program helps students obtain work in the community.

Policies to reduce costs. Tuition/fee waivers for family of clergy, employees and their families. Credit/placement for qualifying scores on AP, IB, CLEP examinations. Work study available nights and weekends.

Payment plans. Credit card, installment payment.

Application procedures. FAFSA, institutional form required. Priority date 3/15; no closing date. Applicants notified on rolling basis starting 3/15.

Contact. Financial aid office: (919) 497-3203
Sean Van Pallandt, Director of Financial Aid
501 North Main Street
Louisburg, NC 27549

Mars Hill College

Mars Hill, North Carolina
www.mhc.edu
Four-year private **Federal Code: 002944**

	Living at home	On-campus
Tuition and fees (2002-2003):	$14,500	$14,500
Room and board:		$5,200
Books and supplies:	$1,000	$1,000
Personal expenses:	$1,000	$1,000
Transportation:	$700	$700

Undergraduate aid. Non-need-based: Scholarships based on academics, athletics, state/district residency.

Merit scholarships. Scholarship and Grant Program offers awards based on merit, SAT/ACT scores, and GPA. Money available for four years, requiring minimum GPA.

Policies to reduce costs. Tuition/fee waivers for employees and their families. Credit/placement for qualifying scores on AP, IB, CLEP examinations. Work study available nights.

Payment plans. Credit card, installment payment.

Application procedures. FAFSA, institutional form required. No deadline. Applicants notified on rolling basis, must reply within 2 week(s) of notification.

Contact. Financial aid office: (828) 689-1123
Scott Miller, Director of Financial Aid
Blackwell Hall, Box 370
Mars Hill, NC 28754

Martin Community College

Williamston, North Carolina
www.martin.cc.nc.us
Two-year public **Federal Code: 007988**

	Living at home
Tuition and fees (2002-2003):	$1,066
Out-of-state:	$5,761
Per-credit charge:	$34
Per-credit out-of-state:	$191
Board only:	$3,024
Books and supplies:	$600
Personal expenses:	$400
Transportation:	$1,160

Undergraduate aid. Need-based: Average financial aid package for full-time students was $366; for part-time $1,875. 61% awarded as scholarships/grants, 39% as loans/jobs. **Non-need-based:** Scholarships based on academics.

Freshman aid. Need-based: Out of 80 full-time freshmen, 80 applied for aid; 79 were judged to have need; of these 79 received aid. Average package met 50% of need. Average scholarship/grant was $3,500; average loan $2,625.

Policies to reduce costs. Tuition/fee waivers for senior citizens, employees and their families. Credit/placement for qualifying scores on AP, CLEP examinations. Work study available nights and for part-time students.

Payment plans. Credit card payment.

Application procedures. FAFSA required. Priority date 5/1; no closing date. Applicants notified on rolling basis starting 5/1.

Contact. Financial aid office: (252) 792-1521 ext. 244
Elvis Jones, Financial Aid Officer
1161 Kehukee Park Road
Williamston, NC 27892-9988

Mayland Community College

Spruce Pine, North Carolina
www.mayland.cc.nc.us
Two-year public **Federal Code: 011197**

	Living at home
Tuition and fees (2002-2003):	$1,056
Out-of-state:	$5,751
Per-credit charge:	$34
Per-credit out-of-state:	$191
Books and supplies:	$750
Personal expenses:	$1,087
Transportation:	$893

Undergraduate aid. Need-based: Need-based aid available for full-time and part-time students.

Policies to reduce costs. Tuition/fee waivers for senior citizens, employees and their families. Credit/placement for qualifying scores on CLEP examinations.

Payment plans. Credit card, deferred payment.

Application procedures. FAFSA, institutional form required. Priority date 3/15; no closing date. Applicants notified on rolling basis starting 6/15.

Contact. Financial aid office: (828) 765-7351
Pamela Ellis, Financial Aid Coordinator
Box 547
Spruce Pine, NC 28777

Meredith College

Raleigh, North Carolina
www.meredith.edu
Four-year private **Federal Code: 002945**

College costs. Fees include use of laptop computer.

	Living at home	On-campus
Tuition and fees:	$18,065	$18,065
Room and board:		$500
Board only:	$1,800	
Books and supplies:	$750	$750
Personal expenses:	$1,250	$1,250
Transportation:	$400	$400

Undergraduate aid. Need-based: Average financial aid package for full-time students was $12,661; for part-time $4,453. 66% awarded as scholarships/grants, 34% as loans/jobs. **Non-need-based:** 48% awarded as scholarships/grants, 52% as loans/jobs. Scholarships based on academics, art, leadership, music/drama, religious affiliation, state/district residency. **Student debt:** 68% of graduating class borrowed to fund education; average debt was $13,939.

Freshman aid. Need-based: Out of 389 full-time freshmen, 288 applied for aid; 230 were judged to have need; of these 230 received aid. Average package met 84% of need. 27 students had full need met. Average scholarship/grant was $11,195; average loan $2,171. **Non-need based:** 19 full-time freshmen with need received non-need scholarships; 124 without need received awards.

Merit scholarships. Presidential Scholarship: 3 per year; $10,000 plus study abroad opportunity; based on academic excellence. Honors Scholarship: 25 per year; $8,000; based on academic excellence. Teaching Fellows Scholarship: 25 per year; $6,500 plus study abroad opportunity; must be a North Carolina Teaching Fellow. Multicultural Fellows Scholarship: 10 per year; $4,000; based on scholastic ability and personal achievement. Emerging Leaders Scholarships: 20 per year; $4,000; based on academic ability and leadership potential.

Policies to reduce costs. Tuition/fee waivers for employees and their families. Credit/placement for qualifying scores on AP, IB, CLEP examinations.

Payment plans. Installment payment.

Application procedures. FAFSA required. CSS Profile required of Early Decision financial aid applicants. Priority date 2/1; no closing date. Applicants notified on rolling basis starting 4/1, must reply by 5/1 or within 4 week(s) of notification. Early decision closing date 10/15.

Contact. Financial aid office: (919) 760-8565
Bill Cox, Director, Financial Assistance
3800 Hillsborough Street
Raleigh, NC 27607-5298

Methodist College

Fayetteville, North Carolina
www.methodist.edu
Four-year private **Federal Code: 002946**

	Living at home	On-campus
Tuition and fees:	$15,850	$15,850
Room and board:		$5,930
Books and supplies:	$800	$800
Personal expenses:	$1,500	$1,500
Transportation:	$950	$400

Undergraduate aid. Need-based: Average financial aid package for full-time students was $16,586; for part-time $15,335. 65% awarded as scholarships/grants, 35% as loans/jobs. **Non-need-based:** 62% awarded as scholarships/grants, 38% as loans/jobs. Scholarships based on academics, alumni affiliation, leadership, music/drama, religious affiliation, state/district residency. **Student debt:** 71% of graduating class borrowed to fund education; average debt was $18,430. **Additional information:** All residential students are guaranteed on-campus work-study.

Freshman aid. Need-based: Out of 381 full-time freshmen, 376 applied for aid; 295 were judged to have need; of these 295 received aid. Average package met 70% of need. 272 students had full need met. Average scholarship/grant was $8,627; average loan $2,363. **Non-need based:** 233 full-time freshmen with need received non-need scholarships; 80 without need received awards.

Merit scholarships. Presidential Scholarship: $3,500-10,000/yr, 3.1+ GPA, 1000+ SAT or 22+ ACT. Merit scholarship: $3,250-4,250, residential freshmen, 2.9+ GPA, 900+ SAT or 19+ ACT, leadership.

Policies to reduce costs. Tuition/fee waivers for senior citizens, family of clergy, employees and their families. Credit/placement for qualifying scores on AP, IB, CLEP examinations.

Payment plans. Credit card, installment, deferred payment.

Application procedures. FAFSA required. Priority date 5/1; closing date 7/1. Applicants notified on rolling basis starting 3/1, must reply within 2 week(s) of notification. **Transfers:** Priority date 5/1; closing date 7/1.

Contact. Bonnie Adamson, Director of Financial Aid
5400 Ramsey Street
Fayetteville, NC 28311-1420

Miller-Motte Technical College

Wilmington, North Carolina
Two-year proprietary
Federal Code: E00896

College costs. Cost of one class is $633 per quarter, 2 classes $1,265 per quarter, 3 classes $1,898 per quarter, 4 classes $2,353 per quarter and 5 classes and over is $2,720 per quarter.

	Living at home
Tuition and fees (2002-2003):	$7,765
Books and supplies:	$900
Personal expenses:	$2,250

Undergraduate aid. All financial aid based on need. 27% awarded as scholarships/grants, 73% as loans/jobs. Need-based aid available for part-time students. **Student debt:** 90% of graduating class borrowed to fund education; average debt was $14,000.

Policies to reduce costs. Tuition at time of enrollment guaranteed for 2 years. Work study available nights and weekends.

Payment plans. Credit card, installment payment.

Application procedures. FAFSA, institutional form required. No deadline.

Contact. Financial aid office: (910) 392-4660
Michele Carroll, Financial Aid Officer
606 South College Road
Wilmington, NC 28403

Mitchell Community College

Statesville, North Carolina
www.mitchell.cc.nc.us
Two-year public
Federal Code: 002947

College costs. Materials fees vary per course.

	Living at home
Tuition and fees (2002-2003):	$1,058
Out-of-state:	$5,753
Per-credit charge:	$34
Per-credit out-of-state:	$191
Books and supplies:	$900
Personal expenses:	$1,448
Transportation:	$2,926

Undergraduate aid. Need-based: Need-based aid available for full-time and part-time students.

Policies to reduce costs. Tuition/fee waivers for senior citizens, employees and their families. Credit/placement for qualifying scores on AP, CLEP examinations. Work study available for part-time students.

Payment plans. Credit card payment.

Application procedures. FAFSA, institutional form required. No deadline. Applicants notified on rolling basis starting 3/1, must reply within 2 week(s) of notification. **Transfers:** No deadline. Students are monitored through NSLDS's Transfer Monitoring List.

Contact. Financial aid office: (704) 878-3256
Candace Cooper, Financial Aid Officer
500 West Broad Street
Statesville, NC 28677

Montgomery Community College

Troy, North Carolina
www.montgomery.cc.nc.us
Two-year public
Federal Code: 008087

	Living at home
Tuition and fees (2002-2003):	$1,085
Out-of-state:	$5,780
Per-credit charge:	$34
Per-credit out-of-state:	$191
Books and supplies:	$1,000
Personal expenses:	$770
Transportation:	$1,386

Undergraduate aid. Need-based: Need-based aid available for full-time and part-time students. **Non-need-based:** Scholarships based on academics.

Policies to reduce costs. Tuition/fee waivers for senior citizens, employees and their families. Credit/placement for qualifying scores on CLEP examinations. Work study available nights and for part-time students.

Payment plans. Credit card payment.

Application procedures. FAFSA, institutional form required. Priority date 7/15; no closing date. Applicants notified on rolling basis starting 6/1. **Transfers:** No deadline.

Contact. Financial aid office: (910) 576-6222
Carolyn Hager, Financial Aid Officer
1011 Page Street
Troy, NC 27371-0787

Montreat College

Montreat, North Carolina
www.montreat.edu
Four-year private
Federal Code: 002948

	Living at home	On-campus
Tuition and fees:	$14,121	$14,121
Room and board:		$4,442
Board only:	$2,500	
Books and supplies:	$800	$800
Personal expenses:	$800	$1,700
Transportation:	$1,000	$1,000

Undergraduate aid. Need-based: Average financial aid package for full-time students was $10,495; for part-time $2,150. 57% awarded as scholarships/grants, 43% as loans/jobs. **Non-need-based:** 70% awarded as scholarships/grants, 30% as loans/jobs. Scholarships based on academics, alumni affiliation, athletics, leadership, music/drama, religious affiliation, state/district residency. **Student debt:** 83% of graduating class borrowed to fund education; average debt was $17,874.

Freshman aid. Need-based: Out of 158 full-time freshmen, 150 applied for aid; 113 were judged to have need; of these 113 received aid. Average scholarship/grant was $4,639; average loan $3,827. **Non-need based:** 84 full-time freshmen with need received non-need scholarships; 37 without need received awards; 48 received athletic scholarships.

Policies to reduce costs. Tuition/fee waivers for senior citizens, employees and their families. Credit/placement for qualifying scores on AP, CLEP examinations. Work study available nights.

Payment plans. Credit card payment.

Application procedures. FAFSA, institutional form required. Priority date 3/15; no closing date. Applicants notified on rolling basis starting 2/15, must reply within 2 week(s) of notification. **Transfers:** Priority date 3/15; no deadline.

Contact. Financial aid office: (800) 545-4656
Lisa Lankford, Dean of Admissions and Financial Aid
Box 1267
Montreat, NC 28757-1267

Mount Olive College

Mount Olive, North Carolina
www.mountolivecollege.edu
Four-year private **Federal Code: 002949**

	Living at home	On-campus
Tuition and fees (2002-2003):	$10,010	$10,010
Room and board:		$4,350
Board only:	$2,000	
Books and supplies:	$700	$700
Personal expenses:	$750	$1,000
Transportation:	$800	

Undergraduate aid. Need-based: Average financial aid package for full-time students was $6,114; for part-time $5,185. 66% awarded as scholarships/grants, 34% as loans/jobs. **Non-need-based:** 49% awarded as scholarships/grants, 51% as loans/jobs. Scholarships based on academics, art, athletics, leadership, music/drama, religious affiliation, state/district residency. **Student debt:** 49% of graduating class borrowed to fund education; average debt was $7,642.

Freshman aid. Need-based: Out of 248 full-time freshmen, 178 applied for aid; 153 were judged to have need; of these 153 received aid. Average package met 73% of need. 35 students had full need met. Average scholarship/grant was $5,989; average loan $1,762. **Non-need based:** 19 full-time freshmen with need received non-need scholarships; 66 without need received awards; 17 received athletic scholarships.

Policies to reduce costs. Tuition/fee waivers for family of clergy, employees and their families. Credit/placement for qualifying scores on AP, CLEP examinations.

Payment plans. Credit card, installment payment.

Application procedures. FAFSA required. Priority date 3/1; no closing date. Applicants notified on rolling basis starting 3/15, must reply within 2 week(s) of notification. **Transfers:** Special scholarship program available for transfers from North Carolina community colleges.

Contact. **Financial aid office:** (919) 658-7164
Diane Graham, Assistant Director of Financial Aid
634 Henderson Street
Mount Olive, NC 28365

Nash Community College

Rocky Mount, North Carolina
www.nash.cc.nc.us
Two-year public **Federal Code: 008557**

	Living at home
Tuition and fees (2002-2003):	$1,058
Out-of-state:	$5,753
Per-credit charge:	$34
Per-credit out-of-state:	$191
Board only:	$2,500
Books and supplies:	$900
Personal expenses:	$2,000
Transportation:	$1,200

Undergraduate aid. Need-based: Average financial aid package for full-time students was $2,827; for part-time $2,004. 99% awarded as scholarships/grants, 1% as loans/jobs. **Non-need-based:** Scholarships based on academics, athletics.

Freshman aid. Need-based: Out of 278 full-time freshmen, 137 applied for aid; 121 were judged to have need; of these 121 received aid. Average package met 100% of need. 121 students had full need met. Average scholarship/grant was $793.

Policies to reduce costs. Tuition/fee waivers for senior citizens, employees and their families. Credit/placement for qualifying scores on AP, IB, CLEP examinations.

Payment plans. Credit card, deferred payment.

Application procedures. FAFSA, institutional form required. Priority date 6/30; no closing date. Applicants notified on rolling basis starting 7/15.

Contact. Tammy Lester, Financial Aid Officer
Box 7488
Rocky Mount, NC 27804-0488

North Carolina Agricultural and Technical State University

Greensboro, North Carolina
www.ncat.edu
Four-year public **Federal Code: 002905**

	Living at home	On-campus
Tuition and fees (2002-2003):	$2,239	$2,239
Out-of-state:	$10,161	$10,161
Room and board:		$4,470
Board only:	$1,850	
Books and supplies:	$800	$800
Personal expenses:	$1,700	$1,700
Transportation:	$1,200	$1,200

Undergraduate aid. Need-based: Average financial aid package for full-time students was $5,238. 36% awarded as scholarships/grants, 64% as loans/jobs. **Non-need-based:** 62% awarded as scholarships/grants, 38% as loans/jobs. Scholarships based on academics, athletics, minority status, music/drama, state/district residency. **Student debt:** 71% of graduating class borrowed to fund education; average debt was $16,044.

Freshman aid. Need-based: Out of 1,770 full-time freshmen, 1,650 applied for aid; 1,344 were judged to have need; of these 1,319 received aid. Average package met 53% of need. 38 students had full need met. Average scholarship/grant was $3,420; average loan $3,087. **Non-need based:** 794 full-time freshmen with need received non-need scholarships; 32 without need received awards; 673 received athletic scholarships.

Policies to reduce costs. Tuition/fee waivers for senior citizens, employees and their families. Credit/placement for qualifying scores on AP, CLEP examinations.

Payment plans. Credit card, installment, deferred payment.

Application procedures. FAFSA required. Priority date 3/15; no closing date. Applicants notified on rolling basis starting 4/1, must reply within 2 week(s) of notification.

Contact. **Financial aid office:** (800) 443-0835
Sherri Avent, Director of Student Financial Aid
1601 East Market Street
Greensboro, NC 27411

North Carolina Central University

Durham, North Carolina
www.nccu.edu
Four-year public **Federal Code: 002950**

	Living at home	On-campus
Tuition and fees (2002-2003):	$2,350	$2,350
Out-of-state:	$10,272	$10,272
Room and board:		$3,284
Books and supplies:	$800	$800

Undergraduate aid. Need-based: Need-based aid available for full-time and part-time students. **Non-need-based:** Scholarships based on academics, alumni affiliation, athletics, minority status, music/drama, state/district residency. **Additional information:** Departmental grants based on need plus other available criteria.

Policies to reduce costs. Tuition/fee waivers for senior citizens, employees and their families. Credit/placement for qualifying scores on AP, CLEP examinations.

Payment plans. Credit card, installment payment.

Application procedures. FAFSA required. Priority date 4/1; no closing date. Applicants notified by 5/1, must reply within 2 week(s) of notification. **Transfers:** Priority date 4/1.

Contact. Sharon Oliver, Director of Student Financial Aid
1801 Fayetteville St.
Durham, NC 27707

North Carolina School of the Arts

Winston-Salem, North Carolina
www.ncarts.edu
Four-year public **Federal Code: 003981**

	Living at home	On-campus
Tuition and fees (2002-2003):	$2,877	$2,877
Out-of-state:	$12,282	$12,282
Room and board:		$4,920
Books and supplies:	$865	$865
Personal expenses:	$832	$1,889

Undergraduate aid. Need-based: Average financial aid package for full-time students was $8,499. 55% awarded as scholarships/grants, 45% as loans/jobs. Need-based aid available for part-time students. **Non-need-based:** 38% awarded as scholarships/grants, 62% as loans/jobs. Scholarships based on academics, art, leadership, minority status, music/drama, state/district residency. **Student debt:** 61% of graduating class borrowed to fund education; average debt was $15,566.

Freshman aid. Need-based: Out of 187 full-time freshmen, 178 applied for aid; 120 were judged to have need; of these 120 received aid. Average package met 74% of need. 5 students had full need met. Average scholarship/grant was $4,009; average loan $2,108. **Non-need based:** 5 full-time freshmen with need received non-need scholarships; 33 without need received awards.

Policies to reduce costs. Tuition/fee waivers for senior citizens, employees and their families. Credit/placement for qualifying scores on AP, IB, CLEP examinations. Work study available nights and weekends.

Application procedures. FAFSA required. Priority date 3/1; no closing date. Applicants notified on rolling basis starting 4/15, must reply within 2 week(s) of notification.

Contact. **Financial aid office:** (336) 770-3297
Jane Kamiab, Director of Financial Aid
1533 South Main Street
Winston-Salem, NC 27127

North Carolina State University

Raleigh, North Carolina
www.ncsu.edu
Four-year public **Federal Code: 002972**

	Living at home	On-campus
Tuition and fees (2002-2003):	$3,452	$3,452
Out-of-state:	$13,444	$13,444
Room and board:		$5,796
Board only:	$2,344	
Books and supplies:	$700	$700
Personal expenses:	$1,150	$1,150
Transportation:	$550	$250

Undergraduate aid. Need-based: Average financial aid package for full-time students was $6,289; for part-time $5,242. 62% awarded as scholarships/grants, 38% as loans/jobs. **Non-need-based:** 47% awarded as scholarships/grants, 53% as loans/jobs. Scholarships based on academics, athletics, state/district residency. **Student debt:** 34% of graduating class borrowed to fund education; average debt was $15,949. **Additional information:** Credit card payments accepted during late registration only.

Freshman aid. Need-based: Out of 3,870 full-time freshmen, 2,209 applied for aid; 1,319 were judged to have need; of these 1,298 received aid. Average package met 85% of need. 268 students had full need met. Average scholarship/grant was $4,739; average loan $1,794. **Non-need based:** 204 full-time freshmen with need received non-need scholarships; 1,155 without need received awards; 62 received athletic scholarships.

Merit scholarships. Freshman Merit Scholarships; students submitting complete application by the November 1 Early Action deadline automatically considered, additional information may be required after initial review.

Policies to reduce costs. Tuition/fee waivers for senior citizens. Credit/placement for qualifying scores on AP, IB, CLEP examinations. Work study available for part-time students.

Payment plans. Credit card, installment payment.

Application procedures. FAFSA, institutional form required. CSS PROFILE recommended for early scholarship consideration. Priority date 3/1; no closing date. Applicants notified on rolling basis starting 2/1, must reply by 5/1 or within 2 week(s) of notification.

Contact. **Financial aid office:** (919) 515-2421
Julia Rice Mallette, Director of Financial Aid
112 Peele Hall, Box 7103
Raleigh, NC 27695-7103

North Carolina Wesleyan College

Rocky Mount, North Carolina
www.ncwc.edu
Four-year private **Federal Code: 002951**

	Living at home	On-campus
Tuition and fees (projected):	$12,225	$12,225
Room and board:		$6,820
Books and supplies:	$675	$675
Transportation:	$1,500	$1,500

Undergraduate aid. Need-based: 69% awarded as scholarships/grants, 31% as loans/jobs. **Non-need-based:** 46% awarded as scholarships/grants, 54% as loans/jobs. Scholarships based on academics, religious affiliation, state/district residency. **Additional information:** Scholarships based on GPA. Various scholarship and leadership awards available.

Policies to reduce costs. Tuition/fee waivers for family of clergy, employees and their families. Credit/placement for qualifying scores on AP, CLEP examinations.

Payment plans. Installment payment.

Application procedures. FAFSA required. Priority date 3/1; no closing date. Applicants notified on rolling basis starting 3/1, must reply within 2 week(s) of notification.

Contact. **Financial aid office:** (252) 985-5295
Brenda Mercer, Director of Financial Aid
3400 North Wesleyan Boulevard
Rocky Mount, NC 27804

Pamlico Community College

Grantsboro, North Carolina
www.pamlico.cc.nc.us
Two-year public **Federal Code: 007031**

	Living at home
Tuition and fees (2002-2003):	$1,043
Out-of-state:	$5,738
Per-credit charge:	$34
Per-credit out-of-state:	$191
Books and supplies:	$380
Personal expenses:	$1,630
Transportation:	$1,370

Undergraduate aid. Additional information: Jobs Training Partner Act and Displaced Homemaker Programs cover tuition, books, fees.

Policies to reduce costs. Tuition/fee waivers for senior citizens.

Application procedures. FAFSA required. No deadline. Applicants notified on rolling basis. **Transfers:** No deadline.

Contact. Sonny Hart, Financial Aid Officer
Highway 306 South
Grantsboro, NC 28529

Peace College

Raleigh, North Carolina
www.peace.edu
Four-year private **Federal Code: 002953**

	Living at home	On-campus
Tuition and fees:	$15,925	$15,925
Room and board:		$5,933
Books and supplies:	$750	$750
Personal expenses:	$2,500	$2,500
Transportation:	$900	$900

Undergraduate aid. Need-based: Need-based aid available for full-time and part-time students. **Non-need-based:** Scholarships based on academics. **Additional information:** Large endowment provides ample scholarship dollars.

Policies to reduce costs. Tuition/fee waivers for children of alumni, senior citizens, family members, family of clergy, employees and their families. Credit/placement for qualifying scores on AP, CLEP examinations. Work study available nights, weekends and for part-time students.

Payment plans. Credit card, installment, deferred payment.

Application procedures. FAFSA required. Priority date 3/15; no closing date. Applicants notified on rolling basis starting 3/1, must reply by 5/1 or within 2 week(s) of notification. **Transfers:** Priority date 3/1; no deadline. Transfer merit scholarships available. Based on transferable credits earned and cumulative college GPA.

Contact. Angela Kirkley, Director of Financial Aid
15 East Peace Street
Raleigh, NC 27604

Pfeiffer University

Misenheimer, North Carolina
www.pfeiffer.edu
Four-year private **Federal Code: 002955**

College costs. $330 health insurance fee.

	Living at home	On-campus
Tuition and fees (2002-2003):	$12,790	$12,790
Room and board:		$5,120
Board only:	$2,322	
Books and supplies:	$750	$750
Personal expenses:	$600	$600
Transportation:	$700	$700

Undergraduate aid. Need-based: Need-based aid available for full-time students. **Non-need-based:** Scholarships based on academics, art, athletics, music/drama, religious affiliation, state/district residency.

Merit scholarships. Honor, Presidential, University, and Legacy Merit Scholarships - from $3,500 to full tuition per year.

Policies to reduce costs. Tuition/fee waivers for family members, family of clergy, employees and their families. Credit/placement for qualifying scores on AP, IB, CLEP examinations. Work study available nights and weekends.

Payment plans. Credit card, installment payment.

Application procedures. FAFSA required. Priority date 5/1; no closing date. Applicants notified on rolling basis starting 3/1, must reply within 2 week(s) of notification. **Transfers:** Priority date 3/15; no deadline.

Contact. Financial aid office: (704) 463-1360 ext. 2070
Lois Williams, Director of Financial Aid
Box 960
Misenheimer, NC 28109

Piedmont Baptist College

Winston-Salem, North Carolina
www.pbc.edu
Five-year private **Federal Code: 002956**

	Living at home	On-campus
Tuition and fees (projected):	$8,380	$8,380
Room and board:		$4,520
Board only:	$754	
Books and supplies:	$500	$500
Personal expenses:	$600	$600
Transportation:	$850	$550

Undergraduate aid. Need-based: Need-based aid available for full-time and part-time students.

Policies to reduce costs. Tuition/fee waivers for family members, family of clergy, employees and their families. Credit/placement for qualifying scores on AP, CLEP examinations. Work study available nights, weekends and for part-time students.

Payment plans. Credit card, installment payment.

Application procedures. Institutional form required. No deadline. Applicants notified on rolling basis starting 3/1. Early decision closing date 11/1. **Transfers:** No deadline.

Contact. Financial aid office: (336) 725-8344 ext.2322
Ronnie Mathis, Financial Aid Officer
716 Franklin Street
Winston-Salem, NC 27101-5133

Piedmont Community College

Roxboro, North Carolina
www.piedmont.cc.nc.us
Two-year public **Federal Code: 009646**

	Living at home
Tuition and fees (2002-2003):	$1,061
Out-of-state:	$5,756
Per-credit charge:	$34
Per-credit out-of-state:	$191
Board only:	$1,500
Books and supplies:	$800
Personal expenses:	$750
Transportation:	$1,116

Policies to reduce costs. Tuition/fee waivers for senior citizens, employees and their families.

Application procedures. FAFSA required. Priority date 4/15; no closing date. Applicants notified on rolling basis, must reply within 2 week(s) of notification. **Transfers:** No deadline.

Contact. Frances Lunsford, Director, Financial Aid
1715 College Drive
Roxboro, NC 27573-1197

Pitt Community College

Greenville, North Carolina
www.pitt.cc.nc.us
Two-year public **Federal Code: 004062**

	Living at home
Tuition and fees (2002-2003):	$1,073
Out-of-state:	$5,768
Per-credit charge:	$34
Per-credit out-of-state:	$191
Books and supplies:	$600
Personal expenses:	$400
Transportation:	$3,200

Undergraduate aid. All financial aid based on need. 87% awarded as scholarships/grants, 13% as loans/jobs. Need-based aid available for part-time students.

Policies to reduce costs. Tuition/fee waivers for senior citizens.

Payment plans. Credit card payment.

Application procedures. FAFSA, institutional form required. Priority date 3/15; closing date 8/24. Applicants notified on rolling basis starting 6/1.

Contact. Financial aid office: (252) 321-4339
Lisa Reichstein, Financial Aid Director
PO Drawer 7007
Greenville, NC 27835-7007

Queens University of Charlotte

Charlotte, North Carolina
www.queens.edu
Four-year private **Federal Code: 002957**

	Living at home	On-campus
Tuition and fees (2002-2003):	$12,290	$12,290
Room and board:		$6,010
Board only:	$1,950	
Books and supplies:	$750	$750
Personal expenses:	$900	$900
Transportation:	$1,250	$500

Undergraduate aid. Need-based: Average financial aid package for full-time students was $9,713; for part-time $6,027. 61% awarded as scholarships/grants, 39% as loans/jobs. **Non-need-based:** 55% awarded as scholarships/grants, 45% as loans/jobs. Scholarships based on academics, alumni affiliation, art, athletics, leadership, minority status, music/drama, religious affiliation, state/district residency. **Student debt:** 52% of graduating class borrowed to fund education; average debt was $14,069.

Freshman aid. Need-based: Out of 211 full-time freshmen, 184 applied for aid; 143 were judged to have need; of these 143 received aid. Average package met 76% of need. 44 students had full need met. Average scholarship/grant was $6,982; average loan $2,364. **Non-need based:** 31 full-time fresh-

men with need received non-need scholarships; 72 without need received awards; 25 received athletic scholarships.

Merit scholarships. Presidential Scholarships based on special application/ recommendations, deadline December; 10 awarded; full tuition.

Policies to reduce costs. Tuition/fee waivers for family members, family of clergy, employees and their families. Credit/placement for qualifying scores on AP, IB, CLEP examinations.

Payment plans. Credit card, installment payment.

Application procedures. FAFSA required. Priority date 3/1; no closing date. Applicants notified on rolling basis starting 3/1, must reply by 5/1 or within 3 week(s) of notification. **Transfers:** Priority date 3/1; no deadline.

Contact. **Financial aid office:** (704) 337-2225
Lauren Mack, Director of Studnet Financial Services
1900 Selwyn Avenue
Charlotte, NC 28274

Randolph Community College

Asheboro, North Carolina
www.randolph.cc.nc.us/randolph
Two-year public **Federal Code: 005447**

	Living at home
Tuition and fees (2002-2003):	$1,058
Out-of-state:	$5,753
Per-credit charge:	$34
Per-credit out-of-state:	$191
Board only:	$1,950
Personal expenses:	$832
Transportation:	$1,305

Undergraduate aid. **Non-need-based:** Scholarships based on academics, leadership, minority status, state/district residency.

Policies to reduce costs. Tuition/fee waivers for senior citizens, employees and their families. Credit/placement for qualifying scores on AP, IB, CLEP examinations. Work study available nights and for part-time students.

Payment plans. Credit card payment.

Application procedures. FAFSA required. Priority date 5/1; no closing date. Applicants notified on rolling basis, must reply within 4 week(s) of notification. **Transfers:** No deadline.

Contact. **Financial aid office:** (336) 633-0222
Box 1009
Asheboro, NC 27204-1009

Richmond Community College

Hamlet, North Carolina
www.richmond.cc.nc.us
Two-year public **Federal Code: 005464**

	Living at home
Tuition and fees (2002-2003):	$1,066
Out-of-state:	$5,761
Per-credit charge:	$34
Per-credit out-of-state:	$191
Board only:	$2,070
Books and supplies:	$600
Personal expenses:	$900
Transportation:	$1,350

Undergraduate aid. **Need-based:** Need-based aid available for full-time and part-time students. **Non-need-based:** Scholarships based on academics, leadership.

Policies to reduce costs. Tuition/fee waivers for senior citizens, employees and their families. Credit/placement for qualifying scores on AP, CLEP examinations. Work study available nights and for part-time students.

Payment plans. Credit card, deferred payment.

Application procedures. FAFSA, institutional form required. Priority date 5/1; no closing date. Applicants notified on rolling basis starting 6/1, must reply within 2 week(s) of notification.

Contact. **Financial aid office:** (910) 582-7108
Beth McQueen, Director of Financial Aid
Box 1189
Hamlet, NC 28345

Roanoke Bible College

Elizabeth City, North Carolina
www.roanokebible.edu
Four-year private **Federal Code: 014101**

	Living at home	On-campus
Tuition and fees:	$6,800	$6,800
Room and board:		$4,400
Books and supplies:	$900	$900
Personal expenses:	$2,500	$2,500
Transportation:	$2,000	$1,500

Undergraduate aid. **Non-need-based:** Scholarships based on academics.

Merit scholarships. Merit based scholarships; full tuition and half tuition available, based on demonstration of exceptional academic ability.

Policies to reduce costs. Tuition/fee waivers for senior citizens, family members, employees and their families. Prepayment discount; credit/ placement for qualifying scores on AP, CLEP examinations.

Payment plans. Installment, deferred payment.

Application procedures. FAFSA, institutional form required. Priority date 4/1; closing date 5/1. Applicants notified by 4/15, must reply within 3 week(s) of notification. **Transfers:** Priority date 3/15.

Contact. Julie Fields, Director of Financial Aid
715 N. Poindexter Street
Elizabeth City, NC 27909

Roanoke-Chowan Community College

Ahoskie, North Carolina
www.roanoke.cc.nc.us
Two-year public **Federal Code: 008613**

	Living at home
Tuition and fees (2002-2003):	$1,065
Out-of-state:	$5,760
Per-credit charge:	$34
Per-credit out-of-state:	$191
Books and supplies:	$680
Personal expenses:	$1,555
Transportation:	$1,620

Undergraduate aid. **Need-based:** 84% awarded as scholarships/grants, 16% as loans/jobs. Need-based aid available for part-time students. **Non-need-based:** Scholarships based on academics.

Policies to reduce costs. Tuition/fee waivers for senior citizens, employees and their families. Credit/placement for qualifying scores on AP, CLEP examinations.

Payment plans. Credit card payment.

Application procedures. FAFSA required. No deadline. Applicants notified on rolling basis starting 7/1.

Contact. **Financial aid office:** (252) 862-1224
Diane Kimbrough, Dean, Student Services
109 Community College Road
Ahoskie, NC 27910-9522

Robeson Community College

Lumberton, North Carolina
Two-year public **Federal Code: 008612**

	Living at home
Tuition and fees (2002-2003):	$1,056
Out-of-state:	$5,751
Per-credit charge:	$34
Per-credit out-of-state:	$191
Books and supplies:	$600
Personal expenses:	$75
Transportation:	$1,041

Undergraduate aid. **Need-based:** Need-based aid available for full-time and part-time students.

Policies to reduce costs. Tuition/fee waivers for senior citizens.

Application procedures. FAFSA required. Priority date 5/15; no closing date. Applicants notified on rolling basis starting 7/31. **Transfers:** No deadline.

Contact. Anna Maynor, Financial Aid Officer
Box 1420
Lumberton, NC 28359

Rockingham Community College

Wentworth, North Carolina
www.rcc.cc.nc.us
Two-year public **Federal Code: 002958**

College costs. Technology fee 1-3 credits is $10 and 4 credits and up is $16.

	Living at home
Tuition and fees (2002-2003):	$1,065
Out-of-state:	$5,760
Per-credit charge:	$34
Per-credit out-of-state:	$191
Books and supplies:	$450
Personal expenses:	$1,000
Transportation:	$1,040

Undergraduate aid. Need-based: Need-based aid available for full-time and part-time students. **Non-need-based:** Scholarships based on academics, art, job skills, leadership, minority status, state/district residency.

Policies to reduce costs. Tuition/fee waivers for senior citizens. Credit/placement for qualifying scores on AP, CLEP examinations.

Payment plans. Credit card, installment, deferred payment.

Application procedures. FAFSA, institutional form required. Priority date 4/15; no closing date. Applicants notified on rolling basis starting 5/30, must reply within 2 week(s) of notification. **Transfers:** Priority date 4/15.

Contact. Linda Estes, Director of Financial Aid
Box 38
Wentworth, NC 27375-0038

Rowan-Cabarrus Community College

Salisbury, North Carolina
www.rccc.cc.nc.us
Two-year public **Federal Code: 005754**

	Living at home
Tuition and fees (2002-2003):	$1,060
Out-of-state:	$5,755
Per-credit charge:	$34
Per-credit out-of-state:	$191

Undergraduate aid. Need-based: Need-based aid available for full-time and part-time students. **Non-need-based:** Scholarships based on academics, job skills, state/district residency.

Policies to reduce costs. Tuition/fee waivers for senior citizens. Credit/placement for qualifying scores on AP, CLEP examinations. Work study available nights and for part-time students.

Payment plans. Credit card, installment payment.

Application procedures. FAFSA required. Priority date 3/15; closing date 5/1. Applicants notified on rolling basis starting 5/1, must reply within 3 week(s) of notification. **Transfers:** No deadline.

Contact. Lisa Ledbetter, Director, Financial Aid
Box 1595
Salisbury, NC 28145

St. Andrews Presbyterian College

Laurinburg, North Carolina
www.sapc.edu
Four-year private **Federal Code: 002967**

College costs. $293 health insurance fee.

	Living at home	On-campus
Tuition and fees (2002-2003):	$14,760	$14,760
Room and board:		$5,410
Books and supplies:	$800	$800
Personal expenses:	$1,750	$850
Transportation:	$1,011	$200

Undergraduate aid. Need-based: Need-based aid available for full-time and part-time students. **Non-need-based:** Scholarships based on academics, athletics, state/district residency.

Policies to reduce costs. Tuition/fee waivers for employees and their families. Credit/placement for qualifying scores on AP, IB, CLEP examinations. Work study available nights, weekends and for part-time students.

Payment plans. Installment, deferred payment.

Application procedures. FAFSA required. Priority date 5/1; no closing date. Applicants notified on rolling basis starting 4/1, must reply within 2 week(s) of notification. **Transfers:** No deadline.

Contact. Financial aid office: (910) 277-5560
Kim Driggers, Director, Student Planning
1700 Dogwood Mile
Laurinburg, NC 28352

St. Augustine's College

Raleigh, North Carolina
www.st-aug.edu
Four-year private **Federal Code: 002968**

	Living at home	On-campus
Tuition and fees (2002-2003):	$8,280	$8,280
Room and board:		$4,960
Books and supplies:	$700	$700
Personal expenses:	$1,258	$1,530
Transportation:	$1,510	$1,810

Undergraduate aid. Need-based: Average financial aid package for full-time students was $11,387; for part-time $1,979. 91% awarded as scholarships/grants, 9% as loans/jobs. **Non-need-based:** 34% awarded as scholarships/grants, 66% as loans/jobs. Scholarships based on academics, art, athletics, leadership, minority status, music/drama, religious affiliation, state/district residency. **Student debt:** 55% of graduating class borrowed to fund education; average debt was $10,416.

Freshman aid. Need-based: Out of 449 full-time freshmen, 449 applied for aid; 446 were judged to have need; of these 446 received aid. Average package met 91% of need. 51 students had full need met. Average loan $2,381. **Non-need based:** 245 full-time freshmen with need received non-need scholarships; 66 without need received awards; 44 received athletic scholarships.

Merit scholarships. Institutional Merit Scholarships based on high school record, evidence of leadership, and SAT score (1000 or better for largest amounts.)

Policies to reduce costs. Tuition/fee waivers for senior citizens, employees and their families. Credit/placement for qualifying scores on AP, IB, CLEP examinations.

Payment plans. Installment payment.

Application procedures. FAFSA, institutional form required. Priority date 4/15; closing date 6/1. Applicants notified on rolling basis starting 5/1, must reply within 2 week(s) of notification. **Transfers:** All transfer students must submit a financial aid transcript.

Contact. Financial aid office: (919) 516-4131
Wanda White, Director of Financial Aid
1315 Oakwood Avenue
Raleigh, NC 27610-2298

Salem College

Winston-Salem, North Carolina
www.salem.edu
Four-year private **Federal Code: 002960**

	Living at home	On-campus
Tuition and fees (2002-2003):	$15,005	$15,005
Room and board:		$8,870
Books and supplies:	$600	$600
Personal expenses:	$1,865	$1,895
Transportation:	$800	$800

Undergraduate aid. Need-based: Average financial aid package for full-time students was $11,752; for part-time $4,889. 60% awarded as scholarships/grants, 40% as loans/jobs. **Non-need-based:** 73% awarded as scholarships/grants, 27% as loans/jobs. Scholarships based on academics, alumni affiliation, leadership, minority status, music/drama, religious affiliation, state/district residency. **Student debt:** 61% of graduating class borrowed to fund education; average debt was $11,367.

Freshman aid. Need-based: Out of 144 full-time freshmen, 122 applied for aid; 76 were judged to have need; of these 76 received aid. Average package met 100% of need. 76 students had full need met. Average scholarship/grant was $10,141; average loan $2,625. **Non-need based:** 54 full-time freshmen with need received non-need scholarships; 38 without need received awards.

Merit scholarships. Various scholarships awarded to students with excellent GPAs, SAT scores, and significant achievements in activities and service.

Policies to reduce costs. Tuition/fee waivers for adults, family of clergy, employees and their families. Credit/placement for qualifying scores on AP, IB, CLEP examinations. Work study available nights, weekends and for part-time students.

Payment plans. Installment payment.

Application procedures. FAFSA required. Priority date 3/1; no closing date. Applicants notified on rolling basis starting 2/12, must reply within 2 week(s) of notification. **Transfers:** No deadline.

Contact. Financial aid office: (336) 721-2808
Julie Setzer, Director of Financial Aid
PO Box 10548
Winston-Salem, NC 27108

Sampson Community College

Clinton, North Carolina
www.sampson.cc.nc.us
Two-year public **Federal Code: 007892**

	Living at home
Tuition and fees (2002-2003):	$1,052
Out-of-state:	$5,747
Per-credit charge:	$34
Per-credit out-of-state:	$191
Books and supplies:	$600
Personal expenses:	$900
Transportation:	$800

Undergraduate aid. Need-based: Need-based aid available for full-time and part-time students. **Non-need-based:** Scholarships based on academics, state/district residency. **Additional information:** Short-term loans available to students waiting for federal aid to be approved. Covers tuition, fees and books only.

Policies to reduce costs. Tuition/fee waivers for senior citizens, employees and their families. Credit/placement for qualifying scores on AP, CLEP examinations.

Payment plans. Credit card, deferred payment.

Application procedures. FAFSA required. Priority date 7/1; no closing date. Applicants notified on rolling basis starting 7/15, must reply within 2 week(s) of notification.

Contact. Financial aid office: (910) 592-8084 ext. 2024
Ruth Scrivner, Director of Financial Aid
PO Box 318
Clinton, NC 28329

Sandhills Community College

Pinehurst, North Carolina
www.sandhills.edu
Two-year public **Federal Code: 002961**

	Living at home
Tuition and fees (2002-2003):	$1,056
Out-of-state:	$5,751
Per-credit charge:	$34
Per-credit out-of-state:	$191
Books and supplies:	$1,000
Personal expenses:	$1,080
Transportation:	$1,872

Undergraduate aid. Need-based: Average financial aid package for full-time students was $3,404; for part-time $1,844. 94% awarded as scholarships/grants, 6% as loans/jobs. **Non-need-based:** 29% awarded as scholarships/grants, 71% as loans/jobs. Scholarships based on academics. **Student debt:** 5% of graduating class borrowed to fund education; average debt was $2,521. **Additional information:** Scholarships available, limited loan capability.

Freshman aid. Need-based: Average package met 68% of need. Average scholarship/grant was $3,501; average loan $1,255.

Merit scholarships. Sandhills Scholars; upper 15% of graduating class; 11 awarded to incoming freshmen.

Policies to reduce costs. Tuition/fee waivers for senior citizens, employees and their families. Credit/placement for qualifying scores on AP, CLEP examinations.

Payment plans. Credit card payment.

Application procedures. FAFSA required. Priority date 6/1; no closing date. Applicants notified on rolling basis starting 2/1, must reply by 8/1 or within 4 week(s) of notification. **Transfers:** Priority date 6/1; no deadline.

Contact. Financial aid office: (910) 695-3743
Kellie Shoemake, Director of Financial Aid
3395 Airport Road
Pinehurst, NC 28374

Shaw University

Raleigh, North Carolina
www.shawuniversity.edu
Four-year private **Federal Code: 002962**

	Living at home	On-campus
Tuition and fees:	$9,178	$9,178
Room and board:		$5,654
Books and supplies:	$700	$700
Personal expenses:	$750	$1,000
Transportation:	$522	$500

Undergraduate aid. Need-based: Average financial aid package for full-time students was $7,634; for part-time $4,405. 59% awarded as scholarships/grants, 41% as loans/jobs. **Non-need-based:** 11% awarded as scholarships/grants, 89% as loans/jobs. Scholarships based on academics, athletics. **Student debt:** 98% of graduating class borrowed to fund education; average debt was $8,486.

Freshman aid. Need-based: Out of 445 full-time freshmen, 445 applied for aid; 418 were judged to have need; of these 418 received aid. Average scholarship/grant was $6,295; average loan $2,468. **Non-need based:** 21 full-time freshmen with need received non-need scholarships; 7 without need received awards; 13 received athletic scholarships.

Merit scholarships. Presidential Scholarship, based on GPA and SAT.

Policies to reduce costs. Tuition/fee waivers for employees and their families. Work study available nights, weekends and for part-time students.

Payment plans. Credit card, installment, deferred payment.

Application procedures. FAFSA, institutional form required. No deadline. Applicants notified on rolling basis starting 4/30.

Contact. Financial aid office: (919) 546-8240
Eric Ingram, Director of Financial Aid
118 East South Street
Raleigh, NC 27601

South College

Asheville, North Carolina
Two-year proprietary
Federal Code: 010264

	Living at home
Tuition and fees (2002-2003):	$9,100
Per-credit charge:	$250
Books and supplies:	$1,050
Personal expenses:	$1,080

Undergraduate aid. All financial aid based on need. Need-based aid available for full-time and part-time students. **Student debt:** 93% of graduating class borrowed to fund education; average debt was $15,505.

Policies to reduce costs. Tuition/fee waivers for employees and their families. Work study available for part-time students.

Payment plans. Credit card, installment payment.

Application procedures. FAFSA required. No deadline. Applicants notified on rolling basis. **Transfers:** No deadline.

Contact. Marty Mehringer, Financial Aid Director
1567 Patton Avenue
Asheville, NC 28806

South Piedmont Community College

Polkton, North Carolina
www.southpiedmont.org
Two-year public **Federal Code: 007985**

	Living at home
Tuition and fees (2002-2003):	$1,073
Out-of-state:	$5,768
Per-credit charge:	$34
Per-credit out-of-state:	$191
Books and supplies:	$650
Personal expenses:	$900
Transportation:	$1,300

Undergraduate aid. Need-based: Need-based aid available for full-time and part-time students. **Additional information:** Small amount of nonfederal scholarship aid available.

Policies to reduce costs. Tuition/fee waivers for senior citizens, employees and their families. Work study available nights and weekends.

Payment plans. Credit card, deferred payment.

Application procedures. FAFSA required. No deadline. Applicants notified on rolling basis.

Contact. Vickie Cameron, Financial Aid Officer
Box 126
Polkton, NC 28135

Southeastern Baptist Theological Seminary

Wake Forest, North Carolina
www.sebts.edu
Four-year private **Federal Code: G02963**

College costs. Seminary students pay $105 a credit hour and $3,150 full-time tuition. Non-Southern Baptist students pay $210 a credit hour and $6,300 full-time tuition.

	Living at home	On-campus
Tuition and fees:	$4,350	$4,350
Room only:		$1,395
Books and supplies:	$600	$600

Undergraduate aid. Additional information: Special endowment awards $300 to all freshmen.

Policies to reduce costs. Tuition/fee waivers for family members.

Payment plans. Installment payment.

Application procedures. Closing date 8/1. Applicants notified on rolling basis. **Transfers:** No deadline.

Contact. Financial aid office: (919) 761-2305
Alan Moseley, Dean of Students
PO Box 1889
Wake Forest, NC 27588

Southeastern Community College

Whiteville, North Carolina
www.southeastern.cc.nc.us
Two-year public **Federal Code: 002964**

	Living at home
Tuition and fees (2002-2003):	$1,090
Out-of-state:	$5,785
Per-credit charge:	$34
Per-credit out-of-state:	$191
Board only:	$2,884
Books and supplies:	$448
Personal expenses:	$1,583
Transportation:	$1,438

Undergraduate aid. Need-based: 94% awarded as scholarships/grants, 6% as loans/jobs. Need-based aid available for part-time students. **Non-need-based:** Scholarships based on academics, athletics, leadership, state/district residency.

Policies to reduce costs. Tuition/fee waivers for senior citizens, employees and their families. Credit/placement for qualifying scores on AP examinations. Work study available for part-time students.

Application procedures. FAFSA required. Priority date 4/3; no closing date. Applicants notified on rolling basis starting 7/1, must reply within 2 week(s) of notification.

Contact. Financial aid office: (910) 642-7141
Doris Caines, Financial Aid Coordinator
Box 151
Whiteville, NC 28472

Southwestern Community College

Sylva, North Carolina
www.southwest.cc.nc.us
Two-year public **Federal Code: 008466**

	Living at home
Tuition and fees (2002-2003):	$1,060
Out-of-state:	$5,755
Per-credit charge:	$34
Per-credit out-of-state:	$191
Books and supplies:	$550
Personal expenses:	$630
Transportation:	$1,650

Undergraduate aid. Need-based: Need-based aid available for full-time and part-time students.

Policies to reduce costs. Tuition/fee waivers for senior citizens. Work study available nights.

Payment plans. Credit card, deferred payment.

Application procedures. FAFSA required. No deadline. Applicants notified on rolling basis starting 5/1, must reply within 2 week(s) of notification.

Contact. Financial aid office: (828) 586-4091 ext. 224
Melody Lawrence, Coordinator of Financial Aid
447 College Drive
Sylva, NC 28779

Stanly Community College

Albemarle, North Carolina
www.stanly.cc.nc.us
Two-year public **Federal Code: 011194**

	Living at home
Tuition and fees (2002-2003):	$1,086
Out-of-state:	$5,781
Per-credit charge:	$34
Per-credit out-of-state:	$191
Board only:	$3,169
Books and supplies:	$800
Personal expenses:	$1,050
Transportation:	$1,975

Undergraduate aid. All financial aid based on need. Need-based aid available for full-time and part-time students.

Policies to reduce costs. Tuition/fee waivers for senior citizens, employees and their families. Credit/placement for qualifying scores on AP examinations. Work study available for part-time students.

Payment plans. Credit card payment.

Application procedures. FAFSA, institutional form required. No deadline. Applicants notified on rolling basis starting 6/1, must reply within 2 week(s) of notification. **Transfers:** No deadline.

Contact. Financial aid office: (704) 991-0231
Cheryn Rowell, Director, Financial Aid
141 College Drive
Albemarle, NC 28001

Surry Community College

Dobson, North Carolina
www.surry.edu
Two-year public **Federal Code: 002970**

	Living at home
Tuition and fees (2002-2003):	$1,056
Out-of-state:	$5,751
Per-credit charge:	$34
Per-credit out-of-state:	$191
Books and supplies:	$700
Personal expenses:	$825
Transportation:	$1,584

Undergraduate aid. Non-need-based: Scholarships based on academics.

Policies to reduce costs. Tuition/fee waivers for senior citizens. Credit/placement for qualifying scores on AP, CLEP examinations.

Payment plans. Credit card payment.

Application procedures. FAFSA, institutional form required. Priority date 5/1; no closing date. Applicants notified on rolling basis starting 6/1, must reply within 2 week(s) of notification.

Contact. Financial aid office: (336) 386-3245
Jamie Childress, Financial Aid Officer
630 South Main Street
Dobson, NC 27017-0304

Tri-County Community College

Murphy, North Carolina
www.tccc.cc.nc.us
Two-year public **Federal Code: 009430**

	Living at home
Tuition and fees (2002-2003):	$1,049
Out-of-state:	$5,744
Per-credit charge:	$34
Per-credit out-of-state:	$191
Books and supplies:	$300
Personal expenses:	$450
Transportation:	$200

Undergraduate aid. All financial aid based on need. 98% awarded as scholarships/grants, 2% as loans/jobs. Need-based aid available for part-time students.

Policies to reduce costs. Tuition/fee waivers for senior citizens, employees and their families. Credit/placement for qualifying scores on AP examinations.

Application procedures. FAFSA required. Priority date 5/31; no closing date. Applicants notified on rolling basis starting 6/1, must reply within 4 week(s) of notification. **Transfers:** No deadline.

Contact. Alicia Tipton, Financial Aid Officer
4600 Highway 64 East
Murphy, NC 28906

University of North Carolina at Asheville

Asheville, North Carolina
www.unca.edu
Four-year public **Federal Code: 002907**

	Living at home	On-campus
Tuition and fees (2002-2003):	$2,957	$2,957
Out-of-state:	$11,362	$11,362
Room and board:		$4,650
Board only:	$750	
Books and supplies:	$700	$700
Personal expenses:	$1,190	$1,190
Transportation:	$1,195	$713

Undergraduate aid. Need-based: Average financial aid package for full-time students was $6,951; for part-time $5,681. 46% awarded as scholarships/grants, 54% as loans/jobs. **Non-need-based:** 28% awarded as scholarships/grants, 72% as loans/jobs. Scholarships based on academics, alumni affiliation, art, athletics, job skills, leadership, minority status, music/drama, state/district residency. **Student debt:** 49% of graduating class borrowed to fund education; average debt was $14,547.

Freshman aid. Need-based: Out of 446 full-time freshmen, 352 applied for aid; 173 were judged to have need; of these 169 received aid. Average package met 79% of need. 65 students had full need met. Average scholarship/grant was $2,675; average loan $2,552. **Non-need based:** 83 full-time freshmen with need received non-need scholarships; 180 without need received awards; 19 received athletic scholarships.

Merit scholarships. North Carolina Teaching Fellows program; outstanding North Carolina high school students with desire and talent to become teachers; $26,000. University Laurels Program; essay, list of co-curricular activities and participation in Laurel's Interview Day; award varies from $500 to full in-state tuition and fees. Western North Carolina Leadership Scholarship; solid academic record and leadership ability; $1,000 renewable. Students must be from one of 24 Western North Carolina counties.

Policies to reduce costs. Tuition/fee waivers for senior citizens, employees and their families. Credit/placement for qualifying scores on AP, IB, CLEP examinations. Work study available nights, weekends and for part-time students.

Payment plans. Deferred payment.

Application procedures. FAFSA required. Priority date 3/1; no closing date. Applicants notified on rolling basis starting 3/15, must reply within 2 week(s) of notification. **Transfers:** No deadline.

Contact. Financial aid office: (828) 251-6535
Scot Schaeffer, Director of Admissions and Financial Aid
CPO#2210, 117 Lipinsky Hall
Asheville, NC 28804-8510

University of North Carolina at Chapel Hill

Chapel Hill, North Carolina
www.unc.edu
Four-year public **Federal Code: 002974**

	Living at home	On-campus
Tuition and fees (2002-2003):	$3,277	$3,277
Out-of-state:	$13,269	$13,269
Room and board:		$5,570
Books and supplies:	$800	$800
Personal expenses:	$1,850	$1,850

Undergraduate aid. Need-based: Average financial aid package for full-time students was $7,824; for part-time $6,233. 65% awarded as scholarships/grants, 35% as loans/jobs. **Non-need-based:** 68% awarded as scholarships/grants, 32% as loans/jobs. Scholarships based on academics, alumni affiliation, art, athletics, leadership, music/drama, religious affiliation, state/district residency. **Student debt:** 23% of graduating class borrowed to fund education; average debt was $11,156.

Freshman aid. Need-based: Out of 3,682 full-time freshmen, 2,605 applied for aid; 1,076 were judged to have need; of these 1,074 received aid. Average package met 100% of need. 877 students had full need met. Average scholarship/grant was $4,920; average loan $2,001. **Non-need based:** 538 full-time freshmen with need received non-need scholarships; 742 without need received awards; 73 received athletic scholarships.

Merit scholarships. Morehead Scholarships; 55 awarded; academic merit, leadership, athletics, moral character; full cost of tuition and expenses. Robertson Scholarships: 15 awarded; academic merit, leadership, community service, multi-cultural interests, full cost of tuition and expenses. Carolina Scholars; 40 awarded; academic merit, leadership, residency specifications; $7,500 - $15,000. Pogue Scholarships; 22 awarded; academic merit, leadership, ethnicity (African American/Native American), North Carolina residency; $7,500. College Fellows Awards; 15 awarded; academic merit, leadership, North Carolina residency; $2,500. Davie Scholarships; 20 awarded; academic merit, leadership; $3,250-$12,000. Jackson Scholarships; 5 awards; academic merit, leadership, North Carolina residency; $2,500. Other academic scholarships; 5 awarded; academic merit, leadership, residency specifications; $2,500, full cost.

Policies to reduce costs. Tuition/fee waivers for senior citizens, employees and their families. Credit/placement for qualifying scores on AP, IB, CLEP examinations.

Payment plans. Credit card, deferred payment.

Application procedures. FAFSA, CSS PROFILE required. Priority date 3/1; no closing date. Applicants notified on rolling basis starting 3/15, must reply by 5/1. **Transfers:** Priority date 3/1.

Contact. Shirley Ort, Director for Office of Student Aid/Associate Provost
Jackson Hall CB #2200
Chapel Hill, NC 27599-2200

University of North Carolina at Charlotte

Charlotte, North Carolina
www.uncc.edu
Four-year public **Federal Code: 002975**

	Living at home	On-campus
Tuition and fees (2002-2003):	$2,460	$2,460
Out-of-state:	$10,680	$10,680
Room and board:		$4,548
Board only:	$1,000	
Books and supplies:	$900	$900
Personal expenses:	$1,200	$1,200
Transportation:	$1,770	$1,050

Undergraduate aid. Need-based: Average financial aid package for full-time students was $7,758; for part-time $7,525. 44% awarded as scholarships/ grants, 56% as loans/jobs. **Non-need-based:** 14% awarded as scholarships/ grants, 86% as loans/jobs. Scholarships based on academics, athletics, leadership. **Student debt:** 54% of graduating class borrowed to fund education; average debt was $17,144.

Freshman aid. Need-based: Out of 2,384 full-time freshmen, 1,517 applied for aid; 1,084 were judged to have need; of these 1,041 received aid. Average package met 71% of need. 243 students had full need met. Average scholarship/grant was $3,373; average loan $2,609. **Non-need based:** 254 full-time freshmen with need received non-need scholarships; 444 without need received awards; 35 received athletic scholarships.

Policies to reduce costs. Tuition/fee waivers for senior citizens. Credit/ placement for qualifying scores on AP, IB, CLEP examinations. Work study available for part-time students.

Payment plans. Credit card, installment payment.

Application procedures. FAFSA required. Priority date 4/1; no closing date. Applicants notified on rolling basis starting 4/1, must reply within 3 week(s) of notification.

Contact. **Financial aid office:** (704) 687-2461
Curtis Whalen, Director of Student Financial Aid
9201 University City Boulevard
Charlotte, NC 28223-0001

University of North Carolina at Greensboro

Greensboro, North Carolina
www.uncg.edu
Four-year public **Federal Code: 002976**

	Living at home	On-campus
Tuition and fees (2002-2003):	$2,545	$2,545
Out-of-state:	$10,995	$10,995
Room and board:		$4,313
Books and supplies:	$1,156	$1,156
Personal expenses:	$1,556	$1,812
Transportation:	$1,866	$458

Undergraduate aid. Need-based: Average financial aid package for full-time students was $9,003; for part-time $10,078. 38% awarded as scholarships/ grants, 62% as loans/jobs. **Non-need-based:** 48% awarded as scholarships/ grants, 52% as loans/jobs. Scholarships based on academics, art, athletics, leadership, music/drama, state/district residency. **Student debt:** 44% of graduating class borrowed to fund education; average debt was $17,075.

Freshman aid. Need-based: Out of 1,993 full-time freshmen, 1,541 applied for aid; 951 were judged to have need; of these 947 received aid. Average package met 79% of need. 403 students had full need met. Average scholarship/grant was $2,222; average loan $2,823. **Non-need based:** 616 full-time freshmen with need received non-need scholarships; 609 without need received awards; 50 received athletic scholarships.

Policies to reduce costs. Tuition/fee waivers for senior citizens, employees and their families. Credit/placement for qualifying scores on AP, CLEP examinations.

Payment plans. Credit card payment.

Application procedures. FAFSA required. Priority date 3/1; no closing date. Applicants notified on rolling basis starting 4/1, must reply within 3 week(s) of notification. **Transfers:** Priority date 3/1.

Contact. Deborah Tollefson, Director of Financial Aid
123 Mossman Building
Greensboro, NC 27402-6166

University of North Carolina at Pembroke

Pembroke, North Carolina
www.uncp.edu
Four-year public **Federal Code: 002954**

	Living at home	On-campus
Tuition and fees (2002-2003):	$2,069	$2,069
Out-of-state:	$9,991	$9,991
Room and board:		$3,845
Board only:	$3,576	
Books and supplies:	$800	$800
Personal expenses:	$1,400	$1,200
Transportation:	$1,480	$1,167

Undergraduate aid. Need-based: Average financial aid package for full-time students was $5,956; for part-time $3,452. 56% awarded as scholarships/ grants, 44% as loans/jobs. **Non-need-based:** 5% awarded as scholarships/ grants, 95% as loans/jobs. Scholarships based on academics, athletics. **Student debt:** 55% of graduating class borrowed to fund education; average debt was $9,732.

Freshman aid. Need-based: Out of 707 full-time freshmen, 590 applied for aid; 466 were judged to have need; of these 455 received aid. Average package met 73% of need. 103 students had full need met. Average scholarship/ grant was $3,967; average loan $2,320. **Non-need based:** 39 full-time freshmen with need received non-need scholarships; 53 without need received awards.

Policies to reduce costs. Tuition/fee waivers for senior citizens, employees and their families. Credit/placement for qualifying scores on AP, CLEP examinations.

Payment plans. Credit card, installment payment.

Application procedures. FAFSA, institutional form required. Closing date 4/15. Applicants notified on rolling basis starting 4/15, must reply within 2 week(s) of notification.

Contact. **Financial aid office:** (910) 521-6255
Bruce Blackmon, Director of Financial Aid
Box 1510
Pembroke, NC 28372

University of North Carolina at Wilmington

Wilmington, North Carolina
www.uncwil.edu
Four-year public **Federal Code: 002984**

	Living at home	On-campus
Tuition and fees (2002-2003):	$2,627	$2,627
Out-of-state:	$10,722	$10,722
Room and board:		$5,142
Books and supplies:	$775	$775
Personal expenses:	$1,200	$1,200
Transportation:	$816	$816

Undergraduate aid. Need-based: Average financial aid package for full-time students was $6,254; for part-time $5,441. 47% awarded as scholarships/ grants, 53% as loans/jobs. **Non-need-based:** 17% awarded as scholarships/ grants, 83% as loans/jobs. Scholarships based on academics, alumni affiliation, art, athletics, leadership, music/drama, state/district residency. **Student debt:** 83% of graduating class borrowed to fund education; average debt was $13,583.

Freshman aid. Need-based: Out of 1,633 full-time freshmen, 842 applied for aid; 491 were judged to have need; of these 491 received aid. Average package met 89% of need. 329 students had full need met. Average scholarship/ grant was $3,315; average loan $2,710. **Non-need based:** 56 received athletic scholarships.

Policies to reduce costs. Tuition/fee waivers for senior citizens, employees and their families. Credit/placement for qualifying scores on AP, CLEP examinations. Work study available nights, weekends and for part-time students.

Payment plans. Credit card, installment, deferred payment.

Application procedures. FAFSA required. No deadline. Applicants notified on rolling basis starting 3/15, must reply within 3 week(s) of notification.

Contact. **Financial aid office:** (910) 962-3177
Emily Bliss, Director of Financial Aid
601 South College Road
Wilmington, NC 28403-3297

Vance-Granville Community College

Henderson, North Carolina
www.vgcc.edu
Two-year public **Federal Code: 009903**

	Living at home
Tuition and fees (2002-2003):	$1,066
Out-of-state:	$5,761
Per-credit charge:	$34
Per-credit out-of-state:	$191
Board only:	$3,170
Books and supplies:	$800
Personal expenses:	$400
Transportation:	$1,200

Undergraduate aid. Need-based: Need-based aid available for full-time and part-time students. **Non-need-based:** Scholarships based on academics.

Policies to reduce costs. Tuition/fee waivers for senior citizens, employees and their families. Credit/placement for qualifying scores on AP, CLEP examinations.

Payment plans. Credit card payment.

Application procedures. FAFSA required. Priority date 7/15; no closing date. Applicants notified on rolling basis starting 5/1, must reply within 2 week(s) of notification. **Transfers:** No deadline.

Contact. Frank Clark, Financial Aid Officer
Box 917
Henderson, NC 27536

Wake Forest University

Winston-Salem, North Carolina
www.wfu.edu
Four-year private **Federal Code: 002978**

College costs. Tuition covers cost of an IBM Thinkpad computer and inkjet printer for freshmen.

	Living at home	On-campus
Tuition and fees (2002-2003):	$24,750	$24,750
Room and board:		$7,190
Board only:	$750	
Books and supplies:	$700	$700
Personal expenses:	$590	$1,200
Transportation:	$260	$370

Undergraduate aid. Need-based: Average financial aid package for full-time students was $19,394; for part-time $15,776. 66% awarded as scholarships/grants, 34% as loans/jobs. **Non-need-based:** 62% awarded as scholarships/grants, 38% as loans/jobs. Scholarships based on academics, art, athletics, leadership, music/drama, religious affiliation, state/district residency. **Student debt:** 28% of graduating class borrowed to fund education; average debt was $24,769.

Freshman aid. Need-based: Out of 973 full-time freshmen, 487 applied for aid; 329 were judged to have need; of these 329 received aid. Average package met 91% of need. 125 students had full need met. Average scholarship/grant was $14,778; average loan $4,809. **Non-need based:** 84 full-time freshmen with need received non-need scholarships; 343 without need received awards; 53 received athletic scholarships.

Merit scholarships. Reynolds Scholarship for extraordinarily capable students; 6 awarded; full tuition, room and board, books, fees for 4 years, also provides for summer study. Joseph G. Gordon Scholarship for underrepresented students with exceptional promise and leadership; 7 awarded; full tuition for 4 years. Carswell Scholarship for students with outstanding qualities of intellect and leadership; 10-12 awarded of between 3/4 and full tuition for 4 years, including summer grant for travel and study projects. Presidential Scholarship for students gifted in areas such as writing, studio art, music theater, debate, leadership, dance, entrepreneurship, and community service; 20 awarded; $11,200 annually for 4 years. Poteat Scholarship for North Carolina residents who are active members of a Baptist Chruch in North Carolina, must make an active contribution to church and society; 18 awarded; $11,200 annually for 4 years. Various smaller programs range up to full tuition.

Policies to reduce costs. Tuition/fee waivers for employees and their families. Credit/placement for qualifying scores on AP, IB examinations.

Payment plans. Installment payment.

Application procedures. FAFSA, CSS PROFILE required. Priority date 3/1; no closing date. Applicants notified by 4/1, must reply by 8/15. Early decision closing date 11/15. **Transfers:** Priority date 2/1; no deadline.

Contact. Financial aid office: (336) 758-5154
W. Wells, Director of Financial Aid
PO Box 7305 Reynolda Station
Winston-Salem, NC 27109

Wake Technical Community College

Raleigh, North Carolina
www.wake.tec.nc.us
Two-year public **Federal Code: 004844**

	Living at home
Tuition and fees (2002-2003):	$1,052
Out-of-state:	$5,747
Per-credit charge:	$34
Per-credit out-of-state:	$191
Board only:	$1,500
Books and supplies:	$1,000
Personal expenses:	$1,350
Transportation:	$1,300

Undergraduate aid. Need-based: 84% awarded as scholarships/grants, 16% as loans/jobs. Need-based aid available for part-time students. **Non-need-based:** 18% awarded as scholarships/grants, 82% as loans/jobs. Scholarships based on academics, job skills, leadership, state/district residency. **Student debt:** 60% of graduating class borrowed to fund education; average debt was $3,000.

Merit scholarships. Refer to college website for local scholarships.

Policies to reduce costs. Tuition/fee waivers for senior citizens, employees and their families. Credit/placement for qualifying scores on AP, CLEP examinations. Work study available for part-time students.

Payment plans. Credit card payment.

Application procedures. FAFSA, institutional form required. Priority date 3/15; no closing date. Applicants notified on rolling basis starting 4/1, must reply within 2 week(s) of notification. **Transfers:** Priority date 3/15; no deadline. Child care grant and NCCCS Grant & Loan Program available.

Contact. Carolyn Braxton, Financial Aid Director
9101 Fayetteville Road
Raleigh, NC 27603

Warren Wilson College

Asheville, North Carolina
www.warren-wilson.edu
Four-year private **Federal Code: 002979**

College costs. All resident students required to work 15 hours per week in college's work program. $2,472 earnings credited toward tuition costs.

	Living at home	On-campus
Tuition and fees:	$16,674	$16,674
Room and board:		$5,120
Board only:	$2,322	
Books and supplies:	$700	$700
Personal expenses:	$840	$775
Transportation:	$841	$775

Undergraduate aid. Need-based: Need-based aid available for full-time and part-time students. **Non-need-based:** Scholarships based on academics, job skills, leadership, state/district residency.

Merit scholarships. Wilson Honor; 1 awarded; $5,000 annually. Warner Honor; 2 awarded; $4,000 annually. Transfer Honor; 2 awarded; $2,000 annually. Sutton Honor; 20 awarded; $1,000 annually. Work Scholarship; 2 awarded; $1,500 annually. Service Scholarship; 2 awarded; $1,500 annually. National Merit; unlimited numbers awarded; $4,000 annually. Valedictorian/Salutatorian Scholarship; 10 awarded; $2,000 annually. North Carolina Presidential Scholarship; 30 awarded; $1,000 annually. All renewable with 3.0 cumulative GPA and successful completion of a minimum of 12 credit hours each semester.

Policies to reduce costs. Tuition/fee waivers for senior citizens, employees and their families. Credit/placement for qualifying scores on AP, CLEP examinations.

Payment plans. Credit card, installment payment.

Application procedures. FAFSA, institutional form required. Priority date 4/1; no closing date. Applicants notified on rolling basis starting 3/1, must reply within 3 week(s) of notification. Early decision closing date 11/15. **Transfers:** Priority date 4/1.

Contact. **Financial aid office:** (828) 771-2082
Kathy Pack, Director of Financial Aid
Office of Admission
Asheville, NC 28815

Wayne Community College

Goldsboro, North Carolina
www.wayne.cc.nc.us
Two-year public **Federal Code: 008216**

	Living at home
Tuition and fees (2002-2003):	$1,060
Out-of-state:	$5,755
Per-credit charge:	$34
Per-credit out-of-state:	$191
Books and supplies:	$800
Personal expenses:	$400
Transportation:	$1,100

Undergraduate aid. Need-based: Need-based aid available for full-time and part-time students. **Non-need-based:** Scholarships based on academics, job skills.

Policies to reduce costs. Tuition/fee waivers for senior citizens, employees and their families. Credit/placement for qualifying scores on AP, CLEP examinations. Work study available nights and for part-time students.

Payment plans. Credit card, deferred payment.

Application procedures. FAFSA, institutional form required. Priority date 3/15; no closing date. Applicants notified on rolling basis starting 6/1, must reply within 2 week(s) of notification. **Transfers:** No deadline.

Contact. **Financial aid office:** (919) 735-5151
Yvonne Goodman, Financial Aid Director
PO Box 8002
Goldsboro, NC 27533-8002

Western Carolina University

Cullowhee, North Carolina
www.wcu.edu
Four-year public **Federal Code: 002981**

	Living at home	On-campus
Tuition and fees (2002-2003):	$2,243	$2,243
Out-of-state:	$9,875	$9,875
Room and board:		$3,424
Board only:	$2,560	
Books and supplies:	$508	$508
Personal expenses:	$1,680	$1,680
Transportation:	$774	$774

Undergraduate aid. Need-based: Average financial aid package for full-time students was $5,970; for part-time $4,436. 44% awarded as scholarships/grants, 56% as loans/jobs. **Non-need-based:** 41% awarded as scholarships/grants, 59% as loans/jobs. Scholarships based on academics, art, athletics, leadership, music/drama, state/district residency. **Student debt:** 43% of graduating class borrowed to fund education; average debt was $15,433.

Freshman aid. Need-based: Out of 1,222 full-time freshmen, 850 applied for aid; 575 were judged to have need; of these 562 received aid. Average package met 67% of need. 379 students had full need met. Average scholarship/grant was $4,230; average loan $2,474. **Non-need based:** 56 full-time freshmen with need received non-need scholarships; 106 without need received awards; 18 received athletic scholarships.

Policies to reduce costs. Tuition/fee waivers for senior citizens, minority students. Credit/placement for qualifying scores on AP, IB, CLEP examinations. Work study available nights and weekends.

Payment plans. Installment payment.

Application procedures. FAFSA, institutional form required. Priority date 3/31; no closing date. Applicants notified on rolling basis starting 4/1. **Transfers:** Priority date 3/31; no deadline.

Contact. **Financial aid office:** (828)227-7290
Nancy Dillard, Director of Student Financial Aid
242 HFR-Administration
Cullowhee, NC 28723

Western Piedmont Community College

Morganton, North Carolina
www.wp.cc.nc.us
Two-year public **Federal Code: 002982**

	Living at home
Tuition and fees (2002-2003):	$1,055
Out-of-state:	$5,750
Per-credit charge:	$34
Per-credit out-of-state:	$191
Books and supplies:	$700
Personal expenses:	$1,200
Transportation:	$1,300

Undergraduate aid. Need-based: Average financial aid package for full-time students was $5,510. 91% awarded as scholarships/grants, 9% as loans/jobs. Need-based aid available for part-time students. **Student debt:** 10% of graduating class borrowed to fund education; average debt was $3,307.

Freshman aid. Need-based: Out of 283 full-time freshmen, 156 applied for aid; 125 were judged to have need; of these 110 received aid. Average package met 68% of need. 11 students had full need met. Average scholarship/grant was $2,405; average loan $1,790. **Non-need based:** 22 full-time freshmen with need received non-need scholarships; 32 without need received awards; 12 received athletic scholarships.

Policies to reduce costs. Tuition/fee waivers for senior citizens, employees and their families. Credit/placement for qualifying scores on AP, IB, CLEP examinations. Work study available for part-time students.

Payment plans. Credit card, deferred payment.

Application procedures. FAFSA required. Priority date 5/1; no closing date. Must reply within 2 week(s) of notification. **Transfers:** Priority date 5/1; no deadline.

Contact. **Financial aid office:** (828) 438-6042
Keith Conley, Director of Financial Aid
1001 Burkemont Avenue
Morganton, NC 28655-4511

Wilkes Community College

Wilkesboro, North Carolina
www.wilkescc.edu
Two-year public **Federal Code: 002983**

	Living at home
Tuition and fees (2002-2003):	$1,066
Out-of-state:	$5,761
Per-credit charge:	$34
Per-credit out-of-state:	$191
Board only:	$1,800
Books and supplies:	$800
Personal expenses:	$400
Transportation:	$400

Undergraduate aid. Need-based: Average financial aid package for full-time students was $1,450; for part-time $700. 97% awarded as scholarships/grants, 3% as loans/jobs. **Non-need-based:** 78% awarded as scholarships/grants, 22% as loans/jobs. Scholarships based on art, leadership, minority status, music/drama, state/district residency. **Student debt:** 2% of graduating class borrowed to fund education; average debt was $3,675.

Freshman aid. Need-based: Out of 345 full-time freshmen, 269 applied for aid; 188 were judged to have need; of these 106 received aid. Average package met 72% of need. 12 students had full need met. Average scholarship/grant was $400; average loan $1,500. **Non-need based:** 16 full-time freshmen with need received non-need scholarships; 102 without need received awards.

Policies to reduce costs. Tuition/fee waivers for senior citizens, employees and their families. Credit/placement for qualifying scores on AP, CLEP examinations. Work study available nights and for part-time students.

Payment plans. Credit card, installment, deferred payment.

Application procedures. FAFSA required. Priority date 5/1; no closing date. Applicants notified on rolling basis starting 5/1, must reply by 8/1. **Transfers:** Priority date 5/1; no deadline.

Contact. **Financial aid office:** (336) 838-6146
Alan Whittington, Director of Financial Aid
1328 Collegiate Drive
Wilkesboro, NC 28697-0120

Wilson Technical Community College

Wilson, North Carolina
www.wilsontech.cc.nc.us
Two-year public **Federal Code: 004845**

	Living at home
Tuition and fees (2002-2003):	$1,052
Out-of-state:	$5,747
Per-credit charge:	$34
Per-credit out-of-state:	$191
Books and supplies:	$600
Personal expenses:	$2,500
Transportation:	$800

Undergraduate aid. **Need-based:** Average financial aid package for full-time students was $3,700; for part-time $3,700. 96% awarded as scholarships/grants, 4% as loans/jobs. **Non-need-based:** 63% awarded as scholarships/grants, 37% as loans/jobs. Scholarships based on academics. **Student debt:** 9% of graduating class borrowed to fund education; average debt was $6,689.

Freshman aid. **Need-based:** Out of 230 full-time freshmen, 207 applied for aid; 142 were judged to have need; of these 99 received aid. Average package met 62% of need. 12 students had full need met. Average scholarship/grant was $3,700; average loan $1,760. **Non-need based:** 17 full-time freshmen with need received non-need scholarships; 10 without need received awards.

Policies to reduce costs. Tuition/fee waivers for senior citizens, employees and their families. Credit/placement for qualifying scores on AP, CLEP examinations.

Payment plans. Credit card, deferred payment.

Application procedures. FAFSA, institutional form required. Priority date 3/15; no closing date. Applicants notified on rolling basis. **Transfers:** No deadline.

Contact. S. Bissette, Financial Aid Officer
Box 4305
Wilson, NC 27893-0305

Wingate University

Wingate, North Carolina
www.wingate.edu
Four-year private **Federal Code: 002985**

	Living at home	On-campus
Tuition and fees (2002-2003):	$14,150	$14,150
Room and board:		$5,720
Board only:	$2,500	
Books and supplies:	$750	$750
Personal expenses:	$900	$900
Transportation:	$700	$700

Undergraduate aid. **Need-based:** Average financial aid package for full-time students was $10,818; for part-time $8,703. 58% awarded as scholarships/grants, 42% as loans/jobs. **Non-need-based:** 75% awarded as scholarships/grants, 25% as loans/jobs. Scholarships based on academics, alumni affiliation, art, athletics, leadership, music/drama, religious affiliation, state/district residency. **Student debt:** 86% of graduating class borrowed to fund education; average debt was $24,000. **Additional information:** Tuition payment plans available with no interest charges for $50 per year enrollment fee. Institutional aid may not be available after June 1.

Freshman aid. **Need-based:** Out of 396 full-time freshmen, 356 applied for aid; 253 were judged to have need; of these 231 received aid. Average package met 60% of need. 2 students had full need met. Average scholarship/grant was $7,800; average loan $2,625. **Non-need based:** 231 full-time freshmen with need received non-need scholarships; 143 without need received awards; 94 received athletic scholarships.

Merit scholarships. Wingate offers Belk Scholarships in $10,000 amounts to top scholars.

Policies to reduce costs. Tuition/fee waivers for employees and their families. Credit/placement for qualifying scores on AP, IB, CLEP examinations.

Payment plans. Installment payment.

Application procedures. FAFSA required. Priority date 5/1; no closing date. Applicants notified on rolling basis starting 3/15, must reply within 4 week(s) of notification. Early decision closing date 12/1. **Transfers:** Priority date 3/1; no deadline. Must submit financial aid transcripts from previous colleges attended.

Contact. **Financial aid office:** (704) 233-8209
Teresa Williams, Director of Financial Planning
Campus Box 3059
Wingate, NC 28174-0157

Winston-Salem State University

Winston-Salem, North Carolina
www.wssu.edu
Four-year public **Federal Code: 002986**

	Living at home	On-campus
Tuition and fees (2002-2003):	$2,063	$2,063
Out-of-state:	$9,059	$9,059
Room and board:		$3,864
Board only:	$1,806	
Books and supplies:	$600	$600
Personal expenses:	$2,100	$2,100
Transportation:	$476	$551

Undergraduate aid. **Need-based:** Average financial aid package for full-time students was $3,925; for part-time $20,777. 55% awarded as scholarships/grants, 45% as loans/jobs. **Non-need-based:** 37% awarded as scholarships/grants, 63% as loans/jobs. Scholarships based on academics, athletics, state/district residency. **Student debt:** 84% of graduating class borrowed to fund education; average debt was $10,500.

Freshman aid. **Need-based:** Out of 614 full-time freshmen, 465 applied for aid; 427 were judged to have need; of these 401 received aid. Average package met 83% of need. 98 students had full need met. Average scholarship/grant was $4,057; average loan $2,265. **Non-need based:** 50 full-time freshmen with need received non-need scholarships; 111 without need received awards; 21 received athletic scholarships.

Policies to reduce costs. Tuition/fee waivers for senior citizens, employees and their families. Credit/placement for qualifying scores on AP, CLEP examinations.

Payment plans. Installment payment.

Application procedures. FAFSA required. Priority date 4/1; no closing date. Applicants notified on rolling basis starting 5/15, must reply within 2 week(s) of notification. **Transfers:** Priority date 4/1; no deadline.

Contact. **Financial aid office:** (336) 750-3280
Thoedore Hindsman, Director of Financial Aid
601 Martin Luther King Jr. Drive
Winston-Salem, NC 27110

North Dakota

Aaker's Business College

Fargo, North Dakota
www.aakers-college.com
Two-year private **Federal Code: 004846**

College costs (2002-2003). $640 per course, network support courses $935, $60 registration fee. Books/supplies: $900. Transportation: $1,098.

Undergraduate aid. All financial aid based on need. Need-based aid available for full-time and part-time students. **Student debt:** 94% of graduating class borrowed to fund education; average debt was $14,000.

Freshman aid. Out of 43 full-time freshmen, 43 applied for aid; 43 were judged to have need; of these 39 received aid. Average scholarship/grant was $900; average loan $2,625.

Policies to reduce costs. Credit/placement for qualifying scores on CLEP examinations.

Application procedures. FAFSA, institutional form required. No deadline. Applicants notified on rolling basis.

Contact. **Financial aid office:** (701) 277-3889
Deb Murray, Financial Aid Director
4012 19th Avenue SW
Fargo, ND 58103

Bismarck State College

Bismarck, North Dakota
www.bismarckstate.com
Two-year public **Federal Code: 002988**

College costs. Full-time annual tuition for residents of Minnesota: $2,790. Full-time annual tuition for residents of South Dakota, Montana, Manitoba, Saskatchewan: $2,642. Full-time annual tuition for residents of Alaska, Arizona, California, Colorado, Hawaii, Idaho, New Mexico, Nevada, Oregon, Utah, Washington, and Wyoming: $3,102. Tuition for Internet courses $115 per-credit-hour.

	Living at home	On-campus
Tuition and fees (2002-2003):	$2,219	$2,219
Out-of-state:	$5,199	$5,199
Per-credit charge:	$69	$69
Per-credit out-of-state:	$183	$183
Room and board:		$3,090
Board only:	$1,500	
Books and supplies:	$700	$700
Personal expenses:	$1,900	$1,900
Transportation:	$800	$800

Undergraduate aid. All financial aid based on need. 29% awarded as scholarships/grants, 71% as loans/jobs. Need-based aid available for part-time students. **Student debt:** 75% of graduating class borrowed to fund education; average debt was $4,640.

Policies to reduce costs. Tuition/fee waivers for minority students, employees and their families. Credit/placement for qualifying scores on CLEP examinations. Work study available nights, weekends and for part-time students.

Payment plans. Credit card, installment payment.

Application procedures. FAFSA, institutional form required. Priority date 4/15; no closing date. Applicants notified on rolling basis starting 6/1, must reply within 3 week(s) of notification. **Transfers:** No deadline. Financial aid based on funds available.

Contact. **Financial aid office:** (701) 224-5494
Jeffrey Jacobs, Director of Financial Aid
PO Box 5587
Bismarck, ND 58506-5587

Dickinson State University

Dickinson, North Dakota
www.dsu.nodak.edu
Four-year public **Federal Code: 002989**

College costs. Tuition for Minnesota residents: $2,554. Tuition for South Dakota, Montana, Manitoba, Saskatchewan residents: $2,752.

	Living at home	On-campus
Tuition and fees (2002-2003):	$2,798	$2,798
Out-of-state:	$6,476	$6,476
Room and board:		$3,200
Board only:	$1,890	
Books and supplies:	$600	$600
Personal expenses:	$1,325	$1,325
Transportation:	$1,325	$1,325

Undergraduate aid. **Need-based:** 40% awarded as scholarships/grants, 60% as loans/jobs. Need-based aid available for part-time students. **Non-need-based:** 27% awarded as scholarships/grants, 73% as loans/jobs. Scholarships based on academics, alumni affiliation, art, athletics, leadership, minority status, music/drama, state/district residency. **Additional information:** Scholarships available to new students, priority deadline December 1; over $638,000 total available.

Policies to reduce costs. Tuition/fee waivers for senior citizens, minority students, employees and their families. Credit/placement for qualifying scores on AP, CLEP examinations. Work study available nights, weekends and for part-time students.

Payment plans. Credit card, installment payment.

Application procedures. FAFSA required. Priority date 3/15; no closing date. Applicants notified on rolling basis starting 5/5, must reply within 2 week(s) of notification. **Transfers:** Priority date 3/15; no deadline.

Contact. **Financial aid office:** (701) 483-2371
Sandy Klein, Director of Financial Aid
PO Box 169
Dickinson, ND 58601-4896

Jamestown College

Jamestown, North Dakota
www.jc.edu
Four-year private **Federal Code: 002990**

	Living at home	On-campus
Tuition and fees:	$8,750	$8,750
Room and board:		$3,850
Board only:	$1,500	
Books and supplies:	$1,000	$1,000
Personal expenses:	$1,300	$1,300
Transportation:	$800	$1,500

Undergraduate aid. **Need-based:** Average financial aid package for full-time students was $7,828; for part-time $3,261. 49% awarded as scholarships/grants, 51% as loans/jobs. **Non-need-based:** 25% awarded as scholarships/grants, 75% as loans/jobs. Scholarships based on academics, art, athletics, leadership, music/drama, religious affiliation. **Student debt:** 92% of graduating class borrowed to fund education; average debt was $17,980.

Freshman aid. **Need-based:** Out of 332 full-time freshmen, 332 applied for aid; 293 were judged to have need; of these 293 received aid. Average package met 69% of need. 34 students had full need met. Average scholarship/grant was $5,133; average loan $3,066. **Non-need based:** 21 full-time freshmen with need received non-need scholarships; 41 without need received awards; 23 received athletic scholarships.

Merit scholarships. Wilson Scholarships for academic merit and leadership; 5 awarded; full tuition. Presidential Scholarships for academic merit and leadership; 10 awarded; $6,000 annually. Honor Scholarships for academic merit and leadership; 50 awarded; $4,500 annually. Arnold Chemistry Scholarships for chemistry majors; 2 awarded; $5,000 annually. Leadership Scholarships for academic merit and leadership; 30 awarded, $3,000 annually.

Policies to reduce costs. Tuition/fee waivers for employees and their families. Credit/placement for qualifying scores on AP, IB, CLEP examinations. Work study available nights, weekends and for part-time students.

Payment plans. Installment payment.

Application procedures. FAFSA, institutional form required. Priority date 6/1; no closing date. Applicants notified on rolling basis starting 6/1, must reply within 6 week(s) of notification. **Transfers:** No deadline.

Contact. **Financial aid office:** (701) 252-3467 ext. 2556
Margery Michael, Director of Financial Aid
6081 College Lane
Jamestown, ND 58405

Lake Region State College

Devils Lake, North Dakota
www.lrsc.nodak.edu
Two-year public **Federal Code: 002991**

College costs. Tuition for Minnesota residents: $2,457. Tuition for South Dakota, Montana, Saskatchewan, Manitoba residents: $2,228.

	Living at home	On-campus
Tuition and fees (2002-2003):	$2,476	$2,476
Out-of-state:	$5,452	$5,452
Per-credit charge:	$74	$74
Per-credit out-of-state:	$198	$198
Room and board:		$3,250
Books and supplies:	$700	$700
Personal expenses:	$1,500	$1,500
Transportation:	$500	$500

Undergraduate aid. All financial aid based on need. Average financial aid package for full-time students was $5,205; for part-time $4,300. 46% awarded as scholarships/grants, 54% as loans/jobs. **Student debt:** 70% of graduating class borrowed to fund education; average debt was $4,000.

Freshman aid. Out of 130 full-time freshmen, 126 applied for aid; 84 were judged to have need; of these 84 received aid. Average package met 89% of need. 52 students had full need met. Average scholarship/grant was $3,045; average loan $2,428.

Policies to reduce costs. Tuition/fee waivers for adults, children of alumni, senior citizens, minority students, employees and their families. Credit/placement for qualifying scores on AP, CLEP examinations. Work study available nights, weekends and for part-time students.

Payment plans. Credit card payment.

Application procedures. FAFSA required. Priority date 4/15; no closing date. Applicants notified on rolling basis starting 5/1, must reply within 2 week(s) of notification. **Transfers:** Priority date 4/15; no deadline.

Contact. **Financial aid office:** (701) 662-1516
Katie Nettell, Director of Financial Aid
1801 North College Drive
Devils Lake, ND 58301-1598

Mayville State University

Mayville, North Dakota
www.mayvillestate.edu
Four-year public **Federal Code: 002993**

College costs. Full-time tuition for Minnesota residents: $2,554. Full-time tuition for South Dakota, Montana, Manitoba, and Saskatchewan residents: $2,753.

	Living at home	On-campus
Tuition and fees (2002-2003):	$3,533	$3,533
Out-of-state:	$7,210	$7,210
Room and board:		$3,366
Board only:	$1,000	
Books and supplies:	$600	$600
Personal expenses:	$2,660	$2,660

Undergraduate aid. **Need-based:** Average financial aid package for full-time students was $6,008. 32% awarded as scholarships/grants, 68% as loans/jobs. Need-based aid available for part-time students. **Non-need-based:** 7% awarded as scholarships/grants, 93% as loans/jobs. Scholarships based on academics, athletics, leadership, minority status, state/district residency. **Student debt:** 89% of graduating class borrowed to fund education; average debt was $15,074.

Freshman aid. **Need-based:** Out of 134 full-time freshmen, 115 applied for aid; 81 were judged to have need; of these 80 received aid. Average package met 85% of need. 36 students had full need met. Average scholarship/grant was $3,014; average loan $2,568. **Non-need based:** 70 full-time freshmen with need received non-need scholarships; 16 without need received awards; 5 received athletic scholarships.

Merit scholarships. Presidential Scholarship; $1,000 to $3,500 per year; based on academic criteria of freshmen from select states.

Policies to reduce costs. Tuition/fee waivers for senior citizens, minority students. Credit/placement for qualifying scores on AP, CLEP examinations. Work study available nights, weekends and for part-time students.

Payment plans. Credit card, installment payment.

Application procedures. FAFSA required. Priority date 4/15; no closing date. Applicants notified on rolling basis starting 5/1, must reply within 2 week(s) of notification. **Transfers:** Priority date 4/15; no deadline.

Contact. Shirley Hanson, Director of Financial Aid
330 Third Street, Northeast
Mayville, ND 58257

Medcenter One College of Nursing

Bismarck, North Dakota
www.medcenterone.com/nursing/nursing.htm
Upper-division private **Federal Code: 009354**

	Living at home	On-campus
Tuition and fees:	$8,500	$8,500
Room only:		$1,800
Books and supplies:	$1,089	$1,089
Personal expenses:	$1,000	$1,000
Transportation:	$585	$585

Undergraduate aid. **Need-based:** Average financial aid package for full-time students was $6,532; for part-time $6,900. 37% awarded as scholarships/grants, 63% as loans/jobs. **Non-need-based:** 13% awarded as scholarships/grants, 87% as loans/jobs. **Student debt:** 82% of graduating class borrowed to fund education; average debt was $9,672.

Policies to reduce costs. Work study available weekends and for part-time students.

Application procedures. FAFSA, institutional form required. Priority date 4/15; no closing date. Applicants notified on rolling basis starting 6/15, must reply within 2 week(s) of notification. **Transfers:** No deadline.

Contact. **Financial aid office:** (701) 323-6270
Janell Thomas, Director/Registrar
512 North Seventh Street
Bismarck, ND 58501

Minot State University

Minot, North Dakota
www.minotstateu.edu
Four-year public **Federal Code: 002994**

College costs. Full-time tuition for Minnesota residents: $2,719. Full-time tuition and fees for South Dakota, Montana, Manitoba, Saskatchewan residents: $2,930.

	Living at home	On-campus
Tuition and fees (2002-2003):	$2,805	$2,805
Out-of-state:	$6,719	$6,719
Room and board:		$3,177
Board only:	$1,190	
Books and supplies:	$700	$700
Personal expenses:	$1,400	$1,715
Transportation:	$750	$750

Undergraduate aid. **Need-based:** Average financial aid package for full-time students was $5,275. 59% awarded as scholarships/grants, 41% as loans/jobs. Need-based aid available for part-time students. **Non-need-based:** 46% awarded as scholarships/grants, 54% as loans/jobs. Scholarships based on academics, alumni affiliation, art, athletics, minority status, music/drama, state/district residency. **Student debt:** 97% of graduating class borrowed to fund education; average debt was $12,922. **Additional information:** Scholarship application deadline is February 15.

Freshman aid. **Need-based:** Out of 477 full-time freshmen, 385 applied for aid; 347 were judged to have need; of these 293 received aid. Average package met 66% of need. 293 students had full need met. Average scholarship/grant was $1,617; average loan $1,431. **Non-need based:** 115 full-time freshmen with need received non-need scholarships.

Policies to reduce costs. Tuition/fee waivers for children of alumni, senior citizens, minority students. Credit/placement for qualifying scores on AP, CLEP examinations. Work study available nights and for part-time students.

Payment plans. Credit card payment.

Application procedures. FAFSA required. Priority date 4/15; no closing date. Applicants notified on rolling basis starting 6/1, must reply within 2 week(s) of notification. **Transfers:** Priority date 4/15; no deadline.

Contact. Dale Gehring, Director of Financial Aid
500 University Avenue West
Minot, ND 58707-5002

Minot State University: Bottineau Campus

Bottineau, North Dakota
www.misu-b.nodak.edu
Two-year public **Federal Code: 002995**

College costs. Tuition for Minnesota residents: $2,457. Tuition for South Dakota, Montana residents: $2,228. Tuition for Canadian province residents: $1,782.

	Living at home	On-campus
Tuition and fees (2002-2003):	$2,295	$2,295
Out-of-state:	$5,271	$5,271
Per-credit charge:	$74	$74
Per-credit out-of-state:	$198	$198
Room and board:		$3,070
Books and supplies:	$600	$600
Personal expenses:	$1,200	$1,200
Transportation:	$600	$600

Undergraduate aid. Need-based: Need-based aid available for full-time and part-time students. **Non-need-based:** Scholarships based on academics, alumni affiliation, athletics, music/drama.

Policies to reduce costs. Tuition/fee waivers for senior citizens, minority students, employees and their families. Work study available nights, weekends and for part-time students.

Application procedures. FAFSA required. Priority date 4/15; no closing date. Applicants notified on rolling basis starting 6/1, must reply within 2 week(s) of notification. **Transfers:** Priority date 4/15; no deadline.

Contact. Financial aid office: (701) 228-5437
Diane Christenson, Financial Aid Officer
105 Simrall Boulevard
Bottineau, ND 58318-1198

North Dakota State College of Science

Wahpeton, North Dakota
www.ndscs.nodak.edu
Two-year public **Federal Code: 002996**

College costs. Full-time tuition for Minnesota residents $2,457. Full-time tuition for South Dakota, Montana, Saskatchewan, Manitoba residents $2,228. Full-time tuition for Alaska, Colorado, Idaho, Nevada, New Mexico, Oregon, Utah, Wyoming residents $2,673.

	Living at home	On-campus
Tuition and fees (2002-2003):	$2,129	$2,129
Out-of-state:	$5,105	$5,105
Per-credit charge:	$74	$74
Per-credit out-of-state:	$198	$198
Room and board:		$3,434
Books and supplies:	$700	$700
Personal expenses:	$900	$1,850
Transportation:	$900	$900

Undergraduate aid. Need-based: Average financial aid package for full-time students was $5,200; for part-time $2,600. 42% awarded as scholarships/grants, 58% as loans/jobs. **Non-need-based:** Scholarships based on academics, athletics, job skills, music/drama, state/district residency. **Student debt:** 70% of graduating class borrowed to fund education; average debt was $6,125.

Freshman aid. Need-based: Out of 630 full-time freshmen, 548 applied for aid; 493 were judged to have need; of these 466 received aid. Average package met 85% of need. 70 students had full need met. Average scholarship/grant was $2,750; average loan $2,250. **Non-need based:** 23 full-time freshmen with need received non-need scholarships; 41 without need received awards; 45 received athletic scholarships.

Policies to reduce costs. Tuition/fee waivers for minority students, employees and their families. Credit/placement for qualifying scores on AP, CLEP examinations. Work study available nights, weekends and for part-time students.

Payment plans. Credit card, installment payment.

Application procedures. FAFSA, institutional form required. Priority date 4/15; no closing date. Applicants notified on rolling basis starting 6/1, must reply within 2 week(s) of notification.

Contact. Financial aid office: (701) 671-2207
Patrick Miller, Director of Financial Aid
800 North 6th Street
Wahpeton, ND 58076

North Dakota State University

Fargo, North Dakota
www.ndsu.edu
Four-year public **Federal Code: 002997**

College costs. Tuition for Minnesota residents: $3,381. Tuition for 20 states in Western Undergraduate Exchange and Midwest Student Exchange Program: $4,356.

	Living at home	On-campus
Tuition and fees (2002-2003):	$3,506	$3,506
Out-of-state:	$8,356	$8,356
Room and board:		$4,175
Board only:	$2,208	
Books and supplies:	$650	$650
Personal expenses:		$2,230
Transportation:		$270

Undergraduate aid. Need-based: Average financial aid package for full-time students was $5,210; for part-time $3,997. 28% awarded as scholarships/grants, 72% as loans/jobs. **Non-need-based:** 20% awarded as scholarships/grants, 80% as loans/jobs. Scholarships based on academics, alumni affiliation, art, athletics, job skills, leadership, minority status, music/drama, religious affiliation, state/district residency. **Student debt:** 69% of graduating class borrowed to fund education; average debt was $19,929.

Freshman aid. Need-based: Out of 1,796 full-time freshmen, 1,470 applied for aid; 993 were judged to have need; of these 990 received aid. Average package met 79% of need. 439 students had full need met. Average scholarship/grant was $3,365; average loan $2,690. **Non-need based:** 359 full-time freshmen with need received non-need scholarships; 328 without need received awards; 26 received athletic scholarships.

Merit scholarships. New Student Scholarships; vary in amount awarded; based on a composite ACT of at least 27 or an SAT of at least 1200, and a cumulative GPA of at least 3.5.

Policies to reduce costs. Tuition/fee waivers for children of alumni, senior citizens, minority students, employees and their families. Credit/placement for qualifying scores on AP, IB, CLEP examinations. Work study available nights and weekends.

Payment plans. Credit card payment.

Application procedures. FAFSA required. Priority date 4/15; no closing date. Applicants notified on rolling basis starting 3/15.

Contact. Financial aid office: (701) 231-7533
Robert Neas, Director of Financial Aid
PO Box 5454
Fargo, ND 58105-5454

Trinity Bible College

Ellendale, North Dakota
www.trinitybiblecollege.edu
Four-year private **Federal Code: 012059**

	Living at home	On-campus
Tuition and fees:	$10,376	$10,376
Room and board:		$4,310
Board only:	$2,120	
Books and supplies:	$660	$660
Personal expenses:	$1,602	$1,602
Transportation:	$430	$1,310

Undergraduate aid. Need-based: 44% awarded as scholarships/grants, 56% as loans/jobs. Need-based aid available for part-time students. **Non-need-based:** 43% awarded as scholarships/grants, 57% as loans/jobs. Scholarships based on academics, alumni affiliation, art, leadership, music/drama, religious affiliation.

Freshman aid. Need-based: Out of 59 full-time freshmen, 59 applied for aid; 58 were judged to have need; of these 58 received aid. Average scholarship/grant was $6,532; average loan $3,727. **Non-need based:** 1 without need received awards.

Policies to reduce costs. Tuition/fee waivers for children of alumni, family members, family of clergy, employees and their families. Tuition at time of enrollment guaranteed for 4 years; credit/placement for qualifying scores on AP, IB, CLEP examinations. Work study available nights, weekends and for part-time students.

Payment plans. Credit card, installment, deferred payment.

Application procedures. FAFSA required. Priority date 3/1; closing date 9/1. Applicants notified on rolling basis starting 3/1, must reply within 3 week(s) of notification.

Contact. **Financial aid office:** (888) 822-2329
Don Flaherty, Financial Aid Director
50 South Sixth Avenue
Ellendale, ND 58436-7150

Turtle Mountain Community College
Belcourt, North Dakota
www.tm.edu
Two-year public

	Living at home
Tuition and fees:	$1,776
Per-credit charge:	$66

Application procedures. FAFSA required. Priority date 4/15; closing date 5/1.

Contact. **Financial aid office:** (701)477-7862
Wanda LaDucer, Financial Aid Director
PO Box 340
Belcourt, ND 58316

University of Mary
Bismarck, North Dakota
www.umary.edu
Four-year private **Federal Code: 002992**

	Living at home	On-campus
Tuition and fees (2002-2003):	$9,500	$9,500
Room and board:		$3,735
Books and supplies:	$610	$610
Personal expenses:	$1,800	$1,800
Transportation:	$1,500	$1,500

Undergraduate aid. **Need-based:** Need-based aid available for full-time and part-time students. **Non-need-based:** Scholarships based on academics, athletics, state/district residency.

Merit scholarships. Presidential Merit Awards; large number awarded; ranging from $1,000-$7,000 annually, guaranteed for 4 years. Athletic and music scholarships; limited number awarded; varying amounts. Music scholarships require audition. Drama/Forensics; limited number; varying amounts.

Policies to reduce costs. Tuition/fee waivers for senior citizens, family members, employees and their families. Credit/placement for qualifying scores on AP, IB, CLEP examinations. Work study available nights, weekends and for part-time students.

Payment plans. Credit card, installment payment.

Application procedures. FAFSA required. Priority date 3/15; no closing date. Applicants notified on rolling basis starting 4/1, must reply within 2 week(s) of notification. **Transfers:** Priority date 5/1.

Contact. **Financial aid office:** (701) 255-7500 ext. 283
Dave Hanson, Director of Student Financial Aid
7500 University Drive
Bismarck, ND 58504-9652

University of North Dakota
Grand Forks, North Dakota
www.und.edu
Four-year public **Federal Code: 003005**

College costs. Tuition for Minnesota residents: $3,381. Tuition for South Dakota, Montana, Saskatchewan, Manitoba residents: $4,431.

	Living at home	On-campus
Tuition and fees (2002-2003):	$3,646	$3,646
Out-of-state:	$8,580	$8,580
Room and board:		$3,987
Board only:	$1,500	
Books and supplies:	$600	$600
Personal expenses:	$2,038	$2,038
Transportation:	$750	$750

Undergraduate aid. **Need-based:** Need-based aid available for full-time and part-time students. **Non-need-based:** Scholarships based on academics, alumni affiliation, art, athletics, job skills, leadership, minority status, music/drama, state/district residency. **Additional information:** 500 freshmen get scholarships each year ranging from $250-$2,500.

Merit scholarships. 15 freshmen will receive $2,500 a year for 4 years; they are either National Merit Finalists listing UND as first choice and in top 10% of graduating class, or in top 10% and have minimum composite of 32 on the ACT. 55 scholarships of $2,000/yr for 4 years provided to students in top 10% of graduating class who are National Merit Semifinalists or have ACT composite of 29-31. 40 students with ACT of 27-28 and in upper 10% of graduating class will receive $1,000 for their freshman year.

Policies to reduce costs. Tuition/fee waivers for minority students, employees and their families. Credit/placement for qualifying scores on AP, IB, CLEP examinations. Work study available nights, weekends and for part-time students.

Payment plans. Credit card payment.

Application procedures. FAFSA required. Priority date 4/15; no closing date. Applicants notified on rolling basis starting 5/15, must reply within 4 week(s) of notification. **Transfers:** No deadline.

Contact. **Financial aid office:** (701) 777-3121
Robin Holden, Director of Student Financial Aid
Enrollment Services
Grand Forks, ND 58202

Valley City State University
Valley City, North Dakota
www.vcsu.edu
Four-year public **Federal Code: 003008**

College costs. Full-time tuition for Minnesota residents: $2,554. Full-time tuition for South Dakota, Montana, Manitoba, Saskatchewan residents: $2,753.

	Living at home	On-campus
Tuition and fees (2002-2003):	$3,588	$3,588
Out-of-state:	$7,265	$7,265
Room and board:		$3,140
Board only:	$1,000	
Books and supplies:	$600	$600
Personal expenses:	$2,684	$2,684

Undergraduate aid. **Need-based:** Average financial aid package for full-time students was $5,204; for part-time $3,157. 37% awarded as scholarships/grants, 63% as loans/jobs. **Non-need-based:** 16% awarded as scholarships/grants, 84% as loans/jobs. Scholarships based on academics, alumni affiliation, athletics, leadership, minority status, music/drama. **Student debt:** 55% of graduating class borrowed to fund education; average debt was $15,563.

Freshman aid. **Need-based:** Out of 183 full-time freshmen, 157 applied for aid; 108 were judged to have need; of these 107 received aid. Average package met 91% of need. 61 students had full need met. Average scholarship/grant was $2,694; average loan $2,513. **Non-need based:** 40 full-time freshmen with need received non-need scholarships; 49 without need received awards; 14 received athletic scholarships.

Policies to reduce costs. Tuition/fee waivers for children of alumni, senior citizens, employees and their families. Work study available nights and weekends.

Payment plans. Credit card payment.

Application procedures. FAFSA required. Priority date 3/15; no closing date. Applicants notified on rolling basis starting 2/1, must reply within 2 week(s) of notification. **Transfers:** Priority date 4/15; no deadline.

Contact. **Financial aid office:** (701) 845-7412
Betty Schumacher, Director of Financial Aid
101 College Street Southwest
Valley City, ND 58072-4098

Williston State College

Williston, North Dakota
www.wsc.nodak.edu
Two-year public **Federal Code: 003007**

College costs. Tuition for Minnesota residents: $2,478. Tuition for South Dakota, Montana, Saskatchewan, Manitoba residents: $1,758.

	Living at home	On-campus
Tuition and fees (2002-2003):	$2,176	$2,176
Out-of-state:	$3,054	$3,054
Per-credit charge:	$68	$68
Per-credit out-of-state:	$101	$101
Room and board:		$2,320
Books and supplies:	$600	$600
Personal expenses:	$500	$500
Transportation:	$550	$550

Undergraduate aid. Need-based: Need-based aid available for full-time and part-time students. **Non-need-based:** Scholarships based on academics, athletics.

Policies to reduce costs. Tuition/fee waivers for senior citizens, minority students, employees and their families. Credit/placement for qualifying scores on AP, CLEP examinations. Work study available nights, weekends and for part-time students.

Payment plans. Credit card payment.

Application procedures. FAFSA required. Priority date 4/15; no closing date. Applicants notified on rolling basis starting 5/15. **Transfers:** Priority date 4/15.

Contact. Financial aid office: (701) 774-4244
Lynn Hagen-Aaberg, Financial Aid Director
Box 1326
Williston, ND 58802-1326

Ohio

ATS Institute of Technology
Highland Heights, Ohio
Two-year proprietary
Federal Code: 034685

College costs (projected). Cost of diploma program is $7,500 per year, including fees; associate degree program is $7,000, including fees.

Application procedures. FAFSA required. Applicants notified on rolling basis.

Contact. **Financial aid office:** (440) 449-1700
Yelena Ksendzovskiy, Financial Aid Director
230 Alpha Park
Highland Heights, OH 44143

Academy of Court Reporting
Cleveland, Ohio
Two-year proprietary
Federal Code: 015150

College costs. Court reporting machine about $1,000.

	Living at home
Tuition and fees (2002-2003):	$6,750
Books and supplies:	$1,350

Undergraduate aid. All financial aid based on need. Need-based aid available for full-time and part-time students.

Application procedures. FAFSA required. Applicants notified on rolling basis.

Contact. **Financial aid office:** (216) 861-3222
Rebecca Burney, Financial Aid Officer
614 Superior Avenue NW
Cleveland, OH 44113

Academy of Court Reporting: Akron
Akron, Ohio
Two-year proprietary
Federal Code: 021521

College costs. Court reporting machine about $1,000.

	Living at home
Tuition and fees (2002-2003):	$6,750
Books and supplies:	$1,350

Undergraduate aid. **Non-need-based:** Scholarships based on academics.

Policies to reduce costs. Work study available for part-time students.

Payment plans. Installment payment.

Application procedures. FAFSA required.

Contact. **Financial aid office:** (330) 867-4030
Lynn Fisher, Director of Financial Aid
2930 West Market Street
Akron, OH 44333

Academy of Court Reporting: Columbus
Columbus, Ohio
Two-year proprietary
Federal Code: 021521

College costs. Court reporting machine about $1,000.

	Living at home
Tuition and fees (2002-2003):	$6,750
Books and supplies:	$1,350

Policies to reduce costs. Tuition at time of enrollment guaranteed for 2 years. Work study available nights and for part-time students.

Application procedures. FAFSA required.

Contact. **Financial aid office:** (330) 867-4030
Lynn Fisher, Director of Financial Aid
630 East Broad Street
Columbus, OH 43215

Antioch College
Yellow Springs, Ohio
www.antioch-college.edu
Four-year private
Federal Code: 003010

	Living at home	On-campus
Tuition and fees (projected):	$22,450	$22,450
Room and board:		$5,770
Books and supplies:	$700	$700
Personal expenses:	$1,250	$1,250

Undergraduate aid. **Non-need-based:** Scholarships based on academics, leadership, minority status. **Additional information:** Middle Income Assistance Program provides interest-free loans to students who qualify for little or no financial aid. If student maintains constant enrollment and graduates within normal time frame, loan forgiven at commencement.

Policies to reduce costs. Tuition/fee waivers for family members, employees and their families. Credit/placement for qualifying scores on AP, IB, CLEP examinations.

Payment plans. Credit card, installment payment.

Application procedures. FAFSA, institutional form required. Priority date 3/1; no closing date. Applicants notified on rolling basis starting 4/1, must reply within 3 week(s) of notification.

Contact. **Financial aid office:** (937) 769-1000
Larry Brickman, Director of Financial Aid Services
795 Livermore Street
Yellow Springs, OH 45387

Antioch University McGregor
Yellow Springs, Ohio
www.mcgregor.edu
Upper-division private
Federal Code: E00553

	Living at home
Tuition and fees (2002-2003):	$10,665
Books and supplies:	$1,133
Transportation:	$792

Undergraduate aid. **Need-based:** Need-based aid available for full-time and part-time students.

Policies to reduce costs. Tuition/fee waivers for employees and their families. Credit/placement for qualifying scores on CLEP examinations.

Payment plans. Credit card, installment payment.

Application procedures. No deadline. Applicants notified on rolling basis.

Contact. **Financial aid office:** (937) 769-1840
Kathy John, Director of Financial Aid
800 Livermore Street
Yellow Springs, OH 45387

Antonelli College
Cincinnati, Ohio
www.antonellic.com
Two-year proprietary
Federal Code: 012891

College costs (2002-2003). Office technology program tuition is $7,725, plus fees; commercial art/interior design program tuition is $9,585, kits and fees not included; photography program tuition is $11,085, kits and fees not included.

Payment plans. Credit card, installment payment.

Application procedures. FAFSA required. No deadline. Applicants notified on rolling basis.

Contact. **Financial aid office:** (513) 241-4338
Leah Elkins, Financial Aid Director
124 East Seventh Street
Cincinnati, OH 45202

Art Academy of Cincinnati

Cincinnati, Ohio
www.artacademy.edu
Four-year private **Federal Code: 003011**

	Living at home
Tuition and fees:	$17,300
Books and supplies:	$1,200
Personal expenses:	$590
Transportation:	$1,140

Undergraduate aid. Need-based: Average financial aid package for full-time students was $8,159; for part-time $4,923. 48% awarded as scholarships/grants, 52% as loans/jobs. **Non-need-based:** 46% awarded as scholarships/grants, 54% as loans/jobs. Scholarships based on academics, alumni affiliation, art. **Additional information:** 40 annual scholarships awarded to entering and transfer students and 50 to continuing students based on spring portfolio competition.

Freshman aid. Need-based: Out of 41 full-time freshmen, 26 applied for aid; 20 were judged to have need; of these 20 received aid. Average package met 50% of need. 4 students had full need met. Average scholarship/grant was $3,772; average loan $3,223. **Non-need based:** 2 full-time freshmen with need received non-need scholarships; 8 without need received awards.

Policies to reduce costs. Tuition/fee waivers for employees and their families. Credit/placement for qualifying scores on AP examinations.

Payment plans. Credit card, installment, deferred payment.

Application procedures. FAFSA required. Priority date 4/1; no closing date. Applicants notified on rolling basis starting 3/1.

Contact. Financial aid office: (513) 562-8751
Karen Geiger, Financial Aid Director
1125 St. Gregory Street
Cincinnati, OH 45202-1700

Art Institute of Cincinnati

Cincinnati, Ohio
www.theartinstituteofcincinnati.com
Two-year proprietary **Federal Code: 014804**

	Living at home
Tuition and fees:	$13,296
Books and supplies:	$2,260

Undergraduate aid. Need-based: Average financial aid package for full-time students was $3,905. **Student debt:** 75% of graduating class borrowed to fund education; average debt was $8,915.

Policies to reduce costs. Tuition at time of enrollment guaranteed for 2 years.

Payment plans. Credit card, installment payment.

Application procedures. FAFSA required. No deadline. Applicants notified on rolling basis starting 9/1, must reply within 1 week(s) of notification. **Transfers:** No deadline.

Contact. Financial aid office: (513) 751-1206
Ennis Jones, Financial Aid Director
1171 East Kemper Road
Cincinatti, OH 45246

Ashland University

Ashland, Ohio
www.ashland.edu
Four-year private **Federal Code: 003012**

	Living at home	On-campus
Tuition and fees (2002-2003):	$17,270	$17,270
Room and board:		$6,212
Board only:	$1,695	
Books and supplies:	$1,000	$1,000
Personal expenses:	$1,461	$1,461
Transportation:	$1,531	$429

Undergraduate aid. Need-based: Average financial aid package for full-time students was $15,818; for part-time $7,560. 61% awarded as scholarships/grants, 39% as loans/jobs. **Non-need-based:** 67% awarded as scholarships/grants, 33% as loans/jobs. Scholarships based on academics, alumni affiliation, art, athletics, job skills, leadership, minority status, music/drama, religious affiliation. **Student debt:** 75% of graduating class borrowed to fund education; average debt was $18,250.

Freshman aid. Need-based: Out of 558 full-time freshmen, 557 applied for aid; 447 were judged to have need; of these 447 received aid. Average package met 90% of need. Average scholarship/grant was $11,396; average loan $3,530. **Non-need based:** 81 without need received awards; 16 received athletic scholarships.

Merit scholarships. Presidential Scholarships for selected applicants with a GPA of 3.75-4.0 and an ACT score from 29-36 or SAT score from 1270-1600, $6,000; GPA of 3.5-3.74 and ACT score from 26-28 or SAT score from 1160-1260, $5,000; GPA of 3.25-3.49 and ACT score from 23-25 or SAT score from 1060-1150, $4,000. Achievement Scholarships for selected applicants with a GPA of 3.0-3.24 and ACT score from 21-22 or SAT score from 970-1050; $2,000.

Policies to reduce costs. Tuition/fee waivers for children of alumni, family members, family of clergy, employees and their families. Credit/placement for qualifying scores on AP, IB, CLEP examinations. Work study available nights and weekends.

Payment plans. Credit card, installment payment.

Application procedures. FAFSA, institutional form required. Priority date 3/15; no closing date. Applicants notified on rolling basis starting 3/15, must reply within 3 week(s) of notification.

Contact. Financial aid office: (419) 289-5002
Stephen Howell, Director of Financial Aid
401 College Avenue
Ashland, OH 44805-9981

Baldwin-Wallace College

Berea, Ohio
www.bw.edu
Four-year private **Federal Code: 003014**

College costs. Conservatory tuition is $20,018.

	Living at home	On-campus
Tuition and fees:	$18,478	$18,478
Room and board:		$6,200
Board only:	$1,323	
Books and supplies:	$798	$798
Personal expenses:	$1,520	$2,300
Transportation:	$1,000	$500

Undergraduate aid. Need-based: Average financial aid package for full-time students was $14,893; for part-time $7,340. 51% awarded as scholarships/grants, 49% as loans/jobs. **Non-need-based:** 54% awarded as scholarships/grants, 46% as loans/jobs. Scholarships based on academics, alumni affiliation, art, leadership, minority status, music/drama, religious affiliation, state/district residency. **Student debt:** 61% of graduating class borrowed to fund education; average debt was $13,688.

Freshman aid. Need-based: Out of 734 full-time freshmen, 669 applied for aid; 549 were judged to have need; of these 549 received aid. Average package met 88% of need. 411 students had full need met. Average scholarship/grant was $6,504; average loan $3,452. **Non-need based:** 509 full-time freshmen with need received non-need scholarships; 173 without need received awards.

Merit scholarships. Presidential Scholarship for all students who graduate in top 5% of high school class and whose test scores and GPA show very strong academic ability; up to $16,500. Trustees Scholarship for all students with cumulative GPA of at least 3.0 or who rank in top 25% of high school class or have minimum 24 ACT or 1100 SAT score; up to $10,500. Griffiths Scholarship for conservatory students who demonstrate outstanding musicianship and talent; up to $4,000. Heritage Award for multicultural students who graduate in top 25% of high school class or have minimum 24 ACT or 1100 SAT score or GPA of 3.0 or higher; up to $4,000. Conservatory merit award for talented conservatory students with financial need. Alumni Scholarship automatically awarded to children and grandchildren of alumni; up to $2,000. Sibling award for full-time student siblings; up to $1,000. Ministerial award for dependent students of qualified ordained United Methodist ministers; up to half tuition.

Policies to reduce costs. Tuition/fee waivers for children of alumni, family of clergy, employees and their families. Credit/placement for qualifying scores on AP, CLEP examinations.

Payment plans. Credit card, installment payment.

Application procedures. FAFSA required. Priority date 5/1; closing date 9/1. Applicants notified on rolling basis starting 2/14, must reply by 5/1 or within 4 week(s) of notification. **Transfers:** Priority date 7/1; closing date 9/15.

Contact. **Financial aid office:** (440) 826-2108
George Rolleston, Director of Financial Aid
275 Eastland Road
Berea, OH 44017-2088

Bluffton College

Bluffton, Ohio
www.bluffton.edu
Four-year private **Federal Code: 003016**

	Living at home	On-campus
Tuition and fees (projected):	$16,730	$16,730
Room and board:		$5,636
Books and supplies:	$500	$500
Personal expenses:	$800	$700
Transportation:	$700	

Undergraduate aid. **Need-based:** Average financial aid package for full-time students was $15,795; for part-time $9,108. 55% awarded as scholarships/grants, 45% as loans/jobs. **Non-need-based:** 70% awarded as scholarships/grants, 30% as loans/jobs. Scholarships based on academics, art, job skills, leadership, minority status. **Student debt:** 69% of graduating class borrowed to fund education; average debt was $20,214. **Additional information:** Tuition Equalization Scholarship Program guarantees qualified students nonrepayable financial aid at least equal to difference between Bluffton College tuition and average tuition at the 3 Ohio public universities with highest tuition. Requirements: minimum 23 ACT or 1050 SAT and rank in top 25% of high school class or 3.0 GPA.

Freshman aid. **Need-based:** Out of 263 full-time freshmen, 248 applied for aid; 229 were judged to have need; of these 229 received aid. Average package met 93% of need. 103 students had full need met. Average scholarship/grant was $12,477; average loan $3,335. **Non-need based:** 30 full-time freshmen with need received non-need scholarships; 30 without need received awards.

Merit scholarships. Academic merit scholarship; tuition equalization scholarship plus $1,000; minimum 3.5 GPA, 25 ACT or 1140 SAT. Academic honors scholarship; TES plus $2,000; minimum 27 ACT or 1220 SAT.

Policies to reduce costs. Tuition/fee waivers for minority students, family of clergy, employees and their families. Credit/placement for qualifying scores on AP, CLEP examinations. Work study available nights, weekends and for part-time students.

Payment plans. Credit card, installment, deferred payment.

Application procedures. FAFSA required. Priority date 5/1; closing date 10/1. Applicants notified on rolling basis starting 3/1, must reply within 3 week(s) of notification. **Transfers:** Institutional non-need based aid for transfer students based on test scores in combination with work at previous institutions or high school academic performance or both.

Contact. **Financial aid office:** (419) 358-3266
Lawrence Matthews, Director of Financial Aid
280 West College Avenue, Suite 1
Bluffton, OH 45817-1196

Bohecker's Business College

Ravenna, Ohio
www.boheckers.com
Two-year proprietary **Federal Code: 016270**

	Living at home
Tuition and fees (2002-2003):	$7,888
Per-credit charge:	$156

Undergraduate aid. All financial aid based on need. Need-based aid available for full-time and part-time students.

Application procedures. FAFSA required. Applicants notified on rolling basis.

Contact. **Financial aid office:** (330) 297-7319
Trudy Young, Financial Aid Director
326 East Main Street
Ravenna, OH 44266

Bowling Green State University

Bowling Green, Ohio
www.bgsu.edu
Four-year public **Federal Code: 003018**

College costs. Campus residents pay $184 residential technology fee.

	Living at home	On-campus
Tuition and fees (2002-2003):	$6,742	$6,742
Out-of-state:	$13,370	$13,370
Room and board:		$6,720
Books and supplies:	$842	$842
Personal expenses:	$1,786	$1,532
Transportation:	$1,834	$610

Undergraduate aid. **Need-based:** Average financial aid package for full-time students was $6,122. 29% awarded as scholarships/grants, 71% as loans/jobs. Need-based aid available for part-time students. **Non-need-based:** 42% awarded as scholarships/grants, 58% as loans/jobs. Scholarships based on academics, alumni affiliation, art, athletics, leadership, minority status, music/drama, state/district residency.

Freshman aid. **Need-based:** Out of 3,586 full-time freshmen, 2,870 applied for aid; 2,116 were judged to have need; of these 2,112 received aid. Average package met 65% of need. 663 students had full need met. Average scholarship/grant was $2,910; average loan $2,594. **Non-need based:** 1,477 full-time freshmen with need received non-need scholarships; 1,158 without need received awards; 81 received athletic scholarships.

Policies to reduce costs. Tuition/fee waivers for senior citizens, employees and their families. Credit/placement for qualifying scores on AP, CLEP examinations.

Payment plans. Credit card, installment payment.

Application procedures. FAFSA required. No deadline. Applicants notified on rolling basis starting 4/15, must reply within 3 week(s) of notification. **Transfers:** No deadline.

Contact. **Financial aid office:** (419) 372-2651
Conrad McRoberts, Director
110 McFall Center
Bowling Green, OH 43403-0085

Bowling Green State University: Firelands College

Huron, Ohio
www.firelands.bgsu.edu
Two-year public **Federal Code: 003018**

	Living at home
Tuition and fees (2002-2003):	$3,626
Out-of-state:	$10,254
Per-credit charge:	$169
Per-credit out-of-state:	$485
Books and supplies:	$728
Personal expenses:	$2,026
Transportation:	$1,306

Undergraduate aid. All financial aid based on need. 33% awarded as scholarships/grants, 67% as loans/jobs. Need-based aid available for part-time students. **Additional information:** Scholarship application deadline May 1. Technology computer loan program available. Based on need, students may receive computer on semester by semester loan basis.

Policies to reduce costs. Tuition/fee waivers for senior citizens, employees and their families. Credit/placement for qualifying scores on AP, CLEP examinations. Work study available for part-time students.

Payment plans. Credit card, installment payment.

Application procedures. FAFSA required. Priority date 3/1; no closing date. Applicants notified on rolling basis starting 4/15, must reply within 2 week(s) of notification. **Transfers:** No deadline.

Contact. **Financial aid office:** (419) 433-5560
Debralee Divers, Director of Admissions and Financial Aid
One University Drive
Huron, OH 44839

Bradford School

Columbus, Ohio
www.bradfordschoolcolumbus.com
Two-year proprietary **Federal Code: 016474**

	Living at home	On-campus
Tuition and fees (2002-2003):	$9,960	$9,960
Room only:		$4,520
Books and supplies:	$900	$900

Undergraduate aid. All financial aid based on need. Need-based aid available for full-time students.

Policies to reduce costs. Tuition/fee waivers for employees and their families. Tuition at time of enrollment guaranteed for 2 years.

Payment plans. Credit card, installment payment.

Application procedures. FAFSA required. No deadline. Applicants notified on rolling basis.

Contact. **Financial aid office:** (614) 416-6200
Julie Freidner, Director of Financial Aid
2469 Stelzer Road
Columbus, OH 43219

Bryant & Stratton College

Cleveland, Ohio
www.bryantstratton.edu
Two-year proprietary **Federal Code: 009343**

	Living at home	On-campus
Tuition and fees (2002-2003):	$10,100	$10,100
Per-credit charge:	$330	$330
Room only:		$3,200
Books and supplies:	$1,000	$1,000
Personal expenses:	$1,384	$1,384
Transportation:	$1,107	$1,107

Undergraduate aid. Need-based: Average financial aid package for full-time students was $4,803; for part-time $3,066. 52% awarded as scholarships/grants, 48% as loans/jobs. **Non-need-based:** Scholarships based on academics. **Student debt:** 83% of graduating class borrowed to fund education; average debt was $13,906.

Freshman aid. Need-based: Out of 59 full-time freshmen, 59 applied for aid; 59 were judged to have need; of these 59 received aid. Average package met 98% of need. 59 students had full need met. Average scholarship/grant was $3,506; average loan $1,718. **Non-need based:** 2 full-time freshmen with need received non-need scholarships.

Policies to reduce costs. Tuition/fee waivers for employees and their families. Work study available nights.

Payment plans. Credit card, installment payment.

Application procedures. FAFSA, institutional form required. Priority date 9/1; closing date 10/31. Applicants notified on rolling basis starting 5/1, must reply within 2 week(s) of notification. **Transfers:** No deadline. By state regulation, Ohio Institutional Grant can be awarded only 3 times a fiscal year.

Contact. **Financial aid office:** (216) 771-1700
Scott Heers, Director of Financial Services
1700 East 13th Street
Cleveland, OH 44114-3203

Bryant & Stratton College: Cleveland West

Parma, Ohio
www.bryantstratton.edu
Two-year proprietary **Federal Code: 015298**

	Living at home
Tuition and fees (2002-2003):	$10,100
Per-credit charge:	$296
Board only:	$1,176
Books and supplies:	$1,050
Personal expenses:	$747
Transportation:	$360

Undergraduate aid. All financial aid based on need. Average financial aid package for full-time students was $10,865; for part-time $5,182. 50% awarded as scholarships/grants, 50% as loans/jobs. **Additional information:** Competitive and matching scholarships offered to high school seniors.

Freshman aid. Out of 89 full-time freshmen, 87 applied for aid; 78 were judged to have need; of these 76 received aid. Average package met 58% of need. Average scholarship/grant was $2,491; average loan $2,221.

Policies to reduce costs. Tuition/fee waivers for employees and their families. Work study available nights and for part-time students.

Payment plans. Credit card, installment payment.

Application procedures. FAFSA required. No deadline. Applicants notified on rolling basis starting 6/1. **Transfers:** Transfer form must be completed for state grant.

Contact. **Financial aid office:** (216) 265-3151
Donna McCullough, Financial Aid Supervisor
12955 Snow Road
Parma, OH 44130-1013

Bryant & Stratton College: Willoughby Hills

Willoughby Hills, Ohio
www.bryantstratton.edu
Two-year proprietary **Federal Code: 022744**

	Living at home
Tuition and fees (2002-2003):	$10,100
Per-credit charge:	$330
Books and supplies:	$1,000
Transportation:	$400

Undergraduate aid. Need-based: Average financial aid package for full-time students was $18,464; for part-time $9,232. 70% awarded as scholarships/grants, 30% as loans/jobs. **Non-need-based:** Scholarships based on academics, athletics. **Student debt:** 95% of graduating class borrowed to fund education; average debt was $14,125.

Freshman aid. Need-based: Out of 48 full-time freshmen, 46 applied for aid; 44 were judged to have need; of these 42 received aid. Average package met 75% of need. 32 students had full need met. **Non-need based:** 4 without need received awards.

Policies to reduce costs. Tuition/fee waivers for employees and their families.

Payment plans. Installment payment.

Application procedures. FAFSA, institutional form required. No deadline. Applicants notified on rolling basis.

Contact. **Financial aid office:** (216) 771-1700
Scott Heers, Financial Aid Director
27557 Chardon Road
Willoughby Hills, OH 44092

Capital University

Columbus, Ohio
www.capital.edu
Four-year private **Federal Code: 003023**

	Living at home	On-campus
Tuition and fees (2002-2003):	$18,980	$18,980
Room and board:		$5,950
Board only:	$2,453	
Books and supplies:	$900	$900
Personal expenses:	$1,834	$1,724
Transportation:	$883	$546

Undergraduate aid. Need-based: Need-based aid available for full-time and part-time students. **Non-need-based:** Scholarships based on academics, alumni affiliation, art, leadership, minority status, music/drama, religious affiliation, state/district residency.

Merit scholarships. Scholarships and grants from $1,000 to full tuition available. Transfer students also eligible for scholarships.

Policies to reduce costs. Tuition/fee waivers for family members, family of clergy, employees and their families. Credit/placement for qualifying scores on AP, CLEP examinations. Work study available nights and weekends.

Payment plans. Installment payment.

Application procedures. FAFSA required. Priority date 2/28; no closing date. Applicants notified on rolling basis starting 3/15, must reply by 5/1 or within 2 week(s) of notification. **Transfers:** Priority date 7/15.

Contact. **Financial aid office:** (614) 236-6926
June Schlabach, Director of Financial Aid and Student Employment
2199 East Main Street
Columbus, OH 43209-2394

Case Western Reserve University

Cleveland, Ohio
www.cwru.edu
Four-year private **Federal Code: E00077**

College costs. Campus residents pay additional $400 technology fee.

	Living at home	On-campus
Tuition and fees (2002-2003):	$22,730	$22,730
Room and board:		$6,750
Board only:	$2,575	
Books and supplies:	$780	$780
Personal expenses:	$1,215	$1,215
Transportation:	$800	

Undergraduate aid. Need-based: Average financial aid package for full-time students was $21,815. 72% awarded as scholarships/grants, 28% as loans/jobs. Need-based aid available for part-time students. **Non-need-based:** 87% awarded as scholarships/grants, 13% as loans/jobs. Scholarships based on academics, art, leadership, music/drama. **Student debt:** 53% of graduating class borrowed to fund education; average debt was $21,830.

Freshman aid. Need-based: Out of 836 full-time freshmen, 675 applied for aid; 525 were judged to have need; of these 525 received aid. Average package met 98% of need. 508 students had full need met. Average scholarship/grant was $15,865; average loan $4,404. **Non-need based:** 463 full-time freshmen with need received non-need scholarships; 231 without need received awards.

Merit scholarships. More than 400 full- and partial-tuition merit scholarships awarded each year.

Policies to reduce costs. Tuition/fee waivers for employees and their families. Credit/placement for qualifying scores on AP, IB examinations.

Payment plans. Credit card, installment payment.

Application procedures. FAFSA, CSS PROFILE required. Priority date 2/1; closing date 4/15. Applicants notified on rolling basis starting 3/15, must reply by 5/1 or within 2 week(s) of notification. Early decision closing date 1/1. **Transfers:** Priority date 5/15; no deadline. Transfers not eligible for CWRU merit-based scholarships.

Contact. Financial aid office: (216) 368-4530
Donald Chenelle, Director of University Financial Aid
Tomlinson Hall
Cleveland, OH 44106

Cedarville University

Cedarville, Ohio
www.cedarville.edu
Four-year private **Federal Code: 003025**

	Living at home	On-campus
Tuition and fees (projected):	$14,010	$14,010
Room and board:		$5,010
Board only:	$2,326	
Books and supplies:	$740	$740
Personal expenses:	$1,050	$1,050

Undergraduate aid. Need-based: Average financial aid package for full-time students was $10,750; for part-time $7,067. 34% awarded as scholarships/grants, 66% as loans/jobs. **Non-need-based:** 72% awarded as scholarships/grants, 28% as loans/jobs. Scholarships based on academics, athletics, leadership, minority status, music/drama.

Freshman aid. Need-based: Out of 857 full-time freshmen, 698 applied for aid; 539 were judged to have need; of these 537 received aid. Average package met 28% of need. 218 students had full need met. Average scholarship/grant was $1,139; average loan $2,309. **Non-need based:** 462 full-time freshmen with need received non-need scholarships; 240 without need received awards; 29 received athletic scholarships.

Policies to reduce costs. Tuition/fee waivers for children of alumni, senior citizens, employees and their families. Prepayment discount; credit/placement for qualifying scores on AP, IB, CLEP examinations. Work study available nights, weekends and for part-time students.

Payment plans. Installment, deferred payment.

Application procedures. FAFSA, institutional form required. Priority date 3/1; no closing date. Applicants notified on rolling basis starting 3/1, must reply within 4 week(s) of notification. **Transfers:** No deadline.

Contact. Financial aid office: (937) 766-7866
Fred Merritt, Director of Financial Aid
251 North Main Street
Cedarville, OH 45314

Central Ohio Technical College

Newark, Ohio
www.newarkcolleges.com/cotc/index.asp
Two-year public **Federal Code: 011046**

	Living at home
Tuition and fees (2002-2003):	$2,904
Out-of-state:	$5,064
Per-credit charge:	$60
Per-credit out-of-state:	$120
Board only:	$1,215
Books and supplies:	$990
Personal expenses:	$2,475
Transportation:	$1,708

Undergraduate aid. All financial aid based on need. Average financial aid package for full-time students was $5,379; for part-time $4,206. 45% awarded as scholarships/grants, 55% as loans/jobs. **Student debt:** 60% of graduating class borrowed to fund education; average debt was $8,084.

Freshman aid. Out of 174 full-time freshmen, 165 applied for aid; 141 were judged to have need; of these 138 received aid. Average scholarship/grant was $3,710; average loan $2,158.

Policies to reduce costs. Tuition/fee waivers for senior citizens, employees and their families. Credit/placement for qualifying scores on CLEP examinations.

Payment plans. Credit card, deferred payment.

Application procedures. FAFSA required. Priority date 4/1; no closing date. Applicants notified on rolling basis starting 5/1, must reply within 3 week(s) of notification. **Transfers:** Priority date 4/1; no deadline.

Contact. Financial aid office: (740) 366-9435
Faith Phillips, Director of Financial Aid
1179 University Drive
Newark, OH 43055

Central State University

Wilberforce, Ohio
www.centralstate.edu
Four-year public **Federal Code: 003026**

	Living at home	On-campus
Tuition and fees (projected):	$4,044	$4,044
Out-of-state:	$8,757	$8,757
Room and board:		$5,727
Board only:	$2,532	
Books and supplies:	$840	$840
Personal expenses:	$933	$933
Transportation:	$648	$648

Undergraduate aid. Need-based: Need-based aid available for full-time and part-time students. **Non-need-based:** Scholarships based on academics, alumni affiliation, art, athletics, leadership, music/drama, religious affiliation.

Policies to reduce costs. Tuition/fee waivers for senior citizens, employees and their families. Credit/placement for qualifying scores on CLEP examinations. Work study available nights, weekends and for part-time students.

Payment plans. Credit card, installment payment.

Application procedures. FAFSA, institutional form required. Priority date 2/15; closing date 8/1. Applicants notified on rolling basis starting 5/1. **Transfers:** No deadline.

Contact. Financial aid office: (937) 376-6579
Veronica Leech, Director of Financial Aid
PO Box 1004
Wilberforce, OH 45384-1004

Chatfield College

St. Martin, Ohio
www.chatfield.edu
Two-year private **Federal Code: 010880**

	Living at home
Tuition and fees (projected):	$6,880
Per-credit charge:	$225
Books and supplies:	$650
Personal expenses:	$1,922
Transportation:	$765

Undergraduate aid. Need-based: Need-based aid available for full-time and part-time students. **Non-need-based:** Scholarships based on academics, leadership. **Additional information:** Institutional grants/scholarships given primarily to first-year students to reduce debt load during initial year.

Policies to reduce costs. Tuition/fee waivers for senior citizens, employees and their families. Credit/placement for qualifying scores on CLEP examinations. Work study available for part-time students.

Payment plans. Credit card, installment, deferred payment.

Application procedures. FAFSA, institutional form required. Priority date 4/25; closing date 8/7. Applicants notified on rolling basis starting 4/1, must reply within 2 week(s) of notification.

Contact. Financial aid office: (513) 875-3344
Rebecca Cluxton, Director of Financial Aid
20918 State Route 251
St. Martin, OH 45118

Cincinnati Bible College and Seminary

Cincinnati, Ohio
www.cincybible.edu
Four-year private **Federal Code: 003029**

	Living at home	On-campus
Tuition and fees (projected):	$7,730	$7,730
Room and board:		$4,740
Books and supplies:	$600	$600
Personal expenses:	$1,950	$1,950
Transportation:	$1,488	$620

Undergraduate aid. Need-based: Need-based aid available for full-time and part-time students.

Policies to reduce costs. Tuition/fee waivers for senior citizens, family members, employees and their families. Prepayment discount; credit/placement for qualifying scores on AP, CLEP examinations.

Payment plans. Credit card, installment payment.

Application procedures. Institutional form required. Priority date 5/1; closing date 9/1. Must reply within 2 week(s) of notification.

Contact. Financial aid office: (513) 244-8100
Carrie Derico, Director of Financial Aid
Box 43200
Cincinnati, OH 45204-3200

Cincinnati College of Mortuary Science

Cincinnati, Ohio
www.ccms.edu
Four-year private **Federal Code: 010906**

	Living at home
Tuition and fees:	$11,875
Books and supplies:	$900
Personal expenses:	$375
Transportation:	$750

Undergraduate aid. All financial aid based on need. Need-based aid available for full-time and part-time students.

Payment plans. Credit card payment.

Application procedures. FAFSA required. Priority date 7/1; no closing date. Applicants notified on rolling basis starting 3/1, must reply within 2 week(s) of notification.

Contact. Financial aid office: (513) 761-2020
Patsy Leon, Financial Aid/Admissions Officer
645 West North Bend Road
Cincinnati, OH 45224-1428

Cincinnati State Technical and Community College

Cincinnati, Ohio
www.cincinnatistate.edu
Two-year public **Federal Code: 010345**

	Living at home
Tuition and fees (2002-2003):	$2,943
Out-of-state:	$5,868
Per-credit charge:	$65
Per-credit out-of-state:	$130
Books and supplies:	$1,200
Personal expenses:	$1,200
Transportation:	$1,500

Undergraduate aid. All financial aid based on need. 70% awarded as scholarships/grants, 30% as loans/jobs. Need-based aid available for part-time students.

Policies to reduce costs. Tuition/fee waivers for senior citizens, employees and their families. Credit/placement for qualifying scores on AP, CLEP examinations. Work study available nights, weekends and for part-time students.

Payment plans. Credit card, installment, deferred payment.

Application procedures. FAFSA required. Priority date 2/15; no closing date. Applicants notified on rolling basis starting 3/15, must reply within 4 week(s) of notification. **Transfers:** No deadline.

Contact. Financial aid office: (513) 569-1530
Dawnia Reck, Director of Student Financial Aid/Scholarships
3520 Central Parkway
Cincinnati, OH 45223-2690

Circleville Bible College

Circleville, Ohio
www.biblecollege.edu
Four-year private **Federal Code: 003030**

	Living at home	On-campus
Tuition and fees (2002-2003):	$8,796	$8,796
Room and board:		$5,098
Books and supplies:	$500	$500
Personal expenses:	$2,606	$1,506
Transportation:	$1,700	$500

Undergraduate aid. Additional information: Religious affiliation tuition discount.

Policies to reduce costs. Tuition/fee waivers for senior citizens, family of clergy, employees and their families. Credit/placement for qualifying scores on AP, CLEP examinations.

Payment plans. Installment payment.

Application procedures. FAFSA, institutional form, CSS PROFILE required. Priority date 4/17; no closing date. Applicants notified on rolling basis starting 5/1, must reply within 2 week(s) of notification. **Transfers:** No deadline.

Contact. Financial aid office: (800) 701-0222
Mike McMurray, Director of Financial Aid
1476 Lancaster Pike
Circleville, OH 43113

Clark State Community College

Springfield, Ohio
www.clark.cc.oh.us
Two-year public **Federal Code: 004852**

	Living at home
Tuition and fees (2002-2003):	$3,102
Out-of-state:	$5,622
Per-credit charge:	$58
Per-credit out-of-state:	$114
Books and supplies:	$800
Personal expenses:	$550
Transportation:	$700

Policies to reduce costs. Tuition/fee waivers for senior citizens, employees and their families. Credit/placement for qualifying scores on CLEP examinations.

Payment plans. Credit card, deferred payment.

Application procedures. FAFSA required. Priority date 6/15; no closing date. Applicants notified on rolling basis. **Transfers:** No deadline.

Contact. **Financial aid office:** (937) 328-6034
Director of Financial Aid
Box 570
Springfield, OH 45501

Cleveland Institute of Art

Cleveland, Ohio
www.cia.edu
Five-year private **Federal Code: 003982**

	Living at home	On-campus
Tuition and fees (2002-2003):	$21,024	$21,024
Room and board:		$6,276
Board only:	$875	
Books and supplies:	$1,100	$1,100
Personal expenses:	$1,030	$1,030
Transportation:	$1,606	$536

Undergraduate aid. Need-based: Average financial aid package for full-time students was $13,692; for part-time $7,421. 52% awarded as scholarships/grants, 48% as loans/jobs. **Non-need-based:** 53% awarded as scholarships/grants, 47% as loans/jobs. Scholarships based on academics, art. **Student debt:** 96% of graduating class borrowed to fund education; average debt was $32,500.

Freshman aid. Need-based: Average package met 66% of need. Average scholarship/grant was $9,159; average loan $3,462. **Non-need based:** 28 without need received awards.

Policies to reduce costs. Tuition/fee waivers for employees and their families. Credit/placement for qualifying scores on AP, IB, CLEP examinations. Work study available nights, weekends and for part-time students.

Payment plans. Credit card payment.

Application procedures. FAFSA, institutional form required. Priority date 3/15; no closing date. Applicants notified on rolling basis starting 3/16, must reply within 4 week(s) of notification. **Transfers:** Priority date 3/15; no deadline.

Contact. **Financial aid office:** (216) 421-7425
Helen Suchy, Director Financial Aid
11141 East Boulevard
Cleveland, OH 44106

Cleveland Institute of Electronics

Cleveland, Ohio
www.cie-wc.edu
Two-year proprietary **Federal Code: 015382**

College costs (2002-2003). Tuition $3,290 per calendar year, two 24-week terms.

Policies to reduce costs. Prepayment discount.

Payment plans. Credit card, installment, deferred payment.

Application procedures. No deadline.

Contact. **Financial aid office:** (216) 781-9400
Marites Capistrano, Director of Financial Aid
1776 East 17th Street
Cleveland, OH 44114-3679

Cleveland Institute of Music

Cleveland, Ohio
www.cim.edu
Four-year private **Federal Code: 003031**

	Living at home	On-campus
Tuition and fees (2002-2003):	$21,445	$21,445
Room and board:		$6,675
Books and supplies:	$900	$900
Personal expenses:	$900	$900
Transportation:	$800	$800

Undergraduate aid. Need-based: Need-based aid available for full-time and part-time students.

Policies to reduce costs. Credit/placement for qualifying scores on AP examinations.

Payment plans. Credit card payment.

Application procedures. FAFSA, institutional form, CSS PROFILE required. Priority date 2/15; no closing date. Applicants notified on rolling basis starting 4/1, must reply by 5/1 or within 2 week(s) of notification.

Contact. **Financial aid office:** (216) 791-500 ext. 262
Beverly Dalheim, Director of Financial Aid
11021 East Boulevard
Cleveland, OH 44106

Cleveland State University

Cleveland, Ohio
www.csuohio.edu
Four-year public **Federal Code: 003032**

	Living at home	On-campus
Tuition and fees (2002-2003):	$5,496	$5,496
Out-of-state:	$10,843	$10,843
Room and board:		$5,880
Board only:	$2,214	
Books and supplies:	$800	$800
Personal expenses:	$1,824	$1,824
Transportation:	$852	$852

Undergraduate aid. Need-based: Average financial aid package for full-time students was $6,557; for part-time $5,487. 38% awarded as scholarships/grants, 62% as loans/jobs. **Non-need-based:** 19% awarded as scholarships/grants, 81% as loans/jobs. Scholarships based on academics, alumni affiliation, art, athletics, job skills, leadership, minority status, music/drama, religious affiliation, state/district residency.

Freshman aid. Need-based: Out of 946 full-time freshmen, 707 applied for aid; 642 were judged to have need; of these 642 received aid. Average package met 50% of need. 19 students had full need met. Average scholarship/grant was $4,718; average loan $2,751. **Non-need based:** 8 full-time freshmen with need received non-need scholarships; 105 without need received awards; 19 received athletic scholarships.

Policies to reduce costs. Tuition/fee waivers for senior citizens, employees and their families. Credit/placement for qualifying scores on AP, IB, CLEP examinations.

Payment plans. Credit card, installment, deferred payment.

Application procedures. FAFSA required. Priority date 2/15; no closing date. Applicants notified on rolling basis starting 4/1, must reply within 4 week(s) of notification.

Contact. **Financial aid office:** (888) 278-6446
Judy Richards, Director of Financial Aid
Rhodes Tower West, Room 204, 1983 East 24th Street
Cleveland, OH 44115-2403

College of Art Advertising

Cincinnati, Ohio
Two-year proprietary **Federal Code: 015963**

	Living at home
Tuition and fees (projected):	$6,855

Undergraduate aid. Need-based: Need-based aid available for full-time and part-time students.

Application procedures. FAFSA required. No deadline.

Contact. **Financial aid office:** (513) 574-1010
Gary Lay, General Manager / Director of Financial Aid
4343 Bridgetown Road
Cincinnati, OH 45211-4427

College of Mount St. Joseph

Cincinnati, Ohio
www.msj.edu
Four-year private **Federal Code: 003033**

	Living at home	On-campus
Tuition and fees (2002-2003):	$15,840	$15,840
Room and board:		$5,470
Books and supplies:	$600	$600
Personal expenses:	$600	$600
Transportation:	$900	$400

Undergraduate aid. Need-based: Average financial aid package for full-time students was $11,200; for part-time $1,480. 61% awarded as scholarships/grants, 39% as loans/jobs. **Non-need-based:** 57% awarded as scholarships/grants, 43% as loans/jobs. Scholarships based on academics, state/district residency. **Student debt:** 80% of graduating class borrowed to fund education; average debt was $8,900.

Freshman aid. Need-based: Out of 268 full-time freshmen, 267 applied for aid; 188 were judged to have need; of these 188 received aid. Average package met 90% of need. 67 students had full need met. Average scholarship/grant was $7,906; average loan $1,652. **Non-need based:** 16 full-time freshmen with need received non-need scholarships; 80 without need received awards.

Policies to reduce costs. Tuition/fee waivers for employees and their families. Credit/placement for qualifying scores on AP, CLEP examinations. Work study available nights and weekends.

Payment plans. Credit card, installment payment.

Application procedures. FAFSA required. Priority date 3/1; no closing date. Applicants notified on rolling basis starting 2/15, must reply by 5/1 or within 4 week(s) of notification. **Transfers:** No deadline.

Contact. Financial aid office: (513) 244-4418
Kathryn Kelly, Director of Financial Aid
5701 Delhi Road
Cincinnati, OH 45233-1672

College of Wooster

Wooster, Ohio
www.wooster.edu
Four-year private **Federal Code: 003037**

	Living at home	On-campus
Tuition and fees (2002-2003):	$23,840	$23,840
Room and board:		$5,960
Board only:	$1,500	
Books and supplies:	$700	$700
Personal expenses:	$600	$600
Transportation:	$150	$150

Undergraduate aid. Need-based: Average financial aid package for full-time students was $20,629; for part-time $4,500. 78% awarded as scholarships/grants, 22% as loans/jobs. **Non-need-based:** 78% awarded as scholarships/grants, 22% as loans/jobs. Scholarships based on academics, leadership, minority status, music/drama, religious affiliation, state/district residency.

Freshman aid. Need-based: Out of 512 full-time freshmen, 407 applied for aid; 334 were judged to have need; of these 334 received aid. Average package met 98% of need. 221 students had full need met. Average scholarship/grant was $15,481; average loan $3,760. **Non-need based:** 65 full-time freshmen with need received non-need scholarships; 170 without need received awards.

Policies to reduce costs. Tuition/fee waivers for employees and their families. Credit/placement for qualifying scores on AP, IB examinations.

Payment plans. Credit card, installment, deferred payment.

Application procedures. FAFSA, institutional form, CSS PROFILE required. Priority date 2/15; no closing date. Applicants notified by 3/15, must reply by 5/1. Early decision closing date 12/1.

Contact. Financial aid office: (330) 263-2317
David Miller, Director of Financial Aid
847 College Avenue
Wooster, OH 44691-2363

Columbus College of Art and Design

Columbus, Ohio
www.ccad.edu
Four-year private **Federal Code: 003039**

	Living at home	On-campus
Tuition and fees (2002-2003):	$17,480	$17,480
Room and board:		$6,300
Board only:	$3,000	
Books and supplies:	$3,000	$3,000
Personal expenses:	$650	$875
Transportation:	$800	$900

Undergraduate aid. Need-based: Average financial aid package for full-time students was $11,226; for part-time $7,722. 58% awarded as scholarships/grants, 42% as loans/jobs. **Non-need-based:** 49% awarded as scholarships/grants, 51% as loans/jobs. Scholarships based on academics, art, state/district residency.

Freshman aid. Need-based: Average package met 65% of need. Average scholarship/grant was $9,027; average loan $4,054.

Policies to reduce costs. Tuition/fee waivers for senior citizens, employees and their families. Credit/placement for qualifying scores on AP examinations. Work study available nights, weekends and for part-time students.

Payment plans. Credit card, installment payment.

Application procedures. FAFSA, institutional form required. Priority date 3/3; closing date 6/2. Applicants notified on rolling basis starting 6/15, must reply within 2 week(s) of notification.

Contact. Financial aid office: (614) 222-3274
Anna Marie Schofield, Director of Financial Aid
107 North Ninth Street
Columbus, OH 43215-3875

Columbus State Community College

Columbus, Ohio
www.cscc.edu
Two-year public **Federal Code: 006867**

	Living at home
Tuition and fees (2002-2003):	$2,960
Out-of-state:	$6,470
Per-credit charge:	$65
Per-credit out-of-state:	$143
Books and supplies:	$1,050
Personal expenses:	$300
Transportation:	$1,450

Undergraduate aid. Need-based: Need-based aid available for full-time and part-time students. **Non-need-based:** Scholarships based on athletics, state/district residency.

Policies to reduce costs. Tuition/fee waivers for senior citizens, employees and their families. Credit/placement for qualifying scores on AP, IB, CLEP examinations. Work study available nights, weekends and for part-time students.

Payment plans. Credit card payment.

Application procedures. FAFSA required. No deadline. Applicants notified on rolling basis starting 4/1.

Contact. Financial aid office: (614) 287-7648
Katie Adams-Bontrager, Director of Financial Aid
550 East Spring Street
Columbus, OH 43216-1609

Cuyahoga Community College: Eastern Campus

Highland Hills, Ohio
www.tri-c.cc.oh.us
Two-year public **Federal Code: 010288**

	Living at home
Tuition and fees (2002-2003):	$1,989
Out-of-district:	$2,628
Out-of-state:	$5,382
Per-credit charge:	$66
Per-credit out-of-district:	$88
Per-credit out-of-state:	$179
Books and supplies:	$675
Personal expenses:	$1,053
Transportation:	$600

Undergraduate aid. Need-based: Average financial aid package for full-time students was $4,870; for part-time $4,363. 83% awarded as scholarships/grants, 17% as loans/jobs. **Non-need-based:** Scholarships based on academics, art, athletics, leadership, music/drama. **Student debt:** 20% of graduating class borrowed to fund education; average debt was $7,300.

Freshman aid. Need-based: Out of 286 full-time freshmen, 162 applied for aid; 162 were judged to have need; of these 162 received aid. Average package met 100% of need. 162 students had full need met. Average scholarship/grant was $4,436; average loan $2,300. **Non-need based:** 9 full-time freshmen with need received non-need scholarships; 4 without need received awards; 4 received athletic scholarships.

Policies to reduce costs. Tuition/fee waivers for senior citizens, employees and their families. Credit/placement for qualifying scores on AP, CLEP examinations.

Payment plans. Credit card, installment, deferred payment.

Application procedures. FAFSA, institutional form required. No deadline. Applicants notified on rolling basis starting 5/1. **Transfers:** No deadline.

Contact. Financial aid office: (216) 987-2211
Armetia DeHart, Director for Financial Aid
4250 Richmond Road
Highland Hills, OH 44122

Cuyahoga Community College: Metropolitan Campus

Cleveland, Ohio
www.tri-c.edu
Two-year public **Federal Code: 003040**

	Living at home
Tuition and fees (2002-2003):	$1,989
Out-of-district:	$2,628
Out-of-state:	$5,382
Per-credit charge:	$66
Per-credit out-of-district:	$88
Per-credit out-of-state:	$179
Books and supplies:	$675
Personal expenses:	$1,053
Transportation:	$600

Undergraduate aid. Need-based: Average financial aid package for full-time students was $5,322; for part-time $4,601. 84% awarded as scholarships/grants, 16% as loans/jobs. **Non-need-based:** Scholarships based on academics, art, athletics, leadership, minority status, music/drama. **Student debt:** 16% of graduating class borrowed to fund education; average debt was $4,754.

Freshman aid. Need-based: Out of 357 full-time freshmen, 283 applied for aid; 283 were judged to have need; of these 283 received aid. Average package met 100% of need. 283 students had full need met. Average scholarship/grant was $6,120; average loan $2,548. **Non-need based:** 4 full-time freshmen with need received non-need scholarships; 1 without need received awards.

Policies to reduce costs. Tuition/fee waivers for senior citizens, employees and their families. Credit/placement for qualifying scores on AP, CLEP examinations. Work study available nights, weekends and for part-time students.

Payment plans. Credit card, installment, deferred payment.

Application procedures. FAFSA, institutional form required. No deadline. Applicants notified on rolling basis starting 5/1. **Transfers:** No deadline.

Contact. Financial aid office: (216) 987-4100
Angela Johnson, Campus Director
2900 Community College Avenue
Cleveland, OH 44115-2878

Cuyahoga Community College: Western Campus

Parma, Ohio
www.tri-c.edu
Two-year public

	Living at home
Tuition and fees (2002-2003):	$1,989
Out-of-district:	$2,628
Out-of-state:	$5,382
Per-credit charge:	$66
Per-credit out-of-district:	$88
Per-credit out-of-state:	$179
Books and supplies:	$675
Personal expenses:	$1,053
Transportation:	$600

Undergraduate aid. Need-based: Average financial aid package for full-time students was $4,248; for part-time $3,998. 75% awarded as scholarships/grants, 25% as loans/jobs. **Non-need-based:** Scholarships based on academics, art, athletics, leadership, minority status, music/drama. **Student debt:** 13% of graduating class borrowed to fund education; average debt was $6,424.

Freshman aid. Need-based: Out of 796 full-time freshmen, 274 applied for aid; 274 were judged to have need; of these 274 received aid. Average package met 100% of need. 274 students had full need met. Average scholarship/grant was $3,874; average loan $2,890. **Non-need based:** 52 full-time freshmen with need received non-need scholarships; 35 without need received awards; 8 received athletic scholarships.

Policies to reduce costs. Tuition/fee waivers for senior citizens, employees and their families. Credit/placement for qualifying scores on AP, CLEP examinations.

Payment plans. Credit card, installment, deferred payment.

Application procedures. FAFSA, institutional form required. No deadline. Applicants notified on rolling basis starting 5/1. **Transfers:** No deadline.

Contact. Financial aid office: (216) 987-5141
Bonnie Guyer, Director of Financial Aid
11000 Pleasant Valley Road
Parma, OH 44130

David N. Myers College

Cleveland, Ohio
www.dnmyers.edu
Four-year private **Federal Code: 003043**

	Living at home
Tuition and fees (2002-2003):	$10,380
Books and supplies:	$800
Personal expenses:	$2,596
Transportation:	$432

Undergraduate aid. Non-need-based: Scholarships based on academics, state/district residency.

Policies to reduce costs. Tuition/fee waivers for employees and their families.

Payment plans. Credit card, installment payment.

Application procedures. FAFSA required. Priority date 4/30; no closing date. Applicants notified on rolling basis starting 5/1, must reply within 4 week(s) of notification. **Transfers:** No deadline.

Contact. Financial aid office: (216) 696-9000
Miria Batig, Director of Financial Aid
112 Prospect Avenue
Cleveland, OH 44115-1096

Davis College

Toledo, Ohio
www.daviscollege.edu
Two-year proprietary **Federal Code: 004855**

	Living at home
Tuition and fees (2002-2003):	$9,035
Per-credit charge:	$199
Board only:	$1,512
Books and supplies:	$750
Personal expenses:	$2,835
Transportation:	$1,356

Undergraduate aid. All financial aid based on need. Need-based aid available for full-time and part-time students.

Policies to reduce costs. Tuition/fee waivers for employees and their families. Work study available nights and weekends.

Payment plans. Credit card, installment payment.

Application procedures. FAFSA required. No deadline. Applicants notified on rolling basis. **Transfers:** No deadline.

Contact. **Financial aid office:** (419) 473-2700
Todd Matthews, Director of Financial Aid
4747 Monroe Street
Toledo, OH 43623

DeVry University: Columbus

Columbus, Ohio
www.devry.cols.edu
Four-year proprietary **Federal Code: 003099**

	Living at home
Tuition and fees:	$10,155
Books and supplies:	$1,100
Personal expenses:	$1,816
Transportation:	$1,438

Undergraduate aid. All financial aid based on need. Average financial aid package for full-time students was $7,409; for part-time $5,402. 26% awarded as scholarships/grants, 74% as loans/jobs.

Freshman aid. Average package met 39% of need. Average scholarship/grant was $3,206; average loan $3,912.

Policies to reduce costs. Tuition/fee waivers for employees and their families.

Payment plans. Credit card, installment, deferred payment.

Application procedures. FAFSA required. No deadline. Applicants notified on rolling basis starting 7/2.

Contact. **Financial aid office:** (614) 253-7291
Cynthia Price, Director of Financial Aid
1350 Alum Creek Drive
Columbus, OH 43209

Defiance College

Defiance, Ohio
www.defiance.edu
Four-year private **Federal Code: 003041**

	Living at home	On-campus
Tuition and fees (2002-2003):	$16,660	$16,660
Room and board:		$5,070
Board only:	$1,220	
Books and supplies:	$600	$600
Personal expenses:	$1,120	$1,120
Transportation:	$1,000	$500

Undergraduate aid. **Need-based:** Average financial aid package for full-time students was $15,477; for part-time $5,709. 69% awarded as scholarships/grants, 31% as loans/jobs. **Non-need-based:** 43% awarded as scholarships/grants, 57% as loans/jobs. Scholarships based on academics, job skills. **Student debt:** 75% of graduating class borrowed to fund education; average debt was $15,493.

Freshman aid. **Need-based:** Out of 203 full-time freshmen, 203 applied for aid; 197 were judged to have need; of these 197 received aid. Average package met 84% of need. Average scholarship/grant was $2,511; average loan $3,057. **Non-need based:** 117 full-time freshmen with need received non-need scholarships; 22 without need received awards.

Merit scholarships. Defiance Scholarship; up to 5 awarded annually; based on minimum high school GPA of 3.8, ACT score of 28 or SAT of 1240, essay, 3 letters of recommendation, interview; full tuition. Presidential Service Leadership award; up to 12 awarded annually; based on minimum high school GPA of 2.5, ACT score of 21, extensive community service background, nomination; half tuition. Pilgrim Scholarship; based on minimum high school GPA of 3.5, ACT score of 26 or SAT of 1170, essay, recommendation letters, interview; half tuition.

Policies to reduce costs. Tuition/fee waivers for adults, senior citizens, employees and their families. Credit/placement for qualifying scores on AP, IB, CLEP examinations. Work study available nights, weekends and for part-time students.

Payment plans. Credit card, installment payment.

Application procedures. FAFSA required. Priority date 3/1; no closing date. Applicants notified on rolling basis starting 3/15, must reply within 3 week(s) of notification.

Contact. **Financial aid office:** (419) 784-4010
Amy Francis, Director of Financial Aid
701 North Clinton Street
Defiance, OH 43512-1695

Denison University

Granville, Ohio
www.denison.edu
Four-year private **Federal Code: 003042**

	Living at home	On-campus
Tuition and fees (2002-2003):	$24,240	$24,240
Room and board:		$6,880
Books and supplies:	$600	$600
Personal expenses:	$1,200	$1,200
Transportation:	$400	$400

Undergraduate aid. **Need-based:** Average financial aid package for full-time students was $21,560. 80% awarded as scholarships/grants, 20% as loans/jobs. Need-based aid available for part-time students. **Non-need-based:** 79% awarded as scholarships/grants, 21% as loans/jobs. Scholarships based on academics, leadership, minority status, music/drama. **Student debt:** 49% of graduating class borrowed to fund education; average debt was $14,077.

Freshman aid. **Need-based:** Out of 633 full-time freshmen, 396 applied for aid; 315 were judged to have need; of these 315 received aid. Average package met 99% of need. 190 students had full need met. Average scholarship/grant was $15,935; average loan $3,127. **Non-need based:** 296 full-time freshmen with need received non-need scholarships; 307 without need received awards.

Merit scholarships. Denison Faculty Scholarship for Achievement for selected secondary school valedictorians and salutatorians; 35 awarded; 75% or full tuition. Tyree Scholarship for highly qualified African-American students; 30 awarded; half tuition. Parajon Scholarship for highly qualified students of Asian, Hispanic, and/or Native American heritage; 60 awarded; half tuition. Alumni Awards for students who have excelled in a particular endeavor (academic record, special talents in the arts, or demonstrated leadership and service to school or community); ranging from 20% to 67% tuition annually. Trustee Scholarship for Achievement for selected secondary school valedictorians and salutatorians; 43 awarded; 75% tuition. Heritage Scholarships (half tuition) for academic achievment. Carr Scholarship; 35 awarded; 75% or full tuition. University Scholarship; 15 awarded; 75% tuition, awarded to highly qualified candidates who are invited into the honors program. Provost awards; 122 awarded; up to 40% tuition.

Policies to reduce costs. Tuition/fee waivers for adults, employees and their families. Credit/placement for qualifying scores on AP, IB, CLEP examinations.

Payment plans. Installment, deferred payment.

Application procedures. FAFSA required. Priority date 2/15; no closing date. Applicants notified on rolling basis starting 4/1, must reply by 5/1 or within 2 week(s) of notification. Early decision closing date 11/15. **Transfers:** No deadline.

Contact. **Financial aid office:** (740) 587-6279
Nancy Hoover, Director of Financial Aid and Student Employment
Box H
Granville, OH 43023

ETI Technical College of Niles

Niles, Ohio
www.eti-college.com
Two-year proprietary **Federal Code: 030790**

College costs. Tuition ranges from $4,620 to $5,940 for associate program academic year.

	Living at home
Tuition and fees (2002-2003):	$5,590
Books and supplies:	$600

Contact. **Financial aid office:** (330) 652-9919
Renee Zuzolo, Director
2076 Youngstown Warren Road
Niles, OH 44446-4398

Edison State Community College

Piqua, Ohio
www.edisonohio.edu
Two-year public **Federal Code: 012750**

	Living at home
Tuition and fees (2002-2003):	$2,760
Out-of-state:	$5,040
Per-credit charge:	$76
Per-credit out-of-state:	$152
Books and supplies:	$921
Personal expenses:	$600
Transportation:	$809

Undergraduate aid. **Non-need-based:** Scholarships based on academics, athletics.

Policies to reduce costs. Tuition/fee waivers for senior citizens, employees and their families. Credit/placement for qualifying scores on AP, CLEP examinations. Work study available nights and weekends.

Payment plans. Credit card, installment, deferred payment.

Application procedures. FAFSA required. Priority date 6/15; no closing date. Applicants notified on rolling basis starting 5/15.

Contact. **Financial aid office:** (937) 778-8600
Lisa Waldrop, Director of Student Financial Aid
1973 Edison Drive
Piqua, OH 45356-9253

Franciscan University of Steubenville

Steubenville, Ohio
www.franciscan.edu
Four-year private **Federal Code: 003036**

	Living at home	On-campus
Tuition and fees (2002-2003):	$14,400	$14,400
Room and board:		$5,200
Board only:	$2,000	
Books and supplies:	$800	$800
Personal expenses:	$1,200	$1,200
Transportation:	$1,500	$1,500

Undergraduate aid. **Need-based:** Average financial aid package for full-time students was $8,570; for part-time $3,898. 41% awarded as scholarships/grants, 59% as loans/jobs. **Non-need-based:** 45% awarded as scholarships/grants, 55% as loans/jobs. Scholarships based on academics. **Student debt:** 76% of graduating class borrowed to fund education; average debt was $22,800.

Freshman aid. **Need-based:** Out of 359 full-time freshmen, 294 applied for aid; 251 were judged to have need; of these 249 received aid. Average package met 60% of need. 52 students had full need met. Average scholarship/grant was $4,704; average loan $4,011. **Non-need based:** 109 full-time freshmen with need received non-need scholarships; 43 without need received awards.

Policies to reduce costs. Tuition/fee waivers for family members, family of clergy, employees and their families. Credit/placement for qualifying scores on AP, IB, CLEP examinations. Work study available nights and weekends.

Payment plans. Credit card, installment payment.

Application procedures. FAFSA required. Priority date 4/15; no closing date. Applicants notified on rolling basis starting 3/1, must reply within 4 week(s) of notification. **Transfers:** Priority date 4/15; closing date 8/1.

Contact. **Financial aid office:** (740) 283-6211
John Herrmann, Financial Aid Director
1235 University Boulevard
Steubenville, OH 43952-1763

Franklin University

Columbus, Ohio
www.franklin.edu
Four-year private **Federal Code: 003046**

	Living at home
Tuition and fees (2002-2003):	$6,420
Board only:	$2,700
Books and supplies:	$600
Personal expenses:	$1,100
Transportation:	$800

Undergraduate aid. **Need-based:** 26% awarded as scholarships/grants, 74% as loans/jobs. Need-based aid available for part-time students. **Non-need-based:** 20% awarded as scholarships/grants, 80% as loans/jobs. Scholarships based on academics, leadership, minority status.

Freshman aid. **Need-based:** Out of 34 full-time freshmen, 26 applied for aid; 24 were judged to have need; of these 21 received aid. Average scholarship/grant was $3,530. **Non-need based:** 21 full-time freshmen with need received non-need scholarships; 2 without need received awards.

Policies to reduce costs. Tuition/fee waivers for employees and their families. Credit/placement for qualifying scores on AP, CLEP examinations.

Payment plans. Credit card, deferred payment.

Application procedures. FAFSA, institutional form required. Priority date 6/15; no closing date. Applicants notified on rolling basis, must reply within 2 week(s) of notification. **Transfers:** One scholarship specifically for transfer students: Transfer Achievement.

Contact. **Financial aid office:** (614) 797-4700
Lee Harrell, Director of Financial Aid
201 South Grant Avenue
Columbus, OH 43215-5399

Gallipolis Career College

Gallipolis, Ohio
www.gallipoliscareercollege.com
Two-year proprietary **Federal Code: 030079**

	Living at home
Tuition and fees (2002-2003):	$5,760
Per-credit charge:	$160
Books and supplies:	$1,200
Personal expenses:	$4,000
Transportation:	$2,500

Application procedures. FAFSA, institutional form required.

Contact. **Financial aid office:** (740) 446-4367
Jeanette Shirey, Financial Aid Administrator
1176 Jackson Pike, Suite 312
Gallipolis, OH 45631

God's Bible School and College

Cincinnati, Ohio
www.gbs.edu
Four-year private **Federal Code: 022205**

	Living at home	On-campus
Tuition and fees (2002-2003):	$4,380	$4,380
Room and board:		$2,900
Books and supplies:	$400	$400
Personal expenses:	$1,275	$800
Transportation:	$1,100	$800

Undergraduate aid. **Additional information:** Institutional work scholarships available.

Policies to reduce costs. Tuition/fee waivers for employees and their families. Prepayment discount; credit/placement for qualifying scores on CLEP examinations.

Payment plans. Credit card, installment, deferred payment.

Application procedures. Priority date 6/1; no closing date. Applicants notified on rolling basis.

Contact. **Financial aid office:** (513) 721-7944
Lori Wagner, Financial Aid Director
1810 Young Street
Cincinnati, OH 45210

Heidelberg College

Tiffin, Ohio
www.heidelberg.edu
Four-year private **Federal Code: 003048**

College costs. Per-credit-hour charge for part-time students and over 17 credits per semester.

	Living at home	On-campus
Tuition and fees (projected):	$13,670	$13,670
Room and board:		$6,336
Board only:	$736	
Books and supplies:	$1,000	$1,000
Personal expenses:	$500	$500
Transportation:	$500	$500

Undergraduate aid. Need-based: Average financial aid package for full-time students was $15,414. 73% awarded as scholarships/grants, 27% as loans/jobs. Need-based aid available for part-time students. **Non-need-based:** 50% awarded as scholarships/grants, 50% as loans/jobs. Scholarships based on academics, music/drama, religious affiliation, state/district residency. **Student debt:** 78% of graduating class borrowed to fund education; average debt was $21,682.

Freshman aid. Need-based: Out of 280 full-time freshmen, 260 applied for aid; 227 were judged to have need; of these 227 received aid. Average package met 83% of need. 80 students had full need met. Average scholarship/grant was $8,879; average loan $3,151. **Non-need based:** 227 full-time freshmen with need received non-need scholarships; 56 without need received awards.

Policies to reduce costs. Tuition/fee waivers for employees and their families. Prepayment discount; credit/placement for qualifying scores on AP, CLEP examinations.

Payment plans. Credit card, installment payment.

Application procedures. FAFSA required. Priority date 3/1; no closing date. Applicants notified on rolling basis starting 3/15, must reply within 2 week(s) of notification.

Contact. **Financial aid office:** (419) 448-2293
Juli Weininger, Director of Financial Aid
310 East Market Street
Tiffin, OH 44883-2462

Hiram College

Hiram, Ohio
www.hiram.edu
Four-year private **Federal Code: 003049**

	Living at home	On-campus
Tuition and fees (2002-2003):	$20,214	$20,214
Room and board:		$6,820
Board only:	$3,620	
Books and supplies:	$600	$600
Personal expenses:	$1,688	$1,688
Transportation:	$844	$844

Undergraduate aid. Need-based: Average financial aid package for full-time students was $17,492; for part-time $6,353. 52% awarded as scholarships/grants, 48% as loans/jobs. **Non-need-based:** 97% awarded as scholarships/grants, 3% as loans/jobs. Scholarships based on academics, alumni affiliation, art, minority status, music/drama, religious affiliation, state/district residency.

Freshman aid. Need-based: Out of 248 full-time freshmen, 220 applied for aid; 208 were judged to have need; of these 207 received aid. Average package met 73% of need. 44 students had full need met. Average scholarship/grant was $10,974; average loan $2,625. **Non-need based:** 156 full-time freshmen with need received non-need scholarships; 28 without need received awards.

Policies to reduce costs. Tuition/fee waivers for children of alumni, family of clergy, employees and their families. Credit/placement for qualifying scores on AP, IB, CLEP examinations. Work study available nights, weekends and for part-time students.

Payment plans. Credit card, installment, deferred payment.

Application procedures. FAFSA required. Priority date 3/1; no closing date. Applicants notified on rolling basis starting 2/15, must reply by 5/1 or within 2 week(s) of notification. Early decision closing date 12/1. **Transfers:** No deadline. Transfer merit scholarships available. Phi Theta Kappa scholarships available.

Contact. **Financial aid office:** (330) 569-5107
Robert Ritz, Director of Student Financial Aid
Teachout Price Hall
Hiram, OH 44234

Hocking Technical College

Nelsonville, Ohio
www.hocking.edu
Two-year public **Federal Code: 007598**

College costs. Fees doubled for out-of-state students.

	Living at home	On-campus
Tuition and fees (2002-2003):	$2,700	$2,700
Out-of-state:	$5,400	$5,400
Per-credit charge:	$55	$55
Per-credit out-of-state:	$130	$130
Room only:		$2,865
Books and supplies:	$1,800	$1,800
Personal expenses:	$510	$1,200
Transportation:	$1,850	$325

Undergraduate aid. Need-based: Need-based aid available for full-time and part-time students. **Non-need-based:** Scholarships based on academics, minority status, state/district residency.

Policies to reduce costs. Tuition/fee waivers for senior citizens, employees and their families. Credit/placement for qualifying scores on AP, CLEP examinations. Work study available nights and weekends.

Payment plans. Credit card, installment payment.

Application procedures. FAFSA, institutional form required. Priority date 2/28; no closing date. Applicants notified on rolling basis starting 4/15. **Transfers:** No deadline. Non-entitlement aid awarded on first-come, first-served basis.

Contact. **Financial aid office:** (740) 753-3591 ext. 2159
Roger Springer, Financial Services Director
3301 Hocking Parkway
Nelsonville, OH 45764-9704

Hondros College

Westerville, Ohio
www.hondroscollege.com
Two-year proprietary

College costs (2002-2003). Tuition for full 2-year associate program $6,750; $225 per 3 credit hour course.

Contact. **Financial aid office:** (614) 508-7200
4140 Executive Parkway
Westerville, OH 43081-3855

ITT Technical Institute: Dayton

Dayton, Ohio
www.itt-tech.edu
Two-year proprietary **Federal Code: 009088**

College costs. Total cost of program varies depending on course of study. Per-credit-hour charge: $347.

Policies to reduce costs. Tuition/fee waivers for employees and their families. Tuition at time of enrollment guaranteed for 2 years.

Payment plans. Credit card, installment payment.

Application procedures. FAFSA, institutional form required. No deadline. Applicants notified on rolling basis.

Contact. **Financial aid office:** (937) 454-2267
Sean Kuhn, Director of Recruitment
3325 Stop Eight Road
Dayton, OH 45414

ITT Technical Institute: Norwood

Norwood, Ohio
www.itt-tech.edu
Two-year proprietary **Federal Code: 023598**

College costs. Total cost of program varies depending on course of study. Per-credit-hour charge: $347.

Policies to reduce costs. Tuition/fee waivers for employees and their families. Tuition at time of enrollment guaranteed for 2 years.

Payment plans. Credit card, installment payment.

Application procedures. FAFSA, institutional form required. No deadline. Applicants notified on rolling basis.

Contact. **Financial aid office:** (513) 531-8300
Susan Spencer, Director of Finance
4750 Wesley Avenue
Norwood, OH 45212

ITT Technical Institute: Strongsville

Strongsville, Ohio
www.itt-tech.edu
Two-year proprietary **Federal Code: 009088**

College costs. Total cost of program varies depending on course of study. Per-credit-hour charge: $347.

Policies to reduce costs. Tuition/fee waivers for employees and their families. Tuition at time of enrollment guaranteed for 2 years.

Payment plans. Credit card, installment payment.

Application procedures. FAFSA, institutional form required. No deadline. Applicants notified on rolling basis.

Contact. **Financial aid office:** (440) 234-9091
Kelly Dellavecchia, Director of Finance
14955 Sprague Road
Strongsville, OH 44136

ITT Technical Institute: Youngstown

Youngstown, Ohio
www.itt-tech.edu
Two-year proprietary **Federal Code: 009837**

College costs. Total cost of program varies depending on course of study. Per-credit-hour charge: $347.

Policies to reduce costs. Tuition/fee waivers for employees and their families. Tuition at time of enrollment guaranteed for 2 years.

Payment plans. Credit card, installment payment.

Application procedures. FAFSA, institutional form required. No deadline. Applicants notified on rolling basis.

Contact. **Financial aid office:** (330) 270-1600
Linda Shirey, Director of Finance
1030 North Meridian Road
Youngstown, OH 44509

International College of Broadcasting

Dayton, Ohio
www.icbcollege.com
Two-year proprietary **Federal Code: 013132**

College costs. $15,700 tuition for associate programs. $8,940 for broadcasting diploma program and $7,380 for recording diploma program. Personal expenses: $2,862.

Undergraduate aid. **Need-based:** Need-based aid available for full-time and part-time students.

Application procedures. FAFSA required. No deadline. Applicants notified on rolling basis starting 11/1.

Contact. **Financial aid office:** (937) 258-8251 ext. 203
Zena Williams, Financial Aid Director
6 South Smithville Road
Dayton, OH 45431

James A. Rhodes State College

Lima, Ohio
www.rhodesstate.edu
Two-year public **Federal Code: 010027**

	Living at home
Tuition and fees (2002-2003):	$3,210
Out-of-state:	$6,360
Per-credit charge:	$70
Per-credit out-of-state:	$140
Board only:	$1,041
Books and supplies:	$945
Personal expenses:	$473
Transportation:	$862

Undergraduate aid. **Need-based:** Average financial aid package for full-time students was $2,889; for part-time $2,889. **Non-need-based:** Scholarships based on academics.

Freshman aid. **Need-based:** Out of 359 full-time freshmen, 296 applied for aid; 296 were judged to have need; of these 214 received aid. Average package met 54% of need. Average scholarship/grant was $1,368.

Policies to reduce costs. Tuition/fee waivers for senior citizens, employees and their families. Credit/placement for qualifying scores on AP examinations. Work study available nights, weekends and for part-time students.

Payment plans. Credit card, installment payment.

Application procedures. FAFSA required. Priority date 4/1; no closing date. Applicants notified on rolling basis starting 5/1, must reply within 2 week(s) of notification. **Transfers:** No deadline.

Contact. **Financial aid office:** (419) 995-8800
Brenda Wakefield, Director of Financial Aid
4240 Campus Drive
Lima, OH 45804

Jefferson Community College

Steubenville, Ohio
www.jeffersoncc.org
Two-year public **Federal Code: 007275**

College costs. Residents of 5 neighboring West Virginia counties eligible for in-state, out-of-district tuition rates.

	Living at home
Tuition and fees (2002-2003):	$2,205
Out-of-district:	$2,355
Out-of-state:	$3,015
Per-credit charge:	$70
Per-credit out-of-district:	$75
Per-credit out-of-state:	$97
Books and supplies:	$700
Personal expenses:	$400
Transportation:	$496

Undergraduate aid. All financial aid based on need. Need-based aid available for full-time and part-time students.

Policies to reduce costs. Tuition/fee waivers for senior citizens, employees and their families. Credit/placement for qualifying scores on CLEP examinations. Work study available nights, weekends and for part-time students.

Payment plans. Credit card, installment payment.

Application procedures. FAFSA, institutional form required. Priority date 6/1; no closing date. Applicants notified on rolling basis starting 6/15.

Contact. **Financial aid office:** (740) 264-5591 ext. 135
Beth Sikole, Director of Student Information
4000 Sunset Boulevard
Steubenville, OH 43952

John Carroll University

University Heights, Ohio
www.jcu.edu
Four-year private **Federal Code: 003050**

	Living at home	On-campus
Tuition and fees (2002-2003):	$19,182	$19,182
Room and board:		$6,564
Board only:	$2,570	
Books and supplies:	$800	$800
Personal expenses:	$500	$500
Transportation:	$1,600	$800

Undergraduate aid. Need-based: Need-based aid available for full-time and part-time students. **Non-need-based:** Scholarships based on academics, state/district residency. **Additional information:** Institutional form for need analysis required from upperclassmen and transfer students only.

Policies to reduce costs. Tuition/fee waivers for employees and their families. Credit/placement for qualifying scores on AP, CLEP examinations.

Payment plans. Credit card, installment payment.

Application procedures. FAFSA required. Priority date 3/1; no closing date. Applicants notified on rolling basis starting 3/1, must reply by 5/1 or within 4 week(s) of notification. **Transfers:** Priority date 3/1; no deadline. 10 renewable scholarships per year for students transferring from local community colleges.

Contact. Financial aid office: (216) 397-4248
Patrick Prosser, Director of Financial Aid
20700 North Park Boulevard
University Heights, OH 44118-4581

Kent State University

Kent, Ohio
www.kent.edu
Four-year public **Federal Code: 003051**

College costs. Overload charge for more than 18 hours $61 per-credit-hour.

	Living at home	On-campus
Tuition and fees (2002-2003):	$6,374	$6,374
Out-of-state:	$12,330	$12,330
Room and board:		$5,570
Board only:	$2,514	
Books and supplies:	$731	$731
Personal expenses:	$1,880	
Transportation:	$1,672	

Undergraduate aid. Need-based: Need-based aid available for full-time and part-time students. **Non-need-based:** Scholarships based on academics, alumni affiliation, art, athletics, leadership, minority status, music/drama, state/district residency.

Merit scholarships. Trustee Scholarship; 500 available; $1,000-$2,500 annually; based on minimum GPA 3.25, ACT scores, leadership activities.

Policies to reduce costs. Tuition/fee waivers for employees and their families. Prepayment discount; credit/placement for qualifying scores on AP, CLEP examinations. Work study available weekends.

Payment plans. Credit card, installment, deferred payment.

Application procedures. FAFSA, institutional form required. Priority date 3/1; no closing date. Applicants notified on rolling basis starting 3/15, must reply within 2 week(s) of notification. **Transfers:** No deadline.

Contact. Financial aid office: (330) 672-2972
Mark Evans, Director of Student Financial Aid
PO Box 5190
Kent, OH 44242-0001

Kent State University: Ashtabula Regional Campus

Ashtabula, Ohio
www.ashtabula.kent.edu
Two-year public **Federal Code: 003051**

	Living at home
Tuition and fees (2002-2003):	$3,674
Out-of-state:	$9,630
Per-credit charge:	$167
Per-credit out-of-state:	$438
Books and supplies:	$700

Undergraduate aid. Need-based: Need-based aid available for full-time and part-time students.

Policies to reduce costs. Tuition/fee waivers for employees and their families. Credit/placement for qualifying scores on AP, CLEP examinations.

Payment plans. Credit card, installment, deferred payment.

Application procedures. FAFSA required. Priority date 2/15; closing date 8/30. Applicants notified on rolling basis starting 6/15, must reply within 3 week(s) of notification.

Contact. Financial aid office: (440) 964-3322
Kelly Sanford, Admissions Counselor
3325 West 13th Street
Ashtabula, OH 44004

Kent State University: East Liverpool Regional Campus

East Liverpool, Ohio
www.kenteliv.kent.edu
Two-year public **Federal Code: 003051**

	Living at home
Tuition and fees (2002-2003):	$3,674
Out-of-state:	$9,360
Per-credit charge:	$167
Per-credit out-of-state:	$438
Books and supplies:	$550
Personal expenses:	$1,315
Transportation:	$885

Undergraduate aid. Non-need-based: Scholarships based on state/district residency.

Policies to reduce costs. Tuition/fee waivers for senior citizens, employees and their families. Credit/placement for qualifying scores on AP, CLEP examinations. Work study available for part-time students.

Payment plans. Credit card, installment, deferred payment.

Application procedures. FAFSA required. Priority date 2/15; no closing date. Applicants notified on rolling basis starting 5/15, must reply within 2 week(s) of notification. **Transfers:** No deadline.

Contact. Financial aid office: (330) 385-3805
Marian Carter, Director of Financial Aid and Registrar
400 East Fourth Street
East Liverpool, OH 43920

Kent State University: Salem Regional Campus

Salem, Ohio
www.salem.kent.edu
Four-year public **Federal Code: 003061**

	Living at home
Tuition and fees (2002-2003):	$3,674
Out-of-state:	$9,630
Books and supplies:	$700
Personal expenses:	$1,500
Transportation:	$900

Undergraduate aid. Need-based: Need-based aid available for full-time and part-time students.

Policies to reduce costs. Tuition/fee waivers for employees and their families. Credit/placement for qualifying scores on AP, CLEP examinations.

Payment plans. Credit card, installment, deferred payment.

Application procedures. FAFSA required. Priority date 2/15; no closing date. Applicants notified on rolling basis starting 7/1, must reply within 2 week(s) of notification. **Transfers:** Priority date 2/15; no deadline.

Contact. Financial aid office: (330) 332-0361
2491 State Route 45 South
Salem, OH 44460

Kent State University: Stark Campus

Canton, Ohio
www.stark.kent.edu
Four-year public **Federal Code: 003054**

	Living at home
Tuition and fees (2002-2003):	$3,674
Out-of-state:	$9,630
Board only:	$2,440
Books and supplies:	$900
Personal expenses:	$1,826
Transportation:	$1,648

Undergraduate aid. All financial aid based on need. 41% awarded as scholarships/grants, 59% as loans/jobs. Need-based aid available for part-time students. **Student debt:** 37% of graduating class borrowed to fund education; average debt was $13,000.

Policies to reduce costs. Tuition/fee waivers for employees and their families. Prepayment discount; credit/placement for qualifying scores on AP, CLEP examinations. Work study available for part-time students.

Payment plans. Credit card, installment, deferred payment.

Application procedures. FAFSA required. Priority date 3/1; no closing date. Applicants notified on rolling basis starting 3/15, must reply within 2 week(s) of notification. **Transfers:** No deadline.

Contact. Financial aid office: (330) 499-9600
Joanne Brown, Financial Aid Officer
6000 Frank Avenue NW
Canton, OH 44720-7599

Kent State University: Trumbull Campus

Warren, Ohio
www.trumbull.kent.edu
Two-year public **Federal Code: 003051**

	Living at home
Tuition and fees (2002-2003):	$3,674
Out-of-state:	$9,630
Per-credit charge:	$167
Per-credit out-of-state:	$438
Books and supplies:	$560
Personal expenses:	$1,484
Transportation:	$940

Undergraduate aid. Need-based: Need-based aid available for full-time and part-time students. **Non-need-based:** Scholarships based on state/district residency.

Policies to reduce costs. Tuition/fee waivers for senior citizens, employees and their families. Prepayment discount; credit/placement for qualifying scores on AP, IB, CLEP examinations.

Payment plans. Credit card, installment, deferred payment.

Application procedures. FAFSA required. Priority date 2/15; no closing date. Applicants notified on rolling basis starting 4/1, must reply within 4 week(s) of notification. **Transfers:** No deadline.

Contact. Financial aid office: (330) 847-0571
Nina Conner, Financial Aid Coordinator
4314 Mahoning Avenue, NW
Warren, OH 44483-1998

Kent State University: Tuscarawas Campus

New Philadelphia, Ohio
www.tusc.kent.edu
Four-year public **Federal Code: 003051**

	Living at home
Tuition and fees (2002-2003):	$3,674
Out-of-state:	$9,630

Undergraduate aid. All financial aid based on need. Need-based aid available for full-time and part-time students.

Policies to reduce costs. Tuition/fee waivers for senior citizens, employees and their families. Credit/placement for qualifying scores on AP, CLEP examinations. Work study available nights, weekends and for part-time students.

Payment plans. Credit card, installment, deferred payment.

Application procedures. FAFSA required. Priority date 2/1; closing date 4/15. Applicants notified on rolling basis starting 4/15, must reply within 3 week(s) of notification. **Transfers:** Financial aid transcripts from all previous institutions required.

Contact. Financial aid office: (330) 339-3391 ext. 47474
Agnes Swigart, Assistant Dean
330 University Drive Northeast
New Philadelphia, OH 44663-9403

Kenyon College

Gambier, Ohio
www.kenyon.edu
Four-year private **Federal Code: 003065**

	Living at home	On-campus
Tuition and fees (2002-2003):	$28,710	$28,710
Room and board:		$4,690
Books and supplies:	$950	$950
Personal expenses:		$640

Undergraduate aid. Need-based: Average financial aid package for full-time students was $21,409. 82% awarded as scholarships/grants, 18% as loans/jobs. **Non-need-based:** 60% awarded as scholarships/grants, 40% as loans/jobs. Scholarships based on academics, leadership, state/district residency. **Student debt:** 47% of graduating class borrowed to fund education; average debt was $20,850.

Freshman aid. Need-based: Out of 440 full-time freshmen, 241 applied for aid; 170 were judged to have need; of these 170 received aid. Average package met 98% of need. 111 students had full need met. Average scholarship/grant was $18,201; average loan $2,105. **Non-need based:** 92 full-time freshmen with need received non-need scholarships; 116 without need received awards.

Merit scholarships. Honor Scholarships, Science Scholarships, African-American Scholarships, Latino Scholarships, and Asian-American Scholarships competitively based on excellence in academic achievement, extracurricular leadership, and community involvement, and range from $11,000-$26,000 annually. Distinguished Academic Scholarships based on academic accomplishment, standardized test results, and extracurricular achievement; $4,000-$12,000. Scholarships for National Merit finalists available.

Policies to reduce costs. Tuition/fee waivers for employees and their families. Credit/placement for qualifying scores on AP, IB examinations. Work study available nights and weekends.

Payment plans. Installment payment.

Application procedures. FAFSA, CSS PROFILE required. Closing date 2/15. Applicants notified by 4/1, must reply by 5/1. Early decision closing date 12/1. **Transfers:** Priority date 2/1; closing date 2/15.

Contact. Financial aid office: (740) 427-5430
Craig Daugherty, Director of Financial Aid
Ransom Hall
Gambier, OH 43022-9623

Kettering College of Medical Arts

Kettering, Ohio
www.kcma.edu
Two-year private **Federal Code: 007035**

	Living at home	On-campus
Tuition and fees (2002-2003):	$6,790	$6,790
Per-credit charge:	$220	$220
Room only:		$1,880
Board only:	$709	
Books and supplies:	$973	$973
Personal expenses:	$2,820	$2,345
Transportation:	$1,521	$1,244

Undergraduate aid. Need-based: Need-based aid available for full-time and part-time students. **Non-need-based:** Scholarships based on academics.

Policies to reduce costs. Tuition/fee waivers for family of clergy, employees and their families. Credit/placement for qualifying scores on AP, CLEP examinations.

Payment plans. Credit card, installment payment.

Application procedures. FAFSA, institutional form required. Priority date 3/31; no closing date. Applicants notified on rolling basis starting 5/15, must reply within 3 week(s) of notification.

Contact. Kim Snell, Director of Student Finance
3737 Southern Boulevard
Kettering, OH 45429-1299

Lake Erie College

Painesville, Ohio
www.lec.edu
Four-year private **Federal Code: 003066**

College costs. Equestrian fee $775 per course.

	Living at home	On-campus
Tuition and fees:	$17,720	$17,720
Room and board:		$5,830
Board only:	$1,000	
Books and supplies:	$530	$530
Personal expenses:	$990	$990
Transportation:	$1,220	$1,220

Undergraduate aid. Need-based: Average financial aid package for full-time students was $14,000; for part-time $4,282. 54% awarded as scholarships/grants, 46% as loans/jobs. **Non-need-based:** 61% awarded as scholarships/grants, 39% as loans/jobs. Scholarships based on academics, alumni affiliation, art, leadership, music/drama, state/district residency. **Student debt:** 74% of graduating class borrowed to fund education; average debt was $17,936.

Freshman aid. Need-based: Out of 133 full-time freshmen, 133 applied for aid; 98 were judged to have need; of these 98 received aid. Average package met 85% of need. 83 students had full need met. Average scholarship/grant was $7,992; average loan $2,409. **Non-need based:** 98 full-time freshmen with need received non-need scholarships; 23 without need received awards.

Merit scholarships. Merit scholarship program based on student GPA.

Policies to reduce costs. Tuition/fee waivers for senior citizens, family members, employees and their families. Prepayment discount; credit/placement for qualifying scores on AP, CLEP examinations.

Payment plans. Credit card, installment payment.

Application procedures. FAFSA required. No deadline. Applicants notified on rolling basis, must reply within 2 week(s) of notification.

Contact. Financial aid office: (440) 639-7879
Jennifer Calhoun, Director of Financial Aid
391 West Washington Street
Painesville, OH 44077-3389

Lakeland Community College

Kirtland, Ohio
www.lakelandcc.edu
Two-year public **Federal Code: 006804**

	Living at home
Tuition and fees (2002-2003):	$2,061
Out-of-district:	$2,519
Out-of-state:	$5,350
Per-credit charge:	$59
Per-credit out-of-district:	$75
Per-credit out-of-state:	$169
Board only:	$1,800
Books and supplies:	$775
Personal expenses:	$1,350
Transportation:	$1,104

Undergraduate aid. Need-based: Need-based aid available for full-time and part-time students. **Non-need-based:** Scholarships based on academics, art, athletics, job skills, leadership, minority status, music/drama, state/district residency. **Additional information:** Loans available for tuition and books.

Policies to reduce costs. Tuition/fee waivers for senior citizens, employees and their families. Credit/placement for qualifying scores on AP, CLEP examinations. Work study available nights, weekends and for part-time students.

Payment plans. Credit card, installment payment.

Application procedures. FAFSA, institutional form required. Priority date 3/1; no closing date. Applicants notified on rolling basis starting 5/1. **Transfers:** Ohio Instructional Grant Transfer Form.

Contact. Financial aid office: (440) 953-7070
Claudette Whitner, Director of Financial Aid
7700 Clocktower Drive
Kirtland, OH 44094

Laura and Alvin Siegal College of Judaic Studies

Beachwood, Ohio
www.siegalcollege.edu
Four-year private **Federal Code: 012838**

	Living at home
Tuition and fees (projected):	$9,775
Books and supplies:	$250

Undergraduate aid. All financial aid based on need. Need-based aid available for full-time and part-time students.

Policies to reduce costs. Tuition/fee waivers for adults, senior citizens, employees and their families. Credit/placement for qualifying scores on IB examinations.

Payment plans. Credit card, installment payment.

Application procedures. Institutional form required. No deadline. Applicants notified on rolling basis. **Transfers:** No deadline.

Contact. Financial aid office: (216) 464-4050 ext. 101
Linda Rosen, Director of Student Services
26500 Shaker Boulevard
Beachwood, OH 44122

Lorain County Community College

Elyria, Ohio
www.lorainccc.edu
Two-year public **Federal Code: 003068**

	Living at home
Tuition and fees (2002-2003):	$2,039
Out-of-district:	$2,457
Out-of-state:	$5,005
Per-credit charge:	$75
Per-credit out-of-district:	$91
Per-credit out-of-state:	$189
Books and supplies:	$955

Undergraduate aid. Need-based: Need-based aid available for full-time and part-time students. **Non-need-based:** Scholarships based on academics.

Merit scholarships. Presidential Scholarships and Trustee Scholarships available.

Policies to reduce costs. Tuition/fee waivers for senior citizens, employees and their families. Credit/placement for qualifying scores on AP, CLEP examinations. Work study available nights, weekends and for part-time students.

Payment plans. Credit card, installment, deferred payment.

Application procedures. FAFSA required. Priority date 8/15; no closing date. Applicants notified on rolling basis starting 7/1, must reply within 3 week(s) of notification. **Transfers:** No deadline.

Contact. Financial aid office: (490) 366-4034
Stephanie Sutton, Manager of Financial Aid
1005 Abbe Road North
Elyria, OH 44035-1691

Lourdes College

Sylvania, Ohio
www.lourdes.edu
Four-year private **Federal Code: 003069**

	Living at home
Tuition and fees (2002-2003):	$14,600
Board only:	$850
Books and supplies:	$590
Personal expenses:	$3,010
Transportation:	$1,080

Undergraduate aid. Need-based: Average financial aid package for full-time students was $12,527; for part-time $4,438. 48% awarded as scholarships/grants, 52% as loans/jobs. **Non-need-based:** 40% awarded as scholarships/grants, 60% as loans/jobs. Scholarships based on academics, art, leadership, music/drama, religious affiliation.

Freshman aid. Need-based: Out of 59 full-time freshmen, 59 applied for aid; 53 were judged to have need; of these 59 received aid. Average package met 87% of need. 18 students had full need met. Average scholarship/grant was $5,395; average loan $2,270. **Non-need based:** 58 full-time freshmen with need received non-need scholarships; 4 without need received awards.

Policies to reduce costs. Tuition/fee waivers for senior citizens, employees and their families. Credit/placement for qualifying scores on AP, CLEP examinations.

Payment plans. Credit card, installment, deferred payment.

Application procedures. FAFSA required. Priority date 3/1; no closing date. Applicants notified on rolling basis starting 5/1, must reply within 2 week(s) of notification.

Contact. Financial aid office: (419) 824-3732
Greg Guzman, Director of Financial Aid
6832 Convent Boulevard
Sylvania, OH 43560-2898

Malone College

Canton, Ohio
www.malone.edu
Four-year private **Federal Code: 003072**

College costs. Per-credit-hour charge applies to under 12 or over 18 credits.

	Living at home	On-campus
Tuition and fees:	$14,995	$14,995
Room and board:		$6,000
Board only:	$1,500	
Books and supplies:	$500	$500
Personal expenses:	$800	$800
Transportation:	$640	$480

Undergraduate aid. Need-based: Average financial aid package for full-time students was $11,397; for part-time $4,735. 57% awarded as scholarships/grants, 43% as loans/jobs. **Non-need-based:** 63% awarded as scholarships/grants, 37% as loans/jobs. Scholarships based on academics, alumni affiliation, athletics, leadership, music/drama, religious affiliation. **Student debt:** 68% of graduating class borrowed to fund education; average debt was $16,330. **Additional information:** Additional financial aid for family members enrolled simultaneously and family of clergy/clergy commitment.

Freshman aid. Need-based: Out of 348 full-time freshmen, 347 applied for aid; 284 were judged to have need; of these 284 received aid. Average package met 83% of need. 57 students had full need met. Average scholarship/grant was $8,948; average loan $2,778. **Non-need based:** 278 full-time freshmen with need received non-need scholarships; 62 without need received awards; 11 received athletic scholarships.

Policies to reduce costs. Tuition/fee waivers for senior citizens, employees and their families. Prepayment discount; credit/placement for qualifying scores on AP, CLEP examinations. Work study available nights and weekends.

Payment plans. Credit card, installment, deferred payment.

Application procedures. FAFSA required. Priority date 3/1; closing date 7/31. Applicants notified on rolling basis starting 3/1, must reply within 2 week(s) of notification.

Contact. Financial aid office: (330) 471-8159
Michael Bole, Director of Financial Aid
515 25th Street Northwest
Canton, OH 44709-3897

Marietta College

Marietta, Ohio
www.marietta.edu
Four-year private **Federal Code: 003073**

	Living at home	On-campus
Tuition and fees (2002-2003):	$20,184	$20,184
Room and board:		$5,774
Board only:	$485	
Books and supplies:	$584	$584
Personal expenses:	$533	$533
Transportation:	$870	$485

Undergraduate aid. Need-based: Average financial aid package for full-time students was $17,455; for part-time $4,648. 67% awarded as scholarships/grants, 33% as loans/jobs. **Non-need-based:** 84% awarded as scholarships/grants, 16% as loans/jobs. Scholarships based on academics, alumni affiliation, art, leadership, minority status, music/drama, state/district residency. **Student debt:** 71% of graduating class borrowed to fund education; average debt was $17,463. **Additional information:** Auditions for music and theater required for competitive scholarships.

Freshman aid. Need-based: Out of 264 full-time freshmen, 240 applied for aid; 203 were judged to have need; of these 203 received aid. Average package met 93% of need. 102 students had full need met. Average scholarship/grant was $7,156; average loan $3,056. **Non-need based:** 174 full-time freshmen with need received non-need scholarships; 32 without need received awards.

Merit scholarships. Dean's Scholarship for selected applicants with minimum 3.25 GPA and 25 ACT or 1150 SAT scores; $4,000-$6,000. President's Scholarships for minimum 3.50 GPA and 27 ACT or 1200 SAT; $6,000-$9,000. Trustees Scholarships for minimum 3.75 GPA and 30 ACT or 1350 SAT; $9,000-13,000. Academic Accomplishment Scholarships for selected minority students; $5,000. Fine Arts Competition and Music Scholarships based on auditions or portfolios; $3,500. Hugh O'Brien Youth Leadership Scholarships; $3,000.

Policies to reduce costs. Tuition/fee waivers for children of alumni, minority students, employees and their families. Credit/placement for qualifying scores on AP, CLEP examinations. Work study available nights and weekends.

Payment plans. Credit card, deferred payment.

Application procedures. FAFSA, institutional form required. Priority date 3/1; closing date 4/15. Applicants notified on rolling basis starting 3/7, must reply within 2 week(s) of notification. **Transfers:** Priority date 4/15; no deadline.

Contact. Financial aid office: (740) 376-4712
Jim Begany, Director of Student Financial Services
215 Fifth Street
Marietta, OH 45750-4005

Marion Technical College

Marion, Ohio
www.mtc.edu
Two-year public **Federal Code: 010736**

	Living at home
Tuition and fees (2002-2003):	$2,844
Out-of-state:	$4,392
Per-credit charge:	$79
Per-credit out-of-state:	$122
Books and supplies:	$1,000
Personal expenses:	$850
Transportation:	$1,200

Undergraduate aid. Non-need-based: Scholarships based on academics.

Merit scholarships. Foundation Scholarship for selected applicants in top 50% of class; full tuition. President's Scholarship for selected applicants in top 50% of class; $1,000. Tech Prep Scholarship for selected graduates of Tech Prep program; $1,000.

Policies to reduce costs. Tuition/fee waivers for senior citizens, employees and their families. Credit/placement for qualifying scores on AP, CLEP examinations. Work study available for part-time students.

Payment plans. Credit card, installment, deferred payment.

Application procedures. FAFSA, institutional form required. Closing date 6/1. Applicants notified on rolling basis. **Transfers:** No deadline.

Contact. **Financial aid office:** (740) 389-4636 ext. 221
R. Andrew Harper, Vice President of Student Services
1467 Mount Vernon Avenue
Marion, OH 43302-5694

MedCentral College of Nursing

Mansfield, Ohio
www.medcentral.edu
Four-year private **Federal Code: 035864**

College costs. Clinical fees are $40 per credit hour.

	Living at home	On-campus
Tuition and fees:	$10,260	$10,260
Room and board:		$1,932

Application procedures. FAFSA required.

Contact. **Financial aid office:** (419) 520-2600
Robert Carlisle, Director of Financial Aid and Student Services
335 Glessner Avenue
Mansfield, OH 44903-2265

Miami University: Hamilton Campus

Hamilton, Ohio
www.ham.muohio.edu
Two-year public **Federal Code: 003079**

College costs. Students paying by the credit hour pay $13 general fee per credit hour.

	Living at home
Tuition and fees (2002-2003):	$3,332
Out-of-state:	$12,056
Per-credit charge:	$125
Per-credit out-of-state:	$488
Books and supplies:	$580
Personal expenses:	$1,732
Transportation:	$896

Undergraduate aid. **Need-based:** Need-based aid available for full-time and part-time students. **Non-need-based:** Scholarships based on academics, athletics, leadership, minority status, state/district residency. **Additional information:** Special gift funds for needy, multicultural students who enter with appropriate academic record. Separate application required for scholarships; closing date January 31.

Policies to reduce costs. Tuition/fee waivers for senior citizens, employees and their families. Credit/placement for qualifying scores on AP, IB, CLEP examinations. Work study available nights, weekends and for part-time students.

Payment plans. Credit card, installment payment.

Application procedures. FAFSA required. Priority date 2/15; no closing date. Applicants notified on rolling basis starting 4/1. **Transfers:** Priority date 2/15; no deadline. Transfer students must complete one semester at Miami University to be considered for scholarships.

Contact. Shelley Helfinstine, Financial Aid Coordinator
1601 Peck Boulevard
Hamilton, OH 45011-3399

Miami University: Middletown Campus

Middletown, Ohio
www.mid.muohio.edu
Two-year public **Federal Code: 003077**

College costs. Students paying by the credit hour pay $13 general fee per credit hour.

	Living at home
Tuition and fees (2002-2003):	$3,332
Out-of-state:	$12,056
Per-credit charge:	$125
Per-credit out-of-state:	$488
Books and supplies:	$600
Personal expenses:	$1,912
Transportation:	$896

Undergraduate aid. All financial aid based on need. Need-based aid available for full-time and part-time students.

Policies to reduce costs. Tuition/fee waivers for employees and their families. Credit/placement for qualifying scores on AP, IB, CLEP examinations. Work study available for part-time students.

Payment plans. Credit card, installment payment.

Application procedures. FAFSA required. Priority date 2/1; no closing date. Applicants notified on rolling basis. **Transfers:** Applicants must file by February 15 to be considered for campus-based aid or alumni scholarships.

Contact. **Financial aid office:** (513) 727-3200
Ellen Hall, Coordinator of Financial Aid
4200 East University Boulevard
Middletown, OH 45042

Miami University: Oxford Campus

Oxford, Ohio
www.muohio.edu
Four-year public **Federal Code: 003077**

College costs. General fees for part-time students $50.58 per credit hour.

	Living at home	On-campus
Tuition and fees (2002-2003):	$7,768	$7,768
Out-of-state:	$16,492	$16,492
Room and board:		$6,240
Board only:	$3,180	
Books and supplies:	$803	$803
Personal expenses:	$2,126	$2,126
Transportation:	$1,104	$432

Undergraduate aid. **Need-based:** Average financial aid package for full-time students was $6,997; for part-time $6,093. 31% awarded as scholarships/grants, 69% as loans/jobs. **Non-need-based:** 46% awarded as scholarships/grants, 54% as loans/jobs. Scholarships based on academics, art, athletics, leadership, minority status, music/drama, state/district residency. **Student debt:** 47% of graduating class borrowed to fund education; average debt was $17,579. **Additional information:** All financial aid awarded through Oxford campus.

Freshman aid. **Need-based:** Out of 3,541 full-time freshmen, 3,507 applied for aid; 1,201 were judged to have need; of these 1,178 received aid. Average package met 65% of need. 283 students had full need met. Average scholarship/grant was $2,970; average loan $2,443. **Non-need based:** 802 full-time freshmen with need received non-need scholarships; 814 without need received awards; 62 received athletic scholarships.

Policies to reduce costs. Tuition/fee waivers for employees and their families. Credit/placement for qualifying scores on AP, IB, CLEP examinations. Work study available nights, weekends and for part-time students.

Payment plans. Credit card, installment, deferred payment.

Application procedures. FAFSA required. Priority date 2/15; no closing date. Applicants notified on rolling basis starting 3/31, must reply by 5/1 or within 3 week(s) of notification. Early decision closing date 11/1. **Transfers:** Institutional merit scholarships not available to transfer students during first year of enrollment.

Contact. **Financial aid office:** (513) 529-8734
Chuck Knepfle, Director of Student Financial Aid
301 South Campus Avenue
Oxford, OH 45056-3434

Miami-Jacobs College

Dayton, Ohio
www.miamijacobs.edu
Two-year proprietary **Federal Code: 003076**

	Living at home
Tuition and fees (2002-2003):	$8,100
Per-credit charge:	$225
Personal expenses:	$2,500
Transportation:	$1,000

Undergraduate aid. All financial aid based on need. Need-based aid available for full-time and part-time students.

Policies to reduce costs. Tuition/fee waivers for employees and their families. Credit/placement for qualifying scores on AP, CLEP examinations.

Payment plans. Credit card, installment, deferred payment.

Application procedures. FAFSA, institutional form required. No deadline. Applicants notified on rolling basis. **Transfers:** No deadline.

Contact. **Financial aid office:** (937) 461-5174
Ron Mills, Director of Financial Aid
110 North Patterson Blvd.
Dayton, OH 45401

Mount Union College

Alliance, Ohio
www.muc.edu
Four-year private **Federal Code: 003083**

	Living at home	On-campus
Tuition and fees (2002-2003):	$17,150	$17,150
Room and board:		$5,070
Books and supplies:	$600	$600
Personal expenses:	$740	$740
Transportation:	$760	$760

Undergraduate aid. Need-based: Average financial aid package for full-time students was $14,667; for part-time $4,805. 67% awarded as scholarships/grants, 33% as loans/jobs. **Non-need-based:** 51% awarded as scholarships/grants, 49% as loans/jobs. Scholarships based on academics, alumni affiliation, art, music/drama, state/district residency. **Student debt:** 60% of graduating class borrowed to fund education; average debt was $15,944.

Freshman aid. Need-based: Out of 578 full-time freshmen, 523 applied for aid; 463 were judged to have need; of these 463 received aid. Average package met 88% of need. 98 students had full need met. Average scholarship/grant was $11,105; average loan $3,798. **Non-need based:** 45 full-time freshmen with need received non-need scholarships; 105 without need received awards.

Policies to reduce costs. Tuition/fee waivers for children of alumni, senior citizens, minority students, family members, family of clergy, employees and their families. Credit/placement for qualifying scores on AP, IB, CLEP examinations. Work study available weekends.

Payment plans. Credit card, installment payment.

Application procedures. FAFSA, institutional form required. Priority date 4/1; no closing date. Applicants notified on rolling basis starting 3/15, must reply within 4 week(s) of notification. **Transfers:** No deadline.

Contact. **Financial aid office:** (330) 823-2674
Sandra Pittenger, Director of Student Financial Services
1972 Clark Avenue
Alliance, OH 44601-3993

Mount Vernon Nazarene University

Mount Vernon, Ohio
www.mvnu.edu
Four-year private **Federal Code: 007085**

College costs. Campus residents and intercollegiate athletes must pay supplemental health insurance fee.

	Living at home	On-campus
Tuition and fees:	$14,280	$14,280
Room and board:		$4,653
Books and supplies:	$900	$900
Personal expenses:	$900	$970
Transportation:	$867	$816

Undergraduate aid. All financial aid based on need. Average financial aid package for full-time students was $9,187; for part-time $1,008. 33% awarded as scholarships/grants, 67% as loans/jobs. **Student debt:** 84% of graduating class borrowed to fund education; average debt was $18,298.

Freshman aid. Out of 349 full-time freshmen, 347 applied for aid; 302 were judged to have need; of these 302 received aid. 52 students had full need met. Average scholarship/grant was $4,347; average loan $4,387.

Policies to reduce costs. Tuition/fee waivers for senior citizens, family members, family of clergy, employees and their families. Credit/placement for qualifying scores on AP, IB, CLEP examinations.

Payment plans. Credit card, installment, deferred payment.

Application procedures. FAFSA, institutional form required. Priority date 3/15; no closing date. Applicants notified on rolling basis starting 2/15, must reply within 2 week(s) of notification.

Contact. **Financial aid office:** (740) 392-6868
Joanne Bowman, Director of Student Financial Planning
800 Martinsburg Road
Mount Vernon, OH 43050

Muskingum Area Technical College

Zanesville, Ohio
www.matc.tec.oh.us
Two-year public **Federal Code: 008133**

	Living at home
Tuition and fees (2002-2003):	$2,901
Out-of-state:	$5,331
Per-credit charge:	$54
Per-credit out-of-state:	$108
Books and supplies:	$675

Undergraduate aid. Need-based: 85% awarded as scholarships/grants, 15% as loans/jobs. Need-based aid available for part-time students. **Non-need-based:** 32% awarded as scholarships/grants, 68% as loans/jobs.

Policies to reduce costs. Tuition/fee waivers for senior citizens, employees and their families. Credit/placement for qualifying scores on CLEP examinations.

Payment plans. Credit card, deferred payment.

Application procedures. FAFSA required. Priority date 5/1; closing date 7/15. Must reply by 9/1.

Contact. **Financial aid office:** (740) 454-2501 ext. 1275
Jennifer Clipner, Financial Aid Director
1555 Newark Road
Zanesville, OH 43701

Muskingum College

New Concord, Ohio
www.muskingum.edu
Four-year private **Federal Code: 003084**

	Living at home	On-campus
Tuition and fees:	$14,800	$14,800
Room and board:		$5,880
Board only:	$1,800	
Books and supplies:	$700	$700
Personal expenses:	$800	$800
Transportation:	$400	$400

Undergraduate aid. Need-based: Need-based aid available for full-time and part-time students. **Non-need-based:** Scholarships based on academics, alumni affiliation, art, minority status, music/drama, religious affiliation, state/district residency. **Additional information:** Scholarship priority date February 1.

Policies to reduce costs. Tuition/fee waivers for children of alumni, minority students, family members, family of clergy, employees and their families. Credit/placement for qualifying scores on AP, CLEP examinations.

Payment plans. Credit card, installment, deferred payment.

Application procedures. FAFSA, institutional form required. Priority date 3/15; no closing date. Applicants notified on rolling basis starting 3/1, must reply by 5/1 or within 2 week(s) of notification. **Transfers:** No deadline.

Contact. **Financial aid office:** (740) 826-8139
Jeff Zellers, Director of Student Financial Services
163 Stormont Street
New Concord, OH 43762-1160

North Central State College

Mansfield, Ohio
www.ncstatecollege.edu
Two-year public **Federal Code: 005313**

	Living at home
Tuition and fees (2002-2003):	$2,836
Out-of-state:	$5,243
Per-credit charge:	$54
Per-credit out-of-state:	$107
Books and supplies:	$705
Personal expenses:	$726
Transportation:	$1,500

Undergraduate aid. All financial aid based on need. Need-based aid available for full-time and part-time students.

Policies to reduce costs. Tuition/fee waivers for senior citizens, employees and their families. Credit/placement for qualifying scores on CLEP examinations.

Payment plans. Credit card, installment, deferred payment.

Application procedures. FAFSA required. Priority date 4/1; no closing date. Applicants notified on rolling basis starting 5/30, must reply within 1 week(s) of notification.

Contact. **Financial aid office:** (419) 755-4899
Doris Smith, Assistant Dean of Financial Aid
Box 698
Mansfield, OH 44901

Northwest State Community College

Archbold, Ohio
www.nscc.cc.oh.us
Two-year public **Federal Code: 008677**

	Living at home
Tuition and fees (2002-2003):	$3,200
Out-of-state:	$6,200
Per-credit charge:	$100
Per-credit out-of-state:	$200
Personal expenses:	$750
Transportation:	$1,200

Undergraduate aid. All financial aid based on need. 61% awarded as scholarships/grants, 39% as loans/jobs. Need-based aid available for part-time students.

Policies to reduce costs. Tuition/fee waivers for senior citizens, employees and their families. Credit/placement for qualifying scores on AP examinations.

Payment plans. Credit card, deferred payment.

Application procedures. FAFSA, institutional form required. Priority date 6/1; no closing date. Applicants notified on rolling basis starting 4/1.

Contact. **Financial aid office:** (419) 267-5511 ext. 326
Paul Sutcliffe, Financial Aid Officer
22600 State Route 34
Archbold, OH 43502

Notre Dame College

Cleveland, Ohio
www.notredamecollege.edu
Four-year private **Federal Code: 003085**

	Living at home	On-campus
Tuition and fees (2002-2003):	$16,052	$16,052
Room and board:		$5,906
Books and supplies:	$1,278	$1,278
Personal expenses:		$808
Transportation:		$550

Undergraduate aid. **Need-based:** Need-based aid available for full-time students. **Non-need-based:** Scholarships based on academics, state/district residency.

Merit scholarships. Merit Scholarships: based on cumulative high school and ACT or SAT I scores; $2,500-$7,500. Presidential Scholarships: awarded to students with cumulative high school GPA of at least 3.9 and ACT composite of at least 27 or SAT I total of at least 1210; $3,000 awarded in addition to Merit Scholarships.

Policies to reduce costs. Tuition/fee waivers for employees and their families. Credit/placement for qualifying scores on AP, CLEP examinations.

Payment plans. Credit card, installment payment.

Application procedures. FAFSA required. Closing date 5/1. Applicants notified on rolling basis starting 1/1, must reply within 2 week(s) of notification.

Contact. Mary McCrystal, Director of Student Financial Assistance
4545 College Road
Cleveland, OH 44121-4293

Oberlin College

Oberlin, Ohio
www.oberlin.edu
Four-year private **Federal Code: 003086**

	Living at home	On-campus
Tuition and fees (2002-2003):	$28,050	$28,050
Room and board:		$6,830
Books and supplies:	$700	$700
Personal expenses:	$900	$900

Undergraduate aid. **Need-based:** Average financial aid package for full-time students was $23,099; for part-time $23,296. 84% awarded as scholarships/grants, 16% as loans/jobs. **Non-need-based:** 78% awarded as scholarships/grants, 22% as loans/jobs. Scholarships based on academics, leadership, music/drama, state/district residency. **Student debt:** 55% of graduating class borrowed to fund education; average debt was $13,034.

Freshman aid. **Need-based:** Out of 719 full-time freshmen, 489 applied for aid; 401 were judged to have need; of these 401 received aid. Average package met 100% of need. 401 students had full need met. Average scholarship/grant was $16,773; average loan $2,333. **Non-need based:** 223 full-time freshmen with need received non-need scholarships; 90 without need received awards.

Merit scholarships. Bonner Scholarship; based on community service. John Frederick Oberlin Scholarship; based on academic merit. Stern Scholarship; based on excellence in sciences. Mary Elizabeth Johnston Scholarship; based on academic merit; available to Ohio residents only. Dean's Scholarship; available to Conservatory of Music students.

Policies to reduce costs. Tuition/fee waivers for employees and their families. Credit/placement for qualifying scores on AP, IB examinations.

Payment plans. Installment, deferred payment.

Application procedures. FAFSA, CSS PROFILE required. Priority date 2/1; closing date 2/15. Applicants notified by 4/15, must reply by 5/1 or within 2 week(s) of notification. Early decision closing date 11/15. **Transfers:** Closing date 3/1. Limited scholarship funding available for transfer students.

Contact. **Financial aid office:** (440) 775-8142
Robert Reddy, Director of Financial Aid
Carnegie Building, 101 North Professor Street
Oberlin, OH 44074

Ohio Business College

Lorain, Ohio
www.ohiobusinesscollege.com
Two-year proprietary **Federal Code: 021585**

	Living at home
Tuition and fees (2002-2003):	$7,440
Per-credit charge:	$145
Books and supplies:	$1,080

Undergraduate aid. **Need-based:** Need-based aid available for full-time and part-time students.

Payment plans. Credit card payment.

Application procedures. FAFSA required. No deadline. Applicants notified on rolling basis.

Contact. Tamara Jones, Regional Financial Aid Manager
1907 North Ridge Road
Lorain, OH 44055

Ohio Business College: Sandusky

Sandusky, Ohio
www.ohiobusinesscollege.com
Two-year proprietary **Federal Code: 021585**

	Living at home
Tuition and fees (2002-2003):	$6,975
Per-credit charge:	$145
Books and supplies:	$1,200

Contact. **Financial aid office:** (419) 627-8345
Andrea Speer, Financial Aid Administrator
4020 Milan Road
Sandusky, OH 44870

Ohio Dominican College

Columbus, Ohio
www.ohiodominican.edu
Four-year private **Federal Code: 003035**

	Living at home	On-campus
Tuition and fees (2002-2003):	$16,200	$16,200
Room and board:		$5,370
Books and supplies:	$665	$665
Personal expenses:	$880	$880
Transportation:	$810	$710

Undergraduate aid. **Need-based:** Need-based aid available for full-time and part-time students. **Non-need-based:** Scholarships based on academics, athletics, state/district residency.

Policies to reduce costs. Tuition/fee waivers for senior citizens, employees and their families. Credit/placement for qualifying scores on AP, IB, CLEP examinations. Work study available nights, weekends and for part-time students.

Payment plans. Credit card, installment, deferred payment.

Application procedures. FAFSA required. Priority date 4/1; no closing date. Applicants notified on rolling basis starting 3/1, must reply within 2 week(s) of notification.

Contact. **Financial aid office:** (614) 251-4640
Cindy Hahn, Director of Financial Aid
1216 Sunbury Road
Columbus, OH 43219

Ohio Institute of Photography and Technology

Dayton, Ohio
www.oipt.com
Two-year proprietary **Federal Code: 013562**

College costs. Tuition costs $11,888 per academic year, including fees and books.

Undergraduate aid. **Need-based:** Need-based aid available for full-time and part-time students.

Policies to reduce costs. Tuition/fee waivers for employees and their families.

Payment plans. Credit card, installment payment.

Application procedures. FAFSA, institutional form required. No deadline. Applicants notified on rolling basis starting 3/1. **Transfers:** No deadline.

Contact. Debra Petrae, Financial Aid Officer
2029 Edgefield Road
Dayton, OH 45439

Ohio Northern University

Ada, Ohio
www.onu.edu
Four-year private **Federal Code: 003089**

College costs. Tuition and fees for engineering $24,900; pharmacy $26,220.

	Living at home	On-campus
Tuition and fees (2002-2003):	$23,310	$23,310
Room and board:		$5,805
Books and supplies:	$900	$900
Personal expenses:	$1,200	$1,400
Transportation:	$600	$400

Undergraduate aid. **Need-based:** Average financial aid package for full-time students was $19,711. 68% awarded as scholarships/grants, 32% as loans/jobs. Need-based aid available for part-time students. **Non-need-based:** 54% awarded as scholarships/grants, 46% as loans/jobs. Scholarships based on academics, art, leadership, music/drama, state/district residency. **Student debt:** 79% of graduating class borrowed to fund education; average debt was $20,740.

Freshman aid. **Need-based:** Out of 533 full-time freshmen, 517 applied for aid; 457 were judged to have need; of these 457 received aid. Average package met 96% of need. 169 students had full need met. Average scholarship/grant was $13,681; average loan $3,991. **Non-need based:** 449 full-time freshmen with need received non-need scholarships; 82 without need received awards.

Merit scholarships. Presidential Scholarship awards up to $24,000 for 3.5 GPA, 30 ACT or 1300 SAT, and on-campus competition. Academic Honors Scholarship awards up to $18,000 for 3.0 GPA, 26 ACT or 1170 SAT, and on-campus competition. Distinguished Achievement Scholarship awards up to $15,000 for 3.2 GPA, 24 ACT or 1070 SAT, on-campus competition, and leadership activities. Deans Scholarship awards $4,000 to $10,000 for 3.3 GPA and 25 ACT or 1140 SAT. Trustees Scholarship awards up to $20,000 for 3.5 GPA, 28 ACT or 1240 SAT and on-campus competition.

Policies to reduce costs. Tuition/fee waivers for children of alumni, family members, family of clergy, employees and their families. Prepayment discount; credit/placement for qualifying scores on AP, IB, CLEP examinations. Work study available nights and weekends.

Payment plans. Credit card, installment payment.

Application procedures. FAFSA, institutional form required. Priority date 4/15; closing date 6/1. Applicants notified on rolling basis starting 2/15, must reply within 2 week(s) of notification.

Contact. **Financial aid office:** (419) 772-2272
Karen Condeni, Vice President/Dean of Admissions and Financial Aid
525 South Main Street
Ada, OH 45810-1599

Ohio State University Agricultural Technical Institute

Wooster, Ohio
Two-year public
Federal Code: 003090

	Living at home	On-campus
Tuition and fees (2002-2003):	$3,963	$3,963
Out-of-state:	$13,386	$13,386
Room only:		$3,900
Books and supplies:	$525	$525
Personal expenses:	$1,034	$3,000
Transportation:	$1,162	$700

Policies to reduce costs. Tuition/fee waivers for employees and their families. Credit/placement for qualifying scores on AP, CLEP examinations.

Payment plans. Installment payment.

Application procedures. No deadline. Applicants notified on rolling basis starting 6/1, must reply within 2 week(s) of notification.

Contact. Barbara LaMoreaux, Coordinator, Financial Aid
1328 Dover Road
Wooster, OH 44691-4099

Ohio State University: Columbus Campus

Columbus, Ohio
www.osu.edu
Four-year public **Federal Code: 003090**

	Living at home	On-campus
Tuition and fees (2002-2003):	$5,691	$5,691
Out-of-state:	$15,114	$15,114
Room and board:		$6,420
Board only:	$2,976	
Books and supplies:	$936	$936
Personal expenses:	$2,286	$2,346
Transportation:	$1,344	$192

Undergraduate aid. Need-based: Average financial aid package for full-time students was $8,211; for part-time $7,061. 35% awarded as scholarships/grants, 65% as loans/jobs. **Non-need-based:** 52% awarded as scholarships/grants, 48% as loans/jobs. Scholarships based on academics, alumni affiliation, art, athletics, job skills, leadership, minority status, music/drama, state/district residency. **Student debt:** 52% of graduating class borrowed to fund education; average debt was $15,011.

Freshman aid. Need-based: Out of 5,940 full-time freshmen, 4,510 applied for aid; 3,067 were judged to have need; of these 3,067 received aid. Average package met 78% of need. 1036 students had full need met. Average scholarship/grant was $3,962; average loan $3,271. **Non-need based:** 2,760 full-time freshmen with need received non-need scholarships; 925 without need received awards; 126 received athletic scholarships.

Policies to reduce costs. Tuition/fee waivers for senior citizens, employees and their families. Credit/placement for qualifying scores on AP, IB, CLEP examinations. Work study available nights, weekends and for part-time students.

Payment plans. Installment payment.

Application procedures. FAFSA required. Priority date 2/15; no closing date. Applicants notified by 4/1, must reply by 5/1 or within 4 week(s) of notification. **Transfers:** Priority date 6/25; no deadline.

Contact. **Financial aid office:** (614) 292-0300
Natala Hart, Director of Office of Student Financial Aid
Third Floor, Lincoln Tower, 1800 Cannon Drive
Columbus, OH 43210

Ohio State University: Lima Campus

Lima, Ohio
www.lima.ohio-state.edu
Four-year public **Federal Code: 003090**

	Living at home
Tuition and fees (2002-2003):	$3,927
Out-of-state:	$13,350
Books and supplies:	$750
Personal expenses:	$400
Transportation:	$810

Undergraduate aid. Need-based: 35% awarded as scholarships/grants, 65% as loans/jobs. Need-based aid available for part-time students. **Non-need-based:** 36% awarded as scholarships/grants, 64% as loans/jobs. Scholarships based on academics.

Policies to reduce costs. Tuition/fee waivers for senior citizens, employees and their families. Credit/placement for qualifying scores on AP, CLEP examinations. Work study available nights and for part-time students.

Application procedures. Priority date 4/1; no closing date. Applicants notified on rolling basis starting 5/1, must reply within 2 week(s) of notification. **Transfers:** Closing date 2/15.

Contact. **Financial aid office:** (419) 995-8299
Diane Douglass, Director for Financial Aid
4240 Campus Drive
Lima, OH 45804-3596

Ohio State University: Mansfield Campus

Mansfield, Ohio
Four-year public **Federal Code: 003090**

	Living at home
Tuition and fees (2002-2003):	$3,927
Out-of-state:	$13,350
Books and supplies:	$525
Personal expenses:	$2,335
Transportation:	$1,100

Undergraduate aid. Need-based: Need-based aid available for full-time and part-time students.

Policies to reduce costs. Tuition/fee waivers for employees and their families. Credit/placement for qualifying scores on AP, CLEP examinations.

Payment plans. Installment payment.

Application procedures. No deadline. Applicants notified on rolling basis starting 5/1, must reply within 2 week(s) of notification.

Contact. Henry Thomas, Coordinator of Admissions and Financial Aid
1680 University Drive
Mansfield, OH 44906

Ohio State University: Marion Campus

Marion, Ohio
Four-year public **Federal Code: 003090**

	Living at home
Tuition and fees (2002-2003):	$3,927
Out-of-state:	$13,350
Books and supplies:	$600
Personal expenses:	$2,600
Transportation:	$1,135

Undergraduate aid. Need-based: Need-based aid available for full-time and part-time students.

Policies to reduce costs. Tuition/fee waivers for employees and their families. Credit/placement for qualifying scores on AP, CLEP examinations.

Payment plans. Installment payment.

Application procedures. No deadline. Applicants notified on rolling basis starting 5/1, must reply within 2 week(s) of notification.

Contact. Dixie Strawser, Financial Aid Officer
1465 Mount Vernon Avenue
Marion, OH 43302

Ohio State University: Newark Campus

Newark, Ohio
Four-year public **Federal Code: 003095**

	Living at home
Tuition and fees (2002-2003):	$3,927
Out-of-state:	$13,350
Books and supplies:	$525
Personal expenses:	$2,276
Transportation:	$1,188

Policies to reduce costs. Tuition/fee waivers for employees and their families. Credit/placement for qualifying scores on AP, CLEP examinations.

Payment plans. Installment payment.

Application procedures. No deadline. Applicants notified on rolling basis starting 5/1, must reply within 2 week(s) of notification.

Contact. Robert Noble, Financial Aid Officer
University Drive
Newark, OH 43055

Ohio Technical College

Cleveland, Ohio
www.ohiotechnicalcollege.com
Two-year proprietary **Federal Code: 011745**

College costs (2002-2003). Tuition for 18-month associate program $17,825; diploma programs range from $9,252 to $15,925. Fees range from $40 to $76 depending on program. Room: $2,781. Books/supplies: $850. Personal expenses: $1,837.

Contact. Denise Schmidt, Director of Financial Aid
1374 East 51st Street
Cleveland, OH 44103-1269

Ohio University

Athens, Ohio
www.ohiou.edu
Four-year public **Federal Code: 003100**

	Living at home	On-campus
Tuition and fees (2002-2003):	$6,336	$6,336
Out-of-state:	$13,818	$13,818
Room and board:		$6,777
Books and supplies:	$798	$798
Personal expenses:	$1,215	$879
Transportation:	$2,898	$1,017

Undergraduate aid. All financial aid based on need. Average financial aid package for full-time students was $6,581; for part-time $5,792. 29% awarded as scholarships/grants, 71% as loans/jobs. **Student debt:** 57% of graduating class borrowed to fund education; average debt was $15,285.

Freshman aid. Out of 3,679 full-time freshmen, 2,884 applied for aid; 1,736 were judged to have need; of these 1,688 received aid. Average package met 65% of need. 334 students had full need met. Average scholarship/grant was $2,381; average loan $2,592.

Policies to reduce costs. Tuition/fee waivers for senior citizens, employees and their families. Credit/placement for qualifying scores on AP, IB, CLEP examinations.

Payment plans. Credit card, installment payment.

Application procedures. FAFSA required. Priority date 3/15; closing date 4/1. Applicants notified on rolling basis starting 4/1, must reply within 3 week(s) of notification.

Contact. Sondra Williams, Director, Student Financial Aid and Scholarships
120 Chubb Hall
Athens, OH 45701-2979

Ohio University: Chillicothe Campus

Chillicothe, Ohio
www.ohiou.edu/chillicothe
Four-year public **Federal Code: 003100**

	Living at home
Tuition and fees (2002-2003):	$3,564
Out-of-state:	$9,150
Books and supplies:	$750
Transportation:	$1,848

Undergraduate aid. Need-based: Need-based aid available for full-time and part-time students.

Policies to reduce costs. Tuition/fee waivers for senior citizens, employees and their families. Credit/placement for qualifying scores on AP, CLEP examinations.

Payment plans. Credit card payment.

Application procedures. FAFSA required. Closing date 4/1. Applicants notified on rolling basis.

Contact. Dennis Bothel, Assistant Director of Student Services
101 University Drive/PO Box 629
Chillicothe, OH 45601

Ohio University: Eastern Campus

St. Clairsville, Ohio
www.eastern.ohiou.edu
Four-year public **Federal Code: 003101**

	Living at home
Tuition and fees (2002-2003):	$3,564
Out-of-state:	$9,150
Transportation:	$1,995

Undergraduate aid. Need-based: Need-based aid available for full-time and part-time students. **Non-need-based:** Scholarships based on academics, alumni affiliation, minority status.

Policies to reduce costs. Tuition/fee waivers for employees and their families.

Payment plans. Credit card, installment payment.

Application procedures. FAFSA required. Closing date 3/1. Applicants notified by 5/15. **Transfers:** Priority date 3/1; closing date 5/1.

Contact. Financial aid office: (740) 695-1720 ext. 209
Kevin Chenoweth, Student Services Manager
45425 National Road West
St. Clairsville, OH 43950

Ohio University: Lancaster Campus

Lancaster, Ohio
www.ohiou.edu/lancaster
Two-year public **Federal Code: 003104**

	Living at home
Tuition and fees (2002-2003):	$3,564
Out-of-state:	$9,150
Per-credit charge:	$108
Per-credit out-of-state:	$280
Books and supplies:	$500
Transportation:	$400

Undergraduate aid. Need-based: 29% awarded as scholarships/grants, 71% as loans/jobs. Need-based aid available for part-time students. **Additional information:** Scholarship application deadline April 1.

Policies to reduce costs. Tuition/fee waivers for employees and their families. Credit/placement for qualifying scores on AP examinations.

Application procedures. FAFSA required. Priority date 2/15; no closing date. Applicants notified on rolling basis, must reply within 2 week(s) of notification.

Contact. Pat Fox, Coordinator, Financial Aid
1570 Granville Pike
Lancaster, OH 43130

Ohio University: Southern Campus at Ironton

Ironton, Ohio
www.southern.ohiou.edu
Four-year public **Federal Code: 003100**

	Living at home
Tuition and fees (2002-2003):	$3,282
Out-of-state:	$4,272
Books and supplies:	$600
Transportation:	$1,800

Undergraduate aid. Need-based: Need-based aid available for full-time and part-time students.

Payment plans. Credit card payment.

Application procedures. FAFSA required. No deadline. Applicants notified on rolling basis.

Contact. Jackie Lundy, Chief Financial Aid Officer
1804 Liberty Avenue
Ironton, OH 45638

Ohio University: Zanesville Campus

Zanesville, Ohio
www.zanesville.ohiou.edu/
Four-year public **Federal Code: 003108**

	Living at home
Tuition and fees (2002-2003):	$3,579
Out-of-state:	$9,165
Books and supplies:	$798
Personal expenses:	$879
Transportation:	$1,017

Policies to reduce costs. Tuition/fee waivers for senior citizens, employees and their families. Credit/placement for qualifying scores on AP examinations.

Payment plans. Credit card, installment payment.

Application procedures. FAFSA required. Priority date 3/15; no closing date. Applicants notified on rolling basis starting 4/15, must reply within 2 week(s) of notification.

Contact. Sharon Lenthe, Financial Aid Director
1425 Newark Road
Zanesville, OH 43701

Ohio Valley College of Technology

East Liverpool, Ohio
www.ohiovalleytech.com
Two-year proprietary **Federal Code: 016261**

College costs. Cost of books included in fees.

	Living at home
Tuition and fees:	$6,890
Transportation:	$500

Undergraduate aid. All financial aid based on need. Need-based aid available for full-time and part-time students.

Policies to reduce costs. Tuition/fee waivers for employees and their families. Credit/placement for qualifying scores on AP examinations.

Payment plans. Credit card, installment payment.

Application procedures. FAFSA required. No deadline. Applicants notified on rolling basis, must reply within 6 week(s) of notification.

Contact. Virginia Hutchison, Financial Aid Officer
16808 St. Clair Avenue, PO Box 7000
East Liverpool, OH 43920

Ohio Wesleyan University

Delaware, Ohio
web.owu.edu
Four-year private **Federal Code: 003109**

	Living at home	On-campus
Tuition and fees (2002-2003):	$24,200	$24,200
Room and board:		$7,010
Board only:	$3,230	
Books and supplies:	$550	$550
Personal expenses:	$500	$500
Transportation:	$100	$800

Undergraduate aid. Need-based: Average financial aid package for full-time students was $20,866; for part-time $6,425. 79% awarded as scholarships/grants, 21% as loans/jobs. **Non-need-based:** 83% awarded as scholarships/grants, 17% as loans/jobs. Scholarships based on academics, alumni affiliation, art, leadership, minority status, music/drama, religious affiliation, state/district residency. **Student debt:** 55% of graduating class borrowed to fund education; average debt was $21,180. **Additional information:** Scholarships awarded based on merits presented in application for admission.

Freshman aid. Need-based: Out of 546 full-time freshmen, 370 applied for aid; 325 were judged to have need; of these 325 received aid. Average package met 90% of need. 93 students had full need met. Average scholarship/grant was $17,074; average loan $2,999. **Non-need based:** 66 full-time freshmen with need received non-need scholarships; 214 without need received awards.

Merit scholarships. Presidential Scholarships; 25 awarded; full tuition. Trustee scholarships; 40 awarded; 75% of tuition. Faculty Scholarships; 140 awarded; 50% of tuition. Community Service Awards; Dean's Award; fine arts, music, theater scholarships; multicultural awards; recognition awards

Policies to reduce costs. Tuition/fee waivers for children of alumni, senior citizens, family of clergy, employees and their families. Prepayment discount; credit/placement for qualifying scores on AP, IB examinations. Work study available nights and weekends.

Payment plans. Credit card, installment payment.

Application procedures. FAFSA, institutional form required. Priority date 3/15; closing date 5/15. Applicants notified on rolling basis starting 1/15, must reply by 5/1. Early decision closing date 12/1.

Contact. Financial aid office: (740) 368-3050
Greg Matthews, Director of Financial Aid
61 South Sandusky Street
Delaware, OH 43015-2398

Otterbein College

Westerville, Ohio
www.otterbein.edu
Four-year private **Federal Code: 003110**

	Living at home	On-campus
Tuition and fees (2002-2003):	$18,993	$18,993
Room and board:		$5,727
Books and supplies:	$600	$600
Personal expenses:	$1,017	$1,017
Transportation:	$806	$531

Undergraduate aid. Non-need-based: Scholarships based on academics, state/district residency.

Policies to reduce costs. Tuition/fee waivers for adults, children of alumni, minority students, family members, family of clergy, employees and their families. Credit/placement for qualifying scores on AP, CLEP examinations. Work study available nights and weekends.

Payment plans. Credit card, installment payment.

Application procedures. FAFSA, CSS PROFILE required. Priority date 4/1; no closing date. Applicants notified on rolling basis starting 2/15, must reply by 5/1. **Transfers:** Transfer students must complete appropriate state grant transfer paperwork.

Contact. Financial aid office: (614) 823-1502
Thomas Yarnell, Director of Financial Aid
One Otterbein College
Westerville, OH 43081

Owens Community College: Findlay Campus

Findlay, Ohio
www.owens.edu
Two-year public

	Living at home
Tuition and fees (2002-2003):	$2,060
Out-of-state:	$3,860
Per-credit charge:	$75
Per-credit out-of-state:	$150
Books and supplies:	$465

Undergraduate aid. Non-need-based: Scholarships based on academics, athletics, state/district residency.

Policies to reduce costs. Tuition/fee waivers for senior citizens, employees and their families. Credit/placement for qualifying scores on AP examinations.

Payment plans. Credit card, installment payment.

Application procedures. FAFSA required. Priority date 3/1; no closing date. Applicants notified on rolling basis starting 4/1.

Contact. Financial aid office: (419) 661-7344
Betsy Johnson, Director of Financial Aid
300 Davis Street
Findlay, OH 45840-3600

Owens Community College: Toledo

Toledo, Ohio
www.owens.edu
Two-year public **Federal Code: 005753**

	Living at home
Tuition and fees (2002-2003):	$2,060
Out-of-state:	$3,860
Per-credit charge:	$75
Per-credit out-of-state:	$150
Books and supplies:	$465

Undergraduate aid. Non-need-based: Scholarships based on academics, athletics, state/district residency.

Policies to reduce costs. Tuition/fee waivers for senior citizens, employees and their families. Credit/placement for qualifying scores on AP examinations.

Payment plans. Credit card, installment payment.

Application procedures. FAFSA required. Priority date 3/1; no closing date. Applicants notified on rolling basis starting 4/1.

Contact. Financial aid office: (419) 661-7343
Betsy Johnson, Director of Financial Aid
Box 10000
Toledo, OH 43699-1947

Pontifical College Josephinum

Columbus, Ohio
www.pcj.edu
Four-year private **Federal Code: 003113**

	Living at home	On-campus
Tuition and fees (2002-2003):	$9,740	$9,740
Room and board:		$5,660
Books and supplies:	$350	$350
Personal expenses:	$2,150	$2,500

Undergraduate aid. All financial aid based on need. Average financial aid package for full-time students was $12,558. Need-based aid available for part-time students. **Student debt:** 10% of graduating class borrowed to fund education; average debt was $27,542.

Freshman aid. Out of 9 full-time freshmen, 8 applied for aid; 5 were judged to have need; of these 5 received aid.

Policies to reduce costs. Credit/placement for qualifying scores on AP, CLEP examinations. Work study available nights and weekends.

Payment plans. Installment payment.

Application procedures. FAFSA, institutional form required. Priority date 6/30; no closing date. Applicants notified on rolling basis starting 8/15, must reply within 2 week(s) of notification. **Transfers:** No deadline.

Contact. Financial aid office: (614) 985-2212
Marky Leichtnam, Director of Financial Aid
7625 North High Street
Columbus, OH 43235-1498

RETS Tech Center

Centerville, Ohio
www.retstechcenter.com
Two-year proprietary **Federal Code: 012267**

College costs (2002-2003). Costs are charged per entire associate degree or diploma program and vary with specific program. Associate programs range from $15,205 to $18,965. Diploma programs range from $7,855 to $8,235. Costs include books, supplies, tools, testing fees. Books/supplies: $950. Personal expenses: $945. Transportation: $900.

Undergraduate aid. All financial aid based on need. Need-based aid available for full-time and part-time students.

Policies to reduce costs. Tuition/fee waivers for employees and their families. Tuition at time of enrollment guaranteed for 2 years; credit/placement for qualifying scores on AP examinations.

Payment plans. Credit card, installment payment.

Application procedures. FAFSA, institutional form required. No deadline. Applicants notified on rolling basis.

Contact. Andrea Sanders, Director of Financial Aid
555 East Alex-Bell Road
Centerville, OH 45459-2712

Rabbinical College of Telshe

Wickliffe, Ohio
Four-year private **Federal Code: 003115**

	Living at home	On-campus
Tuition and fees (2002-2003):	$5,400	$5,400
Room and board:		$2,700
Books and supplies:	$300	$300
Personal expenses:		$1,000
Transportation:		$400

Contact. Financial aid office: (440) 943-5300 ext. 13
Miriam Gester, Director of Financial Aid
28400 Euclid Avenue
Wickliffe, OH 44092-2584

Rosedale Bible College

Irwin, Ohio
www.rosedalebible.org
Two-year private

	Living at home
Tuition and fees:	$3,810
Per-credit charge:	$126

Application procedures. FAFSA, institutional form required. Applicants notified on rolling basis.

Contact. 2270 Rosedale Road
Irwin, OH 43029

School of Advertising Art

Dayton, Ohio
www.saacollege.com
Two-year proprietary **Federal Code: 017160**

College costs. First year tuition for diploma program $13,695, required fees $1,850.

	Living at home
Tuition and fees:	$17,045

Application procedures. FAFSA, institutional form required. Priority date 6/1; no closing date. Applicants notified on rolling basis.

Contact. Heather Mitchell, Financial Aid Director
1725 East David Road
Dayton, OH 45440-1612

Shawnee State University

Portsmouth, Ohio
www.shawnee.edu
Four-year public **Federal Code: 009942**

College costs. Students from some districts in Kentucky and West Virginia pay $4,716 full-time tuition, $131 per-credit hour.

	Living at home	On-campus
Tuition and fees (2002-2003):	$4,050	$4,050
Out-of-state:	$7,146	$7,146
Room and board:		$5,421
Books and supplies:	$900	$900
Personal expenses:	$1,494	$1,494
Transportation:	$1,260	$600

Undergraduate aid. Need-based: Need-based aid available for full-time and part-time students. **Non-need-based:** Scholarships based on academics. **Additional information:** ACT test recommended for scholarship applicants.

Policies to reduce costs. Tuition/fee waivers for senior citizens, employees and their families. Credit/placement for qualifying scores on CLEP examinations.

Payment plans. Credit card, installment payment.

Application procedures. FAFSA, institutional form required. Priority date 6/15; no closing date. Applicants notified on rolling basis starting 5/1, must reply within 4 week(s) of notification.

Contact. Pat Moore, Financial Aid Director
940 Second Street
Portsmouth, OH 45662

Sinclair Community College

Dayton, Ohio
www.sinclair.edu
Two-year public **Federal Code: 003119**

	Living at home
Tuition and fees (2002-2003):	$1,564
Out-of-district:	$2,554
Out-of-state:	$4,219
Per-credit charge:	$35
Per-credit out-of-district:	$57
Per-credit out-of-state:	$94
Books and supplies:	$810
Personal expenses:	$2,000
Transportation:	$473

Undergraduate aid. All financial aid based on need. 90% awarded as scholarships/grants, 10% as loans/jobs. Need-based aid available for part-time students.

Policies to reduce costs. Tuition/fee waivers for senior citizens, employees and their families. Credit/placement for qualifying scores on AP, IB, CLEP examinations. Work study available nights and weekends.

Payment plans. Credit card payment.

Application procedures. FAFSA, institutional form required. Priority date 5/1; closing date 8/1. Applicants notified on rolling basis. **Transfers:** No deadline.

Contact. **Financial aid office:** (937) 512-2765
Kathy Wiesenauer, Director of Financial Aid and Scholarships
444 West Third Street
Dayton, OH 45402-1460

Southeastern Business College

Chillicothe, Ohio
www.careersohio.com
Two-year proprietary **Federal Code: 020568**

College costs. Per-credit-hour cost for Information Technology Administration program is $185.

	Living at home
Tuition and fees:	$6,750
Per-credit charge:	$165
Books and supplies:	$1,300
Personal expenses:	$1,500
Transportation:	$500

Undergraduate aid. All financial aid based on need. Need-based aid available for full-time and part-time students.

Policies to reduce costs. Tuition/fee waivers for employees and their families.

Payment plans. Credit card, installment payment.

Application procedures. FAFSA, institutional form required. Closing date 4/30. Applicants notified by 6/1, must reply within 2 week(s) of notification. **Transfers:** No deadline.

Contact. **Financial aid office:** (740) 774-2063
Jeanette Harris, Financial Aid Representative
1855 Western Avenue
Chillicothe, OH 45601-1038

Southeastern Business College: Lancaster

Lancaster, Ohio
www.careersohio.com
Two-year proprietary **Federal Code: 020568**

	Living at home
Tuition and fees (2002-2003):	$7,200
Per-credit charge:	$150
Books and supplies:	$1,300
Personal expenses:	$1,500
Transportation:	$500

Undergraduate aid. All financial aid based on need. Need-based aid available for full-time and part-time students.

Application procedures. FAFSA, institutional form required. Closing date 4/30. Applicants notified by 6/1, must reply within 2 week(s) of notification.

Contact. **Financial aid office:** (740) 687-6126
Kathy Maloney, Financial Aid Representative
1522 Sheridan Drive
Lancaster, OH 43130-1303

Southern State Community College

Hillsboro, Ohio
www.sscc.edu
Two-year public **Federal Code: 012870**

	Living at home
Tuition and fees (2002-2003):	$2,925
Out-of-state:	$5,715
Per-credit charge:	$75
Per-credit out-of-state:	$147
Board only:	$1,700
Books and supplies:	$1,200
Transportation:	$960

Undergraduate aid. **Need-based:** 59% awarded as scholarships/grants, 41% as loans/jobs. Need-based aid available for part-time students. **Non-need-based:** Scholarships based on academics, art, athletics, music/drama.

Policies to reduce costs. Tuition/fee waivers for senior citizens, employees and their families. Credit/placement for qualifying scores on AP, CLEP examinations. Work study available for part-time students.

Payment plans. Credit card, deferred payment.

Application procedures. FAFSA, institutional form required. Priority date 7/1; closing date 9/1. Applicants notified by 4/15, must reply within 2 week(s) of notification. **Transfers:** Priority date 7/1; no deadline.

Contact. **Financial aid office:** (937) 393-3431 ext. 2611
Janeen Deatley, Financial Aid Director
100 Hobart Drive
Hillsboro, OH 45133

Southwestern College of Business

Dayton, Ohio
www.swcollege.net
Two-year proprietary **Federal Code: 030161**

	Living at home
Tuition and fees (2002-2003):	$6,450

Undergraduate aid. All financial aid based on need. Average financial aid package for full-time students was $4,000. Need-based aid available for part-time students. **Student debt:** 1% of graduating class borrowed to fund education; average debt was $6,500.

Freshman aid. Out of 171 full-time freshmen, 71 applied for aid; 70 were judged to have need; of these 70 received aid. 35 students had full need met.

Application procedures. FAFSA required. No deadline.

Contact. Dameon Monie, Director of Financial Aid
111 West First Street, Suite 1140
Dayton, OH 45402

Southwestern College of Business: Vine Street Campus

Cincinnati, Ohio
Two-year proprietary
Federal Code: 012128

College costs. Quoted tuition is for associate degree programs, fees included. Tuition for diploma programs $4,050, fees included. $4650 tuition, including fees, for Kentucky students attending Kentucky campus.

	Living at home
Tuition and fees (2002-2003):	$5,550
Personal expenses:	$2,500

Application procedures. FAFSA required.

Contact. Sharon Snowden, Financial Aid Director
632 Vine Street
Cincinnati, OH 45202

Stark State College of Technology

Canton, Ohio
www.starkstate.edu
Two-year public
Federal Code: 011141

	Living at home
Tuition and fees (2002-2003):	$3,082
Out-of-state:	$3,982
Per-credit charge:	$91
Per-credit out-of-state:	$121
Books and supplies:	$780

Undergraduate aid. All financial aid based on need. Need-based aid available for full-time and part-time students.

Policies to reduce costs. Tuition/fee waivers for senior citizens, employees and their families. Credit/placement for qualifying scores on AP, CLEP examinations. Work study available nights, weekends and for part-time students.

Payment plans. Credit card, installment payment.

Application procedures. FAFSA, institutional form required. Priority date 5/1; no closing date. Applicants notified on rolling basis starting 7/1. **Transfers:** Priority date 5/1; no deadline.

Contact. Amy Baker, Director of Financial Aid
6200 Frank Avenue NW
Canton, OH 44720

Stautzenberger College

Toledo, Ohio
www.stautzen.com
Two-year proprietary
Federal Code: 004866

College costs. Tuition ranges from $130 to $315 per credit hour depending on program.

	Living at home
Tuition and fees (2002-2003):	$7,090
Per-credit charge:	$125
Books and supplies:	$975
Transportation:	$600

Undergraduate aid. All financial aid based on need. Need-based aid available for full-time and part-time students.

Policies to reduce costs. Tuition/fee waivers for employees and their families.

Payment plans. Credit card, installment, deferred payment.

Application procedures. FAFSA required. No deadline. Applicants notified on rolling basis. **Transfers:** No deadline.

Contact. Mari Huffman, Financial Aid Officer
5355 Southwyck Boulevard
Toledo, OH 43614

Technology Education College

Columbus, Ohio
www.teceducation.com
Two-year proprietary
Federal Code: 011005

College costs. Quoted tuition is academic-year cost of drafting-CAD program. Tuition for other associate degree programs ranges from $6,750 to $8,000 per academic year.

	Living at home	On-campus
Tuition and fees (2002-2003):	$7,155	$7,155
Room only:		$3,120
Books and supplies:	$578	$578
Personal expenses:	$2,600	$1,754

Undergraduate aid. All financial aid based on need. Need-based aid available for full-time and part-time students.

Payment plans. Installment payment.

Application procedures. FAFSA required. No deadline. Applicants notified on rolling basis.

Contact. David Barron, Director of Financial Aid
288 South Hamilton Road
Columbus, OH 43213

Tiffin University

Tiffin, Ohio
www.tiffin.edu
Four-year private
Federal Code: 003121

	Living at home	On-campus
Tuition and fees (2002-2003):	$12,850	$12,850
Room and board:		$5,700
Board only:	$2,600	
Books and supplies:	$1,000	$1,000
Personal expenses:	$1,400	$1,400
Transportation:	$1,150	$1,100

Undergraduate aid. Need-based: Average financial aid package for full-time students was $9,770; for part-time $4,755. 45% awarded as scholarships/grants, 55% as loans/jobs. **Non-need-based:** 25% awarded as scholarships/grants, 75% as loans/jobs. Scholarships based on academics, athletics, music/drama, state/district residency. **Student debt:** 87% of graduating class borrowed to fund education; average debt was $17,125.

Freshman aid. Need-based: Out of 258 full-time freshmen, 253 applied for aid; 221 were judged to have need; of these 221 received aid. Average package met 60% of need. 31 students had full need met. Average scholarship/grant was $4,235; average loan $2,544. **Non-need based:** 215 full-time freshmen with need received non-need scholarships; 41 without need received awards; 21 received athletic scholarships.

Policies to reduce costs. Tuition/fee waivers for senior citizens, employees and their families. Credit/placement for qualifying scores on AP, CLEP examinations.

Payment plans. Credit card, installment, deferred payment.

Application procedures. FAFSA required. Priority date 3/1; no closing date. Applicants notified on rolling basis starting 3/1, must reply within 2 week(s) of notification. **Transfers:** Priority date 3/31; no deadline.

Contact. Financial aid office: (419) 448-3279
Tera Van Doran, Director of Financial Aid
155 Miami Street
Tiffin, OH 44883

Trumbull Business College

Warren, Ohio
www.tbc-trumbullbusiness.com
Two-year proprietary
Federal Code: 013585

College costs. Lab fees additional.

	Living at home
Tuition and fees (projected):	$5,920
Per-credit charge:	$130
Books and supplies:	$936
Personal expenses:	$1,485

Undergraduate aid. Need-based: Need-based aid available for full-time and part-time students.

Application procedures. FAFSA required.

Contact. Financial aid office: (330) 369-3200 ext. 12
Florence Henning, Director of Financial Assistance
3200 Ridge Road
Warren, OH 44484

Union Institute & University

Cincinnati, Ohio
www.tui.edu
Four-year private **Federal Code: 010923**

	Living at home
Tuition and fees (2002-2003):	$9,030
Books and supplies:	$700
Transportation:	$600

Undergraduate aid. Need-based: Need-based aid available for full-time and part-time students. **Non-need-based:** Scholarships based on academics, state/district residency.

Policies to reduce costs. Tuition/fee waivers for employees and their families. Prepayment discount; credit/placement for qualifying scores on AP, CLEP examinations.

Payment plans. Credit card, installment, deferred payment.

Application procedures. FAFSA, institutional form required. Priority date 9/1; closing date 6/30. Applicants notified by 10/15, must reply within 4 week(s) of notification.

Contact. Rob Peifer, Director of Financial Aid
440 East McMillan Street
Cincinnati, OH 45206-1925

University of Akron

Akron, Ohio
www.uakron.edu
Four-year public **Federal Code: 003123**

College costs. Fees for part-time students $32 per-credit-hour. Full-time tuition, Community and Technical College within University of Akron, $4,717.

	Living at home	On-campus
Tuition and fees (2002-2003):	$5,798	$5,798
Out-of-state:	$12,613	$12,613
Room and board:		$6,256
Board only:	$2,200	
Books and supplies:	$704	$704
Personal expenses:	$1,465	$1,484
Transportation:	$1,550	$883

Undergraduate aid. Need-based: Average financial aid package for full-time students was $5,969; for part-time $4,481. 31% awarded as scholarships/grants, 69% as loans/jobs. **Non-need-based:** 70% awarded as scholarships/grants, 30% as loans/jobs. Scholarships based on academics, art, athletics, leadership, minority status, music/drama, religious affiliation, state/district residency.

Freshman aid. Need-based: Out of 3,179 full-time freshmen, 2,427 applied for aid; 2,394 were judged to have need; of these 2,188 received aid. Average package met 47% of need. 253 students had full need met. Average scholarship/grant was $4,103; average loan $2,416. **Non-need based:** 550 full-time freshmen with need received non-need scholarships; 586 without need received awards; 60 received athletic scholarships.

Merit scholarships. Scholarships for Excellence: $9,000 per year; criteria: high school GPA 3.5, class rank top 10%, 27 ACT, 1210 SAT, deadline February 1. Presidential Scholarships: $3,000 per year; criteria same as for Scholarship for Excellence, deadline February 1. Honors Scholarships: $1,400-$2,900 per year; criteria: top 10% of class, GPA 3.5, deadline December 31. Jim and Vanita Oeschlager Leadership Award: $1,000-$13,000 per year; based on leadership and service. National Merit Scholarship: tuition, fees, room and board first year, full tuition second through fourth years; based on selection as National Merit Finalist. Academic Scholarship: $500-$1,500 per year; criteria: upper 20% of high school class, 21 ACT, 3.25 GPA.

Policies to reduce costs. Tuition/fee waivers for senior citizens, employees and their families. Credit/placement for qualifying scores on AP, IB, CLEP examinations. Work study available nights, weekends and for part-time students.

Payment plans. Credit card, installment payment.

Application procedures. FAFSA, institutional form required. Priority date 3/1; no closing date. Applicants notified on rolling basis starting 4/15, must reply within 2 week(s) of notification.

Contact. Financial aid office: (330) 972-7032
Douglas McNutt, Director, Student Financial Aid
302 Buchtel Common
Akron, OH 44325-2001

University of Cincinnati

Cincinnati, Ohio
www.uc.edu
Four-year public **Federal Code: 003125**

	Living at home	On-campus
Tuition and fees (2002-2003):	$6,939	$6,939
Out-of-state:	$17,322	$17,322
Room and board:		$6,774
Board only:	$932	
Books and supplies:	$771	$771
Personal expenses:	$3,699	$3,474
Transportation:	$545	$150

Undergraduate aid. Need-based: Average financial aid package for full-time students was $7,125; for part-time $6,624. 51% awarded as scholarships/grants, 49% as loans/jobs. **Non-need-based:** 5% awarded as scholarships/grants, 95% as loans/jobs.

Freshman aid. Need-based: Out of 3,642 full-time freshmen, 2,634 applied for aid; 2,111 were judged to have need; of these 2,065 received aid. Average package met 57% of need. 257 students had full need met. Average scholarship/grant was $3,888; average loan $1,983. **Non-need based:** 605 full-time freshmen with need received non-need scholarships; 249 without need received awards; 9 received athletic scholarships.

Policies to reduce costs. Tuition/fee waivers for employees and their families. Credit/placement for qualifying scores on AP examinations. Work study available nights, weekends and for part-time students.

Payment plans. Credit card, installment payment.

Application procedures. FAFSA required. No deadline. Applicants notified on rolling basis starting 3/15, must reply within 2 week(s) of notification.

Contact. Financial aid office: (513) 556-6982
Connie Williams, Director, Financial Aid
PO Box 210091
Cincinnati, OH 45221-0091

University of Cincinnati: Clermont College

Batavia, Ohio
www.ucclermont.edu
Two-year public **Federal Code: 003125**

	Living at home
Tuition and fees (2002-2003):	$3,486
Out-of-state:	$8,829
Per-credit charge:	$97
Per-credit out-of-state:	$246
Books and supplies:	$696
Personal expenses:	$2,772
Transportation:	$474

Undergraduate aid. Need-based: Need-based aid available for full-time and part-time students. **Non-need-based:** Scholarships based on academics, state/district residency. **Additional information:** All financial aid applications and awards administered through main campus except in-house loans and scholarships.

Policies to reduce costs. Tuition/fee waivers for senior citizens, employees and their families. Credit/placement for qualifying scores on AP, IB, CLEP examinations.

Payment plans. Credit card payment.

Application procedures. FAFSA required. No deadline. Applicants notified on rolling basis. **Transfers:** No deadline.

Contact. Financial aid office: (513) 732-5284
Shirley Quinn, Financial Aid Officer
4200 Clermont College Drive
Batavia, OH 45103

University of Cincinnati: Raymond Walters College

Cincinnati, Ohio
www.rwc.uc.edu
Two-year public **Federal Code: 003125**

	Living at home
Tuition and fees (2002-2003):	$4,014
Out-of-state:	$10,491
Per-credit charge:	$112
Per-credit out-of-state:	$292
Books and supplies:	$771
Personal expenses:	$3,051
Transportation:	$528

Undergraduate aid. Need-based: Need-based aid available for full-time and part-time students. **Additional information:** All financial aid applications and awards administered through main campus.

Merit scholarships. Dean's scholarships; $1,500 based on GPA (2.5 required), tech prep program participation, 2-page essay; 10 available. Cincinnatus Scholarship Competition; $1,500 to full tuition, room, board and books; must have 26 ACT or be in top 5% of high school class to qualify to compete.

Policies to reduce costs. Tuition/fee waivers for senior citizens, employees and their families. Credit/placement for qualifying scores on AP, IB, CLEP examinations. Work study available nights and for part-time students.

Payment plans. Credit card payment.

Application procedures. FAFSA required. Priority date 3/15; no closing date. Applicants notified on rolling basis starting 3/15, must reply within 2 week(s) of notification. **Transfers:** No deadline.

Contact. **Financial aid office:** (513) 745-5740
Jenny Young, Director of Enrollment Management
9555 Plainfield Road
Cincinnati, OH 45236

University of Dayton

Dayton, Ohio
www.udayton.edu
Four-year private **Federal Code: 003127**

College costs. Estimated cost of books/supplies includes cost of computer. Additional $55 per month for foreign students' health and accident insurance.

	Living at home	On-campus
Tuition and fees:	$18,960	$18,960
Room and board:		$5,890
Books and supplies:	$2,260	$2,260
Personal expenses:	$1,000	$1,000
Transportation:	$500	$300

Undergraduate aid. Need-based: Average financial aid package for full-time students was $9,410; for part-time $6,411. 65% awarded as scholarships/grants, 35% as loans/jobs. **Non-need-based:** 58% awarded as scholarships/grants, 42% as loans/jobs. Scholarships based on academics, alumni affiliation, art, athletics, leadership, music/drama, state/district residency. **Student debt:** 67% of graduating class borrowed to fund education; average debt was $18,897.

Freshman aid. Need-based: Out of 1,736 full-time freshmen, 1,531 applied for aid; 1,119 were judged to have need; of these 1,088 received aid. Average package met 81% of need. 774 students had full need met. Average scholarship/grant was $7,854; average loan $4,018. **Non-need based:** 1,060 full-time freshmen with need received non-need scholarships; 666 without need received awards; 20 received athletic scholarships.

Merit scholarships. President's Scholarships; $1,000 to full tuition; renewable for up to 4 years; based on high school grades, SAT/ACT scores, recommendations.

Policies to reduce costs. Tuition/fee waivers for senior citizens, employees and their families. Credit/placement for qualifying scores on AP, IB, CLEP examinations. Work study available nights, weekends and for part-time students.

Payment plans. Credit card, deferred payment.

Application procedures. FAFSA required. Priority date 3/31; no closing date. Applicants notified by 3/31. **Transfers:** May compete for Transfer Scholarships, which range from $2,500 to $6,000 and are renewable for up to 3 additional years. Selection based on GPA from previous institution.

Contact. **Financial aid office:** (937) 229-4311
Joyce Wilkins, Director of Financial Aid
300 College Park
Dayton, OH 45469-1300

University of Findlay

Findlay, Ohio
www.findlay.edu
Four-year private **Federal Code: 003045**

College costs. Preveterinary students pay additional $1,120; equestrian program students pay additional $3,300. Extra costs for these programs only during first 2 years.

	Living at home	On-campus
Tuition and fees (projected):	$19,952	$19,952
Room and board:		$7,062
Books and supplies:	$700	$700
Personal expenses:		$650
Transportation:	$300	$400

Undergraduate aid. Need-based: Average financial aid package for full-time students was $13,850. 64% awarded as scholarships/grants, 36% as loans/jobs. **Non-need-based:** 74% awarded as scholarships/grants, 26% as loans/jobs. Scholarships based on academics, athletics, music/drama, state/district residency. **Student debt:** 85% of graduating class borrowed to fund education; average debt was $16,500.

Freshman aid. Need-based: Out of 770 full-time freshmen, 534 applied for aid; 463 were judged to have need; of these 463 received aid. Average package met 87% of need. 95 students had full need met. Average scholarship/grant was $8,825; average loan $2,500. **Non-need based:** 82 full-time freshmen with need received non-need scholarships; 45 without need received awards.

Merit scholarships. Full tuition available to select area valedictorian/salutatorians. Automatic academic awards available based on GPA, test scores.

Policies to reduce costs. Tuition/fee waivers for senior citizens, employees and their families. Credit/placement for qualifying scores on AP, CLEP examinations. Work study available nights and weekends.

Payment plans. Credit card, installment payment.

Application procedures. FAFSA required. Priority date 3/1; closing date 8/1. Applicants notified on rolling basis starting 3/1. **Transfers:** Priority date 8/1; no deadline.

Contact. Arman Habegger, Director of Financial Aid
1000 North Main Street
Findlay, OH 45840-3695

University of Northwestern Ohio

Lima, Ohio
www.unoh.edu
Two-year private **Federal Code: 004861**

	Living at home	On-campus
Tuition and fees (2002-2003):	$7,875	$7,875
Per-credit charge:	$160	$160
Room only:		$3,200
Books and supplies:	$1,026	$1,026
Personal expenses:	$1,413	$1,413
Transportation:	$1,667	$1,043

Undergraduate aid. Need-based: Average financial aid package for full-time students was $2,817; for part-time $2,919. 28% awarded as scholarships/grants, 72% as loans/jobs. **Non-need-based:** Scholarships based on academics, job skills, minority status. **Student debt:** 70% of graduating class borrowed to fund education; average debt was $12,334.

Freshman aid. Need-based: Out of 911 full-time freshmen, 25 applied for aid; 4 were judged to have need; of these 3 received aid. Average package met 80% of need. 1 students had full need met. Average scholarship/grant was $6,161. **Non-need based:** 2 full-time freshmen with need received non-need scholarships; 6 without need received awards.

Policies to reduce costs. Tuition/fee waivers for minority students, employees and their families. Tuition at time of enrollment guaranteed for 2 years; credit/placement for qualifying scores on AP, CLEP examinations. Work study available nights and for part-time students.

Payment plans. Credit card, installment payment.

Application procedures. FAFSA required. Priority date 4/1; no closing date. Applicants notified on rolling basis starting 4/30, must reply within 2 week(s) of notification. **Transfers:** No deadline.

Contact. Michael Jones, Director of Financial Aid
1441 North Cable Road
Lima, OH 45805

University of Rio Grande

Rio Grande, Ohio
www.rio.edu
Four-year public **Federal Code: 003116**

College costs. Ohio students pay per-credit-hour community college rates during freshman and sophomore years of $84 in-district (Gallia, Jackson, Meigs, and Vinton counties), $100 out-of-district. In junior and senior years, in-district pays $392 per-credit and $9,486 full-time tuition/fees, out-of-district $400 per-credit and $9,678 full-time tuition/fees for private university rates. West Virginia residents pay $289 per-credit and $7,106 full-time tuition/fees for freshman and sophomore years, out-of-state rates for junior and senior.

	Living at home	On-campus
Tuition and fees (2002-2003):	$2,960	$2,960
Out-of-district:	$3,440	$3,440
Out-of-state:	$10,376	$10,376
Room and board:		$5,392
Books and supplies:	$1,000	$1,000
Personal expenses:	$1,571	$1,571
Transportation:	$2,457	$630

Undergraduate aid. Non-need-based: Scholarships based on academics, alumni affiliation, athletics, leadership, music/drama, state/district residency.

Policies to reduce costs. Tuition/fee waivers for senior citizens, employees and their families. Credit/placement for qualifying scores on AP, CLEP examinations.

Payment plans. Installment payment.

Application procedures. FAFSA, institutional form required. Priority date 3/15; no closing date. Applicants notified on rolling basis starting 1/15, must reply within 3 week(s) of notification.

Contact. Financial aid office: (740) 245-7218
John Hill, Financial Aid Director
218 North College Avenue
Rio Grande, OH 45674

University of Toledo

Toledo, Ohio
www.utoledo.edu
Four-year public **Federal Code: 003131**

	Living at home	On-campus
Tuition and fees (2002-2003):	$5,849	$5,849
Out-of-state:	$14,302	$14,302
Room and board:		$6,630
Board only:	$1,500	
Books and supplies:	$690	$690
Personal expenses:	$2,204	$2,204
Transportation:	$1,270	$560

Undergraduate aid. Need-based: Average financial aid package for full-time students was $6,346; for part-time $6,073. 22% awarded as scholarships/grants, 78% as loans/jobs. **Non-need-based:** 52% awarded as scholarships/grants, 48% as loans/jobs. Scholarships based on academics, athletics, state/district residency. **Student debt:** 65% of graduating class borrowed to fund education; average debt was $20,859. **Additional information:** March priority date for federal aid. Students encouraged to apply as early as December for priority consideration for institutional aid.

Freshman aid. Need-based: Out of 3,698 full-time freshmen, 3,218 applied for aid; 2,340 were judged to have need; of these 2,228 received aid. Average package met 55% of need. 212 students had full need met. Average scholarship/grant was $4,044; average loan $2,878. **Non-need based:** 493 full-time freshmen with need received non-need scholarships; 501 without need received awards; 38 received athletic scholarships.

Merit scholarships. 400 freshman merit scholarships offered annually; awards range from $100 to $4,500 and average $2,000.

Policies to reduce costs. Tuition/fee waivers for employees and their families. Credit/placement for qualifying scores on AP, CLEP examinations.

Payment plans. Credit card, installment, deferred payment.

Application procedures. FAFSA required. Priority date 3/15; no closing date. Applicants notified on rolling basis starting 4/1, must reply within 4 week(s) of notification.

Contact. Financial aid office: (419) 530-2800
Carolyn Baumgartner, Director of Financial Aid
2801 West Bancroft Street
Toledo, OH 43606-3398

Urbana University

Urbana, Ohio
www.urbana.edu
Four-year private **Federal Code: 003133**

	Living at home	On-campus
Tuition and fees (2002-2003):	$12,814	$12,814
Room and board:		$5,140
Board only:	$2,900	
Books and supplies:	$500	$500
Personal expenses:	$508	$508
Transportation:	$150	$150

Undergraduate aid. All financial aid based on need. Need-based aid available for full-time and part-time students.

Policies to reduce costs. Tuition/fee waivers for children of alumni, senior citizens, family members, family of clergy, employees and their families. Tuition at time of enrollment guaranteed for 4 years; credit/placement for qualifying scores on AP, CLEP examinations. Work study available nights and weekends.

Payment plans. Credit card, installment, deferred payment.

Application procedures. FAFSA required. Priority date 4/1; no closing date. Applicants notified on rolling basis starting 2/1, must reply within 4 week(s) of notification. **Transfers:** No deadline.

Contact. Financial aid office: (937) 484-1355
Robin Heise, Director of Financial Aid
579 College Way
Urbana, OH 43078

Ursuline College

Pepper Pike, Ohio
www.ursuline.edu
Four-year private **Federal Code: 003134**

College costs. Additional per credit hour charge for clinical nursing courses.

	Living at home	On-campus
Tuition and fees:	$17,270	$17,270
Room and board:		$5,848
Books and supplies:	$800	$800
Personal expenses:	$850	$850
Transportation:	$1,200	$420

Undergraduate aid. Need-based: Average financial aid package for full-time students was $13,976; for part-time $9,189. 40% awarded as scholarships/grants, 60% as loans/jobs. **Non-need-based:** 34% awarded as scholarships/grants, 66% as loans/jobs. Scholarships based on academics, alumni affiliation, art, athletics, leadership, minority status, religious affiliation.

Freshman aid. Need-based: Out of 94 full-time freshmen, 82 applied for aid; 75 were judged to have need; of these 75 received aid. Average package met 96% of need. 17 students had full need met. Average scholarship/grant was $9,841; average loan $3,652. **Non-need based:** 72 full-time freshmen with need received non-need scholarships; 10 without need received awards; 26 received athletic scholarships.

Merit scholarships. Ursuline Scholarship; 3.3 GPA, 23 ACT/1050 SAT; $3,500 renewable. Ursuline Award; 2.8 GPA, 20 ACT/930 SAT; $2,000 renewable. Presidential Scholarship; 3.7 GPA, 27 ACT/1210 SAT; $6,000 renewable. Dean's Scholarship; 3.3 GPA, 23 ACT/1050 SAT; renewable $3,500. Unlimited number available. Overall scholarship cap of $10,500.

Policies to reduce costs. Tuition/fee waivers for family members, family of clergy, employees and their families. Credit/placement for qualifying scores on AP, CLEP examinations. Work study available nights, weekends and for part-time students.

Payment plans. Credit card, installment payment.

Application procedures. FAFSA, institutional form required. Priority date 3/15; no closing date. Applicants notified on rolling basis starting 3/1, must reply within 4 week(s) of notification. **Transfers:** No deadline.

Contact. **Financial aid office:** (440) 6436-8309
Mary Lynn Perri, Director of Financial Aid
2550 Lander Road
Pepper Pike, OH 44124-4398

Virginia Marti College of Art and Design

Lakewood, Ohio
www.virginiamarticollege.com
Two-year proprietary **Federal Code: 012896**

	Living at home
Tuition and fees (2002-2003):	$12,555
Per-credit charge:	$275
Books and supplies:	$1,025

Undergraduate aid. All financial aid based on need. Need-based aid available for full-time students.

Policies to reduce costs. Tuition/fee waivers for employees and their families. Tuition at time of enrollment guaranteed for 2 years.

Payment plans. Credit card, installment payment.

Application procedures. FAFSA required. No deadline. Applicants notified on rolling basis. **Transfers:** No deadline.

Contact. Jennifer Minkiewicz, Financial Aid Officer
11724 Detroit Avenue
Lakewood, OH 44107

Walsh University

North Canton, Ohio
www.walsh.edu
Four-year private **Federal Code: 003135**

	Living at home	On-campus
Tuition and fees (2002-2003):	$13,870	$13,870
Room and board:		$6,120
Books and supplies:	$1,000	$1,000

Undergraduate aid. Need-based: Average financial aid package for full-time students was $9,778; for part-time $7,677. 43% awarded as scholarships/grants, 57% as loans/jobs. **Non-need-based:** 53% awarded as scholarships/grants, 47% as loans/jobs. Scholarships based on academics, alumni affiliation, athletics, leadership, music/drama, state/district residency. **Student debt:** 82% of graduating class borrowed to fund education; average debt was $18,200.

Freshman aid. Need-based: Out of 302 full-time freshmen, 273 applied for aid; 241 were judged to have need; of these 241 received aid. Average package met 88% of need. 240 students had full need met. Average scholarship/grant was $6,019; average loan $1,627. **Non-need based:** 235 full-time freshmen with need received non-need scholarships; 23 without need received awards; 83 received athletic scholarships.

Merit scholarships. $1,000 for incoming freshmen who have graduated from Catholic high school.

Policies to reduce costs. Tuition/fee waivers for children of alumni, senior citizens, minority students, family members, employees and their families. Credit/placement for qualifying scores on AP, CLEP examinations.

Payment plans. Credit card, installment, deferred payment.

Application procedures. FAFSA, institutional form required. Priority date 3/15; no closing date. Applicants notified on rolling basis starting 3/15, must reply within 4 week(s) of notification. **Transfers:** No deadline.

Contact. Holly Van Gilder, Financial Aid Director
2020 Easton Street, Northwest
North Canton, OH 44720-3396

Washington State Community College

Marietta, Ohio
www.wscc.edu
Two-year public **Federal Code: 010453**

	Living at home
Tuition and fees (2002-2003):	$3,195
Out-of-state:	$6,255
Per-credit charge:	$68
Per-credit out-of-state:	$136
Books and supplies:	$705
Personal expenses:	$4,145
Transportation:	$1,107

Policies to reduce costs. Tuition/fee waivers for senior citizens, employees and their families. Credit/placement for qualifying scores on AP, CLEP examinations.

Payment plans. Credit card, installment payment.

Application procedures. FAFSA, institutional form required. No deadline. Applicants notified on rolling basis starting 5/15, must reply within 2 week(s) of notification.

Contact. Dave Metz, Director of Financial Aid
710 Colegate Drive
Marietta, OH 45750

Wilmington College

Wilmington, Ohio
www.wilmington.edu
Four-year private **Federal Code: 003142**

College costs. 1-6 hours $330 per-credit-hour; 7-11 hours $660 per-credit-hour.

	Living at home	On-campus
Tuition and fees (2002-2003):	$16,564	$16,564
Room and board:		$6,240
Board only:	$1,500	
Books and supplies:	$1,000	$1,000
Personal expenses:	$450	$450
Transportation:	$400	$250

Undergraduate aid. Need-based: Average financial aid package for full-time students was $15,091; for part-time $6,245. 65% awarded as scholarships/grants, 35% as loans/jobs. **Non-need-based:** 47% awarded as scholarships/grants, 53% as loans/jobs. Scholarships based on academics, alumni affiliation, religious affiliation, state/district residency. **Student debt:** 84% of graduating class borrowed to fund education; average debt was $18,996.

Freshman aid. Need-based: Out of 291 full-time freshmen, 276 applied for aid; 254 were judged to have need; of these 254 received aid. Average package met 91% of need. 171 students had full need met. Average scholarship/grant was $10,016; average loan $4,380. **Non-need based:** 50 full-time freshmen with need received non-need scholarships; 37 without need received awards.

Policies to reduce costs. Tuition/fee waivers for children of alumni, family members, family of clergy, employees and their families. Credit/placement for qualifying scores on AP, IB, CLEP examinations.

Payment plans. Credit card, installment, deferred payment.

Application procedures. FAFSA required. Priority date 3/31; closing date 6/1. Applicants notified on rolling basis starting 3/1, must reply by 5/1 or within 2 week(s) of notification.

Contact. **Financial aid office:** (937) 382-6661 ext. 249
Cheryl Louallen, Director of Financial Aid
Box 1325 Pyle Center
Wilmington, OH 45177

Wittenberg University

Springfield, Ohio
www.wittenberg.edu
Four-year private **Federal Code: 003143**

College costs. School of Community Education cost: $277 per credit-hour.

	Living at home	On-campus
Tuition and fees:	$24,948	$24,948
Room and board:		$6,388
Board only:	$3,080	
Books and supplies:	$800	$800
Personal expenses:	$1,000	$1,000
Transportation:	$1,500	$600

Undergraduate aid. All financial aid based on need. Average financial aid package for full-time students was $21,286. 68% awarded as scholarships/grants, 32% as loans/jobs. **Student debt:** 71% of graduating class borrowed to fund education; average debt was $18,623. **Additional information:** Auditions required from applicants for music, theater, and dance scholarships. Portfolio required of applicants for art scholarships.

Freshman aid. Out of 664 full-time freshmen, 559 applied for aid; 474 were judged to have need; of these 474 received aid. Average package met 94% of need. 220 students had full need met. Average scholarship/grant was $17,056; average loan $3,134.

Policies to reduce costs. Tuition/fee waivers for children of alumni, senior citizens, family of clergy, employees and their families. Prepayment discount; credit/placement for qualifying scores on AP examinations.

Payment plans. Installment payment.

Application procedures. FAFSA required. Priority date 3/15; no closing date. Applicants notified on rolling basis starting 2/1, must reply by 5/1 or within 2 week(s) of notification. Early decision closing date 11/15. **Transfers:** Priority date 5/15; no deadline.

Contact. **Financial aid office:** (937) 327-7321
Randy Green, Director of Financial Aid
Ward Street and North Wittenberg
Springfield, OH 45501-0720

Wright State University

Dayton, Ohio
www.wright.edu
Four-year public **Federal Code: 003078**

	Living at home	On-campus
Tuition and fees (2002-2003):	$5,361	$5,361
Out-of-state:	$10,524	$10,524
Room and board:		$5,778
Books and supplies:	$650	$650
Personal expenses:	$1,000	$1,000
Transportation:	$1,310	$600

Undergraduate aid. Need-based: 39% awarded as scholarships/grants, 61% as loans/jobs. Need-based aid available for part-time students. **Non-need-based:** 40% awarded as scholarships/grants, 60% as loans/jobs. **Additional information:** Academic scholarship applications must be submitted by February 1.

Freshman aid. Need-based: Out of 2,306 full-time freshmen, 1,934 applied for aid; 1,274 were judged to have need; of these 1,274 received aid. Average scholarship/grant was $3,502; average loan $2,248. **Non-need based:** 938 full-time freshmen with need received non-need scholarships; 938 without need received awards.

Policies to reduce costs. Tuition/fee waivers for senior citizens, employees and their families. Credit/placement for qualifying scores on AP, CLEP examinations.

Payment plans. Credit card, installment payment.

Application procedures. FAFSA required. Priority date 3/1; no closing date. Applicants notified on rolling basis starting 4/1, must reply within 2 week(s) of notification.

Contact. David Darr, Director of Financial Aid
3640 Colonel Glenn Highway
Dayton, OH 45435

Wright State University: Lake Campus

Celina, Ohio
www.wright.edu
Two-year public **Federal Code: 003078**

	Living at home
Tuition and fees (2002-2003):	$3,738
Out-of-state:	$8,901
Per-credit charge:	$117
Per-credit out-of-state:	$277
Books and supplies:	$843
Personal expenses:	$1,395
Transportation:	$1,461

Undergraduate aid. Need-based: Need-based aid available for full-time and part-time students. **Non-need-based:** Scholarships based on academics, athletics, state/district residency. **Additional information:** Academic scholarship application deadline February 1. All financial aid applications and awards administered by Dayton campus. Monies awarded for both campuses totaled $17,056,000.

Policies to reduce costs. Tuition/fee waivers for senior citizens, employees and their families. Tuition at time of enrollment guaranteed for 2 years; credit/placement for qualifying scores on AP examinations.

Payment plans. Credit card, installment payment.

Application procedures. FAFSA, institutional form required. Priority date 2/15; no closing date. Applicants notified on rolling basis, must reply within 2 week(s) of notification. **Transfers:** No deadline.

Contact. **Financial aid office:** (419) 586-0336
B.J. Hobler, Student Services Office/Registrar and Bursar, Financial Aid
7600 State Route 703
Celina, OH 45822

Xavier University

Cincinnati, Ohio
www.xavier.edu
Four-year private **Federal Code: 003144**

	Living at home	On-campus
Tuition and fees:	$19,290	$19,290
Room and board:		$7,700
Board only:	$1,800	
Books and supplies:	$800	$800
Personal expenses:	$1,000	$1,200
Transportation:	$600	$300

Undergraduate aid. Need-based: Average financial aid package for full-time students was $12,947; for part-time $12,268. 62% awarded as scholarships/grants, 38% as loans/jobs. **Non-need-based:** 67% awarded as scholarships/grants, 33% as loans/jobs. Scholarships based on academics, alumni affiliation, art, athletics, job skills, minority status, music/drama. **Student debt:** 58% of graduating class borrowed to fund education; average debt was $16,711.

Freshman aid. Need-based: Out of 757 full-time freshmen, 582 applied for aid; 434 were judged to have need; of these 434 received aid. Average package met 78% of need. 101 students had full need met. Average scholarship/grant was $10,180; average loan $3,278. **Non-need based:** 74 full-time freshmen with need received non-need scholarships; 284 without need received awards; 48 received athletic scholarships.

Policies to reduce costs. Tuition/fee waivers for senior citizens, minority students, family members, employees and their families. Credit/placement for qualifying scores on AP, IB, CLEP examinations. Work study available nights, weekends and for part-time students.

Payment plans. Credit card, installment, deferred payment.

Application procedures. FAFSA required. Priority date 2/15; no closing date. Applicants notified on rolling basis starting 3/1, must reply by 5/1. **Transfers:** Priority date 4/15; no deadline.

Contact. **Financial aid office:** (513) 745-3142
Paul Calme, Director of Financial Aid
3800 Victory Parkway
Cincinnati, OH 45207-5311

Youngstown State University

Youngstown, Ohio
www.ysu.edu
Four-year public **Federal Code: 003145**

	Living at home	On-campus
Tuition and fees:	$5,472	$5,472
Out-of-district:	$7,774	$7,774
Out-of-state:	$10,652	$10,652
Room and board:		$5,700
Books and supplies:	$840	$840
Personal expenses:	$1,917	$1,917
Transportation:	$1,270	$1,270

Undergraduate aid. Need-based: 32% awarded as scholarships/grants, 68% as loans/jobs. Need-based aid available for part-time students. **Non-need-based:** 94% awarded as scholarships/grants, 6% as loans/jobs. Scholarships based on academics, alumni affiliation, athletics, state/district residency.

Policies to reduce costs. Tuition/fee waivers for senior citizens, employees and their families. Credit/placement for qualifying scores on AP, IB, CLEP examinations.

Payment plans. Credit card, installment, deferred payment.

Application procedures. FAFSA, institutional form required. Priority date 2/15; no closing date. Applicants notified on rolling basis starting 5/30. **Transfers:** No deadline.

Contact. Financial aid office: (330) 941-3505
Elaine Ruse, Director of Scholarships and Financial Aid
One University Plaza
Youngstown, OH 44555-0001

Oklahoma

Bacone College

Muskogee, Oklahoma
www.bacone.edu
Four-year private **Federal Code: 003147**

	Living at home	On-campus
Tuition and fees (2002-2003):	$8,100	$8,100
Room and board:		$5,000
Books and supplies:	$1,000	$1,000
Personal expenses:	$1,000	$500
Transportation:	$500	$250

Undergraduate aid. Non-need-based: Scholarships based on academics, athletics.

Policies to reduce costs. Tuition/fee waivers for employees and their families. Credit/placement for qualifying scores on CLEP examinations.

Payment plans. Credit card, installment payment.

Application procedures. FAFSA required. Priority date 3/31; no closing date. Applicants notified on rolling basis starting 4/1, must reply within 2 week(s) of notification. **Transfers:** Priority date 3/31.

Contact. William Brindle, Associate Financial Aid Director
2299 Old Bacone Road
Muskogee, OK 74403

Cameron University

Lawton, Oklahoma
www.cameron.edu
Four-year public **Federal Code: 003150**

	Living at home	On-campus
Tuition and fees (2002-2003):	$2,340	$2,340
Out-of-state:	$5,493	$5,493
Room and board:		$2,830
Books and supplies:	$690	$690
Personal expenses:	$1,000	$1,000
Transportation:	$2,215	$965

Undergraduate aid. Need-based: 63% awarded as scholarships/grants, 37% as loans/jobs. Need-based aid available for part-time students. **Non-need-based:** 52% awarded as scholarships/grants, 48% as loans/jobs. Scholarships based on academics, athletics.

Policies to reduce costs. Tuition/fee waivers for senior citizens, employees and their families. Credit/placement for qualifying scores on AP, IB, CLEP examinations. Work study available for part-time students.

Payment plans. Credit card payment.

Application procedures. FAFSA, institutional form required. Priority date 6/15; no closing date. Applicants notified on rolling basis starting 7/1, must reply within 2 week(s) of notification. **Transfers:** Academic and financial aid transcripts required.

Contact. Financial aid office: (580) 581-2293
Caryn Pacheco, Director of Financial Assistance
2800 West Gore Boulevard
Lawton, OK 73505

Carl Albert State College

Poteau, Oklahoma
www.carlalbert.edu
Two-year public **Federal Code: 003176**

	Living at home	On-campus
Tuition and fees (2002-2003):	$1,521	$1,521
Out-of-state:	$3,925	$3,925
Per-credit charge:	$36	$36
Per-credit out-of-state:	$116	$116
Room and board:		$2,888
Books and supplies:	$750	$750
Personal expenses:	$1,388	$1,678
Transportation:	$1,391	$1,391

Undergraduate aid. All financial aid based on need. Need-based aid available for full-time and part-time students.

Policies to reduce costs. Tuition/fee waivers for senior citizens, minority students, employees and their families. Credit/placement for qualifying scores on AP examinations. Work study available nights and for part-time students.

Payment plans. Credit card, installment payment.

Application procedures. FAFSA, institutional form required. No deadline. Applicants notified on rolling basis. **Transfers:** No deadline.

Contact. Financial aid office: (918) 647-1343
Robin Benson, Director of Financial Aid
1507 South McKenna
Poteau, OK 74953-5208

East Central University

Ada, Oklahoma
www.ecok.edu
Four-year public **Federal Code: 003154**

	Living at home	On-campus
Tuition and fees (2002-2003):	$2,353	$2,353
Out-of-state:	$5,506	$5,506
Room and board:		$2,646
Books and supplies:	$500	$500
Personal expenses:	$1,500	$1,500
Transportation:	$1,192	$680

Undergraduate aid. Need-based: Need-based aid available for full-time and part-time students. **Non-need-based:** Scholarships based on academics, athletics.

Policies to reduce costs. Tuition/fee waivers for senior citizens, employees and their families. Credit/placement for qualifying scores on AP, IB, CLEP examinations. Work study available for part-time students.

Payment plans. Credit card payment.

Application procedures. FAFSA, institutional form required. Closing date 3/1. Applicants notified on rolling basis starting 4/15, must reply within 2 week(s) of notification. **Transfers:** Closing date 3/1. FAFSA must be in by March 1.

Contact. Marcia Carter, Director of Student Financial Aid
PMBJ8, 1100 East 14th Street
Ada, OK 74820

Eastern Oklahoma State College

Wilburton, Oklahoma
www.eosc.edu
Two-year public **Federal Code: 003155**

	Living at home	On-campus
Tuition and fees (2002-2003):	$1,606	$1,606
Out-of-state:	$4,011	$4,011
Per-credit charge:	$36	$36
Per-credit out-of-state:	$116	$116
Room and board:		$2,784
Books and supplies:	$578	$578
Personal expenses:	$500	$500
Transportation:	$900	$250

Undergraduate aid. Need-based: Need-based aid available for full-time and part-time students.

Policies to reduce costs. Tuition/fee waivers for senior citizens, minority students, unemployed or children of unemployed, employees and their families. Credit/placement for qualifying scores on AP, CLEP examinations.

Payment plans. Credit card, deferred payment.

Application procedures. FAFSA, institutional form required. Priority date 3/1; no closing date. Applicants notified on rolling basis starting 5/1, must reply within 2 week(s) of notification.

Contact. Leah Miller, Director, Financial Aid
1301 West Main Street
Wilburton, OK 74578-4999

Langston University

Langston, Oklahoma
www.lunet.edu
Four-year public **Federal Code: 003157**

	Living at home	On-campus
Tuition and fees (2002-2003):	$2,436	$2,436
Out-of-state:	$5,456	$5,456
Room and board:		$3,404
Board only:	$2,238	
Books and supplies:	$800	$800
Personal expenses:	$2,485	$2,037

Undergraduate aid. All financial aid based on need. Need-based aid available for full-time and part-time students.

Policies to reduce costs. Tuition at time of enrollment guaranteed for 4 years; credit/placement for qualifying scores on AP, CLEP examinations. Work study available for part-time students.

Payment plans. Credit card, installment, deferred payment.

Application procedures. CSS PROFILE required. Priority date 3/1; closing date 5/1. Applicants notified on rolling basis starting 7/15, must reply within 2 week(s) of notification.

Contact. Yvonne Maxwell, Financial Aid Director
Box 728
Langston, OK 73050

Metropolitan College

Oklahoma City, Oklahoma
www.metropolitancollege.edu
Four-year private **Federal Code: 030813**

College costs. Tuition ranges from $4,700 to $6,584. Fees are $50. Books and supplies range from $300 to $1,400, depending on program.

Undergraduate aid. All financial aid based on need. Need-based aid available for full-time and part-time students.

Application procedures. FAFSA required. No deadline.

Contact. Christine Waters, Financial Aid Officer
1900 Northwest Expressway, Suite R302
Oklahoma City, OK 73118

Metropolitan College

Tulsa, Oklahoma
www.metropolitancollege.edu
Four-year private **Federal Code: 030813**

College costs (projected). Tuition and fees $6,534 for court reporting and $6,538 for paralegal per academic year.

Undergraduate aid. All financial aid based on need. Need-based aid available for full-time and part-time students.

Payment plans. Installment payment.

Application procedures. FAFSA required. No deadline. Applicants notified on rolling basis.

Contact. Financial aid office: (918) 627-9300
Marsais Broadway, Director of Financial Aid
10820 E. 45th St. , Ste. #B-101
Tulsa, OK 74146

Murray State College

Tishomingo, Oklahoma
www.msc.cc.ok.us
Two-year public **Federal Code: 003158**

	Living at home	On-campus
Tuition and fees (2002-2003):	$1,631	$1,631
Out-of-state:	$4,035	$4,035
Per-credit charge:	$36	$36
Per-credit out-of-state:	$116	$116
Room and board:		$3,030
Books and supplies:	$600	$600
Personal expenses:	$1,984	$1,984
Transportation:	$922	$512

Policies to reduce costs. Tuition/fee waivers for senior citizens, employees and their families.

Application procedures. Priority date 4/15; no closing date. Applicants notified on rolling basis starting 5/1.

Contact. Financial aid office: (580) 371-2371 ext. 143
Marilyn Schwarz, Financial Aid Director
One Murray Campus
Tishomingo, OK 73460

Northeastern Oklahoma Agricultural and Mechanical College

Miami, Oklahoma
www.neoam.cc.ok.us
Two-year public **Federal Code: 003160**

	Living at home	On-campus
Tuition and fees (2002-2003):	$1,552	$1,552
Out-of-state:	$3,913	$3,913
Per-credit charge:	$36	$36
Per-credit out-of-state:	$116	$116
Room and board:		$3,168
Books and supplies:	$600	$600
Personal expenses:	$1,000	$1,000
Transportation:	$1,077	$673

Undergraduate aid. Need-based: Average financial aid package for full-time students was $4,302; for part-time $2,656. 78% awarded as scholarships/grants, 22% as loans/jobs. **Non-need-based:** 38% awarded as scholarships/grants, 62% as loans/jobs. Scholarships based on academics, art, athletics, leadership, music/drama, state/district residency.

Freshman aid. Need-based: Out of 689 full-time freshmen, 589 applied for aid; 415 were judged to have need; of these 415 received aid. Average package met 77% of need. 83 students had full need met. Average scholarship/grant was $3,094; average loan $1,613. **Non-need based:** 137 full-time freshmen with need received non-need scholarships; 86 without need received awards; 103 received athletic scholarships.

Policies to reduce costs. Tuition/fee waivers for senior citizens, minority students, family members, employees and their families. Credit/placement for qualifying scores on AP, CLEP examinations. Work study available nights, weekends and for part-time students.

Payment plans. Credit card, installment payment.

Application procedures. FAFSA, institutional form required. Priority date 4/1; no closing date. Applicants notified on rolling basis starting 3/1, must reply by 8/30 or within 2 week(s) of notification. **Transfers:** Priority date 4/30. Final academic transcripts are required by FAO.

Contact. Financial aid office: (918) 540-6235
Tammy Higgins, Director of Financial Aid
200 I Street Northeast
Miami, OK 74354-6497

Northeastern State University

Tahlequah, Oklahoma
www.nsuok.edu
Four-year public **Federal Code: 003161**

	Living at home	On-campus
Tuition and fees (2002-2003):	$2,304	$2,304
Out-of-state:	$5,457	$5,457
Room and board:		$2,960
Books and supplies:	$800	$800
Personal expenses:	$625	$625
Transportation:	$800	$600

Undergraduate aid. Need-based: Average financial aid package for full-time students was $7,200; for part-time $3,200. 46% awarded as scholarships/grants, 54% as loans/jobs. **Non-need-based:** 16% awarded as scholarships/grants, 84% as loans/jobs. Scholarships based on academics, alumni affiliation, art, athletics, leadership, minority status, music/drama, state/district residency. **Student debt:** 65% of graduating class borrowed to fund education; average debt was $7,500. **Additional information:** Participates in off-campus job location & development program to assist students with off-campus employers to earn money for college expenses.

Freshman aid. Need-based: Out of 1,145 full-time freshmen, 916 applied for aid; 901 were judged to have need; of these 872 received aid. Average package met 70% of need. 714 students had full need met. Average scholarship/grant was $2,495; average loan $2,600. **Non-need based:** 215 full-time freshmen with need received non-need scholarships; 193 without need received awards; 60 received athletic scholarships.

Merit scholarships. Honors Program; $2,600 per year, up to $6,850 per year for some (minimum 30 ACT required); determined primarily by ACT, minimum 28 ACT and 3.8 high school GPA.

Policies to reduce costs. Tuition/fee waivers for adults, children of alumni, senior citizens, minority students, family members, employees and their families. Credit/placement for qualifying scores on AP, IB, CLEP examinations. Work study available nights, weekends and for part-time students.

Payment plans. Credit card, installment, deferred payment.

Application procedures. FAFSA, institutional form required. Priority date 4/15; no closing date. Applicants notified on rolling basis starting 3/15, must reply within 3 week(s) of notification. **Transfers:** Priority date 1/15; no deadline. State grant deadline is April 30.

Contact. Financial aid office: (918) 456-5511 ext. 3456
Scott Medlin, Director of Student Financial Services
600 North Grand
Tahlequah, OK 74464

Northern Oklahoma College

Tonkawa, Oklahoma
www.north-ok.edu
Two-year public **Federal Code: 003162**

	Living at home	On-campus
Tuition and fees (2002-2003):	$1,529	$1,529
Out-of-state:	$3,933	$3,933
Per-credit charge:	$36	$36
Per-credit out-of-state:	$116	$116
Room and board:		$2,300
Board only:	$1,500	
Books and supplies:	$600	$600
Personal expenses:	$1,000	$1,200
Transportation:	$2,200	$880

Undergraduate aid. Need-based: Need-based aid available for full-time and part-time students.

Policies to reduce costs. Tuition/fee waivers for adults, minority students, unemployed or children of unemployed, employees and their families. Credit/placement for qualifying scores on AP, CLEP examinations.

Payment plans. Credit card payment.

Application procedures. FAFSA, institutional form required. Priority date 6/1; no closing date. Applicants notified on rolling basis starting 4/1. **Transfers:** No deadline.

Contact. Financial aid office: (580) 628-6240
Linda Brown, Director of Financial Aid
Box 310
Tonkawa, OK 74653

Northwestern Oklahoma State University

Alva, Oklahoma
www.nwalva.edu
Four-year public **Federal Code: 003163**

	Living at home	On-campus
Tuition and fees (2002-2003):	$2,293	$2,293
Out-of-state:	$5,446	$5,446
Room and board:		$2,600
Board only:	$1,500	
Books and supplies:	$800	$800
Personal expenses:	$700	$1,100
Transportation:	$550	$750

Undergraduate aid. Need-based: Average financial aid package for full-time students was $3,780; for part-time $3,263. 67% awarded as scholarships/grants, 33% as loans/jobs. **Non-need-based:** 35% awarded as scholarships/grants, 65% as loans/jobs. Scholarships based on academics, alumni affiliation, athletics, leadership, music/drama. **Student debt:** 46% of graduating class borrowed to fund education; average debt was $9,371.

Freshman aid. Need-based: Out of 263 full-time freshmen, 213 applied for aid; 136 were judged to have need; of these 135 received aid. Average package met 89% of need. 45 students had full need met. Average scholarship/grant was $3,039; average loan $1,056. **Non-need based:** 17 full-time freshmen with need received non-need scholarships; 111 without need received awards; 19 received athletic scholarships.

Merit scholarships. Scholarships available to first-time students who establish residence in Alva in order to attend.

Policies to reduce costs. Tuition/fee waivers for children of alumni, senior citizens, family members, employees and their families. Credit/placement for qualifying scores on AP, CLEP examinations. Work study available nights, weekends and for part-time students.

Payment plans. Credit card payment.

Application procedures. FAFSA, institutional form required. Priority date 6/1; no closing date. Applicants notified on rolling basis starting 6/1, must reply within 2 week(s) of notification. **Transfers:** No deadline.

Contact. Financial aid office: (580) 327-8542
Irala Magee, Director of Financial Aid
709 Oklahoma Boulevard
Alva, OK 73717-2799

Oklahoma Baptist University

Shawnee, Oklahoma
www.okbu.edu
Four-year private **Federal Code: 003164**

	Living at home	On-campus
Tuition and fees:	$11,580	$11,580
Room and board:		$3,640
Board only:	$1,000	
Books and supplies:	$650	$650
Personal expenses:	$600	$1,400
Transportation:	$500	$1,000

Undergraduate aid. Need-based: Need-based aid available for full-time and part-time students. **Non-need-based:** Scholarships based on academics, athletics.

Merit scholarships. Prichard Church Vocation Scholarship, in the amount of $1,600, is offered to all students preparing for vocational ministry associated with Southern Baptist Convention.

Policies to reduce costs. Tuition/fee waivers for senior citizens, family of clergy, employees and their families. Credit/placement for qualifying scores on AP, IB, CLEP examinations.

Payment plans. Credit card, installment payment.

Application procedures. FAFSA required. Priority date 3/1; no closing date. Applicants notified on rolling basis starting 4/1, must reply by 5/1 or within 2 week(s) of notification. **Transfers:** Priority date 6/1; no deadline. Students on financial aid suspension from previous institution must complete at least 12 hours with 2.0 GPA to be eligible for aid.

Contact. Financial aid office: (405) 878-2016
Larry Hollingsworth, Director of Student Financial Services
500 West University
Shawnee, OK 74804

Oklahoma Christian University

Oklahoma City, Oklahoma
www.oc.edu
Four-year private **Federal Code: 003165**

	Living at home	On-campus
Tuition and fees:	$13,090	$13,090
Room and board:		$4,636
Board only:	$2,360	
Books and supplies:	$800	$800
Personal expenses:	$1,360	$1,360
Transportation:	$1,360	$1,360

Undergraduate aid. Need-based: Average financial aid package for full-time students was $11,048; for part-time $7,343. **Non-need-based:** Scholarships based on academics, alumni affiliation, athletics, job skills, leadership, minority status, music/drama. **Student debt:** 80% of graduating class borrowed to fund education; average debt was $17,800.

Freshman aid. Need-based: Out of 427 full-time freshmen, 427 applied for aid; 313 were judged to have need; of these 311 received aid. Average package met 54% of need. 66 students had full need met. Average scholarship/grant was $1,633; average loan $2,509. **Non-need based:** 284 full-time freshmen with need received non-need scholarships; 105 without need received awards; 84 received athletic scholarships.

Policies to reduce costs. Tuition/fee waivers for minority students, family members, employees and their families. Prepayment discount; credit/placement for qualifying scores on AP, IB, CLEP examinations. Work study available nights.

Payment plans. Credit card, installment payment.

Application procedures. FAFSA, institutional form required. Priority date 3/15; closing date 8/31. Applicants notified on rolling basis starting 4/1, must reply within 4 week(s) of notification.

Contact. Missi Bryant, Director, Financial Services
Box 11000
Oklahoma City, OK 73136-1100

Oklahoma City Community College

Oklahoma City, Oklahoma
www.occc.edu
Two-year public **Federal Code: 010391**

	Living at home
Tuition and fees (2002-2003):	$1,505
Out-of-state:	$3,909
Per-credit charge:	$36
Per-credit out-of-state:	$116
Books and supplies:	$675
Personal expenses:	$600
Transportation:	$900

Undergraduate aid. Need-based: Average financial aid package for full-time students was $2,575; for part-time $2,575. 63% awarded as scholarships/grants, 37% as loans/jobs. **Non-need-based:** 8% awarded as scholarships/grants, 92% as loans/jobs. Scholarships based on academics, state/district residency. **Student debt:** 20% of graduating class borrowed to fund education; average debt was $9,625.

Freshman aid. Need-based: Out of 1,053 full-time freshmen, 474 applied for aid; 318 were judged to have need; of these 318 received aid. Average package met 68% of need. 25 students had full need met. Average scholarship/grant was $1,980; average loan $2,276. **Non-need based:** 76 full-time freshmen with need received non-need scholarships; 28 without need received awards.

Policies to reduce costs. Tuition/fee waivers for senior citizens, employees and their families. Credit/placement for qualifying scores on AP, IB, CLEP examinations. Work study available nights, weekends and for part-time students.

Payment plans. Credit card, installment payment.

Application procedures. FAFSA, institutional form required. Priority date 7/1; no closing date. Applicants notified on rolling basis starting 5/7. **Transfers:** No deadline. First come-first served, once application materials are complete and accurate.

Contact. Financial aid office: (405) 682-7524
Harold Case, Director of Financial Aid
7777 South May Avenue
Oklahoma City, OK 73159

Oklahoma City University

Oklahoma City, Oklahoma
www.okcu.edu
Four-year private **Federal Code: 003166**

College costs. International students pay $80 international student fee and $30 international house fee annually.

	Living at home	On-campus
Tuition and fees:	$14,030	$14,030
Room and board:		$5,500
Board only:	$2,152	
Books and supplies:	$750	$750
Personal expenses:	$981	$981
Transportation:	$840	$114

Undergraduate aid. Need-based: Average financial aid package for full-time students was $8,796; for part-time $5,588. 21% awarded as scholarships/grants, 79% as loans/jobs. **Non-need-based:** 43% awarded as scholarships/grants, 57% as loans/jobs. Scholarships based on academics, art, athletics, job skills, leadership, music/drama, religious affiliation. **Student debt:** 45% of graduating class borrowed to fund education; average debt was $19,800.

Freshman aid. Need-based: Out of 238 full-time freshmen, 212 applied for aid; 156 were judged to have need; of these 155 received aid. Average scholarship/grant was $654; average loan $2,142. **Non-need based:** 142 full-time freshmen with need received non-need scholarships; 52 without need received awards; 9 received athletic scholarships.

Policies to reduce costs. Tuition/fee waivers for senior citizens, family of clergy, employees and their families. Credit/placement for qualifying scores on AP, IB, CLEP examinations. Work study available nights, weekends and for part-time students.

Payment plans. Credit card, installment, deferred payment.

Application procedures. FAFSA, institutional form required. Priority date 3/3; no closing date. Applicants notified on rolling basis starting 3/15, must reply within 2 week(s) of notification. **Transfers:** Priority date 3/3; no deadline. Financial aid transcripts required from all previously attended institutions whether having received financial aid or not.

Contact. Financial aid office: (405) 521-5211
Molly Roberts, Director of Financial Aid
2501 North Blackwelder
Oklahoma City, OK 73106

Oklahoma Panhandle State University

Goodwell, Oklahoma
www.opsu.edu
Four-year public **Federal Code: 003174**

	Living at home	On-campus
Tuition and fees (2002-2003):	$2,150	$2,150
Out-of-state:	$5,303	$5,303
Room and board:		$2,810
Board only:	$1,200	
Books and supplies:	$180	$180
Personal expenses:	$1,200	$1,598
Transportation:	$1,000	$400

Undergraduate aid. Need-based: Need-based aid available for part-time students. **Non-need-based:** Scholarships based on academics, art, athletics, leadership, minority status, state/district residency.

Policies to reduce costs. Tuition/fee waivers for senior citizens, employees and their families. Credit/placement for qualifying scores on AP, IB, CLEP examinations.

Payment plans. Credit card, installment, deferred payment.

Application procedures. Institutional form required. Priority date 8/25; no closing date. Applicants notified on rolling basis starting 6/15. **Transfers:** No deadline.

Contact. Financial aid office: (580) 349-1582
Mel Riley, Director of Financial Aid
OPSU Admissions
Goodwell, OK 73939-0430

Oklahoma State University

Stillwater, Oklahoma
www.okstate.edu
Four-year public **Federal Code: 003170**

	Living at home	On-campus
Tuition and fees (2002-2003):	$2,960	$2,960
Out-of-state:	$8,014	$8,014
Room and board:		$5,150
Books and supplies:	$900	$900
Personal expenses:		$2,890

Undergraduate aid. **Need-based:** Average financial aid package for full-time students was $7,550; for part-time $4,870. 45% awarded as scholarships/grants, 55% as loans/jobs. **Non-need-based:** 27% awarded as scholarships/grants, 73% as loans/jobs. Scholarships based on academics, alumni affiliation, art, athletics, job skills, leadership, music/drama. **Student debt:** 55% of graduating class borrowed to fund education; average debt was $15,580.

Freshman aid. **Need-based:** Out of 3,159 full-time freshmen, 2,394 applied for aid; 1,270 were judged to have need; of these 1,250 received aid. Average package met 79% of need. 253 students had full need met. Average scholarship/grant was $3,357; average loan $2,532. **Non-need based:** 798 full-time freshmen with need received non-need scholarships; 579 without need received awards; 45 received athletic scholarships.

Policies to reduce costs. Tuition/fee waivers for adults, children of alumni, senior citizens, employees and their families. Credit/placement for qualifying scores on AP, IB, CLEP examinations. Work study available nights, weekends and for part-time students.

Payment plans. Credit card, installment payment.

Application procedures. FAFSA required. No deadline. Applicants notified on rolling basis starting 3/15, must reply within 2 week(s) of notification.

Contact. **Financial aid office:** (405) 744-6604
Charles Bruce, Director of Financial Aid
324 Student Union
Stillwater, OK 74078

Oklahoma State University: Oklahoma City

Oklahoma City, Oklahoma
www.osuokc.edu
Two-year public **Federal Code: 009647**

	Living at home
Tuition and fees (2002-2003):	$1,954
Out-of-state:	$4,744
Per-credit charge:	$50
Per-credit out-of-state:	$143
Books and supplies:	$720

Undergraduate aid. **Non-need-based:** Scholarships based on academics, state/district residency.

Policies to reduce costs. Tuition/fee waivers for adults, senior citizens, minority students, employees and their families. Credit/placement for qualifying scores on AP, CLEP examinations.

Payment plans. Credit card, installment, deferred payment.

Application procedures. FAFSA required. Priority date 7/15; no closing date. Applicants notified on rolling basis starting 8/1, must reply within 2 week(s) of notification. **Transfers:** No deadline.

Contact. **Financial aid office:** (405) 945-8646
Jenny Wilson, Director of Financial Aid
900 North Portland
Oklahoma City, OK 73107-6195

Oklahoma State University: Okmulgee

Okmulgee, Oklahoma
www.osu-okmulgee.edu
Two-year public **Federal Code: 003172**

	Living at home	On-campus
Tuition and fees (2002-2003):	$2,115	$2,115
Out-of-state:	$4,905	$4,905
Per-credit charge:	$50	$50
Per-credit out-of-state:	$143	$143
Room and board:		$4,320
Books and supplies:	$640	$640
Personal expenses:	$850	
Transportation:	$850	

Undergraduate aid. **Need-based:** Need-based aid available for full-time and part-time students.

Policies to reduce costs. Tuition/fee waivers for senior citizens, employees and their families. Credit/placement for qualifying scores on AP, CLEP examinations. Work study available nights, weekends and for part-time students.

Payment plans. Credit card, installment payment.

Application procedures. FAFSA, institutional form required. Priority date 4/1; no closing date. Applicants notified on rolling basis. **Transfers:** No deadline. Requirement of financial aid transcript from any institution(s) attended during transferring academic year.

Contact. **Financial aid office:** (918) 293-5290
Barrett Bell, Director of Enrollment Services
1801 East Fourth Street
Okmulgee, OK 74447-3901

Oklahoma Wesleyan University

Bartlesville, Oklahoma
www.okwu.edu
Four-year private **Federal Code: 003151**

	Living at home	On-campus
Tuition and fees:	$12,150	$12,150
Room and board:		$4,600
Books and supplies:	$650	$650
Personal expenses:	$1,000	$1,000
Transportation:	$1,000	$1,000

Undergraduate aid. **Need-based:** Need-based aid available for full-time and part-time students.

Policies to reduce costs. Tuition/fee waivers for children of alumni, senior citizens, family members, family of clergy, employees and their families. Credit/placement for qualifying scores on AP, CLEP examinations.

Payment plans. Credit card, installment, deferred payment.

Application procedures. FAFSA, institutional form required. Priority date 3/1; no closing date. Applicants notified on rolling basis starting 4/1, must reply by 5/1 or within 2 week(s) of notification.

Contact. **Financial aid office:** (918) 335-6237
Lee Kanakis, Director of Financial Aid
2201 Silver Lake Road
Bartlesville, OK 74006

Oral Roberts University

Tulsa, Oklahoma
www.oru.edu
Four-year private **Federal Code: 003985**

	Living at home	On-campus
Tuition and fees:	$13,970	$13,970
Room and board:		$5,900
Board only:	$3,020	
Books and supplies:	$1,000	$1,000
Personal expenses:	$1,500	$1,500
Transportation:	$1,300	$1,300

Undergraduate aid. **Need-based:** Average financial aid package for full-time students was $12,448; for part-time $3,767. 50% awarded as scholarships/grants, 50% as loans/jobs. **Non-need-based:** 41% awarded as scholarships/grants, 59% as loans/jobs. Scholarships based on academics, alumni affiliation, art, athletics, leadership, minority status, music/drama, religious affiliation.

Student debt: 76% of graduating class borrowed to fund education; average debt was $28,264.

Freshman aid. Need-based: Out of 645 full-time freshmen, 531 applied for aid; 467 were judged to have need; of these 467 received aid. Average package met 90% of need. 249 students had full need met. Average scholarship/grant was $7,096; average loan $5,433. **Non-need based:** 165 full-time freshmen with need received non-need scholarships; 145 without need received awards; 22 received athletic scholarships.

Policies to reduce costs. Tuition/fee waivers for children of alumni, family members, family of clergy, employees and their families. Credit/placement for qualifying scores on AP, CLEP examinations.

Payment plans. Credit card, installment payment.

Application procedures. FAFSA required. Priority date 3/15; no closing date. Applicants notified on rolling basis starting 2/15, must reply within 3 week(s) of notification. **Transfers:** Transfer applicants eligible for some scholarships.

Contact. Financial aid office: (918) 495-6510
Steve Thannickal, Director of Financial Aid
7777 South Lewis Avenue
Tulsa, OK 74171

Redlands Community College

El Reno, Oklahoma
www.redlandscc.edu
Two-year public **Federal Code: 003156**

	Living at home
Tuition and fees (2002-2003):	$1,698
Out-of-state:	$4,102
Per-credit charge:	$36
Per-credit out-of-state:	$116
Books and supplies:	$600
Personal expenses:	$1,200
Transportation:	$700

Undergraduate aid. All financial aid based on need. Need-based aid available for full-time and part-time students.

Policies to reduce costs. Tuition/fee waivers for adults, senior citizens, employees and their families. Credit/placement for qualifying scores on AP, CLEP examinations. Work study available nights and for part-time students.

Payment plans. Credit card, installment, deferred payment.

Application procedures. FAFSA, institutional form required. Priority date 3/30; no closing date. Applicants notified on rolling basis starting 6/1, must reply within 2 week(s) of notification. **Transfers:** Must have financial aid transcripts from all previous post-secondary schools.

Contact. Chris Christian, Financial Aid Officer
1300 Country Club Road
El Reno, OK 73036

Rogers State University

Claremore, Oklahoma
www.rsu.edu
Four-year public **Federal Code: 003168**

	Living at home	On-campus
Tuition and fees (2002-2003):	$2,324	$2,324
Out-of-state:	$5,477	$5,477
Room only:		$3,070
Books and supplies:	$700	$700
Personal expenses:	$1,200	
Transportation:	$1,000	

Undergraduate aid. Need-based: Need-based aid available for full-time and part-time students.

Policies to reduce costs. Tuition/fee waivers for senior citizens. Credit/placement for qualifying scores on CLEP examinations. Work study available nights, weekends and for part-time students.

Payment plans. Credit card, installment, deferred payment.

Application procedures. FAFSA, institutional form required. Priority date 3/1; no closing date. Applicants notified on rolling basis starting 4/1, must reply within 3 week(s) of notification.

Contact. Cynthia Hoyt, Director, Financial Aid
1701 West Will Rogers Boulevard
Claremore, OK 74017

Rose State College

Midwest City, Oklahoma
www.rose.edu
Two-year public **Federal Code: 009185**

	Living at home
Tuition and fees (2002-2003):	$1,532
Out-of-state:	$3,936
Per-credit charge:	$36
Per-credit out-of-state:	$116
Books and supplies:	$625
Personal expenses:	$125
Transportation:	$225

Undergraduate aid. Need-based: 61% awarded as scholarships/grants, 39% as loans/jobs. Need-based aid available for part-time students. **Non-need-based:** Scholarships based on academics, athletics.

Policies to reduce costs. Tuition/fee waivers for senior citizens, employees and their families. Credit/placement for qualifying scores on AP, CLEP examinations. Work study available nights, weekends and for part-time students.

Payment plans. Credit card, installment payment.

Application procedures. FAFSA required. Priority date 6/1; no closing date. Applicants notified on rolling basis starting 3/1, must reply within 4 week(s) of notification.

Contact. Financial aid office: (405) 733-7424
Dean Fisher, Director of Financial Aid
6420 Southeast 15th Street
Midwest City, OK 73110

St. Gregory's University

Shawnee, Oklahoma
www.stgregorys.edu
Four-year private **Federal Code: 003813**

College costs. 14 meals per week offered to commuters for $2,124 per year.

	Living at home	On-campus
Tuition and fees:	$10,450	$10,450
Room only:		$2,680
Board only:	$620	
Books and supplies:	$670	$670
Personal expenses:	$820	$1,836
Transportation:	$134	$390

Undergraduate aid. Need-based: Average financial aid package for full-time students was $8,037. 49% awarded as scholarships/grants, 51% as loans/jobs. Need-based aid available for part-time students. **Non-need-based:** 60% awarded as scholarships/grants, 40% as loans/jobs. Scholarships based on academics, alumni affiliation, art, athletics, job skills, leadership, music/drama, religious affiliation.

Freshman aid. Need-based: Out of 157 full-time freshmen, 157 applied for aid; 123 were judged to have need; of these 123 received aid. Average package met 51% of need. 11 students had full need met. Average scholarship/grant was $6,530; average loan $1,896. **Non-need based:** 72 full-time freshmen with need received non-need scholarships; 43 without need received awards; 30 received athletic scholarships.

Policies to reduce costs. Tuition/fee waivers for family members, family of clergy, employees and their families. Prepayment discount; credit/placement for qualifying scores on AP, IB, CLEP examinations. Work study available nights, weekends and for part-time students.

Payment plans. Credit card, installment payment.

Application procedures. FAFSA, institutional form required. Priority date 4/15; no closing date. Applicants notified on rolling basis starting 2/15, must reply within 2 week(s) of notification.

Contact. Financial aid office: (405) 878-5412
Tammy Kasterke, Director of Financial Aid
1900 West MacArthur Drive
Shawnee, OK 74804

Seminole State College

Seminole, Oklahoma
www.ssc.cc.ok.us
Two-year public **Federal Code: 003178**

	Living at home	On-campus
Tuition and fees (2002-2003):	$1,638	$1,638
Out-of-state:	$4,042	$4,042
Per-credit charge:	$36	$36
Per-credit out-of-state:	$116	$116
Room and board:		$3,605
Books and supplies:	$350	$350
Personal expenses:	$920	$920
Transportation:	$528	$94

Undergraduate aid. Need-based: Need-based aid available for full-time students. **Non-need-based:** Scholarships based on academics, athletics.

Policies to reduce costs. Tuition/fee waivers for senior citizens, employees and their families. Credit/placement for qualifying scores on AP, CLEP examinations.

Payment plans. Credit card payment.

Application procedures. FAFSA, institutional form required. Priority date 5/1; no closing date. Applicants notified on rolling basis starting 3/1, must reply within 4 week(s) of notification. **Transfers:** No deadline.

Contact. Financial aid office: (405) 382-9247
Katherine Benton, Vice President of Fiscal Affairs
2701 Boren Boulevard
Seminole, OK 74868

Southeastern Oklahoma State University

Durant, Oklahoma
www.sosu.edu
Four-year public **Federal Code: 003179**

	Living at home	On-campus
Tuition and fees (2002-2003):	$2,422	$2,422
Out-of-state:	$5,575	$5,575
Room and board:		$2,542
Board only:	$2,046	
Books and supplies:	$600	$600
Personal expenses:	$1,582	$1,312
Transportation:	$1,134	$992

Undergraduate aid. Need-based: Average financial aid package for full-time students was $3,111; for part-time $1,594. 50% awarded as scholarships/grants, 50% as loans/jobs. **Non-need-based:** 34% awarded as scholarships/grants, 66% as loans/jobs. Scholarships based on academics, alumni affiliation, art, athletics, job skills, leadership, minority status, music/drama, religious affiliation, state/district residency. **Student debt:** 54% of graduating class borrowed to fund education; average debt was $10,254.

Freshman aid. Need-based: Out of 598 full-time freshmen, 561 applied for aid; 470 were judged to have need; of these 459 received aid. Average package met 62% of need. 183 students had full need met. Average scholarship/grant was $1,043; average loan $1,163. **Non-need based:** 187 full-time freshmen with need received non-need scholarships; 31 without need received awards; 33 received athletic scholarships.

Policies to reduce costs. Tuition/fee waivers for children of alumni, senior citizens, minority students, employees and their families. Credit/placement for qualifying scores on AP, IB, CLEP examinations. Work study available nights, weekends and for part-time students.

Payment plans. Credit card, deferred payment.

Application procedures. FAFSA, institutional form required. Priority date 3/1; no closing date. Applicants notified on rolling basis starting 5/1, must reply within 2 week(s) of notification.

Contact. Financial aid office: (580) 745-2186
Sherry Foster, Director of Student Financial Aid
1405 N. Fourth Ave., PMB 4225
Durant, OK 74701-0607

Southern Nazarene University

Bethany, Oklahoma
www.snu.edu
Four-year private **Federal Code: 003149**

	Living at home	On-campus
Tuition and fees:	$11,950	$11,950
Room and board:		$4,860
Books and supplies:	$600	$600
Personal expenses:	$1,200	$1,200
Transportation:	$800	$400

Undergraduate aid. Non-need-based: Scholarships based on academics, athletics, state/district residency.

Policies to reduce costs. Tuition/fee waivers for senior citizens, family of clergy, employees and their families. Credit/placement for qualifying scores on AP, CLEP examinations.

Payment plans. Credit card, installment payment.

Application procedures. FAFSA, institutional form required. Priority date 3/1; no closing date. Applicants notified on rolling basis starting 5/1, must reply within 2 week(s) of notification. **Transfers:** Priority date 3/1; no deadline.

Contact. Financial aid office: (405) 491-6406
Chuck Kietzman, Director of Financial Aid
6729 Northwest 39th Expressway
Bethany, OK 73008

Southwestern Christian University

Bethany, Oklahoma
www.sccm.edu
Four-year private **Federal Code: 003180**

	Living at home	On-campus
Tuition and fees (2002-2003):	$7,050	$7,050
Room and board:		$3,500
Books and supplies:	$500	$500
Personal expenses:	$1,200	$1,000
Transportation:	$800	$600

Undergraduate aid. All financial aid based on need. Average financial aid package for full-time students was $7,150. 44% awarded as scholarships/grants, 56% as loans/jobs. Need-based aid available for part-time students. **Student debt:** 77% of graduating class borrowed to fund education; average debt was $16,500.

Freshman aid. Average package met 71% of need. Average scholarship/grant was $2,400; average loan $2,400.

Policies to reduce costs. Tuition/fee waivers for children of alumni, family of clergy, employees and their families. Credit/placement for qualifying scores on CLEP examinations. Work study available nights, weekends and for part-time students.

Payment plans. Credit card, installment payment.

Application procedures. FAFSA required. Priority date 8/1; no closing date. Applicants notified on rolling basis starting 5/1, must reply by 8/1. **Transfers:** No deadline.

Contact. Financial aid office: (405) 789-7661 ext. 3456
Mark Arthur, Director of Financial Aid
Box 340
Bethany, OK 73008

Southwestern Oklahoma State University

Weatherford, Oklahoma
www.swosu.edu
Four-year public **Federal Code: 003181**

	Living at home	On-campus
Tuition and fees (2002-2003):	$2,450	$2,450
Out-of-state:	$5,603	$5,603
Room and board:		$2,765
Board only:	$1,028	
Books and supplies:	$756	$756
Personal expenses:	$996	$996
Transportation:	$1,324	$1,324

Undergraduate aid. Need-based: Average financial aid package for full-time students was $3,377; for part-time $3,425. 45% awarded as scholarships/grants, 55% as loans/jobs. **Non-need-based:** 33% awarded as scholarships/grants, 67% as loans/jobs. Scholarships based on academics, alumni affiliation, art, athletics, music/drama, state/district residency. **Student debt:** 58% of graduating class borrowed to fund education; average debt was $12,222.

Freshman aid. Need-based: Out of 888 full-time freshmen, 664 applied for aid; 526 were judged to have need; of these 517 received aid. Average package met 88% of need. 243 students had full need met. Average scholarship/grant was $1,054; average loan $946. **Non-need based:** 401 full-time freshmen with need received non-need scholarships; 216 without need received awards; 38 received athletic scholarships.

Policies to reduce costs. Tuition/fee waivers for children of alumni, senior citizens, employees and their families. Credit/placement for qualifying scores on AP, IB, CLEP examinations. Work study available for part-time students.

Payment plans. Credit card, installment, deferred payment.

Application procedures. FAFSA, institutional form required. Closing date 3/1. Applicants notified by 3/20, must reply by 4/6. **Transfers:** Priority date 3/1.

Contact. Financial aid office: (508) 774-3786
Thomas Ratliff, Director of Student Financial Services
100 Campus Drive
Weatherford, OK 73096

Tulsa Community College

Tulsa, Oklahoma
www.tulsacc.edu
Two-year public **Federal Code: 009763**

	Living at home
Tuition and fees (2002-2003):	$1,700
Out-of-state:	$4,158
Per-credit charge:	$36
Per-credit out-of-state:	$119
Books and supplies:	$600
Personal expenses:	$900
Transportation:	$780

Undergraduate aid. Need-based: 56% awarded as scholarships/grants, 44% as loans/jobs. Need-based aid available for part-time students. **Non-need-based:** Scholarships based on academics, art, leadership, music/drama, state/district residency.

Policies to reduce costs. Tuition/fee waivers for senior citizens, minority students, employees and their families. Credit/placement for qualifying scores on AP, CLEP examinations. Work study available nights, weekends and for part-time students.

Payment plans. Credit card payment.

Application procedures. FAFSA, institutional form required. Priority date 8/1; no closing date. Applicants notified on rolling basis starting 4/1, must reply within 2 week(s) of notification.

Contact. Financial aid office: (918) 595-7155
Debra MacIntyre, Director of Student Financial Services
6111 East Skelly Drive
Tulsa, OK 74135

Tulsa Welding School

Tulsa, Oklahoma
www.weldingschool.com
Two-year proprietary **Federal Code: 015733**

College costs. Students required to carry accident insurance; $150 through school.

	Living at home
Tuition and fees (2002-2003):	$10,000
Books and supplies:	$450

Undergraduate aid. All financial aid based on need. Need-based aid available for full-time students.

Application procedures. FAFSA required.

Contact. Michael Harter, Chief Executive Officer
2545 East 11th Street
Tulsa, OK 74104-3909

University of Central Oklahoma

Edmond, Oklahoma
www.ucok.edu
Four-year public **Federal Code: 003152**

	Living at home	On-campus
Tuition and fees (2002-2003):	$2,299	$2,299
Out-of-state:	$5,451	$5,451
Room and board:		$3,628
Books and supplies:	$900	$900
Personal expenses:	$2,500	$2,500
Transportation:	$1,960	$980

Undergraduate aid. Need-based: Need-based aid available for full-time students. **Non-need-based:** Scholarships based on academics, alumni affiliation, art, athletics, leadership, minority status, music/drama, state/district residency.

Policies to reduce costs. Tuition/fee waivers for minority students, employees and their families. Credit/placement for qualifying scores on AP, CLEP examinations.

Payment plans. Credit card, deferred payment.

Application procedures. FAFSA, institutional form required. Priority date 5/15; no closing date. Applicants notified on rolling basis starting 4/15, must reply within 3 week(s) of notification.

Contact. Sheila Fugett, Director of Financial Aid
100 North University Drive
Edmond, OK 73034-0151

University of Oklahoma

Norman, Oklahoma
www.ou.edu
Four-year public **Federal Code: 003184**

	Living at home	On-campus
Tuition and fees (2002-2003):	$2,860	$2,860
Out-of-state:	$7,705	$7,705
Room and board:		$5,030
Books and supplies:	$899	$899
Personal expenses:	$2,821	$2,821
Transportation:	$917	$917

Undergraduate aid. Need-based: Average financial aid package for full-time students was $7,880; for part-time $6,094. 33% awarded as scholarships/grants, 67% as loans/jobs. **Non-need-based:** 98% awarded as scholarships/grants, 2% as loans/jobs. Scholarships based on academics, alumni affiliation, art, athletics, leadership, minority status, music/drama, religious affiliation, state/district residency. **Student debt:** 53% of graduating class borrowed to fund education; average debt was $15,841. **Additional information:** Institutional loans are available for early applicants who do not qualify for federal or state need-based aid (middle-income students).

Freshman aid. Need-based: Out of 3,671 full-time freshmen, 2,053 applied for aid; 1,774 were judged to have need; of these 1,774 received aid. Average package met 88% of need. 1561 students had full need met. Average scholarship/grant was $3,418; average loan $2,986. **Non-need based:** 821 full-time freshmen with need received non-need scholarships; 595 without need received awards; 47 received athletic scholarships.

Merit scholarships. President's Leadership Class for leadership: $1,000; 70 awarded. Scholar's Program for academic merit: amounts ranging from $1,000-$1,500; 300 awarded. University Achievement Class for leadership and academics: $1,000; 80 awarded.

Policies to reduce costs. Tuition/fee waivers for children of alumni, senior citizens, minority students, employees and their families. Credit/placement for qualifying scores on AP, IB, CLEP examinations. Work study available nights, weekends and for part-time students.

Payment plans. Credit card, installment payment.

Application procedures. FAFSA, institutional form required. Priority date 3/1; no closing date. Applicants notified on rolling basis starting 3/15, must reply within 6 week(s) of notification. **Transfers:** Transfer leadership resident tuition waiver, transfer academic excellence tuition waiver.

Contact. Financial aid office: (405) 325-5505
Brad Burnett, Director of Financial Aid
1000 Asp Avenue
Norman, OK 73019-4076

University of Science and Arts of Oklahoma

Chickasha, Oklahoma
www.usao.edu
Four-year public **Federal Code: 003167**

	Living at home	On-campus
Tuition and fees (2002-2003):	$2,246	$2,246
Out-of-state:	$5,399	$5,399
Room and board:		$3,630
Board only:	$1,500	
Books and supplies:	$800	$800
Personal expenses:	$1,000	$1,000
Transportation:	$1,800	$1,800

Undergraduate aid. Need-based: Average financial aid package for full-time students was $6,231; for part-time $4,159. 63% awarded as scholarships/grants, 37% as loans/jobs. **Non-need-based:** 50% awarded as scholarships/grants, 50% as loans/jobs. Scholarships based on academics, art, athletics, leadership, music/drama, state/district residency. **Student debt:** 62% of graduating class borrowed to fund education; average debt was $11,299.

Freshman aid. Need-based: Out of 279 full-time freshmen, 266 applied for aid; 210 were judged to have need; of these 210 received aid. Average package met 75% of need. 35 students had full need met. Average scholarship/grant was $4,230; average loan $2,292. **Non-need based:** 11 full-time freshmen with need received non-need scholarships; 45 without need received awards; 11 received athletic scholarships.

Policies to reduce costs. Tuition/fee waivers for senior citizens, employees and their families. Credit/placement for qualifying scores on AP, CLEP examinations. Work study available nights and weekends.

Payment plans. Credit card, installment payment.

Application procedures. FAFSA, institutional form required. Priority date 3/15; no closing date. Applicants notified on rolling basis starting 3/15, must reply within 4 week(s) of notification. **Transfers:** No deadline.

Contact. Financial aid office: (405) 574-1240
Nancy Moats, Director of Financial Aid
1727 W. Alabama
Chickasha, OK 73018-0001

University of Tulsa

Tulsa, Oklahoma
www.utulsa.edu
Four-year private **Federal Code: 003185**

	Living at home	On-campus
Tuition and fees:	$15,736	$15,736
Room and board:		$5,610
Board only:	$1,800	
Books and supplies:	$1,200	$1,200
Personal expenses:	$2,370	$2,370
Transportation:	$1,815	$1,100

Undergraduate aid. Need-based: Average financial aid package for full-time students was $12,922; for part-time $6,838. 43% awarded as scholarships/grants, 57% as loans/jobs. **Non-need-based:** 82% awarded as scholarships/grants, 18% as loans/jobs. Scholarships based on academics, alumni affiliation, art, athletics, leadership, minority status, music/drama, religious affiliation. **Student debt:** 69% of graduating class borrowed to fund education; average debt was $12,171.

Freshman aid. Need-based: Out of 489 full-time freshmen, 436 applied for aid; 234 were judged to have need; of these 233 received aid. Average package met 76% of need. 112 students had full need met. Average scholarship/grant was $3,904; average loan $3,574. **Non-need based:** 200 full-time freshmen with need received non-need scholarships; 126 without need received awards; 65 received athletic scholarships.

Policies to reduce costs. Tuition/fee waivers for employees and their families. Credit/placement for qualifying scores on AP, IB, CLEP examinations. Work study available nights, weekends and for part-time students.

Payment plans. Credit card, installment payment.

Application procedures. FAFSA, institutional form required. Priority date 4/1; no closing date. Applicants notified on rolling basis starting 3/1, must reply by 5/1 or within 2 week(s) of notification. **Transfers:** Priority date 5/1; no deadline.

Contact. Financial aid office: (918) 631-2526
Vicki Hendrickson, Director of Student Financial Services
600 South College Avenue
Tulsa, OK 74104-3189

Vatterott College

Oklahoma City, Oklahoma
www.vatterott-college.com
One-year proprietary **Federal Code: 020693**

College costs. Tuition and fees vary from $6,432 to $7,416 and books, supplies, tools, and equipment fees range from $650 to $1,214 per academic year depending on program.

Undergraduate aid. All financial aid based on need. Need-based aid available for full-time students.

Payment plans. Credit card, deferred payment.

Application procedures. FAFSA required. No deadline.

Contact. Financial aid office: (405) 945-0088
Kelly Harjo, Financial Aid Director
4629 Northwest 23rd Street
Oklahoma City, OK 73127

Western Oklahoma State College

Altus, Oklahoma
www.wosc.edu
Two-year public **Federal Code: 003146**

	Living at home	On-campus
Tuition and fees (2002-2003):	$1,626	$1,626
Out-of-state:	$4,030	$4,030
Per-credit charge:	$36	$36
Per-credit out-of-state:	$116	$116
Room and board:		$3,400
Books and supplies:	$650	$650
Personal expenses:	$1,000	$1,000
Transportation:	$1,350	$1,350

Undergraduate aid. Need-based: Need-based aid available for full-time and part-time students. **Non-need-based:** Scholarships based on academics, alumni affiliation, art, athletics, leadership, music/drama, state/district residency.

Policies to reduce costs. Tuition/fee waivers for senior citizens. Credit/placement for qualifying scores on AP, CLEP examinations. Work study available nights, weekends and for part-time students.

Payment plans. Credit card, installment payment.

Application procedures. FAFSA, institutional form required. Priority date 3/1; no closing date. Applicants notified on rolling basis starting 4/31, must reply within 3 week(s) of notification. **Transfers:** No deadline.

Contact. Financial aid office: (580) 477-7709
Myrna Cross, Director of Financial Aid
2801 North Main Street
Altus, OK 73521

Oregon

Art Institute of Portland

Portland, Oregon
www.aipd.artinstitutes.edu
Four-year proprietary **Federal Code: 007819**

	Living at home
Tuition and fees (2002-2003):	$14,445
Board only:	$2,820
Books and supplies:	$1,194
Personal expenses:	$1,980
Transportation:	$1,065

Undergraduate aid. Need-based: Average financial aid package for full-time students was $3,578; for part-time $2,641. 29% awarded as scholarships/grants, 71% as loans/jobs. **Non-need-based:** 9% awarded as scholarships/grants, 91% as loans/jobs. Scholarships based on art. **Student debt:** 73% of graduating class borrowed to fund education; average debt was $15,600. **Additional information:** Applicants encouraged to apply early for financial aid. Scholarship deadlines range from January 1 to March 1.

Freshman aid. Need-based: Out of 163 full-time freshmen, 153 applied for aid; 115 were judged to have need; of these 115 received aid. Average package met 3% of need. 4 students had full need met. Average scholarship/grant was $1,059; average loan $875. **Non-need based:** 34 full-time freshmen with need received non-need scholarships; 17 without need received awards.

Policies to reduce costs. Tuition/fee waivers for employees and their families. Tuition at time of enrollment guaranteed for 4 years; credit/placement for qualifying scores on AP examinations.

Payment plans. Credit card, installment payment.

Application procedures. FAFSA required. No deadline. Applicants notified on rolling basis starting 1/1, must reply within 5 week(s) of notification. **Transfers:** No deadline.

Contact. Mickey Jacobson, Director of Student Financial Services
1122 NW Davis Street
Portland, OR 97209

Blue Mountain Community College

Pendleton, Oregon
www.bluecc.edu
Two-year public **Federal Code: 003186**

College costs. Washington, Idaho, Nevada, and California state residents pay in-state tuition.

	Living at home
Tuition and fees (projected):	$2,633
Out-of-state:	$5,220
Per-credit charge:	$58
Per-credit out-of-state:	$115
Board only:	$1,800
Books and supplies:	$1,000
Personal expenses:	$390
Transportation:	$900

Undergraduate aid. Need-based: 66% awarded as scholarships/grants, 34% as loans/jobs. Need-based aid available for part-time students. **Non-need-based:** Scholarships based on athletics, music/drama. **Student debt:** 50% of graduating class borrowed to fund education; average debt was $1,914.

Policies to reduce costs. Tuition/fee waivers for senior citizens, employees and their families. Work study available nights, weekends and for part-time students.

Payment plans. Credit card, deferred payment.

Application procedures. FAFSA required. Priority date 3/30; no closing date. Applicants notified on rolling basis starting 4/1, must reply within 2 week(s) of notification. **Transfers:** No deadline.

Contact. Financial aid office: (541) 278-5790
Theresa Bosworth, Director of Financial Aid
Box 100
Pendleton, OR 97801

Central Oregon Community College

Bend, Oregon
www.cocc.edu
Two-year public **Federal Code: 003188**

College costs. All domestic students pay in-district per-credit hour charge after first quarter.

	Living at home	On-campus
Tuition and fees (2002-2003):	$2,274	$2,274
Out-of-district:	$2,454	$2,454
Out-of-state:	$3,864	$3,864
Per-credit charge:	$48	$48
Per-credit out-of-district:	$60	$60
Per-credit out-of-state:	$154	$154
Room and board:		$5,565
Books and supplies:	$900	$900
Personal expenses:	$1,100	$1,100
Transportation:	$1,500	$1,500

Undergraduate aid. Need-based: Average financial aid package for full-time students was $5,719; for part-time $5,009. 52% awarded as scholarships/grants, 48% as loans/jobs. **Non-need-based:** 13% awarded as scholarships/grants, 87% as loans/jobs. Scholarships based on academics, state/district residency. **Student debt:** 35% of graduating class borrowed to fund education; average debt was $7,462. **Additional information:** Institution-sponsored short term loans. Extensive part-time student employment.

Freshman aid. Need-based: Average package met 63% of need. Average scholarship/grant was $3,689; average loan $2,505.

Policies to reduce costs. Tuition/fee waivers for adults, senior citizens, employees and their families. Credit/placement for qualifying scores on AP, CLEP examinations. Work study available nights, weekends and for part-time students.

Payment plans. Credit card, installment payment.

Application procedures. FAFSA required. Priority date 2/28; no closing date. Applicants notified on rolling basis starting 5/1, must reply within 4 week(s) of notification.

Contact. Financial aid office: (541) 383-7260
Laurie Neil, Director of Financial Aid
2600 Northwest College Way
Bend, OR 97701-5998

Chemeketa Community College

Salem, Oregon
www.chemeketa.edu
Two-year public **Federal Code: 003218**

College costs. Domestic out-of-state students pay in-state rate after first quarter.

	Living at home
Tuition and fees (2002-2003):	$1,755
Out-of-state:	$6,075
Per-credit charge:	$43
Per-credit out-of-state:	$149
Board only:	$2,325
Books and supplies:	$1,125
Personal expenses:	$300
Transportation:	$1,125

Undergraduate aid. Need-based: Need-based aid available for full-time students. **Non-need-based:** Scholarships based on academics, athletics.

Policies to reduce costs. Tuition/fee waivers for senior citizens, employees and their families. Credit/placement for qualifying scores on AP, CLEP examinations.

Payment plans. Credit card, deferred payment.

Application procedures. FAFSA required. Priority date 4/1; no closing date. Applicants notified on rolling basis starting 6/30, must reply within 2 week(s) of notification. **Transfers:** Priority date 4/1; closing date 6/30.

Contact. **Financial aid office:** (503) 399-5018
Kathy Campbell, Director of Financial Aid
Box 14007
Salem, OR 97309-7070

Clackamas Community College

Oregon City, Oregon
www.clackamas.cc.or.us
Two-year public **Federal Code: 004878**

College costs. In-state tuition applies to residents of Oregon, Washington, Idaho, Nevada and parts of California.

	Living at home
Tuition and fees (2002-2003):	$2,025
Out-of-state:	$6,480
Per-credit charge:	$41
Per-credit out-of-state:	$140
Books and supplies:	$975
Personal expenses:	$2,250
Transportation:	$855

Undergraduate aid. **Need-based:** 69% awarded as scholarships/grants, 31% as loans/jobs. Need-based aid available for part-time students. **Non-need-based:** Scholarships based on academics, art, athletics, leadership, music/drama. **Additional information:** Institutional tuition rebate guarantee. Frozen tuition rates for new fall students who graduate within 3 years. Any tuition increase levied by college during those 3 years will be refunded to student upon graduation.

Policies to reduce costs. Tuition/fee waivers for senior citizens, employees and their families. Tuition at time of enrollment guaranteed for 2 years; credit/placement for qualifying scores on AP, CLEP examinations. Work study available nights, weekends and for part-time students.

Payment plans. Credit card, installment, deferred payment.

Application procedures. FAFSA required. Priority date 4/10; no closing date. Applicants notified on rolling basis starting 3/15, must reply within 3 week(s) of notification.

Contact. **Financial aid office:** (503) 657-6958 ext. 2422
Mary Jo Jackson, Director, Student Financial Services
19600 South Molalla Avenue
Oregon City, OR 97045

Clatsop Community College

Astoria, Oregon
www.clatsop.cc.or.us
Two-year public **Federal Code: 003189**

	Living at home
Tuition and fees:	$2,430
Out-of-state:	$4,680
Per-credit charge:	$50
Per-credit out-of-state:	$100
Board only:	$2,502
Books and supplies:	$1,050
Personal expenses:	$600
Transportation:	$1,200

Undergraduate aid. **Need-based:** Need-based aid available for full-time and part-time students. **Non-need-based:** Scholarships based on academics.

Merit scholarships. Rochester scholarships awarded to mathematics or science majors; 3.0 GPA minimum; 3 reference letters required; between $3,000 and $5,000; number of awards varies yearly.

Policies to reduce costs. Tuition/fee waivers for senior citizens, family members, employees and their families. Prepayment discount; credit/placement for qualifying scores on CLEP examinations.

Payment plans. Credit card, installment, deferred payment.

Application procedures. FAFSA, institutional form required. Priority date 5/1; no closing date. Applicants notified on rolling basis starting 2/1. **Transfers:** No deadline. Students who apply after July 1 may only be eligible for Pell Grants and loans depending on availability of funds. Reply deadline 1 week before start of classes.

Contact. **Financial aid office:** (503) 338-2322
Sharon Boring, Director of Financial Aid
1653 Jerome Avenue
Astoria, OR 97103

Concordia University

Portland, Oregon
www.cu-portland.edu
Four-year private **Federal Code: 003191**

	Living at home	On-campus
Tuition and fees:	$17,490	$17,490
Room and board:		$5,100
Board only:	$1,600	
Books and supplies:	$500	$500
Personal expenses:	$1,000	$1,000
Transportation:	$500	$500

Undergraduate aid. **Need-based:** 66% awarded as scholarships/grants, 34% as loans/jobs. Need-based aid available for part-time students. **Non-need-based:** 10% awarded as scholarships/grants, 90% as loans/jobs. Scholarships based on academics, athletics, leadership, music/drama, religious affiliation.

Merit scholarships. President's Scholarship: based on Academic Index; $8,000. Regent's Scholarship: calculated from high school GPA and ACT/SAT score; $6,000. University Award: calculated from high school GPA and ACT/SAT score; $4,500. Dean's Award: based on academic index; $5,000.

Policies to reduce costs. Tuition/fee waivers for adults, senior citizens, family of clergy, employees and their families. Credit/placement for qualifying scores on AP, CLEP examinations.

Payment plans. Credit card, installment, deferred payment.

Application procedures. FAFSA required. No deadline. Applicants notified on rolling basis starting 3/15, must reply by 5/1 or within 3 week(s) of notification.

Contact. **Financial aid office:** (503) 280-8514
James Cullen, Financial Aid Director
2811 Northeast Holman Street
Portland, OR 97211

Eastern Oregon University

LaGrande, Oregon
www.eou.edu
Four-year public **Federal Code: 003193**

	Living at home	On-campus
Tuition and fees (2002-2003):	$3,678	$3,678
Out-of-state:	$3,678	$3,678
Room and board:		$5,200
Books and supplies:	$800	$800
Personal expenses:	$700	$1,000
Transportation:	$324	$600

Undergraduate aid. **Need-based:** Average financial aid package for full-time students was $8,163; for part-time $7,460. 45% awarded as scholarships/grants, 55% as loans/jobs. **Non-need-based:** 29% awarded as scholarships/grants, 71% as loans/jobs. Scholarships based on academics, art, leadership, minority status, music/drama, state/district residency. **Student debt:** 62% of graduating class borrowed to fund education; average debt was $13,449.

Freshman aid. **Need-based:** Out of 378 full-time freshmen, 323 applied for aid; 227 were judged to have need; of these 212 received aid. Average package met 44% of need. 89 students had full need met. Average scholarship/grant was $2,993; average loan $2,450. **Non-need based:** 68 full-time freshmen with need received non-need scholarships; 68 without need received awards.

Merit scholarships. University Scholars Scholarships, 65 awards, tuition (renewable). Based on personal essay, recommendations, GPA, activities and awards. Minorities encouraged to apply.

Policies to reduce costs. Tuition/fee waivers for minority students. Credit/placement for qualifying scores on AP, IB, CLEP examinations. Work study available nights, weekends and for part-time students.

Payment plans. Credit card, installment payment.

Application procedures. FAFSA required. Priority date 3/1; no closing date. Applicants notified on rolling basis starting 4/1, must reply within 4 week(s) of notification.

Contact. **Financial aid office:** (541) 962-3393
Rob Clarke, Director of Financial Aid
One University Boulevard
LaGrande, OR 97850

Eugene Bible College
Eugene, Oregon
www.ebc.edu
Four-year private **Federal Code: 015167**

	Living at home	On-campus
Tuition and fees:	$6,990	$6,990
Room and board:		$3,990
Books and supplies:	$525	$525
Transportation:	$700	$700

Undergraduate aid. Need-based: Average financial aid package for full-time students was $5,000; for part-time $3,000. 27% awarded as scholarships/grants, 73% as loans/jobs. **Non-need-based:** 58% awarded as scholarships/grants, 42% as loans/jobs. Scholarships based on academics, leadership, music/drama. **Student debt:** 90% of graduating class borrowed to fund education; average debt was $14,464. **Additional information:** Some early acceptance awards possible for those admitted by May 15. Distance awards to those coming from over 1000 miles away. Some awards for husbands and wives enrolled at same time.

Freshman aid. Need-based: Out of 31 full-time freshmen, 26 applied for aid; 18 were judged to have need; of these 16 received aid. Average package met 18% of need. 9 students had full need met. Average scholarship/grant was $2,000; average loan $2,500. **Non-need based:** 1 full-time freshmen with need received non-need scholarships; 5 without need received awards.

Merit scholarships. Honors award: $300 to all who qualify, based on high school GPA of 3.7 or higher.

Policies to reduce costs. Tuition/fee waivers for family of clergy, employees and their families. Credit/placement for qualifying scores on AP, CLEP examinations. Work study available nights, weekends and for part-time students.

Payment plans. Installment payment.

Application procedures. FAFSA required. Priority date 5/1; no closing date. Applicants notified on rolling basis starting 7/15, must reply within 4 week(s) of notification. **Transfers:** No deadline.

Contact. **Financial aid office:** (800) 322-2638
Rulena Mellor, Director of Financial Aid
2155 Bailey Hill Road
Eugene, OR 97405

George Fox University
Newberg, Oregon
www.georgefox.edu
Four-year private **Federal Code: 003194**

	Living at home	On-campus
Tuition and fees:	$19,810	$19,810
Room and board:		$6,300
Books and supplies:	$600	$600
Personal expenses:	$900	$900
Transportation:	$350	$350

Undergraduate aid. Need-based: Average financial aid package for full-time students was $15,332; for part-time $5,540. 62% awarded as scholarships/grants, 38% as loans/jobs. **Non-need-based:** 56% awarded as scholarships/grants, 44% as loans/jobs. Scholarships based on academics, alumni affiliation, art, minority status, music/drama, religious affiliation, state/district residency. **Additional information:** Audition required for music and drama scholarships.

Freshman aid. Need-based: Out of 318 full-time freshmen, 307 applied for aid; 253 were judged to have need; of these 253 received aid. Average package met 85% of need. 69 students had full need met. Average scholarship/grant was $11,803; average loan $3,232. **Non-need based:** 30 full-time freshmen with need received non-need scholarships; 80 without need received awards.

Merit scholarships. Academic merit awards are based on GPA, SAT/ACT scores and rigor of high school curriculum. Awards range from $2,500-$10,000 per year, renewable based on academic performance.

Policies to reduce costs. Tuition/fee waivers for senior citizens, minority students, family members, family of clergy, employees and their families. Credit/placement for qualifying scores on AP, IB, CLEP examinations.

Payment plans. Installment, deferred payment.

Application procedures. FAFSA required. Priority date 6/15; closing date 2/1. Applicants notified on rolling basis starting 3/1, must reply within 6 week(s) of notification.

Contact. **Financial aid office:** (503) 554-2230
Jenny Getsinger, Director, Financial Aid
414 North Meridian Street
Newberg, OR 97132-2697

ITT Technical Institute: Portland
Portland, Oregon
www.itt-tech.edu
Three-year proprietary **Federal Code: 011852**

College costs. Total program varies depending on course of study. Per-credit-hour charge: $347.

Policies to reduce costs. Tuition/fee waivers for employees and their families.

Payment plans. Credit card, installment payment.

Application procedures. FAFSA, institutional form required. No deadline. Applicants notified on rolling basis.

Contact. Suezi Lyon, Director of Finance
6035 Northeast 78th Court
Portland, OR 97218

Lane Community College
Eugene, Oregon
www.lanecc.edu
Two-year public **Federal Code: 003196**

	Living at home
Tuition and fees (2002-2003):	$1,796
Out-of-state:	$5,981
Per-credit charge:	$38
Per-credit out-of-state:	$131
Board only:	$1,800
Books and supplies:	$795
Personal expenses:	$1,800
Transportation:	$405

Undergraduate aid. Need-based: Need-based aid available for full-time and part-time students. **Non-need-based:** Scholarships based on art, athletics, minority status, music/drama.

Policies to reduce costs. Tuition/fee waivers for senior citizens, employees and their families. Credit/placement for qualifying scores on AP, CLEP examinations. Work study available nights and weekends.

Payment plans. Credit card, installment, deferred payment.

Application procedures. FAFSA required. Priority date 2/15; no closing date. Applicants notified on rolling basis starting 6/1, must reply within 2 week(s) of notification.

Contact. **Financial aid office:** (541) 726-2205
Linda DeWitt, Director of Financial Aid
4000 East 30th Avenue
Eugene, OR 97405

Lewis & Clark College
Portland, Oregon
www.lclark.edu
Four-year private **Federal Code: 003197**

	Living at home	On-campus
Tuition and fees:	$24,686	$24,686
Room and board:		$7,030
Board only:	$3,250	
Books and supplies:	$1,800	$1,800
Personal expenses:	$900	$900
Transportation:	$900	$900

Undergraduate aid. Need-based: Average financial aid package for full-time students was $19,545; for part-time $14,882. 75% awarded as scholarships/grants, 25% as loans/jobs. **Non-need-based:** 90% awarded as scholarships/grants, 10% as loans/jobs. Scholarships based on academics, leadership, music/drama. **Student debt:** 56% of graduating class borrowed to fund education; average debt was $16,412.

Freshman aid. Need-based: Out of 504 full-time freshmen, 333 applied for aid; 271 were judged to have need; of these 270 received aid. Average package met 86% of need. 122 students had full need met. Average scholarship/grant was $16,280; average loan $3,759. **Non-need based:** 108 full-time freshmen with need received non-need scholarships; 98 without need received awards.

Merit scholarships. Neely Scholarship, up to 10 awards, full tuition. Trustee Scholarship, up to 15 awards, half tuition. Deans Scholarships, $4,000-$8,000. Music scholarships, $1,000-$6,000, by audition. Forensic scholarships, $1,000-$5,000, separate application required. Leadership and service awards of $5,000.

Policies to reduce costs. Tuition/fee waivers for family members, employees and their families. Credit/placement for qualifying scores on AP, IB examinations. Work study available nights and weekends.

Payment plans. Credit card payment.

Application procedures. FAFSA required. Priority date 3/1; no closing date. Applicants notified on rolling basis starting 3/1, must reply by 5/1. **Transfers:** Transfers eligible for merit-based Dean's scholarships of up to $7,000, not eligible for Neely or Trustee scholarships. Financial aid transcript form from previous institutions required.

Contact. **Financial aid office:** (503) 768-7090
Glendi Gaddis, Director of Student Financial Services
0615 S.W. Palatine Hill Road
Portland, OR 97219-7899

Linfield College

McMinnville, Oregon
www.linfield.edu
Four-year private **Federal Code: 003198**

	Living at home	On-campus
Tuition and fees (2002-2003):	$20,330	$20,330
Room and board:		$6,553
Board only:	$1,800	
Books and supplies:	$600	$600
Personal expenses:	$1,100	$1,100
Transportation:	$75	$200

Undergraduate aid. Need-based: Need-based aid available for full-time and part-time students. **Non-need-based:** Scholarships based on academics, minority status, music/drama.

Policies to reduce costs. Tuition/fee waivers for senior citizens, employees and their families. Credit/placement for qualifying scores on AP, IB, CLEP examinations. Work study available nights, weekends and for part-time students.

Payment plans. Installment, deferred payment.

Application procedures. FAFSA required. Priority date 2/1; no closing date. Applicants notified by 4/1, must reply by 5/1. **Transfers:** Priority date 3/15; no deadline. Limited number of merit scholarships available for qualified transfer students.

Contact. **Financial aid office:** (503) 883-2225
Dan Preston, Director of Financial Aid and Dean of Enrollment Services
900 SE Baker Street
McMinnville, OR 97218

Linn-Benton Community College

Albany, Oregon
www.linnbenton.edu
Two-year public **Federal Code: 006938**

	Living at home
Tuition and fees (2002-2003):	$2,057
Out-of-state:	$5,972
Per-credit charge:	$43
Per-credit out-of-state:	$130
Books and supplies:	$900
Personal expenses:	$1,080
Transportation:	$1,170

Undergraduate aid. Need-based: 64% awarded as scholarships/grants, 36% as loans/jobs. Need-based aid available for part-time students. **Non-need-based:** Scholarships based on academics, art, job skills, leadership, music/drama, state/district residency.

Policies to reduce costs. Tuition/fee waivers for senior citizens, family members, unemployed or children of unemployed, employees and their families. Credit/placement for qualifying scores on AP, CLEP examinations. Work study available nights, weekends and for part-time students.

Payment plans. Credit card, installment payment.

Application procedures. FAFSA required. Priority date 4/1; no closing date. Applicants notified on rolling basis starting 4/16, must reply within 2 week(s) of notification. **Transfers:** Priority date 4/1; no deadline.

Contact. **Financial aid office:** (541) 917-4850
Lance Popoff, Director of Financial Aid
6500 Southwest Pacific Boulevard
Albany, OR 97321-3779

Marylhurst University

Marylhurst, Oregon
www.marylhurst.edu
Four-year private **Federal Code: 003199**

	Living at home	On-campus
Tuition and fees (2002-2003):	$11,850	$11,850
Room and board:		$6,000
Board only:	$1,500	
Books and supplies:	$600	$600
Personal expenses:	$1,800	
Transportation:	$600	

Undergraduate aid. Need-based: Need-based aid available for full-time and part-time students. **Non-need-based:** Scholarships based on academics.

Policies to reduce costs. Tuition/fee waivers for employees and their families. Credit/placement for qualifying scores on AP, IB, CLEP examinations. Work study available weekends and for part-time students.

Payment plans. Credit card, installment payment.

Application procedures. FAFSA, institutional form required. Priority date 6/1; no closing date. Applicants notified on rolling basis starting 5/1. **Transfers:** No deadline.

Contact. **Financial aid office:** (503) 699-6253
Marlena McKee-Flores, Director of Financial Aid
PO Box 261
Marylhurst, OR 97036-0261

Mount Hood Community College

Gresham, Oregon
Two-year public **Federal Code: 003204**

College costs. Washington State residents pay in-state tuition, plus $11 per-credit additional required fees.

	Living at home
Tuition and fees (2002-2003):	$2,025
Out-of-state:	$7,065
Per-credit charge:	$45
Per-credit out-of-state:	$157
Books and supplies:	$620
Personal expenses:	$540
Transportation:	$820

Undergraduate aid. Non-need-based: Scholarships based on academics.

Policies to reduce costs. Tuition/fee waivers for employees and their families. Credit/placement for qualifying scores on AP, CLEP examinations.

Application procedures. FAFSA, institutional form required. No deadline. Applicants notified on rolling basis starting 2/15, must reply within 4 week(s) of notification.

Contact. Patricia Martin, Associate Dean, Enrollment Services
26000 Southeast Stark Street
Gresham, OR 97030

Multnomah Bible College

Portland, Oregon
www.multnomah.edu
Four-year private **Federal Code: 003206**

	Living at home	On-campus
Tuition and fees:	$10,560	$10,560
Room and board:		$4,650
Board only:	$2,000	
Books and supplies:	$800	$800
Personal expenses:	$1,400	$1,400
Transportation:	$1,200	$1,200

Undergraduate aid. Need-based: Average financial aid package for full-time students was $7,403; for part-time $4,255. 40% awarded as scholarships/grants, 60% as loans/jobs. **Non-need-based:** 25% awarded as scholarships/grants, 75% as loans/jobs. Scholarships based on academics. **Student debt:** 82% of graduating class borrowed to fund education; average debt was $18,885.

Freshman aid. Need-based: Average package met 49% of need. Average scholarship/grant was $4,236; average loan $2,305.

Policies to reduce costs. Tuition/fee waivers for family members, employees and their families. Credit/placement for qualifying scores on AP, IB, CLEP examinations. Work study available nights, weekends and for part-time students.

Payment plans. Credit card, installment payment.

Application procedures. FAFSA, institutional form required. Priority date 3/1; closing date 8/1. Applicants notified on rolling basis starting 4/15, must reply within 3 week(s) of notification. **Transfers:** Priority date 3/1; closing date 8/1.

Contact. Financial aid office: (503) 251-5335
David Allen, Financial Aid Officer
8435 Northeast Glisan Street
Portland, OR 97220-5898

Northwest Christian College

Eugene, Oregon
www.nwcc.edu
Four-year private **Federal Code: 003208**

	Living at home	On-campus
Tuition and fees (2002-2003):	$15,435	$15,435
Room and board:		$5,448
Board only:	$2,175	
Books and supplies:	$750	$750
Personal expenses:	$1,800	$1,650

Undergraduate aid. Need-based: Need-based aid available for full-time and part-time students. **Non-need-based:** Scholarships based on academics, athletics, leadership, music/drama, religious affiliation.

Merit scholarships. Presidential Scholarship: $5,000 per year, superior leadership and achievement and 2 of the following, 3.75 GPA, 1200 SAT, top 15% class rank; Dean's Scholarship: $4,000 per year, superior leadership and achievement and 2 of the following, 3.5 GPA, 1100 SAT, top 33% class rank; Achievement/Leadership Award: $3,000 per year, record of leadership/achievement and 2 of the following 3.0 GPA, 1000 SAT, top 60% class rank; Valedictorian/Salutatorian Scholarship: $6,000 per year, meet criteria for Presidential Scholarship and graduate as valedictorian or salutatorian.

Policies to reduce costs. Tuition/fee waivers for family members, employees and their families. Prepayment discount; credit/placement for qualifying scores on AP, IB, CLEP examinations. Work study available nights and weekends.

Payment plans. Credit card, installment payment.

Application procedures. FAFSA required. Priority date 3/1; no closing date. Applicants notified on rolling basis starting 4/1. **Transfers:** Priority date 3/1; no deadline.

Contact. Financial aid office: (541) 684-7203
Randy Jones, Dean of Admissions and Financial Aid
828 East 11th Avenue
Eugene, OR 97401-3745

Oregon Health Sciences University

Portland, Oregon
www.ohsu.edu
Upper-division public **Federal Code: 004883**

College costs. Tuition shown is for nursing program; costs for other programs vary.

	Living at home	On-campus
Tuition and fees (2002-2003):	$8,395	$8,395
Out-of-state:	$14,617	$14,617
Room only:		$3,560
Books and supplies:	$461	$461
Personal expenses:	$2,285	$2,285
Transportation:	$900	$900

Undergraduate aid. Need-based: Need-based aid available for full-time and part-time students.

Policies to reduce costs. Tuition/fee waivers for minority students, employees and their families.

Payment plans. Credit card, deferred payment.

Application procedures. FAFSA required. Priority date 3/1; no closing date. Applicants notified on rolling basis starting 5/31.

Contact. Director of Financial Aid
3181 SW Sam Jackson Park Road
Portland, OR 97239

Oregon Institute of Technology

Klamath Falls, Oregon
www.oit.edu
Four-year public **Federal Code: 003211**

	Living at home	On-campus
Tuition and fees (2002-2003):	$3,843	$3,843
Out-of-state:	$13,071	$13,071
Room and board:		$5,645
Books and supplies:	$864	$864
Personal expenses:	$2,025	$2,025

Undergraduate aid. All financial aid based on need. Average financial aid package for full-time students was $6,354; for part-time $4,092. 42% awarded as scholarships/grants, 58% as loans/jobs. **Student debt:** 70% of graduating class borrowed to fund education; average debt was $22,394.

Freshman aid. Average package met 43% of need. Average scholarship/grant was $3,679; average loan $2,735.

Policies to reduce costs. Tuition/fee waivers for senior citizens, minority students, employees and their families. Credit/placement for qualifying scores on AP, CLEP examinations. Work study available for part-time students.

Payment plans. Credit card, installment, deferred payment.

Application procedures. FAFSA required. Priority date 3/1; no closing date. Applicants notified on rolling basis starting 4/15, must reply by 9/1 or within 3 week(s) of notification.

Contact. Financial aid office: (541) 885-1280
Tracey Lehmann-Marquit, Director of Financial Aid
3201 Campus Drive
Klamath Falls, OR 97601

Oregon State University

Corvallis, Oregon
www.oregonstate.edu
Four-year public **Federal Code: 003210**

	Living at home	On-campus
Tuition and fees (2002-2003):	$4,014	$4,014
Out-of-state:	$14,898	$14,898
Room and board:		$6,212
Board only:	$3,038	
Books and supplies:	$900	$900
Personal expenses:	$2,355	$2,355
Transportation:	$500	

Undergraduate aid. Non-need-based: Scholarships based on academics, athletics, job skills, leadership, minority status, state/district residency.

Policies to reduce costs. Tuition/fee waivers for employees and their families. Credit/placement for qualifying scores on AP, IB, CLEP examinations.

Payment plans. Installment payment.

Application procedures. FAFSA required. Priority date 2/1; closing date 5/1. Applicants notified on rolling basis starting 4/1, must reply within 3 week(s) of notification. **Transfers:** Priority date 3/1; no deadline.

Contact. Financial aid office: (541) 731-2241
Kate Peterson, Director of Financial Aid
104 Kerr Administration Building
Corvallis, OR 97331-2130

Pacific Northwest College of Art

Portland, Oregon
www.pnca.edu
Four-year private **Federal Code: 003207**

	Living at home
Tuition and fees:	$14,890
Board only:	$1,872
Personal expenses:	$1,951
Transportation:	$852

Undergraduate aid. Need-based: Average financial aid package for full-time students was $9,447; for part-time $4,321. 33% awarded as scholarships/grants, 67% as loans/jobs. **Non-need-based:** 78% awarded as scholarships/grants, 22% as loans/jobs. Scholarships based on academics, art.

Freshman aid. Need-based: Out of 17 full-time freshmen, 14 applied for aid; 14 were judged to have need; of these 14 received aid. Average package met 87% of need. 8 students had full need met. Average scholarship/grant was $3,851; average loan $2,516. **Non-need based:** 2 full-time freshmen with need received non-need scholarships.

Merit scholarships. Leta Kennedy Student Scholarships, total of $10,000, number of awards undetermined, based on artistic merit. Dorothy Lemelson Scholarship, total financial aid-determined cost of attendance ($20,900 in 1999-2000), renewable up to 4 years, 1 award, based on artistic and academic merit. Both highly competitive; deadline March 1.

Policies to reduce costs. Tuition/fee waivers for employees and their families. Credit/placement for qualifying scores on AP examinations. Work study available nights, weekends and for part-time students.

Payment plans. Credit card, installment, deferred payment.

Application procedures. FAFSA required. Priority date 3/1; no closing date. Applicants notified on rolling basis starting 4/1, must reply by 5/1 or within 2 week(s) of notification. **Transfers:** No deadline.

Contact. Jennifer Satalino, Financial Aid
1241 NW Johnson Street
Portland, OR 97209

Pacific University

Forest Grove, Oregon
www.pacificu.edu
Four-year private **Federal Code: 003212**

	Living at home	On-campus
Tuition and fees:	$19,890	$19,890
Room and board:		$5,540
Board only:	$900	
Books and supplies:	$700	$700
Personal expenses:	$900	$900
Transportation:	$500	$500

Undergraduate aid. Need-based: Average financial aid package for full-time students was $16,555; for part-time $15,803. 64% awarded as scholarships/grants, 36% as loans/jobs. **Non-need-based:** 50% awarded as scholarships/grants, 50% as loans/jobs. Scholarships based on academics, art, music/drama, religious affiliation. **Student debt:** 82% of graduating class borrowed to fund education; average debt was $21,547.

Freshman aid. Need-based: Out of 275 full-time freshmen, 266 applied for aid; 213 were judged to have need; of these 213 received aid. Average package met 97% of need. 93 students had full need met. Average scholarship/grant was $11,502; average loan $4,501. **Non-need based:** 41 full-time freshmen with need received non-need scholarships; 46 without need received awards.

Merit scholarships. Honors Scholarship: $9,000; Presidential Scholarship: $8,000; Trustee Scholarship: $7,500; University Scholarship: $6,500, all based on academic merit. Number of awards varies.

Policies to reduce costs. Tuition/fee waivers for family of clergy, employees and their families. Credit/placement for qualifying scores on AP, IB, CLEP examinations. Work study available nights and weekends.

Payment plans. Credit card, installment payment.

Application procedures. FAFSA required. Priority date 2/15; no closing date. Applicants notified on rolling basis starting 3/1.

Contact. **Financial aid office:** (503) 352-2222
Director of Financial Aid
2043 College Way
Forest Grove, OR 97116-1797

Pioneer Pacific College

Wilsonville, Oregon
www.pioneerpacificcollege.com
Two-year proprietary **Federal Code: 016520**

College costs. Costs vary by program, $12,980-$15,766. Quoted annual tuition is for criminal justice.

	Living at home
Tuition and fees (projected):	$7,890
Board only:	$1,112
Personal expenses:	$1,169
Transportation:	$707

Undergraduate aid. All financial aid based on need. Average financial aid package for full-time students was $7,500. 28% awarded as scholarships/grants, 72% as loans/jobs. Need-based aid available for part-time students. **Student debt:** 68% of graduating class borrowed to fund education; average debt was $9,125.

Freshman aid. Out of 114 full-time freshmen, 83 applied for aid; 79 were judged to have need; of these 83 received aid. Average package met 75% of need. 83 students had full need met. Average loan $2,625.

Policies to reduce costs. Tuition/fee waivers for employees and their families. Tuition at time of enrollment guaranteed for 2 years.

Payment plans. Credit card, installment payment.

Application procedures. FAFSA required. No deadline. Applicants notified on rolling basis starting 12/15. **Transfers:** No deadline.

Contact. **Financial aid office:** (503) 682-3903
Stacey Maurer, Financial Aid Director
27501 SW Parkway Avenue
Wilsonville, OR 97070

Portland Community College

Portland, Oregon
www.pcc.edu
Two-year public **Federal Code: 003213**

College costs. Out-of-state students pay in-state tuition after first quarter.

	Living at home
Tuition and fees (2002-2003):	$2,205
Out-of-state:	$8,155
Per-credit charge:	$45
Per-credit out-of-state:	$175
Board only:	$870
Books and supplies:	$1,170
Personal expenses:	$975
Transportation:	$1,035

Undergraduate aid. All financial aid based on need. 46% awarded as scholarships/grants, 54% as loans/jobs. Need-based aid available for part-time students.

Policies to reduce costs. Tuition/fee waivers for senior citizens, employees and their families. Credit/placement for qualifying scores on AP, CLEP examinations. Work study available nights, weekends and for part-time students.

Payment plans. Credit card, installment, deferred payment.

Application procedures. FAFSA required. Priority date 3/1; no closing date. Applicants notified on rolling basis starting 6/1, must reply within 3 week(s) of notification.

Contact. **Financial aid office:** (503) 977-4934
Corbett Gottfried, Director of Financial Aid
Box 19000
Portland, OR 97280-0990

Portland State University

Portland, Oregon
www.pdx.edu
Four-year public **Federal Code: 003216**

	Living at home
Tuition and fees (2002-2003):	$3,885
Out-of-state:	$13,266
Board only:	$2,100
Books and supplies:	$1,200
Personal expenses:	$1,400
Transportation:	$450

Undergraduate aid. Need-based: Average financial aid package for full-time students was $7,484; for part-time $6,434. 26% awarded as scholarships/grants, 74% as loans/jobs. **Non-need-based:** Scholarships based on academics, athletics, state/district residency. **Student debt:** 57% of graduating class borrowed to fund education; average debt was $18,976.

Freshman aid. Need-based: Out of 1,100 full-time freshmen, 696 applied for aid; 504 were judged to have need; of these 487 received aid. Average package met 60% of need. 90 students had full need met. Average scholarship/grant was $3,739; average loan $6,037. **Non-need based:** 225 full-time freshmen with need received non-need scholarships; 90 without need received awards; 15 received athletic scholarships.

Policies to reduce costs. Tuition/fee waivers for senior citizens, minority students, employees and their families. Credit/placement for qualifying scores on AP, CLEP examinations. Work study available nights and weekends.

Payment plans. Credit card, installment payment.

Application procedures. FAFSA required. No deadline. Applicants notified on rolling basis, must reply within 4 week(s) of notification.

Contact. Financial aid office: (503) 725-3461
Samuel Collie, Director of Student Financial Aid
PO Box 751-ADM
Portland, OR 97207-0751

Reed College

Portland, Oregon
www.reed.edu
Four-year private **Federal Code: 003217**

	Living at home	On-campus
Tuition and fees:	$29,200	$29,200
Room and board:		$7,750
Board only:	$1,500	
Books and supplies:	$950	$950
Personal expenses:	$900	$900
Transportation:	$100	$700

Undergraduate aid. All financial aid based on need. Average financial aid package for full-time students was $21,254. 82% awarded as scholarships/grants, 18% as loans/jobs. **Student debt:** 52% of graduating class borrowed to fund education; average debt was $16,758. **Additional information:** College meets demonstrated need of continuing students who have attended Reed minimum of 2 semesters, who file financial aid applications on time, and who maintain satisfactory academic progress. Institutional aid consideration is for a total of 8 semesters.

Freshman aid. Out of 308 full-time freshmen, 228 applied for aid; 182 were judged to have need; of these 170 received aid. Average package met 100% of need. 145 students had full need met. Average scholarship/grant was $20,880; average loan $2,498.

Policies to reduce costs. Tuition/fee waivers for employees and their families. Credit/placement for qualifying scores on AP, IB examinations. Work study available nights and for part-time students.

Payment plans. Installment payment.

Application procedures. FAFSA, institutional form, CSS PROFILE required. Priority date 1/15; closing date 2/1. Applicants notified by 4/1, must reply by 5/1 or within 2 week(s) of notification. Early decision closing date 11/15. **Transfers:** Priority date 2/1; closing date 3/1.

Contact. Financial aid office: (800) 547-4750
Leslie Limper, Director of Financial Aid
3203 Southeast Woodstock Boulevard
Portland, OR 97202-8199

Rogue Community College

Grants Pass, Oregon
www.roguecc.edu
Two-year public **Federal Code: 010071**

College costs. Washington, Montana, Idaho, Nevada and California residents pay in-state tuition.

	Living at home
Tuition and fees (2002-2003):	$2,115
Out-of-state:	$2,565
Per-credit charge:	$47
Per-credit out-of-state:	$57
Books and supplies:	$450
Personal expenses:	$825
Transportation:	$925

Policies to reduce costs. Tuition/fee waivers for unemployed or children of unemployed, employees and their families. Credit/placement for qualifying scores on AP, CLEP examinations.

Payment plans. Credit card, deferred payment.

Application procedures. FAFSA, institutional form required. Priority date 5/1; no closing date. Applicants notified on rolling basis, must reply within 2 week(s) of notification. **Transfers:** Priority date 5/1.

Contact. Anna Manley, Director of Financial Aid
3345 Redwood Highway
Grants Pass, OR 97527

Southern Oregon University

Ashland, Oregon
www.sou.edu
Four-year public **Federal Code: 003219**

	Living at home	On-campus
Tuition and fees (2002-2003):	$3,687	$3,687
Out-of-state:	$11,526	$11,526
Room and board:		$5,665
Board only:	$2,145	
Books and supplies:	$975	$975
Personal expenses:	$2,700	$2,700
Transportation:	$834	$486

Undergraduate aid. Need-based: Average financial aid package for full-time students was $6,942; for part-time $6,721. 38% awarded as scholarships/grants, 62% as loans/jobs. **Non-need-based:** 19% awarded as scholarships/grants, 81% as loans/jobs. Scholarships based on academics, alumni affiliation, art, athletics, leadership, minority status, music/drama, religious affiliation, state/district residency. **Student debt:** 66% of graduating class borrowed to fund education; average debt was $18,044.

Freshman aid. Need-based: Out of 759 full-time freshmen, 585 applied for aid; 460 were judged to have need; of these 460 received aid. Average package met 67% of need. 59 students had full need met. Average scholarship/grant was $5,022; average loan $2,415. **Non-need based:** 24 full-time freshmen with need received non-need scholarships; 119 without need received awards; 10 received athletic scholarships.

Policies to reduce costs. Tuition/fee waivers for senior citizens, minority students, employees and their families. Credit/placement for qualifying scores on AP, IB, CLEP examinations. Work study available nights, weekends and for part-time students.

Payment plans. Credit card, installment payment.

Application procedures. FAFSA required. No deadline. Applicants notified on rolling basis starting 4/1, must reply within 2 week(s) of notification.

Contact. Financial aid office: (541) 552-6161
Peggy Nitsos, Director of Financial Aid
1250 Siskiyou Boulevard
Ashland, OR 97520-5032

Southwestern Oregon Community College

Coos Bay, Oregon
www.socc.edu
Two-year public **Federal Code: 003220**

	Living at home	On-campus
Tuition and fees:	$2,724	$2,724
Per-credit charge:	$54	$54
Room and board:		$4,725
Books and supplies:	$840	$840
Personal expenses:	$540	$540
Transportation:	$840	$420

Undergraduate aid. Need-based: Need-based aid available for full-time and part-time students. **Student debt:** 15% of graduating class borrowed to fund education; average debt was $8,500.

Policies to reduce costs. Tuition/fee waivers for adults, senior citizens, family members, unemployed or children of unemployed, employees and their families. Credit/placement for qualifying scores on AP, CLEP examinations.

Payment plans. Credit card, installment, deferred payment.

Application procedures. FAFSA, institutional form required. Priority date 2/28; closing date 6/30. Applicants notified on rolling basis starting 5/1, must reply within 3 week(s) of notification.

Contact. Robin Bunnell, Associate Dean of Enrollment/Student Services
1988 Newmark
Coos Bay, OR 97420-2956

Treasure Valley Community College

Ontario, Oregon
Two-year public **Federal Code: 003221**

	Living at home	On-campus
Tuition and fees (2002-2003):	$2,240	$2,240
Out-of-state:	$2,739	$2,739
Per-credit charge:	$50	$50
Per-credit out-of-state:	$64	$64
Room and board:		$4,191
Books and supplies:	$420	$420
Personal expenses:	$750	$750
Transportation:	$750	$750

Policies to reduce costs. Tuition/fee waivers for senior citizens, employees and their families. Credit/placement for qualifying scores on AP, CLEP examinations.

Payment plans. Credit card, deferred payment.

Application procedures. FAFSA required. Priority date 4/1; no closing date. Applicants notified on rolling basis starting 5/1.

Contact. Kathy Gibson, Director of Financial Aid
650 College Boulevard
Ontario, OR 97914

Umpqua Community College

Roseburg, Oregon
www.umpqua.edu
Two-year public **Federal Code: 003222**

	Living at home
Tuition and fees (2002-2003):	$1,950
Out-of-state:	$5,012
Per-credit charge:	$42
Per-credit out-of-state:	$110
Board only:	$1,170
Books and supplies:	$750
Personal expenses:	$1,200
Transportation:	$1,050

Undergraduate aid. All financial aid based on need. Need-based aid available for full-time and part-time students.

Policies to reduce costs. Tuition/fee waivers for senior citizens, employees and their families. Credit/placement for qualifying scores on AP, CLEP examinations.

Application procedures. FAFSA required. Priority date 3/1; no closing date. Applicants notified on rolling basis starting 5/1, must reply within 2 week(s) of notification.

Contact. Claudia Justice, Director of Financial Aid
PO Box 967
Roseburg, OR 97470

University of Oregon

Eugene, Oregon
www.uoregon.edu
Four-year public **Federal Code: 003223**

	Living at home	On-campus
Tuition and fees (2002-2003):	$4,404	$4,404
Out-of-state:	$15,933	$15,933
Room and board:		$6,648
Books and supplies:	$675	$675
Personal expenses:	$1,975	$1,975

Undergraduate aid. Need-based: Average financial aid package for full-time students was $7,825; for part-time $7,037. 36% awarded as scholarships/grants, 64% as loans/jobs. **Non-need-based:** 42% awarded as scholarships/grants, 58% as loans/jobs. Scholarships based on academics, athletics. **Student debt:** 40% of graduating class borrowed to fund education; average debt was $22,783.

Freshman aid. Need-based: Out of 3,247 full-time freshmen, 2,399 applied for aid; 1,320 were judged to have need; of these 1,264 received aid. Average package met 63% of need. 484 students had full need met. Average scholarship/grant was $3,836; average loan $3,162. **Non-need based:** 677 full-time freshmen with need received non-need scholarships; 703 without need received awards.

Merit scholarships. Dean Scholarship: freshman non-residents, renewable up to 4 years. Award variable amount based on high school GPA: $5,000 for 4.0 or higher; $4,000 for 3.8-3.99; $3,000 for 3.70-3.79; $2,000 for 3.6-3.69. Freshman residents: $2,000 for 4.0 or higher; $1,000 for all other qualified students. Renewable up to 4 years.

Policies to reduce costs. Tuition/fee waivers for minority students. Credit/placement for qualifying scores on AP, IB, CLEP examinations.

Payment plans. Installment payment.

Application procedures. FAFSA required. Priority date 2/1; closing date 3/1. Applicants notified on rolling basis starting 4/15, must reply within 4 week(s) of notification.

Contact. Financial aid office: (541) 346-3221
Elizabeth Bickford, Associate Director, Financial Aid
Eugene, OR 97403-1217

University of Portland

Portland, Oregon
www.up.edu
Four-year private **Federal Code: 003224**

	Living at home	On-campus
Tuition and fees:	$22,020	$22,020
Room and board:		$6,520
Board only:	$2,000	
Books and supplies:	$700	$700
Personal expenses:	$800	$800
Transportation:	$600	$600

Undergraduate aid. Need-based: Average financial aid package for full-time students was $18,209; for part-time $12,280. 65% awarded as scholarships/grants, 35% as loans/jobs. **Non-need-based:** 93% awarded as scholarships/grants, 7% as loans/jobs. Scholarships based on academics, athletics, music/drama. **Student debt:** 67% of graduating class borrowed to fund education; average debt was $18,739.

Freshman aid. Need-based: Out of 732 full-time freshmen, 616 applied for aid; 452 were judged to have need; of these 452 received aid. Average package met 93% of need. 204 students had full need met. Average scholarship/grant was $12,017; average loan $2,817. **Non-need based:** 270 full-time freshmen with need received non-need scholarships; 244 without need received awards; 26 received athletic scholarships.

Merit scholarships. President's Scholarship; up to $10,000. Holy Cross Scholarship; up to $6,000. Both based on academic excellence, other factors including school and community involvement. Arthur A. Schulte Scholarship; up to $6,000. In all cases, number of awards not limited.

Policies to reduce costs. Tuition/fee waivers for family of clergy, employees and their families. Credit/placement for qualifying scores on AP, IB, CLEP examinations. Work study available nights and weekends.

Payment plans. Installment payment.

Application procedures. FAFSA, institutional form required. Priority date 3/1; no closing date. Applicants notified by 4/1, must reply within 3 week(s) of notification.

Contact. Financial aid office: (503) 943-7311
Tracy Reisinger, Director of Financial Aid
5000 North Willamette Boulevard
Portland, OR 97203-5798

Warner Pacific College

Portland, Oregon
www.warnerpacific.edu
Four-year private **Federal Code: 003225**

	Living at home	On-campus
Tuition and fees:	$16,910	$16,910
Room and board:		$4,990
Board only:	$1,121	
Books and supplies:	$600	$600
Personal expenses:	$2,350	$2,350
Transportation:	$504	$504

Undergraduate aid. Non-need-based: Scholarships based on academics, athletics. **Additional information:** Church scholarship awards matched. SAT II Subject Tests required of scholarship applicants. Scholarship applicants' scores must be received by June 1.

Policies to reduce costs. Tuition/fee waivers for children of alumni, minority students, employees and their families. Credit/placement for qualifying scores on AP, CLEP examinations.

Payment plans. Credit card, installment payment.

Application procedures. FAFSA, CSS PROFILE required. Priority date 6/1; closing date 8/15. Applicants notified on rolling basis starting 4/1, must reply within 4 week(s) of notification.

Contact. Financial aid office: (503) 517-1020
Cindy Pollard, Director of Student Financial Assistance
2219 Southeast 68th Avenue
Portland, OR 97215-4026

Western Baptist College

Salem, Oregon
www.wbc.edu
Four-year private **Federal Code: 001339**

	Living at home	On-campus
Tuition and fees:	$16,075	$16,075
Room and board:		$5,725
Board only:	$2,840	
Books and supplies:	$700	$700
Personal expenses:	$1,500	$1,500
Transportation:	$1,400	$1,400

Undergraduate aid. Need-based: Average financial aid package for full-time students was $12,087; for part-time $8,863. 56% awarded as scholarships/grants, 44% as loans/jobs. **Non-need-based:** 39% awarded as scholarships/grants, 61% as loans/jobs. Scholarships based on academics, alumni affiliation, athletics, leadership, music/drama. **Student debt:** 63% of graduating class borrowed to fund education; average debt was $17,500.

Freshman aid. Need-based: Out of 144 full-time freshmen, 130 applied for aid; 112 were judged to have need; of these 112 received aid. Average package met 69% of need. 24 students had full need met. Average scholarship/grant was $8,148; average loan $4,888. **Non-need based:** 8 full-time freshmen with need received non-need scholarships; 22 without need received awards; 5 received athletic scholarships.

Policies to reduce costs. Tuition/fee waivers for family members, family of clergy, employees and their families. Credit/placement for qualifying scores on AP, CLEP examinations.

Payment plans. Credit card, installment payment.

Application procedures. FAFSA required. Priority date 2/15; no closing date. Applicants notified on rolling basis starting 3/1, must reply within 4 week(s) of notification.

Contact. Financial aid office: (503) 375-7006
Nathan Warthan, Director of Financial Aid
5000 Deer Park Drive SE
Salem, OR 97301-9392

Western Business College

Portland, Oregon
www.western-college.com
Two-year private **Federal Code: 009079**

College costs. $100 per-course online fee for distance learning.

	Living at home
Tuition and fees (2002-2003):	$9,345
Per-credit charge:	$230
Books and supplies:	$750
Personal expenses:	$1,476

Application procedures. FAFSA required. No deadline. Applicants notified on rolling basis.

Contact. Financial aid office: (503) 222-3225 ext. 116
Sharon Hale
425 SW Washington Street
Portland, OR 97204

Western Oregon University

Monmouth, Oregon
www.wou.edu
Four-year public **Federal Code: 003209**

	Living at home	On-campus
Tuition and fees (2002-2003):	$3,720	$3,720
Out-of-state:	$11,772	$11,772
Room and board:		$5,722
Board only:	$1,505	
Books and supplies:	$900	$900
Personal expenses:	$1,400	$1,400
Transportation:	$700	$700

Undergraduate aid. Need-based: Average financial aid package for full-time students was $6,376; for part-time $4,796. 39% awarded as scholarships/grants, 61% as loans/jobs. **Non-need-based:** 15% awarded as scholarships/grants, 85% as loans/jobs. Scholarships based on academics, art, athletics, leadership, minority status, music/drama, state/district residency. **Student debt:** 91% of graduating class borrowed to fund education; average debt was $16,051.

Freshman aid. Need-based: Out of 776 full-time freshmen, 575 applied for aid; 440 were judged to have need; of these 440 received aid. Average package met 71% of need. 72 students had full need met. Average scholarship/grant was $4,003; average loan $2,666. **Non-need based:** 31 full-time freshmen with need received non-need scholarships; 159 without need received awards; 10 received athletic scholarships.

Policies to reduce costs. Tuition/fee waivers for senior citizens, minority students, employees and their families. Credit/placement for qualifying scores on AP, CLEP examinations. Work study available nights, weekends and for part-time students.

Payment plans. Installment, deferred payment.

Application procedures. FAFSA required. Priority date 3/1; no closing date. Applicants notified on rolling basis starting 4/1, must reply within 2 week(s) of notification. **Transfers:** Priority date 3/1; no deadline.

Contact. Financial aid office: (503) 838-8475
Sandra Mountain, Director of Financial Aid
345 North Monmouth Avenue
Monmouth, OR 97361

Willamette University

Salem, Oregon
www.willamette.edu
Four-year private **Federal Code: 003227**

College costs. $40 residence hall activity fee for campus residents; $362 optional health insurance.

	Living at home	On-campus
Tuition and fees:	$25,432	$25,432
Room and board:		$6,600
Books and supplies:	$1,800	$1,800

Undergraduate aid. Need-based: Average financial aid package for full-time students was $21,886; for part-time $7,101. 70% awarded as scholarships/grants, 30% as loans/jobs. **Non-need-based:** Scholarships based on academics, leadership, minority status, music/drama. **Student debt:** 67% of graduating class borrowed to fund education; average debt was $17,660.

Freshman aid. Need-based: Out of 353 full-time freshmen, 281 applied for aid; 226 were judged to have need; of these 226 received aid. Average package met 93% of need. 117 students had full need met. Average scholarship/grant was $16,135; average loan $2,860. **Non-need based:** 59 full-time freshmen with need received non-need scholarships; 116 without need received awards.

Merit scholarships. Presidential Scholarship, $15,000 to full tuition, based on 3.8 GPA, 1350 SAT or 30 ACT, 25 awards. Elmer and Grace Goudy Scholarship, $12,000, based on 3.7 GPA, 1300 SAT or 29 ACT, 40 awards. Willamette University Scholarships for National Merit, National Hispanic and National Achievement Scholars, $10,000 to full tuition, based on PSAT. Multicultural Achievement Scholarships, $5,000-$10,000, based on academic achievement and extracurricular contributions. Willamette Honor Scholarships, $5,000-$10,000, based on superior academic and cocurricular experience. Music, forensics, theater scholarships based on talent. Mark O. Hatfield Scholarship, full tuition, based on excellent academic record and demonstrated commitment to service leadership. Trustee's Scholarship, $18,000, based on 3.85 GPA, 1400 SAT or 32 ACT.

Policies to reduce costs. Tuition/fee waivers for employees and their families. Credit/placement for qualifying scores on AP, IB examinations. Work study available nights, weekends and for part-time students.

Payment plans. Credit card, installment payment.

Application procedures. FAFSA, CSS PROFILE required. CSS PROFILE required of early action applicants. Priority date 2/1; no closing date. Applicants notified by 4/1, must reply by 5/1 or within 2 week(s) of notification.

Contact. Financial aid office: (503) 370-6273
James Eddy, Director of Financial Aid
900 State Street
Salem, OR 97301-3922

Pennsylvania

Academy of Medical Arts and Business

Harrisburg, Pennsylvania
www.acadcampus.com
Two-year proprietary **Federal Code: 022342**

	Living at home
Tuition and fees (2002-2003):	$8,700
Books and supplies:	$1,200
Personal expenses:	$600

Undergraduate aid. All financial aid based on need. Need-based aid available for full-time and part-time students.

Policies to reduce costs. Work study available nights.

Payment plans. Installment payment.

Application procedures. FAFSA required. No deadline. Applicants notified on rolling basis. **Transfers:** State grant deadline for first-time recipients is August 1. Renewal application deadline in May 1.

Contact. **Financial aid office:** (717) 545-4747
Tracy Stewart, Financial Aid Coordinator
2301 Academy Drive
Harrisburg, PA 17112-1012

Albright College

Reading, Pennsylvania
www.albright.edu
Four-year private **Federal Code: 003229**

	Living at home	On-campus
Tuition and fees:	$23,430	$23,430
Room and board:		$7,149
Board only:	$2,000	
Books and supplies:	$800	$800
Personal expenses:	$1,000	$1,000
Transportation:	$600	$200

Undergraduate aid. **Need-based:** Average financial aid package for full-time students was $16,381; for part-time $6,687. 67% awarded as scholarships/grants, 33% as loans/jobs. **Non-need-based:** 40% awarded as scholarships/grants, 60% as loans/jobs. Scholarships based on academics, alumni affiliation, art, leadership, minority status, music/drama, religious affiliation, state/district residency. **Student debt:** 53% of graduating class borrowed to fund education; average debt was $23,377.

Freshman aid. **Need-based:** Out of 453 full-time freshmen, 432 applied for aid; 384 were judged to have need; of these 384 received aid. Average package met 81% of need. 81 students had full need met. Average scholarship/grant was $13,928; average loan $3,577. **Non-need based:** 51 full-time freshmen with need received non-need scholarships; 51 without need received awards.

Policies to reduce costs. Tuition/fee waivers for children of alumni, senior citizens, minority students, family members, employees and their families. Credit/placement for qualifying scores on AP, IB, CLEP examinations. Work study available nights and weekends.

Payment plans. Credit card, installment, deferred payment.

Application procedures. FAFSA required. Priority date 3/1; no closing date. Applicants notified on rolling basis starting 2/15, must reply by 5/1 or within 2 week(s) of notification. **Transfers:** Priority date 6/1; no deadline.

Contact. **Financial aid office:** (610) 921-7515
Mary Ellen Duffy, Director of Financial Aid
PO Box 15234
Reading, PA 19612-5234

Allegheny College

Meadville, Pennsylvania
www.allegheny.edu
Four-year private **Federal Code: 003230**

	Living at home	On-campus
Tuition and fees:	$24,400	$24,400
Room and board:		$5,880
Board only:	$2,100	
Books and supplies:	$700	$700
Personal expenses:	$500	$500
Transportation:	$500	$500

Undergraduate aid. **Need-based:** Average financial aid package for full-time students was $19,120; for part-time $12,983. 73% awarded as scholarships/grants, 27% as loans/jobs. **Non-need-based:** 46% awarded as scholarships/grants, 54% as loans/jobs. Scholarships based on academics, leadership, minority status, state/district residency. **Student debt:** 81% of graduating class borrowed to fund education; average debt was $21,670.

Freshman aid. **Need-based:** Out of 536 full-time freshmen, 465 applied for aid; 398 were judged to have need; of these 398 received aid. Average package met 94% of need. 198 students had full need met. Average scholarship/grant was $14,264; average loan $4,092. **Non-need based:** 77 full-time freshmen with need received non-need scholarships; 122 without need received awards.

Merit scholarships. Trustee Scholarships, up to $12,500 per year, for entering freshmen with rank in top 25% of class.

Policies to reduce costs. Tuition/fee waivers for employees and their families. Prepayment discount; credit/placement for qualifying scores on AP, IB, CLEP examinations. Work study available nights, weekends and for part-time students.

Payment plans. Installment payment.

Application procedures. FAFSA required. Priority date 2/15; no closing date. Applicants notified on rolling basis starting 3/1, must reply by 5/1 or within 4 week(s) of notification. Early decision closing date 1/15. **Transfers:** No deadline. Trustee Scholarships, up to $9,000, available for entering transfer students with high school rank in top 25% of class and high academic achievement in college.

Contact. **Financial aid office:** (800) 835-7780
Robin Szitas, Director of Financial Aid
520 North Main Street
Meadville, PA 16335

Allentown Business School

Allentown, Pennsylvania
www.chooseabs.com
Two-year proprietary **Federal Code: 008889**

College costs (2002-2003). Academic-year tuition varies from $11,000 to $13,500 depending on program. Fees vary by program. Board: $2,985. Personal expenses: $1,131. Transportation: $1,200.

Undergraduate aid. **Need-based:** 29% awarded as scholarships/grants, 71% as loans/jobs. Need-based aid available for part-time students. **Student debt:** 90% of graduating class borrowed to fund education; average debt was $14,000.

Policies to reduce costs. Tuition/fee waivers for employees and their families. Tuition at time of enrollment guaranteed for 2 years. Work study available nights, weekends and for part-time students.

Payment plans. Credit card, installment, deferred payment.

Application procedures. FAFSA, institutional form required. No deadline. Applicants notified on rolling basis. **Transfers:** No deadline.

Contact. Tami Reichard, Director of Financial Aid
1501 Lehigh Street
Allentown, PA 18103

Antonelli Institute of Art and Photography

Erdenheim, Pennsylvania
www.antonelli.org
Two-year proprietary **Federal Code: 007430**

College costs. Tuition for graphic design/commercial art students is $13,200; for photography students $14,800. Required fees $125 Books/supplies: $1,500. Personal expenses: $1,400. Transportation: $1,500.

Undergraduate aid. All financial aid based on need. Average financial aid package for full-time students was $7,180; for part-time $2,300. 40% awarded as scholarships/grants, 60% as loans/jobs. **Student debt:** 85% of graduating class borrowed to fund education; average debt was $6,625.

Freshman aid. Out of 120 full-time freshmen, 82 applied for aid; 81 were judged to have need; of these 81 received aid. Average package met 52% of need. 52 students had full need met. Average scholarship/grant was $5,100; average loan $2,625.

Policies to reduce costs. Tuition/fee waivers for employees and their families. Work study available nights.

Payment plans. Credit card, installment payment.

Application procedures. FAFSA required. No deadline. Applicants notified on rolling basis, must reply within 2 week(s) of notification. **Transfers:** Priority date 3/15; closing date 8/1.

Contact. **Financial aid office:** (215) 836-2222
Eugene Awot, Director of Financial Aid
300 Montgomery Avenue
Erdenheim, PA 19038

Arcadia University

Glenside, Pennsylvania
www.arcadia.edu
Four-year private **Federal Code: 003235**

	Living at home	On-campus
Tuition and fees:	$21,270	$21,270
Room and board:		$8,620
Board only:	$1,500	
Books and supplies:	$700	$700
Personal expenses:	$650	$650
Transportation:	$450	$250

Undergraduate aid. **Need-based:** Need-based aid available for full-time and part-time students. **Non-need-based:** Scholarships based on academics, alumni affiliation, art, leadership. **Additional information:** Early financial aid estimate service offered September through January; may be used before applying for admission. Students should call (888) 232-8373 and request FAST form or download one from www.beaver.edu.

Merit scholarships. Distinguished Scholarships, ranging from $1,000 to full tuition for full-time freshmen. Nearly 37% of new students are recognized annually. Arcadia University Achievement Awards, ranging from $1,000-$6,000 for full-time undergraduates who have demonstrated outstanding leadership, exceptional community/volunteer service or special talents.

Policies to reduce costs. Tuition/fee waivers for children of alumni, senior citizens, employees and their families. Credit/placement for qualifying scores on AP, IB, CLEP examinations.

Payment plans. Credit card, installment, deferred payment.

Application procedures. FAFSA, institutional form required. Priority date 3/1; no closing date. Applicants notified on rolling basis starting 2/15, must reply by 5/1. Early decision closing date 10/15. **Transfers:** Transfer and freshmen students given equal consideration for need-based aid. Beaver College Distinguished Scholarships, $2,000-$8,000 available to transfer students.

Contact. **Financial aid office:** (215) 572-2980
Elizabeth Rihl, Associate Director of Enrollment Management
450 South Easton Road
Glenside, PA 19038-3295

Art Institute of Philadelphia

Philadelphia, Pennsylvania
www.aiph.artinstitutes.edu
Four-year proprietary **Federal Code: 008350**

College costs. One-time activities fee of $50 for bachelor's, $35 for associate.

	Living at home	On-campus
Tuition and fees:	$16,110	$16,110
Room only:		$6,081

Undergraduate aid. **Need-based:** Need-based aid available for full-time and part-time students. **Additional information:** Institute-sponsored scholarships available.

Policies to reduce costs. Tuition/fee waivers for employees and their families. Tuition at time of enrollment guaranteed for 4 years; credit/placement for qualifying scores on IB examinations. Work study available nights, weekends and for part-time students.

Payment plans. Credit card, installment payment.

Application procedures. FAFSA, institutional form required. Closing date 5/1. Applicants notified on rolling basis starting 3/1, must reply within 2 week(s) of notification. **Transfers:** No deadline. Transfer students applying for financial aid must meet standards for satisfactory academic progress as defined by State Grant Program.

Contact. **Financial aid office:** (215) 567-7080 ext. 6392
Colleen Russo, Director of Student Financial Services
1622 Chestnut Street
Philadelphia, PA 19103-5198

Art Institute of Pittsburgh

Pittsburgh, Pennsylvania
www.aip.artinstitutes.edu
Four-year proprietary **Federal Code: 007470**

College costs. Tuition and fees vary according to lock-in date: tuition does not go up as long as students remain enrolled continuously.

	Living at home	On-campus
Tuition and fees (2002-2003):	$14,050	$14,050
Room only:		$4,050
Books and supplies:	$490	$490
Personal expenses:	$1,220	
Transportation:	$360	

Policies to reduce costs. Tuition/fee waivers for employees and their families.

Payment plans. Credit card, installment, deferred payment.

Application procedures. Institutional form required. No deadline. Applicants notified on rolling basis starting 4/15. **Transfers:** No deadline.

Contact. Gayle Knight, Financial Aid Director
420 Boulevard of the Allies
Pittsburgh, PA 15219

Baptist Bible College of Pennsylvania

Clarks Summit, Pennsylvania
www.bbc.edu
Four-year private **Federal Code: 002670**

	Living at home	On-campus
Tuition and fees:	$11,700	$11,700
Room and board:		$4,982
Board only:	$2,500	
Books and supplies:	$600	$600
Personal expenses:	$1,658	$1,144
Transportation:	$600	

Undergraduate aid. **Need-based:** Average financial aid package for full-time students was $4,483; for part-time $1,507. 44% awarded as scholarships/grants, 56% as loans/jobs. **Non-need-based:** Scholarships based on academics, leadership, music/drama, religious affiliation. **Student debt:** 52% of graduating class borrowed to fund education; average debt was $4,262.

Freshman aid. **Need-based:** Out of 155 full-time freshmen, 150 applied for aid; 141 were judged to have need; of these 141 received aid. Average package met 29% of need. 7 students had full need met. Average loan $2,205.

Policies to reduce costs. Tuition/fee waivers for children of alumni, family members, family of clergy, employees and their families. Prepayment discount; credit/placement for qualifying scores on AP, IB, CLEP examinations. Work study available nights and weekends.

Payment plans. Credit card, installment payment.

Application procedures. FAFSA, institutional form required. Closing date 5/1. Applicants notified on rolling basis starting 4/1.

Contact. Tom Pollock, Director of Student Financial Services
538 Venard Road
Clarks Summit, PA 18411-1297

Bloomsburg University of Pennsylvania

Bloomsburg, Pennsylvania
www.bloomu.edu
Four-year public **Federal Code: 003315**

	Living at home	On-campus
Tuition and fees (2002-2003):	$5,550	$5,550
Out-of-state:	$12,118	$12,118
Room and board:		$4,576
Board only:	$1,300	
Books and supplies:	$600	$600
Personal expenses:	$1,410	$1,410
Transportation:	$1,212	$462

Undergraduate aid. **Need-based:** Average financial aid package for full-time students was $11,492. 45% awarded as scholarships/grants, 55% as loans/jobs. Need-based aid available for part-time students. **Non-need-based:** 9% awarded as scholarships/grants, 91% as loans/jobs. Scholarships based on academics, art, athletics, job skills, leadership, minority status, music/drama, state/district residency. **Student debt:** 69% of graduating class borrowed to fund education; average debt was $14,888.

Freshman aid. **Need-based:** Out of 1,478 full-time freshmen, 1,256 applied for aid; 1,005 were judged to have need; of these 955 received aid. Average package met 65% of need. 859 students had full need met. Average scholarship/grant was $3,750; average loan $2,545. **Non-need based:** 287 full-time freshmen with need received non-need scholarships; 33 received athletic scholarships.

Policies to reduce costs. Tuition/fee waivers for minority students, employees and their families. Credit/placement for qualifying scores on AP, CLEP examinations.

Application procedures. FAFSA required. Priority date 3/15; no closing date. Applicants notified on rolling basis starting 4/1. Early decision closing date 11/15.

Contact. Thomas Lyons, Director of Financial Aid
104 Student Service Center, 400 East Second Street
Bloomsburg, PA 17815

Bradford School: Pittsburgh

Pittsburgh, Pennsylvania
www.bradfordschoolpgh.com
Two-year proprietary **Federal Code: 009721**

	Living at home	On-campus
Tuition and fees:	$10,700	$10,700
Room and board:		$5,200

Undergraduate aid. **Need-based:** Need-based aid available for full-time students.

Payment plans. Credit card, installment payment.

Application procedures. FAFSA required.

Contact. **Financial aid office:** (412) 391-6710
Nancy Mitz, Director of Student Services
707 Grant Street, Gulf Tower
Pittsburgh, PA 15219

Bradley Academy for the Visual Arts

York, Pennsylvania
www.bradleyacademy.net
Two-year proprietary **Federal Code: 017171**

	Living at home
Tuition and fees:	$13,320
Per-credit charge:	$370
Books and supplies:	$1,250
Personal expenses:	$2,610

Policies to reduce costs. Tuition/fee waivers for employees and their families. Tuition at time of enrollment guaranteed for 2 years.

Payment plans. Credit card payment.

Application procedures. FAFSA required. Priority date 8/1; no closing date. Applicants notified on rolling basis starting 6/1. **Transfers:** No deadline.

Contact. Fran Stefany, Director of Financial Aid
1409 Williams Road
York, PA 17402

Bryn Athyn College of the New Church

Bryn Athyn, Pennsylvania
www.newchurch.edu/college
Four-year private

	Living at home	On-campus
Tuition and fees:	$7,656	$7,656
Room and board:		$4,956
Books and supplies:	$525	$525
Personal expenses:		$875

Undergraduate aid. **Need-based:** Average financial aid package for full-time students was $6,470. 89% awarded as scholarships/grants, 11% as loans/jobs. **Student debt:** 5% of graduating class borrowed to fund education; average debt was $2,000.

Freshman aid. **Need-based:** Out of 36 full-time freshmen, 21 applied for aid; 21 were judged to have need; of these 21 received aid. Average package met 100% of need. 21 students had full need met. Average scholarship/grant was $5,744; average loan $2,000. **Non-need based:** 2 without need received awards.

Policies to reduce costs. Tuition/fee waivers for senior citizens, family of clergy, employees and their families. Credit/placement for qualifying scores on AP, IB examinations. Work study available nights and weekends.

Payment plans. Credit card, installment payment.

Application procedures. Institutional form required. Closing date 6/1. Applicants notified on rolling basis. **Transfers:** Closing date 6/1.

Contact. **Financial aid office:** (215) 938-2630
Duane Hyatt, Director, Budget and Business Administration
2895 College Drive
Bryn Athyn, PA 19009

Bryn Mawr College

Bryn Mawr, Pennsylvania
www.brynmawr.edu
Four-year private **Federal Code: 003237**

	Living at home	On-campus
Tuition and fees:	$27,520	$27,520
Room and board:		$9,370
Books and supplies:	$1,400	$1,400
Transportation:	$350	$350

Undergraduate aid. All financial aid based on need. Average financial aid package for full-time students was $22,634. 81% awarded as scholarships/grants, 19% as loans/jobs. Need-based aid available for part-time students.

Freshman aid. Out of 305 full-time freshmen, 230 applied for aid; 195 were judged to have need; of these 195 received aid. Average package met 100% of need. 189 students had full need met. Average scholarship/grant was $20,907; average loan $2,815.

Policies to reduce costs. Tuition/fee waivers for employees and their families. Credit/placement for qualifying scores on AP, IB examinations. Work study available for part-time students.

Payment plans. Installment, deferred payment.

Application procedures. FAFSA, CSS PROFILE required. Closing date 2/7. Applicants notified by 3/26, must reply by 5/1. Early decision closing date 11/15. **Transfers:** Closing date 3/15.

Contact. **Financial aid office:** (610) 526-5245
Ethel Desmarais, Director of Financial Aid
101 North Merion Avenue
Bryn Mawr, PA 19010-2899

Bucknell University

Lewisburg, Pennsylvania
www.bucknell.edu
Four-year private **Federal Code: 003238**

College costs. Per-course charge $3,125.

	Living at home	On-campus
Tuition and fees:	$28,960	$28,960
Room and board:		$6,302
Board only:	$2,683	
Books and supplies:	$750	$750
Personal expenses:	$2,234	$2,234
Transportation:	$200	$200

Undergraduate aid. All financial aid based on need. Average financial aid package for full-time students was $18,072. 67% awarded as scholarships/grants, 33% as loans/jobs.

Freshman aid. Out of 917 full-time freshmen, 502 applied for aid; 502 were judged to have need; of these 502 received aid. Average package met 100% of need. Average scholarship/grant was $15,145; average loan $3,937.

Policies to reduce costs. Tuition/fee waivers for employees and their families. Credit/placement for qualifying scores on AP, IB, CLEP examinations. Work study available nights and weekends.

Payment plans. Installment payment.

Application procedures. FAFSA, CSS PROFILE required. Closing date 1/1. Applicants notified by 4/10, must reply by 5/1. Early decision closing date 11/15. **Transfers:** Closing date 4/1. Aid restricted to 2-year college graduates.

Contact. **Financial aid office:** (570) 577-1331
Andrea Leithner, Director of Financial Aid
Freas Hall
Lewisburg, PA 17837-9988

Bucks County Community College

Newtown, Pennsylvania
www.bucks.edu
Two-year public **Federal Code: 003239**

	Living at home
Tuition and fees (2002-2003):	$2,610
Out-of-district:	$5,262
Out-of-state:	$7,898
Per-credit charge:	$78
Per-credit out-of-district:	$156
Per-credit out-of-state:	$234
Board only:	$750
Books and supplies:	$850
Personal expenses:	$1,350
Transportation:	$2,100

Undergraduate aid. **Need-based:** 70% awarded as scholarships/grants, 30% as loans/jobs. Need-based aid available for part-time students. **Non-need-based:** 5% awarded as scholarships/grants, 95% as loans/jobs. Scholarships based on academics.

Policies to reduce costs. Tuition/fee waivers for senior citizens, unemployed or children of unemployed, employees and their families. Credit/placement for qualifying scores on AP, CLEP examinations. Work study available nights, weekends and for part-time students.

Payment plans. Credit card, installment, deferred payment.

Application procedures. FAFSA, institutional form required. Closing date 5/1. Applicants notified on rolling basis starting 6/1.

Contact. **Financial aid office:** (215) 968-8200
Frances McKeown, Director of Financial Aid
275 Swamp Road
Newtown, PA 18940

Butler County Community College

Butler, Pennsylvania
www.bc3.edu
Two-year public **Federal Code: 003240**

College costs. Out-of-county students from a county with no community colleges pay $3,210, $107 per-credit-hour. Out-of-county students from a county with its own community college pay $3,660, $122 per-credit-hour.

	Living at home
Tuition and fees (2002-2003):	$2,100
Out-of-state:	$5,760
Per-credit charge:	$61
Per-credit out-of-state:	$183
Books and supplies:	$800
Personal expenses:	$900
Transportation:	$1,100

Undergraduate aid. **Need-based:** Need-based aid available for full-time and part-time students.

Policies to reduce costs. Tuition/fee waivers for senior citizens, employees and their families. Credit/placement for qualifying scores on AP, CLEP examinations. Work study available for part-time students.

Payment plans. Credit card payment.

Application procedures. FAFSA required. Closing date 4/15.

Contact. **Financial aid office:** (724) 287-8711 ext. 329
Jean Walker, Director of Financial Aid
PO Box 1203
Butler, PA 16003

CHI Institute

Southampton, Pennsylvania
Two-year proprietary **Federal Code: 016146**

College costs. Reported costs are for associate degree program in computer programming. Costs of other programs will vary.

	Living at home
Tuition and fees:	$11,853
Books and supplies:	$765
Transportation:	$300

Undergraduate aid. **Additional information:** Scholarships for graduating seniors. Awards based on institutional scholarship aptitude test and interview with independent committee. Parental income not considered.

Policies to reduce costs. Tuition/fee waivers for employees and their families. Tuition at time of enrollment guaranteed for 2 years.

Payment plans. Credit card, installment payment.

Application procedures. Closing date 9/20. Applicants notified on rolling basis.

Contact. Nicole Gilbert, Financial Aid Officer
520 Street Road
Southampton, PA 18966

Cabrini College

Radnor, Pennsylvania
www.cabrini.edu
Four-year private **Federal Code: 003241**

	Living at home	On-campus
Tuition and fees:	$20,420	$20,420
Room and board:		$8,550
Books and supplies:	$900	$900
Personal expenses:	$1,000	$1,000
Transportation:	$1,625	$600

Undergraduate aid. **Need-based:** Average financial aid package for full-time students was $14,044; for part-time $9,179. 61% awarded as scholarships/grants, 39% as loans/jobs. **Non-need-based:** 69% awarded as scholarships/grants, 31% as loans/jobs. Scholarships based on alumni affiliation. **Student debt:** 79% of graduating class borrowed to fund education; average debt was $17,050.

Freshman aid. **Need-based:** Out of 406 full-time freshmen, 380 applied for aid; 342 were judged to have need; of these 342 received aid. Average package met 47% of need. 69 students had full need met. Average scholarship/grant was $7,804; average loan $2,847. **Non-need based:** 319 full-time freshmen with need received non-need scholarships; 53 without need received awards.

Policies to reduce costs. Tuition/fee waivers for children of alumni, senior citizens, family members, employees and their families. Credit/placement for qualifying scores on AP, IB, CLEP examinations. Work study available nights and weekends.

Payment plans. Credit card, installment payment.

Application procedures. FAFSA required. No deadline. Applicants notified on rolling basis starting 3/1. **Transfers:** No deadline. Achievement scholarships available.

Contact. **Financial aid office:** (610) 902-8420
Michael Colahan, Financial Aid Director
610 King of Prussia Road
Radnor, PA 19087-3698

California University of Pennsylvania

California, Pennsylvania
www.cup.edu
Four-year public **Federal Code: 003316**

	Living at home	On-campus
Tuition and fees (2002-2003):	$5,736	$5,736
Out-of-state:	$12,304	$12,304
Room and board:		$5,176
Board only:	$1,607	
Books and supplies:	$612	$612
Personal expenses:	$1,194	$1,194
Transportation:		$637

Undergraduate aid. **Need-based:** Need-based aid available for full-time and part-time students. **Non-need-based:** Scholarships based on academics, athletics, state/district residency.

Policies to reduce costs. Tuition/fee waivers for senior citizens, minority students, employees and their families. Credit/placement for qualifying scores on AP, CLEP examinations.

Payment plans. Credit card, installment, deferred payment.

Application procedures. FAFSA required. Priority date 5/1; no closing date. Applicants notified on rolling basis starting 4/1, must reply within 2 week(s) of notification.

Contact. **Financial aid office:** (724) 938-4415
Robert Thorn, Director of Financial Aid
250 University Avenue
California, PA 15419-1394

Cambria County Area Community College

Johnstown, Pennsylvania
www.ccacc.cc.pa.us
Two-year public **Federal Code: 031804**

	Living at home
Tuition and fees (2002-2003):	$1,830
Out-of-district:	$3,480
Out-of-state:	$5,130
Per-credit charge:	$55
Per-credit out-of-district:	$110
Per-credit out-of-state:	$165
Board only:	$1,600
Books and supplies:	$500
Personal expenses:	$500
Transportation:	$880

Undergraduate aid. **Need-based:** 74% awarded as scholarships/grants, 26% as loans/jobs. Need-based aid available for part-time students. **Non-need-based:** 24% awarded as scholarships/grants, 76% as loans/jobs. Scholarships based on academics, state/district residency.

Policies to reduce costs. Tuition/fee waivers for employees and their families. Work study available nights and for part-time students.

Payment plans. Installment payment.

Application procedures. FAFSA required. Closing date 5/1. Applicants notified on rolling basis starting 1/1, must reply within 1 week(s) of notification.

Contact. **Financial aid office:** (814) 532-5315
Brenda Coughenour, Director of Financial Aid
PO Box 68
Johnstown, PA 15907-0068

Cambria-Rowe Business College

Johnstown, Pennsylvania
www.crbc.net
Two-year proprietary **Federal Code: 004889**

	Living at home
Tuition and fees (2002-2003):	$6,600
Per-credit charge:	$175
Books and supplies:	$1,000

Undergraduate aid. **Need-based:** Need-based aid available for full-time and part-time students. **Non-need-based:** Scholarships based on academics, leadership.

Merit scholarships. Presidential Grant; 3 awarded; 50% tuition; FBLA Scholarship; 2 awarded; $3,000.

Payment plans. Installment payment.

Application procedures. FAFSA required. Closing date 8/1. Applicants notified on rolling basis. **Transfers:** Closing date 5/1.

Contact. **Financial aid office:** (814) 536-5168
Judy Miller, Financial Aid Adviser
221 Central Avenue
Johnstown, PA 15902

Cambria-Rowe Business College: Indiana

Indiana, Pennsylvania
www.crbc.net
Two-year proprietary **Federal Code: 004889**

College costs. Depending on choice of laptop, fees could be as much as $990.

	Living at home
Tuition and fees:	$7,140

Undergraduate aid. **Need-based:** Need-based aid available for full-time and part-time students.

Application procedures. FAFSA required. No deadline. Applicants notified on rolling basis.

Contact. Judy Miller
422 South 13th Street
Indiana, PA 15701

Career Training Academy

New Kensington, Pennsylvania
www.careerta.com
Two-year proprietary **Federal Code: 026095**

College costs (2002-2003). Total cost of 15-month associate degree program in massage therapy: $18,366 (includes tuition, books, portable massage table, uniforms, lab fees, insurance, graduation fees). Total cost of 15-month associate degree program in medical assistance: $14,572 (includes tuition, books, uniforms, lab fees, insurance, graduation fees). Other diploma programs will vary in cost and required length of study.

Undergraduate aid. All financial aid based on need. Need-based aid available for full-time students. **Additional information:** Work study available after class day.

Policies to reduce costs. Tuition at time of enrollment guaranteed for 2 years; credit/placement for qualifying scores on IB examinations.

Payment plans. Credit card, installment payment.

Application procedures. FAFSA, institutional form required. No deadline.

Contact. Mary Ann Reddy, Financial Services Coordinator
950 Fifth Avenue
New Kensington, PA 15068

Career Training Academy: Monroeville

Monroeville, Pennsylvania
www.careerta.com
Two-year proprietary **Federal Code: 026095**

College costs (2002-2003). Tuition ranges from $3,800 to $15,911 depending on program; required fees range from $75 to $300 depending on program. Books/supplies: $750. Personal expenses: $2,889.

Undergraduate aid. All financial aid based on need. Need-based aid available for full-time and part-time students.

Application procedures. FAFSA, institutional form required.

Contact. 105 Mall Boulevard, Suite 300W
Monroeville, PA 15146

Carlow College

Pittsburgh, Pennsylvania
www.carlow.edu
Four-year private **Federal Code: 003303**

College costs. Part-time and graduate students pay $28 per credit support services fee.

	Living at home	On-campus
Tuition and fees:	$15,264	$15,264
Room and board:		$6,110
Board only:	$1,000	
Books and supplies:	$700	$700
Personal expenses:	$500	$1,000
Transportation:	$500	$500

Undergraduate aid. Need-based: Average financial aid package for full-time students was $12,363; for part-time $4,464. 63% awarded as scholarships/grants, 37% as loans/jobs. **Non-need-based:** 46% awarded as scholarships/grants, 54% as loans/jobs. Scholarships based on academics, athletics, leadership. **Student debt:** 66% of graduating class borrowed to fund education; average debt was $21,446.

Freshman aid. Need-based: Out of 238 full-time freshmen, 236 applied for aid; 235 were judged to have need; of these 235 received aid. Average package met 94% of need. 159 students had full need met. Average scholarship/grant was $9,342; average loan $2,918. **Non-need based:** 159 full-time freshmen with need received non-need scholarships.

Merit scholarships. Full tuition: 3.75 GPA, 1300 SATs; half tuition: 3.5 GPA, 1200 SATs; Presidential: $5,000; 3.25 GPA, 1100 SATs; Valedictorian: $5,000; McAuley: $4,000, 3.25 GPA, 950 SAT, one per Catholic high school in diocese of Pittsburgh, Johnston/Altoona and Greensburg; Messer: $4,000 to math/engineering majors in 3/2 program with Carnegie-Mellon, reviewed individually; Legacy: to daughters or granddaughters of alumnae, requires 3.25 GPA and 900 SAT; Dean's Recognition: 3.25 GPA, SAT of 900 required; Sister Maurice Whalen: to those who submit projects to Pittsburgh Regional Science and Engineering Fair, also requires 3.25 GPA and 1000 SAT. Rose Marie Beard Women of Spirit Honors Scholarship: GPA 3.5 or higher, 1100 SAT or better, ranked in top 15% of high school class, evidence of significant leadership, awards $4,000 for first year for 6 students and is added to any other Carlow-awarded scholarships.

Policies to reduce costs. Tuition/fee waivers for family members, unemployed or children of unemployed, family of clergy, employees and their families. Credit/placement for qualifying scores on AP, IB, CLEP examinations. Work study available for part-time students.

Payment plans. Credit card, installment, deferred payment.

Application procedures. FAFSA required. Priority date 4/1; no closing date. Applicants notified on rolling basis starting 2/15, must reply within 2 week(s) of notification. **Transfers:** May 1 deadline for Pennsylvania State Aid Grant.

Contact. Financial aid office: (412) 578-6058
Natalie Wilson, Director of Student Financial Services
3333 Fifth Avenue
Pittsburgh, PA 15213-3165

Carnegie Mellon University

Pittsburgh, Pennsylvania
www.cmu.edu
Four-year private **Federal Code: 003242**

	Living at home	On-campus
Tuition and fees:	$29,410	$29,410
Room and board:		$8,155
Board only:	$1,130	
Books and supplies:	$895	$895
Personal expenses:	$1,265	$1,265
Transportation:	$540	

Undergraduate aid. Need-based: Average financial aid package for full-time students was $19,732; for part-time $14,413. 62% awarded as scholarships/grants, 38% as loans/jobs. **Non-need-based:** 88% awarded as scholarships/grants, 12% as loans/jobs. Scholarships based on academics, art, leadership, minority status, music/drama, state/district residency. **Student debt:** 52% of graduating class borrowed to fund education; average debt was $19,195. **Additional information:** Early need analysis offered; merit awards available.

Freshman aid. Need-based: Out of 1,365 full-time freshmen, 967 applied for aid; 737 were judged to have need; of these 735 received aid. Average package met 83% of need. 265 students had full need met. Average scholarship/grant was $14,890; average loan $4,021. **Non-need based:** 363 full-time freshmen with need received non-need scholarships; 155 without need received awards.

Policies to reduce costs. Tuition/fee waivers for employees and their families. Credit/placement for qualifying scores on AP examinations. Work study available nights, weekends and for part-time students.

Payment plans. Credit card, installment, deferred payment.

Application procedures. FAFSA, institutional form required. Priority date 2/15; closing date 5/1. Applicants notified by 3/15. Early decision closing date 11/15. **Transfers:** Closing date 5/1.

Contact. Financial aid office: (412) 268-8186
Linda Anderson, Director of Financial Aid
5000 Forbes Avenue
Pittsburgh, PA 15213-3890

Cedar Crest College

Allentown, Pennsylvania
www.cedarcrest.edu
Four-year private **Federal Code: 003243**

College costs. Fee of $300 required of resident students. Part-time evening/weekend per credit hour charge $293.

	Living at home	On-campus
Tuition and fees:	$20,596	$20,596
Room and board:		$7,274
Books and supplies:	$500	$500
Personal expenses:	$500	$500
Transportation:	$500	$500

Undergraduate aid. Need-based: Average financial aid package for full-time students was $15,319; for part-time $4,661. 61% awarded as scholarships/grants, 39% as loans/jobs. **Non-need-based:** 38% awarded as scholarships/grants, 62% as loans/jobs. Scholarships based on academics, alumni affiliation, art, leadership, music/drama. **Student debt:** 95% of graduating class borrowed to fund education; average debt was $20,546.

Freshman aid. Need-based: Out of 185 full-time freshmen, 176 applied for aid; 163 were judged to have need; of these 163 received aid. Average package met 82% of need. 17 students had full need met. Average scholarship/grant was $13,531; average loan $3,417. **Non-need based:** 12 full-time freshmen with need received non-need scholarships; 20 without need received awards.

Merit scholarships. Trustee Tuition Scholarship, full tuition, for seniors with 3.75 or higher cumulative GPA upon completion of 3 consecutive years of full-time study at Cedar Crest College. Presidential Scholarship, up to half tuition, for all incoming freshmen with SAT scores over 1150 and in top 10% of class (renewable for four years with GPA of 3.0). High School Achievement Award of $5,000 per year (renewable for four years with GPA of 3.0) for incoming freshmen with SAT of 1150 and in top 20% of class. Girl Scout Gold Awards of $1,000 per year for recipients of the Girl Scout Gold Award. Art, Dance, and Performing Arts Scholarships of $1,500 per year based on portfolio review, audition, and commitment to the creative process. Governor's School of Excellence Awards of $1,000 per year for graduates of Governor's Schools of Excellence. Hugh O'Brien Youth (HOBY) Awards of $1,000 per year for freshmen who are HOBY alumnae.

Policies to reduce costs. Tuition/fee waivers for children of alumni, family members, employees and their families. Credit/placement for qualifying scores on AP, IB, CLEP examinations. Work study available nights and weekends.

Payment plans. Credit card, installment, deferred payment.

Application procedures. FAFSA, institutional form required. No deadline. Applicants notified on rolling basis starting 11/2, must reply by 5/2 or within 3 week(s) of notification. **Transfers:** No deadline. Certain academic scholarships are available for transfers only, such as the Phi Theta Kappa Scholarship.

Contact. **Financial aid office:** (610) 740-3785
Judith Neyhart, Vice President for Enrollment Advancement
100 College Drive
Allentown, PA 18104-6196

Central Pennsylvania College

Summerdale, Pennsylvania
www.centralpenn.edu
Two-year proprietary **Federal Code: 004890**

College costs. Campus residents pay additional $45 in required fees.

	Living at home	On-campus
Tuition and fees (2002-2003):	$9,810	$9,810
Per-credit charge:	$249	$249
Room and board:		$5,175
Books and supplies:	$810	$810
Personal expenses:	$660	$660
Transportation:	$900	$780

Undergraduate aid. **Need-based:** Need-based aid available for full-time and part-time students. **Non-need-based:** Scholarships based on academics, alumni affiliation, leadership.

Merit scholarships. President's Scholarship: $10,000; to student who has demonstrated outstanding leadership in school and community; Leadership Scholarship: $7,500 each; demonstrated leadership in school and community; Academic Scholarships: $1,500 each; based on high school accomplishments; Summer Start scholarships: $1,200 each for first-time freshmen enrolling in summer quarter and living on campus; Club Scholarship: $3,000; awarded to active member of FBLA, DECA, HOSA, VICA, or TSA. Bachelor's program scholarship: up to $2,000 awarded to Associate Degree graduates from HACC or Central Penn who continue to the Bachelor's level.

Policies to reduce costs. Tuition/fee waivers for employees and their families. Credit/placement for qualifying scores on AP, CLEP examinations. Work study available nights, weekends and for part-time students.

Payment plans. Credit card, installment, deferred payment.

Application procedures. FAFSA, institutional form required. Priority date 3/15; no closing date. Applicants notified on rolling basis starting 2/1, must reply within 2 week(s) of notification.

Contact. **Financial aid office:** (717) 728-2261
Kathy Shepard, Financial Aid Director
College Hill Road
Summerdale, PA 17093-0309

Chatham College

Pittsburgh, Pennsylvania
www.chatham.edu
Four-year private **Federal Code: 003244**

	Living at home	On-campus
Tuition and fees (2002-2003):	$19,742	$19,742
Room and board:		$6,688
Board only:	$3,151	
Books and supplies:	$700	$700
Personal expenses:	$850	$1,000
Transportation:	$850	$500

Undergraduate aid. **Need-based:** Average financial aid package for full-time students was $22,535; for part-time $2,852. 59% awarded as scholarships/grants, 41% as loans/jobs. **Non-need-based:** 80% awarded as scholarships/grants, 20% as loans/jobs. Scholarships based on academics, alumni affiliation, leadership, music/drama. **Student debt:** 99% of graduating class borrowed to fund education; average debt was $18,655.

Freshman aid. **Need-based:** Out of 109 full-time freshmen, 100 applied for aid; 85 were judged to have need; of these 85 received aid. Average package met 72% of need. Average scholarship/grant was $9,370; average loan $3,565. **Non-need based:** 77 full-time freshmen with need received non-need scholarships; 17 without need received awards.

Merit scholarships. Merit scholarship opportunities awarded primarily through on-campus competitions in academics, music, leadership. Alumnae affiliation merit scholarships also available.

Policies to reduce costs. Tuition/fee waivers for employees and their families. Credit/placement for qualifying scores on AP, IB, CLEP examinations. Work study available nights and weekends.

Payment plans. Credit card, installment payment.

Application procedures. FAFSA required. Priority date 5/1; closing date 5/1. Applicants notified on rolling basis starting 2/15, must reply by 5/1 or within 2 week(s) of notification. **Transfers:** No deadline.

Contact. **Financial aid office:** (412) 365-1777
Lynn Jakub, Director of Financial Aid
Woodland Road
Pittsburgh, PA 15232

Chestnut Hill College

Philadelphia, Pennsylvania
www.chc.edu
Four-year private **Federal Code: 003245**

	Living at home	On-campus
Tuition and fees (2002-2003):	$18,150	$18,150
Room and board:		$7,270
Books and supplies:	$1,850	$1,850
Personal expenses:	$1,000	$1,000
Transportation:	$975	$475

Undergraduate aid. **Need-based:** Average financial aid package for full-time students was $12,410. 31% awarded as scholarships/grants, 69% as loans/jobs. Need-based aid available for part-time students. **Non-need-based:** Scholarships based on academics, art, leadership, music/drama. **Student debt:** 85% of graduating class borrowed to fund education; average debt was $16,900.

Freshman aid. **Need-based:** Out of 105 full-time freshmen, 101 applied for aid; 93 were judged to have need; of these 93 received aid. Average package met 82% of need. Average scholarship/grant was $4,100; average loan $2,625. **Non-need based:** 61 full-time freshmen with need received non-need scholarships; 15 without need received awards; 70 received athletic scholarships.

Merit scholarships. 4-year, full-tuition and partial-tuition awards based on academic merit offered. Application priority date is January 15 for merit-based scholarships.

Policies to reduce costs. Tuition/fee waivers for senior citizens, employees and their families. Credit/placement for qualifying scores on AP, IB, CLEP examinations.

Payment plans. Credit card, installment, deferred payment.

Application procedures. FAFSA required. Priority date 4/15; no closing date. Applicants notified on rolling basis starting 3/1, must reply by 5/1. Early decision closing date 12/1. **Transfers:** No deadline.

Contact. **Financial aid office:** (215) 248-7100
Jeanne Cavalieri-Grover, Director of Financial Aid
9601 Germantown Avenue
Philadelphia, PA 19118-2693

Cheyney University of Pennsylvania

Cheyney, Pennsylvania
www.cheyney.edu
Four-year public **Federal Code: 003317**

College costs. Undergraduate Non-resident-DC, DE, MD, NJ, NY residents pay $9,852 for full-time tuition and $411 per credit hour.

	Living at home	On-campus
Tuition and fees (2002-2003):	$5,133	$5,133
Out-of-state:	$11,701	$11,701
Room and board:		$5,390
Books and supplies:	$675	$675
Personal expenses:	$1,472	$1,020
Transportation:	$1,632	$612

Undergraduate aid. **Need-based:** Need-based aid available for full-time and part-time students. **Non-need-based:** Scholarships based on academics, athletics.

Policies to reduce costs. Tuition/fee waivers for minority students, employees and their families.

Payment plans. Credit card, installment payment.

Application procedures. FAFSA required. Priority date 5/1; no closing date. Applicants notified on rolling basis starting 4/1, must reply within 2 week(s) of notification.

Contact. James Brown, Director of Financial Aid
Cheyney and Creek Roads
Cheyney, PA 19319-0019

Churchman Business School

Easton, Pennsylvania
www.churchmanbusiness.com
Two-year proprietary **Federal Code: 014217**

	Living at home
Tuition and fees:	$7,675

Payment plans. Credit card, installment payment.

Application procedures. FAFSA required. No deadline. Applicants notified on rolling basis, must reply by 9/1. **Transfers:** No deadline.

Contact. Pamela Digiacomo, Director of Financial Aid
355 Spring Garden Street
Easton, PA 18042

Commonwealth Technical Institute

Johnstown, Pennsylvania
www.hgac.org
Two-year private

	Living at home	On-campus
Tuition and fees (2002-2003):	$10,492	$10,492
Room and board:		$9,516

Policies to reduce costs. Work study available nights and weekends.

Application procedures. FAFSA required. Closing date 5/1. Applicants notified on rolling basis.

Contact. Financial aid office: (814) 255-8351
Charles Gunby, Financial Aid Administrator
727 Goucher Street
Johnstown, PA 15905-3902

Community College of Allegheny County

Pittsburgh, Pennsylvania
www.ccac.edu
Two-year public

College costs. Additional required fees will vary for out-of-district and out-of-state students.

	Living at home
Tuition and fees:	$2,436
Out-of-district:	$4,581
Out-of-state:	$6,726
Per-credit charge:	$72
Per-credit out-of-district:	$143
Per-credit out-of-state:	$215
Books and supplies:	$600
Personal expenses:	$950
Transportation:	$725

Undergraduate aid. Need-based: 76% awarded as scholarships/grants, 24% as loans/jobs. Need-based aid available for part-time students. **Non-need-based:** 6% awarded as scholarships/grants, 94% as loans/jobs. Scholarships based on academics, athletics.

Policies to reduce costs. Tuition/fee waivers for senior citizens, employees and their families. Credit/placement for qualifying scores on AP, CLEP examinations. Work study available nights and for part-time students.

Payment plans. Credit card, installment, deferred payment.

Application procedures. FAFSA, institutional form required. Priority date 5/1; no closing date. Applicants notified by 5/20.

Contact. Financial aid office: (412) 323-2323
Betty Davis, Assistant Dean of Financial Aid
800 Allegheny Avenue
Pittsburgh, PA 15233

Community College of Beaver County

Monaca, Pennsylvania
www.ccbc.cc.pa.us
Two-year public **Federal Code: 006807**

	Living at home
Tuition and fees (2002-2003):	$2,430
Out-of-district:	$4,920
Out-of-state:	$7,410
Per-credit charge:	$73
Per-credit out-of-district:	$156
Per-credit out-of-state:	$239
Books and supplies:	$600
Personal expenses:	$1,000
Transportation:	$900

Undergraduate aid. Need-based: Need-based aid available for full-time and part-time students. **Non-need-based:** Scholarships based on academics, athletics, state/district residency.

Merit scholarships. Presidential Scholarship, full tuition.

Policies to reduce costs. Tuition/fee waivers for senior citizens, employees and their families. Credit/placement for qualifying scores on AP, CLEP examinations. Work study available for part-time students.

Payment plans. Credit card, installment, deferred payment.

Application procedures. FAFSA, institutional form required. Priority date 5/1; no closing date. Applicants notified on rolling basis starting 8/2, must reply within 2 week(s) of notification.

Contact. Financial aid office: (724) 775-8561 ext. 260
Doug Mahler, Director of Financial Aid
One Campus Drive
Monaca, PA 15061-2588

Community College of Philadelphia

Philadelphia, Pennsylvania
www.ccp.edu
Two-year public **Federal Code: 003249**

	Living at home
Tuition and fees (2002-2003):	$2,770
Out-of-district:	$5,260
Out-of-state:	$7,750
Per-credit charge:	$83
Per-credit out-of-district:	$166
Per-credit out-of-state:	$249
Board only:	$1,004
Books and supplies:	$545
Personal expenses:	$856
Transportation:	$560

Undergraduate aid. All financial aid based on need. 76% awarded as scholarships/grants, 24% as loans/jobs. Need-based aid available for part-time students.

Policies to reduce costs. Tuition/fee waivers for senior citizens, employees and their families. Credit/placement for qualifying scores on AP examinations. Work study available nights, weekends and for part-time students.

Payment plans. Credit card, deferred payment.

Application procedures. FAFSA, institutional form required. Closing date 5/1. Applicants notified on rolling basis. **Transfers:** No deadline.

Contact. Financial aid office: (215) 751-8271
Kim Folkes, Director of Financial Aid
1700 Spring Garden Street
Philadelphia, PA 19130-3991

Consolidated School of Business: Lancaster

Lancaster, Pennsylvania
www.csb.edu
Two-year proprietary **Federal Code: 030299**

College costs. Pre-evaluation placement testing fee $50.

	Living at home
Tuition and fees (2002-2003):	$9,000
Books and supplies:	$1,500

Undergraduate aid. Need-based: Need-based aid available for full-time and part-time students.

Policies to reduce costs. Tuition at time of enrollment guaranteed for 2 years.

Payment plans. Credit card, installment payment.

Application procedures. FAFSA required. No deadline. Applicants notified on rolling basis.

Contact. **Financial aid office:** (717) 394-6211
William Hoyt, Director of Financial Aid
2124 Ambassador Circle
Lancaster, PA 17603

Consolidated School of Business: York

York, Pennsylvania
www.csb.edu
Two-year proprietary **Federal Code: 02289600**

College costs. Pre-evaluation/placement testing fee $50.

	Living at home
Tuition and fees:	$9,300
Books and supplies:	$900

Undergraduate aid. Need-based: Need-based aid available for full-time and part-time students.

Policies to reduce costs. Tuition at time of enrollment guaranteed for 2 years.

Payment plans. Credit card, installment payment.

Application procedures. FAFSA required. No deadline. Applicants notified on rolling basis.

Contact. **Financial aid office:** (717) 764-9550
William Hoyt, Director of Financial Aid
1605 Clugston Road
York, PA 17404

Curtis Institute of Music

Philadelphia, Pennsylvania
www.curtis.edu
Four-year private **Federal Code: 003251**

College costs (projected). All students given full-tuition scholarship. Required fees $1,450; for bachelor of music students $1,550; additional expenses per annum $13,725 (includes books, supplies, living expenses and miscellaneous).

Undergraduate aid. All financial aid based on need. Average financial aid package for full-time students was $10,651. 59% awarded as scholarships/grants, 41% as loans/jobs. **Student debt:** 44% of graduating class borrowed to fund education; average debt was $17,000. **Additional information:** All students accepted on full-tuition scholarship basis.

Freshman aid. Out of 20 full-time freshmen, 15 applied for aid; 15 were judged to have need; of these 15 received aid. Average package met 78% of need. 1 students had full need met. Average scholarship/grant was $6,214; average loan $2,625.

Application procedures. FAFSA, institutional form, CSS PROFILE required. Closing date 3/1. Applicants notified by 4/1, must reply by 5/1.

Contact. Janice Miller, Director, Student Financial Assistance
1726 Locust Street
Philadelphia, PA 19103-6187

DeSales University

Center Valley, Pennsylvania
www.desales.edu
Four-year private **Federal Code: 003986**

College costs. Access/Continuing education per-credit-hour charge of $275.

	Living at home	On-campus
Tuition and fees:	$18,390	$18,390
Room and board:		$7,080
Board only:	$2,750	
Books and supplies:	$800	$800
Personal expenses:	$1,800	$1,800

Undergraduate aid. Need-based: Average financial aid package for full-time students was $12,555; for part-time $1,228. 63% awarded as scholarships/grants, 37% as loans/jobs. **Non-need-based:** 74% awarded as scholarships/grants, 26% as loans/jobs. Scholarships based on academics, leadership, music/drama. **Student debt:** 64% of graduating class borrowed to fund education; average debt was $13,977.

Freshman aid. Need-based: Out of 316 full-time freshmen, 295 applied for aid; 229 were judged to have need; of these 229 received aid. Average package met 78% of need. 113 students had full need met. Average scholarship/grant was $9,450; average loan $2,460. **Non-need based:** 163 full-time freshmen with need received non-need scholarships; 66 without need received awards.

Merit scholarships. Presidential Scholarships for students ranking in top 5% of class and 1300 SAT; full tuition. Trustee Scholarships for students within top 15% of class, minimum 1200 SAT; ranging from $6,000. DeSales Scholarships for students within top 25% of class, minimum 1100 SAT; $4,000.

Policies to reduce costs. Tuition/fee waivers for family members, family of clergy, employees and their families. Credit/placement for qualifying scores on AP, CLEP examinations.

Payment plans. Credit card, installment, deferred payment.

Application procedures. FAFSA, institutional form required. Priority date 2/2; closing date 5/2. Applicants notified on rolling basis starting 2/15, must reply by 5/1 or within 2 week(s) of notification. **Transfers:** Priority date 2/1; no deadline. Transfer scholarships require 3.0 GPA, 8 completed courses. Transfer Opportunity Program (TOP), a grant equal to tuition at participating community college, requires an associate degree to qualify.

Contact. **Financial aid office:** (610) 282-1100 ext. 1287
Peter Rautzhan, Director of Admissions and Financial Aid
2755 Station Avenue
Center Valley, PA 18034-9568

DeVry University: Ft. Washington

Fort Washington, Pennsylvania
Four-year proprietary

	Living at home
Tuition and fees:	$11,265
Books and supplies:	$1,100
Personal expenses:	$1,816
Transportation:	$1,438

Undergraduate aid. All financial aid based on need. Need-based aid available for full-time and part-time students.

Policies to reduce costs. Tuition/fee waivers for employees and their families.

Payment plans. Credit card, installment, deferred payment.

Application procedures. FAFSA required. No deadline. Applicants notified on rolling basis starting 7/2. **Transfers:** No deadline.

Contact. Marie Bennett, Regional Director of Student Finance
501 Office Center Drive, Suite 420
Fort Washington, PA 19034

Dean Institute of Technology

Pittsburgh, Pennsylvania
home.earthlink.net/~deantech
Two-year proprietary **Federal Code: 009186**

College costs. Air-conditioning/refrigeration: 15-month day course $15,300, night course $9,600. 7-month courses in welding or building maintenance $6,105. Electrical technician: 15-month day course or 30-month night course, $15,900. Tools/materials fees not included in tuition.

	Living at home
Tuition and fees (2002-2003):	$15,900
Books and supplies:	$709
Personal expenses:	$1,440
Transportation:	$1,170

Undergraduate aid. Need-based: Need-based aid available for full-time and part-time students.

Policies to reduce costs. Tuition/fee waivers for employees and their families.

Payment plans. Credit card, installment payment.

Application procedures. FAFSA required. Closing date 8/1. Applicants notified on rolling basis, must reply within 8 week(s) of notification.

Contact. Nancy Grom, Director of Financial Aid
1501 West Liberty Avenue
Pittsburgh, PA 15226

Delaware County Community College

Media, Pennsylvania
www.dccc.edu
Two-year public **Federal Code: 007110**

College costs. Required fees vary with program, and with status as in-district, out-of-district, or out-of-state resident.

	Living at home
Tuition and fees (2002-2003):	$1,950
Out-of-district:	$3,900
Out-of-state:	$5,850
Per-credit charge:	$65
Per-credit out-of-district:	$130
Per-credit out-of-state:	$195
Books and supplies:	$750
Personal expenses:	$1,200
Transportation:	$800

Undergraduate aid. Need-based: Need-based aid available for full-time and part-time students. **Additional information:** COPE grants offered to educationally and economically disadvantaged students.

Policies to reduce costs. Tuition/fee waivers for senior citizens, employees and their families. Credit/placement for qualifying scores on AP, CLEP examinations.

Payment plans. Credit card, deferred payment.

Application procedures. FAFSA required. Priority date 5/1; no closing date. Applicants notified on rolling basis starting 6/14.

Contact. Financial aid office: (610) 359-5124
Ray Toole, Director of Financial Aid
901 South Media Line Road
Media, PA 19063

Delaware Valley College

Doylestown, Pennsylvania
www.devalcol.edu
Four-year private **Federal Code: 003252**

College costs. $400 additional "tech fee" for resident students.

	Living at home	On-campus
Tuition and fees:	$19,204	$19,204
Room and board:		$7,372
Books and supplies:	$800	$800
Personal expenses:	$1,100	$1,100
Transportation:	$1,000	$500

Undergraduate aid. Need-based: Average financial aid package for full-time students was $15,583; for part-time $3,450. 73% awarded as scholarships/grants, 27% as loans/jobs. **Non-need-based:** 53% awarded as scholarships/grants, 47% as loans/jobs. Scholarships based on academics, music/drama. **Student debt:** 68% of graduating class borrowed to fund education; average debt was $15,169.

Freshman aid. Need-based: Out of 408 full-time freshmen, 389 applied for aid; 317 were judged to have need; of these 317 received aid. Average package met 79% of need. 143 students had full need met. Average scholarship/grant was $11,770; average loan $3,104. **Non-need based:** 53 full-time freshmen with need received non-need scholarships; 72 without need received awards.

Policies to reduce costs. Tuition/fee waivers for adults, senior citizens, family members, employees and their families. Credit/placement for qualifying scores on AP, CLEP examinations. Work study available nights and weekends.

Payment plans. Credit card, installment, deferred payment.

Application procedures. FAFSA required. Priority date 4/1; no closing date. Applicants notified on rolling basis starting 1/15, must reply by 5/1.

Contact. Financial aid office: (215) 489-2272
Robert Sauer, Director of Financial Aid
700 East Butler Avenue
Doylestown, PA 18901

Dickinson College

Carlisle, Pennsylvania
www.dickinson.edu
Four-year private **Federal Code: 003253**

	Living at home	On-campus
Tuition and fees:	$28,615	$28,615
Room and board:		$7,210
Books and supplies:	$750	$750
Personal expenses:		$1,040
Transportation:		$300

Undergraduate aid. Need-based: Average financial aid package for full-time students was $22,147. 77% awarded as scholarships/grants, 23% as loans/jobs. **Non-need-based:** 81% awarded as scholarships/grants, 19% as loans/jobs. Scholarships based on academics.

Freshman aid. Need-based: Out of 573 full-time freshmen, 338 applied for aid; 306 were judged to have need; of these 306 received aid. Average package met 99% of need. 259 students had full need met. Average scholarship/grant was $16,748; average loan $3,406. **Non-need based:** 41 full-time freshmen with need received non-need scholarships; 55 without need received awards.

Merit scholarships. The John Dickinson and Benjamin Rush Scholarships are awarded to the most academically competitive students; Engage the World Fellowship for selected John Dickinson Scholarship winners.

Policies to reduce costs. Tuition/fee waivers for employees and their families. Credit/placement for qualifying scores on AP, IB examinations.

Payment plans. Credit card, installment, deferred payment.

Application procedures. FAFSA, CSS PROFILE required. Closing date 2/1. Applicants notified by 3/20, must reply by 5/1 or within 2 week(s) of notification. Early decision closing date 11/15. **Transfers:** Priority date 4/1.

Contact. Judith Carter, Director of Financial Aid
PO Box 1773
Carlisle, PA 17013-2896

Drexel University

Philadelphia, Pennsylvania
www.drexel.edu
Five-year private **Federal Code: 003256**

	Living at home	On-campus
Tuition and fees (2002-2003):	$20,020	$20,020
Room and board:		$9,150
Books and supplies:	$650	$650
Personal expenses:	$3,000	$2,000
Transportation:	$1,000	$460

Undergraduate aid. Need-based: Average financial aid package for full-time students was $9,515. 28% awarded as scholarships/grants, 72% as loans/jobs. **Non-need-based:** 74% awarded as scholarships/grants, 26% as loans/jobs. Scholarships based on academics, alumni affiliation, art, athletics, leadership, music/drama. **Student debt:** 100% of graduating class borrowed to fund education; average debt was $21,443.

Freshman aid. Need-based: Out of 2,037 full-time freshmen, 1,894 applied for aid; 1,516 were judged to have need; of these 1,497 received aid. Average package met 76% of need. 347 students had full need met. Average scholarship/grant was $3,934; average loan $5,238. **Non-need based:** 1,459 full-time freshmen with need received non-need scholarships; 358 without need received awards; 39 received athletic scholarships.

Policies to reduce costs. Tuition/fee waivers for children of alumni, family members, employees and their families. Credit/placement for qualifying scores on AP, IB, CLEP examinations.

Payment plans. Credit card, installment, deferred payment.

Application procedures. FAFSA required. Closing date 2/15. Applicants notified on rolling basis starting 4/1. **Transfers:** Priority date 3/2. Scholarships available in amounts up to $8,000. 3.2 cumulative GPA, minimum 30 hours completed at time of application required for eligibility.

Contact. Financial aid office: (215) 895-1626
Douglas Boucher, Director of Financial Aid
3141 Chestnut Street
Philadelphia, PA 19104-2875

DuBois Business College

DuBois, Pennsylvania
www.dbcollege.com
Two-year proprietary **Federal Code: 004893**

	Living at home	On-campus
Tuition and fees (2002-2003):	$6,600	$6,600
Per-credit charge:	$160	$160
Room and board:		$5,850
Board only:	$1,125	
Books and supplies:	$1,000	$1,000
Transportation:	$1,340	

Undergraduate aid. Need-based: Need-based aid available for full-time students.

Policies to reduce costs. Tuition/fee waivers for employees and their families. Credit/placement for qualifying scores on AP examinations.

Payment plans. Installment payment.

Application procedures. FAFSA required. Closing date 8/1. Applicants notified on rolling basis.

Contact. Karen Alderton, Financial Aid Director
One Beaver Drive
DuBois, PA 15801

DuBois Business College: Oil City

Oil City, Pennsylvania
www.dbcollege.com
Two-year proprietary

	Living at home
Tuition and fees (2002-2003):	$6,600
Per-credit charge:	$160
Books and supplies:	$2,500

Application procedures. FAFSA required.

Contact. Karen Alderton, Director of Financial Aid
701 East Third Street
Oil City, PA 16301

Duff's Business Institute

Pittsburgh, Pennsylvania
www.duffsinstitute.com
Two-year proprietary **Federal Code: 007091**

	Living at home
Tuition and fees (2002-2003):	$8,940
Per-credit charge:	$192
Books and supplies:	$400
Personal expenses:	$3,250
Transportation:	$900

Application procedures. Institutional form required.

Contact. Linda Malchano, Director of Financial Aid
100 Forbes Avenue, Suite 1200
Pittsburgh, PA 15222

Duquesne University

Pittsburgh, Pennsylvania
www.duq.edu
Four-year private **Federal Code: 003258**

	Living at home	On-campus
Tuition and fees (2002-2003):	$18,527	$18,527
Room and board:		$7,170
Board only:	$1,500	
Books and supplies:	$550	$550
Personal expenses:	$600	$600
Transportation:	$550	$550

Undergraduate aid. Need-based: Average financial aid package for full-time students was $13,979; for part-time $7,006. 57% awarded as scholarships/grants, 43% as loans/jobs. **Non-need-based:** 77% awarded as scholarships/grants, 23% as loans/jobs. Scholarships based on academics, athletics, minority status, music/drama, religious affiliation. **Student debt:** 64% of graduating class borrowed to fund education; average debt was $17,953.

Freshman aid. Need-based: Out of 1,429 full-time freshmen, 1,407 applied for aid; 961 were judged to have need; of these 961 received aid. Average package met 82% of need. 393 students had full need met. Average scholarship/grant was $9,224; average loan $3,207. **Non-need based:** 776 full-time freshmen with need received non-need scholarships; 354 without need received awards; 76 received athletic scholarships.

Merit scholarships. Competitive scholarships available for academically and/or artistically talented students.

Policies to reduce costs. Tuition/fee waivers for senior citizens, family of clergy, employees and their families. Credit/placement for qualifying scores on AP, IB, CLEP examinations. Work study available nights and weekends.

Payment plans. Credit card, installment, deferred payment.

Application procedures. FAFSA, institutional form required. Closing date 5/1. Applicants notified on rolling basis starting 3/15, must reply within 3 week(s) of notification. Early decision closing date 11/1. **Transfers:** No deadline.

Contact. Financial aid office: (412) 396-6607
Frank Dutkovich, Director of Financial Aid
600 Forbes Avenue
Pittsburgh, PA 15282-0201

East Stroudsburg University of Pennsylvania

East Stroudsburg, Pennsylvania
www.esu.edu
Four-year public **Federal Code: 003320**

	Living at home	On-campus
Tuition and fees (2002-2003):	$5,502	$5,502
Out-of-state:	$12,070	$12,070
Room and board:		$4,290
Books and supplies:	$700	$700
Personal expenses:	$1,131	$1,437
Transportation:	$561	$255

Undergraduate aid. Need-based: Average financial aid package for full-time students was $5,252; for part-time $3,146. 42% awarded as scholarships/grants, 58% as loans/jobs. **Non-need-based:** 2% awarded as scholarships/grants, 98% as loans/jobs. Scholarships based on academics, alumni affiliation, art, athletics, minority status, music/drama. **Student debt:** 69% of graduating class borrowed to fund education; average debt was $19,677.

Freshman aid. Need-based: Out of 971 full-time freshmen, 790 applied for aid; 509 were judged to have need; of these 492 received aid. Average package met 85% of need. 367 students had full need met. Average scholarship/grant was $3,372; average loan $2,507. **Non-need based:** 20 full-time freshmen with need received non-need scholarships; 240 without need received awards; 30 received athletic scholarships.

Policies to reduce costs. Tuition/fee waivers for senior citizens, employees and their families. Credit/placement for qualifying scores on AP, CLEP examinations.

Payment plans. Credit card, installment payment.

Application procedures. FAFSA required. Priority date 3/1; closing date 5/1. Applicants notified by 4/1.

Contact. **Financial aid office:** (570) 422-3340
Georgia Prell, Director of Enrollment Services/ University Registrar
200 Prospect Street
East Stroudsburg, PA 18301-2999

Edinboro University of Pennsylvania

Edinboro, Pennsylvania
www.edinboro.edu
Four-year public **Federal Code: 003321**

	Living at home	On-campus
Tuition and fees (2002-2003):	$5,464	$5,464
Out-of-state:	$7,654	$7,654
Room and board:		$4,634
Books and supplies:	$650	$650
Personal expenses:	$1,635	$1,000
Transportation:	$2,240	$740

Undergraduate aid. Need-based: Average financial aid package for full-time students was $5,482; for part-time $3,596. 46% awarded as scholarships/grants, 54% as loans/jobs. **Non-need-based:** 11% awarded as scholarships/grants, 89% as loans/jobs. Scholarships based on academics, alumni affiliation, art, athletics, job skills, leadership, minority status, music/drama, state/district residency. **Student debt:** 60% of graduating class borrowed to fund education; average debt was $15,623.

Freshman aid. Need-based: Out of 1,416 full-time freshmen, 1,283 applied for aid; 1,001 were judged to have need; of these 980 received aid. Average package met 80% of need. 146 students had full need met. Average scholarship/grant was $1,500; average loan $2,625. **Non-need based:** 75 full-time freshmen with need received non-need scholarships; 170 without need received awards; 7 received athletic scholarships.

Policies to reduce costs. Tuition/fee waivers for senior citizens, employees and their families. Credit/placement for qualifying scores on AP, CLEP examinations. Work study available nights and weekends.

Payment plans. Credit card, installment payment.

Application procedures. FAFSA required. Priority date 3/15; closing date 5/1. Applicants notified by 3/31, must reply within 2 week(s) of notification.

Contact. **Financial aid office:** (888) 611-2680
Dorothy Body, Assistant Vice President for Student Financial Support and Services
Bigger's House
Edinboro, PA 16444

Education Direct: Center for Degree Studies

Scranton, Pennsylvania
educationdirect.com
Two-year proprietary **Federal Code: 004049**

College costs (2002-2003). Cost of degree programs range from $3,166 to $4,626 depending on program. Additional costs to fulfill resident laboratory requirement in technology programs.

Payment plans. Credit card, installment, deferred payment.

Contact. 925 Oak Street
Scranton, PA 18515

Electronic Institutes: Middletown

Middletown, Pennsylvania
www.ei.tec.pa.us
Two-year private **Federal Code: 004886**

	Living at home
Tuition and fees (2002-2003):	$7,950
Board only:	$2,510
Books and supplies:	$325
Personal expenses:	$1,576
Transportation:	$1,690

Undergraduate aid. Need-based: Need-based aid available for full-time students.

Policies to reduce costs. Tuition/fee waivers for employees and their families. Tuition at time of enrollment guaranteed for 2 years.

Application procedures. FAFSA, institutional form required. Priority date 8/1; no closing date. Applicants notified on rolling basis.

Contact. **Financial aid office:** (800) 884-2731
John Huld, Financial Aid Officer
1519 West Harrisburg Pike
Middletown, PA 17057-4851

Elizabethtown College

Elizabethtown, Pennsylvania
www.etown.edu
Four-year private **Federal Code: 003262**

	Living at home	On-campus
Tuition and fees:	$22,500	$22,500
Room and board:		$6,300
Board only:	$1,500	
Books and supplies:	$550	$550
Personal expenses:	$600	$600
Transportation:	$350	$150

Undergraduate aid. Need-based: Average financial aid package for full-time students was $15,897; for part-time $5,377. 71% awarded as scholarships/grants, 29% as loans/jobs. **Non-need-based:** 48% awarded as scholarships/grants, 52% as loans/jobs. Scholarships based on academics, art, minority status, music/drama, religious affiliation. **Student debt:** 80% of graduating class borrowed to fund education; average debt was $19,379.

Freshman aid. Need-based: Out of 464 full-time freshmen, 389 applied for aid; 343 were judged to have need; of these 343 received aid. Average package met 86% of need. 104 students had full need met. Average scholarship/grant was $12,283; average loan $2,955. **Non-need based:** 57 full-time freshmen with need received non-need scholarships; 96 without need received awards.

Merit scholarships. Presidential Scholarships, $12,000 annually, for students in top 2% of class with minimum 1300 SAT score; Provost Scholarships, ranging from $7,750-$10,000 annually, for students in top 10% of class with minimum 1150 SAT; unlimited number awarded. Dean's Scholarships, $3,000-7,500 annually, for students with very strong academic achievement who do not qualify for other merit awards; unlimited number awarded. Music scholarships by audition ranging from $2,000-4,000.

Policies to reduce costs. Tuition/fee waivers for family members, family of clergy, employees and their families. Credit/placement for qualifying scores on AP, IB, CLEP examinations. Work study available nights and weekends.

Payment plans. Credit card, installment, deferred payment.

Application procedures. FAFSA, institutional form required. Priority date 3/15; no closing date. Applicants notified on rolling basis starting 2/15, must reply by 5/1 or within 2 week(s) of notification. **Transfers:** No deadline.

Contact. **Financial aid office:** (717) 361-1404
M. Clarke Paine, Director of Financial Aid
One Alpha Drive
Elizabethtown, PA 17022

Erie Business Center

Erie, Pennsylvania
www.eriebc.com
Two-year proprietary **Federal Code: 004894**

College costs. Equipment/maintenance fee $16 per credit. For summer trimester, room and board $1,240.

	Living at home	On-campus
Tuition and fees (2002-2003):	$6,560	$6,560
Per-credit charge:	$216	$216
Room and board:		$2,480
Books and supplies:	$800	$800

Undergraduate aid. Additional information: Scholarships and veterans' benefits available; Office of Vocational Rehabilitation may provide aid.

Policies to reduce costs. Prepayment discount.

Payment plans. Credit card, installment payment.

Application procedures. Institutional form required. Closing date 8/1. **Transfers:** No deadline.

Contact. Michelle Blount, Financial Aid Director
246 West Ninth Street
Erie, PA 16501

Franklin & Marshall College

Lancaster, Pennsylvania
www.fandm.edu
Four-year private **Federal Code: 003265**

	Living at home	On-campus
Tuition and fees:	$29,060	$29,060
Room and board:		$7,070
Books and supplies:	$700	$700
Personal expenses:		$300
Transportation:		$200

Undergraduate aid. Need-based: Average financial aid package for full-time students was $19,479. 72% awarded as scholarships/grants, 28% as loans/jobs. **Non-need-based:** 61% awarded as scholarships/grants, 39% as loans/jobs. Scholarships based on academics, leadership, music/drama. **Student debt:** 55% of graduating class borrowed to fund education; average debt was $19,656.

Freshman aid. Need-based: Out of 534 full-time freshmen, 292 applied for aid; 232 were judged to have need; of these 232 received aid. Average package met 99% of need. 229 students had full need met. Average scholarship/grant was $17,793; average loan $3,879. **Non-need based:** 14 full-time freshmen with need received non-need scholarships; 116 without need received awards.

Merit scholarships. John Marshall Scholarships: $12,500 awarded annually, independent initiative in intellectual or service areas considered, 50-60 awarded. National Merit Recognition: $18,000 renewable annually, 5 awarded. Presidential Scholarships: $7,500 annually, 70-80 awarded. All based on academic performance, class rank. Buchanan Service Scholarship: $5,000 awarded based on outstanding community service. Gray Scholarship: awarded to outstanding applicants of African-, Latino-, and Asian-American descent, minimizes loans.

Policies to reduce costs. Tuition/fee waivers for employees and their families. Credit/placement for qualifying scores on AP, IB, CLEP examinations.

Payment plans. Installment payment.

Application procedures. FAFSA, CSS PROFILE required. Closing date 2/1. Applicants notified by 4/1, must reply by 5/1. Early decision closing date 11/15. **Transfers:** Closing date 2/1.

Contact. **Financial aid office:** (717) 291-3991
Chris Hanlon, Director of Student Aid
Box 3003
Lancaster, PA 17604-3003

Geneva College

Beaver Falls, Pennsylvania
www.geneva.edu
Four-year private **Federal Code: 003267**

	Living at home	On-campus
Tuition and fees:	$15,480	$15,480
Room and board:		$6,370
Books and supplies:	$700	$700
Personal expenses:	$1,150	$1,150
Transportation:	$2,400	$140

Undergraduate aid. Need-based: Average financial aid package for full-time students was $12,759; for part-time $10,537. 61% awarded as scholarships/grants, 39% as loans/jobs. **Non-need-based:** 27% awarded as scholarships/grants, 73% as loans/jobs. Scholarships based on academics, athletics, music/drama, religious affiliation.

Freshman aid. Need-based: Out of 322 full-time freshmen, 280 applied for aid; 257 were judged to have need; of these 257 received aid. Average package met 78% of need. 44 students had full need met. Average scholarship/grant was $9,172; average loan $2,978. **Non-need based:** 22 full-time freshmen with need received non-need scholarships; 39 without need received awards; 11 received athletic scholarships.

Merit scholarships. Academic scholarships, scholarships for National Merit finalists and semifinalists, grants for members of controlling church and other denominations identified by the college.

Policies to reduce costs. Tuition/fee waivers for minority students, family of clergy, employees and their families. Credit/placement for qualifying scores on AP, IB, CLEP examinations.

Payment plans. Credit card, installment payment.

Application procedures. FAFSA required. Priority date 3/15; no closing date. Applicants notified on rolling basis starting 3/1, must reply by 5/1 or within 4 week(s) of notification.

Contact. Steven Bell, Director of Financial Aid
3200 College Avenue
Beaver Falls, PA 15010

Gettysburg College

Gettysburg, Pennsylvania
www.gettysburg.edu
Four-year private **Federal Code: 003268**

	Living at home	On-campus
Tuition and fees:	$28,624	$28,624
Room and board:		$6,972
Board only:	$2,970	
Books and supplies:	$500	$500
Personal expenses:	$500	$500
Transportation:	$500	$500

Undergraduate aid. Need-based: Average financial aid package for full-time students was $22,415. 81% awarded as scholarships/grants, 19% as loans/jobs. **Non-need-based:** 35% awarded as scholarships/grants, 65% as loans/jobs. Scholarships based on academics, music/drama. **Student debt:** 75% of graduating class borrowed to fund education; average debt was $15,500.

Freshman aid. Need-based: Out of 687 full-time freshmen, 448 applied for aid; 367 were judged to have need; of these 367 received aid. Average package met 100% of need. 367 students had full need met. Average scholarship/grant was $18,570; average loan $3,490. **Non-need based:** 96 full-time freshmen with need received non-need scholarships; 83 without need received awards.

Merit scholarships. Presidential Scholarships based on high school class rank and standardized test scores; number awarded varies.

Policies to reduce costs. Prepayment discount; credit/placement for qualifying scores on AP examinations.

Payment plans. Installment, deferred payment.

Application procedures. FAFSA, CSS PROFILE required. Priority date 2/15; closing date 3/15. Applicants notified by 3/30, must reply by 5/1. Early decision closing date 11/15. **Transfers:** No deadline.

Contact. Ronald Shunk, Director of Financial Aid
Admissions Office-Eisenhower House, 300 North Washington Street
Gettysburg, PA 17325-1484

Gratz College

Melrose Park, Pennsylvania
www.gratzcollege.edu
Four-year private **Federal Code: 004058**

	Living at home
Tuition and fees (projected):	$8,190
Books and supplies:	$550
Personal expenses:	$500

Undergraduate aid. Additional information: Institutional work-study program available.

Policies to reduce costs. Tuition/fee waivers for senior citizens, family members, employees and their families.

Payment plans. Credit card, installment, deferred payment.

Application procedures. FAFSA, institutional form required. Priority date 6/1; no closing date. Applicants notified on rolling basis starting 11/1. **Transfers:** No deadline.

Contact. **Financial aid office:** (215) 635-7300 ext. 163
Karen West, Financial Aid Administrator
7605 Old York Rd.
Melrose Park, PA 19027

Grove City College

Grove City, Pennsylvania
www.gcc.edu
Four-year private **Federal Code: G03269**

	Living at home	On-campus
Tuition and fees:	$9,376	$9,376
Room and board:		$4,852
Board only:	$2,400	
Books and supplies:	$900	$900
Personal expenses:	$350	$350
Transportation:	$250	$250

Undergraduate aid. Need-based: Average financial aid package for full-time students was $5,047. **Non-need-based:** 24% awarded as scholarships/grants, 76% as loans/jobs. Scholarships based on academics. **Student debt:** 40% of graduating class borrowed to fund education; average debt was $19,100. **Additional information:** Institutional aid applications required for institutional scholarships, loans, and student employment.

Freshman aid. Need-based: Out of 580 full-time freshmen, 431 applied for aid; 364 were judged to have need; of these 358 received aid. Average package met 67% of need. 49 students had full need met. Average scholarship/grant was $4,395. **Non-need based:** 197 full-time freshmen with need received non-need scholarships; 132 without need received awards.

Merit scholarships. Trustee Scholarship Test Program, full tuition, on-campus academic test required; 12 awarded. Presidential Scholarships, $1,650, for all valedictorians in class of 30 or more, salutatorians in class of 175 or more, and awarded to National Merit Finalist. Engineering Scholarships, $2,500: 4 awarded.

Policies to reduce costs. Tuition/fee waivers for employees and their families. Credit/placement for qualifying scores on AP, IB examinations.

Application procedures. Institutional form required. Closing date 4/15. Applicants notified by 6/10. Early decision closing date 11/15. **Transfers:** Closing date 12/15.

Contact. **Financial aid office:** (724) 458-3300
Patty Peterson, Director of Financial Aid
100 Campus Drive
Grove City, PA 16127-2104

Gwynedd-Mercy College

Gwynedd Valley, Pennsylvania
www.gmc.edu
Four-year private **Federal Code: 003270**

College costs. Tuition and fees for nursing and allied health programs $16,600; $370 per-credit-hour charge. $200 required fee for non-residents.

	Living at home	On-campus
Tuition and fees (2002-2003):	$15,825	$15,825
Room and board:		$7,210
Board only:	$3,500	
Books and supplies:	$450	$450
Personal expenses:	$1,500	$1,000
Transportation:	$1,500	$500

Undergraduate aid. Need-based: Average financial aid package for full-time students was $13,236. 70% awarded as scholarships/grants, 30% as loans/jobs. Need-based aid available for part-time students. **Non-need-based:** Scholarships based on academics. **Student debt:** 80% of graduating class borrowed to fund education; average debt was $15,510.

Freshman aid. Need-based: Out of 263 full-time freshmen, 257 applied for aid; 190 were judged to have need; of these 181 received aid. Average package met 85% of need. 147 students had full need met. Average scholarship/grant was $9,718; average loan $3,268. **Non-need based:** 131 full-time freshmen with need received non-need scholarships; 67 without need received awards.

Merit scholarships. Presidential scholarship, $10,000: must have SAT scores of 1200 or above and be in top 30% of class to be eligible, essay required, Feb. 15 deadline. Connelly Scholarship, $6,000 - $7,000, must have SAT scores of 1100 or above and be in top 50% of class to be eligible. Mother Mary Bernard Scholarship, $4,500 - $5,000, must have SAT scores of 1000 or above, be in top 50% of class, and have documented leadership experience to be eligible. Yearly scholarship for Catholic school graduates, $2,000 (tuition incentive grant).

Policies to reduce costs. Tuition/fee waivers for senior citizens, employees and their families. Credit/placement for qualifying scores on AP, CLEP examinations.

Payment plans. Credit card, installment payment.

Application procedures. FAFSA, institutional form required. Priority date 3/15; no closing date. Applicants notified on rolling basis starting 3/1, must reply by 5/1 or within 2 week(s) of notification. **Transfers:** Priority date 3/15.

Contact. Barbara Kaufmann, Director of Student Financial Aid
Sumneytown Pike
Gwynedd Valley, PA 19437-0901

Harrisburg Area Community College

Harrisburg, Pennsylvania
www.hacc.edu
Two-year public **Federal Code: 003273**

College costs. Required fees $270 for out-of-district and out-of-state students.

	Living at home
Tuition and fees (2002-2003):	$2,325
Out-of-district:	$4,440
Out-of-state:	$6,555
Per-credit charge:	$71
Per-credit out-of-district:	$141
Per-credit out-of-state:	$212
Books and supplies:	$900
Personal expenses:	$800
Transportation:	$1,450

Undergraduate aid. Need-based: Need-based aid available for full-time and part-time students. **Non-need-based:** Scholarships based on academics.

Policies to reduce costs. Tuition/fee waivers for employees and their families. Credit/placement for qualifying scores on AP, IB, CLEP examinations.

Payment plans. Credit card, installment payment.

Application procedures. FAFSA, institutional form required. Priority date 5/15; no closing date. Applicants notified on rolling basis starting 7/1, must reply within 4 week(s) of notification.

Contact. Sherrill Goodlive, Director of Financial Aid
1 HACC Drive, Cooper 206
Harrisburg, PA 17110-2999

Haverford College

Haverford, Pennsylvania
www.haverford.edu
Four-year private **Federal Code: 003274**

College costs. Freshmen subject to a 1-time fee of $160.

	Living at home	On-campus
Tuition and fees:	$28,880	$28,880
Room and board:		$9,020
Books and supplies:	$890	$890
Personal expenses:		$1,270
Transportation:		$150

Undergraduate aid. All financial aid based on need. Average financial aid package for full-time students was $23,550. 84% awarded as scholarships/grants, 16% as loans/jobs. **Student debt:** 42% of graduating class borrowed to fund education; average debt was $15,253.

Freshman aid. Out of 311 full-time freshmen, 168 applied for aid; 132 were judged to have need; of these 132 received aid. Average package met 100% of need. 132 students had full need met. Average scholarship/grant was $20,754; average loan $1,896.

Policies to reduce costs. Tuition/fee waivers for employees and their families. Credit/placement for qualifying scores on AP, IB examinations. Work study available nights and weekends.

Payment plans. Installment, deferred payment.

Application procedures. FAFSA, CSS PROFILE required. CSS required for all students wishing to be considered for institutional funds. Closing date 1/31. Applicants notified by 4/8, must reply by 5/1. Early decision closing date 11/15. **Transfers:** Closing date 3/1.

Contact. David Hoy, Director of Financial Aid
370 Lancaster Avenue
Haverford, PA 19041-1392

Holy Family University

Philadelphia, Pennsylvania
www.hfc.edu
Four-year private **Federal Code: 003275**

	Living at home
Tuition and fees (2002-2003):	$14,490
Books and supplies:	$640
Personal expenses:	$3,110
Transportation:	$900

Undergraduate aid. Need-based: 44% awarded as scholarships/grants, 56% as loans/jobs. **Non-need-based:** 33% awarded as scholarships/grants, 67% as loans/jobs. Scholarships based on academics, alumni affiliation, athletics. **Student debt:** 62% of graduating class borrowed to fund education; average debt was $17,125.

Freshman aid. Need-based: Out of 224 full-time freshmen, 190 applied for aid; 174 were judged to have need; of these 174 received aid. Average package met 86% of need. 56 students had full need met. Average scholarship/grant was $5,090. **Non-need based:** 22 full-time freshmen with need received non-need scholarships; 22 without need received awards; 24 received athletic scholarships.

Policies to reduce costs. Tuition/fee waivers for senior citizens, family of clergy, employees and their families. Credit/placement for qualifying scores on AP, IB, CLEP examinations. Work study available nights and weekends.

Payment plans. Credit card, installment, deferred payment.

Application procedures. FAFSA, institutional form required. Priority date 3/1; no closing date. Applicants notified on rolling basis starting 4/1, must reply within 2 week(s) of notification. **Transfers:** No deadline.

Contact. Financial aid office: (215) 637-5538
Janice Hetrick, Director of Financial Aid
Grant and Frankford Avenues
Philadelphia, PA 19114-2094

ICM School of Business & Medical Careers

Pittsburgh, Pennsylvania
www.icmschool.com
Two-year proprietary **Federal Code: 007436**

	Living at home
Tuition and fees (2002-2003):	$11,260
Books and supplies:	$1,200

Contact. 10 Wood Street
Pittsburgh, PA 15222

ITT Technical Institute: Bensalem

Bensalem, Pennsylvania
www.itt-tech.edu
Two-year proprietary

College costs. Total program varies depending on course of study. Per-credit-hour charge: $347.

Contact. Robert Russo, Director of Finance
3330 Tillman Drive
Bensalem, PA 19020

ITT Technical Institute: Mechanicsburg

Mechanicsburg, Pennsylvania
www.itt-tech.edu
Two-year proprietary **Federal Code: 007329**

College costs. Total program varies depending on course of study. Per-credit-hour charge: $347.

Policies to reduce costs. Tuition/fee waivers for employees and their families. Tuition at time of enrollment guaranteed for 2 years.

Payment plans. Credit card, installment payment.

Application procedures. FAFSA, institutional form required. No deadline. Applicants notified on rolling basis.

Contact. Kirsten Zabiewrowsky, Director of Finance
5020 Louise Drive
Mechanicsburg, PA 17055

ITT Technical Institute: Monroeville

Monroeville, Pennsylvania
www.itt-tech.edu
Two-year proprietary **Federal Code: 009837**

College costs. Total program varies depending on course of study. Per-credit-hour charge: $347.

Policies to reduce costs. Tuition/fee waivers for employees and their families. Tuition at time of enrollment guaranteed for 2 years.

Payment plans. Credit card, installment payment.

Application procedures. FAFSA, institutional form required. No deadline. Applicants notified on rolling basis.

Contact. Nora Murphy, Director of Finance
105 Mall Boulevard, Suite 200E
Monroeville, PA 15146

ITT Technical Institute: Pittsburgh

Pittsburgh, Pennsylvania
www.itt-tech.edu
Two-year proprietary **Federal Code: 009837**

College costs. Total program varies depending on course of study. Per-credit-hour charge: $347.

Policies to reduce costs. Tuition/fee waivers for employees and their families. Tuition at time of enrollment guaranteed for 2 years.

Payment plans. Credit card, installment payment.

Application procedures. FAFSA, institutional form required. No deadline. Applicants notified on rolling basis.

Contact. Janet Davidson, Director of Finance
Eight Parkway Center
Pittsburgh, PA 15220

Immaculata University

Immaculata, Pennsylvania
www.immaculata.edu
Four-year private **Federal Code: 003276**

	Living at home	On-campus
Tuition and fees (2002-2003):	$16,400	$16,400
Room and board:		$7,600
Board only:	$2,800	
Books and supplies:	$1,000	$1,000
Personal expenses:	$1,500	$1,500
Transportation:	$2,300	$800

Undergraduate aid. Need-based: Average financial aid package for full-time students was $10,000; for part-time $3,600. 25% awarded as scholarships/grants, 75% as loans/jobs. **Non-need-based:** Scholarships based on academics, alumni affiliation, leadership, minority status, music/drama, religious affiliation, state/district residency. **Student debt:** 60% of graduating class borrowed to fund education; average debt was $17,125.

Freshman aid. Need-based: Out of 111 full-time freshmen, 111 applied for aid; 101 were judged to have need; of these 101 received aid. Average package met 60% of need. 21 students had full need met. Average scholarship/grant was $2,500; average loan $2,625. **Non-need based:** 101 full-time freshmen with need received non-need scholarships; 20 without need received awards.

Policies to reduce costs. Tuition/fee waivers for senior citizens, family members, employees and their families. Tuition at time of enrollment guaranteed for 4 years; credit/placement for qualifying scores on AP, IB, CLEP examinations. Work study available nights, weekends and for part-time students.

Payment plans. Credit card, installment, deferred payment.

Application procedures. FAFSA, institutional form required. Priority date 2/15; closing date 4/15. Applicants notified on rolling basis starting 1/1, must reply within 2 week(s) of notification.

Contact. **Financial aid office:** (610) 647-4400 ext. 3026
Peter Lysionek, Director of Financial Aid
Box 642
Immaculata, PA 19345

Indiana University of Pennsylvania

Indiana, Pennsylvania
www.iup.edu
Four-year public **Federal Code: 003277**

	Living at home	On-campus
Tuition and fees (2002-2003):	$5,541	$5,541
Out-of-state:	$12,109	$12,109
Room and board:		$4,524
Books and supplies:	$800	$800
Transportation:	$500	

Undergraduate aid. **Need-based:** Average financial aid package for full-time students was $6,669; for part-time $7,052. 46% awarded as scholarships/grants, 54% as loans/jobs. **Non-need-based:** 19% awarded as scholarships/grants, 81% as loans/jobs. Scholarships based on academics, alumni affiliation, art, athletics, leadership, minority status, music/drama, state/district residency. **Student debt:** 60% of graduating class borrowed to fund education; average debt was $16,319.

Freshman aid. **Need-based:** Out of 2,578 full-time freshmen, 2,184 applied for aid; 1,676 were judged to have need; of these 1,645 received aid. Average package met 85% of need. 1289 students had full need met. Average scholarship/grant was $3,682; average loan $2,573. **Non-need based:** 553 full-time freshmen with need received non-need scholarships; 227 without need received awards; 28 received athletic scholarships.

Policies to reduce costs. Tuition/fee waivers for senior citizens, employees and their families. Prepayment discount; credit/placement for qualifying scores on AP, IB, CLEP examinations. Work study available nights, weekends and for part-time students.

Payment plans. Credit card, installment payment.

Application procedures. FAFSA required. Closing date 4/15. Applicants notified on rolling basis starting 3/15.

Contact. **Financial aid office:** (724) 357-2218
Christine Zuzack, Director of Financial Aid
117 John Sutton Hall, 1011 South Dr
Indiana, PA 15705-1088

Information Computer Systems Institute

Allentown, Pennsylvania
Two-year proprietary
Federal Code: 022552

College costs. Tuition for associate-degree program (15 months): $16,202. Books/supplies: $800.

Undergraduate aid. **Need-based:** Need-based aid available for full-time and part-time students.

Application procedures. FAFSA required. No deadline. Applicants notified on rolling basis.

Contact. 2201 Hangar Place
Allentown, PA 18103

Juniata College

Huntingdon, Pennsylvania
www.juniata.edu
Four-year private **Federal Code: 003279**

	Living at home	On-campus
Tuition and fees:	$22,760	$22,760
Room and board:		$6,290
Board only:	$1,650	
Books and supplies:	$450	$450
Transportation:	$600	$250

Undergraduate aid. **Need-based:** Average financial aid package for full-time students was $17,938. 76% awarded as scholarships/grants, 24% as loans/jobs. Need-based aid available for part-time students. **Non-need-based:** 59% awarded as scholarships/grants, 41% as loans/jobs. Scholarships based on academics, alumni affiliation, art, leadership, minority status, music/drama, religious affiliation, state/district residency. **Student debt:** 78% of graduating class borrowed to fund education; average debt was $16,553.

Freshman aid. **Need-based:** Out of 374 full-time freshmen, 335 applied for aid; 289 were judged to have need; of these 289 received aid. Average package met 93% of need. 175 students had full need met. Average scholarship/grant was $14,651; average loan $2,965. **Non-need based:** 270 full-time freshmen with need received non-need scholarships; 45 without need received awards.

Merit scholarships. arts scholarships, environmental responsibility scholarships, leadership scholarships, service and peacemaking scholarships: each awarding 1 full tuition, room and board, 2 full tuition, nominated by alumni; friendship scholarships: $2,000 awarded to international student; Calvert Ellis scholarships: $10,000-12,000 for high high school GPA or SAT scores; Juniata Presidential scholarships: $7,500-9,500 for high high school GPA or SAT scores; Juniata transfer scholarships: $8,500 for a transfer student member of Phi Theta Kappa from a 2-year college; JC transfer scholarships: $5,000-7,000 for 2-year college transfers with high GPA; Juniata PAR (program for area residents) scholarships: half tuition for area residents (non-traditional and others); Frederick & Mary Beckley scholarship: for a left-handed student; Richard M. Simpson scholarship: $11,000 for a Pennsylvania resident with high grades; North American Indian scholarship: (need-based) up to $10,000 for a Native American; Ray Day scholarship: up to $5,000 for a minority student; John & Irene Dale scholarship: $3,000 for an information technology student; Robert Steele Memorial scholarship: (need-based) up to $4,000 for a medical/science student; Metz scholarship: up to $5,000 for intended major in business/economics; Anna Groninger Smith Memorial scholarship: (need-based) up to $4,000 for a woman in business studies; W & M Donham scholarships: up to $2,000 for New England residents majoring in business/economics; Alumni scholarships: up to $5,000 for children of alumni; Church of the Brethren scholarships: up to $5,000 for Church of the Brethren members in various majors; Dorothy Baker Johnson Memorial scholarship: up to $4,000 for women aiming for careers that will require an advanced degree; Charles & Floretta Gibson scholarships: (need-based) for excellent character; Sam Hayes Jr. scholarship: (need-based) up to $1,500 for a Pennsylvania FFA or 4H member

Policies to reduce costs. Tuition/fee waivers for adults, senior citizens, employees and their families. Credit/placement for qualifying scores on AP, IB examinations.

Payment plans. Installment payment.

Application procedures. FAFSA, CSS PROFILE required. Priority date 3/1; no closing date. Applicants notified on rolling basis starting 12/1, must reply within 2 week(s) of notification. Early decision closing date 11/15. **Transfers:** Juniata Transfer Scholarships; Juniata PhiTheta Kappa Transfer Scholarship.

Contact. **Financial aid office:** (814) 641-3142
Randall Rennell, Director of Student Financial Planning
18th and Moore Streets
Huntingdon, PA 16652

Keystone College

La Plume, Pennsylvania
www.keystone.edu
Four-year private **Federal Code: 003280**

	Living at home	On-campus
Tuition and fees:	$13,850	$13,850
Room and board:		$7,400
Board only:	$1,500	
Books and supplies:	$800	$800
Personal expenses:	$1,500	$1,000
Transportation:	$1,500	$500

Undergraduate aid. **Need-based:** Average financial aid package for full-time students was $17,100; for part-time $2,500. 74% awarded as scholarships/grants, 26% as loans/jobs. **Non-need-based:** 7% awarded as scholarships/grants, 93% as loans/jobs. Scholarships based on academics, art, job skills, leadership. **Student debt:** 93% of graduating class borrowed to fund education; average debt was $16,125.

Freshman aid. **Need-based:** Out of 411 full-time freshmen, 312 applied for aid; 312 were judged to have need; of these 307 received aid. Average package met 87% of need. 268 students had full need met. Average scholarship/grant was $12,500; average loan $2,625. **Non-need based:** 98 full-time freshmen with need received non-need scholarships; 8 without need received awards.

Merit scholarships. Academic Excellence Scholarship offers one-half tuition up to full tuition to all full-time, first-time students in the top 5% of their class with SAT scores of 1100 or above. Presidential Scholarship of up to $7,000 each year based on class rank and SAT/ACT scores. Trustee Scholarship of up to $6,000 each year based on class rank and SAT/ACT scores. Leadership Award of up to $4,000 each year to students demonstrating non-athletic leadership skills in high school.

Policies to reduce costs. Tuition/fee waivers for adults, children of alumni, senior citizens, family members, employees and their families. Credit/placement for qualifying scores on AP, IB, CLEP examinations. Work study available nights, weekends and for part-time students.

Payment plans. Installment payment.

Application procedures. FAFSA required. Priority date 5/1; no closing date. Applicants notified on rolling basis starting 2/1, must reply by 5/1 or within 3 week(s) of notification. **Transfers:** Priority date 5/1; closing date 8/1.

Contact. **Financial aid office:** (570) 945-6955
Ginger Kline, Director of Financial Aid
One College Green
La Plume, PA 18440-1099

King's College

Wilkes-Barre, Pennsylvania
www.kings.edu
Four-year private **Federal Code: 003282**

	Living at home	On-campus
Tuition and fees:	$19,060	$19,060
Room and board:		$7,930
Board only:	$2,050	
Books and supplies:	$850	$850
Personal expenses:	$2,000	$1,500
Transportation:	$950	$450

Undergraduate aid. Need-based: Average financial aid package for full-time students was $13,626; for part-time $4,651. 74% awarded as scholarships/grants, 26% as loans/jobs. **Non-need-based:** 37% awarded as scholarships/grants, 63% as loans/jobs. Scholarships based on academics, leadership. **Student debt:** 82% of graduating class borrowed to fund education; average debt was $16,000. **Additional information:** Most minority students receive some King's aid in the form of a diversity scholarship.

Freshman aid. Need-based: Out of 409 full-time freshmen, 385 applied for aid; 348 were judged to have need; of these 346 received aid. Average package met 76% of need. 72 students had full need met. Average scholarship/grant was $6,814; average loan $3,219. **Non-need based:** 234 full-time freshmen with need received non-need scholarships; 43 without need received awards.

Policies to reduce costs. Tuition/fee waivers for senior citizens, family members, employees and their families. Credit/placement for qualifying scores on AP, IB, CLEP examinations. Work study available nights, weekends and for part-time students.

Payment plans. Credit card, installment, deferred payment.

Application procedures. FAFSA, institutional form required. Priority date 2/15; no closing date. Applicants notified on rolling basis starting 3/1, must reply within 2 week(s) of notification. **Transfers:** No deadline.

Contact. **Financial aid office:** (570) 208-5868
Ellen McGuire, Director of Financial Aid
133 North River Street
Wilkes-Barre, PA 18711

Kutztown University of Pennsylvania

Kutztown, Pennsylvania
www.kutztown.edu
Four-year public **Federal Code: 003322**

	Living at home	On-campus
Tuition and fees (2002-2003):	$5,477	$5,477
Out-of-state:	$12,045	$12,045
Room and board:		$4,682
Books and supplies:	$800	$800
Personal expenses:	$1,750	$1,750
Transportation:	$1,352	

Undergraduate aid. Need-based: Average financial aid package for full-time students was $5,831; for part-time $3,505. 44% awarded as scholarships/grants, 56% as loans/jobs. **Non-need-based:** 8% awarded as scholarships/grants, 92% as loans/jobs. Scholarships based on academics, alumni affiliation, art, athletics, leadership, minority status, music/drama, state/district residency. **Student debt:** 75% of graduating class borrowed to fund education; average debt was $13,978.

Freshman aid. Need-based: Out of 1,692 full-time freshmen, 1,414 applied for aid; 924 were judged to have need; of these 924 received aid. Average package met 70% of need. 658 students had full need met. Average scholarship/grant was $3,816; average loan $2,350. **Non-need based:** 68 full-time freshmen with need received non-need scholarships; 94 without need received awards; 16 received athletic scholarships.

Policies to reduce costs. Tuition/fee waivers for minority students, employees and their families. Credit/placement for qualifying scores on AP, IB, CLEP examinations. Work study available nights, weekends and for part-time students.

Payment plans. Credit card, installment, deferred payment.

Application procedures. FAFSA required. Priority date 2/15; no closing date. Applicants notified on rolling basis starting 3/30.

Contact. **Financial aid office:** (610) 683-4077
Anita Faust, Director of Financial Aid
Admissions Center
Kutztown, PA 19530-0730

La Roche College

Pittsburgh, Pennsylvania
www.laroche.edu
Four-year private **Federal Code: 003987**

	Living at home	On-campus
Tuition and fees:	$15,620	$15,620
Room and board:		$6,474
Board only:	$2,464	
Books and supplies:	$800	$800
Personal expenses:	$900	$900
Transportation:	$400	$400

Undergraduate aid. Need-based: Average financial aid package for full-time students was $11,750. 51% awarded as scholarships/grants, 49% as loans/jobs. **Non-need-based:** 64% awarded as scholarships/grants, 36% as loans/jobs. Scholarships based on academics.

Freshman aid. Need-based: Out of 295 full-time freshmen, 212 applied for aid; 182 were judged to have need; of these 182 received aid. Average package met 90% of need. 118 students had full need met. Average scholarship/grant was $2,000; average loan $3,000. **Non-need based:** 182 full-time freshmen with need received non-need scholarships; 69 without need received awards.

Policies to reduce costs. Tuition/fee waivers for employees and their families. Credit/placement for qualifying scores on AP, CLEP examinations.

Payment plans. Credit card, installment, deferred payment.

Application procedures. FAFSA, institutional form required. Priority date 3/1; closing date 5/1. Applicants notified on rolling basis starting 3/1, must reply within 2 week(s) of notification.

Contact. **Financial aid office:** (412) 536-1120
John Matsko, Director of Financial Aid
9000 Babcock Boulevard
Pittsburgh, PA 15237

La Salle University

Philadelphia, Pennsylvania
www.lasalle.edu
Four-year private **Federal Code: 003287**

	Living at home	On-campus
Tuition and fees:	$22,960	$22,960
Room and board:		$8,200
Books and supplies:	$500	$500
Personal expenses:	$2,000	$1,000

Undergraduate aid. Need-based: Average financial aid package for full-time students was $15,519; for part-time $6,122. **Non-need-based:** Scholarships based on academics, athletics. **Student debt:** 71% of graduating class borrowed to fund education; average debt was $15,528.

Freshman aid. Need-based: Average scholarship/grant was $12,999; average loan $2,910.

Merit scholarships. Christian Brothers Scholarship: full tuition, based on academics and extracurricular leadership. Community Service Scholarship: half tuition, based on involvement in community service and academics. Mission Grant: $4,000, for graduate of Catholic high school, 2.75 GPA or ranked in top 50% of class.

Policies to reduce costs. Tuition/fee waivers for family of clergy, employees and their families. Credit/placement for qualifying scores on AP, CLEP examinations. Work study available nights and weekends.

Payment plans. Credit card, installment, deferred payment.

Application procedures. FAFSA required. Priority date 2/15; no closing date. Applicants notified on rolling basis starting 11/15. **Transfers:** Priority date 2/15.

Contact. Michael Wisnieski, Director of Financial Aid
1900 West Olney Avenue
Philadelphia, PA 19141-1199

Lackawanna College

Scranton, Pennsylvania
www.lackawanna.edu
Two-year private **Federal Code: 003283**

	Living at home
Tuition and fees (2002-2003):	$8,800
Per-credit charge:	$280
Books and supplies:	$832
Personal expenses:	$4,126

Undergraduate aid. Need-based: Average financial aid package for full-time students was $6,153; for part-time $3,075. 45% awarded as scholarships/grants, 55% as loans/jobs. **Non-need-based:** Scholarships based on academics, athletics, leadership. **Student debt:** 82% of graduating class borrowed to fund education; average debt was $8,625.

Freshman aid. Need-based: Out of 231 full-time freshmen, 222 applied for aid; 202 were judged to have need; of these 195 received aid. Average package met 52% of need. 1 students had full need met. Average scholarship/grant was $3,933; average loan $2,830. **Non-need based:** 16 full-time freshmen with need received non-need scholarships; 2 without need received awards; 1 received athletic scholarships.

Policies to reduce costs. Tuition/fee waivers for senior citizens, family members, employees and their families. Credit/placement for qualifying scores on CLEP examinations.

Payment plans. Credit card, installment, deferred payment.

Application procedures. FAFSA, institutional form required. Priority date 5/1; no closing date. Applicants notified on rolling basis starting 5/1. **Transfers:** No deadline.

Contact. Financial aid office: (570) 961-7859
Babara Hapeman, Director of Financial Aid
501 Vine Street
Scranton, PA 18509

Lafayette College

Easton, Pennsylvania
www.lafayette.edu
Four-year private **Federal Code: 003284**

	Living at home	On-campus
Tuition and fees:	$27,328	$27,328
Room and board:		$8,418
Books and supplies:	$600	$600
Personal expenses:	$1,500	$925
Transportation:		$100

Undergraduate aid. Need-based: Average financial aid package for full-time students was $20,609; for part-time $4,391. 85% awarded as scholarships/grants, 15% as loans/jobs. **Non-need-based:** 49% awarded as scholarships/grants, 51% as loans/jobs. Scholarships based on academics, leadership, state/district residency. **Student debt:** 46% of graduating class borrowed to fund education; average debt was $17,380. **Additional information:** Parent loans, of up to $7,500 annually, are available with college absorbing interest while student is enrolled. Family has 8 years after graduation to repay. Not limited to those demonstrating need.

Freshman aid. Need-based: Out of 580 full-time freshmen, 405 applied for aid; 337 were judged to have need; of these 332 received aid. Average package met 97% of need. 326 students had full need met. Average scholarship/grant was $18,947; average loan $2,777. **Non-need based:** 59 full-time freshmen with need received non-need scholarships; 57 without need received awards.

Merit scholarships. Marquis Scholarships, $12,500 annually, based on academic merit, 60 awarded (per class). Trustee Scholarship, $7,500 annually, based on academic merit, 32 awarded (per class).

Policies to reduce costs. Tuition/fee waivers for employees and their families. Prepayment discount; credit/placement for qualifying scores on AP examinations.

Payment plans. Installment, deferred payment.

Application procedures. FAFSA, CSS PROFILE required. Closing date 2/1. Applicants notified on rolling basis starting 3/15, must reply by 5/1. Early decision closing date 11/1. **Transfers:** Closing date 6/1.

Contact. Arlina DeNardo, Director of Student Financial Aid
118 Markle Hall
Easton, PA 18042-1770

Lancaster Bible College

Lancaster, Pennsylvania
www.lbc.edu
Four-year private **Federal Code: 003285**

	Living at home	On-campus
Tuition and fees (2002-2003):	$10,775	$10,775
Room and board:		$5,010
Books and supplies:	$700	$700
Personal expenses:	$1,750	$1,750
Transportation:	$1,050	$750

Undergraduate aid. Need-based: Average financial aid package for full-time students was $7,969; for part-time $5,644. 58% awarded as scholarships/grants, 42% as loans/jobs. **Non-need-based:** 13% awarded as scholarships/grants, 87% as loans/jobs. Scholarships based on academics, alumni affiliation, leadership, music/drama, state/district residency. **Student debt:** 75% of graduating class borrowed to fund education; average debt was $13,409.

Freshman aid. Need-based: Out of 131 full-time freshmen, 127 applied for aid; 102 were judged to have need; of these 101 received aid. Average package met 60% of need. 6 students had full need met. Average scholarship/grant was $5,165; average loan $2,705. **Non-need based:** 57 full-time freshmen with need received non-need scholarships; 22 without need received awards.

Merit scholarships. Child of Full-time Christian Worker Scholarship is available to dependent students where major wage earner or head of household is in full-time Christian work. Scholarship is 50 percent reduction in tuition, room and board. The reduction includes federal and state aid and other institutional scholarships. Remainder of reduction paid by school.

Policies to reduce costs. Tuition/fee waivers for children of alumni, senior citizens, family members, family of clergy, employees and their families. Prepayment discount; credit/placement for qualifying scores on AP, CLEP examinations. Work study available nights, weekends and for part-time students.

Payment plans. Credit card, installment payment.

Application procedures. FAFSA, institutional form required. Priority date 5/2; no closing date. Applicants notified on rolling basis starting 3/15, must reply within 3 week(s) of notification.

Contact. Financial aid office: (717) 560-8254
Karen Fox, Director of Financial Aid
901 Eden Road
Lancaster, PA 17608-3403

Lebanon Valley College of Pennsylvania

Annville, Pennsylvania
www.lvc.edu
Four-year private **Federal Code: 003288**

	Living at home	On-campus
Tuition and fees:	$20,660	$20,660
Room and board:		$6,110
Board only:	$1,280	
Books and supplies:	$700	$700
Personal expenses:	$610	
Transportation:	$730	

Undergraduate aid. Need-based: Average financial aid package for full-time students was $16,144; for part-time $2,250. 72% awarded as scholarships/grants, 28% as loans/jobs. **Non-need-based:** 47% awarded as scholarships/grants, 53% as loans/jobs. Scholarships based on academics, alumni affiliation, music/drama. **Student debt:** 74% of graduating class borrowed to fund education; average debt was $19,686.

Freshman aid. Need-based: Out of 425 full-time freshmen, 383 applied for aid; 340 were judged to have need; of these 340 received aid. Average package met 81% of need. 92 students had full need met. Average scholarship/grant was $5,541; average loan $3,157. **Non-need based:** 291 full-time freshmen with need received non-need scholarships; 68 without need received awards.

Merit scholarships. Vickroy scholarship; half tuition; automatic for admitted applicants in top 10% of graduating class. Leadership scholarship; one-third tuition; automatic for admitted applicants in top 20% of graduating class. Achievement scholarship; one-quarter tuition; automatic for admitted applicants in top 30% of graduating class. Students with SAT scores of 1100+ may interview for any of the academic scholarships.

Policies to reduce costs. Tuition/fee waivers for children of alumni, employees and their families. Credit/placement for qualifying scores on AP, IB, CLEP examinations. Work study available nights and weekends.

Payment plans. Credit card, installment payment.

Application procedures. FAFSA, institutional form required. Priority date 3/1; no closing date. Applicants notified on rolling basis starting 3/1, must reply by 5/1 or within 2 week(s) of notification.

Contact. Financial aid office: (717) 867-6126
Jennifer Liedtka, Director, Financial Aid
101 North College Avenue
Annville, PA 17003

Lehigh Carbon Community College

Schnecksville, Pennsylvania
www.lccc.edu
Two-year public **Federal Code: 006810**

	Living at home
Tuition and fees:	$2,475
Out-of-district:	$4,635
Out-of-state:	$6,795
Per-credit charge:	$72
Per-credit out-of-district:	$144
Per-credit out-of-state:	$216
Board only:	$1,000
Books and supplies:	$1,200
Personal expenses:	$700
Transportation:	$1,300

Undergraduate aid. Need-based: 69% awarded as scholarships/grants, 31% as loans/jobs. Need-based aid available for part-time students. **Non-need-based:** 12% awarded as scholarships/grants, 88% as loans/jobs. Scholarships based on academics, athletics, leadership, state/district residency.

Policies to reduce costs. Tuition/fee waivers for employees and their families. Credit/placement for qualifying scores on AP, CLEP examinations. Work study available nights and for part-time students.

Payment plans. Credit card, installment payment.

Application procedures. FAFSA required. Closing date 5/2. Applicants notified on rolling basis starting 5/2, must reply within 2 week(s) of notification. **Transfers:** Closing date 5/3.

Contact. Financial aid office: (610) 799-1133
Marian Snyder, Director of Financial Aid
4525 Education Park Drive
Schnecksville, PA 18078

Lehigh University

Bethlehem, Pennsylvania
www.lehigh.edu
Four-year private **Federal Code: 003289**

College costs. Additional $250 fee for engineering students.

	Living at home	On-campus
Tuition and fees:	$27,430	$27,430
Room and board:		$7,400
Board only:	$2,730	
Books and supplies:	$800	$800
Personal expenses:	$1,210	$1,210

Undergraduate aid. Need-based: Average financial aid package for full-time students was $22,737; for part-time $14,388. 73% awarded as scholarships/grants, 27% as loans/jobs. **Non-need-based:** 39% awarded as scholarships/grants, 61% as loans/jobs. Scholarships based on academics, art, athletics, leadership, music/drama. **Student debt:** 52% of graduating class borrowed to fund education; average debt was $16,972.

Freshman aid. Need-based: Out of 1,144 full-time freshmen, 667 applied for aid; 497 were judged to have need; of these 495 received aid. Average package met 99% of need. 211 students had full need met. Average scholarship/grant was $15,870; average loan $3,174. **Non-need based:** 61 full-time freshmen with need received non-need scholarships; 81 without need received awards; 7 received athletic scholarships.

Merit scholarships. Dean's Scholarships for $10,000 per year for students who excel academically and demonstrate leadership skills. Baker Scholarship for $2,500 per year for students who demonstrate excellence in music or theater and have a superior academic record. Choral Arts Scholarships for $2,500 for students with singing talent. President's Scholarships for full tuition for fifth year of study for seniors with 3.5 GPA and minimum 90 credits completed at institution.

Policies to reduce costs. Tuition/fee waivers for employees and their families. Credit/placement for qualifying scores on AP, IB examinations.

Payment plans. Installment payment.

Application procedures. FAFSA, CSS PROFILE required. Applicants notified by 3/30, must reply by 5/1 or within 3 week(s) of notification. Early decision closing date 11/15. **Transfers:** Closing date 4/15.

Contact. Financial aid office: (610) 758-3181
William Stanford, Director of Financial Aid
27 Memorial Drive West
Bethlehem, PA 18015-3094

Lincoln University

Lincoln University, Pennsylvania
www.lincoln.edu
Four-year public **Federal Code: 003290**

College costs. Additional $458 required fees for out-of-state students.

	Living at home	On-campus
Tuition and fees (2002-2003):	$6,094	$6,094
Out-of-state:	$9,074	$9,074
Room and board:		$5,584
Books and supplies:	$350	$350
Personal expenses:	$900	$915
Transportation:	$500	$500

Undergraduate aid. Need-based: Average financial aid package for full-time students was $11,000; for part-time $4,000. 45% awarded as scholarships/grants, 55% as loans/jobs. **Non-need-based:** 35% awarded as scholarships/grants, 65% as loans/jobs. Scholarships based on academics, alumni affiliation, leadership, music/drama. **Student debt:** 75% of graduating class borrowed to fund education; average debt was $22,000.

Freshman aid. Need-based: Out of 475 full-time freshmen, 452 applied for aid; 430 were judged to have need; of these 430 received aid. Average package met 85% of need. 344 students had full need met. Average scholarship/grant was $5,500; average loan $2,625. **Non-need based:** 65 full-time freshmen with need received non-need scholarships; 48 without need received awards.

Policies to reduce costs. Tuition/fee waivers for children of alumni, employees and their families. Credit/placement for qualifying scores on AP, IB examinations. Work study available nights, weekends and for part-time students.

Payment plans. Credit card, installment payment.

Application procedures. FAFSA required. Closing date 5/1. Applicants notified on rolling basis starting 4/1, must reply within 2 week(s) of notification.

Contact. Financial aid office: (800) 561-2606
Shirley Silva-Paige, Director of Financial Aid
Lincoln Hall
Lincoln University, PA 19352-0999

Lock Haven University of Pennsylvania

Lock Haven, Pennsylvania
www.lhup.edu
Four-year public **Federal Code: 003323**

	Living at home	On-campus
Tuition and fees (2002-2003):	$5,606	$5,606
Out-of-state:	$10,174	$10,174
Room and board:		$4,744
Books and supplies:	$700	$700
Personal expenses:	$1,338	$1,498

Undergraduate aid. Need-based: Average financial aid package for full-time students was $5,965; for part-time $2,200. 48% awarded as scholarships/grants, 52% as loans/jobs. **Non-need-based:** 8% awarded as scholarships/

grants, 92% as loans/jobs. Scholarships based on academics, alumni affiliation, art, athletics, leadership, minority status, music/drama, state/district residency. **Student debt:** 74% of graduating class borrowed to fund education; average debt was $16,742.

Freshman aid. Need-based: Out of 1,101 full-time freshmen, 1,060 applied for aid; 978 were judged to have need; of these 978 received aid. Average package met 73% of need. 469 students had full need met. Average scholarship/grant was $3,900; average loan $2,500. **Non-need based:** 180 full-time freshmen with need received non-need scholarships; 118 without need received awards; 55 received athletic scholarships.

Policies to reduce costs. Tuition/fee waivers for senior citizens, minority students, employees and their families. Credit/placement for qualifying scores on AP, IB, CLEP examinations.

Payment plans. Installment payment.

Application procedures. FAFSA, institutional form required. Priority date 3/15; no closing date. Applicants notified on rolling basis starting 3/1, must reply by 5/1 or within 2 week(s) of notification. **Transfers:** Priority date 4/1; no deadline.

Contact. **Financial aid office:** (877) 405-3057
William Irwin, Director of Financial Aid
Akeley Hall
Lock Haven, PA 17745

Luzerne County Community College

Nanticoke, Pennsylvania
www.luzerne.edu
Two-year public **Federal Code: 006811**

	Living at home
Tuition and fees (2002-2003):	$2,280
Out-of-district:	$4,290
Out-of-state:	$6,300
Per-credit charge:	$67
Per-credit out-of-district:	$134
Per-credit out-of-state:	$201
Books and supplies:	$600
Personal expenses:	$625
Transportation:	$500

Undergraduate aid. Need-based: Need-based aid available for full-time and part-time students.

Policies to reduce costs. Tuition/fee waivers for senior citizens, employees and their families. Credit/placement for qualifying scores on AP, CLEP examinations.

Payment plans. Credit card, installment payment.

Application procedures. FAFSA, institutional form required. Priority date 4/15; no closing date. Applicants notified on rolling basis starting 7/1. **Transfers:** No deadline.

Contact. **Financial aid office:** (570) 740-0395
Mary Kosin, Director of Financial Aid
1333 South Prospect Street
Nanticoke, PA 18634-9804

Lycoming College

Williamsport, Pennsylvania
www.lycoming.edu
Four-year private **Federal Code: 003293**

	Living at home	On-campus
Tuition and fees:	$21,523	$21,523
Room and board:		$5,866
Books and supplies:	$800	$800
Personal expenses:		$800
Transportation:		$600

Undergraduate aid. Need-based: Average financial aid package for full-time students was $16,676; for part-time $8,925. 75% awarded as scholarships/grants, 25% as loans/jobs. **Non-need-based:** 38% awarded as scholarships/grants, 62% as loans/jobs. Scholarships based on academics, art, music/drama. **Student debt:** 93% of graduating class borrowed to fund education; average debt was $15,200.

Freshman aid. Need-based: Out of 373 full-time freshmen, 360 applied for aid; 301 were judged to have need; of these 301 received aid. Average package met 80% of need. 56 students had full need met. Average scholarship/grant was $13,283; average loan $3,175. **Non-need based:** 33 full-time freshmen with need received non-need scholarships; 39 without need received awards.

Policies to reduce costs. Tuition/fee waivers for minority students, family members, family of clergy, employees and their families. Credit/placement for qualifying scores on AP, IB, CLEP examinations. Work study available nights, weekends and for part-time students.

Payment plans. Installment payment.

Application procedures. FAFSA, institutional form required. Priority date 4/15; closing date 5/1. Applicants notified on rolling basis starting 3/15, must reply by 5/1 or within 4 week(s) of notification. **Transfers:** Priority date 4/15; no deadline.

Contact. **Financial aid office:** (570) 321-4040
Wendy Mahonski, Director of Financial Aid
700 College Place
Williamsport, PA 17701

Manor College

Jenkintown, Pennsylvania
www.manor.edu
Two-year private **Federal Code: 003294**

College costs. Tuition for allied health program is $10,130 per year, $315 per-credit-hour.

	Living at home	On-campus
Tuition and fees:	$10,110	$10,110
Per-credit charge:	$220	$220
Room and board:		$4,900
Board only:	$1,348	
Books and supplies:	$564	$564
Personal expenses:	$1,124	$787
Transportation:	$2,244	$860

Undergraduate aid. All financial aid based on need. Average financial aid package for full-time students was $6,525; for part-time $3,072. 59% awarded as scholarships/grants, 41% as loans/jobs. **Student debt:** 92% of graduating class borrowed to fund education; average debt was $6,625.

Freshman aid. Out of 152 full-time freshmen, 132 applied for aid; 120 were judged to have need; of these 120 received aid. Average package met 40% of need. 36 students had full need met. Average scholarship/grant was $3,500; average loan $2,625.

Policies to reduce costs. Tuition/fee waivers for senior citizens, family of clergy, employees and their families. Credit/placement for qualifying scores on AP, CLEP examinations. Work study available nights, weekends and for part-time students.

Payment plans. Credit card, installment, deferred payment.

Application procedures. FAFSA, institutional form required. Priority date 5/2; no closing date. Applicants notified on rolling basis starting 3/2, must reply within 2 week(s) of notification. **Transfers:** No deadline. Require a financial aid transcript and academic transcript prior to packaging financial aid.

Contact. I. Jerry Czenstuch, Director of Financial Aid
700 Fox Chase Road
Jenkintown, PA 19046

Marywood University

Scranton, Pennsylvania
www.marywood.edu
Four-year private **Federal Code: 003296**

	Living at home	On-campus
Tuition and fees:	$19,300	$19,300
Room and board:		$8,134
Books and supplies:	$700	$700
Personal expenses:	$700	$700
Transportation:	$900	$500

Undergraduate aid. Need-based: Average financial aid package for full-time students was $17,000; for part-time $12,425. 53% awarded as scholarships/grants, 47% as loans/jobs. **Non-need-based:** 81% awarded as scholarships/grants, 19% as loans/jobs. Scholarships based on academics, alumni affiliation, art, leadership, minority status, music/drama.

Freshman aid. Need-based: Out of 310 full-time freshmen, 308 applied for aid; 294 were judged to have need; of these 294 received aid. Average package met 81% of need. 82 students had full need met. Average scholarship/

grant was $12,919; average loan $2,977. **Non-need based:** 46 without need received awards.

Merit scholarships. Presidential Scholarships, full tuition, for students with SAT scores of at least 1300 and rank in upper tenth of graduating class. IHM Scholarships for students with SAT scores of 1150 or more and rank in the upper fifth of high school class. Marywood grants for students with demonstrated academic ability. Talent awards for students who demonstrate proficency in music, art or theater and major in 1 of those areas. Other non-need-based merit scholarships available. See Web site.

Policies to reduce costs. Tuition/fee waivers for senior citizens, family members, family of clergy, employees and their families. Credit/placement for qualifying scores on AP, IB, CLEP examinations. Work study available nights, weekends and for part-time students.

Payment plans. Credit card, installment, deferred payment.

Application procedures. FAFSA, institutional form required. Priority date 2/15; no closing date. Applicants notified on rolling basis starting 3/1, must reply by 5/1 or within 3 week(s) of notification.

Contact. Financial aid office: (570) 348-6225
Stanley Skrutski, Director of Financial Aid
2300 Adams Avenue
Scranton, PA 18509-1598

McCann School of Business: Pottsville

Pottsville, Pennsylvania
www.mccannschool.com
Two-year proprietary **Federal Code: 004898**

	Living at home
Tuition and fees (2002-2003):	$7,425

Contact. Joyce Zaleski, Financial Aid Director
2650 Woodglen Road
Pottsville, PA 17901

McCann School of Business: Sunbury

Sunbury, Pennsylvania
www.mccannschool.com
Two-year proprietary **Federal Code: 004898**

	Living at home
Tuition and fees (2002-2003):	$7,095
Per-credit charge:	$156

Contact. Joyce Zaleski, Financial Aid Director
225 Market Street ,Third Floor
Sunbury, PA 17801

Median School of Allied Health Careers

Pittsburgh, Pennsylvania
www.medianschool.com
Two-year proprietary **Federal Code: 008568**

College costs (2002-2003). Tuition and fees vary per program from $9,190 to $20,495. Additional charges vary per program from $460 to $1,845. Affiliated dorm charges $6,000. Board: $2,707. Books/supplies: $1,100. Personal expenses: $1,602. Transportation: $788.

Undergraduate aid. Non-need-based: Scholarships based on academics.

Merit scholarships. Five $1,000 scholarships, to commuters. Two $2,000 scholarships, to students not living at home. Scholarships are non-need, based on results of examination given at school in January and March.

Policies to reduce costs. Tuition at time of enrollment guaranteed for 2 years. Work study available nights and for part-time students.

Application procedures. FAFSA required. No deadline. Applicants notified on rolling basis. **Transfers:** No deadline. PHEAA state grant deadline is 0501 for prior recipients.

Contact. Financial aid office: (800) 570-0693
Donna Durr, Financial Aid Coordinator
125 Seventh Street
Pittsburgh, PA 15222-3400

Mercyhurst College

Erie, Pennsylvania
www.mercyhurst.edu
Four-year private **Federal Code: 003297**

	Living at home	On-campus
Tuition and fees (projected):	$16,980	$16,980
Room and board:		$6,414
Books and supplies:	$1,100	$1,100
Personal expenses:	$1,250	$1,000
Transportation:	$500	$300

Undergraduate aid. Need-based: Average financial aid package for full-time students was $12,165; for part-time $6,566. 45% awarded as scholarships/grants, 55% as loans/jobs. **Non-need-based:** 43% awarded as scholarships/grants, 57% as loans/jobs. Scholarships based on academics, art, athletics, leadership, minority status, music/drama, religious affiliation. **Student debt:** 95% of graduating class borrowed to fund education; average debt was $16,596.

Freshman aid. Need-based: Out of 1,119 full-time freshmen, 1,076 applied for aid; 898 were judged to have need; of these 898 received aid. Average package met 90% of need. 719 students had full need met. Average scholarship/grant was $7,736; average loan $2,442. **Non-need based:** 674 full-time freshmen with need received non-need scholarships; 22 without need received awards; 14 received athletic scholarships.

Policies to reduce costs. Tuition/fee waivers for adults, children of alumni, minority students, family members, unemployed or children of unemployed, employees and their families. Prepayment discount; credit/placement for qualifying scores on AP, IB, CLEP examinations. Work study available nights and weekends.

Payment plans. Credit card, installment payment.

Application procedures. FAFSA, institutional form required. Priority date 5/1; no closing date. Applicants notified on rolling basis starting 2/15, must reply by 5/1 or within 2 week(s) of notification. **Transfers:** No deadline.

Contact. Financial aid office: (814) 824-2471
Jim Theeuwes, Director of Financial Aid
501 East 38th Street
Erie, PA 16546-0001

Messiah College

Grantham, Pennsylvania
www.messiah.edu
Four-year private **Federal Code: 003298**

	Living at home	On-campus
Tuition and fees:	$19,550	$19,550
Room and board:		$6,340
Board only:	$2,960	
Books and supplies:	$740	$740
Personal expenses:	$1,100	$1,100
Transportation:	$580	$580

Undergraduate aid. Need-based: Average financial aid package for full-time students was $12,398; for part-time $8,531. 53% awarded as scholarships/grants, 47% as loans/jobs. **Non-need-based:** 56% awarded as scholarships/grants, 44% as loans/jobs. Scholarships based on academics, alumni affiliation, art, leadership, music/drama, religious affiliation. **Student debt:** 74% of graduating class borrowed to fund education; average debt was $16,885.

Freshman aid. Need-based: Out of 764 full-time freshmen, 665 applied for aid; 548 were judged to have need; of these 548 received aid. Average package met 72% of need. 98 students had full need met. Average scholarship/grant was $5,021; average loan $2,632. **Non-need based:** 459 full-time freshmen with need received non-need scholarships; 183 without need received awards.

Policies to reduce costs. Tuition/fee waivers for adults, children of alumni, senior citizens, minority students, family members, family of clergy, employees and their families. Credit/placement for qualifying scores on AP, IB, CLEP examinations. Work study available nights.

Payment plans. Credit card, installment payment.

Application procedures. FAFSA required. Priority date 4/1; no closing date. Applicants notified on rolling basis starting 3/15, must reply by 5/1 or within 4 week(s) of notification. Early decision closing date 10/15.

Contact. Financial aid office: (717) 691-6007
Greg Gearhart, Director of Financial Aid
One College Avenue
Grantham, PA 17027-0800

Metropolitan Career Center

Philadelphia, Pennsylvania
http://www.metropolitancareercenter.org
Two-year private **Federal Code: 031091**

College costs. Books and supplies included in cost of tuition.

	Living at home
Tuition and fees:	$8,490
Per-credit charge:	$274
Personal expenses:	$1,890

Undergraduate aid. Need-based: Need-based aid available for full-time and part-time students.

Application procedures. FAFSA required.

Contact. Financial aid office: (215) 568-9215 ext. 314
Rhonda Moore, Financial Aid Officer
100 South Broad Street, Suite 830
Philadelphia, PA 19110

Millersville University of Pennsylvania

Millersville, Pennsylvania
www.millersville.edu
Four-year public **Federal Code: 003325**

	Living at home	On-campus
Tuition and fees (2002-2003):	$5,547	$5,547
Out-of-state:	$12,115	$12,115
Room and board:		$5,230
Board only:	$1,254	
Books and supplies:	$700	$700
Personal expenses:	$1,047	$1,047
Transportation:	$700	$400

Undergraduate aid. Need-based: Average financial aid package for full-time students was $5,672; for part-time $4,027. 52% awarded as scholarships/grants, 48% as loans/jobs. **Non-need-based:** 16% awarded as scholarships/grants, 84% as loans/jobs. Scholarships based on academics, athletics, minority status. **Student debt:** 65% of graduating class borrowed to fund education; average debt was $11,092.

Freshman aid. Need-based: Out of 1,245 full-time freshmen, 1,049 applied for aid; 632 were judged to have need; of these 611 received aid. Average package met 81% of need. 142 students had full need met. Average scholarship/grant was $3,630; average loan $2,325. **Non-need based:** 163 full-time freshmen with need received non-need scholarships; 342 without need received awards; 30 received athletic scholarships.

Policies to reduce costs. Tuition/fee waivers for senior citizens, employees and their families. Credit/placement for qualifying scores on AP, CLEP examinations. Work study available nights, weekends and for part-time students.

Payment plans. Credit card, installment payment.

Application procedures. FAFSA required. Closing date 3/15. Applicants notified by 6/1, must reply within 2 week(s) of notification. **Transfers:** No deadline.

Contact. Financial aid office: (717) 872-3026
Kendra Feigert, Director of Financial Aid
PO Box 1002
Millersville, PA 17551-0302

Montgomery County Community College

Blue Bell, Pennsylvania
www.mc3.edu
Two-year public **Federal Code: 004452**

College costs. Required fees for out-of-county students $600; for out-of-state $900.

	Living at home
Tuition and fees (projected):	$2,640
Out-of-district:	$4,950
Out-of-state:	$7,260
Per-credit charge:	$78
Per-credit out-of-district:	$155
Per-credit out-of-state:	$232
Board only:	$1,830
Books and supplies:	$980

Undergraduate aid. Need-based: Average financial aid package for full-time students was $2,117; for part-time $1,368. 73% awarded as scholarships/grants, 27% as loans/jobs. **Non-need-based:** Scholarships based on academics. **Student debt:** 10% of graduating class borrowed to fund education; average debt was $4,458.

Freshman aid. Need-based: Out of 1,571 full-time freshmen, 666 applied for aid; 449 were judged to have need; of these 327 received aid. Average package met 18% of need. 24 students had full need met. Average scholarship/grant was $1,580; average loan $1,159. **Non-need based:** 34 full-time freshmen with need received non-need scholarships; 59 without need received awards.

Policies to reduce costs. Tuition/fee waivers for senior citizens, employees and their families. Credit/placement for qualifying scores on AP, CLEP examinations. Work study available nights, weekends and for part-time students.

Payment plans. Credit card, installment payment.

Application procedures. FAFSA, institutional form required. Closing date 5/1. Applicants notified on rolling basis starting 2/1. **Transfers:** Priority date 5/1; no deadline.

Contact. Cindy Haney, Director of Financial Aid
340 DeKalb Pike
Blue Bell, PA 19422-0758

Moravian College

Bethlehem, Pennsylvania
www.moravian.edu
Four-year private **Federal Code: 003301**

	Living at home	On-campus
Tuition and fees:	$22,058	$22,058
Room and board:		$7,095
Board only:	$2,600	
Books and supplies:	$700	$700
Personal expenses:	$1,630	$1,270
Transportation:	$1,710	$400

Undergraduate aid. Need-based: Average financial aid package for full-time students was $15,199; for part-time $10,884. 63% awarded as scholarships/grants, 37% as loans/jobs. **Non-need-based:** 32% awarded as scholarships/grants, 68% as loans/jobs. Scholarships based on academics, alumni affiliation, leadership, minority status, music/drama, religious affiliation.

Freshman aid. Need-based: Out of 317 full-time freshmen, 276 applied for aid; 235 were judged to have need; of these 235 received aid. Average package met 84% of need. 53 students had full need met. Average scholarship/grant was $12,616; average loan $3,251. **Non-need based:** 32 full-time freshmen with need received non-need scholarships; 70 without need received awards.

Merit scholarships. Comenius Scholarship: ranging from $8,000 to full-tuition. Founders Scholarship: $2,000-$8,000, for top 25%, 1150 SAT. Trustee Scholarship: $7,000-10,000, must be National Honor Society member and in top 20% of class. Other scholarships available for minority students specifically.

Policies to reduce costs. Tuition/fee waivers for children of alumni, minority students, family of clergy, employees and their families. Credit/placement for qualifying scores on AP, IB, CLEP examinations. Work study available nights and weekends.

Payment plans. Installment payment.

Application procedures. FAFSA, CSS PROFILE required. Priority date 2/15; closing date 3/15. Applicants notified by 4/1, must reply by 5/1 or within 2 week(s) of notification. Early decision closing date 2/1. **Transfers:** Priority date 4/1; no deadline.

Contact. **Financial aid office:** (610) 861-1330
Stephen Cassel, Director of Financial Aid
1200 Main Street
Bethlehem, PA 18018

Mount Aloysius College

Cresson, Pennsylvania
www.mtaloy.edu
Four-year private **Federal Code: 003302**

	Living at home	On-campus
Tuition and fees:	$15,280	$15,280
Room and board:		$5,700
Board only:	$1,500	
Books and supplies:	$1,400	$1,400
Personal expenses:	$2,750	$2,750

Undergraduate aid. Need-based: Average financial aid package for full-time students was $9,000. 52% awarded as scholarships/grants, 48% as loans/jobs. Need-based aid available for part-time students. **Non-need-based:** Scholarships based on academics, alumni affiliation, athletics, leadership, music/drama. **Student debt:** 90% of graduating class borrowed to fund education; average debt was $17,125.

Freshman aid. Need-based: Out of 279 full-time freshmen, 279 applied for aid; 269 were judged to have need; of these 269 received aid. Average package met 88% of need. Average scholarship/grant was $3,000. **Non-need based:** 10 full-time freshmen with need received non-need scholarships.

Policies to reduce costs. Tuition/fee waivers for children of alumni, family members, unemployed or children of unemployed. Credit/placement for qualifying scores on AP, CLEP examinations. Work study available nights and weekends.

Payment plans. Credit card, installment payment.

Application procedures. FAFSA required. Priority date 2/15; closing date 5/1. Applicants notified on rolling basis starting 2/15, must reply within 4 week(s) of notification. **Transfers:** No deadline.

Contact. **Financial aid office:** (814) 886-6357
Stacy Schenk, Financial Aid Director
7373 Admiral Peary Highway
Cresson, PA 16630

Muhlenberg College

Allentown, Pennsylvania
www.muhlenberg.edu
Four-year private **Federal Code: 003304**

	Living at home	On-campus
Tuition and fees:	$24,945	$24,945
Room and board:		$6,540
Board only:	$2,035	
Books and supplies:	$750	$750
Personal expenses:	$1,700	$1,700
Transportation:	$1,360	$300

Undergraduate aid. Need-based: Average financial aid package for full-time students was $16,023; for part-time $4,431. 78% awarded as scholarships/grants, 22% as loans/jobs. **Non-need-based:** 54% awarded as scholarships/grants, 46% as loans/jobs. Scholarships based on academics, music/drama. **Student debt:** 73% of graduating class borrowed to fund education; average debt was $16,848. **Additional information:** Merit scholarships for academic and extracurricular achievement.

Freshman aid. Need-based: Out of 549 full-time freshmen, 322 applied for aid; 235 were judged to have need; of these 235 received aid. Average package met 97% of need. 223 students had full need met. Average scholarship/grant was $12,819; average loan $2,971. **Non-need based:** 68 full-time freshmen with need received non-need scholarships; 182 without need received awards.

Merit scholarships. Presidential Scholarship for academic excellence: up to $10,000; Dana Associates Honors Program for academic excellence and critical thinking based on special application: $3,000; Muhlenberg Scholar Honors Program for academic excellence: $3,000; R.J. Fellows Honors Program for academic excellence and activism: $3,000.

Policies to reduce costs. Tuition/fee waivers for employees and their families. Prepayment discount; credit/placement for qualifying scores on AP, CLEP examinations.

Application procedures. FAFSA, institutional form, CSS PROFILE required. Closing date 2/15. Applicants notified by 4/1, must reply by 5/1. Early decision closing date 1/15. **Transfers:** Transfers awarded aid on a funds-available basis after returning students and freshmen have been served.

Contact. **Financial aid office:** (484) 664-3175
Gregory Mitton, Director of Financial Aid
2400 West Chew Street
Allentown, PA 18104

Neumann College

Aston, Pennsylvania
www.neumann.edu
Four-year private **Federal Code: 003988**

	Living at home	On-campus
Tuition and fees:	$16,410	$16,410
Room and board:		$7,480
Board only:	$3,080	
Books and supplies:	$1,300	$1,300
Personal expenses:	$2,000	$1,700
Transportation:	$900	$500

Undergraduate aid. All financial aid based on need. Average financial aid package for full-time students was $15,000; for part-time $3,000. 53% awarded as scholarships/grants, 47% as loans/jobs. **Student debt:** 75% of graduating class borrowed to fund education; average debt was $17,000.

Freshman aid. Out of 370 full-time freshmen, 350 applied for aid; 350 were judged to have need; of these 350 received aid. Average scholarship/grant was $10,000; average loan $2,800.

Policies to reduce costs. Tuition/fee waivers for employees and their families. Credit/placement for qualifying scores on AP, CLEP examinations.

Payment plans. Credit card, installment, deferred payment.

Application procedures. FAFSA required. No deadline. Applicants notified on rolling basis.

Contact. **Financial aid office:** (610) 558-5520
Joseph Henderson, Director of Financial Aid
One Neumann Drive
Aston, PA 19014-1298

New Castle School of Trades

Pulaski, Pennsylvania
www.ncstrades.com
Two-year proprietary **Federal Code: 007780**

College costs. Figure given is for school's entire 15-month course of study.

	Living at home
Tuition and fees:	$13,090
Books and supplies:	$1,000

Undergraduate aid. Need-based: Need-based aid available for full-time and part-time students.

Contact. Trudy Sotter, Financial Aid
4164 US 422
Pulaski, PA 16143-9721

Newport Business Institute

Lower Burrell, Pennsylvania
www.newportbusiness.com
Two-year private **Federal Code: 004901**

	Living at home
Tuition and fees (projected):	$8,250
Books and supplies:	$825

Undergraduate aid. Need-based: Need-based aid available for full-time and part-time students. **Non-need-based:** Scholarships based on academics, leadership.

Policies to reduce costs. Tuition/fee waivers for employees and their families.

Payment plans. Credit card, installment payment.

Application procedures. FAFSA required. Closing date 5/1. Applicants notified on rolling basis starting 5/1.

Contact. Rosemary Leipertz, Director of Financial Aid
945 Greensburg Road
Lower Burrell, PA 15068

Newport Business Institute

Williamsport, Pennsylvania
www.newportbusiness.com
Two-year proprietary **Federal Code: 004914**

College costs. $600 per class.

	Living at home
Tuition and fees (2002-2003):	$7,575
Books and supplies:	$900

Application procedures. FAFSA required. No deadline. Applicants notified on rolling basis.

Contact. Susan Craigo, Assistant
941 West Third Street
Williamsport, PA 17701

Northampton County Area Community College

Bethlehem, Pennsylvania
www.northampton.edu
Two-year public **Federal Code: 007191**

College costs. In-district students pay a $18 fee per credit hour. In state (out of district) pay $42 fee per credit hour. Out of state pay $66 fee per credit hour.

	Living at home	On-campus
Tuition and fees (2002-2003):	$2,550	$2,550
Out-of-district:	$4,560	$4,560
Out-of-state:	$6,570	$6,570
Per-credit charge:	$67	$67
Per-credit out-of-district:	$134	$134
Per-credit out-of-state:	$201	$201
Room and board:		$5,204
Board only:	$2,381	
Books and supplies:	$1,000	$1,000
Personal expenses:	$1,550	$950

Undergraduate aid. All financial aid based on need. Average financial aid package for full-time students was $1,760; for part-time $880. 71% awarded as scholarships/grants, 29% as loans/jobs.

Policies to reduce costs. Tuition/fee waivers for senior citizens, unemployed or children of unemployed, employees and their families. Credit/placement for qualifying scores on AP, CLEP examinations. Work study available nights, weekends and for part-time students.

Payment plans. Credit card, installment payment.

Application procedures. FAFSA, institutional form required. Priority date 3/31; no closing date. Applicants notified on rolling basis starting 6/1, must reply within 2 week(s) of notification.

Contact. **Financial aid office:** (610) 861-5510
Cindy King, Director of Financial Aid
3835 Green Pond Road
Bethlehem, PA 18020

Oakbridge Academy of Arts

Lower Burrell, Pennsylvania
www.oakbridgeacademy.com
Two-year private **Federal Code: 015063**

	Living at home
Tuition and fees (projected):	$8,750
Books and supplies:	$1,000
Personal expenses:	$4,123

Undergraduate aid. All financial aid based on need. Need-based aid available for full-time and part-time students.

Policies to reduce costs. Tuition/fee waivers for employees and their families.

Application procedures. FAFSA required. Closing date 5/1. Applicants notified on rolling basis.

Contact. **Financial aid office:** (724) 335-5336
Melissa Mathobel, Financial Aid Director
1250 Greensburg Road
Lower Burrell, PA 15068

Orleans Technical Institute - Center City Campus

Philadelphia, Pennsylvania
Two-year private

College costs. Tuition for full associate program (28 months) $20,300.

	Living at home
Tuition and fees:	$8,875
Books and supplies:	$2,000

Undergraduate aid. **Need-based:** Need-based aid available for full-time and part-time students.

Policies to reduce costs. Tuition/fee waivers for employees and their families.

Payment plans. Credit card, installment payment.

Application procedures. FAFSA, institutional form required. No deadline. Applicants notified on rolling basis.

Contact. **Financial aid office:** (215) 854-1822
Financial Aid Director
1845 Walnut Street, 7th Floor
Philadelphia, PA 19103-4707

PJA School

Upper Darby, Pennsylvania
www.pjaschool.com
Two-year proprietary **Federal Code: 023013**

College costs. Books and materials included in cost of tuition.

	Living at home
Tuition and fees:	$7,930
Per-credit charge:	$245
Personal expenses:	$2,067
Transportation:	$607

Undergraduate aid. All financial aid based on need. Need-based aid available for full-time and part-time students. **Additional information:** PJA works with various funding agencies, including the Office of Vocational Rehabilitation, Delaware County Office of Employment and Training, Chester County Office of Employment and Training, Philadelphia Workforce Development Corporation, and Veteran's Administration. PJA also offers an interest-free payment plan.

Policies to reduce costs. Tuition at time of enrollment guaranteed for 2 years.

Payment plans. Installment payment.

Application procedures. FAFSA, institutional form required. No deadline. Applicants notified on rolling basis.

Contact. Mary Rose, Director of Financial Aid
7900 West Chester Pike
Upper Darby, PA 19082

Peirce College

Philadelphia, Pennsylvania
www.peirce.edu
Four-year private **Federal Code: 003309**

College costs. If student takes one course at a time, $100 technology fee per course.

	Living at home
Tuition and fees:	$11,800
Books and supplies:	$900
Personal expenses:	$1,500
Transportation:	$1,200

Undergraduate aid. All financial aid based on need. Average financial aid package for full-time students was $3,500; for part-time $2,000. 54% awarded as scholarships/grants, 46% as loans/jobs. **Student debt:** 80% of graduating class borrowed to fund education; average debt was $13,200.

Additional information: Tuition discounts available for full-time students employed as public servants.

Freshman aid. Out of 34 full-time freshmen, 26 applied for aid; 23 were judged to have need; of these 23 received aid. Average package met 26% of need. 26 students had full need met. Average scholarship/grant was $1,500; average loan $4,000.

Policies to reduce costs. Tuition/fee waivers for children of alumni, family members, employees and their families. Credit/placement for qualifying scores on AP, IB, CLEP examinations. Work study available for part-time students.

Payment plans. Credit card, installment, deferred payment.

Application procedures. FAFSA, institutional form required. Priority date 4/15; no closing date. Applicants notified on rolling basis, must reply within 3 week(s) of notification. **Transfers:** No deadline.

Contact. **Financial aid office:** (215) 670-9370
Lisa Gargiulo, Supervisor, Student Financial Services
1420 Pine Street
Philadelphia, PA 19102

Penn Commercial, Inc.

Washington, Pennsylvania
www.penn-commercial.com
Two-year proprietary **Federal Code: 004902**

College costs. Quoted costs are for computer management program. Tuition and fees range from $6,000 to $8,500 per academic year depending on program.

	Living at home
Tuition and fees (2002-2003):	$7,665
Per-credit charge:	$150
Books and supplies:	$945
Personal expenses:	$2,438

Contact. Jenny Slesh, Financial Aid Director
82 South Main Street
Washington, PA 15301

Penn State Abington

Abington, Pennsylvania
www.abington.psu.edu
Four-year public **Federal Code: 003329**

	Living at home
Tuition and fees (2002-2003):	$8,238
Out-of-state:	$12,596
Board only:	$1,800
Books and supplies:	$816
Personal expenses:	$1,854
Transportation:	$990

Undergraduate aid. Need-based: Average financial aid package for full-time students was $7,711; for part-time $7,298. 58% awarded as scholarships/grants, 42% as loans/jobs. **Non-need-based:** 24% awarded as scholarships/grants, 76% as loans/jobs. Scholarships based on academics, alumni affiliation, athletics, minority status. **Student debt:** 69% of graduating class borrowed to fund education; average debt was $17,900.

Freshman aid. Need-based: Out of 788 full-time freshmen, 642 applied for aid; 459 were judged to have need; of these 440 received aid. Average package met 63% of need. 19 students had full need met. Average scholarship/grant was $4,388; average loan $2,421. **Non-need based:** 58 full-time freshmen with need received non-need scholarships; 143 without need received awards.

Policies to reduce costs. Tuition/fee waivers for senior citizens, employees and their families. Credit/placement for qualifying scores on AP, IB, CLEP examinations.

Payment plans. Deferred payment.

Application procedures. FAFSA required. Priority date 2/15; no closing date. Applicants notified on rolling basis starting 2/15. **Transfers:** Priority date 4/15; no deadline. Schools required to obtain student aid information through National Student Loan Data System (NSLDS).

Contact. 106 Sutherland
Abington, PA 19001

Penn State Altoona

Altoona, Pennsylvania
www.aa.psu.edu
Four-year public **Federal Code: 003329**

	Living at home	On-campus
Tuition and fees (2002-2003):	$8,248	$8,248
Out-of-state:	$12,606	$12,606
Room and board:		$6,550
Board only:	$1,800	
Books and supplies:	$816	$816
Personal expenses:	$1,854	$2,016
Transportation:	$990	$378

Undergraduate aid. Need-based: Average financial aid package for full-time students was $9,909; for part-time $7,830. 52% awarded as scholarships/grants, 48% as loans/jobs. **Non-need-based:** 30% awarded as scholarships/grants, 70% as loans/jobs. Scholarships based on academics, alumni affiliation, athletics, minority status. **Student debt:** 69% of graduating class borrowed to fund education; average debt was $17,900.

Freshman aid. Need-based: Out of 1,344 full-time freshmen, 1,084 applied for aid; 838 were judged to have need; of these 819 received aid. Average package met 70% of need. 60 students had full need met. Average scholarship/grant was $3,950; average loan $2,660. **Non-need based:** 214 full-time freshmen with need received non-need scholarships; 208 without need received awards.

Policies to reduce costs. Tuition/fee waivers for senior citizens, employees and their families. Credit/placement for qualifying scores on AP, IB, CLEP examinations. Work study available nights and weekends.

Payment plans. Deferred payment.

Application procedures. FAFSA required. Priority date 2/15; no closing date. Applicants notified on rolling basis starting 2/15. **Transfers:** Priority date 4/15; no deadline. Schools required to obtain student aid information through National Student Loan Data System (NSLDS).

Contact. E108 E. Raymond Smith Building
Altoona, PA 16601-3760

Penn State Beaver

Monaca, Pennsylvania
www.br.psu.edu
Two-year public **Federal Code: 003329**

	Living at home	On-campus
Tuition and fees (2002-2003):	$8,130	$8,130
Out-of-state:	$12,380	$12,380
Per-credit charge:	$313	$313
Per-credit out-of-state:	$502	$502
Room and board:		$6,550
Board only:	$1,800	
Books and supplies:	$816	$816
Personal expenses:	$1,854	$2,016
Transportation:	$990	$378

Undergraduate aid. Need-based: Average financial aid package for full-time students was $8,541; for part-time $7,724. 54% awarded as scholarships/grants, 46% as loans/jobs. **Non-need-based:** 37% awarded as scholarships/grants, 63% as loans/jobs. Scholarships based on academics, alumni affiliation, athletics, minority status. **Student debt:** 69% of graduating class borrowed to fund education; average debt was $17,900.

Freshman aid. Need-based: Out of 274 full-time freshmen, 224 applied for aid; 181 were judged to have need; of these 177 received aid. Average package met 68% of need. 10 students had full need met. Average scholarship/grant was $3,832; average loan $2,455. **Non-need based:** 35 full-time freshmen with need received non-need scholarships; 38 without need received awards.

Policies to reduce costs. Tuition/fee waivers for senior citizens, employees and their families. Credit/placement for qualifying scores on AP, IB, CLEP examinations. Work study available nights and weekends.

Payment plans. Deferred payment.

Application procedures. FAFSA required. Priority date 2/15; no closing date. Applicants notified on rolling basis starting 2/15. **Transfers:** Priority date 4/15; no deadline. Schools required to obtain student aid information through National Student Loan Data System (NSLDS).

Contact. 100 University Drive
Monaca, PA 15061-2799

Penn State Berks

Reading, Pennsylvania
www.bk.psu.edu
Four-year public **Federal Code: 003329**

	Living at home	On-campus
Tuition and fees (2002-2003):	$8,248	$8,248
Out-of-state:	$12,606	$12,606
Room and board:		$6,550
Board only:	$1,800	
Books and supplies:	$816	$816
Personal expenses:	$1,854	$2,016
Transportation:	$990	$378

Undergraduate aid. Need-based: Average financial aid package for full-time students was $8,918; for part-time $6,326. 52% awarded as scholarships/grants, 48% as loans/jobs. **Non-need-based:** 33% awarded as scholarships/grants, 67% as loans/jobs. Scholarships based on academics, alumni affiliation, athletics, minority status. **Student debt:** 69% of graduating class borrowed to fund education; average debt was $17,900.

Freshman aid. Need-based: Out of 808 full-time freshmen, 632 applied for aid; 413 were judged to have need; of these 389 received aid. Average package met 67% of need. 32 students had full need met. Average scholarship/grant was $3,812; average loan $2,571. **Non-need based:** 120 full-time freshmen with need received non-need scholarships; 176 without need received awards.

Policies to reduce costs. Tuition/fee waivers for senior citizens, employees and their families. Credit/placement for qualifying scores on AP, IB, CLEP examinations. Work study available nights.

Payment plans. Credit card, deferred payment.

Application procedures. FAFSA required. Priority date 2/15; no closing date. Applicants notified on rolling basis starting 2/15. **Transfers:** Priority date 4/15; no deadline. Schools required to obtain student aid information through National Student Loan Data System (NSLDS).

Contact. 14 Perkins Student Center
Reading, PA 19610-6009

Penn State Delaware County

Media, Pennsylvania
www.de.psu.edu
Two-year public **Federal Code: 006922**

	Living at home
Tuition and fees (2002-2003):	$8,120
Out-of-state:	$12,370
Per-credit charge:	$313
Per-credit out-of-state:	$502
Board only:	$1,800
Books and supplies:	$816
Personal expenses:	$1,854
Transportation:	$990

Undergraduate aid. Need-based: Average financial aid package for full-time students was $7,886; for part-time $6,787. 56% awarded as scholarships/grants, 44% as loans/jobs. **Non-need-based:** 31% awarded as scholarships/grants, 69% as loans/jobs. Scholarships based on academics, alumni affiliation, athletics, minority status. **Student debt:** 69% of graduating class borrowed to fund education; average debt was $17,900.

Freshman aid. Need-based: Out of 433 full-time freshmen, 318 applied for aid; 220 were judged to have need; of these 208 received aid. Average package met 65% of need. 9 students had full need met. Average scholarship/grant was $4,349; average loan $2,332. **Non-need based:** 50 full-time freshmen with need received non-need scholarships; 81 without need received awards.

Policies to reduce costs. Tuition/fee waivers for senior citizens, employees and their families. Credit/placement for qualifying scores on AP, IB, CLEP examinations. Work study available nights.

Payment plans. Credit card, deferred payment.

Application procedures. FAFSA required. Priority date 2/15; no closing date. Applicants notified on rolling basis starting 2/15. **Transfers:** Priority date 4/15; no deadline. Schools required to obtain student aid information through National Student Loan Data System (NSLDS).

Contact. 25 Yearsley Mill Road
Media, PA 19063-5596

Penn State Dubois

DuBois, Pennsylvania
www.ds.psu.edu
Two-year public **Federal Code: 003335**

	Living at home
Tuition and fees (2002-2003):	$8,110
Out-of-state:	$12,360
Per-credit charge:	$313
Per-credit out-of-state:	$502
Board only:	$1,800
Books and supplies:	$816
Personal expenses:	$1,854
Transportation:	$990

Undergraduate aid. Need-based: Average financial aid package for full-time students was $9,744; for part-time $7,490. 58% awarded as scholarships/grants, 42% as loans/jobs. **Non-need-based:** 47% awarded as scholarships/grants, 53% as loans/jobs. Scholarships based on academics, alumni affiliation, athletics, minority status. **Student debt:** 69% of graduating class borrowed to fund education; average debt was $17,900.

Freshman aid. Need-based: Out of 236 full-time freshmen, 210 applied for aid; 180 were judged to have need; of these 179 received aid. Average package met 73% of need. 20 students had full need met. Average scholarship/grant was $3,948; average loan $2,500. **Non-need based:** 86 full-time freshmen with need received non-need scholarships; 32 without need received awards.

Policies to reduce costs. Tuition/fee waivers for senior citizens, employees and their families. Credit/placement for qualifying scores on AP, IB, CLEP examinations. Work study available nights, weekends and for part-time students.

Payment plans. Deferred payment.

Application procedures. FAFSA required. No deadline. Applicants notified on rolling basis starting 2/15. **Transfers:** Priority date 4/15; no deadline. Schools required to obtain student aid information through National Student Loan Data System (NSLDS).

Contact. 101 Hiller
DuBois, PA 15801

Penn State Erie, The Behrend College

Erie, Pennsylvania
www.pserie.psu.edu
Four-year public **Federal Code: 003329**

	Living at home	On-campus
Tuition and fees (2002-2003):	$8,382	$8,382
Out-of-state:	$15,740	$15,740
Room and board:		$6,130
Board only:	$1,800	
Books and supplies:	$816	$816
Personal expenses:	$1,854	$2,016
Transportation:	$990	$378

Undergraduate aid. Need-based: Average financial aid package for full-time students was $9,959; for part-time $6,795. 48% awarded as scholarships/grants, 52% as loans/jobs. **Non-need-based:** 38% awarded as scholarships/grants, 62% as loans/jobs. Scholarships based on academics, alumni affiliation, athletics, minority status. **Student debt:** 69% of graduating class borrowed to fund education; average debt was $17,900.

Freshman aid. Need-based: Out of 828 full-time freshmen, 719 applied for aid; 555 were judged to have need; of these 542 received aid. Average package met 69% of need. 41 students had full need met. Average scholarship/grant was $3,682; average loan $2,641. **Non-need based:** 188 full-time freshmen with need received non-need scholarships; 131 without need received awards.

Policies to reduce costs. Tuition/fee waivers for senior citizens, employees and their families. Credit/placement for qualifying scores on AP, IB, CLEP examinations. Work study available nights, weekends and for part-time students.

Payment plans. Deferred payment.

Application procedures. FAFSA required. Priority date 2/15; no closing date. Applicants notified on rolling basis starting 2/15. **Transfers:** Priority date 4/15; no deadline. Schools required to obtain student aid information through National Student Loan Data System (NSLDS).

Contact. Jane Brady, Assistant Director of Financial Aid
5091 Station Road
Erie, PA 16563-0105

Penn State Fayette

Uniontown, Pennsylvania
www.fe.psu.edu
Two-year public **Federal Code: 003329**

	Living at home
Tuition and fees (2002-2003):	$8,110
Out-of-state:	$12,360
Per-credit charge:	$313
Per-credit out-of-state:	$502
Board only:	$1,800
Books and supplies:	$816
Personal expenses:	$1,854
Transportation:	$990

Undergraduate aid. Need-based: Average financial aid package for full-time students was $9,002; for part-time $8,219. 55% awarded as scholarships/grants, 45% as loans/jobs. **Non-need-based:** 30% awarded as scholarships/grants, 70% as loans/jobs. Scholarships based on academics, alumni affiliation, athletics, minority status. **Student debt:** 69% of graduating class borrowed to fund education; average debt was $17,900.

Freshman aid. Need-based: Out of 186 full-time freshmen, 178 applied for aid; 136 were judged to have need; of these 134 received aid. Average package met 68% of need. 1 students had full need met. Average scholarship/grant was $3,549; average loan $2,311. **Non-need based:** 64 full-time freshmen with need received non-need scholarships; 33 without need received awards.

Policies to reduce costs. Tuition/fee waivers for senior citizens, employees and their families. Credit/placement for qualifying scores on AP, IB, CLEP examinations. Work study available nights and weekends.

Payment plans. Deferred payment.

Application procedures. FAFSA required. Priority date 2/15; no closing date. Applicants notified on rolling basis starting 2/15. **Transfers:** Priority date 4/15; no deadline. Schools required to obtain student aid information through National Student Loan Data System (NSLDS).

Contact. 108 Williams Building
Uniontown, PA 15401-0519

Penn State Harrisburg

Middletown, Pennsylvania
www.hbg.psu.edu
Upper-division public **Federal Code: 003329**

	Living at home	On-campus
Tuition and fees (2002-2003):	$8,362	$8,362
Out-of-state:	$15,720	$15,720
Room only:		$3,070
Board only:	$1,800	
Books and supplies:	$816	$816
Personal expenses:	$1,854	$2,016
Transportation:	$990	$378

Undergraduate aid. Need-based: Average financial aid package for full-time students was $11,055; for part-time $8,513. 48% awarded as scholarships/grants, 52% as loans/jobs. **Non-need-based:** 19% awarded as scholarships/grants, 81% as loans/jobs. Scholarships based on academics, alumni affiliation, athletics, minority status. **Student debt:** 69% of graduating class borrowed to fund education; average debt was $17,900.

Freshman aid. Need-based: Out of 9 full-time freshmen, 6 applied for aid; 4 were judged to have need; of these 4 received aid. Average package met 71% of need. 1 students had full need met. Average scholarship/grant was $2,975; average loan $2,625. **Non-need based:** 2 full-time freshmen with need received non-need scholarships; 2 without need received awards.

Policies to reduce costs. Tuition/fee waivers for senior citizens, employees and their families. Credit/placement for qualifying scores on AP, IB, CLEP examinations. Work study available nights and for part-time students.

Payment plans. Deferred payment.

Application procedures. FAFSA required. Priority date 2/15; no closing date. Applicants notified on rolling basis starting 2/15. **Transfers:** Priority date 4/15; no deadline. Schools required to obtain student aid information through National Student Loan Data System (NSLDS).

Contact. Anna Griswold, Assistant Vice Provost for Student Aid
Swatapa Building, 777 West Harrisburg Pike
Middletown, PA 17057-4898

Penn State Hazleton

Hazleton, Pennsylvania
www.hn.psu.edu
Two-year public **Federal Code: 003338**

	Living at home	On-campus
Tuition and fees (2002-2003):	$8,120	$8,120
Out-of-state:	$12,370	$12,370
Per-credit charge:	$313	$313
Per-credit out-of-state:	$502	$502
Room and board:		$6,550
Board only:	$1,800	
Books and supplies:	$816	$816
Personal expenses:	$1,854	$2,016
Transportation:	$990	$378

Undergraduate aid. Need-based: Average financial aid package for full-time students was $8,951; for part-time $5,343. 54% awarded as scholarships/grants, 46% as loans/jobs. **Non-need-based:** 37% awarded as scholarships/grants, 63% as loans/jobs. Scholarships based on academics, alumni affiliation, athletics, minority status. **Student debt:** 69% of graduating class borrowed to fund education; average debt was $17,900.

Freshman aid. Need-based: Out of 531 full-time freshmen, 448 applied for aid; 351 were judged to have need; of these 341 received aid. Average package met 69% of need. 18 students had full need met. Average scholarship/grant was $3,856; average loan $2,629. **Non-need based:** 73 full-time freshmen with need received non-need scholarships; 73 without need received awards.

Policies to reduce costs. Tuition/fee waivers for senior citizens, employees and their families. Credit/placement for qualifying scores on AP, IB, CLEP examinations. Work study available nights and weekends.

Payment plans. Deferred payment.

Application procedures. FAFSA required. Priority date 2/15; no closing date. Applicants notified on rolling basis starting 2/15. **Transfers:** Priority date 4/15; no deadline. Schools required to obtain student aid information through National Student Loan Data System (NSLDS).

Contact. 110 Admin. Building, 76 University Drive
Hazleton, PA 18202

Penn State Lehigh Valley

Fogelsville, Pennsylvania
www.lv.psu.edu
Four-year public **Federal Code: 003329**

	Living at home
Tuition and fees (2002-2003):	$8,130
Out-of-state:	$12,380
Board only:	$1,800
Books and supplies:	$816
Personal expenses:	$1,854
Transportation:	$990

Undergraduate aid. Need-based: Average financial aid package for full-time students was $8,243; for part-time $9,123. 54% awarded as scholarships/grants, 46% as loans/jobs. **Non-need-based:** 31% awarded as scholarships/grants, 69% as loans/jobs. Scholarships based on academics, alumni affiliation, athletics, minority status. **Student debt:** 69% of graduating class borrowed to fund education; average debt was $17,900.

Freshman aid. Need-based: Out of 187 full-time freshmen, 140 applied for aid; 105 were judged to have need; of these 105 received aid. Average package met 67% of need. 8 students had full need met. Average scholarship/grant was $3,771; average loan $2,465. **Non-need based:** 28 full-time freshmen with need received non-need scholarships; 37 without need received awards.

Policies to reduce costs. Tuition/fee waivers for senior citizens, employees and their families. Credit/placement for qualifying scores on AP, IB, CLEP examinations.

Payment plans. Deferred payment.

Application procedures. FAFSA required. Priority date 2/15; no closing date. Applicants notified on rolling basis starting 2/15. **Transfers:** Priority date 4/15; no deadline. Schools required to obtain student aid information through National Student Loan Data System (NSLDS).

Contact. 8380 Mohr Lane, Academic Building
Fogelsville, PA 18051-9999

Penn State McKeesport

McKeesport, Pennsylvania
www.mk.psu.edu
Two-year public **Federal Code: 003329**

	Living at home	On-campus
Tuition and fees (2002-2003):	$8,110	$8,110
Out-of-state:	$12,360	$12,360
Per-credit charge:	$313	$313
Per-credit out-of-state:	$502	$502
Room and board:		$6,130
Board only:	$1,800	
Books and supplies:	$816	$816
Personal expenses:	$1,854	$2,016
Transportation:	$990	$378

Undergraduate aid. Need-based: Average financial aid package for full-time students was $8,586; for part-time $9,057. 57% awarded as scholarships/grants, 43% as loans/jobs. **Non-need-based:** 34% awarded as scholarships/grants, 66% as loans/jobs. Scholarships based on academics, alumni affiliation, athletics, minority status. **Student debt:** 69% of graduating class borrowed to fund education; average debt was $17,900.

Freshman aid. Need-based: Out of 339 full-time freshmen, 292 applied for aid; 237 were judged to have need; of these 233 received aid. Average package met 67% of need. 12 students had full need met. Average scholarship/grant was $4,205; average loan $2,616. **Non-need based:** 68 full-time freshmen with need received non-need scholarships; 56 without need received awards.

Policies to reduce costs. Tuition/fee waivers for senior citizens, employees and their families. Credit/placement for qualifying scores on AP, IB, CLEP examinations. Work study available nights and weekends.

Payment plans. Deferred payment.

Application procedures. FAFSA required. Priority date 2/15; no closing date. Applicants notified on rolling basis starting 2/15. **Transfers:** Priority date 4/15. Schools required to obtain student aid information through National Student Loan Data System (NSLDS).

Contact. 101 Frable Building, 4000 University Drive
McKeesport, PA 15132

Penn State Mont Alto

Mont Alto, Pennsylvania
www.ma.psu.edu
Two-year public **Federal Code: 003340**

	Living at home	On-campus
Tuition and fees (2002-2003):	$8,120	$8,120
Out-of-state:	$12,370	$12,370
Per-credit charge:	$313	$313
Per-credit out-of-state:	$502	$502
Room and board:		$6,550
Board only:	$1,800	
Books and supplies:	$816	$816
Personal expenses:	$1,854	$2,016
Transportation:	$990	$378

Undergraduate aid. Need-based: Average financial aid package for full-time students was $10,032; for part-time $8,730. 55% awarded as scholarships/grants, 45% as loans/jobs. **Non-need-based:** 34% awarded as scholarships/grants, 66% as loans/jobs. Scholarships based on academics, alumni affiliation, athletics, minority status. **Student debt:** 69% of graduating class borrowed to fund education; average debt was $17,900.

Freshman aid. Need-based: Out of 336 full-time freshmen, 280 applied for aid; 222 were judged to have need; of these 217 received aid. Average package met 73% of need. 13 students had full need met. Average scholarship/grant was $4,447; average loan $2,475. **Non-need based:** 92 full-time freshmen with need received non-need scholarships; 48 without need received awards.

Policies to reduce costs. Tuition/fee waivers for senior citizens, employees and their families. Credit/placement for qualifying scores on AP, IB, CLEP examinations. Work study available nights, weekends and for part-time students.

Payment plans. Deferred payment.

Application procedures. FAFSA required. Priority date 2/15; no closing date. Applicants notified on rolling basis starting 2/15. **Transfers:** Priority date 4/15; no deadline. Schools required to obtain student aid information through National Student Loan Data System (NSLDS).

Contact. 1 Campus Drive
Mont Alto, PA 17237-9703

Penn State New Kensington

Upper Burrell, Pennsylvania
www.nk.psu.edu
Two-year public **Federal Code: 003329**

	Living at home
Tuition and fees (2002-2003):	$8,120
Out-of-state:	$12,370
Per-credit charge:	$313
Per-credit out-of-state:	$502
Board only:	$1,800
Books and supplies:	$816
Personal expenses:	$1,854
Transportation:	$990

Undergraduate aid. Need-based: Average financial aid package for full-time students was $8,182; for part-time $8,081. 53% awarded as scholarships/grants, 47% as loans/jobs. **Non-need-based:** 47% awarded as scholarships/grants, 53% as loans/jobs. Scholarships based on academics, alumni affiliation, athletics, minority status. **Student debt:** 69% of graduating class borrowed to fund education; average debt was $17,900.

Freshman aid. Need-based: Out of 240 full-time freshmen, 212 applied for aid; 162 were judged to have need; of these 153 received aid. Average package met 69% of need. 7 students had full need met. Average scholarship/grant was $3,395; average loan $2,330. **Non-need based:** 55 full-time freshmen with need received non-need scholarships; 39 without need received awards.

Policies to reduce costs. Tuition/fee waivers for senior citizens, employees and their families. Credit/placement for qualifying scores on AP, CLEP examinations. Work study available nights, weekends and for part-time students.

Payment plans. Deferred payment.

Application procedures. FAFSA required. Priority date 2/15; no closing date. Applicants notified on rolling basis starting 2/15. **Transfers:** Priority date 4/15; no deadline. Schools required to obtain student aid information through National Student Loan Data System (NSLDS).

Contact. 3550 Seventh Street Road, Route 780
Upper Burrell, PA 15068-1798

Penn State Schuylkill - Capital College

Schuylkill Haven, Pennsylvania
www.sl.psu.edu
Four-year public **Federal Code: 003343**

	Living at home	On-campus
Tuition and fees (2002-2003):	$7,154	$7,154
Out-of-state:	$10,896	$10,896
Room and board:		$5,780
Board only:	$1,800	
Books and supplies:	$864	$864
Personal expenses:	$1,854	$2,016
Transportation:	$990	$378

Undergraduate aid. Need-based: Average financial aid package for full-time students was $9,802; for part-time $7,803. 57% awarded as scholarships/grants, 43% as loans/jobs. **Non-need-based:** 39% awarded as scholarships/grants, 61% as loans/jobs. Scholarships based on academics, alumni affiliation, athletics, minority status. **Student debt:** 69% of graduating class borrowed to fund education; average debt was $17,900.

Freshman aid. Need-based: Out of 273 full-time freshmen, 248 applied for aid; 205 were judged to have need; of these 198 received aid. Average package met 69% of need. 17 students had full need met. Average scholarship/grant was $4,040; average loan $2,521. **Non-need based:** 76 full-time fresh-

men with need received non-need scholarships; 42 without need received awards.

Policies to reduce costs. Tuition/fee waivers for senior citizens, employees and their families. Credit/placement for qualifying scores on AP, IB, CLEP examinations.

Payment plans. Deferred payment.

Application procedures. FAFSA required. Priority date 2/15; no closing date. Applicants notified on rolling basis starting 2/15. **Transfers:** Priority date 4/15; no deadline. Schools required to obtain student aid information through National Student Loan Data System (NSLDS).

Contact. 200 University Drive, A102 Administration Building
Schuylkill Haven, PA 17972

Penn State Shenango

Sharon, Pennsylvania
www.shenango.psu.edu
Two-year public **Federal Code: 003329**

	Living at home
Tuition and fees (2002-2003):	$8,120
Out-of-state:	$12,370
Per-credit charge:	$313
Per-credit out-of-state:	$502
Board only:	$1,800
Books and supplies:	$816
Personal expenses:	$1,854
Transportation:	$990

Undergraduate aid. Need-based: Average financial aid package for full-time students was $9,370; for part-time $7,689. 55% awarded as scholarships/grants, 45% as loans/jobs. **Non-need-based:** 27% awarded as scholarships/grants, 73% as loans/jobs. Scholarships based on academics, alumni affiliation, athletics, minority status. **Student debt:** 69% of graduating class borrowed to fund education; average debt was $17,900.

Freshman aid. Need-based: Out of 152 full-time freshmen, 145 applied for aid; 126 were judged to have need; of these 125 received aid. Average package met 72% of need. 11 students had full need met. Average scholarship/grant was $3,984; average loan $2,361. **Non-need based:** 46 full-time freshmen with need received non-need scholarships; 19 without need received awards.

Policies to reduce costs. Tuition/fee waivers for senior citizens, employees and their families. Credit/placement for qualifying scores on AP, IB, CLEP examinations. Work study available nights, weekends and for part-time students.

Payment plans. Deferred payment.

Application procedures. FAFSA required. Priority date 2/15; no closing date. Applicants notified on rolling basis starting 2/15. **Transfers:** Priority date 4/15; no deadline. Schools required to obtain student aid information through National Student Loan Data System (NSLDS).

Contact. 147 Shenango Avenue
Sharon, PA 16146-1597

Penn State University Park

University Park, Pennsylvania
www.psu.edu
Four-year public **Federal Code: 003329**

	Living at home	On-campus
Tuition and fees (2002-2003):	$8,382	$8,382
Out-of-state:	$17,610	$17,610
Room and board:		$6,130
Board only:	$1,800	
Books and supplies:	$816	$816
Personal expenses:	$1,854	$2,016
Transportation:	$990	$378

Undergraduate aid. Need-based: Average financial aid package for full-time students was $10,954; for part-time $8,014. 47% awarded as scholarships/grants, 53% as loans/jobs. **Non-need-based:** 46% awarded as scholarships/grants, 54% as loans/jobs. Scholarships based on academics, alumni affiliation, athletics, minority status. **Student debt:** 69% of graduating class borrowed to fund education; average debt was $17,900.

Freshman aid. Need-based: Out of 6,115 full-time freshmen, 4,420 applied for aid; 2,719 were judged to have need; of these 2,573 received aid. Average package met 71% of need. 344 students had full need met. Average scholarship/grant was $4,329; average loan $2,731. **Non-need based:** 1,290 full-time freshmen with need received non-need scholarships; 1,516 without need received awards; 117 received athletic scholarships.

Policies to reduce costs. Tuition/fee waivers for senior citizens, employees and their families. Credit/placement for qualifying scores on AP, CLEP examinations. Work study available nights, weekends and for part-time students.

Payment plans. Credit card, installment, deferred payment.

Application procedures. FAFSA required. Priority date 2/15; no closing date. Applicants notified on rolling basis starting 2/15. **Transfers:** Priority date 4/15; no deadline. Schools required to obtain student aid information through National Student Loan Data System (NSLDS).

Contact. Anna Griswold, Assistant Vice Provost for Student Aid
201 Shields Building
University Park, PA 16804-3000

Penn State Wilkes-Barre

Lehman, Pennsylvania
www.wb.psu.edu
Four-year public **Federal Code: 003329**

	Living at home
Tuition and fees (2002-2003):	$8,130
Out-of-state:	$12,380
Board only:	$1,800
Books and supplies:	$816
Personal expenses:	$1,854
Transportation:	$990

Undergraduate aid. Need-based: Average financial aid package for full-time students was $7,673; for part-time $8,169. 53% awarded as scholarships/grants, 47% as loans/jobs. **Non-need-based:** 48% awarded as scholarships/grants, 52% as loans/jobs. Scholarships based on academics, alumni affiliation, athletics, minority status. **Student debt:** 69% of graduating class borrowed to fund education; average debt was $17,900.

Freshman aid. Need-based: Out of 242 full-time freshmen, 208 applied for aid; 155 were judged to have need; of these 151 received aid. Average package met 68% of need. 14 students had full need met. Average scholarship/grant was $3,232; average loan $2,434. **Non-need based:** 37 full-time freshmen with need received non-need scholarships; 44 without need received awards.

Policies to reduce costs. Tuition/fee waivers for senior citizens, employees and their families. Credit/placement for qualifying scores on AP, IB, CLEP examinations. Work study available nights and weekends.

Payment plans. Deferred payment.

Application procedures. FAFSA required. Priority date 2/15; no closing date. Applicants notified on rolling basis starting 2/15. **Transfers:** Priority date 4/15; no deadline. Schools required to obtain student aid information through National Student Loan Data System (NSLDS).

Contact. Box PSU
Lehman, PA 18627-0217

Penn State Worthington Scranton

Dunmore, Pennsylvania
www.sn.psu.edu
Two-year public **Federal Code: 003344**

	Living at home
Tuition and fees (2002-2003):	$8,110
Out-of-state:	$12,360
Per-credit charge:	$313
Per-credit out-of-state:	$502
Board only:	$1,800
Books and supplies:	$816
Personal expenses:	$1,854
Transportation:	$990

Undergraduate aid. Need-based: Average financial aid package for full-time students was $8,092; for part-time $7,745. 53% awarded as scholarships/grants, 47% as loans/jobs. **Non-need-based:** 26% awarded as scholarships/grants, 74% as loans/jobs. Scholarships based on academics, alumni affiliation, athletics, minority status. **Student debt:** 69% of graduating class borrowed to fund education; average debt was $17,900.

Freshman aid. **Need-based:** Out of 271 full-time freshmen, 235 applied for aid; 185 were judged to have need; of these 183 received aid. Average package met 66% of need. 9 students had full need met. Average scholarship/grant was $3,637; average loan $2,468. **Non-need based:** 39 full-time freshmen with need received non-need scholarships; 42 without need received awards.

Policies to reduce costs. Tuition/fee waivers for senior citizens, employees and their families. Credit/placement for qualifying scores on AP, IB, CLEP examinations. Work study available nights, weekends and for part-time students.

Payment plans. Deferred payment.

Application procedures. FAFSA required. Priority date 2/15; no closing date. Applicants notified on rolling basis starting 2/15. **Transfers:** Priority date 4/15; no deadline. Schools required to obtain student aid information through National Student Loan Data System (NSLDS).

Contact. 120 Ridge View Drive
Dunmore, PA 18512-1699

Penn State York

York, Pennsylvania
www.yk.psu.edu
Two-year public **Federal Code: 003347**

	Living at home
Tuition and fees (2002-2003):	$8,110
Out-of-state:	$12,360
Per-credit charge:	$313
Per-credit out-of-state:	$502
Board only:	$1,800
Books and supplies:	$816
Personal expenses:	$1,854
Transportation:	$990

Undergraduate aid. **Need-based:** Average financial aid package for full-time students was $7,932; for part-time $7,727. 55% awarded as scholarships/grants, 45% as loans/jobs. **Non-need-based:** 32% awarded as scholarships/grants, 68% as loans/jobs. Scholarships based on academics, alumni affiliation, athletics, minority status. **Student debt:** 69% of graduating class borrowed to fund education; average debt was $17,900.

Freshman aid. **Need-based:** Out of 294 full-time freshmen, 246 applied for aid; 178 were judged to have need; of these 177 received aid. Average package met 65% of need. 11 students had full need met. Average scholarship/grant was $3,502; average loan $2,491. **Non-need based:** 55 full-time freshmen with need received non-need scholarships; 61 without need received awards.

Policies to reduce costs. Tuition/fee waivers for senior citizens, employees and their families. Credit/placement for qualifying scores on AP, IB, CLEP examinations. Work study available nights, weekends and for part-time students.

Payment plans. Deferred payment.

Application procedures. FAFSA required. Priority date 2/15; no closing date. Applicants notified on rolling basis starting 2/15. **Transfers:** Priority date 4/15; no deadline. Schools required to obtain student aid information through National Student Loan Data System (NSLDS).

Contact. 1031 Edgecomb Avenue
York, PA 17403-3398

Pennsylvania College of Technology

Williamsport, Pennsylvania
www.pct.edu
Four-year public **Federal Code: 003395**

	Living at home	On-campus
Tuition and fees (2002-2003):	$9,540	$9,540
Out-of-state:	$11,730	$11,730
Room and board:		$5,942
Board only:	$1,500	
Books and supplies:	$900	$900
Personal expenses:	$2,200	$2,200
Transportation:		$150

Undergraduate aid. **Need-based:** 57% awarded as scholarships/grants, 43% as loans/jobs. Need-based aid available for part-time students. **Non-need-based:** Scholarships based on academics, alumni affiliation.

Policies to reduce costs. Tuition/fee waivers for employees and their families. Credit/placement for qualifying scores on AP, CLEP examinations.

Payment plans. Deferred payment.

Application procedures. FAFSA, institutional form required. Priority date 4/1; no closing date. Applicants notified on rolling basis starting 6/1, must reply by 7/1 or within 4 week(s) of notification.

Contact. **Financial aid office:** (570) 327-4766
Ben Comfort, Director of Financial Aid
One College Avenue
Williamsport, PA 17701

Pennsylvania Institute of Culinary Arts

Pittsburgh, Pennsylvania
www.paculinary.com
Two-year proprietary **Federal Code: 030068**

College costs. The total cost of the 16-month culinary program, including all fees, ranges from $32,795 to $34,089. Board: $2,448. Books/supplies: $3,107. Transportation: $480.

Undergraduate aid. All financial aid based on need. Average financial aid package for full-time students was $6,125; for part-time $6,125. 20% awarded as scholarships/grants, 80% as loans/jobs. **Student debt:** 80% of graduating class borrowed to fund education; average debt was $36,125.

Policies to reduce costs. Tuition/fee waivers for employees and their families. Tuition at time of enrollment guaranteed for 2 years.

Payment plans. Credit card, installment payment.

Application procedures. FAFSA, institutional form required. No deadline. Applicants notified on rolling basis. **Transfers:** No deadline.

Contact. **Financial aid office:** (412) 566-2433 ext. 4226
Jennifer Burns, Financial Aid Manager
717 Liberty Avenue
Pittsburgh, PA 15222

Pennsylvania Institute of Technology

Media, Pennsylvania
www.pit.edu
Two-year private **Federal Code: 010998**

	Living at home
Tuition and fees:	$8,700
Per-credit charge:	$291
Books and supplies:	$900

Undergraduate aid. **Need-based:** Need-based aid available for full-time and part-time students. **Non-need-based:** Scholarships based on academics, leadership.

Merit scholarships. Presidential Scholarship, half tuition scholarship for current high school graduates. SAT scores required.

Policies to reduce costs. Tuition/fee waivers for employees and their families. Credit/placement for qualifying scores on AP, CLEP examinations. Work study available nights, weekends and for part-time students.

Payment plans. Credit card, installment payment.

Application procedures. FAFSA, institutional form required. Closing date 8/1. Applicants notified on rolling basis starting 7/1. **Transfers:** No deadline.

Contact. **Financial aid office:** (610) 892-1520
Sandy Shaffer, Director of Financial Aid
800 Manchester Avenue
Media, PA 19063-4098

Philadelphia Biblical University

Langhorne, Pennsylvania
www.pbu.edu
Four-year private **Federal Code: 003351**

	Living at home	On-campus
Tuition and fees:	$12,745	$12,745
Room and board:		$5,650
Books and supplies:	$750	$750
Personal expenses:	$900	$900
Transportation:	$1,000	$1,000

Undergraduate aid. Need-based: Average financial aid package for full-time students was $8,330; for part-time $4,765. 62% awarded as scholarships/grants, 38% as loans/jobs. **Non-need-based:** 58% awarded as scholarships/grants, 42% as loans/jobs. Scholarships based on academics, leadership, music/drama. **Student debt:** 70% of graduating class borrowed to fund education; average debt was $13,000.

Freshman aid. Need-based: Out of 175 full-time freshmen, 137 applied for aid; 113 were judged to have need; of these 113 received aid. Average package met 62% of need. 10 students had full need met. Average scholarship/grant was $7,175; average loan $2,565. **Non-need based:** 5 full-time freshmen with need received non-need scholarships; 35 without need received awards.

Policies to reduce costs. Tuition/fee waivers for employees and their families. Prepayment discount; credit/placement for qualifying scores on AP, CLEP examinations. Work study available nights, weekends and for part-time students.

Payment plans. Credit card, installment payment.

Application procedures. FAFSA required. Priority date 5/1; no closing date. Applicants notified on rolling basis starting 3/15. **Transfers:** No deadline.

Contact. **Financial aid office:** (215) 702-4246
William Kellaris, Director of Financial Aid
200 Manor Avenue
Langhorne, PA 19047-2990

Philadelphia University

Philadelphia, Pennsylvania
www.philau.edu
Four-year private **Federal Code: 003354**

	Living at home	On-campus
Tuition and fees:	$20,022	$20,022
Room and board:		$7,392
Board only:	$1,500	
Books and supplies:	$1,000	$1,000
Personal expenses:	$803	$782
Transportation:	$2,000	$1,500

Undergraduate aid. Need-based: Average financial aid package for full-time students was $13,519; for part-time $6,726. 61% awarded as scholarships/grants, 39% as loans/jobs. **Non-need-based:** 93% awarded as scholarships/grants, 7% as loans/jobs. Scholarships based on academics, athletics, leadership. **Student debt:** 67% of graduating class borrowed to fund education; average debt was $25,258.

Freshman aid. Need-based: Out of 614 full-time freshmen, 526 applied for aid; 447 were judged to have need; of these 447 received aid. Average package met 72% of need. 54 students had full need met. Average scholarship/grant was $9,940; average loan $3,130. **Non-need based:** 42 full-time freshmen with need received non-need scholarships; 162 without need received awards; 8 received athletic scholarships.

Policies to reduce costs. Tuition/fee waivers for employees and their families. Credit/placement for qualifying scores on AP, CLEP examinations.

Payment plans. Credit card, installment payment.

Application procedures. FAFSA required. Priority date 4/15; no closing date. Applicants notified on rolling basis starting 2/15, must reply within 3 week(s) of notification.

Contact. Lisa Cooper, Director of Financial Aid
School House Lane & Henry Avenue
Philadelphia, PA 19144-5497

Pittsburgh Institute of Aeronautics

Pittsburgh, Pennsylvania
www.piainfo.org
Two-year private **Federal Code: 005310**

	Living at home
Tuition and fees (2002-2003):	$8,631
Books and supplies:	$900
Personal expenses:	$400
Transportation:	$800

Undergraduate aid. Need-based: Need-based aid available for full-time students.

Policies to reduce costs. Tuition/fee waivers for employees and their families. Credit/placement for qualifying scores on CLEP examinations.

Payment plans. Installment payment.

Application procedures. FAFSA required. Priority date 5/1; no closing date. Applicants notified on rolling basis.

Contact. Darla Mroski, Assistant Director of Finance
Box 10897
Pittsburgh, PA 15236-0897

Pittsburgh Technical Institute: Boyd School Division

Oakdale, Pennsylvania
www.pittsburghtechnical.com
Two-year proprietary **Federal Code: 007437**

College costs. Tuition varies by program.

Undergraduate aid. All financial aid based on need. Average financial aid package for full-time students was $7,271. 40% awarded as scholarships/grants, 60% as loans/jobs. Need-based aid available for part-time students. **Student debt:** 92% of graduating class borrowed to fund education; average debt was $15,314.

Freshman aid. Out of 1,036 full-time freshmen, 932 applied for aid; 932 were judged to have need; of these 932 received aid. Average package met 60% of need. 174 students had full need met. Average scholarship/grant was $3,604; average loan $2,625.

Policies to reduce costs. Tuition/fee waivers for family members, employees and their families. Tuition at time of enrollment guaranteed for 2 years; credit/placement for qualifying scores on CLEP examinations.

Payment plans. Credit card, installment, deferred payment.

Application procedures. FAFSA, institutional form required. No deadline. Applicants notified on rolling basis.

Contact. **Financial aid office:** (412) 809-5140
Terry Farrell, Senior Vice President of Financial Aid
1111 McKee Road
Oakdale, PA 15071-3205

Point Park College

Pittsburgh, Pennsylvania
www.ppc.edu
Four-year private **Federal Code: 003357**

College costs. Cost of tuition in bachelor of arts and bachelor of fine arts programs within conservatory of performing arts: $15560 or $437 per credit hour.

	Living at home	On-campus
Tuition and fees:	$15,180	$15,180
Room and board:		$6,660
Books and supplies:	$700	$700
Personal expenses:	$750	$500
Transportation:	$700	

Undergraduate aid. Need-based: Average financial aid package for full-time students was $11,728; for part-time $6,150. 47% awarded as scholarships/grants, 53% as loans/jobs. **Non-need-based:** 26% awarded as scholarships/grants, 74% as loans/jobs. Scholarships based on academics, alumni affiliation, art, athletics, leadership, music/drama. **Student debt:** 96% of graduating class borrowed to fund education; average debt was $8,209.

Freshman aid. Need-based: Out of 328 full-time freshmen, 306 applied for aid; 261 were judged to have need; of these 261 received aid. Average package met 75% of need. 63 students had full need met. Average scholarship/grant was $7,681; average loan $3,806. **Non-need based:** 24 full-time freshmen with need received non-need scholarships; 159 without need received awards; 5 received athletic scholarships.

Policies to reduce costs. Tuition/fee waivers for children of alumni, senior citizens, family members, unemployed or children of unemployed, employees and their families. Credit/placement for qualifying scores on AP, IB, CLEP examinations. Work study available nights and weekends.

Payment plans. Credit card, installment, deferred payment.

Application procedures. FAFSA required. Priority date 5/1; no closing date. Applicants notified on rolling basis starting 2/1, must reply within 3 week(s) of notification. **Transfers:** Priority date 5/1; no deadline.

Contact. **Financial aid office:** (412) 392-3935
Sandra Cronin, Director of Financial Aid
201 Wood Street
Pittsburgh, PA 15222-1984

Reading Area Community College

Reading, Pennsylvania
www.racc.cc.pa.us
Two-year public **Federal Code: 010388**

College costs. Additional fees for out-of-district students $150.

	Living at home
Tuition and fees:	$2,760
Out-of-district:	$5,100
Per-credit charge:	$59
Per-credit out-of-district:	$118
Per-credit out-of-state:	$176
Books and supplies:	$500
Personal expenses:	$1,200
Transportation:	$800

Policies to reduce costs. Tuition/fee waivers for senior citizens, employees and their families. Credit/placement for qualifying scores on AP, CLEP examinations.

Payment plans. Credit card, installment, deferred payment.

Application procedures. FAFSA, institutional form required. Priority date 7/1; no closing date. Applicants notified on rolling basis starting 4/15, must reply within 2 week(s) of notification.

Contact. Benjamin Rosenberger, Financial Aid Coordinator
10 South Second Street
Reading, PA 19603-1706

Robert Morris University

Moon Township, Pennsylvania
www.rmu.edu
Four-year private **Federal Code: 001746**

	Living at home	On-campus
Tuition and fees:	$13,484	$13,484
Room and board:		$6,954
Board only:	$2,734	
Books and supplies:	$800	$800
Personal expenses:	$1,950	$1,000
Transportation:	$2,740	$1,000

Undergraduate aid. **Need-based:** Average financial aid package for full-time students was $8,254; for part-time $1,556. 54% awarded as scholarships/grants, 46% as loans/jobs. **Non-need-based:** Scholarships based on academics, athletics.

Freshman aid. **Need-based:** Out of 477 full-time freshmen, 465 applied for aid; 402 were judged to have need; of these 402 received aid. Average package met 79% of need. 108 students had full need met. Average scholarship/grant was $10,504; average loan $1,163. **Non-need based:** 195 full-time freshmen with need received non-need scholarships; 41 received athletic scholarships.

Policies to reduce costs. Tuition/fee waivers for family members, employees and their families. Credit/placement for qualifying scores on AP, CLEP examinations. Work study available weekends and for part-time students.

Payment plans. Credit card, installment, deferred payment.

Application procedures. FAFSA required. No deadline. Applicants notified on rolling basis starting 3/1, must reply within 3 week(s) of notification. **Transfers:** No deadline.

Contact. **Financial aid office:** (412) 299-2450
Shari Payne, Director of Financial Aid
881 Narrows Run Road
Moon Township, PA 15108-1189

Rosedale Technical Institute

Pittsburgh, Pennsylvania
www.rosedaletech.org
Two-year private **Federal Code: 012050**

	Living at home
Tuition and fees:	$10,040

Undergraduate aid. **Need-based:** Need-based aid available for full-time students.

Application procedures. FAFSA required. Closing date 8/1.

Contact. Kathleen Stein, Director of Financial Aid
4634 Browns Hill Road
Pittsburgh, PA 15217

Rosemont College

Rosemont, Pennsylvania
www.rosemont.edu
Four-year private **Federal Code: 003360**

	Living at home	On-campus
Tuition and fees (2002-2003):	$17,600	$17,600
Room and board:		$7,700
Board only:	$2,650	
Books and supplies:	$1,000	$1,000
Personal expenses:	$800	$800
Transportation:	$925	$175

Undergraduate aid. **Need-based:** Average financial aid package for full-time students was $17,939. Need-based aid available for part-time students. **Non-need-based:** Scholarships based on academics, alumni affiliation, art, religious affiliation. **Student debt:** 60% of graduating class borrowed to fund education; average debt was $16,500.

Freshman aid. **Need-based:** Out of 74 full-time freshmen, 62 applied for aid; 54 were judged to have need; of these 54 received aid. Average package met 94% of need. 35 students had full need met. Average scholarship/grant was $12,513; average loan $2,914. **Non-need based:** 37 full-time freshmen with need received non-need scholarships; 16 without need received awards.

Policies to reduce costs. Tuition/fee waivers for adults, children of alumni, senior citizens, family members, family of clergy, employees and their families. Credit/placement for qualifying scores on AP, IB examinations. Work study available nights, weekends and for part-time students.

Payment plans. Credit card, installment payment.

Application procedures. FAFSA required. Priority date 3/1; no closing date. Applicants notified on rolling basis starting 2/15, must reply by 5/1 or within 4 week(s) of notification. **Transfers:** Priority date 6/1; no deadline. Not eligible for the same institutional merit funds as first year students; must have made academic progress at previous school.

Contact. Judith Rile, Director of Financial Aid
1400 Montgomery Avenue
Rosemont, PA 19010

St. Charles Borromeo Seminary - Overbrook

Wynnewood, Pennsylvania
Four-year private

	Living at home	On-campus
Tuition and fees (2002-2003):	$9,150	$9,150
Room and board:		$6,260
Books and supplies:	$800	$800
Personal expenses:		$500

Undergraduate aid. **Additional information:** Scholarships offered to full-time students studying for priesthood.

Policies to reduce costs. Tuition/fee waivers for minority students, unemployed or children of unemployed, family of clergy, employees and their families. Credit/placement for qualifying scores on AP, IB examinations. Work study available nights and weekends.

Payment plans. Installment, deferred payment.

Application procedures. FAFSA required. Closing date 4/1. Applicants notified on rolling basis, must reply within 4 week(s) of notification.

Contact. **Financial aid office:** (610) 785-6582
Bonnie Behm, Financial Aid Coordinator
100 East Wynnewood Road
Wynnewood, PA 19096

St. Joseph's University

Philadelphia, Pennsylvania
www.sju.edu
Four-year private **Federal Code: 003367**

College costs. Tuition may vary based on major.

	Living at home	On-campus
Tuition and fees:	$24,330	$24,330
Room and board:		$9,350
Board only:	$3,220	
Books and supplies:	$800	$800
Personal expenses:	$2,030	$1,800

Undergraduate aid. Need-based: Average financial aid package for full-time students was $11,300. 59% awarded as scholarships/grants, 41% as loans/jobs. **Non-need-based:** Scholarships based on art, athletics. **Student debt:** 65% of graduating class borrowed to fund education; average debt was $11,131.

Freshman aid. Need-based: Out of 1,032 full-time freshmen, 958 applied for aid; 730 were judged to have need; of these 730 received aid. Average package met 80% of need. 402 students had full need met. Average scholarship/grant was $7,650; average loan $3,312. **Non-need based:** 609 full-time freshmen with need received non-need scholarships; 195 without need received awards; 60 received athletic scholarships.

Policies to reduce costs. Tuition/fee waivers for employees and their families. Credit/placement for qualifying scores on AP examinations. Work study available nights and weekends.

Payment plans. Credit card, installment, deferred payment.

Application procedures. FAFSA required. Priority date 2/15; no closing date. Applicants notified on rolling basis starting 3/15, must reply by 5/1. **Transfers:** No deadline. Financial aid for transfers subject to availability of funds.

Contact. **Financial aid office:** (610) 660-1555
Eileen Tucker, Director of Financial Aid
5600 City Avenue
Philadelphia, PA 19131-1395

St. Vincent College

Latrobe, Pennsylvania
www.stvincent.edu
Four-year private **Federal Code: 003368**

	Living at home	On-campus
Tuition and fees:	$19,370	$19,370
Room and board:		$6,440
Board only:	$2,000	
Books and supplies:	$1,500	$1,500

Undergraduate aid. Need-based: Average financial aid package for full-time students was $15,143; for part-time $4,713. 74% awarded as scholarships/grants, 26% as loans/jobs. **Non-need-based:** 43% awarded as scholarships/grants, 57% as loans/jobs. Scholarships based on academics, athletics, leadership, minority status, music/drama.

Freshman aid. Need-based: Out of 318 full-time freshmen, 318 applied for aid; 268 were judged to have need; of these 268 received aid. Average package met 91% of need. 59 students had full need met. Average scholarship/grant was $11,691; average loan $3,122. **Non-need based:** 36 full-time freshmen with need received non-need scholarships; 47 without need received awards; 27 received athletic scholarships.

Merit scholarships. Academic Merit Scholarship available ranging from $1,000 to $11,000, based on high school GPA, class rank, and SAT scores. Students in top ten percent of their high school class are eligible for the Wimmer Scholarship, based on exam, top scorer is awarded full tuition, next four scorers are awarded between $12,000 and a full scholarship. Leadership Merit Grant ranges from $500 to $3,000, based on extracurricular activities and recommendations.

Policies to reduce costs. Tuition/fee waivers for senior citizens, employees and their families. Credit/placement for qualifying scores on AP, IB, CLEP examinations. Work study available weekends and for part-time students.

Payment plans. Credit card, installment payment.

Application procedures. FAFSA required. Priority date 3/1; closing date 5/1. Applicants notified on rolling basis starting 3/1, must reply within 2 week(s) of notification.

Contact. **Financial aid office:** (800) 782-5549
David Collins, Assistant Vice President, Admission and Financial Aid
300 Fraser Purchase Road
Latrobe, PA 15650-2690

Schuylkill Institute of Business & Technology

Pottsville, Pennsylvania
www.sibtinpa.com
Two-year proprietary **Federal Code: 014984**

College costs (projected). Programs cost a total of between $7,100 and $25,000 and last between 9 and 24 months. Transportation: $2,712.

Undergraduate aid. All financial aid based on need. Average financial aid package for full-time students was $10,000. 40% awarded as scholarships/grants, 60% as loans/jobs. Need-based aid available for part-time students. **Student debt:** 65% of graduating class borrowed to fund education; average debt was $12,000.

Freshman aid. Out of 155 full-time freshmen, 140 applied for aid; 140 were judged to have need; of these 140 received aid. 80 students had full need met. Average loan $2,625.

Policies to reduce costs. Tuition/fee waivers for employees and their families. Tuition at time of enrollment guaranteed for 2 years.

Payment plans. Credit card, installment payment.

Application procedures. FAFSA required. Closing date 7/31. Applicants notified by 10/1, must reply by 10/15. **Transfers:** No deadline.

Contact. Valerie Wessner, Financial Aid Director
171 Red Horse Road
Pottsville, PA 17901

Seton Hill University

Greensburg, Pennsylvania
www.setonhill.edu
Four-year private **Federal Code: 003362**

	Living at home	On-campus
Tuition and fees:	$18,930	$18,930
Room and board:		$6,100
Books and supplies:	$1,000	$1,000
Personal expenses:	$2,200	$2,400

Undergraduate aid. Need-based: Average financial aid package for full-time students was $15,500; for part-time $5,500. 70% awarded as scholarships/grants, 30% as loans/jobs. **Non-need-based:** 15% awarded as scholarships/grants, 85% as loans/jobs. Scholarships based on academics, alumni affiliation, art, athletics, job skills, leadership, music/drama. **Student debt:** 66% of graduating class borrowed to fund education; average debt was $20,900. **Additional information:** Presidential scholarships available. Awards range up to one half of tuition per year. Scholarships for Girl Scout Gold awardees, Hugh O'Brien Youth, Governor's School of Excellence participants, and Maureen O'Brien Leadership award.

Freshman aid. Need-based: Out of 212 full-time freshmen, 210 applied for aid; 197 were judged to have need; of these 197 received aid. Average package met 75% of need. 26 students had full need met. Average scholarship/grant was $13,000; average loan $3,276. **Non-need based:** 41 full-time freshmen with need received non-need scholarships; 7 without need received awards; 7 received athletic scholarships.

Merit scholarships. Half tuition, for students in top 10% of high school class. One-third tuition, for students in top 20% of high school class. 25% of tuition, top 30% of class.

Policies to reduce costs. Tuition/fee waivers for adults, senior citizens, family members, family of clergy, employees and their families. Credit/placement for qualifying scores on AP, IB, CLEP examinations. Work study available weekends and for part-time students.

Payment plans. Credit card, installment, deferred payment.

Application procedures. FAFSA, institutional form required. Priority date 4/1; no closing date. Applicants notified on rolling basis starting 12/1, must reply within 2 week(s) of notification. **Transfers:** Scholarship available for full-time transfer students with cumulative 3.5 GPA.

Contact. **Financial aid office:** (724) 838-4293
Maryann Dudas, Director of Financial Aid
Seton Hill Drive
Greensburg, PA 15601

Shippensburg University of Pennsylvania

Shippensburg, Pennsylvania
www.ship.edu
Four-year public **Federal Code: 003326**

	Living at home	On-campus
Tuition and fees (2002-2003):	$5,502	$5,502
Out-of-state:	$12,070	$12,070
Room and board:		$4,864
Books and supplies:	$750	$750
Personal expenses:	$1,904	$1,904
Transportation:	$2,000	

Undergraduate aid. Need-based: Average financial aid package for full-time students was $5,863; for part-time $4,917. 47% awarded as scholarships/grants, 53% as loans/jobs. **Non-need-based:** 12% awarded as scholarships/grants, 88% as loans/jobs. Scholarships based on academics, athletics. **Student debt:** 67% of graduating class borrowed to fund education; average debt was $15,707.

Freshman aid. Need-based: Out of 1,507 full-time freshmen, 1,254 applied for aid; 817 were judged to have need; of these 786 received aid. Average package met 75% of need. 187 students had full need met. Average scholarship/grant was $3,746; average loan $2,532. **Non-need based:** 89 full-time freshmen with need received non-need scholarships; 142 without need received awards; 65 received athletic scholarships.

Policies to reduce costs. Tuition/fee waivers for senior citizens, employees and their families. Credit/placement for qualifying scores on AP, IB, CLEP examinations.

Payment plans. Installment payment.

Application procedures. FAFSA required. Priority date 3/15; no closing date. Applicants notified on rolling basis, must reply within 2 week(s) of notification.

Contact. **Financial aid office:** (717) 477-1131
Peter D'Annabale, Director of Financial Aid
1871 Old Main Drive
Shippensburg, PA 17257-2299

Slippery Rock University of Pennsylvania

Slippery Rock, Pennsylvania
www.sru.edu
Four-year public **Federal Code: 003327**

	Living at home	On-campus
Tuition and fees (2002-2003):	$5,548	$5,548
Out-of-state:	$12,116	$12,116
Room and board:		$4,400
Board only:	$1,858	
Books and supplies:	$640	$640
Personal expenses:	$500	$1,000
Transportation:	$755	$255

Undergraduate aid. Need-based: Average financial aid package for full-time students was $6,162; for part-time $4,935. 48% awarded as scholarships/grants, 52% as loans/jobs. **Non-need-based:** 18% awarded as scholarships/grants, 82% as loans/jobs. Scholarships based on academics, alumni affiliation, art, athletics, job skills, minority status, music/drama, state/district residency. **Student debt:** 77% of graduating class borrowed to fund education; average debt was $19,455. **Additional information:** May 1 closing date for Pennsylvania state grants.

Freshman aid. Need-based: Out of 1,435 full-time freshmen, 1,321 applied for aid; 946 were judged to have need; of these 923 received aid. Average package met 83% of need. 478 students had full need met. Average scholarship/grant was $2,835. **Non-need based:** 260 full-time freshmen with need received non-need scholarships; 287 without need received awards; 42 received athletic scholarships.

Policies to reduce costs. Tuition/fee waivers for senior citizens, employees and their families. Credit/placement for qualifying scores on AP, IB, CLEP examinations. Work study available nights, weekends and for part-time students.

Payment plans. Credit card, installment payment.

Application procedures. FAFSA required. Priority date 5/1; no closing date. Applicants notified on rolling basis starting 3/15, must reply within 2 week(s) of notification.

Contact. **Financial aid office:** (724) 738-2044
Patricia Hladio, Director of Financial Aid
Maltby Center/Slippery Rock University
Slippery Rock, PA 16057

South Hills School of Business & Technology

State College, Pennsylvania
www.southhills.edu
Two-year proprietary **Federal Code: 013263**

	Living at home
Tuition and fees:	$10,125
Per-credit charge:	$279
Board only:	$2,500
Books and supplies:	$1,500
Personal expenses:	$2,500
Transportation:	$1,001

Undergraduate aid. All financial aid based on need. Average financial aid package for full-time students was $4,625; for part-time $2,625. 42% awarded as scholarships/grants, 58% as loans/jobs.

Freshman aid. Out of 471 full-time freshmen, 471 applied for aid; 471 were judged to have need; of these 471 received aid. Average package met 75% of need.

Policies to reduce costs. Tuition/fee waivers for employees and their families.

Payment plans. Installment payment.

Application procedures. FAFSA required. Closing date 8/1. Applicants notified on rolling basis starting 7/1. **Transfers:** No deadline.

Contact. **Financial aid office:** (814) 234-7755
Harriet Arndt, Director Financial Aid
480 Waupelani Drive
State College, PA 16801-4516

South Hills School of Business and Technology

Altoona, Pennsylvania
www.southhills.edu
Two-year proprietary **Federal Code: 010281**

College costs. Tuition $3,350 per term; fees $25 per term. Full cost of associate degree programs, including tuition, fees and books, ranges from $11,650 to $27,322 depending on number of terms in program. Books/supplies: $600.

Contact. Joan Graffi, Director of Financial Aid
508 58th Street
Altoona, PA 16602

Swarthmore College

Swarthmore, Pennsylvania
www.swarthmore.edu
Four-year private **Federal Code: 003370**

	Living at home
Tuition and fees:	$28,802
Books and supplies:	$960
Personal expenses:	$940

Undergraduate aid. Need-based: Average financial aid package for full-time students was $25,032. 85% awarded as scholarships/grants, 15% as loans/jobs. **Non-need-based:** 65% awarded as scholarships/grants, 35% as loans/jobs. Scholarships based on academics, leadership, state/district residency. **Student debt:** 33% of graduating class borrowed to fund education; average debt was $12,759. **Additional information:** School meets 100% of demonstrated financial need for all students.

Freshman aid. Need-based: Out of 371 full-time freshmen, 232 applied for aid; 179 were judged to have need; of these 179 received aid. Average package met 100% of need. 179 students had full need met. Average scholarship/grant was $21,656; average loan $1,853. **Non-need based:** 2 without need received awards.

Policies to reduce costs. Tuition/fee waivers for employees and their families. Credit/placement for qualifying scores on AP, IB examinations.

Payment plans. Installment payment.

Application procedures. FAFSA, institutional form, CSS PROFILE required. Closing date 2/15. Applicants notified by 4/1, must reply by 5/1. Early decision closing date 11/15. **Transfers:** Closing date 4/7.

Contact. **Financial aid office:** (610) 328-8358
Laura Talbot, Director of Financial Aid
500 College Avenue
Swarthmore, PA 19081

Talmudical Yeshiva of Philadelphia

Philadelphia, Pennsylvania
Four-year private **Federal Code: 012523**

College costs. $75 fee for yeshiva linen.

	Living at home	On-campus
Tuition and fees (2002-2003):	$5,600	$5,600
Room and board:		$5,000
Books and supplies:	$900	$900

Undergraduate aid. Need-based: 81% awarded as scholarships/grants, 19% as loans/jobs.

Policies to reduce costs. Tuition/fee waivers for employees and their families. Credit/placement for qualifying scores on IB examinations.

Payment plans. Installment payment.

Application procedures. FAFSA required. Priority date 8/1; closing date 5/1. Applicants notified on rolling basis starting 3/15, must reply within 2 week(s) of notification.

Contact. **Financial aid office:** (215) 477-1000
Uri Mandelbaum, Registrar/Director Student Financial Aid
6063 Drexel Road
Philadelphia, PA 19131

Temple University

Philadelphia, Pennsylvania
www.temple.edu
Four-year public **Federal Code: 003371**

	Living at home	On-campus
Tuition and fees (2002-2003):	$8,062	$8,062
Out-of-state:	$14,316	$14,316
Room and board:		$7,112
Books and supplies:	$800	$800
Personal expenses:	$2,440	$4,404
Transportation:	$1,850	

Undergraduate aid. Need-based: Average financial aid package for full-time students was $10,715; for part-time $7,247. 49% awarded as scholarships/grants, 51% as loans/jobs. **Non-need-based:** 41% awarded as scholarships/grants, 59% as loans/jobs. Scholarships based on academics, art, athletics, music/drama. **Student debt:** 70% of graduating class borrowed to fund education; average debt was $20,807.

Freshman aid. Need-based: Out of 3,160 full-time freshmen, 2,990 applied for aid; 2,275 were judged to have need; of these 2,215 received aid. Average package met 82% of need. 593 students had full need met. Average scholarship/grant was $4,404; average loan $2,662. **Non-need based:** 992 full-time freshmen with need received non-need scholarships; 715 without need received awards; 35 received athletic scholarships.

Policies to reduce costs. Tuition/fee waivers for employees and their families. Credit/placement for qualifying scores on AP, IB, CLEP examinations. Work study available nights and weekends.

Payment plans. Credit card, installment, deferred payment.

Application procedures. FAFSA required. Closing date 3/1. Applicants notified on rolling basis starting 2/15, must reply by 5/1 or within 3 week(s) of notification. **Transfers:** Priority date 3/1; no deadline.

Contact. **Financial aid office:** (215) 204-2244
John Morris, Director, Student Financial Services
1801 North Broad Street (041-09)
Philadelphia, PA 19122-6096

Thiel College

Greenville, Pennsylvania
www.thiel.edu
Four-year private **Federal Code: 003376**

	Living at home	On-campus
Tuition and fees:	$14,296	$14,296
Room and board:		$6,584
Books and supplies:	$600	$600
Personal expenses:	$1,500	$1,600

Undergraduate aid. Need-based: Average financial aid package for full-time students was $14,214; for part-time $4,770. 68% awarded as scholarships/grants, 32% as loans/jobs. **Non-need-based:** 31% awarded as scholarships/grants, 69% as loans/jobs. Scholarships based on academics, alumni affiliation, art, leadership, music/drama, religious affiliation. **Student debt:** 87% of graduating class borrowed to fund education; average debt was $19,150.

Freshman aid. Need-based: Out of 404 full-time freshmen, 387 applied for aid; 326 were judged to have need; of these 326 received aid. Average package met 78% of need. 51 students had full need met. Average scholarship/grant was $9,180; average loan $3,379. **Non-need based:** 75 full-time freshmen with need received non-need scholarships; 52 without need received awards.

Policies to reduce costs. Tuition/fee waivers for adults, senior citizens, family members, family of clergy, employees and their families. Credit/placement for qualifying scores on AP, CLEP examinations. Work study available nights and weekends.

Payment plans. Credit card, installment payment.

Application procedures. FAFSA required. Closing date 3/1. Applicants notified on rolling basis starting 2/1, must reply within 2 week(s) of notification. **Transfers:** Priority date 6/1; no deadline.

Contact. **Financial aid office:** (724) 589-2250
Cynthia Farrell, Director of Financial Aid
75 College Avenue
Greenville, PA 16125

University of Pennsylvania

Philadelphia, Pennsylvania
www.upenn.edu
Four-year private **Federal Code: 003378**

	Living at home	On-campus
Tuition and fees:	$29,318	$29,318
Room and board:		$8,642
Board only:	$3,134	
Books and supplies:	$760	$760
Personal expenses:	$1,576	$1,576
Transportation:	$300	$300

Undergraduate aid. All financial aid based on need. Average financial aid package for full-time students was $23,875. 66% awarded as scholarships/grants, 34% as loans/jobs. **Student debt:** 44% of graduating class borrowed to fund education; average debt was $20,247.

Freshman aid. Out of 2,426 full-time freshmen, 1,289 applied for aid; 983 were judged to have need; of these 983 received aid. Average package met 100% of need. 983 students had full need met. Average scholarship/grant was $19,686; average loan $5,266.

Policies to reduce costs. Tuition/fee waivers for employees and their families. Prepayment discount; credit/placement for qualifying scores on AP, IB examinations. Work study available nights, weekends and for part-time students.

Payment plans. Installment payment.

Application procedures. FAFSA, institutional form, CSS PROFILE required. Priority date 2/15; no closing date. Applicants notified by 4/1, must reply by 5/1. Early decision closing date 11/1. **Transfers:** Priority date 3/15; closing date 3/15.

Contact. **Financial aid office:** (215) 898-1988
William Schilling, Director of Financial Aid
One College Hall
Philadelphia, PA 19104

University of Pittsburgh

Pittsburgh, Pennsylvania
www.pitt.edu
Four-year public **Federal Code: 008815**

	Living at home	On-campus
Tuition and fees (2002-2003):	$8,528	$8,528
Out-of-state:	$17,336	$17,336
Room and board:		$6,470
Board only:	$1,800	
Books and supplies:	$500	$500
Personal expenses:	$1,000	$1,000
Transportation:	$600	$400

Undergraduate aid. Need-based: Average financial aid package for full-time students was $10,798. 30% awarded as scholarships/grants, 70% as loans/jobs. Need-based aid available for part-time students. **Non-need-based:** 65% awarded as scholarships/grants, 35% as loans/jobs. Scholarships based on academics, athletics. **Student debt:** 60% of graduating class borrowed to fund education; average debt was $20,154.

Freshman aid. Need-based: Out of 3,112 full-time freshmen, 2,535 applied for aid; 1,846 were judged to have need; of these 1,748 received aid. Average package met 88% of need. 386 students had full need met. Average scholarship/grant was $4,459; average loan $3,499. **Non-need based:** 1,007 full-time freshmen with need received non-need scholarships; 439 without need received awards; 79 received athletic scholarships.

Merit scholarships. Academic Scholarships available with a range of awards from $1,000 to full tuition, room and board. These scholarships can be renewed for up to 4 years with a 3.0 GPA.

Policies to reduce costs. Tuition/fee waivers for employees and their families. Credit/placement for qualifying scores on AP, IB, CLEP examinations. Work study available nights and weekends.

Payment plans. Credit card, installment, deferred payment.

Application procedures. FAFSA, institutional form required. Priority date 3/1; no closing date. Applicants notified on rolling basis starting 3/15. **Transfers:** Priority date 5/1; no deadline. Transfer students not eligible for freshman scholarships.

Contact. Financial aid office: (412) 624-7488
Betsy Porter, Director, Office of Admissions and Financial Aid
4227 Fifth Avenue, 1st Floor, Alumni Hall
Pittsburgh, PA 15260

University of Pittsburgh at Bradford

Bradford, Pennsylvania
www.upb.pitt.edu
Four-year public **Federal Code: 003380**

College costs. Nursing program tuition $8,882 and per-credit-hour $301 in-state, tuition $19,376 and per-credit-hour $640 out-of-state. These figures are not inclusive of fees and room and board. This is for tuition only.

	Living at home	On-campus
Tuition and fees (2002-2003):	$8,452	$8,452
Out-of-state:	$17,260	$17,260
Room and board:		$5,470
Books and supplies:	$800	$800
Personal expenses:	$800	$800
Transportation:	$1,200	$800

Undergraduate aid. Need-based: 49% awarded as scholarships/grants, 51% as loans/jobs. Need-based aid available for part-time students. **Non-need-based:** 55% awarded as scholarships/grants, 45% as loans/jobs. Scholarships based on academics, minority status, state/district residency. **Student debt:** 72% of graduating class borrowed to fund education; average debt was $18,364.

Policies to reduce costs. Tuition/fee waivers for employees and their families. Credit/placement for qualifying scores on AP, IB, CLEP examinations. Work study available nights, weekends and for part-time students.

Payment plans. Credit card, installment payment.

Application procedures. FAFSA required. Priority date 3/1; no closing date. Applicants notified on rolling basis starting 4/1, must reply within 4 week(s) of notification. **Transfers:** No deadline. Transfers must meet academic policy guidelines.

Contact. Financial aid office: (814) 362-7550
Melissa Ibanez, Director of Financial Aid
300 Campus Drive
Bradford, PA 16701

University of Pittsburgh at Greensburg

Greensburg, Pennsylvania
www.pitt.edu/~upg
Four-year public **Federal Code: 003381**

	Living at home	On-campus
Tuition and fees (2002-2003):	$8,468	$8,468
Out-of-state:	$17,276	$17,276
Room and board:		$5,600
Books and supplies:	$600	$600
Personal expenses:	$1,100	$1,110
Transportation:	$1,100	$700

Undergraduate aid. Need-based: 47% awarded as scholarships/grants, 53% as loans/jobs. Need-based aid available for part-time students. **Non-need-based:** Scholarships based on academics, leadership.

Policies to reduce costs. Tuition/fee waivers for senior citizens, employees and their families. Credit/placement for qualifying scores on AP, CLEP examinations. Work study available nights and weekends.

Payment plans. Credit card, installment payment.

Application procedures. FAFSA, institutional form required. Priority date 3/1; closing date 5/1. Applicants notified on rolling basis starting 4/1, must reply within 3 week(s) of notification. **Transfers:** Priority date 3/1.

Contact. Financial aid office: (724) 836-9880
Brandi Darr, Director of Admissions and Financial Aid
1150 Mount Pleasant Road
Greensburg, PA 15601

University of Pittsburgh at Johnstown

Johnstown, Pennsylvania
www.upj.pitt.edu
Four-year public **Federal Code: 003382**

	Living at home	On-campus
Tuition and fees (2002-2003):	$8,470	$8,470
Out-of-state:	$17,278	$17,278
Room and board:		$5,570
Books and supplies:	$800	$800
Personal expenses:	$1,000	$1,000

Undergraduate aid. Need-based: Average financial aid package for full-time students was $7,046; for part-time $3,857. 53% awarded as scholarships/grants, 47% as loans/jobs. **Non-need-based:** 29% awarded as scholarships/grants, 71% as loans/jobs. Scholarships based on academics, athletics, leadership, minority status. **Student debt:** 83% of graduating class borrowed to fund education; average debt was $17,894.

Freshman aid. Need-based: Out of 794 full-time freshmen, 679 applied for aid; 599 were judged to have need; of these 555 received aid. Average package met 60% of need. 86 students had full need met. Average scholarship/grant was $3,906; average loan $3,892. **Non-need based:** 192 full-time freshmen with need received non-need scholarships; 29 without need received awards; 14 received athletic scholarships.

Policies to reduce costs. Tuition/fee waivers for employees and their families. Credit/placement for qualifying scores on AP, IB, CLEP examinations.

Payment plans. Credit card, installment, deferred payment.

Application procedures. FAFSA required. Closing date 4/1. Applicants notified on rolling basis starting 3/15, must reply within 2 week(s) of notification.

Contact. Financial aid office: (800) 881-5544
Julie Salem, Director of Financial Aid
450 Schoolhouse Road, 157 Blackington Hall
Johnstown, PA 15904-1200

University of Pittsburgh at Titusville

Titusville, Pennsylvania
www.upt.pitt.edu
Two-year public **Federal Code: 003383**

	Living at home	On-campus
Tuition and fees (2002-2003):	$7,702	$7,702
Out-of-state:	$15,628	$15,628
Per-credit charge:	$242	$242
Per-credit out-of-state:	$508	$508
Room and board:		$6,248
Books and supplies:	$800	$800
Personal expenses:	$1,600	$1,600
Transportation:	$350	$250

Undergraduate aid. Need-based: Average financial aid package for full-time students was $10,464; for part-time $4,025. 71% awarded as scholarships/grants, 29% as loans/jobs. **Non-need-based:** 15% awarded as scholarships/grants, 85% as loans/jobs. Scholarships based on academics, athletics, state/district residency. **Student debt:** 100% of graduating class borrowed to fund education; average debt was $8,295.

Freshman aid. Need-based: Out of 187 full-time freshmen, 178 applied for aid; 153 were judged to have need; of these 153 received aid. Average package met 86% of need. 20 students had full need met. Average scholarship/grant was $7,434; average loan $3,025. **Non-need based:** 7 without need received awards; 3 received athletic scholarships.

Merit scholarships. $2,000 merit scholarships: up to 5 for the top 5 students with science as a major. Renewable with a 3.0 GPA and continued science major. 6 Presidential scholarships of $2,000 each awarded based on high school academic record.

Policies to reduce costs. Tuition/fee waivers for adults, unemployed or children of unemployed, employees and their families. Credit/placement for qualifying scores on AP examinations. Work study available nights and weekends.

Payment plans. Credit card, installment payment.

Application procedures. FAFSA required. Closing date 5/1. Applicants notified on rolling basis starting 2/1, must reply within 3 week(s) of notification. **Transfers:** Priority date 5/1; no deadline. PA residents by May 1 for PHEAA. Transfer students must have completed 24 credits to renew.

Contact. Financial aid office: (814) 827-4421
Melissa Gabriel, Director of Financial Aid
UPT Admissions Office
Titusville, PA 16354

University of Scranton

Scranton, Pennsylvania
www.scranton.edu
Four-year private **Federal Code: 003384**

	Living at home	On-campus
Tuition and fees:	$21,408	$21,408
Room and board:		$9,156
Board only:	$1,900	
Books and supplies:	$900	$900
Personal expenses:	$1,100	$1,140
Transportation:	$900	$450

Undergraduate aid. All financial aid based on need. Average financial aid package for full-time students was $14,346; for part-time $6,213. 70% awarded as scholarships/grants, 30% as loans/jobs. **Student debt:** 62% of graduating class borrowed to fund education; average debt was $15,000.

Freshman aid. Out of 960 full-time freshmen, 824 applied for aid; 664 were judged to have need; of these 651 received aid. Average package met 75% of need. 103 students had full need met. Average scholarship/grant was $11,383; average loan $2,840.

Policies to reduce costs. Tuition/fee waivers for senior citizens, family members, employees and their families. Credit/placement for qualifying scores on AP, IB, CLEP examinations. Work study available nights and weekends.

Payment plans. Credit card, installment payment.

Application procedures. FAFSA required. Priority date 2/15; no closing date. Applicants notified on rolling basis starting 3/1, must reply by 5/1 or within 2 week(s) of notification. **Transfers:** No deadline. Institutional grants available based on financial need.

Contact. William Burke, Director of Financial Aid
800 Linden Street
Scranton, PA 18510-4699

University of the Sciences in Philadelphia

Philadelphia, Pennsylvania
www.usip.edu
Four-year private **Federal Code: 003353**

	Living at home	On-campus
Tuition and fees (2002-2003):	$19,338	$19,338
Room and board:		$7,950
Books and supplies:	$700	$700
Personal expenses:	$800	$800
Transportation:	$1,060	$400

Undergraduate aid. Need-based: Average financial aid package for full-time students was $11,762. 29% awarded as scholarships/grants, 71% as loans/jobs. Need-based aid available for part-time students. **Non-need-based:** 27% awarded as scholarships/grants, 73% as loans/jobs. Scholarships based on academics, athletics. **Student debt:** 67% of graduating class borrowed to fund education; average debt was $28,225.

Freshman aid. Need-based: Average package met 62% of need. Average scholarship/grant was $4,300; average loan $2,625.

Policies to reduce costs. Tuition/fee waivers for employees and their families. Credit/placement for qualifying scores on AP, IB, CLEP examinations.

Payment plans. Credit card, installment payment.

Application procedures. FAFSA required. Priority date 3/15; closing date 3/15. Applicants notified on rolling basis starting 1/15, must reply by 5/1 or within 2 week(s) of notification.

Contact. Financial aid office: (215) 596-8894
Nick Flocco, Director of Financial Aid
600 South 43rd Street
Philadelphia, PA 19104-4495

Valley Forge Christian College

Phoenixville, Pennsylvania
www.vfcc.edu
Four-year private **Federal Code: 003306**

	Living at home	On-campus
Tuition and fees:	$9,592	$9,592
Room and board:		$4,860
Board only:	$2,085	
Books and supplies:	$700	$700
Personal expenses:	$1,166	$1,166
Transportation:	$850	$750

Undergraduate aid. Need-based: Average financial aid package for full-time students was $6,877; for part-time $4,486. 44% awarded as scholarships/grants, 56% as loans/jobs. **Non-need-based:** 23% awarded as scholarships/grants, 77% as loans/jobs. Scholarships based on academics, leadership, music/drama, religious affiliation, state/district residency.

Freshman aid. Need-based: Out of 194 full-time freshmen, 172 applied for aid; 158 were judged to have need; of these 158 received aid. Average package met 51% of need. 9 students had full need met. Average scholarship/grant was $4,110; average loan $2,410. **Non-need based:** 7 full-time freshmen with need received non-need scholarships; 33 without need received awards.

Merit scholarships. Trustee's Scholarship, President's Scholarship, Dean's Scholarship, Professor's Scholarship ranging from full tuition/mininum 3.56 GPA, 1300 SAT or 29 ACT, and upper 10% class rank, to $1,000-$2,000 for minimum 3.5 GPA and minimum 1030 SAT or 22 ACT, application required, renewable with maintenance.of 3.5 GPA.

Policies to reduce costs. Tuition/fee waivers for senior citizens, family members, family of clergy, employees and their families. Credit/placement for qualifying scores on AP, CLEP examinations. Work study available nights, weekends and for part-time students.

Payment plans. Credit card, installment payment.

Application procedures. FAFSA required. Priority date 5/1; no closing date. Applicants notified on rolling basis starting 3/15, must reply within 3 week(s) of notification.

Contact. **Financial aid office:** (610) 917-1498
Evie Meyer, Director of Financial Aid
1401 Charlestown Road
Phoenixville, PA 19460

Villanova University

Villanova, Pennsylvania
www.villanova.edu
Four-year private **Federal Code: 003388**

College costs. Quoted tuition is for School of Liberal Arts. Tuition $26,300 for School of Sciences and Nursing; $28,180 for School of Engineering (includes laptop program); $27,400 for School of Commerce and Finance (includes laptop program and Wall Street Journal).

	Living at home	On-campus
Tuition and fees:	$26,850	$26,850
Room and board:		$8,810
Books and supplies:	$800	$800
Personal expenses:	$900	$900
Transportation:	$2,100	$400

Undergraduate aid. Need-based: Average financial aid package for full-time students was $17,641; for part-time $6,839. 58% awarded as scholarships/grants, 42% as loans/jobs. **Non-need-based:** 65% awarded as scholarships/grants, 35% as loans/jobs. Scholarships based on academics, athletics, leadership, minority status. **Student debt:** 53% of graduating class borrowed to fund education; average debt was $28,217. **Additional information:** Financial aid deadline February 15 for FAFSA, March 8 for institutional application.

Freshman aid. Need-based: Out of 1,582 full-time freshmen, 1,051 applied for aid; 761 were judged to have need; of these 748 received aid. Average package met 81% of need. 101 students had full need met. Average scholarship/grant was $12,976; average loan $3,283. **Non-need based:** 169 full-time freshmen with need received non-need scholarships; 256 without need received awards; 35 received athletic scholarships.

Policies to reduce costs. Tuition/fee waivers for senior citizens, employees and their families. Credit/placement for qualifying scores on AP, IB examinations. Work study available nights and weekends.

Application procedures. FAFSA, institutional form required. Closing date 2/15. Applicants notified by 4/1, must reply by 5/1. **Transfers:** No deadline. FAFSA application must be submitted by February 15, institution's own form must be submitted by March 8.

Contact. **Financial aid office:** (610) 519-4010
Bonnie Lee Behm, Director of Financial Assistance
800 Lancaster Avenue
Villanova, PA 19085-1672

Washington and Jefferson College

Washington, Pennsylvania
www.washjeff.edu
Four-year private **Federal Code: 003389**

	Living at home	On-campus
Tuition and fees:	$23,260	$23,260
Room and board:		$6,310
Board only:	$1,910	
Books and supplies:	$600	$600
Personal expenses:	$700	$700
Transportation:	$200	$195

Undergraduate aid. Need-based: Average financial aid package for full-time students was $15,229; for part-time $5,000. 75% awarded as scholarships/grants, 25% as loans/jobs. **Non-need-based:** 69% awarded as scholarships/grants, 31% as loans/jobs. Scholarships based on academics.

Freshman aid. Need-based: Out of 328 full-time freshmen, 286 applied for aid; 286 were judged to have need; of these 240 received aid. Average package met 89% of need. 106 students had full need met. Average scholarship/grant was $7,684; average loan $3,534. **Non-need based:** 166 full-time freshmen with need received non-need scholarships; 68 without need received awards.

Policies to reduce costs. Tuition/fee waivers for adults, employees and their families. Credit/placement for qualifying scores on AP, CLEP examinations.

Payment plans. Credit card, installment payment.

Application procedures. FAFSA required. Priority date 2/15; no closing date. Applicants notified on rolling basis starting 3/1, must reply by 5/1. Early decision closing date 12/1.

Contact. **Financial aid office:** (724) 223-6019
Nancy Sninksy, Director of Financial Aid
60 South Lincoln Street
Washington, PA 15301

Waynesburg College

Waynesburg, Pennsylvania
www.waynesburg.edu
Four-year private **Federal Code: 003391**

	Living at home	On-campus
Tuition and fees:	$13,850	$13,850
Room and board:		$5,520
Board only:	$2,000	
Books and supplies:	$900	$900
Personal expenses:	$1,200	$1,700
Transportation:	$1,200	$400

Undergraduate aid. Need-based: Average financial aid package for full-time students was $11,120. 69% awarded as scholarships/grants, 31% as loans/jobs. Need-based aid available for part-time students. **Non-need-based:** Scholarships based on academics, alumni affiliation, job skills, leadership, religious affiliation, state/district residency. **Student debt:** 74% of graduating class borrowed to fund education; average debt was $14,500.

Freshman aid. Need-based: Out of 317 full-time freshmen, 311 applied for aid; 298 were judged to have need; of these 298 received aid. Average package met 82% of need. 92 students had full need met. Average scholarship/grant was $7,359; average loan $2,779.

Merit scholarships. Presidential Honor Scholarship, $4,500 annually; Honor Scholarship, $3,000 annually; College Leadership Program, $1,000-$1,600 annually; all for outstanding students; A.B. Miller Scholarship, $6,000-$8,000 annually.

Policies to reduce costs. Tuition/fee waivers for family members, employees and their families. Credit/placement for qualifying scores on AP, IB, CLEP examinations. Work study available nights.

Payment plans. Credit card, installment payment.

Application procedures. FAFSA, institutional form required. Priority date 3/15; no closing date. Applicants notified on rolling basis starting 2/15, must reply within 2 week(s) of notification. **Transfers:** Priority date 3/15.

Contact. **Financial aid office:** (724) 852-3208
Matthew Stokan, Director of Financial Aid
51 West College Street
Waynesburg, PA 15370

West Chester University of Pennsylvania

West Chester, Pennsylvania
www.wcupa.edu
Four-year public **Federal Code: 003328**

	Living at home	On-campus
Tuition and fees (2002-2003):	$5,468	$5,468
Out-of-state:	$12,036	$12,036
Room and board:		$5,146
Books and supplies:	$800	$800
Personal expenses:	$1,368	$1,368
Transportation:	$1,620	$1,020

Undergraduate aid. Need-based: Need-based aid available for full-time and part-time students. **Non-need-based:** Scholarships based on academics, athletics, minority status, music/drama.

Policies to reduce costs. Tuition/fee waivers for senior citizens, minority students, employees and their families. Credit/placement for qualifying scores on AP, CLEP examinations. Work study available nights, weekends and for part-time students.

Payment plans. Credit card, installment payment.

Application procedures. FAFSA required. Priority date 3/1; no closing date. Applicants notified on rolling basis starting 4/15, must reply within 3 week(s) of notification.

Contact. **Financial aid office:** (610) 436-2627
Dana Parker, Director of Financial Aid
Messikomer Hall
West Chester, PA 19383

Western School of Health and Business Careers

Pittsburgh, Pennsylvania
www.westernschool.com
Two-year proprietary **Federal Code: 022023**

College costs (2002-2003). Depending on program, cost ranges from $8,000 to $28,800, includes lab fees, books, and registration fee.

Undergraduate aid. Need-based: Need-based aid available for full-time students.

Application procedures. FAFSA required. No deadline. Applicants notified on rolling basis.

Contact. Eileen Randolph, Director of Financial Aid
421 Seventh Avenue
Pittsburgh, PA 15219

Westmoreland County Community College

Youngwood, Pennsylvania
wccc4me.org
Two-year public **Federal Code: 010176**

	Living at home
Tuition and fees:	$1,770
Out-of-district:	$3,630
Out-of-state:	$5,340
Per-credit charge:	$57
Per-credit out-of-district:	$119
Per-credit out-of-state:	$176
Books and supplies:	$600
Transportation:	$1,000

Undergraduate aid. Need-based: Need-based aid available for full-time and part-time students. **Non-need-based:** Scholarships based on academics.

Policies to reduce costs. Tuition/fee waivers for senior citizens, employees and their families. Credit/placement for qualifying scores on AP, CLEP examinations. Work study available nights and for part-time students.

Payment plans. Credit card, installment payment.

Application procedures. FAFSA, institutional form required. No deadline. Applicants notified on rolling basis starting 5/1. **Transfers:** No deadline.

Contact. **Financial aid office:** (724) 925-4063
Gary Means, Director of Financial Aid
400 Armbrust Road
Youngwood, PA 15697-1895

Widener University

Chester, Pennsylvania
www.widener.edu
Four-year private **Federal Code: 003313**

College costs. $700 additional fee for engineering students.

	Living at home	On-campus
Tuition and fees:	$21,500	$21,500
Room and board:		$8,050
Board only:	$1,800	
Books and supplies:	$800	$800
Personal expenses:	$1,035	$1,035
Transportation:	$1,080	$225

Undergraduate aid. Need-based: Average financial aid package for full-time students was $18,481; for part-time $16,239. 68% awarded as scholarships/grants, 32% as loans/jobs. **Non-need-based:** 58% awarded as scholarships/grants, 42% as loans/jobs. Scholarships based on academics, leadership, music/drama.

Freshman aid. Need-based: Out of 642 full-time freshmen, 609 applied for aid; 552 were judged to have need; of these 552 received aid. Average package met 91% of need. 45 students had full need met. Average scholarship/grant was $12,536; average loan $4,728. **Non-need based:** 87 full-time freshmen with need received non-need scholarships; 89 without need received awards.

Merit scholarships. Presidential Scholarships: for one-fourth, one-third, one-half tuition; renewable based on high school SAT and GPA. Transfer Scholarships: ranging from $2,000 to $5,000, for resident or commuter transfer students based on GPA; Music Scholarship based on performance.

Policies to reduce costs. Tuition/fee waivers for senior citizens, family members, employees and their families. Credit/placement for qualifying scores on AP, IB examinations.

Payment plans. Credit card, installment payment.

Application procedures. FAFSA, institutional form required. Priority date 2/15; no closing date. Applicants notified on rolling basis starting 3/15, must reply within 4 week(s) of notification.

Contact. **Financial aid office:** (610) 499-4174
Walter Cathie, Dean of University Financial Aid
One University Place
Chester, PA 19013

Wilkes University

Wilkes-Barre, Pennsylvania
www.wilkes.edu
Four-year private **Federal Code: 003394**

	Living at home	On-campus
Tuition and fees:	$19,630	$19,630
Room and board:		$8,430
Board only:	$1,500	
Books and supplies:	$900	$900
Personal expenses:	$1,000	$600
Transportation:	$800	$800

Undergraduate aid. Need-based: Average financial aid package for full-time students was $12,286. 63% awarded as scholarships/grants, 37% as loans/jobs. Need-based aid available for part-time students. **Non-need-based:** 76% awarded as scholarships/grants, 24% as loans/jobs. Scholarships based on academics, leadership, minority status, music/drama.

Freshman aid. Need-based: Out of 407 full-time freshmen, 388 applied for aid; 350 were judged to have need; of these 349 received aid. Average package met 78% of need. 54 students had full need met. Average scholarship/grant was $10,858; average loan $1,896. **Non-need based:** 51 without need received awards.

Policies to reduce costs. Tuition/fee waivers for children of alumni, senior citizens, family members, employees and their families. Credit/placement for qualifying scores on AP, CLEP examinations.

Payment plans. Credit card, installment, deferred payment.

Application procedures. FAFSA, institutional form required. Priority date 3/1; no closing date. Applicants notified on rolling basis starting 2/21.

Contact. **Financial aid office:** (570) 408-4346
Rachael Lohman, Director of Financial Aid
Chase Hall/184 South River Street
Wilkes-Barre, PA 18766

Williamson Free School of Mechanical Trades

Media, Pennsylvania
www.williamsonschool.org
Three-year private

College costs (2002-2003). All students receive full scholarships covering tuition, room and board, and textbooks. Required fees, $985.

Application procedures. No deadline.

Contact. Ed Bailey, Director of Enrollments
106 South New Middletown Road
Media, PA 19063

Wilson College

Chambersburg, Pennsylvania
www.wilson.edu
Four-year private **Federal Code: 003396**

	Living at home	On-campus
Tuition and fees (2002-2003):	$15,630	$15,630
Room and board:		$6,790
Board only:	$1,000	
Books and supplies:	$800	$800
Personal expenses:	$400	$400
Transportation:	$1,425	$200

Undergraduate aid. Need-based: Average financial aid package for full-time students was $15,159; for part-time $7,405. 68% awarded as scholarships/grants, 32% as loans/jobs. **Non-need-based:** 59% awarded as scholarships/grants, 41% as loans/jobs. Scholarships based on academics, alumni affiliation, leadership, music/drama, religious affiliation, state/district residency. **Student debt:** 100% of graduating class borrowed to fund education; average debt was $16,246.

Freshman aid. Need-based: Out of 82 full-time freshmen, 62 applied for aid; 49 were judged to have need; of these 49 received aid. Average package met 83% of need. 17 students had full need met. Average scholarship/grant was $12,077; average loan $2,847. **Non-need based:** 6 full-time freshmen with need received non-need scholarships; 31 without need received awards.

Merit scholarships. Half-tuition scholarships for full-time students who are members of Presbyterian Church, USA.

Policies to reduce costs. Tuition/fee waivers for employees and their families. Credit/placement for qualifying scores on AP, CLEP examinations. Work study available nights, weekends and for part-time students.

Payment plans. Credit card, installment payment.

Application procedures. FAFSA, institutional form required. Closing date 4/30. Applicants notified on rolling basis starting 2/15. **Transfers:** One-quarter tuition scholarships available to transfer articulation students who hold associate degrees from Harrisburg Area Community College, Hagerstown Community College, Central Penn College, Luzerne County Community College, Lehigh Carbon Community College and Harcum College.

Contact. Financial aid office: (717)262-2016
Linda Brittain, Director of Financial Aid
1015 Philadelphia Avenue
Chambersburg, PA 17201-1285

York College of Pennsylvania

York, Pennsylvania
www.ycp.edu
Four-year private **Federal Code: 003399**

	Living at home	On-campus
Tuition and fees:	$8,550	$8,550
Room and board:		$5,950
Books and supplies:	$600	$600
Personal expenses:	$500	$1,000
Transportation:	$750	$500

Undergraduate aid. Need-based: Average financial aid package for full-time students was $6,625; for part-time $3,832. 48% awarded as scholarships/grants, 52% as loans/jobs. **Non-need-based:** 13% awarded as scholarships/grants, 87% as loans/jobs. Scholarships based on academics, music/drama. **Student debt:** 65% of graduating class borrowed to fund education; average debt was $15,792.

Freshman aid. Need-based: Out of 922 full-time freshmen, 748 applied for aid; 582 were judged to have need; of these 541 received aid. Average package met 72% of need. 149 students had full need met. Average scholarship/grant was $3,708; average loan $2,397. **Non-need based:** 128 full-time freshmen with need received non-need scholarships; 75 without need received awards.

Merit scholarships. Trustee Scholarships: full tuition, for students with top 20% class rank and SATs over 1200, 5 awarded. Residential Scholarships: half tuition, to top student in each department, 9 awarded. Valedictorian and Salutatorian Scholarships: half tuition, unlimited number awarded. Dean's Academic Scholarship: one-third tuition, to students with top 40% class rank, SATs over 1150, 130 awarded.

Policies to reduce costs. Tuition/fee waivers for employees and their families. Credit/placement for qualifying scores on AP, IB, CLEP examinations.

Payment plans. Deferred payment.

Application procedures. FAFSA, institutional form required. Priority date 3/1; no closing date. Applicants notified on rolling basis starting 2/15, must reply within 4 week(s) of notification. **Transfers:** No deadline.

Contact. Financial aid office: (717) 849-1682
Calvin Williams, Director of Financial Aid
Country Club Road
York, PA 17405-7199

Puerto Rico

Atlantic College

Guaynabo, Puerto Rico
www.atlanticcollege-pr.com
Four-year private **Federal Code: 016871**

	Living at home
Tuition and fees (2002-2003):	$3,830
Books and supplies:	$500

Undergraduate aid. All financial aid based on need. Need-based aid available for full-time and part-time students.

Policies to reduce costs. Tuition at time of enrollment guaranteed for 4 years. Work study available nights.

Payment plans. Installment payment.

Application procedures. FAFSA required. No deadline. Applicants notified on rolling basis. **Transfers:** No deadline.

Contact. Janice Rivera, Director
PO Box 3918
Guaynabo, PR 00970

Bayamon Central University

Bayamon, Puerto Rico
www.ucb.edu.pr
Four-year private **Federal Code: 010015**

	Living at home
Tuition and fees (2002-2003):	$3,740
Board only:	$2,079
Books and supplies:	$565
Personal expenses:	$1,950
Transportation:	$720

Undergraduate aid. All financial aid based on need. Need-based aid available for full-time and part-time students.

Policies to reduce costs. Tuition/fee waivers for employees and their families. Credit/placement for qualifying scores on AP, CLEP examinations. Work study available nights and for part-time students.

Payment plans. Installment, deferred payment.

Application procedures. FAFSA, institutional form required. Priority date 4/30; closing date 8/1. Applicants notified by 6/1, must reply by 8/20. **Transfers:** Priority date 5/30; no deadline.

Contact. **Financial aid office:** (787) 786-3030 ext. 2116
Viviana Cintrón, Director of Financial Aid Office
PO Box 1725
Bayamon, PR 00960-1725

Columbia College

Caguas, Puerto Rico
www.columbiaco.edu
Four-year proprietary **Federal Code: 013517**

	Living at home
Tuition and fees (projected):	$4,800
Personal expenses:	$600
Transportation:	$207

Undergraduate aid. All financial aid based on need. Average financial aid package for full-time students was $7,260; for part-time $7,260. 97% awarded as scholarships/grants, 3% as loans/jobs.

Freshman aid. Average scholarship/grant was $4,300.

Policies to reduce costs. Tuition/fee waivers for employees and their families. Tuition at time of enrollment guaranteed for 4 years. Work study available nights and for part-time students.

Payment plans. Credit card, deferred payment.

Application procedures. FAFSA, institutional form required. Closing date 6/30. Applicants notified on rolling basis.

Contact. **Financial aid office:** (787) 743-4041
Virginia Guang, Financial Aid Administrator
PO Box 8517
Caguas, PR 00726

Conservatory of Music of Puerto Rico

San Juan, Puerto Rico
www.cmpr.edu
Four-year public **Federal Code: 010819**

	Living at home
Tuition and fees (2002-2003):	$1,760
Out-of-state:	$1,760
Books and supplies:	$400
Personal expenses:	$450
Transportation:	$650

Undergraduate aid. All financial aid based on need. Average financial aid package for full-time students was $3,178. 68% awarded as scholarships/grants, 32% as loans/jobs. Need-based aid available for part-time students.

Freshman aid. Average package met 52% of need. Average scholarship/grant was $2,639; average loan $3,045.

Policies to reduce costs. Tuition/fee waivers for employees and their families. Credit/placement for qualifying scores on AP examinations. Work study available nights.

Payment plans. Credit card, deferred payment.

Application procedures. FAFSA, institutional form required. Priority date 6/30; no closing date. Applicants notified on rolling basis starting 8/30. **Transfers:** Closing date 4/15.

Contact. **Financial aid office:** (787) 751-0160 ext. 230
Jorge Medina, Financial Aid Officer
U.P. Roosevelt No. 350, Rafael Lamar
San Juan, PR 00918

Escuela de Artes Plasticas de Puerto Rico

San Juan, Puerto Rico
www.eap.edu.pr
Four-year public **Federal Code: 017345**

	Living at home
Tuition and fees (2002-2003):	$1,794
Books and supplies:	$2,250
Personal expenses:	$1,750
Transportation:	$500

Undergraduate aid. All financial aid based on need. 98% awarded as scholarships/grants, 2% as loans/jobs. Need-based aid available for part-time students.

Freshman aid. Out of 57 full-time freshmen, 57 applied for aid; 57 were judged to have need; of these 57 received aid.

Payment plans. Deferred payment.

Application procedures. FAFSA, institutional form required. Closing date 5/12. Applicants notified by 7/11.

Contact. Marion Munoz, Financial Aid Officer
PO Box 9021112
San Juan, PR 00902-1112

Huertas Junior College

Caguas, Puerto Rico
Two-year proprietary **Federal Code: 014105**

	Living at home
Tuition and fees (projected):	$5,148
Per-credit charge:	$118
Books and supplies:	$800
Personal expenses:	$800
Transportation:	$800

Policies to reduce costs. Tuition/fee waivers for employees and their families. Tuition at time of enrollment guaranteed for 2 years.

Payment plans. Installment payment.

Application procedures. FAFSA, institutional form required. No deadline. Applicants notified on rolling basis.

Contact. Magaly Gonzalez, Director of Financial Aid Office
PO Box 8429
Caguas, PR 00726

Humacao Community College

Humacao, Puerto Rico
Two-year private
Federal Code: 014952

	Living at home
Tuition and fees (2002-2003):	$3,775
Per-credit charge:	$95
Books and supplies:	$750
Personal expenses:	$900
Transportation:	$375

Undergraduate aid. All financial aid based on need. 89% awarded as scholarships/grants, 11% as loans/jobs. Need-based aid available for part-time students.

Freshman aid. Out of 144 full-time freshmen, 138 applied for aid; 128 were judged to have need; of these 50 received aid.

Policies to reduce costs. Tuition/fee waivers for employees and their families. Work study available nights and for part-time students.

Payment plans. Installment, deferred payment.

Application procedures. FAFSA required. Priority date 1/1; closing date 6/30. Applicants notified on rolling basis starting 3/4. **Transfers:** No deadline.

Contact. **Financial aid office:** (787) 852-1430 ext. 28
Brendly Rodriguez, Financial Aid Officer
PO Box 9139
Humacao, PR 00792

ICPR Junior College

San Juan, Puerto Rico
www.icprjc.edu
Two-year proprietary
Federal Code: 011940

	Living at home
Tuition and fees (2002-2003):	$4,470
Per-credit charge:	$120
Board only:	$1,649
Books and supplies:	$926
Personal expenses:	$3,364
Transportation:	$1,324

Undergraduate aid. **Need-based:** 95% awarded as scholarships/grants, 5% as loans/jobs. **Non-need-based:** Scholarships based on state/district residency.

Policies to reduce costs. Tuition/fee waivers for children of alumni, family members, employees and their families.

Payment plans. Credit card, installment, deferred payment.

Application procedures. FAFSA, institutional form required. Closing date 4/15. Applicants notified on rolling basis starting 11/15. **Transfers:** No deadline.

Contact. Rosa Hernandez, Financial Aid Director
PO Box 190304
San Juan, PR 00919-0304

Inter American University of Puerto Rico: Barranquitas Campus

Barranquitas, Puerto Rico
www.br.inter.edu
Four-year private
Federal Code: 005027

	Living at home
Tuition and fees (2002-2003):	$4,150
Board only:	$1,200
Books and supplies:	$640
Personal expenses:	$880
Transportation:	$600

Policies to reduce costs. Tuition/fee waivers for adults, minority students. Tuition at time of enrollment guaranteed for 4 years.

Payment plans. Credit card, deferred payment.

Application procedures. FAFSA required. Closing date 4/30. Applicants notified on rolling basis, must reply within 2 week(s) of notification.

Contact. Eduardo Fontanez, Director of Financial Aid
PO Box 517
Barranquitas, PR 00794

Inter American University of Puerto Rico: Bayamon Campus

Bayamon, Puerto Rico
www.bc.inter.edu
Four-year private
Federal Code: 003938

	Living at home
Tuition and fees (2002-2003):	$4,150

Undergraduate aid. **Non-need-based:** Scholarships based on academics.

Payment plans. Credit card, installment, deferred payment.

Application procedures. FAFSA, institutional form required. Priority date 3/15; closing date 4/28. Applicants notified on rolling basis starting 5/10. **Transfers:** No deadline.

Contact. **Financial aid office:** (787) 279-4100
Jaime Falcon, Director of Financial Aid
500 Dr. John Will Harris Rd.
Bayamon, PR 00957

Inter American University of Puerto Rico: Fajardo Campus

Fajardo, Puerto Rico
www.inter.edu/fajardoi.html
Four-year private
Federal Code: 010763

	Living at home
Tuition and fees (2002-2003):	$4,150
Books and supplies:	$640
Transportation:	$600

Policies to reduce costs. Tuition/fee waivers for senior citizens. Credit/placement for qualifying scores on AP, CLEP examinations.

Payment plans. Credit card, deferred payment.

Application procedures. FAFSA, institutional form required. Closing date 4/30. Applicants notified on rolling basis. Early decision closing date 2/15.

Contact. Lydia Santiago, Dean Of Administration
PO Box 70003
Fajardo, PR 00738

Inter American University of Puerto Rico: Guayama Campus

Guayama, Puerto Rico
www.inter.edu
Four-year private
Federal Code: 010764

	Living at home
Tuition and fees (2002-2003):	$4,150
Board only:	$1,200
Books and supplies:	$640
Transportation:	$880

Undergraduate aid. All financial aid based on need. Average financial aid package for full-time students was $2,105; for part-time $243. 74% awarded as scholarships/grants, 26% as loans/jobs.

Freshman aid. Out of 441 full-time freshmen, 413 applied for aid; 395 were judged to have need; of these 380 received aid. Average package met 12% of need. Average scholarship/grant was $388; average loan $69.

Policies to reduce costs. Work study available nights, weekends and for part-time students.

Payment plans. Credit card, deferred payment.

Application procedures. FAFSA, institutional form required. Closing date 4/29. Applicants notified by 6/15, must reply by 7/30. **Transfers:** No deadline.

Contact. **Financial aid office:** (787) 864-2222 ext. 2206
Jose Vechini Rodriguez, Director of Financial Aid
PO Box 10004
Guayama, PR 00785

Inter American University of Puerto Rico: Metropolitan Campus

San Juan, Puerto Rico
metro.inter.edu
Four-year private **Federal Code: 017202**

	Living at home
Tuition and fees (2002-2003):	$4,316
Board only:	$1,200
Books and supplies:	$640
Personal expenses:	$880
Transportation:	$600

Undergraduate aid. All financial aid based on need. 57% awarded as scholarships/grants, 43% as loans/jobs. Need-based aid available for part-time students.

Policies to reduce costs. Tuition/fee waivers for employees and their families. Credit/placement for qualifying scores on AP examinations. Work study available nights and weekends.

Payment plans. Deferred payment.

Application procedures. Institutional form required. Closing date 4/30. Applicants notified on rolling basis.

Contact. **Financial aid office:** (787) 250-1912 ext. 2185
Glenda Diaz, Director of Financial Aid
Box 191293
San Juan, PR 00919-1293

Inter American University of Puerto Rico: San German Campus

San German, Puerto Rico
www.sg.inter.edu
Four-year private **Federal Code: 00714**

	Living at home	On-campus
Tuition and fees (2002-2003):	$4,166	$4,166
Room and board:		$2,400
Books and supplies:	$890	$890
Personal expenses:	$880	$880
Transportation:	$600	$600

Undergraduate aid. **Need-based:** Need-based aid available for full-time and part-time students. **Non-need-based:** Scholarships based on academics, athletics.

Policies to reduce costs. Tuition/fee waivers for employees and their families. Tuition at time of enrollment guaranteed for 4 years; credit/placement for qualifying scores on AP, CLEP examinations. Work study available nights and weekends.

Payment plans. Credit card, installment, deferred payment.

Application procedures. FAFSA, institutional form required. Closing date 5/13. Applicants notified on rolling basis, must reply by 8/1.

Contact. Maria Lugo, Director of Financial Aid
Box 5100
San German, PR 00683

Pontifical Catholic University of Puerto Rico

Ponce, Puerto Rico
www.pucpr.edu
Four-year private **Federal Code: 003936**

	Living at home	On-campus
Tuition and fees (2002-2003):	$4,236	$4,236
Room and board:		$2,840
Board only:	$1,700	
Books and supplies:	$600	$600
Personal expenses:	$1,216	$1,216
Transportation:	$552	$408

Undergraduate aid. **Need-based:** 22% awarded as scholarships/grants, 78% as loans/jobs. Need-based aid available for part-time students. **Non-need-based:** Scholarships based on academics, athletics.

Policies to reduce costs. Tuition/fee waivers for family of clergy, employees and their families. Credit/placement for qualifying scores on AP examinations. Work study available nights, weekends and for part-time students.

Payment plans. Credit card, installment, deferred payment.

Application procedures. FAFSA, institutional form required. Priority date 5/1; no closing date. Applicants notified by 7/1, must reply within 4 week(s) of notification. **Transfers:** Priority date 5/8; no deadline. Distribution of awards based on availability of funds when application received.

Contact. Margaret Alustiza, Director of Student Aid
2250 Las Americas Avenue, Suite 284
Ponce, PR 00717-0777

Technological College of San Juan

San Juan, Puerto Rico
Two-year public
Federal Code: 010567

	Living at home
Tuition and fees:	$2,885
Out-of-state:	$2,885
Per-credit charge:	$85
Books and supplies:	$621
Personal expenses:	$920
Transportation:	$840

Undergraduate aid. All financial aid based on need. 97% awarded as scholarships/grants, 3% as loans/jobs. Need-based aid available for part-time students.

Policies to reduce costs. Tuition/fee waivers for employees and their families. Tuition at time of enrollment guaranteed for 2 years; credit/placement for qualifying scores on AP examinations.

Payment plans. Credit card, installment, deferred payment.

Application procedures. FAFSA, institutional form required. Closing date 9/30. Applicants notified by 10/30. **Transfers:** Financial aid transcripts.

Contact. **Financial aid office:** (787) 250-7111 ext. 2286
Maria de los A. Quinones, Director of Financial Aid
180 Jose R. Oliver Avenue
San Juan, PR 00918

Turabo University

Gurabo, Puerto Rico
www.suagm.edu/ut
Four-year private **Federal Code: 011719**

	Living at home
Tuition and fees (2002-2003):	$4,649
Books and supplies:	$600
Personal expenses:	$2,620
Transportation:	$1,350

Undergraduate aid. **Non-need-based:** Scholarships based on academics, athletics.

Policies to reduce costs. Tuition/fee waivers for employees and their families. Credit/placement for qualifying scores on AP, CLEP examinations.

Payment plans. Credit card, installment, deferred payment.

Application procedures. FAFSA required. Priority date 5/30; no closing date. Applicants notified by 7/30.

Contact. **Financial aid office:** (787) 743-7979 ext. 4350
Carmen Rivera, Admissions and Financial Aid Director
PO Box 3030
Gurabo, PR 00778

Universidad Metropolitana

Rio Piedras, Puerto Rico
www.suagm.edu/UMET
Four-year private **Federal Code: 025875**

	Living at home
Tuition and fees (2002-2003):	$4,190
Books and supplies:	$700
Personal expenses:	$2,620
Transportation:	$1,350

Policies to reduce costs. Tuition/fee waivers for employees and their families. Credit/placement for qualifying scores on AP, CLEP examinations. Work study available nights.

Payment plans. Credit card, installment payment.

Application procedures. FAFSA required. Priority date 5/30; no closing date. Applicants notified by 7/30.

Contact. **Financial aid office:** (787) 766-1717 ext . 6587
Evelyn Robledo, Admissions and Financial Aid Director
Apartado 21150
Rio Piedras, PR 00928

Universidad Politecnica de Puerto Rico

Hato Rey, Puerto Rico
www.pupr.edu
Five-year private **Federal Code: 014055**

College costs (2002-2003). Tuition based on program per-credit-hour charges (business administration $120, engineering $130, architecture $145) plus fees: $506. Books/supplies: $1,000. Personal expenses: $1,848. Transportation: $984.

Undergraduate aid. Need-based: Need-based aid available for full-time and part-time students. **Non-need-based:** Scholarships based on academics, music/drama.

Policies to reduce costs. Tuition/fee waivers for employees and their families.

Payment plans. Credit card, installment, deferred payment.

Application procedures. FAFSA, institutional form required. Closing date 6/30. Applicants notified by 7/15.

Contact. Lydia Cruz, Director of Financial Aid
PO Box 192017
San Juan, PR 00918

Universidad del Este

Carolina, Puerto Rico
www.suagm.edu
Four-year private **Federal Code: 011718**

	Living at home
Tuition and fees (2002-2003):	$4,190
Books and supplies:	$700
Personal expenses:	$2,620
Transportation:	$1,350

Undergraduate aid. Non-need-based: Scholarships based on academics, athletics.

Policies to reduce costs. Tuition/fee waivers for employees and their families. Credit/placement for qualifying scores on AP examinations.

Payment plans. Credit card, installment payment.

Application procedures. FAFSA, institutional form required. Priority date 5/30; no closing date. Applicants notified by 7/30. **Transfers:** No deadline.

Contact. **Financial aid office:** (787) 257-7373 ext. 3401
Clotilde Santiago, Admissions and Financial Aid Director
PO Box 2010
Carolina, PR 00983

University of Puerto Rico at Humacao

Humacao, Puerto Rico
www.upr.clu.edu
Four-year public **Federal Code: 003942**

	Living at home
Tuition and fees (2002-2003):	$1,245
Board only:	$3,600
Books and supplies:	$1,200
Personal expenses:	$1,000
Transportation:	$1,080

Undergraduate aid. Need-based: Average financial aid package for full-time students was $4,293; for part-time $2,930. 92% awarded as scholarships/grants, 8% as loans/jobs. **Non-need-based:** Scholarships based on academics, athletics, music/drama.

Freshman aid. Need-based: Out of 882 full-time freshmen, 760 applied for aid; 760 were judged to have need; of these 760 received aid. Average package met 50% of need. Average scholarship/grant was $4,211; average loan $2,600.

Policies to reduce costs. Tuition/fee waivers for employees and their families.

Payment plans. Credit card, deferred payment.

Application procedures. FAFSA, institutional form required. Closing date 7/31. Applicants notified by 9/10, must reply by 9/17 or within 2 week(s) of notification.

Contact. Larry Cruz, Director of Financial Aid
CUH Station
Humacao, PR 00791

University of Puerto Rico at Ponce

Ponce, Puerto Rico
http://upr-ponce.upr.edu
Four-year public **Federal Code: 009652**

	Living at home
Tuition and fees (2002-2003):	$2,245
Out-of-state:	$3,400
Books and supplies:	$1,200
Personal expenses:	$800
Transportation:	$1,080

Policies to reduce costs. Tuition/fee waivers for employees and their families. Credit/placement for qualifying scores on AP examinations.

Payment plans. Credit card, installment, deferred payment.

Application procedures. FAFSA, institutional form required. Closing date 5/30. Applicants notified by 10/15.

Contact. Carmelo Montes, Financial Aid Officer
Box 7186
Ponce, PR 00732

University of Puerto Rico at Utuado

Utuado, Puerto Rico
http://upr-utuado.upr.clu.edu
Four-year public **Federal Code: 010922**

	Living at home
Tuition and fees (2002-2003):	$1,095
Books and supplies:	$1,200
Personal expenses:	$1,000

Undergraduate aid. All financial aid based on need. 93% awarded as scholarships/grants, 7% as loans/jobs. Need-based aid available for part-time students.

Policies to reduce costs. Tuition/fee waivers for employees and their families.

Payment plans. Deferred payment.

Application procedures. FAFSA, institutional form required. Priority date 5/31; no closing date. Applicants notified on rolling basis starting 9/30, must reply within 4 week(s) of notification. **Transfers:** Priority date 5/30; closing date 6/15. Closing date for Pell grant applicants is May 1.

Contact. Edgar Salva, Financial Assistance Officer
Box 2500
Utuado, PR 00641

University of Puerto Rico: Bayamon University College

Bayamon, Puerto Rico
www.uprb.upr.edu
Four-year public **Federal Code: 010975**

	Living at home
Tuition and fees (2002-2003):	$1,095
Books and supplies:	$800
Personal expenses:	$600
Transportation:	$700

Policies to reduce costs. Tuition/fee waivers for family members, employees and their families.

Payment plans. Deferred payment.

Application procedures. Institutional form required. Closing date 6/15. Applicants notified by 7/12, must reply within 4 week(s) of notification. **Transfers:** Closing date 7/12.

Contact. Anilda González, Director of Financial Aid
174 State Road #170 Parque Industrial Minillas
Bayamon, PR 00959

University of Puerto Rico: Carolina Regional College

Carolina, Puerto Rico
http://cunic-net.upr.clu.edu
Four-year public **Federal Code: 003942**

	Living at home
Tuition and fees (2002-2003):	$1,605
Books and supplies:	$1,800
Personal expenses:	$1,000
Transportation:	$810

Undergraduate aid. All financial aid based on need. Need-based aid available for full-time and part-time students.

Policies to reduce costs. Tuition/fee waivers for employees and their families. Credit/placement for qualifying scores on AP, CLEP examinations.

Payment plans. Deferred payment.

Application procedures. FAFSA, institutional form required. Closing date 5/15. **Transfers:** Closing date 5/16.

Contact. **Financial aid office:** (787) 769-0188
Lucy Rodriguez, Financial Aid Officer/Director
Box 4800
Carolina, PR 00984-4800

University of Puerto Rico: Cayey University College

Cayey, Puerto Rico
wwwcuc.upr.clu.edu
Four-year public **Federal Code: 007206**

	Living at home
Tuition and fees (2002-2003):	$1,245
Books and supplies:	$1,200
Personal expenses:	$1,000
Transportation:	$1,080

Undergraduate aid. All financial aid based on need. 96% awarded as scholarships/grants, 4% as loans/jobs. Need-based aid available for part-time students.

Policies to reduce costs. Tuition/fee waivers for employees and their families. Tuition at time of enrollment guaranteed for 4 years; credit/placement for qualifying scores on AP examinations. Work study available nights and weekends.

Payment plans. Credit card, installment, deferred payment.

Application procedures. FAFSA required. Closing date 6/30. Applicants notified by 7/30, must reply by 7/30. **Transfers:** Priority date 1/30; closing date 2/28.

Contact. Hector Maldonado, Director of Financial Aid
Antonio R. Barcelo Avenue
Cayey, PR 00736

University of Puerto Rico: Mayaguez Campus

Mayaguez, Puerto Rico
www.uprm.edu
Four-year public **Federal Code: 003944**

	Living at home	On-campus
Tuition and fees (2002-2003):	$1,245	$1,245
Room and board:		$6,620
Board only:	$1,800	
Books and supplies:	$1,000	$1,000
Personal expenses:	$800	
Transportation:	$1,000	

Policies to reduce costs. Tuition/fee waivers for employees and their families. Credit/placement for qualifying scores on AP examinations.

Payment plans. Installment, deferred payment.

Application procedures. FAFSA, institutional form required. Closing date 6/30. Applicants notified by 9/30, must reply within 2 week(s) of notification. **Transfers:** No deadline.

Contact. **Financial aid office:** (787) 265-1920
Ana Rodriguez, Director of Financial Aid
Box 9021
Mayaguez, PR 00681-9021

University of Puerto Rico: Medical Sciences Campus

San Juan, Puerto Rico
www.rcm.upr.edu
Four-year public **Federal Code: 003945**

	Living at home
Tuition and fees (2002-2003):	$2,098
Board only:	$1,500
Books and supplies:	$1,200
Personal expenses:	$800
Transportation:	$500

Undergraduate aid. All financial aid based on need. Need-based aid available for full-time and part-time students.

Policies to reduce costs. Tuition/fee waivers for employees and their families. Credit/placement for qualifying scores on AP examinations.

Payment plans. Installment, deferred payment.

Application procedures. FAFSA, institutional form required. Priority date 4/30; closing date 6/15. Applicants notified on rolling basis starting 8/1, must reply within 2 week(s) of notification.

Contact. **Financial aid office:** (787) 758-2525 ext. 3205
Cruz Figueroa, Director, Financial Aid
Box 365067
San Juan, PR 00936-5067

University of Puerto Rico: Rio Piedras Campus

San Juan, Puerto Rico
www.rrp.upr.edu
Four-year public **Federal Code: 007108**

College costs. Students who provide evidence of private medical insurance exempt from $529 health service fee.

	Living at home	On-campus
Tuition and fees (2002-2003):	$1,095	$1,095
Out-of-state:	$2,475	$2,475
Room and board:		$6,620
Books and supplies:	$1,200	$1,200
Personal expenses:	$1,000	$1,000
Transportation:	$1,000	$1,000

Undergraduate aid. All financial aid based on need. Need-based aid available for full-time and part-time students. **Additional information:** Tuition fees waived for honor students, athletes, members of music chorus, and others with special talents.

Policies to reduce costs. Tuition/fee waivers for employees and their families. Credit/placement for qualifying scores on AP examinations.

Payment plans. Credit card, installment, deferred payment.

Application procedures. FAFSA, institutional form required. Closing date 5/31. Applicants notified by 9/7.

Contact. Luz Santiago, Director of Financial Aid
Box 23344
San Juan, PR 00931-3344

University of the Sacred Heart

Santurce, Puerto Rico
www.sagrado.edu
Four-year private **Federal Code: 003937**

	Living at home	On-campus
Tuition and fees (2002-2003):	$4,780	$4,780
Room only:		$1,800
Board only:	$3,766	
Books and supplies:	$1,250	$1,250
Personal expenses:	$2,010	$2,010
Transportation:	$1,976	$1,954

Undergraduate aid. Need-based: Need-based aid available for full-time and part-time students. **Non-need-based:** Scholarships based on academics, athletics.

Policies to reduce costs. Tuition/fee waivers for family of clergy, employees and their families. Credit/placement for qualifying scores on AP examinations.

Payment plans. Credit card, deferred payment.

Application procedures. FAFSA, institutional form required. Closing date 5/30. Applicants notified on rolling basis starting 6/15, must reply by 8/30. **Transfers:** No deadline.

Contact. Luis Aquiles, Director, Financial Aid
PO Box 12383
San Juan, PR 00914-0383

Rhode Island

Brown University

Providence, Rhode Island
www.brown.edu
Four-year private **Federal Code: 003401**

	Living at home	On-campus
Tuition and fees (projected):	$29,846	$29,846
Room and board:		$8,096
Board only:	$3,066	
Books and supplies:	$1,000	$1,000
Personal expenses:	$1,306	$1,306

Undergraduate aid. All financial aid based on need. Need-based aid available for full-time and part-time students.

Policies to reduce costs. Prepayment discount; credit/placement for qualifying scores on AP, IB examinations.

Payment plans. Installment payment.

Application procedures. FAFSA, institutional form, CSS PROFILE required. Closing date 2/1. Applicants notified by 4/1, must reply by 5/1. **Transfers:** Closing date 4/15.

Contact. **Financial aid office:** (401) 863-2721
Michael Bartini, Director of Financial Aid
45 Prospect Street
Providence, RI 02912

Bryant College

Smithfield, Rhode Island
www.bryant.edu
Four-year private **Federal Code: 003402**

College costs. Tuition includes personal use of laptop computer for freshman and sophomores.

	Living at home	On-campus
Tuition and fees:	$22,458	$22,458
Room and board:		$8,546
Board only:	$2,500	
Books and supplies:	$900	$900
Personal expenses:	$1,000	$1,000
Transportation:	$1,500	$200

Undergraduate aid. Need-based: Average financial aid package for full-time students was $13,740; for part-time $4,517. 65% awarded as scholarships/grants, 35% as loans/jobs. **Non-need-based:** 37% awarded as scholarships/grants, 63% as loans/jobs. Scholarships based on academics, alumni affiliation, athletics, minority status. **Student debt:** 72% of graduating class borrowed to fund education; average debt was $20,597.

Freshman aid. Need-based: Out of 718 full-time freshmen, 584 applied for aid; 466 were judged to have need; of these 466 received aid. Average package met 74% of need. 91 students had full need met. Average scholarship/grant was $5,477; average loan $3,914. **Non-need based:** 449 full-time freshmen with need received non-need scholarships; 238 without need received awards; 10 received athletic scholarships.

Policies to reduce costs. Tuition/fee waivers for family members, employees and their families. Credit/placement for qualifying scores on AP, IB, CLEP examinations. Work study available nights and weekends.

Application procedures. FAFSA, institutional form required. Closing date 2/15. Applicants notified by 3/24, must reply by 5/1. Early decision closing date 11/15. **Transfers:** Closing date 4/1.

Contact. **Financial aid office:** (401) 232-6020
John Canning, Director of Financial Aid
1150 Douglas Pike
Smithfield, RI 02917

Community College of Rhode Island

Warwick, Rhode Island
www.ccri.cc.ri.us
Two-year public **Federal Code: 004916**

	Living at home
Tuition and fees (2002-2003):	$2,014
Out-of-state:	$5,428
Per-credit charge:	$83
Per-credit out-of-state:	$248
Books and supplies:	$700
Personal expenses:	$1,000
Transportation:	$720

Undergraduate aid. Need-based: Need-based aid available for full-time and part-time students. **Non-need-based:** Scholarships based on athletics.

Policies to reduce costs. Tuition/fee waivers for senior citizens, unemployed or children of unemployed, employees and their families. Credit/placement for qualifying scores on AP, CLEP examinations. Work study available nights, weekends and for part-time students.

Payment plans. Credit card, installment, deferred payment.

Application procedures. FAFSA, institutional form required. Priority date 3/1; no closing date. Applicants notified on rolling basis starting 5/1, must reply within 2 week(s) of notification.

Contact. **Financial aid office:** (401) 825-2281
Christine Jenkins, Assistant Dean, Enrollment Services
400 East Avenue
Warwick, RI 02886

Johnson & Wales University

Providence, Rhode Island
www.jwu.edu
Four-year private **Federal Code: 003404**

College costs (2002-2003). Culinary program $17,652, hospitality program $15,393, equine program $17,652, business program $14,562, school of technology program $15,246. Annual required fees $630, room and board $6,366. Optional weekend meal plan $786. Books/supplies: $750. Personal expenses: $500. Transportation: $750.

Undergraduate aid. Non-need-based: Scholarships based on academics, alumni affiliation, job skills, leadership.

Policies to reduce costs. Tuition/fee waivers for employees and their families. Tuition at time of enrollment guaranteed for 4 years; credit/placement for qualifying scores on AP, CLEP examinations.

Payment plans. Credit card, installment payment.

Application procedures. FAFSA required. No deadline. Applicants notified on rolling basis starting 3/1, must reply within 2 week(s) of notification. **Transfers:** No deadline. Transfer scholarships available.

Contact. **Financial aid office:** (800) 342-5598 ext. 4648
Lynn Robinson, Director of Financial Aid
8 Abbott Park Place
Providence, RI 02903-3703

Providence College

Providence, Rhode Island
www.providence.edu
Four-year private **Federal Code: 003406**

College costs. $207 per-credit-hour charges for evening division classes only.

	Living at home	On-campus
Tuition and fees:	$22,179	$22,179
Room and board:		$8,500

Undergraduate aid. Need-based: Average financial aid package for full-time students was $14,582. 67% awarded as scholarships/grants, 33% as loans/jobs. **Non-need-based:** 70% awarded as scholarships/grants, 30% as loans/jobs. Scholarships based on academics, athletics, minority status. **Student debt:** 65% of graduating class borrowed to fund education; average debt was $19,850. **Additional information:** Tuition Payment Agreement Plan (TPA) provides families with monthly payment plan that divides charges into 10 monthly installments.

Freshman aid. **Need-based:** Out of 878 full-time freshmen, 671 applied for aid; 481 were judged to have need; of these 481 received aid. Average package met 88% of need. 58 students had full need met. Average scholarship/grant was $9,200; average loan $4,425. **Non-need based:** 60 full-time freshmen with need received non-need scholarships; 109 without need received awards; 25 received athletic scholarships.

Policies to reduce costs. Tuition/fee waivers for senior citizens, minority students, family members, family of clergy, employees and their families. Credit/placement for qualifying scores on AP, IB, CLEP examinations. Work study available nights, weekends and for part-time students.

Payment plans. Installment payment.

Application procedures. FAFSA, CSS PROFILE required. Closing date 2/1. Applicants notified by 4/7, must reply by 5/1. **Transfers:** Priority date 4/15; no deadline.

Contact. **Financial aid office:** (401) 865-2286
Herbert D'Arcy, Executive Director, Financial Aid
549 River Avenue, Harkins Hall 222
Providence, RI 02918-0001

Rhode Island College

Providence, Rhode Island
www.ric.edu
Four-year public **Federal Code: 003407**

	Living at home	On-campus
Tuition and fees (2002-2003):	$3,761	$3,761
Out-of-state:	$9,525	$9,525
Room and board:		$6,136
Board only:	$1,800	
Books and supplies:	$600	$600
Personal expenses:	$1,120	$1,120
Transportation:	$1,000	$400

Undergraduate aid. **Non-need-based:** Scholarships based on academics, alumni affiliation, art, music/drama.

Policies to reduce costs. Tuition/fee waivers for senior citizens, unemployed or children of unemployed, employees and their families. Credit/placement for qualifying scores on AP, CLEP examinations.

Payment plans. Credit card, installment payment.

Application procedures. FAFSA, institutional form required. Priority date 3/1; no closing date. Applicants notified on rolling basis starting 3/15, must reply within 3 week(s) of notification. **Transfers:** Priority date 5/15; no deadline.

Contact. James Hanbury, Director of Financial Aid
600 Mount Pleasant Avenue
Providence, RI 02908

Rhode Island School of Design

Providence, Rhode Island
www.risd.edu
Four-year private **Federal Code: 003409**

College costs. Additional costs vary by program.

	Living at home	On-campus
Tuition and fees:	$26,199	$26,199
Room and board:		$7,366

Policies to reduce costs. Tuition/fee waivers for employees and their families. Credit/placement for qualifying scores on AP examinations.

Payment plans. Installment, deferred payment.

Application procedures. CSS PROFILE required. Closing date 2/15. Applicants notified by 4/1, must reply by 5/1. **Transfers:** Closing date 4/7. Transfer students with previous undergraduate degree not eligible for scholarship aid.

Contact. Peter Riefler, Director of Financial Aid
Two College Street
Providence, RI 02903-2791

Roger Williams University

Bristol, Rhode Island
www.rwu.edu
Four-year private **Federal Code: 003410**

College costs. Tuition differential for architecture program: $2856. Students living on campus pay additional $346 in required fees.

	Living at home	On-campus
Tuition and fees:	$20,840	$20,840
Room and board:		$9,290
Board only:	$825	
Books and supplies:	$700	$700
Personal expenses:	$526	$506
Transportation:	$800	$540

Undergraduate aid. **Need-based:** Average financial aid package for full-time students was $14,500; for part-time $6,340. 65% awarded as scholarships/grants, 35% as loans/jobs. **Non-need-based:** 59% awarded as scholarships/grants, 41% as loans/jobs. Scholarships based on academics. **Student debt:** 65% of graduating class borrowed to fund education; average debt was $16,366.

Freshman aid. **Need-based:** Out of 981 full-time freshmen, 885 applied for aid; 730 were judged to have need; of these 730 received aid. Average package met 80% of need. 527 students had full need met. Average scholarship/grant was $7,200; average loan $5,700. **Non-need based:** 136 full-time freshmen with need received non-need scholarships; 136 without need received awards.

Policies to reduce costs. Tuition/fee waivers for employees and their families. Credit/placement for qualifying scores on AP, CLEP examinations. Work study available nights and weekends.

Payment plans. Credit card, installment payment.

Application procedures. FAFSA, CSS PROFILE required. Closing date 2/1. Applicants notified on rolling basis starting 3/19, must reply by 5/1 or within 2 week(s) of notification. Early decision closing date 12/1.

Contact. **Financial aid office:** (401) 254-3100
Lynn Fawthrop, Vice President of Enrollment Management and Retention
One Old Ferry Road
Bristol, RI 02809

Salve Regina University

Newport, Rhode Island
www.salve.edu
Four-year private **Federal Code: 003411**

	Living at home	On-campus
Tuition and fees (2002-2003):	$19,410	$19,410
Room and board:		$8,400
Board only:	$2,900	
Books and supplies:	$700	$700
Personal expenses:		$1,000
Transportation:		$640

Undergraduate aid. **Need-based:** Average financial aid package for full-time students was $14,533; for part-time $6,697. 62% awarded as scholarships/grants, 38% as loans/jobs. **Non-need-based:** 19% awarded as scholarships/grants, 81% as loans/jobs. Scholarships based on academics, music/drama. **Student debt:** 76% of graduating class borrowed to fund education; average debt was $19,375.

Freshman aid. **Need-based:** Out of 529 full-time freshmen, 421 applied for aid; 367 were judged to have need; of these 367 received aid. Average package met 76% of need. Average scholarship/grant was $11,311; average loan $2,890. **Non-need based:** 10 full-time freshmen with need received non-need scholarships.

Merit scholarships. Dean's, Trustee's, and Presidential scholarships are available to students who rank in the top 20% of their class and meet SAT criteria.

Policies to reduce costs. Tuition/fee waivers for family members, employees and their families. Credit/placement for qualifying scores on AP, IB, CLEP examinations. Work study available nights, weekends and for part-time students.

Payment plans. Credit card payment.

Application procedures. FAFSA, institutional form, CSS PROFILE required. Priority date 3/1; no closing date. Applicants notified on rolling basis starting 4/1, must reply by 5/1 or within 2 week(s) of notification. **Trans-**

fers: Priority date 3/1; no deadline. Must provide financial aid transcripts from previous institutions attended.

Contact. **Financial aid office:** (401) 341-2901
Aida Mirante, Director of Financial Aid
100 Ochre Point Avenue
Newport, RI 02840-4192

University of Rhode Island

Kingston, Rhode Island
www.uri.edu
Four-year public **Federal Code: 003414**

	Living at home	On-campus
Tuition and fees (2002-2003):	$5,854	$5,854
Out-of-state:	$15,324	$15,324
Room and board:		$7,361
Board only:	$1,598	
Books and supplies:	$600	$600
Personal expenses:	$1,576	$1,576

Undergraduate aid. Need-based: Average financial aid package for full-time students was $8,965; for part-time $5,242. 32% awarded as scholarships/grants, 68% as loans/jobs. **Non-need-based:** 9% awarded as scholarships/grants, 91% as loans/jobs. Scholarships based on academics, alumni affiliation, athletics, leadership, minority status, music/drama. **Student debt:** 64% of graduating class borrowed to fund education; average debt was $14,000.

Freshman aid. Need-based: Out of 2,282 full-time freshmen, 1,928 applied for aid; 1,638 were judged to have need; of these 1,539 received aid. Average package met 72% of need. 1046 students had full need met. Average scholarship/grant was $3,070; average loan $4,637. **Non-need based:** 568 full-time freshmen with need received non-need scholarships; 160 without need received awards; 128 received athletic scholarships.

Merit scholarships. Centennial Scholarship, 525 awarded per year, up to full tuition for full-time students with 3.0 GPA or better, 1120 SAT score, 1150 for engineering and pharmacy in top third of class.

Policies to reduce costs. Tuition/fee waivers for senior citizens, unemployed or children of unemployed, employees and their families. Credit/placement for qualifying scores on AP, CLEP examinations.

Application procedures. FAFSA required. Priority date 3/1; no closing date. Applicants notified on rolling basis starting 3/20, must reply by 5/1 or within 2 week(s) of notification.

Contact. Harry Amaral, Director of Financial Aid
14 Upper College Road
Kingston, RI 02881-1391

Zion Bible Institute

Barrington, Rhode Island
www.zbi.edu
Four-year private **Federal Code: 035705**

	Living at home	On-campus
Tuition and fees:	$3,853	$3,853
Room and board:		$4,180

Contact. Patricia Stauffer, Financial Aid Director
27 Middle Highway
Barrington, RI 02806

South Carolina

Aiken Technical College

Aiken, South Carolina
www.atc.edu
Two-year public **Federal Code: 010056**

College costs. Residents of Richmond and Columbia Counties (GA) pay $1,992 tuition, $83 per-credit-hour plus additional $30 per year fee. Other out-of-state students pay additional $88 required fee per year.

	Living at home
Tuition and fees (2002-2003):	$2,142
Out-of-district:	$2,358
Out-of-state:	$5,886
Per-credit charge:	$83
Per-credit out-of-district:	$92
Per-credit out-of-state:	$239
Books and supplies:	$450
Personal expenses:	$900
Transportation:	$1,125

Undergraduate aid. Need-based: Need-based aid available for full-time and part-time students. **Non-need-based:** Scholarships based on academics, leadership, state/district residency.

Merit scholarships. John D. Bryan Criminal Justice; $500 annually; 1 awarded. Vernon Ford Scholarships, $750 annually; 8 awarded; for candidates with minimum GPA of 3.0.

Policies to reduce costs. Tuition/fee waivers for senior citizens. Credit/placement for qualifying scores on AP, CLEP examinations. Work study available nights, weekends and for part-time students.

Payment plans. Credit card payment.

Application procedures. FAFSA required. Priority date 5/1; closing date 6/30. Applicants notified on rolling basis starting 4/1, must reply within 4 week(s) of notification. **Transfers:** No deadline.

Contact. Financial aid office: (803) 593-9231
Amanda Chittum, Director of Financial Aid
Drawer 696
Aiken, SC 29802

Anderson College

Anderson, South Carolina
www.ac.edu
Four-year private **Federal Code: 003418**

	Living at home	On-campus
Tuition and fees:	$13,115	$13,115
Room and board:		$5,445
Books and supplies:	$1,400	$1,400
Personal expenses:	$1,750	$1,750
Transportation:	$2,250	$1,750

Undergraduate aid. Need-based: Average financial aid package for full-time students was $7,843; for part-time $845. 74% awarded as scholarships/grants, 26% as loans/jobs. **Non-need-based:** 47% awarded as scholarships/grants, 53% as loans/jobs. Scholarships based on academics, alumni affiliation, art, athletics, leadership, minority status, music/drama, religious affiliation, state/district residency. **Student debt:** 81% of graduating class borrowed to fund education; average debt was $14,135.

Freshman aid. Need-based: Out of 327 full-time freshmen, 327 applied for aid; 327 were judged to have need; of these 327 received aid. Average package met 84% of need. 214 students had full need met. Average scholarship/grant was $3,502; average loan $2,142. **Non-need based:** 327 full-time freshmen with need received non-need scholarships; 85 without need received awards; 20 received athletic scholarships.

Policies to reduce costs. Tuition/fee waivers for adults, children of alumni, senior citizens, family members, family of clergy, employees and their families. Credit/placement for qualifying scores on AP, CLEP examinations.

Payment plans. Credit card, installment payment.

Application procedures. FAFSA required. Priority date 3/1; closing date 7/1. Applicants notified on rolling basis starting 3/1, must reply within 2 week(s) of notification.

Contact. Financial aid office: (864) 231-2070
Jeff Holliday, Director of Financial Aid
316 Boulevard
Anderson, SC 29621

Benedict College

Columbia, South Carolina
www.benedict.edu
Four-year private **Federal Code: 003420**

	Living at home	On-campus
Tuition and fees:	$11,586	$11,586
Room and board:		$5,434
Books and supplies:	$1,000	$1,000
Personal expenses:	$2,000	$1,400
Transportation:	$1,400	$800

Undergraduate aid. Need-based: Need-based aid available for full-time and part-time students.

Policies to reduce costs. Tuition/fee waivers for senior citizens. Credit/placement for qualifying scores on CLEP examinations.

Payment plans. Installment payment.

Application procedures. FAFSA required. Priority date 4/15; no closing date. Applicants notified on rolling basis starting 4/15.

Contact. Financial aid office: (803) 253-5105
Sul Black, Director of Financial Aid
1600 Harden Street
Columbia, SC 29204

Central Carolina Technical College

Sumter, South Carolina
www.cctech.edu
Two-year public **Federal Code: 003995**

College costs. In-state students in natural resources management and environmental engineering program pay $1,992 tuition and $83 per-credit-hour, regardless of county.

	Living at home
Tuition and fees (2002-2003):	$2,092
Out-of-district:	$2,480
Out-of-state:	$4,604
Per-credit charge:	$83
Per-credit out-of-district:	$99
Per-credit out-of-state:	$188
Books and supplies:	$600

Undergraduate aid. All financial aid based on need. Need-based aid available for full-time and part-time students.

Policies to reduce costs. Tuition/fee waivers for senior citizens. Credit/placement for qualifying scores on AP, CLEP examinations. Work study available nights and for part-time students.

Payment plans. Credit card payment.

Application procedures. FAFSA required. Priority date 6/15; no closing date. Applicants notified on rolling basis, must reply within 2 week(s) of notification.

Contact. Financial aid office: (803) 778-6668
William Whitlock, Director of Financial Aid
506 North Guignard Drive
Sumter, SC 29150

Charleston Southern University

Charleston, South Carolina
www.csuniv.edu
Four-year private **Federal Code: 003419**

	Living at home	On-campus
Tuition and fees:	$14,426	$14,426
Room and board:		$5,544
Books and supplies:	$1,000	$1,000

Undergraduate aid. Need-based: Average financial aid package for full-time students was $10,613; for part-time $8,481. 56% awarded as scholarships/grants, 44% as loans/jobs. **Non-need-based:** 57% awarded as scholarships/grants, 43% as loans/jobs. Scholarships based on academics, alumni affiliation, art, athletics, leadership, music/drama, religious affiliation, state/district residency.

Freshman aid. Need-based: Out of 647 full-time freshmen, 380 applied for aid; 321 were judged to have need; of these 321 received aid. Average package met 75% of need. 78 students had full need met. Average scholarship/grant was $8,130; average loan $2,651. **Non-need based:** 67 full-time freshmen with need received non-need scholarships; 86 without need received awards; 35 received athletic scholarships.

Policies to reduce costs. Tuition/fee waivers for employees and their families. Credit/placement for qualifying scores on AP, IB, CLEP examinations. Work study available nights and weekends.

Payment plans. Credit card, installment payment.

Application procedures. FAFSA required. Priority date 4/15; no closing date. Applicants notified on rolling basis starting 2/1, must reply within 1 week(s) of notification.

Contact. Financial aid office: (843) 863-7050
Ellen Green, Director of Financial Aid
9200 University Boulevard
Charleston, SC 29423

Claflin University

Orangeburg, South Carolina
www.claflin.edu
Four-year private **Federal Code: 003424**

	Living at home	On-campus
Tuition and fees (2002-2003):	$8,940	$8,940
Room and board:		$4,800
Board only:	$1,814	
Books and supplies:	$800	$800
Personal expenses:	$200	$200

Undergraduate aid. Need-based: Need-based aid available for full-time students.

Policies to reduce costs. Tuition/fee waivers for family of clergy, employees and their families. Credit/placement for qualifying scores on AP, CLEP examinations.

Payment plans. Credit card, installment, deferred payment.

Application procedures. FAFSA, institutional form required. Priority date 4/15; no closing date. Applicants notified on rolling basis starting 5/15, must reply within 2 week(s) of notification.

Contact. Sheri Jefferson, Director of Financial Aid
400 Magnolia Street
Orangeburg, SC 29115

Clemson University

Clemson, South Carolina
www.clemson.edu
Four-year public **Federal Code: 003425**

College costs. Students in colleges of business, behavioral sciences, and engineering and sciences must own personal computer, $1,800 estimated allowance. Tuition/fees excludes lab fees.

	Living at home	On-campus
Tuition and fees (2002-2003):	$6,244	$6,244
Out-of-state:	$13,342	$13,342
Room and board:		$4,454
Board only:	$2,170	
Books and supplies:	$768	$768
Personal expenses:	$1,640	$1,640
Transportation:	$3,544	$2,194

Undergraduate aid. Need-based: Average financial aid package for full-time students was $8,518; for part-time $5,527. 37% awarded as scholarships/grants, 63% as loans/jobs. **Non-need-based:** 61% awarded as scholarships/grants, 39% as loans/jobs. Scholarships based on academics, athletics, leadership, minority status, music/drama, state/district residency.

Freshman aid. Need-based: Out of 2,464 full-time freshmen, 1,486 applied for aid; 956 were judged to have need; of these 930 received aid. Average package met 84% of need. 453 students had full need met. Average scholarship/grant was $3,112; average loan $2,774. **Non-need based:** 832 full-time freshmen with need received non-need scholarships; 1,183 without need received awards; 72 received athletic scholarships.

Policies to reduce costs. Tuition/fee waivers for senior citizens. Credit/placement for qualifying scores on AP, IB, CLEP examinations.

Payment plans. Credit card, installment payment.

Application procedures. FAFSA required. Priority date 4/1; no closing date. Applicants notified on rolling basis starting 4/1, must reply within 3 week(s) of notification. **Transfers:** Transfer students must earn 12 semester hours before being considered for institutional scholarship.

Contact. Financial aid office: (864) 656-2280
Marvin Carmichael, Director of Student Financial Aid
105 Sikes Hall
Clemson, SC 29634-5124

Coastal Carolina University

Conway, South Carolina
www.coastal.edu
Four-year public **Federal Code: 003451**

	Living at home	On-campus
Tuition and fees (2002-2003):	$4,430	$4,430
Out-of-state:	$11,840	$11,840
Room and board:		$5,610
Books and supplies:	$744	$744
Personal expenses:	$1,562	$1,562
Transportation:	$984	$936

Undergraduate aid. Need-based: Average financial aid package for full-time students was $6,717; for part-time $3,508. 33% awarded as scholarships/grants, 67% as loans/jobs. **Non-need-based:** 29% awarded as scholarships/grants, 71% as loans/jobs. Scholarships based on academics, art, athletics, leadership, music/drama, state/district residency. **Student debt:** 60% of graduating class borrowed to fund education; average debt was $15,090.

Freshman aid. Need-based: Out of 934 full-time freshmen, 687 applied for aid; 574 were judged to have need; of these 574 received aid. Average package met 54% of need. 215 students had full need met. Average scholarship/grant was $3,069; average loan $8,707. **Non-need based:** 118 full-time freshmen with need received non-need scholarships; 241 without need received awards; 39 received athletic scholarships.

Policies to reduce costs. Tuition/fee waivers for senior citizens, employees and their families. Credit/placement for qualifying scores on AP, IB, CLEP examinations. Work study available nights, weekends and for part-time students.

Payment plans. Credit card, installment, deferred payment.

Application procedures. FAFSA required. Priority date 4/1; no closing date. Applicants notified on rolling basis starting 3/1, must reply by 5/1 or within 3 week(s) of notification.

Contact. Financial aid office: (843) 349-2313
Glenn Hanson, Director of Financial Aid
Box 261954
Conway, SC 29528-6054

Coker College

Hartsville, South Carolina
www.coker.edu
Four-year private **Federal Code: 003427**

	Living at home	On-campus
Tuition and fees (2002-2003):	$15,565	$15,565
Room and board:		$5,196
Board only:	$800	
Books and supplies:	$900	$900
Personal expenses:	$550	$550

Undergraduate aid. Need-based: Average financial aid package for full-time students was $14,514; for part-time $9,160. 54% awarded as scholarships/grants, 46% as loans/jobs. **Non-need-based:** 95% awarded as scholarships/grants, 5% as loans/jobs. Scholarships based on academics, art, athletics, music/drama. **Student debt:** 77% of graduating class borrowed to fund education; average debt was $10,949. **Additional information:** Endowed scholarship program for qualified applicants. June 1 deadline for filing South Carolina Tuition Grant forms.

Freshman aid. Need-based: Out of 116 full-time freshmen, 116 applied for aid; 100 were judged to have need; of these 100 received aid. Average

package met 92% of need. 34 students had full need met. Average scholarship/grant was $5,344; average loan $3,949. **Non-need based:** 99 full-time freshmen with need received non-need scholarships; 16 without need received awards; 7 received athletic scholarships.

Merit scholarships. Scholarships for Excellence; awarded on a competitive basis to students showing potential for continued high performance and leadership; up to $17,000 per year; candidates may be invited to campus for interviews. President's Scholarships; based upon SAT or ACT score and high school GPA; up to $7,500 per year. Dean's Scholarships; based upon SAT or ACT score and high school GPA; up to $7,000 per year. Departmental Scholarships; Art, Dance, Music, Theater, Biology, and Chemistry scholarships to talented students; Language and Literature/ creative writing scholarship; range from $500 to $4,000 per year; Art, Dance, Music, and Theater scholarships require an audition or portfolio; some departments require an interview. Intercollegiate athletics scholarships available in all 12 sponsored sports, including baseball, basketball, cross-country, golf, soccer, and tennis for men and basketball, cross-country, soccer, softball, tennis, and volleyball for women; work-awards are available to qualified student-trainers. Valedictorian Scholarships; $500 per year to students ranked number one in their class at the end of their junior year or first semester of their senior year.

Policies to reduce costs. Tuition/fee waivers for adults, children of alumni, employees and their families. Credit/placement for qualifying scores on AP, IB, CLEP examinations. Work study available nights and weekends.

Payment plans. Credit card, installment payment.

Application procedures. FAFSA required. Priority date 4/1; closing date 6/1. Applicants notified on rolling basis starting 12/1, must reply by 5/1 or within 3 week(s) of notification. **Transfers:** No deadline.

Contact. Betty Williams, Director of Financial Aid
300 East College Avenue
Hartsville, SC 29550

College of Charleston
Charleston, South Carolina
www.cofc.edu
Four-year public **Federal Code: 003428**

	Living at home	On-campus
Tuition and fees (2002-2003):	$4,556	$4,556
Out-of-state:	$10,290	$10,290
Room and board:		$5,075
Books and supplies:	$851	$851
Personal expenses:	$2,976	$2,976
Transportation:	$1,944	$658

Undergraduate aid. Need-based: Average financial aid package for full-time students was $8,324; for part-time $7,283. 47% awarded as scholarships/grants, 53% as loans/jobs. **Non-need-based:** 61% awarded as scholarships/grants, 39% as loans/jobs. Scholarships based on academics, alumni affiliation, art, athletics, music/drama. **Student debt:** 43% of graduating class borrowed to fund education; average debt was $15,135.

Freshman aid. Need-based: Out of 1,999 full-time freshmen, 1,138 applied for aid; 763 were judged to have need; of these 736 received aid. Average package met 71% of need. 251 students had full need met. Average scholarship/grant was $3,330; average loan $2,305. **Non-need based:** 556 full-time freshmen with need received non-need scholarships; 650 without need received awards; 29 received athletic scholarships.

Merit scholarships. Foundation Scholarships based on high school performance, test scores, and leadership qualities, no additional application required; ranging from $1,000-$4,000 annually for up to 4 years. Numerous other scholarships available by application.

Policies to reduce costs. Tuition/fee waivers for senior citizens, employees and their families. Credit/placement for qualifying scores on AP, IB, CLEP examinations.

Payment plans. Credit card, installment payment.

Application procedures. FAFSA required. Priority date 3/15; no closing date. Applicants notified on rolling basis starting 4/10, must reply within 8 week(s) of notification. **Transfers:** No aid available to transfer students who enroll for first time in summer school.

Contact. Financial aid office: (843) 953-5540
Donald Griggs, Director of Financial Assistance and Veteran's Affairs
66 George Street
Charleston, SC 29424-0001

Columbia College
Columbia, South Carolina
www.columbiacollegesc.edu
Four-year private **Federal Code: 003430**

	Living at home	On-campus
Tuition and fees (2002-2003):	$16,620	$16,620
Room and board:		$5,240
Board only:	$3,240	
Books and supplies:	$700	$700
Personal expenses:	$2,000	$2,150
Transportation:	$1,450	$1,250

Undergraduate aid. Non-need-based: Scholarships based on academics, athletics.

Merit scholarships. Scholarships for freshmen; 2 awarded; full tuition. Presidental Scholarships; $5,000 annually. Trustees Scholarships; ranging from $1,000-$3,000 annually. Leadership Scholarships; $3,000 annually. For all who meet academic qualifications.

Policies to reduce costs. Tuition/fee waivers for family of clergy, employees and their families. Credit/placement for qualifying scores on AP, CLEP examinations.

Application procedures. FAFSA required. Priority date 4/1; no closing date. Applicants notified on rolling basis starting 3/15, must reply within 2 week(s) of notification. **Transfers:** Priority date 4/15; no deadline. Must meet institutional standards of satisfactory academic progress.

Contact. Financial aid office: (803) 786-3612
Anita Kaminer Elliott, Director of Financial Aid
1301 Columbia College Drive
Columbia, SC 29203-5998

Columbia International University
Columbia, South Carolina
www.ciu.edu
Four-year private **Federal Code: 003429**

	Living at home	On-campus
Tuition and fees (2002-2003):	$10,688	$10,688
Room and board:		$4,940
Books and supplies:	$800	$800
Personal expenses:	$100	$100
Transportation:	$2,210	

Undergraduate aid. Need-based: Average financial aid package for full-time students was $8,397; for part-time $5,254. 39% awarded as scholarships/grants, 61% as loans/jobs. **Non-need-based:** 52% awarded as scholarships/grants, 48% as loans/jobs. Scholarships based on academics, state/district residency. **Student debt:** 78% of graduating class borrowed to fund education; average debt was $13,350. **Additional information:** Spouse scholarship program; special short quarter scholarships for missionaries on furlough.

Freshman aid. Need-based: Average package met 45% of need. Average scholarship/grant was $5,031; average loan $4,015.

Policies to reduce costs. Tuition/fee waivers for children of alumni, minority students, family of clergy, employees and their families. Credit/placement for qualifying scores on AP, CLEP examinations. Work study available nights, weekends and for part-time students.

Payment plans. Credit card, installment, deferred payment.

Application procedures. FAFSA, institutional form required. Closing date 3/17. Applicants notified on rolling basis starting 4/1, must reply within 4 week(s) of notification. **Transfers:** FASFA required by June 30 to federal processor for state need-based aid. State aid requires one-year residency prior to award in most cases. Non-need-based state aid requires graduation from a state high school.

Contact. Mary Bisesi, Director of Financial Aid
PO Box 3122
Columbia, SC 29230-3122

Converse College

Spartanburg, South Carolina
www.converse.edu
Four-year private **Federal Code: 003431**

	Living at home	On-campus
Tuition and fees:	$18,915	$18,915
Room and board:		$5,795
Board only:	$1,500	
Books and supplies:	$650	$650
Personal expenses:	$500	$1,000
Transportation:	$800	$500

Undergraduate aid. **Need-based:** Average financial aid package for full-time students was $15,053; for part-time $5,385. 74% awarded as scholarships/grants, 26% as loans/jobs. **Non-need-based:** 81% awarded as scholarships/grants, 19% as loans/jobs. Scholarships based on academics, alumni affiliation, art, athletics, leadership, music/drama. **Student debt:** 58% of graduating class borrowed to fund education; average debt was $18,131.

Freshman aid. **Need-based:** Average package met 93% of need. Average scholarship/grant was $14,218; average loan $2,475.

Policies to reduce costs. Tuition/fee waivers for employees and their families. Credit/placement for qualifying scores on AP, IB, CLEP examinations.

Payment plans. Credit card payment.

Application procedures. FAFSA required. Priority date 5/1; no closing date. Applicants notified on rolling basis starting 2/20, must reply by 5/1 or within 2 week(s) of notification. Early decision closing date 11/15.

Contact. Margaret Collins, Director of Scholarships and Financial Assistance
580 East Main Street
Spartanburg, SC 29302-0006

Denmark Technical College

Denmark, South Carolina
www.den.tec.sc.us
Two-year public **Federal Code: 005363**

	Living at home	On-campus
Tuition and fees (2002-2003):	$2,152	$2,152
Out-of-state:	$4,144	$4,144
Per-credit charge:	$83	$83
Per-credit out-of-state:	$166	$166
Room and board:		$3,096
Books and supplies:	$750	$750
Personal expenses:	$2,000	$2,000
Transportation:	$1,200	$1,000

Undergraduate aid. **Need-based:** Need-based aid available for full-time and part-time students.

Policies to reduce costs. Tuition/fee waivers for senior citizens.

Application procedures. FAFSA required. No deadline. Applicants notified on rolling basis starting 6/1, must reply within 2 week(s) of notification.

Contact. Clara Moses, Director of Financial Aid
Solomon Blatt Boulevard
Denmark, SC 29042

Erskine College

Due West, South Carolina
www.erskine.edu
Four-year private **Federal Code: 003432**

	Living at home	On-campus
Tuition and fees:	$17,367	$17,367
Room and board:		$5,799
Books and supplies:	$800	$800
Personal expenses:	$2,300	$1,015

Undergraduate aid. **Need-based:** Average financial aid package for full-time students was $16,500; for part-time $2,000. 84% awarded as scholarships/grants, 16% as loans/jobs. **Non-need-based:** 82% awarded as scholarships/grants, 18% as loans/jobs. Scholarships based on academics, alumni affiliation, athletics, leadership, minority status, music/drama, religious affiliation, state/district residency. **Student debt:** 65% of graduating class borrowed to fund education; average debt was $10,000. **Additional information:** Filing deadline 5/1 for institutional form, 6/30 for state form.

Freshman aid. **Need-based:** Out of 217 full-time freshmen, 206 applied for aid; 175 were judged to have need; of these 175 received aid. Average package met 80% of need. 52 students had full need met. Average scholarship/grant was $8,000; average loan $2,000. **Non-need based:** 126 full-time freshmen with need received non-need scholarships; 31 without need received awards; 46 received athletic scholarships.

Merit scholarships. E.B. Kennedy Scholarship; $22,221; 2 awarded. Daniel Stinson Bell Scholarship; $15,700; based on Christian commitment, academic achievement, character, service; 3 awarded. Erskine College Academic Excellence Sholarship; $10,000; 1 awarded. Luke and Amelia Solomon Scholarship; $6,000; based on Christian commitment, academic excellence, leadership, community service; 1 awarded.

Policies to reduce costs. Tuition/fee waivers for children of alumni, family members, family of clergy, employees and their families. Credit/placement for qualifying scores on AP, IB, CLEP examinations. Work study available nights and weekends.

Payment plans. Credit card, installment payment.

Application procedures. FAFSA, institutional form required. Priority date 2/15; closing date 5/1. Applicants notified on rolling basis starting 12/15. **Transfers:** Priority date 4/1; closing date 5/1. Must submit academic transcripts from previous schools. South Carolina residents must have earned 24 hours in previous year to receive SC tuition grant and 30 hours plus 3.0 GPS to receive the Life Scholarship.

Contact. **Financial aid office:** (864) 379-8832
Becky Pressley, Director of Financial Aid
2 Washington Street
Due West, SC 29639-0176

Florence-Darlington Technical College

Florence, South Carolina
www.fdtc.edu
Two-year public **Federal Code: 003990**

	Living at home
Tuition and fees (2002-2003):	$2,102
Out-of-district:	$2,364
Out-of-state:	$4,198
Per-credit charge:	$83
Per-credit out-of-district:	$94
Per-credit out-of-state:	$170
Books and supplies:	$300
Personal expenses:	$300

Undergraduate aid. **Need-based:** Need-based aid available for full-time and part-time students. **Non-need-based:** Scholarships based on academics.

Policies to reduce costs. Tuition/fee waivers for senior citizens, employees and their families. Credit/placement for qualifying scores on AP, IB, CLEP examinations. Work study available for part-time students.

Payment plans. Credit card payment.

Application procedures. FAFSA required. Priority date 5/1; no closing date. Applicants notified on rolling basis starting 7/1, must reply within 2 week(s) of notification. **Transfers:** No deadline.

Contact. William Whitlock, Director of Financial Assistance
PO Box 100548
Florence, SC 29501-0548

Forrest Junior College

Anderson, South Carolina
www.forrestcollege.com
Two-year proprietary **Federal Code: 004924**

	Living at home
Tuition and fees (2002-2003):	$4,560
Per-credit charge:	$95

Undergraduate aid. All financial aid based on need. Need-based aid available for full-time and part-time students.

Policies to reduce costs. Work study available nights, weekends and for part-time students.

Payment plans. Credit card, installment, deferred payment.

Application procedures. FAFSA required. No deadline. Applicants notified on rolling basis starting 4/30, must reply by 5/31 or within 4 week(s) of notification. **Transfers:** No deadline.

Contact. Kathy Montgomery, Director of Financial Aid
601 East River Street
Anderson, SC 29624

Francis Marion University

Florence, South Carolina
www.fmarion.edu
Four-year public **Federal Code: 009226**

	Living at home	On-campus
Tuition and fees (2002-2003):	$4,340	$4,340
Out-of-state:	$8,530	$8,530
Room and board:		$4,082
Board only:	$2,151	
Books and supplies:	$760	$760
Personal expenses:	$2,062	$2,257
Transportation:	$2,080	$1,311

Undergraduate aid. Need-based: 90% awarded as scholarships/grants, 10% as loans/jobs. Need-based aid available for part-time students. **Non-need-based:** 25% awarded as scholarships/grants, 75% as loans/jobs. Scholarships based on academics, alumni affiliation, minority status, music/drama, religious affiliation.

Policies to reduce costs. Tuition/fee waivers for senior citizens, employees and their families. Credit/placement for qualifying scores on AP, CLEP examinations. Work study available nights and weekends.

Payment plans. Credit card payment.

Application procedures. FAFSA, institutional form required. Priority date 3/1; no closing date. Applicants notified on rolling basis starting 4/15. **Transfers:** Priority date 3/1; no deadline. Institutional scholarships available after 1 semester completed in residence.

Contact. Kathryn Phillips, Director of Financial Assistance
PO Box 100547
Florence, SC 29501-0547

Furman University

Greenville, South Carolina
www.furman.edu
Four-year private **Federal Code: 003434**

	Living at home	On-campus
Tuition and fees (2002-2003):	$21,262	$21,262
Room and board:		$5,664
Board only:	$2,016	
Books and supplies:	$670	$670
Personal expenses:	$560	$670
Transportation:	$1,097	$920

Undergraduate aid. Need-based: Average financial aid package for full-time students was $18,349; for part-time $4,870. 73% awarded as scholarships/grants, 27% as loans/jobs. **Non-need-based:** 85% awarded as scholarships/grants, 15% as loans/jobs. Scholarships based on academics, alumni affiliation, art, athletics, leadership, minority status, music/drama, religious affiliation, state/district residency. **Student debt:** 36% of graduating class borrowed to fund education; average debt was $17,741. **Additional information:** 5-point comprehensive education financing plan includes financial aid packaging, money management counseling, debt management counseling, outside scholarship coordination, and summer job-match program.

Freshman aid. Need-based: Out of 738 full-time freshmen, 655 applied for aid; 355 were judged to have need; of these 355 received aid. Average package met 91% of need. 216 students had full need met. Average scholarship/grant was $13,367; average loan $3,761. **Non-need based:** 99 full-time freshmen with need received non-need scholarships; 252 without need received awards; 42 received athletic scholarships.

Merit scholarships. Over 100 renewable merit scholarships offered to entering freshmen, including 4 Herman W. Lay Scholarships for room, board and tuition, 10 Duke Scholarships for full tuition, 30 Founders (half-tuition) Scholarships and 35 Bell Tower Scholarships (quarter-tuition).

Policies to reduce costs. Tuition/fee waivers for employees and their families. Credit/placement for qualifying scores on AP, IB examinations. Work study available nights and weekends.

Payment plans. Installment payment.

Application procedures. FAFSA, institutional form required. Closing date 1/15. Applicants notified by 3/15, must reply by 5/1. Early decision closing date 11/15. **Transfers:** Closing date 6/1. For South Carolina Tuition Grant Tuition, must have earned 24 credits in previous year. For Life Scholarship, must have earned 3.0 cumulative GPA and 30 credits earned.

Contact. Financial aid office: (864) 294-2204
Martin Carney, Director of Financial Aid
3300 Poinsett Highway
Greenville, SC 29613

Horry-Georgetown Technical College

Conway, South Carolina
www.hgtc.edu
Two-year public **Federal Code: 004925**

	Living at home
Tuition and fees (2002-2003):	$2,112
Out-of-district:	$2,904
Out-of-state:	$4,224
Per-credit charge:	$83
Per-credit out-of-district:	$116
Per-credit out-of-state:	$171
Books and supplies:	$400

Undergraduate aid. Need-based: Need-based aid available for full-time and part-time students. **Additional information:** Participates in South Carolina lottery tuition assistance program. Full-time technical college students who are state residents receive assistance for tuition not covered by federal or need-based grants.

Policies to reduce costs. Tuition/fee waivers for senior citizens.

Payment plans. Credit card payment.

Application procedures. FAFSA required. Priority date 4/1; closing date 5/1. Applicants notified by 7/1.

Contact. Neyle Lyerly, Director of Financial Aid
Highway 501 East
Conway, SC 29526-1966

ITT Technical Institute: Greenville

Greenville, South Carolina
www.itt-tech.edu
Two-year proprietary **Federal Code: 023598**

College costs. Total program varies depending on course of study. Per-credit-hour charge: $347.

Policies to reduce costs. Tuition/fee waivers for employees and their families. Tuition at time of enrollment guaranteed for 2 years.

Payment plans. Credit card, installment payment.

Application procedures. FAFSA, institutional form required. No deadline. Applicants notified on rolling basis.

Contact. Jan Tallman, Director of Finance
One Marcus Drive, Patewood Business Center, Building 4, Suite 402
Greenville, SC 29615

Johnson & Wales University

Charleston, South Carolina
www.jwu.edu
Four-year private **Federal Code: 003404**

College costs. Tuition for the Hospitality College is $13,713.

	Living at home	On-campus
Tuition and fees (2002-2003):	$17,616	$17,616
Room only:		$4,129
Books and supplies:	$750	$750
Personal expenses:	$1,250	

Undergraduate aid. All financial aid based on need. Need-based aid available for full-time students. **Additional information:** Academic scholarships awarded based on SAT or ACT scores.

Application procedures. FAFSA required. No deadline.

Contact. **Financial aid office:** (401) 598-1468
Lynn Robinson, Director, Financial Aid
701 East Bay Street
Charleston, SC 29403

Lander University

Greenwood, South Carolina
www.lander.edu
Four-year public **Federal Code: 003435**

	Living at home	On-campus
Tuition and fees (2002-2003):	$4,704	$4,704
Out-of-state:	$9,648	$9,648
Room and board:		$4,648
Board only:	$1,550	
Books and supplies:	$820	$820
Personal expenses:	$1,250	$1,850
Transportation:	$850	$500

Undergraduate aid. Need-based: Average financial aid package for full-time students was $4,400; for part-time $3,553. 44% awarded as scholarships/grants, 56% as loans/jobs. **Non-need-based:** 54% awarded as scholarships/grants, 46% as loans/jobs. Scholarships based on academics. **Student debt:** 49% of graduating class borrowed to fund education; average debt was $12,500. **Additional information:** For more information, email finaid@lander.edu.

Freshman aid. Need-based: Out of 489 full-time freshmen, 343 applied for aid; 245 were judged to have need; of these 235 received aid. Average package met 60% of need. 131 students had full need met. Average scholarship/grant was $1,495; average loan $2,625.

Policies to reduce costs. Tuition/fee waivers for senior citizens, employees and their families. Credit/placement for qualifying scores on AP, CLEP examinations. Work study available weekends and for part-time students.

Payment plans. Credit card, installment payment.

Application procedures. FAFSA required. Priority date 4/15; no closing date. Applicants notified on rolling basis starting 4/15, must reply within 4 week(s) of notification. **Transfers:** No deadline.

Contact. **Financial aid office:** (864) 388-8340
Stephen Schnaiter, Director of Financial Aid
Stanley Avenue
Greenwood, SC 29649-2099

Limestone College

Gaffney, South Carolina
www.limestone.edu
Four-year private **Federal Code: 003436**

	Living at home	On-campus
Tuition and fees:	$12,300	$12,300
Room and board:		$5,400
Books and supplies:	$1,250	$1,250
Personal expenses:	$4,450	$1,450
Transportation:	$2,375	$1,300

Undergraduate aid. Need-based: Average financial aid package for full-time students was $8,007; for part-time $6,574. 52% awarded as scholarships/grants, 48% as loans/jobs. **Non-need-based:** 43% awarded as scholarships/grants, 57% as loans/jobs. Scholarships based on academics, alumni affiliation, art, athletics, job skills, leadership, music/drama, religious affiliation, state/district residency. **Student debt:** 84% of graduating class borrowed to fund education; average debt was $7,752.

Freshman aid. Need-based: Out of 146 full-time freshmen, 145 applied for aid; 120 were judged to have need; of these 120 received aid. Average package met 62% of need. 31 students had full need met. Average scholarship/grant was $4,966; average loan $2,345. **Non-need based:** 25 full-time freshmen with need received non-need scholarships; 26 without need received awards; 15 received athletic scholarships.

Merit scholarships. Presidential Scholarship; full tuition; SAT above 1300, GPA 3.5 or above; 1 available. Academic Dean Scholarships; partial tuition; based on academic achievement (GPA 3.0 or above). Founders Scholarships; partial tuition; GPA 2.75 or above. R.S. Campbell Scholarship; SAT above 1100, GPA 3.25 or above; 1 available. Leadership Scholarship; partial tuition; based on evidence of student leadership. Drada Hoover Scholarship; SAT 1200 or higher; GPA 3.5; top 10% of graduating class.

Policies to reduce costs. Tuition/fee waivers for employees and their families. Credit/placement for qualifying scores on AP, CLEP examinations.

Payment plans. Credit card, installment payment.

Application procedures. FAFSA required. Priority date 5/1; closing date 7/1. Applicants notified on rolling basis starting 1/15, must reply within 2 week(s) of notification. **Transfers:** Priority date 5/1; no deadline.

Contact. **Financial aid office:** (800) 795-7151 ext. 4598
Virginia Hickey, Director of Financial Aid
1115 College Drive
Gaffney, SC 29340-3799

Medical University of South Carolina

Charleston, South Carolina
www.musc.edu
Upper-division public **Federal Code: 003438**

College costs. College of Health Professions: in-state $7,146 tuition/fees, $298 per-credit-hour; out-of-state $19,948 tuition/fees, $831 per-credit-hour. College of Nursing: in-state $6,686 tuition/fees, $303 per-credit-hour; out-of-state $18,308 tuition/fees, $847 per-credit-hour. Other fees vary by program. Books/supplies: $825. Personal expenses: $250.

Undergraduate aid. Need-based: Average financial aid package for full-time students was $7,893; for part-time $7,075. 13% awarded as scholarships/grants, 87% as loans/jobs. **Non-need-based:** 13% awarded as scholarships/grants, 87% as loans/jobs. Scholarships based on academics, alumni affiliation, leadership, state/district residency.

Policies to reduce costs. Tuition/fee waivers for senior citizens, minority students, employees and their families. Credit/placement for qualifying scores on CLEP examinations.

Payment plans. Credit card payment.

Application procedures. FAFSA, institutional form required. Priority date 3/17; no closing date. **Transfers:** Priority date 3/17; no deadline.

Contact. **Financial aid office:** (843) 792-2536
Pearl Givens, Director, Financial Aid
41 Bee Street
Charleston, SC 29425

Midlands Technical College

Columbia, South Carolina
www.midlandstech.com
Two-year public **Federal Code: 003993**

	Living at home
Tuition and fees (2002-2003):	$2,117
Out-of-district:	$2,665
Out-of-state:	$6,361
Per-credit charge:	$83
Per-credit out-of-district:	$106
Per-credit out-of-state:	$259
Books and supplies:	$400
Personal expenses:	$676
Transportation:	$772

Policies to reduce costs. Tuition/fee waivers for senior citizens, employees and their families. Credit/placement for qualifying scores on CLEP examinations.

Payment plans. Credit card payment.

Application procedures. FAFSA required. Priority date 4/15; no closing date. Applicants notified on rolling basis, must reply within 2 week(s) of notification.

Contact. Margaret Hunt, Director of Student Aid
PO Box 2408
Columbia, SC 29202

Miller-Motte Technical College

Charleston, South Carolina
www.miller-motte.com
Two-year proprietary

	Living at home
Tuition and fees:	$7,500

Application procedures. FAFSA, institutional form required. Applicants notified on rolling basis.

Contact. Marla Bunn, Financial Aid Director
8085 Rivers Avenue, Suite E
Charleston, SC 29406

Morris College

Sumter, South Carolina
www.morris.edu
Four-year private **Federal Code: 003439**

	Living at home	On-campus
Tuition and fees (2002-2003):	$6,993	$6,993
Room and board:		$3,410
Board only:	$1,700	
Books and supplies:	$1,000	$1,000
Personal expenses:	$1,300	$1,100
Transportation:	$1,200	$1,200

Undergraduate aid. All financial aid based on need. Average financial aid package for full-time students was $10,700; for part-time $5,300. 49% awarded as scholarships/grants, 51% as loans/jobs. **Student debt:** 98% of graduating class borrowed to fund education; average debt was $13,125. **Additional information:** Students encouraged to complete FAFSA on the web.

Freshman aid. Out of 273 full-time freshmen, 269 applied for aid; 269 were judged to have need; of these 269 received aid. Average package met 84% of need. 28 students had full need met. Average scholarship/grant was $750; average loan $2,625.

Policies to reduce costs. Credit/placement for qualifying scores on CLEP examinations. Work study available nights and weekends.

Payment plans. Credit card, installment, deferred payment.

Application procedures. FAFSA, institutional form required. Priority date 3/30; no closing date. Applicants notified on rolling basis starting 5/30, must reply within 2 week(s) of notification.

Contact. **Financial aid office:** (803) 934-3238
Sandra Gibson, Financial Aid Officer
100 West College Street
Sumter, SC 29150-3599

Newberry College

Newberry, South Carolina
www.newberry.edu
Four-year private **Federal Code: 003440**

	Living at home	On-campus
Tuition and fees (2002-2003):	$16,360	$16,360
Room and board:		$4,910
Board only:	$2,230	
Books and supplies:	$800	$800
Personal expenses:	$1,195	$1,195
Transportation:	$800	$800

Undergraduate aid. Need-based: Average financial aid package for full-time students was $12,318; for part-time $5,941. 67% awarded as scholarships/grants, 33% as loans/jobs. **Non-need-based:** 56% awarded as scholarships/grants, 44% as loans/jobs. Scholarships based on academics, athletics. **Student debt:** 98% of graduating class borrowed to fund education; average debt was $13,477.

Freshman aid. Need-based: Out of 193 full-time freshmen, 176 applied for aid; 161 were judged to have need; of these 161 received aid. Average package met 71% of need. 38 students had full need met. Average scholarship/grant was $9,513; average loan $3,095. **Non-need based:** 28 full-time freshmen with need received non-need scholarships; 63 without need received awards; 24 received athletic scholarships.

Policies to reduce costs. Tuition/fee waivers for employees and their families. Credit/placement for qualifying scores on AP, IB, CLEP examinations.

Payment plans. Credit card, installment payment.

Application procedures. FAFSA, institutional form required. Priority date 3/1; closing date 5/1. Applicants notified on rolling basis starting 3/1, must reply within 2 week(s) of notification.

Contact. Cathryn Stockweather, Director of Financial Aid
2100 College Street
Newberry, SC 29108

North Greenville College

Tigerville, South Carolina
www.ngc.edu
Four-year private **Federal Code: 003441**

College costs. Commuter students pay $100 less in fees.

	Living at home	On-campus
Tuition and fees:	$9,300	$9,300
Room and board:		$5,280
Books and supplies:	$1,000	$1,000
Personal expenses:	$2,000	$2,000
Transportation:	$2,210	$2,110

Undergraduate aid. All financial aid based on need. Average financial aid package for full-time students was $8,000; for part-time $700. 82% awarded as scholarships/grants, 18% as loans/jobs. **Student debt:** 50% of graduating class borrowed to fund education; average debt was $3,500.

Freshman aid. Out of 412 full-time freshmen, 390 applied for aid; 300 were judged to have need; of these 295 received aid. Average package met 70% of need. 75 students had full need met. Average scholarship/grant was $1,000; average loan $2,625.

Policies to reduce costs. Tuition/fee waivers for children of alumni, family members, family of clergy, employees and their families. Credit/placement for qualifying scores on AP, IB, CLEP examinations.

Payment plans. Credit card, installment payment.

Application procedures. FAFSA required. Priority date 6/1; closing date 6/30. Applicants notified on rolling basis starting 8/1, must reply within 2 week(s) of notification. **Transfers:** No deadline.

Contact. **Financial aid office:** (864) 977-7050
Mike Jordan, Director of Financial Aid
Box 1892
Tigerville, SC 29688-7177

Northeastern Technical College

Cheraw, South Carolina
www.netc.edu
Two-year public **Federal Code: 007602**

	Living at home
Tuition and fees (2002-2003):	$2,092
Out-of-district:	$2,188
Out-of-state:	$3,700
Per-credit charge:	$83
Per-credit out-of-district:	$87
Per-credit out-of-state:	$150
Books and supplies:	$900
Personal expenses:	$2,000
Transportation:	$3,000

Undergraduate aid. Need-based: 96% awarded as scholarships/grants, 4% as loans/jobs.

Policies to reduce costs. Tuition/fee waivers for senior citizens. Credit/placement for qualifying scores on AP, CLEP examinations.

Payment plans. Credit card payment.

Application procedures. FAFSA required. No deadline. Applicants notified on rolling basis, must reply within 8 week(s) of notification.

Contact. Sheryl Marshall, Coordinator of Student Financial Assistance
Drawer 1007
Cheraw, SC 29520

Orangeburg-Calhoun Technical College

Orangeburg, South Carolina
www.octech.edu
Two-year public **Federal Code: 006815**

	Living at home
Tuition and fees (2002-2003):	$2,007
Out-of-district:	$2,511
Out-of-state:	$3,855
Per-credit charge:	$83
Per-credit out-of-district:	$194
Per-credit out-of-state:	$160
Books and supplies:	$400
Personal expenses:	$500
Transportation:	$300

Undergraduate aid. All financial aid based on need. Need-based aid available for full-time and part-time students.

Policies to reduce costs. Tuition/fee waivers for senior citizens. Credit/placement for qualifying scores on CLEP examinations.

Payment plans. Credit card payment.

Application procedures. FAFSA, institutional form required. Priority date 6/1; no closing date. Applicants notified on rolling basis starting 5/1, must reply within 2 week(s) of notification. **Transfers:** Priority date 6/1; no deadline. Financial aid transcripts required of mid-year transfers prior to disbursement of aid.

Contact. Financial aid office: (803) 535-1249
Chris Dooley, Financial Aid Coordinator
3250 St. Matthews Road
Orangeburg, SC 29118-8299

Piedmont Technical College

Greenwood, South Carolina
www.ptc.edu
Two-year public **Federal Code: 003992**

College costs. Tuition for students from counties contributing partial support $2,280 full-time, $95 per-credit-hour.

	Living at home
Tuition and fees (2002-2003):	$2,092
Out-of-district:	$2,548
Out-of-state:	$3,748
Per-credit charge:	$83
Per-credit out-of-district:	$102
Per-credit out-of-state:	$152
Books and supplies:	$850
Personal expenses:	$200
Transportation:	$450

Undergraduate aid. All financial aid based on need. Average financial aid package for full-time students was $6,000; for part-time $1,500. 67% awarded as scholarships/grants, 33% as loans/jobs. **Student debt:** 20% of graduating class borrowed to fund education; average debt was $10,150.

Freshman aid. Average package met 50% of need. Average scholarship/grant was $2,282; average loan $1,912.

Policies to reduce costs. Tuition/fee waivers for senior citizens, employees and their families. Credit/placement for qualifying scores on AP, IB, CLEP examinations. Work study available nights, weekends and for part-time students.

Payment plans. Credit card payment.

Application procedures. FAFSA required. Priority date 5/1; no closing date. Applicants notified on rolling basis starting 6/1, must reply within 2 week(s) of notification. **Transfers:** No deadline.

Contact. Financial aid office: (864) 941-8365
Deborah Williams, Director of Financial Aid
Box 1467
Greenwood, SC 29648

Presbyterian College

Clinton, South Carolina
www.presby.edu
Four-year private **Federal Code: 003445**

	Living at home	On-campus
Tuition and fees:	$20,110	$20,110
Room and board:		$6,326
Board only:	$2,586	
Books and supplies:	$933	$933
Personal expenses:	$2,333	$2,333
Transportation:	$1,169	$1,169

Undergraduate aid. Need-based: Average financial aid package for full-time students was $19,578; for part-time $7,722. 77% awarded as scholarships/grants, 23% as loans/jobs. **Non-need-based:** 87% awarded as scholarships/grants, 13% as loans/jobs. Scholarships based on academics, alumni affiliation, art, athletics, leadership, minority status, music/drama, religious affiliation. **Student debt:** 68% of graduating class borrowed to fund education; average debt was $15,481.

Freshman aid. Need-based: Out of 315 full-time freshmen, 314 applied for aid; 207 were judged to have need; of these 207 received aid. Average package met 82% of need. 16 students had full need met. Average scholarship/grant was $16,753; average loan $3,183. **Non-need based:** 106 full-time freshmen with need received non-need scholarships; 107 without need received awards; 16 received athletic scholarships.

Merit scholarships. Academic and leadership scholarships, applications by December 5; number and amounts awarded vary; music awards based on audition.

Policies to reduce costs. Tuition/fee waivers for employees and their families. Credit/placement for qualifying scores on AP, IB, CLEP examinations.

Payment plans. Credit card, installment payment.

Application procedures. FAFSA, institutional form required. Priority date 3/1; no closing date. Applicants notified on rolling basis starting 3/26, must reply by 5/1.

Contact. Financial aid office: (864)833-8290
Judi Gillespie, Director of Financial Aid
Box 975
Clinton, SC 29325-9989

South Carolina State University

Orangeburg, South Carolina
www.scsu.edu
Four-year public **Federal Code: 003446**

	Living at home	On-campus
Tuition and fees (2002-2003):	$4,556	$4,556
Out-of-state:	$8,820	$8,820
Room and board:		$3,568
Board only:	$1,500	
Books and supplies:	$1,000	$1,000
Personal expenses:	$700	$700
Transportation:	$300	$100

Undergraduate aid. Need-based: Need-based aid available for full-time students. **Non-need-based:** Scholarships based on academics, athletics.

Policies to reduce costs. Tuition/fee waivers for senior citizens. Credit/placement for qualifying scores on AP examinations.

Payment plans. Credit card, installment, deferred payment.

Application procedures. FAFSA required. Priority date 5/1; no closing date. Applicants notified on rolling basis starting 6/15, must reply by 8/1 or within 4 week(s) of notification. **Transfers:** Must provide documentation on amount of state aid received, and which semesters it was received, prior to transfer.

Contact. Margaret Black, Director of Financial Aid
300 College Street NE
Orangeburg, SC 29117

Southern Wesleyan University

Central, South Carolina
www.swu.edu
Four-year private **Federal Code: 003422**

	Living at home	On-campus
Tuition and fees:	$14,090	$14,090
Room and board:		$4,950
Board only:	$500	
Books and supplies:	$900	$900
Personal expenses:	$700	$900
Transportation:	$950	$700

Undergraduate aid. Need-based: Average financial aid package for full-time students was $10,192; for part-time $6,387. 58% awarded as scholarships/grants, 42% as loans/jobs. **Non-need-based:** 46% awarded as scholarships/grants, 54% as loans/jobs. Scholarships based on academics, athletics, leadership, minority status, music/drama, religious affiliation. **Student debt:** 88% of graduating class borrowed to fund education; average debt was $7,239.

Freshman aid. Need-based: Average package met 77% of need. Average scholarship/grant was $9,209; average loan $1,947.

Policies to reduce costs. Tuition/fee waivers for senior citizens, family of clergy, employees and their families. Credit/placement for qualifying scores on AP, IB, CLEP examinations.

Payment plans. Credit card, installment, deferred payment.

Application procedures. FAFSA, institutional form required. Priority date 6/30; no closing date. Applicants notified on rolling basis starting 2/1, must reply within 2 week(s) of notification. **Transfers:** No deadline.

Contact. Financial aid office: (800) 289-1292
Jeff Dennis, Financial Aid Director
PO Box 1020
Central, SC 29630-1020

Spartanburg Methodist College

Spartanburg, South Carolina
www.smcsc.edu
Two-year private **Federal Code: 003447**

	Living at home	On-campus
Tuition and fees:	$8,870	$8,870
Per-credit charge:	$235	$235
Room and board:		$4,796
Books and supplies:	$800	$800
Personal expenses:	$1,800	$1,800
Transportation:	$1,000	$1,000

Undergraduate aid. Need-based: Average financial aid package for full-time students was $10,158; for part-time $2,342. 80% awarded as scholarships/grants, 20% as loans/jobs. **Non-need-based:** 75% awarded as scholarships/grants, 25% as loans/jobs. Scholarships based on academics, athletics, job skills, leadership, music/drama, religious affiliation, state/district residency. **Student debt:** 53% of graduating class borrowed to fund education; average debt was $2,421. **Additional information:** College strives to meet 100% of established financial need of all students.

Freshman aid. Need-based: Out of 358 full-time freshmen, 340 applied for aid; 337 were judged to have need; of these 337 received aid. Average package met 89% of need. 291 students had full need met. Average scholarship/grant was $2,814; average loan $2,420. **Non-need based:** 329 full-time freshmen with need received non-need scholarships; 16 without need received awards; 81 received athletic scholarships.

Merit scholarships. Camak Scholars, $4,100; Trustees Scholars, $3,500; Presidential Scholars, $3,000; Faculty Achievement, $2,400

Policies to reduce costs. Tuition/fee waivers for adults, children of alumni, senior citizens, unemployed or children of unemployed, family of clergy, employees and their families. Credit/placement for qualifying scores on AP, CLEP examinations. Work study available nights, weekends and for part-time students.

Payment plans. Credit card, installment payment.

Application procedures. FAFSA, institutional form required. Priority date 6/30; closing date 8/23. Applicants notified on rolling basis starting 2/1, must reply within 2 week(s) of notification. **Transfers:** Priority date 6/30; closing date 8/23. Students must pass the equivalent of 12 hours if full time.

Contact. Financial aid office: (864) 587-4000
Carolyn Sparks, Director of Financial Aid
1200 Textile Road
Spartanburg, SC 29301

Spartanburg Technical College

Spartanburg, South Carolina
www.stcsc.edu
Two-year public **Federal Code: 003994**

	Living at home
Tuition and fees (2002-2003):	$2,132
Out-of-district:	$2,630
Out-of-state:	$4,332
Per-credit charge:	$83
Per-credit out-of-district:	$104
Per-credit out-of-state:	$175
Books and supplies:	$600

Undergraduate aid. Need-based: Need-based aid available for full-time and part-time students. **Additional information:** Participates in South Carolina lottery tuition assistance program. Full-time technical college students who are state residents receive assistance for tuition not covered by federal or need-based grants.

Policies to reduce costs. Tuition/fee waivers for senior citizens. Credit/placement for qualifying scores on AP examinations.

Payment plans. Credit card payment.

Application procedures. Priority date 2/28; closing date 5/1. Applicants notified on rolling basis starting 5/1.

Contact. Nancy Garmroth, Coordinator of Student Aid
Box 4386
Spartanburg, SC 29305

Technical College of the Lowcountry

Beaufort, South Carolina
www.tclonline.org
Two-year public **Federal Code: 009910**

	Living at home
Tuition and fees (2002-2003):	$2,142
Out-of-state:	$3,860
Per-credit charge:	$83
Per-credit out-of-state:	$155
Books and supplies:	$425
Personal expenses:	$1,600
Transportation:	$1,050

Undergraduate aid. Need-based: Need-based aid available for full-time students. **Additional information:** State lottery aid may be available to South Carolina residents attending two year technical institutions.

Policies to reduce costs. Tuition/fee waivers for senior citizens, employees and their families. Credit/placement for qualifying scores on AP, CLEP examinations.

Payment plans. Credit card, deferred payment.

Application procedures. No deadline. Applicants notified on rolling basis starting 7/1.

Contact. Claretha Singleton, Coordinator of Financial Aid
921 South Ribaut Road
Beaufort, SC 29901-1288

The Citadel

Charleston, South Carolina
www.citadel.edu
Four-year public **Federal Code: 003423**

College costs. Students in Corps of Cadets required to pay $879 in fees which include laundry and dry cleaning charges and infirmary fees. Freshmen also pay $4,780 deposit and upperclassmen pay $1,520 deposit for uniforms, books, and supplies.

	Living at home	On-campus
Tuition and fees (2002-2003):	$4,067	$4,067
Out-of-state:	$11,538	$11,538
Room and board:		$4,575

Undergraduate aid. Need-based: Average financial aid package for full-time students was $6,048. 48% awarded as scholarships/grants, 52% as loans/jobs. Need-based aid available for part-time students. **Non-need-based:** 66% awarded as scholarships/grants, 34% as loans/jobs. Scholarships based on academics, alumni affiliation, athletics, leadership, music/drama, state/district residency. **Student debt:** 59% of graduating class borrowed to fund education; average debt was $13,901.

Freshman aid. Need-based: Out of 520 full-time freshmen, 415 applied for aid; 285 were judged to have need; of these 274 received aid. Average package met 85% of need. 105 students had full need met. Average scholarship/grant was $6,986; average loan $2,487. **Non-need based:** 172 full-time freshmen with need received non-need scholarships; 46 without need received awards; 65 received athletic scholarships.

Policies to reduce costs. Tuition/fee waivers for senior citizens, employees and their families. Credit/placement for qualifying scores on AP, CLEP examinations.

Payment plans. Credit card, deferred payment.

Application procedures. FAFSA required. Priority date 3/17; no closing date. Applicants notified by 4/15, must reply within 2 week(s) of notification. **Transfers:** Closing date 1/15.

Contact. Financial aid office: (843) 953-5187
Henry Fuller, Director of Financial Aid
171 Moultrie Street
Charleston, SC 29409

Tri-County Technical College
Pendleton, South Carolina
www.tctc.edu
Two-year public **Federal Code: 004926**

	Living at home
Tuition and fees (2002-2003):	$2,007
Out-of-district:	$2,415
Out-of-state:	$5,495
Per-credit charge:	$83
Per-credit out-of-district:	$100
Per-credit out-of-state:	$229
Books and supplies:	$650

Undergraduate aid. Need-based: Need-based aid available for full-time and part-time students. **Non-need-based:** Scholarships based on academics, state/district residency. **Additional information:** Deadline for application to institutional scholarships April 2.

Merit scholarships. General and departmental scholarships competitively awarded, some with special qualification criteria, such as student's career field or place of residency; over 125 awarded.

Policies to reduce costs. Tuition/fee waivers for senior citizens. Credit/placement for qualifying scores on AP, CLEP examinations. Work study available nights and for part-time students.

Payment plans. Credit card payment.

Application procedures. FAFSA required. Priority date 6/30; no closing date. Applicants notified on rolling basis starting 6/15, must reply within 2 week(s) of notification. **Transfers:** No deadline.

Contact. Financial aid office: (864) 646-8361
Stuart Spires, Director, Student Aid
Box 587
Pendleton, SC 29670

Trident Technical College
Charleston, South Carolina
www.tridenttech.edu
Two-year public **Federal Code: 004920**

	Living at home
Tuition and fees (2002-2003):	$2,092
Out-of-district:	$2,332
Out-of-state:	$4,492
Per-credit charge:	$83
Per-credit out-of-district:	$93
Per-credit out-of-state:	$183
Books and supplies:	$650

Undergraduate aid. Need-based: Need-based aid available for full-time and part-time students.

Policies to reduce costs. Tuition/fee waivers for senior citizens. Credit/placement for qualifying scores on AP, CLEP examinations.

Payment plans. Credit card payment.

Application procedures. FAFSA required. No deadline. Applicants notified on rolling basis, must reply within 6 week(s) of notification.

Contact. Cindy Seabrook, Director of Student Financial Aid
Box 118067
Charleston, SC 29423

University of South Carolina
Columbia, South Carolina
www.sc.edu
Four-year public **Federal Code: 0034480**

College costs. Health professions (pharmacy, health, nursing) have higher undergraduate fees.

	Living at home	On-campus
Tuition and fees (2002-2003):	$4,984	$4,984
Out-of-state:	$13,104	$13,104
Room and board:		$5,038
Board only:	$2,500	
Books and supplies:	$607	$607
Personal expenses:	$2,514	$2,514
Transportation:	$1,446	$1,679

Undergraduate aid. Need-based: Average financial aid package for full-time students was $8,263; for part-time $6,902. 32% awarded as scholarships/grants, 68% as loans/jobs. **Non-need-based:** 42% awarded as scholarships/grants, 58% as loans/jobs. Scholarships based on academics, alumni affiliation, art, athletics, job skills, leadership, minority status, music/drama, religious affiliation, state/district residency. **Student debt:** 70% of graduating class borrowed to fund education; average debt was $15,260.

Freshman aid. Need-based: Out of 3,186 full-time freshmen, 1,977 applied for aid; 1,383 were judged to have need; of these 1,383 received aid. Average package met 74% of need. 365 students had full need met. Average scholarship/grant was $3,058; average loan $2,916. **Non-need based:** 929 full-time freshmen with need received non-need scholarships; 1,587 without need received awards; 92 received athletic scholarships.

Policies to reduce costs. Tuition/fee waivers for senior citizens, employees and their families. Credit/placement for qualifying scores on AP, IB, CLEP examinations. Work study available nights, weekends and for part-time students.

Payment plans. Credit card, installment, deferred payment.

Application procedures. FAFSA required. Priority date 4/1; no closing date. Applicants notified on rolling basis starting 5/1. **Transfers:** Priority date 4/1.

Contact. Financial aid office: (803) 777-8134
Ed Miller, Director of Financial Aid and Scholarships
Office of Undergraduate Admissions
Columbia, SC 29208

University of South Carolina at Aiken
Aiken, South Carolina
www.usca.edu
Four-year public **Federal Code: 003449**

	Living at home	On-campus
Tuition and fees (2002-2003):	$4,470	$4,470
Out-of-state:	$9,334	$9,334
Room and board:		$4,220
Books and supplies:	$800	$800
Personal expenses:	$1,500	$1,500
Transportation:	$1,500	$1,500

Undergraduate aid. Need-based: Need-based aid available for full-time and part-time students.

Policies to reduce costs. Tuition/fee waivers for senior citizens, employees and their families. Credit/placement for qualifying scores on AP, CLEP examinations.

Payment plans. Credit card, deferred payment.

Application procedures. FAFSA required. Priority date 3/15; no closing date. Applicants notified on rolling basis starting 5/20, must reply within 2 week(s) of notification. **Transfers:** Financial aid transcripts from previous institutions.

Contact. Glenn Shumpert, Director of Financial Aid
471 University Parkway
Aiken, SC 29801

University of South Carolina at Lancaster

Lancaster, South Carolina
http://usclancaster.sc.edu
Two-year public **Federal Code: 003453**

	Living at home
Tuition and fees (2002-2003):	$3,130
Out-of-state:	$7,378
Per-credit charge:	$120
Per-credit out-of-state:	$297
Books and supplies:	$500
Personal expenses:	$938
Transportation:	$1,176

Policies to reduce costs. Tuition/fee waivers for senior citizens, minority students, employees and their families. Credit/placement for qualifying scores on AP, CLEP examinations.

Payment plans. Credit card payment.

Application procedures. FAFSA required. Priority date 4/15; no closing date. Applicants notified on rolling basis starting 6/1, must reply within 2 week(s) of notification.

Contact. Financial aid office: (803) 313-7069
Leah Sturgis, Director of Financial Aid
Box 889
Lancaster, SC 29721

University of South Carolina at Spartanburg

Spartanburg, South Carolina
www.uscs.edu
Four-year public **Federal Code: 006951**

	Living at home	On-campus
Tuition and fees (2002-2003):	$4,838	$4,838
Out-of-state:	$9,730	$9,730
Room and board:		$4,700
Books and supplies:	$650	$650
Transportation:	$1,510	

Undergraduate aid. Need-based: Need-based aid available for full-time and part-time students. **Non-need-based:** Scholarships based on academics, athletics, minority status, state/district residency. **Additional information:** Out-of-state students who are recipients of financial aid may qualify for out-of-state fee waiver. Educational benefits available to veterans and children of deceased/disabled veterans.

Policies to reduce costs. Tuition/fee waivers for senior citizens. Credit/placement for qualifying scores on AP, IB, CLEP examinations. Work study available nights, weekends and for part-time students.

Payment plans. Credit card, deferred payment.

Application procedures. FAFSA, institutional form required. Priority date 3/1; closing date 7/15. Applicants notified on rolling basis starting 5/1, must reply within 2 week(s) of notification. **Transfers:** Students eligible for financial assistance for total of 5 years or 10 full-time semesters at all postsecondary institutions attended for the bachelor's degree, and 5 full-time semesters of enrollment for associate's degree in nursing.

Contact. Financial aid office: (864) 503-5340
Kim Jenerette, Director of Financial Aid and Scholarships
800 University Way
Spartanburg, SC 29303

University of South Carolina at Sumter

Sumter, South Carolina
www.uscsumter.edu
Two-year public **Federal Code: 003426**

	Living at home
Tuition and fees (2002-2003):	$3,080
Out-of-state:	$7,328
Per-credit charge:	$120
Per-credit out-of-state:	$297
Books and supplies:	$500
Personal expenses:	$938
Transportation:	$1,176

Undergraduate aid. All financial aid based on need. Need-based aid available for part-time students.

Policies to reduce costs. Tuition/fee waivers for senior citizens, employees and their families. Credit/placement for qualifying scores on AP, CLEP examinations. Work study available nights, weekends and for part-time students.

Payment plans. Credit card, installment payment.

Application procedures. FAFSA, institutional form required. Closing date 4/1. Applicants notified by 6/1, must reply within 2 week(s) of notification.

Contact. Sue Sims, Director, Financial Aid
200 Miller Road
Sumter, SC 29150-2498

University of South Carolina at Union

Union, South Carolina
www.sc.edu/union
Two-year public **Federal Code: 004927**

	Living at home
Tuition and fees (2002-2003):	$3,030
Out-of-state:	$7,278
Per-credit charge:	$120
Per-credit out-of-state:	$297
Books and supplies:	$625
Personal expenses:	$1,140
Transportation:	$1,264

Policies to reduce costs. Tuition/fee waivers for senior citizens. Credit/placement for qualifying scores on AP, CLEP examinations. Work study available nights, weekends and for part-time students.

Payment plans. Credit card, installment, deferred payment.

Application procedures. FAFSA required. Priority date 4/15; no closing date. Applicants notified on rolling basis starting 7/15, must reply within 2 week(s) of notification.

Contact. Bobby Holcombe, Financial Aid Director
PO Drawer 729
Union, SC 29379

University of South Carolina: Salkehatchie Regional Campus

Allendale, South Carolina
uscsalkehatchie.sc.edu
Two-year public **Federal Code: 003454**

	Living at home
Tuition and fees (2002-2003):	$3,130
Out-of-state:	$7,378
Per-credit charge:	$120
Per-credit out-of-state:	$297
Books and supplies:	$635
Personal expenses:	$1,159
Transportation:	$1,264

Undergraduate aid. Need-based: Need-based aid available for full-time and part-time students. **Non-need-based:** Scholarships based on academics.

Policies to reduce costs. Tuition/fee waivers for senior citizens. Credit/placement for qualifying scores on AP, IB, CLEP examinations. Work study available nights, weekends and for part-time students.

Payment plans. Credit card payment.

Application procedures. FAFSA required. Priority date 4/30; no closing date. Applicants notified on rolling basis starting 6/1. **Transfers:** No deadline.

Contact. Julie Hadwin, Director of Financial Aid
PO Box 617
Allendale, SC 29810

Voorhees College

Denmark, South Carolina
www.voorhees.edu
Four-year private **Federal Code: 003455**

	Living at home	On-campus
Tuition and fees (2002-2003):	$6,880	$6,880
Room and board:		$3,516
Books and supplies:	$600	$600
Personal expenses:	$1,365	$1,365
Transportation:	$1,500	$1,500

Undergraduate aid. Need-based: Need-based aid available for full-time and part-time students.

Policies to reduce costs. Tuition/fee waivers for employees and their families.

Payment plans. Installment payment.

Application procedures. FAFSA, institutional form required. Priority date 4/15; no closing date. Applicants notified on rolling basis starting 4/1, must reply within 2 week(s) of notification. **Transfers:** Priority date 4/15.

Contact. Financial aid office: (803) 703-7109
Carolyn White, Director of Enrollment Management
PO Box 678
Denmark, SC 29042

Williamsburg Technical College

Kingstree, South Carolina
www.wiltech.edu
Two-year public **Federal Code: 009322**

	Living at home
Tuition and fees (2002-2003):	$2,112
Out-of-state:	$3,912
Per-credit charge:	$83
Per-credit out-of-state:	$158
Books and supplies:	$750
Personal expenses:	$1,300
Transportation:	$1,588

Undergraduate aid. All financial aid based on need. Need-based aid available for full-time and part-time students. **Additional information:** Tuition waivers for children of war veterans.

Policies to reduce costs. Tuition/fee waivers for senior citizens, employees and their families. Credit/placement for qualifying scores on AP, CLEP examinations. Work study available for part-time students.

Payment plans. Credit card payment.

Application procedures. FAFSA, institutional form required. Closing date 5/1. Applicants notified on rolling basis starting 5/1, must reply within 4 week(s) of notification. **Transfers:** No deadline.

Contact. Financial aid office: (843) 355-4167
Bridgett Wilson, Veterans Affairs, Financial Aid Director
601 Martin Luther King Jr. Avenue
Kingstree, SC 29556-4197

Winthrop University

Rock Hill, South Carolina
www.winthrop.edu
Four-year public **Federal Code: 003456**

	Living at home	On-campus
Tuition and fees (2002-2003):	$5,600	$5,600
Out-of-state:	$10,310	$10,310
Room and board:		$4,470
Board only:	$2,658	
Books and supplies:	$750	$750
Personal expenses:	$1,236	$1,236
Transportation:	$123	$1,236

Undergraduate aid. Need-based: Average financial aid package for full-time students was $6,384; for part-time $4,100. 44% awarded as scholarships/grants, 56% as loans/jobs. **Non-need-based:** 42% awarded as scholarships/grants, 58% as loans/jobs. Scholarships based on academics, art, athletics, music/drama, state/district residency. **Student debt:** 61% of graduating class borrowed to fund education; average debt was $16,700. **Additional information:** Academic scholarships from $1,500 to full tuition and board awarded to approximately one-third of entering freshman class each year.

Freshman aid. Need-based: Out of 940 full-time freshmen, 672 applied for aid; 498 were judged to have need; of these 473 received aid. Average package met 66% of need. 175 students had full need met. Average scholarship/grant was $4,126; average loan $2,138. **Non-need based:** 180 full-time freshmen with need received non-need scholarships; 263 without need received awards; 29 received athletic scholarships.

Merit scholarships. Music scholarships and athletic grants, amounts vary. International Baccalaureate Scholarship for students who graduate with IB diploma; full tuition.

Policies to reduce costs. Tuition/fee waivers for senior citizens, employees and their families. Credit/placement for qualifying scores on AP, IB, CLEP examinations. Work study available for part-time students.

Payment plans. Credit card, installment, deferred payment.

Application procedures. FAFSA required. Priority date 3/1; no closing date. Applicants notified on rolling basis starting 4/1, must reply within 2 week(s) of notification. **Transfers:** Transfer students are not eligible for academic scholarship their first year.

Contact. Betty Whalen, Director, Financial Resource Center
701 Oakland Avenue
Rock Hill, SC 29733

Wofford College

Spartanburg, South Carolina
www.wofford.edu
Four-year private **Federal Code: 003457**

College costs. $190 fee for health services required of campus residents.

	Living at home	On-campus
Tuition and fees:	$20,610	$20,610
Room and board:		$6,100
Board only:	$2,384	
Books and supplies:	$851	$851
Personal expenses:	$1,110	$1,110
Transportation:	$932	$690

Undergraduate aid. Need-based: Average financial aid package for full-time students was $15,796; for part-time $14,577. 81% awarded as scholarships/grants, 19% as loans/jobs. **Non-need-based:** 84% awarded as scholarships/grants, 16% as loans/jobs. Scholarships based on academics, athletics, leadership, music/drama, religious affiliation, state/district residency. **Student debt:** 56% of graduating class borrowed to fund education; average debt was $12,470.

Freshman aid. Need-based: Out of 297 full-time freshmen, 210 applied for aid; 163 were judged to have need; of these 163 received aid. Average package met 92% of need. 89 students had full need met. Average scholarship/grant was $14,262; average loan $3,129. **Non-need based:** 74 full-time freshmen with need received non-need scholarships; 138 without need received awards; 59 received athletic scholarships.

Policies to reduce costs. Tuition/fee waivers for employees and their families. Credit/placement for qualifying scores on AP, IB, CLEP examinations.

Payment plans. Installment payment.

Application procedures. FAFSA required. Priority date 3/15; no closing date. Applicants notified on rolling basis starting 3/25, must reply by 5/1. Early decision closing date 11/15.

Contact. **Financial aid office:** (864) 597-4149
Donna Hawkins, Director of Financial Aid
429 North Church Street
Spartanburg, SC 29303-3663

York Technical College

Rock Hill, South Carolina
www.yorktech.com
Two-year public **Federal Code: 003996**

	Living at home
Tuition and fees (2002-2003):	$2,092
Out-of-district:	$2,500
Out-of-state:	$5,188
Per-credit charge:	$83
Per-credit out-of-district:	$100
Per-credit out-of-state:	$212
Books and supplies:	$900

Undergraduate aid. **Need-based:** Average financial aid package for full-time students was $3,359; for part-time $2,193. 99% awarded as scholarships/grants, 1% as loans/jobs. **Non-need-based:** 99% awarded as scholarships/grants, 1% as loans/jobs.

Freshman aid. **Need-based:** Out of 445 full-time freshmen, 347 applied for aid; 194 were judged to have need; of these 187 received aid. Average package met 40% of need. 2 students had full need met. Average scholarship/grant was $2,401. **Non-need based:** 12 full-time freshmen with need received non-need scholarships; 7 received athletic scholarships.

Policies to reduce costs. Tuition/fee waivers for senior citizens. Credit/placement for qualifying scores on AP, CLEP examinations. Work study available nights and for part-time students.

Payment plans. Credit card, installment payment.

Application procedures. FAFSA required. Priority date 7/1; no closing date. Applicants notified on rolling basis starting 7/1. **Transfers:** Priority date 6/1; no deadline.

Contact. **Financial aid office:** (803) 327-8005
Regina Venson, Financial Aid Department Manager
452 South Anderson Road
Rock Hill, SC 29730

South Dakota

Augustana College

Sioux Falls, South Dakota
www.augie.edu
Four-year private **Federal Code: 003458**

	Living at home	On-campus
Tuition and fees:	$16,972	$16,972
Room and board:		$5,026
Books and supplies:	$700	$700
Personal expenses:	$400	$800
Transportation:	$400	$200

Undergraduate aid. Need-based: Average financial aid package for full-time students was $13,811; for part-time $6,747. 61% awarded as scholarships/grants, 39% as loans/jobs. **Non-need-based:** 61% awarded as scholarships/grants, 39% as loans/jobs. Scholarships based on academics, alumni affiliation, art, athletics, leadership, minority status, music/drama, religious affiliation. **Student debt:** 79% of graduating class borrowed to fund education; average debt was $17,292.

Freshman aid. Need-based: Out of 417 full-time freshmen, 366 applied for aid; 301 were judged to have need; of these 301 received aid. Average package met 95% of need. 56 students had full need met. Average scholarship/grant was $10,176; average loan $4,600. **Non-need based:** 113 full-time freshmen with need received non-need scholarships; 113 without need received awards; 121 received athletic scholarships.

Policies to reduce costs. Tuition/fee waivers for children of alumni, senior citizens, family members, employees and their families. Prepayment discount; credit/placement for qualifying scores on AP, IB, CLEP examinations. Work study available nights, weekends and for part-time students.

Payment plans. Credit card, installment payment.

Application procedures. FAFSA, institutional form required. Priority date 3/1; no closing date. Applicants notified on rolling basis starting 3/15, must reply within 3 week(s) of notification. **Transfers:** Priority date 3/1; no deadline.

Contact. Financial aid office: (605) 274-5216
Brenda Murtha, Director of Financial Aid
2001 South Summit Avenue
Sioux Falls, SD 57197-9990

Black Hills State University

Spearfish, South Dakota
www.bhsu.edu
Four-year public **Federal Code: 003459**

College costs. Recprocity for Minnesota residents. $98 per-credit-hour charge for Western Undergraduate Exchange students. $98 per credit hour charge for adjacent state residents.

	Living at home	On-campus
Tuition and fees (2002-2003):	$3,931	$3,931
Out-of-state:	$8,181	$8,181
Room and board:		$3,740
Board only:	$1,232	
Books and supplies:	$600	$600
Personal expenses:	$1,252	$1,252
Transportation:	$850	$850

Undergraduate aid. All financial aid based on need. Need-based aid available for full-time and part-time students.

Policies to reduce costs. Tuition/fee waivers for senior citizens, employees and their families. Credit/placement for qualifying scores on AP, CLEP examinations.

Payment plans. Credit card, installment, deferred payment.

Application procedures. FAFSA required. Priority date 3/1; no closing date. Applicants notified on rolling basis starting 5/15, must reply within 3 week(s) of notification.

Contact. Deb Henriksen, Director of Financial Aid
University Street Box 9502
Spearfish, SD 57799-9502

Dakota State University

Madison, South Dakota
www.dsu.edu
Four-year public **Federal Code: 003463**

College costs. Reciprocity for Minnesota residents. $98 per credit hour charge for Western Undergraduate Exchange Students. $98 per credit hour charge for adjacent state residents.

	Living at home	On-campus
Tuition and fees (2002-2003):	$4,042	$4,042
Out-of-state:	$8,292	$8,292
Room and board:		$3,260
Books and supplies:	$600	$600
Transportation:	$420	$320

Undergraduate aid. Need-based: Average financial aid package for full-time students was $5,297; for part-time $4,395. 27% awarded as scholarships/grants, 73% as loans/jobs. **Non-need-based:** 20% awarded as scholarships/grants, 80% as loans/jobs. Scholarships based on academics, alumni affiliation, art, athletics, leadership, minority status, music/drama, state/district residency. **Student debt:** 78% of graduating class borrowed to fund education; average debt was $18,416. **Additional information:** Application deadline for grants and scholarships is 3/1. No deadline for loan and job applications.

Freshman aid. Need-based: Out of 340 full-time freshmen, 297 applied for aid; 227 were judged to have need; of these 223 received aid. **Non-need based:** 56 without need received awards.

Policies to reduce costs. Tuition/fee waivers for adults, senior citizens, family of clergy, employees and their families. Credit/placement for qualifying scores on AP, CLEP examinations.

Payment plans. Credit card, deferred payment.

Application procedures. FAFSA, institutional form required. Priority date 3/1; no closing date. Applicants notified on rolling basis starting 4/1, must reply within 2 week(s) of notification. **Transfers:** Priority date 3/1.

Contact. Financial aid office: (605) 256-5152
Rosie Jamison, Financial Aid Director
820 North Washington Avenue
Madison, SD 57042

Dakota Wesleyan University

Mitchell, South Dakota
www.dwu.edu
Four-year private **Federal Code: 003461**

	Living at home	On-campus
Tuition and fees (projected):	$13,398	$13,398
Room and board:		$4,416
Board only:	$1,866	
Books and supplies:	$800	$800
Personal expenses:	$1,200	$1,200
Transportation:	$600	$600

Undergraduate aid. Need-based: Average financial aid package for full-time students was $11,061; for part-time $3,420. 43% awarded as scholarships/grants, 57% as loans/jobs. **Non-need-based:** Scholarships based on academics, alumni affiliation, art, athletics, leadership, minority status, music/drama, religious affiliation. **Student debt:** 95% of graduating class borrowed to fund education; average debt was $13,925.

Freshman aid. Need-based: Out of 148 full-time freshmen, 148 applied for aid; 148 were judged to have need; of these 148 received aid. Average package met 74% of need. 7 students had full need met. Average scholarship/grant was $4,442; average loan $3,293. **Non-need based:** 74 full-time freshmen with need received non-need scholarships; 72 received athletic scholarships.

Merit scholarships. Academic Scholarships awarded based on combination of ACT scores and GPA. Awarded for four years.

Policies to reduce costs. Tuition/fee waivers for senior citizens, employees and their families. Prepayment discount; credit/placement for qualifying scores on AP, IB, CLEP examinations. Work study available nights and weekends.

Payment plans. Credit card, installment, deferred payment.

Application procedures. FAFSA required. Priority date 4/1; no closing date. Applicants notified on rolling basis starting 3/1, must reply within 2 week(s) of notification. **Transfers:** Priority date 4/1; no deadline.

Contact. **Financial aid office:** (605) 995-2654
Wilma Hjellum, Manager of Student Financial Aid
1200 West University Avenue
Mitchell, SD 57301-4398

Kilian Community College

Sioux Falls, South Dakota
kcc.cc.sd.us
Two-year private **Federal Code: 015000**

	Living at home
Tuition and fees (projected):	$5,385
Per-credit charge:	$175
Board only:	$300
Books and supplies:	$100
Personal expenses:	$600
Transportation:	$600

Undergraduate aid. Need-based: 38% awarded as scholarships/grants, 62% as loans/jobs. Need-based aid available for part-time students. **Non-need-based:** 0% awarded as scholarships/grants, 100% as loans/jobs. Scholarships based on academics, leadership.

Policies to reduce costs. Tuition/fee waivers for senior citizens, employees and their families. Credit/placement for qualifying scores on CLEP examinations. Work study available nights and for part-time students.

Payment plans. Credit card, installment payment.

Application procedures. FAFSA, institutional form required. No deadline. Applicants notified on rolling basis, must reply within 2 week(s) of notification. **Transfers:** No deadline.

Contact. **Financial aid office:** (605) 336-1711
Glen Poppinga, Director of Financial Aid
224 North Phillips Avenue
Sioux Falls, SD 57104-6014

Mitchell Technical Institute

Mitchell, South Dakota
www.mitchelltech.com
Two-year public **Federal Code: 008284**

College costs (2002-2003). Tuition varies depending on program. Fees, $1,177. Books/supplies: $800. Personal expenses: $750. Transportation: $900.

Undergraduate aid. Need-based: Need-based aid available for full-time and part-time students.

Application procedures. FAFSA required. No deadline. Applicants notified on rolling basis, must reply within 3 week(s) of notification.

Contact. Grant Uecker, Financial Aid Coordinator
821 North Capital
Mitchell, SD 57301

Mount Marty College

Yankton, South Dakota
www.mtmc.edu
Four-year private **Federal Code: 003465**

	Living at home	On-campus
Tuition and fees:	$13,586	$13,586
Room and board:		$4,670
Board only:	$540	
Books and supplies:	$600	$600
Personal expenses:	$970	$1,350
Transportation:	$846	$846

Undergraduate aid. Need-based: Average financial aid package for full-time students was $12,118; for part-time $4,006. 51% awarded as scholarships/grants, 49% as loans/jobs. **Non-need-based:** 26% awarded as scholarships/grants, 74% as loans/jobs. Scholarships based on academics, art, athletics, leadership, music/drama, religious affiliation. **Student debt:** 82% of graduating class borrowed to fund education; average debt was $19,140. **Additional information:** Prestige scholarships application deadline 2/1.

Freshman aid. Need-based: Average package met 76% of need. Average scholarship/grant was $4,833; average loan $3,500.

Policies to reduce costs. Tuition/fee waivers for family members, family of clergy, employees and their families. Credit/placement for qualifying scores on AP, IB, CLEP examinations. Work study available nights and weekends.

Payment plans. Credit card, installment payment.

Application procedures. FAFSA, institutional form required. Priority date 3/1; no closing date. Applicants notified on rolling basis starting 3/15, must reply within 2 week(s) of notification.

Contact. **Financial aid office:** (605) 668-1589
Kenneth Kocer, Director of Financial Assistance
1105 West Eighth Street
Yankton, SD 57078

National American University: Rapid City

Rapid City, South Dakota
www.national.edu
Four-year proprietary **Federal Code: 00405700**

	Living at home	On-campus
Tuition and fees (2002-2003):	$10,155	$10,155
Room and board:		$3,525
Board only:	$1,800	
Books and supplies:	$1,125	$1,125
Personal expenses:		$1,053
Transportation:	$1,092	$897

Undergraduate aid. All financial aid based on need. Need-based aid available for full-time and part-time students.

Policies to reduce costs. Tuition/fee waivers for family members, unemployed or children of unemployed, employees and their families. Credit/placement for qualifying scores on AP, IB, CLEP examinations. Work study available nights, weekends and for part-time students.

Payment plans. Credit card, installment payment.

Application procedures. FAFSA, institutional form required. No deadline. Applicants notified on rolling basis, must reply within 4 week(s) of notification. **Transfers:** No deadline.

Contact. Cheryl Bullinger, Director of Financial Aid
PO Box 1780
Rapid City, SD 57709

Northern State University

Aberdeen, South Dakota
www.northern.edu
Four-year public **Federal Code: 003466**

College costs. Reciprocity agreement applies to Minnesota residents. Members Western Undergraduate Exchange pay $99 per credit hour. $98 per-credit-hour charge for adjacent state residents.

	Living at home	On-campus
Tuition and fees (2002-2003):	$3,875	$3,875
Out-of-state:	$8,125	$8,125
Room and board:		$3,234
Books and supplies:	$650	$650
Personal expenses:	$2,350	$2,350
Transportation:	$825	$825

Undergraduate aid. Need-based: Need-based aid available for full-time and part-time students. **Non-need-based:** Scholarships based on academics, athletics, state/district residency.

Policies to reduce costs. Tuition/fee waivers for senior citizens. Credit/placement for qualifying scores on AP, CLEP examinations.

Payment plans. Credit card, deferred payment.

Application procedures. FAFSA required. Priority date 3/1; no closing date. Applicants notified on rolling basis starting 5/1, must reply within 2 week(s) of notification. **Transfers:** Financial aid transcript(s) required from all schools previously attended.

Contact. Sharon Kienow, Director of Student Financial Assistance
1200 South Jay Street
Aberdeen, SD 57401-7198

Presentation College

Aberdeen, South Dakota
www.presentation.edu
Four-year private **Federal Code: 003467**

	Living at home	On-campus
Tuition and fees (2002-2003):	$9,073	$9,073
Room and board:		$4,150
Board only:	$1,545	
Books and supplies:	$1,250	$1,250
Personal expenses:	$620	$620
Transportation:	$980	$980

Undergraduate aid. Need-based: Need-based aid available for full-time and part-time students.

Policies to reduce costs. Tuition/fee waivers for employees and their families. Credit/placement for qualifying scores on CLEP examinations. Work study available nights and weekends.

Payment plans. Credit card, installment payment.

Application procedures. FAFSA required. Priority date 4/1; no closing date. Applicants notified on rolling basis starting 5/1, must reply within 2 week(s) of notification. **Transfers:** Priority date 4/1; no deadline.

Contact. **Financial aid office:** (605) 229-8429
Val Weisser, Financial Aid Director
1500 North Main Street
Aberdeen, SD 57401

Sinte Gleska University

Rosebud, South Dakota
www.sinte.edu
Four-year public **Federal Code: 014303**

	Living at home
Tuition and fees:	$2,250
Books and supplies:	$500
Personal expenses:	$500
Transportation:	$900

Undergraduate aid. Need-based: Need-based aid available for full-time and part-time students.

Application procedures. FAFSA required. No deadline.

Contact. William Hay, Director of Financial Aid
Box 490
Rosebud, SD 57570

South Dakota School of Mines and Technology

Rapid City, South Dakota
www.sdsmt.edu
Four-year public **Federal Code: 003470**

College costs. Reciprocity with Minnesota residents. $98 per credit hour charge for Western Undergraduate Exchange members. $98 per credit hour charge for adjacent state residents.

	Living at home	On-campus
Tuition and fees (2002-2003):	$3,959	$3,959
Out-of-state:	$8,209	$8,209
Room and board:		$3,484
Board only:	$1,000	
Books and supplies:	$850	$850
Personal expenses:	$1,250	$1,250
Transportation:	$750	$650

Undergraduate aid. Need-based: Average financial aid package for full-time students was $5,598; for part-time $3,760. 33% awarded as scholarships/grants, 67% as loans/jobs. **Non-need-based:** 97% awarded as scholarships/grants, 3% as loans/jobs. Scholarships based on academics, athletics, leadership. **Additional information:** Closing date for scholarship applications February 3.

Freshman aid. Need-based: Out of 410 full-time freshmen, 384 applied for aid; 207 were judged to have need; of these 203 received aid. Average package met 79% of need. 72 students had full need met. Average scholarship/grant was $3,695; average loan $2,118. **Non-need based:** 84 full-time freshmen with need received non-need scholarships; 80 without need received awards; 22 received athletic scholarships.

Merit scholarships. Presidential Scolarship; 5 awarded; $100 to $5,000. Surbeck Scholars; 2 awarded; $7,000. All based on ACT/SAT scores, high school GPA and class rank.

Policies to reduce costs. Tuition/fee waivers for adults, senior citizens. Credit/placement for qualifying scores on AP, CLEP examinations. Work study available nights, weekends and for part-time students.

Payment plans. Credit card, installment, deferred payment.

Application procedures. FAFSA required. Priority date 3/15; no closing date. Applicants notified on rolling basis starting 5/1, must reply within 3 week(s) of notification. **Transfers:** No deadline.

Contact. **Financial aid office:** (605) 394-2274
David Martin, Director of Financial Aid
501 East St. Joseph Street
Rapid City, SD 57701

South Dakota State University

Brookings, South Dakota
www.sdstate.edu
Four-year public **Federal Code: 003471**

College costs. Reciprocity for Minnesota residents. $98 per credit hour for Western Undergraduate Exchange members. $98 per-credit-hour charge for adjacent state residents.

	Living at home	On-campus
Tuition and fees (2002-2003):	$3,833	$3,833
Out-of-state:	$8,083	$8,083
Room and board:		$3,373
Board only:	$1,304	
Books and supplies:	$700	$700
Personal expenses:	$1,866	$1,568
Transportation:	$1,080	$900

Undergraduate aid. Need-based: Average financial aid package for full-time students was $6,912. 27% awarded as scholarships/grants, 73% as loans/jobs. Need-based aid available for part-time students. **Non-need-based:** 27% awarded as scholarships/grants, 73% as loans/jobs. Scholarships based on academics, athletics, state/district residency. **Student debt:** 70% of graduating class borrowed to fund education; average debt was $16,297. **Additional information:** Awards financial aid to approximately 84% of all freshmen and approximately 84% of all undergraduates.

Freshman aid. Need-based: Average package met 86% of need. Average scholarship/grant was $3,040; average loan $2,470.

Merit scholarships. Academic scholarships for first-year freshmen at the university, college, and departmental levels based on academic performance in high school; application priority deadline January 25; 350-400 awarded; ranging from $200-$5,000; 75% of funds reserved for sophomores, juniors and seniors. Athletic, music, and theater scholarships require separate applications. New first-year students with a 24+ ACT composite are eligible for a $1,000 per year renewable academic scholarship.

Policies to reduce costs. Tuition/fee waivers for senior citizens, employees and their families. Credit/placement for qualifying scores on AP, IB, CLEP examinations.

Payment plans. Credit card payment.

Application procedures. FAFSA required. Priority date 3/1; no closing date. Applicants notified on rolling basis starting 4/1, must reply within 3 week(s) of notification. **Transfers:** Priority date 3/1; no deadline. Students must request that a financial aid transcipt be sent to SDSU from each post-secondary school previously attended. Request forms available from SDSU and at most other college financial aid offices.

Contact. Jay Larsen, Director of Financial Aid
Box 2201
Brookings, SD 57007-0649

Southeast Technical Institute

Sioux Falls, South Dakota
www.southeasttech.com
Two-year public **Federal Code: 008285**

College costs. $400 laptop fee required for some students.

	Living at home
Tuition and fees (2002-2003):	$3,019
Per-credit charge:	$56
Per-credit out-of-state:	$56
Board only:	$1,800
Books and supplies:	$700
Personal expenses:	$1,350
Transportation:	$900

Undergraduate aid. All financial aid based on need. Need-based aid available for full-time and part-time students.

Policies to reduce costs. Credit/placement for qualifying scores on AP, IB examinations.

Payment plans. Credit card, installment payment.

Application procedures. FAFSA required. Priority date 5/1; no closing date. Applicants notified on rolling basis starting 5/1, must reply within 3 week(s) of notification. **Transfers:** No deadline.

Contact. **Financial aid office:** (605) 367-4465
David Vikander, Financial Aid Officer
2320 North Career Avenue
Sioux Falls, SD 57107

University of Sioux Falls

Sioux Falls, South Dakota
www.usiouxfalls.edu
Four-year private **Federal Code: 003469**

	Living at home	On-campus
Tuition and fees (projected):	$13,900	$13,900
Room and board:		$4,150
Books and supplies:	$640	$640
Personal expenses:	$600	$2,000
Transportation:	$1,000	$800

Undergraduate aid. **Need-based:** Need-based aid available for full-time and part-time students. **Non-need-based:** Scholarships based on academics, alumni affiliation, art, athletics, job skills, leadership, minority status, music/drama, religious affiliation, state/district residency.

Policies to reduce costs. Tuition/fee waivers for senior citizens, employees and their families. Prepayment discount; credit/placement for qualifying scores on AP, CLEP examinations.

Payment plans. Credit card payment.

Application procedures. FAFSA required. Priority date 3/1; no closing date. Applicants notified on rolling basis starting 3/1, must reply within 2 week(s) of notification. **Transfers:** Priority date 3/1; no deadline.

Contact. **Financial aid office:** (605) 331-6623
Ruth Hanson, Director of Financial Aid
1101 West 22nd Street
Sioux Falls, SD 57105-1699

University of South Dakota

Vermillion, South Dakota
www.usd.edu
Four-year public **Federal Code: 003474**

College costs. Recoprocity for Minnesota residents. $98 per-credit-hour charge for Western Undergraduate Exchange members. $98 per-credit-hour charge for adjacent state residents.

	Living at home	On-campus
Tuition and fees (2002-2003):	$3,872	$3,872
Out-of-state:	$8,122	$8,122
Room and board:		$3,409
Books and supplies:	$700	$700
Personal expenses:	$1,200	$1,200
Transportation:	$700	$700

Undergraduate aid. **Need-based:** Average financial aid package for full-time students was $6,565; for part-time $6,565. 44% awarded as scholarships/grants, 56% as loans/jobs. **Non-need-based:** Scholarships based on academics, art, athletics, leadership, music/drama. **Student debt:** 82% of graduating class borrowed to fund education; average debt was $17,294.

Freshman aid. **Need-based:** Out of 989 full-time freshmen, 957 applied for aid; 579 were judged to have need; of these 576 received aid. Average package met 85% of need. 331 students had full need met. Average scholarship/grant was $3,013; average loan $2,588. **Non-need based:** 472 full-time freshmen with need received non-need scholarships; 284 without need received awards; 28 received athletic scholarships.

Policies to reduce costs. Tuition/fee waivers for senior citizens, employees and their families. Credit/placement for qualifying scores on AP, CLEP examinations.

Payment plans. Credit card, installment payment.

Application procedures. FAFSA required. Priority date 3/1; no closing date. Applicants notified on rolling basis starting 5/1, must reply within 2 week(s) of notification.

Contact. Julie Pier, Director of Student Financial Aid
414 East Clark Street
Vermillion, SD 57069-2390

Western Dakota Technical Institute

Rapid City, South Dakota
www.westerndakotatech.org
Two-year public **Federal Code: 010170**

College costs (projected). Total program cost ranges from $3,200 - $8,000 depending on course of study. Books/supplies: $816. Personal expenses: $1,353. Transportation: $1,220.

Undergraduate aid. **Need-based:** Need-based aid available for full-time and part-time students.

Policies to reduce costs. Tuition/fee waivers for employees and their families. Credit/placement for qualifying scores on AP, CLEP examinations. Work study available nights, weekends and for part-time students.

Payment plans. Credit card, installment, deferred payment.

Application procedures. FAFSA required. Priority date 4/20; no closing date. Applicants notified on rolling basis starting 6/30, must reply within 2 week(s) of notification.

Contact. **Financial aid office:** (605) 394-4034
Starla Russell, Financial Aid Coordinator
800 Mickelson Drive
Rapid City, SD 57703

Tennessee

American Baptist College of ABT Seminary

Nashville, Tennessee
www.abcnash.edu
Four-year private **Federal Code: 010460**

	Living at home	On-campus
Tuition and fees:	$4,360	$4,360
Room only:		$1,600
Books and supplies:	$440	$440

Undergraduate aid. Need-based: Need-based aid available for full-time students.

Application procedures. FAFSA required. No deadline. Applicants notified on rolling basis, must reply within 2 week(s) of notification.

Contact. Marcella Lockhart, Director of Enrollment Management
1800 Baptist World Center Drive
Nashville, TN 37207

Aquinas College

Nashville, Tennessee
www.aquinas-tn.edu
Four-year private **Federal Code: 003477**

College costs. Additional $40 per-credit hour for nursing classes. Additional required fees for nursing and teacher education programs.

	Living at home
Tuition and fees (2002-2003):	$11,180
Board only:	$2,025
Books and supplies:	$1,000
Personal expenses:	$1,500
Transportation:	$1,500

Undergraduate aid. Need-based: Average financial aid package for full-time students was $7,300; for part-time $5,100. 61% awarded as scholarships/ grants, 39% as loans/jobs. **Non-need-based:** 7% awarded as scholarships/ grants, 93% as loans/jobs. Scholarships based on academics. **Student debt:** 83% of graduating class borrowed to fund education; average debt was $15,000.

Freshman aid. Need-based: Average package met 67% of need. Average scholarship/grant was $1,500; average loan $2,250.

Policies to reduce costs. Tuition/fee waivers for employees and their families. Credit/placement for qualifying scores on AP, CLEP examinations. Work study available nights and for part-time students.

Payment plans. Credit card, installment payment.

Application procedures. FAFSA required. Priority date 3/15; no closing date. Applicants notified on rolling basis starting 3/1, must reply within 2 week(s) of notification.

Contact. Financial aid office: (615) 297-7545 ext. 442
Zelena O'Sullivan, Director of Financial Aid
4210 Harding Road
Nashville, TN 37205-2086

Austin Peay State University

Clarksville, Tennessee
www.apsu.edu
Four-year public **Federal Code: 003478**

	Living at home	On-campus
Tuition and fees (2002-2003):	$3,454	$3,454
Out-of-state:	$10,412	$10,412
Room and board:		$3,820
Books and supplies:	$800	$800
Personal expenses:	$1,972	$1,972
Transportation:	$1,382	$760

Undergraduate aid. Need-based: Need-based aid available for full-time and part-time students. **Non-need-based:** Scholarships based on academics, art, athletics, leadership, minority status, music/drama, state/district residency.

Policies to reduce costs. Tuition/fee waivers for senior citizens, employees and their families. Credit/placement for qualifying scores on AP, CLEP examinations.

Payment plans. Credit card, installment, deferred payment.

Application procedures. FAFSA required. Priority date 4/1; no closing date. Applicants notified on rolling basis starting 4/15, must reply within 2 week(s) of notification. **Transfers:** Priority date 4/1; no deadline.

Contact. Financial aid office: (931) 221-7907
Darolyn Parks-Porter, Student Financial Aid
Box 4548
Clarksville, TN 37044

Belmont University

Nashville, Tennessee
www.belmont.edu
Four-year private **Federal Code: 003479**

	Living at home	On-campus
Tuition and fees:	$15,954	$15,954
Room and board:		$6,032
Books and supplies:	$791	$791
Personal expenses:	$1,700	$1,700
Transportation:	$900	$900

Undergraduate aid. Need-based: Average financial aid package for full-time students was $2,649; for part-time $2,735. 32% awarded as scholarships/ grants, 68% as loans/jobs. **Non-need-based:** Scholarships based on academics, art, athletics, leadership, music/drama, religious affiliation, state/district residency. **Student debt:** 57% of graduating class borrowed to fund education; average debt was $15,954.

Freshman aid. Need-based: Out of 487 full-time freshmen, 408 applied for aid; 238 were judged to have need; of these 229 received aid. Average package met 34% of need. 54 students had full need met. Average scholarship/ grant was $2,043; average loan $2,284. **Non-need based:** 127 full-time freshmen with need received non-need scholarships; 113 without need received awards; 20 received athletic scholarships.

Policies to reduce costs. Tuition/fee waivers for senior citizens, family members, family of clergy, employees and their families. Credit/placement for qualifying scores on AP, IB, CLEP examinations.

Payment plans. Credit card, installment payment.

Application procedures. FAFSA, CSS PROFILE required. Priority date 3/15; no closing date. Applicants notified on rolling basis starting 3/15, must reply by 5/1 or within 2 week(s) of notification. **Transfers:** Scholarships available.

Contact. Financial aid office: (615) 460-6403
Paula Gill, Director of Student Financial Services
1900 Belmont Boulevard
Nashville, TN 37212-3757

Bethel College

McKenzie, Tennessee
www.bethel-college.edu
Four-year private **Federal Code: 003480**

	Living at home	On-campus
Tuition and fees:	$9,630	$9,630
Room and board:		$5,080
Books and supplies:	$1,050	$1,050
Personal expenses:		$1,000
Transportation:	$700	

Undergraduate aid. Need-based: Need-based aid available for full-time and part-time students. **Non-need-based:** Scholarships based on academics, athletics, music/drama, religious affiliation, state/district residency.

Policies to reduce costs. Tuition/fee waivers for senior citizens, employees and their families. Credit/placement for qualifying scores on AP, CLEP examinations. Work study available nights and weekends.

Payment plans. Credit card, installment payment.

Application procedures. FAFSA, institutional form required. Priority date 3/3; closing date 6/30. Applicants notified on rolling basis starting 3/1. **Transfers:** Financial aid transcripts from previously attended institutions required.

Contact. **Financial aid office:** (610) 799-1133
Laura Bateman, Director of Financial Aid
325 Cherry Avenue
McKenzie, TN 38201

Bryan College

Dayton, Tennessee
www.bryan.edu
Four-year private **Federal Code: 003536**

	Living at home	On-campus
Tuition and fees:	$13,500	$13,500
Room and board:		$4,400
Board only:	$1,300	
Books and supplies:	$900	$900
Personal expenses:	$600	$1,100
Transportation:	$1,100	$1,100

Undergraduate aid. Need-based: Average financial aid package for full-time students was $10,949. 44% awarded as scholarships/grants, 56% as loans/jobs. Need-based aid available for part-time students. **Non-need-based:** 78% awarded as scholarships/grants, 22% as loans/jobs. Scholarships based on academics, alumni affiliation, art, athletics, job skills, leadership, music/drama. **Student debt:** 63% of graduating class borrowed to fund education; average debt was $14,703.

Freshman aid. Need-based: Out of 126 full-time freshmen, 125 applied for aid; 96 were judged to have need; of these 96 received aid. Average package met 77% of need. 20 students had full need met. Average scholarship/grant was $3,553; average loan $2,958. **Non-need based:** 96 full-time freshmen with need received non-need scholarships; 30 without need received awards; 30 received athletic scholarships.

Policies to reduce costs. Tuition/fee waivers for adults, children of alumni, family of clergy, employees and their families. Credit/placement for qualifying scores on AP, IB, CLEP examinations. Work study available for part-time students.

Payment plans. Installment payment.

Application procedures. Institutional form required. Priority date 5/1; no closing date. Applicants notified on rolling basis starting 2/15, must reply within 2 week(s) of notification. **Transfers:** No deadline.

Contact. **Financial aid office:** (423) 775-7339
Anne Rader, Director of Financial Aid
PO Box 7000
Dayton, TN 37321-7000

Carson-Newman College

Jefferson City, Tennessee
www.cn.edu
Four-year private **Federal Code: 003481**

	Living at home	On-campus
Tuition and fees:	$13,620	$13,620
Room and board:		$4,800
Books and supplies:	$600	$600
Personal expenses:	$750	$800
Transportation:	$1,200	$1,000

Undergraduate aid. Need-based: Average financial aid package for full-time students was $11,722; for part-time $5,248. 69% awarded as scholarships/grants, 31% as loans/jobs. **Non-need-based:** 59% awarded as scholarships/grants, 41% as loans/jobs. Scholarships based on academics, art, athletics, leadership, minority status, music/drama, religious affiliation. **Student debt:** 65% of graduating class borrowed to fund education; average debt was $16,413.

Freshman aid. Need-based: Out of 431 full-time freshmen, 425 applied for aid; 299 were judged to have need; of these 299 received aid. Average package met 76% of need. 63 students had full need met. Average scholarship/grant was $9,535; average loan $3,462. **Non-need based:** 56 full-time freshmen with need received non-need scholarships; 114 without need received awards; 33 received athletic scholarships.

Policies to reduce costs. Tuition/fee waivers for adults, senior citizens, minority students, family members, family of clergy, employees and their families. Credit/placement for qualifying scores on AP, CLEP examinations. Work study available nights, weekends and for part-time students.

Payment plans. Credit card, installment payment.

Application procedures. FAFSA, institutional form required. Priority date 4/1; no closing date. Applicants notified on rolling basis starting 2/1, must reply within 2 week(s) of notification.

Contact. Don Elia, Director of Financial Aid
1646 Russell Avenue
Jefferson City, TN 37760

Chattanooga State Technical Community College

Chattanooga, Tennessee
www.cstcc.cc.tn.us
Two-year public **Federal Code: 003998**

	Living at home
Tuition and fees (2002-2003):	$1,771
Out-of-state:	$6,563
Per-credit charge:	$68
Per-credit out-of-state:	$275
Books and supplies:	$450
Personal expenses:	$1,700
Transportation:	$1,600

Policies to reduce costs. Tuition/fee waivers for senior citizens, employees and their families. Credit/placement for qualifying scores on AP, CLEP examinations.

Payment plans. Credit card payment.

Application procedures. FAFSA required. Priority date 6/1; no closing date. Applicants notified on rolling basis starting 4/1, must reply within 2 week(s) of notification.

Contact. **Financial aid office:** (423) 697-4402
Mary Knaff, Financial Aid Director
4501 Amnicola Highway
Chattanooga, TN 37406

Christian Brothers University

Memphis, Tennessee
www.cbu.edu
Four-year private **Federal Code: 003482**

	Living at home	On-campus
Tuition and fees:	$17,490	$17,490
Room and board:		$5,100
Board only:	$1,500	
Books and supplies:	$675	$675
Personal expenses:	$1,537	$1,537
Transportation:	$659	$659

Undergraduate aid. Need-based: Average financial aid package for full-time students was $11,887; for part-time $6,122. 44% awarded as scholarships/grants, 56% as loans/jobs. **Non-need-based:** 66% awarded as scholarships/grants, 34% as loans/jobs. Scholarships based on academics, athletics, state/district residency. **Student debt:** 69% of graduating class borrowed to fund education; average debt was $16,579. **Additional information:** ROTC scholarships available to qualified applicants.

Freshman aid. Need-based: Out of 235 full-time freshmen, 195 applied for aid; 191 were judged to have need; of these 191 received aid. Average package met 79% of need. 36 students had full need met. Average scholarship/grant was $6,249; average loan $2,926. **Non-need based:** 189 full-time freshmen with need received non-need scholarships; 86 without need received awards; 32 received athletic scholarships.

Policies to reduce costs. Tuition/fee waivers for children of alumni, employees and their families. Credit/placement for qualifying scores on AP, CLEP examinations.

Payment plans. Credit card, installment, deferred payment.

Application procedures. FAFSA required. Priority date 2/15; no closing date. Applicants notified on rolling basis starting 3/30, must reply by 5/1 or within 2 week(s) of notification. **Transfers:** No deadline.

Contact. **Financial aid office:** (901) 321-3305
Jim Shannon, Director of Student Financial Resources
650 East Parkway South
Memphis, TN 38104-5581

Cleveland State Community College

Cleveland, Tennessee
www.clevelandstatecc.edu
Two-year public **Federal Code: 003999**

	Living at home
Tuition and fees (2002-2003):	$1,731
Out-of-state:	$6,523
Per-credit charge:	$68
Per-credit out-of-state:	$275
Books and supplies:	$600
Personal expenses:	$900
Transportation:	$1,008

Undergraduate aid. Need-based: Average financial aid package for full-time students was $2,088; for part-time $1,854. 78% awarded as scholarships/grants, 22% as loans/jobs. **Non-need-based:** 72% awarded as scholarships/grants, 28% as loans/jobs. Scholarships based on athletics, minority status.

Freshman aid. Need-based: Average package met 75% of need. Average scholarship/grant was $2,152; average loan $1,082.

Policies to reduce costs. Tuition/fee waivers for senior citizens, employees and their families. Credit/placement for qualifying scores on AP, CLEP examinations.

Payment plans. Credit card, installment payment.

Application procedures. FAFSA required. Priority date 6/15; no closing date. Applicants notified on rolling basis starting 7/1, must reply within 2 week(s) of notification.

Contact. Financial aid office: (423) 478-6215
Geraldine Parks, Director of Financial Aid
Box 3570
Cleveland, TN 37320-3570

Columbia State Community College

Columbia, Tennessee
www.coscc.cc.tn.us
Two-year public **Federal Code: 003483**

	Living at home
Tuition and fees (2002-2003):	$1,731
Out-of-state:	$6,523
Per-credit charge:	$68
Per-credit out-of-state:	$275
Books and supplies:	$2,813
Personal expenses:	$625
Transportation:	$820

Undergraduate aid. Need-based: Need-based aid available for full-time and part-time students. **Non-need-based:** Scholarships based on academics, athletics, state/district residency.

Policies to reduce costs. Tuition/fee waivers for senior citizens. Credit/placement for qualifying scores on AP, CLEP examinations.

Application procedures. FAFSA, institutional form required. Closing date 3/15. Applicants notified on rolling basis starting 5/15, must reply within 2 week(s) of notification.

Contact. David Ogden, Director, Financial Assistance
Box 1315
Columbia, TN 38402

Crichton College

Memphis, Tennessee
www.crichton.edu
Four-year private **Federal Code: 009982**

	Living at home	On-campus
Tuition and fees (2002-2003):	$10,920	$10,920
Room only:		$3,400
Board only:	$900	
Books and supplies:	$750	$750
Personal expenses:	$900	$900
Transportation:	$2,340	$2,340

Undergraduate aid. Need-based: Average financial aid package for full-time students was $6,729; for part-time $4,390. 39% awarded as scholarships/grants, 61% as loans/jobs. **Non-need-based:** 21% awarded as scholarships/grants, 79% as loans/jobs. Scholarships based on academics, alumni affiliation, athletics, leadership, music/drama, religious affiliation, state/district residency. **Student debt:** 71% of graduating class borrowed to fund education; average debt was $16,653.

Freshman aid. Need-based: Out of 38 full-time freshmen, 34 applied for aid; 29 were judged to have need; of these 27 received aid. Average package met 24% of need. 10 students had full need met. Average scholarship/grant was $3,898; average loan $2,268. **Non-need based:** 23 full-time freshmen with need received non-need scholarships; 12 without need received awards; 4 received athletic scholarships.

Merit scholarships. Crichton Singers (ensemble); $600-$2,000 for up to four years; audition and 2.50 cumulative GPA. New Direction (drama group); $600-$2,000 for up to four years; audition and 2.50 cumulative GPA. Enhanced Campus Life (athletics); $600-$2,000 for up to four years; tryouts. All vary in number awarded based on demand.

Policies to reduce costs. Tuition/fee waivers for adults, children of alumni, minority students, employees and their families. Credit/placement for qualifying scores on AP, IB, CLEP examinations. Work study available nights, weekends and for part-time students.

Payment plans. Credit card, installment payment.

Application procedures. FAFSA, institutional form required. Priority date 3/31; no closing date. Applicants notified on rolling basis starting 3/1, must reply within 2 week(s) of notification. **Transfers:** Priority date 3/31; no deadline.

Contact. Financial aid office: (901) 320-9787
Dede Pirtle, Director of Financial Aid
255 North Highland, Attn: Admissions
Memphis, TN 38111

Draughons Junior College of Business: Nashville

Nashville, Tennessee
www.draughons.org
Two-year proprietary **Federal Code: 004934**

	Living at home
Tuition and fees (2002-2003):	$5,365
Per-credit charge:	$225
Books and supplies:	$500

Undergraduate aid. All financial aid based on need. 36% awarded as scholarships/grants, 64% as loans/jobs. Need-based aid available for part-time students. **Student debt:** 36% of graduating class borrowed to fund education; average debt was $8,000. **Additional information:** Financial aid form for in-state applicants must be filed before 5/1.

Policies to reduce costs. Tuition/fee waivers for employees and their families. Credit/placement for qualifying scores on CLEP examinations. Work study available nights.

Payment plans. Credit card, installment payment.

Application procedures. FAFSA required. No deadline. Applicants notified on rolling basis. **Transfers:** Students must notify Tennessee Student Assistance Corporation of institutional change before appropriate deadlines.

Contact. Financial aid office: (615) 361-7555
Bob Hobart, Director of Financial Aid
340 Plus Park at Pavilion Boulevard
Nashville, TN 37217

Draughons Junior College: Clarksville

Clarksville, Tennessee
www.draughons.org
Two-year proprietary **Federal Code: 004934**

	Living at home
Tuition and fees (projected):	$6,125
Per-credit charge:	$200
Books and supplies:	$700

Contact. Linda Cumby
1860 Wilma Rudolph Boulevard
Clarksville, TN 37040

Dyersburg State Community College

Dyersburg, Tennessee
www.dscc.edu
Two-year public **Federal Code: 006835**

	Living at home
Tuition and fees (2002-2003):	$1,741
Out-of-state:	$6,533
Per-credit charge:	$68
Per-credit out-of-state:	$275
Board only:	$1,628
Books and supplies:	$600
Personal expenses:	$630
Transportation:	$1,776

Undergraduate aid. Need-based: Average financial aid package for full-time students was $3,671; for part-time $2,669. 79% awarded as scholarships/grants, 21% as loans/jobs. **Non-need-based:** Scholarships based on academics, athletics, job skills, leadership, minority status, music/drama, state/district residency. **Student debt:** 12% of graduating class borrowed to fund education; average debt was $1,615.

Policies to reduce costs. Tuition/fee waivers for senior citizens, employees and their families. Credit/placement for qualifying scores on AP, CLEP examinations. Work study available nights and for part-time students.

Payment plans. Credit card payment.

Application procedures. FAFSA required. Priority date 3/1; no closing date. Applicants notified on rolling basis starting 3/1, must reply within 2 week(s) of notification. **Transfers:** No deadline.

Contact. Financial aid office: (731) 286-3238
Sandra Rockett, Director of Financial Aid
1510 Lake Road
Dyersburg, TN 38024

East Tennessee State University

Johnson City, Tennessee
www.etsu.edu
Four-year public **Federal Code: 003487**

	Living at home	On-campus
Tuition and fees (2002-2003):	$3,311	$3,311
Out-of-state:	$10,269	$10,269
Room and board:		$3,898
Board only:	$2,168	
Books and supplies:	$850	$850
Personal expenses:	$3,883	$3,883

Undergraduate aid. Need-based: Average financial aid package for full-time students was $4,584; for part-time $4,721. 45% awarded as scholarships/grants, 55% as loans/jobs. **Non-need-based:** 45% awarded as scholarships/grants, 55% as loans/jobs. Scholarships based on academics, alumni affiliation, art, athletics, job skills, leadership, minority status, music/drama, religious affiliation, state/district residency. **Student debt:** 35% of graduating class borrowed to fund education; average debt was $18,003. **Additional information:** Housing costs payable by installment.

Freshman aid. Need-based: Out of 1,474 full-time freshmen, 580 applied for aid; 418 were judged to have need; of these 399 received aid. Average package met 84% of need. 86 students had full need met. Average scholarship/grant was $2,992; average loan $1,759. **Non-need based:** 140 full-time freshmen with need received non-need scholarships; 105 without need received awards; 25 received athletic scholarships.

Policies to reduce costs. Tuition/fee waivers for senior citizens, employees and their families. Credit/placement for qualifying scores on AP, IB, CLEP examinations.

Payment plans. Credit card, deferred payment.

Application procedures. FAFSA required. Priority date 4/15; no closing date. Applicants notified on rolling basis starting 4/30, must reply within 3 week(s) of notification.

Contact. Financial aid office: (423) 439-4300
Margaret Miller, Director of Financial Aid
Box 70731
Johnson City, TN 37614-0731

Fisk University

Nashville, Tennessee
www.fisk.edu
Four-year private **Federal Code: 003490**

	Living at home	On-campus
Tuition and fees:	$11,235	$11,235
Room and board:		$5,770
Board only:	$2,240	
Books and supplies:	$1,000	$1,000
Personal expenses:	$1,800	$1,800
Transportation:	$1,500	$2,163

Undergraduate aid. All financial aid based on need. Average financial aid package for full-time students was $13,000. 43% awarded as scholarships/grants, 57% as loans/jobs. Need-based aid available for part-time students.

Freshman aid. Out of 217 full-time freshmen, 206 applied for aid; 195 were judged to have need; of these 195 received aid. Average package met 50% of need. 7 students had full need met. Average scholarship/grant was $3,600; average loan $2,625.

Policies to reduce costs. Tuition/fee waivers for employees and their families. Credit/placement for qualifying scores on IB examinations.

Payment plans. Credit card payment.

Application procedures. FAFSA required. Priority date 3/1; closing date 7/1. Applicants notified on rolling basis starting 4/1, must reply within 2 week(s) of notification. **Transfers:** Priority date 3/1.

Contact. Financial aid office: (615) 329-8585
Mark Adkins, Director of Financial Affairs
1000 17th Avenue N.
Nashville, TN 37208-3051

Freed-Hardeman University

Henderson, Tennessee
www.fhu.edu
Four-year private **Federal Code: 003492**

	Living at home	On-campus
Tuition and fees:	$11,046	$11,046
Room and board:		$5,520
Books and supplies:	$1,000	$1,000
Personal expenses:		$1,342
Transportation:		$900

Undergraduate aid. Need-based: Average financial aid package for full-time students was $11,220. 49% awarded as scholarships/grants, 51% as loans/jobs. Need-based aid available for part-time students. **Non-need-based:** Scholarships based on academics, art, athletics, leadership, minority status, music/drama, state/district residency. **Student debt:** 84% of graduating class borrowed to fund education; average debt was $17,692.

Freshman aid. Need-based: Out of 414 full-time freshmen, 325 applied for aid; 276 were judged to have need; of these 276 received aid. Average package met 86% of need. 146 students had full need met. Average scholarship/grant was $3,826; average loan $4,425. **Non-need based:** 130 full-time freshmen with need received non-need scholarships; 39 without need received awards; 50 received athletic scholarships.

Policies to reduce costs. Tuition/fee waivers for senior citizens, family of clergy, employees and their families. Credit/placement for qualifying scores on AP, IB, CLEP examinations. Work study available nights, weekends and for part-time students.

Payment plans. Credit card, installment payment.

Application procedures. FAFSA required. Priority date 4/1; no closing date. Applicants notified on rolling basis starting 3/1, must reply within 4 week(s) of notification. **Transfers:** Priority date 4/1.

Contact. Financial aid office: (731) 989-6662
Larry Cyr, Director of Financial Aid
158 East Main Street
Henderson, TN 38340

ITT Technical Institute: Knoxville

Knoxville, Tennessee
www.itt-tech.edu
Three-year proprietary **Federal Code: 030734**

College costs. Total program varies depending on course of study. Per-credit-hour charge: $347.

Policies to reduce costs. Tuition/fee waivers for employees and their families.

Payment plans. Credit card, installment payment.

Application procedures. FAFSA, institutional form required. No deadline. Applicants notified on rolling basis.

Contact. Kelly Armstrong, Director of Finance
10208 Technology Drive
Knoxville, TN 37932

ITT Technical Institute: Memphis

Memphis, Tennessee
www.itt-tech.edu
Two-year proprietary **Federal Code: 007557**

College costs. Total program varies depending on course of study. Per-credit-hour charge: $347.

Policies to reduce costs. Tuition/fee waivers for employees and their families. Tuition at time of enrollment guaranteed for 2 years.

Payment plans. Credit card, installment payment.

Application procedures. FAFSA, institutional form required. No deadline. Applicants notified on rolling basis.

Contact. Heather Lindsay, Director of Finance
1255 Lynnfield Road, Suite 192
Memphis, TN 38119

ITT Technical Institute: Nashville

Nashville, Tennessee
www.itt-tech.edu
Three-year proprietary **Federal Code: 023598**

College costs. Total program varies depending on course of study. Per-credit-hour charge: $347.

Policies to reduce costs. Tuition/fee waivers for employees and their families.

Payment plans. Credit card, installment payment.

Application procedures. FAFSA, institutional form required. No deadline. Applicants notified on rolling basis.

Contact. James Blackburn, Director of Finance
441 Donelson Pike
Nashville, TN 37214-8029

Jackson State Community College

Jackson, Tennessee
www.jscc.edu
Two-year public **Federal Code: 004937**

	Living at home
Tuition and fees (2002-2003):	$1,751
Out-of-state:	$6,543
Per-credit charge:	$68
Per-credit out-of-state:	$275
Board only:	$2,170
Books and supplies:	$800
Personal expenses:	$762
Transportation:	$1,996

Undergraduate aid. Need-based: Average financial aid package for full-time students was $2,043; for part-time $3,065. 97% awarded as scholarships/grants, 3% as loans/jobs. **Non-need-based:** 86% awarded as scholarships/grants, 14% as loans/jobs. Scholarships based on academics, art, athletics, job skills, leadership, minority status, music/drama. **Student debt:** 1% of graduating class borrowed to fund education; average debt was $1,513.

Freshman aid. Need-based: Out of 650 full-time freshmen, 508 applied for aid; 348 were judged to have need; of these 354 received aid. Average package met 78% of need. 17 students had full need met. Average scholarship/grant was $3,641; average loan $270. **Non-need based:** 36 full-time freshmen with need received non-need scholarships; 20 without need received awards; 25 received athletic scholarships.

Policies to reduce costs. Tuition/fee waivers for adults, senior citizens, minority students, employees and their families. Credit/placement for qualifying scores on AP, CLEP examinations. Work study available nights, weekends and for part-time students.

Payment plans. Credit card, deferred payment.

Application procedures. FAFSA, institutional form required. Priority date 4/1; no closing date. Applicants notified on rolling basis starting 6/1, must reply within 2 week(s) of notification.

Contact. Financial aid office: (731) 425-2605
Dewana Latimer, Director of Financial Aid
2046 North Parkway
Jackson, TN 38301

John A. Gupton College

Nashville, Tennessee
www.guptoncollege.com
Two-year private **Federal Code: 008859**

	Living at home	On-campus
Tuition and fees (projected):	$5,297	$5,297
Per-credit charge:	$150	$150
Room only:		$3,400
Books and supplies:	$850	$850

Undergraduate aid. All financial aid based on need. 38% awarded as scholarships/grants, 62% as loans/jobs. Need-based aid available for part-time students. **Student debt:** 61% of graduating class borrowed to fund education; average debt was $13,250.

Payment plans. Credit card, installment payment.

Application procedures. FAFSA required. No deadline. Applicants notified on rolling basis. **Transfers:** No deadline.

Contact. Financial aid office: (615) 327-3927
B. Steven Spann, President/CFO
1616 Church Street
Nashville, TN 37203-2920

Johnson Bible College

Knoxville, Tennessee
www.jbc.edu
Four-year private **Federal Code: 003495**

College costs. Part-time students pay mandatory fee of $18.75 per hour.

	Living at home	On-campus
Tuition and fees:	$5,850	$5,850
Out-of-state:	$5,850	$5,850
Room and board:		$3,710
Books and supplies:	$1,000	$1,000
Personal expenses:	$1,660	$1,930
Transportation:	$1,600	$1,300

Undergraduate aid. Need-based: Average financial aid package for full-time students was $2,561; for part-time $1,968. 66% awarded as scholarships/grants, 34% as loans/jobs. **Non-need-based:** 51% awarded as scholarships/grants, 49% as loans/jobs. Scholarships based on academics, leadership, minority status, music/drama, religious affiliation. **Student debt:** 58% of graduating class borrowed to fund education; average debt was $7,911. **Additional information:** J.B.C. has an additional work program for students who do not qualify for federal work-study.

Freshman aid. Need-based: Out of 179 full-time freshmen, 175 applied for aid; 173 were judged to have need; of these 173 received aid. Average package met 33% of need. Average scholarship/grant was $1,346; average loan $1,015. **Non-need based:** 87 full-time freshmen with need received non-need scholarships.

Policies to reduce costs. Tuition/fee waivers for minority students, family members, family of clergy, employees and their families. Credit/placement for qualifying scores on AP, CLEP examinations. Work study available nights, weekends and for part-time students.

Payment plans. Credit card, installment, deferred payment.

Application procedures. FAFSA, institutional form required. No deadline. Applicants notified by 4/30, must reply within 2 week(s) of notification. **Transfers:** No deadline.

Contact. **Financial aid office:** (865) 251-2303
Janette Overton, Financial Aid Director
7900 Johnson Drive
Knoxville, TN 37998-0001

King College

Bristol, Tennessee
www.king.edu
Four-year private **Federal Code: 003496**

	Living at home	On-campus
Tuition and fees:	$17,040	$17,040
Room and board:		$5,460
Board only:	$1,600	
Books and supplies:	$600	$600
Transportation:	$2,640	$1,000

Undergraduate aid. Need-based: Average financial aid package for full-time students was $14,330; for part-time $7,860. 61% awarded as scholarships/grants, 39% as loans/jobs. **Non-need-based:** 86% awarded as scholarships/grants, 14% as loans/jobs. Scholarships based on academics, art, athletics, job skills, music/drama. **Student debt:** 14% of graduating class borrowed to fund education; average debt was $3,366.

Freshman aid. Need-based: Average package met 65% of need. Average scholarship/grant was $6,090; average loan $3,639.

Policies to reduce costs. Tuition/fee waivers for senior citizens, family of clergy, employees and their families. Credit/placement for qualifying scores on AP, CLEP examinations. Work study available nights, weekends and for part-time students.

Payment plans. Credit card, installment payment.

Application procedures. FAFSA required. Priority date 3/1; no closing date. Applicants notified on rolling basis starting 3/1, must reply within 4 week(s) of notification. **Transfers:** Aid not offered if student failed to make satisfactory progress at previous school.

Contact. **Financial aid office:** (423) 652-4725
Suzanne Booher, Financial Aid Director
1350 King College Road
Bristol, TN 37620-2699

Lambuth University

Jackson, Tennessee
www.lambuth.edu
Four-year private **Federal Code: 003498**

	Living at home	On-campus
Tuition and fees:	$11,590	$11,590
Room and board:		$5,178
Board only:	$2,884	
Books and supplies:	$800	$800
Personal expenses:	$1,316	$1,360
Transportation:	$1,300	$1,200

Undergraduate aid. Need-based: Average financial aid package for full-time students was $10,425; for part-time $3,000. 63% awarded as scholarships/grants, 37% as loans/jobs. **Non-need-based:** 50% awarded as scholarships/grants, 50% as loans/jobs. Scholarships based on academics, athletics, job skills, leadership, music/drama, religious affiliation. **Student debt:** 85% of graduating class borrowed to fund education; average debt was $11,000. **Additional information:** Part-time students eligible for federal and state aid, but not institutional aid.

Freshman aid. Need-based: Out of 194 full-time freshmen, 194 applied for aid; 135 were judged to have need; of these 135 received aid. Average package met 76% of need. 38 students had full need met. Average scholarship/grant was $5,935; average loan $2,231. **Non-need based:** 14 full-time freshmen with need received non-need scholarships; 59 without need received awards; 18 received athletic scholarships.

Merit scholarships. Hyde Scholarships require admission acceptance deadline of 2/1, ACT 30+, GPA 3.5+; 2 full scholarships, highly competitive. Presidential Scholarships require deadline of 2/1, ACT 29+, GPA 3.5+; must maintain 3.25 to retain 4-year awards near tuition for first-time freshmen. Bishop's Scholarship requires firm intentions of entering ministry in Methodist Church, GPA 3.0+, ACT 20+. Dean's Scholarship requires GPA 3.0+, ACT 25+. Scholar Athlete/Performance Awards require admission by 2/15, GPA 2.0+, ACT 18+.

Policies to reduce costs. Tuition/fee waivers for adults, senior citizens, family of clergy, employees and their families. Credit/placement for qualifying scores on AP, IB, CLEP examinations. Work study available nights, weekends and for part-time students.

Payment plans. Credit card, installment, deferred payment.

Application procedures. FAFSA, institutional form required. Priority date 2/1; no closing date. Applicants notified on rolling basis starting 12/15, must reply by 5/1 or within 3 week(s) of notification.

Contact. **Financial aid office:** (731) 425-3330
Lisa Warmath, Director of Financial Aid
705 Lambuth Boulevard
Jackson, TN 38301-5296

Lane College

Jackson, Tennessee
www.lanecollege.edu
Four-year private **Federal Code: 003499**

	Living at home	On-campus
Tuition and fees (2002-2003):	$6,570	$6,570
Room and board:		$4,080
Books and supplies:	$550	$550
Personal expenses:	$675	$675
Transportation:	$630	$405

Undergraduate aid. Need-based: Average financial aid package for full-time students was $7,852; for part-time $4,136. 65% awarded as scholarships/grants, 35% as loans/jobs. **Non-need-based:** Scholarships based on academics, athletics. **Student debt:** 98% of graduating class borrowed to fund education; average debt was $19,297.

Freshman aid. Need-based: Out of 299 full-time freshmen, 295 applied for aid; 277 were judged to have need; of these 277 received aid. Average package met 79% of need. 42 students had full need met. Average scholarship/grant was $5,345; average loan $2,237. **Non-need based:** 2 received athletic scholarships.

Policies to reduce costs. Tuition/fee waivers for employees and their families. Credit/placement for qualifying scores on AP, CLEP examinations.

Payment plans. Credit card, installment, deferred payment.

Application procedures. FAFSA required. Priority date 4/1; no closing date. Applicants notified on rolling basis starting 3/31, must reply within 2 week(s) of notification.

Contact. **Financial aid office:** (731) 426-7537
Ursula Singleton, Director of Financial Aid
545 Lane Avenue
Jackson, TN 38301

Lee University

Cleveland, Tennessee
www.leeuniversity.edu
Four-year private **Federal Code: 003500**

College costs. Required fees reported are for on-campus residents; required fees for commuters $160.

	Living at home	On-campus
Tuition and fees (2002-2003):	$8,300	$8,300
Room and board:		$4,910
Board only:	$1,224	
Books and supplies:	$650	$650
Personal expenses:	$885	$1,180
Transportation:	$1,150	$1,184

Undergraduate aid. Need-based: Average financial aid package for full-time students was $7,273; for part-time $4,834. 45% awarded as scholarships/grants, 55% as loans/jobs. **Non-need-based:** 56% awarded as scholarships/grants, 44% as loans/jobs. Scholarships based on academics, alumni affiliation, athletics, leadership, minority status, music/drama, religious affiliation, state/district residency. **Student debt:** 65% of graduating class borrowed to fund education; average debt was $20,621.

Freshman aid. Need-based: Out of 834 full-time freshmen, 494 applied for aid; 419 were judged to have need; of these 419 received aid. Average package met 59% of need. 91 students had full need met. Average scholarship/grant was $5,222; average loan $2,842. **Non-need based:** 64 full-time freshmen with need received non-need scholarships; 347 without need received awards; 63 received athletic scholarships.

Policies to reduce costs. Tuition/fee waivers for senior citizens, family members, employees and their families. Credit/placement for qualifying scores on AP, CLEP examinations. Work study available nights and weekends.

Payment plans. Credit card, installment, deferred payment.

Application procedures. FAFSA, institutional form required. Priority date 4/15; no closing date. Applicants notified on rolling basis starting 2/1, must reply within 3 week(s) of notification. **Transfers:** No deadline.

Contact. **Financial aid office:** (423) 614-8034
Michael Ellis, Director of Student Financial Aid
1120 North Ocoee Street
Cleveland, TN 37311

Lipscomb University

Nashville, Tennessee
www.lipscomb.edu
Four-year private **Federal Code: 003486**

	Living at home	On-campus
Tuition and fees:	$12,600	$12,600
Room and board:		$5,590

Undergraduate aid. All financial aid based on need. Need-based aid available for full-time and part-time students.

Policies to reduce costs. Tuition/fee waivers for family of clergy, employees and their families. Credit/placement for qualifying scores on AP, IB, CLEP examinations. Work study available nights, weekends and for part-time students.

Payment plans. Credit card, installment payment.

Application procedures. FAFSA required. Priority date 2/28; no closing date. Applicants notified on rolling basis starting 2/15, must reply by 5/1 or within 2 week(s) of notification.

Contact. **Financial aid office:** (615) 269-1791
Jeff Dale, Director of Student Financial Assistance
3901 Granny White Pike
Nashville, TN 37204-3951

Maryville College

Maryville, Tennessee
www.maryvillecollege.edu
Four-year private **Federal Code: 003505**

	Living at home	On-campus
Tuition and fees (2002-2003):	$18,835	$18,835
Room and board:		$5,900
Board only:	$2,920	
Books and supplies:	$600	$600
Personal expenses:	$750	$750
Transportation:	$500	$650

Undergraduate aid. **Need-based:** Average financial aid package for full-time students was $17,427; for part-time $8,816. 74% awarded as scholarships/grants, 26% as loans/jobs. **Non-need-based:** 70% awarded as scholarships/grants, 30% as loans/jobs. Scholarships based on academics, art, leadership, minority status, music/drama, religious affiliation, state/district residency.

Freshman aid. **Need-based:** Out of 246 full-time freshmen, 246 applied for aid; 204 were judged to have need; of these 204 received aid. Average package met 90% of need. 53 students had full need met. Average scholarship/grant was $13,336; average loan $4,373. **Non-need based:** 32 full-time freshmen with need received non-need scholarships; 42 without need received awards.

Merit scholarships. Presidential Scholarship, full tuition, awarded for leadership and academic ability. Dean's Scholarship, consisting of half tuition and room grant, awarded to entering freshman with 3.5 GPA.

Policies to reduce costs. Tuition/fee waivers for employees and their families. Credit/placement for qualifying scores on AP, IB, CLEP examinations.

Payment plans. Credit card, installment payment.

Application procedures. FAFSA required. Priority date 3/1; no closing date. Applicants notified on rolling basis starting 3/15, must reply within 4 week(s) of notification. Early decision closing date 11/15. **Transfers:** No deadline.

Contact. **Financial aid office:** (865) 981-8100
Richard Brand, Director of Financial Aid
502 East Lamar Alexander Parkway
Maryville, TN 37804-5907

Memphis College of Art

Memphis, Tennessee
www.mca.edu
Four-year private **Federal Code: 003507**

	Living at home
Tuition and fees:	$14,760
Books and supplies:	$1,300
Personal expenses:	$1,000
Transportation:	$1,350

Undergraduate aid. **Need-based:** Average financial aid package for full-time students was $9,000; for part-time $3,500. 39% awarded as scholarships/grants, 61% as loans/jobs. **Non-need-based:** 43% awarded as scholarships/grants, 57% as loans/jobs. Scholarships based on academics, art. **Student debt:** 90% of graduating class borrowed to fund education; average debt was $20,000. **Additional information:** Students considered for institutional resources through admissions application process.

Freshman aid. **Need-based:** Out of 69 full-time freshmen, 60 applied for aid; 54 were judged to have need; of these 54 received aid. Average package met 97% of need. 46 students had full need met. Average scholarship/grant was $3,000; average loan $3,500. **Non-need based:** 54 full-time freshmen with need received non-need scholarships; 9 without need received awards.

Merit scholarships. Full tuition award: merit, 1 available. Half tuition award: merit, 6 available. All renewable.

Policies to reduce costs. Tuition/fee waivers for employees and their families. Credit/placement for qualifying scores on AP, IB, CLEP examinations.

Payment plans. Credit card, installment, deferred payment.

Application procedures. FAFSA required. Priority date 4/1; no closing date. Applicants notified on rolling basis, must reply within 3 week(s) of notification. **Transfers:** Grants of $1,000 awarded to students who attended accredited junior or community college earning at least 30 credit hours.

Contact. **Financial aid office:** (901) 272-5136
Cindy Stanley, Director of Financial Aid
Overton Park, 1930 Poplar Avenue
Memphis, TN 38104-2764

Middle Tennessee State University

Murfreesboro, Tennessee
www.mtsu.edu
Four-year public **Federal Code: 003510**

	Living at home	On-campus
Tuition and fees (2002-2003):	$3,442	$3,442
Out-of-state:	$10,400	$10,400
Room and board:		$4,230
Books and supplies:	$600	$600
Personal expenses:	$1,046	$1,046
Transportation:	$2,350	$750

Undergraduate aid. **Need-based:** Average financial aid package for full-time students was $4,880; for part-time $4,755. 28% awarded as scholarships/grants, 72% as loans/jobs. **Non-need-based:** 97% awarded as scholarships/grants, 3% as loans/jobs. Scholarships based on academics, athletics, leadership, minority status, music/drama. **Student debt:** 9% of graduating class borrowed to fund education; average debt was $17,938. **Additional information:** Application filing deadline for scholarships February 15.

Freshman aid. **Need-based:** Out of 1,578 full-time freshmen, 1,578 applied for aid; 1,019 were judged to have need; of these 947 received aid. Average package met 83% of need. 359 students had full need met. Average scholarship/grant was $2,850; average loan $2,278. **Non-need based:** 279 full-time freshmen with need received non-need scholarships; 289 without need received awards; 54 received athletic scholarships.

Policies to reduce costs. Tuition/fee waivers for senior citizens, employees and their families. Credit/placement for qualifying scores on AP, IB, CLEP examinations. Work study available nights, weekends and for part-time students.

Payment plans. Credit card, installment, deferred payment.

Application procedures. FAFSA required. Priority date 3/15; closing date 5/15. Applicants notified on rolling basis starting 4/1, must reply within 2 week(s) of notification.

Contact. **Financial aid office:** (615) 898-2830
David Hutton, Director of Student Financial Aid
208 Cope Administration Building
Murfreesboro, TN 37132

Miller-Motte Technical College

Clarksville, Tennessee
www.miller-motte.com/clarksvillemain.html
Two-year proprietary **Federal Code: 026142**

	Living at home
Tuition and fees:	$7,300
Books and supplies:	$900
Personal expenses:	$1,350
Transportation:	$900

Undergraduate aid. All financial aid based on need. Need-based aid available for full-time and part-time students.

Policies to reduce costs. Tuition/fee waivers for employees and their families. Tuition at time of enrollment guaranteed for 2 years. Work study available nights, weekends and for part-time students.

Payment plans. Credit card, installment payment.

Application procedures. FAFSA, institutional form required. No deadline. Applicants notified on rolling basis. **Transfers:** No deadline.

Contact. **Financial aid office:** (931) 553-0071
Donna Green, F/A Director
1820 Business Park Drive
Clarksville, TN 37040

Milligan College

Milligan College, Tennessee
www.milligan.edu
Four-year private **Federal Code: 003511**

	Living at home	On-campus
Tuition and fees (2002-2003):	$14,340	$14,340
Room and board:		$4,370
Board only:	$2,200	
Books and supplies:	$600	$600
Personal expenses:	$1,154	$1,020
Transportation:	$896	$1,350

Undergraduate aid. All financial aid based on need. Average financial aid package for full-time students was $14,993; for part-time $8,316. 51% awarded as scholarships/grants, 49% as loans/jobs.

Freshman aid. Out of 165 full-time freshmen, 155 applied for aid; 132 were judged to have need; of these 132 received aid. Average package met 70% of need. 93 students had full need met. Average scholarship/grant was $1,577; average loan $2,319.

Policies to reduce costs. Tuition/fee waivers for employees and their families. Prepayment discount; credit/placement for qualifying scores on AP, CLEP examinations.

Payment plans. Credit card, installment payment.

Application procedures. FAFSA, institutional form required. Priority date 3/1; no closing date. Applicants notified on rolling basis starting 3/1, must reply within 2 week(s) of notification. **Transfers:** Priority date 3/1.

Contact. **Financial aid office:** (423) 461-8967
Nancy Beverly, Director of Financial Aid
Box 210
Milligan College, TN 37682

Nashville Auto-Diesel College

Nashville, Tennessee
www.nadcedu.com
One-year proprietary **Federal Code: 007440**

College costs (2002-2003). Full program costs range from $15,500 to $20,995 for diploma programs; $17,995 to $20,995 for associate programs. Includes books, tools, test fees.

Undergraduate aid. All financial aid based on need. Need-based aid available for full-time students.

Policies to reduce costs. Work study available nights and weekends.

Payment plans. Credit card, installment payment.

Application procedures. FAFSA required. No deadline. Applicants notified on rolling basis.

Contact. **Financial aid office:** (615) 650-8202
Norman Minick, Director of Financial Aid
1524 Gallatin Road
Nashville, TN 37206

National College of Business & Technology: Tennessee

Nashville, Tennessee
www.ncbt.edu
Two-year proprietary **Federal Code: 003726**

	Living at home
Tuition and fees (projected):	$6,186
Per-credit charge:	$162
Books and supplies:	$900
Personal expenses:	$3,259

Undergraduate aid. All financial aid based on need. Need-based aid available for full-time and part-time students.

Application procedures. FAFSA required. No deadline.

Contact. Pamela Cotton, Director of Financial Aid and Compliance Officer
PO Box 6400
Roanoke, VA 24017

Northeast State Technical Community College

Blountville, Tennessee
www.NortheastState.edu
Two-year public **Federal Code: 005378**

	Living at home
Tuition and fees (2002-2003):	$1,762
Out-of-state:	$6,554
Per-credit charge:	$68
Per-credit out-of-state:	$275
Board only:	$3,600
Books and supplies:	$700
Personal expenses:	$2,400
Transportation:	$1,260

Undergraduate aid. **Need-based:** Average financial aid package for full-time students was $2,234; for part-time $2,283. 82% awarded as scholarships/grants, 18% as loans/jobs. **Non-need-based:** 86% awarded as scholarships/grants, 14% as loans/jobs. Scholarships based on academics, alumni affiliation, art, job skills, leadership, minority status, music/drama, religious affiliation. **Student debt:** 67% of graduating class borrowed to fund education; average debt was $4,350.

Freshman aid. **Need-based:** Out of 646 full-time freshmen, 443 applied for aid; 313 were judged to have need; of these 292 received aid. Average package met 75% of need. 57 students had full need met. Average scholarship/grant was $2,828; average loan $1,733. **Non-need based:** 104 full-time freshmen with need received non-need scholarships; 93 without need received awards.

Policies to reduce costs. Tuition/fee waivers for senior citizens, employees and their families. Credit/placement for qualifying scores on AP, CLEP examinations. Work study available nights and for part-time students.

Payment plans. Credit card payment.

Application procedures. FAFSA required. Priority date 3/31; no closing date. Applicants notified on rolling basis starting 3/1, must reply within 3 week(s) of notification. **Transfers:** No deadline.

Contact. **Financial aid office:** (423) 323-0252
Cruzita Lucero, Director of Financial Aid
Box 246
Blountville, TN 37617-0246

Nossi College of Art

Goodlettsville, Tennessee
www.nossi.com
Two-year private **Federal Code: 017347**

College costs (projected). Tuition for first year (3 semesters) $9,535; required fees $325; estimated cost of books and supplies $1,800.

Undergraduate aid. Need-based: Need-based aid available for full-time and part-time students.

Payment plans. Installment payment.

Contact. Mary Kidd, Financial Aid Director
907 Rivergate Parkway, Building E-6
Goodlettsville, TN 37072

O'More College of Design

Franklin, Tennessee
www.omorecollege.edu
Four-year private **Federal Code: 014663**

	Living at home
Tuition and fees:	$10,790
Books and supplies:	$750

Undergraduate aid. All financial aid based on need. 86% awarded as scholarships/grants, 14% as loans/jobs. Need-based aid available for part-time students.

Payment plans. Credit card, installment payment.

Application procedures. FAFSA, institutional form required. Priority date 4/1; closing date 7/30. Applicants notified on rolling basis starting 8/1. **Transfers:** Priority date 5/1; no deadline.

Contact. Amy Shelton, Financial Aid Director
423 South Margin Street
Franklin, TN 37064-0908

Pellissippi State Technical Community College

Knoxville, Tennessee
www.pstcc.edu
Two-year public **Federal Code: 012693**

	Living at home
Tuition and fees (2002-2003):	$1,761
Out-of-state:	$6,553
Per-credit charge:	$68
Per-credit out-of-state:	$275
Books and supplies:	$500
Personal expenses:	$1,500
Transportation:	$1,650

Undergraduate aid. Need-based: Need-based aid available for full-time and part-time students. **Non-need-based:** Scholarships based on academics, art, minority status, music/drama.

Policies to reduce costs. Tuition/fee waivers for senior citizens, employees and their families. Credit/placement for qualifying scores on AP, IB, CLEP examinations. Work study available nights, weekends and for part-time students.

Payment plans. Credit card, deferred payment.

Application procedures. FAFSA required. Priority date 5/1; no closing date. Applicants notified on rolling basis starting 6/30, must reply within 2 week(s) of notification.

Contact. Financial aid office: (423) 694-6565
Pat Peace, Director of Financial Aid and Veterans Affairs
Box 22990
Knoxville, TN 37933-0990

Remington College: Southeast College of Technology

Memphis, Tennessee
www.educationamerica.com
Two-year proprietary **Federal Code: E00768**

College costs (2002-2003). Tuition for 72-week associate programs $22,272; bachelor's programs additional $11,025 (for additional 72 weeks).

Undergraduate aid. All financial aid based on need. Average financial aid package for full-time students was $5,125. 48% awarded as scholarships/grants, 52% as loans/jobs. Need-based aid available for part-time students.

Freshman aid. Out of 117 full-time freshmen, 117 applied for aid; 111 were judged to have need; of these 111 received aid. Average package met 49% of need. Average scholarship/grant was $4,000; average loan $3,062.

Policies to reduce costs. Tuition/fee waivers for employees and their families.

Payment plans. Credit card, installment payment.

Application procedures. FAFSA, institutional form required. Applicants notified on rolling basis, must reply within 2 week(s) of notification. **Transfers:** No deadline.

Contact. Judy Stott, Director of Financial services
2731 Nonconnah Boulevard, Suite 160
Memphis, TN 38132

Rhodes College

Memphis, Tennessee
www.rhodes.edu
Four-year private **Federal Code: 003519**

	Living at home	On-campus
Tuition and fees:	$22,578	$22,578
Room and board:		$6,382
Board only:	$1,500	
Books and supplies:	$760	$760
Personal expenses:	$400	$1,200
Transportation:	$500	$720

Undergraduate aid. Need-based: Average financial aid package for full-time students was $16,054; for part-time $16,719. 79% awarded as scholarships/grants, 21% as loans/jobs. **Non-need-based:** 70% awarded as scholarships/grants, 30% as loans/jobs. Scholarships based on academics, art, minority status, music/drama, religious affiliation. **Student debt:** 48% of graduating class borrowed to fund education; average debt was $15,100. **Additional information:** Auditions required for theater and music achievement awards and art achievement awards. Interviews recommended for merit scholarships.

Freshman aid. Need-based: Out of 439 full-time freshmen, 262 applied for aid; 192 were judged to have need; of these 188 received aid. Average package met 87% of need. 81 students had full need met. Average scholarship/grant was $11,678; average loan $3,423. **Non-need based:** 120 full-time freshmen with need received non-need scholarships; 125 without need received awards.

Policies to reduce costs. Tuition/fee waivers for employees and their families. Credit/placement for qualifying scores on AP, IB examinations. Work study available nights and weekends.

Payment plans. Credit card, installment payment.

Application procedures. FAFSA, CSS PROFILE required. Priority date 3/1; no closing date. Applicants notified by 4/10, must reply by 5/1 or within 2 week(s) of notification. Early decision closing date 11/1.

Contact. Financial aid office: (901) 843-3810
Forrest Stuart, Director of Financial Aid
2000 North Parkway
Memphis, TN 38112

Roane State Community College

Harriman, Tennessee
www.roanestate.edu
Two-year public **Federal Code: 009914**

	Living at home
Tuition and fees (2002-2003):	$1,745
Out-of-state:	$6,537
Per-credit charge:	$68
Per-credit out-of-state:	$275
Books and supplies:	$500
Personal expenses:	$750
Transportation:	$1,440

Undergraduate aid. Need-based: Need-based aid available for full-time and part-time students. **Non-need-based:** Scholarships based on academics, art, athletics, leadership, music/drama, state/district residency.

Policies to reduce costs. Tuition/fee waivers for senior citizens, employees and their families. Credit/placement for qualifying scores on AP, CLEP examinations. Work study available nights, weekends and for part-time students.

Payment plans. Credit card, deferred payment.

Application procedures. FAFSA, institutional form required. Priority date 4/1; no closing date. Applicants notified on rolling basis starting 5/1.

Contact. Joy Goldberg, Director of Scholarships and Financial Aid
276 Patton Lane
Harriman, TN 37748

South College

Knoxville, Tennessee
www.southcollegetn.edu
Two-year proprietary **Federal Code: 004938**

College costs. Tuition $9,300 for physical therapy assistance, occupational therapy assistance, network administration programs.

	Living at home
Tuition and fees (2002-2003):	$9,300
Books and supplies:	$900
Personal expenses:	$1,200
Transportation:	$1,200

Undergraduate aid. All financial aid based on need. Need-based aid available for full-time and part-time students.

Policies to reduce costs. Credit/placement for qualifying scores on AP examinations.

Payment plans. Installment, deferred payment.

Application procedures. FAFSA, institutional form required. Priority date 5/31; no closing date. Applicants notified on rolling basis.

Contact. Larry Broadwater, Financial Aid Officer
720 North Fifth Avenue
Knoxville, TN 37917

Southern Adventist University

Collegedale, Tennessee
www.southern.edu
Four-year private **Federal Code: 003518**

	Living at home	On-campus
Tuition and fees:	$12,800	$12,800
Room and board:		$4,280
Board only:	$2,000	
Books and supplies:	$900	$900
Personal expenses:	$1,500	$1,500
Transportation:	$550	$500

Undergraduate aid. Need-based: Average financial aid package for full-time students was $9,121; for part-time $9,117. 43% awarded as scholarships/grants, 57% as loans/jobs. **Non-need-based:** 72% awarded as scholarships/grants, 28% as loans/jobs. Scholarships based on academics, alumni affiliation, art, leadership, music/drama. **Student debt:** 65% of graduating class borrowed to fund education; average debt was $14,900.

Freshman aid. Need-based: Out of 475 full-time freshmen, 451 applied for aid; 307 were judged to have need; of these 307 received aid. Average package met 57% of need. 34 students had full need met. Average scholarship/grant was $4,012; average loan $3,135. **Non-need based:** 314 full-time freshmen with need received non-need scholarships; 178 without need received awards.

Merit scholarships. Freshman scholarship based on combination of high school GPA, ACT/SAT scores, leadership positions held.

Policies to reduce costs. Tuition/fee waivers for senior citizens, family members, family of clergy, employees and their families. Prepayment discount; credit/placement for qualifying scores on AP, CLEP examinations. Work study available for part-time students.

Payment plans. Credit card, installment, deferred payment.

Application procedures. FAFSA required. Priority date 3/31; no closing date. Applicants notified on rolling basis starting 4/15, must reply within 2 week(s) of notification. **Transfers:** Priority date 3/31; no deadline.

Contact. Financial aid office: (423) 238-2835
Marc Grundy, Director of Student Finance
Box 370
Collegedale, TN 37315-0370

Southwest Tennessee Community College

Memphis, Tennessee
www.southwest.tn.edu
Two-year public **Federal Code: 010439**

	Living at home
Tuition and fees (2002-2003):	$1,751
Out-of-state:	$6,543
Per-credit charge:	$64
Per-credit out-of-state:	$275
Personal expenses:	$1,400
Transportation:	$600

Undergraduate aid. All financial aid based on need. 96% awarded as scholarships/grants, 4% as loans/jobs. Need-based aid available for part-time students. **Additional information:** State grants available to eligible students who apply by 4/1.

Policies to reduce costs. Tuition/fee waivers for senior citizens, minority students, employees and their families. Credit/placement for qualifying scores on AP, CLEP examinations.

Payment plans. Credit card, deferred payment.

Application procedures. FAFSA required. Priority date 4/15; no closing date. Applicants notified on rolling basis starting 6/1, must reply within 4 week(s) of notification. **Transfers:** Priority date 4/15; no deadline.

Contact. Financial aid office: (901) 333-5960
Daniel Miller, Director of Financial Aid
P.O. Box 780
Memphis, TN 38101-0780

Tennessee State University

Nashville, Tennessee
www.tnstate.edu
Four-year public **Federal Code: 003522**

	Living at home	On-campus
Tuition and fees (2002-2003):	$3,252	$3,252
Out-of-state:	$10,210	$10,210
Room and board:		$3,990
Books and supplies:	$875	$875
Personal expenses:	$2,100	$2,800
Transportation:	$800	$800

Undergraduate aid. Need-based: Average financial aid package for full-time students was $3,844; for part-time $3,874. 51% awarded as scholarships/grants, 49% as loans/jobs. **Non-need-based:** Scholarships based on academics. **Student debt:** 20% of graduating class borrowed to fund education; average debt was $11,275.

Freshman aid. Need-based: Out of 1,288 full-time freshmen, 704 applied for aid; 574 were judged to have need; of these 561 received aid. Average package met 82% of need. 69 students had full need met. Average scholarship/grant was $1,521; average loan $530. **Non-need based:** 138 full-time freshmen with need received non-need scholarships; 82 without need received awards; 10 received athletic scholarships.

Policies to reduce costs. Tuition/fee waivers for senior citizens, minority students. Credit/placement for qualifying scores on AP, CLEP examinations.

Payment plans. Credit card, deferred payment.

Application procedures. FAFSA required. Priority date 4/1; no closing date. Applicants notified on rolling basis starting 7/10, must reply within 2 week(s) of notification.

Contact. Brenda Burney, Director of Financial Aid
3500 John A. Merritt Boulevard
Nashville, TN 37209-1561

Tennessee Technological University

Cookeville, Tennessee
www.tntech.edu
Four-year public **Federal Code: 003523**

	Living at home	On-campus
Tuition and fees (2002-2003):	$3,266	$3,266
Out-of-state:	$10,224	$10,224
Room and board:		$4,798
Books and supplies:	$700	$700
Personal expenses:		$840
Transportation:		$700

Undergraduate aid. Need-based: Average financial aid package for full-time students was $3,620; for part-time $3,940. 47% awarded as scholarships/grants, 53% as loans/jobs. **Non-need-based:** 42% awarded as scholarships/grants, 58% as loans/jobs. Scholarships based on academics, alumni affiliation, art, athletics, leadership, minority status, music/drama, religious affiliation, state/district residency. **Student debt:** 37% of graduating class borrowed to fund education; average debt was $13,903. **Additional information:** Tuition and/or fee waivers available for children of public school teachers (Tennessee).

Freshman aid. Need-based: Out of 1,378 full-time freshmen, 1,002 applied for aid; 593 were judged to have need; of these 579 received aid. Average package met 79% of need. 136 students had full need met. **Non-need based:** 230 full-time freshmen with need received non-need scholarships; 265 without need received awards; 75 received athletic scholarships.

Merit scholarships. Presidential Scholarship; $5,000 renewable annually. National Merit Finalist Scholarship; 9 awarded.

Policies to reduce costs. Tuition/fee waivers for senior citizens, minority students, employees and their families. Credit/placement for qualifying scores on AP, CLEP examinations. Work study available nights, weekends and for part-time students.

Payment plans. Credit card, installment, deferred payment.

Application procedures. FAFSA required. Priority date 3/15; no closing date. Applicants notified on rolling basis starting 3/15, must reply within 2 week(s) of notification.

Contact. Financial aid office: (931) 372-3073
Raymond Holbrook, Director of Student Financial Aid
Office of Admissions
Cookeville, TN 38505

Tennessee Wesleyan College

Athens, Tennessee
www.twcnet.edu
Four-year private **Federal Code: 003525**

	Living at home	On-campus
Tuition and fees:	$11,340	$11,340
Room and board:		$4,600
Books and supplies:	$800	$800
Personal expenses:	$1,000	$1,000
Transportation:	$1,200	$1,000

Undergraduate aid. Need-based: Average financial aid package for full-time students was $7,980; for part-time $7,327. 59% awarded as scholarships/grants, 41% as loans/jobs. **Non-need-based:** 51% awarded as scholarships/grants, 49% as loans/jobs. Scholarships based on academics, athletics, leadership, minority status, music/drama, religious affiliation.

Freshman aid. Need-based: Out of 131 full-time freshmen, 109 applied for aid; 91 were judged to have need; of these 91 received aid. Average package met 69% of need. 21 students had full need met. Average scholarship/grant was $6,246; average loan $2,105. **Non-need based:** 15 full-time freshmen with need received non-need scholarships; 21 without need received awards; 25 received athletic scholarships.

Policies to reduce costs. Tuition/fee waivers for children of alumni, minority students, family members, family of clergy, employees and their families. Credit/placement for qualifying scores on AP, IB, CLEP examinations. Work study available nights, weekends and for part-time students.

Payment plans. Credit card, installment, deferred payment.

Application procedures. FAFSA, institutional form required. No deadline. Applicants notified on rolling basis starting 4/1, must reply within 2 week(s) of notification. **Transfers:** No deadline.

Contact. Financial aid office: (423) 746-5215
Robert Perry, Financial Aid Director
Box 40
Athens, TN 37371

Trevecca Nazarene University

Nashville, Tennessee
www.trevecca.edu
Four-year private **Federal Code: 003526**

	Living at home	On-campus
Tuition and fees:	$11,960	$11,960
Room and board:		$5,588
Board only:	$3,066	
Books and supplies:	$772	$772
Personal expenses:	$1,501	$1,264
Transportation:	$1,144	$846

Undergraduate aid. Need-based: Average financial aid package for full-time students was $10,449; for part-time $5,045. 19% awarded as scholarships/grants, 81% as loans/jobs. **Non-need-based:** 42% awarded as scholarships/grants, 58% as loans/jobs. Scholarships based on academics, alumni affiliation, athletics, leadership, music/drama, religious affiliation. **Student debt:** 59% of graduating class borrowed to fund education; average debt was $15,059.

Freshman aid. Need-based: Out of 231 full-time freshmen, 168 applied for aid; 132 were judged to have need; of these 132 received aid. Average package met 37% of need. 115 students had full need met. Average scholarship/grant was $4,035; average loan $3,540. **Non-need based:** 120 full-time freshmen with need received non-need scholarships; 38 without need received awards; 33 received athletic scholarships.

Policies to reduce costs. Tuition/fee waivers for employees and their families. Credit/placement for qualifying scores on AP, CLEP examinations.

Payment plans. Credit card, installment payment.

Application procedures. FAFSA required. Priority date 3/1; no closing date. Applicants notified on rolling basis starting 3/20.

Contact. Financial aid office: (615) 248-1242
Eddie White, Assistant Director of Financial Aid
333 Murfreesboro Road
Nashville, TN 37210

Tusculum College

Greeneville, Tennessee
www.tusculum.edu
Four-year private **Federal Code: 003527**

	Living at home	On-campus
Tuition and fees (2002-2003):	$13,700	$13,700
Room and board:		$5,290
Books and supplies:	$500	$500

Undergraduate aid. Need-based: Need-based aid available for full-time and part-time students. **Non-need-based:** Scholarships based on academics, athletics, job skills, leadership, music/drama, religious affiliation, state/district residency.

Policies to reduce costs. Tuition/fee waivers for employees and their families. Credit/placement for qualifying scores on AP, CLEP examinations. Work study available nights, weekends and for part-time students.

Payment plans. Credit card, installment payment.

Application procedures. FAFSA, institutional form required. Priority date 2/1; no closing date. Applicants notified on rolling basis starting 3/1, must reply within 3 week(s) of notification.

Contact. Pat Shannon, Director of Financial Aid
60 Shiloh Road
Greeneville, TN 37743

Union University

Jackson, Tennessee
www.uu.edu
Four-year private **Federal Code: 003528**

	Living at home	On-campus
Tuition and fees (projected):	$14,450	$14,450
Room and board:		$4,640
Books and supplies:	$600	$600

Undergraduate aid. **Need-based:** 53% awarded as scholarships/grants, 47% as loans/jobs. Need-based aid available for part-time students. **Non-need-based:** 65% awarded as scholarships/grants, 35% as loans/jobs. Scholarships based on academics, alumni affiliation, art, athletics, leadership, music/drama, religious affiliation. **Student debt:** 41% of graduating class borrowed to fund education; average debt was $16,272.

Freshman aid. **Need-based:** Out of 386 full-time freshmen, 361 applied for aid; 239 were judged to have need; of these 237 received aid. Average scholarship/grant was $1,855; average loan $2,497. **Non-need based:** 232 full-time freshmen with need received non-need scholarships; 40 without need received awards; 30 received athletic scholarships.

Policies to reduce costs. Tuition/fee waivers for children of alumni, minority students, family members, family of clergy, employees and their families. Credit/placement for qualifying scores on AP, IB, CLEP examinations. Work study available nights and weekends.

Payment plans. Credit card, installment, deferred payment.

Application procedures. FAFSA, institutional form required. Priority date 1/15; no closing date. Applicants notified on rolling basis starting 2/15, must reply by 5/1 or within 2 week(s) of notification.

Contact. **Financial aid office:** (731) 661-5015
Bryan Nelson, Director of Financial Aid
1050 Union University Drive
Jackson, TN 38305-3697

University of Memphis

Memphis, Tennessee
www.memphis.edu
Four-year public **Federal Code: 003509**

	Living at home	On-campus
Tuition and fees (2002-2003):	$3,704	$3,704
Out-of-state:	$10,858	$10,858
Room and board:		$5,496
Books and supplies:	$850	$850
Personal expenses:	$715	$715
Transportation:	$825	$500

Undergraduate aid. **Need-based:** Average financial aid package for full-time students was $3,758; for part-time $5,244. **Student debt:** 29% of graduating class borrowed to fund education; average debt was $19,525.

Freshman aid. **Need-based:** Out of 1,704 full-time freshmen, 1,442 applied for aid; 1,141 were judged to have need; of these 1,052 received aid. Average package met 78% of need. 110 students had full need met. Average scholarship/grant was $3,951; average loan $2,171. **Non-need based:** 490 full-time freshmen with need received non-need scholarships; 142 without need received awards; 53 received athletic scholarships.

Policies to reduce costs. Tuition/fee waivers for senior citizens, employees and their families. Credit/placement for qualifying scores on AP, CLEP examinations. Work study available for part-time students.

Payment plans. Credit card, installment payment.

Application procedures. FAFSA required. Priority date 3/1; no closing date. Applicants notified on rolling basis starting 3/1, must reply within 2 week(s) of notification.

Contact. **Financial aid office:** (901) 678-4825
Charles Boudreau, Director of Student Financial Aid
Memphis, TN 38152

University of Tennessee Health Science Center

Memphis, Tennessee
www.utmem.edu
Upper-division public **Federal Code: 006725**

College costs. Quoted costs are for medical technology program. Costs of other programs will vary by program.

	Living at home	On-campus
Tuition and fees (2002-2003):	$5,025	$5,025
Out-of-state:	$16,494	$16,494
Room only:		$3,600
Books and supplies:	$1,097	$1,097
Personal expenses:	$1,455	$1,527
Transportation:	$1,305	$1,370

Undergraduate aid. **Need-based:** Need-based aid available for full-time and part-time students. **Additional information:** Scholarships available to defray out-of-state portion of fees charged to out-of-state minority students.

Policies to reduce costs. Tuition/fee waivers for minority students, employees and their families.

Payment plans. Credit card, installment payment.

Application procedures. Institutional form required. No deadline. Applicants notified on rolling basis starting 4/15, must reply within 2 week(s) of notification.

Contact. 800 Madison Avenue
Memphis, TN 38163

University of Tennessee: Chattanooga

Chattanooga, Tennessee
www.utc.edu
Four-year public **Federal Code: 003529**

	Living at home	On-campus
Tuition and fees (2002-2003):	$3,550	$3,550
Out-of-state:	$10,570	$10,570
Room only:		$2,680
Board only:	$2,415	
Books and supplies:	$800	$800
Personal expenses:	$1,182	$1,182
Transportation:	$1,298	$1,298

Undergraduate aid. **Need-based:** Average financial aid package for full-time students was $8,240; for part-time $6,250. 38% awarded as scholarships/grants, 62% as loans/jobs. **Non-need-based:** 48% awarded as scholarships/grants, 52% as loans/jobs. Scholarships based on academics, alumni affiliation, art, athletics, job skills, minority status, music/drama. **Student debt:** 45% of graduating class borrowed to fund education; average debt was $14,350.

Freshman aid. **Need-based:** Out of 1,176 full-time freshmen, 799 applied for aid; 519 were judged to have need; of these 448 received aid. Average package met 79% of need. 192 students had full need met. Average scholarship/grant was $3,615; average loan $2,555. **Non-need based:** 334 full-time freshmen with need received non-need scholarships; 277 without need received awards; 88 received athletic scholarships.

Policies to reduce costs. Tuition/fee waivers for senior citizens, employees and their families. Credit/placement for qualifying scores on AP, CLEP examinations.

Payment plans. Credit card, installment, deferred payment.

Application procedures. FAFSA, institutional form required. Priority date 3/1; closing date 2/1. Applicants notified on rolling basis starting 3/1, must reply within 2 week(s) of notification. **Transfers:** Priority date 3/1.

Contact. **Financial aid office:** (423) 425-4677
Jonathan Looney, Director of Financial Aid
131 Hooper Hall
Chattanooga, TN 37403

University of Tennessee: Knoxville

Knoxville, Tennessee
www.tennessee.edu
Four-year public **Federal Code: 003530**

College costs. Out-of-state students pay additional required fees.

	Living at home	On-campus
Tuition and fees (2002-2003):	$4,056	$4,056
Out-of-state:	$12,158	$12,158
Room and board:		$4,512
Board only:	$2,048	
Books and supplies:	$998	$998
Personal expenses:	$2,260	$2,002
Transportation:	$2,278	$2,494

Undergraduate aid. All financial aid based on need. Need-based aid available for full-time and part-time students. **Additional information:** Application priority date for scholarships 2/1.

Policies to reduce costs. Tuition/fee waivers for senior citizens, employees and their families. Credit/placement for qualifying scores on AP, IB, CLEP examinations. Work study available nights and weekends.

Payment plans. Credit card, installment, deferred payment.

Application procedures. FAFSA required. Priority date 3/1; no closing date. Applicants notified on rolling basis starting 4/1, must reply within 3 week(s) of notification. **Transfers:** Transfer students must provide financial aid transcripts from all colleges previously attended regardless of whether any aid was received.

Contact. Jeff Gerkin, Director of Financial Aid
320 Student Services Building
Knoxville, TN 37996-0230

University of Tennessee: Martin

Martin, Tennessee
www.utm.edu
Four-year public **Federal Code: 003531**

	Living at home	On-campus
Tuition and fees (2002-2003):	$3,498	$3,498
Out-of-state:	$10,518	$10,518
Room and board:		$3,980
Board only:	$1,070	
Books and supplies:	$900	$900
Personal expenses:	$1,672	$1,672
Transportation:	$860	$736

Undergraduate aid. All financial aid based on need. Average financial aid package for full-time students was $7,001; for part-time $6,201. 52% awarded as scholarships/grants, 48% as loans/jobs. **Student debt:** 44% of graduating class borrowed to fund education; average debt was $12,750.

Freshman aid. Average package met 73% of need. Average scholarship/grant was $4,117; average loan $3,426.

Policies to reduce costs. Tuition/fee waivers for senior citizens, employees and their families. Credit/placement for qualifying scores on AP, IB, CLEP examinations.

Payment plans. Credit card, deferred payment.

Application procedures. FAFSA required. Priority date 3/1; no closing date. Applicants notified on rolling basis starting 5/1, must reply within 2 week(s) of notification. **Transfers:** Priority date 3/1; no deadline.

Contact. **Financial aid office:** (731) 587-7040
Bobbie McClain, Director of Student Financial Assistance
200 Hall Moody Administration Building
Martin, TN 38238

University of the South

Sewanee, Tennessee
www.sewanee.edu
Four-year private **Federal Code: 003534**

	Living at home	On-campus
Tuition and fees:	$24,335	$24,335
Room and board:		$6,725
Board only:	$2,690	
Books and supplies:	$550	$550
Personal expenses:	$810	$810

Undergraduate aid. Non-need-based: Scholarships based on academics, leadership, minority status, religious affiliation.

Merit scholarships. Benedict Scholars Program for exceptional freshmen; 3 full cost scholarships. Wilkins Scholarships for outstanding incoming freshmen; 25 awarded, half tuition.

Policies to reduce costs. Tuition/fee waivers for employees and their families. Credit/placement for qualifying scores on AP examinations.

Payment plans. Installment payment.

Application procedures. FAFSA, institutional form required. Priority date 3/1; no closing date. Applicants notified by 4/1, must reply within 4 week(s) of notification. Early decision closing date 11/15. **Transfers:** Priority date 3/1; no deadline.

Contact. David Gelinas, Director of Financial Aid
735 University Avenue
Sewanee, TN 37383

Vanderbilt University

Nashville, Tennessee
www.vanderbilt.edu
Four-year private **Federal Code: 003535**

College costs. Health insurance fee $468 for students who do not have own insurance. Engineering lab fee $600.

	Living at home	On-campus
Tuition and fees:	$28,440	$28,440
Room and board:		$9,457

Undergraduate aid. Need-based: Average financial aid package for full-time students was $27,981. 77% awarded as scholarships/grants, 23% as loans/jobs. **Non-need-based:** 92% awarded as scholarships/grants, 8% as loans/jobs. Scholarships based on academics, minority status, music/drama, state/district residency. **Student debt:** 38% of graduating class borrowed to fund education; average debt was $24,023. **Additional information:** Various payment plans available.

Freshman aid. Need-based: Out of 1,576 full-time freshmen, 817 applied for aid; 654 were judged to have need; of these 631 received aid. Average package met 99% of need. 622 students had full need met. Average scholarship/grant was $19,685; average loan $4,861. **Non-need based:** 360 full-time freshmen with need received non-need scholarships; 357 without need received awards; 62 received athletic scholarships.

Policies to reduce costs. Tuition/fee waivers for employees and their families. Credit/placement for qualifying scores on AP, IB examinations.

Payment plans. Installment, deferred payment.

Application procedures. FAFSA, CSS PROFILE required. Priority date 2/1; no closing date. Applicants notified on rolling basis starting 4/1, must reply by 5/1. Early decision closing date 11/1. **Transfers:** Priority date 4/15; no deadline.

Contact. David Mohning, Director, Student Financial Aid
2305 West End Avenue
Nashville, TN 37203-1727

Volunteer State Community College

Gallatin, Tennessee
www.volstate.edu
Two-year public **Federal Code: 009912**

	Living at home
Tuition and fees (2002-2003):	$1,741
Out-of-state:	$6,533
Per-credit charge:	$73
Per-credit out-of-state:	$280
Board only:	$2,120
Books and supplies:	$800
Personal expenses:	$400
Transportation:	$2,150

Undergraduate aid. Need-based: 70% awarded as scholarships/grants, 30% as loans/jobs. Need-based aid available for part-time students. **Non-need-based:** 87% awarded as scholarships/grants, 13% as loans/jobs. Scholarships based on academics, art, athletics, leadership, minority status, music/drama, religious affiliation, state/district residency.

Policies to reduce costs. Tuition/fee waivers for senior citizens, minority students, employees and their families. Credit/placement for qualifying scores on AP, CLEP examinations. Work study available for part-time students.

Payment plans. Credit card, deferred payment.

Application procedures. FAFSA required. Priority date 4/15; no closing date. Applicants notified on rolling basis, must reply within 2 week(s) of notification. **Transfers:** Priority date 4/15; no deadline.

Contact. **Financial aid office:** (615) 452-8600 ext. 3456
Sue Pedigo, Director of Financial Aid
1480 Nashville Pike
Gallatin, TN 37066

Walters State Community College

Morristown, Tennessee
www.ws.edu
Two-year public **Federal Code: 008863**

	Living at home
Tuition and fees (2002-2003):	$1,771
Out-of-state:	$6,563
Per-credit charge:	$68
Per-credit out-of-state:	$275
Books and supplies:	$750
Personal expenses:	$1,050
Transportation:	$1,410

Undergraduate aid. Need-based: Need-based aid available for full-time and part-time students. **Non-need-based:** Scholarships based on academics, athletics, music/drama, state/district residency.

Policies to reduce costs. Tuition/fee waivers for senior citizens, minority students, employees and their families. Credit/placement for qualifying scores on AP, CLEP examinations.

Payment plans. Credit card payment.

Application procedures. FAFSA required. No deadline. Applicants notified on rolling basis.

Contact. Financial aid office: (423) 585-6811
Bob Creswell, Director of Financial Aid
500 South Davy Crockett Parkway
Morristown, TN 37813-6899

Texas

ATI-Career Training Center

Dallas, Texas
www.aticareertraining.com
Two-year proprietary **Federal Code: 025966**

College costs. One-time comprehensive rate per program: medical assisting and dental assisting: $10,899; respiratory therapy technology, $28,493; graphic design, $15,030; information technology and networking, $17,310; graphic-aided design, $12,014; business administration technology, $11,796; and electronic technology, $16,260.

Undergraduate aid. All financial aid based on need. Average financial aid package for full-time students was $5,125. **Additional information:** Limited work-study positions available during school hours.

Payment plans. Credit card, installment payment.

Application procedures. FAFSA, institutional form required.

Contact. Karen Eilert, Director of Financial Aid
10003 Technology Boulevard, West
Dallas, TX 75220

Abilene Christian University

Abilene, Texas
www.acu.edu
Four-year private **Federal Code: 003537**

	Living at home	On-campus
Tuition and fees:	$13,290	$13,290
Room and board:		$5,080
Board only:	$2,920	
Books and supplies:	$800	$800
Personal expenses:	$1,578	$1,578
Transportation:	$1,137	$1,137

Undergraduate aid. Need-based: Average financial aid package for full-time students was $10,633; for part-time $6,989. 54% awarded as scholarships/grants, 46% as loans/jobs. **Non-need-based:** 37% awarded as scholarships/grants, 63% as loans/jobs. Scholarships based on academics, art, athletics, leadership, minority status, music/drama, religious affiliation, state/district residency. **Student debt:** 72% of graduating class borrowed to fund education; average debt was $25,845. **Additional information:** Early estimate service is available.

Freshman aid. Need-based: Out of 1,028 full-time freshmen, 1,027 applied for aid; 568 were judged to have need; of these 566 received aid. Average package met 76% of need. 267 students had full need met. Average scholarship/grant was $7,431; average loan $2,652. **Non-need based:** 546 full-time freshmen with need received non-need scholarships; 208 without need received awards; 27 received athletic scholarships.

Merit scholarships. Presidential Scholarship; half or full tuition; based on interview, ACT or SAT scores. Heritage Award; $1,000 per year; based on Church of Christ, ACT or SAT scores. Transfer Scholarship; $1,000-$2,000; based on GPA.

Policies to reduce costs. Tuition/fee waivers for employees and their families. Credit/placement for qualifying scores on AP, IB, CLEP examinations.

Payment plans. Credit card, installment payment.

Application procedures. FAFSA, institutional form required. Priority date 3/1; no closing date. Applicants notified on rolling basis starting 4/1.

Contact. Gary West, Director of Student Financial Services
ACU Box 29000
Abilene, TX 79699

Alvin Community College

Alvin, Texas
www.alvincollege.edu
Two-year public **Federal Code: 003539**

	Living at home
Tuition and fees (2002-2003):	$782
Out-of-district:	$1,262
Out-of-state:	$1,802
Per-credit charge:	$16
Per-credit out-of-district:	$32
Per-credit out-of-state:	$50
Board only:	$1,857
Books and supplies:	$800
Personal expenses:	$1,274
Transportation:	$1,777

Undergraduate aid. All financial aid based on need. Need-based aid available for full-time and part-time students. **Additional information:** Short-term loans available.

Policies to reduce costs. Tuition/fee waivers for senior citizens, employees and their families. Credit/placement for qualifying scores on AP, CLEP examinations. Work study available nights and for part-time students.

Payment plans. Credit card, installment payment.

Application procedures. FAFSA required. Priority date 6/30; no closing date. Applicants notified on rolling basis, must reply within 4 week(s) of notification.

Contact. Dora Sims, Director of Student Financial Aid and Placement
3110 Mustang Road
Alvin, TX 77511-4898

Amarillo College

Amarillo, Texas
www.actx.edu
Two-year public **Federal Code: 003540**

	Living at home
Tuition and fees (2002-2003):	$861
Out-of-district:	$1,191
Out-of-state:	$2,046
Per-credit charge:	$21
Per-credit out-of-district:	$32
Per-credit out-of-state:	$61
Board only:	$1,513
Books and supplies:	$800
Personal expenses:	$1,084
Transportation:	$1,287

Undergraduate aid. Non-need-based: Scholarships based on academics, state/district residency.

Policies to reduce costs. Tuition/fee waivers for employees and their families. Credit/placement for qualifying scores on AP, CLEP examinations.

Payment plans. Credit card, installment payment.

Application procedures. FAFSA, institutional form required. Priority date 6/15; no closing date. Applicants notified on rolling basis starting 6/15, must reply within 2 week(s) of notification.

Contact. Financial aid office: (806) 371-5310
Director of Financial Aid
Box 447
Amarillo, TX 79178

Amberton University

Garland, Texas
www.amberu.edu
Upper-division private **Federal Code: 014925**

	Living at home
Tuition and fees:	$6,000
Books and supplies:	$500

Policies to reduce costs. Tuition/fee waivers for employees and their families. Credit/placement for qualifying scores on CLEP examinations.

Payment plans. Deferred payment.

Application procedures. No deadline.

Contact. Melinda Reagan, Executive Vice President
1700 Eastgate Drive
Garland, TX 75041-5595

Angelina College
Lufkin, Texas
www.angelina.edu
Two-year public **Federal Code: 006661**

College costs. Students taking 1-3 credits pay higher per-credit-hour charge.

	Living at home	On-campus
Tuition and fees:	$840	$840
Out-of-district:	$1,170	$1,170
Out-of-state:	$1,770	$1,770
Per-credit charge:	$21	$21
Per-credit out-of-district:	$32	$32
Per-credit out-of-state:	$52	$52
Room and board:		$3,900
Board only:	$2,240	
Books and supplies:	$950	$950
Personal expenses:	$1,328	$1,328
Transportation:	$2,304	$576

Undergraduate aid. All financial aid based on need. 97% awarded as scholarships/grants, 3% as loans/jobs. Need-based aid available for part-time students.

Freshman aid. Out of 893 full-time freshmen, 732 applied for aid; 711 were judged to have need; of these 698 received aid.

Policies to reduce costs. Tuition/fee waivers for senior citizens, employees and their families. Credit/placement for qualifying scores on AP, CLEP examinations. Work study available nights and for part-time students.

Payment plans. Credit card, installment payment.

Application procedures. FAFSA, institutional form required. Priority date 7/15; no closing date. Applicants notified on rolling basis starting 7/15.

Contact. **Financial aid office:** (936) 633-5291
Rebecca Innerarity, Director of Financial Aid
Box 1768
Lufkin, TX 75902-1768

Angelo State University
San Angelo, Texas
www.angelo.edu
Four-year public **Federal Code: 003541**

	Living at home	On-campus
Tuition and fees (2002-2003):	$3,022	$3,022
Out-of-state:	$9,562	$9,562
Room and board:		$4,810
Books and supplies:	$600	$600
Personal expenses:	$1,440	$1,440

Undergraduate aid. Need-based: Average financial aid package for full-time students was $3,735. 51% awarded as scholarships/grants, 49% as loans/jobs. Need-based aid available for part-time students. **Non-need-based:** 47% awarded as scholarships/grants, 53% as loans/jobs. Scholarships based on academics, leadership. **Student debt:** 53% of graduating class borrowed to fund education; average debt was $15,000.

Freshman aid. Need-based: Out of 1,184 full-time freshmen, 960 applied for aid; 653 were judged to have need; of these 652 received aid. Average package met 81% of need. 579 students had full need met. Average scholarship/grant was $2,028; average loan $1,870. **Non-need based:** 583 full-time freshmen with need received non-need scholarships; 76 without need received awards; 18 received athletic scholarships.

Merit scholarships. 1 of every 6 students receives Carr Academic Scholarship program; average award $2,200 per semester. Special Academic Scholarships available for undergraduates planning on majoring in chemistry/biochemistry, mathematics, physics, French, German.

Policies to reduce costs. Tuition/fee waivers for senior citizens. Credit/placement for qualifying scores on AP, CLEP examinations. Work study available nights, weekends and for part-time students.

Payment plans. Credit card, installment payment.

Application procedures. FAFSA, institutional form required. Priority date 5/1; no closing date. Applicants notified on rolling basis starting 3/1. **Transfers:** Priority date 5/2; no deadline.

Contact. **Financial aid office:** (800) 946-8627
Lyn Wheeler, Director of Financial Aid
PO Box 11014 ASU Station
San Angelo, TX 76909

Arlington Baptist College
Arlington, Texas
www.abconline.edu
Four-year private **Federal Code: 014305**

	Living at home	On-campus
Tuition and fees (projected):	$4,640	$4,640
Room and board:		$3,600
Board only:	$1,100	
Books and supplies:	$800	$800
Personal expenses:	$800	$720
Transportation:	$600	$600

Undergraduate aid. All financial aid based on need. Average financial aid package for full-time students was $5,113. 38% awarded as scholarships/grants, 62% as loans/jobs. Need-based aid available for part-time students. **Student debt:** 65% of graduating class borrowed to fund education; average debt was $8,500.

Freshman aid. Out of 36 full-time freshmen, 36 applied for aid; 36 were judged to have need; of these 36 received aid.

Policies to reduce costs. Tuition/fee waivers for family members, family of clergy. Credit/placement for qualifying scores on AP, CLEP examinations.

Payment plans. Credit card, installment, deferred payment.

Application procedures. FAFSA required. Priority date 8/15; no closing date. Applicants notified on rolling basis. **Transfers:** No deadline.

Contact. David Clogston, Business Manager
3001 West Division
Arlington, TX 76012

Austin Business College
Austin, Texas
www.austinbusinesscollege.org
Two-year proprietary **Federal Code: 014536**

College costs (2002-2003). Tuition for full associate degree program (91 quarter credits) $15,925; books $1,608. Tuition for certificate programs (36-50.5 quarter credits) ranges from $6,300 to $8,838; books $617-$1,126. Registration fee $100; lab fee $300. Books/supplies: $913.

Contact. 2101 IH 35 South, Third Floor
Austin, TX 78741

Austin College
Sherman, Texas
www.austincollege.edu
Four-year private **Federal Code: 003543**

College costs. Board only (on-campus meal plan): $3,722.

	Living at home	On-campus
Tuition and fees:	$17,925	$17,925
Room only:		$3,100
Board only:	$1,500	
Books and supplies:	$800	$800
Personal expenses:	$950	$950
Transportation:	$250	$250

Undergraduate aid. Need-based: Average financial aid package for full-time students was $16,704; for part-time $5,536. 72% awarded as scholarships/grants, 28% as loans/jobs. **Non-need-based:** 57% awarded as scholarships/grants, 43% as loans/jobs. Scholarships based on academics, alumni affiliation, art, leadership, music/drama, religious affiliation, state/district residency. **Student debt:** 74% of graduating class borrowed to fund education; average debt was $22,462.

Freshman aid. Need-based: Out of 348 full-time freshmen, 263 applied for aid; 209 were judged to have need; of these 209 received aid. Average package met 98% of need. 141 students had full need met. Average scholarship/

grant was $13,026; average loan $4,008. **Non-need based:** 43 full-time freshmen with need received non-need scholarships; 119 without need received awards.

Merit scholarships. 10 full-tuition Presidental Scholarships: 3.25 overall GPA required, 3.50 GPA for the final two years. 15 Leadership Institute Merit-Based Scholarships: 4 year value of $40,000, 3.0 GPA required. Sara Bernice Moseley Scholarship for Outstanding Presbyterian Students: $2,000-$10,000 per year; must remain in good academic standing, active in ministry or service to others. Distinguished Alumni Scholarship: $10,000 per year; 3.0 GPA required. One Trustee Fellowship: tuition, room and board, books and fees, finalists selected by interview process, 3.25 GPA by end of freshman year and 3.5 required thereafter.

Policies to reduce costs. Tuition/fee waivers for employees and their families. Credit/placement for qualifying scores on AP, IB, CLEP examinations. Work study available nights and weekends.

Payment plans. Installment payment.

Application procedures. FAFSA, institutional form required. Priority date 4/1; no closing date. Applicants notified on rolling basis starting 3/1, must reply by 5/1. Early decision closing date 12/1.

Contact. **Financial aid office:** (903) 813-2900
Laurie Coulter, Director of Financial Aid
900 North Grand, Suite 6N
Sherman, TX 75090-4400

Austin Community College

Austin, Texas
www.austincc.edu
Two-year public **Federal Code: 012015**

	Living at home
Tuition and fees (2002-2003):	$1,326
Out-of-district:	$2,796
Out-of-state:	$5,496
Per-credit charge:	$32
Per-credit out-of-district:	$81
Per-credit out-of-state:	$171
Board only:	$1,906
Books and supplies:	$750
Personal expenses:	$1,310
Transportation:	$998

Undergraduate aid. Need-based: Need-based aid available for full-time and part-time students.

Policies to reduce costs. Tuition/fee waivers for senior citizens, employees and their families. Credit/placement for qualifying scores on AP, CLEP examinations.

Payment plans. Credit card, installment payment.

Application procedures. FAFSA, institutional form required. Closing date 4/2. Applicants notified on rolling basis starting 6/1, must reply within 2 week(s) of notification.

Contact. **Financial aid office:** (512) 223-7940
Terry Bazan, Director, Financial Assistance
5930 Middle Fiskville Road
Austin, TX 78752-4390

Austin Graduate School of Theology

Austin, Texas
www.austingrad.edu
Upper-division private **Federal Code: 017322**

	Living at home
Tuition and fees (2002-2003):	$4,500
Books and supplies:	$400
Personal expenses:	$1,584
Transportation:	$1,071

Undergraduate aid. Need-based: Need-based aid available for full-time and part-time students. **Non-need-based:** Scholarships based on academics. **Additional information:** Generous scholarships for students taking at least 12 hours. Federal work study program available. Institutional work study program (need-based) available.

Policies to reduce costs. Tuition/fee waivers for family of clergy, employees and their families. Credit/placement for qualifying scores on CLEP examinations.

Payment plans. Installment payment.

Application procedures. FAFSA, institutional form required. Priority date 7/1; closing date 8/1. **Transfers:** If seeking government loan or grant must submit financial aid transcripts from previous institution.

Contact. **Financial aid office:** (512) 476-2772
Dave Arthur, Vice President
1909 University Avenue
Austin, TX 78705

Baylor University

Waco, Texas
www.baylor.edu
Four-year private **Federal Code: 003545**

	Living at home	On-campus
Tuition and fees:	$18,500	$18,500
Room and board:		$5,634
Board only:	$1,533	
Books and supplies:	$1,460	$1,460
Personal expenses:	$1,590	$1,744
Transportation:	$1,566	$1,344

Undergraduate aid. Need-based: Average financial aid package for full-time students was $11,518; for part-time $6,470. 50% awarded as scholarships/grants, 50% as loans/jobs. **Non-need-based:** 46% awarded as scholarships/grants, 54% as loans/jobs. Scholarships based on academics, art, athletics, job skills, leadership, music/drama.

Freshman aid. Need-based: Out of 2,601 full-time freshmen, 2,243 applied for aid; 1,290 were judged to have need; of these 1,283 received aid. Average package met 71% of need. 272 students had full need met. Average scholarship/grant was $8,790; average loan $2,799. **Non-need based:** 903 full-time freshmen with need received non-need scholarships; 886 without need received awards; 70 received athletic scholarships.

Merit scholarships. President's Baylor Scholarship, $28,000, for 4 years. Provost's Baylor Scholarship, $20,000, for 4 years. Achievement Baylor Scholarship, $8,000, for 4 years. Above scholarships (unlimited number) based on high school rank and SAT/ACT scores. Regent's Baylor scholarship, full-tuition, limited to National Merit finalists who list Baylor as first choice; unlimited number.

Policies to reduce costs. Tuition/fee waivers for family of clergy, employees and their families. Tuition at time of enrollment guaranteed for 4 years; credit/placement for qualifying scores on AP, IB, CLEP examinations.

Payment plans. Installment payment.

Application procedures. FAFSA required. Priority date 3/1; no closing date. Applicants notified on rolling basis starting 3/1, must reply by 5/1 or within 2 week(s) of notification. **Transfers:** Priority date 3/1; no deadline.

Contact. **Financial aid office:** (800) 229-5678
Cliff Neel, Director of Scholarships and Student Financial Aid
Box 97056
Waco, TX 76798-7056

Blinn College

Brenham, Texas
www.blinn.edu
Two-year public **Federal Code: 003549**

	Living at home	On-campus
Tuition and fees:	$1,480	$1,480
Out-of-state:	$4,210	$4,210
Per-credit charge:	$19	$19
Per-credit out-of-district:	$31	$31
Per-credit out-of-state:	$110	$110
Room and board:		$4,300
Books and supplies:	$720	$720
Personal expenses:	$1,094	$1,094
Transportation:	$306	$412

Undergraduate aid. Need-based: Need-based aid available for full-time and part-time students.

Policies to reduce costs. Tuition/fee waivers for senior citizens, employees and their families. Credit/placement for qualifying scores on AP, CLEP examinations.

Payment plans. Credit card, installment payment.

Application procedures. FAFSA, institutional form required. Priority date 6/1; no closing date. Applicants notified on rolling basis starting 7/1.

Contact. **Financial aid office:** (979) 830-4144
Scot Mertz, Director of Financial Aid
902 College Avenue
Brenham, TX 77833

Border Institute of Technology

El Paso, Texas
www.bitelp.com
Two-year proprietary **Federal Code: 012982**

	Living at home
Tuition and fees:	$8,530
Per-credit charge:	$140
Books and supplies:	$900
Transportation:	$1,400

Contact. Hector Martinez, Financial Aid Director
9611 Acer Avenue
El Paso, TX 79925-6744

Brazosport College

Lake Jackson, Texas
www.brazosport.edu
Two-year public **Federal Code: 007287**

	Living at home
Tuition and fees:	$860
Out-of-district:	$1,570
Out-of-state:	$2,660
Per-credit charge:	$20
Per-credit out-of-district:	$35
Per-credit out-of-state:	$82
Board only:	$2,480
Books and supplies:	$702
Personal expenses:	$1,070
Transportation:	$840

Undergraduate aid. **Need-based:** Average financial aid package for full-time students was $1,778; for part-time $987. **Non-need-based:** Scholarships based on academics, art, job skills, leadership, music/drama, state/district residency.

Freshman aid. **Need-based:** Out of 270 full-time freshmen, 133 applied for aid; 76 were judged to have need; of these 75 received aid. Average package met 49% of need. **Non-need based:** 6 full-time freshmen with need received non-need scholarships; 30 without need received awards.

Policies to reduce costs. Tuition/fee waivers for employees and their families. Credit/placement for qualifying scores on AP, CLEP examinations. Work study available for part-time students.

Payment plans. Credit card, installment payment.

Application procedures. FAFSA, institutional form required. Priority date 7/1; no closing date. Applicants notified on rolling basis starting 5/1. **Transfers:** No deadline.

Contact. **Financial aid office:** (979) 230-3377
Anne Walker, Director of Enrollment Management and Financial Aid
500 College Drive
Lake Jackson, TX 77566

Brookhaven College

Farmers Branch, Texas
www.dcccd.edu/bhc
Two-year public **Federal Code: 014471**

	Living at home
Tuition and fees (2002-2003):	$780
Out-of-district:	$1,380
Out-of-state:	$2,280
Per-credit charge:	$26
Per-credit out-of-district:	$46
Per-credit out-of-state:	$76
Board only:	$1,500
Books and supplies:	$800
Personal expenses:	$920
Transportation:	$1,330

Undergraduate aid. **Additional information:** Some tuition waivers available based upon state residency.

Policies to reduce costs. Credit/placement for qualifying scores on CLEP examinations.

Payment plans. Credit card payment.

Application procedures. FAFSA required. Priority date 6/1; no closing date. Applicants notified on rolling basis.

Contact. Kathryn Kelley-Novak, Director of Financial Aid
3939 Valley View Lane
Farmers Branch, TX 75244

Cedar Valley College

Lancaster, Texas
www.dcccd.edu/cvc
Two-year public **Federal Code: 014035**

	Living at home
Tuition and fees (2002-2003):	$780
Out-of-district:	$1,380
Out-of-state:	$2,280
Per-credit charge:	$26
Per-credit out-of-district:	$46
Per-credit out-of-state:	$76
Books and supplies:	$600
Personal expenses:	$1,045
Transportation:	$1,330

Policies to reduce costs. Credit/placement for qualifying scores on CLEP examinations.

Payment plans. Credit card payment.

Application procedures. FAFSA required. Priority date 5/1; no closing date. Applicants notified on rolling basis.

Contact. Frank Ellis, Director of Financial Aid
3030 North Dallas Avenue
Lancaster, TX 75134

Central Texas College

Killeen, Texas
www.ctcd.cc.tx.us
Two-year public **Federal Code: 004003**

College costs. Minimum out-of-state per-credit hour charge $500 for first credit hour.

	Living at home	On-campus
Tuition and fees:	$660	$660
Out-of-district:	$810	$810
Out-of-state:	$2,250	$2,250
Per-credit charge:	$22	$22
Per-credit out-of-district:	$27	$27
Per-credit out-of-state:	$75	$75
Room and board:		$3,200
Books and supplies:	$1,140	$1,140
Personal expenses:	$1,380	$1,200
Transportation:	$637	$637

Undergraduate aid. All financial aid based on need. Need-based aid available for full-time and part-time students.

Policies to reduce costs. Tuition/fee waivers for senior citizens, employees and their families. Credit/placement for qualifying scores on AP, CLEP examinations. Work study available nights, weekends and for part-time students.

Payment plans. Credit card, installment payment.

Application procedures. FAFSA, institutional form required. Priority date 7/1; no closing date. Applicants notified on rolling basis starting 3/1, must reply within 4 week(s) of notification. **Transfers:** Priority date 7/1; no deadline.

Contact. **Financial aid office:** (254) 526-1508
Annabelle Smith, Director of Student Financial Aid
Box 1800
Killeen, TX 76540

Cisco Junior College

Cisco, Texas
www.cisco.cc.tx.us
Two-year public **Federal Code: 003553**

	Living at home	On-campus
Tuition and fees (projected):	$1,668	$1,668
Out-of-district:	$1,884	$1,884
Out-of-state:	$2,251	$2,251
Per-credit charge:	$26	$26
Per-credit out-of-district:	$34	$34
Per-credit out-of-state:	$46	$46
Room and board:		$3,240
Board only:	$1,785	
Books and supplies:	$800	$800
Personal expenses:	$1,986	$1,986
Transportation:	$950	$950

Policies to reduce costs. Tuition/fee waivers for employees and their families. Credit/placement for qualifying scores on CLEP examinations.

Payment plans. Credit card, installment payment.

Application procedures. FAFSA required. Priority date 8/15; no closing date. Applicants notified on rolling basis starting 8/15. **Transfers:** Student must complete verification process with college before award can be made even if he/she has award letter from previous institution. Must submit student aid report in duplicate to determine eligibility for financial assistance.

Contact. Dianne Pharr, Director of Financial Aid
Route 3, Box 3
Cisco, TX 76437

Clarendon College

Clarendon, Texas
www.clarendoncollege.edu
Two-year public **Federal Code: 003554**

	Living at home	On-campus
Tuition and fees (2002-2003):	$1,080	$1,080
Out-of-district:	$1,500	$1,500
Out-of-state:	$1,830	$1,830
Per-credit charge:	$36	$36
Per-credit out-of-district:	$50	$50
Per-credit out-of-state:	$61	$61
Room and board:		$2,500
Board only:	$1,250	
Books and supplies:	$800	$800
Personal expenses:	$2,075	$2,075
Transportation:	$1,230	$1,230

Undergraduate aid. Need-based: Average financial aid package for full-time students was $2,060; for part-time $1,723. 73% awarded as scholarships/grants, 27% as loans/jobs. **Non-need-based:** Scholarships based on academics, art, athletics, music/drama, state/district residency. **Student debt:** 5% of graduating class borrowed to fund education; average debt was $1,318.

Freshman aid. Need-based: Out of 122 full-time freshmen, 89 applied for aid; 80 were judged to have need; of these 85 received aid. Average package met 75% of need. 4 students had full need met. Average scholarship/grant was $2,663; average loan $299. **Non-need based:** 53 full-time freshmen with need received non-need scholarships; 27 without need received awards; 23 received athletic scholarships.

Policies to reduce costs. Tuition/fee waivers for senior citizens. Credit/placement for qualifying scores on CLEP examinations. Work study available weekends.

Payment plans. Credit card, installment payment.

Application procedures. FAFSA, institutional form required. Priority date 7/1; closing date 8/28. Applicants notified on rolling basis starting 8/1, must reply by 8/15 or within 2 week(s) of notification. **Transfers:** No deadline.

Contact. Financial aid office: (806) 874-3571
Marian Wilmoth, Financial Aid Coordinator
PO Box 968
Clarendon, TX 79226

Coastal Bend College

Beeville, Texas
www.coastalbend.edu
Two-year public **Federal Code: 003546**

	Living at home	On-campus
Tuition and fees (2002-2003):	$1,124	$1,124
Out-of-district:	$1,724	$1,724
Out-of-state:	$1,844	$1,844
Per-credit charge:	$32	$32
Per-credit out-of-district:	$57	$57
Per-credit out-of-state:	$50	$50
Room and board:		$1,920
Books and supplies:	$600	$600
Personal expenses:	$1,500	$1,500
Transportation:	$1,498	$424

Undergraduate aid. Need-based: Average financial aid package for full-time students was $2,153; for part-time $1,076. 97% awarded as scholarships/grants, 3% as loans/jobs. **Non-need-based:** Scholarships based on academics, leadership.

Freshman aid. Need-based: Out of 509 full-time freshmen, 352 applied for aid; 352 were judged to have need; of these 352 received aid. Average package met 90% of need. 300 students had full need met. Average scholarship/grant was $2,153. **Non-need based:** 52 full-time freshmen with need received non-need scholarships; 100 without need received awards.

Policies to reduce costs. Tuition/fee waivers for senior citizens. Credit/placement for qualifying scores on AP, CLEP examinations.

Payment plans. Credit card, installment payment.

Application procedures. FAFSA, institutional form required. Priority date 4/1; no closing date. Applicants notified on rolling basis starting 5/1, must reply within 2 week(s) of notification.

Contact. Financial aid office: (361) 354-2238
Mary Mixson, Director of Financial Aid
3800 Charco Road
Beeville, TX 78102

College of Biblical Studies-Houston

Houston, Texas
www.cbshouston.edu
Four-year private **Federal Code: 034224**

College costs. $7,500 tuition for bachelor degree program, plus $100 fee. Lower division programs, $75 per-credit-hour and $75 fee.

Contact. Artis Lovelady, Financial Aid Officer
6000 Dale Carnegie Drive
Houston, TX 77036

College of Saint Thomas More

Fort Worth, Texas
www.cstm.edu
Four-year private **Federal Code: 031894**

College costs. Tuition includes Rome program.

	Living at home
Tuition and fees:	$12,000
Books and supplies:	$500

Undergraduate aid. Need-based: Need-based aid available for full-time and part-time students.

Policies to reduce costs. Work study available nights.

Contact. Financial aid office: (817) 923-8459
Stephen Matuszak, Financial Aid Department
3020 Lubbock Avenue
Fort Worth, TX 76109

College of the Mainland

Texas City, Texas
www.com.edu
Two-year public **Federal Code: 007096**

	Living at home
Tuition and fees (2002-2003):	$645
Out-of-district:	$1,215
Out-of-state:	$1,755
Per-credit charge:	$14
Per-credit out-of-district:	$36
Per-credit out-of-state:	$54
Board only:	$1,993
Books and supplies:	$800
Personal expenses:	$1,087
Transportation:	$1,287

Undergraduate aid. All financial aid based on need. Need-based aid available for full-time and part-time students.

Policies to reduce costs. Tuition/fee waivers for senior citizens, employees and their families. Credit/placement for qualifying scores on AP, CLEP examinations. Work study available nights, weekends and for part-time students.

Payment plans. Credit card, installment, deferred payment.

Application procedures. FAFSA, institutional form required. No deadline. Applicants notified on rolling basis. **Transfers:** Priority date 8/1; no deadline.

Contact. **Financial aid office:** (409) 938-1211 ext. 274
Rebecca Miles, Director of Financial Aid
1200 Amburn Road
Texas City, TX 77591

Collin County Community College District

Plano, Texas
www.ccccd.edu
Two-year public **Federal Code: 016792**

	Living at home
Tuition and fees (2002-2003):	$934
Out-of-district:	$1,174
Out-of-state:	$2,224
Per-credit charge:	$21
Per-credit out-of-district:	$29
Per-credit out-of-state:	$64
Board only:	$1,995
Books and supplies:	$550
Personal expenses:	$1,230
Transportation:	$1,910

Undergraduate aid. **Need-based:** Average financial aid package for full-time students was $3,274; for part-time $1,906. 69% awarded as scholarships/grants, 31% as loans/jobs. **Non-need-based:** 21% awarded as scholarships/grants, 79% as loans/jobs. Scholarships based on art, athletics, music/drama, state/district residency. **Student debt:** 7% of graduating class borrowed to fund education; average debt was $3,637.

Freshman aid. **Need-based:** Out of 1,601 full-time freshmen, 1,040 applied for aid; 1,038 were judged to have need; of these 730 received aid. Average package met 30% of need. 14 students had full need met. Average scholarship/grant was $2,238; average loan $1,926. **Non-need based:** 225 full-time freshmen with need received non-need scholarships; 1,089 without need received awards; 52 received athletic scholarships.

Policies to reduce costs. Tuition/fee waivers for senior citizens. Credit/placement for qualifying scores on AP, CLEP examinations. Work study available nights, weekends and for part-time students.

Payment plans. Credit card, installment payment.

Application procedures. FAFSA, institutional form required. Priority date 6/1; no closing date. Applicants notified on rolling basis starting 6/1, must reply within 2 week(s) of notification. **Transfers:** Priority date 6/1; no deadline. Applicants must have 2.0 GPA cumulative and less than 90 transferable credit hours.

Contact. **Financial aid office:** (972) 881-5760
Debra Wilkison, Director of Financial Aid
2800 East Spring Creek Parkway
Plano, TX 75094

Commonwealth Institute of Funeral Service

Houston, Texas
www.commonwealthinst.org
Two-year private **Federal Code: 003556**

College costs (2002-2003). Full program costs: $8,100 for associate program; $5,850 for certificate program. Board: $1,470. Books/supplies: $1,183. Personal expenses: $1,102. Transportation: $2,408.

Undergraduate aid. All financial aid based on need. Need-based aid available for full-time and part-time students.

Policies to reduce costs. Credit/placement for qualifying scores on AP, CLEP examinations.

Payment plans. Installment payment.

Application procedures. FAFSA required. Priority date 7/10; no closing date. Applicants notified on rolling basis starting 7/12. **Transfers:** No deadline.

Contact. **Financial aid office:** (281) 873-0262
Dennis Christie, Director of Financial Aid
415 Barren Springs Drive
Houston, TX 77090-5913

Concordia University at Austin

Austin, Texas
www.concordia.edu
Four-year private **Federal Code: 003557**

	Living at home	On-campus
Tuition and fees (2002-2003):	$14,410	$14,410
Room and board:		$6,150
Books and supplies:	$600	$600
Personal expenses:	$1,050	$1,050
Transportation:	$650	$650

Undergraduate aid. **Need-based:** Average financial aid package for full-time students was $10,370; for part-time $4,467. 62% awarded as scholarships/grants, 38% as loans/jobs. **Non-need-based:** 44% awarded as scholarships/grants, 56% as loans/jobs. Scholarships based on academics, leadership, music/drama, religious affiliation. **Student debt:** 67% of graduating class borrowed to fund education; average debt was $18,674.

Freshman aid. **Need-based:** Out of 181 full-time freshmen, 171 applied for aid; 132 were judged to have need; of these 132 received aid. Average package met 80% of need. 132 students had full need met. Average scholarship/grant was $9,823; average loan $2,250. **Non-need based:** 106 full-time freshmen with need received non-need scholarships; 30 without need received awards.

Policies to reduce costs. Tuition/fee waivers for adults, family of clergy, employees and their families. Credit/placement for qualifying scores on AP, IB, CLEP examinations.

Payment plans. Credit card, deferred payment.

Application procedures. FAFSA, institutional form required. Priority date 4/15; closing date 7/1. Applicants notified on rolling basis starting 3/1, must reply within 2 week(s) of notification. **Transfers:** Financial aid transcripts from all previously attended trade/technical schools and colleges/universities required.

Contact. Patricia Jost, Director of Financial Assistance
3400 Interstate 35 North
Austin, TX 78705-2799

Criswell College

Dallas, Texas
www.criswell.edu
Four-year private

	Living at home
Tuition and fees (2002-2003):	$5,480
Books and supplies:	$500

Policies to reduce costs. Tuition/fee waivers for family of clergy, employees and their families. Prepayment discount; credit/placement for qualifying scores on AP examinations.

Payment plans. Credit card, installment payment.

Application procedures. CSS PROFILE required. Priority date 6/1; no closing date. Applicants notified on rolling basis.

Contact. **Financial aid office:** (214) 828-1325
Kirk Spencer, Director of Financial Aid
4010 Gaston Avenue
Dallas, TX 75246-1537

Dallas Baptist University

Dallas, Texas
www.dbu.edu
Four-year private **Federal Code: 003560**

	Living at home	On-campus
Tuition and fees (2002-2003):	$10,350	$10,350
Room and board:		$4,140
Board only:	$1,500	
Books and supplies:	$900	$900
Personal expenses:	$1,575	$1,575
Transportation:	$2,016	$616

Undergraduate aid. **Need-based:** Average financial aid package for full-time students was $9,529; for part-time $4,993. 41% awarded as scholarships/grants, 59% as loans/jobs. **Non-need-based:** 42% awarded as scholarships/grants, 58% as loans/jobs. Scholarships based on academics, alumni affiliation, art, athletics, job skills, leadership, music/drama, religious affiliation.

Freshman aid. **Need-based:** Out of 268 full-time freshmen, 247 applied for aid; 165 were judged to have need; of these 165 received aid. Average package met 97% of need. 76 students had full need met. Average scholarship/grant was $2,627; average loan $2,375. **Non-need based:** 144 full-time freshmen with need received non-need scholarships; 61 without need received awards; 28 received athletic scholarships.

Policies to reduce costs. Tuition/fee waivers for children of alumni, family members, family of clergy, employees and their families. Credit/placement for qualifying scores on AP, CLEP examinations. Work study available nights, weekends and for part-time students.

Payment plans. Credit card, installment, deferred payment.

Application procedures. FAFSA, institutional form required. Priority date 3/15; no closing date. Applicants notified on rolling basis, must reply within 2 week(s) of notification.

Contact. **Financial aid office:** (214) 333-5363
Lee French, Director of Financial Aid
3000 Mountain Creek Parkway
Dallas, TX 75211-9299

Dallas Christian College

Dallas, Texas
www.dallas.edu
Four-year private **Federal Code: 006941**

	Living at home	On-campus
Tuition and fees (2002-2003):	$6,500	$6,500
Room and board:		$4,100
Books and supplies:	$600	$600
Transportation:	$800	$250

Undergraduate aid. **Need-based:** Average financial aid package for full-time students was $4,327; for part-time $3,025. 48% awarded as scholarships/grants, 52% as loans/jobs. **Non-need-based:** 67% awarded as scholarships/grants, 33% as loans/jobs. **Student debt:** 68% of graduating class borrowed to fund education; average debt was $6,029.

Freshman aid. **Need-based:** Out of 31 full-time freshmen, 31 applied for aid; 14 were judged to have need; of these 14 received aid. **Non-need based:** 7 full-time freshmen with need received non-need scholarships; 6 without need received awards.

Policies to reduce costs. Tuition/fee waivers for family of clergy, employees and their families. Credit/placement for qualifying scores on AP, CLEP examinations.

Payment plans. Credit card, installment payment.

Application procedures. FAFSA, institutional form required. Closing date 4/15. Applicants notified on rolling basis, must reply within 2 week(s) of notification.

Contact. Robin Walker, Financial Aid Officer
2700 Christian Parkway
Dallas, TX 75234-7299

Dallas Institute of Funeral Service

Dallas, Texas
www.dallasinstitute.edu
One-year private **Federal Code: 010761**

College costs. Tuition $10,000 for 15-month associate program, $4,000 for 6-month funeral director program. Student activity fee $100 for each program. Personal expenses: $1,190. Transportation: $1,200.

Payment plans. Installment payment.

Application procedures. No deadline. Applicants notified on rolling basis.

Contact. Lance Mason, Director of Financial Aid
3909 South Buckner Boulevard
Dallas, TX 75227

DeVry University: Irving

Dallas, Texas
www.dal.devry.edu
Four-year proprietary **Federal Code: 010139**

	Living at home
Tuition and fees:	$10,125
Books and supplies:	$1,100
Personal expenses:	$1,750
Transportation:	$1,422

Undergraduate aid. All financial aid based on need. Average financial aid package for full-time students was $6,831; for part-time $5,676. 16% awarded as scholarships/grants, 84% as loans/jobs.

Freshman aid. Average package met 32% of need. Average scholarship/grant was $2,991; average loan $3,810.

Policies to reduce costs. Tuition/fee waivers for employees and their families.

Payment plans. Credit card, installment, deferred payment.

Application procedures. FAFSA required. No deadline. Applicants notified on rolling basis starting 7/1. **Transfers:** No deadline.

Contact. Nga Phan, Director, Financial Aid
4800 Regent Boulevard
Dallas, TX 75063-2440

Del Mar College

Corpus Christi, Texas
www.delmar.edu
Two-year public **Federal Code: 003563**

	Living at home
Tuition and fees (projected):	$1,160
Out-of-district:	$1,910
Out-of-state:	$2,870
Per-credit charge:	$23
Per-credit out-of-district:	$62
Per-credit out-of-state:	$94
Board only:	$1,778
Books and supplies:	$800
Personal expenses:	$978
Transportation:	$1,306

Undergraduate aid. All financial aid based on need. 80% awarded as scholarships/grants, 20% as loans/jobs. Need-based aid available for part-time students.

Policies to reduce costs. Tuition/fee waivers for senior citizens, employees and their families. Credit/placement for qualifying scores on AP, CLEP examinations. Work study available nights, weekends and for part-time students.

Payment plans. Credit card, installment payment.

Application procedures. FAFSA required. Priority date 5/1; no closing date. Applicants notified on rolling basis starting 7/1, must reply within 2 week(s) of notification.

Contact. **Financial aid office:** (361) 698-1293
Enrique Garcia, Assistant Dean of Financial Aid
101 Baldwin Boulevard
Corpus Christi, TX 78404-3897

East Texas Baptist University

Marshall, Texas
www.etbu.edu
Four-year private **Federal Code: 003564**

	Living at home	On-campus
Tuition and fees:	$10,290	$10,290
Room and board:		$3,594
Board only:	$1,800	
Books and supplies:	$800	$800
Personal expenses:	$1,211	$1,211
Transportation:	$695	$632

Undergraduate aid. Need-based: Average financial aid package for full-time students was $8,468; for part-time $4,694. 63% awarded as scholarships/grants, 37% as loans/jobs. **Non-need-based:** 64% awarded as scholarships/grants, 36% as loans/jobs. Scholarships based on academics, alumni affiliation, leadership, music/drama, religious affiliation. **Student debt:** 70% of graduating class borrowed to fund education; average debt was $10,340.

Freshman aid. Need-based: Out of 338 full-time freshmen, 294 applied for aid; 269 were judged to have need; of these 269 received aid. Average package met 85% of need. 109 students had full need met. Average scholarship/grant was $5,301; average loan $2,639. **Non-need based:** 153 full-time freshmen with need received non-need scholarships; 57 without need received awards.

Policies to reduce costs. Tuition/fee waivers for employees and their families. Credit/placement for qualifying scores on AP, IB, CLEP examinations. Work study available nights, weekends and for part-time students.

Payment plans. Credit card, installment payment.

Application procedures. FAFSA, institutional form required. Priority date 6/1; no closing date. Applicants notified on rolling basis starting 1/15, must reply within 3 week(s) of notification. **Transfers:** Priority date 6/1. Not eligible for scholarships based on ACT/SAT tests.

Contact. Financial aid office: (903) 923-2138
Katherine Evans, Director of Financial Aid
1209 North Grove
Marshall, TX 75670-1498

Eastfield College

Mesquite, Texas
www.efc.dcccd.edu
Two-year public **Federal Code: 008510**

	Living at home
Tuition and fees (2002-2003):	$780
Out-of-district:	$1,380
Out-of-state:	$2,280
Per-credit charge:	$26
Per-credit out-of-district:	$46
Per-credit out-of-state:	$76
Books and supplies:	$400
Personal expenses:	$935
Transportation:	$1,170

Undergraduate aid. Need-based: Need-based aid available for full-time and part-time students.

Merit scholarships. Lecroy Scholars Program; 5-10 awarded; $2,400 ($600 per semester); based on demonstrated church, community or academic leadership and GPA 3.0; requires enrollment in 12 hours for awarding semester and participation in Lecroy Scholars events. Erin Tierney Kramp Encouragement Program; 2 awarded; $2,400 ($600 per semester); based on demonstrated courage in the face of adversity, moral character, leadership, and high academic standards; requires enrollment in 8 hours for awarding semester, and maintenance of high academic standards.

Policies to reduce costs. Tuition/fee waivers for senior citizens. Credit/placement for qualifying scores on AP, IB, CLEP examinations. Work study available nights, weekends and for part-time students.

Payment plans. Credit card, deferred payment.

Application procedures. FAFSA, institutional form required. Priority date 5/1; no closing date. Applicants notified on rolling basis starting 4/15.

Contact. Financial aid office: (972) 860-7188
Reva Rattan, Dean of Financial Aid
3737 Motley Drive
Mesquite, TX 75150

El Centro College

Dallas, Texas
www.ecc.dcccd.edu
Two-year public **Federal Code: 004453**

	Living at home
Tuition and fees (2002-2003):	$780
Out-of-district:	$1,380
Out-of-state:	$2,280
Per-credit charge:	$26
Per-credit out-of-district:	$46
Per-credit out-of-state:	$76
Books and supplies:	$750
Personal expenses:	$600
Transportation:	$400

Undergraduate aid. Need-based: Need-based aid available for full-time and part-time students. **Additional information:** Interview required for financial aid applicants.

Merit scholarships. Rising Star Scholarships available to Dallas County high school graduates in top 40% of class with financial need.

Policies to reduce costs. Tuition/fee waivers for senior citizens, minority students, unemployed or children of unemployed, employees and their families. Credit/placement for qualifying scores on AP, IB, CLEP examinations.

Payment plans. Credit card, installment payment.

Application procedures. FAFSA required. Priority date 5/1; no closing date. Applicants notified on rolling basis, must reply within 2 week(s) of notification. **Transfers:** Financial aid transcript may be required from previous institutions attended.

Contact. Financial aid office: (214) 860-2099
John Wells, Director of Financial Aid
Main and Lamar Streets
Dallas, TX 75202

El Paso Community College

El Paso, Texas
www.epcc.edu
Two-year public **Federal Code: 010387**

	Living at home
Tuition and fees (projected):	$1,312
Out-of-state:	$1,890
Per-credit charge:	$29
Per-credit out-of-state:	$55
Books and supplies:	$545
Personal expenses:	$1,223
Transportation:	$1,505

Undergraduate aid. Non-need-based: Scholarships based on academics, athletics.

Policies to reduce costs. Tuition/fee waivers for senior citizens, employees and their families. Credit/placement for qualifying scores on AP, IB, CLEP examinations. Work study available nights, weekends and for part-time students.

Payment plans. Credit card payment.

Application procedures. FAFSA, institutional form required. Priority date 5/1; no closing date. Applicants notified on rolling basis starting 7/1, must reply within 2 week(s) of notification. **Transfers:** Priority date 5/1; no deadline.

Contact. Financial aid office: (915) 831-2566
Linda Gonzalez-Hensge, Director of Student Financial Services
Box 20500
El Paso, TX 79998

Frank Phillips College

Borger, Texas
www.fpc.cc.tx.us
Two-year public **Federal Code: 003568**

	Living at home	On-campus
Tuition and fees (projected):	$1,687	$1,687
Out-of-district:	$2,017	$2,017
Out-of-state:	$2,248	$2,248
Per-credit charge:	$24	$24
Per-credit out-of-district:	$35	$35
Per-credit out-of-state:	$43	$43
Room and board:		$2,849
Books and supplies:	$605	$605
Personal expenses:	$1,310	$985
Transportation:	$1,376	$710

Undergraduate aid. Need-based: Need-based aid available for full-time and part-time students. **Non-need-based:** Scholarships based on academics, athletics, music/drama. **Additional information:** Some Texas fire department and police department personnel, active duty military personnel, children of military missing in action may qualify for reduced or waived tuition.

Policies to reduce costs. Tuition/fee waivers for senior citizens, employees and their families. Credit/placement for qualifying scores on AP, IB, CLEP examinations. Work study available nights, weekends and for part-time students.

Payment plans. Credit card, installment payment.

Application procedures. FAFSA, institutional form required. Applicants notified on rolling basis, must reply within 2 week(s) of notification. **Transfers:** Financial aid transcripts from prior school required for midyear transfer.

Contact. Financial aid office: (800) 687-2056 ext. 718
Linda Kunce, Director Financial Aid
Box 5118
Borger, TX 79008-5118

Galveston College

Galveston, Texas
www.gc.edu
Two-year public **Federal Code: 004972**

College costs. In-state students pay $50 for 1-6 credits; out-of-state students pay $300 for 1-10 credits. Required fees range from $46 to $355 depending on number of credits taken (1 to 20 credits).

	Living at home
Tuition and fees (2002-2003):	$240
Out-of-state:	$900
Per-credit charge:	$8
Per-credit out-of-state:	$30
Board only:	$2,304
Books and supplies:	$848
Personal expenses:	$1,334
Transportation:	$1,464

Undergraduate aid. All financial aid based on need. 92% awarded as scholarships/grants, 8% as loans/jobs. Need-based aid available for part-time students.

Policies to reduce costs. Tuition/fee waivers for senior citizens, employees and their families. Credit/placement for qualifying scores on AP, CLEP examinations. Work study available for part-time students.

Payment plans. Credit card, installment payment.

Application procedures. FAFSA required. Priority date 5/9; no closing date. Applicants notified on rolling basis starting 6/1. **Transfers:** No deadline.

Contact. Financial aid office: (409) 763-6551 ext. 235
Midge Berlowe, Director of Financial Aid
4015 Avenue Q
Galveston, TX 77550

Grayson County College

Denison, Texas
www.grayson.edu
Two-year public **Federal Code: 003570**

	Living at home	On-campus
Tuition and fees (2002-2003):	$1,020	$1,020
Out-of-district:	$1,200	$1,200
Out-of-state:	$2,340	$2,340
Per-credit charge:	$34	$34
Per-credit out-of-district:	$40	$40
Per-credit out-of-state:	$78	$78
Room and board:		$3,180
Board only:	$1,792	
Books and supplies:	$504	$504
Personal expenses:	$1,192	$1,192
Transportation:	$1,458	$1,458

Undergraduate aid. Need-based: Need-based aid available for full-time and part-time students. **Additional information:** Short term loans available.

Policies to reduce costs. Credit/placement for qualifying scores on CLEP examinations.

Payment plans. Credit card payment.

Application procedures. FAFSA required. No deadline. Applicants notified on rolling basis, must reply within 5 week(s) of notification.

Contact. Financial aid office: (903) 463-8642
David Akins, Director of Financial Aid
6101 Grayson Drive
Denison, TX 75020

Hallmark Institute of Aeronautics

San Antonio, Texas
www.hallmarkinstitute.com
Two-year proprietary **Federal Code: 010509**

College costs. Tuition for full associate program in airframe technology or powerplant technology $14,684; combined program $20,215. Tuition for diploma programs ranges from $12,181 to $17,384. Costs include books, equipment and supplies. Registration fee $100. Course fees vary. International students pay additional 8%.

Undergraduate aid. Need-based: Average financial aid package for full-time students was $5,500. 23% awarded as scholarships/grants, 77% as loans/jobs. **Student debt:** 98% of graduating class borrowed to fund education; average debt was $10,200.

Policies to reduce costs. Tuition at time of enrollment guaranteed for 2 years.

Payment plans. Credit card, installment payment.

Contact. 8901 Wetmore Road
San Antonio, TX 78216

Hallmark Institute of Technology

San Antonio, Texas
www.hallmarkinstitute.com
Two-year proprietary **Federal Code: 010509**

College costs (2002-2003). Costs for associate programs range from $13,577-$22,000; diploma programs range from $9,456-$11,635. (International students pay additional 8%.) Includes books, equipment, supplies. Additional registration fee $100 for all programs.

Undergraduate aid. Need-based: Average financial aid package for full-time students was $5,500. 41% awarded as scholarships/grants, 59% as loans/jobs. **Student debt:** 98% of graduating class borrowed to fund education; average debt was $10,200.

Policies to reduce costs. Tuition at time of enrollment guaranteed for 2 years; credit/placement for qualifying scores on CLEP examinations.

Payment plans. Credit card, installment payment.

Application procedures. FAFSA required. No deadline. Applicants notified on rolling basis. **Transfers:** No deadline.

Contact. **Financial aid office:** (210) 690-9000
Grace Calixto, Director of Financial Aid
10401 IH 10 West
San Antonio, TX 78230-1737

Hardin-Simmons University

Abilene, Texas
www.hsutx.edu
Four-year private **Federal Code: 003571**

	Living at home	On-campus
Tuition and fees:	$12,176	$12,176
Room and board:		$3,699
Board only:	$750	
Books and supplies:	$750	$750
Personal expenses:	$450	$1,482
Transportation:	$900	$1,056

Undergraduate aid. Need-based: Average financial aid package for full-time students was $10,950; for part-time $6,679. 64% awarded as scholarships/grants, 36% as loans/jobs. **Non-need-based:** Scholarships based on academics, art, job skills, leadership, music/drama, religious affiliation. **Student debt:** 74% of graduating class borrowed to fund education; average debt was $19,959.

Freshman aid. Need-based: Out of 437 full-time freshmen, 415 applied for aid; 282 were judged to have need; of these 282 received aid. Average package met 20% of need. 56 students had full need met. Average scholarship/grant was $4,314; average loan $2,371. **Non-need based:** 152 full-time freshmen with need received non-need scholarships; 62 without need received awards.

Merit scholarships. Academic scholarships ranging from $1,000 to $2,000 per semester available for students with composite scores of 25 and above on ACT, or 1140 and above on SAT I.

Policies to reduce costs. Tuition/fee waivers for family members, employees and their families. Tuition at time of enrollment guaranteed for 4 years; credit/placement for qualifying scores on AP, CLEP examinations.

Payment plans. Credit card, installment payment.

Application procedures. FAFSA required. Priority date 3/15; no closing date. Applicants notified on rolling basis starting 1/1. **Transfers:** Full-time transfer students with more than 24 transferable hours and 3.25 GPA may qualify for $1,000 per semester academic scholarship for tuition only. Renewal requires 3.0 cumulative GPA.

Contact. **Financial aid office:** (915) 670-1331
Shane Davidson, Associate Vice President of Enrollment Services
PO Box 16050
Abilene, TX 79698

Hill College

Hillsboro, Texas
www.hill-college.cc.tx.us
Two-year public **Federal Code: 003573**

	Living at home	On-campus
Tuition and fees (2002-2003):	$1,030	$1,030
Out-of-district:	$1,270	$1,270
Out-of-state:	$1,670	$1,670
Per-credit charge:	$22	$22
Per-credit out-of-district:	$30	$30
Per-credit out-of-state:	$30	$30
Room and board:		$2,680
Board only:	$3,916	
Books and supplies:	$900	$900
Personal expenses:	$1,107	$1,107
Transportation:	$1,379	$829

Undergraduate aid. Need-based: Need-based aid available for full-time and part-time students. **Non-need-based:** Scholarships based on academics, athletics.

Policies to reduce costs. Tuition/fee waivers for senior citizens, employees and their families. Credit/placement for qualifying scores on AP, CLEP examinations. Work study available for part-time students.

Payment plans. Credit card, installment payment.

Application procedures. FAFSA, institutional form required. Priority date 8/1; no closing date. Applicants notified on rolling basis. **Transfers:** No deadline.

Contact. Nancy Holland, Director of Student Financial Aid
Box 619
Hillsboro, TX 76645

Houston Baptist University

Houston, Texas
www.hbu.edu
Four-year private **Federal Code: 003576**

	Living at home	On-campus
Tuition and fees:	$11,355	$11,355
Room and board:		$4,443
Books and supplies:	$700	$700
Personal expenses:	$1,370	$1,400
Transportation:	$1,260	$1,260

Undergraduate aid. Need-based: Average financial aid package for full-time students was $9,699; for part-time $10,415. 53% awarded as scholarships/grants, 47% as loans/jobs. **Non-need-based:** 38% awarded as scholarships/grants, 62% as loans/jobs. Scholarships based on academics, alumni affiliation, art, athletics, leadership, music/drama, religious affiliation. **Student debt:** 46% of graduating class borrowed to fund education; average debt was $12,203.

Freshman aid. Need-based: Out of 252 full-time freshmen, 148 applied for aid; 127 were judged to have need; of these 127 received aid. Average package met 59% of need. 22 students had full need met. Average scholarship/grant was $6,501; average loan $2,126. **Non-need based:** 9 full-time freshmen with need received non-need scholarships; 21 without need received awards; 1 received athletic scholarships.

Policies to reduce costs. Tuition/fee waivers for senior citizens, family of clergy, employees and their families. Tuition at time of enrollment guaranteed for 4 years; credit/placement for qualifying scores on AP, IB, CLEP examinations.

Payment plans. Credit card, installment payment.

Application procedures. FAFSA, institutional form required. Priority date 3/1; closing date 4/15. Applicants notified on rolling basis starting 4/15, must reply within 3 week(s) of notification.

Contact. Sherry Byrd, Director Financial Aid
7502 Fondren Road
Houston, TX 77074-3298

Houston Community College System

Houston, Texas
www.hccs.edu
Two-year public **Federal Code: 010422**

	Living at home
Tuition and fees (projected):	$1,290
Out-of-district:	$2,610
Out-of-state:	$3,510
Per-credit charge:	$43
Per-credit out-of-district:	$87
Per-credit out-of-state:	$117

Undergraduate aid. Need-based: Need-based aid available for full-time and part-time students.

Policies to reduce costs. Tuition/fee waivers for senior citizens, employees and their families. Credit/placement for qualifying scores on AP, CLEP examinations. Work study available nights and weekends.

Payment plans. Credit card, installment payment.

Application procedures. FAFSA required. Priority date 8/15; no closing date. Applicants notified on rolling basis starting 6/1, must reply within 2 week(s) of notification.

Contact. Alex Prince, Chief Financial Aid Officer
3100 Main
Houston, TX 77266-7517

Howard College

Big Spring, Texas
www.howardcollege.edu
Two-year public **Federal Code: 003574**

	Living at home	On-campus
Tuition and fees (2002-2003):	$991	$991
Out-of-district:	$1,281	$1,281
Out-of-state:	$1,661	$1,661
Per-credit charge:	$23	$23
Per-credit out-of-district:	$32	$32
Per-credit out-of-state:	$45	$45
Room and board:		$3,000
Board only:	$1,800	
Books and supplies:	$500	$500
Personal expenses:	$875	$1,330
Transportation:	$800	$800

Undergraduate aid. Need-based: Need-based aid available for full-time and part-time students. **Non-need-based:** Scholarships based on academics, athletics, leadership, music/drama.

Policies to reduce costs. Tuition/fee waivers for senior citizens, employees and their families. Credit/placement for qualifying scores on AP, CLEP examinations. Work study available for part-time students.

Payment plans. Credit card, installment payment.

Application procedures. FAFSA, institutional form required. Priority date 4/1; no closing date. Applicants notified on rolling basis starting 7/15, must reply within 2 week(s) of notification. **Transfers:** Priority date 4/1.

Contact. **Financial aid office:** (915) 264-5083
Ann Duncan, Director of Financial Aid
1001 Birdwell Lane
Big Spring, TX 79720

Howard Payne University

Brownwood, Texas
www.hputx.edu
Four-year private **Federal Code: 003575**

College costs. Flat rate of $4850 per semester for 9 or more credits; $250 per credit for less than 9 credits.

	Living at home	On-campus
Tuition and fees (2002-2003):	$10,500	$10,500
Room and board:		$3,870
Board only:	$1,500	
Books and supplies:	$700	$700
Personal expenses:	$1,200	$1,406
Transportation:	$850	$700

Undergraduate aid. Need-based: Need-based aid available for full-time and part-time students. **Non-need-based:** Scholarships based on academics, alumni affiliation, art, job skills, music/drama.

Policies to reduce costs. Tuition/fee waivers for senior citizens, family of clergy, employees and their families. Credit/placement for qualifying scores on AP, CLEP examinations.

Payment plans. Credit card, installment, deferred payment.

Application procedures. FAFSA, institutional form required. Priority date 3/1; no closing date. Applicants notified on rolling basis starting 3/30, must reply within 3 week(s) of notification.

Contact. **Financial aid office:** (915) 649-8015
Glenda Huff, Director of Student Financial Aid
1000 Fisk Avenue
Brownwood, TX 76801

Huston-Tillotson College

Austin, Texas
www.htc.edu
Four-year private **Federal Code: 003577**

	Living at home	On-campus
Tuition and fees:	$8,236	$8,236
Room and board:		$5,027
Board only:	$1,411	
Books and supplies:	$645	$645
Personal expenses:	$1,332	$1,332
Transportation:	$825	$825

Undergraduate aid. Need-based: Average financial aid package for full-time students was $11,198; for part-time $3,652. 51% awarded as scholarships/grants, 49% as loans/jobs. **Non-need-based:** Scholarships based on academics, athletics, music/drama, religious affiliation. **Student debt:** 69% of graduating class borrowed to fund education; average debt was $22,125.

Freshman aid. Need-based: Out of 122 full-time freshmen, 118 applied for aid; 118 were judged to have need; of these 118 received aid. Average package met 72% of need. 25 students had full need met. Average scholarship/grant was $3,121; average loan $2,704. **Non-need based:** 20 full-time freshmen with need received non-need scholarships; 7 without need received awards; 41 received athletic scholarships.

Policies to reduce costs. Tuition/fee waivers for employees and their families. Prepayment discount.

Payment plans. Credit card, installment, deferred payment.

Application procedures. FAFSA, institutional form required. Priority date 3/15; closing date 5/1. Applicants notified on rolling basis, must reply within 2 week(s) of notification.

Contact. Bronte Jones, Director of Financial Aid
900 Chicon Street
Austin, TX 78702

ITT Technical Institute: Arlington

Arlington, Texas
Two-year proprietary **Federal Code: 016496**

College costs. Total program varies depending on course of study. Per-credit-hour charge: $347.

Policies to reduce costs. Tuition/fee waivers for employees and their families. Tuition at time of enrollment guaranteed for 2 years.

Payment plans. Credit card, installment payment.

Application procedures. FAFSA, institutional form required. No deadline. Applicants notified on rolling basis.

Contact. Director of Finance
551 Ryan Plaza Drive
Arlington, TX 76017

ITT Technical Institute: Austin

Austin, Texas
www.itt-tech.edu
Two-year proprietary **Federal Code: 007329**

College costs. Total program varies depending on course of study. Per-credit-hour charge: $347.

Policies to reduce costs. Tuition/fee waivers for employees and their families. Tuition at time of enrollment guaranteed for 2 years.

Payment plans. Credit card, installment payment.

Application procedures. FAFSA, institutional form required. No deadline. Applicants notified on rolling basis.

Contact. Tom Pruitt, Director of Finance
6330 Highway 290 East, Suite 150
Austin, TX 78723

ITT Technical Institute: Houston

Houston, Texas
Two-year proprietary
Federal Code: 016497

College costs. Total program varies depending on course of study. Per-credit-hour charge: $347.

Policies to reduce costs. Tuition/fee waivers for employees and their families. Tuition at time of enrollment guaranteed for 2 years.

Payment plans. Credit card, installment payment.

Application procedures. FAFSA, institutional form required. No deadline. Applicants notified on rolling basis.

Contact. Sandy Wilkerson, Director of Finance
2950 South Gessner
Houston, TX 77063-3751

ITT Technical Institute: Houston North

Houston, Texas
www.itt-tech.edu
Two-year proprietary
Federal Code: 007329

College costs. Total program varies depending on course of study. Per-credit-hour charge: $347.

Policies to reduce costs. Tuition/fee waivers for employees and their families. Tuition at time of enrollment guaranteed for 2 years.

Payment plans. Credit card, installment payment.

Application procedures. FAFSA, institutional form required. No deadline. Applicants notified on rolling basis.

Contact. Linda Trammel, Director of Finance
15621 Blue Ash Drive, Suite 160
Houston, TX 77090-5818

ITT Technical Institute: Houston South

Houston, Texas
www.itt-tech.edu
Two-year proprietary
Federal Code: 007329

College costs. Total program varies depending on course of study. Per-credit-hour charge: $347.

Policies to reduce costs. Tuition/fee waivers for employees and their families. Tuition at time of enrollment guaranteed for 2 years.

Payment plans. Credit card, installment payment.

Application procedures. Institutional form required. No deadline. Applicants notified on rolling basis.

Contact. Belinda Balsano, Director of Finance
2222 Bay Area Boulevard
Houston, TX 77058

ITT Technical Institute: San Antonio

San Antonio, Texas
www.itt-tech.edu
Two-year proprietary
Federal Code: 030714

College costs. Total program varies depending on course of study. Per-credit-hour charge: $347.

Policies to reduce costs. Tuition/fee waivers for employees and their families. Tuition at time of enrollment guaranteed for 2 years.

Payment plans. Credit card, installment payment.

Application procedures. FAFSA, institutional form required. No deadline. Applicants notified on rolling basis.

Contact. Christine Gray, Director of Finance
5700 Northwest Parkway
San Antonio, TX 78249

International Business College

Lubbock, Texas
www.ibclubbock.com
Two-year proprietary

College costs. Costs vary by program. Computer office specialist program $8,714.

Contact. Christina Pearson, Director of Financial Aid
4630 50th Street, Suite 100
Lubbock, TX 79414-3509

Jacksonville College

Jacksonville, Texas
www.jacksonville-college.edu
Two-year private
Federal Code: 003579

	Living at home	On-campus
Tuition and fees (2002-2003):	$4,805	$4,805
Per-credit charge:	$150	$150
Room and board:		$2,628
Board only:	$2,142	
Books and supplies:	$800	$800
Personal expenses:	$1,767	$1,135
Transportation:	$1,287	$698

Undergraduate aid. Non-need-based: Scholarships based on academics, athletics, music/drama, religious affiliation, state/district residency.

Policies to reduce costs. Tuition/fee waivers for family of clergy, employees and their families.

Payment plans. Credit card, installment payment.

Application procedures. FAFSA required. Priority date 6/10; no closing date. Applicants notified on rolling basis. **Transfers:** No deadline.

Contact. Financial aid office: (903) 586-2518
Don Compton, Financial Aid Officer
105 B.J. Albritton Drive
Jacksonville, TX 75766-4759

Jarvis Christian College

Hawkins, Texas
www.jarvis.edu
Four-year private
Federal Code: 003637

	Living at home	On-campus
Tuition and fees:	$5,550	$5,550
Room and board:		$3,485
Board only:	$1,875	
Books and supplies:	$600	$600
Personal expenses:	$950	$950
Transportation:	$800	$800

Undergraduate aid. Need-based: Need-based aid available for full-time and part-time students. **Non-need-based:** Scholarships based on academics, athletics, religious affiliation. **Additional information:** High school transcript required for scholarship consideration.

Policies to reduce costs. Tuition/fee waivers for family of clergy, employees and their families. Credit/placement for qualifying scores on AP, IB, CLEP examinations. Work study available nights, weekends and for part-time students.

Payment plans. Credit card, installment, deferred payment.

Application procedures. FAFSA required. Priority date 6/30; no closing date. Applicants notified on rolling basis starting 5/1, must reply within 2 week(s) of notification. **Transfers:** Priority date 4/15; no deadline.

Contact. Financial aid office: (903) 769-5741
Harold Abney, Director of Admission and Financial Aid
PO Box 1470
Hawkins, TX 75765-1470

Kilgore College

Kilgore, Texas
www.kilgorecc.edu
Two-year public **Federal Code: 003580**

College costs. Cited required fees are for in-district students. Required fees $750 for out-of-district and out-of-state students.

	Living at home	On-campus
Tuition and fees (2002-2003):	$930	$930
Out-of-district:	$1,590	$1,590
Out-of-state:	$2,070	$2,070
Per-credit charge:	$14	$14
Per-credit out-of-district:	$36	$36
Per-credit out-of-state:	$52	$52
Room and board:		$2,950
Books and supplies:	$600	$600
Personal expenses:	$1,200	$1,200

Undergraduate aid. Need-based: Average financial aid package for full-time students was $4,250; for part-time $3,000. 97% awarded as scholarships/grants, 3% as loans/jobs. **Non-need-based:** Scholarships based on academics, alumni affiliation, art, athletics, job skills, leadership, music/drama, state/district residency. **Student debt:** 1% of graduating class borrowed to fund education; average debt was $2,500. **Additional information:** State of Texas grants available for honor graduates with unmet needs.

Freshman aid. Need-based: Out of 1,108 full-time freshmen, 887 applied for aid; 665 were judged to have need; of these 597 received aid. Average package met 40% of need. Average scholarship/grant was $4,250. **Non-need based:** 179 full-time freshmen with need received non-need scholarships; 265 without need received awards; 57 received athletic scholarships.

Merit scholarships. Presidential Scholarships: 20 available; ACT 25 or top 10% of senior class; tuition, fees and books for 4 semesters; renewable at 2.5 GPA. Exemptions for valedictorians. Educational aid exemptions.

Policies to reduce costs. Tuition/fee waivers for senior citizens, unemployed or children of unemployed, employees and their families. Credit/placement for qualifying scores on AP, CLEP examinations. Work study available for part-time students.

Payment plans. Credit card, installment payment.

Application procedures. FAFSA, institutional form required. Closing date 6/1. Applicants notified on rolling basis starting 3/1, must reply within 2 week(s) of notification. **Transfers:** No deadline. Transfer students must submit financial aid transcript from previous school plus all appropriate internal aid forms.

Contact. **Financial aid office:** (903) 983-8183
Annette Morgan, Director of Financial Aid
1100 Broadway
Kilgore, TX 75662-3299

Lamar State College at Orange

Orange, Texas
www.lsco.edu
Two-year public **Federal Code: 016748**

	Living at home
Tuition and fees (2002-2003):	$2,488
Out-of-state:	$9,028
Board only:	$1,942
Books and supplies:	$560
Personal expenses:	$1,562
Transportation:	$3,044

Undergraduate aid. All financial aid based on need. Average financial aid package for full-time students was $4,000; for part-time $1,750. 98% awarded as scholarships/grants, 2% as loans/jobs.

Freshman aid. Out of 237 full-time freshmen, 234 applied for aid; 225 were judged to have need; of these 219 received aid. 6 students had full need met. Average scholarship/grant was $3,800.

Policies to reduce costs. Tuition/fee waivers for senior citizens, employees and their families. Credit/placement for qualifying scores on AP, CLEP examinations. Work study available for part-time students.

Payment plans. Credit card, installment, deferred payment.

Application procedures. FAFSA, institutional form required. Priority date 4/1; no closing date. Applicants notified on rolling basis starting 5/15, must reply within 2 week(s) of notification. **Transfers:** No deadline.

Contact. **Financial aid office:** (409) 882-3317
Kerry Olson, Director of Financial Aid
410 West Front Street
Orange, TX 77630

Lamar State College at Port Arthur

Port Arthur, Texas
www.lamarpa.edu
Two-year public **Federal Code: 016666**

	Living at home
Tuition and fees:	$2,664
Out-of-state:	$10,398
Per-credit charge:	$68
Per-credit out-of-state:	$304
Board only:	$2,097
Books and supplies:	$643
Personal expenses:	$1,597
Transportation:	$3,220

Undergraduate aid. All financial aid based on need. Need-based aid available for full-time and part-time students.

Policies to reduce costs. Tuition/fee waivers for senior citizens. Credit/placement for qualifying scores on AP, CLEP examinations. Work study available nights, weekends and for part-time students.

Payment plans. Credit card, installment payment.

Application procedures. FAFSA, institutional form required. Priority date 4/1; no closing date. Applicants notified on rolling basis starting 4/15, must reply within 2 week(s) of notification.

Contact. **Financial aid office:** (409) 984-6203
Diane Hargett, Director of Financial Aid
Box 310
Port Arthur, TX 77641-0310

Lamar University

Beaumont, Texas
www.lamar.edu
Four-year public **Federal Code: 003581**

	Living at home	On-campus
Tuition and fees (2002-2003):	$3,076	$3,076
Out-of-state:	$9,616	$9,616
Room and board:		$5,010
Books and supplies:	$640	$640
Personal expenses:	$1,746	$1,746
Transportation:	$1,862	$1,862

Undergraduate aid. All financial aid based on need. Average financial aid package for full-time students was $792; for part-time $924. 54% awarded as scholarships/grants, 46% as loans/jobs. **Student debt:** 18% of graduating class borrowed to fund education; average debt was $6,625.

Freshman aid. Out of 1,208 full-time freshmen, 918 applied for aid; 590 were judged to have need; of these 590 received aid. Average package met 10% of need. 94 students had full need met.

Policies to reduce costs. Tuition/fee waivers for senior citizens, employees and their families. Credit/placement for qualifying scores on AP, CLEP examinations. Work study available for part-time students.

Payment plans. Credit card, installment payment.

Application procedures. FAFSA, institutional form required. Priority date 4/1; no closing date. Applicants notified on rolling basis starting 6/15, must reply within 2 week(s) of notification. **Transfers:** No deadline.

Contact. **Financial aid office:** (409) 880-8450
Jill Rowley, Director of Financial Aid
Box 10009
Beaumont, TX 77705

Laredo Community College

Laredo, Texas
www.laredo.edu
Two-year public **Federal Code: 003582**

	Living at home	On-campus
Tuition and fees (2002-2003):	$1,116	$1,116
Out-of-district:	$1,776	$1,776
Out-of-state:	$2,556	$2,556
Per-credit charge:	$22	$22
Per-credit out-of-district:	$44	$44
Per-credit out-of-state:	$70	$70
Room only:		$2,020
Board only:	$2,982	
Books and supplies:	$500	$500
Personal expenses:	$1,150	$1,173
Transportation:	$1,834	$1,812

Policies to reduce costs. Tuition/fee waivers for senior citizens, employees and their families. Credit/placement for qualifying scores on AP, CLEP examinations.

Application procedures. FAFSA, institutional form required. Priority date 5/1; no closing date. Applicants notified on rolling basis.

Contact. Rick Moreno, Director of Financial Aid
West End Washington Street
Laredo, TX 78040

LeTourneau University

Longview, Texas
www.letu.edu
Four-year private **Federal Code: 003584**

College costs. 0-6 hours is $250 per credit; 7-11 hours is $550 per credit

	Living at home	On-campus
Tuition and fees:	$14,190	$14,190
Room and board:		$5,820
Board only:	$2,750	
Books and supplies:	$1,040	$1,040
Personal expenses:	$965	$965
Transportation:	$1,040	$1,040

Undergraduate aid. Need-based: Average financial aid package for full-time students was $10,256; for part-time $4,485. 39% awarded as scholarships/grants, 61% as loans/jobs. **Non-need-based:** 15% awarded as scholarships/grants, 85% as loans/jobs. Scholarships based on academics, alumni affiliation, leadership. **Student debt:** 70% of graduating class borrowed to fund education; average debt was $20,055.

Freshman aid. Need-based: Out of 242 full-time freshmen, 234 applied for aid; 170 were judged to have need; of these 167 received aid. Average package met 87% of need. 37 students had full need met. Average scholarship/grant was $3,261; average loan $2,558. **Non-need based:** 46 full-time freshmen with need received non-need scholarships; 48 without need received awards.

Merit scholarships. Honor scholarship, GPA 3.0-3.29, ACT minimum score 25 or SAT minimum score 1150; up to $1,000 per year. Dean's Scholarship, GPA 3.3-3.59, ACT minimum 27 or SAT minimum 1200; up to $2,000 per year. Presidential Scholarship, GPA 3.60 and up, ACT minimum score 29 or SAT minimum score 1300; up to $3,000 per year.

Policies to reduce costs. Tuition/fee waivers for family of clergy, employees and their families. Credit/placement for qualifying scores on AP, IB, CLEP examinations. Work study available nights and weekends.

Payment plans. Credit card, installment, deferred payment.

Application procedures. FAFSA required. Priority date 2/15; no closing date. Applicants notified on rolling basis starting 3/1, must reply within 3 week(s) of notification. **Transfers:** Priority date 2/15; no deadline.

Contact. **Financial aid office:** (903) 233-3430
Delinda Hall, Director of Financial Aid
PO Box 7001
Longview, TX 75607

Lee College

Baytown, Texas
www.lee.edu
Two-year public **Federal Code: 003583**

	Living at home
Tuition and fees (2002-2003):	$712
Out-of-district:	$1,252
Out-of-state:	$1,492
Per-credit charge:	$14
Per-credit out-of-district:	$32
Per-credit out-of-state:	$40
Board only:	$2,414
Books and supplies:	$600
Personal expenses:	$1,248
Transportation:	$897

Undergraduate aid. Need-based: Need-based aid available for full-time and part-time students. **Non-need-based:** Scholarships based on academics, art, athletics, job skills, music/drama.

Policies to reduce costs. Tuition/fee waivers for senior citizens, employees and their families. Credit/placement for qualifying scores on AP, CLEP examinations. Work study available for part-time students.

Payment plans. Credit card, installment, deferred payment.

Application procedures. FAFSA required. Priority date 4/1; no closing date. Applicants notified on rolling basis starting 6/1.

Contact. Sharon Mullins, Financial Aid Officer
Box 818
Baytown, TX 77522

Lon Morris College

Jacksonville, Texas
www.lonmorris.edu
Two-year private **Federal Code: 003585**

	Living at home	On-campus
Tuition and fees (2002-2003):	$7,600	$7,600
Room and board:		$4,600
Books and supplies:	$450	$450
Personal expenses:	$400	$1,500
Transportation:	$200	$1,000

Undergraduate aid. Need-based: Average financial aid package for full-time students was $9,365; for part-time $9,785. 84% awarded as scholarships/grants, 16% as loans/jobs. **Non-need-based:** 72% awarded as scholarships/grants, 28% as loans/jobs. Scholarships based on academics, athletics. **Student debt:** 38% of graduating class borrowed to fund education; average debt was $3,093.

Freshman aid. Need-based: Out of 198 full-time freshmen, 198 applied for aid; 191 were judged to have need; of these 191 received aid. Average package met 91% of need. 51 students had full need met. Average scholarship/grant was $9,575; average loan $2,381. **Non-need based:** 52 full-time freshmen with need received non-need scholarships; 22 without need received awards; 15 received athletic scholarships.

Policies to reduce costs. Tuition/fee waivers for minority students, family members, family of clergy, employees and their families. Prepayment discount; credit/placement for qualifying scores on AP, IB, CLEP examinations.

Payment plans. Credit card, installment payment.

Application procedures. FAFSA, institutional form required. Priority date 6/1; no closing date. Applicants notified on rolling basis starting 4/1, must reply within 3 week(s) of notification. **Transfers:** Priority date 6/1; closing date 8/1.

Contact. **Financial aid office:** (903) 589-4061
Kris Marquis, Financial Aid Director
800 College Avenue
Jacksonville, TX 75766

Lubbock Christian University

Lubbock, Texas
www.lcu.edu
Four-year private **Federal Code: 003586**

	Living at home	On-campus
Tuition and fees (2002-2003):	$10,992	$10,992
Room and board:		$4,160
Board only:	$2,100	
Books and supplies:	$450	$450
Personal expenses:	$1,750	$1,750
Transportation:	$1,402	$1,562

Undergraduate aid. Need-based: Average financial aid package for full-time students was $10,006; for part-time $5,020. 47% awarded as scholarships/grants, 53% as loans/jobs. **Non-need-based:** 29% awarded as scholarships/grants, 71% as loans/jobs. Scholarships based on academics, art, athletics, music/drama, religious affiliation. **Student debt:** 65% of graduating class borrowed to fund education; average debt was $17,910.

Freshman aid. Need-based: Out of 289 full-time freshmen, 274 applied for aid; 237 were judged to have need; of these 237 received aid. Average package met 79% of need. 39 students had full need met. Average scholarship/grant was $7,175; average loan $2,509. **Non-need based:** 29 full-time freshmen with need received non-need scholarships; 47 without need received awards; 15 received athletic scholarships.

Policies to reduce costs. Tuition/fee waivers for employees and their families. Credit/placement for qualifying scores on AP, IB, CLEP examinations. Work study available nights, weekends and for part-time students.

Payment plans. Credit card, installment payment.

Application procedures. FAFSA, institutional form required. Priority date 6/1; no closing date. Applicants notified on rolling basis starting 3/1, must reply within 2 week(s) of notification. **Transfers:** No deadline.

Contact. Financial aid office: (806) 720-7176
Tia Clary, Director of Financial Aid
5601 19th Street
Lubbock, TX 79407

MTI College of Business and Technology

Houston, Texas
www.mti-tex.com
Two-year proprietary **Federal Code: 015823**

College costs. Cost of full associate degree programs (17 months) ranges from $18,500 to $21,500; 13.5-month diploma program $17,200; 7-month certificate program $7,400. Books and other fees included.

Application procedures. FAFSA required.

Contact. 7277 Regency Square Boulevard
Houston, TX 77036

MTI College of Business and Technology

Houston, Texas
www.mti-tex.com
Two-year proprietary **Federal Code: 022452**

College costs. Cost of full associate degree programs (17 months) ranges from $18,500 to $21,500; 13.5-month diploma program $17,200, 7-month certificate $7,400. Books and other fees included.

Contact. 1275 Space Park Drive
Houston, TX 77058

McLennan Community College

Waco, Texas
www.mclennan.edu
Two-year public **Federal Code: 003590**

	Living at home
Tuition and fees (2002-2003):	$1,410
Out-of-district:	$1,560
Out-of-state:	$3,210
Per-credit charge:	$34
Per-credit out-of-district:	$39
Per-credit out-of-state:	$94
Board only:	$1,854
Books and supplies:	$725
Personal expenses:	$1,596
Transportation:	$1,879

Undergraduate aid. Non-need-based: Scholarships based on athletics. **Additional information:** Individuals selected for Tartan Scholar's Program receive a prestigious academic scholarship.

Policies to reduce costs. Tuition/fee waivers for employees and their families. Credit/placement for qualifying scores on AP, CLEP examinations.

Payment plans. Credit card, installment payment.

Application procedures. FAFSA required. Priority date 6/1; no closing date. Applicants notified on rolling basis starting 5/1.

Contact. Financial aid office: (254) 299-8698
James Kubacak, Director of Financial Aid
1400 College Drive
Waco, TX 76708

McMurry University

Abilene, Texas
www.mcm.edu
Four-year private **Federal Code: 003591**

	Living at home	On-campus
Tuition and fees (projected):	$12,446	$12,446
Room and board:		$5,025
Board only:	$1,866	
Books and supplies:	$640	$640
Personal expenses:	$1,880	$1,880
Transportation:	$902	$650

Undergraduate aid. Need-based: Average financial aid package for full-time students was $13,061; for part-time $6,301. 57% awarded as scholarships/grants, 43% as loans/jobs. **Non-need-based:** 73% awarded as scholarships/grants, 27% as loans/jobs. Scholarships based on academics, art, music/drama, religious affiliation. **Student debt:** 58% of graduating class borrowed to fund education; average debt was $14,715.

Freshman aid. Need-based: Out of 322 full-time freshmen, 322 applied for aid; 244 were judged to have need; of these 244 received aid. Average package met 63% of need. 77 students had full need met. Average scholarship/grant was $9,687; average loan $2,775. **Non-need based:** 184 full-time freshmen with need received non-need scholarships; 76 without need received awards.

Policies to reduce costs. Tuition/fee waivers for senior citizens, family of clergy, employees and their families. Credit/placement for qualifying scores on AP, CLEP examinations. Work study available nights, weekends and for part-time students.

Payment plans. Credit card, installment payment.

Application procedures. FAFSA, institutional form required. Priority date 3/15; no closing date. Applicants notified on rolling basis starting 2/1, must reply within 3 week(s) of notification. **Transfers:** No deadline.

Contact. Financial aid office: (915) 793-4712
Kathyrn Martin, Director of Financial Aid
South 14th and Sayles Boulevard
Abilene, TX 79697-0001

Midland College

Midland, Texas
www.midland.edu
Two-year public **Federal Code: 009797**

	Living at home	On-campus
Tuition and fees (projected):	$1,260	$1,260
Out-of-district:	$1,320	$1,320
Out-of-state:	$1,920	$1,920
Per-credit charge:	$36	$36
Per-credit out-of-district:	$38	$38
Per-credit out-of-state:	$58	$58
Room and board:		$3,260
Board only:	$1,340	
Books and supplies:	$666	$666
Personal expenses:	$1,450	$1,450
Transportation:	$1,223	$1,223

Undergraduate aid. Need-based: Need-based aid available for full-time and part-time students. **Non-need-based:** Scholarships based on academics, state/district residency.

Merit scholarships. Abell-Hangar Foundations Scholarships; varying amounts; renewable; available for full-time or part-time study to any Midland High, Midland Lee, or Greenwood High School graduate.

Policies to reduce costs. Tuition/fee waivers for senior citizens, employees and their families. Credit/placement for qualifying scores on AP, CLEP examinations.

Payment plans. Credit card, installment, deferred payment.

Application procedures. FAFSA required. Priority date 5/1; no closing date. Applicants notified on rolling basis starting 5/15, must reply within 2 week(s) of notification. **Transfers:** Priority date 5/1; no deadline.

Contact. **Financial aid office:** (432) 685-4733
Leticia Williams, Director of Financial Aid
3600 North Garfield
Midland, TX 79705

Midwestern State University

Wichita Falls, Texas
www.mwsu.edu
Four-year public **Federal Code: 003592**

	Living at home	On-campus
Tuition and fees (2002-2003):	$4,808	$4,808
Out-of-state:	$11,348	$11,348
Room and board:		$4,434
Board only:	$1,803	
Books and supplies:	$900	$900
Personal expenses:	$1,090	$1,090
Transportation:	$1,016	$1,016

Undergraduate aid. Need-based: Need-based aid available for full-time and part-time students.

Policies to reduce costs. Credit/placement for qualifying scores on AP, CLEP examinations. Work study available for part-time students.

Payment plans. Credit card, installment, deferred payment.

Application procedures. FAFSA, institutional form required. Priority date 6/1; no closing date. Applicants notified on rolling basis starting 3/1, must reply within 2 week(s) of notification.

Contact. **Financial aid office:** (940) 397-4214
Kathy Pennartz, Director of Financial Aid
3410 Taft Boulevard
Wichita Falls, TX 76308

Mountain View College

Dallas, Texas
www.mvc.dcccd.edu
Two-year public **Federal Code: 008503**

	Living at home
Tuition and fees (2002-2003):	$780
Out-of-district:	$1,380
Out-of-state:	$2,280
Per-credit charge:	$26
Per-credit out-of-district:	$46
Per-credit out-of-state:	$76
Books and supplies:	$800
Personal expenses:	$1,045
Transportation:	$1,330

Undergraduate aid. Non-need-based: Scholarships based on academics.

Policies to reduce costs. Tuition/fee waivers for adults, senior citizens, employees and their families. Credit/placement for qualifying scores on AP, CLEP examinations.

Payment plans. Credit card, installment payment.

Application procedures. FAFSA, institutional form required. Priority date 5/1; no closing date. Applicants notified on rolling basis starting 6/1.

Contact. **Financial aid office:** (214) 860-8688
Glenda Hall, Director of Financial Aid
4849 West Illinois Avenue
Dallas, TX 75211

North Central Texas College

Gainesville, Texas
www.nctc.edu
Two-year public **Federal Code: 003558**

	Living at home	On-campus
Tuition and fees (2002-2003):	$900	$900
Out-of-district:	$1,380	$1,380
Out-of-state:	$2,100	$2,100
Per-credit charge:	$30	$30
Per-credit out-of-district:	$46	$46
Per-credit out-of-state:	$70	$70
Room and board:		$2,800
Board only:	$1,500	
Books and supplies:	$1,050	$1,050
Personal expenses:	$1,300	$1,300
Transportation:	$1,200	$920

Undergraduate aid. All financial aid based on need. Need-based aid available for full-time and part-time students.

Policies to reduce costs. Tuition/fee waivers for employees and their families. Credit/placement for qualifying scores on AP, CLEP examinations. Work study available nights and for part-time students.

Payment plans. Credit card, installment payment.

Application procedures. FAFSA required. Priority date 5/1; no closing date. Applicants notified on rolling basis starting 6/1, must reply within 4 week(s) of notification.

Contact. Janet Dragoo, Director of Financial Aid
1525 West California
Gainesville, TX 76240

North Harris Montgomery Community College District

Houston, Texas
www.nhmccd.cc.edu
Two-year public **Federal Code: 011145**

	Living at home
Tuition and fees (2002-2003):	$1,014
Out-of-district:	$2,214
Out-of-state:	$2,664
Per-credit charge:	$28
Per-credit out-of-district:	$68
Per-credit out-of-state:	$83
Board only:	$1,800
Books and supplies:	$600
Personal expenses:	$1,000
Transportation:	$1,480

Undergraduate aid. Need-based: 86% awarded as scholarships/grants, 14% as loans/jobs. **Non-need-based:** Scholarships based on academics.

Policies to reduce costs. Tuition/fee waivers for senior citizens, employees and their families. Credit/placement for qualifying scores on AP, CLEP examinations.

Payment plans. Credit card, installment payment.

Application procedures. FAFSA, institutional form required. Priority date 4/15; no closing date. Applicants notified on rolling basis starting 7/1. **Transfers:** Priority date 4/15; no deadline.

Contact. Financial aid office: (281) 260-3588
Donna Smith, Director of Financial Aid and Scholarships
250 North Sam Houston Parkway East
Houston, TX 77060-2000

North Lake College

Irving, Texas
nlc.dcccd.edu
Two-year public **Federal Code: 014036**

	Living at home
Tuition and fees (2002-2003):	$780
Out-of-district:	$1,380
Out-of-state:	$2,280
Per-credit charge:	$26
Per-credit out-of-district:	$46
Per-credit out-of-state:	$76
Books and supplies:	$600

Undergraduate aid. Need-based: 88% awarded as scholarships/grants, 12% as loans/jobs. Need-based aid available for part-time students. **Non-need-based:** 12% awarded as scholarships/grants, 88% as loans/jobs.

Policies to reduce costs. Tuition/fee waivers for senior citizens, employees and their families. Credit/placement for qualifying scores on CLEP examinations.

Payment plans. Credit card, deferred payment.

Application procedures. FAFSA required. Priority date 5/1; no closing date. Applicants notified on rolling basis.

Contact. Financial aid office: (972) 273-3321
Paul Felix, Director of Financial Aid
5001 North MacArthur Boulevard
Irving, TX 75038-3899

Northeast Texas Community College

Mount Pleasant, Texas
www.ntcc.cc.tx.us
Two-year public **Federal Code: 016396**

	Living at home	On-campus
Tuition and fees (2002-2003):	$1,194	$1,194
Out-of-district:	$1,644	$1,644
Out-of-state:	$1,944	$1,944
Per-credit charge:	$18	$18
Per-credit out-of-district:	$33	$33
Per-credit out-of-state:	$43	$43
Room and board:		$2,900
Books and supplies:	$600	$600
Personal expenses:	$1,477	$1,477
Transportation:	$1,272	$1,272

Undergraduate aid. Need-based: Need-based aid available for full-time and part-time students. **Non-need-based:** Scholarships based on academics, art, athletics, job skills, music/drama, state/district residency.

Policies to reduce costs. Tuition/fee waivers for senior citizens, employees and their families. Credit/placement for qualifying scores on CLEP examinations.

Payment plans. Credit card, installment payment.

Application procedures. FAFSA, institutional form required. Priority date 6/1; no closing date. Applicants notified on rolling basis starting 6/1.

Contact. Financial aid office: (903) 572-1911 ext. 207
Patricia Durst, Director of Financial Aid
Box 1307
Mount Pleasant, TX 75456-1307

Northwest Vista College

San Antonio, Texas
www.accd.edu
Two-year public **Federal Code: 033723**

	Living at home
Tuition and fees (2002-2003):	$1,118
Out-of-district:	$1,883
Out-of-state:	$3,473
Per-credit charge:	$30
Per-credit out-of-district:	$56
Per-credit out-of-state:	$109
Board only:	$1,122
Books and supplies:	$900
Personal expenses:	$1,561
Transportation:	$1,225

Undergraduate aid. Need-based: Need-based aid available for full-time and part-time students. **Non-need-based:** Scholarships based on academics, leadership.

Policies to reduce costs. Tuition/fee waivers for senior citizens, employees and their families. Work study available nights, weekends and for part-time students.

Payment plans. Credit card, installment payment.

Application procedures. FAFSA required. Priority date 4/1; no closing date. Applicants notified on rolling basis, must reply within 2 week(s) of notification. **Transfers:** Priority date 4/1; no deadline.

Contact. Financial aid office: (210) 348-2100
Noe Ortiz, Financial Aid Director
3535 North Ellison Drive
San Antonio, TX 78251

Northwood University: Texas Campus

Cedar Hill, Texas
www.northwood.edu
Four-year private **Federal Code: 013040**

	Living at home	On-campus
Tuition and fees (2002-2003):	$13,461	$13,461
Room and board:		$5,788
Board only:	$2,823	
Books and supplies:	$1,107	$1,107
Personal expenses:	$1,774	$1,774
Transportation:	$1,950	$1,275

Undergraduate aid. Need-based: Average financial aid package for full-time students was $11,334; for part-time $2,630. 63% awarded as scholarships/grants, 37% as loans/jobs. **Non-need-based:** 60% awarded as scholarships/grants, 40% as loans/jobs. Scholarships based on academics, alumni affiliation, athletics, state/district residency. **Student debt:** 73% of graduating class borrowed to fund education; average debt was $18,487.

Freshman aid. Need-based: Out of 218 full-time freshmen, 196 applied for aid; 174 were judged to have need; of these 174 received aid. Average package met 66% of need. 34 students had full need met. Average scholarship/grant was $7,680; average loan $2,695. **Non-need based:** 165 full-time freshmen with need received non-need scholarships; 3 received athletic scholarships.

Merit scholarships. Merit Scholarships; $3,000 - $5,000; unlimited number awarded; all based on test scores and GPA.

Policies to reduce costs. Tuition/fee waivers for children of alumni, family members, employees and their families. Credit/placement for qualifying scores on AP, IB, CLEP examinations. Work study available nights, weekends and for part-time students.

Payment plans. Installment payment.

Application procedures. FAFSA required. No deadline. Applicants notified on rolling basis starting 4/1, must reply within 2 week(s) of notification. **Transfers:** No deadline.

Contact. Michael Rhodes, Director of Traditional Financial Aid
1114 West FM 1382
Cedar Hill, TX 75104

Odessa College

Odessa, Texas
www.odessa.edu
Two-year public **Federal Code: 003596**

	Living at home	On-campus
Tuition and fees:	$1,042	$1,042
Out-of-district:	$1,342	$1,342
Out-of-state:	$1,642	$1,642
Per-credit charge:	$22	$22
Per-credit out-of-district:	$32	$32
Per-credit out-of-state:	$42	$42
Room and board:		$2,900
Board only:	$1,781	
Books and supplies:	$800	$800
Personal expenses:	$996	$996
Transportation:	$856	$646

Policies to reduce costs. Credit/placement for qualifying scores on AP, CLEP examinations.

Payment plans. Credit card, deferred payment.

Application procedures. FAFSA required. Priority date 5/1; no closing date. Applicants notified on rolling basis starting 6/15.

Contact. Financial aid office: (915) 335-6429
Tanya Hughes, Director of Financial Aid
201 West University
Odessa, TX 79764-7127

Our Lady of the Lake University of San Antonio

San Antonio, Texas
www.ollusa.edu
Four-year private **Federal Code: 003598**

	Living at home	On-campus
Tuition and fees (2002-2003):	$13,842	$13,842
Room and board:		$4,862
Books and supplies:	$720	$720
Personal expenses:	$1,570	$1,730
Transportation:	$1,020	$816

Undergraduate aid. Non-need-based: Scholarships based on academics, alumni affiliation, art, music/drama.

Merit scholarships. General Academic; 1,205 awarded yearly (renewable); Art/fine arts and music; 4 awarded yearly (renewable); Children of faculty/staff; 60 awarded yearly (renewable). All based on GPA scores and high school record.

Policies to reduce costs. Tuition/fee waivers for employees and their families. Credit/placement for qualifying scores on AP, CLEP examinations.

Payment plans. Credit card, installment payment.

Application procedures. FAFSA required. No deadline. Applicants notified on rolling basis starting 2/15, must reply within 3 week(s) of notification. **Transfers:** Priority date 2/15; no deadline.

Contact. Guadalupe Valdez, Director of Financial Aid
411 Southwest 24th Street
San Antonio, TX 78207-4689

Palo Alto College

San Antonio, Texas
www.accd.edu
Two-year public **Federal Code: 016615**

	Living at home
Tuition and fees (2002-2003):	$1,118
Out-of-district:	$1,883
Out-of-state:	$3,473
Per-credit charge:	$30
Per-credit out-of-district:	$56
Per-credit out-of-state:	$109
Books and supplies:	$500

Undergraduate aid. All financial aid based on need. Need-based aid available for full-time and part-time students.

Policies to reduce costs. Credit/placement for qualifying scores on CLEP examinations.

Payment plans. Credit card, installment payment.

Application procedures. FAFSA required. Priority date 3/31; closing date 6/1. Applicants notified on rolling basis starting 5/31.

Contact. Financial aid office: (210) 921-5316
Lamar Duarte, Director of Financial Aid
1400 West Villaret
San Antonio, TX 78224

Panola College

Carthage, Texas
www.panola.edu
Two-year public **Federal Code: 003600**

	Living at home	On-campus
Tuition and fees:	$1,170	$1,170
Out-of-district:	$1,860	$1,860
Out-of-state:	$2,250	$2,250
Per-credit charge:	$21	$21
Per-credit out-of-district:	$44	$44
Per-credit out-of-state:	$57	$57
Room and board:		$3,090
Board only:	$2,000	
Books and supplies:	$650	$650
Personal expenses:	$1,500	$1,200
Transportation:	$1,200	$975

Undergraduate aid. Need-based: Average financial aid package for full-time students was $6,000; for part-time $2,000. 98% awarded as scholarships/grants, 2% as loans/jobs. **Non-need-based:** 96% awarded as scholarships/grants, 4% as loans/jobs. Scholarships based on academics, art, athletics, leadership, music/drama.

Freshman aid. Need-based: Average package met 85% of need. Average scholarship/grant was $500.

Policies to reduce costs. Tuition/fee waivers for senior citizens, employees and their families. Credit/placement for qualifying scores on AP, CLEP examinations. Work study available nights, weekends and for part-time students.

Payment plans. Credit card, deferred payment.

Application procedures. FAFSA, institutional form required. Priority date 6/1; no closing date. Applicants notified on rolling basis starting 2/1, must reply within 1 week(s) of notification. **Transfers:** Priority date 6/1; no deadline.

Contact. Financial aid office: (903) 693-2039
Tommy Young, Financial Aid Director
1109 West Panola Street
Carthage, TX 75633

Paris Junior College

Paris, Texas
paris.cc.tx.us
Two-year public **Federal Code: 003601**

	Living at home	On-campus
Tuition and fees (projected):	$1,170	$1,170
Out-of-district:	$1,740	$1,740
Out-of-state:	$2,640	$2,640
Per-credit charge:	$32	$32
Per-credit out-of-district:	$50	$50
Per-credit out-of-state:	$80	$80
Room and board:		$3,210
Books and supplies:	$400	$400

Undergraduate aid. Need-based: Need-based aid available for full-time and part-time students. **Non-need-based:** Scholarships based on athletics, music/drama.

Policies to reduce costs. Tuition/fee waivers for senior citizens, employees and their families. Credit/placement for qualifying scores on CLEP examinations.

Application procedures. FAFSA required. Priority date 6/1; no closing date. Applicants notified on rolling basis starting 6/1.

Contact. Linda Slawson, Director of Financial Aid
2400 Clarksville Street
Paris, TX 75460

Paul Quinn College

Dallas, Texas
www.pqc.edu
Four-year private **Federal Code: 003602**

	Living at home	On-campus
Tuition and fees:	$5,200	$5,200
Room and board:		$3,800
Books and supplies:	$800	$800
Personal expenses:	$350	$500
Transportation:	$400	$700

Policies to reduce costs. Tuition/fee waivers for minority students, family members, employees and their families.

Payment plans. Installment payment.

Application procedures. FAFSA, institutional form required. No deadline. Applicants notified on rolling basis starting 7/15, must reply by 5/1 or within 2 week(s) of notification. **Transfers:** Priority date 5/1.

Contact. Victoria Carson, Director of Financial Aid
3837 Simpson Stuart Road
Dallas, TX 75241

Prairie View A&M University

Prairie View, Texas
www.pvamu.edu
Four-year public **Federal Code: 003630**

	Living at home	On-campus
Tuition and fees (2002-2003):	$3,304	$3,304
Out-of-state:	$9,844	$9,844
Room and board:		$5,810
Board only:	$2,031	
Books and supplies:	$730	$730
Personal expenses:	$1,998	$1,813
Transportation:	$3,037	$2,611

Undergraduate aid. Need-based: Average financial aid package for full-time students was $6,920. 36% awarded as scholarships/grants, 64% as loans/jobs. Need-based aid available for part-time students. **Non-need-based:** 5% awarded as scholarships/grants, 95% as loans/jobs. Scholarships based on academics, athletics. **Student debt:** 75% of graduating class borrowed to fund education; average debt was $20,000.

Freshman aid. Need-based: Out of 994 full-time freshmen, 951 applied for aid; 888 were judged to have need; of these 888 received aid. Average package met 75% of need. Average scholarship/grant was $3,300; average loan $2,625. **Non-need based:** 301 full-time freshmen with need received non-need scholarships; 93 without need received awards; 15 received athletic scholarships.

Policies to reduce costs. Tuition/fee waivers for senior citizens, employees and their families. Credit/placement for qualifying scores on AP, CLEP examinations. Work study available nights and weekends.

Payment plans. Credit card, installment, deferred payment.

Application procedures. FAFSA, institutional form required. Closing date 4/1. Applicants notified by 6/1, must reply by 8/1. **Transfers:** Priority date 4/1. Minimum 2.0 GPA from all colleges attended required to be considered for financial aid.

Contact. A. D. James, Executive Director of Financial Aid
Box 3089
Prairie View, TX 77446-0188

Ranger College

Ranger, Texas
www.ranger.cc.tx.us
Two-year public **Federal Code: 003603**

College costs. Additional fees: $20 per year required fee for out-of-district and out-of-state students;$50 nonrefundable dorm reservation fee for dorm residents; $10 testing fee for vocational nursing applicants.

	Living at home	On-campus
Tuition and fees (2002-2003):	$1,210	$1,210
Out-of-state:	$1,390	$1,390
Per-credit charge:	$28	$28
Per-credit out-of-state:	$34	$34
Room and board:		$2,810
Books and supplies:	$450	$450
Personal expenses:	$810	$810
Transportation:	$1,200	$1,000

Policies to reduce costs. Credit/placement for qualifying scores on CLEP examinations.

Payment plans. Installment payment.

Application procedures. FAFSA, institutional form required. Closing date 7/24. Applicants notified on rolling basis, must reply within 2 week(s) of notification.

Contact. Donny Purvis, Financial Aid Director
College Circle
Ranger, TX 76470

Remington College: Dallas

Garland, Texas
www.educationamerica.com
Two-year proprietary **Federal Code: 030121**

College costs (2002-2003). Tuition for full 18-month associate programs: $24,885 for most programs, $14,250 for business technology. Tuition for 8-month diploma program in medical assisting $8,500. Registration fee $50. Books and supplies included. Personal expenses: $3,360.

Contact. 1800 Eastgate Drive
Garland, TX 75041

Remington College: Houston

Houston, Texas
www.educationamerica.com
Two-year proprietary **Federal Code: E00672**

College costs (2002-2003). Cost of tuition, books, tools and lab fees for all full associate programs (18 months): $25,872. Medical assisting diploma program (8 months): $9,240. Registration fee $50. Board: $2,817. Personal expenses: $1,764. Transportation: $1,935.

Undergraduate aid. Need-based: Need-based aid available for full-time and part-time students. **Non-need-based:** Scholarships based on state/district residency.

Policies to reduce costs. Tuition/fee waivers for employees and their families. Tuition at time of enrollment guaranteed for 2 years. Work study available nights.

Payment plans. Credit card, installment payment.

Application procedures. FAFSA, institutional form required. No deadline. Applicants notified on rolling basis. **Transfers:** No deadline.

Contact. Jill Brown, Director, Financial Services
3110 Hayes Road, 380
Houston, TX 77082

Rice University

Houston, Texas
www.rice.edu
Four-year private **Federal Code: 003604**

	Living at home	On-campus
Tuition and fees (2002-2003):	$18,316	$18,316
Room and board:		$7,480
Board only:	$2,980	
Books and supplies:	$600	$600
Personal expenses:	$1,550	$1,550
Transportation:	$950	$300

Undergraduate aid. Need-based: Average financial aid package for full-time students was $15,498. 82% awarded as scholarships/grants, 18% as loans/jobs. Need-based aid available for part-time students. **Non-need-based:** 69% awarded as scholarships/grants, 31% as loans/jobs. Scholarships based on academics, alumni affiliation, art, athletics, leadership, music/drama, state/district residency. **Student debt:** 62% of graduating class borrowed to fund education; average debt was $12,705. **Additional information:** Freshman tuition guaranteed not to increase beyond rate of inflation up to 6 years at Rice. Subsequent raises in tuition do not affect students already enrolled. Loan portion of financial aid packages capped at $2,475 for each year of student's enrollment (up to 4 years).

Freshman aid. Need-based: Out of 700 full-time freshmen, 456 applied for aid; 222 were judged to have need; of these 222 received aid. Average package met 100% of need. 222 students had full need met. Average scholarship/grant was $13,209; average loan $2,368. **Non-need based:** 130 full-time freshmen with need received non-need scholarships; 201 without need received awards; 69 received athletic scholarships.

Policies to reduce costs. Tuition/fee waivers for employees and their families. Credit/placement for qualifying scores on AP, IB examinations. Work study available nights and weekends.

Payment plans. Installment, deferred payment.

Application procedures. FAFSA, CSS PROFILE required. Priority date 3/1; no closing date. Applicants notified by 4/15, must reply by 5/1. Early decision closing date 11/1. **Transfers:** Closing date 4/1.

Contact. Financial aid office: (713) 348-4958
Julia Benz, Director, Student Financial Services
6100 Main Street, MS17
Houston, TX 77251-1892

Richland College

Dallas, Texas
www.rlc.dcccd.edu
Two-year public **Federal Code: 008504**

	Living at home
Tuition and fees (2002-2003):	$780
Out-of-district:	$1,380
Out-of-state:	$2,280
Per-credit charge:	$26
Per-credit out-of-district:	$46
Per-credit out-of-state:	$76
Books and supplies:	$350
Personal expenses:	$935

Undergraduate aid. Need-based: 72% awarded as scholarships/grants, 28% as loans/jobs. Need-based aid available for part-time students. **Non-need-based:** Scholarships based on art, leadership, music/drama.

Policies to reduce costs. Tuition/fee waivers for senior citizens, employees and their families. Credit/placement for qualifying scores on AP, CLEP examinations. Work study available nights and for part-time students.

Payment plans. Credit card, installment payment.

Application procedures. FAFSA required. Priority date 5/2; no closing date. Applicants notified on rolling basis starting 6/1, must reply within 2 week(s) of notification.

Contact. Financial aid office: (972) 238-6188
David Ximenez, Director of Financial Aid
12800 Abrams Road
Dallas, TX 75243-2199

St. Edward's University

Austin, Texas
www.stedwards.edu
Four-year private **Federal Code: 003621**

	Living at home	On-campus
Tuition and fees:	$14,710	$14,710
Room and board:		$6,018
Books and supplies:	$864	$864
Personal expenses:	$2,040	$2,040
Transportation:	$816	$816

Undergraduate aid. Need-based: Average financial aid package for full-time students was $10,873; for part-time $5,010. 60% awarded as scholarships/grants, 40% as loans/jobs. **Non-need-based:** 23% awarded as scholarships/grants, 77% as loans/jobs. Scholarships based on academics, alumni affiliation, art, athletics, job skills, leadership, music/drama, religious affiliation. **Student debt:** 62% of graduating class borrowed to fund education; average debt was $21,627.

Freshman aid. Need-based: Out of 448 full-time freshmen, 355 applied for aid; 275 were judged to have need; of these 274 received aid. Average package met 77% of need. 43 students had full need met. Average scholarship/grant was $8,741; average loan $2,712. **Non-need based:** 136 full-time freshmen with need received non-need scholarships; 33 without need received awards; 30 received athletic scholarships.

Merit scholarships. Full-time students can apply for university scholarships after completion of one fall semester at SEU. Awarded scholarships disbursed following year. Academic scholarships require 3.5 SEU GPA. Service scholarships require 2.75 GPA, significant community service involvement. Award amounts range from $500 to $6,000.

Policies to reduce costs. Tuition/fee waivers for employees and their families. Credit/placement for qualifying scores on AP, IB, CLEP examinations. Work study available for part-time students.

Payment plans. Credit card, installment, deferred payment.

Application procedures. FAFSA required. Priority date 4/15; no closing date. Applicants notified on rolling basis starting 2/1, must reply by 6/1 or within 2 week(s) of notification. **Transfers:** Priority date 4/15; no deadline.

Contact. **Financial aid office:** (512) 448-8520
Doris Constantine, Director of Student Financial Services
3001 South Congress Avenue
Austin, TX 78704

St. Mary's University

San Antonio, Texas
www.stmarytx.edu
Four-year private **Federal Code: 003623**

College costs. All students provided with a laptop, which is replaced with a new laptop junior year, as part of tuition.

	Living at home	On-campus
Tuition and fees:	$16,492	$16,492
Room and board:		$5,952
Board only:	$2,155	
Books and supplies:	$1,500	$1,500
Personal expenses:	$1,177	$1,177
Transportation:	$600	$600

Undergraduate aid. Need-based: Average financial aid package for full-time students was $12,207; for part-time $5,310. 59% awarded as scholarships/grants, 41% as loans/jobs. **Non-need-based:** 67% awarded as scholarships/grants, 33% as loans/jobs. Scholarships based on academics, alumni affiliation, athletics, leadership, music/drama. **Student debt:** 81% of graduating class borrowed to fund education; average debt was $24,949.

Freshman aid. Need-based: Out of 667 full-time freshmen, 534 applied for aid; 481 were judged to have need; of these 481 received aid. Average package met 53% of need. 140 students had full need met. Average scholarship/grant was $6,744; average loan $3,426. **Non-need based:** 346 full-time freshmen with need received non-need scholarships; 52 without need received awards; 49 received athletic scholarships.

Policies to reduce costs. Tuition/fee waivers for employees and their families. Prepayment discount; credit/placement for qualifying scores on AP, CLEP examinations. Work study available nights and weekends.

Payment plans. Credit card, installment, deferred payment.

Application procedures. FAFSA required. Priority date 2/15; no closing date. Applicants notified on rolling basis starting 5/1, must reply within 2 week(s) of notification.

Contact. David Krause, Director of Financial Assistance
One Camino Santa Maria
San Antonio, TX 78228

St. Philip's College

San Antonio, Texas
www.accd.edu/spc
Two-year public **Federal Code: 003608**

	Living at home
Tuition and fees (2002-2003):	$1,118
Out-of-district:	$1,883
Out-of-state:	$3,473
Per-credit charge:	$30
Per-credit out-of-district:	$56
Per-credit out-of-state:	$109
Board only:	$1,350
Books and supplies:	$900
Personal expenses:	$2,185
Transportation:	$1,225

Undergraduate aid. Need-based: 70% awarded as scholarships/grants, 30% as loans/jobs. Need-based aid available for part-time students. **Non-need-based:** Scholarships based on academics.

Policies to reduce costs. Tuition/fee waivers for senior citizens, employees and their families. Credit/placement for qualifying scores on AP, CLEP examinations. Work study available nights, weekends and for part-time students.

Payment plans. Credit card, installment payment.

Application procedures. FAFSA required. Priority date 3/1; no closing date. Applicants notified on rolling basis starting 7/15.

Contact. **Financial aid office:** (210) 531-3272
Diego Bernal, Director of Financial Aid
1801 Martin Luther King Drive
San Antonio, TX 78203

Sam Houston State University

Huntsville, Texas
www.shsu.edu
Four-year public **Federal Code: 003606**

	Living at home	On-campus
Tuition and fees (2002-2003):	$3,382	$3,382
Out-of-state:	$9,922	$9,922
Room and board:		$4,090
Books and supplies:	$650	$650
Personal expenses:	$1,500	$1,500
Transportation:	$2,482	$1,176

Undergraduate aid. Need-based: Average financial aid package for full-time students was $552; for part-time $3,840. 51% awarded as scholarships/grants, 49% as loans/jobs. **Non-need-based:** 27% awarded as scholarships/grants, 73% as loans/jobs. Scholarships based on academics, athletics. **Student debt:** 52% of graduating class borrowed to fund education; average debt was $13,251.

Freshman aid. Need-based: Out of 1,606 full-time freshmen, 1,070 applied for aid; 74 were judged to have need; of these 711 received aid. Average scholarship/grant was $3,939; average loan $2,238. **Non-need based:** 279 full-time freshmen with need received non-need scholarships; 234 without need received awards; 58 received athletic scholarships.

Policies to reduce costs. Credit/placement for qualifying scores on AP, IB, CLEP examinations.

Payment plans. Credit card, installment payment.

Application procedures. FAFSA required. Priority date 3/31; closing date 5/31. Applicants notified on rolling basis starting 6/1, must reply within 4 week(s) of notification. **Transfers:** Priority date 3/31; closing date 5/31.

Contact. **Financial aid office:** (936) 294-1724
Patty Mabry, Director of Financial Aid
PO Box 2418
Huntsville, TX 77341-2418

San Antonio College

San Antonio, Texas
www.accd.edu/sac
Two-year public **Federal Code: 009163**

	Living at home
Tuition and fees (2002-2003):	$1,118
Out-of-district:	$1,883
Out-of-state:	$3,473
Per-credit charge:	$30
Per-credit out-of-district:	$56
Per-credit out-of-state:	$109
Books and supplies:	$800
Personal expenses:	$1,627
Transportation:	$1,500

Undergraduate aid. Need-based: 78% awarded as scholarships/grants, 22% as loans/jobs. **Non-need-based:** 3% awarded as scholarships/grants, 97% as loans/jobs. **Additional information:** Leveraging Educational Assistance Partnership (LEAP), public student incentive grant, towards excellence access and success grants (Texas and Texas II grants) available.

Policies to reduce costs. Credit/placement for qualifying scores on AP, CLEP examinations. Work study available nights, weekends and for part-time students.

Payment plans. Credit card payment.

Application procedures. Priority date 3/1; no closing date. Applicants notified by 7/1.

Contact. **Financial aid office:** (210) 733-2150
Tom Campos, Director of Student Financial Services
1300 San Pedro Avenue
San Antonio, TX 78212-4299

San Jacinto College: Central Campus

Pasadena, Texas
www.sjcd.cc.tx.us
Two-year public **Federal Code: 003609**

	Living at home
Tuition and fees (2002-2003):	$946
Out-of-district:	$1,486
Out-of-state:	$2,146
Per-credit charge:	$20
Per-credit out-of-district:	$38
Per-credit out-of-state:	$60
Board only:	$3,580
Books and supplies:	$830
Personal expenses:	$1,908
Transportation:	$1,418

Policies to reduce costs. Credit/placement for qualifying scores on CLEP examinations.

Application procedures. FAFSA, institutional form required. Priority date 6/1; no closing date. Applicants notified on rolling basis.

Contact. Elena Olivier, Financial Aid Director
8060 Spencer Highway
Pasadena, TX 77505-5999

Schreiner University

Kerrville, Texas
www.schreiner.edu
Four-year private **Federal Code: 003610**

	Living at home	On-campus
Tuition and fees (2002-2003):	$13,002	$13,002
Room and board:		$6,654
Board only:	$2,550	
Books and supplies:	$800	$800
Personal expenses:	$1,500	$1,500
Transportation:	$1,200	$1,200

Undergraduate aid. Need-based: Average financial aid package for full-time students was $12,528; for part-time $8,030. 65% awarded as scholarships/grants, 35% as loans/jobs. **Non-need-based:** 52% awarded as scholarships/grants, 48% as loans/jobs. Scholarships based on academics, alumni affiliation, art, job skills, leadership, music/drama, religious affiliation. **Student debt:** 68% of graduating class borrowed to fund education; average debt was $17,954.

Freshman aid. Need-based: Out of 205 full-time freshmen, 131 applied for aid; 117 were judged to have need; of these 117 received aid. Average package met 66% of need. 20 students had full need met. Average scholarship/grant was $9,689; average loan $2,196. **Non-need based:** 12 full-time freshmen with need received non-need scholarships; 14 without need received awards.

Merit scholarships. Awards for students with exceptional academic achievement and leadership abilities requiring 3.5 GPA and a 1100 SAT I or 24 ACT; 66 awarded after participation in the Schreiner Scholars program; partial and full tuition.

Policies to reduce costs. Tuition/fee waivers for employees and their families. Prepayment discount; credit/placement for qualifying scores on AP, IB, CLEP examinations.

Payment plans. Installment payment.

Application procedures. FAFSA, institutional form required. Priority date 4/1; no closing date. Applicants notified on rolling basis starting 12/15, must reply within 2 week(s) of notification. **Transfers:** Priority date 12/15. SAT I or ACT scores required for applicants transferring with fewer than 15 hours. Interviews required of applicants with less than 2.0 GPA.

Contact. Financial aid office: (800) 343-4919
Kevin Catron, Director of Financial Aid
2100 Memorial Boulevard
Kerrville, TX 78028-5697

South Plains College

Levelland, Texas
www.southplainscollege.edu
Two-year public **Federal Code: 003611**

	Living at home	On-campus
Tuition and fees:	$1,550	$1,550
Out-of-district:	$1,910	$1,910
Out-of-state:	$2,390	$2,390
Per-credit charge:	$26	$26
Per-credit out-of-district:	$38	$38
Per-credit out-of-state:	$54	$54
Room and board:		$2,600
Board only:	$800	
Books and supplies:	$580	$580
Personal expenses:	$1,100	$1,100
Transportation:	$700	$700

Undergraduate aid. Need-based: Need-based aid available for full-time and part-time students. **Non-need-based:** Scholarships based on academics, athletics.

Policies to reduce costs. Tuition/fee waivers for senior citizens. Credit/placement for qualifying scores on AP, CLEP examinations.

Payment plans. Credit card, installment payment.

Application procedures. FAFSA required. Priority date 6/10; no closing date. Applicants notified on rolling basis starting 6/30, must reply within 2 week(s) of notification. **Transfers:** Priority date 6/10; no deadline.

Contact. Jim Ann Batenhorst, Director of Financial Aid
1401 College Avenue
Levelland, TX 79336

South Texas Community College

McAllen, Texas
www.stcc.cc.tx.us
Two-year public **Federal Code: 031034**

	Living at home
Tuition and fees (2002-2003):	$1,447
Out-of-district:	$1,707
Out-of-state:	$3,365

Contact. PO Box 9701
McAllen, TX 78502-9701

Southern Methodist University

Dallas, Texas
www.smu.edu
Four-year private **Federal Code: 003613**

	Living at home	On-campus
Tuition and fees (2002-2003):	$21,942	$21,942
Room and board:		$7,954
Books and supplies:	$576	$576
Personal expenses:	$1,000	$1,100
Transportation:	$842	$126

Undergraduate aid. Need-based: Average financial aid package for full-time students was $20,885; for part-time $7,748. 73% awarded as scholarships/grants, 27% as loans/jobs. **Non-need-based:** 68% awarded as scholarships/grants, 32% as loans/jobs. Scholarships based on academics, art, athletics, leadership, music/drama, religious affiliation, state/district residency. **Student debt:** 47% of graduating class borrowed to fund education; average debt was $18,693.

Freshman aid. Need-based: Out of 1,380 full-time freshmen, 660 applied for aid; 505 were judged to have need; of these 505 received aid. Average package met 99% of need. 225 students had full need met. Average scholarship/grant was $13,764; average loan $2,546. **Non-need based:** 414 full-time freshmen with need received non-need scholarships; 554 without need received awards; 62 received athletic scholarships.

Policies to reduce costs. Tuition/fee waivers for family of clergy, employees and their families. Credit/placement for qualifying scores on AP, IB, CLEP examinations.

Payment plans. Installment, deferred payment.

Application procedures. FAFSA required. Priority date 2/1; no closing date. Applicants notified on rolling basis starting 3/15. **Transfers:** Priority date 4/1. Merit scholarships available for community college and senior institution honor transfers. Students entering without scholarship aid will receive need-based aid up to cost of tuition.

Contact. **Financial aid office:** (214) 768-2068
Michael Novak, Executive Director of Enrollment Services
Box 750296
Dallas, TX 75275-0296

Southwest Texas Junior College

Uvalde, Texas
www.swtjc.cc.tx.us
Two-year public **Federal Code: 003614**

	Living at home	On-campus
Tuition and fees (2002-2003):	$1,185	$1,185
Out-of-district:	$1,560	$1,560
Out-of-state:	$2,265	$2,265
Per-credit charge:	$24	$24
Per-credit out-of-district:	$37	$37
Per-credit out-of-state:	$60	$60
Room and board:		$2,320
Books and supplies:	$500	$500
Personal expenses:	$1,017	$745
Transportation:	$572	$710

Undergraduate aid. Need-based: Need-based aid available for full-time and part-time students.

Policies to reduce costs. Tuition/fee waivers for senior citizens. Credit/placement for qualifying scores on AP, CLEP examinations.

Application procedures. FAFSA required. Priority date 6/15; no closing date. Applicants notified on rolling basis starting 5/1, must reply within 2 week(s) of notification.

Contact. Ismael Talavera, Director of Financial Aid
Garner Field Road
Uvalde, TX 78801

Southwest Texas State University

San Marcos, Texas
www.swt.edu
Four-year public **Federal Code: 003615**

	Living at home	On-campus
Tuition and fees:	$4,016	$4,016
Out-of-state:	$11,096	$11,096
Room and board:		$5,310
Board only:	$2,808	
Books and supplies:	$750	$750
Personal expenses:	$1,650	$1,950
Transportation:	$1,020	$880

Undergraduate aid. Need-based: Average financial aid package for full-time students was $7,384; for part-time $6,134. 40% awarded as scholarships/grants, 60% as loans/jobs. **Non-need-based:** 26% awarded as scholarships/grants, 74% as loans/jobs. Scholarships based on academics, art, athletics, leadership, music/drama, state/district residency. **Student debt:** 55% of graduating class borrowed to fund education; average debt was $15,002.

Freshman aid. Need-based: Out of 2,434 full-time freshmen, 1,461 applied for aid; 947 were judged to have need; of these 913 received aid. Average package met 80% of need. 301 students had full need met. Average scholarship/grant was $4,707; average loan $2,251. **Non-need based:** 345 full-time freshmen with need received non-need scholarships; 387 without need received awards; 56 received athletic scholarships.

Merit scholarships. Roy and Joan C. Mitte Foundation Scholarships, $5,050, 25 awarded, based on National Merit Competition finalist/semi-finalist status or valedictorian/salutatorian of high school class, or in top 5% of graduating class; President's Endowed Scholarships, $1,000, 9 awarded, based on minimum ACT score of 24 or SAT score of 1000, rank in upper 25% of high school class; Freshmen Program Scholarships, $200-$700, 10 awarded, based on ACT/SAT scores, high school grades, high school leadership activities.

Policies to reduce costs. Tuition/fee waivers for employees and their families. Credit/placement for qualifying scores on AP, IB, CLEP examinations.

Payment plans. Credit card, installment payment.

Application procedures. FAFSA required. Priority date 4/1; no closing date. Applicants notified on rolling basis starting 5/1, must reply within 3 week(s) of notification.

Contact. **Financial aid office:** (512) 245-2315
Mariko Gomez, Director of Financial Aid
429 North Guadalupe Street
San Marcos, TX 78666-5709

Southwestern Adventist University

Keene, Texas
www.swau.edu
Four-year private **Federal Code: 003619**

	Living at home	On-campus
Tuition and fees:	$11,156	$11,156
Room and board:		$5,270
Board only:	$1,614	
Books and supplies:	$700	$700
Personal expenses:	$966	$1,040
Transportation:	$770	$780

Undergraduate aid. Need-based: Need-based aid available for full-time and part-time students. **Non-need-based:** Scholarships based on academics, athletics, leadership, music/drama.

Policies to reduce costs. Tuition/fee waivers for senior citizens, family members, employees and their families. Prepayment discount; credit/placement for qualifying scores on AP, IB, CLEP examinations.

Payment plans. Credit card, installment payment.

Application procedures. FAFSA, institutional form required. Priority date 3/15; no closing date. Applicants notified on rolling basis starting 4/15.

Contact. **Financial aid office:** (817) 645-3921 ext. 262
Patty Norwood, Financial Aid Director
Box 567
Keene, TX 76059

Southwestern Assemblies of God University

Waxahachie, Texas
www.sagu.edu
Four-year private **Federal Code: 003616**

	Living at home	On-campus
Tuition and fees (projected):	$8,400	$8,400
Room and board:		$4,770
Books and supplies:	$612	$612
Personal expenses:	$1,479	$1,479
Transportation:	$1,611	$1,275

Policies to reduce costs. Tuition/fee waivers for family members, family of clergy, employees and their families. Prepayment discount; credit/placement for qualifying scores on AP, CLEP examinations.

Payment plans. Credit card, installment payment.

Application procedures. FAFSA, institutional form required. Priority date 3/1; closing date 6/1. Applicants notified on rolling basis starting 6/1, must reply within 2 week(s) of notification.

Contact. Matt Dufrene, Director of Financial Aid
1200 Sycamore Street
Waxahachie, TX 75165

Southwestern University

Georgetown, Texas
www.southwestern.edu
Four-year private **Federal Code: 003620**

	Living at home	On-campus
Tuition and fees (2002-2003):	$17,570	$17,570
Room and board:		$6,240
Board only:	$1,700	
Books and supplies:	$700	$700
Personal expenses:	$1,000	$770
Transportation:	$400	$210

Undergraduate aid. Need-based: Average financial aid package for full-time students was $15,038. 67% awarded as scholarships/grants, 33% as loans/jobs. **Non-need-based:** 82% awarded as scholarships/grants, 18% as loans/jobs. Scholarships based on academics, art, music/drama, religious affiliation. **Student debt:** 48% of graduating class borrowed to fund education; average debt was $17,505. **Additional information:** Southwestern has instituted our STAR loan program, a family loan program combining the ability to borrow up to $22,500 annually with the benefit of a fixed, monthly payment plan. There are 2 types of STAR loans: Gold STAR, a subsidized program for students who ranked in top 10% of high school class or received Southwestern academic merit scholarship, and Silver STAR, an unsubsidized program.

Freshman aid. **Need-based:** Out of 342 full-time freshmen, 247 applied for aid; 190 were judged to have need; of these 190 received aid. Average package met 100% of need. 190 students had full need met. Average scholarship/grant was $12,116; average loan $3,008. **Non-need based:** 97 full-time freshmen with need received non-need scholarships; 87 without need received awards.

Merit scholarships. Southwestern offers 2 merit scholarships: University Scholar at $3,000 per year, and Southwestern Scholar at $5,000 per year. Students who meet criteria are guaranteed award if they apply by deadline. Competitive awards range from $7,500 per year to full tuition, room, and board.

Policies to reduce costs. Tuition/fee waivers for family of clergy, employees and their families. Credit/placement for qualifying scores on AP, IB, CLEP examinations. Work study available nights and weekends.

Payment plans. Installment, deferred payment.

Application procedures. FAFSA, institutional form required. Closing date 3/1. Applicants notified on rolling basis starting 2/15, must reply by 5/1. Early decision closing date 11/1. **Transfers:** Priority date 3/1; closing date 5/15.

Contact. **Financial aid office:** (512) 863-1259
James Gaeta, Director of Financial Aid
1001 East University Avenue
Georgetown, TX 78626

Stephen F. Austin State University

Nacogdoches, Texas
www.sfasu.edu
Four-year public **Federal Code: 003624**

College costs. Tuition for AR and LA residents: $3510 plus fees.

	Living at home	On-campus
Tuition and fees:	$3,433	$3,433
Out-of-state:	$10,513	$10,513
Room and board:		$4,800
Board only:	$600	
Books and supplies:	$840	$840
Personal expenses:	$1,309	$1,309
Transportation:	$1,361	$1,361

Undergraduate aid. **Need-based:** Average financial aid package for full-time students was $7,038; for part-time $4,522. 46% awarded as scholarships/grants, 54% as loans/jobs. **Non-need-based:** Scholarships based on academics, alumni affiliation, art, athletics, leadership, music/drama, state/district residency. **Student debt:** 59% of graduating class borrowed to fund education; average debt was $9,142.

Freshman aid. **Need-based:** Out of 1,961 full-time freshmen, 1,500 applied for aid; 1,037 were judged to have need; of these 1,019 received aid. Average package met 78% of need. 242 students had full need met. Average scholarship/grant was $4,698; average loan $2,028. **Non-need based:** 601 full-time freshmen with need received non-need scholarships; 227 without need received awards; 64 received athletic scholarships.

Merit scholarships. Academic Excellence Scholarship Program: $2,000 per year; rank in top 10% of high school class or top quartile class with 1100 SAT or 24 ACT; renewable with earned 3.5 GPA. Three Dugas full support scholarships: $4,000 per semester; active member of School of Honors (minimum 1220 SAT, 27 ACT or very good grades and high class standing; 3.25 GPA maintenance). Up to 11 University Scholars Program awards: $1,000 per semester; minimum 1220 SAT, 27 ACT; 3.0 GPA maintenance. One Student Foundation Association Leadership Scholarship: amounts vary; successful recipient has demonstrated leadership capabilities and academic achievement throughout high school career.

Policies to reduce costs. Credit/placement for qualifying scores on AP, IB, CLEP examinations.

Payment plans. Credit card, installment payment.

Application procedures. FAFSA, institutional form required. Priority date 4/1; closing date 4/15. Applicants notified on rolling basis starting 5/1, must reply within 2 week(s) of notification.

Contact. **Financial aid office:** (936) 468-2403
Mike O'Rear, Director of Financial Aid
Box 13051, SFA Station
Nacogdoches, TX 75962-3051

Sul Ross State University

Alpine, Texas
www.sulross.edu
Four-year public **Federal Code: 003625**

	Living at home	On-campus
Tuition and fees (2002-2003):	$3,032	$3,032
Out-of-state:	$9,572	$9,572
Room and board:		$3,850
Board only:	$1,862	
Books and supplies:	$678	$678
Personal expenses:	$1,214	$1,576
Transportation:	$969	$678

Undergraduate aid. **Need-based:** Average financial aid package for full-time students was $3,901; for part-time $2,929. 58% awarded as scholarships/grants, 42% as loans/jobs. **Non-need-based:** 50% awarded as scholarships/grants, 50% as loans/jobs. Scholarships based on academics, alumni affiliation, leadership. **Student debt:** 31% of graduating class borrowed to fund education; average debt was $2,885.

Freshman aid. **Need-based:** Out of 323 full-time freshmen, 260 applied for aid; 232 were judged to have need; of these 260 received aid. Average loan $3,300. **Non-need based:** 14 without need received awards.

Policies to reduce costs. Tuition/fee waivers for employees and their families. Credit/placement for qualifying scores on AP, CLEP examinations.

Payment plans. Installment payment.

Application procedures. FAFSA, institutional form required. Priority date 5/1; no closing date. Applicants notified on rolling basis starting 5/1, must reply within 2 week(s) of notification. **Transfers:** Priority date 5/1; no deadline.

Contact. **Financial aid office:** (915) 837-8055
Rowena Gallego, Director Student Financial Assistance
Box C-2
Alpine, TX 79832

Tarleton State University

Stephenville, Texas
Four-year public **Federal Code: 003631**

College costs. Reported costs are for main campus; required fees at Center/Fort Hood may vary.

	Living at home	On-campus
Tuition and fees (2002-2003):	$3,152	$3,152
Out-of-state:	$9,692	$9,692
Room and board:		$4,496
Books and supplies:	$719	$719
Personal expenses:	$1,094	$2,156
Transportation:	$506	$404

Undergraduate aid. **Need-based:** Average financial aid package for full-time students was $7,372; for part-time $4,692. 46% awarded as scholarships/grants, 54% as loans/jobs. **Non-need-based:** 31% awarded as scholarships/grants, 69% as loans/jobs. **Student debt:** 61% of graduating class borrowed to fund education; average debt was $17,667.

Freshman aid. **Need-based:** Out of 1,143 full-time freshmen, 736 applied for aid; 545 were judged to have need; of these 822 received aid. Average package met 55% of need. 450 students had full need met. Average scholarship/grant was $3,573; average loan $1,951. **Non-need based:** 269 full-time freshmen with need received non-need scholarships; 282 without need received awards; 48 received athletic scholarships.

Policies to reduce costs. Tuition/fee waivers for senior citizens, employees and their families. Credit/placement for qualifying scores on AP, CLEP examinations. Work study available for part-time students.

Payment plans. Credit card, installment payment.

Application procedures. FAFSA required. Priority date 4/1; no closing date. Applicants notified on rolling basis, must reply within 2 week(s) of notification. **Transfers:** No deadline.

Contact. **Financial aid office:** (254) 968-9070
Betty Murray, Director, Student Financial Aid
Box T-0030
Stephenville, TX 76402

Tarrant County College

Fort Worth, Texas
www.tccd.edu
Two-year public **Federal Code: 003626**

	Living at home
Tuition and fees (2002-2003):	$1,115
Out-of-district:	$1,475
Out-of-state:	$4,415
Per-credit charge:	$30
Per-credit out-of-district:	$42
Per-credit out-of-state:	$140
Board only:	$1,000
Books and supplies:	$1,100
Personal expenses:	$1,500
Transportation:	$1,800

Undergraduate aid. **Non-need-based:** Scholarships based on academics.

Policies to reduce costs. Tuition/fee waivers for employees and their families. Credit/placement for qualifying scores on AP, CLEP examinations.

Payment plans. Credit card, installment payment.

Application procedures. FAFSA, institutional form required. Priority date 4/15; no closing date. Applicants notified on rolling basis starting 3/1, must reply within 2 week(s) of notification.

Contact. Claire Roemer, Director of Financial Aid
1500 Houston Street
Fort Worth, TX 76102

Temple College

Temple, Texas
www.templejc.edu
Two-year public **Federal Code: 003627**

	Living at home
Tuition and fees (2002-2003):	$1,410
Out-of-district:	$2,130
Out-of-state:	$3,990
Per-credit charge:	$26
Per-credit out-of-district:	$50
Per-credit out-of-state:	$112
Board only:	$2,256
Books and supplies:	$850
Personal expenses:	$1,266
Transportation:	$1,298

Undergraduate aid. All financial aid based on need. Need-based aid available for full-time and part-time students.

Policies to reduce costs. Tuition/fee waivers for senior citizens, employees and their families. Credit/placement for qualifying scores on AP, IB, CLEP examinations. Work study available nights and for part-time students.

Payment plans. Credit card payment.

Application procedures. FAFSA required. Priority date 6/1; no closing date. Applicants notified on rolling basis starting 5/1, must reply within 4 week(s) of notification. **Transfers:** No deadline.

Contact. **Financial aid office:** (254) 298-8321
Lanette Wigginton, Director of Financial Aid
2600 South First Street
Temple, TX 76504-7435

Texarkana College

Texarkana, Texas
www.texarkanacollege.edu
Two-year public **Federal Code: 003628**

College costs. Arkansas and Oklahoma residents pay out-of-district rates. Out-of-state per-credit-hour charge varies depending on number of credits taken.

	Living at home
Tuition and fees:	$930
Out-of-district:	$1,380
Out-of-state:	$1,880
Per-credit charge:	$25
Per-credit out-of-district:	$38
Per-credit out-of-state:	$58
Books and supplies:	$750
Personal expenses:	$1,200
Transportation:	$750

Undergraduate aid. **Need-based:** 97% awarded as scholarships/grants, 3% as loans/jobs. Need-based aid available for part-time students. **Non-need-based:** Scholarships based on academics, athletics.

Policies to reduce costs. Tuition/fee waivers for senior citizens, employees and their families. Credit/placement for qualifying scores on AP, CLEP examinations. Work study available nights, weekends and for part-time students.

Payment plans. Credit card, installment payment.

Application procedures. FAFSA, institutional form required. Priority date 5/15; no closing date. Applicants notified on rolling basis starting 3/1. **Transfers:** No deadline.

Contact. Dawna Vise, Director of Financial Aid
2500 North Robison Road
Texarkana, TX 75599

Texas A&M International University

Laredo, Texas
www.tamiu.edu
Four-year public **Federal Code: 009651**

	Living at home	On-campus
Tuition and fees:	$3,301	$3,301
Out-of-state:	$10,381	$10,381
Room only:		$3,120
Board only:	$1,879	
Books and supplies:	$1,000	$1,000
Personal expenses:	$1,438	$2,027
Transportation:	$1,420	$813

Undergraduate aid. **Need-based:** Need-based aid available for full-time and part-time students. **Non-need-based:** Scholarships based on academics. **Additional information:** 80 percent of all students receive aid.

Policies to reduce costs. Tuition/fee waivers for senior citizens. Credit/placement for qualifying scores on AP, IB, CLEP examinations. Work study available nights and for part-time students.

Payment plans. Credit card, installment payment.

Application procedures. FAFSA, institutional form required. Priority date 3/15; no closing date. Applicants notified on rolling basis starting 7/15, must reply within 2 week(s) of notification.

Contact. **Financial aid office:** (956) 326-2225
Laura Elizondo, Director of Financial Aid
5201 University Boulevard
Laredo, TX 78041-1900

Texas A&M University

College Station, Texas
www.tamu.edu
Four-year public **Federal Code: 003632**

	Living at home	On-campus
Tuition and fees (2002-2003):	$4,748	$4,748
Out-of-state:	$11,288	$11,288
Room and board:		$6,030
Board only:	$2,757	
Books and supplies:	$802	$802
Personal expenses:	$1,522	$1,522
Transportation:	$532	$532

Undergraduate aid. Need-based: Average financial aid package for full-time students was $8,415; for part-time $6,241. 51% awarded as scholarships/grants, 49% as loans/jobs. **Non-need-based:** 24% awarded as scholarships/grants, 76% as loans/jobs. Scholarships based on academics, alumni affiliation, art, athletics, job skills, leadership, music/drama, state/district residency. **Student debt:** 29% of graduating class borrowed to fund education; average debt was $14,418. **Additional information:** Short-term loans available. Out-of-state students awarded academic scholarships of $1,000 or more are eligible for waiver of out-of-state tuition.

Freshman aid. Need-based: Out of 6,392 full-time freshmen, 3,383 applied for aid; 1,851 were judged to have need; of these 1,825 received aid. Average package met 71% of need. 1144 students had full need met. Average scholarship/grant was $7,238; average loan $2,484. **Non-need based:** 1,552 full-time freshmen with need received non-need scholarships; 1,309 without need received awards.

Policies to reduce costs. Tuition/fee waivers for senior citizens, employees and their families. Credit/placement for qualifying scores on AP, IB, CLEP examinations. Work study available nights, weekends and for part-time students.

Payment plans. Credit card, installment payment.

Application procedures. FAFSA, institutional form required. No deadline. Applicants notified on rolling basis starting 4/1, must reply within 4 week(s) of notification. **Transfers:** Must provide previous financial aid transcript.

Contact. Financial aid office: (979) 845-3236
Arnold Trejo, Executive Director of Student Financial Aid
PO Box 30014
College Station, TX 77842-3014

Texas A&M University-Commerce

Commerce, Texas
www.tamu-commerce.edu
Four-year public **Federal Code: 003565**

	Living at home	On-campus
Tuition and fees (2002-2003):	$3,224	$3,224
Out-of-state:	$9,764	$9,764
Room and board:		$4,786
Board only:	$980	
Books and supplies:	$900	$900
Personal expenses:	$1,470	$1,470
Transportation:	$1,170	$1,170

Undergraduate aid. Need-based: Average financial aid package for full-time students was $6,642; for part-time $4,846. 50% awarded as scholarships/grants, 50% as loans/jobs. **Student debt:** 62% of graduating class borrowed to fund education; average debt was $15,575. **Additional information:** Work-study also available for full-time students.

Freshman aid. Need-based: Out of 669 full-time freshmen, 523 applied for aid; 393 were judged to have need; of these 377 received aid. Average package met 72% of need. 120 students had full need met. Average scholarship/grant was $5,353; average loan $1,635. **Non-need based:** 181 without need received awards; 16 received athletic scholarships.

Policies to reduce costs. Tuition/fee waivers for senior citizens. Credit/placement for qualifying scores on AP, IB, CLEP examinations. Work study available for part-time students.

Payment plans. Credit card, installment, deferred payment.

Application procedures. FAFSA, institutional form required. Priority date 5/1; no closing date. Applicants notified on rolling basis starting 6/1, must reply within 2 week(s) of notification. **Transfers:** Closing date 10/1.

Contact. John Patton, Director of Financial Aid
Box 3011
Commerce, TX 75429-3011

Texas A&M University-Corpus Christi

Corpus Christi, Texas
www.tamucc.edu
Four-year public **Federal Code: 011161**

	Living at home	On-campus
Tuition and fees (2002-2003):	$3,418	$3,418
Out-of-state:	$9,958	$9,958
Room and board:		$7,020
Board only:	$1,753	
Books and supplies:	$600	$600
Personal expenses:	$965	$1,179
Transportation:	$1,286	$737

Undergraduate aid. Need-based: Average financial aid package for full-time students was $6,320; for part-time $4,840. 55% awarded as scholarships/grants, 45% as loans/jobs. **Non-need-based:** 17% awarded as scholarships/grants, 83% as loans/jobs. Scholarships based on academics, art, athletics, music/drama. **Student debt:** 33% of graduating class borrowed to fund education; average debt was $9,642.

Freshman aid. Need-based: Out of 1,001 full-time freshmen, 713 applied for aid; 506 were judged to have need; of these 481 received aid. Average package met 79% of need. 97 students had full need met. Average scholarship/grant was $4,395; average loan $2,322. **Non-need based:** 95 full-time freshmen with need received non-need scholarships; 118 without need received awards; 33 received athletic scholarships.

Policies to reduce costs. Tuition/fee waivers for senior citizens, employees and their families. Credit/placement for qualifying scores on AP, IB, CLEP examinations.

Payment plans. Credit card, installment, deferred payment.

Application procedures. FAFSA, institutional form required. Closing date 4/1. Applicants notified on rolling basis starting 5/1, must reply within 2 week(s) of notification.

Contact. Financial aid office: (361) 825-2338
Dalinda Zeriali, Financial Assistance Director
6300 Ocean Drive
Corpus Christi, TX 78412

Texas A&M University-Galveston

Galveston, Texas
www.tamug.edu
Four-year public **Federal Code: 003632**

	Living at home	On-campus
Tuition and fees (projected):	$3,642	$3,642
Out-of-state:	$10,888	$10,888
Room and board:		$4,692
Board only:	$2,014	
Books and supplies:	$896	$896
Personal expenses:	$1,020	$1,020
Transportation:	$846	$846

Undergraduate aid. Need-based: Average financial aid package for full-time students was $7,612. 49% awarded as scholarships/grants, 51% as loans/jobs. Need-based aid available for part-time students. **Non-need-based:** 7% awarded as scholarships/grants, 93% as loans/jobs. Scholarships based on academics, state/district residency. **Student debt:** 31% of graduating class borrowed to fund education; average debt was $7,885.

Freshman aid. Need-based: Out of 409 full-time freshmen, 253 applied for aid; 207 were judged to have need; of these 196 received aid. Average package met 73% of need. 97 students had full need met. Average scholarship/grant was $4,459; average loan $1,839. **Non-need based:** 50 full-time freshmen with need received non-need scholarships; 8 without need received awards.

Policies to reduce costs. Credit/placement for qualifying scores on AP, IB, CLEP examinations.

Payment plans. Installment payment.

Application procedures. FAFSA, institutional form required. Priority date 4/1; no closing date. Applicants notified on rolling basis starting 6/1, must reply within 2 week(s) of notification.

Contact. **Financial aid office:** (409) 740-4500
Dennis Carlton, Director of Financial Aid
PO Box 1675
Galveston, TX 77553-1675

Texas A&M University-Kingsville

Kingsville, Texas
www.tamuk.edu
Four-year public **Federal Code: 003639**

	Living at home	On-campus
Tuition and fees (projected):	$2,982	$2,982
Out-of-state:	$9,192	$9,192
Room and board:		$3,966
Board only:	$1,844	
Books and supplies:	$614	$614
Personal expenses:	$1,594	$2,108
Transportation:	$1,840	$1,476

Undergraduate aid. Need-based: Average financial aid package for full-time students was $6,500; for part-time $4,570. 30% awarded as scholarships/grants, 70% as loans/jobs. **Non-need-based:** Scholarships based on academics, leadership. **Student debt:** 46% of graduating class borrowed to fund education; average debt was $2,867.

Freshman aid. Need-based: Out of 1,532 full-time freshmen, 1,194 applied for aid; 987 were judged to have need; of these 987 received aid. Average package met 82% of need. 692 students had full need met. Average scholarship/grant was $6,625; average loan $3,875. **Non-need based:** 304 full-time freshmen with need received non-need scholarships.

Policies to reduce costs. Tuition/fee waivers for senior citizens, employees and their families. Credit/placement for qualifying scores on AP, CLEP examinations.

Payment plans. Credit card, installment payment.

Application procedures. FAFSA required. Applicants notified on rolling basis.

Contact. **Financial aid office:** (361) 593-3911
Arturo Pecos, Director of Financial Aid Programs
MSC 105
Kingsville, TX 78363-8201

Texas A&M University-Texarkana

Texarkana, Texas
www.tamut.edu
Upper-division public **Federal Code: 031703**

	Living at home
Tuition and fees (2002-2003):	$2,502
Out-of-state:	$9,042
Books and supplies:	$860
Personal expenses:	$1,488
Transportation:	$1,864

Undergraduate aid. All financial aid based on need. Need-based aid available for full-time and part-time students.

Policies to reduce costs. Tuition/fee waivers for senior citizens. Credit/placement for qualifying scores on CLEP examinations.

Payment plans. Credit card, installment payment.

Application procedures. FAFSA, institutional form required. Priority date 5/1; closing date 11/1. Applicants notified on rolling basis, must reply within 6 week(s) of notification. **Transfers:** Priority date 5/1; closing date 11/1. Must have completed minimum of 54 semester hours of transferable college credit to apply for financial aid. Notified applicants must reply within 45 days from date of award letter. Exceptions made on individual basis. March 1 financial aid deadline for scholarships.

Contact. Marilyn Raney, Director of Financial Aid
2600 North Robinson Road
Texarkana, TX 75505

Texas A&M University: Baylor College of Dentistry

Dallas, Texas
www.tambcd.edu
Upper-division public **Federal Code: 004948**

College costs. Additional required fees: $2,289 for books, instruments and supplies.

	Living at home
Tuition and fees (2002-2003):	$4,028
Out-of-state:	$11,601
Board only:	$3,100
Personal expenses:	$2,700
Transportation:	$1,900

Undergraduate aid. Need-based: Average financial aid package for full-time students was $9,791. 23% awarded as scholarships/grants, 77% as loans/jobs. Need-based aid available for part-time students. **Non-need-based:** Scholarships based on academics. **Student debt:** 69% of graduating class borrowed to fund education; average debt was $27,197.

Application procedures. FAFSA, institutional form required. Priority date 3/15; no closing date. Applicants notified on rolling basis starting 6/1, must reply within 2 week(s) of notification. **Transfers:** Priority date 3/15; no deadline.

Contact. Kay Egbert, Director of Student Aid
PO Box 660677
Dallas, TX 75266-0677

Texas Christian University

Fort Worth, Texas
www.tcu.edu
Four-year private **Federal Code: 003636**

	Living at home	On-campus
Tuition and fees (2002-2003):	$16,340	$16,340
Room and board:		$5,302
Books and supplies:	$720	$720
Personal expenses:		$1,920
Transportation:		$600

Undergraduate aid. Need-based: Average financial aid package for full-time students was $12,268; for part-time $8,546. 52% awarded as scholarships/grants, 48% as loans/jobs. **Non-need-based:** 70% awarded as scholarships/grants, 30% as loans/jobs. Scholarships based on academics, art, athletics, leadership, music/drama, religious affiliation.

Freshman aid. Need-based: Out of 1,449 full-time freshmen, 852 applied for aid; 610 were judged to have need; of these 607 received aid. Average package met 73% of need. 318 students had full need met. Average scholarship/grant was $8,569; average loan $3,617. **Non-need based:** 160 full-time freshmen with need received non-need scholarships; 303 without need received awards; 50 received athletic scholarships.

Policies to reduce costs. Tuition/fee waivers for adults, family of clergy, employees and their families. Credit/placement for qualifying scores on AP, IB, CLEP examinations.

Payment plans. Credit card, installment payment.

Application procedures. FAFSA, institutional form required. Closing date 5/1. Applicants notified on rolling basis starting 3/1. **Transfers:** Priority date 6/1.

Contact. **Financial aid office:** (817) 257-7858
Michael Scott, Director of Scholarships and Student Financial Aid
TCU Box 297013
Fort Worth, TX 76129

Texas College

Tyler, Texas
www.texascollege.edu
Four-year private **Federal Code: 003638**

	Living at home	On-campus
Tuition and fees (2002-2003):	$5,930	$5,930
Room and board:		$2,930
Books and supplies:	$420	$420
Personal expenses:	$1,714	$1,714
Transportation:	$722	$628

Policies to reduce costs. Tuition/fee waivers for family of clergy, employees and their families. Work study available nights.

Payment plans. Credit card, installment, deferred payment.

Application procedures. FAFSA required. Priority date 4/1; no closing date. Applicants notified on rolling basis starting 5/1, must reply within 2 week(s) of notification. **Transfers:** Priority date 4/1.

Contact. **Financial aid office:** (903) 593-8311 ext. 2269
Lois Bowie, Financial Aid Officer
2404 North Grand Avenue
Tyler, TX 75712-4500

Texas Lutheran University

Seguin, Texas
www.tlu.edu
Four-year private **Federal Code: 003641**

	Living at home	On-campus
Tuition and fees (2002-2003):	$14,550	$14,550
Room and board:		$4,442
Board only:	$1,330	
Books and supplies:	$670	$670
Personal expenses:	$1,100	$1,100
Transportation:	$880	$728

Undergraduate aid. Need-based: Average financial aid package for full-time students was $13,991; for part-time $7,788. 71% awarded as scholarships/grants, 29% as loans/jobs. **Non-need-based:** 77% awarded as scholarships/grants, 23% as loans/jobs. Scholarships based on academics, alumni affiliation, art, athletics, job skills, leadership, music/drama, religious affiliation. **Student debt:** 60% of graduating class borrowed to fund education; average debt was $21,500.

Freshman aid. Need-based: Out of 371 full-time freshmen, 357 applied for aid; 239 were judged to have need; of these 239 received aid. Average package met 86% of need. 207 students had full need met. Average scholarship/grant was $13,952; average loan $3,380. **Non-need based:** 234 full-time freshmen with need received non-need scholarships; 117 without need received awards.

Merit scholarships. Pacesetter Award for College Excellence; 50 awarded; $22,000-$48,000; highly selective criteria. Janota Scholarship for Valedictorian/Salutatorian; 20 awarded; $22,000.

Policies to reduce costs. Tuition/fee waivers for children of alumni, employees and their families. Credit/placement for qualifying scores on AP, IB, CLEP examinations. Work study available nights, weekends and for part-time students.

Payment plans. Credit card, installment payment.

Application procedures. FAFSA required. Priority date 4/1; no closing date. Applicants notified on rolling basis starting 3/1, must reply within 2 week(s) of notification. **Transfers:** Priority date 4/1; no deadline.

Contact. **Financial aid office:** (830) 372-8075
Erma Nieto, Director of Financial Aid and Admission
1000 West Court Street
Seguin, TX 78155-5999

Texas Southern University

Houston, Texas
www.tsu.edu
Four-year public **Federal Code: 003642**

	Living at home	On-campus
Tuition and fees (2002-2003):	$2,630	$2,630
Out-of-state:	$8,960	$8,960
Room and board:		$4,500
Board only:	$1,500	
Books and supplies:	$500	$500
Personal expenses:	$1,700	$1,700
Transportation:	$1,400	$1,400

Undergraduate aid. All financial aid based on need. Average financial aid package for full-time students was $1,200; for part-time $1,200. **Student debt:** 64% of graduating class borrowed to fund education; average debt was $23,000.

Freshman aid. Out of 1,395 full-time freshmen, 1,263 applied for aid; 1,191 were judged to have need; of these 1,219 received aid. 410 students had full need met. Average scholarship/grant was $4,700; average loan $2,625.

Policies to reduce costs. Tuition/fee waivers for minority students. Credit/placement for qualifying scores on AP, CLEP examinations. Work study available nights, weekends and for part-time students.

Payment plans. Credit card, installment, deferred payment.

Application procedures. FAFSA required. Priority date 5/1; no closing date. Applicants notified on rolling basis starting 6/1. **Transfers:** Priority date 4/1; closing date 8/30.

Contact. **Financial aid office:** (713) 313-7802
Albert Tezno, Director of Financial Aid
3100 Cleburne Street
Houston, TX 77004

Texas State Technical College: Marshall

Marshall, Texas
www.marshall.tstc.edu
Two-year public

	Living at home
Tuition and fees (2002-2003):	$2,124
Out-of-state:	$5,244

Application procedures. FAFSA required. Priority date 6/1; no closing date.

Contact. 2400 East End Boulevard South
Marshall, TX 75672

Texas State Technical College: Waco

Waco, Texas
www.waco.tstc.edu
Two-year public **Federal Code: 003634**

	Living at home	On-campus
Tuition and fees (2002-2003):	$1,967	$1,967
Out-of-state:	$5,087	$5,087
Per-credit charge:	$48	$48
Per-credit out-of-state:	$152	$152
Room and board:		$4,301
Books and supplies:	$751	$751
Personal expenses:	$1,899	$1,899
Transportation:	$1,283	$731

Undergraduate aid. All financial aid based on need. Average financial aid package for full-time students was $7,436; for part-time $7,617. 45% awarded as scholarships/grants, 55% as loans/jobs. **Student debt:** 29% of graduating class borrowed to fund education; average debt was $8,200.

Freshman aid. Out of 1,440 full-time freshmen, 871 applied for aid; 835 were judged to have need; of these 784 received aid. Average package met 56% of need. 91 students had full need met. Average scholarship/grant was $3,536; average loan $2,416.

Policies to reduce costs. Credit/placement for qualifying scores on AP, IB, CLEP examinations. Work study available nights, weekends and for part-time students.

Payment plans. Credit card, installment payment.

Application procedures. FAFSA required. Priority date 6/1; no closing date. Applicants notified on rolling basis starting 5/15. **Transfers:** Priority date 6/1.

Contact. **Financial aid office:** (254) 867-4814
Jackie Adler, Director, Financial Aid
3801 Campus Drive
Waco, TX 76705

Texas State Technical College: West Texas

Sweetwater, Texas
www.sweetwater.tstc.edu
Two-year public **Federal Code: 009932**

	Living at home	On-campus
Tuition and fees (2002-2003):	$2,094	$2,094
Out-of-state:	$5,214	$5,214
Per-credit charge:	$48	$48
Per-credit out-of-state:	$152	$152
Room and board:		$3,200
Books and supplies:	$1,100	$1,100
Personal expenses:	$650	$650

Undergraduate aid. **Need-based:** Need-based aid available for full-time and part-time students. **Non-need-based:** Scholarships based on academics.

Policies to reduce costs. Tuition/fee waivers for senior citizens. Work study available nights, weekends and for part-time students.

Payment plans. Credit card, installment, deferred payment.

Application procedures. FAFSA, institutional form required. Priority date 5/1; no closing date. Applicants notified on rolling basis starting 7/1.

Contact. Greg Torres, Director of Financial Aid
300 College Drive
Sweetwater, TX 79556

Texas Tech University

Lubbock, Texas
www.ttu.edu
Four-year public **Federal Code: 003644**

	Living at home	On-campus
Tuition and fees (2002-2003):	$3,867	$3,867
Out-of-state:	$10,407	$10,407
Room and board:		$5,497
Books and supplies:	$800	$800
Personal expenses:	$1,180	$1,748
Transportation:	$1,367	$1,321

Undergraduate aid. **Need-based:** Average financial aid package for full-time students was $710; for part-time $4,412. 50% awarded as scholarships/grants, 50% as loans/jobs. **Non-need-based:** 31% awarded as scholarships/grants, 69% as loans/jobs. Scholarships based on academics, art, athletics, job skills, leadership, music/drama.

Freshman aid. **Need-based:** Out of 4,075 full-time freshmen, 2,538 applied for aid; 1,229 were judged to have need; of these 1,209 received aid. Average package met 57% of need. 136 students had full need met. Average scholarship/grant was $3,911; average loan $2,218. **Non-need based:** 79 full-time freshmen with need received non-need scholarships; 583 without need received awards; 52 received athletic scholarships.

Merit scholarships. Presidential Plus Scholarship; $10,000 per year up to 5 years; awarded to National Merit Finalists who select Texas Tech as school of choice. Texas Tech Select Scholarship; $1,000 per year up to 5 years (may be combined with other merit scholarship offers); awarded to National Merit Semi-Finalists who come to Texas Tech as freshmen. Presidential Endowed Scholarship; $4,000 per year for up to 5 years; awarded to incoming freshmen in top 10% of high school graduating class who score SAT composite 1400 or ACT 31. Honors Endowed Scholarship; $2,500 per year up to 5 years; awarded to incoming freshmen in top 10% of high school graduating class who score SAT composite 1300 or ACT 29. McFadden Scholars Scholarship (or University Scholars Scholarship); $1,500 per year up to 4 years; awarded to incoming freshmen in top 10% of high school graduating class who score a composite SAT 1250 or ACT 28. Superior Scholastic Achievement Scholarship; $1,000 per year up to four years; awarded to incoming freshmen in top 10% of high school graduating class who score composite SAT 1200 or ACT 26.

Policies to reduce costs. Credit/placement for qualifying scores on AP, IB, CLEP examinations.

Payment plans. Credit card, installment payment.

Application procedures. FAFSA, institutional form required. Priority date 3/1; no closing date. Applicants notified on rolling basis starting 3/1, must reply within 2 week(s) of notification. **Transfers:** Priority date 3/1.

Contact. **Financial aid office:** (806) 742-3681
Edwin Earl Hudgins, Director of Financial Aid
Box 45005
Lubbock, TX 79409-5005

Texas Wesleyan University

Fort Worth, Texas
www.txwesleyan.edu
Four-year private **Federal Code: 003645**

	Living at home	On-campus
Tuition and fees (2002-2003):	$11,276	$11,276
Room and board:		$3,990
Board only:	$3,166	
Books and supplies:	$675	$675
Personal expenses:	$1,590	$1,590
Transportation:	$796	$734

Undergraduate aid. All financial aid based on need. 54% awarded as scholarships/grants, 46% as loans/jobs. Need-based aid available for part-time students.

Policies to reduce costs. Tuition/fee waivers for employees and their families. Credit/placement for qualifying scores on AP, CLEP examinations.

Payment plans. Credit card, installment, deferred payment.

Application procedures. FAFSA, institutional form required. Priority date 4/15; no closing date. Applicants notified on rolling basis starting 4/15, must reply within 2 week(s) of notification. **Transfers:** No deadline.

Contact. Dean Carpenter, Director of Financial Aid
1201 Wesleyan Street
Fort Worth, TX 76105-1536

Texas Woman's University

Denton, Texas
www.twu.edu
Four-year public **Federal Code: 003646**

	Living at home	On-campus
Tuition and fees (2002-2003):	$3,432	$3,432
Out-of-state:	$9,882	$9,882
Room and board:		$4,428
Board only:	$1,944	
Books and supplies:	$720	$720
Personal expenses:	$963	$1,683
Transportation:	$1,008	$720

Policies to reduce costs. Tuition/fee waivers for senior citizens. Credit/placement for qualifying scores on AP, CLEP examinations.

Payment plans. Credit card, installment payment.

Application procedures. FAFSA, institutional form required. Priority date 4/1; no closing date. Applicants notified on rolling basis starting 4/1, must reply within 2 week(s) of notification.

Contact. **Financial aid office:** (940) 898-3050
Governor Jackson, Director of Financial Aid
Box 425589
Denton, TX 76204-5589

Trinity University

San Antonio, Texas
www.trinity.edu
Four-year private **Federal Code: 003647**

	Living at home	On-campus
Tuition and fees (2002-2003):	$17,854	$17,854
Room and board:		$7,040
Board only:	$1,744	
Books and supplies:	$600	$600
Personal expenses:	$1,102	$1,102
Transportation:		$1,000

Undergraduate aid. **Need-based:** Average financial aid package for full-time students was $14,518. 74% awarded as scholarships/grants, 26% as loans/jobs. **Non-need-based:** 47% awarded as scholarships/grants, 53% as loans/jobs. Scholarships based on academics, music/drama.

Freshman aid. **Need-based:** Out of 674 full-time freshmen, 639 applied for aid; 290 were judged to have need; of these 289 received aid. Average package met 90% of need. 189 students had full need met. Average scholarship/grant was $11,066; average loan $2,739. **Non-need based:** 215 full-time freshmen with need received non-need scholarships; 297 without need received awards.

Policies to reduce costs. Tuition/fee waivers for employees and their families. Credit/placement for qualifying scores on AP, IB examinations.

Application procedures. FAFSA, CSS PROFILE required. Priority date 2/1; no closing date. Applicants notified by 4/1, must reply by 5/1 or within 4 week(s) of notification. Early decision closing date 11/1. **Transfers:** Priority date 5/1; no deadline.

Contact. **Financial aid office:** (210) 999-8315
Terri Reik, Director of Financial Aid
715 Stadium Drive
San Antonio, TX 78212

Trinity Valley Community College

Athens, Texas
www.tvcc.edu
Two-year public **Federal Code: 003572**

	Living at home	On-campus
Tuition and fees (projected):	$900	$900
Out-of-district:	$1,600	$1,600
Out-of-state:	$2,250	$2,250
Per-credit charge:	$15	$15
Per-credit out-of-district:	$30	$30
Per-credit out-of-state:	$60	$60
Room and board:		$3,486
Board only:	$1,950	
Books and supplies:	$435	$435
Personal expenses:	$980	$980
Transportation:	$1,005	$895

Undergraduate aid. Need-based: Need-based aid available for full-time and part-time students. **Non-need-based:** Scholarships based on academics, athletics.

Policies to reduce costs. Tuition/fee waivers for adults, senior citizens, employees and their families. Credit/placement for qualifying scores on AP, CLEP examinations. Work study available nights and weekends.

Payment plans. Credit card, installment payment.

Application procedures. FAFSA, institutional form required. Priority date 7/1; no closing date. Applicants notified on rolling basis starting 7/1, must reply within 2 week(s) of notification. **Transfers:** No deadline. Students on suspension at previous institution ineligible to receive aid.

Contact. Financial aid office: (903) 675-6233
Julie Lively, Director of Financial Aid
100 Cardinal Drive
Athens, TX 75751

Tyler Junior College

Tyler, Texas
www.tjc.edu
Two-year public **Federal Code: 003648**

	Living at home	On-campus
Tuition and fees (2002-2003):	$1,130	$1,130
Out-of-district:	$1,760	$1,760
Out-of-state:	$2,060	$2,060
Per-credit charge:	$15	$15
Per-credit out-of-district:	$36	$36
Per-credit out-of-state:	$46	$46
Room and board:		$3,700
Board only:	$875	
Books and supplies:	$600	$600
Personal expenses:	$1,312	$1,312
Transportation:	$2,002	$1,001

Undergraduate aid. Need-based: Need-based aid available for full-time and part-time students. **Non-need-based:** Scholarships based on academics, alumni affiliation, art, athletics, leadership, music/drama.

Policies to reduce costs. Tuition/fee waivers for senior citizens. Credit/placement for qualifying scores on AP, IB, CLEP examinations. Work study available for part-time students.

Payment plans. Credit card, installment payment.

Application procedures. FAFSA, institutional form required. Priority date 6/1; no closing date. Applicants notified on rolling basis starting 3/1, must reply within 2 week(s) of notification. **Transfers:** Priority date 6/1. Financial aid transcript required if student enrolled same year elsewhere.

Contact. Financial aid office: (903) 510-2646
Devon Wiggins, Director of Student Financial Aid and Scholarship
Box 9020
Tyler, TX 75711-9020

University of Dallas

Irving, Texas
www.udallas.edu
Four-year private **Federal Code: 003651**

	Living at home	On-campus
Tuition and fees:	$18,062	$18,062
Room and board:		$6,494
Books and supplies:	$850	$850
Personal expenses:	$2,950	$2,950

Undergraduate aid. Need-based: Average financial aid package for full-time students was $14,409; for part-time $8,350. 71% awarded as scholarships/grants, 29% as loans/jobs. **Non-need-based:** 76% awarded as scholarships/grants, 24% as loans/jobs. Scholarships based on academics, alumni affiliation, art, leadership, music/drama. **Additional information:** Aid available for Rome semester.

Freshman aid. Need-based: Out of 310 full-time freshmen, 297 applied for aid; 190 were judged to have need; of these 190 received aid. Average package met 77% of need. 46 students had full need met. Average scholarship/grant was $10,458; average loan $4,484. **Non-need based:** 168 full-time freshmen with need received non-need scholarships; 102 without need received awards.

Policies to reduce costs. Tuition/fee waivers for family members, employees and their families. Credit/placement for qualifying scores on AP, IB, CLEP examinations.

Payment plans. Credit card, installment payment.

Application procedures. FAFSA, institutional form required. Priority date 3/1; no closing date. Applicants notified on rolling basis starting 3/20, must reply within 2 week(s) of notification. **Transfers:** Priority date 4/1; closing date 7/15.

Contact. Financial aid office: (972) 721-5266
Curt Eley, Dean of Enrollment Management
1845 East Northgate
Irving, TX 75062-4736

University of Houston

Houston, Texas
www.uh.edu
Four-year public **Federal Code: 003652**

	Living at home	On-campus
Tuition and fees (projected):	$3,648	$3,648
Out-of-state:	$11,658	$11,658
Room and board:		$5,694
Books and supplies:	$900	$900
Personal expenses:	$1,758	$1,758
Transportation:	$1,368	$1,368

Undergraduate aid. Need-based: Average financial aid package for full-time students was $11,340; for part-time $4,200. 45% awarded as scholarships/grants, 55% as loans/jobs. **Non-need-based:** 10% awarded as scholarships/grants, 90% as loans/jobs. Scholarships based on athletics, job skills. **Student debt:** 27% of graduating class borrowed to fund education; average debt was $12,988. **Additional information:** 45-day and 90-day institutional loans available.

Freshman aid. Need-based: Average package met 83% of need. Average scholarship/grant was $5,250; average loan $2,900.

Policies to reduce costs. Tuition/fee waivers for senior citizens, employees and their families. Credit/placement for qualifying scores on AP, IB, CLEP examinations. Work study available for part-time students.

Payment plans. Credit card, installment payment.

Application procedures. FAFSA required. Priority date 4/1; no closing date. Applicants notified on rolling basis starting 4/5, must reply within 4 week(s) of notification.

Contact. Financial aid office: (713) 743-1010
Robert Sheridan, Director of Scholarships and Financial Aid
122 E. Cullen Building
Houston, TX 77204-2023

University of Houston: Clear Lake

Houston, Texas
www.uhcl.edu
Upper-division public **Federal Code: 011711**

	Living at home
Tuition and fees (2002-2003):	$4,324
Out-of-state:	$10,864
Board only:	$1,739
Books and supplies:	$750
Personal expenses:	$3,053
Transportation:	$2,145

Undergraduate aid. Need-based: Need-based aid available for full-time and part-time students.

Policies to reduce costs. Work study available nights, weekends and for part-time students.

Payment plans. Installment payment.

Application procedures. FAFSA, institutional form required. Priority date 4/2; no closing date. Applicants notified on rolling basis starting 6/2, must reply within 4 week(s) of notification. **Transfers:** Priority date 5/1; no deadline.

Contact. Financial aid office: (281) 283-2481
Lynda McKendree, Director, Financial Aid/Veterans Affairs
2700 Bay Area Boulevard
Houston, TX 77058-1080

University of Houston: Downtown

Houston, Texas
www.uhd.edu
Four-year public **Federal Code: 003612**

	Living at home
Tuition and fees (2002-2003):	$2,684
Out-of-state:	$9,224
Board only:	$2,319
Personal expenses:	$957
Transportation:	$1,975

Undergraduate aid. Need-based: Average financial aid package for full-time students was $4,417. 67% awarded as scholarships/grants, 33% as loans/jobs. Need-based aid available for part-time students. **Non-need-based:** 39% awarded as scholarships/grants, 61% as loans/jobs. Scholarships based on academics, leadership, state/district residency.

Freshman aid. Need-based: Out of 841 full-time freshmen, 753 applied for aid; 413 were judged to have need; of these 407 received aid. Average package met 61% of need. 43 students had full need met. Average scholarship/grant was $4,452; average loan $1,139. **Non-need based:** 15 full-time freshmen with need received non-need scholarships; 71 without need received awards.

Policies to reduce costs. Tuition/fee waivers for senior citizens. Credit/placement for qualifying scores on AP, IB, CLEP examinations. Work study available nights, weekends and for part-time students.

Payment plans. Credit card, installment payment.

Application procedures. FAFSA, institutional form required. Priority date 4/1; no closing date. Applicants notified on rolling basis starting 6/1, must reply within 4 week(s) of notification.

Contact. Director of Financial Aid
One Main Street
Houston, TX 77002

University of Houston: Victoria

Victoria, Texas
www.uhv.edu
Upper-division public **Federal Code: 013231**

	Living at home
Tuition and fees (2002-2003):	$3,060
Out-of-state:	$9,330
Board only:	$3,575
Books and supplies:	$750
Personal expenses:	$1,827
Transportation:	$2,384

Undergraduate aid. Need-based: Average financial aid package for full-time students was $6,328; for part-time $5,120. 45% awarded as scholarships/grants, 55% as loans/jobs. **Non-need-based:** 10% awarded as scholarships/grants, 90% as loans/jobs. Scholarships based on academics. **Additional information:** Short-term loans available at registration.

Policies to reduce costs. Tuition/fee waivers for senior citizens, employees and their families. Work study available nights, weekends and for part-time students.

Payment plans. Credit card, installment payment.

Application procedures. FAFSA, institutional form required. Priority date 4/15; no closing date. Applicants notified on rolling basis starting 6/1, must reply within 3 week(s) of notification. **Transfers:** Priority date 4/15; no deadline.

Contact. Financial aid office: (361) 570-4131
Carolyn Mallory, Financial Aid Coordinator
3007 North Ben Wilson
Victoria, TX 77901-4450

University of Mary Hardin-Baylor

Belton, Texas
www.umhb.edu
Four-year private **Federal Code: 003588**

	Living at home	On-campus
Tuition and fees (2002-2003):	$10,640	$10,640
Room and board:		$4,039
Board only:	$2,046	
Books and supplies:	$750	$750
Personal expenses:	$1,588	$1,588
Transportation:	$1,058	$1,058

Undergraduate aid. Need-based: Average financial aid package for full-time students was $8,026; for part-time $6,013. 55% awarded as scholarships/grants, 45% as loans/jobs. **Non-need-based:** 44% awarded as scholarships/grants, 56% as loans/jobs. Scholarships based on academics. **Student debt:** 72% of graduating class borrowed to fund education; average debt was $17,125.

Freshman aid. Need-based: Out of 469 full-time freshmen, 442 applied for aid; 326 were judged to have need; of these 326 received aid. Average package met 74% of need. 67 students had full need met. Average scholarship/grant was $5,019; average loan $2,656. **Non-need based:** 220 full-time freshmen with need received non-need scholarships; 114 without need received awards.

Policies to reduce costs. Tuition/fee waivers for children of alumni, minority students, family members, family of clergy, employees and their families. Credit/placement for qualifying scores on AP, CLEP examinations.

Payment plans. Credit card, deferred payment.

Application procedures. FAFSA, institutional form required. Priority date 3/1; no closing date. Applicants notified on rolling basis starting 3/1, must reply within 2 week(s) of notification. **Transfers:** Priority date 3/1.

Contact. Financial aid office: (254) 295-4517
Ron Brown, Director of Financial Aid
Box 8004
Belton, TX 76513

University of North Texas

Denton, Texas
www.unt.edu
Four-year public **Federal Code: 003594**

	Living at home	On-campus
Tuition and fees (2002-2003):	$3,565	$3,565
Out-of-state:	$10,105	$10,105
Room and board:		$4,597
Board only:	$3,720	
Books and supplies:	$600	$600
Personal expenses:	$1,650	$1,650
Transportation:	$1,800	$800

Undergraduate aid. Need-based: Average financial aid package for full-time students was $6,050; for part-time $5,259. 37% awarded as scholarships/grants, 63% as loans/jobs. **Non-need-based:** 27% awarded as scholarships/grants, 73% as loans/jobs. Scholarships based on academics, alumni affiliation, art, athletics, leadership, music/drama, state/district residency. **Student debt:** 37% of graduating class borrowed to fund education; average debt was $16,523.

Freshman aid. Need-based: Out of 2,951 full-time freshmen, 1,851 applied for aid; 1,105 were judged to have need; of these 1,070 received aid. Average package met 75% of need. 22 students had full need met. Average scholarship/grant was $4,133; average loan $1,555. **Non-need based:** 342 full-time freshmen with need received non-need scholarships; 512 without need received awards; 53 received athletic scholarships.

Policies to reduce costs. Tuition/fee waivers for employees and their families. Credit/placement for qualifying scores on AP, IB, CLEP examinations. Work study available nights and weekends.

Payment plans. Credit card, installment payment.

Application procedures. FAFSA required. Priority date 6/1; no closing date. Applicants notified on rolling basis starting 4/1.

Contact. Financial aid office: (940) 565-2016
Carolyn Cunningham, Director of Financial Aid
1401 West Prairie, Suite 309
Denton, TX 76203

University of St. Thomas

Houston, Texas
www.stthom.edu
Four-year private **Federal Code: 003654**

	Living at home	On-campus
Tuition and fees:	$15,112	$15,112
Room and board:		$6,840
Board only:	$2,954	
Books and supplies:	$800	$800
Personal expenses:	$1,696	$1,696
Transportation:	$1,628	$1,628

Undergraduate aid. Need-based: Average financial aid package for full-time students was $11,832; for part-time $6,951. 76% awarded as scholarships/grants, 24% as loans/jobs. **Non-need-based:** 56% awarded as scholarships/grants, 44% as loans/jobs. Scholarships based on academics. **Student debt:** 62% of graduating class borrowed to fund education; average debt was $20,685.

Freshman aid. Need-based: Out of 274 full-time freshmen, 205 applied for aid; 173 were judged to have need; of these 172 received aid. Average package met 71% of need. 27 students had full need met. Average scholarship/grant was $10,692; average loan $2,531. **Non-need based:** 53 full-time freshmen with need received non-need scholarships; 79 without need received awards.

Policies to reduce costs. Tuition/fee waivers for family of clergy, employees and their families. Credit/placement for qualifying scores on AP, IB, CLEP examinations.

Payment plans. Credit card, installment payment.

Application procedures. FAFSA required. Priority date 3/1; no closing date. Applicants notified on rolling basis starting 3/1, must reply within 4 week(s) of notification. **Transfers:** Priority date 3/1; no deadline.

Contact. Financial aid office: (713) 525-2170
Maria Shaulis, Dean of Scholarships and Financial Aid
3800 Montrose Boulevard
Houston, TX 77006-4696

University of Texas Health Science Center at San Antonio

San Antonio, Texas
www.uthscsa.edu
Upper-division public **Federal Code: 003659**

College costs. Some costs vary by program; cited annual costs are representative of typical allied health programs.

	Living at home
Tuition and fees (2002-2003):	$2,700
Out-of-state:	$9,200
Books and supplies:	$850
Personal expenses:	$1,100
Transportation:	$1,025

Undergraduate aid. Additional information: Students strongly advised to provide parental information on need analysis form regardless of dependency status.

Payment plans. Installment payment.

Application procedures. FAFSA, institutional form required. Priority date 3/15; no closing date. Applicants notified on rolling basis. **Transfers:** No deadline.

Contact. Robert Lawson, Director of Student Financial Aid
7703 Floyd Curl Drive
San Antonio, TX 78229

University of Texas Medical Branch at Galveston

Galveston, Texas
www.utmb.edu
Upper-division public **Federal Code: 013976**

College costs. Additional required fees vary per program. Class and laboratory fees vary per course.

	Living at home	On-campus
Tuition and fees (2002-2003):	$1,668	$1,668
Out-of-state:	$7,938	$7,938
Room only:		$2,024
Board only:	$3,636	
Books and supplies:	$1,261	$1,261
Personal expenses:	$5,052	$5,052
Transportation:	$3,324	$2,820

Undergraduate aid. Need-based: 15% awarded as scholarships/grants, 85% as loans/jobs. Need-based aid available for part-time students. **Non-need-based:** 3% awarded as scholarships/grants, 97% as loans/jobs. Scholarships based on academics, minority status, state/district residency.

Policies to reduce costs. Credit/placement for qualifying scores on IB, CLEP examinations. Work study available nights, weekends and for part-time students.

Payment plans. Credit card, installment, deferred payment.

Application procedures. FAFSA, institutional form required. No deadline. Applicants notified on rolling basis, must reply within 4 week(s) of notification. **Transfers:** No deadline. Students should correct FAFSA to add UTMB, Title IV code 013976.

Contact. Financial aid office: (409) 772-4952
Betty Hazelbaker, Director of Student Financial Aid
301 University Boulevard
Galveston, TX 77555-1305

University of Texas Southwestern Medical Center at Dallas

Dallas, Texas
www.utsouthwestern.edu
Upper-division public **Federal Code: 010019**

	Living at home
Tuition and fees (2002-2003):	$2,345
Out-of-state:	$8,885
Books and supplies:	$703

Undergraduate aid. Need-based: Need-based aid available for full-time and part-time students.

Policies to reduce costs. Credit/placement for qualifying scores on AP, CLEP examinations. Work study available nights, weekends and for part-time students.

Payment plans. Credit card, installment payment.

Application procedures. FAFSA required. Priority date 3/15; no closing date. Applicants notified on rolling basis starting 4/15, must reply within 2 week(s) of notification. **Transfers:** No deadline.

Contact. Financial aid office: (214) 648-3611
Charles Kettlewell, Registrar and Director of Financial Aid
5323 Harry Hines Boulevard
Dallas, TX 75390-9162

University of Texas at Arlington

Arlington, Texas
www.uta.edu
Four-year public **Federal Code: 003656**

	Living at home	On-campus
Tuition and fees (2002-2003):	$4,123	$4,123
Out-of-state:	$10,663	$10,663
Room and board:		$4,607
Board only:	$1,961	
Books and supplies:	$600	$600
Personal expenses:	$1,500	$1,200
Transportation:	$1,960	$1,960

Undergraduate aid. Need-based: Average financial aid package for full-time students was $7,831; for part-time $5,894. 43% awarded as scholarships/grants, 57% as loans/jobs. **Non-need-based:** 35% awarded as scholarships/grants, 65% as loans/jobs. Scholarships based on academics, art, athletics, job skills, leadership, music/drama. **Student debt:** 46% of graduating class borrowed to fund education; average debt was $12,741.

Freshman aid. Need-based: Average package met 85% of need. Average scholarship/grant was $4,868; average loan $2,552.

Merit scholarships. Academic Scholarships: $1,000-$4,000 per year, renewable, based on minimum SAT 1050 or ACT 22, top 25% of high school class.

Policies to reduce costs. Tuition/fee waivers for employees and their families. Credit/placement for qualifying scores on AP, IB, CLEP examinations. Work study available nights and weekends.

Payment plans. Credit card, installment payment.

Application procedures. FAFSA required. Priority date 6/1; no closing date. Applicants notified on rolling basis starting 5/1, must reply within 3 week(s) of notification. **Transfers:** Priority date 6/1. To receive Texas grant, student must have either received Texas grant at prior school or completed associates degree at prior school.

Contact. Financial aid office: (817) 272-3561
Karen Krause, Director
Box 19111
Arlington, TX 76019

University of Texas at Austin

Austin, Texas
www.utexas.edu
Four-year public **Federal Code: 003658**

College costs. Additional fees required for some programs.

	Living at home	On-campus
Tuition and fees (2002-2003):	$3,950	$3,950
Out-of-state:	$10,490	$10,490
Room and board:		$5,975
Books and supplies:	$722	$722
Personal expenses:	$1,954	$1,954
Transportation:	$748	$748

Undergraduate aid. Need-based: Average financial aid package for full-time students was $7,470. 42% awarded as scholarships/grants, 58% as loans/jobs. Need-based aid available for part-time students. **Non-need-based:** 57% awarded as scholarships/grants, 43% as loans/jobs. Scholarships based on academics, art, athletics, job skills, leadership, music/drama, state/district residency.

Freshman aid. Need-based: Out of 7,208 full-time freshmen, 5,120 applied for aid; 3,980 were judged to have need; of these 3,870 received aid. Average package met 93% of need. 3520 students had full need met. Average scholarship/grant was $5,630; average loan $3,100. **Non-need based:** 1,120 without need received awards.

Policies to reduce costs. Tuition/fee waivers for senior citizens, employees and their families. Credit/placement for qualifying scores on AP, IB, CLEP examinations. Work study available nights.

Payment plans. Credit card, installment payment.

Application procedures. FAFSA required. Priority date 4/1; no closing date. Applicants notified on rolling basis starting 4/1, must reply within 4 week(s) of notification.

Contact. Financial aid office: (512) 475-6282
Lawrence Burt, Director of Student Financial Services
John Hargis Hall D0700
Austin, TX 78712-1111

University of Texas at Brownsville

Brownsville, Texas
www.utb.edu
Four-year public **Federal Code: 030646**

	Living at home
Tuition and fees (2002-2003):	$2,674
Out-of-state:	$9,214
Board only:	$4,770
Books and supplies:	$534
Personal expenses:	$2,188
Transportation:	$1,368

Undergraduate aid. Need-based: Need-based aid available for full-time and part-time students.

Policies to reduce costs. Tuition/fee waivers for employees and their families. Credit/placement for qualifying scores on AP examinations.

Payment plans. Installment payment.

Application procedures. FAFSA required. Priority date 4/1; closing date 8/15. Applicants notified on rolling basis, must reply within 4 week(s) of notification.

Contact. Financial aid office: (956) 544-8277
Mari Chapa, Director of Financial Aid
80 Fort Brown
Brownsville, TX 78520

University of Texas at Dallas

Richardson, Texas
www.utdallas.edu
Four-year public **Federal Code: 009741**

College costs. Additional fees required for some programs.

	Living at home	On-campus
Tuition and fees (2002-2003):	$4,775	$4,775
Out-of-state:	$11,315	$11,315
Room and board:		$5,914
Board only:	$1,987	
Books and supplies:	$1,000	$1,000
Personal expenses:	$680	$1,671
Transportation:	$1,884	$1,884

Undergraduate aid. Need-based: Average financial aid package for full-time students was $9,376; for part-time $7,417. 44% awarded as scholarships/grants, 56% as loans/jobs. **Non-need-based:** 26% awarded as scholarships/grants, 74% as loans/jobs. Scholarships based on academics, state/district residency.

Freshman aid. Need-based: Out of 872 full-time freshmen, 510 applied for aid; 350 were judged to have need; of these 350 received aid. Average package met 82% of need. 224 students had full need met. Average scholarship/grant was $4,053; average loan $1,460. **Non-need based:** 167 full-time freshmen with need received non-need scholarships; 93 without need received awards.

Merit scholarships. Eugene McDermott Scholars Program Awards; 20 awarded; full tuition and fees plus domestic and international travel costs for enhancement of scholar's education; based on being in top 10% of high school class, high scores on entrance exams, evidence of leadership abilities.

Policies to reduce costs. Tuition/fee waivers for senior citizens. Credit/placement for qualifying scores on AP, IB, CLEP examinations. Work study available weekends.

Payment plans. Credit card, installment payment.

Application procedures. FAFSA required. Priority date 3/12; closing date 4/30. Applicants notified by 4/15, must reply within 4 week(s) of notification. **Transfers:** Priority date 4/1.

Contact. Financial aid office: (972) 883-2941
Maria Ramos, Director of Financial Aid
Office of Admissions
Richardson, TX 75083

University of Texas at El Paso

El Paso, Texas
www.utep.edu
Four-year public **Federal Code: 003661**

College costs. Mexican citizens who show need may qualify for in-state tuition.

	Living at home	On-campus
Tuition and fees:	$3,312	$3,312
Out-of-state:	$9,852	$9,852
Room only:		$2,655
Board only:	$1,600	
Books and supplies:	$842	$842
Personal expenses:	$2,946	$2,946
Transportation:	$1,597	$1,597

Undergraduate aid. Need-based: Average financial aid package for full-time students was $7,761; for part-time $7,380. 46% awarded as scholarships/grants, 54% as loans/jobs. **Non-need-based:** Scholarships based on academics, alumni affiliation, art, athletics, job skills, leadership, minority status, music/drama, religious affiliation, state/district residency. **Student debt:** 35% of graduating class borrowed to fund education; average debt was $7,305. **Additional information:** Emergency loans available.

Freshman aid. Need-based: Out of 2,225 full-time freshmen, 1,656 applied for aid; 1,302 were judged to have need; of these 1,284 received aid. Average package met 79% of need. 451 students had full need met. Average scholarship/grant was $3,752; average loan $2,774. **Non-need based:** 70 full-time freshmen with need received non-need scholarships; 170 without need received awards; 46 received athletic scholarships.

Policies to reduce costs. Credit/placement for qualifying scores on AP, CLEP examinations.

Payment plans. Credit card, installment, deferred payment.

Application procedures. FAFSA, institutional form required. Priority date 3/15; no closing date. Applicants notified by 6/30, must reply within 2 week(s) of notification.

Contact. Linda Gonzalez-Hensgen, Director of Financial Aid
500 West University Avenue
El Paso, TX 79968

University of Texas at San Antonio

San Antonio, Texas
www.utsa.edu
Four-year public **Federal Code: 010115**

	Living at home	On-campus
Tuition and fees (projected):	$3,700	$3,700
Out-of-state:	$10,240	$10,240
Room and board:		$6,442
Board only:	$1,100	
Books and supplies:	$514	$514
Personal expenses:	$1,878	$1,878
Transportation:	$2,563	$2,563

Undergraduate aid. Need-based: Need-based aid available for full-time students. **Non-need-based:** Scholarships based on academics, job skills.

Policies to reduce costs. Tuition/fee waivers for senior citizens, employees and their families. Credit/placement for qualifying scores on AP, CLEP examinations. Work study available weekends.

Payment plans. Credit card, installment payment.

Application procedures. FAFSA required. Priority date 3/15; closing date 8/30. Applicants notified by 3/15, must reply within 4 week(s) of notification.

Contact. Lisa Blazer, Director of Student Financial Aid
6900 North Loop 1604 West
San Antonio, TX 78249

University of Texas at Tyler

Tyler, Texas
www.uttyler.edu
Four-year public **Federal Code: 011163**

College costs. Students may rent on-campus apartment from private company; $250-$600 per month.

	Living at home
Tuition and fees (projected):	$3,472
Out-of-state:	$9,952
Board only:	$2,912
Books and supplies:	$700
Personal expenses:	$1,210
Transportation:	$1,575

Undergraduate aid. Need-based: Average financial aid package for full-time students was $1,575; for part-time $1,449. 41% awarded as scholarships/grants, 59% as loans/jobs. **Non-need-based:** 77% awarded as scholarships/grants, 23% as loans/jobs. Scholarships based on academics, music/drama. **Student debt:** 47% of graduating class borrowed to fund education; average debt was $2,140. **Additional information:** Apply early for all programs.

Freshman aid. Need-based: Out of 292 full-time freshmen, 288 applied for aid; 172 were judged to have need; of these 128 received aid. Average scholarship/grant was $1,357; average loan $1,026. **Non-need based:** 64 full-time freshmen with need received non-need scholarships; 118 without need received awards.

Policies to reduce costs. Tuition/fee waivers for senior citizens, employees and their families. Credit/placement for qualifying scores on AP, IB, CLEP examinations. Work study available for part-time students.

Payment plans. Credit card, installment payment.

Application procedures. FAFSA required. Priority date 4/1; no closing date. Applicants notified on rolling basis starting 4/15, must reply within 3 week(s) of notification. **Transfers:** Priority date 4/1.

Contact. Financial aid office: (903) 566-7180
Candice Garner, Director of Financial Aid
3900 University Boulevard
Tyler, TX 75799

University of Texas of the Permian Basin

Odessa, Texas
www.utpb.edu
Four-year public **Federal Code: 009930**

College costs. New Mexico resident tuition $3,300 full time, $110 per credit hour.

	Living at home	On-campus
Tuition and fees (2002-2003):	$3,202	$3,202
Out-of-state:	$9,742	$9,742
Room only:		$1,720
Books and supplies:	$555	$555
Personal expenses:	$1,375	$1,375
Transportation:	$1,452	$1,452

Undergraduate aid. Need-based: Average financial aid package for full-time students was $7,444; for part-time $4,099. 49% awarded as scholarships/grants, 51% as loans/jobs. **Non-need-based:** 50% awarded as scholarships/grants, 50% as loans/jobs. Scholarships based on academics. **Student debt:** 76% of graduating class borrowed to fund education; average debt was $16,168.

Freshman aid. Need-based: Out of 166 full-time freshmen, 156 applied for aid; 113 were judged to have need; of these 111 received aid. Average package met 86% of need. 53 students had full need met. Average scholarship/grant was $5,452; average loan $2,236. **Non-need based:** 17 full-time freshmen with need received non-need scholarships; 39 without need received awards.

Policies to reduce costs. Tuition/fee waivers for senior citizens. Credit/placement for qualifying scores on AP, CLEP examinations. Work study available nights and weekends.

Payment plans. Credit card, installment payment.

Application procedures. FAFSA, institutional form required. Priority date 5/1; no closing date. Applicants notified on rolling basis starting 6/1, must reply within 2 week(s) of notification.

Contact. Financial aid office: (915) 552-2620
Robert Vasquez, Director of Financial Aid and Placement
4901 East University Boulevard
Odessa, TX 79762

University of Texas-Houston Health Science Center

Houston, Texas
www.uth.tmc.edu
Upper-division public **Federal Code: 013956**

College costs (2002-2003). Nursing program students must attend for full calendar year (fall, spring, summer semesters). Full-time tuition: $3,375 in-state, $13,230 out-of-state; required fees $672; room in college-operated apartment complex $6,060. Estimated expenses for calendar year: books and supplies $1,050, transportation $2,724, personal expenses $2,964, room and board for off-campus commuters $14,328.

Undergraduate aid. All financial aid based on need. Average financial aid package for full-time students was $12,457. 21% awarded as scholarships/grants, 79% as loans/jobs. Need-based aid available for part-time students. **Student debt:** 90% of graduating class borrowed to fund education; average debt was $14,530.

Policies to reduce costs. Credit/placement for qualifying scores on AP examinations.

Payment plans. Credit card, installment payment.

Application procedures. FAFSA, institutional form required. No deadline. Applicants notified on rolling basis starting 6/1. **Transfers:** No deadline.

Contact. **Financial aid office:** (713) 500-3860
Carl Gordon, Director of Student Financial Aid
Box 20036
Houston, TX 77225

University of Texas: Pan American

Edinburg, Texas
www.panam.edu
Four-year public **Federal Code: 003599**

College costs. Mexican citizens may be eligible for in-state tuition rates.

	Living at home	On-campus
Tuition and fees (2002-2003):	$2,719	$2,719
Out-of-state:	$8,989	$8,989
Room and board:		$5,286
Board only:	$1,444	
Books and supplies:	$564	$564
Personal expenses:	$902	$902
Transportation:	$757	$549

Undergraduate aid. **Need-based:** Average financial aid package for full-time students was $6,915; for part-time $4,704. 68% awarded as scholarships/grants, 32% as loans/jobs. **Non-need-based:** 98% awarded as scholarships/grants, 2% as loans/jobs. Scholarships based on alumni affiliation, art, athletics, job skills, leadership, music/drama, state/district residency. **Student debt:** 84% of graduating class borrowed to fund education; average debt was $11,625.

Freshman aid. **Need-based:** Average package met 71% of need. Average scholarship/grant was $6,706; average loan $495.

Policies to reduce costs. Tuition/fee waivers for senior citizens, employees and their families. Credit/placement for qualifying scores on AP, CLEP examinations.

Payment plans. Credit card, installment payment.

Application procedures. FAFSA, CSS PROFILE required. Closing date 2/28. Applicants notified on rolling basis starting 3/1, must reply within 2 week(s) of notification.

Contact. **Financial aid office:** (956) 381-2501
Michele Alvarado, Director of Financial Services
1201 West University Drive
Edinburg, TX 78541

University of the Incarnate Word

San Antonio, Texas
www.uiw.edu
Four-year private **Federal Code: 003578**

	Living at home	On-campus
Tuition and fees (2002-2003):	$14,328	$14,328
Room and board:		$5,510
Board only:	$1,187	
Books and supplies:	$800	$800
Personal expenses:	$1,430	$1,430
Transportation:	$1,060	$845

Undergraduate aid. **Need-based:** Average financial aid package for full-time students was $11,957; for part-time $6,505. 52% awarded as scholarships/grants, 48% as loans/jobs. **Non-need-based:** 37% awarded as scholarships/grants, 63% as loans/jobs. Scholarships based on academics, alumni affiliation, art, athletics, job skills, leadership, minority status, music/drama, religious affiliation. **Student debt:** 66% of graduating class borrowed to fund education; average debt was $27,267. **Additional information:** Students encouraged to pursue outside scholarship programs.

Freshman aid. **Need-based:** Out of 399 full-time freshmen, 342 applied for aid; 303 were judged to have need; of these 303 received aid. Average package met 44% of need. 115 students had full need met. Average scholarship/grant was $5,380; average loan $2,791. **Non-need based:** 192 full-time freshmen with need received non-need scholarships; 34 without need received awards; 3 received athletic scholarships.

Policies to reduce costs. Tuition/fee waivers for senior citizens, family of clergy, employees and their families. Credit/placement for qualifying scores on AP, CLEP examinations.

Payment plans. Credit card, installment payment.

Application procedures. FAFSA, institutional form required. Priority date 4/1; no closing date. Applicants notified on rolling basis starting 3/1, must reply within 2 week(s) of notification. **Transfers:** No deadline.

Contact. **Financial aid office:** (210) 829-6008
Amy Carcanagues, Director of Financial Assistance
4301 Broadway
San Antonio, TX 78209-6397

Victoria College

Victoria, Texas
www.victoriacollege.edu
Two-year public **Federal Code: 003662**

	Living at home
Tuition and fees (2002-2003):	$924
Out-of-district:	$1,224
Out-of-state:	$1,974
Per-credit charge:	$20
Per-credit out-of-district:	$30
Per-credit out-of-state:	$55
Books and supplies:	$482
Personal expenses:	$1,098
Transportation:	$725

Policies to reduce costs. Tuition/fee waivers for employees and their families. Credit/placement for qualifying scores on AP, CLEP examinations. Work study available for part-time students.

Payment plans. Credit card, installment payment.

Application procedures. FAFSA, institutional form required. Priority date 4/15; no closing date. Applicants notified on rolling basis.

Contact. **Financial aid office:** (361) 572-6415
Lauri Voss, Director of Financial Aid
2200 East Red River
Victoria, TX 77901

Wayland Baptist University

Plainview, Texas
www.wbu.edu
Four-year private **Federal Code: 003663**

	Living at home	On-campus
Tuition and fees (2002-2003):	$8,450	$8,450
Room and board:		$3,256
Board only:	$2,700	
Books and supplies:	$586	$586
Personal expenses:	$1,094	$1,228
Transportation:	$812	$800

Undergraduate aid. Need-based: Average financial aid package for full-time students was $9,208; for part-time $4,916. 61% awarded as scholarships/grants, 39% as loans/jobs. **Non-need-based:** 32% awarded as scholarships/grants, 68% as loans/jobs. Scholarships based on academics, alumni affiliation, art, athletics, job skills, leadership, minority status, music/drama, religious affiliation.

Freshman aid. Need-based: Out of 182 full-time freshmen, 181 applied for aid; 139 were judged to have need; of these 139 received aid. Average package met 76% of need. 32 students had full need met. Average scholarship/grant was $5,490; average loan $4,105. **Non-need based:** 133 full-time freshmen with need received non-need scholarships; 18 without need received awards; 13 received athletic scholarships.

Policies to reduce costs. Tuition/fee waivers for senior citizens, employees and their families. Credit/placement for qualifying scores on AP, IB, CLEP examinations.

Payment plans. Credit card, installment payment.

Application procedures. FAFSA, institutional form required. Priority date 5/1; no closing date. Applicants notified on rolling basis starting 2/15, must reply within 4 week(s) of notification.

Contact. Financial aid office: (806) 291-3524
Bob Womack, Director of Financial Aid
1900 West Seventh Street
Plainview, TX 79072

West Texas A&M University

Canyon, Texas
www.wtamu.edu
Four-year public **Federal Code: 003665**

College costs. Out-of-state students from border counties pay in-state tuition. Tuition reduction plan available to students from border states.

	Living at home	On-campus
Tuition and fees (projected):	$3,306	$3,306
Out-of-state:	$12,021	$12,021
Room and board:		$4,309
Board only:	$2,140	
Books and supplies:	$750	$750
Personal expenses:	$1,110	$1,574
Transportation:	$1,610	$898

Undergraduate aid. Need-based: Average financial aid package for full-time students was $5,770; for part-time $5,663. 48% awarded as scholarships/grants, 52% as loans/jobs. **Non-need-based:** 30% awarded as scholarships/grants, 70% as loans/jobs. Scholarships based on academics, alumni affiliation, art, athletics, leadership, music/drama, state/district residency. **Additional information:** Scholarship deadline February 1.

Freshman aid. Need-based: Out of 792 full-time freshmen, 579 applied for aid; 439 were judged to have need; of these 433 received aid. Average package met 79% of need. 431 students had full need met. Average scholarship/grant was $3,426; average loan $1,979. **Non-need based:** 266 full-time freshmen with need received non-need scholarships; 122 without need received awards; 41 received athletic scholarships.

Policies to reduce costs. Tuition/fee waivers for senior citizens, employees and their families. Credit/placement for qualifying scores on AP, IB, CLEP examinations. Work study available for part-time students.

Payment plans. Credit card, installment payment.

Application procedures. FAFSA required. Priority date 5/1; closing date 2/1. Applicants notified on rolling basis starting 3/1, must reply within 2 week(s) of notification. **Transfers:** No deadline. Must provide financial aid transcripts through last semester of attendance. All academic transcripts must be on file.

Contact. Financial aid office: (806) 651-2055
Jim Reed, Director of Student Financial Aid
2501 Fourth Avenue, WTAMU Box 60907
Canyon, TX 79016-0001

Western Technical Institute

El Paso, Texas
www.wti-ep.com
Two-year proprietary **Federal Code: 014535**

College costs (2002-2003). Tuition for full associate programs ranges from $17,010 to $20,790; certificate programs range from $7,045 to $10,395. Registration fee $100.

Undergraduate aid. All financial aid based on need. Need-based aid available for full-time and part-time students. **Student debt:** 6% of graduating class borrowed to fund education; average debt was $5,000.

Policies to reduce costs. Tuition/fee waivers for employees and their families.

Payment plans. Credit card, installment, deferred payment.

Application procedures. FAFSA required. No deadline. Applicants notified on rolling basis.

Contact. Financial aid office: (915) 532-3737 ext. 105
Jennifer Phillips, Financial Aid Director
1000 Texas Avenue
El Paso, TX 79901

Western Texas College

Snyder, Texas
wtc.cc.tx.us
Two-year public **Federal Code: 009549**

	Living at home	On-campus
Tuition and fees (2002-2003):	$1,380	$1,380
Out-of-district:	$1,550	$1,550
Out-of-state:	$1,680	$1,680
Per-credit charge:	$27	$27
Per-credit out-of-district:	$32	$32
Per-credit out-of-state:	$37	$37
Room and board:		$3,464
Books and supplies:	$350	$350
Personal expenses:	$900	$900
Transportation:	$960	$960

Undergraduate aid. Need-based: Average financial aid package for full-time students was $4,500; for part-time $2,000. 95% awarded as scholarships/grants, 5% as loans/jobs. **Non-need-based:** Scholarships based on academics, art, athletics, leadership, music/drama, state/district residency.

Freshman aid. Need-based: Out of 123 full-time freshmen, 123 applied for aid; 65 were judged to have need; of these 65 received aid. Average package met 75% of need. 20 students had full need met. **Non-need based:** 30 full-time freshmen with need received non-need scholarships.

Policies to reduce costs. Tuition/fee waivers for senior citizens, employees and their families. Credit/placement for qualifying scores on AP, CLEP examinations.

Payment plans. Credit card, installment payment.

Application procedures. FAFSA, institutional form required. Priority date 8/2; no closing date. Applicants notified on rolling basis starting 6/1, must reply within 2 week(s) of notification.

Contact. Financial aid office: (915) 573-8511 ext. 309
Kathy Hall, Director of Student Financial Aid
6200 College Avenue
Snyder, TX 79549

Wharton County Junior College

Wharton, Texas
www.wcjc.edu
Two-year public **Federal Code: 003668**

	Living at home	On-campus
Tuition and fees (projected):	$1,440	$1,440
Out-of-district:	$2,250	$2,250
Out-of-state:	$3,030	$3,030
Per-credit charge:	$48	$48
Per-credit out-of-district:	$75	$75
Per-credit out-of-state:	$101	$101
Room and board:		$2,860
Books and supplies:	$650	$650
Personal expenses:	$2,420	$1,520
Transportation:	$1,300	

Undergraduate aid. Need-based: Need-based aid available for full-time and part-time students. **Non-need-based:** Scholarships based on academics, athletics.

Policies to reduce costs. Tuition/fee waivers for employees and their families. Credit/placement for qualifying scores on AP, CLEP examinations.

Application procedures. FAFSA required. Priority date 6/1; no closing date. Applicants notified on rolling basis starting 8/1, must reply by 8/15. **Transfers:** Priority date 6/1; closing date 7/1.

Contact. Richard Hyde, Director of Financial Aid
911 Boling Highway
Wharton, TX 77488-0080

Wiley College

Marshall, Texas
www.wileyc.edu
Four-year private **Federal Code: 003669**

College costs. Required fees include book and computer laptop fees. Additional $118 in required fees for on-campus residents.

	Living at home	On-campus
Tuition and fees (2002-2003):	$7,160	$7,160
Room and board:		$3,824
Board only:	$3,708	
Books and supplies:	$600	$600
Personal expenses:	$1,190	$944
Transportation:	$2,010	$536

Undergraduate aid. All financial aid based on need. Need-based aid available for full-time and part-time students.

Policies to reduce costs. Tuition/fee waivers for family of clergy, employees and their families.

Payment plans. Installment payment.

Application procedures. FAFSA, institutional form required. Priority date 6/1; no closing date. Applicants notified on rolling basis starting 6/15.

Contact. Reggie Brazzle, Director of Financial Aid
711 Wiley Avenue
Marshall, TX 75670

Brigham Young University

Provo, Utah
www.byu.edu
Four-year private **Federal Code: 003670**

College costs. Undergraduate tuition additional $140 for non-members of The Church of Jesus Christ of Latter-day Saints. Per-credit-hour charge additional $82 for non-members.

	Living at home	On-campus
Tuition and fees (projected):	$3,150	$3,150
Out-of-state:	$4,740	$4,740
Room and board:		$4,900
Books and supplies:	$1,110	$1,110
Personal expenses:	$1,550	$1,550
Transportation:	$1,370	$1,370

Undergraduate aid. Need-based: Average financial aid package for full-time students was $3,853; for part-time $3,966. 59% awarded as scholarships/grants, 41% as loans/jobs. **Non-need-based:** 71% awarded as scholarships/grants, 29% as loans/jobs. Scholarships based on academics, art, athletics, leadership, minority status, music/drama. **Student debt:** 50% of graduating class borrowed to fund education; average debt was $11,000. **Additional information:** More than 8,500 employment positions for students.

Freshman aid. Need-based: Out of 4,901 full-time freshmen, 1,590 applied for aid; 447 were judged to have need; of these 265 received aid. Average package met 30% of need. 30 students had full need met. Average scholarship/grant was $1,720; average loan $1,082. **Non-need based:** 514 without need received awards; 55 received athletic scholarships.

Policies to reduce costs. Tuition/fee waivers for employees and their families. Credit/placement for qualifying scores on AP, IB examinations.

Payment plans. Deferred payment.

Application procedures. FAFSA, institutional form required. Closing date 4/15. Applicants notified by 7/1. **Transfers:** Must provide financial aid transcript.

Contact. Financial aid office: (801) 422-4104
Paul Conrad, Director of Financial Aid
A-153 ASB
Provo, UT 84602-1110

College of Eastern Utah

Price, Utah
Two-year public
Federal Code: 003676

	Living at home	On-campus
Tuition and fees (2002-2003):	$1,630	$1,630
Out-of-state:	$5,762	$5,762
Room and board:		$3,268
Books and supplies:	$750	$750
Personal expenses:	$1,275	$1,179
Transportation:	$1,534	$1,378

Undergraduate aid. Need-based: Need-based aid available for full-time and part-time students. **Non-need-based:** Scholarships based on academics, art, athletics, leadership, minority status, music/drama, religious affiliation, state/district residency.

Policies to reduce costs. Tuition/fee waivers for senior citizens, family members, employees and their families. Credit/placement for qualifying scores on AP, CLEP examinations. Work study available nights and weekends.

Payment plans. Credit card payment.

Application procedures. FAFSA, institutional form required. Priority date 3/1; no closing date. Applicants notified on rolling basis starting 3/15, must reply within 2 week(s) of notification. **Transfers:** No deadline.

Contact. Financial aid office: (435) 613-5207
Bill Osborn, Financial Aid Director
451 East 400 North
Price, UT 84501

Dixie State College of Utah

St. George, Utah
www.dixie.edu
Two-year public **Federal Code: 003671**

	Living at home	On-campus
Tuition and fees (2002-2003):	$1,758	$1,758
Out-of-state:	$6,052	$6,052
Per-credit charge:	$55	$55
Per-credit out-of-state:	$240	$240
Room and board:		$2,880
Board only:	$3,256	
Books and supplies:	$700	$700
Personal expenses:	$3,232	$3,232

Undergraduate aid. Need-based: Need-based aid available for full-time students. **Non-need-based:** Scholarships based on academics, alumni affiliation, art, athletics, leadership, minority status, music/drama.

Policies to reduce costs. Tuition/fee waivers for senior citizens, employees and their families. Credit/placement for qualifying scores on AP, CLEP examinations. Work study available nights, weekends and for part-time students.

Payment plans. Credit card, installment payment.

Application procedures. FAFSA required. Priority date 4/1; no closing date. Applicants notified on rolling basis starting 5/1, must reply within 2 week(s) of notification.

Contact. Financial aid office: (435) 652-7575
Peggy Leavitt, Director of Financial Aid
225 South 700 East
St. George, UT 84770-3876

ITT Technical Institute: Murray

Murray, Utah
www.itt-tech.edu
Three-year proprietary **Federal Code: 016774**

College costs. Total program varies depending on course of study. Per-credit-hour charge: $347.

Policies to reduce costs. Tuition/fee waivers for employees and their families.

Payment plans. Credit card, installment payment.

Application procedures. FAFSA, institutional form required. No deadline. Applicants notified on rolling basis.

Contact. Director of Finance
920 West LeVoy Drive
Murray, UT 84123

LDS Business College

Salt Lake City, Utah
www.ldsbc.edu
Two-year private **Federal Code: 003672**

	Living at home	On-campus
Tuition and fees:	$2,326	$2,326
Per-credit charge:	$97	$97
Room only:		$2,236
Board only:	$2,250	
Books and supplies:	$850	$850
Personal expenses:	$1,400	$1,400
Transportation:	$950	$950

Undergraduate aid. Need-based: 50% awarded as scholarships/grants, 50% as loans/jobs. Need-based aid available for part-time students. **Non-need-based:** Scholarships based on academics, leadership.

Merit scholarships. Service scholarships for The Church of Jesus Christ of Latter-day Saints missionaries who have returned from mission within past year. Covers half tuition for one semester.

Policies to reduce costs. Tuition/fee waivers for family of clergy, employees and their families. Credit/placement for qualifying scores on AP, IB, CLEP examinations.

Payment plans. Credit card, installment payment.

Application procedures. FAFSA required. No deadline. Applicants notified on rolling basis starting 3/1, must reply within 3 week(s) of notification. **Transfers:** No deadline.

Contact. **Financial aid office:** (801) 524-8110
Doug Horne, Financial Aid Administrator
411 East South Temple
Salt Lake City, UT 84111-1392

Salt Lake Community College

Salt Lake City, Utah
www.slcc.edu
Two-year public **Federal Code: 005220**

	Living at home
Tuition and fees (2002-2003):	$1,890
Out-of-state:	$5,800
Books and supplies:	$1,035
Personal expenses:	$1,275
Transportation:	$495

Undergraduate aid. Need-based: Need-based aid available for full-time and part-time students. **Non-need-based:** Scholarships based on academics, alumni affiliation, art, athletics, leadership, music/drama.

Policies to reduce costs. Tuition/fee waivers for adults, senior citizens, minority students, employees and their families. Credit/placement for qualifying scores on AP, CLEP examinations.

Payment plans. Credit card, installment payment.

Application procedures. FAFSA, institutional form required. Priority date 5/1; no closing date. Applicants notified on rolling basis starting 5/1, must reply within 4 week(s) of notification.

Contact. **Financial aid office:** (801) 957-4145
Cristi Easton, Director of Financial Aid
4600 South Redwood Road
Salt Lake City, UT 84130-0808

Snow College

Ephraim, Utah
www.snow.edu
Two-year public **Federal Code: 003679**

College costs. Western Undergraduate Exchange students pay $1,884 tuition.

	Living at home	On-campus
Tuition and fees (2002-2003):	$1,522	$1,522
Out-of-state:	$6,080	$6,080
Room and board:		$3,770
Books and supplies:	$530	$530
Personal expenses:	$700	$900
Transportation:	$600	$550

Undergraduate aid. Need-based: Average financial aid package for full-time students was $3,296; for part-time $2,202. 70% awarded as scholarships/grants, 30% as loans/jobs. **Non-need-based:** 88% awarded as scholarships/grants, 12% as loans/jobs. Scholarships based on academics, athletics, state/district residency.

Freshman aid. Need-based: Average scholarship/grant was $589; average loan $1,998.

Policies to reduce costs. Tuition/fee waivers for employees and their families. Credit/placement for qualifying scores on AP, CLEP examinations.

Payment plans. Credit card, deferred payment.

Application procedures. FAFSA, institutional form required. Priority date 3/1; closing date 7/15. Applicants notified on rolling basis starting 8/1, must reply within 1 week(s) of notification. **Transfers:** Priority date 3/15; closing date 6/15. F.A.T. required for midyear transfers.

Contact. **Financial aid office:** (435) 283-7132
Jack Dalene, Director of Financial Aid
150 East College Avenue
Ephraim, UT 84627

Southern Utah University

Cedar City, Utah
www.suu.edu
Four-year public **Federal Code: 003678**

	Living at home	On-campus
Tuition and fees (2002-2003):	$2,350	$2,350
Out-of-state:	$7,344	$7,344
Room and board:		$3,674
Board only:	$1,606	
Books and supplies:	$1,036	$1,036
Personal expenses:	$1,700	$1,700
Transportation:	$1,418	$1,418

Undergraduate aid. Need-based: Average financial aid package for full-time students was $4,463; for part-time $3,484. 56% awarded as scholarships/grants, 44% as loans/jobs. **Non-need-based:** 15% awarded as scholarships/grants, 85% as loans/jobs. Scholarships based on academics, art, athletics, job skills, leadership, music/drama, state/district residency. **Student debt:** 60% of graduating class borrowed to fund education; average debt was $11,081.

Freshman aid. Need-based: Average package met 62% of need. Average scholarship/grant was $2,543; average loan $2,228.

Policies to reduce costs. Tuition/fee waivers for employees and their families. Credit/placement for qualifying scores on AP, CLEP examinations.

Payment plans. Credit card payment.

Application procedures. FAFSA, institutional form required. No deadline. Applicants notified on rolling basis starting 2/1.

Contact. **Financial aid office:** (435) 586-7735
Paul Morris, Director of Financial Aid
351 West Center Street
Cedar City, UT 84720

University of Utah

Salt Lake City, Utah
www.utah.edu
Four-year public **Federal Code: 003675**

	Living at home	On-campus
Tuition and fees (2002-2003):	$3,324	$3,324
Out-of-state:	$10,182	$10,182
Room and board:		$5,140
Board only:	$1,944	
Books and supplies:	$1,086	$1,086
Personal expenses:	$810	
Transportation:	$366	

Undergraduate aid. Need-based: Average financial aid package for full-time students was $6,310; for part-time $5,200. **Non-need-based:** Scholarships based on academics, art, athletics, job skills, leadership, minority status, music/drama. **Student debt:** 58% of graduating class borrowed to fund education; average debt was $12,300.

Freshman aid. Need-based: Out of 2,309 full-time freshmen, 1,380 applied for aid; 733 were judged to have need; of these 641 received aid. Average package met 66% of need. 95 students had full need met. Average scholarship/grant was $3,750; average loan $2,327. **Non-need based:** 128 full-time freshmen with need received non-need scholarships; 90 without need received awards; 3 received athletic scholarships.

Policies to reduce costs. Tuition/fee waivers for senior citizens, employees and their families. Credit/placement for qualifying scores on AP, IB examinations. Work study available nights and weekends.

Payment plans. Credit card, deferred payment.

Application procedures. FAFSA required. Priority date 3/15; no closing date. Applicants notified on rolling basis starting 4/24.

Contact. **Financial aid office:** (801) 581-6211
Kent Larson, Director of Financial Aid
201 S. 1460 E, Room 250S
Salt Lake City, UT 84112

Utah Career College

West Jordan, Utah
www.utahcollege.com
Two-year proprietary **Federal Code: 011166**

College costs (2002-2003). Tuition $220-$245 per credit hour. Tuition for full associate degree programs (72-84 weeks) ranges from $19,800 to $22,540; books and lab fees $180-$330 per quarter. Diploma programs (48-60 weeks) range from $13,640 to $15,190; books and lab fees $175-$370 per quarter. Books/supplies: $785. Personal expenses: $2,529.

Undergraduate aid. All financial aid based on need. Need-based aid available for full-time and part-time students.

Policies to reduce costs. Tuition/fee waivers for employees and their families.

Payment plans. Credit card, installment payment.

Application procedures. FAFSA, institutional form required. No deadline. Applicants notified on rolling basis starting 7/1, must reply within 2 week(s) of notification. **Transfers:** No deadline.

Contact. **Financial aid office:** (801) 304-4224
Whitney Hannah, Director of Financial Aid
1902 West 7800 South
West Jordan, UT 84088

Utah State University

Logan, Utah
www.usu.edu
Four-year public **Federal Code: 003677**

	Living at home	On-campus
Tuition and fees (2002-2003):	$2,898	$2,898
Out-of-state:	$8,199	$8,199
Room and board:		$4,220
Books and supplies:	$750	$750
Personal expenses:	$1,545	$1,545
Transportation:	$1,055	$1,080

Undergraduate aid. All financial aid based on need. Average financial aid package for full-time students was $4,830; for part-time $3,500. 46% awarded as scholarships/grants, 54% as loans/jobs. **Student debt:** 49% of graduating class borrowed to fund education; average debt was $11,700.

Freshman aid. Out of 2,459 full-time freshmen, 1,112 applied for aid; 848 were judged to have need; of these 814 received aid. Average package met 55% of need. 92 students had full need met. Average scholarship/grant was $2,675; average loan $2,300.

Policies to reduce costs. Tuition/fee waivers for senior citizens, employees and their families. Credit/placement for qualifying scores on AP, IB, CLEP examinations.

Payment plans. Credit card, installment, deferred payment.

Application procedures. FAFSA, institutional form required. No deadline. Applicants notified on rolling basis starting 4/1, must reply within 4 week(s) of notification. **Transfers:** No deadline.

Contact. **Financial aid office:** (435) 797-0173
Judy Lecheminant, Director of Financial Aid
0160 Old Main Hill
Logan, UT 84322-0160

Utah Valley State College

Orem, Utah
www.uvsc.edu
Two-year public **Federal Code: 004027**

	Living at home
Tuition and fees (2002-2003):	$2,196
Out-of-state:	$6,802
Books and supplies:	$670
Personal expenses:	$650
Transportation:	$650

Undergraduate aid. **Need-based:** 46% awarded as scholarships/grants, 54% as loans/jobs. Need-based aid available for part-time students. **Non-need-based:** 6% awarded as scholarships/grants, 94% as loans/jobs. Scholarships based on academics, alumni affiliation, art, athletics, leadership, minority status, music/drama. **Student debt:** 27% of graduating class borrowed to fund education; average debt was $4,837.

Policies to reduce costs. Tuition/fee waivers for employees and their families. Credit/placement for qualifying scores on AP, IB, CLEP examinations. Work study available weekends and for part-time students.

Payment plans. Credit card, deferred payment.

Application procedures. FAFSA, institutional form required. Priority date 5/1; closing date 6/15. Applicants notified on rolling basis starting 4/1, must reply within 2 week(s) of notification.

Contact. **Financial aid office:** (801) 863-8442
Michael Francis, Assistant Vice President for Business Services
800 West University Parkway
Orem, UT 84058-5999

Weber State University

Ogden, Utah
www.weber.edu
Four-year public **Federal Code: 003680**

	Living at home	On-campus
Tuition and fees (2002-2003):	$2,426	$2,426
Out-of-state:	$7,292	$7,292
Room and board:		$5,160
Books and supplies:	$900	$900
Personal expenses:	$1,275	$1,275
Transportation:	$1,108	$1,108

Undergraduate aid. All financial aid based on need. Average financial aid package for full-time students was $5,300; for part-time $1,810. 44% awarded as scholarships/grants, 56% as loans/jobs. **Student debt:** 65% of graduating class borrowed to fund education; average debt was $10,500.

Freshman aid. Out of 1,934 full-time freshmen, 1,547 applied for aid; 1,284 were judged to have need; of these 1,101 received aid. Average package met 84% of need. 859 students had full need met. Average scholarship/grant was $3,125; average loan $1,825.

Policies to reduce costs. Tuition/fee waivers for senior citizens, employees and their families. Prepayment discount; credit/placement for qualifying scores on AP, IB, CLEP examinations. Work study available nights, weekends and for part-time students.

Payment plans. Credit card, installment, deferred payment.

Application procedures. FAFSA, institutional form required. Priority date 3/1; no closing date. Applicants notified on rolling basis starting 3/15, must reply within 2 week(s) of notification.

Contact. **Financial aid office:** (801) 626-7569
Richard Effiong, Director of Financial Aid
1137 University Circle
Ogden, UT 84408-1137

Westminster College

Salt Lake City, Utah
www.westminstercollege.edu
Four-year private **Federal Code: 003681**

	Living at home	On-campus
Tuition and fees (2002-2003):	$15,990	$15,990
Room and board:		$4,820
Books and supplies:	$900	$900
Personal expenses:	$2,700	$2,125

Undergraduate aid. **Need-based:** Average financial aid package for full-time students was $13,573; for part-time $8,694. 60% awarded as scholarships/grants, 40% as loans/jobs. **Non-need-based:** 67% awarded as scholarships/grants, 33% as loans/jobs. Scholarships based on academics, alumni affiliation, art, minority status, music/drama, religious affiliation. **Student debt:** 65% of graduating class borrowed to fund education; average debt was $16,500.

Freshman aid. **Need-based:** Out of 312 full-time freshmen, 312 applied for aid; 217 were judged to have need; of these 217 received aid. Average package met 89% of need. 75 students had full need met. Average scholarship/grant was $9,982; average loan $3,315. **Non-need based:** 32 full-time freshmen with need received non-need scholarships; 95 without need received awards.

Policies to reduce costs. Tuition/fee waivers for employees and their families. Credit/placement for qualifying scores on AP, IB, CLEP examinations. Work study available nights, weekends and for part-time students.

Payment plans. Credit card, installment, deferred payment.

Application procedures. FAFSA required. Priority date 4/15; no closing date. Applicants notified on rolling basis starting 3/30, must reply within 3 week(s) of notification. **Transfers:** No deadline.

Contact. Ruth Henneman, Director of Financial Aid
1840 South 1300 East
Salt Lake City, UT 84105

Vermont

Bennington College

Bennington, Vermont
www.bennington.edu
Four-year private **Federal Code: 003682**

	Living at home	On-campus
Tuition and fees:	$28,770	$28,770
Room and board:		$7,140
Board only:	$3,200	
Books and supplies:	$800	$800
Personal expenses:	$1,700	$1,700
Transportation:		$800

Undergraduate aid. Need-based: Average financial aid package for full-time students was $20,119; for part-time $13,893. 75% awarded as scholarships/grants, 25% as loans/jobs. **Non-need-based:** 69% awarded as scholarships/grants, 31% as loans/jobs. Scholarships based on academics. **Student debt:** 79% of graduating class borrowed to fund education; average debt was $17,100.

Freshman aid. Need-based: Out of 171 full-time freshmen, 122 applied for aid; 110 were judged to have need; of these 110 received aid. Average package met 74% of need. 6 students had full need met. Average scholarship/grant was $16,035; average loan $2,417. **Non-need based:** 4 full-time freshmen with need received non-need scholarships; 33 without need received awards.

Merit scholarships. Bennington College offers four-year merit-based awards to its most outstanding students. Awards up to $10,000 per year, which are sustained throughout the students' time at Bennington. Selection is based on a review of the application materials; there is no separate merit-application process. The number of and amount of awards varies depending on the strength of the applicant pool.

Policies to reduce costs. Credit/placement for qualifying scores on IB examinations.

Payment plans. Installment payment.

Application procedures. FAFSA, institutional form, CSS PROFILE required. CSS profile required of early decision applicants only. Priority date 3/1; no closing date. Applicants notified by 4/1, must reply by 5/1 or within 2 week(s) of notification. Early decision closing date 11/15. **Transfers:** Priority date 3/1.

Contact. Financial aid office: (802) 440-4325
Meg Woolmington, Director of Financial Aid
One College Drive
Bennington, VT 05201-6001

Burlington College

Burlington, Vermont
www.burlingtoncollege.edu
Four-year private **Federal Code: 012183**

	Living at home	On-campus
Tuition and fees (projected):	$13,125	$13,125
Room only:		$5,750
Board only:	$2,250	
Books and supplies:	$600	$600
Personal expenses:	$900	
Transportation:	$1,800	

Undergraduate aid. All financial aid based on need. Average financial aid package for full-time students was $9,600; for part-time $5,822. 35% awarded as scholarships/grants, 65% as loans/jobs. **Student debt:** 55% of graduating class borrowed to fund education; average debt was $14,870.

Freshman aid. Out of 24 full-time freshmen, 18 applied for aid; 17 were judged to have need; of these 17 received aid. Average package met 53% of need. 2 students had full need met. Average scholarship/grant was $5,473; average loan $3,486.

Policies to reduce costs. Tuition/fee waivers for senior citizens, employees and their families. Credit/placement for qualifying scores on AP, IB, CLEP examinations. Work study available nights, weekends and for part-time students.

Payment plans. Credit card, installment payment.

Application procedures. FAFSA required. Priority date 6/1; closing date 8/1. Applicants notified on rolling basis starting 4/1, must reply by 8/1. **Transfers:** No deadline.

Contact. Financial aid office: (802) 862-9610
Karan Lapan, Financial Aid Adviser
95 North Avenue
Burlington, VT 05401

Castleton State College

Castleton, Vermont
www.castleton.edu
Four-year public **Federal Code: 003683**

College costs. New England Board of Higher Education rate for students from other New England states: 150% of Vermont resident tuition. Available to degree candidates in academic areas not offered by educational institutions in their home states.

	Living at home	On-campus
Tuition and fees (2002-2003):	$5,504	$5,504
Out-of-state:	$11,716	$11,716
Room and board:		$5,782
Board only:	$1,500	
Books and supplies:	$800	$800
Personal expenses:	$600	$600
Transportation:	$800	$300

Undergraduate aid. Need-based: Average financial aid package for full-time students was $7,600; for part-time $4,800. 35% awarded as scholarships/grants, 65% as loans/jobs. **Non-need-based:** 15% awarded as scholarships/grants, 85% as loans/jobs. Scholarships based on academics, alumni affiliation, art, leadership, music/drama, state/district residency. **Student debt:** 76% of graduating class borrowed to fund education; average debt was $15,700.

Freshman aid. Need-based: Out of 386 full-time freshmen, 340 applied for aid; 273 were judged to have need; of these 266 received aid. Average package met 78% of need. 114 students had full need met. Average scholarship/grant was $3,800; average loan $2,750. **Non-need based:** 4 full-time freshmen with need received non-need scholarships; 40 without need received awards.

Policies to reduce costs. Tuition/fee waivers for senior citizens, employees and their families. Credit/placement for qualifying scores on AP, CLEP examinations.

Payment plans. Credit card, installment payment.

Application procedures. FAFSA required. Priority date 3/15; no closing date. Applicants notified on rolling basis starting 1/1, must reply by 5/1 or within 2 week(s) of notification.

Contact. Financial aid office: (802) 468-1286
Bill Allen, Dean of Enrollment
Seminary Street
Castleton, VT 05735

Champlain College

Burlington, Vermont
www.champlain.edu
Four-year private **Federal Code: 003684**

	Living at home	On-campus
Tuition and fees (2002-2003):	$12,295	$12,295
Room and board:		$8,400
Board only:	$3,380	
Books and supplies:	$600	$600
Personal expenses:	$500	$600
Transportation:	$750	

Undergraduate aid. Need-based: Average financial aid package for full-time students was $8,377; for part-time $5,924. 46% awarded as scholarships/grants, 54% as loans/jobs. **Non-need-based:** 8% awarded as scholarships/grants, 92% as loans/jobs. Scholarships based on academics, leadership.

Freshman aid. Need-based: Out of 388 full-time freshmen, 289 applied for aid; 244 were judged to have need; of these 244 received aid. Average package met 62% of need. 28 students had full need met. Average scholarship/grant was $5,593; average loan $3,112. **Non-need based:** 6 full-time freshmen with need received non-need scholarships; 68 without need received awards.

Merit scholarships. Champlain offers competitive, non-need-based academic/community service scholarships; application deadline is Jan. 15.

Policies to reduce costs. Tuition/fee waivers for senior citizens, employees and their families. Credit/placement for qualifying scores on AP, IB, CLEP examinations. Work study available nights and weekends.

Payment plans. Credit card, installment payment.

Application procedures. FAFSA, institutional form required. Priority date 5/1; no closing date. Applicants notified on rolling basis starting 3/1, must reply within 2 week(s) of notification. **Transfers:** No deadline.

Contact. **Financial aid office:** (802) 860-2730
David Myette, Director of Financial Aid
163 South Willard Street
Burlington, VT 05402-0670

College of St. Joseph in Vermont

Rutland, Vermont
www.csj.edu
Four-year private **Federal Code: 003685**

	Living at home	On-campus
Tuition and fees (2002-2003):	$12,200	$12,200
Room and board:		$6,400
Books and supplies:	$600	$600
Personal expenses:	$900	$900
Transportation:	$750	$550

Undergraduate aid. Need-based: Need-based aid available for full-time and part-time students. **Non-need-based:** Scholarships based on academics, athletics.

Policies to reduce costs. Tuition/fee waivers for children of alumni, senior citizens, family members, employees and their families. Credit/placement for qualifying scores on AP, IB examinations. Work study available nights and weekends.

Payment plans. Credit card, installment, deferred payment.

Application procedures. FAFSA, institutional form required. Priority date 3/1; no closing date. Applicants notified on rolling basis starting 3/15, must reply within 2 week(s) of notification. **Transfers:** Priority date 3/1.

Contact. **Financial aid office:** (802) 773-5900 ext. 218
Renee Henry, Financial Aid Director
71 Clement Road
Rutland, VT 05701-3899

Community College of Vermont

Waterbury, Vermont
www.ccv.edu
Two-year public **Federal Code: 011167**

College costs. New England Board of Higher Education rate for students from other New England states: 150% of Vermont resident tuition. Available to degree candidates in academic areas not offered by educational institutions in their home states.

	Living at home
Tuition and fees (2002-2003):	$4,240
Out-of-state:	$8,380
Per-credit charge:	$138
Per-credit out-of-state:	$276
Board only:	$620
Books and supplies:	$600
Personal expenses:	$96
Transportation:	$800

Policies to reduce costs. Tuition/fee waivers for senior citizens, employees and their families. Credit/placement for qualifying scores on CLEP examinations.

Payment plans. Credit card payment.

Application procedures. FAFSA, institutional form required. No deadline. Applicants notified on rolling basis starting 9/1, must reply within 3 week(s) of notification. **Transfers:** No deadline.

Contact. John Sweeney, Director for Financial Aid
103 South Main Street
Waterbury, VT 05676-0120

Goddard College

Plainfield, Vermont
www.goddard.edu
Four-year private **Federal Code: 003686**

College costs. Annual tuition for distance learning bachelor of arts $8,550; annual room and board for 16 days a year (8 days a semester) distance learning students spend on campus $720. Per-credit-hour charge: $285. Books/supplies: $765. Personal expenses: $1,127. Transportation: $600.

Undergraduate aid. Need-based: Need-based aid available for full-time students. **Non-need-based:** Scholarships based on academics, art, job skills, leadership, music/drama, state/district residency.

Merit scholarships. $2,000 incentive grant offered to all students.

Policies to reduce costs. Tuition/fee waivers for employees and their families. Credit/placement for qualifying scores on AP, IB, CLEP examinations. Work study available nights and weekends.

Payment plans. Credit card, deferred payment.

Application procedures. FAFSA required. Applicants notified on rolling basis starting 4/15, must reply within 4 week(s) of notification. **Transfers:** No deadline.

Contact. **Financial aid office:** (802) 454-8311
Beverly Jene, Director of Financial Aid
123 Pitkin Road
Plainfield, VT 05667

Green Mountain College

Poultney, Vermont
www.greenmtn.edu
Four-year private **Federal Code: 003687**

	Living at home	On-campus
Tuition and fees (2002-2003):	$19,170	$19,170
Room and board:		$5,980
Books and supplies:	$600	$600
Personal expenses:	$850	$850

Undergraduate aid. Need-based: Need-based aid available for full-time and part-time students. **Non-need-based:** Scholarships based on academics, athletics. **Additional information:** Service/recognition awards available to all students. Academic scholarships can be earned for work performed at the college.

Merit scholarships. Scholarships for art, performing arts, writing, global citizenship, leadership, service; ranging from $500-$3,000 renewable annually.

Policies to reduce costs. Tuition/fee waivers for family members, family of clergy, employees and their families. Credit/placement for qualifying scores on AP, IB, CLEP examinations.

Payment plans. Installment payment.

Application procedures. FAFSA required. Priority date 2/15; no closing date. Applicants notified on rolling basis starting 3/1, must reply by 5/1 or within 4 week(s) of notification.

Contact. **Financial aid office:** (802) 287-8210
Michael Falvey, Assistant Director of Financial Aid
One College Circle
Poultney, VT 05764

Johnson State College

Johnson, Vermont
www.jsc.vsc.edu
Four-year public **Federal Code: 003688**

College costs. New England Board of Higher Education rate for students from other New England states: 150% of Vermont resident tuition. Available to degree candidates in academic areas not offered by educational institutions in their home states.

	Living at home	On-campus
Tuition and fees (2002-2003):	$5,504	$5,504
Out-of-state:	$11,716	$11,716
Room and board:		$5,684
Books and supplies:	$600	$600
Personal expenses:	$650	$650
Transportation:		$300

Undergraduate aid. **Need-based:** Need-based aid available for full-time and part-time students. **Non-need-based:** Scholarships based on academics.

Policies to reduce costs. Tuition/fee waivers for senior citizens, family members, employees and their families. Credit/placement for qualifying scores on AP, CLEP examinations.

Payment plans. Credit card, installment, deferred payment.

Application procedures. FAFSA required. Priority date 3/1; no closing date. Applicants notified on rolling basis starting 4/1, must reply within 3 week(s) of notification. **Transfers:** Financial aid transcripts from previously attended colleges required.

Contact. **Financial aid office:** (800) 635-2356
Penny Howrigan, Associate Dean of Enrollment Services
337 College Hill
Johnson, VT 05656

Landmark College

Putney, Vermont
www.landmark.edu
Two-year private **Federal Code: 017157**

College costs. Computer required. Cost through school $2,000.

	Living at home	On-campus
Tuition and fees:	$35,300	$35,300
Room and board:		$6,000
Books and supplies:	$900	$900
Personal expenses:		$1,500
Transportation:		$750

Undergraduate aid. All financial aid based on need. Need-based aid available for full-time and part-time students. **Additional information:** Students encouraged to apply to their state departments of vocational rehabilitation for additional financial assistance.

Policies to reduce costs. Work study available nights, weekends and for part-time students.

Application procedures. FAFSA, institutional form required. Priority date 3/1; no closing date. Applicants notified on rolling basis starting 4/1, must reply within 3 week(s) of notification. **Transfers:** No deadline.

Contact. Cathy Mullins, Director of Financial Aid
River Road South
Putney, VT 05346

Lyndon State College

Lyndonville, Vermont
www.lyndonstate.edu
Four-year public **Federal Code: 003689**

College costs. New England Board of Higher Education rate for students from other New England states: 150% of Vermont resident tuition. Available to degree candidates in academic areas not offered by educational institutions in their home states.

	Living at home	On-campus
Tuition and fees (2002-2003):	$5,504	$5,504
Out-of-state:	$11,716	$11,716
Room and board:		$5,782
Board only:	$1,000	
Books and supplies:	$600	$600
Personal expenses:	$600	$600
Transportation:	$300	$300

Undergraduate aid. **Need-based:** Need-based aid available for full-time and part-time students. **Non-need-based:** Scholarships based on academics, leadership.

Policies to reduce costs. Tuition/fee waivers for senior citizens, family members, employees and their families. Prepayment discount; credit/placement for qualifying scores on AP, IB, CLEP examinations. Work study available nights, weekends and for part-time students.

Payment plans. Credit card payment.

Application procedures. FAFSA required. Priority date 2/1; no closing date. Applicants notified on rolling basis starting 4/1, must reply within 2 week(s) of notification. **Transfers:** Priority date 2/1; no deadline.

Contact. **Financial aid office:** (802) 626-6218
Tanya Bradley, Director of Financial Aid
1001 College Road
Lyndonville, VT 05851

Marlboro College

Marlboro, Vermont
www.marlboro.edu
Four-year private **Federal Code: 003690**

	Living at home	On-campus
Tuition and fees:	$21,630	$21,630
Room and board:		$7,425
Board only:	$2,000	
Books and supplies:	$600	$600

Undergraduate aid. **Need-based:** Need-based aid available for full-time and part-time students. **Non-need-based:** Scholarships based on academics, art, leadership, music/drama, state/district residency.

Merit scholarships. 50th Anniversary Scholarships; $6,000; academic merit of incoming freshmen. Presidential Scholarship; $6,000; academic merit of incoming transfer students.

Policies to reduce costs. Tuition/fee waivers for children of alumni, senior citizens, employees and their families. Credit/placement for qualifying scores on AP, IB, CLEP examinations. Work study available for part-time students.

Payment plans. Credit card payment.

Application procedures. FAFSA, CSS PROFILE required. Priority date 3/1; no closing date. Applicants notified by 4/1, must reply by 5/1 or within 2 week(s) of notification. Early decision closing date 11/15.

Contact. **Financial aid office:** (802) 258-9312
Julia Dower, Associate Director of Financial Aid
PO Box A, South Road
Marlboro, VT 05344-0300

Middlebury College

Middlebury, Vermont
www.middlebury.edu
Four-year private **Federal Code: 003691**

College costs. $200 student activity fee also required.

	On-campus
Comprehensive fee:	$35,900
Books and supplies:	$750
Personal expenses:	$1,000

Undergraduate aid. All financial aid based on need. Average financial aid package for full-time students was $26,979. 77% awarded as scholarships/grants, 23% as loans/jobs. **Student debt:** 47% of graduating class borrowed to fund education; average debt was $21,751. **Additional information:** College maintains need-blind admissions policy and meets full demonstrated financial need of students who qualify for admission, to degree resources permit.

Freshman aid. Out of 586 full-time freshmen, 314 applied for aid; 218 were judged to have need; of these 218 received aid. Average package met 100% of need. 218 students had full need met. Average scholarship/grant was $20,653; average loan $3,879.

Policies to reduce costs. Tuition/fee waivers for employees and their families. Credit/placement for qualifying scores on AP, IB examinations. Work study available nights and weekends.

Payment plans. Credit card, installment payment.

Application procedures. FAFSA, institutional form, CSS PROFILE required. Priority date 11/15; closing date 12/31. Applicants notified by 4/1, must reply by 5/1. Early decision closing date 11/15. **Transfers:** Closing date 3/1.

Contact. **Financial aid office:** (802) 443-5158
Robert Donaghey, Director of Financial Aid
The Emma Willard House
Middlebury, VT 05753-6002

New England Culinary Institute

Montpelier, Vermont
www.neci.edu
Two-year proprietary **Federal Code: 015904**

College costs. Tuition, fees, supplies, room and board will vary with program. Associate and bachelor's program tuition ranges from $13,080-$20,450.

	Living at home	On-campus
Tuition and fees (projected):	$13,470	$13,470
Room and board:		$4,520
Board only:	$1,620	
Books and supplies:	$1,000	$1,000
Transportation:	$1,500	$1,500

Undergraduate aid. Need-based: Average financial aid package for full-time students was $12,143; for part-time $12,143. 22% awarded as scholarships/grants, 78% as loans/jobs. **Non-need-based:** 9% awarded as scholarships/grants, 91% as loans/jobs. **Student debt:** 85% of graduating class borrowed to fund education; average debt was $20,376.

Freshman aid. Non-need based: 10 without need received awards.

Merit scholarships. Second Generation Scholarship; $1,000 awarded to students recommended by alumni. James Beard Foundation; $1,000 - $2,000 awarded to students. Massachusetts Restaurant Association; up to $2,500 awarded. National Restaurant Association; up to $2,000 awarded.

Policies to reduce costs. Credit/placement for qualifying scores on IB examinations. Work study available nights.

Payment plans. Credit card, installment payment.

Application procedures. FAFSA required. No deadline. Applicants notified on rolling basis.

Contact. Financial aid office: (802) 223-6324
David Coates, Chief Financial Officer
250 Main Street
Montpelier, VT 05602

New England Culinary Institute: Essex Junction

Essex Junction, Vermont
www.neci.edu
Two-year proprietary **Federal Code: 022540**

	Living at home	On-campus
Tuition and fees:	$20,840	$20,840
Room and board:		$5,525
Board only:	$1,620	
Books and supplies:	$1,000	$1,000
Transportation:	$1,500	$1,500

Undergraduate aid. Need-based: Average financial aid package for full-time students was $12,128; for part-time $12,128. 22% awarded as scholarships/grants, 78% as loans/jobs. **Non-need-based:** 4% awarded as scholarships/grants, 96% as loans/jobs. **Student debt:** 85% of graduating class borrowed to fund education; average debt was $20,376.

Freshman aid. Non-need based: 2 without need received awards.

Merit scholarships. Second Generation Scholarship; $1,000 awarded to students recommended by alumni. James Beard Foundation; $1,000 - $2,000 awarded to students. Massachusetts Restaurant Association; up to $2,500 awarded. National Restaurant Association; up to $2,000 awarded.

Policies to reduce costs. Credit/placement for qualifying scores on IB examinations. Work study available nights.

Application procedures. FAFSA required. No deadline. Applicants notified on rolling basis.

Contact. Financial aid office: (802) 223-6324
David Coodes, Chief Financial Officer
48 1/2 Park Street
Essex Junction, VT 05452

Norwich University

Northfield, Vermont
www.norwich.edu
Four-year private **Federal Code: 003692**

College costs. Military students pay an additional $1,120 per year for cadet uniform for first and second year.

	Living at home	On-campus
Tuition and fees (2002-2003):	$17,010	$17,010
Room and board:		$6,372
Books and supplies:	$500	$500
Personal expenses:	$400	$400
Transportation:	$400	$400

Undergraduate aid. Need-based: Need-based aid available for full-time and part-time students. **Non-need-based:** Scholarships based on academics, leadership, music/drama. **Additional information:** Winners of ROTC scholarships receive full room and board at no expense; must maintain a 2.75 GPA. Renewable up to 4 years.

Policies to reduce costs. Tuition/fee waivers for employees and their families. Prepayment discount; credit/placement for qualifying scores on AP, CLEP examinations.

Payment plans. Credit card, installment payment.

Application procedures. FAFSA, institutional form, CSS PROFILE required. Priority date 3/1; no closing date. Applicants notified on rolling basis starting 12/15. Early decision closing date 11/15.

Contact. Karen McGrath, Dean of Enrollment Management
65 South Main Street
Northfield, VT 05663

St. Michael's College

Colchester, Vermont
www.smcvt.edu
Four-year private **Federal Code: 003694**

	Living at home	On-campus
Tuition and fees:	$22,519	$22,519
Room and board:		$7,680
Books and supplies:	$800	$800
Personal expenses:	$220	$220
Transportation:	$400	$400

Undergraduate aid. Need-based: Average financial aid package for full-time students was $17,145. 74% awarded as scholarships/grants, 26% as loans/jobs. Need-based aid available for part-time students. **Non-need-based:** 51% awarded as scholarships/grants, 49% as loans/jobs. Scholarships based on academics, athletics. **Student debt:** 83% of graduating class borrowed to fund education; average debt was $16,420.

Freshman aid. Need-based: Out of 527 full-time freshmen, 462 applied for aid; 349 were judged to have need; of these 349 received aid. Average package met 93% of need. 269 students had full need met. Average scholarship/grant was $10,743; average loan $3,831. **Non-need based:** 121 full-time freshmen with need received non-need scholarships; 111 without need received awards; 5 received athletic scholarships.

Merit scholarships. State Scholarships; $10,000; renewable annually; based on combined SAT score of 1200, 3.5 average in a college prep program; other factors such as leadership and community service considered. St. Michael's College Presidential Scholarships; full tuition; 4 awarded; requires Vermont residency.

Policies to reduce costs. Tuition/fee waivers for family members, employees and their families. Credit/placement for qualifying scores on AP, IB, CLEP examinations. Work study available nights, weekends and for part-time students.

Payment plans. Installment payment.

Application procedures. FAFSA, institutional form required. CSS Profile should be submitted by students who apply for early action and wish early estimate on aid. Closing date 3/15. Applicants notified by 4/10, must reply by 5/1 or within 2 week(s) of notification. **Transfers:** Closing date 3/15.

Contact. Nelberta Lund, Director of Financial Aid
One Winooski Park
Colchester, VT 05439

Southern Vermont College

Bennington, Vermont
www.svc.edu
Four-year private **Federal Code: 003693**

	Living at home	On-campus
Tuition and fees (2002-2003):	$11,695	$11,695
Room and board:		$5,990
Board only:	$2,250	
Books and supplies:	$750	$750
Personal expenses:	$550	$690
Transportation:	$900	$600

Undergraduate aid. Need-based: Average financial aid package for full-time students was $12,580; for part-time $5,968. 62% awarded as scholarships/grants, 38% as loans/jobs. **Non-need-based:** 29% awarded as scholarships/grants, 71% as loans/jobs. Scholarships based on academics, leadership. **Additional information:** Financial aid provided through Vermont Student Assistance Corporation (VSAC).

Freshman aid. Need-based: Out of 86 full-time freshmen, 73 applied for aid; 62 were judged to have need; of these 62 received aid. Average package met 90% of need. 13 students had full need met. Average scholarship/grant was $10,720; average loan $2,560. **Non-need based:** 1 without need received awards.

Merit scholarships. Everett Scholarship; based on academic merit, from $1,000-$5,000, deadline March 1, renewable. Leadership Scholarships awarded to 10 first-time freshmen, $1,000, renewable annually.

Policies to reduce costs. Tuition/fee waivers for senior citizens, employees and their families. Prepayment discount; credit/placement for qualifying scores on AP, CLEP examinations. Work study available nights and weekends.

Payment plans. Credit card, installment payment.

Application procedures. FAFSA, institutional form required. Priority date 5/1; no closing date. Applicants notified on rolling basis starting 3/1, must reply by 5/1 or within 2 week(s) of notification. **Transfers:** Priority date 5/1. $1,000 need-based transfer scholarship available for each transfer.

Contact. Financial aid office: (877) 563-6076
Yvonne Whitaker, Director of Financial Aid Services
982 Mansion Drive
Bennington, VT 05201

Sterling College

Craftsbury Common, Vermont
www.sterlingcollege.edu
Four-year private **Federal Code: 014991**

College costs. Students receive $1,200 tuition and book credit in exchange for work done on campus.

	Living at home	On-campus
Tuition and fees (2002-2003):	$14,750	$14,750
Room and board:		$5,670
Books and supplies:	$600	$600
Personal expenses:		$500
Transportation:		$200

Undergraduate aid. Need-based: Average financial aid package for full-time students was $10,920. 58% awarded as scholarships/grants, 42% as loans/jobs. Need-based aid available for part-time students. **Non-need-based:** 9% awarded as scholarships/grants, 91% as loans/jobs. Scholarships based on academics, leadership, state/district residency. **Student debt:** 73% of graduating class borrowed to fund education; average debt was $18,464.

Freshman aid. Need-based: Average package met 81% of need. Average scholarship/grant was $7,589; average loan $2,136.

Merit scholarships. Achievement Scholarships: $700-$1,200; demonstration of a significant life achievement. Vermont Scholarship: $1,000-$2,000; applicants who live in the state of Vermont. Bounder Scholarship: $30-$500; applicants who live west of the Mississippi or in the Deep South. Presidential Scholarship: $500-$5,000; applicants who have performed well academically, pursued some degree of activity in environmental, outdoor leadership, or resource management. SCA Award: $1,000; alumni of Student Conservation Association. Transfer Award: $1,000; transfer students for transfer costs.

Policies to reduce costs. Tuition/fee waivers for employees and their families. Work study available nights, weekends and for part-time students.

Payment plans. Credit card, installment payment.

Application procedures. FAFSA, institutional form required. Priority date 3/15; no closing date. Applicants notified on rolling basis starting 5/1, must reply within 2 week(s) of notification. **Transfers:** No deadline.

Contact. Financial aid office: (800) 648-3591
Edward Houston, Director of Financial Aid
PO Box 72
Craftsbury Common, VT 05827-0072

University of Vermont

Burlington, Vermont
www.uvm.edu
Four-year public **Federal Code: 003696**

College costs. Additional $20 fee for on-campus students.

	Living at home	On-campus
Tuition and fees (2002-2003):	$8,994	$8,994
Out-of-state:	$21,484	$21,484
Room and board:		$6,378
Board only:	$2,146	
Books and supplies:	$696	$696
Personal expenses:	$1,039	$1,039

Undergraduate aid. Need-based: Average financial aid package for full-time students was $12,867; for part-time $8,709. 60% awarded as scholarships/grants, 40% as loans/jobs. **Non-need-based:** 42% awarded as scholarships/grants, 58% as loans/jobs. Scholarships based on academics, art, athletics. **Student debt:** 45% of graduating class borrowed to fund education; average debt was $22,425.

Freshman aid. Need-based: Out of 1,839 full-time freshmen, 1,272 applied for aid; 989 were judged to have need; of these 985 received aid. Average package met 98% of need. 967 students had full need met. Average scholarship/grant was $10,220; average loan $4,571. **Non-need based:** 59 full-time freshmen with need received non-need scholarships; 323 without need received awards; 23 received athletic scholarships.

Merit scholarships. Merit and need-based scholarships offered to both Vermont and out-of-state residents. Merit program for out-of-state students, Presidential Scholarship, designed for high-quality students based upon academic work in secondary school. Vermont Scholars Program, for top tier of academically qualified Vermont residents. No separate application required to apply for UVM-based scholarships. Green and Gold Scholarships available to top Vermont high school students; each high school in state nominates one student.

Policies to reduce costs. Tuition/fee waivers for senior citizens, employees and their families. Credit/placement for qualifying scores on AP, IB, CLEP examinations. Work study available nights, weekends and for part-time students.

Payment plans. Credit card, installment payment.

Application procedures. FAFSA required. Priority date 2/10; closing date 3/15. Applicants notified on rolling basis starting 3/15, must reply within 4 week(s) of notification. Early decision closing date 11/1. **Transfers:** Priority date 2/10; no deadline.

Contact. Financial aid office: (802) 656-3156
Donald Honeman, Director of Admissions and Financial Aid
194 South Prospect Street
Burlington, VT 05401-3596

Vermont Technical College

Randolph Center, Vermont
www.vtc.edu
Four-year public **Federal Code: 003698**

College costs. New England Board of Higher Education rate for students from other New England states: 150% of Vermont resident tuition. Available to degree candidates in academic areas not offered by educational institutions in their home states.

	Living at home	On-campus
Tuition and fees (2002-2003):	$6,488	$6,488
Out-of-state:	$12,208	$12,208
Room and board:		$5,782
Board only:	$990	
Books and supplies:	$750	$750
Personal expenses:	$650	$650
Transportation:	$700	$350

Undergraduate aid. Need-based: Need-based aid available for full-time and part-time students. **Non-need-based:** Scholarships based on academics.

Merit scholarships. VTC Presidential Scholarship awarded to 5 non-residents, $2,000. VTC Scholars program, full tuition for 2 years (excluding room and board) awarded to 4 Vermont students.

Policies to reduce costs. Tuition/fee waivers for employees and their families. Credit/placement for qualifying scores on AP, CLEP examinations. Work study available nights and weekends.

Payment plans. Installment, deferred payment.

Application procedures. FAFSA required. Priority date 3/1; no closing date. Applicants notified on rolling basis starting 3/15, must reply within 2 week(s) of notification. **Transfers:** Priority date 3/1.

Contact. **Financial aid office:** (800) 965-8790
Cathy McCullough, Director of Financial Aid
PO Box 500
Randolph Center, VT 05061-0500

Woodbury College

Montpelier, Vermont
www.woodbury-college.edu
Four-year private **Federal Code: 014348**

	Living at home
Tuition and fees (2002-2003):	$12,840
Books and supplies:	$600
Personal expenses:	$2,400

Undergraduate aid. Need-based: Need-based aid available for full-time and part-time students. **Student debt:** 70% of graduating class borrowed to fund education; average debt was $28,000.

Policies to reduce costs. Work study available nights, weekends and for part-time students.

Application procedures. FAFSA required.

Contact. Marcy Spaulding, Director of Financial Aid
660 Elm Street
Montpelier, VT 05602

Virginia

Art Institute of Washington

Arlington, Virginia
www.aiw.artinstitutes.edu
Four-year proprietary

	Living at home
Tuition and fees (projected):	$14,670

Undergraduate aid. Need-based: Need-based aid available for part-time students.

Application procedures. FAFSA, institutional form required.

Contact. Lisa Reed, Director of Financial and Administrative Services
1820 North Fort Myer Drive
Arlington, VA 22209-1802

Averett University

Danville, Virginia
www.averett.edu
Four-year private **Federal Code: 003702**

College costs. BBA program $250 per-credit-hour.

	Living at home	On-campus
Tuition and fees (2002-2003):	$16,800	$16,800
Room and board:		$5,150
Board only:	$800	
Books and supplies:	$750	$750
Personal expenses:	$1,435	$1,450
Transportation:	$300	

Undergraduate aid. Need-based: Average financial aid package for full-time students was $13,002; for part-time $5,755. 63% awarded as scholarships/grants, 37% as loans/jobs. **Non-need-based:** 61% awarded as scholarships/grants, 39% as loans/jobs. Scholarships based on academics, art, leadership, music/drama, religious affiliation, state/district residency. **Student debt:** 96% of graduating class borrowed to fund education; average debt was $11,947.

Freshman aid. Need-based: Out of 199 full-time freshmen, 179 applied for aid; 169 were judged to have need; of these 169 received aid. Average package met 70% of need. 27 students had full need met. Average scholarship/grant was $9,425; average loan $3,370. **Non-need based:** 24 full-time freshmen with need received non-need scholarships; 29 without need received awards.

Policies to reduce costs. Tuition/fee waivers for children of alumni, senior citizens, family members, family of clergy, employees and their families. Credit/placement for qualifying scores on AP, IB, CLEP examinations. Work study available nights, weekends and for part-time students.

Payment plans. Credit card, installment payment.

Application procedures. FAFSA required. Priority date 4/1; no closing date. Applicants notified on rolling basis starting 3/1, must reply within 2 week(s) of notification.

Contact. Financial aid office: (434) 791-5890
Carl Bradsher, Dean of Financial Assistance
420 West Main Street
Danville, VA 24541

Blue Ridge Community College

Weyers Cave, Virginia
www.br.vccs.edu
Two-year public **Federal Code: 006819**

	Living at home
Tuition and fees (2002-2003):	$1,355
Out-of-state:	$5,733
Per-credit charge:	$40
Per-credit out-of-state:	$186
Books and supplies:	$600
Personal expenses:	$900
Transportation:	$1,200

Undergraduate aid. Need-based: Need-based aid available for full-time and part-time students. **Non-need-based:** Scholarships based on academics, job skills, leadership, minority status.

Policies to reduce costs. Tuition/fee waivers for senior citizens. Credit/placement for qualifying scores on AP, CLEP examinations.

Payment plans. Credit card payment.

Application procedures. FAFSA, institutional form required. Priority date 5/1; no closing date. Applicants notified on rolling basis starting 5/30, must reply within 2 week(s) of notification.

Contact. Financial aid office: (540) 234-9261 ext. 2223
Robert Clemmer, Financial Aid Officer
Box 80
Weyers Cave, VA 24486-9989

Bluefield College

Bluefield, Virginia
www.bluefield.edu
Four-year private **Federal Code: 003703**

	Living at home	On-campus
Tuition and fees (projected):	$10,165	$10,165
Room and board:		$5,410
Board only:	$2,025	
Books and supplies:	$900	$900
Personal expenses:	$600	$900
Transportation:	$3,150	$980

Undergraduate aid. Need-based: Average financial aid package for full-time students was $7,229; for part-time $5,673. 64% awarded as scholarships/grants, 36% as loans/jobs. **Non-need-based:** 28% awarded as scholarships/grants, 72% as loans/jobs. Scholarships based on academics, art, athletics, leadership, music/drama, religious affiliation. **Student debt:** 57% of graduating class borrowed to fund education; average debt was $6,764.

Freshman aid. Need-based: Out of 201 full-time freshmen, 142 applied for aid; 127 were judged to have need; of these 127 received aid. Average package met 73% of need. 17 students had full need met. Average scholarship/grant was $6,285; average loan $2,443. **Non-need based:** 13 full-time freshmen with need received non-need scholarships; 38 without need received awards.

Policies to reduce costs. Tuition/fee waivers for adults, senior citizens, family of clergy, employees and their families. Credit/placement for qualifying scores on AP, CLEP examinations.

Payment plans. Credit card, installment payment.

Application procedures. FAFSA, institutional form required. Priority date 3/10; no closing date. Applicants notified on rolling basis, must reply within 3 week(s) of notification. **Transfers:** Scholarships of up to $2,000 per year available.

Contact. Financial aid office: (276) 326-4215
Debbie Checchio, Director of Financial Aid
3000 College Drive
Bluefield, VA 24605

Bridgewater College

Bridgewater, Virginia
www.bridgewater.edu
Four-year private **Federal Code: 003704**

	Living at home	On-campus
Tuition and fees:	$16,990	$16,990
Room and board:		$8,160
Board only:	$4,160	
Books and supplies:	$860	$860
Personal expenses:	$990	$990
Transportation:	$900	$400

Undergraduate aid. Need-based: Average financial aid package for full-time students was $15,822; for part-time $4,225. 75% awarded as scholarships/grants, 25% as loans/jobs. **Non-need-based:** 50% awarded as scholarships/grants, 50% as loans/jobs. Scholarships based on academics, minority status, music/drama, religious affiliation. **Student debt:** 73% of graduating class borrowed to fund education; average debt was $20,055. **Additional information:** GED required of home-schooled students applying for Title IV federal aid.

Freshman aid. Need-based: Out of 406 full-time freshmen, 363 applied for aid; 307 were judged to have need; of these 307 received aid. Average package met 88% of need. 62 students had full need met. Average scholarship/grant was $12,355; average loan $3,830. **Non-need based:** 307 full-time freshmen with need received non-need scholarships; 98 without need received awards.

Merit scholarships. President's Merit ACE Plus Award, full tuition, for rank in top 5% of high school class, minimum SAT score of 1350 or ACT score of 30, based on academic achievement and difficulty of curriculum. President's Merit Ace Award, $12,000, for rank in top 5% of class, minimum SAT of 1250 or ACT of 28, based on academic achievement and difficulty of curriculum. McKinney Scholarship, $12,000, for graduates of Carroll County, MD, high schools who rank in top 10% of class with minimum SAT of 1250 or ACT of 28. McKinney ACE Scholarships, $4,000 to $10,000 depending on class rank and/or SAT/ACT scores.

Policies to reduce costs. Tuition/fee waivers for senior citizens, employees and their families. Credit/placement for qualifying scores on AP, IB examinations. Work study available nights, weekends and for part-time students.

Application procedures. FAFSA required. Priority date 3/1; no closing date. Applicants notified on rolling basis starting 3/15, must reply within 2 week(s) of notification. **Transfers:** McKinney ACE merit scholarships available to students with 12 or more transferable credits; $4,000 to $10,000 based on GPA and test scores.

Contact. **Financial aid office:** (540) 828-5377
J. Vern Fairchilds, Director of Financial Aid
402 East College Street
Bridgewater, VA 22812-1599

Bryant & Stratton College

Virginia Beach, Virginia
www.bryantstratton.edu
Two-year proprietary **Federal Code: 010061**

College costs. Technology fee $100 per semester. Course fee $15 per credit hour for books.

	Living at home
Tuition and fees:	$9,900
Per-credit charge:	$330
Books and supplies:	$750
Personal expenses:	$1,560
Transportation:	$738

Undergraduate aid. Need-based: 43% awarded as scholarships/grants, 57% as loans/jobs. Need-based aid available for part-time students. **Non-need-based:** 8% awarded as scholarships/grants, 92% as loans/jobs. **Student debt:** 99% of graduating class borrowed to fund education; average debt was $14,125.

Policies to reduce costs. Tuition/fee waivers for employees and their families. Credit/placement for qualifying scores on AP, CLEP examinations. Work study available nights and for part-time students.

Payment plans. Credit card, installment payment.

Application procedures. FAFSA required. No deadline. Applicants notified on rolling basis. **Transfers:** No deadline.

Contact. **Financial aid office:** (757) 499-7900
Anita Wyche, Director of Financial Aid
301 Centre Pointe Drive
Virginia Beach, VA 23462-4417

Christendom College

Front Royal, Virginia
www.christendom.edu
Four-year private

	Living at home	On-campus
Tuition and fees (2002-2003):	$12,650	$12,650
Room and board:		$4,800
Books and supplies:	$500	$500
Personal expenses:	$300	$300
Transportation:		$400

Undergraduate aid. Need-based: Average financial aid package for full-time students was $9,630. 47% awarded as scholarships/grants, 53% as loans/jobs. **Non-need-based:** Scholarships based on academics. **Student debt:** 43% of graduating class borrowed to fund education; average debt was $11,380. **Additional information:** Christendom accepts no direct federal aid, nor does it participate in indirect programs of federal aid.

Freshman aid. Need-based: Out of 93 full-time freshmen, 69 applied for aid; 42 were judged to have need; of these 42 received aid. Average package met 90% of need. 42 students had full need met. Average scholarship/grant was $3,368; average loan $3,685. **Non-need based:** 17 full-time freshmen with need received non-need scholarships; 27 without need received awards.

Policies to reduce costs. Tuition/fee waivers for family members, family of clergy, employees and their families. Prepayment discount; credit/placement for qualifying scores on AP examinations.

Payment plans. Credit card, installment payment.

Application procedures. Institutional form required. Priority date 4/1; closing date 6/1. Applicants notified on rolling basis starting 2/1, must reply within 4 week(s) of notification.

Contact. Alisa Polk, Financial Aid Officer
134 Christendom Drive
Front Royal, VA 22630

College of Health Sciences

Roanoke, Virginia
www.chs.edu
Four-year private **Federal Code: 009893**

College costs. Tuition for physician assistant program: $30,000 for full 2-year program.

	Living at home	On-campus
Tuition and fees (2002-2003):	$6,600	$6,600
Room only:		$2,000
Books and supplies:	$800	$800
Personal expenses:	$2,100	$2,100
Transportation:	$1,900	$900

Undergraduate aid. Need-based: Need-based aid available for full-time and part-time students. **Non-need-based:** Scholarships based on academics.

Merit scholarships. Commonwealth Award for all full-time Virginia students; $2,400. Merit Awards available to full-time out-of-state students based on SAT/GPA; amounts vary.

Policies to reduce costs. Tuition/fee waivers for employees and their families. Credit/placement for qualifying scores on AP, CLEP examinations.

Payment plans. Credit card payment.

Application procedures. FAFSA, institutional form required. Priority date 2/20; no closing date. Applicants notified on rolling basis starting 5/1, must reply within 2 week(s) of notification. **Transfers:** No deadline.

Contact. Deborah Johnson, Financial Aid Officer
Box 13186
Roanoke, VA 24031-3186

College of William and Mary

Williamsburg, Virginia
www.wm.edu
Four-year public **Federal Code: 003705**

College costs. Out-of-state students pay an additional $30 in fees.

	Living at home	On-campus
Tuition and fees (2002-2003):	$5,088	$5,088
Out-of-state:	$19,256	$19,256
Room and board:		$5,489
Board only:	$2,170	
Books and supplies:	$800	$800
Personal expenses:	$970	$970
Transportation:	$600	

Undergraduate aid. Need-based: Average financial aid package for full-time students was $8,154. 57% awarded as scholarships/grants, 43% as loans/jobs. **Non-need-based:** 35% awarded as scholarships/grants, 65% as loans/jobs. Scholarships based on academics, athletics, leadership. **Student debt:** 26% of graduating class borrowed to fund education; average debt was $19,762.

Freshman aid. Need-based: Out of 1,317 full-time freshmen, 632 applied for aid; 344 were judged to have need; of these 344 received aid. Average package met 82% of need. 108 students had full need met. Average scholarship/grant was $6,805; average loan $2,523. **Non-need based:** 40 full-time freshmen with need received non-need scholarships; 317 without need received awards; 71 received athletic scholarships.

Policies to reduce costs. Tuition/fee waivers for senior citizens, employees and their families. Credit/placement for qualifying scores on AP, IB examinations.

Payment plans. Installment payment.

Application procedures. FAFSA, CSS PROFILE required. CSS profile required of early decision applicants only. Priority date 2/15; closing date 3/15. Applicants notified by 4/1, must reply by 5/1 or within 4 week(s) of notification. Early decision closing date 11/1.

Contact. **Financial aid office:** (757) 221-2420
Edward Irish, Director of Student Financial Aid
PO Box 8795
Williamsburg, VA 23187-8795

Danville Community College

Danville, Virginia
www.dcc.vccs.edu
Two-year public **Federal Code: 003758**

	Living at home
Tuition and fees (2002-2003):	$1,319
Out-of-state:	$5,697
Per-credit charge:	$40
Per-credit out-of-state:	$186
Books and supplies:	$700
Personal expenses:	$1,328
Transportation:	$1,800

Undergraduate aid. All financial aid based on need. 94% awarded as scholarships/grants, 6% as loans/jobs. Need-based aid available for part-time students.

Policies to reduce costs. Tuition/fee waivers for senior citizens. Credit/placement for qualifying scores on AP, CLEP examinations. Work study available for part-time students.

Payment plans. Credit card payment.

Application procedures. FAFSA required. Priority date 6/1; no closing date. Applicants notified on rolling basis starting 5/1, must reply within 2 week(s) of notification. **Transfers:** Priority date 6/1; no deadline. Limited aid available to transfer students admitted in spring semester.

Contact. **Financial aid office:** (434) 797-8439
Else Liggon, Coordinator of Financial Aid
1008 South Main Street
Danville, VA 24541

DeVry University: Crystal City

Arlington, Virginia
www.crys.devry.edu
Four-year proprietary

	Living at home
Tuition and fees:	$11,265
Books and supplies:	$1,100
Personal expenses:	$1,550
Transportation:	$1,422

Undergraduate aid. All financial aid based on need. Average financial aid package for full-time students was $3,091; for part-time $2,653. 13% awarded as scholarships/grants, 87% as loans/jobs.

Freshman aid. Out of 279 full-time freshmen, 279 applied for aid; 249 were judged to have need; of these 249 received aid. Average package met 28% of need. 5 students had full need met. Average scholarship/grant was $2,257; average loan $2,462.

Policies to reduce costs. Tuition/fee waivers for employees and their families.

Payment plans. Credit card, installment, deferred payment.

Application procedures. FAFSA required. No deadline. Applicants notified on rolling basis starting 7/1. **Transfers:** No deadline.

Contact. Roberta McDevitt, Director of Student Finance
2341 Jefferson Davis Highway
Arlington, VA 22202

ECPI College of Technology

Virginia Beach, Virginia
www.ecpi.edu
Two-year proprietary **Federal Code: 010198**

College costs. Required fee is for books.

	Living at home
Tuition and fees (2002-2003):	$9,300
Personal expenses:	$1,120
Transportation:	$630

Undergraduate aid. Need-based: Need-based aid available for full-time and part-time students.

Application procedures. No deadline. Applicants notified on rolling basis.

Contact. Jeff Arthur, Vice President of Financial Aid
5555 Greenwich Road, Suite 300
Virginia Beach, VA 23462-6542

ECPI Technical College: Roanoke

Roanoke, Virginia
www.ecpi.net
Two-year proprietary **Federal Code: 017205**

College costs. Required fee is for books.

	Living at home
Tuition and fees (2002-2003):	$9,300
Personal expenses:	$2,072
Transportation:	$630

Undergraduate aid. Need-based: Need-based aid available for full-time and part-time students.

Application procedures. FAFSA required. No deadline. Applicants notified on rolling basis.

Contact. **Financial aid office:** (540) 563-8080
Elmer Haas, Director
5234 Airport Road
Roanoke, VA 24012

Eastern Mennonite University

Harrisonburg, Virginia
www.emu.edu
Four-year private **Federal Code: 003708**

	Living at home	On-campus
Tuition and fees (2002-2003):	$16,370	$16,370
Room and board:		$5,350
Board only:	$3,000	
Books and supplies:	$700	$700
Personal expenses:	$800	$800

Undergraduate aid. Need-based: Average financial aid package for full-time students was $13,140; for part-time $5,100. 55% awarded as scholarships/grants, 45% as loans/jobs. **Non-need-based:** 77% awarded as scholarships/grants, 23% as loans/jobs. Scholarships based on academics, alumni affiliation, music/drama, religious affiliation, state/district residency. **Student debt:** 91% of graduating class borrowed to fund education; average debt was $19,300.

Freshman aid. Need-based: Out of 208 full-time freshmen, 205 applied for aid; 199 were judged to have need; of these 199 received aid. Average package met 91% of need. 47 students had full need met. Average scholarship/grant was $9,720; average loan $4,100. **Non-need based:** 92 full-time freshmen with need received non-need scholarships; 61 without need received awards.

Merit scholarships. President's Scholarship for GPA of 3.9 or higher; Academic Achievement Scholarship for minimum 3.2 GPA; University Grant for minimum 2.5 GPA; minimum SAT score of 920 or ACT score of 20 required for all scholarships. Amounts based on GPA and test scores; no limit on number of awards. Full-tuition scholarships available for 2 honors program applicants with highest test scores and GPA; half-tuition scholarships available for next 10 candidates.

Policies to reduce costs. Tuition/fee waivers for employees and their families. Credit/placement for qualifying scores on AP, IB, CLEP examinations. Work study available nights, weekends and for part-time students.

Payment plans. Credit card, installment payment.

Application procedures. FAFSA required. Priority date 3/15; no closing date. Applicants notified on rolling basis starting 3/1. **Transfers:** No deadline. Financial aid transcripts from previous colleges required.

Contact. Financial aid office: (540) 432-4137
Michele Hensley, Director of Financial Assistance
1200 Park Road
Harrisonburg, VA 22802-2462

Eastern Shore Community College

Melfa, Virginia
www.es.vccs.edu
Two-year public **Federal Code: 003748**

	Living at home
Tuition and fees (2002-2003):	$1,349
Out-of-state:	$5,727
Per-credit charge:	$40
Per-credit out-of-state:	$186
Books and supplies:	$500
Personal expenses:	$1,196
Transportation:	$1,440

Policies to reduce costs. Tuition/fee waivers for senior citizens. Credit/placement for qualifying scores on CLEP examinations.

Payment plans. Credit card payment.

Application procedures. FAFSA required. Priority date 5/1; no closing date. Applicants notified on rolling basis starting 6/1, must reply within 2 week(s) of notification.

Contact. P. Bryan Smith, Financial Aid Officer
29300 Lankford Highway
Melfa, VA 23410-9755

Emory & Henry College

Emory, Virginia
www.ehc.edu
Four-year private **Federal Code: 003709**

	Living at home	On-campus
Tuition and fees:	$15,900	$15,900
Room and board:		$6,050
Board only:	$1,500	
Books and supplies:	$700	$700
Personal expenses:	$700	$700
Transportation:	$1,100	

Undergraduate aid. All financial aid based on need. Average financial aid package for full-time students was $11,913; for part-time $6,531. 68% awarded as scholarships/grants, 32% as loans/jobs. **Student debt:** 51% of graduating class borrowed to fund education; average debt was $9,412. **Additional information:** Virginia residents eligible for additional in-state tuition grants.

Freshman aid. Out of 237 full-time freshmen, 182 applied for aid; 151 were judged to have need; of these 151 received aid. Average package met 83% of need. 13 students had full need met. Average scholarship/grant was $5,061; average loan $3,226.

Policies to reduce costs. Tuition/fee waivers for employees and their families. Credit/placement for qualifying scores on AP, IB examinations.

Payment plans. Credit card, installment payment.

Application procedures. FAFSA required. Priority date 4/1; closing date 8/1. Applicants notified on rolling basis starting 2/1, must reply within 4 week(s) of notification. Early decision closing date 12/1.

Contact. Financial aid office: (276) 944-6115
Scarlett Cortner, Coordinator, Financial Aid
Box 10
Emory, VA 24327

Ferrum College

Ferrum, Virginia
www.ferrum.edu
Four-year private **Federal Code: 003711**

	Living at home	On-campus
Tuition and fees:	$15,640	$15,640
Room and board:		$5,600
Board only:	$1,500	
Books and supplies:	$800	$800
Personal expenses:	$1,130	$1,300
Transportation:	$700	$430

Undergraduate aid. Need-based: Need-based aid available for full-time and part-time students. **Non-need-based:** Scholarships based on academics, leadership, music/drama, religious affiliation, state/district residency.

Merit scholarships. President Scholarships for freshmen with a minimum high school GPA of 3.0, minimum combined SAT score of 1000, renewable for 4 years based on maintaining minimum 2.75 GPA; ranging from $5,400-$7,800. Community Activity Scholarships based on commitment to student organizations and activities (excluding athletics), minimum of 2.5 GPA and 900 combined SAT required.

Policies to reduce costs. Tuition/fee waivers for senior citizens, family members, family of clergy, employees and their families. Credit/placement for qualifying scores on AP, CLEP examinations. Work study available nights and weekends.

Payment plans. Credit card, installment payment.

Application procedures. FAFSA required. Priority date 4/1; no closing date. Applicants notified on rolling basis starting 3/1. **Transfers:** Priority date 4/1.

Contact. Financial aid office: (540) 365-4282
Sheila Nelson-Hensley, Director of Financial Aid
Spilman-Daniel House
Ferrum, VA 24088

George Mason University

Fairfax, Virginia
www.gmu.edu
Four-year public **Federal Code: 003749**

	Living at home	On-campus
Tuition and fees (2002-2003):	$4,416	$4,416
Out-of-state:	$13,716	$13,716
Room and board:		$5,600
Board only:	$3,120	
Books and supplies:	$750	$750
Personal expenses:	$1,284	$1,284
Transportation:	$1,439	$1,180

Undergraduate aid. **Need-based:** Average financial aid package for full-time students was $6,770; for part-time $4,046. 44% awarded as scholarships/grants, 56% as loans/jobs. **Non-need-based:** 20% awarded as scholarships/grants, 80% as loans/jobs. Scholarships based on academics, athletics, minority status, music/drama, state/district residency. **Student debt:** 41% of graduating class borrowed to fund education; average debt was $14,174.

Freshman aid. **Need-based:** Out of 2,225 full-time freshmen, 1,504 applied for aid; 894 were judged to have need; of these 805 received aid. Average package met 63% of need. 534 students had full need met. Average scholarship/grant was $4,788; average loan $2,906. **Non-need based:** 291 full-time freshmen with need received non-need scholarships; 300 without need received awards; 38 received athletic scholarships.

Policies to reduce costs. Tuition/fee waivers for senior citizens, employees and their families. Credit/placement for qualifying scores on AP, CLEP examinations.

Payment plans. Credit card, installment, deferred payment.

Application procedures. FAFSA required. Priority date 3/1; no closing date. Applicants notified on rolling basis starting 4/1, must reply within 3 week(s) of notification.

Contact. Jevita de Freitas, Director, Student Financial Planning
4400 University Drive, MSN 3A4
Fairfax, VA 22030

Hampden-Sydney College

Hampden-Sydney, Virginia
www.hsc.edu
Four-year private **Federal Code: 003713**

	Living at home	On-campus
Tuition and fees (2002-2003):	$19,893	$19,893
Room and board:		$6,722
Books and supplies:	$900	$900
Personal expenses:		$900

Undergraduate aid. **Need-based:** Need-based aid available for full-time students. **Non-need-based:** Scholarships based on academics, leadership, state/district residency.

Merit scholarships. Allan Scholarship, $16,000 annually; Venable Scholarship, $12,000 annually; Patrick Henry Scholarship, $8,000 annually; Achievement Awards, $5,000 annually. All based on academic prowess.

Policies to reduce costs. Tuition/fee waivers for employees and their families. Credit/placement for qualifying scores on AP, IB examinations.

Payment plans. Credit card, installment payment.

Application procedures. FAFSA, CSS PROFILE required. Priority date 3/1; closing date 5/1. Applicants notified by 3/15, must reply by 5/1 or within 3 week(s) of notification. Early decision closing date 11/15.

Contact. **Financial aid office:** (434) 223-6119
Keith Wellings, Director of Financial Aid
Box 667
Hampden-Sydney, VA 23943

Hampton University

Hampton, Virginia
www.hamptonu.edu
Four-year private **Federal Code: 003714**

	Living at home	On-campus
Tuition and fees (2002-2003):	$12,252	$12,252
Room and board:		$5,828
Board only:	$1,500	
Books and supplies:	$750	$750
Personal expenses:	$1,050	$1,103
Transportation:	$1,323	$1,260

Undergraduate aid. **Need-based:** Average financial aid package for full-time students was $8,539; for part-time $4,828. 25% awarded as scholarships/grants, 75% as loans/jobs. **Non-need-based:** 76% awarded as scholarships/grants, 24% as loans/jobs. Scholarships based on academics, athletics, leadership, music/drama. **Student debt:** 62% of graduating class borrowed to fund education; average debt was $23,000.

Freshman aid. **Need-based:** Out of 1,272 full-time freshmen, 1,027 applied for aid; 727 were judged to have need; of these 584 received aid. Average package met 28% of need. 400 students had full need met. Average scholarship/grant was $3,656; average loan $2,453. **Non-need based:** 413 full-time freshmen with need received non-need scholarships; 258 without need received awards; 46 received athletic scholarships.

Policies to reduce costs. Tuition/fee waivers for employees and their families. Credit/placement for qualifying scores on AP, IB, CLEP examinations.

Payment plans. Credit card, deferred payment.

Application procedures. FAFSA required. Priority date 3/1; no closing date. Applicants notified on rolling basis starting 4/1, must reply within 2 week(s) of notification.

Contact. **Financial aid office:** (757) 727-5332
Cassondra Costa, Financial Aid Director
Hampton, VA 23668

Hollins University

Roanoke, Virginia
www.hollins.edu
Four-year private **Federal Code: 003715**

	Living at home	On-campus
Tuition and fees (2002-2003):	$18,450	$18,450
Room and board:		$6,875
Books and supplies:	$600	$600
Personal expenses:		$850
Transportation:	$800	$800

Undergraduate aid. **Need-based:** Average financial aid package for full-time students was $15,737. 71% awarded as scholarships/grants, 29% as loans/jobs. Need-based aid available for part-time students. **Non-need-based:** Scholarships based on academics, alumni affiliation, art, leadership, music/drama, state/district residency. **Student debt:** 64% of graduating class borrowed to fund education; average debt was $13,477.

Freshman aid. **Need-based:** Out of 202 full-time freshmen, 198 applied for aid; 132 were judged to have need; of these 132 received aid. Average package met 81% of need. 26 students had full need met. Average scholarship/grant was $12,095; average loan $3,979. **Non-need based:** 93 full-time freshmen with need received non-need scholarships; 66 without need received awards.

Merit scholarships. Hollins Scholar Awards, full tuition, 3 awarded; Trustee Awards, $10,500-$13,000; Presidential Awards, $7,500-$10,000; all based on outstanding academic merit. Faculty Recognition Awards, $4,000-$7,000, 75-100 awarded, based on academic merit, leadership skills, special achievements; Endowed Scholarships, more than 100 awarded, $500 to $5,000, based on GPA, need, special interests; Alumni Scholarships, $500-$1,000.

Policies to reduce costs. Tuition/fee waivers for employees and their families. Credit/placement for qualifying scores on AP, IB examinations. Work study available nights, weekends and for part-time students.

Payment plans. Credit card, installment payment.

Application procedures. FAFSA required. Priority date 2/15; closing date 3/1. Applicants notified on rolling basis starting 3/15, must reply by 5/1 or within 3 week(s) of notification. Early decision closing date 12/1. **Transfers:** Priority date 7/1; closing date 7/15.

Contact. **Financial aid office:** (540) 362-6332
Rebecca Eckstein, Director of Scholarships and Financial Assistance
Box 9707
Roanoke, VA 24020-1707

ITT Technical Institute: Norfolk

Norfolk, Virginia
www.itt-tech.edu
Three-year proprietary **Federal Code: 007327**

College costs. Total program varies depending on course of study. Per-credit-hour charge: $347.

Policies to reduce costs. Tuition/fee waivers for employees and their families.

Payment plans. Credit card, installment payment.

Application procedures. FAFSA, institutional form required. No deadline. Applicants notified on rolling basis.

Contact. Marsha Miller, Director of Finance
863 Glenrock Road
Norfolk, VA 23502

ITT Technical Institute: Richmond

Richmond, Virginia
www.itt-tech.edu
Two-year proprietary **Federal Code: 022865**

College costs. Total program varies depending on course of study. Per-credit-hour charge: $347. Books/supplies: $3,100.

Policies to reduce costs. Tuition/fee waivers for employees and their families. Tuition at time of enrollment guaranteed for 2 years.

Payment plans. Credit card, installment payment.

Application procedures. FAFSA, institutional form required. No deadline. Applicants notified on rolling basis.

Contact. Tara Phillips, Director of Finance
300 Gateway Centre Parkway
Richmond, VA 23235

J. Sargeant Reynolds Community College

Richmond, Virginia
www.jsr.vccs.edu
Two-year public **Federal Code: 003759**

	Living at home
Tuition and fees (2002-2003):	$1,812
Out-of-state:	$6,189
Per-credit charge:	$60
Per-credit out-of-state:	$206
Board only:	$1,600
Books and supplies:	$1,000
Personal expenses:	$900
Transportation:	$900

Undergraduate aid. **Need-based:** 96% awarded as scholarships/grants, 4% as loans/jobs. Need-based aid available for part-time students. **Non-need-based:** Scholarships based on academics.

Merit scholarships. J. Sargeant Reynolds Community College Local Board Scholarship for area high school students with minimum 3.0 GPA; 23 awarded; full tuition. Eric and Jeanette Lipman Endowed Scholarship based on academic excellence; number and amount awarded varies. Central Fidelity Bank Scholarship for first-year students with minimum 2.5 cumulative GPA; 2 awarded; $1,500. Dennis Foundation Scholarship, preference given to dependents of former employees of Dominion Oil Company or presently employed Woodfin Oil Company, academic excellence major consideration; number and amount awarded vary. Numerous other scholarships available.

Policies to reduce costs. Tuition/fee waivers for senior citizens. Credit/placement for qualifying scores on AP, IB, CLEP examinations. Work study available nights, weekends and for part-time students.

Payment plans. Credit card payment.

Application procedures. FAFSA required. Priority date 6/30; no closing date. Applicants notified on rolling basis starting 7/15, must reply within 2 week(s) of notification.

Contact. **Financial aid office:** (804) 371-3137
Barry Davis, Director of Financial Aid
Admissions and Records
Richmond, VA 23285-5622

James Madison University

Harrisonburg, Virginia
www.jmu.edu
Four-year public **Federal Code: 003721**

	Living at home	On-campus
Tuition and fees (2002-2003):	$4,288	$4,288
Out-of-state:	$11,472	$11,472
Room and board:		$5,568
Books and supplies:	$750	$750
Personal expenses:		$1,250
Transportation:		$1,674

Undergraduate aid. **Need-based:** Average financial aid package for full-time students was $5,754; for part-time $5,394. 30% awarded as scholarships/grants, 70% as loans/jobs. **Non-need-based:** 23% awarded as scholarships/grants, 77% as loans/jobs. Scholarships based on academics, alumni affiliation, art, athletics, leadership, minority status, music/drama, state/district residency. **Student debt:** 52% of graduating class borrowed to fund education; average debt was $11,786.

Freshman aid. **Need-based:** Out of 3,283 full-time freshmen, 2,305 applied for aid; 1,123 were judged to have need; of these 951 received aid. Average package met 43% of need. 753 students had full need met. Average scholarship/grant was $3,280; average loan $2,847. **Non-need based:** 464 full-time freshmen with need received non-need scholarships; 133 without need received awards; 732 received athletic scholarships.

Merit scholarships. See university website for scholarship information.

Policies to reduce costs. Tuition/fee waivers for senior citizens, employees and their families. Credit/placement for qualifying scores on AP, IB, CLEP examinations. Work study available nights and weekends.

Payment plans. Credit card, installment payment.

Application procedures. FAFSA required. Priority date 3/1; no closing date. Applicants notified on rolling basis starting 4/1, must reply within 4 week(s) of notification. **Transfers:** Priority date 3/1; no deadline.

Contact. **Financial aid office:** (540) 568-7820
Lisa Turner, Director of Financial Aid and Scholarships
Sonner Hall MSC 0101
Harrisonburg, VA 22807

Johnson & Wales University: Norfolk

Norfolk, Virginia
www.jwu.edu
Four-year private **Federal Code: 003404**

College costs. Culinary program tuition is $18,444.

	Living at home	On-campus
Tuition and fees:	$16,914	$16,914
Room and board:		$6,621
Books and supplies:	$750	$750
Personal expenses:	$1,250	

Application procedures. FAFSA required. Priority date 1/1; no closing date. Applicants notified on rolling basis, must reply within 4 week(s) of notification.

Contact. Margo Simmons, Assistant Director of Financial Aid
2428 Almeda Avenue, Suite 316
Norfolk, VA 23513

Liberty University

Lynchburg, Virginia
www.liberty.edu
Four-year private **Federal Code: 010392**

	Living at home	On-campus
Tuition and fees (projected):	$12,020	$12,020
Room and board:		$5,200
Books and supplies:	$800	$800
Personal expenses:	$850	$850
Transportation:	$1,850	$1,850

Undergraduate aid. Need-based: Average financial aid package for full-time students was $7,815; for part-time $4,605. 38% awarded as scholarships/grants, 62% as loans/jobs. **Non-need-based:** 81% awarded as scholarships/grants, 19% as loans/jobs. Scholarships based on academics, athletics, leadership, music/drama, state/district residency.

Freshman aid. Need-based: Out of 1,559 full-time freshmen, 1,504 applied for aid; 1,199 were judged to have need; of these 1,198 received aid. Average package met 60% of need. 107 students had full need met. Average scholarship/grant was $3,172; average loan $2,551. **Non-need based:** 1,186 full-time freshmen with need received non-need scholarships; 348 without need received awards; 64 received athletic scholarships.

Merit scholarships. Liberty Academic Achievement Scholarship; Based on combination of high school grades and standardized test scores. Students may qualify for up to $6,000. Additional $3,500 could be applied if student is also accepted into the Honors Program.

Policies to reduce costs. Tuition/fee waivers for family of clergy, employees and their families. Credit/placement for qualifying scores on AP, CLEP examinations.

Payment plans. Credit card, installment payment.

Application procedures. FAFSA required. Priority date 3/1; no closing date. Applicants notified on rolling basis, must reply within 3 week(s) of notification.

Contact. **Financial aid office:** (434) 582-2270
Rhonda Allbeck, Director of Student Financial Aid
1971 University Boulevard
Lynchburg, VA 24502

Longwood University

Farmville, Virginia
www.longwood.edu
Four-year public **Federal Code: 003719**

College costs. Required laptop computer for first year students $2,000.

	Living at home	On-campus
Tuition and fees:	$5,877	$5,877
Out-of-state:	$11,803	$11,803
Room and board:		$5,298
Board only:	$2,112	
Books and supplies:	$700	$700
Personal expenses:	$1,200	$1,200
Transportation:	$1,000	$1,000

Undergraduate aid. Need-based: Average financial aid package for full-time students was $6,325. 48% awarded as scholarships/grants, 52% as loans/jobs. Need-based aid available for part-time students. **Non-need-based:** 23% awarded as scholarships/grants, 77% as loans/jobs. Scholarships based on academics, alumni affiliation, art, athletics, music/drama. **Student debt:** 85% of graduating class borrowed to fund education; average debt was $13,915.

Freshman aid. Need-based: Out of 878 full-time freshmen, 623 applied for aid; 384 were judged to have need; of these 384 received aid. Average package met 70% of need. 59 students had full need met. Average scholarship/grant was $3,584; average loan $2,982. **Non-need based:** 26 full-time freshmen with need received non-need scholarships; 207 without need received awards; 23 received athletic scholarships.

Merit scholarships. Longwood Scholars, 5 awarded, $1,200. Admissions Scholarships, 40 awarded, $500. Hull Education, 10 awarded, full tuition (in-state rates) and fees. Longwood Honors, 5 awarded, $1,000. Citizen Scholars, 4 awards, $6,000. All awards based on grades and test scores.

Policies to reduce costs. Tuition/fee waivers for senior citizens, employees and their families. Credit/placement for qualifying scores on AP, IB, CLEP examinations.

Payment plans. Installment payment.

Application procedures. FAFSA required. Priority date 3/1; no closing date. Applicants notified on rolling basis starting 4/1, must reply within 2 week(s) of notification.

Contact. **Financial aid office:** (434) 395-2077
Karen Schirabeck, Director of Financial Aid
201 High Street
Farmville, VA 23909-1898

Lynchburg College

Lynchburg, Virginia
www.lynchburg.edu
Four-year private **Federal Code: 003720**

	Living at home	On-campus
Tuition and fees (2002-2003):	$20,165	$20,165
Room and board:		$4,600
Books and supplies:	$500	$500
Personal expenses:		$440
Transportation:	$390	$430

Undergraduate aid. Non-need-based: Scholarships based on academics, state/district residency.

Policies to reduce costs. Tuition/fee waivers for adults, employees and their families. Prepayment discount; credit/placement for qualifying scores on AP, CLEP examinations.

Payment plans. Credit card, installment payment.

Application procedures. FAFSA required. Priority date 3/1; no closing date. Applicants notified on rolling basis starting 3/1. Early decision closing date 11/15. **Transfers:** Priority date 7/1; no deadline.

Contact. Michelle Davis, Coordinator of Financial Aid
1501 Lakeside Drive
Lynchburg, VA 24501

Mary Baldwin College

Staunton, Virginia
www.mbc.edu
Four-year private **Federal Code: 003723**

	Living at home	On-campus
Tuition and fees:	$19,409	$19,409
Room and board:		$5,525
Board only:	$2,000	
Books and supplies:	$700	$700
Personal expenses:	$1,200	$1,200
Transportation:	$400	$400

Undergraduate aid. Need-based: Average financial aid package for full-time students was $18,010; for part-time $7,955. 68% awarded as scholarships/grants, 32% as loans/jobs. **Non-need-based:** 42% awarded as scholarships/grants, 58% as loans/jobs. Scholarships based on academics, leadership, state/district residency. **Student debt:** 67% of graduating class borrowed to fund education; average debt was $19,332.

Freshman aid. Need-based: Out of 244 full-time freshmen, 219 applied for aid; 188 were judged to have need; of these 186 received aid. Average package met 89% of need. 34 students had full need met. Average scholarship/grant was $12,575; average loan $2,935. **Non-need based:** 22 full-time freshmen with need received non-need scholarships; 50 without need received awards.

Policies to reduce costs. Tuition/fee waivers for children of alumni, employees and their families. Credit/placement for qualifying scores on AP, IB, CLEP examinations.

Payment plans. Credit card, installment payment.

Application procedures. FAFSA required. Priority date 5/15; no closing date. Applicants notified on rolling basis starting 2/1. Early decision closing date 11/15. **Transfers:** No deadline.

Contact. **Financial aid office:** (540) 887-7022
Jacquelyn Elliott-Wonderley, Director of Financial Aid/Associate Dean of Admissions
Office of Admissions
Staunton, VA 24401

Mary Washington College

Fredericksburg, Virginia
www.mwc.edu
Four-year public **Federal Code: 003746**

	Living at home	On-campus
Tuition and fees:	$4,688	$4,688
Out-of-state:	$12,436	$12,436
Room and board:		$5,478
Board only:	$2,044	
Books and supplies:	$900	$900
Personal expenses:	$1,730	$1,678
Transportation:	$1,690	$1,034

Undergraduate aid. Need-based: Average financial aid package for full-time students was $5,326; for part-time $2,300. 37% awarded as scholarships/grants, 63% as loans/jobs. **Non-need-based:** 20% awarded as scholarships/grants, 80% as loans/jobs. Scholarships based on academics, art, leadership, minority status, music/drama, state/district residency. **Student debt:** 72% of graduating class borrowed to fund education; average debt was $13,100.

Freshman aid. Need-based: Out of 885 full-time freshmen, 653 applied for aid; 408 were judged to have need; of these 392 received aid. Average package met 64% of need. 35 students had full need met. Average scholarship/grant was $2,840; average loan $2,515. **Non-need based:** 141 full-time freshmen with need received non-need scholarships; 140 without need received awards.

Merit scholarships. Alumni Scholarship Program; students offered early decision and Honors Admission are automatically considered. No separate application is needed. Scholarships range from $500 to $3,400. One Virginia resident will receive tuition, fees, room and board up to $10,000. All scholarships are renewable.

Policies to reduce costs. Credit/placement for qualifying scores on AP, IB, CLEP examinations. Work study available nights, weekends and for part-time students.

Payment plans. Installment payment.

Application procedures. FAFSA required. Priority date 3/1; no closing date. Applicants notified by 4/15, must reply by 5/1 or within 2 week(s) of notification.

Contact. **Financial aid office:** (540) 654-2468
Deborah Harber, Senior Associate Dean for Financial Aid
1301 College Avenue
Fredericksburg, VA 22401-5358

Marymount University

Arlington, Virginia
www.marymount.edu
Four-year private **Federal Code: 003724**

College costs. Room and board phone data wiring fee of $270 required.

	Living at home	On-campus
Tuition and fees:	$16,438	$16,438
Room and board:		$7,230
Books and supplies:	$500	$500
Personal expenses:	$900	$900
Transportation:	$750	$470

Undergraduate aid. Need-based: Average financial aid package for full-time students was $12,623; for part-time $5,300. 60% awarded as scholarships/grants, 40% as loans/jobs. **Non-need-based:** 64% awarded as scholarships/grants, 36% as loans/jobs. Scholarships based on academics, alumni affiliation, leadership, state/district residency. **Student debt:** 61% of graduating class borrowed to fund education; average debt was $14,915.

Freshman aid. Need-based: Out of 361 full-time freshmen, 324 applied for aid; 231 were judged to have need; of these 230 received aid. Average package met 82% of need. 53 students had full need met. Average scholarship/grant was $7,331; average loan $2,713. **Non-need based:** 159 full-time freshmen with need received non-need scholarships; 84 without need received awards.

Merit scholarships. Freshman Academic Scholarship: requires GPA of 3.0 or better and good test scores.

Policies to reduce costs. Tuition/fee waivers for children of alumni, senior citizens, family members, employees and their families. Prepayment discount; credit/placement for qualifying scores on AP, IB, CLEP examinations.

Payment plans. Credit card, deferred payment.

Application procedures. FAFSA required. Priority date 3/1; no closing date. Applicants notified on rolling basis starting 3/15, must reply within 2 week(s) of notification. **Transfers:** Academic scholarships available; apply by May 1.

Contact. **Financial aid office:** (703) 284-1530
Debbie Raines, Director of Financial Aid
2807 North Glebe Road
Arlington, VA 22207-4299

Mountain Empire Community College

Big Stone Gap, Virginia
www.me.vccs.edu
Two-year public **Federal Code: 009629**

	Living at home
Tuition and fees (2002-2003):	$1,394
Out-of-state:	$5,772
Per-credit charge:	$40
Per-credit out-of-state:	$186
Books and supplies:	$600
Transportation:	$1,000

Undergraduate aid. Need-based: 97% awarded as scholarships/grants, 3% as loans/jobs. Need-based aid available for part-time students. **Non-need-based:** Scholarships based on academics, state/district residency. **Additional information:** The college does not participate in loan programs. All financial aid is grant, scholarship, or work study.

Merit scholarships. Presidential Honor Scholarship for valedictorian or salutatorian; full tuition. Dean's Academic Honor Award for top 10 in graduating class; ranging from $500-$1,000.

Policies to reduce costs. Tuition/fee waivers for senior citizens. Credit/placement for qualifying scores on AP, IB, CLEP examinations. Work study available for part-time students.

Payment plans. Credit card payment.

Application procedures. FAFSA required. Priority date 5/1; no closing date. Applicants notified on rolling basis starting 1/1. **Transfers:** Priority date 5/1; no deadline.

Contact. **Financial aid office:** (276) 523-2400
Perry Carroll, Director of Enrollment Services
Drawer 700
Big Stone Gap, VA 24219

National College of Business & Technology: Bluefield

Bluefield, Virginia
www.ncbt.edu
Two-year proprietary **Federal Code: 003726**

	Living at home
Tuition and fees (projected):	$6,186
Per-credit charge:	$162
Books and supplies:	$1,200

Undergraduate aid. All financial aid based on need. Need-based aid available for full-time and part-time students.

Policies to reduce costs. Tuition/fee waivers for employees and their families.

Payment plans. Credit card payment.

Application procedures. FAFSA required. No deadline. Applicants notified on rolling basis starting 9/1.

Contact. Pamela Cotton, Director of Financial Aid and Compliance Officer
PO Box 6400
Roanoke, VA 24017

National College of Business & Technology: Charlottesville

Charlottesville, Virginia
www.ncbt.edu
Two-year proprietary **Federal Code: 003726**

	Living at home
Tuition and fees (projected):	$6,186
Per-credit charge:	$162
Books and supplies:	$1,200

Undergraduate aid. All financial aid based on need. Need-based aid available for full-time and part-time students.

Policies to reduce costs. Tuition/fee waivers for employees and their families.

Payment plans. Credit card payment.

Application procedures. FAFSA required. No deadline. Applicants notified on rolling basis.

Contact. Pamela Cotton, Director of Financial Aid and Compliance Officer
PO Box 6400
Roanoke, VA 24017

National College of Business & Technology: Danville

Danville, Virginia
www.ncbt.edu
Two-year proprietary **Federal Code: 003726**

	Living at home
Tuition and fees (projected):	$5,625
Per-credit charge:	$155
Books and supplies:	$1,200

Undergraduate aid. All financial aid based on need. Need-based aid available for full-time and part-time students.

Policies to reduce costs. Tuition/fee waivers for employees and their families.

Payment plans. Credit card payment.

Application procedures. FAFSA required. No deadline. Applicants notified on rolling basis starting 9/1.

Contact. Pamela Cotton, Director of Financial Aid and Compliance Officer
PO Box 6400
Roanoke, VA 24017

National College of Business & Technology: Harrisonburg

Harrisonburg, Virginia
www.ncbt.edu
Two-year proprietary **Federal Code: 003726**

	Living at home
Tuition and fees (projected):	$6,186
Per-credit charge:	$162
Books and supplies:	$1,200

Undergraduate aid. All financial aid based on need. Need-based aid available for full-time and part-time students.

Policies to reduce costs. Tuition/fee waivers for employees and their families.

Payment plans. Credit card payment.

Application procedures. FAFSA required. No deadline. Applicants notified on rolling basis starting 9/1.

Contact. Pamela Cotton, Director of Financial Aid and Compliance Officer
PO Box 6400
Roanoke, VA 24017

National College of Business & Technology: Lynchburg

Lynchburg, Virginia
www.ncbt.edu
Two-year proprietary **Federal Code: 010489**

	Living at home
Tuition and fees (projected):	$6,186
Per-credit charge:	$162
Books and supplies:	$1,200

Undergraduate aid. All financial aid based on need. Need-based aid available for full-time and part-time students.

Policies to reduce costs. Tuition/fee waivers for employees and their families.

Payment plans. Credit card payment.

Application procedures. FAFSA required. No deadline. Applicants notified on rolling basis starting 9/1.

Contact. **Financial aid office:** (540) 986-1000
Pamela Cotton, Director of Financial Aid and Compliance Officer
PO Box 6400
Roanoke, VA 24017

National College of Business & Technology: Martinsville

Martinsville, Virginia
www.ncbt.edu
Two-year private **Federal Code: 003726**

	Living at home
Tuition and fees (projected):	$6,186
Per-credit charge:	$162
Books and supplies:	$1,200

Undergraduate aid. All financial aid based on need. Need-based aid available for full-time and part-time students.

Policies to reduce costs. Tuition/fee waivers for employees and their families.

Payment plans. Credit card payment.

Application procedures. FAFSA required. No deadline. Applicants notified on rolling basis.

Contact. Pamela Cotton, Director of Financial Aid and Compliance Officer
PO Box 6400
Roanoke, VA 24017

National College of Business & Technology: Roanoke

Roanoke, Virginia
www.ncbt.edu
Four-year proprietary **Federal Code: 003726**

	Living at home
Tuition and fees (projected):	$6,186
Books and supplies:	$1,200

Undergraduate aid. All financial aid based on need. Need-based aid available for full-time and part-time students.

Policies to reduce costs. Tuition/fee waivers for employees and their families.

Payment plans. Credit card payment.

Application procedures. FAFSA required. No deadline. Applicants notified on rolling basis. **Transfers:** No deadline.

Contact. Pamela Cotton, Financial Aid Director and Compliance Officer
Box 6400
Roanoke, VA 24017-0400

Norfolk State University

Norfolk, Virginia
www.nsu.edu
Four-year public **Federal Code: 003765**

	Living at home	On-campus
Tuition and fees (projected):	$3,840	$3,840
Out-of-state:	$13,260	$13,260
Room and board:		$5,882
Board only:	$2,080	
Books and supplies:	$1,000	$1,000
Personal expenses:	$2,700	$2,700

Undergraduate aid. Need-based: Average financial aid package for full-time students was $4,830; for part-time $3,284. 46% awarded as scholarships/grants, 54% as loans/jobs. **Non-need-based:** Scholarships based on academics, religious affiliation, state/district residency. **Student debt:** 85% of graduating class borrowed to fund education; average debt was $15,869.

Freshman aid. Need-based: Average package met 77% of need. Average scholarship/grant was $3,252; average loan $2,625.

Policies to reduce costs. Tuition/fee waivers for senior citizens, employees and their families. Credit/placement for qualifying scores on AP, CLEP examinations. Work study available nights and weekends.

Payment plans. Credit card, installment, deferred payment.

Application procedures. FAFSA required. Priority date 4/15; no closing date. Applicants notified on rolling basis starting 2/1. **Transfers:** Priority date 4/15; closing date 4/15.

Contact. Financial aid office: (757) 823-8381
Estherine Harding, Director of Financial Aid
700 Park Avenue
Norfolk, VA 23504

Old Dominion University

Norfolk, Virginia
www.odu.edu
Four-year public **Federal Code: 003728**

	Living at home	On-campus
Tuition and fees (2002-2003):	$4,264	$4,264
Out-of-state:	$13,294	$13,294
Room and board:		$5,498
Board only:	$2,262	
Books and supplies:	$700	$700
Personal expenses:	$1,838	$1,838
Transportation:	$1,000	$1,000

Undergraduate aid. Need-based: Average financial aid package for full-time students was $6,916; for part-time $4,817. 48% awarded as scholarships/grants, 52% as loans/jobs. **Non-need-based:** 26% awarded as scholarships/grants, 74% as loans/jobs. Scholarships based on academics, alumni affiliation, art, athletics, leadership, minority status, music/drama, state/district residency. **Student debt:** 80% of graduating class borrowed to fund education; average debt was $16,500. **Additional information:** Students with combined SAT-I of 1180 and 3.25 GPA who apply by December 1 given priority scholarship consideration.

Freshman aid. Need-based: Out of 1,701 full-time freshmen, 1,440 applied for aid; 930 were judged to have need; of these 900 received aid. Average package met 67% of need. 300 students had full need met. Average scholarship/grant was $4,381; average loan $2,425. **Non-need based:** 319 full-time freshmen with need received non-need scholarships; 197 without need received awards; 57 received athletic scholarships.

Policies to reduce costs. Tuition/fee waivers for senior citizens, employees and their families. Credit/placement for qualifying scores on AP, IB, CLEP examinations. Work study available for part-time students.

Payment plans. Credit card, installment, deferred payment.

Application procedures. FAFSA required. Priority date 2/15; closing date 3/15. Applicants notified on rolling basis starting 3/15, must reply within 2 week(s) of notification. **Transfers:** Priority date 2/15; closing date 3/15. Aid available through Virginia transfer grant.

Contact. Financial aid office: (757) 683-3633
Betty Diamond, Director of Financial Aid
108 Rollins Hall, 5215 Hampton Boulevard
Norfolk, VA 23529

Paul D. Camp Community College

Franklin, Virginia
www.pc.vccs.edu
Two-year public **Federal Code: 009159**

	Living at home
Tuition and fees (2002-2003):	$1,304
Out-of-state:	$5,682
Per-credit charge:	$40
Per-credit out-of-state:	$186
Books and supplies:	$500
Personal expenses:	$900
Transportation:	$900

Undergraduate aid. Need-based: Need-based aid available for full-time and part-time students.

Policies to reduce costs. Tuition/fee waivers for senior citizens. Credit/placement for qualifying scores on AP, CLEP examinations. Work study available nights and for part-time students.

Payment plans. Credit card payment.

Application procedures. FAFSA, institutional form required. Closing date 8/1. Applicants notified on rolling basis starting 7/25, must reply within 2 week(s) of notification. **Transfers:** Priority date 7/30; no deadline.

Contact. Financial aid office: (757) 569-6718
Nita Holt, Financial Aid Coordinator
100 North College Drive
Franklin, VA 23851-0737

Piedmont Virginia Community College

Charlottesville, Virginia
www.pvcc.edu
Two-year public **Federal Code: 009928**

	Living at home
Tuition and fees (2002-2003):	$1,326
Out-of-state:	$5,704
Per-credit charge:	$40
Per-credit out-of-state:	$186
Board only:	$1,500
Books and supplies:	$900
Personal expenses:	$1,850
Transportation:	$1,650

Undergraduate aid. All financial aid based on need. 93% awarded as scholarships/grants, 7% as loans/jobs. Need-based aid available for part-time students.

Policies to reduce costs. Tuition/fee waivers for senior citizens. Credit/placement for qualifying scores on AP, CLEP examinations. Work study available for part-time students.

Payment plans. Credit card payment.

Application procedures. FAFSA, institutional form required. Priority date 3/30; no closing date. Applicants notified on rolling basis starting 5/1.

Contact. Financial aid office: (434) 961-5405
Esther Freix, Coordinator of Financial Aid
501 College Drive
Charlottesville, VA 22902-7589

Radford University

Radford, Virginia
www.radford.edu
Four-year public **Federal Code: 003732**

	Living at home	On-campus
Tuition and fees (2002-2003):	$3,344	$3,344
Out-of-state:	$9,792	$9,792
Room and board:		$5,442
Board only:	$2,170	
Books and supplies:	$650	$650
Personal expenses:	$2,900	$1,400
Transportation:	$800	$600

Undergraduate aid. Need-based: Need-based aid available for full-time and part-time students. **Non-need-based:** Scholarships based on academics, athletics. **Additional information:** Student's need and grades considered.

Top consideration given to those with greatest need and who apply by deadline.

Merit scholarships. RU Foundation funds full scholarships for outstanding freshman.

Policies to reduce costs. Tuition/fee waivers for senior citizens, employees and their families. Credit/placement for qualifying scores on AP, CLEP examinations. Work study available nights and weekends.

Payment plans. Installment payment.

Application procedures. FAFSA required. Priority date 3/1; no closing date. Applicants notified on rolling basis starting 4/15, must reply within 2 week(s) of notification.

Contact. **Financial aid office:** (540) 831-5408
Barbara Porter, Director of Financial Aid
Radford University Admissions, Martin Hall
Radford, VA 24142

Randolph-Macon College

Ashland, Virginia
www.rmc.edu
Four-year private **Federal Code: 003733**

College costs. $1,983 per course.

	Living at home	On-campus
Tuition and fees (2002-2003):	$20,045	$20,045
Room and board:		$5,715
Books and supplies:	$600	$600
Personal expenses:	$550	$550
Transportation:	$650	$350

Undergraduate aid. Need-based: Average financial aid package for full-time students was $14,858; for part-time $13,288. 66% awarded as scholarships/grants, 34% as loans/jobs. **Non-need-based:** 65% awarded as scholarships/grants, 35% as loans/jobs. Scholarships based on academics, alumni affiliation, leadership, minority status, religious affiliation, state/district residency. **Student debt:** 61% of graduating class borrowed to fund education; average debt was $18,125.

Freshman aid. Need-based: Out of 377 full-time freshmen, 296 applied for aid; 235 were judged to have need; of these 235 received aid. Average package met 88% of need. 74 students had full need met. Average scholarship/grant was $11,171; average loan $3,805. **Non-need based:** 52 full-time freshmen with need received non-need scholarships; 132 without need received awards.

Merit scholarships. Over 400 scholarships awarded to outstanding applicants based on school record and ACT or SAT scores. Grants range from $5,000-$15,000.

Policies to reduce costs. Tuition/fee waivers for family members, family of clergy, employees and their families. Credit/placement for qualifying scores on AP, IB, CLEP examinations.

Payment plans. Installment payment.

Application procedures. FAFSA required. Priority date 2/1; closing date 3/1. Applicants notified by 4/1, must reply by 5/1 or within 2 week(s) of notification. Early decision closing date 12/1.

Contact. **Financial aid office:** (804) 752-7529
Mary Neal, Director of Financial Aid
Box 5005
Ashland, VA 23005-5505

Randolph-Macon Woman's College

Lynchburg, Virginia
www.rmwc.edu
Four-year private **Federal Code: 003734**

College costs. $200 telecommunications fee required of campus residents.

	Living at home	On-campus
Tuition and fees (2002-2003):	$19,080	$19,080
Room and board:		$7,560
Books and supplies:	$800	$800
Personal expenses:	$1,000	$1,000
Transportation:	$500	$500

Undergraduate aid. Need-based: Average financial aid package for full-time students was $18,381; for part-time $9,997. 70% awarded as scholarships/grants, 30% as loans/jobs. **Non-need-based:** 75% awarded as scholarships/grants, 25% as loans/jobs. Scholarships based on academics, alumni affiliation, art, leadership, minority status, music/drama, religious affiliation, state/district residency. **Student debt:** 67% of graduating class borrowed to fund education; average debt was $20,385. **Additional information:** Endowment of over $110 million enables college to offer approximately $2 million annually to incoming first-year students. Grants range from $500 to full tuition. Student must reapply each year.

Freshman aid. Need-based: Out of 206 full-time freshmen, 162 applied for aid; 133 were judged to have need; of these 133 received aid. Average package met 90% of need. 55 students had full need met. Average scholarship/grant was $15,466; average loan $2,461. **Non-need based:** 34 full-time freshmen with need received non-need scholarships; 71 without need received awards.

Merit scholarships. Gottwald Scholarship, full tuition plus travel stipend, based on academic profile, 12 awarded.

Policies to reduce costs. Tuition/fee waivers for adults, family of clergy, employees and their families. Credit/placement for qualifying scores on AP, IB, CLEP examinations. Work study available nights, weekends and for part-time students.

Payment plans. Installment, deferred payment.

Application procedures. FAFSA required. Priority date 3/1; no closing date. Applicants notified on rolling basis starting 3/1, must reply by 5/1 or within 2 week(s) of notification. Early decision closing date 11/15. **Transfers:** Priority date 2/1.

Contact. Sharon Wilkes, Director of Financial Planning and Analysis
2500 Rivermont Avenue
Lynchburg, VA 24503-1526

Rappahannock Community College

Glenns, Virginia
www.rcc.vccs.edu
Two-year public **Federal Code: 009160**

	Living at home
Tuition and fees (2002-2003):	$1,334
Out-of-state:	$5,712
Per-credit charge:	$40
Per-credit out-of-state:	$186
Books and supplies:	$690
Personal expenses:	$1,500
Transportation:	$1,560

Undergraduate aid. Need-based: Need-based aid available for full-time and part-time students.

Policies to reduce costs. Tuition/fee waivers for senior citizens. Credit/placement for qualifying scores on AP, CLEP examinations.

Payment plans. Credit card payment.

Application procedures. FAFSA, institutional form required. Priority date 5/15; no closing date. Applicants notified on rolling basis starting 6/30.

Contact. Carolyn Ward, Financial Aid Officer
12745 College Drive
Glenns, VA 23149

Richard Bland College

Petersburg, Virginia
www.rbc.edu
Two-year public **Federal Code: 003707**

	Living at home
Tuition and fees (2002-2003):	$1,742
Out-of-state:	$7,410
Per-credit charge:	$69
Per-credit out-of-state:	$311
Board only:	$2,000
Books and supplies:	$650
Personal expenses:	$1,200
Transportation:	$1,000

Undergraduate aid. Need-based: Average financial aid package for full-time students was $2,000; for part-time $1,000. 95% awarded as scholarships/

grants, 5% as loans/jobs. **Non-need-based:** Scholarships based on academics, state/district residency.

Merit scholarships. Presidential Scholarships, average $1,000, for full-time first-time Virginia residents, based on minimum 3.5 high school GPA.

Policies to reduce costs. Tuition/fee waivers for senior citizens, employees and their families. Credit/placement for qualifying scores on AP, CLEP examinations. Work study available for part-time students.

Payment plans. Credit card payment.

Application procedures. FAFSA, institutional form required. Priority date 5/1; no closing date. Applicants notified by 6/1, must reply within 2 week(s) of notification.

Contact. **Financial aid office:** (804) 862-6223
Tony Jones, Director of Financial Aid
11301 Johnson Road
Petersburg, VA 23805

Roanoke College

Salem, Virginia
www.roanoke.edu
Four-year private **Federal Code: 003736**

College costs. Telecommunications fee $250 for campus residents. Part-time students pay $915 per course.

	Living at home	On-campus
Tuition and fees (2002-2003):	$19,716	$19,716
Room and board:		$6,338
Board only:	$750	
Books and supplies:	$650	$650
Personal expenses:	$600	$600
Transportation:	$600	$600

Undergraduate aid. **Need-based:** Average financial aid package for full-time students was $17,370; for part-time $6,754. 69% awarded as scholarships/grants, 31% as loans/jobs. **Non-need-based:** 89% awarded as scholarships/grants, 11% as loans/jobs. Scholarships based on academics, minority status, music/drama, religious affiliation, state/district residency. **Student debt:** 70% of graduating class borrowed to fund education; average debt was $16,760.

Freshman aid. **Need-based:** Out of 460 full-time freshmen, 351 applied for aid; 348 were judged to have need; of these 346 received aid. Average package met 92% of need. 80 students had full need met. Average scholarship/grant was $14,165; average loan $3,787. **Non-need based:** 313 full-time freshmen with need received non-need scholarships; 96 without need received awards.

Merit scholarships. William Beard Scholarship, full tuition, room and board, 2 awarded; Bittle Scholarship, full tuition, 6 awarded; Baughman Scholarship, half tuition, 25 awarded; Roanoke College Scholarship, $3,000-$6,000, variable number of awards; all based on superior academics and leadership ability.

Policies to reduce costs. Tuition/fee waivers for adults, senior citizens, employees and their families. Credit/placement for qualifying scores on AP, IB, CLEP examinations. Work study available nights, weekends and for part-time students.

Payment plans. Credit card, installment payment.

Application procedures. FAFSA required. Priority date 3/1; no closing date. Applicants notified on rolling basis starting 12/25, must reply within 2 week(s) of notification. Early decision closing date 11/15. **Transfers:** No deadline.

Contact. **Financial aid office:** (540) 375-2235
Thomas Blair, Director of Financial Aid
221 College Lane
Salem, VA 24153-3794

Shenandoah University

Winchester, Virginia
www.su.edu
Four-year private **Federal Code: 003737**

	Living at home	On-campus
Tuition and fees (2002-2003):	$17,510	$17,510
Room and board:		$6,600
Board only:	$650	
Books and supplies:	$1,000	$1,000
Personal expenses:	$1,500	$1,500
Transportation:	$600	$600

Undergraduate aid. **Need-based:** Average financial aid package for full-time students was $12,107; for part-time $3,638. 41% awarded as scholarships/grants, 59% as loans/jobs. **Non-need-based:** 68% awarded as scholarships/grants, 32% as loans/jobs. Scholarships based on academics, job skills, music/drama, religious affiliation, state/district residency. **Student debt:** 65% of graduating class borrowed to fund education; average debt was $13,698.

Freshman aid. **Need-based:** Out of 323 full-time freshmen, 226 applied for aid; 218 were judged to have need; of these 218 received aid. Average package met 85% of need. 54 students had full need met. Average scholarship/grant was $3,957; average loan $3,095. **Non-need based:** 77 full-time freshmen with need received non-need scholarships; 77 without need received awards.

Policies to reduce costs. Tuition/fee waivers for family of clergy, employees and their families. Credit/placement for qualifying scores on AP, IB, CLEP examinations.

Payment plans. Credit card, installment, deferred payment.

Application procedures. FAFSA required. Priority date 3/1; no closing date. Applicants notified on rolling basis starting 3/1, must reply within 2 week(s) of notification. **Transfers:** Priority date 3/1; no deadline.

Contact. **Financial aid office:** (540) 665-4538
Nancy Bragg, Director of Financial Aid
1460 University Drive
Winchester, VA 22601-5195

Southside Virginia Community College

Alberta, Virginia
www.sv.vccs.edu
Two-year public **Federal Code: 008661**

	Living at home
Tuition and fees (2002-2003):	$1,364
Out-of-state:	$5,742
Per-credit charge:	$40
Per-credit out-of-state:	$186
Board only:	$1,500
Books and supplies:	$866
Personal expenses:	$1,602
Transportation:	$1,950

Undergraduate aid. **Need-based:** 98% awarded as scholarships/grants, 2% as loans/jobs. Need-based aid available for part-time students. **Non-need-based:** Scholarships based on academics.

Merit scholarships. Guaranteed Academic Merit Award, $1,000, for high school graduates within college's service area with 3.0 GPA who do not receive at least $1,000 in need-based aid.

Policies to reduce costs. Tuition/fee waivers for senior citizens. Credit/placement for qualifying scores on AP, CLEP examinations. Work study available nights and for part-time students.

Payment plans. Credit card payment.

Application procedures. FAFSA, institutional form required. Priority date 6/1; closing date 8/1. Applicants notified on rolling basis starting 6/15. **Transfers:** State aid limited to in-state residents.

Contact. **Financial aid office:** (434) 736-2026
Brent Richey, Director of Financial Aid
109 Campus Drive
Alberta, VA 23821

Southwest Virginia Community College

Richlands, Virginia
www.sw.vccs.edu
Two-year public **Federal Code: 007260**

	Living at home
Tuition and fees (2002-2003):	$1,349
Out-of-state:	$5,727
Per-credit charge:	$40
Per-credit out-of-state:	$186
Board only:	$1,000
Books and supplies:	$650
Personal expenses:	$1,250
Transportation:	$1,200

Policies to reduce costs. Tuition/fee waivers for senior citizens. Credit/placement for qualifying scores on AP, CLEP examinations.

Payment plans. Credit card payment.

Application procedures. FAFSA, institutional form required. Priority date 5/30; no closing date. Applicants notified on rolling basis starting 7/1.

Contact. Roderick Moore, Director of Admissions, Records and Financial Aid
Box SVCC
Richlands, VA 24641-1510

Sweet Briar College

Sweet Briar, Virginia
www.sbc.edu
Four-year private **Federal Code: 003742**

	Living at home	On-campus
Tuition and fees:	$19,900	$19,900
Room and board:		$8,040
Books and supplies:	$600	$600
Personal expenses:	$750	$750
Transportation:	$600	$600

Undergraduate aid. Need-based: Need-based aid available for full-time and part-time students. **Non-need-based:** Scholarships based on academics, art, music/drama, state/district residency.

Merit scholarships. Founders and Prothro Scholarships, up to $15,000; Commonwealth Scholarships, up to $13,000; International Scholarships, up to $12,500, for international students of traditional college age who intend to study at Sweet Briar for 4 years and live in residence halls; Betty Bean Black Scholarships, up to $12,000; Sweet Briar Scholarships, up to $9,000, for students with special talents in specific area. All awards based on academic qualifications; all renewable annually with maintenance of specified GPA.

Policies to reduce costs. Tuition/fee waivers for adults, senior citizens, employees and their families. Credit/placement for qualifying scores on AP, IB examinations. Work study available nights, weekends and for part-time students.

Payment plans. Credit card, installment payment.

Application procedures. FAFSA required. Priority date 3/1; no closing date. Applicants notified on rolling basis starting 3/1, must reply by 5/1 or within 2 week(s) of notification. Early decision closing date 12/1. **Transfers:** Closing date 7/15.

Contact. Bobbi Carpenter, Director of Financial Aid
Box B
Sweet Briar, VA 24595

Thomas Nelson Community College

Hampton, Virginia
www.tncc.vccs.edu
Two-year public **Federal Code: 006871**

	Living at home
Tuition and fees (2002-2003):	$1,325
Out-of-state:	$5,703
Per-credit charge:	$40
Per-credit out-of-state:	$186
Books and supplies:	$1,053
Personal expenses:	$1,171
Transportation:	$978

Undergraduate aid. Need-based: Need-based aid available for full-time and part-time students.

Policies to reduce costs. Tuition/fee waivers for senior citizens. Credit/placement for qualifying scores on AP, CLEP examinations. Work study available nights and for part-time students.

Payment plans. Credit card payment.

Application procedures. FAFSA, institutional form required. Priority date 5/1; no closing date. Applicants notified on rolling basis starting 6/1, must reply within 2 week(s) of notification.

Contact. Financial aid office: (757) 825-2848
Pamela Turner, Coordinator of Financial Aid
Box 9407
Hampton, VA 23670

Tidewater Tech

Virginia Beach, Virginia
www.tidetech.com
Two-year proprietary **Federal Code: 016538**

College costs (2002-2003). Annual tuition varies from $10,000 to $15,680, depending on program.

Contact. Financial aid office: (757) 340-2121
Denice Bright, Financial Aid Officer
2697 Dean Drive, Suite 100
Virginia Beach, VA 23452

University of Richmond

University of Richmond, Virginia
www.richmond.edu
Four-year private **Federal Code: 003744**

	Living at home	On-campus
Tuition and fees (2002-2003):	$24,980	$24,980
Room and board:		$5,160
Board only:	$2,380	
Books and supplies:	$900	$900

Undergraduate aid. Need-based: Average financial aid package for full-time students was $17,657; for part-time $13,278. 82% awarded as scholarships/grants, 18% as loans/jobs. **Non-need-based:** 68% awarded as scholarships/grants, 32% as loans/jobs. Scholarships based on academics, athletics, minority status, music/drama, religious affiliation. **Student debt:** 39% of graduating class borrowed to fund education; average debt was $16,115. **Additional information:** Interview required for University, Oldham, Ethyl, and CIGNA. Undergraduate research grants available.

Freshman aid. Need-based: Out of 776 full-time freshmen, 413 applied for aid; 261 were judged to have need; of these 260 received aid. Average package met 98% of need. 135 students had full need met. Average scholarship/grant was $15,696; average loan $1,876. **Non-need based:** 38 full-time freshmen with need received non-need scholarships; 183 without need received awards; 65 received athletic scholarships.

Merit scholarships. Over 50 merit-based scholarships available, ranging from one-half to full tuition.

Policies to reduce costs. Tuition/fee waivers for employees and their families. Credit/placement for qualifying scores on AP, IB, CLEP examinations. Work study available nights and weekends.

Payment plans. Credit card, installment payment.

Application procedures. FAFSA, institutional form required. Closing date 2/25. Applicants notified by 4/1, must reply by 5/1 or within 4 week(s) of notification. Early decision closing date 11/15.

Contact. Cindy Deffenbaugh, Director of Student Financial Aid
28 Westhampton Way
University of Richmond, VA 23173

University of Virginia

Charlottesville, Virginia
www.virginia.edu
Four-year public **Federal Code: 003745**

	Living at home	On-campus
Tuition and fees (2002-2003):	$4,780	$4,780
Out-of-state:	$19,990	$19,990
Room and board:		$5,231
Books and supplies:	$900	$900
Personal expenses:	$1,610	$1,610

Undergraduate aid. Need-based: Average financial aid package for full-time students was $11,462; for part-time $9,910. 72% awarded as scholarships/grants, 28% as loans/jobs. **Non-need-based:** 47% awarded as scholarships/grants, 53% as loans/jobs. Scholarships based on academics, athletics, leadership, minority status, state/district residency. **Student debt:** 32% of graduating class borrowed to fund education; average debt was $13,536.

Freshman aid. Need-based: Out of 2,976 full-time freshmen, 1,551 applied for aid; 689 were judged to have need; of these 640 received aid. Average package met 91% of need. 365 students had full need met. Average scholarship/grant was $8,389; average loan $3,167. **Non-need based:** 108 full-time freshmen with need received non-need scholarships; 747 without need received awards; 117 received athletic scholarships.

Policies to reduce costs. Tuition/fee waivers for senior citizens, employees and their families. Credit/placement for qualifying scores on AP, IB examinations.

Payment plans. Installment payment.

Application procedures. FAFSA, institutional form required. Priority date 3/1; no closing date. Applicants notified by 4/5, must reply by 5/1. Early decision closing date 11/1.

Contact. Financial aid office: (434) 982-6000
Yvonne Hubbard, Director, Student Financial Services
Office of Admission
Charlottesville, VA 22904-4160

University of Virginia's College at Wise

Wise, Virginia
www.uvawise.edu
Four-year public **Federal Code: 003747**

	Living at home	On-campus
Tuition and fees (2002-2003):	$3,844	$3,844
Out-of-state:	$11,604	$11,604
Room and board:		$5,701
Board only:	$750	
Books and supplies:	$638	$638
Personal expenses:	$882	$882
Transportation:	$1,100	$660

Undergraduate aid. Need-based: Average financial aid package for full-time students was $5,043; for part-time $2,521. 67% awarded as scholarships/grants, 33% as loans/jobs. **Non-need-based:** 44% awarded as scholarships/grants, 56% as loans/jobs. Scholarships based on academics, alumni affiliation, art, athletics, job skills, leadership, music/drama, religious affiliation, state/district residency. **Student debt:** 65% of graduating class borrowed to fund education; average debt was $6,245.

Freshman aid. Need-based: Out of 327 full-time freshmen, 298 applied for aid; 229 were judged to have need; of these 229 received aid. Average package met 95% of need. 217 students had full need met. Average scholarship/grant was $3,538; average loan $1,589. **Non-need based:** 117 full-time freshmen with need received non-need scholarships; 40 without need received awards; 44 received athletic scholarships.

Policies to reduce costs. Tuition/fee waivers for senior citizens. Prepayment discount; credit/placement for qualifying scores on AP examinations. Work study available nights, weekends and for part-time students.

Payment plans. Credit card, installment payment.

Application procedures. FAFSA required. Priority date 2/1; no closing date. Applicants notified on rolling basis starting 2/1, must reply within 4 week(s) of notification. **Transfers:** Priority date 4/1.

Contact. Financial aid office: (540) 328-0103
Bill Wendle, Assistant Director of Financial Aid
One College Avenue
Wise, VA 24293

Virginia Commonwealth University

Richmond, Virginia
www.vcu.edu
Four-year public **Federal Code: 003735**

	Living at home	On-campus
Tuition and fees (2002-2003):	$3,918	$3,918
Out-of-state:	$14,888	$14,888
Room and board:		$5,374
Board only:	$1,500	
Books and supplies:	$800	$800
Personal expenses:	$2,370	$2,370
Transportation:	$2,090	$2,090

Undergraduate aid. Need-based: Average financial aid package for full-time students was $6,457; for part-time $4,072. 47% awarded as scholarships/grants, 53% as loans/jobs. **Non-need-based:** 23% awarded as scholarships/grants, 77% as loans/jobs. Scholarships based on academics, alumni affiliation, art, athletics, music/drama, state/district residency. **Student debt:** 68% of graduating class borrowed to fund education; average debt was $19,895.

Freshman aid. Need-based: Out of 2,740 full-time freshmen, 2,199 applied for aid; 1,523 were judged to have need; of these 1,508 received aid. Average package met 51% of need. 83 students had full need met. Average scholarship/grant was $3,531; average loan $2,818. **Non-need based:** 426 full-time freshmen with need received non-need scholarships; 542 without need received awards; 52 received athletic scholarships.

Merit scholarships. Undergraduate Scholars Program: merit-based scholarships to up to 10% of freshman class; renewable up to 4 years. Dianne Nunnally Collins Scholarship: 1 awarded; in-state tuition, fees, room and board, books. Presidential Scholarship: 15 awarded; in-state tuition, fees, room and board. Provost's Scholarship: 50 awarded; in-state tuition, fees. Dean's Scholarship: 80 awarded; half in-state tuition and fees. Phi Theta Kappa Scholarship for Phi Theta Kappa members at Virginia community colleges who transfer to VCU: 5 awarded; half in-state tuition and fees. Reynolds Metals Scholarship for dependents of eligible Reynolds Metals employees in Virginia: 5 awarded; in-state tuition and fees.

Policies to reduce costs. Tuition/fee waivers for senior citizens, employees and their families. Credit/placement for qualifying scores on AP, IB, CLEP examinations. Work study available nights, weekends and for part-time students.

Payment plans. Credit card, installment payment.

Application procedures. FAFSA required. Priority date 4/1; no closing date. Applicants notified on rolling basis starting 4/1, must reply by 5/1 or within 4 week(s) of notification. Early decision closing date 11/1. **Transfers:** Virginia Transfer Grant program available.

Contact. Financial aid office: (804) 828-6669
Director, Financial Aid
Box 842526
Richmond, VA 23284-2526

Virginia Highlands Community College

Abingdon, Virginia
www.vhcc.edu
Two-year public **Federal Code: 007099**

	Living at home
Tuition and fees (2002-2003):	$1,327
Out-of-state:	$5,705
Per-credit charge:	$40
Per-credit out-of-state:	$186
Books and supplies:	$610
Personal expenses:	$950
Transportation:	$1,400

Policies to reduce costs. Tuition/fee waivers for senior citizens. Credit/placement for qualifying scores on AP, CLEP examinations.

Payment plans. Credit card payment.

Application procedures. FAFSA required. No deadline. Applicants notified on rolling basis starting 5/1.

Contact. Patty Fullen, Financial Aid Officer
Box 828
Abingdon, VA 24210-0828

Virginia Intermont College

Bristol, Virginia
www.vic.edu
Four-year private **Federal Code: 003752**

	Living at home	On-campus
Tuition and fees (projected):	$13,863	$13,863
Room and board:		$5,470
Books and supplies:	$820	$820
Personal expenses:	$2,190	$2,190
Transportation:	$3,000	$3,000

Undergraduate aid. All financial aid based on need. Average financial aid package for full-time students was $11,034; for part-time $6,182. 56% awarded as scholarships/grants, 44% as loans/jobs. **Student debt:** 69% of graduating class borrowed to fund education; average debt was $17,125.

Freshman aid. Average package met 56% of need. Average scholarship/grant was $6,686; average loan $2,854.

Policies to reduce costs. Tuition/fee waivers for family members, employees and their families. Credit/placement for qualifying scores on AP, IB, CLEP examinations. Work study available nights, weekends and for part-time students.

Payment plans. Credit card, installment payment.

Application procedures. FAFSA, institutional form required. Priority date 4/15; closing date 6/30. Applicants notified on rolling basis starting 3/15, must reply within 2 week(s) of notification. **Transfers:** No deadline. Limited to a certain number of units of state aid.

Contact. **Financial aid office:** (540) 466-7871
Nancy Roberts, Director of Financial Aid
1013 Moore Street
Bristol, VA 24201

Virginia Military Institute

Lexington, Virginia
www.vmi.edu
Four-year public **Federal Code: 003753**

College costs. Additional $1,278 fee for uniforms, laundry, haircuts. Security deposit $200.

	Living at home	On-campus
Tuition and fees (2002-2003):	$5,385	$5,385
Out-of-state:	$17,172	$17,172
Room and board:		$5,055
Books and supplies:	$650	$650
Personal expenses:		$1,000
Transportation:		$750

Undergraduate aid. **Need-based:** Average financial aid package for full-time students was $12,369. 73% awarded as scholarships/grants, 27% as loans/jobs. **Non-need-based:** 83% awarded as scholarships/grants, 17% as loans/jobs. Scholarships based on academics, athletics, leadership, minority status, music/drama, state/district residency. **Student debt:** 50% of graduating class borrowed to fund education; average debt was $13,000.

Freshman aid. **Need-based:** Out of 359 full-time freshmen, 229 applied for aid; 173 were judged to have need; of these 168 received aid. Average package met 90% of need. 107 students had full need met. Average scholarship/grant was $9,655; average loan $3,923. **Non-need based:** 16 full-time freshmen with need received non-need scholarships; 93 without need received awards; 25 received athletic scholarships.

Merit scholarships. Institute Scholarship, up to $19,830, 10-12 awarded, for superior academic performance, demonstrated character and leadership, extracurricular activities; 3.7 high school GPA, minimum 1250 on SAT or 27 on ACT, rank in top 5% of class.

Policies to reduce costs. Credit/placement for qualifying scores on AP, IB examinations. Work study available nights and weekends.

Payment plans. Installment payment.

Application procedures. FAFSA required. Closing date 3/1. Applicants notified on rolling basis starting 3/15, must reply by 5/1 or within 4 week(s) of notification. Early decision closing date 11/15.

Contact. **Financial aid office:** (540) 464-7208
Timothy Golden, Director of Financial Aid
Office of Admissions
Lexington, VA 24450-9967

Virginia Polytechnic Institute and State University

Blacksburg, Virginia
www.vt.edu
Four-year public **Federal Code: 003754**

College costs. Out-of-state required fees $955.

	Living at home	On-campus
Tuition and fees (projected):	$5,095	$5,095
Out-of-state:	$14,979	$14,979
Room and board:		$4,084
Board only:	$2,020	
Books and supplies:	$896	$896
Personal expenses:	$1,750	$1,750
Transportation:	$754	$754

Undergraduate aid. **Need-based:** Average financial aid package for full-time students was $6,983. 39% awarded as scholarships/grants, 61% as loans/jobs. Need-based aid available for part-time students. **Non-need-based:** Scholarships based on art, athletics.

Freshman aid. **Need-based:** Out of 4,714 full-time freshmen, 3,155 applied for aid; 2,081 were judged to have need; of these 2,007 received aid. Average package met 61% of need. 173 students had full need met. Average scholarship/grant was $3,322; average loan $2,930. **Non-need based:** 501 full-time freshmen with need received non-need scholarships; 1,345 without need received awards; 64 received athletic scholarships.

Policies to reduce costs. Tuition/fee waivers for employees and their families. Credit/placement for qualifying scores on AP, IB, CLEP examinations. Work study available nights, weekends and for part-time students.

Payment plans. Installment payment.

Application procedures. FAFSA required. Priority date 3/11; no closing date. Applicants notified on rolling basis starting 3/30, must reply by 5/1 or within 4 week(s) of notification. Early decision closing date 11/1. **Transfers:** Priority date 2/1; closing date 3/1. Based on family EFC per FAFSA and available resources.

Contact. **Financial aid office:** (540) 231-9555
Barry Simmons, Director of Financial Aid
201 Burruss Hall
Blacksburg, VA 24061-0202

Virginia State University

Petersburg, Virginia
www.vsu.edu
Four-year public **Federal Code: 003764**

	Living at home	On-campus
Tuition and fees (2002-2003):	$3,554	$3,554
Out-of-state:	$10,248	$10,248
Room and board:		$5,694
Board only:	$2,290	
Books and supplies:	$700	$700
Personal expenses:	$532	$532
Transportation:	$800	$400

Undergraduate aid. **Need-based:** Average financial aid package for full-time students was $7,975; for part-time $3,525. 47% awarded as scholarships/grants, 53% as loans/jobs. **Non-need-based:** 34% awarded as scholarships/grants, 66% as loans/jobs. Scholarships based on academics, art, athletics, music/drama, state/district residency. **Student debt:** 86% of graduating class borrowed to fund education; average debt was $18,500. **Additional information:** Strongly recommend that students apply for scholarship assistance through federal, state, local and private agencies.

Freshman aid. **Need-based:** Out of 1,129 full-time freshmen, 1,072 applied for aid; 1,072 were judged to have need; of these 1,072 received aid. Average package met 70% of need. Average scholarship/grant was $3,926; average loan $5,525. **Non-need based:** 94 full-time freshmen with need received non-need scholarships; 193 without need received awards; 10 received athletic scholarships.

Merit scholarships. Presidential Scholarships: 3.2 GPA, SAT 1100 or ACT 24; $7,000. Provost's Scholarships: 3.0 GPA, SAT 1000 or ACT 21; $3,500. Fine and Performing Arts Scholarships: outstanding talent in music or fine arts, audition or portfolio may be required, recommendation required; $1,500. Math, Science, and Technology Scholarships: 3.0 GPA, above average ability in math, science, or technology, recommendation and essay required; $1,500.

Policies to reduce costs. Tuition/fee waivers for senior citizens, employees and their families. Credit/placement for qualifying scores on AP, CLEP examinations. Work study available nights, weekends and for part-time students.

Payment plans. Credit card payment.

Application procedures. FAFSA, institutional form required. Priority date 3/31; closing date 5/1. Applicants notified on rolling basis starting 5/1, must reply within 2 week(s) of notification. **Transfers:** Priority date 3/1; closing date 5/1.

Contact. **Financial aid office:** (804) 524-5990
Henry Debose, Director of Financial Aid
One Hayden Street
Petersburg, VA 23806

Virginia Union University

Richmond, Virginia
www.vuu.edu
Four-year private **Federal Code: 003766**

	Living at home	On-campus
Tuition and fees (2002-2003):	$11,630	$11,630
Room and board:		$5,236
Books and supplies:	$500	$500
Personal expenses:	$1,000	$1,000
Transportation:	$800	$500

Undergraduate aid. Need-based: Need-based aid available for full-time and part-time students. **Non-need-based:** Scholarships based on academics, athletics, state/district residency.

Policies to reduce costs. Tuition/fee waivers for employees and their families. Credit/placement for qualifying scores on AP, IB, CLEP examinations. Work study available nights, weekends and for part-time students.

Payment plans. Credit card, installment, deferred payment.

Application procedures. FAFSA required. Priority date 4/27; no closing date. Applicants notified on rolling basis starting 5/1, must reply within 2 week(s) of notification. **Transfers:** Priority date 4/27; no deadline. Student must submit a financial aid transcript from all prior schools attended before receiving aid.

Contact. **Financial aid office:** (804) 257-5882
Phenie Golatt, Director of Financial Aid
1500 North Lombardy Street
Richmond, VA 23220

Virginia Wesleyan College

Norfolk, Virginia
www.vwc.edu
Four-year private **Federal Code: 003767**

College costs. Damage deposit of $75 for residents.

	Living at home	On-campus
Tuition and fees:	$19,200	$19,200
Room and board:		$6,150
Books and supplies:	$750	$750
Personal expenses:	$1,800	$1,800
Transportation:	$1,630	$1,300

Undergraduate aid. Need-based: Average financial aid package for full-time students was $16,366; for part-time $3,509. 27% awarded as scholarships/grants, 73% as loans/jobs. **Non-need-based:** 74% awarded as scholarships/grants, 26% as loans/jobs. Scholarships based on academics, art, leadership, music/drama, religious affiliation, state/district residency.

Freshman aid. Need-based: Out of 297 full-time freshmen, 273 applied for aid; 223 were judged to have need; of these 223 received aid. Average package met 84% of need. 60 students had full need met. Average scholarship/grant was $3,167; average loan $3,121. **Non-need based:** 223 full-time freshmen with need received non-need scholarships; 50 without need received awards.

Merit scholarships. Wesleyan Scholars; $9,000 to the full comprehensive fee, 10 awarded; based on SAT scores, GPA, high school class rank, and competition results. Presidential Scholars based on SAT, GPA, and high school class rank; $7,000. Academic Dean Scholars based on complete academic record; ranging from $1,000-$6,000. Transfer Student Scholarships for students with excellent GPA and a minimum of 3-4 semesters of full-time work; $1,000-$7,000. Leadership Scholarships for students with demonstrated leadership positions, school, community, and church; $1,000-$6,000.

Policies to reduce costs. Tuition/fee waivers for adults, family of clergy, employees and their families. Credit/placement for qualifying scores on AP, IB, CLEP examinations.

Payment plans. Credit card, installment payment.

Application procedures. FAFSA required. No deadline. Applicants notified on rolling basis starting 2/15, must reply by 5/1 or within 2 week(s) of notification. **Transfers:** Priority date 3/1; no deadline. 4 semester maximum of special aid available for students who graduated with a 3.0 GPA and earned an associate degree from a local community college. Must enroll full time and maintain 2.5 GPA minimum.

Contact. **Financial aid office:** (757) 455-3345
Eugenia Hickman, Director of Financial Aid
1584 Wesleyan Drive
Norfolk/Virginia Beach, VA 23502-5599

Virginia Western Community College

Roanoke, Virginia
www.vw.vccs.edu
Two-year public **Federal Code: 003760**

	Living at home
Tuition and fees (2002-2003):	$1,319
Out-of-state:	$5,697
Per-credit charge:	$40
Per-credit out-of-state:	$186
Books and supplies:	$550
Personal expenses:	$1,200
Transportation:	$800

Undergraduate aid. Need-based: Need-based aid available for full-time and part-time students. **Non-need-based:** Scholarships based on academics.

Policies to reduce costs. Tuition/fee waivers for senior citizens. Credit/placement for qualifying scores on AP examinations.

Payment plans. Credit card payment.

Application procedures. FAFSA required. No deadline. Applicants notified on rolling basis starting 4/1.

Contact. **Financial aid office:** (540) 857-7331
Larry Ewing, Financial Aid Officer
Box 14007
Roanoke, VA 24038

Washington and Lee University

Lexington, Virginia
www.wlu.edu
Four-year private **Federal Code: 003768**

	Living at home	On-campus
Tuition and fees (2002-2003):	$21,175	$21,175
Room and board:		$5,913
Books and supplies:	$1,000	$1,000
Personal expenses:		$1,395

Undergraduate aid. Need-based: Average financial aid package for full-time students was $16,928. 81% awarded as scholarships/grants, 19% as loans/jobs. **Non-need-based:** 70% awarded as scholarships/grants, 30% as loans/jobs. Scholarships based on academics. **Student debt:** 33% of graduating class borrowed to fund education; average debt was $15,634. **Additional information:** Honor Scholarship annual competition through Admissions Office, deadline for complete application December 15.

Freshman aid. Need-based: Out of 488 full-time freshmen, 204 applied for aid; 131 were judged to have need; of these 129 received aid. Average package met 99% of need. 115 students had full need met. Average scholarship/grant was $16,318; average loan $2,322. **Non-need based:** 34 full-time freshmen with need received non-need scholarships; 130 without need received awards.

Policies to reduce costs. Tuition/fee waivers for employees and their families. Credit/placement for qualifying scores on AP, IB examinations.

Payment plans. Credit card payment.

Application procedures. FAFSA, CSS PROFILE required. Priority date 2/1; no closing date. Applicants notified by 4/1, must reply by 5/1. Early decision closing date 12/1. **Transfers:** Transfer students are awarded institutional funds only after commitments to enrolled students are met. Notification usually in late summer.

Contact. **Financial aid office:** (540) 458-8715
John DeCourcy, Director of Student Financial Aid
116 North Main Street
Lexington, VA 24450-0303

Washington

Art Institute of Seattle

Seattle, Washington
www.ais.edu
Two-year proprietary **Federal Code: 016210**

	Living at home	On-campus
Tuition and fees (projected):	$15,480	$15,480
Per-credit charge:	$344	$344
Room and board:		$8,355
Board only:	$2,205	
Books and supplies:	$975	$975
Personal expenses:	$2,265	$2,265
Transportation:	$1,065	$1,065

Undergraduate aid. Need-based: Average financial aid package for full-time students was $4,151. 32% awarded as scholarships/grants, 68% as loans/jobs. Need-based aid available for part-time students. **Non-need-based:** 11% awarded as scholarships/grants, 89% as loans/jobs. Scholarships based on academics, art.

Policies to reduce costs. Tuition/fee waivers for employees and their families. Tuition at time of enrollment guaranteed for 2 years; credit/placement for qualifying scores on AP, IB, CLEP examinations. Work study available nights, weekends and for part-time students.

Payment plans. Credit card, installment, deferred payment.

Application procedures. FAFSA, institutional form required. Priority date 4/15; no closing date. Applicants notified on rolling basis, must reply within 4 week(s) of notification. **Transfers:** No deadline.

Contact. Financial aid office: (206) 239-2261
Lydia Tanevski, Director of Student Financial Services
2323 Elliott Avenue
Seattle, WA 98121

Bastyr University

Kenmore, Washington
www.bastyr.edu
Upper-division private **Federal Code: 016059**

College costs. Quoted tuition is for nutrition, psychology, herbal science, and exercise and wellness programs. Acupuncture and Oriental medicine program tuition/fees $15,950.

	Living at home
Tuition and fees (2002-2003):	$12,150
Books and supplies:	$1,100

Undergraduate aid. All financial aid based on need. Need-based aid available for full-time and part-time students.

Policies to reduce costs. Tuition/fee waivers for employees and their families. Work study available nights and weekends.

Application procedures. FAFSA, institutional form required. Priority date 6/1; no closing date. Applicants notified on rolling basis starting 5/15, must reply within 2 week(s) of notification. **Transfers:** No deadline.

Contact. Financial aid office: (425) 602-3074
Richard Dent, Director of Student Enrollment
14500 Juanita Drive NE
Kenmore, WA 98028

Bellevue Community College

Bellevue, Washington
www.bcc.ctc.edu
Two-year public **Federal Code: 003769**

	Living at home
Tuition and fees (2002-2003):	$2,115
Out-of-state:	$7,323
Per-credit charge:	$64
Per-credit out-of-state:	$236
Books and supplies:	$690
Personal expenses:	$1,824
Transportation:	$1,212

Undergraduate aid. Need-based: 62% awarded as scholarships/grants, 38% as loans/jobs. Need-based aid available for part-time students. **Non-need-based:** Scholarships based on academics, athletics.

Policies to reduce costs. Tuition/fee waivers for senior citizens, employees and their families. Credit/placement for qualifying scores on AP examinations. Work study available nights, weekends and for part-time students.

Payment plans. Credit card, installment payment.

Application procedures. FAFSA, institutional form required. Priority date 4/13; no closing date. Applicants notified on rolling basis starting 8/1.

Contact. Sherri Ballantyne, Director of Financial Aid
3000 Landerholm Circle SE
Bellevue, WA 98007-6484

Central Washington University

Ellensburg, Washington
www.cwu.edu
Four-year public **Federal Code: 003771**

	Living at home	On-campus
Tuition and fees (2002-2003):	$3,792	$3,792
Out-of-state:	$11,781	$11,781
Room and board:		$5,410
Board only:	$2,088	
Books and supplies:	$690	$690
Personal expenses:	$1,944	$1,944
Transportation:	$1,212	$1,212

Undergraduate aid. Need-based: Average financial aid package for full-time students was $4,092; for part-time $3,025. 50% awarded as scholarships/grants, 50% as loans/jobs. **Non-need-based:** Scholarships based on academics, alumni affiliation, art, athletics, job skills, leadership, minority status, music/drama, religious affiliation, state/district residency. **Student debt:** 62% of graduating class borrowed to fund education; average debt was $22,382.

Freshman aid. Need-based: Out of 1,246 full-time freshmen, 872 applied for aid; 564 were judged to have need; of these 543 received aid. Average package met 80% of need. 53 students had full need met. Average scholarship/grant was $4,697; average loan $3,040. **Non-need based:** 515 without need received awards; 16 received athletic scholarships.

Policies to reduce costs. Tuition/fee waivers for senior citizens, employees and their families. Credit/placement for qualifying scores on AP, IB, CLEP examinations.

Payment plans. Credit card payment.

Application procedures. FAFSA required. Priority date 3/1; no closing date. Applicants notified on rolling basis starting 4/15, must reply within 4 week(s) of notification. **Transfers:** Equal Opportunity Grant available for junior-level transfers from selected Washington counties. May receive up to $2,500/year for three years.

Contact. Financial aid office: (509) 963-1611
Agnes Canedo, Director of Financial Aid
400 East 8th Avenue
Ellensburg, WA 98926-7463

Centralia College

Centralia, Washington
www.centralia.ctc.edu
Two-year public **Federal Code: 003772**

	Living at home
Tuition and fees (2002-2003):	$2,118
Out-of-state:	$2,515
Per-credit charge:	$63
Per-credit out-of-state:	$76
Books and supplies:	$690
Transportation:	$1,224

Undergraduate aid. All financial aid based on need. Average financial aid package for full-time students was $3,047. 89% awarded as scholarships/grants, 11% as loans/jobs. Need-based aid available for part-time students.

Policies to reduce costs. Tuition/fee waivers for senior citizens, unemployed or children of unemployed, employees and their families. Credit/placement for qualifying scores on AP, IB, CLEP examinations.

Payment plans. Credit card, deferred payment.

Application procedures. FAFSA, institutional form required. Priority date 5/15; no closing date. Applicants notified on rolling basis starting 7/10, must reply within 2 week(s) of notification. **Transfers:** No deadline.

Contact. **Financial aid office:** (360) 736-9391 ext. 234
Tracy Smothers, Financial Aid Director
600 West Locust
Centralia, WA 98531

Clark College

Vancouver, Washington
www.clark.edu
Two-year public **Federal Code: 003773**

	Living at home
Tuition and fees (2002-2003):	$2,242
Out-of-state:	$2,639
Per-credit charge:	$69
Per-credit out-of-state:	$82
Board only:	$1,998
Books and supplies:	$745
Personal expenses:	$1,921
Transportation:	$1,162

Undergraduate aid. **Need-based:** 73% awarded as scholarships/grants, 27% as loans/jobs. Need-based aid available for part-time students. **Non-need-based:** 42% awarded as scholarships/grants, 58% as loans/jobs. Scholarships based on academics, art, athletics, leadership, minority status, music/drama, state/district residency.

Merit scholarships. More than $300,000 in merit and program-based scholarships available as part of Clark College scholarship application process. Scholarships range in size from $500 to full tuition. Scholarship opportunities available in all areas of study. Recipients selected from those completing Clark's Standard Scholarship application form available through college's website.

Policies to reduce costs. Tuition/fee waivers for senior citizens, unemployed or children of unemployed, employees and their families. Credit/placement for qualifying scores on AP, CLEP examinations. Work study available nights, weekends and for part-time students.

Payment plans. Credit card payment.

Application procedures. FAFSA required. Priority date 5/1; no closing date. Applicants notified on rolling basis starting 6/15, must reply within 2 week(s) of notification. **Transfers:** No deadline.

Contact. **Financial aid office:** (360) 992-2153
Michael Johnson, Director of Financial Aid
1800 East McLoughlin Boulevard
Vancouver, WA 98663-3598

Cornish College of the Arts

Seattle, Washington
www.cornish.edu
Four-year private **Federal Code: 012315**

	Living at home
Tuition and fees:	$18,600
Books and supplies:	$1,800
Personal expenses:	$2,000
Transportation:	$800

Undergraduate aid. **Need-based:** Need-based aid available for full-time and part-time students. **Non-need-based:** Scholarships based on academics.

Policies to reduce costs. Tuition/fee waivers for employees and their families. Credit/placement for qualifying scores on AP, CLEP examinations. Work study available nights, weekends and for part-time students.

Payment plans. Credit card, installment, deferred payment.

Application procedures. FAFSA, institutional form required. Priority date 2/15; no closing date. Applicants notified on rolling basis starting 4/15, must reply by 5/1 or within 2 week(s) of notification.

Contact. **Financial aid office:** (206) 726-5014
Cynthia Richardson, Director for Financial Aid
1000 Lenora
Seattle, WA 98121

Crown College

Tacoma, Washington
www.crowncollege.edu
Four-year private

	Living at home
Tuition and fees:	$8,085
Books and supplies:	$700

Undergraduate aid. All financial aid based on need. Need-based aid available for full-time students.

Payment plans. Credit card, installment payment.

Application procedures. FAFSA required.

Contact. **Financial aid office:** (253) 531-3123
Monika Lehrbach, Director of Financial Aid
8739 South Hosmer
Tacoma, WA 98444-1836

DeVry University: Seattle

Federal Way, Washington
www.sea.devry.edu
Four-year proprietary

	Living at home
Tuition and fees:	$11,325
Books and supplies:	$1,100
Personal expenses:	$1,996
Transportation:	$1,612

Undergraduate aid. All financial aid based on need. Average financial aid package for full-time students was $5,091; for part-time $4,201. 14% awarded as scholarships/grants, 86% as loans/jobs.

Freshman aid. Average package met 34% of need. Average scholarship/grant was $2,964; average loan $4,059.

Policies to reduce costs. Tuition/fee waivers for employees and their families.

Payment plans. Credit card, installment, deferred payment.

Application procedures. FAFSA required. No deadline. Applicants notified on rolling basis. **Transfers:** No deadline.

Contact. Diane Rooney, Assistant Director of Student Finance
3600 South 344th Way
Federal Way, WA 98001-2995

Eastern Washington University

Cheney, Washington
www.ewu.edu
Four-year public **Federal Code: 003775**

	Living at home	On-campus
Tuition and fees (2002-2003):	$3,579	$3,579
Out-of-state:	$11,856	$11,856
Room and board:		$5,226
Books and supplies:	$690	$690
Personal expenses:	$1,908	$1,908
Transportation:	$1,188	$1,188

Undergraduate aid. Need-based: Average financial aid package for full-time students was $13,749; for part-time $8,676. 40% awarded as scholarships/grants, 60% as loans/jobs. **Non-need-based:** 55% awarded as scholarships/grants, 45% as loans/jobs. Scholarships based on academics, alumni affiliation, athletics, minority status, music/drama, state/district residency. **Student debt:** 68% of graduating class borrowed to fund education; average debt was $17,891. **Additional information:** Prepaid tuition plan available to Washington state residents.

Freshman aid. Need-based: Out of 1,291 full-time freshmen, 1,281 applied for aid; 937 were judged to have need; of these 925 received aid. Average package met 37% of need. 235 students had full need met. Average scholarship/grant was $3,648; average loan $2,116. **Non-need based:** 300 full-time freshmen with need received non-need scholarships; 124 without need received awards; 38 received athletic scholarships.

Merit scholarships. Killin Scholarship, $3,500, three awards, academic excellence (3.7 GPA, 1100 SAT); Honors Scholarship, $2,500, 38 awards, academic excellence; Presidential Scholarship, $2,000, 75 awards, GPA, SAT, early admission

Policies to reduce costs. Tuition/fee waivers for senior citizens, employees and their families. Prepayment discount; credit/placement for qualifying scores on AP, IB, CLEP examinations. Work study available nights, weekends and for part-time students.

Payment plans. Credit card, installment payment.

Application procedures. FAFSA required. Priority date 2/15; no closing date. Applicants notified on rolling basis starting 4/1, must reply within 4 week(s) of notification. **Transfers:** Educational Opportunity Grant(EOG); financially needy, placebound students with AA or junior status, $2500 renewable, rolling priority, first-come, first-served at end of each month beginning April 1, ending September 30.

Contact. Financial aid office: (509) 359-2314
Bruce Defrates, Director of Financial Aid
101 Sutton Hall
Cheney, WA 99004-2447

Edmonds Community College

Lynnwood, Washington
www.edcc.edu
Two-year public **Federal Code: 005001**

	Living at home
Tuition and fees (2002-2003):	$2,106
Out-of-state:	$7,314
Per-credit charge:	$63
Per-credit out-of-state:	$235
Board only:	$2,088
Books and supplies:	$690
Personal expenses:	$1,824
Transportation:	$1,212

Undergraduate aid. Need-based: Need-based aid available for full-time and part-time students. **Non-need-based:** Scholarships based on athletics.

Policies to reduce costs. Tuition/fee waivers for senior citizens, employees and their families. Credit/placement for qualifying scores on AP examinations. Work study available nights and for part-time students.

Payment plans. Credit card payment.

Application procedures. FAFSA, institutional form required. Priority date 5/1; no closing date. Applicants notified on rolling basis starting 6/1, must reply within 4 week(s) of notification.

Contact. Financial aid office: (425) 640-1457
Rae-Ellen Berthelsen, Associate Dean Financial Aid
20000 68th Avenue West
Lynnwood, WA 98036

Everett Community College

Everett, Washington
www.everettcc.edu
Two-year public **Federal Code: 003776**

	Living at home
Tuition and fees (2002-2003):	$1,970
Out-of-state:	$7,178
Per-credit charge:	$63
Per-credit out-of-state:	$229
Board only:	$3,100
Books and supplies:	$690
Personal expenses:	$1,824
Transportation:	$1,171

Undergraduate aid. All financial aid based on need. 83% awarded as scholarships/grants, 17% as loans/jobs. Need-based aid available for part-time students.

Policies to reduce costs. Tuition/fee waivers for senior citizens, employees and their families. Credit/placement for qualifying scores on AP, IB, CLEP examinations. Work study available nights, weekends and for part-time students.

Payment plans. Credit card payment.

Application procedures. FAFSA, institutional form required. Priority date 5/1; no closing date. Applicants notified on rolling basis starting 7/31, must reply within 2 week(s) of notification. **Transfers:** Priority date 5/1; no deadline.

Contact. Financial aid office: (425) 388-9280
Christina Castorena, Director of Financial Aid
2000 Tower Street
Everett, WA 98201-1352

Evergreen State College

Olympia, Washington
www.evergreen.edu
Four-year public **Federal Code: 008155**

	Living at home	On-campus
Tuition and fees (2002-2003):	$3,590	$3,590
Out-of-state:	$12,413	$12,413
Room and board:		$5,610
Board only:	$2,190	
Books and supplies:	$780	$780
Personal expenses:	$1,818	$1,818
Transportation:	$1,704	$1,188

Undergraduate aid. Need-based: Average financial aid package for full-time students was $9,175; for part-time $7,084. 43% awarded as scholarships/grants, 57% as loans/jobs. **Non-need-based:** 18% awarded as scholarships/grants, 82% as loans/jobs. Scholarships based on academics, state/district residency. **Student debt:** 51% of graduating class borrowed to fund education; average debt was $13,000. **Additional information:** Application deadline for merit and cultural diversity scholarships February 1; for other aid February 15. Minority students may apply for tuition and fee waiver scholarships; amount of award equal to in-state tuition and fees. Discount waiver for employees. To meet priority deadline for required financial aid forms, official results of FAFSA must be received by March 15.

Freshman aid. Need-based: Out of 462 full-time freshmen, 256 applied for aid; 181 were judged to have need; of these 168 received aid. Average package met 77% of need. 62 students had full need met. Average scholarship/grant was $4,396; average loan $2,113. **Non-need based:** 70 full-time freshmen with need received non-need scholarships; 9 without need received awards; 41 received athletic scholarships.

Policies to reduce costs. Tuition/fee waivers for employees and their families. Credit/placement for qualifying scores on AP, IB, CLEP examinations.

Payment plans. Credit card, installment payment.

Application procedures. FAFSA, institutional form required. Priority date 2/15; closing date 3/15. Applicants notified on rolling basis starting 4/15, must reply within 4 week(s) of notification.

Contact. Financial aid office: 360-867-6205
Marla Skelley, Director of Financial Aid
2700 Evergreen Parkway NW
Olympia, WA 98505

Gonzaga University

Spokane, Washington
www.gonzaga.edu
Four-year private **Federal Code: 003778**

	Living at home	On-campus
Tuition and fees:	$20,735	$20,735
Room and board:		$5,960
Board only:	$1,030	
Books and supplies:	$750	$750
Personal expenses:	$1,750	$1,750
Transportation:	$1,200	$1,200

Undergraduate aid. Need-based: Average financial aid package for full-time students was $12,525; for part-time $2,818. 63% awarded as scholarships/grants, 37% as loans/jobs. **Non-need-based:** 66% awarded as scholarships/grants, 34% as loans/jobs. Scholarships based on academics, alumni affiliation, athletics, leadership, minority status, music/drama. **Student debt:** 72% of graduating class borrowed to fund education; average debt was $21,174.

Freshman aid. Need-based: Out of 905 full-time freshmen, 814 applied for aid; 616 were judged to have need; of these 615 received aid. Average package met 84% of need. 127 students had full need met. Average scholarship/grant was $11,244; average loan $4,118. **Non-need based:** 250 full-time freshmen with need received non-need scholarships; 180 without need received awards; 27 received athletic scholarships.

Policies to reduce costs. Tuition/fee waivers for senior citizens, family members, family of clergy, employees and their families. Credit/placement for qualifying scores on AP, IB, CLEP examinations.

Payment plans. Credit card, installment, deferred payment.

Application procedures. FAFSA required. Priority date 2/1; no closing date. Applicants notified on rolling basis starting 3/1, must reply by 5/1 or within 3 week(s) of notification.

Contact. Financial aid office: (509) 323-6582
Thayne McCulloh, Dean of Student Financial Services
502 East Boone Avenue
Spokane, WA 99258-0001

Grays Harbor College

Aberdeen, Washington
www.ghc.ctc.edu
Two-year public **Federal Code: 003779**

	Living at home
Tuition and fees (2002-2003):	$2,088
Out-of-state:	$7,296
Per-credit charge:	$63
Per-credit out-of-state:	$235
Books and supplies:	$850

Undergraduate aid. Need-based: Need-based aid available for full-time and part-time students. **Non-need-based:** Scholarships based on academics, art, athletics, leadership, music/drama.

Policies to reduce costs. Tuition/fee waivers for adults, senior citizens, minority students, unemployed or children of unemployed, employees and their families. Prepayment discount; credit/placement for qualifying scores on AP, CLEP examinations. Work study available nights, weekends and for part-time students.

Payment plans. Credit card payment.

Application procedures. FAFSA, institutional form required. Priority date 5/1; no closing date. Applicants notified on rolling basis starting 5/15.

Contact. Financial aid office: (360) 538-4081
Everett Brackett, Director of Financial Aid
1620 Edward P. Smith Drive
Aberdeen, WA 98520

Green River Community College

Auburn, Washington
www.greenriver.edu
Two-year public **Federal Code: 003780**

	Living at home
Tuition and fees (2002-2003):	$2,163
Out-of-state:	$2,559
Per-credit charge:	$63
Per-credit out-of-state:	$76
Board only:	$2,524
Books and supplies:	$870
Personal expenses:	$1,076
Transportation:	$1,285

Undergraduate aid. All financial aid based on need. Need-based aid available for full-time and part-time students.

Policies to reduce costs. Tuition/fee waivers for senior citizens, employees and their families.

Payment plans. Credit card payment.

Application procedures. FAFSA, institutional form required. Priority date 4/15; no closing date. Applicants notified on rolling basis starting 6/30, must reply within 2 week(s) of notification. **Transfers:** No deadline.

Contact. Financial aid office: (253) 833-9111 ext. 2440
Mary Edington, Director of Financial Aid
12401 Southeast 320th Street
Auburn, WA 98092

Henry Cogswell College

Everett, Washington
www.henrycogswell.edu
Four-year private **Federal Code: 016175**

	Living at home
Tuition and fees:	$14,400
Board only:	$1,968
Personal expenses:	$1,720
Transportation:	$1,144

Undergraduate aid. All financial aid based on need. Average financial aid package for full-time students was $4,746; for part-time $4,068. 40% awarded as scholarships/grants, 60% as loans/jobs. **Student debt:** 18% of graduating class borrowed to fund education; average debt was $11,416. **Additional information:** Many students qualify for tuition reimbursement from industry employers.

Freshman aid. Out of 16 full-time freshmen, 11 applied for aid; 6 were judged to have need; of these 6 received aid. 5 students had full need met. Average scholarship/grant was $2,275; average loan $2,625.

Policies to reduce costs. Tuition/fee waivers for unemployed or children of unemployed, employees and their families. Tuition at time of enrollment guaranteed for 4 years; credit/placement for qualifying scores on AP, IB, CLEP examinations. Work study available nights and for part-time students.

Payment plans. Credit card, installment, deferred payment.

Application procedures. FAFSA, institutional form required. Priority date 3/1; no closing date. Applicants notified on rolling basis starting 1/1, must reply within 4 week(s) of notification. **Transfers:** No deadline.

Contact. Financial aid office: (425) 258-3351
Kelley Campbell, Financial Aid Director
3002 Colby Ave.
Everett, WA 98201

Heritage College

Toppenish, Washington
www.heritage.edu
Four-year private **Federal Code: 003777**

	Living at home
Tuition and fees:	$8,440
Board only:	$2,046
Personal expenses:	$1,896
Transportation:	$1,532

Undergraduate aid. Need-based: Average financial aid package for full-time students was $11,012; for part-time $5,324. 59% awarded as scholarships/

grants, 41% as loans/jobs. **Non-need-based:** 21% awarded as scholarships/grants, 79% as loans/jobs. Scholarships based on academics, leadership, minority status. **Student debt:** 48% of graduating class borrowed to fund education; average debt was $14,959.

Freshman aid. Need-based: Out of 63 full-time freshmen, 58 applied for aid; 56 were judged to have need; of these 56 received aid. Average package met 72% of need. 4 students had full need met. Average scholarship/grant was $8,018; average loan $1,753.

Policies to reduce costs. Tuition/fee waivers for senior citizens, employees and their families. Credit/placement for qualifying scores on CLEP examinations. Work study available nights, weekends and for part-time students.

Payment plans. Credit card, installment, deferred payment.

Application procedures. FAFSA, institutional form required. Priority date 2/10; no closing date. Applicants notified on rolling basis, must reply within 4 week(s) of notification.

Contact. **Financial aid office:** (509) 865-8502
Laura Pendleton, Director of Financial Aid Operations
3240 Fort Road
Toppenish, WA 98948-9599

ITT Technical Institute: Bothell

Bothell, Washington
www.itt-tech.edu
Two-year proprietary **Federal Code: 030718**

College costs. Total program varies depending on course of study. Per-credit-hour charge: $347.

Policies to reduce costs. Tuition/fee waivers for employees and their families. Tuition at time of enrollment guaranteed for 2 years.

Payment plans. Credit card, installment payment.

Application procedures. FAFSA, institutional form required. No deadline. Applicants notified on rolling basis.

Contact. Terri O'Dell, Director of Finance
2525 223rd Street S.E.
Bothell, WA 98021

ITT Technical Institute: Seattle

Seattle, Washington
www.itt-tech.edu
Three-year proprietary **Federal Code: 008443**

College costs. Total program varies depending on course of study. Per-credit-hour charge: $347.

Policies to reduce costs. Tuition/fee waivers for employees and their families.

Payment plans. Credit card, installment payment.

Application procedures. FAFSA, institutional form required. No deadline. Applicants notified on rolling basis.

Contact. Lisa Loffin, Director of Finance
12720 Gateway Drive, Suite 100
Seattle, WA 98168

ITT Technical Institute: Spokane

Spokane, Washington
www.itt-tech.edu
Two-year proprietary **Federal Code: 030718**

College costs. Total program varies depending on course of study. Per-credit-hour charge: $347.

Policies to reduce costs. Tuition/fee waivers for employees and their families. Tuition at time of enrollment guaranteed for 2 years.

Payment plans. Credit card, installment payment.

Application procedures. FAFSA, institutional form required. No deadline. Applicants notified on rolling basis.

Contact. Helen Horton, Director of Finance
North 1050 Argonne Road
Spokane, WA 99212

Lake Washington Technical College

Kirkland, Washington
www.lwtc.ctc.edu
Two-year public **Federal Code: 005373**

College costs. Class fees vary by program. U.S. students pay additional $30 per credit, international students pay additional $59 per credit for first 5 credit-hours.

	Living at home
Tuition and fees (2002-2003):	$1,629
Per-credit charge:	$26
Per-credit out-of-state:	$26
Board only:	$2,172
Books and supplies:	$720
Personal expenses:	$1,896
Transportation:	$1,260

Undergraduate aid. Need-based: Need-based aid available for full-time and part-time students.

Policies to reduce costs. Tuition/fee waivers for senior citizens, employees and their families. Credit/placement for qualifying scores on CLEP examinations. Work study available for part-time students.

Payment plans. Credit card payment.

Application procedures. FAFSA, institutional form required. Priority date 4/15; no closing date. Applicants notified on rolling basis. **Transfers:** No deadline.

Contact. Bill Chaney, Director of Financial Aid
11605 132nd Avenue, NE
Kirkland, WA 98034

Lower Columbia College

Longview, Washington
www.lcc.ctc.edu
Two-year public **Federal Code: 003782**

	Living at home
Tuition and fees (2002-2003):	$2,091
Out-of-state:	$7,279
Per-credit charge:	$66
Per-credit out-of-state:	$238
Books and supplies:	$750
Personal expenses:	$1,200
Transportation:	$1,050

Policies to reduce costs. Tuition/fee waivers for adults, senior citizens, unemployed or children of unemployed, employees and their families. Credit/placement for qualifying scores on AP, CLEP examinations.

Payment plans. Credit card, deferred payment.

Application procedures. Institutional form, CSS PROFILE required. Priority date 5/1; no closing date. Applicants notified on rolling basis starting 4/21, must reply within 2 week(s) of notification. **Transfers:** State need grant awards transfer with student, if previously awarded at another WA institution, SEOG usually not available to transfer students. Student employment, loans, Pell Grant available.

Contact. **Financial aid office:** (360) 442-2311
James Gorman, Financial Aid Officer
1600 Maple
Longview, WA 98632-0310

North Seattle Community College

Seattle, Washington
www.northseattle.edu
Two-year public **Federal Code: 009704**

	Living at home
Tuition and fees (2002-2003):	$2,108
Out-of-state:	$7,315
Per-credit charge:	$63
Per-credit out-of-state:	$234
Books and supplies:	$700
Personal expenses:	$1,864
Transportation:	$1,235

Undergraduate aid. **Need-based:** Need-based aid available for full-time and part-time students.

Policies to reduce costs. Tuition/fee waivers for senior citizens, unemployed or children of unemployed, employees and their families. Credit/placement for qualifying scores on IB, CLEP examinations. Work study available nights, weekends and for part-time students.

Payment plans. Credit card, installment payment.

Application procedures. FAFSA, institutional form required. Priority date 4/30; closing date 8/29. Applicants notified on rolling basis starting 8/1, must reply within 2 week(s) of notification.

Contact. **Financial aid office:** (206) 528-4700
Suzanne Scheldt, Director of Financial Aid
9600 College Way North
Seattle, WA 98103

Northwest Aviation College

Auburn, Washington
www.afsnac.com
Two-year private

College costs (2002-2003). Program cost $37,662; includes tuition, books, materials, aircraft rental.

Contact. 506 23rd Northeast
Auburn, WA 98002

Northwest College

Kirkland, Washington
www.nwcollege.edu
Four-year private **Federal Code: 003783**

	Living at home	On-campus
Tuition and fees (2002-2003):	$12,853	$12,853
Room and board:		$5,996
Books and supplies:	$850	$850
Personal expenses:	$1,760	$1,760
Transportation:	$1,060	$300

Undergraduate aid. **Need-based:** Average financial aid package for full-time students was $10,207; for part-time $6,591. 49% awarded as scholarships/grants, 51% as loans/jobs. **Non-need-based:** 35% awarded as scholarships/grants, 65% as loans/jobs. Scholarships based on academics, art, athletics, leadership, music/drama, religious affiliation. **Student debt:** 93% of graduating class borrowed to fund education; average debt was $20,374.

Freshman aid. **Need-based:** Out of 174 full-time freshmen, 126 applied for aid; 107 were judged to have need; of these 107 received aid. Average package met 72% of need. 27 students had full need met. Average scholarship/grant was $7,974; average loan $2,685. **Non-need based:** 15 full-time freshmen with need received non-need scholarships; 31 without need received awards; 14 received athletic scholarships.

Policies to reduce costs. Tuition/fee waivers for senior citizens, family members, family of clergy, employees and their families. Credit/placement for qualifying scores on AP, IB, CLEP examinations. Work study available nights, weekends and for part-time students.

Payment plans. Credit card, installment, deferred payment.

Application procedures. FAFSA, institutional form required. Priority date 3/1; no closing date. Applicants notified on rolling basis starting 4/15, must reply within 4 week(s) of notification.

Contact. **Financial aid office:** (425) 889-5210
Lana Walter, Director of Financial Aid
Box 579
Kirkland, WA 98083-0579

Olympic College

Bremerton, Washington
www.oc.ctc.edu
Two-year public **Federal Code: 003784**

	Living at home
Tuition and fees (2002-2003):	$2,163
Out-of-state:	$7,371
Per-credit charge:	$63
Per-credit out-of-state:	$235
Books and supplies:	$600
Personal expenses:	$1,197
Transportation:	$1,026

Undergraduate aid. **Need-based:** 75% awarded as scholarships/grants, 25% as loans/jobs. Need-based aid available for part-time students. **Non-need-based:** Scholarships based on academics, state/district residency.

Policies to reduce costs. Tuition/fee waivers for senior citizens, employees and their families. Credit/placement for qualifying scores on AP, IB, CLEP examinations. Work study available nights and for part-time students.

Payment plans. Credit card, installment payment.

Application procedures. FAFSA, institutional form required. No deadline. Applicants notified on rolling basis starting 6/1, must reply within 2 week(s) of notification.

Contact. **Financial aid office:** (360) 475-7160
Nick Rengler, Associate Dean, Student Financial Services
1600 Chester Avenue
Bremerton, WA 98337-1699

Pacific Lutheran University

Tacoma, Washington
www.plu.edu
Four-year private **Federal Code: 003785**

	Living at home	On-campus
Tuition and fees (2002-2003):	$18,500	$18,500
Room and board:		$5,870
Board only:	$1,998	
Books and supplies:	$672	$672
Personal expenses:	$1,908	$1,908
Transportation:	$1,188	$100

Undergraduate aid. **Need-based:** Average financial aid package for full-time students was $15,392; for part-time $10,886. 59% awarded as scholarships/grants, 41% as loans/jobs. **Non-need-based:** 61% awarded as scholarships/grants, 39% as loans/jobs. Scholarships based on academics, alumni affiliation, art, leadership, music/drama, state/district residency. **Student debt:** 18% of graduating class borrowed to fund education; average debt was $20,585.

Freshman aid. **Need-based:** Out of 579 full-time freshmen, 505 applied for aid; 400 were judged to have need; of these 397 received aid. Average package met 94% of need. 230 students had full need met. Average scholarship/grant was $5,960; average loan $4,137. **Non-need based:** 264 full-time freshmen with need received non-need scholarships; 91 without need received awards.

Policies to reduce costs. Tuition/fee waivers for employees and their families. Prepayment discount; credit/placement for qualifying scores on AP, IB, CLEP examinations. Work study available for part-time students.

Payment plans. Credit card, installment payment.

Application procedures. FAFSA required. Priority date 1/31; no closing date. Applicants notified on rolling basis starting 4/1, must reply by 5/1 or within 4 week(s) of notification.

Contact. **Financial aid office:** (253) 535-7134
Kay Soltis, Director of Financial Aid
Office of Admissions
Tacoma, WA 98447-0003

Peninsula College

Port Angeles, Washington
www.pc.ctc.edu
Two-year public **Federal Code: 003786**

	Living at home	On-campus
Tuition and fees (2002-2003):	$2,070	$2,070
Out-of-state:	$2,467	$2,467
Per-credit charge:	$63	$63
Per-credit out-of-state:	$76	$76
Room and board:		$5,388
Books and supplies:	$795	$795
Personal expenses:	$1,320	$1,320
Transportation:	$1,260	$1,260

Undergraduate aid. Need-based: Need-based aid available for full-time and part-time students. **Non-need-based:** Scholarships based on academics, athletics, job skills.

Policies to reduce costs. Tuition/fee waivers for senior citizens, unemployed or children of unemployed, employees and their families. Credit/placement for qualifying scores on AP, CLEP examinations.

Payment plans. Credit card, deferred payment.

Application procedures. FAFSA, institutional form required. Priority date 4/1; no closing date. Applicants notified on rolling basis starting 6/1, must reply within 2 week(s) of notification. **Transfers:** No deadline.

Contact. Financial aid office: (360) 417-6391
Cheryl Reid, Director of Financial Aid
1502 East Lauridsen Boulevard
Port Angeles, WA 98362

Renton Technical College

Renton, Washington
www.renton-tc.ctc.edu
Two-year public **Federal Code: 014001**

	Living at home
Tuition and fees (2002-2003):	$2,322
Out-of-state:	$2,322
Books and supplies:	$690
Personal expenses:	$1,825
Transportation:	$1,209

Undergraduate aid. All financial aid based on need. Need-based aid available for full-time and part-time students.

Policies to reduce costs. Credit/placement for qualifying scores on CLEP examinations.

Payment plans. Credit card payment.

Application procedures. FAFSA, institutional form required. No deadline. Applicants notified on rolling basis.

Contact. Financial aid office: (425) 235-5841
Janet Riebe, Director of Financial Aid
3000 Northeast Fourth Street
Renton, WA 98056-4195

St. Martin's College

Lacey, Washington
www.stmartin.edu
Four-year private **Federal Code: 003794**

	Living at home	On-campus
Tuition and fees (projected):	$17,950	$17,950
Room and board:		$5,300
Board only:	$2,172	
Books and supplies:	$720	$720
Personal expenses:	$1,896	$1,896
Transportation:	$1,260	$1,260

Undergraduate aid. Need-based: Average financial aid package for full-time students was $14,659; for part-time $10,579. 53% awarded as scholarships/grants, 47% as loans/jobs. **Non-need-based:** 31% awarded as scholarships/grants, 69% as loans/jobs. Scholarships based on academics, alumni affiliation, athletics, music/drama.

Freshman aid. Need-based: Average package met 89% of need. Average scholarship/grant was $12,225; average loan $3,069.

Merit scholarships. Valedictorian Scholarships; awarded after competitive interviews of high school valedictorians; 2 available; full scholarships.

Policies to reduce costs. Tuition/fee waivers for children of alumni, family members, employees and their families. Credit/placement for qualifying scores on AP, CLEP examinations. Work study available nights, weekends and for part-time students.

Payment plans. Credit card, installment, deferred payment.

Application procedures. FAFSA required. Priority date 3/1; no closing date. Applicants notified on rolling basis starting 3/15, must reply within 3 week(s) of notification. **Transfers:** Priority date 3/1; no deadline.

Contact. Financial aid office: (360) 438-4397
Rebecca Wonderly, Director of Financial Aid
5300 Pacific Avenue Southeast
Lacey, WA 98503

Seattle Central Community College

Seattle, Washington
www.seattlecentral.org
Two-year public **Federal Code: 003787**

	Living at home
Tuition and fees (2002-2003):	$2,143
Out-of-state:	$7,351
Per-credit charge:	$63
Per-credit out-of-state:	$234
Board only:	$543
Books and supplies:	$720
Personal expenses:	$1,896
Transportation:	$1,260

Undergraduate aid. Need-based: Need-based aid available for full-time and part-time students.

Policies to reduce costs. Tuition/fee waivers for senior citizens, unemployed or children of unemployed, employees and their families. Tuition at time of enrollment guaranteed for 2 years. Work study available nights, weekends and for part-time students.

Payment plans. Credit card payment.

Application procedures. FAFSA required. Priority date 4/30; closing date 8/27. Applicants notified on rolling basis, must reply within 2 week(s) of notification.

Contact. Joan Ray, Assistant Dean, Financial Student Services
1701 Broadway
Seattle, WA 98122

Seattle Pacific University

Seattle, Washington
www.spu.edu
Four-year private **Federal Code: 003788**

	Living at home	On-campus
Tuition and fees (2002-2003):	$17,682	$17,682
Room and board:		$6,660
Board only:	$1,024	
Books and supplies:	$690	$690
Personal expenses:	$945	$1,383
Transportation:	$648	$648

Undergraduate aid. Need-based: Average financial aid package for full-time students was $14,980; for part-time $11,310. 52% awarded as scholarships/grants, 48% as loans/jobs. **Non-need-based:** 81% awarded as scholarships/grants, 19% as loans/jobs. Scholarships based on academics, alumni affiliation, art, athletics, leadership, minority status, music/drama, religious affiliation. **Student debt:** 64% of graduating class borrowed to fund education; average debt was $18,354.

Freshman aid. Need-based: Out of 600 full-time freshmen, 499 applied for aid; 374 were judged to have need; of these 369 received aid. Average package met 76% of need. 83 students had full need met. Average scholarship/grant was $10,891; average loan $4,836. **Non-need based:** 176 without need received awards; 5 received athletic scholarships.

Policies to reduce costs. Tuition/fee waivers for children of alumni, senior citizens, family of clergy, employees and their families. Credit/placement for qualifying scores on AP, IB, CLEP examinations.

Payment plans. Credit card, installment payment.

Application procedures. FAFSA required. Priority date 1/31; no closing date. Applicants notified on rolling basis starting 4/15, must reply within 4 week(s) of notification.

Contact. **Financial aid office:** (206) 281-2061
Vickie Rekow, Director of Financial Aid
3307 Third Avenue West
Seattle, WA 98119-1997

Seattle University

Seattle, Washington
www.seattleu.edu
Four-year private **Federal Code: 003790**

College costs. $200 admission fee, $80 matriculation fee required. $419 per-credit-hour flat rate for part-time less than 12 credits. $80 per-credit-hour charge for credit by examination. $80 per-credit-hour charge for validation of field experience. $55 removal fee for incompletes.

	Living at home	On-campus
Tuition and fees (2002-2003):	$18,855	$18,855
Room and board:		$6,627
Board only:	$846	
Books and supplies:	$945	$945
Personal expenses:	$162	$162
Transportation:	$1,245	$1,245

Undergraduate aid. Need-based: Average financial aid package for full-time students was $18,926; for part-time $11,789. 53% awarded as scholarships/grants, 47% as loans/jobs. **Non-need-based:** 59% awarded as scholarships/grants, 41% as loans/jobs. Scholarships based on academics, alumni affiliation, athletics, leadership, minority status, music/drama, state/district residency. **Student debt:** 67% of graduating class borrowed to fund education; average debt was $17,299.

Freshman aid. Need-based: Out of 679 full-time freshmen, 658 applied for aid; 471 were judged to have need; of these 467 received aid. Average package met 89% of need. 217 students had full need met. Average scholarship/grant was $10,592; average loan $4,127. **Non-need based:** 180 full-time freshmen with need received non-need scholarships; 71 without need received awards; 27 received athletic scholarships.

Merit scholarships. Sullivan Leadership Award for entering freshmen of Oregon, Washington, or Idaho residency; service, leadership, strong academics (3.5 GPA) important; 6 awarded; full tuition, room and board for 4 years. Presidential Scholarship; $11,000 annually for 4 years. Trustee Scholarship; $8,000 annually for 4 years. Campion Scholarship; $5,000 annually for 4 years; for first-time freshmen of U.S. citizenship or permanent resident status; strong academic and extracurricular records important.

Policies to reduce costs. Tuition/fee waivers for family of clergy, employees and their families. Credit/placement for qualifying scores on AP, IB, CLEP examinations. Work study available nights and weekends.

Payment plans. Credit card, installment payment.

Application procedures. FAFSA required. Priority date 2/1; no closing date. Applicants notified on rolling basis starting 4/1, must reply by 5/1 or within 4 week(s) of notification. **Transfers:** Closing date 3/1.

Contact. Jim White, Director of Financial Aid
900 Broadway
Seattle, WA 98122-4340

South Seattle Community College

Seattle, Washington
www.southseattle.edu
Two-year public **Federal Code: 009706**

	Living at home
Tuition and fees (2002-2003):	$2,063
Out-of-state:	$7,287
Per-credit charge:	$63
Per-credit out-of-state:	$234
Board only:	$1,926
Books and supplies:	$690
Personal expenses:	$1,824
Transportation:	$1,212

Undergraduate aid. Need-based: Need-based aid available for full-time and part-time students. **Non-need-based:** Scholarships based on academics, state/district residency.

Policies to reduce costs. Tuition/fee waivers for senior citizens, unemployed or children of unemployed, employees and their families. Credit/placement for qualifying scores on AP, IB, CLEP examinations. Work study available for part-time students.

Payment plans. Credit card payment.

Application procedures. FAFSA, institutional form required. No deadline. Applicants notified on rolling basis starting 7/1.

Contact. **Financial aid office:** (206) 764-5317
Everett Brackett, Financial Aid Director
6000 16th Avenue Southwest
Seattle, WA 98106-1499

Spokane Community College

Spokane, Washington
www.scc.spokane.cc.wa.us
Two-year public **Federal Code: 003793**

	Living at home
Tuition and fees (2002-2003):	$2,077
Out-of-state:	$2,475
Per-credit charge:	$63
Per-credit out-of-state:	$76
Board only:	$2,100
Books and supplies:	$750
Personal expenses:	$3,012
Transportation:	$1,125

Undergraduate aid. Non-need-based: Scholarships based on athletics.

Policies to reduce costs. Tuition/fee waivers for senior citizens, unemployed or children of unemployed, employees and their families. Credit/placement for qualifying scores on AP examinations.

Payment plans. Credit card, deferred payment.

Application procedures. FAFSA, institutional form required. Priority date 4/1; no closing date. Applicants notified on rolling basis starting 6/1, must reply within 2 week(s) of notification. **Transfers:** No deadline.

Contact. Sue Jarvis, Director of Financial Aid
North 1810 Greene Street
Spokane, WA 99217-5399

Spokane Falls Community College

Spokane, Washington
www.sfcc.spokane.cc.wa.us
Two-year public **Federal Code: 009544**

	Living at home
Tuition and fees (2002-2003):	$2,077
Out-of-state:	$2,475
Per-credit charge:	$63
Per-credit out-of-state:	$76
Board only:	$2,100
Books and supplies:	$750
Personal expenses:	$3,012
Transportation:	$1,125

Undergraduate aid. Non-need-based: Scholarships based on athletics.

Policies to reduce costs. Tuition/fee waivers for senior citizens, unemployed or children of unemployed, employees and their families. Credit/placement for qualifying scores on AP examinations.

Payment plans. Credit card, installment payment.

Application procedures. FAFSA, institutional form required. Priority date 4/1; no closing date. Applicants notified on rolling basis starting 5/15, must reply within 2 week(s) of notification.

Contact. Karen Driscoll, Director of Financial Aid
West 3410 Fort George Wright Drive
Spokane, WA 99224

Trinity Lutheran College

Issaquah, Washington
www.tlc.edu
Four-year private **Federal Code: 013525**

	Living at home	On-campus
Tuition and fees (2002-2003):	$9,590	$9,590
Room and board:		$5,350
Books and supplies:	$642	$642
Personal expenses:	$1,704	$1,818
Transportation:	$1,134	$1,134

Undergraduate aid. Non-need-based: Scholarships based on academics, art, leadership, music/drama.

Policies to reduce costs. Tuition/fee waivers for family of clergy, employees and their families. Prepayment discount; credit/placement for qualifying scores on AP, CLEP examinations.

Payment plans. Credit card, installment payment.

Application procedures. FAFSA, institutional form required. Priority date 5/1; no closing date. Applicants notified on rolling basis starting 5/15. **Transfers:** No deadline.

Contact. Financial aid office: (425) 961-5514
Susan Dalgleish, Director of Financial Aid
4221 228th Avenue SE
Issaquah, WA 98029

University of Puget Sound

Tacoma, Washington
www.ups.edu
Four-year private **Federal Code: 003797**

	Living at home	On-campus
Tuition and fees (2002-2003):	$23,945	$23,945
Room and board:		$6,140
Books and supplies:	$750	$750
Personal expenses:	$1,300	$1,300
Transportation:	$500	$500

Undergraduate aid. Need-based: Average financial aid package for full-time students was $18,963. 60% awarded as scholarships/grants, 40% as loans/jobs. Need-based aid available for part-time students. **Non-need-based:** 79% awarded as scholarships/grants, 21% as loans/jobs. Scholarships based on academics, alumni affiliation, art, leadership, music/drama. **Student debt:** 59% of graduating class borrowed to fund education; average debt was $24,272. **Additional information:** Cooperative education allows qualified upperclassmen to alternate semesters of full-time study and full-time work.

Freshman aid. Need-based: Out of 666 full-time freshmen, 483 applied for aid; 390 were judged to have need; of these 390 received aid. Average package met 92% of need. 178 students had full need met. Average scholarship/grant was $10,433; average loan $5,125. **Non-need based:** 341 full-time freshmen with need received non-need scholarships; 164 without need received awards.

Merit scholarships. Wyatt Trustee Scholarship, $9,000 annually; Trustee Scholarships, $8,000 annually; President's Scholarships, $5,000 annually; Dean's Scholarships, $3,000 annually; all admitted freshmen considered on basis of admission application materials; renewable for 3 additional years.

Policies to reduce costs. Tuition/fee waivers for employees and their families. Credit/placement for qualifying scores on AP, IB examinations.

Payment plans. Installment payment.

Application procedures. FAFSA required. Closing date 2/1. Applicants notified on rolling basis starting 3/15, must reply within 2 week(s) of notification. Early decision closing date 11/15. **Transfers:** Priority date 3/1; no deadline. Institutional application also required.

Contact. Financial aid office: (253) 879-3214
Maggie Mittuch, Director of Student Financial Services
1500 North Warner Street
Tacoma, WA 98416-1062

University of Washington

Seattle, Washington
www.washington.edu
Four-year public **Federal Code: 003798**

	Living at home	On-campus
Tuition and fees (2002-2003):	$4,636	$4,636
Out-of-state:	$15,337	$15,337
Room and board:		$6,570
Books and supplies:	$798	$798
Personal expenses:	$2,187	$2,187
Transportation:	$396	$396

Undergraduate aid. Need-based: Average financial aid package for full-time students was $9,784. 53% awarded as scholarships/grants, 47% as loans/jobs. **Non-need-based:** 37% awarded as scholarships/grants, 63% as loans/jobs. Scholarships based on academics, alumni affiliation, art, athletics, music/drama. **Student debt:** 51% of graduating class borrowed to fund education; average debt was $14,500. **Additional information:** Tuition not due until third week of term.

Freshman aid. Need-based: Out of 4,708 full-time freshmen, 3,154 applied for aid; 1,748 were judged to have need; of these 1,541 received aid. Average package met 87% of need. 684 students had full need met. Average scholarship/grant was $6,670; average loan $2,722. **Non-need based:** 603 full-time freshmen with need received non-need scholarships; 394 without need received awards.

Policies to reduce costs. Tuition/fee waivers for senior citizens. Credit/placement for qualifying scores on AP, IB examinations. Work study available nights and weekends.

Payment plans. Credit card, installment payment.

Application procedures. FAFSA required. Priority date 2/28; no closing date. Applicants notified on rolling basis starting 4/1, must reply within 3 week(s) of notification. **Transfers:** Priority date 2/28; no deadline.

Contact. Kay Lewis, Director, Financial Aid
1410 NE Campus Parkway, Box 355852
Seattle, WA 98195-5840

Walla Walla College

College Place, Washington
www.wwc.edu
Four-year private **Federal Code: 003799**

College costs. $370 per-credit-hour charge if above 16 credits.

	Living at home	On-campus
Tuition and fees (projected):	$16,944	$16,944
Room and board:		$4,605
Board only:	$2,235	
Books and supplies:	$810	$810
Personal expenses:	$1,950	$1,950
Transportation:	$1,500	$1,500

Undergraduate aid. Need-based: Average financial aid package for full-time students was $13,641; for part-time $10,802. 37% awarded as scholarships/grants, 63% as loans/jobs. **Non-need-based:** 79% awarded as scholarships/grants, 21% as loans/jobs. Scholarships based on academics, leadership, music/drama. **Student debt:** 73% of graduating class borrowed to fund education; average debt was $22,090.

Freshman aid. Need-based: Out of 276 full-time freshmen, 267 applied for aid; 200 were judged to have need; of these 200 received aid. Average package met 89% of need. 63 students had full need met. Average scholarship/grant was $4,299; average loan $3,636. **Non-need based:** 182 full-time freshmen with need received non-need scholarships; 87 without need received awards.

Policies to reduce costs. Tuition/fee waivers for senior citizens, family of clergy, employees and their families. Credit/placement for qualifying scores on AP, IB, CLEP examinations.

Payment plans. Credit card, installment payment.

Application procedures. FAFSA, institutional form required. No deadline. Applicants notified on rolling basis starting 3/15.

Contact. Cassie Ragenovich, Director of Student Financial Services
204 South College Avenue
College Place, WA 99324-3000

Walla Walla Community College

Walla Walla, Washington
www.wwcc.edu
Two-year public **Federal Code: 005006**

	Living at home
Tuition and fees (2002-2003):	$2,138
Out-of-state:	$3,154
Per-credit charge:	$67
Per-credit out-of-state:	$67
Personal expenses:	$450
Transportation:	$200

Undergraduate aid. Need-based: 64% awarded as scholarships/grants, 36% as loans/jobs. Need-based aid available for part-time students. **Non-need-based:** Scholarships based on academics, athletics, music/drama.

Policies to reduce costs. Tuition/fee waivers for senior citizens, unemployed or children of unemployed, employees and their families. Credit/placement for qualifying scores on AP, CLEP examinations. Work study available nights and for part-time students.

Payment plans. Credit card, installment payment.

Application procedures. FAFSA, institutional form required. Priority date 3/1; no closing date. Applicants notified on rolling basis starting 7/15, must reply within 2 week(s) of notification.

Contact. Financial aid office: (509) 527-4301
Terri Johnson, Director of Financial Aid
500 Tausick Way
Walla Walla, WA 99362-9270

Washington State University

Pullman, Washington
www.wsu.edu
Four-year public **Federal Code: 003800**

	Living at home	On-campus
Tuition and fees (2002-2003):	$4,864	$4,864
Out-of-state:	$12,659	$12,659
Room and board:		$5,530
Books and supplies:	$710	$710
Personal expenses:	$1,962	$1,962
Transportation:	$1,212	$1,212

Undergraduate aid. Need-based: Average financial aid package for full-time students was $8,874; for part-time $8,266. 42% awarded as scholarships/grants, 58% as loans/jobs. **Non-need-based:** 29% awarded as scholarships/grants, 71% as loans/jobs. Scholarships based on academics, alumni affiliation, art, athletics, job skills, leadership, minority status, music/drama, religious affiliation, state/district residency. **Student debt:** 80% of graduating class borrowed to fund education; average debt was $15,000.

Freshman aid. Need-based: Out of 2,581 full-time freshmen, 2,135 applied for aid; 1,710 were judged to have need; of these 1,605 received aid. Average package met 98% of need. 537 students had full need met. Average scholarship/grant was $4,337; average loan $2,939. **Non-need based:** 1,061 full-time freshmen with need received non-need scholarships; 735 without need received awards; 73 received athletic scholarships.

Policies to reduce costs. Tuition/fee waivers for senior citizens, employees and their families. Credit/placement for qualifying scores on AP, IB, CLEP examinations. Work study available nights, weekends and for part-time students.

Payment plans. Credit card payment.

Application procedures. FAFSA required. Priority date 3/1; no closing date. Applicants notified on rolling basis starting 4/15. **Transfers:** President's Scholarship available for transfer students with minimum 3.9 GPA.

Contact. Wayne Sparks, Director of Student Financial Aid
370 Lighty Student Services Bldg., PO Box 641067
Pullman, WA 99164-1067

Wenatchee Valley College

Wenatchee, Washington
www.wvc.ctc.edu
Two-year public **Federal Code: 003801**

	Living at home
Tuition and fees (2002-2003):	$2,079
Out-of-state:	$2,476
Per-credit charge:	$63
Per-credit out-of-state:	$76
Books and supplies:	$678
Personal expenses:	$714
Transportation:	$1,008

Undergraduate aid. Need-based: 69% awarded as scholarships/grants, 31% as loans/jobs. Need-based aid available for part-time students. **Non-need-based:** Scholarships based on academics, athletics. **Student debt:** 25% of graduating class borrowed to fund education; average debt was $10,023.

Policies to reduce costs. Tuition/fee waivers for senior citizens, employees and their families. Credit/placement for qualifying scores on AP examinations.

Payment plans. Credit card payment.

Application procedures. FAFSA required. Closing date 4/2. Applicants notified by 7/2, must reply within 3 week(s) of notification.

Contact. Financial aid office: (509) 664-2567
Financial Aid Director
1300 Fifth Street
Wenatchee, WA 98801-1799

Western Washington University

Bellingham, Washington
www.wwu.edu
Four-year public **Federal Code: 003802**

	Living at home	On-campus
Tuition and fees (2002-2003):	$3,702	$3,702
Out-of-state:	$11,901	$11,901
Room and board:		$5,648
Board only:	$948	
Books and supplies:	$720	$720
Personal expenses:	$1,317	$1,890
Transportation:	$1,131	$1,131

Undergraduate aid. Need-based: Average financial aid package for full-time students was $7,854; for part-time $8,937. 48% awarded as scholarships/grants, 52% as loans/jobs. **Non-need-based:** 15% awarded as scholarships/grants, 85% as loans/jobs. Scholarships based on academics, alumni affiliation, art, athletics, leadership, minority status, music/drama, state/district residency. **Student debt:** 57% of graduating class borrowed to fund education; average debt was $15,050. **Additional information:** Short-term student loans ranging from $100 to $1,000 available on a quarterly basis.

Freshman aid. Need-based: Out of 2,209 full-time freshmen, 2,209 applied for aid; 806 were judged to have need; of these 774 received aid. Average package met 80% of need. 274 students had full need met. Average scholarship/grant was $4,154; average loan $2,500. **Non-need based:** 61 full-time freshmen with need received non-need scholarships; 365 without need received awards; 25 received athletic scholarships.

Policies to reduce costs. Tuition/fee waivers for senior citizens, minority students, employees and their families. Credit/placement for qualifying scores on AP, IB examinations.

Payment plans. Credit card, installment payment.

Application procedures. FAFSA required. Priority date 2/15; no closing date. Applicants notified on rolling basis starting 3/20, must reply within 3 week(s) of notification. **Transfers:** Some state aid not available for out-of-state transfer students.

Contact. Financial aid office: (360) 650-3470
Clara Capron, Director of Student Financial Resources
Old Main 200
Bellingham, WA 98225-9009

Whitman College

Walla Walla, Washington
www.whitman.edu
Four-year private **Federal Code: 003803**

	Living at home	On-campus
Tuition and fees (2002-2003):	$24,274	$24,274
Room and board:		$6,550
Books and supplies:	$1,000	$1,000

Undergraduate aid. Need-based: Average financial aid package for full-time students was $17,950; for part-time $15,850. 72% awarded as scholarships/grants, 28% as loans/jobs. **Non-need-based:** 80% awarded as scholarships/grants, 20% as loans/jobs. Scholarships based on academics, art, leadership, minority status, music/drama, state/district residency. **Student debt:** 60% of graduating class borrowed to fund education; average debt was $15,000.

Freshman aid. Need-based: Out of 379 full-time freshmen, 244 applied for aid; 164 were judged to have need; of these 164 received aid. Average package met 97% of need. 124 students had full need met. Average scholarship/grant was $13,000; average loan $2,650. **Non-need based:** 117 full-time freshmen with need received non-need scholarships; 68 without need received awards.

Policies to reduce costs. Tuition/fee waivers for employees and their families. Credit/placement for qualifying scores on AP, IB examinations. Work study available nights, weekends and for part-time students.

Payment plans. Installment payment.

Application procedures. FAFSA, CSS PROFILE required. Priority date 11/15; closing date 2/1. Applicants notified on rolling basis starting 12/20, must reply by 2/15. Early decision closing date 11/15.

Contact. Financial aid office: (509) 527-5178
Varga Fox, Director of Financial Aid Services
515 Boyer Avenue
Walla Walla, WA 99362-2046

Whitworth College

Spokane, Washington
www.whitworth.edu
Four-year private **Federal Code: 003804**

	Living at home	On-campus
Tuition and fees (2002-2003):	$18,798	$18,798
Room and board:		$6,050
Board only:	$2,169	
Books and supplies:	$720	$720
Personal expenses:	$1,899	$2,023
Transportation:	$1,248	$1,248

Undergraduate aid. Need-based: Average financial aid package for full-time students was $16,510; for part-time $4,736. 65% awarded as scholarships/grants, 35% as loans/jobs. **Non-need-based:** 71% awarded as scholarships/grants, 29% as loans/jobs. Scholarships based on academics, alumni affiliation, art, music/drama, religious affiliation.

Freshman aid. Need-based: Out of 433 full-time freshmen, 426 applied for aid; 308 were judged to have need; of these 308 received aid. Average package met 88% of need. 6 students had full need met. Average scholarship/grant was $12,504; average loan $3,832. **Non-need based:** 29 full-time freshmen with need received non-need scholarships; 110 without need received awards.

Merit scholarships. Merit scholarships based on GPA, SAT/ACT scores and class rank, $4,000-$8,500; unlimited until March 1, 2002.

Policies to reduce costs. Tuition/fee waivers for children of alumni, senior citizens, family of clergy, employees and their families. Credit/placement for qualifying scores on AP, IB, CLEP examinations.

Payment plans. Credit card, installment payment.

Application procedures. FAFSA required. Priority date 3/1; no closing date. Applicants notified on rolling basis starting 4/1, must reply by 5/1 or within 4 week(s) of notification. **Transfers:** Priority date 4/1; no deadline.

Contact. Financial aid office: (509) 777-3215
Wendy Olson, Director of Financial Aid
300 West Hawthorne Road
Spokane, WA 99251-0002

West Virginia

Alderson-Broaddus College

Philippi, West Virginia
www.ab.edu
Four-year private **Federal Code: 003806**

	Living at home	On-campus
Tuition and fees (projected):	$16,155	$16,155
Room and board:		$5,300
Books and supplies:	$700	$700
Personal expenses:	$1,250	$1,250
Transportation:	$850	$650

Undergraduate aid. Need-based: Need-based aid available for full-time and part-time students. **Non-need-based:** Scholarships based on academics, athletics, music/drama.

Policies to reduce costs. Tuition/fee waivers for family members, employees and their families. Credit/placement for qualifying scores on AP, CLEP examinations. Work study available nights and weekends.

Payment plans. Credit card payment.

Application procedures. FAFSA required. Priority date 3/1; no closing date. Applicants notified on rolling basis. **Transfers:** Priority date 8/1; no deadline.

Contact. Financial aid office: (304) 457-6354
Brian Weingart, Director of Financial Aid
College Hill
Philippi, WV 26416

Appalachian Bible College

Bradley, West Virginia
www.abc.edu
Four-year private **Federal Code: 007544**

	Living at home	On-campus
Tuition and fees (2002-2003):	$7,390	$7,390
Room and board:		$3,540
Books and supplies:	$600	$600

Undergraduate aid. Need-based: Average financial aid package for full-time students was $3,250; for part-time $1,014. 69% awarded as scholarships/grants, 31% as loans/jobs.

Freshman aid. Need-based: Out of 58 full-time freshmen, 58 applied for aid; 58 were judged to have need; of these 58 received aid. Average package met 84% of need. Average scholarship/grant was $2,225; average loan $2,500.

Policies to reduce costs. Tuition/fee waivers for children of alumni, senior citizens, family members, family of clergy, employees and their families. Credit/placement for qualifying scores on AP, CLEP examinations. Work study available for part-time students.

Payment plans. Credit card, installment payment.

Application procedures. FAFSA, institutional form required. Priority date 6/15; no closing date. Applicants notified on rolling basis starting 6/15, must reply by 8/1 or within 4 week(s) of notification.

Contact. Financial aid office: (304) 877-6428 ext. 3247
Shirley Carfrey, Director of Financial Aid
Box ABC
Bradley, WV 25818-1353

Bethany College

Bethany, West Virginia
www.bethanywv.edu
Four-year private **Federal Code: 003808**

	Living at home	On-campus
Tuition and fees (2002-2003):	$12,566	$12,566
Room and board:		$6,000
Books and supplies:	$400	$400
Personal expenses:	$1,000	$800
Transportation:	$1,200	$600

Undergraduate aid. Need-based: Average financial aid package for full-time students was $16,750. 64% awarded as scholarships/grants, 36% as loans/jobs. **Non-need-based:** 88% awarded as scholarships/grants, 12% as loans/jobs. Scholarships based on academics, alumni affiliation, leadership, music/drama, religious affiliation. **Student debt:** 76% of graduating class borrowed to fund education; average debt was $18,000. **Additional information:** Scholarships available for travel program.

Freshman aid. Need-based: Out of 350 full-time freshmen, 350 applied for aid; 307 were judged to have need; of these 307 received aid. Average package met 86% of need. 183 students had full need met. Average loan $2,800. **Non-need based:** 265 full-time freshmen with need received non-need scholarships; 42 without need received awards.

Policies to reduce costs. Tuition/fee waivers for children of alumni, family of clergy, employees and their families. Credit/placement for qualifying scores on AP, IB, CLEP examinations.

Payment plans. Credit card, installment payment.

Application procedures. FAFSA, institutional form required. Priority date 4/1; closing date 5/1. Applicants notified on rolling basis starting 3/1, must reply within 3 week(s) of notification. **Transfers:** Priority date 4/1; no deadline.

Contact. Financial aid office: (304) 829-7141
Jeffrey DeRubbo, Director of Financial Aid
Office of Admission
Bethany, WV 26032-0428

Bluefield State College

Bluefield, West Virginia
www.bluefield.wvnet.edu
Four-year public **Federal Code: 003809**

	Living at home
Tuition and fees (2002-2003):	$2,598
Out-of-state:	$6,296
Board only:	$2,120
Books and supplies:	$800
Personal expenses:	$840
Transportation:	$1,200

Undergraduate aid. Need-based: Average financial aid package for full-time students was $4,700; for part-time $4,700. 65% awarded as scholarships/grants, 35% as loans/jobs. **Non-need-based:** 43% awarded as scholarships/grants, 57% as loans/jobs. Scholarships based on academics, alumni affiliation, athletics, leadership, minority status, state/district residency. **Student debt:** 47% of graduating class borrowed to fund education; average debt was $7,200.

Freshman aid. Need-based: Out of 392 full-time freshmen, 310 applied for aid; 275 were judged to have need; of these 275 received aid. Average package met 70% of need. 65 students had full need met. Average scholarship/grant was $2,900; average loan $2,400. **Non-need based:** 45 full-time freshmen with need received non-need scholarships; 60 without need received awards; 25 received athletic scholarships.

Policies to reduce costs. Tuition/fee waivers for senior citizens, employees and their families. Credit/placement for qualifying scores on AP, CLEP examinations. Work study available nights, weekends and for part-time students.

Payment plans. Credit card, deferred payment.

Application procedures. FAFSA, institutional form required. Closing date 3/1. Applicants notified on rolling basis starting 6/1. **Transfers:** Priority date 3/1; no deadline.

Contact. Financial aid office: (304) 327-4020
Tom Isle, Director of Financial Aid
219 Rock Street
Bluefield, WV 24701

Concord College

Athens, West Virginia
www.concord.edu
Four-year public **Federal Code: 003810**

	Living at home	On-campus
Tuition and fees (2002-2003):	$2,963	$2,963
Out-of-state:	$6,648	$6,648
Room and board:		$4,628
Board only:	$750	
Books and supplies:	$650	$650
Personal expenses:	$1,000	$1,000
Transportation:	$969	$455

Undergraduate aid. Non-need-based: Scholarships based on academics, alumni affiliation, art, athletics, job skills, leadership, minority status, music/drama, state/district residency. **Additional information:** Room and board may be paid in 2 installments each semester: 60% at registration, 40% six weeks later. March 1 is priority deadline for state forms. April 15 is priority deadline for FAFSA.

Policies to reduce costs. Tuition/fee waivers for employees and their families. Credit/placement for qualifying scores on AP, CLEP examinations.

Payment plans. Credit card, installment payment.

Application procedures. FAFSA, institutional form required. Applicants notified on rolling basis starting 3/1, must reply within 2 week(s) of notification.

Contact. Patricia Harmon, Director of Financial Aid
1000 Vermillion Street
Athens, WV 24712-1000

Corinthian Schools: National Institute of Technology

Cross Lanes, West Virginia
www.cci.edu
Two-year proprietary **Federal Code: 010356**

College costs (2002-2003). Electronics program $18,662. Network administration program $17,791. Medical business and clinical specialist $10,751. Cost of books $1,158 for electronics, $884 for network administration, $289 for medical.

Undergraduate aid. Need-based: Need-based aid available for full-time students. **Non-need-based:** Scholarships based on academics, art.

Policies to reduce costs. Tuition/fee waivers for employees and their families.

Payment plans. Credit card, installment payment.

Application procedures. FAFSA required. No deadline. Applicants notified on rolling basis.

Contact. Aimee Swtizer, Finance Director
5514 Big Tyler Road
Cross Lanes, WV 25313

Davis and Elkins College

Elkins, West Virginia
www.davisandelkins.edu
Four-year private **Federal Code: 003811**

	Living at home	On-campus
Tuition and fees:	$14,688	$14,688
Room and board:		$5,926
Books and supplies:	$750	$750

Undergraduate aid. Need-based: Average financial aid package for full-time students was $10,238; for part-time $9,056. 59% awarded as scholarships/grants, 41% as loans/jobs. **Non-need-based:** 48% awarded as scholarships/grants, 52% as loans/jobs. Scholarships based on academics, alumni affiliation, art, athletics, leadership, music/drama. **Student debt:** 80% of graduating class borrowed to fund education; average debt was $14,000.

Freshman aid. Need-based: Out of 185 full-time freshmen, 157 applied for aid; 157 were judged to have need; of these 157 received aid. Average package met 80% of need. 32 students had full need met. Average scholarship/grant was $7,432; average loan $2,227. **Non-need based:** 18 full-time freshmen with need received non-need scholarships; 42 without need received awards; 22 received athletic scholarships.

Policies to reduce costs. Tuition/fee waivers for employees and their families. Credit/placement for qualifying scores on AP, IB, CLEP examinations. Work study available nights and weekends.

Payment plans. Credit card, installment payment.

Application procedures. FAFSA required. Priority date 3/1; no closing date. Applicants notified on rolling basis starting 1/1, must reply within 2 week(s) of notification.

Contact. Financial aid office: (304) 637-1373
Susan Wilson, Director of Financial Aid
100 Campus Drive
Elkins, WV 26241

Eastern West Virginia Community and Technical College

Moorefield, West Virginia
www.eastern.wvnet.edu
Two-year public

	Living at home
Tuition and fees (2002-2003):	$1,560
Out-of-state:	$5,484
Per-credit charge:	$65
Per-credit out-of-state:	$229

Undergraduate aid. Need-based: Need-based aid available for full-time and part-time students.

Application procedures. FAFSA, institutional form required. Priority date 6/1; no closing date. Applicants notified on rolling basis.

Contact. Robert Eagle, Director of Financial Aid
HC 65, Box 402
Moorefield, WV 26836

Fairmont State College

Fairmont, West Virginia
www.fscwv.edu
Four-year public **Federal Code: 003812**

	Living at home	On-campus
Tuition and fees (2002-2003):	$2,636	$2,636
Out-of-state:	$6,210	$6,210
Room and board:		$4,522
Board only:	$2,264	
Books and supplies:	$500	$500
Personal expenses:	$500	$500
Transportation:	$1,000	$1,350

Undergraduate aid. All financial aid based on need. Average financial aid package for full-time students was $4,841; for part-time $4,809. 52% awarded as scholarships/grants, 48% as loans/jobs. **Student debt:** 87% of graduating class borrowed to fund education; average debt was $7,871.

Freshman aid. Average package met 59% of need. Average scholarship/grant was $3,162; average loan $1,801.

Policies to reduce costs. Tuition/fee waivers for adults, children of alumni, senior citizens, minority students, employees and their families. Credit/placement for qualifying scores on AP, CLEP examinations. Work study available nights and weekends.

Payment plans. Credit card, installment, deferred payment.

Application procedures. FAFSA required. Closing date 3/1. Applicants notified on rolling basis starting 4/15, must reply within 2 week(s) of notification. **Transfers:** Academic transcripts required.

Contact. Financial aid office: (304) 367-4213
Kaye Widney, Director of Financial Aid/Scholarships
1201 Locust Avenue
Fairmont, WV 26554

Glenville State College

Glenville, West Virginia
www.glenville.edu
Four-year public **Federal Code: 003813**

	Living at home	On-campus
Tuition and fees (2002-2003):	$2,700	$2,700
Out-of-state:	$6,480	$6,480
Room and board:		$4,540
Books and supplies:	$800	$800
Personal expenses:	$1,244	$1,224
Transportation:	$1,500	$1,500

Undergraduate aid. Need-based: Need-based aid available for full-time and part-time students. **Non-need-based:** Scholarships based on academics, art, athletics, music/drama.

Policies to reduce costs. Tuition/fee waivers for employees and their families. Credit/placement for qualifying scores on AP, CLEP examinations. Work study available nights, weekends and for part-time students.

Payment plans. Credit card, installment payment.

Application procedures. FAFSA required. Priority date 3/1; no closing date. Applicants notified on rolling basis starting 4/1, must reply within 3 week(s) of notification.

Contact. Financial aid office: (304) 462-4103
Karen Lay, Financial Aid Officer
200 High Street
Glenville, WV 26351-1292

Huntington Junior College

Huntington, West Virginia
www.huntingtonjuniorcollege.edu
Two-year proprietary **Federal Code: 009047**

College costs. Tuition includes books.

	Living at home
Tuition and fees (projected):	$5,850

Payment plans. Installment payment.

Application procedures. No deadline. Applicants notified on rolling basis.

Contact. Financial aid office: (304) 697-7550
Darlene Cummings, Financial Aid Officer
900 Fifth Avenue
Huntington, WV 25701

International Academy of Design and Technology

Fairmont, West Virginia
www.iadtwv.com
Two-year proprietary **Federal Code: 010217**

College costs (2002-2003). All costs for 18 month programs include lab fees, books and supplies. Computer information management program $22,474. E-commerce program $22,525. Visual communications program $22,525.

Undergraduate aid. Need-based: Need-based aid available for full-time and part-time students. **Non-need-based:** Scholarships based on academics. **Additional information:** Financial aid applicants notified of award 1-3 days after financial aid office receives all necessary information.

Policies to reduce costs. Tuition/fee waivers for employees and their families. Tuition at time of enrollment guaranteed for 2 years. Work study available nights and weekends.

Payment plans. Credit card, installment payment.

Application procedures. FAFSA required. No deadline.

Contact. Financial aid office: (304) 534-5677
Laurie Butts, Controller
2000 Green River Drive
Fairmont, WV 26554

Marshall University

Huntington, West Virginia
www.marshall.edu
Four-year public **Federal Code: 003815**

	Living at home	On-campus
Tuition and fees (2002-2003):	$2,984	$2,984
Out-of-state:	$7,986	$7,986
Room and board:		$5,442
Board only:	$1,500	
Books and supplies:	$800	$800
Personal expenses:	$208	$1,092
Transportation:	$1,020	$570

Undergraduate aid. Need-based: Average financial aid package for full-time students was $6,376; for part-time $4,631. 41% awarded as scholarships/grants, 59% as loans/jobs. **Non-need-based:** 92% awarded as scholarships/grants, 8% as loans/jobs. Scholarships based on academics, art, athletics, minority status, music/drama, state/district residency. **Student debt:** 53% of graduating class borrowed to fund education; average debt was $15,484.

Freshman aid. Need-based: Out of 1,456 full-time freshmen, 1,230 applied for aid; 864 were judged to have need; of these 853 received aid. Average package met 58% of need. 369 students had full need met. Average scholarship/grant was $4,046; average loan $3,230. **Non-need based:** 541 full-time freshmen with need received non-need scholarships; 357 without need received awards; 73 received athletic scholarships.

Merit scholarships. Michael Perry Scholarship, $500 to incoming freshmn with 3.2 high school GPA and 20 ACT score; $750 to incoming freshman with 3.5 high school GPA and 23 ACT, or 3.2 GPA and 25 ACT, all one year only; Presidential Scholarship, $1,250 (renewable pending maintenance of 3.5 cumulative college GPA) to incoming freshman with 3.5 high school GPA and 25 ACT score; John Marshall Scholarship, tuition waiver plus $1,250 stipend (renewable yearly pending maintenance of 3.5 cumulative college GPA) to incoming freshman with 3.5 high school GPA and 30 ACT score. All subject to fund availability. Yeager scholarship, full tuition and fees, full room & board, book allowance, stipend, personal computer for use during program, and $4,000 toward study abroad. Competitive minimum ACT 28/SAT 1260. High school students apply by 12/1.

Policies to reduce costs. Tuition/fee waivers for employees and their families. Credit/placement for qualifying scores on AP, IB, CLEP examinations.

Payment plans. Credit card, installment, deferred payment.

Application procedures. FAFSA required. Priority date 3/1; no closing date. Applicants notified on rolling basis starting 5/1, must reply within 2 week(s) of notification. **Transfers:** Priority date 1/1; no deadline. Should be making normal academic progress toward graduation.

Contact. Jack Toney, Director of Financial Aid
1 John Marshall Drive
Huntington, WV 25755

Mountain State College

Parkersburg, West Virginia
www.mountainstate.org
Two-year proprietary **Federal Code: 005008**

	Living at home
Tuition and fees (2002-2003):	$7,165
Books and supplies:	$600

Policies to reduce costs. Tuition at time of enrollment guaranteed for 2 years; credit/placement for qualifying scores on CLEP examinations.

Payment plans. Installment, deferred payment.

Application procedures. FAFSA required. No deadline. Applicants notified on rolling basis.

Contact. Financial aid office: (304) 485-5487
Faye Wagoner, Director of Financial Aid
Spring at 16th Street
Parkersburg, WV 26101-3993

Mountain State University

Beckley, West Virginia
www.mountainstate.edu
Four-year private **Federal Code: 003807**

	Living at home	On-campus
Tuition and fees (2002-2003):	$4,560	$4,560
Room and board:		$4,962
Board only:	$1,600	
Books and supplies:	$825	$825
Personal expenses:	$1,340	$1,340
Transportation:	$350	

Undergraduate aid. Need-based: Average financial aid package for full-time students was $6,000; for part-time $4,800. 30% awarded as scholarships/grants, 70% as loans/jobs. **Non-need-based:** 3% awarded as scholarships/grants, 97% as loans/jobs. Scholarships based on academics, alumni affiliation, athletics, leadership.

Freshman aid. Need-based: Out of 625 full-time freshmen, 575 applied for aid; 546 were judged to have need; of these 546 received aid. Average package met 45% of need. 21 students had full need met. Average scholarship/grant was $3,300; average loan $2,350. **Non-need based:** 11 full-time freshmen with need received non-need scholarships; 25 without need received awards.

Policies to reduce costs. Tuition/fee waivers for employees and their families. Credit/placement for qualifying scores on AP, IB, CLEP examinations. Work study available nights and for part-time students.

Payment plans. Credit card, installment payment.

Application procedures. FAFSA, institutional form required. Priority date 3/1; no closing date. Applicants notified on rolling basis starting 3/1, must reply within 2 week(s) of notification.

Contact. Financial aid office: (304) 253-7351 ext. 1443
Sue Pack, Director of Financial Aid
PO Box 9003
Beckley, WV 25802-9003

Ohio Valley College

Vienna, West Virginia
www.ovc.edu
Four-year private **Federal Code: 003819**

	Living at home	On-campus
Tuition and fees:	$10,676	$10,676
Room and board:		$5,224
Board only:	$750	
Books and supplies:	$700	$700
Personal expenses:	$750	$750
Transportation:	$1,000	$750

Undergraduate aid. Need-based: Need-based aid available for full-time and part-time students. **Non-need-based:** Scholarships based on academics, athletics, job skills, leadership, music/drama.

Policies to reduce costs. Tuition/fee waivers for senior citizens, employees and their families. Credit/placement for qualifying scores on AP, CLEP examinations.

Payment plans. Credit card, installment payment.

Application procedures. FAFSA required. Priority date 2/15; no closing date. Applicants notified on rolling basis starting 3/15, must reply within 4 week(s) of notification. **Transfers:** No deadline.

Contact. Financial aid office: (304) 865-6077
Marjorie Lyons, Director of Financial Aid
#1 Campus View Drive
Vienna, WV 26105

Potomac State College of West Virginia University

Keyser, West Virginia
www.psc.wvu.edu
Two-year public **Federal Code: 003829**

	Living at home	On-campus
Tuition and fees (2002-2003):	$2,192	$2,192
Out-of-state:	$7,246	$7,246
Per-credit charge:	$102	$102
Per-credit out-of-state:	$313	$313
Room and board:		$4,450
Books and supplies:	$700	$700
Personal expenses:	$1,120	$1,120
Transportation:	$640	$640

Undergraduate aid. Need-based: Need-based aid available for full-time and part-time students. **Non-need-based:** Scholarships based on academics, athletics, leadership.

Policies to reduce costs. Tuition/fee waivers for adults, employees and their families. Credit/placement for qualifying scores on AP, CLEP examinations. Work study available nights and weekends.

Payment plans. Credit card, installment payment.

Application procedures. FAFSA required. Priority date 2/15; no closing date. Applicants notified on rolling basis starting 4/1, must reply within 2 week(s) of notification.

Contact. Financial aid office: (304) 788-6852
Robert Eagle, Director of Financial Aid
1 Grand Central Park, Suite 2090
Keyser, WV 26726

Salem International University

Salem, West Virginia
www.salemiu.edu
Four-year private **Federal Code: 003820**

	Living at home	On-campus
Tuition and fees (2002-2003):	$13,930	$13,930
Room and board:		$4,632
Board only:	$960	
Books and supplies:	$660	$660
Personal expenses:	$320	$320
Transportation:	$320	$320

Undergraduate aid. Need-based: Average financial aid package for full-time students was $15,213; for part-time $4,562. 60% awarded as scholarships/grants, 40% as loans/jobs. **Non-need-based:** 92% awarded as scholarships/grants, 8% as loans/jobs. Scholarships based on academics. **Student debt:** 45% of graduating class borrowed to fund education; average debt was $14,449.

Freshman aid. Need-based: Out of 51 full-time freshmen, 39 applied for aid; 33 were judged to have need; of these 33 received aid. Average package met 99% of need. 14 students had full need met. Average scholarship/grant was $5,101; average loan $4,548. **Non-need based:** 3 full-time freshmen with need received non-need scholarships; 17 without need received awards; 16 received athletic scholarships.

Merit scholarships. Scholarships based on high school GPA, standardized test scores; extensive amount awarded. Breed-related awards for students in the equine career and industry management program. Awards for academically excellent GED diploma recipients.

Policies to reduce costs. Tuition/fee waivers for senior citizens, employees and their families. Prepayment discount; credit/placement for qualifying scores on AP, IB, CLEP examinations. Work study available nights, weekends and for part-time students.

Payment plans. Credit card, installment payment.

Application procedures. FAFSA required. Priority date 4/15; no closing date. Applicants notified on rolling basis starting 2/15, must reply within 4 week(s) of notification. **Transfers:** No deadline.

Contact. Charlotte Lake, Director of Financial Aid
223 West Main Street
Salem, WV 26426

Shepherd College

Shepherdstown, West Virginia
www.shepherd.edu
Four-year public **Federal Code: 003822**

	Living at home	On-campus
Tuition and fees (2002-2003):	$2,866	$2,866
Out-of-state:	$6,982	$6,982
Room and board:		$4,738
Board only:	$1,235	
Books and supplies:	$800	$800
Personal expenses:	$1,275	$1,275
Transportation:	$1,500	$1,000

Undergraduate aid. Need-based: Average financial aid package for full-time students was $7,435; for part-time $6,438. 41% awarded as scholarships/grants, 59% as loans/jobs. **Non-need-based:** 19% awarded as scholarships/grants, 81% as loans/jobs. Scholarships based on academics, art, athletics, job skills, leadership, minority status, music/drama, state/district residency. **Student debt:** 60% of graduating class borrowed to fund education; average debt was $12,618.

Freshman aid. Need-based: Out of 705 full-time freshmen, 573 applied for aid; 358 were judged to have need; of these 335 received aid. Average package met 64% of need. 62 students had full need met. Average scholarship/grant was $3,155; average loan $2,383. **Non-need based:** 39 full-time freshmen with need received non-need scholarships; 88 without need received awards; 35 received athletic scholarships.

Merit scholarships. Rubye Clyde and Burkhart Scholarships; $5,000; 4 awarded, renewable awarded each year based on GPA of 3.5 and ACT of 30 or higher or SAT of 1270. Alumni Scholarships; 2 awarded each year to incoming students, minimum GPA 3.5 and ACT of 30 or SAT of 1270.

Policies to reduce costs. Tuition/fee waivers for senior citizens, minority students, employees and their families. Credit/placement for qualifying scores on AP, IB, CLEP examinations. Work study available nights, weekends and for part-time students.

Payment plans. Credit card payment.

Application procedures. FAFSA required. Priority date 3/1; no closing date. Applicants notified on rolling basis starting 3/25, must reply within 2 week(s) of notification. **Transfers:** Priority date 3/1; no deadline. Reciprocity tuition for 50 graduates of specified Maryland community colleges, tuition waivers of scholarships available through admissions.

Contact. **Financial aid office:** (304) 876-5470
Elizabeth Sturm, Director of Financial Aid
P.O. Box 3210
Shepherdstown, WV 25443-3210

Southern West Virginia Community and Technical College

Mount Gay, West Virginia
www.southern.wvnet.edu
Two-year public **Federal Code: 003816**

	Living at home
Tuition and fees (2002-2003):	$1,560
Out-of-state:	$5,484
Per-credit charge:	$65
Per-credit out-of-state:	$229
Books and supplies:	$450
Personal expenses:	$900

Undergraduate aid. Need-based: Need-based aid available for full-time and part-time students.

Policies to reduce costs. Tuition/fee waivers for employees and their families. Credit/placement for qualifying scores on AP, CLEP examinations.

Application procedures. FAFSA required. No deadline. Applicants notified on rolling basis.

Contact. Merle Dempsey, Financial Aid Director
Box 2900 Dempsey Branch Road
Mount Gay, WV 25637

University of Charleston

Charleston, West Virginia
www.ucwv.edu
Four-year private **Federal Code: 003818**

	Living at home	On-campus
Tuition and fees:	$17,400	$17,400
Room and board:		$5,980
Books and supplies:	$700	$700
Personal expenses:	$1,800	$500
Transportation:		$250

Undergraduate aid. Need-based: Need-based aid available for full-time and part-time students. **Non-need-based:** Scholarships based on academics, art, athletics, leadership, music/drama.

Policies to reduce costs. Tuition/fee waivers for employees and their families. Tuition at time of enrollment guaranteed for 4 years; credit/placement for qualifying scores on AP, IB, CLEP examinations. Work study available nights, weekends and for part-time students.

Payment plans. Credit card, installment payment.

Application procedures. FAFSA required.

Contact. **Financial aid office:** (304) 257-4750
Janet Ruge, Director of Financial Aid
2300 MacCorkle Avenue SE
Charleston, WV 25304

Valley College of Technology

Martinsburg, West Virginia
www.vct.edu
Two-year proprietary **Federal Code: G26094**

College costs. Quoted tuition for associate. Certificates' tuition $6,130 for office technology program and $6,890 for business technology program.

	Living at home
Tuition and fees (2002-2003):	$6,320
Per-credit charge:	$190
Personal expenses:	$3,120

Undergraduate aid. Need-based: 46% awarded as scholarships/grants, 54% as loans/jobs. Need-based aid available for part-time students. **Student debt:** 73% of graduating class borrowed to fund education; average debt was $4,445.

Freshman aid. Need-based: Out of 64 full-time freshmen, 59 applied for aid; 59 were judged to have need; of these 59 received aid. Average package met 60% of need. Average loan $2,625.

Payment plans. Credit card, installment payment.

Application procedures. FAFSA, institutional form required. No deadline. Applicants notified on rolling basis. **Transfers:** No deadline.

Contact. **Financial aid office:** (304) 263-0979
Tangene Umstead, Financial Aid Administrator
287 Aikens Center
Martinsburg, WV 25401

West Liberty State College

West Liberty, West Virginia
www.wlsc.edu
Four-year public **Federal Code: 003823**

	Living at home	On-campus
Tuition and fees (2002-2003):	$2,516	$2,516
Out-of-state:	$6,248	$6,248
Room and board:		$3,540
Board only:	$1,500	
Books and supplies:	$800	$800
Personal expenses:	$1,000	$1,000
Transportation:	$1,080	$840

Undergraduate aid. Need-based: Average financial aid package for full-time students was $5,592; for part-time $3,824. 45% awarded as scholarships/grants, 55% as loans/jobs. **Non-need-based:** 25% awarded as scholarships/grants, 75% as loans/jobs. Scholarships based on academics, alumni affiliation, art, athletics, leadership, music/drama. **Student debt:** 69% of graduating class borrowed to fund education; average debt was $12,874. **Additional information:** Non-need based student employment available at food service, college union, bookstore, and tutoring office. Resident assistant and campus security jobs also available.

Freshman aid. Need-based: Out of 467 full-time freshmen, 388 applied for aid; 224 were judged to have need; of these 300 received aid. Average package met 79% of need. 133 students had full need met. Average scholarship/ grant was $3,712; average loan $2,472. **Non-need based:** 181 full-time freshmen with need received non-need scholarships; 35 without need received awards; 14 received athletic scholarships.

Policies to reduce costs. Tuition/fee waivers for senior citizens, employees and their families. Credit/placement for qualifying scores on AP, CLEP examinations. Work study available nights and weekends.

Payment plans. Credit card, installment, deferred payment.

Application procedures. FAFSA required. Priority date 3/1; no closing date. Applicants notified on rolling basis starting 2/15, must reply within 2 week(s) of notification. **Transfers:** Financial aid transcript required from all previous colleges attended regardless of whether aid was received.

Contact. **Financial aid office:** (304) 336-8016
Scott Cook, Financial Aid Director
Box 295
West Liberty, WV 26074-0295

West Virginia Business College

Nutter Fort, West Virginia
www.wvbusinesscollege.com
Two-year proprietary **Federal Code: 010861**

College costs. Associate degree program costs $13,000 for entire 2-year program.

	Living at home
Tuition and fees (projected):	$6,500
Books and supplies:	$475
Transportation:	$2,000

Contact. 116 Pennsylvania Avenue
Nutter Fort, WV 26301

West Virginia Business College

Wheeling, West Virginia
www.wvbusinesscollege.com
Two-year proprietary **Federal Code: 010861**

College costs. Associate degree program costs $13,500.

	Living at home
Tuition and fees (projected):	$7,500

Contact. Teresa Warren, Financial Aid Manager
1052 Main Street
Wheeling, WV 26003

West Virginia Junior College

Morgantown, West Virginia
www.wvjc.com
Two-year proprietary **Federal Code: 005007**

College costs. Cost of books/supplies included in tuition/fees.

	Living at home
Tuition and fees (2002-2003):	$8,475
Personal expenses:	$2,529

Undergraduate aid. Need-based: Need-based aid available for full-time and part-time students.

Application procedures. FAFSA required. No deadline. Applicants notified on rolling basis.

Contact. 148 Willey Street
Morgantown, WV 26505

West Virginia Junior College: Charleston

Charleston, West Virginia
www.wvjc.com
Two-year proprietary **Federal Code: 010573**

	Living at home
Tuition and fees:	$9,375

Undergraduate aid. Need-based: Need-based aid available for full-time and part-time students.

Application procedures. FAFSA required. No deadline. Applicants notified on rolling basis.

Contact. 1000 Virginia Street East
Charleston, WV 25301

West Virginia Northern Community College

Wheeling, West Virginia
www.northern.wvnet.edu
Two-year public **Federal Code: 010920**

	Living at home
Tuition and fees (2002-2003):	$1,680
Out-of-state:	$5,352
Per-credit charge:	$70
Per-credit out-of-state:	$223
Books and supplies:	$500
Personal expenses:	$1,153
Transportation:	$1,024

Undergraduate aid. Need-based: Need-based aid available for full-time and part-time students.

Policies to reduce costs. Tuition/fee waivers for adults, senior citizens, employees and their families. Credit/placement for qualifying scores on AP, CLEP examinations.

Payment plans. Credit card, installment payment.

Application procedures. FAFSA, institutional form required. Priority date 3/15; no closing date. Applicants notified on rolling basis starting 3/10.

Contact. **Financial aid office:** (304) 233-5900 ext. 4262
Janet Fike, Director, Financial Aid
1704 Market Street
Wheeling, WV 26003

West Virginia State College

Institute, West Virginia
www.wvsc.edu
Four-year public **Federal Code: 003826**

	Living at home	On-campus
Tuition and fees (2002-2003):	$2,562	$2,562
Out-of-state:	$5,892	$5,892
Room and board:		$4,300
Board only:	$1,983	
Books and supplies:	$664	$664
Personal expenses:	$1,168	$1,065
Transportation:	$1,299	$498

Undergraduate aid. All financial aid based on need. 54% awarded as scholarships/grants, 46% as loans/jobs. Need-based aid available for part-time students.

Policies to reduce costs. Tuition/fee waivers for employees and their families. Credit/placement for qualifying scores on AP, IB, CLEP examinations. Work study available nights, weekends and for part-time students.

Payment plans. Credit card, installment, deferred payment.

Application procedures. FAFSA required. Priority date 3/1; closing date 6/15. Applicants notified on rolling basis starting 2/15, must reply within 2 week(s) of notification.

Contact. **Financial aid office:** (304) 766-3131
Mary Blizzard, Director of Financial Aid
Campus Box 197
Institute, WV 25112-1000

West Virginia University

Morgantown, West Virginia
www.wvu.edu
Four-year public **Federal Code: 003827**

	Living at home	On-campus
Tuition and fees (2002-2003):	$3,240	$3,240
Out-of-state:	$9,710	$9,710
Room and board:		$5,398
Books and supplies:	$720	$720
Personal expenses:	$940	$1,208
Transportation:	$1,227	$1,035

Undergraduate aid. Need-based: Average financial aid package for full-time students was $7,125; for part-time $6,306. 39% awarded as scholarships/grants, 61% as loans/jobs. **Non-need-based:** 36% awarded as scholarships/grants, 64% as loans/jobs. Scholarships based on academics, alumni affiliation, art, athletics, leadership, minority status, music/drama, state/district residency. **Additional information:** February 1 closing date for freshman scholarships.

Freshman aid. Need-based: Out of 3,978 full-time freshmen, 2,369 applied for aid; 1,587 were judged to have need; of these 1,523 received aid. Average package met 89% of need. 685 students had full need met. Average scholarship/grant was $3,235; average loan $2,696. **Non-need based:** 807 full-time freshmen with need received non-need scholarships; 1,124 without need received awards; 35 received athletic scholarships.

Merit scholarships. Scholars Program designed to encourage state's outstanding students to attend university and remain in West Virginia as well as to attract outstanding students nationally; 2,800 awarded; comprehensive scholarships total $4.5 million annually.

Policies to reduce costs. Tuition/fee waivers for senior citizens, minority students, employees and their families. Credit/placement for qualifying scores on AP, IB, CLEP examinations. Work study available nights, weekends and for part-time students.

Payment plans. Credit card, installment, deferred payment.

Application procedures. FAFSA required. Priority date 2/15; closing date 3/1. Applicants notified on rolling basis starting 3/15, must reply within 2 week(s) of notification.

Contact. Financial aid office: (800) 344-9881
Leslie Carpenter, Director of Financial Aid
Admissions and Records Office
Morgantown, WV 26506-6009

West Virginia University Institute of Technology

Montgomery, West Virginia
www.wvutech.edu
Four-year public **Federal Code: 003825**

	Living at home	On-campus
Tuition and fees (2002-2003):	$3,066	$3,066
Out-of-state:	$7,664	$7,664
Room and board:		$4,896
Books and supplies:	$800	$800
Personal expenses:	$1,100	$1,600
Transportation:	$1,100	$800

Undergraduate aid. Need-based: Need-based aid available for full-time students. **Additional information:** Room and board may be deferred for up to 60 days. First 50% due in 30 days.

Policies to reduce costs. Tuition/fee waivers for employees and their families. Credit/placement for qualifying scores on AP, CLEP examinations. Work study available nights, weekends and for part-time students.

Payment plans. Credit card, installment payment.

Application procedures. FAFSA, institutional form required. Priority date 2/1; closing date 4/1. Applicants notified on rolling basis, must reply within 3 week(s) of notification.

Contact. Financial aid office: (304) 442-3228
Nina Morton, Director of Financial Aid
405 Fayette Pike
Montgomery, WV 25136-2436

West Virginia University at Parkersburg

Parkersburg, West Virginia
www.wvup.edu
Four-year public **Federal Code: 003828**

	Living at home
Tuition and fees (2002-2003):	$1,548
Out-of-state:	$4,944
Books and supplies:	$500
Personal expenses:	$1,270
Transportation:	$1,100

Undergraduate aid. Non-need-based: Scholarships based on academics, state/district residency.

Policies to reduce costs. Credit/placement for qualifying scores on AP, CLEP examinations.

Payment plans. Credit card, installment payment.

Application procedures. FAFSA required. Priority date 3/1; no closing date. Applicants notified on rolling basis, must reply within 2 week(s) of notification.

Contact. Financial aid office: (304) 424-8210
August Kafer, Coordinator of Financial Aid
300 Campus Drive
Parkersburg, WV 26104-8647

West Virginia Wesleyan College

Buckhannon, West Virginia
www.wvwc.edu
Four-year private **Federal Code: 003830**

College costs. Required fees include laptop leasing.

	Living at home	On-campus
Tuition and fees (projected):	$19,600	$19,600
Room and board:		$5,200
Board only:	$2,500	
Books and supplies:	$600	$600
Personal expenses:	$1,500	$1,500
Transportation:	$750	$750

Undergraduate aid. Need-based: Need-based aid available for full-time students. **Non-need-based:** Scholarships based on academics, alumni affiliation, art, athletics, music/drama, religious affiliation.

Policies to reduce costs. Tuition/fee waivers for family of clergy, employees and their families. Credit/placement for qualifying scores on AP, CLEP examinations. Work study available nights and weekends.

Payment plans. Credit card, installment payment.

Application procedures. FAFSA required. Priority date 2/15; no closing date. Applicants notified on rolling basis. Early decision closing date 12/1. **Transfers:** Priority date 3/15; no deadline. Financial aid transcripts required from all institutions previously attended.

Contact. Financial aid office: (304) 473-8080
Robert Skinner, Admission and Financial Planning
59 College Avenue
Buckhannon, WV 26201-2998

Wheeling Jesuit University

Wheeling, West Virginia
www.wju.edu
Four-year private **Federal Code: 003831**

	Living at home	On-campus
Tuition and fees (2002-2003):	$18,290	$18,290
Room and board:		$5,610
Board only:	$800	
Books and supplies:	$600	$600
Personal expenses:	$800	$600
Transportation:	$500	$500

Undergraduate aid. Need-based: Average financial aid package for full-time students was $15,155; for part-time $4,662. 36% awarded as scholarships/grants, 64% as loans/jobs. **Non-need-based:** 62% awarded as scholarships/grants, 38% as loans/jobs. Scholarships based on academics, alumni affiliation, art, athletics, job skills, leadership, minority status, music/drama, religious affiliation. **Student debt:** 60% of graduating class borrowed to fund education; average debt was $12,645.

Freshman aid. Need-based: Out of 295 full-time freshmen, 291 applied for aid; 243 were judged to have need; of these 242 received aid. Average package met 95% of need. 95 students had full need met. Average scholarship/grant was $4,905; average loan $3,062. **Non-need based:** 231 full-time freshmen with need received non-need scholarships; 48 without need received awards; 45 received athletic scholarships.

Policies to reduce costs. Tuition/fee waivers for senior citizens, family members; employees and their families. Tuition at time of enrollment guaranteed for 4 years; credit/placement for qualifying scores on AP, CLEP examinations. Work study available nights, weekends and for part-time students.

Payment plans. Credit card, installment payment.

Application procedures. FAFSA, institutional form required. Priority date 3/1; no closing date. Applicants notified on rolling basis starting 3/15, must reply within 2 week(s) of notification. **Transfers:** No deadline.

Contact. Financial aid office: (304) 243-2304
Christie Tomczyk, Director of Financial Aid
316 Washington Avenue
Wheeling, WV 26003-6295

Wisconsin

Alverno College

Milwaukee, Wisconsin
www.alverno.edu
Four-year private **Federal Code: 003832**

	Living at home	On-campus
Tuition and fees (2002-2003):	$12,750	$12,750
Room and board:		$4,960
Books and supplies:	$800	$800
Personal expenses:	$1,700	$1,700
Transportation:	$700	$500

Undergraduate aid. Need-based: 59% awarded as scholarships/grants, 41% as loans/jobs. Need-based aid available for part-time students. **Non-need-based:** 2% awarded as scholarships/grants, 98% as loans/jobs. Scholarships based on academics, alumni affiliation, leadership, minority status, music/drama.

Policies to reduce costs. Tuition/fee waivers for employees and their families. Credit/placement for qualifying scores on AP, IB, CLEP examinations. Work study available nights, weekends and for part-time students.

Payment plans. Credit card, installment, deferred payment.

Application procedures. FAFSA, institutional form required. Closing date 4/15. Applicants notified on rolling basis starting 4/1, must reply within 2 week(s) of notification. **Transfers:** No deadline. Scholarships ranging from $2,150 to $3,150 available based on minimum 2.5 college GPA for students with at least 12 college credits.

Contact. Financial aid office: (414) 382-6040
Mark Levine, Director, Student Financial Planning/Resources
3400 South 43rd Street
Milwaukee, WI 53234-3922

Bellin College of Nursing

Green Bay, Wisconsin
www.bcon.edu
Four-year private **Federal Code: 006639**

	Living at home
Tuition and fees (2002-2003):	$11,525
Board only:	$1,100
Books and supplies:	$560
Personal expenses:	$665
Transportation:	$900

Undergraduate aid. Need-based: Need-based aid available for full-time and part-time students. **Non-need-based:** Scholarships based on academics. **Additional information:** Freshmen and sophomores receive aid through University of Wisconsin-Green Bay. Juniors and seniors receive aid through Bellin College of Nursing.

Merit scholarships. Merit Scholarship based on academics (high school GPA, ACT scores), no application form required, number awarded varies; ranging from $1,000-$2,500 annually, renewable conditionally. Dr. Fergus Scholarship for Merit Scholarship recipient: 1 awarded, approximately $2,500 renewable annually.

Policies to reduce costs. Credit/placement for qualifying scores on AP, CLEP examinations. Work study available nights, weekends and for part-time students.

Payment plans. Installment payment.

Application procedures. FAFSA required. Priority date 3/1; no closing date. Applicants notified on rolling basis starting 4/1, must reply within 2 week(s) of notification. **Transfers:** Students with 4-year degrees ineligible for all federal and state grant programs.

Contact. Financial aid office: (920) 433-5801
Lena Terry, Director of Financial Aid
725 South Webster Avenue
Green Bay, WI 54305

Beloit College

Beloit, Wisconsin
www.beloit.edu
Four-year private **Federal Code: 003835**

	Living at home	On-campus
Tuition and fees (2002-2003):	$23,236	$23,236
Room and board:		$5,268
Books and supplies:	$400	$400
Personal expenses:		$900

Undergraduate aid. Need-based: Average financial aid package for full-time students was $17,839. 79% awarded as scholarships/grants, 21% as loans/jobs. **Non-need-based:** 49% awarded as scholarships/grants, 51% as loans/jobs. Scholarships based on academics, leadership, minority status, music/drama. **Student debt:** 56% of graduating class borrowed to fund education; average debt was $14,942.

Freshman aid. Need-based: Out of 304 full-time freshmen, 274 applied for aid; 215 were judged to have need; of these 215 received aid. Average package met 100% of need. 215 students had full need met. Average scholarship/grant was $12,956; average loan $1,775. **Non-need based:** 153 full-time freshmen with need received non-need scholarships; 25 without need received awards.

Merit scholarships. Presidential Scholarship based on application and mandatory interviews; $40,000 over 4 years.

Policies to reduce costs. Tuition/fee waivers for adults, family members, employees and their families. Credit/placement for qualifying scores on AP, CLEP examinations.

Payment plans. Credit card, installment payment.

Application procedures. FAFSA, institutional form required. Priority date 3/1; no closing date. Applicants notified on rolling basis starting 2/1, must reply by 5/1 or within 2 week(s) of notification. **Transfers:** No deadline.

Contact. Financial aid office: (608) 363-2663
Jane Hessian, Director of Financial Aid
700 College Street
Beloit, WI 53511-5595

Blackhawk Technical College

Janesville, Wisconsin
www.blackhawk.edu
Two-year public **Federal Code: 005390**

College costs. Materials fees vary by program; minimum $3.85 per course.

	Living at home
Tuition and fees (2002-2003):	$2,111
Out-of-state:	$15,512
Per-credit charge:	$67
Per-credit out-of-state:	$514
Board only:	$2,120
Books and supplies:	$900
Personal expenses:	$1,100
Transportation:	$880

Undergraduate aid. Need-based: Average financial aid package for full-time students was $5,735. 55% awarded as scholarships/grants, 45% as loans/jobs. Need-based aid available for part-time students. **Student debt:** 60% of graduating class borrowed to fund education; average debt was $4,834.

Policies to reduce costs. Tuition/fee waivers for adults, children of alumni, senior citizens, minority students, family members, unemployed or children of unemployed, family of clergy, employees and their families.

Payment plans. Credit card, deferred payment.

Application procedures. Priority date 4/1; closing date 6/15. Applicants notified on rolling basis starting 4/15, must reply within 2 week(s) of notification.

Contact. Financial aid office: (608) 757-7664
Burdette Richter, Financial Aid Officer
Box 5009
Janesville, WI 53547

Bryant & Stratton College

Milwaukee, Wisconsin
www.bryantstratton.edu
Two-year proprietary **Federal Code: 005009**

	Living at home
Tuition and fees:	$9,900
Per-credit charge:	$330
Books and supplies:	$750

Policies to reduce costs. Tuition/fee waivers for employees and their families. Credit/placement for qualifying scores on AP, CLEP examinations. Work study available nights.

Payment plans. Credit card, installment payment.

Application procedures. FAFSA required. No deadline. Applicants notified on rolling basis, must reply within 2 week(s) of notification.

Contact. Financial aid office: (414) 276-5200
Greg Bradner, Business Director
310 W. Wisconsin Avenue, Suite 500
Milwaukee, WI 53203

Cardinal Stritch University

Milwaukee, Wisconsin
www.stritch.edu
Four-year private **Federal Code: 003837**

	Living at home	On-campus
Tuition and fees (2002-2003):	$13,580	$13,580
Room and board:		$4,990
Books and supplies:	$500	$500
Personal expenses:	$1,200	$1,200
Transportation:	$800	$350

Undergraduate aid. Need-based: Need-based aid available for full-time and part-time students. **Non-need-based:** Scholarships based on academics, art, athletics, music/drama.

Policies to reduce costs. Tuition/fee waivers for family members, employees and their families. Credit/placement for qualifying scores on AP, IB, CLEP examinations.

Payment plans. Credit card, installment payment.

Application procedures. FAFSA, institutional form required. No deadline. Applicants notified on rolling basis starting 3/1, must reply within 3 week(s) of notification.

Contact. Financial aid office: (414) 410-4048
John Mueller, Director of Financial Aid
6801 North Yates Road
Milwaukee, WI 53217-7516

Carroll College

Waukesha, Wisconsin
www.cc.edu
Four-year private **Federal Code: 003838**

	Living at home	On-campus
Tuition and fees (2002-2003):	$16,750	$16,750
Room and board:		$5,170
Board only:	$2,039	
Books and supplies:	$760	$760
Personal expenses:	$2,222	$1,280
Transportation:	$1,675	$928

Undergraduate aid. Need-based: Average financial aid package for full-time students was $12,532. 72% awarded as scholarships/grants, 28% as loans/jobs. Need-based aid available for part-time students. **Non-need-based:** 43% awarded as scholarships/grants, 57% as loans/jobs. Scholarships based on academics, alumni affiliation, art, leadership, minority status, music/drama, religious affiliation, state/district residency. **Student debt:** 78% of graduating class borrowed to fund education; average debt was $16,200.

Freshman aid. Need-based: Out of 550 full-time freshmen, 545 applied for aid; 409 were judged to have need; of these 409 received aid. Average package met 90% of need. 327 students had full need met. Average scholarship/grant was $11,222; average loan $2,743. **Non-need based:** 245 full-time freshmen with need received non-need scholarships; 132 without need received awards.

Merit scholarships. Trustee Scholarship; $30,000 (renewable; $7,500 per year). Voorhees Scholarship; $28,000 (renewable; $7,000 per year). Charles Caroll Scholarship; $26,000 (renewable; $6,500 per year). Presidential Scholarship; $24,000 (renewable; $6,000 per year). Pioneer Scholarship; $22,000 (renewable; $5,500 per year). Hilger Scholarship; $20,000 (renewable; $5,000 per year).

Policies to reduce costs. Tuition/fee waivers for children of alumni, family members, employees and their families. Credit/placement for qualifying scores on AP, IB, CLEP examinations. Work study available nights and weekends.

Payment plans. Credit card, installment payment.

Application procedures. FAFSA required. Priority date 4/15; no closing date. Applicants notified on rolling basis starting 2/15, must reply by 5/1 or within 2 week(s) of notification. **Transfers:** Priority date 4/15.

Contact. Financial aid office: (262) 524-7296
Dawn Thomas, Director of Student Financial Services
100 North East Avenue
Waukesha, WI 53186-9988

Carthage College

Kenosha, Wisconsin
www.carthage.edu
Four-year private **Federal Code: 003839**

	Living at home	On-campus
Tuition and fees:	$20,150	$20,150
Room and board:		$6,070
Board only:	$2,080	
Books and supplies:	$750	$750
Personal expenses:	$1,500	$1,500
Transportation:	$1,000	$1,000

Undergraduate aid. Need-based: Average financial aid package for full-time students was $16,277. 53% awarded as scholarships/grants, 47% as loans/jobs. Need-based aid available for part-time students. **Non-need-based:** 74% awarded as scholarships/grants, 26% as loans/jobs. Scholarships based on academics, alumni affiliation, art, leadership, minority status, music/drama, religious affiliation.

Freshman aid. Need-based: Out of 612 full-time freshmen, 593 applied for aid; 490 were judged to have need; of these 490 received aid. Average package met 91% of need. Average scholarship/grant was $7,679; average loan $4,708. **Non-need based:** 400 full-time freshmen with need received non-need scholarships; 12 without need received awards.

Policies to reduce costs. Tuition/fee waivers for children of alumni, family members, family of clergy, employees and their families. Prepayment discount; credit/placement for qualifying scores on AP, IB, CLEP examinations.

Payment plans. Installment payment.

Application procedures. FAFSA required. Priority date 2/15; no closing date. Applicants notified on rolling basis starting 3/1. **Transfers:** Priority date 2/15.

Contact. Financial aid office: (262) 551-6001
Bill Henderson, Director of Financial aid
2001 Alford Park Drive
Kenosha, WI 53140-1994

Chippewa Valley Technical College

Eau Claire, Wisconsin
www.cvtc.edu
Two-year public **Federal Code: 005304**

College costs. Materials fees vary by program; minimum $3.50 per course.

	Living at home
Tuition and fees (2002-2003):	$2,116
Out-of-state:	$15,517
Per-credit charge:	$67
Per-credit out-of-state:	$514
Board only:	$2,254
Books and supplies:	$853
Personal expenses:	$1,370
Transportation:	$821

Undergraduate aid. Need-based: Need-based aid available for full-time and part-time students.

Merit scholarships. TOP Grant: $250 per semester, up to $1,000 total. Must be enrolled full time in Wisconsin technical college within three years of graduating from a Wisconsin high school. May not have received more than 18 credits at Wisconsin technical school since high school graduation. Must maintain minimum semester 2.0 GPA. Must enroll in occupational associate degree or one-two year technical diploma program.

Policies to reduce costs. Credit/placement for qualifying scores on AP, CLEP examinations. Work study available nights, weekends and for part-time students.

Payment plans. Credit card, installment payment.

Application procedures. FAFSA required. Priority date 3/15; no closing date. Applicants notified on rolling basis starting 6/1, must reply within 2 week(s) of notification. **Transfers:** No deadline.

Contact. **Financial aid office:** (715) 833-6250
Mary Gorud, Financial Aid Officer
620 West Clairemont Avenue
Eau Claire, WI 54701-6162

College of Menominee Nation

Keshena, Wisconsin
www.menominee.edu
Two-year private **Federal Code: 031251**

	Living at home
Tuition and fees:	$4,075
Per-credit charge:	$135

Application procedures. FAFSA required. Applicants notified on rolling basis.

Contact. Regina Prey, Financial Aid Director
S 172 Highway 47/55
Keshena, WI 54135

Columbia College of Nursing

Milwaukee, Wisconsin
www.ccon.edu
Four-year private **Federal Code: 003838**

	Living at home	On-campus
Tuition and fees (2002-2003):	$15,165	$15,165
Room and board:		$4,340
Board only:	$1,970	
Books and supplies:	$734	$734
Personal expenses:	$2,144	$1,234
Transportation:	$1,618	$897

Undergraduate aid. **Need-based:** Need-based aid available for full-time and part-time students. **Non-need-based:** Scholarships based on academics, alumni affiliation, art, leadership, minority status, music/drama, religious affiliation, state/district residency. **Additional information:** Students must apply to and meet financial aid requirements of Carroll College.

Policies to reduce costs. Tuition/fee waivers for employees and their families. Credit/placement for qualifying scores on AP, IB, CLEP examinations. Work study available nights and weekends.

Payment plans. Credit card, installment payment.

Application procedures. FAFSA required. No deadline. Applicants notified on rolling basis starting 2/15, must reply by 5/1 or within 2 week(s) of notification. **Transfers:** No deadline.

Contact. **Financial aid office:** (262) 524-7296
Tim Opgenorth, Director of Financial Services, Carroll College
Mount Mary College Enrollment Office; 2900 N. Menominee River Parkway
Milwaukee, WI 53222-4597

Concordia University Wisconsin

Mequon, Wisconsin
www.cuw.edu
Four-year private **Federal Code: 003842**

	Living at home	On-campus
Tuition and fees (projected):	$15,575	$15,575
Room and board:		$5,790
Books and supplies:	$750	$750
Personal expenses:	$2,785	$1,710
Transportation:	$600	$140

Undergraduate aid. **Need-based:** Average financial aid package for full-time students was $11,900. 85% awarded as scholarships/grants, 15% as loans/jobs. Need-based aid available for part-time students. **Non-need-based:** 59% awarded as scholarships/grants, 41% as loans/jobs. Scholarships based on academics, state/district residency.

Freshman aid. **Need-based:** Out of 358 full-time freshmen, 326 applied for aid; 282 were judged to have need; of these 282 received aid. Average package met 70% of need. 83 students had full need met. Average scholarship/grant was $11,000; average loan $2,200. **Non-need based:** 133 full-time freshmen with need received non-need scholarships; 32 without need received awards.

Policies to reduce costs. Tuition/fee waivers for children of alumni, family of clergy, employees and their families. Credit/placement for qualifying scores on AP, IB, CLEP examinations. Work study available nights and weekends.

Payment plans. Credit card, installment payment.

Application procedures. FAFSA, institutional form required. Priority date 5/1; no closing date. Applicants notified on rolling basis starting 1/15, must reply within 3 week(s) of notification.

Contact. Carol Masse, Director of Financial Aid
12800 North Lake Shore Drive
Mequon, WI 53097

Edgewood College

Madison, Wisconsin
www.edgewood.edu
Four-year private **Federal Code: 003848**

	Living at home	On-campus
Tuition and fees (2002-2003):	$14,200	$14,200
Room and board:		$5,364
Board only:	$1,100	
Books and supplies:	$750	$750
Personal expenses:	$1,720	$1,720
Transportation:	$500	$330

Undergraduate aid. **Need-based:** Average financial aid package for full-time students was $11,313; for part-time $7,101. 48% awarded as scholarships/grants, 52% as loans/jobs. **Non-need-based:** 36% awarded as scholarships/grants, 64% as loans/jobs. Scholarships based on academics, alumni affiliation, art, leadership, minority status, music/drama, religious affiliation. **Additional information:** Auditions required for music scholarships, portfolios required for fine arts scholarships, essays required for a number of institutional scholarships, including AHANA Student Advancement Award, Alumni Association Scholarship, O'Connor Memorial Scholarship.

Freshman aid. **Need-based:** Out of 270 full-time freshmen, 234 applied for aid; 197 were judged to have need; of these 197 received aid. Average package met 80% of need. 36 students had full need met. Average scholarship/grant was $8,425; average loan $2,617. **Non-need based:** 25 full-time freshmen with need received non-need scholarships; 68 without need received awards.

Policies to reduce costs. Tuition/fee waivers for employees and their families. Credit/placement for qualifying scores on AP, IB, CLEP examinations. Work study available nights, weekends and for part-time students.

Payment plans. Installment payment.

Application procedures. FAFSA, institutional form required. Priority date 3/15; no closing date. Applicants notified on rolling basis starting 4/1, must reply within 2 week(s) of notification. **Transfers:** No deadline.

Contact. Scott Flanagan, Dean of Admissions and Financial Aid
1000 Edgewood College Drive
Madison, WI 53711

Fox Valley Technical College

Appleton, Wisconsin
www.fvtc.edu
Two-year public **Federal Code: 009744**

College costs. Materials fees vary by program; minimum $3.50 per course.

	Living at home
Tuition and fees (2002-2003):	$2,202
Out-of-state:	$15,603
Per-credit charge:	$67
Per-credit out-of-state:	$514
Books and supplies:	$600
Transportation:	$300

Policies to reduce costs. Tuition/fee waivers for senior citizens.

Payment plans. Credit card, deferred payment.

Application procedures. FAFSA required. Priority date 3/1; no closing date. Applicants notified on rolling basis.

Contact. **Financial aid office:** (920) 735-5719
Virginia Muenster, Financial Aid Officer
1825 North Bluemound Drive
Appleton, WI 54912-2277

Herzing College

Madison, Wisconsin
www.herzing.edu
Two-year proprietary **Federal Code: 009621**

College costs (2002-2003). Tuition for three semesters. For associate degrees: $11,140 for computer, electronics and telecommunications program, $11,055 for CAD drafting program, $12,085 for computer information systems program, $12,165 for computer network technology program. For bachelor's degrees: $10,560 for technology management program, $12,085 for computer information systems program.

Application procedures. FAFSA required. No deadline. Applicants notified on rolling basis.

Contact. 5218 East Terrace Drive
Madison, WI 53718

ITT Technical Institute: Green Bay

Green Bay, Wisconsin
www.itt-tech.edu
Two-year proprietary

College costs. Total program varies depending on course of study. Per-credit-hour charge: $347.

Contact. 470 Security Boulevard
Green Bay, WI 54313

ITT Technical Institute: Greenfield

Greenfield, Wisconsin
www.itt-tech.edu
Three-year proprietary **Federal Code: 030875**

College costs. Total program varies depending on course of study. Per-credit-hour charge: $347.

Policies to reduce costs. Tuition/fee waivers for employees and their families.

Payment plans. Credit card, installment payment.

Application procedures. FAFSA, institutional form required. No deadline. Applicants notified on rolling basis.

Contact. Diana Vandagrifft, Director of Finance
6300 W. Layton Avenue
Greenfield, WI 53220-4612

Lac Courte Oreilles Ojibwa Community College

Hayward, Wisconsin
www.lco-college.edu
Two-year public **Federal Code: 017199**

	Living at home
Tuition and fees:	$3,540
Out-of-state:	$3,540
Per-credit charge:	$110
Per-credit out-of-state:	$110
Transportation:	$500

Undergraduate aid. Need-based: Need-based aid available for full-time students.

Policies to reduce costs. Tuition/fee waivers for senior citizens.

Payment plans. Installment payment.

Application procedures. FAFSA required. No deadline. Applicants notified on rolling basis.

Contact. Agnes Fleming, Financial Aid Officer
13466 West Trepania Road
Hayward, WI 54843

Lakeland College

Sheboygan, Wisconsin
www.lakeland.edu
Four-year private **Federal Code: 003854**

	Living at home	On-campus
Tuition and fees:	$14,325	$14,325
Room and board:		$5,440
Board only:	$750	
Books and supplies:	$500	$500
Personal expenses:	$750	$750
Transportation:	$700	$700

Undergraduate aid. Need-based: Need-based aid available for full-time and part-time students. **Non-need-based:** Scholarships based on academics.

Policies to reduce costs. Tuition/fee waivers for senior citizens, employees and their families. Tuition at time of enrollment guaranteed for 4 years; prepayment discount; credit/placement for qualifying scores on AP, IB, CLEP examinations. Work study available nights, weekends and for part-time students.

Payment plans. Credit card, installment payment.

Application procedures. FAFSA, institutional form required. Priority date 5/1; closing date 7/1. Applicants notified on rolling basis starting 2/1, must reply within 2 week(s) of notification. **Transfers:** Priority date 5/1; closing date 7/1.

Contact. **Financial aid office:** (920) 565-1297
Donald Seymour, Director of Financial Aid
Box 359
Sheboygan, WI 53082

Lakeshore Technical College

Cleveland, Wisconsin
www.gotoltc.edu
Two-year public **Federal Code: 009194**

College costs. Materials fees vary by program; minimum $3.50 per course.

	Living at home
Tuition and fees (2002-2003):	$2,270
Out-of-state:	$15,671
Per-credit charge:	$67
Per-credit out-of-state:	$514
Books and supplies:	$1,000
Personal expenses:	$1,625
Transportation:	$1,100

Undergraduate aid. All financial aid based on need. 56% awarded as scholarships/grants, 44% as loans/jobs. Need-based aid available for part-time students.

Policies to reduce costs. Tuition/fee waivers for senior citizens. Credit/placement for qualifying scores on AP, CLEP examinations. Work study available nights and for part-time students.

Payment plans. Credit card, installment, deferred payment.

Application procedures. FAFSA, institutional form required. Priority date 6/1; no closing date. Applicants notified on rolling basis starting 6/1, must reply within 3 week(s) of notification.

Contact. **Financial aid office:** (920) 693-1118
Mary Moede, Financial Aid Manager
1290 North Avenue
Cleveland, WI 53015-9761

Lawrence University

Appleton, Wisconsin
www.lawrence.edu
Four-year private **Federal Code: 003856**

	Living at home	On-campus
Tuition and fees (2002-2003):	$23,667	$23,667
Room and board:		$5,457
Books and supplies:	$555	$555
Personal expenses:	$951	$951
Transportation:		$300

Undergraduate aid. Need-based: Average financial aid package for full-time students was $20,421. 73% awarded as scholarships/grants, 27% as loans/jobs. Need-based aid available for part-time students. **Non-need-based:** 83% awarded as scholarships/grants, 17% as loans/jobs. Scholarships based on academics, minority status, music/drama, state/district residency. **Student debt:** 69% of graduating class borrowed to fund education; average debt was $16,927. **Additional information:** The first $1,000 (aggregate) of independently-sponsored scholarships received by a needy student will reduce student's loan or work-study commitment. Half of scholarships in excess of $1,000 will offset loan or work-study.

Freshman aid. Need-based: Out of 348 full-time freshmen, 252 applied for aid; 217 were judged to have need; of these 217 received aid. Average package met 100% of need. 217 students had full need met. Average scholarship/grant was $16,188; average loan $3,502. **Non-need based:** 75 full-time freshmen with need received non-need scholarships; 102 without need received awards.

Merit scholarships. Trustee Scholarships $10,000 per year; Presidential Scholarships $7,500 per year; Alumni Scholarships $5,000 per year; Conservatory Scholarships $2,000-$10,000 per year. Students must participate in one of two weekend scholarship competitions.

Policies to reduce costs. Tuition/fee waivers for employees and their families. Prepayment discount; credit/placement for qualifying scores on AP, IB examinations. Work study available nights, weekends and for part-time students.

Payment plans. Installment payment.

Application procedures. FAFSA, institutional form required. Priority date 3/15; no closing date. Applicants notified on rolling basis starting 3/15, must reply by 5/1 or within 2 week(s) of notification. Early decision closing date 11/15. **Transfers:** Priority date 4/15; no deadline.

Contact. Financial aid office: (920) 832-6583
Steven Syverson, Dean of Admissions and Financial Aid
Box 599
Appleton, WI 54912-0599

Maranatha Baptist Bible College

Watertown, Wisconsin
www.mbbc.edu
Four-year private **Federal Code: 016394**

	Living at home	On-campus
Tuition and fees (2002-2003):	$7,440	$7,440
Room and board:		$4,200
Board only:	$1,060	
Books and supplies:	$570	$570
Personal expenses:	$1,700	$1,700
Transportation:	$1,090	$1,090

Undergraduate aid. Need-based: Need-based aid available for full-time and part-time students. **Non-need-based:** Scholarships based on academics.

Policies to reduce costs. Tuition/fee waivers for family of clergy, employees and their families. Credit/placement for qualifying scores on AP, CLEP examinations. Work study available for part-time students.

Payment plans. Installment payment.

Application procedures. FAFSA required. Priority date 3/1; no closing date. Applicants notified on rolling basis starting 2/1, must reply within 2 week(s) of notification. **Transfers:** Financial aid transcript or equivalent required.

Contact. Financial aid office: (920) 206-2318
Randy Hibbs, Financial Aid Administrator
745 West Main Street
Watertown, WI 53094

Marian College of Fond du Lac

Fond du Lac, Wisconsin
www.mariancollege.edu
Four-year private **Federal Code: 003861**

	Living at home	On-campus
Tuition and fees (2002-2003):	$14,195	$14,195
Room and board:		$4,800
Books and supplies:	$700	$700
Personal expenses:	$1,230	$1,230
Transportation:	$1,000	$500

Undergraduate aid. Need-based: Average financial aid package for full-time students was $15,490; for part-time $9,727. 50% awarded as scholarships/grants, 50% as loans/jobs. **Non-need-based:** 65% awarded as scholarships/grants, 35% as loans/jobs. Scholarships based on academics, state/district residency. **Student debt:** 85% of graduating class borrowed to fund education; average debt was $19,500.

Freshman aid. Need-based: Out of 244 full-time freshmen, 235 applied for aid; 205 were judged to have need; of these 205 received aid. Average package met 93% of need. 92 students had full need met. Average scholarship/grant was $5,361; average loan $3,093. **Non-need based:** 194 full-time freshmen with need received non-need scholarships; 26 without need received awards.

Merit scholarships. Academic Achievement Award, 7 awards, $7,500 based on 3.5 GPA or higher, 25 ACT, top 15% of class; Presidential Scholarship $5,000 based on 3.1 GPA or higher, top 20% of class; Naber Leadership Scholarship $3,000, based on 2.5 GPA or higher, top 50% of class.

Policies to reduce costs. Tuition/fee waivers for senior citizens, family members, employees and their families. Credit/placement for qualifying scores on AP, IB, CLEP examinations. Work study available nights, weekends and for part-time students.

Payment plans. Credit card, installment payment.

Application procedures. FAFSA, institutional form required. Priority date 3/1; no closing date. Applicants notified on rolling basis starting 3/1, must reply within 4 week(s) of notification. **Transfers:** No deadline.

Contact. Financial aid office: (920) 923-7614
Debra McKinney, Director of Financial Aid
45 South National Avenue
Fond du Lac, WI 54935-4699

Marquette University

Milwaukee, Wisconsin
www.marquette.edu
Four-year private **Federal Code: 003863**

	Living at home	On-campus
Tuition and fees:	$20,724	$20,724
Room and board:		$6,842
Board only:	$1,260	
Books and supplies:	$900	$900
Personal expenses:	$1,350	$1,350
Transportation:	$1,280	$300

Undergraduate aid. Need-based: Average financial aid package for full-time students was $16,400; for part-time $6,943. 63% awarded as scholarships/grants, 37% as loans/jobs. **Non-need-based:** 66% awarded as scholarships/grants, 34% as loans/jobs. Scholarships based on academics, art, athletics, leadership, minority status, music/drama, religious affiliation, state/district residency.

Freshman aid. Need-based: Out of 1,856 full-time freshmen, 1,695 applied for aid; 1,210 were judged to have need; of these 1,208 received aid. Average package met 91% of need. 641 students had full need met. Average scholarship/grant was $10,664; average loan $3,521. **Non-need based:** 443 full-time freshmen with need received non-need scholarships; 370 without need received awards; 27 received athletic scholarships.

Merit scholarships. Ignatius Scholarships; $4,000-$10,000. College Scholarships; $5,000. Raynor Scholarships; 5 awarded; full tuition. National Merit Scholarships; $2,000.

Policies to reduce costs. Tuition/fee waivers for senior citizens, employees and their families. Credit/placement for qualifying scores on AP, IB, CLEP examinations. Work study available nights, weekends and for part-time students.

Payment plans. Installment payment.

Application procedures. FAFSA required. CSS profile required of applicants for Marquette University Ignacius Scholarship. Priority date 3/1; closing date 3/1. Applicants notified by 4/1, must reply by 5/1 or within 3 week(s) of notification. **Transfers:** Transfer scholarships available.

Contact. **Financial aid office:** (414) 288-0200
Daniel Goyette, Director of Student Financial Aid
P.O. Box 1881
Milwaukee, WI 53201-1881

Mid-State Technical College

Wisconsin Rapids, Wisconsin
www.mstc.edu
Two-year public **Federal Code: 005380**

College costs. Materials fees vary by program; minimum $3.50 per course.

	Living at home
Tuition and fees (2002-2003):	$2,106
Out-of-state:	$15,507
Per-credit charge:	$67
Per-credit out-of-state:	$514
Board only:	$2,102
Books and supplies:	$790
Personal expenses:	$1,277
Transportation:	$765

Undergraduate aid. **Need-based:** Average financial aid package for full-time students was $6,198; for part-time $5,347. 63% awarded as scholarships/grants, 37% as loans/jobs. **Non-need-based:** 37% awarded as scholarships/grants, 63% as loans/jobs. Scholarships based on academics, leadership.

Freshman aid. **Need-based:** Out of 890 full-time freshmen, 623 applied for aid; 511 were judged to have need; of these 511 received aid. Average scholarship/grant was $3,827. **Non-need based:** 186 full-time freshmen with need received non-need scholarships; 447 without need received awards.

Policies to reduce costs. Tuition/fee waivers for senior citizens. Work study available nights, weekends and for part-time students.

Payment plans. Credit card, installment, deferred payment.

Application procedures. FAFSA required. No deadline. Applicants notified on rolling basis starting 5/30, must reply within 2 week(s) of notification. **Transfers:** No deadline.

Contact. **Financial aid office:** (715) 422-5501
Mary Green, Financial Aid Officer
500 32nd Street North
Wisconsin Rapids, WI 54494

Milwaukee Area Technical College

Milwaukee, Wisconsin
www.milwaukee.tec.wi.us
Two-year public **Federal Code: 003866**

College costs. Materials fees vary by program. Minimum materials fee $3.85 per course. College parallel (transfer) program: per-credit-hour $99 in-state, $418.63 out-of-state.

	Living at home
Tuition and fees (2002-2003):	$2,185
Out-of-state:	$15,586
Per-credit charge:	$67
Per-credit out-of-state:	$514
Board only:	$2,124
Books and supplies:	$790
Personal expenses:	$1,290
Transportation:	$775

Undergraduate aid. All financial aid based on need. Need-based aid available for full-time and part-time students.

Policies to reduce costs. Tuition/fee waivers for senior citizens.

Payment plans. Credit card, installment, deferred payment.

Application procedures. FAFSA required. Priority date 3/15; no closing date. Applicants notified on rolling basis starting 4/15.

Contact. **Financial aid office:** (414) 297-6279
Al Pinckney, Director of Financial Aid
700 West State Street
Milwaukee, WI 53233

Milwaukee Institute of Art & Design

Milwaukee, Wisconsin
www.miad.edu
Four-year private **Federal Code: 014203**

	Living at home	On-campus
Tuition and fees (2002-2003):	$20,030	$20,030
Room and board:		$6,400
Books and supplies:	$1,650	$1,650
Personal expenses:	$1,624	$1,624
Transportation:	$1,624	$1,624

Undergraduate aid. **Need-based:** Average financial aid package for full-time students was $14,115; for part-time $12,130. 46% awarded as scholarships/grants, 54% as loans/jobs. **Non-need-based:** 26% awarded as scholarships/grants, 74% as loans/jobs. Scholarships based on academics, art, leadership. **Student debt:** 100% of graduating class borrowed to fund education; average debt was $33,505.

Freshman aid. **Need-based:** Out of 128 full-time freshmen, 123 applied for aid; 112 were judged to have need; of these 112 received aid. Average package met 76% of need. 34 students had full need met. Average scholarship/grant was $8,209; average loan $6,173. **Non-need based:** 6 full-time freshmen with need received non-need scholarships; 16 without need received awards.

Merit scholarships. One full admission scholarship; several half admission scholarships; Miller Brewing Company Scholarship: 2 half tuition; MIAD Scholarship: several $2,500 to $5,000; Academic Achievement Scholarship: several. All awards based on portfolio and grade point average.

Policies to reduce costs. Tuition/fee waivers for employees and their families. Credit/placement for qualifying scores on AP, CLEP examinations. Work study available nights, weekends and for part-time students.

Payment plans. Installment, deferred payment.

Application procedures. FAFSA required. Priority date 3/1; no closing date. Applicants notified on rolling basis starting 4/1, must reply by 5/1 or within 4 week(s) of notification.

Contact. **Financial aid office:** (414) 291-3272
Lloyd Mueller, Director of Financial Aid
273 East Erie Street
Milwaukee, WI 53202

Milwaukee School of Engineering

Milwaukee, Wisconsin
www.msoe.edu
Four-year private **Federal Code: 003868**

College costs. $1,140 technology package required for all first-year students.

	Living at home	On-campus
Tuition and fees:	$23,034	$23,034
Room and board:		$5,445
Board only:	$1,950	
Books and supplies:	$1,320	$1,320
Personal expenses:	$1,680	$1,680
Transportation:	$1,285	$1,285

Undergraduate aid. **Need-based:** Average financial aid package for full-time students was $15,348; for part-time $4,606. 44% awarded as scholarships/grants, 56% as loans/jobs. **Non-need-based:** 62% awarded as scholarships/grants, 38% as loans/jobs. Scholarships based on academics, state/district residency. **Student debt:** 75% of graduating class borrowed to fund education; average debt was $3,000. **Additional information:** More than 90% of full time students receive financial assistance. More than 60% receive academic scholarships.

Freshman aid. **Need-based:** Out of 438 full-time freshmen, 434 applied for aid; 365 were judged to have need; of these 365 received aid. Average package met 77% of need. 41 students had full need met. Average scholarship/grant was $4,032; average loan $4,147. **Non-need based:** 363 full-time freshmen with need received non-need scholarships; 68 without need received awards.

Merit scholarships. President Scholarship: full tuition, high academic standing, 5 awards.

Policies to reduce costs. Tuition/fee waivers for employees and their families. Credit/placement for qualifying scores on AP, IB, CLEP examinations. Work study available nights and weekends.

Payment plans. Credit card, installment payment.

Application procedures. FAFSA required. Priority date 3/15; no closing date. Applicants notified on rolling basis starting 3/1, must reply within 2 week(s) of notification.

Contact. **Financial aid office:** (414) 277-7223
Louis LaSota, Director of Financial Aid
1025 North Broadway
Milwaukee, WI 53202-3109

Moraine Park Technical College

Fond du Lac, Wisconsin
www.morainepark.edu
Two-year public **Federal Code: 005303**

College costs. Materials fees vary by program; minimum $3.50 per course.

	Living at home
Tuition and fees (2002-2003):	$2,106
Out-of-state:	$15,507
Per-credit charge:	$67
Per-credit out-of-state:	$514
Books and supplies:	$900

Undergraduate aid. **Need-based:** Need-based aid available for full-time and part-time students. **Non-need-based:** Scholarships based on academics, job skills, leadership, minority status, state/district residency.

Policies to reduce costs. Credit/placement for qualifying scores on CLEP examinations. Work study available nights, weekends and for part-time students.

Payment plans. Credit card, installment, deferred payment.

Application procedures. FAFSA, institutional form required. Priority date 5/1; no closing date. Applicants notified on rolling basis starting 6/15, must reply within 2 week(s) of notification.

Contact. **Financial aid office:** (920) 929-2123
Karen Zuehlke, Financial Aid Specialist
235 North National Avenue
Fond du Lac, WI 54935

Mount Mary College

Milwaukee, Wisconsin
www.mtmary.edu
Four-year private **Federal Code: 003869**

	Living at home	On-campus
Tuition and fees (2002-2003):	$14,165	$14,165
Room and board:		$4,974
Board only:	$1,680	
Books and supplies:	$800	$800
Personal expenses:	$1,280	$1,280
Transportation:	$900	$900

Undergraduate aid. **Need-based:** Average financial aid package for full-time students was $11,200; for part-time $6,964. 46% awarded as scholarships/grants, 54% as loans/jobs. **Non-need-based:** 31% awarded as scholarships/grants, 69% as loans/jobs. Scholarships based on academics, alumni affiliation, art, leadership, music/drama. **Student debt:** 68% of graduating class borrowed to fund education; average debt was $21,799.

Freshman aid. **Need-based:** Out of 107 full-time freshmen, 98 applied for aid; 90 were judged to have need; of these 90 received aid. Average package met 74% of need. 11 students had full need met. Average scholarship/grant was $8,482; average loan $3,047. **Non-need based:** 4 full-time freshmen with need received non-need scholarships; 28 without need received awards.

Policies to reduce costs. Tuition/fee waivers for senior citizens, family members, family of clergy, employees and their families. Credit/placement for qualifying scores on AP, IB, CLEP examinations. Work study available nights, weekends and for part-time students.

Payment plans. Credit card, installment payment.

Application procedures. FAFSA required. Priority date 3/1; no closing date. Applicants notified on rolling basis starting 1/1, must reply within 2 week(s) of notification.

Contact. **Financial aid office:** (414) 256-1258
Debra Duff, Director of Financial Aid
2900 North Menomonee River Parkway
Milwaukee, WI 53222

Nicolet Area Technical College

Rhinelander, Wisconsin
www.nicoletcollege.edu
Two-year public **Federal Code: 008919**

College costs. Materials fees vary by program; minimum $3.50 per course. College parallel (transfer) program: per-credit-hour $94 in-state, $304 out-of-state.

	Living at home
Tuition and fees (2002-2003):	$2,087
Out-of-state:	$15,488
Per-credit charge:	$67
Per-credit out-of-state:	$514
Board only:	$2,056
Books and supplies:	$760
Personal expenses:	$1,249
Transportation:	$748

Policies to reduce costs. Credit/placement for qualifying scores on AP, CLEP examinations.

Payment plans. Credit card, deferred payment.

Application procedures. FAFSA, institutional form required. Priority date 4/15; no closing date. Applicants notified on rolling basis starting 6/1, must reply within 2 week(s) of notification.

Contact. **Financial aid office:** (715) 365-4423
William Peshel, Director of Financial Aid
Box 518
Rhinelander, WI 54501

Northland College

Ashland, Wisconsin
www.northland.edu
Four-year private **Federal Code: 003875**

	Living at home	On-campus
Tuition and fees:	$17,650	$17,650
Room and board:		$5,100
Board only:	$3,020	
Books and supplies:	$600	$600
Personal expenses:	$1,200	$1,200
Transportation:	$500	$500

Undergraduate aid. **Need-based:** Average financial aid package for full-time students was $15,203. 65% awarded as scholarships/grants, 35% as loans/jobs. Need-based aid available for part-time students. **Non-need-based:** 18% awarded as scholarships/grants, 82% as loans/jobs. Scholarships based on academics, alumni affiliation, leadership, minority status, music/drama. **Student debt:** 84% of graduating class borrowed to fund education; average debt was $15,676.

Freshman aid. **Need-based:** Average package met 82% of need. Average scholarship/grant was $12,038; average loan $2,659.

Policies to reduce costs. Tuition/fee waivers for senior citizens, employees and their families. Credit/placement for qualifying scores on AP, IB, CLEP examinations. Work study available nights and weekends.

Payment plans. Credit card, installment payment.

Application procedures. FAFSA, institutional form required. Priority date 4/15; no closing date. Applicants notified on rolling basis starting 3/1, must reply by 5/1 or within 4 week(s) of notification.

Contact. Tracey Roseth, Director of Financial Aid
1411 Ellis Avenue
Ashland, WI 54806

Ripon College

Ripon, Wisconsin
www.ripon.edu
Four-year private **Federal Code: 003884**

	Living at home	On-campus
Tuition and fees:	$19,940	$19,940
Room and board:		$5,055
Board only:	$2,500	
Books and supplies:	$500	$500
Personal expenses:	$650	$650
Transportation:	$700	$300

Undergraduate aid. Need-based: Average financial aid package for full-time students was $18,573. 75% awarded as scholarships/grants, 25% as loans/jobs. Need-based aid available for part-time students. **Non-need-based:** 80% awarded as scholarships/grants, 20% as loans/jobs. Scholarships based on academics, alumni affiliation, art, leadership, minority status, music/drama, religious affiliation, state/district residency. **Student debt:** 75% of graduating class borrowed to fund education; average debt was $15,565. **Additional information:** Our institution strives to meet 100% of students' demonstrated financial need for all four years.

Freshman aid. Need-based: Out of 250 full-time freshmen, 241 applied for aid; 193 were judged to have need; of these 193 received aid. Average package met 100% of need. 193 students had full need met. Average scholarship/grant was $15,547; average loan $2,751. **Non-need based:** 48 without need received awards.

Merit scholarships. Pickard Scholarships: full tuition(1); $60,000 (10); both types by invitation only. Presidential Scholarships: $48,000; minimum 3.8 GPA, top 5% of class, ACT 30, SAT (V+M) 1340, by invitation only. Knop Scholars Program: $50,000 (2); physics major, 3.5 GPA, top 10% of class, interview, by invitation only. Faculty Scholarships: $40,000; 3.76 GPA, ACT 29, SAT 1300. Dean's Scholarships: $28,000; 3.51 GPA, ACT 27, SAT 1220. Founder's Scholarships: $24,000; 3.36 GPA, ACT 25, SAT 1140. Honor Scholarships: $20,000; 3.2 GPA, ACT 24, SAT 1110. US Army ROTC Scholarships: $64,000+. Diversity Scholarships: $60,000; application required. Forensics Academic Scholarships: $40,000; 3.5 GPA, ACT 27, SAT 1220, interview. Valedictorian Scholarships: $24,000. Art Scholarships: $20,000 maximum award; portfolio. Theatre Scholarships: $20,000 maximum; interview. Music Scholarships: $20,000; audition. Leadership Awards: $20,000; application required. Badger Boy/Girl Scholarships: $16,000 maximum award. Legacy Awards: $8,000. ACE Awards: $8,000. United Church of Christ Scholarships: $8,000; application required.

Policies to reduce costs. Tuition/fee waivers for children of alumni, family members, employees and their families. Tuition at time of enrollment guaranteed for 4 years; credit/placement for qualifying scores on AP, IB examinations. Work study available nights and weekends.

Payment plans. Installment payment.

Application procedures. FAFSA required. Priority date 3/1; no closing date. Applicants notified on rolling basis starting 3/1, must reply within 2 week(s) of notification. **Transfers:** No deadline.

Contact. **Financial aid office:** (920) 748-8101
Michelle Krajnik, Director of Financial Aid
300 Seward Street
Ripon, WI 54971

St. Norbert College

De Pere, Wisconsin
www.snc.edu
Four-year private **Federal Code: 003892**

	Living at home	On-campus
Tuition and fees (2002-2003):	$19,084	$19,084
Room and board:		$5,472
Books and supplies:	$450	$450
Personal expenses:	$750	$750
Transportation:	$500	$350

Undergraduate aid. Need-based: Average financial aid package for full-time students was $14,718; for part-time $4,656. 67% awarded as scholarships/grants, 33% as loans/jobs. **Non-need-based:** 47% awarded as scholarships/grants, 53% as loans/jobs. Scholarships based on academics, art, leadership, minority status, music/drama, state/district residency. **Student debt:** 74% of graduating class borrowed to fund education; average debt was $16,059.

Freshman aid. Need-based: Out of 499 full-time freshmen, 397 applied for aid; 330 were judged to have need; of these 330 received aid. Average package met 88% of need. 133 students had full need met. Average scholarship/grant was $11,325; average loan $3,399. **Non-need based:** 50 full-time freshmen with need received non-need scholarships; 146 without need received awards.

Merit scholarships. Trustees Distinguished Scholarship; based on high school courses, grades, class rank (top 10%), ACT/SAT scores (ACT 27 or higher), essay to scholarship committee; $28,000-$34,000 over 4 years. Presidential Scholarship; based on college prep background, class rank in top 20% of class, minimum ACT of 25, various high school activities, community service projects and leadership recognition; $24,000-$26,000 over 4 years. John F. Kennedy Scholarship; based on college prep background, class rank in top 40% of class, minimum ACT of 22, community service, work experience, leadership positions; $18,000-$22,000 over 4 years.

Policies to reduce costs. Tuition/fee waivers for employees and their families. Credit/placement for qualifying scores on AP, IB, CLEP examinations. Work study available nights, weekends and for part-time students.

Payment plans. Deferred payment.

Application procedures. FAFSA, institutional form required. Priority date 3/1; no closing date. Applicants notified on rolling basis starting 3/15, must reply within 2 week(s) of notification. Early decision closing date 12/1. **Transfers:** Priority date 3/1; no deadline.

Contact. **Financial aid office:** (920) 403-3071
Jeff Zahn, Director of Financial Aid
100 Grant Street
De Pere, WI 54115-2099

Silver Lake College

Manitowoc, Wisconsin
www.sl.edu
Four-year private **Federal Code: 003850**

	Living at home	On-campus
Tuition and fees:	$14,350	$14,350
Room only:		$4,100
Books and supplies:	$600	$600
Personal expenses:	$1,080	$1,080
Transportation:	$1,000	$1,000

Undergraduate aid. Need-based: Average financial aid package for full-time students was $6,443; for part-time $5,179. 48% awarded as scholarships/grants, 52% as loans/jobs. **Non-need-based:** 53% awarded as scholarships/grants, 47% as loans/jobs. Scholarships based on academics, athletics, leadership, music/drama. **Student debt:** 41% of graduating class borrowed to fund education; average debt was $18,216.

Freshman aid. Need-based: Out of 33 full-time freshmen, 33 applied for aid; 32 were judged to have need; of these 32 received aid. Average package met 67% of need. 1 students had full need met. Average scholarship/grant was $7,491; average loan $2,313. **Non-need based:** 32 full-time freshmen with need received non-need scholarships.

Merit scholarships. Presidential Scholarship based on academics, $4,250 per year (renewable). Religious Service Award based on church-related activities, $500 per year (renewable).

Policies to reduce costs. Tuition/fee waivers for children of alumni, senior citizens, employees and their families. Credit/placement for qualifying scores on AP, CLEP examinations. Work study available nights, weekends and for part-time students.

Payment plans. Credit card, installment, deferred payment.

Application procedures. FAFSA, institutional form required. Priority date 4/15; no closing date. Applicants notified on rolling basis starting 5/1.

Contact. **Financial aid office:** (920) 686-6122
Mary Beth Kornely, Director Student Financial Aid
2406 South Alverno Road
Manitowoc, WI 54220

University of Wisconsin-Baraboo/Sauk County

Baraboo, Wisconsin
www.baraboo.uwc.edu
Two-year public **Federal Code: 003897**

College costs. Minnesota reciprocity tuition: $2,708 full-time, $113 per-credit-hour.

	Living at home
Tuition and fees (2002-2003):	$2,916
Out-of-state:	$11,616
Per-credit charge:	$113
Per-credit out-of-state:	$475
Board only:	$1,522
Books and supplies:	$515
Personal expenses:	$992
Transportation:	$836

Undergraduate aid. Need-based: Need-based aid available for full-time and part-time students. **Non-need-based:** Scholarships based on academics, art, leadership, music/drama.

Merit scholarships. Campus scholarship program offering non-need based awards ranging from $250 to full tuition.

Policies to reduce costs. Tuition/fee waivers for senior citizens. Credit/placement for qualifying scores on AP, IB, CLEP examinations. Work study available nights and for part-time students.

Payment plans. Installment, deferred payment.

Application procedures. FAFSA, institutional form required. Priority date 4/15; no closing date. Applicants notified on rolling basis starting 4/15, must reply within 3 week(s) of notification.

Contact. Marilyn Krump, Director of Financial Aid
1006 Connie Road
Baraboo, WI 53913-1098

University of Wisconsin-Barron County

Rice Lake, Wisconsin
www.barron.uwc.edu
Two-year public **Federal Code: 003897**

College costs. Minnesota reciprocity tuition: $2,708 full-time, $113 per-credit-hour.

	Living at home
Tuition and fees (2002-2003):	$2,896
Out-of-state:	$11,596
Per-credit charge:	$113
Per-credit out-of-state:	$475
Books and supplies:	$150

Undergraduate aid. Need-based: Need-based aid available for full-time and part-time students.

Policies to reduce costs. Credit/placement for qualifying scores on AP, CLEP examinations.

Payment plans. Installment, deferred payment.

Application procedures. FAFSA required. Priority date 4/15; no closing date. Applicants notified on rolling basis starting 6/1.

Contact. Dale Fenton, Director of Student Services
1800 College Drive
Rice Lake, WI 54868

University of Wisconsin-Eau Claire

Eau Claire, Wisconsin
www.uwec.edu
Four-year public **Federal Code: 003917**

College costs. Tuition includes textbook rental. Minnesota reciprocity tuition $3,424; per credit hour charge $143.

	Living at home	On-campus
Tuition and fees (2002-2003):	$3,722	$3,722
Out-of-state:	$13,768	$13,768
Room and board:		$3,910
Books and supplies:	$330	$330
Personal expenses:	$1,050	$1,480
Transportation:	$950	$950

Undergraduate aid. Need-based: Average financial aid package for full-time students was $5,830; for part-time $5,422. 36% awarded as scholarships/grants, 64% as loans/jobs. **Non-need-based:** 13% awarded as scholarships/grants, 87% as loans/jobs. Scholarships based on academics, art, leadership, minority status, music/drama, state/district residency. **Student debt:** 61% of graduating class borrowed to fund education; average debt was $14,386.

Freshman aid. Need-based: Out of 2,126 full-time freshmen, 1,462 applied for aid; 789 were judged to have need; of these 776 received aid. Average package met 77% of need. 597 students had full need met. Average scholarship/grant was $3,379; average loan $2,949. **Non-need based:** 171 full-time freshmen with need received non-need scholarships; 311 without need received awards.

Merit scholarships. Chancellor's Award: 6 awards of full, in-state tuition for 1 year; Dean's Awards: 20 awards of $1,000; Wisconsin Academic Excellence Scholars for selected high school valedictorians: $2,250, renewable; National Merit Scholarship finalists: full, in-state fees, for top 25% of high school class with ACT composite of 25 or more, though some require ACT of 28 or 30.

Policies to reduce costs. Tuition/fee waivers for senior citizens. Credit/placement for qualifying scores on AP, IB, CLEP examinations.

Payment plans. Installment payment.

Application procedures. FAFSA required. Priority date 4/15; no closing date. Applicants notified on rolling basis starting 4/15, must reply within 3 week(s) of notification.

Contact. Kathleen Sahlhoff, Director of Financial Aid
112 Schofield Hall
Eau Claire, WI 54701

University of Wisconsin-Fond du Lac

Fond du Lac, Wisconsin
www.fdl.wwc.edu
Two-year public

College costs. Minnesota reciprocity tuition: $2,456 full-time, $102 per-credit-hour.

	Living at home
Tuition and fees (2002-2003):	$2,646
Out-of-state:	$10,090
Per-credit charge:	$101
Per-credit out-of-state:	$411
Board only:	$1,315
Books and supplies:	$455
Personal expenses:	$810
Transportation:	$705

Undergraduate aid. Need-based: Need-based aid available for full-time and part-time students.

Policies to reduce costs. Tuition/fee waivers for senior citizens. Credit/placement for qualifying scores on AP, CLEP examinations.

Payment plans. Installment, deferred payment.

Application procedures. FAFSA, institutional form required. Priority date 4/15; no closing date. Applicants notified on rolling basis starting 6/1, must reply within 2 week(s) of notification. **Transfers:** Priority date 4/1; no deadline.

Contact. Jill Nicholas, Director of Admissions and Financial Aid
400 University Drive
Fond du Lac, WI 54935-2998

University of Wisconsin-Fox Valley

Menasha, Wisconsin
www.uwfoxvalley.uwc.edu
Two-year public

College costs. Minnesota reciprocity tuition: $2,708 full-time, $113 per-credit-hour.

	Living at home
Tuition and fees (2002-2003):	$2,906
Out-of-state:	$11,606
Per-credit charge:	$113
Per-credit out-of-state:	$475
Books and supplies:	$455
Personal expenses:	$810
Transportation:	$705

Undergraduate aid. Need-based: Need-based aid available for full-time and part-time students.

Policies to reduce costs. Tuition/fee waivers for senior citizens. Credit/placement for qualifying scores on AP, CLEP examinations.

Payment plans. Credit card, installment, deferred payment.

Application procedures. FAFSA required. Priority date 4/15; no closing date. Applicants notified on rolling basis starting 6/1, must reply within 3 week(s) of notification.

Contact. Rhonda Uschan, Director
1478 Midway Road
Menasha, WI 54952-2850

University of Wisconsin-Green Bay

Green Bay, Wisconsin
www.uwgb.edu
Four-year public **Federal Code: 003899**

College costs. Minnesota annual reciprocity tuition: $3,108; $130 per credit hour.

	Living at home	On-campus
Tuition and fees (2002-2003):	$4,024	$4,024
Out-of-state:	$14,070	$14,070
Room and board:		$4,212
Books and supplies:	$500	$500
Personal expenses:	$600	$1,400
Transportation:	$750	$450

Undergraduate aid. Need-based: Average financial aid package for full-time students was $6,666; for part-time $7,160. 45% awarded as scholarships/grants, 55% as loans/jobs. **Non-need-based:** 10% awarded as scholarships/grants, 90% as loans/jobs. Scholarships based on academics, art, athletics, leadership, music/drama. **Additional information:** Auditions required for music and theater scholarships.

Freshman aid. Need-based: Out of 889 full-time freshmen, 734 applied for aid; 460 were judged to have need; of these 449 received aid. Average package met 77% of need. 168 students had full need met. Average scholarship/grant was $3,445; average loan $2,725. **Non-need based:** 136 full-time freshmen with need received non-need scholarships; 53 without need received awards; 13 received athletic scholarships.

Policies to reduce costs. Tuition/fee waivers for senior citizens. Prepayment discount; credit/placement for qualifying scores on AP, IB, CLEP examinations.

Payment plans. Installment payment.

Application procedures. FAFSA required. Priority date 4/1; no closing date. Applicants notified on rolling basis starting 11/1, must reply within 3 week(s) of notification. **Transfers:** Priority date 4/1; no deadline.

Contact. Financial aid office: (920) 465-2075
Ron Ronnenberg, Director of Financial Aid and Student Employment
2420 Nicolet Drive
Green Bay, WI 54311-7001

University of Wisconsin-La Crosse

La Crosse, Wisconsin
www.uwlax.edu
Four-year public **Federal Code: 003919**

College costs. Minnesota reciprocity tuition: $3,425 full-time, $143 per-credit-hour. Required fees include textbook rental. Additional tuition for occupational therapy and physician assistant programs.

	Living at home	On-campus
Tuition and fees (2002-2003):	$3,804	$3,804
Out-of-state:	$13,850	$13,850
Room and board:		$3,800
Books and supplies:	$200	$200
Personal expenses:	$1,330	$1,800
Transportation:	$140	$250

Undergraduate aid. Need-based: Average financial aid package for full-time students was $5,658; for part-time $3,506. 38% awarded as scholarships/grants, 62% as loans/jobs. **Non-need-based:** 5% awarded as scholarships/grants, 95% as loans/jobs. Scholarships based on academics, art, leadership, minority status. **Student debt:** 55% of graduating class borrowed to fund education; average debt was $14,306.

Freshman aid. Need-based: Out of 1,572 full-time freshmen, 1,131 applied for aid; 905 were judged to have need; of these 890 received aid. Average package met 91% of need. 774 students had full need met. Average scholarship/grant was $2,016; average loan $2,212. **Non-need based:** 35 full-time freshmen with need received non-need scholarships; 201 without need received awards.

Policies to reduce costs. Tuition/fee waivers for senior citizens, minority students. Credit/placement for qualifying scores on AP, IB, CLEP examinations. Work study available nights, weekends and for part-time students.

Payment plans. Credit card, installment payment.

Application procedures. FAFSA, institutional form required. Priority date 3/15; no closing date. Applicants notified on rolling basis starting 4/15, must reply by 5/10 or within 3 week(s) of notification.

Contact. Financial aid office: (608) 785-8604
Jim Finn, Director of Financial Aid
1725 State Street, Room 115 Main Hall
La Crosse, WI 54601

University of Wisconsin-Madison

Madison, Wisconsin
www.wisc.edu
Four-year public **Federal Code: 003895**

College costs. Minnesota reciprocity tuition: $5,420 full-time, $226 per-credit-hour.

	Living at home	On-campus
Tuition and fees (2002-2003):	$4,423	$4,423
Out-of-state:	$18,424	$18,424
Room and board:		$5,700
Board only:	$1,500	
Books and supplies:	$660	$660
Personal expenses:	$1,550	$1,550
Transportation:	$100	$340

Undergraduate aid. Need-based: Need-based aid available for full-time and part-time students. **Non-need-based:** Scholarships based on academics, athletics, state/district residency.

Policies to reduce costs. Credit/placement for qualifying scores on AP, IB, CLEP examinations.

Application procedures. FAFSA, institutional form required. No deadline. Applicants notified on rolling basis starting 4/1, must reply within 2 week(s) of notification.

Contact. Financial aid office: (608) 262-3060
Steve Van Ess, Director Student Financial Services
716 Landgon Street
Madison, WI 53706-1400

University of Wisconsin-Manitowoc

Manitowoc, Wisconsin
www.manitowoc.uwc.edu
Two-year public **Federal Code: 003897**

College costs. Minnesota reciprocity tuition: $2,708 full-time, $113 per-credit-hour.

	Living at home
Tuition and fees (2002-2003):	$2,864
Out-of-state:	$11,564
Per-credit charge:	$113
Per-credit out-of-state:	$475
Board only:	$1,476
Books and supplies:	$515
Personal expenses:	$990
Transportation:	$800

Policies to reduce costs. Credit/placement for qualifying scores on AP examinations. Work study available nights and for part-time students.

Payment plans. Credit card, installment, deferred payment.

Application procedures. FAFSA, institutional form required. Priority date 3/1; no closing date. Applicants notified on rolling basis starting 5/1, must reply within 2 week(s) of notification.

Contact. Michael Herrity, Director of Student Services
705 Viebahn Street
Manitowoc, WI 54220-6699

University of Wisconsin-Marathon County

Wausau, Wisconsin
www.uwmc.uwc.edu
Two-year public

College costs. Minnesota reciprocity tuition: $2,708 full time, $113 per-credit-hour.

	Living at home	On-campus
Tuition and fees (2002-2003):	$2,904	$2,904
Out-of-state:	$11,604	$11,604
Per-credit charge:	$113	$113
Per-credit out-of-state:	$475	$475
Room and board:		$3,390
Books and supplies:	$700	$700
Personal expenses:	$810	$900
Transportation:	$705	$550

Undergraduate aid. All financial aid based on need. Need-based aid available for full-time and part-time students.

Policies to reduce costs. Tuition/fee waivers for senior citizens. Credit/placement for qualifying scores on AP, IB, CLEP examinations. Work study available nights and for part-time students.

Payment plans. Installment, deferred payment.

Application procedures. FAFSA, institutional form required. Priority date 4/15; no closing date. Applicants notified on rolling basis starting 6/1, must reply within 3 week(s) of notification.

Contact. Nolan Beck, Director of Student Services
518 South Seventh Avenue
Wausau, WI 54401-5396

University of Wisconsin-Marinette

Marinette, Wisconsin
www.marinette.uwc.edu
Two-year public **Federal Code: 003897**

College costs. Minnesota reciprocity tuition: $2,708 full-time tuition, $113 per-credit-hour.

	Living at home
Tuition and fees (2002-2003):	$2,854
Out-of-state:	$11,554
Per-credit charge:	$113
Per-credit out-of-state:	$475
Books and supplies:	$455
Personal expenses:	$810
Transportation:	$705

Undergraduate aid. Need-based: Need-based aid available for full-time and part-time students.

Policies to reduce costs. Credit/placement for qualifying scores on AP, CLEP examinations. Work study available nights, weekends and for part-time students.

Payment plans. Credit card, installment, deferred payment.

Application procedures. FAFSA required. Priority date 4/1; no closing date. Applicants notified on rolling basis starting 6/1. **Transfers:** No deadline.

Contact. Cynthia Bailey, Director of Student Services
750 West Bay Shore Street
Marinette, WI 54143

University of Wisconsin-Milwaukee

Milwaukee, Wisconsin
www.uwm.edu
Four-year public **Federal Code: 003896**

College costs. Minnesota reciprocity tuition: $5,585 full-time, $233 per-credit-hour. Additional tuition for communication science/disorders and occupational therapy programs.

	Living at home	On-campus
Tuition and fees (2002-2003):	$4,353	$4,353
Out-of-state:	$17,105	$17,105
Room and board:		$4,850
Board only:	$2,150	
Books and supplies:	$700	$700
Personal expenses:	$1,388	$1,388
Transportation:	$1,008	

Policies to reduce costs. Tuition/fee waivers for senior citizens. Credit/placement for qualifying scores on AP, CLEP examinations.

Payment plans. Installment payment.

Application procedures. No deadline. Applicants notified on rolling basis starting 4/15.

Contact. Financial aid office: (414) 229-6300
Mary Roggeman, Director of Financial Aid
Box 749
Milwaukee, WI 53201

University of Wisconsin-Oshkosh

Oshkosh, Wisconsin
www.uwosh.edu
Four-year public **Federal Code: 003920**

College costs. Minnesota reciprocity tuition: $3,884 full-time, $143 per-credit-hour.

	Living at home	On-campus
Tuition and fees (2002-2003):	$3,460	$3,460
Out-of-state:	$13,506	$13,506
Room and board:		$3,970
Books and supplies:	$600	$600
Personal expenses:	$2,000	$2,000
Transportation:	$1,100	$420

Undergraduate aid. Need-based: Average financial aid package for full-time students was $5,100; for part-time $3,550. 40% awarded as scholarships/grants, 60% as loans/jobs. **Non-need-based:** Scholarships based on academics, alumni affiliation, art, leadership, minority status, music/drama, state/district residency. **Student debt:** 55% of graduating class borrowed to fund education; average debt was $14,000.

Freshman aid. Need-based: Out of 1,680 full-time freshmen, 1,140 applied for aid; 627 were judged to have need; of these 627 received aid. Average package met 55% of need. 349 students had full need met. Average scholarship/grant was $2,300; average loan $2,625. **Non-need based:** 283 full-time freshmen with need received non-need scholarships; 50 without need received awards.

Policies to reduce costs. Credit/placement for qualifying scores on AP, IB, CLEP examinations.

Payment plans. Installment payment.

Application procedures. FAFSA required. Priority date 3/15; no closing date. Applicants notified on rolling basis starting 5/1, must reply within 2 week(s) of notification. **Transfers:** Must send financial aid transcript to university.

Contact. Financial aid office: (920) 424-3377
Beatrice Contreras, Director of Financial Aid
800 Algoma Boulevard
Oshkosh, WI 54901-8602

University of Wisconsin-Parkside

Kenosha, Wisconsin
www.uwp.edu
Four-year public **Federal Code: 005015**

College costs. Minnesota reciprocity tuition: $3,426 full-time, $143 per-credit-hour.

	Living at home	On-campus
Tuition and fees (2002-2003):	$3,532	$3,532
Out-of-state:	$13,578	$13,578
Room and board:		$5,256
Board only:	$1,800	
Books and supplies:	$770	$770
Personal expenses:	$1,144	$1,356
Transportation:	$850	$850

Undergraduate aid. Need-based: Average financial aid package for full-time students was $5,953; for part-time $5,175. 54% awarded as scholarships/grants, 46% as loans/jobs. **Non-need-based:** 48% awarded as scholarships/grants, 52% as loans/jobs. Scholarships based on academics, art, athletics, music/drama. **Student debt:** 62% of graduating class borrowed to fund education; average debt was $12,500.

Freshman aid. Need-based: Out of 564 full-time freshmen, 422 applied for aid; 259 were judged to have need; of these 242 received aid. Average package met 72% of need. 108 students had full need met. Average scholarship/grant was $4,055; average loan $2,620. **Non-need based:** 78 full-time freshmen with need received non-need scholarships; 35 without need received awards; 14 received athletic scholarships.

Policies to reduce costs. Tuition/fee waivers for senior citizens. Credit/placement for qualifying scores on AP, IB, CLEP examinations. Work study available nights, weekends and for part-time students.

Payment plans. Installment payment.

Application procedures. FAFSA required. Priority date 4/1; no closing date. Applicants notified on rolling basis starting 3/1, must reply within 2 week(s) of notification.

Contact. Financial aid office: (262) 595-2574
Randy McCready, Director of Scholarships and Financial Aid
P.O. Box 2000
Kenosha, WI 53141-2000

University of Wisconsin-Platteville

Platteville, Wisconsin
www.uwplatt.edu
Four-year public **Federal Code: 003921**

College costs. Minnesota reciprocity tuition: $3,425 full-time, $143 per credit hour. Required fees include textbook rental.

	Living at home	On-campus
Tuition and fees (2002-2003):	$3,720	$3,720
Out-of-state:	$13,766	$13,766
Room and board:		$3,978
Books and supplies:	$300	$300
Personal expenses:	$930	$1,170
Transportation:	$870	$410

Undergraduate aid. All financial aid based on need. Average financial aid package for full-time students was $4,836. 21% awarded as scholarships/grants, 79% as loans/jobs. Need-based aid available for part-time students. **Student debt:** 61% of graduating class borrowed to fund education; average debt was $10,030.

Policies to reduce costs. Credit/placement for qualifying scores on AP, CLEP examinations. Work study available nights and weekends.

Payment plans. Installment payment.

Application procedures. FAFSA required. Priority date 3/15; no closing date. Applicants notified on rolling basis starting 6/1, must reply within 2 week(s) of notification.

Contact. Financial aid office: (608) 342-1836
Liz Tucker, Director of Financial Aid
One University Plaza
Platteville, WI 53818

University of Wisconsin-Richland

Richland Center, Wisconsin
richland.uwc.edu
Two-year public **Federal Code: 003897**

College costs. Required fees include book rental costs. Minnesota reciprocity tuition: $2,708 full-time; $113 per-credit-hour.

	Living at home	On-campus
Tuition and fees (2002-2003):	$3,052	$3,052
Out-of-state:	$11,752	$11,752
Per-credit charge:	$113	$113
Per-credit out-of-state:	$475	$475
Room only:		$2,790
Board only:	$1,485	
Books and supplies:	$515	$515
Personal expenses:	$990	$1,390
Transportation:	$800	$800

Undergraduate aid. All financial aid based on need. Need-based aid available for full-time and part-time students.

Policies to reduce costs. Tuition/fee waivers for senior citizens. Credit/placement for qualifying scores on AP, IB, CLEP examinations. Work study available nights, weekends and for part-time students.

Payment plans. Credit card, installment payment.

Application procedures. FAFSA required. Priority date 4/15; no closing date. Applicants notified on rolling basis starting 5/15, must reply within 3 week(s) of notification.

Contact. John Poole, Director of Student Services
1200 Highway 14 West
Richland Center, WI 53581

University of Wisconsin-River Falls

River Falls, Wisconsin
www.uwrf.edu
Four-year public **Federal Code: 003923**

College costs. Required fees include textbook rental. Minnesota reciprocity tuition: $3,425 full-time, $143 per-credit-hour.

	Living at home	On-campus
Tuition and fees (2002-2003):	$3,670	$3,670
Out-of-state:	$13,716	$13,716
Room and board:		$3,690
Books and supplies:	$200	$200
Personal expenses:	$1,106	$1,106
Transportation:	$1,006	$1,006

Undergraduate aid. All financial aid based on need. Need-based aid available for full-time and part-time students.

Policies to reduce costs. Tuition/fee waivers for senior citizens. Credit/placement for qualifying scores on AP, IB, CLEP examinations.

Payment plans. Installment payment.

Application procedures. FAFSA, institutional form required. Priority date 3/15; no closing date. Applicants notified on rolling basis starting 4/1, must reply within 3 week(s) of notification.

Contact. Dave Woodward, Director of Financial Aid
410 South Third Street
River Falls, WI 54022-5001

University of Wisconsin-Rock County

Janesville, Wisconsin
www.rock.uwc.edu
Two-year public **Federal Code: 003897**

College costs. Minnesota reciprocity tuition: $2,708 full-time, $113 per-credit-hour.

	Living at home
Tuition and fees (2002-2003):	$3,090
Out-of-state:	$11,794
Per-credit charge:	$113
Per-credit out-of-state:	$475
Books and supplies:	$500
Personal expenses:	$810
Transportation:	$705

Undergraduate aid. All financial aid based on need. Need-based aid available for full-time and part-time students.

Policies to reduce costs. Credit/placement for qualifying scores on AP, CLEP examinations. Work study available nights, weekends and for part-time students.

Payment plans. Credit card, installment, deferred payment.

Application procedures. FAFSA, institutional form required. Priority date 4/15; no closing date. Applicants notified on rolling basis starting 6/1, must reply within 3 week(s) of notification.

Contact. **Financial aid office:** (608) 758-6523
Amber Culver, Senior Student Services Coordinator
2909 Kellogg Avenue
Janesville, WI 53546-5699

University of Wisconsin-Stevens Point

Stevens Point, Wisconsin
www.uwsp.edu
Four-year public **Federal Code: 003924**

College costs. Required fees include textbook rental. Minnesota reciprocity tuition: $3,424 full-time, $143 per-credit-hour.

	Living at home	On-campus
Tuition and fees (2002-2003):	$3,632	$3,632
Out-of-state:	$13,678	$13,678
Room and board:		$3,616
Board only:	$1,990	
Books and supplies:	$450	$450
Personal expenses:	$1,830	$1,730
Transportation:	$340	$250

Undergraduate aid. Need-based: Average financial aid package for full-time students was $5,817; for part-time $4,294. 36% awarded as scholarships/grants, 64% as loans/jobs. **Non-need-based:** 20% awarded as scholarships/grants, 80% as loans/jobs. Scholarships based on academics. **Student debt:** 63% of graduating class borrowed to fund education; average debt was $13,396.

Freshman aid. Need-based: Out of 1,520 full-time freshmen, 1,242 applied for aid; 652 were judged to have need; of these 600 received aid. Average package met 92% of need. 495 students had full need met. Average scholarship/grant was $3,247; average loan $2,803. **Non-need based:** 77 full-time freshmen with need received non-need scholarships; 128 without need received awards.

Policies to reduce costs. Credit/placement for qualifying scores on AP, IB, CLEP examinations.

Payment plans. Installment payment.

Application procedures. FAFSA required. Priority date 3/15; closing date 7/15. Applicants notified on rolling basis starting 5/1, must reply within 4 week(s) of notification. **Transfers:** No deadline.

Contact. Philip George, Director of Financial Aid
Student Services Center
Stevens Point, WI 54481

University of Wisconsin-Stout

Menomonie, Wisconsin
www.uwstout.edu
Four-year public **Federal Code: 003915**

College costs. Required fees include textbook rental. Minnesota reciprocity tuition $3,425. Per credit hour charge $143.

	Living at home	On-campus
Tuition and fees (2002-2003):	$3,777	$3,777
Out-of-state:	$13,823	$13,823
Room and board:		$3,830
Board only:	$460	
Books and supplies:	$272	$272
Personal expenses:	$1,339	$1,648
Transportation:	$803	$803

Undergraduate aid. Need-based: Average financial aid package for full-time students was $6,197; for part-time $6,548. 34% awarded as scholarships/grants, 66% as loans/jobs. **Non-need-based:** 14% awarded as scholarships/grants, 86% as loans/jobs. Scholarships based on academics. **Student debt:** 67% of graduating class borrowed to fund education; average debt was $15,714.

Freshman aid. Need-based: Out of 1,203 full-time freshmen, 919 applied for aid; 611 were judged to have need; of these 611 received aid. Average package met 86% of need. 228 students had full need met. Average scholarship/grant was $3,606; average loan $3,243. **Non-need based:** 238 full-time freshmen with need received non-need scholarships; 124 without need received awards.

Merit scholarships. Wisconsin Academic Excellence Scholarship, $2,250 selected by high school. National Merit Finalist Scholarship, $2,000; automatically awarded to NMSQT finalist. National Merit Semifinalist Scholarship, $1,000; automatically awarded to NMSQT semifinalist. Chancellor's Academic Honor Scholarship, $1,000; automatically awarded to top 5% of high school class with ACT of 25 who enroll by July 15th.

Policies to reduce costs. Tuition/fee waivers for senior citizens. Credit/placement for qualifying scores on AP, IB, CLEP examinations. Work study available nights, weekends and for part-time students.

Payment plans. Credit card, installment payment.

Application procedures. FAFSA required. Priority date 4/1; no closing date. Applicants notified on rolling basis starting 4/1, must reply within 4 week(s) of notification. **Transfers:** Priority date 4/1; no deadline.

Contact. **Financial aid office:** (715) 232-1363
Beth Resech, Director of Financial Aid
Menomonie, WI 54751

University of Wisconsin-Superior

Superior, Wisconsin
www.uwsuper.edu
Four-year public **Federal Code: 003925**

College costs. Minnesota reciprocity tuition: $3,425 full-time, $143 per-credit-hour.

	Living at home	On-campus
Tuition and fees (2002-2003):	$3,461	$3,461
Out-of-state:	$13,971	$13,971
Room and board:		$3,962
Books and supplies:	$670	$670
Personal expenses:	$1,440	$1,440
Transportation:	$670	$670

Undergraduate aid. Need-based: Average financial aid package for full-time students was $8,020; for part-time $7,663. 42% awarded as scholarships/grants, 58% as loans/jobs. **Non-need-based:** 24% awarded as scholarships/grants, 76% as loans/jobs. Scholarships based on academics, state/district residency. **Student debt:** 55% of graduating class borrowed to fund education; average debt was $14,261. **Additional information:** Tuition Assistance Program (TAP) available to non-resident students on limited basis.

Freshman aid. Need-based: Out of 269 full-time freshmen, 191 applied for aid; 130 were judged to have need; of these 127 received aid. 70 students had full need met. Average scholarship/grant was $4,267; average loan $1,945. **Non-need based:** 48 full-time freshmen with need received non-need scholarships; 19 without need received awards.

Policies to reduce costs. Tuition/fee waivers for minority students. Credit/placement for qualifying scores on AP, IB, CLEP examinations. Work study available nights and weekends.

Payment plans. Credit card, installment payment.

Application procedures. FAFSA required. Priority date 4/15; no closing date. Applicants notified on rolling basis starting 11/1, must reply by 5/1 or within 2 week(s) of notification.

Contact. **Financial aid office:** (715) 394-8200
Anne Podgorak, Director of Financial Aid
Belknap and Catlin
Superior, WI 54880

University of Wisconsin-Washington County

West Bend, Wisconsin
washington.uwc.edu
Two-year public **Federal Code: 003897**

College costs. Minnesota reciprocity tuition: $2,708 full-time, $113 per-credit-hour.

	Living at home
Tuition and fees (2002-2003):	$2,944
Out-of-state:	$11,644
Per-credit charge:	$113
Per-credit out-of-state:	$475
Board only:	$1,522
Books and supplies:	$552
Personal expenses:	$930
Transportation:	$836

Undergraduate aid. Need-based: Need-based aid available for full-time and part-time students. **Non-need-based:** Scholarships based on academics.

Policies to reduce costs. Credit/placement for qualifying scores on AP, IB, CLEP examinations.

Payment plans. Installment, deferred payment.

Application procedures. FAFSA required. Priority date 4/15; no closing date. Applicants notified on rolling basis starting 4/30, must reply within 3 week(s) of notification.

Contact. Financial aid office: (262) 335-5207
Janet Brown, Director of Student Services
400 University Drive
West Bend, WI 53095

University of Wisconsin-Waukesha

Waukesha, Wisconsin
waukesha.uwc.edu
Two-year public **Federal Code: 003897**

College costs. Minnesota reciprocity tuition: $2,708 full-time; $113 per-credit-hour.

	Living at home
Tuition and fees (2002-2003):	$2,862
Out-of-state:	$11,562
Per-credit charge:	$113
Per-credit out-of-state:	$475
Books and supplies:	$500
Personal expenses:	$1,000
Transportation:	$800

Undergraduate aid. Need-based: Need-based aid available for full-time and part-time students. **Non-need-based:** Scholarships based on academics, leadership, minority status, music/drama.

Freshman aid. Non-need based: 7 without need received awards.

Merit scholarships. University of Wisconsin-Waukesha Scholarship Program: numerous scholarships; amounts based on different criteria.

Policies to reduce costs. Credit/placement for qualifying scores on AP, CLEP examinations. Work study available nights, weekends and for part-time students.

Payment plans. Credit card, installment, deferred payment.

Application procedures. FAFSA required. Priority date 4/15; no closing date. Applicants notified on rolling basis starting 5/15, must reply within 3 week(s) of notification.

Contact. Financial aid office: (262) 521-5210
Judy Becker, Coordinator of Financial Aid
1500 University Drive
Waukesha, WI 53188

University of Wisconsin-Whitewater

Whitewater, Wisconsin
www.uww.edu
Four-year public **Federal Code: 003926**

College costs. Minnesota reciprocity tuition: $3,425 full-time, $143 per-credit-hour. Required fees include textbook rental.

	Living at home	On-campus
Tuition and fees (2002-2003):	$3,737	$3,737
Out-of-state:	$13,783	$13,783
Room and board:		$4,010
Board only:	$700	
Books and supplies:	$650	$650
Personal expenses:	$1,550	$1,550
Transportation:	$800	$800

Undergraduate aid. All financial aid based on need. Average financial aid package for full-time students was $6,411. 31% awarded as scholarships/grants, 69% as loans/jobs. **Student debt:** 86% of graduating class borrowed to fund education; average debt was $10,451.

Policies to reduce costs. Credit/placement for qualifying scores on AP, CLEP examinations.

Payment plans. Installment payment.

Application procedures. FAFSA required. Priority date 3/15; no closing date. Applicants notified on rolling basis starting 4/15, must reply within 2 week(s) of notification.

Contact. Financial aid office: (262) 472-1130
Carol Miller, Director Financial Aid
800 West Main Street
Whitewater, WI 53190-1791

Viterbo University

La Crosse, Wisconsin
www.viterbo.edu
Four-year private **Federal Code: 003911**

	Living at home	On-campus
Tuition and fees (2002-2003):	$14,300	$14,300
Room and board:		$4,910
Board only:	$2,750	
Books and supplies:	$650	$650
Personal expenses:	$1,100	$1,600
Transportation:	$700	$700

Undergraduate aid. Need-based: Average financial aid package for full-time students was $11,826; for part-time $7,945. 60% awarded as scholarships/grants, 40% as loans/jobs. **Non-need-based:** 52% awarded as scholarships/grants, 48% as loans/jobs. Scholarships based on academics, alumni affiliation, art, athletics, leadership, minority status, music/drama. **Student debt:** 84% of graduating class borrowed to fund education; average debt was $15,678.

Freshman aid. Need-based: Out of 352 full-time freshmen, 312 applied for aid; 281 were judged to have need; of these 281 received aid. Average package met 86% of need. 60 students had full need met. Average scholarship/grant was $8,574; average loan $2,252. **Non-need based:** 26 full-time freshmen with need received non-need scholarships; 53 without need received awards; 3 received athletic scholarships.

Policies to reduce costs. Tuition/fee waivers for employees and their families. Credit/placement for qualifying scores on AP, IB, CLEP examinations. Work study available nights and weekends.

Payment plans. Credit card, installment payment.

Application procedures. FAFSA required. Priority date 3/15; no closing date. Applicants notified on rolling basis starting 3/15, must reply within 2 week(s) of notification. **Transfers:** No deadline.

Contact. Financial aid office: (608) 796-3900
Terry Norman, Director of Financial Aid
815 South Ninth Street
La Crosse, WI 54601

Waukesha County Technical College

Pewaukee, Wisconsin
www.wctc.edu
Two-year public **Federal Code: 005294**

College costs. Materials fees range from $3.50 - $200 depending on program.

	Living at home
Tuition and fees (2002-2003):	$2,126
Out-of-state:	$15,527
Per-credit charge:	$67
Per-credit out-of-state:	$514
Board only:	$2,130
Books and supplies:	$690
Personal expenses:	$1,290
Transportation:	$880

Undergraduate aid. Non-need-based: Scholarships based on academics.

Policies to reduce costs. Tuition/fee waivers for senior citizens.

Payment plans. Credit card, installment, deferred payment.

Application procedures. FAFSA, institutional form required. No deadline. Applicants notified on rolling basis.

Contact. Financial aid office: (262) 691-5436
Tom Rabe, Director of Financial Aid
800 Main Street
Pewaukee, WI 53072

Western Wisconsin Technical College

La Crosse, Wisconsin
www.wwtc.edu
Two-year public **Federal Code: 003840**

College costs. Materials fees vary by program; minimum $3.50 per course.

	Living at home	On-campus
Tuition and fees (2002-2003):	$2,151	$2,151
Out-of-state:	$15,552	$15,552
Per-credit charge:	$67	$67
Per-credit out-of-state:	$514	$514
Room only:		$1,940
Books and supplies:	$832	$832
Personal expenses:	$2,206	$2,206
Transportation:	$782	

Undergraduate aid. Need-based: Average financial aid package for full-time students was $5,238; for part-time $4,033. **Additional information:** Nights and weekends are limited.

Freshman aid. Need-based: Out of 616 full-time freshmen, 483 applied for aid; 410 were judged to have need; of these 410 received aid. Average package met 74% of need. 57 students had full need met. Average scholarship/grant was $3,680; average loan $1,960. **Non-need based:** 5 full-time freshmen with need received non-need scholarships; 73 without need received awards.

Policies to reduce costs. Credit/placement for qualifying scores on AP examinations. Work study available nights, weekends and for part-time students.

Payment plans. Credit card, deferred payment.

Application procedures. FAFSA, institutional form required. Priority date 3/1; no closing date. Applicants notified on rolling basis starting 4/1.

Contact. Financial aid office: (608) 785-9302
Julie McConaughey, Student Financial Services Manager
PO Box 908
La Crosse, WI 54602-0908

Wisconsin Indianhead Technical College

Shell Lake, Wisconsin
www.witc.edu
Two-year public **Federal Code: 011824**

College costs. Materials fees vary by program; minimum $3.50 per course. Additional fees vary by campus among college's four campuses.

	Living at home
Tuition and fees (2002-2003):	$2,106
Out-of-state:	$15,507
Per-credit charge:	$67
Per-credit out-of-state:	$514
Board only:	$2,088
Books and supplies:	$808
Personal expenses:	$1,128
Transportation:	$680

Undergraduate aid. Need-based: Need-based aid available for full-time and part-time students. **Non-need-based:** Scholarships based on state/district residency.

Policies to reduce costs. Tuition/fee waivers for senior citizens. Credit/placement for qualifying scores on CLEP examinations. Work study available nights, weekends and for part-time students.

Payment plans. Credit card, installment, deferred payment.

Application procedures. FAFSA required. Applicants notified on rolling basis.

Contact. Financial aid office: (715) 468-2815 ext. 2246
Shane Evenson, Director, Financial Aid
505 Pine Ridge Drive
Shell Lake, WI 54871

Wisconsin Lutheran College

Milwaukee, Wisconsin
www.wlc.edu
Four-year private **Federal Code: 014658**

	Living at home	On-campus
Tuition and fees:	$15,846	$15,846
Room and board:		$5,580
Board only:	$1,500	
Books and supplies:	$650	$650
Personal expenses:	$1,180	$1,460
Transportation:	$600	$300

Undergraduate aid. Need-based: Average financial aid package for full-time students was $13,268; for part-time $5,675. 69% awarded as scholarships/grants, 31% as loans/jobs. **Non-need-based:** 61% awarded as scholarships/grants, 39% as loans/jobs. Scholarships based on academics, art, leadership, minority status, music/drama, state/district residency. **Student debt:** 65% of graduating class borrowed to fund education; average debt was $13,667.

Freshman aid. Need-based: Out of 158 full-time freshmen, 139 applied for aid; 130 were judged to have need; of these 130 received aid. Average package met 83% of need. 33 students had full need met. Average scholarship/grant was $9,338; average loan $2,406. **Non-need based:** 16 full-time freshmen with need received non-need scholarships; 25 without need received awards.

Merit scholarships. Presidential Scholarship, $8,000-$8,500, based on ACT score of 27 or higher plus top 10% of HS class or GPA of 3.7, no limit on number of awards. Academic Scholarship, $7,500, based on ACT score of 24 or higher and top 25% of high school class or GPA of 3.4

Policies to reduce costs. Tuition/fee waivers for employees and their families. Credit/placement for qualifying scores on AP, CLEP examinations. Work study available nights and weekends.

Payment plans. Installment payment.

Application procedures. FAFSA, institutional form required. Priority date 3/1; no closing date. Applicants notified on rolling basis starting 3/15, must reply within 2 week(s) of notification. **Transfers:** Transfer scholarship and transfer grant available for qualifying students.

Contact. Financial aid office: (414) 443-8856
Linda Loeffel, Director of Financial Aid
8800 West Bluemound Road
Milwaukee, WI 53226-4699

Wyoming

Casper College

Casper, Wyoming
www.caspercollege.edu
Two-year public **Federal Code: 003928**

College costs. Students from Western Undergraduate Exchange schools and Nebraska residents pay $1,848 tuition per year.

	Living at home	On-campus
Tuition and fees (2002-2003):	$1,368	$1,368
Out-of-state:	$3,816	$3,816
Per-credit charge:	$51	$51
Per-credit out-of-state:	$153	$153
Room and board:		$3,060
Books and supplies:	$500	$500
Personal expenses:	$450	$900
Transportation:	$450	$450

Undergraduate aid. Need-based: Need-based aid available for full-time and part-time students. **Non-need-based:** Scholarships based on academics, art, athletics, leadership, music/drama, state/district residency. **Additional information:** Athletic scholarships offered in rodeo and livestock judging, basketball and volleyball.

Policies to reduce costs. Tuition/fee waivers for senior citizens, employees and their families. Credit/placement for qualifying scores on AP, CLEP examinations.

Payment plans. Credit card, installment payment.

Application procedures. FAFSA, institutional form required. Priority date 3/15; closing date 8/10. Applicants notified on rolling basis starting 6/1.

Contact. Darry Voigt, Director of Financial Aid
125 College Drive
Casper, WY 82601

Central Wyoming College

Riverton, Wyoming
www.cwc.edu
Two-year public **Federal Code: 005018**

College costs. Students from Western Undergraduate Exchange schools and Nebraska residents pay $1,854 tuition per year.

	Living at home	On-campus
Tuition and fees (2002-2003):	$1,636	$1,636
Out-of-state:	$4,084	$4,084
Per-credit charge:	$51	$51
Per-credit out-of-state:	$153	$153
Room and board:		$3,690
Board only:	$1,800	
Books and supplies:	$700	$700
Personal expenses:	$750	$1,000
Transportation:	$500	$600

Undergraduate aid. Need-based: 68% awarded as scholarships/grants, 32% as loans/jobs. Need-based aid available for part-time students. **Non-need-based:** Scholarships based on academics, alumni affiliation, art, athletics, leadership, minority status, music/drama, state/district residency. **Student debt:** 37% of graduating class borrowed to fund education; average debt was $7,089.

Merit scholarships. Honors Scholarships, in-state tuition and general fees plus $300 book stipend, for graduating high-school seniors with minimum 3.5 cumulative GPA or minimum ACT composite 25; Seniors Scholarships, in-state tuition, for graduating high school seniors with 3.0-3.49 cumulative GPA or minimum ACT composite 22; Full Ride academic scholarships, in-state tuition, general fees, room and board, books and supplies, for Wyoming National Merit finalists.

Policies to reduce costs. Tuition/fee waivers for senior citizens, employees and their families. Credit/placement for qualifying scores on AP, CLEP examinations. Work study available nights, weekends and for part-time students.

Payment plans. Credit card, installment, deferred payment.

Application procedures. FAFSA, institutional form required. Priority date 4/15; no closing date. Applicants notified on rolling basis starting 5/1, must reply within 2 week(s) of notification.

Contact. Financial aid office: (307) 855-2150
Jacque Burns, Financial Aid Officer
2660 Peck Avenue
Riverton, WY 82501

Eastern Wyoming College

Torrington, Wyoming
ewc.cc.wy.us
Two-year public **Federal Code: 003929**

College costs. Students from Western Undergraduate Exchange schools and Nebraska residents pay $1,848 tuition per year.

	Living at home	On-campus
Tuition and fees (2002-2003):	$1,736	$1,736
Out-of-state:	$4,184	$4,184
Per-credit charge:	$51	$51
Per-credit out-of-state:	$153	$153
Room and board:		$2,946
Books and supplies:	$675	$675
Personal expenses:	$525	$1,200
Transportation:	$475	$700

Undergraduate aid. Need-based: Need-based aid available for full-time and part-time students. **Non-need-based:** Scholarships based on academics, art, athletics, leadership, music/drama. **Additional information:** Installment payment plan on room and board contracts offered.

Policies to reduce costs. Tuition/fee waivers for children of alumni, senior citizens, employees and their families. Credit/placement for qualifying scores on AP, IB, CLEP examinations. Work study available nights, weekends and for part-time students.

Payment plans. Credit card, installment payment.

Application procedures. FAFSA, institutional form required. Priority date 3/15; no closing date. Applicants notified on rolling basis starting 1/1, must reply within 2 week(s) of notification.

Contact. Financial aid office: (800) 658-3195 ext. 8325
Billy Bates, Dean of Student Services
3200 West C Street
Torrington, WY 82240

Laramie County Community College

Cheyenne, Wyoming
www.lccc.cc.wy.us
Two-year public **Federal Code: 009259**

College costs. Students from Western Undergraduate Exchange schools and Nebraska residents pay $2,268 tuition per year.

	Living at home	On-campus
Tuition and fees (2002-2003):	$1,620	$1,620
Out-of-state:	$4,068	$4,068
Per-credit charge:	$51	$51
Per-credit out-of-state:	$153	$153
Room and board:		$4,192
Books and supplies:	$560	$560
Personal expenses:	$1,500	$1,800
Transportation:	$560	$740

Undergraduate aid. Need-based: Need-based aid available for full-time and part-time students.

Policies to reduce costs. Tuition/fee waivers for senior citizens, employees and their families. Credit/placement for qualifying scores on AP, CLEP examinations.

Payment plans. Credit card, deferred payment.

Application procedures. FAFSA, institutional form required. Priority date 4/1; no closing date. Applicants notified on rolling basis starting 6/1, must reply within 2 week(s) of notification.

Contact. Dennis Schraeder, Director of Financial Aid
1400 East College Drive
Cheyenne, WY 82007

Sheridan College

Sheridan, Wyoming
www.sheridan.edu
Two-year public **Federal Code: 003930**

College costs. Students from Western Undergraduate Exchange schools pay $1,848 tuition per year.

	Living at home	On-campus
Tuition and fees (2002-2003):	$1,584	$1,584
Out-of-state:	$4,032	$4,032
Per-credit charge:	$51	$51
Per-credit out-of-state:	$153	$153
Room and board:		$3,620
Board only:	$1,900	
Books and supplies:	$600	$600
Personal expenses:	$1,000	$1,000
Transportation:	$640	$640

Undergraduate aid. Need-based: Average financial aid package for full-time students was $4,630; for part-time $2,265. 70% awarded as scholarships/grants, 30% as loans/jobs. **Non-need-based:** 67% awarded as scholarships/grants, 33% as loans/jobs. Scholarships based on academics, athletics.

Freshman aid. Need-based: Out of 320 full-time freshmen, 251 applied for aid; 123 were judged to have need; of these 122 received aid. Average package met 52% of need. 16 students had full need met. Average scholarship/grant was $2,373; average loan $1,619. **Non-need based:** 71 full-time freshmen with need received non-need scholarships; 21 without need received awards; 23 received athletic scholarships.

Merit scholarships. Merit scholarships, in-state tuition and fees, for graduating high school students with minimum composite ACT score of 25 or minimum SAT of 1120; renewable.

Policies to reduce costs. Tuition/fee waivers for senior citizens, employees and their families. Credit/placement for qualifying scores on AP, CLEP examinations. Work study available nights, weekends and for part-time students.

Payment plans. Credit card, installment, deferred payment.

Application procedures. FAFSA, institutional form required. Priority date 3/1; no closing date. Applicants notified on rolling basis, must reply within 3 week(s) of notification. **Transfers:** No deadline.

Contact. Financial aid office: (307) 674-6446 ext. 6141
Mike Collins, Director of Finance
PO Box 1500
Sheridan, WY 82801-1500

University of Wyoming

Laramie, Wyoming
www.uwyo.edu
Four-year public **Federal Code: 003932**

College costs. Computer technology fees vary by program ($50 for engineering, $25 for education, $20 for all others).

	Living at home	On-campus
Tuition and fees:	$3,090	$3,090
Out-of-state:	$8,940	$8,940
Room and board:		$5,546
Board only:	$2,063	
Books and supplies:	$1,000	$1,000
Personal expenses:	$1,000	$2,000
Transportation:	$347	$679

Undergraduate aid. Need-based: Average financial aid package for full-time students was $7,467. 43% awarded as scholarships/grants, 57% as loans/jobs. Need-based aid available for part-time students. **Non-need-based:** 63% awarded as scholarships/grants, 37% as loans/jobs. Scholarships based on academics, alumni affiliation, art, athletics, leadership, minority status, music/drama, religious affiliation, state/district residency. **Student debt:** 57% of graduating class borrowed to fund education; average debt was $18,311.

Freshman aid. Need-based: Out of 1,707 full-time freshmen, 1,354 applied for aid; 736 were judged to have need; of these 727 received aid. Average package met 74% of need. 487 students had full need met. Average scholarship/grant was $3,823; average loan $4,194. **Non-need based:** 329 full-time freshmen with need received non-need scholarships; 546 without need received awards; 78 received athletic scholarships.

Merit scholarships. Western Heritage Scholarship; number awarded and packages vary, President's Honor Scholarship; number awarded varies; undergraduate fees and tuition. Numerous other scholarships based on academic achievement.

Policies to reduce costs. Tuition/fee waivers for senior citizens, employees and their families. Credit/placement for qualifying scores on AP, IB, CLEP examinations. Work study available for part-time students.

Payment plans. Credit card, installment payment.

Application procedures. FAFSA required. Priority date 2/1; no closing date. Applicants notified on rolling basis starting 3/15, must reply within 3 week(s) of notification. **Transfers:** Priority date 2/1; no deadline.

Contact. Financial aid office: (307) 766-2116
David Gruen, Director of Student Financial Aid
Knight Hall 146
Laramie, WY 82071

Western Wyoming Community College

Rock Springs, Wyoming
www.wwcc.cc.wy.us
Two-year public **Federal Code: 003933**

College costs. Students from Western Undergraduate Exchange schools and Nebraska residents pay $2,098 tuition per year.

	Living at home	On-campus
Tuition and fees (2002-2003):	$1,474	$1,474
Out-of-state:	$3,920	$3,920
Per-credit charge:	$62	$62
Per-credit out-of-state:	$164	$164
Room and board:		$3,128
Books and supplies:	$500	$500

Undergraduate aid. Need-based: 63% awarded as scholarships/grants, 37% as loans/jobs. Need-based aid available for part-time students. **Non-need-based:** 57% awarded as scholarships/grants, 43% as loans/jobs. Scholarships based on academics, art, athletics, music/drama, state/district residency.

Policies to reduce costs. Tuition/fee waivers for adults, senior citizens, employees and their families. Credit/placement for qualifying scores on AP, IB, CLEP examinations. Work study available for part-time students.

Payment plans. Credit card, installment, deferred payment.

Application procedures. FAFSA, institutional form required. Priority date 4/1; no closing date. Applicants notified on rolling basis starting 5/15, must reply within 2 week(s) of notification.

Contact. Financial aid office: (307) 382-1643
Stacee Hanson, Financial Aid Director
Box 428
Rock Springs, WY 82902

Academic scholarships

Alabama

Alabama State University
Athens State University
Auburn University
Auburn University at Montgomery
Birmingham-Southern College
Bishop State Community College
Calhoun Community College
Central Alabama Community College
Chattahoochee Valley Community College
Enterprise State Junior College
Faulkner University
Gadsden State Community College
George C. Wallace State Community College
  Selma
Harry M. Ayers State Technical College
Huntingdon College
J. F. Drake State Technical College
Jacksonville State University
Jefferson Davis Community College
Jefferson State Community College
Judson College
Lurleen B. Wallace Junior College
Northeast Alabama Community College
Northwest-Shoals Community College
Oakwood College
Samford University
Snead State Community College
Southeastern Bible College
Southern Christian University
Spring Hill College
Stillman College
Talladega College
Troy State University
Troy State University Dothan
Troy State University in Montgomery
Tuskegee University
University of Alabama
University of Alabama
  Birmingham
  Huntsville
University of Mobile
University of Montevallo
University of North Alabama
University of South Alabama
University of West Alabama
Wallace State Community College at Hanceville

Alaska

Alaska Bible College
Alaska Pacific University
University of Alaska
  Anchorage
  Fairbanks

Arizona

Arizona State University
Arizona Western College
Eastern Arizona College
Embry-Riddle Aeronautical University: Prescott Campus
Northern Arizona University
Pima Community College
Prescott College
Scottsdale Community College
South Mountain Community College
Southwestern College
University of Arizona
Yavapai College

Arkansas

Arkansas State University
Arkansas State University
  Beebe
  Mountain Home
Arkansas Tech University
Central Baptist College
Harding University
Henderson State University
Hendrix College
John Brown University
Lyon College
Mid-South Community College
Mississippi County Community College
North Arkansas College
Northwest Arkansas Community College
Ouachita Baptist University
Philander Smith College
Phillips Community College of the University of Arkansas
Rich Mountain Community College
Southeast Arkansas College
Southern Arkansas University
Southern Arkansas University Tech
University of Arkansas
University of Arkansas
  Community College at Batesville
  Community College at Hope
  Fort Smith
  Monticello
  Pine Bluff
University of Central Arkansas
University of the Ozarks
Williams Baptist College

California

Art Institute
  of California - Orange County
  of California: Los Angeles
Azusa Pacific University
Bethany College
Bethesda Christian University
Biola University
California Baptist University
California College of Arts and Crafts
California Institute of Technology
California Institute of the Arts
California Maritime Academy
California Polytechnic State University: San Luis Obispo
California State Polytechnic University: Pomona
California State University
  Chico
  Dominguez Hills
  Fresno
  Fullerton
  Long Beach
  Monterey Bay
  Northridge
  Stanislaus
Chapman University
Christian Heritage College
Claremont McKenna College
College of the Canyons
College of the Siskiyous
Columbia College
Concordia University
Deep Springs College
Dominican University of California
East Los Angeles College
Fashion Institute of Design and Merchandising
Fashion Institute of Design and Merchandising
  San Diego
  San Francisco
Glendale Community College
Golden Gate University
Golden West College
Harvey Mudd College
Holy Names College
Hope International University
Humboldt State University
La Sierra University
Marymount College
Master's College
Menlo College
Mills College
Modesto Junior College
Monterey Institute of International Studies
Mount San Jacinto College
National Hispanic University
Occidental College
Ohlone College
Orange Coast College
Otis College of Art and Design
Patten University
Pepperdine University
Pitzer College
Point Loma Nazarene University
Riverside Community College
St. Mary's College of California
Samuel Merritt College
San Diego State University
San Joaquin Delta College
Santa Clara University
Santa Rosa Junior College
Scripps College
Simpson College
Sonoma State University
Taft College
University of California
  Berkeley
  Irvine
  Los Angeles
  Riverside
  San Diego
  Santa Cruz
University of La Verne
University of Redlands
University of San Diego
University of San Francisco
University of Southern California
University of the Pacific
Vanguard University of Southern California
Westwood College of Technology
  Inland Empire
Whittier College
Woodbury University
Yuba Community College District

Colorado

Arapahoe Community College
Colorado Christian University
Colorado College
Colorado Mountain College
  Alpine Campus
  Spring Valley Campus
  Timberline Campus
Colorado School of Mines
Colorado State University
Colorado State University
  Pueblo
Colorado Technical University
Fort Lewis College
Front Range Community College
Mesa State College
Metropolitan State College of Denver
Morgan Community College
Otero Junior College
Regis University
Remington College
  Colorado Springs
Rocky Mountain College of Art & Design
Trinidad State Junior College
University of Colorado
  Boulder
  Colorado Springs
  Denver
  Health Sciences Center
University of Denver
University of Northern Colorado

Connecticut

Albertus Magnus College
Briarwood College
Central Connecticut State University
Eastern Connecticut State University
Fairfield University
Housatonic Community College
International College of Hospitality Management
Mitchell College
Norwalk Community College
Quinebaug Valley Community College
Quinnipiac University
Sacred Heart University
St. Joseph College
Southern Connecticut State University
Trinity College
Tunxis Community College
University of Bridgeport
University of Connecticut
University of Hartford
University of New Haven
Western Connecticut State University

Delaware

Delaware State University
Delaware Technical and Community College
  Owens Campus
  Stanton/Wilmington Campus
University of Delaware
Wilmington College

District of Columbia

American University
Catholic University of America
Corcoran College of Art and Design
Gallaudet University
George Washington University
Trinity College

Florida

Art Institute of Fort Lauderdale
Baptist College of Florida
Barry University
Bethune-Cookman College
Broward Community College
Carlos Albizu University
Chipola Junior College
Eckerd College
Edward Waters College
Embry-Riddle Aeronautical University
Flagler College
Florida Agricultural and Mechanical University
Florida Atlantic University
Florida College
Florida Gulf Coast University
Florida Institute of Technology
Florida International University
Florida Keys Community College
Florida Metropolitan University
  Melbourne Campus
Florida Southern College
Florida State University
Gulf Coast Community College
Hobe Sound Bible College
Indian River Community College
International Academy of Design and Technology
International College
Jacksonville University
Jones College
Lake City Community College
Lake-Sumter Community College
Manatee Community College
Miami-Dade Community College
New College of Florida
Northwood University
  Florida Campus
Nova Southeastern University
Okaloosa-Walton Community College
Palm Beach Atlantic University
Palm Beach Community College
Pasco-Hernando Community College
Pensacola Junior College
Polk Community College

Rollins College
St. Leo University
St. Petersburg College
St. Thomas University
Santa Fe Community College
Schiller International University
Seminole Community College
South Florida Community College
Southeastern College of the Assemblies of God
Stetson University
Tallahassee Community College
University of Central Florida
University of Florida
University of Miami
University of North Florida
University of South Florida
University of Tampa
University of West Florida
Warner Southern College
Webber International University

Georgia

Agnes Scott College
Albany State University
Andrew College
Armstrong Atlantic State University of Atlanta
Atlanta College of Art
Augusta State University
Berry College
Brenau University
Brewton-Parker College
Clark Atlanta University
Clayton College and State University
Columbus State University
Covenant College
Dalton State College
Darton College
DeKalb Technical College
East Georgia College
Emmanuel College
Emory University
Floyd College
Fort Valley State University
Georgia College and State University
Georgia Institute of Technology
Georgia Southern University
Georgia Southwestern State University
Georgia State University
Herzing College
Kennesaw State University
LaGrange College
Macon State College
Medical College of Georgia
Mercer University
Middle Georgia College
Morehouse College
Morris Brown College
North Georgia College & State University
Oglethorpe University
Oxford College of Emory University
Paine College
Piedmont College
Reinhardt College
Savannah College of Art and Design
Savannah State University
Savannah Technical College
Shorter College
South Georgia College
Southern Polytechnic State University
Spelman College
State University of West Georgia
Thomas University
Toccoa Falls College
Truett-McConnell College
University of Georgia
Valdosta State University
Waycross College
Wesleyan College
West Georgia Technical College
Young Harris College

Hawaii

Brigham Young University-Hawaii
Chaminade University of Honolulu
Hawaii Pacific University
University of Hawaii
- Honolulu Community College
- Manoa
- West Oahu

Idaho

Albertson College of Idaho
Boise Bible College
Boise State University
Brigham Young University - Idaho
Eastern Idaho Technical College
Idaho State University
Lewis-Clark State College
North Idaho College
Northwest Nazarene University
University of Idaho

Illinois

Augustana College
Aurora University
Benedictine University
Black Hawk College
Blackburn College
Bradley University
Carl Sandburg College
Chicago State University
City Colleges of Chicago
- Kennedy-King College
- Malcolm X College

College of DuPage
College of Lake County
Columbia College Chicago
Concordia University
Danville Area Community College
De Paul University
Dominican University
East-West University
Eastern Illinois University
Elgin Community College
Elmhurst College
Eureka College
Governors State University
Greenville College
Harrington Institute of Interior Design
Highland Community College
Illinois College
Illinois Eastern Community Colleges
- Frontier Community College
- Lincoln Trail College
- Olney Central College
- Wabash Valley College

Illinois Institute of Technology
Illinois State University
Illinois Wesleyan University
Joliet Junior College
Judson College
Kaskaskia College
Kendall College
Kishwaukee College
Knox College
Lake Forest College
Lake Land College
Lewis University
Lexington College
Lincoln College
Lincoln Land Community College
Loyola University of Chicago
MacMurray College
McHenry County College
McKendree College
Millikin University
Monmouth College
Moody Bible Institute
Moraine Valley Community College
Morrison Institute of Technology
National-Louis University
North Central College
North Park University
Northeastern Illinois University
Northern Illinois University
Northwestern Business College
Oakton Community College
Olivet Nazarene University
Parkland College
Principia College
Quincy University
Rend Lake College
Richland Community College
Robert Morris College: Chicago
Rock Valley College
Rockford College
Roosevelt University
St. Francis Medical Center College of Nursing
St. Xavier University
Sauk Valley Community College
School of the Art Institute of Chicago
South Suburban College of Cook County
Southeastern Illinois College
Southern Illinois University Carbondale
Southwestern Illinois College
Spoon River College
Springfield College in Illinois
Trinity Christian College
Trinity International University
Triton College
University of Chicago
University of Illinois
- Chicago
- Springfield
- Urbana-Champaign

University of St. Francis
VanderCook College of Music
Waubonsee Community College
Western Illinois University
Wheaton College
William Rainey Harper College

Indiana

Ancilla College
Anderson University
Ball State University
Bethel College
Butler University
Calumet College of St. Joseph
DePauw University
Earlham College
Franklin College
Goshen College
Grace College
Hanover College
Huntington College
Indiana Institute of Technology
Indiana State University
Indiana University
- Bloomington
- East
- Kokomo
- Northwest
- South Bend
- Southeast

Indiana University-Purdue University Fort Wayne
Indiana University-Purdue University Indianapolis
Indiana Wesleyan University
Manchester College
Marian College
Oakland City University
Purdue University
Purdue University
- Calumet
- North Central Campus

Rose-Hulman Institute of Technology
St. Joseph's College
Saint Mary's College
St. Mary-of-the-Woods College
Taylor University
Taylor University: Fort Wayne
Tri-State University
University of Evansville
University of Indianapolis
University of St. Francis
University of Southern Indiana
Valparaiso University
Vincennes University
Wabash College

Iowa

Allen College
American Institute of Business
Briar Cliff University
Buena Vista University
Central College
Clarke College
Coe College
Cornell College
Des Moines Area Community College
Dordt College
Drake University
Ellsworth Community College
Emmaus Bible College
Faith Baptist Bible College and Theological Seminary
Franciscan University
Graceland University
Grand View College
Grinnell College
Hamilton College
- Cedar Rapids
- Mason City

Hawkeye Community College
Iowa State University
Iowa Wesleyan College
Kaplan College
Loras College
Luther College
Maharishi University of Management
Mercy College of Health Sciences
Morningside College
Mount Mercy College
North Iowa Area Community College
Northeast Iowa Community College
Northwestern College
St. Ambrose University
St. Luke's College
Simpson College
Southeastern Community College
- North Campus

University of Dubuque
University of Iowa
University of Northern Iowa
Upper Iowa University
Vatterott College
Waldorf College
Wartburg College
Western Iowa Tech Community College
William Penn University

Kansas

Allen County Community College
Baker University
Barclay College
Barton County Community College
Benedictine College
Bethany College
Bethel College
Butler County Community College
Central Christian College
Dodge City Community College
Donnelly College
Emporia State University
Garden City Community College
Hesston College
Highland Community College
Hutchinson Community College
Independence Community College
Johnson County Community College
Kansas City Kansas Community College
Kansas State University
Kansas Wesleyan University
Labette Community College
McPherson College
MidAmerica Nazarene University
Newman University
North Central Kansas Technical College
Ottawa University
Pratt Community College
St. Mary College

Seward County Community College
Southwestern College
Sterling College
Tabor College
University of Kansas
University of Kansas Medical Center
Washburn University of Topeka
Wichita State University

Kentucky
Asbury College
Beckfield College
Bellarmine University
Brescia University
Centre College
Clear Creek Baptist Bible College
Cumberland College
Daymar College
Georgetown College
Hopkinsville Community College
Jefferson Community College
Kentucky Christian College
Kentucky Mountain Bible College
Lexington Community College
Maysville Community College
Mid-Continent College
Morehead State University
Murray State University
National College of Business & Technology
- Danville
- Florence
- Lexington
- Pikeville
- Richmond

Pikeville College
Prestonsburg Community College
St. Catharine College
Southeast Community College
Spalding University
Spencerian College: Lexington
Thomas More College
Transylvania University
Union College
University of Kentucky
University of Louisville

Louisiana
Centenary College of Louisiana
Delgado Community College
Dillard University
Louisiana College
Louisiana State University
- Alexandria

Louisiana State University and Agricultural and Mechanical College
Loyola University New Orleans
McNeese State University
Nicholls State University
Northwestern State University
Our Lady of Holy Cross College
- Baton Rouge

St. Joseph Seminary College
Southeastern Louisiana University
Southern University and Agricultural and Mechanical College
Tulane University
University of Louisiana at Monroe
University of New Orleans
Xavier University of Louisiana

Maine
Bowdoin College
College of the Atlantic
Husson College
Maine College of Art
New England School of Communications
St. Joseph's College
Thomas College
University of Maine
University of Maine
- Augusta
- Farmington
- Fort Kent
- Machias
- Presque Isle

University of New England
University of Southern Maine

Maryland
Allegany College
Baltimore Hebrew University
Baltimore International College
Bowie State University
Capitol College
Carroll Community College
Cecil Community College
Chesapeake College
College of Notre Dame of Maryland
College of Southern Maryland
Columbia Union College
Community College of Baltimore County
- Essex

Coppin State College
Frederick Community College
Frostburg State University
Goucher College
Hood College
Johns Hopkins University
Johns Hopkins University: Peabody Conservatory of Music
Loyola College in Maryland
Maryland Institute College of Art
McDaniel College
Montgomery College
- Rockville Campus

Mount St. Mary's College
St. Mary's College of Maryland
Salisbury University
Towson University
University of Maryland
- Baltimore County
- College Park
- University College

Villa Julie College
Washington Bible College
Washington College
Wor-Wic Community College

Massachusetts
Ai The New England Institute of Art and Design
American International College
Anna Maria College
Art Institute of Boston at Lesley University
Assumption College
Atlantic Union College
Babson College
Bay Path College
Becker College
Benjamin Franklin Institute of Technology
Bentley College
Berklee College of Music
Berkshire Community College
Boston College
Boston University
Brandeis University
Bridgewater State College
Cape Cod Community College
Clark University
College of the Holy Cross
Dean College
Elms College
Emerson College
Emmanuel College
Endicott College
Fisher College
Fitchburg State College
Framingham State College
Gordon College
Hampshire College
Hellenic College/Holy Cross
Laboure College
Lasell College
Lesley University
Marian Court College
Massachusetts College of Art
Massachusetts College of Liberal Arts
Massachusetts College of Pharmacy and Health Sciences
Massachusetts Maritime Academy
Merrimack College
Mount Holyoke College
New England Conservatory of Music
Newbury College
Nichols College
Northeastern University
Pine Manor College
Regis College
Salem State College
Simmons College
Simon's Rock College of Bard
Smith College
Stonehill College
Suffolk University
Tufts University
University of Massachusetts
- Amherst
- Boston
- Dartmouth
- Lowell

Wentworth Institute of Technology
Western New England College
Westfield State College
Wheaton College
Worcester Polytechnic Institute

Michigan
Adrian College
Alma College
Alpena Community College
Andrews University
Aquinas College
Baker College
- of Auburn Hills
- of Cadillac
- of Clinton Township
- of Jackson
- of Muskegon
- of Owosso
- of Port Huron

Bay de Noc Community College
Calvin College
Central Michigan University
Cleary University
College for Creative Studies
Concordia University
Cornerstone University
Davenport University
- Eastern Region
- Midland

Davenport University - Western Region
Eastern Michigan University
Ferris State University
Finlandia University
Glen Oaks Community College
Gogebic Community College
Grace Bible College
Grand Rapids Community College
Grand Valley State University
Hillsdale College
Hope College
Jackson Community College
Kalamazoo College
Kellogg Community College
Kettering University
Lansing Community College
Lawrence Technological University
Macomb Community College
Madonna University
Marygrove College
Michigan State University
Michigan Technological University
Mid Michigan Community College
Monroe County Community College
Montcalm Community College
Mott Community College
Northern Michigan University
Northwestern Michigan College
Northwood University
Oakland Community College
Oakland University
Reformed Bible College
Saginaw Valley State University
Schoolcraft College
Siena Heights University
Southwestern Michigan College
Spring Arbor University
University of Michigan
University of Michigan
- Dearborn
- Flint

Walsh College of Accountancy and Business Administration
Washtenaw Community College
Wayne State University
Western Michigan University
William Tyndale College

Minnesota
Augsburg College
Bemidji State University
Bethany Lutheran College
Bethel College
Brown College
Carleton College
College of St. Benedict
College of St. Catherine
College of St. Scholastica
College of Visual Arts
Concordia College: Moorhead
Concordia University: St. Paul
Crossroads College
Crown College
Fergus Falls Community College
Gustavus Adolphus College
Hamline University
Itasca Community College
Macalester College
Martin Luther College
Metropolitan State University
Minnesota State College - Southeast Technical
Minnesota State University
- Mankato
- Moorhead

National American University
- St. Paul

North Central University
North Hennepin Community College
Northland Community & Technical College
Northwestern College
Oak Hills Christian College
Pine Technical College
Rainy River Community College
Rasmussen College
- Mankato
- St. Cloud

St. Cloud Technical College
St. John's University
St. Mary's University of Minnesota
St. Olaf College
Southwest State University
University of Minnesota
- Crookston
- Duluth
- Morris
- Twin Cities

University of St. Thomas
Vermilion Community College
Winona State University

Mississippi
Alcorn State University
Blue Mountain College
Coahoma Community College
Delta State University
Holmes Community College
Itawamba Community College
Magnolia Bible College
Millsaps College

Mississippi College
Mississippi Gulf Coast Community College
Perkinston
Mississippi State University
Mississippi University for Women
Mississippi Valley State University
Pearl River Community College
Rust College
University of Mississippi
University of Mississippi Medical Center

Missouri

Avila University
Blue River Community College
Calvary Bible College
Central Methodist College
Central Missouri State University
Columbia College
Conception Seminary College
Cottey College
Crowder College
Culver-Stockton College
Deaconess College of Nursing
Drury University
East Central College
Evangel University
Fontbonne College
Hannibal-LaGrange College
Harris Stowe State College
Jefferson College
Kansas City Art Institute
Lincoln University
Lindenwood University
Longview Community College
Maple Woods Community College
Maryville University of Saint Louis
Mineral Area College
Missouri Baptist University
Missouri Southern State College
Missouri Valley College
Missouri Western State College
Moberly Area Community College
North Central Missouri College
Northwest Missouri State University
Ozark Christian College
Penn Valley Community College
Rockhurst University
St. Charles Community College
St. Louis Christian College
St. Louis College of Pharmacy
St. Louis University
Southeast Missouri State University
Southwest Baptist University
Southwest Missouri State University
St. Louis Community College
Forest Park
Stephens College
Three Rivers Community College
Truman State University
University of Missouri
Columbia
Kansas City
Rolla
St. Louis
Washington University in St. Louis
Webster University
Westminster College
William Jewell College
William Woods University

Montana

Carroll College
Dawson Community College
Flathead Valley Community College
Miles Community College
Montana State University
Billings
Bozeman
Montana Tech of the University of Montana
Rocky Mountain College
University of Great Falls
University of Montana-Missoula
University of Montana: Western

Nebraska

Bellevue University
Central Community College
Chadron State College
Clarkson College
College of Saint Mary
Concordia University
Creative Center
Creighton University
Dana College
Doane College
Grace University
Hastings College
Metropolitan Community College
Mid Plains Community College Area
Midland Lutheran College
Nebraska Christian College
Nebraska Methodist College of Nursing and Allied Health
Nebraska Wesleyan University
Northeast Community College
Peru State College
Southeast Community College
Beatrice Campus
Lincoln Campus
Milford Campus
Union College
University of Nebraska
Kearney
Lincoln
Omaha
Vatterott College
Wayne State College
Western Nebraska Community College
York College

Nevada

Sierra Nevada College
Truckee Meadows Community College
University of Nevada
Las Vegas
Reno
Western Nevada Community College

New Hampshire

Chester College of New England
Colby-Sawyer College
Daniel Webster College
Franklin Pierce College
Hesser College
Keene State College
New England College
Plymouth State College
Rivier College
St. Anselm College
Southern New Hampshire University
Thomas More College of Liberal Arts
University of New Hampshire
University of New Hampshire at Manchester

New Jersey

Berkeley College
Bloomfield College
Burlington County College
Caldwell College
Centenary College
The College of New Jersey
College of St. Elizabeth
Cumberland County College
Drew University
Felician College
Georgian Court College
Kean University
Mercer County Community College
Monmouth University
Montclair State University
New Jersey Institute of Technology
Ocean County College
Passaic County Community College
Ramapo College of New Jersey
Richard Stockton College of New Jersey
Rider University
Rowan University
Rutgers, The State University of New Jersey
Camden Regional Campus
New Brunswick Regional Campus
Newark Regional Campus
St. Peter's College
Salem Community College
Seton Hall University
Somerset Christian College
Stevens Institute of Technology
Union County College
Warren County Community College
William Paterson University of New Jersey

New Mexico

Albuquerque Technical-Vocational Institute
College of Santa Fe
College of the Southwest
Eastern New Mexico University
New Mexico Highlands University
New Mexico Institute of Mining and Technology
New Mexico Military Institute
New Mexico State University
Alamogordo
St. John's College
San Juan College
Southwestern Indian Polytechnic Institute
University of New Mexico
Western New Mexico University

New York

Adelphi University
Adirondack Community College
Albany College of Pharmacy
Alfred University
Bard College
Berkeley College
Berkeley College of New York City
Briarcliffe College
Bryant & Stratton Business Institute
Albany
Syracuse
Canisius College
Cayuga County Community College
Cazenovia College
City University of New York
Baruch College
Brooklyn College
City College
College of Staten Island
Hunter College
John Jay College of Criminal Justice
Queens College
Clarkson University
College of Aeronautics
College of Mount St. Vincent
College of New Rochelle
Concordia College
Cooper Union for the Advancement of Science and Art
Culinary Institute of America
D'Youville College
Daemen College
Dominican College of Blauvelt
Dowling College
Eastman School of Music of the University of Rochester
Elmira College
Eugene Lang College/New School University
Finger Lakes Community College
Fordham University
Fulton-Montgomery Community College
Hamilton College
Hartwick College
Hilbert College
Hobart and William Smith Colleges
Hofstra University
Houghton College
Iona College
Ithaca College
Jamestown Business College
Jamestown Community College
Jefferson Community College
Keuka College
Laboratory Institute of Merchandising
Le Moyne College
Long Island University
C. W. Post Campus
Southampton College
Manhattan College
Manhattan School of Music
Manhattanville College
Mannes College of Music
Marist College
Marymount College of Fordham University
Marymount Manhattan College
Medaille College
Metropolitan College of New York
Molloy College
Monroe College
Mount St. Mary College
Nassau Community College
Nazareth College of Rochester
New York Institute of Technology
New York University
Niagara County Community College
Niagara University
Nyack College
Onondaga Community College
Pace University
Pace University: Pleasantville/Briarcliff
Parsons School of Design
Paul Smith's College
Phillips Beth Israel School of Nursing
Polytechnic University
Pratt Institute
Rensselaer Polytechnic Institute
Roberts Wesleyan College
Rochester Institute of Technology
Russell Sage College
Sage College of Albany
St. Bonaventure University
St. John Fisher College
St. John's University
St. Joseph's College
St. Joseph's College: Suffolk Campus
St. Lawrence University
Schenectady County Community College
School of Visual Arts
State University of New York
Albany
Binghamton
Buffalo
College at Brockport
College at Buffalo
College at Cortland
College at Fredonia
College at Geneseo
College at Old Westbury
College at Oneonta
College at Plattsburgh
College at Potsdam
College of Agriculture and Technology at Cobleskill
College of Agriculture and Technology at Morrisville
College of Environmental Science and Forestry
Farmingdale
Institute of Technology at Utica/Rome
Maritime College
New Paltz
Oswego
Purchase
Stony Brook
Suffolk County Community College

Syracuse University
Tompkins-Cortland Community College
Trocaire College
Union College
University of Rochester
Utica College
Villa Maria College of Buffalo
Wagner College
Webb Institute
Wells College
Westchester Business Institute
Westchester Community College

North Carolina

Alamance Community College
Appalachian State University
Asheville Buncombe Technical Community College
Barton College
Beaufort County Community College
Belmont Abbey College
Blue Ridge Community College
Brevard College
Brunswick Community College
Campbell University
Cape Fear Community College
Carteret Community College
Catawba College
Catawba Valley Community College
Central Carolina Community College
Chowan College
Coastal Carolina Community College
College of the Albemarle
Davidson College
Davidson County Community College
Duke University
Durham Technical Community College
East Carolina University
Edgecombe Community College
Elizabeth City State University
Elon University
Forsyth Technical Community College
Gardner-Webb University
Gaston College
Greensboro College
Guilford College
Haywood Community College
High Point University
Isothermal Community College
James Sprunt Community College
Johnson C. Smith University
Johnston Community College
Lees-McRae College
Lenoir Community College
Lenoir-Rhyne College
Livingstone College
Mars Hill College
Martin Community College
Meredith College
Methodist College
Montgomery Community College
Montreat College
Mount Olive College
Nash Community College
North Carolina Agricultural and Technical State University
North Carolina Central University
North Carolina School of the Arts
North Carolina State University
North Carolina Wesleyan College
Peace College
Pfeiffer University
Queens University of Charlotte
Randolph Community College
Richmond Community College
Roanoke Bible College
Roanoke-Chowan Community College
Rockingham Community College
Rowan-Cabarrus Community College
St. Andrews Presbyterian College
St. Augustine's College
Salem College
Sampson Community College
Sandhills Community College
Shaw University
Southeastern Community College
Stanly Community College
Surry Community College
University of North Carolina
  Asheville
  Chapel Hill
  Charlotte
  Greensboro
  Pembroke
  Wilmington
Vance-Granville Community College
Wake Forest University
Wake Technical Community College
Warren Wilson College
Wayne Community College
Western Carolina University
Wilson Technical Community College
Wingate University
Winston-Salem State University

North Dakota

Bismarck State College
Dickinson State University
Jamestown College
Lake Region State College
Mayville State University
Minot State University
Minot State University: Bottineau Campus
North Dakota State College of Science
North Dakota State University
Trinity Bible College
University of Mary
University of North Dakota
Valley City State University
Williston State College

Ohio

Academy of Court Reporting
  Akron
Antioch College
Art Academy of Cincinnati
Ashland University
Baldwin-Wallace College
Bluffton College
Bowling Green State University
Bowling Green State University: Firelands College
Bryant & Stratton College
Bryant & Stratton College
  Willoughby Hills
Capital University
Case Western Reserve University
Cedarville University
Central Ohio Technical College
Central State University
Chatfield College
Cincinnati State Technical and Community College
Circleville Bible College
Cleveland Institute of Art
Cleveland State University
College of Mount St. Joseph
College of Wooster
Columbus College of Art and Design
Cuyahoga Community College
  Eastern Campus
  Metropolitan Campus
  Western Campus
David N. Myers College
Defiance College
Denison University
Edison State Community College
Franciscan University of Steubenville
Franklin University
Heidelberg College
Hiram College
Hocking Technical College
James A. Rhodes State College
Jefferson Community College
John Carroll University
Kent State University
Kent State University
  Stark Campus
  Tuscarawas Campus
Kenyon College
Kettering College of Medical Arts
Lake Erie College
Lakeland Community College
Lorain County Community College
Lourdes College
Malone College
Marietta College
Marion Technical College
Miami University
  Hamilton Campus
  Oxford Campus
Mount Union College
Mount Vernon Nazarene University
Muskingum College
Northwest State Community College
Notre Dame College
Oberlin College
Ohio Dominican College
Ohio Northern University
Ohio State University
  Columbus Campus
  Lima Campus
Ohio University
Ohio University
  Eastern Campus
Ohio Wesleyan University
Otterbein College
Owens Community College
  Findlay Campus
  Toledo
Pontifical College Josephinum
Shawnee State University
Sinclair Community College
Southern State Community College
Tiffin University
Union Institute & University
University of Akron
University of Cincinnati
  Clermont College
University of Dayton
University of Findlay
University of Northwestern Ohio
University of Rio Grande
University of Toledo
Urbana University
Ursuline College
Walsh University
Wilmington College
Wittenberg University
Wright State University: Lake Campus
Xavier University
Youngstown State University

Oklahoma

Bacone College
Cameron University
Carl Albert State College
East Central University
Langston University
Northeastern Oklahoma Agricultural and Mechanical College
Northeastern State University
Northwestern Oklahoma State University
Oklahoma Baptist University
Oklahoma Christian University
Oklahoma City Community College
Oklahoma City University
Oklahoma Panhandle State University
Oklahoma State University
Oklahoma State University
  Oklahoma City
Oral Roberts University
Redlands Community College
Rose State College
St. Gregory's University
Seminole State College
Southeastern Oklahoma State University
Southern Nazarene University
Southwestern Christian University
Southwestern Oklahoma State University
Tulsa Community College
University of Central Oklahoma
University of Oklahoma
University of Science and Arts of Oklahoma
University of Tulsa
Western Oklahoma State College

Oregon

Central Oregon Community College
Chemeketa Community College
Clackamas Community College
Clatsop Community College
Concordia University
Eastern Oregon University
Eugene Bible College
George Fox University
Lewis & Clark College
Linfield College
Linn-Benton Community College
Marylhurst University
Mount Hood Community College
Multnomah Bible College
Northwest Christian College
Oregon Institute of Technology
Oregon State University
Pacific Northwest College of Art
Pacific University
Portland State University
Southern Oregon University
Umpqua Community College
University of Oregon
University of Portland
Warner Pacific College
Western Baptist College
Western Oregon University
Willamette University

Pennsylvania

Albright College
Allegheny College
Arcadia University
Baptist Bible College of Pennsylvania
Bloomsburg University of Pennsylvania
Bucks County Community College
California University of Pennsylvania
Cambria County Area Community College
Cambria-Rowe Business College
Carlow College
Carnegie Mellon University
Cedar Crest College
Central Pennsylvania College
Chatham College
Chestnut Hill College
Cheyney University of Pennsylvania
Community College of Allegheny County
Community College of Beaver County
Delaware Valley College
DeSales University
Dickinson College
Drexel University
Duquesne University
East Stroudsburg University of Pennsylvania
Edinboro University of Pennsylvania
Elizabethtown College
Franklin & Marshall College
Geneva College
Gettysburg College
Grove City College
Gwynedd-Mercy College
Harrisburg Area Community College
Holy Family University
Immaculata University
Indiana University of Pennsylvania
Juniata College
Keystone College
King's College
Kutztown University of Pennsylvania
La Roche College
La Salle University
Lackawanna College
Lafayette College
Lancaster Bible College

Lebanon Valley College of Pennsylvania
Lehigh Carbon Community College
Lehigh University
Lincoln University
Lock Haven University of Pennsylvania
Lycoming College
Manor College
Marywood University
Median School of Allied Health Careers
Mercyhurst College
Messiah College
Millersville University of Pennsylvania
Montgomery County Community College
Moravian College
Mount Aloysius College
Muhlenberg College
Newport Business Institute
Northampton County Area Community College
Peirce College
Penn State
- Abington
- Altoona
- Beaver
- Berks
- Delaware County
- Dubois
- Erie, The Behrend College
- Fayette
- Harrisburg
- Hazleton
- Lehigh Valley
- McKeesport
- Mont Alto
- New Kensington
- Schuylkill - Capital College
- Shenango
- University Park
- Wilkes-Barre
- Worthington Scranton
- York

Pennsylvania College of Technology
Pennsylvania Institute of Technology
Philadelphia Biblical University
Philadelphia University
Point Park College
Robert Morris University
Rosemont College
St. Vincent College
Seton Hill University
Shippensburg University of Pennsylvania
Slippery Rock University of Pennsylvania
Swarthmore College
Temple University
Thiel College
University of Pittsburgh
University of Pittsburgh
- Bradford
- Greensburg
- Johnstown
- Titusville

University of Scranton
University of the Sciences in Philadelphia
Valley Forge Christian College
Villanova University
Washington and Jefferson College
Waynesburg College
West Chester University of Pennsylvania
Westmoreland County Community College
Widener University
Wilkes University
Wilson College
York College of Pennsylvania

Puerto Rico

Inter American University of Puerto Rico
- Bayamon Campus
- San German Campus

Pontifical Catholic University of Puerto Rico
Turabo University
Universidad del Este
Universidad Metropolitana
Universidad Politecnica de Puerto Rico
University of Puerto Rico
- Bayamon University College
- Cayey University College
- Humacao
- Mayaguez Campus
- Utuado

University of the Sacred Heart

Rhode Island

Bryant College
Johnson & Wales University
Providence College
Rhode Island College
Roger Williams University
Salve Regina University
University of Rhode Island

South Carolina

Aiken Technical College
Anderson College
Charleston Southern University
The Citadel
Clemson University
Coastal Carolina University
Coker College
College of Charleston
Columbia College
Columbia International University
Converse College
Erskine College
Florence-Darlington Technical College
Francis Marion University
Furman University
Lander University
Limestone College
Medical University of South Carolina
Morris College
Newberry College
North Greenville College
Piedmont Technical College
Presbyterian College
South Carolina State University
Southern Wesleyan University
Spartanburg Methodist College
Tri-County Technical College
University of South Carolina
University of South Carolina
- Salkehatchie Regional Campus
- Spartanburg
- Union

Williamsburg Technical College
Winthrop University
Wofford College

South Dakota

Augustana College
Black Hills State University
Dakota State University
Dakota Wesleyan University
Kilian Community College
Mount Marty College
Northern State University
South Dakota School of Mines and Technology
South Dakota State University
Southeast Technical Institute
University of Sioux Falls
University of South Dakota

Tennessee

Aquinas College
Austin Peay State University
Belmont University
Bethel College
Bryan College
Carson-Newman College
Christian Brothers University
Columbia State Community College
Crichton College
Dyersburg State Community College
East Tennessee State University
Fisk University
Freed-Hardeman University
Jackson State Community College
Johnson Bible College
King College
Lambuth University
Lane College
Lee University
Lipscomb University
Maryville College
Memphis College of Art
Middle Tennessee State University
Milligan College
- Tennessee

Northeast State Technical Community College
O'More College of Design
Pellissippi State Technical Community College
Rhodes College
Roane State Community College
Southern Adventist University
Southwest Tennessee Community College
Tennessee State University
Tennessee Technological University
Tennessee Wesleyan College
Trevecca Nazarene University
Tusculum College
Union University
University of Tennessee
- Chattanooga
- Knoxville
- Martin

University of the South
Vanderbilt University
Volunteer State Community College
Walters State Community College

Texas

Abilene Christian University
Alvin Community College
Amarillo College
Angelina College
Angelo State University
Austin College
Austin Graduate School of Theology
Baylor University
Brazosport College
Central Texas College
Clarendon College
Coastal Bend College
College of the Mainland
Commonwealth Institute of Funeral Service
Concordia University at Austin
Dallas Baptist University
East Texas Baptist University
El Paso Community College
Frank Phillips College
Galveston College
Hardin-Simmons University
Hill College
Houston Baptist University
Howard College
Howard Payne University
Huston-Tillotson College
Jacksonville College
Jarvis Christian College
Kilgore College
Lee College
LeTourneau University
Lon Morris College
Lubbock Christian University
McMurry University
Midland College
Mountain View College
North Central Texas College
North Harris Montgomery Community College District
Northeast Texas Community College
Northwest Vista College
Northwood University: Texas Campus
Our Lady of the Lake University of San Antonio
Palo Alto College
Panola College
Paul Quinn College
Prairie View A&M University
Rice University
St. Edward's University
St. Mary's University
St. Philip's College
Sam Houston State University
Schreiner University
South Plains College
Southern Methodist University
Southwest Texas State University
Southwestern Adventist University
Southwestern University
Stephen F. Austin State University
Sul Ross State University
Tarrant County College
Texarkana College
Texas A&M International University
Texas A&M University
Texas A&M University
- Baylor College of Dentistry
- Corpus Christi
- Galveston
- Kingsville
- Texarkana

Texas Christian University
Texas Lutheran University
Texas Southern University
Texas State Technical College
- Waco
- West Texas

Texas Tech University
Texas Wesleyan University
Trinity University
Trinity Valley Community College
Tyler Junior College
University of Dallas
University of Houston
- Downtown
- Victoria

University of Mary Hardin-Baylor
University of North Texas
University of St. Thomas
University of Texas
- Arlington
- Austin
- Dallas
- El Paso
- Medical Branch at Galveston
- of the Permian Basin
- San Antonio
- Tyler

University of the Incarnate Word
Wayland Baptist University
West Texas A&M University
Western Technical Institute
Western Texas College
Wharton County Junior College

Utah

Brigham Young University
College of Eastern Utah
Dixie State College of Utah
LDS Business College
Salt Lake Community College
Snow College
Southern Utah University
University of Utah
Utah State University
Utah Valley State College
Westminster College

Vermont

Bennington College
Castleton State College

Champlain College
College of St. Joseph in Vermont
Goddard College
Green Mountain College
Johnson State College
Lyndon State College
Marlboro College
Norwich University
St. Michael's College
Southern Vermont College
Sterling College
University of Vermont
Vermont Technical College

Virginia

Averett University
Blue Ridge Community College
Bluefield College
Bridgewater College
Christendom College
College of Health Sciences
College of William and Mary
Eastern Mennonite University
Emory & Henry College
Ferrum College
George Mason University
Hampden-Sydney College
Hampton University
Hollins University
J. Sargeant Reynolds Community College
James Madison University
Liberty University
Longwood University
Lynchburg College
Mary Baldwin College
Mary Washington College
Marymount University
Mountain Empire Community College
- Bluefield
- Charlottesville
- Danville
- Harrisonburg
- Lynchburg
- Martinsville
- Roanoke

Norfolk State University
Old Dominion University
Piedmont Virginia Community College
Radford University
Randolph-Macon College
Randolph-Macon Woman's College
Richard Bland College
Roanoke College
Shenandoah University
Southside Virginia Community College
Southwest Virginia Community College
Sweet Briar College
University of Richmond
University of Virginia
University of Virginia's College at Wise
Virginia Commonwealth University
Virginia Intermont College
Virginia Military Institute
Virginia State University
Virginia Union University
Virginia Wesleyan College
Virginia Western Community College
Washington and Lee University

Washington

Art Institute of Seattle
Bellevue Community College
Central Washington University
Centralia College
Clark College
Cornish College of the Arts
Eastern Washington University
Everett Community College
Evergreen State College
Gonzaga University
Grays Harbor College
Henry Cogswell College
Heritage College
Northwest College
Olympic College
Pacific Lutheran University
Peninsula College
St. Martin's College
Seattle Pacific University
Seattle University
South Seattle Community College
Trinity Lutheran College
University of Puget Sound
University of Washington
Walla Walla College
Walla Walla Community College
Washington State University
Wenatchee Valley College
Western Washington University
Whitman College
Whitworth College

West Virginia

Alderson-Broaddus College
Bethany College
Bluefield State College
Concord College
Corinthian Schools: National Institute of Technology
Davis and Elkins College
Fairmont State College
Glenville State College
International Academy of Design and Technology
Marshall University
Mountain State University
Ohio Valley College
Potomac State College of West Virginia University
Salem International University
Shepherd College
University of Charleston
West Liberty State College
West Virginia State College
West Virginia University
West Virginia University at Parkersburg
West Virginia Wesleyan College
Wheeling Jesuit University

Wisconsin

Alverno College
Bellin College of Nursing
Beloit College
Cardinal Stritch University
Carroll College
Carthage College
Columbia College of Nursing
Concordia University Wisconsin
Edgewood College
Lakeland College
Lakeshore Technical College
Lawrence University
Maranatha Baptist Bible College
Marian College of Fond du Lac
Marquette University
Mid-State Technical College
Milwaukee Institute of Art & Design
Milwaukee School of Engineering
Moraine Park Technical College
Mount Mary College
Northland College
Ripon College
St. Norbert College
Silver Lake College
University of Wisconsin
- Baraboo/Sauk County
- Eau Claire
- Green Bay
- La Crosse
- Madison
- Oshkosh
- Parkside
- Richland
- River Falls
- Stevens Point
- Stout
- Superior
- Washington County
- Waukesha
- Whitewater

Viterbo University
Waukesha County Technical College
Wisconsin Lutheran College

Wyoming

Casper College
Central Wyoming College
Eastern Wyoming College
Sheridan College
University of Wyoming
Western Wyoming Community College

Art scholarships

Alabama
Athens State University
Auburn University at Montgomery
Birmingham-Southern College
Chattahoochee Valley Community College
Enterprise State Junior College
Huntingdon College
Jacksonville State University
Jefferson State Community College
Judson College
Lurleen B. Wallace Junior College
Northeast Alabama Community College
Northwest-Shoals Community College
Snead State Community College
University of Alabama
University of Alabama
Birmingham
Huntsville
University of Mobile
University of Montevallo
University of North Alabama
University of South Alabama

Alaska
University of Alaska
Fairbanks

Arizona
Arizona State University
Eastern Arizona College
Northern Arizona University
Pima Community College
University of Arizona

Arkansas
Arkansas State University
Arkansas Tech University
Harding University
Henderson State University
Hendrix College
Lyon College
North Arkansas College
Ouachita Baptist University
Southern Arkansas University
University of Arkansas
University of Arkansas
Pine Bluff
University of the Ozarks
Williams Baptist College

California
Art Institute
of California - Orange County
California Baptist University
California College of Arts and Crafts
California Institute of the Arts
California Polytechnic State University: San Luis Obispo
California State Polytechnic University: Pomona
California State University
Chico
Long Beach
Stanislaus
Chapman University
College of the Canyons
College of the Siskiyous
Concordia University
Irvine Valley College
Master's College
Otis College of Art and Design
Point Loma Nazarene University
Riverside Community College
San Diego State University
Santa Rosa Junior College
Sonoma State University
University of California
Riverside
San Diego
Santa Cruz
University of La Verne
University of Redlands
University of San Diego
University of Southern California
Whittier College

Colorado
Colorado Christian University
Colorado State University
Colorado State University
Pueblo
Fort Lewis College
Mesa State College
Metropolitan State College of Denver
Rocky Mountain College of Art & Design
University of Colorado
Boulder
Colorado Springs
Denver
University of Denver

Connecticut
Albertus Magnus College
Eastern Connecticut State University
Fairfield University
Quinebaug Valley Community College
Sacred Heart University
University of Connecticut
University of Hartford

Delaware
University of Delaware

District of Columbia
Corcoran College of Art and Design
George Washington University

Florida
Barry University
Broward Community College
Chipola Junior College
Eckerd College
Florida Agricultural and Mechanical University
Florida International University
Florida Keys Community College
Florida Southern College
Jacksonville University
Lake-Sumter Community College
Manatee Community College
Miami-Dade Community College
Okaloosa-Walton Community College
Palm Beach Atlantic University
Rollins College
St. Leo University
St. Petersburg College
Santa Fe Community College
Seminole Community College
Stetson University
Tallahassee Community College
University of Miami
University of South Florida
University of Tampa
University of West Florida

Georgia
Andrew College
of Atlanta
Atlanta College of Art
Augusta State University
Berry College
Brenau University
Clark Atlanta University
Covenant College
Darton College
Emmanuel College
Emory University
Floyd College
Georgia College and State University
Georgia Institute of Technology
Georgia Southern University
Georgia State University
LaGrange College
Mercer University
Middle Georgia College
Morris Brown College
North Georgia College & State University
Piedmont College
Reinhardt College
Savannah College of Art and Design
Shorter College
University of Georgia
Wesleyan College
Young Harris College

Hawaii
Brigham Young University-Hawaii
University of Hawaii
Manoa

Idaho
Albertson College of Idaho
Idaho State University
Lewis-Clark State College

Illinois
American Academy of Art
Augustana College
Black Hawk College
Bradley University
Carl Sandburg College
College of DuPage
Columbia College Chicago
De Paul University
Eastern Illinois University
Elgin Community College
Elmhurst College
Greenville College
Illinois College
Illinois Institute of Art
Illinois State University
Illinois Wesleyan University
Knox College
Lake Forest College
Lewis University
Lincoln College
Loyola University of Chicago
MacMurray College
McKendree College
Millikin University
Monmouth College
North Central College
North Park University
Northeastern Illinois University
Olivet Nazarene University
Parkland College
Quincy University
Rend Lake College
Robert Morris College: Chicago
School of the Art Institute of Chicago
South Suburban College of Cook County
Southeastern Illinois College
Southern Illinois University Carbondale
Springfield College in Illinois
Trinity Christian College
University of St. Francis
Western Illinois University
Wheaton College
William Rainey Harper College

Indiana
Bethel College
Grace College
Huntington College
Indiana State University
Indiana University
Bloomington
Southeast
Indiana University-Purdue University Fort Wayne
Indiana Wesleyan University
Manchester College
Marian College
Oakland City University
St. Mary-of-the-Woods College
Taylor University
University of Evansville
University of Indianapolis
University of St. Francis
University of Southern Indiana
Valparaiso University
Vincennes University
Wabash College

Iowa
Central College
Clarke College
Coe College
Cornell College
Dordt College
Drake University
Ellsworth Community College
Franciscan University
Graceland University
Grand View College
Iowa State University
Iowa Wesleyan College
Kirkwood Community College
Luther College
Morningside College
Mount Mercy College
North Iowa Area Community College
St. Ambrose University
Simpson College
University of Northern Iowa
Waldorf College

Kansas
Allen County Community College
Baker University
Bethany College
Bethel College
Emporia State University
Garden City Community College
Highland Community College
Kansas City Kansas Community College
Kansas State University
Kansas Wesleyan University
McPherson College
MidAmerica Nazarene University
Ottawa University
Pratt Community College
St. Mary College
Sterling College
Tabor College
University of Kansas
Wichita State University

Kentucky
Bellarmine University
Cumberland College
Georgetown College
Jefferson Community College
Louisville Technical Institute
Murray State University
Spencerian College: Lexington
Transylvania University
Union College
University of Louisville

Louisiana
Centenary College of Louisiana
Louisiana College
Louisiana State University and Agricultural and Mechanical College
Loyola University New Orleans
Northwestern State University
University of Louisiana at Monroe
Xavier University of Louisiana

Maine
Maine College of Art
University of Maine

University of Maine
  Augusta
  Machias
  Presque Isle

Maryland

Bowie State University
Chesapeake College
College of Notre Dame of Maryland
Community College of Baltimore County
  Essex
Goucher College
Maryland College of Art and Design
Maryland Institute College of Art
Montgomery College
  Rockville Campus
St. Mary's College of Maryland
Salisbury University
Towson University
University of Maryland
  Baltimore County
  College Park
Villa Julie College

Massachusetts

Art Institute of Boston at Lesley University
Boston University
Endicott College
Massachusetts College of Art
Massachusetts College of Liberal Arts
Regis College
Salem State College
University of Massachusetts
  Amherst
  Boston
  Lowell

Michigan

Adrian College
Alma College
Alpena Community College
Aquinas College
Calvin College
Central Michigan University
College for Creative Studies
Concordia University
Eastern Michigan University
Ferris State University
Glen Oaks Community College
Gogebic Community College
Grand Rapids Community College
Grand Valley State University
Hillsdale College
Hope College
Jackson Community College
Kalamazoo College
Madonna University
Marygrove College
Monroe County Community College
Northern Michigan University
Northwestern Michigan College
Siena Heights University
Southwestern Michigan College
Spring Arbor University
University of Michigan
University of Michigan
  Dearborn
  Flint
Western Michigan University

Minnesota

Augsburg College
Bemidji State University
Bethany Lutheran College
Bethel College
College of St. Benedict
College of St. Scholastica
College of Visual Arts
Minnesota State University
  Mankato
Riverland Community College: A Technical and Community College
St. John's University
St. Mary's University of Minnesota
Southwest State University
University of Minnesota
  Twin Cities
Winona State University

Mississippi

Delta State University
Itawamba Community College
Millsaps College
Mississippi State University
University of Mississippi

Missouri

Avila University
Central Missouri State University
Columbia College
Cottey College
Crowder College
Culver-Stockton College
Drury University
Evangel University
Fontbonne College
Hannibal-LaGrange College
Jefferson College
Kansas City Art Institute
Lincoln University
Lindenwood University
Maryville University of Saint Louis
Mineral Area College
Missouri Southern State College
Missouri Western State College
St. Charles Community College
St. Louis University
Southeast Missouri State University
Southwest Baptist University
Southwest Missouri State University
St. Louis Community College
  Forest Park
Truman State University
University of Missouri
  Columbia
  Kansas City
  St. Louis
Webster University
William Jewell College
William Woods University

Montana

Dawson Community College
Montana State University
  Billings
  Bozeman
Rocky Mountain College
University of Montana-Missoula
University of Montana: Western

Nebraska

Central Community College
Chadron State College
Creative Center
Creighton University
Dana College
Doane College
Hastings College
Mid Plains Community College Area
Midland Lutheran College
Nebraska Wesleyan University
Northeast Community College
Peru State College
Southeast Community College
  Beatrice Campus
University of Nebraska
  Lincoln
  Omaha
Wayne State College
Western Nebraska Community College

Nevada

Sierra Nevada College
Truckee Meadows Community College
University of Nevada
  Las Vegas
  Reno

New Hampshire

Chester College of New England
Colby-Sawyer College
Keene State College
New England College
University of New Hampshire

New Jersey

Bloomfield College
Caldwell College
College of St. Elizabeth
Drew University
Felician College
Georgian Court College
Monmouth University
Montclair State University
Richard Stockton College of New Jersey
Rider University
Rutgers, The State University of New Jersey
  New Brunswick Regional Campus
  Newark Regional Campus
Union County College

New Mexico

College of Santa Fe
Eastern New Mexico University
University of New Mexico

New York

Adelphi University
Alfred University
Canisius College
City University of New York
  Brooklyn College
  College of Staten Island
College of New Rochelle
Daemen College
Hartwick College
Hobart and William Smith Colleges
Houghton College
Long Island University
  C. W. Post Campus
  Southampton College
Molloy College
Nassau Community College
Nazareth College of Rochester
Parsons School of Design
Pratt Institute
Rensselaer Polytechnic Institute
Roberts Wesleyan College
Rochester Institute of Technology
St. Bonaventure University
St. John's University
State University of New York
  Binghamton
  College at Buffalo
  College at Plattsburgh
  College at Potsdam
  New Paltz
  Purchase
Syracuse University
Villa Maria College of Buffalo

North Carolina

Appalachian State University
Barton College
Brevard College
College of the Albemarle
Davidson College
Duke University
East Carolina University
Elon University
Greensboro College
Guilford College
Meredith College
Mount Olive College
North Carolina School of the Arts
Pfeiffer University
Queens University of Charlotte
Rockingham Community College
St. Augustine's College
University of North Carolina
  Asheville
  Chapel Hill
  Greensboro
  Wilmington
Wake Forest University
Western Carolina University
Wilkes Community College
Wingate University

North Dakota

Dickinson State University
Jamestown College
Minot State University
North Dakota State University
Trinity Bible College
University of North Dakota

Ohio

Art Academy of Cincinnati
Ashland University
Baldwin-Wallace College
Bluffton College
Bowling Green State University
Bowling Green State University: Firelands College
Capital University
Case Western Reserve University
Central State University
Cleveland Institute of Art
Cleveland State University
Columbus College of Art and Design
Cuyahoga Community College
  Eastern Campus
  Metropolitan Campus
  Western Campus
Hiram College
Kent State University
Lake Erie College
Lakeland Community College
Lourdes College
Marietta College
Miami University
  Oxford Campus
Mount Union College
Mount Vernon Nazarene University
Muskingum College
Ohio Northern University
Ohio State University
  Columbus Campus
Ohio University
Ohio Wesleyan University
Pontifical College Josephinum
Southern State Community College
University of Akron
University of Dayton
Ursuline College
Xavier University

Oklahoma

Carl Albert State College
Northeastern Oklahoma Agricultural and Mechanical College
Northeastern State University
Oklahoma City University
Oklahoma Panhandle State University
Oklahoma State University
Oral Roberts University
St. Gregory's University
Southeastern Oklahoma State University
Southwestern Oklahoma State University
Tulsa Community College
University of Central Oklahoma
University of Oklahoma
University of Science and Arts of Oklahoma
University of Tulsa
Western Oklahoma State College

Oregon
Art Institute of Portland
Clackamas Community College
Eastern Oregon University
George Fox University
Lane Community College
Linn-Benton Community College
Pacific Northwest College of Art
Pacific University
Southern Oregon University
Western Oregon University

Pennsylvania
Albright College
Arcadia University
Bloomsburg University of Pennsylvania
Carnegie Mellon University
Cedar Crest College
Chestnut Hill College
Drexel University
East Stroudsburg University of Pennsylvania
Edinboro University of Pennsylvania
Elizabethtown College
Indiana University of Pennsylvania
Juniata College
Keystone College
Kutztown University of Pennsylvania
Lehigh University
Lock Haven University of Pennsylvania
Lycoming College
Marywood University
Mercyhurst College
Messiah College
Northampton County Area Community College
Oakbridge Academy of Arts
Point Park College
Rosemont College
St. Joseph's University
Seton Hill University
Slippery Rock University of Pennsylvania
Temple University
Thiel College

Puerto Rico
Humacao Community College

Rhode Island
Rhode Island College

South Carolina
Anderson College
Charleston Southern University
Coastal Carolina University
Coker College
College of Charleston
Converse College
Furman University
Limestone College
Presbyterian College
University of South Carolina
Winthrop University

South Dakota
Augustana College
Dakota State University
Dakota Wesleyan University
Mount Marty College
University of Sioux Falls
University of South Dakota

Tennessee
Austin Peay State University
Belmont University
Bryan College
Carson-Newman College
East Tennessee State University
Freed-Hardeman University
Jackson State Community College
King College
Lipscomb University
Maryville College
Memphis College of Art
Northeast State Technical Community College
Pellissippi State Technical Community College
Rhodes College
Roane State Community College
Southern Adventist University
Tennessee Technological University
Union University
University of Tennessee
  Chattanooga
  Knoxville
Volunteer State Community College

Texas
Abilene Christian University
Angelina College
Austin College
Baylor University
Brazosport College
Clarendon College
College of the Mainland
Collin County Community College District
Dallas Baptist University
Galveston College
Hardin-Simmons University
Houston Baptist University
Howard Payne University
Kilgore College
Lee College
Lubbock Christian University
McMurry University
Northeast Texas Community College
Our Lady of the Lake University of San Antonio
Panola College
Rice University
Richland College
St. Edward's University
Schreiner University
Southern Methodist University
Southwest Texas State University
Southwestern University
Stephen F. Austin State University
Texas A&M University
Texas A&M University
  Corpus Christi
Texas Christian University
Texas Lutheran University
Texas Tech University
Tyler Junior College
University of Dallas
University of North Texas
University of Texas
  Arlington
  Austin
  El Paso
  Pan American
University of the Incarnate Word
Wayland Baptist University
West Texas A&M University
Western Technical Institute
Western Texas College

Utah
Brigham Young University
College of Eastern Utah
Dixie State College of Utah
Salt Lake Community College
Southern Utah University
University of Utah
Utah State University
Utah Valley State College
Westminster College

Vermont
Castleton State College
Goddard College
Marlboro College
University of Vermont

Virginia
Averett University
Bluefield College
Hollins University
James Madison University
Longwood University
Mary Washington College
Old Dominion University
Randolph-Macon Woman's College
Sweet Briar College
University of Virginia's College at Wise
Virginia Commonwealth University
Virginia Polytechnic Institute and State University
Virginia State University
Virginia Wesleyan College

Washington
Art Institute of Seattle
Central Washington University
Clark College
Everett Community College
Grays Harbor College
Northwest College
Pacific Lutheran University
Seattle Pacific University
Trinity Lutheran College
University of Puget Sound
University of Washington
Washington State University
Western Washington University
Whitman College
Whitworth College

West Virginia
Concord College
Corinthian Schools: National Institute of Technology
Davis and Elkins College
Fairmont State College
Glenville State College
Marshall University
Shepherd College
University of Charleston
West Liberty State College
West Virginia University
West Virginia Wesleyan College
Wheeling Jesuit University

Wisconsin
Cardinal Stritch University
Carroll College
Carthage College
Columbia College of Nursing
Edgewood College
Marquette University
Milwaukee Institute of Art & Design
Mount Mary College
Ripon College
St. Norbert College
University of Wisconsin
  Baraboo/Sauk County
  Eau Claire
  Green Bay
  La Crosse
  Oshkosh
  Parkside
  Richland
  River Falls
Viterbo University
Wisconsin Lutheran College

Wyoming
Casper College
Central Wyoming College
Eastern Wyoming College
University of Wyoming
Western Wyoming Community College

Music/drama scholarships

Alabama

Auburn University at Montgomery
Birmingham-Southern College
Chattahoochee Valley Community College
Enterprise State Junior College
Faulkner University
Huntingdon College
Jacksonville State University
Jefferson State Community College
Judson College
Lurleen B. Wallace Junior College
Northeast Alabama Community College
Northwest-Shoals Community College
Samford University
Snead State Community College
University of Alabama
University of Alabama
  Birmingham
  Huntsville
University of Mobile
University of Montevallo
University of North Alabama
University of South Alabama
University of West Alabama
Wallace State Community College at Hanceville

Arizona

Arizona State University
Eastern Arizona College
Northern Arizona University
Pima Community College
South Mountain Community College
Southwestern College
University of Arizona

Arkansas

Arkansas State University
Arkansas State University
  Beebe
Arkansas Tech University
Harding University
Henderson State University
Hendrix College
John Brown University
Lyon College
Mississippi County Community College
North Arkansas College
Northwest Arkansas Community College
Southern Arkansas University
University of Arkansas
University of Arkansas
  Fort Smith
  Monticello
  Pine Bluff
University of Central Arkansas
University of the Ozarks
Williams Baptist College

California

Azusa Pacific University
Bethany College
Bethesda Christian University
Biola University
California Baptist University
California Institute of the Arts
California Polytechnic State University: San Luis Obispo
California State Polytechnic University: Pomona
California State University
  Chico
  Fresno
  Long Beach
  Stanislaus
Chapman University
Christian Heritage College
College of the Canyons
College of the Siskiyous
Concordia University
Dominican University of California
Holy Names College
Irvine Valley College
La Sierra University
Master's College
Mount San Jacinto College
Occidental College
Point Loma Nazarene University
Riverside Community College
San Diego State University
Santa Clara University
Santa Rosa Junior College
Simpson College
Sonoma State University
University of California
  Riverside
  San Diego
  Santa Cruz
University of La Verne
University of Redlands
University of San Diego
University of Southern California
University of the Pacific
Whittier College
Yuba Community College District

Colorado

Colorado Christian University
Colorado School of Mines
Colorado State University
Colorado State University
  Pueblo
Fort Lewis College
Mesa State College
Metropolitan State College of Denver
University of Colorado
  Boulder
  Denver
University of Denver
University of Northern Colorado

Connecticut

Albertus Magnus College
Eastern Connecticut State University
Fairfield University
Sacred Heart University
University of Connecticut
University of Hartford

Delaware

Delaware State University
University of Delaware

District of Columbia

American University
Catholic University of America
George Washington University

Florida

Barry University
Bethune-Cookman College
Broward Community College
Chipola Junior College
Daytona Beach Community College
Eckerd College
Florida International University
Florida Southern College
Gulf Coast Community College
Indian River Community College
Jacksonville University
Lake-Sumter Community College
Manatee Community College
Miami-Dade Community College
Okaloosa-Walton Community College
Palm Beach Atlantic University
Rollins College
St. Leo University
St. Petersburg College
Santa Fe Community College
Seminole Community College
South Florida Community College
Southeastern College of the Assemblies of God
Stetson University
Tallahassee Community College
University of Florida
University of Miami
University of North Florida
University of South Florida
University of Tampa
University of West Florida
Warner Southern College
Webber International University

Georgia

Agnes Scott College
Andrew College
Augusta State University
Berry College
Brenau University
Clark Atlanta University
Clayton College and State University
Covenant College
Darton College
Emmanuel College
Emory University
Georgia College and State University
Georgia Institute of Technology
Georgia Southern University
Georgia State University
Kennesaw State University
LaGrange College
Mercer University
Middle Georgia College
North Georgia College & State University
Oglethorpe University
Paine College
Piedmont College
Savannah College of Art and Design
Savannah State University
Shorter College
Toccoa Falls College
Truett-McConnell College
University of Georgia
Wesleyan College
Young Harris College

Hawaii

Brigham Young University-Hawaii
Hawaii Pacific University
University of Hawaii
  Manoa

Idaho

Albertson College of Idaho
Boise Bible College
Boise State University
Idaho State University
Lewis-Clark State College
North Idaho College
University of Idaho

Illinois

Augustana College
Aurora University
Benedictine University
Black Hawk College
Bradley University
College of DuPage
College of Lake County
Columbia College Chicago
Concordia University
De Paul University
Eastern Illinois University
Elgin Community College
Elmhurst College
Greenville College
Illinois College
Illinois State University
Illinois Wesleyan University
Judson College
Kishwaukee College
Knox College
Lake Forest College
Lewis University
Lincoln College
Loyola University of Chicago
MacMurray College
McHenry County College
McKendree College
Millikin University
Monmouth College
Moody Bible Institute
North Central College
North Park University
Northeastern Illinois University
Olivet Nazarene University
Parkland College
Quincy University
Rend Lake College
St. Xavier University
South Suburban College of Cook County
Southeastern Illinois College
Southern Illinois University Carbondale
Springfield College in Illinois
Trinity Christian College
Trinity International University
VanderCook College of Music
Western Illinois University
Wheaton College
William Rainey Harper College

Indiana

American Conservatory of Music
Anderson University
Ball State University
Bethel College
Goshen College
Grace College
Hanover College
Huntington College
Indiana Institute of Technology
Indiana State University
Indiana University
  Bloomington
  Southeast
Indiana Wesleyan University
Manchester College
Marian College
Oakland City University
Purdue University
St. Joseph's College
St. Mary-of-the-Woods College
Taylor University
University of Evansville
University of Indianapolis
University of Southern Indiana
Valparaiso University
Vincennes University
Wabash College

Iowa

Central College
Clarke College
Coe College
Cornell College
Dordt College
Drake University
Ellsworth Community College
Emmaus Bible College
Franciscan University
Graceland University
Grand View College
Iowa State University
Iowa Wesleyan College
Iowa Western Community College
Kirkwood Community College
Loras College
Luther College
Maharishi University of Management
Morningside College

Mount Mercy College
North Iowa Area Community College
St. Ambrose University
Simpson College
Southwestern Community College
University of Dubuque
University of Northern Iowa
Waldorf College
Wartburg College
William Penn University

Kansas
Allen County Community College
Baker University
Barclay College
Benedictine College
Bethany College
Bethel College
Central Christian College
Emporia State University
Garden City Community College
Hesston College
Highland Community College
Kansas City Kansas Community College
Kansas State University
Kansas Wesleyan University
MidAmerica Nazarene University
Newman University
Ottawa University
Pratt Community College
St. Mary College
Southwestern College
Sterling College
Tabor College
University of Kansas
Wichita State University

Kentucky
Asbury College
Bellarmine University
Centre College
Cumberland College
Georgetown College
Kentucky Christian College
Kentucky Mountain Bible College
Morehead State University
Murray State University
Pikeville College
Spencerian College: Lexington
Transylvania University
Union College
University of Kentucky
University of Louisville

Louisiana
Centenary College of Louisiana
Louisiana College
Louisiana State University and Agricultural and Mechanical College
Loyola University New Orleans
Northwestern State University
Southeastern Louisiana University
University of Louisiana at Monroe
Xavier University of Louisiana

Maine
University of Maine
University of Maine
Augusta
Machias
Presque Isle
University of Southern Maine

Maryland
Bowie State University
College of Notre Dame of Maryland
Columbia Union College
Community College of Baltimore County
Essex
Goucher College
Johns Hopkins University: Peabody Conservatory of Music
Montgomery College
Rockville Campus
St. Mary's College of Maryland
Salisbury University
Towson University
University of Maryland
Baltimore County
College Park
Villa Julie College

Massachusetts
Anna Maria College
Atlantic Union College
Berklee College of Music
Boston University
Cape Cod Community College
Emerson College
Gordon College
Massachusetts College of Liberal Arts
Merrimack College
New England Conservatory of Music
Northeastern University
Regis College
Salem State College
Stonehill College
University of Massachusetts
Amherst
Boston

Michigan
Adrian College
Alma College
Alpena Community College
Andrews University
Calvin College
Central Michigan University
Concordia University
Cornerstone University
Eastern Michigan University
Ferris State University
Glen Oaks Community College
Gogebic Community College
Grace Bible College
Grand Rapids Community College
Grand Valley State University
Hillsdale College
Hope College
Jackson Community College
Kalamazoo College
Macomb Community College
Madonna University
Marygrove College
Monroe County Community College
Northern Michigan University
Northwestern Michigan College
Saginaw Valley State University
Schoolcraft College
Siena Heights University
Southwestern Michigan College
University of Michigan
University of Michigan
Dearborn
Flint
Wayne State University
Western Michigan University
William Tyndale College

Minnesota
Augsburg College
Bemidji State University
Bethany Lutheran College
Bethel College
College of St. Benedict
College of St. Scholastica
Concordia College: Moorhead
Concordia University: St. Paul
Crossroads College
Crown College
Fergus Falls Community College
Gustavus Adolphus College
Martin Luther College
Minnesota State University
Mankato
North Central University
Northwestern College
Riverland Community College: A Technical and Community College
St. John's University
St. Mary's University of Minnesota
Southwest State University
University of Minnesota
Twin Cities
University of St. Thomas
Winona State University

Mississippi
Delta State University
Itawamba Community College
Millsaps College
Mississippi Gulf Coast Community College
Perkinston
Mississippi State University
Pearl River Community College
Rust College
University of Mississippi

Missouri
Avila University
Central Methodist College
Central Missouri State University
Columbia College
Cottey College
Crowder College
Culver-Stockton College
Drury University
East Central College
Evangel University
Fontbonne College
Hannibal-LaGrange College
Harris Stowe State College
Lincoln University
Lindenwood University
Mineral Area College
Missouri Baptist University
Missouri Southern State College
Missouri Western State College
Moberly Area Community College
North Central Missouri College
Rockhurst University
St. Charles Community College
St. Louis Christian College
St. Louis University
Southeast Missouri State University
Southwest Baptist University
Southwest Missouri State University
St. Louis Community College
Forest Park
Truman State University
University of Missouri
Columbia
Kansas City
Rolla
St. Louis
Webster University
William Jewell College
William Woods University

Montana
Carroll College
Dawson Community College
Miles Community College
Montana State University
Billings
Bozeman
Rocky Mountain College
University of Montana-Missoula
University of Montana: Western

Nebraska
Central Community College
Chadron State College
College of Saint Mary
Dana College
Doane College
Grace University
Hastings College
Mid Plains Community College Area
Midland Lutheran College
Nebraska Wesleyan University
Peru State College
Southeast Community College
Beatrice Campus
University of Nebraska
Lincoln
Omaha
Wayne State College
Western Nebraska Community College
York College

Nevada
Truckee Meadows Community College
University of Nevada
Las Vegas
Reno

New Hampshire
Colby-Sawyer College
Franklin Pierce College
Keene State College
New England College
Plymouth State College
University of New Hampshire

New Jersey
Caldwell College
The College of New Jersey
Drew University
Georgian Court College
Montclair State University
Richard Stockton College of New Jersey
Rider University
Rowan University
Rutgers, The State University of New Jersey
New Brunswick Regional Campus
William Paterson University of New Jersey

New Mexico
College of Santa Fe
College of the Southwest
Eastern New Mexico University
New Mexico Highlands University
University of New Mexico

New York
Adelphi University
Alfred University
Canisius College
City University of New York
Brooklyn College
College of Staten Island
Queens College
Concordia College
Eastman School of Music of the University of Rochester
Elmira College
Genesee Community College
Hartwick College
Hobart and William Smith Colleges
Houghton College
Ithaca College
Jamestown Community College
Long Island University
C. W. Post Campus
Manhattan School of Music
Mannes College of Music
Marist College
Molloy College
Nassau Community College
Nazareth College of Rochester
Niagara University
Nyack College
Rensselaer Polytechnic Institute
Roberts Wesleyan College
St. Bonaventure University
St. John's University
Skidmore College

State University of New York
- Binghamton
- Buffalo
- College at Buffalo
- College at Plattsburgh
- College at Potsdam
- New Paltz
- Purchase

Syracuse University
Villa Maria College of Buffalo
Wagner College

North Carolina

Appalachian State University
Barton College
Brevard College
Campbell University
Catawba College
Chowan College
College of the Albemarle
Davidson College
East Carolina University
Elon University
Gardner-Webb University
Greensboro College
Guilford College
High Point University
Isothermal Community College
Lees-McRae College
Lenoir-Rhyne College
Meredith College
Methodist College
Montreat College
Mount Olive College
North Carolina Agricultural and Technical State University
North Carolina Central University
North Carolina School of the Arts
Pfeiffer University
Queens University of Charlotte
St. Augustine's College
Salem College
University of North Carolina
- Asheville
- Chapel Hill
- Greensboro
- Wilmington

Wake Forest University
Western Carolina University
Wilkes Community College
Wingate University

North Dakota

Dickinson State University
Jamestown College
Minot State University
Minot State University: Bottineau Campus
North Dakota State College of Science
North Dakota State University
Trinity Bible College
University of North Dakota
Valley City State University

Ohio

Ashland University
Baldwin-Wallace College
Bowling Green State University
Bowling Green State University: Firelands College
Capital University
Case Western Reserve University
Cedarville University
Central State University
Cleveland State University
College of Wooster
Cuyahoga Community College
- Eastern Campus
- Metropolitan Campus
- Western Campus

Denison University
Heidelberg College
Hiram College
Kent State University
Kent State University
- Stark Campus

Lake Erie College
Lakeland Community College
Lourdes College
Malone College
Marietta College
Miami University
- Oxford Campus

Mount Union College
Muskingum College
Oberlin College
Ohio Northern University
Ohio State University
- Columbus Campus

Ohio Wesleyan University
Pontifical College Josephinum
Southern State Community College
Tiffin University
University of Akron
University of Dayton
University of Findlay
University of Rio Grande
Urbana University
Walsh University
Xavier University

Oklahoma

Carl Albert State College
Northeastern Oklahoma Agricultural and Mechanical College
Northeastern State University
Northwestern Oklahoma State University
Oklahoma Christian University
Oklahoma City University
Oklahoma State University
Oral Roberts University
St. Gregory's University
Southeastern Oklahoma State University
Southwestern Christian University
Southwestern Oklahoma State University
Tulsa Community College
University of Central Oklahoma
University of Oklahoma
University of Science and Arts of Oklahoma
University of Tulsa
Western Oklahoma State College

Oregon

Blue Mountain Community College
Clackamas Community College
Concordia University
Eastern Oregon University
Eugene Bible College
George Fox University
Lane Community College
Lewis & Clark College
Linfield College
Linn-Benton Community College
Northwest Christian College
Pacific University
Southern Oregon University
University of Portland
Western Baptist College
Western Oregon University
Willamette University

Pennsylvania

Albright College
Baptist Bible College of Pennsylvania
Bloomsburg University of Pennsylvania
Carnegie Mellon University
Cedar Crest College
Chatham College
Chestnut Hill College
Delaware Valley College
DeSales University
Drexel University
Duquesne University
East Stroudsburg University of Pennsylvania
Edinboro University of Pennsylvania
Elizabethtown College
Franklin & Marshall College
Geneva College
Gettysburg College
Immaculata University
Indiana University of Pennsylvania
Juniata College
Kutztown University of Pennsylvania
Lancaster Bible College
Lebanon Valley College of Pennsylvania
Lehigh University
Lincoln University
Lock Haven University of Pennsylvania
Lycoming College
Marywood University
Mercyhurst College
Messiah College
Moravian College
Mount Aloysius College
Muhlenberg College
Philadelphia Biblical University
Point Park College
St. Vincent College
Seton Hill University
Slippery Rock University of Pennsylvania
Temple University
Thiel College
Valley Forge Christian College
West Chester University of Pennsylvania
Widener University
Wilkes University
Wilson College
York College of Pennsylvania

Puerto Rico

Humacao Community College
Universidad Politecnica de Puerto Rico
University of Puerto Rico
- Humacao

Rhode Island

Rhode Island College
Salve Regina University
University of Rhode Island

South Carolina

Anderson College
Charleston Southern University
The Citadel
Clemson University
Coastal Carolina University
Coker College
College of Charleston
Converse College
Erskine College
Francis Marion University
Furman University
Limestone College
Morris College
Presbyterian College
Southern Wesleyan University
Spartanburg Methodist College
University of South Carolina
Winthrop University
Wofford College

South Dakota

Augustana College
Dakota State University
Dakota Wesleyan University
Mount Marty College
University of Sioux Falls
University of South Dakota

Tennessee

Austin Peay State University
Belmont University
Bethel College
Bryan College
Carson-Newman College
Crichton College
Dyersburg State Community College
East Tennessee State University
Freed-Hardeman University
Jackson State Community College
Johnson Bible College
King College
Lambuth University
Lee University
Lipscomb University
Maryville College
Middle Tennessee State University
Milligan College
Northeast State Technical Community College
Pellissippi State Technical Community College
Rhodes College
Roane State Community College
Southern Adventist University
Tennessee Technological University
Tennessee Wesleyan College
Trevecca Nazarene University
Tusculum College
Union University
University of Tennessee
- Chattanooga
- Knoxville
- Martin

Vanderbilt University
Volunteer State Community College
Walters State Community College

Texas

Abilene Christian University
Angelina College
Austin College
Baylor University
Brazosport College
Clarendon College
College of the Mainland
Collin County Community College District
Concordia University at Austin
Dallas Baptist University
East Texas Baptist University
Frank Phillips College
Galveston College
Hardin-Simmons University
Houston Baptist University
Howard College
Howard Payne University
Huston-Tillotson College
Jacksonville College
Kilgore College
Lee College
Lubbock Christian University
McMurry University
Northeast Texas Community College
Our Lady of the Lake University of San Antonio
Panola College
Paris Junior College
Paul Quinn College
Rice University
Richland College
St. Edward's University
St. Mary's University
Schreiner University
Southern Methodist University
Southwest Texas State University
Southwestern Adventist University
Southwestern University
Stephen F. Austin State University
Texas A&M University
Texas A&M University
- Corpus Christi

Texas Christian University
Texas Lutheran University
Texas Tech University
Trinity University
Tyler Junior College
University of Dallas
University of North Texas

University of Texas
- Arlington
- Austin
- El Paso
- Pan American
- Tyler

University of the Incarnate Word
Wayland Baptist University
West Texas A&M University
Western Technical Institute
Western Texas College

Utah
Brigham Young University
College of Eastern Utah
Dixie State College of Utah
Salt Lake Community College
Southern Utah University
University of Utah
Utah State University
Utah Valley State College
Westminster College

Vermont
Castleton State College
Goddard College
Marlboro College
Norwich University

Virginia
Averett University
Bluefield College
Bridgewater College
Eastern Mennonite University
Emory & Henry College
Ferrum College
George Mason University
Hampton University
Hollins University
James Madison University
Liberty University
Longwood University
Mary Washington College
Old Dominion University
Randolph-Macon Woman's College
Roanoke College
Shenandoah University
Sweet Briar College
University of Richmond
University of Virginia's College at Wise
Virginia Commonwealth University
Virginia Military Institute
Virginia State University
Virginia Wesleyan College

Washington
Central Washington University
Clark College
Eastern Washington University
Everett Community College
Gonzaga University
Grays Harbor College
Northwest College
Pacific Lutheran University
St. Martin's College
Seattle Pacific University
Seattle University
Trinity Lutheran College
University of Puget Sound
University of Washington
Walla Walla College
Walla Walla Community College
Washington State University
Western Washington University
Whitman College
Whitworth College

West Virginia
Alderson-Broaddus College
Bethany College
Concord College
Davis and Elkins College
Fairmont State College
Glenville State College
Marshall University
Ohio Valley College
Shepherd College
University of Charleston
West Liberty State College
West Virginia University
West Virginia Wesleyan College
Wheeling Jesuit University

Wisconsin
Alverno College
Beloit College
Cardinal Stritch University
Carroll College
Carthage College
Columbia College of Nursing
Edgewood College
Lawrence University
Marquette University
Mount Mary College
Northland College
Ripon College
St. Norbert College
Silver Lake College
University of Wisconsin
- Baraboo/Sauk County
- Eau Claire
- Green Bay
- Oshkosh
- Parkside
- Richland
- River Falls
- Waukesha

Viterbo University
Wisconsin Lutheran College

Wyoming
Casper College
Central Wyoming College
Eastern Wyoming College
University of Wyoming
Western Wyoming Community College

ROTC scholarships

Alabama
Alabama State University
Auburn University
Birmingham-Southern College
Faulkner University
Huntingdon College
Jacksonville State University
Marion Military Institute
Samford University
Troy State University
Troy State University in Montgomery
Tuskegee University
University of Alabama
University of Alabama
  Birmingham
  Huntsville
University of Mobile
University of Montevallo
University of North Alabama
University of South Alabama

Alaska
University of Alaska
  Fairbanks

Arizona
Arizona State University
Embry-Riddle Aeronautical University: Prescott Campus
Northern Arizona University
University of Arizona

Arkansas
Arkansas State University
Arkansas Tech University
Harding University
Hendrix College
John Brown University
University of Arkansas
University of Arkansas
  Pine Bluff
University of Central Arkansas

California
Azusa Pacific University
Biola University
California Polytechnic State University: San Luis Obispo
California State Polytechnic University: Pomona
Pepperdine University
San Diego State University
San Jose State University
Santa Clara University
University of California
  Berkeley
  Irvine
  Los Angeles
University of San Diego
University of San Francisco
University of Southern California

Colorado
Colorado School of Mines
Colorado State University
Colorado State University
  Pueblo
Colorado Technical University
Regis University
University of Colorado
  Boulder
  Colorado Springs
University of Northern Colorado

Connecticut
Eastern Connecticut State University
Southern Connecticut State University

Delaware
Delaware State University
University of Delaware

District of Columbia
American University
George Washington University
Georgetown University

Florida
Bethune-Cookman College
Chipola Junior College
Eckerd College
Embry-Riddle Aeronautical University
Florida Institute of Technology
Florida Southern College
Jacksonville University
University of Central Florida
University of Florida
University of South Florida
University of Tampa
University of West Florida

Georgia
Albany State University
Augusta State University
Clark Atlanta University
Fort Valley State University
Georgia College and State University
Georgia Institute of Technology
Georgia Southern University
LaGrange College
Mercer University
Morehouse College
North Georgia College & State University
Paine College
Thomas University
University of Georgia
Valdosta State University

Hawaii
Chaminade University of Honolulu
Hawaii Pacific University
University of Hawaii
  Manoa

Idaho
Boise State University
Northwest Nazarene University
University of Idaho

Illinois
Benedictine University
Chicago State University
Elgin Community College
Governors State University
Illinois Institute of Technology
Illinois State University
Kaskaskia College
Lewis University
Loyola University of Chicago
Northern Illinois University
Olivet Nazarene University
Rock Valley College
Southern Illinois University Carbondale
University of Illinois
  Chicago
Western Illinois University
Wheaton College

Indiana
Ball State University
Bethel College
DePauw University
Indiana State University
Purdue University
Rose-Hulman Institute of Technology
Saint Mary's College
University of Notre Dame
Valparaiso University

Iowa
Allen College
Coe College
Drake University
Iowa State University
University of Dubuque
University of Northern Iowa

Kansas
Baker University
Kansas State University
McPherson College
MidAmerica Nazarene University
St. Mary College
University of Kansas

Kentucky
Asbury College
Bellarmine University
Centre College
Georgetown College
Morehead State University
Spalding University
Spencerian College: Lexington
Thomas More College
Transylvania University
University of Kentucky
University of Louisville

Louisiana
Dillard University
Louisiana College
Louisiana State University and Agricultural and Mechanical College
Loyola University New Orleans
Northwestern State University
Tulane University
University of Louisiana at Monroe

Maine
University of Maine

Maryland
Bowie State University
Coppin State College
Johns Hopkins University
Loyola College in Maryland
McDaniel College
Mount St. Mary's College
University of Maryland
  Baltimore
  College Park
Villa Julie College

Massachusetts
Boston College
Boston University
Clark University
College of the Holy Cross
Harvard College
Nichols College
Stonehill College
University of Massachusetts
  Amherst
  Dartmouth
  Lowell
Western New England College
Worcester Polytechnic Institute

Michigan
Central Michigan University
Eastern Michigan University
Ferris State University
Michigan State University
Michigan Technological University
Northern Michigan University
University of Michigan
Western Michigan University

Minnesota
College of St. Benedict
College of St. Scholastica
Gustavus Adolphus College
Minnesota State University
  Mankato
Riverland Community College: A Technical and Community College
St. John's University
University of Minnesota
  Crookston
  Duluth
  Twin Cities
University of St. Thomas

Mississippi
Alcorn State University
Delta State University
Mississippi State University
Mississippi University for Women
Mississippi Valley State University
University of Mississippi

Missouri
Central Missouri State University
Columbia College
Evangel University
Rockhurst University
St. Louis University
Southeast Missouri State University
Southwest Baptist University
Southwest Missouri State University
Truman State University
University of Missouri
  Columbia
  Rolla
  St. Louis
Washington University in St. Louis
Wentworth Military Academy
Westminster College

Montana
Montana State University
  Bozeman
University of Montana-Missoula

Nebraska
Creighton University
Dana College
Nebraska Methodist College of Nursing and Allied Health
University of Nebraska
  Omaha

Nevada
University of Nevada
  Reno

New Hampshire
Southern New Hampshire University
University of New Hampshire

New Jersey
New Jersey Institute of Technology
Princeton University
Rowan University
Seton Hall University
Stevens Institute of Technology

New Mexico
New Mexico Military Institute
University of New Mexico

New York
Alfred University
Canisius College
Clarkson University
Cornell University
D'Youville College
Dowling College
Elmira College
Fordham University
Hofstra University
Ithaca College
Le Moyne College
Manhattan College
Mount St. Mary College
Nazareth College of Rochester
Niagara University
Rensselaer Polytechnic Institute

Roberts Wesleyan College
Rochester Institute of Technology
St. Bonaventure University
St. John's University
St. Lawrence University
Skidmore College
State University of New York
- College at Brockport
- College at Fredonia
- College at Geneseo
- College at Potsdam
- Maritime College

Syracuse University
Union College

North Carolina
Appalachian State University
Campbell University
Davidson College
Duke University
East Carolina University
Elizabeth City State University
Elon University
Johnson C. Smith University
Lenoir-Rhyne College
Livingstone College
Methodist College
North Carolina Agricultural and Technical State University
North Carolina State University
Pfeiffer University
St. Augustine's College
Shaw University
Wake Forest University
Winston-Salem State University

North Dakota
North Dakota State University
University of North Dakota

Ohio
Bowling Green State University
Capital University
Cedarville University
Central State University
Cleveland State University
College of Mount St. Joseph
Columbus College of Art and Design
John Carroll University
Kent State University
Kent State University
- Stark Campus

Mount Union College
Ohio Northern University
Ohio State University
- Columbus Campus

Ohio University
University of Akron
University of Dayton
University of Toledo
Ursuline College
Xavier University
Youngstown State University

Oklahoma
Cameron University
Langston University
Oklahoma Baptist University
Oklahoma Christian University
Oklahoma State University
Oral Roberts University
Southern Nazarene University
University of Central Oklahoma
University of Oklahoma

Oregon
Oregon State University
Portland State University
University of Portland
Western Oregon University

Pennsylvania
Bloomsburg University of Pennsylvania
Bucknell University
Dickinson College
Drexel University
Duquesne University
Edinboro University of Pennsylvania
Indiana University of Pennsylvania
King's College
La Salle University
Lafayette College
Lebanon Valley College of Pennsylvania
Lehigh University
Lock Haven University of Pennsylvania
Marywood University
Mercyhurst College
Moravian College
Penn State
- Abington
- Altoona
- Beaver
- Berks
- Delaware County
- Dubois
- Erie, The Behrend College
- Fayette
- Harrisburg
- Hazleton
- Lehigh Valley
- McKeesport
- Mont Alto
- New Kensington
- Schuylkill - Capital College
- Shenango
- University Park
- Wilkes-Barre
- Worthington Scranton
- York

St. Joseph's University
St. Vincent College
Shippensburg University of Pennsylvania
Slippery Rock University of Pennsylvania
Temple University
University of Scranton
Villanova University
Waynesburg College
Widener University

Puerto Rico
Humacao Community College
University of Puerto Rico
- Mayaguez Campus

Rhode Island
Bryant College
Providence College
Salve Regina University
University of Rhode Island

South Carolina
Charleston Southern University
The Citadel
Clemson University
Converse College
Furman University
Limestone College
Morris College
Newberry College
Presbyterian College
South Carolina State University
University of South Carolina
University of South Carolina
- Spartanburg

Wofford College

South Dakota
Black Hills State University
South Dakota School of Mines and Technology
South Dakota State University

Tennessee
Austin Peay State University
Carson-Newman College
East Tennessee State University
King College
Middle Tennessee State University
Rhodes College
Tennessee Technological University
University of Tennessee
- Knoxville
- Martin

Texas
Angelo State University
Baylor University
McMurry University
Rice University
St. Edward's University
St. Mary's University
Sam Houston State University
Southern Methodist University
Southwest Texas State University
Stephen F. Austin State University
Texas A&M University
Texas Christian University
Texas Tech University
University of Dallas
University of Houston
University of North Texas
University of Texas
- Arlington
- Austin
- El Paso
- Pan American

University of the Incarnate Word
Western Technical Institute

Utah
Brigham Young University
Utah State University
Westminster College

Vermont
Norwich University
St. Michael's College
University of Vermont

Virginia
George Mason University
Hampden-Sydney College
Hampton University
Longwood University
Old Dominion University
Radford University
University of Richmond
Virginia Commonwealth University
Virginia Military Institute
Virginia Polytechnic Institute and State University
Virginia State University
Virginia Union University

Washington
Central Washington University
Eastern Washington University
Gonzaga University
Pacific Lutheran University
Seattle Pacific University
Seattle University
Washington State University
Whitworth College

West Virginia
Marshall University
University of Charleston
West Virginia State College

Wisconsin
Carroll College
Marian College of Fond du Lac
Marquette University
Milwaukee School of Engineering
Ripon College
St. Norbert College
University of Wisconsin
- La Crosse
- Madison
- Stevens Point
- Whitewater

Viterbo University

Wyoming
University of Wyoming

Athletic scholarships

Archery

California
College of the Redwoods M

Texas
Texas A&M University W

Badminton

Kentucky
St. Catharine College M

New Jersey
New Jersey Institute of Technology M

Baseball

Alabama
Alabama Agricultural and Mechanical University M
Alabama State University M
Auburn University M
Auburn University at Montgomery M
Bevill State Community College M
Birmingham-Southern College M
Central Alabama Community College M
Chattahoochee Valley Community College M
Concordia College M
Enterprise State Junior College M
Gadsden State Community College M
George C. Wallace State Community College
Selma M
Jacksonville State University M
James H. Faulkner State Community College M
Jefferson Davis Community College M
Jefferson State Community College M
Lurleen B. Wallace Junior College M
Miles College M
Northwest-Shoals Community College M
Samford University M
Selma University M
Shelton State Community College M
Snead State Community College M
Spring Hill College M
Talladega College M
Troy State University M
Tuskegee University M
University of Alabama M
University of Alabama
Birmingham M
Huntsville M
University of Mobile M
University of Montevallo M
University of North Alabama M
University of South Alabama M
University of West Alabama M
Wallace State Community College at Hanceville M

Arizona
Arizona State University M
Arizona Western College M
Central Arizona College M
Cochise College M
Eastern Arizona College M
Glendale Community College M
Pima Community College M
Scottsdale Community College M
South Mountain Community College M
University of Arizona M
Yavapai College M

Arkansas
Arkansas State University M
Arkansas Tech University M
Harding University M
Henderson State University M
Lyon College M
Ouachita Baptist University M
Southern Arkansas University M
University of Arkansas M
University of Arkansas
Fort Smith M
Little Rock M
University of Central Arkansas M
Williams Baptist College M

California
Azusa Pacific University M
Biola University M
California Baptist University M
California Polytechnic State University: San Luis Obispo M
California State Polytechnic University: Pomona M
California State University
Chico M
Fresno M
Fullerton M
Long Beach M
Los Angeles M
Northridge M
Sacramento M
San Bernardino M
Stanislaus M
Concordia University M,W
Grossmont Community College M
Loyola Marymount University M
Master's College M
Patten University M
Pepperdine University M
Point Loma Nazarene University M
St. Mary's College of California M
San Diego City College W
San Diego State University M
San Jose State University M
Santa Clara University M
Stanford University M
University of California
Berkeley M
Irvine M
Los Angeles M
Riverside M
Santa Barbara M
University of San Diego M
University of San Francisco M
University of Southern California M
University of the Pacific M
Vanguard University of Southern California M
Yuba Community College District M

Colorado
Colorado School of Mines M
Mesa State College M
Metropolitan State College of Denver M
Otero Junior College M
Regis University M
Trinidad State Junior College M
University of Denver M
University of Northern Colorado M

Connecticut
Central Connecticut State University M
Fairfield University M
Manchester Community College W
Mitchell College M
Quinnipiac University M
Teikyo Post University M
University of Bridgeport M
University of Connecticut M
University of Hartford M
University of New Haven M

Delaware
Delaware State University M
Delaware Technical and Community College
Owens Campus M
Stanton/Wilmington Campus M
University of Delaware M
Wilmington College M

District of Columbia
George Washington University M
Georgetown University M
Howard University M

Florida
Barry University M
Bethune-Cookman College M
Broward Community College M
Chipola Junior College M
Daytona Beach Community College M
Eckerd College M
Edward Waters College M
Embry-Riddle Aeronautical University M
Flagler College M
Florida Atlantic University M
Florida College M
Florida Gulf Coast University M
Florida Institute of Technology M
Florida International University M
Florida Southern College M
Florida State University M
Gulf Coast Community College M
Hillsborough Community College M
Indian River Community College M
Jacksonville University M
Lake City Community College M
Lake-Sumter Community College M
Manatee Community College M
Miami-Dade Community College M
Northwood University
Florida Campus M
Nova Southeastern University M
Okaloosa-Walton Community College M
Palm Beach Atlantic University M
Palm Beach Community College M
Pasco-Hernando Community College M
Pensacola Junior College M
Polk Community College M
Rollins College M
St. Leo University M
St. Petersburg College M
St. Thomas University M
Santa Fe Community College M
Stetson University M
Tallahassee Community College M
University of Central Florida M
University of Florida M
University of Miami M
University of North Florida M
University of South Florida M
University of Tampa M
University of West Florida M
Warner Southern College M
Webber International University M

Georgia
Abraham Baldwin Agricultural College M
Albany State University M
Andrew College M
Armstrong Atlantic State University M
Augusta State University M
Berry College M
Brewton-Parker College M
Columbus State University M
Darton College M
Emmanuel College M
Georgia College and State University M
Georgia Institute of Technology M
Georgia Perimeter College M
Georgia Southern University M
Georgia Southwestern State University M
Georgia State University M
Gordon College M
Kennesaw State University M
Mercer University M
Middle Georgia College M
Paine College M
Savannah State University M
Shorter College M
Southern Polytechnic State University M
State University of West Georgia M
Thomas University M
Truett-McConnell College M
University of Georgia M
Valdosta State University M
Young Harris College M

Hawaii
Hawaii Pacific University M
University of Hawaii
Manoa M

Idaho
Albertson College of Idaho M
College of Southern Idaho M
Lewis-Clark State College M
Northwest Nazarene University M

Illinois
Black Hawk College M
Bradley University M
Carl Sandburg College M
Chicago State University M
College of Lake County M
Danville Area Community College M
Eastern Illinois University M
Elgin Community College M
Highland Community College M
Illinois Central College M
Illinois Eastern Community Colleges
Lincoln Trail College M
Olney Central College M
Wabash Valley College M
Illinois Institute of Technology M
Illinois State University M
John A. Logan College M
Judson College M
Kankakee Community College M
Kaskaskia College M
Kishwaukee College M
Lake Land College M
Lewis and Clark Community College M
Lewis University M
Lincoln College M
McHenry County College M
McKendree College M
Moraine Valley Community College M
Northwestern University M
Olivet Nazarene University M
Parkland College M
Quincy University M
Rend Lake College M
Robert Morris College: Chicago M
St. Xavier University M
Sauk Valley Community College M
South Suburban College of Cook County M
Southeastern Illinois College M
Southern Illinois University Carbondale M
Southern Illinois University Edwardsville M
Southwestern Illinois College M
Springfield College in Illinois M
Trinity Christian College M
Trinity International University M
University of Illinois
Chicago M
Urbana-Champaign M
University of St. Francis M
Western Illinois University M

Indiana
Ancilla College M
Ball State University M
Bethel College M
Butler University M
Calumet College of St. Joseph M
Goshen College M
Grace College M
Huntington College M
Indiana Institute of Technology M
Indiana State University M
Indiana University
Bloomington M
Southeast M
Indiana University-Purdue University Fort Wayne M
Indiana University-Purdue University Indianapolis M
Indiana Wesleyan University M
Marian College M
Oakland City University M
Purdue University M
St. Joseph's College M
Taylor University M
University of Evansville M
University of Indianapolis M
University of Notre Dame M
University of St. Francis M
University of Southern Indiana M
Valparaiso University M
Vincennes University M

Iowa
Briar Cliff University M
Clinton Community College M
Des Moines Area Community College M
Dordt College M
Ellsworth Community College M
Franciscan University M
Graceland University M
Grand View College M
Indian Hills Community College M
Iowa Central Community College M
Iowa Lakes Community College M
Iowa Wesleyan College M
Iowa Western Community College M
Kirkwood Community College M
Morningside College M
Muscatine Community College M
North Iowa Area Community College M
Northwestern College M
St. Ambrose University M
Scott Community College M
Southwestern Community College M
University of Iowa M
University of Northern Iowa M
Waldorf College M
William Penn University M

Kansas
Allen County Community College M
Baker University M
Barton County Community College M
Benedictine College M
Bethany College M
Butler County Community College M
Central Christian College M
Cloud County Community College M
Dodge City Community College M
Emporia State University M
Fort Scott Community College M
Friends University M
Garden City Community College M
Hesston College M
Highland Community College M
Hutchinson Community College M
Independence Community College M
Johnson County Community College M
Kansas City Kansas Community College M
Kansas State University M
Kansas Wesleyan University M
Labette Community College M
MidAmerica Nazarene University M
Newman University M
Ottawa University M
Pittsburg State University M
Pratt Community College M
Seward County Community College M
Sterling College M
Tabor College M
University of Kansas M
Washburn University of Topeka M
Wichita State University M

Kentucky
Alice Lloyd College M
Bellarmine University M
Brescia University M
Campbellsville University M
Cumberland College M
Georgetown College M
Kentucky Wesleyan College M
Lindsey Wilson College M
Mid-Continent College M
Morehead State University M
Murray State University M
Pikeville College M
St. Catharine College M
Spalding University M
Union College M
University of Kentucky M
University of Louisville M

Louisiana
Centenary College of Louisiana M
Grambling State University M
Louisiana State University
Shreveport M
Louisiana State University and Agricultural and Mechanical College M
Louisiana Tech University M
McNeese State University M
Nicholls State University M
Northwestern State University M
Southeastern Louisiana University M
Southern University and Agricultural and Mechanical College M
Tulane University M
University of Louisiana at Lafayette M
University of Louisiana at Monroe M
University of New Orleans M

Maine
University of Maine M

Maryland
Anne Arundel Community College M
Chesapeake College M
College of Southern Maryland M
Columbia Union College M
Community College of Baltimore County
Catonsville M
Dundalk M
Essex M
Coppin State College M
Garrett College M
Hagerstown Community College M
Mount St. Mary's College M
Towson University M
University of Maryland
Baltimore County M
College Park M

Massachusetts
American International College M
Dean College M
Fisher College W
Northeastern University M
University of Massachusetts
Amherst M

Michigan
Aquinas College M
Central Michigan University M
Concordia University M
Eastern Michigan University M
Glen Oaks Community College M
Grand Rapids Community College M
Grand Valley State University M
Hillsdale College M
Kellogg Community College M
Macomb Community College M
Michigan State University M
Northwood University M
Oakland University M
Saginaw Valley State University M
Siena Heights University M
University of Michigan M
Wayne State University M

Minnesota
Bethany Lutheran College M
Concordia University: St. Paul M
Minnesota State University
Mankato M
St. Cloud State University M
Southwest State University M
University of Minnesota
Crookston M
Duluth M
Twin Cities M,W
Winona State University M

Mississippi
Alcorn State University M
Delta State University M
Holmes Community College M
Itawamba Community College M
Mississippi State University M
Mississippi Valley State University M
Northwest Mississippi Community College M
University of Mississippi M
University of Southern Mississippi M

Missouri
Avila University M
Central Methodist College M
Central Missouri State University M
College of the Ozarks M
Crowder College M
Culver-Stockton College M
Evangel University M
Hannibal-LaGrange College M
Harris Stowe State College M
Jefferson College M
Lincoln University M
Lindenwood University M
Longview Community College M
Maple Woods Community College M
Mineral Area College M
Missouri Baptist University M
Missouri Southern State College M
Missouri Valley College M
Missouri Western State College M
North Central Missouri College M
Research College of Nursing M
Rockhurst University M
St. Charles Community College M
St. Louis University M
Southeast Missouri State University M
Southwest Baptist University M
Southwest Missouri State University M
St. Louis Community College
Forest Park M
Three Rivers Community College M
Truman State University M
University of Missouri
Columbia M
Rolla M
St. Louis M
William Jewell College M
William Woods University M

Montana
Miles Community College M

Nebraska
Bellevue University M
Concordia University M
Creighton University M
Dana College M
Doane College M
Hastings College M
Mid Plains Community College Area M
Midland Lutheran College M
Peru State College M
University of Nebraska
Kearney M
Lincoln M
Omaha M
Wayne State College M
Western Nebraska Community College M
York College M

Nevada
University of Nevada
Las Vegas M
Reno M

New Hampshire
Franklin Pierce College M
Hesser College M

New Jersey
Bloomfield College M
Brookdale Community College M
Caldwell College M
Fairleigh Dickinson University
Metropolitan Campus M
Mercer County Community College M
Monmouth University M
New Jersey Institute of Technology M
Rider University M
Rutgers, The State University of New Jersey
New Brunswick Regional Campus M
St. Peter's College M
Salem Community College M
Seton Hall University M
Sussex County Community College M

New Mexico
College of the Southwest M
Eastern New Mexico University M
New Mexico Highlands University M
New Mexico Junior College M
New Mexico Military Institute M
New Mexico State University M
University of New Mexico M

New York
Adelphi University M
Briarcliffe College M
Canisius College M
City University of New York
Baruch College W
Borough of Manhattan Community College W
Queens College M
Concordia College M
Dominican College of Blauvelt M
Dowling College M
Fordham University M
Hofstra University M
Iona College M
Le Moyne College M
Long Island University
C. W. Post Campus M
Manhattan College M
Marist College M
Mercy College M
Molloy College M
Monroe Community College M
New York Institute of Technology M
Niagara University M
Nyack College M
Pace University M
Pace University: Pleasantville/Briarcliff M
St. Bonaventure University M

St. John's University M
State University of New York
Albany M
Binghamton M
Buffalo M
Health Science Center at Stony Brook M
Stony Brook M
Wagner College M

North Carolina

Appalachian State University M
Barton College M
Belmont Abbey College M
Brevard College M
Campbell University M
Catawba College M
Davidson College M
Duke University M
East Carolina University M
Elon University M
Gardner-Webb University M
High Point University M
Lenoir Community College M
Lenoir-Rhyne College M
Louisburg College M
Mars Hill College M
Montreat College M
Mount Olive College M
North Carolina Agricultural and Technical State University M
North Carolina State University M
Pfeiffer University M
Pitt Community College M
St. Andrews Presbyterian College M
St. Augustine's College M
Shaw University M
Southeastern Community College M
University of North Carolina
Asheville M
Chapel Hill M
Charlotte M
Greensboro M
Pembroke M
Wilmington M
Wake Forest University M
Western Carolina University M
Wingate University M

North Dakota

Dickinson State University M
Jamestown College M
Mayville State University M
Minot State University M
Minot State University: Bottineau Campus M
North Dakota State University M
University of Mary M
University of North Dakota M
Valley City State University M
Williston State College M

Ohio

Ashland University M
Bowling Green State University M
Cedarville University M
Cleveland State University M
Kent State University M
Lakeland Community College M
Malone College M
Miami University
Oxford Campus M
Mount Vernon Nazarene University M
Ohio Dominican College M
Ohio State University
Columbus Campus M
Ohio University M
Shawnee State University M
Sinclair Community College M
Tiffin University M
University of Akron M
University of Cincinnati M
University of Dayton M
University of Findlay M
University of Rio Grande M
University of Toledo M
Urbana University M
Walsh University M
Wright State University M
Xavier University M
Youngstown State University M

Oklahoma

Bacone College M
Cameron University M
Carl Albert State College M
East Central University M
Eastern Oklahoma State College M
Northeastern Oklahoma Agricultural and Mechanical College M
Northeastern State University M
Northern Oklahoma College M
Northwestern Oklahoma State University M
Oklahoma Baptist University M
Oklahoma City University M
Oklahoma State University M
Oklahoma Wesleyan University M
Oral Roberts University M
Redlands Community College M
Rose State College M
Seminole State College M
Southeastern Oklahoma State University M
Southern Nazarene University M
Southwestern Oklahoma State University M
University of Central Oklahoma M
University of Oklahoma M
University of Science and Arts of Oklahoma M
Western Oklahoma State College M

Oregon

Blue Mountain Community College M
Chemeketa Community College M
Clackamas Community College M
Concordia University M
Lane Community College M
Linn-Benton Community College M
Mount Hood Community College M
Oregon Institute of Technology M
Oregon State University M
Portland State University M
Southwestern Oregon Community College M
Treasure Valley Community College M
University of Portland M
Western Baptist College M

Pennsylvania

California University of Pennsylvania M
Drexel University M
Duquesne University M
East Stroudsburg University of Pennsylvania M
Geneva College M
Indiana University of Pennsylvania M
Kutztown University of Pennsylvania M
La Salle University M
Lackawanna College M
Lehigh Carbon Community College W
Lehigh University M
Lock Haven University of Pennsylvania M
Mercyhurst College M
Millersville University of Pennsylvania M
Penn State
University Park M
Philadelphia University M
Point Park College M
St. Joseph's University M
St. Vincent College M
Shippensburg University of Pennsylvania M
Slippery Rock University of Pennsylvania M
Temple University M
University of Pittsburgh M
University of the Sciences in Philadelphia M
Villanova University M
West Chester University of Pennsylvania M

Puerto Rico

Inter American University of Puerto Rico
Bayamon Campus M
Metropolitan Campus M
San German Campus M
Turabo University M
Universidad Metropolitana M,W
University of Puerto Rico
Carolina Regional College M
Cayey University College M
Mayaguez Campus M

Rhode Island

University of Rhode Island M

South Carolina

Anderson College M
Charleston Southern University M
The Citadel M
Claflin University M
Clemson University M
Coastal Carolina University M
Coker College M
College of Charleston M
Erskine College M
Francis Marion University M
Furman University M
Lander University M
Limestone College M
Morris College M
North Greenville College M
Presbyterian College M
Southern Wesleyan University M
Spartanburg Methodist College M
University of South Carolina M
University of South Carolina
Aiken M
Spartanburg M
Voorhees College M
Winthrop University M
Wofford College M

South Dakota

Dakota State University M
Dakota Wesleyan University M
Mount Marty College M
National American University
Rapid City M
South Dakota State University M
University of Sioux Falls M
University of South Dakota M

Tennessee

Austin Peay State University M
Belmont University M
Bethel College M
Carson-Newman College M
Chattanooga State Technical Community College M
Christian Brothers University M
Cleveland State Community College M
Columbia State Community College M
Crichton College M
Dyersburg State Community College M
East Tennessee State University M
Freed-Hardeman University M
Jackson State Community College M
King College M
Lambuth University M
Lee University M
Lipscomb University M
Middle Tennessee State University M
Milligan College M
Roane State Community College M
Southwest Tennessee Community College M
Tennessee Technological University M
Tennessee Wesleyan College M
Trevecca Nazarene University M
Tusculum College M
Union University M
University of Memphis M
University of Tennessee
Knoxville M
Martin M
Vanderbilt University M
Volunteer State Community College M
Walters State Community College M

Texas

Abilene Christian University M
Alvin Community College M
Angelina College M
Baylor University M
Blinn College M
Cisco Junior College W
Clarendon College M
Collin County Community College District M
Dallas Baptist University M
El Paso Community College M
Frank Phillips College M
Galveston College M
Hill College M
Houston Baptist University M
Jarvis Christian College M
Lamar University M
Laredo Community College M
Lon Morris College M
Lubbock Christian University M
McLennan Community College M
North Central Texas College M
Northwood University: Texas Campus M
Odessa College M
Paris Junior College M
Prairie View A&M University M
Ranger College M
Rice University M
St. Edward's University M
St. Mary's University M
Sam Houston State University M
Southwest Texas State University M
Southwestern Adventist University M
Tarleton State University M
Texas A&M University M
Texas A&M University
Corpus Christi M,W
Kingsville M
Texas Christian University M
Texas Southern University M
Texas Tech University M
University of Houston M
University of Texas
Arlington M
Austin M
Pan American M
University of the Incarnate Word M
Wayland Baptist University M
West Texas A&M University M
Western Texas College M
Wharton County Junior College M

Utah

Brigham Young University M
College of Eastern Utah M
Dixie State College of Utah M
Salt Lake Community College M
Snow College M
Southern Utah University M
University of Utah M
Utah Valley State College M

Virginia

Bluefield College M
College of William and Mary M
George Mason University M
James Madison University M
Liberty University M
Longwood University M
Norfolk State University M

Old Dominion University M
Radford University M
University of Richmond M
University of Virginia M
University of Virginia's College at Wise M
Virginia Commonwealth University M
Virginia Intermont College M
Virginia Military Institute M
Virginia Polytechnic Institute and State University M

Washington

Central Washington University M
Centralia College M
Edmonds Community College M
Everett Community College M
Gonzaga University M
Grays Harbor College M
Green River Community College M
Lower Columbia College M
Olympic College M
Peninsula College W
St. Martin's College M
Spokane Community College M
University of Washington M
Walla Walla Community College M
Washington State University M
Wenatchee Valley College M

West Virginia

Alderson-Broaddus College M
Bluefield State College M
Concord College M
Davis and Elkins College M
Marshall University M
Ohio Valley College M
Potomac State College of West Virginia University M
Salem International University M
Shepherd College M
University of Charleston M
West Liberty State College M
West Virginia State College M
West Virginia University M
West Virginia University Institute of Technology M
West Virginia Wesleyan College M

Wisconsin

Cardinal Stritch University M
University of Wisconsin
  Milwaukee M
  Parkside M
Viterbo University M

Basketball

Alabama

Alabama Agricultural and Mechanical University M,W
Alabama State University M,W
Athens State University M
Auburn University M,W
Auburn University at Montgomery M,W
Bevill State Community College M,W
Birmingham-Southern College M,W
Concordia College M,W
Enterprise State Junior College M,W
Faulkner University M
Gadsden State Community College M,W
George C. Wallace State Community College
  Dothan M
  Selma M,W
Jacksonville State University M,W
James H. Faulkner State Community College M,W
Jefferson Davis Community College M
Judson College W
Lawson State Community College M,W
Lurleen B. Wallace Junior College M,W
Marion Military Institute M
Miles College M,W
Northwest-Shoals Community College M,W
Samford University M,W
Selma University M,W
Shelton State Community College M,W
Snead State Community College M,W
Spring Hill College M,W
Talladega College M,W
Troy State University M,W
Tuskegee University M,W
University of Alabama M,W
University of Alabama
  Birmingham M,W
  Huntsville M,W
University of Mobile M,W
University of Montevallo M,W
University of North Alabama M,W
University of South Alabama M,W
University of West Alabama M,W
Wallace State Community College at Hanceville M,W

Alaska

University of Alaska
  Anchorage M,W
  Fairbanks M,W

Arizona

Arizona State University M,W
Arizona Western College M
Central Arizona College M,W
Cochise College M,W
Eastern Arizona College M,W
Glendale Community College M,W
Northern Arizona University M,W
Pima Community College M,W
Scottsdale Community College M,W
South Mountain Community College M,W
University of Arizona M,W
Yavapai College M,W

Arkansas

Arkansas State University M,W
Arkansas Tech University M,W
Harding University M,W
Henderson State University M,W
John Brown University M,W
Lyon College M,W
North Arkansas College M,W
Ouachita Baptist University M,W
Philander Smith College M,W
Southern Arkansas University M,W
University of Arkansas M,W
University of Arkansas
  Fort Smith M,W
  Little Rock M
  Monticello M,W
  Pine Bluff M,W
University of Central Arkansas M,W
Williams Baptist College M,W

California

Azusa Pacific University M,W
Bethany College M,W
Biola University M,W
California Baptist University M,W
California Polytechnic State University: San Luis Obispo M,W
California State Polytechnic University: Pomona M,W
California State University
  Bakersfield M
  Chico M,W
  Fresno M,W
  Fullerton M,W
  Long Beach M,W
  Los Angeles M,W
  Northridge M,W
  Sacramento M,W
  San Bernardino M,W
  Stanislaus M,W
Christian Heritage College M,W
Concordia University M,W
Dominican University of California M,W
Fresno Pacific University M,W
Grossmont Community College M,W
Holy Names College M,W
Hope International University M,W
Humboldt State University M,W
Loyola Marymount University M,W
Master's College M,W
Patten University M,W
Pepperdine University M,W
Point Loma Nazarene University M,W
St. Mary's College of California M,W
San Diego State University M,W
San Jose State University M,W
Santa Clara University M,W
Stanford University M,W
University of California
  Berkeley M,W
  Irvine M,W
  Los Angeles M,W
  Riverside M,W
  Santa Barbara M,W
University of San Diego M,W
University of San Francisco M,W
University of Southern California M,W
University of the Pacific M,W
Vanguard University of Southern California M,W
Yuba Community College District M,W

Colorado

Colorado Christian University M,W
Colorado School of Mines M,W
Colorado State University M,W
Colorado State University
  Pueblo M,W
Fort Lewis College M,W
Mesa State College M,W
Metropolitan State College of Denver M,W
Otero Junior College M,W
Regis University M,W
Trinidad State Junior College M
University of Colorado
  Boulder M,W
  Colorado Springs M,W
University of Denver M,W
University of Northern Colorado M,W

Connecticut

Capital Community College M,W
Central Connecticut State University M,W
Fairfield University M,W
Mitchell College M,W
Quinnipiac University M,W
Sacred Heart University M,W
Southern Connecticut State University M,W
Teikyo Post University M,W
University of Bridgeport M,W
University of Connecticut M,W
University of Hartford M,W
University of New Haven M,W

Delaware

Delaware State University M,W
Delaware Technical and Community College
  Stanton/Wilmington Campus M,W
University of Delaware M,W
Wilmington College M,W

District of Columbia

American University M,W
George Washington University M,W
Georgetown University M,W
Howard University M,W
University of the District of Columbia M,W

Florida

Barry University M,W
Bethune-Cookman College M,W
Broward Community College M,W
Chipola Junior College M,W
Daytona Beach Community College M,W
Eckerd College M,W
Edward Waters College M,W
Embry-Riddle Aeronautical University M
Flagler College M,W
Florida Agricultural and Mechanical University M
Florida Atlantic University M,W
Florida College M
Florida Institute of Technology M,W
Florida International University M,W
Florida Southern College M,W
Florida State University M,W
Gulf Coast Community College M,W
Hillsborough Community College M,W
Indian River Community College M,W
Jacksonville University M,W
Manatee Community College M
Miami-Dade Community College M,W
Nova Southeastern University M,W
Okaloosa-Walton Community College M,W
Palm Beach Atlantic University M,W
Palm Beach Community College M,W
Pasco-Hernando Community College M
Pensacola Junior College M,W
Polk Community College M
Rollins College M,W
St. Leo University M,W
St. Petersburg College M,W
St. Thomas University M
Santa Fe Community College M,W
Stetson University M,W
Tallahassee Community College M,W
University of Central Florida M,W
University of Florida M,W
University of Miami M,W
University of North Florida M,W
University of South Florida M,W
University of Tampa M,W
University of West Florida M,W
Warner Southern College M,W
Webber International University M,W

Georgia

Abraham Baldwin Agricultural College M
Albany State University M,W
Andrew College M,W
Armstrong Atlantic State University M,W
Augusta State University M,W
Berry College M,W
Brewton-Parker College M,W
Clark Atlanta University M,W
Clayton College and State University M,W
Columbus State University M,W
Covenant College M,W
Darton College W
Emmanuel College M,W
Fort Valley State University M,W
Georgia College and State University M,W
Georgia Institute of Technology M,W
Georgia Perimeter College M,W
Georgia Southern University M,W

Georgia Southwestern State University M,W
Georgia State University M,W
Kennesaw State University M,W
Mercer University M,W
Middle Georgia College M,W
Morehouse College M
North Georgia College & State University M,W
Paine College M,W
Reinhardt College M,W
Savannah State University M,W
Shorter College M,W
Southern Polytechnic State University M,W
State University of West Georgia M,W
Truett-McConnell College M,W
University of Georgia M,W
Valdosta State University M,W

Hawaii

Brigham Young University-Hawaii M
Chaminade University of Honolulu M
Hawaii Pacific University M
University of Hawaii
  Hilo M
  Manoa M,W

Idaho

Albertson College of Idaho M,W
Boise State University M,W
College of Southern Idaho M,W
Idaho State University M,W
Lewis-Clark State College M,W
North Idaho College M,W
Northwest Nazarene University M,W
University of Idaho M,W

Illinois

Black Hawk College M,W
Black Hawk College
  East Campus M,W
Bradley University M,W
Carl Sandburg College M,W
Chicago State University M,W
City Colleges of Chicago
  Kennedy-King College M,W
  Malcolm X College M,W
  Wright College M,W
College of Lake County M,W
Danville Area Community College M,W
De Paul University M,W
Eastern Illinois University M,W
Elgin Community College M,W
Highland Community College M,W
Illinois Central College M,W
Illinois Eastern Community Colleges
  Lincoln Trail College M,W
  Olney Central College M,W
  Wabash Valley College M,W
Illinois Institute of Technology M,W
Illinois State University M,W
John A. Logan College M,W
Judson College M,W
Kankakee Community College M,W
Kaskaskia College M,W
Kendall College M,W
Kishwaukee College M,W
Lake Land College M,W
Lewis and Clark Community College M,W
Lewis University M,W
Lincoln College M,W
Lincoln Land Community College M,W
Loyola University of Chicago M,W
McHenry County College M,W
McKendree College M,W
Moraine Valley Community College M,W
Northwestern University M,W
Olivet Nazarene University M,W
Parkland College M,W
Quincy University M,W
Rend Lake College M,W
Robert Morris College: Chicago M,W
St. Xavier University M
Sauk Valley Community College M,W
Shawnee Community College M,W
South Suburban College of Cook County M,W
Southeastern Illinois College M,W
Southern Illinois University Carbondale M,W
Southern Illinois University Edwardsville M,W
Southwestern Illinois College M,W
Trinity Christian College M,W
Trinity International University M,W
University of Illinois
  Chicago M,W
  Springfield M,W
  Urbana-Champaign M,W
University of St. Francis M,W
Waubonsee Community College M,W
Western Illinois University M,W

Indiana

Ancilla College M,W
Ball State University M,W
Bethel College M,W
Butler University M,W
Calumet College of St. Joseph M,W
Goshen College M,W
Grace College M,W
Huntington College M,W
Indiana Institute of Technology M,W
Indiana State University M,W
Indiana University
  Bloomington M,W
  Southeast M,W
Indiana University-Purdue University Fort Wayne M,W
Indiana University-Purdue University Indianapolis M,W
Indiana Wesleyan University M,W
Marian College M,W
Oakland City University M,W
Purdue University M,W
Purdue University
  Calumet M,W
St. Joseph's College M,W
St. Mary-of-the-Woods College W
Taylor University M,W
Taylor University: Fort Wayne M,W
University of Evansville M,W
University of Indianapolis M,W
University of Notre Dame M,W
University of St. Francis M,W
University of Southern Indiana M,W
Valparaiso University M,W
Vincennes University M,W

Iowa

Briar Cliff University M,W
Clinton Community College M
Des Moines Area Community College M,W
Dordt College M,W
Drake University M,W
Ellsworth Community College M,W
Franciscan University M,W
Graceland University M,W
Grand View College M,W
Indian Hills Community College M
Iowa Central Community College M,W
Iowa Lakes Community College M,W
Iowa State University M,W
Iowa Wesleyan College M,W
Iowa Western Community College M,W
Kirkwood Community College M,W
Marshalltown Community College M,W
Morningside College M,W
Muscatine Community College M
North Iowa Area Community College M,W
Northwestern College M,W
St. Ambrose University M,W
Scott Community College M
Southwestern Community College M,W
University of Iowa M,W
University of Northern Iowa M,W
Waldorf College M,W
William Penn University M,W

Kansas

Allen County Community College M,W
Baker University M,W
Barton County Community College M,W
Benedictine College M,W
Bethany College M,W
Bethel College M,W
Butler County Community College M,W
Central Christian College M,W
Cloud County Community College M,W
Dodge City Community College M,W
Emporia State University M,W
Fort Hays State University M,W
Fort Scott Community College M,W
Friends University M,W
Garden City Community College M,W
Hesston College M,W
Highland Community College M,W
Hutchinson Community College M,W
Independence Community College M,W
Johnson County Community College M,W
Kansas City Kansas Community College M,W
Kansas State University M,W
Kansas Wesleyan University M,W
Labette Community College M,W
McPherson College M,W
MidAmerica Nazarene University M,W
Newman University M,W
Ottawa University M,W
Pittsburg State University M,W
Pratt Community College M,W
St. Mary College M,W
Seward County Community College M,W
Southwestern College M,W
Sterling College M,W
Tabor College M,W
University of Kansas M,W
Washburn University of Topeka M,W
Wichita State University M,W

Kentucky

Alice Lloyd College M,W
Bellarmine University M,W
Brescia University M,W
Campbellsville University M,W
Cumberland College M,W
Georgetown College M,W
Kentucky Wesleyan College M,W
Lindsey Wilson College M,W
Morehead State University M,W
Murray State University M,W
Pikeville College M,W
St. Catharine College M,W
Spalding University M,W
Union College M,W
University of Kentucky M,W
University of Louisville M,W

Louisiana

Centenary College of Louisiana M,W
Dillard University M,W
Grambling State University M,W
Louisiana State University and Agricultural and Mechanical College M,W
Louisiana Tech University M,W
McNeese State University M,W
Nicholls State University M,W
Northwestern State University M,W
Southeastern Louisiana University M,W
Southern University and Agricultural and Mechanical College M,W
Tulane University M,W
University of Louisiana at Lafayette M,W
University of Louisiana at Monroe M,W
University of New Orleans M,W
Xavier University of Louisiana M,W

Maine

University of Maine M,W
University of Maine
  Augusta M,W

Maryland

Allegany College M,W
Anne Arundel Community College M,W
Bowie State University M,W
Chesapeake College M,W
College of Southern Maryland M
Columbia Union College M,W
Community College of Baltimore County
  Catonsville M,W
  Dundalk M,W
  Essex M,W
Coppin State College M,W
Garrett College M,W
Hagerstown Community College M,W
Howard Community College M,W
Loyola College in Maryland M,W
Morgan State University M,W
Mount St. Mary's College M,W
Towson University M,W
University of Maryland
  Baltimore County M,W
  College Park M,W

Massachusetts

American International College M,W
Assumption College M,W
Bentley College M,W
Boston College M,W
Boston University M,W
College of the Holy Cross M,W
Dean College M,W
Merrimack College M,W
Mount Ida College M
Northeastern University M,W
Roxbury Community College M
Stonehill College M,W
University of Massachusetts
  Amherst M,W
  Lowell M,W

Michigan

Alpena Community College M,W
Aquinas College M,W
Central Michigan University M,W
Concordia University M,W
Cornerstone University M,W
Eastern Michigan University M,W
Ferris State University M,W
Glen Oaks Community College M,W
Gogebic Community College M,W
Grand Rapids Community College M,W
Grand Valley State University M,W
Hillsdale College M,W
Kellogg Community College M,W
Lansing Community College M,W
Macomb Community College M,W
Michigan State University M,W
Michigan Technological University M,W
Mott Community College M,W
Northern Michigan University M,W
Northwood University M,W
Oakland Community College M,W
Oakland University M,W
Saginaw Valley State University M,W
Schoolcraft College M,W
Siena Heights University M,W
Spring Arbor University M,W
University of Michigan M,W
University of Michigan
  Dearborn M,W

Wayne State University M,W
Western Michigan University M,W

Minnesota

Bemidji State University M,W
Bethany Lutheran College M,W
Concordia University: St. Paul M,W
Minnesota State University
Mankato M,W
Moorhead M,W
St. Cloud State University M,W
Southwest State University M,W
University of Minnesota
Crookston M,W
Duluth M,W
Morris M,W
Twin Cities M,W
Winona State University M,W

Mississippi

Alcorn State University M,W
Coahoma Community College M,W
Delta State University M,W
Holmes Community College M,W
Itawamba Community College M,W
Mary Holmes College M,W
Mississippi Gulf Coast Community College
Perkinston M,W
Mississippi State University M,W
Mississippi University for Women W
Mississippi Valley State University M,W
Northwest Mississippi Community College M,W
University of Mississippi M,W
University of Southern Mississippi M,W

Missouri

Avila University M,W
Central Methodist College M,W
Central Missouri State University M,W
College of the Ozarks M,W
Columbia College M,W
Cottey College W
Crowder College W
Culver-Stockton College M,W
Drury University M,W
Evangel University M,W
Hannibal-LaGrange College M,W
Harris Stowe State College M,W
Jefferson College W
Lincoln University M,W
Lindenwood University M,W
Mineral Area College M,W
Missouri Baptist University M,W
Missouri Southern State College M,W
Missouri Valley College M,W
Missouri Western State College M,W
Moberly Area Community College M,W
North Central Missouri College M,W
Penn Valley Community College M
Research College of Nursing M,W
Rockhurst University M,W
St. Louis University M,W
Southeast Missouri State University M,W
Southwest Baptist University M,W
Southwest Missouri State University M,W
St. Louis Community College
Forest Park M,W
Meramec M,W
Three Rivers Community College M,W
Truman State University M,W
University of Missouri
Columbia M,W
Kansas City M,W
Rolla M,W
St. Louis M,W
William Jewell College M,W
William Woods University W

Montana

Carroll College M,W
Dawson Community College M,W
Miles Community College M,W
Montana State University
Billings M,W
Bozeman M,W
Montana Tech of the University of Montana M,W
Rocky Mountain College M,W
University of Great Falls M,W
University of Montana-Missoula M,W
University of Montana: Western M,W

Nebraska

Bellevue University M
Central Community College M
Chadron State College M,W
College of Saint Mary W
Concordia University M,W
Creighton University M,W
Dana College M,W
Doane College M,W
Hastings College M,W
Mid Plains Community College Area M,W
Midland Lutheran College M,W
Nebraska College of Technical Agriculture M,W
Northeast Community College M,W
Peru State College M,W
Southeast Community College
Beatrice Campus M,W
University of Nebraska
Kearney M,W
Lincoln M,W
Omaha M,W
Wayne State College M,W
Western Nebraska Community College M,W
York College M,W

Nevada

University of Nevada
Las Vegas M,W
Reno M,W

New Hampshire

Franklin Pierce College M,W
Hesser College M,W
St. Anselm College M,W
Southern New Hampshire University M,W
University of New Hampshire M,W

New Jersey

Bloomfield College M,W
Brookdale Community College M,W
Caldwell College M,W
Essex County College M,W
Fairleigh Dickinson University
Metropolitan Campus M,W
Felician College M,W
Georgian Court College W
Mercer County Community College M,W
Monmouth University M,W
New Jersey Institute of Technology M,W
Rider University M,W
Rutgers, The State University of New Jersey
New Brunswick Regional Campus M,W
St. Peter's College M,W
Salem Community College W
Seton Hall University M,W

New Mexico

Eastern New Mexico University M,W
New Mexico Highlands University M,W
New Mexico Junior College M,W
New Mexico Military Institute M
New Mexico State University M,W
University of New Mexico M,W
Western New Mexico University M,W

New York

Adelphi University M,W
Canisius College M,W
City University of New York
Queens College M,W
Concordia College M,W
Daemen College M,W
Dominican College of Blauvelt M,W
Dowling College M,W
Fordham University M,W
Genesee Community College M,W
Globe Institute of Technology M
Hofstra University M,W
Houghton College M,W
Iona College M,W
Le Moyne College M,W
Long Island University
C. W. Post Campus M,W
Southampton College M,W
Manhattan College M,W
Marist College M,W
Mercy College M,W
Molloy College M,W
Monroe Community College M
New York Institute of Technology M
Niagara County Community College M
Niagara University M,W
Nyack College M,W
Pace University M,W
Pace University: Pleasantville/Briarcliff M,W
Paul Smith's College M,W
Roberts Wesleyan College M,W
Sage College of Albany M,W
St. Bonaventure University M,W
St. John's University M,W
State University of New York
Albany M,W
Binghamton M,W
Buffalo M,W
College of Technology at Alfred M,W
Stony Brook M,W
Syracuse University M,W
Wagner College M,W

North Carolina

Appalachian State University M,W
Barber-Scotia College M,W
Barton College M,W
Belmont Abbey College M,W
Brevard College M,W
Campbell University M,W
Catawba College M,W
Davidson College M,W
Duke University M,W
East Carolina University M,W
Elizabeth City State University M,W
Elon University M,W
Fayetteville State University M,W
Gardner-Webb University M,W
High Point University M,W
Johnson C. Smith University M,W
Lees-McRae College M,W
Lenoir Community College M
Lenoir-Rhyne College M,W
Livingstone College M,W
Louisburg College M,W
Mars Hill College M,W
Montreat College M,W
Mount Olive College M,W
North Carolina Agricultural and Technical State University M,W
North Carolina Central University M,W
North Carolina State University M,W
Pfeiffer University M,W
Queens University of Charlotte M,W
St. Andrews Presbyterian College M,W
St. Augustine's College M,W
Shaw University M,W
University of North Carolina
Asheville M,W
Chapel Hill M,W
Charlotte M,W
Greensboro M,W
Pembroke M,W
Wilmington M,W
Wake Forest University M,W
Western Carolina University M,W
Wingate University M,W
Winston-Salem State University M,W

North Dakota

Bismarck State College M,W
Dickinson State University M,W
Jamestown College M,W
Lake Region State College M,W
Mayville State University M,W
Minot State University M,W
Minot State University: Bottineau Campus M,W
North Dakota State College of Science M,W
North Dakota State University M,W
University of Mary M,W
University of North Dakota M,W
Valley City State University M,W
Williston State College M,W

Ohio

Ashland University M,W
Bowling Green State University M,W
Cedarville University M,W
Central State University M,W
Cincinnati State Technical and Community College M,W
Clark State Community College M,W
Cleveland State University M,W
Columbus State Community College M,W
Edison State Community College M,W
Kent State University M,W
Lakeland Community College M,W
Malone College M,W
Miami University
Oxford Campus M,W
Mount Vernon Nazarene University M,W
Ohio Dominican College M,W
Ohio State University
Columbus Campus M,W
Ohio University M,W
Owens Community College
Findlay Campus M,W
Toledo M,W
Shawnee State University M,W
Sinclair Community College M,W
Southern State Community College M,W
Tiffin University M,W
University of Akron M,W
University of Cincinnati M,W
University of Dayton M,W
University of Findlay M,W
University of Rio Grande M,W
University of Toledo M,W
Urbana University M,W
Ursuline College W
Walsh University M,W
Wright State University M,W
Xavier University M,W
Youngstown State University M,W

Oklahoma

Bacone College M,W
Cameron University M,W
Carl Albert State College M,W
East Central University M,W
Eastern Oklahoma State College M,W
Northeastern Oklahoma Agricultural and Mechanical College M,W
Northeastern State University M,W
Northern Oklahoma College M,W
Northwestern Oklahoma State University M,W

Oklahoma Baptist University M,W
Oklahoma Christian University M,W
Oklahoma City University M,W
Oklahoma Panhandle State University M,W
Oklahoma State University M,W
Oklahoma Wesleyan University M,W
Oral Roberts University M,W
Redlands Community College M,W
Rose State College M,W
St. Gregory's University M,W
Seminole State College M,W
Southeastern Oklahoma State University M,W
Southern Nazarene University M,W
Southwestern Oklahoma State University M,W
University of Central Oklahoma M,W
University of Oklahoma M,W
University of Science and Arts of Oklahoma M,W
University of Tulsa M,W
Western Oklahoma State College M,W

Oregon

Blue Mountain Community College M,W
Chemeketa Community College M,W
Clackamas Community College M,W
Concordia University M,W
Lane Community College M,W
Linn-Benton Community College M,W
Mount Hood Community College M,W
Northwest Christian College M
Oregon Institute of Technology M,W
Oregon State University M,W
Portland Community College M,W
Portland State University M,W
Southern Oregon University M,W
Southwestern Oregon Community College M,W
Treasure Valley Community College M,W
University of Oregon M,W
University of Portland M,W
Western Baptist College M,W

Pennsylvania

Bloomsburg University of Pennsylvania M,W
California University of Pennsylvania M,W
Carlow College W
Cheyney University of Pennsylvania M,W
Community College of Beaver County M
Drexel University M,W
Duquesne University M,W
East Stroudsburg University of Pennsylvania M,W
Edinboro University of Pennsylvania M,W
Geneva College M,W
Holy Family University M,W
Indiana University of Pennsylvania M,W
Kutztown University of Pennsylvania M,W
La Salle University M,W
Lackawanna College M,W
Lock Haven University of Pennsylvania M,W
Manor College M,W
Mercyhurst College M,W
Millersville University of Pennsylvania M,W
Penn State
University Park M,W
Philadelphia University M,W
Point Park College M,W
Robert Morris University M,W
St. Joseph's University M,W
St. Vincent College M,W
Seton Hill University M,W
Shippensburg University of Pennsylvania M,W
Slippery Rock University of Pennsylvania M,W
Temple University M,W
University of Pittsburgh M,W
University of Pittsburgh
Johnstown M,W
Titusville M
University of the Sciences in Philadelphia M,W
Villanova University M,W
West Chester University of Pennsylvania M,W

Puerto Rico

Bayamon Central University M,W
Inter American University of Puerto Rico
Bayamon Campus M,W
Fajardo Campus M
Guayama Campus M,W
Metropolitan Campus M,W
San German Campus M,W
Turabo University M,W
Universidad del Este M,W
Universidad Metropolitana M,W
University of Puerto Rico
Bayamon University College M,W
Carolina Regional College M,W
Cayey University College M,W
Mayaguez Campus M,W
Ponce M,W
Utuado M,W
University of the Sacred Heart M

Rhode Island

Bryant College M,W
Providence College M,W
University of Rhode Island M,W

South Carolina

Anderson College M,W
Charleston Southern University M,W
The Citadel M
Claflin University M,W
Clemson University M,W
Coastal Carolina University M,W
Coker College M,W
College of Charleston M,W
Converse College W
Erskine College M,W
Francis Marion University M,W
Furman University M,W
Lander University M,W
Limestone College M,W
Morris College M,W
North Greenville College M,W
Presbyterian College M,W
South Carolina State University M,W
Southern Wesleyan University M,W
Spartanburg Methodist College M,W
University of South Carolina M,W
University of South Carolina
Aiken M,W
Spartanburg M,W
Voorhees College M,W
Winthrop University M,W
Wofford College M,W

South Dakota

Augustana College M,W
Black Hills State University M,W
Dakota State University M,W
Dakota Wesleyan University M,W
Mount Marty College M,W
Northern State University M,W
South Dakota School of Mines and Technology M,W
South Dakota State University M,W
University of Sioux Falls M,W
University of South Dakota M,W

Tennessee

Austin Peay State University M,W
Belmont University M,W
Bethel College M,W
Bryan College M,W
Carson-Newman College M,W
Chattanooga State Technical Community College M,W
Christian Brothers University M,W
Cleveland State Community College M,W
Columbia State Community College M,W
Crichton College M
Dyersburg State Community College M,W
East Tennessee State University M,W
Freed-Hardeman University M,W
Jackson State Community College M,W
King College M,W
Lambuth University M,W
Lane College M,W
Lee University M,W
Lipscomb University M,W
Middle Tennessee State University M,W
Milligan College M,W
Roane State Community College M,W
Southwest Tennessee Community College M,W
Tennessee State University M,W
Tennessee Technological University M,W
Tennessee Wesleyan College M,W
Trevecca Nazarene University M,W
Tusculum College M,W
Union University M,W
University of Memphis M,W
University of Tennessee
Chattanooga M,W
Knoxville M,W
Martin M,W
Vanderbilt University M,W
Volunteer State Community College M,W
Walters State Community College M,W

Texas

Abilene Christian University M,W
Angelina College M,W
Angelo State University M,W
Baylor University M,W
Blinn College M,W
Clarendon College M,W
Collin County Community College District M,W
Frank Phillips College M,W
Hill College M,W
Houston Baptist University M,W
Jacksonville College M,W
Jarvis Christian College M,W
Kilgore College M,W
Lamar University M,W
Lee College M
Lon Morris College M,W
Lubbock Christian University M,W
McLennan Community College M,W
Midland College M,W
Midwestern State University M,W
Odessa College M,W
Panola College M,W
Paris Junior College M,W
Prairie View A&M University M,W
Ranger College M,W
Rice University M,W
St. Edward's University M,W
St. Mary's University M,W
Sam Houston State University M,W
South Plains College M,W
Southern Methodist University M,W
Southwest Texas State University M,W
Southwestern Adventist University M,W
Stephen F. Austin State University M,W
Tarleton State University M,W
Texas A&M University M,W
Texas A&M University
Commerce M,W
Corpus Christi M,W
Kingsville M,W
Texas Christian University M,W
Texas Southern University M,W
Texas Tech University M,W
Texas Woman's University W
Trinity Valley Community College M,W
Tyler Junior College M,W
University of Houston M,W
University of North Texas M,W
University of Texas
Arlington M,W
Austin M,W
Pan American M,W
San Antonio M,W
University of the Incarnate Word M,W
Wayland Baptist University M,W
West Texas A&M University M,W
Western Texas College W

Utah

Brigham Young University M,W
College of Eastern Utah M,W
Dixie State College of Utah M,W
Salt Lake Community College M,W
Snow College M,W
Southern Utah University M,W
University of Utah M,W
Utah State University M,W,
Utah Valley State College M,W
Weber State University M,W

Vermont

College of St. Joseph in Vermont M,W
Green Mountain College M,W
St. Michael's College M,W
University of Vermont M,W

Virginia

Bluefield College M,W
College of William and Mary M,W
George Mason University M,W
Hampton University M,W
James Madison University M,W
Liberty University M,W
Longwood University M,W
Norfolk State University M,W
Old Dominion University M,W
Radford University M,W
University of Richmond M,W
University of Virginia M,W
University of Virginia's College at Wise M,W
Virginia Commonwealth University M,W
Virginia Intermont College M,W
Virginia Military Institute M
Virginia Polytechnic Institute and State University M,W
Virginia State University M,W
Virginia Union University M,W

Washington

Central Washington University M,W
Centralia College M,W
Clark College M,W
Eastern Washington University M,W
Edmonds Community College M,W
Everett Community College M,W
Evergreen State College M,W
Gonzaga University M,W
Grays Harbor College M,W
Green River Community College M,W
Lower Columbia College M,W
North Seattle Community College M,W
Northwest College M,W
Olympic College M,W
St. Martin's College M,W
Seattle Pacific University M,W
Seattle University M,W
Spokane Community College M,W
University of Washington M,W

Walla Walla Community College M,W
Washington State University M,W
Wenatchee Valley College M,W
Western Washington University M,W

West Virginia
Alderson-Broaddus College M,W
Bluefield State College M,W
Concord College M,W
Davis and Elkins College M,W
Fairmont State College M,W
Glenville State College M,W
Marshall University M,W
Mountain State University M
Ohio Valley College M,W
Potomac State College of West Virginia University M,W
Salem International University M,W
Shepherd College M,W
University of Charleston M,W
West Liberty State College M,W
West Virginia State College M,W
West Virginia University M,W
West Virginia University Institute of Technology M,W
West Virginia Wesleyan College M,W
Wheeling Jesuit University M,W

Wisconsin
Cardinal Stritch University M,W
Marquette University M,W
Silver Lake College W
University of Wisconsin
Green Bay M,W
Madison M,W
Milwaukee M,W
Parkside M,W
Viterbo University M,W

Wyoming
Casper College M,W
Eastern Wyoming College M
Sheridan College M,W
University of Wyoming M,W
Western Wyoming Community College M,W

Bowling

Arkansas
University of Arkansas
Pine Bluff W

Delaware
Delaware State University W

Florida
Bethune-Cookman College W

Illinois
McKendree College M,W

Indiana
Vincennes University M,W

Kansas
Wichita State University M,W

Kentucky
Pikeville College M,W

Maryland
Coppin State College W
Morgan State University W

Michigan
Aquinas College M,W
Saginaw Valley State University M

Mississippi
Alcorn State University W
Mississippi Valley State University M,W

Missouri
Lindenwood University M,W

Nebraska
University of Nebraska
Lincoln W

North Carolina
North Carolina Central University M,W
St. Augustine's College W
Shaw University W

Pennsylvania
Bucks County Community College M

Texas
Prairie View A&M University W
Texas Southern University W

Boxing

Connecticut
Southern Connecticut State University M

Louisiana
Southern University and Agricultural and Mechanical College W

Puerto Rico
Universidad Metropolitana M,W

Cheerleading

Alabama
Athens State University W
George C. Wallace State Community College
Selma M,W
James H. Faulkner State Community College M,W
Northwest-Shoals Community College M,W

Arkansas
University of Central Arkansas M,W

Delaware
University of Delaware M,W

Florida
Nova Southeastern University M,W
Pensacola Junior College M,W
University of Central Florida M,W
Warner Southern College M,W
Webber International University M,W

Idaho
North Idaho College M,W

Illinois
Lincoln College M,W
McKendree College M,W
Olivet Nazarene University M,W

Indiana
Grace College M,W
Marian College M,W
University of St. Francis M,W

Iowa
Drake University M,W
Iowa Western Community College M,W
St. Ambrose University M,W
Waldorf College M,W
William Penn University M,W

Kansas
Allen County Community College M,W
Benedictine College M,W
Dodge City Community College M,W
Emporia State University M,W
Garden City Community College M,W
Labette Community College M,W
MidAmerica Nazarene University M,W
Pratt Community College M,W
Seward County Community College M,W
Southwestern College M,W
Tabor College M,W
Washburn University of Topeka M,W

Kentucky
Bellarmine University M,W
Cumberland College M,W
Murray State University M,W
Union College M,W

Louisiana
Southeastern Louisiana University M,W

Mississippi
Northwest Mississippi Community College M,W

Missouri
Avila University W
Evangel University M,W
Harris Stowe State College W
Lindenwood University M,W
Missouri Southern State College M,W
Moberly Area Community College M,W
St. Louis University M,W

Montana
Miles Community College W

Nebraska
Hastings College W
Southeast Community College
Beatrice Campus W

New York
Nyack College M,W

North Carolina
Brunswick Community College W
Campbell University W
Gardner-Webb University M,W
Lees-McRae College M,W
Methodist College M
North Carolina State University M,W

Ohio
Kent State University M,W
Tiffin University M,W

Oklahoma
Northeastern Oklahoma Agricultural and Mechanical College M,W
Oklahoma Christian University W
Oklahoma City University M,W
Rose State College M,W
Southeastern Oklahoma State University W
Southwestern Oklahoma State University M,W
University of Science and Arts of Oklahoma M,W
University of Tulsa M,W
Western Oklahoma State College M,W

Oregon
Southwestern Oregon Community College M,W

Pennsylvania
Geneva College W
Kutztown University of Pennsylvania W
Lackawanna College W

South Carolina
Anderson College W
Limestone College M,W
Morris College M,W
North Greenville College M,W
Spartanburg Methodist College M,W

South Dakota
Dakota Wesleyan University M,W

Tennessee
Bethel College M,W
Freed-Hardeman University W
Lambuth University M,W
Tennessee Technological University M,W
Tennessee Wesleyan College W
University of Memphis M,W

Texas
Clarendon College W
East Texas Baptist University M,W
Houston Baptist University M,W
Tyler Junior College M,W

Utah
Brigham Young University M,W

Virginia
James Madison University M,W
Liberty University M,W
Old Dominion University M,W

Washington
Walla Walla Community College W

West Virginia
Mountain State University M,W
West Virginia University M,W

Wyoming
University of Wyoming M,W

Cricket

New York
Pace University: Pleasantville/Briarcliff W

Pennsylvania
Haverford College M
Penn State
Delaware County W

Tennessee
University of Tennessee
Knoxville M,W

Cross-country

Alabama
Alabama Agricultural and Mechanical University M,W
Alabama State University M,W
Auburn University M,W
Birmingham-Southern College M,W
Jacksonville State University M,W
Lurleen B. Wallace Junior College M,W
Miles College M,W
Northwest-Shoals Community College M
Samford University M,W
Spring Hill College M,W
Troy State University M,W
University of Alabama M,W
University of Alabama
Birmingham W
Huntsville M,W

University of Mobile M,W
University of North Alabama M,W
University of South Alabama M,W
University of West Alabama M,W
Wallace State Community College at Hanceville M,W

Alaska
University of Alaska
Anchorage M,W
Fairbanks M,W

Arizona
Arizona State University M,W
Central Arizona College M,W
Gateway Community College M,W
Glendale Community College M,W
Northern Arizona University M,W
Pima Community College M,W
Scottsdale Community College M,W
University of Arizona M,W
Yavapai College W

Arkansas
Arkansas State University M,W
Arkansas Tech University W
Harding University M,W
Henderson State University W
Lyon College M,W
Southern Arkansas University W
University of Arkansas M,W
University of Arkansas
Little Rock M,W
Pine Bluff M,W

California
Azusa Pacific University M,W
Biola University M,W
California Baptist University M,W
California Polytechnic State University: San Luis Obispo M,W
California State Polytechnic University: Pomona M,W
California State University
Chico M,W
Fresno M,W
Fullerton M,W
Long Beach M,W
Los Angeles M,W
Northridge M,W
Sacramento M,W
Stanislaus M,W
Concordia University M,W
Fresno Pacific University M,W
Holy Names College M,W
Humboldt State University M,W
Loyola Marymount University M,W
Master's College M,W
Pepperdine University M,W
Point Loma Nazarene University M,W
St. Mary's College of California M,W
San Diego State University W
San Jose State University M,W
Santa Clara University M,W
Stanford University M
University of California
Berkeley M,W
Irvine M,W
Los Angeles M,W
Riverside M,W
Santa Barbara M,W
University of San Diego M,W
University of San Francisco M,W
University of Southern California M,W
University of the Pacific W
Vanguard University of Southern California M,W
Yuba Community College District M,W

Colorado
Colorado Christian University M,W
Colorado School of Mines M,W
Colorado State University M,W
Fort Lewis College M,W
Mesa State College W
University of Colorado
Boulder M,W
Colorado Springs M,W
University of Northern Colorado W

Connecticut
Central Connecticut State University M,W
Quinnipiac University M,W
Teikyo Post University M
University of Connecticut M,W
University of Hartford M,W
University of New Haven M,W

District of Columbia
American University M,W
George Washington University M,W
Georgetown University M,W
Howard University M,W

Florida
Bethune-Cookman College M,W
Eckerd College W
Embry-Riddle Aeronautical University M,W
Flagler College M,W
Florida Atlantic University M,W
Florida Institute of Technology M,W
Florida Southern College M,W
Florida State University M,W
Jacksonville University M,W
Nova Southeastern University W
Palm Beach Atlantic University M,W
Stetson University M,W
University of Central Florida M,W
University of Florida M,W
University of Miami M,W
University of North Florida M,W
University of South Florida M,W
University of Tampa M,W
University of West Florida M,W
Warner Southern College M,W
Webber International University M,W

Georgia
Albany State University M,W
Augusta State University M,W
Berry College M,W
Brenau University W
Clark Atlanta University M,W
Clayton College and State University M,W
Columbus State University M,W
Covenant College M,W
Georgia College and State University M,W
Georgia Institute of Technology M,W
Georgia Southern University W
Georgia State University M,W
Kennesaw State University M,W
Mercer University M,W
Morehouse College M
Paine College M,W
Reinhardt College M,W
Savannah State University W
Shorter College M,W
State University of West Georgia M,W
Truett-McConnell College M,W
University of Georgia M,W
Valdosta State University M,W

Hawaii
Brigham Young University-Hawaii M,W
Chaminade University of Honolulu M,W
Hawaii Pacific University M,W
University of Hawaii
Hilo M,W
Manoa W

Idaho
Boise State University M,W
College of Southern Idaho M,W
Idaho State University M,W
Lewis-Clark State College M,W
Northwest Nazarene University M,W
University of Idaho M,W

Illinois
Bradley University M,W
Chicago State University M,W
College of Lake County M,W
Danville Area Community College M,W
De Paul University M,W
Eastern Illinois University M,W
Illinois Institute of Technology M,W
Illinois State University M,W
Judson College M,W
Kendall College M,W
Lewis University M,W
Lincoln College M,W
Loyola University of Chicago M,W
McKendree College M,W
Moraine Valley Community College M,W
Northwestern University W
Olivet Nazarene University M,W
Rend Lake College M
Robert Morris College: Chicago M,W
St. Xavier University W
Sauk Valley Community College M,W
South Suburban College of Cook County M,W
Southern Illinois University Carbondale M,W
Southern Illinois University Edwardsville M,W
Trinity Christian College M,W
University of Illinois
Chicago M,W
Urbana-Champaign M,W
University of St. Francis W
Waubonsee Community College M,W
Western Illinois University M,W

Indiana
Ball State University M,W
Bethel College M,W
Butler University M,W
Goshen College M,W
Grace College M,W
Huntington College M,W
Indiana State University M,W
Indiana University
Bloomington M,W
Indiana University-Purdue University Fort Wayne M,W
Indiana University-Purdue University Indianapolis M,W
Indiana Wesleyan University M,W
Marian College M,W
Oakland City University M,W
Purdue University M,W
St. Joseph's College M,W
Taylor University M,W
University of Evansville M,W
University of Indianapolis M,W
University of Notre Dame M,W
University of St. Francis M,W
University of Southern Indiana M,W
Valparaiso University M,W
Vincennes University M,W

Iowa
Briar Cliff University M,W
Dordt College M,W
Drake University M,W
Franciscan University M,W
Graceland University M,W
Grand View College M,W
Iowa State University M,W
Morningside College M,W
Northwestern College M,W
St. Ambrose University M,W
University of Iowa M,W
University of Northern Iowa M,W
William Penn University M,W

Kansas
Allen County Community College M,W
Baker University M,W
Barton County Community College M,W
Benedictine College M,W
Bethany College M,W
Butler County Community College M,W
Central Christian College M,W
Cloud County Community College M,W
Emporia State University M,W
Fort Hays State University M,W
Garden City Community College M,W
Highland Community College M,W
Hutchinson Community College M,W
Johnson County Community College M,W
Kansas City Kansas Community College M,W
Kansas State University M,W
Kansas Wesleyan University M,W
McPherson College M,W
MidAmerica Nazarene University M,W
Ottawa University M,W
Pittsburg State University M,W
Pratt Community College M,W
Southwestern College M,W
Sterling College M,W
Tabor College M,W
University of Kansas M,W
Wichita State University M,W

Kentucky
Bellarmine University M,W
Campbellsville University M,W
Cumberland College M,W
Georgetown College M,W
Lindsey Wilson College M,W
Mid-Continent College M,W
Murray State University M,W
Pikeville College M,W
University of Kentucky M,W
University of Louisville M,W

Louisiana
Centenary College of Louisiana M,W
Dillard University M,W
Louisiana State University and Agricultural and Mechanical College M,W
Louisiana Tech University M,W
McNeese State University M,W
Nicholls State University M,W
Northwestern State University M,W
Southeastern Louisiana University M,W
Southern University and Agricultural and Mechanical College M,W
Tulane University M,W
University of Louisiana at Lafayette M,W
University of Louisiana at Monroe M,W
University of New Orleans M,W

Maine
University of Maine M,W

Maryland
Anne Arundel Community College M,W
Bowie State University M,W
Columbia Union College M,W
Coppin State College M,W
Hagerstown Community College M,W
Loyola College in Maryland M,W
Morgan State University M,W
Mount St. Mary's College M,W
Towson University M,W
University of Maryland
Baltimore County M,W

Massachusetts
Boston College W
Boston University M,W
Merrimack College W
Northeastern University M,W
University of Massachusetts
  Amherst M,W
  Lowell M,W

Michigan
Aquinas College M,W
Central Michigan University M,W
Cornerstone University M,W
Eastern Michigan University M,W
Ferris State University M,W
Grand Rapids Community College M,W
Grand Valley State University M,W
Hillsdale College M,W
Lansing Community College M,W
Macomb Community College M,W
Michigan State University M,W
Mott Community College M,W
Northern Michigan University W
Northwood University M,W
Oakland Community College M,W
Oakland University M,W
Saginaw Valley State University M,W
Schoolcraft College W
Siena Heights University M,W
Spring Arbor University M,W
University of Michigan M,W
Wayne State University M,W
Western Michigan University M,W

Minnesota
Concordia University: St. Paul M,W
Minnesota State University
  Mankato M,W
  Moorhead M,W
St. Cloud State University M,W
University of Minnesota
  Duluth M,W
  Twin Cities M,W
Winona State University W

Mississippi
Alcorn State University M,W
Delta State University W
Mississippi State University W
Mississippi Valley State University M,W
University of Mississippi M,W
University of Southern Mississippi M,W

Missouri
Central Methodist College M,W
Central Missouri State University M,W
Drury University M,W
Evangel University M,W
Lindenwood University M,W
Missouri Baptist University M,W
Missouri Southern State College M,W
Missouri Valley College M,W
Northwest Missouri State University M,W
Research College of Nursing M,W
St. Louis University M,W
Southeast Missouri State University M,W
Southwest Baptist University M,W
Southwest Missouri State University M,W
Truman State University M,W
University of Missouri
  Columbia M,W
  Kansas City M,W
  Rolla M,W
William Jewell College M,W

Montana
Flathead Valley Community College M,W
Montana State University
  Billings M,W
  Bozeman M,W
University of Montana-Missoula M,W

Nebraska
College of Saint Mary W
Concordia University M,W
Creighton University M,W
Dana College M,W
Doane College M,W
Hastings College M,W
Midland Lutheran College M,W
University of Nebraska
  Kearney M,W
  Lincoln M,W
  Omaha W
Wayne State College M,W
York College M,W

Nevada
University of Nevada
  Las Vegas W
  Reno W

New Hampshire
University of New Hampshire W

New Jersey
Bloomfield College M
Fairleigh Dickinson University
  Metropolitan Campus M,W
Felician College M,W
Georgian Court College W
Monmouth University M,W
Rider University M,W
Rutgers, The State University of New Jersey
  New Brunswick Regional Campus M,W
St. Peter's College M,W
Seton Hall University M,W

New Mexico
Eastern New Mexico University M,W
New Mexico Highlands University M,W
New Mexico State University M,W
University of New Mexico M,W

New York
Adelphi University M,W
Canisius College M,W
Daemen College M,W
Dominican College of Blauvelt M,W
Fordham University M,W
Hofstra University M,W
Houghton College M,W
Iona College M
Le Moyne College M,W
Long Island University
  C. W. Post Campus M,W
Manhattan College M,W
Marist College M,W
Mercy College M,W
Molloy College M,W
New York Institute of Technology M,W
Niagara University M,W
Nyack College M,W
Pace University M,W
Pace University: Pleasantville/Briarcliff M,W
Roberts Wesleyan College M,W
St. John's University M,W
State University of New York
  Albany M,W
  Binghamton M,W
  Buffalo M,W
  College of Technology at Alfred M,W
  Stony Brook M,W
Syracuse University M,W
Wagner College M,W

North Carolina
Appalachian State University M,W
Barton College M,W
Belmont Abbey College M,W
Brevard College M,W
Campbell University M,W
Catawba College M,W
Davidson College M,W
East Carolina University M,W
Elon University M,W
Fayetteville State University M,W
Gardner-Webb University M,W
High Point University M,W
Johnson C. Smith University M,W
Lees-McRae College M,W
Lenoir-Rhyne College M,W
Livingstone College M,W
Mars Hill College M,W
Montreat College M,W
Mount Olive College M,W
North Carolina Agricultural and Technical State University M,W
North Carolina Central University M,W
North Carolina State University M,W
Pfeiffer University M,W
Queens University of Charlotte M,W
St. Andrews Presbyterian College M,W
St. Augustine's College M,W
Shaw University M,W
University of North Carolina
  Asheville M,W
  Chapel Hill M,W
  Charlotte M,W
  Greensboro M,W
  Pembroke M,W
  Wilmington M,W
Wake Forest University M,W
Western Carolina University M,W
Wingate University M,W
Winston-Salem State University M,W

North Dakota
Dickinson State University M,W
Jamestown College M,W
Minot State University M,W
North Dakota State University M,W
University of Mary M,W
University of North Dakota M,W
Valley City State University M,W

Ohio
Ashland University M,W
Bowling Green State University M,W
Cedarville University M,W
Cleveland State University W
Kent State University M,W
Malone College M,W
Miami University
  Oxford Campus M,W
Ohio State University
  Columbus Campus M,W
Ohio University M,W
Shawnee State University M,W
Tiffin University M,W
University of Akron M,W
University of Dayton M,W
University of Findlay M,W
University of Rio Grande M,W
University of Toledo M,W
Walsh University M,W
Wright State University M,W
Xavier University M,W
Youngstown State University M,W

Oklahoma
East Central University M,W
Oklahoma Baptist University M,W
Oklahoma Christian University M,W
Oklahoma Panhandle State University M,W
Oklahoma State University M,W
Oral Roberts University M,W
St. Gregory's University M,W
Southeastern Oklahoma State University W
Southern Nazarene University M,W
Southwestern Oklahoma State University W
University of Central Oklahoma M,W
University of Oklahoma M,W
University of Tulsa M,W

Oregon
Chemeketa Community College M,W
Clackamas Community College M,W
Lane Community College M,W
Mount Hood Community College M,W
Oregon Institute of Technology M,W
Portland State University M,W
Southern Oregon University M,W
University of Oregon M,W
University of Portland M,W

Pennsylvania
Bloomsburg University of Pennsylvania W
Cheyney University of Pennsylvania M,W
Duquesne University M,W
East Stroudsburg University of Pennsylvania M,W
Edinboro University of Pennsylvania M,W
Geneva College M,W
Holy Family University W
Indiana University of Pennsylvania M,W
Kutztown University of Pennsylvania M,W
La Salle University M,W
Lehigh University M,W
Lock Haven University of Pennsylvania M,W
Mercyhurst College M,W
Millersville University of Pennsylvania M,W
Penn State
  University Park M,W
Point Park College M,W
Robert Morris University M,W
St. Joseph's University M,W
St. Vincent College M,W
Seton Hill University M,W
Shippensburg University of Pennsylvania M,W
Slippery Rock University of Pennsylvania M,W
University of Pittsburgh M,W
University of the Sciences in Philadelphia M,W
Villanova University M,W
West Chester University of Pennsylvania M,W

Puerto Rico
Bayamon Central University M,W
Inter American University of Puerto Rico
  Bayamon Campus M,W
  Guayama Campus M,W
  San German Campus M,W
Turabo University M,W
Universidad del Este M,W
University of Puerto Rico
  Carolina Regional College M,W
  Cayey University College M,W
  Mayaguez Campus M,W
  Ponce M,W
University of the Sacred Heart M,W

Rhode Island
Providence College M,W
University of Rhode Island M,W

South Carolina
Anderson College M,W
Charleston Southern University M,W

The Citadel M,W
Clemson University M,W
Coastal Carolina University M,W
Coker College M,W
College of Charleston M,W
Converse College W
Erskine College M,W
Francis Marion University M,W
Furman University M,W
Lander University W
Limestone College M,W
Morris College M,W
North Greenville College M,W
Presbyterian College M,W
South Carolina State University M,W
Southern Wesleyan University M,W
Spartanburg Methodist College M,W
University of South Carolina W
University of South Carolina
Aiken M,W
Spartanburg M,W
Voorhees College M,W
Winthrop University M,W
Wofford College M,W

South Dakota

Augustana College M,W
Black Hills State University M,W
Dakota Wesleyan University M,W
Mount Marty College M,W
South Dakota School of Mines and Technology M,W
South Dakota State University M,W
University of Sioux Falls M,W
University of South Dakota M,W

Tennessee

Austin Peay State University M,W
Belmont University M,W
Bethel College M,W
Carson-Newman College M,W
East Tennessee State University M,W
Freed-Hardeman University M,W
Lambuth University M,W
Lee University M,W
Lipscomb University M,W
Middle Tennessee State University M,W
Milligan College M,W
Tennessee Technological University M,W
Tennessee Wesleyan College W
Tusculum College M,W
Union University M,W
University of Memphis M,W
University of Tennessee
Chattanooga M,W
Knoxville M,W
Martin W
Vanderbilt University W

Texas

Abilene Christian University M,W
Angelo State University M,W
Baylor University M,W
Dallas Baptist University W
Lamar University M,W
Northwood University: Texas Campus M,W
Odessa College W
Rice University M,W
Sam Houston State University M,W
South Plains College M,W
Southern Methodist University M,W
Southwest Texas State University M,W
Stephen F. Austin State University M,W
Tarleton State University M,W
Texas A&M University M,W
Texas A&M University
Commerce M,W
Texas Christian University M,W
Texas Southern University M,W
Texas Tech University M,W
University of Houston M,W
University of Texas
Arlington M,W
Austin M,W
San Antonio M,W
University of the Incarnate Word M,W
Wayland Baptist University M,W
West Texas A&M University M,W

Utah

Brigham Young University M,W
University of Utah M,W
Utah State University M,W
Weber State University M,W

Vermont

Champlain College W
University of Vermont M,W

Virginia

College of William and Mary M,W
George Mason University M,W
Hampton University M,W
James Madison University M,W
Liberty University M,W
Longwood University M,W
Norfolk State University M,W
Radford University M,W
University of Richmond W
University of Virginia M,W
University of Virginia's College at Wise M,W
Virginia Commonwealth University M,W
Virginia Military Institute M,W
Virginia Polytechnic Institute and State University M,W
Virginia State University M,W

Washington

Central Washington University M,W
Clark College M,W
Eastern Washington University M,W
Everett Community College M,W
Evergreen State College M,W
Gonzaga University M,W
Northwest College M,W
St. Martin's College M,W
Seattle Pacific University M,W
Seattle University M,W
Spokane Community College M,W
University of Washington M,W
Washington State University M,W
Western Washington University M,W

West Virginia

Alderson-Broaddus College M,W
Bluefield State College M,W
Concord College M,W
Davis and Elkins College M,W
Glenville State College M,W
Marshall University M,W
Ohio Valley College M
Salem International University M,W
University of Charleston M,W
West Liberty State College M,W
West Virginia University M,W
West Virginia Wesleyan College M,W
Wheeling Jesuit University M,W

Wisconsin

Marquette University M,W
University of Wisconsin
Green Bay M,W
Madison M,W
Milwaukee M,W
Parkside M,W

Wyoming

University of Wyoming M,W

Diving

Alabama

Auburn University M,W
University of Alabama M,W

Alaska

University of Alaska
Fairbanks W

Arizona

Arizona State University M,W
Northern Arizona University W
University of Arizona M,W

Arkansas

John Brown University M,W
Ouachita Baptist University M,W

California

Biola University W
California Baptist University M,W
California State University
Fresno W
Northridge M,W
College of the Redwoods M
Pepperdine University W
San Diego State University W
San Jose State University W
Stanford University M,W
University of California
Berkeley M,W
Irvine M,W
University of San Diego W
University of Southern California M,W

Colorado

Colorado State University W
University of Denver M,W

Connecticut

Central Connecticut State University W
Fairfield University M,W
Southern Connecticut State University M
University of Connecticut M,W

District of Columbia

American University M,W
George Washington University M,W
Howard University M,W

Florida

Florida State University M,W
Indian River Community College M,W
University of Florida M,W
University of Miami M,W

Georgia

Georgia Institute of Technology M,W
Georgia Southern University W
University of Georgia M,W

Hawaii

University of Hawaii
Manoa M,W

Illinois

Illinois Institute of Technology M,W
Illinois State University W
Lincoln College M,W
Northwestern University M,W
Southern Illinois University Carbondale M,W
University of Illinois
Chicago M,W
Urbana-Champaign W
Western Illinois University M,W

Indiana

Ball State University M,W
Indiana University
Bloomington M,W
Indiana University-Purdue University
Indianapolis M,W
Purdue University M,W
University of Evansville M,W
University of Notre Dame M,W
Valparaiso University M,W

Iowa

University of Iowa M,W

Kansas

University of Kansas W

Kentucky

University of Kentucky M,W
University of Louisville M,W

Louisiana

Tulane University W

Maine

University of Maine M,W

Maryland

Loyola College in Maryland M,W
Towson University M,W
University of Maryland
Baltimore County M,W

Massachusetts

Boston College W
Boston University M,W
Northeastern University W
University of Massachusetts
Amherst M,W

Michigan

Eastern Michigan University M,W
Grand Rapids Community College M,W
Grand Valley State University M,W
Hillsdale College W
Michigan State University M,W
Oakland University M,W
University of Michigan M,W
Wayne State University M,W

Minnesota

Minnesota State University
Mankato M,W
Moorhead M
St. Cloud State University M,W
University of Minnesota
Twin Cities M,W

Mississippi

Delta State University M,W

Missouri

Drury University M,W
Lindenwood University M,W
St. Louis University M,W
Southwest Missouri State University M
University of Missouri
Columbia M,W

Nebraska

University of Nebraska
Kearney W
Lincoln W

Nevada

University of Nevada
Las Vegas M
Reno W

New Hampshire

University of New Hampshire W

New Jersey

Rider University M,W

Rutgers, The State University of New Jersey
New Brunswick Regional Campus M,W
St. Peter's College M,W

New Mexico
Southwestern Indian Polytechnic Institute M
University of New Mexico W

New York
Fordham University M,W
Iona College M,W
Marist College M,W
Niagara University M,W
St. Bonaventure University M,W
St. John's University M,W
State University of New York
Binghamton M,W
Buffalo M,W
Stony Brook M,W
Syracuse University M,W

North Carolina
Davidson College M,W
East Carolina University M,W
North Carolina State University M,W
University of North Carolina
Chapel Hill W
Wilmington M,W

North Dakota
University of North Dakota W

Ohio
Ashland University M,W
Bowling Green State University M,W
Cleveland State University M,W
Miami University
Oxford Campus M,W
Ohio State University
Columbus Campus M,W
Ohio University M,W
University of Findlay M,W
University of Toledo M,W
Wright State University M,W

Pennsylvania
Indiana University of Pennsylvania M,W
La Salle University M,W
Lehigh University M,W
Lock Haven University of Pennsylvania W
Slippery Rock University of Pennsylvania M,W
University of Pittsburgh M,W
Villanova University W

Rhode Island
University of Rhode Island M,W

South Carolina
Clemson University M,W
College of Charleston M,W
University of South Carolina M,W

South Dakota
South Dakota State University M,W
University of South Dakota M,W

Tennessee
University of Tennessee
Knoxville M,W

Texas
Southern Methodist University M,W
Texas A&M University M,W
Texas Christian University M,W
University of Houston W
University of Texas
Austin M,W

Utah
Brigham Young University M,W
University of Utah M,W

Virginia
George Mason University M,W
James Madison University M,W
Old Dominion University M,W
University of Richmond W
University of Virginia M,W
Virginia Military Institute M
Virginia Polytechnic Institute and State University M,W

West Virginia
West Virginia University M,W

Wisconsin
University of Wisconsin
Green Bay M,W
Madison M,W
Milwaukee M,W

Wyoming
University of Wyoming M,W

Equestrian

California
California State University
Fresno W

Georgia
Thomas University M,W

Indiana
St. Mary-of-the-Woods College W

Kansas
Kansas State University W

Kentucky
Murray State University M,W

Massachusetts
Mount Ida College M,W

Missouri
William Woods University M,W

Nebraska
Nebraska College of Technical Agriculture M,W

New York
Dowling College W
Molloy College M,W
Vassar College W

North Carolina
St. Andrews Presbyterian College M,W

Oklahoma
Oklahoma State University W

South Carolina
Anderson College M,W
University of South Carolina W

Texas
Texas A&M University W
West Texas A&M University W

Virginia
Virginia Intermont College M,W

Fencing

California
California State University
Fullerton M,W
Stanford University M,W

Illinois
Northwestern University W

Indiana
University of Notre Dame M,W

Michigan
Wayne State University M,W

New Jersey
Fairleigh Dickinson University
Metropolitan Campus W
New Jersey Institute of Technology M,W
Rutgers, The State University of New Jersey
New Brunswick Regional Campus M,W

New York
City University of New York
Queens College W
St. John's University M,W

North Carolina
North Carolina State University M,W

Ohio
Cleveland State University M,W
Ohio State University
Columbus Campus M,W

Pennsylvania
Penn State
University Park M,W
Temple University W

Field Hockey

California
Stanford University W
University of California
Berkeley W
University of the Pacific W

Connecticut
Fairfield University W
Quinnipiac University W
University of Connecticut W

Delaware
University of Delaware W

District of Columbia
American University W

Illinois
Northwestern University W

Indiana
Ball State University W

Iowa
University of Iowa W

Kentucky
Bellarmine University W
University of Louisville W

Louisiana
Tulane University M

Maine
University of Maine W

Maryland
Towson University W
University of Maryland
College Park W

Massachusetts
American International College W
Bentley College W
Boston College W
Boston University W
Northeastern University W
University of Massachusetts
Amherst W

Michigan
Central Michigan University W
Michigan State University W
University of Michigan W

Missouri
Lindenwood University W
St. Louis University W
Southwest Missouri State University W

New Hampshire
Franklin Pierce College W
University of New Hampshire W

New Jersey
Monmouth University W
Rider University W
Rutgers, The State University of New Jersey
New Brunswick Regional Campus W

New York
Hofstra University W
Houghton College W
Long Island University
C. W. Post Campus W
State University of New York
Albany W
Syracuse University W

North Carolina
Appalachian State University W
Catawba College W
Davidson College W
Duke University W
University of North Carolina
Chapel Hill W
Wake Forest University W

Ohio
Kent State University W
Miami University
Oxford Campus W
Ohio State University
Columbus Campus W
Ohio University W

Pennsylvania
Bloomsburg University of Pennsylvania W
Drexel University W
East Stroudsburg University of Pennsylvania W
Indiana University of Pennsylvania W
Kutztown University of Pennsylvania W
La Salle University W
Lehigh University W
Lock Haven University of Pennsylvania W
Mercyhurst College W
Millersville University of Pennsylvania W
Penn State
University Park W
Philadelphia University W
St. Joseph's University W

Shippensburg University of Pennsylvania W
Slippery Rock University of Pennsylvania W
Temple University W
Villanova University W
West Chester University of Pennsylvania W

Rhode Island
Providence College W
University of Rhode Island W

Vermont
University of Vermont W

Virginia
College of William and Mary W
James Madison University W
Longwood University W
Old Dominion University W
Radford University W
University of Richmond W
University of Virginia W
Virginia Commonwealth University W

West Virginia
Davis and Elkins College W

Football (non-tackle)

Connecticut
Trinity College M

Georgia
Clark Atlanta University M,W

Missouri
Lincoln University M

New York
City University of New York
Hunter College W
State University of New York
College at Cortland M

Football (tackle)

Alabama
Alabama Agricultural and Mechanical University M
Alabama State University M
Auburn University M
Jacksonville State University M
Miles College M
Samford University M
Troy State University M
Tuskegee University M
University of Alabama M
University of Alabama
Birmingham M
University of North Alabama M
University of West Alabama M

Arizona
Arizona State University M
Arizona Western College M
Eastern Arizona College M
Glendale Community College M
Northern Arizona University M
Pima Community College M
Scottsdale Community College M
University of Arizona M

Arkansas
Arkansas State University M
Arkansas Tech University M
Harding University M
Henderson State University M
Ouachita Baptist University M
Southern Arkansas University M
University of Arkansas M
University of Arkansas
Monticello M
Pine Bluff M
University of Central Arkansas M

California
Azusa Pacific University M
California Polytechnic State University:
San Luis Obispo M
California State University
Fresno M
Sacramento M
Grossmont Community College M
Humboldt State University M
St. Mary's College of California M
San Diego State University M
San Jose State University M
Stanford University M
University of California
Berkeley M
Los Angeles M
University of Southern California M
Yuba Community College District M

Colorado
Colorado School of Mines M
Colorado State University M
Fort Lewis College M
Mesa State College M
University of Colorado
Boulder M
University of Northern Colorado M

Connecticut
Sacred Heart University M
Southern Connecticut State University M
University of Connecticut M
University of New Haven M

Delaware
Delaware State University M
University of Delaware M

District of Columbia
Georgetown University M
Howard University M

Florida
Bethune-Cookman College M
Florida Agricultural and Mechanical University M
Florida Atlantic University M
Florida State University M
University of Central Florida M
University of Florida M
University of Miami M
University of South Florida M
Webber International University M

Georgia
Albany State University M
Clark Atlanta University M
Fort Valley State University M
Georgia Institute of Technology M
Georgia Military College M
Georgia Southern University M
Middle Georgia College M,W
Morehouse College M
Savannah State University M
State University of West Georgia M
University of Georgia M
Valdosta State University M

Hawaii
University of Hawaii
Manoa M

Idaho
Boise State University M
Idaho State University M
University of Idaho M

Illinois
Eastern Illinois University M
Illinois State University M
McKendree College M
Northwestern University M
Olivet Nazarene University M
Quincy University M
St. Xavier University M
Southern Illinois University Carbondale M
Trinity International University M
University of Illinois
Springfield W
Urbana-Champaign M
University of St. Francis M
Western Illinois University M

Indiana
Ball State University M
Indiana State University M
Indiana University
Bloomington M
Purdue University M
St. Joseph's College M
Taylor University M
University of Indianapolis M
University of Notre Dame M
University of St. Francis M

Iowa
Briar Cliff University M
Ellsworth Community College M
Graceland University M
Iowa Central Community College M
Iowa State University M
Iowa Wesleyan College M
Morningside College M
North Iowa Area Community College M
Northwestern College M
St. Ambrose University M
University of Iowa M
University of Northern Iowa M
Waldorf College M
William Penn University M

Kansas
Baker University M
Benedictine College M
Bethany College M
Bethel College M
Butler County Community College M
Dodge City Community College M
Emporia State University M
Fort Hays State University M
Fort Scott Community College M
Friends University M
Garden City Community College M
Highland Community College M
Hutchinson Community College M
Independence Community College M
Kansas State University M
Kansas Wesleyan University M
McPherson College M
MidAmerica Nazarene University M
Ottawa University M
Pittsburg State University M
St. Mary College M
Southwestern College M
Sterling College M
Tabor College M
University of Kansas M
Washburn University of Topeka M

Kentucky
Campbellsville University M
Cumberland College M
Georgetown College M
Kentucky Wesleyan College M
Murray State University M
Pikeville College M
Union College M
University of Kentucky M
University of Louisville M

Louisiana
Grambling State University M
Louisiana State University and Agricultural and Mechanical College M
Louisiana Tech University M
McNeese State University M
Nicholls State University M
Northwestern State University M
Southern University and Agricultural and Mechanical College M
Tulane University M
University of Louisiana at Lafayette M
University of Louisiana at Monroe M

Maine
University of Maine M

Maryland
Bowie State University M
Morgan State University M
Towson University M
University of Maryland
College Park M

Massachusetts
American International College M
Boston College M
Dean College M
Massachusetts Institute of Technology W
Northeastern University M
University of Massachusetts
Amherst M

Michigan
Central Michigan University M
Eastern Michigan University M
Ferris State University M
Grand Rapids Community College M
Grand Valley State University M
Hillsdale College M
Michigan State University M
Michigan Technological University M
Northern Michigan University M
Northwood University M
Saginaw Valley State University M
University of Michigan M
Wayne State University M
Western Michigan University M

Minnesota
Bemidji State University M
Concordia University: St. Paul M
Minnesota State University
Mankato M
Moorhead M
St. Cloud State University M
Southwest State University M
University of Minnesota
Crookston M
Duluth M
Morris M
Twin Cities M,W
Winona State University M

Mississippi
Alcorn State University M
Coahoma Community College M
Delta State University M
Holmes Community College M
Itawamba Community College M
Mississippi Gulf Coast Community College
Perkinston M
Mississippi State University M
Mississippi Valley State University M
Northwest Mississippi Community College M
University of Mississippi M
University of Southern Mississippi M

Missouri
Avila University M

Central Methodist College M
Central Missouri State University M
Culver-Stockton College M
Evangel University M
Lindenwood University M
Missouri Southern State College M
Missouri Valley College M
Missouri Western State College M
Northwest Missouri State University M
Southeast Missouri State University M
Southwest Baptist University M
Truman State University M
University of Missouri
Columbia M
Rolla M
William Jewell College M

Montana
Carroll College M
Montana State University
Bozeman M
Montana Tech of the University of Montana M
Rocky Mountain College M
University of Montana-Missoula M
University of Montana: Western M

Nebraska
Chadron State College M
Concordia University M
Dana College M
Doane College M
Hastings College M
Midland Lutheran College M
Peru State College M
University of Nebraska
Kearney M
Lincoln M
Omaha M
Wayne State College M

Nevada
University of Nevada
Las Vegas M
Reno M

New Hampshire
University of New Hampshire M

New Jersey
Monmouth University M
Rutgers, The State University of New Jersey
New Brunswick Regional Campus M

New Mexico
Eastern New Mexico University M
New Mexico Highlands University M
New Mexico Military Institute M
New Mexico State University M
University of New Mexico M
Western New Mexico University M

New York
Hofstra University M
St. John's University M
State University of New York
Albany M
Buffalo M
College of Technology at Alfred M
Health Science Center at Stony Brook M
Stony Brook M
Syracuse University M

North Carolina
Appalachian State University M
Catawba College M
Davidson College M
Duke University M
East Carolina University M
Elizabeth City State University M
Elon University M
Fayetteville State University M
Gardner-Webb University M
Johnson C. Smith University M
Lenoir-Rhyne College M
Livingstone College M
Mars Hill College M
North Carolina Agricultural and Technical State University M
North Carolina Central University M
North Carolina State University M
St. Augustine's College M
University of North Carolina
Chapel Hill M
Wake Forest University M
Western Carolina University M
Wingate University M
Winston-Salem State University M

North Dakota
Dickinson State University M
Jamestown College M
Mayville State University M
Minot State University M
North Dakota State College of Science M
North Dakota State University M
University of Mary M
University of North Dakota M
Valley City State University M

Ohio
Ashland University M
Bowling Green State University M
Kent State University M
Malone College M
Miami University
Oxford Campus M
Ohio State University
Columbus Campus M
Ohio University M
Tiffin University M
University of Akron M
University of Cincinnati M
University of Findlay M
University of Toledo M
Urbana University M
Walsh University M
Wilmington College W
Youngstown State University M

Oklahoma
East Central University M
Northeastern Oklahoma Agricultural and Mechanical College M
Northeastern State University M
Northwestern Oklahoma State University M
Oklahoma Panhandle State University M
Oklahoma State University M
Southeastern Oklahoma State University M
Southwestern Oklahoma State University M
University of Central Oklahoma M
University of Oklahoma M
University of Tulsa M

Oregon
Oregon State University M
Portland State University M
Southern Oregon University M
University of Oregon M

Pennsylvania
Bloomsburg University of Pennsylvania M
California University of Pennsylvania M
Cheyney University of Pennsylvania M
East Stroudsburg University of Pennsylvania M
Edinboro University of Pennsylvania M
Geneva College M
Indiana University of Pennsylvania M
Kutztown University of Pennsylvania M
Lackawanna College M
Lehigh University M
Lock Haven University of Pennsylvania M
Mercyhurst College M
Millersville University of Pennsylvania M
Penn State
University Park M
Robert Morris University M
Shippensburg University of Pennsylvania M
Slippery Rock University of Pennsylvania M
Temple University M
University of Pittsburgh M
Villanova University M
West Chester University of Pennsylvania M

Rhode Island
University of Rhode Island M

South Carolina
Charleston Southern University M
The Citadel M
Clemson University M
Coastal Carolina University M
Furman University M
North Greenville College M
Presbyterian College M
South Carolina State University M
University of South Carolina M
Wofford College M

South Dakota
Augustana College M
Black Hills State University M
Dakota State University M
Dakota Wesleyan University M
Northern State University M
South Dakota School of Mines and Technology M
South Dakota State University M
University of Sioux Falls M
University of South Dakota M

Tennessee
Bethel College M
Carson-Newman College M
East Tennessee State University M
Lambuth University M
Lane College M
Middle Tennessee State University M
Tennessee State University M
Tennessee Technological University M
Tusculum College M
University of Memphis M
University of Tennessee
Chattanooga M
Knoxville M
Martin M
Vanderbilt University M

Texas
Abilene Christian University M
Angelo State University M
Baylor University M
Blinn College M
Kilgore College M
Midwestern State University M
Prairie View A&M University M
Ranger College M
Rice University M
Sam Houston State University M
Southern Methodist University M
Southwest Texas State University M
Stephen F. Austin State University M
Tarleton State University M
Texas A&M University M
Texas A&M University
Commerce M
Kingsville M
Texas Christian University M
Texas Southern University M
Texas Tech University M
Trinity Valley Community College M
Tyler Junior College M
University of Houston M
University of North Texas M
University of Texas
Austin M
West Texas A&M University M

Utah
Brigham Young University M
Dixie State College of Utah M
Snow College M
Southern Utah University M
University of Utah M
Utah State University M
Weber State University M

Virginia
College of William and Mary M
Hampton University M
James Madison University M
Liberty University M
Norfolk State University M
University of Richmond M
University of Virginia M
University of Virginia's College at Wise M
Virginia Military Institute M
Virginia Polytechnic Institute and State University M
Virginia State University M
Virginia Union University M

Washington
Central Washington University M
Eastern Washington University M
University of Washington M
Washington State University M
Western Washington University M

West Virginia
Concord College M
Fairmont State College M
Glenville State College M
Marshall University M
Shepherd College M
University of Charleston M
West Liberty State College M
West Virginia State College M
West Virginia University M
West Virginia University Institute of Technology M
West Virginia Wesleyan College M

Wisconsin
University of Wisconsin
Madison M

Wyoming
University of Wyoming M

Golf

Alabama
Alabama State University M,W
Auburn University M,W
Birmingham-Southern College M,W
Central Alabama Community College M
Gadsden State Community College M
Jacksonville State University M,W
James H. Faulkner State Community College M,W
Northwest-Shoals Community College M
Samford University M,W
Spring Hill College M,W
Troy State University M,W

University of Alabama M,W
University of Alabama
Birmingham M,W
University of Mobile M,W
University of Montevallo M,W
University of North Alabama M
University of South Alabama M,W
Wallace State Community College at
Hanceville M

Arizona
Arizona State University M,W
Central Arizona College M
Gateway Community College M,W
Glendale Community College M
Northern Arizona University W
Pima Community College M,W
Scottsdale Community College M
University of Arizona M,W

Arkansas
Arkansas State University M,W
Arkansas Tech University M
Lyon College M,W
Ouachita Baptist University M
University of Arkansas M,W
University of Arkansas
Little Rock M,W
Pine Bluff M,W
Williams Baptist College M

California
Bethany College M
California State University
Bakersfield M
Chico M
Fresno M
Long Beach M,W
Northridge M
Sacramento M
San Bernardino M
Stanislaus M
Holy Names College M
Loyola Marymount University M
Master's College M
Pepperdine University M,W
Point Loma Nazarene University M
St. Mary's College of California M,W
San Diego State University M,W
San Jose State University M,W
Santa Clara University M,W
Stanford University M,W
University of California
Berkeley M,W
Irvine M,W
Los Angeles M,W
Santa Barbara M
University of San Diego M
University of San Francisco M,W
University of Southern California M,W
University of the Pacific M

Colorado
Colorado Christian University M
Colorado School of Mines M,W
Colorado State University M,W
Colorado State University
Pueblo M
Fort Lewis College M
Mesa State College W
Regis University M
Trinidad State Junior College M,W
University of Colorado
Boulder M,W
Colorado Springs M
University of Denver W
University of Northern Colorado M,W

Connecticut
Central Connecticut State University M
Quinnipiac University M
University of Connecticut M
University of Hartford M,W

District of Columbia
American University M
George Washington University M
Georgetown University M

Florida
Barry University M,W
Bethune-Cookman College M,W
Daytona Beach Community College W
Eckerd College M
Embry-Riddle Aeronautical University
M
Flagler College M
Florida Atlantic University M,W
Florida Gulf Coast University M,W
Florida International University W
Florida Southern College M,W
Florida State University M,W
Jacksonville University M,W
Lake City Community College W
Northwood University
Florida Campus M,W
Nova Southeastern University M,W
Palm Beach Atlantic University M
Rollins College M,W
St. Petersburg College W
St. Thomas University M
Stetson University M,W
University of Central Florida M,W
University of Florida M,W
University of Miami W
University of North Florida M
University of South Florida M,W
University of Tampa M
University of West Florida M,W
Warner Southern College M,W
Webber International University M,W

Georgia
Abraham Baldwin Agricultural College
M
Andrew College M,W
Armstrong Atlantic State University M
Augusta State University M,W
Berry College M,W
Clayton College and State University M
Columbus State University M
Darton College M,W
Georgia College and State University M
Georgia Institute of Technology M
Georgia Southern University M
Georgia State University M,W
Kennesaw State University M
Mercer University M,W
Reinhardt College M
Shorter College W
Thomas University M
University of Georgia M,W
Valdosta State University M

Hawaii
University of Hawaii
Hilo M
Manoa M,W

Idaho
Albertson College of Idaho M,W
Boise State University M,W
Idaho State University M,W
Lewis-Clark State College M,W
Northwest Nazarene University M
University of Idaho M,W

Illinois
Black Hawk College M
Bradley University M,W
Chicago State University M,W
College of Lake County M
Danville Area Community College
M,W
De Paul University M
Eastern Illinois University M,W
Elgin Community College M
Highland Community College M,W
Illinois State University M,W
John A. Logan College M,W
Kishwaukee College M,W
Lewis and Clark Community College M
Lewis University M,W
Lincoln College M,W
Loyola University of Chicago M,W
McKendree College M,W
Moraine Valley Community College M
Northwestern University M,W
Olivet Nazarene University M
Parkland College M
Quincy University M,W
Rend Lake College M,W
Sauk Valley Community College M
Southern Illinois University Carbondale
M,W
Southern Illinois University
Edwardsville W
Springfield College in Illinois M
University of Illinois
Urbana-Champaign M,W
University of St. Francis M,W
Waubonsee Community College M
Western Illinois University M

Indiana
Ancilla College M
Ball State University M
Bethel College M
Butler University M,W
Goshen College M
Grace College M
Huntington College M,W
Indiana University
Bloomington M,W
Indiana University-Purdue University
Indianapolis M
Indiana Wesleyan University M
Marian College M,W
Oakland City University M,W
Purdue University M,W
St. Joseph's College M,W
Taylor University M
University of Evansville M,W
University of Indianapolis M,W
University of Notre Dame M,W
University of St. Francis M
University of Southern Indiana M,W
Vincennes University M

Iowa
Briar Cliff University M,W
Clinton Community College M,W
Dordt College M
Drake University M
Ellsworth Community College M,W
Franciscan University M
Graceland University M,W
Grand View College M,W
Indian Hills Community College M
Iowa Central Community College M,W
Iowa Lakes Community College M,W
Iowa State University M,W
Iowa Wesleyan College M,W
Kirkwood Community College M
Marshalltown Community College M,W
Morningside College M,W
Muscatine Community College M,W
North Iowa Area Community College
M,W
Northwestern College M,W
St. Ambrose University M,W
Scott Community College M,W
University of Iowa M,W
University of Northern Iowa M,W
Waldorf College M,W
William Penn University M

Kansas
Allen County Community College M,W
Baker University M,W
Barton County Community College M
Benedictine College M,W
Bethany College M
Central Christian College M,W
Cloud County Community College M
Dodge City Community College M,W
Friends University M
Hutchinson Community College M
Johnson County Community College M
Kansas City Kansas Community
College M
Kansas State University M,W
Kansas Wesleyan University M,W
Newman University M,W
Ottawa University M
Pittsburg State University M
Pratt Community College M,W
Southwestern College M,W
Tabor College M,W
University of Kansas M,W
Washburn University of Topeka M
Wichita State University M,W

Kentucky
Bellarmine University M,W
Brescia University M,W
Campbellsville University M,W
Cumberland College M,W
Georgetown College M,W
Kentucky Wesleyan College M,W
Lindsey Wilson College M,W
Morehead State University M
Murray State University M,W
Pikeville College M,W
St. Catharine College M,W
Union College M,W
University of Kentucky M,W
University of Louisville M

Louisiana
Centenary College of Louisiana M,W
Grambling State University M
Louisiana State University and
Agricultural and Mechanical College
M,W
Louisiana Tech University M
McNeese State University M,W
Nicholls State University M
Northwestern State University M
Southeastern Louisiana University M
Southern University and Agricultural
and Mechanical College M,W
Tulane University M,W
University of Louisiana at Lafayette M
University of Louisiana at Monroe M
University of New Orleans M,W

Maryland
College of Southern Maryland M,W
Loyola College in Maryland M
Mount St. Mary's College M,W
Towson University M
University of Maryland
College Park M,W

Michigan
Aquinas College M,W
Cornerstone University M
Eastern Michigan University M,W
Ferris State University M,W
Glen Oaks Community College M,W
Grand Rapids Community College M
Grand Valley State University M,W
Hillsdale College M
Lansing Community College M
Michigan State University M,W
Mott Community College M
Northern Michigan University M
Northwood University M,W
Oakland Community College M
Oakland University M,W
Saginaw Valley State University M
Siena Heights University M
Spring Arbor University M
University of Michigan M,W
Wayne State University M
Western Michigan University W

Minnesota
Bethany Lutheran College M,W
Concordia University: St. Paul W
Minnesota State University
Mankato M,W
Moorhead W
St. Cloud State University M,W
Southwest State University W
University of Minnesota
Twin Cities M,W
Winona State University M,W

Mississippi
Alcorn State University M,W
Delta State University M
Itawamba Community College M
Mississippi Gulf Coast Community College
Perkinston M
Mississippi State University M,W
Mississippi Valley State University M,W
Northwest Mississippi Community College M,W
University of Mississippi M,W
University of Southern Mississippi M,W

Missouri
Avila University W
Central Methodist College M,W
Central Missouri State University M
Culver-Stockton College M,W
Drury University M,W
Evangel University M,W
Hannibal-LaGrange College M
Lincoln University M
Lindenwood University M,W
Missouri Baptist University M
Missouri Southern State College M
Missouri Valley College M,W
Missouri Western State College M
Penn Valley Community College M
Research College of Nursing M,W
Rockhurst University M,W
Southeast Missouri State University M
Southwest Baptist University M
Southwest Missouri State University M,W
Truman State University M,W
University of Missouri
Columbia M,W
Kansas City M,W
Rolla M
St. Louis M,W
William Jewell College W
William Woods University M,W

Montana
Carroll College W
Miles Community College M,W
Montana State University
Bozeman W
Montana Tech of the University of Montana M,W
Rocky Mountain College W
University of Montana-Missoula W
University of Montana: Western M,W

Nebraska
Chadron State College W
College of Saint Mary W
Concordia University M,W
Creighton University M,W
Doane College M,W
Hastings College M,W
Mid Plains Community College Area M
Midland Lutheran College M,W
Nebraska College of Technical Agriculture M,W
Northeast Community College M,W
Southeast Community College
Beatrice Campus M
University of Nebraska
Kearney M,W
Lincoln M,W
Wayne State College M,W
York College M,W

Nevada
University of Nevada
Las Vegas M
Reno M,W

New Jersey
Brookdale Community College M
Caldwell College M,W
Fairleigh Dickinson University
Metropolitan Campus M
Monmouth University M,W
Rider University M
Rutgers, The State University of New Jersey
New Brunswick Regional Campus M,W
St. Peter's College M
Seton Hall University M

New Mexico
College of the Southwest M,W
New Mexico Junior College M
New Mexico Military Institute M
New Mexico State University M,W
University of New Mexico M,W
Western New Mexico University M,W

New York
Adelphi University M,W
Canisius College M
City University of New York
Queens College M
Daemen College M
Dominican College of Blauvelt M
Dowling College M
Hofstra University M,W
Iona College M
Le Moyne College M
Manhattan College M
Mercy College M
Niagara University M
Nyack College M
Pace University M,W
Pace University: Pleasantville/Briarcliff M,W
St. Bonaventure University M
St. John's University M
State University of New York
Albany W
Binghamton M
Wagner College M,W

North Carolina
Appalachian State University M,W
Barton College M
Belmont Abbey College M
Brevard College M
Campbell University M,W
Catawba College M
Catawba Valley Community College M
Davidson College M
Duke University M,W
East Carolina University M,W
Elon University M,W
Fayetteville State University M
Gardner-Webb University M,W
High Point University M
Johnson C. Smith University M
Lees-McRae College M
Lenoir-Rhyne College M
Livingstone College M
Louisburg College M
Mars Hill College M
Montreat College M
Mount Olive College M
North Carolina Central University M,W
North Carolina State University M,W
Pfeiffer University M,W
Pitt Community College M,W
Queens University of Charlotte M,W
St. Andrews Presbyterian College M
St. Augustine's College M,W
University of North Carolina
Chapel Hill M,W
Charlotte M
Greensboro M,W
Pembroke M
Wilmington M,W
Wake Forest University M,W
Western Carolina University M,W
Wingate University M,W

North Dakota
Dickinson State University M,W
Jamestown College M,W
Minot State University M
North Dakota State University W
University of North Dakota M,W

Ohio
Ashland University M,W
Bowling Green State University M,W
Cedarville University M
Central State University M,W
Cleveland State University M,W
Kent State University M,W
Lakeland Community College M,W
Malone College M,W
Miami University
Oxford Campus M
Mount Vernon Nazarene University M
Ohio State University
Columbus Campus M,W
Ohio University M
Shawnee State University M
Sinclair Community College M
Tiffin University M,W
University of Akron M
University of Dayton M,W
University of Findlay M,W
University of Toledo M,W
Urbana University M
Ursuline College W
Walsh University M,W
Wright State University M
Xavier University M,W
Youngstown State University M,W

Oklahoma
Cameron University M
East Central University M
Northeastern State University M,W
Oklahoma Baptist University M,W
Oklahoma Christian University M
Oklahoma City University M,W
Oklahoma Panhandle State University M,W
Oklahoma State University M,W
Oklahoma Wesleyan University M
Oral Roberts University M,W
St. Gregory's University M,W
Seminole State College M,W
Southern Nazarene University M,W
Southwestern Oklahoma State University M,W
University of Central Oklahoma M
University of Oklahoma M,W
University of Tulsa M,W

Oregon
Oregon State University M,W
Portland State University M,W
University of Oregon M,W
University of Portland M,W

Pennsylvania
Duquesne University M
Holy Family University M
Indiana University of Pennsylvania M
Kutztown University of Pennsylvania W
La Salle University M,W
Lackawanna College M,W
Lehigh University M
Mercyhurst College M,W
Millersville University of Pennsylvania M
Penn State
University Park M,W
Philadelphia University M
Robert Morris University M
St. Joseph's University M
St. Vincent College M,W
Seton Hill University M,W
Slippery Rock University of Pennsylvania M,W
Temple University M
University of the Sciences in Philadelphia M,W
West Chester University of Pennsylvania M

Rhode Island
University of Rhode Island M

South Carolina
Anderson College M,W
Charleston Southern University M,W
The Citadel M,W
Clemson University M
Coastal Carolina University M,W
Coker College M
College of Charleston M,W
Francis Marion University M
Furman University M,W
Limestone College M,W
Morris College M
North Greenville College M
Presbyterian College M
South Carolina State University M
Southern Wesleyan University M
Spartanburg Methodist College M
University of South Carolina M,W
University of South Carolina
Aiken M
Winthrop University M,W
Wofford College M,W

South Dakota
Dakota State University M
Dakota Wesleyan University M,W
Mount Marty College M,W
Northern State University W
University of Sioux Falls M,W

Tennessee
Austin Peay State University M,W
Belmont University M,W
Bethel College M
Carson-Newman College M
Christian Brothers University M
Cleveland State Community College M,W
East Tennessee State University M,W
Freed-Hardeman University M,W
King College M
Lambuth University M
Lee University M
Lipscomb University M,W
Middle Tennessee State University M,W
Milligan College M
Tennessee Technological University M,W
Tennessee Wesleyan College M
Trevecca Nazarene University M,W
Tusculum College M,W
Union University M
University of Memphis M,W
University of Tennessee
Chattanooga M,W
Knoxville M,W
Martin M
Vanderbilt University M,W
Walters State Community College M,W

Texas
Abilene Christian University M

Baylor University M,W
Lamar University M,W
Lon Morris College M
McLennan Community College M
Midland College M
Northwood University: Texas Campus M,W
Odessa College M
Paris Junior College M
Prairie View A&M University M,W
Rice University M
St. Edward's University M
St. Mary's University M
Sam Houston State University M,W
Southern Methodist University M,W
Southwest Texas State University M,W
Stephen F. Austin State University M
Texas A&M University M,W
Texas A&M University
Commerce M
Corpus Christi W
Texas Christian University M,W
Texas Southern University M,W
Texas Tech University M,W
Texas Wesleyan University M
Tyler Junior College M,W
University of Houston M
University of North Texas M,W
University of Texas
Arlington M
Austin M,W
San Antonio M
University of the Incarnate Word M,W
West Texas A&M University M,W
Western Texas College M

Utah
Brigham Young University M,W
Dixie State College of Utah M
Southern Utah University M
University of Utah M
Utah State University M
Weber State University M,W

Virginia
Bluefield College M
George Mason University M
Hampton University M,W
James Madison University M,W
Liberty University M
Longwood University M,W
Old Dominion University M,W
Radford University M,W
University of Virginia M
Virginia Commonwealth University M
Virginia Intermont College M
Virginia Military Institute M
Virginia Polytechnic Institute and State University M
Virginia Union University M,W

Washington
Centralia College W
Eastern Washington University M,W
Edmonds Community College M,W
Gonzaga University M,W
Grays Harbor College M,W
Green River Community College M
Lower Columbia College M
St. Martin's College M,W
Spokane Community College M,W
University of Washington M,W
Walla Walla Community College M,W
Washington State University M,W
Western Washington University M,W

West Virginia
Bluefield State College M
Concord College M
Davis and Elkins College M
Glenville State College M,W
Marshall University M,W
Ohio Valley College M
Potomac State College of West Virginia University M,W
University of Charleston M
West Liberty State College M,W
West Virginia University Institute of Technology M
West Virginia Wesleyan College M
Wheeling Jesuit University M,W

Wisconsin
Marquette University M
University of Wisconsin
Green Bay M
Madison M,W
Parkside M

Wyoming
Eastern Wyoming College M
University of Wyoming M,W

Gymnastics

Alabama
Auburn University W
University of Alabama W

Alaska
University of Alaska
Anchorage W

Arizona
Arizona State University W
University of Arizona W

California
California Polytechnic State University: San Luis Obispo W
California State University
Fullerton W
San Jose State University W
University of California
Berkeley M,W
Los Angeles W
Santa Barbara W

Colorado
University of Denver W

Connecticut
Southern Connecticut State University M
University of Bridgeport W

District of Columbia
George Washington University W
Howard University M,W

Florida
University of Florida W

Georgia
University of Georgia W

Idaho
Boise State University W

Illinois
Illinois State University W
University of Illinois
Chicago M,W
Urbana-Champaign M,W

Indiana
Ball State University W

Iowa
Iowa State University W
University of Iowa M,W

Kansas
Fort Hays State University M

Kentucky
University of Kentucky W

Louisiana
Centenary College of Louisiana W
Louisiana State University and Agricultural and Mechanical College W

Maryland
Columbia Union College M,W
Towson University W
University of Maryland
College Park W

Michigan
Eastern Michigan University W
Michigan State University M,W
University of Michigan M,W
Western Michigan University W

Minnesota
University of Minnesota
Twin Cities M,W
Winona State University W

Missouri
Southeast Missouri State University W
University of Missouri
Columbia W

Nebraska
University of Nebraska
Lincoln M,W

New Hampshire
University of New Hampshire W

New Jersey
Rutgers, The State University of New Jersey
New Brunswick Regional Campus W

North Carolina
North Carolina State University M,W
University of North Carolina
Chapel Hill W

Ohio
Bowling Green State University W
Kent State University W
Ohio State University
Columbus Campus M,W

Oklahoma
University of Oklahoma M,W

Oregon
Oregon State University W

Pennsylvania
Penn State
University Park M,W
Temple University M,W
University of Pittsburgh W
West Chester University of Pennsylvania W

Rhode Island
University of Rhode Island W

Tennessee
Southern Adventist University M,W

Texas
Texas Woman's University W

Utah
Brigham Young University W
Southern Utah University W
University of Utah W
Utah State University W

Virginia
College of William and Mary M,W
James Madison University M,W

Washington
Seattle Pacific University W

West Virginia
West Virginia University W

Handball

Illinois
Western Illinois University W

Ice hockey

Alabama
University of Alabama
Huntsville M

Alaska
University of Alaska
Anchorage M
Fairbanks M

Colorado
Colorado College M
University of Denver M,W

Connecticut
Fairfield University M
Quinnipiac University M,W
Sacred Heart University M
University of Connecticut M,W

Indiana
University of Notre Dame M

Iowa
Dordt College M

Maine
University of Maine M,W

Massachusetts
American International College M
Bentley College M
Boston College M
Boston University W
Merrimack College M
Northeastern University M,W
University of Massachusetts
Amherst M
Lowell M

Michigan
Ferris State University M
Michigan State University M
Michigan Technological University M
Northern Michigan University M
University of Michigan M
Wayne State University M,W
Western Michigan University M

Minnesota
Bemidji State University M
Minnesota State University
Mankato M,W
St. Cloud State University M
University of Minnesota
Duluth M,W
Twin Cities M,W

Missouri
Lindenwood University M,W

Nebraska
University of Nebraska
Omaha M

New Hampshire
University of New Hampshire M,W

New York
Canisius College M
Clarkson University M,W
Monroe Community College M
Niagara University M,W
Paul Smith's College M
Rensselaer Polytechnic Institute M
St. Lawrence University M,W

North Dakota
Minot State University: Bottineau Campus M
University of North Dakota M,W

Ohio
Bowling Green State University M
Ohio State University
Columbus Campus M,W
University of Findlay M,W

Pennsylvania
Mercyhurst College M,W

Rhode Island
Providence College M,W

Vermont
University of Vermont M

Wisconsin
University of Wisconsin
Madison M,W

Judo

Hawaii
Hawaii Tokai International College M,W

Kentucky
Cumberland College M,W

New York
Nassau Community College M,W
Polytechnic University M,W

Puerto Rico
Turabo University M,W
University of Puerto Rico
Cayey University College M,W
Humacao M,W

Lacrosse

California
Stanford University W

Colorado
University of Denver M,W

Connecticut
Central Connecticut State University W
Fairfield University M,W
Mitchell College M
Quinnipiac University M,W
University of Hartford M
University of New Haven W

Delaware
University of Delaware M,W

District of Columbia
American University W
Georgetown University M,W

Illinois
Northwestern University W

Indiana
Butler University M
University of Notre Dame M,W

Maryland
Anne Arundel Community College M,W
Community College of Baltimore County
Catonsville M,W
Dundalk M,W
Essex M,W
Johns Hopkins University M,W
Loyola College in Maryland M,W
Mount St. Mary's College M,W
Towson University M,W
University of Maryland
Baltimore County M,W
College Park M,W

Massachusetts
American International College W
Boston College W
Boston University W
Dean College M
Mount Ida College M
University of Massachusetts
Amherst M,W
Lowell M

Missouri
Lindenwood University M,W

New Hampshire
University of New Hampshire W

New Jersey
Monmouth University W
Rutgers, The State University of New Jersey
New Brunswick Regional Campus M,W

New York
Adelphi University M,W
Canisius College M,W
Dominican College of Blauvelt M,W
Dowling College M
Hofstra University M,W
Le Moyne College M,W
Long Island University
C. W. Post Campus M,W
Southampton College M
Manhattan College M,W
Marist College M,W
Molloy College M
Monroe Community College M
New York Institute of Technology M
Niagara University W
Pace University M
Pace University: Pleasantville/Briarcliff M
State University of New York
Albany M,W
Binghamton M,W
Health Science Center at Stony Brook M,W
Stony Brook M,W
Syracuse University M,W
Wagner College W

North Carolina
Catawba College M
Davidson College W
Duke University M
Lees-McRae College M
Mars Hill College M
Pfeiffer University M,W
Queens University of Charlotte M,W
St. Andrews Presbyterian College M
University of North Carolina
Chapel Hill M,W
Wingate University M

Ohio
Ohio State University
Columbus Campus M,W

Pennsylvania
Drexel University M
Duquesne University W
East Stroudsburg University of Pennsylvania W
Indiana University of Pennsylvania W
La Salle University W
Lehigh University M,W
Lock Haven University of Pennsylvania W
Mercyhurst College M,W
Millersville University of Pennsylvania W
Penn State
University Park M,W
Philadelphia University W
St. Joseph's University M
St. Vincent College M,W
Shippensburg University of Pennsylvania W
Temple University W
West Chester University of Pennsylvania M,W

South Carolina
Limestone College M,W

Tennessee
Vanderbilt University W

Virginia
College of William and Mary W
James Madison University W
Longwood University W
Old Dominion University W
Radford University M
University of Richmond W
University of Virginia M,W
Virginia Military Institute M
Virginia Polytechnic Institute and State University W

West Virginia
Wheeling Jesuit University M

Wisconsin
University of Wisconsin
Madison W

Rifle

Alabama
Birmingham-Southern College W
Jacksonville State University M,W

Alaska
University of Alaska
Fairbanks M,W

California
University of San Francisco M,W

Georgia
Mercer University M,W
North Georgia College & State University M,W

Illinois
De Paul University W

Kentucky
Morehead State University M,W
Murray State University M,W
University of Kentucky M,W

Louisiana
Centenary College of Louisiana M,W

Mississippi
University of Mississippi W

Missouri
Lindenwood University M,W
University of Missouri
Kansas City M,W

Nebraska
University of Nebraska
Lincoln W

Nevada
University of Nevada
Reno M,W

Ohio
University of Akron M,W
Xavier University M,W

Pennsylvania
Duquesne University M,W

Tennessee
Austin Peay State University W
Tennessee Technological University M,W
University of Memphis M,W
University of Tennessee
Martin M,W

Virginia
George Mason University M,W
Virginia Military Institute M

West Virginia
West Virginia University M,W

Rodeo

Alabama
University of West Alabama M,W

Arizona
Central Arizona College M,W
Cochise College M,W

Arkansas
University of Arkansas
Monticello M,W

Idaho
Boise State University M,W
College of Southern Idaho M,W

Kansas
Fort Hays State University M,W
Garden City Community College M,W
Pratt Community College M,W

Kentucky
Murray State University M,W

Louisiana
McNeese State University M,W

Minnesota
University of Minnesota
Crookston M,W

Mississippi
Northwest Mississippi Community College M,W

Missouri
Missouri Valley College M,W

Montana
Dawson Community College M,W
Miles Community College M,W

Montana State University
Bozeman M,W
University of Montana-Missoula M,W
University of Montana: Western M,W

Nebraska
Nebraska College of Technical Agriculture M,W
Southeast Community College
Beatrice Campus M,W

Nevada
Western Nevada Community College M,W

New Mexico
Eastern New Mexico University M,W

North Dakota
Dickinson State University M,W

Oklahoma
Eastern Oklahoma State College M,W
Northeastern Oklahoma Agricultural and Mechanical College M,W
Northwestern Oklahoma State University M,W
Oklahoma Panhandle State University M,W
Southeastern Oklahoma State University M,W
Southwestern Oklahoma State University M,W

Oregon
Blue Mountain Community College M,W
Eastern Oregon University M,W

South Dakota
National American University
Rapid City M,W
Western Dakota Technical Institute M,W

Tennessee
University of Tennessee
Martin M,W

Texas
Cisco Junior College M,W
Clarendon College M,W
Howard College M,W
North Central Texas College M,W
Odessa College M,W
South Plains College M,W
Southwest Texas Junior College M,W
Tarleton State University M,W
Western Texas College M,W

Utah
Dixie State College of Utah M,W

Washington
Walla Walla Community College M,W

Wyoming
Casper College M,W
Central Wyoming College M,W
Eastern Wyoming College M,W
University of Wyoming M,W

Rowing (crew)

California
California State University
Sacramento W
Humboldt State University W
Loyola Marymount University W
San Diego State University W
University of California
Berkeley M,W
University of Southern California W

Delaware
University of Delaware W

District of Columbia
George Washington University M,W

Florida
Barry University W
Florida Institute of Technology M,W
Jacksonville University M,W
University of Central Florida W
University of Miami W
University of Tampa W

Indiana
Indiana University
Bloomington W
University of Notre Dame W

Iowa
University of Iowa W

Kansas
Kansas State University W
University of Kansas W

Kentucky
Murray State University M,W
University of Louisville W

Massachusetts
Boston University M,W
Northeastern University M,W
University of Massachusetts
Amherst W

Michigan
Eastern Michigan University W
Michigan State University W
University of Michigan W

Nebraska
Creighton University W

New Hampshire
University of New Hampshire W

New Jersey
Rutgers, The State University of New Jersey
New Brunswick Regional Campus M,W

New York
Dowling College M,W
Fordham University W
State University of New York
Buffalo W
Syracuse University M,W

North Carolina
Duke University W
University of North Carolina
Chapel Hill W

Ohio
Ohio State University
Columbus Campus W

Oklahoma
University of Tulsa W

Pennsylvania
Drexel University M,W
Duquesne University W
Mercyhurst College M,W
Robert Morris University W
Temple University M,W

South Carolina
Clemson University W

Tennessee
University of Tennessee
Knoxville W

Texas
Southern Methodist University W
University of Texas
Austin W

Virginia
University of Virginia W

Washington
Washington State University W
Western Washington University M,W

West Virginia
University of Charleston M,W
West Virginia University W

Wisconsin
University of Wisconsin
Madison M,W

Rugby

California
University of California
Berkeley M

Illinois
Eastern Illinois University W

Ohio
Tiffin University M

Skiing

Alaska
Alaska Pacific University M,W
University of Alaska
Anchorage M,W
Fairbanks M,W

Colorado
Colorado Mountain College
Alpine Campus M,W
Spring Valley Campus M,W
Timberline Campus M,W
University of Colorado
Boulder M,W
University of Denver M,W

Georgia
Armstrong Atlantic State University M,W

Idaho
Albertson College of Idaho M,W

Massachusetts
University of Massachusetts
Amherst M,W

Michigan
Michigan Technological University W
Northern Michigan University M,W

Minnesota
University of Minnesota
Twin Cities M,W

Montana
Montana State University
Bozeman W
Rocky Mountain College M,W

Nevada
Sierra Nevada College M,W
University of Nevada
Reno M,W

New Hampshire
University of New Hampshire M,W

New Mexico
University of New Mexico M,W

New York
Paul Smith's College M,W

North Carolina
Lees-McRae College M,W

Tennessee
Carson-Newman College M,W

Utah
University of Utah M,W

Vermont
University of Vermont M,W

West Virginia
Davis and Elkins College M,W

Wisconsin
University of Wisconsin
Green Bay M,W

Soccer

Alabama
Auburn University W
Auburn University at Montgomery M,W
Birmingham-Southern College M,W
Samford University W
Shelton State Community College W
Spring Hill College M,W
University of Alabama W
University of Alabama
Birmingham M,W
Huntsville M,W
University of Mobile M,W
University of Montevallo M,W
University of North Alabama W
University of South Alabama W
Wallace State Community College at Hanceville M

Arizona
Arizona State University W
Arizona Western College M
Cochise College W
Glendale Community College M,W
Northern Arizona University W
Pima Community College M,W
Scottsdale Community College M
South Mountain Community College M
University of Arizona W
Yavapai College M

Arkansas
Arkansas State University W
Harding University W
John Brown University M,W
Lyon College M,W
Ouachita Baptist University M,W
University of Arkansas W
University of Arkansas
Little Rock M,W
Williams Baptist College M

California
Azusa Pacific University M,W
Biola University M,W
California Baptist University M,W
California Polytechnic State University:
San Luis Obispo M

California State Polytechnic University: Pomona M,W
California State University
- Bakersfield M,W
- Chico M,W
- Fresno M,W
- Fullerton M,W
- Los Angeles M,W
- Northridge M
- Sacramento M,W
- San Bernardino M,W
- Stanislaus M,W

Christian Heritage College M
Concordia University M,W
Dominican University of California M,W
Fresno Pacific University M
Grossmont Community College W
Holy Names College M,W
Hope International University M,W
Humboldt State University M,W
Loyola Marymount University M,W
Master's College M,W
Pepperdine University W
Point Loma Nazarene University M
St. Mary's College of California M,W
San Diego State University M,W
San Jose State University M
Santa Clara University M,W
Stanford University M,W
University of California
- Berkeley M,W
- Irvine M,W
- Los Angeles M,W
- Santa Barbara M,W

University of San Diego M,W
University of San Francisco M,W
University of Southern California W
University of the Pacific W
Vanguard University of Southern California M,W
Yuba Community College District M,W

Colorado

Colorado Christian University M,W
Colorado College W
Colorado School of Mines M
Colorado State University
- Pueblo M,W

Fort Lewis College M,W
Mesa State College W
Metropolitan State College of Denver M,W
Regis University W
University of Colorado
- Boulder W
- Colorado Springs M

University of Denver M,W
University of Northern Colorado W

Connecticut

Central Connecticut State University M,W
Fairfield University M,W
Mitchell College M,W
Quinnipiac University M,W
Southern Connecticut State University M,W
Teikyo Post University M,W
University of Bridgeport M,W
University of Connecticut M,W
University of Hartford M,W
University of New Haven M,W

Delaware

Delaware Technical and Community College
- Stanton/Wilmington Campus M,W

Goldey-Beacom College M
University of Delaware M,W

District of Columbia

American University M,W
George Washington University M,W
Georgetown University M,W
Howard University M

Florida

Barry University M,W
Eckerd College M,W
Embry-Riddle Aeronautical University M,W
Flagler College M,W
Florida Atlantic University M,W
Florida Institute of Technology M
Florida International University M,W
Florida Southern College M,W
Florida State University W
Jacksonville University M,W
Northwood University
- Florida Campus M,W

Nova Southeastern University M,W
Palm Beach Atlantic University M,W
Polk Community College W
Rollins College M,W
St. Leo University M,W
St. Thomas University M,W
Stetson University M,W
University of Central Florida M,W
University of Florida W
University of Miami W
University of North Florida M,W
University of South Florida M,W
University of Tampa M,W
University of West Florida M,W
Warner Southern College M,W
Webber International University M,W

Georgia

Andrew College M,W
Berry College M,W
Brenau University W
Brewton-Parker College M,W
Clayton College and State University M,W
Covenant College M,W
Emmanuel College M,W
Georgia Perimeter College M,W
Georgia Southern University M,W
Georgia State University M,W
Gordon College M
Mercer University M,W
Morehouse College M
North Georgia College & State University M,W
Reinhardt College M,W
Shorter College M,W
Thomas University M,W
Truett-McConnell College M,W
University of Georgia W
Young Harris College M,W

Hawaii

Hawaii Pacific University M,W
University of Hawaii
- Manoa W

Idaho

Albertson College of Idaho M,W
Boise State University W
Idaho State University W
Northwest Nazarene University M,W
University of Idaho W

Illinois

Bradley University M
College of Lake County M,W
De Paul University M,W
Eastern Illinois University M,W
Elgin Community College M,W
Illinois State University W
Judson College M,W
Kendall College M,W
Kishwaukee College M
Lewis and Clark Community College M,W
Lewis University M,W
Lincoln College M,W
Lincoln Land Community College M
Loyola University of Chicago M,W
McHenry County College M
McKendree College M,W
Moraine Valley Community College M,W
Northwestern University M,W
Olivet Nazarene University M,W
Parkland College M,W
Quincy University M,W
Robert Morris College: Chicago M,W
St. Xavier University M,W
South Suburban College of Cook County M
Southern Illinois University Edwardsville M,W
Southwestern Illinois College M
Springfield College in Illinois M,W
Trinity Christian College M,W
Trinity International University M,W
University of Illinois
- Chicago M
- Springfield M

University of St. Francis M,W
Waubonsee Community College M,W
Western Illinois University M,W

Indiana

Bethel College M
Butler University M,W
Calumet College of St. Joseph W
Goshen College M,W
Grace College M,W
Huntington College M,W
Indiana Institute of Technology M,W
Indiana State University W
Indiana University
- Bloomington M,W

Indiana University-Purdue University Fort Wayne M,W
Indiana University-Purdue University Indianapolis M,W
Indiana Wesleyan University M,W
Marian College M,W
Oakland City University M,W
Purdue University W
St. Joseph's College M,W
St. Mary-of-the-Woods College W
Taylor University M,W
Taylor University: Fort Wayne M
University of Evansville M,W
University of Indianapolis M,W
University of Notre Dame W
University of St. Francis M,W
University of Southern Indiana M,W
Valparaiso University M,W

Iowa

Briar Cliff University M,W
Clinton Community College M,W
Dordt College M,W
Drake University M,W
Franciscan University M,W
Graceland University M,W
Grand View College M,W
Iowa Central Community College M,W
Iowa State University W
Iowa Wesleyan College M,W
Kirkwood Community College M
Morningside College M,W
Muscatine Community College M,W
Northwestern College M,W
St. Ambrose University M,W
Scott Community College M,W
University of Iowa W
University of Northern Iowa W
Waldorf College M,W
William Penn University M,W

Kansas

Allen County Community College M,W
Baker University M,W
Barton County Community College M,W
Benedictine College M,W
Bethany College M,W
Bethel College M,W
Central Christian College M,W
Cloud County Community College M,W
Emporia State University W
Friends University M,W
Hesston College M
Johnson County Community College M
Kansas City Kansas Community College M
Kansas Wesleyan University M,W
MidAmerica Nazarene University M,W
Newman University M,W
Ottawa University M,W
St. Mary College M,W
Southwestern College M,W
Sterling College M,W
Tabor College M,W
University of Kansas W
Washburn University of Topeka W

Kentucky

Bellarmine University M,W
Brescia University M,W
Campbellsville University M
Cumberland College M,W
Georgetown College M,W
Kentucky Wesleyan College M,W
Lindsey Wilson College M,W
Mid-Continent College M
Morehead State University W
Murray State University W
St. Catharine College M,W
Spalding University M,W
Union College M,W
University of Kentucky M,W
University of Louisville M,W

Louisiana

Centenary College of Louisiana M,W
Louisiana College M
Louisiana State University and Agricultural and Mechanical College W
McNeese State University W
Nicholls State University W
Southeastern Louisiana University W
Tulane University W
University of Louisiana at Lafayette W
University of Louisiana at Monroe W

Maine

University of Maine M,W

Maryland

Anne Arundel Community College M,W
Chesapeake College M,W
College of Southern Maryland M,W
Columbia Union College M,W
Community College of Baltimore County
- Catonsville M,W
- Dundalk M,W
- Essex M,W

Hagerstown Community College M
Loyola College in Maryland M,W
Mount St. Mary's College M,W
Towson University M,W
University of Maryland
- Baltimore County M,W
- College Park M,W

Massachusetts

American International College W
Bentley College M,W
Boston College M,W
Boston University M,W
Dean College M,W
Merrimack College W
Mount Ida College M,W
Northeastern University M,W

University of Massachusetts
Amherst M,W
Lowell M,W

Michigan
Aquinas College M,W
Central Michigan University W
Concordia University M,W
Cornerstone University M,W
Eastern Michigan University W
Grand Rapids Community College W
Grand Valley State University W
Michigan State University M,W
Northern Michigan University W
Northwood University M,W
Oakland University M,W
Saginaw Valley State University M,W
Schoolcraft College M,W
Siena Heights University M,W
Spring Arbor University M,W
University of Michigan M,W
Western Michigan University M,W

Minnesota
Bemidji State University W
Bethany Lutheran College M,W
Concordia University: St. Paul W
Minnesota State University
Mankato W
Moorhead W
St. Cloud State University W
Southwest State University W
University of Minnesota
Crookston W
Duluth W
Morris W
Twin Cities W
Winona State University W

Mississippi
Alcorn State University W
Holmes Community College M
Mississippi State University W
University of Mississippi W
University of Southern Mississippi W

Missouri
Avila University M,W
Central Methodist College M,W
Central Missouri State University W
Columbia College M
Culver-Stockton College M,W
Drury University M,W
Hannibal-LaGrange College M,W
Harris Stowe State College M,W
Lincoln University M
Lindenwood University M,W
Missouri Baptist University M,W
Missouri Southern State College M,W
Missouri Valley College M,W
Northwest Missouri State University W
Research College of Nursing M,W
Rockhurst University M,W
St. Louis University M,W
Southeast Missouri State University W
Southwest Baptist University M,W
Southwest Missouri State University M,W
St. Louis Community College
Forest Park M
Meramec M,W
Truman State University M,W
University of Missouri
Columbia W
Kansas City M
Rolla M,W
St. Louis M,W
William Jewell College M,W
William Woods University M,W

Montana
Carroll College W
Flathead Valley Community College M
Montana State University
Billings M,W
Rocky Mountain College W
University of Montana-Missoula W

Nebraska
Bellevue University M,W
College of Saint Mary W
Concordia University M,W
Creighton University M,W
Dana College M,W
Doane College M,W
Hastings College M,W
Midland Lutheran College W
York College M,W

Nevada
University of Nevada
Las Vegas M,W
Reno W

New Hampshire
Franklin Pierce College M,W
Hesser College M,W
Southern New Hampshire University M,W
University of New Hampshire M,W

New Jersey
Bloomfield College M,W
Caldwell College M,W
Essex County College M
Fairleigh Dickinson University
Metropolitan Campus M,W
Felician College M,W
Georgian Court College W
Mercer County Community College M,W
Monmouth University M,W
New Jersey Institute of Technology M,W
Rider University M,W
Rutgers, The State University of New Jersey
New Brunswick Regional Campus M,W
St. Peter's College M,W
Seton Hall University M,W
Sussex County Community College W

New Mexico
College of the Southwest M,W
New Mexico Highlands University W
University of New Mexico M,W

New York
Adelphi University M,W
Bryant & Stratton Business Institute
Syracuse M,W
Canisius College M,W
City University of New York
Queens College W
Concordia College M,W
Daemen College M,W
Dominican College of Blauvelt M,W
Dowling College M
Fordham University M,W
Genesee Community College W
Hartwick College M
Hofstra University M,W
Houghton College M,W
Iona College M
Jamestown Community College M
Le Moyne College M,W
Long Island University
C. W. Post Campus M,W
Southampton College M,W
Manhattan College M,W
Marist College M,W
Mercy College M
Molloy College M,W
Monroe Community College M,W
New York Institute of Technology M,W
Niagara University M,W
Nyack College M,W
Pace University W
Pace University: Pleasantville/Briarcliff W
Paul Smith's College M,W
Roberts Wesleyan College M,W
St. Bonaventure University M,W
St. John's University M,W
State University of New York
Albany M,W
Binghamton M,W
Buffalo M,W
College at Oneonta M
Stony Brook M,W
Syracuse University M,W
Wagner College W

North Carolina
Appalachian State University M
Barton College M,W
Belmont Abbey College M,W
Brevard College M,W
Campbell University M,W
Catawba College M,W
Davidson College M,W
Duke University M,W
East Carolina University M,W
Elon University M,W
Gardner-Webb University M,W
High Point University M,W
Lees-McRae College M,W
Lenoir-Rhyne College M,W
Louisburg College M,W
Mars Hill College M,W
Montreat College M,W
Mount Olive College M,W
North Carolina State University M,W
Pfeiffer University M,W
Queens University of Charlotte M,W
St. Andrews Presbyterian College M,W
University of North Carolina
Asheville M,W
Chapel Hill M,W
Charlotte M,W
Greensboro M,W
Pembroke M
Wilmington M,W
Wake Forest University M,W
Western Carolina University W
Wingate University M,W

North Dakota
Jamestown College W
North Dakota State University W
University of Mary M,W
University of North Dakota W

Ohio
Ashland University M,W
Bowling Green State University M,W
Bryant & Stratton College
Willoughby Hills M
Cedarville University M,W
Cleveland State University M
Kent State University W
Lakeland Community College M
Malone College M,W
Miami University
Oxford Campus W
Mount Vernon Nazarene University M,W
Ohio Dominican College M,W
Ohio State University
Columbus Campus M,W
Shawnee State University M,W
Southern State Community College M
Tiffin University M,W
University of Akron M
University of Dayton M,W
University of Findlay M,W
University of Rio Grande M,W
University of Toledo W
Urbana University M,W
Ursuline College W
Walsh University M,W
Wright State University M
Xavier University M,W
Youngstown State University W

Oklahoma
East Central University W
Northeastern State University M,W
Northern Oklahoma College M,W
Oklahoma Christian University M,W
Oklahoma City University M,W
Oklahoma State University W
Oklahoma Wesleyan University M,W
Oral Roberts University M,W
St. Gregory's University M,W
Southern Nazarene University M,W
Southwestern Oklahoma State University M,W
University of Oklahoma W
University of Science and Arts of Oklahoma M,W
University of Tulsa M,W

Oregon
Concordia University M,W
Oregon Institute of Technology W
Oregon State University M,W
Portland State University W
Southern Oregon University W
Southwestern Oregon Community College M,W
University of Oregon W
University of Portland M,W
Western Baptist College M,W

Pennsylvania
Bloomsburg University of Pennsylvania M,W
California University of Pennsylvania M,W
Carlow College W
Drexel University M,W
Duquesne University M,W
East Stroudsburg University of Pennsylvania M,W
Edinboro University of Pennsylvania W
Geneva College M,W
Holy Family University M,W
Indiana University of Pennsylvania W
Kutztown University of Pennsylvania M,W
La Salle University M,W
Lehigh University M,W
Lock Haven University of Pennsylvania M,W
Manor College M,W
Mercyhurst College M,W
Millersville University of Pennsylvania M,W
Penn State
University Park M,W
Philadelphia University M,W
Point Park College M
Robert Morris University M,W
St. Joseph's University M,W
St. Vincent College M,W
Seton Hill University M,W
Shippensburg University of Pennsylvania M,W
Slippery Rock University of Pennsylvania M,W
Temple University M,W
University of Pittsburgh M,W
Villanova University M,W
West Chester University of Pennsylvania M,W

Puerto Rico
Inter American University of Puerto Rico
Bayamon Campus M
Guayama Campus M
San German Campus M
Turabo University M

University of Puerto Rico
  Cayey University College M
  Mayaguez Campus M

Rhode Island
Providence College M,W
University of Rhode Island M,W

South Carolina
Anderson College M,W
Charleston Southern University M,W
The Citadel M,W
Clemson University M,W
Coastal Carolina University M,W
Coker College M,W
College of Charleston M,W
Converse College W
Erskine College M,W
Francis Marion University M,W
Furman University M,W
Lander University M,W
Limestone College M,W
North Greenville College M,W
Presbyterian College M,W
Southern Wesleyan University M,W
Spartanburg Methodist College M,W
University of South Carolina M,W
University of South Carolina
  Aiken M
  Spartanburg M,W
Winthrop University M
Wofford College M,W

South Dakota
Augustana College W
Dakota State University M,W
Mount Marty College M,W
National American University
  Rapid City M,W
South Dakota State University W
University of Sioux Falls M,W
University of South Dakota W

Tennessee
Belmont University M,W
Bethel College M,W
Bryan College M,W
Carson-Newman College M,W
Christian Brothers University M,W
East Tennessee State University W
Freed-Hardeman University M,W
King College M,W
Lambuth University M,W
Lee University M,W
Lipscomb University M,W
Middle Tennessee State University W
Milligan College M,W
Tennessee Technological University W
Tennessee Wesleyan College M,W
Trevecca Nazarene University M,W
Tusculum College M,W
Union University M
University of Memphis M,W
University of Tennessee
  Chattanooga W
  Knoxville W
  Martin W
Vanderbilt University M,W

Texas
Angelo State University W
Baylor University W
Dallas Baptist University W
Hill College W
Jarvis Christian College M
Lon Morris College M
Midwestern State University M,W
Northwood University: Texas Campus M,W
Rice University W
St. Edward's University M,W
St. Mary's University M,W
Southern Methodist University M,W
Southwest Texas State University W
Stephen F. Austin State University W
Texas A&M University W
Texas A&M University
  Commerce W
  Corpus Christi W
Texas Christian University W
Texas Tech University W
Texas Woman's University W
Tyler Junior College M
University of Houston W
University of North Texas W
University of Texas
  Austin W
University of the Incarnate Word M,W
West Texas A&M University M,W

Utah
Brigham Young University W
Dixie State College of Utah W
University of Utah W
Utah State University W

Vermont
College of St. Joseph in Vermont M,W
Green Mountain College M,W
University of Vermont M,W

Virginia
Bluefield College M,W
College of William and Mary M,W
George Mason University M,W
James Madison University M,W
Liberty University M,W
Longwood University M
Old Dominion University M,W
Radford University M,W
University of Richmond M,W
University of Virginia M,W
Virginia Commonwealth University M,W
Virginia Intermont College M,W
Virginia Military Institute M
Virginia Polytechnic Institute and State University M,W

Washington
Central Washington University W
Clark College M,W
Eastern Washington University W
Edmonds Community College M,W
Everett Community College M,W
Evergreen State College M,W
Gonzaga University M,W
Grays Harbor College M
Green River Community College M
Lower Columbia College W
Northwest College M
Seattle Pacific University M
Seattle University M,W
Spokane Community College M,W
University of Washington M,W
Walla Walla Community College M,W
Washington State University W
Wenatchee Valley College M,W
Western Washington University M,W

West Virginia
Alderson-Broaddus College M
Concord College M,W
Davis and Elkins College M,W
Marshall University M,W
Ohio Valley College M
Potomac State College of West Virginia University M,W
Salem International University M
Shepherd College M,W
University of Charleston M,W
West Virginia University M,W
West Virginia Wesleyan College M,W
Wheeling Jesuit University M,W

Wisconsin
Cardinal Stritch University M,W
Marquette University M,W
University of Wisconsin
  Green Bay M,W
  Madison M,W
  Milwaukee M,W
  Parkside M,W
Viterbo University M,W

Wyoming
University of Wyoming W

Softball

Alabama
Alabama State University W
Athens State University W
Auburn University W
Bevill State Community College W
Birmingham-Southern College W
Central Alabama Community College W
Chattahoochee Valley Community College W
Concordia College W
Enterprise State Junior College W
Faulkner University W
Gadsden State Community College W
George C. Wallace State Community College
  Selma W
Jacksonville State University W
James H. Faulkner State Community College W
Jefferson State Community College W
Judson College W
Lurleen B. Wallace Junior College W
Miles College W
Northwest-Shoals Community College W
Samford University W
Shelton State Community College W
Snead State Community College W
Spring Hill College W
Troy State University W
University of Alabama W
University of Alabama
  Birmingham W
  Huntsville W
University of Mobile W
University of North Alabama W
University of West Alabama W
Wallace State Community College at Hanceville W

Arizona
Arizona State University W
Arizona Western College W
Central Arizona College W
Eastern Arizona College W
Glendale Community College W
Pima Community College W
Scottsdale Community College W
South Mountain Community College W
University of Arizona W

Arkansas
Henderson State University W
Southern Arkansas University W
University of Arkansas W
University of Arkansas
  Monticello W

California
Azusa Pacific University W
Bethany College W
Biola University W
California Baptist University W
California Polytechnic State University: San Luis Obispo W
California State University
  Bakersfield W
  Fresno W
  Fullerton W
  Long Beach W
  Northridge W
  San Bernardino W
  Stanislaus W
Concordia University W
Dominican University of California W
Grossmont Community College W
Hope International University W
Humboldt State University W
Loyola Marymount University W
Master's College W
Point Loma Nazarene University W
St. Mary's College of California W
San Diego State University W
San Jose State University W
Santa Clara University W
Stanford University W
University of California
  Berkeley W
  Los Angeles W
  Riverside W
  Santa Barbara W
University of San Diego W
University of the Pacific W
Vanguard University of Southern California W
Yuba Community College District W

Colorado
Colorado School of Mines W
Colorado State University W
Fort Lewis College W
Mesa State College W
Otero Junior College W
Regis University W
University of Colorado
  Colorado Springs W
University of Northern Colorado W

Connecticut
Central Connecticut State University W
Fairfield University W
Mitchell College W
Quinnipiac University W
Southern Connecticut State University W
Teikyo Post University W
University of Bridgeport W
University of Connecticut W
University of New Haven W

Delaware
Delaware State University W
Delaware Technical and Community College
  Owens Campus W
Goldey-Beacom College W
University of Delaware W
Wilmington College W

Florida
Barry University W
Bethune-Cookman College W
Broward Community College W
Chipola Junior College W
Daytona Beach Community College W
Eckerd College W
Edward Waters College W
Florida Atlantic University W
Florida Gulf Coast University W
Florida Institute of Technology W
Florida Southern College W
Florida State University W
Gulf Coast Community College W
Hillsborough Community College W
Indian River Community College W
Jacksonville University W
Lake City Community College W
Lake-Sumter Community College W
Manatee Community College W

Miami-Dade Community College W
Northwood University
Florida Campus W
Nova Southeastern University W
Okaloosa-Walton Community College W
Palm Beach Community College W
Pasco-Hernando Community College W
Pensacola Junior College W
Polk Community College W
Rollins College W
St. Leo University W
St. Petersburg College W
St. Thomas University W
Santa Fe Community College W
Stetson University W
Tallahassee Community College W
University of Central Florida W
University of Florida W
University of North Florida W
University of South Florida W
University of Tampa W
University of West Florida W
Warner Southern College W
Webber International University W

Georgia

Abraham Baldwin Agricultural College W
Albany State University W
Andrew College W
Armstrong Atlantic State University W
Augusta State University W
Brewton-Parker College W
Columbus State University W
Darton College W
Emmanuel College W
Georgia College and State University W
Georgia Institute of Technology W
Georgia Perimeter College W
Georgia Southern University W
Georgia Southwestern State University W
Georgia State University W
Gordon College W
Kennesaw State University W
Mercer University W
Middle Georgia College W
North Georgia College & State University W
Paine College W
South Georgia College W
State University of West Georgia W
Thomas University W
Valdosta State University W
Young Harris College W

Hawaii

Brigham Young University-Hawaii W
Chaminade University of Honolulu W
Hawaii Pacific University W
University of Hawaii
Hilo W
Manoa W

Idaho

Albertson College of Idaho W
North Idaho College W
Northwest Nazarene University W

Illinois

Black Hawk College W
Bradley University W
Carl Sandburg College W
College of Lake County W
Danville Area Community College W
De Paul University W
Eastern Illinois University W
Elgin Community College W
Highland Community College W
Illinois Central College W
Illinois Eastern Community Colleges
Lincoln Trail College W
Olney Central College W
Wabash Valley College W
Illinois State University W
John A. Logan College W
Judson College W
Kankakee Community College W
Kaskaskia College W
Kishwaukee College W
Lake Land College W
Lewis University W
Lincoln College W
Lincoln Land Community College W
Loyola University of Chicago W
McHenry County College W
McKendree College W
Moraine Valley Community College W
Northwestern University W
Olivet Nazarene University W
Parkland College W
Quincy University W
Rend Lake College W
Robert Morris College: Chicago W
St. Xavier University W
Sauk Valley Community College W
Shawnee Community College W
South Suburban College of Cook County W
Southeastern Illinois College W
Southern Illinois University Carbondale W
Southern Illinois University Edwardsville W
Southwestern Illinois College W
Springfield College in Illinois W
Trinity Christian College W
Trinity International University W
University of Illinois
Chicago W
Springfield W
University of St. Francis W
Waubonsee Community College W
Western Illinois University W

Indiana

Ancilla College W
Ball State University W
Bethel College W
Butler University W
Calumet College of St. Joseph W
Goshen College W
Grace College W
Huntington College W
Indiana Institute of Technology W
Indiana State University W
Indiana University
Bloomington W
Indiana University-Purdue University Fort Wayne W
Indiana University-Purdue University Indianapolis W
Indiana Wesleyan University W
Marian College W
Oakland City University M,W
Purdue University W
St. Joseph's College W
St. Mary-of-the-Woods College W
Taylor University W
University of Evansville W
University of Indianapolis W
University of Notre Dame W
University of St. Francis W
University of Southern Indiana W
Valparaiso University W

Iowa

Briar Cliff University W
Clinton Community College W
Dordt College W
Drake University W
Ellsworth Community College W
Franciscan University W
Graceland University W
Grand View College W
Indian Hills Community College W
Iowa Central Community College W
Iowa Lakes Community College W
Iowa State University W
Iowa Wesleyan College W
Iowa Western Community College W
Kirkwood Community College W
Marshalltown Community College W
Morningside College W
North Iowa Area Community College W
Northwestern College W
St. Ambrose University W
Scott Community College W
Southwestern Community College W
University of Iowa W
University of Northern Iowa W
Waldorf College W
William Penn University W

Kansas

Allen County Community College W
Baker University W
Barton County Community College W
Benedictine College W
Bethany College W
Butler County Community College W
Central Christian College W
Cloud County Community College W
Dodge City Community College W
Emporia State University W
Fort Hays State University W
Fort Scott Community College W
Friends University W
Garden City Community College W
Highland Community College W
Hutchinson Community College W
Independence Community College W
Johnson County Community College W
Kansas City Kansas Community College W
Kansas Wesleyan University W
Labette Community College W
McPherson College W
MidAmerica Nazarene University W
Newman University W
Ottawa University W
Pittsburg State University W
Pratt Community College W
St. Mary College W
Seward County Community College W
Southwestern College W
Sterling College W
Tabor College W
University of Kansas W
Washburn University of Topeka W
Wichita State University W

Kentucky

Alice Lloyd College W
Bellarmine University W
Brescia University W
Campbellsville University W
Cumberland College W
Georgetown College W
Kentucky Wesleyan College W
Lindsey Wilson College W
Mid-Continent College W
Pikeville College W
St. Catharine College W
Spalding University W
Union College W
University of Kentucky W

Louisiana

Centenary College of Louisiana W
Louisiana State University and Agricultural and Mechanical College W
Louisiana Tech University W
McNeese State University W
Nicholls State University W
Northwestern State University W
Southeastern Louisiana University W
Southern University and Agricultural and Mechanical College W
University of Louisiana at Lafayette W
University of Louisiana at Monroe W

Maine

University of Maine W
University of Maine
Augusta M,W

Maryland

Anne Arundel Community College W
Bowie State University W
Chesapeake College W
College of Southern Maryland W
Columbia Union College W
Community College of Baltimore County
Catonsville W
Dundalk W
Essex W
Coppin State College W
Hagerstown Community College W
Morgan State University W
Mount St. Mary's College W
Towson University W
University of Maryland
Baltimore County W
College Park W

Massachusetts

American International College W
Bentley College W
Boston College W
Boston University W
Dean College W
Merrimack College W
Mount Ida College W
University of Massachusetts
Amherst W

Michigan

Alpena Community College W
Aquinas College W
Central Michigan University W
Concordia University W
Cornerstone University W
Eastern Michigan University W
Ferris State University W
Glen Oaks Community College W
Grand Valley State University W
Hillsdale College W
Kellogg Community College W
Michigan State University W
Northwood University W
Oakland Community College W
Oakland University W
Saginaw Valley State University W
Siena Heights University W
Spring Arbor University W
University of Michigan W
Wayne State University W
Western Michigan University W

Minnesota

Bemidji State University W
Bethany Lutheran College W
Concordia University: St. Paul W
Minnesota State University
Mankato W
Moorhead W
St. Cloud State University W
Southwest State University W
University of Minnesota
Crookston W
Duluth W
Twin Cities W
Winona State University W

Mississippi

Alcorn State University W
Delta State University W
Holmes Community College W
Itawamba Community College W

Mississippi Gulf Coast Community College
Perkinston W
Mississippi State University W
Mississippi University for Women W
Mississippi Valley State University W
Northwest Mississippi Community College W
University of Mississippi W
University of Southern Mississippi W

Missouri
Avila University W
Central Methodist College W
Central Missouri State University W
Columbia College W
Culver-Stockton College W
Evangel University W
Hannibal-LaGrange College W
Lincoln University W
Lindenwood University W
Missouri Baptist University W
Missouri Southern State College W
Missouri Valley College W
Missouri Western State College W
North Central Missouri College W
Northwest Missouri State University W
St. Charles Community College W
St. Louis University W
Southeast Missouri State University W
Southwest Baptist University W
Southwest Missouri State University W
St. Louis Community College
Forest Park W
Meramec W
Truman State University W
University of Missouri
Columbia W
Kansas City W
Rolla W
St. Louis W
William Jewell College W
William Woods University W

Montana
Montana State University
Billings W

Nebraska
Bellevue University W
College of Saint Mary W
Concordia University W
Creighton University W
Dana College W
Doane College W
Hastings College W
Mid Plains Community College Area W
Midland Lutheran College W
Peru State College W
University of Nebraska
Kearney W
Lincoln W
Omaha W
Wayne State College W
Western Nebraska Community College W
York College W

Nevada
University of Nevada
Las Vegas W
Reno W

New Hampshire
Franklin Pierce College W
Hesser College W

New Jersey
Bloomfield College W
Brookdale Community College W
Caldwell College W
Fairleigh Dickinson University
Metropolitan Campus W
Felician College W
Georgian Court College W
Mercer County Community College W
Monmouth University W
Rider University W
Rutgers, The State University of New Jersey
New Brunswick Regional Campus W
St. Peter's College W
Salem Community College W
Seton Hall University W

New Mexico
Eastern New Mexico University W
New Mexico Highlands University W
New Mexico State University W
University of New Mexico W
Western New Mexico University W

New York
Adelphi University W
Canisius College W
City University of New York
Queens College W
Concordia College W
Dominican College of Blauvelt W
Dowling College W
Fordham University W
Hofstra University W
Iona College W
Le Moyne College W
Long Island University
C. W. Post Campus M,W
Southampton College W
Manhattan College W
Marist College W
Mercy College W
Molloy College W
New York Institute of Technology W
Niagara University W
Nyack College W
Pace University W
Pace University: Pleasantville/Briarcliff W
St. Bonaventure University W
St. John's University W
State University of New York
Albany W
Binghamton W
Buffalo W
Stony Brook W
Syracuse University W
Wagner College W

North Carolina
Barber-Scotia College W
Barton College W
Belmont Abbey College W
Brevard College W
Campbell University W
Catawba College W
East Carolina University W
Elon University W
Fayetteville State University W
Gardner-Webb University W
Johnson C. Smith University W
Lees-McRae College W
Lenoir-Rhyne College W
Louisburg College W
Mars Hill College W
Montreat College W
Mount Olive College W
North Carolina Central University W
Pfeiffer University W
Queens University of Charlotte W
St. Andrews Presbyterian College W
St. Augustine's College W
Shaw University W
Southeastern Community College W
University of North Carolina
Chapel Hill W
Charlotte W
Greensboro W
Pembroke W
Wilmington W
Wingate University W
Winston-Salem State University W

North Dakota
Dickinson State University W
Jamestown College W
Mayville State University W
Minot State University W
North Dakota State University W
University of Mary W
University of North Dakota W
Valley City State University W

Ohio
Ashland University W
Bowling Green State University W
Cedarville University W
Cleveland State University W
Kent State University W
Lakeland Community College W
Malone College W
Miami University
Oxford Campus W
Mount Vernon Nazarene University W
Ohio Dominican College W
Ohio State University
Columbus Campus W
Ohio University W
Shawnee State University W
Southern State Community College W
Tiffin University W
University of Akron W
University of Dayton W
University of Findlay W
University of Rio Grande W
University of Toledo W
Urbana University W
Ursuline College W
Walsh University W
Wright State University W
Youngstown State University W

Oklahoma
Bacone College W
Cameron University W
Carl Albert State College W
East Central University W
Eastern Oklahoma State College W
Northeastern Oklahoma Agricultural and Mechanical College W
Northeastern State University W
Northern Oklahoma College M,W
Oklahoma Baptist University W
Oklahoma Christian University W
Oklahoma City University W
Oklahoma Panhandle State University M,W
Oklahoma State University W
Rose State College W
St. Gregory's University W
Seminole State College W
Southeastern Oklahoma State University W
Southern Nazarene University W
Southwestern Oklahoma State University W
University of Central Oklahoma W
University of Oklahoma W
University of Science and Arts of Oklahoma W
University of Tulsa W
Western Oklahoma State College W

Oregon
Blue Mountain Community College W
Clackamas Community College W
Concordia University W
Northwest Christian College W
Oregon Institute of Technology W
Oregon State University W
Portland State University W
Southern Oregon University W
Southwestern Oregon Community College W
University of Oregon W

Pennsylvania
Bloomsburg University of Pennsylvania W
California University of Pennsylvania W
Carlow College W
Community College of Beaver County W
Drexel University W
East Stroudsburg University of Pennsylvania W
Edinboro University of Pennsylvania W
Geneva College W
Holy Family University W
Indiana University of Pennsylvania W
Kutztown University of Pennsylvania W
La Salle University W
Lackawanna College W
Lock Haven University of Pennsylvania W
Mercyhurst College W
Millersville University of Pennsylvania W
Penn State
University Park W
Philadelphia University W
Point Park College W
Robert Morris University W
St. Joseph's University W
St. Vincent College W
Seton Hill University W
Shippensburg University of Pennsylvania W
Slippery Rock University of Pennsylvania W
Temple University W
University of Pittsburgh W
University of the Sciences in Philadelphia W
Villanova University W
West Chester University of Pennsylvania W

Puerto Rico
Inter American University of Puerto Rico
Bayamon Campus M,W
Guayama Campus M,W
Universidad Metropolitana M,W
University of Puerto Rico
Carolina Regional College W
Cayey University College M
Mayaguez Campus W
Ponce M,W

Rhode Island
Providence College W
University of Rhode Island W

South Carolina
Anderson College W
Charleston Southern University W
Claflin University W
Coastal Carolina University W
Coker College W
College of Charleston W
Erskine College W
Francis Marion University W
Furman University W
Lander University W
Limestone College W
Morris College W
North Greenville College W
Presbyterian College W
South Carolina State University W
Southern Wesleyan University W
Spartanburg Methodist College W
University of South Carolina W
University of South Carolina
Aiken W
Spartanburg W
Voorhees College W

Winthrop University W

South Dakota
Augustana College W
Dakota State University W
Dakota Wesleyan University W
Mount Marty College W
Northern State University W
South Dakota State University W
University of Sioux Falls W
University of South Dakota W

Tennessee
Austin Peay State University W
Belmont University W
Bethel College W
Carson-Newman College W
Christian Brothers University W
Cleveland State Community College W
Dyersburg State Community College W
East Tennessee State University W
Freed-Hardeman University W
Jackson State Community College W
Lambuth University W
Lee University W
Lipscomb University W
Middle Tennessee State University W
Milligan College W
Roane State Community College W
Southwest Tennessee Community College W
Tennessee Technological University W
Tennessee Wesleyan College W
Trevecca Nazarene University W
Tusculum College W
Union University W
University of Tennessee
Chattanooga W
Knoxville W
Martin W
Volunteer State Community College W
Walters State Community College W

Texas
Abilene Christian University W
Alvin Community College W
Angelo State University W
Baylor University W
Blinn College M
Collin County Community College District W
Galveston College W
Hill College W
Houston Baptist University W
Lon Morris College W
Midland College W
Northwood University: Texas Campus W
Odessa College W
Paris Junior College W
Prairie View A&M University W
Ranger College W
St. Edward's University W
Sam Houston State University W
Southwest Texas State University W
Stephen F. Austin State University W
Tarleton State University W
Texas A&M University W
Texas A&M University
Kingsville W
Texas Tech University W
Texas Woman's University W
University of Houston W
University of Texas
Arlington W
Austin W
University of the Incarnate Word W
Western Texas College W

Utah
College of Eastern Utah W
Dixie State College of Utah W
Snow College W
Southern Utah University W
University of Utah W
Utah State University W
Utah Valley State College W

Vermont
University of Vermont W

Virginia
Bluefield College W
George Mason University W
Hampton University W
James Madison University W
Longwood University W
Norfolk State University W
Radford University W
University of Virginia W
University of Virginia's College at Wise W
Virginia Intermont College W
Virginia Polytechnic Institute and State University W
Virginia Union University W

Washington
Central Washington University W
Centralia College W
Edmonds Community College W
Everett Community College W
Grays Harbor College W
Green River Community College W
Lower Columbia College W
Olympic College W
St. Martin's College W
Seattle University W
Spokane Community College W
University of Washington W
Walla Walla Community College W
Wenatchee Valley College W
Western Washington University W

West Virginia
Alderson-Broaddus College W
Bluefield State College W
Concord College W
Davis and Elkins College W
Marshall University W
Mountain State University W
Potomac State College of West Virginia University W
Salem International University W
Shepherd College W
University of Charleston W
West Liberty State College W
West Virginia State College W
West Virginia University Institute of Technology W
West Virginia Wesleyan College W

Wisconsin
Cardinal Stritch University W
University of Wisconsin
Green Bay W
Madison W
Parkside W
Viterbo University W

Squash

Nebraska
University of Nebraska
Lincoln W

New York
Fordham University M

Pennsylvania
Carnegie Mellon University M

Swimming

Alabama
Auburn University M,W
Spring Hill College M,W
University of Alabama M,W

Arizona
Arizona State University M,W
Northern Arizona University M,W
University of Arizona M,W

Arkansas
Henderson State University M,W
John Brown University M,W
Ouachita Baptist University M,W
University of Arkansas W
University of Arkansas
Little Rock M,W

California
Biola University W
California Baptist University M,W
California State University
Bakersfield M,W
Fresno W
Northridge M,W
San Bernardino M,W
Grossmont Community College M,W
Loyola Marymount University W
Pepperdine University W
San Diego State University W
San Jose State University W
Stanford University M,W
University of California
Berkeley M,W
Irvine M,W
Los Angeles W
Santa Barbara M,W
University of San Diego W
University of Southern California M,W
University of the Pacific M,W

Colorado
Colorado School of Mines M,W
Colorado State University W
Metropolitan State College of Denver M,W
University of Denver M,W
University of Northern Colorado W

Connecticut
Central Connecticut State University W
Fairfield University M,W
Southern Connecticut State University M
University of Connecticut M,W

Delaware
University of Delaware W

District of Columbia
American University M,W
George Washington University M,W
Howard University M,W

Florida
Broward Community College M,W
Eckerd College M,W
Florida Atlantic University M,W
Florida State University M,W
Indian River Community College M,W
Rollins College M,W
University of Florida M,W
University of Miami M,W
University of North Florida W
University of Tampa M,W

Georgia
Darton College M,W
Georgia Institute of Technology M,W
Georgia Southern University W
University of Georgia M,W

Hawaii
University of Hawaii
Manoa M,W

Illinois
Eastern Illinois University M,W
Illinois Institute of Technology M,W
Illinois State University W
Lewis University M,W
Lincoln College M,W
Northwestern University M,W
Southern Illinois University Carbondale M,W
University of Illinois
Chicago M,W
Urbana-Champaign W
Western Illinois University M,W

Indiana
Ball State University M,W
Indiana University
Bloomington M,W
Indiana University-Purdue University Indianapolis M,W
Purdue University M,W
University of Evansville M,W
University of Indianapolis M,W
University of Notre Dame M,W
Valparaiso University M,W
Vincennes University M,W

Iowa
Iowa State University W
University of Iowa M,W
University of Northern Iowa W

Kansas
University of Kansas W

Kentucky
Cumberland College M,W
University of Kentucky M,W
University of Louisville M,W

Louisiana
Centenary College of Louisiana W
Louisiana State University and Agricultural and Mechanical College M,W
Tulane University W
University of Louisiana at Monroe M,W
University of New Orleans M,W

Maine
University of Maine W

Maryland
Loyola College in Maryland M,W
Towson University M,W
University of Maryland
Baltimore County M,W
College Park M,W

Massachusetts
Bentley College M,W
Boston College W
Boston University M,W
Northeastern University W
University of Massachusetts
Amherst M,W
Lowell M

Michigan
Eastern Michigan University M,W
Grand Rapids Community College M,W
Grand Valley State University M,W
Hillsdale College W
Michigan State University M,W
Northern Michigan University W
Oakland University M,W
University of Michigan M,W
Wayne State University M,W

Minnesota
Minnesota State University
Mankato M,W
St. Cloud State University M,W
University of Minnesota
Twin Cities M,W

Mississippi
Delta State University M,W

Missouri
Drury University M,W
Lindenwood University M,W
St. Louis University M,W
Southwest Missouri State University M
Truman State University M,W
University of Missouri
Columbia M,W
Rolla M

Nebraska
University of Nebraska
Kearney W
Lincoln W

Nevada
University of Nevada
Las Vegas M,W
Reno W

New Hampshire
University of New Hampshire W

New Jersey
New Jersey Institute of Technology M,W
Rider University M,W
Rutgers, The State University of New Jersey
New Brunswick Regional Campus M,W
St. Peter's College M,W
Seton Hall University M,W

New Mexico
New Mexico State University W

New York
Adelphi University M,W
Canisius College W
City University of New York
Queens College M,W
Fordham University M,W
Iona College M
Manhattan College W
Marist College M,W
Monroe Community College M,W
Niagara University M,W
St. Bonaventure University M,W
St. John's University M,W
State University of New York
Binghamton M,W
Buffalo M,W
Stony Brook M,W
Syracuse University M,W
Wagner College W

North Carolina
Catawba College W
Davidson College M,W
East Carolina University M,W
Gardner-Webb University W
Mars Hill College W
North Carolina Agricultural and Technical State University W
North Carolina State University M,W
Pfeiffer University W
University of North Carolina
Chapel Hill M,W
Wilmington M,W
Wingate University W

North Dakota
University of North Dakota M,W

Ohio
Ashland University M,W
Bowling Green State University M,W
Cleveland State University M,W
Miami University
Oxford Campus M,W
Ohio State University
Columbus Campus M,W
Ohio University M,W
University of Akron W
University of Findlay M,W
University of Toledo M,W
Walsh University W
Wright State University M,W
Xavier University M,W
Youngstown State University W

Oregon
Oregon State University W

Pennsylvania
Bloomsburg University of Pennsylvania M,W
Drexel University M,W
Duquesne University M,W
East Stroudsburg University of Pennsylvania W
Edinboro University of Pennsylvania W
Indiana University of Pennsylvania M,W
Kutztown University of Pennsylvania M,W
La Salle University M,W
Lehigh University M,W
Lock Haven University of Pennsylvania W
Millersville University of Pennsylvania W
Penn State
University Park M,W
Shippensburg University of Pennsylvania M,W
Slippery Rock University of Pennsylvania M,W
University of Pittsburgh M,W
Villanova University W
West Chester University of Pennsylvania M,W

Puerto Rico
Bayamon Central University M,W
Inter American University of Puerto Rico
Bayamon Campus M,W
Turabo University M,W
University of Puerto Rico
Mayaguez Campus M,W
University of the Sacred Heart M,W

Rhode Island
University of Rhode Island M,W

South Carolina
Clemson University M,W
College of Charleston M,W
Limestone College W
University of South Carolina M,W

South Dakota
South Dakota State University M,W
University of South Dakota M,W

Tennessee
University of Tennessee
Knoxville M,W

Texas
Rice University W
Southern Methodist University M,W
Texas A&M University M,W
Texas Christian University M,W
University of Houston W
University of North Texas W
University of Texas
Austin M,W

Utah
Brigham Young University M,W
University of Utah M,W

Virginia
George Mason University M,W
James Madison University M,W
Old Dominion University M,W
University of Richmond W
University of Virginia M,W
Virginia Military Institute M
Virginia Polytechnic Institute and State University M,W

Washington
Central Washington University M,W
Evergreen State College M,W
Seattle University M,W
University of Washington M,W
Washington State University W

West Virginia
Salem International University M,W
University of Charleston M,W
West Virginia University M,W
West Virginia Wesleyan College M,W
Wheeling Jesuit University M,W

Wisconsin
University of Wisconsin
Green Bay M,W
Madison M,W
Milwaukee M,W

Wyoming
University of Wyoming M,W

Synchronized swimming

Alabama
University of Alabama
Birmingham W

California
Stanford University W

Massachusetts
Wheaton College W

Minnesota
Carleton College W

New Jersey
Richard Stockton College of New Jersey W

New York
Canisius College W
Keuka College W

Ohio
Ohio State University
Columbus Campus W
Walsh University W

Table tennis

Arizona
South Mountain Community College M,W

North Carolina
East Carolina University M
Gardner-Webb University M

Puerto Rico
Inter American University of Puerto Rico
Bayamon Campus M,W
Metropolitan Campus M,W
Universidad del Este M,W
Universidad Metropolitana M,W
University of Puerto Rico
Carolina Regional College M,W
Cayey University College M,W
Mayaguez Campus M,W
Ponce M,W

Tennis

Alabama
Alabama Agricultural and Mechanical University M,W
Alabama State University M,W
Auburn University M,W
Auburn University at Montgomery M,W
Birmingham-Southern College M,W
Central Alabama Community College M,W
Jacksonville State University M,W
James H. Faulkner State Community College M,W
Jefferson Davis Community College M,W
Judson College W
Miles College M,W
Northwest-Shoals Community College W
Samford University M,W
Snead State Community College W
Spring Hill College M,W
Troy State University M,W
University of Alabama M,W
University of Alabama
Birmingham M,W
Huntsville M,W
University of Mobile W
University of Montevallo W
University of North Alabama M,W
University of South Alabama M,W
Wallace State Community College at Hanceville M,W

Arizona
Arizona State University M,W
Gateway Community College M,W
Glendale Community College M,W
Northern Arizona University M,W
Pima Community College M,W
Scottsdale Community College M,W
South Mountain Community College M,W
University of Arizona M,W

Arkansas
Arkansas State University W
Arkansas Tech University W
Harding University M,W
Henderson State University W
John Brown University M,W
Lyon College M,W
Ouachita Baptist University M,W
Southern Arkansas University W
University of Arkansas M,W
University of Arkansas
Little Rock M,W

California
Azusa Pacific University M
Biola University W
California Polytechnic State University: San Luis Obispo M,W
California State Polytechnic University: Pomona M,W

California State University
Bakersfield W
Fresno M,W
Fullerton W
Long Beach W
Los Angeles M,W
Northridge W
Sacramento M,W
Dominican University of California M,W
Grossmont Community College M,W
Hope International University M,W
Loyola Marymount University M,W
Marymount College M,W
Pepperdine University M,W
Point Loma Nazarene University M,W
St. Mary's College of California M,W
San Diego State University M,W
San Jose State University W
Santa Clara University M,W
Stanford University M,W
University of California
Berkeley M,W
Irvine M,W
Los Angeles M,W
Riverside M,W
Santa Barbara M,W
University of San Diego M,W
University of San Francisco M,W
University of Southern California M,W
University of the Pacific M,W
Vanguard University of Southern California M,W
Yuba Community College District M,W

Colorado

Colorado Christian University M,W
Colorado School of Mines M,W
Colorado State University W
Colorado State University
Pueblo M,W
Mesa State College M,W
Metropolitan State College of Denver M,W
University of Colorado
Boulder M,W
Colorado Springs M,W
University of Denver M,W
University of Northern Colorado M,W

Connecticut

Fairfield University M,W
Quinnipiac University M,W
University of Connecticut M,W
University of Hartford M,W
University of New Haven W

Delaware

Delaware State University M,W

District of Columbia

American University M,W
George Washington University M,W
Georgetown University W
Howard University M,W

Florida

Barry University M,W
Bethune-Cookman College M,W
Broward Community College M,W
Eckerd College M,W
Embry-Riddle Aeronautical University M,W
Flagler College M,W
Florida Atlantic University M,W
Florida Gulf Coast University M,W
Florida International University W
Florida Southern College M,W
Florida State University M,W
Hillsborough Community College W
Jacksonville University M,W
Northwood University
Florida Campus M,W
Palm Beach Atlantic University M,W
Pasco-Hernando Community College W
Polk Community College W
Rollins College M,W
St. Leo University M,W
St. Thomas University M,W
Stetson University M,W
University of Central Florida M,W
University of Florida M,W
University of Miami M,W
University of North Florida M,W
University of South Florida M,W
University of Tampa W
University of West Florida M,W
Webber International University M,W

Georgia

Abraham Baldwin Agricultural College M,W
Albany State University M
Armstrong Atlantic State University M,W
Augusta State University M,W
Berry College M,W
Brenau University W
Clark Atlanta University M,W
Clayton College and State University W
Columbus State University M,W
Darton College M,W
Emmanuel College M,W
Fort Valley State University M,W
Georgia College and State University M,W
Georgia Institute of Technology M,W
Georgia Perimeter College M,W
Georgia Southern University M,W
Georgia Southwestern State University M,W
Georgia State University M,W
Gordon College W
Kennesaw State University W
Mercer University M,W
Middle Georgia College W
Morehouse College M
North Georgia College & State University M,W
Reinhardt College M,W
Savannah State University W
Shorter College M,W
South Georgia College W
Southern Polytechnic State University M
Thomas University W
University of Georgia M,W
Valdosta State University M,W
Young Harris College W

Hawaii

Brigham Young University-Hawaii M,W
Chaminade University of Honolulu M,W
Hawaii Pacific University M,W
University of Hawaii
Hilo M,W
Manoa M,W

Idaho

Albertson College of Idaho M,W
Boise State University M,W
Idaho State University M,W
Lewis-Clark State College M,W
University of Idaho M,W

Illinois

Bradley University M,W
Chicago State University M,W
College of Lake County M,W
De Paul University M,W
Eastern Illinois University M,W
Elgin Community College M,W
Illinois Eastern Community Colleges
Olney Central College M
Illinois State University M,W
Judson College M,W
Lake Land College M,W
Lewis and Clark Community College M,W
Lewis University M,W
McHenry County College M,W
McKendree College M,W
Moraine Valley Community College W
Northwestern University M,W
Olivet Nazarene University M,W
Quincy University M,W
Rend Lake College W
Robert Morris College: Chicago W
Sauk Valley Community College M,W
Southern Illinois University Carbondale M,W
Southern Illinois University
Edwardsville M,W
Southwestern Illinois College M,W
Springfield College in Illinois W
University of Illinois
Chicago M,W
Springfield M,W
Urbana-Champaign M,W
University of St. Francis M,W
Waubonsee Community College M,W
Western Illinois University M,W

Indiana

Ball State University M,W
Bethel College M,W
Butler University M,W
Goshen College M,W
Grace College M,W
Huntington College M,W
Indiana State University M,W
Indiana University
Bloomington M,W
Indiana University-Purdue University
Fort Wayne M,W
Indiana University-Purdue University
Indianapolis M,W
Indiana Wesleyan University M,W
Marian College M,W
Purdue University M,W
Taylor University M,W
University of Evansville M,W
University of Indianapolis M,W
University of Notre Dame M,W
University of St. Francis W
University of Southern Indiana M,W
Valparaiso University M,W
Vincennes University M

Iowa

Dordt College M,W
Drake University M,W
Graceland University M,W
Iowa State University W
Northwestern College M,W
St. Ambrose University M,W
University of Iowa M,W
University of Northern Iowa W

Kansas

Baker University M,W
Barton County Community College M,W
Benedictine College M,W
Bethany College M,W
Bethel College M,W
Butler County Community College M,W
Central Christian College M,W
Emporia State University M,W
Fort Hays State University W
Friends University M,W
Hutchinson Community College M,W
Independence Community College M,W
Johnson County Community College M,W
Kansas State University W
Kansas Wesleyan University M,W
Labette Community College W
Pratt Community College M,W
Seward County Community College M,W
Southwestern College M,W
Tabor College M,W
University of Kansas W
Washburn University of Topeka M,W
Wichita State University M,W

Kentucky

Bellarmine University M,W
Brescia University W
Campbellsville University M,W
Cumberland College M,W
Georgetown College M,W
Kentucky Wesleyan College W
Lindsey Wilson College M,W
Morehead State University M,W
Murray State University M,W
Pikeville College M,W
University of Kentucky M,W
University of Louisville M,W

Louisiana

Centenary College of Louisiana M,W
Dillard University M,W
Grambling State University M,W
Louisiana State University and Agricultural and Mechanical College M,W
Louisiana Tech University W
McNeese State University W
Nicholls State University W
Northwestern State University W
Southeastern Louisiana University M,W
Southern University and Agricultural and Mechanical College M,W
Tulane University M,W
University of Louisiana at Lafayette M,W
University of Louisiana at Monroe M,W
University of New Orleans M,W
Xavier University of Louisiana M,W

Maryland

College of Southern Maryland M,W
Community College of Baltimore County
Catonsville M,W
Essex M,W
Coppin State College M,W
Loyola College in Maryland M,W
Morgan State University M,W
Mount St. Mary's College M,W
Towson University M,W
University of Maryland
Baltimore County M,W
College Park W

Massachusetts

Boston College W
Boston University W
Merrimack College W
University of Massachusetts
Amherst W
Lowell M,W

Michigan

Aquinas College M,W
Eastern Michigan University W
Ferris State University M,W
Glen Oaks Community College W
Grand Rapids Community College M,W
Grand Valley State University M,W
Hillsdale College M,W
Michigan State University M,W
Michigan Technological University W
Northern Michigan University W
Northwood University M,W
Oakland Community College W
Oakland University W
Saginaw Valley State University W
Spring Arbor University M,W
University of Michigan M,W
Wayne State University M,W

Western Michigan University M,W

Minnesota
Bemidji State University W
Minnesota State University
Mankato M,W
Moorhead W
St. Cloud State University M,W
Southwest State University W
University of Minnesota
Duluth M,W
Twin Cities M,W
Winona State University M,W

Mississippi
Alcorn State University M,W
Blue Mountain College W
Delta State University M,W
Holmes Community College M,W
Mississippi State University M,W
Mississippi University for Women W
Mississippi Valley State University M,W
Northwest Mississippi Community College M,W
University of Mississippi M,W
University of Southern Mississippi M,W

Missouri
Drury University M,W
Evangel University M,W
Lincoln University W
Lindenwood University M,W
Missouri Southern State College W
Missouri Western State College W
Northwest Missouri State University M,W
Research College of Nursing M,W
Rockhurst University M,W
St. Louis University M,W
Southeast Missouri State University W
Southwest Baptist University M,W
Southwest Missouri State University M,W
Truman State University M,W
University of Missouri
Columbia W
Kansas City M,W
Rolla M
St. Louis M,W
William Jewell College M,W

Montana
Montana State University
Billings M,W
Bozeman M,W
University of Montana-Missoula M,W

Nebraska
Concordia University M,W
Creighton University M,W
Hastings College M,W
Midland Lutheran College M,W
University of Nebraska
Kearney M,W
Lincoln M,W

Nevada
University of Nevada
Las Vegas M,W
Reno M,W

New Hampshire
Franklin Pierce College M,W

New Jersey
Caldwell College M,W
Fairleigh Dickinson University
Metropolitan Campus M,W
Monmouth University M,W
New Jersey Institute of Technology M,W
Rider University M,W
Rutgers, The State University of New Jersey
New Brunswick Regional Campus M,W
St. Peter's College M,W
Seton Hall University W

New Mexico
College of Santa Fe M,W
Eastern New Mexico University W
New Mexico Military Institute M
New Mexico State University M,W
University of New Mexico M,W
Western New Mexico University M,W

New York
Adelphi University M,W
City University of New York
Queens College M,W
Concordia College M,W
Dowling College M,W
Fordham University M,W
Hofstra University M,W
Iona College M,W
Le Moyne College M,W
Long Island University
C. W. Post Campus W
Manhattan College M,W
Marist College M,W
Mercy College M
Molloy College W
Niagara University M,W
Pace University M,W
Pace University: Pleasantville/Briarcliff M,W
St. Bonaventure University M,W
St. John's University M,W
State University of New York
Albany W
Binghamton M,W
Buffalo M,W
Stony Brook M,W
Syracuse University W
Wagner College M,W

North Carolina
Appalachian State University M,W
Barton College M,W
Belmont Abbey College M,W
Campbell University M,W
Catawba College M,W
Davidson College M,W
Duke University M,W
East Carolina University M,W
Elon University M,W
Fayetteville State University W
Gardner-Webb University M,W
High Point University M,W
Johnson C. Smith University M
Lees-McRae College M,W
Livingstone College M
Mars Hill College M,W
Montreat College M,W
Mount Olive College M,W
North Carolina Agricultural and Technical State University M,W
North Carolina Central University M,W
North Carolina State University M,W
Pfeiffer University M,W
Queens University of Charlotte M,W
St. Andrews Presbyterian College W
St. Augustine's College M,W
Shaw University M,W
University of North Carolina
Asheville M,W
Chapel Hill M,W
Charlotte M,W
Greensboro M,W
Wilmington M,W
Wake Forest University M,W
Western Carolina University W
Wingate University M,W
Winston-Salem State University M,W

North Dakota
University of Mary M,W
University of North Dakota W

Ohio
Bowling Green State University M,W
Cedarville University M,W
Cleveland State University M,W
Malone College M,W
Miami University
Oxford Campus W
Ohio Dominican College M,W
Ohio State University
Columbus Campus M,W
Shawnee State University W
Sinclair Community College M,W
Tiffin University M,W
University of Akron M,W
University of Dayton M,W
University of Findlay M,W
University of Toledo M,W
Walsh University M,W
Wright State University M,W
Xavier University M,W
Youngstown State University M,W

Oklahoma
Cameron University M,W
East Central University M,W
Northeastern State University W
Oklahoma Baptist University M,W
Oklahoma Christian University M,W
Oklahoma City University M,W
Oklahoma State University M,W
Oral Roberts University M,W
St. Gregory's University W
Seminole State College M,W
Southeastern Oklahoma State University M,W
Southern Nazarene University M,W
University of Central Oklahoma M,W
University of Oklahoma M,W
University of Science and Arts of Oklahoma M,W
University of Tulsa M,W

Oregon
Portland State University W
Southern Oregon University W
University of Oregon M,W
University of Portland M,W

Pennsylvania
Bloomsburg University of Pennsylvania W
California University of Pennsylvania W
Carlow College W
Cheyney University of Pennsylvania M,W
Drexel University M
Duquesne University M,W
East Stroudsburg University of Pennsylvania M,W
Edinboro University of Pennsylvania M,W
Geneva College W
Indiana University of Pennsylvania W
Kutztown University of Pennsylvania M,W
La Salle University M,W
Lehigh University M,W
Mercyhurst College M,W
Millersville University of Pennsylvania M,W
Penn State
University Park M,W
Philadelphia University M,W
Robert Morris University M,W
St. Joseph's University M,W
St. Vincent College M
Seton Hill University M,W
Shippensburg University of Pennsylvania W
Slippery Rock University of Pennsylvania M,W
Temple University M,W
University of Pittsburgh W
University of the Sciences in Philadelphia M,W
West Chester University of Pennsylvania M,W

Puerto Rico
Inter American University of Puerto Rico
Bayamon Campus M,W
San German Campus M,W
Turabo University M,W
Universidad del Este M,W
University of Puerto Rico
Bayamon University College M,W
Carolina Regional College M,W
Cayey University College M
Mayaguez Campus M,W
Ponce M,W
University of the Sacred Heart M

Rhode Island
University of Rhode Island W

South Carolina
Anderson College M,W
Charleston Southern University M,W
The Citadel M
Clemson University M,W
Coastal Carolina University M,W
Coker College M,W
College of Charleston M,W
Converse College W
Erskine College M,W
Francis Marion University M,W
Furman University M,W
Lander University M
Limestone College M,W
Morris College M,W
North Greenville College M,W
Presbyterian College M,W
South Carolina State University M,W
Spartanburg Methodist College M,W
University of South Carolina M,W
University of South Carolina
Aiken M
Spartanburg M,W
Winthrop University M,W
Wofford College M,W

South Dakota
Dakota State University M,W
Northern State University W
University of Sioux Falls M,W

Tennessee
Austin Peay State University M,W
Belmont University M,W
Bethel College M,W
Bryan College M,W
Carson-Newman College M,W
East Tennessee State University M,W
Freed-Hardeman University M,W
King College M,W
Lambuth University M,W
Lee University M,W
Lipscomb University M,W
Middle Tennessee State University M,W
Milligan College M,W
Tennessee Technological University M,W
Tennessee Wesleyan College M,W
Tusculum College M,W
Union University M,W
University of Memphis M,W
University of Tennessee
Chattanooga M,W
Knoxville M,W
Martin M,W
Vanderbilt University M,W

Texas
Abilene Christian University M,W
Baylor University M,W
Collin County Community College District M,W
Dallas Baptist University W
Lamar University M,W
Laredo Community College M,W
Lee College W
McLennan Community College W
Midwestern State University M,W
North Central Texas College W
Prairie View A&M University M,W
Rice University M,W
St. Edward's University M,W
St. Mary's University M,W
Sam Houston State University W
Southern Methodist University M,W
Southwest Texas State University W
Stephen F. Austin State University W
Tarleton State University W
Texas A&M University M,W
Texas A&M University
    Corpus Christi M,W
    Kingsville M,W
Texas Christian University M,W
Texas Southern University M,W
Texas Tech University M,W
Texas Woman's University W
Tyler Junior College M,W
University of Houston W
University of North Texas W
University of Texas
    Arlington M,W
    Austin M,W
    San Antonio M,W
University of the Incarnate Word M,W
West Texas A&M University M,W

Utah
Brigham Young University M,W
Southern Utah University W
University of Utah M,W
Utah State University M,W
Weber State University M,W

Virginia
Bluefield College M,W
College of William and Mary M,W
George Mason University M,W
Hampton University M,W
James Madison University M,W
Liberty University M,W
Longwood University M,W
Old Dominion University M,W
Radford University M,W
University of Richmond W
University of Virginia M,W
University of Virginia's College at Wise M,W
Virginia Commonwealth University M,W
Virginia Intermont College M,W
Virginia Military Institute M
Virginia Polytechnic Institute and State University M,W
Virginia Union University M,W

Washington
Eastern Washington University M,W
Gonzaga University M,W
Green River Community College M,W
Lower Columbia College W
Spokane Community College M,W
University of Washington M,W
Washington State University W

West Virginia
Bluefield State College M,W
Concord College M,W
Davis and Elkins College M,W
Marshall University W
Potomac State College of West Virginia University M,W
Salem International University M,W
University of Charleston M,W
West Liberty State College M,W
West Virginia University M,W
West Virginia University Institute of Technology M,W
West Virginia Wesleyan College M,W

Wisconsin
Marquette University M,W
University of Wisconsin
    Green Bay M,W
    Madison M,W
    Milwaukee W

Wyoming
University of Wyoming W

Track and field

Alabama
Alabama Agricultural and Mechanical University M,W
Alabama State University M,W
Auburn University M,W
Gadsden State Community College M,W
Lawson State Community College M
Miles College M,W
Samford University M,W
Troy State University M,W
University of Alabama M,W
University of Alabama
    Birmingham W
University of North Alabama M,W
University of South Alabama M,W
Wallace State Community College at Hanceville M,W

Arizona
Arizona State University M,W
Central Arizona College M,W
Glendale Community College M,W
Northern Arizona University M,W
Pima Community College M,W
Scottsdale Community College M,W
University of Arizona M,W

Arkansas
Arkansas State University M,W
Arkansas Tech University W
Harding University M,W
University of Arkansas M,W
University of Arkansas
    Little Rock M,W
    Pine Bluff M,W

California
Azusa Pacific University M,W
Biola University M,W
California Polytechnic State University: San Luis Obispo M,W
California State Polytechnic University: Pomona M,W
California State University
    Bakersfield M,W
    Chico M,W
    Fresno M,W
    Fullerton M,W
    Long Beach M,W
    Los Angeles M,W
    Northridge M,W
    Sacramento M,W
    Stanislaus M,W
Concordia University M,W
Fresno Pacific University M,W
Humboldt State University M,W
Point Loma Nazarene University M,W
San Diego State University W
Stanford University M,W
University of California
    Berkeley M,W
    Irvine M,W
    Los Angeles M,W
    Riverside M,W
    Santa Barbara M,W
University of Southern California M,W
Vanguard University of Southern California M,W
Yuba Community College District M,W

Colorado
Colorado School of Mines M,W
Colorado State University M,W
University of Colorado
    Boulder M,W
    Colorado Springs M,W
University of Northern Colorado M,W

Connecticut
Central Connecticut State University M,W
Quinnipiac University M,W
Southern Connecticut State University M
University of Connecticut M,W
University of New Haven M,W

Delaware
Delaware State University M,W
University of Delaware W

District of Columbia
American University M,W
Georgetown University M,W
Howard University M,W

Florida
Bethune-Cookman College M,W
Edward Waters College M
Florida Agricultural and Mechanical University M,W
Florida Atlantic University W
Florida International University M,W
Florida State University M,W
Jacksonville University W
University of Central Florida W
University of Florida M,W
University of Miami M,W
University of North Florida M,W
University of South Florida M,W
Warner Southern College M,W
Webber International University M,W

Georgia
Albany State University M,W
Berry College M,W
Fort Valley State University M,W
Georgia Institute of Technology M,W
Georgia Southern University W
Georgia State University W
Morehouse College M
Paine College M,W
Savannah State University M,W
Shorter College M,W
University of Georgia M,W

Hawaii
University of Hawaii
    Manoa M,W

Idaho
Boise State University M,W
Idaho State University M,W
Northwest Nazarene University M,W
University of Idaho M,W

Illinois
Bradley University W
Chicago State University M,W
Danville Area Community College M,W
De Paul University M,W
Eastern Illinois University M,W
Illinois State University M,W
Lewis University M,W
Loyola University of Chicago M,W
McKendree College M,W
Olivet Nazarene University M,W
Robert Morris College: Chicago W
Southern Illinois University Carbondale M,W
Southern Illinois University Edwardsville M,W
Trinity Christian College M,W
University of Illinois
    Chicago M,W
    Urbana-Champaign M,W
University of St. Francis W
Western Illinois University M,W

Indiana
Ball State University M,W
Goshen College M,W
Grace College M,W
Huntington College M,W
Indiana State University M,W
Indiana University
    Bloomington M,W
Indiana University-Purdue University Fort Wayne M,W
Indiana Wesleyan University M,W
Marian College M,W
Purdue University M,W
Purdue University
    Calumet W
St. Joseph's College M,W
Taylor University M,W
University of Indianapolis M,W
University of Notre Dame M,W
University of St. Francis M,W
Valparaiso University M,W
Vincennes University M,W

Iowa
Briar Cliff University M,W
Dordt College M,W
Drake University M,W
Franciscan University M,W
Graceland University M,W
Iowa State University M,W
Iowa Wesleyan College M,W
Morningside College M,W
Northwestern College M,W
St. Ambrose University M,W
University of Iowa M,W
University of Northern Iowa M,W
William Penn University M,W

Kansas
Allen County Community College M,W
Baker University M,W
Barton County Community College M,W
Benedictine College M,W
Bethany College M,W
Bethel College M,W
Butler County Community College M,W
Cloud County Community College M,W
Emporia State University M,W
Fort Hays State University M,W
Garden City Community College M,W
Highland Community College M,W
Hutchinson Community College M,W
Independence Community College M,W
Johnson County Community College M,W
Kansas City Kansas Community College M,W
Kansas State University M,W
Kansas Wesleyan University M,W
McPherson College M,W
MidAmerica Nazarene University M,W
Ottawa University M,W
Pittsburg State University M,W
Pratt Community College M,W
Southwestern College M,W

Sterling College M,W
Tabor College M,W
University of Kansas M,W
Wichita State University M,W

Kentucky

Bellarmine University M,W
Cumberland College M,W
Lindsey Wilson College M,W
Murray State University M,W
University of Kentucky M,W
University of Louisville M,W

Louisiana

Grambling State University M,W
Louisiana State University and Agricultural and Mechanical College M,W
Louisiana Tech University M,W
McNeese State University M,W
Nicholls State University M,W
Northwestern State University M,W
Southeastern Louisiana University M,W
Southern University and Agricultural and Mechanical College M,W
Tulane University W
University of Louisiana at Lafayette M,W
University of Louisiana at Monroe M,W
University of New Orleans M,W

Maine

University of Maine M,W

Maryland

Bowie State University M,W
Columbia Union College M,W
Coppin State College M,W
Hagerstown Community College M,W
Morgan State University M,W
Mount St. Mary's College M,W
Towson University M,W
University of Maryland
  Baltimore County M,W
  College Park M,W

Massachusetts

Bentley College M,W
Boston College M,W
Boston University M,W
Northeastern University M,W
University of Massachusetts
  Amherst M,W
  Lowell M,W

Michigan

Aquinas College M,W
Central Michigan University M,W
Eastern Michigan University M,W
Ferris State University M,W
Grand Rapids Community College M,W
Grand Valley State University M,W
Hillsdale College W
Macomb Community College M,W
Michigan State University M,W
Northwood University M,W
Saginaw Valley State University M,W
Siena Heights University M,W
University of Michigan M,W
Western Michigan University M,W

Minnesota

Bemidji State University M,W
Concordia University: St. Paul M,W
Minnesota State University
  Mankato M,W
  Moorhead M,W
St. Cloud State University M,W
University of Minnesota
  Duluth M,W
  Twin Cities M,W
Winona State University W

Mississippi

Alcorn State University M,W
Holmes Community College M
Mississippi State University M,W
Mississippi Valley State University M,W
University of Mississippi M,W
University of Southern Mississippi M,W

Missouri

Central Methodist College M,W
Central Missouri State University M,W
Evangel University M,W
Harris Stowe State College W
Lincoln University M,W
Lindenwood University M,W
Missouri Southern State College M,W
Missouri Valley College M,W
Southeast Missouri State University M,W
Southwest Missouri State University M,W
Truman State University M,W
University of Missouri
  Columbia M,W
  Kansas City M,W
  Rolla M,W
William Jewell College M,W

Montana

Montana State University
  Bozeman M,W
University of Montana-Missoula M,W

Nebraska

Chadron State College M,W
Concordia University M,W
Dana College M,W
Doane College M,W
Hastings College M,W
Midland Lutheran College M,W
University of Nebraska
  Kearney M,W
  Lincoln M,W
Wayne State College M,W
York College M,W

Nevada

University of Nevada
  Las Vegas W
  Reno W

New Hampshire

University of New Hampshire W

New Jersey

Essex County College M,W
Fairleigh Dickinson University
  Metropolitan Campus M,W
Felician College M,W
Monmouth University M,W
Rider University M,W
Rutgers, The State University of New Jersey
  New Brunswick Regional Campus M,W
St. Peter's College M,W
Seton Hall University M,W

New Mexico

Eastern New Mexico University M,W
New Mexico Military Institute M
New Mexico State University W
University of New Mexico M,W

New York

Adelphi University M,W
Fordham University M,W
Houghton College M,W
Iona College M
Long Island University
  C. W. Post Campus M,W
Manhattan College M,W
Marist College M,W
New York Institute of Technology M,W
Pace University M,W
Pace University: Pleasantville/Briarcliff M,W
Roberts Wesleyan College M,W
St. John's University M,W
State University of New York
  Albany M,W
  Binghamton M,W
  Buffalo M,W
  College of Technology at Alfred M,W
  Stony Brook M,W
Syracuse University M,W
Wagner College M,W

North Carolina

Appalachian State University M,W
Brevard College M,W
Campbell University M,W
Davidson College M,W
East Carolina University M,W
Fayetteville State University W
Gardner-Webb University M,W
High Point University M
Johnson C. Smith University M,W
Lees-McRae College M,W
Livingstone College M,W
Mars Hill College M,W
North Carolina Agricultural and Technical State University M,W
North Carolina Central University M,W
North Carolina State University M,W
St. Augustine's College M,W
Shaw University M,W
University of North Carolina
  Asheville M,W
  Chapel Hill M,W
  Charlotte M,W
  Pembroke M
  Wilmington M,W
Wake Forest University M,W
Western Carolina University M,W
Winston-Salem State University M,W

North Dakota

Dickinson State University M,W
Jamestown College M,W
Minot State University M,W
North Dakota State University M,W
University of Mary M,W
University of North Dakota M,W
Valley City State University M,W

Ohio

Ashland University M,W
Bowling Green State University M,W
Cedarville University M,W
Central State University M,W
Kent State University M,W
Malone College M,W
Miami University
  Oxford Campus M,W
Ohio State University
  Columbus Campus M,W
Ohio University M,W
Tiffin University M,W
University of Akron M,W
University of Findlay M,W
University of Rio Grande M,W
University of Toledo M,W
Walsh University M,W
Youngstown State University M,W

Oklahoma

Oklahoma Baptist University M,W
Oklahoma Christian University M,W
Oklahoma State University M,W
Oral Roberts University M,W
Southern Nazarene University M,W
University of Central Oklahoma M,W
University of Oklahoma M,W
University of Tulsa M,W

Oregon

Chemeketa Community College M,W
Clackamas Community College M,W
Lane Community College M,W
Mount Hood Community College M,W
Oregon Institute of Technology M,W
Portland State University M,W
Southern Oregon University M,W
Southwestern Oregon Community College M,W
University of Oregon M,W
University of Portland M,W

Pennsylvania

Cheyney University of Pennsylvania M,W
Duquesne University M,W
East Stroudsburg University of Pennsylvania M,W
Edinboro University of Pennsylvania M,W
Geneva College M,W
Indiana University of Pennsylvania M,W
Kutztown University of Pennsylvania M,W
La Salle University M,W
Lehigh University M,W
Lock Haven University of Pennsylvania M,W
Millersville University of Pennsylvania M,W
Penn State
  University Park M,W
Robert Morris University M,W
St. Joseph's University M,W
Shippensburg University of Pennsylvania M,W
Slippery Rock University of Pennsylvania M,W
Temple University M,W
University of Pittsburgh M,W
Villanova University M,W
West Chester University of Pennsylvania M,W

Puerto Rico

Bayamon Central University M,W
Inter American University of Puerto Rico
  Bayamon Campus M,W
  Fajardo Campus M,W
  Guayama Campus M,W
  Metropolitan Campus M,W
  San German Campus M,W
Turabo University M,W
Universidad del Este M,W
Universidad Metropolitana M,W
University of Puerto Rico
  Bayamon University College M,W
  Carolina Regional College M,W
  Cayey University College M,W
  Mayaguez Campus M,W
  Ponce M,W
  Utuado M,W
University of the Sacred Heart M,W

Rhode Island

Providence College M,W
University of Rhode Island M,W

South Carolina

Anderson College M,W
Charleston Southern University M,W
The Citadel M,W
Claflin University M,W
Clemson University M,W
Coastal Carolina University M,W
Francis Marion University M,W
Furman University M,W
Morris College M,W
South Carolina State University M,W
University of South Carolina M,W
Voorhees College M,W

Winthrop University M,W
Wofford College W

South Dakota
Augustana College M,W
Black Hills State University M,W
Dakota Wesleyan University M,W
Mount Marty College M,W
Northern State University M,W
South Dakota School of Mines and Technology M,W
South Dakota State University M,W
University of Sioux Falls M,W
University of South Dakota M,W

Tennessee
Austin Peay State University W
Belmont University M,W
Bethel College M,W
East Tennessee State University M,W
Middle Tennessee State University M,W
Tennessee Technological University W
University of Memphis M,W
University of Tennessee
- Chattanooga M,W
- Knoxville M,W
- Martin M,W

Vanderbilt University W

Texas
Abilene Christian University M,W
Angelo State University M,W
Baylor University M,W
Dallas Baptist University W
Jarvis Christian College M,W
Lamar University M,W
Northwood University: Texas Campus M,W
Odessa College W
Prairie View A&M University M,W
Ranger College M,W
Rice University M,W
Sam Houston State University M,W
South Plains College M,W
Southern Methodist University M,W
Southwest Texas State University M,W
Stephen F. Austin State University M,W
Tarleton State University M,W
Texas A&M University M,W
Texas A&M University
- Commerce M,W
- Corpus Christi M,W

Texas Christian University M,W
Texas Southern University M,W
Texas Tech University M,W
University of Houston M,W
University of North Texas M,W
University of Texas
- Arlington M,W
- Austin M,W
- San Antonio M,W

Wayland Baptist University M,W

Utah
Brigham Young University M,W
Southern Utah University M,W
University of Utah M,W
Utah State University M,W
Utah Valley State College M,W
Weber State University M,W

Vermont
University of Vermont W

Virginia
College of William and Mary M,W
George Mason University M,W
Hampton University M,W
James Madison University M,W
Liberty University M,W
Norfolk State University M,W
Radford University M,W
University of Richmond W
University of Virginia M,W
Virginia Commonwealth University M,W
Virginia Military Institute M,W
Virginia Polytechnic Institute and State University M,W
Virginia Union University M,W

Washington
Central Washington University M,W
Clark College M,W
Eastern Washington University M,W
Grays Harbor College M,W
Northwest College M,W
St. Martin's College M,W
Seattle Pacific University M,W
Seattle University M,W
Spokane Community College M,W
University of Washington M,W
Washington State University M,W
Western Washington University M,W

West Virginia
Glenville State College M,W
Marshall University M,W
University of Charleston M,W
West Liberty State College M,W
West Virginia State College M,W
West Virginia University M,W
West Virginia Wesleyan College M,W
Wheeling Jesuit University M,W

Wisconsin
Marquette University M,W
University of Wisconsin
- Madison M,W
- Milwaukee M,W
- Parkside M,W

Wyoming
University of Wyoming M,W

Triathlon

New York
Suffolk County Community College W

North Carolina
Warren Wilson College M,W

Volleyball

Alabama
Alabama Agricultural and Mechanical University W
Alabama State University W
Auburn University W
Bevill State Community College W
Birmingham-Southern College W
Central Alabama Community College W
Gadsden State Community College W
Jacksonville State University W
James H. Faulkner State Community College M,W
Judson College W
Lawson State Community College W
Miles College W
Northwest-Shoals Community College W
Samford University W
Spring Hill College W
Talladega College W
Tuskegee University W
University of Alabama W
University of Alabama
- Birmingham W
- Huntsville W

University of Montevallo W
University of North Alabama W
University of South Alabama W
University of West Alabama W
Wallace State Community College at Hanceville W

Alaska
University of Alaska
- Anchorage W
- Fairbanks W

Arizona
Arizona State University W
Arizona Western College W
Eastern Arizona College W
Embry-Riddle Aeronautical University: Prescott Campus W
Glendale Community College W
Northern Arizona University W
Pima Community College W
Scottsdale Community College W
University of Arizona W
Yavapai College W

Arkansas
Arkansas State University W
Arkansas Tech University W
Harding University W
Henderson State University W
John Brown University W
Lyon College W
Ouachita Baptist University W
Southern Arkansas University W
University of Arkansas W
University of Arkansas
- Fort Smith W
- Little Rock W
- Pine Bluff W

University of Central Arkansas W
Williams Baptist College W

California
Azusa Pacific University W
Bethany College M,W
Biola University W
California Baptist University M,W
California Polytechnic State University: San Luis Obispo W
California State Polytechnic University: Pomona W
California State University
- Bakersfield W
- Chico W
- Fresno W
- Fullerton W
- Long Beach M,W
- Los Angeles W
- Northridge M,W
- Sacramento W
- San Bernardino W
- Stanislaus W

Christian Heritage College W
Concordia University W
Dominican University of California W
Fresno Pacific University W
Grossmont Community College M,W
Holy Names College W
Hope International University M,W
Humboldt State University W
Loyola Marymount University W
Master's College W
Pepperdine University M,W
Point Loma Nazarene University W
St. Mary's College of California W
San Diego State University M,W
San Jose State University W
Santa Clara University W
Stanford University M,W
University of California
- Berkeley W
- Irvine M,W
- Los Angeles M,W
- Riverside W
- Santa Barbara M,W

University of San Diego W
University of San Francisco W
University of Southern California M,W
University of the Pacific M,W
Vanguard University of Southern California W
Yuba Community College District W

Colorado
Colorado Christian University W
Colorado School of Mines W
Colorado State University W
Colorado State University
- Pueblo W

Fort Lewis College W
Mesa State College W
Metropolitan State College of Denver W
Otero Junior College W
Regis University W
Trinidad State Junior College W
University of Colorado
- Boulder W
- Colorado Springs W

University of Denver W
University of Northern Colorado W

Connecticut
Central Connecticut State University W
Fairfield University W
Mitchell College W
Quinnipiac University W
Teikyo Post University W
University of Bridgeport W
University of Connecticut W
University of Hartford W
University of New Haven M,W

Delaware
Delaware State University W
University of Delaware W
Wilmington College W

District of Columbia
American University W
George Washington University W
Georgetown University W
Howard University W

Florida
Barry University W
Bethune-Cookman College W
Broward Community College W
Eckerd College M,W
Embry-Riddle Aeronautical University W
Flagler College W
Florida Agricultural and Mechanical University W
Florida Atlantic University W
Florida College W
Florida Institute of Technology W
Florida International University W
Florida Southern College W
Florida State University W
Hillsborough Community College W
Indian River Community College W
Jacksonville University W
Lake-Sumter Community College W
Manatee Community College W
Miami-Dade Community College W
Northwood University
- Florida Campus W

Nova Southeastern University W
Palm Beach Atlantic University W
Palm Beach Community College W
Pasco-Hernando Community College W
Pensacola Junior College W
Polk Community College W
Rollins College W
St. Leo University W
St. Petersburg College W
St. Thomas University W
Stetson University W
University of Central Florida W
University of Florida W
University of Miami W
University of North Florida W

University of South Florida W
University of Tampa W
University of West Florida W
Warner Southern College W
Webber International University W

Georgia

Abraham Baldwin Agricultural College W
Albany State University W
Armstrong Atlantic State University W
Augusta State University W
Brenau University W
Brewton-Parker College W
Covenant College W
Fort Valley State University W
Georgia Institute of Technology W
Georgia Southern University W
Georgia Southwestern State University W
Georgia State University W
Mercer University W
Paine College W
State University of West Georgia W
University of Georgia W
Valdosta State University W

Hawaii

Brigham Young University-Hawaii W
Chaminade University of Honolulu W
Hawaii Pacific University W
University of Hawaii
Hilo W
Manoa M,W

Idaho

Albertson College of Idaho W
Boise State University W
College of Southern Idaho W
Idaho State University W
Lewis-Clark State College W
North Idaho College W
Northwest Nazarene University W
University of Idaho W

Illinois

Black Hawk College W
Black Hawk College
East Campus W
Bradley University W
Carl Sandburg College W
Chicago State University W
College of Lake County W
Danville Area Community College W
De Paul University W
Dominican University W
Eastern Illinois University W
Elgin Community College W
Highland Community College W
Illinois Central College W
Illinois Eastern Community Colleges
Lincoln Trail College W
Wabash Valley College W
Illinois Institute of Technology W
Illinois State University W
John A. Logan College W
Judson College W
Kankakee Community College W
Kaskaskia College W
Kendall College M,W
Kishwaukee College W
Lake Land College W
Lewis and Clark Community College W
Lewis University M,W
Lincoln College W
Loyola University of Chicago M,W
McHenry County College W
McKendree College W
Moraine Valley Community College W
Northwestern University W
Olivet Nazarene University W
Parkland College W
Quincy University M,W
Rend Lake College W
Robert Morris College: Chicago W
St. Xavier University W
Sauk Valley Community College W
Shawnee Community College W
South Suburban College of Cook County W
Southern Illinois University Carbondale W
Southern Illinois University Edwardsville W
Southwestern Illinois College W
Springfield College in Illinois W
Trinity Christian College M,W
Trinity International University M,W
University of Illinois
Chicago W
Springfield W
Urbana-Champaign W
University of St. Francis W
Waubonsee Community College W
Western Illinois University W

Indiana

Ball State University M,W
Bethel College W
Butler University W
Goshen College W
Grace College W
Huntington College W
Indiana State University W
Indiana University
Bloomington W
Southeast W
Indiana University-Purdue University Fort Wayne M,W
Indiana University-Purdue University Indianapolis W
Indiana Wesleyan University W
Marian College W
Oakland City University W
Purdue University W
St. Joseph's College W
Taylor University: Fort Wayne W
University of Evansville W
University of Indianapolis W
University of Notre Dame W
University of St. Francis W
University of Southern Indiana W
Valparaiso University W
Vincennes University W

Iowa

Briar Cliff University W
Clinton Community College W
Des Moines Area Community College W
Dordt College W
Drake University W
Ellsworth Community College W
Franciscan University W
Graceland University M,W
Grand View College W
Indian Hills Community College W
Iowa Central Community College W
Iowa Lakes Community College W
Iowa State University W
Iowa Wesleyan College W
Iowa Western Community College W
Kirkwood Community College W
Morningside College W
Muscatine Community College W
North Iowa Area Community College W
Northwestern College W
St. Ambrose University M,W
Scott Community College W
Southwestern Community College W
University of Iowa W
University of Northern Iowa W
Waldorf College W
William Penn University W

Kansas

Allen County Community College W
Baker University W
Barton County Community College W
Benedictine College W
Bethany College W
Bethel College W
Butler County Community College W
Central Christian College W
Cloud County Community College W
Dodge City Community College W
Emporia State University W
Fort Hays State University W
Fort Scott Community College W
Friends University W
Garden City Community College W
Hesston College W
Highland Community College W
Hutchinson Community College W
Independence Community College W
Johnson County Community College W
Kansas City Kansas Community College W
Kansas State University W
Kansas Wesleyan University W
Labette Community College W
McPherson College W
MidAmerica Nazarene University W
Newman University W
Ottawa University W
Pittsburg State University W
Pratt Community College W
St. Mary College W
Seward County Community College W
Southwestern College W
Sterling College W
Tabor College W
University of Kansas W
Washburn University of Topeka W
Wichita State University W

Kentucky

Bellarmine University W
Brescia University W
Campbellsville University W
Cumberland College W
Georgetown College W
Kentucky Wesleyan College W
Lindsey Wilson College W
Morehead State University W
Murray State University W
Pikeville College W
Spalding University W
Union College W
University of Kentucky W
University of Louisville W

Louisiana

Centenary College of Louisiana W
Dillard University M,W
Louisiana State University and Agricultural and Mechanical College W
Louisiana Tech University W
McNeese State University W
Nicholls State University W
Northwestern State University W
Southeastern Louisiana University W
Southern University and Agricultural and Mechanical College W
Tulane University W
University of Louisiana at Monroe W
University of New Orleans W

Maine

University of Maine W

Maryland

Bowie State University W
College of Southern Maryland W
Community College of Baltimore County
Catonsville W
Dundalk W
Essex W
Coppin State College W
Garrett College W
Hagerstown Community College W
Loyola College in Maryland W
Morgan State University W
Towson University W
University of Maryland
Baltimore County W
College Park W

Massachusetts

American International College W
Bentley College W
Boston College W
Dean College W
Merrimack College W
Mount Ida College M
Northeastern University W
University of Massachusetts
Lowell W

Michigan

Alpena Community College W
Aquinas College W
Central Michigan University W
Concordia University W
Cornerstone University W
Eastern Michigan University W
Ferris State University W
Glen Oaks Community College W
Grand Rapids Community College W
Grand Valley State University W
Hillsdale College W
Kellogg Community College W
Lansing Community College W
Macomb Community College W
Michigan State University W
Michigan Technological University W
Mott Community College W
Northern Michigan University W
Northwood University W
Oakland Community College W
Oakland University W
Saginaw Valley State University W
Schoolcraft College W
Siena Heights University W
Spring Arbor University W
University of Michigan W
University of Michigan
Dearborn W
Wayne State University W
Western Michigan University W

Minnesota

Bemidji State University W
Bethany Lutheran College W
Concordia University: St. Paul W
Minnesota State University
Mankato W
Moorhead W
St. Cloud State University W
Southwest State University W
University of Minnesota
Crookston W
Duluth W
Morris W
Twin Cities W
Winona State University W

Mississippi

Alcorn State University W
Mississippi State University W
Mississippi University for Women W
Mississippi Valley State University W
University of Mississippi W
University of Southern Mississippi W

Missouri

Avila University M,W
Central Methodist College W
Central Missouri State University W
College of the Ozarks W
Columbia College W
Cottey College W
Culver-Stockton College W
Drury University W
Evangel University W

Hannibal-LaGrange College W
Harris Stowe State College W
Jefferson College W
Lindenwood University M,W
Longview Community College W
Mineral Area College W
Missouri Baptist University M,W
Missouri Southern State College W
Missouri Valley College M,W
Missouri Western State College W
Northwest Missouri State University W
Research College of Nursing W
Rockhurst University W
St. Louis University W
Southeast Missouri State University W
Southwest Baptist University W
Southwest Missouri State University W
St. Louis Community College
  Forest Park W
Three Rivers Community College W
Truman State University W
University of Missouri
  Columbia W
  Kansas City W
  St. Louis W
William Jewell College W
William Woods University M,W

Montana

Carroll College W
Montana State University
  Billings W
  Bozeman W
Montana Tech of the University of Montana W
Rocky Mountain College W
University of Great Falls W
University of Montana-Missoula W
University of Montana: Western W

Nebraska

Bellevue University W
Central Community College W
Chadron State College W
College of Saint Mary W
Concordia University W
Creighton University W
Dana College W
Doane College W
Hastings College W
Mid Plains Community College Area W
Midland Lutheran College W
Nebraska College of Technical Agriculture M,W
Northeast Community College W
Peru State College W
Southeast Community College
  Beatrice Campus W
University of Nebraska
  Kearney W
  Lincoln W
  Omaha W
Wayne State College W
Western Nebraska Community College W

Nevada

University of Nevada
  Las Vegas W
  Reno W

New Hampshire

Franklin Pierce College W
Hesser College M,W
University of New Hampshire W

New Jersey

Bloomfield College W
Fairleigh Dickinson University
  Metropolitan Campus W
Georgian Court College W
New Jersey Institute of Technology M,W
Rider University W
Rutgers, The State University of New Jersey
  New Brunswick Regional Campus W
  Newark Regional Campus M
St. Peter's College W
Seton Hall University W

New Mexico

College of the Southwest W
Eastern New Mexico University W
New Mexico Highlands University W
New Mexico State University W
University of New Mexico W
Western New Mexico University W

New York

Adelphi University W
Canisius College W
City University of New York
  Queens College M,W
Concordia College M,W
Daemen College W
Dominican College of Blauvelt W
Dowling College W
Fordham University W
Genesee Community College W
Hofstra University W
Houghton College W
Iona College W
Le Moyne College W
Long Island University
  C. W. Post Campus W
  Southampton College M,W
Manhattan College W
Marist College M
Mercy College W
Molloy College W
New York Institute of Technology W
Niagara University W
Nyack College W
Pace University W
Pace University: Pleasantville/Briarcliff W
Roberts Wesleyan College M,W
Sage College of Albany W
St. Bonaventure University W
St. John's University W
State University of New York
  Albany W
  Binghamton W
  Buffalo W
  Stony Brook W
Syracuse University W
Wagner College W

North Carolina

Appalachian State University W
Barber-Scotia College W
Barton College W
Brevard College W
Campbell University W
Catawba College W
Davidson College W
Duke University W
East Carolina University W
Elon University W
Fayetteville State University W
Gardner-Webb University W
High Point University W
Johnson C. Smith University W
Lees-McRae College M,W
Lenoir Community College W
Lenoir-Rhyne College W
Livingstone College W
Mars Hill College W
Montreat College W
Mount Olive College W
North Carolina Agricultural and Technical State University W
North Carolina Central University W
North Carolina State University W
Pfeiffer University W
Pitt Community College W
Queens University of Charlotte W
St. Andrews Presbyterian College W
St. Augustine's College W
Shaw University W
Southeastern Community College W
University of North Carolina
  Asheville W
  Chapel Hill W
  Charlotte W
  Greensboro W
  Pembroke W
  Wilmington W
Wake Forest University W
Western Carolina University W
Wingate University W
Winston-Salem State University W

North Dakota

Bismarck State College W
Dickinson State University W
Jamestown College W
Lake Region State College W
Mayville State University W
Minot State University W
Minot State University: Bottineau Campus W
North Dakota State College of Science W
North Dakota State University W
University of Mary W
University of North Dakota W
Valley City State University W
Williston State College W

Ohio

Ashland University W
Bowling Green State University W
Cedarville University W
Central State University W
Clark State Community College W
Cleveland State University W
Kent State University W
Lakeland Community College W
Malone College W
Miami University
  Oxford Campus W
Mount Vernon Nazarene University W
Ohio Dominican College W
Ohio State University
  Columbus Campus M,W
Ohio University W
Shawnee State University W
Sinclair Community College W
Southern State Community College W
Tiffin University W
University of Akron W
University of Dayton W
University of Findlay M,W
University of Rio Grande W
University of Toledo W
Urbana University W
Ursuline College W
Walsh University W
Wright State University W
Xavier University W
Youngstown State University W

Oklahoma

Cameron University W
Northeastern Oklahoma Agricultural and Mechanical College W
Oklahoma Wesleyan University W
Oral Roberts University W
Redlands Community College W
Southeastern Oklahoma State University W
Southern Nazarene University W
University of Central Oklahoma W
University of Oklahoma W
University of Tulsa W

Oregon

Blue Mountain Community College W
Chemeketa Community College W
Clackamas Community College W
Concordia University W
Lane Community College W
Linn-Benton Community College W
Mount Hood Community College W
Oregon Institute of Technology W
Oregon State University W
Portland State University W
Southern Oregon University W
Southwestern Oregon Community College W
Treasure Valley Community College W
University of Oregon W
University of Portland W
Western Baptist College W

Pennsylvania

California University of Pennsylvania W
Carlow College W
Cheyney University of Pennsylvania W
Community College of Beaver County W
Duquesne University W
East Stroudsburg University of Pennsylvania W
Edinboro University of Pennsylvania W
Indiana University of Pennsylvania W
Kutztown University of Pennsylvania W
La Salle University W
Lackawanna College W
Lehigh University W
Lock Haven University of Pennsylvania W
Mercyhurst College M,W
Millersville University of Pennsylvania W
Penn State
  University Park M,W
Philadelphia University W
Point Park College W
Robert Morris University W
St. Vincent College W
Seton Hill University W
Shippensburg University of Pennsylvania W
Slippery Rock University of Pennsylvania W
University of Pittsburgh W
University of Pittsburgh
  Titusville W
University of the Sciences in Philadelphia W
Villanova University W
West Chester University of Pennsylvania W

Puerto Rico

Bayamon Central University M,W
Inter American University of Puerto Rico
  Bayamon Campus M,W
  Metropolitan Campus M,W
  San German Campus M,W
Turabo University M,W
Universidad del Este M,W
Universidad Metropolitana M,W
University of Puerto Rico
  Bayamon University College M,W
  Carolina Regional College M,W
  Mayaguez Campus M,W
  Ponce M,W
  Utuado M,W
University of the Sacred Heart M,W

Rhode Island

University of Rhode Island W

South Carolina

Anderson College W
Charleston Southern University W
The Citadel W
Clemson University W
Coastal Carolina University W
Coker College W

College of Charleston W
Converse College W
Francis Marion University W
Furman University W
Lander University W
Limestone College W
Morris College W
North Greenville College W
Presbyterian College W
South Carolina State University W
Southern Wesleyan University W
Spartanburg Methodist College W
University of South Carolina W
University of South Carolina
Aiken W
Spartanburg W
Voorhees College W
Winthrop University W
Wofford College W

South Dakota
Augustana College W
Black Hills State University W
Dakota State University W
Dakota Wesleyan University W
Mount Marty College W
National American University
Rapid City W
South Dakota School of Mines and Technology W
South Dakota State University W
University of Sioux Falls W
University of South Dakota W

Tennessee
Austin Peay State University W
Belmont University W
Bethel College W
Bryan College W
Carson-Newman College W
Christian Brothers University W
East Tennessee State University W
Freed-Hardeman University W
King College W
Lambuth University W
Lane College W
Lee University W
Lipscomb University W
Middle Tennessee State University W
Milligan College W
Tennessee Technological University W
Tennessee Wesleyan College W
Trevecca Nazarene University W
Tusculum College W
Union University W
University of Memphis W
University of Tennessee
Chattanooga W
Knoxville W
Martin W

Texas
Abilene Christian University W
Alvin Community College W
Angelo State University W
Baylor University W
Blinn College W
Clarendon College W
Collin County Community College District W
Dallas Baptist University W
Frank Phillips College W
Galveston College W
Hill College W
Houston Baptist University W
Jacksonville College W
Jarvis Christian College W
Lamar University W
Laredo Community College W
Lee College W
Lon Morris College W
Lubbock Christian University W
Midwestern State University W
North Central Texas College W
Panola College W
Prairie View A&M University W
Rice University W
St. Edward's University W
St. Mary's University W
Sam Houston State University W
Southern Methodist University W
Southwest Texas State University W
Southwestern Adventist University W
Stephen F. Austin State University W
Tarleton State University W
Texas A&M University W
Texas A&M University
Commerce W
Corpus Christi W
Kingsville W
Texas Christian University W
Texas Southern University W
Texas Tech University W
Texas Woman's University W
Tyler Junior College W
University of Houston W
University of North Texas W
University of Texas
Arlington W
Austin W
San Antonio W
University of the Incarnate Word W
Wayland Baptist University W
West Texas A&M University W
Wharton County Junior College W

Utah
Brigham Young University M,W
College of Eastern Utah W
Dixie State College of Utah W
Salt Lake Community College W
Snow College W
University of Utah W
Utah State University W
Utah Valley State College W
Weber State University W

Virginia
Bluefield College W
College of William and Mary W
George Mason University M,W
Hampton University W
James Madison University W
Liberty University W
Norfolk State University W
Radford University W
University of Virginia W
University of Virginia's College at Wise W
Virginia Commonwealth University W
Virginia Polytechnic Institute and State University W
Virginia Union University W

Washington
Central Washington University W
Centralia College W
Clark College W
Eastern Washington University W
Edmonds Community College W
Everett Community College W
Evergreen State College W
Gonzaga University W
Grays Harbor College W
Green River Community College W
Lower Columbia College W
Northwest College W
Olympic College W
St. Martin's College W
Seattle Pacific University W
Seattle University W
Spokane Community College W
University of Washington W
Walla Walla Community College W
Washington State University W
Western Washington University W

West Virginia
Alderson-Broaddus College W
Concord College W
Davis and Elkins College W
Glenville State College W
Marshall University W
Mountain State University W
Ohio Valley College W
Potomac State College of West Virginia University W
Salem International University W
Shepherd College W
University of Charleston W
West Liberty State College W
West Virginia University W
West Virginia University Institute of Technology W
West Virginia Wesleyan College W
Wheeling Jesuit University W

Wisconsin
Marquette University W
University of Wisconsin
Green Bay W
Madison W
Milwaukee M,W
Parkside W
Viterbo University W

Wyoming
Casper College W
Eastern Wyoming College W
Sheridan College W
University of Wyoming W
Western Wyoming Community College W

Water polo

California
California Baptist University M,W
California State University
Bakersfield W
Long Beach M
Grossmont Community College M,W
Loyola Marymount University M,W
Pepperdine University M
San Diego State University W
San Jose State University W
Santa Clara University M,W
Stanford University M,W
University of California
Berkeley M,W
Irvine M,W
Los Angeles M,W
University of Southern California M,W
University of the Pacific M,W

District of Columbia
George Washington University M

Florida
Broward Community College W
Florida Atlantic University W

Hawaii
Brigham Young University-Hawaii M
Chaminade University of Honolulu M
University of Hawaii
Manoa W

Indiana
Indiana University
Bloomington W

Michigan
University of Michigan W

New York
City University of New York
Queens College M,W
Fordham University M
Hartwick College W
Marist College W
Wagner College W

Pennsylvania
Mercyhurst College M,W
Slippery Rock University of Pennsylvania M,W

Puerto Rico
University of Puerto Rico
Mayaguez Campus M

West Virginia
Salem International University M,W

Wyoming
Western Wyoming Community College M

Weight lifting

New York
City University of New York
York College M,W

Oklahoma
Northeastern Oklahoma Agricultural and Mechanical College M,W

Puerto Rico
Technological College of San Juan M,W
Turabo University M,W
Universidad del Este M
Universidad Metropolitana M
University of Puerto Rico
Carolina Regional College M,W
Cayey University College M

Wrestling

Arizona
Arizona State University M
Embry-Riddle Aeronautical University: Prescott Campus M

California
California Polytechnic State University: San Luis Obispo M
California State University
Bakersfield M
Fresno M
Fullerton M
Stanford University M

Colorado
Colorado School of Mines M
Colorado State University
Pueblo M
University of Northern Colorado M

Connecticut
Southern Connecticut State University M

Delaware
Delaware State University M

District of Columbia
American University M
Howard University M

Idaho
Boise State University M
North Idaho College M

Illinois
City Colleges of Chicago
Wright College M
College of Lake County M
Eastern Illinois University M
Lincoln College M

Northwestern University M
Southern Illinois University
Edwardsville M
Southwestern Illinois College M
University of Illinois
Urbana-Champaign M
Waubonsee Community College M

Indiana

Indiana University
Bloomington M
Purdue University M
University of Indianapolis M

Iowa

Briar Cliff University M
Ellsworth Community College M
Iowa Central Community College M
Iowa State University M
Northwestern College M
University of Iowa M
University of Northern Iowa M
Waldorf College M
William Penn University M

Kansas

Fort Hays State University M
Labette Community College M

Kentucky

Cumberland College M,W

Maryland

University of Maryland
College Park M

Massachusetts

American International College M
Babson College M
Boston University M

Michigan

Central Michigan University M
Eastern Michigan University M
Grand Rapids Community College M
Michigan State University M
University of Michigan M

Minnesota

Minnesota State University
Mankato M
Moorhead M
St. Cloud State University M
Southwest State University M
University of Minnesota
Morris M,W
Twin Cities M

Missouri

Central Missouri State University M
Lindenwood University M
Missouri Baptist University M
Missouri Valley College M,W
St. Louis Community College
Meramec M
Truman State University M
University of Missouri
Columbia M

Nebraska

Chadron State College M
Dana College M
University of Nebraska
Kearney M
Lincoln M
Omaha M

New Jersey

Rider University M
Rutgers, The State University of New Jersey
New Brunswick Regional Campus M

New York

Hofstra University M
Niagara County Community College M
State University of New York
Binghamton M
Buffalo M
Wagner College M

North Carolina

Appalachian State University M
Campbell University M
Davidson College M
Duke University M
Gardner-Webb University M
North Carolina Agricultural and Technical State University M
North Carolina State University M
University of North Carolina
Chapel Hill M
Greensboro M
Pembroke M

North Dakota

Dickinson State University M
Jamestown College M
North Dakota State University M
University of Mary M

Ohio

Ashland University M
Cleveland State University M
Cuyahoga Community College
Western Campus M
Kent State University M
Ohio State University
Columbus Campus M
Ohio University M
University of Findlay M

Oklahoma

Oklahoma State University M
University of Central Oklahoma M
University of Oklahoma M

Oregon

Clackamas Community College M
Oregon State University M
Portland State University M
Southern Oregon University M
University of Oregon M

Pennsylvania

Bloomsburg University of Pennsylvania M
California University of Pennsylvania M
Cheyney University of Pennsylvania M
Drexel University M
Duquesne University M
East Stroudsburg University of Pennsylvania M
Edinboro University of Pennsylvania M
Kutztown University of Pennsylvania M
Lehigh University M
Lock Haven University of Pennsylvania M
Mercyhurst College M
Millersville University of Pennsylvania M
Penn State
University Park M
Shippensburg University of Pennsylvania M
Slippery Rock University of Pennsylvania M
University of Pittsburgh M
University of Pittsburgh
Johnstown M

Puerto Rico

Inter American University of Puerto Rico
Bayamon Campus M
University of Puerto Rico
Bayamon University College M
Cayey University College M
Mayaguez Campus M
University of the Sacred Heart M

South Carolina

Anderson College M
The Citadel M
Spartanburg Methodist College M

South Dakota

Augustana College M
Dakota Wesleyan University M
Northern State University M
South Dakota State University M

Tennessee

Carson-Newman College M
University of Tennessee
Chattanooga M

Virginia

George Mason University M
James Madison University M
Norfolk State University M
Old Dominion University M
University of Virginia M
Virginia Military Institute M
Virginia Polytechnic Institute and State University M

Washington

Central Washington University M

West Virginia

West Liberty State College M
West Virginia University M

Wisconsin

University of Wisconsin
Madison M
Parkside M

Wyoming

University of Wyoming M
Western Wyoming Community College M

Alphabetical Index

Selected Books and Software from the College Board

Annual college directories

The College Board College Handbook with *Real Stuff* CD-ROM, 2004. Over 2 million copies sold. The only one-volume guide to all U.S. two- and four-year colleges. 2,200 pages, paperbound. **Item# 006941** $27.95

The College Board Scholarship Handbook with *Real Stuff* CD-ROM, 2004. Over 2,100 real scholarships, grants, internships, and loans for undergraduate students. 620 pages, paperbound. **Item# 006984** $26.95

The College Board College Cost & Financial Aid Handbook, 2004. Detailed cost and financial aid information at 3,100 two- and four-year institutions; includes indexed information on college scholarships. 800 pages, paperbound. **Item# 006976** $23.95

The College Board Index of Majors and Graduate Degrees, 2004. "A comprehensive, no-nonsense guide"—the *New York Times*. Covers 900 major fields of study at all degree levels: undergraduate, graduate, and professional, including law, medicine, and dentistry. 740 pages, paperbound. **Item# 006968** $23.95

The College Board International Student Handbook of U.S. Colleges, 2004. Provides students with information they need to apply for study at 2,500 U.S. colleges, including costs, required tests, financial aid, ESL programs. 360 pages, paperbound. **Item# 006992** $27.95

Test prep for College Board programs

10 Real SAT®s, Third Edition. 10 real, complete SATs for student practice, with test-taking tips from the test makers themselves. Also includes a mini-SAT on CD-ROM. 700 pages, paperbound. **Item# 006860** $19.95

Real SAT II: Subject Tests. The only source of real SAT II practice questions from cover to cover. 700 pages, paperbound. **Item# 007034** $18.95

APCD® in Spanish Language, 2001. Designed to assist and reinforce classroom teaching, this CD helps students prepare with interactive review and problem-solving strategies. Features audio component. **Item# 201894** $49.00

APCD® in Calculus AB, 2000. A valuable study tool that complements classroom materials and also provides practice exam review with analysis of answers and scores. **Item# 201907** $49.00

APCD® in U.S. History, 1998. This CD augments classroom instruction and materials with multiple-choice practice tests and essay tutorials. **Item# 201865** $49.00

APCD® in European History, 1999. Reinforcement and review of classroom materials includes maps, timelines, practice tests, and essay tutorials. **Item# 201891** $49.00

APCD® in English Language, 1999. Designed to supplement classroom and home assignments, this CD provides essay tutorials, guidelines, and practice tests. **Item# 201889** $49.00

APCD® in English Literature, 1998. A thorough exam review offering essay tutorials and multiple-choice practice, this CD is designed to complement written preparation materials provided in the classroom. **Item# 201864** $49.00

One-on-One with the SAT™. (Version 2.3) Valuable advice and test-taking strategies from the SAT test makers, plus the opportunity to take a real, complete SAT and hundreds of additional practice questions on computer. (Home version—Windows® and Macintosh®) **Item# 006747** $29.95

The CLEP® Official Study Guide 2004–15th Edition. Qualifying scores on CLEP exams can earn credit at over 2,900 colleges. Only guide to cover all 34 CLEP exams with sample questions for all 34 exams. 500 pages, paperbound. **Item# 007026** $22.00

General guidance for students and parents

The College Application Essay, Sarah Myers McGinty. Application essay policies of more than 180 institutions, types of questions asked, plus 40 actual questions and analyses of 6 essays. 131 pages, paperbound. **Item# 005759** $12.95

Campus Visits and College Interviews, Zola Dincin Schneider. Newly revised 2nd edition (2002). Why they are important, when to visit, what to look for, questions usually asked, much more. 162 pages, paperbound. **Item# 006755** $12.95

The College Board Guide to 150 Popular College Majors. One-of-a-kind reference to majors in 17 fields, with related information on typical courses, high school preparation, much more. 377 pages, paperbound. **Item# 004000** $16.00

The Parents' Guide to Paying for College, Gerald Krefetz. Expert advice from a well-known investment analyst and financial consultant on covering college costs, with case studies. 158 pages, paperbound. **Item# 006046** $14.95

Order Form

Dept. GSP1203A

Mail order form to: College Board Publications, Dept. GSP1203A, P.O. Box 869010, Plano, TX 75074 *(payment must accompany all orders)*
***or* phone:** 800 323-7155, M–F, 8 a.m.–9 p.m. Eastern Time *(credit card orders only)*
***or* fax 24 hours, 7 days a week to:** 888 321-7183 *(purchase orders above $25 and credit card orders)*
***or* online** through the College Board Store at www.collegeboard.com *(credit card orders only)*

Item No.	Title	Price	Amount
	Annual college directories		
006984	Scholarship Handbook with *Real Stuff* CD-ROM, 2004	$26.95	
006941	The College Handbook, with *Real Stuff* CD-ROM, 2004	$27.95	
006976	College Cost & Financial Aid Handbook, 2004	$23.95	
006968	Index of Majors and Graduate Degrees, 2004	$23.95	
006992	International Student Handbook of U.S. Colleges, 2004	$27.95	
995694	2004 Scholarship 3-book set: *College Handbook, Scholarship Handbook, College Cost & Financial Aid Handbook*	$67.00	
995692	2004 Classic 3-book set: *College Handbook, Index of Majors, College Cost & Financial Aid Handbook*	$65.00	
	Test prep for College Board programs		
201907	AP® CD-ROM in Calculus AB, 2000	$49.00	
201864	AP CD-ROM in English Literature, 1998	$49.00	
201865	AP CD-ROM in U.S. History, 1998	$49.00	
201891	AP CD-ROM in European History, 1999	$49.00	
201889	AP CD-ROM in English Language, 1999	$49.00	
201894	AP CD-ROM in Spanish Language, 2001	$49.00	
006860	10 Real SAT®s, Third Edition	$19.95	
006747	One-on-One with the SAT® (Home version, Windows®/Macintosh®)	$29.95	
007026	The CLEP® Official Study Guide, 2004–15th Edition	$22.00	
007034	Real SAT II: Subject Tests	$18.95	
	General guidance for students and parents		
005759	The College Application Essay	$12.95	
006755	Campus Visits and College Interviews, 2nd edition	$12.95	
004000	College Board Guide to 150 Popular College Majors	$16.00	
006046	The Parents' Guide to Paying for College	$14.95	
		Subtotal	**$**
		Shipping and handling	$
		Total	**$**
		Sales Tax: *(IL,CA,FL,GA,TN,PA,DC,MA,TX,VA,Can.)*	$
		Grand Total	**$**

Shipping and Handling

$0	–	$20.00	=	$4.00
$20.01	–	$40.00	=	$5.00
$40.01	–	$60.00	=	$6.00
$60.01+	=	10% of dollar value of order		

❑ Enclosed is my check or money order made payable to the ***College Board*** ❑ Enclosed is my purchase order above $25

❑ Please charge my ❑ MasterCard ❑ Visa ❑ American Express ❑ Discover

card number exp. date: month / year cardholder's signature

Allow two weeks from receipt of order for delivery.

SHIP TO:

Name *Street Address (no P. O. Box numbers, please)*

City *State* ( ) *Telephone*